138

Webster's New World Encyclopedia

CONCISE EDITION

Webster's New World Encyclopedia

CONCISE EDITION

MACMILLAN · U S A

Macmillan
A Prentice Hall Macmillan Company
15 Columbus Circle
New York, NY 10023

Webster's new world encyclopedia concise edition. – 1st ed.
    p. cm.
Based on *Webster's new world encyclopedia*.
ISBN 0-671-85017-2
1. Encyclopedias and dictionaries.   I. Webster's new world encyclopedia.
AG5.W3875 1994   94-914024
031–dc20   CIP

First edition

Set in Century Old Style

Typeset and page make-up by Roger Walker/Graham Harmer
Manufactured in the United States of America

10 9 8 7 6 5 4 3 2 1

First Macmillan Edition

Editors

Editors
Stephen P Elliott
Hilary McGlynn

Editorial Assistant
Avril Cridlan

Design
Terence Caven
Behram Kapadia

Cartography
Ruth Jones

Production
Tony Ballsdon

Contributors

Owen Adikibi PhD
Lesley and Roy Adkins
Christine Avery PhD
John Ayto MA
Paul Bahn
Bernard Balleine
Tia Cockerell LLB
Sue Cusworth
Nigel Davis MSc
Ian D Derbyshire PhD
J Denis Derbyshire PhD, FBIM
Col Michael Dewar
Dougal Dixon BSc, MSc
Nigel Dudley
George du Boulay FRCR, FRCP, Hon FACR
Ingrid von Essen
Eric Farge
Anna Farkas
Peter Fleming PhD
Kent Fedorowich BA, MA, PhD
Derek Gjertsen BA
Lawrence Garner BA
Wendy Grossman
Joseph Harrison BA, PhD
Michael Hitchcock PhD
Stuart Holroyd
Gerald M D Howat
MA, MLitt, PhD, FRHistC
H G Jerrard PhD
Robin Kerrod FRAS
Charles Kidd
Stephen Kite B Arch, RIBA
Peter Lafferty MSc
Mike Lewis MBCS
Graham Ley MPhil
Carol Lister PhD, FSS

Graham Littler BSc, MSc, FSS
Robin Maconie MA
Morven MacKillop
Tom McArthur PhD
Isabel Miller BA PhD
Karin Mogg MSc PhD
Bob Moore PhD
David Munro PhD
Joanne O'Brien
Maureen O'Connor
Roger Owen MA, DPhil
Robert Paisley PhD
Martin Palmer
David Penfold PhD, MBCS
Paulette Pratt
Michael Pudlo MSc, PhD
Tim Pulleine
Chris Rhys
Ian Ridpath FRAS
Adrian Room MA
Simon Ross
Julian Rowe PhD
Paul Rowntree MA
Jack Schofield BA, MA
Emma Shackleton
Mark Slade MA
Steve Smyth
Jennifer Speake MPhil
Joe Staines
Glyn Stone
Calum Storrie
Michael Thum
Norman Vance, PhD,
Professor of English, Univ. of Sussex
Stephen Webster BSc, MPhil
Liz Whitelegg BSc

How to Use This Book

Arrangement of Entries

Entries are ordered alphabetically, as if there were no spaces between words. Thus, entries for words beginning "gold" follow the order:

> gold
> Golden Fleece
> goldfinch

However, we have avoided a purely mechanical alphabetization in cases where a different order corresponds more with human logic. For example, sovereigns with the same name are grouped according to country and then by number, so that King George II of England is placed before George III of England, and not next to King George II of Greece. Words beginning "Mc" and "Mac" are treated as if they begin "Mac"; and "St" and "Saint" are both treated as if they were spelled "Saint."

Foreign Names

Names of foreign sovereigns and places are usually shown in their English form, except where the foreign name is more familiar; thus, there are entries for Charles V of Spain, but Juan Carlos (not John Charles), and for Florence, not Firenze. Cross references have been provided in cases where confusion is possible.

Cross References

These are shown by a ◊ symbol immediately preceding the reference. Cross-referencing is selective; a cross reference is shown when another entry contains material directly relevant to the subject matter of an entry, and where the reader may not otherwise think of looking. Common alternative spellings, where there is no agreed upon consistent form, are also shown.

Units

SI (metric) units are used throughout for scientific entries. Measurements of distances, temperatures, sizes, and so on, usually include both the US measurement and the metric equivalent. Entries are also included for a wide variety of measurements no longer in common use.

Science and Technology

These entries are generally placed under the name by which they are better known, with the technical term given as a cross reference. To make it easier for the nonspecialist to understand, technical terms are frequently explained when used within the text of an entry, even though they may have their own entry elsewhere.

Chinese Names

Pinyin, the preferred system for transcribing Chinese names of people and places, is generally used: thus there is an entry at Mao Zedong, not Mao Tsetung; an exception is made for a few names that are more familiar in their former (Wade-Giles) form, such as Sun Yat-sen and Chiang Kai-shek. Where confusion is likely, Wade-Giles forms are given as cross references.

Webster's New World Encyclopedia

CONCISE EDITION

Aalto Alvar 1898–1976. Finnish architect and designer. One of Finland's first Modernists, he had a unique architectural style, characterized by asymmetry, curved walls, and contrast of natural materials. He invented a new form of laminated bent-plywood furniture 1932 and won many design awards for household and industrial items.

aardvark (Afrikaans "earth pig") nocturnal mammal *Orycteropus afer*, order Tubulidentata, found in central and S Africa. A timid, defenseless animal about the size of a pig, it has a long head, piglike snout, and large asinine ears. It feeds on termites, which it licks up with its long sticky tongue.

aardwolf nocturnal mammal *Proteles cristatus* of the ◊hyena family, Hyaenidae. It is found in E and S Africa, usually in the burrows of the aardvark, and feeds on termites.

Aarhus (Danish *Århus*) second-largest city of Denmark, on the E coast overlooking the Kattegat; population (1990) 261,400. It is the capital of Aarhus county in Jylland (Jutland) and a shipping and commercial center.

Aaron *c.* 13th century BC. In the Old Testament, the elder brother of Moses and co-leader of the ◊Hebrews in their march from Egypt to the Promised Land of Canaan. He made the Golden Calf for the Hebrews to worship when they despaired of Moses' return from Mount Sinai, but he was allowed to continue as high priest. All his descendants are hereditary high priests, called the *cohanim*, or cohens, and maintain a special place in worship and ceremony in the synagogue.

Aaron Hank (Henry Louis) 1934– . US baseball player and all-time home-run leader. In the course of his career, primarily with the Milwaukee and Atlanta Braves, he won the National League batting title twice, 1955 and 1959. In 1957, as a member of the World Championship team, he was named the National League's most valuable player. His greatest achievement was breaking Babe Ruth's lifetime record of 714 home runs; by the time of his retirement in 1976, Aaron had hit a total of 755 home runs. He was elected to the Baseball Hall of Fame in 1982.

abacus method of calculating with a handful of stones on "a flat surface" (Latin *abacus*), familiar to the Greeks and Romans, and used by earlier peoples, possibly even in ancient Babylon; it still survives in the more sophisticated bead-frame form of the Russian *schoty* and the Japanese *soroban*. The abacus has been superseded by the electronic calculator.

abalone edible marine snail of the worldwide genus *Haliotis*, family Haliotidae. Abalones have flattened, oval, spiraled shells, which have holes around the outer edge and a bluish mother-of-pearl lining. This lining is used in ornamental work.

Abbadid dynasty 11th century. Muslim dynasty based in Seville, Spain, which lasted from 1023 until 1091. The dynasty was founded by Abu-el-Kasim Mohammed Ibn Abbad, who led the townspeople against the Berbers when the Spanish caliphate fell. The dynasty continued under Motadid (1042–1069) and Motamid (1069–1091) when the city was taken by the ◊Almoravids.

Abbas I *the Great c.* 1557–1629. Shah of Persia from 1588. He expanded Persian territory by conquest, defeating the Uzbeks near Herat 1597 and also the Turks. The port of Bandar-Abbas is named after him. At his death his empire reached from the river Tigris to the Indus. He was a patron of the arts.

Abbasid dynasty family of rulers of the Islamic empire, whose ◊caliphs reigned in Baghdad 750–1258. They were descended from Abbas, the prophet Mohammed's uncle, and some of them, such as Harun al-Rashid and Mamun (reigned 813–33), were outstanding patrons of cultural development. Later their power dwindled, and in 1258 Baghdad was burned by the Tatars.

Abbey Edwin Austin 1852–1911. US artist and illustrator. Born in Philadelphia, Abbey was educated by private tutors and later studied at the Pennsylvania Academy of Fine Arts. His illustrations, first published in *Harper's Weekly*, earned him a national reputation and commissions to illustrate many popular books. Living much of his later life in England, he was elected to the Royal Academy and the US National Academy of Design and received the French Legion of Honor. Among his works are the murals he painted for the Boston Public Library depicting the quest for the Holy Grail.

Abd al-Malik Ibn Marwan 647–705. Caliph who reigned 685–705. Based in Damascus, he waged military campaigns to unite Muslim groups and battled against the Greeks. He instituted a purely Arab coinage and replaced Syriac, Coptic, and Greek with Arabic as the language for his lands. His reign was turbulent but succeeded in extending and strengthening the power of the Omayyad dynasty. He was also a patron of the arts.

Abd el-Krim el-Khettabi 1881–1963. Moroccan chief known as the "Wolf of the ◊Riff." With his brother Mohammed, he led the ***Riff revolt*** against the French and Spanish invaders, inflicting disastrous defeat on the Spanish at Anual in 1921, but surrendered to a large French army under Pétain in 1926. Banished to the island of Réunion, he was released in 1947 and died in voluntary exile in Cairo.

abdomen in invertebrates, the part of the body below the ◊thorax, containing the digestive organs; in insects and other arthropods, it is the hind part of the body. In mammals, the abdomen is separated from the thorax by the diaphragm, a sheet of muscular tissue; in arthropods, commonly by a narrow constriction. In insects and spiders, the abdomen is characterized by the absence of limbs.

Abdul-Hamid II 1842–1918. Last sultan of Turkey 1876–1909. In 1908 the ◊Young Turks under Enver

Pasha forced Abdul-Hamid to restore the constitution of 1876 and in 1909 insisted on his deposition. He died in confinement. For his part in the ◊Armenian massacres suppressing the revolt of 1894–96 he was known as "the Great Assassin"; his actions still motivate Armenian violence against the Turks.

Abdul-Jabbar Kareem 1947– . US basketball player who played for the Milwaukee Bucks 1969–75 and the Los Angeles Lakers 1975–89. He held the record for being named professional basketball's most valuable player six times over the period between 1971 and 1980. A center at 7 ft 2 in tall, he was noted for his "sky hook" shot. He led the University of California at Los Angeles (UCLA) to the National Collegiate Athletic Association (NCAA) championship 1967–69.

Abdullah ibn Hussein 1882–1951. King of Jordan from 1946. He worked with the British guerrilla leader T E ◊Lawrence in the Arab revolt of World War I. Abdullah became king of Trans-Jordan 1946; on the incorporation of Arab Palestine (after the 1948–49 Arab–Israeli War) he renamed the country the Hashemite Kingdom of Jordan. He was assassinated.

Abdullah Sheik Mohammed 1905–1982. Indian politician, known as the "Lion of Kashmir." He headed the struggle for constitutional government against the Maharajah of Kashmir, and in 1948, following a coup, became prime minister. He agreed to the accession of the state to India, but was dismissed and imprisoned from 1953 (with brief intervals) until 1966, when he called for Kashmiri self-determination. He became chief minister of Jammu and Kashmir 1975, accepting the sovereignty of India.

Abel in the Old Testament, the second son of Adam and Eve; as a shepherd, he made burnt offerings of meat to God which were more acceptable than the fruits offered by his brother Cain; he was killed by the jealous Cain.

Abel John Jacob 1857–1938. US biochemist, discoverer of ◊adrenaline. He studied the chemical composition of body tissues, and this led, in 1898, to the discovery of adrenaline, the first hormone to be identified, which Abel called epinephrine. He later became the first to isolate ◊amino acids from blood.

Abelard Peter 1079–1142. French scholastic philosopher who worked on logic and theology. His romantic liaison with his pupil ◊Héloïse caused a medieval scandal. Details of his controversial life are contained in the autobiographical *Historia Calamitatum Mearum/The History of My Misfortunes*.

Aberdeen city and seaport on the E coast of Scotland, administrative headquarters of Grampian Region; population (1991) 201,100. Industries include agricultural machinery, paper, and textiles; fishing; shipbuilding; granite-quarrying; and engineering. There are shore-based maintenance and service depots for the North Sea oil rigs. Aberdeen is Scotland's third-largest city.

aberration of starlight apparent displacement of a star from its true position, due to the combined effects of the speed of light and the speed of the Earth in orbit around the Sun (about 18.5 mi per sec/30 km per sec).

Abidja'n port and former capital (until 1983) of the Republic of Ivory Coast, W Africa; population (1982) 1,850,000. Products include coffee, palm oil, cocoa, and timber (mahogany). Yamoussoukro became the new capital 1983, but was not internationally recognized as such until 1992.

Abilene city in central Texas, SW of Fort Worth; seat of Taylor County; population (1990) 106,650. It is a center for oil-drilling equipment. Abilene was founded 1881 as the terminus for the Texas and Pacific Railroad.

Abkhazia autonomous republic in Georgia, situated on the Black Sea
capital Sukhumi
area 3,320 sq mi/8,600 sq km
products tin, fruit, tobacco
population (1989) 526,000
history The region has been the scene of secessionist activity on the part of the minority Muslim Abkhazi community since 1989, culminating in the republic's declaration of independence 1992. Georgian troops invaded and took control Aug 1992, but secessionist guerrillas subsequently gained control of the northern half of the republic.

ablative in the grammar of certain inflected languages, such as Latin, the ablative case is the form of a noun, pronoun, or adjective used to indicate the agent in passive sentences or the instrument, manner, or place of the action described by the verb.

abolitionism in US and UK history, a movement culminating in the late 18th and early 19th centuries that aimed first to end the slave trade, and then to abolish the institution of ◊slavery and to emancipate slaves.

Aboriginal art art of the Australian Aborigines. Traditionally this was largely religious and directed toward portraying the stories of the Dreamtime. Perishable materials were used, such as in bark painting and carved trees and logs, and apart from some sheltered cave paintings and rock engravings few early works survive. Abstract patterns and stylized figures predominate.

aborigine (Latin *ab origine* "from the beginning") any indigenous inhabitant of a region or country. The word often refers to the original peoples of areas colonized by Europeans, and especially to ◊Australian Aborigines.

abortion ending of a pregnancy before the fetus is developed sufficiently to survive outside the uterus. Loss of a fetus at a later gestational age is termed premature stillbirth. Abortion may be accidental (miscarriage) or deliberate (termination of pregnancy).

In 1989 an antiprogesterone pill was introduced in France, under the name RU 486. Within 24 hours of ingestion, it leads to the expulsion of the fetus from the uterus, and can be used at an earlier stage in pregnancy. The pill is also an effective contraceptive when taken up to 72 hours after intercourse.

Abortion as a means of birth control has long been the subject of controversy. The argument centers largely upon whether a woman should legally be permitted to have an abortion, and that being so, under what circumstances. Another aspect is whether, and to what extent, the law should protect the fetus. Those who oppose abortion generally believe that human life begins at the moment of conception, when a sperm fertilizes an egg. This is the view held, for example, by the Roman Catholic Church. Those who support unrestricted legal abortion may believe in a woman's right to choose whether she wants a child, and may take into account the large numbers of deaths and injuries from back-street abortions that are thus avoided. Others approve abortion for specific reasons. For example, if a woman's life or health is jeopardized, abortion may be recommended; and if there is a strong likelihood that the child will be born with severe mental or physical handicap. Other grounds for abortion include preg-

Aboriginal art
Aboriginal rock
painting.

nancy resulting from sexual assault such as rape or incest. In the US in 1989, a Supreme Court decision gave state legislatures the right to introduce some restrictions on the unconditional right, established by the Supreme Court in an earlier decision (*Roe* v *Wade*), for any woman to decide to have an abortion.

Abraham *c.* 2300 BC. In the Old Testament, founder of the Jewish nation. In his early life he was called Abram. God promised him heirs and land for his people in Canaan (Israel), renamed him Abraham ("father of many nations"), and tested his faith by a command (later retracted) to sacrifice his son Isaac.

Abraham, Plains of plateau near Québec, Canada, where the British commander ◊Wolfe defeated the French under ◊Montcalm, Sept 13, 1759, during the French and Indian War (1754–63). The outcome of the battle established British supremacy in Canada.

Abrams v US US Supreme Court decision 1919 dealing with First Amendment rights in instances of sedition or espionage. Abrams, convicted of publishing pamphlets criticizing the US role in World War I and encouraging resistance to the war, appealed to the Supreme Court for protection under the right to free speech. The Court upheld the 1918 Sedition Law, ruling that Congress had the right to restrict speech that had a "tendency" toward harmful results. A famous dissent was filed by Justices Holmes and Brandeis.

abrasive substance used for cutting and polishing or for removing small amounts of the surface of hard materials. There are two types: natural and artificial abrasives, and their hardness is measured using the Mohs' scale. Natural abrasives include quartz, sandstone, pumice, diamond, and corundum; artificial abrasives include rouge, whiting, and carborundum.

Abruzzi mountainous region of S central Italy, comprising the provinces of L'Aquila, Chieti, Pescara, and Teramo; area 4,169 sq mi/10,800 sq km; population (1990) 1,272,000; capital L'Aquila. Gran Sasso d'Italia,

9,564 ft/2,914 m, is the highest point of the ◊Apennines.

Absalom in the Old Testament, the favorite son of King David; when defeated in a revolt against his father he fled on a mule, but caught his hair in a tree branch and was killed by Joab, one of David's officers.

absolute zero lowest temperature theoretically possible, zero degrees Kelvin (0K), equivalent to −459.67°F/−273.15°C, at which molecules are motionless. Although the third law of ◊thermodynamics indicates the impossibility of reaching absolute zero exactly, a temperature of 2×10^{-9}K (two billionths of a degree above absolute zero) was produced 1989 by Finnish scientists. Near absolute zero, the physical properties of some materials change substantially (see ◊cryogenics); for example, some metals lose their electrical resistance and become superconductive.

absolutism or *absolute monarchy* system of government in which the ruler or rulers have unlimited power. The principle of an absolute monarch, given a right to rule by God (see ◊divine right of kings), was extensively used in Europe during the 17th and 18th centuries. Absolute monarchy is contrasted with limited or constitutional monarchy, in which the sovereign's powers are defined or limited.

absorption in science, the taking up of one substance by another, such as a liquid by a solid (ink by blotting paper) or a gas by a liquid (ammonia by water). In biology, absorption describes the passing of nutrients or medication into and through tissues such as intestinal walls and blood vessels. In physics, absorption is the phenomenon by which a substance retains radiation of particular wavelengths; for example, a piece of blue glass absorbs all visible light except the wavelengths in the blue part of the spectrum; it also refers to the partial loss of energy resulting from light and other electromagnetic waves passing through a medium. In nuclear physics, absorption is the capture by elements, such as boron, of neutrons produced by fission in a reactor.

abstract art nonrepresentational art. Ornamental art without figurative representation occurs in most cultures. The modern abstract movement in sculpture and painting emerged in Europe and North America between 1910 and 1920. Two approaches produce different abstract styles: images that have been "abstracted" from nature to the point where they no longer reflect a conventional reality and nonobjective, or "pure," art forms, supposedly without reference to reality.

Abstract Expressionism US movement in abstract art that emphasized the act of painting, the expression inherent in paint itself, and the interaction of artist, paint, and canvas. Abstract Expressionism emerged in New York in the early 1940s. Arshile Gorky, Franz Kline, Jackson Pollock, and Mark Rothko are associated with the movement.

Absurd, Theatre of the avant-garde drama originating with a group of playwrights in the 1950s, including Beckett, Ionesco, Genet, and Pinter. Their work expressed the belief that in a godless universe human existence has no meaning or purpose and therefore all communication breaks down. Logical construction and argument gives way to irrational and illogical speech and to its ultimate conclusion, silence, as in Beckett's play *Breath* 1970.

Abu Bakr or *Abu-Bekr* 573–634. "Father of the virgin," name used by Abd-el-Ka'aba from about 618 when the prophet Mohammed married his daughter Ayesha. He was a close adviser to Mohammed in the period 622–32. On the prophet's death, he became the first ◊caliph, adding Mesopotamia to the Muslim world and instigating expansion into Iraq and Syria.

Abu Dhabi sheikdom in SW Asia, on the Persian Gulf, capital of the ◊United Arab Emirates; area 26,000 sq mi/67,350 sq km; population (1982 est) 516,000. Formerly under British protection, it has been ruled since 1971 by Sheik Sultan Zayed bin al-Nahayan, who is also president of the Supreme Council of Rulers of the United Arab Emirates.

Abu Simbel former site of two ancient temples cut into the rock on the banks of the Nile in S Egypt during the reign of Ramses II, commemorating him and his wife Nefertari. The temples were moved, in sections, 1966–67 before the site was flooded by the Aswan High Dam.

abyssal plain broad expanse of sea floor lying 2–4 mi/3–6 km below sea level. Abyssal plains are found in all the major oceans, and they extend from bordering continental rises to mid-oceanic ridges.

abyssal zone dark ocean region 6,500–19,500 ft/2,000–6,000 m deep; temperature 39°F/4°C. Three-quarters of the area of the deep ocean floor lies in the abyssal zone, which is too far from the surface for photosynthesis to take place. Some fish and crustaceans living there are blind or have their own light sources. The region above is the bathyal zone; the region below, the hadal zone.

Abyssinia former name of ◊Ethiopia.

abzyme in biotechnology, an artificially created antibody that can be used like an enzyme to accelerate reactions.

AC in physics, abbreviation for ◊*alternating current*.

acacia any of a large group of shrubs and trees of the genus *Acacia* of the legume family Leguminosae. Acacias include the thorn trees of the African savanna and the gum arabic tree *A. senegal* of N Africa, and several North American species of the SW US and Mexico. Acacias are found in warm regions of the world, particularly Australia.

Academy Award annual award in many categories, given since 1927 by the American Academy of Motion Picture Arts and Sciences (founded by Louis B Mayer of Metro-Goldwyn-Mayer 1927). Arguably the film community's most prestigious accolade, the award is a gold-plated statuette, which has been nicknamed "Oscar" since 1931.

Academy, French or *Académie Française* literary society concerned with maintaining the purity of the French language, founded by ◊Richelieu 1635. Membership is limited to 40 "Immortals" at a time.

acanthus any herbaceous plant of the genus *Acanthus* with handsome lobed leaves. Twenty species are found in the Mediterranean region and Old World

---

Academy Awards: recent winners

1983   Best Picture: *Terms of Endearment*; Best Director: James L Brooks *Terms of Endearment*; Best Actor: Robert Duvall *Tender Mercies*; Best Actress: Shirley MacLaine *Terms of Endearment*

1984   Best Picture: *Amadeus*; Best Director: Milos Forman *Amadeus*; Best Actor: F Murray Abraham *Amadeus*; Best Actress: Sally Field *Places in the Heart*

1985   Best Picture: *Out of Africa*; Best Director: Sidney Pollack *Out of Africa*; Best Actor: William Hurt *Kiss of the Spider Woman*; Best Actress: Geraldine Page *The Trip to Bountiful*

1986   Best Picture: *Platoon*; Best Director: Oliver Stone *Platoon*; Best Actor: Paul Newman *The Color of Money*; Best Actress: Marlee Matlin *Children of a Lesser God*

1987   Best Picture: *The Last Emperor*; Best Director: Bernardo Bertolucci *The Last Emperor*; Best Actor: Michael Douglas *Wall Street*; Best Actress: Cher *Moonstruck*

1988   Best Picture: *Rain Man*; Best Director: Barry Levinson *Rain Man*; Best Actor: Dustin Hoffman *Rain Man*; Best Actress: Jodie Foster *The Accused*

1989   Best Picture: *Driving Miss Daisy*; Best Director: Oliver Stone *Born on the Fourth of July*; Best Actor: Daniel Day-Lewis *My Left Foot*; Best Actress: Jessica Tandy *Driving Miss Daisy*

1990   Best Picture: *Dances with Wolves*; Best Director: Kevin Costner *Dances with Wolves*; Best Actor: Jeremy Irons *Reversal of Fortune*; Best Actress: Kathy Bates *Misery*

1991   Best Picture: *The Silence of the Lambs*; Best Director: Jonathan Demme *The Silence of the Lambs*; Best Actor: Anthony Hopkins *The Silence of the Lambs*; Best Actress: Jodie Foster *The Silence of the Lambs*

1992   Best Picture: *Unforgiven*; Best Director: Clint Eastwood *Unforgiven*; Best Actor: Al Pacino *Scent of a Woman*; Best Actress: Emma Thompson *Howards End*

tropics, including bear's breech *A. mollis*, whose leaves were used as a motif in Classical architecture, especially on Corinthian columns.

a cappella (Italian "in the style of the chapel") choral music sung without instrumental accompaniment. It is characteristic of ◊gospel music, ◊doo-wop, and the evangelical Christian church movement.

Acapulco or *Acapulco de Juarez* port and holiday resort in S Mexico; population (1990) 592,200. There is deep-sea fishing, and tropical products are exported. Acapulco was founded 1550 and was Mexico's major Pacific coast port until about 1815. Sometimes called the Riviera of Mexico, it attracts many tourists to its beaches, luxury hotels, and gambling casinos.

acceleration rate of change of the velocity of a moving body. It is usually measured in feet per second per second (ft s^{-2}) or meters per second per second (m s^{-2}). Because velocity is a ◊vector quantity (possessing both magnitude and direction) a body traveling at constant speed may be said to be accelerating if its direction of motion changes. According to Newton's second law of motion, a body will accelerate only if it is acted upon by an unbalanced, or resultant, ◊force.

Acceleration due to gravity is the acceleration of a body falling freely under the influence of the Earth's gravitational field; it varies slightly at different latitudes and altitudes. The value adopted internationally for gravitational acceleration is 32.174 ft s^{-2}/9.806 m s^{-2}.

accelerator in physics, a device to bring charged particles (such as protons and electrons) up to high speeds and energies, at which they can be of use in industry, medicine, and pure physics. At low energies, accelerated particles can be used to produce the image on a television screen and generate X-rays (by means of a ◊cathode-ray tube), destroy tumor cells, or kill bacteria. When high-energy particles collide with other particles, the fragments formed reveal the nature of the fundamental forces of nature.

accent way of speaking that identifies a person with a particular country, region, language, social class, or some mixture of these.

acclimation or *acclimatization* the physiological changes induced in an organism by exposure to new environmental conditions. When humans move to higher altitudes, for example, the number of red blood cells rises to increase the oxygen-carrying capacity of the blood in order to compensate for the lower levels of oxygen in the air.

accordion musical instrument of the reed organ type comprising left and right wind chests connected by flexible bellows. The right hand plays melody on a piano-style keyboard while the left hand has a system of push buttons for selecting single notes or chord harmonies.

accounting the principles and practice of systematically recording, presenting, and interpreting financial accounts; financial record keeping and management of businesses and other organizations, from balance sheets to policy decisions, for tax or operating purposes. Forms of inflation accounting, such as CCA (current cost accounting) and CPP (current purchasing power) are aimed at providing valid financial comparisons over a period in which money values change.

In the 20th century, especially in the US, the role of accounting has expanded into the realm of decision making, traditionally reserved to the economist. The accountant's role had been one of recording economic events for the purposes of stewardship. The increasing complexity of business organizations has led accountants into the areas of providing information to decision makers and even to prediction and analysis, both historically the function of economists.

accusative in the grammar of some inflected languages, such as Latin, Greek, and Russian, the accusative case is the form of a noun, pronoun, or adjective used when it is the direct object of a verb. The accusative is also used for the object of certain prepositions.

Acer genus of trees and shrubs of the temperate regions of the northern hemisphere with over 115 species, many of them popular garden specimens in Australia. *Acer* includes ◊sycamore and ◊maple.

acetaldehyde common name for ethanal.

acetate common name for ethanoate.

acetic acid common name for ◊ethanoic acid.

acetone common name for ◊propanone.

acetylene common name for ◊ethyne.

Achaea in ancient Greece, an area of the N Peloponnese. The *Achaeans* were the predominant society during the ◊Mycenaean period and are said by Homer to have taken part in the siege of Troy.

Achaean League union in 275 BC of most of the cities of the N Peloponnese, which managed to defeat ◊Sparta, but was itself defeated by the Romans 146 BC.

Achaemenid dynasty family ruling the Persian Empire 550–330 BC, and named after Achaemenes, ancestor of Cyrus the Great, founder of the empire. His successors included Cambyses, Darius I, Xerxes, and Darius III, who, as the last Achaemenid ruler, was killed after defeat in battle against Alexander the Great 330 BC.

Achebe Chinua 1930– . Nigerian novelist whose themes include the social and political impact of European colonialism on African people, and the problems of newly independent African nations. His novels include the widely acclaimed *Things Fall Apart* 1958 and *Anthills of the Savannah* 1987.

achene dry, one-seeded ◊fruit that develops from a single ◊ovary and does not split open to disperse the seed. Achenes commonly occur in groups—for example, the fruiting heads of buttercup *Ranunculus* and clematis. The outer surface may be smooth, spiny, ribbed, or tuberculate, depending on the species.

Acheson Dean (Gooderham) 1893–1971. US politician. As undersecretary of state 1945–47 in ◊Truman's Democratic administration, he was associated with George C Marshall in preparing the ◊Marshall Plan, and succeeded him as secretary of state 1949–53. Acheson's foreign policy was widely criticized by Republican members of Congress, especially Senator ◊McCarthy, for an alleged weak response to Communist advances in SE Asia, especially after the outbreak of the Korean War. He advocated containment of the Soviet Union. He survived a vote calling for his resignation, but left the State Department in 1952 following the election of ◊Eisenhower. His books include *Power and Diplomacy* 1958 and *Present at the Creation* 1969, which won the Pulitzer prize for history.

Achilles Greek hero of Homer's *Iliad*. He was the son of Peleus, king of the Myrmidons in Thessaly, and of the sea nymph Thetis, who rendered him invulnerable, except for the heel by which she held him, by dipping him in the river Styx. Achilles killed ◊Hector at the climax of the *Iliad*, and according to subsequent Greek

acid rain

As industry has expanded since the industrial revolution, the quantity of waste gases and smoke given off by factories has increased enormously. As a result more and more chemical pollutants are being added to the atmosphere. Fossil fuels, such as coal, oil, and gas, contain sulfur which is given off when they are burned. The chemicals produced can alter the acidity of the rain and cause severe damage to plant life, lakes, and the water supply.

A tree is damaged in a number of ways. The bark and leaves are damaged by the direct effects. The change in pH of the ground water makes the roots less effective. Fewer nutrients pass up into the tree, making it more susceptible to damage. Leaves and needles fall off and the crowns thin and die.

Sulfur dioxide (SO_2) and nitrogen oxides are given off with the smoke when fossil fuels burn.

H_2SO_4

HNO_3

SO_2

NO_2

Some of the gases go directly into plants and into the ground, but most are oxidized to sulfuric acid (H_2SO_4) and nitric acid (HNO_3). These acids, dissolved in rainwater, rain down often a great distance away.

Direct effects of chemicals in the atmosphere are felt within a few miles of the emission. These include the deterioration of buildings and harm to human health.

Indirect effects, due to chemical changes in the ground water, can be felt thousands of miles away.

Sometimes lime is dropped into an acid lake to neutralize it, but this is only a temporary measure.

Acidity is measured in pH. The lower the pH value the higher the acidity. In a lake (or river) affected by acid rain, different creatures die at different pH values.

death in lakes and rivers

1. Crustaceans and snails die
2. Salmon and trout die
3. Sensitive insects die
4. Whitefish and grayling die
5. Perch and pike die
6. Eel die

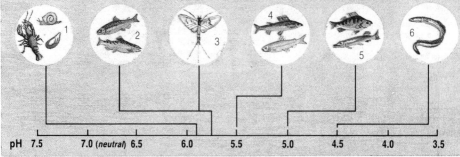

| pH | 7.5 | 7.0 (neutral) | 6.5 | 6.0 | 5.5 | 5.0 | 4.5 | 4.0 | 3.5 |

legends was himself killed by Paris, who shot a poisoned arrow into Achilles' heel.

Achilles tendon tendon pinning the calf muscle to the heel bone. It is one of the largest in the human body.

achromatic lens combination of lenses made from materials of different refractive indexes, constructed in such a way as to minimize chromatic aberration (which in a single lens causes colored fringes around images because the lens diffracts the different wavelengths in white light to slightly different extents).

acid compound that, in solution in an ionizing solvent (usually water), gives rise to hydrogen ions (H⁺ or protons). In modern chemistry, acids are defined as substances that are proton donors and accept electrons to form ◊ionic bonds. Acids react with ◊bases to form salts, and they act as solvents. Strong acids are corrosive; dilute acids have a sour or sharp taste, although in some organic acids this may be partially masked by other flavor characteristics.

acid rain acidic rainfall, thought to be caused principally by the release into the atmosphere of sulfur dioxide (SO_2) and oxides of nitrogen. Sulfur dioxide is formed by the burning of fossil fuels, such as coal, that contain high quantities of sulfur; nitrogen oxides are contributed from various industrial activities and from automobile exhaust fumes.

aclinic line the magnetic equator, an imaginary line near the equator, where the compass needle balances horizontally, the attraction of the north and south magnetic poles being equal.

acne skin eruption, mainly occurring among adolescents and young adults, caused by inflammation of the sebaceous glands which secrete an oily substance (sebum), the natural lubricant of the skin. Sometimes the openings of the glands become blocked and they swell; the contents decompose and pimples form on the face, back, and chest.

Aconcagua extinct volcano in the Argentine Andes; the highest peak in the Americas, 22,834 ft/6,960 m. It was first climbed by Edward Fitzgerald's expedition 1897.

acoustic ohm unit of acoustic impedance (the ratio of the sound pressure on a surface to the sound flux through the surface). It is analogous to the ohm as the unit of electrical impedance.

acoustics in general, the experimental and theoretical science of sound and its transmission; in particular, that branch of the science that has to do with the phenomena of sound in a particular space such as a room or theater.

acquired immune deficiency syndrome full name for the disease ◊AIDS.

acquittal in law, the setting free of someone charged with a crime after a trial.

It follows a verdict of "not guilty" and prevents retrial of a defendant on the same charges under the US Constitution.

acre traditional English land measure equal to 4,840 square yards (4,047 sq m/0.405 ha). Originally meaning a field, it was the size that a yoke of oxen could plow in a day.

Acre or *'Akko* seaport in Israel; population (1983) 37,000. Taken by the Crusaders 1104, it was captured by Saladin 1187 and retaken by Richard I (the Lionheart) 1191. Napoleon failed in a siege 1799. British field marshal Allenby captured the port 1918. From being part of British-mandated Palestine, it became part of Israel 1948.

acronym word formed from the initial letters and/or syllables of other words, intended as a pronounceable abbreviation; for example, NATO (*N*orth *A*tlantic *T*reaty *O*rganization) and radar (*ra*dio *d*etecting *a*nd *r*anging).

acropolis (Greek "high city") citadel of an ancient Greek town. The Acropolis of Athens contains the ruins of the Parthenon and surrounding complexes, built there during the days of the Athenian empire. The term is also used for analogous structures, as in the massive granite-built ruins of Great ◊Zimbabwe.

acrostic (Greek "at the extremity of a line or row") a number of lines of writing, usually verse, whose initial letters (read downward) form a word, phrase, or sentence. A *single acrostic* is formed by the initial letters of lines only; a *double acrostic* is formed by the first and last letters.

acrylic acid common name for propenoic acid.

acrylic fiber synthetic fiber often used as a substitute for wool. It was first developed 1947 but not produced in great volumes until the 1950s. Strong and warm, acrylic fiber is often used for casual and athletic wear, and as linings for boots and gloves.

actinide any of a series of 15 radioactive metallic chemical elements with atomic numbers 89 (actinium) to 103 (lawrencium). Elements 89 to 95 occur in nature; the rest of the series are synthesized elements only. Actinides are grouped together because of their chemical similarities (for example, they are all bivalent), the properties differing only slightly with atomic number. The series is set out in a band in the ◊periodic table of the elements, as are the ◊lanthanides.

actinium (Greek *aktis* "ray") white, radioactive, metallic element, the first of the actinide series, symbol Ac, atomic number 89, atomic weight 227; it is a weak emitter of high-energy alpha particles. Actinium occurs with uranium and radium in ◊pitchblende and other ores, and can be synthesized by bombarding radium with neutrons. The longest-lived isotope, Ac-227, has a half-life of 21.8 years (all the other isotopes have very short half-lives). Actinium was discovered in 1899 by the French chemist André Debierne.

action and reaction in physical mechanics, equal and opposite effects produced by a force acting on an object. For example, the pressure of expanding gases from the burning of fuel in a rocket engine (a force) produces an equal and opposite reaction, which causes the rocket to move.

action painting or *gesture painting* in US art, a dynamic school of Abstract Expressionism. It emphasized the importance of the physical act of painting, sometimes expressed with both inventiveness and aggression, and on occasion performed for the camera. Jackson ◊Pollock was the leading exponent.

Actium, Battle of naval battle in which Octavian defeated the combined fleets of ◊Mark Antony and ◊Cleopatra 31 BC to become the undisputed ruler of the Roman world (as the emperor ◊Augustus). The site is at Akri, a promontory in W Greece.

activity in physics, the number of particles emitted in one second by a radioactive source. The term is used to describe the radioactivity or the potential danger of that source. The unit of activity is the becquerel (Bq), named after the French physicist Antoine Henri Becquerel.

act of Congress in the US, a bill or resolution passed by both houses of Congress (the Senate and the House of Representatives), which becomes law with the signature of the president. If vetoed by the presi-

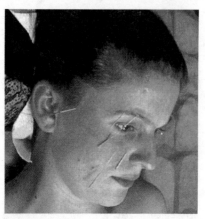

acupuncture A patient being treated for persistent headaches by acupuncture.

dent, it may still become law if it returns to Congress again and is passed by a majority of two-thirds in each house.

act of God legal term meaning some sudden and irresistible act of nature that could not reasonably have been foreseen or prevented, such as floods, storms, earthquakes, or sudden death.

Actors Studio theater workshop in New York City, established 1947 by Cheryl Crawford and Elia Kazan. Under Lee Strasberg, who became artistic director 1948, it became known for the study of Konstantin Stanislavsky's ◊Method acting.

actuary mathematician who makes statistical calculations concerning human life expectancy and other risks, on which insurance premiums are based.

The professional body in the US is the Society of Actuaries, formed 1949 by a merger of two earlier bodies.

acupuncture system of inserting long, thin metal needles into the body at predetermined points to relieve pain, as an anesthetic in surgery, and to assist healing. The needles are rotated manually or electrically. The method, developed in ancient China and increasingly popular in the West, is thought to work by somehow stimulating the brain's own painkillers, the ◊endorphins.

acute angle an angle between 0° and 90°; that is, an amount of turn that is less than a quarter of a circle.

AD in the Christian calendar, abbreviation for *Anno Domini* (Latin "in the year of the Lord"); used with dates.

ADA high-level computer-programming language, developed and owned by the US Department of Defense, designed for use in situations in which a computer directly controls a process or machine, such as a military aircraft. The language took more than five years to specify, and became commercially available only in the late 1980s. It is named after English mathematician Ada Augusta ◊Byron.

Adam (Hebrew *adham* "man") in the Old Testament, founder of the human race. Formed by God from dust and given the breath of life, Adam was placed in the Garden of Eden, where ◊Eve was created from his rib and given to him as a companion. Because she tempted him, he tasted the forbidden fruit of the Tree of Knowledge of Good and Evil, for which trespass they were expelled from the Garden.

Adams Abigail Smith 1744–1818. First lady to US president John Adams and public figure. She married

lawyer John Adams of Boston 1764; one of their children, John Quincy Adams, would become the sixth US president. A strong supporter of the cause of American independence, she joined her husband on diplomatic missions to Paris and London after the Revolutionary War. As wife of the US vice president 1789–97 and later president 1797–1801, she was widely respected.

Adams Ansel 1902–1984. US photographer known for his printed images of dramatic landscapes and organic forms of the American West. He was associated with the zone system of exposure estimation.

In 1916 Adams made his first trip to Yosemite National Park, and for the rest of his life the High Sierras were a major focus of his work. Although he first became a professional musician, in the late 1920s he turned to professional photography. Light and texture were important elements in his photographs. Adams worked to establish photography as a fine art. He founded the first museum collection of photography, at New York City's Museum of Modern Art 1937. His love of nature also carried over into his work as a conservationist and director of the Sierra Club from 1936.

Adams Charles Francis 1807–1886. US political leader, journalist, and diplomat. Adams was born in Boston, the son of John Quincy Adams. After graduation from Harvard, he studied law with Daniel Webster. As a respected historian and abolitionist, he established the *Boston Whig* and accepted the vice-presidential nomination of the Free Soil party 1848. He later joined the Republican party. After service in the US House of Representatives 1858–61, he was appointed US minister to England by Lincoln. He unsuccessfully sought the 1872 Republican nomination for president.

Adams John 1735–1826. 2nd president of the US 1797–1801, and vice president 1789–97. He was a member of the Continental Congress 1774–78 and signed the Declaration of Independence. In 1779 he went to France and negotiated the treaty of 1783 that ended the American Revolution. In 1785 he became the first US ambassador in London.

He was born in Quincy, Massachusetts.

Adams John Couch 1819–1892. English astronomer who mathematically deduced the existence of the planet Neptune 1845 from the effects of its gravitational pull on the motion of Uranus, although it was not found until 1846 by J G Galle. Adams also studied the Moon's motion, the Leonid meteors, and terrestrial magnetism.

Adams John Quincy 1767–1848. 6th president of the US 1825–29. Eldest son of President John Adams, he was born in Quincy, Massachusetts, and became US minister in The Hague, Berlin, St Petersburg, and London. He negotiated the Treaty of Ghent and the ◊War of 1812 (fought between Britain and the US) on generous terms for the US. In 1817 he became ◊Monroe's secretary of state, formulated the ◊Monroe Doctrine 1823, and was elected president by the House of Representatives, despite receiving fewer votes than his main rival, Andrew ◊Jackson. As president, Adams was an advocate of strong federal government.

Adams Richard 1920– . English novelist. A civil servant 1948–72, he wrote *Watership Down* 1972, a tale of a rabbit community, which is read by adults and children. Later novels include *Shardik* 1974, *The Plague Dogs* 1977, and *Girl on a Swing* 1980.

Adams Samuel 1722–1803. US politician, second cousin of President John Adams. He was the chief instigator of the Boston Tea Party (see ◊American Revolution). He was also a signatory to the Declaration of Independence, served in the ◊Continental Congress, and anticipated the French emperor Napoleon in calling the British a "nation of shopkeepers."

adaptation in biology, any change in the structure or function of an organism that allows it to survive and reproduce more effectively in its environment. In ◊evolution, adaptation is thought to occur as a result of random variation in the genetic makeup of organisms (produced by ◊mutation and ◊recombination) coupled with ◊natural selection.

adaptive radiation in evolution, the formation of several species, with ◊adaptations to different ways of life, from a single ancestral type. Adaptive radiation is likely to occur whenever members of a species migrate to a new habitat with unoccupied ecological niches. It is thought that the lack of competition in such niches allows sections of the migrant population to develop new adaptations, and eventually to become new species.

The colonization of newly formed volcanic islands has led to the development of many unique species. The 13 species of Darwin's finch on the Galápagos Islands, for example, are probably descended from a single species from the South American mainland. The parent stock evolved into different species that now occupy a range of diverse niches.

Addams Charles 1912–1988. US cartoonist, creator of the ghoulish family featured in the *New Yorker* magazine. A successful television comedy series in the 1960s and two feature-length films in the 1990s were based on the cartoon.

Addams Jane 1860–1935. US social reformer and feminist, who in 1889 cofounded and led Hull House, a settlement house in the slums of Chicago. It was one of the earliest community centers and served as a model for others throughout the US. Innovative services such as day care were provided. She was vice president of the National American Women Suffrage Association 1911–14, led the Woman's Peace Party and the first

Adams John Quincy Adams, 6th president of the USA, painted by Chapel.

Women's Peace Congress 1915, and was president of the Women's International League for Peace and Freedom 1919. She was a US leader in attempts to reform child-labor laws.

addax light-colored ◊antelope *Addax nasomaculatus* of the family Bovidae. It lives in the Sahara desert where it exists on scanty vegetation without drinking. It is about 3.5 ft/1.1 m at the shoulder, and both sexes have spirally twisted horns.

adder European venomous snake, the common ◊viper *Vipera berus*. Growing to about 24 in/60 cm in length, it has a thick body, triangular head, a characteristic V-shaped mark on its head and, often, zigzag markings along the back. It feeds on small mammals and lizards. The puff adder *Bitis arietans* is a large, yellowish, thick-bodied viper up to 5 ft/1.6 m long, living in Africa and Arabia.

addiction state of dependence on drugs, alcohol, or other substances. Symptoms include uncontrolled craving, tolerance, and symptoms of withdrawal when access is denied. Habitual use produces changes in chemical processes in the brain; when the substance is withheld, severe neurological manifestations, even death, may follow. These are reversed by the administration of the addictive substance, and mitigated by a gradual reduction in dosage.

Addis Ababa or *Adis Abeba* capital of Ethiopia; population (1984) 1,413,000. It was founded 1887 by Menelik, chief of Shoa, who ascended the throne of Ethiopia 1889. His former residence, Menelik Palace, is now occupied by the government.

Addison Joseph 1672–1719. English writer. In 1704 he celebrated ◊Marlborough's victory at Blenheim in a poem, "The Campaign," and subsequently held political appointments, including undersecretary of state and secretary to the Lord-Lieutenant of Ireland 1708. In 1709 he contributed to the *Tatler* magazine, begun by Richard ◊Steele, with whom he was cofounder 1711 of the *Spectator*.

Addison's disease rare deficiency or failure of the ◊adrenal glands to produce corticosteroid hormones; it is treated with hormones. The condition, formerly fatal, is characterized by anemia, weakness, low blood pressure, and brownish pigmentation of the skin.

additive in food, any natural or artificial chemical added to prolong the shelf life of processed foods (salt or nitrates), alter the color or flavor of food, or improve its food value (vitamins or minerals). Many chemical additives are used and they are subject to regulation, since individuals may be affected by constant exposure even to traces of certain additives and may suffer side effects ranging from headaches and ◊hyperactivity to cancer.

They must be listed on labels of foods sold in the US so consumers may be aware of those they cannot tolerate. The natural food movement has grown enormously in the 1970s and 1980s, as increasing awareness of the dangers of additives sent consumers looking for additive-free foods.

Artificial sweeteners are used in a range of products for diabetics and for weight loss or weight control. *Nutrients* may be added to replace or enhance food value. Minerals and vitamins are the most common, especially where the diet would otherwise be deficient, leading to diseases such as beriberi and pellagra. *Preservatives* are primarily antioxidants and antimicrobials that control natural oxidation and the action of microorganisms. See ◊food technology. *Emulsifiers* and *surfactants* regulate the consistency of fats in prepared food and on the surface of the food in contact with the air. *Thickeners*, primarily vegetable gums, regulate the consistency of food. Pectin acts in this way on fruit products. *Leavening agents* lighten the texture of baked goods without the use of yeasts. Sodium bicarbonate is an example. *Acidulants* sharpen the taste of foods but may also perform a buffering function in the control of acidity. *Bleaching agents* assist in the aging of flours. *Anticaking agents* prevent powdered products coagulating into solid lumps. *Humectants* control the humidity of the product by absorbing and retaining moisture. *Clarifying agents* are used in fruit juices, vinegars, and other fermented liquids. Gelatin is the most common. *Firming agents* restore the texture of vegetables that may be damaged during processing. *Foam regulators* are used in beer to provide a controlled "head" on top of the poured product.

Adelaide capital and industrial city of South Australia; population (1990) 1,049,100. Industries include oil refining, shipbuilding, and the manufacture of electrical goods and automobiles. Grain, wool, fruit, and wine are exported. Founded 1836, Adelaide was named after William IV's queen.

Aden (Arabic *'Adan*) main port and commercial center of Yemen, on a rocky peninsula at the SW corner of Arabia, commanding the entrance to the Red Sea; population (1984) 318,000. The city's economy is based on oil refining, fishing, and shipping. A British territory from 1839, Aden became part of independent South Yemen 1967; it was the capital of South Yemen until 1990.

history After annexation by Britain, Aden and its immediately surrounding area (47 sq mi/121 sq km) were developed as a ship-refueling station following the opening of the Suez Canal 1869. It was a colony 1937–63 and then, after a period of transitional violence among rival nationalist groups and British forces, was combined with the former Aden protectorate (112,000 sq mi/290,000 sq km) to create the Southern Yemen People's Republic 1967, which was renamed the People's Democratic Republic of Yemen 1970–90.

Adenauer Konrad 1876–1967. German Christian Democrat politician, chancellor of West Germany 1949–63. With the French president de Gaulle he achieved the postwar reconciliation of France and Germany and strongly supported all measures designed to strengthen the Western bloc in Europe.

adenoids masses of lymphoid tissue, similar to ◊tonsils, located in the upper part of the throat, behind the nose. They are part of a child's natural defenses against the entry of germs but usually shrink and disappear by the age of ten.

adhesive substance that sticks two surfaces together. Natural adhesives (glues) include gelatin in its crude industrial form (made from bones, hide fragments, and fish offal) and vegetable gums. Synthetic adhesives include thermoplastic and thermosetting resins, which are often stronger than the substances they join; mixtures of ◊epoxy resin and hardener that set by chemical reaction; and elastomeric (stretching) adhesives for flexible joints. Superglues are fast-setting adhesives used in very small quantities.

adipose tissue type of ◊connective tissue of vertebrates that serves as an energy reserve, and also pads some organs. It is commonly called fat tissue, and consists of large spherical cells filled with fat. In mammals, major layers are in the inner layer of skin and around the kidneys and heart.

Adirondacks mountainous area in NE New York, rising to 5,344 ft/1,629 m at Mount Marcy; the source of the Hudson and Ausable rivers; named after an Indian tribe. The Adirondacks area occupies about 25% of the state of New York, and a state park occupies more than 500 million acres/200 million hectares. Thickly wooded, the region is noted for scenery, health resorts such as Saranac Lake, and sports facilities such as those at Lake Placid, where the 1932 and 1980 winter Olympic Games were held.

adjective grammatical ◊part of speech for words that describe nouns (for example, *new* and *beautiful*, as in "a new hat" and "a beautiful day"). Adjectives generally have three degrees (grades or levels for the description of relationships): the positive degree (*new, beautiful*), the comparative degree (*newer, more beautiful*), and the superlative degree (*newest, most beautiful*).

Adler Alfred 1870–1937. Austrian psychologist. Adler saw the "will to power" as more influential in accounting for human behavior than the sexual drive theory. A dispute over this theory led to the dissolution of his ten-year collaboration with ◊Freud.

Adler Cyrus 1863–1940. US educator and public figure. In 1892 he was appointed curator at the Smithsonian Institution and later served as its librarian and assistant secretary. From 1908 until his death, he was president of Dropsie College and a leader of the American Jewish Committee. His appeal for protection of the rights of religious ethnic minorities was adopted in the final text of the Treaty of Versailles after World War I.

administrative law law concerning the powers and control of government agencies or those agencies granted statutory powers of administration.

admiral highest-ranking naval officer. In the US Navy, in descending order, the ranks of admiral are: fleet admiral, admiral, vice admiral, and rear admiral.

admiral any of several species of butterfly in the same family (Nymphalidae) as the tortoiseshells. The red admiral *Vanessa atalanta*, wingspan 2.5 in/6 cm, is found worldwide in the northern hemisphere. It migrates south each year from northern areas to subtropical zones.

adobe in architecture, building with earth bricks. The formation of earth bricks ("adobe") and the construction of walls by enclosing earth within molds (*pisé de terre*) are the two principal methods of earth building. The techniques are commonly found in Spain, Latin America, and the SW US.

Adonis in Greek mythology, a beautiful youth loved by the goddess ◊Aphrodite. He was killed while boar-hunting but was allowed to return from the underworld for six months every year to rejoin her. The anemone sprang from his blood.

adoption permanent legal transfer of parental rights and duties in respect of a child from one person to another.

State laws determine processes for adoption, rights of adoptees (such as access to information about natural parents), and inheritance rights.

adrenal gland or *suprarenal gland* gland situated on top of the kidney. The adrenals are soft and yellow, and consist of two parts: the cortex and medulla. The *cortex* (outer part) secretes various steroid hormones, controls salt and water metabolism, and regulates the use of carbohydrates, proteins, and fats. The *medulla* (inner part) secretes the hormones adrenaline and noradrenaline, which, during times of stress, cause the heart to beat faster and harder, increase blood flow to the heart and muscle cells, and dilate airways in the lungs, thereby delivering more oxygen to cells throughout the body and in general preparing the body for "fight or flight."

adrenaline or *epinephrine* hormone secreted by the medulla of the ◊adrenal glands.

Adrian IV (Nicholas Breakspear) *c.* 1100–1159. Pope 1154–59, the only British pope. He secured the execution of Arnold of Brescia, crowned Frederick I Barbarossa as German emperor, refused Henry II's request that Ireland should be granted to the English crown in absolute ownership, and was at the height of a quarrel with the emperor when he died.

Adriatic Sea large arm of the Mediterranean Sea, lying NW to SE between the Italian and the Balkan peninsulas. The western shore is Italian; the eastern is Croatian, Yugoslav, and Albanian. The sea is about 500 mi/805 km long, and its area is 52,220 sq mi/ 135,250 sq km.

adultery voluntary sexual intercourse between a married person and someone other than his or her legal partner.

Adventist person who believes that Christ will return to make a second appearance on the Earth. Expectation of the Second Coming of Christ is found in New Testament writings generally. Adventist views are held in particular by the ◊Seventh-Day Adventist church (with 1.5 million members in 200 countries), Christadelphians, the Jehovah's Witnesses, the Four Square Gospel Alliance, the Advent Christian church, and the Evangelical Adventist church.

adverb grammatical ◊part of speech for words that modify or describe verbs ("she ran *quickly*"), adjectives ("a *beautifully* clear day"), and adverbs ("they did it *really* well"). Most adverbs are formed from adjectives or past participles by adding -*ly* (*quick: quickly*) or -*ally* (*automatic: automatically*).

advertising any of various methods used by a company to increase the sales of its products or to promote a brand name.

advocate (Latin *advocatus*, one summoned to one's aid, especially in a court of law) professional pleader in a court of justice.

More common terms are attorney, ◊lawyer, or counsel, but advocate is retained in such countries as Scotland and France, whose legal systems are based on Roman law.

Aegean civilization the cultures of Bronze Age Greece, including the ◊*Minoan civilization* of Crete and the ◊*Mycenaean civilization* of the E Peloponnese.

Aegean Islands islands of the Aegean Sea, but more specifically a region of Greece comprising the Dodecanese islands, the Cyclades islands, Lesvos, Samos, and Chios; area 3,523 sq mi/9,122 sq km; population (1991) 460,800.

Aegean Sea branch of the Mediterranean between Greece and Turkey; the Dardanelles connect it with the Sea of Marmara. The numerous islands in the Aegean Sea include Crete, the Cyclades, the Sporades, and the Dodecanese. There is political tension between Greece and Turkey over sea limits claimed by Greece around such islands as Lesvos, Chios, Samos, and Kos.

Aelfric *c.* 955–1020. Anglo-Saxon writer and abbot, author of two collections of *Catholic Homilies* 990–92, sermons, and the *Lives of the Saints* 996–97, written in vernacular Old English prose.

Aeneas in Classical legend, a Trojan prince who became the ancestral hero of the Romans. According to ◊Homer, he was the son of Anchises and the goddess Aphrodite. During the Trojan War he owed his life to the frequent intervention of the gods. The legend on which Virgil's epic poem the *Aeneid* is based describes his escape from Troy and his eventual settlement in Latium, on the Italian peninsula.

Aeneid Latin narrative poem or epic by ◊Virgil in 12 books, composed in the traditional Homeric meter of hexameters. Written during the last 10 years of the poet's life (29–19 BC), it celebrates Roman imperial values in the role of its Trojan hero, ◊Aeneas, who is destined to found a new city in Italy. After the fall of ◊Troy, Aeneas wanders the Mediterranean with his companions until, landing in North Africa, he falls in love with Dido, Queen of Carthage. He later deserts her and establishes the Trojans in Latium, where the king of the Latini offers him his daughter, Lavinia, in marriage. He is opposed by Turnus, a rival suitor, but eventually kills the latter in singlehanded combat. The poem is indebted to many predecessors (Apollonius of Rhodes, and the Latin writers Ennius and ◊Lucretius) in addition to ◊Homer's *Odyssey* and *Iliad*.

Aeolian harp wind-blown instrument consisting of a shallow soundbox supporting gut strings at low tension and tuned to the same pitch. It produces an eerie harmony that rises and falls with the changing pressure of the wind. It was common in parts of central Europe during the 19th century.

aerial or *antenna* in radio and television broadcasting, a conducting device that radiates or receives electromagnetic waves. The design of an aerial depends principally on the wavelength of the signal. Long waves (hundreds of meters in wavelength) may employ long wire aerials; short waves (several centimeters in wavelength) may employ rods and dipoles; microwaves may also use dipoles—often with reflectors arranged like a toast rack—or highly directional parabolic dish aerials. Because microwaves travel in straight lines, giving line-of-sight communication, microwave aerials are usually located at the tops of tall masts or towers.

aerobics (Greek "air" and "life") exercises for cardiovascular fitness. A strenuous application of movement to raise the heart rate to 120 beats per minute or more for sessions of 5–20 minutes' duration, 3–5 times per week.

aerodynamics branch of fluid physics that studies the forces exerted by air or other gases in motion—for example, the airflow around bodies (such as land vehicles, bullets, rockets, and aircraft) moving at speed through the atmosphere. For maximum efficiency, the aim is usually to design the shape of an object to produce a streamlined flow, with a minimum of turbulence in the moving air.

aeronautics science of travel through the Earth's atmosphere, including aerodynamics, aircraft structures, jet and rocket propulsion, and aerial navigation.

aerosol particles of liquid or solid suspended in a gas. Fog is a common natural example. Aerosol cans contain a substance such as scent or cleaner packed under pressure with a device for releasing it as a fine spray. Most aerosols used chlorofluorocarbons (CFCs) as propellants until these were found to cause destruction of the ◊ozone layer in the stratosphere.

Aeschines lived 4th century BC. Orator of ancient Athens, a rival of ◊Demosthenes.

Aeschylus c. 525–c. 456 BC. Athenian dramatist, who developed Greek tragedy by introducing the second actor, thus enabling true dialogue and dramatic action to occur independently of the chorus. Ranked with ◊Euripides and ◊Sophocles as one of the three great tragedians, Aeschylus composed some 90 plays between 500 and 456 BC, of which seven complete tragedies survive in his name: *Persians* 472 BC, *Seven Against Thebes* 467 BC, *Suppliants* 463 BC, the *Oresteia* trilogy (*Agamemnon, Libation-Bearers,* and *Eumenides*) 458 BC, and *Prometheus Bound* (of uncertain date and authorship).

Aesir principal gods of Norse mythology—Odin, Thor, Balder, Loki, Freya, and Tyr—whose dwelling place was Asgard.

Aesop by tradition, a writer of Greek fables. According to the historian Herodotus, he lived in the mid-6th century BC and was a slave of a Samian. The fables, which are ascribed to him, were collected at a later date and are anecdotal stories using animal characters to illustrate moral or satirical points.

Aesthetic movement English artistic movement of the late 19th century, dedicated to the doctrine of "art for art's sake"—that is, art as self-sufficient, not needing to justify its existence by serving any particular use. Artists associated with the movement include Aubrey Beardsley and James Whistler. The writer Oscar Wilde was, in his twenties, an exemplary Aesthete.

Aetolia district of ancient Greece on the NW of the gulf of Corinth. The *Aetolian League* was a confederation of the cities of Aetolia, which, following the death of Alexander the Great, became the chief rival of Macedonian power and the Achaean League. In 189 BC the Aetolians were forced to accept a treaty as subject allies of Rome.

affidavit legal document, used in court applications and proceedings, in which a person swears that certain facts are true.

affirmative action government policy of positive discrimination that favors members of minority ethnic groups and women in such areas as employment and education, designed to counter the effects of long-term

---

Afghanistan
Republic of
(*Jamhuria Afghanistan*)

area 251,707 sq mi/652,090 sq km
capital Kabul
cities Kandahar, Herat, Mazar-i-Sharif
physical mountainous in center and NE, plains in N and SW
environment an estimated 95% of the urban population is without access to sanitation services
features Hindu Kush mountain range (Khyber and Salang passes, Wakhan salient and Panjshir Valley), Amu Darya (Oxus) River, Helmand River, Lake Saberi
head of state Burhanuddin Rabbani from 1992
head of government Gulbuddin Hekmatyar from 1993
political system emergent democracy
political parties Homeland Party (Hezb-i-Watan, formerly People's Democratic Party of Afghanistan, PDPA) Marxist-Leninist; Hezb-i-Islami and Jamiat-i-Islami, Islamic fundamentalist mujaheddin; National Liberation Front, moderate mujaheddin
exports dried fruit, natural gas, fresh fruits, carpets; small amounts of rare minerals, karakul lambskins, Afghan coats

currency afgháni
population (1992) 18,052,000 (more than 5 million became refugees after 1979); growth rate 0.6% p.a.
life expectancy (1986) men 43, women 41
languages Pushtu, Dari (Persian)
religion Muslim (80% Sunni, 20% Shi'ite)
literacy men 39%, women 8% (1985 est)
GNP $3.3 bn (1985); $275 per head
GDP $1.86 bn; $111 per head

chronology
1747 Afghanistan became an independent emirate.
1839–42 and 1878–80 Afghan Wars instigated by Britain to counter the threat to British India from expanding Russian influence in Afghanistan.
1919 Afghanistan recovered full independence following Third Afghan War.
1953 Lt-Gen Daud Khan became prime minister and introduced reform program.
1963 Daud Khan forced to resign and constitutional monarchy established.
1973 Monarchy overthrown in coup by Daud Khan.
1978 Daud Khan ousted by Taraki and the PDPA.
1979 Taraki replaced by Hafizullah Amin; USSR entered country to prop up government; it installed Babrak Karmal in power. Amin executed.
1986 Replacement of Karmal as leader by Dr Najibullah Ahmadzai. Partial Soviet troop withdrawal.
1988 New non-Marxist constitution adopted.
1989 Complete withdrawal of Soviet troops; state of emergency imposed in response to intensification of civil war.
1991 US and Soviet military aid withdrawn. Mujaheddin began talks with Russians and Kabul government.
1992 April: Najibullah government overthrown. June: after a succession of short-term presidents, Burhanuddin Rabbani named interim head of state; Islamic law introduced. Sept: Hezb-i-Islami barred from government participation after shell attacks on Kabul. Dec: Rabbani elected president for two-year term by constituent assembly.
1993 Jan: renewed bombardment of Kabul by Hezb-i- Islami and other rebel forces. Interim parliament appointed by constituent assembly. March: peace agreement signed between Rabbani and dissident mujaheddin leader Gulbuddin Hekmatyar, under which Hekmatyar became prime minister.

discrimination against them. In Europe, Sweden, Belgium, the Netherlands, and Italy actively promote affirmative action through legal and financial incentives.

affluent society society in which most people have money left over after satisfying their basic needs such as food and shelter. They are then able to decide how to spend their excess ("disposable") income, and become "consumers." The term was popularized by the US economist John Kenneth ◊Galbraith.

Afghan native to or an inhabitant of Afghanistan. The dominant group, particularly in Kabul, are the Pathans. The Tajiks, a smaller ethnic group, are predominantly traders and farmers in the province of Herat and around Kabul. The Hazaras, another farming group, are found in the southern mountain ranges of the Hindu Kush. The Uzbeks and Turkomen are farmers and speak Altaic-family languages. The smallest Altaic minority are the Kirghiz, who live in the Pamir. Baluchi nomads live in the south, and Nuristani farmers live in the mountains of the northeast.

Afghan hound breed of fast hunting dog resembling the ◊saluki, though more thickly coated, first introduced to the West by British army officers serving on India's North-West Frontier along the Afghanistan border in the late 19th century. The Afghan hound is about 28 in/70 cm tall and has a long, silky coat.

Afghanistan mountainous, landlocked country in S central Asia, bounded N by Tajikistan, Turkmenistan, and Uzbekistan; W by Iran; and S and E by Pakistan and China.

Afghan Wars three wars waged between Britain and Afghanistan to counter the threat to British India from expanding Russian influence in Afghanistan.
First Afghan War 1838–42, when the British garrison at Kabul was wiped out.
Second Afghan War 1878–80, when General Roberts captured Kabul and relieved Kandahar. *Third Afghan War* 1919, when peace followed the dispatch by the UK of the first airplane ever seen in Kabul.

AFL–CIO abbreviation for ◊*American Federation of Labor and Congress of Industrial Organizations.*

Africa second largest of the continents, three times the area of Europe
area 11,620,451 sq mi/30,097,000 sq km
largest cities (population over 1 million) Cairo, Algiers, Lagos, Kinshasa, Abidjan, Cape Town, Nairobi, Casablanca, El Gîza, Addis Ababa, Luanda, Dar es Salaam, Ibadan, Douala, Mogadishu
features Great Rift Valley, containing most of the great lakes of E Africa (except Lake Victoria); Atlas Mountains in the NW; Drakensberg mountain range in the SE; Sahara Desert (world's largest desert) in the N; Namib, Kalahari, and Great Karoo deserts in the S; Nile, Zaïre, Niger, Zambezi, Limpopo, Volta, and Orange rivers
physical dominated by a uniform central plateau comprising a southern tableland with a mean altitude of 3,000 ft/1,070 m that falls northward to a lower elevated plain with a mean altitude of 1,300 ft/400 m. Although there are no great alpine regions or extensive coastal plains, Africa has a mean altitude of 2,000 ft/610 m, two times greater than Europe's. The highest points are Mount Kilimanjaro 19,364 ft/5,900 m and Mount Kenya 17,058 ft/5,200 m; the lowest point is Lac Assal in Djibouti −471 ft/−144 m. Compared with other continents, Africa has few broad estuaries or inlets and therefore has proportionately the shortest coastline (15,000 mi/24,000 km). The geographical

extremities of the continental mainland are Cape Hafun in the E, Cape Almadies in the W, Ras Ben Sekka in the N, and Cape Agulhas in the S. The Sahel is a narrow belt of savanna and scrub forest which covers 1.7 billion acres/700 million hectares of W and central Africa; 75% of the continent lies within the tropics.

African National Congress (ANC) multiracial nationalist organization formed in South Africa 1912 to extend the franchise to the whole population and end all racial discrimination there. Its president is Nelson ◊Mandela. Although originally nonviolent, the ANC was banned by the government from 1960 to Jan 1990, and in exile in Mozambique developed a military wing, *Umkhonto we Sizwe*, which engaged in sabotage and guerrilla training. The armed struggle was suspended Aug 1990 after the organization's headquarters were moved from Zambia to Johannesburg. Talks between the ANC and the South African government have taken place intermittently since Dec 1991, with the proposed aim of creating a nonracial constitution. In Oct 1992, accusations of inhumane treatment of prisoners held in ANC camps outside South Africa led Mandela to institute an inquiry and promise an end to such abuses.

African violet herbaceous plant *Saintpaulia ionantha* from tropical central and E Africa, with velvety green leaves and scentless purple flowers. Different colors and double varieties have been bred.

Afrikaans language an official language (with English) of the Republic of South Africa and Namibia. Spoken mainly by the Afrikaners—descendants of Dutch and other 17th-century colonists—it is a variety of the Dutch language, modified by circumstance and the influence of German, French, and other immigrant as well as local languages. It became a standardized written language about 1875.

Afrika Korps German army in the western desert of North Africa 1941–43 during World War II, commanded by Field Marshal Erwin Rommel. It was driven out of North Africa by May 1943.

Afrikaner (formerly known as *Boer*) inhabitant of South Africa descended from the original Dutch, Flemish, and ◊Huguenot settlers of the 17th century. Comprising approximately 60% of the white population in South Africa, they were originally farmers but have now become mainly urbanized. Their language is Afrikaans.

afterbirth in mammals, the placenta and other material, including blood and membranes, expelled from the uterus soon after birth. In the natural world it is often eaten.

afterburning method of increasing the thrust of a gas turbine (jet) airplane engine by spraying additional fuel into the hot exhaust duct between the turbojet and the tailpipe where it ignites. Used for short-term increase of power during takeoff, or during combat in military aircraft.

afterimage persistence of an image on the retina of the eye after the object producing it has been removed. This leads to persistence of vision, a necessary phenomenon for the illusion of continuous movement in films and television. The term is also used for the persistence of sensations other than vision.

Aga Khan IV 1936– . Spiritual head (*imam*) of the *Ismaili* Muslim sect (see ◊Islam). He succeeded his grandfather 1957.

Agamemnon in Greek legend, a Greek hero, son of Atreus, king of Mycenae, and brother of ◊Menelaus.

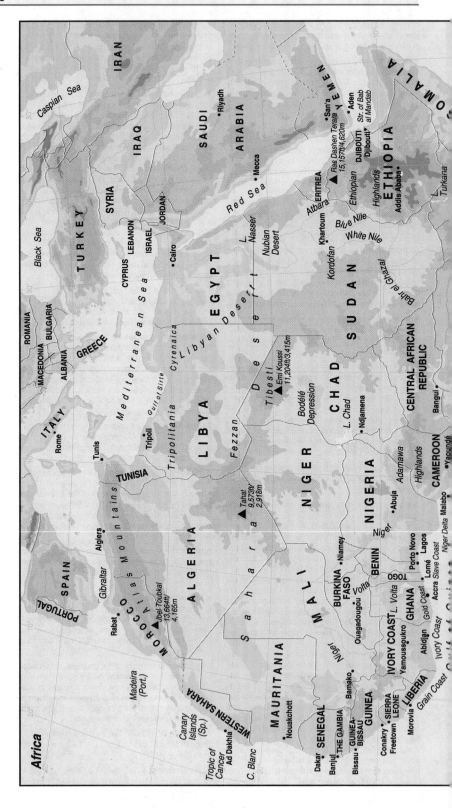

Africa

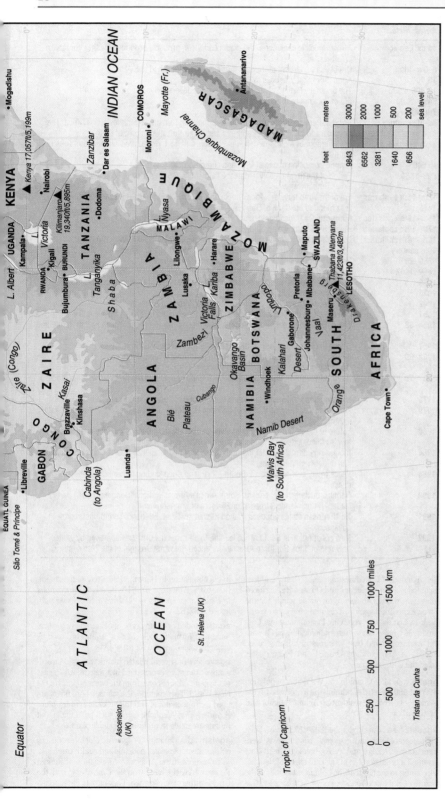

Equator

ATLANTIC

OCEAN

EQUATL GUINEA
São Tomé & Príncipe

GABON
•Libreville

CONGO
Brazzaville•
Kinshasa

ZAIRE

Zaïre (Congo)

Kasai

Cabinda
(to Angola)

Luanda•

ANGOLA

Bié
Plateau

Cubango

Shaba

ZAMBIA

Zambezi

RWANDA
Bujumbura• •Kigali
BURUNDI

Tanganyika

L. Albert

UGANDA
Kampala•

Victoria

KENYA
▲Kenya 17,057ft/5,199m
•Nairobi
Kilimanjaro▲
19,340ft/5,895m

TANZANIA
•Dodoma

MALAWI
Nyasa
Lilongwe•

Lusaka•

L.
Kariba

Victoria
Falls

MOZAMBIQUE

Harare•

ZIMBABWE

Vaal

Limpopo

NAMIBIA

Okavango
Basin

Windhoek•

Kalahari
Desert

BOTSWANA

Gaborone•

Maputo•
SWAZILAND
•Mbabane
Pretoria•
Johannesburg•
Maseru•
LESOTHO
▲Thabana Ntlenyana
11,423ft/3,482m

Drakensberg

SOUTH

AFRICA

Cape Town•

Namib Desert

Walvis Bay
(to South Africa)

Orange

•Mogadishu

INDIAN OCEAN

Zanzibar
•Dar es Salaam

COMOROS
Moroni •

Mayotte (Fr.)

Mozambique Channel

MADAGASCAR
•Antananarivo

feet   meters
9843   3000
6562   2000
3281   1000
1640   500
656   200
        sea level

St. Helena (UK)

•Ascension
(UK)

Tropic of Capricorn

Tristan da Cunha

0   250   500   750   1000 miles
0   500   1000 1500 km

Africa: history	
14 million BC	Africa, which is considered the *cradle continent*, probably produced the first humanlike creatures.
3–5 million	Direct line of descent of modern humans was established in E Africa.
15,000	Agriculture first practiced in Egypt.
10,000–2000	The originally fertile Sahara became a barrier desert between north and south.
5450–2500	Era of Saharan rock and cave paintings.
7th century **BC–6th century** AD	Assyria, Persia, Greece, Rome, and Byzantium in turn made conquests in N Africa. The Egyptian and black African traditions met in the Nubian kingdom of Kush.
320 BC–AD **50**	The kingdom of Axum flourished in Ethiopia and gave rise to the later legend of Prester John.
AD **640**	Islamic expansion began in N, E, and central Africa.
300–1500	Period of the great medieval states: Ghana, Mali, Songhai, Benin, Ife, and the culture of Great Zimbabwe.
12th–15th centuries	Era of the Arab travelers: for example, Ibn Batuta; and of trade, for example, Kilwa.
1488	Diaz rounded the Cape of Good Hope.
15th–16th centuries	European sea trade in gold, ivory, timber, and pepper.
17th–19th centuries	Height of the Atlantic and Indian Ocean slave trade.
18th–19th centuries	European travelers in Africa: Park, Livingstone, Stanley, Speke, Mary Kingsley.
19th century	Colonial wars against well-organized native states: Ashanti, Dahomey, Zululand.
1880–90	Peak of European colonization in the *scramble for Africa*.
1899–1902	South African War, the first large-scale war between whites in Africa.
1920	League of Nations mandate system introduced the idea of European trusteeship.
1936	Italy's conquest of Ethiopia.
1942	World War II reached its turning point in the Battles of Alamein.
1951	Libya became the first independent state to be declared by the United Nations.
1954–62	The fight for independence in Algeria precipitated the end of the French Fourth Republic 1958.
1957	Ghana became independent, the first of the revived black nation states.
1952–60	Mau-Mau movement in Kenya began the ousting of white settlers south of the Sahara.
1963	Organization of African Unity (OAU) founded.
1967–70	Revolt of Biafra within the federation of Nigeria constituted the first civil war in a modern black state.
1975	Mozambique's independence led to the end of dictatorship in Portugal.
1979	Zimbabwe's achievement of independence left South Africa as the last white-ruled state in Africa.
1980	Future of the OAU doubtful due to division over Western Sahara and Libyan aggression toward Chad. Extensive food shortages in many parts of central and E Africa.
1984	Increasing internal disaster in South Africa leading to violence between black population and minority white groups.
1988	Peace treaty between Angola, South Africa, and Cuba leading to Namibia's independence.
1990	Namibia declared independent. South Africa's African National Congress (ANC) party leader Nelson Mandela freed after 26 years of imprisonment.
1991	North African states opposed Iraq on Kuwait invasion. Ethiopia's communist regime collapsed.
1992	New constitution in South Africa leading to all-races majority rule approved by whites-only referendum. Southern Africa experienced the worst drought of the 20th century.

He married ◊Clytemnestra, and their children included Electra, Iphigenia, and Orestes. He sacrificed Iphigenia in order to secure favorable winds for the Greek expedition against Troy and after a ten years' siege sacked the city, receiving Priam's daughter Cassandra as a prize. On his return home, he and Cassandra were murdered by Clytemnestra and her lover, Aegisthus. His children Orestes and Electra later killed the guilty couple.

Agana capital of Guam in the W Pacific; population (1990) 1,139. It is the administrative center of the island, bordered by residential Agana Heights and Apra Harbor.

Agassiz Jean Louis Rodolphe 1807–1873. Swiss-born US paleontologist and geologist. His interests were comparative zoology and Ice Age geology. In 1832 he accepted a professorship at the University of Neuchâtel; coming to the US 1846, he became a member of the faculty of Harvard. Agassiz, known as a conservative in his opposition to Darwin, conducted many expeditions to the American West. His massive *Contributions to the Natural History of the United States* was published 1857–62.

agate banded or cloudy type of ◊chalcedony, a silica, SiO_2, that forms in rock cavities. Agates are used as ornamental stones and for art objects.

agave any of several related plants with stiff sword-shaped spiny leaves arranged in a rosette. All species of the genus *Agave* come from the warmer parts of the New World. They include *A. sisalina*, whose fibers are used for rope making, and the Mexican century plant *A. americana*. Alcoholic drinks such as ◊tequila and pulque are made from the sap of agave plants.

ageism discrimination against older people in employment, pensions, housing, and health care.

To combat it the American Association of Retired Persons (AARP) has 30 million members, and the Gray Panthers were formed. They have been responsible for legislation forbidding employers to discriminate; for example, it is illegal in the US to let age be a factor to fail to employ people aged 40–69, to dismiss them, or to reduce their working conditions or wages.

Agent Orange selective ◊weedkiller, notorious for its use in the 1960s during the Vietnam War by US forces to eliminate ground cover which could protect enemy forces. It was subsequently discovered to contain highly poisonous ◊dioxin. Thousands of US troops who had handled it later developed cancer or fathered deformed babies.

age-sex graph graph of the population of an area.

aggression in biology, behavior used to intimidate or injure another organism (of the same or of a different species), usually for the purposes of gaining a territory, a mate, or food. Aggression often involves an escalating series of threats aimed at intimidating an opponent without having to engage in potentially dangerous physical contact. Aggressive signals include roaring by wapiti (American elk), snarling by dogs, the fluffing up of feathers by birds, and the raising of fins by some species of fish.

Agincourt, Battle of battle of the Hundred Years' War in which Henry V of England defeated the French on Oct 25, 1415, mainly through the overwhelming superiority of the English longbow. The French lost more than 6,000 men to about 1,600 English casualties. As a result of the battle, Henry gained France and the French princess, Catherine of Valois, as his wife. The village of Agincourt (modern *Azincourt*) is south of Calais, in N France.

aging in common usage, the period of deterioration of the physical condition of a living organism that leads to death; in biological terms, the entire life process.

agitprop (Russian "agitation propaganda") Soviet government bureau established Sept 1920 in charge of Communist agitation and propaganda. The idea was developed by later left-wing groups in the West for the use of theater and other entertainment to convey political messages.

Agnew Spiro Theodore 1918– . US vice president 1969–73. A Republican, he was governor of Maryland 1966–69, and vice president under ◊Nixon. He took the lead in a campaign against the press and opponents of the ◊Vietnam War. Although he was one of the few administration officials not to be implicated in the ◊Watergate affair, he resigned 1973, shortly before pleading "no contest" to a charge of income-tax evasion.

agnosticism belief that the existence of God cannot be proven; that in the nature of things the individual cannot know anything of what lies behind or beyond the world of natural phenomena. The term was coined 1869 by T H ◊Huxley.

agora in an ancient Greek town, the public meeting place and market, equivalent to the Roman ◊forum. The limits were marked with boundary stones, and trade was regulated. The Agora at Athens contained an altar to the 12 Olympian gods; sanctuaries of Zeus, Apollo, and Hephaestus; the mint; administrative offices of state; fountain houses; shops; and covered arcades (stoas).

agoraphobia ◊phobia involving fear of open spaces and crowded places. The anxiety produced can be so severe that some sufferers are confined to their homes for many years.

Agra city of Uttar Pradesh, India, on the river Jumna, 100 mi/160 km SE of Delhi; population (1981) 747,318. A commercial and university center, it was the capital of the Mogul empire 1527–1628, from which period the Taj Mahal dates.

agribusiness commercial farming on an industrial scale, often financed by companies whose main interests lie outside agriculture; for example, multinational corporations. Agribusiness farms are mechanized, large in size, highly structured, and reliant on chemicals.

Agricola Gnaeus Julius AD 37–93. Roman general and politician. Born in Provence, he became consul AD 77, and then governor of Britain AD 78–85. He extended Roman rule to the Firth of Forth in Scotland and won the battle of Mons Graupius. His fleet sailed around the north of Scotland and proved Britain an island.

agriculture the practice of farming, including the cultivation of the soil (for raising crops) and the raising of domesticated animals. Crops are for human nourishment, animal fodder, or commodities such as cotton and sisal. Animals are raised for wool, milk, leather, dung (as fuel), or meat. The units for managing agricultural production vary from small holdings and individually owned farms to corporate-run farms and collective farms run by entire communities.

Agriculture developed in the Middle East and Egypt at least 10,000 years ago. Farming communities soon became the base for society in China, India, Europe, Mexico, and Peru, then spread throughout the world. Reorganization along more scientific and productive lines took place in Europe in the 18th century in response to dramatic population growth. Mechanization made considerable progress in the US and Europe during the 19th century. After World War II, there was an explosive growth in the use of agricultural chemicals: herbicides, insecticides, fungicides, and fertilizers. In the 1960s there was development of high-yielding species, especially in the ◊*green revolution* of the Third World, and the industrialized countries began intensive farming of cattle, poultry, and pigs. In the 1980s, hybridization by genetic engineering methods and pest control by the use of chemicals plus ◊pheromones were developed. However, there was also a reaction against some forms of intensive agriculture because of the pollution and habitat destruction caused. One result of this was a growth of alternative methods, including organic agriculture.

Agrippa Marcus Vipsanius 63–12 BC. Roman general and admiral, instrumental in the successful campaigns and rise to power of ◊Augustus. He commanded the victorious fleet at the battle of ◊Actium and married Augustus's daughter Julia.

agronomy study of crops and soils, a branch of agricultural science. Agronomy includes such topics as selective breeding (of plants and animals), irrigation, pest control, and soil analysis and modification.

Ahab c. 875–854 BC. King of Israel. His empire included the suzerainty of Moab, and Judah was his subordinate ally, but his kingdom was weakened by constant wars with Syria. By his marriage with Jezebel, princess of Sidon, Ahab introduced into Israel the worship of the Phoenician god Baal, thus provoking the hostility of Elijah and other prophets. Ahab died in battle against the Syrians at Ramoth Gilead.

Ahasuerus (Latinized Hebrew form of the Persian *Khshayarsha*, Greek *Xerxes*) name of several Per-

AIDS

Many questions remain to be answered on the effects of the human immuno-deficiency virus (HIV). It is not known if the virus can remain dormant indefinitely. Nor is it understood why some people remain sympton–free for many years, while others develop intermediate symptoms, such as persistent generalized lymphadenopathy (swollen glands), fever, increased susceptibility to disease, lethargy, diarrhoea, unexplained weight loss, and night sweats.

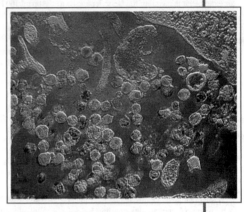

HIV (colored orange) binds to a protein (CD4) on the inside surface of human T4 lymphocytes. These blood cells have a key role in the immune system. Once inside the T4 cell, the virus uses the enzyme reverse transcriptase to insert its genetic material into the host's DNA. This provirus may remain latent for years. When it multiplies, it destroys the T4 cell and matures as it is released into the blood.

glycoprotein, GP120

lipia membrane (fat)

glycoprotein, GP41

core protein, P24

the AIDS virus in cross-section

core protein, P18

genetic template, RNA

reverse transcriptase

AIDS is the name given to a constellation of opportunistic infections—bacterial, viral, fungal and parasitic diseases and tumors. HIV also acts directly to destroy blood and other cells of the body.

digestive tract
Severe thrush affecting the mouth and esophagus makes eating difficult. Chronic diarrhoea and opportunistic intestinal infection can lead to dehydration and malnutrition.

lungs
Lung diseases, such as tuberculosis, are characteristic of AIDS, and *Pneumocystis carinii*, rarely affecting healthy individuals, is common.

skin
Kaposi's sarcoma, a skin cancer usually seen in elderly men, occurs in AIDS in a highly malignant form. Other skin conditions include rashes and eczema.

central nervous system
Compromised immunity, the indirect cause of disease, increases the risk of encephalitis and tumor, Dementia complex is a direct result of HIV infection. The virus causes widespread damage to the central nervous system, with progressive intellectual, neuromuscular, and psychological dysfunction

pregnancy
HIV can be transmitted across the placenta or during birth; and both mother and baby are at increased risk of developing full-blown AIDS.

a cure?
Drugs are being used to treat HIV and opportunistic infection, but they cause severe side effects and so far do not actually cure AIDS; second-generation anti-viral drugs are still undergoing development. The search continues for a reliable AIDS vaccine.

sian kings in the Bible, notably the husband of Esther. Traditionally it was also the name of the Wandering Jew.

Ahmad Shah Durrani 1724–1773. Founder and first ruler of Afghanistan. Elected shah in 1745, he had conquered the Punjab by 1751 and defeated the Marathapeople's confederacy at Panipat, Punjab, in 1761.

Ahmedabad or *Ahmadabad* capital of Gujarat, India; population (1981) 2,515,195. It is a cotton-manufacturing center, and has many sacred buildings of the Hindu, Muslim, and Jain faiths.

Ahriman in Zoroastrianism, the supreme evil spirit, lord of the darkness and death, waging war with his counterpart Ahura Mazda (Ormuzd) until a time when human beings choose to lead good lives and Ahriman is finally destroyed.

Ahura Mazda or *Ormuzd* in Zoroastrianism, the spirit of supreme good. As god of life and light he will finally prevail over his enemy, Ahriman.

AI abbreviation for ◊*artificial intelligence*.

aid, foreign financial and other assistance given by richer, usually industrialized, countries to war-damaged or developing states.

AIDS (acronym for *acquired immune deficiency syndrome*) the gravest of the sexually transmitted diseases, or ◊STDs. It is caused by the human immunodeficiency virus (HIV), now known to be a ◊retrovirus, an organism first identified 1983. HIV is transmitted in body fluids, mainly blood and sexual secretions.

The HIV virus originated in Africa. In the US, 230,179 cases were reported up to June 1992, with 152,153 deaths, 66% of all cases. One million Americans are thought to be infected with the virus. Recent evidence indicates that the presence of other diseases, especially syphilis, is linked to the full-blown development of AIDS.

Aiken Howard 1900– . US mathematician and computer pioneer. In 1939, in conjunction with engineers from ◊IBM, he started work on the design of an automatic calculator using standard business-machine components. In 1944 the team completed one of the first computers, the Automatic Sequence Controlled Calculator (known as the Mark 1), a programmable computer controlled by punched paper tape and using punched cards.

aikido Japanese art of self-defense; one of the ◊martial arts. Two main systems of aikido are tomiki and uyeshiba.

ailanthus any tree or shrub of the genus *Ailanthus* of the quassia family. All have compound leaves made up of pointed leaflets and clusters of small greenish flowers with an unpleasant smell. The tree of heaven *A. altissima*, native to E Asia, is grown worldwide as an ornamental. It can grow to 100 ft/30 m in height and 3 ft/1 m in diameter.

Ailey Alvin 1931–1989. US dancer, choreographer, and director whose Alvin Ailey City Center Dance Theater, formed 1958, was the first truly interracial dance company and opened dance to a wider audience. Ailey studied modern, ethnic, jazz, and academic dance, and his highly individual work celebrates rural and urban black America in pieces like *Blues Suite* 1958 and the company signature piece *Revelations* 1960.

Ainu aboriginal people of Japan, driven north in the 4th century AD by ancestors of the Japanese. They

aircraft carrier
Aerial photograph showing aircraft positioned on the deck of the USS Saratoga.

now number about 25,000, inhabiting Japanese and Russian territory on Sakhalin, Hokkaido, and the Kuril Islands. Their language has no written form, and is unrelated to any other.

air conditioning system that controls the state of the air inside a building or vehicle. A complete air-conditioning unit controls the temperature and humidity of the air, removes dust and odors from it, and circulates it by means of a fan. US inventor W H Carrier developed the first effective air-conditioning unit 1902 for a New York printing plant.

aircraft any aeronautical vehicle, which may be lighter than air (supported by buoyancy) or heavier than air (supported by the dynamic action of air on its surfaces). ◊Balloons and ◊airships are lighter-than-air craft. Heavier-than-air craft include the airplane, glider, autogyro, and helicopter.

aircraft carrier oceangoing naval vessel with a broad, flat-topped deck for launching and landing military aircraft; an effort to provide a floating military base for warplanes too far from home for refueling, repairing, reconnaissance, escorting, and various attack and defense operations.

air-cushion vehicle (ACV) craft that is supported by a layer, or cushion, of high-pressure air. The ◊hovercraft is one form of ACV.

Airedale terrier breed of large ◊terrier dog, about 2 ft/60 cm tall, with a rough red-brown coat. It originated about 1850 in England, as a cross of the otter hound and Irish and Welsh terriers.

airplane powered heavier-than-air craft supported in flight by fixed wings. Airplanes can be propelled by the thrust of a jet engine, a rocket engine, or airscrew (propeller), as well as combinations of these. They must be designed aerodynamically, as streamlining ensures maximum flight efficiency. The shape of a plane depends on its use and operating speed—aircraft operating at well below the speed of sound need

Akihito Emperor Akihito of Japan and his wife on their wedding day, 1959.

not be as streamlined as supersonic aircraft. The Wright brothers flew the first powered plane (a biplane) in Kitty Hawk, North Carolina, 1903. For the history of aircraft and aviation, see ◊flight.

air pollution contamination of the atmosphere caused by the discharge, accidental or deliberate, of a wide range of toxic airborne substances. Often the amount of the released substance is relatively high in a certain locality, so the harmful effects become more noticeable. The cost of preventing any discharge of pollutants into the air is prohibitive, so attempts are more usually made to reduce gradually the amount of discharge and to disperse this as quickly as possible by using a very tall chimney, or by intermittent release.

California's Clean Air Act 1988 aims to reduce exhaust emissions of carbon monoxide, nitrogen oxides, hydrocarbons and other precursors of smog in increasingly stringent phases.

air sac in birds, a thin-walled extension of the lungs. There are nine of these and they extend into the abdomen and bones, effectively increasing lung capacity. In mammals, it is another name for the alveoli in the lungs, and in some insects, for widenings of the trachea.

airship or *dirigible* any aircraft that is lighter than air and power-driven, consisting of an elliptical balloon that forms the streamlined envelope or hull and has below it the propulsion system (propellers), steering mechanism, and space for crew, passengers, and/or cargo. The balloon section is filled with lighter-than-air gas, either the nonflammable helium or, before helium was industrially available in large enough quantities, the easily ignited and flammable hydrogen. The envelope's form is maintained by internal pressure in the nonrigid (blimp) and semirigid (in which the nose and tail sections have a metal framework connected by a rigid keel) types. The rigid type (zeppelin) maintains its form using an internal metal framework. Airships have been used for luxury travel, polar exploration, warfare, and advertising.

Ajaccio capital and second-largest port of Corsica; population (1990) 59,300. Founded by the Genoese 1492, it was the birthplace of Napoleon; it has been French since 1768.

Ajax Greek hero in Homer's *Iliad*. Son of Telamon, king of Salamis, he was second only to Achilles among the Greek heroes in the Trojan War. According to subsequent Greek legends, Ajax went mad with jealousy when ◊Agamemnon awarded the armor of the dead Achilles to ◊Odysseus. He later committed suicide in shame.

Ajman smallest of the seven states that make up the ◊United Arab Emirates; area 96 sq mi/250 sq km; population (1985) 64,318.

AK abbreviation for the state of ◊*Alaska*.

Akbar Jalal ud-Din Mohammed 1542–1605. Mogul emperor of N India from 1556, when he succeeded his father. He gradually established his rule throughout N India. He is considered the greatest of the Mogul emperors, and the firmness and wisdom of his rule won him the title "Guardian of Mankind"; he was a patron of the arts.

à Kempis Thomas see ◊Thomas à Kempis, religious writer.

Ake v Oklahoma a US Supreme Court decision 1985 dealing with the right of indigent defendants to the "raw materials" needed for an adequate defense. The case was an appeal of the conviction of Glen Ake, a diagnosed paranoid schizophrenic, who had been denied psychiatric assistance by the court during his trial. The Supreme Court ruled that Ake had not been granted due process because his unstable condition, which could have been remedied by treatment, had helped to determine his sentence. The case used the same constitutional grounds to require court-appointed psychiatrists for indigent defendants as an earlier decision had to guarantee court-appointed attorneys.

Akhenaton another name for ◊Ikhnaton, pharaoh of Egypt.

Akhetaton capital of ancient Egypt established by the monotheistic pharaoh ◊Ikhnaton as the center for his cult of the Aton, the sun's disk; it is the modern Tell el Amarna 190 mi/300 km S of Cairo. Ikhnaton's palace had formal enclosed gardens. After his death it was abandoned, and the ◊*Amarna tablets*, found in the ruins, were probably discarded by his officials.

Akihito 1933– . Emperor of Japan from 1989, succeeding his father Hirohito (Showa). His reign is called the Heisei ("achievement of universal peace") era.

Akkad northern Semitic people who conquered the Sumerians in 2350 BC and ruled Mesopotamia. The ancient city of Akkad in central Mesopotamia, founded by ◊Sargon I, was an imperial center in the late 3rd millennium BC; the site is unidentified, but it was on the Euphrates.

Akron city in Ohio, on the Cuyahoga River, 35 mi/56 km SE of Cleveland; population (1990) 660,000. Known as the "Rubber Capital of the World," it is home to the headquarters of several major tire and rubber companies, although production there had ended by 1982.

The city is also a major trucking center and the site of the University of Akron. Akron was first settled 1807. Dr B F Goodrich established a rubber factory 1870, and the industry grew immensely with the rising demand for tires from about 1910.

Aksum ancient Greek-influenced Semitic kingdom that flourished in the 1st–6th centuries AD and covered a large part of modern Ethiopia as well as the Sudan. The ruins of its capital, also called Aksum, lie NW of Aduwa, but the site has been developed as a modern city.

al- for Arabic names beginning *al-*, see rest of name; for example, for "al-Fatah", see ◊Fatah, al-.

AL abbreviation for the state of ◊*Alabama*.

Alabama state in S US; nickname Heart of Dixie/Cotton State
area 51,994 sq mi/134,700 sq km
capital Montgomery
cities Birmingham, Mobile, Huntsville, Tuscaloosa
physical the state comprises the Cumberland Plateau in the N; the Black Belt, or Canebrake (excellent cotton-growing country), in the center; S of this, the coastal plain of Piney Woods

features rivers: Alabama, Tennessee; Appalachian mountains, George Washington Carver Museum at the Tuskegee Institute (a college founded for blacks by Booker T Washington); White House of the Confederacy at Montgomery; George C Marshall Space Flight Center at Huntsville; annual Mardi Gras celebration at Mobile; Helen Keller's birthplace at Tuscumbia

products cotton (no longer the prime crop, but still important), soybeans, peanuts, wood products, coal, livestock, poultry, iron, chemicals, textiles, paper

population (1990) 4,040,600

famous people Hank Aaron, Tallulah Bankhead, Nat King Cole, W C Handy, Helen Keller, Joe Louis, Willie Mays, Jesse Owens, Leroy "Satchel" Paige, George C Wallace, Booker T Washington, Hank Williams

history first settled by the French in the early 18th century; ceded to Britain 1763; passed to the US 1783 and became a state 1819. It was one of the ◊Confederate States in the American Civil War, and Montgomery was the first capital of the Confederacy. Birmingham became the South's leading industrial center in the late 19th century. Alabama was in the forefront of the civil rights movement in the 1950s and 1960s: Martin Luther ◊King, Jr, led a successful boycott of segregated Montgomery buses in 1955; school integration began in the early 1960s despite the opposition of Governor George C Wallace; the 1965 Selma march resulted in federal voting-rights legislation.

alabaster naturally occurring fine-grained white or light-colored translucent form of ◊gypsum, often streaked or mottled. It is a soft material, used for carvings, and ranks second on the Mohs' scale of hardness.

Alain-Fournier adopted name of Henri-Alban Fournier 1886–1914. French novelist. His haunting semiautobiographical fantasy *Le Grand Meaulnes/The Lost Domain* 1913 was a cult novel of the 1920s and 1930s. His life is intimately recorded in his correspondence with his brother-in-law Jacques Rivière. He was killed in action on the Meuse in World War I.

Alamein, El, Battles of in World War II, two decisive battles in the western desert, N Egypt. In the *First Battle of El Alamein* July 1–27, 1942, the British 8th Army under Auchinleck held the German and Italian forces under Rommel. In the *Second Battle of El Alamein* Oct 23–Nov 4, 1942, Montgomery defeated Rommel.

Alamo, the mission fortress in San Antonio, Texas,. It was besieged Feb 23–March 6, 1836, by ◊Santa Anna and 4,000 Mexicans; they killed the garrison of about 180, including Davy ◊Crockett and Jim ◊Bowie.

The struggle against such overwhelming odds made the battle of the Alamo a rallying point for the settlers in the Texas War of Independence from Mexico.

Alanbrooke Alan Francis Brooke, 1st Viscount Alanbrooke 1883–1963. British army officer, Chief of Staff in World War II, and largely responsible for the strategy that led to the German defeat.

Alaric *c.* 370–410. King of the Visigoths. In 396 he invaded Greece and retired with much booty to Illyria. In 400 and 408 he invaded Italy, and in 410 captured and sacked Rome, but died the same year on his way to invade Sicily.

Alaska largest state of the US, on the northwest extremity of North America, separated from the lower 48 states by British Columbia; nickname Last Frontier

Alabama

total area 591,004 sq mi/1,530,700 sq km
land area 570,833 sq mi/1,478,457 sq km
capital Juneau
cities Anchorage, Fairbanks, Fort Yukon, Holy Cross, Nome

physical much of Alaska is mountainous and includes Mount McKinley (Denali), 20,322 ft/6,194 m, the highest peak in North America, surrounded by Denali National Park. Caribou (descended from 2,000 reindeer imported from Siberia in early 1900s) thrive in the Arctic tundra, and elsewhere there are extensive forests

features Yukon River; Rocky Mountains, including Mount McKinley and Mount Katmai, a volcano that erupted 1912 and formed the Valley of Ten Thousand Smokes (from which smoke and steam still escape and which is now a national monument); Arctic Wild Life Range, with the only large herd of indigenous North American caribou; Little Diomede Island, which is only 2.5 mi/4 km from Russian Big Diomede/Ratmanov Island. The chief railroad line runs from Seward to Fairbanks, which is linked by highway (via Canada) with Seattle; near Fairbanks is the University of Alaska

products oil, natural gas, coal, copper, iron, gold, tin, fur, salmon fisheries and canneries, lumber

population (1990) 550,000; including 9% American Indians, Aleuts, and Inuits

history various groups of Indians crossed the Bering land bridge 60,000–15,000 years ago; the Eskimo began to settle the Arctic coast from Siberia about 2000 BC; the Aleuts settled the Aleutian archipelago about 1000 BC. The first European to visit Alaska was Vitus Bering 1741. Alaska was a Russian colony from 1744 until purchased by the US 1867 for $7,200,000; gold was discovered five years later. It became a state 1959. A congressional act 1980 gave environmental protection to 104 million acres/42 million hectares. Valuable mineral resources have been exploited from 1968, especially in the Prudhoe Bay area to the SE of Point Barrow. An oil pipeline (1977) runs from Prud-

Alaska

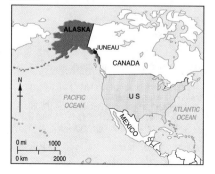

hoe Bay to the port of Valdez. Oil spill from a tanker in Prince William Sound caused great environmental damage 1989. Under construction is an underground natural-gas pipeline to Chicago and San Francisco.

albacore name loosely applied to several species of fishes found in warm regions of the Atlantic and Pacific oceans, in particular to a large tuna, *Thunnus alalunga*, and to several other species of the mackerel family.

Albania country in SE Europe, bounded N and E by Yugoslavia, E by Macedonia, SE by Greece, and W and SW by the Adriatic Sea.

Albanian person of Albanian culture from Albania and the surrounding area. The Albanian language belongs to a separate group within the Indo-European family and has an estimated 4 million speakers. There are both Christian and Muslim Albanians, the latter having been converted by the Ottoman Turks. Albanians comprise the majority of Kosovo in Yugoslavia and are in conflict with the Serbs, for whom the province is historically and culturally significant.

Alban, St died AD 303. First Christian martyr in England. In 793 King Offa founded a monastery on the site of Alban's martyrdom, around which the city of St Albans grew up.

Albany capital of New York State, situated on the west bank of the Hudson River, about 140 mi/225 km N of New York City; population (1990) 101,000. With Schenectady and Troy it forms a metropolitan area, population (1980) 794,298. First reached by Henry Hudson during his 1609 voyage up the river since named for him, Albany, a deepwater port, began as the Dutch trading post Fort Nassau 1614 and was soon the settlement of Fort Orange. It was renamed Albany 1664 when the English took control and incorporated 1686. After the revolution, in 1797, the state capital was moved there from New York City. The completion of the Erie Canal 1825 fostered its economic development. A massive government complex, the Empire State Plaza, was built in the 1960s.

Albany city on the Flint River, Georgia, SE of Columbus; seat of Dougherty County; population (1990) 78,100. It is a commercial center for the production of pecans and peanuts, chemicals, lumber, and other industrial products.

albatross large seabird, genus *Diomedea*, with long narrow wings adapted for gliding and a wingspan of up to 10 ft/3 m, mainly found in the southern hemisphere. It belongs to the order Procellariiformes, the same group as petrels and shearwaters.

Albee Edward 1928– . US playwright. His internationally performed plays are associated with the Theatre of the ◊Absurd and include *The Zoo Story* 1960, *The American Dream* 1961, *Who's Afraid of Virginia Woolf?* 1962 (his most successful play; also filmed with Elizabeth Taylor and Richard Burton as the quarrel-

---

Albania Republic of
(*Republika e Shqipërisë*)

area 11,097 sq mi/28,748 sq km
capital Tiranë
cities Shkodër, Elbasan, Vlorë, chief port Durrës
physical mainly mountainous, with rivers flowing E–W, and a narrow coastal plain
features Dinaric Alps, with wild boar and wolves
head of state Sali Berisha from 1992
head of government Alexander Meksi from 1992
political system emergent democracy
political parties Democratic Party of Albania (PSDS), moderate, market-oriented; Socialist Party of Albania (PSS), ex-communist; Human Rights Union (HMU), Greek minority party
exports crude oil, bitumen, chrome, iron ore, nickel, coal, copper wire, tobacco, fruit, vegetables

currency lek
population (1992) 3,357,000; growth rate 1.9% p.a.
life expectancy men 69, women 73
languages Albanian, Greek
religion Muslim 70%, although all religion banned 1967–90
literacy 75% (1986)
GNP $2.8 bn (1986 est); $900 per head
GDP $1.3 bn; $543 per head

chronology
c. 1468 Albania made part of the Ottoman Empire.
1912 Independence achieved from Turkey.
1925 Republic proclaimed.
1928–39 Monarchy of King Zog.
1939–44 Under Italian and then German rule.
1946 Communist republic proclaimed under the leadership of Enver Hoxha.
1949 Admitted into Comecon.
1961 Break with Khrushchev's USSR.
1967 Albania declared itself the "first atheist state in the world".
1978 Break with "revisionist" China.
1985 Death of Hoxha.
1987 Normal diplomatic relations restored with Canada, Greece, and West Germany.
1988 Attendance of conference of Balkan states for the first time since the 1930s.
1990 One-party system abandoned; first opposition party formed.
1991 Party of Labor of Albania (PLA) won first multiparty elections; Ramiz Alia reelected president; three successive governments formed. PLA renamed PSS.
1992 Presidential elections won by PSDS; Sali Berisha elected president. Alia and other former communist officials charged with corruption and abuse of power; totalitarian and communist parties banned.
1993 Jan: Nexhmije Hoxha, widow of Enver Hoxha, sentenced to nine years' imprisonment for misuse of government funds 1985–90.

ing, alcoholic, academic couple 1966), and *Tiny Alice* 1965. *A Delicate Balance* 1966 and *Seascape* 1975 both won Pulitzer prizes.

Albéniz Isaac 1860–1909. Spanish composer and pianist, born in Caltalonia. He composed the suite *Iberia* and other piano pieces, making use of traditional Spanish melodies.

Albert Prince Consort 1819–1861. Husband of British Queen ◊Victoria from 1840; a patron of the arts, science, and industry. Albert was the second son of the Duke of Saxe Coburg-Gotha and first cousin to Queen Victoria, whose chief adviser he became. He planned the Great Exhibition of 1851; the profit was used to buy the sites in London of all the South Kensington museums and colleges and the Royal Albert Hall, built 1871. He died of typhoid.

Alberta province of W Canada
area 255,223 sq mi/661,200 sq km
capital Edmonton
cities Calgary, Lethbridge, Medicine Hat, Red Deer
physical the Rocky Mountains; dry, treeless prairie in the center and S; toward the N this merges into a zone of poplar, then mixed forest. The valley of the Peace River is the northernmost farming land in Canada (except for Inuit pastures), and good grazing lands lie in the foothills of the Rockies
features Banff, Elk Island, Jasper, Waterton Lake, and Wood Buffalo national parks; annual Calgary stampede; extensive dinosaur finds near Drumheller
products coal; wheat, barley, oats, sugar beet in the S; cattle; oil and natural gas
population (1986) 2,375,000
history in the 17th century much of its area was part of a grant to the ◊Hudson's Bay Company for the fur trade, and the first trading posts were established in the late 18th century. The grant was bought by Canada 1869, and Alberta became a province 1905. After an oil strike in 1947, Alberta became a major oil and gas producer.

Albigenses heretical sect of Christians (associated with the Cathars) who flourished in S France near Albi and Toulouse during the 11th–13th centuries. They adopted the Manichean belief in the duality of good and evil and pictured Jesus as being a rebel against the cruelty of an omnipotent God.

albinism rare hereditary condition in which the body has no tyrosinase, one of the enzymes that form the pigment melanin, normally found in the skin, hair, and eyes. As a result, the hair is white and the skin and eyes are pink. The skin and eyes are abnormally sensitive to light, and vision is often impaired. The condition occurs among all human and animal groups.

Albinoni Tomaso 1671–1751. Italian Baroque composer and violinist, whose work was studied and adapted by ◊Bach. He composed over 40 operas.

Albion ancient name for Britain used by the Greeks and Romans. It was mentioned by Pytheas of Massilia (4th century BC), and is probably of Celtic origin, but the Romans, having in mind the white cliffs of Dover, assumed it to be derived from *albus* (white).

Alboin 6th century. King of the Lombards about 561–573. At that time the Lombards were settled north of the Alps. Early in his reign he attacked the Gepidae, a Germanic tribe occupying present-day Romania, killing their king and taking his daughter Rosamund to be his wife. About 568 he crossed the Alps to invade Italy, conquering the country as far S as Rome. He was murdered at the instigation of his wife, after he forced

Alberta

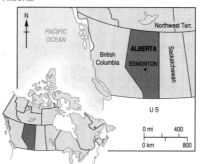

her to drink wine from a cup made from her father's skull.

albumin any of a group of sulfur-containing ◊proteins. The best known is in the form of egg white; others occur in milk, and as a major component of serum. Many vegetables and fluids also contain albumins. They are soluble in water and dilute salt solutions, and are coagulated by heat.

Albuquerque largest city of New Mexico, situated E of the Rio Grande, in the Pueblo district; population (1990) 384,750. Founded 1706, it was named after Afonso de Albuquerque. It is a resort and industrial center, specializing in electronic products and aerospace equipment. Sandia Laboratories here is engaged in high-technology defense and space-related projects. The University of New Mexico was founded here 1889. Kirkland Air Force Base is nearby.

Albuquerque Afonso de 1453–1515. Viceroy and founder of the Portuguese East Indies with strongholds in Ceylon, Goa, and Malacca 1508–15, when the king of Portugal replaced him by his worst enemy. He died at sea on the way home when his ship *Flor del Mar* was lost between Malaysia and India.

Alcaeus *c.* 611–*c.* 580 BC. Greek lyric poet. Born at Mytilene in Lesvos, he was a member of a family opposed to the ruling tyrants, and spent time in exile. The surviving fragments of his poems deal with politics, drinking, and love. The Alcaic stanza is named after him.

alcázar Moorish palace in Spain; one of five in Toledo defended by the Nationalists against the Republicans for 71 days in 1936 during the Spanish ◊Civil War.

alchemy (Arabic *al-Kimya*) supposed technique of transmuting base metals, such as lead and mercury, into silver and gold by the philosopher's stone, a hypothetical substance, to which was also attributed the power to give eternal life.

Alcibiades 450–404 BC. Athenian politician and general. He organized a confederation of Peloponnesian states against Sparta that collapsed after the battle of Mantinea 418 BC. Although accused of profaning the ◊Eleusinian Mysteries, he was eventually accepted as the commander of the Athenian fleet. He achieved several victories such as Cyzicus 410 BC, before his forces were defeated at Notium 406. He was murdered in Phrygia by the Persians.

alcohol any member of a group of organic chemical compounds characterized by the presence of one or more aliphatic OH (hydroxyl) groups in the molecule, and which form ◊esters with acids. The main uses of alcohols are as solvents for gums, resins, lacquers, and varnishes; in the making of dyes; for essential oils in perfumery; and for medical substances in pharmacy. Alcohol (ethanol) is produced naturally in the ◊fermentation process and is consumed as part of alcoholic beverages.

alcoholic beverage any drink containing alcohol, often used for its intoxicating effects. Ethyl alcohol, a colorless liquid (C_2H_5OH) is the basis of all common intoxicants. Foods rich in sugars, such as grapes, produce this alcohol as a natural product of decay, called fermentation.

Alcoholics Anonymous (AA) voluntary self-help organization established 1934 in the US to combat alcoholism; branches now exist in many other countries.

Alcott Louisa May 1832–1888. US author. Her children's classic *Little Women* 1869 drew on her own home circumstances, the heroine Jo being a partial self-portrait.

Born in Germantown, Pennsylvania, she spent most of her life in Concord, Massachusetts, the daughter of transcendentalist and educator Amos Bronson Alcott (1799–1888). She was educated in her home by her father and, occasionally, by family friends Ralph Waldo Emerson and Henry David Thoreau. Alcott began writing to help earn money for the family. Her first book *Flower Fables* 1848; her first success was *Hospital Sketches* 1863. The publication of *Little Women* was followed by *Little Men* 1871. She also wrote *Eight Cousins* 1875, *Under the Lilacs* 1879, and *A Garland for Girls* 1888.

Alcuin (Flaccus Albinus Alcuinus) 735–804. English scholar. Born in York, he went to Rome 780, and in 782 took up residence at Charlemagne's court in Aachen. From 796 he was abbot of Tours. He disseminated Anglo-Saxon scholarship, organized education and learning in the Frankish empire, gave a strong impulse to the Carolingian Renaissance, and was a prominent member of Charlemagne's academy.

alder any tree or shrub of the genus *Alnus*, in the birch family Betulaceae, found mainly in cooler parts of the northern hemisphere and characterized by toothed leaves and catkins.

Sitka alder *A. sinuata* and red alder *A. rubra* are common to W North America.

Aldrin Edwin (Eugene "Buzz") 1930– . US astronaut who landed on the Moon with Neil ◊Armstrong during the *Apollo 11* mission in July 1969, becoming the second person to set foot on the Moon.

aleatory music (Latin *alea* "dice") method of composition (pioneered by John ◊Cage) dating from about 1945 in which the elements are assembled by chance by using, for example, dice or computer.

Aleppo (Syrian *Halab*) ancient city in NW Syria; population (1981) 977,000. There has been a settlement on the site for at least 4,000 years.

Aleutian Islands volcanic island chain in the N Pacific, stretching 1,200 mi/1,900 km SW of Alaska, of which it forms part; population 6,000 Aleuts (most of whom belong to the Orthodox Church, plus a large US defense establishment). There are 14 large and more than 100 small islands running along the Aleutian Trench. The islands are mountainous, barren, and treeless; they are ice-free all year but are often foggy, with only about 25 days of sunshine recorded annually.

Alexander eight popes, including:

Alexander III (Orlando Barninelli) died 1181. Pope 1159–81. His authority was opposed by Frederick I

Barbarossa, but Alexander eventually compelled him to render homage 1178. He supported Henry II of England in his invasion of Ireland, but imposed penance on him after the murder of Thomas à ◊Becket.

Alexander VI (Rodrigo Borgia) 1431–1503. Pope 1492–1503. Of Spanish origin, he bribed his way to the papacy, where he furthered the advancement of his illegitimate children, who included Cesare and Lucrezia ◊Borgia. When ◊Savonarola preached against his corrupt practices Alexander had him executed.

Alexander three tsars of Russia:

Alexander I 1777–1825. Tsar from 1801. Defeated by Napoleon at Austerlitz 1805, he made peace at Tilsit 1807, but economic crisis led to a break with Napoleon's ◊continental system and the opening of Russian ports to British trade; this led to Napoleon's ill-fated invasion of Russia 1812. After the Congress of Vienna 1815, Alexander hoped through the Holy Alliance with Austria and Prussia to establish a new Christian order in Europe.

After Napoleon's defeat Russia controlled the Congress Kingdom of Poland, for which a constitution was provided.

Alexander II 1818–1881. Tsar from 1855. He embarked on reforms of the army, the government, and education, and is remembered as "the Liberator" for his emancipation of the serfs 1861, but he lacked the personnel to implement his reforms. However, the revolutionary element remained unsatisfied, and Alexander became increasingly autocratic and reactionary. He was assassinated by an anarchistic terrorist group, the ◊Nihilists.

Alexander III 1845–1894. Tsar from 1881, when he succeeded his father, Alexander II. He pursued a reactionary policy, promoting Russification and persecuting the Jews. He married Dagmar (1847–1928), daughter of Christian IX of Denmark and sister of Queen Alexandra of Britain, 1866.

Alexander three kings of Scotland:

Alexander I c. 1078–1124. King of Scotland from 1107, known as *the Fierce*. He ruled to the north of the rivers Forth and Clyde while his brother and successor David ruled to the south. He assisted Henry I of England in his campaign against Wales 1114, but defended the independence of the church in Scotland. Several monasteries, including the abbeys of Inchcolm and Scone, were established by him.

Alexander II 1198–1249. King of Scotland from 1214, when he succeeded his father William the Lion. Alexander supported the English barons in their struggle with King John after ◊Magna Carta.

Alexander III 1241–1285. King of Scotland from 1249, son of Alexander II. In 1263, by military defeat of Norwegian forces, he extended his authority over the Western Isles, which had been dependent on Norway. He strengthened the power of the central Scottish government.

Alexander I Karageorgevich 1888–1934. Regent of Serbia 1912–21 and king of Yugoslavia 1921–34, as dictator from 1929. Second son of ◊Peter I, King of Serbia, he was declared regent for his father 1912 and on his father's death became king of the state of South Slavs—Yugoslavia—that had come into being 1918.

Alexander Nevski, St 1220–1263. Russian military leader, son of the grand duke of Novgorod. In 1240 he defeated the Swedes on the banks of the Neva (hence

Nevski), and 1242 defeated the Teutonic Knights on the frozen Lake Peipus.

Alexander Severus AD 208–235. Roman emperor from 222, when he succeeded his cousin Heliogabalus. He attempted to involve the Senate more closely in administration, and was the patron of the jurists Ulpian and Paulus, and the historian Cassius Dio. His campaign against the Persians 232 achieved some success, but in 235, on his way to defend Gaul against German invaders, he was killed in a mutiny.

Alexander the Great 356–323 BC. King of Macedonia and conqueror of the large Persian empire. As commander of the vast Macedonian army he conquered Greece 336. He defeated the Persian king Darius in Asia Minor 333, then moved on to Egypt, where he founded Alexandria. He defeated the Persians again in Assyria 331, then advanced further east to reach the Indus. He conquered the Punjab before diminished troops forced his retreat.

Alexandra 1872–1918. Last tsarina of Russia 1894–1917. She was the former Princess Alix of Hessen and granddaughter of Britain's Queen Victoria. She married ◊Nicholas II and, from 1907, fell under the spell of ◊Rasputin, a "holy man" brought to the palace to try to cure her son of hemophilia. She was shot with the rest of her family by the Bolsheviks in the Russian Revolution.

Alexandria city in central Louisiana on the Red River, NW of Baton Rouge; seat of Rapides parish; population (1990) 49,188.

Alexandria or *El Iskandariya* city, chief port, and second-largest city of Egypt, situated between the Mediterranean and Lake Maryut; population (1986) 5,000,000. It is linked by canal with the Nile and is an industrial city (oil refining, gas processing, and cotton and grain trading). Founded 331 BC by Alexander the Great, Alexandria was the capital of Egypt for over 1,000 years.

Alexandria, Library of library in Alexandria, Egypt, founded 330 BC by ◊Ptolemy I and further expanded by Ptolemy II. It was the world's first state-funded scientific institution, and comprised a museum, teaching facilities, and a library that contained 700,000 scrolls, including much ancient Greek literature. It was burned down AD 640 at the time of the Arab conquest.

Alexandria, school of group of writers and scholars of Alexandria who made the city the chief center of culture in the Western world from about 331 BC to AD 642. They include the poets Callimachus, Apollonius Rhodius, and Theocritus; Euclid, pioneer of geometry; Eratosthenes, the geographer; Hipparchus, who developed a system of trigonometry; the astronomer Ptolemy, who gave his name to the Ptolemaic system of astronomy that endured for over 1,000 years; and the Jewish philosopher Philo. The Gnostics and Neoplatonists also flourished in Alexandria.

Alexeev Vasiliy 1942– . Soviet weight lifter who broke 80 world records 1970–77, a record for any sport. He was Olympic super-heavyweight champion twice, world champion seven times. He retired after the 1980 Olympics.

Alexius five Byzantine emperors, including:

Alexius I (Comnenus) 1048–1118. Byzantine emperor 1081–1118. The Latin (W European) Crusaders helped him repel Norman and Turkish invasions, and he devoted great skill to buttressing the threatened empire. His daughter Anna Comnena chronicled his reign.

Alexius III (Angelos) died *c.* 1210. Byzantine emperor 1195–1203. He gained power by deposing and blinding his brother Isaac II, but Isaac's Venetian allies enabled him and his son Alexius IV to regain power as coemperors.

Alexius IV (Angelos) 1182–1204. Byzantine emperor from 1203, when, with the aid of the army of the Fourth Crusade, he deposed his uncle Alexius III. He soon lost the support of the Crusaders (by that time occupying Constantinople) and was overthrown and murdered by another Alexius, Alexius Mourtzouphlus (son-in-law of Alexius III) 1204, an act which

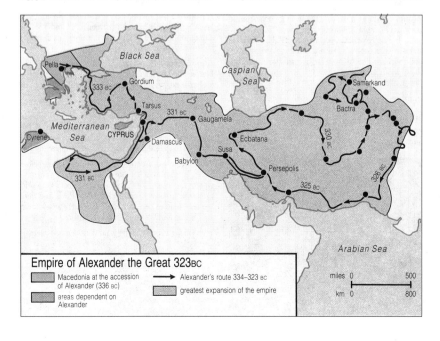

Empire of Alexander the Great 323BC

- ▨ Macedonia at the accession of Alexander (336 BC)
- ▨ areas dependent on Alexander
- ➡ Alexander's route 334–323 BC
- ▨ greatest expansion of the empire

miles 0   500
km 0   800

the Crusaders used as a pretext to sack the city the same year.

alfalfa or *lucerne* perennial tall herbaceous plant *Medicago sativa* of the pea family Leguminosae. It is native to Eurasia and bears spikes of small purple flowers in late summer. It is now a major fodder crop, generally processed into hay, meal, or silage. Alfalfa sprouts, the sprouted seeds, have become a popular salad ingredient.

Alfonso X *el Sabio* ("the Wise") 1221–1284. King of Castile from 1252. His reign was politically unsuccessful but he contributed to learning: he made Castilian the official language of the country and commissioned a history of Spain and an encyclopedia, as well as several translations from Arabic concerning, among other subjects, astronomy and games.

Alfonso XII 1857–1885. King of Spain from 1875, son of ◊Isabella II. He assumed the throne after a period of republican government following his mother's flight and effective abdication 1868. His rule was peaceful. He ended the civil war started by the Carlists and drafted a constitution, both 1876.

Alfonso XIII 1886–1941. King of Spain 1886–1931. He assumed power 1906 and married Princess Ena, granddaughter of Queen Victoria of the United Kingdom, in the same year. He abdicated 1931 soon after the fall of the Primo de Rivera dictatorship 1923–30 (which he supported), and Spain became a republic. His assassination was attempted several times.

Alfred *the Great* c. 848–c. 900. King of Wessex from 871. He defended England against Danish invasion, founded the first English navy, and put into operation a legal code. He encouraged the translation of works from Latin (some he translated himself), and promoted the development of the ◊Anglo-Saxon Chronicle.

algae (singular *alga*) diverse group of plants (including those commonly called seaweeds) that shows great variety of form, ranging from single-celled forms to multicellular seaweeds of considerable size and complexity.

Algarve (Arabic *al-gharb* "the west") ancient kingdom in S Portugal, the modern district of Faro, a popular holiday resort; population (1981) 323,500. Industries include agriculture, fishing, wine, mining, and tourism. The Algarve began to be wrested from the ◊Moors in the 12th century and was united with Portugal as a kingdom 1253.

algebra system of arithmetic applying to any set of nonnumerical symbols (usually letters), and the axioms and rules by which they are combined or operated upon; sometimes known as *generalized arithmetic.*

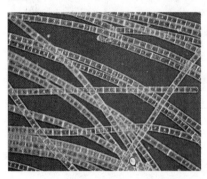

algae Microscopic view of green filamentary algae.

Algeciras Conference international conference held Jan–April 1906 when France, Germany, Britain Russia, and Austria–Hungary, together with the US, Spain, the Low Countries, Portugal, and Sweden, met to settle the question of Morocco. The conference was prompted by increased German demands in what had traditionally been seen as a French area of influence, but it resulted in a reassertion of Anglo-French friendship and the increased isolation of Germany. France and Spain gained control of Morocco.

Algeria country in N Africa, bounded E by Tunisia and Libya, SE by Niger, SW by Mali and Mauritania, NW by Morocco, and N by the Mediterranean Sea.

Algiers (Arabic *al-Jazair*, French *Alger*) capital of Algeria, situated on the narrow coastal plain between the Atlas Mountains and the Mediterranean; population (1984) 2,442,300.

Algiers, Battle of bitter conflict in Algiers 1954–62 between the Algerian nationalist population and the French colonial army and French settlers. The conflict ended with Algerian independence 1962.

ALGOL (acronym for *algorithmic language*) in computing, an early high-level programming language, developed in the 1950s and 1960s for scientific applications. A general-purpose language, ALGOL is best suited to mathematical work and has an algebraic style. Although no longer in common use, it has greatly influenced more recent languages, such as ADA and PASCAL.

Algonquian a group of languages spoken by North American Indians of the Eastern Woodland zone S and E of Hudson Bay. Algonquian includes over 20 languages spoken by American Indians of the NE coast as well as by the Cree, Arapaho, Blackfoot, Cheyenne, Ojibwa, and Fox.

algorithm procedure or series of steps that can be used to solve a problem. In computer science, it describes the logical sequence of operations to be performed by a program. A ◊flow chart is a visual representation of an algorithm.

Alhambra fortified palace in Granada, Spain, built by Moorish kings mainly between 1248 and 1354. It stands on a rocky hill and is the finest example of Moorish architecture.

Ali c. 598–660. 4th caliph of Islam. He was born in Mecca, the son of Abu Talib, uncle to the prophet Mohammed, who gave him his daughter Fatima in marriage. On Mohammed's death 632, Ali had a claim to succeed him, but this was not conceded until 656. After a stormy reign, he was assassinated. Around Ali's name the controversy has raged between the Sunni and the Shiites (see ◊Islam), the former denying his right to the caliphate and the latter supporting it.

Ali Mohammed. Adopted name of Cassius Marcellus Clay, Jr, 1942– . US boxer. Olympic light-heavyweight champion 1960, he went on to become world professional heavyweight champion 1964, and was the only man to regain the title twice. He was known for his fast footwork and extrovert nature.

alien in law, a person who is not a citizen of a particular nation.

In the US, federal legislation determines which aliens may legally enter a country or reside in it; their rights at law, both civil and criminal; and the processes and conditions by which they may become citizens.

alimentary canal in animals, the tube through which food passes; it extends from the mouth to the

Algeria Democratic and
Popular Republic of
(*al-Jumhuriya al- Jazairiya
ad-Dimuqratiya ash-Shabiya*)

area 919,352 sq mi/2,381,741 sq km
capital al-Jazair (Algiers)
cities Qacentina/Constantine; ports are Ouahran/Oran,
Annaba/Bône
physical coastal plains backed by mountains in N; Sahara
desert in S
features Atlas mountains, Barbary Coast, Chott Melrhir
depression, Hoggar mountains
head of state Liamiwe Zeroual from 1994
head of government Redha Malek from 1993
political system semi-military rule
political parties National Liberation Front (FLN), nationalist socialist; Socialist Forces Front (FSS), Berber- based
exports oil, natural gas, iron, wine, olive oil
currency dinar

population (1990 est) 25,715,000 (83% Arab, 17%
Berber); growth rate 3.0% p.a.
life expectancy men 59, women 62
languages Arabic (official); Berber, French
religion Sunni Muslim (state religion)
literacy men 63%, women 37% (1985 est)
GDP $64.6 bn; $2,796 per head

chronology
1954 War for independence from France led by the FLN.
1962 Independence achieved from France. Republic
declared. Ahmed Ben Bella elected prime minister.
1963 Ben Bella elected Algeria's first president.
1965 Ben Bella deposed by military, led by Colonel Houari
Boumédienne.
1976 New constitution approved.
1978 Death of Boumédienne.
1979 Benjedid Chadli elected president. Ben Bella released
from house arrest. FLN adopted new party structure.
1981 Algeria helped secure release of US prisoners in Iran.
1983 Chadli reelected.
1988 Riots in protest at government policies; 170 killed.
Reform program introduced. Diplomatic relations with Egypt
restored.
1989 Constitutional changes proposed, leading to limited
political pluralism.
1990 Fundamentalist Islamic Salvation Front (FIS) won
Algerian municipal and provincial elections.
1991 Dec: FIS won first round of multiparty elections.
1992 Jan: Chadli resigned; military took control of government; Mohammed Boudiaf became president; FIS leaders
detained. Feb: State of emergency declared. March: FIS
ordered to disband. June: Boudiaf assassinated.
1993 Worsening civil strife; assassinations of politicians
and other prominent political figures.
1994 Liamiwe Zeroual, defense minister and former general,
appointed president with broad powers.

anus. It is a complex organ, adapted for ◊digestion. In
human adults, it is about 30 ft/9 m long, consisting of
the mouth cavity, pharynx, esophagus, stomach, and
the small and large intestines.

alimony in the US, money allowance given by court
order to a former spouse after separation or ◊divorce.
The right has been extended to relationships outside
marriage and is colloquially termed palimony.
Alimony is separate and distinct from court orders for
child support.

Ali Pasha Mehmed Emin 1815–1871. Grand vizier
(chief minister) of the Ottoman empire 1855–56,
1858–59, 1861, and 1867–71, noted for his attempts to
westernize the Ottoman Empire.

alkali (Arabic *al-qualīy* "ashes") in chemistry, a compound classed as a ◊base that is soluble in water. Alkalis neutralize acids and are soapy to the touch. The
hydroxides of metals are alkalis; those of sodium
(sodium hydroxide, NaOH) and of potassium (potassium hydroxide, KOH) being chemically powerful;
both were derived from the ashes of plants.

alkali metal any of a group of six metallic elements
with similar chemical bonding properties: lithium,
sodium, potassium, rubidium, cesium, and francium.
They form a linked group in the ◊periodic table of the
elements. They are univalent (have a valence of one)
and of very low density (lithium, sodium, and potassium float on water); in general they are reactive, soft,
low-melting-point metals. Because of their reactivity
they are only found as compounds in nature.

alkaline-earth metal any of a group of six metallic
elements with similar bonding properties: beryllium,
magnesium, calcium, strontium, barium, and radium.
They form a linked group in the ◊periodic table of the
elements. They are strongly basic, bivalent (have a
valence of two), and occur in nature only in compounds.

alkaloid any of a number of physiologically active
and frequently poisonous substances contained in
some plants. They are usually organic bases and contain nitrogen. They form salts with acids and, when
soluble, give alkaline solutions.

Allah Islamic name for God.

Allahabad ("city of god") historic city in Uttar
Pradesh state, NE India, 360 mi/580 km SE of Delhi, on
the Yamuna River where it meets the Ganges and the
mythical Seraswati River; population (1981) 642,000.
A Hindu religious event, the festival of the jar of nectar
of immortality (Khumbh Mela), is held here every 12
years with the participants washing away sin and
sickness by bathing in the rivers.

Allegheny Mountains range over 500mi/800km
long extending from Pennsylvania to Virginia, rising
to more than 4,900 ft/1,500 m and averaging 2,500
ft/750 m. The mountains are a major source of timber,
coal, iron, and limestone. They initially hindered western migration, the first settlement to the west being
Marietta 1788.

allegory in literature, the description or illustration
of one thing in terms of another; a work of poetry or

alpaca The alpaca is related to the llama, and has been known since 200 BC.

prose in the form of an extended ◊metaphor or parable that makes use of symbolic fictional characters.

Allen Ethan 1738–1789. US military leader who founded the "Green Mountain Boys" 1770. At the outbreak of the American Revolution 1775 they joined with Benedict ◊Arnold and captured Fort Ticonderoga, the first victory for the American side. Captured by the British in the subsequent invasion of Canada, Allen continued his campaign for Vermont's independence after his release in 1778. He died before it achieved statehood in 1791.

Allen Woody. Adopted name of Allen Stewart Konigsberg 1935– . US film writer, director, and actor, known for his cynical, witty, often self-deprecating parody and offbeat humor. His film *Annie Hall* 1975 won him three Academy Awards.

His film career began with *What's New Pussycat?* 1965, which he wrote and in which he acted. Other films include *Take the Money and Run* 1969, *Bananas* 1971, *Play It Again, Sam* 1972, *Sleeper* 1973, *Love and Death* 1975, *Interiors* 1978, *Manhattan* 1979, *Stardust Memories* 1982, *Midsummer Night's Sex Comedy* 1982, *Zelig* 1983, *Broadway Danny Rose* 1984, *Purple Rose of Cairo* 1985, *Hannah and Her Sisters* 1986, and *Radio Days* 1987, *Alice* (1990), and *Husbands and Wives* (1992). His play *Don't Drink the Water* appeared on Broadway 1966. Allegations of child molestation and court battles followed his 1992 break with longtime companion Mia Farrow.

Allende Gossens Salvador 1908–1973. Chilean Marxist politician, president from 1970 until his death during a military coup in 1973.

Allentown city in E Pennsylvania, on the Lehigh River, just NW of Philadelphia; population (1990) 105,090. It is an industrial center for textiles, machinery, and electronic equipment. During the American Revolution it was a center for munitions production.

allergy special sensitivity of the body that makes it react, with an exaggerated response of the natural immune defense mechanism, especially with ◊histamines, to the introduction of an otherwise harmless foreign substance (*allergen*).

Allies, the in World War I, the 23 countries allied against the Central Powers (Germany, Austria-Hungary, Turkey, and Bulgaria), including France, Italy,

Russia, the UK, Australia and other Commonwealth nations, and, in the latter part of the war, the US; and in World War II, the 49 countries allied against the ◊Axis Powers (Germany, Italy, and Japan), including France, the UK, Australia and other Commonwealth nations, the US, and the USSR.

alligator reptile of the genus *Alligator*, related to the crocodile. There are two species: *A. mississipiensis*, the Mississippi alligator of the southern states of the US, and *A. sinensis* from the swamps of the lower Chang Jiang River in China. The former grows to about 12 ft/4 m, but the latter only to 5 ft/1.5 m. Alligators lay their eggs in sand; they swim well with lashing movements of the tail; they feed on fish and mammals but seldom attack people.

alliteration in poetry and prose, the use, within a line or phrase, of words beginning with the same sound, as in "Two tired toads trotting to Tewkesbury." It was a common device in Old English poetry, and its use survives in many traditional phrases, such as *dead as a doornail, pretty as a picture.*

allopathy the usual contemporary method of treating disease, using therapies designed to counteract the manifestations of the disease. In strict usage, allopathy is the opposite of ◊homeopathy.

alloy metal blended with some other metallic or nonmetallic substance to give it special qualities, such as resistance to corrosion, greater hardness, or tensile strength. Useful alloys include bronze, brass, cupronickel, duralumin, German silver, gunmetal, pewter, solder, steel, and stainless steel.

All Saints' Day or *All-Hallows* or *Hallowmas* festival on Nov 1 for all Christian saints and martyrs who have no special day of their own.

All Souls' Day festival in the Roman Catholic Church, held on Nov 2 (following All Saints' Day) in the conviction that through prayer and self-denial the faithful can hasten the deliverance of souls expiating their sins in purgatory.

allspice spice prepared from the dried berries of the evergreen pimento tree or West Indian pepper tree *Pimenta dioica* of the myrtle family, cultivated chiefly in Jamaica. It has an aroma similar to that of a mixture of cinnamon, cloves, and nutmeg.

alluvial deposit layer of broken rocky matter, or sediment, formed from material that has been carried in suspension by a river or stream and dropped as the velocity of the current changes. River plains and deltas are made entirely of alluvial deposits, but smaller pockets can be found in the beds of upland torrents.

alluvial fan roughly triangular sedimentary formation found at the base of slopes. An alluvial fan results when a sediment-laden stream or river rapidly deposits its load of gravel and silt as its speed is reduced on entering a plain.

Alma-Ata (formerly until 1921 *Vernyi*) capital of Kazakhstan; population (1991) 1,151,300. Industries include engineering, printing, tobacco processing, textile manufacturing, and leather products.

Almohad Berber dynasty 1130–1269 founded by the Berber prophet Mohammed ibn Tumart (*c.* 1080–1130). The Almohads ruled much of Morocco and Spain, which they took by defeating the ◊Almoravids; they later took the area that today forms Algeria and Tunis. Their policy of religious "purity" involved the forced conversion and massacre of the Jewish population of Spain. The Almohads were themselves defeated by the Christian kings of Spain 1212, and in Morocco 1269.

almond tree *Prunus amygdalus*, family Rosaceae, related to the peach and apricot. Dessert almonds are the kernels of the fruit of the sweet variety *P. amygdalus dulcis*, which is also the source of a low-cholesterol culinary oil. Oil of bitter almonds, from the variety *P. amygdalus amara*, is used in flavoring. Almond oil is also used for cosmetics, perfumes, and fine lubricants.

Almoravid Berber dynasty 1056–1147 founded by the prophet Abdullah ibn Tashfin, ruling much of Morocco and Spain in the 11th–12th centuries. The Almoravids came from the Sahara and in the 11th century began laying the foundations of an empire covering the whole of Morocco and parts of Algeria; their capital was the newly founded Marrakesh. In 1086 they defeated Alfonso VI of Castile to gain much of Spain. They were later overthrown by the ◊Almohads.

aloe plant of the genus *Aloe* of African plants, family Liliaceae, distinguished by their long, fleshy, spiny-edged leaves. The drug usually referred to as "bitter aloes" is a powerful cathartic prepared from the juice of the leaves of several of the species.

alpaca domesticated South American hoofed mammal *Lama pacos* of the camel family, found in Chile, Peru, and Bolivia, and herded at high elevations in the Andes. It is bred mainly for its long, fine, silky wool, and stands about 3 ft/1 m tall at the shoulder with neck and head another 2 ft/60 cm.

alpha and omega first (α) and last (Ω) letters of the Greek alphabet, a phrase hence meaning the beginning and end, or sum total, of anything.

alphabet set of conventional symbols used for writing, based on a correlation between individual symbols and spoken sounds, so called from *alpha* (α) and *beta* (β), the names of the first two letters of the Classical Greek alphabet. The earliest known alphabet is from Palestine, about 1700 BC. Alphabetic writing now takes many forms—for example, the Hebrew *aleph-beth* and the Arabic script, both written from right to left; the Devanagari script of the Hindus, in which the symbols "hang" from a line common to all the symbols; and the Greek alphabet, with the first clearly delineated vowel symbols.

Alpha Centauri or *Rigil Kent* brightest star in the constellation Centaurus and the third brightest star in the sky. It is actually a triple star (see ◊binary star); the two brighter stars orbit each other every 80 years, and the third, Proxima Centauri, is the closest star to the Sun, 4.2 light-years away, 0.1 light-years closer than the other two.

alphanumeric data data made up of any of the letters of the alphabet and any digit from 0 to 9. The classification of data according to the type or types of character contained enables computer ◊validation systems to check the accuracy of data: a computer can be programmed to reject entries that contain the wrong type of character. For example, a person's name would be rejected if it contained any numeric data, and a bank-account number would be rejected if it contained any alphabetic data. A car's registration number, by comparison, would be expected to contain alphanumeric data but no punctuation marks.

alpha particle positively charged, high-energy particle emitted from the nucleus of a radioactive ◊atom. It is one of the products of the spontaneous disintegration of radioactive elements (see ◊radioactivity) such as radium and thorium, and is identical with the nucleus of a helium atom—that is, it consists of two protons and two neutrons. The process of emission, *alpha decay*, transforms one element into another, decreasing the atomic (or proton) number by two and the atomic mass (or nucleon number) by four.

Alps mountain chain, the barrier between N Italy and France, Germany and Austria.

Famous peaks include **Mont Blanc**, the highest at 15,777 ft/4,809 m, first climbed by Jacques Balmat and Michel Paccard 1786; **Matterhorn** in the Pennine Alps, 14,694 ft/4,479 m, first climbed by Edward Whymper 1865 (four of the party of seven were killed when a rope broke during their descent); **Eiger** in the Bernese Alps/Oberland, 13,030 ft/3,970 m, with a near-vertical rock wall on the north face, first climbed 1858; **Jungfrau**, 13,673 ft/4,166 m; and **Finsteraarhorn** 14,027 ft/4,275 m. *Famous passes* include **Brenner**, the lowest, Austria/Italy; **Great St Bernard**, one of the highest, 8,113 ft/2,472 m, Italy/Switzerland (by which Napoleon marched into Italy 1800); **Little St Bernard**, Italy/France (which Hannibal is thought to have used); and **St Gotthard**, S Switzerland, which Suvorov used when ordered by the tsar to withdraw his troops from Italy. All have been superseded by all-weather road/rail tunnels. The Alps extend down the Adriatic coast into Slovenia, Croatia, Bosnia-Herzegovina, Yugoslavia, and N Albania with the Julian and Dinaric Alps.

Alsace region of France; area 3,204 sq mi/8,300 sq km; population (1986) 1,600,000. It consists of the *départements* of Bas-Rhin and Haut-Rhin, and its capital is Strasbourg.

Alsace-Lorraine area of NE France, lying west of the river Rhine. It forms the French regions of ◊Alsace and ◊Lorraine. The former iron and steel industries are being replaced by electronics, chemicals, and precision engineering. The German dialect spoken does not have equal rights with French, and there is autonomist sentiment.

Alsatian breed of dog known officially from 1977 as the *German shepherd*. It is about 26 in/63 cm tall

Alps *The French Alps, showing left to right, Aiguille du Chardonnet, Aiguille Verte, and Aiguille du Dru.*

and has a wolflike appearance, a thick coat with many varieties of coloring, and a distinctive gait. Alsatians are used as police dogs because of their high intelligence.

Altai territory of the Russian Federation, in SW Siberia; area 101,043 sq mi/261,700 sq km; capital Barnaul; population (1985) 2,744,000. Industries include mining, light engineering, chemicals, and timber. Altai was colonized by the Russians from the 18th century.

Altair or *Alpha Aquilae* brightest star in the constellation Aquila and the 12th brightest star in the sky. It is a white star 16 light-years away and forms the so-called Summer Triangle with the stars Deneb (in the constellation Cygnus) and Vega (in Lyra).

Altamira caves decorated with Paleolithic wall paintings, the first such to be discovered, 1879. The paintings are realistic depictions of bison, deer, and horses in polychrome (several colors). The caves are near the village of Santillana del Mar in Santander province, N Spain; other well-known Paleolithic cave paintings are in ◊Lascaux, SW France.

alternating current (AC) electric current that flows for an interval of time in one direction and then in the opposite direction, that is, a current that flows in alternately reversed directions through or around a circuit. Electric energy is usually generated as alternating current in a power station, and alternating currents may be used for both power and lighting.

alternative energy energy from sources that are renewable and ecologically safe, as opposed to sources that are nonrenewable with toxic byproducts, such as coal, oil, or gas (fossil fuels), and uranium (for nuclear power). The most important alternative energy source is flowing water, harnessed as ◊hydroelectric power. Other sources include the oceans' tides and waves (see tidal power station and ◊wave power), wind (harnessed by windmills and wind turbines), the Sun (◊solar energy), and the heat trapped in the Earth's crust (◊geothermal energy).

alternative medicine see ◊medicine, alternative.

alternator electricity ◊generator that produces an alternating current.

Althing parliament of Iceland, established about 930, the oldest in the world. It was dissolved 1800, revived 1843 as an advisory body, and became a legislative body again 1874. It has an upper and a lower house comprising one-third and two-thirds of its members respectively.

altimeter instrument used in aircraft that measures altitude, or height above sea level. The common type is a form of aneroid ◊barometer, which works by sensing the differences in air pressure at different altitudes. This must continually be recalibrated because of the change in air pressure with changing weather conditions. The ◊radar altimeter measures the height of the aircraft above the ground, measuring the time it takes for radio pulses emitted by the aircraft to be reflected. Radar altimeters are essential features of automatic and blind-landing systems.

Altiplano densely populated upland plateau of the Andes of South America, stretching from S Peru to NW Argentina. The height of the Altiplano is 10,000–13,000 ft/3,000–4,000 m.

Altman Robert 1925– . US maverick film director. His antiwar comedy *M*A*S*H* 1970 was a critical and commercial success; subsequent films include *McCabe and Mrs Miller* 1971, *The Long Goodbye* 1973, *Nashville* 1975, *Popeye* 1980, and *The Player* 1992.

Alton city in W Illinois, on the Mississippi River, just NE of St Louis, Missouri; population (1980) 34,171. Alton is an industrial center with flour mills and oil refineries. It was the site of the Lincoln–Douglas debates 1858.

Altoona city in S central Pennsylvania, in the Allegheny Mountains, NW of Harrisburg; population (1980) 57,078. It is a railroad manufacturing and repair center, and there is coal mining. The first steel railroad tracks in the US were laid from Pittsburgh to Altoona.

alum any double sulfate of a monovalent metal or radical (such as sodium, potassium, or ammonium) and a trivalent metal (such as aluminum or iron). The commonest alum is the double sulfate of potassium and aluminum,

$$K_2Al_2(SO_4)_4 \cdot 24H_2O$$

a white crystalline powder that is readily soluble in water. It is used in curing animal skins. Other alums are used in papermaking and to fix dye in the textile industry.

aluminum lightweight, silver-white, ductile and malleable, metallic element, symbol Al, atomic number 13, atomic weight 26.9815. It is the third most abundant element (and the most abundant metal) in the Earth's crust, of which it makes up about 8.1% by mass. It oxidizes rapidly, the layer of oxide on its surface making it highly resistant to tarnish, and is an excellent conductor of electricity. In its pure state aluminum is a weak metal, but when combined with elements such as copper, silicon, or magnesium it forms alloys of great strength. In nature it is found only in the combined state in many minerals, and is prepared commercially from the ore bauxite.

Alva or *Alba* Ferdinand Alvarez de Toledo, duke of 1508–1582. Spanish politician and general. He successfully commanded the Spanish armies of the Holy Roman emperor Charles V and his son Philip II of Spain. In 1567 he was appointed governor of the Netherlands, where he set up a reign of terror to suppress Protestantism and the revolt of the Netherlands. In 1573 he was recalled at his own request. He later led a successful expedition against Portugal 1580–81.

Alvarado Pedro de 1485–1541. Spanish conquistador, ruler of Guatemala 1524–41. Alvarado joined Hernán ◊Cortés' army 1519 and became his principal captain during the conquest of New Spain. Left in command at Tenochtitlán, Mexico, he provoked the Aztec rebellion which resulted in the death of ◊Montezuma II 1520. He conquered Guatemala 1523–24 and was its governor and captain general until his death. He also attacked Ecuador 1534 in a bid for a share of the former Inca empire, but was paid off.

alveolus (plural *alveoli*) one of the many thousands of tiny air sacs in the ◊lungs in which exchange of oxygen and carbon dioxide takes place between air and the bloodstream.

Alzheimer's disease common manifestation of ◊dementia, thought to afflict one in 20 people over 65. Attacking the brain's "gray matter," it is a disease of mental processes rather than physical function, characterized by memory loss and progressive intellectual impairment.

AM in physics, abbreviation for *amplitude modulation*, one way in which radio waves are altered for the transmission of broadcasting signals. AM is constant in frequency, and varies the amplitude of the transmitting wave in accordance with the signal being broadcast.

a.m. or **A.M.** abbreviation for **ante meridiem** (Latin "before noon").

Amalekite in the Old Testament, a member of an ancient Semitic people of SW Palestine and the Sinai peninsula. According to Exodus 17 they harried the rear of the Israelites after their crossing of the Red Sea, were defeated by Saul and David, and were destroyed in the reign of Hezekiah.

amalgam any alloy of mercury with other metals. Most metals will form amalgams, except iron and platinum. Amalgam is used in dentistry for filling teeth, and usually contains copper, silver, and zinc as the main alloying ingredients. This amalgam is pliable when first mixed and then sets hard, but the mercury leaches out and may cause a type of heavy-metal poisoning.

Amarna tablets collection of Egyptian clay tablets with cuneiform inscriptions, found in the ruins of the ancient city of ◊Akhetaton on the east bank of the Nile. Most of the tablets, which comprise royal archives and letters of 1411–1375 BC, are in the British Museum.

Amazon South American river, the world's second longest, 4,080 mi/6,570 km, and the largest in volume of water. Its main headstreams, the Marañón and the Ucayali, rise in central Peru and unite to flow E across Brazil for about 2,500 mi/4,000 km. It has 30,000 mi/48,280 km of navigable waterways, draining 2,750,000 sq mi/7,000,000 sq km, nearly half the South American landmass. It reaches the Atlantic on the equator, its estuary 50 mi/80 km wide, discharging a volume of water so immense that 40 mi/64 km out to sea, fresh water remains at the surface. The Amazon basin covers 3,000,000 sq mi/7,500,000 sq km, of which 2,000,000 sq mi/5,000,000 sq km is tropical forest containing 30% of all known plant and animal species (80,000 known species of trees, 3,000 known species of land vertebrates, 2,000 freshwater fish). It is the wettest region on Earth; average rainfall 8.3 ft/2.54 m a year.

Amazon in Greek legend, a member of a group of female warriors living near the Black Sea, who cut off their right breasts to use the bow more easily. Their queen, Penthesilea, was killed by Achilles at the siege of Troy. The term Amazon has come to mean a large, strong woman.

Amazonian Indian an indigenous inhabitant of the Amazon River Basin in South America. The majority of the societies are kin-based; traditional livelihood includes hunting and gathering, fishing, and shifting cultivation. A wide range of indigenous languages are spoken. Numbering perhaps 2.5 million in the 16th century, they had been reduced to perhaps one-tenth of that number by the 1820s. Their rain forests are being destroyed for mining and ranching, and Indians are being killed, transported, or assimilated.

Amazon Pact treaty signed 1978 by Bolivia, Brazil, Colombia, Ecuador, Guyana, Peru, Suriname, and Venezuela to protect and control the industrial or commercial development of the Amazon River.

ambassador officer of the highest rank in the diplomatic service, who represents the head of one sovereign state at the court or capital of another.

amber fossilized resin from coniferous trees of the Middle Tertiary period. It is often washed ashore on

River Amazon

the Baltic coast with plant and animal specimens preserved in it; many extinct species have been found preserved in this way. It ranges in color from red to yellow, and is used to make jewelry.

amblyopia reduced vision without apparent eye disorder.

Ambrose, St *c.* 340–397. One of the early Christian leaders and theologians known as the Fathers of the Church. Feast day Dec 7.

ambrosia food of the gods, which was supposed to confer eternal life upon all who ate it.

ameba any of a number of one-celled organisms, especially of the genus *Amoeba*, that move and feed by extensions of their colorless gelatinous protoplasm. They reproduce by ◊binary fission. Some members of the genus *Entamoeba* are harmful parasites. See also ◊amebiasis.

amen Hebrew word signifying affirmation ("so be it"), commonly used at the close of a Jewish or Christian prayer or hymn. As used by Jesus in the New Testament it was traditionally translated "verily."

Amenhotep III King of Egypt (*c.* 1400 BC) who built great monuments at Thebes, including the temples at Luxor. Two portrait statues at his tomb were known to the Greeks as the colossi of Memnon; one was cracked, and when the temperature changed at dawn it gave out an eerie sound, then thought supernatural. His son **Amenhotep IV** changed his name to ◊Ikhnaton.

America the W hemisphere of the Earth, containing the continents of North America and South America. This great landmass extends from the Arctic to the Antarctic, from beyond 75° N to past 55° S. The area is about 16 million sq mi/42 million sq km, and the estimated population is over 500 million. Politically, it consists of 36 nations and US, British, French, and Dutch dependencies.

American Civil War 1861–65; see ◊Civil War, American.

American Federation of Labor and Congress of Industrial Organizations (AFL–CIO) federation of North American labor unions, representing (1992) about 20% of the work force in North America.

American Indians: major tribes

Area	Tribe
North America	
Arctic	Inuit, Aleut
Sub-Arctic	Algonquin, Cree, Ottawa
NE Woodlands	Huron, Iroquois, Mohican, Shawnee
SE Woodlands	Cherokee, Choctaw, Creek, Hopewell, Natchez, Seminole
Great Plains	Blackfoot, Cheyenne, Comanche, Pawnee, Sioux
NW Coast	Chinook, Tlingit, Tsimshian
Desert West	Apache, Navaho, Pueblo, Hopi, Mohave, Shoshone
Central America	Maya, Aztec, Olmec
South America	
Eastern	Carib, Xingu
Central	Guaraní, Miskito
Western	Araucanian, Aymara, Chimú, Inca, Jivaro, Quechua

American Indian any of the aboriginal peoples of the Americas; the Arctic peoples (Inuit and Aleut) are often included, especially by the Bureau of Indian Affairs (BIA) of the Department of the Interior, responsible for overseeing policy on US Indian life, their reservations, education, and social welfare.

American Revolution revolt 1775–83 of the British North American colonies that resulted in the establishment of the United States of America. It was caused by colonial opposition to British economic exploitation and by the unwillingness of the colonists to pay for a standing army. It was also fueled by the colonists' antimonarchist sentiment and a desire to participate in the policies affecting them.

American Samoa see ◊Samoa, American.

America's Cup international yacht-racing trophy named after the US schooner *America*, owned by J L Stevens, who won a race around the Isle of Wight 1851.

americium radioactive metallic element of the ◊actinide series, symbol Am, atomic number 95, atomic weight 243.13; it was first synthesized 1944. It occurs in nature in minute quantities in ◊pitchblende and other uranium ores, where it is produced from the decay of neutron-bombarded plutonium, and is the element with the highest atomic number that occurs in nature. It is synthesized in quantity only in nuclear reactors by the bombardment of plutonium with neutrons. Its longest-lived isotope is Am-243, with a half-life of 7,650 years.

amethyst variety of ◊quartz, SiO_2, colored violet by the presence of small quantities of impurities such as manganese or iron; used as a semiprecious stone. Amethysts are found chiefly in the Ural Mountains, India, the US, Uruguay, and Brazil.

Amhara member of an ethnic group comprising approximately 25% of the polulation of Ethiopia; 13 million (1987). The Amhara are traditionally farmers. They speak Amharic, a language of the Semitic branch of the Afro-Asiatic family. Most are members of the Ethiopian Christian Church.

Amida Buddha the "Buddha of immeasurable light." Japanese name for *Amitābha*, the Buddha venerated in Pure Land Buddhism. He presides over the Western Paradise (the Buddha-land of his own creation), and through his unlimited compassion and power to save, true believers can achieve enlightenment and be reborn.

American Revolution: chronology

1773	A government tax on tea led Massachusetts citizens disguised as North American Indians to board British ships carrying tea and throw it into Boston harbor, the Boston Tea Party.
1774–75	The First Continental Congress was held in Philadelphia to call for civil disobedience in reply to British measures such as the Intolerable Acts, which closed the port of Boston and quartered British troops in private homes.
1775 April 19	Hostilities began at Lexington and Concord, Massachusetts. The first shots were fired when British troops, sent to seize illegal military stores and arrest rebel leaders John Hancock and Samuel Adams, were attacked by the local militia (minutemen).
May 10	Fort Ticonderoga, New York, was captured from the British.
June 17	The colonialists were defeated in the first battle of the Revolution, the Battle of Bunker Hill (which actually took place on Breed's Hill, nearby); George Washington was appointed colonial commander in chief soon afterward.
1776 July 4	The Second Continental Congress issued the Declaration of Independence, which specified some of the colonists' grievances and proclaimed an independent government.
Aug 27	Washington was defeated at Long Island and was forced to evacuate New York and retire to Pennsylvania.
Dec 26	Washington recrossed the Delaware River and defeated the British at Trenton, New Jersey.
1777 Jan 3	Washington defeated the British at Princeton, New Jersey.
Sept 11–Oct 4	British general William Howe defeated Washington at Brandywine and Germantown and occupied Philadelphia.
Oct 17	British general John Burgoyne surrendered at Saratoga, New York, and was therefore unable to link up with Howe.
1777–78	Washington wintered at Valley Forge, Pennsylvania, enduring harsh conditions and seeing many of his troops leave to return to their families.
1778	France, with the support of its ally Spain, entered the war on the US side (John Paul Jones led a French-sponsored naval unit).
1780 May 12	The British captured Charleston, South Carolina, one of a series of British victories in the South, but alienated support by enforcing conscription.
1781 Oct 19	British general Charles Cornwallis, besieged in Yorktown, Virginia, by Washington and the French fleet, surrendered.
1782	Peace negotiations opened.
1783 Sept 3	The Treaty of Paris recognized American independence.

Amin (Dada) Idi 1926– . Ugandan politician, president 1971–79. He led the coup that deposed Milton Obote 1971, expelled the Asian community 1972, and exercised a reign of terror over his people. He fled to Libya when insurgent Ugandan and Tanzanian troops invaded the country 1979.

amino acid water-soluble organic ◊molecule, mainly composed of carbon, oxygen, hydrogen, and nitrogen, containing both a basic amino group (NH_2) and an acidic carboxyl (COOH) group. When two or more amino acids are joined together, they are known as ◊peptides; ◊proteins are made up of interacting polypeptides (peptide chains consisting of more than three amino acids) and are folded or twisted in characteristic shapes.

Amis Kingsley 1922– . English novelist and poet. His works include *Lucky Jim* 1954, a comic portrayal of life in a provincial university, and *Take a Girl Like You* 1960. He won the UK's Booker Prize 1986 for *The Old Devils*. He is the father of Martin Amis.

Amis Martin 1949– . English novelist. His works are characterized by their savage wit and include *The Rachel Papers* 1974, *Money* 1984, *London Fields* 1989, and *Time's Arrow* 1991.

Amman capital and chief industrial center of Jordan; population (1986) 1,160,000. It is a major communications center, linking historic trade routes across the Middle East.

ammeter instrument that measures electric current, usually in ◊amperes.

Ammon in Egyptian mythology, the king of the gods, the equivalent of Zeus (Roman Jupiter). The name is also spelled Amen/Amun, as in the name of the pharaoh Tutankh*amen*. In art, he is represented as a ram, as a man with a ram's head, or as a man crowned with feathers. He had temples at Siwa oasis, Libya, and at Thebes, Egypt; his oracle at Siwa was patronized by the Classical Greeks.

ammonia NH_3 colorless pungent-smelling gas, lighter than air and very soluble in water. It is made on an industrial scale by the ◊Haber process, and used mainly to produce nitrogenous fertilizers, some explosives, and nitric acid.

ammonium chloride or *sal ammoniac* NH_4Cl a volatile salt that forms white crystals around volcanic craters. It is prepared synthetically for use in "dry-cell" batteries, fertilizers, and dyes.

amnesia loss or impairment of memory. As a clinical condition it may be caused by disease or injury to the brain, or by shock; in some cases it may be a symptom of an emotional disorder.

Amnesty International human-rights organization established in the UK 1961 to campaign for the release of political prisoners worldwide; it is politically unaligned. Amnesty International has 700,000 members, and section offices in 43 countries. The organization was awarded the Nobel Peace Prize 1977.

amniocentesis sampling the amniotic fluid surrounding a fetus in the womb for diagnostic purposes. It is used to detect Down's syndrome and other genetic abnormalities.

Amos book of the Old Testament written *c.* 750 BC. One of the ◊prophets, Amos was a shepherd who foretold the destruction of Israel because of the people's abandonment of their faith.

amp in physics, abbreviation for ampere, a unit of electrical current.

amethyst Quartz colored with impurities such as iron or manganese gives a violet color to amethyst.

ampere SI unit (abbreviation amp, symbol A) of electrical current. Electrical current is measured in a similar way to water current, in terms of an amount per unit time; one ampere represents a flow of about 6.28×10^{18} ◊electrons per second, or a rate of flow of charge of one coulomb per second.

Ampère's rule rule developed by French physicist André Ampère connecting the direction of an electric current and its associated magnetic currents. It states that if a person were traveling along a current-carrying wire in the direction of conventional current flow (from the positive to the negative terminal), and carrying a magnetic compass, then the north pole of the compass needle would be deflected to the left-hand side.

amphetamine or *speed* powerful synthetic ◊stimulant. Benzedrine was the earliest amphetamine marketed, used as a pep pill in World War II to help soldiers overcome fatigue, and until the 1970s amphetamines were prescribed by doctors as an appetite suppressant for weight loss; as an antidepressant, to induce euphoria; and as a stimulant, to increase alertness. Indications for its use today are very restricted because of severe side effects, including addiction and distorted behavior. It is a sulfate or phosphate form of $C_9H_{13}N$.

amphibian (Greek "double life") member of the vertebrate class Amphibia, which generally spend their larval (tadpole) stage in fresh water, transferring to land at maturity (after ◊metamorphosis) and generally returning to water to breed. Like fish and reptiles, they continue to grow throughout life, and cannot maintain a temperature greatly differing from that of their environment. The class includes caecilians (wormlike in appearance), salamanders, frogs, and toads.

amphitheater large oval or circular building used by the Romans for gladiatorial contests, fights of wild animals, and other similar events. It is a structure with an open space surrounded by rising rows of seats. The arena of an amphitheater is completely surrounded by the seats of the spectators, hence the name (Greek *amphi* "around"). The ◊Colosseum in Rome, completed AD 80, held 50,000 spectators.

amplifier electronic device that magnifies the strength of a signal, such as a radio signal. The ratio of output signal strength to input signal strength is called the *gain* of the amplifier. As well as achieving high gain, an amplifier should be free from distortion and able to operate over a range of frequencies. Practical amplifiers are usually complex circuits, although simple amplifiers can be built from single transistors or valves.

amplitude maximum displacement of an oscillation from the equilibrium position. For a wave motion, it is the height of a crest (or the depth of a trough). With a

Amsterdam Tall brick canal-side houses of up to six or seven floors, with pointed gables, have been built in Amsterdam, the capital of the Netherlands, since the 17th century.

sound wave, for example, amplitude corresponds to the intensity (loudness) of the sound. In AM (amplitude modulation) radio broadcasting, the required audio-frequency signal is made to modulate (vary slightly) the amplitude of a continuously transmitted radio carrier wave.

amplitude modulation (AM) method by which radio waves are altered for the transmission of broadcasting signals. AM waves are constant in frequency, but the amplitude of the transmitting wave varies in accordance with the signal being broadcast.

ampulla in the inner ◊ear, a slight swelling at the end of each semicircular canal, able to sense the motion of the head. The sense of balance largely depends on sensitive hairs within the ampulla responding to movements of fluid within the canal.

Amritsar industrial city in the Punjab, India; population (1981) 595,000. It is the holy city of ◊Sikhism, with the Guru Nanak University (named after the first Sikh guru) and the Golden Temple, from which armed demonstrators were evicted by the Indian army under General Dayal 1984, 325 being killed. Subsequently, Indian prime minister Indira Gandhi was assassinated in reprisal. In 1919 the city was the scene of the Amritsar Massacre.

Amritsar Massacre also called *Jallianwallah Bagh massacre* the killing of 379 Indians (and wounding of 1,200) in Amritsar, at the site of a Sikh religious shrine in the Punjab 1919. British troops under General Edward Dyer (1864–1927) opened fire without warning on a crowd of some 10,000, assembled to protest against the arrest of two Indian National Congress leaders.

Amsterdam capital of the Netherlands; population (1990) 695,100. Canals cut through the city link it with the North Sea and the Rhine, and as a Dutch port it is second only to Rotterdam. There is shipbuilding, printing, food processing, banking, and insurance.

Amundsen Roald 1872–1928. Norwegian explorer who in 1903–06 became the first person to navigate the ◊Northwest Passage. Beaten to the North Pole by

US explorer Robert Peary 1910, he reached the South Pole ahead of Captain Scott 1911.

Amur river in E Asia. Formed by the Argun and Shilka rivers, the Amur enters the Sea of Okhotsk. At its mouth at Nikolevsk it is 10 mi/16 km wide. For much of its course of over 2,730 mi/4,400 km it forms, together with its tributary, the Ussuri, the boundary between Russia and China.

Anabaptist member of any of various 16th-century radical Protestant sects. They believed in adult rather than child baptism, and sought to establish utopian communities. Anabaptist groups spread rapidly in N Europe, particularly in Germany, and were widely persecuted.

anabatic wind warm wind that blows uphill in steep-sided valleys in the early morning. As the sides of a valley warm up in the morning the air above is also warmed and rises up the valley to give a gentle breeze. By contrast, a katabatic wind is cool and blows down a valley at night.

anabolic steroid any ◊hormone of the ◊steroid group that stimulates tissue growth. Its use in medicine is limited to the treatment of some anemias and breast cancers; it may help to break up blood clots. Side effects include aggressive behavior, masculinization in women, and, in children, reduced height.

It is used in sports, such as weight lifting and track and field, to increase muscle bulk for greater strength and stamina but it is widely condemned because of dangerous side effects. In 1988 the Canadian sprinter Ben Johnson was stripped of an Olympic gold medal for having taken anabolic steroids.

anaconda South American snake *Eunectes murinus*, a member of the python and boa family, the Boidae. One of the largest snakes, growing to 30 ft/9 m or more, it is found in and near water, where it lies in wait for the birds and animals on which it feeds. The anaconda is not venomous, but kills its prey by coiling round it and squeezing until the creature suffocates.

Anaheim city in SW California, SE of Los Angeles; industries include electronic and farm equipment and processed foods; population (1990) 266,406. Disneyland amusement park is here. Anaheim was settled by German immigrants 1858 as a wine-producing community.

Analects the most important of the four books that contain the teachings and ideas of ◊Confucianism.

analog (of a quantity or device) changing continuously; by contrast a ◊digital quantity or device varies in series of distinct steps. For example, an analog clock measures time by means of a continuous movement of hands around a dial, whereas a digital clock measures time with a numerical display that changes in a series of discrete steps.

analog signal in electronics, current or voltage that conveys or stores information, and varies continuously in the same way as the information it represents. Analog signals are prone to interference and distortion.

analytic in philosophy, a term derived from ◊Kant: the converse of ◊synthetic.

analytic geometry another name for ◊coordinate geometry.

anarchism (Greek *anarkhos* "without ruler") political belief that society should have no government, laws, police, or other authority, but should be a free association of all its members. It does not mean "without order"; most theories of anarchism imply an order of a very strict and symmetrical kind, but they maintain that such order can be achieved by cooperation. Anarchism must not be confused with nihilism (a purely negative and destructive activity directed against society); anarchism is essentially a pacifist movement.

Anastasia 1901–1918. Russian Grand Duchess, youngest daughter of ◊Nicholas II. During the Russian Revolution she was presumed shot with her parents by the Bolsheviks after the Revolution of 1917, but it has been alleged that Anastasia escaped.

anatomy study of the structure of the body and its component parts, especially the ◊human body, as distinguished from physiology, which is the study of bodily functions.

Anaximander c. 610–c. 546 BC. Greek astronomer and philosopher. He claimed that the Earth was a cylinder three times wider than it is deep, motionless at the center of the universe, and he is credited with drawing the first geographical map. He said that the celestial bodies were fire seen through holes in the hollow rims of wheels encircling the Earth. According to Anaximander, the first animals came into being from moisture and the first humans grew inside fish, emerging once fully developed.

ancestor worship religious rituals and beliefs oriented toward deceased members of a family or group, as a symbolic expression of values or in the belief that the souls of the dead remain involved in this world and are capable of influencing current events.

Anchorage port and largest city of Alaska, at the head of Cook Inlet; population (1990) 226,340. Established 1918, Anchorage is an important center of administration, communication, and commerce. Oil and gas extraction and fish canning are also important to the local economy.

Two US military bases are nearby—Fort Richardson and Elmendorf Air Force Base. Alaska Pacific University and a branch of the University of Alaska are here. The Fur Rendezvous winter carnival is an annual event. The 1964 earthquake that killed 114 people was the most powerful in North American recorded history—8.4 on the Richter scale.

anchovy small fish *Engraulis encrasicholus* of the ◊herring family. It is fished extensively, being abundant in the Mediterranean, and is also found on the Atlantic coast of Europe and in the Black Sea. It grows to 8 in/20 cm.

ancien régime the old order; the feudal, absolute monarchy in France before the French Revolution 1789.

ancient art art of prehistoric cultures and the ancient civilizations around the Mediterranean that predate the Classical world of Greece and Rome: for example, Sumerian and Aegean art. Artifacts range from simple relics of the Paleolithic period, such as pebbles carved with symbolic figures, to the sophisticated art forms of ancient Egypt and Assyria: for example, mural paintings, sculpture, and jewelry.

Andalusia (Spanish ***Andalucía***) fertile autonomous region of S Spain, including the provinces of Almería, Cádiz, Córdoba, Granada, Huelva, Jaén, Málaga, and Seville; area 33,698 sq mi/87,300 sq km; population (1986) 6,876,000. Málaga, Cádiz, and Algeciras are the chief ports and industrial centers. The ***Costa del Sol*** on the south coast has many tourist resorts, including Marbella and Torremolinos.

Andaman and Nicobar Islands two groups of islands in the Bay of Bengal, between India and Myan-

mar, forming a Union Territory of the Republic of India; capital Port Blair; area 3,204 sq mi/8,300 sq km; population (1991) 278,000. The economy is based on fishing, timber, rubber, fruit, and rice.

Andean Indian any indigenous inhabitant of the Andes range in South America, stretching from Ecuador to Peru to Chile, and including both the coast and the highlands. Many Andean civilizations developed in this region from local fishing-hunting-farming societies, all of which predated the ◊Inca, who consolidated the entire region and ruled from about 1200 to the 1530s, when the Spanish arrived and conquered. The earliest pan-Andean civilization was the Chavin, about 1200–800 BC, which was followed by large and important coastal city-states, such as the Mochica, the Chimú, the Nazca, and the Paracas. The region was dominated by the Tiahuanaco when the Inca started to expand, took them and outlying peoples into their empire, and imposed the Quechua language on all. It is now spoken by over 10 million people and is a member of the Andean-Equaorial family.

Andersen Hans Christian 1805–1875. Danish writer of fairy tales, such as "The Ugly Duckling," "The Snow Queen," "The Little Mermaid," and "The Emperor's New Clothes." A gothic inventiveness, strong sense of wonder, and a redemptive evocation of material and spiritual poverty have given these stories perennial and universal appeal; they have been translated into many languages. He also wrote adult novels and travel books.

Anderson city in E central Indiana, NE of Indianapolis; seat of Madison County; population (1990) 59,500. Industries include automobile accessories and paper products.

Anderson Carl David 1905–1991. US physicist who discovered the positive electron (positron) in 1932; he shared the Nobel Prize for Physics in 1936.

Anderson Marian 1902–1993. US contralto whose voice was remarkable for its range and richness. She toured Europe 1930, but in 1939 she was barred from singing at Constitution Hall, Washington, DC, because she was black. In 1955 she sang at the Metropolitan Opera, the first black singer to appear there. In 1958 she was appointed an alternate (deputizing) delegate to the United Nations.

Following her bar from Constitution Hall, Eleanor Roosevelt and others organized a concert at the Lincoln Memorial; it was attended by 75,000 people.

Anderson Maxwell 1888–1959. US playwright, noted for *What Price Glory?* 1924, a realistic portrayal of the American soldier in action during World War I, co-written with Laurence Stallings. He won a Pulitzer Prize for his comedic prose satire *Both Your Houses* 1933. Most of his plays had moral and social problems as themes.

Anderson Sherwood 1876–1941. US writer, a member of the Chicago Group, who was encouraged by Theodore Dreiser and Carl Sandburg. He was best known for his sensitive, experimental, and poetic novels of the desperation of small-town Midwestern life, such as in his most noted work, *Winesburg, Ohio* 1919. Born in Camden, Ohio, Anderson joined the army at age 17 and then worked in a factory before leaving his wife and job and going to Chicago. His works include *Windy McPherson's Son* 1916, *Poor White* 1920, *Dark Laughter* 1925, *Hello Towns* 1929, and *Puzzled America* 1935. He also is known for his short-story collections and autobiographical works.

Andes great mountain system or *cordillera* that forms the western fringe of South America, extending through some 67° of latitude and the republics of Colombia, Venezuela, Ecuador, Peru, Bolivia, Chile, and Argentina. The mountains exceed 12,000 ft/3,600 m for half their length of 4,000 mi/6,500 km.

andesite volcanic igneous rock, intermediate in silica content between rhyolite and basalt. It is characterized by a large quantity of feldspar ◊minerals, giving it a light color. Andesite erupts from volcanoes at destructive plate margins (where one plate of the Earth's surface moves beneath another; see ◊plate tectonics), including the Andes, from which it gets its name.

Andhra Pradesh state in E central India
area 106,845 sq mi/276,700 sq km
capital Hyderabad
cities Secunderabad
products rice, sugar cane, tobacco, groundnuts, cotton
population (1991) 66,304,900
languages Telugu, Urdu, Tamil
history formed 1953 from the Telegu-speaking areas of Madras, and enlarged 1956 from the former Hyderabad state.

Andorra landlocked country in the E Pyrenees, bounded N by France and S by Spain.

Andrea del Sarto (Andrea d'Agnola di Francesco) 1486–1531. Italian Renaissance painter active in Florence, one of the finest portraitists and religious painters of his time. His style is serene and noble, characteristic of High Renaissance art.

Andrew (full name Andrew Albert Christian Edward) 1960– . Prince of the UK, Duke of York, second son of Queen Elizabeth II. He married Sarah Ferguson 1986; their first daughter, Princess Beatrice, was born 1988, and their second daughter, Princess Eugenie, was born 1990. The couple separated 1992. Prince Andrew is a naval helicopter pilot.

Andrews Julie. Adopted name of Julia Elizabeth Wells 1935– . British-born US singer and actress. A child performer with her mother and stepfather in British music halls, she first appeared in the US in the Broadway production *The Boy Friend* 1954. She was the original Eliza Doolittle in *My Fair Lady* 1956. In 1960 she appeared in Lerner and Loewe's *Camelot* on Broadway. Her films include *Mary Poppins* 1964, *The Americanization of Emily* 1963, *The Sound of Music* 1965, *10* 1980, and *Victor/Victoria* 1982.

Andrew, St New Testament apostle. According to tradition, he went with John to Ephesus, preached in Scythia, and was martyred at Patras on an X-shaped cross (*St Andrew's cross*). He is the patron saint of Scotland. Feast day Nov 30.

Androcles traditionally, a Roman slave who fled from a cruel master into the African desert, where he encountered and withdrew a thorn from the paw of a crippled lion. Recaptured and sentenced to combat a lion in the arena, he found his adversary was his old friend. The emperor Tiberius was said to have freed them both.

Andromache in Greek legend, the loyal wife of ◊Hector and mother of Astyanax. After the fall of Troy she was awarded to Neoptolemus, Achilles' son; she later married a Trojan seer called Helenus. Andromache is the heroine of Homer's

Andromeda galaxy galaxy 2.2 million light-years away from Earth in the constellation Andromeda, and the most distant object visible to the naked eye. It is the largest member of the Local Group of galaxies. Like the Milky Way, it is a spiral orbited by several companion galaxies but contains about twice as many stars. It is about 200,000 light-years across.

Andropov Yuri 1914–1984. Soviet communist politician, president of the USSR 1983–84. As chief of the KGB 1967–82, he established a reputation for efficiently suppressing dissent.

Andorra Principality of
(*Principat d'Andorra*)

area 181 sq mi/468 sq km
capital Andorra-la-Vella
cities Les Escaldes
physical mountainous, with narrow valleys

features the E Pyrenees, Valira River
heads of state Joan Marti i Alanis (bishop of Urgel, Spain) and François Mitterrand (president of France)
head of government Oscar Riba Reig from 1989
political system semi-feudal co-principality
political party Democratic Party of Andorra
exports main industries tourism and tobacco
currency French franc and Spanish peseta
population (1992) 57,100 (30% Andorrans, 61% Spanish, 6% French)
languages Catalan (official); Spanish, French
religion Roman Catholic
literacy 100% (1987)
GDP $300 million (1985)
chronology
1278 Treaty signed making Spanish bishop and French count joint rulers of Andorra (through marriage the king of France later inherited the count's right).
1970 Extension of franchise to third-generation female and second-generation male Andorrans.
1976 First political organization (Democratic Party of Andorra) formed.
1977 Franchise extended to first-generation Andorrans.
1981 First prime minister appointed by General Council.
1982 With the appointment of an Executive Council, executive and legislative powers were separated.
1991 Links with European Community (EC) formalized.
1993 First constitution approved in a referendum.

anemia condition caused by a shortage of hemoglobin, the oxygen-carrying component of red blood cells. The main symptoms are fatigue, pallor, breathlessness, palpitations, and poor resistance to infection. Treatment depends on the cause.

anemometer device for measuring wind speed and liquid flow. The most basic form, the **cup-type anemometer**, consists of cups at the ends of arms, which rotate when the wind blows. The speed of rotation indicates the wind speed.

anemone any plant of the genus *Anemone* of the buttercup family Ranunculaceae. The function of petals is performed by its sepals. The garden anemone *A. coronaria* is white, blue, red, or purple.

The white or lavender-tinged wood anemone *A. quinquefolia* grows in open woods, flowering in spring.

anesthetic drug that produces loss of sensation or consciousness; the resulting state is anesthesia, in which the patient is insensitive to stimuli. Anesthesia may also happen as a result of nerve disorder.

aneurysm weakening in the wall of an artery, causing it to balloon outwards, with the risk of rupture and serious, often fatal, blood loss. If detected in time and accessible, some aneurysms can be excised.

angel (Greek *angelos* "messenger") in Jewish, Christian, and Muslim belief, a supernatural being intermediate between God and humans. The Christian hierarchy has nine orders: **Seraphim**, **Cherubim**, **Thrones** (who contemplate God and reflect his glory), **Dominations**, **Virtues**, **Powers** (who regulate the stars and the universe), **Principalities**, **Archangels**, and **Angels** (who minister to humanity). In traditional Catholic belief every human being has a guardian angel. The existence of angels was reasserted by Pope John Paul II 1986.

angel dust popular name for the anesthetic **phencyclidine**, a depressant drug.

Angel Falls highest waterfalls in the world, on the river Caroni in the tropical rain forest of Bolivar Region, Venezuela; total height 3,210 ft/978 m. They were named after the aviator and prospector James Angel who flew over the falls and crash-landed nearby 1935.

angelfish any of a number of unrelated fishes. The freshwater **angelfish**, genus *Pterophyllum*, of South America, is a tall, side-to-side flattened fish with a striped body, up to 10 in/26 cm long, but usually smaller in captivity. The **angelfish** or **monkfish** of the genus *Squatina* is a bottom-living shark up to 6 ft/1.8 m long with a body flattened from top to bottom. The **marine angelfishes**, *Pomacanthus* and others, are long narrow-bodied fish with spiny fins, often brilliantly colored, up to 2 ft/60 cm long, living around coral reefs in the tropics.

Angelico Fra (Guido di Pietro) *c.* 1400–1455. Italian painter of religious scenes, active in Florence. He was a monk and painted a series of frescoes at the monastery of San Marco, Florence, begun after 1436. He also produced several altarpieces in a simple style.

Angelou Maya (born Marguerite Johnson) 1928– . US novelist, poet, playwright, and short-story writer. Her powerful autobiographical works, *I Know Why the Caged Bird Sings* 1970 and its three sequels, tell of the struggles toward physical and spiritual liberation of a black woman growing up in the South.

angina or **angina pectoris** severe pain in the chest due to impaired blood supply to the heart muscle because a coronary artery is narrowed. Faintness and difficulty in breathing accompany the pain. Treatment is by drugs, such as nitroglycerin and amyl nitrite; rest is important.

angiosperm flowering plant in which the seeds are enclosed within an ovary, which ripens to a fruit. Angiosperms are divided into monocotyledons (single seed leaf in the embryo) and dicotyledons (two seed leaves in the embryo). They include the majority of flowers, herbs, grasses, and trees except conifers.

Angle member of the Germanic tribe that invaded Britain in the 5th century; see ◊Anglo-Saxon.

angle in mathematics, the amount of turn or rotation; it may be defined by a pair of rays (half-lines) that share a common endpoint but do not lie on the same line. Angles are measured in ◊degrees (°) or radians (rads)—a complete turn or circle being 360° or 2π rads.

Angles are classified generally by their degree measures: *acute angles* are less than 90°; *right angles* are exactly 90° (a quarter turn); *obtuse angles* are greater than 90° but less than 180°; *reflex angles* are greater than 180° but less than 360°.

angle of declination angle at a particular point on the Earth's surface between the direction of the true or geographic North Pole and the magnetic north pole. The angle of declination has varied over time because of the slow drift in the position of the magnetic north pole.

angler any of an order of fishes Lophiiformes, with flattened body and broad head and jaws. Many species have small, plantlike tufts on their skin. These act as camouflage for the fish as it waits, either floating among seaweed or lying on the sea bottom, twitching the enlarged tip of the threadlike first ray of its dorsal fin to entice prey.

Anglo-Irish Agreement or *Hillsborough Agreement* concord reached 1985 between the UK prime minister Margaret Thatcher and Irish prime minister Garret FitzGerald. One sign of the improved relations between the two countries was increased cooperation between police and security forces across

angler *Angler fish entice their prey into their large mouths by means of a fishing rod—a modified dorsal ray with a fleshy lure at its tip.*

the border with Northern Ireland. The pact also gave the Irish Republic a greater voice in the conduct of Northern Ireland's affairs. However, the agreement was rejected by Northern Ireland Unionists as a step toward renunciation of British sovereignty. In March 1988 talks led to further strengthening of the agreement.

Anglo-Saxon one of the several Germanic invaders (Angles, Saxons, and Jutes) who conquered much of Britain between the 5th and 7th centuries. After the conquest kingdoms were set up, which are commonly referred to as the *Heptarchy*; these were united in the early 9th century under the overlordship of Wessex. The Norman invasion 1066 brought Anglo-Saxon rule to an end.

The Jutes probably came from the Rhineland and not, as was formerly believed, from Jutland. The Angles and Saxons came from Schleswig–Holstein, and may have united before invading. There was probably considerable intermarriage with the Romanized Celts of ancient Britain, although the latter's language and civilization almost disappeared. The English-speaking peoples of Britain, Australia, New Zealand, and the US are often referred to today as Anglo-Saxons, but the term is inaccurate, since the Welsh,

Scots, and Irish are mainly of Celtic or Norse descent, and by the 1980s fewer than 15% of Americans were of British descent.

Anglo-Saxon Chronicle history of England from the Roman invasion to the 11th century, in the form of a series of chronicles written in Old English by monks, begun in the 9th century (during the reign of King Alfred), and continuing to the 12th century.

Anglo-Saxon language group of dialects spoken by the ◊Anglo-Saxon peoples who, in the 5th–7th centuries, invaded and settled in Britain (in what became England and Lowland Scotland). Anglo-Saxon is traditionally known as Old English. See ◊English language.

Angola country in SW Africa, bounded W by the Atlantic ocean, N and NE by Zaire, E by Zambia, and S by Namibia. The Cabinda enclave, a district of Angola, is bounded W by the Atlantic Ocean, N by the river Congo, and E and S by Zaire.

Angry Young Men group of British writers who emerged about 1950 after the creative hiatus that followed World War II. They included Kingsley Amis, John Wain, John Osborne, and Colin Wilson. Also linked to the group were Iris Murdoch and Kenneth Tynan.

Angola People's Republic of
(*República Popular de Angola*)

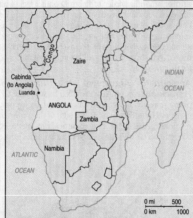

area 481,226 sq mi/1,246,700 sq km
capital and chief port Luanda
cities Lobito and Benguela, also ports; Huambo, Lubango
physical narrow coastal plain rises to vast interior plateau with rain forest in NW; desert in S
features Cuanza, Cuito, Cubango, and Cunene rivers; Cabinda enclave
head of state and government José Eduardo dos Santos from 1979
political system socialist republic
political parties People's Movement for the Liberation of Angola–Workers' Party (MPLA–PT), Marxist-Leninist; National Union for the Total Independence of Angola (UNITA); National Front for the Liberation of Angola (FNLA)
exports oil, coffee, diamonds, palm oil, sisal, iron ore, fish
currency kwanza
population (1992) 10,609,000 (largest ethnic group Ovimbundu); growth rate 2.5% p.a.
life expectancy men 40, women 44
languages Portuguese (official); Bantu dialects

religions Roman Catholic 68%, Protestant 20%, animist 12%
literacy 20%
GDP $2.7 bn; $432 per head

chronology
1951 Angola became an overseas territory of Portugal.
1956 First independence movement formed, the MPLA.
1961 Unsuccessful independence rebellion.
1962 Second nationalist movement formed, the FNLA.
1966 Third nationalist movement formed, UNITA.
1975 Independence achieved from Portugal. Transitional government of independence formed from representatives of MPLA, FNLA, UNITA, and Portuguese government. MPLA proclaimed People's Republic of Angola under the presidency of Dr Agostinho Neto. FNLA and UNITA proclaimed People's Democratic Republic of Angola.
1976 MPLA gained control of most of the country. South African troops withdrawn, but Cuban units remained.
1977 MPLA restructured to become MPLA–PT.
1979 Death of Neto, succeeded by José Eduardo dos Santos.
1980 UNITA guerrillas, aided by South Africa, continued raids against the Luanda government and bases of the South West Africa People's Organization (SWAPO) in Angola.
1984 South Africa promised to withdraw its forces if the Luanda government guaranteed that areas vacated would not by filled by Cuban or SWAPO units (the Lusaka Agreement).
1985 South African forces officially withdrawn.
1986 Further South African raids into Angola. UNITA continued to receive South African support.
1988 Peace treaty, providing for the withdrawal of all foreign troops, signed with South Africa and Cuba.
1989 Cease-fire agreed with UNITA broke down and guerrilla activity restarted.
1990 Peace offer by rebels. Return to multiparty politics promised.
1991 Peace agreement signed, civil war between MPLA–PT and UNITA officially ended. Amnesty for all political prisoners.
1992 MPLA–PT's general-election victory fiercely disputed by UNITA, plunging the country into renewed civil war. UNITA offered, and eventually accepted, seats in the new government, but fighting continued.
1993 Fighting continued. Key city fell to UNITA. MPLA–PT made power-sharing agreement with UNITA. Dos Santos government recognized by US.

angst (German "anxiety") an emotional state of anxiety without a specific cause. In ◊Existentialism, the term refers to general human anxiety at having free will, that is, of being responsible for one's actions.

angstrom unit (symbol Å) of length equal to 10^{-10} meter or one-ten-millionth of a millimeter, used for atomic measurements and the wavelengths of electromagnetic radiation. It is named after the Swedish scientist A J Ångström.

Ångström Anders Jonas 1814–1874. Swedish astrophysicist who worked in spectroscopy and solar physics. In 1861 Ångström identified the presence of hydrogen in the Sun. His major work *Recherches sur le spectre solaire* 1868, an atlas of solar spectra, presented the measurements of 1,000 spectral lines expressed in units of one-ten-millionth of a millimeter, the unit which later became the angstrom.

Anguilla island in the E Caribbean
area 62 sq mi/160 sq km
capital The Valley
features white coral-sand beaches; 80% of its coral reef has been lost through tourism (pollution and souvenir sales)
exports lobster, salt
currency Eastern Caribbean dollar
population (1988) 7,000
languages English, Creole
government from 1982, governor, executive council, and legislative house of assembly
history a British colony from 1650, Anguilla was long associated with St Christopher–Nevis but revolted against alleged domination by the larger island and in 1969 declared itself a republic. A small British force restored order, and Anguilla retained a special position at its own request; since 1980 it has been a separate dependency of the UK.

angular momentum see ◊momentum.

Anhui or *Anhwei* province of E China, watered by the Chang Jiang (Yangtze River)
area 54,000 sq mi/139,900 sq km
capital Hefei
products cereals in the N; cotton, rice, tea in the S
population (1990) 56,181,000.

animal or *metazoan* member of the kingdom Animalia, one of the major categories of living things, the science of which is *zoology*. Animals are all heterotrophs (they obtain their energy from organic substances produced by other organisms); they have eukaryotic cells (the genetic material is contained within a distinct nucleus) bounded by a thin cell membrane rather than the thick cell wall of plants. Most animals are capable of moving around for at least part of their life cycle.

animal behavior the scientific study of the behavior of animals, either by comparative psychologists (with an interest mainly in the psychological processes involved in the control of behavior) or by ethologists (with an interest in the biological context and relevance of behavior).

animism in psychology and physiology, the view of human personality that attributes human life and behavior to a force distinct from matter. In religious theory, the conception of a spiritual reality behind the material one: for example, beliefs in the soul as a shadowy duplicate of the body capable of independent activity, both in life and death. In anthropology, the concept of spirits residing in all natural phenomena and objects.

Anguilla

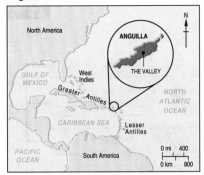

anise plant *Pimpinella anisum*, of the carrot family Umbelliferae, whose fragrant seeds are used to flavor foods. Aniseed oil is used in cough medicines.

Ankara (formerly *Angora*) capital of Turkey; population (1990) 2,559,500. Industries include cement, textiles, and leather products. It replaced Istanbul (then in Allied occupation) as capital 1923.

Annamese member of the majority ethnic group in Vietnam, comprising 90% of the population. The Annamese language is distinct from Vietnamese, though it has been influenced by Chinese and has loan words from Khmer. Their religion combines elements of Buddhism, Confucianism, and Taoism, as well as ancestor worship.

Annapolis seaport and capital of Maryland; population (1984) 31,900. It was named after Princess (later Queen) Anne 1695. The State House, built 1772–80, is the oldest US state capitol in continuous legislative use. It was in session here Nov 1783–Jun 1784 that ◊Congress received George ◊Washington's resignation as commander in chief 1783 and ratified the peace treaty that ended the Revolutionary War. The US Naval Academy is here, and John Paul ◊Jones is buried in the chapel crypt.

Annapurna mountain 26,502 ft/8,075 m in the Himalayas, Nepal. The north face was first climbed by a French expedition (Maurice Herzog) 1950 and the south by a British team 1970.

Ann Arbor city in SE Michigan, W of Dearborn and Detroit, on the Huron River; seat of Washtenaw county; population (1990) 109,600. It is a center for medical, aeronautical, nuclear, and chemical research, and the site of the University of Michigan (1837).

Anne 1665–1714. Queen of Great Britain and Ireland 1702–14. She was the second daughter of James, Duke of York, who became James II, and Anne Hyde. She succeeded William III 1702. Events of her reign include the War of the Spanish Succession, Marlborough's victories at Blenheim, Ramillies, Oudenarde, and Mal- plaquet, and the union of the English and Scottish parliaments 1707. Anne was succeeded by George I.

Anne (full name Anne Elizabeth Alice Louise) 1950– . Princess of the UK, second child of Queen Elizabeth II, declared Princess Royal 1987. She is an excellent horsewoman, winning a gold medal at the 1976 Olympics, and is actively involved in global charity work, especially for children. In 1973 she married Capt Mark Phillips (1949–); they separated 1989 and were divorced 1992. In Dec 1992 she married Commander Tim Laurence.

animal The animal kingdom is divided into 18 major groups or phyla.

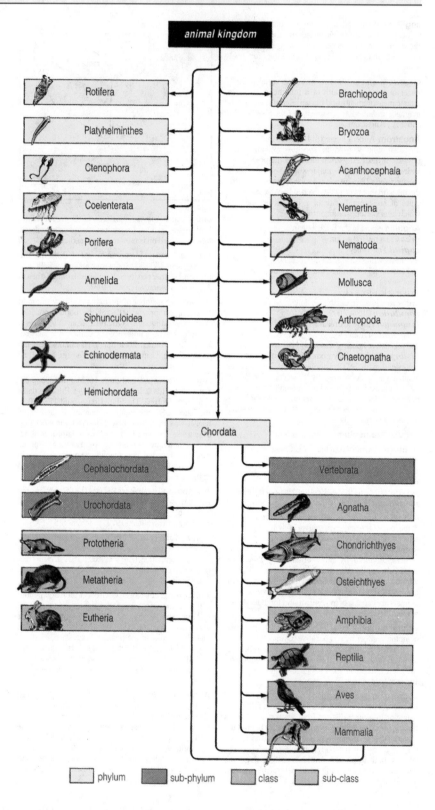

animal kingdom

Rotifera

Platyhelminthes

Ctenophora

Coelenterata

Porifera

Annelida

Siphunculoidea

Echinodermata

Hemichordata

Brachiopoda

Bryozoa

Acanthocephala

Nemertina

Nematoda

Mollusca

Arthropoda

Chaetognatha

Chordata

Cephalochordata

Urochordata

Prototheria

Metatheria

Eutheria

Vertebrata

Agnatha

Chondrichthyes

Osteichthyes

Amphibia

Reptilia

Aves

Mammalia

☐ phylum ☐ sub-phylum ☐ class ☐ sub-class

annelid any segmented worm of the phylum Annelida. Annelids include earthworms, leeches, and marine worms such as lugworms.

Anne of Austria 1601–1666. Queen of France from 1615 and regent 1643–61. Daughter of Philip III of Spain, she married Louis XIII of France (whose chief minister, Cardinal Richelieu, worked against her). On her husband's death she became regent for their son, Louis XIV, until his majority.

She chose her lover ◊Mazarin as her chief minister.

Anne of Cleves 1515–1557. Fourth wife of ◊Henry VIII of England 1540. She was the daughter of the Duke of Cleves, and was recommended to Henry as a wife by Thomas ◊Cromwell, who wanted an alliance with German Protestantism against the Holy Roman Empire. Henry did not like her looks, had the marriage declared void after six months, pensioned her, and had Cromwell beheaded.

Anne of Denmark 1574–1619. Queen consort of James VI of Scotland (later James I of Great Britain 1603). She was the daughter of Frederick II of Denmark and Norway, and married James 1589. Anne was suspected of Catholic leanings and was notably extravagant.

Anniston city in E Alabama, NE of Birmingham; seat of Calhoun county; population (1990) 26,600. The site of iron mines, its industries include iron products as well as textiles and chemicals.

anno Domini (Latin "in the year of our Lord") in the Christian chronological system, refers to dates since the birth of Jesus, denoted by the letters AD. There is no year 0, so AD 1 follows immediately after the year 1 BC (before Christ). The system became the standard reckoning in the Western world after being adopted by the English historian Bede in the 8th century. The abbreviations CE (Common Era) and BCE (before Common Era) are often used instead by scholars and writers as objective, rather than religious, terms.

annual plant plant that completes its life cycle within one year, during which time it germinates, grows to maturity, bears flowers, produces seed, and then dies.

annual rings or **growth rings** concentric rings visible on the wood of a cut tree trunk or other woody stem. Each ring represents a period of growth when new ◊xylem is laid down to replace tissue being converted into wood (secondary xylem). The wood formed from xylem produced in the spring and early summer has larger and more numerous vessels than the wood formed from xylem produced in autumn when growth is slowing down. The result is a clear boundary between the pale spring wood and the denser, darker autumn wood. Annual rings may be used to estimate the age of the plant (see ◊dendrochronology), although occasionally more than one growth ring is produced in a given year.

Annunciation in the New Testament, the announcement to Mary by the archangel Gabriel that she was to be the mother of Christ; the feast of the Annunciation is March 25 (also known as Lady Day).

anode the positive electrode toward which negative particles (anions, electrons) move within a device such as the cells of a battery, electrolytic cells, and diodes.

anodizing process that increases the resistance to ◊corrosion of a metal, such as aluminum, by building up a protective oxide layer on the surface. The natural corrosion resistance of aluminum is provided by a thin film of aluminum oxide; anodizing increases the thickness of this film and thus the corrosion protection.

anorexia lack of desire to eat, especially the pathological condition of **anorexia nervosa**, usually found in adolescent girls and young women, who may be obsessed with the desire to lose weight. Compulsive eating, or ◊bulimia, often accompanies anorexia.

Anouilh Jean 1910–1987. French dramatist. His plays, influenced by the Neo-Classical tradition, include *Antigone* 1942, *L'Invitation au château/Ring Round the Moon* 1947, *Colombe* 1950, and *Becket* 1959, about St Thomas à Becket and Henry II.

Anschluss (German "union") the annexation of Austria with Germany, accomplished by the German chancellor Adolf Hitler March 12, 1938.

Austria was occupied jointly by the Allies until 1955, when it declared independence as a republic.

Anselm, St *c.* 1033–1109. Medieval priest and philosopher. As abbot from 1078, he made the abbey of Bec in Normandy, France, a center of scholarship in Europe. He was appointed archbishop of Canterbury by William II of England 1093, but was later forced into exile. He holds an important place in the development of ◊Scholasticism.

In his *Proslogion* he developed the ontological proof of theism, which infers God's existence from our capacity to conceive of a perfect being. His major work, *Cur deus homo?/Why Did God Become Man?*, treats the subject of the Atonement. He was canonized 1494.

ant insect belonging to the family Formicidae, and to the same order (Hymenoptera) as bees and wasps. Ants are characterized by a conspicuous "waist" and elbowed antennae. About 10,000 different species are known; all are social in habit, and all construct nests of various kinds. Ants are found in all parts of the world, except the polar regions. It is estimated that there are about 10 million billion ants.

Antabuse proprietary name for disulfiram, a synthetic chemical used in the treatment of alcoholism. It produces unpleasant side effects if combined with alcohol, such as nausea, headaches, palpitations, and collapse. The "Antabuse effect" is produced coincidentally by certain antibiotics.

antacid any substance that neutralizes stomach acid, such as sodium bicarbonate or magnesium hydroxide ("milk of magnesia"). Antacids are weak ◊bases, swallowed as solids or emulsions. They may be taken between meals to relieve symptoms of hyperacidity, such as pain, bloating, nausea, and "heartburn." Excessive or prolonged need for antacids should be investigated medically.

Antananarivo (formerly **Tananarive**) capital of Madagascar, on the interior plateau, with a rail link to Tamatave; population (1986) 703,000. Industries include tobacco, food processing, leather goods, and clothing.

Antarctica continent surrounding the South Pole, arbitrarily defined as the region lying S of the Antarctic Circle. Occupying 10% of the world's surface, Antarctica contains 90% of the world's ice and 70% of its fresh water

area 5,400,000 sq mi/13,900,000 sq km (the size of Europe and the US combined)

features Mount Erebus on Ross Island is the world's southernmost active volcano; the Ross Ice Shelf is formed by several glaciers coalescing in the Ross Sea

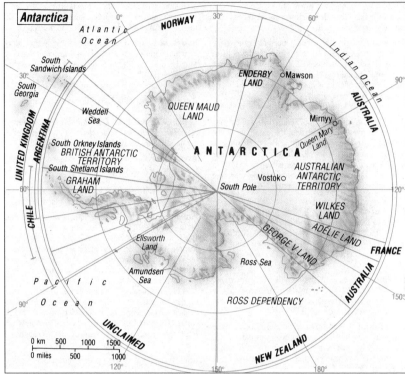

Antarctica

Atlantic Ocean · 0° · NORWAY · 30° · 60°

South Sandwich Islands

South Georgia

Indian Ocean

ENDERBY LAND · Mawson

90°

Weddell Sea

QUEEN MAUD LAND

Mirnyy

AUSTRALIA

UNITED KINGDOM · ARGENTINA

South Orkney Islands
BRITISH ANTARCTIC TERRITORY
South Shetland Islands

ANTARCTICA

Queen Mary Land

GRAHAM LAND

Vostok

AUSTRALIAN ANTARCTIC TERRITORY

South Pole

CHILE

WILKES LAND

ADÉLIE LAND

FRANCE

Ellsworth Land

GEORGE V LAND

Ross Sea

AUSTRALIA

150°

Amundsen Sea

Pacific Ocean

90°

ROSS DEPENDENCY

UNCLAIMED

0 km 500 1000 1500
0 miles 500 1000

120° · NEW ZEALAND · 150° · 180°

---

physical formed of two blocks of rock with an area of about 3,000,000 sq mi/8,000,000 sq km, Antarctica is covered by a cap of ice that flows slowly toward its 14,000 mi/22,400 km coastline, reaching the sea in high ice cliffs. The most southerly shores are near the 78th parallel in the Ross and Weddell seas. E Antarctica is a massive block of ancient rocks that surface in the Transantarctic Mountains of Victoria Land. Separated by a deep channel, W Antarctica is characterized by the mountainous regions of Graham Land, the Antarctic Peninsula, Palmer Land, and Ellsworth Land; the highest peak is Vinson Massif (16,866 ft/5,139 m).

Antarctic Circle imaginary line that encircles the South Pole at latitude 66° 32' S. The line encompasses the continent of Antarctica and the Antarctic Ocean.

Antarctic Peninsula mountainous peninsula of W Antarctica extending 1,200 mi/1,930 km N toward South America; originally named *Palmer Land* after a US navigator, Captain Nathaniel Palmer, who was the first to explore the region 1820. It was claimed by Britain 1832, Argentina 1940, and Chile 1942. Its name was changed to the Antarctic Peninsula 1964.

Antarctic Treaty international agreement aiming to promote scientific research and keep Antarctica free from conflict. It dates from 1961 and in 1991 a 50-year ban on mining activity was secured.

anteater *The anteater is a relative of the sloths, armadillos, and pangolins.*

Antares or *Alpha Scorpii* brightest star in the constellation Scorpius and the 15th brightest star in the sky. It is a red supergiant several hundred times larger than the Sun and perhaps 10,000 times as luminous, lies about 300 light-years away, and fluctuates, slightly in brightness.

anteater mammal of the family Myrmecophagidae, order Edentata, native to Mexico, Central America, and tropical South America. An anteater lives almost entirely on ants and termites. It has toothless jaws, an extensile tongue, and claws for breaking into the nests of its prey.

antelope any of numerous kinds of even-toed, hoofed mammals belonging to the cow family, Bovidae. Most antelopes are lightly built and good runners. They are grazers or browsers, and chew the cud. They range in size from the dik-diks and duikers, only 1 ft/30 cm high, to the eland, which can be 6 ft/1.8 m at the shoulder.

antenna in zoology, an appendage ("feeler") on the head. Insects, centipedes, and millipedes each have one pair of antennae but there are two pairs in crustaceans, such as shrimps. In insects, the antennae are involved with the senses of smell and touch; they are frequently complex structures with large surface areas that increase the ability to detect scents.

antenna in radio and television, another name for ◊aerial.

anther in a flower, the terminal part of a stamen in which the ◊pollen grains are produced. It is usually borne on a slender stalk or filament, and has two lobes, each containing two chambers, or pollen sacs, within which the pollen is formed.

Antarctica: chronology

1773–74	English explorer James Cook first sailed in Antarctic seas, but exploration was difficult before the development of iron ships able to withstand ice pressure.
1819–21	Antarctica was circumnavigated by Russian explorer Fabian Bellingshausen.
1823	British navigator James Weddell sailed into the sea now named after him.
1841–42	Scottish explorer James Ross sighted the Great Ice Barrier now named after him.
1895	Norwegian explorer Carsten Borchgrevink was one of the first landing party on the continent.
1898	Borchgrevink's British expedition first wintered in Antarctica.
1901–04	English explorer Robert Scott first penetrated the interior of the continent.
1907–08	English explorer Ernest Shackleton came within 113 mi/182 km of the Pole.
1911	Norwegian explorer Roald Amundsen reached the Pole, Dec 14, overland with dogs.
1912	Scott reached the Pole, Jan 18, initially aided by ponies.
1928–29	US naval officer Richard Byrd made the first flight to the Pole.
1935	US explorer Lincoln Ellsworth (1880–1951) first flew across Antarctica.
1946–48	US explorer Finn Ronne's expedition proved the Antarctic to be one continent.
1957–58	English explorer Vivian Fuchs made the first overland crossing.
1959	A Soviet expedition crossed from the West Ice Shelf to the Pole; the International Antarctic Treaty suspended all territorial claims, reserving an area south of 60°S latitude for peaceful purposes.
1961–62	The Bentley Trench was discovered, which suggested that there may be an Atlantic–Pacific link beneath the continent.
1966–67	Specially protected areas were established internationally for animals and plants.
1979	Fossils of apelike humanoids resembling E Africa's Proconsul were found 300 mi/500 km from the Pole.
1980	International Convention on the exploitation of resources—oil, gas, fish, and krill.
1982	The first circumnavigation of Earth (Sept 2, 1979–Aug 29, 1982) via the Poles was completed by English explorers Ranulph Fiennes and Charles Burton.
1990	The longest unmechanized crossing (3,182 mi/6,100 km) was made by a six-person international team, using only skis and dogs.
1991	The Antarctic Treaty imposing a 50-year ban on mining activity was secured.
1992–93	Norwegian lawyer Erling Kagge skied unassisted to South Pole from Berkner Island in Weddell Sea; Ranulph Fiennes and Michael Stroud crossed Antarctic continent on foot, unassisted, but had to be rescued before reaching ultimate destination of Scott's Base.

Anthony Susan B(rownell) 1820–1906. US pioneering campaigner for women's rights who also worked for the antislavery and temperance movements. Her causes included equality of pay for women teachers, married women's property rights, and women's suffrage. In 1869, with Elizabeth Cady ◊Stanton, she founded the National Woman Suffrage Association.

Anthony, St c. 251–356. Also known as Anthony of Thebes. He was the founder of Christian monasticism. At the age of 20, he renounced all his possessions and began a hermetic life of study and prayer, later seeking further solitude in a cave in the desert.

anthracite (from Greek *anthrax*, "coal") hard, dense, shiny variety of ◊coal, containing over 90% carbon and a low percentage of ash and impurities, which causes it to burn without flame, smoke, or smell.

anthrax cattle and sheep disease occasionally transmitted to humans, usually via infected hides and fleeces. It may develop as black skin pustules or severe pneumonia. Treatment is with antibiotics.

The causative agent is a bacillus (*Bacillus anthracis*).

anthropology (Greek *anthropos* "man" and *logos* "discourse") study of humankind, which developed following 19th-century evolutionary theory to investigate the human species, past and present, physically, socially, and culturally.

The four subdisciplines are physical anthropology, linguistics, cultural anthropology, and archeology.

anthropomorphism the attribution of human characteristics to animals, inanimate objects, or deities. It appears in the mythologies of many cultures and as a literary device in fables and allegories.

antibiotic drug that kills or inhibits the growth of bacteria and fungi. It is derived from living organisms such as fungi or bacteria, which distinguishes it from synthetic antimicrobials.

antibody a protein molecule produced in the blood by B-lymphocytes (see ◊lymphocyte). Antibodies bind specific foreign agents that invade the body, tagging them for destruction by phagocytes (white blood cells that engulf and destroy invaders) or activating a chemical system that renders them harmless. Each antibody is specific for a particular ◊antigen (the molecular pattern unique to a foreign substance).

Antichrist in Christian theology, the opponent of Christ. The appearance of the Antichrist was believed to signal the Second Coming, at which Christ would conquer his opponent. The concept may stem from the

Anthony Early American feminist Susan B Anthony began campaigning for women's rights 1852.

idea of conflict between Light and Darkness, which is present in Persian, Babylonian, and Jewish literature and which influenced early Christian thought.

anticoagulant substance that suppresses the formation of blood clots. Common anticoagulants are heparin, produced by the liver and lungs, and derivatives of coumarin. Anticoagulants are used medically in treating heart attacks, for example. They are also produced by blood-feeding animals, such as mosquitoes, leeches, and vampire bats, to keep the victim's blood flowing.

anticonvulsant any drug used to prevent epileptic seizures (convulsions or fits); see ◊epilepsy.

antidepressant any drug used to relieve symptoms in depressive illness. The two main groups are the tricyclic antidepressants (TCADs) and the monoamine oxidase inhibitors (MAOIs), which act by altering chemicals available to the central nervous system. Both may produce serious side effects and are restricted.

antifreeze substance added to a water-cooling system (for example, that of a car) to prevent it freezing in cold weather.

The most common types of antifreeze contain the chemical ethylene ◊glycol, or (HOCH$_2$CH$_2$OH), an organic alcohol with a freezing point of about –5°F/15°C. The addition of this chemical depresses the freezing point of water significantly. A solution containing 33.5% by volume of ethylene glycol will not freeze until about –4°F/–20°C. A 50% solution will not freeze until –31°F/–35°C.

antigen any substance that causes the production of ◊antibodies by the body's immune system. Common antigens include the proteins carried on the surface of bacteria, viruses, and pollen grains. The proteins of incompatible blood groups or tissues also act as antigens, which has to be taken into account in medical procedures such as blood transfusions and organ transplants.

Antigone in Greek legend, a daughter of Jocasta, by her son ◊Oedipus. She is the subject of a tragedy by ◊Sophocles.

Antigonus 382–301 BC. A general of Alexander the Great after whose death 323 BC Antigonus made himself master of Asia Minor. He was defeated and killed by ◊Seleucus I at the battle of Ipsus.

Antigua and Barbuda country comprising three islands in the E Caribbean (Antigua, Barbuda, and uninhabited Redonda).

antihistamine any substance that counteracts the effects of ◊histamine. Antihistamines may be naturally produced (such as vitamin C and epinephrin) or synthesized (pseudepinephrin).

anti-inflammatory any substance that reduces swelling in soft tissues. Antihistamines relieve allergic reactions; aspirin and NSAIDs are effective in joint and musculoskeletal conditions; rubefacients (counterirritant liniments) ease painful joints, tendons, and muscles.

Antilles group of West Indian islands, divided N–S into the ***Greater Antilles*** (Cuba, Jamaica, Haiti–Dominican Republic, Puerto Rico) and ***Lesser Antilles***, subdivided into the Leeward Islands (Virgin Islands, St Christopher–Nevis, Antigua and Barbuda, Anguilla, Montserrat, and Guadeloupe) and

---

Antigua and Barbuda
State of

area Antigua 108 sq mi/280 sq km, Barbuda 62 sq mi/161 sq km, plus Redonda 0.4 sq mi/1 sq km
capital and chief port St John's
cities Codrington (on Barbuda)
physical low-lying tropical islands of limestone and coral with some higher volcanic outcrops; no rivers and low rainfall result in frequent droughts and deforestation
features Antigua is the largest of the Leeward Islands; Redonda is an uninhabited island of volcanic rock rising to 1,000 ft/305 m
head of state Elizabeth II from 1981, represented by governor general

head of government Vere C Bird from 1981
political system liberal democracy
political parties Antigua Labour Party (ALP), moderate, left of center; Progressive Labour Movement (PLM), left of center
exports sea-island cotton, rum, lobsters
currency Eastern Caribbean dollar
population (1992) 64,500; growth rate 1.3% p.a.
life expectancy 70 years
language English
media no daily newspaper; weekly papers all owned by political parties
religion Christian (mostly Anglican)
literacy 90% (1985)
GDP $173 million (1985); $2,200 per head

chronology
1493 Antigua visited by Christopher Columbus.
1632 Antigua colonized by English settlers.
1667 Treaty of Breda formally ceded Antigua to Britain.
1871–1956 Antigua and Barbuda administered as part of the Leeward Islands federation.
1967 Antigua and Barbuda became an associated state within the Commonwealth, with full internal independence.
1971 PLM won the general election by defeating the ALP.
1976 PLM called for early independence, but ALP urged caution. ALP won the general election.
1981 Independence from Britain achieved.
1983 Assisted US invasion of Grenada.
1984 ALP won a decisive victory in the general election.
1985 ALP reelected.
1989 Another sweeping general election victory for the ALP under Vere Bird.
1991 Bird remained in power despite calls for his resignation.

the Windward Islands (Dominica, Martinique, St Lucia, St Vincent and the Grenadines, Barbados, and Grenada).

antimatter in physics, a form of matter in which most of the attributes (such as electrical charge, magnetic moment, and spin) of ◊elementary particles are reversed.

antimony silver-white, brittle, semimetallic element (a metalloid), symbol Sb (from Latin *stibium*), atomic number 51, atomic weight 121.75. It occurs chiefly as the ore stibnite, and is used to make alloys harder; it is also used in photosensitive substances in color photography, optical electronics, fireproofing, pigment, and medicine. It was employed by the ancient Egyptians in a mixture to protect the eyes from files.

Antioch ancient capital of the Greek kingdom of Syria, founded 300 BC by ◊Seleucus I in memory of his father Antiochus, and famed for its splendor and luxury. Under the Roman and Byzantine empires it was an early center of Christianity. It was captured by the Arabs 637. After a five-month siege 1098 Antioch was taken by the crusaders, who held it until 1268. The site is now occupied by the Turkish town of Antakya.

Antiochus thirteen kings of Sytria of the Seleucid dynasty, including:

Antiochus I *c.* 324–*c.* 261 BC. King of Syria from 281 BC, son of Seleucus I, one of the generals of Alexander the Great. He earned the title of Antiochus Soter, or Savior, by his defeat of the Gauls in Galatia 276.

Antiochus II *c.* 286–*c.* 246 BC. King of Syria 261–246 BC, son of Antiochus I. He was known as Antiochus Theos, the Divine. During his reign the eastern provinces broke away from the Graeco-Macedonian rule and set up native princes. He made peace with Egypt by marrying the daughter of Ptolemy Philadelphus, but was a tyrant among his own people.

Antiochus III the Great *c.* 241–187 BC. King of Syria from 223 BC, nephew of Antiochus II. He secured a loose control over Armenia and Parthia 209, overcame Bactria, received the homage of the Indian king of the Kabul valley, and returned by way of the Persian Gulf 204. He took possession of Palestine, entering Jerusalem 198. He crossed into NW Greece, but was decisively defeated by the Romans at Thermopylae 191 and at Magnesia 190. The Peace of Apamea 188 BC confined Seleucid rule to Asia.

Antiochus IV *c.* 215–164 BC. King of Syria from 175 BC, known as Antiochus Epiphanes, the Illustrious, son of Antiochus III. He occupied Jerusalem about 170, seizing much of the Temple treasure, and instituted worship of the Greek type in the Temple in an attempt to eradicate Judaism. This produced the revolt of the Hebrews under the Maccabees; Antiochus died before he could suppress it.

Antiochus XIII 1st century BC. King of Syria 69–65 BC, the last of the Seleucid dynasty. During his reign Syria was made a Roman province by Pompey the Great.

antiphony in music, a form of composition using widely spaced choirs or groups of instruments to create perspectives in sound. It was developed in 17th-century Venice by Giovanni Gabrieli and his pupil Heinrich Schütz.

antipope rival claimant to the elected pope for the leadership of the Roman Catholic Church, for instance in the Great Schism 1378–1417 when there were rival popes in Rome and Avignon.

antipyretic any drug, such as aspirin, used to reduce fever.

anti-Semitism literally, prejudice against Semitic people (see ◊Semite), but in practice it has meant prejudice or discrimination against, and persecution of, the Jews as an ethnic group. Historically this was practiced for almost 2,000 years by European Christians. Anti-Semitism was a tenet of Hitler's Germany, and in the Holocaust 1933–45 about 6 million Jews died in concentration camps and in local extermination ◊pogroms, such as the siege of the Warsaw ghetto. In eastern Europe, as well as in Islamic nations, anti-Semitism exists and is promulgated by neofascist groups. It is a form of ◊racism.

In the 20th century, fascism and the Nazi Party's application of racial theories led to organized persecution and genocide. After World War II, the creation of Israel 1948 provoked Palestinian anti-Zionism, backed by the Arab world. Anti-Semitism is still fostered by extreme right-wing groups, such as the National Front in the UK and France, the Neo-Nazis in the US and Germany, and the Palestine Liberation Organization in the Arab nations.

antiseptic any substances that kills or inhibits the growth of microorganisms. The use of antiseptics was pioneered by Joseph ◊Lister. He used carbolic acid (◊phenol), which is a weak antiseptic; substances such as TCP are derived from this.

antispasmodic any drug that reduces motility, the spontaneous action of the muscle walls. Anticholinergics are a type of antispasmodic that act indirectly by way of the autonomic nervous system, which controls involuntary movement. Other drugs act directly on the smooth muscle to relieve spasm (contraction).

antitrust laws in economics, regulations preventing or restraining trusts, monopolies, or any business practice considered to be unfair or uncompetitive. In the US, antitrust laws prevent mergers and acquisitions that might create a monopoly situation or ones in which restrictive practices might be stimulated.

antiviral any drug that acts against viruses, usually preventing them from multiplying. Most viral infections are not susceptible to antibiotics. Antivirals have been difficult drugs to develop, and do not necessarily cure viral diseases.

antivivisection opposition to vivisection, that is, experiments on living animals, which is practiced in the pharmaceutical and cosmetics industries on the grounds that it may result in discoveries of importance to medical science. Antivivisectionists argue that it is immoral to inflict pain on helpless creatures, and that it is unscientific because results achieved with animals may not be paralleled with human beings.

Antivivisectionist groups, now joined by animal rights activists, sometimes take illegal action to draw attention to their cause.

antler "horn" of a deer, often branched, and made of bone rather than horn. Antlers, unlike true horns, are shed and regrown each year. Reindeer of both sexes grow them, but in all other types of deer, only the males have antlers.

ant lion larva of one of the insects of the family Myrmeleontidae, order Neuroptera, which traps ants by waiting at the bottom of a pit dug in loose, sandy soil. Ant lions are mainly tropical, but also occur in parts of Europe and in the US, where they are called doodlebugs.

Antonine Wall Roman line of fortification built AD 142. It was the Roman Empire's northwest frontier, between the Clyde and Forth rivers, Scotland. It was defended until *c.* 200.

Antoninus Pius AD 86–161. Roman emperor who had been adopted 138 as Hadrian's heir, and succeeded him later that year. He enjoyed a prosperous reign, during which the Antonine Wall was built. His daughter married his successor ◊Marcus Aurelius Antoninus.

Antonioni Michelangelo 1912– . Italian film director, famous for his subtle presentations of neuroses and personal relationships among the leisured classes. His elliptical approach to narrative is best seen in *L'Avventura* 1959.

antonymy near or precise oppositeness between or among words. *Good* and *evil* are antonyms, and therefore *evil* and *bad* are synonyms in this context.

Antrim county of Northern Ireland
area 1,092 sq mi/2,830 sq km
cities Belfast (county town), Larne (port)
features Giant's Causeway of natural hexagonal basalt columns, which, in legend, was built to enable the giants to cross between Ireland and Scotland; Antrim borders Lough Neagh, and is separated from Scotland by the North Channel, 20 mi/30 km wide
products potatoes, oats, linen, synthetic textiles
population (1981) 642,000.

Antwerp (Flemish *Antwerpen*, French *Anvers*) port in Belgium on the river Scheldt, capital of the province of Antwerp; population (1991) 467,500. One of the world's busiest ports, it has shipbuilding, oil-refining, petrochemical, textile, and diamond-cutting industries. The home of the artist Rubens is preserved, and many of his works are in the Gothic cathedral. The province of Antwerp has an area of 1,119 sq mi/2,900 sq km; population (1987) 1,588,000.

Anubis in Egyptian mythology, the jackal-headed god of the dead, son of Osiris. Anubis presided over the funeral cult, including embalming, and led the dead to judgment.

anus opening at the end of the alimentary canal that allows undigested food and associated materials to pass out of an animal. It is found in all types of multicellular animal except the coelenterates (sponges) and the platyhelminthes (flatworms), which have a mouth only.

anxiety emotional state of fear or apprehension. Anxiety is a normal response to potentially dangerous situations. Abnormal anxiety can either be free-floating, experienced in a wide range of situations, or it may be phobic, when the sufferer is excessively afraid of an object or situation.

ANZAC (acronym for *Australian and New Zealand Army Corps*) general term for all troops of both countries serving in World War I and to some extent those in World War II.

Anzio seaport and resort on the W coast of Italy, 33 mi/53 km SE of Rome; population (1984) 25,000. It is the site of the Roman town of Antium and the birthplace of the emperor Nero.

Anzio, Battle of in World War II, the beachhead invasion of Italy Jan 22–May 23, 1944, by Allied troops; failure to use information gained by deciphering German codes led to Allied troops being stranded temporarily after German attacks.

aorta the chief ◊artery, the dorsal blood vessel carrying oxygenated blood from the left ventricle of the heart in birds and mammals. It branches to form smaller arteries, which in turn supply all body organs except the lungs. Loss of elasticity in the aorta provides evidence of ◊atherosclerosis, which may lead to heart disease.

apache member of a group of North ◊American Indian peoples who lived as hunters in the Southwest. They are related to the Navaho, and now number about 10,000, living in reservations in Arizona, SW Oklahoma, and New Mexico. They were known as fierce raiders and horse warriors in the 18th and 19th centuries. Apache also refers to any of several southern Athabaskan languages and dialects spoken by these people.

apartheid racial-segregation policy of the government of South Africa, which was legislated 1948, when the Afrikaner National Party gained power. Nonwhites (Bantu, Coloured or mixed, or Indian) do not share full rights of citizenship with the 4.5 million whites (for example, the 23 million black people cannot vote in parliamentary elections), and many public facilities and institutions were until 1990 (and in some cases remain) restricted to the use of one race only; the establishment of ◊Black National States is another manifestation of apartheid. In 1991 President de Klerk repealed the key elements of apartheid legislation.

apatosaurus large plant-eating dinosaur, formerly called **brontosaurus**, which flourished about 145 million years ago. Up to 69 ft/21 m long and 30 tons in weight, it stood on four elephantlike legs and had a long tail, long neck, and small head. It probably snipped off low-growing vegetation with peglike front teeth, and swallowed it whole to be ground by pebbles in the stomach.

ape ◊primate of the family Pongidae, closely related to humans, including gibbon, orangutan, chimpanzee, and gorilla.

Apennines chain of mountains stretching the length of the Italian peninsula. A continuation of the Maritime Alps, from Genoa it swings across the peninsula to Ancona on the east coast, and then back to the west coast and into the "toe" of Italy. The system is continued over the Strait of Messina along the N Sicilian coast, then across the Mediterranean Sea in a series of islands to the Atlas Mountains of N Africa. The highest peak is Gran Sasso d'Italia at 9,560 ft/2,914 m.

aphasia difficulty in speaking, writing, and reading, usually caused by damage to the brain.

aphid any of the family of small insects, Aphididae, in the order Homoptera, that live by sucking sap from plants. There are many species, often adapted to particular plants.

Aphrodite in Greek mythology, the goddess of love (Roman Venus, Phoenician Astarte, Babylonian Ishtar); said to be either a daughter of Zeus (in Homer) or sprung from the foam of the sea (in Hesiod). She was the unfaithful wife of Hephaestus, the god of fire, and the mother of Eros.

Apia capital and port of Western ◊Samoa, on the N coast of Upolu Island, in the W Pacific; population (1981) 33,000. It was the final home of the writer Robert Louis Stevenson from 1888 to 1894.

Apis ancient Egyptian god with a human body and a bull's head, linked with Osiris (and later merged with him into the Ptolemaic god Serapis); his cult centers were Memphis and Heliopolis, where sacred bulls were mummified.

Apocrypha appendix to the Old Testament of the Bible, not included in the final Hebrew canon but recognized by Roman Catholics. There are also disputed New Testament texts known as Apocrypha.

Apollo in Greek and Roman mythology, the god of sun, music, poetry, prophecy, agriculture, and pastoral life, and leader of the Muses. He was the twin child (with ◊Artemis) of Zeus and Leto. Ancient statues show Apollo as the embodiment of the Greek ideal of male beauty. His chief cult centers were his supposed birthplace on the island of Delos, in the Cyclades, and Delphi.

Apollonius of Perga c. 260–c. 190 BC. Greek mathematician, called "the Great Geometer." In his work *Conic Sections* he showed that a plane intersecting a cone will generate an ellipse, a parabola, or a hyperbola, depending on the angle of intersection. In astronomy, he used a system of circles called epicycles and deferents to explain the motion of the planets; this system, as refined by Ptolemy, was used until the Renaissance.

Apollonius of Rhodes lived 3rd century BC. Greek poet, author of the epic *Argonautica*, which tells the story of Jason and the Argonauts and their quest for the Golden Fleece.

Apollo project US space project to land a person on the Moon, achieved July 20, 1969, when Neil Armstrong was the first to set foot there. He was accompanied on the Moon's surface by Col Edwin E Aldrin, Jr; Michael Collins remained in the orbiting command module.

apoplexy alternate name for ◊stroke.

apostle in the New Testament, any of the chosen 12 ◊disciples sent out by Jesus after his resurrection to preach the Gospel. In the earliest days of Christianity the term was extended to include some who had never known Jesus in the flesh, notably St Paul.

Apostles' Creed one of the three ancient ◊creeds of the Christian church.

apostolic succession doctrine in the Christian church that certain spiritual powers were received by the first apostles directly from Jesus, and have been handed down in the ceremony of "laying on of hands" from generation to generation of bishops.

apostrophe mark (') used in written English and some other languages. In English it serves primarily to indicate either a missing letter (*mustn't* for *must not*) or number ('*47* for *1947*), or grammatical possession ("*John's* camera," "*women's* dresses"). It is often omitted in proper names (Publishers Association, Actors Studio, *Collins Dictionary*). Many people otherwise competent in writing have great difficulty with the apostrophe, which has never been stable at any point in its history.

apothecary person who prepares and dispenses medicines; a pharmacist.

Appalachians mountain system of E North America, stretching about 1,500 mi/2,400 km from Alabama to Québec, composed of ancient eroded rocks and rounded peaks. The chain separates the Mississippi–Missouri lowlands from the Atlantic coastal plain and includes the Allegheny, Catskill, White, and Blue Ridge mountains, the last having the highest peak, Mount Mitchell, 6,712 ft/2,045 m. The E edge has a fall line to the coastal plain where Philadelphia, Baltimore, and Washington stand. The Appalachians are heavily forested and have deposits of coal and other minerals.

Apollo project US astronaut Edwin Aldrin, the second astronaut to walk on the Moon, on July 20, 1969.

apparent depth depth that a transparent material such as water or glass appears to have when viewed from above. This is less than its real depth because of the ◊refraction that takes place when light passes into a less dense medium. The ratio of the real depth to the apparent depth of a transparent material is equal to its refractive index.

appeasement historically, the conciliatory policy adopted by the British government, in particular under Neville Chamberlain, toward the Nazi and Fascist dictators in Europe in the 1930s in an effort to maintain peace. It was strongly opposed by Winston Churchill, but the ◊Munich Agreement 1938 was almost universally hailed as its justification. Appeasement ended when Germany occupied Bohemia–Moravia March 1939.

War was declared after Germany attacked Poland Sept 1939, the beginning of World War II.

appendicitis inflammation of the appendix, a small, blind extension of the bowel in the lower right abdomen. In an acute attack, the pus-filled appendix may burst, causing a potentially lethal spread of infection. Treatment is by removal (appendectomy).

appendix area of the mammalian gut, associated with the digestion of cellulose. In herbivores it may be large, containing millions of bacteria that secrete enzymes to digest grass. No vertebrate can produce the type of digestive enzyme that will digest cellulose, the main constituent of plant cell walls. Those herbivores that rely on cellulose for their energy have all evolved specialist mechanisms to make use of the correct type of bacteria.

apple fruit of *Malus pumila*, a tree of the family Rosaceae. There are several hundred varieties of cultivated apples, grown all over the world, which may be divided into eating, cooking, and cider apples. All are derived from the wild crab apple.

Appleton city in E central Wisconsin, northwest of Oshkosh, on the Fox River; seat of Outagamie country; population (1990) 65,700. It is a manufacturing center for paper products. Founded 1847, it claims to have the world's first hydroelectric plant, built 1882.

appliqué embroidery used to create pictures or patterns by "applying" pieces of material onto a background fabric. The pieces are cut into the appropriate shapes and sewn on, providing decoration for wall hangings, furnishing textiles, and clothes.

Appomattox village in Virginia, scene of the surrender April 9, 1865, of the Confederate army under Robert E Lee to the Union army under Ulysses S Grant, which ended the American Civil War.

appropriate technology simple or small-scale machinery and tools that, because they are cheap and easy to produce and maintain, may be of most use in the developing world; for example, hand plows and simple looms. This equipment may be used to supplement local crafts and traditional skills to encourage small-scale industrialization.

apricot fruit of *Prunus armeniaca*, a tree of the rose family Rosaceae, closely related to the almond, peach, plum, and cherry. It has yellow-fleshed fruit.

April Fools' Day the first day of April, when it is customary in W Europe and the US to expose people to ridicule by a practical joke, causing them to believe some falsehood or to go on a fruitless errand.

a priori (Latin "from what comes before") in logic, an argument that is known to be true, or false, without reference to experience; the converse of ◊a posteriori.

Apuleius Lucius lived 2nd century AD. Roman lawyer, philosopher, and author of *Metamorphoses*, or *The Golden Ass*.

Aqaba, Gulf of gulf extending for 100 mi/160 km between the Negev and the Red Sea; its coastline is uninhabited except at its head, where the frontiers of Israel, Egypt, Jordan, and Saudi Arabia converge. The two ports of Eilat (Israeli "Elath") and Aqaba, Jordan's only port, are situated here.

aquaculture another name for ◊fish farming.

aqualung or *scuba* underwater breathing apparatus worn by divers, developed in the early 1940s by French diver Jacques Cousteau. Compressed- air cylinders strapped to the diver's back are regulated by a valve system and by a mouth tube to provide air to the diver at the same pressure as that of the surrounding water (which increases with the depth).

aquamarine blue variety of the mineral ◊beryl. A semiprecious gemstone, it is used in jewelry.

Aquarius zodiacal constellation a little south of the celestial equator near Pegasus. Aquarius is represented as a man pouring water from a jar. The Sun passes through Aquarius from late Feb to early March. In astrology, the dates for Aquarius are between about Jan 20 and Feb 18.

aquatint printmaking technique, usually combined with ◊etching to produce areas of subtle tone as well as more precisely etched lines. Aquatint became common in the late 18th century.

aqueduct any artificial channel or conduit for water, often an elevated structure of stone, wood, or iron built for conducting water across a valley. The Greeks built a tunnel 4,200 ft/1,280 m long near Athens, 2,500 years ago. Many Roman aqueducts are still standing, for example the one at Nîmes in S France, built about AD 18 (which is 160 ft/48 m high).

aqueous humor watery fluid found in the space between the cornea and lens of the vertebrate eye. Similar to blood serum in composition, it is renewed every four hours.

aquifer any rock formation containing water. The rock of an aquifer must be porous and permeable (full of interconnected holes) so that it can absorb water. Aquifers supply ◊artesian wells, and are actively sought in arid areas as sources of drinking and irrigation water.

Aquila constellation on the celestial equator (see ◊celestial sphere). Its brightest star is first-magnitude ◊Altair, flanked by the stars Beta and Gamma Aquilae. It is represented by an eagle.

Aquinas St Thomas *c.* 1226–1274. Neapolitan philosopher and theologian, the greatest figure of the school of ◊Scholasticism. He was a Dominican monk, known as the "Angelic Doctor." In 1879 his works were recognized as the basis of Catholic theology. His *Summa contra Gentiles/Against the Errors of the Infi-*

aqueduct *Pont du Gard, Roman aqueduct near Nîmes, S France.*

dels 1259–64 argues that reason and faith are compatible. He assimilated the philosophy of Aristotle into Christian doctrine.

Aquino (Maria) Corazon (born Cojuangco) 1933– . President of the Philippines 1986–92. She was instrumental in the nonviolent overthrow of President Ferdinand Marcos 1986. As president, she sought to rule in a conciliatory manner, but encountered opposition from left (communist guerrillas) and right (army coup attempts), and her land reforms were seen as inadequate.

The daughter of a sugar baron, she studied in the US and in 1956 married the politician Benigno Aquino (1933–1983). The chief political opponent of the right-wing president Marcos, he was assassinated by a military guard at Manila airport on his return from exile. Corazon Aquino was drafted by the opposition to contest the Feb 1986 presidential election and claimed victory over Marcos, accusing the government of voting fraud. She led a nonviolent "people's power" campaign, which overthrew Marcos Feb 25. A devout Roman Catholic, Aquino enjoyed strong church backing in her 1986 campaign. The US provided strong support as well and was instrumental in turning back a 1989 coup attempt. In 1991 she announced she would not enter the 1992 presidential elections.

Aquitaine region of SW France; capital Bordeaux; area 15,942 sq mi/41,300 sq km; population (1986) 2,718,000. It comprises the *départements* of Dordogne, Gironde, Landes, Lot-et-Garonne, and Pyrénées-Atlantiques. Red wines (Margaux, St Julien) are produced in the Médoc district, bordering the Gironde. Aquitaine was an English possession 1152–1452.

AR abbreviation for the state of ◊*Arkansas*.

Arab any of a Semitic (see ◊Semite) people native to the Arabian peninsula, but now settled throughout North Africa and the nations of the Middle East.

arabesque in ballet, a pose in which the dancer stands on one leg, straight or bent, with the other leg raised behind, fully extended. The arms are held in a harmonious position to give the longest possible line from fingertips to toes.

Arabian Nights tales in oral circulation among Arab storytellers from the 10th century, probably having their roots in India. They are also known as *The Thousand and One Nights* and include "Ali Baba," "Aladdin," "Sinbad the Sailor," and "The Old Man of the Sea."

Arabian Sea northwestern branch of the ◊Indian Ocean.

Arabic language major Semitic language of the Hamito-Semitic family of W Asia and North Africa, originating among the Arabs of the Arabian peninsula. It is spoken today by about 120 million people in the Middle East and N Africa. Arabic script is written from right to left.

Arabic numerals or *Hindu-Arabic numerals* the symbols 0, 1, 2, 3, 4, 5, 6, 7, 8, 9, early forms of which were in use among the Arabs before being adopted by the peoples of Europe during the Middle Ages in place of ◊Roman numerals. The symbols appear to have originated in India and probably reached Europe by way of Spain.

Arab-Israeli Wars series of wars between Israel and various Arab states in the Middle East since the founding of the state of Israel 1948.
First Arab-Israeli War May 15, 1948–Jan 13/March 24, 1949. As soon as the independent state of Israel had been proclaimed by the Jews, it was invaded by combined Arab forces. The Israelis defeated them and went on to annex territory until they controlled 75% of what had been Palestine under British mandate.
Second Arab-Israeli War Oct 29–Nov 4, 1956. After Egypt had taken control of the Suez Canal and blockaded the Straits of Tiran, Israel, with British and French support, invaded and captured Sinai and the Gaza Strip, from which it withdrew under heavy US pressure after the entry of a United Nations force.
Third Arab-Israeli War June 5–10, 1967, the *Six-Day War*. It resulted in the Israeli capture of the Golan Heights from Syria; the eastern half of Jerusalem and the West Bank from Jordan; and, in the south, the Gaza Strip and Sinai peninsula as far as the Suez Canal.
Fourth Arab-Israeli War Oct 6–24, 1973, the "October War" or *Yom Kippur War*, so called because the Israeli forces were taken by surprise on the Day of ◊Atonement. It started with the recrossing of the Suez Canal by Egyptian forces who made initial gains, though there was some later loss of ground by the Syrians in the north.
Fifth Arab-Israeli War From 1978 the presence of Palestinian guerrillas in Lebanon led to Arab raids on Israel and Israeli retaliatory incursions, but on June 6, 1982, Israel launched a full-scale invasion. By June 14 Beirut was encircled, and ◊Palestine Liberation Organization (PLO) and Syrian forces were evacuated (mainly to Syria) Aug 21–31, but in Feb 1985 there was a unilateral Israeli withdrawal from the country without any gain or losses incurred. Israel maintains a "security zone" in S Lebanon and supports the South Lebanese Army militia as a buffer against Palestinian guerrilla incursions.

Arab League organization of Arab states established in Cairo 1945 to promote Arab unity, primarily in opposition to Israel. The original members were Egypt, Syria, Iraq, Lebanon, Transjordan (Jordan 1949), Saudi Arabia, and Yemen. In 1979 Egypt was suspended and the league's headquarters transferred to Tunis in protest against the Egypt-Israeli peace, but Egypt was readmitted as a full member May 1989, and in March 1990 its headquarters returned to Cairo.

Arab Monetary Fund (AMF) money reserve established 1976 by 20 Arab states plus the Palestine Liberation Organization to provide a mechanism for promoting greater stability in exchange rates and to coordinate Arab economic and monetary policies. It operates mainly by regulating petrodollars within the Arab community to make member countries less dependent on the West for the handling of their surplus money. The fund's headquarters are in Abu Dhabi in the United Arab Emirates.

Arachne (Greek "spider") in Greek legend, a Lydian woman who was so skillful a weaver that she challenged the goddess ◊Athena to a contest. Athena tore Arachne's beautiful tapestries to pieces and Arachne hanged herself. She was transformed into a spider, and her weaving became a cobweb.

arachnid or *arachnoid* type of arthropod, including spiders, scorpions, and mites. They differ from insects in possessing only two main body regions, the cephalothorax and the abdomen.

Arafat Yassir 1929– . Palestinian nationalist politician, cofounder of al-◊Fatah 1956 and president of the ◊Palestine Liberation Organization (PLO) from 1969. His support for Saddam Hussein after Iraq's invasion of Kuwait 1990 weakened his international standing, but he has since been influential in Middle East peace talks, and in 1993 was part of a historic agreement with Israel.

arch *The Arch of Titus from c. AD 81 on the Via Sacra in the Forum, Rome.*

Aragón autonomous region of NE Spain including the provinces of Huesca, Teruel, and Zaragoza; area 18,412 sq mi/47,700 sq km; population (1986) 1,215,000. Its capital is Zaragoza, and products include almonds, figs, grapes, and olives. Aragón was an independent kingdom 1035–1479

Aral Sea inland sea divided between Kazakhstan and Uzbekistan, the world's fourth-largest lake; former area 24,000 sq mi/62,000 sq km, but decreasing. Water from its tributaries, the Amu Darya and Syr Darya, has been diverted for irrigation and city use, and the sea is disappearing, with long-term consequences for the climate.

Aramaic language Semitic language of the Hamito-Semitic family of W Asia, the everyday language of Palestine 2,000 years ago, during the Roman occupation and the time of Jesus.

Aran Islands three rocky islands (Inishmore, Inishmaan, Inisheer) in the mouth of Galway Bay, Republic of Ireland; population approximately 4,600. The capital is Kilronan. J M ◊Synge used the language of the islands in his plays.

Ararat double-peaked mountain on the Turkish-Iranian border; the higher, Great Ararat, 16,854 ft/5,137 m, was the reputed resting place of Noah's Ark after the Flood.

Arawak member of an indigenous American people of the Caribbean and NE Amazon Basin. Arawaks lived mainly by shifting cultivation in tropical forests. They were driven out of many West Indian islands by another American Indian people, the Caribs, shortly before the arrival of the Spanish in the 16th century. Subsequently, their numbers on Hispaniola declined from some 4 million in 1492 to a few thousand after their exploitation by the Spanish in their search for gold; the remainining few were eradicated by disease (smallpox was introduced 1518). Arawakan languages belong to the Andean-Equatorial group.

Arbil Kurdish city in a province of the same name in N Iraq; population (1985) 334,000. Occupied since Assyrian times, it was the site of a battle 331 BC at which Alexander the Great defeated the Persians under Darius III. In 1974 Arbil became the capital of a Kurdish autonomous region set up by the Iraqi government.

arbitration submission of a dispute to a third, unbiased party for settlement. It may be personal litigation, a labor-union issue, or an international dispute.

arbor vitae any of several coniferous trees or shrubs of the genus *Thuja* of the cypress family, having flattened branchlets covered in overlapping aromatic green scales. In North America, the northern white cedar *T. occidentalis* and the western red cedar *T. plicata* are representatives. The Chinese or Oriental species *T. orientalis*, reaching 60 ft/18 m in height, is grown widely as an ornamental.

arc in geometry, a section of a curved line or circle. A circle has three types of arc: a *semicircle*, which is exactly half of the circle; *minor arcs*, which are less than the semicircle; and *major arcs*, which are greater than the semicircle.

Arc de Triomphe arch at the head of the Champs Elysées in the Place de l'Etoile, Paris, France, begun by Napoleon 1806 and completed 1836. It was intended to commemorate Napoleon's victories of 1805–06 and commissioned from Jean Chalgrin (1739–1811). Beneath it rests France's "Unknown Soldier."

arch curved structure of masonry that supports the weight of material over an open space, as in a bridge or doorway. The first arches consisted of several wedge-shaped stones supported by their mutual pressure. The term is also applied to any curved structure that is an arch in form only.

Archaean or *Archaeozoic* the earliest eon of geological time; the first part of the Precambrian, from the formation of Earth up to about 2,500 million years ago. It was a time when no life existed, and with every new discovery of ancient life its upper boundary is being pushed further back.

archaeopteryx extinct primitive bird, known from fossilized remains, about 160 million years old, found in limestone deposits in Bavaria, Germany. It is popularly known as "the first bird," although some earlier bird ancestors are now known. It was about the size of a crow and had feathers and wings, but in many respects its skeleton is reptilian (teeth and a long, bony tail) and very like some small meat-eating dinosaurs of the time.

archbishop in the Christian church, a bishop of superior rank who has authority over other bishops in his jurisdiction and often over an ecclesiastical province. The office exists in the Roman Catholic, Eastern Orthodox, and Anglican churches.

archeology study of history (primarily but not exclusively the prehistoric and ancient periods), based on the examination of physical remains. Principal activities include preliminary field (or site) surveys, excavation (where necessary), and the classification, dating, and interpretation of finds. Since 1958 radiocarbon dating has been used to establish the age of archeological strata and associated materials.

archery use of the bow and arrow, originally in hunting and warfare, now as a competitive sport. The world governing body is the Fédération Internationale de Tir à l'Arc (FITA) founded 1931. In competitions, results are based on double FITA rounds; that is, 72 arrows at each of four targets at 90, 70, 50, and 30 meters(70, 60, 50, and 30 for women). The best possible score is 2,880.

Organizations in the US include the National Archery Association 1879 and, for actual hunting with the bow, the National Field Archery Association 1940.

Archimedes *c.* 287–212 BC. Greek mathematician who made major discoveries in geometry, hydrostatics, and mechanics. He formulated a law of fluid displacement (Archimedes' principle), and is credited with the invention of the Archimedes screw, a cylindrical device for raising water.

Archimedes' principle in physics, law stating that an object totally or partly submerged in a fluid displaces a volume of fluid that weighs the same as the apparent loss in weight of the object (which, in turn, equals the upward force, or upthrust, experienced by that object). It was discovered by the Greek mathematician Archimedes.

Archimedes screw one of the earliest kinds of pump, thought to have been invented by Archimedes. It consists of a spiral screw revolving inside a close-fitting cylinder. It is used, for example, to raise water for irrigation.

archipelago group of islands, or an area of sea containing a group of islands. The islands of an archipelago are usually volcanic in origin, and they sometimes represent the tops of peaks in areas around continental margins flooded by the sea.

Archipenko Alexander 1887–1964. Ukrainian-born abstract sculptor who lived in France from 1908 and in the US from 1923. He pioneered Cubist works composed of angular forms and spaces and later experimented with clear plastic and sculptures incorporating lights.

architecture art of designing structures. The term covers the design of the visual appearance of structures; their internal arrangements of space; selection of external and internal building materials; design or selection of natural and artificial lighting systems, as well as mechanical, electrical, and plumbing systems; and design or selection of decorations and furnishings. Architectural style may emerge from evolution of techniques and styles particular to a culture in a given time period with or without identifiable individuals as architects, or may be attributed to specific individuals or groups of architects working together on a project.

Neo-Gothic The late 19th century saw a fussy Gothic revival in Europe and the US, particularly evident in churches (Ralph Adams Cram's work in the US—for example, St John the Divine, New York) and public buildings (Charles Barry's work in the Houses of Parliament, London).

Art Nouveau This architecture arising at the end of the 19th century countered Neo-Gothic, using sinuous, flowing shapes for buildings, room plans, and interior design. The style is characterized by the work of Charles Rennie Mackintosh in Scotland (Glasgow Art School) and Antonio Gaudi in Spain (Church of the Holy Family, Barcelona), and design elements were used especially in France but also in England and the US.

Modernist This architecture is also known as Functionalism or the International Style. It began in the 1900s with the Vienna school and the German

Arctic exploration: chronology	
60,000– 35,000 BC	Ancestors of the Inuit and American Indians began migration from Siberia to North America by the lost land bridge of Beringia.
320 BC	Pytheas, a Greek sailor contemporary with Alexander the Great, possibly reached Iceland.
9th–10th centuries AD	Vikings colonized Iceland and Greenland, which then had a much warmer climate.
c. **1000**	Norwegian sailor Leif Ericsson reached Baffin Island (NE of Canada) and Labrador.
1497	Genoese pilot Giovanni Caboto first sought the Northwest Passage as a trade route around North America for Henry VII of England.
1553	English navigator Richard Chancellor tried to find the Northeast Passage around Siberia and first established direct English trade with Russia.
1576	English sailor Martin Frobisher reached Frobisher Bay, but found only *fools' gold* (iron pyrites) for Elizabeth I of England.
1594–97	Dutch navigator Willem Barents made three expeditions in search of the Northeast Passage.
1607	English navigator Henry Hudson failed to cross the Arctic Ocean, but his reports of whales started the northern whaling industry.
1670	Hudson's Bay Company started the fur trade in Canada.
1728	Danish navigator Vitus Bering passed the Bering Strait.
1829–33	Scottish explorer John Ross discovered the North Magnetic Pole.
1845	The mysterious disappearance of English explorer John Franklin's expedition to the Northwest Passage stimulated further exploration.
1878–79	Swedish navigator Nils Nordensköld was the first European to discover the Northeast Passage.
1893–96	Norwegian explorer Fridtjof Nansen's ship *Fram* drifted across the Arctic while locked in the ice, proving that no Arctic continent existed.
1903–06	Norwegian explorer Roald Amundsen sailed through the Northwest Passage.
1909	US explorers Robert Peary, Matt Henson, and four Inuit reached the North Pole on April 2.
1926 May 9	US explorers Richard Byrd and Floyd Bennett flew to the Pole.
May 12	Italian aviator Umberto Nobile and Amundsen crossed the Pole (Spitzbergen–Alaska) in the airship *Norge*.
1954	Scandinavian Airlines launched the first regular commercial flights over the short-cut polar route.
1958	The US submarine *Nautilus* crossed the Pole beneath the ice.
1960	From this date a Soviet nuclear-powered icebreaker kept open a 2,500 mi/4,000 km Asia–Europe passage along the north coast of Siberia for 150 days a year.
1969	Wally Herbert of the British Transarctic Expedition made the first surface crossing, by dog sled, of the Arctic Ocean (Alaska–Spitzbergen).
1977	The Soviet icebreaker *Arktika* made the first surface voyage to the Pole.
1982	English explorers Ranulph Fiennes and Charles Burton completed the first circumnavigation of the Earth via the Poles, Sept 2 1979–Aug 29 1982.
1988	Canadian and Soviet skiers attempted the first overland crossing from the USSR to Canada via the Pole.
1993	International research project established to develop a geographical information system covering the biological resources of the Arctic.

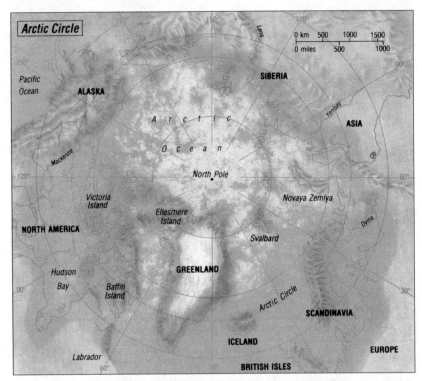

Arctic Circle

Pacific Ocean
ALASKA
SIBERIA
Arctic
Ocean
ASIA
Mackenzie
North Pole
Victoria Island
Novaya Zemlya
Ellesmere Island
NORTH AMERICA
Svalbard
Hudson Bay
GREENLAND
Baffin Island
Arctic Circle
SCANDINAVIA
ICELAND
EUROPE
Labrador
BRITISH ISLES

Bauhaus but was also seen in the US, Scandinavia, and France. It used spare line and form, an emphasis on rationalism, and the elimination of ornament. It makes great use of technological advances in materials such as glass, steel, and concrete and of construction techniques that allow flexibility of design. Notable practitioners include Frank Lloyd Wright, Mies van der Rohe, and Le Corbusier. Modern architecture also furthered the notion of the planning of extensive multibuilding projects and of whole towns or communities.

Post-Modernist This architecture emerged in the US, Japan, and Europe in the 1980s, with one trend toward high-tech forms and another reverting back to using simplified or geometric elements from earlier styles to decorate traditional forms.

arc lamp or *arc light* electric light that uses the illumination of an electric arc maintained between two electrodes. The British scientist Humphry Davy developed an arc lamp 1808, and its main use in recent years has been in cinema projectors. The lamp consists of two carbon electrodes, between which a very high voltage is maintained. Electric current arcs (jumps) between the two, creating a brilliant light.

Arctic, the that part of the northern hemisphere surrounding the ◊North Pole; arbitrarily defined as the region lying N of the Arctic Circle (66° 32') or N of the tree line. There is no Arctic continent; the greater part of the region comprises the Arctic Ocean, which is the world's smallest ocean. Arctic climate, fauna, and flora extend over the islands and northern edges of continental landmasses that surround the Arctic Ocean (Svalbard, Iceland, Greenland, Siberia, Scandinavia, Alaska, and Canada). *area* 14,000,000 sq mi/36,000,000 sq km *physical* Pack-ice floating on the Arctic Ocean occupies almost the entire region

between the North Pole and the coasts of North America and Eurasia, covering an area that ranges in diameter from 1,900 mi/3,000 km to 2,500 mi/4,000 km. The pack-ice reaches a maximum extent in Feb when its outer limit (influenced by the cold Labrador Current and the warm Gulf Stream) varies from 50°N along the coast of Labrador to 75°N in the Barents Sea N of Scandinavia. In spring the pack-ice begins to break up into ice floes which are carried by the south-flowing Greenland Current to the Atlantic Ocean. Arctic ice is at its minimum area in Aug. The greatest concentration of icebergs in Arctic regions is found in Baffin Bay. They are derived from the glaciers of W Greenland, then carried along Baffin Bay and down into the N Atlantic where they melt off Labrador and Newfoundland. *See table p. 51*

Arctic Circle imaginary line that encircles the North Pole at latitude 66° 32' N. Within this line there is at least one day in the summer during which the Sun never sets, and at least one day in the winter during which the Sun never rises.

Arctic Ocean ocean surrounding the North Pole; area 5,400,000 sq mi/14,000,000 sq km. Because of the Siberian and North American rivers flowing into it, it has low salinity and freezes readily.

Arcturus or *Alpha Boötis* brightest star in the constellation Boötes and the fourth-brightest star in the sky. Arcturus is a red giant about 28 times larger than the Sun and 70 times more luminous, 36 light-years away from Earth.

Ardennes wooded plateau in NE France, SE Belgium, and N Luxembourg, cut through by the river Meuse; also a *département* of ◊Champagne-Ardenne. There was heavy fighting here in World Wars I and II (see ◊Bulge, Battle of the).

Argentina Republic of
(*República Argentina*)

area 1,073,116 sq mi/2,780,092 sq km
capital Buenos Aires (to move to Viedma)
cities Rosario, Córdoba, Tucumán, Mendoza, Santa Fé; ports are La Plata and Bahía Blanca
physical mountains in W, forest and savanna in N, pampas (treeless plains) in E central area, Patagonian plateau in S; rivers: Colorado, Salado, Paraná, Uruguay, Río de la Plata estuary
territories part of Tierra del Fuego; disputed claims to S Atlantic islands and part of Antarctica
environment an estimated 7,700 sq mi/20,000 sq km of land has been swamped with salt water
features Andes mountains, with Aconcagua the highest peak in the W hemisphere; Iguaçú Falls
head of state and government Carlos Menem from 1989
political system emergent democratic federal republic
political parties Radical Civic Union Party (UCR), moderate centrist; Justicialist Party, right-wing Peronist
exports livestock products, cereals, wool, tannin, peanuts, linseed oil, minerals (coal, copper, molybdenum, gold, silver, lead, zinc, barium, uranium); the country has huge resources of oil, natural gas, hydroelectric power
currency peso = 10,000 australs (which it replaced 1992)
population (1992) 33,070,000 (mainly of Spanish or Italian

origin, only about 30,000 American Indians surviving); growth rate 1.5% p.a.
life expectancy men 66, women 73
languages Spanish (official); English, Italian, German, French
religion Roman Catholic (state-supported)
literacy men 96%, women 95% (1985 est)
GDP $70.1 bn (1990); $2,162 per head

chronology
1816 Independence achieved from Spain, followed by civil wars.
1946 Juan Perón elected president, supported by his wife "Evita."
1952 Evita Perón died.
1955 Perón overthrown and civilian administration restored.
1966 Coup brought back military rule.
1973 A Peronist party won the presidential and congressional elections. Perón returned from exile in Spain as president, with his third wife, Isabel, as vice president.
1974 Perón died, succeeded by Isabel.
1976 Coup resulted in rule by a military junta led by Lt-Gen Jorge Videla. Congress dissolved, and hundreds of people, including Isabel Perón, detained.
1976–83 Ferocious campaign against left-wing elements, the "dirty war."
1978 Videla retired. Succeeded by General Roberto Viola, who promised a return to democracy.
1981 Viola died suddenly. Replaced by General Leopoldo Galtieri.
1982 With a deteriorating economy, Galtieri sought popular support by ordering an invasion of the British-held Falkland Islands. After losing the short war, Galtieri was removed and replaced by General Reynaldo Bignone.
1983 Amnesty law passed and democratic constitution of 1853 revived. General elections won by Raúl Alfonsín and the UCR. Armed forces under scrutiny.
1984 National Commission on the Disappearance of Persons (CONADEP) reported on over 8,000 people who had disappeared during the "dirty war" of 1976–83.
1985 A deteriorating economy forced Alfonsín to seek help from the International Monetary Fund and introduce an austerity program.
1986 Unsuccessful attempt on Alfonsín's life.
1988 Unsuccessful army coup.
1989 Carlos Menem, of the Justicialist Party, elected president.
1990 Full diplomatic relations with the UK restored. Menem elected Justicialist Party leader. Revolt by army officers thwarted.
1992 New currency introduced.

are metric unit of area, equal to 100 square meters(119.6 sq yd); 100 ares make one ◊hectare.

Arecibo site in Puerto Rico of the world's largest single-dish ◊radio telescope, 1,000 ft/305 m in diameter. It is built in a natural hollow and uses the rotation of the Earth to scan the sky.

Ares in Greek mythology, the god of war, equivalent to the Roman ◊Mars. The son of Zeus and Hera, he was worshiped chiefly in Thrace.

Aretino Pietro 1492–1556. Italian writer. He earned his living, both in Rome and Venice, by publishing satirical pamphlets while under the protection of a highly placed family. His *Letters* 1537–57 are a unique record of the cultural and political events of his time, and illustrate his vivacious, exuberant character. He also wrote poems and comedies.

Argentina country in South America, bounded W and S by Chile, N by Bolivia, and E by Paraguay, Brazil, Uruguay, and the Atlantic Ocean.

argon colorless, odorless, nonmetallic, gaseous element, symbol Ar, atomic number 18, atomic weight 39.948. It is grouped with the ◊inert gases, since it was long believed not to react with other substances, but observations now indicate that it can be made to combine with boron fluoride to form compounds. It constitutes almost 1% of the Earth's atmosphere, and was discovered 1894 by British chemists John Rayleigh (1842–1919) and William Ramsay (1852–1916) after all oxygen and nitrogen had been removed chemically from a sample of air. It is used in electric discharge tubes and argon lasers.

Argonauts in Greek legend, the band of heroes who accompanied ◊Jason when he set sail in the *Argo* to find the ◊Golden Fleece.

Arizona

Argos city in ancient Greece, at the head of the Gulf of Nauplia, which was once a cult center of the goddess Hera. In the Homeric age the name "Argives" was sometimes used instead of "Greeks." In the Classical period Argos repeatedly, but unsuccessfully, contested supremacy in S Greece with ◊Sparta.

Argus in Greek mythology, a giant with 100 eyes. When he was killed by Hermes, Hera transplanted his eyes into the tail of her favorite bird, the peacock.

aria solo vocal piece in an opera or oratorio, often in three sections, the third repeating the first after a contrasting central section.

Ariadne in Greek legend, the daughter of Minos, King of Crete. When ◊Theseus came from Athens as one of the sacrificial victims offered to the ◊Minotaur, she fell in love with him and gave him a ball of thread, which enabled him to find his way out of the labyrinth.

Arianism a system of Christian theology that gave God the Father primacy over Christ. It was founded about 310 by ◊Arius, and condemned as heretical at the Council of Nicaea 325.

arid region in earth science, a region that is very dry and has little vegetation. Aridity depends on temperature, rainfall, and evaporation, and so is difficult to quantify, but an arid area is usually defined as one that receives less than 10 in/250 mm of rainfall each year. (By comparison, New York City receives 44 in/112 cm per year.) There are arid regions in North Africa, Pakistan, Australia, the US, and elsewhere. Very arid regions are ◊deserts.

Aries zodiacal constellation in the northern hemisphere between Pisces and Taurus, near Auriga, represented as the legendary ram whose golden fleece was sought by Jason and the Argonauts. Its most distinctive feature is a curve of three stars of decreasing brightness. The brightest of these is Hamal or Alpha Arietis, 65 light-years from Earth.

Ariosto Ludovico 1474–1533. Italian poet who wrote Latin poems and comedies on Classical lines, including the poem *Orlando Furioso* 1516, published 1532, an epic treatment of the *Roland* story, the perfect poetic expression of the Italian Renaissance.

Aristarchus of Samos c. 320–c. 250 BC. Greek astronomer. The first to argue that the Earth moves around the Sun, he was ridiculed for his beliefs. He was also the first astronomer to estimate the sizes of the Sun and Moon and their distances from the Earth.

Aristides c. 530–468 BC. Athenian politician. He was one of the ten Athenian generals at the battle of ◊Marathon 490 BC and was elected chief archon, or magistrate. Later he came into conflict with the democratic leader Themistocles, and was exiled about 483 BC. He returned to fight against the Persians at Salamis 480 BC and in the following year commanded the Athenians at Plataea. As commander of the Athenian fleet he established the alliance of Ionian states known as the Delian League.

aristocracy (Greek *aristos* "best," *kratos* "power") social elite or system of political power associated with landed wealth, as in western Europe; monetary wealth, as in Carthage and Venice; or religious superiority, as with the Brahmins in India. The Prussian (Junker) aristocracy based its legitimacy not only on landed wealth but also on service to the state. Aristocracies are also usually associated with monarchy but have frequently been in conflict with the sovereign over their respective rights and privileges. In Europe, their economic base was undermined during the 19th century by inflation and falling agricultural prices, leading to their demise as a political force after 1914.

Aristophanes c. 448–380 BC. Greek comedic dramatist. Of his 11 extant plays (of a total of over 40), the early comedies are remarkable for the violent satire with which he ridiculed the democratic war leaders. He also satirized contemporary issues such as the new learning of Socrates in *The Clouds* 423 BC and the power of women in ◊*Lysistrata* 411 BC. The chorus plays a prominent role, frequently giving the play its title, as in *The Wasps* 422 BC, *The Birds* 414 BC, and *The Frogs* 405 BC.

Aristotle 384–322 BC. Greek philosopher who advocated reason and moderation. He maintained that sense experience is our only source of knowledge, and that by reasoning we can discover the essences of things, that is, their distinguishing qualities. In his works on ethics and politics, he suggested that human happiness consists in living in conformity with nature. He derived his political theory from the recognition that mutual aid is natural to humankind, and refused to set up any one constitution as universally ideal. Of Aristotle's works some 22 treatises survive, dealing with logic, metaphysics, physics, astronomy, meteorology, biology, psychology, ethics, politics, and literary criticism.

His works were lost to Europe after the decline of Rome, but they were reintroduced in the Middle Ages by Arab and Jewish scholars and became the basis of medieval ◊scholasticism.

arithmetic branch of mathematics concerned with the study of numbers and their properties. The fundamental operations of arithmetic are addition, subtraction, multiplication, and division. Raising to powers (for example, squaring or cubing a number), the extraction of roots (for example, square roots), percentages, fractions, and ratios are developed from these operations.

arithmetic mean the average of a set of n numbers, obtained by adding the numbers and dividing by n. For example, the arithmetic mean of the set of 5 numbers 1, 3, 6, 8, and 12 is $(1 + 3 + 6 + 8 + 12)/5 = 30/5 = 6$.

arithmetic progression or *arithmetic sequence* sequence of numbers or terms that have a common difference between any one term and the next in the sequence. For example, 2, 7, 12, 17, 22, 27, … is an arithmetic sequence with a common difference of 5.

Arius c. 256–336. Egyptian priest whose ideas gave rise to ◊Arianism, a Christian belief which denied the complete divinity of Jesus.

Arizona state in SW US; nickname Grand Canyon State
area 113,500 sq mi/294,100 sq km
capital Phoenix

cities Tucson, Scottsdale, Tempe, Mesa, Glendale, Flagstaff

physical Colorado Plateau in the N and E, desert basins and mountains in the S and W, Colorado River, Grand Canyon

features Grand Canyon National Park (the multicolored-rock gorge through which the Colorado River flows, 4–18 mi/6–29 km wide, up to 1.1 mi/1.7 km deep, and 217 mi/350 km long); Organ Pipe Cactus National Monument Park; deserts: Painted (including the Petrified Forest of fossil trees), Gila, Sonoran; dams: Roosevelt, Hoover; old London Bridge (transported 1971 to the tourist resort of Lake Havasu City)

products cotton under irrigation, livestock, copper, molybdenum, silver, electronics, aircraft

population (1990) 3,665,000; including 4.5% American Indians (Navaho, Hopi, Apache), who by treaty own 25% of the state

famous people Cochise, Wyatt Earp, Geronimo, Barry Goldwater, Zane Grey, Percival Lowell, Frank Lloyd Wright

history part of New Spain 1715; part of Mexico 1824; passed to the US after Mexican War 1848; territory 1863; statehood achieved 1912.

Arkansas state in S central US; nickname Wonder State/Land of Opportunity

area 53,191 sq mi/137,800 sq km

capital Little Rock

cities Fort Smith, Pine Bluff, Fayetteville

physical Ozark Mountains and plateau in the W, lowlands in the E; Arkansas River; many lakes

features Hot Springs National Park

products cotton, soybeans, rice, oil, natural gas, bauxite, timber, processed foods

population (1990) 2,350,700

famous people Johnny Cash, Bill Clinton, J William Fulbright, Douglas MacArthur, Winthrop Rockefeller

history explored by Hernando de Soto 1541; European settlers 1648, who traded with local Indians; part of Louisiana Purchase 1803; statehood achieved 1836.

Arkansas

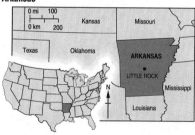

Arkwright Richard 1732–1792. English inventor and manufacturing pioneer who developed a machine for spinning cotton (he called it a "spinning frame") 1768. He set up a water-powered spinning factory 1771 and installed steam power in another factory 1790.

Arlington county in Virginia, and suburb of Washington, DC; population (1990) 170,900. It is the site of the National Cemetery for the dead of the US wars. The grounds were first used as a military cemetery 1864 during the American Civil War. By 1975, 165,142 military, naval, and civilian persons had been buried there, including the ◊Unknown Soldier of both world wars, President John F Kennedy, and his brother Robert Kennedy.

Arlington city in N Texas, located between Dallas and Fort Worth; population (1990) 261,700. Industries include machinery, paper products, steel, automobile assembly, rubber, and chemicals.

armadillo mammal of the family Dasypodidae, with an armor of bony plates on its back. Some 20 species live between Texas and Patagonia and range in size from the fairy armadillo at 5 in/13 cm to the giant armadillo, 4.5 ft/1.5 m long. Armadillos feed on insects, snakes, fruit, and carrion. Some can roll into an armored ball if attacked; others rely on burrowing for protection.

Armageddon in the New Testament (Revelation 16), the site of the final battle between the nations that will end the world; it has been identified with ◊Megiddo in Israel.

armature in a motor or generator, the wire-wound coil that carries the current and rotates in a magnetic field. (In alternating-current machines, the armature is sometimes stationary.) The pole piece of a permanent magnet or electromagnet and the moving, iron part of a ◊solenoid, especially if the latter acts as a switch, may also be referred to as armatures.

Armenia country in W Asia, bounded E by Azerbaijan, N by Georgia, W by Turkey, and S by Iran.

Armenian member of the largest ethnic group inhabiting Armenia. There are Armenian minorities in Azerbaijan, as well as in Turkey and Iran. Christianity was introduced to the ancient Armenian kingdom in the 3rd century. There are 4–5 million speakers of Armenian, which belongs to the Indo-European family of languages.

Armenian church form of Christianity adopted in Armenia in the 3rd century. The Catholicos, or exarch, is the supreme head, and Echmiadzin (near Yerevan) is his traditional seat.

Armenian language one of the main divisions of the Indo-European language family. Old Armenian, the classic literary language, is still used in the liturgy of the Armenian Church. Armenian was not written down until the 5th century AD, when an alphabet of 36 (now 38) letters was evolved. Literature flourished in the 4th to 14th centuries, revived in the 18th, and continued throughout the 20th.

Contemporary Armenian, with modified grammar and enriched with words from other languages, is used by a group of 20th-century writers.

Armenian massacres series of massacres of Armenians by Turkish soldiers between 1895 and 1915. Reforms promised to Armenian Christians by Turkish rulers never materialized; unrest broke out and there were massacres by Turkish troops 1895. Again in 1909 and 1915, the Turks massacred altogether more than a million Armenians and deported others into the N Syrian desert, where they died of starvation; those who could fled to Russia or Persia. Only some 100,000 were left.

Arminius 17 BC–AD 19. German chieftain. An ex-soldier of the Roman army, he annihilated a Roman force

armadillo The horny bands and plates of the armadillo serve as armor.

Armenia Republic of

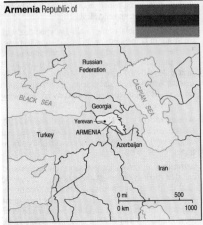

area 11,500 sq mi/29,800 sq km
capital Yerevan
cities Kumayri (formerly Leninakan)
physical mainly mountainous (including Mount Ararat), wooded
features State Academia Theatre of Opera and Ballet; Yerevan Film Studio
head of state Levon Ter-Petrossian from 1990
head of government Gagik Arutyunyan from 1991
political system emergent democracy

products copper, molybdenum, cereals, cotton, silk
population (1992) 3,426,000 (90% Armenian, 5% Azeri, 2% Russian, 2% Kurd)
language Armenian
religion traditionally Armenian Christian

chronology
1918 Became an independent republic.
1920 Occupied by the Red Army.
1936 Became a constituent republic of the USSR.
1988 Feb: demonstrations in Yerevan called for transfer of Nagorno-Karabakh from Azerbaijan to Armenian control. Dec: earthquake claimed around 25,000 lives and caused extensive damage.
1989 Jan–Nov: strife-torn Nagorno-Karabakh placed under direct rule from Moscow. Pro-autonomy Armenian National Movement founded. Nov: civil war erupted with Azerbaijan over Nagorno-Karabakh.
1990 March: Armenia boycotted USSR constitutional referendum. Aug: nationalists secured control of Armenian supreme soviet; former dissident Levon Ter-Petrossian indirectly elected president; independence declared. Nakhichevan republic affected by Nagorno-Karabakh dispute.
1991 March: overwhelming support for independence in referendum. Dec: Armenia joined new Commonwealth of Independent States; Nagorno-Karabakh declared its independence; Armenia granted diplomatic recognition by US.
1992 Admitted into United Nations and the Conference on Security and Cooperation in Europe. Conflict over Nagorno-Karabakh worsened.

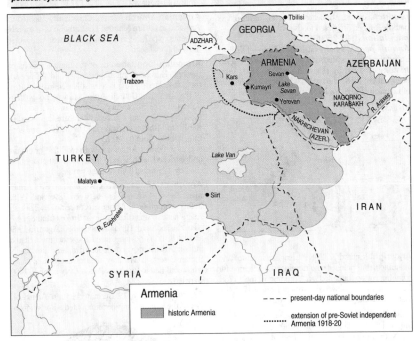

Armenia

historic Armenia

– – – present-day national boundaries

········· extension of pre-Soviet independent Armenia 1918-20

led by Varus in the Teutoburger Forest area AD 9, and saved Germany from becoming a Roman province. He was later treacherously killed by some of his kinsmen.

Arminius Jacobus. Latinized name of Jakob Harmensen 1560–1609. Dutch Protestant priest who founded Arminianism, a school of Christian theology opposed to Calvin's doctrine of predestination. His views were developed by Simon Episcopius

(1583–1643). Arminianism is the basis of Wesleyan ◊Methodism.

armistice cessation of hostilities while awaiting a peace settlement. "The Armistice" refers specifically to the end of World War I between Germany and the Allies Nov 11, 1918. On June 22, 1940, French representatives signed an armistice with Germany in the same railroad carriage at Compiègne as in 1918. No

Armstrong US jazz trumpeter and singer Louis Armstrong, pictured at the back with his Hot Seven band in the 1920s.

armistice was signed with either Germany or Japan 1945; both nations surrendered and there was no provision for the suspension of fighting. The Korean armistice, signed at Panmunjom July 27, 1953, terminated the Korean War 1950–53.

Armistice Day anniversary of the armistice signed Nov 11, 1918, ending World War I.

In the US this holiday is now called Veterans' Day.

armor body protection worn in battle. Body armor is depicted in Greek and Roman art. Chain mail was developed in the Middle Ages but the craft of the armorer in Europe reached its height in design in the 15th century, when knights, and to some extent, their horses, were encased in plate armor that still allowed freedom of movement. Medieval Japanese armor was articulated, made of iron, gilded metal, leather, and silk. Contemporary bulletproof vests and riot gear are forms of armor. The term is used in a modern context to refer to a mechanized armored vehicle, such as a tank.

armored personnel carrier (APC) wheeled or tracked military vehicle designed to transport up to ten people. Armored to withstand small-arms fire and shell splinters, it is used on battlefields.

Armstrong Henry (born Henry Jackson) "Homicide Hank" 1912–1988. US boxer. He was the only man to hold world titles at three different weights simultaneously. Between May and Nov 1938 he held the featherweight, welterweight, and lightweight titles. He retired in 1945 and became a Baptist minister.

Armstrong Louis ("Satchmo") 1901–1971. US jazz cornet and trumpet player and singer. His Chicago recordings in the 1920s with the Hot Five and Hot Seven brought him recognition for his warm and pure trumpet tone, his skill at improvisation, and his quirky, gravelly voice. From the 1930s he also appeared in films.

Armstrong Neil Alden 1930– . US astronaut. In 1969, he became the first person to set foot on the Moon, and said, "That's one small step for a man, one giant leap for mankind." The Moon landing was part of the ◊Apollo project.

army organized military force for fighting on the ground. A national army is used to further a political policy by force either within the state or on the territory of another state. Most countries have a national army, maintained by taxation, and raised either by conscription (compulsory military service) or voluntarily (paid professionals). Private armies may be employed by individuals and groups.

Arnhem, Battle of in World War II, airborne operation by the Allies, Sept 17–26, 1944, to secure a bridgehead over the Rhine, thereby opening the way for a thrust toward the Ruhr and a possible early end to the war. It was only partially successful, with 7,600 casualties. Arnhem is a city in the Netherlands, on the Rhine SE of Utrecht; population (1991) 131,700. It produces salt, chemicals, and pharmaceuticals.

Arnold Benedict 1741–1801. US soldier and military strategist who, during the American Revolution, won the turning-point battle at Saratoga 1777 for the Americans. He is chiefly remembered as a traitor to the American side, having plotted to betray the strategic post at West Point to the British.

Arnold Matthew 1822–1888. English poet and critic. His poems, characterized by their elegiac mood and pastoral themes, include *The Forsaken Merman* 1849, *Thyrsis* 1867 (commemorating his friend Arthur Hugh Clough), *Dover Beach* 1867, and *The Scholar Gypsy* 1853. Arnold's critical works include *Essays in Criticism* 1865 and 1888, and *Culture and Anarchy* 1869, which attacks 19th-century philistinism.

Arp Hans or Jean 1887–1966. French abstract painter and sculptor. He was one of the founders of the ◊Dada movement about 1917, and later was associated with the Surrealists. His innovative wood sculptures use organic shapes in bright colors.

Arrhenius Svante August 1859–1927. Swedish scientist, the founder of physical chemistry. Born near Uppsala, he became a professor at Stockholm in 1895, and made a special study of electrolysis. He wrote *Worlds in the Making* and *Destinies of the Stars*, and in 1903 received the Nobel Prize for Chemistry. In 1905 he pre-

artesian well *In an artesian well, water rises from an underground water-containing rock layer under its own pressure.*

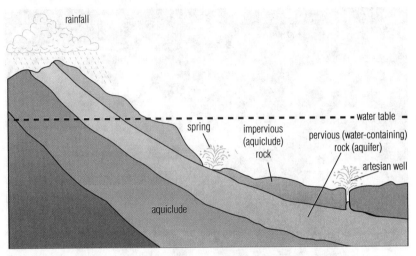

artesian well In an artesian well, water rises from an underground water-containing rock layer under its own pressure.

rainfall

water table

spring

impervious (aquiclude) rock

pervious (water-containing) rock (aquifer)

artesian well

aquiclude

dicted global warming as a result of carbon dioxide emission from burning fossil fuels.

arrhythmia disturbance of the natural rhythm of the heart. There are various kinds of arrhythmia, some innocent, some indicative of heart disease.

arrowroot starchy substance derived from the roots and tubers of various tropical plants with thick, clumpy roots. The true arrowroot *Maranta arundinacea* was used by the Indians of South America as an antidote against the effects of poisoned arrows.

arsenic brittle, grayish-white, semimetallic element (a metalloid), symbol As, atomic number 33, atomic weight 74.92. It occurs in many ores and occasionally in its elemental state, and is widely distributed, being present in minute quantities in the soil, the sea, and the human body. In larger quantities, it is poisonous. The chief source of arsenic compounds is as a byproduct from metallurgical processes. It is used in making semiconductors, alloys, and solders.

arson malicious and willful setting fire to property. Often arson is a crime committed to claim insurance benefits fraudulently.

art in the broadest sense, all the processes and products of human skill, imagination, and invention; the opposite of nature. In contemporary usage, definitions of art usually reflect aesthetic criteria, and the term may encompass literature, music, drama, painting, and sculpture. Popularly, the term is most commonly used to refer to the visual arts. In Western culture, aesthetic criteria introduced by the ancient Greeks still influence our perceptions and judgments of art.

Art Deco popular and pervasive style in art and architecture named after a 1925 French exhibition of modern art, noted for streamlined shapes and geometric forms. It was popular particularly in France and the US, where it was used extensively in the 1920s and 1930s, in urban architecture such as the Chrysler Building, New York City; in interior design such as in Radio City Music Hall, New York City; and in notable designs for streamlined trains, automobiles, and airplanes. It also influenced industrial design in products such as chinaware, radios, textiles, home furnishings, jewelry, and printed matter. Its use in film sets and costumes helped promote a fascination with Modernism that culminated in the 1939–40 World's Fair in New York City. From the 1970s, a revival of interest in the

designs and designers, notably Raymond Loewy, name the style, which in its time was called *moderne*.

Artemis in Greek mythology, the goddess of chastity, the young of all creatures, the Moon, and the hunt (Roman Diana). She is the twin sister of ◊Apollo and was worshiped at cult centers throughout the Greek world, one of the largest of which was at ◊Ephesus. Her great temple there, reconstructed several times in antiquity, was one of the ◊Seven Wonders of the World.

arteriosclerosis hardening of the arteries, with thickening and loss of elasticity. It is associated with smoking, aging, and a diet high in saturated fats. The term is used loosely as a synonym for ◊atherosclerosis.

artery vessel that carries blood from the heart to the rest of the body. It is built to withstand considerable pressure, having thick walls that are impregnated with muscle and elastic fibers. During contraction of the heart muscles, arteries expand in diameter to allow for the sudden increase in pressure that occurs; the resulting ◊pulse or pressure wave can be felt at the wrist. Not all arteries carry oxygenated (oxygen-rich) blood; the pulmonary arteries convey deoxygenated (oxygen-poor) blood from the heart to the lungs.

artesian well well that is supplied with water rising from an underground water-saturated rock layer (◊aquifer). The water rises from the aquifer under its own pressure. Such a well may be drilled into an aquifer that is confined by impermeable rocks both above and below. If the water table (the top of the region of water saturation) in that aquifer is above the level of the well head, hydrostatic pressure will force the water to the surface.

The name comes from Artois (Latin *Artesium*), a historical region of N France, on the Strait of Dover, where the phenomenon was first observed.

arthritis inflammation of the joints, with pain, swelling, and restricted motion. Many conditions may cause arthritis, including ◊gout and trauma to the joint.

arthropod member of the phylum Arthropoda; an invertebrate animal with jointed legs and a segmented body with a horny or chitinous casing (exoskeleton), which is shed periodically and replaced as the animal grows. Included are arachnids such as spiders and

artificial respiration

This technique, popularly known as the "kiss of life," is the most effective way of reestablishing an oxygen supply in an unconscious person who has stopped breathing.

Any person who fails to breathe spontaneously requires immediate resuscitation. Warning signs include absence of chest movements and blue-gray pallor. If the vital air supply is interrupted for more than four minutes, brain, heart, and other tissues begin to suffer irreversible damage.

Often the mouth and throat are blocked by blood, stomach contents, or dentures. The victim's head should be turned to one side, which may clear the airway. Any obstruction can be removed manually. If the person is still not breathing artificial resuscitation should be started at once.

When an unconscious person is placed in the prone position the tongue may drop into the back of the throat, obstructing the airway and preventing air from reaching the lungs. An open airway must be established before artificial respiration is given. The head is tilted backward until neck and chest are in line. Then the jaw is extended to lift the tongue. The position is maintained by keeping one hand on the forehead and the other under the chin.

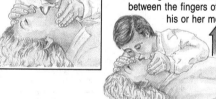

An airtight seal is created by pinching the victim's nostrils between the fingers of one hand and placing the lips around his or her mouth. The lungs are expanded with steady, gentle breaths, and the chest rises visibly. Exhalation occurs naturally as the victim's mouth is uncovered. For adults, the procedure is repeated 12–16 times per minute.

As soon as spontaneous breathing recommences the victim should be placed in the recovery position. This keeps the airway clear. An unconscious person should never be left unattended.

The lips are placed around the nose and mouth of an infant to obtain an airtight seal. No more than little puffs are required to fill the lungs, at a rate of 20 per minute.

mites, as well as crustaceans, millipedes, centipedes, and insects.

Arthur 6th century AD. Legendary British king and hero in stories of ◊Camelot and the quest for the ◊Holy Grail. Arthur is said to have been born in Tintagel, Cornwall, and buried in Glastonbury, Somerset. He may have been a Romano-Celtic leader against pagan Saxon invaders.

Arthur Chester Alan 1830–1886. 21st president of the US 1881–85, a Republican. In 1880 he was chosen as James ◊Garfield's vice president, and was his successor when Garfield was assassinated the following year.

artichoke either of two plants of the composite or sunflower family Compositae. The **common** or **globe artichoke** *Cynara scolymus* is native to the Mediterranean, and is a form of thistle. It is tall, with purplish blue flowers; the bracts of the unopened flower are eaten. The **Jerusalem artichoke** *Helianthus tuberosus* is a sunflower, native to North America. It has edible tubers, and its common name is a corruption of the Italian for sunflower, *girasole*.

article grammatical ◊part of speech. There are two articles in English: the **definite article** *the*, which serves to specify or identify a noun (as in "This is *the* book I need"), and the **indefinite article** *a* or (before vowels) *an*, which indicates a single unidentified noun ("They gave me *a* piece of paper and *an* envelope").

artificial insemination (AI) introduction by instrument of semen from a sperm bank or donor into the female reproductive tract to bring about fertilization. Originally used by animal breeders to improve stock with sperm from high-quality males, in the 20th century it has been developed for use in humans, to help the infertile. In ◊in vitro fertilization, the egg is fertilized in a test tube and then implanted in the womb. In zygote intrafallopian transfer (ZIFT) the mixed egg and sperm are reintroduced into the fallopian tube.

The sperm for artificial insemination may come from the husband (AIH) or a donor (AID).

artificial intelligence (AI) branch of science concerned with creating computer programs that can perform actions comparable with those of an intelligent human. Current AI research covers such areas as planning (for robot behavior), language understanding, pattern recognition, and knowledge representation.

artificial respiration maintenance of breathing when the natural process is suspended. If breathing is permanently suspended, as in paralysis, an **iron lung** is used; in cases of electric shock or apparent drowning, for example, the first choice is the expired-air method, the **kiss of life** by mouth-to-mouth breathing until natural breathing is resumed.

artillery collective term for military ◊firearms too heavy to be carried. Artillery can be mounted on ships or airplanes and includes cannons and missile launchers.

Art Nouveau art style of about 1890–1910 in Europe, named after a shop in Paris that opened 1895, which makes marked use of sinuous lines, stylized flowers and foliage, and flame shapes. In England, it appears in the illustrations of Aubrey Beardsley; in Spain, in the architecture of Antonio Gaudí; in France, in the architecture of Hector Guimard and the art glass of René Lalique; in Belgium, in the houses and design of Victor Horta; in the US, in the lamps and metalwork of Louis Comfort Tiffany; and in Scotland, in the interior and exterior designs of Charles Rennie Mackintosh.

Art Nouveau was also known as **Jugendstil** in Germany and **Stile Liberty** in Italy, after the fashionable London department store.

Arts and Crafts movement English social movement, largely antimachine in spirit, based in design and architecture and founded by William ◊Morris in the latter half of the 19th century. It was supported by the architect A W Pugin and by John ◊Ruskin and stressed the importance of handcrafting. The ◊Art Nouveau style succeeded it.

Aruba island in the Caribbean, the westernmost of the Lesser Antilles; an overseas part of the Netherlands
area 75 sq mi/193 sq km
population (1989) 62,400
history Aruba obtained separate status from the other Netherlands Antilles 1986 and has full internal autonomy.

Arunachal Pradesh state of India, in the Himalayas on the borders of Tibet and Myanmar
area 32,270 sq mi/83,600 sq km
capital Itanagar
products rubber, coffee, spices, fruit, timber
population (1991) 858,400
languages 50 different dialects
history formerly nominally part of Assam, known as the renamed Arunachal Pradesh ("Hills of the Rising Sun"). It became a state 1986.

Aryan Indo-European family of languages: also the hypothetical parent language of an ancient people who are believed to have lived between central Asia and E Europe and to have reached Persia and India in one direction and Europe in another, sometime in the 2nd century BC, diversifying into the various Indo-European language speakers of later times. In ◊Nazi Germany Hitler and other theorists erroneously propagated the idea of the Aryans as a white-skinned, blue-eyed, fair-haired master race.

Aryan languages 19th-century name for the ◊Indo-European languages; the languages of the Aryan peoples of India. The name Aryan is no longer used by language scholars because of its association with the Nazi concept of white supremacy.

asbestos any of several related minerals of fibrous structure that offer great heat resistance because of their nonflammability and poor conductivity. Commercial asbestos is generally made from olivine, a ◊serpentine mineral, tremolite (a white ◊amphibole), and riebeckite (a blue amphibole, also known as crocidolite when in its fibrous form). Asbestos usage is now strictly controlled because exposure to its dust can cause cancer.

Ascension British island of volcanic origin in the S Atlantic, a dependency of ◊St Helena since 1922; population (1982) 1,625. The chief settlement is Georgetown.

Ascension Day or **Holy Thursday** in the Christian calendar, the feast day commemorating Jesus' ascension into heaven. It is the 40th day after Easter.

ASCII (acronym for **American standard code for information interchange**) in computing, a coding system in which numbers are assigned to letters, digits, and punctuation symbols. Although computers work in binary number code, ASCII numbers are usually quoted as decimal or hexadecimal numbers. For example, the decimal number 45 (binary 0101101) represents a hyphen, and 65 (binary 1000001) a capital A. The first 32 codes are used for control functions, such as carriage return and backspace.

ascorbic acid $C_6H_8O_6$ or *vitamin C* a relatively simple organic acid found in fresh fruits and vegetables.

It is soluble in water and destroyed by prolonged boiling, so soaking or overcooking of vegetables reduces their vitamin C content. Lack of ascorbic acid results in scurvy.

ASEAN acronym for ◊*Association of South East Asian Nations*.

asexual reproduction in biology, reproduction that does not involve the manufacture and fusion of sex cells, nor the necessity for two parents. The process carries a clear advantage in that there is no need to search for a mate nor to develop complex pollinating mechanisms; every asexual organism can reproduce on its own. Asexual reproduction can therefore lead to a rapid population buildup.

Asgard in Scandinavian mythology, the place where the gods lived. It was reached by a bridge called Bifrost, the rainbow.

Ashcan school group of US painters active about 1908–14, also known as *The Eight*. Members included Robert Henri (1865–1929), George Luks (1867–1933), William Glackens (1870–1938), Everett Shinn (1876–1953), and John Sloan (1871–1951). Their style is realist; their subjects centered on city life, the poor, and the outcast.

Ashe Arthur Robert, Jr 1943–1993. US tennis player and coach. He won the US national men's singles title at Forest Hills and the first US Open 1968. Known for his exceptionally strong serve, Ashe turned professional 1969. He won the Australian men's title 1970 and Wimbledon 1975. Cardiac problems ended his playing career 1979, but he continued his involvement with the sport as captain of the US Davis Cup team. In 1992 he launched a fund-raising campaign to combat AIDS, which he had contracted from a blood transfusion.

Born in Richmond, Virginia, Ashe entered the University of California at Los Angeles (UCLA) on a tennis scholarship 1962 and took the National Collegiate Athletic Association (NCAA) men's singles and doubles titles 1966.

Ashikaga in Japanese history, the family who held the office of ◊shogun 1338–1573, a period of civil wars. Nō drama evolved under the patronage of Ashikaga shoguns. Relations with China improved intermittently and there was trade with Korea. The last (15th) Ashikaga shogun was ousted by Oda Nobunaga at the start of the ◊Momoyama period. The Ashikaga belonged to the ◊Minamoto clan.

Ashkenazi (plural *Ashkenazim*) a Jew of German or E European descent, as opposed to a Sephardi, of Spanish, Portuguese, or N African descent.

Ashkenazy Vladimir 1937– . Russian-born pianist and conductor. His keyboard technique differs slightly from standard Western technique. In 1962 he was joint winner of the Tchaikovsky Competition with John Ogdon. He excels in Rachmaninov, Prokofiev, and Liszt.

Ashkhabad capital of Turkmenistan; population (1989) 402,000. Industries include glass, carpets ("Bukhara" carpets are made here), cotton; the spectacular natural setting has been used by the film-making industry.

Ashland city in NE Kentucky, on the Ohio River, E of Louisville; population (1990) 23,600. Industries include chemicals, coal, oil, limestone, coke, petroleum products, steel, clothing, and leather goods.

ashram Indian community whose members lead a simple life of discipline and self-denial and devote themselves to social service. Noted ashrams are those founded by Mahatma Gandhi at Wardha and the poet Rabindranath Tagore at Santiniketan.

Ashwander v Tennessee Valley Authority (TVA) a US Supreme Court decision 1936 dealing with the government's authority to utilize navigable waterways as public property. The debate arose over the contracted sale of excess electricity produced by the TVA's Wilson Dam. Power companies unaccustomed to government competition in the industry filed suit to have the TVA contracts canceled. The Court ruled that since the government had acquired the electricity legally, through the exercise of its right to dam waterways, it had full right to dispose of its property.

Ash Wednesday first day of Lent, the period in the Christian calendar leading up to Easter; in the Roman Catholic Church the foreheads of the congregation are marked with a cross in ash, as a sign of penitence.

Asia largest of the continents, occupying one-third of the total land surface of the world
area 17,000,000 sq mi/44,000,000 sq km
largest cities (population over 5 million) Tokyo, Shanghai, Osaka, Beijing, Seoul, Calcutta, Bombay, Jakarta, Bangkok, Tehran, Hong Kong, Delhi, Tianjin, Karachi
features Mount Everest, at 29,118 ft/8,872 m is the world's highest mountain; Dead Sea at –1,293 ft/–394 m is the world's lowest point below sea level; rivers (over 2,000 mi/3,200 km) include Chiang Jiang (Yangtze), Huang He (Yellow), Ob-Irtysh, Amur, Lena, Mekong, Yenisei; lakes (over 7,000 sq mi/18,000 sq km) include Caspian Sea (the largest lake in the world), Aral Sea, Baikal (largest freshwater lake in Eurasia), Balkhash; deserts include the Gobi, Takla Makan, Syrian Desert, Arabian Desert, Negev
physical lying in the eastern hemisphere, Asia extends from the Arctic Circle to just over 10° S of the equator. The Asian mainland, which forms the greater part of the Eurasian continent, lies entirely in the northern hemisphere and stretches from Cape Chelyubinsk at its northern extremity to Cape Piai at the southern tip of the Malay Peninsula. From Dezhneva Cape in the E, the mainland extends W over more than 165° longitude to Cape Baba in Turkey.

Asia Minor historical name for *Anatolia*, the Asian part of Turkey.

Asian native to or an inhabitant of the continent of Asia, which is the contiguous landmass east of the Ural Mountains, the traditional boundary between Europe and Asia. The region is culturally heterogenous with numerous distinctive ethnic and sociolinguistic groups, totaling over half the Earth's human population (including China, India, and Japan). Asians are of three main racial stocks: Mongoloid in the east; Caucasoid in the west; and Negroid in the Philippines and off-shore islands of the Indian Ocean. The Indians of the Americas were Asian migrants to the New World during the last Ice Age.

Asian Development Bank (ADB) bank founded 1966 to stimulate growth in Asia and the Far East by administering direct loans and technical assistance. Members include 30 countries within the region and 14 countries of W Europe and North America. The headquarters are in Manila, Philippines.

Asia-Pacific Economic Cooperation Conference (APEC) trade group comprising 12 Pacific Asian countries, formed Nov 1989 to promote multi-

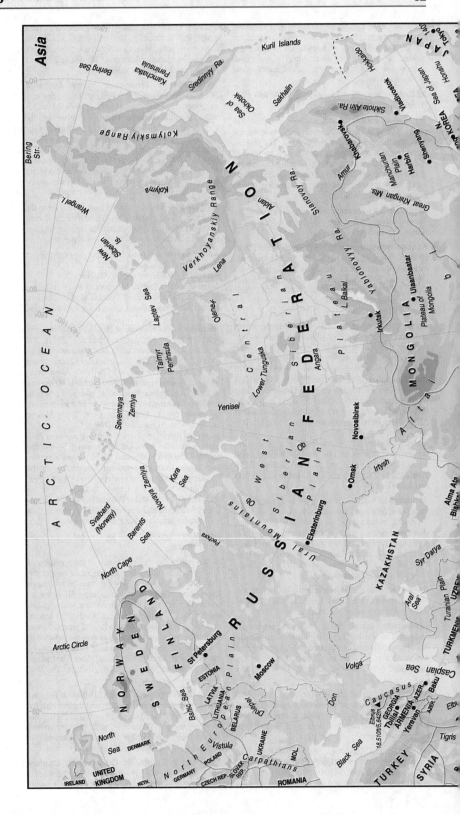

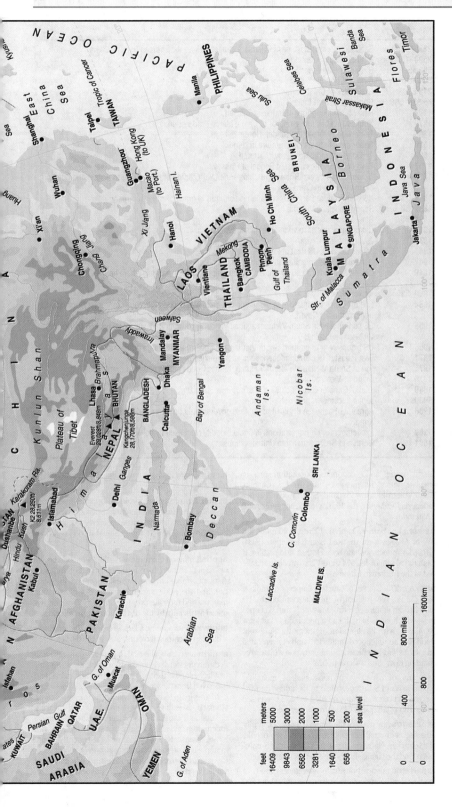

Asia: history

2800–2200 BC	Sage kings, earliest Chinese legendary dynasty; civilization spread to all of China.
2500–1500 BC	Indus Valley civilization.
563 BC	Birth of the Buddha.
551 BC	Birth of Confucius.
215 BC	Great Wall of China begun.
AD 320–550	Gupta dynasty in India.
1192	First Muslim kingdom of India established.
1279	Kublai Khan became emperor of China; Marco Polo visited.
1395	Tamerlane defeated the Golden Horde.
1526	Babur established Mogul empire in N India.
1600s	English East India Company chartered.
1757	Clive defeated the nawab of Bengal at Plassey.
1839–42	Opium War between Britain and China ended with ceding of Hong Kong to Britain and opening of treaty ports in China.
1854	US Commodore Perry forced Japanese shogun to grant commercial treaty.
1857–58	Sepoy Rebellion in India.
1894–95	Sino-Japanese War.
1912	Qin dynasty overthrown in republican revolution in China.
1931	Japan invaded China.
1941	Japan attacked US fleet at Pearl Harbor.
1947	India and Pakistan gained independence.
1949	Chiang Kai-shek forced by Chinese communists to flee to Taiwan, where he set up a US-backed Republic of China.
1950–53	Korean War.
1954	End of French colonialism in Indochina: Vietnam was divided into the communist North and the noncommunist South.
1955	US sent to advise South Vietnam against Vietcong communist insurgents, backed by North Vietnam and China.
1965	US troops sent to support South Vietnamese government in large numbers.
1971	East Pakistan declared independence as Bangladesh.
1975	Fall of South Vietnam to North Vietnam. Khmer Rouge seized power in Cambodia.
1976	Death of Mao Zedong.
1980	Trial of Gang of Four (including Mao's widow Jiang Qing).
1980s	Japan became world's richest nation.
1986	Agreement between British and Chinese governments on future 1997 administration of Hong Kong.
1989	Prodemocracy demonstrations in China bloodily repressed by government troops.
1991	North and South Korea join United Nations.

lateral trade and economic cooperation among member states. Its members are the US, Canada, Japan, Australia, New Zealand, South Korea, Brunei, Indonesia, Malaysia, the Philippines, Singapore, and Thailand.

Asmara or *Asmera* capital of Eritrea; 40 mi/64 km SW of Massawa on the Red Sea; population (1984) 275,385. Products include beer, clothes, and textiles. It has a naval school. In 1974 unrest here precipitated the end of the Ethiopian Empire.

Asoka c. 273–232 BC. ◊Mauryan emperor of India c. 268–232 BC, the greatest of the Mauryan rulers. He inherited an empire covering most of N and S central India which, at its height, had a population of at least 30 million, with its capital at ◊Pataliputra. A devout Buddhist, he renounced militarism and concentrated on establishing an efficient administration with a large standing army and a secret police.

asp any of several venomous snakes, including *Vipera aspis* of S Europe, allied to the adder, and the Egyptian cobra *Naja haje*, reputed to have been used by the Egyptian queen Cleopatra for her suicide.

asparagus any plant of the genus *Asparagus*, family Liliaceae, with small scalelike leaves and many needle-like branches. Native to Eurasia, *A. officinalis* is cultivated, and the young shoots are eaten as a vegetable.

aspartame noncarbohydrate sweetener used in foods under the tradename Nutrasweet. It is about 200 times as sweet as sugar and, unlike saccharine, has no aftertaste.

aspen any of several species of ◊poplar tree, genus *Populus*. The European quaking aspen *P. tremula* has flattened leafstalks that cause the leaves to flutter with every breeze. The soft, light-colored wood is used for matches and paper pulp.

asphalt mineral mixture containing semisolid brown or black ◊bitumen, used in the construction industry. Asphalt is mixed with rock chips to form paving material, and the purer varieties are used for insulating material and for waterproofing masonry. It can be produced artificially by the distillation of ◊petroleum.

asphyxia suffocation; a lack of oxygen that produces a buildup of carbon dioxide waste in the tissues.

aspirin acetylsalicylic acid, a popular pain-relieving drug (analgesic) developed in the early 20th century for headaches and arthritis. It inhibits prostaglandins, and is derived from the white willow tree *Salix alba*.

In the long term, even moderate use may cause stomach bleeding, kidney damage, and hearing defects, and aspirin is no longer considered suitable for children under 12, because of a suspected link with a rare disease, Reye's syndrome (consequently, acetaminophen is often substituted). However, recent medical research suggests that an aspirin a day may be of value in preventing heart attack (myocardial infarction) and thrombosis.

Asquith Herbert Henry, 1st Earl of Oxford and Asquith 1852–1928. British Liberal politician, prime minister 1908–16. As chancellor of the Exchequer he introduced old-age pensions 1908. He limited the powers of the House of Lords and attempted to give Ireland Home Rule.

During World War I, his attitude of "wait and see" was not adapted to all-out war, and in Dec 1916 he was replaced by Lloyd George. In 1918 the Liberal election defeat led to the eclipse of the party.

ass any of several horselike, odd-toed, hoofed mammals of the genus *Equus*, family Equidae. Species include the African wild ass *E. asinus*, and the Asian wild ass *E. hemionus*. They differ from horses in their smaller size, larger ears, tufted tail, and characteristic bray. Donkeys and burros are domesticated asses.

Assad Hafez al 1930– . Syrian Ba'athist politician, president from 1971. He became prime minister after a bloodless military coup 1970, and the following year was the first president to be elected by popular vote. Having suppressed dissent, he was reelected 1978, 1985, and 1992. He is a Shia (Alawite) Muslim.

Assam state of NE India
area 30,262 sq mi/78,400 sq km
capital Dispur
cities Guwahati
products half India's tea is grown and half its oil produced here; rice, jute, sugar, cotton, coal
population (1991) 24,294,600, including 12 million Assamese (Hindus), 5 million Bengalis (chiefly Muslim immigrants from Bangladesh), Nepalis, and 2 million indigenous people (Christian and traditional religions)
language Assamese
history a thriving region from 1000 BC; Assam migrants came from China and Myanmar (Burma). After Burmese invasion 1826, Britain took control and made Assam a separate province 1874; it was included in the Dominion of India, except for most of the Muslim district of Silhet, which went to Pakistan 1947. Ethnic unrest started in the 1960s when Assamese was declared the official language. After protests, the Gara, Khasi, and Jainitia tribal hill districts became the state of Meghalaya 1971; the Mizo hill district became the Union Territory of Mizoram 1972. There were massacres of Muslim Bengalis by Hindus 1983. In 1987 members of the Bodo ethnic group began fighting for a separate homeland. Direct rule was imposed by the Indian government Nov 1990 following separatist violence from the Marxist-militant United Liberation Front of Assam (ULFA), which had extorted payments from tea-exporting companies. In March 1991 it was reported that the ULFA, operating from the jungles of Myanmar, had been involved in 97 killings, mainly of Congress I politicians, since Nov 27, 1990.

assassination murder, usually of a political, royal, or public person. The term derives from the order of the Assassins, a Muslim sect that, in the 11th and 12th centuries, murdered officials to further its political ends.

assembly language low-level computer-programming language closely related to a computer's internal codes. It consists chiefly of a set of short sequences of letters (mnemonics), which are translated, by a program called an assembler, into machine code for the computer's ◊central processing unit (CPU) to follow directly. In assembly language, for example, "JMP" means "jump" and "LDA" means "load accumulator." Assembly code is used by programmers who need to write very fast or efficient programs.

assembly line method of mass production in which a product is built up step-by-step by successive workers adding one part at a time.

assize in medieval Europe, the passing of laws, either by the king with the consent of nobles, as in the Constitutions of ◊Clarendon 1164 by Henry II of England, or as a complete system, such as the *Assizes of Jerusalem*, a compilation of the law of the feudal kingdom of Jerusalem in the 13th century.

Association of South East Asian Nations (ASEAN) regional alliance formed in Bangkok 1967; it took over the nonmilitary role of the Southeast Asia Treaty Organization 1975. Its members are Indonesia, Malaysia, the Philippines, Singapore, Thailand, and (from 1984) Brunei; its headquarters are in Jakarta, Indonesia.

Assyria empire in the Middle East *c* 2500–612 BC, in N Mesopotamia (now Iraq); early capital Ashur, later Nineveh. It was initially subject to Sumer and intermittently to Babylon. The Assyrians adopted in the main the Sumerian religion and structure of society. At its greatest extent the empire included Egypt and stretched from the E Mediterranean coast to the head of the Persian Gulf. *See map p. 66*

Astaire Fred. Adopted name of Frederick Austerlitz 1899–1987. US dancer, actor, singer, and choreographer who starred in numerous films, including *Top Hat* 1935, *Easter Parade* 1948, and *Funny Face* 1957, many containing inventive sequences he designed and choreographed himself. He made ten classic films with the most popular of his dancing partners, Ginger Rogers. He later played straight dramatic roles in such films as *On the Beach* 1959.

Astarte alternate name for the Babylonian and Assyrian goddess ◊Ishtar.

astatine nonmetallic, radioactive element, symbol At, atomic number 85, atomic weight 210. It is a member of the ◊halogen group, and is very rare in nature. Astatine is highly unstable, with at least 19 isotopes; the longest lived has a half-life of about eight hours.

aster any plant of the large genus *Aster*, family Compositae, belonging to the same subfamily as the daisy. All asters have starlike flowers with yellow centers and outer rays (not petals) varying from blue and purple to white and the genus comprises a great variety of size. Many are cultivated as garden flowers, including the Michaelmas daisy *A. nova-belgii*.

asterisk starlike punctuation mark (*) used to link the asterisked word with a note at the bottom of a page, and in place of certain letters in a word (usually a ◊taboo word).

asteroid or *minor planet* any of many thousands of small bodies, composed of rock and iron, that orbit the Sun. Most lie in a belt between the orbits of Mars and Jupiter, and are thought to be fragments left over from the formation of the ◊Solar System. About 100,000 may exist, but their total mass is only a few hundredths the mass of the Moon.

asthenosphere division of the Earth's structure lying beneath the ◊lithosphere, at a depth of approximately 45 mi/70 km to 160 mi/260 km. It is thought to be the soft, partially molten layer of the ◊mantle on which the rigid plates of the Earth's surface move to produce the motions of ◊plate tectonics.

asthma difficulty in breathing due to spasm of the bronchi (air passages) in the lungs. Attacks may be provoked by allergy, infection, stress, or emotional

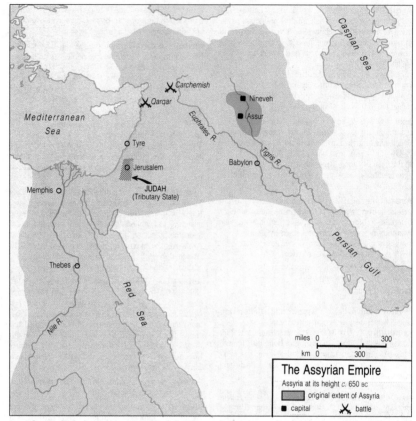

The Assyrian Empire

Assyria at its height *c.* 650 BC

original extent of Assyria

■ capital ✗ battle

upset. It may also be increasing as a result of air pollution and occupational hazards. Treatment is with ◊bronchodilators to relax the bronchial muscles and thereby ease the breathing, and in severe cases by inhaled ◊steroids that reduce inflammation of the bronchi.

astigmatism aberration occurring in lenses, including that in the eye. It results when the curvature of the lens differs in two perpendicular planes, so that rays in one plane may be in focus while rays in the other are not. With astigmatic eyesight, the vertical and horizontal cannot be in focus at the same time; correction is by the use of a cylindrical lens that reduces the overall focal length of one plane so that both planes are seen in sharp focus.

Aston Francis William 1877–1945. English physicist who developed the mass spectrometer, which separates ◊isotopes by projecting their ions (charged atoms) through a magnetic field. He received the Nobel Prize for Chemistry 1922.

Astor John Jacob 1763–1848. German-born US merchant who founded the monopolistic American Fur Company 1808. His subsidiary enterprise, the Pacific Fur Company, was created 1881 following the US government's Louisiana Purchase 1803 facilitating trade with the West. He founded Astoria, now in Oregon, as his trading post at the mouth of the Columbia River.

astrolabe ancient navigational instrument, forerunner of the sextant. Astrolabes usually consisted of a flat disk with a sighting rod that could be pivoted to point at the Sun or bright stars. From the altitude of

the Sun or star above the horizon, the local time could be estimated.

astrology (Greek *astron* "star" *legein* "speak") study of the relative position of the planets and stars in the belief that they influence events on Earth. The astrologer casts a ◊horoscope based on the time and place of the subject's birth. Astrology has no proven scientific basis, but has been widespread since ancient times. Western astrology is based on the 12 signs of the zodiac; Chinese astrology is based on a 60-year cycle and lunar calendar.

astronaut person making flights into space; the term *cosmonaut* is used in the West for any astronaut from the former Soviet Union.

astronomical unit unit (symbol AU) equal to the mean distance of the Earth from the Sun: 92,955,800 mi/149,597,870 km. It is used to describe planetary distances. Light travels this distance in approximately 8.3 minutes.

astronomy science of the celestial bodies: the Sun, the Moon, and the planets; the stars and galaxies; and all other objects in the universe. It is concerned with their positions, motions, distances, and physical conditions and with their origins and evolution. Astronomy thus divides into fields such as astrophysics, celestial mechanics, and cosmology. See also ◊gamma-ray astronomy, ◊infrared astronomy, ◊radio astronomy, ◊ultraviolet astronomy, and ◊X-ray astronomy.

astrophysics study of the physical nature of stars, galaxies, and the universe. It began with the development of spectroscopy in the 19th century, which allowed astronomers to analyze the composition of stars from their light. Astrophysicists view the universe as a vast natural laboratory in which they can study matter under conditions of temperature, pressure, and density that are unattainable on Earth.

Asturias autonomous region of N Spain; area 4,092 sq mi/10,600 sq km; population (1986) 1,114,000. Half of Spain's coal comes from the mines of Asturias. Agricultural produce includes corn, fruit, and livestock. Oviedo and Gijón are the main industrial towns.

Asturias Miguel Angel 1899–1974. Guatemalan author and diplomat. He published poetry, Guatemalan legends, and novels, such as *El señor presidente/The President* 1946, *Men of Corn* 1949, and *Strong Wind* 1950, attacking Latin-American dictatorships and "Yankee imperialism." Nobel Prize 1967.

Asunción capital and port of Paraguay, on the Paraguay River; population (1984) 729,000. It produces textiles, footwear, and food products. Founded 1537, it was the first Spanish settlement in the La Plata region.

Aswan winter resort town in Upper Egypt; population (1985) 183,000. It is near the High Dam, built 1960–70, which keeps the level of the Nile constant throughout the year without flooding. It produces steel and textiles.

Atacama Desert desert in N Chile; area about 31,000 sq mi/80,000 sq km. There are mountains inland, and the coastal area is rainless and barren. The desert has silver and copper mines, and extensive nitrate deposits.

Atahualpa c. 1502–1533. Last emperor of the Incas of Peru. He was taken prisoner 1532 when the Spaniards arrived and agreed to pay a substantial ransom, but he was accused of plotting against the conquistador Pizarro and was sentenced to be burned. On his consenting to Christian baptism, the sentence was commuted to strangulation.

Atatürk Kemal. Name assumed 1934 by Mustafa Kemal Pasha 1881–1938. (Atatúrk "Father of the Turks") Turkish politician and general, first president of Turkey from 1923. After World War I he established a provisional rebel government and in 1921–22 the Turkish armies under his leadership expelled the Greeks who were occupying Turkey. He was the founder of the modern republic, which he ruled as virtual dictator, with a policy of consistent and radical westernization.

atavism (Latin *atavus* "ancestor") in ◊genetics, the reappearance of a characteristic not apparent in the immediately preceding generations; in psychology, the manifestation of primitive forms of behavior.

ataxia loss of muscular coordination due to neurological damage or disease.

Athanasian creed one of the three ancient ◊creeds of the Christian church. Mainly a definition of the Trinity and Incarnation, it was written many years after the death of Athanasius, but was attributed to him as the chief upholder of Trinitarian doctrine.

Athanasius, St 298–373. Bishop of Alexandria, supporter of the doctrines of the Trinity and Incarnation. He was a disciple of St Anthony the hermit, and an opponent of ◊Arianism in the great Arian controversy. Following the official condemnation of Arianism at the Council of Nicaea 325, Athanasius was appointed bishop of Alexandria 328. The Athanasian creed was

astronaut US astronaut Bruce McCandless floats free above the Earth in his crewed maneuvring unit Feb 7, 1984.

not actually written by him, although it reflects his views.

atheism nonbelief in, or the positive denial of, the existence of a God or gods. A related concept is ◊agnosticism.

Athelstan c. 895–939. King of the Mercians and West Saxons. Son of Edward the Elder and grandson of Alfred the Great, he was crowned king 925 at Kingston upon Thames. He subdued parts of Cornwall and Wales, and defeated the Welsh, Scots, and Danes at Brunanburh 937.

Athena in Greek mythology, the goddess of war, wisdom, and the arts and crafts (Roman Minerva), who was supposed to have sprung fully grown from the head of Zeus. In Homer's *Odyssey*, she is the protectress of ◊Odysseus and his son Telemachus. Her chief cult center was Athens, where the ◊Parthenon was dedicated to her.

Athens city in NE Georgia, on the Oconee River, NE of Atlanta; seat of Clarke County; population (1980) 42,549. The University of Georgia was established here 1801. Industries include cotton and electrical products.

Athens (Greek *Athinai*) capital city of Greece and of ancient Attica; population (1981) 885,000. metropolitan area (1991) 3,096,800. Situated 5 mi/8 km NE of its port of Piraeus on the Gulf of Aegina, it is built around

Atatürk The maker of modern Turkey, Kemal Atatürk was a dictator who introduced many social and administrative reforms that affected Turkish religion, justice, education, language, and the status of women.

Athens *View of Athens, capital of Greece, from Philopapou Hill.*

the rocky hills of the Acropolis 555 ft/169 m and the Areopagus 368 ft/112 m, and is overlooked from the NE by the hill of Lycabettus, 909 ft/277 m high. It lies in the S of the central plain of Attica, watered by the mountain streams of Cephissus and Ilissus. It has less green space than any other European capital (4%) and severe air and noise pollution.

atherosclerosis thickening and hardening of the walls of the arteries, associated with atheroma.

athletics collectively, all the sports, exercises, and contests that utilize and promote such physical skills as speed, agility, and stamina.

Atlanta capital and largest city of Georgia; population (1990) 394,000, metropolitan area 2,010,000. It lies founded 1837 and was partly destroyed by General ◊Sherman 1864. There are Ford and Lockheed assembly plants, and it is the headquarters of Coca-Cola. In 1990 it was chosen as the host city for the 1996 summer Olympic Games.

Atlanta is also the financial, trade, and convention center for the SE US and has one of the busiest and most automated US airports. Educational institutions include Atlanta University, Emory University, the Georgia Institute of Technology, and Georgia State University. The city grew considerably in importance after 1900.

Atlantic, Battle of the continuous battle fought in the Atlantic Ocean during World War II by the sea and air forces of the Allies and Germany, to control the supply routes to the UK. The number of U-boats destroyed by the Allies during the war was nearly 800. At least 2,200 convoys of 75,000 merchant ships crossed the Atlantic, protected by US naval forces. Before the US entry into the war 1941, destroyers were supplied to the British under the Lend-Lease Act 1941.

Atlantic City seaside resort in New Jersey; population (1990) 38,000. Formerly a family resort, Atlantic City has become a center for casino gambling, which

was legalized 1978. It is noted for its "boardwalk" and for being the basis of the Monopoly board game; the Miss America contest has been held here since 1921.

Atlantic Ocean ocean lying between Europe and Africa to the E and the Americas to the W, probably named after the legendary island continent of ◊Atlantis; area of basin 31,500,000 sq mi/81,500,000 sq km; including the Arctic Ocean and Antarctic seas, 41,000,000 sq mi/106,200,000 sq km. The average depth is 2 mi/3 km; greatest depth the Milwaukee Depth in the Puerto Rico Trench 28,374 ft/8,648 m. The *Mid-Atlantic Ridge*, of which the Azores, Ascension, St Helena, and Tristan da Cunha form part, divides it from N to S. Lava welling up from this central area annually increases the distance between South America and Africa. The N Atlantic is the saltiest of the main oceans and has the largest tidal range.

Atlantis legendary island continent, said to have sunk following underwater convulsions. Although the ◊Atlantic Ocean is probably named after it, the structure of the sea bottom rules out its ever having existed there. The Greek philosopher Plato created an imaginary early history for it.

Atlas in Greek mythology, one of the ◊Titans who revolted against the gods; as a punishment, Atlas was compelled to support the heavens on his head and shoulders. Growing weary, he asked ◊Perseus to turn him into stone, and he was transformed into Mount Atlas.

Atlas Mountains mountain system of NW Africa, stretching 1,500 mi/2,400 km from the Atlantic coast of Morocco to the Gulf of Gabes, Tunisia, and lying between the Mediterranean on the N and the Sahara on the S. The highest peak is Mount Toubkal 13,670 ft/4,167 m.

atmosphere mixture of gases that surrounds the Earth, prevented from escaping by the pull of the Earth's gravity. Atmospheric pressure decreases with

Composition of the atmosphere

gas	symbol	volume (%)	role
nitrogen	N_2	78.08	cycled through human activities and through the action of microorganisms on animal and plant waste
oxygen	O_2	20.94	cycled mainly through the respiration of animals and plants and through the action of photosynthesis
carbon dioxide	CO_2	0.03	cycled through respiration and photosynthesis in exchange reactions with oxygen. It is also a product of burning fossil fuels
argon	Ar	0.093	chemically inert and with only a few industrial uses
neon	Ne	0.0018	as argon
helium	He	0.0005	as argon
krypton	Kr	trace	as argon
xenon	Xe	trace	as argon
ozone	O_3	0.00006	a product of oxygen molecules split into single atoms by the Sun's radiation and unaltered oxygen molecules
hydrogen	H_2	0.00005	unimportant

height in the atmosphere. In its lowest layer, the atmosphere consists of nitrogen (78%) and oxygen (21%), both in molecular form (two atoms bounded together). The other 1% is largely argon, with very small quantities of other gases, including water vapor and carbon dioxide. The atmosphere plays a major part in the various cycles of nature (the ◊water cycle, ◊carbon cycle, and ◊nitrogen cycle). It is the principal industrial source of nitrogen, oxygen, and argon, which are obtained by fractional distillation of liquid air.

atom smallest unit of matter that can take part in a chemical reaction, and which cannot be broken down chemically into anything simpler. An atom is made up of protons and neutrons in a central nucleus surrounded by electrons (see ◊atomic structure). The atoms of the various elements differ in atomic number, atomic weight, and chemical behavior. There are 109 different types of atom, corresponding with the 109 known elements as listed in the ◊periodic table of the elements.

atomic bomb bomb deriving its explosive force from nuclear fission (see ◊nuclear energy) as a result of a neutron chain reaction, developed in the 1940s in the US into a usable weapon.

atomic clock timekeeping device regulated by various periodic processes occurring in atoms and molecules, such as atomic vibration or the frequency of absorbed or emitted radiation.

atomic mass unit or *dalton unit* (symbol amu or u) unit of mass that is used to measure the relative mass of atoms and molecules. It is equal to one-twelfth of the mass of a carbon-12 atom, which is equivalent to the mass of a proton or 1.66×10^{-27} kg. The atomic weight of an atom has no units; thus oxygen-16 has an atomic mass of 16 daltons but an atomic weight of 16.

atomic number or *proton number* the number (symbol Z) of protons in the nucleus of an atom. It is equal to the positive charge on the nucleus. In a neutral atom, it is also equal to the number of electrons surrounding the nucleus. The 109 elements are arranged in the ◊periodic table of the elements according to their atomic number.

atomic radiation energy given out by disintegrating atoms during ◊radioactive decay, whether natural or synthesized. The energy may be in the form of fast-moving particles, known as ◊alpha particles and ◊beta particles, or in the form of high-energy electromagnetic waves known as ◊gamma radiation. Overlong exposure to atomic radiation can lead to ◊radiation sickness. Radiation biology studies the effect of radiation on living organisms.

atomic structure internal structure of an ◊atom. The core of the atom is the *nucleus*, a dense body only one ten-thousandth the diameter of the atom itself. The simplest nucleus, that of hydrogen, comprises a single stable positively charged particle, the *proton*.

atomic bomb Giant waterspout at Bikini Island in the W Pacific after the explosion of a US atomic bomb in an underwater test.

Nuclei of other elements contain more protons and additional particles, called *neutrons*, of about the same mass as the proton but with no electrical charge. Each element has its own characteristic nucleus with a unique number of protons, the atomic number. The number of neutrons may vary. Where atoms of a single element have different numbers of neutrons, they are called ◊isotopes. Although some isotopes tend to be unstable and exhibit ◊radioactivity, they all have identical chemical properties.

The nucleus is surrounded by a number of moving *electrons* each of which has a negative charge equal to the positive charge on a proton, but which weighs only 1/1,839 times as much. In a neutral atom, the nucleus is surrounded by the same number of electrons as it contains protons. According to ◊quantum theory, the position of an electron is uncertain: it may be found at any point. However, it is more likely to be found in some places than others. The region of space in which an electron is most likely to be found is called an orbital. The chemical properties of an element are determined by the ease with which its atoms can gain or lose electrons from its outer orbitals. High-energy physics research has discovered the existence of subatomic particles (see ◊particle physics) other than the proton, neutron, and electron. More than 300 kinds of particle are now known, and these are classified into several classes according to their mass, electric charge, spin, magnetic moment, and interaction. The ◊elementary particles, which include the electron, are indivisible and may be regarded as the fundamenal units of matter; the *hadrons*, such as the proton and neutron, are composite particles made up of either two or three elementary particles called quarks. Atoms are held together by the electrical forces of attraction between each negative electron and the positive protons within the nucleus: The latter repel one another with enormous forces; a nucleus holds together only because an even stronger force, called the *strong nuclear force*, attracts the protons and neutrons to one another. The strong force acts over a very short range—the protons and neutrons must be in virtual contact with one another If, therefore, a fragment of a complex nucleus, containing some protons, becomes only slightly loosened form the main group of neutrons and protons, the natural repulsion between the protons will cause this fragment to fly apart from the rest of the nucleus at high speed. It is by such fragmentation of atomic nuclei (nuclear ◊fission) that nuclear energy is released.

Aton in ancient Egypt, the Sun's disk as an emblem of the single deity whose worship was promoted by ◊Ikhnaton in an attempt to replace the many gods traditionally worshiped.

atonality music in which there is an apparent absence of ◊key; often associated with an expressionist style.

atonement in Christian theology, the doctrine that Jesus suffered on the cross to bring about reconciliation and forgiveness between God and humanity.

Atonement, Day of Jewish holy day (*Yom Kippur*) held on the tenth day of Tishri (Sept–Oct), the first month of the Jewish year. It is a day of fasting, penitence, and cleansing from sin, ending the Ten Days of Penitence that follow *Rosh Hashanah*, the Jewish New Year.

ATP abbreviation for *adenosine triphosphate*, a nucleotide molecule found in all cells. It can yield large amounts of energy, and is used to drive the thousands of biological processes needed to sustain life, growth,

movement, and reproduction. Green plants use light energy to manufacture ATP as part of the process of ◊photosynthesis. In animals, ATP is formed by the breakdown of glucose molecules, usually obtained from the carbohydrate component of a diet, in a series of reactions termed ◊respiration. It is the driving force behind muscle contraction and the synthesis of complex molecules needed by individual cells.

atrium in architecture, an open inner courtyard. Originally the central court or main room of an ancient Roman house, open to the sky, often with a shallow pool to catch water.

atrophy in medicine, a diminution in size and function, or output, of a body tissue or organ. It is usually due to nutritional impairment, disease, or disuse (muscle).

atropine alkaloid derived from belladonna, a plant with toxic properties. It acts as an anticholinergic, inhibiting the passage of certain nerve impulses. As atropine sulfate, it is administered as a mild antispasmodic drug.

Attenborough Richard 1923– . English actor, director, and producer. He began his acting career in war films and comedies. His films include *Brighton Rock* 1947 and *10 Rillington Place* 1970 (as actor), and *Oh! What a Lovely War* 1969, *Gandhi* (which won eight Academy Awards) 1982, *Cry Freedom* 1987, and *Chaplin* 1992 (as director).

Attica (Greek *Attiki*) region of Greece comprising Athens and the district around it; area 1,305 sq mi/3,381 sq km. It is renowned for its language, art, and philosophical thought in Classical times. It is a prefecture of modern Greece with Athens as its capital.

Attila c. 406–453. King of the Huns in an area from the Alps to the Caspian Sea from 434, known to later Christian history as the "Scourge of God." He twice attacked the Eastern Roman Empire to increase the quantity of tribute paid to him, 441–443 and 447–449, and then attacked the Western Roman Empire 450–452.

Attleboro city in SE Massachusetts, NW of New Bedford; population (1990) 38,400. Industries include jewelry, tools, silver products, electronics, and paper goods.

Attlee Clement (Richard), 1st Earl 1883–1967. British Labour politician. In the coalition government during World War II he was Lord Privy Seal 1940–42, dominions secretary 1942–43, and Lord President of the Council 1943–45, as well as deputy prime minister from 1942. As prime minister 1945–51 he introduced a sweeping program of nationalization and a whole new system of social services.

attorney person who represents another in legal matters. In the US, attorney is the formal title for a lawyer. See also ◊power of attorney.

attorney general principal law officer. In the US, the principal officer of the federal government or of a state. Attorneys general act as chief officers for criminal and civil law and as chief legal representatives of their governments in government operations.

attrition in earth science, the process by which particles of rock being transported by river, wind, or sea are rounded and gradually reduced in size by being struck against one another.

Atwood Margaret (Eleanor) 1939– . Canadian novelist, short-story writer, and poet. Her novels, which often treat feminist themes with wit and irony, include *The Edible Woman* 1969, *Life Before Man* 1979, *Bodily Harm* 1981, *The Handmaid's Tale* 1986, and *Cat's Eye* 1989.

Auburn city in SW Maine, on the Androscoggin River, W of Lewiston; seat of Androscoggin County; population (1990) 24,300. Industries include shoes, textiles, poultry, livestock, and bricks.

Auckland largest city in New Zealand, situated in N North Island; population (1991) 315,900. It fills the isthmus that separates its two harbors (Waitemata and Manukau), and its suburbs spread N across the Harbor Bridge. It is the country's chief port and leading industrial center, having iron and steel plants, engineering, automobile assembly, textiles, food processing, sugar refining, and brewing.

Auden W(ystan) H(ugh) 1907–1973. English-born US poet. He wrote some of his most original poetry, such as *Look, Stranger!* 1936, in the 1930s when he led the influential left-wing literary group that included Louis MacNeice, Stephen Spender, and Cecil Day Lewis. He moved to the US 1939, became a US citizen 1946, and adopted a more conservative and Christian viewpoint, for example in *The Age of Anxiety* 1947.

audiometer electrical instrument used to test hearing.

audit official inspection of a company's accounts by a qualified accountant as required by law each year to ensure that the company balance sheet reflects the true state of its affairs.

auditory canal tube leading from the outer ◊ear opening to the eardrum. It is found only in animals whose eardrums are located inside the skull, principally mammals and birds.

Audubon John James 1785–1851. US naturalist and artist. In 1827, after extensive travels and observations of birds, he published the first part of his *Birds of North America*, with a remarkable series of color plates. Later he produced a similar work on North American quadrupeds.

Augean stables in Greek legend, the stables of Augeas, king of Elis in southern Greece. One of the labors of ◊Heracles was to clean out the stables, which contained 3,000 cattle and had never been cleaned before. He was given only one day to do the labor, and so he diverted the river Alpheus through their yard.

Augsburg, Confession of statement of the Protestant faith as held by the German Reformers, composed by Philip Melanchthon. Presented to the holy Roman emperor Charles V, at the conference known as the Diet of Augsburg 1530, it is the creed of the modern Lutheran church.

augur member of a college of Roman priests who interpreted the will of the gods from signs or "auspices" such as the flight of birds, the condition of entrails of sacrificed animals, and the direction of thunder and lightning. Their advice was sought before battle and on other important occasions. Consuls and other high officials had the right to consult the auspices themselves, and a campaign was said to be conducted "under the auspices" of the general who had consulted the gods.

Augusta capital of Maine, located in the SW part of the state, on the Kennebec River, NE of Lewiston and Auburn; population (1990) 21,300. Industries include cotton, timber, and textiles.

Augusta city in E central Georgia, on the Savannah River on the South Carolina border; seat of Richmond County; population (1990) 44,600. It is a manufacturing city and terminal for river barges. Industries include textiles and other cotton products and building materials. Established 1736 as Fort Augusta, an Indian trading post, it was the site of several battles during the Revolutionary War and served as Georgia's capital 1786–95.

Augustan Age golden age of the Roman emperor ◊Augustus, during which art and literature flourished. The name is also given to later periods which used Classical ideals, such as that of Queen Anne in England.

Augustine of Hippo, St 354–430. One of the early Christian leaders and writers known as the Fathers of the Church. He was converted to Christianity by Ambrose in Milan and became bishop of Hippo (modern Annaba, Algeria) 396. Among Augustine's many writings are his *Confessions*, a spiritual autobiography, and *De Civitate Dei/The City of God*, vindicating the Christian church and divine providence in 22 books.

Augustine, St ?–605. first archbishop of Canterbury, England. He was sent from Rome to convert England to Christianity by Pope Gregory I. He landed at Ebbsfleet in Kent 597 and soon after baptized Ethelbert, King of Kent, along with many of his subjects. He was consecrated bishop of the English at Arles in the same year, and appointed archbishop 601, establishing his see at Canterbury. Feast day May 26.

Augustus 63 BC–AD 14. Title of Octavian (Gaius Julius Caesar Octavianus), first of the Roman emperors. He joined forces with Mark Antony and Lepidus in the Second Triumvirate. Following Mark Antony's liaison with the Egyptian queen Cleopatra, Augustus defeated her troops at Actium 31 BC. As emperor (from 27 BC) he reformed the government of the empire, the

Augustus Marble sculpture of Augustus, the first of a long series of Roman emperors.

army, and Rome's public services and was a patron of the arts. The period of his rule is known as the ◊Augustan Age.

auk any member of the family Alcidae, consisting of marine diving birds including razorbills, puffins, murres, and guillemots. Confined to the northern hemisphere, they feed on fish and use their wings to "fly" underwater in pursuit.

Aung San 1916–1947. Burmese (Myanmar) politician. He was a founder and leader of the Anti-Fascist People's Freedom League, which led Burma's fight for independence from Great Britain. During World War II he collaborated first with Japan and then with the UK. In 1947 he became head of Burma's provisional government but was assassinated the same year by political opponents. His daughter ◊Suu Kyi (1945–) spearheaded a nonviolent prodemocracy movement in Myanmar (formerly Burma) from 1988.

Aurangzeb or **Aurungzebe** 1618–1707. Mogul emperor of N India from 1658. Third son of ◊Shah Jahan, he made himself master of the court by a palace revolution.His reign was the most brilliant period of the Mogul dynasty, but his despotic tendencies and Muslim fanaticism aroused much opposition. His latter years were spent in war with the princes of Rajputana and the Marathas and Sikhs. His drive south into the Deccan overextended Mogul resources.

Aurelian Roman emperor from 270. A successful soldier, he was chosen emperor by his troops on the death of Claudius II. He defeated the Goths and Vandals, defeated and captured ◊Zenobia of Palmyra, and was planning a campaign against Parthia when he was numbered. The *Aurelian Wall*, a fortification surrounding Rome, was built by Aurelian 271. It was made of concrete, and substantial ruins exist. The *Aurelian Way* ran from Rome through Pisa and Genoa to Antipolis (Antibes) in Gaul.

Auric Georges 1899–1983. French composer. He was one of the musical group called *Les Six*. Auric composed a comic opera, several ballets, and incidental music to films of Jean Cocteau.

Aurignacian in archeology, an Old Stone Age culture that came between the Mousterian and the Solutrian in the Upper Paleolithic. The name is derived from a cave at Aurignac in the Pyrenees of France. The earliest cave paintings are attributed to the Aurignacian peoples of W Europe about 16,000 BC.

aurora colored light in the night sky near the Earth's magnetic poles, called *aurora borealis* ("northern lights") in the northern hemisphere and *aurora australis* in the southern hemisphere. Although auroras are usually restricted to the polar skies, fluctuations in the ◊solar wind occasionally cause them to be visible at lower latitudes. An aurora is usually in the form of a luminous arch with its apex toward the magnetic pole followed by arcs, bands, rays, curtains, and coronas, usually green but often showing shades of blue and red, and sometimes yellow or white. Auroras are caused at heights of over 60 mi/100 km by a fast stream of charged particles from solar flares and low-density "holes" in the Sun's corona. These are guided by the Earth's magnetic field toward the north and south magnetic poles, where they enter the upper atmosphere and bombard the gases in the atmosphere, causing them to emit visible light.

The French philosopher Gassendi coined the term "northern dawn" 1621.

Aurora in Roman mythology, the goddess of the dawn. Her Greek equivalent is Eos.

Aurora city in NE Illinois, on the Fox River, W of Chicago; population (1990) 99,600. Industries include transportation equipment, glass, and chemicals. Aurora was a pioneer in the use of electric street lights.

Auschwitz (Polish *Oswiecim*) town near Kraków in Poland, the site of a notorious ◊concentration camp used by the Nazis in World War II to exterminate Jews and other political and social minorities, as part of the "final solution." Each of the four gas chambers could hold 6,000 people.

Austen Jane 1775–1817. English novelist who described her raw material as "three or four families in a Country Village." *Sense and Sensibility* was published 1811, *Pride and Prejudice* 1813, *Mansfield Park* 1814, *Emma* 1816, *Northanger Abbey* and *Persuasion* 1818, all anonymously. She observed speech and manners with wit and precision, revealing her characters' absurdities in relation to high standards of integrity and appropriateness.

Austerlitz, Battle of battle on Dec 2, 1805, in which the French forces of Emperor Napoleon defeated those of Alexander I of Russia and Francis II of Austria at a small town in the Czech Republic (formerly in Austria), 12 mi/19 km E of Brno.

Austin capital of Texas, on the Colorado River; population (1990) 465,600. It is a center for electronic and scientific research. It is the home of the University of Texas and the Lyndon B Johnson Library and Museum. The state capitol, 308 ft/94 m high, is the largest of any state. Austin was founded 1838 and developed as a stop on the Chisholm cattle-drive trail in the 1860s.

Austin Stephen Fuller 1793–1836. American pioneer and political leader. A settler in Texas 1821, he was a supporter of the colony's autonomy and was imprisoned 1833–35 for his opposition to Mexican rule. Released during the Texas revolution, he campaigned for US support. After the end of the war 1836, he was appointed secretary of state of the independent Republic of Texas but died shortly afterwards.

The state capital of Austin was named in his honor.

Australasia loosely applied geographical term, usually meaning Australia, New Zealand, and neighboring islands.

Australia country occupying all of the Earth's smallest continent, situated S of Indonesia, between the Pacific and Indian oceans.

Australian Aborigine any of the 500 groups of indigenous inhabitants of the continent of Australia, who migrated to this region from S Asia about 40,000 years ago. They are dark-skinned Caucasoids, with fair hair in childhood and heavy dark beards and body hair in adult males. They were hunters and gatherers, living throughout the continent in small kin-based groups before European settlement. Several hundred different languages developed, including Aranda (Arunta), spoken in central Australia, and Murngin, spoken in Arnhem Land. In recent years a movement for the recognition of Aborigine rights has begun, with campaigns against racial discrimination in housing, education, wages, and medical facilities.

Australian Antarctic Territory islands and territories south of 60° S, between 160° E and 45° E longitude, excluding Adélie Land; area 2,332,984 sq mi/6,044,000 sq km of land and 29,259 sq mi/75,800 sq km of ice shelf. The population on the Antarctic continent is limited to research personnel.

Australian Capital Territory territory ceded to Australia by New South Wales 1911 to provide the

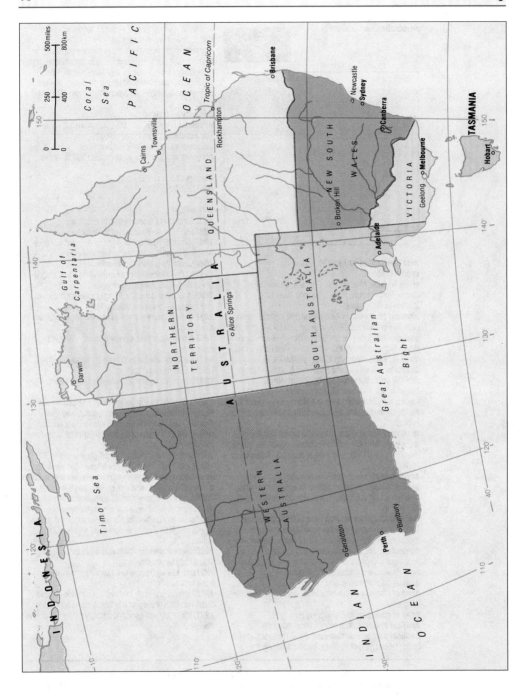

Australia Commonwealth of

area 2,966,136 sq mi/7,682,300 sq km
capital Canberra
cities Adelaide, Alice Springs, Brisbane, Darwin, Melbourne, Perth, Sydney, Hobart, Geelong, Newcastle, Townsville, Wollongong
physical the world's smallest, flattest, and driest continent (40% lies in the tropics, 30% is desert, and 30% is marginal grazing); Great Sandy Desert; Gibson Desert; Great Victoria Desert; Simpson Desert; the Great Barrier Reef (largest coral reef in the world, stretching 1,250 mi/2,000 km off E coast of Queensland); Great Dividing Range and Australian Alps in the E (Mount Kosciusko, 7,136 ft/2,229 m, Australia's highest peak). The fertile SE region is watered by the Darling, Lachlan, Murrumbridgee, and Murray rivers; rivers in the interior are seasonal. Lake Eyre basin and Nullarbor Plain in the S
territories Norfolk Island, Christmas Island, Cocos (Keeling) Islands, Ashmore and Cartier Islands, Coral Sea Islands, Heard Island and McDonald Islands, Australian Antarctic Territory
environment an estimated 75% of Australia's northern tropical rain forest has been cleared for agriculture or urban development since Europeans first settled there in the early 19th century
features Ayers Rock; Arnhem Land; Gulf of Carpentaria; Cape York Peninsula; Great Australian Bight; unique animal species include the kangaroo, koala, platypus, wombat, Tasmanian devil, and spiny anteater; of 800 species of bird, the budgerigar, cassowary, emu, kookaburra, lyre bird, and black swan are also unique as a result of Australia's long isolation from other continents
head of state Elizabeth II from 1952, represented by governor general
head of government Paul Keating from 1991
political system federal constitutional monarchy
political parties Australian Labor Party, moderate left of center; Liberal Party of Australia, moderate, liberal, free

enterprise; National Party of Australia (formerly Country Party), centrist non-metropolitan
exports world's largest exporter of sheep, wool, diamonds, alumina, coal, lead and refined zinc ores, and mineral sands; other exports include cereals, beef, veal, mutton, lamb, sugar, nickel (world's second-largest producer), iron ore; principal trade partners are Japan, the US, and EC member states
currency Australian dollar
population (1992) 17,562,000; growth rate 1.5% p.a.
life expectancy men 75, women 80
languages English, Aboriginal languages
religions Anglican 26%, other Protestant 17%, Roman Catholic 26%
literacy 98.5.% (1988)
GDP $286.9 bn (1992)

chronology
1901 Creation of Commonwealth of Australia.
1927 Seat of government moved to Canberra.
1942 Statute of Westminster Adoption Act gave Australia autonomy from UK in internal and external affairs.
1944 Liberal Party founded by Robert Menzies.
1951 Australia joined New Zealand and the US as a signatory to the ANZUS Pacific security treaty.
1966 Menzies resigned after being Liberal prime minister for 17 years, and was succeeded by Harold Holt.
1967 A referendum was passed giving Aborigines full citizenship rights.
1968 John Gorton became prime minister after Holt's death.
1971 Gorton succeeded by William McMahon, heading a Liberal–Country Party coalition.
1972 Gough Whitlam became prime minister, leading a Labor government.
1975 Senate blocked the government's financial legislation; Whitlam dismissed by the governor general, who invited Malcolm Fraser to form a Liberal–Country Party caretaker government. This action of the governor general, John Kerr, was widely criticized.
1978 Northern Territory attained self-government.
1983 Labor Party, returned to power under Bob Hawke, convened meeting of employers and unions to seek consensus on economic policy to deal with growing unemployment.
1986 Australia Act passed by UK government, eliminating last vestiges of British legal authority in Australia.
1988 Labor foreign minister Bill Hayden appointed governor general designate. Free-trade agreement with New Zealand signed.
1990 Hawke won record fourth election victory, defeating Liberal Party by small majority.
1991 Paul Keating became new Labor Party leader and prime minister.
1992 Keating's popularity declined as economic problems continued. Oath of allegiance to British crown abandoned.
1993 Labor Party won general election, entering fifth term of office.

site of ◊Canberra, with Jervis Bay port, ceded 1915; area 926 sq mi/2,400 sq km; population (1987) 261,000.

Austria landlocked country in central Europe, bounded E by Hungary, S by Slovenia and Italy, W by Switzerland and Liechtenstein, NW by Germany, and N by the Czech and Slovak republics. *See panel p. 76*

Austrian Succession, War of the war 1740–48 between Austria (supported by England and Holland) and Prussia (supported by France and Spain).

1740 The Holy Roman emperor Charles VI died and the succession of his daughter Maria Theresa was disputed by a number of European powers. Frederick the Great of Prussia seized Silesia from Austria. *1743* At Dettingen an army of British, Austrians, and Hanoverians under the command of George II was victorious over the French. *1745* An Austro-English army was defeated at Fontenoy but British naval superiority was confirmed, and there were gains in the Americas and India. *1748* The war was ended by the Treaty of Aix-la-Chapelle.

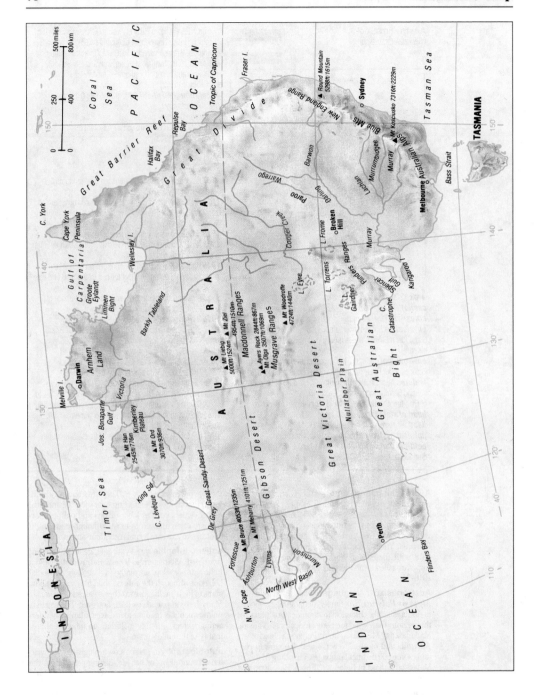

Austria Republic of (*Republik Österreich*)

area 32,374 sq mi/83,500 sq km
capital Vienna
cities Graz, Linz, Salzburg, Innsbruck
physical landlocked mountainous state, with Alps in W and S and low relief in E where most of the population is concentrated
environment Hainburg, the largest primeval forest left in Europe, under threat from a dam project (suspended 1990)
features Austrian Alps (including Grossglockner and Brenner and Semmering passes); Lechtaler and Allgauer Alps N of river Inn; Carnic Alps on Italian border; river Danube
head of state Thomas Klestil from 1992
head of government Franz Vranitzky from 1986
political system democratic federal republic
political parties Socialist Party of Austria (SPÖ), democratic socialist; Austrian People's Party (ÖVP), progres-

sive centrist; Freedom Party of Austria (FPÖ), moderate left of center; United Green Party of Austria (VGÖ), conservative ecological; Green Alternative Party (ALV), radical ecological
exports lumber, textiles, clothing, iron and steel, paper, machinery and transport equipment, foodstuffs
currency schilling
population (1992) 7,857,000; growth rate 0.1% p.a.
life expectancy men 70, women 77
language German
religions Roman Catholic 85%, Protestant 6%
literacy 98% (1983)
GDP $184.7 bn (1992)

chronology
1867 Emperor Franz Josef established dual monarchy of Austria–Hungary.
1914 Archduke Franz Ferdinand assassinated by a Serbian nationalist; Austria–Hungary invaded Serbia, precipitating World War I.
1918 Habsburg empire ended; republic proclaimed.
1938 Austria incorporated into German Third Reich by Hitler (the *Anschluss*).
1945 Under Allied occupation, constitution of 1920 reinstated and coalition government formed by the SPÖ and the ÖVP.
1955 Allied occupation ended, and the independence of Austria formally recognized.
1966 ÖVP in power with Josef Klaus as chancellor.
1970 SPÖ formed a minority government, with Dr Bruno Kreisky as chancellor.
1983 Kreisky resigned and was replaced by Dr Fred Sinowatz, leading a coalition.
1986 Dr Kurt Waldheim elected president. Sinowatz resigned, succeeded by Franz Vranitzky. No party won an overall majority; Vranitzky formed a coalition of the SPÖ and the ÖVP, with ÖVP leader, Dr Alois Mock, as vice chancellor.
1989 Austria sought European Community membership.
1990 Vranitzky reelected.
1991 Bid for EC membership endorsed by the Community.
1992 Thomas Klestil elected president, replacing Waldheim.

Austro-Hungarian Empire the Dual Monarchy established by the Hapsburg Franz Joseph 1867 between his empire of Austria and his kingdom of Hungary (including territory that became Czechoslovakia as well as parts of Poland, the Ukraine, Romania, Yugoslavia, and Italy). It collapsed autumn 1918 with the end of World War I. Only two king-emperors ruled: Franz Joseph 1867–1916 and Charles 1916–18.

Austronesian languages (also known as *Malayo-Polynesian*) family of languages spoken in Malaysia, the Indonesian archipelago, parts of the region that was formerly Indochina, Taiwan, Madagascar, Melanesia, and Polynesia (excluding Australia and most of New Guinea). The group contains some 500 distinct languages, including Malay in Malaysia, Bahasa in Indonesia, Fijian, Hawaiian, and Maori.

autarchy national economic policy that aims at achieving self-sufficiency and eliminating the need for imports (by imposing tariffs, for example). Such a goal may be difficult, if not impossible, for a small country. Countries that take protectionist measures and try to prevent free trade are sometimes described as autarchical.

authoritarianism rule of a country by a dominant elite who repress opponents and the press to maintain

their own wealth and power. They are frequently indifferent to activities not affecting their security, and rival power centers such as labor unions and political parties, are often allowed to exist, although under tight control. An extreme form is ◊totalitarianism.

autism, infantile rare syndrome, generally present from birth, characterized by a withdrawn state and a failure to develop normally in language or social behavior, although the autistic child may, rarely, show signs of high intelligence in other areas, such as music. Many have impaired intellect, however. The cause is unknown, but is thought to involve a number of interacting factors, possibly including an inherent abnormality of the child's brain.

autobiography a person's own biography, or written account of his or her life, distinguished from the journal or diary by being a connected narrative, and from memoirs by dealing less with contemporary events and personalities. *The Boke of Margery Kempe* about 1432–36 is the oldest known autobiography in English.

auto-da-fé (Portuguese "act of faith") religious ceremony, including a procession, solemn mass, and sermon, which accompanied the sentencing of heretics by the Spanish ◊Inquisition before they were handed over to the secular authorities for punishment, usually burning.

autoimmunity in medicine, condition where the body's immune responses are mobilized not against "foreign" matter, such as invading germs, but against the body itself. Diseases considered to be of autoimmune origin include ◊myasthenia gravis, rheumatoid ◊arthritis, and ◊lupus erythematosus.

automatic pilot control device that keeps an airplane flying automatically on a given course at a given height and speed. Devised by US business executive Lawrence Sperry 1912, the automatic pilot contains a set of ◊gyroscopes that provide references for the plane's course. Sensors detect when the plane deviates from this course and send signals to the control surfaces—the ailerons, elevators, and rudder—to take the appropriate action. Autopilot is also used in missiles. Most airliners cruise on automatic pilot, also called autopilot and gyropilot, for much of the time.

automation widespread use of self-regulating machines in industry. Automation involves the addition of control devices, using electronic sensing and computing techniques, which often follow the pattern of human nervous and brain functions, to already mechanized physical processes of production and distribution; for example, steel processing, mining, chemical production, and road, rail, and air control.

automaton mechanical figure imitating human or animal performance. Automatons are usually designed for aesthetic appeal as opposed to purely functional robots. The earliest recorded automaton is an Egyptian wooden pigeon of 400 BC.

automobile or *car* a small, driver-guided, passenger-carrying motor vehicle; originally the automated version of the horse-drawn carriage, meant to convey people and their goods over streets and roads. Most are four-wheeled and have water-cooled, piston-type internal-combustion engines fueled by gasoline or diesel. Variations have existed for decades that use ingenious and often nonpolluting power plants, but the automobile industry long ago settled on this general formula for the consumer market. Experimental and sports models are streamlined, energy-efficient, and hand-built.

automobile racing competitive racing of motor vehicles. It has forms as diverse as hill-climbing, stock-car racing, rallying, sports-car racing, and Formula One Grand Prix racing. The first organized race was from Paris to Rouen 1894.

autonomic nervous system in mammals, the part of the ◊nervous system that controls the involuntary activities of the smooth muscles (of the digestive tract, blood vessels), the heart, and the glands. The *sympathetic* system responds to stress, when it speeds the heart rate, increases blood pressure and generally prepares the body for action. The *parasympathetic* system is more important when the body is at rest, since it slows the heart rate, decreases blood pressure, and stimulates the digestive system.

autonomy in politics, term used to describe political self-government of a state or, more commonly, a subdivision of a state. Autonomy may be based upon cultural or ethnic differences and often leads eventually to independence.

autopsy or *post-mortem* examination of the internal organs and tissues of a dead body, performed to try to establish the cause of death.

autosuggestion conscious or unconscious acceptance of an idea as true, without demanding rational proof, but with potential subsequent effect for good or ill. Pioneered by the French psychotherapist Emile Coué (1857–1926) in healing, it is used in modern psychotherapy to conquer nervous habits and dependence on tobacco, alcohol, and so on.

Auvergne ancient province of central France and a modern region comprising the *départements* of Allier, Cantal, Haute-Loire, and Puy-de-Dôme
area 10,036 sq mi/26,000 sq km
population (1986) 1,334,000
capital Clermont-Ferrand
physical mountainous, composed chiefly of volcanic rocks in several masses
products cattle, wheat, wine, and cheese
history named after the ancient Gallic Avenni tribe whose leader, Vercingetorix, led a revolt against the Romans 52 BC. In the 14th century the Auvergne was divided into a duchy, dauphiny, and countship. The duchy and dauphiny were united by the dukes of Bourbon before being confiscated by Francis I 1527. The countship united with France 1615.

Auxerre capital of Yvonne *département*, France, 106 mi/170 km SE of Paris, on the river Yvonne; population (1990) 40,600. The Gothic cathedral, founded 1215, has exceptional sculptures and stained glass.

avalanche fall of a mass of snow and ice down a steep slope. Avalanches occur because of the unstable nature of snow masses in mountain areas.

Avalokiteśvara in Mahāyāna Buddhism, one of the most important bodhisattvas, seen as embodying compassion. Known as *Guanyin* in China and *Kannon* in Japan, he is one of the attendants of Amida Buddha.

avant-garde in the arts, those artists or works that are in the forefront of new developments in their media. The term was introduced (as was "reactionary") after the French Revolution, when it was used to describe any socialist political movement.

avatar in Hindu mythology, the descent of a deity to Earth in a visible form, for example the ten avatars of ◊Vishnu.

Avedon Richard 1923– . US photographer. A fashion photographer with *Harper's Bazaar* magazine in New York from the mid-1940s, he moved to *Vogue* 1965. He later became the highest-paid fashion and advertising photographer in the world. He became associated with *The New Yorker* 1993. Using large-format cameras, his work consists of intensely realistic images, chiefly portraits.

Ave Maria Christian prayer to the Virgin Mary, which takes its name from the archangel Gabriel's salutation to the Virgin Mary when announcing that she would be the mother of the Messiah (Luke 11:28).

average in statistics, a term used inexactly to indicate the typical member of a set of data. It usually refers to the ◊arithmetic mean. The term is also used to refer to the middle member of the set when it is sorted in ascending or descending order (the ◊median), and the most commonly occurring item of data (the ◊mode), as in "the average family."

Averroës (Arabic *Ibn Rushd*) 1126–1198. Arabian philosopher who argued for the eternity of matter and against the immortality of the individual soul. His philosophical writings, including commentaries on Aristotle and on Plato's *Republic*, became known to the West through Latin translations. He influenced Christian and Jewish writers into the Renaissance, and reconciled Islamic and Greek thought in that philosophic truth comes through reason. St Thomas Aquinas opposed this position.

aviation see ◊flight for the history of aviation and airplanes.

Avicenna (Arabic *Ibn Sina*) 979–1037. Arabian philosopher and physician. He was the most renowned philosopher of medieval Islam. His *Canon Medicinae* was a standard work for many centuries. His philosophical writings were influenced by al-Farabi, Aristotle, and the Neoplatonists, and in turn influenced the scholastics of the 13th century.

Avignon city in Provence, France, capital of Vaucluse *département*, on the river Rhône NW of Marseilles; population (1990) 89,400. An important Gallic and Roman city, it has a 12th-century bridge (only half still standing), a 13th-century cathedral, 14th-century walls, and two palaces built during the residence here of the popes, Le Palais Vieux (1334–42) and Le Palais Nouveau (1342–52). Avignon was papal property 1348–1791.

avocado tree *Persea americana* of the laurel family, native to Central America. Its dark-green, thick-skinned, pear-shaped fruit has buttery-textured flesh and is used in salads.

Avogadro's number or *Avogadro's constant* the number of carbon atoms in 12 g of the carbon-12 isotope (6.022137×10^{23}). The atomic weight of any element, expressed in grams, contains this number of atoms. It is named after Amadeo Avogadro.

avoirdupois system of weights based on the pound (0.45 kg), which consists of 16 ounces, each of 16 drams, with each dram equal to 27.34 grains (1.772 g).

Avon any of several rivers in England and Scotland. The Avon in Warwickshire is associated with Shakespeare.

AWACS (acronym for *Airborne Warning And Control System*) surveillance system that incorporates a long-range surveillance and detection radar mounted on a Boeing E-3 sentry aircraft. It was used with great success in the 1991 Gulf War.

Axelrod Julius 1912– . US neuropharmacologist who shared the 1970 Nobel Prize for Medicine with the biophysicists Bernard Katz and Ulf von Euler (1905–1983) for his work on neurotransmitters (the chemical messengers of the brain).

axiom in mathematics, a statement that is assumed to be true and upon which theorems are proved by using logical deduction; for example, two straight lines cannot enclose a space. The Greek mathematician Euclid used a series of axioms that he considered could not be demonstrated in terms of simpler concepts to prove his geometrical theorems.

axis (plural *axes*) in geometry, one of the reference lines by which a point on a graph may be located. The horizontal axis is usually referred to as the *x*-axis, and the vertical axis as the *y*-axis. The term is also used to refer to the imaginary line about which an object may be said to be symmetrical (*axis of symmetry*) – for example, the diagonal of a square—or the line about which an object may revolve (*axis of rotation*).

Axis alliance of Nazi Germany and Fascist Italy before and during World War II. The *Rome–Berlin Axis* was formed 1936, when Italy was being threatened with sanctions because of its invasion of Ethiopia (Abyssinia). It became a full military and political alliance May 1939. A ten-year alliance among Germany, Italy, and Japan (*Rome–Berlin–Tokyo Axis*) was signed Sept 1940 and was subsequently joined by Hungary, Bulgaria, Romania, and the puppet states of Slovakia and Croatia. The Axis collapsed with the fall of Mussolini and the surrender of Italy 1943 and Germany and Japan 1945.

axon long threadlike extension of a ◊nerve cell that conducts electrochemical impulses away from the cell body toward other nerve cells, or toward an effector organ such as a muscle. Axons terminate in ◊synapses with other nerve cells, muscles, or glands.

Axum alternative transliteration of ◊Aksum, an ancient kingdom in Ethiopia.

ayatollah honorific title awarded to Shiite Muslims in Iran by popular consent, as, for example, to Ayatollah Ruhollah ◊Khomeini.

Ayckbourn Alan 1939– . English playwright. His prolific output, characterized by comic dialogue and experiments in dramatic structure, includes *The Norman Conquests* (a trilogy) 1974, *A Woman in Mind* 1986, *Henceforward* 1987, and *Man of the Moment* 1988.

aye-aye nocturnal tree-climbing prosimian *Daubentonia madagascariensis* of Madagascar, related to the lemurs. It is just over 3 ft/1 m long, including a tail 20 in/50 cm long.

Ayer A(lfred) J(ules) 1910–1989. English philosopher. He wrote *Language, Truth and Logic* 1936, an exposition of the theory of "logical positivism," presenting a criterion by which meaningful statements (essentially truths of logic, as well as statements derived from experience) could be distinguished from meaningless metaphysical utterances (for example, claims that there is a God or that the world external to our own minds is illusory).

Ayers Rock vast ovate mass of pinkish rock in Northern Territory, Australia; 1,110 ft/335 m high and 6 mi/9 km around. It is named after Henry Ayers, a premier of South Australia.

Ayesha 611–678. Third and favorite wife of the prophet Mohammed, who married her when she was nine. Her father, Abu Bakr, became ◊caliph on Mohammed's death 632. She bitterly opposed the later succession to the caliphate of Ali, who had once accused her of infidelity.

Aymara member of an American Indian people of Bolivia and Peru, builders of a great culture, who were conquered first by the Incas and then by the Spaniards. Today 1.4 million Aymara farm and herd llamas and alpacas in the highlands; their language, belonging to the Andean-Equatorial language family, survives, and their Roman Catholicism incorporates elements of their old beliefs.

AZ abbreviation for the state of *Arizona*.

azalea any of various deciduous flowering shrubs, genus *Rhododendron*, of the heath family Ericaceae. There are several species native to Asia and North America, and from these many cultivated varieties have been derived. Azaleas are closely related to the evergreen ◊rhododendrons of the same genus.

Azerbaijan country in W Asia, bounded S by Iran, E by the Caspian Sea, W by Armenia and Georgia, and N by Russia.

Azerbaijan, Iranian two provinces of NW Iran, *Eastern Azerbaijan* (capital Tabriz), population (1986) 4,114,000, and *Western Azerbaijan* (capital Orúmiyeh), population (1986) 1,972,000. Azerbaijanis in Iran, as in the Republic of Azerbaijan, are mainly Shiite Muslim ethnic Turks, descendants of followers of the Khans from the Mongol Empire.

Azilian archeological period following the close of the Old Stone (Paleolithic) Age and regarded as one of the cultures of the Mesolithic Age. It was first recognized at Mas d'Azil, a village in Ariège, France.

Azores group of nine islands in the N Atlantic, belonging to Portugal; area 867 sq mi/2,247 sq km; population (1987) 254,000. They are outlying peaks of the Mid-Atlantic Ridge and are volcanic in origin. The

Ayers Rock The world's largest monolith, Ayers Rock in Northern Territory, Australia, is sacred to Aboriginal peoples of the area.

Azerbaijan Republic of

area 33,400 sq mi/86,600 sq km
capital Baku
cities Gyandzha (formerly Kirovabad), Sumgait
physical Caspian Sea; the country ranges from semidesert to the Caucasus Mountains
head of state Geidar Aliyev from 1993
head of government Suret Guseinov from 1993
political system emergent democracy
political parties Republican Democratic Party, ex-communist-dominated; Popular Front, democratic nationalist; Islamic Party, fundamentalist
products oil, iron, copper, fruit, vines, cotton, silk, carpets
population (1990) 7,145,600 (83% Azeri, 6% Russian, 6% Armenian)

language Turkic
religion traditionally Shi'ite Muslim

chronology
1917–18 A member of the anti-Bolshevik Transcaucasian Federation.
1918 Became an independent republic.
1920 Occupied by the Red Army.
1922–36 Formed part of the Transcaucasian Federal Republic with Georgia and Armenia.
1936 Became a constituent republic of the USSR.
1988 Riots followed Nagorno-Karabakh's request for transfer to Armenia.
1989 Jan–Nov: strife-torn Nagorno-Karabakh placed under direct rule from Moscow. Azerbaijan Popular Front established. Nov: civil war erupted with Armenia.
1990 Jan: Soviet troops dispatched to Baku to restore order. Aug: communists won parliamentary elections. Nakhichevan republic affected by Nagorno-Karabakh dispute.
1991 Aug: Azeri leadership supported attempted anti-Gorbachev coup in Moscow; independence declared. Sept: former communist Ayaz Mutalibov elected president. Dec: joined new Commonwealth of Independent States; Nagorno-Karabakh declared independence.
1992 Jan: admitted into Conference on Security and Cooperation in Europe; March: Mutalibov resigned; Azerbaijan became a member of the United Nations; accorded diplomatic recognition by the US. June: Albulfaz Elchibey, leader of the Popular Front, elected president; renewed campaign against Armenia in the fight for Nagorno-Karabakh.
1993 Prime Minister Rakham Guseinov resigned. President Elchibey ousted, replaced by former Communist Party leader Geidar Aliyev. Suret Guseinov appointed prime minister.

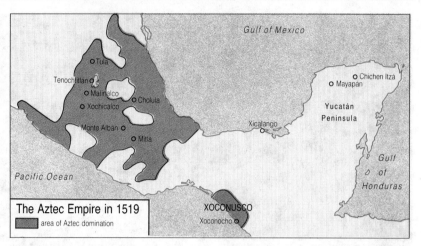

The Aztec Empire in 1519

area of Aztec domination

capital is Ponta Delgada on the main island, San Miguel.

Azov (Russian *Azovskoye More*) inland sea of Europe forming a gulf in the NE of the Black Sea, between Ukraine and Russia; area 14,500 sq mi/37,555 sq km. Principal ports include Rostov-on-Don, Kerch, and Taganrog. Azov is a good source of freshwater fish.

AZT or *retrovir* or *zidovudine* trademark for azidothymidine, an antiviral drug used in the treatment of ◊AIDS.

Aztec member of an ancient Mexican civilization that migrated south into the valley of Mexico in the 12th century, and in 1325 began reclaiming lake marshland to build their capital, Tenochtitlán, on the site of present-day Mexico City. Under Montezuma I (reigned from 1440), the Aztecs created a tribute empire in central Mexico. After the conquistador Cortès landed 1519, Montezuma II (reigned from 1502) was killed and Tenochtitlán subsequently destroyed. Nahuatl is the Aztec language; it belongs to the Uto-Aztecan family of languages.

B

Baader-Meinhof gang popular name for the West German left-wing guerrilla group the *Rote Armee Fraktion*/Red Army Faction, active from 1968 against what it perceived as US imperialism. The three main founding members were Andreas Baader (1943–77), Gudrun Ensslin, and Ulrike Meinhof (1934–76).

Baal divine title given to their chief male gods by the Phoenicians, or Canaanites. Their worship as fertility gods, often orgiastic and of a phallic character, was strongly denounced by the Hebrew prophets.

Baalbek city of ancient Syria, now in Lebanon, 36 mi/60 km NE of Beirut. It was originally a center of Baal worship. The Greeks identified Baal with Helios, the Sun, and renamed Baalbek *Heliopolis*. Its ruins, including Roman temples, survive; the Temple of Bacchus, built in the 2nd century AD, is still almost intact.

Ba'ath Party ruling political party in Iraq and Syria. Despite public support of pan-Arab unity and its foundations 1943 as a party of Arab nationalism, its ideology has been so vague that it has fostered widely differing (and often opposing) parties in Syria and Iraq.

Babangida Ibrahim 1941– . Nigerian politician and soldier, president from 1985. He became head of the Nigerian army in 1983 and in 1985 led a coup against President Buhari, assuming the presidency himself. He has promised a return to civilian rule.

Babbage Charles 1792–1871. English mathematician who devised a precursor of the computer. He designed an analytical engine, a general-purpose mechanical computing device for performing different calculations according to a program input on punched cards (an idea borrowed from the Jacquard loom). This device was never built, but it embodied many of the principles on which present digital computers are based.

Babbit metal soft, white metal, an ◊alloy of tin, lead, copper, and antimony, used to reduce friction in bearings, developed by the US inventor Isaac Babbit 1839.

Babbitt Milton 1916– . US composer. After studying with Roger Sessions he developed a personal style of serialism influenced by jazz. He was a leading composer of electronic music using the 1960 RCA Mark II synthesizer, which he helped to design.

Babel Hebrew name for the city of ◊Babylon, chiefly associated with the *Tower of Babel* which, in the

Genesis story in the Old Testament, was erected in the plain of Shinar by the descendants of Noah. It was a ziggurat, or staged temple, seven stories high (300 ft/ 100 m) with a shrine of Marduk on the summit. It was built by Nabopolassar, father of Nebuchadnezzar, and was destroyed when Sennacherib sacked the city 689 BC.

Babington Anthony 1561–1586. English traitor who hatched a plot to assassinate Elizabeth I and replace her with ◊Mary Queen of Scots; its discovery led to Mary's execution and his own.

Babism religious movement founded during the 1840s by Mirza Ali Mohammad ("the Bab"). An offshoot of Islam, its main difference lies in the belief that Mohammed was not the last of the prophets. The movement split into two groups after the death of the Bab; Baha'ullah, the leader of one of these groups, founded the ◊Baha'i faith.

Babi Yar ravine near Kiev, Ukraine, where more than 100,000 people (80,000 Jews; the others were Poles, Russians, and Ukrainians) were killed by the Nazis 1941. The site was ignored until the Soviet poet Yevtushenko wrote a poem called "Babi Yar" 1961 in protest at plans for a sports center on the site.

baboon large monkey, genus *Papio*, with a long doglike muzzle and large canine teeth, spending much of its time on the ground in open country. Males, with head and body up to 3.5 ft/1.1 m long, are larger than females and dominant males rule the "troops" in which baboons live. They inhabit Africa and SW Arabia.

Babylon capital of ancient Babylonia, on the bank of the lower Euphrates River. The site is now in Iraq, 55 mi/88 km S of Baghdad and 5 mi/8 km N of Hilla, which is built chiefly of bricks from the ruins of Babylon. The *Hanging Gardens of Babylon*, one of the ◊Seven Wonders of the World, were probably erected on a vaulted stone base, the only stone construction in the mud-brick city. They formed a series of terraces, irrigated by a hydraulic system.

Bacall Lauren. Adopted name of Betty Joan Perske 1924– . Striking US actress who became an overnight star when cast by Howard Hawks opposite Humphrey Bogart in *To Have and Have Not* 1944. She and Bogart married in 1945 and starred together in *The Big Sleep* 1946 and several other films. She also appeared in *The Cobweb* 1955, *Harper* 1966, and *The Shootist* 1976.

Bacchus in Greek and Roman mythology, the god of fertility (see ◊Dionysus) and of wine; his rites (the *Bacchanalia*) were orgiastic.

Bach Johann Christian 1735–1782. German composer, the 11th son of J S Bach, who became celebrated in Italy as a composer of operas. In 1762 he was invited to London, where he became music master to the royal

baboon Hamadryas baboon of Ethiopia, Somalia, and southern Saudi Arabia.

family. He remained in England until his death, enjoying great popularity both as composer and performer.

Bach Johann Sebastian 1685–1750. German composer. He was a master of ◊counterpoint, and his music epitomizes the Baroque polyphonic style. His orchestral music includes the six *Brandenburg Concertos*, other concertos for keyboard instrument and violin, and four orchestral suites. Bach's keyboard music, for ◊clavier and organ, his fugues, and his choral music are of equal importance. He also wrote chamber music and songs.

bacillus member of a group of rodlike ◊bacteria that occur everywhere in the soil and air. Some are responsible for diseases such as anthrax or for causing food spoilage.

backgammon board game for two players, often used in gambling. It was known in Mesopotamia, Greece, and Rome and in medieval England.

Bacon Francis 1561–1626. English politician, philosopher, and essayist. He became Lord Chancellor 1618, and the same year confessed to bribe-taking, was fined £40,000 (which was later remitted by the king), and spent four days in the Tower of London. His works include *Essays* 1597, characterized by pith and brevity; *The Advancement of Learning* 1605, a seminal work discussing scientific method; the *Novum Organum* 1620, in which he redefined the task of natural science, seeing it as a means of empirical discovery and a method of increasing human power over nature; and *The New Atlantis* 1626, describing a utopian state in which scientific knowledge is systematically sought and exploited.

His writing helped to inspire the founding of the ◊Royal Society.

Bacon Francis 1909–1992. British painter, born in Dublin. He moved to London in 1925 and taught himself to paint. He practiced abstract art, then developed a distorted Expressionist style with tortured figures presented in loosely defined space. From 1945 he focused on studies of figures, as in his series of screaming popes based on the portrait of Innocent X by Velázquez.

Bacon Nathaniel 1647–1676. American colonial leader and wealthy plantation owner. An advocate of social reform in Virginia and an opponent of Governor William ◊Berkeley, he gained wide public support and was proclaimed "General of Virginia."

Bacon Roger 1214–1292. English philosopher, scientist, and a teacher at Oxford University. He was interested in alchemy, the biological and physical sciences, and magic. Many discoveries have been credited to him, including the magnifying lens. He foresaw the extensive use of gunpowder and mechanical automobiles, boats, and planes.

badger The American badger is slightly smaller than its Eurasian cousin.

bacteria (singular *bacterium*) microscopic unicellular organisms with prokaryotic cells (see ◊prokaryote). They usually reproduce by ◊binary fission (dividing into two equal parts), and since this may occur approximately every 20 minutes, a single bacterium is potentially capable of producing 16 million copies of itself in a day. It is thought that 1–10% of the world's bacteria have been identified.

Bactria former region of central Asia (now divided among Afghanistan, Pakistan, and Tajikistan) which was partly conquered by ◊Alexander the Great. During the 3rd–6th centuries BC it was a center of East-West trade and cultural exchange.

Bactrian species of ◊camel *Camelus bactrianus* found in the Gobi Desert in Central Asia. Body fat is stored in two humps on the back. It has very long winter fur which is shed in ragged lumps. The head and body length is about 10 ft/3 m, and the camel is up to 6.8 ft/2.1 m tall at the shoulder. Most Bactrian camels are domesticated and are used as beasts of burden in W Asia.

Baden former state of SW Germany, which had Karlsruhe as its capital. Baden was captured from the Romans in 282 by the Alemanni; later it became a margravate and in 1806, a grand duchy. A state of the German empire 1871–1918, then a republic, and under Hitler a *Gau* (province), it was divided between the *Länder* of Württemberg-Baden and Baden in 1945 and in 1952 made part of ◊Baden-Württemberg.

Baden-Powell Robert Stephenson Smyth, 1st Baron Baden-Powell 1857–1941. British general, founder of the Scout Association. He fought in defense of Mafeking (now Mafikeng) during the Boer War. After 1907 he devoted his time to developing the Scout movement, which rapidly spread throughout the world. He was created a peer in 1929.

Baden-Württemberg administrative region (German *Land*) of Germany
area 13,819 sq mi/ 35,800 sq km
capital Stuttgart
cities Mannheim, Karlsruhe, Freiburg, Heidelberg, Heilbronn, Pforzheim, Ulm
physical Black Forest; Rhine boundary S and W; source of the river Danube; see also ◊Swabia
products wine, jewelry, watches, clocks, musical instruments, textiles, chemicals, iron, steel, electrical equipment, surgical instruments
population (1988) 9,390,000
history formed 1952 (following a plebiscite) by the merger of the *Länder* Baden, Württemberg-Baden, and Württemberg-Hohenzollern.

badger large mammal of the weasel family with molar teeth of a crushing type adapted to a partly vegetable diet, and short strong legs with long claws suitable for digging. The Eurasian *common badger Meles meles* is about 3 ft/1 m long, with long, coarse, grayish hair on the back, and a white face with a broad black stripe along each side. Mainly a woodland animal, it is harmless and nocturnal, and spends the day in a system of burrows called a "sett." It feeds on roots, a variety of fruits and nuts, insects, worms, mice, and young rabbits.

badminton racket game similar to lawn ◊tennis but played on a smaller court and with a shuttlecock instead of a ball. The object of the game is to prevent the opponent from being able to return the shuttlecock.

Badoglio Pietro 1871–1956. Italian soldier and Fascist politician. A veteran of campaigns against the peoples of Tripoli and Cyrenaica, in 1935 he became commander in chief in Ethiopia, adopting ruthless

badminton

A volleying game played on an indoor court with rackets and a shuttlecock. It is played as singles or pairs and the object is to play the shuttle over the raised net and to score points by grounding the shuttle in the opponent's half of the court or by forcing an error. Only the server can score points. A game is won when one side reaches 15 points (11 in women's singles).

Shuttles

Shuttles come in two forms. They can be either synthetic or made with 16 goose feathers. The feathered cock is the one used in major tournament play while the plastic cock is used at junior level and for practice.

Service

The shuttle is dropped from the hand onto the racket and the service must be underhand and hit over the net. Overhand serving, like that in lawn tennis, is not permitted in badminton.

grips

(2) backhand

(1) forehand

Grips

There are three forms of grip which should be adopted: (1) the forehand grip (2) the backhand grip and (3) the frying pan grip, for smashes

(3) frying pan

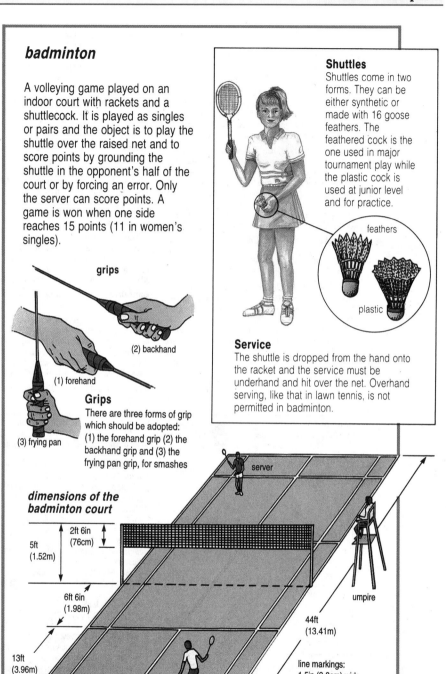

feathers

plastic

dimensions of the badminton court

server

2ft 6in (76cm)

5ft (1.52m)

6ft 6in (1.98m)

umpire

44ft (13.41m)

13ft (3.96m)

receiver

line markings: 1.5in (3.8cm) wide

2ft 6in (76.2cm)

long service line for doubles

17ft (5.18m)

back boundary line, or long service line for singles

20ft (6.09m)

measures to break patriot resistance. He was created viceroy of Ethiopia and duke of Addis Ababa in 1936. He resigned during the disastrous campaign into Greece 1940 and succeeded Mussolini as prime minister of Italy from July 1943 to June 1944, negotiating the armistice with the Allies.

Baekeland Leo Hendrik 1863–1944. Belgian-born US chemist. He invented Bakelite, the first commercial plastic, made from formaldehyde and ◊phenol. He later made a photographic paper, Velox, which could be developed in artificial light.

Baez Joan 1941– . US folk singer and pacifist activist whose pure soprano in the early 1960s popularized traditional English and American folk songs such as "Silver Dagger" and "We Shall Overcome" (an anthem of the civil-rights movement). She helped Bob Dylan at the start of his career and has recorded many of his songs. She founded the Institute for the Study of Non-Violence in Carmel, California, 1965.

Baffin William 1584–1622 English explorer and navigator. In 1616 he and Robert Bylot explored Baffin Bay, NE Canada, and reached latitude 77° 45' N, which for 236 years remained the "furthest north."

Baffin Island island in the Northwest Territories, area 195,875 sq mi/507,450 sq km *features* largest island in the Canadian Arctic; mountains rise above 6,000 ft/ 2,000 m, and there are several large lakes. The northernmost part of the strait separating Baffin Island from Greenland forms Baffin Bay, the southern end is Davis Strait. It is named after William Baffin, who carried our research here 1614 during his search for the ◊Northwest Passage.

Baghdad historic city and capital of Iraq, on the river Tigris; population (1985) 4,649,000. Industries include oil refining, distilling, tanning, tobacco processing, and the manufacture of textiles and cement. Founded 762, it became Iraq's capital 1921. During the Gulf War 1991, the UN coalition forces bombed it in repeated air raids and destroyed much of the city.

bagpipe ancient wind instrument used outdoors and incorporating a number of reed pipes powered from a single inflated bag. Known in Roman times, it is found in various forms throughout Europe including Ireland and Greece. The most famous, that of the Highlands, is the Scottish national instrument.

Baha'i religion founded in the 19th century from a Muslim splinter group, ◊Babism, by the Persian Baha'ullah. His message in essence was that all great religious leaders are manifestations of the unknowable God and all scriptures are sacred. There is no priesthood: all Baha'is are expected to teach and to work toward world unification. There are about 4.5 million Baha'is worldwide.

Bahamas country comprising a group of about 700 islands and about 2,400 uninhabited islets and cays in the Caribbean, 50 mi/80 km from the SE coast of Florida. They extend for about 760 mi/1,223 km from NW to SE, but only 22 of the islands are inhabited.

Bahrain country comprising a group of islands in the Persian Gulf, between Saudi Arabia and Iran.

Baikal (Russian *Baykal Ozero*) freshwater lake in S Siberia, Russia, the largest in Asia, and the eighth largest in the world (area 12,150 sq mi/31,500 sq km); also the deepest in the world (up to 5,700 ft/1,640 m). Fed by more than 300 rivers, it is drained only by the Lower Angara. It has fisheries and is rich in fauna.

Baird John Logie 1888–1946. Scottish electrical engineer who pioneered television. In 1925 he gave the first

---

Bahamas
Commonwealth of the

area 5,352 sq mi/13,864 sq km
capital Nassau on New Providence
cities Alice Town, Andros Town, Hope Town, Spanish Wells, Freeport, Moss Town, George Town
physical comprises 700 tropical coral islands and about 1,000 cays
features desert islands: only 30 are inhabited; Blue Holes of Andros, the world's longest and deepest submarine caves; the Exumas are a narrow spine of 365 islands
principal islands Andros, Grand Bahama, Great Abaco, Eleuthera, New Providence, Berry Islands, Biminis, Great

Inagua, Acklins, Exumas, Mayaguana, Crooked Island, Long Island, Cat Island, Rum Cay, Watling (San Salvador) Island
head of state Elizabeth II from 1973, represented by governor-general
head of government Hubert Ingraham from 1992
political system constitutional monarchy
political parties Progressive Liberal Party (PLP), centrist; Free National Movement (FNM), center-left
exports cement, pharmaceuticals, petroleum products, crawfish, salt, aragonite, rum, pulpwood; over half the islands' employment comes from tourism
currency Bahamian dollar
population (1990 est) 251,000; growth rate 1.8% p.a.
languages English and some Creole
media three independent daily newspapers
religions 29% Baptist, 23% Anglican, 22% Roman Catholic
literacy 95% (1986)
GDP $2.7 bn (1987); $11,261 per head
chronology
1964 Independence achieved from Britain.
1967 First national assembly elections; Lynden Pindling became prime minister.
1972 Constitutional conference to discuss full independence.
1973 Full independence achieved.
1983 Allegations of drug trafficking by government ministers.
1984 Deputy prime minister and two cabinet ministers resigned. Pindling denied any personal involvement and was endorsed as party leader.
1987 Pindling reelected despite claims of frauds.
1992 FNM led by Hubert Ingraham won absolute majority in assembly elections and succeeded Pindling.

Bahrain State of
(*Dawlat al Bahrayn*)

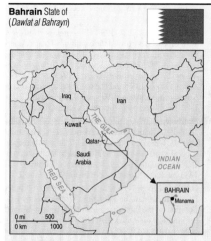

area 266 sq mi/688 sq km
capital Manama on the largest island (also called Bahrain)
cities Muharraq, Jidd Hafs, Isa Town; oil port Mina Sulman
physical 35 islands, composed largely of sand-covered
limestone; generally poor and infertile soil; flat and hot
environment a wildlife park on Bahrain preserves the
endangered oryx; most of the south of the island is preserved
for the ruling family's falconry
features causeway linking Bahrain to mainland Saudi
Arabia; Sitra island is a communications center for the lower

Persian Gulf and has a satellite-tracking station
head of state and government Sheik Isa bin Sulman al-
Khalifa from 1961
political system absolute emirate
political parties none
exports oil, natural gas, aluminum, fish
currency Bahrain dinar
population (1990 est) 512,000 (two-thirds are nationals);
growth rate 4.4% p.a.
life expectancy men 67, women 71
languages Arabic (official), Farsi, English, Urdu
religion 85% Muslim (Shi'ite 60%, Sunni 40%)
literacy men 79%, women 64% (1985 est)
GDP $3.5 bn (1987); $7,772 per head

chronology
1861 Became British protectorate.
1968 Britain announced its intention to withdraw its forces.
Bahrain formed, with Qatar and the Trucial States, the Federation of Arab Emirates.
1971 Qatar and the Trucial States withdrew from the federation and Bahrain became an independent state.
1973 New constitution adopted, with an elected national
assembly.
1975 Prime minister resigned and national assembly dissolved. Emir and his family assumed virtually absolute
power.
1986 Gulf University established in Bahrain. A causeway
was opened linking the island with Saudi Arabia.
1988 Bahrain recognized Afghan rebel government.
1991 Bahrain joined United Nations coalition that ousted
Iraq from its occupation of Kuwait.

public demonstration of television and in 1926 pioneered fiber optics, radar (in advance of Robert ◊Wat-
son-Watt), and "noctovision," a system for seeing at
night by using infrared rays.

He also developed video recording on both wax
records and magnetic steel disks (1926–27), color TV
(1925–28), 3-D color TV (1925–46), and transatlantic
TV (1928). In 1944 he developed facsimile television
and demonstrated the world's first all-electronic color
and 3-D color receiver (500 lines).

Baker James (Addison), III 1930– . US Republican
politician. Under President Reagan, he was White
House chief of staff 1981–85 and treasury secretary
1985–88. After managing George Bush's successful
presidential campaign 1988, Baker was appointed secretary of state 1989 and played a prominent role in the
1990–91 Gulf crisis and the subsequent search for a
lasting Middle East peace settlement. In 1992 he left
the State Department to become White House chief of
staff and to oversee Bush's reelection campaign.

Bakersfield city in S California, NE of Santa Barbara, on the Kern river; the seat of Kern County; population (1990) 174,800. It is known for its oil wells and
oil products. Oil was first discovered 1899.

Baker v Carr a US Supreme Court decision 1962
dealing with the responsibility of federal courts to
hear suits against unconstitutional electoral apportionment. The petitioner filed suit against the Tennessee legislature, which, by neglecting to
reapportion the state seats according to demographic
changes, had allowed a disparity to develop between
the voting powers of urban and rural residents. The
Court did not decide whether this constituted an
infraction of the 14th Amendment right to equal protection. Instead, it empowered federal courts to rule in
state apportionment suits.

Baku capital city of the Republic of Azerbaijan,

industrial port (oil refining) on the Caspian Sea; population (1987) 1,741,000. It is a major oil center and is
linked by pipelines with Batumi on the Black Sea. In
Jan 1990 there were violent clashes between the Azeri
majority and the Armenian minority, and Soviet
troops were sent to the region; over 13,000 Armenians
subsequently fled from the city. In early March 1992,
opposition political forces sponsored protests in the
city that led to the resignation of President Mutalibov.

Balaclava, Battle of in the Crimean War, an engagement on Oct 25, 1854, near a town in Ukraine, 6 mi/10
km SE of Sevastopol. It was the scene of the ill-timed
Charge of the Light Brigade of British cavalry
against the Russian entrenched artillery. Of the 673
soldiers who took part, there were 272 casualties. *Balaclava helmets* were knitted hoods worn here by
soldiers in the bitter weather.

balance apparatus for weighing or measuring mass.
The various types include the *beam balance* consisting of a centrally pivoted lever with pans hanging
from each end, and the *spring balance*, in which the
object to be weighed stretches (or compresses) a vertical coil spring fitted with a pointer that indicates the
weight on a scale. Kitchen scales are balances.

balance of nature in ecology, the idea that there is
an inherent equilibrium in most ◊ecosystems, with
plants and animals interacting so as to produce a
stable, continuing system of life on earth. Organisms
in the ecosystem are adapted to each other—for example, waste products produced by one species are used
by another and resources used by some are replenished by others; the oxygen needed by animals is produced by plants while the waste product of animal
respiration, carbon dioxide, is used by plants as a raw
material in photosynthesis. The nitrogen cycle, the
water cycle, and the control of animal populations by
natural predators are other examples. The activities of

Baldwin US author James Baldwin focused his eloquence and passion on the subject of race in America.

human beings can, and frequently do, disrupt the balance of nature.

balance of payments in economics, an account of a country's debit and credit transactions with other countries. Items are divided into the *current account*, which includes both visible trade (imports and exports of goods) and invisible trade (services such as transport, tourism, interest, and dividends), and the *capital account*, which includes investment in and out of the country, international grants, and loans. Deficits or surpluses on these accounts are brought into balance by buying and selling reserves of foreign currencies.

balance of power in politics, the theory that the best way of ensuring international order is to have power so distributed among states that no single state is able to achieve a dominant position. The term, which may also refer more simply to the actual distribution of power, is one of the most enduring concepts in international relations. Since the development of nuclear weapons, it has been asserted that the balance of power has been replaced by a *balance of terror*.

Balanchine George 1904–1983. Russian-born US choreographer. After leaving the USSR in 1924, he worked with ◊Diaghilev in France. Moving to the US in 1933, he became a major influence on dance, starting the New York City Ballet in 1948. He was the most influential 20th-century choreographer of ballet in the US. He developed an "American Neo-Classic" dance style and made the New York City Ballet one of the world's great companies. He also pioneered choreography in Hollywood films.

Balboa Vasco Núñez de 1475–1519. Spanish ◊conquistador. He founded a settlement at Darien (now Panama) 1511 and crossed the Isthmus in search of gold, reaching the Pacific Ocean (which he called the South Sea) on Sept 25, 1513, after a 25-day expedition. He was made admiral of the Pacific and governor of Panama but was removed by Spanish court intrigue, imprisoned, and executed.

Balder in Norse mythology, the son of Odin and Freya and husband of Nanna, and the best, wisest, and most loved of all the gods. He was killed, at ◊Loki's instigation, by a twig of mistletoe shot by the blind god Hodur.

Baldwin James 1924–1987. US writer, born in New York City, who portrayed the condition of black Americans in contemporary society. His works include the novels *Go Tell It on the Mountain* 1953, *Another Country* 1962, and *Just Above My Head* 1979; the play *The Amen Corner* 1955; and the autobiographical essays *Notes of a Native Son* 1955 and *The Fire Next Time* 1963. He was active in the civil-rights movement.

Baldwin Stanley, 1st Earl Baldwin of Bewdley 1867–1947. British Conservative politician, prime minister 1923–24, 1924–29, and 1935–37; he weathered the general strike 1926, secured complete adult suffrage 1928, and handled the ◊abdication crisis of Edward VIII 1936, but failed to prepare Britain for World War II.

Baldwin I 1058–1118. King of Jerusalem from 1100. A French nobleman, he joined his brother Godfrey de Bouillon on the First Crusade in 1096 and established the kingdom of Jerusalem in 1100. It was destroyed by Islamic conquest in 1187.

Balearic Islands (Spanish *Baleares*) group of Mediterranean islands forming an autonomous region of Spain; including ◊Majorca, ◊Minorca, ◊Ibiza, Cabrera, and Formentera
area 1,930 sq mi/5,000 sq km
capital Palma de Mallorca
products figs, olives, oranges, wine, brandy, coal, iron, slate; tourism is crucial
population (1986) 755,000
history a Roman colony from 123 BC, the Balearic Islands were an independent Moorish kingdom 1009–1232; they were conquered by Aragon 1343.

Balfour Arthur James, 1st Earl of Balfour 1848–1930. British Conservative politician, prime minister 1902–05 and foreign secretary 1916–19, when he issued the Balfour Declaration 1917 and was involved in peace negotiations after World War I, signing the Treaty of Versailles.

Balfour Declaration letter, dated Nov 2, 1917, from the British foreign secretary A J Balfour to Lord Rothschild (chair, British Zionist Federation) stating: "HM government view with favour the establishment in Palestine of a national home for the Jewish people." It led to the foundation of Israel 1948.

Bali island of Indonesia, E of Java, one of the Sunda Islands
area 2,240 sq mi/5,800 sq km
capital Denpasar
physical volcanic mountains
features Balinese dancing, music, drama; 1 million tourists a year (1990)
products gold and silver work, woodcarving, weaving, copra, salt, coffee
population (1989) 2,787,000
history Bali's Hindu culture goes back to the 7th century; the Dutch gained control of the island by 1908.

Balkans (Turkish "mountains") peninsula of SE Europe, stretching into the Mediterranean Sea between the Adriatic and Aegean seas, comprising Albania, Bosnia-Herzegovina, Bulgaria, Croatia, Greece, Romania, Slovenia, the part of Turkey in Europe, and Yugoslavia. It is joined to the rest of Europe by an isthmus 750 mi/1,200 km wide between Rijeka on the W and the mouth of the Danube on the Black Sea to the E.

Balkan Wars two wars 1912–13 and 1913 (preceding World War I) which resulted in the expulsion by the Balkan states of Ottoman Turkey from Europe, except for a small area around Istanbul.

Ball Lucille 1911–1989. US comedy actress, famed as TV's Lucy. She began her film career as a bit player 1933, and appeared in dozens of movies over the next few years, including *Room Service* 1938 (with the Marx Brothers) and *Fancy Pants* 1950 (with Bob Hope). From 1951 to 1957 she starred with her husband, Cuban bandleader Desi Arnaz, in "I Love Lucy," the first US television show filmed before an audience. It was followed by "The Lucy Show" 1962–68 and "Here's Lucy" 1968–74.

Her TV success limited her film output after 1950; her later films include *Mame* 1974. The television series are still transmitted in many countries.

ballad popular poem that tells a story. Of simple metrical form and dealing with some strongly emotional event, the ballad is halfway between the lyric and the epic. Most English ballads date from the 15th century. Poets of the Romantic movement both in England and in Germany were greatly influenced by the ballad revival, as seen in, for example, the *Lyrical Ballads* 1798 of Wordsworth and Coleridge. Other later forms are the "broadsheets," with a satirical or political motive, and the testamentary "hanging" ballads of the condemned criminal.

ballade in music, an instrumental piece based on a story; a form used in piano works by ◊Chopin and ◊Liszt. In literature, a poetic form developed in France in the later Middle Ages from the ballad, generally consisting of one or more groups of three stanzas of seven or eight lines each, followed by a shorter stanza or envoy, the last line being repeated as a chorus.

ball-and-socket joint a joint allowing considerable movement in three dimensions, for instance the joint between the pelvis and the femur. To facilitate movement, such joints are lubricated by cartilage and synovial fluid. The bones are kept in place by ligaments and moved by muscles.

Ballard J(ames) G(raham) 1930– . English novelist whose works include science fiction on the theme of disaster, such as *The Drowned World* 1962 and *High-Rise* 1975; the partly autobiographical *Empire of the Sun* 1984, dealing with his internment in China during World War II; and the autobiographical novel *The Kindness of Women* 1991.

Ballesteros Seve(riano) 1957– . Spanish golfer who came to prominence 1976 and has won several leading tournaments in the US, including the Masters Tournament 1980 and 1983. He has also won the British Open three times: in 1979, 1984, and 1988.

ballet theatrical representation in dance form in which music also plays a major part in telling a story or conveying a mood. Some such form of entertainment existed in ancient Greece, but Western ballet as we know it today first appeared in Italy. From there it was brought by Catherine de' Medici to France in the form of a spectacle combining singing, dancing, and declamation. In the 20th century Russian ballet has had a vital influence on the Classical tradition in the West, and ballet developed further in the US through the work of George Balanchine and the American Ballet Theater, and in the UK through the influence of Marie Rambert. ◊Modern dance is a separate development.

ballistics study of the motion and impact of projectiles such as bullets, bombs, and missiles. For projectiles from a gun, relevant exterior factors include temperature, barometric pressure, and wind strength; and for nuclear missiles these extend to such factors as the speed at which the Earth turns.

Baltic Sea

balloon lighter-than-air craft that consists of a gasbag filled with gas lighter than the surrounding air and an attached basket, or gondola, for carrying passengers and/or instruments. In 1783, the first successful human ascent was in Paris, in a hot-air balloon designed by the ◊Montgolfier brothers Joseph Michel and Etienne Jacques. In 1785, a hydrogen-filled balloon designed by French physicist Jacques Charles traveled across the English Channel.

ballot the process of voting in an election. In political elections in democracies ballots are usually secret: voters indicate their choice of candidate on a voting slip that is placed in a sealed ballot box or by pulling levers on a machine in a voting booth. *Ballot rigging* is a term used to describe elections that are fraudulent because of interference with the voting process or the counting of ◊votes.

ballroom dancing collective term for social dances such as the ◊foxtrot, quickstep, ◊tango, and ◊waltz.

ball valve valve that works by the action of external pressure raising a ball and thereby opening a hole.

balsam any of various garden plants of the genus *Impatiens* of the balsam family. They are usually annuals with spurred red or white flowers and pods that burst and scatter their seeds when ripe. In medicine and perfumery, balsam refers to various oily or gummy aromatic plant resins, such as balsam of Peru from the Central American tree *Myroxylon pereirae*.

Baltic Sea large shallow arm of the North Sea, extending NE from the narrow Skagerrak and Kattegat, between Sweden and Denmark, to the Gulf of Bothnia between Sweden and Finland. Its coastline is 5,000 mi/8,000 km long, and its area, including the gulfs of Riga, Finland, and Bothnia, is 163,000 sq mi/422,300 sq km. Its shoreline is shared by Denmark, Germany, Poland, the Baltic States, Russia, Finland, and Sweden.

Baltic States collective name for the states of ◊Estonia, ◊Latvia, and ◊Lithuania, former constituent republics of the USSR (from 1940). They regained independence Sept 1991.

Baltimore industrial port and largest city in Maryland, on the W shore of Chesapeake Bay, NE of Washington, DC; population (1990) 736,000. Industries include shipbuilding, oil refining, food processing, and the manufacture of steel, chemicals, and aerospace equipment.

It is the seat of Johns Hopkins University. The inner harbor area has the National Aquarium, a 30-story

Bandaranaike In 1960 Sri Lankan politician Sirimavo Bandaranaike became the world's first woman prime minister.

World Trade Center, and the first commissioned warship of the US Navy, dating from 1797. It was named after the founder of Maryland, Lord Baltimore (1579–1632). The city of Baltimore dates from 1729 and was incorporated 1797. At Fort McHenry, Francis Scott Key wrote the poem "The Star-Spangled Banner." The writer Edgar Allan Poe and the baseball player Babe Ruth lived here.

Baltistan region in the Karakoram range of NE Kashmir, held by Pakistan since 1949. It is the home of Balti Muslims of Tibetan origin. The chief town is Skardu, but Ghyari is of greater significance to Muslims as the site of a mosque built by Sayyid Ali Hamadani, a Persian who brought the Shia Muslim religion to Baltistan in the 14th century.

Baluchistan mountainous desert area, comprising a province of Pakistan, part of the Iranian province of Sistán and Balúchestan, and a small area of Afghanistan. The Pakistani province has an area of 134,019 sq mi/347,200 sq km and a population (1985) of 4,908,000; its capital is Quetta. Sistán and Balúchestan has an area of 70,098 sq mi/181,600 sq km and a popu-

Bangkok the Royal Palace in Bangkok contains within its 6,200-ft perimeter walls fine temples, including the Chapel Royal of the Emerald Buddha.

lation (1986) of 1,197,000; its capital is Zahedan. The port of Gwadar in Pakistan is strategically important, situated on the Indian Ocean and the Strait of Hormuz.

The common religion of the Baluch (or Baluchi) people is Islam, and they speak Baluchi, a member of the Iranian branch of the Indo-European language family. In the drier areas they make use of tents, moving when it becomes too arid. Although they practice nomadic pastoralism, many are settled agriculturalists.

Balzac Honoré de 1799–1850. French novelist. His first success was *Les Chouans/The Chouans* and *La Physiologie du mariage/The Physiology of Marriage* 1829, inspired by Walter Scott. This was the beginning of the long series of novels *La Comédie humaine/The Human Comedy*. He also wrote the Rabelaisian *Contes drolatiques/Ribald Tales* 1833.

Bamako capital and port of Mali on the river Niger; population (1976) 400,000. It produces pharmaceuticals, chemicals, textiles, tobacco, and metal products.

bamboo any of numerous plants of the subgroup Bambuseae within the grass family Gramineae, mainly found in tropical and subtropical regions. Some species grow as tall as 120 ft/36 m. The stems are hollow and jointed and can be used in furniture, house, and boat construction. The young shoots are edible; paper is made from the stem.

banana any of several treelike tropical plants of the genus *Musa*, family Musaceae, which grow up to 25 ft/8 m high. The edible banana is the fruit of a sterile hybrid form.

band music group, usually falling into a special category: for example, *military*, comprising woodwind, brass, and percussion; *brass*, solely of brass and percussion; *marching*, a variant of brass; *dance* and *swing*, often like a small orchestra; *jazz*, with no fixed instrumentation; *rock* and *pop*, generally electric guitar, bass, and drums, variously augmented; and *steel*, from the West Indies, in which percussion instruments made from oil drums sound like marimbas.

Banda Hastings Kamuzu 1902– . Malawi politician, president from 1966. He led his country's independence movement and was prime minister of Nyasaland (the former name of Malawi) from 1963. He became Malawi's first president 1966 and 1971 was named president for life; his rule has been authoritarian. Despite civil unrest during 1992, he has resisted calls for free, multiparty elections.

Bandaranaike Sirimavo (born Ratwatte) 1916– . Sri Lankan politician who succeeded her husband Solomon Bandaranaike to become the world's first female prime minister, 1960–65 and 1970–77, but was expelled from parliament 1980 for abuse of her powers while in office.

Bandaranaike Solomon West Ridgeway Dias 1899–1959. Sri Lankan nationalist politician. In 1952 he founded the Sri Lanka Freedom party and in 1956 became prime minister, pledged to a socialist program and a neutral foreign policy. He failed to satisfy extremists and was assassinated by a Buddhist monk.

Bandar Seri Begawan (formerly until 1970 *Brunei Town*) capital and largest city of Brunei, 9 mi/14 km from the mouth of the Brunei River; population (1987 est) 56,300.

bandicoot small marsupial mammal inhabiting Australia and New Guinea. There are about 11 species, family Peramelidae, rat- or rabbit-sized and living in burrows. They have long snouts, eat insects, and are nocturnal. A related group, the rabbit bandicoots or bilbys, is reduced to a single species that is now endangered and protected by law.

Bandung commercial city and capital of Jawa Barat province on the island of Java, Indonesia; population (1980) 1,463,000. Bandung is the third-largest city in Indonesia and was the administrative center when the country was the Netherlands East Indies.

Bangalore capital of Karnataka state, S India; population (1981) 2,600,000. Industries include electronics, aircraft and machine-tools construction, and coffee.

Bangkok capital and port of Thailand, on the river Chao Phraya; population (1990) 6,019,000. Products include paper, ceramics, cement, textiles, and aircraft. It is the headquarters of the Southeast Asia Treaty Organization (SEATO).

Bangladesh country in southern Asia, bounded N, W, and E by India, SE by Myanmar, and S by the Bay of Bengal.

Bangui capital and port of the Central African Republic, on the river Ubangi; population (1988) 597,000. Industries include beer, cigarettes, office machinery, and timber and metal products.

banjo resonant stringed musical instrument, with a long fretted neck and circular drum-type sound box covered on the topside only by stretched skin (now usually plastic). It is played with a plectrum.

Banjul capital and chief port of Gambia, on an island at the mouth of the river Gambia; population (1983) 44,536. Established 1816 as a settlement for freed slaves, it was known as Bathurst until 1973.

bank financial institution that uses funds deposited with it to lend money to companies or individuals, and also provides financial services to its customers.

Bank of Commerce and Credit International (BCCI) international bank, founded 1972. By 1990 BCCI had offices in 69 countries, $15 billion in deposits, and $20 billion in assets. In July 1991 evidence of widespread systematic fraud at BCCI led regulators in 7 countries to seize the bank's assets, and its operations in most of the remaining 62 countries were then also shut down. A subsequent investigation resulted in a New York criminal indictment of the institution and four of its units, and the arrest of some 20 BCCI officials in Abu Dhabi for alleged fraud.

bankruptcy process by which the property of a person (in legal terms, an individual or corporation)

Bangladesh
People's Republic of
(*Gana Prajatantri Bangladesh*)
(formerly *East Pakistan*)

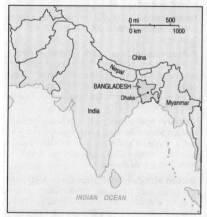

area 55,585 sq mi/144,000 sq km
capital Dhaka (formerly Dacca)
cities ports Chittagong, Khulna
physical flat delta of rivers Ganges (Padma) and Brahmaputra (Jamuna), the largest estuarine delta in the world; annual rainfall of 100 in/2,540 mm; some 75% of the land is less than 10 ft/3 m above sea level; hilly in extreme SE and NE
environment deforestation on the slopes of the Himalayas increases the threat of flooding in the coastal lowlands of Bangladesh, which are also subject to devastating monsoon storms. The building of India's Farakka Barrage has reduced the flow of the Ganges in Bangladesh and permitted salt water to intrude further inland. Increased salinity has destroyed fisheries, contaminated drinking water, and damaged forests
head of state Abdur Rahman Biswas from 1991
head of government Begum Khaleda Zia from 1991
political system emergent democratic republic
political parties Bangladesh Nationalist Party (BNP),

Islamic, right of center; Awami League, secular, moderate socialist; Jatiya Dal (National Party), Islamic nationalist
exports jute, tea, garments, fish products
currency taka
population (1991 est) 107,992,100; growth rate 2.17% p.a.; just over 1 million people live in small ethnic groups in the tropical Chittagong Hill Tracts, Mymensingh, and Sylhet districts
life expectancy men 50, women 52
language Bangla (Bengali)
religions Sunni Muslim 85%, Hindu 14%
literacy men 43%, women 22% (1985 est)
GDP $17.6 bn (1987); $172 per head

chronology
1947 Formed into eastern province of Pakistan on partition of British India.
1970 Half a million killed in flood.
1971 Bangladesh emerged as independent nation, under leadership of Sheik Mujibur Rahman, after civil war.
1975 Mujibur Rahman assassinated. Martial law imposed.
1976–77 Maj Gen Zia ur-Rahman assumed power.
1978–79 Elections held and civilian rule restored.
1981 Assassination of Maj Gen Zia.
1982 Lt Gen Ershad assumed power in army coup. Martial law reimposed.
1986 Elections held but disputed. Martial law ended.
1987 State of emergency declared in response to opposition demonstrations.
1988 Assembly elections boycotted by main opposition parties. State of emergency lifted. Islam made state religion. Monsoon floods left 30 million homeless and thousands dead.
1989 Power devolved to Chittagong Hill Tracts to end 14-year conflict between local people and army-protected settlers.
1990 Following mass antigovernment protests, President Ershadm resigned; Shahabuddin Ahmad became interim president.
1991 Feb: elections resulted in coalition government with BNP dominant. April: cyclone killed around 139,000 and left up to 10 million homeless. Sept: parliamentary government restored; Abdur Rahman Biswas elected president.

baobab *The Australian baobab, or gourd tree, grows in NW Australia.*

baobab tree of the genus *Adansonia*, family Bombacaceae. It has rootlike branches, hence its nickname "upside-down" tree, and a disproportionately thick girth, up to 30 ft/9 m in diameter. The pulp of its fruit is edible and is known as monkey bread. Baobabs may live for 1,000 years and are found in Africa and Australia.

baptism immersion in or sprinkling with water as a religious rite of initiation. It was practiced long before the beginning of Christianity. In the Christian baptism ceremony, sponsors or godparents make vows on behalf of the child, which are renewed by the child at confirmation. It is one of the seven sacraments. The *amrit* ceremony in Sikhism is sometimes referred to as baptism.

Baptist member of any of several Protestant and evangelical Christian sects that practice baptism by immersion only upon profession of faith. Baptists seek their authority in the Bible. They originated among English Dissenters who took refuge in the Netherlands in the early 17th century, and spread by emigration and, later, missionary activity. Of the world total of approximately 31 million, some 26.5 million are in the US and 265,000 in the UK.

bar unit of pressure equal to 10^5 pascals or 10^6 dynes/cm^2, approximately 750 mmHg or 0.987 atm. Its diminutive, the ***millibar*** (one-thousandth of a bar), is commonly used by meteorologists.

Barabbas in the New Testament, a condemned robber released by Pilate at Passover instead of Jesus to appease a mob.

Barbados island country in the Caribbean, one of the Lesser Antilles. It is about 300 mi/483 km N of Venezuela.

Barbarossa nickname "red beard" given to the Holy Roman emperor ◊Frederick I, and also to two brothers, Horuk and Khair-ed-Din, who were Barbary pirates. Horuk was killed by the Spaniards 1518; Khair-ed-Din took Tunis 1534 and died in Constantinople 1546.

Barbary ape tailless, yellowish-brown macaque monkey *Macaca sylvanus*, found in the mountains and wilds of Algeria and Morocco. It was introduced to Gibraltar, where legend has it that the British will leave if the ape colony dies out.

barbed wire cheap fencing material made of strands of galvanized wire (see ◊galvanizing), twisted together with sharp barbs at close intervals. In 1873 an American, Joseph Glidden, devised a machine to mass-produce barbed wire. Its use on the open grasslands of 19th-century America led to range warfare between farmers and cattle ranchers; the latter used to drive their herds cross-country.

Barber Samuel 1910–1981. US composer of a Neo-Classical, later somewhat dissonant style, whose works include *Adagio for Strings* 1936 and the opera *Vanessa* 1958, which won him one of his two Pulitzer prizes. Another Barber opera, *Antony and Cleopatra* 1966, was commissioned for the opening of the new Metropolitan Opera House at Lincoln Center, New York City. Barber's music is lyrical and fastidiously worked. His later works include *The Lovers* 1971.

barberry any spiny shrub of the genus *Berberia* of the barberry family, having sour red berries and yellow flowers. These shrubs are often used as hedges. The barberry family (Berberidaceae) also includes plants such as the May apple *Podophyllum peltatum* of the E North American woodlands.

unable to pay debts is taken away under a court order and divided fairly among the person's creditors, after preferential payments such as taxes and wages. Proceedings may be instituted either by the debtor (voluntary bankruptcy) or by any creditor for a substantial sum (involuntary bankruptcy). Until "discharged," a bankrupt is severely restricted in financial activities.

Banks Nathaniel Prentiss 1816–1894. US politician and American Civil War general. He was Speaker of the US House of Representatives 1854–57. At the outbreak of the war 1861, he was appointed major general in command of the Department of Annapolis. Defeated by Stonewall ◊Jackson in the Shenandoah Valley, he was sent to New Orleans 1863, taking command of the Department of the Gulf. He led the ill-fated Red River expedition 1864.

Bannister Roger Gilbert 1929– . English track and field athlete, the first person to run a mile in under four minutes. He achieved this feat at Oxford, England, on May 6, 1954, in a time of 3 min 59.4 sec.

bantam small variety of domestic chicken. Bantams can either be a small version of one of the large breeds, or a separate type. Some are prolific layers. Bantam cocks have a reputation as spirited fighters.

Banting Frederick Grant 1891–1941. Canadian physician who discovered a technique for isolating the hormone insulin 1921 when, experimentally, he and his colleague Charles ◊Best tied off the ducts of the ◊pancreas to determine the function of the cells known as the islets of Langerhans. This allowed for the treatment of diabetes. Banting and John J R Macleod (1876–1935), his mentor, shared the 1923 Nobel Prize for Medicine, and Banting divided his prize with Best.

Bantu languages group of related languages belonging to the Niger-Congo family, spoken widely over the greater part of Africa south of the Sahara, including Swahili, Xhosa, and Zulu. Meaning "people" in Zulu, the word Bantu itself illustrates a characteristic use of prefixes: *mu-ntu* "man," *ba-ntu* "people."

Bantustan or ***homeland*** name until 1978 for a ◊Black National State in the Republic of South Africa.

barbershop in music, a style of unaccompanied close-harmony singing of sentimental ballads, revived in the US during the 19th century. Traditionally sung by four male voices, since the 1970s it has developed as a style of ◊a cappella choral singing for both male and female voices.

Barbie Klaus 1913–1991. German Nazi, a member of the ◊SS from 1936. During World War II he was involved in the deportation of Jews from the occupied Netherlands 1940–42 and in tracking down Jews and Resistance workers in France 1942–45. He was arrested 1983 and convicted of crimes against humanity in France 1987.

barbiturate hypnosedative drug, commonly known as a "sleeping pill," consisting of any salt or ester of barbituric acid $C_4H_4O_3N_2$. They work by depressing brain activity. Most barbiturates, being highly addictive, are no longer prescribed and are listed as controlled substances.

Barbizon school French school of landscape painters of the mid-19th century, based at Barbizon in the forest of Fontainebleau. Members included Jean-François Millet, Diaz de la Peña (1807–1876), and Théodore Rousseau (1812–1867). They aimed to paint fresh, realistic scenes, sketching and painting their subjects in the open air.

Barbour Philip Pendleton 1783–1841. US jurist and political leader. He served as Speaker of the House in the US House of Representatives 1821–23. A strong supporter of states' rights, he was appointed federal district judge by President ◊Jackson 1830. He served on the US Supreme Court 1836–41, consistently ruling in favor of the prerogative of the states over federal authority.

Barbuda one of the islands that form the state of ◊Antigua and Barbuda.

Barcelona capital, industrial city (textiles, engineering, chemicals), and port of Catalonia, NE Spain; population (1991) 1,653,200. As the chief center of anarchism and Catalonian nationalism, it was prominent in the overthrow of the monarchy 1931 and was the last city of the republic to surrender to Franco 1939. In 1992 the city hosted the Summer Olympics.

bar code pattern of bars and spaces that can be read by a computer. Bar codes are widely used in retailing, industrial distribution, and public libraries. The code is read by a scanning device; the computer determines the code from the widths of the bars and spaces.

Bardeen John 1908–1991. US physicist who won a Nobel Prize 1956, with Walter Brattain and William Shockley, for the development of the transistor 1948. In 1972 he became the first double winner of a Nobel Prize in the same subject (with Leon Cooper and John Schrieffer) for his work on superconductivity.

Bardot Brigitte 1934– . French film actress whose sensual appeal did much to popularize French cinema internationally. Her films include *Et Dieu créa la femme/And God Created Woman* 1950, *Viva Maria* 1965, and *Shalako* 1968.

Barenboim Daniel 1942– . Israeli pianist and conductor, born in Argentina. Pianist/conductor with the English Chamber Orchestra from 1964, he became conductor of the New York Philharmonic Orchestra 1970 and musical director of the Orchestre de Paris 1975. Appointed artistic and musical director of the Opéra de la Bastille, Paris, July 1987, he was dismissed from his post July 1989, a few months before its opening, for

---

Barbados

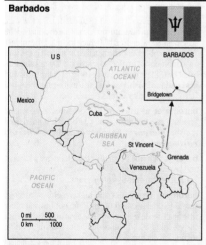

area 430 sq km/166 sq mi
capital Bridgetown
cities Speightstown, Holetown, Oistins
physical most easterly island of the West Indies; surrounded by coral reefs; subject to hurricanes June–Nov
features highest point Mount Hillaby 1,115 ft/340 m
head of state Elizabeth II from 1966, represented by governor-general Hugh Springer from 1984
head of government prime minister Erskine Lloyd Sandiford from 1987
political system constitutional monarchy
political parties Barbados Labor Party (BLP), moderate, left of center; Democratic Labor Party (DLP), moderate, left of center; National Democratic Party (NDP), center
exports sugar, rum, electronic components, clothing, cement
currency Barbados dollar
population (1990 est) 260,000; growth rate 0.5% p.a.
life expectancy men 70, women 75
languages English and Bajan (Barbadian English dialect)
media two independent daily newspapers
religions 70% Anglican, 9% Methodist, 4% Roman Catholic
literacy 99% (1984)
GDP $1.4 bn (1987); $5,449 per head

chronology
1627 Became British colony; developed as a sugar-plantation economy, initially on basis of slavery.
1834 Slaves freed.
1951 Universal adult suffrage introduced. BLP won general election.
1954 Ministerial government established.
1961 Independence achieved from Britain. DLP, led by Errol Barrow, in power.
1966 Barbados achieved full independence within Commonwealth. Barrow became the new nation's first prime minister.
1972 Diplomatic relations with Cuba established.
1976 BLP, led by Tom Adams, returned to power.
1983 Barbados supported US invasion of Grenada.
1985 Adams died; Bernard St John became prime minister.
1986 DLP, led by Barrow, returned to power.
1987 Barrow died; Erskine Lloyd Sandiford became prime minister.
1989 New NDP opposition formed.
1991 DLP, under Erskine Sandiford, won general election.

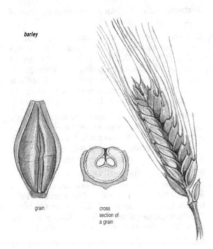

barley *Barley was first cultivated in Egypt about 5000 BC.*

barley

grain

cross section of a grain

reasons which he claimed were more political than artistic. His dismissal was the subject of a highly publicized and controversial dispute. In 1991 he became director of the Chicago Symphony Orchestra. He is a celebrated interpreter of Mozart and Beethoven.

Barents Willem *c.* 1550–1597. Dutch explorer and navigator. He made three expeditions to seek the ◊Northeast Passage; he died on the last voyage. The Barents Sea, part of the Arctic Ocean N of Norway, is named after him.

barium soft, silver-white, metallic element, symbol Ba, atomic number 56, atomic weight 137.33. It is one of the alkaline-earth metals, found in nature as barium carbonate and barium sulfate. As the sulfate it is used in medicine: taken as a suspension (a "barium meal"), its progress is followed by using X-rays to reveal abnormalities of the alimentary canal. Barium is also used in alloys, pigments, and safety matches and, with strontium, forms the emissive surface in cathode-ray tubes. It was first discovered in barytes or heavy spar.

bark protective outer layer on the stems and roots of woody plants, composed mainly of dead cells. To allow for expansion of the stem, the bark is continually added to from within, and the outer surface often becomes fissured or is shed as scales. The bark from the cork oak *Quercus suber* is economically important and harvested commercially. The spice ◊cinnamon and the drugs cascara (used as a laxative and stimulant) and ◊quinine all come from bark.

barley cereal belonging to the grass family (Gramineae). Cultivated barley *Hordeum vulgare* comprises three main varieties—six-rowed, four-rowed, and two-rowed. Barley was one of the earliest cereals to be cultivated, about 5000 BC in Egypt, and no other cereal can thrive in so wide a range of climatic conditions; polar barley is sown and reaped well within the Arctic Circle in Europe. Barley is no longer much used in bread-making, but it is used in soups and stews and as a starch. Its high-protein form finds a wide use for animal feeding, and its low-protein form is used in brewing and distilling alcoholic beverages.

Barlow Joel 1754–1812. US poet and diplomat. A member of the literary circle the "Connecticut Wits," he published an epic entitled *The Vision of Columbus* 1787. As US consul in Algiers 1795–97, he gained the release of American hostages taken by the Barbary

pirates operating against US and European shipping. On diplomatic mission to France 1811 he died while accompanying Napoleon in his retreat from Russia 1812.

bar mitzvah in Judaism, initiation of a boy, which takes place at the age of 13, into the adult Jewish community; less common is the *bat* or *bas mitzvah* for girls aged 12. The child reads a passage from the Torah in the synagogue on the Sabbath and is subsequently regarded as a full member of the congregation.

Barnabas, St in the New Testament, a "fellow laborer" with St Paul; he went with St Mark on a missionary journey to Cyprus, his birthplace. Feast day June 11.

barnacle marine crustacean of the subclass Cirripedia. The larval form is free-swimming, but when mature, it fixes itself by the head to rock or floating wood. The animal then remains attached, enclosed in a shell through which the cirri (modified legs) protrude to sweep food into the mouth. Barnacles include the stalked *goose barnacle* Lepas anatifera found on ships' bottoms, and the *acorn barnacles*, such as *Balanus balanoides*, common on rocks.

Barnard Christiaan (Neethling) 1922– . South African surgeon who performed the first human heart transplant 1967 in Cape Town. The patient, 54-year-old Louis Washkansky, lived for 18 days.

Barnard's star second closest star to the Sun, six light-years away in the constellation Ophiuchus. It is a faint red dwarf of 10th magnitude, visible only through a telescope. It is named after the US astronomer Edward E Barnard (1857–1923), who discovered 1916 that it has the fastest proper motion of any star, crossing 1 degree of sky every 350 years.

Barnum Phineas T(aylor) 1810–1891. US showman. In 1871, after an adventurous career, he established the "Greatest Show on Earth" (which included the midget "Tom Thumb") comprising a circus, a menagerie, and an exhibition of "freaks," conveyed in 100 rail automobiles. In 1881, it merged with its chief competitor and has continued to this day as the Ringling Brothers and Barnum and Bailey Circus.

barometer instrument that measures atmospheric pressure as an indication of weather. Most often used are the *mercury barometer* and the *aneroid barometer*.

baron rank in the peerage of the UK, above a baronet and below a viscount.
Life peers are always of this rank.

baron any member of the higher nobility, a direct vassal (feudal servant) of the king, not bearing other titles such as duke or count. The term originally meant the vassal of a lord, but acquired its present meaning in the 12th century.

baronet British order of chivalry below the rank of baron, but above that of knight, created 1611 by James I to finance the settlement of Ulster. It is a hereditary honor, although women cannot succeed to a baronetcy. A baronet does not have a seat in the House of Lords but is entitled to the style *Sir* before his name. The sale of baronetcies was made illegal 1937.

Barons' Wars civil wars in England: *1215–17* between King ◊John and his barons, over his failure to honor ◊Magna Carta *1264–67* between ◊Henry III (and the future ◊Edward I) and his barons (led by Simon de ◊Montfort) *1264* May 14 **Battle of Lewes**

at which Henry III was defeated and captured *1265* Aug 4 Simon de Montfort was defeated by the future Edward I at Evesham and killed.

Baroque style of art and architecture characterized by extravagance in ornament, asymmetry of design, and great expressiveness. It dominated European *art* for most of the 17th century, with artists such as the painter Rubens and the sculptor Bernini. In *architecture*, it often involved large-scale designs, such as Bernini's piazza in Rome and the palace of Versailles in France. In *music*, the Baroque period lasted from about 1600 to 1750, and its composers included Monteverdi, Vivaldi, J S Bach, and Handel.

barracuda large predatory fish *Sphyraena barracuda* found in the warmer seas of the world. It can grow over 6 ft/2 m long and has a superficial resemblance to a pike. Young fish shoal, but the older ones are solitary. The barracuda has very sharp shearing teeth and may attack people.

Barranquilla seaport in N Colombia, on the Magdalena River; population (1985) 1,120,900. Products include chemicals, tobacco, textiles, furniture, and footwear.

Barras Paul François Jean Nicolas, Count 1755–1829. French revolutionary. He was elected to the National Convention 1792 and helped to overthrow Robespierre 1794. In 1795 he became a member of the ruling Directory (see ◊French Revolution). In 1796 he brought about the marriage of his former mistress, Joséphine de Beauharnais, with Napoleon and assumed dictatorial powers. After Napoleon's coup d'état Nov 19, 1799, Barras fell into disgrace.

barrel a unit of liquid capacity, the value of which depends on the liquid being measured. It is used for petroleum, a barrel of which contains 42 gallons/159 liters; a barrel of alcohol contains 49.9 gallons/189 liters.

Barrett Browning Elizabeth 1806–1861. English poet. In 1844 she published *Poems* (including "The Cry of the Children"), which led to her friendship with and secret marriage to Robert Browning 1846. The *Sonnets from the Portuguese* 1847 were written during their courtship. Later works include *Casa Guidi Windows* 1851 and the poetic novel *Aurora Leigh* 1857.

Barrie J(ames) M(atthew) 1860–1937. Scottish playwright and novelist, author of *The Admirable Crichton* 1902 and the children's fantasy *Peter Pan* 1904.

barrier island long island of sand, lying offshore and parallel to the coast. Some are over 60 mi/100 km in length. Most barrier islands are derived from marine sands piled up by shallow longshore currents that sweep sand parallel to the seashore. Others are derived from former spits, connected to land and built up by drifted sand, that were later severed from the mainland.

barrier reef ◊coral reef that lies offshore, separated from the mainland by a shallow lagoon.

barrow burial mound, usually composed of earth but sometimes of stones, examples of which are found in many parts of the world. The two main types are *long*, dating from the New Stone Age, or Neolithic, and *round*, dating from the later Mesolithic peoples of the early Bronze Age.

Barrow northernmost town in the US, at Point Barrow, Alaska; the world's largest Eskimo settlement. Population (1990) 3,469. There is oil at nearby Prudhoe Bay, and the US Naval Research Laboratory is in the vicinity. Barrow developed as a whaling center about 1900.

Barrymore US family of actors, the children of British-born Maurice Barrymore and Georgie Drew, both stage personalities.
Lionel Barrymore (1878–1954) first appeared on the stage with his grandmother, Mrs John Drew, 1893. He played numerous film roles from 1909, including *A Free Soul* 1931 and *Grand Hotel* 1932, but was perhaps best known for his annual radio portrayal of Scrooge in Dickens's *A Christmas Carol*.
Ethel Barrymore (1879–1959) played with the British actor Henry Irving in London 1898 and 1928 opened the Ethel Barrymore Theater in New York; she also appeared in many films from 1914, including *None but the Lonely Heart* 1944.
John Barrymore (1882–1942), a flamboyant actor who often appeared on stage and screen with his brother and sister. In his early years he was a Shakespearean actor. From 1923 he acted almost entirely in films, including *Dinner at Eight* 1933, and became a screen idol, nicknamed "The Profile."

Barth John 1930– . US novelist and short-story writer who was influential in the "academic" experimental movement of the 1960s. His works are usually interwoven fictions based on language games, since he is concerned with the relationship of language and reality. They include the novels *The Sot-Weed Factor* 1960, *Giles Goat-Boy* 1966, *Letters* 1979, *Sabbatical: A Romance* 1982, and *The Tidewater Tales* 1987. He also wrote the novella *Chimera* 1972 and *Lost in the Funhouse* 1968, a collection of short stories.

Bartholomew, St in the New Testament, one of the apostles. Some legends relate that after the Crucifixion he took Christianity to India; others that he was a missionary in Anatolia and Armenia, where he suffered martyrdom by being flayed alive. Feast day Aug 24.

Bartók Béla 1881–1945. Hungarian composer who developed a personal musical language, combining folk elements with mathematical concepts of tone and rhythmic proportion. His large output includes six string quartets, concertos, an opera, and graded teaching pieces for piano.

Bartolommeo Fra, also called *Baccio della Porta* c. 1472–c. 1517. Italian religious painter of the High Renaissance, active in Florence. His painting of *The Last Judgment* 1499 (Museo di San Marco, Florence) influenced Raphael.

Barton Clara 1821–1912. US health worker, founder of the American Red Cross 1881 and its president until 1904. A volunteer nurse, she tended the casualties of the American Civil War 1861–65 and in 1864 General Benjamin Butler named her superintendent of nurses for his forces.

Baryshnikov Mikhail 1948– . Latvian-born dancer, now based in the US. He joined the Kirov Ballet 1967 and became one of its most brilliant soloists. After defecting from the Soviet Union "on artistic, not political grounds" while on tour in Canada 1974, he danced with various companies, and later joined the American Ballet Theater (ABT) as principal dancer, partnering Gelsey Kirkland. He left to join the New York City Ballet 1978–80, but rejoined ABT as director 1980–90. From 1990 he has danced for various companies.

Barzun Jacques Martin 1907– . French-born US historian and educator whose specialty was 19th-century

Base

binary (base 2)	octal (base 8)	decimal (base 10)	hexadecimal (base 16)
0	0	0	0
1	1	1	1
10	2	2	2
11	3	3	3
100	4	4	4
101	5	5	5
110	6	6	6
111	7	7	7
1000	10	8	8
1001	11	9	9
1010	12	10	A
1011	13	11	B
1100	14	12	C
1101	15	13	D
1110	16	14	E
1111	17	15	F
10000	20	16	10
11111111	377	255	FF
11111010001	3721	2001	7D1

European intellectual life. His book *The Modern Researcher* 1970 is recognized as a classic study of historical method. Among his many historical works is *Romanticism and the Modern Ego* 1943.

basal metabolic rate (BMR) amount of energy needed by an animal just to stay alive. It is measured when the animal is awake but resting, and includes the energy required to keep the heart beating, sustain breathing, repair tissues, and keep the brain and nerves functioning. Measuring the animal's consumption of oxygen gives an accurate value for BMR, because oxygen is needed to release energy from food.

basalt commonest volcanic ◊igneous rock, and the principal rock type on the ocean floor; it is basic, that is, it contains relatively little silica: about 50%. It is usually dark gray but can also be green, brown, or black.

base in mathematics, the number of different single-digit symbols used in a particular number system. In our usual (decimal) counting system of numbers (with symbols 0, 1, 2, 3, 4, 5, 6, 7, 8, 9) the base is 10. In the binary number system, which has only the symbols 1 and 0, the base is two. A base is also a number that, when raised to a particular power (that is, when multiplied by itself a particular number of times as in $10^2 = 10 \times 10 = 100$), has a ◊logarithm equal to the power. For example, the logarithm of 100 to the base ten is 2. In geometry, the term is used to denote the line or area on which a polygon or solid stands.

base in chemistry, a substance that accepts protons, such as the hydroxide ion (OH$^-$) and ammonia (NH$_3$). Bases react with acids to give a salt. Those that dissolve in water are called ◊alkalis.

baseball a bat-and-ball game between two teams, played on a field called a diamond, because of the arrangement of the bases. Bats, balls, and gloves constitute the basic equipment. The game is divided into nine innings. During the "top" half of each inning the home team plays defense and the visiting team, offense. In the "bottom" half, the roles are reversed. There are nine defensive positions: the pitcher, who stands on a mound 60.5 ft/18.4 m from home plate; the catcher, who crouches behind home plate; the first, second, and third basemen, who stand at or near their respective bases (90 ft/27.4 m apart), which together with home plate form the diamond-shaped infield; the shortstop, who covers the infield between second and third bases; and the right, center, and left fielders, whose domain is the outfield, the dimensions of which vary from stadium to stadium. The highest-level professional teams are divided into the American league (AL) and the National League (NL). The league champions meet annually in the World Series.

Basel or *Basle* (French *Bâle*) financial, commercial, and industrial city (dyes, vitamins, agrochemicals, dietary products, genetic products) in Switzerland; population (1990) 171,000. Basel was a strong military station under the Romans. In 1501 it joined the Swiss confederation and later developed as a center for the Reformation.

basenji breed of dog originating in Central Africa, where it is used as a hunter. About 1.3 ft/41 cm tall, it has a wrinkled forehead, curled tail, and short glossy coat. It is remarkable because it has no true bark.

Bashkir autonomous republic of Russia, with the Ural Mountains on the east
area 55,430 sq mi/143,600 sq km
capital Ufa
products minerals, oil, natural gas
population (1982) 3,876,000
languages Russian, Bashkir (about 25%)
history annexed by Russia 1557; became the first Soviet autonomous republic 1919. Since 1989 Bashkirs have demanded greater independence.

Bashō Adopted name of Matsuo Munefusa 1644–1694. Japanese poet who was a master of the *haiku*, a 17-syllable poetic form with lines of 5, 7, and 5 syllables, which he infused with subtle allusiveness. His *Oku-no-hosomichi/The Narrow Road to the Deep North* 1694, an account of a visit to northern and western Honshū, consists of haiku interspersed with prose passages.

BASIC (acronym for *beginner's all-purpose symbolic instruction code*) high-level computer-programming language, developed 1964, originally designed to take advantage of multiuser systems (which can be used by many people at the same time). The language is relatively easy to learn and is popular among microcomputer users.

Basie Count (William) 1904–1984. US jazz band leader, pianist, and organist who developed the big-band sound and a simplified, swinging style of music. He led impressive groups of musicians in a career spanning more than 50 years. Basie's compositions include "One O'Clock Jump" and "Jumpin' at the Woodside."

basil or *sweet basil* plant *Ocimum basilicum* of the mint family Labiatae. A native of the tropics, it is cultivated in Europe as a culinary herb. *See illustration p. 96*

Baseball

Recent World Series Champions

1984	Detroit Tigers (AL)
1985	Kansas City Royals (AL)
1986	New York Mets (NL)
1987	Minnesota Twins (AL)
1988	Los Angeles Dodgers (NL)
1989	Oakland Athletics (AL)
1990	Cincinnati Reds (NL)
1991	Minnesota Twins (AL)
1992	Toronto Blue Jays (AL)
1993	Toronto Blue Jays (AL)

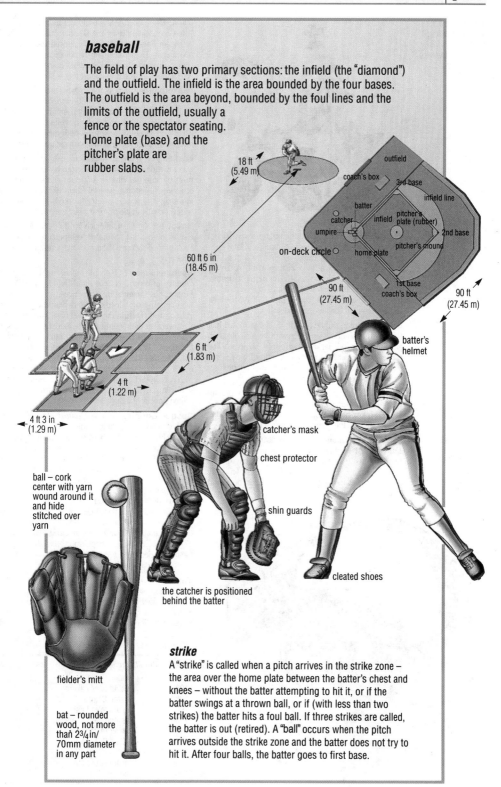

baseball

The field of play has two primary sections: the infield (the "diamond") and the outfield. The infield is the area bounded by the four bases. The outfield is the area beyond, bounded by the foul lines and the limits of the outfield, usually a fence or the spectator seating. Home plate (base) and the pitcher's plate are rubber slabs.

18 ft (5.49 m)

outfield

coach's box

3rd base

infield line

batter

pitcher's plate (rubber)

catcher

infield

umpire

2nd base

pitcher's mound

on-deck circle

home plate

60 ft 6 in (18.45 m)

90 ft (27.45 m)

1st base

coach's box

90 ft (27.45 m)

6 ft (1.83 m)

batter's helmet

4 ft (1.22 m)

4 ft 3 in (1.29 m)

catcher's mask

chest protector

ball – cork center with yarn wound around it and hide stitched over yarn

shin guards

cleated shoes

the catcher is positioned behind the batter

fielder's mitt

bat – rounded wood, not more than 2³/₄ in/ 70mm diameter in any part

strike

A "strike" is called when a pitch arrives in the strike zone – the area over the home plate between the batter's chest and knees – without the batter attempting to hit it, or if the batter swings at a thrown ball, or if (with less than two strikes) the batter hits a foul ball. If three strikes are called, the batter is out (retired). A "ball" occurs when the pitch arrives outside the strike zone and the batter does not try to hit it. After four balls, the batter goes to first base.

basil Basil is a member of the mint family grown in many areas of the world as a cooking herb.

Basil II *c.* 958–1025. Byzantine emperor from 976. His achievement as emperor was to contain, and later decisively defeat, the Bulgarians, earning for himself the title "Bulgar-Slayer" after a victory 1014. After the battle he blinded almost all 15,000 of the defeated, leaving only a few men with one eye to lead their fellows home. The Byzantine empire had reached its largest extent at the time of his death.

basilica Roman public building; a large roofed hall flanked by columns, generally with an aisle on each side, used for judicial or other public business. The earliest known basilica, at Pompeii, dates from the 2nd century BC. This architectural form was adopted by the early Christians for their churches.

Basilicata mountainous region of S Italy, comprising the provinces of Potenza and Matera; area 3,860 sq mi/10,000 sq km; population (1990) 624,500. Its capital is Potenza. It was the Roman province of Lucania.

basilisk Central and South American lizard, genus *Basiliscus*. It is able to run on its hind legs when traveling fast (about 7 mph/11 kph) and may dash a short distance across the surface of water. The male has a well developed crest on the head, body, and tail.

basilisk The basilisk of Central and South America is a lizard of the iguana family.

Basil, St *c.* 330–379. Cappadocian monk, known as "the Great," founder of the Basilian monks. Elected bishop of Caesarea 370, Basil opposed the heresy of ◊Arianism. He wrote many theological works and composed the "Liturgy of St Basil," in use in the Eastern Orthodox Church. His feast day is Jan 2.

basketball ball game between two teams of five players, played on both indoor and outdoor rectangular courts. Players move the ball by passing it or by dribbling it (bouncing it on the floor) while running. Basketball is played worldwide by both men and women and, with soccer, is one of the two most popular sports.

basketry ancient craft (Mesolithic–Neolithic) used to make a wide range of objects (from baskets to furniture) by interweaving or braiding rushes, cane, or other equally strong, natural fibers. Wickerwork is a more rigid type of basketry worked onto a sturdy frame, usually made from strips of willow.

Basov Nikolai Gennadievich 1912– . Soviet physicist who in 1953, with his compatriot Aleksandr Prokhorov, developed the microwave amplifier called a ◊maser.

Basque member of a people inhabiting the ◊Basque Country of central N Spain and the extreme SW of France. The Basques are a pre-Indo-European people who largely maintained their independence until the 19th century. During the Spanish Civil War 1936–39, they were on the republican side defeated by Franco. Their language (*Euskara*) is unrelated to any other language. The Basque separatist movement ETA (*Euskadi ta Askatasuna*, "Basque Nation and Liberty") and the French organization Iparretarrak ("ETA fighters from the North Side") have engaged in guerrilla activity from 1968 in an attempt to secure a united Basque state.

Basque Country (Basque *Euskal Herria*) homeland of the Basque people in the W Pyrenees, divided by the Franco-Spanish border. The Spanish Basque Country (Spanish *País Vasco*) is an autonomous region (created 1979) of central N Spain, comprising the provinces of Vizcaya, Alava, and Guipúzcoa (Basque *Bizkaia*, *Araba*, and *Gipuzkoa*); area 2,818 sq mi/7,300 sq km; population (1988) 2,176,790. The French Basque Country (French *Pays Basque*) comprises the *département* of Pyrénées-Atlantiques, including the arrondissements of Labourd, Basse-Navarre, and Soule (Basque *Lapurdi*, *Nafarroa Beherea*, and *Zuberoa*); area 4770 sq mi/7,633 sq km; population (1981) 555,700. To Basque nationalists *Euskal Herria* also includes the autonomous Spanish province of Navarre.

Basra (Arabic *al-Basrah*) principal port in Iraq, in the Shatt-al-Arab delta, 60 ml/97 km from the Persian Gulf, founded in the 7th century; population (1991) 850,000. Exports include wool, oil, cereal, and dates. Aerial bombing during the 1991 Gulf War destroyed

Basketball	
Recent NBA Champions	
1984	Boston Celtics
1985	Los Angeles Lakers
1986	Boston Celtics
1987	Los Angeles Lakers
1988	Los Angeles Lakers
1989	Detroit Pistons
1990	Detroit Pistons
1991	Chicago Bulls
1992	Chicago Bulls
1993	Chicago Bulls

basketball

An indoor sport played on a court by five members per side. The object is, via a series of dribbling and passing moves with the hands, to get the ball into the opposing half of the court and score goals by tossing the ball into the opposing basket.

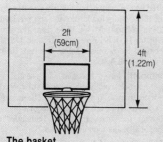

2ft
(59cm)

4ft
(1.22m)

The basket

The basket is a piece of netting which hangs from a metal rim and is open at both ends to allow the ball to pass through. The rim is attached to a backboard and points can be scored by bouncing the ball off the backboard and into the basket.

Play

Play is started with a jumpball. Two players, one from each team, face each other and the referee tosses the ball into the air between the two players, who attempt to tap the ball to a teammate. The ball can only be played after it has reached its greatest height. A player in the jumpball can only play the ball twice, after which it must be played to a player not involved.

Free throw

A free throw is awarded to a player who has been fouled by an opponent. The throw must be taken from the free-throw line. The opposing team must not impede the throw and must not stand within the key (restricted area). The number of free throws awarded depends upon the type of foul.

dimensions of the international court

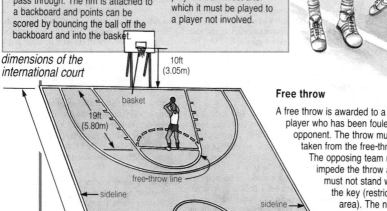

basket

10ft
(3.05m)

19ft
(5.80m)

free-throw line

sideline

sideline

94ft
(28.6m)

key

50ft
(15.24m)

bridges, factories, power stations, water-treatment plants, sewage-treatment plants, and the port. A Shiite rebellion March 1991 was crushed by the Iraqi army, causing further death and destruction.

bass long-bodied scaly sea fish *Morone labrax* found in the N Atlantic and Mediterranean. They grow to 3 ft/1 m, and are often seen in shoals.

Basse-Normandie or *Lower Normandy* coastal region of NW France lying between Haute-Normandie and Brittany (Bretagne). It includes the *départements* of Calvados, Manche, and Orne; area 6,794 sq mi/ 17,600 sq km; population (1986) 1,373,000. Its capital is Caen. Apart from stock farming, dairy farming, and textiles, the area produces Calvados (apple brandy).

basset type of dog with a long low body, wrinkled forehead, and long pendulous ears, originally bred in France for hunting hares.

Basseterre capital and port of St Christopher–Nevis, in the Leeward Islands; population (1980) 14,000. Industries include data processing, rum, clothes, and electrical components.

bassoon double-reed ◊woodwind instrument, the bass of the oboe family. It doubles back on itself in a tube about 7.5 ft/2.5 m long. Its tone is rich and deep.

Bass Strait channel between Australia and Tasmania, named after British explorer George Bass; oil was discovered here in the 1960s.

Bastille castle of St Antoine, built about 1370 as part of the fortifications of Paris. It was made a state prison by Cardinal ◊Richelieu and was stormed by the mob that set the French Revolution in motion July 14, 1789. Only seven prisoners were found in the castle when it was stormed; the governor and most of the garrison were killed, and the Bastille was razed.

Basutoland former name for ◊Lesotho, a kingdom in S Africa.

bat flying mammal in which the forelimbs are developed as wings capable of rapid and sustained flight. There are two main groups of bats: *megabats*, or *flying foxes*, which eat fruit, and *microbats*, which mainly eat insects. Although by no means blind, many microbats rely largely on echolocation for navigation and finding prey, sending out pulses of high-pitched sound and listening for the echo. Bats are nocturnal, and those native to temperate countries hibernate in winter. There are about 1,000 species of bats forming the order Chiroptera, making this the second-largest mammalian order; bats make up nearly one-quarter of the world's mammals. Although bats are widely distributed, bat populations have declined alarmingly and many species are now endangered.

Bataan peninsula in Luzon, the Philippines, which was defended against the Japanese in World War II by US and Filipino troops under General MacArthur Jan 1–April 9, 1942. MacArthur was evacuated, but some 67,000 Allied prisoners died on the *Bataan Death March* to camps in the interior.

Batak member of the several distinct but related peoples of N Sumatra in Indonesia. Numbering approximately 2.5 million, the Batak speak languages belonging to the Austronesian family.

Bath historic city in Avon, England; population (1991) 79,900.
features Hot springs; the ruins of the baths after which it is named, as well as a great temple, are the finest Roman remains in Britain. Excavations 1979

revealed thousands of coins and "curses," offered at a place which was thought to be the link between the upper and lower worlds. The Gothic Bath Abbey has an unusually decorated west front and fan vaulting. There is much 18th-century architecture, notably the Royal Crescent by John Wood. The Assembly Rooms 1771 were destroyed in an air raid 1942 but reconstructed 1963. The University of Technology was established 1966. The Bath Festival Orchestra is based here.
history The Roman city of Aquae Sulis ("waters of Sul"—the British goddess of wisdom) was built in the first 20 years after the Roman invasion. In medieval times the hot springs were crown property, administered by the church, but the city was transformed in the 18th century to a fashionable spa, presided over by "Beau" ◊Nash. At his home here the astronomer William Herschel discovered Uranus 1781. Visitors included the novelists Tobias Smollett, Henry Fielding, and Jane Austen.

batholith large, irregular, deep-seated mass of igneous rock, usually granite, with an exposed surface of more than 40 sq mi/100 sq km. The mass forms by the intrusion or upswelling of magma (molten rock) through the surrounding rock. Batholiths form the core of all major mountain ranges.

Bath, Order of the British order of knighthood, believed to have been founded in the reign of Henry IV (1399–1413). Formally instituted 1815, it included civilians from 1847 and women from 1970.

Báthory Stephen 1533–1586. King of Poland, elected by a diet convened 1575 and crowned 1576. Báthory succeeded in driving the Russian troops of Ivan the Terrible out of his country. His military successes brought potential conflicts with Sweden, but he died before these developed.

bathyal zone upper part of the ocean, which lies on the continental shelf at a depth of between 650 ft/ 200 m and 6,500 ft/2,000 m.

bathyscaph or *bathyscaphe* or *bathyscape* deep-sea diving apparatus used for exploration at great depths in the ocean. In 1960, Jacques Piccard and Don Walsh took the bathyscaph *Trieste* to a depth of 35,820 ft/10,917 m in the Challenger Deep in the ◊Mariana Trench off the island of Guam in the Pacific Ocean.

batik Javanese technique of hand-applied color design for fabric; areas to be left undyed in a color are sealed with wax. Practiced throughout Indonesia, the craft was introduced to the West by Dutch traders.

Batista Fulgencio 1901–1973. Cuban dictator 1933–44, when he stood down, and again 1952–59, after seizing power in a coup. His authoritarian methods enabled him to jail his opponents and amass a large personal fortune. He was overthrown by rebel forces led by Fidel ◊Castro 1959.

battery any energy-storage device allowing release of electricity on demand. It is made up of one or more electrical ◊cells. Primary-cell batteries are disposable; secondary-cell batteries, or accumulators, are rechargeable. Primary-cell batteries are an extremely uneconomical form of energy, since they produce only 2% of the power used in their manufacture.
The lead–acid *car battery* is a secondary-cell battery. The car's generator continually recharges the battery. It consists of sets of lead (positive) and lead peroxide (negative) plates in an electrolyte of sulfuric acid (battery acid).
The introduction of rechargeable nickel–cadmium batteries has revolutionized portable electronic news-

gathering (sound recording, video) and information processing (computing). These batteries offer a stable, short-term source of power free of noise and other electrical hazards.

Battle Creek city in S Michigan, directly E of Kalamazoo; population (1990) 53,540. It became known as the cereal capital of the world after J H Kellogg, W K Kellogg, and C W Post established dry cereal and grain factories here. Battle Creek was also a station on the ◊Underground Railroad.

baud in engineering, a unit of telegraph signaling speed equal to one pulse per second; also the number of bits per second that can be transmitted in a computer system.

Baudelaire Charles Pierre 1821–1867. French poet whose work combined rhythmical and musical perfection with a morbid romanticism and eroticism, finding beauty in decadence and evil. His first book of verse was *Les Fleurs du mal/◊Flowers of Evil* 1857.

Baudouin 1930–1993. King of the Belgians 1951–93. In 1950 his father, ◊Leopold III, abdicated and Baudouin was known until his succession July 1951 as *Le Prince Royal*. In 1960 he married Fabiola de Mora y Aragón (1928–), member of a Spanish noble family. He was succeeded by his brother Albert.

Bauhaus German school of Modern architecture and design founded 1919 by the architect Walter ◊Gropius at Weimar in Germany in an attempt to fuse all arts, design, architecture, and crafts into a unified whole. Moved to Dessau under political pressure 1925, it was closed by the Nazis 1933 because of "decadence." Associated with the Bauhaus were the artists Klee and Kandinsky and the architect Mies van der Rohe.

Baum L(yman) Frank 1856–1919. US writer, author of the children's fantasy *The Wonderful Wizard of Oz* 1900 and its 13 sequels. The series was continued by another author after his death. The film *The Wizard of Oz* 1939 with Judy Garland became a US classic.

bauxite principal ore of ◊aluminium, consisting of a mixture of hydrated aluminum oxides and hydroxides, generally contaminated with compounds of iron, which give it a red color. To produce aluminum the ore is processed into a white powder (alumina), which is then smelted by passing a large electric current through it. Chief producers of bauxite are Australia, Guinea, Jamaica, Russia, Kazakhstan, Suriname, and Brazil.

Bavaria (German *Bayern*) administrative region (German *Land*) of Germany
area 27,252 sq mi/70,600 sq km
capital Munich
cities Nuremberg, Augsburg, Würzburg, Regensburg
features largest of the German *Länder*; forms the Danube basin; festivals at Bayreuth and Oberammergau *products* beer, electronics, electrical engineering, optics, automobiles, aerospace, chemicals, plastics, oil refining, textiles, glass, toys
population (1988) 11,000,000
famous people Lucas Cranach, Adolf Hitler, Franz Josef Strauss, Richard Strauss
religion 70% Roman Catholic, 26% Protestant
history the last king, Ludwig III, abdicated 1918, and Bavaria declared itself a republic.

bay various species of ◊laurel, genus *Laurus*. The aromatic evergreen leaves are used for flavoring in cooking. There is also a golden-leaved variety.

Bayeux Tapestry linen hanging made about 1067–70, which gives a vivid pictorial record of the invasion of England by William I (the Conqueror) 1066. It is an embroidery rather than a true tapestry, sewn with woolen threads in blue, green, red, and yellow, 231 ft/70 m long and 20 in/50 cm wide, and containing 72 separate scenes with descriptive wording in Latin. It is exhibited at the museum of Bayeaux in Normandy, France.

Bay of Pigs inlet on the S coast of Cuba about 90 mi/145 km SW of Havana. It was the site of an unsuccessful invasion attempt by 1,500 US-sponsored Cuban exiles April 17–20, 1961; 1,173 were taken prisoner.

bayonet short sword attached to the muzzle of a firearm. The bayonet was placed inside the barrel of the muzzleloading muskets of the late 17th century. The *sock* or ring bayonet, invented 1700, allowed a weapon to be fired without interruption, leading to the demise of the pike.

Bayreuth city in Bavaria, S Germany, where opera festivals are held every summer; population (1983) 71,000. It was the home of composer Richard ◊Wagner, and the Wagner theater was established 1876.

BC in the Christian calendar, abbreviation for *before Christ*, used with dates.

BCE abbreviation for *before the Common Era*, used with dates (instead of BC).

BCG (abbreviation for *bacillus of Calmette and Guérin*) bacillus used as a vaccine to confer active immunity to ◊tuberculosis (TB).

Beach Boys, the US pop group formed 1961. They began as exponents of vocal-harmony surf music with Chuck Berry guitar riffs (their hits include "Surfin' USA" 1963 and "Help Me, Rhonda" 1965), but the compositions, arrangements, and production by Brian Wilson (1942–) became highly complex under the influence of psychedelic rock, peaking with "Good Vibrations" 1966. Wilson spent most of the next 20 years in retirement but returned with a solo album 1988.

beagle short-haired hound with pendant ears, sickle tail, and a bell-like voice for hunting hares on foot ("beagling").

beak horn-covered projecting jaws of a bird, or other horny jaws such as those of the tortoise or octopus. The beaks of birds are adapted by shape and size to specific diets.

beam balance instrument for measuring mass (or weight). A simple form consists of a beam pivoted at its midpoint with a pan hanging at each end. The mass to be measured, in one pan, is compared with a variety of standard masses placed in the other. When the beam is balanced, the masses' turning effects or moments under gravity, and hence the masses themselves, are equal.

bean any seed of numerous leguminous plants. Beans are rich in nitrogenous or protein matter and are grown both for human consumption and as food for cattle and horses. Varieties of bean are grown throughout Europe, the US, South America, China, Japan, SE Asia, and Australia.

bear large mammal with a heavily built body, short powerful limbs, and a very short tail. Bears breed once a year, producing one to four cubs. In northern regions they hibernate, and the young are born in the winter den. They are found mainly in North America and N Asia. The skin of the polar bear is black to conserve 80–90% of the solar energy trapped and channeled down the hollow hairs of its fur.

Beatles, the (left to right) John Lennon, Ringo Starr, George Harrison, and Paul McCartney at the start of their career 1963.

bear in business, a speculator who sells stocks or shares on the stock exchange expecting a fall in the price in order to buy them back at a profit, the opposite of ◊bull. In a bear market, prices fall, and bears prosper.

Beard Charles Austin 1874–1948. US historian and a leader of the Progressive movement, active in promoting political and social reform. As a chief exponent of critical economic history, he published *An Economic Interpretation of the Constitution of the United States* 1913 and *The Economic Origins of Jeffersonian Democracy* 1915. With his wife, Mary, he wrote *A Basic History of the United States* 1944, long a standard textbook in the US.

bearing device used in a machine to allow free movement between two parts, typically the rotation of a shaft in a housing. *Ball bearings* consist of two rings, one fixed to a housing, one to the rotating shaft. Between them is a set, or race, of steel balls. They are widely used to support shafts, as in the spindle in the hub of a bicycle wheel.

bearing the direction of a fixed point, or the path of a moving object, from a point of observation on the Earth's surface, expressed as an angle from the north. Bearings are taken by ◊compass and are measured in degrees (°), given as three-digit numbers increasing clockwise. For instance, north is 000°, northeast is 045°, south is 180°, and southwest is 225°.

Beat Generation or *Beat movement* beatniks of the 1950s and 1960s, usually in their teens and early twenties, who rejected conventional lifestyles and opted for life on the road, drug experimentation, and antimaterialist values; and the associated literary movement whose members included William S Burroughs, Lawrence Ferlinghetti, Allen ◊Ginsberg, and Jack ◊Kerouac (who is credited with coining the term).

beatification in the Catholic church, the first step toward ◊canonization. Persons who have been beatified can be prayed to, and the title "Blessed" can be put before their names.

Beatitudes in the New Testament, the sayings of Jesus reported in Matthew 6: 1–12 and Luke 6: 20–38, depicting the spiritual qualities that characterize members of the Kingdom of God.

Beatles, the English pop group 1960–70. The members, all born in Liverpool, were John ◊Lennon (1940–1980, rhythm guitar, vocals), Paul ◊McCartney (1942– , bass, vocals), George Harrison (1943– , lead guitar, vocals), and Ringo Starr (formerly Richard Starkey, 1940– , drums). Using songs written largely by Lennon and McCartney, the Beatles dominated rock music and pop culture in the 1960s.

In addition to experimenting with a wide range of musical styles, they greatly influenced subsequent bands, made films and toured extensively. Their hit songs include "She Loves You" 1963, "Can't Buy Me Love" 1964, and "Yesterday" 1965. Their films include *A Hard Day's Night* 1964, *Help!* 1965, and the animated feature *Yellow Submarine* 1968, for which they provided the soundtrack. The Beatles continued to have an impact on the dress, hair, lifestyle, and thought of young people even after they pursued separate careers.

Beaton Cecil 1904–1980. English portrait and fashion photographer, designer, illustrator, diarist, and conversationalist. He produced portrait studies and also designed scenery and costumes for ballets, and sets for plays and films.

Beatrix 1936– . Queen of the Netherlands. The eldest daughter of Queen ◊Juliana, she succeeded to the throne on her mother's abdication 1980. In 1966 she married West German diplomat Claus von Amsberg (1926–), who was created Prince of the Netherlands. Her heir is Prince Willem Alexander (1967–).

Beatty Warren. Adopted name of Warren Beaty 1937– . US actor, director, and producer, popular for such films as *Splendor in the Grass* 1961, *Bonnie and Clyde* 1967, *Heaven Can Wait* 1978, *Reds* 1981 (Academy Award for Best Producer), *Dick Tracy* 1990, and *Bugsy* 1992. He is the brother of the actress Shirley MacLaine.

Beaufort Henry 1375–1447. English priest, bishop of Lincoln from 1398, of Winchester from 1405. As chancellor of England, he supported his half brother Henry IV and made enormous personal loans to Henry V to finance war against France. As a guardian of Henry VI from 1421, he was in effective control of the country until 1426. In the same year he was created a cardinal. In 1431 he crowned Henry VI as king of France in Paris.

Beaufort scale system of recording wind velocity, devised by Francis Beaufort 1806. It is a numerical scale ranging from 0 to 17, calm being indicated by 0 and a hurricane by 12; 13–17 indicate degrees of hurricane force.

Beaumarchais Pierre Augustin Caron de 1732–1799. French dramatist. His great comedies *Le Barbier de Seville/The Barber of Seville* 1775 and *Le Mariage de Figaro/The Marriage of Figaro* (1778, but prohibited until 1784) form the basis of operas by ◊Rossini and ◊Mozart.

Beaumont city and port in SE Texas, on the Neches River, NE of Houston; seat of Jefferson County; population (1990) 114,320. It is an oil-processing center for the surrounding oil fields and a shipping point via the Sabine–Neches canal to the Gulf of Mexico; other industries include shipbuilding and paper production.

In 1901, when a successful oil well was drilled at Spindletop Field, the modern oil industry began in the West.

Beaumont Francis 1584–1616. English dramatist and poet. From about 1608 he collaborated with John Fletcher. Their joint plays include *Philaster* 1610, *The Maid's Tragedy* about 1611, and *A King and No King* about 1611. *The Woman Hater* about 1606 and *The Knight of the Burning Pestle* about 1607 are ascribed to Beaumont alone.

Beauvoir Simone de 1908–1986. French socialist, feminist, and writer who taught philosophy at the Sorbonne university in Paris 1931–43. Her book *Le Deuxième sexe/The Second Sex* 1949 became a seminal work for many feminists.

beaver aquatic rodent *Castor fiber* with webbed hind feet, a broad flat scaly tail, and thick waterproof fur. It has very large incisor teeth and fells trees to feed on the bark and to use the logs to construct the "lodge" in which the young are reared, food is stored, and where much of the winter is spent.

Beaverbrook (William) Max(well) Aitken, 1st Baron Beaverbrook 1879–1964. British financier, newspaper proprietor, and politician, born in Canada. He bought a majority interest in the *Daily Express* 1919, founded the *Sunday Express* 1921, and bought the London *Evening Standard* 1929. He served in Lloyd George's World War I cabinet and Churchill's World War II cabinet.

bebop or *bop* hot jazz style, rhythmically complex, virtuosic, and highly improvisational, developed in New York 1940–55 by Charlie Parker, Dizzy Gillespie, Thelonius Monk, and other black musicians disaffected with dance bands.

Becker Boris 1967– . German tennis player. In 1985, at the age of 17, he became the youngest winner of a singles title at Wimbledon. He has won the title three times and helped West Germany to win the Davis Cup 1988 and 1989. He also won the US Open 1989.

Becket St Thomas à 1118–1170. English priest and politician. He was chancellor to ◊Henry II 1155–62, when he was appointed archbishop of Canterbury. The interests of the church soon conflicted with those of the crown and Becket was assassinated; he was canonized 1172.

He resisted Henry's attempts to regulate relations between church and state, and was murdered by four knights before the altar of Canterbury cathedral.

Beckett Samuel 1906–1989. Irish novelist and dramatist who wrote in French and English. His *En attendant Godot/Waiting for Godot* 1952 is possibly the most universally known example of Theatre of the ◊Absurd, in which life is taken to be meaningless. This genre is taken to further extremes in *Fin de Partie/Endgame* 1957 and *Happy Days* 1961. Nobel Prize for Literature 1969.

becquerel SI unit (symbol Bq) of ◊radioactivity, equal to one radioactive disintegration (change in the nucleus of an atom when a particle or ray is given off) per second.

Becquerel Antoine Henri 1852–1908. French physicist who discovered penetrating radiation coming from uranium salts, the first indication of ◊radioactivity, and shared a Nobel Prize with Marie and Pierre ◊Curie 1903.

bed in geology, a single ◊sedimentary rock unit with a distinct set of physical characteristics or contained fossils, readily distinguishable from those of beds above and below. Well-defined partings called *bedding planes* separate successive beds or strata.

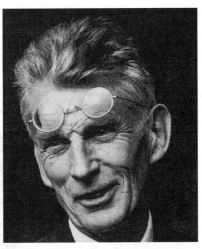

Beckett Irish novelist and dramatist Samuel Beckett, winner of the Nobel Prize for Literature 1969.

bedbug flattened wingless red-brown insect *Cimex lectularius* with piercing mouthparts. It hides by day in crevices or bedclothes, and emerges at night to suck human blood.

Bede c. 673–735. English theologian and historian, known as *the Venerable Bede*, active in Durham and Northumbria. He wrote many scientific, theological, and historical works. His *Historia Ecclesiastica Gentis Anglorum/Ecclesiastical History of the English People* 731 is a seminal source for early English history.

Bedlam (abbreviation of *Bethlehem*) the earliest mental hospital in Europe. The hospital was opened in the 14th century in London and is now sited in Surrey. It is now used as a slang word meaning chaos.

Bedouin (Arabic "desert-dweller") Arab of any of the nomadic peoples occupying the deserts of Arabia and N Africa, now becoming increasingly settled. Their traditional trade was rearing horses and camels.

bee four-winged insect of the superfamily Apoidea in the order Hymenoptera, usually with a sting. There are over 12,000 species, of which fewer than 1 in 20 are social in habit. The *hive bee* or *honeybee Apis mellifera* establishes perennial colonies of about 80,000, the majority being infertile females (workers), with a few larger fertile males (drones), and a single very large fertile female (the queen). Worker bees live for no more than a few weeks, while a drone may live a few months, and a queen several years. Queen honeybees lay two kinds of eggs: fertilized, female eggs, which have two sets of chromosomes and develop into workers or queens, and unfertilized, male eggs, which have only one set of chromosomes and develop into drones. *See illustration p. 102*

beech genus of trees *Fagus*, of the family Fagaceae. Of the ten species in this genus only one is native to North America; others grow in Europe. The American beech *F. grandifolia* grows to 100 ft/30 m, with blue-gray bark; a broad, rounded crown; and leaves that are lanceolate, serrate, triangular, and edible.

Beecham Thomas 1879–1961. British conductor and impresario. He established the Royal Philharmonic Orchestra 1946 and fostered the works of composers such as Dellus, Sibellus, and Richard Strauss.

Beecher Lyman 1775–1863. US Congregational and Presbyterian minister, one of the most popular pulpit orators of his time. He was the father of Harriet Beecher ◊Stowe and Henry Ward Beecher.

bee The honeybee lives in colonies of 40,000–80,000 workers, 200 drones, and 1 queen.

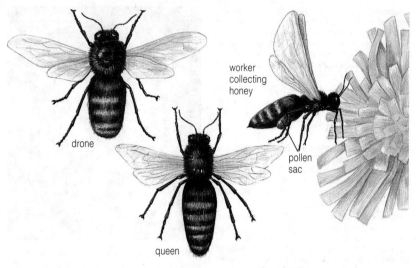

worker collecting honey

drone

pollen sac

queen

As a pastor in Connecticut and Boston, he preached against nitarianism and Roman Catholicism and contributed to the development of the New Haven theology of evangelical Calvinism.

Beelzebub (Hebrew "lord of the flies") in the New Testament, the leader of the devils, sometimes identified with Satan and sometimes with his chief assistant (see ◊devil). In the Old Testament Beelzebub was a fertility god worshiped by the Philistines and other Semitic groups (Baal).

beer alcoholic drink made from water and malt (fermented barley or other grain), flavored with hops. Beer contains between 1% and 6% alcohol. One of the oldest alcoholic drinks, it was brewed in ancient China, Egypt, and Babylon.

The distinction between beer (containing hops) and ale (without hops) was made in medieval times. Beer is now a generic term including pilsner and lager. Stout is top fermented but is sweet and strongly flavored with roasted grain; lager (German "store") is a light beer, bottom fermented and matured over a longer period. Modern ales, like beer, are made with hops but fermented more rapidly at relatively high temperatures. In the US light beers are made with more water, fewer calories and less alcohol.

Begin Israeli prime minister Menachem Begin.

Beersheba industrial town in Israel; population (1987) 115,000. It is the chief center of the Negev Desert and has been a settlement from the Stone Age.

beet plant of the genus *Beta* of the goosefoot family Chenapodiaceae. The common beet *B. vulgaris* is used in one variety to produce sugar, and another, the mangelwurzel, is grown as cattle fodder. The beetroot, or red beet, *B. rubra* is a salad plant.

Beethoven Ludwig van 1770–1827. German composer and pianist whose mastery of musical expression in every genre made him the dominant influence on 19th-century music. Beethoven's repertoire includes concert overtures; the opera *Fidelio*; 5 piano concertos and 2 for violin (1 unfinished); 32 piano sonatas, including the *Moonlight* and *Appassionata*; 17 string quartets; the *Mass in D* (*Missa solemnis*); and 9 symphonies, as well as many youthful works. He usually played his own piano pieces and conducted his orchestral works until he was hampered by deafness 1801; nevertheless he continued to compose.

beetle common name of insects in the order Coleoptera (Greek "sheath-winged") with leathery forewings folding down in a protective sheath over the membranous hindwings, which are those used for flight. They pass through a complete metamorphosis. They include some of the largest and smallest of all insects: the largest is the *Hercules beetle Dynastes hercules* of the South American rain forests, 6 in/15 cm long; the smallest is only 0.02 in/0.05 cm long. Comprising more than 50% of the animal kingdom, beetles number some 370,000 named species, with many not yet described.

Begin Menachem 1913–1992. Israeli politician. He was leader of the extremist Irgun Zvai Leumi organization in Palestine from 1942, and prime minister of Israel 1977–83, as head of the right-wing Likud party. In 1978 Begin shared a Nobel Peace Prize with President Sadat of Egypt for work on the ◊Camp David Agreements for a Middle East peace settlement.

begonia any plant of the genus *Begonia* of the tropical and subtropical family Begoniaceae. Begonias have fleshy and succulent leaves, and some have large, brilliant flowers. There are numerous species native to the tropics, in particular South America and India.

Behan Brendan 1923–1964. Irish dramatist. His early experience of prison and knowledge of the workings of the ◊IRA (recounted in his autobiography *Borstal Boy* 1958) provided him with two recurrent themes in his plays. *The Quare Fellow* 1954 was followed by the tragicomedy *The Hostage* 1958, first written in Gaelic.

behaviorism school of psychology originating in the US, of which the leading exponent was John B ◊Watson. Behaviorists maintain that all human activity can ultimately be explained in terms of conditioned reactions or reflexes and habits formed in consequence. Leading behaviorists include Ivan ◊Pavlov and B F ◊Skinner.

behavior therapy in psychology, the application of behavioral principles, derived from learning theories, to the treatment of clinical conditions such as ◊phobias, ◊obsessions, and sexual and interpersonal problems. For example, in treating a phobia the person is taken into the feared situation in gradual steps. Over time, the fear typically reduces, and the problem becomes less acute.

behemoth in the Old Testament (Job 40), an animal cited by God as evidence of his power; usually thought to refer to the hippopotamus. It is used proverbially to mean any giant and powerful creature.

Behring Emil von 1854–1917. German physician who discovered that the body produces antitoxins, substances able to counteract poisons released by bacteria. Using this knowledge, he developed new treatments for diseases such as ◊diphtheria.

Beiderbecke Bix (Leon Bismarck) 1903–1931. US jazz cornetist, composer, and pianist. A romantic soloist with the bands of King Oliver, Louis Armstrong, and Paul Whiteman, Beiderbecke was the first acknowledged white jazz innovator. He was influenced by the Classical composers Claude Debussy, Maurice Ravel, and Igor Stravinsky.

Beijing or *Peking* capital of China; part of its northeast border is formed by the Great Wall of China; population (1989) 6,800,000. The municipality of Beijing has an area of 6,871 sq mi/17,800 sq km and a population (1990) of 10,819,000. Industries include textiles, petrochemicals, steel, and engineering.

Beirut or *Beyrouth* capital and port of ◊Lebanon, devastated by civil war in the 1970s and 1980s, when it was occupied by armies of neighboring countries; population (1988 est) 1,500,000.

Bekka, the or *El Beqa'a* governorate of E Lebanon separated from Syria by the Anti-Lebanon Mountains. Zahlé and the ancient city of Baalbek are the chief towns. The Bekka Valley was of strategic importance in the Syrian struggle for control of N Lebanon. In the early 1980s the valley was penetrated by Shia Muslims who established an extremist Hezbollah stronghold with the support of Iranian Revolutionary Guards.

Belarus or *Byelorussia* or *Belorussia* country in E central Europe, bounded S by Ukraine, E by Russia, W by Poland, and N by Latvia and Lithuania.

Belau, Republic of (formerly *Palau*) self-governing island group in Micronesia
area 193 sq mi/500 sq km
capital Koror
features 26 larger islands (8 inhabited) and about 300 islets
population (1990) 15,100

Belarus
Republic of

area 80,100 sq mi/207,600 sq km
capital Minsk (Mensk)
cities Gomel, Vitebsk, Mogilev, Bobruisk, Grodno, Brest
physical more than 25% forested; rivers W Dvina, Dnieper and its tributaries, including the Pripet and Beresina; the Pripet Marshes in the E; mild and damp climate
environment large areas contaminated by fallout from Chernobyl
features Belovezhskaya Pushcha (scenic forest reserve)
head of state Stanislav Shushkevich from 1991
head of government Vyacheslav Kebich from 1990

political system emergent democracy
political parties Byelorussian Popular Front (Adradzhenne), moderate nationalist; Byelorussian Ecological Union (BEU); Byelorussian Social Democratic Party, moderate left of center; Christian Democratic Union of Belarus, centrist; Communist Party, left-wing
products peat, agricultural machinery, fertilizers, glass, textiles, leather, salt, electrical goods, meat, dairy produce
currency rouble and dukat
population (1992) 10,321,000 (77% Byelorussian "Eastern Slavs," 13% Russian, 4% Polish, 1% Jewish)
languages Byelorussian, Russian
religions Roman Catholic, Russian Orthodox, with Baptist and Muslim minorities

chronology
1918–19 Briefly independent from Russia.
1937–41 More than 100,000 people were shot in mass executions ordered by Stalin.
1941–44 Occupied by Nazi Germany.
1945 Became a founding member of the United Nations.
1986 April: fallout from the Chernobyl nuclear reactor in Ukraine contaminated a large area.
1989 Byelorussian Popular Front established as well as a more extreme nationalist organization, the Tolaka group.
1990 Sept: Byelorussian established as state language and republican sovereignty declared.
1991 April: Minsk hit by nationalist-backed general strike. Aug: declared independence from Soviet Union; Communist Party suspended. Sept: reformist Shushkevich elected president. Dec: Commonwealth of Independent States formed in Minsk; Belarus accorded diplomatic recognition by US.
1992 Jan: admitted into Conference on Security and Cooperation in Europe. May: protocols signed with US agreeing to honor START disarmament treaty.

history Spain held the islands from about 1600, and sold them to Germany 1899. Japan seized them in World War I, administered them by League of Nations mandate, and used them as a naval base during World War II. They were captured by the US 1944, and became part of the US Trust Territory of the Pacific Islands three years later. Belau became internally self-governing 1980. It is the only remaining member of the Trust Territory.

bel canto (Italian "beautiful song") in music, an 18th-century Italian style of singing with emphasis on perfect technique and beautiful tone. The style reached its peak in the operas of Rossini, Donizetti, and Bellini.

Belfast industrial port (shipbuilding, engineering, electronics, textiles, tobacco) and capital of Northern Ireland since 1920; population (1985) 300,000 (Protestants form the majority in E Belfast, Catholics in the W). Since 1968 the city has been heavily damaged by civil disturbances.

Belgium country in W Europe, bounded N by the Netherlands, NW by the North Sea, S and W by France, E by Luxembourg and Germany.

Belgrade (Serbo-Croatian *Beograd*) capital of Yugoslavia and Serbia, and Danube river port linked with the port of Bar on the Adriatic Sea; population (1981) 1,470,000. Industries include light engineering, food processing, textiles, pharmaceuticals, and electrical goods.

Belisarius *c.* 505–565. Roman general under Emperor ◊Justinian I. He won major victories over the Persians in 530 and the Vandals in 533 when he sacked Carthage. Later he invaded Sicily and fought a series of campaigns against the Goths in Italy.

Belize country in Central America, bounded N by Mexico, W and S by Guatemala, and E by the Caribbean Sea.

Belize City chief port of Belize, and capital until 1970; population (1991) 46,000. After the city was destroyed by a hurricane 1961 it was decided to move the capital inland, to Belmopan.

Bell Alexander Graham 1847–1922. Scottish-born US scientist and inventor of the telephone. He patented his invention 1876, and later experimented with a type of

Belgium Kingdom of (French *Royaume de Belgique*, Flemish *Koninkrijk België*)

area 11,784 sq mi/30,510 sq km
capital Brussels
cities Ghent, Liège, Charleroi, Bruges, Mons, Namur, Leuven; ports are Antwerp, Ostend, Zeebrugge
physical fertile coastal plain in NW, central rolling hills rise eastward, hills and forest in SE
environment a 1989 government report judged the drinking water in Flanders to be "seriously substandard" and more than half the rivers and canals in that region to be in a "very bad" condition
features Ardennes Forest; rivers Scheldt and Meuse
head of state King Albert from 1993
head of government Jean-Luc Dehaene from 1992
political system liberal democracy
political parties Flemish Christian Social Party (CVP), center-left; French Social Christian Party (PSC), center-left; Flemish Socialist Party (SP), left of center; French Socialist Party (PS), left of center; Flemish Liberal Party (PVV), moderate centrist; French Liberal Reform Party (PRL), moderate centrist; Flemish People's Party (VU), federalist; Flemish Green Party (Agalev); French Green Party (Ecolo)
exports iron, steel, textiles, manufactured goods, petrochemicals, plastics, vehicles, diamonds
currency Belgian franc

population (1992) 10,021,000 (comprising Flemings and Walloons); growth rate 0.1% p.a.
life expectancy men 72, women 78
languages in the N (Flanders) Flemish (a Dutch dialect, known as *Vlaams*) 55%; in the S (Wallonia) Walloon (a French dialect) 32%; bilingual 11%; German (E border) 0.6%; all are official
religion Roman Catholic 75%
literacy 98% (1984)
GDP $218.7 bn (1992)

chronology
1830 Belgium became an independent kingdom.
1914 Invaded by Germany.
1940 Again invaded by Germany.
1948 Belgium became founding member of Benelux Customs Union.
1949 Belgium became founding member of Council of Europe and NATO.
1951 Leopold III abdicated in favor of his son Baudouin.
1952 Belgium became founding member of European Coal and Steel Community.
1957 Belgium became founding member of the European Economic Community.
1971 Steps toward regional autonomy taken.
1972 German-speaking members included in the cabinet for the first time.
1973 Linguistic parity achieved in government appointments.
1974 Leo Tindemans became prime minister. Separate regional councils and ministerial committees established.
1978 Wilfried Martens succeeded Tindemans as prime minister.
1980 Open violence over language divisions. Regional assemblies for Flanders and Wallonia and a three-member executive for Brussels created.
1981 Short-lived coalition led by Mark Eyskens was followed by the return of Martens.
1987 Martens head of caretaker government after breakup of coalition.
1988 Following a general election, Martens formed a new CVP–PS–SP–PSC–VU coalition.
1992 Martens-led coalition collapsed; Jean-Luc Dehaene formed a new CVP-led coalition.
1993 Federal system adopted, based on Flanders, Wallonia, and Brussels. King Baudoin died and was succeeded by his brother Prince Albert of Liege.

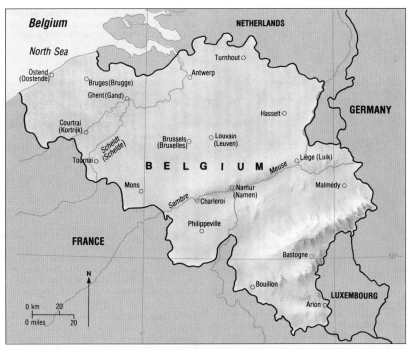

Belgium

North Sea

NETHERLANDS

Turnhout ○

Ostend ○
(Oostende)
Bruges (Brugge) ○
Antwerp ○

Ghent (Gand) ○

Hasselt ○

GERMANY

Courtrai
(Kortrijk) ○
Brussels ○
(Bruxelles)
Louvain ○
(Leuven)

Scheldt
(Schelde)
Tournai ○
Liège (Luik) ○
Meuse

B E L G I U M

Mons ○
Namur ○
(Namen)
Malmédy ○

Sambre
Charleroi ○

Philippeville ○

FRANCE

N

Bastogne ○

Bouillon ○

LUXEMBOURG
Arlon ○

0 km   20
0 miles   20

Belize
(formerly **British Honduras**)

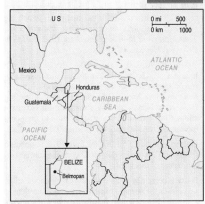

US

0 mi   500
0 km   1000

ATLANTIC
OCEAN

Mexico

Honduras

Guatemala
CARIBBEAN
SEA

PACIFIC
OCEAN

BELIZE
● Belmopan

area 8,864 sq mi/22,963 sq km
capital Belmopan
cities ports Belize City, Dangriga, Punta Gorda; Orange
Walk, Corozal
physical tropical swampy coastal plain, Maya Mountains in
S; over 90% forested
environment since 1981 Belize has developed an extensive
system of national parks and reserves to protect large areas
of tropical forest, coastal mangrove, and offshore islands.
Forestry has been replaced by agriculture and ecotourism,
which are now the most important sectors of the economy;
world's first jaguar reserve created 1986 in the Cockscomb
Mountains
features world's second longest barrier reef; Maya ruins
head of state Elizabeth II from 1981, represented by governor-general

head of government Manuel Esquivel from 1993
political system constitutional monarchy
political parties People's United Party (PUP), left of center;
United Democratic Party (UDP), moderate conservative
exports sugar, citrus fruits, rice, fish products, bananas
currency Belize dollar
population (1992) 196,000 (including Mayan minority in
the interior); growth rate 2.5% p.a.
life expectancy (1988) 60
languages English (official); Spanish (widely spoken),
native Creole dialects
media no daily newspaper; several independent weekly
tabloids
religions Roman Catholic 60%, Protestant 35%
literacy 93% (1988)
GDP $247 million (1988); $1,220 per head

chronology
1862 Belize (British Honduras) became a British colony.
1954 Constitution adopted, providing for limited internal
self-government. General election won by George Price.
1964 Self-government achieved from the UK (universal
adult suffrage introduced).
1965 Two-chamber national assembly introduced, with
Price as prime minister.
1970 Capital moved from Belize City to Belmopan.
1973 British Honduras became Belize.
1975 British troops sent to defend the disputed frontier with
Guatemala.
1980 United Nations called for full independence.
1981 Full independence achieved. Price became prime
minister.
1984 Price defeated in general election. Manuel Esquivel
formed the government. The UK reaffirmed its undertaking to
defend the frontier.
1989 Price and the PUP won the general election.
1991 Diplomatic relations with Guatemala established.
1993 In general election UDP defeated PUP. Manuel
Esquivel returned as prime minister.

Bell Alexander Graham Bell, Scottish scientist and inventor of the telephone.

phonograph and, in aeronautics, invented the tricycle undercarriage.

Born in Edinburgh, Bell was educated at the universities of Edinburgh and London and studied under his father, who developed a method for teaching the deaf to speak. In 1870 the family moved to Canada and Bell came to the US, where he opened a school 1872 for teachers of the deaf in Boston. In 1873 he began teaching vocal physiology at Boston University. He became a US citizen 1882. Bell also worked on converting sea water to drinking water and on air conditioning and sheep breeding.

belladonna or *deadly nightshade* poisonous plant *Atropa belladonna*, found in Europe and Asia. The dried powdered leaves contain ◊alkaloids. Belladonna extract acts medicinally as an anticholinergic (blocking the passage of certain nerve impulses), and is highly toxic in large doses.

Bellamy Edward 1850–1898. US author and social critic. In 1888, deeply concerned with the social problems of the day, he published *Looking Backward: 2000–1887*, a utopian novel. A huge bestseller, it inspired wide public support for Bellamy's political program of state socialism. He published a second utopian novel, *Equality* 1897.

Belleville city in SW Illinois, SE of East St Louis; seat of St Clair County; population (1990) 42,800. Industries include coal, beer, furnaces and boilers, and clothing.

bellflower general name for many plants of the family Campanulaceae, especially those of the genus *Campanula*. The white, pink, or blue flowers are bell-shaped and showy. The varied leaf bluebell *C. rotundifolia* grows in northern North America and Europe.

Bellingham city and port in NW Washington, just S of the Canadian border, on Bellingham Bay in the Strait of Georgia; population (1990) 52,180. It is a port of entry for the logging and paper industry; there are also shipbuilding and food processing industries.

Bellini family of Italian Renaissance painters. Jacopo and his sons Gentile and Giovanni were founders of the Venetian school in the 15th and early 16th centuries.

Bellini Vincenzo 1801–1835. Italian opera composer whose lyrical, melodic treatments of classic themes include *La Sonnambula* 1831, *Norma* 1831, and *I Puritani* 1835.

Bellow Saul 1915– . Canadian-born US novelist. Novels such as *Herzog* 1964, *Humboldt's Gift* 1975, and *The Dean's December* 1982 show his method of inhabiting the consciousness of a central character, frequently a Jewish-American intellectual, to portray an individual's frustration with the ongoing events of an indifferent society. His finely styled works and skilled characterizations won him the Nobel Prize for Literature 1976. Later works include *Him with His Foot in His Mouth* (1984) and *More Die of Heartbreak* (1987).

Bellow moved 1924 to the US with this family and graduated from Northwestern University 1937. He taught at various colleges, including Princeton, Bard, and the University of Chicago. He won the National Book Award 1954, 1965, and 1971 and a Pulitzer prize 1976.

Bellows George Wesley 1882–1925. US painter known for the vigorous style of his portrayals of the drama of street life and sport. His most famous works, such as *Stag at Sharkey's* 1909, show the violence and excitement of illegal boxing matches. Taught by Robert ◊Henri, he became the youngest academician of his time.

Bell's theorem hypothesis of British physicist John Bell, that an unknown force, of which space, time, and motion are all aspects, continues to link separate parts of the universe that were once united, and that this force travels faster than the speed of light.

Belmondo Jean-Paul 1933– . French film actor who became a star in Jean-Luc Godard's *A bout de souffle/Breathless* 1959. He is best known for his racy personality in French vehicles, many of which he produced. His other films include *Cartouche* 1962, *That Man from Rio* 1964, *The Brain* 1968, *Borsalino* 1970, and *Stavisky* 1974.

Belmont August 1816–1890. German-born US financier, who became the ◊Rothschilds' exclusive representative in the US when he established a private bank in New York 1837. Belmont was a leading member of New York City society's most exclusive clique (the "400") and was instrumental in financing the costs of the Mexican War (1846–48).

Belmopan capital of ◊Belize from 1970; population (1991) 4,000. It replaced Belize City as the administrative center of the country.

Belo Horizonte industrial city (steel, engineering, textiles) in SE Brazil, capital of the fast-developing state of Minas Gerais; population (1991) 2,103,300. Built in the 1890s, it was Brazil's first planned modern city.

Beloit city in SE Wisconsin, on the Rock River, SE of Madison; population (1990) 35,600. Industries include electrical machinery, shoes, generators, and diesel engines.

Belorussia alternate form of ◊Belarus, a country in E central Europe.

Belsen site of a Nazi ◊concentration camp in Lower Saxony, Germany.

Belshazzar in the Old Testament, the last king of Babylon, son of Nebuchadnezzar. During a feast (known as *Belshazzar's Feast*) he saw a message, interpreted by ◊Daniel as prophesying the fall of Babylon and death of Belshazzar.

All of this is said to have happened on the same night that the city was invaded by the Medes and Persians (539 BC).

Bemba member of a people native to NE Zambia and neighboring areas of Zaire and Zimbabwe, although many reside in urban areas such as Lusaka and Copperbelt. They number about three million. The Bemba language belongs to the Bantu branch of the Niger–Congo family.

Ben Ali Zine el Abidine 1936– . Tunisian politician, president from 1987. After training in France and the US, he returned to Tunisia and became director-general of national security. He was made minister of the interior and then prime minister under the aging president for life, Habib ◊Bourguiba, whom he deposed 1987 by a bloodless coup with the aid of ministerial colleagues. He ended the personality cult established by Bourguiba and moved toward a pluralist political system.

Benares alternative transliteration of ◊Varanasi, a holy city in India.

Ben Bella Ahmed 1916– . Algerian politician. He was leader of the National Liberation Front (FLN) from 1952, the first prime minister of independent Algeria 1962–63, and its first president 1963–65. In 1965 Ben Bella was overthrown by Col Houari ◊Boumédienne and detained until 1979. In 1985 he founded a new party, Mouvement pour la Démocratie en Algérie, and returned to Algeria 1990 after nine years in exile.

bends popular name for a paralytic affliction of deep-sea divers, arising from too rapid a release of nitrogen from solution in their blood. If a diver surfaces too quickly, nitrogen that had dissolved in the blood under increasing water pressure is suddenly released, forming bubbles in the bloodstream and causing paralysis. Immediate treatment is compression and slow decompression in a special chamber.

Benedictine order religious order of monks and nuns in the Roman Catholic Church, founded by St ◊Benedict at Subiaco, Italy, in the 6th century. It had a strong influence on medieval learning and reached the height of its prosperity early in the 14th century.

There are Benedictine monasteries in the US in Latrobe, Pennsylvania, and St Meinrad, Indiana. In 1985 there were 9,453 monks and 7,911 nuns living in Benedictine convents.

Benedict, St c. 480–c. 547. Founder of Christian monasticism in the West and of the ◊Benedictine order. He founded the monastery of Monte Cassino, Italy. Here he wrote out his rule for monastic life, and was visited shortly before his death by the Ostrogothic king Totila, whom he converted to the Christian faith. His feast day is July 11.

benefice in the early Middle Ages, a donation of land or money to the Christian church as an act of devotion; from the 12th century, the term came to mean the income enjoyed by clergy.

Benelux (acronym from *Belgium, the Netherlands, and Luxembourg*) customs union agreed by Belgium, the Netherlands, and Luxembourg 1948, fully effective 1960. It was the precursor of the European Community.

Beneš Eduard 1884–1948. Czechoslovak politician. He worked with Tomáš ◊Masaryk toward Czechoslovak nationalism from 1918 and was foreign minister and representative at the League of Nations. He was president of the republic from 1935 until forced to resign by the Germans; he headed a government in exile in London during World War II. He returned home as president 1945 but resigned again after the Communist coup 1948.

Bengal former province of British India, divided 1947 into ◊West Bengal, a state of India, and East Bengal, from 1972 ◊Bangladesh. A famine in 1943, caused by a slump in demand for jute and a bad harvest, resulted in over 3 million deaths.

Bengal, Bay of part of the Indian Ocean lying between the east coast of India and the west coast of Myanmar (Burma) and the Malay Peninsula. The Irrawaddy, Ganges, and Brahmaputra rivers flow into the bay. The principal islands are to be found in the Andaman and Nicobar groups.

Bengali person of Bengali culture from Bangladesh and India (W Bengal, Tripura). There are 80–150 million speakers of Bengali, an Indo-Iranian language belonging to the Indo-European family. It is the official language of Bangladesh and of the state of Bengal and is also used by emigrant Bangladeshi and Bengali communities in such countries as the US and the UK. Bengalis in Bangladesh are predominantly Muslim, whereas those in India are mainly Hindu.

Benghazi or *Banghazi* historic city and industrial port in N Libya on the Gulf of Sirte; population (1982) 650,000. It was controlled by Turkey between the 16th century and 1911, and by Italy 1911–42; it was a major naval supply base during World War II.

Ben-Gurion David. Adopted name of David Gruen 1886–1973. Israeli statesman and socialist politician, one of the founders of the state of Israel, the country's first prime minister 1948–53, and again 1955–63.

Benin country in W Africa, bounded E by Nigeria, N by Niger and Burkina Faso, W by Togo, and S by the Gulf of Guinea. *See panel p. 108*

Benin former African kingdom 1200–1897, now a province of Nigeria. It reached the height of its power in the 14th–17th centuries when it ruled the area between the Niger Delta and Lagos.

Benjamin Judah Philip 1811–1884. US Confederate official. Holding office in the US Senate 1852–61, he

Bellini The Doge Leonardo Loredan (c. 1501), painted by Giovanni Bellini, National Gallery, London.

Benin People's Republic of
(*République Populaire du Bénin*)

area 43,472 sq mi/112,622 sq km
capital Porto Novo (official), Cotonou (de facto)
cities Abomey, Natitingou, Parakou; chief port Cotonou
physical flat to undulating terrain; hot and humid in S; semiarid in N
features coastal lagoons with fishing villages on stilts; Niger River in NE
head of state and government Nicéphore Soglo from 1991
political system socialist pluralist republic
political parties Party of the People's Revolution of Benin (PRPB); other parties from 1990

exports cocoa, peanuts, cotton, palm oil, petroleum, cement, sea products
currency CFA franc
population (1992) 4,928,000; growth rate 3% p.a.
life expectancy men 42, women 46
languages French (official); Fon 47% and Yoruba 9% in south; six major tribal languages in north
religions animist 65%, Christian 17%, Muslim 13%
literacy men 37%, women 16% (1985 est)
GDP $1.6 bn (1987); $365 per head

chronology
1851 Under French control.
1958 Became self-governing dominion within the French Community.
1960 Independence achieved from France.
1960–72 Acute political instability, with switches from civilian to military rule.
1972 Military regime established by General Mathieu Kerekou.
1974 Kerekou announced that the country would follow a path of "scientific socialism."
1975 Name of country changed from Dahomey to Benin.
1977 Return to civilian rule under a new constitution.
1980 Kerekou formally elected president by the national revolutionary assembly.
1989 Marxist-Leninism dropped as official ideology. Strikes and protests against Kerekou's rule mounted; demonstrations banned and army deployed against protesters.
1990 Referendum support for multiparty politics.
1991 Multiparty elections held. Kerekou defeated in presidential elections by Nicéphore Soglo.

was a proponent of secession of the South and resigned from office at the outbreak of the American Civil War. As one of the leaders of the Confederacy, he served as attorney general, secretary of war, and secretary of state.

Ben Nevis highest mountain in the British Isles (4,406 ft/1,343 m), in the Grampian Mountains, Scotland.

bent or **bent grass** any grasses of the genus *Agrostis*. Creeping bent grass *A. stolonifera*, also known as fiorin, is common in N North America and Eurasia, including lowland Britain. It spreads by ◊stolons and bears large attractive panicles of yellow or purple flowers on thin stalks. It is often used on lawns and golf courses.

Bentham Jeremy 1748–1832. English philosopher, legal and social reformer, and founder of ◊utilitarianism. The essence of his moral philosophy is found in the pronouncement of his *Principles of Morals and Legislation* (written 1780, published 1789): that the object of all legislation should be "the greatest happiness for the greatest number."

Benton Thomas Hart 1782–1858. US political leader. He was elected to the US Senate 1820, where he served for the next 30 years. He distinguished himself as an outspoken opponent of the Bank of the United States and the extension of slavery as well as a strong supporter of westward expansion.

Benton Harbor city in SW Michigan, NE of Chicago, Illinois, which is across Lake Michigan; population (1990) 12,820. Industries include iron and other metal products and food processing. The religious sect, House of David, was established here 1903.

Benz Karl Friedrich 1844–1929. German automobile engineer who produced the world's first gasoline-driven motor vehicle. He built his first model engine 1878 and the gasoline-driven automobile 1885.

benzene C_6H_6 clear liquid hydrocarbon of characteristic odor, occurring in coal tar. It is used as a solvent and in the synthesis of many chemicals.

benzoic acid C_6H_5COOH white crystalline solid, sparingly soluble in water, that is used as a preservative for certain foods and as an antiseptic. It is obtained chemically by the direct oxidation of benzaldehyde and occurs in certain natural resins, some essential oils, and as hippuric acid.

Beowulf Anglo-Saxon poem (composed *c.* 700), the only complete surviving example of Germanic folk epic. It exists in a single manuscript copied about 1000 in the Cottonian collection of the British Museum.

Berber member of a non-Semitic Caucasoid people of North Africa who since prehistoric times inhabited Barbary, the Mediterranean coastlands from Egypt to the Atlantic. Their language, present-day Berber (a member of the Afro-Asiatic language family), is spoken by about one-third of Algerians and nearly two-thirds of Moroccans, 10 million people. Berbers are mainly agricultural, but some are still nomadic.

Bérégovoy Pierre 1925–1993. French socialist politician, prime minister from 1992. A close ally of François ◊Mitterrand, he was named Chief of Staff 1981 after managing the successful presidential campaign. He was social affairs minister 1982–84 and finance minister 1984–86 and 1988–92.

Berg Alban 1885–1935. Austrian composer. He studied under Arnold ◊Schoenberg and was associated with him as one of the leaders of the serial, or 12-tone, school of composition. His output includes orchestral, chamber, and vocal music as well as two operas, *Wozzeck* 1925, a grim story of working-class life, and the unfinished *Lulu* 1929–35.

Berg Paul 1926– . US molecular biologist. In 1972, using gene-splicing techniques developed by others,

Berg spliced and combined into a single hybrid ◊DNA from an animal tumor virus (SV40) and DNA from a bacterial virus. Berg's work aroused fears in other workers and excited continuing controversy. For his work on recombinant DNA, he shared the 1980 Nobel Prize for Chemistry with Walter ◊Gilbert and Frederick ◊Sanger.

Bergius Friedrich Karl Rudolph 1884–1949. German research chemist who invented processes for converting coal into oil and wood into sugar. He shared a Nobel Prize 1931 with Carl Bosch for his part in inventing and developing high-pressure industrial methods.

Bergman Ingmar 1918– . Swedish stage producer (from the 1930s) and film director (from the 1950s), regarded by many as one of the great masters of modern cinema. His work deals with complex moral, psychological, and metaphysical problems and is tinged with pessimism. His films include *Wild Strawberries* 1957, *The Seventh Seal* 1957, *Persona* 1966, *Autumn Sonata* 1978, and *Fanny and Alexander* 1982.

Bergman Ingrid 1917–1982. Swedish actress whose films include *Intermezzo* 1939, *Casablanca* 1943, *For Whom the Bell Tolls* 1943, and *Gaslight* 1944, for which she won an Academy Award.

Beria Lavrenti 1899–1953. Soviet politician who in 1938 became minister of the interior and head of the Soviet police force that imprisoned, liquidated, and transported millions of Soviet citizens. On Stalin's death 1953, he attempted to seize power but was foiled and shot after a secret trial. Apologists for Stalin have blamed Beria for the atrocities committed by Soviet police during Stalin's dictatorship.

Bering Vitus 1681–1741. Danish explorer, the first European to sight Alaska. He died on Bering Island in the Bering Sea, both named after him, as is the Bering Strait, which separates Asia (Russia) from North America (Alaska).

Bering Sea section of the N Pacific between Alaska and Siberia, from the Aleutian Islands north to the Bering Strait.

Bering Strait strait between Alaska and Siberia, linking the N Pacific and Arctic oceans.

Berkeley city on San Francisco Bay in California; population (1990) 102,700. It is the site of an acclaimed branch of the University of California, noted for its nuclear research at the Lawrence Berkeley Laboratory. Berkeley was settled 1853.

Berkeley Busby. Adopted name of William Berkeley Enos 1895–1976. US choreographer and film director who used ingenious and extravagant sets and teams of female dancers to create large-scale kaleidoscopic patterns through movement and costume when filmed from above, as in *Gold Diggers of 1933* and *Footlight Parade* 1933.

Berkeley Sir William 1606–1677. British colonial administrator in North America, governor of the colony of Virginia 1641–77. Siding with the Royalists during the English Civil War, he was removed from the governorship by Oliver Cromwell 1652. He was reappointed 1660 by Charles II after the Restoration of the monarchy. However, growing opposition to him in the colony culminated in ◊Bacon's Rebellion 1676 and in 1677 Berkeley was removed from office for his brutal repression of that uprising.

He was knighted by Charles I in 1639.

berkelium synthesized, radioactive, metallic element of the actinide series, symbol Bk, atomic number 97, atomic weight 247.

It was first produced 1949 by Glenn Seaborg and his team, at the University of California at Berkeley, after which it is named.

Berlin industrial city (machine tools, electrical goods, paper, printing) and capital of the Federal Republic of Germany; population (1990) 3,102,500. The Berlin Wall divided the city from 1961 to 1989, but in Oct 1990 Berlin became the capital of a unified Germany, once more with East and West Berlin reunited as the 16th *Land* (state) of the Federal Republic.

Berlin Irving. Adopted name of Israel Baline 1888–1989. Russian-born US songwriter whose more than 1,500 songs include such hits as "Alexander's Ragtime Band" 1911, "Always" 1925, "God Bless America" 1917 (published 1939), and "White Christmas" 1942, and the musicals *Top Hat* 1935, *Annie Get Your Gun* 1946, and *Call Me Madam* 1950. He also provided songs for films like *Blue Skies* 1946 and *Easter Parade* 1948.

Berlin blockade in June 1948, the closing of entry to Berlin from the west by Soviet forces. It was an attempt to prevent the other Allies (the US, France, and the UK) unifying the western part of Germany. The British and US forces responded by sending supplies to the city by air for over a year (the *Berlin airlift*). In May 1949 the blockade was lifted; the airlift continued until Sept. The blockade marked the formal division of the city into Eastern and Western sectors.

Berlin, Congress of congress of the European powers (Russia, Turkey, Austria–Hungary, the UK,

Berlin 1945–89

French sector		US sector
British sector		Soviet sector

Berlin Wall The day after the breaching of the Berlin Wall on Nov 9, 1989, unarmed East German soldiers were positioned at the Brandenburg Gate.

France, Italy, and Germany) held in Berlin 1878 to determine the boundaries of the Balkan states after the Russo-Turkish war 1877–78.

Berlin Wall dividing barrier between East and West Berlin 1961–89, erected by East Germany to prevent East Germans from leaving for West Germany. Escapers were shot on sight.

Berlioz (Louis) Hector 1803–1869. French romantic composer, the founder of modern orchestration.

Much of his music was inspired by drama and literature and has a theatrical quality. He wrote symphonic works, such as *Symphonie fantastique* 1830–31 and *Roméo et Juliette* 1839; dramatic cantatas including *La Damnation de Faust* 1846 and *L'Enfance du Christ* 1854; sacred music; and three operas.

berm on a beach, a ridge of sand or pebbles running parallel to the water's edge, formed by the action of the waves on beach material. Sand and pebbles are deposited at the farthest extent of swash (advance of water) on that particular beach. Berms can also be formed well up a beach following a storm, when they are known as *storm berms*.

Bermuda British colony in the NW Atlantic Ocean
area 21 sq mi/54 sq km
capital and chief port Hamilton
features consists of about 150 small islands, of which 20 are inhabited, linked by bridges and causeways; Britain's oldest colony
products Easter lilies, pharmaceuticals; tourism and banking are important
currency Bermuda dollar
population (1988) 58,100
language English
religion Christian
government under the constitution of 1968, Bermuda is a fully self-governing British colony, with a governor (Lord Waddington from 1992), senate, and elected House of Assembly (premier from 1982 John Swan, United Bermuda Party)
history the islands were named after Juan de Bermudez, who visited them 1515 and were settled by British colonists 1609. Indian and African slaves were transported from 1616 and soon outnumbered the white settlers. Racial violence 1977 led to intervention, at the request of the government, by British troops.

Bern (French *Berne*) capital of Switzerland and of Bern canton, in W Switzerland on the Aare River; population (1990) 134,600; canton 945,600. It joined the Swiss confederation 1353 and became the capital 1848. Industries include textiles, chocolate, pharmaceuticals, light metal and electrical goods.

Bernadette, St 1844–1879. French saint, born in ◊Lourdes in the French Pyrenees. In Feb 1858 she had a vision of the Virgin Mary in a grotto, and it became a center of pilgrimage. Many sick people who were dipped in the water of a spring there were said to have been cured. Her feast day is April 16.

Bernadotte Jean-Baptiste Jules 1764–1844. Marshal in Napoleon's army who in 1818 became ◊Charles XIV of Sweden. Hence, Bernadotte is the family name of the present royal house of Sweden.

Bernard Claude 1813–1878. French physiologist and founder of experimental medicine. Bernard first demonstrated that digestion is not restricted to the stomach, but takes place throughout the small intestine. He discovered the digestive input of the pancreas, several functions of the liver, and the vasomotor nerves which dilate and contract the blood vessels and thus regulate body temperature. This led him to the concept of the *milieu intérieur* ("internal environment") whose stability is essential to good health.

Bernard of Clairvaux, St 1090–1153. Christian founder in 1115 of Clairvaux monastery in Champagne, France. He reinvigorated the ◊Cistercian order, preached in support of the Second Crusade in 1146, and had the scholastic philosopher Abelard condemned for heresy. He is often depicted with a beehive. His feast day is Aug 20.

Bernard of Menthon, St or *Bernard of Montjoux* 923–1008. Christian priest, founder of the hospices for travelers on the Alpine passes that bear his name. The large, heavily built *St Bernard* dogs, formerly employed to find travelers lost in the snow, were also named after him. He is the patron saint of mountaineers. His feast day is May 28.

Bernhardt Sarah. Adopted name of Rosine Bernard 1845–1923. French actress who dominated the stage of her day, frequently performing at the Comédie-Française in Paris. She excelled in tragic roles, including Cordelia in Shakespeare's *King Lear*, the title role in Racine's *Phèdre*, and the male roles of Hamlet and of Napoleon's son in Edmond ◊Rostand's *L'Aiglon*.

Bernini Giovanni Lorenzo 1598–1680. Italian sculptor, architect, and painter, a leading figure in the development of the Baroque style. His work in Rome includes the colonnaded piazza in front of St Peter's Basilica (1656), fountains (as in the Piazza Navona), and papal monuments. His sculpture includes *The Ecstasy of St Theresa* 1645–52 (Sta Maria della Vittoria, Rome) and numerous portrait busts.

Bernoulli's principle law stating that the speed of a fluid varies inversely with pressure, an increase in speed producing a decrease in pressure (such as a drop in hydraulic pressure as the fluid speeds up flowing through a constriction in a pipe) and vice versa. The principle also explains the pressure differences on

Bermuda

each surface of an airfoil, which gives lift to the wing of an aircraft. The principle was named after Swiss mathematician and physicist Daniel Bernoulli.

Bernstein Leonard 1918–1990. US composer, conductor, and pianist, one of the most energetic and versatile of US musicians in the 20th century. His works, which established a vogue for realistic, contemporary themes, include symphonies such as *The Age of Anxiety* 1949, ballets such as *Fancy Free* 1944, and scores for musicals, including *Wonderful Town* 1953, *West Side Story* 1957, and *Mass* 1971 in memory of President J F Kennedy.

Born in Lawrence, Massachusetts, he was educated at Harvard University and the Curtis Institute of Music. From 1958 to 1970 he was musical director of the New York Philharmonic. Among his other works are *Jeremiah* 1944, *Facsimile* 1946, *Candide* 1956, and the *Chichester Psalms* 1965.

berry fleshy, many-seeded ◊fruit that does not split open to release the seeds. The outer layer of tissue, the exocarp, forms an outer skin that is often brightly colored to attract birds to eat the fruit and thus disperse the seeds. Examples of berries are the tomato and the grape.

Berry Chuck (Charles) 1926– . US musician. He made his first recording, of the song "Maybellene," at Chess Records in Chicago 1955. Widely promoted by New York disk jockey Alan Freed, it became an early rock-and-roll classic. Recognized as one of the fathers of rock and roll, Berry enjoyed a revival of popularity in the 1970s and 1980s.

Bertolucci Bernardo 1940– . Italian film director whose work combines political and historical perspectives with an elegant and lyrical visual appeal. His films include *The Spider's Stratagem* 1970, *Last Tango in Paris* 1972, *1900* 1976, *The Last Emperor* 1987 (for which he received an Academy Award), and *The Sheltering Sky* 1990.

beryl mineral, beryllium aluminum silicate, $Be_3Al_2Si_6O_{18}$, which forms crystals chiefly in granite. It is the chief ore of beryllium. Two of its gem forms are aquamarine (light-blue crystals) and emerald (dark-green crystals).

Well-formed crystals of up to 200 tons have been found.

beryllium hard, light-weight, silver-white, metallic element, symbol Be, atomic number 4, atomic weight 9.012. It is one of the ◊alkaline-earth metals, with chemical properties similar to those of magnesium; in nature it is found only in combination with other elements. It is used to make sturdy, light alloys and to control the speed of neutrons in nuclear reactors. Beryllium oxide was discovered in 1798 by French chemist Louis-Nicolas Vauquelin (1763–1829), but the element was not isolated until 1828, by Friedrich Wöhler and Antoine-Alexandre-Brutus Bussy independently.

The name comes from Latin *beryllus*.

Berzelius Jöns Jakob 1779–1848. Swedish chemist who accurately determined more than 2,000 relative atomic and molecular masses. He devised (1813–14) the system of chemical symbols and formulae now in use and proposed oxygen as a reference standard for atomic masses. His discoveries include the elements cerium (1804), selenium (1817), and thorium (1828); he was the first to prepare silicon in its amorphous form and to isolate zirconium. The words *isomerism allotropy*, and *protein* were coined by him.

Berry The rock and roll songs of Chuck Berry are classics of the genre.

Bessarabia region in SE Europe, divided between Moldova and Ukraine. Bessarabia was annexed by Russia 1812, but broke away at the Russian Revolution to join Romania. The cession was confirmed by the Allies, but not by Russia, in a Paris treaty of 1920; the USSR reoccupied it 1940 and divided it between the Moldavian and Ukrainian republics (now independent Moldova and Ukraine). Romania recognized the position in the 1947 peace treaty.

Bessel Friedrich Wilhelm 1784–1846. German astronomer and mathematician, the first person to find the approximate distance to a star by direct methods when he measured the ◊parallax (annual displacement) of the star 61 Cygni in 1838. In mathematics, he introduced the series of functions now known as *Bessel functions*.

Bessemer process the first cheap method of making ◊steel, invented by Henry Bessemer in England 1856. It has since been superseded by more efficient steel-making processes, such as the basic-oxygen process. In the Bessemer process compressed air is blown into the bottom of a converter, a furnace shaped like a cement mixer, containing molten pig iron. The excess carbon in the iron burns out, other impurities form a slag, and the furnace is emptied by tilting.

beta-blocker any of a class of drugs that block impulses that stimulate certain nerve endings (beta receptors) serving the heart muscles. This reduces the heart rate and the force of contraction, which in turn reduces the amount of oxygen (and therefore the blood supply) required by the heart. Beta-blockers are banned from use in competitive sports. They may be useful in the treatment of angina, arrhythmia, and raised blood pressure, and following myocardial infarctions. They must be withdrawn from use gradually.

beta particle electron ejected with great velocity from a radioactive atom that is undergoing spontaneous disintegration. Beta particles do not exist in the nucleus but are created on disintegration, *beta decay*, when a neutron converts to a proton to emit an electron. The process transforms one element into another, increasing the atomic number by one while the mass number remains the same.

Betelgeuse or *Alpha Orionis* red supergiant star in the constellation of Orion and the tenth brightest star in the sky, although its brightness varies. It is over 300 times the diameter of the Sun, about the same size as the orbit of Mars, is over 10,000 times as luminous as the Sun, and lies 650 light-years from Earth.

betel nut fruit of the areca palm *Areca catechu*, used together with lime and betel pepper as a masticatory stimulant by peoples of the East and Papua New Guinea. Chewing it results in blackened teeth and a mouth stained deep red.

Bethe Hans Albrecht 1906– . German-born US physicist who worked on the first atomic bomb. He was awarded a Nobel Prize 1967 for his discoveries concerning energy production in stars.

Bethlehem city in E Pennsylvania; population (1990) 71,428. Its former steel industry has been replaced by high technology. Lehigh University is here. Bethlehem was founded 1741 by German immigrants.

Bethlehem (Hebrew *Beit-Lahm*) town on the west bank of the river Jordan, S of Jerusalem; population (1980) 14,000. It was occupied by Israel 1967. In the Bible it is mentioned as the birthplace of King David and Jesus.

Bettelheim Bruno 1903–1990. Austrian-born US child psychologist. At the University of Chicago he founded a treatment center for emotionally disturbed children based on the principle of a supportive home environment. Among his most influential books are *Love Is Not Enough* 1950, *Truants from Life* 1954, and *Children of the Dream* 1962.

Bhagavad-Gītā (Hindu "the Song of the Blessed") religious and philosophical Sanskrit poem, dating from around 300 BC, forming an episode in the sixth book of the *Mahābhārata*, one of the two great Hindu epics. It is the supreme religious work of Hinduism.

Bhopal industrial city (textiles, chemicals, electrical goods, jewelry) and capital of Madhya Pradesh, central India; population (1981) 672,000. Nearby Bhimbetka Caves, discovered 1973, have the world's largest collection of prehistoric paintings, about 10,000 years old. In 1984 some 2,600 people died from an escape of the poisonous gas methyl isocyanate from a factory owned by US company Union Carbide; another 300,000 suffer from long-term health problems.

Bhumibol Adulyadej 1927– . King of Thailand from 1946. Born in the US and educated in Bangkok and Switzerland, he succeeded to the throne on the assassination of his brother. In 1973 he was active, with popular support, in overthrowing the military government of Marshal Thanom Kittikachorn and thus ended a sequence of army-dominated regimes in power from 1932.

Bhutan mountainous, landlocked country in the eastern Himalayas (SE Asia), bounded N and W by Tibet (China) and to the S and E by India.

Bhutto Benazir 1953– . Pakistani politician, leader of the Pakistan People's Party (PPP) from 1984 (in exile until 1986), and prime minister of Pakistan 1988–90, when the opposition maneuvered her from office and charged her with corruption. In May 1991 new charges were brought against her. She was the first female leader of a Muslim state.

Bhutto Zulfikar Ali 1928–1979. Pakistani politician, president 1971–73; prime minister from 1973 until the 1977 military coup led by General ◊Zia ul-Haq. In 1978 Bhutto was sentenced to death for conspiring to

Bhutan
Kingdom of (*Druk-yul*)

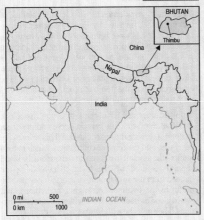

area 17,954 sq mi/46,500 sq km
capital Thimbu (Thimphu)
cities Paro, Punakha, Mongar
physical occupies southern slopes of the Himalayas; cut by valleys formed by tributaries of the Brahmaputra; thick forests in S
features Gangkar Punsum (24,700 ft/7,529 m) is one of the world's highest unclimbed peaks
head of state and government Jigme Singye Wangchuk from 1972
political system absolute monarchy

political parties none officially; illegal Bhutan People's Party (BPP)
exports timber, talc, fruit and vegetables, cement, distilled spirits, calcium carbide
currency ngultrum; also Indian currency
population (1992) 1,511,000; growth rate 2% p.a. (75% Ngalops and Sharchops, 25% Nepalese)
life expectancy men 44, women 43
languages Dzongkha (official, a Tibetan dialect), Sharchop, Bumthap, Nepali, and English
media one daily newspaper (*Kuensel*), published in Dzongkha, English, and Nepali editions; it gives the government's point of view
religions 75% Lamaistic Buddhist (state religion), 25% Hindu
literacy 5%
GDP $250 million (1987); $170 per head

chronology
1865 Trade treaty with Britain signed.
1907 First hereditary monarch installed.
1910 Anglo-Bhutanese Treaty signed.
1949 Indo-Bhutan Treaty of Friendship signed.
1952 King Jigme Dorji Wangchuk installed.
1953 National assembly established.
1959 4,000 Tibetan refugees given asylum.
1968 King established first cabinet.
1972 King died and was succeeded by his son Jigme Singye Wangchuk.
1979 Tibetan refugees told to take Bhutanese citizenship or leave; most stayed.
1983 Bhutan became a founding member of the South Asian Regional Association for Cooperation.
1988 King imposed "code of conduct" suppressing Nepalese customs.
1990 Hundreds of people allegedly killed during pro-democracy demonstrations.

The Bible

The Books of the Old Testament			The Books of the New Testament		
name of book	chapters	date written	name of book	chapters	date written
The Pentateuch or the Five Books of Moses			The Gospels		
Genesis	50	mid-8th century BC	Matthew	28	before AD 70
Exodus	40	950–586 BC	Mark	16	before AD 70
Leviticus	27	mid-7th century BC	Luke	24	AD 70–80
Numbers	36	850–650 BC	John	21	AD 90–100
Deuteronomy	34	mid-7th century BC	The Acts	28	AD 70–80
Joshua	24	c. 550 BC	Romans	16	AD 120
Judges	21	c. 550 BC	1 Corinthians	16	AD 57
Ruth	4	end 3rd century BC	2 Corinthians	13	AD 57
1 Samuel	31	c. 900 BC	Galatians	6	AD 53
2 Samuel	24	c. 900 BC	Ephesians	6	AD 140
1 Kings	22	550–600 BC	Philippians	4	AD 63
2 Kings	25	550–600 BC	Colossians	4	AD 140
1 Chronicles	29	c. 300 BC	1 Thessalonians	5	AD 50–54
2 Chronicles	36	c. 300 BC	2 Thessalonians	3	AD 50–54
Ezra	10	c. 450 BC	1 Timothy	6	before AD 64
Nehemiah	13	c. 450 BC	2 Timothy	4	before AD 64
Esther	10	c. 200 BC	Titus	3	before AD 64
Job	42	600–400 BC	Philemon	1	AD 60–62
Psalms	150	6th–2nd century BC	Hebrews	13	AD 80–90
Proverbs	31	350–150 BC	James	5	before AD 52
Ecclesiastes	12	c. 200 BC	1 Peter	5	before AD 64
Song of Solomon	8	3rd century BC	2 Peter	3	before AD 64
Isaiah	66	end 3rd century BC	1 John	5	AD 90–100
Jeremiah	52	604 BC	2 John	1	AD 90–100
Lamentations	5	586–536 BC	3 John	1	AD 90–100
Ezekiel	48	6th century BC	Jude	1	AD 75–80
Daniel	12	c. 166 BC	Revelation	22	AD 81–96
Hosea	14	c. 732 BC			
Joel	3	c. 500 BC			
Amos	9	775–750 BC			
Obadiah	1	6th–3rd century BC			
Jonah	4	600–200 BC			
Micah	7	end 3rd century BC			
Nahum	3	c. 626 BC			
Habakkuk	3	c. 600 BC			
Zephaniah	3	3rd century BC			
Haggai	2	c. 520 BC			
Zechariah	14	c. 520 BC			
Malachi	4	c. 430 BC			

murder a political opponent and was hanged the following year. He was the father of Benazir Bhutto.

Biafra, Republic of African state proclaimed in 1967 when fears that Nigerian central government was increasingly in the hands of the rival Hausa tribe led the predominantly Ibo Eastern Region of Nigeria to secede under Lt Col Odumegwu Ojukwu. On the proclamation of Biafra, civil war ensued with the rest of the federation. In a bitterly fought campaign federal forces confined the Biafrans to a shrinking area of the interior by 1968, and by 1970 Biafra ceased to exist.

Bible the sacred book of the Jewish and Christian religions. The Hebrew Bible, recognized by both Jews and Christians, is called the ◊*Old Testament* by Christians. The ◊*New Testament* comprises books recognized by the Christian church from the 4th century as canonical. The Roman Catholic Bible also includes the ◊*Apocrypha.*

bicarbonate of soda or *baking soda* (technical name *sodium hydrogencarbonate*) NaHCO$_3$ white crystalline solid that neutralizes acids and is used in medicine to treat acid indigestion. It is also used in baking powders and effervescent drinks.

Bichat Marie François Xavier 1771–1802. French physician and founder of ◊histology, the study of tissues. He studied the organs of the body, their structure, and the ways in which they are affected by disease. This led to his discovery and naming of "tissue," a basic biological and medical concept; he identified 21 types. He argued that disease does not affect the whole organ but only certain of its constituent tissues.

bicycle pedal-driven two-wheeled vehicle used in ◊cycling. It consists of a metal frame mounted on two large wire-spoked wheels, with handlebars in front and a seat between the front and back wheels. The bicycle is an energy-efficient, nonpolluting form of transport, and it is estimated that 800 million bicycles are in use throughout the world—outnumbering automobiles three to one. China, India, Denmark, and the Netherlands are countries with a high use of bicycles. More than 10% of road spending in the Netherlands is on cycleways and bicycle parking.

Biddle Nicholas 1786–1844. US financier and public figure. An expert in international commerce, he was appointed a director of the Bank of the United States by President James Monroe 1819 and became president of the bank 1822. An extreme fiscal conservative, Biddle became the focus of Andrew ◊Jackson's campaigns against the power of the bank in 1828 and 1832. After the withdrawal of the bank's federal charter 1836, he remained its president under a state charter.

biennial plant plant that completes its life cycle in two years. During the first year it grows vegetatively and the surplus food produced is stored in its perennating organ, usually the root. In the following year these food reserves are used for the production of leaves, flowers, and seeds, after which the plant dies. Many root vegetables are biennials, including the carrot *Daucus carota* and parsnip *Pastinaca sativa*. Some garden plants that are grown as biennials are actually perennials, for example, the wallflower *Cheiranthus cheiri*.

Bienville Jean Baptiste Le Moyne, Sieur de 1680–1768. French colonial administrator, governor of the North American colony of Louisiana 1706–13, 1717–23, and 1733–43. During his first term he founded the settlement at Mobile in Alabama and in his second term established the Louisiana colonial capital at New Orleans. During his final term Bienville was drawn into a costly and ultimately unsuccessful war with the Indians of the lower Mississippi Valley.

Bierstadt Albert 1830–1902. German-born US landscape painter. His spectacular panoramas of the American wilderness fell out of favor after his death until interest in the Hudson River School rekindled late in the century. A classic work is *Thunderstorm in the Rocky Mountains* 1859 (Museum of Fine Arts, Boston).

His *Discovery of the Hudson* hangs in the Capitol in Washington, DC.

big-band jazz ◊swing music created in the late 1930s and 1940s by bands of 13 or more players, such as those of Duke ◊Ellington and Benny ◊Goodman. Big-band jazz relied on fixed arrangements, where there is more than one instrument to some of the parts, rather than improvisation. Big bands were mainly dance bands, and they ceased to be economically viable in the 1950s.

Big Bang in astronomy, the hypothetical "explosive" event that marked the origin of the universe as we know it. At the time of the Big Bang, the entire universe was squeezed into a hot, superdense state. The Big Bang explosion threw this compacted material outward, producing the expanding universe (see ◊red shift). The cause of the Big Bang is unknown; observations of the current rate of expansion of the universe suggest that it took place about 10–20 billion years ago. The Big Bang theory began modern ◊cosmology.

Big Dipper American name for the seven brightest and most prominent stars in the constellation ◊Ursa Major, which in outline resemble a large dipper.

Bihar or *Behar* state of NE India
area 67,125 sq mi/ 173,900 sq km
capital Patna
features river Ganges in the N, Rajmahal Hills in the S
products copper, iron, coal, rice, jute, sugar cane, grain, oilseed
population (1991) 86,338,900
languages Hindi, Bihari
famous people Chandragupta, Asoka
history the ancient kingdom of Magadha roughly corresponded to central and S Bihar. Many Bihari people were massacred as a result of their protest at the establishment of Bangladesh 1971.

Bihari member of a N Indian people, also living in Bangladesh, Nepal, and Pakistan, and numbering over 40 million. The Bihari are mainly Muslim. The Bihari language is related to Hindi and has several widely varying dialects. It belongs to the Indic branch of the Indo-European family. Many Bihari were massacred during the formation of Bangladesh, which they opposed.

Bikini atoll in the ◊Marshall Islands, W Pacific, where the US carried out 23 atomic- and hydrogen-bomb tests (some underwater) 1946–58.

Biko Steve (Stephen) 1946–1977. South African civil-rights leader. An active opponent of ◊apartheid, he was arrested in Sept 1977; he died in detention six days later. After his death in the custody of South African police, he became a symbol of the antiapartheid movement.

bilateralism in economics, a trade agreement between two countries or groups of countries in which they give each other preferential treatment. Usually the terms agreed result in balanced trade and are favored by countries with limited foreign exchange reserves. Bilateralism is incompatible with free trade.

bile brownish fluid produced by the liver. In most vertebrates, it is stored in the gall bladder and emptied into the small intestine as food passes through. Bile consists of bile salts, bile pigments, cholesterol, and lecithin. *Bile salts* assist in the breakdown and absorption of fats; *bile pigments* are the breakdown products of old red blood cells that are passed into the gut to be eliminated with the feces.

billiards indoor game played, normally by two players, with tapered poles (called cues) and composition balls (one red, two white) on a rectangular table covered with a green, feltlike cloth (baize) without pockets. A variation popular in England is played on a table with six pockets, one at each corner and in each of the long sides at the middle. Scoring strokes are made by sinking the red ball, sinking the opponent's ball, or sinking another ball off one of these two. The cannon (when the cue ball hits the two other balls on the table) is another scoring stroke.

Billings city in S central Montana, on the N shore of the Yellowstone River; seat of Yellowstone County; population (1990) 81,100. It is a center for transporting livestock and animal products and for vegetable and grain processing. Nearby, to the SE, is Big Horn Indian reservation where the Battle of Little Big Horn took place 1876.

billion the cardinal number represented by a 1 followed by nine zeros (1,000,000,000 or 10^9), equivalent to a thousand million.

bill of lading document giving proof of particular goods having been loaded on a ship. The person to whom the goods are being sent normally needs to show the bill of lading in order to obtain the release of the goods. For air freight, there is an *airway bill.*

Bill of Rights in the US, the first ten amendments to the US Constitution, incorporated 1791:

1 guarantees freedom of worship, of speech, of the press, of assembly, and to petition the government; *2* grants the right to keep and bear arms; *3* prohibits billeting of soldiers in private homes in peacetime; *4* forbids unreasonable search and seizure; *5* guarantees none be "deprived of life, liberty or property without due process of law" or compelled in any criminal case to be a witness against himself or herself; *6* grants the right to speedy trial, to call witnesses, and to have defense counsel; *7* grants the right to trial by jury of one's peers; *8* prevents the infliction of excessive bail or fines, or "cruel and unusual punishment"; *9, 10* provide a safeguard to the states and people for all rights not specifically delegated to the central government.

Billy the Kid nickname of William H Bonney 1859–1881. US outlaw, a leader in the 1878 Lincoln County cattle war in New Mexico, who allegedly killed his first victim at 12 and was reputed to have killed 21 men by age 22, when he died.

Biloxi port in Mississippi; population (1990) 46,300. Chief occupations include tourism and seafood canning. Named after a local Indian people, Biloxi was founded 1719 by the French. The city suffered heavy damage from Hurricane Camille 1969, but rebuilding was rapid.

binary fission in biology, a form of ◊asexual reproduction, whereby a single-celled organism, such as the ameba, divides into two smaller "daughter" cells. It can also occur in a few simple multicellular organisms, such as sea anemones, producing two smaller sea anemones of equal size.

binary star pair of stars moving in orbit around their common center of mass. Observations show that most stars are binary, or even multiple—for example, the nearest star system to the Sun, ◊Alpha Centauri.

binary weapon in chemical warfare, weapon consisting of two substances that in isolation are harmless but when mixed together form a poisonous nerve gas. They are loaded into the delivery system separately and combine after launch.

binding energy in physics, the amount of energy needed to break the nucleus of an atom into the neutrons and protons of which it is made.

Bingham George Caleb 1811–1879. US painter. The influence of the Hudson River School is evident in such frontier landscapes as *Fur Traders Descending the Missouri* 1845.

Binghamton city in S central New York State, where the Chenango River meets the Susquehanna River; population (1990) 53,000. Industries include electronic, computer, and camera equipment and textiles. Johnson City and Endicott, directly to the W on the Susquehanna River, form the Triple Cities with Binghamton.

binoculars optical instrument for viewing an object in magnification with both eyes; for example, field glasses and opera glasses. Binoculars consist of two telescopes containing lenses and prisms, which produce a stereoscopic effect as well as magnifying the image. Use of prisms has the effect of "folding" the light path, allowing for a compact design.

binomial in mathematics, an expression consisting of two terms, such as $a + b$ or $a - b$.

binomial system of nomenclature in biology, the system in which all organisms are identified by a two-part Latinized name. Devised by the biologist ◊Linnaeus, it is also known as the Linnaean system. The first name is capitalized and identifies the ◊genus; the second identifies the ◊species within that genus.

biochemistry science concerned with the chemistry of living organisms: the structure and reactions of proteins (such as enzymes), nucleic acids, carbohydrates, and lipids.

biodegradable capable of being broken down by living organisms, principally bacteria and fungi. In biodegradable substances, such as food and sewage, the natural processes of decay lead to compaction and liquefaction, and to the release of nutrients that are then recycled by the ecosystem. Nonbiodegradable substances, such as glass, heavy metals, and most types of plastic, present serious problems of disposal.

Billy the Kid
Although few details of his life are known, US outlaw Billy the Kid became the symbol of the discontented of his day.

biodiversity (contraction of *biological diversity*) measure of the variety of the Earth's animal, plant, and microbial species; of genetic differences within species; and of the ecosystems that support those species. Its maintenance is important for ecological stability and as a resource for research into, for example, new drugs and crops. Research suggests that biodiversity is far greater than previously realized, especially among smaller organisms—for instance, it is thought that only 1–10% of the world's bacterial species have been identified. In the 20th century, however, the destruction of habitats is believed to have resulted in the most severe and rapid loss of diversity in the history of the planet.

bioengineering the application of engineering to biology and medicine. Common applications include the design and use of artificial limbs, joints, and organs, including hip joints and heart valves.

biofeedback modification or control of a biological system by its results or effects. For example, a change in the position or ◊trophic level of one species affects all levels above it.

biofeedback in medicine, the use of electrophysiological monitoring devices to "feed back" information about internal processes and thus facilitate conscious control. Developed in the US in the 1960s, independently by neurophysiologist Barbara Brown and neuropsychiatrist Joseph Kamiya, the technique is effective in alleviating hypertension and preventing associated organic and physiological dysfunctions.

biofuel any solid, liquid, or gaseous fuel produced from organic (once living) matter, either directly from plants or indirectly from industrial, commercial, domestic, or agricultural wastes. There are three main ways for the development of biofuels: the burning of dry organic wastes (such as household refuse, industrial and agricultural wastes, straw, wood, and peat); the fermentation of wet wastes (such as animal dung)

Biology: chronology

c. 500 BC	First studies of the structure and behavior of animals, by the Greek Alcmaeon of Creton.
c. 450	Hippocrates of Cos undertook the first detailed studies of human anatomy.
c. 350	Aristotle laid down the basic philosophy of the biological sciences and outlined a theory of evolution.
c. 300	Theophrastus carried out the first detailed studies of plants.
c. AD 175	Galen established the basic principles of anatomy and physiology.
c. 1500	Leonardo da Vinci studied human anatomy to improve his drawing ability and produced detailed anatomical drawings.
1628	William Harvey described the circulation of the blood and the function of the heart as a pump.
1665	Robert Hooke used a microscope to describe the cellular structure of plants.
1672	Marcelle Malphigi undertook the first studies in embryology by describing the development of a chicken egg.
1677	Anthony van Leeuwenhoek greatly improved the microscope and used it to describe spermatozoa as well as many microorganisms.
1736	Carolus (Carl) Linnaeus published his systematic classification of plants, so establishing taxonomy.
1768–79	James Cook's voyages of discovery in the Pacific revealed an undreamed-of diversity of living species, prompting the development of theories to explain their origin.
1796	Edward Jenner established the practice of vaccination against smallpox, laying the foundations for theories of antibodies and immune reactions.
1809	Jean-Baptiste Lamarck advocated a theory of evolution through inheritance of acquired characters.
1839	Theodor Schwann proposed that all living matter is made up of cells.
1857	Louis Pasteur established that microorganisms are responsible for fermentation, creating the discipline of microbiology.
1859	Charles Darwin published *On the Origin of Species*, expounding his theory of the evolution of species by natural selection.
1866	Gregor Mendel pioneered the study of inheritance with his experiments on peas, but achieved little recognition.
1883	August Weismann proposed his theory of the continuity of the germ plasm.
1900	Mendel's work was rediscovered and the science of genetics founded.
1935	Konrad Lorenz published the first of many major studies of animal behavior, which founded the discipline of ethology.
1953	James Watson and Francis Crick described the molecular structure of the genetic material DNA.
1964	William Hamilton recognized the importance of inclusive fitness, so paving the way for the development of sociobiology.
1975	Discovery of endogenous opiates (the brain's own painkillers) opened up a new phase in the study of brain chemistry.
1976	Har Gobind Khorana and his colleagues constructed the first artificial gene to function naturally when inserted into a bacterial cell, a major step in genetic engineering.
1992	Researchers at the University of California stimulated the multiplication of isolated brain cells of mice, overturning the axiom that mammalian brains cannot produce replacement cells once birth has taken place. The world's largest organism, a honey fungus with underground hyphae (filaments) spreading across 1,480 acres/600 hectares, was discovered in Washington State.

---

in the absence of oxygen to produce biogas (containing up to 60% methane), or the fermentation of sugar cane or corn to produce alcohol; and energy forestry (producing fast-growing wood for fuel).

biogeography study of how and why plants and animals are distributed around the world, in the past as well as in the present; more specifically, a theory describing the geographical distribution of ◊species developed by Robert MacArthur and US zoologist Edward O Wilson. The theory argues that for many species, ecological specializations mean that suitable habitats are patchy in their occurrence. Thus for a dragonfly, ponds in which to breed are separated by large tracts of land, and for edelweiss adapted to alpine peaks the deep valleys between cannot be colonized.

biography account of a person's life. When it is written by that person, it is an ◊autobiography. Biography may consist simply of the factual details of a person's life told in chronological order, but has generally become a matter of interpretation as well as historical accuracy. Unofficial biographies (not sanctioned by the subject) have frequently led to legal disputes over both interpretation and facts.

Bioko island in the Bight of Bonny, W Africa, part of Equatorial Guinea; area 786 sq mi/2,017 sq km; products include coffee, cacao, and copra; population (1983) 57,190. Formerly a Spanish possession, as *Fernando Po*, it was known 1973–79 as *Macías Nguema Bijogo*.

biological clock regular internal rhythm of activity, produced by unknown mechanisms, and not dependent on external time signals. Such clocks are known to exist in almost all animals, and also in many plants, fungi, and unicellular organisms. In higher organisms, there appears to be a series of clocks of graded importance. For example, although body temperature and activity cycles in human beings are normally "set" to 24 hours, the two cycles may vary independently, showing that two clock mechanisms are involved.

Exposing humans to bright light can change the biological clock and help, for example, people suffering from ◊seasonal affective disorder.

biological warfare the use of living organisms, or of infectious material derived from them, to bring about death or disease in humans, animals, or plants. At least ten countries have this capability.

biological weathering form of ◊weathering caused by the activities of living organisms—for example, the growth of roots or the burrowing of animals. Tree roots are probably the most significant agents of biological weathering as they are capable of prizing apart rocks by growing into cracks and joints.

biology science of life. Strictly speaking, biology includes all the life sciences—for example, anatomy and physiology, cytology, zoology and botany, ecology, genetics, biochemistry and biophysics, animal behavior, embryology, and plant breeding. During the 1990s an important focus of biological research will be the international ◊Human Genome Project, which will attempt to map the entire genetic code contained in the 23 pairs of human chromosomes.

bioluminescence production of light by living organisms. It is a feature of many deep-sea fishes, crustaceans, and other marine animals. On land, bioluminescence is seen in some nocturnal insects such as glowworms and fireflies, and in certain bacteria and fungi. Light is usually produced by the oxidation of luciferin, a reaction catalyzed by the ◊enzyme luciferase. This reaction is unique, being the only known biological oxidation that does not produce heat. Animal luminescence is involved in communication, camouflage, or the luring of prey, but its function in other organisms is unclear.

biomass the total mass of living organisms present in a given area. It may be specified for a particular species (such as earthworm biomass) or for a general category (such as herbivore biomass). Estimates also exist for the entire global plant biomass. Measurements of biomass can be used to study interactions between organisms, the stability of those interactions, and variations in population numbers.

biome broad natural assemblage of plants and animals shaped by common patterns of vegetation and climate. Examples include the tundra biome and the desert biome.

biomechanics study of natural structures to improve those produced by humans. For example, mother-of-pearl is structurally superior to fiberglass, and deer antlers have outstanding durability because they are composed of microscopic fibers. Such natural structures may form the basis of high-tech composites.

bionics (from "biological electronics") design and development of electronic or mechanical artificial systems that imitate those of living things. The bionic arm, for example, is an artificial limb (◊prosthesis) that uses electronics to amplify minute electrical signals generated in body muscles to work electric motors, which operate the joints of the fingers and wrist.

biophysics application of physical laws to the properties of living organisms. Examples include using the principles of ◊mechanics to calculate the strength of bones and muscles, and ◊thermodynamics to study plant and animal energetics.

biopsy removal of a living tissue sample from the body for diagnostic examination.

biorhythm rhythmic change, mediated by ◊hormones, in the physical state and activity patterns of certain plants and animals that have seasonal activities. Examples include winter hibernation, spring flowering or breeding, and periodic migration. The hormonal changes themselves are often a response to changes in day length (◊photoperiodism); they signal the time of year to the animal or plant. Other biorhythms are innate and continue even if external stimuli such as day length are removed. These include a 24-hour or ◊circadian rhythm, a 28-day or circalunar rhythm (corresponding to the phases of the Moon), and even a year-long rhythm in some organisms.

biosphere the narrow zone that supports life on our planet. It is limited to the waters of the Earth, a fraction of its crust, and the lower regions of the atmosphere.

BioSphere 2 (BS2) ecological test project, a "planet in a bottle," in Arizona. Under a glass dome, several different habitats are recreated, with representatives of nearly 4,000 species, including eight humans, sealed in the biosphere for two years from summer 1991 to see how effectively the recycling of air, water, and waste can work in an enclosed environment and whether a stable ecosystem can be created; ultimately BS2 is a prototype space colony. The four men and four women emerged Sept 26, 1993.

biosynthesis synthesis of organic chemicals from simple inorganic ones by living cells—for example, the conversion of carbon dioxide and water to glucose by plants during ◊photosynthesis. Other biosynthetic reactions produce cell constituents including proteins and fats.

biotechnology industrial use of living organisms to manufacture food, drugs, or other products. The brewing and baking industries have long relied on the yeast microorganism for ◊fermentation purposes, while the dairy industry employs a range of bacteria and fungi to convert milk into cheeses and yogurts. ◊Enzymes, whether extracted from cells or produced artificially, are central to most biotechnological applications.

biotin or *vitamin H* vitamin of the B complex, found in many different kinds of food; egg yolk, liver, legumes, and yeast contain large amounts. Its absence from the diet may lead to dermatitis.

bird of paradise
The male blue bird of paradise displays to the female high up in the tree canopy.

bird This diagram shows a representative species from each of the 29 orders.

bird classification

Struthioniformes
ostrich

Casuariformes
cassowary

Tinamiformes
tinamous

Gaviiformes
diver

Sphenisciforme
penguin

Ciconiiformes
stork

Falconiformes
falcon

Gruiformes
crane

Columbiformes
pigeon

Cuculiformes
cuckoo

Caprimulgiformes
nightjar

Coliiformes
mousebird

Coraciformes
kingfisher

Passeriformes
starling

Passeriformes
lark

Rheiformes
rhea

Apterygiformes
kiwi

Podicipediformes
grebe

Procellariiformes
petrel

Pelecaniformes
pelican

Anseriformes
goose

Galliformes
pheasant

Charadriiformes
plover

Psittaciformes
parrot

Strigiformes
owl

Sphenisciformes
swift

Trogoniformes
trogon

Piciformes
woodpecker

Passeriformes
thrush

biotite dark mica, $K(Mg, Fe)_3Al\ Si_3O_{10}(OH, F)_2$, a common silicate mineral. It is brown to black with shiny surfaces, and like all micas, it splits into very thin flakes along its one perfect cleavage. Biotite is a mineral of igneous rocks such as granites, and metamorphic rocks such as schists and gneisses.

birch any tree of the genus *Betula*, including about 40 species found in cool temperate parts of the northern hemisphere. Birches grow rapidly, and their hard, beautiful wood is used for veneers and cabinetwork.

Paper birch *B. papyrifera* is native to the N half of North America.

bird backboned animal of the class Aves, the biggest group of land vertebrates, characterized by warm blood, feathers, wings, breathing through lungs, and egg-laying by the female. There are nearly 8,500 species of birds.

bird of paradise one of 40 species of crowlike birds, family Paradiseidae, native to New Guinea and neighboring islands. Females are generally drably colored, but the males have bright and elaborate plumage used in courtship display. Hunted almost to extinction for their plumage, they are now subject to conservation.

Birdseye Clarence 1886–1956. US inventor who pioneered food refrigeration processes. While working as a fur trader in Labrador 1912–16 he was struck by the ease with which food could be preserved in an Arctic climate. Back in the US he found that the same effect could be obtained by rapidly freezing prepared food between two refrigerated metal plates. To market his products he founded the General Sea Foods Co. 1924, which he sold to General Foods 1929.

Birendra Bir Bikram Shah Dev 1945– . King of Nepal from 1972, when he succeeded his father Mahendra; he was formally crowned 1975. King Birendra has overseen Nepal's return to multiparty politics and introduced a new constitution 1990.

Birmingham industrial city in the West Midlands, second-largest city of the UK; population (1991 est) 934,900, metropolitan area 2,632,000. Industries include motor vehicles, machine tools, aerospace control systems, plastics, chemicals, and food.

Birmingham commercial and industrial city (iron, steel, chemicals, building materials, computers, cotton textiles) and largest city in Alabama; population (1990) 266,000.

birth control another name for ◊family planning; see also ◊contraceptive.

birth rate the number of live births per year per thousand of the population. Birth rate is a factor in demographic transition. It is sometimes called *crude birth rate* because it takes in the whole population, including men and women who are too old to bear children.

Biscay, Bay of bay of the Atlantic Ocean between N Spain and W France, known for rough seas and exceptionally high tides.

bishop (Greek "overseer") priest next in rank to an archbishop in the Roman Catholic, Eastern Orthodox, Anglican, or Episcopal churches. A bishop has charge of a district called a *diocese*.

Bishops with more limited authority have the highest rank in certain Lutheran denominations and in the Methodist church.

Bismarck capital of North Dakota, on the Missouri river in Burleigh County, in the southern part of the state; population (1990) 49,200. It is a shipping point

Bismarck Prusso-German politician Prince Otto von Bismarck, known as the Iron Chancellor, came to prominence after the collapse of the revolution of 1848.

for the region's agricultural and livestock products from surrounding farms and for oil products from nearby oil wells.

Bismarck Otto Eduard Leopold, Prince von 1815–1898. German politician, prime minister of Prussia 1862–90 and chancellor of the German Empire 1871–90. He pursued an aggressively expansionist policy, waging wars against Denmark 1863–64, Austria 1866, and France 1870–71, which brought about the unification of Germany.

Bismarck Archipelago group of over 200 islands in the SW Pacific Ocean, part of ◊Papua New Guinea; area 19,200 sq mi/49,660 sq km. The largest island is New Britain.

bismuth hard, brittle, pinkish-white, metallic element, symbol Bi, atomic number 83, atomic weight 208.98. It has the highest atomic number of all the stable elements (the elements from atomic number 84 up are radioactive). Bismuth occurs in ores and occasionally as a free metal (◊native metal). It is a poor conductor of heat and electricity and is used in alloys of low melting point and in medical compounds to soothe gastric ulcers. The name comes from the Latin *besemutum*, from the earlier German *Wismut*.

bison large, hoofed mammal of the bovine family. There are two species, both brown. The *European bison* or *wisent Bison bonasus*, of which only a few protected herds survive, is about 7 ft/2 m high and weighs up to 2,500 lb/1,100 kg. The *North American bison* (often known as "buffalo") *B. bison* is slightly smaller, with a heavier mane and more sloping hindquarters. Formerly roaming the prairies in vast numbers, it was almost exterminated in the 19th century, but survives in protected areas.

Bissau capital and chief port of Guinea-Bissau, on an island at the mouth of the Geba River; population (1988) 125,000. Originally a fortified slave-trading center, Bissau became a free port 1869.

bit (contraction of *b*inary dig*it*) in computing, a single binary digit, either 0 or 1. A bit is the smallest unit of data stored in a computer; all other data must be coded into a pattern of individual bits. A ◊byte represents sufficient computer memory to store a single character of data and usually contains eight bits. For example, in the ◊ASCII code system used by most microcomputers the capital letter A would be stored in a single byte of memory as the bit pattern 01000001.

Bithynia district of NW Asia that became a Roman province 74 BC.

bittern any of several small herons, in particular the common bittern *Botaurus stellaris* of Europe and Asia. It is shy, stoutly built, has a streaked camouflage pattern and a loud, booming call. An inhabitant of marshy country, it is now quite rare in Britain.

bitumen impure mixture of hydrocarbons, including such deposits as petroleum, asphalt, and natural gas, although sometimes the term is restricted to a soft kind of pitch resembling asphalt.

bivalve marine or freshwater mollusk whose body is enclosed between two shells hinged together by a ligament on the dorsal side of the body.

Bizet Georges (Alexandre César Léopold) 1838–1875. French composer of operas, among them *Les Pêcheurs de perles/The Pearl Fishers* 1863, and *La jolie Fille de Perth/The Fair Maid of Perth* 1866. He also wrote the concert overture *Patrie* and incidental music to Daudet's *L'Arlésienne*. His operatic masterpiece *Carmen* was produced a few months before his death 1875.

black English term first used 1625 to describe West Africans, now used to refer to Africans south of the Sahara and to people of African descent living outside Africa. In some countries such as the UK (but not in North America) the term is sometimes also used for people originally from the Indian subcontinent, for Australian Aborigines, and for peoples of Melanesia.

Black Hugo LaFayette 1886–1971. US jurist. He was elected to the US Senate 1926 and despite his earlier association with the Ku Klux Klan, distinguished himself as a progressive populist. He was appointed to the US Supreme Court by F D Roosevelt 1937, resigning shortly before his death.

blackberry prickly shrub *Rubus fruticosus* of the rose family, closely allied to raspberries and dewberries, that is native to northern parts of Europe. It produces pink or white blossoms and edible, black, compound fruits.

The North American blackberry *R. allegheniensis* has white blossoms and grows wild in Canada and E US.

blackbird bird *Turdus merula* of the thrush family. The male is black with a yellow bill and eyelids, the female dark brown with a dark beak. About 10 in/25 cm long, it lays three to five blue-green eggs with brown spots. Its song is rich and flutelike.

black body in physics, a hypothetical object that completely absorbs all thermal (heat) radiation striking it. It is also a perfect emitter of thermal radiation.

black box popular name for the unit containing an airplane's flight and voice recorders. These monitor the plane's behavior and the crew's conversation, thus providing valuable clues to the cause of a disaster. The box is nearly indestructible and usually painted orange for easy recovery. The name also refers to any compact electronic device that can be quickly connected or disconnected as a unit.

Black Death great epidemic of bubonic ◊plague that ravaged Europe in the 14th century, killing between one-third and half of the population. The cause of the plague was the bacterium *Pasteurella pestis*, transmitted by fleas borne by migrating Asian black rats. The name Black Death was first used in England in the early 19th century.

Blackfoot member of a Plains ◊American Indian people, some 10,000 in number and consisting of three subtribes: the Blackfoot proper, the Blood, and the Piegan, who live in Montana, Saskatchewan, and Alberta. They were skilled, horse-riding buffalo hunters until their territories were settled by Europeans. Their name derives from their black moccasins. Their language belongs to the Algonquian family.

Black Forest (German *Schwarzwald*) mountainous region of coniferous forest in Baden-Württemberg, W Germany. Bounded to the W and S by the Rhine, which separates it from the Vosges, it has an area of 1,800 sq mi/4,660 sq km and rises to 4,905 ft/1,493 m in the Feldberg. Parts of the forest have recently been affected by ◊acid rain.

Black Hawk or ***Black Sparrow Hawk*** (Sauk name ***Makataimeshekiakiak***) 1767–1838. North American Sauk Indian leader. A principal opponent of the cession of Indian lands to the US government, he sided with the British during the War of 1812 and joined his people in their removal to Iowa at the end of the war. In 1832 he led a large contingent back to Illinois to resettle the Sauk homeland. Defeated by Illinois militia in the bloody "Black Hawk War," he was captured and permanently exiled to Iowa.

black hole object in space whose gravity is so great that nothing can escape from it, not even light. Thought to form when massive stars shrink at the ends of their lives, a black hole sucks in more matter, including other stars, from the space around it. Matter that falls into a black hole is squeezed to infinite density at the center of the hole. Black holes can be detected because gas falling toward them becomes so hot that it emits X-rays.

Black Hole of Calcutta incident in Anglo-Indian history: according to tradition, the nawab (ruler) of Bengal confined 146 British prisoners on the night of June 20, 1756, in one small room, of whom only 23 allegedly survived. Later research reduced the death count to 43, assigning negligence rather than intention.

blackmail criminal offense of extorting money with menaces or threats of detrimental action, such as exposure of some misconduct on the part of the victim.

Black Monday worldwide stockmarket crash that began Oct 19, 1987, prompted by the announcement of worse-than-expected US trade figures and the response by US Secretary of the Treasury James Baker, who indicated that the sliding dollar needed to decline further. This caused a world panic as fears of the likely impact of a US recession were voiced by the major industrialized countries. Between Oct 19 and 23, the New York Stock Exchange fell by 33%, the London Stock Exchange Financial Times 100 Index by 25%, the European index by 17%, and Tokyo by 12%. The expected world recession did not occur; by the end of 1988 it was clear that the main effect had been a steadying in stock market activity and only a slight slowdown in world economic growth.

Blackmun Harry Andrew 1908– . US Supreme Court associate justice 1970– . A conservative in his early years on the Court, he became more moderate during the later part of his tenure.

Black Muslim member of a religious group founded 1929 in the US and led, from 1934, by Elijah Mohammed (then Elijah Poole) (1897–1975) after he had a vision of ◊Allah. Its growth from 1946 as a black separatist organization was due to Malcolm X (1926–1965), the son of a Baptist minister who, in 1964, broke away and founded his own Organization for African-American Unity, preaching "active self-defense." Under the leadership of Louis Farrakhan, the movement underwent a recent revival.

Black National State area in the Republic of South Africa set aside for development toward self-government by black Africans in accordance with ◊apartheid. Before 1980 these areas were known as **black homelands** or **bantustans**. They make up less than 14% of the country and tend to be in arid areas (though some have mineral wealth) and may be in scattered blocks. Those that achieved nominal independence are Transkei 1976, Bophuthatswana 1977, Venda 1979, and Ciskei 1981. They are not recognized outside South Africa because of their racial basis.

Black Power movement toward black separatism in the US during the 1960s, embodied in the **Black Panther Party** founded 1966 by Huey Newton and Bobby Seale. Its declared aim was the establishment of a separate black state in the US established by a black plebiscite under the aegis of the United Nations. Following a National Black Political Convention 1972, a National Black Assembly was established to exercise pressure on the Democratic and Republican parties.

Black Sea (Russian **Chernoye More**) inland sea in SE Europe, linked with the seas of Azov and Marmara, and via the Dardanelles strait with the Mediterranean. Uranium deposits beneath it are among the world's largest. It is heavily polluted by agricultural fertilizers.

Black September guerrilla splinter group of the ◊Palestine Liberation Organization formed 1970. Operating from bases in Syria and Lebanon, it was responsible for the kidnappings at the Munich Olympics 1972 that led to the deaths of 11 Israelis, and more recent hijack and bomb attempts. The group is named after the month in which Palestinian guerrillas were expelled from Jordan by King Hussein.

Blackshirts term widely used to describe fascist paramilitary organizations. Originating with Mussolini's fascist Squadristi in the 1920s, it was also applied to the Nazi SS (*Schutzstaffel*) and to the followers of Oswald Mosley's British Union of Fascists.

blacksnake any of several species of snake. The blacksnake *Pseudechis porphyriacus* is a venomous snake of the cobra family found in damp forests and swamps in E Australia. The blacksnake *Coluber constrictor* from E US, is a relative of the European grass snake, growing up to 4 ft/1.2 m long, and without venom.

Black Stone in Islam, the sacred stone built into the east corner of the Kaaba which is a focal point of the *hajj*, or pilgrimage, to Mecca. There are a number of stories concerning its origin, one of which states that it was sent to Earth at the time of the first man, Adam; Mohammed declared that it was given to Abraham by Gabriel. It has been suggested that it is of meteoric origin.

Black Thursday day of the Wall Street stock market crash Oct 29, 1929, which precipitated the ◊Depression in the US and throughout the world.

black widow North American spider *Latrodectus mactans*. The male is small and harmless, but the female is 0.5 in/1.3 cm long with a red patch below the abdomen and a powerful venomous bite. The bite causes pain and fever in human victims, but they usually recover.

bladder hollow elastic-walled organ in the ◊urinary systems of some fishes, most amphibians, some reptiles, and all mammals. Urine enters the bladder through two ureters, one leading from each kidney, and leaves it through the urethra.

Black Sea

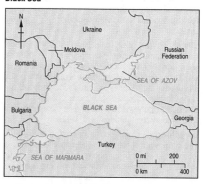

bladderwort any of a large genus *Utricularia* of carnivorous aquatic plants of the family Lentibulariaceae. They have leaves with bladders that entrap small aquatic animals.

Blaine James Gillespie 1830–1893. US politician and diplomat. Elected to the US House of Representatives 1862, he became Speaker 1868. Unsuccessful in the Republican presidential nominations 1876 and 1880, he served briefly as President Garfield's secretary of state. Gaining the Republican presidential nomination 1884, he was defeated by Grover Cleveland. During the B Harrison administration 1889–93, Blaine again served as secretary of state.

Blake William 1757–1827. English poet, artist, engraver, and visionary. His lyrics, as in *Songs of Innocence* 1789 and *Songs of Experience* 1794 express spiritual wisdom in radiant imagery and symbolism. Prophetic books like *The Marriage of Heaven and Hell* 1790, *America* 1793, and *Milton* 1804 yield their meaning to careful study. He created a new composite art form in engraving and hand-coloring his own works.

blank verse in literature, the unrhymed iambic pentameter or ten-syllable line of five stresses. First used by the Italian Gian Giorgio Trissino in his tragedy *Sofonisba* 1514–15, it was introduced to England about 1540 by the Earl of Surrey and developed by Christopher Marlowe. More recent exponents of blank verse in English include Thomas Hardy, T S Eliot, and Robert Frost.

Blanqui Louis Auguste 1805–1881. French revolutionary politician. He formulated the theory of the "dictatorship of the proletariat," used by Karl Marx, and spent a total of 33 years in prison for insurrection. Although in prison, he was elected president of the Commune of Paris 1871. His followers, the Blanquists, joined with the Marxists 1881.

Blantyre-Limbe chief industrial and commercial center of Malawi, in the Shire highlands; population (1987) 331,600. It produces tea, coffee, rubber, tobacco, and textiles.

Blarney small town in County Cork, Republic of Ireland, possessing, inset in the wall of the 15th-century castle, the **Blarney Stone**, reputed to give persuasive speech to those kissing it.

blasphemy (Greek "evil-speaking") written or spoken insult directed against religious belief or sacred things with deliberate intent to outrage believers.

There are numerous laws in the US against blasphemy, but they are rarely enforced.

blast furnace smelting furnace in which temperature is raised by the injection of an air blast. It is used to extract metals from their ores, chiefly pig iron from iron ore.

Blaue Reiter, der ("the Blue Rider") group of German Expressionist painters based in Munich, some of whom had left *die ◊Brücke*. They were interested in the value of colors, in folk art, and in the necessity of painting "the inner, spiritual side of nature," but styles were highly varied. Wassily ◊Kandinsky and Franz Marc published a book of their views 1912, and there were two exhibitions 1911, 1912.

bleaching decolorization of colored materials. The two main types of bleaching agent are the *oxidizing bleaches*, which bring about the ◊oxidation of pigments and include the ultraviolet rays in sunshine, hydrogen peroxide, and chlorine in household bleaches; and the *reducing bleaches*, which bring about reduction and include sulfur dioxide.

blenny any fish of the family Blenniidae, mostly small fishes found near rocky shores, with elongated slimy bodies tapering from head to tail, no scales, and long pelvic fins set far forward.

Bligh William 1754–1817. English sailor who accompanied Captain James ◊Cook on his second voyage around the world 1772–74, and in 1787 commanded HMS *Bounty* on an expedition to the Pacific. On the return voyage the crew mutinied 1789, and Bligh was cast adrift in a boat with 18 men. He was appointed governor of New South Wales 1805, where his discipline again provoked a mutiny 1808 (the Rum Rebellion). He returned to Britain, and was made an admiral 1811.

blight any of a number of plant diseases caused mainly by parasitic species of ◊fungus, which produce a whitish appearance on leaf and stem surfaces—for instance, *potato blight Phytophthora infestans*. General damage caused by aphids or pollution is sometimes known as blight.

blimp airship: any self-propelled, lighter-than-air craft that can be steered. A blimp with a soft frame is also called a *dirigible*; a ◊*zeppelin* is rigid-framed.

blind spot area where the optic nerve and blood vessels pass through the retina of the ◊eye. No visual image can be formed as there are no light-sensitive cells in this part of the retina. Thus the organism is blind to objects that fall in this part of the visual field.

Blitzkrieg (German "lightning war") swift military campaign, as used by Germany at the beginning of World War II 1939–41. The abbreviated *Blitz* was applied to the attempted saturation bombing of London by the German air force between Sept 1940 and May 1941.

Blixen Karen, born Karen Dinesen 1885–1962. Danish writer. Her autobiography *Out of Africa* 1937 is based on her experience of running a coffee plantation in Kenya. She wrote fiction, mainly in English, under the adopted name Isak Dinesen.

Bloch Konrad 1912– . German-born US chemist whose research concerned cholesterol. Making use of the ◊radioisotope carbon-14 (the radioactive form of carbon), Bloch was able to follow the complex steps by which the body chemically transforms acetic acid into cholesterol. For his work in this field Bloch shared the 1964 Nobel Prize for Medicine with Feodor Lynen (1911–1979).

blockade cutting-off of a place by hostile forces by land, sea, or air so as to prevent any movement to or fro, in order to compel a surrender without attack or to achieve some other political aim (for example, the ◊Berlin blockade 1948).

Block and tackle type of ◊pulley

Bloemfontein capital of the Orange Free State and judicial capital of the Republic of South Africa; population (1985) 204,000. Founded 1846, the city produces canned fruit, glassware, furniture, and plastics.

blood liquid circulating in the arteries, veins, and capillaries; the term also refers to the corresponding fluid in those invertebrates that possess a closed ◊circulatory system. Blood carries nutrients and oxygen to individual cells and removes waste products, such as carbon dioxide. It is also important in the immune response and, in many animals, in the distribution of heat throughout the body.

blood group any of the blood groups into which blood is classified according to antigenic activity. Red blood cells of one individual may carry molecules on their surface that act as ◊antigens in another individual whose red blood cells lack these molecules. The two main antigens are designated A and B. These give rise to four blood groups: having A only (A), having B only (B), having both (AB), and having neither (O). Each of these groups may or may not contain the ◊rhesus factor. Correct typing of blood groups is vital in transfusion, since incompatible types of donor and recipient blood will result in blood clotting, with possible death of the recipient.

bloodhound ancient breed of dog. Black and tan in color, it has long, pendulous ears and distinctive wrinkled head and face. It grows to a height of about 26 in/65 cm at the shoulder. The breed originated as a hunting dog in Belgium in the Middle Ages, and its excellent powers of scent have been employed in tracking and criminal detection from very early times.

blood pressure pressure, or tension, of the blood against the inner walls of blood vessels, especially the arteries, due to the muscular pumping activity of the heart. Abnormally high blood pressure (see ◊hypertension) may be associated with various conditions or arise with no obvious cause; abnormally low blood pressure (hypotension) occurs in ◊shock and after excessive fluid or blood loss from any cause.

blood test laboratory evaluation of a blood sample. There are numerous blood tests, from simple typing to establish the ◊blood group to sophisticated biochemical assays of substances, such as hormones, present in the blood only in minute quantities.

blood vessel specialized tube that carries blood around the body of multicellular animals. Blood vessels are highly evolved in vertebrates, where the three main types—the arteries, veins, and capillaries—are all adapted for their particular role within the body.

Bloomer Amelia Jenks 1818–1894. US campaigner for women's rights. In 1849, when unwieldy crinolines were the fashion, she introduced a knee-length skirt combined with loose trousers gathered at the ankles, which became known as *bloomers* (also called "rational dress").

Bloomington city in S central Indiana, SW of Indianapolis; seat of Monroe County; population (1990) 42,100. It is an exporter of limestone from nearby quarries. It is also a center for the manufacture of electrical products and lifts.

Indiana University 1820 is located here.

Bloomington city in central Illinois, SE of Peoria; seat of McLean County; population (1990) 42,200. It is in the middle of a rich farming and livestock raising area.

Illinois Wesleyan University 1850 is located here.

Bloomsbury Group group of writers and artists based in Bloomsbury, London. The group included the artists Duncan Grant and Vanessa Bell, and the writers Lytton ◊Strachey and Leonard (1880–1969) and Virginia ◊Woolf.

blowfly any fly of the genus *Calliphora*, also known as bluebottle, or of the related genus *Lucilia*, when it is greenbottle. It lays its eggs in dead flesh, on which the maggots feed.

blubber thick layer of ◊fat under the skin of marine mammals, which provides an energy store and an effective insulating layer, preventing the loss of body heat to the surrounding water. Blubber has been used (when boiled down) in engineering, food processing, cosmetics, and printing, but all of these products can now be produced synthetically, thus saving the lives of animals.

Bluebeard folktale character, popularized by the writer Charles ◊Perrault in France about 1697, and historically identified with Gilles de Rais. Bluebeard murdered six wives for disobeying his command not to enter a locked room, but was himself killed before he could murder the seventh.

blueberry any of various North American acid-soil shrubs of the genus *Vaccinium* of the heath family. The genus also includes huckleberries, bilberries, deerberries, and cranberries, many of which resemble each other and are difficult to distinguish from blueberries. All have small, elliptical short-stalked leaves, slender green or reddish twigs, and whitish bell-like blossoms. Only true blueberries, however, have tiny granular speckles on their twigs. Blueberries have black or blue edible fruits, often covered with a white powder.

bluebird three species of a North American bird, genus *Sialia*, belonging to the thrush subfamily, Turdinae. The eastern bluebird *S. sialis* is regarded as the herald of spring. About 7 in/18 cm long, it has a reddish breast, the upper plumage being sky-blue, and a distinctive song.

bluegrass dense, spreading grass of the genus *Poa*, which is blue-tinted and grows in clumps. Various species are known from the northern hemisphere. Kentucky bluegrass *P. pratensis*, introduced to the US from Europe, provides pasture for horses.

blue-green algae or *cyanobacteria* single-celled, primitive organisms that resemble bacteria in their internal cell organization, sometimes joined together in colonies or filaments. Blue-green algae are among the oldest known living organisms and, with bacteria, belong to the kingdom Monera; remains have been found in rocks up to 3.5 billion years old. They are widely distributed in aquatic habitats, on the damp surfaces of rocks and trees, and in the soil.

Blue Mountains part of the ◊Great Dividing Range, New South Wales, Australia, ranging 2,000–3,600 ft/600–1,100 m and blocking Sydney from the interior until the crossing 1813 by surveyor William Lawson, Gregory Blaxland, and William Wentworth.

Blue Nile (Arabic *Bahr el Azraq*) river rising in the mountains of Ethiopia. Flowing W then N for 1,250 mi/2,000 km, it eventually meets the White Nile at Khartoum.

The river is dammed at Roseires where a hydro-electric scheme produces 70% of Sudan's electricity.

blueprint photographic process used for copying engineering drawings and architectural plans, so called because it produces a white copy of the original against a blue background.

Blue Ridge Mountains range extending from West Virginia to Georgia, and including Mount Mitchell 6,712 ft/2,045 m; part of the ◊Appalachians.

blues African-American music that originated in the rural American South in the late 19th century, characterized by a 12-bar construction and frequently melancholy lyrics. The guitar has been the dominant instrument; harmonica and piano are also common. Blues guitar and vocal styles have played a vital part in the development of jazz, rock, and pop music in general.

Blum Léon 1872–1950. French politician. He was converted to socialism by the ◊Dreyfus affair 1899 and in 1936 became the first socialist prime minister of France. He was again premier for a few weeks 1938. Imprisoned under the ◊Vichy government 1942 as a danger to French security, he was released by the Allies 1945. He again became premier for a few weeks 1946.

boa any of various nonvenomous snakes of the family Boidae, found mainly in tropical and subtropical parts of the New World. Boas feed mainly on small mammals and birds. They catch these in their teeth or kill them by constriction (crushing the creature within their coils until it suffocates). The boa constrictor *Constrictor constrictor* can grow up to 18.5 ft/5.5 m long, but rarely reaches more than 12 ft/4 m. Other boas include the anaconda and the emerald tree boa *Boa canina*, about 6 ft/2 m long and bright green.

boar wild member of the pig family, such as the Eurasian wild boar *Sus scrofa*, from which domestic pig breeds derive. The wild boar is sturdily built, being 4.5 ft/1.5 m long and 3 ft/1 m high, and possesses formidable tusks. Of gregarious nature and mainly woodland-dwelling, it feeds on roots, nuts, insects, and some carrion.

boat people illegal emigrants traveling by sea, especially those Vietnamese who left their country after the takeover of South Vietnam 1975 by North Vietnam. Some 160,000 Vietnamese fled to Hong Kong, many being attacked at sea by Thai pirates, and in 1989 50,000 remained there in cramped, squalid refugee camps. The UK government began forced repatriation 1990.

bobcat cat *Felis rufa* living in a variety of habitats from S Canada through to S Mexico. It is similar to the lynx, but only 2.5 ft/75 cm long, with reddish fur and less well-developed ear tufts.

bobsledding the sport of racing steel-bodied, steerable toboggans, crewed by two or four people, down mountain ice-chutes at speeds of up to 80 mph/130 kph. It was introduced as an Olympic event in 1924, and world championships have been held every year since 1931. Included among the major bobsledding events are the Olympic Championships (the four-crew event was introduced at the 1924 Winter Olympics and the two-crew in 1932); also the World Championships (the four-crew championship introduced in 1924 and the two-crew in 1931); in Olympic years winners automatically become world champions.

Boca Raton city in SE Florida, on the Atlantic Ocean, N of Miami; population (1990) 61,500. Although it is mainly a resort and residential area, there is some light industry.

Boccaccio Giovanni 1313–1375. Italian poet, chiefly known for the collection of tales called the ◊*Decameron* 1348–53.

Boccioni Umberto 1882–1916. Italian painter and sculptor. One of the founders of the ◊Futurist movement, he was a pioneer of abstract art.

Bodhidharma 6th century AD. Indian Buddhist and teacher. He entered China from S India about 520 and was the founder of the Ch'an school. Ch'an focuses on contemplation leading to intuitive meditation, a direct pointing to and stilling of the human mind. In the 20th century, the Japanese variation, ◊Zen, has attracted many followers in the West.

Bodin Jean 1530–1596. French political philosopher whose six-volume *De la République* 1576 is considered the first work on political economy.

Boeing US military and commercial aircraft manufacturer. Among the models Boeing has produced are the B-Flying 17 Fortress, 1935; the B-52 Stratofortress, 1952; the Chinook helicopter, 1961; the first jetliner, the Boeing 707, 1957; the ◊jumbo jet or Boeing 747, 1969; and the ◊jetfoil, 1975.

Boeotia ancient district of central Greece, of which ◊Thebes was the chief city. The *Boeotian League* (formed by ten city-states in the 6th century BC) superseded ◊Sparta in the leadership of Greece in the 4th century BC.

Boer Dutch settler or descendant of Dutch and Huguenot settlers in South Africa; see also ◊Afrikaner.

Boer War the second of the ◊South African Wars 1899–1902, waged between Dutch settlers in South Africa and the British.

Boethius Anicius Manilus Severinus 480–524. Roman philosopher. While imprisoned on suspicion of treason by the emperor ◊Theodoric the Great, he wrote treatises on music and mathematics and *De Consolatione Philosophiae/The Consolation of Philosophy*, a dialogue in prose. It was translated into European languages during the Middle Ages; English translations by Alfred the Great, Geoffrey Chaucer, and Queen Elizabeth I.

bog type of wetland where decomposition is slowed down and dead plant matter accumulates as ◊peat. Bogs develop under conditions of low temperature, high acidity, low nutrient supply, stagnant water, and oxygen deficiency. Typical bog plants are sphagnum moss, rushes, and cotton grass; insectivorous plants such as sundews and bladderworts are common in bogs (insect prey make up for the lack of nutrients).

Bogart Humphrey 1899–1957. US film actor who achieved fame as the gangster in *The Petrified Forest* 1936. He became an international cult figure as the tough, romantic "loner" in such films as *The Maltese Falcon* 1941 and *Casablanca* 1943, a status resurrected in the 1960s and still celebrated today. He won an Academy Award for his role in *The African Queen* 1952.

Bogomil member of a sect of Christian heretics who originated in 10th-century Bulgaria and spread throughout the Byzantine empire. Their name derives from Bogomilus, or Theophilus, probably a Greek Orthodox priest who taught in Bulgaria 927–950. Despite persecution, they were expunged by the Ottomans only after the fall of Constantinople 1453.

Bogotá capital of Colombia, South America; 8,660 ft/2,640 m above sea level on the edge of the plateau of the E Cordillera; population (1985) 4,185,000. It was founded 1538.

Bohemia area of the Czech Republic, a kingdom of central Europe from the 9th century. It was under Hapsburg rule 1526–1918, when it was included in Czechoslovakia. The name Bohemia derives from the Celtic Boii, its earliest known inhabitants.

Bohr Aage 1922– . Danish physicist who produced a new model of the nucleus 1952, known as the collective model. For this work, he shared the 1975 Nobel Prize for Physics. He was the son of Niels Bohr.

Bohr Niels Henrik David 1885–1962. Danish physicist. His theoretic work produced a new model of atomic structure, now called the Bohr model, and helped establish the validity of ◊quantum theory.

boiler any vessel that converts water into steam. Boilers are used in conventional power stations to generate steam to feed steam ◊turbines, which drive the electricity generators. They are also used in steamships, which are propelled by steam turbines, and in steam locomotives. Every boiler has a furnace in which fuel (coal, oil, or gas) is burned to produce hot gases, and a system of tubes in which heat is transferred from the gases to the water.

boiling point for any given liquid, the temperature at which the application of heat raises the temperature of the liquid no further, but converts it into vapor.

Boise capital of Idaho, located in the W part of the state, on the Boise River in the western foothills of the Rocky Mountains; population (1990) 125,700. It serves as a center for the farm and livestock products of the region and has meatpacking and food-processing industries; steel and lumber products are also manufactured.

Bokassa Jean-Bédel 1921– . President of the Central African Republic 1966–79 and later self-proclaimed emperor 1977–79. Commander in chief from 1963, in Dec 1965 he led the military coup that gave him the presidency. On Dec 4, 1976, he proclaimed the Central African Empire and one year later crowned himself as emperor for life.

His regime was characterized by arbitrary state violence and cruelty. Overthrown in 1979, Bokassa was in exile until 1986. Upon his return he was sentenced to death, but this was commuted to life imprisonment 1988.

bolero Spanish dance in triple time for a solo dancer or a couple, usually with castanet accompaniment. It was used as the title of a one-act ballet score by Ravel, choreographed by Nijinsky for Ida Rubinstein 1928.

Boleyn Anne 1507–1536. Queen of England, the woman for whom Henry VIII broke with the pope and founded the Church of England (see ◊Reformation). Second wife of Henry, she was married to him 1533 and gave birth to the future Queen Elizabeth I in the same year. Accused of adultery and incest with her half brother (a charge invented by Thomas ◊Cromwell), she was beheaded.

Bolger Jim (James) Brendan 1935– . New Zealand politician and prime minister from 1990. A successful sheep and cattle farmer, Bolger was elected to Parliament 1972. He held a variety of cabinet posts under Robert Muldoon's leadership 1977–84 and was an effective, if uncharismatic, leader of the opposition from March 1986, taking the National Party to electoral victory Oct 1990. His subsequent failure to honor election pledges, leading to cuts in welfare provision, led to a sharp fall in his popularity.

Bolívar Simón 1783–1830. South American nationalist, leader of revolutionary armies, known as *the Liberator*. He fought the Spanish colonial forces in

Bolivia Republic of
(*República de Bolivia*)

area 424,052 sq mi/1,098,581 sq km
capital La Paz (seat of government), Sucre (legal capital and seat of judiciary)
cities Santa Cruz, Cochabamba, Oruro, Potosí
physical high plateau (Altiplano) between mountain ridges (cordilleras); forest and lowlands (llano) in the E
features Andes, lakes Titicaca (the world's highest navigable lake, 12,500 ft/3,800 m) and Poopó; La Paz is world's highest capital city (11,800 ft/3,600 m)
head of state and government Gonzalo Sanchez de Lozada from 1993
political system emergent democratic republic
political parties National Revolutionary Movement (MNR), center right; Movement of the Revolutionary Left (MIR), left of center; Solidarity Civil Union (UCS), radical free-market; Nationalist Democratic Action (ADN), right of center
exports tin, antimony (second largest world producer), other nonferrous metals, oil, gas (piped to Argentina), agricultural products, coffee, sugar, cotton
currency boliviano
population (1992) 7,739,000; (Quechua 25%, Aymara

17%, mestizo (mixed) 30%, European 14%); growth rate 2.7% p.a.
life expectancy men 51, women 54
languages Spanish, Aymara, Quechua (all official)
religion Roman Catholic 95% (state-recognized)
literacy men 84%, women 65% (1985 est)
GDP $4.2 bn (1987); $617 per head

chronology
1825 Liberated from Spanish rule by Simón Bolívar; independence achieved (formerly known as Upper Peru).
1952 Dr Víctor Paz Estenssoro elected president.
1956 Dr Hernán Siles Zuazo became president.
1960 Estenssoro returned to power.
1964 Army coup led by the vice president, General René Barrientos.
1966 Barrientos became president.
1967 Uprising, led by "Che" Guevara, put down with US help.
1969 Barrientos killed in plane crash, replaced by Vice President Siles Salinas. Army coup deposed him.
1970 Army coup put General Juan Torres González in power.
1971 Torres replaced by Col Hugo Banzer Suárez.
1973 Banzer promised a return to democratic government.
1974 Attempted coup prompted Banzer to postpone elections and ban political and labor-union activity.
1978 Elections declared invalid after allegations of fraud.
1980 More inconclusive elections followed by another coup, led by General Luis García. Allegations of corruption and drug trafficking led to cancellation of US and EC aid.
1981 García forced to resign. Replaced by General Celso Torrelio Villa.
1982 Torrelio resigned. Replaced by military junta led by General Guido Vildoso. Because of worsening economy, Vildoso asked congress to install a civilian administration. Dr Siles Zuazo chosen as president.
1983 Economic aid from US and Europe resumed.
1984 New coalition government formed by Siles. Abduction of president by right-wing officers. The president undertook a five-day hunger strike as an example to the nation.
1985 President Siles resigned. Election result inconclusive; Dr Paz Estenssoro chosen by congress as president.
1989 Jaime Paz Zamora (MIR) elected president in power-sharing arrangement with Hugo Banzer Suárez, pledged to maintain fiscal and monetary discipline and preserve free-market policies.
1993 MNR won congressional and presidential elections; Gonzalo Sanchez de Lozada succeeded Zamora.

several uprisings and eventually liberated his native Venezuela 1821, Colombia and Ecuador 1822, Peru 1824, and Bolivia (a new state named after him, formerly Upper Peru) 1825.

Bolivia landlocked country in central Andes mountains in South America, bounded N and E by Brazil, SE by Paraguay, S by Argentina, and W by Chile and Peru.

Bolkiah Hassanal 1946– . Sultan of Brunei from 1967, following the abdication of his father, Omar Ali Saifuddin (1916–1986). As absolute ruler, Bolkiah also assumed the posts of prime minister and defense minister on independence 1984.

Böll Heinrich 1917–1985. German novelist. A radical Catholic and anti-Nazi, he attacked Germany's political past and the materialism of its contemporary society. His many publications include poems, short stories, and novels which satirized West German society, for example *Billard um Halbzehn/Billiards at Half-Past Nine* 1959 and *Gruppenbild mit Dame/Group Portrait with Lady* 1971. Nobel Prize for Literature 1972.

boll weevil small American beetle *Anthonomus grandis* of the weevil group. The female lays her eggs in the unripe pods or "bolls" of the cotton plant, and on these the larvae feed, causing great destruction.

Bologna industrial city and capital of Emilia-Romagna, Italy, 50 mi/80 km N of Florence; population (1988) 427,000. It was the site of an Etruscan town, later of a Roman colony, and became a republic in the 12th century. It came under papal rule 1506 and was united with Italy 1860.

Bolshevik (from Russian *bolshinstvo* "a majority") member of the majority of the Russian Social Democratic Party who split from the Mensheviks 1903. The Bolsheviks, under ◊Lenin, advocated the destruction of capitalist political and economic institutions, and the setting-up of a socialist state with power in the hands of the workers. The Bolsheviks set the ◊Russian Revolution 1917 in motion. They changed their name to the Russian Communist Party 1918.

They maintained power after the Civil War 1918–21.

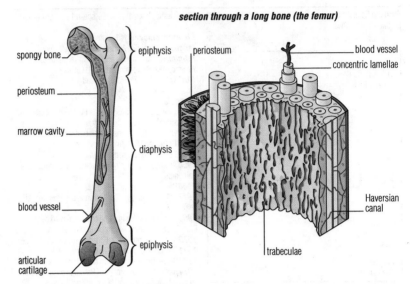

bone Bone is a network of fibrous material impregnated with mineral salts and as strong as reinforced concrete.

section through a long bone (the femur)

spongy bone
epiphysis
periosteum
blood vessel
concentric lamellae
periosteum
marrow cavity
diaphysis
blood vessel
epiphysis
Haversian canal
articular cartilage
trabeculae

Bolt Robert (Oxton) 1924– . British dramatist, known for his historical plays, such as *A Man for All Seasons* 1960 (filmed 1967) about Thomas More, and for his screenplays, including *Lawrence of Arabia* 1962 and *Dr Zhivago* 1965.

Boltzmann constant in physics, the constant (symbol k) that relates the kinetic energy (energy of motion) of a gas atom or molecule to temperature. Its value is 1.380662×10^{-23} joules per Kelvin. It is equal to the gas constant R, divided by ◊Avogadro's number.

bomb container filled with explosive or chemical material and generally used in warfare. There are also ◊incendiary bombs and nuclear bombs and missiles (see ◊nuclear warfare). Any object designed to cause damage by explosion can be called a bomb (car bombs, letter bombs). Initially dropped from airplanes (from World War I), bombs were in World War II also launched by rocket (◊V1, V2). The 1960s saw the development of missiles that could be launched from aircraft, land sites, or submarines. In the 1970s laser guidance systems were developed to hit small targets with accuracy.

Bombay industrial port (textiles, engineering, pharmaceuticals, diamonds), commercial center, and capital of Maharashtra, W India; population (1981) 8,227,000. It is the center of the Hindi film industry.

Bonaparte Corsican family of Italian origin that gave rise to the Napoleonic dynasty: see ◊Napoleon I, ◊Napoleon II, and ◊Napoleon III. Others were the brothers and sister of Napoleon I: *Joseph* (1768–1844), whom Napoleon made king of Naples 1806 and Spain 1808; *Lucien* (1775–1840), whose handling of the Council of Five Hundred on Nov 10, 1799, ensured Napoleon's future; *Louis* (1778–1846), the father of Napoleon III, who was made king of Holland 1806–10; *Caroline* (1782–1839), who married Joachim ◊Murat 1800; and *Jerome* (1784–1860), made king of Westphalia 1807.

bond in chemistry, the result of the forces of attraction that hold together atoms of an element or elements to form a molecule. The principal types of bonding are ◊ionic, covalent, ◊metallic, and ◊intermolecular (such as hydrogen bonding).

bond in commerce, a security issued by a government, local authority, company, bank, or other institution on fixed interest. Usually a long-term security, a bond may be irredeemable (with no date of redemption), secured (giving the investor a claim on the company's property or on a part of its assets), or unsecured (not protected by a lien). Property bonds are nonfixed securities with the yield fixed to property investment. See also ◊Eurobond.

bone hard connective tissue comprising the ◊skeleton of most vertebrate animals. It consists of a network of collagen fibers impregnated with mineral salts (largely calcium phosphate and calcium carbonate), a combination that gives the bone great strength, comparable in some cases with that of reinforced concrete. Enclosed within this solid matrix are bone cells, blood vessels, and nerves. The interior of the long bones of the limbs consists of a spongy matrix filled with a soft marrow that produces blood cells.

bone china or *softpaste* semiporcelain made of 5% bone ash added to 95% kaolin; first made in the West in imitation of Chinese porcelain, whose formula was kept secret by the Chinese.

bone marrow in vertebrates, soft tissue in the center of some large bones that manufactures red and white blood cells.

bone marrow substance found inside the cavity of bones. In early life it produces red blood cells but later on lipids (fat) accumulate and its color changes from red to yellow.

Boniface VIII Benedict Caetani *c.* 1228–1303. Pope from 1294. He clashed unsuccessfully with Philip IV of France over his taxation of the clergy, and also with Henry III of England.

Boniface, St 680–754. English Benedictine monk, known as the "Apostle of Germany"; originally named Wynfrith. After a missionary journey to Frisia 716, he was given the task of bringing Christianity to Germany 718 by Pope Gregory II, and was appointed archbishop of Mainz 746. He returned to Frisia 754 and was martyred near Dockum. His feast day is June 5.

bonito any of various species of medium-sized tuna, predatory fish of the genus *Sarda*, in the mackerel family. The ocean bonito *Katsuwonus pelamis* grows to 3 ft/1 m and is common in tropical seas. The Atlantic bonito *Sarda sarda* is found in the Mediterranean and tropical Atlantic and grows to the same length but has a narrower body.

Bonn industrial city (chemicals, textiles, plastics, aluminum) and seat of government of the Federal Republic of Germany, 15 mi/18 km SSE of Cologne, on the left bank of the Rhine; population (1988) 292,000.

Bonnard Pierre 1867–1947. French Post-Impressionist painter. With other members of *les Nabis*, he explored the decorative arts (posters, stained glass, furniture). He painted domestic interiors and nudes.

Bonneville Salt Flats bed of a prehistoric lake in Utah, of which the Great Salt Lake is the surviving remnant. The flats, near the Nevada border, have been used to set many land speed records.

Bonney William H see ◊Billy the Kid.

Bonnie and Clyde Bonnie Parker (1911–1934) and Clyde Barrow (1900–1934). Infamous US criminals who carried out a series of small-scale robberies in Texas, Oklahoma, New Mexico, and Missouri between Aug 1932 and May 1934. They were eventually betrayed and then killed in a police ambush.

bonsai (Japanese "bowl cultivation") art of producing miniature trees by selective pruning. It originated in China many centuries ago and later spread to Japan. Some specimens in China are about 1,000 years old and some in the imperial Japanese collection are more than 300 years old.

Bonus Army or *Bonus Expeditionary Force* in US history, a march on Washington, DC, by unemployed ex-servicemen during the great ◊Depression to lobby Congress for immediate cash payment of a promised war veterans' bonus.

boogie-woogie jazz played on the piano, using a repeated motif for the left hand. It was common in the US from around 1900 to the 1950s. Boogie-woogie players included Pinetop Smith (1904–1929), Meade "Lux" Lewis (1905–1964), and Jimmy Yancey (1898–1951). Rock-and-roll pianist Jerry Lee Lewis adapted the style.

bookbinding securing of the pages of a book between protective covers by sewing and/or gluing. Cloth binding was first introduced 1822, but from the mid-20th century synthetic bindings were increasingly employed, and most hardcover books are bound by machine.

bookkeeping process of recording commercial transactions in a systematic and established procedure. These records provide the basis for the preparation of accounts.

booklouse any of numerous species of tiny wingless insects of the order Psocoptera, especially *Atropus pulsatoria*, which lives in books and papers, feeding on starches and molds.

Boole George 1815–1864. English mathematician whose work *The Mathematical Analysis of Logic* 1847 established the basis of modern mathematical logic, and whose *Boolean algebra* can be used in designing computers.

boomerang hand-thrown, flat wooden hunting missile shaped in a curved angle, formerly used throughout the world but developed by the Australian Aborigines to a great degree of diversity and elaboration. It is used to kill game and as a weapon or, in the case of the returning boomerang, as recreation.

Boone Daniel 1734–1820. US pioneer who explored the Wilderness Road (East Virginia–Kentucky) 1775 and paved the way for the first westward migration of settlers.

Boone was born in Pennsylvania and spent most of his youth in North Carolina. During the American Revolution, he led militias against Indians allied with the British. He was captured by a Shawnee war party and so impressed the chief that he was adopted by the tribe. He left the Indians and continued to explore westward.

Booth Edwin Thomas 1833–1893. US actor. He was one of America's most acclaimed Shakespearean performers, famous for his portrayal of Hamlet. As lead actor, theater manager, and producer, he successfully brought to the New York stage numerous Shakespearean tragedies. His career suffered in the wake of the public disgrace of his brother John Wilkes ◊Booth, who assassinated President Lincoln 1865.

Booth John Wilkes 1839–1865. US actor and fanatical Confederate sympathizer who assassinated President Abraham ◊Lincoln April 14, 1865; he escaped with a broken leg and was later shot in a barn in Virginia when he refused to surrender.

He had earlier conceived a plan to kidnap Lincoln and decided to kill him in vengeance when the plan failed.

Boothe Claire see ◊Luce, Claire Boothe.

bootlegging illegal manufacture, distribution, or sale of a product. The term originated in the US, when the sale of alcohol to American Indians was illegal and bottles were hidden for sale in the legs of the jackboots of unscrupulous traders. The term was later used for all illegal liquor sales during the period of ◊Prohibition in the US 1920–33, and is often applied to unauthorized commercial tape recordings and the copying of computer software.

Bophuthatswana Republic of; self-governing black "homeland" within South Africa
area 15,571 sq mi/40,330 sq km
capital Mmbatho or Sun City, a casino resort frequented by many white South Africans
features divided into six "blocks"
exports platinum, chromium, vanadium, asbestos, manganese
currency South African rand
population (1985) 1,627,000
languages Setswana, English
religion Christian
government executive president elected by the Assembly: Chief Lucas Mangope
recent history first "independent" Black National State from 1977, but not recognized by any country other than South Africa.

Bora-Bora one of the 14 Society Islands of French Polynesia; situated 140 mi/225 km NW of Tahiti; area 15 sq mi/39 sq km; population (1977) 2,500. Exports include mother-of-pearl, fruit, and tobacco.

borax hydrous sodium borate, $Na_2B_4O_7 \cdot 10H_2O$, found as soft, whitish crystals or encrustations on the shores of hot springs and in the dry beds of salt lakes in arid regions, where it occurs with other borates, halite, and ◊gypsum. It is used in bleaches and washing powders.

Bordeaux port on the river Garonne, capital of Aquitaine, SW France, a center for the wine trade, oil refining, and aeronautics and space industries; population (1990) 213,300. Bordeaux was under the English crown for three centuries until 1453. In 1870, 1914, and 1940 the French government was moved here because of German invasion.

Borelli Giovanni Alfonso 1608–1679. Italian scientist who explored the links between physics and medicine and showed how mechanical principles could be applied to animal ◊physiology. This approach, known as iatrophysics, has proved basic to understanding how the mammalian body works.

Borg Björn (Rune) 1956– . Swedish tennis player who won the men's singles title at Wimbledon five times 1976–80, a record since the abolition of the challenge system 1922. He also won six French Open singles titles 1974–75 and 1978–81 inclusive. In 1990 Borg announced plans to return to professional tennis, but he enjoyed little competitive success 1991–92.

Borges Jorge Luis 1899–1986. Argentine poet and short-story writer, an exponent of ◊magic realism. In 1961 he became director of the National Library, Buenos Aires, and was professor of English literature at the university there. He is known for his fantastic and paradoxical work *Ficciones/Fictions* 1944.

Borgia Cesare 1476–1507. Italian general, illegitimate son of Pope ◊Alexander VI. Made a cardinal at 17 by his father, he resigned to become captain-general of the papacy, campaigning successfully against the city republics of Italy. Ruthless and treacherous in war, he was an able ruler (the model for Machiavelli's *The Prince*), but his power crumbled on the death of his father. He was a patron of artists, including Leonardo da Vinci.

Borgia Lucrezia 1480–1519. Duchess of Ferrara from 1501. She was the illegitimate daughter of Pope ◊Alexander VI and sister of Cesare Borgia. She was married at 12 and again at 13 to further her father's ambitions, both marriages being annulled by him. At 18 she was married again, but her husband was murdered in 1500 on the order of her brother, with whom (as well as with her father) she was said to have committed incest. Her final marriage was to the Duke of Este, the son and heir of the Duke of Ferrara. She made the court a center of culture and was a patron of authors and artists such as Ariosto and Titian.

boric acid or *boracic acid* H_3BO_3, acid formed by the combination of hydrogen and oxygen with nonmetallic boron. It is a weak antiseptic and is used in the manufacture of glass and enamels. It is also an efficient insecticide against ants and cockroaches.

Borlaug Norman Ernest 1914– . US microbiologist and agronomist. He developed high-yielding varieties of wheat and other grain crops to be grown in Third World countries, and was the first to use the term "Green Revolution." Nobel Prize for Peace 1970.

Bormann Martin 1900–1945. German Nazi leader. He took part in the abortive Munich putsch (uprising) 1923 and rose to high positions in the Nazi (National Socialist) Party, becoming deputy party leader May 1941.

Born Max 1882–1970. German physicist who received a Nobel Prize 1954 for fundamental work on the ◊quantum theory. He left Germany for the UK during the Nazi era.

Borneo third-largest island in the world, one of the Sunda Islands in the W Pacific; area 290,000 sq mi/754,000 sq km. It comprises the Malaysian territories of *Sabah* and ◊*Sarawak,* ◊*Brunei,* and, occupying by far the largest part, the Indonesian territory of ◊*Kalimantan.* It is mountainous and densely forested. In coastal areas the people of Borneo are mainly of Malaysian origin, with a few Chinese, and the interior is inhabited by the indigenous Dyaks. It was formerly under both Dutch and British colonial influence until Sarawak was formed 1841.

Bornu kingdom of the 9th–19th centuries to the west and south of Lake Chad, W central Africa. Converted to Islam in the 11th century, Bornu reached its greatest strength in the 15th–18th centuries. From 1901 it was absorbed in the British, French, and German colonies in this area, which became the states of Niger, Cameroon, and Nigeria. The largest section of ancient Bornu is now the *state of Bornu* in Nigeria.

Borodin Alexander Porfir'yevich 1833–1887. Russian composer. Born in St Petersburg, the illegitimate son of a Russian prince, he became by profession an expert in medical chemistry, but in his spare time devoted himself to music. His principal work is the opera *Prince Igor,* left unfinished; it was completed by Rimsky-Korsakov and Glazunov and includes the Polovtsian Dances.

boron nonmetallic element, symbol B, atomic number 5, atomic weight 10.811. In nature it is found only in compounds, as with sodium and oxygen in borax. It exists in two allotropic forms (see ◊allotropy): brown amorphous powder and very hard, brilliant crystals. Its compounds are used in the preparation of boric acid, water softeners, soaps, enamels, glass, and pottery glazes. In alloys it is used to harden steel. Because it absorbs slow neutrons, it is used to make boron carbide control rods for nuclear reactors. It is a necessary trace element in the human diet. The element was named by Humphry Davy, who isolated it 1808, from *bor*ax + -on, as in carb*on*.

Borromini Francesco 1599–1667. Italian Baroque architect, one of the two most important (with ◊Bernini, his main rival) in 17th-century Rome. Whereas Bernini designed in a florid, expansive style, his pupil Borromini developed a highly idiosyncratic and austere use of the Classical language of architecture. His genius may be seen in the cathedrals of San Carlo 1641 and San Ivo 1660 and the oratorio of St Filippo Neri 1650.

borzoi large breed of dog originating in Russia, 2.5 ft/75 cm or more at the shoulder. It is of the greyhound type, white with darker markings, with a thick, silky coat.

Bosch Carl 1874–1940. German metallurgist and chemist. He developed Fritz Haber's small-scale technique for the production of ammonia into an industrial high-pressure process that made use of water gas as a source of hydrogen; see ◊Haber process. He shared the Nobel Prize for Chemistry 1931 with Friedrich Bergius.

Bosch Hieronymus (Jerome) 1460–1516. Early Dutch painter. His fantastic visions of weird and hellish creatures, as shown in *The Garden of Earthly Delights* about 1505–10 (Prado, Madrid), show astonishing imagination and a complex imagery. His religious subjects focused not on the holy figures but on the mass of ordinary witnesses, placing the religious event in a contemporary Dutch context and creating cruel caricatures of human sinfulness.

Bosnia-Herzegovina Serbo-Croatian *Bosna-Hercegovina* country in central Europe, bounded N and W by Croatia, E by the Yugoslavian republic of Serbia, and E and S by the Yugoslavian republic of Montenegro.

Bosnian Crisis period of international tension 1908 when Austria attempted to capitalize on Turkish weakness after the ◊Young Turk revolt by annexing the provinces of Bosnia and Herzegovina. Austria

Bosnia-Herzegovina
Republic of

area 19,745 sq mi/51,129 sq km
capital Sarajevo
cities Banja Luka, Mostar, Prijedor, Tuzla, Zenica
physical barren, mountainous country
features part of the Dinaric Alps, limestone gorges
population (1992) 4,397,000 including 44% Muslims, 33% Serbs, 17% Croats; a complex patchwork of ethnically mixed communities
head of state Alija Izetbegović from 1990
head of government Mile Akmadžīc from 1992
political system emergent democracy
political parties Party of Democratic Action (SDA), Muslim-oriented; Serbian Democratic Party (SDS), Serbian nationalist; Christian Democratic Union (HDS), centrist; League of Communists, left-wing
products citrus fruits and vegetables; iron, steel, and leather goods; textiles
language Serbian variant of Serbo-Croatian
religions Sunni Muslim, Serbian Orthodox, Roman Catholic

chronology
1918 Incorporated in the future Yugoslavia.
1941 Occupied by Nazi Germany.
1945 Became republic within Yugoslav Socialist Federation.
1980 Upsurge in Islamic nationalism.
1990 Ethnic violence erupted between Muslims and Serbs. Nov–Dec: communists defeated in multiparty elections; coalition formed by Serb, Muslim, and Croatian parties.
1991 May: Serbia–Croatia conflict spread disorder into Bosnia-Herzegovina. Aug: Serbia revealed plans to annex the SE part of the republic. Sept: Serbian enclaves established by force. Oct: "sovereignty" declared. Nov: plebiscite by Serbs favored remaining within Yugoslavia; Serbs and Croats established autonomous communities.
1992 Feb–March: Muslims and Croats voted overwhelmingly in favor of independence; referendum boycotted by Serbs. April: US and EC recognized Bosnian independence. Ethnic hostilities escalated, with Serb forces occupying E and Croatian forces much of W; state of emergency declared; all-out civil war. May: admitted to United Nations. June: UN forces drafted into Sarajevo to break three-month siege of city by Serbs. Accusations of "ethnic cleansing" being practiced, particularly by Serbs. Oct: UN ban on military flights over Bosnia-Herzegovina. First British troops deployed.
1993 UN–EC peace plan introduced, failed. US began airdrops of food and medical supplies.

obtained Russian approval in exchange for conceding Russian access to the Bosporus straits.

Bosporus (Turkish *Karadeniz Bogåazi*) strait 17 mi/27 km long, joining the Black Sea with the Sea of Marmara and forming part of the water division between Europe and Asia; its name may be derived from the Greek legend of ◊Io. Istanbul stands on its west side. The *Bosporus Bridge* 1973, 5,320 ft/1,621 m, links Istanbul and Anatolia (the Asian part of Turkey). In 1988 a second bridge across the straits was opened, linking Asia and Europe.

Boston industrial and commercial center, capital of Massachusetts; population (1990) 574,300; metropolitan area 4,171,600. It is a publishing center and industrial port on Massachusetts Bay, but the economy is dominated by financial and health services and government. Boston and Northeastern universities are here. Harvard University and the Massachusetts Institute of Technology are in neighboring Cambridge, across the Charles River.

features Faneuil Hall, Old North Church, Paul Revere house, USS *Constitution* ("Old Ironsides"), New England Aquarium, Museum of Science, J F Kennedy National Historic Site

history founded by Puritans 1630, Boston was a center of opposition to British trade restrictions, culminating in the Boston Tea Party 1773. After the first shots of the American Revolution in 1775 at nearby Lexington and Concord, the Battle of Bunker Hill was fought outside the city. The British withdrew from the city 1776. In the 19th century, Boston became the metropolis of New England. Urban redevelopment and the growth of service industries have compensated for the city's industrial decline.

Boston Tea Party protest 1773 by colonists in Massachusetts, against the tea tax imposed on them by the British government before the ◊American Revolution.

Boswell James 1740–1795. Scottish biographer and diarist. He was a member of Samuel ◊Johnson's London Literary Club and the two men traveled to Scotland together 1773, as recorded in Boswell's *Journal of the Tour to the Hebrides* 1785. His classic English biography *Life of Samuel Johnson* was published 1791.

botanical garden place where a wide range of plants is grown, providing the opportunity to see a botanical diversity not likely to be encountered naturally. Among the earliest forms of botanical garden was the *physic garden*, devoted to the study and growth of medicinal plants; an example is the Chelsea Physic Garden in London, established 1673 and still in existence. Following increased botanical exploration, botanical gardens were used to test the commercial potential of new plants being sent back from all parts of the world.

botany the study of plants. It is subdivided into a number of specialized studies, such as the identification and classification of plants (taxonomy), their external formation (plant morphology), their internal arrangement (plant anatomy), their microscopic examination (plant histology), their functioning and life history (plant physiology), and their distribution over the Earth's surface in relation to their surroundings (plant ecology). Paleobotany concerns the study of fossil plants, while economic botany deals with the utility of plants. Horticulture, agriculture, and forestry are branches of botany.

Botswana Republic of

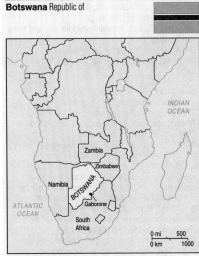

area 225,000 sq mi/582,000 sq km
capital Gaborone
cities Mahalpye, Serowe, Tutume, Francistown
physical desert in SW, plains in E, fertile lands and swamp in N
environment the Okavango Swamp is threatened by plans to develop the area for mining and agriculture
features Kalahari Desert in SW; Okavango Swamp in N, remarkable for its wildlife; Makgadikgadi salt pans in E; diamonds mined at Orapa and Jwaneng in partnership with De Beers of South Africa

head of state and government Quett Ketamile Joni Masire from 1980
political system democratic republic
political parties Botswana Democratic Party (BDP), moderate centrist; Botswana National Front (BNF), moderate, left of center
exports diamonds (third largest producer in world), copper, nickel, meat products, textiles
currency pula
population (1992) 1,359,000 (Bamangwato 80%, Bangwaketse 20%); growth rate 3.5% p.a.
life expectancy (1988) 59 years
languages English (official), Setswana (national)
religions Christian 50%, animist 50%
literacy (1988) 84%
GDP $2.0 bn (1988); $1,611 per head

chronology
1885 Became a British protectorate.
1960 New constitution created a legislative council.
1963 End of rule by High Commission.
1965 Capital transferred from Mafeking to Gaborone. Internal self-government achieved. Sir Seretse Khama elected head of government.
1966 Independence achieved from Britain. New constitution came into effect; name changed from Bechuanaland to Botswana; Seretse Khama elected president.
1980 Seretse Khama died; succeeded by Vice President Quett Masire.
1984 Masire reelected.
1985 South African raid on Gaborone.
1987 Joint permanent commission with Mozambique established, to improve relations.
1989 The BDP and Masire reelected.

Botany Bay inlet on the east coast of Australia, 5 mi/ 8 km S of Sydney, New South Wales. Chosen 1787 as the site for a penal colony, it proved unsuitable. Sydney now stands on the site of the former settlement. The name Botany Bay continued to be popularly used for any convict settlement in Australia.

Botha P(ieter) W(illem) 1916– . South African politician, prime minister from 1978. Botha initiated a modification of ◊apartheid, which later slowed in the face of Afrikaner (Boer) opposition. In 1984 he became the first executive state president. In 1989 he unwillingly resigned both party leadership and presidency after suffering a stroke, and was succeeded by F W de Klerk.

Botswana landlocked country in central southern Africa, bounded S and SE by South Africa, W and N by Namibia, and NE by Zimbabwe.

Botticelli Sandro 1445–1510. Florentine painter of religious and mythological subjects. He was patronized by the ruling ◊Medici family, for whom he painted *Primavera* 1478 and *The Birth of Venus* about 1482–84 (both in the Uffizi, Florence). From the 1490s he was influenced by the religious fanatic ◊Savonarola and developed a harshly expressive and emotional style.

botulism rare, often fatal type of ◊food poisoning. Symptoms include muscular paralysis and disturbed breathing and vision. It is caused by a toxin produced by the bacterium *Clostridium botulinum*, sometimes found in improperly canned food.

Boucher François 1703–1770. French Rococo painter, court painter from 1765. He was much patronized for his lighthearted, decorative scenes: for example *Diana Bathing* 1742 (Louvre, Paris).

Boudicca Queen of the Iceni (native Britons), often referred to by the Latin form *Boadicea*. Her husband, King Prasutagus, had been a tributary of the Romans, but on his death AD 60 the territory of the Iceni was violently annexed. Boudicca was scourged and her daughters raped. Boudicca raised the whole of SE England in revolt, and before the main Roman armies could return from campaigning in Wales she burned Londinium (London), Verulamium (St Albans), and Camolodunum (Colchester). Later the Romans under governor Suetonius Paulinus defeated the British between London and Chester; they were virtually annihilated and Boudicca poisoned herself.

Bougainville Louis Antoine de 1729–1811. French navigator. After service with the French in Canada during the Seven Years' War, he made the first French circumnavigation of the world 1766–69 and the first systematic observations of longitude.

bougainvillea any plant of the genus of South American tropical vines *Bougainvillea*, of the four o'clock family Nyctaginaceae, now cultivated in warm countries throughout the world for the red and purple bracts that cover the flowers. They are named after the French navigator Louis Bougainville.

Boulanger Nadia (Juliette) 1887–1979. French music teacher and conductor. A pupil of Fauré, and admirer of Stravinsky, she included among her composition pupils at the American Conservatory in Fontainebleau (from 1921) Aaron Copland, Roy Harris, Walter Piston, and Philip Glass.

She was the first woman to conduct the Royal Philharmonic, London, 1937 and the Boston Symphony, the New York Philharmonic, and the Philadelphia Orchestra 1938.

Boulder city in N central Colorado, NW of Denver, in the eastern foothills of the Rocky Mountains; population (1990) 83,300. A center of scientific research, especially space research, it also has agriculture, mining, and tourism.

It is the site of the University of Colorado 1876.

Boulez Pierre 1925– . French composer and conductor. He studied with ◊Messiaen and promoted contemporary music with a series of innovative *Domaine Musical* concerts and recordings in the 1950s, as conductor of the BBC Symphony and New York Philharmonic orchestras during the 1970s, and as founder and director of IRCAM, a music research studio in Paris opened 1977.

Boumédienne Houari. Adopted name of Mohammed Boukharouba 1925–1978. Algerian politician who brought the nationalist leader Ben Bella to power by a revolt 1962 and superseded him as president in 1965 by a further coup.

Bounty, Mutiny on the. Naval mutiny in the Pacific 1789 against British captain William ◊Bligh.

Bourbon dynasty French royal house (succeeding that of ◊Valois), beginning with Henry IV and ending with Louis XVI, with a brief revival under Louis XVIII, Charles X, and Louis Philippe. The Bourbons also ruled Spain almost uninterruptedly from Philip V to Alfonso XIII and were restored in 1975 (◊Juan Carlos); at one point they also ruled Naples and several Italian duchies. The Grand Duke of Luxembourg is also a Bourbon by male descent.

Bourdon gauge instrument for measuring pressure, patented by French watchmaker Eugène Bourdon 1849. The gauge contains a C-shaped tube, closed at one end. When the pressure inside the tube increases, the tube uncurls slightly causing a small movement at its closed end. A system of levers and gears magnifies this movement and turns a pointer, which indicates the pressure on a circular scale. Bourdon gauges are often fitted to cylinders of compressed gas used in industry and hospitals.

Bourgeois Léon Victor Auguste 1851–1925. French politician. Entering politics as a Radical, he was prime minister in 1895, and later served in many cabinets. He was one of the pioneer advocates of the League of Nations. He was awarded the Nobel Peace Prize 1920.

bourgeoisie (French) the middle classes. The French word originally meant "the freemen of a borough." It came to mean the whole class above the workers and peasants, and below the nobility. Bourgeoisie (and *bourgeois*) has also acquired a contemptuous sense, implying commonplace, philistine respectability. By socialists it is applied to the whole propertied class, as distinct from the proletariat.

Bourguiba Habib ben Ali 1903– . Tunisian politician, first president of Tunisia 1957–87. Educated at the University of Paris, he became a journalist and was frequently imprisoned by the French for his nationalist aims as leader of the Néo-Destour party. He became prime minister 1956, president (for life from 1974) and prime minister of the Tunisian republic 1957; he was overthrown in a bloodless coup 1987.

Boutros-Ghali Boutros 1922– . Egyptian diplomat and politician, deputy prime minister 1991–92. He worked toward peace in the Middle East in the foreign ministry posts he held 1977–91. He became secretary-general of the United Nations Jan 1992, and during his first year of office had to deal with the war in Bosnia-Herzegovina and famine in Somalia.

Bouvines, Battle of victory for Philip II (Philip Augustus) of France in 1214, near the village of Bouvines in Flanders, over the Holy Roman emperor Otto IV and his allies. The battle, one of the most decisive in medieval Europe, ensured the succession of Frederick II as emperor and confirmed Philip as ruler of the whole of N France and Flanders; it led to the renunciation of all English claims to the region.

Bow Clara 1905–1965. US film actress known as a "Jazz Baby" and the "It Girl" after her portrayal of a glamorous flapper in the silent film *It* 1927.

She made a smooth transition to sound with *The Wild Party* 1929. Other films include *Down to the Sea in Ships* 1925; *The Plastic Age, Kid Boots, Mantrap,* and *Dancing Mothers,* all 1926; *Rough House Rosie* 1927; *Red Hair* and *Three Weekends,* both 1928; and *The Saturday Night Kid* 1929. She made her last film *Hoopla* 1933 and retired to her husband's ranch in Nevada.

Bowditch Nathaniel 1773–1838. US astronomer. He wrote *The New American Practical Navigator* 1802, having discovered many inaccuracies in the standard navigation guide of the day. His *Celestial Mechanics* 1829–39 was a translation of the first four volumes of French astronomer Pierre Laplace's *Traité de mécanique céleste* 1799–1825.

Bowdler Thomas 1754–1825. British editor whose prudishly expurgated versions of Shakespeare and other authors gave rise to the verb *bowdlerize*.

Bowdoin James 1726–1790. American public official. A supporter of American independence, he was elected to the Massachusetts General Court 1753, chosen as a member of the Governor's Council 1757, and served on the Massachusetts Executive Council

Botticelli The Madonna of the Eucharist *(c. 1472), Isabella Stewart Gardner Museum, Boston. Botticelle's ecclesiastical commissions included work for many of Florence's major churches and for the Sistine Chapel in Rome. His allegorical paintings, produced for the Medicis, were influenced by humanist writers and epitomize the spirit of the Renaissance.*

1775–76. He was president of the state constitutional convention 1779–80 and governor 1785–87.

Bowdoin College in Brunswick, Maine, is named in his honor.

Bowie David. Adopted name of David Jones 1947– . English pop singer, songwriter, and actor whose career has been a series of image changes. His hits include "Jean Genie" 1973, "Rebel, Rebel" 1974, "Golden Years" 1975, and "Underground" 1986. He has acted in plays and films, including Nicolas Roeg's *The Man Who Fell to Earth* 1976.

Bowie James "Jim" 1796–1836. US frontiersman and folk hero. A colonel in the Texan forces during the Mexican War, he is said to have invented the single-edge, guarded hunting and throwing knife known as a *Bowie knife*. He was killed in the battle of the ◊Alamo.

bowling indoor sport in which a ball is rolled into a target of standing pins. There are many forms of the sport, but the term "bowling" usually refers to the most popular variety, tenpin. The ball used in tenpin bowling is sometimes plastic but more commonly hard rubber. An official ball (one allowed in league play) must weigh 10–16 lb/4.5–7.3 kg and may not exceed 8.6 in/21.8 cm in diameter. Finger holes are drilled into each ball. Methods of gripping differ from bowler to bowler but most common is the underhand three-finger grip (thumb, middle finger, and ring finger).

bowls a lawn bowling game played on a bowling green and indoors.

box any of several small evergreen trees and shrubs, genus *Buxus*, of the family Buxaceae, with small, leathery leaves. Some species are used as hedge plants and for shaping into garden ornaments.

boxer breed of dog, about 2 ft/60 cm tall, with a smooth coat and a set-back nose. The tail is usually docked. Boxers are usually brown but may be brindled or white.

Boxer member of the *I ho ch'üan* ("Righteous Harmonious Fists"), a society of Chinese nationalists dedicated to fighting European influence. The *Boxer Rebellion* or *Uprising* 1900 was instigated by the empress ◊Zi Xi. European and US legations in Beijing were besieged and thousands of Chinese Christian converts and missionaries murdered. An international punitive force was dispatched, Beijing was captured Aug 14, 1900, and China agreed to pay a large indemnity.

Brahms German composer Brahms in his study.

boxfish or *trunkfish*, any fish of the family Ostraciodontidae, with scales that are hexagonal bony plates fused to form a box covering the body, only the mouth and fins being free of the armor. Boxfishes swim slowly. The cowfish, genus *Lactophrys*, with two "horns" above the eyes, is a member of this group.

boxing fighting with gloved fists, almost entirely a male sport. The sport dates from the 18th century, when fights were fought with bare knuckles and untimed rounds. Each round ended with a knockdown. Fighting with gloves became the accepted form in the latter part of the 19th century after the formulation of the Queensberry Rules 1867.

Boxing has school, amateur, semiprofessional, and professional matches.

Boyd-Orr John 1880–1971. British nutritionist and health campaigner. He was awarded the Nobel Prize for Peace in 1949 in recognition of his work toward alleviating world hunger.

Boyle's law law stating that the volume of a given mass of gas at a constant temperature is inversely proportional to its pressure. For example, if the pressure of a gas doubles, its volume will be reduced by a half, and vice versa. The law was discovered in 1662 by Irish physicist and chemist Robert Boyle.

Brabant (Flemish *Braband*) former duchy of W Europe, comprising the Dutch province of ◊North Brabant and the Belgian provinces of Brabant and Antwerp. They were divided when Belgium became independent 1830. The present-day Belgian province of Brabant has an area of 1,312 sq mi/3,400 sq km and a population (1987) of 2,245,900.

brachiopod any member of the phylum Brachiopoda, marine invertebrates with two shells, resembling but totally unrelated to bivalves. There are about 300 living species; they were much more numerous in past geological ages. They are suspension feeders, ingesting minute food particles from water. A single internal organ, the iophophore, handles feeding, aspiration, and excretion.

bracken large fern, especially *Pteridium aquilinum*, abundant in the northern hemisphere. A perennial rootstock throws up coarse fronds.

bracket fungus any ◊fungus of the class Basidiomycetes, with fruiting bodies that grow like shelves from trees.

bract leaflike structure in whose axil a flower or inflorescence develops. Bracts are generally green and smaller than the true leaves. However, in some plants they may be brightly colored and conspicuous, taking over the role of attracting pollinating insects to the flowers, whose own petals are small; examples include poinsettia *Euphorbia pulcherrima* and bougainvillea.

Bradenton city in W Florida, on the S shores of Tampa Bay, SW of Tampa; seat of Manatee County; population (1990) 43,800. It is a resort center during the winter months. Some travertine, a sparkling sheet of calcium carbonate formed on cave walls and floors, is quarried here.

Bradford William 1590–1657. British colonial administrator in America, the first governor of Plymouth colony, Massachusetts, 1621–57. As one of the Pilgrim Fathers he sailed for America aboard the *Mayflower* 1620 and was among the signatories of the Mayflower Compact, the first written constitution in the New World. His memoirs, *History of Plimoth Plantation*, are an important source for the colony's early history.

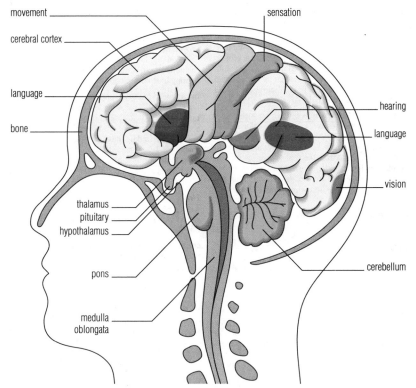

movement

cerebral cortex

language

bone

thalamus
pituitary
hypothalamus

pons

medulla
oblongata

sensation

hearing

language

vision

cerebellum

brain Cross section of a human brain, showing the surface of the right half of the cerebrum and sections through the midbrain, pons, medulla oblongata, and cerebellum.

Bradley Omar Nelson 1893–1981. US general in World War II. In 1943 he commanded the 2nd US Corps in their victories in Tunisia and Sicily, leading to the surrender of 250,000 Axis troops, and in 1944 led the US troops in the invasion of France. His command, as the 12th Army Group, grew to 1.3 million troops, the largest US force ever assembled.

Born in Clark, Missouri, Bradley graduated from West Point 1915 and served in World War I. After World War II, he headed the Veterans Administration 1945–47, was chief of staff of the US Army 1948–49, and was the first chairman of the joint chiefs of staff 1949–53. He was appointed general of the army 1950 and retired from the army 1953. He wrote his memoirs in *A Soldier's Story* 1951.

Brahma in Hinduism, the creator of the cosmos, who forms with Vishnu and Siva the Trimurti, or three aspects of the absolute spirit.

Brahman in Hinduism, the supreme being, an abstract, impersonal world-soul into whom the *atman*, or individual soul, will eventually be absorbed when its cycle of rebirth is ended.

Brahmanism earliest stage in the development of ◊Hinduism. Its sacred scriptures are the ◊Vedas, with their accompanying literature of comment and explanation known as Brahmanas, Aranyakas, and Upanishads.

Brahmaputra river in Asia 1,800 mi/2,900 km long, a tributary of the Ganges.

Brahms Johannes 1833–1897. German composer, pianist, and conductor. Considered one of the greatest composers of symphonic music and of songs, his works include four symphonies, lieder (songs), concertos for piano and for violin, chamber music, sonatas,

and the choral *A German Requiem* 1868. He performed and conducted his own works.

Braille system of writing for the blind. Letters are represented by a combination of raised dots on paper or other materials, which are then read by touch. It was invented in 1829 by *Louis Braille* (1809–1852), who became blind at the age of three.

brain in higher animals, a mass of interconnected ◊nerve cells, forming the anterior part of the ◊central nervous system, whose activities it coordinates and controls. In ◊vertebrates, the brain is contained by the skull. An enlarged portion of the upper spinal cord, the *medulla oblongata*, contains centers for the control of respiration, heartbeat rate and strength, and blood pressure. Overlying this is the *cerebellum*, which is concerned with coordinating complex muscular processes such as maintaining posture and moving limbs. The cerebral hemispheres (*cerebrum*) are paired outgrowths of the front end of the forebrain, in early vertebrates mainly concerned with the senses, but in higher vertebrates greatly developed and involved in the integration of all sensory input and motor output, and in intelligent behavior.

brake device used to slow down or stop the movement of a moving body or vehicle. The mechanically applied caliper brake used on bicycles uses a scissor action to press hard rubber blocks against the wheel rim. The main braking system of an automobile works hydraulically: when the driver depresses the brake pedal, liquid pressure forces pistons to apply brakes on each wheel.

Bramante Donato *c.* 1444–1514. Italian Renaissance architect and artist. Inspired by Classical designs, he was employed by Pope Julius II in rebuilding part of the Vatican and St Peter's in Rome.

bramble any prickly bush of a genus *Rubus* belonging to the rose family Rosaceae. Examples are ◊blackberry, raspberry, and dewberry.

Brancusi Constantin 1876–1957. Romanian sculptor, active in Paris from 1904, a pioneer of abstract forms and conceptual art. He developed increasingly simplified natural or organic forms, such as the sculpted head that gradually came to resemble an egg (*Sleeping Muse* 1910, Musée National d'Art Moderne, Paris).

Brandeis Louis Dembitz 1856–1941. US jurist. As a crusader for progressive causes, he helped draft social-welfare and labor legislation. In 1916, with his appointment to the US Supreme Court by President Wilson, he became the first Jewish justice and maintained his support of individual rights in his opposition to the 1917 Espionage Act and in his dissenting opinion in the first wiretap case, *Olmstead* v *US* 1928.

Brandenburg administrative *Land* (state) of Germany
area 10,000 sq mi/25,000 sq km
capital Potsdam
cities Cottbus, Brandenburg, Frankfurt-on-Oder
products iron and steel, paper, pulp, metal products, semiconductors
population (1990) 2,700,000
history the Hohenzollern rulers who took control of Brandenburg 1415 later acquired the powerful duchy of Prussia and became emperors of Germany. At the end of World War II, Brandenburg lost over 5,000 sq mi/12,950 sq km of territory when Poland advanced its frontier to the line of the Oder and Neisse rivers. The remainder, which became a region of East Germany, was divided 1952 into the districts of Frankfurt-on-Oder, Potsdam, and Cottbus. When Germany was reunited 1990, Brandenburg reappeared as a state of the Federal Republic.

Brando Marlon 1924– . US actor whose casual style, mumbling speech, and use of Method acting earned him a place as a distinctive actor. He won best-actor Academy Awards for *On the Waterfront* 1954 and *The Godfather* 1972.

Brandt Willy. Adopted name of Karl Herbert Frahm 1913–1992. German socialist politician, federal chancellor (premier) of West Germany 1969–74. He played a key role in the remolding of the Social Democratic Party (SPD) as a moderate socialist force (leader 1964–87). As mayor of West Berlin 1957–66, Brandt became internationally known during the Berlin Wall crisis 1961. Nobel Peace Prize 1971.

He resigned from the chancellorship 1974 following the discovery that an aide had been an East German spy. Brandt continued to wield considerable influence in the SPD, in particular over the party's new radical left wing. He chaired the Brandt Commission on Third World problems 1977–83 and was a member of the European Parliament 1979–83.

brandy (Dutch *brandewijn* "burnt wine") alcoholic drink distilled from fermented grape juice (wine). The best-known examples are produced in France, notably Armagnac and Cognac. Brandy can also be prepared from other fruits, for example, apples (Calvados) and cherries (Kirschwasser). Brandies contain up to 55% alcohol.

Braque Georges 1882–1963. French painter who, with Picasso, founded the Cubist movement around 1907–10. They worked together at L'Estaque in the south of France and in Paris. Braque began to experiment in collages and invented a technique of gluing paper, wood, and other materials to canvas. His later work became more decorative.

Brasília capital of Brazil from 1960, 3,000 ft/1,000 m above sea level; population (1991) 1,841,000. It was designed by Lucio Costa (1902–1963), with Oscar Niemeyer as chief architect, as a completely new city to bring life to the interior.

brass metal ◊alloy of copper and zinc, with not more than 5% or 6% of other metals. The zinc content ranges from 20% to 45%, and the color of brass varies accordingly from coppery to whitish yellow. Brasses are characterized by the ease with which they may be shaped and machined; they are strong and ductile, resist many forms of corrosion, and are used for electrical fittings, ammunition cases, screws, household fittings, and ornaments.

Brassica genus of plants of the family Cruciferae. The most familiar species is the common cabbage *Brassica oleracea*, with its varieties broccoli, cauliflower, kale, and brussels sprouts.

brass instrument in music, any instrument made of brass or other metal, which is directly blown through a "cup" or "funnel" mouthpiece.

In the symphony orchestra they comprise: the *French horn*, a descendant of the natural hunting horn, valved, and curved into a circular loop, with a wide bell; the *trumpet*, a cylindrical tube curved into an oblong, with a narrow bell and three valves (the state *fanfare trumpet* has no valves); the *trombone*, an instrument with a "slide" to vary the effective length of the tube (the *sackbut*, common from the 14th century, was its forerunner); the *tuba*, normally the lowest toned instrument of the orchestra, which is valved and with a very wide bore to give sonority, and a bell that points upward. In the brass band (in descending order of pitch) they comprise: the *cornet*, three-valved instrument, looking like a shorter, broader trumpet, and with a wider bore; the *flugelhorn*, valved instrument, rather similar in range to the cornet; the *tenor horn*, B-flat *baritone*, *euphonium*, *trombone*, and *bombardon* (bass tuba). A brass band normally also includes bass and side drums, triangle, and cymbals.

Bratislava (German *Pressburg*) industrial port (engineering, chemicals, oil refining) in the Slovak Republic, on the river Danube; population (1991) 441,500. It was the capital of Hungary 1526–1784 and is now capital of the Slovak Republic.

Brattain Walter Houser 1902–1987. US physicist. In 1956 he was awarded a Nobel Prize jointly with William Shockley and John Bardeen for their work on the development of the transistor, which replaced the comparatively costly and clumsy vacuum tube in electronics.

He was born in Amoy, China, the son of a teacher. From 1929 to 1967 he was on the staff of Bell Telephone Laboratories.

Braun Eva 1910–1945. German mistress of Adolf Hitler. Secretary to Hitler's photographer and personal friend, Heinrich Hoffmann, she became Hitler's mistress in the 1930s and married him in the air-raid shelter of the Chancellery in Berlin on April 29, 1945. The next day they committed suicide together.

Brazil largest country in South America (almost half the continent), bounded SW by Uruguay, Argentina, Paraguay and Bolivia; W by Peru and Colombia; N by Venezuela, Guyana, Suriname, and French Guiana; and NE and SE by the Atlantic Ocean.

Brazil Federative Republic of
(*República Federativa do Brasil*)

area 3,285,618 sq mi/8,511,965 sq km
capital Brasília
cities São Paulo, Belo Horizonte, Curitiba, Manaus, Fortaleza; ports are Rio de Janeiro, Belém, Recife, Pôrto Alegre, Salvador
physical the densely forested Amazon basin covers the northern half of the country with a network of rivers; the south is fertile; enormous energy resources, both hydroelectric (Itaipú dam on the Paraná, and Tucuruí on the Tocantins) and nuclear (uranium ores)
environment Brazil has one-third of the world's tropical rain forest. It contains 55,000 species of flowering plants (the greatest variety in the world) and 20% of all the world's bird species. During the 1980s at least 7% of the Amazon rain forest was destroyed by settlers who cleared the land for cultivation and grazing
features Mount Roraima, Xingu National Park; Amazon delta; Rio harbor
head of state and government Itamar Franco from 1992
political system emergent democratic federal republic
political parties Social Democratic Party (PDS), moderate, left of center; Brazilian Democratic Movement Party (PMDB), center-left; Liberal Front Party (PFL), moderate, left of center; Workers' Party (PT), left of center; National Reconstruction Party (PRN), center-right
exports coffee, sugar, soybeans, cotton, textiles, timber, motor vehicles, iron, chrome, manganese, tungsten, and other ores, as well as quartz crystals, industrial diamonds, gemstones; the world's sixth largest arms exporter

currency cruzado (introduced 1986; value = 100 cruzeiros, the former unit); inflation 1990 was 1,795%
population (1992) 151,381,000 (including 200,000 Indians, survivors of 5 million, especially in Rondônia and Mato Grosso, mostly living on reservations); growth rate 2.2% p.a.
life expectancy men 61, women 66
languages Portuguese (official); 120 Indian languages
religions Roman Catholic 89%; Indian faiths
literacy men 79%, women 76% (1985 est)
GDP $352 bn (1988); $2,434 per head

chronology
1822 Independence achieved from Portugal; ruled by Dom Pedro, son of the refugee King John VI of Portugal.
1889 Monarchy abolished and republic established.
1891 Constitution for a federal state adopted.
1930 Dr Getúlio Vargas became president.
1945 Vargas deposed by the military.
1946 New constitution adopted.
1951 Vargas returned to office.
1954 Vargas committed suicide.
1956 Juscelino Kubitschek became president.
1960 Capital moved to Brasília.
1961 João Goulart became president.
1964 Bloodless coup made General Castelo Branco president; he assumed dictatorial powers, abolishing free political parties.
1967 New constitution adopted. Branco succeeded by Marshal da Costa e Silva.
1969 Da Costa e Silva resigned and a military junta took over.
1974 General Ernesto Geisel became president.
1978 General Baptista de Figueiredo became president.
1979 Political parties legalized again.
1984 Mass calls for a return to fully democratic government.
1985 Tancredo Neves became first civilian president in 21 years. Neves died and was succeeded by the vice president, José Sarney.
1988 New constitution approved, transferring power from the president to the congress. Measures announced to halt large-scale burning of Amazonian rain forest for cattle grazing.
1989 Forest Protection Service and Ministry for Land Reform abolished. International concern over how much of the Amazon has been burned. Fernando Collor (PRN) elected president Dec, pledging free-market economic policies.
1990 Government won the general election offset by mass abstentions.
1992 Collor charged with corruption and replaced by Vice President Itamar Franco. Hosted Earth Summit.
1993 Collor indicted for "passive corruption."

Brazil nut seed, rich in oil and highly nutritious, of the gigantic South American tree *Bertholletia excelsa*. The seeds are enclosed in a hard outer casing, each fruit containing 10–20 seeds arranged like the segments of an orange. The timber of the tree is also valuable.

brazing method of joining two metals by melting an ◊alloy into the joint. It is similar to soldering but takes place at a much higher temperature. Copper and silver alloys are widely used for brazing, at temperatures up to about 1,650°F/900°C.

Brazzaville capital of the Congo, industrial port (foundries, railroad repairs, shipbuilding, shoes, soap, furniture, bricks) on the river Zaïre, opposite Kinshasa; population (1984) 595,000. There is a cathedral

1892 and the Pasteur Institute 1908. It stands on Pool Malebo (Stanley Pool).

bread food baked from a kneaded dough or batter made with ground cereals, usually wheat, and water; many other ingredients may be added. The dough may be unleavened or raised (usually with yeast).

breadfruit fruit of the tropical trees *Artocarpus communis* and *A. altilis* of the mulberry family Moraceae. It is highly nutritious and when baked is said to taste like bread. It is native to many South Pacific islands.

bream deep-bodied, flattened fish *Abramis brama* of the carp family, growing to about 1.6 ft/50 cm, typically found in lowland rivers across Europe.

breast The human breast or mammary gland.

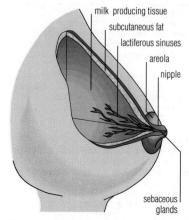

milk producing tissue
subcutaneous fat
lactiferous sinuses
areola
nipple

sebaceous glands

The name bream is also applied to porgies, small-mouthed, deep-bodied marine fishes of the family Sparidae. The pinfish bream *Lagodon rhomboides* is found from Cape Cod S to the Gulf of Mexico. Several members of the North American sunfish family are also popularly referred to as bream.

breast one of a pair of organs on the upper front of the human female, also known as a ◊mammary gland. Each of the two breasts contains milk-producing cells, and a network of tubes or ducts that lead to an opening in the nipple.

Breasted James Henry 1865–1935. US Orientalist. Well known as the author of textbooks and popular works on the history of the ancient Near East, Breasted founded the University of Chicago Oriental Institute, funded by John D Rockefeller, as a center of American archeological research. He published *A History of Egypt* 1905, and directed the Chicago expedition to Egypt and Sudan 1905–07.

Breathalyzer trademark for an instrument for on-the-spot checking by police of the amount of alcohol consumed by a suspect driver. The driver breathes into a plastic bag connected to a tube containing a chemical (such as a diluted solution of potassium dichromate in 50% sulfuric acid) that changes color in the presence of alcohol. Another method is to use a gas chromatograph, again from a breath sample.

breathing in terrestrial animals, the muscular movements whereby air is taken into the lungs and then expelled, a form of gas exchange. Breathing is sometimes referred to as external respiration, for true respiration is a cellular (internal) process.

Brecht Bertolt 1898–1956. German dramatist and poet who aimed to destroy the "suspension of disbelief" usual in the theater and to express Marxist ideas. He adapted John Gay's *Beggar's Opera* as *Die Dreigroschenoper/The Threepenny Opera* 1928, set to music by Kurt Weill. Later plays include *Mutter Courage/Mother Courage* 1941, set during the Thirty Years' War, and *Der kaukasische Kreidekreis/The Caucasian Chalk Circle* 1949.

Breda, Treaty of 1667 treaty that ended the Second Anglo-Dutch War (1664–67). By the terms of the treaty, England gained New Amsterdam, which was renamed New York.

breeder reactor in nuclear physics, a reactor in which more fissionable material is produced (breeding) than is consumed in running it. Breeder reactors are typically operated by and for the military to produce

plutonium-239, the fissile material used in the nuclear weapons industry. Although uranium-235 is fissile, it comprises less than 1% of uranium ore, an amount too small to supply the weapons industry. Therefore, non-fissile uranium-238, which is plentiful, comprising 99% of uranium ore, is used instead, in breeder reactors, to manufacture fissile plutonium-239.

breeding in biology, the crossing and selection of animals and plants to change the characteristics of an existing breed or cultivar (variety), or to produce a new one.

Bremen industrial port (iron, steel, oil refining, chemicals, aircraft, shipbuilding, cars) in Germany, on the river Weser 43 mi/69 km from the open sea; population (1988) 522,000.

Bremen administrative region (German *Land*) of Germany, consisting of the cities of Bremen and Bremerhaven; area 154 sq mi/400 sq km; population (1988) 652,000.

Bremerton city in W Washington, SW of Seattle and NW of Tacoma, on an inlet of Puget Sound; population (1990) 38,100. It serves as a port for the area's fish, dairy, and lumber products. Tourism is also important to the economy.

Brendel Alfred 1931– . Austrian pianist, known for his fastidious and searching interpretations of Beethoven, Schubert, and Liszt. He is the author of *Musical Thoughts and Afterthoughts* 1976 and *Music Sounded Out* 1990.

Brennan William Joseph, Jr 1906– . US jurist and associate justice of the US Supreme Court 1956–90. He wrote many important Supreme Court majority decisions that assured the freedoms set forth in the First Amendment and established the rights of minority groups. He is especially noted for writing the majority opinion in *Baker* v *Carr* 1962, in which state voting reapportionment ensured "one person, one vote," and in *US* v *Eichman* 1990, which ruled that the law banning desecration of the flag was a violation of the right to free speech as provided for in the First Amendment.

Born in Newark, New Jersey, Brennan graduated from the University of Pennsylvania and Harvard Law School. A New Jersey superior court 1949–52 and supreme court 1952–56 judge, he was appointed to the US Supreme Court by President Eisenhower. Considered a moderate liberal, his vote was usually cast with the majority during the years of the Court under Chief Justice Earl ◊Warren, but he became a key liberal influence when the court majority, under chief justices ◊Burger and ◊Rehnquist, shifted to the conservative side in the 1980s. He retired from the Court 1990, citing health reasons.

Brenner Sidney 1927– . South African scientist, one of the pioneers of genetic engineering. Brenner discovered messenger ◊RNA (a link between ◊DNA and the ◊ribosomes in which proteins are synthesized) 1960.

Brenner Pass lowest of the Alpine passes, 4,495 ft/ 1,370 m; it leads from Trentino–Alto Adige, Italy, to the Austrian Tirol, and is 12 mi/19 km long.

Brescia (ancient *Brixia*) historic and industrial city (textiles, engineering, firearms, metal products) in N Italy, 52 mi/84 km E of Milan; population (1988) 199,000. It has medieval walls and two cathedrals (12th and 17th century).

Brest naval base and industrial port (electronics, engineering, chemicals) on *Rade de Brest* (Brest Roads), a great bay at the western extremity of Brittany, France; population (1983) 201,000. Occupied as a U-boat base by the Germans 1940–44, the city was destroyed by Allied bombing and rebuilt.

Brest-Litovsk, Treaty of bilateral treaty signed March 3, 1918, between Russia and Germany, Austria–Hungary, and their allies. Under its terms, Russia agreed to recognize the independence of Georgia, Ukraine, Poland, and the Baltic States, and to pay heavy compensation. Under the Nov 1918 Armistice that ended World War I, it was annulled, since Russia was one of the winning allies.

Breton André 1896–1966. French author, among the leaders of the ◊Dada art movement. *Les Champs magnétiques/Magnetic Fields* 1921, an experiment in automatic writing, was one of the products of the movement. He was also a founder of ◊Surrealism, publishing *Le Manifeste de surréalisme/Surrealist Manifesto* 1924. Other works include *Najda* 1928, the story of his love affair with a medium.

Breton language member of the Celtic branch of the Indo-European language family; the language of Brittany in France, related to Welsh and Cornish, and descended from the speech of Celts who left Britain as a consequence of the Anglo-Saxon invasions of the 5th and 6th centuries. Officially neglected for centuries, Breton is now a recognized language of France.

Bretton Woods township in New Hampshire, where the United Nations Monetary and Financial Conference was held in 1944 to discuss postwar international payments problems. The agreements reached on financial assistance and measures to stabilize exchange rates led to the creation of the International Bank for Reconstruction and Development in 1945 and the International Monetary Fund (IMF).

There were 44 nations represented at the conference, which considered proposals by the US, UK, and Canadian governments. The IMF became a specialized agency of the UN 1947. The "Bretton Woods" system was based on a policy of fixed exchange rates, the elimination of exchange restrictions, currency convertibility, and a multilateral system of international payments.

Breuer Marcel 1902–1981. Hungarian-born architect and designer who studied and taught at the ◊Bauhaus school in Germany. His tubular steel chair 1925 was the first of its kind. He moved to England, then to the US, where he was in partnership with Walter Gropius 1937–40. His buildings show an affinity with natural materials; the best known is the Bijenkorf, Rotterdam, the Netherlands (with Elzas) 1953.

brewing making of beer, ale, or other alcoholic beverage from ◊malt and ◊barley by steeping (mashing), boiling, and fermenting.

Mashing the barley releases its sugars. Yeast is then added, which contains the enzymes needed to convert the sugars into ethanol (alcohol) and carbon dioxide. Hops are added to give a bitter taste.

Brezhnev Leonid Ilyich 1906–1982. Soviet leader. A protégé of Stalin and Khrushchev, he came to power (after he and ◊Kosygin forced Khrushchev to resign) as general secretary of the Soviet Communist Party (CPSU) 1964–82 and was president 1977–82. Domestically he was conservative; abroad the USSR was established as a military and political superpower during the Brezhnev era, extending its influence in Africa and Asia.

Brian known as *Brian Boru* ("Brian of the Tribute") 926–1014. High king of Ireland from 976, who took Munster, Leinster, and Connacht to become ruler of all

Ireland. He defeated the Norse at Clontarf, thus ending Norse control of Dublin, although he was himself killed. He was the last high king with jurisdiction over most of Scotland. His exploits were celebrated in several chronicles.

Briand Aristide 1862–1932. French radical socialist politician. He was prime minister 1909–11, 1913, 1915–17, 1921–22, 1925–26 and 1929, and foreign minister 1925–32. In 1925 he concluded the ◊Locarno Pact (settling Germany's western frontier) and in 1928 the ◊Kellogg–Briand Pact renouncing war; in 1930 he outlined a scheme for a United States of Europe.

bribery corruptly receiving or agreeing to receive, giving or promising to give, any gift, loan, fee, reward, or advantage as an inducement or reward to persons in certain positions of trust. For example, it is an offense to improperly influence in this way judges or other judicial officers, members and officers of public bodies, or voters at public elections.

brick common building material, rectangular in shape, made of clay that has been fired in a kiln. Bricks are made by kneading a mixture of crushed clay and other materials into a stiff mud and extruding it into a ribbon. The ribbon is cut into individual bricks, which are fired at a temperature of up to about 1,800°F/1,000°C. Bricks may alternatively be pressed into shape in molds.

bridge structure that provides a continuous path or road over water, valleys, ravines, or above other roads. The basic designs and composites of these are based on the way they bear the weight of the structure and its load. *Beam*, or *girder*, bridges are supported at each end by the ground with the weight thrusting downward. *Cantilever* bridges are a complex form of girder. *Arch* bridges thrust outward but downward at their ends; they are in compression. *Suspension* bridges use cables under tension to pull inward against anchorages on either side of the span, so that the roadway hangs from the main cables by the network of vertical cables. The *cable-stayed* bridge relies on diagonal cables connected directly between the bridge deck and supporting towers at each end. Some bridges are too low to allow traffic to pass beneath easily, so they are designed with movable parts, like swing and draw bridges.

Today the longest spans are suspension bridges, with the measurement referring only to that part of the bridge actually suspended by cables.

bridge card game derived from whist. First played among members of the Indian Civil Service about 1900, bridge was brought to England in 1903 and played at the Portland Club in 1908. It is played in two forms: auction bridge and ◊contract bridge.

Bridgeport city in Connecticut, on Long Island Sound; population (1990) 141,700. Industries include metal goods, electrical appliances, and aircraft, but many factories closed in the 1970s. The university was established 1927. The P T Barnum Museum and Tom Thumb statues are here. Bridgeport was settled 1639.

Bridges Harry 1901–1990. Australian-born US labor leader. In 1931 he formed a labor union of clockworkers and in 1934, after police opened fire on a picket line and killed two strikers, he organized a successful general strike. He was head of the International Longshoremen's and Warehousemen's Union for many years.

Bridgetown port and capital of Barbados; population (1987) 8,000. Sugar is exported through the nearby deep-water port. Bridgetown was founded 1628.

brigade military formation consisting of a minimum of two battalions, but more usually three or more, as well as supporting arms. There are typically about 5,000 soldiers in a brigade, which is commanded by a brigadier general. Two or more brigades form a division.

brine common name for a solution of sodium chloride (NaCl) in water. Brines are used extensively in the food-manufacturing industry for canning vegetables, pickling vegetables (sauerkraut manufacture), and curing meat. Industrially, brine is the source from which chlorine, caustic soda (sodium hydroxide), and sodium carbonate are made.

Brinell hardness test test of the hardness of a substance according to the area of indentation made by a 0.4 in/10 mm hardened steel or sintered tungsten carbide ball under standard loading conditions in a test machine. The resulting Brinell number is equal to the load (kg) divided by the surface area (mm^2) and is named after its inventor Swedish metallurgist Johann Brinell.

Brisbane industrial port (brewing, engineering, tanning, tobacco, shoes; oil pipeline from Moonie), capital of Queensland, E Australia, near the mouth of Brisbane River, dredged to carry oceangoing ships; population (1990) 1,301,700.

Bristol industrial port (aircraft engines, engineering, microelectronics, tobacco, chemicals, paper, printing), administrative headquarters of Avon, SW England; population (1991 est) 370,300. The old docks have been redeveloped for housing, industry, yachting facilities, and the National Lifeboat Museum. Further developments include a new city center, with Brunel's Temple Meads railroad station at its focus, and a weir across the Avon nearby to improve the waterside environment.

Bristol city located in Virginia and Tennessee (the border runs through the center of the city), NE of Knoxville; population (1990) 23,400 (Tennessee), 18,400 (Virginia). This dual city is divided politically, but one unit economically. Industries include lumber, steel, office machines, pharmaceuticals, missile parts, and textiles.

Bristol city in central Connecticut, SW of Hartford; population (1990) 60,600. Known as the clockmaking capital of the US, its products also include tools and machinery parts.

Britain another name for ◊Great Britain.

Britain, ancient period in the history of the British Isles (excluding Ireland) from prehistory to the Roman occupation. After the last glacial retreat of the Ice Age about 15,000 BC, Britain was inhabited by hunters who

British Columbia

became neolithic farming villagers. They built stone circles and buried their chiefs in ◊barrow mounds. Around 400 BC Britain was conquered by the ◊Celts and 54 BC by the Romans under Julius Caesar; ◊Boudicca led an uprising against their occupation.

Britain, Battle of World War II air battle between German and British air forces over Britain lasting July 10–Oct 31, 1940.

British Antarctic Territory colony created 1962 and comprising all British territories south of latitude 60° S: the South Orkney Islands, the South Shetland Islands, the Antarctic Peninsula and all adjacent lands, and Coats Land, extending to the South Pole; total land area 170,874 sq mi/660,000 sq km; population (exclusively scientific personnel) about 300.

British Broadcasting Corporation (BBC) the UK state-owned broadcasting network. It operates television and national and local radio stations, and is financed solely by the sale of television viewing licenses; it is not allowed to carry advertisements. Overseas radio broadcasts (World Service) have a government subsidy.

The BBC was converted from a private company (established 1922) to a public body 1927.

British Columbia province of Canada on the Pacific Ocean
area 365,851 sq mi/947,800 sq km
capital Victoria
cities Vancouver, Prince George, Kamloops, Kelowna
physical Rocky Mountains and Coast Range; deeply indented coast; rivers include the Fraser and Columbia; over 80 lakes; more than half the land is forested
products fruit and vegetables; timber and wood products; fish; coal, copper, iron, lead; oil and natural gas; hydroelectricity
population (1991) 3,185,900
history Captain Cook explored the coast 1778; a British colony was founded on Vancouver Island 1849, and the gold rush of 1858 extended settlement to the mainland; it became a province 1871. In 1885 the Canadian Pacific Railroad linking British Columbia to the east coast was completed.

British Empire various territories all over the world conquered or colonized by Britain from about 1600, most now independent or ruled by other powers; the British Empire was at its largest at the end of World War I, with over 25% of the world's population and area. The ◊Commonwealth is composed of former and remaining territories of the British Empire.

The first successful British colony was Jamestown, Virginia, founded 1607. British settlement spread up and down the east coast of North America and by 1664, when the British secured New Amsterdam (New York) from the Dutch, continuous colonies existed from the present South Carolina to what is now New Hampshire. The attempt of George III and his minister Lord North to coerce the colonists into paying special taxes to Britain roused them to resistance, which came to a head in the ◊American Revolution 1775–81 and led to the creation of the United States of America from the 13 English colonies then lost.

Colonies and trading posts were set up in many parts of the world by the British, who also captured them from other European empire builders. Settlements were made in Gambia and on the Gold Coast of Africa 1618; in Bermuda 1609 and other islands of the West Indies; Jamaica was taken from Spain 1655; in Canada, Acadia (Nova Scotia) was secured from France by the Treaty of Utrecht 1713, which recognized Newfoundland and Hudson Bay (as well as

British Empire

current name	colonial names and history	colonized	independent
India	British E India Company 18th century–1858	18th century	1947
Pakistan	British E India Company 18th century–1858	18th century	1947
Sri Lanka	Portuguese, Dutch 1602–1796; Ceylon 1802–1972	16th century	1948
Ghana	Gold Coast	1618	1957
Nigeria		1861	1960
Cyprus	Turkish to 1878, then British rule	1878	1960
Sierra Leone	British protectorate	1788	1961
Tanzania	German E Africa to 1921; British mandate from League of Nations/UN as Tanganyika	19th century	1961
Jamaica	Spanish to 1655	16th century	1962
Trinidad & Tobago	Spanish 1532–1797; British 1797–1962	1532	1962
Uganda	British protectorate	1894	1962
Kenya	British colony from 1920	1895	1963
Malaysia	British interests from 1786; Federation of Malaya 1957–63	1874	1963
Malawi	British protectorate of Nyasaland 1907–53; Federation of Rhodesia & Nyasaland 1953–64	1891	1964
Malta	French 1798–1814	1798	1964
Zambia	N Rhodesia—British protectorate; Federation of Rhodesia & Nyasaland 1953–64	1924	1964
The Gambia		1888	1965
Singapore	Federation of Malaya 1963–65	1858	1965
Guyana	Dutch to 1796; British Guiana 1796–1966	1620	1966
Botswana	Bechuanaland—British protectorate	1885	1966
Lesotho	Basutoland	1868	1966
Bangladesh	British E India Co. 18th cent.–1858; British India 1858–1947; E Pakistan 1947–71	18th century	1971
Zimbabwe	S Rhodesia from 1923; UDI under Ian Smith 1965–79	1895	1980

Gibraltar in Europe) as British. New France (Québec), Cape Breton Island, and Prince Edward Island became British as a result of the Seven Years' War 1756–63. In the Far East, the British East India Company, chartered 1600, set up trading posts. The company steadily increased its possessions up to the eve of the ◊Sepoy Rebellion 1857. Although this revolt was put down, it resulted in the taking over of the government of British India by the crown 1858; Queen Victoria was proclaimed empress of India Jan 1, 1877. Ceylon (now Sri Lanka) had also been annexed to the British East India Company 1796, and Burma (now Myanmar), after a series of Anglo-Burmese Wars from 1824, became a province of British India 1886. Burma and Ceylon became independent 1948 and the republic of Sri Lanka dates from 1972. British India, as the two dominions of India and Pakistan, was given independence in 1947. In 1950 India became a republic but remained a member of the Commonwealth. Constitutional development in Canada started with an act of 1791 which set up Lower Canada (Québec), mainly French-speaking, and Upper Canada (Ontario), mainly English-speaking. Discontent led to rebellion in both Canadas 1837. After the suppression of these uprisings, Lord Durham was sent out to advise on the affairs of British North America. In accordance with his recommendations, the two Canadas were united 1840 and given a representative legislative council. With the British North America Act 1867, the self-governing dominion of Canada came into existence. In New Zealand and Australia, colonization began with the need for a penal settlement after the loss of the original American colonies. The first shipload of British convicts landed in Australia 1788 on the site of the future city of Sydney. New South Wales was opened to free settlers 1819, and in 1853 transportation of convicts was abolished. An act of Parliament created the federal commonwealth of Aus-

tralia, an independent dominion, 1901. New Zealand was created a dominion 1907. The Cape of Good Hope in South Africa was occupied by two English captains 1620, but neither the home government nor the East India Company was interested. The Dutch occupied it from 1650 until 1795 when, French revolutionary armies having occupied the Dutch Republic, the British seized it to keep it from the French. Under the Treaty of Paris 1814 Britain bought it from the Netherlands. It was proclaimed a British colony 1843. The need to find new farmland and establish independence from British rule led a body of Boers (Dutch "farmers") from the Cape to make the Great Trek northeast 1836, to found Transvaal and Orange Free State. Conflict between the British government and the Boers culminated in the Boer War 1899–1902, which brought Transvaal and Orange Free State under British sovereignty. Given self-government 1907, they were formed, with Cape Colony and Natal, into the Union of South Africa 1910. The British South Africa Company, chartered 1889, extended British influence over Southern Rhodesia and Northern Rhodesia; with Nyasaland, the Rhodesias were formed into a federation 1953–63 with representative government. Uganda was made a British protectorate 1894. Kenya became a colony 1920. In W Africa, Sierra Leone colony was founded 1788 with the cession of a strip of land to provide a home for liberated slaves; a protectorate was established over the hinterland 1896. British influence in Nigeria began through the activities of the National Africa Company (the Royal Niger Company from 1886), which bought Lagos from an African chief 1861; in 1900 the two protectorates of N and S Nigeria were proclaimed. In 1921–22, under League of Nations mandate, some German colonies were ceded to Britain: Tanganyika was transferred to British administration, SW Africa to South Africa; and Cameroons and Togoland were divided between Britain and France. The establishment of the greater part of Ireland as the Irish Free State, with dominion status, occurred 1922. A new constitution 1937 dropped the name and declared Ireland (Eire) to be a "sovereign independent state"; in 1949 Ireland became a republic outside the Commonwealth, though remaining in a special relationship with Britain.

British Honduras former name (until 1973) of ◊Belize.

British Indian Ocean Territory British colony in the Indian Ocean directly administered by the Foreign and Commonwealth Office. It consists of the Chagos Archipelago some 1,200 mi/1,900 km NE of Mauritius
area 23 sq mi/60 sq km
features lagoons; US naval and air base on Diego Garcia
products copra, salt fish, tortoiseshell
population (1982) 3,000
history purchased 1965 for $3 million by Britain from Mauritius to provide a joint US/UK base. The islands of Aldabra, Farquhar, and Desroches, some 300 mi/485 km N of Madagascar, originally formed part of the British Indian Ocean Territory but were returned to the administration of the Seychelles 1976.

British Isles group of islands off the northwest coast of Europe, consisting of Great Britain (England, Wales, and Scotland), Ireland, the Channel Islands, the Orkney and Shetland islands, the Isle of Man, and many other islands that are included in various counties, such as the Isle of Wight, Scilly Isles, Lundy Island, and the Inner and Outer Hebrides. The islands are divided from Europe by the North Sea, Strait of Dover, and the English Channel, and face the Atlantic to the W.

British Museum largest museum of the UK. Founded in 1753, it opened in London in 1759. Rapid additions led to the constuction of the present buildings (1823–47). In 1881 the Natural History Museum was transferred to South Kensington.

British Somaliland British protectorate comprising over 67,980 sq mi/176,000 sq km of territory on the Somali coast of E Africa from 1884 until the independence of Somalia 1960. British authorities were harassed by Somali nationalists under the leadership of Mohammed bin Abdullah Hassan.

British Virgin Islands part of the ◊Virgin Islands group in the West Indies.

Brittany (French *Bretagne*, Breton *Breiz*) region of NW France in the Breton peninsula between the Bay of Biscay and the English Channel; area 10,499 sq mi/27,200 sq km; capital Rennes; population (1987) 2,767,000. A farming region, it includes the *départements* of Côtes-du-Nord, Finistère, Ille-et-Vilaine, and Morbihan.
   history Brittany was the Gallo-Roman province of Armorica after being conquered by Julius Caesar 56 BC. It was devastated by Norsemen after the Roman withdrawal. Established under the name of Brittany in the 5th century AD by Celts fleeing the Anglo-Saxon invasion of Britain, it became a strong, expansionist state that maintained its cultural and political independence, despite pressure from the Carolingians, Normans, and Capetians. In 1171, the duchy of Brittany was inherited by Geoffrey, son of Henry II of England, and remained in the Angevin dynasty's possession until 1203, when Geoffrey's son Arthur was murdered by King ◊John, and the title passed to the Capetian Peter of Dreux. Under the Angevins, feudalism was introduced, and French influence

increased under the Capetians. By 1547 it had been formally annexed by France, and the ◊Breton language was banned in education. A separatist movement developed after World War II, and there has been guerrilla activity.

Britten (Edward) Benjamin 1913–1976. English composer. He often wrote for the individual voice; for example, the role in the opera *Peter Grimes* 1945, based on verses by George Crabbe, was created for Peter Pears. Among his many works are the *Young Person's Guide to the Orchestra* 1946; the chamber opera *The Rape of Lucretia* 1946; *Billy Budd* 1951; *A Midsummer Night's Dream* 1960; and *Death in Venice* 1973.

Brno industrial city (chemicals, arms, textiles, machinery) in the Czech Republic; population (1991) 388,000. Now the second largest city in the Czech Republic, Brno was formerly the capital of the Austrian crown land of Moravia.

broadbill primitive perching bird of the family Eurylaimidae, found in Africa and S Asia. Broadbills are forest birds and are often found near water. They are gregarious and noisy, have brilliant coloration and wide bills, and feed largely on insects.

broadcasting the transmission of sound and vision programs by ◊radio and ◊television. In the US, broadcasting licenses are issued to public organizations and competing commercial companies by the Federal Communications Commission.

Broadway major avenue in New York running from the tip of Manhattan NW and crossing Times Square at 42nd Street, at the heart of the theater district, where Broadway is known as "the Great White Way." New York theaters situated outside this area are described as *off-Broadway*, those even smaller and farther away are *off-off-Broadway*.

broccoli variety of ◊cabbage.

Brockton city in SW Massachusetts, S of Boston; population (1990) 92,800. Industries include footwear, tools, and electronic equipment.

Brodsky Joseph 1940– . Russian poet who emigrated to the US in 1972. His work, often dealing with themes of exile, is admired for its wit and economy of language, particularly in its use of understatement. Many of his poems, written in Russian, have been translated into English (*A Part of Speech* 1980). More recently he has also written in English. He was awarded the Nobel Prize for Literature in 1987 and became US poet laureate 1991.

Broglie Louis de, 7th Duc de Broglie 1892–1987. French theoretical physicist. He established that all subatomic particles can be described either by particle equations or by wave equations, thus laying the foundations of wave mechanics. He was awarded the 1929 Nobel Prize for Physics.

bromeliad any tropical or subtropical plant of the pineapple family Bromeliaceae, usually with stiff leathery leaves and bright flower spikes.

bromine dark, reddish-brown, nonmetallic element, a volatile liquid at room temperature, symbol Br, atomic number 35, atomic weight 79.904. It is a member of the ◊halogen group, has an unpleasant odor, and is very irritating to mucous membranes. Its salts are known as bromides.

bronchiole small-bore air tube found in the vertebrate lung responsible for delivering air to the main respiratory surfaces. Bronchioles lead off from the larger bronchus and branch extensively before terminating in the many thousand alveoli that form the bulk of lung tissue.

bronchitis inflammation of the bronchi (air passages) of the lungs, usually caused initially by a viral infection, such as a cold or flu. It is aggravated by environmental pollutants, especially smoking, and results in a persistent cough, irritated mucus-secreting glands, and large amounts of sputum.

bronchodilator drug that relieves obstruction of the airways by causing the bronchi and bronchioles to relax and widen. It is most useful in the treatment of ◊asthma.

bronchus one of a pair of large tubes (bronchii) branching off from the windpipe and passing into the vertebrate lung. Apart from their size, bronchii differ from the bronchioles in possessing cartilaginous rings, which give rigidity and prevent collapse during breathing movements.

Bronson Charles. Adopted name of Charles Bunchinsky 1921– . US film actor. His films are mainly violent thrillers such as *Death Wish* 1974. He was one of *The Magnificent Seven* 1960.

Brontë three English novelists, daughters of a Yorkshire parson. ***Charlotte*** (1816–1855), notably with *Jane Eyre* 1847 and *Villette* 1853, reshaped autobiographical material into vivid narrative. ***Emily*** (1818–1848) in *Wuthering Heights* 1847 expressed the intensity and nature mysticism which also pervades her poetry (*Poems* 1846). The more modest talent of ***Anne*** (1820–1849) produced *Agnes Grey* 1847 and *The Tenant of Wildfell Hall* 1848.

brontosaurus former name of a type of large, plant-eating dinosaur, now better known as ◊apatosaurus.

Bronx, the borough of New York City, NE of Harlem River; area 42 sq mi/109 sq km; population (1990) 1,169,000. Largely residential, it is named after an early Dutch settler, James Bronck. The New York Zoological Society and Gardens are here, popularly called the Bronx Zoo and the Bronx Botanical Gardens.

bronze alloy of copper and tin, yellow or brown in color. It is harder than pure copper, more suitable for ◊casting, and also resists ◊corrosion. Bronze may contain as much as 25% tin, together with small amounts of other metals, mainly lead.

Bronze Age stage of prehistory and early history when copper and bronze became the first metals worked extensively and used for tools and weapons. It developed out of the Stone Age, preceded the Iron Age, and may be dated 5000–1200 BC in the Middle East and about 2000–500 BC in Europe. Recent discoveries in Thailand suggest that the Far East, rather than the Middle East, was the cradle of the Bronze Age.

Brooke Rupert (Chawner) 1887–1915. English poet, symbol of the World War I "lost generation." His five war sonnets, the best known of which is "The Patriot," were published posthumously. Other notable works include "Grantchester" and "The Great Lover."

Brooklyn borough of New York City, occupying the southwest end of Long Island. It is linked to Manhattan Island by the Brooklyn-Battery Tunnel, the Brooklyn Bridge 1883, and the Williamsburg and the Manhattan bridges, and to Staten Island by the Verrazano-Narrows Bridge 1964. There are more than 60 parks of which Prospect is the largest. There is also a museum, botanical garden, and a beach and amusement area at Coney Island.

Brooks Louise 1906–1985. US actress, known for her roles in silent films such as *A Girl in Every Port* 1928

and *Die Büchse der Pandora/Pandora's Box* and *Das Tagebuch einer Verlorenen/Diary of a Lost Girl*, both 1929 and both directed by G W Pabst. At 25 she had appeared in 17 films. She retired from the screen 1938.

Brooks Mel. Adopted name of Melvin Kaminsky 1926– . US film director and comedian, known for madcap and slapstick verbal humor. He became well known with his record album *The 2,000-Year-Old Man* 1960. His films include *The Producers* 1968, *Blazing Saddles* 1974, *Young Frankenstein* 1975, *History of the World Part I* 1981, and *To Be or Not to Be* 1983.

Brown Charles Brockden 1771–1810. US novelist and magazine editor. He introduced the American Indian into fiction and is called the "father of the American novel" for his *Wieland* 1798, *Ormond* 1799, *Edgar Huntly* 1799, and *Arthur Mervyn* 1800. His works also pioneered the Gothic and fantastic traditions in US fiction.

Brown James 1928– . US rhythm-and-blues and soul singer, a pioneer of funk. Staccato horn arrangements and shouted vocals characterize his hits, which include "Please, Please, Please" 1956, "Papa's Got a Brand New Bag" 1965, and "Say It Loud, I'm Black and I'm Proud" 1968. In that year his TV appearance appealing for calm succeeded in restraining race riots in US cities.

Brown John 1800–1859. US slavery abolitionist. With 18 men, on the night of Oct 16, 1859, he seized the government arsenal at Harper's Ferry in W Virginia, apparently intending to distribute weapons to runaway slaves who would then defend a mountain stronghold, which Brown hoped would become a republic of former slaves. On Oct 18 the arsenal was stormed by US Marines under Col Robert E ◊Lee. Brown was tried and hanged on Dec 2, becoming a martyr and the hero of the popular song "John Brown's Body" *c.* 1860.

brown dwarf hypothetical object less massive than a star, but heavier than a planet. Brown dwarfs would not have enough mass to ignite nuclear reactions at their centers but would shine by heat released during their contraction from a gas cloud. Because of the difficulty of detection, no brown dwarfs have been spotted with certainty, but some astronomers believe that vast numbers of them may exist throughout the Galaxy.

Brownian motion the continuous random motion of particles in a fluid medium (gas or liquid) as they are subjected to impact from the molecules of the medium. The phenomenon was explained by German physicist Albert Einstein in 1905 but was probably observed as long ago as 1827 by the Scottish botanist Robert Brown. It provides evidence for the ◊kinetic theory of matter.

Browning Robert 1812–1889. English poet, married to Elizabeth Barrett Browning. His work is characterized by the use of dramatic monologue and an interest in obscure literary and historical figures. It includes the play *Pippa Passes* 1841 and the poems "The Pied Piper of Hamelin" 1842, "My Last Duchess" 1842, "Home Thoughts from Abroad" 1845, and "Rabbi Ben Ezra" 1864.

Brownshirts the SA (*Sturmabteilung*), or Storm Troops, the private army of the German Nazi party, who derived their name from the color of their uniform.

Brownsville city in S Texas on the Rio Grande just before it flows into the Gulf of Mexico, S of Corpus Christi and N of Matamoros, Mexico; seat of Cameron County; population (1990) 99,000. It is a port of entry to

Brunei Islamic Sultanate of
(*Negara Brunei Darussalam*)

area 2,225 sq mi/5,765 sq km
capital Bandar Seri Begawan
cities Tutong, Seria, Kuala Belait
physical flat coastal plain with hilly lowland in W and
mountains in E; 75% of the area is forested; the Limbang
valley splits Brunei in two, and its cession to Sarawak 1890
is disputed by Brunei
features Temburong, Tutong, and Belait rivers; Mount
Pagon (6,070 ft/1,850 m)

head of state and of government HM Muda Hassanal
Bolkiah Mu'izzaddin Waddaulah, Sultan of Brunei, from 1967
political system absolute monarchy
political party Brunei National United Party (BNUP)
exports liquefied natural gas (world's largest producer) and
oil, both expected to be exhausted by the year 2000
currency Brunei dollar
population (1990 est) 372,000 (65% Malay, 20% Chinese
– few Chinese granted citizenship); growth rate 12% p.a.
life expectancy 74 years
languages Malay (official), Chinese (Hokkien), English
religion 60% Muslim (official)
literacy 95%
GDP $3.4 bn (1985); $20,000 per head

chronology
1888 Brunei became a British protectorate.
1941–45 Occupied by Japan.
1959 Written constitution made Britain responsible for
defence and external affairs.
1962 Sultan began rule by decree.
1963 Proposal to join Malaysia abandoned.
1967 Sultan abdicated in favor of his son, Hassanal Bolkiah.
1971 Brunei given internal self-government.
1975 United Nations resolution called for independence for
Brunei.
1984 Independence achieved from Britain, with Britain
maintaining a small force to protect the oil and gas fields.
1985 A "loyal and reliable" political party, the Brunei
National Democratic Party (BNDP), legalized.
1986 Death of former sultan, Sir Omar. Formation of multi-
ethnic BNUP.
1988 BNDP banned.

the US; industries include chemicals and food products; tourism is also important. Originally Fort Taylor
1846, it was an important Confederate port during the
Civil War.

Bruce one of the chief Scottish noble houses. ◊Robert I
(Robert the Bruce) and his son, David II, were both
kings of Scotland descended from Robert de Bruis
(died 1094), a Norman knight who arrived in England
with William the Conqueror 1066.

Bruce Robert. King of Scotland; see ◊Robert I.

Brücke, die German Expressionist art movement
1905–13, formed in Dresden. Ernst Ludwig Kirchner
was one of its founders, and Emil Nolde was a member
1906–07. Influenced by African art, they strove for
spiritual significance, using raw colors to express different emotions. In 1911 the ◊*Blaue Reiter* took over as
the leading group in German art.

Brüderhof Christian Protestant sect with beliefs
similar to the ◊Mennonites. They live in groups of families (single persons are assigned to a family), marry
only within the sect (divorce is not allowed), and retain
a "modest" dress for women (cap or headscarf, and long
skirts). In the US they are known as Hutterites.

They originated as an Anabaptist sect in Moravia in
1529. Jacob Hutter, a Swiss minister, was their leader
until martyred 1536. They survived relentless persecution in the 16th and 17th centuries.

Brueghel family of Flemish painters. *Pieter
Brueghel the Elder* (*c.* 1525–69) was one of the
greatest artists of his time. He painted satirical and
humorous pictures of peasant life, many of which
include symbolic details illustrating folly and inhu-
manity, and a series of Months (five survive), including *Hunters in the Snow* (Kunsthistorisches Museum,
Vienna).

Bruges (Flemish *Brugge*) historic city in NW Belgium; capital of W Flanders province, 10 mi/16 km from
the North Sea, with which it is connected by canal; population (1991) 117,100. Bruges was the capital of
medieval ◊Flanders and was the chief European wool
manufacturing town as well as its chief market. The
contemporary port handles coal, iron ore, oil, and fish;
local industries include lace, textiles, paint, steel, beer,
furniture, and motors.

Brummell Beau (George Bryan) 1778–1840. British
dandy and leader of fashion. He introduced long
trousers as conventional day and evening wear for men.
A friend of the Prince of Wales, the future George IV, he
later quarrelled with him. Gambling losses drove him
in 1816 to exile in France, where he died in an asylum.

Brundtland Gro Harlem 1939– . Norwegian Labor
politician. Environment minister 1974–76, she briefly
took over as prime minister 1981 and was elected
prime minister 1986 and again 1990. She chaired the
World Commission on Environment and Development
which produced the Brundtland Report, published as
Our Common Future 1987. In 1992 she resigned as
leader of the Norwegian Labor Party, a post she had
held since 1981.

Brunei country comprising two enclaves on the NW
coast of the island of Borneo, bounded on the landward
side by Sarawak and to the NW by the South China Sea.

Brunel Isambard Kingdom 1806–1859. British
engineer and inventor. In 1833 he became engineer to
the Great Western Railroad, which adopted the 7 ft/2.1
m gauge on his advice. He built the Clifton Suspension
Bridge over the river Avon at Bristol and the Saltash
Bridge over the river Tamar near Plymouth. His shipbuilding designs include the *Great Western* 1838, the
first steamship to cross the Atlantic regularly; the

Great Britain 1845, the first large iron ship to have a screw propeller; and the *Great Eastern* 1858, which laid the first transatlantic telegraph cable.

Bruno, St 1030–1101. German founder of the monastic Catholic ◊Carthusian order. He was born in Cologne, became a priest, and controlled the cathedral school of Rheims 1057–76. Withdrawing to the mountains near Grenoble after an ecclesiastical controversy, he founded the monastery at Chartreuse in 1084. Feast day Oct 6.

Brunswick (German *Braunschweig*) industrial city (chemical engineering, precision engineering, food processing) in Lower Saxony, Germany; population (1988) 248,000. It was one of the chief cities of N Germany in the Middle Ages and a member of the ◊Hanseatic League. It was capital of the duchy of Brunswick from 1671.

Brussels (Flemish *Brussel*, French *Bruxelles*) capital of Belgium, industrial city (lace, textiles, machinery, and chemicals); population (1987) 974,000 (80% French-speaking, the suburbs Flemish-speaking). It is the headquarters of the European Economic Community (EEC) and since 1967 of the international secretariat of ◊NATO. First settled in the 6th century, and a city from 1312, Brussels became the capital of the Spanish Netherlands 1530 and of Belgium 1830.

Brussels sprout one of the small edible buds along the stem of a variety (*Brassica oleracea* var. *gemmifera*) of ◊cabbage.

Brussels, Treaty of pact of economic, political, cultural, and military alliance established March 17, 1948, for 50 years, by the UK, France, and the Benelux countries, joined by West Germany and Italy 1955. It was the forerunner of the North Atlantic Treaty Organization and the European Community.

Brutus Marcus Junius *c.* 78–42 BC. Roman senator and general, a supporter of ◊Pompey (against ◊Caesar) in the civil war. Pardoned by Caesar and raised to high office by him, he nevertheless plotted Caesar's assassination to restore the purity of the Republic. Brutus committed suicide when he was defeated (with ◊Cassius) by ◊Mark Antony, Caesar's lieutenant, at Philippi 42 BC.

Bryan city in E Texas, NW of Houston; seat of Brazos County; population (1990) 55,000. Its industries include the manufacture of cotton gins.

Bryan William Jennings 1860–1925. US politician who campaigned unsuccessfully for the presidency three times: as the Populist and Democratic nominee 1896, as an antiimperialist Democrat tariff reformer 1908. He served as President Wilson's secretary of state 1913–15. In the early 1920s he was a leading fundamentalist and opponent of Clarence ◊Darrow in the Scopes monkey trial. He died shortly after from the strain.

Bryant William Cullen 1794–1878. US poet and literary figure. His most famous poem, "Thanatopsis," was published 1817. He was co-owner and co-editor of the *New York Evening Post* 1829–78 and was involved in Democratic party politics. However, his resolute opposition to slavery converted him to Republicanism at the inception of the party 1856.

Brynner Yul 1915–1985. Actor, in the US from 1940, who made a shaven head his trademark. He played the king in *The King and I* both on stage from 1951 and on film 1956 (Academy Award) and was the leader of *The Magnificent Seven* 1960.

bryophyte member of the Bryophyta, a division of the plant kingdom containing three classes: the Hepaticae (liverwort), Musci (◊moss), and Anthocerotae (hornwort). Bryophytes are generally small, low-growing, terrestrial plants with no vascular (water-conducting) system as in higher plants. Their life cycle shows a marked alternation of generations. Bryophytes chiefly occur in damp habitats and require water for the dispersal of the male gametes (antherozoids).

bubble chamber in physics, a device for observing the nature and movement of atomic particles, and their interaction with radiations. It is a vessel filled with a superheated liquid through which ionizing particles move and collide. The paths of these particles are shown by strings of bubbles, which can be photographed and studied. By using a pressurized liquid medium instead of a gas, it overcomes drawbacks inherent in the earlier ◊cloud chamber. It was invented by US physicist Donald Glaser 1952.

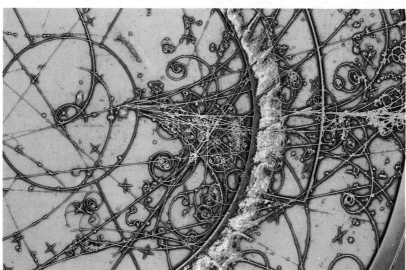

bubble chamber
Artificially colored bubble chamber photograph taken at CERN, the European particle physics laboratory outside Geneva.

***Budapest** The parliament building on the eastern side of the Danube River.*

Buber Martin 1878–1965. Austrian-born Israeli philosopher, a Zionist and advocate of the reappraisal of ancient Jewish thought in contemporary terms. His book *I and Thou* 1923 posited a direct dialogue between the individual and God; it had great impact on Christian and Jewish theology. When forced by the Nazis to abandon a professorship in comparative religion at Frankfurt, he went to Jerusalem and taught social philosophy at the Hebrew University 1937–51.

bubonic plague epidemic disease of the Middle Ages; see ◊plague and ◊Black Death.

Bucaramanga industrial and commercial city (coffee, tobacco, cacao, cotton) in N central Colombia; population (1985) 493,929. It was founded by the Spanish 1622.

buccaneer member of any of various groups of seafarers who plundered Spanish ships and colonies on the Spanish American coast in the 17th century. Unlike true pirates, they were acting on (sometimes spurious) commission.

Buchanan James 1791–1868. 15th president of the US 1857–61, a Democrat. He was a member of the US House of Representatives 1821–31 and was US minister to Russia 1832–34, when he was elected to the Senate. Adhering to a policy of compromise on the issue of slavery, he left his Senate seat to serve as US secretary of state during the Mexican War (1846–48). Nominated by the Democrats and elected president 1856, he could do little to avert the secession of the South over the issue of slavery, precipitating the outbreak of the Civil War 1861.

Bucharest (Romanian *Bucureşti*) capital and largest city of Romania; population (1985) 1,976,000, the conurbation of Bucharest district having an area of 587 sq mi/1,520 sq km and a population of 2,273,000. It was originally a citadel built by Vlad the Impaler (see ◊Dracula) to stop the advance of the Ottoman invasion in the 14th century. Bucharest became the capital of the princes of Wallachia 1698 and of Romania 1861. Savage fighting took place in the city during Romania's 1989 revolution.

Buchenwald site of a Nazi ◊concentration camp 1937–45 at a village NE of Weimar, E Germany.

Buchner Eduard 1860–1917. German chemist who researched the process of fermentation. In 1897 he observed that fermentation could be produced mechanically, by cell-free extracts. Buchner argued that it was not the whole yeast cell that produced fermentation, but only the presence of the enzyme he named zymase. Nobel Prize 1907.

Buck Pearl S(ydenstricker) 1892–1973. US novelist. Daughter of missionaries to China, she spent much of her life there and wrote novels about Chinese life, such as *East Wind–West Wind* 1930 and *The Good Earth* 1931, for which she received a Pulitzer prize 1932. She received the Nobel Prize for Literature 1938.

She wanted to make the East understandable to the West.

Buckingham Palace London home of the British sovereign, built 1703 for the duke of Buckingham, but bought by George III 1762 and reconstructed by John ◊Nash 1821–36; a new front was added 1913.

buckminsterfullerene form of carbon, made up of molecules (buckyballs) consisting of 60 carbon atoms arranged in 12 pentagons and 20 hexagons to form a perfect sphere. It was named after the US architect and engineer Richard Buckminster Fuller because of its structural similarity to the geodesic dome that he designed. See ◊fullerene.

buckwheat any of several plants of the genus *Fagopyrum*, family Polygonaceae. The name usually refers to *F. esculentum*, which grows to about 3 ft/1 m and can grow on poor soil in a short summer. The highly nutritious black, triangular seeds (groats) are consumed by both animals and humans. They can be eaten either cooked whole or or as a cracked meal (kasha) or ground into flour, often made into pancakes.

bud undeveloped shoot usually enclosed by protective scales; inside is a very short stem and numerous undeveloped leaves, or flower parts, or both. Terminal buds are found at the tips of shoots, while axillary buds develop in the axils of the leaves, often remaining dormant unless the terminal bud is removed or damaged. Adventitious buds may be produced anywhere on the plant, their formation sometimes stimulated by an injury, such as that caused by pruning.

Budapest capital of Hungary, industrial city (chemicals, textiles) on the river Danube; population (1989) 2,115,000. Buda, on the right bank of the Danube, became the Hungarian capital 1867 and was joined with Pest, on the left bank, 1872.

Buddha "enlightened one," title of Prince *Gautama Siddhārtha c.* 563–483 BC. Religious leader, founder of Buddhism, born at Lumbini in Nepal. At the age of 29 he left his wife and son and a life of luxury, to escape from the material burdens of existence. After six years of austerity he realized that asceticism, like overindulgence, was futile, and chose the middle way of meditation. He became enlightened under a bo, or bodhi, tree near Buddh Gaya in Bihar, India. He began teaching at Varanasi, and founded the Sangha, or order of monks. He spent the rest of his life traveling around N India, and died at Kusinagara in Uttar Pradesh.

Buddhism one of the great world religions, which originated in India about 500 BC. It derives from the teaching of the Buddha, who is regarded as one of a series of such enlightened beings; there are no gods. The chief doctrine is that of *karma*, good or evil deeds meeting an appropriate reward or punishment either in this life or (through reincarnation) a long succession of lives. The main divisions in Buddhism are *Theravāda* (or Hīnayāna) in SE Asia and *Mahāyāna* in N Asia; *Lamaism* in Tibet and *Zen* in Japan are among the many Mahāyāna sects. Its symbol is the lotus. There are over 247.5 million Buddhists worldwide.

budding type of ◊asexual reproduction in which an outgrowth develops from a cell to form a new individual. Most yeasts reproduce in this way.

Budge Donald 1915– . US tennis player. He was the first to perform the Grand Slam when he won the Wimbledon, French, US, and Australian championships all in 1938.

He won 14 Grand Slam events.

budget estimate of income and expenditure for some future period, used in financial planning.

National budgets set out estimates of government income and expenditure and generally include projected changes in taxation and growth. Interim budgets are not uncommon, in particular, when dramatic changes in economic conditions occur. Governments will sometimes construct a budget deficit or surplus as part of macroeconomic policy.

budget deficit the amount of shortfall that occurs when expenditures exceed revenues. While individuals and private enterprises can have budget deficits, the most economically significant deficit is the federal budget deficit. The deficit must be covered through the sale of government securities on the financial market or through the printing of money. Since printing money would be unacceptably inflationary, the government sells bonds and other financial instruments, promising to repay the face value plus interest in a specified time. The accumulation of obligations constitutes the ◊national debt.

Buenos Aires capital and industrial city of Argentina, on the south bank of the Rio de la Plata; population (1991) 2,961,000, metropolitan area 7,950,400. It was founded 1536, and became the capital 1853.

buffalo either of two species of wild cattle. The Asiatic water buffalo *Bubalis bubalis* is found domesticated throughout S Asia and wild in parts of India and Nepal. It likes moist conditions. Usually gray or black, up to 6 ft/1.8 m high, both sexes carry large horns. The African

Buddha 13th-century Thai bronze Buddha.

buffalo *Syncerus caffer* is found in Africa, south of the Sahara, where there is grass, water, and cover in which to retreat. There are a number of subspecies, the biggest up to 5 ft/1.6 m high, and black, with massive horns set close together over the head. The name is also commonly applied to the American ◊bison.

Buffalo industrial port in New York State, at the east end of Lake Erie; population (1990) 328,100. It is linked with New York City by the New York State Barge Canal. Grain from Buffalo's elevators is shipped overseas via the St Lawrence Seaway. An industrial city, Buffalo was hard hit by the closing of steel mills and auto factories in the late 1970s and early 1980s. The State University of New York at Buffalo and Canisius College are here. Settled in 1780, Buffalo was burned by the British during the War of 1812 but was soon rebuilt and flourished with the completion of the Erie Canal 1825.

buffer mixture of chemical compounds chosen to maintain a steady ◊pH. The commonest buffers consist of a mixture of a weak organic acid and one of its salts or a mixture of acid salts of phosphoric acid. The addition of either an acid or a base causes a shift in the chemical equilibrium, thus keeping the pH constant.

bug in computing, an error in a program. It can be an error in the logical structure of a program or a syntax error, such as a spelling mistake. Some bugs cause a program to fail immediately; others remain dormant, causing problems only when a particular combination of events occurs. The process of finding and removing errors from a program is called *debugging*.

bug in entomology, an insect belonging to the order Hemiptera. All these have two pairs of wings with forewings partly thickened. They also have piercing mouthparts adapted for sucking the juices of plants or animals, the "beak" being tucked under the body when not in use.

bugle MU in music, a valveless brass instrument with a shorter tube and less flared bell than the trumpet. Constructed of copper plated with brass, it has long been used as a military instrument for giving a range of signals based on the tones of a harmonic series. The bugle is conical whereas the trumpet is cylindrical.

Bulawayo industrial city and railroad junction in Zimbabwe; population (1982) 415,000. It lies at an altitude of 4,450 ft/1,355 m on the river Matsheumlope, a tributary of the Zambezi, and was founded on the site of the kraal (enclosed village), burned down 1893, of the Matabele chief, Lobenguela. It produces agricultural and electrical equipment. The former capital of Matabeleland, Bulawayo developed with the exploitation of gold mines in the neighborhood.

bulb underground bud with fleshy leaves containing a reserve food supply and with roots growing from its base. Bulbs function in vegetative reproduction and are characteristic of many monocotyledonous plants such as the daffodil, snowdrop, and onion. Bulbs are grown on a commercial scale in temperate countries, such as England and the Netherlands.

Bulfinch Charles 1763–1844. US architect. He became one of New England's leading architects after his design for the Massachusetts State House was accepted 1787. He designed the Hollis Street Church, Harvard's University Hall, the Massachusetts General Hospital, and the Connecticut State House. In 1817 he was appointed architect of the US Capitol by President Monroe.

Bulganin Nikolai 1895–1975. Soviet politician and military leader. His career began in 1918 when he joined the Cheka, the Soviet secret police. He helped to organize Moscow's defense in World War II, became a marshal of the USSR 1947, and was minister of defense 1947–49 and 1953–55. On the fall of Malenkov he became prime minister (chair of Council of Ministers) 1955–58 until ousted by Khrushchev.

Bulgaria country in SE Europe, bounded N by Romania, W by Yugoslavia, SW by Macedonia, S by Greece, SE by Turkey, and E by the Black Sea.

Bulgarian member of an ethnic group living mainly in Bulgaria. There are 8–8.5 million speakers of Bulgarian, a Slavic language belonging to the Indo-European family. The Bulgarians use the Cyrillic alphabet and are known for their folk arts.

Bulge, Battle of the or *Ardennes offensive* in World War II, Hitler's plan, code-named "Watch on the Rhine," for a breakthrough by his field marshal Rundstedt aimed at the US line in the ◊Ardennes Dec 16, 1944–Jan 28, 1945. There were 77,000 Allied casualties and 130,000 German, including Hitler's last powerful reserve, his Panzer elite. Although US troops were encircled for some weeks at Bastogne, the German counteroffensive failed.

bulimia (Greek "ox hunger") condition of continuous, uncontrolled hunger. Considered a counteraction to stress or depression, this eating disorder is found chiefly in young women. When compensated for by forced vomiting or overdoses of laxatives, the condition is called *bulimia nervosa*. It is sometimes associated with ◊anorexia.

bull speculator who buys stocks or shares on the stock exchange expecting a rise in the price in order to sell them later at a profit, the opposite of a ◊bear. In a bull market, prices rise and bulls profit.

bull or *papal bull* document or edict issued by the pope; so called from the circular seals (medieval Latin *bulla*) attached to them. Some of the most celebrated bulls include Leo X's condemnation of Luther 1520 and Pius IX's proclamation of papal infallibility 1870.

Bull John. Imaginary figure personifying England; see ◊John Bull.

bulldog British dog of ancient but uncertain origin. The head is broad and square, with deeply wrinkled cheeks, small folded ears, and the nose laid back between the eyes. The bulldog grows to about 18 in/45 cm at the shoulder.

bullfighting the national sport of Spain (where there are more than 400 bullrings), which is also popular in Mexico, Portugal, and much of Latin America. It involves the ritualized taunting of a bull in a circular ring, until its eventual death at the hands of the matador. Originally popular in Greece and Rome, it was introduced into Spain by the Moors in the 11th century.

bullfinch Eurasian finch *Pyrrhula pyrrhula*, with a thick head and neck and short heavy bill. It is small and blue-gray or black, the males being reddish and the females brown on the breast. Bullfinches are 6 in/15 cm long, and usually seen in pairs. They feed on tree buds as well as seeds and berries, and are usually seen in woodland. They also live in the Aleutians and on the Alaska mainland.

Bull Run, Battles of in the American Civil War, two victories for the Confederate army under General Robert E Lee at *Manassas* Junction, NE Virginia: *First Battle of Bull Run* July 21, 1861; *Second Battle of Bull Run* Aug 29–30, 1862.

In the First Battle of Bull Run 34,000 Confederate troops routed 30,000 Union troops and challenged the North's complacent expectation of quick victory. In the Second Battle of Bull Run, Lee led 54,000 soldiers in a victory over Union forces, routing 63,000 Northern troops and opening an invasion route to the North.

bull terrier heavily built, smooth-coated breed of dog, usually white, originating as a cross between a terrier and a bulldog. It grows to about 16 in/40 cm tall and was formerly used in bull-baiting. Pit bull terriers are used in illegal dog fights.

Bülow Bernhard, Prince von 1849–1929. German diplomat and politician. He was chancellor of the German Empire 1900–09 under Kaiser Wilhelm II and, holding that self-interest was the only rule for any state, adopted attitudes to France and Russia that unintentionally reinforced the trend toward opposing European power groups: the ◊Triple Entente (Britain, France, Russia) and the ◊Triple Alliance (Germany, Austria–Hungary, Italy).

He resigned after losing the confidence of Emperor William II and the Reichstag.

bulrush any of a number of marsh plants (especially of the genus *Scirpus*) belonging to the ◊sedge family, having long, slender, solid stems tipped with brown spikelets of tiny flowers. Bulrushes are used in basketmaking and thatching.

bumblebee any large ◊bee, 1–2 in/2–5 cm, usually dark-colored but banded with yellow, orange, or white, belonging to the genus *Bombus*.

Bunche Ralph 1904–1971. US diplomat. Grandson of a slave, he was principal director of the UN Department of Trusteeship 1947–54 and UN undersecretary acting as mediator in Palestine 1948-49 and as special representative in the Congo 1960. He taught at Harvard and Howard universities and was involved in the planning of the ◊United Nations. In 1950 he was awarded the Nobel Prize for Peace, the first awarded to a black man.

Bulgaria Republic of
(*Republika Bulgaria*)

area 42,812 sq mi/110,912 sq km
capital Sofia
cities Plovdiv, Ruse; Black Sea ports Burgas and Varna
physical lowland plains in N and SE separated by mountains that cover three-quarters of the country
environment pollution has virtually eliminated all species of fish once caught in the Black Sea. Vehicle-exhaust emissions in Sofia have led to dust concentrations more than twice the medically accepted level
features key position on land route from Europe to Asia; Black Sea coast; Balkan and Rhodope mountains; Danube River in N
head of state Zhelyu Zhelev from 1990
head of government Lyuben Berov from 1992
political system emergent democratic republic
political parties Union of Democratic Forces (UDF), right of center; Bulgarian Socialist Party (BSP), left-wing, ex-communist; Movement for Rights and Freedoms (MRF), centrist

exports textiles, leather, chemicals, nonferrous metals, timber, machinery, tobacco, cigarettes (world's largest exporter)
currency lev
population (1990 est) 8,978,000 (including 900,000–1,500,000 ethnic Turks, concentrated in S and NE); growth rate 0.1% p.a.
life expectancy men 69, women 74
languages Bulgarian, Turkish
religions Eastern Orthodox Christian 90%, Sunni Muslim 10%
literacy 98%
GDP $25.4 bn (1987); $2,836 per head

chronology
1908 Bulgaria became a kingdom independent of Turkish rule.
1944 Soviet invasion of German-occupied Bulgaria.
1946 Monarchy abolished and communist-dominated people's republic proclaimed.
1947 Soviet-style constitution adopted.
1949 Death of Georgi Dimitrov, the communist government leader.
1954 Election of Todor Zhivkov as Communist Party general secretary; made nation a loyal satellite of USSR.
1971 Constitution modified; Zhivkov elected president.
1985–89 Large administrative and personnel changes made haphazardly under Soviet stimulus.
1987 New electoral law introduced multicandidate elections.
1989 Program of "Bulgarianization" resulted in mass exodus of Turks to Turkey. Nov: Zhivkov ousted by Petar Mladenov. Dec: opposition parties allowed to form.
1990 April: BCP renamed Bulgarian Socialist Party (BSP). Aug: Dr Zhelyu Zhelev elected president. Nov: government headed by Andrei Lukanov resigned, replaced Dec by coalition led by Dimitur Popov.
1991 July: new constitution adopted. Oct: UDF beat BSP in general election by narrow margin; formation of first noncommunist, UDF-minority government under Filip Dimitrov.
1992 Zhelev became Bulgaria's first directly elected president. Relations with West greatly improved. Dimitrov resigned after vote of no confidence; replaced by Lyuben Berov and nonparty government.

Bunker Hill, Battle of the first significant engagement in the ◊American Revolution, June 17, 1775, near a small hill in Charlestown (now part of Boston), Massachusetts; the battle actually took place on Breed's Hill. Although the colonists were defeated they were able to retreat to Boston and suffered fewer casualties than the British.

The failure to defeat the rebels soundly resulted in the replacement of General Thomas ◊Gage as British commander.

Bunsen Robert Wilhelm von 1811–1899. German chemist credited with the invention of the *Bunsen burner*. His name is also given to the carbon-zinc electric cell, which he invented 1841 for use in arc lamps. In 1859 he discovered two new elements, cesium and ribidium.

Bunshaft Gordon 1909–1990. US architect whose Modernist buildings include the first to be completely enclosed in curtain walling (walls which hang from a rigid steel frame), the Lever Building 1952 in New York. He also designed the Heinz Company's UK headquarters 1965 at Hayes Park, London.

Buntline Ned. Adopted name of US author Edward Z C ◊Judson.

Buñuel Luis 1900–1983. Spanish ◊Surrealist film director. He collaborated with Salvador Dali on *Un

Chien andalou/An Andalusian Dog 1928 and *L'Age d'or/The Golden Age* 1930 and established his solo career with *Los olvidados/The Young and the Damned* 1950. His works are often anticlerical, with black humor and erotic imagery.

Bunyan John 1628–1688. English author. A Baptist, he was imprisoned in Bedford 1660–72 for unlicensed preaching. During a second jail sentence 1675 he started to write *The Pilgrim's Progress*, the first part of which was published 1678. Other works include *Grace Abounding* 1666, *The Life and Death of Mr Badman* 1680, and *The Holy War* 1682.

buoy floating object used to mark channels for shipping or warn of hazards to navigation. Buoys come in different shapes, such as a pole (spar buoy), cylinder (car buoy), and cone (nun buoy). Light buoys carry a small tower surmounted by a flashing lantern, and bell buoys house a bell, which rings as the buoy moves up and down with the waves. Mooring buoys are heavy and have a ring on top to which a ship can be tied.

buoyancy lifting effect of a fluid on a body wholly or partly immersed in it. This was studied by ◊Archimedes in the 3rd century BC.

bur or *burr* in botany, a type of "false fruit" or pseudocarp, surrounded by numerous hooks; for instance, that of burdock *Arctium*, where the hooks are formed from bracts surrounding the flowerhead. Burs catch in the feathers or fur of passing animals, and thus may be dispersed over considerable distances.

Burbage Richard *c.* 1567–1619. English actor, thought to have been ◊Shakespeare's original Hamlet, Othello, and Lear. He also appeared in first productions of works by Ben Jonson, Thomas Kyd, and John Webster. His father *James Burbage* (*c.* 1530–1597) built the first English playhouse, known as "the Theatre"; his brother **Cuthbert Burbage** (*c.* 1566–1636) built the original ◊Globe Theatre 1599 in London.

burbot long, rounded fish *Lota lota* of the cod family, the only one living entirely in fresh water. Up to 3 ft/1 m long, it lives on the bottom of clear lakes and rivers, often in holes or under rocks, throughout Europe, Asia, and North America.

bureaucracy organization whose structure and operations are governed to a high degree by written rules and a hierarchy of offices; in its broadest sense, all forms of administration, and in its narrowest, rule by officials.

Burgenland federal state of SE Austria, extending S from the Danube along the western border of the Hungarian plain; area 1,544 sq mi/4,000 sq km; population (1989) 267,200. It is a largely agricultural region adjoining the Neusiedler See, and produces timber, fruit, sugar, wine, lignite, antimony, and limestone. Its capital is Eisenstadt.

Burger Warren Earl 1907– . US jurist and chief justice of the United States 1969-86. His term in the US Supreme Court was marked by a conservative turn in civil-rights matters. His majority decision in the Watergate tapes case *US* v *Nixon* 1974 was instrumental in bringing about Nixon's resignation. Born in St Paul, Minnesota, Burger was educated at the University of Minnesota and was admitted to the bar 1931. President Eisenhower appointed him judge of the US Court of Appeals 1956. In 1969 Burger was named to the US Supreme Court, succeeding Chief Justice Earl Warren. Burger retired from the Court 1986 and was succeeded by William Rehnquist.

Burgess Anthony. Adopted name of Anthony John Burgess Wilson 1917–1993. British novelist, critic, and composer. His prolific work includes *A Clockwork Orange* 1962, set in a future London terrorized by teenage gangs, and the panoramic *Earthly Powers* 1980. His vision has been described as bleak and pessimistic, but his work is also comic and satiric, as in his novels featuring the poet Enderby.

Burgess Shale Site site of unique fossil-bearing rock formations created 530 million years ago by a mud slide, in Yoho National Park, British Columbia. The shales in this corner of the Rocky Mountains contain more than 120 species of marine invertebrate fossils. Although discovered 1909 by US geologist Charles Walcott, the Burgess Shales have only recently been used as evidence in the debate concerning the evolution of life. In *Wonderful Life* 1990 Stephen Jay Gould drew attention to a body of scientific opinion interpreting the fossil finds as evidence of parallel early evolutionary trends extinguished by chance rather than natural selection.

burgh (burh or borough) term originating in Germanic lands in the 9th–10th centuries referring to a fortified settlement, usually surrounding a monastery or castle. Later, it was used to mean new towns, or towns that enjoyed particular privileges relating to

government and taxation and whose citizens were called **burghers**.

burgher term used from the 11th century to describe citizens of burghs who were freemen of a burgh, and had the right to participate in its government. They usually had to possess a house within the burgh.

Burgoyne John 1722–1792. British general and dramatist. He served in the American War of Independence and surrendered 1777 to the colonists at Saratoga, New York State, in one of the pivotal battles of the war. He wrote comedies, among them *The Maid of the Oaks* 1775 and *The Heiress* 1786. He figures in George Bernard Shaw's play *The Devil's Disciple* 1896.

Burgundy ancient kingdom and duchy in the valleys of the rivers Saône and Rhône, France. The Burgundi were a Teutonic tribe that overran the country about 400. From the 9th century to the death of Duke ◊Charles the Bold 1477, Burgundy was the nucleus of a powerful principality. On Charles's death the duchy was incorporated into France. The capital of Burgundy was Dijon. Today the region to which it corresponds is Bourgogne.

Burgundy region centered around the valleys of the Rhône and Saône rivers in E France and SW Germany, partly corresponding with modern Bourgogne. Settled by the Teutonic Burgundi around AD 443, and brought under Frankish control 534, Burgundy played a central role in the medieval history of NW Europe. It was divided among various groups between the 9th and 11th centuries, splitting into a duchy in the west, controlled by French ◊Carolingians, while the rest became a county in the ◊Holy Roman Empire. The duchy was acquired by the Capetian king Robert the Pious 1002, and until 1361 it was the most important and loyal fiefdom in the realm. Duchy and county were reunited 1384, and in the 15th century this wealthy region was the glittering capital of European court culture.

Burgundy (French *Bourgogne*) region of France that includes the *départements* of Côte-d'Or, Nièvre, Sâone-et-Loire, and Yonne; area 12,198 sq mi/31,600 sq km; population (1986) 1,607,000. Its capital is Dijon.

Burke Edmund 1729–1797. British Whig politician and political theorist, born in Dublin, Ireland. In Parliament from 1765, he opposed the government's attempts to coerce the American colonists, for example in *Thoughts on the Present Discontents* 1770, and supported the emancipation of Ireland, but denounced the French Revolution, for example in *Reflections on the Revolution in France* 1790.

Burke's Peerage popular name of the *Genealogical and Heraldic History of the Peerage, Baronetage, and Knightage of the United Kingdom*, first issued by John Burke 1826. The most recent edition was 1970.

Burkina Faso (formerly Upper Volta) landlocked country in W Africa, bounded E by Niger, NW and W by Mali, S by Ivory Coast, Ghana, Togo, and Benin.

burlesque in the 17th and 18th centuries, a form of satirical comedy parodying a particular play or dramatic genre. For example, John ◊Gay's *The Beggar's Opera* 1728 is a burlesque of 18th-century opera, and Richard Brinsley ◊Sheridan's *The Critic* 1777 satirizes the sentimentality in contemporary drama. In the US from the mid-19th century, burlesque referred to a sex and comedy show invented by Michael Bennett Leavitt 1866 with acts including acrobats, singers, and comedians. During the 1920s striptease was intro-

Burkina Faso The People's
Democratic Republic of
(formerly **Upper Volta**)

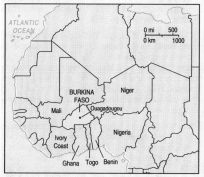

area 105,811 sq mi/274,122 sq km
capital Ouagadougou
cities Bobo-Dioulasso, Koudougou
physical landlocked plateau with hills in W and SE; headwaters of the river Volta; semiarid in N, forest and farmland in S
environment tropical savanna subject to overgrazing and deforestation
features linked by rail to Abidjan in Ivory Coast, Burkina Faso's only outlet to the sea
head of state and government Blaise Compaoré from 1987
political system transitional
political parties Organization for Popular Democracy–Workers' Movement (ODP–MT), nationalist left-wing; FP–Popular Front
exports cotton, groundnuts, livestock, hides, skins, sesame, cereals
currency CFA franc

population (1990 est) 8,941,000; growth rate 2.4% p.a.
life expectancy men 44, women 47
languages French (official); about 50 native Sudanic languages spoken by 90% of population
religions animist 53%, Sunni Muslim 36%, Roman Catholic 11%
literacy men 21%, women 6% (1985 est)
GDP $1.6 bn (1987); $188 per head

chronology
1958 Became a self-governing republic within the French Community.
1960 Independence from France, with Maurice Yaméogo as the first president.
1966 Military coup led by Col Lamizana. Constitution suspended, political activities banned, and a supreme council of the armed forces established.
1969 Ban on political activities lifted.
1970 Referendum approved a new constitution leading to a return to civilian rule.
1974 After experimenting with a mixture of military and civilian rule, Lamizana reassumed full power.
1977 Ban on political activities removed. Referendum approved a new constitution based on civilian rule.
1978 Lamizana elected president.
1980 Lamizana overthrown in bloodless coup led by Col Zerbo.
1982 Zerbo ousted in a coup by junior officers. Major Ouédraogo became president and Thomas Sankara prime minister.
1983 Sankara seized complete power.
1984 Upper Volta renamed Burkina Faso, "land of upright men".
1987 Sankara killed in coup led by Blaise Compaoré.
1989 New government party ODP–MT formed by merger of other progovernment parties. Coup against Compaoré foiled.
1991 New constitution approved. Compaoré reelected president.
1992 Multiparty elections won by FP–Popular Front.

duced in order to counteract the growing popularity of the movies; Gypsy Rose Lee was the most famous stripper.

Burlington city in N central North Carolina, NW of Durham; population (1990) 39,500. Industries include textiles, chemicals, furniture, and agricultural products.

Burlington city in NW Vermont, on the E shore of Lake Champlain; seat of Chittenden County; population (1990) 39,100. It is a port of entry to the US; industries include computer parts, steel, marble, lumber, dairy products, and tourism. It was a naval base during the War of 1812.

It is the site of the University of Vermont 1791.

Burma former name (to 1989) of ◊Myanmar.

Burman member of the largest ethnic group in Myanmar (formerly Burma). The Burmans, speakers of a Sino-Tibetan language, migrated from the hills of Tibet, settling in the areas around Mandalay by the 11th century AD.

Burma War war 1942–45 during which Burma (now ◊Myanmar) was occupied by Japan. Initially supported by ◊Aung San's Burma National Army, the Japanese captured Rangoon and Mandalay 1942, forcing the withdrawal of General Alexander's British forces to India. During 1943, Chindit guerrilla resistance was organized and after a year's heavy fighting at Imphal and Kohima, British, Commonwealth,

American, and Chinese nationalist troops reopened the "Burma Road" between India and China Jan 1945. Rangoon was recaptured May 1945.

burn in medicine, destruction of body tissue by extremes of temperature, corrosive chemicals, electricity, or radiation. *First-degree burns* may cause reddening; *second-degree burns* cause blistering and irritation but usually heal spontaneously; *third-degree burns* are disfiguring and may be life-threatening.

Burnett Frances (Eliza) Hodgson 1849–1924. English writer who emigrated with her family to the US 1865. Her novels for children include the rags-to-riches tale *Little Lord Fauntleroy* 1886 and the sentimental *The Secret Garden* 1909.

Burney Frances (Fanny) 1752–1840. English novelist and diarist, daughter of musician Dr Charles Burney (1726–1814). She achieved success with *Evelina*, published anonymously 1778, became a member of Dr ◊Johnson's circle, received a post at court from Queen Charlotte, and in 1793 married the French émigré General d'Arblay. She published three further novels, *Cecilia* 1782, *Camilla* 1796, and *The Wanderer* 1814; her diaries and letters appeared 1842.

Burnham Forbes 1923–1985. Guyanese Marxist–Leninist politician. He was prime minister 1964–80, leading the country to independence 1966 and declaring it the world's first cooperative republic 1970. He was executive president 1980–85. Resistance to the US landing in Grenada 1983 was said to be due to his fore-warning the Grenadans of the attack.

Burns Robert 1759–1796. Scottish poet who used the Scots dialect at a time when it was not considered suitably "elevated" for literature. Burns's first volume, *Poems, Chiefly in the Scottish Dialect*, appeared 1786. In addition to his poetry, Burns wrote or adapted many songs, including "Auld Lang Syne."

Burnside Ambrose Everett 1824–1881. US military leader and politician. He was appointed brigadier general in the Union army soon after the outbreak of the Civil War 1861. Named as George ◊McClellan's successor as commander of the Army of the Potomac, Burnside served briefly in that position before being transferred to the West. He was governor of Rhode Island 1866–69 and US senator 1874–81.

Burr Aaron 1756–1836. US politician, Republican vice president 1800–04, in which year he killed his political rival Alexander ◊Hamilton in a duel. In 1807 Burr was tried and acquitted of treason charges, which implicated him variously in a scheme to conquer Mexico, or part of Florida, or to rule over a seceded Louisiana.

Burroughs Edgar Rice 1875–1950. US novelist. He wrote *Tarzan of the Apes* 1914, the story of an aristocratic child lost in the jungle and reared by apes, and followed it with over 20 more books about the Tarzan character. He also wrote a series of novels about life on Mars. He was born in Chicago.

Burroughs William S 1914– . US novelist. He "dropped out" and, as part of the ◊Beat Generation, wrote *Junkie* 1953, describing his addiction to heroin; *The Naked Lunch* 1959; *The Soft Machine* 1961; and

Dead Fingers Talk 1963. His later novels include *Queer* and *Mind Wars*, both 1985.

He was born in St Louis, Missouri.

Bursa city in NW Turkey, with a port at Mudania; population (1990) 834,600. It was the capital of the Ottoman Empire 1326–1423.

Burton Richard Francis 1821–1890. British explorer and translator (he knew 35 Oriental languages). He traveled mainly in the Middle East and NE Africa, often disguised as a Muslim; made two attempts to find the source of the Nile, 1855 and 1857–58 (on the second, with John Speke, he reached Lake Tanganyika); and wrote many travel books. He translated Oriental erotica and the *Arabian Nights* 1885–88.

Burton Richard. Adopted name of Richard Jenkins 1925–1984. Welsh actor of stage and screen. He had a rich, dramatic voice. Films in which he appeared with his wife Elizabeth ◊Taylor include *Cleopatra* 1962 and *Who's Afraid of Virginia Woolf?* 1966. Among his later films are *Equus* 1977 and *Nineteen Eighty-Four* 1984.

He also won acclaim for his stage performances in both Shakespearian and contemporary dramas throughout his film career.

Burundi country in E central Africa, bounded N by Rwanda, W by Zaire, SW by Lake Tanganyika, and SE and E by Tanzania.

Bush George Herbert Walker 1924– . 41st president of the US 1989–93. A Republican, he was director of the Central Intelligence Agency (CIA) 1976–81 and US vice president 1981–89. In 1989, as president, he visited Eastern European countries undergoing reform, held a summit meeting at Malta with Soviet president Gorbachev, and sent US troops to Panama to oust that

Burundi Republic of
(*Republika y'Uburundi*)

area 10,744 sq mi/27,834 sq km
capital Bujumbura
cities Gitega, Bururi, Ngozi, Muyinga
physical landlocked grassy highland straddling watershed of Nile and Congo
features Lake Tanganyika, Great Rift Valley
head of government Sylvie Kinigi from 1993
political system one-party military republic
political party Union for National Progress (UPRONA), nationalist socialist
exports coffee, cotton, tea, nickel, hides, livestock, cigarettes, beer, soft drinks; there are 500 million tons of peat reserves in the basin of the Akanyaru River
currency Burundi franc
population (1990 est) 5,647,000 (of whom 15% are the

Nilotic Tutsi, still holding most of the land and political power; 1% are Pygmy Twa, and the remainder Bantu Hutu); growth rate 2.8% p.a.
life expectancy men 45, women 48
languages Kirundi (a Bantu language) and French (both official), Kiswahili
religions Roman Catholic 62%, Protestant 5%, Muslim 1%, animist 32%
literacy men 43%, women 26% (1985)
GDP $1.1 bn (1987); $230 per head

chronology
1962 Separated from Ruanda-Urundi, as Burundi, and given independence as a monarchy under King Mwambutsa IV.
1966 King deposed by his son Charles, who became Ntare V; he was in turn deposed by his prime minister, Capt Michel Micombero, who declared Burundi a republic.
1972 Ntare V killed, allegedly by the Hutu ethnic group. Massacres of 150,000 Hutus by the rival Tutsi ethnic group, of which Micombero was a member.
1973 Micombero made president and prime minister.
1974 UPRONA declared the only legal political party, with the president as its secretary general.
1976 Army coup deposed Micombero. Col Jean-Baptiste Bagaza appointed president by the Supreme Revolutionary Council.
1981 New constitution adopted, providing for a national assembly.
1984 Bagaza elected president as sole candidate.
1987 Bagaza deposed in coup Sept. Maj Pierre Buyoya headed new Military Council for National Redemption.
1988 Some 24,000 majority Hutus killed by Tutsis.
1992 New constitution approved by referendum.
1993 Melchior Ndadaye, a Hutu, elected president, but killed in Oct during attempted military coup.

country's drug-trafficking president, Manuel Noriega. Bush led the UN coalition and sent US forces to Saudi Arabia to prepare for a military strike after Iraq annexed Kuwait 1990. In Jan 1991, he led the coalition war against Iraq that forced Saddam Hussein to remove his troops from Kuwait. He was instrumental in convincing Israel and several of its traditional Arab enemies to convene for a historic face-to-face meeting in Spain in Nov 1991. Domestic economic problems in 1991–92 were followed by his defeat in the 1992 presidential elections by Democrat Bill Clinton.

bushel dry measure used for grain and fruit, equal to eight gallons (2,219.36 cu in/36.37 l) in the UK; some US states have different standards according to the goods measured. One bushel equals four pecks.

bushido chivalric code of honor of the Japanese military caste, the ◊samurai. Bushido means "the way of the warrior"; the code stresses simple living, self-discipline, and bravery.

Bushman former name for the ◊Kung, San, and other hunter-gatherer groups (for example, the Gikwe, Heikom, and Sekhoin) living in and around the Kalahari Desert in southern Africa. They number approximately 50,000 and speak San and other languages of the Khoisan family. They are characteristically small-statured and brown-skinned.

bushmaster large snake *Lachesis muta*. It is a type of pit viper, and is related to the rattlesnakes. Up to 12 ft/4 m long, it is found in wooded areas of South and Central America and is the largest venomous snake in the New World. When alarmed, it produces a noise by vibrating its tail among dry leaves.

business cycle period of time that includes a peak and trough of economic activity, as measured by a country's national income. In Keynesian economics, one of the main roles of the government is to smooth out the peaks and troughs of the business cycle by intervening in the economy, thus minimizing "overheating" and "stagnation."

Bustamante (William) Alexander (born Clarke) 1884–1977. Jamaican socialist politician. As leader of the Labor Party, he was the first prime minister of independent Jamaica 1962–67.

butane one of two gaseous alkanes (paraffin hydrocarbons) having the same formula but differing in structure. Normal butane is derived from natural gas; isobutane is a byproduct of petroleum manufacture. Liquefied under pressure, it is used as a fuel for industrial and domestic purposes (for example, in portable cookers).

Buthelezi Chief Gatsha 1928– . Zulu leader and politician, chief minister of KwaZulu, a black "homeland" in the Republic of South Africa from 1970. He is the founder (1975) and president of ◊Inkatha, a paramilitary organization for attaining a nonracial democratic political system. He has been accused of complicity in the factional violence between Inkatha and ◊African National Congress supporters that has continued to rack the townships despite his signing of a peace accord with ANC leader, Nelson Mandela, Sept 1991.

Butler Samuel 1835–1902. English author who made his name 1872 with a satiric attack on contemporary utopianism, *Erewhon* (*nowhere* reversed), but is now remembered for his autobiographical *The Way of All Flesh* written 1872–85 and published 1903.

Butte mining town in Montana, in the Rocky Mountains; population (1990) 33,900. Butte was founded

1864 during a rush for gold, soon exhausted; copper was found some 20 years later on what was called "the richest hill on earth." The last mine closed 1983. Butte is the seat of the Montana College of Mineral Science and Technology.

butter solid, edible yellowish fat made from whole milk. Making butter by hand, which is done by skimming off the cream and churning it, was traditionally a convenient means of preserving milk.

Salted butter has a longer shelf-life than sweet butter, salt being added as a preservative.

buttercup plant of the genus *Ranunculus* of the buttercup family with divided leaves and yellow flowers.

Species include the swamp buttercup *R. septentrionaiis* of the US.

butterfly insect belonging, like moths, to the order Lepidoptera, in which the wings are covered with tiny scales, often brightly colored. There are some 15,000 species of butterfly, many of which are under threat throughout the world because of the destruction of habitat.

butterfly fish any of several fishes, not all related. The freshwater butterfly fish *Pantodon buchholzi* of W Africa can leap from the water and glide for a short distance on its large winglike pectoral fins. Up to 4 in/10 cm long, it lives in stagnant water. The tropical marine butterfly fishes, family Chaetodontidae, are brightly colored with laterally flattened bodies, often with long snouts which they poke into crevices in rocks and coral when feeding.

buyer's market market having an excess of goods and services on offer and where prices are likely to be declining. The buyer benefits from the wide choice and competition available.

buzzard any of a number of species of medium-sized hawks with broad wings, often seen soaring. The *common buzzard Buteo buteo* of Europe and Asia is about 1.8 ft/55 cm long with a wingspan of over 4 ft/1.2 m. It preys on a variety of small animals up to the size of a rabbit.

Byatt A(ntonia) S(usan) 1936– . English novelist and critic. Her fifth novel, *Possession*, won the 1990

butterfly

An adult female cabbage white lays her eggs on the underside of a cabbage leaf. The caterpillars that emerge are "feeding and growing machines." They look quite unlike the winged adults. In autumn, the caterpillars cease feeding, rest on a tree or post, and form a cocoon around themselves. The following spring, the young adults emerge, mate, then die.

As the adult emerges from the cocoon its wings fill with blood and harden.

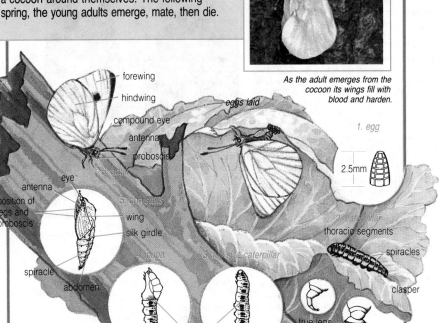

forewing

hindwing

eggs laid

compound eye

antenna

proboscis

6. adult

eye

antenna

position of legs and proboscis

5. chrysalis

wing

silk girdle

spiracle

abdomen

4. pupa

3. autumn-late caterpillar

life cycle stages

silk girdles

1. egg

2.5mm

2. caterpillar

thoracic segments

spiracles

clasper

true legs

false legs

development timescale					sheds skin		earliest emergence		
stage	1	2			3 & 4		5	can remain pupating for up to 6 months ▶	6
weeks	1	2	3	4	5	6	7	8	34

Caterpillars have simple eyes and biting mouthparts. They bite off pieces of leaves with their jaws. Adult butterflies have large, compound eyes and sucking mouthparts, with which they feed on nectar.

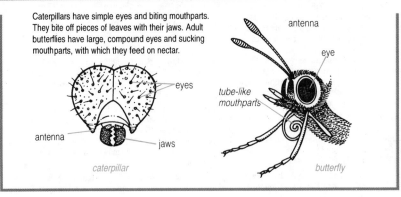

antenna

eye

tube-like mouthparts

eyes

antenna

jaws

caterpillar

butterfly

Booker Prize. *The Virgin in the Garden* 1978 is a confident, zestfully handled account of a varied group of characters putting on a school play during Coronation year, 1953. It has a sequel, *Still Life* 1985.

Byblos ancient Phoenician city (modern Jebeil), 20 mi/32 km N of Beirut, Lebanon. Known to the Assyrians and Babylonians as *Gubla*, it had a thriving export of cedar and pinewood to Egypt as early as 1500 BC. In Roman times it boasted an amphitheater, baths, and a temple, and was known for its celebration of the resurrection of Adonis, worshiped as a god of vegetation.

Byelorussia alternate form of ◊Belarus, a country in E central Europe.

Byelorussian or *Belorussian* "White Russian" native of Belarus. Byelorussian, a Balto-Slavic language belonging to the Indo-European family, is spoken by about 10 million people, including some in Poland. It is written in the Cyrillic script. Byelorussian literature dates to the 11th century AD.

Byrd Richard Evelyn 1888–1957. US aviator and explorer. The first to fly over the North Pole (1926), he also flew over the South Pole (1929) and led five overland expeditions in Antarctica.

At the request of President Franklin Roosevelt, he took command of the US Antarctic Service. Byrd maintained that new techniques could be used as supplements to traditional methods, rather than as replacements for them. In holding this view, he disagreed with Norwegian explorer Roald ◊Amundsen.

Byrds, the US pioneering folk-rock group 1964–73. Emulated for their 12-string guitar sound, as on the hits "Mr Tambourine Man" (a 1965 version of Bob Dylan's song) and "Eight Miles High" 1966, they moved toward country rock in the late 1960s, setting another trend.

Byron Augusta Ada 1815–1851. English mathematician, a pioneer in writing programs for Charles ◊Babbage's analytical engine. In 1983 a new, high-level computer language, ADA, was named after her. She was the daughter of the poet Lord Byron.

Byron George Gordon, 6th Baron Byron 1788–1824. English poet who became the symbol of Romanticism and political liberalism throughout Europe in the 19th century. His reputation was established with the first two cantos of *Childe Harold* 1812. Later works include *The Prisoner of Chillon* 1816, *Beppo* 1818, *Mazeppa* 1819, and, most notably, the satirical *Don Juan* 1819–24. He left England in 1816, spending most of his later life in Italy.

byte sufficient computer memory to store a single character of data. The character is stored in the byte of memory as a pattern of ◊bits (binary digits), using a code such as ◊ASCII. A byte usually contains eight

Byron A portrait of Lord Byron by Richard Westall (1813), National Gallery, London.

bits—for example, the capital letter F can be stored as the bit pattern 01000110.

Byzantine Empire the *Eastern Roman Empire* 395–1453, with its capital at Constantinople (formerly Byzantium, modern Istanbul).

Byzantine style style in the visual arts and architecture that originated in the 4th–5th centuries in Byzantium (the capital of the Eastern Roman Empire) and spread to Italy, throughout the Balkans, and to Russia, where it survived for many centuries. It is characterized by heavy stylization, strong linear emphasis, the use of rigid artistic stereotypes and rich colors such as gold. Byzantine artists excelled in mosaic work and manuscript painting. In architecture, the dome supported on pendentives was in widespread use.

Byzantium (modern Istanbul) ancient Greek city on the Bosporus, founded as a colony of the Greek city of Megara on an important strategic site at the entrance to the Black Sea in about 660 BC. In AD 330 the capital of the Roman Empire was transferred there by Constantine the Great, who renamed it ◊Constantinople.

C high-level general-purpose computer-programming language popular on minicomputers and microcomputers. Developed in the early 1970s from an earlier language called BCPL, C was first used as the language of the operating system ◊Unix, though it has since become widespread beyond Unix. It is useful for writing fast and efficient systems programs, such as operating systems (which control the operations of the computer).

c. abbreviation for *circa* (Latin "about"); used with dates that are uncertain.

C abbreviation for *centum* (Latin "hundred"); *century, centigrade,* ◊*Celsius.*

C °C symbol for ◊Celsius (temperature scale), formerly called centigrade.

CA abbreviation for the state of ◊California.

cabbage plant *Brassica oleracea* of the cress family Cruciferae, allied to the turnip and wild mustard, or charlock. It is a table vegetable, cultivated as early as 2000 BC, and the numerous commercial varieties include kale, Brussels sprouts, common cabbage, savoy, cauliflower, sprouting broccoli, and kohlrabi.

cabinet in government, a group of ministers that act as advisers to a country's executive. Cabinet members generally advise on, decide, or administer the government's policy. The US cabinet consists of the secretaries (heads) of the executive departments, appointed by the president and confirmed by the Senate. The secretaries are not members of Congress; they are advisers to the president. In the UK, the cabinet system originated under the Stuart monarchs; under William III it became customary for the king to select his ministers from the party with a parliamentary majority. The chief royal adviser was called the prime minister.

cable car method of transporting passengers up steep slopes by cable. In the *cable railway*, passenger automobiles are hauled along rails by a cable wound by a powerful winch. A pair of cars usually operates together on the funicular principle, one going up as the other goes down. The other main type is the *aerial cable car*, where the passenger car is suspended from a trolley that runs along an aerial cableway.

Cable News Network (CNN) international television news channel; the 24-hour service was founded 1980 by US entrepreneur Ted Turner and has its headquarters in Atlanta, Georgia. It established its global reputation 1991 with eyewitness accounts from Baghdad of the beginning of the Gulf War.

cable television distribution of broadcast signals through cable relay systems. Narrow-band systems were originally used to deliver services to areas with poor regular reception; systems with wider bands, using coaxial and fiber-optic cable, are increasingly used for distribution and development of home-based interactive services.

Cabot Sebastian 1474–1557. Italian navigator and cartographer, the second son of Giovanni ◊Caboto. He explored the Brazilian coast and the Rio de la Plata for the Holy Roman Emperor Charles V 1526–30.

Caboto Giovanni or *John Cabot* 1450–1498. Italian navigator. Commissioned, with his three sons, by Henry VII of England to discover unknown lands, he arrived at Cape Breton Island on June 24, 1497, thus becoming the first European to reach the North American mainland (he thought he was in NE Asia). In 1498 he sailed again, touching Greenland, and probably died on the voyage.

cacao tropical American evergreen tree *Theobroma cacao* of the Sterculia family, now also cultivated in W Africa and Sri Lanka. Its seeds are cocoa beans, from which ◊cocoa and chocolate are prepared.

cactus (plural *cacti*) plant of the family Cactaceae, although the term is commonly applied to many different succulent and prickly plants. True cacti have a woody axis (central core) overlaid with an enlarged fleshy stem, which assumes various forms and is usually covered with spines (actually reduced leaves). They all have special adaptations to growing in dry areas.

CAD (acronym for *computer-aided design*) the use of computers in creating and editing design drawings. CAD also allows such things as automatic testing of designs and multiple or animated three-dimensional views of designs. CAD systems are widely used in architecture, electronics, and engineering, for example in the motor-vehicle industry, where automobiles designed with the assistance of computers are now commonplace. A related development is ◊CAM (computer-assisted manufacturing).

Cadiz Spanish city and naval base, capital and seaport of the province of Cadiz, standing on Cadiz Bay, an inlet of the Atlantic, 64 mi/103 km S of Seville; population (1991) 156,600. After the discovery of the Americas 1492, Cadiz became one of Europe's most vital trade ports. The English adventurer Francis ◊Drake burned a Spanish fleet here 1587 to prevent the sailing of the ◊Armada.

cadmium soft, silver-white, ductile, and malleable metallic element, symbol Cd, atomic number 48, atomic weight 112.40. Cadmium occurs in nature as a sulfide or carbonate in zinc ores. It is a toxic metal that, because of industrial dumping, has become an environmental pollutant. It is used in batteries, electroplating, and as a constituent of alloys used for bearings with low coefficients of friction; it is also a constituent of an alloy with a very low melting point.

Cadmus in Greek legend, a Phoenician from Tyre, brother of ◊Europa. He founded the city of Thebes in Greece. Obeying the oracle of ◊Athena, Cadmus killed the sacred dragon that guarded the spring of Ares. He sowed the teeth of the dragon, from which sprang a multitude of fierce warriors who fought among themselves; the survivors were considered to be the ancestors of the Theban aristocracy.

Caesar powerful family of ancient Rome, which included Gaius Julius Caesar, whose grand-nephew and adopted son ◊Augustus assumed the name of Caesar and passed it on to his adopted son ◊Tiberius. From then on, it was used by the successive emperors, becoming a title of the Roman rulers. The titles "tsar" in Russia and "kaiser" in Germany were both derived from the name Caesar.

Caesar Gaius Julius *c.* 100–44 BC. Roman statesman and general. He formed with ◊Pompey and ◊Crassus the First Triumvirate 60 BC. He conquered Gaul 58–50 and invaded Britain 55 and 54. He fought against Pompey 49–48, defeating him at Pharsalus. After a period in Egypt Caesar returned to Rome as dictator from 46. He was assassinated by conspirators on the ◊Ides of March 44.

Caesarea ancient city in Palestine (now Qisarya). It was built by Herod the Great 22–12 BC, who also constructed an artificial harbor (*portus Augusti*). Caesarea was the administrative capital of the province of Judea.

Caesarean section surgical operation to deliver a baby by cutting through the mother's abdominal and intrauterine walls. It may be recommended for almost any obstetric complication implying a threat to mother or baby.

caffeine ◊alkaloid organic substance found in tea, coffee, and kola nuts; it stimulates the heart and central nervous system. When isolated, it is a bitter crystalline compound, $C_8H_{10}N_4O_2$. Too much caffeine (more than six average cups of tea or coffee a day) can be detrimental to health.

Cage John 1912–1992. US composer. A pupil of Arnold ◊Schoenberg, he maintained that all sounds should be available for musical purposes; for example, he used 24 radios, tuned to random stations, in *Imaginary Landscape No 4* 1951. He also worked to reduce the control of the composer over the music, introducing randomness (◊aleatory music) and inexactitude and allowing sounds to "be themselves." Cage's unconventional ideas have had a profound impact on 20th-century music.

Cagliari capital and port of Sardinia, Italy, on the Gulf of Cagliari; population (1988) 222,000.

Cagney James 1899–1986. US actor who moved to films from Broadway. Usually associated with gangster roles (*The Public Enemy* 1931), he was an actor of great versatility, playing Bottom in *A Midsummer Night's Dream* 1935 and singing and dancing in *Yankee Doodle Dandy* 1942.

He starred in *Mr Roberts* 1955, and *One Two Three* 1961 was his last film before retirement; but in 1981 he came back for *Ragtime*.

Cain in the Old Testament, the first-born son of Adam and Eve. Motivated by jealousy, he murdered his brother Abel because the latter's sacrifice was more acceptable to God than his own.

Cain James M(allahan) 1892–1977. US novelist. He was the author of *The Postman Always Rings Twice* 1934, *Mildred Pierce* 1941, and *Double Indemnity* 1943, which all became classic motion pictures. These novels epitomized the "hard-boiled" fiction of the 1930s and 1940s.

Caine Michael. Adopted name of Maurice Micklewhite 1933– . English actor, an accomplished performer with an enduring Cockney streak. His films include *Alfie* 1966, *The Man Who Would Be King* 1975, *Educating Rita* 1983, and *Hannah and Her Sisters* 1986.

Caesar The campaigns of military commander Gaius Julius Caesar extended and consolidated the boundaries of the Roman Empire and facilitated his rise to dictator.

cairn Scottish breed of ◊terrier. Shaggy, short-legged, and compact, it can be sandy, grayish brindle, or red. It was formerly used for flushing out foxes and badgers.

Cairo capital of Egypt, on the east bank of the river Nile 8 mi/13 km above the apex of the delta and 100 mi/160 km from the Mediterranean; the largest city in Africa and in the Middle East; population (1985) 6,205,000; metropolitan area (1987) 13,300,000. An earthquake in a suburb of the city Oct 1992 left over 500 dead. *history* El Fustat (Old Cairo) was founded by Arabs about 642, Al Qahira about 1000 by the ◊Fatimid ruler Gowhar. Cairo was the capital of the Ayyubid dynasty, one of whose sultans, Saladin, built the Citadel in the late 1100s.

Cajun member of a French-speaking community of Louisiana, descended from French-Canadians who, in the 18th century, were driven there from Nova Scotia (then known as Acadia, from which the name Cajun comes). *Cajun music* has a lively rhythm and features steel guitar, fiddle, and accordion.

CAL (acronym for *computer-assisted learning*) the use of computers in education and training: the computer displays instructional material to a student and asks questions about the information given; the student's answers determine the sequence of the lessons.

Calabria mountainous earthquake region occupying the "toe" of Italy, comprising the provinces of Catanzaro, Cosenza, and Reggio; capital Catanzaro; area 5,829 sq mi/15,100 sq km; population (1990) 2,153,700. Reggio is the industrial center.

calamine $Zn_4Si_2O_7(OH)_2 \cdot H_2O$ native zinc silicate, an ore of zinc. The term also refers to a pink powder of zinc oxide mixed with 0.5% ferric oxide, used in lotions and ointments as a topical astringent.

Calamity Jane nickname of Martha Jane Burke c. 1852–1903. US heroine of Deadwood, South Dakota. She worked as a teamster, transporting supplies to the mining camps, adopted male dress, and, as an excellent shot, promised "calamity" to any aggressor. Many fictional accounts of the Wild West featured her exploits.

calcination ◊oxidation of metals by burning in air.

calcite colorless, white, or light-colored common rock-forming mineral, calcium carbonate, $CaCO_3$. It is the main constituent of ◊limestone and marble and forms many types of invertebrate shell.

calcium soft, silvery-white metallic element, symbol Ca, atomic number 20, atomic weight 40.08. It is one of

California

the ◊alkaline-earth metals. It is the fifth most abundant element (the third most abundant metal) in the Earth's crust. It is found mainly as its carbonate $CaCO_3$, which occurs in a fairly pure condition as chalk and limestone (see ◊calcite). Calcium is an essential component of bones, teeth, shells, milk, and leaves, and it forms 1.5% of the human body by mass.

calculus branch of mathematics that permits the manipulation of continuously varying quantities, used in practical problems involving such matters as changing speeds, problems of flight, varying stresses in the framework of a bridge, and alternating current theory. *Integral calculus* deals with the method of summation or adding together the effects of continuously varying quantities. *Differential calculus* deals in a similar way with rates of change. Many of its applications arose from the study of the gradients of the tangents to curves.

Calcutta largest city of India, on the river Hooghly, the westernmost mouth of the river Ganges, some 80 mi/130 km N of the Bay of Bengal. It is the capital of West Bengal; population (1981) 9,166,000. It is chiefly a commercial and industrial center (engineering, shipbuilding, jute, and other textiles). Calcutta was the seat of government of British India 1773–1912. There is severe air pollution.

Calder Alexander 1898–1976. US abstract sculptor, the inventor of *mobiles*, suspended shapes that move in the lightest current of air. In the 1920s he began making wire sculptures and *stabiles* (static mobiles), colored abstract shapes attached by lines of wire. Huge versions adorn Lincoln Center in New York City and UNESCO in Paris.

caldera in geology, a very large basin-shaped ◊crater. Calderas are found at the tops of volcanoes, where the original peak has collapsed into an empty chamber beneath. The basin, many times larger than the original volcanic vent, may be flooded, producing a crater lake, or the flat floor may contain a number of small volcanic cones, produced by volcanic activity after the collapse.

Calderón de la Barca Pedro 1600–1681. Spanish dramatist and poet. After the death of Lope de Vega in 1635, he was considered to be the leading Spanish dramatist. Most celebrated of the 118 plays is the philosophical *La vida es sueño/Life is a Dream* 1635.

calendar division of the ◊year into months, weeks, and days and the method of ordering the years. From year one, an assumed date of the birth of Jesus, dates are calculated backward (BC "before Christ" or BCE "before common era") and forward (AD, Latin *anno Domini* "in the year of the Lord," or CE "common era"). The *lunar month* (period between one new moon and the next) naturally averages 29.5 days, but the Western calendar uses for convenience a *calendar*

month with a complete number of days, 30 or 31 (Feb has 28). For adjustments, since there are slightly fewer than six extra hours a year left over, they are added to Feb as a 29th day every fourth year (*leap year*), century years being excepted unless they are divisible by 400. For example, 1896 was a leap year; 1900 was not. 1996 is the next leap year.

Calgary city in Alberta, Canada, on the Bow River, in the foothills of the Rocky Mountains; at 3,440 ft/1,048 m it is one of the highest Canadian cities; population (1986) 671,000. It is the center of a large agricultural region and is the oil and financial center of Alberta and W Canada. The 1988 Winter Olympic Games were held here.

It has oil-linked and agricultural industries, such as fertilizer factories and flour mills, and is also a tourist center; the annual Calgary Exhibition and Stampede is held in July. The University of Calgary became independent of the University of Alberta 1966.

Calhoun John C(aldwell) 1782–1850. US politician; vice president 1825–33 under Andrew Jackson. Throughout his vice presidency, he was a defender of strong states' rights against an overpowerful federal government and of the institution of slavery. He served in the US Senate 1842–43 and 1845–50, where he continued to espouse the right of states to legislate on slavery.

Cali city in SW Colombia, in the Cauca Valley 3,200 ft/975 m above sea level; population (1985) 1,398,276. Cali was founded 1536. It has textile, sugar, and engineering industries.

California Pacific-coast state of the US; nicknamed the Golden State (originally because of its gold mines, more recently because of its orange groves and sunshine)
area 158,685 sq mi/411,100 sq km
capital Sacramento
cities Los Angeles, San Diego, San Francisco, San José, Fresno
physical Sierra Nevada, including Yosemite and Sequoia national parks, Lake Tahoe, Mount Whitney (14,500 ft/4,418 m, the highest mountain in the lower 48 states); the Coast Range; Death Valley (282 ft/86 m below sea level, the lowest point in the western hemisphere); Colorado and Mohave deserts; Monterey Peninsula; Salton Sea; the San Andreas fault; huge, offshore underwater volcanoes with tops 5 mi/8 km across
features California Institute of Technology (Caltech); Lawrence Berkeley and Lawrence Livermore laboratories of the University of California, which share particle physics and nuclear weapons research with Los Alamos; Stanford University, which has the Hoover Institute and is the powerhouse of ◊Silicon Valley; Paul Getty art museum at Malibu, built in the style of a Roman villa; Hollywood
products leading agricultural state with fruit (peaches, citrus, grapes in the valley of the San Joaquin and Sacramento rivers), nuts, wheat, vegetables, cotton, and rice, all mostly grown by irrigation, the water being carried by immense concrete-lined canals to the Central and Imperial valleys; beef cattle; timber; fish; oil; natural gas; aerospace technology; electronics (Silicon Valley); food processing; films and television programs; great reserves of energy (geothermal) in the hot water that lies beneath much of the state
population (1990) 29,760,000, the most populous state of the US (69.9% white; 25.8% Hispanic; 9.6% Asian and Pacific islander, including many Vietnamese; 7.4% black; 0.8% American Indian)

famous people Luther Burbank, Walt Disney, William Randolph Hearst, Jack London, Marilyn Monroe, Richard Nixon, Ronald Reagan, John Steinbeck
history colonized by Spain 1769; ceded to the US after the Mexican War 1848; became a state 1850. The discovery of gold in the Sierra Nevada Jan 1848 was followed by the gold rush 1849–56.

The completion of the first transcontinental railroad 1869 fostered economic development. The Los Angeles area flourished with the growth of the film industry after 1910, oil discoveries in the early 1920s, and the development of aircraft plants and shipyards during World War II. Some 100,000 Californians of Japanese ancestry were interned during the war. California became the nation's most populous state in 1962. Northern California benefited from the growth of the electronics industry from the 1970s in what came to be called Silicon Valley. The state's economy suffered during the early 1990s as the defense industries declined. Devastating earthquakes occurred in the San Francisco Bay (1989) and San Fernando Valley – Los Angeles (1993) areas

California current cold ocean ◊current in the E Pacific Ocean flowing southward down the W coast of North America. It is part of the North Pacific gyre (a vast, circular movement of ocean water).

californium synthesized, radioactive, metallic element of the actinide series, symbol Cf, atomic number 98, atomic weight 251. It is produced in very small quantities and used in nuclear reactors as a neutron source. The longest-lived isotope, Cf-251, has a half-life of 800 years.

Caligula Gaius Caesar AD 12–41. Roman emperor, son of Germanicus and successor to Tiberius AD 37. Caligula was a cruel tyrant and was assassinated by an officer of his guard. He is believed to have been mentally unstable.

calipers instrument used for measuring the thickness or diameter of objects—for example, the internal and external diameter of pipes. Some calipers are made like a drawing compass, having two legs, often curved, pivoting about a screw at one end. The ends of the legs are placed in contact with the object to be measured, and the gap between the ends is then measured against a rule. The slide caliper looks like an adjustable wrench, and carries a scale for direct measuring, usually with a ◊vernier scale for accuracy.

caliph title of civic and religious heads of the world of Islam. The first caliph was ◊Abu Bakr. Nominally elective, the office became hereditary, held by the Ummayyad dynasty 661–750 and then by the ◊Abbasid dynasty. After the death of the last Abbasid (1258), the title was claimed by a number of Muslim chieftains in Egypt, Turkey, and India. The most powerful of these were the Turkish sultans of the Ottoman Empire.

Callaghan (Leonard) James, Baron Callaghan 1912– . British Labour politician. As chancellor of the Exchequer 1964–67, he introduced corporation and capital-gains taxes, and resigned following devaluation. He was home secretary 1967–70 and prime minister 1976–79 in a period of increasing economic stress.

Callao chief commercial and fishing port of Peru, 7 mi/12 km SW of Lima; population (1988) 318,000. Founded 1537, it was destroyed by an earthquake 1746. It is Peru's main naval base, and produces fertilizers.

Callas Maria. Adopted name of Maria Kalogeropoulos 1923–1977. US lyric soprano, born in New York of Greek parents. With a voice of fine range and a gift for dramatic expression, she excelled in operas including *Norma, La Sonnambula, Madame Butterfly, Aïda, Lucia di Lammermoor,* and *Medea.*

Callicrates 5th century BC. Athenian architect (with Ictinus) of the ◊Parthenon on the Acropolis.

calligraphy art of handwriting, regarded in China and Japan as the greatest of the visual arts, and playing a large part in Islamic art because the depiction of the human and animal form is forbidden.

Callimachus 310–240 BC. Greek poet and critic known for his epigrams. Born in Cyrene, he taught in Alexandria, Egypt, where he is reputed to have been head of the great library.

Callisto second largest moon of Jupiter, 3,000 mi/4,800 km in diameter, orbiting every 16.7 days at a distance of 1.2 million mi/1.9 million km from the planet. Its surface is covered with large craters.

callus in botany, a tissue that forms at a damaged plant surface. Composed of large, thin-walled ◊parenchyma cells, it grows over and around the wound, eventually covering the exposed area. In animals, a callus is a thickened pad of skin, formed where there is repeated rubbing against a hard surface. In humans, calluses often develop on the hands and feet of those involved in heavy manual work.

Calmette Albert 1863–1933. French bacteriologist. A student of Pasteur, he developed (with Camille Guérin, 1872–1961) the ◊BCG vaccine against tuberculosis in 1921.

calorie c.g.s unit of heat, now replaced by the ◊joule (one calorie is approximately 4.2 joules). It is the heat required to raise the temperature of one gram of water by 1°C. In dietetics, the Calorie or kilocalorie is equal to 1,000 calories.

calorimeter instrument used in physics to measure heat. A simple calorimeter consists of a heavy copper vessel that is polished (to reduce heat losses by radiation) and covered with insulating material (to reduce losses by convection and conduction).

Calvary in the New Testament, the site of Jesus' crucifixion at Jerusalem. Two chief locations are suggested: the site where the Church of the Sepulchre now stands, and the hill beyond the Damascus gate.

Calvert George, Baron Baltimore 1579–1632. English politician who founded the North American colony of Maryland 1632. As a supporter of colonization, he was granted land in Newfoundland 1628 but, finding the climate too harsh, obtained a royal charter for the more temperate Maryland 1632.

Calvin John (also known as *Cauvin* or *Chauvin*) 1509–1564. French-born Swiss Protestant church reformer and theologian. He was a leader of the Reformation in Geneva and set up a strict religious community there. His theological system is known as Calvinism, and his church government as ◊Presbyterianism. Calvin wrote (in Latin) *Institutes of the Christian Religion* 1536 and commentaries on the New Testament and much of the Old Testament.

Calvin Melvin 1911– . US chemist who, using radioactive carbon-14 as a tracer, determined the biochemical processes of ◊photosynthesis, in which green plants use ◊chlorophyll to convert carbon dioxide and water into sugar and oxygen. Nobel Prize 1961.

Calvinism Christian doctrine as interpreted by John Calvin and adopted in Scotland, parts of Switzerland, and the Netherlands; by the ◊Puritans in England and

New England; and by the subsequent Congregational and Presbyterian churches in the US. Its central doctrine is predestination, under which certain souls (the elect) are predestined by God through the sacrifice of Jesus to salvation, and the rest to damnation. Although Calvinism is rarely accepted today in its strictest interpretation, the 20th century has seen a Neo-Calvinist revival through the work of Karl Barth.

Calypso in Greek legend, a sea ◊nymph who waylaid the homeward-bound ◊Odysseus for seven years.

calypso West Indian satirical ballad with a syncopated beat. Calypso is a traditional song form of Trinidad, a feature of its annual carnival, with roots in W African praise singing. It was first popularized in the US by Harry Belafonte (1927–) in 1956. Mighty Sparrow (1935–) is Trinidad's best-known calypso singer.

cam part of a machine that converts circular motion to linear motion or vice versa. The *edge cam* in an automobile engine is in the form of a rounded projection on a shaft, the camshaft. When the camshaft turns, the cams press against linkages (plungers or followers) that open the valves in the cylinders.

CAM (acronym for *computer-aided manufacturing*) the use of computers to control production processes; in particular, the control of machine tools and ◊robots in factories. In some factories, the whole

design and production system has been automated by linking ◊CAD (computer-aided design) to CAM.

Cambodia (formerly *Khmer Republic* 1970–76, *Democratic Kampuchea* 1976–79, and *People's Republic of Kampuchea* 1979–89) country in SE Asia, bounded N and NW by Thailand, N by Laos, E and SE by Vietnam, and SW by the Gulf of Thailand.

Cambrai, Battles of two battles in World War I at Cambrai in NE France:
First Battle Nov–Dec 1917, the city was almost captured by the British when large numbers of tanks were used for the first time. *Second Battle* Aug 26–Oct 5, 1918, the city was taken during the final British offensive.

Cambrian period of geological time 570–510 million years ago; the first period of the Paleozoic era. All invertebrate animal life appeared, and marine algae were widespread. The earliest fossils with hard shells, such as trilobites, date from this period.

Cambridge city in England, on the river Cam (a river sometimes called by its earlier name, Granta), 50 mi/80 km N of London; population (1989) 101,000. It is the administrative headquarters of Cambridgeshire. The city is centered on Cambridge University (founded 12th century), whose outstanding buildings, including Kings College Chapel, back onto the river. Present-day

---

Cambodia State of
(formerly *Khmer Republic* 1970–76,
Democratic Kampuchea 1976–79,
People's Republic of Kampuchea
1979–89)

area 69,880 sq mi/181,035 sq km
capital Phnom Penh
cities Battambang, the seaport Kompong Som
physical mostly flat forested plains with mountains in SW and N; Mekong River runs N–S
features ruins of ancient capital Angkor; Lake Tonle Sap
head of state Prince (King from 1993) Norodom Sihanouk from 1991
head of government Prince Norodom Ranariddh from 1993
political system transitional
political parties Cambodian People's Party (CPP), reform socialist (formerly the communist Kampuchean People's Revolutionary Party [KPRP]); Party of Democratic Kampuchea (Khmer Rouge), ultranationalist communist; Khmer People's National Liberation Front (KPNLF), anticommunist; United Front for an Independent, Neutral,

Peaceful, and Cooperative Cambodia (FUNCINPEC), moderate centrist
exports rubber, rice, pepper, wood, cattle
currency Cambodian riel
population (1992) 8,974,000; growth rate 2.2% p.a.
life expectancy men 42, women 45
languages Khmer (official), French
religion Theravāda Buddhist 95%
literacy men 78%, women 39% (1980 est)
GDP $592 million (1987); $83 per head

chronology
1863–1941 French protectorate.
1941–45 Occupied by Japan.
1946 Recaptured by France.
1953 Independence achieved from France.
1970 Prince Sihanouk overthrown by US-backed Lon Nol.
1975 Lon Nol overthrown by Khmer Rouge.
1976–78 Khmer Rouge introduced an extreme communist program, forcing urban groups into rural areas and bringing over 2.5 million deaths from famine, disease, and maltreatment.
1978–79 Vietnamese invasion and installation of Heng Samrin government.
1982 The three main anti-Vietnamese resistance groups formed an alliance under Prince Sihanouk.
1987 Vietnamese troop withdrawal began.
1989 Sept: completion of Vietnamese withdrawal. Nov: United Nations peace proposal rejected by Phnom Penh government.
1991 Oct: Peace agreement signed in Paris, providing for a UN Transitional Authority in Cambodia (UNTAC) to administer country in transition period in conjunction with all-party Supreme National Council; communism abandoned. Nov: Sihanouk returned as head of state.
1992 Political prisoners released; freedom of speech and party formation restored. Oct: Khmer Rouge refused to disarm in accordance with peace process. Dec: UN Security Council voted to impose limited trade embargo on area of country controlled by Khmer Rouge guerrillas.
1993 Free general elections resulted in win by FUNCINPEC over the CPP. Sihanouk became king. Prince Norodom Ranariddh, FUNCINPEC leader, appointed prime minister

Cameroon Republic of
(*République du Cameroun*)

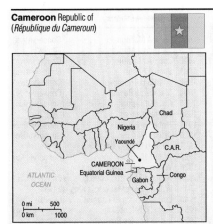

area 183,638 sq mi/475,440 sq km
capital Yaoundé
cities chief port Douala; Nkongsamba, Garova
physical desert in far north in the Lake Chad basin, mountains in W, dry savanna plateau in the intermediate area, and dense tropical rain forest in S
environment the Korup National Park preserves 500 sq mi/1,300 sq km of Africa's fast-disappearing tropical rain forest. Scientists have identified nearly 100 potentially useful chemical substances produced naturally by the plants of this forest
features Mount Cameroon 13,358 ft/4,070 m, an active volcano on the coast, W of the Adamawa Mountains
head of state and of government Paul Biya from 1982
political system emergent democratic republic
political parties Democratic Assembly of the Cameroon People (RDPC), nationalist, left of center; Social Democratic Front (SDF), center-left; Social Movement for New Democracy (MSND), left of center; Union of the Peoples of Cameroon (UPC), left of center
exports cocoa, coffee, bananas, cotton, timber, rubber, groundnuts, gold, aluminum, crude oil
currency CFA franc
population (1992) 12,662,000; growth rate 2.7% p.a.
life expectancy men 49, women 53
languages French and English in pidgin variations (official); there has been some discontent with the emphasis on French—there are 163 indigenous peoples with their own African languages
media heavy government censorship
religions Roman Catholic 35%, animist 25%, Muslim 22%, Protestant 18%
literacy men 68%, women 45% (1985 est)
GDP $12.7 bn (1987); $1,170 per head

chronology
1884 Treaty signed establishing German rule.
1916 Captured by Allied forces in World War I.
1922 Divided between Britain and France.
1946 French Cameroon and British Cameroons made UN trust territories.
1960 French Cameroon became the independent Republic of Cameroon. Ahmadou Ahidjo elected president.
1961 Northern part of British Cameroon merged with Nigeria and southern part joined the Republic of Cameroon to become the Federal Republic of Cameroon.
1966 One-party regime introduced.
1972 New constitution made Cameroon a unitary state, the United Republic of Cameroon.
1973 New national assembly elected.
1982 Ahidjo resigned and was succeeded by Paul Biya.
1983 Biya began to remove his predecessor's supporters; accused by Ahidjo of trying to create a police state. Ahidjo went into exile in France.
1984 Biya reelected; defeated a plot to overthrow him. Country's name changed to Republic of Cameroon.
1988 Biya reelected.
1990 Widespread public disorder. Biya granted amnesty to political prisoners.
1991 Constitutional changes made.
1992 Ruling RDPC won in first multiparty elections in 28 years. Biya's presidential victory challenged by opposition.

industries include the manufacture of scientific instruments, radios, electronics, paper, flour milling, and fertilizers.

Cambridge city in Massachusetts; population (1990) 95,802. Industries include paper and publishing. Harvard University 1636 (the oldest educational institution in the US, named after John Harvard [1607–1638], who bequeathed his library to it along with half his estate), Massachusetts Institute of Technology (1861), and the John F Kennedy School of Government (part of Harvard) are here, as well as a park named after Kennedy.

Cambyses 6th century BC. King of Persia 529–522 BC. Succeeding his father Cyrus, he assassinated his brother Smerdis and conquered Egypt in 525 BC. There he outraged many of the local religious customs and was said to have become insane. He died in Syria.

Camden industrial city of New Jersey, on the Delaware River; population (1990) 87,500. The city is linked with Philadelphia, Pennsylvania, by the Benjamin Franklin suspension bridge (1926). The Walt ◊Whitman House, where the poet lived 1884–92, is now a museum.

Camden Town Group school of British painters 1911–13, based in Camden, London, inspired by W R Sickert. The work of Spencer Gore (1878–1914) and Harold Gilman (1876–1919) is typical of the group, rendering everyday town scenes in Post-Impressionist style.

camel large cud-chewing mammal of the even-toed hoofed order Artiodactyla. Unlike typical ruminants, it has a three-chambered stomach. It has two toes which have broad soft soles for walking on sand, and hooves resembling nails. There are two species, the single-humped *Arabian camel Camelus dromedarius* and the twin-humped **Bactrian camel *C. bactrianus*** from Asia. They carry a food reserve of fatty tissue in the hump, can go without drinking for long periods, can feed on salty vegetation, and can withstand extremes of heat and cold, thus being well adapted to desert conditions.

camellia any oriental evergreen shrub with roselike flowers of the genus *Camellia*, tea family Theaceae. Numerous species, including *C. japonica* and *C. reticulata*, have been introduced into Europe, the US, and Australia.

Camelot legendary seat of King ◊Arthur.
A possible site is the Iron Age hill fort of South Cadbury Castle in Somerset, England, where excavations from 1967 have revealed remains dating from 3000 BC to AD 1100, including those of a large 6th-century settlement, the time ascribed to Arthur.

cameo small relief carving of semiprecious stone, shell, or glass. A pale-colored surface layer is carved to reveal a darker ground. Fine cameos were produced in ancient Greece and Rome, during the Renaissance, and in the Victorian era. They were used for decorating goblets and vases, and as jewelry.

camera apparatus used in ◊photography, consisting of a lens system set in a light-proof box inside of which a sensitized film or plate can be placed. The lens collects rays of light reflected from the subject and brings them together as a sharp image on the film; it has marked numbers known as apertures, or f-stops, that reduce or increase the amount of light. Apertures also control depth of field. A shutter controls the amount of time light has to affect the film. There are small-, medium-, and large-format cameras; the format refers to the size of recorded image and the dimensions of the print obtained.

camera obscura darkened box with a tiny hole for projecting the inverted image of the scene outside on to a screen inside. For its development as a device for producing photographs, see ◊photography.

Cameron Simon 1799–1889. US political leader. He served two partial terms in the US Senate 1845–49 and 1857–60. A supporter of Abraham Lincoln at the 1860 Republican nominating convention, he was appointed secretary of war at the outbreak of the American Civil War 1861. A dismal failure in that position, Cameron was named minister to Russia 1862. After the end of the war 1865 he returned to the Senate 1867–77.

Cameroon country in W Africa, bounded NW by Nigeria; NE by Chad; E by the Central African Republic; S by Congo, Gabon, and Equatorial Guinea; and W by the Atlantic. *See panel p. 159*

Camorra Italian secret society formed about 1820 by criminals in the dungeons of Naples and continued once they were freed. It dominated politics from 1848, was suppressed 1911, but many members eventually surfaced in the US ◊Mafia. The Camorra still operates in the Naples area.

camouflage colors or structures that allow an animal to blend with its surroundings to avoid detection by other animals. Camouflage can take the form of matching the background color, of countershading (darker on top, lighter below, to counteract natural shadows), or of irregular patterns that break up the outline of the animal's body. More elaborate camouflage involves closely resembling a feature of the natural environment, as with the stick insect; this is closely akin to ◊mimicry.

Camp Walter Chauncey 1859–1925. US football coach who was responsible for instituting some of the most basic rules of the game of American football, including team size, field dimensions, and the four-down system. He also initiated the tradition of selecting an annual all-American football team.

Campania agricultural region (wheat, citrus, wine, vegetables, tobacco) of S Italy, including the volcano ◊Vesuvius; area 5,250 sq mi/13,600 sq km; population (1990) 5,853,900. The capital is Naples; industrial centers include Benevento, Caserta, and Salerno. There are ancient sites at Pompeii, Herculaneum, and Paestum.

campanile originally a bell tower erected near, or attached to, a church or town hall in Italy. The leaning tower of Pisa is an example; another is the great campanile of Florence, 275 ft/90 m high.

They were used as components of 19th-century American factory architecture in New England.

Campbell Malcolm 1885–1948. British racing driver who once held both land- and water-speed records. He set the land-speed record nine times, pushing it up to 301.1 mph/484.8 kph at Bonneville Flats, Utah, in 1935, and broke the water-speed record three times,

Canada: prime ministers		
1867	John A Macdonald	(Conservative)
1873	Alexander Mackenzie	(Liberal)
1878	John A Macdonald	(Conservative)
1891	John J Abbott	(Conservative)
1892	John S D Thompson	(Conservative)
1894	Mackenzie Bowell	(Conservative)
1896	Charles Tupper	(Conservative)
1896	Wilfred Laurier	(Liberal)
1911	Robert L Borden	(Conservative)
1920	Arthur Meighen	(Conservative)
1921	William Lyon Mackenzie King	(Liberal)
1926	Arthur Meighen	(Conservative)
1926	William Lyon Mackenzie King	(Liberal)
1930	Richard Bedford Bennett	(Conservative)
1935	William Lyon Mackenzie King	(Liberal)
1948	Louis Stephen St Laurent	(Liberal)
1957	John G Diefenbaker	(Conservative)
1963	Lester Bowles Pearson	(Liberal)
1968	Pierre Elliot Trudeau	(Liberal)
1979	Joseph Clark	(Progressive Conservative)
1980	Pierre Elliot Trudeau	(Liberal)
1984	John Turner	(Liberal)
1984	Brian Mulroney	(Progressive Conservative)
1993	Kim Campbell	(Progressive Conservative)
1993	Jean Chretien	(Liberal)

the best being 141.74 mph/228.2 kph on Coniston Water, England, in 1939. His automobile and boat were both called *Bluebird*.

Camp David official country home of US presidents, situated in the Appalachian mountains; it was originally named Shangri-la by F D Roosevelt, but was renamed Camp David by Eisenhower (after his grandson).

Camp David Agreements two framework agreements signed 1978 by Israeli prime minister Begin and Egyptian president Sadat at Camp David, Maryland, US, under the guidance of US president Carter, covering an Egypt–Israel peace treaty and phased withdrawal of Israel from Sinai, which was completed 1982, and an overall Middle East settlement including the election by the West Bank and Gaza Strip Palestinians of a "self-governing authority." The latter issue has stalled repeatedly over questions of who should represent the Palestinians and what form the self-governing body should take.

camphor $C_{10}H_{16}O$ volatile, aromatic ◊ketone substance obtained from the camphor tree *Cinnamomum camphora*. It is distilled from chips of the wood, and is used in insect repellents and medicinal inhalants and liniments, and in the manufacture of celluloid.

Campo-Formio, Treaty of peace settlement 1797 during the Revolutionary Wars between Napoleon and Austria, by which France gained the region that is now Belgium and Austria was compensated with Venice and part of an area that now reaches into Slovenia and Croatia.

Camus Albert 1913–1960. Algerian-born French writer. A journalist in France, he was active in the Resistance during World War II. His novels, which owe much to ◊existentialism, include *L'Etranger/The Outsider* 1942, *La Peste/The Plague* 1948, and *L'Homme révolté/The Rebel* 1952. He was awarded the Nobel Prize for Literature 1957.

Canada

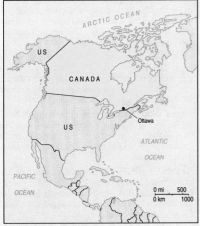

area 3,849,674 sq mi/9,970,610 sq km
capital Ottawa
cities Toronto, Montréal, Vancouver, Edmonton, Calgary, Winnipeg, Quebec, Hamilton, Saskatoon, Halifax
physical mountains in W, with low-lying plains in interior and rolling hills in E. Climate varies from temperate in S to arctic in N
environment sugar maples are dying in E Canada as a result of increasing soil acidification; nine rivers in Nova Scotia are now too acid to support salmon or trout reproduction
features St Lawrence Seaway, Mackenzie River; Great Lakes; Arctic Archipelago; Rocky Mountains; Great Plains or Prairies; Canadian Shield; Niagara Falls; the world's second largest country
head of state Elizabeth II from 1952, represented by governor-general
head of government Jean Chretien from 1993
political system federal constitutional monarchy
political parties Progressive Conservative Party, free-enterprise, right of center; Liberal Party, nationalist, centrist; New Democratic Party (NDP), moderate left of center
exports wheat, timber, pulp, newsprint, fish (salmon), furs (ranched fox and mink exceed the value of wild furs), oil, natural gas, aluminum, asbestos (world's second largest producer), coal, copper, iron, zinc, nickel (world's largest producer), uranium (world's largest producer), motor vehi-

cles and parts, industrial and agricultural machinery, fertilizers, chemicals
currency Canadian dollar
population (1992) 27,737,000—including 300,000 North American Indians, of whom 75% live on more than 2,000 reservations in Ontario and the four Western provinces; some 300,000 Métis (people of mixed race) and 19,000 Inuit of whom 75% live in the Northwest Territories. Over half Canada's population lives in Ontario and Québec. Growth rate 1.1% p.a.
life expectancy men 72, women 79
languages English, French (both official; about 70% speak English, 20% French, and the rest are bilingual); there are also North American Indian languages and the Inuit Inuktitut
religion Roman Catholic 46%, Protestant 35%
literacy 99%
GDP $562 bn (1992)

chronology
1867 Dominion of Canada founded.
1949 Newfoundland joined Canada.
1957 Progressive Conservatives returned to power after 22 years in opposition.
1961 NDP formed.
1963 Liberals elected under Lester Pearson.
1968 Pearson succeeded by Pierre Trudeau.
1979 Joe Clark, leader of the Progressive Conservatives, formed a minority government; defeated on budget proposals.
1980 Liberals under Trudeau returned with a large majority. Québec referendum rejected demand for independence.
1982 Canada Act removed Britain's last legal control over Canadian affairs; "patriation" of Canada's constitution.
1983 Clark replaced as leader of the Progressive Conservatives by Brian Mulroney.
1984 Trudeau retired and was succeeded as Liberal leader and prime minister by John Turner. Progressive Conservatives won the federal election with a large majority, and Mulroney became prime minister.
1988 Conservatives reelected with reduced majority on platform of free trade with the US.
1989 Free-trade agreement signed. Turner resigned as Liberal Party leader, and Ed Broadbent as NDP leader.
1990 Collapse of Meech Lake accord. Canada joined the coalition opposing Iraq's invasion of Kuwait.
1992 Gradual withdrawal of Canadian forces in Europe announced. Self-governing homeland for Inuit approved. Constitutional reform package, the Charlottetown Accord, rejected in national referendum.
1993 Mulroney resigned leadership of Conservative Party; Kim Campbell, the new party leader, became prime minister. Oct: Conservatives defeated in general election. Liberal leader Jean Chretien became prime minister.

Canaan ancient region between the Mediterranean and the Dead Sea, called in the Bible the "Promised Land" of the Israelites. It was occupied as early as the 3rd millennium BC by the Canaanites, a Semitic-speaking people who were known to the Greeks of the 1st millennium BC as Phoenicians. The capital was Ebla (now Tell Mardikh, Syria).

Canada country occupying the northern part of the North American continent, bounded S by the US, N by the Arctic Ocean, NW by Alaska, E by the Atlantic Ocean, and W by the Pacific Ocean. *See table p. 162*

canal artificial waterway constructed for drainage, irrigation, or navigation. *Irrigation canals* carry water for irrigation from rivers, reservoirs, or wells, and are designed to maintain an even flow of water over the whole length. *Navigation and ship canals* are constructed at one level between ◊locks,

and frequently link with rivers or sea inlets to form a waterway system. The Suez Canal 1869 and the Panama Canal 1914 eliminated long trips around continents and dramatically shortened shipping routes.

Irrigation canals, dug from ancient times, provided flood control as well as neolithic farming villages with an expanded area of rich alluvial soil, especially in the Tigris-Euphrates valley and along the Nile, where agricultural surpluses eventually allowed for the rise of civilizations. Navigation canals developed after irrigation and drainage canals; often they link two waterways and were at first level and shallow. Soon, those with inclined planes had towpaths along which men and animals towed vessels from one level to the next. Locks were invented to allow passage where great variations in level exist. By the 20th century mechanized tows and self-propelled barges were in use.

Canaletto Antonio (Giovanni Antonio Canale) 1697–1768. Italian painter celebrated for his paintings of views (*vedute*) of Venice (his native city) and of the river Thames and London 1746–56.

Canaries current cold ocean current in the North Atlantic Ocean flowing SW from Spain along the NW coast of Africa. It meets the northern equatorial current at a latitude of 20° N.

canary bird *Serinus canaria* of the finch family, found wild in the Canary Islands and Madeira. It is greenish with a yellow underside. Canaries have been bred as cage birds in Europe since the 15th century, and many domestic varieties are yellow or orange.

Canary Islands (Spanish *Canarias*) group of volcanic islands 60 mi/100 km off the NW coast of Africa, forming the Spanish provinces of Las Palmas and Santa Cruz de Tenerife
area 2,818 sq mi/7,300 sq km
population (1986) 1,615,000
features The chief centers are Santa Cruz on Tenerife (which also has the highest peak in extracontinental Spain, Pico de Teide, 12,186 ft/3,713 m), and Las Palmas on Gran Canaria. The province of Santa Cruz comprises Tenerife, Palma, Gomera, and Hierro; the province of Las Palmas comprises Gran Canaria, Lanzarote, and Fuerteventura. There are also six uninhabited islets. The Northern Hemisphere Observatory (1981) is on the island of La Palma, the first in the world to be controlled remotely.

Canberra capital of Australia (since 1908), situated in the Australian Capital Territory, enclosed within New South Wales, on a tributary of the Murrumbidgee River; area (Australian Capital Territory including the port at Jervis Bay) 939 sq mi/2,432 sq km; population (1988) 297,300.

cancer group of diseases characterized by abnormal proliferation of cells. Cancer (malignant) cells are usually degenerate, capable only of reproducing themselves (tumor formation). Malignant cells tend to spread from their site of origin by traveling through the bloodstream or lymphatic system.

Cancer faintest of the zodiacal constellations (its brightest stars are fourth magnitude). It lies in the northern hemisphere, between Leo and Gemini, and is represented as a crab. Cancer's most distinctive feature is the star cluster Praesepe, popularly known as the Beehive. The Sun passes through the constellation during late July and early Aug. In astrology, the dates for Cancer are between about June 22 and July 22.

candela SI unit (symbol cd) of luminous intensity, which replaced the old units of candle and standard candle. It measures the brightness of a light itself rather than the amount of light falling on an object, which is called *illuminance* and measured in ◊lux.

Candide satire by ◊Voltaire, published 1759. The hero experiences extremes of fortune in the company of Dr Pangloss, a personification of the popular belief of the time (partly based on a misunderstanding of ◊Leibniz) that "all is for the best in the best of all possible worlds." Voltaire exuberantly demonstrates that this idea is absurd and inhumane.

cane reedlike stem of various plants such as the sugar cane, bamboo, and, in particular, the group of palms called rattans, consisting of the genus *Calamus* and its allies. Their slender stems are dried and used for making walking sticks, baskets, and furniture.

Canes Venatici constellation of the northern hemisphere near Ursa Major, identified with the hunting dogs of ◊Boötes, the herder. Its stars are faint, and it contains the Whirlpool galaxy (M51), the first spiral galaxy to be recognized.

Canetti Elias 1905– . Bulgarian-born writer. He was exiled from Austria as a Jew 1938 and settled in England 1939. His books, written in German, include *Die Blendung/Auto da Fé* 1935. He was awarded the Nobel Prize for Literature 1981.

canine in mammalian carnivores, any of the long, often pointed teeth found at the front of the mouth between the incisors and premolars. Canine teeth are used for catching prey, for killing, and for tearing flesh. They are absent in herbivores such as rabbits and sheep, and are much reduced in humans.

Canis Major brilliant constellation of the southern hemisphere, identified with one of the two dogs following at the heel of Orion. Its main star, ◊Sirius, is the brightest star in the sky.

Canis Minor small constellation along the celestial equator, identified with the second of the two dogs of Orion (the other dog is Canis Major). Its brightest star is Procyon.

Cannes Film Festival international film festival held every year in Cannes, France.
A number of important prizes are awarded, including the Palme d'Or (Golden Palm) for the best film.

canning food preservation in hermetically sealed containers by the application of heat. Originated by Nicolas Appert in France 1809 with glass containers, it was developed by Peter Durand in England 1810 with cans made of sheet steel thinly coated with tin to delay corrosion. Cans for beer and soft drinks are now generally made of aluminum.

Cannizzaro Stanislao 1826–1910. Italian chemist who revived interest in the work of Avogadro that had, in 1811, revealed the difference between ◊atoms and ◊molecules, and so established atomic and molecular weights as the basis of chemical calculations.

Cannon Annie Jump 1863–1941. US astronomer who, from 1896, worked at Harvard College Observatory and carried out revolutionary work on the classification of stars by examining their spectra. Her system, still used today, has spectra arranged according to temperature and runs from O through B, A, F, G, K, and M. O-type stars are the hottest, with surface temperatures of over 25,000 K.

canon in theology, the collection of writings that is accepted as authoritative in a given religion, such as the *Tripitaka* in Theravāda Buddhism. In the Christian church, it comprises the books of the ◊Bible.

canon in music, an echo form for two or more parts repeating and following a leading melody at regular time intervals to achieve a harmonious effect. It is often found in Classical music, for example ◊Vivaldi and J S ◊Bach.

canonical hours in the Catholic church, seven set periods of devotion: *matins and lauds, prime, terce, sext, nones, evensong* or *vespers*, and *compline.*

canonization in the Catholic church, the admission of one of its members to the Calendar of ◊Saints. The evidence of the candidate's exceptional piety is contested before the Congregation for the Causes of Saints by the Promotor Fidei, popularly known as the *devil's advocate.* Papal ratification of a favorable verdict results in ◊beatification, and full sainthood (conferred in St Peter's basilica, the Vatican) follows after further proof.

canon law rules and regulations of the Christian church, especially the Greek Orthodox, Roman Catholic, and Anglican churches. Its origin is sought in the declarations of Jesus and the apostles. In 1983 Pope John Paul II issued a new canon law code reducing offenses carrying automatic excommunication, extending the grounds for annulment of marriage, removing the ban on marriage with non-Catholics, and banning labor union and political activity by priests.

Canopus or *Alpha Carinae* second brightest star in the sky (after Sirius), lying in the constellation Carina. It is a yellow-white supergiant about 120 light-years from Earth, and thousands of times more luminous than the Sun.

Canova Antonio 1757–1822. Italian Neo-Classical sculptor, based in Rome from 1781. He received commissions from popes, kings, and emperors for his highly finished marble portrait busts and groups. He made several portraits of Napoleon.

Canova was born near Treviso. His reclining marble *Pauline Borghese* 1805–07 (Borghese Gallery, Rome) is a fine example of cool, polished Classicism. He executed the tombs of popes Clement XIII, Pius VII, and Clement XIV. His marble sculptures include *Cupid and Psyche* (Louvre, Paris) and *The Three Graces* (Victoria and Albert Museum, London).

Cantabria autonomous region of N Spain; area 2,046 sq mi/5,300 sq km; population (1986) 525,000. The capital is Santander. From the coastline on the Bay of Biscay it rises to the Cantabrian Mountains. Mining is the major industry.

cantaloupe any of several small varieties of muskmelon *Cucumis melo*, distinguished by their round, ribbed fruits with orange-colored flesh.

cantata in music, an extended work for voices, from the Italian, meaning "sung," as opposed to ◊sonata ("sounded") for instruments. A cantata can be sacred or secular, sometimes uses solo voices, and usually has orchestral accompaniment. The first printed collection of sacred cantata texts dates from 1670.

Canterbury historic cathedral city in Kent, England, on the river Stour, 62 mi/100 km SE of London; population (1984) 39,000. In 597 King Ethelbert welcomed ◊Augustine's mission to England here, and the city has since been the metropolis of the Anglican Communion and seat of the archbishop of Canterbury.

Canterbury, archbishop of primate of all England, archbishop of the Church of England (Anglican), and first peer of the realm, ranking next to royalty. He crowns the sovereign, has a seat in the House of Lords, and is a member of the Privy Council. He is appointed by the prime minister.

cantilever beam or structure that is fixed at one end only, though it may be supported at some point along

its length; for example, a diving board. The cantilever principle, widely used in construction engineering, eliminates the need for a second main support at the free end of the beam, allowing for more elegant structures and reducing the amount of materials required. Many large-span bridges have been built on the cantilever principle.

canton in France, an administrative district, a subdivision of the *arrondissement*; in Switzerland, one of the 23 subdivisions forming the Confederation.

Canton alternate spelling of Kwangchow or ◊Guangzhou, a city in China.

Canton city in NE Ohio, SE of Akron; seat of Stark County; population (1990) 84,161. Its products include office equipment, ceramics, and steel. The home of President William McKinley is here, as is the Football Hall of Fame.

cantor (Latin *cantare* "to sing") in Judaism, the prayer leader and choir master in a synagogue; the cantor is not a rabbi, and the position can be held by any lay person.

Canute c. 995–1035. King of England from 1016, Denmark from 1018, and Norway from 1028. Having invaded England 1013 with his father, Sweyn, king of Denmark, he was acclaimed king on his father's death 1014 by his ◊Viking army. Canute defeated ◊Edmund II Ironside at Assandun, Essex, 1016, and became king of all England on Edmund's death. He succeeded his brother Harold as king of Denmark 1018, compelled King Malcolm to pay homage by invading Scotland about 1027, and conquered Norway 1028. He was succeeded by his illegitimate son Harold I.

canyon (Spanish *cañon* "tube") deep, narrow valley or gorge running through mountains. Canyons are formed by stream down-cutting, usually in arid areas, where the stream or river receives water from outside the area.

capacitor or *condenser* device for storing electric charge, used in electronic circuits; it consists of two or more metal plates separated by an insulating layer called a dielectric.

Cape Canaveral promontory on the Atlantic coast of Florida, 228 mi/367 km N of Miami, used as a rocket launch site by ◊NASA.

First mentioned 1513, it was known 1963–73 as Cape Kennedy, to honor Pres J F Kennedy after his assassination. The ◊Kennedy Space Center is nearby.

Cape Cod hook-shaped peninsula in SE Massachusetts, 60 mi/100 km long and 1–20 mi/1.6–32 km wide. Its beaches and woods make it a popular tourist area. It is separated from the rest of the state by the Cape Cod Canal. The islands of Martha's Vineyard and Nantucket are just S of the cape.

Cape Horn southernmost point of South America, in the Chilean part of the archipelago of ◊Tierra del Fuego; notorious for gales and heavy seas. It was named 1616 by Dutch explorer Willem Schouten (1580–1625) after his birthplace (Hoorn).

Capella or *Alpha Aurigae* brightest star in the constellation Auriga and the sixth brightest star in the sky. It consists of a pair of yellow giant stars 41 light-years from Earth, orbiting each other every 104 days.

Cape of Good Hope South African headland forming a peninsula between Table Bay and False Bay, Cape Town. The first European to sail around it was Bartholomew Diaz 1488. Formerly named Cape of Storms, it was given its present name by King John II of Portugal.

Cape Verde Republic of
(*República de Cabo Verde*)

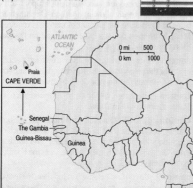

head of state Mascarenhas Monteiro from 1991
head of government Carlos Viega from 1991
political system socialist pluralist state
political parties African Party for the Independence of
Cape Verde (PAICV), African nationalist; Movement for
Democracy (MPD)
exports bananas, salt, fish
currency Cape Verde escudo
population (1992) 346,000 (including 100,000 Angolan
refugees); growth rate 1.9% p.a.
life expectancy men 57, women 61
language Creole dialect of Portuguese
religion Roman Catholic 80%
literacy men 61%, women 39% (1985)
GDP $158 million (1987); $454 per head

chronology
15th century First settled by Portuguese.
1951–74 Ruled as an overseas territory by Portugal.
1974 Moved toward independence through a transitional
Portuguese–Cape Verde government.
1975 Independence achieved from Portugal. National
people's assembly elected. Aristides Pereira became the first
president.
1980 Constitution adopted providing for eventual union
with Guinea-Bissau.
1981 Union with Guinea-Bissau abandoned and the constitution amended; became one-party state.
1991 First multiparty elections held. New party, MPD, won
majority in assembly. Pereira replaced by Mascarenhas
Monteiro.

area 1,557 sq mi/4,033 sq km
capital Praia
cities Mindelo, Sal-Rei, Porto Novo
physical archipelago of ten volcanic islands 350 mi/565 km
W of Senegal; the windward (Barlavento) group includes
Santo Antão, São Vicente, Santa Luzia, São Nicolau, Sal,
and Boa Vista; the leeward (Sotovento) group comprises
Maio, São Tiago, Fogo, and Brava; all but Santa Luzia are
inhabited
features strategic importance guaranteed by its domination
of western shipping lanes; Sal, Boa Vista, and Maio lack
water supplies but have fine beaches

Cape Province (Afrikaans *Kaapprovinsie*)
largest province of the Republic of South Africa,
named after the Cape of Good Hope
area 247,638 sq mi/641,379 sq km, excluding Walvis
Bay
capital Cape Town
cities Port Elizabeth, East London, Kimberley, Gra-
hamstown, Stellenbosch
physical Orange River, Drakensberg, Table Mountain (highest point Maclear's Beacon, 3,567 ft/1,087 m);
Great Karoo Plateau, Walvis Bay
products fruit, vegetables, wine, meat, ostrich feathers, diamonds, copper, asbestos, manganese
population (1985) 5,041,000; officially including
44% Colored; 31% black; 25% white; 0.6% Asian
history Dutch traders established the first European
settlement on the Cape 1652, but it was taken by
the British 1795, after the French Revolutionary
armies had occupied the Netherlands, and was sold to
Britain for £6 million 1814. The Cape achieved self-
government 1872. It was an original province of the
Union 1910.

caper trailing shrub *Capparis spinosa*, native to the
Mediterranean and belonging to the family Cappari-
daceae. Its flower buds are preserved in vinegar as a
condiment.

Capet Hugh 938–996. King of France from 987, when
he claimed the throne on the death of Louis V. He
founded the *Capetian dynasty*, of which various
branches continued to reign until the French Revolution, for example, ◊Valois and ◊Bourbon.

Cape Town (Afrikaans *Kaapstad*) port and oldest
city (founded 1652) in South Africa, situated in the SW
on Table Bay; population (1985) 776,617. Industries
include horticulture and trade in wool, wine, fruit,
grain, and oil. It is the legislative capital of the Republic
of South Africa and capital of Cape Province.

Cape Verde group of islands in the Atlantic, W of
Senegal (W Africa).

capillary narrowest blood vessel in vertebrates,
0.008–0.02 mm in diameter, barely wider than a
red blood cell. Capillaries are distributed as *beds*,
complex networks connecting arteries and veins. Capillary walls are extremely thin, consisting of a single
layer of cells, and so nutrients, dissolved gases, and
waste products can easily pass through them. This
makes the capillaries the main area of exchange
between the fluid (◊lymph) bathing body tissues and
the blood.

capillary in physics, a very narrow, thick-walled
tube, usually made of glass, such as in a thermometer.
Properties of fluids, such as surface tension and viscosity, can be studied using capillary tubes.

capital in architecture, a stone placed on the top of a
column, pier, or pilaster, and usually wider on the
upper surface than the diameter of the supporting
shaft. A capital consists of three parts: the top
member, called the *abacus*, a block that acts as the
supporting surface to the superstructure; the middle
portion, known as the bell or *echinus*; and the lower
part, called the necking or *astragal*.

capital in economics, accumulated or inherited
wealth held in the form of assets (such as stocks and
shares, property, and bank deposits). In stricter terms,
capital is defined as the stock of goods used in the production of other goods, and may be *fixed capital*
(such as buildings, plant, and machinery) that is
durable, or *circulating capital* (raw materials and
components) that is used up quickly.

capitalism economic system in which the principal
means of production, distribution, and exchange are in
private (individual or corporate) hands and competi-
tively operated for profit. A *mixed economy* com-

bines the private enterprise of capitalism and a degree of state monopoly, as in nationalized industries.

capital punishment punishment by death. Capital punishment is retained in 92 countries and territories (1990), including the US (37 states), China, and Islamic countries. It was abolished in the UK 1965 for all crimes except treason. Methods of execution include electrocution, lethal gas, hanging, shooting, lethal injection, garrotting, and decapitation.

In the US, the Supreme Court declared capital punishment unconstitutional 1972 (as a cruel and unusual punishment) but decided 1976 that this was not so in all circumstances. It was therefore reintroduced in some states, and in 1990 there were more than 2,000 prisoners on death row (awaiting execution) in the US. The first state to abolish capital punishment was Michigan 1847.

Capone Al(phonse "Scarface") 1898–1947. US gangster. During the ◊Prohibition period, he built a formidable criminal organization in Chicago. He was brutal in his pursuit of dominance, killing seven members of a rival gang in the St Valentine's Day massacre. He was imprisoned 1931–39 for income-tax evasion, the only charge that could be sustained against him.

Capote Truman. Adopted name of Truman Streckfus Persons 1924–1984. US novelist, journalist, and playwright. He wrote *Breakfast at Tiffany's* 1958; set a trend with the first "nonfiction novel," *In Cold Blood* 1966, reconstructing a Kansas killing; and mingled recollection and fiction in *Music for Chameleons* 1980.

Cappadocia ancient region of Asia Minor, in E central Turkey. It was conquered by the Persians 584 BC but in the 3rd century BC became an independent kingdom. The region was annexed as a province of the Roman Empire AD 17.

Capra Frank 1897–1991. Italian-born US film director. His satirical, populist comedies, which often have the common man pitted against corrupt corporations, were hugely successful in the Depression years of the 1930s. He won Academy Awards for *It Happened One Night* 1934, *Mr Deeds Goes to Town* 1936, and *You Can't Take It with You* 1938. Among his other classic films are *Mr Smith Goes to Washington* 1939, and *It's a Wonderful Life* 1946.

Capricornus zodiacal constellation in the southern hemisphere next to Sagittarius. It is represented as a fish-tailed goat, and its brightest stars are third magnitude. The Sun passes through it late Jan to mid-Feb. In astrology, the dates for Capricornus (popularly known as Capricorn) are between about Dec 22 and Jan 19.

capsule in botany, a dry, usually many-seeded fruit formed from an ovary composed of two or more fused ◊carpels, which splits open to release the seeds. The same term is used for the spore-containing structure of mosses and liverworts; this is borne at the top of a long stalk or seta.

capuchin monkey of the genus *Cebus* found in Central and South America, so called because the hairs on the head resemble the cowl of a Capuchin monk. Capuchins live in small groups, feed on fruit and insects, and have a long tail that is semiprehensile and can give support when climbing through the trees.

Capuchin member of the Franciscan order of monks in the Roman Catholic church, instituted by the Italian monk Matteo di Bassi (died 1552), who wished to return to the literal observance of the rule of St Francis. The Capuchin rule was drawn up 1529 and the

order recognized by the pope 1619. The name was derived from the French term for the brown habit and pointed hood (*capuche*) that they wore. The order has been involved in missionary activity.

Caracalla Marcus Aurelius Antoninus AD 186–217. Roman emperor. He succeeded his father Septimius ◊Severus AD 211 and, with the support of the army, he murdered his brother Geta 212 to become sole ruler of the empire. During his reign, Roman citizenship was given to all subjects of the empire. He was assassinated 217.

Caracas chief city and capital of Venezuela, situated on the slopes of the Andes Mountains, 8 mi/13 km S of its port La Guaira on the Caribbean coast; population of metropolitan area (1989) 3,373,100. Founded 1567, it is now a large industrial and commercial center, notably for oil companies.

carat unit for measuring the mass of precious stones, derived from the Arabic word *quirrat*, meaning "seed." Originally, 1 carat was the weight of a carob seed; it is now taken as 0.00705 oz/0.2 g, and is part of the troy system of weights. Also, an alternate spelling of ◊karat.

Caravaggio Michelangelo Merisi da 1573–1610. Italian early Baroque painter, active in Rome 1592–1606, then in Naples, and finally in Malta. His life was as dramatic as his art (he had to leave Rome after killing a man). He created a forceful style, using contrasts of light and shade and focusing closely on the subject figures, sometimes using dramatic foreshortening.

caraway herb *Carum carvi* of the carrot family Umbelliferae. Native to northern temperate Eurasian regions, it is grown for its spicy, aromatic seeds, which are used in cooking, medicine, and perfumery.

carbide compound of carbon and one other chemical element, usually a metal, silicon, or boron.

carbohydrate chemical compound composed of carbon, hydrogen, and oxygen, with the basic formula $C_m(H_2O)_n$, and related compounds with the same basic structure but modified ◊functional groups. As sugar and starch, carbohydrates form a major energy-providing part of the human diet.

carbolic acid common name for the aromatic compound ◊phenol.

carbon nonmetallic element, symbol C, atomic number 6, atomic weight 12.011. It is one of the most widely distributed elements, both inorganically and organically, and occurs in combination with other elements in all plants and animals. The atoms of carbon can link with one another in rings or chains, giving rise to innumerable complex compounds. It occurs in nature (1) in the pure state in three crystalline forms of graphite, diamond, and various fullerenes; (2) as calcium carbonate ($CaCO_3$) in carbonaceous rocks such as chalk and limestone; (3) as carbon dioxide (CO_2) in the atmosphere; and (4) as hydrocarbons in the fossil fuels petroleum, coal, and natural gas. Noncrystalline forms of pure carbon include charcoal and coal.

Carbonari secret revolutionary society in S Italy in the first half of the 19th century that advocated constitutional government. The movement spread to N Italy but support dwindled after the formation of ◊Mazzini's nationalist Young Italy movement, although it helped prove the way for the unification of Italy (see ◊Risorgimento).

carbonate CO_3^{2-} ion formed when carbon dioxide dissolves in water; any salt formed by this ion and another chemical element, usually a metal.

carbon cycle As
there is only a limited
amount of carbon in
the Earth and its
atmosphere, carbon
must be continuously
recycled if life is to
continue.

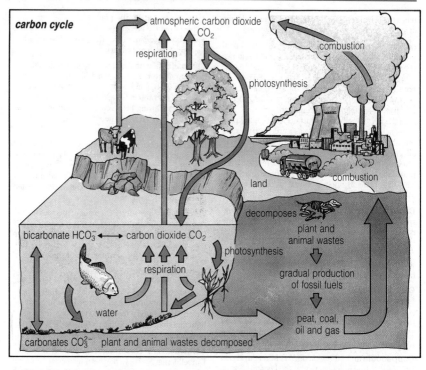

carbon cycle

carbonation in earth science, a form of chemical ◊weathering caused by rainwater that has absorbed carbon dioxide from the atmosphere and formed a weak carbonic acid. The slightly acidic rainwater is then capable of dissolving certain minerals in rocks. ◊Limestone is particularly vulnerable to this form of weathering.

carbon cycle the sequence by which carbon circulates and is recycled through the natural world. The carbon element from carbon dioxide in the atmosphere is taken up during the process of ◊photosynthesis, and the oxygen component is released back into the atmosphere. Some of this carbon becomes locked up in coal and petroleum and other sediments. Carbon (as carbon dioxide) is released during aerobic respiration of plants and animals. New carbon also enters the atmosphere during volcanic eruptions. Today, the carbon cycle is being altered by the increased consumption of fossil fuels and the burning of large tracts of tropical forests, as a result of which levels of carbon dioxide are building up in the atmosphere and probably contributing to the ◊greenhouse effect.

carbon dating alternate name for ◊radiocarbon dating.

carbon dioxide CO_2 colorless, odorless gas, slightly soluble in water and denser than air. It is formed by the complete oxidation of carbon.

carbon fiber fine, black, silky filament of pure carbon produced by heat treatment from a special grade of Courtelle acrylic fiber, used for reinforcing plastics. The resulting composite is very stiff and, weight for weight, has four times the strength of high-tensile steel. It is used in the aerospace industry, automobiles, and electrical and sports equipment.

Carboniferous period of geological time 363–290 million years ago, the fifth period of the Paleozoic era.

In the US it is divided into two periods: the Mississippian (lower) and the Pennsylvanian (upper). Typical of the lower-Carboniferous rocks are shallow-water ◊limestones, while upper-Carboniferous rocks have ◊delta deposits with ◊coal (hence the name). Amphibians were abundant, and reptiles evolved during this period.

carbon monoxide CO colorless, odorless gas formed when carbon is oxidized in a limited supply of air. It is a poisonous constituent of automobile exhaust fumes, forming a stable compound with hemoglobin in the blood, thus preventing the hemoglobin from transporting oxygen to the body tissues.

Carborundum trademark for a very hard, black abrasive, consisting of silicon carbide (SiC), an artificial compound of carbon and silicon. It is harder than ◊corundum but not as hard as ◊diamond.

carbuncle in medicine, a bacterial infection of the skin, similar to a boil but deeper and more widespread. It is treated with drawing salves, lancing, or antibiotics.

carburetion any process involving chemical combination with carbon, especially the mixing or charging of a gas, such as air, with volatile compounds of carbon (gasoline, kerosene, or fuel oil) in order to increase potential heat energy during combustion. Carburetion applies to combustion in the cylinders of reciprocating gasoline engines of the types used in aircraft, road vehicles, or marine vessels. The device by which the liquid fuel is atomized and mixed with air is called a *carburetor*.

Carchemish (now Karkamis, Turkey) center of the ◊Hittite New Empire (c. 1400–1200 BC) on the river Euphrates, 50 mi/80 km NE of Aleppo, and taken by Sargon II of Assyria 717 BC. Nebuchadnezzar II of Babylon defeated the Egyptians here 605 BC.

carcinogen any agent that increases the chance of a cell becoming cancerous (see ◊cancer), including various chemical compounds, some viruses, X-rays, and other forms of ionizing radiation. The term is often used more narrowly to mean chemical carcinogens only.

carcinoma malignant ◊tumor arising from the skin, the glandular tissues, or the mucous membranes that line the gut and lungs.

Cárdenas Lázaro 1895–1970. Mexican center-left politician and general, president 1934–40. A civil servant in early life, Cárdenas took part in the revolutionary campaigns 1915–29 that followed the fall of President Díaz (1830–1915). As president of the republic, he attempted to achieve the goals of the revolution by building schools, distributing land to the peasants, and developing transport and industry. He was minister of defense 1943–45.

cardiac pertaining to the ◊heart.

Cardiff (Welsh *Caerdydd*) capital of Wales (from 1955) and administrative headquarters of South and Mid Glamorgan, at the mouth of the Taff, Rhymney, and Ely rivers; population (1991) 272,600. Besides steelworks, there are car-component, flour-milling, paper, cigar, and other industries.

Cardin Pierre 1922– . French pioneering fashion designer whose clothes are bold and fantastic. He was the first to launch menswear (1960) and ready-to-wear collections (1963) and has given his name to a perfume.

cardinal in the Roman Catholic church, the highest rank next to the pope. Cardinals act as an advisory body to the pope and elect him. Their red hat is the badge of office. The number of cardinals has varied; there were 151 in 1989.

cardinal number in mathematics, one of the series of numbers 0, 1, 2, 3, 4, ... Cardinal numbers relate to quantity, whereas ordinal numbers (first, second, third, fourth, ...) relate to order.

Cardozo Benjamin Nathan 1870–1938. US jurist and Supreme Court justice. He was appointed to the US Supreme Court by President Hoover 1932. During the F D Roosevelt administration, he upheld the constitutionality of New Deal programs to counter the depression of 1929 conveyed in such famous cases as *Ashwander* v *Tennessee Valley Authority* 1936.

Carib member of a group of ◊American Indian people of the N coast of South America and the islands of the S West Indies in the Caribbean. Those who moved N to take the islands from the Arawak Indians were alleged by the conquering Spaniards to be fierce cannibals. In 1796, the English in the West Indies deported most of them to Roatan Island, off Honduras. Carib languages belong to the Ge-Pano-Carib family.

Caribbean Community and Common Market (CARICOM) organization for economic and foreign policy coordination in the Caribbean region, established by the Treaty of Chaguaramas 1973 to replace the former Caribbean Free Trade Association. Its members are Antigua and Barbuda, Bahamas, Barbados, Belize, Dominica, Grenada, Guyana, Jamaica, Montserrat, St Christopher–Nevis, St Lucia, St Vincent and the Grenadines, and Trinidad and Tobago. The British Virgin Islands and the Turks and Caicos Islands are associate members, and the Dominican Republic, Haiti, Mexico, Puerto Rico, Suriname, and Venezuela are observers. CARICOM headquarters are in Kingston, Jamaica.

Caribbean Sea W part of the Atlantic Ocean between the S coast of North America and the N coasts of S America. Central America is to the W and the West Indies are the islands within the sea, which is about 1,700 mi/2,740 km long and 400–900 mi/650–1,500 km wide. It is from here that the ◊Gulf Stream turns toward Europe.

caribou the ◊reindeer of North America.

caricature exaggerated portrayal of individuals or types, aiming to ridicule or otherwise expose the subject. Classical and medieval examples survive. Artists of the 18th, 19th, and 20th centuries have often used caricature as a way of satirizing society and politics. Notable exponents include the French artist Honoré Daumier and the German George Grosz.

CARICOM acronym for ◊ *Caribbean Community and Common Market*.

caries decay and disintegration, usually of the substance of teeth (cavity) or bone. It is caused by acids produced when the bacteria that live in the mouth break down sugars in the food. Fluoride, a low sugar intake, and regular brushing are all protective. Caries form mainly in the 45 minutes following an intake of sugary food, so the most dangerous diet for the teeth is one in which frequent sugary snacks and drinks are consumed.

Carina constellation of the southern hemisphere, represented as a ship's keel. Its brightest star is Canopus; it also contains Eta Carinae, a massive and highly luminous star embedded in a gas cloud, perhaps 8,000 light-years away. It has varied unpredictably in the past; some astronomers think it is likely to explode as a supernova within 10,000 years.

Carinthia (German *Kärnten*) federal province of Alpine SE Austria, bordering Italy and Slovenia in the S; area 3,667 sq mi/9,500 sq km; population (1987) 542,000. The capital is Klagenfurt. It was an independent duchy from 976 and a possession of the Hapsburg dynasty 1276–1918.

Carl XVI Gustaf 1946– . King of Sweden from 1973. He succeeded his grandfather Gustaf VI, his father having been killed in an airplane crash 1947. Under the new Swedish constitution, which became effective on his grandfather's death, the monarchy was stripped of all power at his accession.

Carlisle city in S Pennsylvania, in the Cumberland Valley, SW of Harrisburg; seat of Cumberland County; population (1990) 18,400. Industries include electronics and steel products. The US Army War College and Dickinson College are here.

Carlos I 1863–1908. King of Portugal, of the Braganza-Coburg line, from 1889 until he was assassinated in Lisbon with his elder son Luis. He was succeeded by his younger son Manuel.

Carlos Don 1545–1568. Spanish prince. Son of Philip II, he was recognized as heir to the thrones of Castile and Aragon but became mentally unstable and had to be placed under restraint following a plot to assassinate his father. His story was the subject of plays by Friedrich von Schiller, Vittorio Alfieri, Thomas Otway, and others.

Carlos four kings of Spain; see ◊Charles.

Carlow county in the Republic of Ireland, in the province of Leinster; county town Carlow; area 347 sq mi/900 sq km; population (1991) 40,900. Mostly flat except for mountains in the S, the land is fertile, and well suited to dairy farming.

Carlson Chester 1906–1968. US scientist who invented ◊xerography. A research worker with Bell Telephone, he lost his job 1930 during the Depression and set to work on his own to develop an efficient copying machine. By 1938 he had invented the Xerox photocopier.

Carlsson Ingvar (Gösta) 1934– . Swedish socialist politician, leader of the Social Democratic Party, deputy prime minister 1982–86 and prime minister 1986–91.

Carlucci Frank (Charles) 1930– . US politician. A former diplomat and deputy director of the CIA, he was national security adviser 1986–87 and defense secretary 1987–89 under President Reagan, supporting Soviet–US arms reduction.

Carlyle Thomas 1795–1881. Scottish essayist and social historian. His works include *Sartor Resartus* 1833–34, describing his loss of Christian belief; *The French Revolution* 1837; *Chartism* 1839; and *Past and Present* 1843. His prose style was idiosyncratic, encompassing grand, thunderous rhetoric and deliberate obscurity.

Carmelite order mendicant order of friars in the Roman Catholic church. The order was founded on Mount Carmel in Palestine by Berthold, a crusader from Calabria, about 1155, and spread to Europe in the 13th century. The Carmelites have devoted themselves largely to missionary work and mystical theology. They are known as *White Friars* because of the white overmantle they wear (over a brown habit).

carnation any of numerous double-flowered cultivated varieties of a plant *Dianthus caryophyllus* of the pink family. The flowers smell like cloves; they are divided into flake, bizarre, and picotees, according to whether the petals exhibit one or more colors on their white ground, have the color dispersed in strips, or have a colored border to the petals.

carnauba palm *Copernicia cerifera*, native to South America. It produces fine timber and a hard wax, used for polishes and lipsticks.

Carnegie Andrew 1835–1919. US industrialist and philanthropist, born in Scotland, who developed the Pittsburgh iron and steel industries, making the US the world's leading producer. He endowed public libraries, education, and various research trusts.

Carnegie Dale 1888–1955. US author and teacher who wrote the best-selling self-help book *How to Win Friends and Influence People* 1937.

carnelian semiprecious gemstone variety of ◊chalcedony consisting of quartz (silica) with iron impurities, which give it a translucent red color. It is found mainly in Brazil, India, and Japan.

carnivore animal that eats other animals. Although the term is sometimes confined to those that eat the flesh of ◊vertebrate prey, it is often used more broadly to include any animal that eats other animals, even microscopic ones. Carrion-eaters may or may not be included.

The mammalian order Carnivora includes civet cats, raccoons, cats, dogs, and bears.

Carnot Lazare Nicolas Marguerite 1753–1823. French general and politician. A member of the National Convention in the French Revolution, he organized the armies of the republic. He was war minister 1800–01 and minister of the interior 1815 under Napoleon. His work on fortification, *De la Défense de places fortes* 1810, became a military textbook. Minister of the interior during the ◊Hundred Days, he was proscribed at the restoration of the monarchy and retired to Germany.

Carnot cycle series of changes in the physical condition of a gas in a reversible heat engine, necessarily in the following order: (1) isothermal expansion (without change of temperature), (2) adiabatic expansion (without change of heat content), (3) isothermal compression, and (4) adiabatic compression.

carnotite potassium uranium vanadate, $K_2(UO_2)_2(VO_4)_2 \cdot 3H_2O$, a radioactive ore of vanadium and uranium with traces of radium. A yellow powdery mineral, it is mined chiefly in the Colorado Plateau; Radium Hill, Australia; and Shaba, Zaire.

carob small Mediterranean tree *Ceratonia siliqua* of the legume family Leguminosae. Its pods, 8 in/20 cm long, are used as animal fodder; they are also the source of a chocolate substitute.

carol song that in medieval times was associated with a round dance; now those that are sung at annual festivals, such as Easter and Christmas.

Carol I 1839–1914. First king of ◊Romania 1881–1914. A prince of the house of Hohenzollern-Sigmaringen, he was invited to become prince of Romania, then part of the Ottoman Empire, 1866. In 1877, in alliance with Russia, he declared war on Turkey, and the Congress of Berlin 1878 recognized Romanian independence.

Carol II 1893–1953. King of Romania 1930–40. Son of King Ferdinand, he married Princess Helen of Greece and they had a son, Michael. In 1925 he renounced the succession because of his affair with Elena Lupescu and went into exile in Paris. Michael succeeded to the throne 1927, but in 1930 Carol returned to Romania and was proclaimed king. In 1938 he introduced a new constitution under which he practically became an absolute ruler. He was forced to abdicate by the pro-Nazi ◊Iron Guard Sept 1940, went to Mexico, and married his mistress 1947.

Carolines scattered archipelago in Micronesia, Pacific Ocean, consisting of over 500 coral islets; area 463 sq mi/1,200 sq km. The chief islands are Ponape, Kusai, and Truk in the E group, and Yap and Belau in the W group.

Carolingian dynasty Frankish dynasty descending from ◊Pepin the Short (died 768) and named after his son Charlemagne; its last true ruler was Louis V of France (reigned 966–87), who was followed by Hugh ◊Capet, first ruler of the Capetian dynasty.

carotene naturally occurring pigment of the ◊carotenoid group. Carotenes produce the orange, yellow, and red colors of carrots, tomatoes, oranges, and crustaceans.

Carothers Wallace 1896–1937. US chemist who carried out research into polymerization. By 1930 he had discovered that some polymers were fiber-forming, and in 1937 he produced ◊nylon.

carp fish *Cyprinus carpio* found all over the world. It commonly grows to 1.8 ft/50 cm and 7 lb/3 kg, but may be even larger. It lives in lakes, ponds, and slow rivers. The wild form is drab, but cultivated forms may be golden, or may have few large scales (mirror carp) or be scaleless (leather carp). *Koi* carp are highly prized and can grow up to 3 ft/1 m long with a distinctive pink, red, white, or black coloring.

Carpaccio Vittorio 1450/60–1525/26. Italian painter known for scenes of his native Venice. His series *The Legend of St Ursula* 1490–98 (Accademia, Venice) is full of detail of contemporary Venetian life. His other great series is the lives of saints George and Jerome 1502–07 (S Giorgio degli Schiavoni, Venice).

Carpathian Mountains central European mountain system, forming a semicircle through Slovakia–Poland–Ukraine–Romania, 900 mi/1,450 km long. The central **Tatra Mountains** on the Slovak–Polish frontier include the highest peak, Gerlachovka, 8,737 ft/2,663 m.

carpel female reproductive unit in flowering plants (◊angiosperms). It usually comprises an ◊ovary containing one or more ovules, the stalk or style, and a ◊stigma at its top which receives the pollen. A flower may have one or more carpels, and they may be separate or fused together. Collectively the carpels of a flower are known as the gynoecium.

Carpenter John 1948– . US director of horror and science-fiction films, notable for such films as *Dark Star* 1974 and *Assault on Precinct 13* 1976.

carpet thick textile fabric, generally made of wool, used for covering floors and stairs. There is a long tradition of fine handmade carpets in the Middle East, India, Pakistan, and China. Western carpets are machine-made. Carpets and rugs have also often been made in the home as a pastime, cross and tent stitch on canvas being widely used in the 18th and 19th centuries.

carpetbagger in US history, derogatory name for any of the entrepreneurs and politicians from the North who moved to the Southern states during ◊Reconstruction 1861–65 after the Civil War, to exploit the chaotic conditions for their own benefit.

Carracci Italian family of painters in Bologna, whose forte was murals and ceilings. The foremost of them, *Annibale Carracci* (1560–1609), decorated the Farnese Palace, Rome, with a series of mythological paintings united by simulated architectural ornamental surrounds (completed 1604).

Carrel Alexis 1873–1944. US surgeon born in France, whose experiments paved the way for organ transplant. Working at the Rockefeller Institute, New York City, he devised a way of joining blood vessels end to end (anastomosing). This was a key move in the development of transplant surgery, as was his work on keeping organs viable outside the body, for which he was awarded the Nobel Prize for Medicine 1912.

Carrhae, Battle of battle 53 BC in which the invading Roman general Crassus was defeated and killed by the Parthians. The ancient town of Carrhae is near Haran, Turkey.

Carroll Charles 1737–1832. American public official who, as a member of the Continental Congress, was one of the signatories of the Declaration of Independence 1776. He was one of Maryland's first US senators 1789–92.

Carroll Lewis. Adopted name of Charles Lutwidge Dodgson 1832–1898. English author of children's classics *Alice's Adventures in Wonderland* 1865 and its sequel *Through the Looking-Glass* 1872. Among later works was the mock-heroic nonsense poem *The Hunting of the Snark* 1876. An Oxford don, he also published mathematical works.

carrot hardy European biennial *Daucus carota* of the family Umbelliferae. Cultivated since the 16th century for its edible root, it has a high sugar content and also contains ◊carotene, which is converted by the human liver to vitamin A.

Carson Kit (Christopher) 1809–68. US frontier settler, guide, and Indian agent, who later fought for the federal side in the Civil War. Carson City, Nevada, was named after him.

Carson Rachel 1907–1964. US naturalist. An aquatic biologist with US Fish and Wildlife Service 1936–49, she then became its editor-in-chief until 1952. In 1951 she published *The Sea Around Us* and in 1963 *Silent Spring*, attacking the indiscriminate use of pesticides.

Carson City capital of Nevada; population (1990) 40,400. Settled as a trading post 1851, it was named after the frontier guide Kit Carson 1858. It flourished as a boom town after the discovery of the nearby Comstock silver-ore lode 1859.

Cartagena or *Cartagena de los Indes* port, industrial center, and capital of the department of Bolivar, NW Colombia; population (1985) 531,000. Plastics and chemicals are produced here.

cartel (German *Kartell* "a group") agreement among national or international firms to fix prices for their products. A cartel may restrict supply (output) to raise prices in order to increase member profits. It therefore represents a form of ◊oligopoly. ◊OPEC, for example, is an oil cartel.

Carter Elliott (Cook) 1908– . US composer. His early work shows the influence of Igor ◊Stravinsky, but after 1950 his music became increasingly intricate and densely written in a manner resembling Charles ◊Ives. He invented "metrical modulation," which allows different instruments or groups to stay in touch while playing at different speeds. He wrote four string quartets, the *Symphony for Three Orchestras* 1967, and the song cycle *A Mirror on Which to Dwell* 1975.

Carter Jimmy (James Earl) 1924– . 39th president of the US 1977–81, a Democrat. In 1976 he narrowly wrested the presidency from Gerald Ford. Features of his presidency were the return of the Panama Canal Zone to Panama, the Camp David Agreements for peace in the Middle East, and the Iranian seizure of US embassy hostages. He was defeated by Ronald Reagan 1980.

Born in Plains, Georgia; he served in the navy, studied nuclear physics, and after a spell as a peanut farmer entered politics 1953.

Cartesian coordinates in ◊coordinate geometry, components used to define the position of a point by its perpendicular distance from a set of two or more axes, or reference lines. For a two-dimensional area defined by two axes at right angles (a horizontal x-axis and a vertical y-axis), the coordinates of a point are given by its perpendicular distances from the y-axis and x-axis, written in the form (x,y). For example, a point P that lies three units from the y-axis and four units from the x-axis has Cartesian coordinates (3,4). In three-dimensional coordinate geometry, points are located with reference to a third, z-axis, mutually at right angles to the x and y axes.

Carthage ancient Phoenician port in N Africa founded by colonists from Tyre in the late 9th century BC; it lay 10 mi/16 km N of Tunis, Tunisia. A leading trading center, it was in conflict with Greece from the 6th century BC, and then with Rome, and was destroyed by Roman forces 146 BC at the end of the ◊*Punic Wars*. About 45 BC, Roman colonists settled in Carthage, and it became the wealthy capital of the province of Africa. After its capture by the Vandals AD 439 it was little more than a pirate stronghold. From 533 it formed part of the Byzantine Empire until its final destruction by Arabs 698, during their conquest in the name of Islam.

Carthusian order Roman Catholic order of monks and, later, nuns, founded by St Bruno 1084 at Chartreuse, near Grenoble, France. Living chiefly in unbroken silence, they ate one vegetarian meal a day and supported themselves by their own labors; the rule is still one of severe austerity.

Cartier Georges Étienne 1814–1873. French-Canadian politician. He fought against the British in the rebellion 1837, was elected to the Canadian parliament 1848, and was joint prime minister with John A Macdonald 1858–62. He brought Québec into the Canadian federation 1867.

Cartier Jacques 1491–1557. French navigator who was the first European to sail up the St Lawrence River 1534. He named the site of Montréal.

Cartier-Bresson Henri 1908– . French photographer, considered one of the greatest photographic artists. His documentary work was shot in black and white, using a small-format camera. His work is remarkable for its tightly structured composition and his ability to capture the decisive moment.

cartilage flexible bluish-white connective ◊tissue made up of the protein collagen. In cartilaginous fish it forms the skeleton; in other vertebrates it forms the greater part of the embryonic skeleton, and is replaced by ◊bone in the course of development, except in areas of wear such as bone endings, and the disks between the backbones. It also forms structural tissue in the larynx, nose, and external ear of mammals.

caryatid The Erechtheon, Porch of the Caryatids, situated near the Parthenon, Athens.

cartography art and practice of drawing ◊maps.

cartoon humorous or satirical drawing or ◊carica-ture; a cartoon strip or ◊comic strip; traditionally, the base design for a large fresco, mosaic, or tapestry, transferred to wall or canvas by tracing or picking out (pouncing). Surviving examples include Leonardo da Vinci's *Virgin and St Anne* (National Gallery, London).

Cartwright Edmund 1743–1823. British inventor. He patented the power loom 1785, built a weaving mill 1787, and patented a wool-combing machine 1789.

Caruso Enrico 1873–1921. Italian operatic tenor. In 1902 he starred, with Nellie Melba, in Puccini's *La Bohème*. He was one of the first opera singers to profit from phonograph recordings.

Carver George Washington 1864–1943. US agricul-tural chemist. Born a slave in Missouri, he was kid-napped and raised by his former owner, Moses Carver. He devoted his life to improving the economy of the US South and the condition of blacks. He advocated the diversification of crops, promoted peanut production, and was a pioneer in the field of plastics.

Carver was honored as one of America's most influ-ential and innovative agronomists.

caryatid building support or pillar in the shape of a woman, the name deriving from the Karyatides, who were priestesses at the temple of Artemis at Karyai; the male equivalent is a *telamon* or *atlas*.

Casablanca (Arabic *Dar el-Beida*) port, commer-cial and industrial center on the Atlantic coast of Morocco; population (1982) 2,139,000. It trades in fish, phosphates, and manganese. The Great Hassan II Mosque, completed 1989, is the world's largest; it is built on a platform (430,000 sq ft/40,000 sq m) jutting out over the Atlantic, with walls 200 ft/60 m high, topped by a hydraulic sliding roof, and a minaret 574 ft/175 m high.

Casals Pablo 1876–1973. Catalan cellist, composer, and conductor. As a cellist, he was celebrated for his interpretations of J S Bach's unaccompanied suites. He left Spain 1939 to live in Prades, in the French Pyre-nees, where he founded an annual music festival. In 1956 he moved to Puerto Rico, where he launched the Casals Festival 1957, and toured extensively in the US. He wrote instrumental and choral works, including the Christmas oratorio *The Manger*.

He married three times; his first wife was the Por-tuguese cellist Guilhermina Suggia (1888–1950).

Casanova de Seingalt Giovanni Jacopo 1725–1798. Italian adventurer, spy, violinist, librarian, and, accord-ing to his *Memoirs*, one of the world's great lovers. From 1774 he was a spy in the Venetian police service. In 1782 a libel got him into trouble, and after more wanderings he was appointed 1785 librarian to Count Waldstein at his castle of Dûx in Bohemia. Here Casanova wrote his *Memoirs* (published 1826–38, although the complete text did not appear until 1960–61).

Cascade Range volcanic mountains in the western US and Canada, extending 700 mi/1,120 km from N California through Oregon and Washington to the Fraser River. They include Mount St Helens and Mount Rainier (the highest peak, 14,408 ft/4,392 m), which is noteworthy for its glaciers. The mountains are the most active in the US, excluding Alaska and Hawaii.

casein main protein of milk, from which it can be sep-arated by the action of acid, the enzyme rennin, or bac-teria (souring); it is also the main component of cheese.

Casein is used commercially in cosmetics, in glues, and as a sizing for coating paper.

Casement Roger David 1864–1916. Irish nationalist. While in the British consular service, he exposed the ruthless exploitation of the people of the Belgian Congo and Peru, for which he was knighted 1911 (degraded 1916). He was hanged for treason by the British for his involvement in the Irish nationalist cause.

Cash Johnny 1932– . US country singer, songwriter, and guitarist. His early hits, recorded for Sun Records in Memphis, Tennessee, include the million-selling "I Walk the Line" 1956. Many of his songs have become classics.

cash crop crop grown solely for sale rather than for the farmer's own use, for example, coffee, cotton, or sugar beet. Many Third World countries grow cash crops to meet their debt repayments rather than grow food for their own people. The price for these crops depends on financial interests, such as those of the multinational companies and the International Mone-tary Fund.

cashew tropical American tree *Anacardium occiden-tale*, family Anacardiaceae. Extensively cultivated in India and Africa, it produces poisonous kidney-shaped nuts that become edible after being roasted.

cash flow input of cash required to cover all expenses of a business, whether revenue or capital. Alternatively, the actual or prospective balance between the various outgoing and incoming move-ments which are designated in total, positive or nega-tive according to which is greater.

cashmere natural fiber originating from the wool of the goats of Kashmir, India, used for shawls, scarves, sweaters, and coats. It can also be made artifi-cially.

Casper city in E central Wyoming, on the North Platte River, NW of Cheyenne; seat of Natrona County; population (1990) 46,700. The largest city in Wyoming, it serves as the marketing center for the region's live-stock and petroleum products.

Caspian Sea world's largest inland sea, divided between Iran, Azerbaijan, Russia, Kazakhstan, and Turkmenistan; area about 155,000 sq mi/400,000 sq km, with a maximum depth of 3,250 ft/1,000 m. The chief ports are Astrakhan and Baku. Drainage in the N and damming of the Volga and Ural rivers for hydro-electric power left the sea approximately 90 ft/28 m below sea level. In June 1991 opening of sluices in the dams caused the water level to rise dramatically, threatening towns and industrial areas.

Cass Lewis 1782–1866. US political leader and diplo-mat. He was appointed secretary of war 1831 by Pres-ident Jackson, and served as US minister to France 1836–42. He was the unsuccessful Democratic presi-dential candidate in 1848, returning to the Senate 1849–57. In the Buchanan administration 1856–60, he served as secretary of state 1857–60.

Cassandra in Greek legend, the daughter of ◊Priam, king of Troy. Her prophecies (for example, of the fall of Troy) were never believed, because she had rejected the love of the god Apollo. She was murdered with ◊Agamemnon by his wife Clytemnestra, having been awarded as a prize to the Greek hero on his sacking of Troy.

Cassatt Mary 1845–1926. US Impressionist painter and printmaker. In 1868 she settled in Paris. Her popu-lar, colorful pictures of mothers and children show the

Cassatt The Bath (1891–92), US artist Mary Cassatt.

then-new influence of Japanese prints, for example *The Bath* 1891–92 (Art Institute, Chicago).

Born to a wealthy Philadelphia family, in 1868 she settled in Paris and exhibited with the Impressionists 1879–81, 1886, the only American to do so. She also excelled in etching and pastels. Her work, always respected in France, has gained recognition in the US in recent years, the largest collection being on view at the Philadelphia Art Museum.

cassava or *manioc* plant *Manihot utilissima*, belonging to the spurge family Euphorbiaceae. Native to South America, it is now widely grown throughout the tropics for its starch-containing roots, from which tapioca and bread are made.

Cassini joint space probe of the US agency NASA and the European Space Agency to the planet Saturn. *Cassini* is scheduled to be launched 1997 and to go into orbit around Saturn 2004, dropping off a subprobe, *Huygens*, to land on Saturn's largest moon, Titan.

Cassiopeia prominent constellation of the northern hemisphere, named after the mother of Andromeda. It has a distinctive W-shape, and contains one of the most powerful radio sources in the sky, Cassiopeia A, the remains of a ◊supernova (star explosion).

Cassius Gaius died 42 BC. Roman soldier, one of the conspirators who killed Julius ◊Caesar 44 BC. He fought with Pompey against Caesar, and was pardoned after the battle of Pharsalus 48, but became a leader in the conspiracy of 44. After Caesar's death he joined Brutus, and committed suicide after their defeat at ◊Philippi 42 BC.

Castagno Andrea del *c.* 1421–1457. Italian Renaissance painter, active in Florence. In his frescoes in Sta Apollonia, Florence, he adapted the pictorial space to the architectural framework and followed ◊Masaccio's lead in perspective.

castanets Spanish percussion instrument made of two hollowed wooden shells, clapped in the hand to produce a rhythmic accompaniment to dance.

caste (Portuguese *casta* "race") stratification of Hindu society into four main groups: *Brahmans* (priests), *Kshatriyas* (nobles and warriors), *Vaisyas* (traders and farmers), and *Sudras* (servants); plus a fifth group, *Harijan* (untouchables). No upward or downward mobility exists, as in classed societies. The system dates from ancient times, and there are more than 3,000 subdivisions.

Castiglione Baldassare, Count Castiglione 1478–1529. Italian author and diplomat who described the perfect Renaissance gentleman in *Il Cortegiano/The Courtier* 1528.

Castile kingdom founded in the 10th century, occupying the central plateau of Spain. Its union with ◊Aragon 1479, based on the marriage of ◊Ferdinand and Isabella, effected the foundation of the Spanish state, which at the time was occupied and ruled by the ◊Moors. Castile comprised the two great basins separated by the Sierra de Gredos and the Sierra de Guadarrama, known traditionally as Old and New Castile. The area now forms the regions of ◊Castilla–León and ◊Castilla–La Mancha.

Castilian language member of the Romance branch of the Indo-European language family, originating in NW Spain, in the provinces of Old and New Castile. It is the basis of present-day standard Spanish (see ◊Spanish language) and is often seen as the same language, the terms *castellano* and *español* being used interchangeably in both Spain and the Spanish-speaking countries of the Americas.

Castilla–La Mancha autonomous region of central Spain; area 30,571 sq mi/79,200 sq km; population (1986) 1,665,000. It includes the provinces of Albacete, Ciudad Real, Cuenca, Guadalajara, and Toledo. Irrigated land produces grain and chickpeas, and merino sheep graze here.

Castilla–León autonomous region of central Spain; area 36,323 sq mi/94,100 sq km; population (1986) 2,600,000. It includes the provinces of Ávila, Burgos, León, Palencia, Salamanca, Segovia, Soria, Valladolid,

castle

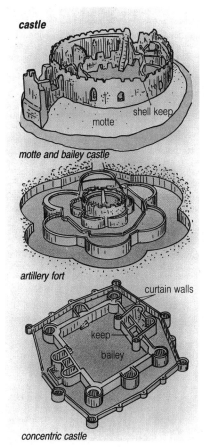

motte and bailey castle

shell keep

motte

artillery fort

curtain walls

keep

bailey

concentric castle

castle *(far left) Three stages in the development of the castle.*

castle *(top) Stokesay Castle in Shropshire, England, built between the 12th and 13th centuries. (bottom) Bodiam Castle, built by Sir Edward Dalyngrigge in the 14th century.*

and Zamora. Irrigated land produces wheat and rye. Cattle, sheep, and fighting bulls are bred in the uplands.

casting process of producing solid objects by pouring molten material into a shaped mold and allowing it to cool. Casting is used to shape such materials as glass and plastics, as well as metals and alloys.

cast iron cheap but invaluable constructional material, most commonly used for automobile engine blocks. Cast iron is partly refined pig (crude) ◊iron, which is very fluid when molten and highly suitable for shaping by casting; it contains too many impurities (for example, carbon) to be readily shaped in any other way. Solid cast iron is heavy and can absorb great shock but is very brittle.

castle private fortress of a king or noble. The earliest castles in Britain were built following the Norman Conquest, and the art of castle building reached a peak in the 13th century. By the 15th century, the need for castles for domestic defense had largely disappeared, and the advent of gunpowder made them largely useless against attack. See also ◊château.

castor-oil plant tall, tropical and subtropical shrub *Ricinus communis* of the spurge family Euphorbiaceae. The seeds, in North America called castor beans, yield the purgative castor oil and also ricin, one of the most powerful poisons known, which can be targeted to destroy cancer cells, while leaving normal cells untouched.

castration removal of the testicles. Male domestic animals may be castrated to prevent reproduction, to make them larger or more docile, or to remove a disease site.

Castries port and capital of St Lucia, on the NW coast of the island in the Caribbean; population (1988) 53,000. It produces textiles, chemicals, tobacco, and wood and rubber products.

Castro (Ruz) Fidel 1927– . Cuban communist politician, prime minister 1959–76 and president from 1976. He led two unsuccessful coups against the right-wing Batista regime and led the revolution that overthrew the dictator 1959. He raised the standard of living for most Cubans but dealt harshly with dissenters.

Castro built a strong military force and attempted to export his revolution to other Latin American countries. *See illustration p. 174*

cat small, domesticated, carnivorous mammal *Felis catus*, often kept as a pet or for catching small pests such as rodents. Found in many color variants, it may have short, long, or no hair, but the general shape and size is constant. All cats walk on the pads of their toes, and have retractile claws. They have strong limbs, large eyes, and acute hearing. The canine teeth are long and well-developed, as are the shearing teeth in the side of the mouth.

catacomb underground cemetery, such as the catacombs of the early Christians. Examples include those beneath the basilica of St Sebastian in Rome, where bodies were buried in niches in the walls of the tunnels.

Catalan language member of the Romance branch of the Indo-European language family, an Iberian language closely related to Provençal in France. It is spoken in Catalonia in NE Spain, the Balearic Islands, Andorra, and a corner of SW France.

Catalonia (Spanish *Cataluña*, Catalan *Catalunya*) autonomous region of NE Spain; area

Castro (Ruz) The Cuban revolutionary and premier Fidel Castro.

12,313 sq mi/31,900 sq km; population (1986) 5,977,000. It includes Barcelona (the capital), Gerona, Lérida, and Tarragona. Industries include wool and cotton textiles; hydroelectric power is produced.

French Catalonia is the adjacent *département* of Pyrénées-Orientales.

catalyst substance that alters the speed of, or makes possible, a chemical or biochemical reaction but remains unchanged at the end of the reaction. ◊Enzymes are natural biochemical catalysts. In practice most catalysts are used to speed up reactions.

catalytic converter device fitted to the exhaust system of a motor vehicle in order to reduce toxic emissions from the engine. It converts harmful exhaust products to relatively harmless ones by passing the exhaust gases over a mixture of catalysts coated on a metal or ceramic honeycomb (a structure that increases the surface area and therefore the amount of active catalyst with which the exhaust gases will come into contact). *Oxidation catalysts* (small amounts of precious palladium and platinum metals) convert hydrocarbons (unburnt fuel) and carbon monoxide into carbon dioxide and water, while *three-way catalysts* (platinum and rhodium metals) convert nitrogen oxide gases into nitrogen and oxygen.

catamaran (Tamil "tied log") twin-hulled sailing vessel, based on the aboriginal craft of South America and the Indies, made of logs lashed together, with an outrigger. A similar vessel with three hulls is known as a trimaran. Automobile ferries with a wave-piercing catamaran design are also in use in parts of Europe and North America. They have a pointed main hull and two outriggers and travel at a speed of 35 knots (52.5 mph/84.5 kph).

cataract eye disease in which the crystalline lens or its capsule becomes opaque, causing blindness. Fluid accumulates between the fibers of the lens and gives place to deposits of ◊albumin. These coalesce into rounded bodies, the lens fibers break down, and areas of the lens or the lens capsule become filled with opaque products of degeneration.

catastrophe theory mathematical theory developed by René Thom in 1972, in which he showed that the growth of an organism proceeds by a series of gradual changes that are triggered by, and in turn trigger, large-scale changes or "catastrophic" jumps. It also has applications in engineering—for example, the gradual strain on the structure of a bridge that can eventually result in a sudden collapse—and has been extended to economic and psychological events.

catchment area area from which water is collected by a river and its tributaries. In the social sciences the term may be used to denote the area from which people travel to obtain a particular service or product, such as the area from which a school draws its pupils.

catechism teaching by question and answer on the Socratic method, but chiefly as a means of instructing children in the basics of the Christian creed. A person being instructed in this way in preparation for baptism or confirmation is called a *catechumen*.

category in philosophy, a fundamental concept applied to being that cannot be reduced to anything more elementary. Aristotle listed ten categories: substance, quantity, quality, relation, place, time, position, state, action, and passion.

caterpillar larval stage of a ◊butterfly or ◊moth. Wormlike in form, the body is segmented, may be hairy, and often has scent glands. The head has strong biting mandibles, silk glands, and a spinneret.

catfish fish belonging to the order Siluriformes, in which barbels (feelers) on the head are well-developed, so giving a resemblance to the whiskers of a cat. Catfishes are found worldwide, mainly but not exclusively in fresh water, and are plentiful in South America.

cathedral (Latin *cathedra*, "seat" or "throne") Christian church containing the throne of a bishop or archbishop, which is usually situated on the south side of the choir. A cathedral is governed by a dean and chapter.

There are cathedrals in most of the important cities of the world, built in a wide variety of architectural styles.

Catherine I 1684–1727. Empress of Russia from 1725. A Lithuanian peasant, born Martha Skavronsky, she married a Swedish dragoon and eventually became the mistress of Peter the Great. In 1703 she was rechristened Katarina Alexeievna. The tsar divorced his wife 1711 and married Catherine 1712. She accompanied him on his campaigns, and showed tact and shrewdness. In 1724 she was proclaimed empress, and after Peter's death 1725 she ruled capably with the help of her ministers. She allied Russia with Austria and Spain in an anti-English bloc.

Catherine II *the Great* 1729–1796. Empress of Russia from 1762, and daughter of the German prince of Anhalt-Zerbst. In 1745, she married the Russian grand duke Peter. Catherine was able to dominate him; six months after he became Tsar Peter III 1762, he was murdered in a coup and Catherine ruled alone. During her reign Russia extended its boundaries to include territory from wars with the Turks 1768–74, 1787–92, and from the partitions of Poland 1772, 1793, and 1795, as well as establishing hegemony over the Black Sea.

She admired and aided the French *Encyclopédistes*.

Catherine de' Medici 1519–1589. French queen consort of Henry II, whom she married 1533; daughter of Lorenzo de' Medici, Duke of Urbino; and mother of Francis II, Charles IX, and Henry III. At first outshone by Henry's mistress Diane de Poitiers (1490–1566), she became regent 1560–63 for Charles IX and remained in power until his death 1574.

Catherine of Alexandria, St Christian martyr. According to legend she disputed with 50 scholars, refusing to give up her faith and marry Emperor Maxentius. Her emblem is a wheel, on which her persecutors tried to kill her (the wheel broke and she was beheaded). Feast day Nov 25.

Catherine of Aragon 1485–1536. First queen of Henry VIII of England, 1509–33, and mother of Mary I. Catherine had married Henry's elder brother Prince Arthur 1501 and on his death 1502 was betrothed to

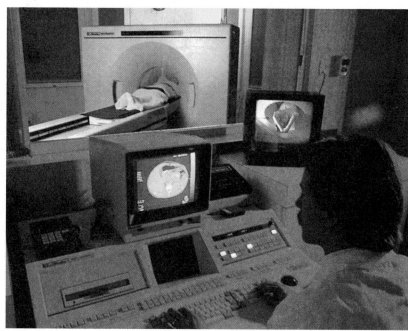

Henry, marrying him on his accession. She failed to produce a male heir and Henry divorced her without papal approval, thus creating the basis for the English ◊Reformation.

Catherine of Siena 1347–1380. Italian mystic, born in Siena. She persuaded Pope Gregory XI to return to Rome from Avignon 1376. In 1375 she is said to have received on her body the stigmata, the impression of Jesus' wounds. Her *Dialogue* is a classic mystical work. Feast day April 29.

Catherine of Valois 1401–1437. Queen of Henry V of England, whom she married 1420; the mother of Henry VI. After the death of Henry V, she secretly married Owen Tudor (*c.* 1400–1461) about 1425, and their son Edmund Tudor became the father of Henry VII.

catheter fine tube inserted into the body to introduce or remove fluids. The original catheter was the urinary one, passed by way of the urethra (the duct that leads urine away from the bladder). In today's practice, catheters can be inserted into blood vessels, either in the limbs or trunk, to provide blood samples and local pressure measurements, and to deliver drugs and/or nutrients directly into the bloodstream.

cathode in electronics, the part of an electronic device in which electrons are generated. In a thermionic valve, electrons are produced by the heating effect of an applied current; in a photoelectric cell, they are produced by the interaction of light and a semiconducting material. The cathode is kept at a negative potential relative to the device's other electrodes (anodes) in order to ensure that the liberated electrons stream away from the cathode and toward the anodes.

cathode-ray tube vacuum tube in which a beam of electrons is produced and focused onto a fluorescent screen. It is an essential component of television receivers, computer visual display terminals, and ◊oscilloscopes.

Catholic church whole body of the Christian church, though usually referring to the Roman Catholic church (see ◊Roman Catholicism).

Catiline (Lucius Sergius Catilina) *c.* 108–62 BC. Roman politician. Twice failing to be elected to the consulship in 64/63 BC, he planned a military coup, but ◊Cicero exposed his conspiracy. He died at the head of the insurgents.

Catlin George 1796–1872. US explorer and artist. Born in Wilkes-Barre, Pennsylvania, Catlin briefly practiced law before embarking on a career as a portrait painter. His deep interest in the Indians of the West then led him to travel widely, recording pictorially the lifeways and customs of the tribes of the Rocky Mountains and Great Plains 1832–40.

Cato Marcus Porcius. Known as "the Censor" 234–149 BC. Roman politician. Having significantly developed Roman rule in Spain, Cato was appointed ◊censor 184 BC. He acted severely, taxing luxuries and heavily revising the senatorial and equestrian lists.

CAT scan or *CT scan* (acronym for *computerized axial tomography*) sophisticated method of X-ray imaging. Quick and noninvasive, CAT scanning is used in medicine as an aid to diagnosis, helping to pinpoint problem areas without the need for exploratory surgery. It is also used in archeology to examine mummies.

Catskills US mountain range, mainly in SE New York W of the Hudson River. The highest point is Slide mountain 4,204 ft/1,281 m. Long a vacation and resort center for New York City residents, the Catskills offer hiking, skiing, hunting and fishing, and the picturesque trails and scenes of woods, waterfalls, lakes, and streams that have attracted such painters as Frederic Church and Thomas Cole. It is the setting for *Rip Van Winkle*, one of Washington Irving's most popular tales.

cattle any large, ruminant, even-toed, hoofed mammal of the genus *Bos*, family Bovidae, including

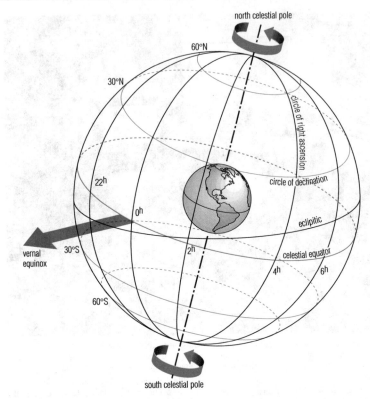

celestial sphere
*The main features of
the celestial sphere.*

north celestial pole

60°N

30°N

circle of right ascension

circle of declination

22ʰ

0ʰ

eclipitic

vernal
equinox

30°S

2ʰ

celestial equator

4ʰ

6ʰ

60°S

south celestial pole

wild species such as the yak, gaur, gayal, banteng, and kouprey, as well as domestic breeds. Asiatic water buffaloes *Bubalus*, African buffaloes *Syncerus*, and American bison *Bison* are not considered true cattle. Cattle are bred for meat (beef cattle) or milk (dairy cattle).

Catullus Gaius Valerius *c*. 84–54 BC. Roman lyric poet, who wrote in a variety of meters and forms, from short narratives and hymns to epigrams. Born in Verona, N Italy, he moved with ease through the literary and political society of late republican Rome. His love affair with the woman he called Lesbia provided the inspiration for many of his poems.

Caucasoid referring to one of the three major varieties (see ◊race) of humans, *Homo sapiens sapiens*, including the indigenous peoples of Europe, the Near East, North Africa, India, and Australia. Caucasoids exhibit the widest range of variation in physical traits, including straight to curly hair; fair to dark skin; blue, hazel, and brown eyes; blond, red, brown, and black hair; medium to heavy beard and body hair; small to high-bridged noses; medium to thin lips. The term was coined by the German anthropologist J F Blumenbach (1752–1840), who erroneously theorized that they originated in the Caucasus region. See also ◊Mongoloid, ◊Negroid.

Caucasus series of mountain ranges between the Caspian and Black seas, in the republics of Russia, Georgia, Armenia, and Azerbaijan; 750 mi/1,200 km long. The highest peak is Elbruz, 18,480 ft/5,633 m.

caucus in the US, a closed meeting of regular party members; for example, to choose a candidate for office. The term was originally used in the 18th century in Boston, Massachusetts.

cauliflower variety of ◊cabbage *Brassica oleracea*, distinguished by its large, flattened head of fleshy, aborted flowers. It is similar to broccoli but less hardy.

causality in philosophy, a consideration of the connection between cause and effect, usually referred to as the "causal relationship." If an event is assumed to have a cause, two important questions arise: what is the relationship between cause and effect, and must it follow that every event is caused? The Scottish philosopher David Hume considered these questions to be, in principle, unanswerable.

cauterization in medicine, the use of special instruments to burn or fuse small areas of body tissue to destroy dead cells, prevent the spread of infection, or seal tiny blood vessels to minimize blood loss during surgery.

Cavaco Silva Anibal 1939– . Portuguese politician, finance minister 1980–81, and prime minister and Social Democratic Party (PSD) leader from 1985. Under his leadership Portugal joined the European Community 1985 and the Western European Union 1988.

cavalier horseman of noble birth, but mainly used to describe a male supporter of Charles I in the English Civil War (Cavalier), typically with courtly dress and long hair (as distinct from a Roundhead); also a supporter of Charles II after the Restoration.

Cavalier poets poets of Charles I's court, including Thomas Carew, Robert Herrick, Richard Lovelace, and John Suckling. They wrote witty, lighthearted love lyrics.

Cavalli (Pietro) Francesco 1602–1676. Italian composer, organist at St Mark's, Venice, and the first to make opera a popular entertainment with such works as *Xerxes* 1654, later performed in honor of Louis XIV's wedding in Paris. Twenty-seven of his operas survive.

cave roofed-over cavity in the Earth's crust usually produced by the action of underground water or by waves on a seacoast. Caves of the former type commonly occur in areas underlain by limestone, such as Kentucky and many Balkan regions, where the rocks are soluble in water. A *pothole* is a vertical hole in rock caused by water descending a crack; it is thus open to the sky.

Cavendish Henry 1731–1810. English physicist. He discovered hydrogen (which he called "inflammable air") 1766, and determined the compositions of water and of nitric acid.

caviar salted roe (eggs) of sturgeon, salmon, and other fishes. Caviar is prepared by beating and straining the egg sacs until the eggs are free from fats and then adding salt. Russia and Iran are the main exporters of the most prized variety of caviar, derived from Caspian Sea sturgeon. Iceland produces various high-quality, lower-priced caviars.

cavitation ◊erosion of rocks caused by the forcing of air into cracks. Cavitation results from the pounding of waves on the coast and the swirling of turbulent river currents, and exerts great pressure, eventually causing rocks to break apart.

cavity in dentistry, decay of tooth enamel by the acids produced by mouth bacteria. Continuing decay undermines the inner tooth and attacks the nerve, causing toothache. Measures can be taken to save teeth by cleaning out the decay (drilling) and filling the tooth with a plastic substance such as silver amalgam or covering the cavity with an inlay or crown.

Cavour Camillo Benso di, Count 1810–1861. Italian nationalist politician. He was the editor of *Il* ◊*Risorgimento* from 1847. As prime minister of Piedmont 1852–59 and 1860–61, he enlisted the support of Britain and France for the concept of a united Italy achieved 1861; after expelling the Austrians 1859, he assisted Garibaldi in liberating southern Italy 1860.

Caxton William *c.* 1422–1491. The first English printer. He learned the art of printing in Cologne, Germany, 1471 and set up a press in Belgium where he produced the first book printed in English, his own version of a French romance, *Recuyell of the Historyes of Troye* 1474. Returning to England 1476, he established himself in London, where he produced the first book printed in England, *Dictes or Sayengis of the Philosophres* 1477.

A typeface is named for him.

Cayenne capital and chief port of French Guiana, on Cayenne Island, NE South America, at the mouth of the river Cayenne; population (1990) 41,700.

cayenne pepper condiment derived from the dried fruits of various species of ◊capsicum (especially *Capsicum frutescens*), a tropical American genus of plants of the family Solanaceae. It is wholly distinct in its origin from black or white pepper, which is derived from an East Indian plant (*Piper nigrum*).

cayman or *caiman* large reptile, resembling the ◊crocodile.

Cayman Islands British island group in the West Indies
area 100 sq mi/260 sq km

features comprises three low-lying islands: Grand Cayman, Cayman Brac, and Little Cayman
government governor, executive council, and legislative assembly
exports seawhip coral, a source of prostaglandins; shrimps; honey; jewelry
currency CI dollar
population (1988) 22,000
language English
history discovered by Chrisopher Columbus 1503; acquired by Britain following the Treaty of Madrid 1670; a dependency of Jamaica 1863, In 1962 the islands became a separate colony, although the inhabitants chose to remain British. From that date, changes in legislation attracted foreign banks and the Caymans are now an international financial center and tax haven as well as a tourist resort.

CD abbreviation for *Corps Diplomatique* (French "Diplomatic Corps"); ◊*compact disk*, *certificate of deposit*.

CD-ROM (abbreviation for *compact-disk read-only memory*) computer storage device developed from the technology of the audio ◊compact disk. It consists of a plastic-coated metal disk, on which binary digital information is etched in the form of microscopic pits. This can then be read optically by passing a light beam over the disk. CD-ROMs typically hold about 550 ◊megabytes of data, and are used in distributing large amounts of text and graphics, such as encyclopedias, catalogs, and technical manuals.

Ceaușescu Nicolae 1918–1989. Romanian politician, leader of the Romanian Communist Party (RCP), in power 1965–89. He pursued a policy line independent of and critical of the USSR. He appointed family members, including his wife *Elena Ceaușescu*, to senior state and party posts, and governed in an increasingly repressive manner, zealously implementing schemes that impoverished the nation. The Ceaușescus were overthrown in a bloody revolutionary coup Dec 1989 and executed.

Cebu chief city and port of the island of Cebu in the Philippines; population (1990) 610,400; area of the island 1,964 sq mi/5,086 sq km. The oldest city of the Philippines, Cebu was founded as San Miguel 1565 and became the capital of the Spanish Philippines.

cedar any of an Old World genus *Cedrus* of coniferous trees of the pine family Pinaceae. The *cedar of Lebanon* C. *libani* grows to great heights and age in the mountains of Syria and Asia Minor. Of the historic

cedar *The true cedars are evergreen conifers growing from the Mediterranean to the Himalayas.*

forests on Mount Lebanon itself, only a few stands of trees remain.

Cedar Falls city in NE Iowa, on the Cedar River, W of Waterloo; population (1990) 35,000. Industries include farm and other heavy equipment, rotary pumps, and tools.

Cedar Rapids city in E Iowa; population (1990) 108,800. It produces communications equipment, construction machinery, and processed foods. Coe College is here. Cedar Rapids was settled 1837.

Celebes English name for ◊Sulawesi, an island of Indonesia.

celery Old World plant *Apium graveolens* of the carrot family Umbelliferae. It grows wild in ditches and salt marshes and has a coarse texture and acrid taste. Cultivated varieties of celery are grown under cover to make them less bitter.

celestial mechanics the branch of astronomy that deals with the calculation of the orbits of celestial bodies, their gravitational attractions (such as those that produce the Earth's tides), and also the orbits of artificial satellites and space probes. It is based on the laws of motion and gravity laid down by Isaac ◊Newton.

celestial sphere imaginary sphere surrounding the Earth, on which the celestial bodies seem to lie. The positions of bodies such as stars, planets, and galaxies are specified by their coordinates on the celestial sphere. The equivalents of latitude and longitude on the celestial sphere are called declination and right ascension (which is measured in hours from 0 to 24). The *celestial poles* lie directly above the Earth's poles, and the *celestial equator* lies over the Earth's equator. The celestial sphere appears to rotate once around the Earth each day, actually a result of the rotation of the Earth on its axis. *See illustration p. 176*

celiac disease deficiency disease, usually in young children, due to disorder of the absorptive surface of the small intestine. It is mainly associated with an intolerance to gluten (a constituent of wheat) and characterized by diarrhea and malnutrition.

cell in biology, a discrete, membrane-bound portion of living matter, the smallest unit capable of an independent existence. All living organisms consist of one or more cells, with the exception of ◊viruses. Bacteria, protozoa, and many other microorganisms consist of single cells, whereas a human is made up of billions of cells. Essential features of a cell are the membrane, which encloses it and restricts the flow of substances in and out; the jellylike material within, often known as ◊protoplasm; the ◊ribosomes, which carry out protein synthesis; and the ◊DNA, which forms the hereditary material.

cell division the process by which a cell divides, either ◊meiosis, associated with sexual reproduction, or ◊mitosis, associated with growth, cell replacement, or repair. Both forms involve the duplication of DNA and the splitting of the nucleus.

cell, electrical or *voltaic cell* or *galvanic cell* device in which chemical energy is converted into electrical energy; the popular name is ◊"battery" but this actually refers to a collection of cells in one unit. The reactive chemicals of a *primary cell* cannot be replenished, whereas *secondary cells*—such as storage batteries—are rechargeable: their chemical reactions can be reversed and the original condition restored by applying an electric current. It is dangerous to attempt to recharge a primary cell.

Cellini Benvenuto 1500–1571. Italian sculptor and goldsmith working in the Mannerist style; author of an arrogant autobiography (begun 1558). Among his works are a graceful bronze *Perseus* 1545–54 (Loggia dei Lanzi, Florence) and a gold salt cellar made for Francis I of France 1540–43 (Kunsthistorisches Museum, Vienna), topped by nude reclining figures.

cello abbreviation for *violoncello*, a member of the violin family and fourth member of a string quartet. The cello has been much in demand as a solo instrument because of its exceptional range and brilliance of tone, and its repertoire extends from Bach to Beethoven, Dvořák, and Elgar.

cellophane transparent wrapping film made from wood ◊cellulose, widely used for packaging, first produced by Swiss chemist Jacques Edwin Brandenberger 1908.

cellular phone or *cellphone* mobile radio telephone, one of a network connected to the telephone system by a computer-controlled communication system. Service areas are divided into small "cells," about 3 mi/5 km across, each with a separate low-power transmitter.

cellulite fatty compound alleged by some dietitians to be produced in the body by liver disorder and to cause lumpy deposits on the hips and thighs. Medical opinion generally denies its existence, attributing the lumpy appearance to a type of subcutaneous fat deposit.

celluloid transparent or translucent, highly flammable, plastic material (a thermoplastic) made from cellulose nitrate and camphor. It was once used for toilet articles, novelties, and photographic film, but has now been replaced by the nonflammable substance cellulose acetate.

cellulose complex ◊carbohydrate composed of long chains of glucose units. It is the principal constituent of the cell wall of higher plants, and a vital ingredient in the diet of many ◊herbivores. Molecules of cellulose are organized into long, unbranched microfibrils that give support to the cell wall. No mammal produces the enzyme (cellulase) necessary for digesting cellulose; mammals such as rabbits and cows are only able to digest grass because the bacteria present in their gut manufacture the appropriate enzyme.

Celsius scale of temperature, previously called centigrade, in which the range from freezing to boiling of water is divided into 100 degrees, freezing point being 0 degrees and boiling point 100 degrees.

Celt member of an Indo-European people that originated in Alpine Europe and spread to the Iberian peninsula and beyond. They were ironworkers and farmers. In the 1st century BC they were defeated by the Roman Empire and by Germanic tribes and confined largely to Britain, Ireland, and N France.

Celtic art style of art that originated about 500 BC, probably on the Rhine, and spread as the Celts moved westward to Gaul and the British Isles and southward to Italy and Turkey. Celtic manuscript illumination and sculpture from Ireland and Anglo-Saxon Britain of the 6th–8th centuries has intricate spiral and geometric ornament, as in *The Book of Kells* (Trinity College, Dublin) and the *Lindisfarne Gospels* (British Museum, London).

Celtic languages branch of the Indo-European family, divided into two groups: the *Brythonic* or *P-Celtic* (Welsh, Cornish, Breton, and Gaulish) and the *Goidelic* or *Q-Celtic* (Irish, Scottish, and Manx

cell

Cells are the building units of living things. Most of them are tiny, measuring less than .03 mm in diameter. Animal and plant cells have similar internal structures and composition, but plant cells, because of their rigid cellulose walls, are more regular in shape. Animal cells lack chloroplasts, the photosynthesizing structures of plant cells.

In animal and plant embryos, all cells tend to be identical, but gradually they change into various distinct types.

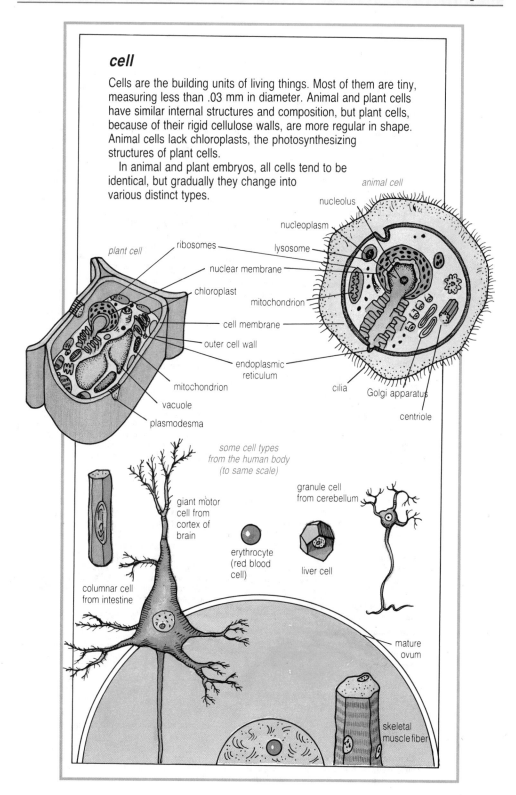

animal cell

nucleolus

nucleoplasm

plant cell

ribosomes

lysosome

nuclear membrane

chloroplast

mitochondrion

cell membrane

outer cell wall

endoplasmic reticulum

mitochondrion

cilia

Golgi apparatus

vacuole

centriole

plasmodesma

some cell types from the human body (to same scale)

giant motor cell from cortex of brain

granule cell from cerebellum

erythrocyte (red blood cell)

liver cell

columnar cell from intestine

mature ovum

skeletal muscle fiber

Gaelic). Celtic languages once stretched from the Black Sea to Britain, but have been in decline for centuries, limited to the so-called "Celtic fringe" of western Europe.

cement any bonding agent used to unite particles in a single mass or to cause one surface to adhere to another. *Portland cement* is a powder obtained from burning together a mixture of lime (or chalk) and clay, and when mixed with water and sand or gravel, turns into mortar or concrete. In geology, a chemically precipitated material such as carbonate that occupies the interstices of clastic rocks is called cement.

Cenozoic or *Caenozoic* era of geological time that began 65 million years ago and is still in process. It is divided into the Tertiary and Quaternary periods. The Cenozoic marks the emergence of mammals as a dominant group, including humans, and the formation of the mountain chains of the Himalayas and the Alps.

censorship suppression by authority of material considered immoral, heretical, subversive, libelous, damaging to state security, or otherwise offensive. It is generally more stringent under totalitarian or strongly religious regimes and in wartime.

censorship, film control of the content and presentation of films. Film censorship dates back almost as far as the cinema. In Britain, censorship was established in 1912, in the US 1922. In some countries, self-regulation of the industry has not been regarded as sufficient; in the USSR, for example, state censorship forbade the treatment of certain issues.

census official count of the population of a country, originally for military call-up and taxation, later for assessment of social trends as other information regarding age, sex, and occupation of each individual was included. They may become unnecessary as computerized databanks are developed.

The first US census was taken in 1790.

centaur in Greek mythology, a creature half-human and half-horse. Centaurs were supposed to live in Thessaly, and be wild and lawless; the mentor of Heracles, Chiron, was an exception.

Centaurus large bright constellation of the southern hemisphere, represented as a centaur. Its brightest star, ◊Alpha Centauri, is a triple star and contains the closest star to the Sun, Proxima Centauri. Omega Centauri, the largest and brightest globular cluster of stars in the sky, is 16,000 light-years away.

center of gravity the point in an object about which its weight is evenly balanced. In a uniform gravitational field, this is the same as the center of mass.

centigrade former name for the ◊Celsius temperature scale.

centipede jointed-legged animal of the group Chilopoda, members of which have a distinct head and a single pair of long antennae. Their bodies are composed of segments (which may number nearly 200), each of similar form and bearing a single pair of legs. Most are small, but the tropical *Scolopendra gigantea* may reach 1 ft/30 cm in length. *Millipedes*, class Diplopoda, have fewer segments (up to 100), but have two pairs of legs on each.

CENTO abbreviation for ◊*Central Treaty Organization.*

Central African Federation or (CAF) grouping imposed by the British government 1953, incorporating the territories of Nyasaland and Northern and Southern Rhodesia. Although it established representative government along federal and multiracial lines, an underlying function was to prevent the spread of Afrikaner nationalism into central Africa. It was dismembered 1963 in the face of African demands for independence in Nyasaland and Northern Rhodesia, and the intransigence of the minority white community in Southern Rhodesia.

Central African Republic landlocked country in Central Africa, bordered NE and E by Sudan, S by Zaire and the Congo, W by Cameroon, and NW by Chad.

Central America the part of the Americas that links Mexico with the Isthmus of Panama, comprising Belize, Costa Rica, El Salvador, Guatemala, Honduras, Nicaragua, and Panama. It is also an isthmus, crossed by mountains that form part of the Cordilleras, rising to a maximum height of 13,845 ft/4,220 m. There are numerous active volcanoes. Central America is about 200,000 sq mi/523,000 sq km in area and has a population (1980) estimated at 22,700,000, mostly Indians or mestizos (of mixed white-Indian ancestry). Tropical agricultural products and other basic commodities and raw materials are exported.

Central American Common Market CACM (*Mercado Común Centroamericana* MCCA) economic alliance established 1960 by El Salvador, Guatemala, Honduras (seceded 1970), and Nicaragua; Costa Rica joined 1962. Formed to encourage economic development and cooperation between the smaller Central American nations and to attract industrial capital, CACM failed to live up to early expectations: nationalist interests remained strong and by the mid-1980s political instability in the region and border conflicts between members were hindering its activities.

Central Asian Republics group of five republics: ◊Kazakhstan, ◊Kyrgyzstan, ◊Tajikistan, ◊Turkmenistan, and ◊Uzbekistan. Formerly part of the Soviet Union, their independence was recognized 1991. They comprise a large part of the geographical region of Turkestan and are the home of large numbers of Muslims.

Central Command military strike force consisting of units from the US army, navy, and air force, which operates in the Middle East and North Africa. Its headquarters are in Fort McDill, Florida. It was established 1979, following the Iranian hostage crisis and the Soviet invasion of Afghanistan, and was known as the Rapid Deployment Force until 1983. It commanded coalition forces in the Gulf War 1991.

Plagued by organizational problems, interservice rivalries, equipment shortages, and lack of access to bases in the Middle East, it was reorganized by President Reagan in 1983 as the US Central Command.

Central Intelligence Agency (CIA) US intelligence organization established 1947. It has actively intervened overseas, generally to undermine left-wing regimes or to protect US financial interests; for example, in the Congo (now Zaire) and Nicaragua. From 1980 all covert activity by the CIA has by law to be reported to Congress, preferably beforehand, and must be authorized by the president. In 1990 the CIA's estimated budget was $10–12 billion. Robert James Woolsey became CIA director 1993.

central nervous system (CNS) the part of the nervous system that coordinates various body functions. It has a high concentration of nerve-cell bodies and synapses (junctions between ◊nerve cells). In ◊vertebrates, the CNS consists of a brain and a dorsal nerve cord (the spinal cord) enclosed and protected within

Central African Republic
(*République Centrafricaine*)

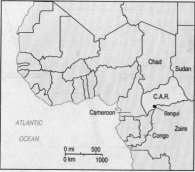

area 240,260 sq mi/622,436 sq km
capital Bangui
cities Berbérati, Bouar, Bossangoa
physical landlocked flat plateau, with rivers flowing N and S, and hills in NE and SW; dry in N, rain forest in SW
environment an estimated 87% of the urban population is without access to safe drinking water
features Kotto and Mbali river falls; the Oubangui River rises 20 ft/6 m at Bangui during the wet season (June–Nov)
head of state André Kolingba from 1981
head of government Enoch Derant Lakoue from 1993
political system one-party military republic
political parties Central African Democratic Assembly (RDC), nationalist; all political activity has been banned since the 1981 coup, but the main opposition groups, although passive, still exist. They are the Patriotic Front Ubangi Workers' Party (FPO-PT), the Central African Movement for National Liberation (MCLN), and the Movement for the Liberation of the Central African People (MPLC)

exports diamonds, uranium, coffee, cotton, timber, tobacco
currency CFA franc
population (1992)2,930,000 (more than 80 ethnic groups); growth rate 2.3% p.a.
life expectancy men 41, women 45
languages Sangho (national), French (official), Arabic, Hunsa, and Swahili
religions Protestant 25%, Roman Catholic 25%, Muslim 10%, animist 10%
literacy men 53%, women 29% (1985 est)
GDP $1 bn (1987); $374 per head

chronology
1960 Central African Republic achieved independence from France; David Dacko elected president.
1962 The republic made a one-party state.
1965 Dacko ousted in military coup led by Col Bokassa.
1966 Constitution rescinded and national assembly dissolved.
1972 Bokassa declared himself president for life.
1977 Bokassa made himself emperor of the Central African Empire.
1979 Bokassa deposed by Dacko following violent repressive measures by the self-styled emperor, who went into exile.
1981 Dacko deposed in a bloodless coup, led by General André Kolingba, and an all-military government established.
1983 Clandestine opposition movement formed.
1984 Amnesty for all political party leaders announced. President Mitterrand of France paid a state visit.
1985 New constitution promised, with some civilians in the government.
1986 Bokassa returned from France, expecting to return to power; he was imprisoned and his trial started. General Kolingba reelected. New constitution approved by referendum.
1988 Bokassa found guilty and received death sentence, later commuted to life imprisonment.
1992 Abortive debate held on political reform; multiparty elections promised but then postponed.
1993 Enoch Derant Lakoue appointed prime minister.

the spinal column. In worms, insects, and crustaceans, it consists of a paired ventral nerve cord with concentrations of nerve-cell bodies, known as ◊*ganglia* in each segment, and a small brain in the head.

Central Powers originally the signatories of the ◊Triple Alliance 1882: Germany, Austria-Hungary, and Italy. During World War I, Italy remained neutral before joining the ◊Allies.

central processing unit (CPU) main component of a computer, the part that executes individual program instructions and controls the operation of other parts. It is sometimes called the central processor or, when contained on a single integrated circuit, a microprocessor. *See illustration p. 182*

Central Treaty Organization (CENTO) military alliance that replaced the Baghdad Pact 1959; it collapsed when the withdrawal of Iran, Pakistan, and Turkey 1979 left the UK as the only member.

Centre region of N central France; area 15,131 sq mi/ 39,200 sq km; population (1986) 2,324,000. Centre includes the *départements* of Cher, Eure-et-Loire, Indre, Indre-et-Loire, Loire-et-Cher, and Loiret. Its capital is Orléans.

centrifugal force useful concept in physics, based on an apparent (but not real) force. It may be regarded as a force that acts radially outward from a spinning or orbiting object, thus balancing the ◊centripetal force (which is real). For an object of mass m moving

with a velocity v in a circle of radius r, the centrifugal force F equals mv^2/r (outward).

centrifuge apparatus that rotates at high speeds, causing substances inside it to be thrown outward. One use is for separating mixtures of substances of different densities.

centripetal force force that acts radially inward on an object moving in a curved path. For example, with a weight whirled in a circle at the end of a length of string, the centripetal force is the tension in the string. For an object of mass m moving with a velocity v in a circle of radius r, the centripetal force F equals mv^2/r (inward). The reaction to this force is the ◊centrifugal force.

cephalopod any predatory marine mollusk of the class Cephalopoda, with the mouth and head surrounded by tentacles. Cephalopods are the most intelligent, the fastest-moving, and the largest of all animals without backbones, and there are remarkable luminescent forms which swim or drift at great depths. They have the most highly developed nervous and sensory systems of all invertebrates, the eye in some closely paralleling that found in vertebrates. Examples include octopus, squid, and cuttlefish. Shells are rudimentary or absent in most cephalopods.

Cepheus constellation of the north polar region, named after King Cepheus of Greek mythology, husband of Cassiopeia and father of Andromeda. It contains the Garnet Star (Mu Cephei), a red supergiant of

CPU

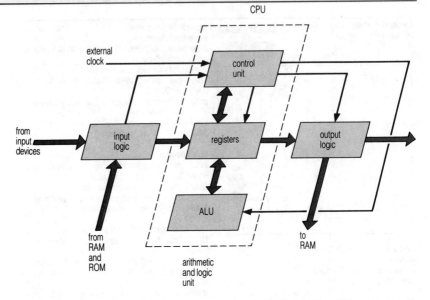

external clock

control unit

from input devices

input logic

registers

output logic

ALU

from RAM and ROM

to RAM

arithmetic and logic unit

variable brightness that is one of the reddest-colored stars known, and Delta Cephei, prototype of the Cepheid variables.

ceramic nonmetallic mineral (clay) used to form articles that are then fired at high temperatures. Ceramics are divided into heavy clay products (bricks, roof tiles, drainpipes, sanitary ware), refractories or high-temperature materials (linings for furnaces used to manufacture steel, fuel elements in nuclear reactors), and pottery, which uses kaolinite, ball clay, china stone, and flint. Superceramics, such as silicon carbide, are lighter, stronger, and more heat-resistant than steel for use in motor and aircraft engines and have to be cast to shape since they are too hard to machine.

The earliest ceramics date back to the beginning of the Neolithic in the Near East, Asia, the Americas, Europe, and Africa.

Cerberus in Greek mythology, the three-headed dog guarding the entrance to ◊Hades, the underworld.

cereal grass grown for its edible, nutrient-rich, starchy seeds. The term refers primarily to wheat, oats, rye, and barley, but may also refer to corn, millet, and rice. Cereals contain about 75% complex carbohydrates and 10% protein, plus fats and fiber (roughage). They store well. If all the world's cereal crop were consumed as whole-grain products directly by humans, everyone could obtain adequate protein and carbohydrate; however, a large proportion of cereal production in affluent nations is used as animal feed to boost the production of meat, dairy products, and eggs.

cerebellum part of the brain of ◊vertebrate animals which controls muscular movements, balance, and coordination. It is relatively small in lower animals such as newts and lizards, but large in birds since flight demands precise coordination. The human cerebellum is also well developed, because of the need for balance when walking or running, and for coordinated hand movements.

cerebral hemorrhage or ***apoplectic fit*** in medicine, a ◊stroke in which a blood vessel bursts in the brain, caused by factors such as high blood pressure combined with hardening of the arteries, or chronic poisoning with lead or alcohol. It may cause death or damage parts of the brain, leading to paralysis or mental impairment. The effects are usually long-term and the condition may recur.

cerebral palsy any nonprogressive abnormality of the brain caused by oxygen deprivation before birth, injury during birth, hemorrhage, meningitis, viral infection, or faulty development. It is characterized by muscle spasm, weakness, lack of coordination, and impaired movement. Intelligence is not always affected.

cerebrovascular accident (CVA) alternate name for ◊stroke.

cerebrum part of the vertebrate ◊brain, formed from the two paired cerebral hemispheres. In birds and mammals it is the largest part of the brain. It is covered with an infolded layer of gray matter, the cerebral cortex, which integrates brain functions. The cerebrum coordinates the senses, and is responsible for learning and other higher mental faculties.

Ceres the largest asteroid, 584 mi/940 km in diameter, and the first to be discovered (by Italian astronomer Giuseppe Piazzi 1801). Ceres orbits the Sun every 4.6 years at an average distance of 257 million mi/414 million km. Its mass is about one-seventieth of that of the Moon.

Ceres in Roman mythology, the goddess of agriculture, equivalent to the Greek ◊Demeter.

Cerf Bennett Alfred 1898–1971. US editor and publisher. In 1925 he co-purchased the rights to the Modern Library series, and subsequently founded Random House 1927. The company grew to be one of the world's largest publishing houses.

cerium malleable and ductile, gray, metallic element, symbol Ce, atomic number 58, atomic weight 140.12. It is the most abundant member of the lanthanide series, and is used in alloys, electronic components, nuclear fuels, and lighter flints. It was discovered 1804 by the Swedish chemists Jöns Berzelius and Wilhelm Hisinger (1766–1852), and, independently, by Martin Klaproth. The element was named after the then recently discovered asteroid Ceres.

Cézanne Mountains in Provence *(c. 1886),* National Gallery, London.

CERN nuclear research organization founded 1954 as a cooperative enterprise among European governments. It has laboratories at Meyrin, near Geneva, Switzerland. It was originally known as the *Conseil Européen pour la Recherche Nucléaire* but subsequently renamed *Organisation Euro-péenne pour la Recherche Nucléaire*, although still familiarly known as CERN. It houses the world's largest particle ◊accelerator, the ◊Large Electron–Positron Collider (LEP), with which notable advances have been made in ◊particle physics.

Cervantes Saavedra, Miguel de 1547–1616. Spanish novelist, playwright, and poet whose masterpiece *Don Quixote* (in full *El ingenioso hidalgo Don Quixote de la Mancha*) was published 1605. In 1613, his *Novelas ejemplares/Exemplary Novels* appeared, followed by *Viaje del Parnaso/The Voyage to Parnassus* 1614. A spurious second part of *Don Quixote* prompted Cervantes to bring out his own second part 1615, often considered superior to the first in construction and characterization.

cervix (Latin "neck") abbreviation for *cervix uteri*, the neck of the womb.

cesium (Latin *caesius* "bluish-gray") soft, silvery-white, ductile, metallic element, symbol Cs, atomic number 55, atomic weight 132.905. It is one of the ◊alkali metals, and is the most electropositive of all the elements. In air it ignites spontaneously, and it reacts vigorously with water. It is used in the manufacture of photoelectric cells.

Cetewayo HF (Cetshwayo) *c.* 1826–1884. King of Zululand, South Africa, 1873–83, whose rule was threatened by British annexation of the Transvaal 1877. Although he defeated the British at Isandhlwana 1879, he was later that year defeated by them at Ulundi. Restored to his throne 1883, he was then expelled by his subjects.

Cetus constellation straddling the celestial equator (see ◊celestial sphere), represented as a sea monster. Cetus contains the long-period variable star ◊Mira, and Tau Ceti, one of the nearest stars visible with the naked eye.

Ceylon former name (until 1972) of ◊Sri Lanka.

Cézanne Paul 1839–1906. French Post-Impressionist painter, a leading figure in the development of modern art. He broke away from the Impressionists' spontaneous vision to develop a style that captured not only light and life, but the structure of natural forms in landscapes, still lifes, portraits, and his series of bathers.

CFC abbreviation for ◊*chlorofluorocarbon*.

Chaco province of Argentina; area 38,458 sq mi/99,633 sq km; population (1991) 838,300. Its capital is Resistencia, in the SE. The chief crop is cotton.

Chad landlocked country in central N Africa, bounded N by Libya, E by Sudan, S by the Central African Republic, and W by Cameroon, Nigeria, and Niger. *See panel p. 184*

Chad, Lake lake on the NE boundary of Nigeria. It once varied in extent between rainy and dry seasons from 20,000 sq mi/50,000 sq km to 7,000 sq mi/20,000 sq km, but a series of droughts 1979–89 reduced its area by 80%. The S Chad irrigation project used the lake waters to irrigate the surrounding desert, but the 2,500 mi/4,000 km of canals dug for the project are now permanently dry because of the shrinking size of the lake. The Lake Chad basin is being jointly developed for oil and natron by Cameroon, Chad, Niger, and Nigeria.

Chadli Benjedid 1929– . Algerian socialist politician, president 1979–92. An army colonel, he supported Boumédienne in the overthrow of Ben Bella 1965, and succeeded Boumédienne 1979, pursuing more moderate policies. Chadli resigned Jan 1992 following a victory for Islamic fundamentalists in the first round of assembly elections.

Chad Republic of
(*République du Tchad*)

area 495,624 sq mi/1,284,000 sq km
capital Ndjamena (formerly Fort Lamy)
cities Sarh, Moundou, Abéché
physical landlocked state with mountains and part of Sahara Desert in N; moist savanna in S; rivers in S flow NW to Lake Chad
head of state Idriss Deby from 1990
head of government Fuidel Mounyar (interim) 1993
political system emergent democratic republic
political parties National Union for Independence and Revolution (UNIR), nationalist; Alliance for Democracy and Progress (RDP), center-left; Union for Democracy and Progress (UPDT), center-left
exports cotton, meat, livestock, hides, skins
currency CFA franc
population (1992) 5,961,000; growth rate 2.3% p.a. Nomadic tribes move N–S seasonally in search of water
life expectancy men 42, women 45
languages French, Arabic (both official), over 100 African languages spoken
religions Muslim 44% (N), Christian 33%, animist 23% (S)
literacy men 40%, women 11% (1985 est)
GDP $980 million (1986); $186 per head

chronology
1960 Independence achieved from France, with François Tombalbaye as president.
1963 Violent opposition in the Muslim north, led by the Chadian National Liberation Front (Frolinat), backed by Libya.
1968 Revolt quelled with France's help.
1975 Tombalbaye killed in military coup led by Félix Malloum. Frolinat continued its resistance.
1978 Malloum tried to find a political solution by bringing the former Frolinat leader Hissène Habré into his government but they were unable to work together.
1979 Malloum forced to leave the country; an interim government was set up under General Goukouni. Habré continued his opposition with his Army of the North (FAN).
1981 Habré now in control of half the country. Goukouni fled and set up a "government in exile."
1983 Habré's regime recognized by the Organization for African Unity (OAU), but in the north Goukouni's supporters, with Libya's help, fought on. Eventually a cease-fire was agreed, with latitude 16°N dividing the country.
1984 Libya and France agreed to a withdrawal of forces.
1985 Fighting between Libyan-backed and French-backed forces intensified.
1987 Chad, France, and Libya agreed on cease-fire proposed by OAU.
1988 Full diplomatic relations with Libya restored.
1989 Libyan troop movements reported on border; Habré reelected, amended constitution.
1990 President Habré ousted in coup led by Idriss Deby. New constitution adopted.
1991 Several antigovernment coups foiled.
1992 Antigovernment coup foiled. Two new opposition parties approved.
1993 Fuidel Mounyar chosen as transitional prime minister pending multiparty elections.

Chadwick James 1891–1974. British physicist. In 1932 he discovered the particle in the nucleus of an atom that became known as the neutron because it has no electric charge. He received the Nobel Prize for Physics 1935.

chaffinch bird *Fringilla coelebs* of the finch family, common throughout much of Europe and W Asia. About 6 in/15 cm long, the male is olive-brown above, with a bright chestnut breast, a bluish-gray cap, and two white bands on the upper part of the wing; the female is duller.

Chagall Marc 1887–1985. Russian-born French painter and designer; much of his highly colored, fantastic imagery was inspired by the village life of his boyhood and by Jewish and Russian folk tradition. He also designed stained glass, mosaics (for Israel's Knesset in the 1960s), the ceiling of the Paris Opera House 1964, tapestries, and stage sets. He was an original figure, often seen as a precursor of Surrealism, as in *The Dream* (Metropolitan Museum of Art, New York).

Chain Ernst Boris 1906–1979. German-born British biochemist who worked on the development of ◊penicillin. Chain fled to Britain from the Nazis 1933. After the discovery of penicillin by Alexander Fleming, Chain worked to isolate and purify it. For this work, he shared the 1945 Nobel Prize for Medicine with Fleming and Howard Florey. Chain also discovered penicillinase, an enzyme that destroys penicillin.

chain reaction in chemistry, a succession of reactions, usually involving ◊free radicals, where the products of one stage are the reactants of the next. A chain reaction is characterized by the continual generation of reactive substances.

chain reaction in nuclear physics, a fission reaction that is maintained because neutrons released by the splitting of some atomic nuclei themselves go on to split others, releasing even more neutrons. Such a reaction can be controlled (as in a nuclear reactor) by using moderators to absorb excess neutrons. Uncontrolled, a chain reaction produces a nuclear explosion (as in an atomic bomb).

Chalatenango department on the northern frontier of El Salvador; area 968 sq mi/2,507 sq km; population (1981) 235,700. The capital is Chalatenango.

Chalcedon, Council of ecumenical council of the early Christian church, convoked 451 by the Roman emperor Marcian, and held at Chalcedon (now Kadiköy, Turkey). The council, attended by over 500 bishops, resulted in the *Definition of Chalcedon*, an agreed doctrine for both the eastern and western churches.

chalcedony form of quartz, SiO_2, in which the crystals are so fine-grained that they are impossible to distinguish with a microscope (cryptocrystalline). Agate, onyx, and carnelian are ◊gem varieties of chalcedony.

chalcopyrite copper iron sulfide, $CuFeS_2$, the most common ore of copper. It is brassy yellow in color and may have an iridescent surface tarnish. It occurs in many different types of mineral vein, in rocks ranging from basalt to limestone.

chalk soft, fine-grained, whitish rock composed of calcium carbonate, $CaCO_3$, extensively quarried for use in cement, lime, and mortar, and in the manufacture of cosmetics and toothpaste. **Blackboard chalk** in fact consists of ◊gypsum (calcium sulfate, $CaSO_4 \cdot 2H_2$).

Chamberlain (Arthur) Neville 1869–1940. British Conservative politician, son of Joseph Chamberlain. He was prime minister 1937–40; his policy of appeasement toward the fascist dictators Mussolini and Hitler (with whom he concluded the ◊Munich Agreement 1938) failed to prevent the outbreak of World War II. He resigned 1940 following the defeat of the British forces in Norway.

In 1938 Chamberlain went to Munich, Germany, and negotiated with Hitler on the Czechoslovak question. He was ecstatically received on his return and claimed that the Munich Agreement brought "peace in our time". However, Germany advanced against British allies and within a year Britain was at war.

Chamberlain (Joseph) Austen 1863–1937. British Conservative politician, elder son of Joseph Chamberlain; as foreign secretary 1924–29 he negotiated the Pact of Locarno, for which he won the Nobel Peace Prize 1925, and signed the ◊Kellogg–Briand pact to outlaw war 1928.

Chamberlain Owen 1920– . US physicist whose graduate studies were interrupted by wartime work on the Manhattan Project at Los Alamos. After World War II, working with Italian physicist Emilio Segrè, he discovered the existence of the antiproton. Both men were awarded the Nobel Prize for Physics 1959.

Chamberlain Wilt (Wilton Norman) 1936– . US basketball player who set a record by averaging 50.4 points a game during the 1962 season, and was the only man to score 100 points in a game. He played professionally for the Philadelphia Warriors, Philadelphia 76ers, Los Angeles Lakers, and briefly for the ◊Harlem Globetrotters. Playing against the New York Knickerbockers 1962 he became the only man to score 100 points in a National Basketball Association (NBA) game. He was the only center to lead the league in assists. He led the league in scoring 1960–66, was NBA Most Valuable Player 1960, 1966–68, and retired 1973 after a 13-year career.

chamber music music suitable for performance in a small room or chamber, rather than in the concert hall, and usually written for instrumental combinations, played with one instrument to a part, as in the string quartet.

chameleon any of some 80 or so species of lizard of the family Chameleontidae. Some species have highly developed color-changing abilities, which are caused by changes in the intensity of light, of temperature, and of emotion altering the dispersal of pigment granules in the layers of cells beneath the outer skin.

chamois goatlike mammal *Rupicapra rupicapra* found in mountain ranges of S Europe and Asia Minor. It is brown, with dark patches running through the eyes, and can be up to 2.6 ft/80 cm high. Chamois are very sure-footed, and live in herds of up to 30 members.

Chamorro Violeta Barrios de *c.* 1939– . President of Nicaragua from 1990. With strong US support, she was elected to be the candidate for the National Oppo-

Chagall Don Quixote *(1975), private collection, by French painter Marc Chagall.*

sition Union (UNO) 1989, winning the presidency from David Ortega Saavedra Feb 1990 and thus ending the period of Sandinista rule.

champagne sparkling white wine invented by Dom Pérignon, a Benedictine monk, 1668. It is made from a blend of grapes (*pinot noir* and *pinot chardonnay*) grown in the Marne River region around Reims and Epernay, in Champagne, NE France. After a first fermentation, sugar and yeast are added to the still wine, which, when bottled, undergoes a second fermentation to produce the sparkle. Sugar syrup may be added to make the wine sweet (*sec*) or dry (*brut*).

Champagne-Ardenne region of NE France; area 9,882 sq mi/25,600 sq km; population (1986) 1,353,000. Its capital is Reims, and it comprises the *départements* of Ardennes, Aube, Marne, and Haute-Marne. It has sheep and dairy farming and vineyards.

Champaign city in E central Illinois, directly W of Urbana; population (1990) 63,500. Industries include

chameleon Meller's chameleon of the savanna of Tanzania and Malawi is the largest chameleon found outside Madagascar, about 1.7 ft/55 cm long.

electronic equipment, academic clothing, and air-conditioning equipment. Together with Urbana, it is the site of the University of Illinois.

Champion v Ames US Supreme Court decision 1903 that gave judicial sanction to the use of federal police power. Champion, arrested for shipping lottery tickets across state lines, in violation of the Federal Lottery Act 1895, filed suit against the federal government, arguing that the act infringed on the police power of the states. The Court upheld the Lottery Act 5 to 4, ruling that the federal government had the right to use its regulatory and prohibitive powers in the interest of the public good.

Champlain Samuel de 1567–1635. French pioneer, soldier, and explorer in Canada. Having served in the army of Henry IV and on an expedition to the West Indies, he began his exploration of Canada 1603. In a third expedition 1608 he founded and named Québec, and was appointed lieutenant governor of French Canada 1612.

Champlain, Lake lake in NE US (extending some 6 mi/10 km into Canada) on the New York–Vermont border; length 125 mi/201 km; area 430 sq mi/692 sq km. It is linked by canal to the St Lawrence and Hudson rivers.

Champollion Jean François, le Jeune 1790–1832. French Egyptologist who in 1822 deciphered Egyptian hieroglyphics with the aid of the ◊Rosetta Stone.

chance likelihood, or ◊probability, of an event taking place, expressed as a fraction or percentage. For example, the chance that a tossed coin will land heads up is 50%.

Chandigarh city of N India, in the foothills of the Himalayas; population (1981) 421,000. It is also a Union Territory; area 44 sq mi/114 sq km; population (1991) 640,725.

Chandler Happy (Albert Benjamin) 1898–1991. US politician and sports administrator. He was governor of Kentucky 1934–39 and 1955–59. After his first term as governor he resigned to enter the US Senate. In 1945 Chandler was appointed baseball commissioner but resigned 1951, mainly because of personality conflicts with several team owners.

Chandler Raymond 1888–1959. US crime writer who created the hard-boiled private eye Philip Marlowe in books that include *The Big Sleep* 1939, *Farewell, My Lovely* 1940, and *The Long Goodbye* 1954.

Many of his books have been made into popular Hollywood films. He also wrote numerous screenplays, notably *Double Indemnity* 1944 and *Strangers on a Train* 1951.

Chandragupta Maurya ruler of N India *c.* 325–*c.* 297 BC, founder of the Mauryan dynasty. He overthrew the Nanda dynasty 325 and then conquered the Punjab 322 after the death of ◊Alexander the Great, expanding his empire west to Persia. He is credited with having united most of India.

Chanel Coco (Gabrielle) 1883–1971. French fashion designer, creator of the "little black dress," informal cardigan suit, costume jewelry, and perfumes.

Chaney Lon (Alonso) 1883–1930. US star of silent films, often in grotesque or monstrous roles such as *The Phantom of the Opera* 1925. A master of makeup, he was nicknamed "the Man of a Thousand Faces." He sometimes used extremely painful devices for added effect, as in the title role in *The Hunchback of Notre Dame* 1923, when he carried over 70 lb/30 kg of costume in the form of a heavy hump and harness.

Chaney Lon, Jr (Creighton) 1906–1973. US actor (son of Lon Chaney) who gave an acclaimed performance as Lennie in *Of Mice and Men* 1940. He went on to star in many 1940s horror films, including the title role in *The Wolf Man* 1941. His other work includes *My Favorite Brunette* 1947 and *The Haunted Palace* 1963.

Changchun industrial city and capital of Jilin province, China; population (1989) 2,020,000. Machinery and motor vehicles are manufactured. It is also the center of an agricultural district.

Chang Jiang or *Yangtze Kiang* longest river of China, flowing about 3,900 mi/6,300 km from Tibet to the Yellow Sea. It is a main commercial waterway.

Changsha port on the river Chang Jiang, capital of Hunan province, China; population (1989) 1,300,000. It trades in rice, tea, timber, and nonferrous metals; works antimony, lead, and silver; and produces chemicals, electronics, porcelain, and embroideries.

Channel Islands group of islands in the English Channel, off the NW coast of France; they are a possession of the British crown. They comprise the islands of Jersey, Guernsey, Alderney, Great and Little Sark, with the lesser Herm, Brechou, Jethou, and Lihou.

Channel Tunnel tunnel built beneath the English Channel, linking Britain and mainland Europe. It comprises twin rail tunnels, 31 mi/50 km long and 24 ft/ 7.3 m in diameter, located 130 ft/40 m beneath the seabed. Specially designed shuttle trains carrying automobiles and trucks will run between terminals at Folkestone, Kent, England, and Sangatte, W of Calais, France. It was begun 1986, and the French and English sections were linked Dec 1990. It was officially opened May 6, 1994.

Channing William Ellery 1780–1842. US minister and theologian. He became a leader of the Unitarian movement 1819, opposing the strict Calvinism of the New England Congregationalist churches. He was an instrumental figure in the establishment of the American Unitarian Association. In his later years, Channing devoted his energies to abolitionism in its campaign to end the institution of slavery.

Chanson de Roland early 12th-century epic poem which tells of the real and imaginary deeds of Roland and other knights of Charlemagne, and their last stand against the Basques at Roncesvalles.

chant singing of a formula, usually by a group, for confidence or spiritual improvement. Chants can be secular or religious, both Western and Eastern. Ambrosian and ◊Gregorian chants are forms of ◊plainsong melody.

chapel place of worship used by some Christian denominations; also, a part of a building used for Christian worship. A large church or cathedral may have several chapels.

Chaplin Charlie (Charles Spencer) 1889–1977. English film actor and director. He made his reputation as a tramp with a smudge moustache, bowler hat, and twirling cane in silent comedies from the mid-1910s, including *The Rink* 1916, *The Kid* 1920, and *The Gold Rush* 1925. His work often contrasts buffoonery with pathos, and his later films combine dialogue with mime and music, as in *The Great Dictator* 1940 and *Limelight* 1952. He was one of cinema's most popular and greatest stars. *See illustration p. 188*

Chapman John ("Johnny Appleseed") 1774–1845. US pioneer and folk hero, credited with establishing orchards throughout the Midwest by planting seeds

Channel tunnel

The rail link between the UK and France has the potential to reduce the travel time between London and Paris to about three hours, matching the total time of a journey by air. An Anglo-French consortium raised monry for work to begin at both ends of the projected route in 1987, and the tunnel was officially opened in May 1994.

The machines used to bore the Channel tunnel each weigh almost 500 tons. They have rotating heads with tungsten-carbide "picks," and special trains travel behind them to deliver equipment and remove debris. 700,000 concrete segments will form the tunnel lining, and trackwork, mechanical and electrical equipment and signals will be installed.▶

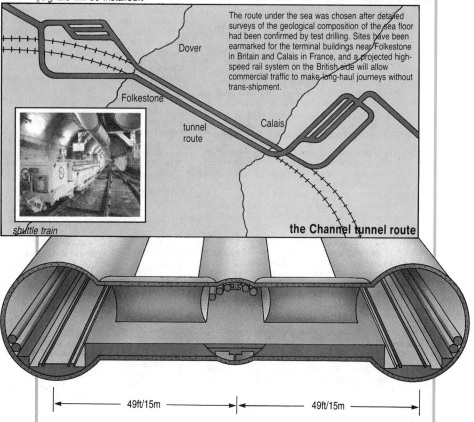

Dover

Folkestone

tunnel route

Calais

The route under the sea was chosen after detailed surveys of the geological composition of the sea floor had been confirmed by test drilling. Sites have been earmarked for the terminal buildings near Folkestone in Britain and Calais in France, and a projected high-speed rail system on the British side will allow commercial traffic to make long-haul journeys without trans-shipment.

shuttle train   the Channel tunnel route

|← 49ft/15m →|← 49ft/15m →|

There are two main tunnels, each carrying trains traveling in one direction only. Between them is a service tunnel, supplying fresh air to the system. Special precautions are being taken to prevent rabid animals from using the tunnel to reach Britain, which is rabies-free.

Chaplin English actor Charlie Chaplin, probably the most famous comic actor in cinema history, seen here with Jackie Coogan in The Kid 1920.

as he traveled. Famous as the subject of local legends and folk tales, Chapman was described as a religious visionary with boundless generosity.

charcoal black, porous form of ◊carbon, produced by heating wood or other organic materials in the absence of air. It is used as a fuel in the smelting of metals such as copper and zinc, and by artists for making black line drawings. *Activated charcoal* has been powdered and dried so that it presents a much increased surface area for adsorption; it is used for filtering and purifying liquids and gases—for example, in drinking-water filters and gas masks.

Chardin Jean-Baptiste-Siméon 1699–1779. French painter of naturalistic still lifes and quiet domestic scenes that recall the Dutch tradition. His work is a complete contrast to that of his contemporaries, the Rococo painters. He developed his own technique using successive layers of paint to achieve depth of tone and is generally considered one of the finest exponents of the genre.

charge-coupled device (CCD) device for forming images electronically, using a layer of silicon that releases electrons when struck by incoming light. The electrons are stored in pixels and read off into a computer at the end of the exposure. CCDs have now almost entirely replaced photographic film for applications such as astrophotography where extreme sensitivity to light is paramount.

charged particle beam high-energy beam of electrons or protons. Such beams are being developed as weapons.

Charge of the Light Brigade disastrous attack by the British Light Brigade of cavalry against the Russian entrenched artillery on Oct 25, 1854, during the Crimean War at the Battle of ◊Balaclava.

chariot horse-drawn carriage with two wheels, used in ancient Egypt, Greece, and Rome, for fighting, processions, and races; it is thought to have originated in Asia. Typically, the fighting chariot contained a driver and a warrior, who would fight on foot, with the chariot providing rapid mobility.

charismatic movement late 20th-century movement within the Christian church that emphasizes the role of the Holy Spirit in the life of the individual

believer and in the life of the church. See ◊Pentecostal movement.

Charlemagne Charles I *the Great* 742–814. King of the Franks from 768 and Holy Roman emperor from 800. By inheritance (his father was ◊Pepin the Short) and extensive campaigns of conquest, he united most of W Europe by 804, when after 30 years of war the Saxons came under his control. He reformed the legal, judicial, and military systems; established schools; and promoted Christianity, commerce, agriculture, arts, and literature. In his capital, Aachen, scholars gathered from all over Europe.

Charles (Mary) Eugenia 1919– . Dominican politician, prime minister from 1980; cofounder and first leader of the centrist Dominica Freedom Party (DFP). Two years after Dominica's independence the DFP won the 1980 general election and she became the Caribbean's first female prime minister.

Charles Jacques Alexandre César 1746–1823. French physicist who studied gases and made the first ascent in a hydrogen-filled balloon 1783. His work on the expansion of gases led to the formulation of ◊Charles's law.

Charles Ray 1930– . US singer, songwriter, and pianist whose first hits were "I've Got A Woman" 1955, "What'd I Say" 1959, and "Georgia on My Mind" 1960. He has recorded gospel, blues, rock, soul, country, and rhythm and blues.

Charles I 1600–1649. King of Great Britain and Ireland from 1625, son of James I of England (James VI of Scotland). He accepted the petition of right 1628 but then dissolved Parliament and ruled without a parliament 1629–40. His advisers were Strafford and Laud, who persecuted the Puritans and provoked the Scots to revolt. The ◊Short Parliament, summoned 1640, refused funds, and the ◊Long Parliament later that year rebelled. Charles declared war on Parliament 1642 but surrendered 1646 and was beheaded 1649. He was the father of Charles II.

Charles II 1630–1685. King of Great Britain and Ireland from 1660, when Parliament accepted the restoration of the monarchy after the collapse of Cromwell's Commonwealth; son of Charles I. His chief minister Clarendon, who arranged his marriage 1662 with Catherine of Braganza, was replaced 1667 with the Cabal of advisers. His plans to restore Catholicism in Britain led to war with the Netherlands 1672–74 in support of Louis XIV of France and a break with Parliament, which he dissolved 1681. He was succeeded by James II.

Charles (full name Charles Philip Arthur George) 1948– . Prince of the UK, heir to the British throne, and Prince of Wales since 1958 (invested 1969). He is the first-born child of Queen Elizabeth II and the Duke of Edinburgh. He studied at Trinity College, Cambridge, 1967–70, before serving in the Royal Air Force and Royal Navy. He is the first royal heir since 1659 to have an English wife, Lady Diana Spencer, daughter of the 8th Earl Spencer. They have two sons and heirs, William (1982–) and Henry (1984–). Amid much publicity, Charles and Diana separated 1992.

Charles I king of France, better known as the Holy Roman emperor ◊Charlemagne.

Charles II *the Bald* king of France, see ◊Charles II, Holy Roman emperor.

Charles III *the Simple* 879–929. King of France 893–922, son of Louis the Stammerer. He was crowned

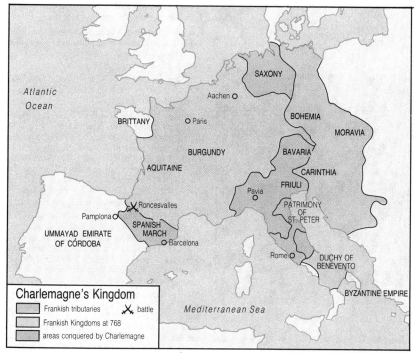

Charlemagne's Kingdom

- Frankish tributaries   ✗ battle
- Frankish Kingdoms at 768
- areas conquered by Charlemagne

at Reims. In 911 he ceded what later became the duchy of Normandy to the Norman chief Rollo.

Charles V *the Wise* 1337–1380. King of France from 1364. He was regent during the captivity of his father, John II, in England 1356–60, and became king on John's death. He reconquered nearly all France from England 1369–80.

Charles VI *the Mad* or *the Well-Beloved* 1368–1422. King of France from 1380, succeeding his father Charles V; he was under the regency of his uncles until 1388. He became mentally unstable 1392, and civil war broke out between the dukes of Orléans and Burgundy. Henry V of England invaded France 1415, conquering Normandy, and in 1420 forced Charles to sign the Treaty of Troyes, recognizing Henry as his successor.

Charles VII 1403–1461. King of France from 1429. Son of Charles VI, he was excluded from the succession by the Treaty of Troyes, but recognized by the south of France. In 1429 Joan of Arc raised the siege of Orléans and had him crowned at Reims. He organized France's first standing army and by 1453 had expelled the English from all of France except Calais.

Charles X 1757–1836. King of France from 1824. Grandson of Louis XV and brother of Louis XVI and Louis XVIII, he was known as the comte d'Artois before his accession. He fled to England at the beginning of the French Revolution, and when he came to the throne on the death of Louis XVIII, he attempted to reverse the achievements of the revolution. A revolt ensued 1830, and he again fled to England.

Charles I Holy Roman emperor, better known as ◊Charlemagne.

Charles II *the Bald* 823–877. Holy Roman emperor from 875 and (as Charles II) king of France from 843. Younger son of Louis I (the Pious), he warred against his eldest brother, Emperor Lothair I. The Treaty of Verdun 843 made him king of the West Frankish Kingdom (now France and the Spanish Marches).

Charles III *the Fat* 839–888. Holy Roman emperor 881–87; he became king of the West Franks 885, thus uniting for the last time the whole of Charlemagne's dominions, but was deposed.

Charles IV 1316–1378. Holy Roman emperor from 1355 and king of Bohemia from 1346. Son of John of Luxembourg, king of Bohemia, he was elected king of Germany 1346 and ruled all Germany from 1347. He was the founder of the first German university in Prague 1348.

Charles V 1500–1558. Holy Roman emperor 1519–56. Son of Philip of Burgundy and Joanna of Castile, he inherited vast possessions, which led to rivalry from Francis I of France, whose alliance with the Ottoman Empire brought Vienna under siege 1529 and 1532. Charles was also in conflict with the Protestants in Germany until the Treaty of Passau 1552, which allowed the Lutherans religious liberty. *See illustration p. 190*

Charles VI 1685–1740. Holy Roman emperor from 1711, father of ◊Maria Theresa, whose succession to his Austrian dominions he tried to ensure, and himself claimant to the Spanish throne 1700, thus causing the War of the ◊Spanish Succession.

Charles VII 1697–1745. Holy Roman emperor from 1742, opponent of ◊Maria Theresa's claim to the Austrian dominions of Charles VI.

Charles (Karl Franz Josef) 1887–1922. Emperor of Austria and king of Hungary from 1916, the last of the Hapsburg emperors. He succeeded his great-uncle Franz Josef 1916 but was forced to withdraw to Switzerland 1918, although he refused to abdicate. In 1921 he attempted unsuccessfully to regain the crown of Hungary and was deported to Madeira.

Charles V Holy
Roman emperor and
king of Spain Charles
V aimed to preserve
the medieval idea of
the empire.

Charles III 1716–1788. King of Spain from 1759. Son of Philip V, he became duke of Parma 1732 and conquered Naples and Sicily 1734. On the death of his half brother Ferdinand VI (1713–1759), he became king of Spain, handing over Naples and Sicily to his son Ferdinand (1751–1825). At home, he reformed state finances, strengthened the armed forces, and expelled the Jesuits. During his reign, Spain was involved in the Seven Years' War with France against England. This led to the loss of Florida 1763, which was only regained when Spain and France supported the colonists during the American Revolution.

Charles IV 1748–1819. King of Spain from 1788, when he succeeded his father, Charles III; he left the government in the hands of his wife and her lover, the minister Manuel de Godoy (1767–1851). In 1808 Charles was induced to abdicate by Napoleon's machinations in favor of his son Ferdinand VII (1784–1833), who was subsequently deposed by Napoleon's brother Joseph. Charles was awarded a pension by Napoleon and died in Rome.

Charles VIII 1408–1470. King of Sweden from 1448. He was elected regent of Sweden 1438, when Sweden broke away from Denmark and Norway. He stepped down 1441 when Christopher III of Bavaria (1418–1448) was elected king, but after his death became king. He was twice expelled by the Danes and twice restored.

Charles IX 1550–1611. King of Sweden from 1604, the youngest son of Gustavus Vasa. In 1568 he and his brother John led the rebellion against Eric XIV (1533–1577); John became king as John III and attempted to catholicize Sweden, and Charles led the opposition. John's son Sigismund, king of Poland and a Catholic, succeeded to the Swedish throne 1592, and Charles led the Protestants. He was made regent 1595 and deposed Sigismund 1599. Charles was elected king of Sweden 1604 and was involved in unsuccessful wars with Russia, Poland, and Denmark. He was the father of Gustavus Adolphus.

Charles X 1622–1660. King of Sweden from 1654, when he succeeded his cousin Christina. He waged

war with Poland and Denmark and in 1657 invaded Denmark by leading his army over the frozen sea.

Charles XII 1682–1718. King of Sweden from 1697, when he succeeded his father, Charles XI. From 1700 he was involved in wars with Denmark, Poland, and Russia.

Charles XIII 1748–1818. King of Sweden from 1809, when he was elected; he became the first king of Sweden and Norway 1814.

Charles XIV (Jean Baptiste Jules Bernadotte) 1763–1844. King of Sweden and Norway from 1818. A former marshal in the French army, in 1810 he was elected crown prince of Sweden under the name of Charles John (Carl Johan). Loyal to his adopted country, he brought Sweden into the alliance against Napoleon 1813, as a reward for which Sweden received Norway. He was the founder of the present dynasty.

Charles Albert 1798–1849. King of Sardinia from 1831. He showed liberal sympathies in early life, and after his accession introduced some reforms. On the outbreak of the 1848 revolution he granted a constitution and declared war on Austria. His troops were defeated at Custozza and Novara. In 1849 he abdicated in favor of his son Victor Emmanuel and retired to a monastery, where he died.

Charles Edward Stuart the *Young Pretender* or *Bonnie Prince Charlie* 1720–1788. British prince, grandson of James II and son of James, the Old Pretender. In the Jacobite rebellion 1745 Charles won the support of the Scottish Highlanders; his army invaded England to claim the throne but was beaten back by the duke of Cumberland and routed at Culloden 1746. Charles went into exile.

With a price of £30,000 on his head, Charles Edward fled to France, eventually settling in Italy 1766.

Charles Martel *c.* 688–741. Frankish ruler (Mayor of the Palace) of the E Frankish kingdom from 717 and the whole kingdom from 731. His victory against the Moors at Moussais-la-Bataille near Tours 732 earned him his nickname of Martel, "the Hammer," because he halted the Islamic advance by the ◊Moors into Europe.

Charles River Bridge v Warren Bridge US Supreme Court decision 1837 dealing with the interpretation of corporate charters and states' power to regulate corporations. The owners of the Charles River toll bridge, in fear of economic competition, sued for an injunction against the building of the Warren Bridge, which the state of Massachusetts had authorized. They claimed that their 1785 charter implied the exclusive right to bridge the river; the state was impairing that contract by sanctioning a second bridge. The Court ruled implicit rights to be invalid and declared that ambiguous clauses must be interpreted in favor of the public over the corporation.

Charles's law law stating that the volume of a given mass of gas at constant pressure is directly proportional to its absolute temperature (temperature in kelvin). It was discovered by French physicist Jacques Charles 1787, and independently by French chemist Joseph Gay-Lussac 1802.

Charles the Bold Duke of Burgundy 1433–1477. Son of Philip the Good, he inherited Burgundy and the Low Countries from him 1465. He waged wars attempting to free the duchy from dependence on France and restore it as a kingdom. He was killed in battle.

Charleston capital and chief city of West Virginia, on the Kanawha River; population (1990) 57,300. It is the center of a region that produces coal, natural gas, salt, clay, timber, and oil, and it is an important chemical-producing center. Charleston developed from a fort built 1788.

Charleston main port and city of South Carolina; population (1990) 80,400. Industries include textiles, clothing, and paper products. A nuclear-submarine naval base and an air-force base are nearby. The city dates from 1670.

Charleston back-kicking dance of the 1920s that originated in Charleston, South Carolina, and became an American craze.

Charlotte city in North Carolina, on the border with South Carolina; population (1990) 395,900. Industries include data processing, textiles, chemicals, machinery, and food products. It was the gold-mining center of the country until gold was discovered in California 1849.

Charlotte Amalie capital, tourist resort, and free port of the US Virgin Islands, on the island of St Thomas; population (1980) 11,756. Boat building and rum distilling are among the economic activities. It was founded 1672 by the Danish West India Company.

Charlottesville city in central Virginia, in the Blue Ridge mountain foothills, NW of Richmond, on the Rivanna River; seat of Albemarle County; population (1990) 40,300. Tourism is important, and some textiles are manufactured.

Charlottesville is the site of the University of Virginia, established 1819 by Thomas Jefferson. Jefferson's home, Monticello, is nearby, as is President James Monroe's home, Ash Lawn.

Charlottetown capital of Prince Edward Island, Canada; population (1986) 16,000. The city trades in textiles, fish, timber, vegetables, and dairy produce. It was founded by French settlers in the 1720s.

Charon in Greek mythology, the boatman who ferried the dead over the rivers Acheron and Styx to ◊Hades, the underworld. A coin placed on the tongue of the dead paid for their passage.

Charybdis In Greek legend, a whirlpool formed by a monster of the same name on one side of the narrow straits of Messina, Sicily, opposite the monster Scylla.

Chase Salmon Portland 1808–1873. US public official and chief justice of the US. He held a US Senate seat 1849–55 and 1860; helped found the Republican Party 1854–56; was elected governor of Ohio 1855; became Abraham Lincoln's secretary of the treasury 1861; and was appointed chief justice of the US Supreme Court 1864. He presided over the impeachment trial of President A ◊Johnson 1868.

chasing indentation of a design on metal by small chisels and hammers. This method of decoration was familiar in ancient Egypt, Assyria, and Greece; it is used today on fine silverware.

château country house or important residence in France. The term originally applied to a French medieval castle, and the château was first used as a domestic building in the late 15th century; by the reign of Louis XIII (1610–43) fortifications such as moats and keeps were no longer used for defensive purposes, but merely as decorative features. The Loire valley contains some fine examples of châteaux.

Chateaubriand François René, vicomte de 1768–1848. French author. In exile from the French Revolution 1794–99, he wrote *Atala* 1801 (after his

château The château of Azay le Rideau, France.

encounters with North American Indians) and the autobiographical *René*, which formed part of *Le Génie du Christianisme/The Genius of Christianity* 1802. He later wrote *Mémoires d'outre tombe/Memoirs from Beyond the Tomb* 1849–50.

Chattanooga city in Tennessee, on the Tennessee River; population (1990) 152,500. It is the focus of the ◊Tennessee Valley Authority area. Developed as a salt-trading center after 1835, it now produces chemicals, textiles, and metal products. The Hunter Museum of Art and a campus of the University of Tennessee are here. Chattanooga was laid out 1838 after Cherokee Indians were removed from the area. Union forces captured it from the Confederacy 1863.

Chatwin Bruce 1940–1989. English writer. His works include *The Songlines* 1987, written after living with Aborigines; the novel *Utz* 1988, a novel about a manic porcelain collector in Prague; and travel pieces and journalism collected in *What Am I Doing Here* 1989.

Chaucer Geoffrey *c.* 1340–1400. English poet. *The Canterbury Tales*, a collection of stories told by a group of pilgrims on their way to Canterbury, reveals his knowledge of human nature and his stylistic variety, from urbane and ironic to simple and bawdy. Early allegorical poems, including *The Book of the Duchess*, were influenced by French poems like the *Roman de la Rose*. His *Troilus and Criseyde* is a substantial narrative poem about the tragic betrayal of an idealized courtly love.

chauvinism warlike, often unthinking patriotism, as exhibited by Nicholas Chauvin, one of Napoleon I's veterans and his fanatical admirer. In the mid-20th century the expression *male chauvinism* was coined to mean an assumed superiority of the male sex over the female.

Chávez Carlos 1899–1978. Mexican composer. A student of the piano and of the complex rhythms of his country's folk music, he founded the Mexico Symphony Orchestra. He composed a number of ballets, seven symphonies, and concertos for both violin and piano.

Chayefsky (Sidney) Paddy 1923–1981. US writer. He established his reputation with the television plays *Marty* 1955 (for which he won an Oscar when he turned it into a film) and *Bachelor Party* 1957. He also won Oscars for *The Hospital* 1971 and *Network* 1976.

Chernobyl *The damage caused to one of the nuclear reactors in the 1986 accident at the Chernobyl power station near Kiev, Ukraine.*

People Live 1943, *The Housebreaker of Shady Hill* 1958, *The Brigadier and the Golf Widow* 1964, and *Stories of John Cheever* 1978 (Pulitzer prize). Among his novels are *Bullet Park* 1969 and *Oh What a Paradise It Seems* 1982.

Chekhov Anton (Pavlovich) 1860–1904. Russian dramatist and writer of short stories. His plays concentrate on the creation of atmosphere and delineation of internal development, rather than external action. His first play, *Ivanov* 1887, was a failure, as was *The Seagull* 1896 until revived by Stanislavsky 1898 at the Moscow Art Theater, for which Chekhov went on to write his finest plays: *Uncle Vanya* 1899, *The Three Sisters* 1901, and *The Cherry Orchard* 1904.

chelate chemical compound whose molecules consist of one or more metal atoms or charged ions joined to chains of organic residues by coordinate (or dative covalent) chemical ♢bonds.

Chelyabinsk industrial city and capital of Chelyabinsk region, W Siberia, Russia; population (1987) 1,119,000. It has iron and engineering works and makes chemicals, motor vehicles, and aircraft.

chemical equation method of indicating the reactants and products of a chemical reaction by using chemical symbols and formulae. A chemical equation gives two basic pieces of information: (1) the reactants (on the left-hand side) and products (right-hand side); and (2) the reacting proportions (stoichiometry) — that is, how many units of each reactant and product are involved. The equation must balance; that is, the total number of atoms of a particular element on the left-hand side must be the same as the number of atoms of that element on the right-hand side.

chemical warfare use in war of gaseous, liquid, or solid substances intended to have a toxic effect on humans, animals, or plants. Together with ♢biological warfare, it was banned by the Geneva Protocol 1925 and the United Nations in 1989 also voted for a ban. The total US stockpile 1989 was estimated at 30,000 metric tons and the Soviet stockpile at 50,000 metric tons. In June 1990, the US and USSR agreed bilaterally to reduce their stockpile to 5,000 metric tons each by 2002. The US began replacing its stocks with new nerve-gas ♢binary weapons.

chemical weathering form of ♢weathering brought about by a chemical change in the rocks affected. Chemical weathering involves the "rotting," or breakdown, of the minerals within a rock, and usually produces a claylike residue (such as kaolinite and bauxite). Some chemicals are dissolved and carried away from the weathering source.

chemistry science concerned with the composition of matter and of the changes that take place in it under certain conditions.

chemotherapy any medical treatment with chemicals. It usually refers to treatment of cancer with cytotoxic and other drugs. The term was coined by the German bacteriologist Paul Ehrlich for the use of synthetic chemicals against infectious diseases.

Chengdu or ***Chengtu*** ancient city, capital of Sichuan province, China; population (1989) 2,780,000. It is a busy rail junction and has railroad workshops, and textile, electronics, and engineering industries. It has well-preserved temples.

Cherenkov Pavel 1904– . Soviet physicist. In 1934 he discovered ***Cherenkov radiation***; this occurs as a bluish light when charged atomic particles pass

check an order written by the drawer to a commercial or central bank to pay a specific sum on demand.

checkers board game played on a ♢chess board. Each of the two players has 12 men (disk-shaped pieces), and attempts either to capture all the opponent's men or to block their movements.

Checkpoint Charlie Western-controlled crossing point for non-Germans between West Berlin and East Berlin, opened 1961 as the only crossing point between the Allied and Soviet sectors. Its dismantling in June 1990 was seen as a symbol of the ending of the ♢Cold War.

cheese food made from the ***curds*** (solids) of soured milk from cows, sheep, or goats, separated from the ***whey*** (liquid), then salted, put into molds, and pressed into firm blocks. Cheese is ripened with bacteria or surface fungi, and kept for a time to mature before eating.

cheetah large wild cat *Acinonyx jubatus* native to Africa, Arabia, and SW Asia, but now rare in some areas. Yellowish with black spots, it has a slim lithe build. It is up to 3 ft/1 m tall at the shoulder, and up to 5 ft/1.5 m long. It can reach 70 mph/110 kph, but tires after about 400 yd/365 m. Cheetahs live in open country where they hunt small antelopes, hares, and birds.

Cheever John 1912–1982. US writer whose stories and novels focus on the ironies of upper-middle-class life in suburban America. His short stories were frequently published in *The New Yorker*. His first novel was *The Wapshot Chronicle* 1957, for which he won the National Book Award. Others include *Falconer* 1977.

Cheever was born in Quincy, Massachusetts. His collections of short stories include *The Way Some*

through water or other media at a speed in excess of that of light. He shared a Nobel Prize 1958 with his colleagues Ilya ◊Frank and Igor Tamm for work resulting in a cosmic-ray counter.

Cherenkov discovered that this effect was independent of any medium and depended for its production on the passage of high-velocity electrons. The phenomenon has also been claimed as the discovery of the French scientist Lucien Mallet.

Chernobyl city in central Ukraine; site of a nuclear power station. In April 1986 a leak, caused by overheating, occurred in a nonpressurized boiling-water nuclear reactor. The resulting clouds of radioactive isotopes were traced as far away as the UK; over 250 people were killed in the short term, and thousands of square miles contaminated.

Cherokee member of a North ◊American Indian people, formerly living in the S Allegheny Mountains of what is now Alabama, the Carolinas, Georgia, and Tennessee. Their scholarly leader Sequoyah (*c.* 1770–1843) devised the syllabary used for writing their language. Their language belongs to the Macro-Siouan family.

In 1829 they were transported to a reservation in Oklahoma, by forced march, the Trail of Tears, by order of President Andrew Jackson as a punishment for aiding the British during the American Revolution. In 1984, they were permitted to reestablish a tribal center in North Carolina.

cherry any of various trees of the genus *Prunus*, belonging to the rose family. Cherry trees are distinguished from plums and apricots by their fruits, which are spherical and smooth and not covered with a bloom. They grow best in deep fertile soil.

Most cultivated cherries come from Europe. The common chokecherry *P. virginiana* is a widespread wild cherry tree of the US.

Chesapeake Bay largest of the inlets on the Atlantic coast of the US, bordered by Maryland and Virginia. It is about 200 mi/320 km in length and 4–40 mi/6–64 km in width.

The Chesapeake Bay Bridge Tunnel connects both Virginia shores; farther north the Chesapeake Bay Bridge links the W Maryland shore near Annapolis to Kent Island.

chess board game originating as early as the 2nd century AD. Two players use 16 pieces each, on a board of 64 squares of alternating color, to try to force the opponent into a position where the main piece (the king) is threatened and cannot move to another position without remaining threatened.

Chesterfield Philip Dormer Stanhope, 4th Earl of Chesterfield 1694–1773. English politician and writer, author of *Letters to his Son* 1774. A member of the literary circle of Swift, Pope, and Bolingbroke, he incurred the wrath of Dr Samuel ◊Johnson by failing to carry out an offer of patronage.

Chesterton G(ilbert) K(eith) 1874–1936. English novelist, essayist, and satirical poet, author of a series of novels featuring as detective a naive priest, Father Brown. Other novels include *The Napoleon of Notting Hill* 1904 and *The Man Who Knew Too Much* 1922.

chestnut tree of the genus *Castanea*, belonging to the beech family Fagaceae. The Spanish or sweet chestnut *C. sativa* produces edible nuts inside husks; its timber is also valuable. ◊Horse chestnuts are quite distinct, belonging to the genus *Aesculus*, family Hippocastanaceae.

the way each piece can move

arrangement of the chessmen

chess The names of chess pieces reflect the game's long history; the eight pawns (foot soldiers) are in front of the king and queen, two bishops, two knights, and two rooks (or castles).

Chetnik member of a Serbian nationalist group that operated underground during the German occupation of Yugoslavia during World War II. Led by Col Draza Mihailović, the Chetniks initially received aid from the Allies, but this was later transferred to the communist partisans led by Tito. The term has also popularly been applied to Serb militia forces in the 1991–92 Yugoslav civil war.

Chevalier Maurice 1888–1972. French singer and actor. He began as dancing partner to the revue artiste Mistinguett at the Folies-Bergère, and made numerous films including *Innocents of Paris* 1929 (which revived his song "Louise"), *The Merry Widow* 1934, and *Gigi* 1958.

chewing gum gummy confectionery to be chewed not swallowed. It is composed mainly of chicle (milky juice of the tropical sapodilla tree *Achras zapota* of Central America), usually flavored with mint, sweetened, and pressed flat. The first patent was taken out in the US in 1871. *Bubble gum* is a variety that allows chewers to blow bubbles.

Cheyenne capital of Wyoming, located in the SE part of the state, just N of the Colorado border in the foothills of the Laramie Mountains; population (1990) 50,000. An agricultural and transportation center, its industries include oil refining, fertilizers, electronics, restaurant equipment, and ceramics. Tourism is also important to the economy.

Chiang Ching alternative transliteration of ◊Jiang Qing, Chinese actress, third wife of Mao Zedong.

Chiang Ching-kuo 1910–1988. Taiwanese politician, son of Chiang Kai-shek, prime minister 1971–78, president 1978–88.

Chiang Kai-shek (Pinyin *Jiang Jie Shi*) 1887–1975. Chinese nationalist ◊Guomindang (Kuomintang) general and politician, president of China 1928–31 and 1943–49, of Taiwan from 1949, where he set up a US-supported right-wing government on his expulsion from the mainland by the communist forces. He was a commander in the civil war that lasted from the end of imperial rule 1911 to the Second ◊Sino-Japanese War and beyond,

Chiang Kai-shek
Chinese nationalist leader Chiang Kai-shek helped to unite China in the 1920s and fought a bitter war with the communist Mao Zedong before being driven out of mainland China to Taiwan in 1949.

having split with the communist leader Mao Zedong 1927.

Chicago financial and industrial city in Illinois, on Lake Michigan. It is the third largest US city; population (1990) 2,783,700, metropolitan area 8,065,000. Industries include iron, steel, chemicals, electrical goods, machinery, meatpacking and food processing, publishing, and fabricated metals. The once famous stockyards are now closed.

Chicano citizen or resident of the US of Mexican descent. The term was originally used for those who became US citizens after the ◊Mexican War.

Chichen Itzá Toltec city situated among the Mayan city-states of Yucatán, Mexico. It flourished AD 900–1200 and displays Classic and Post-Classic architecture of the Toltec style. The site has temples with sculptures and color reliefs, an observatory, and a sacred well into which sacrifices, including human beings, were cast.

Chichen Itzá
Archeological site in Mexico and sacred center of the Mayas for 700 years.

chickenpox or *varicella* common acute disease, caused by a virus of the ◊herpes group and transmitted by airborne droplets. Chickenpox chiefly attacks children under the age of ten. The incubation period is two to three weeks. One attack normally gives immunity for life.

chickpea annual plant *Cicer arietinum*, family Leguminosae, which is grown for food in India and the Middle East. Its short, hairy pods contain edible pealike seeds.

Chico city in N California, NW of Sacramento; population (1990) 40,000. Situated in the fertile Sacramento Valley, a farming region, its industries include food processing and lumber products.

chigger or *harvest mite* scarlet or rusty brown ◊mite of the family Trombiculidae, common in summer and autumn. Their tiny red larvae cause intensely irritating bites.

chihuahua smallest breed of dog, 10 in/15 cm high, developed in the US from Mexican origins. It may weigh only 2.2 lb/1 kg. The domed head and wide-set ears are characteristic, and the skull is large compared to the body. It can be almost any color, and occurs in both smooth (or even hairless) and long-coated varieties.

Chihuahua capital of Chihuahua state, Mexico, 800 mi/1,285 km NW of Mexico City; population (1984) 375,000. Founded 1707, it is the center of a mining district and has textile mills.
The University of Chihuahua is here. The revolutionary leader Pancho Villa had his headquarters here during the early 20th century, and his home is a tourist attraction.

chilblain painful inflammation of the skin of the feet, hands, or ears, due to cold. The parts turn red, swell, itch violently, and are very tender. In bad cases, the skin cracks, blisters, or ulcerates.

Child Lydia Maria 1802–1880. US writer, social critic, and feminist, author of the popular women's guides *The Frugal Housewife* 1829 and *The Mother's Book* 1831. With her husband, David Child, she worked for the abolition of slavery, advocating educational support for black Americans. The Childs edited the weekly *National Anti-Slavery Standard* 1840–44.

child abuse the molesting of children by parents and other adults. It can give rise to various criminal charges and has become a growing concern since the early 1980s.

Child, Convention on the Rights of the United Nations document designed to make the well-being of children an international obligation. It was adopted 1989 and covers children from birth up to 18.

Children's Crusade ◊crusade by some 10,000 children from France, the Low Countries, and Germany, in 1212, to recapture Jerusalem for Christianity. Motivated by religious piety, many of them were sold into slavery or died of disease.

children's literature works specifically written for children. The earliest known illustrated children's book in English is *Goody Two Shoes* 1765, possibly written by Oliver Goldsmith. *Fairy tales* were originally part of a vast range of oral literature, credited only to the writer who first recorded them, such as Charles Perrault. During the 19th century several writers, including Hans Christian Andersen, wrote original stories in the fairy tale genre; others, such as the Grimm brothers, collected (and sometimes adapted) existing stories.

Chile South American country, bounded N by Peru and Bolivia, E by Argentina, and S and W by the Pacific Ocean.

Chilean Revolution in Chile, the presidency of Salvador ◊Allende 1970–73, the western hemisphere's first democratically elected Marxist-oriented president of an independent state.

chili the pod, or powder made from the pod, of a variety of ◊capsicum, *Capsicum frutescens*, a hot, red pepper. It is widely used in cooking.

Chimbote largest fishing port in Peru; population (1981) 216,000. Sugar and fish products are exported; other industries include iron and steel.

chimera in biology, an organism composed of tissues that are genetically different. Chimeras can develop naturally if a ◊mutation occurs in a cell of a developing embryo, but are more commonly produced artificially by implanting cells from one organism into the embryo of another.

chimera or *chimaera* in Greek mythology, a fire-breathing animal with a lion's head, a goat's body, and a tail in the form of a snake; hence any apparent hybrid of two or more creatures. The chimera was killed by the hero Bellerophon on the winged horse Pegasus.

chimpanzee highly intelligent African ape *Pan troglodytes* that lives mainly in rain forests but sometimes in wooded savanna. Chimpanzees are covered in thin but long black body hair, except for the face, hands, and feet, which may have pink or black skin. They normally walk on all fours, supporting the front of the body on the knuckles of the fingers, but can stand or walk upright for a short distance. They can grow to 4.5 ft/1.4 m tall, and weigh up to 110 lb/50 kg. They are strong and climb well, but spend time on the ground, living in loose social groups. The bulk of the diet is fruit, with some leaves, insects, and occasional meat. Chimpanzees can use "tools," fashioning twigs to extract termites from their nests.

Chile Republic of
República de Chile)

area 292,257 sq mi/756,950 sq km
capital Santiago
cities Concepción, Viña del Mar, Temuco; ports Valparaíso, Antofagasta, Arica, Iquique, Punta Arenas
physical Andes mountains along E border, Atacama Desert in N, fertile central valley, grazing land and forest in S
territories Easter Island, Juan Fernández Islands, part of Tierra del Fuego, claim to part of Antarctica
features Atacama Desert is one of the driest regions in the world
head of state and government Patricio Aylwin from 1990

political system emergent democratic republic
political parties Christian Democratic Party (PDC), moderate centrist; National Renewal Party (RN), right-wing
exports copper (world's leading producer), iron, molybdenum (world's second largest producer), nitrate, pulp and paper, steel products, fishmeal, fruit
currency peso
population (1992) 13,599,000 (the majority are of European origin or are mestizos, of mixed American Indian and Spanish descent); growth rate 1.6% p.a.
life expectancy men 64, women 73
language Spanish
religion Roman Catholic 89%
literacy 94% (1988)
GDP $18.9 bn (1987); $6,512 per head

chronology
1818 Achieved independence from Spain.
1964 PDC formed government under Eduardo Frei.
1970 Dr Salvador Allende became the first democratically elected Marxist president; he embarked on an extensive program of nationalization and social reform.
1973 Government overthrown by the CIA-backed military, led by General Augusto Pinochet. Allende killed. Policy of repression began during which all opposition was put down and political activity banned.
1983 Growing opposition to the regime from all sides, with outbreaks of violence.
1988 Referendum on whether Pinochet should serve a further term resulted in a clear "No" vote.
1989 President Pinochet agreed to constitutional changes to allow pluralist politics. Patricio Aylwin (PDC) elected president (his term would begin 1990); Pinochet remained as army commander in chief.
1990 Aylwin reached accord on end to military junta government. Pinochet censured by president.
1992 Future US–Chilean free-trade agreement announced.

China People's Republic of
(*Zhonghua Renmin Gonghe Guo*)

area 3,599,975 sq mi/9,596,960 sq km
capital Beijing (Peking)
cities Chongqing (Chungking), Shenyang (Mukden), Wuhan, Nanjing (Nanking), Harbin; ports Tianjin (Tientsin), Shanghai, Qingdao (Tsingtao), Lüda (Lü-ta), Guangzhou (Canton)
physical two-thirds of China is mountains or desert (N and W); the low-lying E is irrigated by rivers Huang He (Yellow River), Chang Jiang (Yangtze-Kiang), Xi Jiang (Si Kiang)
features Great Wall of China; Gezhouba Dam; Ming Tombs; Terracotta Warriors (Xi'ain); Gobi Desert; world's most populous country
head of state Jiang Zemin from 1993
head of government Li Peng from 1987
political system communist republic
political party Chinese Communist Party (CCP), Marxist-Leninist-Maoist
exports tea, livestock and animal products, silk, cotton, oil, minerals (China is the world's largest producer of tungsten and antimony), chemicals, light industrial goods
currency yuan
population (1992) 1,165,888,000 (the majority are Han or ethnic Chinese; the 67 million of other ethnic groups, including Tibetan, Uigur, and Zhuang, live in border areas). The number of people of Chinese origin outside China, Taiwan, and Hong Kong is estimated at 15–24 million. Growth rate 1.2% p.a.
life expectancy men 67, women 69
languages Chinese, including Mandarin (official), Cantonese, and other dialects
religions officially atheist, but traditionally Taoist, Confucianist, and Buddhist; Muslim 13 million; Catholic 3–6 million (divided between the "patriotic" church established 1958 and the "loyal" church subject to Rome); Protestant 3 million
literacy men 82%, women 66% (1985 est)
GDP $293.4 bn (1987); $274 per head

chronology
1949 People's Republic of China proclaimed by Mao Zedong.
1954 Soviet-style constitution adopted.
1956–57 Hundred Flowers Movement encouraged criticism of then government.
1958–60 Great Leap Forward commune experiment to achieve "true communism."
1960 Withdrawal of Soviet technical advisers.
1962 Sino-Indian border war.
1962–65 Economic recovery program under Liu Shaoqi; Maoist "socialist education movement" rectification campaign.
1966–69 Great Proletarian Cultural Revolution; Liu Shaoqi overthrown.
1969 Ussuri River border clashes with USSR.
1970–76 Reconstruction under Mao and Zhou Enlai.
1971 Entry into United Nations.
1972 US president Nixon visited Beijing.
1975 New state constitution. Unveiling of Zhou's "Four Modernizations" program.
1976 Deaths of Zhou Enlai and Mao Zedong; appointment of Hua Guofeng as prime minister and Communist Party chair. Vice Premier Deng Xiaoping in hiding. Gang of Four arrested.
1977 Rehabilitation of Deng Xiaoping.
1979 Economic reforms introduced. Diplomatic relations opened with US. Punitive invasion of Vietnam.
1980 Zhao Ziyang appointed prime minister.
1981 Hu Yaobang succeeded Hua Guofeng as party chair. Imprisonment of Gang of Four.
1982 New state constitution adopted.
1984 "Enterprise management" reforms for industrial sector.
1986 Student prodemocracy demonstrations.
1987 Hu was replaced as party leader by Zhao, with Li Peng as prime minister. Deng left Politburo but remained influential.
1988 Yang Shangkun replaced Li Xiannian as state president. Economic reforms encountered increasing problems; inflation rocketed.
1989 Over 2,000 killed in prodemocracy student demonstrations in Tiananmen Square; international sanctions imposed.
1991 March: European Community and Japanese sanctions lifted. May: normal relations with USSR resumed. Sept: UK prime minister John Major visited Beijing. Nov: relations with Vietnam normalized.
1992 China promised to sign 1968 Nuclear Non-Proliferation Treaty. Historic visit by Japan's emperor.
1993 Jiang Zemin, Chinese Communist Party general secretary, set to replace Yang Shangkun as president.

Chimu South American civilization that flourished on the coast of Peru from about 1250 to about 1470, when it was conquered by the Incas. The Chimu people produced fine work in gold, realistic portrait pottery, savage fanged feline images in clay, and possibly a system of writing or recording by painting patterns on beans. They built aqueducts carrying water many miles, and the huge, mazelike city of Chan Chan, 14 sq mi/36 sq km, on the coast near Trujillo.

China the largest country in E Asia, bounded N by Mongolia; NW by Tajikistan, Kyrgyzstan, Kazakhstan, and Afghanistan; SW by India, Nepal, and Bhutan; S by Myanmar (Burma), Laos, and Vietnam; SE by the South China Sea; E by the East China Sea, North Korea, and Yellow Sea; NE by Russia. *See table* *p. 198*

China Sea area of the Pacific Ocean bordered by China, Vietnam, Borneo, the Philippines, and Japan. Various groups of small islands and shoals, including the Paracels, 300 mi/500 km E of Vietnam, have been disputed by China and other powers because they lie in oil-rich areas.

chinchilla South American rodent *Chinchilla laniger* found in high, rather barren areas of the Andes in Bolivia and Chile. About the size of a small rabbit, it has long ears and a long bushy tail, and shelters in rock crevices. These gregarious animals have thick, soft, silver-gray fur, and were hunted almost to extinc-

China "People's power" thwarted: students confront troops in peaceful demonstrations in Tiananmen Square, Beijing, June 1989; shortly afterward the military attacked, and killed over 2,000 unarmed protesters.

tion for it. They are now farmed and protected in the wild.

Chinese native to or an inhabitant of China and Taiwan, or a person of Chinese descent. The Chinese comprise more than 25% of the world's population, and the Chinese language (Mandarin) is the largest member of the Sino-Tibetan family.

Chinese art the painting and sculpture of China. From the Bronze Age to the Cultural Revolution, Chinese art shows a stylistic unity unparalleled in any other culture. From about the 1st century AD Buddhism inspired much sculpture and painting. The *Han dynasty* (206 BC– AD 220) produced outstanding metalwork, ceramics, and sculpture. The *Song dynasty* (960–1278) established standards of idyllic landscape and nature painting in a delicate calligraphic style. *See illustration p. 199*

Chinese language language or group of languages of the Sino-Tibetan family, spoken in China, Taiwan, Hong Kong, Singapore, and Chinese communities throughout the world. Varieties of spoken Chinese differ greatly, but all share a written form using thousands of ideographic symbols—characters—which have changed little in 2,000 years. Nowadays, *putonghua* ("common speech"), based on the educated Beijing dialect known as Mandarin Chinese, is promoted throughout China as the national spoken and written language.

Chinese Revolution series of great political upheavals in China 1911–49 that eventually led to Communist Party rule and the establishment of the People's Republic of China. In 1912, a nationalist revolt overthrew the imperial Manchudynasty. Led by Sun Yat-sen 1923–25 and by Chiang Kai-shek 1925–49, the nationalists, or Guomindang, were increasing challenged by the growing communist movement. The 6,000 mi/10,000 km *Long March* to the NW by the communists 1934–35 to escape from attacks by the Guomindang forces resulted in Mao Zedong's emergence as communist leader. During World War II 1939–45, the various Chinese political groups pooled military resources against the Japanese invaders. After World War II, the conflict reignited

into open civil war 1946–49, until the Guomindang were defeated at Nanking and forced to flee to Taiwan. Communist rule was established in the People's Republic of China under the leadership of Mao.

chinook warm dry wind that blows downhill on the eastern side of the Rocky Mountains of North America. It often occurs in winter and spring when it produces a rapid thaw, and so is important to the agriculture of the area.

chip or *silicon chip* another name for an ◊*integrated circuit*, a complete electronic circuit on a slice of silicon (or other semiconductor) crystal only a few millimeterssquare.

chipmunk any of several species of small ground squirrel with characteristic stripes along its side. Chipmunks live in North America and E Asia, in a variety of habitats, usually wooded, and take shelter in burrows. They have pouches in their cheeks for carrying food. They climb well but spend most of their time on or near the ground.

Chippendale Thomas *c.* 1718–1779. English furniture designer. He set up his workshop in St Martin's Lane, London 1753. His book *The Gentleman and Cabinet Maker's Director* 1754, was a significant contribution to furniture design. He favored Louis XVI, Chinese, Gothic, and Neo-Classical styles, and worked mainly in mahogany.

Chirac Jacques 1932– . French conservative politician, prime minister 1974–76 and 1986–88. He established the neo-Gaullist Rassemblement pour la République (RPR) 1976, and became mayor of Paris 1977.

Chirico Giorgio de 1888–1978. Italian painter born in Greece, whose style presaged Surrealism in its use of enigmatic imagery and dreamlike settings, for example, *Nostalgia of the Infinite* 1911, Museum of Modern Art, New York.

Chiron unusual Solar-System object orbiting between Saturn and Uranus, discovered 1977 by US astronomer Charles T Kowal (1940–). Initially classified as an asteroid, it is now believed to be a giant

China: dynasties

dynasty	dates	major events
Hsia	1994–1523 BC	agriculture, bronze, first writing
Shang or Yin	1523–1027	first major dynasty; first Chinese calendar
Chou	1027–255	developed society using money, iron, written laws; age of Confucius
Qin	255–206	unification after period of Warring States, building of Great Wall begun, roads built
Han	AD 206–220	first centralized and effectively administered empire; introduction of Buddhism
San Kuo	220–265	division into three parts, prolonged fighting (Three Kingdoms) and eventual victory of Wei over Chu and Wu; Confucianism superseded by Buddhism and Taoism
Tsin	265–420	beginning of Hun invasions in the north
Sui	581–618	reunification; barbarian invasions stopped; Great Wall refortified
T'ang	618–906	centralized government; empire greatly extended; period of excellence in sculpture, painting and poetry
Wu Tai (Five Dynasties)	907–960	economic depression and loss of territory in northern China, central Asia, and Korea; first use of paper money
Song	960–1279	period of calm and creativity; printing developed (movable type); central government restored; northern and western frontiers neglected and Mongol incursions begun
Yüan	1260–1368	beginning of Mongol rule in China, under Kublai Khan; Marco Polo visited China; dynasty brought to an end by widespread revolts, centered in Mongolia
Ming	1368–1644	Mongols driven out by native Chinese, Mongolia captured by 2nd Ming emperor; period of architectural development; Beijing flourished as new capital
Manchu	1644–1912	China once again under non-Chinese rule, the Qing conquered by nomads from Manchuria; trade with the West; culture flourished, but conservatism eventually led to the dynasty's overthrow by nationalistic revolutionaries led by Sun Yatsen

cometary nucleus about 120 mi/200 km across, composed of ice with a dark crust of carbon dust.

chiropractic technique of manipulation of the spine and other parts of the body, based on the principle that disorders are attributable to aberrations in the functioning of the nervous system, which manipulation can correct.

Chisholm Jesse *c.* 1806–*c.* 1868. US pioneer who gained a reputation as a resourceful guide, trader, and military scout during the early 19th century. He established one of the main paths of the yearly Texas cattle drive, known among cowboys as the "Chisholm Trail." Ranging over the southern part of the Great Plains, he customarily followed a route from the Mexican border to Kansas, ending at the market town of Abilene.

Chisholm v Georgia landmark case 1793 in which the US Supreme Court ruled that states are not immune from suits brought by citizens of other states. Alexander Chisholm, a South Carolinian, sued Georgia for payment on Georgia state bonds that were confiscated during the American Revolution. Georgia ignored the case, claiming it was not in federal jurisdiction, but the Supreme Court ruled that Georgia must appear in court to answer the charges. This decision frightened state governments as the number of similar suits grew across the nation. In response to fears about this economic danger to states' survival, the 11th Amendment, passed in 1798, reversed the Chisholm decision.

Chişinău (Russian *Kishinev*) capital of Moldova, situated in a rich agricultural area; population (1989) 565,000. It is a commercial and cultural center; industries include cement, food processing, tobacco, and textiles.

Chissano Joaquim 1939– . Mozambique nationalist politician, president from 1986; foreign minister 1975–86. In Oct 1992 Chissano signed a peace accord

with the leader of the rebel Mozambique National Resistance (MNR) party, bringing to an end 16 years of civil war.

Chittagong city and port in Bangladesh, 10 mi/16 km from the mouth of the Karnaphuli River, on the Bay of Bengal; population (1981) 1,388,476. Industries include steel, engineering, chemicals, and textiles.

chive or **chives** bulbous perennial European plant *Allium schoenoprasum* of the lily family Liliaceae. It has long, tubular leaves and dense, round flower heads in blue or lilac, and is used as a garnish for salads.

chlamydia single-celled bacterium that can live only parasitically in animal cells. Chlamydiae are thought to be descendants of bacteria that have lost certain metabolic processes. In humans, they cause ◊trachoma, a disease found mainly in the tropics (a leading cause of blindness); venereally transmitted chlamydiae cause genital and urinary infections.

chloramphenicol the first broad-spectrum antibiotic to be used commercially. It was discovered 1947 in a Venezuelan soil sample containing the bacillus *Streptomyces venezuelae*, which produces the antibiotic substance $C_{11}H_{12}Cl_2N_2O_5$, now synthesized. Because of its toxicity, its use is limited to treatment of life-threatening infections, such as meningitis and typhoid fever.

chlorate any salt derived from an acid containing both chlorine and oxygen and possessing the negative ion ClO^-, ClO_2^{2-}, ClO_3^-, or ClO_4^{4-}. Common chlorates are those of sodium, potassium, and barium. Certain chlorates are used in weedkillers.

chloride Cl^- negative ion formed when hydrogen chloride dissolves in water, and any salt containing this ion, commonly formed by the action of hydrochloric acid (HCl) on various metals or by direct combination of a metal and chlorine. Sodium chloride (NaCl) is common table salt.

chlorine greenish-yellow, gaseous, nonmetallic element with a pungent odor, symbol Cl, atomic number 17, atomic weight 35.453. It is a member of the ◊halogen group and is widely distributed, in combination with the ◊alkali metals, as chlorates or chlorides.

chlorofluorocarbon (CFC) synthetic chemical that is odorless, nontoxic, nonflammable, and chemically inert. CFCs have been used as propellants in ◊aerosol cans, as refrigerants in refrigerators and air conditioners, and in the manufacture of foam packaging. They are partly responsible for the destruction of the ◊ozone layer. In June 1990 representatives of 93 nations, including the US and the UK, agreed to phase out production of CFCs and various other ozone-depleting chemicals by the end of the 20th century.

chloroform (technical name *trichloromethane*) CCl₃ clear, colorless, toxic, carcinogenic liquid with a characteristic pungent, sickly sweet smell and taste, formerly used as an anesthetic (now superseded by less harmful substances). It is used as a solvent and in the synthesis of organic chemical compounds.

chlorophyll green pigment present in most plants; it is responsible for the absorption of light energy during ◊photosynthesis. The pigment absorbs the red and blue-violet parts of sunlight but reflects the green, thus giving plants their characteristic color.

chocolate powder, syrup, confectionery, or beverage derived from cacao seeds. See ◊cocoa and chocolate.

cholecystectomy surgical removal of the ◊gallbladder. It is carried out when gallstones or infection lead to inflammation of the gallbladder, which may then be removed either via a laparotomy or by ◊endoscopy; the latter method, which performs the operation without making a large wound, is increasing in popularity.

cholera any of several intestinal diseases, especially *Asiatic cholera*, an infection caused by a bacterium *Vibrio cholerae*, transmitted in contaminated water and characterized by violent diarrhea and vomiting. It is prevalent in many tropical areas.

cholesterol white, crystalline ◊sterol found throughout the body, especially in fats, blood, nerve tissue, and bile; it is also provided in the diet by foods such as eggs, meat, and butter. A high level of cholesterol in the blood is thought to contribute to atherosclerosis (hardening of the arteries).

Chomsky Noam 1928– . US professor of linguistics. He proposed a theory of transformational generative grammar, which attracted widespread interest because of the claims it made about the relationship between language and the mind and the universality of an underlying language structure. He has been a leading critic of the imperialist tendencies of the US government.

Chongjin port and capital of North Hamgyong province on the northeast coast of North Korea; population (1984) 754,000. Timber, iron, and textiles are exported; there is steel, pig iron, and fish processing.

Chongqing or *Chungking*, also known as *Pahsien* city in Sichuan province, China, that stands at the confluence of the ◊Chang Jiang and Jialing Jiang rivers; population (1984) 2,733,700. Industries include iron, steel, chemicals, synthetic rubber, and textiles.

Chopin Frédéric (François) 1810–1849. Polish composer and pianist. He made his debut as a pianist at the age of eight. As a performer, Chopin revolutionized the technique of pianoforte-playing, turning the hands

Chinese art Part of the Sacred Way to the Ming tombs (30 mi/50 km from Beijing) is lined with statues of courtiers, soldiers, politicians, and animals.

outward and favoring a light, responsive touch. His compositions for piano, which include two concertos and other works with orchestra, are characterized by great volatility of mood, and rhythmic fluidity.

He died Oct 17, 1849, and was buried in Père Lachaise cemetery in Paris.

Chopin Kate 1851–1904. US novelist and short-story writer. Her novel *The Awakening* 1899, the story of a married New Orleans woman's awakening to her sexuality, is now regarded as a classic of feminist sensibility.

chord in geometry, a straight line joining any two points on a curve. The chord that passes through the center of a circle (its longest chord) is the diameter. The longest and shortest chords of an ellipse (a regular oval) are called the major and minor axes respectively.

chord in music, a group of three or more notes sounded together. The resulting combination of tones may be either harmonious or dissonant.

chordate animal belonging to the phylum Chordata, which includes vertebrates, sea squirts, amphioxi, and others. All these animals, at some stage of their lives, have a supporting rod of tissue (notochord or backbone) running down their bodies.

chorea disease of the nervous system marked by involuntary movements of the face muscles and limbs, formerly called St Vitus's dance. ◊*Huntington's chorea* is also characterized by such movements.

chorion villus sampling (CVS) ◊biopsy of a small sample of placental tissue, carried out in early pregnancy at 10–12 weeks' gestation. Since the placenta forms from embryonic cells, the tissue obtained can be tested to reveal genetic abnormality in the fetus. The advantage of CVS over ◊amniocentesis is that it provides an earlier diagnosis, so that if any abnormality is discovered, and the parents opt for an abortion, it can be carried out more safely.

choroid black layer found at the rear of the ◊eye beneath the retina. By absorbing light that has already passed through the retina, it stops back-reflection and so aids vision.

Chou En-lai alternative transliteration of ◊Zhou Enlai.

Christianity: chronology

1st century	The Christian church is traditionally said to have originated at Pentecost, and separated from the parent Jewish religion by the declaration of saints Barnabas and Paul that the distinctive rites of Judaism were not necessary for entry into the Christian church.
3rd century	Christians were persecuted under the Roman emperors Severus, Decius, and Diocletian.
312	Emperor Constantine established Christianity as the religion of the Roman Empire.
4th century	A settled doctrine of Christian belief evolved, with deviating beliefs condemned as heresies. Questions of discipline threatened disruption within the Church; to settle these, Constantine called the Council of Arles 314, followed by the councils of Nicaea 325 and Constantinople 381.
5th century	Councils of Ephesus 431 and Chalcedon 451. Christianity was carried northward by such figures as saints Columba and Augustine.
800	Holy Roman Emperor Charlemagne crowned by the pope. The church assisted the growth of the feudal system of which it formed the apex.
1054	The Eastern Orthodox Church split from the Roman Catholic Church.
11th–12th centuries	Secular and ecclesiastical jurisdiction were often in conflict; for example, Emperor Henry IV and Pope Gregory VII, Henry II of England and his archbishop Becket.
1096–1291	The church supported a series of wars in the Middle East, called the Crusades.
1233	The Inquisition was established to suppress heresy.
14th century	Increasing worldliness (against which the foundation of the Dominican and Franciscan monastic orders was a protest) and ecclesiastical abuses led to dissatisfaction and the appearance of the reformers Wycliffe and Huss.
15th–17th centuries	Thousands of women were accused of witchcraft, tortured, and executed.
early 16th century	The Renaissance brought a reexamination of Christianity in N Europe by the humanists Erasmus, More, and Colet.
1517	The German priest Martin Luther started the Reformation, an attempt to return to a pure form of Christianity, and became leader of the Protestant movement.
1519–64	In Switzerland the Reformation was carried out by Calvin and Zwingli.
1529	Henry VIII renounced papal supremacy and proclaimed himself head of the Church of England.
1545–63	The Counter-Reformation was initiated by the Catholic church at the Council of Trent.
1560	The Church of Scotland was established according to Calvin's Presbyterian system.
17th century	Jesuit missionaries established themselves in China and Japan. Puritans, Quakers, and other sects seeking religious freedom established themselves in North America.
18th century	During the Age of Reason, Christian dogmas were questioned, and intellectuals began to examine society in purely secular terms. In England and America, religious revivals occurred among the working classes in the form of Methodism and the Great Awakening. In England the Church of England suffered the loss of large numbers of Nonconformists.
19th century	The evolutionary theories of Darwin and the historical criticism of the Bible challenged the Book of Genesis. Missionaries converted people in Africa and Asia, suppressing indigenous faiths and cultures.
1948	The World Council of Churches was founded as part of the ecumenical movement to reunite various Protestant sects and, to some extent, the Protestant churches and the Catholic church.
1950s–80s	Protestant evangelicism grew rapidly in the US, spread by television.
1969	A liberation theology of freeing the poor from oppression emerged in South America, and attracted papal disapproval.
1972	The United Reformed Church was formed by the union of the Presbyterian Church in England and the Congregational Church. In the US, the 1960s–70s saw the growth of cults, some of them nominally Christian, which were a source of social concern.
1980s	The Roman Catholic Church played a major role in the liberalization of the Polish government; and in the USSR the Orthodox Church and other sects were tolerated and even encouraged under President Gorbachev.
1989	Barbara Harris, first female bishop, ordained in the US.
1993	Synod for the Church of England accepts the ordination of women.

chow chow breed of dog originating in China in ancient times. About 1.5 ft/45 cm tall, it has a broad neck and head, round catlike feet, a soft woolly undercoat with a coarse outer coat, and a mane. Its coat should be of one color, and it has an unusual blue-black tongue.

Chrétien de Troyes lived second half of the 12th century. French poet, born in Champagne. His epics, which introduced the concept of the ◊Holy Grail, include *Lancelot, ou le chevalier de la charrette*; *Perceval, ou le conte du Graal*, written for Philip, Count of Flanders; *Erec*; *Yvain, ou le chevalier au Lion*; and other Arthurian romances.

Christ the ◊Messiah as prophesied in the Hebrew Bible, or Old Testament.

Christian follower of ◊Christianity, the religion derived from the teachings of Jesus. In the New Testament (Acts 11:26) it is stated that the first to be called Christians were the disciples in Antioch (now Antakya, Turkey).

Christian I 1426–1481. King of Denmark from 1448, and founder of the Oldenburg dynasty. In 1450 he established the union of Denmark and Norway that lasted until 1814.

Christian IV 1577–1648. King of Denmark and Norway from 1588. He sided with the Protestants in the Thirty Years' War (1618–48), and founded Christiania (now Oslo, capital of Norway). He was succeeded by Frederick II 1648.

Christian IX 1818–1906. King of Denmark from 1863. His daughter Alexandra married Edward VII of the UK and another, Dagmar, married Tsar Alexander III of Russia; his second son, George, became king of Greece. In 1864 he lost the duchies of Schleswig and Holstein after a war with Austria and Prussia.

Christian X 1870–1947. King of Denmark and Iceland from 1912, when he succeeded his father Frederick VIII. He married Alexandrine, Duchess of Mecklenburg-Schwerin, and was popular for his democratic attitude. During World War II he was held prisoner by the Germans in Copenhagen. He was succeeded by Frederick IX.

Christianity world religion derived from the teaching of Jesus in the first third of the 1st century, with a present-day membership of about 1 billion. It is divided into groups or denominations that differ in some areas of belief and practice. Its main divisions are the ◊Roman Catholic, ◊Eastern Orthodox, and ◊Protestant churches. *beliefs* Christians believe in one God with three aspects: God the Father, God the Son (Jesus), and God the Holy Spirit, who is the power of God working in the world. God created everything that exists and showed his love for the world by coming to Earth as Jesus, and suffering and dying in order to be reconciled with humanity. Christians believe that three days after his death by crucifixion Jesus was raised to life by God's power, appearing many times in bodily form to his followers, and that he is now alive in the world through the Holy Spirit. Christians speak of the sufferings they may have to endure because of their faith, and the reward of everlasting life in God's presence which is promised to those who have faith in Jesus Christ and who live according to his teaching.

Christian Science or *the Church of Christ, Scientist* sect established in the US by Mary Baker Eddy 1879. Christian Scientists believe that since God is good and is a spirit, matter and evil are not ultimately real. Consequently they refuse all medical treatment. The church has its own daily newspaper, the *Christian Science Monitor*.

Christie Agatha (born Miller) 1890–1976. English detective novelist who created the characters Hercule Poirot and Miss Jane Marple. She wrote more than 70 novels, including *The Murder of Roger Ackroyd* 1926 and *Ten Little Indians* 1939. Her play *The Mousetrap*, which opened in London 1952, is the longest continuous running show in the world.

Christina 1626–1689. Queen of Sweden 1632–54. Succeeding her father Gustavus Adolphus at the age of six, she assumed power 1644, but disagreed with the former regent Oxenstjerna. Refusing to marry, she eventually nominated her cousin Charles Gustavus (Charles X) as her successor. As a secret convert to Roman Catholicism, which was then illegal in Sweden, she had to abdicate 1654, and went to live in Rome, twice returning to Sweden unsuccessfully to claim the throne.

Christmas Christian religious holiday, observed throughout the Western world on Dec 25 and traditionally marked by feasting and gift-giving. In the Christian church, it is the day on which the birth of Jesus is celebrated, although the actual birth date is unknown. Many of its customs have a non-Christian origin and were adapted from celebrations of the winter solstice.

Christophe Henri 1767–1820. West Indian slave, one of the leaders of the revolt against the French 1791, who was proclaimed king of Haiti 1811. His government distributed plantations to military leaders. He shot himself when his troops deserted him because of his alleged cruelty.

Christopher, St patron saint of travelers. His feast day, July 25, was dropped from the Roman Catholic liturgical calendar 1969.

chromatic scale musical scale proceeding by semitones. All 12 notes in the octave are used rather than the 7 notes of the diatonic scale.

chromatography technique for separating or analyzing a mixture of gases, liquids, or dissolved substances. This is brought about by means of two immiscible substances, one of which (*the mobile phase*) transports the sample mixture through the other (*the stationary phase*). The mobile phase may be a gas or a liquid; the stationary phase may be a liquid or a solid, and may be in a column, on paper, or in a thin layer on a glass or plastic support. The components of the mixture are absorbed or impeded by the stationary phase to different extents and therefore become separated. The technique is used for both qualitative and quantitive analyzes in biology and chemistry.

chromite $FeCr_2O_3$, iron chromium oxide, the main chromium ore. It is one of the spinel group of minerals, and crystallizes in dark-colored octahedra of the cubic system. Chromite is usually found in association with ultrabasic and basic rocks; in Cyprus, for example, it occurs with ◊serpentine, and in South Africa it forms continuous layers in a layered intrusion.

chromium hard, brittle, gray-white, metallic element, symbol Cr, atomic number 24, atomic weight 51.996. It takes a high polish, has a high melting point, and is very resistant to corrosion. It is used in chromium electroplating, in the manufacture of stainless steel and other alloys, and as a catalyst. Its compounds are used for tanning leather and for ◊alums. In human nutrition it is a vital trace element. In nature, it occurs chiefly as chrome iron ore or chromite ($FeCr_2O_4$). Kazakhstan, Zimbabwe, and Brazil are sources.

chromosome structure in a cell nucleus that carries the ◊genes. Each chromosome consists of one very long strand of DNA, coiled and folded to produce a compact body. The point on a chromosome where a particular gene occurs is known as its locus. Most higher organisms have two copies of each chromosome (they are ◊diploid) but some have only one (they are haploid). There are 46 chromosomes in a normal human cell. See also ◊mitosis and ◊meiosis.

chronic in medicine, term used to describe a condition that is of slow onset and then runs a prolonged course, such as rheumatoid arthritis or chronic bronchitis. In contrast, an *acute* condition develops quickly and may be of relatively short duration.

chronic fatigue syndrome medical condition characterized by long-term fatigue, irritability, confusion, and, often, inflammation of the brain. It is thought to be caused by a virus, an abnormality of the immune system, or a lack of hormones in the brain and endocrine system. It is called "Yuppie flu" because it is found most often in professional women— and sometimes men—in their thirties.

Chronicles two books of the Old Testament containing genealogy and history.

Chronicles, medieval books modeled on the Old Testament Books of Chronicles. Until the later Middle

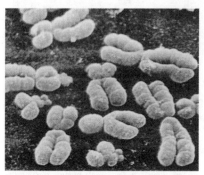

chromosome False-color electron-microscope view of a group of human chromosomes.

Ages, they were usually written in Latin by clerics, who borrowed extensively from one another.

chronometer instrument for measuring time precisely, originally used at sea. It is designed to remain accurate through all conditions of temperature and pressure. The first accurate marine chronometer, capable of an accuracy of half a minute a year, was made 1761 by John Harrison in England.

The term is now applied to scientific timekeeping devices.

chrysanthemum any plant of the genus *Chrysanthemum* of the family Compositae, with about 200 species. There are hundreds of cultivated varieties, whose exact wild ancestry is uncertain. In the Far East the common chrysanthemum has been cultivated for more than 2,000 years and is the imperial emblem of Japan. Chrysanthemums may be grown from seed, but are more usually propagated by cutting or division.

They were introduced into the West in 1789.

Chrysler Walter Percy 1875–1940. US industrialist. After World War I, he became president of the independent Maxwell Motor Company and went on to found the Chrysler Corporation 1925. By 1928 he had acquired Dodge and Plymouth, making Chrysler Corporation one of the largest US motor-vehicle manufacturers.

Chuang member of the largest minority group in China, numbering about 15 million. They live in S China, where they cultivate rice fields. Their religion includes elements of ancestor worship. The Chuang language belongs to the Tai family.

chub any of several large minnows of the carp family. Creek chub *Semotelusatromaculatus*, up to 12 in/30 cm, is found widely in North American streams. Also, any of a number of small-mouthed marine fishes of the family Kyphosidae.

Chubu mountainous coastal region of central Honshu Island, Japan; area 25,791 sq mi/66,774 sq km; population (1986) 20,694,000. The chief city is Nagoya.

Chugoku SW region of Honshu Island, Japan; area 12,314 sq mi/31,881 sq km; population (1986) 7,764,000. The chief city is ◊Hiroshima.

Chun Doo-hwan 1931– . South Korean military ruler who seized power 1979, president 1981–88 as head of the newly formed Democratic Justice Party.

church building designed as a Christian place of worship. Churches were first built in the 3rd century, when persecution ceased under the Holy Roman emperor Constantine. The original church design was based on the Roman ◊basilica, with a central nave, aisles either side, and an apse at one end.

Churchill Randolph (Henry Spencer) 1849–1895. British Conservative politician, chancellor of the Exchequer and leader of the House of Commons 1886; father of Winston Churchill.

He married Jennie Jerome (1854–1921), daughter of a wealthy New Yorker, 1874.

Churchill Winston (Leonard Spencer) 1874–1965. British Conservative politician, prime minister 1940–45 and 1951–55. In Parliament from 1900, as a Liberal until 1923, he held a number of ministerial offices, including First Lord of the Admiralty 1911–15 and chancellor of the Exchequer 1924–29. Absent from the cabinet in the 1930s, he returned Sept 1939 to lead a coalition government 1940–45, negotiating with Allied leaders in World War II to achieve the unconditional surrender of Germany 1945; he led a Conservative government 1951–55. He received the Nobel Prize for Literature 1953.

He was born at Blenheim Palace, the elder son of Lord Randolph Churchill. During the Boer War he was a war correspondent and made a dramatic escape from imprisonment in Pretoria. In 1900 he was elected Conservative member of Parliament for Oldham, but he disagreed with Chamberlain's tariff-reform policy and joined the Liberals. In 1911 he was appointed First Lord of the Admiralty. In 1915–16 he served in the trenches in France but then resumed his parliamentary duties and was minister of munitions under Lloyd George 1917, when he was concerned with the development of the tank. After the armistice he was secretary for war 1918–21 and then as colonial secretary played a leading part in the establishment of the Irish Free State. During the postwar years he was active in support of the Whites (anti-Bolsheviks) in Russia. From 1929 to 1939 he was out of office as he disagreed with the Conservatives on India, rearmament, and Chamberlain's policy of appeasement. On the first day of World War II he went back to his old post at the Admiralty. In May 1940 he was called to the premiership as head of an all-party administration and made a much quoted "blood, tears, toil, and sweat" speech to the House of Commons. He had a close relationship with US president F D Roosevelt and in Aug 1941 concluded the Atlantic Charter with him. In Feb 1945 he met Stalin and Roosevelt at Yalta and agreed on the final plans for victory. On May 8 he announced the unconditional surrender of Germany. On May 23,

church The ground plan of a typical large cathedral church is in the shape of an elongated cross.

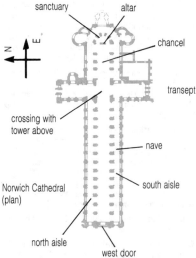

Norwich Cathedral (plan)

sanctuary   altar

chancel

transept

crossing with tower above

nave

south aisle

north aisle

west door

Churchill British prime minister Winston Churchill, March 1944.

1945, the coalition was dissolved, and Churchill formed a caretaker government drawn mainly from the Conservatives. Defeated in the general election in July, he became leader of the opposition until the election Oct 1951, in which he again became prime minister. In April 1955 he resigned and retired to paint. After he died his paintings were exhibited in several shows, including a major retrospective in New York City in the 1980s.

Church of England established form of Christianity in England, a member of the Anglican Communion. It was dissociated from the Roman Catholic Church 1534. There were approximately 1,100,000 regular worshipers in 1988.

history 2nd century Christianity arrived in England during the Roman occupation.

597 St Augustine became the first archbishop of Canterbury.

1529–34 At the *Reformation* the chief change was political: the sovereign (Henry VIII) replaced the pope as head of the church and assumed the right to appoint archbishops and bishops.

1536–40 The monasteries were closed down.

1549 First publication of the *Book of Common Prayer*, the basis of worship throughout the Anglican Church.

1563–1604 The *Thirty-Nine Articles*, the Church's doctrinal basis, were drawn up, enforced by Parliament, and revised.

17th–18th centuries Colonizers took the Church of England to North America (where three US bishops were consecrated after the American Revolution, and whose successors still lead the Episcopal Church in the US), Australia, New Zealand, and India.

19th century Missionaries were active in Africa. The *Oxford Movement* eventually developed into Anglo-Catholicism.

20th century There were moves toward reunion with the Methodist and Roman Catholic churches. The *ordination of women* was accepted by some overseas Anglican churches, for example the US Episcopal Church 1976.

CIA abbreviation for the US ◊ *Central Intelligence Agency*.

cicada any of several insects of the family Cicadidae. Most species are tropical, but a few occur in Europe and North America. Young cicadas live underground, for up to 17 years in some species. The adults live on trees, whose juices they suck. The males produce a loud, almost continuous, chirping by vibrating membranes in resonating cavities in the abdomen.

Cicero Marcus Tullius 106–43 BC. Roman orator, writer, and politician. His speeches and philosophical and rhetorical works are models of Latin prose, and his letters provide a picture of contemporary Roman life. As consul 63 BC he exposed the Roman politician Catiline's conspiracy in four major orations.

Cid, El Rodrigo Diaz de Bivar 1040–1099. Spanish soldier, nicknamed *El Cid* ("the lord") by the ◊ Moors. Born in Castile of a noble family, he fought against the king of Navarre and won his nickname *el Campeador* ("the Champion") by killing the Navarrese champion in single combat. Essentially a mercenary, fighting both with and against the Moors, he died while defending ◊ Valencia against them, and in subsequent romances became Spain's national hero.

cider juice pressed from apples as a beverage or for making vinegar. In the US, hard cider refers to fermented apple juice drunk as an alcoholic beverage. Alcoholic cider is produced in large quantities in the Americas, France, and England.

Cierva Juan de la 1895–1936. Spanish engineer. In trying to produce an aircraft that would not stall and could fly slowly, he invented the ◊ autogiro, the forerunner of the helicopter but differing from it in having unpowered rotors that revolve freely.

cigar compact roll of cured tobacco leaves, contained in a binder leaf, which in turn is surrounded by a wrapper leaf. The cigar was originally a sheath of palm leaves filled with tobacco, smoked by the Indians of Central America. Cigar smoking was introduced into Spain soon after 1492 and spread all over Europe in the next few centuries. From about 1890 cigar smoking was gradually supplanted in popularity by cigarette smoking.

The best cigars are still hand-rolled in Cuba, hence Havanas.

cigarette thin paper tube stuffed with shredded tobacco for smoking, now usually plugged with a filter. The first cigarettes were the *papelitos* smoked in South America about 1750. The habit spread to Spain and then throughout the world; today it is the most general form of tobacco smoking, although it is dangerous to the health of both smokers and nonsmokers who breathe in the smoke.

cilia (singular *cilium*) small threadlike organs on the surface of some cells, composed of contractile fibers that produce rhythmic waving movements. Some single-celled organisms move by means of cilia. In multicellular animals, they keep lubricated surfaces clear of debris. They also move food in the digestive tracts of some invertebrates.

Cilicia ancient region of Asia Minor, now forming part of Turkey, situated between the Taurus Mountains and the Mediterranean. Access from the N across the Taurus range is through the *Cilician Gates*, a strategic pass that has been used for centuries as part of a trade route linking Europe and the Middle East.

Cimabue Giovanni (Cenni de Peppi) *c.* 1240–1302. Italian painter, active in Florence, traditionally styled the "father of Italian painting." His paintings retain the golden background of Byzantine art but the figures have a new naturalism. Among the works attributed to him are *Madonna and Child* (Uffizi, Florence), a huge Gothic image of the Virgin that nevertheless has a novel softness and solidity that points forward to Giotto.

Cincinnati city and port in Ohio, on the Ohio River; population (1990) 364,000. Chief industries include machinery, clothing, furniture making, wine, chemicals, and meatpacking. Founded 1788, Cincinnati became a city 1819. It attracted large numbers of European immigrants, particularly Germans, during the 19th century. Proctor and Gamble, a household-products manufacturer, has its headquarters here. Xavier University and the University of Cincinnati are here, and it has a major symphony orchestra. William Howard Taft, 27th president of the US, was born in Cincinnati.

Cincinnatus Lucius Quintus 5th century BC. Roman general. Appointed dictator 458 BC, he defeated the Aequi (an Italian people) in a brief campaign, then resumed life as a yeoman farmer.

cinema 20th-century form of art and entertainment consisting of "moving pictures" in either black and white or color, projected onto a screen. Cinema borrows from the other arts, such as music, drama, and literature, but is entirely dependent for its origins on technological developments, including the technology of action photography, projection, sound reproduction, and film processing and printing (see ◊photography).

CinemaScope trade name for a wide-screen process using anamorphic lenses, in which images are compressed during filming and then extended during projection over a wide curved screen. The first film to be made in CinemaScope was *The Robe* 1953.

cinéma vérité filmmaking that aims to capture truth on film by observing, recording, and presenting real events and situations as they occur without major directorial, editorial, or technical control.

Cinerama wide-screen process devised 1937 by Fred Waller of Paramount's special-effects department. Originally three 35-mm cameras and three projectors were used to record and project a single image. Three aspects of the image were recorded and then projected on a large curved screen with the result that the images blended together to produce an illusion of vastness. The first Cinerama film was *How the West Was Won* 1962. It was eventually abandoned in favor of a single-lens 70-mm process.

cinnabar mercuric sulfide, HgS, the only commercially useful ore of mercury. It is deposited in veins and impregnations near recent volcanic rocks and hot springs. The mineral itself is used as a red pigment, commonly known as *vermilion*. Cinnabar is found in the US (California), Spain (Almadén), Peru, Italy, and Slovenia.

cinnamon dried inner bark of a tree *Cinnamomum zeylanicum* of the laurel family, grown in India and Sri Lanka. The bark is ground to make the spice used in curries and confectionery. Oil of cinnamon is obtained from waste bark and is used as flavoring in food and medicine.

Cinque Ports group of ports in S England, originally five, Sandwich, Dover, Hythe, Romney, and Hastings, later including Rye, Winchelsea, and others. Probably founded in Roman times, they rose to importance after the Norman conquest and until the end of the 15th century were bound to supply the ships and men necessary against invasion.

circadian rhythm metabolic rhythm found in most organisms, which generally coincides with the 24-hour day. Its most obvious manifestation is the regular cycle of sleeping and waking, but body temperature and the concentration of ◊hormones that influence mood and behavior also vary over the day. In humans, alteration of habits (such as rapid air travel around the world) may result in the circadian rhythm being out of phase with actual activity patterns, causing malaise until it has had time to adjust.

Circe in Greek mythology, an enchantress living on the island of Aeaea. In Homer's *Odyssey*, she turned the followers of ◊Odysseus into pigs. Odysseus, bearing the herb moly provided by Hermes to protect him from the same fate, forced her to release his men.

circle perfectly round shape, the path of a point that moves so as to keep a constant distance from a fixed point (the center). Each circle has a *radius* (the distance from any point on the circle to the center), a *circumference* (the boundary of the circle), *diameters* (straight lines crossing the circle through the center), *chords* (lines joining two points on the circumference), *tangents* (lines that touch the circumference at one point only), *sectors* (regions inside the circle between two radii), and *segments* (regions between a chord and the circumference).

circuit in physics or electrical engineering, an arrangement of electrical components through which a current can flow. There are two basic circuits, series and parallel. In a series circuit, the components are connected end to end so that the current flows through all components one after the other. In a parallel circuit, components are connected side by side so that part of the current passes through each component. A circuit diagram shows in graphical form how components are connected together, using standard symbols for the components.

circuit breaker switching device designed to protect an electric circuit from excessive current. It has the

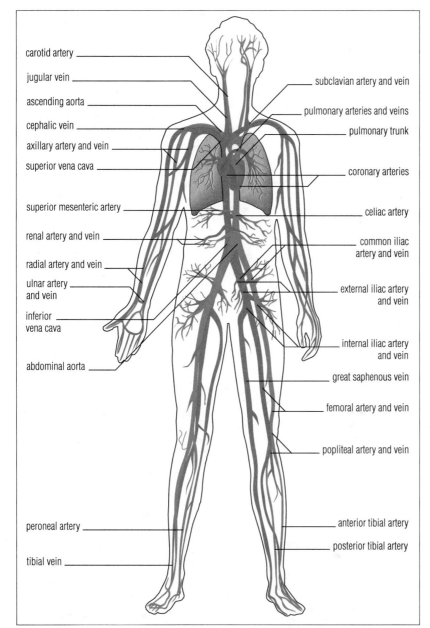

carotid artery

jugular vein

ascending aorta

cephalic vein

axillary artery and vein

superior vena cava

superior mesenteric artery

renal artery and vein

radial artery and vein

ulnar artery
and vein

inferior
vena cava

abdominal aorta

peroneal artery

tibial vein

subclavian artery and vein

pulmonary arteries and veins

pulmonary trunk

coronary arteries

celiac artery

common iliac
artery and vein

external iliac artery
and vein

internal iliac artery
and vein

great saphenous vein

femoral artery and vein

popliteal artery and vein

anterior tibial artery

posterior tibial artery

circulatory system
Blood flows through
60,000 mi/96,500 km
of arteries and veins,
supplying oxygen and
nutrients to organs
and limbs.

same action as a ◊fuse, and many houses now have a circuit breaker between the incoming main supply and the domestic circuits. Circuit breakers usually work by means of ◊solenoids. Those at electricity-generating stations have to be specially designed to prevent dangerous arcing (the release of luminous discharge) when the high-voltage supply is switched off. They may use an air blast or oil immersion to quench the arc.

circulatory system system of vessels in an animal's body that transports essential substances (blood or other circulatory fluid) to and from the different parts of the body. Except for simple animals such

as sponges and coelenterates (jellyfishes, sea anemones, corals), all animals have a circulatory system.

circumcision surgical removal of all or part of the foreskin (prepuce) of the penis, usually performed on the newborn; it is practiced among Jews and Muslims. In some societies in Africa and the Middle East, female circumcision or clitoridectomy (removal of the labia minora and/or clitoris) is practiced on adolescents as well as babies; it is illegal in the West.

circumference in geometry, the curved line that encloses a curved plane figure, for example a ◊circle or an ellipse. Its length varies according to the nature of the curve, and may be ascertained by the appropriate formula. The circumference of a circle is πd or $2\pi r$, where d is the diameter of the circle, r is its radius, and π is the constant pi, approximately equal to 3.1416.

circumnavigation sailing around the world. The first ship to sail around the world was the *Victoria*, one of a Spanish squadron of five vessels that sailed from Seville Aug 1519 under the Portuguese navigator Ferdinand Magellan.

circus entertainment, often held in a large tent ("big top"), involving performing animals, acrobats, and clowns. In 1871 Phineas T ◊Barnum created the "Greatest Show on Earth" in the US. The popularity of animal acts decreased in the 1980s. Originally, in Roman times, a circus was an arena for chariot races and gladiatorial combats.

cirque French name for a corrie, a steep-sided hollow in a mountainside.

cirrhosis any degenerative disease in an organ of the body, especially the liver, characterized by excessive development of connective tissue, causing scarring and painful swelling. Cirrhosis of the liver may be caused by an infection such as viral hepatitis, by chronic alcoholism or drug use, blood disorder, or malnutrition. If cirrhosis is diagnosed early, it can be arrested by treating the cause; otherwise it will progress to jaundice, edema, vomiting of blood, coma, and death.

CIS abbreviation for ◊*Commonwealth of Independent States*, established 1992 by 11 former Soviet republics.

Cisalpine Gaul region of the Roman province of Gallia (N Italy) S of the Alps; *Transalpine Gaul*, the region N of the Alps, comprised what is now Belgium, France, the Netherlands, and Switzerland.

Ciskei, Republic of Bantu homeland in South Africa, which became independent 1981, although this is not recognized by any other country
area 2,974 sq mi/7,700 sq km
capital Bisho
features one of the two homelands of the Xhosa people created by South Africa (the other is Transkei)
products wheat, sorghum, sunflower, vegetables, timber, metal products, leather, textiles
population (1985) 925,000
language Xhosa
government president (Brig Oupa Gqozo from 1990), with legislative and executive councils
recent history In Sept 1992 Ciskei troops fired on African National Congress (ANC) demonstrators demanding the ousting of the territory's military leader, Brig Gqozo; 28 people were slain and about 200 injured. Brig Gqozo had assumed power in a military takeover 1990. Initially sympathetic to the aims of the ANC, he had pledged to restore civilian rule and called for the reincorporation of Ciskei into South Africa. Subsequently, he turned against the organization and has been accused of repressing its supporters.

Cistercian order Roman Catholic monastic order established at Cîteaux 1098 by St Robert de Champagne, abbot of Molesme, as a stricter form of the Benedictine order. Living mainly by agricultural labor, the Cistercians made many advances in farming methods in the Middle Ages. The *Trappists*, so called from the original house at La Trappe in Normandy (founded by Dominique de Rancé 1664), followed a particularly strict version of the rule.

CITES (abbreviation for *Convention on International Trade in Endangered Species*) international agreement under the auspices of the IUCN with the aim of regulating trade in ◊endangered species of animals and plants. The agreement came into force 1975 and by 1991 had been signed by 110 states. It prohibits any trade in a category of 8,000 highly endangered species and controls trade in a further 30,000 species.

citizens' band (CB) short-range radio communication facility (around 27 MHz) used by members of the public in the US and many European countries to talk to one another or call for emergency assistance.

citizenship status as a member of a state. In most countries citizenship may be acquired either by birth or by naturalization. The status confers rights such as voting and the protection of the law and also imposes responsibilities such as military service, in some countries.

citric acid $HOOCCH_2C(OH)(COOH)CH_2COOH$ organic acid widely distributed in the plant kingdom; it is found in high concentrations in citrus fruits and has a sharp, sour taste. At one time it was commercially prepared from concentrated lemon juice, but now the main source is the fermentation of sugar with certain molds.

citronella lemon-scented oil used in cosmetics and insect repellents, obtained from the S Asian grass *Cymbopogon nardus*.

citrus any tree or shrub of the genus *Citrus*, family Rutaceae. Citruses are found in Asia and other warm parts of the world. They are evergreen and aromatic, and several species—the orange, lemon, lime, citron, and grapefruit—are cultivated for fruit.

Ciudad Juárez city on the Rio Grande, in Chihuahua, N Mexico, on the US border; population (1990) 797,650. It is a center for cotton.

civet small to medium-sized carnivorous mammal found in Africa and Asia, belonging to the family Viverridae, which also includes ◊*mongooses* and ◊*genets*. Distant relations of cats, they generally have longer jaws and more teeth. All have a scent gland in the inguinal (groin) region. Extracts from this gland are taken from the *African civet Civettictis civetta* and used in perfumery.

civil aviation the operation of passenger and freight transport by air. With increasing traffic, control of air space is a major problem. The Federal Aviation Agency (FAA) is responsible for regulating development of aircraft, air navigation, traffic control, and communications in the US. The Civil Aeronautics Board is the US authority prescribing safety regulations and investigating accidents. The world's largest airline was the Soviet Union's government-owned Aeroflot (split among republics 1992), which operated 1,300 aircraft over 620,000 mi/1 million km of routes and carried over 110 million passengers a year.

civil disobedience deliberate breaking of laws considered unjust, a form of nonviolent direct action; the term was coined by the US writer Henry Thoreau in an essay of that name 1849. It was advocated by Mahatma ◊Gandhi to prompt peaceful withdrawal of British power from India. Civil disobedience has since been employed by, for instance, the US civil-rights movement in the 1960s and the peace movement in the 1980s.

civil engineering branch of engineering that is concerned with the construction of roads, bridges, aqueducts, waterworks, tunnels, canals, irrigation works, and harbors.

civil law legal system based on ◊Roman law. It is one of the two main European legal systems, ◊English (common) law being the other. Civil law may also mean the law relating to matters other than criminal law, such as ◊contract and ◊tort.

civil rights rights of the individual citizen. In many countries they are specified (as in the Bill of Rights of the US constitution) and guaranteed by law to ensure equal treatment for all citizens. In the US, the struggle to obtain civil rights for former slaves and their descendants, both through legislation and in practice, has been a major theme since the Civil War.

Civil Rights Cases five Supreme Court cases 1883 that tested the Civil Rights Act of 1875, which guaranteed protection from racial discrimination by private citizens. Congress considered this protection implicit in the 13th and 14th Amendments, but the Court disagreed. According to an 8–1 ruling, the 13th Amendment only prohibited forced servitude while the 14th Amendment protected citizens only from discrimination by the state, not by private individuals. The Civil Rights Act was struck down, a decision not reversed until 1964.

civil-rights movement general term for efforts by US blacks to improve their status in society after World War II. Following their significant contribution to the national effort in wartime, they began a sustained campaign for full civil rights, which challenged racial discrimination. Despite favorable legislation such as the Civil Rights Act 1964 and the 1965 Voting Rights Act, growing discontent among urban blacks in northern states led to outbreaks of civil disorder, such as the Watts riots in Los Angeles, Aug 1965. Another riot in the city 1992, following the acquittal of policemen charged with beating a black motorist, were seen as demonstrating the unsatisfactory progress of black civil rights..

civil service the body of administrative staff appointed to carry out the policy of a government. In the US, federal employees are restricted in the role they may play in political activity, and they retain their posts (except at senior levels) when there is a change in administration.

civil war war between rival groups within the same country.

Civil War, American also called the *War Between the States* war 1861–65 between the Southern or Confederate States of America and the Northern or Union States. The former wished to maintain certain "states' rights," in particular the right to determine state law on the institution of slavery, and claimed the right to secede from the Union; the latter fought primarily to maintain the Union, with slave emancipation (proclaimed 1863) a secondary issue.

The issue of slavery had brought to a head longstanding social and economic differences between the two oldest sections of the country. A series of political crises was caused by the task of determining whether newly admitted states, such as California, should permit or prohibit slavery in their state constitutions. The political parties in the late 1850s came to represent only sectional interests—Democrats in the South, Republicans in the North. This breakdown of an underlying national political consensus (which had previously sustained national parties) led to the outbreak of hostilities, only a few weeks after the inauguration of the first Republican president, Abraham Lincoln.

Civil War, English in British history, the conflict between King Charles I and the Royalists (Cavaliers) on one side and the Parliamentarians (also called Roundheads) under Oliver ◊Cromwell on the other. Their differences centered on the king's unconstitutional acts but became a struggle over the relative powers of crown and Parliament. Hostilities began 1642 and a series of Royalist defeats (Marston Moor 1644, Naseby 1645) culminated in Charles's capture 1647 and execution 1649. The war continued until the final defeat of Royalist forces at Worcester 1651. Cromwell became Protector (ruler) from 1651 until his death 1658.

Civil War, Spanish war 1936–39 precipitated by a military revolt led by General Franco against the Republican government. Inferior military capability led to the gradual defeat of the Republicans by 1939, and the establishment of Franco's dictatorship.

Clair René. Adopted name of René-Lucien Chomette 1898–1981. French filmmaker, originally a poet, novelist, and journalist. His *Sous les toits de Paris/Under the Roofs of Paris* 1930 was one of the first sound films. His other films include *Entr'acte* 1924, *Le Million* 1931, and *A nous la Liberté* 1931.

clam common name for a ◊bivalve mollusk. The giant clam *Tridacna gigas* of the Indopacific can grow to 3 ft/1 m across in 50 years and weigh, with the shell, 1,000 lb/500 kg.

clan social grouping based on ◊kinship. Some traditional societies are organized by clans, which are either matrilineal or patrilineal, and whose members must marry into another clan in order to avoid inbreeding.

Clapton Eric 1945– . English blues and rock guitarist, singer, and songwriter. Originally a blues purist, then one of the pioneers of heavy rock with Cream 1966–68, he returned to the blues after making the landmark album *Layla and Other Assorted Love Songs* 1970 by Derek and the Dominos. Solo albums include *Journeyman* 1989 and the acoustic *Unplugged* 1992.

Clarendon Edward Hyde, 1st Earl of Clarendon 1609–1674. English politician and historian, chief adviser to Charles II 1651–67. A member of Parliament 1640, he joined the Royalist side 1641. The *Clarendon Code* 1661–65, a series of acts passed by the government, was directed at Nonconformists (or Dissenters) and were designed to secure the supremacy of the Church of England.

In retirement he wrote the *History of the Rebellion and Civil Wars in England* 1702–04.

Clare, St c. 1194–1253. Christian saint. Born in Assisi, Italy, at 18 she became a follower of St Francis, who founded for her the convent of San Damiano. Here she gathered the first members of the *Order of Poor Clares*. In 1958 she was proclaimed the patron saint of television by Pius XII, since in 1252 she saw from her convent sickbed the Christmas services being held in the Basilica of St Francis in Assisi. Feast day Aug 12.

clarinet musical ◊woodwind instrument, developed in Germany in the 18th century, with a single reed and a cylindrical tube, broadening at the end. At the lower end of its range it has a rich "woody" tone, which becomes increasingly brilliant toward the upper register. Its ability both to blend and to contrast with other instruments make it popular for chamber music and as a solo instrument. It is also heard in military and concert bands and as a jazz instrument.

Clark George Rogers 1752–1818. American military leader and explorer. He was made commander of the Virginia frontier militia at the outbreak of the American Revolution 1775. During 1778–79 he led an attack on the Indian allies of the British to the west of the Ohio River and founded a settlement at the site of Louisville, Kentucky.

Clark Jim (James) 1936–1968. Scottish-born automobile racing driver, one of the finest in the postwar era. He was twice world champion in 1963 and 1965.

Clark Joe (Joseph) Charles 1939– . Canadian Progressive Conservative politician who became party leader 1976, and May 1979 defeated Pierre ◊Trudeau at the polls to become the youngest prime minister in Canada's history. Following the rejection of his government's budget, he was defeated in a second election Feb 1980. He became secretary of state for external affairs (foreign minister) 1984 in the ◊Mulroney government.

Clark Kenneth, Lord Clark 1903–1983. British art historian, director of the National Gallery, London, 1934–45. His books include *Leonardo da Vinci* 1939 and *The Nude* 1956.

Clarksville city in N Tennessee, at the confluence of the Cumberland and Red rivers, NW of Nashville; population (1980) 54,777. Industries include tobacco products, clothing, air-conditioning and heating equipment, rubber, and cheese.

class in biological classification, a group of related ◊orders. For example, all mammals belong to the class Mammalia and all birds to the class Aves. Thus, the class Angiospermae (flowering plants) includes numerous plant orders such as Rosales (currants, acacias, roses, and others). The class Reptilia (reptiles) includes the orders Crocodilia and Chelonia (turtles) among others.

class action in law, a court procedure where one or more claimants represent a larger group of people who are all making the same kind of claim against the same defendant. The court's decision is binding on all the members of the group.

classical economics school of economic thought that dominated 19th-century thinking. It originated with Adam ◊Smith's *The Wealth of Nations* 1776, which embodied many of the basic concepts and principles of the Classical school. Smith's theories were further developed in the writings of John Stuart Mill and David Ricardo. Central to the theory were economic freedom, competition, and laissez faire government. The idea that economic growth could best be promoted by free trade, unassisted by government, was in conflict with ◊mercantilism.

Classicism in art, music, and literature, a style that emphasizes the qualities traditionally considered characteristic of ancient Greek and Roman art, that is, reason, balance, objectivity, restraint, and strict adherence to form. The term Classicism (also ◊Neo-Classicism) is often used to characterize the culture of 18th-century Europe, and contrasted with 19th-century Romanticism.

classification in biology, the arrangement of organisms into a hierarchy of groups on the basis of their similarities in biochemical, anatomical, or physiological characters. The basic grouping is a ◊species, several of which may constitute a ◊genus, which in turn are grouped into families, and so on up through orders, classes, phyla (in plants, sometimes called divisions), to kingdoms.

Claude Lorrain (Claude Gelée) 1600–1682. French landscape painter, active in Rome from 1627. His distinctive, luminous, Classical style had great impact on late 17th- and 18th-century taste. His subjects are mostly mythological and historical, with insignificant figures lost in great expanses of poetic scenery, as in *The Enchanted Castle* 1664 (National Gallery, London).

Claudian (Claudius Claudianus) *c.* 370–404. Last of the great Latin poets of the Roman Empire, probably born in Alexandria, Egypt. He wrote official panegyrics, epigrams, and the mythological epic *The Rape of Proserpine*.

Claudius Tiberius Claudius Nero 10 BC–AD 54. Nephew of ◊Tiberius, made Roman emperor by his troops AD 41, after the murder of his nephew ◊Caligula. Claudius was a scholar, historian, and able administrator. During his reign the Roman empire was considerably extended, and in 43 he took part in the invasion of Britain.

Clausius Rudolf Julius Emanuel 1822. German physicist, one of the founders of the science of thermodynamics. In 1850 be enunciated its second law: heat cannot pass from a colder to a hotter body.

claustrophobia ◊phobia involving fear of enclosed spaces.

clavichord stringed keyboard instrument, common in Renaissance Europe and in 18th-century Germany. Notes are sounded by a metal blade striking the string. The clavichord was a forerunner of the pianoforte.

clavicle the collarbone of many vertebrates. In humans it is vulnerable to fracture; falls involving a sudden force on the arm may result in very high stresses passing into the chest region by way of the clavicle and other bones.

claw hard, hooked, pointed outgrowth of the digits of mammals, birds, and most reptiles. Claws are composed of the protein keratin, and grow continuously from a bundle of cells in the lower skin layer. Hooves and nails are modified structures with the same origin as claws.

clay very fine-grained ◊sedimentary deposit that has undergone a greater or lesser degree of consolidation. When moistened it is plastic, and it hardens on heating, which renders it impermeable. It may be white, gray, red, yellow, blue, or black, depending on its composition. Clay minerals consist largely of hydrous silicates of aluminum and magnesium together with iron, potassium, sodium, and organic substances. The crystals of clay minerals have a layered structure, capable of holding water, and are responsible for its plastic properties. According to international classification, in mechanical analysis of soil, clay has a grain size of less than 0.00008 in/0.002 mm.

Clay Henry 1777–1852. US politician. He stood unsuccessfully three times for the presidency: as a Democratic-Republican 1824, as a National Republican 1832, and as a Whig 1844. He supported the war of 1812 against Britain and tried to hold the Union together on the slavery issue by the Missouri Compromise of 1820, and again in the compromise of 1850. He was secretary of state 1825–29, and devised an "American system" for the national economy.

Claude Lorrain
Jacob with Laban
and his Daughters
*(1676) by French
landscape painter
Claude Lorrain.*

Clearwater city in W central Florida, on the Gulf of Mexico, NW of St Petersburg; seat of Pinellas County; population (1990) 98,800. Industries include tourism, citrus fruits, fishing, electronics, and flowers.

cleavage in geology, the tendency of a rock, especially slate, to split along parallel or subparallel planes that result from realignment of component minerals during deformation or metamorphism.

Cleese John 1939– . English actor and comedian who has written for and appeared in both television programs and films. On British television, he is particularly associated with the comedy series "Monty Python's Flying Circus" and "Fawlty Towers". His films include *Monty Python and the Holy Grail* 1974, *Life of Brian* 1979, and *A Fish Called Wanda* 1988.

Cleisthenes lived 6th century BC. Athenian statesman, he was exiled with his family, the Alcmaeonidae, and intrigued and campaigned against the Athenian tyrants, the Pisistratids. After their removal in 510 BC he developed a popular faction in favor of democracy, which was established by his reforms over the next decade.

clematis any temperate woody climbing plant of the genus *Clematis* with showy flowers. Clematis are a member of the buttercup family, Ranunculaceae.

Rock clematis *C. verticillaris* grows in woods and thickets in most of shady E North America.

Clemenceau Georges 1841–1929. French politician and journalist (prominent in the defense of Alfred ◊Dreyfus). He was prime minister 1906–09 and 1917–20. After World War I he presided over the peace conference in Paris that drew up the Treaty of ◊Versailles, but failed to secure for France the Rhine as a frontier.

Clemens Samuel Langhorne. Real name of the US writer Mark ◊Twain.

Clement VII 1478–1534. Pope 1523–34. He refused to allow the divorce of Henry VIII of England and Catherine of Aragon. Illegitimate son of a brother of Lorenzo de' Medici, the ruler of Florence, he commissioned monuments for the Medici chapel in Florence from the Renaissance artist Michelangelo.

Clemente Roberto (Walker) 1934–1972. Puerto Rican–born US baseball player who played for the Pittsburgh Pirates 1955–72. He had a career batting average of .317, was the 11th player in history to reach 3,000 hits, and was an outstanding right fielder. He died in a plane crash while flying to aid Nicaraguan earthquake victims.

Clement of Rome, St lived late 1st century AD. One of the early Christian leaders and writers known as the Fathers of the Church. According to tradition he was the third or fourth bishop of Rome, and a disciple of St Peter. He wrote a letter addressed to the church at Corinth (First Epistle of Clement), and many other writings have been attributed to him.

Cleon 5th century BC. Athenian politician and general in the ◊Peloponnesian War. He became "leader of the people" after the death of ◊Pericles to whom he was opposed. He was an aggressive imperialist and advocated a vigorous war policy against the Spartans. He was killed by the Spartans at the battle at Amphipolis 422 BC.

Cleopatra c. 68–30 BC. Queen of Egypt 51–48 and 47–30 BC. When the Roman general Julius Caesar arrived in Egypt, he restored her to the throne from which she had been ousted. Cleopatra and Caesar became lovers and she went with him to Rome. After Caesar's assassination 44 BC she returned to Alexandria and resumed her position as queen of Egypt. In 41 BC she was joined there by Mark Antony, one of Rome's rulers. In 31 BC Rome declared war on Egypt and scored a decisive victory in the naval Battle of Actium off the W coast of Greece. Cleopatra fled with her 60 ships to Egypt; Antony abandoned the struggle and followed her. Both he and Cleopatra committed suicide.

Cleopatra's Needle either of two ancient Egyptian granite obelisks erected at Heliopolis in the 15th century BC by Thothmes III, and removed to Alexandria by the Roman emperor Augustus about 14 BC. They

Clinton *The 42nd president of the United States of America, Bill Clinton, a Democrat. 1993–* .

have no connection with Cleopatra's reign. One of the pair was taken to England 1878 and erected on the Victoria Embankment in London. The other was given by the khedive of Egypt to the US and erected in Central Park, New York, in 1881.

clerihew humorous verse form invented by Edmund Clerihew Bentley, characterized by a first line consisting of a person's name.

Cleveland largest city of Ohio, US, on Lake Erie at the mouth of the river Cuyahoga; population (1990) 505,600, metropolitan area 2,759,800. Its chief industries are iron and steel and petroleum refining.

Iron ore from the Lake Superior region and coal from Ohio and Pennsylvania mines are brought here. Other manufactured goods include machine tools, auto and airplane parts, hardware, trucks, electronic equipment, and appliances. Cleveland has art and natural-history museums, a world-famous symphony orchestra, and Case Western University. It was surveyed 1796 and grew rapidly after a canal linked Lake Erie to the Ohio River 1832. John D Rockefeller established Standard Oil in Cleveland 1870. After surviving a financial crisis in 1978, Cleveland sought vigorously to broaden its economy.

Cleveland (Stephen) Grover 1837–1908. 22nd and 24th president of the US, 1885–89 and 1893–97; the first Democratic president elected after the Civil War and the only president to hold office for two nonconsecutive terms. He attempted to check corruption in the civil service and reduce tariffs. These policies provoked political opposition, and he was defeated by Republican Benjamin Harrison 1888. He was returned to office 1892 and supported the Sherman Silver Purchase Act, which permitted free silver coinage and may have caused the economic panic of 1893. He was a noninterventionist but in 1895 initiated arbitration that settled a boundary dispute between Britain and Venezuela. An unswerving conservative, he refused to involve the government in economic affairs but used federal troops to end the Pullman strike 1894.

Clift (Edward) Montgomery 1920–1966. US film and theater actor. A star of the late 1940s and 1950s in films such as *Red River* 1948, *A Place in the Sun* 1951, and *From Here to Eternity* 1953, he was disfigured in an automobile accident in 1957 but continued to make films. He played the title role in *Freud* 1962.

climate weather conditions at a particular place over a period of time. Climate encompasses all the meteorological elements and the factors that influence them. The primary factors that determine the variations of climate over the surface of the Earth are (a) the effect of latitude and the tilt of the Earth's axis to the plane of the orbit about the Sun (66.5°); (b) the large-scale movements of different wind belts over the Earth's surface; (c) the temperature difference between land and sea;

(d) contours of the ground; and (e) location of the area in relation to ocean currents. Catastrophic variations to climate may be caused by the impact of another planetary body, or by clouds resulting from volcanic activity. The most important local or global meteorological changes brought about by human activity are those linked with ◊ozone depleters and the ◊greenhouse effect.

climatology study of climate, its global variations and causes.

clinical ecology in medicine, ascertaining environmental factors involved in illnesses, particularly those manifesting nonspecific symptoms such as fatigue, depression, allergic reactions, and immune system malfunctions, and prescribing means of avoiding or minimizing these effects.

clinical psychology discipline dealing with the understanding and treatment of health problems, particularly mental disorders. The main problems dealt with include anxiety, phobias, depression, obsessions, sexual and marital problems, drug and alcohol dependence, childhood behavioral problems, psychoses (such as schizophrenia), mental handicap, and brain damage (such as dementia).

Clinton Bill (William Jefferson) 1946– . 42nd president of the US 1993– . A Democrat, he served as governor of Arkansas 1979–81 and 1983–93, establishing a liberal and progressive reputation. After winning the 1992 nomination for president, he chose Al Gore as his running mate. The 1992 campaign centered on the problems of the US economy, with Clinton successfully challenging the incumbent George Bush while weathering criticism of his avoidance of the military draft and other "character" issues. Clinton began his administration with ambitious plans for deficit reduction, military reforms, and health care restructuring; all were met by strong opposition. Despite lack of support among Democrats, he was able to secure approval of the North American Free Trade Agreement (NAFTA) in late 1993.

Clinton De Witt 1769–1828. American political leader. After serving in the US Senate 1802–03, he was elected mayor of New York City 1803–15 and governor of New York from 1817. A strong promoter of the Erie Canal, he was instrumental in the initiation of that project, completed 1825.

cloisonné ornamental craft technique in which thin metal strips are soldered in a pattern onto a metal surface, and the resulting compartments (*cloisons*) filled with colored ◊enamels and fired. The technique was probably developed in the Byzantine Middle East and traded to Asia and Europe. Cloisonné vases and brooches were made in medieval Europe, but the technique was perfected in Japan and China during the 17th, 18th, and 19th centuries.

Close Glenn 1948– . US actress who received Academy Award nominations for her roles as the embittered "other woman" in *Fatal Attraction* 1987 and as the scheming antiheroine of *Dangerous Liaisons* 1988. She played Gertrude in Franco Zeffirelli's film of *Hamlet* 1990 and appeared as an opera star in *Meeting Venus* 1991.

closed shop any company or firm, public corporation, or other body that requires its employees to be members of the appropriate labor union. Usually demanded by unions, the closed shop may be preferred by employers as simplifying negotiation, but it was condemned by the European Court of Human Rights 1981.

cloud water vapor condensed into minute water particles that float in masses in the atmosphere. Clouds, like fogs or mists, which occur at lower levels, are formed by the cooling of air containing water vapor, which generally condenses around tiny dust particles.

cloud chamber apparatus for tracking ionized particles. It consists of a vessel fitted with a piston and filled with air or other gas, supersaturated with water vapor. When the volume of the vessel is suddenly expanded by moving the piston outward, the vapor cools and a cloud of tiny droplets forms on any nuclei, dust, or ions present. As fast-moving ionizing particles collide with the air or gas molecules, they show as visible tracks.

Clouet François *c.* 1515–1572. French portrait painter who succeeded his father Jean Clouet as court painter. He worked in the Italian style of Mannerism. His half-nude portrait of Diane de Poitiers, *The Lady in Her Bath c.* 1570 (National Gallery, Washington), is also thought to be a likeness of Marie Touchet, mistress of Charles IX.

Clouet Jean (known as ***Janet***) 1486–1541. French artist, court painter to Francis I. His portraits and drawings, often compared to Holbein's, show an outstanding naturalism.

clove dried, unopened flower bud of the clove tree *Eugenia caryophyllus*. A member of the myrtle family Myrtaceae, the clove tree is a native of the Moluccas. Cloves are used for flavoring in cooking and confectionery. Oil of cloves, which has tonic and carminative qualities, is employed in medicine. The aromatic quality of cloves is shared to a large degree by the leaves, bark, and fruit of the tree.

clover any of an Old World genus *Trifolium* of low-growing leguminous plants, usually with compound leaves of three leaflets and small flowers in dense heads. Sweet clover refers to various species belonging to the related genus *Melilotus*.

Red clover *T. pratense* and white clover *T. repens* now grow widely in the US. The most common honey is made from clover and the most important source of fodder is red clover.

Clovis 465–511. Merovingian king of the Franks from 481. He succeeded his father Childeric as king of the Salian (northern) Franks; defeated the Gallo-Romans (Romanized Gauls) near Soissons 486, ending their rule in France; and defeated the Alemanni, a confederation of Germanic tribes, near Cologne 496. He embraced Christianity and subsequently proved a powerful defender of orthodoxy against the Arian Visigoths, whom he defeated at Poitiers 507. He made Paris his capital.

clutch any device for disconnecting rotating shafts, used especially in a car's transmission system. In an automobile with a manual gearbox, the driver depresses the clutch when changing gear, thus disconnecting the engine from the gearbox.

Clytemnestra in Greek legend, the wife of ◊Agamemnon. With her lover Aegisthus, she murdered her husband on his return from the Trojan War and was in turn killed by her son Orestes.

cm symbol for ***centimeter***.

coal black or blackish mineral substance formed from the compaction of ancient plant matter in tropical swamp conditions. It is used as a fuel and in the chemical industry. Coal is classified according to the proportion of carbon it contains. The main types are ◊***anthracite*** (shiny, with more than 90% carbon),

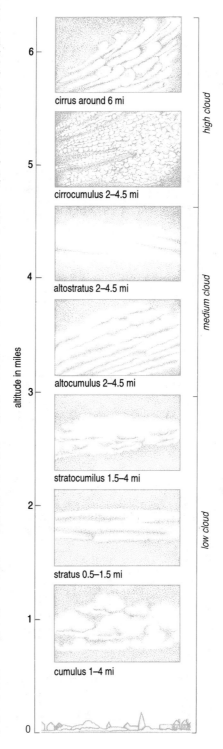

cloud *Standard types of cloud.*

cirrus around 6 mi

cirrocumulus 2–4.5 mi

altostratus 2–4.5 mi

altocumulus 2–4.5 mi

stratocumilus 1.5–4 mi

stratus 0.5–1.5 mi

cumulus 1–4 mi

altitude in miles

high cloud

medium cloud

low cloud

coastal erosion

The sea erodes the land by the constant battering of waves. The force of the waves creates a hydraulic effect, compressing air to form explosive pockets in the rocks and cliffs. The waves also have an abrasive effect, flinging rocks and pebbles against the cliff faces and wearing them away.

In areas where there are beaches, the waves cause longshore drift, in which sand and stone fragments are carried in a particular direction parallel to the shore.

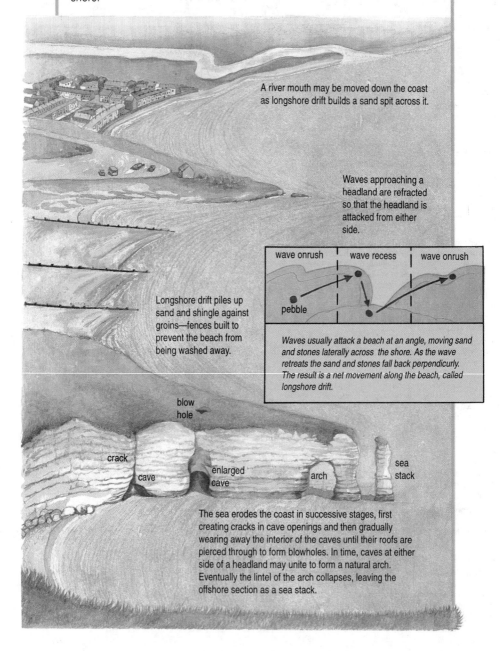

A river mouth may be moved down the coast as longshore drift builds a sand spit across it.

Waves approaching a headland are refracted so that the headland is attacked from either side.

wave onrush | wave recess | wave onrush

pebble

Waves usually attack a beach at an angle, moving sand and stones laterally across the shore. As the wave retreats the sand and stones fall back perpendicurly. The result is a net movement along the beach, called longshore drift.

Longshore drift piles up sand and shingle against groins—fences built to prevent the beach from being washed away.

blow hole

crack

cave

enlarged cave

arch

sea stack

The sea erodes the coast in successive stages, first creating cracks in cave openings and then gradually wearing away the interior of the caves until their roofs are pierced through to form blowholes. In time, caves at either side of a headland may unite to form a natural arch. Eventually the lintel of the arch collapses, leaving the offshore section as a sea stack.

bituminous coal (shiny and dull patches, more than 80% carbon), and *lignite* (woody, grading into peat, 70% carbon). Coal burning is one of the main causes of ◊acid rain.

coal gas gas produced when coal is destructively distilled or heated out of contact with the air. Its main constituents are methane, hydrogen, and carbon monoxide. Coal gas has been superseded by ◊natural gas for domestic purposes.

coal mining extraction of coal (a ◊sedimentary rock) from the Earth's crust. Coal mines may be opencast, adit, or deepcast. The least expensive is opencast but this results in scars on the landscape.

coastal erosion the erosion of the land by the constant battering of the sea's waves. This produces two effects. The first is a hydraulic effect, in which the force of the wave compresses air pockets in coastal rocks and cliffs, and the air then expands explosively. The second is the effect of corrasion, in which rocks and pebbles are flung against the cliffs, wearing them away. Frost shattering (or freeze-thaw), caused by the expansion of frozen seawater in cavities, and ◊biological weathering, caused by the burrowing of rock-boring mollusks, also result in the breakdown of the rock.

coastal protection measures taken to prevent ◊coastal erosion. Many stretches of coastline are so severely affected by erosion that beaches are swept away, threatening the livelihood of seaside resorts, and buildings become unsafe.

coati or *coatimundi* any of several species of carnivores of the genus *Nasua*, in the same family, Procyonidae, as the raccoons. A coati is a good climber and has long claws, a long tail, a good sense of smell, and a long, flexible piglike snout used for digging. Coatis live in packs in the forests of South and Central America.

coaxial cable electric cable that consists of a solid or stranded central conductor insulated from and surrounded by a solid or braided conducting tube or sheath. It can transmit the high-frequency signals used in television, telephone, and other telecommunications transmissions.

cobalt hard, lustrous, gray, metallic element, symbol Co, atomic number 27, atomic weight 58.933. It is found in various ores and occasionally as a free metal, sometimes in metallic meteorite fragments. It is used in the preparation of magnetic, wear-resistant, and high-strength alloys; its compounds are used in inks, paints, and varnishes.

cobalt ore cobalt is extracted from a number of minerals, the main ones being *smaltite*, $(CoNi)As_3$; *linnaeite*, Co_3S_4; *cobaltite*, CoAsS; and *glaucodot*, $(CoFe)AsS$.

Cobb Ty(rus Raymond), nicknamed "the Georgia Peach" 1886–1961. US baseball player, one of the greatest batters and base runners of all time. He played for Detroit and Philadelphia 1905–28, and won the American League batting average championship 12 times. He holds the record for runs scored (2,254) and lifetime batting average (.367). He had 4,191 hits in his career—a record that stood for almost 60 years.

COBOL (acronym for *common business-oriented language*) high-level computer-programming language, designed in the late 1950s for commercial data-processing problems; it has become the major language in this field. COBOL features powerful facilities for file handling and business arithmetic. Program instructions written in this language make extensive use of words and look very much like English sentences. This makes COBOL one of the easiest languages to learn and understand.

cobra any of several poisonous snakes, especially the genus *Naja*, of the family Elapidae, found in Africa and S Asia, species of which can grow from 3 ft/1 m to over 14 ft/4.3 m. The neck stretches into a hood when the snake is alarmed. Cobra venom contains nerve toxins powerful enough to kill humans.

Coca-Cola trade name of a sweetened, carbonated drink, originally made with coca leaves and flavored with cola nuts, and containing caramel and caffeine. Invented in 1886, Coca-Cola was sold in every state of the US by 1895 and in 155 countries by 1987.

As a rule, Fanta, an orange-flavored soda made by Coca-Cola, preceded the cola-flavored soda in the Third World. With the increased presence of Americans in Third World nations, US imperialism became known as Coca-Colonialism.

cocaine alkaloid $C_{17}H_{21}NO_4$ extracted from the leaves of the coca tree. It has limited medical application, mainly as a local anesthetic agent that is readily absorbed by mucous membranes (lining tissues) of the nose and throat. It is both toxic and addictive. Its use as a stimulant is illegal. ◊Crack is a derivative of cocaine.

coccus (plural *cocci*) member of a group of globular bacteria, some of which are harmful to humans. The cocci contain the subgroups *streptococci*, where the bacteria associate in straight chains, and *staphylococci*, where the bacteria associate in branched chains.

Cochise c. 1812–1874. Apache Indian leader who campaigned relentlessly against white settlement of his territory. Unjustly arrested by US authorities 1850, he escaped from custody and took American hostages, whom he later executed. Joining forces with the Mimbreño Apache, he successfully fought off a large force of California settlers 1862. Finally apprehended by General George Crook 1871, Cochise made peace with the US government the following year.

cochlea part of the inner ◊ear. It is equipped with approximately 10,000 hair cells, which move in response to sound waves and thus stimulate nerve cells to send messages to the brain. In this way they turn vibrations of the air into electrical signals.

cockatiel Australian parrot *Nymphicus hollandicus*, about 8 in/20 cm long, with grayish plumage, yellow cheeks, a long tail, and a crest like a cockatoo. Cockatiels are popular as pets and aviary birds.

cockatoo any of several crested parrots, especially of the genus *Cacatua*. They usually have light-colored plumage with tinges of red, yellow, or orange on the face, and an erectile crest on the head. They are native to Australia, New Guinea, and nearby islands.

cobra The Indian cobra feeds on rodents, lizards, and frogs.

cock-of-the-rock
The Guyanan cock-of-
the-rock lives in
forested ravines in N
South America.

Cockcroft John Douglas 1897–1967. British physicist. In 1932 he and the Irish physicist Ernest Walton succeeded in splitting the nucleus of an atom for the first time. In 1951 they were jointly awarded a Nobel Prize.

cockle any of over 200 species of bivalve mollusk with ribbed, heart-shaped shells. Some are edible and are sold in W European markets.

The Atlantic strawberry cockle *Americardia media*, about 1 in/2.5 cm across, is a common E North American species.

cock-of-the-rock South American bird of the genus *Rupicola*. It belongs to the family Cotingidae, which also includes the cotingas and umbrella birds. There are two species: *R. peruviana*, the Andean cock-of-the-rock, and *R. rupicola*, the Guyanan cock-of-the-rock. The male has brilliant orange plumage including the head crest, the female is a duller brown. Males display at a communal breeding area.

cockroach any of numerous insects of the family Blattidae, distantly related to mantises and grasshoppers. There are 3,500 species, mainly in the tropics. They have long antennae and biting mouthparts. They can fly, but rarely do so.

cocoa and chocolate food products made from the ◊cacao (or cocoa) bean, fruit of a tropical tree *Theobroma cacao*, now cultivated mainly in Africa. Chocolate as a drink was introduced to Europe from the New World by the Spanish in the 16th century; eating chocolate was first produced in the late 18th century. Cocoa and chocolate are widely used in confectionery and drinks.

coconut fruit of the coconut palm *Cocos nucifera* of the family Arecaceae, which grows throughout the lowland tropics. The fruit has a large outer husk of fibers, which is split off and used for coconut matting and ropes. Inside this is the nut exported to temperate countries. Its hard shell contains white flesh and coconut milk, both of which are nourishing and palatable.

Cocos Islands or *Keeling Islands* group of 27 small coral islands in the Indian Ocean, about 1,720 mi/2,770 km NW of Perth, Australia; area 5.5 sq mi/14 sq km; population (1986) 616. They are owned by Australia.

Cocteau Jean 1889–1963. French poet, dramatist, and film director. A leading figure in European Modernism, he worked with Picasso, Diaghilev, and Stravinsky. He produced many volumes of poetry; ballets such as *Le Boeuf sur le toit/The Ox on the Roof* 1920; plays, for example, *Orphée/Orpheus* 1926; and a mature novel of bourgeois French life, *Les Enfants terribles/Children of the Game* 1929, which he made into a film 1950.

cod any fish of the family Gadoidea, especially the Atlantic cod, *Gadus morhua* found in the N Atlantic and Baltic. It is brown to gray with spots, white below, and can grow to 5 ft/1.5 m.

codeine opium derivative that provides analgesia in mild to moderate pain. It also suppresses the cough center of the brain. It is an alkaloid, derived from morphine but less toxic and addictive.

cod-liver oil oil obtained by subjecting the fresh livers of cod to pressure at a temperature of about 185°F/85°C. It is highly nutritious, being a valuable source of the vitamins A and D; overdose can be harmful.

Cody (William Frederick) "Buffalo Bill" 1846–1917. US scout and performer. From 1883 he toured the US and Europe with a Wild West show which featured the recreation of Indian attacks and, for a time, the cast included Chief ◊Sitting Bull as well as Annie ◊Oakley. His nickname derives from a time when he had a contract to supply buffalo carcasses to railroad laborers (over 4,000 in 18 months).

He was a heavy drinker and a trusting investor; he died in poverty after seeing his exploits recounted and exaggerated in novels of the West.

coefficient the number part in front of an algebraic term, signifying multiplication. For example, in the expression $4x^2 + 2xy - x$, the coefficient of x^2 is 4 (because $4x^2$ means $4 \times x^2$), that of xy is 2, and that of x is -1 (because $-1 \times x = -x$).

coefficient of relationship the probability that any two individuals share a given gene by virtue of being descended from a common ancestor. In sexual reproduction of diploid species, an individual shares half its genes with each parent, with its offspring, and (on average) with each sibling; but only a quarter (on average) with its grandchildren or its siblings' offspring; an eighth with its great-grandchildren, and so on.

coelacanth lobe-finned fish *Latimeria chalumnae* up to 6 ft/2 m long. It has bone and muscle at the base of the fins, and is distantly related to the freshwater lobefins, which were the ancestors of all land animals with backbones. Coelacanths live in deep water (650 ft/200 m) around the Comoros Islands, off the coast of Madagascar. They were believed to be extinct until one was caught in 1938.

coelenterate any freshwater or marine organism of the phylum Coelenterata, having a body wall composed of two layers of cells. They also possess stinging cells. Examples are jellyfish, hydra, and coral.

Coetzee J(ohn) M 1940– . South African author whose novel *In the Heart of the Country* 1975 dealt with the rape of a white woman by a black man. In 1983 he won Britain's prestigious Booker Prize for *The Life and Times of Michael K*.

coffee drink made from the roasted and ground bean-like seeds found inside the red berries of any of several species of shrubs of the genus *Coffea*, originally native to Ethiopia and now cultivated throughout the tropics. It contains a stimulant, ◊caffeine.

cognition in psychology, a general term covering the functions involved in synthesizing information—for example, perception (seeing, hearing, and so on), attention, memory, and reasoning.

cognitive therapy treatment for emotional disorders such as ◊depression and ◊anxiety, developed by Professor Aaron T Beck in the US. This approach encourages the patient to challenge the distorted and unhelpful thinking that is characteristic of these problems. The treatment includes ◊behavior therapy and has been most helpful for people suffering from depression.

Cohan George M(ichael) 1878–1942. US composer. His Broadway hit musical *Little Johnny Jones* 1904 included his songs "Give My Regards to Broadway" and "Yankee Doodle Boy." "You're a Grand Old Flag" 1906 further associated him with popular patriotism, as did his World War I song "Over There" 1917.

Cohan Robert Paul 1925– . US choreographer and founder of the London Contemporary Dance Theater 1969–87; now artistic director of the Contemporary Dance Theater. He was a student of Martha ◊Graham and co-director of her company 1966–69. His works include *Waterless Method of Swimming Instruction* 1974 and *Mass for Man* 1985.

coherence in physics, property of two or more waves of a beam of light or other electromagnetic radiation having the same frequency and the same ◊phase, or a constant phase difference.

cohesion in physics, a phenomenon in which interaction between two surfaces of the same material in contact makes them cling together (with two different materials the similar phenomenon is called adhesion). According to kinetic theory, cohesion is caused by attraction between particles at the atomic or molecular level. ◊Surface tension, which causes liquids to form spherical droplets, is caused by cohesion.

coin form of money. The right to make and issue coins is a state monopoly, and the great majority are tokens in that their face value is greater than that of the metal of which they consist.

coke clean, light fuel produced when ◊coal is strongly heated in an airtight oven. Coke contains 90% carbon and makes an useful domestic and industrial fuel (used, for example, in the iron and steel industries).

cola or **kola** any tropical tree of the genus *Cola*, especially *C. acuminata*, family Sterculiaceae. The nuts are chewed in W Africa for their high caffeine content, and in the West are used to flavor soft drinks.

Colbert Claudette. Adopted name of Claudette Lily Cauchoin 1905– . French-born film actress who lived in Hollywood from childhood. She was ideally cast in sophisticated, romantic roles, but had a natural instinct for comedy and appeared in several of Hollywood's finest, including *It Happened One Night* 1934 and *The Palm Beach Story* 1942.

Colbert Jean-Baptiste 1619–1683. French politician, chief minister to Louis XIV, and controller-general (finance minister) from 1665. He reformed the Treasury, promoted French industry and commerce by protectionist measures, and tried to make France a naval power equal to England or the Netherlands, while favoring a peaceful foreign policy.

Cody US Wild West performer Buffalo Bill Cody.

cold, common minor disease of the upper respiratory tract, caused by a variety of viruses. Symptoms are headache, chill, nasal discharge, sore throat, and occasionally cough. Research indicates that the virulence of a cold depends on psychological factors and either a reduction or an increase of social or work activity, as a result of stress, in the previous six months.

cold-blooded of animals, dependent on the surrounding temperature.

cold fusion in nuclear physics, the fusion of atomic nuclei at room temperature. Were cold fusion to become possible it would provide a limitless, cheap, and pollution-free source of energy, and it has therefore been the subject of research around the world. In 1989, Martin Fleischmann (1927–) and Stanley Pons (1943–) of the University of Utah claimed that they

coelacanth The coelacanth is the sole survivor of an ancient group of fishes and is found only in deep trenches of the

had achieved cold fusion in the laboratory, but their results could not be substantiated.

Cold Harbor, Battle of American Civil War engagement near Richmond, Virginia, June 1–12, 1864, in which the Confederate army under Robert E ◊Lee repulsed Union attacks under Ulysses S ◊Grant, inflicting as many as 6,000 casualties in an hour and forcing Grant to adopt a siege of Petersburg. This demonstrated the tenacity of the Confederate forces late in the war and kept Grant's army largely stationary until April 1865.

Colditz city in E Germany, near Leipzig, site of a castle used as a high-security prisoner-of-war camp (Oflag IVC) in World War II. Among daring escapes was that of British Captain Patrick Reid (1910–1990) and others Oct 1942. It became a museum 1989. In 1990 the castle was converted to a hotel.

Cold War Ideological, political, and economic tensions 1945–90 between the USSR and Eastern Europe on the one hand and the US and Western Europe on the other. The Cold War was exacerbated by propaganda, covert activity by intelligence agencies, and economic sanctions; it intensified at times of conflict anywhere in the world. Arms-reduction agreements between the US and USSR in the late 1980s, and a diminution of Soviet influence in Eastern Europe, symbolized by the opening of the Berlin Wall 1989, led to a reassessment of positions, and the "war" officially ended 1990.

Coleridge Samuel Taylor 1772–1834. English poet, one of the founders of the Romantic movement. A friend of Southey and Wordsworth, he collaborated with the latter on *Lyrical Ballads* 1798. His poems include "The Rime of the Ancient Mariner," "Christabel," and "Kubla Khan"; critical works include *Biographia Literaria*.

Colette Sidonie-Gabrielle 1873–1954. French writer. At 20 she married Henri Gauthier-Villars, a journalist known as "Willy," under whose name and direction her four "Claudine" novels, based on her own early life, were written. Divorced 1906, she worked as a striptease and mime artist for a while, but continued to write. Works from this later period include *Chéri* 1920, *La Fin de Chéri/The End of Chéri* 1926, and *Gigi* 1944.

Colfax Schuyler 1823–1885. US political leader. He was elected to the US House of Representatives 1854 and served as Speaker of the House 1863–69. A radical Republican, Colfax was elected vice president for President Grant's first term 1869–73. He was not renominated because of charges of corruption and financial improprieties.

colitis inflammation of the colon (large intestine) with diarrhea (often bloody). It may be caused by food poisoning or some types of bacterial dysentery.

collage (French "gluing" or "pasting") technique of pasting paper and other materials to create a picture. Several artists in the early 20th century used collage: Jean (or Hans) Arp, Georges Braque, Max Ernst, and Kurt Schwitters, among others.

collagen strong, rubbery ◊protein that plays a major structural role in the bodies of ◊vertebrates. Collagen supports the ear flaps and the tip of the nose in humans, as well as being the main constituent of tendons and ligaments. Bones are made up of collagen, with the mineral calcium phosphate providing increased rigidity.

collective bargaining process whereby management, representing an employer, and a labor union, representing employees, agree to negotiate jointly terms and conditions of employment. Agreements can be company-based or industry-wide.

collective farm (Russian *kolkhoz*) farm in which a group of farmers pool their land, domestic animals, and agricultural implements, retaining as private property enough only for the members' own requirements. The profits of the farm are divided among its members. In cooperative farming, farmers retain private ownership of the land.

collective security system for achieving international stability by an agreement among all states to unite against any aggressor. Such a commitment was embodied in the post–World War I League of Nations and also in the United Nations, although the League was not, and the UN has not yet been, able to live up to the ideals of its founders.

collective unconscious in psychology, the shared pool of memories inherited from ancestors that Carl Jung suggested coexists with individual ◊unconscious recollections. He thought it could affect individuals both for ill, in precipitating mental disturbance, and for good, in prompting achievements (for example, in the arts).

collectivization policy pursued by the Soviet leader Stalin in the USSR after 1928 to reorganize agriculture by taking land into state ownership or creating ◊collective farms. Much of this was achieved during the first two Five-Year Plans but only with much coercion and loss of life among the peasantry.

College Station city in E central Texas, NW of Houston, adjoining the city of Bryan; population (1990) 52,500. Texas A & M University is here.

collenchyma plant tissue composed of relatively elongated cells with thickened cell walls, in particular at the corners where adjacent cells meet. It is a supporting and strengthening tissue found in nonwoody plants, mainly in the stems and leaves.

collie sheepdog originally bred in Britain. The rough and smooth collies are about 2 ft/60 cm tall and have long narrow heads and muzzles. They may be light to dark brown or silver-gray, with black and white markings. The border collie is a working dog, often black and white, about 20 in/50 cm tall, with a dense coat. The bearded collie is about the same size, and is rather like an Old English sheepdog in appearance.

Collier Lesley 1947– . British ballerina, a principal dancer of the Royal Ballet from 1972. She created roles in Kenneth MacMillan's *Anastasia* 1971 and *Four Seasons* 1975, Hans van Manen's *Four Schumann Pieces* 1975, Frederick Ashton's *Rhapsody*, and Glen Tetley's *Dance of Albiar* both 1980.

Collins Phil(lip David Charles) 1951– . English pop singer, drummer, and actor. A member of the group Genesis from 1970, he has also pursued a successful middle-of-the-road solo career since 1981, with hits (often new versions of old songs) including "In the Air Tonight" 1981 and "Groovy Kind of Love" 1988.

Collins Michael 1890–1922. Irish nationalist. He was a Sinn Féin leader, a founder and director of intelligence of the Irish Republican Army 1919, minister for finance in the provisional government of the Irish Free State 1922 (see ◊Ireland, Republic of), commander of the Free State forces in the civil war, and for ten days head of state before being killed by Irishmen opposed to the partition treaty with Britain.

Collins (William) Wilkie 1824–1889. English author of mystery and suspense novels. He wrote *The*

Woman in White 1860 (with its fat villain Count Fosco), often called the first English detective novel, and *The Moonstone* 1868 (with Sergeant Cuff, one of the first detectives in English literature).

collision theory theory that explains how chemical reactions take place and why rates of reaction alter. For a reaction to occur the reactant particles must collide. Only a certain fraction of the total collisions cause chemical change; these are called *fruitful collisions*. The fruitful collisions have sufficient energy (activation energy) at the moment of impact to break the existing bonds and form new bonds, resulting in the products of the reaction. Increasing the concentration of the reactants and raising the temperature bring about more collisions and therefore more fruitful collisions, increasing the rate of reaction.

colloid substance composed of extremely small particles of one material (the dispersed phase) evenly and stably distributed in another material (the continuous phase). The size of the dispersed particles (1–1,000 nanometers across) is less than that of particles in suspension but greater than that of molecules in true solution. Colloids involving gases include *aerosols* (dispersions of liquid or solid particles in a gas, as in

fog or smoke) and *foams* (dispersions of gases in liquids). Those involving liquids include *emulsions* (in which both the dispersed and the continuous phases are liquids) and *sols* (solid particles dispersed in a liquid). Sols in which both phases contribute to a molecular three-dimensional network have a jellylike form and are known as *gels*, gelatin, starch "solution," and silica gel are common examples.

Collor de Mello Fernando 1949– . Brazilian politician, president 1990–92. He founded the center-right National Reconstruction Party (PRN) 1989 and won that year's presidential election by promising to root out government corruption and entrenched privileges. However, rumors of his misconduct led to his constitutional removal from office by a vote of impeachment 1992.

Cologne (German *Köln*) industrial and commercial port in North Rhine–Westphalia, Germany, on the left bank of the Rhine, 22 mi/35 km SE of Düsseldorf; population (1988) 914,000. To the N is the Ruhr coal field, on which many of Cologne's industries are based. They include motor vehicles, freight cars, chemicals, and machine tools. Cologne is an important transshipment center.

Colombia Republic of
(*República de Colombia*)

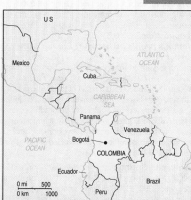

area 440,715 sq mi/1,141,748 sq km
capital Santa Fé de Bogotá
cities Medellín, Cali, Bucaramanga; ports Barranquilla, Cartagena, Buenaventura
physical the Andes mountains run N–S; flat coastland in W and plains (llanos) in E; Magdalena River runs N to Caribbean Sea; includes islands of Providencia, San Andrés, and Mapelo
features Zipaquira salt mine and underground cathedral; Lake Guatavita, source of the legend of "El Dorado"
head of state and government Cesar Gaviria Trujillo from 1990
political system emergent democratic republic
political parties Liberal Party (PL), centrist; April 19 Movement (M-19); National Salvation Movement; Conservative Party, right of center
exports emeralds (world's largest producer), coffee (world's second largest producer), cocaine (country's largest export), bananas, cotton, meat, sugar, oil, skins, hides, tobacco
currency peso
population (1992) 33,392,800 (mestizo 68%, white 20%, Amerindian 1%); growth rate 2.2% p.a.

life expectancy men 61, women 66; Indians 34
language Spanish
religion Roman Catholic 95%
literacy men 89%, women 87% (1987); Indians 40%
GDP $31.9 bn (1987); $1,074 per head

chronology
1886 Full independence achieved from Spain. Conservatives in power.
1930 Liberals in power.
1946 Conservatives in power.
1948 Left-wing mayor of Bogotá assassinated; widespread outcry.
1949 Start of civil war, "La Violencia," during which over 250,000 people died.
1957 Hoping to halt the violence, Conservatives and Liberals agreed to form a National Front, sharing the presidency.
1970 National Popular Alliance (ANAPO) formed as a left-wing opposition to the National Front.
1974 National Front accord temporarily ended.
1975 Civil unrest because of disillusionment with the government.
1978 Liberals, under Julio Turbay, revived the accord and began an intensive fight against drug dealers.
1982 Liberals maintained their control of congress but lost the presidency. The Conservative president, Belisario Betancur, granted guerrillas an amnesty and freed political prisoners.
1984 Minister of justice assassinated by drug dealers; campaign against them stepped up.
1986 Virgilio Barco Vargas, Liberal, elected president by record margin.
1989 Drug cartel assassinated leading presidential candidate; Vargas declared antidrug war; bombing campaign by drug traffickers killed hundreds; police killed José Rodríguez Gacha, one of the most wanted cartel leaders.
1990 Cesar Gaviria Trujillo elected president. Liberals maintained control of congress.
1991 New constitution prohibited extradition of Colombians wanted for trial in other countries; several leading drug traffickers arrested. Oct: Liberal Party won general election.
1992 One of the drug cartel leaders, Pablo Escobar, escaped from prison. State of emergency declared in Nov.
1993 Escobar continued to defy government; shot dead in Dec.

Colombia country in South America, bounded N by the Caribbean Sea, W by the Pacific Ocean, NW corner by Panama, E and NE by Venezuela, SE by Brazil, and SW by Peru and Ecuador. *See panel p. 212*

Colombo capital and principal seaport of Sri Lanka, on the W coast near the mouth of the Kelani River; population (1990) 615,000, Greater Colombo about 1,000,000. It trades in tea, rubber, and cacao. It has iron- and steelworks and an oil refinery.

Colombo Matteo Realdo *c.* 1516–1559. Italian anatomist who discovered pulmonary circulation, the process of blood circulating from the heart to the lungs and back.

Colombo Plan plan for cooperative economic and social development in Asia and the Pacific, established 1950. The 26 member countries are Afghanistan, Australia, Bangladesh, Bhutan, Cambodia, Canada, Fiji, India, Indonesia, Iran, Japan, South Korea, Laos, Malaysia, Maldives, Myanmar (Burma), Nepal, New Zealand, Pakistan, Papua New Guinea, Philippines, Singapore, Sri Lanka, Thailand, UK, and US. They meet annually to discuss economic and development plans such as irrigation, hydroelectric schemes, and technical training.

Colón second largest city in Panama, at the Caribbean end of the Panama Canal; population (1990) 140,900. It has a special economic zone (created 1948) used by foreign companies to avoid taxes on completed products in their home countries; $2 billion worth of goods passed through the zone in 1987, from dozens of countries and 600 companies. Unemployment in the city of Colón, outside the zone, was over 25% in 1991.

colon in anatomy, the part of the large intestine between the cecum and rectum, where water and mineral salts are absorbed from digested food, and the residue formed into feces or fecal pellets.

colon in punctuation, a mark (:) commonly used before a direct quotation (She said: "Leave it out") or a list, or to add detail to a statement ("That is his cat: the fluffy white one").

colonialism another name for ◊*imperialism.*

colophon decorative device on the title page or spine of a book, the trademark of the individual publisher. Originally a colophon was an inscription on the last page of a book giving the writer or printer's name and the place and year of publication.

color quality or wavelength of light emitted or reflected from an object. Visible white light consists of electromagnetic radiation of various wavelengths, and if a beam is refracted through a prism, it can be spread out into a spectrum, in which the various colors correspond to different wavelengths. From long to short wavelengths (from about 700 to 400 nanometers) the colors are red, orange, yellow, green, blue, indigo, and violet.

Colorado river in North America, rising in the Rocky Mountains and flowing 1,450 mi/2,333 km to the Gulf of California through Colorado, Utah, Arizona (including the Grand Canyon), and N Mexico. The many dams along its course, including Hoover and Glen Canyon, provide power and irrigation water, but have destroyed wildlife and scenery, and very little water now reaches the sea. To the W of the river in SE California is the *Colorado Desert*, an arid area of 2,000 sq mi/5,000 sq km. Its tributaries include the Gunnison, Green, Little Colorado, and Gila rivers. The Imperial Valley is irrigated by the Colorado River.

Colorado

Colorado state in W central US; nickname Centennial State
area 104,104 sq mi/269,700 sq km
capital Denver
cities Colorado Springs, Aurora, Lakewood, Fort Collins, Greeley, Pueblo
physical Great Plains in the E; the main ranges of the Rocky Mountains (more than 14,000 ft/4,300 m); high plateaus of the Colorado Basin in the W
features Rocky Mountain National Park; Pike's Peak; prehistoric cliff dwellings of the Mesa Verde National Park; Garden of the Gods (natural sandstone sculptures); Dinosaur and Great Sand Dunes national monuments; mining "ghost" towns; ski resorts, including Aspen, Vail, Steamboat Springs; US Air Force Academy
products cereals, meat and dairy products, oil, coal, molybdenum, uranium, iron, steel, machinery
population (1990) 3,294,400
famous people Jack Dempsey, Douglas Fairbanks
history first visited by Spanish explorers in the 16th century; claimed for Spain 1706; east portion passed to the US 1803 as part of the Louisiana Purchase, the rest in 1845 and 1848 as a result of the Mexican War. It attracted fur traders, and Denver was founded following the discovery of gold 1858. Colorado became a state 1876. Irrigated agriculture, ranching, tourism and outdoor sports, energy development, and the establishment of military bases fueled rapid growth after World War II.

Colorado Springs city in Colorado, 75 mi/120 km SE of Denver; population (1990) 281,100. At an altitude of about 6,000 ft/1,800 m, and surrounded by magnificent scenery, it was founded as a health resort 1871. A gold strike at nearby Cripple Creek 1892 aided its growth.

color blindness hereditary defect of vision that reduces the ability to discriminate certain colors, usually red and green. The condition is sex-linked, affecting men more than women.

coloring food ◊additive used to alter or improve the color of processed foods. Colorings include artificial colors, such as tartrazine and amaranth, which are made from petrochemicals, and the "natural" colors such as chlorophyll, caramel, and carotene. Some of the natural colors are actually synthetic copies of the naturally occurring substances, and some of these, notably the synthetically produced caramels, may be injurious to health.

Colosseum amphitheater in ancient Rome, begun by the emperor Vespasian to replace the one destroyed by fire during the reign of Nero, and completed by his son Titus AD 80. It was 615 ft/187 m long and 160 ft/49 m high, and seated 50,000 people. Early Christians were martyred there by lions and gladiators. It could be flooded for mock sea battles.

Colossus of Rhodes bronze statue of Apollo erected at the entrance to the harbor at ◊Rhodes 292–280 BC. Said to have been about 100 ft/30 m high, it was counted as one of the Seven Wonders of the World, but in 224 BC fell as a result of an earthquake.

Colt Samuel 1814–1862. US gunsmith, who in 1835 invented the revolver, a handgun that bears his name.

Coltrane John (William) 1926–1967. US jazz saxophonist who first came to prominence 1955 with the Miles ◊Davis quintet, later playing with Thelonious Monk 1957. He was a powerful and individual artist, whose performances featured much experimentation. His 1960s quartet was highly regarded for its innovations in melody and harmony.

Columba, St 521–597. Irish Christian abbot, missionary to Scotland. He was born in County Donegal of royal descent, and founded monasteries and churches in Ireland. In 563 he sailed with 12 companions to ◊Iona, and built a monastery there that was to play a leading part in the conversion of Britain. Feast day June 9.

Columban, St 543–615. Irish Christian abbot. He was born in Leinster, studied at Bangor, and about 585 went to the Vosges, France, with 12 other monks and founded the monastery of Luxeuil. Later, he preached in Switzerland, then went to Italy, where he built the abbey of Bobbio in the Apennines. Feast day Nov 23.

Columbia city in central Missouri, NE of Jefferson City, seat of Boone County; population (1990) 69,100. It is the site of the University of Missouri 1853 and Stephens College 1833.

Columbia river in W North America, 1,215 mi/1,950 m in length. It rises in British Columbia and flows through Washington to the Pacific below Astoria, after forming much of the boundary between Washington and Oregon. This fast-running river has enormous hydroelectric potential and is harnessed for irrigation and power by the Grand Coulee and other major dams. Although it is famous for salmon fishing, the catch is now much reduced. The mouth of the Columbia was discovered 1792. The explorer David Thompson followed it from its source to its mouth 1811.

Columbia capital of South Carolina, on the Congaree River; population (1990) 98,100. Manufacturing includes textiles, plastics, electrical goods, fertilizers, and hosiery, but the chief product is fuel assemblies for nuclear reactors. The main campus of the University of South Carolina is here. Columbia was laid out as the state capital 1786. It was burned by Union troops 1865, near the close of the Civil War.

columbine any plant of the genus *Aquilegia* of the buttercup family Ranunculaceae. All are perennial herbs with divided leaves and flowers with spurred petals.

The eastern columbine *A. canadensis*, with red flowers, is native to E North America.

columbium (Cb) former name for the chemical element ◊niobium. The name is still used occasionally in metallurgy.

Columbus capital of Ohio, on the rivers Scioto and Olentangy; population (1990) 632,900. It has coal-field and natural gas resources nearby; its industries include the manufacture of automobiles, planes, missiles, and electrical goods.

Columbus city in W central Georgia, SW of Macon, across the Chattahoochee River from Phenix City,

Alabama; seat of Muscogee County; population (1990) 179,300. Industries include processed food, machinery, iron and steel, textiles, cotton, and peanuts. It is a distribution center for surrounding farmlands, and lies just N of the US Army infantry base Fort Benning.

Columbus Christopher (Spanish *Cristóbal Colón*) 1451–1506. Italian navigator and explorer who made four voyages to the New World: 1492 to San Salvador Island, Cuba, and Haiti; 1493–96 to Guadaloupe, Montserrat, Antigua, Puerto Rico, and Jamaica; 1498 to Trinidad and the mainland of South America; 1502–04 to Honduras and Nicaragua. Believing that Asia could be reached by sailing westward, he eventually won the support of King Ferdinand and Queen Isabella of Spain and set off on his first voyage from Palos Aug 3, 1492, with three small ships, the *Niña*, the *Pinta*, and his flagship the *Santa Maria*. Land was sighted Oct 12, probably Watling Island (now San Salvador Island), and within a few weeks he reached Cuba and Haiti, returning to Spain March 1493.

Columbus Day (Oct 12), a US public holiday, is named for him.

column in architecture, a structure, round or polygonal in plan, erected vertically as a support for some part of a building. Cretan paintings reveal the exis-

major comets

name	first recorded sighting	orbital period(years)	interesting facts
Halley's comet	240 BC	76	parent of Eta Aquarid and Orionid meteor showers
Comet Tempel-Tuttle	AD 1366	33	parent of Leonid meteors
Biela's comet	1772	6.6	broke in half 1846; not seen since 1852
Encke's comet	1786	3.3	parent of Taurid meteors
Comet Swift-Tuttle	1862	130	parent of Perseid meteors
Comet Ikeya-Seki	1965	880	so-called *Sun-grazing* comet, passed 300,000 mi/500,000 km above surface of Sun on Oct 21, 1965
Comet Kohoutek	1973		observed from space by Skylab astronauts; period too long to calculate accurately
Comet West	1975	500,000	nucleus broke into four parts
Comet Bowell	1980		ejected from Solar System after close encounter with Jupiter
Comet IRAS–Araki–Alcock	1983		passed only 2.8 million mi/4.5 million km from Earth on May 11, 1983; period too long to calculate accurately
Comet Austin	1989		passed 20 million mi/32 million km from Earth 1990

tence of wooden columns in Aegean architecture in about 1500 BC. The Hittites, Assyrians, and Egyptians also used wooden columns, and they are a feature of the monumental architecture of China and Japan. In Classical architecture there are five principal types of column; see ◊order.

coma in medicine, a state of deep unconsciousness from which the subject cannot be roused and in which the subject does not respond to pain. Possible causes include head injury, liver failure, cerebral hemorrhage, and drug overdose.

Comaneci Nadia 1961– . Romanian gymnast. She won three gold medals at the 1976 Olympics at the age of 14, and was the first gymnast to record a perfect score of 10 in international competition. Upon retirement she became a coach of the Romanian team, but defected to Canada 1989.

combine harvester or *combine* machine used for harvesting cereals and other crops, so called because it combines the actions of reaping (cutting the crop) and threshing (beating the ears so that the grain separates).

combustion burning, defined in chemical terms as the rapid combination of a substance with oxygen, accompanied by the evolution of heat and usually light. A slow-burning candle flame and the explosion of a mixture of gasoline vapor and air are extreme examples of combustion.

Comecon (acronym for *Council for Mutual Economic Assistance*, or *CMEA*) economic organization 1949–91, linking the USSR with Bulgaria, Czechoslovakia, Hungary, Poland, Romania, East Germany (1950–90), Mongolia (from 1962), Cuba (from 1972), and Vietnam (from 1978), with Yugoslavia as an associated member. Albania also belonged 1949–61. Its establishment was prompted by the ◊Marshall Plan.

Comédie Française French national theater (for both comedy and tragedy) in Paris, founded 1680 by Louis XIV. Its base is the Salle Richelieu on the right bank of the river Seine, and the Théatre de l'Odéon, on the left bank, is a testing ground for avant-garde ideas.

comedy in the simplest terms, a literary work, usually dramatic, with a happy or amusing ending, as opposed to ◊tragedy. The comic tradition has undergone many changes since its Greek and Roman roots; although some comedies are timeless, such as those of Shakespeare and Molière, others are very representative of a particular era, relying upon topical allusion and current fashion.

comet small, icy body orbiting the Sun, usually on a highly elliptical path. A comet consists of a central nucleus a few miles across, and has been likened to a dirty snowball because it consists mostly of ice mixed with dust. As the comet approaches the Sun the nucleus heats up, releasing gas and dust which form a tenuous coma, up to 60,000 mi/100,000 km wide, around the nucleus. Gas and dust stream away from the coma to form one or more tails, which may extend for millions of miles.

comic book publication in strip-cartoon form. Comic books are usually aimed at children, although in Japan, Latin America, and Europe millions of adults read them. Artistically sophisticated adult comics and *graphic novels* are produced in the US and several European countries, notably France. Comic books developed from ◊comic strips in newspapers or, like those of Walt ◊Disney, as spinoffs from animated cartoon films.

comic strip or *strip cartoon* sequence of several frames of drawings in ◊cartoon style.

Cominform (acronym for *Communist Information Bureau*) organization 1947–56 established by Soviet politician Andrei Zhdanov (1896–1948) to exchange information between European communist parties. Yugoslavia was expelled 1948.

Comintern acronym from *Communist International*.

comma punctuation mark (,) most commonly used to mark off a phrase or noun in apposition, mark off a subordinate clause or phrase, or separate items in a list.

commando member of a specially trained, highly mobile military unit. The term originated in South Africa in the 19th century, where it referred to Boer military reprisal raids against Africans and, in the South African Wars, against the British. Commando units have often carried out operations behind enemy lines.

commedia dell'arte popular form of Italian improvised comic drama in the 16th and 17th centuries, performed by trained troupes of actors and involving stock characters and situations. It exerted considerable influence on writers such as Molière and Carlo Goldoni, and on the genres of pantomime, harlequinade, and the Punch and Judy show. It laid the foundation for a tradition of mime, strong in France, that has continued with the contemporary mime of Jean-Louis Barrault and Marcel Marceau.

commodity something produced for sale. Commodities may be consumer goods, such as radios, or producer goods, such as copper bars. *Commodity markets* deal in raw or semiraw materials that are amenable to grading and that can be stored for considerable periods without deterioration.

Commodus Lucius Aelius Aurelius 161–192. Roman emperor from 180, son of Marcus Aurelius Antoninus. He was a tyrant, spending lavishly on gladiatorial combats, confiscating the property of the wealthy, persecuting the Senate, and renaming Rome "Colonia Commodiana." There were many attempts against his life, and he was finally strangled at the instigation of his mistress and advisers, who had discovered themselves on the emperor's death list.

Common Agricultural Policy (CAP) system that allows the member countries of the European Community (EC) jointly to organize and control agricultural production within their boundaries. The objectives of the CAP were outlined in the Treaty of Rome: to increase agricultural productivity, to provide a fair standard of living for farmers and their employees, to stabilize markets, and to assure the availability of supply at a price that was reasonable to the consumer. The CAP is increasingly criticized for its role in creating overproduction, and consequent environmental damage, and for the high price of food subsidies.

common law that part of the English law not embodied in legislation. It consists of rules of law based on common custom and usage and on judicial decisions. English common law became the basis of law in the US and many other English-speaking countries.

common logarithm another name for a ◊logarithm to the base ten.

Common Market popular name for the *European Economic Community*; see ◊European Community (EC).

Commons, House of the lower but more powerful of the two parts of the British and Canadian ◊parliaments.

commonwealth body politic founded on law for the common "weal" or good. Political philosophers of the 17th century, such as Thomas Hobbes and John Locke, used the term to mean an organized political community. In Britain it was specifically applied to the regime (*the Commonwealth*) of Oliver ◊Cromwell 1649–60.

Commonwealth of Independent States (CIS) successor body to the ◊Union of Soviet Socialist

---

Commonwealth, British

country	date joined	country	date joined	country	date joined
in Africa		Falkland Islands	1931	**in Australasia and the Pacific**	
Botswana	1966	Grenada	1974	Australia	1931
British Indian Ocean Territory	1965	Guyana	1966	Cook Islands	1931
Gambia	1965	Jamaica	1962	Norfolk Island	1931
Ghana	1957	Montserrat	1931	Kiribati	1979
Kenya	1963	St Christopher–Nevis	1983	Nauru	1968
Lesotho	1966	St Lucia	1979	New Zealand	1931
Malawi	1964	St Vincent and		Niue	1931
Mauritius	1968	the Grenadines	1979	Papua New Guinea	1975
Namibia	1990	Trinidad and Tobago	1962	Pitcairn Islands	1931
Nigeria	1960	Turks and Caicos Islands	1931	Solomon Islands	1978
St Helena	1931			Tokelau	1931
Seychelles	1976	**in the Antarctic**		Tonga	1970
Sierra Leone	1961	Australian Antarctic Territory	1936	Tuvalu	1978
Swaziland	1968	British Antarctic Territory	1931	Vanuatu	1980
Tanzania	1961	Falkland Islands		Western Samoa	1970
Uganda	1962	Dependencies	1931		
Zambia	1964	Ross Dependency	1931	**in Europe**	
Zimbabwe	1980			Channel Islands	1931
		in Asia		Guernsey	
in the Americas		Bangladesh	1972	Jersey	
Anguilla	1931	Brunei	1984	Cyprus	1961
Antigua and Barbuda	1981	Hong Kong	1931	Gibraltar	1931
Bahamas	1973	India	1947	Malta	1964
Barbados	1966	Malaysia	1957	Isle of Man	1931
Belize	1982	Maldives	1982	United Kingdom	1931
Bermuda	1931	Pakistan	1947†	England	
British Virgin Islands	1931	Singapore	1965	Northern Ireland	
Canada	1931	Sri Lanka	1948	Scotland	
Cayman Islands	1931			Wales	
Dominica	1978	† left 1972 and rejoined 1989			

Republics, initially formed as a new commonwealth of Slav republics on Dec 8, 1991, by the presidents of the Russian Federation, Belarus, and Ukraine. On Dec 21, eight of the nine remaining non-Slav republics— Moldova, Tajikistan, Armenia, Azerbaijan, Turkmenistan, Kazakhstan, Kyrgyzstan, and Uzbekistan—joined the CIS at a meeting held in Kazakhstan's capital, Alma Ata. The CIS formally came into existence in Jan 1992 after President Gorbachev had resigned and the Soviet government had voted itself out of existence. It has no real, formal political institutions and its role is uncertain. Its headquarters are in Minsk (Mensk), Belarus.

Commonwealth, the (British) voluntary association of 50 countries and their dependencies that once formed part of the ◊British Empire and are now independent sovereign states. They are all regarded as "full members of the Commonwealth." Additionally, there are some 20 territories that are not completely sovereign and remain dependencies of the UK or another of the fully sovereign members, and are regarded as "Commonwealth countries." Heads of government meet every two years, apart from those of Nauru and Tuvalu; however, Nauru and Tuvalu have the right to participate in all functional activities. The Commonwealth has no charter nor constitution, and is founded more on tradition and sentiment than on political or economic factors.

commune group of people or families living together, sharing resources and responsibilities.

communication in biology, the signaling of information by one organism to another, usually with the intention of altering the recipient's behavior. Signals used in communication may be *visual* (such as the human smile or the display of colorful plumage in birds), *auditory* (for example, the whines or barks of a dog), *olfactory* (such as the odors released by the scent glands of a deer), *electrical* (as in the pulses emitted by electric fish), or *tactile* (for example, the nuzzling of male and female elephants).

communications satellite relay station in space for sending telephone, television, telex, and other messages around the world. Messages are sent to and from the satellites via ground stations. Most communications satellites are in ◊geostationary orbit, appearing to hang fixed over one point on the Earth's surface.

Communion, Holy in the Christian church, another name for the ◊Eucharist.

communism (French *commun* "common general") revolutionary socialism based on the theories of the political philosophers Karl Marx and Friedrich Engels, emphasizing common ownership of the means of production and a planned economy. The principle held is that each should work according to his or her capacity and receive according to his or her needs. Politically, it seeks the overthrow of capitalism through a proletarian revolution. The first communist state was the USSR after the revolution of 1917. Revolutionary socialist parties and groups united to form communist parties in other countries. After World War II, communism was enforced in those countries that came under Soviet occupation. China emerged after 1961 as a rival to the USSR in world communist leadership, and other countries attempted to adapt communism to their own needs. The late 1980s saw a movement for more individual freedoms in many communist countries, culminating in the abolition or overthrow of communist rule in Eastern European

countries and Mongolia, and further state repression in China. The failed hard-line coup in the USSR against President Gorbachev 1991 resulted in the effective abandonment of communism there.

Communism Peak alternate form of Pik ◊Kommunizma, the highest mountain in the ◊Pamirs.

community in the social sciences, the sense of identity, purpose, and companionship that comes from belonging to a particular place, organization, or social group. The concept dominated sociological thinking in the first half of the 20th century and inspired the academic discipline of *community studies*.

commutative operation in mathematics, an operation that is independent of the order of the numbers or symbols concerned. For example, addition is commutative: the result of adding $4 + 2$ is the same as that of adding $2 + 4$; subtraction is not, as $4 - 2 = 2$, but $2 - 4 = -2$. Compare ◊associative operation and ◊distributive operation.

Comoros group of islands in the Indian Ocean between Madagascar and the E coast of Africa. Three of them Njazidja—Nzwani, and Mwali—form the republic of Comoros; the fourth island, Mayotte, is a French dependency. *See panel p. 224*

compact disk or *CD* disk for storing digital information, about 4.5 in/12 cm across, mainly used for music, when it can have over an hour's playing time. Entirely different from a conventional LP (long-playing) phonograph record, the compact disk is made of aluminum with a transparent plastic coating; the metal disk underneath is etched by a ◊laser beam with microscopic pits that carry a digital code representing the sounds. During playback, a laser beam reads the code and produces signals that are changed into near-exact replicas of the original sounds. *See illustration p. 224*

company in the army, a subunit of a battalion. It consists of about 120 soldiers and is commanded by a captain in the US army and by a major in the British army. Four or five companies make a battalion.

comparative advantage law of international trade first elaborated by English economist David Ricardo showing that trade becomes worthwhile if the cost of production of particular items differs between one country and another.

compass any instrument for finding direction. The most commonly used is a magnetic compass, consisting of a thin piece of magnetic material with the north-seeking pole indicated, free to rotate on a pivot and mounted on a compass card on which the points of the compass are marked. When the compass is properly adjusted and used, the north-seeking pole will point to the magnetic north, from which true north can be found from tables of magnetic corrections.

A compass (or pair of compasses) is also an instrument used for drawing circles or taking measurements, consisting of a pair of pointed legs connected by a central pivot. *See illustration p. 225*

compiler computer program that translates programs written in a ◊high-level language into machine code (the form in which they can be run by the computer). The compiler translates each high-level instruction into several machine-code instructions— in a process called *compilation*—and produces a complete independent program that can be run by the computer as often as required, without the original source program being present.

complement the set of the elements within the universal set that are not contained in the designated set.

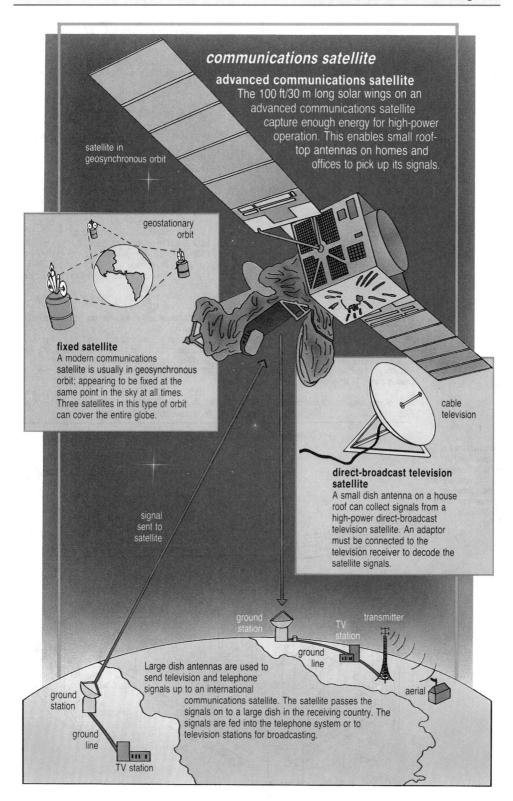

communications satellite

advanced communications satellite
The 100 ft/30 m long solar wings on an advanced communications satellite capture enough energy for high-power operation. This enables small roof-top antennas on homes and offices to pick up its signals.

satellite in geosynchronous orbit

geostationary orbit

fixed satellite
A modern communications satellite is usually in geosynchronous orbit; appearing to be fixed at the same point in the sky at all times. Three satellites in this type of orbit can cover the entire globe.

cable television

direct-broadcast television satellite
A small dish antenna on a house roof can collect signals from a high-power direct-broadcast television satellite. An adaptor must be connected to the television receiver to decode the satellite signals.

signal sent to satellite

ground station

TV station

transmitter

ground line

Large dish antennas are used to send television and telephone signals up to an international communications satellite. The satellite passes the signals on to a large dish in the receiving country. The signals are fed into the telephone system or to television stations for broadcasting.

aerial

ground station

ground line

TV station

Comoros
Federal Islamic Republic of
(*Jumhurīyat al-Qumur al-Itthādīyah al-Islāmīyah*)

area 719 sq mi/1,862 sq km
capital Moroni
cities Mutsamudu, Domoni, Fomboni
physical comprises the volcanic islands of Njazídja, Nzwani, and Mwali (formerly Grande Comore, Anjouan, Moheli); at N end of Mozambique Channel
features active volcano on Njazídja; poor tropical soil
head of state Said Mohammad Djohar (interim administration) from 1989
head of government Halidi Abderamane Ibrahim from 1993

political system emergent democracy
political parties Comoran Union for Progress (Udzima), nationalist Islamic; National Union for Congolese Democracy (UNDC), left of center; Popular Democratic Movement (MDP), centrist
exports copra, vanilla, cocoa, sisal, coffee, cloves, essential oils
currency CFA franc
population (1992) 497,000; growth rate 3.1% p.a.
life expectancy men 48, women 52
languages Arabic (official), Comorian (Swahili and Arabic dialect), Makua, French
religions Muslim (official) 86%, Roman Catholic 14%
literacy 15%
GDP $198 million (1987); $468 per head

chronology
1975 Independence achieved from France, but island of Mayotte remained part of France. Ahmed Abdallah elected president. The Comoros joined the United Nations.
1976 Abdallah overthrown by Ali Soilih.
1978 Soilih killed by mercenaries working for Abdallah. Islamic republic proclaimed and Abdallah elected president.
1979 The Comoros became a one-party state; powers of the federal government increased.
1985 Constitution amended to make Abdallah head of government as well as head of state.
1989 Abdallah killed by French mercenaries who took control of government; under French and South African pressure, mercenaries left Comoros, turning authority over to French administration and interim president Said Mohammad Djohar.
1990 Antigovernment coup foiled.
1992 Third transitional government appointed. Second antigovernment coup foiled.
1993 General election failed to provide any one party with overall assembly majority. President Djohar appointed Halidi Abderamane Ibrahim prime minister.

compact disk The compact disk is a digital storage device; music is recorded as a series of etched pits representing numbers in digital code.

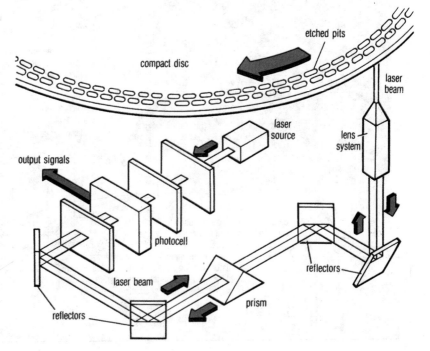

For example, if the universal set is the set of all positive whole numbers and the designated set S is the set of all even numbers, then the complement of S (denoted S') is the set of all odd numbers.

complementary angles two angles that add up to 90°.

complex in psychology, a group of ideas and feelings that have become repressed because they are distasteful to the person in whose mind they arose, but are still active in the depths of the person's unconscious mind, continuing to affect his or her life and actions, even though he or she is no longer fully aware of their existence. Typical examples include the ◊Oedipus complex and the inferiority complex.

complex number in mathematics, a number written in the form $a + ib$, where a and b are ◊real numbers and i is the square root of –1 (that is, $i^2 = -1$); i used to be known as the "imaginary" part of the complex number. Some equations in algebra, such as those of the form $x^2 + 5 = 0$, cannot be solved without recourse to complex numbers, because the real numbers do not include square roots of negative numbers.

component in mathematics, one of the vectors produced when a single vector is resolved into two or more parts. The vector sum of the components gives the original vector.

composite in industry, any purpose-designed engineering material created by combining single materials with complementary properties into a composite form. Most composites have a structure in which one component consists of discrete elements, such as fibers, dispersed in a continuous matrix. For example, lengths of asbestos, glass, or carbon steel, or "whiskers" (specially grown crystals a few millimeterslong) of substances such as silicon carbide may be dispersed in plastics, concrete, or steel.

Composite in Classical architecture, one of the five types of ◊column. See ◊order.

composite function in mathematics, a function made up of two or more other functions carried out in sequence, usually denoted by * or °, as in the relation $(f * g) x = f[g(x)]$.

compost organic material decomposed by bacteria under controlled conditions to make a nutrient-rich natural fertilizer for use in gardening or farming. A well-made compost heap reaches a high temperature during the composting process, killing most weed seeds that might be present.

As the ◊decomposers feed, they raise the temperature in the center of the compost as high as 150°F/66°C.

compound chemical substance made up of two or more ◊elements bonded together, so that they cannot be separated by physical means. Compounds are held together by ionic or covalent bonds.

compound interest interest calculated by computing the rate against the original capital plus reinvested interest each time the interest becomes due. When simple interest is calculated, only the interest on the original capital is added.

Compromise of 1850 in US history, legislative proposals designed to resolve the sectional conflict between North and South over the admission of California to the Union 1850. Slavery was prohibited in California, but a new fugitive slave law was passed to pacify the slave states. The Senate debate on the compromise lasted nine months: acceptance temporarily revitalized the Union.

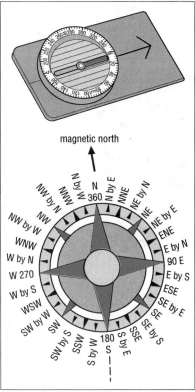

compass As early as 2500 BC, the Chinese were using pieces of magnetic rock, magnetite, as simple compasses.

magnetic north

Compton Arthur Holly 1892–1962. US physicist known for his work on X-rays. Working at Chicago 1923 he found that X-rays scattered by such light elements as carbon increased their wavelengths. Compton concluded from this unexpected result that X-rays were displaying both wavelike and particlelike properties, since named the **Compton effect**. He shared a Nobel Prize 1927 with Scottish physicist Charles Wilson (1869–1959).

computer programmable electronic device that processes data and performs calculations and other symbol-manipulation tasks. There are three types: the ◊**digital computer**, which manipulates information coded in binary numbers (see binary number system); the **analog computer**, which works with continuously varying quantities; and the **hybrid computer**, which has characteristics of both analog and digital computers.

computer-aided design use of computers to create and modify design drawings; see ◊CAD.

computer-aided manufacturing use of computers to regulate production processes in industry; see ◊CAM.

computer-assisted learning use of computers in education and training; see ◊CAL.

computer game or *video game* any computer-controlled game in which the computer (sometimes) opposes the human player. Computer games typically employ fast, animated graphics on a ◊VDU (visual display unit), and synthesized sound.

computer graphics use of computers to display and manipulate information in pictorial form. The output

computer A desktop computer is made of a number of connected units, dealing with input, display, processing, reading, output, and connection to other computers.

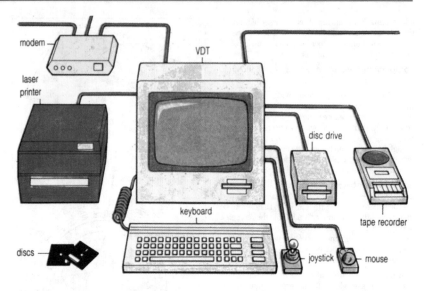

modem

laser printer

VDT

disc drive

keyboard

tape recorder

discs

joystick

mouse

may be as simple as a pie chart, or as complex as an animated sequence in a science-fiction film, or a seemingly three-dimensional engineering blueprint. Input may be achieved by scanning an image, by drawing with a mouse or stylus on a graphics tablet, or by drawing directly on the screen with a light pen. The drawing is stored in the computer as ◊raster graphics or ◊vector graphics. Computer graphics are increasingly used in computer-aided design (◊CAD), and to generate models and simulations in engineering, meteorology, medicine and surgery, and other fields of science.

computer literacy ability to understand and make use of computer technology in an everyday context.

computer simulation representation of a real-life situation in a computer program. For example, the program might simulate the flow of customers arriving at a bank. The user can alter variables, such as the number of cashiers on duty, and see the effect.

computer terminal the device whereby the operator communicates with the computer; see ◊terminal.

Comte Auguste 1798–1857. French philosopher regarded as the founder of sociology, a term he coined 1830. He sought to establish sociology as an intellectual discipline, using a scientific approach ("positivism") as the basis of a new science of social order and social development.

computer graphics An image of air flow over an F-16 jet fighter aircraft produced on a Cray supercomputer.

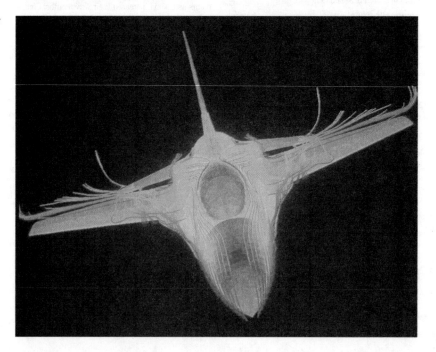

computing: chronology

1614	John Napier invented logarithms.
1615	William Oughtred invented the slide rule.
1623	Wilhelm Schickard (1592–1635) invented the mechanical calculating machine.
1645	Blaise Pascal produced a calculator.
1672–74	Gottfried Leibniz built his first calculator, the Stepped Reckoner.
1801	Joseph-Marie Jacquard developed an automatic loom controlled by punch cards.
1820	The first mass-produced calculator, the Arithometer, was developed by Charles Thomas de Colmar (1785–1870).
1822	Charles Babbage completed his first model for the difference engine.
1830s	Babbage created the first design for the analytical engine.
1890	Herman Hollerith developed the punched-card ruler for the US census.
1936	Alan Turing published the mathematical theory of computing.
1938	Konrad Zuse constructed the first binary calculator, using Boolean algebra.
1939	US mathematician and physicist J V Atanasoff (1903–) became the first to use electronic means for mechanizing arithmetical operations.
1943	The Colossus electronic code-breaker was developed at Bletchley Park, England. The Harvard University Mark I or Automatic Sequence Controlled Calculator (partly financed by IBM) became the first program-controlled calculator.
1946	ENIAC (acronym for electronic numerator, integrator, analyzer, and computer), the first general purpose, fully electronic digital computer, was completed at the University of Pennsylvania.
1948	Manchester University (England) Mark I, the first stored-program computer, was completed. William Shockley of Bell Laboratories invented the transistor.
1951	Launch of Ferranti Mark I, the first commercially produced computer. Whirlwind, the first real-time computer, was built for the US air-defense system. Grace Murray Hopper of Remington Rand invented the compiler computer program.
1952	EDVAC (acronym for electronic discrete variable computer) was completed at the Institute for Advanced Study, Princeton (by John Von Neumann and others).
1953	Magnetic core memory was developed.
1958	The first integrated circuit was constructed.
1963	The first minicomputer was built by Digital Equipment (DEC). The first electronic calculator was built by Bell Punch Company.
1964	Launch of IBM System/360, the first compatible family of computers. John Kemeny and Thomas Kurtz of Dartmouth College invented BASIC (beginner's all-purpose symbolic instruction code), a computer language similar to FORTRAN.
1965	The first supercomputer, the Control Data CD6600, was developed.
1971	The first microprocessor, the Intel 4004, was announced.
1974	CLIP–4, the first computer with a parallel architecture, was developed by John Backus at IBM.
1975	Altair 8800, the first personal computer (PC), or microcomputer, was launched.
1981	The Xerox Star system, the first WIMP system (acronym for windows, icons, menus, and pointing devices), was developed. IBM launched the IBM PC.
1984	Apple launched the Macintosh computer.
1985	The Inmos T414 transputer, the first *off-the-shelf* microprocessor for building parallel computers, was announced.
1988	The first optical microprocessor, which uses light instead of electricity, was developed.
1989	Wafer-scale silicon memory chips, able to store 200 million characters, were launched.
1990	Microsoft released Windows 3, a popular windowing environment for PCs.
1991	IBM developed world's fastest high-capacity memory computer chip, SRAM (static random access memory), able to send or receive 8 billion bits of information per second.
1992	Philips launched the CD-I (compact disk-interactive) player, based on CD audio technology, to provide interactive multimedia programs for the home user.
1993	Intel launched the Pentium chip containing 3.1 million transistors and capable of 100 MIPs (millions of instructions per second).

Conakry capital and chief port of the Republic of Guinea; population (1983) 705,300. It is on the island of Tumbo, linked with the mainland by a causeway and by rail with Kankan, 300 mi/480 km to the NE. Bauxite and iron ore are mined nearby.

concave lens converging ◊lens—that is, a parallel beam of light gets wider as it passes through such a lens. A concave lens is thinner at its center than at the edges.

concentration camp prison camp for civilians in wartime or under totalitarian rule. The first concentration camps were devised by the British during the Second Boer War in South Africa 1899 for the detention of Afrikaner women and children (with the subsequent deaths of more than 20,000 people). A system of hundreds of concentration camps was developed by

the Nazis in Germany and occupied Europe (1933–45) to imprison Jews and political and ideological opponents after Hitler became chancellor Jan 1933. The most infamous camps in World War II were the extermination camps of Auschwitz, Belsen, Dachau, Maidanek, Sobibor, and Treblinka. The total number of people who died at the camps exceeded 6 million, and some inmates were subjected to medical experimentation before being killed.

concertina portable reed organ related to the ◊accordion but smaller in size and rounder in shape, with buttons for keys. It was invented in England in the 19th century.

concerto composition, usually in three movements, for solo instrument (or instruments) and orchestra. It developed during the 18th century from the ***con-***

certo grosso form for string orchestra, in which a group of solo instruments is contrasted with a full orchestra.

conciliar movement in the history of the Christian church, a 15th-century attempt to urge the supremacy of church councils over the popes, with regard to the ◊Great Schism and the reformation of the church. Councils were held in Pisa 1409, Constance 1414–18, Pavia-Siena 1423–24, Basle 1431–49, and Ferrara-Florence-Rome 1438–47.

conclave secret meeting, in particular the gathering of cardinals in Rome to elect a new pope. They are locked away in the Vatican Palace until they have reached a decision. The result of each ballot is announced by a smoke signal—black for an undecided vote and white when the choice is made.

Concord capital of New Hampshire, in the S central part of the state, on the Merrimack River, N of Manchester; population (1990) 36,000. Industries include granite, leather goods, electrical equipment, printed products, and wood products.

concordance book containing an alphabetical list of the important words in a major work, with reference to the places in which they occur. The first concordance was one for the Latin Vulgate Bible compiled by a Dominican monk in the 13th century.

concordat agreement regulating relations between the papacy and a secular government, for example, that for France between Pius VII and the emperor Napoleon, which lasted 1801–1905; Mussolini's concordat, which lasted 1929–78 and safeguarded the position of the church in Italy; and one of 1984 in Italy in which Roman Catholicism ceased to be the Italian state religion.

Concorde the only supersonic airliner, which cruises at Mach 2, or twice the speed of sound, about 1,350 mph/2,170 kph. Concorde, the result of Anglo-French cooperation, made its first flight 1969 and entered commercial service seven years later. It is 202 ft/62 m long and has a wingspan of nearly 84 ft/26 m.

concrete building material composed of cement, stone, sand, and water. It has been used since Egyptian and Roman times. During the 20th century, it has been increasingly employed as an economical alternative to materials such as brick and wood.

concurrent lines two or more lines passing through a single point; for example, the diameters of a circle are all concurrent at the center of the circle.

Condé Louis de Bourbon, Prince of Condé 1530–1569. Prominent French ◊Huguenot leader, founder of the house of Condé and uncle of Henry IV of France. He fought in the wars between Henry II and the Holy Roman emperor Charles V, including the defense of Metz.

Condé Louis II 1621–1686. Prince of Condé called the *Great Condé*. French commander who won brilliant victories during the Thirty Years' War at Rocroi 1643 and Lens 1648, but rebelled 1651 and entered the Spanish service. Pardoned 1660, he commanded Louis XIV's armies against the Spanish and the Dutch.

condensation in organic chemistry, a reaction in which two organic compounds combine to form a larger molecule, accompanied by the removal of a smaller molecule (usually water). This is also known as an addition–elimination reaction. Polyamides (such as nylon) and polyesters (such as Terylene) are made by condensation ◊polymerization.

condenser in optics, a ◊lens or combination of lenses with a short focal length used for concentrating a light source onto a small area, as used in a slide projector or microscope substage lighting unit. A condenser can also be made using a concave mirror.

conditioning in psychology, two major principles of behavior modification. In *classical conditioning*, described by Ivan Pavlov, a new stimulus can evoke an automatic response by being repeatedly associated with a stimulus that naturally provokes a response. For example, the sound of a bell repeatedly associated with food will eventually trigger salivation, even if sounded without food being presented. In *operant conditioning*, described by US psychologists Edward Lee Thorndike (1874–1949) and Burrhus Frederic Skinner, the frequency of a voluntary response can be increased by following it with a reinforcer or reward.

condom or *sheath* or *prophylactic* barrier contraceptive, made of rubber, which fits over an erect penis and holds in the sperm produced by ejaculation. It is an effective means of preventing pregnancy if used carefully, preferably with a ◊spermicide. A condom with spermicide is 97% effective; one without spermicide is 85% effective. Condoms also give protection against sexually transmitted diseases, including AIDS.

condominium joint rule of a territory by two or more states, for example, Kanton and Enderbury islands in the South Pacific Phoenix group (under the joint control of Britain and the US for 50 years from 1939).

The term has also come into use in North America to describe a type of joint property ownership of, for example, apartment buildings.

condor large bird, a New World vulture *Vultur gryphus*, with wingspan up to 10 ft/3 m, weight up to 28 lb/13 kg, and length up to 3.8 ft/1.2 m. It is black, with some white on the wings and a white frill at the base of the neck. It lives in the Andes and along the South American coast, and feeds on carrion. The Californian condor *Gymnogyps californianus* is a similar bird, on the verge of extinction.

Condorcet Marie Jean Antoine Nicolas Caritat, Marquis de Condorcet 1743–1794. French philosopher, mathematician, and politician, associated with the *Encyclopédistes*. One of the Girondins, he opposed the execution of Louis XVI, and was imprisoned and poisoned himself. While in prison, he wrote *Esquisse d'un tableau des progrès de l'esprit humain/Historical Survey of the Progress of Human Understanding* 1795, which envisaged inevitable future progress, though not the perfectibility of human nature.

conductance ability of a material to carry an electrical current, usually given the symbol G. For a direct current, it is the reciprocal of ◊resistance: a conductor of resistance R has a conductance of $1/R$. For an alternating current, conductance is the resistance R divided by the ◊impedance Z: $G = R/Z$. Conductance was formerly expressed in reciprocal ohms (or mhos); the SI unit is the siemens (S).

conductor any material that conducts heat or electricity (as opposed to an insulator, or nonconductor). A good conductor has a high electrical or heat conductivity, and is generally a substance rich in free electrons such as a metal. A poor conductor (such as the nonmetals glass and porcelain) has few free electrons. Carbon is exceptional in being nonmetallic and yet (in some of its forms) a relatively good conductor of heat

Confederacy 1861–65

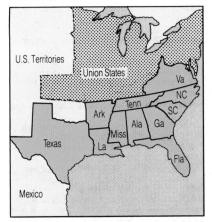

and electricity. Substances such as silicon and germanium, with intermediate conductivities that are improved by heat, light, or voltage, are known as ◊semiconductors.

cone in geometry, a solid or surface consisting of the set of all straight lines passing through a fixed point (the vertex) and the points of a circle or ellipse whose plane does not contain the vertex.

cone in botany, the reproductive structure of the conifers and cycads; also known as a ◊strobilus. It consists of a central axis surrounded by numerous, overlapping, scalelike, modified leaves (sporophylls) that bear the reproductive organs. Usually there are separate male and female cones, the former bearing pollen sacs containing pollen grains, and the larger female cones bearing the ovules that contain the ova or egg cells. The pollen is carried from male to female cones by the wind (anemophily). The seeds develop within the female cone and are released as the scales open in dry atmospheric conditions, which favor seed dispersal.

Confederacy in US history, popular name for the *Confederate States of America*, the government established by 7 (later 11) Southern states in Feb 1861 when they seceded from the Union, precipitating the ◊Civil War. Richmond, Virginia, was the capital, and Jefferson Davis the president. The Confederacy fell after its army was defeated 1865 and General Robert E Lee surrendered.

Confederation, Articles of in US history, the initial means by which the 13 former British colonies created a form of national government. Ratified 1781, the articles established a unicameral legislature, Congress, with limited powers of raising revenue, regulating currency, and conducting foreign affairs. But because the individual states retained significant autonomy, the confederation was unmanageable. The articles were superseded by the US Constitution 1788.

confession in religion, the confession of sins, practiced in Roman Catholic, Orthodox, and most Far Eastern Christian churches, and since the early 19th century revived in Anglican and Lutheran churches. The Lateran Council of 1215 made auricular confession (self-accusation by the penitent to a priest, who in Catholic doctrine is divinely invested with authority to give absolution) obligatory once a year.

confirmation rite practiced by a number of Christian denominations, including Roman Catholic, Anglican,

and Orthodox, in which a previously baptized person is admitted to full membership in the church. In Reform Judaism there is often a confirmation service several years after the bar or bat mitzvah (initiation into the congregation).

Confucianism body of beliefs and practices based on the Chinese classics and supported by the authority of the philosopher Confucius. The origin of things is seen in the union of *yin* and *yang*, the passive and active principles. Human relationships follow the patriarchal pattern. For more than 2,000 years Chinese political government, social organization, and individual conduct was shaped by Confucian principles. In 1912, Confucian philosophy, as a basis for government, was dropped by the state.

congenital disease in medicine, a disease that is present at birth. It is not necessarily genetic in origin; for example, congenital herpes may be acquired by the baby as it passes through the mother's birth canal.

conger any large marine eel of the family Congridae, especially the genus *Conger*. Conger eels live in shallow water, hiding in crevices during the day and active by night, feeding on fish and crabs. They are valued for food and angling.

The American conger *C. oceanicus* grows to 4.5 ft/ 1.4 m in length.

conglomerate in mineralogy, coarse clastic ◊sedimentary rock, composed of rounded fragments (clasts) of pre-existing rocks cemented in a finer matrix, usually sand.

Congo country in W central Africa, bounded N by Cameroon and the Central African Republic, E and S by Zaire, W by the Atlantic Ocean, and NW by Gabon. *See panel p. 230*

Congregationalism form of church government adopted by those Protestant Christians known as Congregationalists, who let each congregation manage its own affairs, like the people of the Old Testament. The first Congregationalists established themselves in London and were called the Brownists after Robert Browne, who in 1581 defined the congregational principle. They opposed King James I and were supporters of Oliver ◊Cromwell. They became one of the most important forces in the founding of New England.

Congress national legislature of the US, consisting of the House of Representatives (435 members, apportioned to the states of the Union on the basis of population, and elected for two-year terms) and the Senate (100 senators, 2 for each state, elected for six years, one-third elected every two years). Both representatives and senators are elected by direct popular vote. Congress meets in Washington, DC, in the Capitol Building. An ◊act of Congress is a bill passed by both houses.

Congress of Racial Equality (CORE) US nonviolent civil-rights organization, founded Chicago 1942.

Congreve William 1670–1729. English dramatist and poet. His first success was the comedy *The Old Bachelor* 1693, followed by *The Double Dealer* 1694, *Love for Love* 1695, the tragedy *The Mourning Bride* 1697, and *The Way of the World* 1700. His plays, which satirize the social affectations of the time, are characterized by elegant wit and wordplay.

congruent in geometry, having the same shape and size, as applied to two-dimensional or solid figures. With plane congruent figures, one figure will fit on top of the other exactly, though this may first require rotation and/or reflection of one of the figures.

Congo
Republic of
(*République du Congo*)

ATLANTIC

OCEAN

C.A.R.

Cameroon
Equatorial Guinea
Gabon   Zaire
CONGO
Cabinda   Brazzaville
(to Angola)

0 mi   500
0 km   1000

area 132,012 sq mi/342,000 sq km
capital Brazzaville
cities chief port Pointe-Noire; N'Kayi, Loubomo
physical narrow coastal plain rises to central plateau, then falls into northern basin; Zaïre (Congo) River on the border with Zaire; half the country is rain forest
environment an estimated 93% of the rural population is without access to safe drinking water
features 70% of the population lives in Brazzaville, Pointe-Noire, or in towns along the railway linking these two places
head of state Pascal Lissouba from 1992
head of government Jacques-Joachim Thumbi-Opango from 1993
political system emergent democracy
political parties Pan-African Union for Social Democracy (UPADS), moderate left of center; Congolese Labor Party (PCT), (Marxist-Leninist ideology abandoned 1990) left-wing; Congolese Movement for Democracy and Integral

Development (MCDDI), moderate centrist; Rally for Democracy and Development (RDD), nationalist, center-left.
exports timber, petroleum, cocoa, sugar
currency CFA franc
population (1992) 2,692,000 (chiefly Bantu); growth rate 2.6% p.a.
life expectancy men 45, women 48
languages French (official); many African languages
religions animist 50%, Christian 48%, Muslim 2%
literacy men 79%, women 55% (1985 est)
GDP $2.1 bn (1983); $500 per head

chronology
1910 Became part of French Equatorial Africa.
1960 Achieved independence from France, with Abbé Youlou as the first president.
1963 Youlou forced to resign. New constitution approved, with Alphonse Massamba-Débat as president.
1964 The Congo became a one-party state.
1968 Military coup, led by Capt Marien Ngouabi, ousted Massamba-Débat.
1970 A Marxist state, the People's Republic of the Congo, was announced, with the PCT as the only legal party.
1977 Ngouabi assassinated. Col Yhombi-Opango became president.
1979 Yhombi-Opango handed over the presidency to the PCT, who chose Col Denis Sassou-Nguessou as his successor.
1984 Sassou-Nguessou elected for another five-year term.
1990 The PCT abandoned Marxist-Leninism and promised multiparty politics.
1991 1979 constitution suspended. Country renamed the Republic of Congo.
1992 New constitution approved and multiparty elections held, giving UPADS the most assembly seats. Pascal Lissouba elected president.
1993 Ethnic conflicts intensified, and economy disintegrated.

conifer tree or shrub of the class Coniferales, in the gymnosperm or naked-seed-bearing group of plants. They are often pyramidal in form, with leaves that are either scaled or made up of needles; most are evergreen. Conifers include pines, spruces, firs, yews, junipers, monkey puzzles, and larches.

conjugate angles two angles that add up to 360°.

conjugation in biology, the bacterial equivalent of sexual reproduction. A fragment of the ◊DNA from one bacterium is passed along a thin tube, the pilus, into the cell of another bacterium.

conjunction grammatical ◊part of speech that serves to connect words, phrases, and clauses. Coordinating conjunctions link parts of equal grammatical value; *and, but,* and *or* are the most common. Subordinating conjunctions link subordinate clauses to the main clause in a sentence; among the most common are *if, when,* and *though.*

conjunction in astronomy, the alignment of two celestial bodies as seen from Earth. A superior planet (or other object) is in conjunction when it lies behind the Sun. An ◊inferior planet (or other object) comes to *inferior conjunction* when it passes between the Earth and the Sun; it is at *superior conjunction* when it passes behind the Sun. *Planetary conjunction* takes place when a planet is closely aligned with another celestial object, such as the Moon, a star, or another planet.

conjunctivitis inflammation of the conjunctiva, the delicate membrane that lines the inside of the eyelids

and covers the front of the eye. It may be caused by infection, allergy, or other irritant.

Conkling Roscoe 1829–1888. US political leader, one of the founders of the Republican Party 1854. He served in the US House of Representatives 1859–63 and 1865–67, and in the US Senate 1867–81. A radical Republican, Conkling was an active prosecutor in President A ◊Johnson's impeachment trial.

Connecticut state in NE US; nickname Constitution State/Nutmeg State
area 5,018 sq mi/13,000 sq km
capital Hartford
physical highlands in the NW; Connecticut River
features Yale University; Mystic Seaport (reconstruction of 19th-century village, with restored ships)
products dairy, poultry, and market-garden products; tobacco, watches, clocks, silverware, helicopters, jet engines, nuclear submarines, hardware and locks, electrical and electronic equipment, guns and ammunition, optical instruments. Hartford is the center of the nation's insurance industry
population (1990) 3,287,100
famous people Benedict Arnold, Phineas T Barnum, Jonathan Edwards, Nathan Hale, Katharine Hepburn, Charles Ives, Edward H Land, Eugene O'Neill, Wallace Stevens, Harriet Beecher Stowe, Mark Twain, Eli Whitney
history Dutch navigator Adriaen Block was the first European to record the area 1614, and in 1633 Dutch colonists built a trading post near modern Hartford but it soon was settled by Puritan colonists from

Massachusetts 1635. It was one of the original 13 colonies and became a state 1788. It prospered in the 19th century from shipbuilding, whaling, and growing industry. In the 20th century it became an important supplier of military equipment. Connecticut is second to Alaska among states in personal income per capita. Many of New York City's most affluent residential suburbs are in SW Connecticut.

connective tissue in animals, tissue made up of a noncellular substance, the ◊extracellular matrix, in which some cells are embedded. Skin, bones, tendons, cartilage, and adipose tissue (fat) are the main connective tissues. There are also small amounts of connective tissue in organs such as the brain and liver, where they maintain shape and structure.

Connery Sean 1930– . Scottish film actor, the first and best interpreter of James Bond in several films based on the novels of Ian Fleming. His films include *Dr No* 1962, *From Russia with Love* 1963, *Marnie* 1964, *Goldfinger* 1964, *Diamonds Are Forever* 1971, *A Bridge Too Far* 1977, *The Name of the Rose* 1986, and *The Untouchables* 1987 (Academy Award).

Connors Jimmy 1952– . US tennis player who won the Wimbledon title 1974 and 1982, and subsequently won ten Grand Slam events. He was one of the first players to popularize the two-handed backhand.

conquistador any of the early Spanish explorers and adventurers in the Americas, such as Hernán Cortés (Mexico) and Francisco Pizarro (Peru).

Conrad Joseph. Adopted name of Teodor Jozef Conrad Korzeniowski 1857–1924. English novelist, born in the Ukraine of Polish parents. He joined the French merchant marine at the age of 17 and first learned English at 21. His greatest works include the novels *Lord Jim* 1900, *Nostromo* 1904, *The Secret Agent* 1907, and *Under Western Eyes* 1911, and the short stories "Heart of Darkness" 1902 and "The Shadow Line" 1917. These combine a vivid sensuous evocation of various lands and seas with a rigorous, humane scrutiny of moral dilemmas, pitfalls, and desperation.

Conrad I King of the Germans from 911, when he succeeded Louis the Child, the last of the German Carolingians. During his reign the realm was harassed by ◊Magyar invaders.

Conrad II King of the Germans from 1024, Holy Roman emperor from 1027. He ceded the Sleswick (Schleswig) borderland, south of the Jutland peninsula, to King Canute, but extended his rule into Lombardy and Burgundy.

Conrad III 1093–1152. Holy Roman emperor from 1138, the first king of the Hohenstaufen dynasty. Throughout his reign there was a fierce struggle between his followers, the *Ghibellines*, and the *Guelphs*, the followers of Henry the Proud, duke of Saxony and Bavaria (1108–1139), and later of his son Henry the Lion (1129–1195).

Conrad V (Conradin) 1252–1268. Son of Conrad IV, recognized as king of the Germans, Sicily, and Jerusalem by German supporters of the Hohenstaufens 1254. He led Ghibelline forces against Charles of Anjou at the battle of Tagliacozzo, N Italy 1266, and was captured and executed.

conscription legislation for all able-bodied male citizens (and female in some countries, such as Israel) to serve with the armed forces. It originated in France 1792, and in the 19th and 20th centuries became the established practice in almost all European states.

Connecticut

Modern conscription systems often permit alternative national service for conscientious objectors.

In the US conscription (the **draft**) was introduced during the Civil War—by the Confederates 1862 and by the Union side 1863. In World War I a Selective Service Act was passed 1917, then again 1940 in anticipation of US entry into World War II. It remained in force (except for 15 months 1947–48) until after the US withdrawal from Vietnam 1973, although the system was changed to a lottery based on a registrant's birthday. This was done to rectify the inequities stemming from the deferment system that had allowed college students to delay their service. In 1980 Carter restored registration for a possible military draft for men at 18, but his proposal that it be extended to women was rejected by Congress. The US now has a policy based on all-volunteer armed forces.

conservation in the life sciences, action taken to protect and preserve the natural world, usually from pollution, overexploitation, and other harmful features of human activity. The late 1980s saw a great increase in public concern for the environment, with membership in conservation groups, such as the Sierra Club, the Nature Conservancy, and Friends of the Earth, rising sharply. Globally the most important issues include the depletion of atmospheric ozone by the action of chlorofluorocarbons (CFCs), the buildup of carbon dioxide in the atmosphere (thought to contribute to an intensification of the ◊greenhouse effect), and the destruction of the tropical rain forests (see ◊deforestation).

conservatism approach to government favoring the maintenance of existing institutions and identified with a number of Western political parties, such as the US Republican, British Conservative, German Christian Democratic, and Australian Liberal parties. It

Connery Scottish actor Sean Connery shot to fame as the first James Bond in Doctor No 1962.

tends to be explicitly nondoctrinaire and pragmatic but generally emphasizes free-enterprise capitalism, minimal government intervention in the economy, rigid law and order, and the importance of national traditions.

Constable John 1776–1837. English landscape painter. He painted scenes of his native Suffolk, including *The Haywain* 1821 (National Gallery, London), as well as castles, cathedrals, landscapes, and coastal scenes in other parts of Britain. Constable inherited the Dutch tradition of somber realism, in particular the style of Jacob Ruisdael, but he aimed to capture the momentary changes of nature as well as to create monumental images of British scenery, such as *The White Horse* 1819 (Frick Collection, New York) and *Flatford Mill* 1825.

Constance, Council of council held by the Roman Catholic church 1414–17 in Constance, Germany. It elected Pope Martin V, which ended the Great Schism 1378–1417 when there were rival popes in Rome and Avignon.

constant in mathematics, a fixed quantity or one that does not change its value in relation to ◊variables. For example, in the algebraic expression $y^2 = 5x - 3$, the numbers 3 and 5 are constants. In physics, certain quantities are regarded as universal constants, such as the speed of light in a vacuum.

Constantine II 1940– . King of the Hellenes (Greece). In 1964 he succeeded his father Paul I, went into exile 1967, and was formally deposed 1973.

He married Princess Anne-Marie of Denmark in 1964.

Constantine the Great *c.* AD 280–337. First Christian emperor of Rome and founder of Constantinople. He defeated Maxentius, joint emperor of Rome AD 312, and in 313 formally recognized Christianity. As sole emperor of the west of the empire, he defeated Licinius, emperor of the east, to become ruler of the Roman world 324. He presided over the church's first council at Nicaea 325. Constantine moved his capital to Byzantium on the Bosporus 330, renaming it Constantinople (now Istanbul).

Constantinople former name (330–1453) of Istanbul, Turkey. It was named after the Roman emperor Constantine the Great when he enlarged the Greek city of Byzantium 328 and declared it the capital of the ◊Byzantine Empire 330. Its elaborate fortifications enabled it to resist a succession of sieges, but it was captured by crusaders 1204, and was the seat of a Latin (Western European) kingdom until recaptured by the Greeks 1261. An attack by the Turks 1422 proved unsuccessful, but it was taken by another Turkish army May 29, 1453, after nearly a year's siege, and became the capital of the Ottoman Empire.

constellation one of the 88 areas into which the sky is divided for the purposes of identifying and naming celestial objects. The first constellations were simple, arbitrary patterns of stars in which early civilizations visualized gods, sacred beasts, and mythical heroes.

constitution body of fundamental laws of a state, laying down the system of government and defining the relations of the legislature, executive, and judiciary to each other and to the citizens. Since the French Revolution almost all countries (the UK is an exception) have adopted written constitutions; that of the US (1787) is the oldest.

Constructivism revolutionary art movement founded in Moscow 1917 by the Russians Naum

◊Gabo, his brother Antoine Pevsner (1886–1962), and Vladimir Tatlin (1885–1953). Tatlin's abstract sculptures, using wood, metal, and clear plastic, were hung on walls or suspended from ceilings. Gabo and Pevsner soon left the USSR and joined the European avant-garde.

consul chief magistrate of ancient Rome after the expulsion of the last king 510 BC. The consuls were two annually elected magistrates, both of equal power; they jointly held full civil power in Rome and the chief military command in the field. After the establishment of the Roman Empire the office became purely honorary.

consumer price index yearly index of the cost of goods and services to the consumer needed for an average standard of living. See also ◊producer price index.

Consumers Union private organization formed to protect consumers' interests, usually in terms of quality and safety.

consumption in economics, the purchase of goods and services for final use, as opposed to spending by firms on capital goods, known as capital formation.

In national accounting, it means a country's total expenditure over a given period (usually a year) on goods and services, including expenditure on raw materials and defense.

consumption in medicine, former name for the disease ◊tuberculosis.

contact lens lens, made of soft or hard plastic, that is worn in contact with the cornea and conjunctiva of the eye, beneath the eyelid, to correct defective vision. In special circumstances, contact lenses may be used as protective shells or for cosmetic purposes, such as changing eye color.

Contadora Group alliance formed among Colombia, Mexico, Panama, and Venezuela Jan 1983 to establish a general peace treaty for Central America. It was named after Contadora, the island of the Pearl Group in the Gulf of Panama where the first meeting was held.

contempt of court behavior that shows lack of respect for the authority of a court of law, such as disobeying a court order, breach of an injunction, or improper use of legal documents. Behavior that disrupts, prejudices, or interferes with court proceedings either inside or outside the courtroom may also be contempt. The court may punish contempt with a fine or imprisonment.

continent any one of the seven large landmasses of the Earth, as distinct from the oceans. They are Asia, Africa, North America, South America, Europe, Australia, and Antarctica. Continents are constantly moving and evolving (see ◊plate tectonics). A continent does not end at the coastline; its boundary is the edge of the shallow continental shelf, which may extend several hundred or miles out to sea.

Continental Congress in US history, the federal legislature of the original 13 states, acting as a provisional revolutionary government during the ◊American Revolution. It convened in Philadelphia from 1774 until 1789, when the US Constitution was adopted. The Second Continental Congress, convened May 1775, was responsible for drawing up the ◊Declaration of Independence and, in 1777, the Articles of Confederation. The Congress authorized an army to resist the British and issued paper money to finance the war

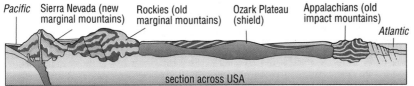

Pacific | Sierra Nevada (new marginal mountains) | Rockies (old marginal mountains) | Ozark Plateau (shield) | Appalachians (old impact mountains) | Atlantic

section across USA

continent *The North American continent, composed of the wide area of the Ozark plateau shield, is growing in the west as a result of collision with the Pacific plate.*

effort. It also oversaw the deliberations of the Constitutional Convention.

continental drift in geology, the theory that, about 250–200 million years ago, the Earth consisted of a single large continent (◊Pangaea), which subsequently broke apart to form the continents known today. The theory was proposed 1912 by German meteorologist Alfred Wegener, but such vast continental movements could not be satisfactorily explained until the study of ◊plate tectonics in the 1960s.

continental rise the portion of the ocean floor rising gently from the abyssal plain toward the steeper continental slope. The continental rise is a depositional feature formed from sediments transported down the slope mainly by turbidity currents. Much of the continental rise consists of coalescing submarine alluvial fans bordering the continental slope.

continental shelf the submerged edge of a continent, a gently sloping plain that extends into the ocean. It typically has a gradient of less than 1°. When the angle of the sea bed increases to 1°–5° (usually several hundred miles away from land), it becomes known as the *continental slope*.

continental slope sloping, submerged portion of a continent. It extends downward from the edge of the continental shelf. In some places, such as south of the Aleutian Islands of Alaska, continental slopes extend directly to the ocean deeps or abyssal plain. In others, such as the E coast of North America, they grade into the gentler continental rises that in turn grade into the abyssal plains.

Continental System system of economic preference and protection within Europe 1806–13 created by the French emperor Napoleon in order to exclude British trade. Apart from its function as economic warfare, the system also reinforced the French economy at the expense of other European states. It failed owing to British naval superiority.

continuo abbreviation for *basso continuo*; in music, the bass line on which a keyboard player, often accompanied by a bass stringed instrument, built up a harmonic accompaniment in 17th-century Baroque music.

continuous data data that can take any of an infinite number of values between whole numbers and so may not be measured completely accurately. This type of data contrasts with ◊discrete data, in which the variable can only take one of a finite set of values. For example, the sizes of apples on a tree form continuous data, whereas the numbers of apples form discrete data.

Contra member of a Central American right-wing guerrilla force attempting to overthrow the democratically elected Nicaraguan Sandinista government 1979–90. The Contras, many of them mercenaries or former members of the deposed dictator Somoza's guard (see ◊Nicaraguan Revolution), operated mainly from bases outside Nicaragua, mostly in Honduras, with covert US funding, as revealed by the ◊Irangate hearings 1986–87.

contrabassoon larger version of the ◊bassoon, sounding an octave lower.

contraceptive any drug, device, or technique that prevents pregnancy. The contraceptive pill (the ◊Pill) contains female hormones that interfere with egg production or the first stage of pregnancy. The "morning-after" pill can be taken up to 72 hours after unprotected intercourse. Barrier contraceptives include ◊condoms (sheaths) and ◊diaphragms, also called caps or Dutch caps; they prevent the sperm entering the cervix (neck of the womb). ◊Intrauterine devices, also known as IUDs or coils, cause a slight inflammation of the lining of the womb; this prevents the fertilized egg from becoming implanted. See also ◊family planning.

contract agreement between two or more parties that will be enforced by law according to the intention of the parties.

In a contract each party mutually obliges himself or herself to the other for exchange of property or performance for a consideration.

contract bridge card game first played 1925. From 1930 it quickly outgrew auction bridge in popularity.

control experiment essential part of a scientifically valid experiment, designed to show that the factor being tested is actually responsible for the effect observed. In the control experiment all factors, apart from the one under test, are exactly the same as in the test experiments, and all the same measurements are

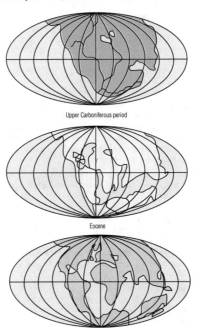

continental drift
The drifting continents.

Upper Carboniferous period

Eocene

Lower Quaternary

carried out. In drug trials, a placebo (a harmless substance) is given alongside the substance being tested in order to compare effects.

convection heat energy transfer that involves the movement of a fluid (gas or liquid). According to ◊kinetic theory, molecules of fluid in contact with the source of heat expand and tend to rise within the bulk of the fluid. Less energetic, cooler molecules sink to take their place, setting up convection currents. This is the principle of natural convection in many domestic hot-water systems and space heaters.

convectional rainfall rainfall associated with hot climates, resulting from the uprising of convection currents of warm air. Air that has been warmed by the extreme heat of the ground surface rises to great heights and is abruptly cooled. The water vapor carried by the air condenses and rain falls heavily. Convectional rainfall is usually accompanied by a thunderstorm.

convertiplane vertical takeoff and landing craft (VTOL) with rotors on its wings that spin horizontally for takeoff, but tilt to spin in a vertical plane for forward flight.

convex lens converging ◊lens—that is, a parallel beam of light passing through it converges and is eventually brought to a focus; it can therefore produce a real image on a screen. Such a lens is wider at its center than at the edges.

conveyor device used for transporting materials. Widely used throughout industry is the **conveyor belt**, usually a rubber or fabric belt running on rollers. Trough-shaped belts are used, for example in mines, for transporting ores and coal. **Chain conveyors** are also used in coal mines to remove coal from the cutting machines. Overhead endless chain conveyors are used to carry components and bodies in car-assembly works. Other types include **bucket conveyors** and **screw conveyors**, powered versions of the ◊Archimedes' screw.

convoy system grouping of ships to sail together under naval escort in wartime. In World War I (1914–18) navy escort vessels were at first used only to accompany troopships, but the convoy system was adopted for merchant shipping when the unrestricted German submarine campaign began 1917. In World War II (1939–45) the convoy system was widely used by the Allies to keep the Atlantic sea lanes open.

convulsion series of violent contractions of the muscles over which the patient has no control. It may be associated with loss of consciousness. Convulsions may arise from any one of a number of causes, including brain disease (such as ◊epilepsy), injury, high fever, poisoning, and electrocution.

Cook, Mount highest point, 12,353 ft/3,764 m, of the Southern Alps, a range of mountains running through New Zealand.

Cook James 1728–1779. British naval explorer. After surveying the St Lawrence 1759, he made three voyages: 1768–71 to Tahiti, New Zealand, and Australia; 1772–75 to the South Pacific; and 1776–79 to the South and North Pacific, attempting to find the Northwest Passage and charting the Siberian coast. He was killed in Hawaii.

Cook Thomas 1808–1892. Pioneer British travel agent and founder of Thomas Cook & Son. He introduced traveler's checks (then called "circular notes") in the early 1870s.

Cooke Alistair 1908– . British-born US journalist. He is best known for his writings interpreting US his-

tory and culture and for his role as television host of "Omnibus" and "Masterpiece Theatre."

Cooke Sam 1931–1964. US soul singer and songwriter who began his career as a gospel singer and turned to pop music 1956. His hits include "You Send Me" 1957 and "Wonderful World" 1960 (re-released 1986). His smooth tenor voice gilded some indifferent material, but his own song "A Change Is Gonna Come" 1965 is a moving civil-rights anthem.

cooking heat treatment of food to make it more palatable, digestible, and safe. It breaks down connective tissue in meat, making it tender, and softens the cellulose in plant tissue. Some nutrients may be lost in the process, but this does not affect the overall nutritional value of a balanced diet.

Cook Islands group of six large and a number of smaller Polynesian islands 1,600 mi/2,600 km NE of Auckland, New Zealand; area 112 sq mi/290 sq km; population (1991) 19,000. Their main products include fruit, copra, and crafts. They became a self-governing overseas territory of New Zealand 1965.

Cook Strait strait dividing North Island and South Island, New Zealand. A submarine cable carries electricity from South to North Island.

Cooley's anemia alternate name for ◊thalassemia.

Coolidge (John) Calvin 1872–1933. 30th president of the US 1923–29, a Republican. As governor of Massachusetts 1919, he was responsible for crushing a Boston police strike. As Warren ◊Harding's vice president 1921–23, he succeeded to the presidency on Harding's death (Aug 2, 1923). He won the 1924 presidential election, and his period of office was marked by economic growth.

Coolidge declined to run for reelection in 1928, supporting his secretary of the interior, Herbert ◊Hoover, who won the presidency.

Cooper Gary 1901–1962. US film actor. He epitomized the lean, true-hearted American, slow of speech but capable of outdoing the "bad guys" in *Lives of a Bengal Lancer* 1935, *Mr Deeds Goes to Town* (Academy Award for best picture 1936), *Sergeant York* 1940 (Academy Award for best actor 1941), and *High Noon* (Academy Award for best actor 1952).

Cooper James Fenimore 1789–1851. US writer, considered the first great US novelist. He wrote about 50 novels, mostly about the frontier, wilderness life, and the sea. He is best remembered for his ◊Leatherstocking Tales, a series of five novels: *The Pioneers* 1823, *The Last of the Mohicans* 1826, *The Prairie* 1827, *The Pathfinder* 1840, and *The Deerslayer* 1841. All describe the adventures of the frontier hero Natty Bumppo before and after the American Revolution.

Cooper Leon 1930– . US physicist who in 1955 began work on the puzzling phenomenon of ◊superconductivity. He proposed that at low temperatures electrons would be bound in pairs (since known as *Cooper pairs*) and in this state electrical resistance to their flow through solids would disappear. He shared the 1972 Nobel Prize for Physics with John ◊Bardeen and John Schrieffer (1931–).

cooperative movement the banding together of groups of people for mutual assistance in trade, manufacture, the supply of credit, housing, or other services. The original principles of the cooperative movement were laid down 1844 by the Rochdale Pioneers, under the influence of Robert Owen, and by Charles Fourier in France.

coordinate geometry or *analytical geometry* system of geometry in which points, lines, shapes, and surfaces are represented by algebraic expressions. In plane (two-dimensional) coordinate geometry, the plane is usually defined by two axes at right angles to each other, the horizontal *x*-axis and the vertical *y*-axis, meeting at O, the origin. A point on the plane can be represented by a pair of ◊Cartesian coordinates, which define its position in terms of its distance along the *x*-axis and along the *y*-axis from O. These distances are respectively the *x* and *y* coordinates of the point.

coot any of various freshwater birds of the genus *Fulica* in the rail family. Coots are about 1.2 ft/38 cm long, and mainly black. They have a white bill, extending up the forehead in a plate, and big feet with lobed toes.

Copenhagen (Danish *København*) capital of Denmark, on the islands of Zealand and Amager; population (1990) 1,337,100 (including suburbs).

Copernicus Nicolaus 1473–1543. Polish astronomer who believed that the Sun, not the Earth, is at the center of the Solar System, thus defying the Christian church doctrine of the time. For 30 years he worked on the hypothesis that the rotation and the orbital motion of the Earth were responsible for the apparent movement of the heavenly bodies. His great work *De Revolutionibus Orbium Coelestium/About the Revolutions of the Heavenly Spheres* was not published until the year of his death.

Copland Aaron 1900–1990. US composer. His early works, such as his piano concerto 1926, were in the jazz idiom but he gradually developed a gentler style with a regional flavor drawn from American folk music. Among his works are the ballets *Billy the Kid* 1939, *Rodeo* 1942, *Appalachian Spring* 1944 (based on a poem by Hart Crane), and *Inscape for Orchestra* 1967.

copper orange-pink, very malleable and ductile, metallic element, symbol Cu (from Latin *cuprum*), atomic number 29, atomic weight 63.546. It is used for its durability, pliability, high thermal and electrical conductivity, and resistance to corrosion.

copper ore any mineral from which copper is extracted, including native copper, Cu; chalcocite, Cu_2S; chalcopyrite, $CuFeS_2$; bornite, Cu_5FeS_4; azurite, $Cu_3(CO_3)_2(OH)_2$; malachite, $Cu_2CO_3(OH)_2$; and chrysocolla, $CuSiO_3 \cdot 2H_2O$.

Coppola Francis Ford 1939– . US film director and screenwriter. He directed *The Godfather* 1972, which became one of the biggest money-making films of all time, and its sequels *The Godfather Part II* 1974, which garnered seven Academy Awards, and *The Godfather Part III* 1990. His other films include *Apocalypse Now* 1979, *One From the Heart* 1982, *Rumblefish* 1983, *The Outsiders* 1983, and *Tucker: The Man and His Dream* 1988.

copra dried meat from the kernel of the ◊coconut, used to make coconut oil.

Copt descendant of those ancient Egyptians who adopted Christianity in the 1st century and refused to convert to Islam after the Arab conquest. They now form a small minority (about 5%) of Egypt's population. *Coptic* is a member of the Hamito-Semitic language family. It is descended from the language of the ancient Egyptians and is the ritual language of the Coptic Christian church. It is written in the Greek alphabet with some additional characters derived from ◊demotic script.

Copenhagen
Sailing boats moored in the Nyhavn, close to the old Royal Market in central Copenhagen, capital of Denmark.

copulation act of mating in animals with internal ◊fertilization. Male mammals have a ◊penis or other organ that is used to introduce spermatozoa into the reproductive tract of the female. Most birds transfer sperm by pressing their cloacas (the openings of their reproductive tracts) together.

copyright law applying to literary, musical, and artistic works (including plays, recordings, films, photographs, radio and television broadcasts, and, in the US and the UK, computer programs), which prevents the reproduction of the work, in whole or in part, without the author's consent.

In the US (since 1989) copyright lasts for a holder's lifetime plus 50 years, or a flat 75 years for a company copyright. It must be registered with the US Copyright Office of the Library of Congress to bring a court action. Works first federally copyrighted before 1978 must still be renewed in the 28th year to receive the second term of 47 years or it will fall into the public domain at the end of the 28th year. Various conditions apply to works published before 1989 and those between Jan 1, 1978, and March 1, 1989. For specific information, contact the Copyright Office, Library of Congress, Washington, DC.

coral marine invertebrate of the class Anthozoa in the phylum Cnidaria, which also includes sea anemones and jellyfish. It has a skeleton of lime (calcium carbonate) extracted from the surrounding water. Corals exist in warm seas, at moderate depths with sufficient light. Some coral is valued for decoration or jewelry, for example, Mediterranean red coral *Corallumrubrum*.

Coral Sea or *Solomon Sea* part of the Pacific Ocean bounded by NE Australia, New Guinea, the Solomon Islands, Vanuatu, and New Caledonia. It contains numerous coral islands and reefs. The Coral Sea Islands are a territory of Australia; they comprise scattered reefs and islands over an area of about 386,000 sq mi/1,000,000 sq km. They are uninhabited except for a meteorological station on Willis Island. The ◊Great Barrier Reef lies along its W edge, just off the E coast of Australia.

In the World War II Battle of the Coral Sea, May 7–8, 1942, the US fleet prevented the Japanese from landing in SE New Guinea and thus threatening Australia.

Corbett Gentleman Jim (James John) 1866–1933. US boxer who gained the heavyweight title in his 1892 New Orleans fight with reigning champion John L Sul-

Córdoba The Spanish city was once a Moorish settlement and its cathedral was originally built as a mosque.

livan. It was the first title bout to be fought with gloves and according to the Marquess of Queensberry rules. Corbett held the title until his defeat 1897 by Robert Fitzsimmons.

cordillera group of mountain ranges and their valleys, all running in a specific direction, formed by the continued convergence of two tectonic plates (see ◊plate tectonics) along a line.

The whole western section of North America, including the Rocky Mountains and the coastal ranges parallel to the contact between the North American and the Pacific plates, is called the Western Cordillera.

Córdoba capital of Córdoba province, Spain, on the river Guadalquivir; population (1991) 309,000. Paper, textiles, and copper products are manufactured here. It has many Moorish remains, including the mosque, now a cathedral, founded by 'Abd-ar-Rahman I 785, which is one of the largest Christian churches in the world. Córdoba was probably founded by the Carthaginians; it was held by the Moors 711–1236.

core in earth science, the innermost part of the Earth. It is divided into an inner core, the upper boundary of which is 1,060 mi/1,700 km from the center, and an outer core, 1,130 mi/1,820 km thick. Both parts are thought to consist of iron-nickel alloy, with the inner core being solid and the outer core being semisolid. The temperature may be 5,400°F/3,000°C.

CORE (acronym from *Congress of Racial Equality*) US nonviolent civil-rights organization, founded in Chicago 1942.

Corfu (Greek *Kérkyra*) northernmost and second largest of the Ionian islands of Greece, off the coast of Epirus in the Ionian Sea; area 414 sq mi/1,072 sq km; population (1981) 96,500. Its businesses include tourism, fruit, olive oil, and textiles. Its largest town is the port of Corfu (Kérkyra), population (1981) 33,560. Corfu was colonized by the Corinthians about 700 BC. Venice held it 1386–1797, Britain 1815–64.

coriander pungent fresh herb, the Eurasian plant *Coriandrum sativum*, a member of the parsley family Umbelliferae; also a spice: the dried ripe fruit. The spice is used commercially as a flavoring in meat prod-

ucts, bakery goods, tobacco, gin, liqueurs, chili, and curry powder. Both are much used in cooking in the Middle East, India, Mexico, and China.

Corinth (Greek *Kórinthos*) port in Greece, on the isthmus connecting the Peloponnese with the mainland; population (1981) 22,650. The rocky isthmus is bisected by the 4 mi/6.5 km Corinth canal, opened 1893. The site of the ancient city-state of Corinth lies 4.5 mi/7 km SW of the port.

Corinthian in Classical architecture, one of the five types of column; see ◊order.

cork light, waterproof outer layers of the bark of the stems and roots of almost all trees and shrubs. The cork oak *Quercus suber*, a native of S Europe and N Africa, is cultivated in Spain and Portugal; the exceptionally thick outer layers of its bark provide the cork that is used commercially.

corm short, swollen, underground plant stem, surrounded by protective scale leaves, as seen in the genus *Crocus*. It stores food, provides a means of ◊vegetative reproduction, and acts as a perennating organ.

cormorant any of various diving seabirds, mainly of the genus *Phalacrocorax*, about 3 ft/90 cm long, with webbed feet, long neck, hooked beak, and glossy black plumage. There are some 30 species of cormorant worldwide, including a flightless form *Nannopterum harrisi* in the Galápagos Islands. Cormorants generally feed on fish and shellfish. Some species breed on inland lakes and rivers.

corn cultivated New World plant *Zea mays* of the grass family, with the grain borne on cobs enclosed in husks. It is also called maize or Indian corn. It was domesticated by 6,000 BC in Mesoamerica, where it grew wild. It became the staple crop for the ◊Neolithic farming villages of Mexico and ◊civilizations of Mexico and Peru; it was cultivated throughout most of the New World at the point of European contact. It was brought to Europe, Asia, and Africa by the colonizing powers, but its use is mainly for animal feed in those regions. In the US, a corn monoculture dominates the Midwest, where many hybrids have been developed for both human food and animal feed. Today it is grown extensively in all subtropical and warm temperate regions, and its range has been extended to colder zones by hardy varieties developed in the 1960s.

cornea transparent front section of the vertebrate ◊eye. The cornea is curved and behaves as a fixed lens, so that light entering the eye is partly focused before it reaches the lens.

Corneille Pierre 1606–1684. French dramatist. His many tragedies, such as *Oedipe* 1659, glorify the strength of will governed by reason, and established the French Classical dramatic tradition for the next two centuries. His first play, *Mélite*, was performed 1629, followed by others that gained him a brief period of favor with Cardinal Richelieu. *Le Cid* 1636 was attacked by the Academicians, although it received public acclaim. Later plays were based on Aristotle's unities.

Cornell Katherine 1898–1974. German-born US actress. Her first major success came with an appearance on Broadway in *Nice People* 1921. This debut was followed by a long string of New York stage successes, several of which were directed by her husband, Guthrie McClintic. From 1930 she began to produce her own plays; the most famous of them, *The Barretts of Wimpole Street* 1931, was later taken on tour and produced for television 1956.

cornet brass band instrument. It is like a shorter, broader trumpet, with a wider bore and mellower tone, and without fixed notes. Notes of different pitch are obtained by overblowing and by means of three pistons.

cornflower plant *Centaurea cyanus* of the family Compositae. It is distinguished from the knapweeds by its deep azure-blue flowers. Formerly a common weed in N European wheat fields, it is now commonly grown in gardens as a herbaceous plant.

Cornforth John Warcup 1917– . Australian chemist. Using ◊radioisotopes as markers, he found out how cholesterol is manufactured in the living cell and how enzymes synthesize chemicals that are mirror images of each other (optical ◊isomers). He shared a Nobel Prize 1975 with Swiss chemist Vladimir Prelog (1906–).

Cornish language extinct member of the ◊Celtic languages, a branch of the Indo-European language family, spoken in Cornwall, England, until 1777. Written Cornish first appeared in 10th-century documents; some religious plays were written in Cornish in the 15th and 16th centuries, but later literature is scanty, consisting mainly of folk tales and verses. In recent years the language has been revived in a somewhat reconstructed form by members of the Cornish nationalist movement.

cornstarch purified, fine, powdery starch made from corn, used as a thickener in cooking and to make corn syrup commercially.

cornucopia (Latin "horn of plenty") in Greek mythology, one of the horns of the goat Amaltheia, which was caused by Zeus to refill itself indefinitely with food and drink. In paintings, the cornucopia is depicted as a horn-shaped container spilling over with fruit and flowers.

Cornwall county in SW England including the Isles of ◊Scilly (Scillies)
area (excluding Scillies) 1,370 sq mi/3,550 sq km
cities Truro (administrative headquarters), Camborne, Launceston; resorts of Bude, Falmouth, Newquay, Penzance, St Ives

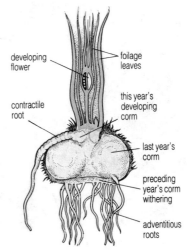

developing flower

foilage leaves

contractile root

this year's developing corm

last year's corm

preceding year's corm withering

adventitious roots

corm *Corms, found in plants such as the gladiolus and crocus, are underground storage organs.*

physical Bodmin Moor (including Brown Willy 1,375 ft/419 m); Land's End peninsula; St Michael's Mount; rivers Tamar, Fowey, Fal, Camel
features Poldhu, site of first transatlantic radio signal 1901. The Stannary or Tinners' Parliament has six members from each of the four Stannary towns: Losthwithiel, Launceston, Helston, and Truro. The flag of St Piran, a white St George's cross on a black ground, is used by separatists
products electronics, spring flowers, tin (mined since Bronze Age, some workings renewed 1960s, though the industry has all but disappeared), kaolin (St Austell), fish
population (1991) 469,300
famous people John Betjeman, Humphry Davy, Daphne Du Maurier, William Golding
history the Stannary, established in the 11th century, ceased to meet 1752 but its powers were rescinded at Westminster, and it was revived 1974 as a separatist movement.

Cornwallis Charles, 1st Marquess 1738–1805. British general in the ◊American Revolution until 1781, when his defeat at Yorktown led to final surrender and ended the war. He then served as governor-general of India and viceroy of Ireland.

corolla a collective name for the petals of a flower. In some plants the petal margins are partially or completely fused to form a *corolla tube*, for example in morning glories *Convolvulus*.

corona faint halo of hot (about 3,600,000°F/ 2,000,000°C) and tenuous gas around the Sun, which boils from the surface. It is visible at solar ◊eclipses or through a *coronagraph*, an instrument that blocks light from the Sun's brilliant disk. Gas flows away from the corona to form the ◊solar wind. *See illustration p. 238*

Coronado Francisco de *c.* 1500–1554. Spanish explorer who sailed to the New World 1535 in search of gold. In 1540 he set out with several hundred men from the Gulf of California on an exploration of what are today the Southern states. Although he failed to discover any gold, his expedition came across the impressive Grand Canyon of the Colorado and introduced the use of the horse to the indigenous Indians.

coronary artery disease (Latin *corona* "crown," from the arteries' encircling of the heart) condition in which the fatty deposits of ◊atherosclerosis form in

corona The corona, the Sun's outer atmosphere, can be seen only during a total solar eclipse.

the coronary arteries that supply the heart muscle, making them too narrow.

coronation ceremony of investing a sovereign with the emblems of royalty, as a symbol of inauguration in office. Since the coronation of Harold 1066, English sovereigns have been crowned in Westminster Abbey, London.

Corot Jean-Baptiste-Camille 1796–1875. French painter, creator of a distinctive landscape style with cool colors and soft focus. His early work, including Italian scenes in the 1820s, influenced the Barbizon school of painters. Like them, Corot worked outdoors, but he also continued a conventional academic tradition with more romanticized paintings.

corporal punishment physical punishment of wrongdoers—for example, by whipping. It is still used as a punishment for criminals in many countries, especially under Islamic law. Corporal punishment of children by parents is illegal in some countries, including Sweden, Finland, Denmark, and Norway.

corporation a number of people grouped together in a legally constituted joint enterprise, usually for the conduct of business and for tax advantages. Types of corporations include publicly traded corporations, which sell stock to the public to raise capital, and privately held corporations. Corporations are legal entities filed with state governments and distinct from the individuals who manage their affairs or the owners of their stock. Only about 15% of the businesses in the US are corporations, but they produce 80% of sales.

corporation tax tax levied on a company's profits by public authorities. It is a form of income tax, and rates vary according to country, but there is usually a flat rate. It is a large source of revenue for governments.

Corpus Christi feast celebrated in the Roman Catholic and Orthodox churches, and to some extent in the Anglican church, on the Thursday after Trinity Sunday. It was instituted in the 13th century through the devotion of St Juliana, prioress of Mount Cornillon, near Liège, Belgium, in honor of the Real Presence of Christ in the Eucharist.

Corpus Christi city and port in SE Texas, on the Gulf of Mexico at the mouth of the river Nueces, SE of San Antonio; seat of Nueces County; population (1990) 257,500. Its main industries are oil refining and shipping, commercial fishing, and the processing and ship-

ping of agricultural products. Corpus Christi was originally a small trading post.

It was used as a base by General Zachary Taylor during the Mexican–American War 1845–58 and was captured by Union troops 1864 during the Civil War.

corrasion the grinding away of solid rock surfaces by particles carried by water, ice, and wind. It is generally held to be the most significant form of ◊erosion. As the eroding particles are carried along they become eroded themselves due to the process of ◊attrition.

Correggio Antonio Allegri da *c.* 1494–1534. Italian painter of the High Renaissance whose style followed the Classical grandeur of Leonardo and Titian but anticipated the Baroque in its emphasis on movement, softer forms, and contrasts of light and shade.

correlation the degree of relationship between two sets of information. If one set of data increases at the same time as the other, the relationship is said to be positive or direct. If one set of data increases as the other decreases, the relationship is negative or inverse. Correlation can be shown by plotting a best-fit line on a ◊scatter diagram.

corrosion the eating away and eventual destruction of metals and alloys by chemical attack. The rusting of ordinary iron and steel is the most common form of corrosion. Rusting takes place in moist air, when the iron combines with oxygen and water to form a brown-orange deposit of ◊rust (hydrated iron oxide). The rate of corrosion is increased where the atmosphere is polluted with sulfur dioxide. Salty road and air conditions accelerate the rusting of automobile bodies.

corrosion in earth science, an alternate name for ◊solution, the process by which water dissolves rocks such as limestone.

corsair pirate based on the N African Barbary Coast. From the 16th century onward the corsairs plundered shipping in the Mediterranean and Atlantic, holding hostages for ransom or selling them as slaves. Although many punitive expeditions were sent against them, they were not suppressed until France occupied Algiers 1830.

Corsica (French *Corse*) island region of France, in the Mediterranean off the W coast of Italy, N of Sardinia; it comprises the *départements* of Haute Corse and Corse du Sud
area 3,358 sq mi/8,700 sq km
capital Ajaccio (port)
physical mountainous; ◊maquis vegetation
features Corsica's mountain bandits were eradicated 1931, but the tradition of the vendetta or blood feud lingers. The island is the main base of the Foreign Legion
government its special status involves a 61-member regional parliament with the power to scrutinize French National Assembly bills applicable to the island and propose amendments
products wine, olive oil
population (1986) 249,000, including just under 50% native Corsicans. There are about 400,000 *émigrés*, mostly in Mexico and Central America, who return to retire
languages French (official); the majority speak Corsican, an Italian dialect
famous people Napoleon

Cortés Hernán (Ferdinand) 1485–1547. Spanish conquistador. He conquered the Aztec empire 1519–21, and secured Mexico for Spain.

cortex in biology, the outer layer of a structure such as the brain, kidney, or adrenal gland. In botany the cortex includes non-specialized cells lying just beneath the surface cells of the root and stem.

cortisone natural corticosteroid produced by the ◊adrenal gland, now synthesized for its antiinflammatory qualities and used in the treatment of rheumatoid arthritis.

Cortona Pietro da. Italian Baroque painter.

corundum native aluminum oxide, Al_2O_3, the hardest naturally occurring mineral known apart from diamond (corundum rates 9 on the Mohs' scale of hardness); lack of ◊cleavage also increases its durability. Its crystals are barrel-shaped prisms of the trigonal system. Varieties of gem-quality corundum are *ruby* (red) and *sapphire* (any color other than red, usually blue). Poorer-quality and synthetic corundum is used in industry, for example as an ◊abrasive.

Cosby Bill (William Henry) 1937– . US comedian and actor. His portrayal of the dashing, handsome secret agent in the television series "I Spy" 1965–68 won him three Emmy awards and revolutionized the way in which blacks were presented on screen. His sardonic humor, based on wry observations of domestic life and parenthood, found its widest audience in "The Cosby Show" 1984–92, which consistently topped the national ratings and provided new role models for young African Americans. It also made him one of the richest performers in show business.

cosecant in trigonometry, a ◊function of an angle in a right-angled triangle found by dividing the length of the hypotenuse (the longest side) by the length of the side opposite the angle. Thus the cosecant of an angle *A*, usually shortened to cosec *A*, is always greater than (or equal to) 1. It is the reciprocal of the sine of the angle, that is, cosec $A = 1/\sin A$.

Cosgrave Liam 1920– . Irish Fine Gael politician, prime minister of the Republic of Ireland 1973–77. As party leader 1965–77, he headed a Fine Gael–Labor coalition government from 1973. Relations between the Irish and UK governments improved under his premiership.

Cosgrave William Thomas 1880–1965. Irish politician. He took part in the ◊Easter Rising 1916 and sat in the Sinn Féin cabinet of 1919–21. Head of the Free State government 1922–33, he founded and led the Fine Gael opposition 1933–44. His eldest son is Liam Cosgrave.

cosine in trigonometry, a ◊function of an angle in a right-angled triangle found by dividing the length of the side adjacent to the angle by the length of the hypotenuse (the longest side). It is usually shortened to *cos*.

cosine rule in trigonometry, a rule that relates the sides and angles of triangles. The rule has the formula $a^2 = b^2 + c^2 - 2bc \cos A$ where *a*, *b*, and *c* are the sides of the triangle, and *A* is the angle opposite *a*.

cosmic radiation streams of high-energy particles from outer space, consisting of protons, alpha particles, and light nuclei, which collide with atomic nuclei

Costa Rica
Republic of
(*República de Costa Rica*)

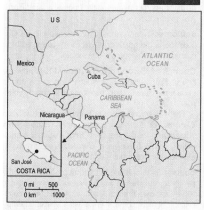

area 19,735 sq mi/ 51,100 sq km
capital San José
cities ports Limón, Puntarenas
physical high central plateau and tropical coasts; Costa Rica was once entirely forested, containing an estimated 5% of the Earth's flora and fauna. By 1983 only 17% of the forest remained; half of the arable land had been cleared for cattle ranching, which led to landlessness, unemployment (except for 2,000 politically powerful families), and soil erosion; the massive environmental destruction also caused incalculable loss to the gene pool
environment one of the leading centers of conservation in Latin America, with more than 10% of the country protected by national parks, and tree replanting proceeding at a rate of 60 sq mi/150 sq km per year
features Poas Volcano; Guayabo pre-Colombian ceremonial site

head of state and government Rafael Calderón from 1990
political system liberal democracy
political parties National Liberation Party (PLN), left of center; Christian Socialist Unity Party (PUSC), centrist coalition; ten minor parties
exports coffee, bananas, cocoa, sugar, beef
currency colón
population (1992) 3,161,000 (including 1,200 Guaymi Indians); growth rate 2.6% p.a.
life expectancy men 71, women 76
language Spanish (official)
religion Roman Catholic 95%
literacy men 94%, women 93% (1985 est)
GDP $4.3 bn (1986); $1,550 per head

chronology
1821 Independence achieved from Spain.
1949 New constitution adopted. National army abolished. José Figueres, cofounder of the PLN, elected president; he embarked on ambitious socialist program.
1958–73 Mainly conservative administrations.
1974 PLN regained the presidency and returned to socialist policies.
1978 Rodrigo Carazo, conservative, elected president. Sharp deterioration in the state of the economy.
1982 Luis Alberto Monge (PLN) elected president. Harsh austerity program introduced to rebuild the economy. Pressure from the US to abandon neutral stance and condemn Sandinista regime in Nicaragua.
1983 Policy of neutrality reaffirmed.
1985 Following border clashes with Sandinista forces, a US-trained antiguerrilla guard formed.
1986 Oscar Arias Sánchez won the presidency on a neutralist platform.
1987 Arias won Nobel Prize for Peace for devising a Central American peace plan.
1990 Rafael Calderón (PUSC) elected president.

in the Earth's atmosphere, and produce secondary nuclear particles (chiefly mesons, such as pions and muons) that shower the Earth.

cosmology study of the structure of the universe. Modern cosmology began in the 1920s with the discovery that the universe is expanding, which suggested that it began in an explosion, the ◊Big Bang. An alternative—now discarded—view, the ◊steady-state theory, claimed that the universe has no origin, but is expanding because new matter is being continually created.

Cossack member of any of several, formerly horse-raising groups of S and SW Russia, Ukraine, and Poland, predominantly of Russian or Ukrainian origin, who took in escaped serfs and lived in independent communal settlements (military brotherhoods) from the 15th to the 19th century. Later they held land in return for military service in the cavalry under Russian and Polish rulers. After 1917, the various Cossack communities were incorporated into the Soviet administrative and collective system.

Costa Rica country in Central America, bounded N by Nicaragua, SE by Panama, E by the Caribbean Sea, and W by the Pacific Ocean. *See panel p. 239*

cost-benefit analysis process whereby a project is assessed for its social and welfare benefits in addition to considering the financial return on investment. For example, this might take into account the environmental impact of an industrial plant or convenience for users of a new railroad. A major difficulty is finding a way to quantify net social costs and benefits.

Costello Elvis. Adopted name of Declan McManus 1954– . English rock singer, songwriter, and guitarist whose intricate yet impassioned lyrics have made him one of Britain's foremost songwriters. The great stylistic range of his work was evident from his 1977 debut *My Aim Is True* and was further extended 1993 when he collaborated with the Classical Brodsky Quartet on the song cycle *The Juliet Letters*.

Costner Kevin 1955– . US film actor. He first achieved top-ranking success with his role as law-enforcer Elliot Ness, in the 1987 film version of the 1960s television series "The Untouchables." Increasingly identified with the embodiment of idealism and high principle, Costner went on to direct and star in *Dances With Wolves* 1990, a Western sympathetic to the native American Indian, which won several Academy Awards. Subsequent films include *Robin Hood: Prince of Thieves* 1991, *JFK* 1991, *The Bodyguard* 1992, and *A Perfect World* 1993

cost of living see ◊consumer price index.

cotangent in trigonometry, a ◊function of an angle in a right-angled triangle found by dividing the length of the side adjacent to the angle by the length of the side opposite it. It is usually written as cotan or cot, and it is the reciprocal of the tangent of the angle, so that cot $A = 1/\tan A$, where A is the angle in question.

Cotonou chief port and largest city of Benin, on the Bight of Benin; population (1982) 487,000. Palm products and timber are exported. Although not the official capital, it is the seat of the president, and the main center of commerce and politics.

Cotopaxi (Quechua "shining peak") active volcano, situated to the S of Quito in Ecuador. It is 19,347 ft/5,897 m high and was first climbed 1872.

Cotten Joseph 1905– . US actor, intelligent and low-keyed, who was brought into films by Orson Welles.

Cotten gave outstanding performances in *Citizen Kane* 1941, *The Magnificent Ambersons* 1942, and *The Third Man* 1949.

cotton tropical and subtropical herbaceous plant of the genus *Gossypium* of the mallow family Malvaceae. Fibers surround the seeds inside the ripened fruits, or bolls, and these are spun into yarn for cloth.

Cotton John 1585–1652. English-born American religious leader. In Puritan views led to charges of heterodoxy being filed against him 1633. In the same year, he immigrated to the Massachusetts Bay Colony, where he was named teacher of Boston's First Congregational Church. A powerful force in the colony, he published widely circulated sermons and theological works.

cotton gin machine that separates cotton fibers from the seed boll. Production of the gin (then called an en*gin*e) by its US inventor Eli Whitney 1793 was a milestone in textile history.

cotton spinning creating thread or fine yarn from the cotton plant by spinning the raw fiber contained within the seedpods. The fiber is separated from the pods by a machine called a ◊cotton gin. It is then cleaned and the fibers are separated out (carding). Finally the fibers are drawn out to the desired length and twisted together to form strong thread.

cottonwood any of several North American poplars of the genus *Populus*, with seeds topped by a thick tuft of silky hairs. The eastern cottonwood *P. deltoides*, growing to 100 ft/30 m, is native to the eastern US. The name cottonwood is also given to the downy-leaved Australian tree *Bedfordia salaoina*.

cougar another name for the ◊puma, a large North American cat.

coulomb SI unit (symbol C) of electrical charge. One coulomb is the quantity of electricity conveyed by a current of one ◊ampere in one second.

Council of Europe body constituted 1949 in Strasbourg, France (still its headquarters), to secure "a greater measure of unity between the European countries."

The widest association of European states, it has a *Committee* of foreign ministers, a *Parliamentary Assembly* (with members from national parliaments), and a *European Commission* investigating violations of human rights.

counseling approach to treating problems, usually psychological ones, in which clients are encouraged to solve their own problems with support from a counselor. There is some overlap with ◊psychotherapy although counseling is less concerned with severe psychological disorders.

counterpoint in music, the art of combining different forms of an original melody with apparent freedom and yet to harmonious effect. Giovanni Palestrina and J S ◊Bach were masters of counterpoint.

Counter-Reformation movement initiated by the Catholic church at the Council of Trent 1545–63 to counter the spread of the ◊Reformation. Extending into the 17th century, its dominant forces included the rise of the Jesuits as an educating and missionary group and the deployment of the Spanish ◊Inquisition in other countries.

count rate number of particles emitted per unit time by a radioactive source. It is measured by a counter, such as a ◊Geiger counter, or ratemeter.

courtship display
The courtship display of gulls, with neck arching and sky-pointing.

country and western or *country music* popular music of the US South and West; it evolved from the folk music of the English, Irish, and Scottish settlers and has a strong blues influence. Characteristic instruments are the steel guitar, mandolin, and fiddle.

county administrative unit of a country or state. In the US a county is a subdivision of a state; the power of counties differs widely among states. In the UK it is nowadays synonymous with "shire," although historically the two had different origins. Many of the English counties can be traced back to Saxon times. The republic of Ireland has 26 geographical and 27 administrative counties.

coup d'état or *coup* forcible takeover of the government of a country by elements from within that country, generally carried out by violent or illegal means. It differs from a revolution in typically being carried out by a small group (for example, of army officers or opposition politicians) to install its leader as head of government, rather than being a mass uprising by the people.

Courbet Gustave 1819–1877. French artist, a portrait, genre, and landscape painter. Reacting against academic trends, both Classicist and Romantic, he sought to establish a new realism based on contemporary life. His *Burial at Ornans* 1850 (Louvre, Paris), showing ordinary working people gathered around a village grave, shocked the public and the critics with its "vulgarity."

Courrèges André 1923– . French fashion designer who is credited with inventing the miniskirt 1964. His "space-age" designs—square-shaped short skirts and trousers—were copied worldwide in the 1960s.

Court Margaret (born Smith) 1942– . Australian tennis player. The most prolific winner in the women's game, she won a record 64 Grand Slam titles, including 25 at singles.

courtship behavior exhibited by animals as a prelude to mating. The behavior patterns vary considerably from one species to another, but are often ritualized forms of behavior not obviously related to courtship or mating (for example, courtship feeding in birds).

court tennis racket and ball game played in France from about the 12th century, over a central net in an indoor court, but with a sloping roof let into each end and one side of the court, against which the ball may be hit. It is now played in several countries including the US, but there are very few courts. Basic scoring is as for ◊tennis, but with various modifications. It is the game on which tennis was based.

Cousteau Jacques Yves 1910– . French oceanographer, known for his researches in command of the *Calypso* from 1951, his film and television documentaries, and his many books; he pioneered the invention of the aqualung 1943 and techniques in underwater filming.

covalence in chemistry, a form of ◊valence in which two atoms unite by sharing electrons in pairs, so that each atom provides half the shared electrons (see also ◊bond).

Coventry industrial city in West Midlands, England; population (1984 est) 314,100. Manufacturing includes automobiles, electronic equipment, machine tools, and agricultural machinery. The poet Philip Larkin was born here.

Coward Noël 1899–1973. English playwright, actor, producer, director, and composer, who epitomized the witty and sophisticated man of the theater. From his first success with *The Young Idea* 1923, he wrote and appeared in plays and comedies on both sides of the Atlantic such as *Hay Fever* 1925, *Private Lives* 1930 with Gertrude Lawrence, *Design for Living* 1933, and *Blithe Spirit* 1941.

Cox Jacob Dolson 1828–1900. Canadian-born US educator and public figure. After service in the US Congress 1876–79, Cox was president of the University of Cincinnati 1885–89. He was elected governor of Ohio 1866 and served as secretary of the interior (1869–70) under President Grant.

coyote wild dog *Canis latrans*, in appearance like a small wolf, living from Alaska to Central America and east to New York. Its head and body are about 3 ft/ 90 cm long and brown, flecked with gray or black. Coyotes live in open country and can run at 40 mph/

65 kph. Their main foods are rabbits and rodents. Although persecuted by humans for over a century, the species is very successful.

CPR abbreviation for *cardiopulmonary ◊resuscitation*.

crab any decapod (ten-legged) crustacean of the division Brachyura, with a broad, rather round, upper body shell (carapace) and a small ◊abdomen tucked beneath the body. Crabs are related to lobsters and crayfish. Mainly marine, some crabs live in fresh water or on land. They are alert carnivores and scavengers. They have a typical sideways walk, and strong pincers on the first pair of legs, the other four pairs being used for walking. Periodically, the outer shell is cast to allow for growth. The name "crab" is sometimes used for similar arthropods, such as the horseshoe crab, which is neither a true crab nor a crustacean.

There are many species of true crabs worldwide. The North American blue crab *Callinectes sapidus*, called the soft-shelled crab after molting, is about 6 in/15 cm wide. It is extensively fished along the Atlantic and Gulf coasts. Other true crabs include fiddler crabs (Uca), the males of which have one enlarged claw to wave at and attract females, and spider crabs, with small bodies and very long legs, including the Japanese spider crab *Macrocheira kaemperi* with a leg span of 11 ft/3.4 m. Hermit crabs (division Anomura) have a soft, spirally twisted abdomen and make their homes in empty shells of sea snails for protection. Some tropical hermit crabs are found a considerable distance from the sea. The robber crab *Birgus latro* grows large enough to climb palm trees and feed on coconuts.

crab apple any of 25 species of wild ◊apple trees (genus *Malus*), native to temperate regions of the northern hemisphere. Numerous varieties of cultivated apples have been derived from *M. pumila*, the common native crab apple of SE Europe and central Asia. The fruit of native species is smaller and more bitter than that of cultivated varieties and is used in crab-apple jelly.

Crab nebula cloud of gas 6,000 light-years from Earth, in the constellation Taurus. It is the remains of a star that exploded as a ◊supernova (observed as a brilliant point of light on Earth 1054). At its center is a ◊pulsar that flashes 30 times a second. The name comes from its crablike shape.

crack street name for a chemical derivative (bicarbonate) of ◊cocaine in hard, crystalline lumps; it is heated and inhaled (smoked) as a stimulant. Crack

was first used in San Francisco in the early 1980s and is highly addictive.

cracking reaction in which a large alkane molecule is broken down by heat into a smaller alkane and a small alkene molecule. The reaction is carried out at a high temperature (1100°F/600°C or higher) and often in the presence of a catalyst. Cracking is a commonly used process in the ◊petrochemical industry.

Cracow alternate form of ◊Kraków, a Polish city.

crag in previously glaciated areas, a large lump of rock that a glacier has been unable to wear away. As the glacier passed up and over the crag, weaker rock on the far side was largely protected from erosion and formed a tapering ridge, or *tail*, of debris.

Cranach Lucas 1472–1553. German painter, etcher, and woodcut artist, a leading light in the German Renaissance. He painted many full-length nudes and precise and polished portraits, such as *Martin Luther* 1521 (Uffizi, Florence).

cranberry any of several trailing evergreen plants of the genus *Vaccinium* in the heath family Ericaceae, allied to bilberries and blueberries. They grow in marshy places and bear small, acid, crimson berries, high in vitamin C, used for making sauce and jelly.

crane in engineering, a machine for raising, lowering, or placing in position heavy loads. The three main types are the jib crane, the overhead traveling crane, and the tower crane. Most cranes have the machinery mounted on a revolving turntable. This may be mounted on trucks or be self-propelled, often being fitted with caterpillar tracks.

crane in zoology, a large, wading bird of the family Gruidae, with long legs and neck, and powerful wings. Cranes are marsh- and plains-dwelling birds, feeding on plants as well as insects and small animals. They fly well and are usually migratory. Their courtship includes frenzied, leaping dances. They are found in all parts of the world except South America.

Crane (Harold) Hart 1899–1932. US poet. His long mystical poem *The Bridge* 1930 uses the Brooklyn Bridge as a symbol. In his work he attempted to link humanity's present with its past, in an epic continuum. He drowned after jumping overboard from a steamer bringing him back to the US after a visit to Mexico.

Crane Stephen 1871–1900. US writer who introduced grim realism into the US novel. His book *The Red Badge of Courage* 1895 deals vividly with the US Civil War.

Born in Newark, New Jersey, Crane became a journalist. His first novel, self-published, *Maggie: A Girl of the Streets* 1893, was rejected by many editors because of its unpleasant subject of New York slum life. His free-verse poetry is collected in *The Black Riders* 1895. His critically acclaimed short stories include "The Open Boat," based on a true experience of shipwreck during a journalistic assignment to Cuba 1897.

craniotomy operation to remove or turn back a small flap of skull bone to give access to the living brain.

cranium the dome-shaped area of the vertebrate skull, consisting of several fused plates, that protects the brain. Fossil remains of the human cranium have aided the development of theories concerning human evolution.

crankshaft essential component of piston engines that converts the up-and-down (reciprocating) motion of the pistons into useful rotary motion. The auto-

crane The whooping crane Grus americana *of N America is exceedingly rare in the wild.*

crater *Aerial view of Meteor Crater, near Winslow, Arizona.*

mobile crankshaft carries a number of cranks. The pistons are connected to the cranks by connecting rods and ◊bearings; when the pistons move up and down, the connecting rods force the offset crank pins to describe a circle, thereby rotating the crankshaft.

Crassus Marcus Licinius *c.* 108–53 BC. Roman general who crushed the ◊Spartacus uprising 71 BC. In 60 BC he joined with Caesar and Pompey in the First Triumvirate and obtained command in the east 55 BC. Invading Mesopotamia, he was defeated by the Parthians at the battle of Carrhae, captured, and put to death.

crater bowl-shaped depression, usually round and with steep sides. Craters are formed by explosive events such as the eruption of a volcano or by the impact of a meteorite. A ◊caldera is a much larger feature.

craton or *shield* core of a continent, a vast tract of highly deformed ◊metamorphic rock around which the continent has been built. Intense mountain-building periods shook these shield areas in Precambrian times before stable conditions set in.

Crawford Joan. Adopted name of Lucille Le Seur 1908–1977. US film actress who became a star with her performance as a flapper (liberated young woman) in *Our Dancing Daughters* 1928. Later she appeared as a sultry, often suffering, mature woman. Her films include *Mildred Pierce* 1945 (for which she won an Academy Award), *Password* 1947, and *Whatever Happened to Baby Jane?* 1962.

Craxi Bettino 1934– . Italian socialist politician, leader of the Italian Socialist Party (PSI) 1976–93, prime minister 1983–87.

crayfish freshwater decapod (ten-limbed) crustacean belonging to several families structurally similar to, but smaller than, the lobster. Crayfish are brownish-green scavengers and are found in all parts of the world except Africa. They are edible, and some species are farmed.

The spiny lobster *Palinurus vulgaris*, is sometimes called crayfish; it is actually a marine lobster without pincers, and grows up to 20 in/50 cm long.

Crazy Horse 1849–1877. Sioux Indian chief, one of the Indian leaders at the massacre of ◊Little Bighorn. He was killed when captured.

creationism theory concerned with the origins of matter and life, claiming, as does the Bible in Genesis, that the world and humanity were created by a supernatural Creator, not more than 6,000 years ago. It was developed in response to Darwin's theory of ◊evolution; it is not recognized by most scientists as having a factual basis.

Crécy, Battle of first major battle of the Hundred Years' War 1346. Philip VI of France was defeated by Edward III of England at the village of Crécy-en-Ponthieu, now in Somme *département*, France, 11 mi/18 km NE of Abbeville.

credit in economics, means by which goods or services are obtained without immediate payment, usually by agreeing to pay interest. The three main forms are *consumer credit* (usually extended to individuals by retailers), *bank credit* (such as overdrafts or personal loans), and *trade credit* (common in the commercial world both within countries and internationally).

credit card card issued by a credit company, retail outlet, or bank, which enables the holder to obtain goods or services on credit (usually to a specified limit), payable on specified terms. The first credit card was introduced 1950 in the US.

Cree member of a North American Indian people whose language belongs to the Algonquian family. The Cree are distributed over a vast area in Canada from Québec to Alberta. In the US the majority of Cree live in the Rocky Boys reservation in Montana. Cree and Ojibwa languages are closely related and are spoken by around 50,000 people.

creed in general, any system of belief; in the Christian church the verbal confessions of faith expressing the accepted doctrines of the church. The different forms are the ◊Apostles' Creed, the ◊Nicene Creed, and the ◊Athanasian Creed. The only creed recognized by the Orthodox Church is the Nicene Creed.

creep in civil and mechanical engineering, the property of a solid, typically a metal, under continuous stress that causes it to deform below its yield point (the point at which any elastic solid normally stretches without any increase in load or stress). Lead, tin, and zinc, for example, exhibit creep at ordinary temperatures, as seen in the movement of the lead sheeting on the roofs of old buildings.

cremation disposal of the dead by burning. The custom was universal among ancient Indo-European peoples, for example, the Greeks, Romans, and Teutons. It was discontinued among Christians until the late 19th century because of their belief in the bodily resurrection of the dead. Overcrowded urban cemeteries gave rise to its revival in the West. It has remained the usual method of disposal in the East.

Creole in the West Indies and Spanish America, originally someone of European descent born in the New World; later someone of mixed European and African descent. In Louisiana and other states on the Gulf of Mexico, it applies either to someone of French or Spanish descent or (popularly) to someone of mixed French or Spanish and African descent.

Also, a patois or dialect based on French, Dutch, or English, as spoken in the West Indies.

Creole language any ◊pidgin language that has ceased to be simply a trade jargon in ports and markets and has become the mother tongue of a particular community. Many Creoles have developed into distinct languages with literatures of their own; for example, Jamaican Creole, Haitian Creole, Krio in Sierra Leone, and Tok Pisin, now the official language of Papua New Guinea.

creosote black, oily liquid derived from coal tar, used as a wood preservative. Medicinal creosote, which is transparent and oily, is derived from wood tar.

crescent curved shape of the Moon when it appears less than half-illuminated. It also refers to any object or symbol resembling the crescent Moon. Often associated with Islam, it was first used by the Turks on their standards after the capture of Constantinople 1453, and appears on the flags of many Muslim countries. The **Red Crescent** is the Muslim equivalent of the Red Cross.

cress any of several plants of the Cruciferae family, characterized by a pungent taste. The common European garden cress *Lepidium sativum* is cultivated worldwide.

Cresson Edith 1934– . French politician and founder member of the Socialist Party, prime minister 1991–92. Cresson held successive ministerial portfolios in François Mitterrand's government 1981–86 and 1988–90. Her government was troubled by a struggling economy, a series of strikes, and unrest in many of the country's poor suburban areas, which eventually forced her resignation.

Cretaceous period of geological time 146–65 million years ago. It is the last period of the Mesozoic era, during which angiosperm (seed-bearing) plants evolved, and dinosaurs reached a peak before their almost complete extinction at the end of the period. Chalk is a typical rock type of the second half of the period.

Crete (Greek *Kríti*) largest Greek island in the E Mediterranean Sea, 62 mi/100 km SE of mainland Greece
area 3,234 sq mi/8,378 sq km
capital Khaniá (Canea)
cities Iráklion (Heraklion), Rethymnon, Aghios Nikolaos
products citrus fruit, olives, wine
population (1991) 536,900
language Cretan dialect of Greek
history it has remains of the ◊Minoan civilization 3000–1400 BC (see ◊Knossos) and was successively under Roman, Byzantine, Venetian, and Turkish rule. The island was annexed by Greece 1913.

crevasse deep crack in the surface of a glacier; it can reach several meters in depth. Crevasses often occur where a glacier flows over the break of a slope, because the upper layers of ice are unable to stretch and cracks result. Crevasses may also form at the edges of glaciers owing to friction with the bedrock.

crib death see ◊sudden infant death syndrome (SIDS).

Crick Francis 1916– . British molecular biologist. From 1949 he researched the molecular structure of DNA, and the means whereby characteristics are transmitted from one generation to another. For this work he was awarded a Nobel Prize (with Maurice ◊Wilkins and James ◊Watson) 1962.

cricket in zoology, an insect belonging to any of various families, especially the Grillidae, of the order Orthoptera. Crickets are related to grasshoppers. They have somewhat flattened bodies and long antennae. The males make a chirping noise by rubbing together special areas on the forewings. The females have a long needlelike egg-laying organ (ovipositor). There are some 900 species known worldwide.

cricket bat-and-ball game between two teams of 11 players each. It is played with a small solid ball and long flat-sided wooden bats, on a round or oval field, at the center of which is a finely mown pitch, 22 yd/20 m long. At each end of the pitch is a wicket made up of three upright wooden sticks (stumps), surmounted by two smaller sticks (bails). The object of the game is to score more runs than the opposing team. A run is normally scored by the batsman striking the ball and exchanging ends with his or her partner until the ball is returned by a fielder, or by hitting the ball to the boundary line for an automatic four or six runs.

Crimea N peninsula on the Black Sea, an autonomous republic of ◊Ukraine; formerly a region (1954–91)
area 10,425 sq mi/27,000 sq km
capital Simferopol
cities Sevastopol, Yalta
features mainly steppe, but S coast is a holiday resort
products iron, oil
population 2.5 million (70% Russian, despite return of 150,000 Tatars since 1989)
history Crimea was under Turkish rule 1475–1774; a subsequent brief independence was ended by Russian annexation 1783. Crimea was the republic of Taurida 1917–20 and the Crimean Autonomous Soviet Republic from 1920 until occupied by Germany 1942–44. It was then reduced to a region, its Tatar people being deported to Uzbekistan for collaboration. Although they were exonerated 1967 and some were allowed to return, others were forcibly re-exiled 1979. A drift back to their former homeland began 1987 and a federal ruling 1988 confirmed their right to residency.

cricket

A good captain will position fielders according to the strength of the opposition's batsmen, the state of the pitch, and the stage the match has reached. An attacking field, with fielders close in to the batsmen, is employed when using a fast bowler. A defensive field with the fielders spread out around the boundary, is used when the batting team needs a lot of runs but has few overs remaining. With this type of field, only singles or twos are generally scored. Tactical fielding is more evident in one-day matches when each side plays a limited number of overs.

the pitch

fielding positions

The fielding positions shown are those available to the defending captain.

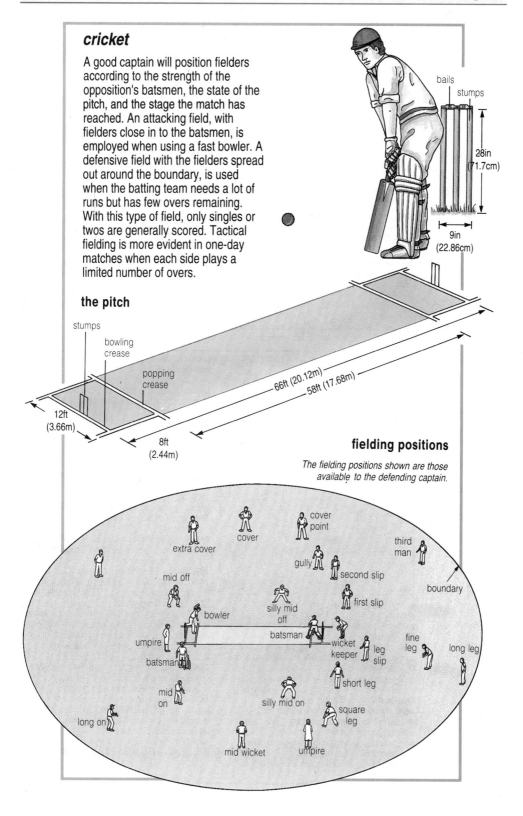

Since 1991 the Crimea has sought to gain independence from the Ukraine; the latter has resisted all secessionist moves.

Crimean War war 1853–56 between Russia and the allied powers of England, France, Turkey, and Sardinia. The war arose from British and French mistrust of Russia's ambitions in the Balkans. It began with an allied Anglo-French expedition to the Crimea to attack the Russian Black Sea city of Sevastopol. The battles of the river Alma, ◊Balaclava (including the charge of the Light Brigade), and Inkerman 1854 led to a siege which, owing to military mismanagement, lasted for a year until Sept 1855. The war was ended by the Treaty of Paris 1856. The scandal surrounding French and British losses through disease led to the organization of proper military nursing services by Florence Nightingale.

crime, organized illegal operations run like a large business. The best-known such organization is the ◊Mafia. For the history of US organized crime, see gangsterism. Japanese gangsters are called *yakuza*.

criminal law body of law that defines the public wrongs (crimes) that are punishable by the state and establishes methods of prosecution and punishment. It is distinct from ◊civil law, which deals with legal relationships between individuals (including organizations), such as contract law.

Criminal offenses are either ◊felonies or ◊misdemeanors. Felonies are more likely to require a formal charge, called an indictment, by a grand jury. Punishments include imprisonment, fines, suspended terms of imprisonment, probation, and ◊community service.

crith unit of mass used for weighing gases. One crith is the mass of one liter of hydrogen gas (H_2) at standard temperature and pressure.

critical angle in optics, for a ray of light passing from a denser to a less dense medium (such as from glass to air), the smallest angle of incidence at which the emergent ray grazes the surface of the denser medium—at an angle of refraction of 90°.

critical mass in nuclear physics, the minimum mass of fissile material that can undergo a continuous ◊chain reaction. Below this mass, too many ◊neutrons escape from the surface for a chain reaction to carry on; above the critical mass, the reaction may accelerate into a nuclear explosion.

critical path analysis procedure used in the management of complex projects to minimize the amount of time taken. The analysis shows which subprojects can run in parallel with each other, and which have to be completed before other subprojects can follow on. By identifying the time required for each separate subproject and the relationship between the subprojects, it is possible to produce a planning schedule showing when each subproject should be started and finished in order to complete the whole project most efficiently. Complex projects may involve hundreds of subprojects, and computer ◊applications packages for critical

---

Croatia
Republic of

area 21,824 sq mi/56,538 sq km
capital Zagreb
cities chief port: Rijeka (Fiume); other ports: Zadar, Sibenik, Split, Dubrovnik
physical Adriatic coastline with large islands; very mountainous, with part of the Karst region and the Julian and Styrian Alps; some marshland
features popular sea resorts along the extensive Adriatic coastline
head of state Franjo Tudjman from 1990
head of government Nikica Valentić from 1993
political system emergent democracy
political parties Christian Democratic Union (HDZ), right-wing, nationalist; Coalition of National Agreement, centrist; Communist Party, reform-communist
products cereals, potatoes, tobacco, fruit, livestock, metal goods, textiles

currency Croatian dinar
population (1992) 4,808,000 including 75% Croats, 12% Serbs, and 1% Slovenes
language Croatian variant of Serbo-Croatian
media no official censorship but no press or TV independent of government
religions Roman Catholic (Croats); Orthodox Christian (Serbs)
GNP $7.9 bn (1990); $1,660 per head

chronology
1918 Became part of the kingdom that united the Serbs, Croats, and Slovenes.
1929 The kingdom of Croatia, Serbia, and Slovenia became Yugoslavia. Croatia continued its campaign for autonomy.
1941 Became a Nazi puppet state following German invasion.
1945 Became constituent republic of Yugoslavia.
1970s Separatist demands resurfaced. Crackdown against anti-Serb separatist agitators.
1989 Formation of opposition parties permitted.
1990 April–May: Communists defeated by Tudjman-led Croatian Democratic Union (HDZ) in first free election since 1938. Sept: "sovereignty" declared.
1991 Feb: assembly called for Croatia's secession. March: Serb-dominated Krajina announced secession from Croatia. June: Croatia declared independence; military conflict with Serbia; internal civil war ensued. Oct: Croatia formally seceded from Yugoslavia.
1992 Jan: United Nations peace accord reached in Sarajevo; Croatia's independence recognized by the European Community. March–April: UN peacekeeping force of 14,000 drafted into Croatia. May: became a member of the United Nations. Aug: Tudjman directly elected president; HDZ won assembly elections. Sept: Tudjman requested withdrawal of UN forces on expiry of mandate 1993.
1993 Jan: Croatian forces launched offensive to retake parts of Serb-held Krajina, violating the 1992 UN peace accord.

path analysis are widely used to help reduce the time and effort involved in their analysis.

critical temperature temperature above which a particular gas cannot be converted into a liquid by pressure alone. It is also the temperature at which a magnetic material loses its magnetism (the Curie temperature or point).

Croat member of the majority ethnic group in ◊Croatia. Their language is generally considered to be identical to that of the Serbs, hence Serbo-Croatian.

Croatia (Serbo-Croatian *Hrvatska*) country in central Europe, bounded N by Slovenia and Hungary, W by the Adriatic Sea, and E by Bosnia-Herzegovina and the Yugoslavian republic of Serbia.

crochet craft technique similar to both knitting and lacemaking, in which one hooked needle is used to produce a loosely looped network of wool or cotton.

Crockett Davy 1786–1836. US folk hero, born in Tennessee, a Democratic Congressman 1827–31 and 1833–35. A series of books, of which he may have been part-author, made him into a mythical hero of the frontier, but their Whig associations cost him his office. He died in the battle of the ◊Alamo during the War of Texan Independence.

crocodile large aquatic carnivorous reptile of the family Crocodiliae, related to alligators and caymans, but distinguished from them by a more pointed snout and a notch in the upper jaw into which the fourth tooth in the lower jaw fits. Crocodiles can grow up to 20 ft/6 m, and have long, powerful tails that propel them when swimming. They can live up to 100 years.

crocus any plant of the genus *Crocus* of the iris family Iridaceae, native to N parts of the Old World, especially S Europe and Asia Minor. It has single yellow, purple, or white flowers and narrow, pointed leaves.

Croesus 6th century BC. Last king of Lydia *c.* 560–546 BC, famed for his wealth. Dominant over the Greek cities of the Asia Minor coast, he was defeated and captured by ◊Cyrus the Great and Lydia was absorbed into the Persian empire.

Crohn's disease or *regional ileitis* chronic inflammatory bowel disease. It tends to flare up for a few days at a time, causing diarrhea, abdominal cramps, loss of appetite, and mild fever. The cause of Crohn's disease is unknown, although stress may be a factor.

Cro-Magnon prehistoric human *Homo sapiens sapiens* believed to be ancestral to Europeans, the first skeletons of which were found 1868 in the Cro-Magnon cave near Les Eyzies, in the Dordogne region of France. They are thought to have superseded the Neanderthals in the Middle East, Africa, Europe, and Asia about 40,000 years ago. Although modern in skeletal form, they were more robust in build than some present-day humans. They hunted bison, reindeer, and horses, and are associated with Upper Paleolithic cultures, which produced fine flint and bone tools, jewelry, and naturalistic cave paintings.

Cromwell Oliver 1599–1658. English general and politician, Puritan leader of the Parliamentary side in the ◊Civil War. He raised cavalry forces (later called *Ironsides*) which aided the victories at Edgehill 1642 and Marston Moor 1644, and organized the New Model Army, which he led (with General Fairfax) to victory at Naseby 1645. He declared Britain a republic ("the Commonwealth") 1649, following the execution

crocodile The estuarine or saltwater crocodile, of India, SE Asia, and Australasia, is one of the largest and most dangerous of its family.

of Charles I. As Lord Protector (ruler) from 1653, Cromwell established religious toleration and raised Britain's prestige in Europe on the basis of an alliance with France against Spain.

Cronkite Walter 1916– . US broadcast journalist who was anchorperson of the national evening news program for CBS, a US television network, from 1962 to 1981.

Cronus or *Kronos* in Greek mythology, ruler of the world and one of the ◊Titans. He was the father of Zeus, who overthrew him.

Crookes William 1832–1919. English scientist whose many chemical and physical discoveries included the metallic element thallium 1861, the radiometer 1875, and the Crookes high-vacuum tube used in X-ray techniques.

crop any plant product grown or harvested for human use. Over 80 crops are grown worldwide, providing people with the majority of their food and supplying fibers, rubber, pharmaceuticals, dyes, and other materials. Crops grown for export are ◊cash crops. A catch crop is one grown in the interval between two main crops.

crop rotation system of regularly changing the crops grown on a piece of land. The crops are grown in a particular order to utilize and add to the nutrients in the soil and to prevent the buildup of insect and fungal pests. Including a legume crop, such as peas or beans, in the rotation helps build up nitrate in the soil because the roots contain bacteria capable of fixing nitrogen from the air.

croquet outdoor game played with mallets and balls on a level hooped lawn measuring 90 ft/27 m by 60 ft/18 m. Played in France in the 16th and 17th centuries, it gained popularity in the US and England in the 1850s.

Crosby Bing (Harry Lillis) 1904–1977. US film actor and singer who achieved world success with his distinctive style of crooning in such songs as "Pennies from Heaven" 1936 (featured in a film of the same name) and "White Christmas" 1942. He won an acting Oscar for *Going My Way* 1944, and made a series of "Road" film comedies with Dorothy Lamour and Bob ◊Hope, the last being *Road to Hong Kong* 1962.

cross symbol of the Christian religion, in widespread use since the 3rd century. It is a symbol of the crucifixion of Jesus and the central significance of his suffering, death, and resurrection. The Latin cross is the most commonly used; other types are the Greek cross, St Anthony's cross, and St Andrew's cross. Symbolic crosses were used by pre-Christian cultures, for example the ancient Egyptian ankh (St Anthony's cross with a loop at the top), symbol of life, and the swastika, used by Hindus, Buddhists, Celts, and N American Indians before it was adopted by the Nazis.

crossword puzzle in which a grid of open and blacked-out squares must be filled with interlocking words, to be read horizontally and vertically, according to numbered clues. The first crossword was devised by Arthur Wynne of Liverpool, England, in the *New York World* 1913.

croup inflammation (usually viral) of a child's larynx and trachea, with croaking breathing and hoarse coughing.

crow any of 35 species of the genus *Corvus*, family Corvidae, which also includes jays and magpies. Ravens belong to the same genus as crows. Crows are usually about 1.5 ft/45 cm long, black, with a strong bill feathered at the base, and omnivorous with a bias toward animal food. They are considered to be very intelligent.

crucifixion death by fastening to a cross, a form of capital punishment used by the ancient Romans, Persians, and Carthaginians, and abolished by the Roman emperor Constantine. Specifically, *the Crucifixion* refers to the execution by the Romans of ◊Jesus in this manner.

Cruelty, Theater of theory advanced by Antonin Artaud in his book *Le Théâtre et son double* 1938 and adopted by a number of writers and directors. It aims to shock the audience into an awareness of basic, primitive human nature through the release of feelings usually repressed by conventional behavior.

cruise missile long-range guided missile that has a terrain-seeking radar system and flies at moderate speed and low altitude. It is descended from the German V1 of World War II. Initial trials in the 1950s demonstrated the limitations of cruise missiles, which included high fuel consumption and relatively slow speeds (when compared to intercontinental ballistic missiles—ICBMs) as well as inaccuracy and a small warhead. Improvements to guidance systems by the use of terrain-contour matching (TERCOM) ensured pinpoint accuracy on low-level flights after launch from a mobile ground launcher (ground-launched cruise missile—GLCM), from an aircraft (air-launched cruise missile—ALCM), or from a submarine or ship (sea-launched cruise missile—SLCM).

crusade European war against non-Christians and heretics, sanctioned by the pope; in particular, *the Crusades*, a series of wars 1096–1291 undertaken by European rulers to recover Palestine from the Muslims. Motivated by religious zeal, the desire for land, and the trading ambitions of the major Italian cities, the Crusades were varied in their aims and effects.

crust the outermost part of the structure of Earth, consisting of two distinct parts, the oceanic crust and the continental crust. The *oceanic crust* is on average about 6.2 mi/10 km thick and consists mostly of basaltic types of rock. By contrast, the *continental crust* is largely made of granite and is more complex in its structure. Because of the movements of ◊plate tectonics, the oceanic crust is in no place older than about 200 million years. However, parts of the continental crust are over 3 billion years old.

crustacean one of the class of arthropods that includes crabs, lobsters, shrimps, pillbugs, and barnacles. The external skeleton is made of protein and chitin hardened with lime. Each segment bears a pair of appendages that may be modified as sensory feelers (antennae), as mouthparts, or as swimming, walking, or grasping structures.

cryogenics science of very low temperatures (approaching ◊absolute zero), including the production of very low temperatures and the exploitation of special properties associated with them, such as the disappearance of electrical resistance (◊superconductivity).

cryolite rare granular crystalline mineral (sodium aluminum fluoride), Na_3AlF_6, used in the electrolytic reduction of ◊bauxite to aluminum. It is chiefly found in Greenland.

Cryolite also occurs in Colorado at Pike's Peak.

cryptography science of creating and reading codes; for example, those produced by the Enigma coding machine used by the Germans in World War II, and those used in commerce by banks encoding electronic fund-transfer messages, and by business firms sending computer-conveyed memos between headquarters, and in the growing field of electronic mail. No method of encrypting is completely unbreakable, but decoding can be made extremely complex and time consuming.

crystal substance with an orderly three-dimensional arrangement of its atoms or molecules, thereby creating an external surface of clearly defined smooth faces having characteristic angles between them. Examples are table salt and quartz.

crystallography the scientific study of crystals. In 1912 it was found that the shape and size of the repeating atomic patterns (unit cells) in a crystal could be determined by passing X-rays through a sample. This method, known as ◊X-ray diffraction, opened up an entirely new way of "seeing" atoms. It has been found that many substances have a unit cell that exhibits all the symmetry of the whole crystal; in table salt (sodium chloride, NaCl), for instance, the unit cell is an exact cube.

CSCE abbreviation for ◊*Conference on Security and Cooperation in Europe*.

CT abbreviation for the state of ◊*Connecticut*.

Ctesiphon ruined royal city of the Parthians, and later capital of the Sassanian Empire, 12 mi/19 km SE of Baghdad, Iraq. A palace of the 4th century still has its throne room standing, spanned by a single vault of unreinforced brickwork some 80 ft/24 m across.

cu abbreviation for *cubic* (measure).

Cuba island country in the Caribbean Sea, the largest of the West Indies, off the S coast of Florida and to the E of Mexico.

cube in geometry, a regular solid figure whose faces are all squares. It has 6 equal-area faces and 12 equal-length edges. If the length of one edge is l, the volume V of the cube is given by $V = l^3$ and its surface area A by $A = 6l^2$.

cubic equation any equation in which the largest power of x is x^3. For example, $x^3 + 3x^2y + 4y^2 = 0$ is a cubic equation.

cubic measure measure of volume, indicated either by the word "cubic" followed by a linear measure, as in "cubic foot," or the word "cubed" after a linear measure, as in "meter cubed."

Cubism revolutionary movement in early 20th-century painting, pioneering abstract art. Its founders, Georges Braque and Pablo Picasso, were admirers of Paul Cézanne and were inspired by his attempt to create

Cuba
Republic of
(*República de Cuba*)

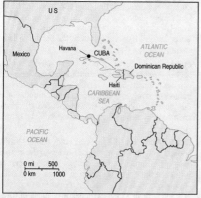

0 mi 500
0 km 1000

area 42,820 sq mi/110,860 sq km
capital Havana
cities Santiago de Cuba, Camagüey
physical comprises Cuba, the largest and westernmost of
the West Indies, and smaller islands including Isle of Youth;
low hills; Sierra Maestra mountains in SE
features 2,100 mi/3,380 km of coastline, with deep bays,
sandy beaches, coral islands and reefs; more than 1,600
islands surround the Cuban mainland
head of state and government Fidel Castro Ruz from
1959
political system communist republic
political party Communist Party of Cuba (PCC), Marxist-
Leninist
exports sugar, tobacco, coffee, nickel, fish
currency Cuban peso
population (1992) 10,848,000; 37% are white of Spanish
descent, 51% mulatto, and 11% are of African origin; growth
rate 0.6% p.a.
life expectancy men 72, women 75
language Spanish
religions Roman Catholic 85%; also Episcopalians and
Methodists
literacy men 96%, women 95% (1988)
disposable national income $15.8 bn (1983); $1,590 per
head

chronology
1492 Christopher Columbus landed in Cuba and claimed it
for Spain.
1898 US defeated Spain in Spanish-American War; Spain
gave up all claims to Cuba.
1901 Cuba achieved independence; Tomás Estrada Palma
became first president of the Republic of Cuba.
1933 Fulgencia Batista seized power.
1944 Batista retired.
1952 Batista seized power again to begin an oppressive
regime.
1953 Fidel Castro led an unsuccessful coup against Batista.
1956 Second unsuccessful coup by Castro.
1959 Batista overthrown by Castro. Constitution of 1940
replaced by a "Fundamental Law," making Castro prime minister, his brother Raúl Castro his deputy, and "Che" Guevara
his number three.
1960 All US businesses in Cuba appropriated without compensation; US broke off diplomatic relations.
1961 US sponsored an unsuccessful invasion at the Bay of
Pigs. Castro announced that Cuba had become a communist
state, with a Marxist-Leninist program of economic development.
1962 Cuba expelled from the Organization of American
States. Soviet nuclear missiles installed but subsequently
removed from Cuba at US insistence.
1965 Cuba's sole political party renamed Cuban Communist
Party (PCC). With Soviet help, Cuba began to make considerable economic and social progress.
1972 Cuba became a full member of the Moscow-based
Council for Mutual Economic Assistance.
1976 New socialist constitution approved; Castro elected
president.
1976-81 Castro became involved in extensive international
commitments, sending troops as Soviet surrogates, particularly to Africa.
1984 Castro tried to improve US-Cuban relations by discussing exchange of US prisoners in Cuba for Cuban "undesirables" in the US.
1988 Peace accord with South Africa signed, agreeing to
withdrawal of Cuban troops from Angola.
1989 Reduction in Cuba's overseas military activities.
1991 Soviet troops withdrawn.
1992 Castro affirmed continuing support of communism.
1993 First direct parliamentary vote held. Communist seats
were uncontested and all candidates won their seats. Mysterious epidemic swept the country, possibly linked to malnutrition.

a structure on the surface of the canvas. About 1907–10
in France the Cubists began to "abstract" images from
nature, gradually releasing themselves from the imitation of reality. Cubism announced that a work of art
exists in its own right rather than as a representation of
the real world, and it attracted such artists as Juan Gris,
Fernand Léger, and Robert Delaunay.

cubit earliest known unit of length, which originated
between 2800 and 2300 BC. It is approximately 20.6 in/
50.5 cm long, which is about the length of the human
forearm measured from the tip of the middle finger to
the elbow.

cuckoo species of bird, any of about 200 members of
the family Cuculidae, especially the Eurasian cuckoo
Cuculus canorus, whose name derives from its characteristic call. Somewhat hawklike, it is about 1.1 ft/33
cm long, bluish-gray and barred beneath (females
sometimes reddish), and has a long, typically rounded
tail. Cuckoos feed on insects, including hairy caterpillars that are distasteful to most birds. It is a "brood
parasite," laying its eggs singly, at intervals of about
48 hours, in the nests of small insectivorous birds. As

soon as the young cuckoo hatches, it ejects all other
young birds or eggs from the nest and is tended by its
"foster parents" until fledging. American species
hatch and rear their own young.

cucumber trailing annual plant *Cucumis sativus* of
the gourd family Cucurbitaceae, producing long,
green-skinned fruit with crisp, translucent, edible
flesh. Small cucumbers, called gherkins, usually the
fruit of *C. anguria*, are often pickled.

Cugnot Nicolas-Joseph 1728–1804. French engineer
who produced the first high-pressure steam engine.
While serving in the French army, he was asked to
design a steam-operated gun carriage. After several
years, he produced a three-wheeled, high-pressure carriage capable of carrying 400 gallons/1,800 liters of
water and four passengers at a speed of 3 mph/5 kph.
Although he worked further on the carriage, the political upheavals of the French revolutionary era
obstructed progress and his invention was ignored.

Cukor George 1899–1983. US film director. He moved
to the cinema from the theater and was praised for his

skilled handling of such stars as Greta ◊Garbo (in *Camille* 1937) and Katharine Hepburn (in *The Philadelphia Story* 1940). He won an Academy Award for the direction of *My Fair Lady* 1964.

His films were usually sophisticated dramas or light comedies.

cultural anthropology or *social anthropology* subdiscipline of anthropology that analyzes human culture and society, the nonbiological and behavioral aspects of humanity. Two principal branches are ethnography (the study at first hand of living cultures) and ethnology (the comparison of cultures using ethnographic evidence).

Cultural Revolution Chinese mass movement 1966–69 begun by Communist Party chair Mao Zedong, directed against the upper middle class—bureaucrats, artists, and academics—who were killed, imprisoned, humiliated, or "resettled." Intended to "purify" Chinese communism, it was also an attempt by Mao to renew his political and ideological pre-eminence inside China. Half a million people are estimated to have been killed.

culture in biology, the growing of living cells and tissues in laboratory conditions.

culture in sociology and anthropology, the way of life of a particular society or group of people, including patterns of thought, beliefs, behavior, customs, traditions, rituals, dress, and language, as well as art, music, and literature. Sociologists and anthropologists use culture as a key concept in describing and analyzing human societies.

Cuman member of a powerful alliance of Turkic-speaking peoples of the Middle Ages, which dominated the steppes in the 11th and 12th centuries and built an empire reaching from the river Volga to the Danube.

Cumberland city in NW Maryland, in the Allegheny Mountains, on the Potomac River, directly S of Johnstown, Pennsylvania; seat of Allegheny County; population (1990) 23,700. Its industries include the mining and shipping of coal, sheet metal, iron products, and tires. It was first an Indian village and then a trading post and fort before it was incorporated 1815.

cumin seedlike fruit of the herb *Cuminum cyminum* of the carrot family Umbelliferae, with a bitter flavor. It is used as a spice in cooking.

cummings e e. Literary signature of Edward Estlin Cummings 1894–1962. US poet and novelist. He made his reputation with collections of poetry such as *Tulips and Chimneys* 1923. At first the poems gained notoriety for their idiosyncratic punctuation and typography (using only lowercase letters, for example), but their lyric power has gradually been recognized.

cuneiform ancient writing system formed of combinations of wedge-shaped strokes, usually impressed on clay. It was probably invented by the Sumerians, and was in use in Mesopotamia as early as the middle of the 4th millennium BC.

Cupid in Roman mythology, the god of love, identified with the Greek ◊Eros.

cuprite Cu_2O ore (copper(I) oxide), found in crystalline form or in earthy masses. It is red to black in color, and is often called ruby copper.

cupronickel copper alloy (75% copper and 25% nickel), used in hardware products and for coinage.

US coins made with cupronickel include the dime, quarter, half-dollar, and dollar.

Curaçao island in the West Indies, one of the ◊Netherlands Antilles; area 171 sq mi/444 sq km; population (1988) 148,500. The principal industry, dating from 1918, is the refining of Venezuelan petroleum. Curaçao was colonized by Spain 1527, annexed by the Dutch West India Company 1634, and gave its name from 1924 to the group of islands renamed the Netherlands Antilles 1948. Its capital is the port of Willemstad.

curare black, resinous poison extracted from the bark and juices of various South American trees and plants. Originally used on arrowheads by Amazonian hunters to paralyze prey, it blocks nerve stimulation of the muscles. Alkaloid derivatives (called curarines) are used in medicine as muscle relaxants during surgery.

Curia Romana the judicial and administrative bodies through which the pope carries on the government of the Roman Catholic church. It includes certain tribunals; the chancellery, which issues papal bulls; various offices including that of the cardinal secretary of state; and the Congregations, or councils of cardinals, each with a particular department of work.

Curie Marie (born Sklodovska) 1867–1934. Polish scientist. In 1898 she reported the possible existence of a new, powerfully radioactive element in pitchblende ores. Her husband, Pierre (1859–1906) abandoned his own researches to assist her, and in the same year they announced the existence of polonium and radium. They isolated the pure elements 1902. Both scientists refused to take out a patent on their discovery and were jointly awarded the Davy Medal 1903 and the Nobel Prize for Physics 1903, with Antoine ◊Becquerel. Marie Curie wrote a *Treatise on Radioactivity* 1910, and was awarded the Nobel Prize for Chemistry 1911.

curium synthesized, radioactive, metallic element of the *actinide* series, symbol Cm, atomic number 96, atomic weight 247. It is produced by bombarding plutonium or americium with neutrons. Its longest-lived isotope has a half-life of 1.7×10^7 years.

Curium is used to generate heat and power in satellites or in remote places. Named in 1946 for Pierre and Marie Curie by Glenn Seaborg, it was first synthesized in 1944 by Seaborg at the University of California at Berkeley, by analogy with the corresponding ◊lanthanide, gadolinium (see ◊periodic table of the elements).

Curley James Michael 1874–1958. US Democratic politician. He was a member of the US House of Representatives 1912–14, several times mayor of Boston between 1914 and 1934, when he was elected governor. He lost a bid for the US Senate 1936 and did not hold political office again until elected to the House 1942. His fourth and last mayoral term began 1946, during which time he spent six months in federal prison on a mail-fraud conviction.

curling game played on ice with stones; sometimes described as "bowls on ice." One of the national games of Scotland, it has spread to many countries. It can also be played on artificial (cement or asphalt) ponds.

currant berry of a small seedless variety of cultivated grape *Vitis vinifera*. Currants are grown on a large scale in Greece and California and used dried in cooking and baking. Because of the similarity of the fruit, the name currant is also given to several species of shrubs in the genus *Ribes*, family Grossulariaceae.

current flow of a body of water or air, or of heat, moving in a definite direction. Ocean currents are fast-

flowing currents of seawater generated by the wind or by variations in water density between two areas. They are partly responsible for transferring heat from the equator to the poles and thereby evening out the global heat imbalance. There are three basic types of ocean current: *drift currents* are broad and slow-moving; *stream currents* are narrow and swift-moving; and *upwelling currents* bring cold, nutrient-rich water from the ocean bottom.

current account in economics, that part of the balance of payments concerned with current transactions, as opposed to capital movements. It includes trade (visibles) and service transactions, such as investment, insurance, shipping, and tourism (invisibles). The state of the current account is regarded as a barometer of overall economic health.

current, electric see ◊electric current.

Curtis Tony. Adopted name of Bernard Schwartz 1925– . US film actor who starred in the 1950s and 1960s in such films as *The Vikings* 1958 and *The Boston Strangler* 1968, as well as specializing in light comedies such as *Some Like It Hot* 1959, with Jack Lemmon and Marilyn Monroe.

Curtiss Glenn Hammond 1878–1930. US aeronautical inventor, pioneer aviator, and aircraft designer. In 1908 he made the first public flights in the US, including the 1-mile flight. He belonged to Alexander Graham Bell's Aerial Experiment Association 1907–09 and established the first flying school 1909. In 1910 Curtiss staged his sensational flight down the Hudson River from Albany to New York City.

Curtiz Michael. Adopted name of Mihaly Kertész 1888–1962. Hungarian-born film director who worked in Austria, Germany, and France before moving to the US in 1926, where he made several films with Errol Flynn. He directed *Mildred Pierce* 1945, which revitalized Joan Crawford's career, and *Casablanca* 1942 (Academy Award).

curve in geometry, the ◊locus of a point moving according to specified conditions. The circle is the locus of all points equidistant from a given point (the center). Other common geometrical curves are the ◊ellipse, ◊parabola, and ◊hyperbola, which are also produced when a cone is cut by a plane at different angles.

Curzon Line Polish-Soviet frontier proposed after the Russo-Polish war 1919–20. It was based on the eastward limit of areas with a predominantly Polish population and acquired its name 1920 after the British foreign secretary, Lord Curzon, suggested that the Poles, who had invaded the USSR, should retire to this line pending a peace conference. The frontier established 1945 in general follows the Curzon Line.

Cushing Harvey Williams 1869–1939. US neurologist who pioneered neurosurgery. He developed a range of techniques for the surgical treatment of brain tumors, and also studied the link between the ◊pituitary gland and conditions such as dwarfism.

Cushing's syndrome condition in which the body chemistry is upset by excessive production of ◊steroid hormones from the adrenal cortex.

cusp point where two branches of a curve meet and the tangents to each branch coincide.

Custer George A(rmstrong) 1839–1876. US Civil War general, the Union's youngest brigadier general as a result of a brilliant war record. He campaigned against the Sioux from 1874, and was killed with a detachment

Custer US Civil War general George Armstrong Custer, remembered for his last stand at the Battle of Little Big Horn, 1876.

of his troops by the forces of Sioux chief Sitting Bull in the Battle of Little Bighorn, Montana: also called *Custer's last stand*, June 25, 1876.

Some historians accuse Custer of a reckless desire to advance his career. He had been reduced in rank in the regular army at the end of the Civil War.

Cuthbert, St died 687. Christian saint. A shepherd in Northumbria, England, he entered the monastery of Melrose, Scotland, after receiving a vision. He traveled widely as a missionary and because of his alleged miracles was known as the "wonderworker of Britain."

cuticle the horny noncellular surface layer of many invertebrates such as insects; in botany, the waxy surface layer on those parts of plants that are exposed to the air, continuous except for ◊stomata and lenticels. All types are secreted by the cells of the ◊epidermis. A cuticle reduces water loss and, in arthropods, acts as an ◊exoskeleton.

cuttlefish any of a family, Sepiidae, of squidlike cephalopods with an internal calcareous shell (cuttlebone). The common cuttle *Sepia officinalis* of the Atlantic and Mediterranean is up to 1 ft/30 cm long. It swims actively by means of the fins into which the sides of its oval, flattened body are expanded, and jerks itself backward by shooting a jet of water from its "siphon."

Cuyp Aelbert 1620–1691. Dutch painter of countryside scenes, seascapes, and portraits. His idyllically peaceful landscapes are bathed in golden light; for example, *A Herdsman with Cows by a River* (about 1650, National Gallery, London). His father, *Jacob Gerritsz Cuyp* (1594–1652), was also a landscape and portrait painter.

Cuzco city in S Peru, capital of Cuzco department, in the Andes Mountains, over 11,000 ft/3,350 m above sea level and 350 mi/560 km SE of Lima; population (1988) 255,000. It was founded in the 11th century as the ancient capital of the ◊Inca empire and was captured by the Spanish conqueror Francisco Pizarro 1533.

CVA abbreviation for *cerebrovascular accident*; see ◊stroke.

cwt symbol for ◊*hundredweight*, a unit of weight equal to 100 lb (45.36 kg) in the US and 112 lb (50.8 kg) in the UK and Canada.

cyanide ion derived from hydrogen cyanide (HCN), and any salt containing this ion (produced when

hydrogen cyanide is neutralized by alkalis), such as potassioum cyanide (KCN). The principal cyanides are potassium cyanide, sodium cyanide, calcium cyanide, mercury cyanide, gold cyanide, and copper cyanide. Certain cyanides are poisons.

cyanocobalamin chemical name for ◊vitamin B_{12}, which is normally produced by microorganisms in the gut. The richest natural source is raw liver. The deficiency disease, pernicious anemia, is the poor development of red blood cells with possible degeneration of the spinal chord. Sufferers develop extensive bruising and recover slowly from even minor injuries.

cybernetics (Greek *kubernan* "to steer") science concerned with how systems organize, regulate, and reproduce themselves, and also how they evolve and learn. In the laboratory, inanimate objects are created that behave like living systems. Applications range from the creation of electronic artificial limbs to the running of the fully automated factory where decision-making machines operate up to managerial level.

cyclamen any plant of the genus *Cyclamen* of perennial plants of the primrose family Primulaceae, with heart-shaped leaves and petals that are twisted at the base and bent back. The flowers are usually white or pink, and several species are cultivated.

cycle in physics, a sequence of changes that moves a system away from, and then back to, its original state. An example is a vibration that moves a particle first in one direction and then in the opposite direction, with the particle returning to its original position at the end of the vibration.

cycling riding a ◊bicycle for sport, pleasure, or transport. Cycle racing can take place on oval artificial tracks, on the road, or across country (cyclo-cross).

cycloid in geometry, a curve resembling a series of arches traced out by a point on the circumference of a circle that rolls along a straight line. Its applications include the study of the motion of wheeled vehicles along roads and tracks.

cyclone alternate name for a ◊depression, an area of low atmospheric pressure. A severe cyclone that forms in the tropics is called a tropical cyclone or ◊hurricane.

Cyclops in Greek mythology, one of a race of Sicilian giants, who had one eye in the middle of the forehead and lived as shepherds. ◊Odysseus blinded the Cyclops Polyphemus in Homer's *Odyssey*.

Cygnus large prominent constellation of the northern hemisphere, named after its shape (Latin "swan"). Its brightest star is first-magnitude ◊Deneb.

cylinder in geometry, a tubular solid figure with a circular base. In everyday use, the term applies to a *right cylinder*, the curved surface of which is at right angles to the base.

cymbal ancient musical instrument of percussion, consisting of a shallow circular brass dish held at the center; either used in pairs clashed together or singly, struck with a beater. Smaller finger cymbals or *crotala*, used by Debussy and Stockhausen, are more solid and pure in tone. Turkish or "buzz" cymbals have loose rivets to extend the sound.

Cymbeline or *Cunobelin* 1st century AD. King of the Catuvellauni AD 5–40, who fought unsuccessfully against the Roman invasion of Britain. His capital was at Colchester.

Cynic school of Greek philosophy (Cynicism), founded in Athens about 400 BC by Antisthenes, a disciple of

Cyprus Greek
Republic of Cyprus
(*Kypriakí Dimokratía*) in the south, and
Turkish Republic of Northern
Cyprus (*Kibris Cumhuriyeti*) in the north

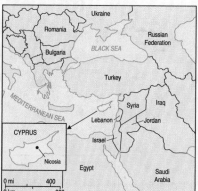

area 3,571 sq mi/9,251 sq km, 37% in Turkish hands
capital Nicosia (divided between Greeks and Turks)
cities ports Limassol, Larnaca, Paphos (Greek); Morphou,
and ports Kyrenia and Famagusta (Turkish)
physical central plain between two E–W mountain ranges
features archeological and historic sites; Mount Olympus
6,406 ft/1,953 m (highest peak); beaches
heads of state and government Glafkos Clerides
(Greek) from 1993, Rauf Denktaş (Turkish) from 1974
political system democratic divided republic
political parties Democratic Front (DIKO), center-left; Progressive Party of the Working People (AKEL), socialist;
Democratic Rally (DISY), centrist; Socialist Party (EDEK),
socialist; *Turkish zone*: National Unity Party (NUP), Communal Liberation Party (CLP), Republican Turkish Party (RTP),
New British Party (NBP)
exports citrus, grapes, raisins, Cyprus sherry, potatoes,
clothing, footwear
currency Cyprus pound and Turkish lira

population (1992) 580,000 (Greek Cypriot 78%, Turkish
Cypriot 18%); growth rate 1.2% p.a.
life expectancy men 72, women 76
languages Greek and Turkish (official), English
religions Greek Orthodox 78%, Sunni Muslim 18%
literacy 99% (1984)
GDP $3.7 bn (1987); $5,497 per head

chronology
1878 Came under British administration.
1955 Guerrilla campaign began against the British for
enosis (union with Greece), led by Archbishop Makarios and
General Grivas.
1956 Makarios and enosis leaders deported.
1959 Compromise agreed and Makarios returned to be
elected president of an independent Greek-Turkish Cyprus.
1960 Independence achieved from Britain, with Britain
retaining its military bases.
1963 Turks set up their own government in northern Cyprus.
Fighting broke out between the two communities.
1964 United Nations peacekeeping force installed.
1971 Grivas returned to start a guerrilla war against the
Makarios government.
1974 Grivas died. Military coup deposed Makarios, who
fled to Britain. Nicos Sampson appointed president. Turkish
army sent to northern Cyprus to confirm Turkish Cypriots'
control; military regime in southern Cyprus collapsed;
Makarios returned. Northern Cyprus declared itself the Turkish Federated State of Cyprus (TFSC), with Rauf Denktaş as
president.
1977 Makarios died; succeeded by Spyros Kyprianou.
1983 An independent Turkish Republic of Northern Cyprus
proclaimed but recognized only by Turkey.
1984 UN peace proposals rejected.
1985 Summit meeting between Kyprianou and Denktaş
failed to reach agreement.
1988 Georgios Vassiliou elected president. Talks with
Denktaş began, under UN auspices.
1989 Peace talks abandoned.
1992 UN-sponsored peace talks collapsed.
1993 Democratic Rally leader Glafkos Clerides narrowly
won presidential election.

Socrates, who advocated a stern and simple morality
and a complete disregard of pleasure and comfort.

cypress any coniferous tree or shrub of the genera
Cupressus and *Chamaecyparis*, family Cupressaceae.
There are about 20 species, originating from temperate regions of the northern hemisphere. They have
minute, scalelike leaves and small cones made up of
woody, wedge-shaped scales and containing an aromatic resin.

Cyprian, St *c.* 210–258. Christian martyr, one of the
earliest Christian writers, and bishop of Carthage
about 249. He wrote a treatise on the unity of the
church. Feast day Sept 16.

Cyprus island in the Mediterranean Sea, off the S
coast of Turkey and W coast of Syria. *See map p. 254*

Cyrano de Bergerac Savinien 1619–1655. French
writer. He joined a corps of guards at 19 and performed heroic feats which brought him fame. He is the
hero of a classic play by Edmond ◊Rostand, in which
his excessively long nose is used as a counterpoint to
his chivalrous character.

Cyrenaica area of E Libya, colonized by the Greeks
in the 7th century BC; later held by the Egyptians,
Romans, Arabs, Turks, and Italians. Present cities in
the region are Benghazi, Derna, and Tobruk.

Cyril and Methodius, Sts two brothers, both Christian saints: Cyril 826–869 and Methodius 815–885.
Born in Thessalonica, they were sent as missionaries to
what is today Moravia. They invented a Slavonic alphabet, and translated the Bible and the liturgy from Greek
to Slavonic. The language (known as **Old Church
Slavonic**) remained in use in churches and for literature among Bulgars, Serbs, and Russians up to the 17th
century. The *cyrillic alphabet* is named after Cyril
and may have been invented by him. Feast day Feb 14.

Cyrus the Great died 529 BC. Founder of the Persian
Empire. As king of Persia, he was originally subject to
the ◊Medes, whose empire he overthrew 550 BC. He
captured ◊Croesus 546 BC, and conquered ◊Lydia,
adding Babylonia (including Syria and Palestine) to
his empire 539 BC, allowing exiled Jews to return to Jer-
sualem. He died fighting in Afghanistan.

cystic fibrosis hereditary disease involving defects
of various tissues, including the sweat glands, the
mucous glands of the bronchi (air passages), and the
pancreas. The sufferer experiences repeated chest
infections and digestive disorders and generally fails
to thrive. In 1989 the gene for cystic fibrosis was identified by teams of researchers in Michigan and
Toronto, Canada. This discovery promises more reliable diagnosis of the disease in babies before birth.

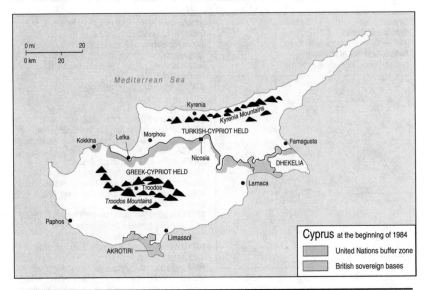

Cyprus at the beginning of 1984

| | United Nations buffer zone |
| | British sovereign bases |

Czech Republic
(*Česká Republika*)

area 30,461 sq mi/78,864 sq km
capital Prague
cities Brno, Ostrava, Olomouc, Liberec, Plzeň, Ustí nad Labem, Hradec Králové
physical mountainous; rivers: Morava, Labe (Elbe), Vltava (Moldau)
environment considered the most polluted country in E Europe. Pollution is worst in N Bohemia, which produces coal and coal-generated electricity. Up to 20 times the permissible level of sulphur dioxide is released over Prague, where 75% of the drinking water fails to meet the country's health standards
features summer and winter resort areas in Western Carpathian, Bohemian, and Sudetic mountain ranges
head of state Václav Havel from 1993
head of government Václav Klaus from 1993
political system emergent democracy
political parties Civic Democratic Party (CDP), right of center; Civic Movement (CM), left of center; Communist

Party (CPCZ), left-wing; Czechoslovak People's Party, centrist nationalist
exports machinery, vehicles, coal, iron and steel, chemicals, glass, ceramics, clothing
currency koruna
population (1991) 10,298,700 (with German and other minorities); growth rate 0.4% p.a.
life expectancy men 68, women 75
languages Czech (official)
religions Roman Catholic (75%), Protestant, Hussite, Orthodox
literacy 100%

chronology
1526–1918 Under Habsburg domination.
1918 Independence achieved from Austro-Hungarian Empire; Czechs joined Slovaks in forming Czechoslovakia as independent nation.
1948 Communists assumed power in Czechoslovakia.
1969 Czech Socialist Republic created under new federal-constitution.
1989 Nov: pro-democracy demonstrations in Prague; new political parties formed, including Czech-based Civic Forum under Václav Havel; Communist Party stripped of powers; political parties legalized. Dec: new "grand coalition" government formed, including former dissidents; Havel appointed state president. Amnesty granted to 22,000 prisoners; calls for USSR to withdraw troops.
1990 July: Havel reelected president in multiparty elections.
1991 Civic Forum split into CDP and CM; evidence of increasing Czech and Slovak separatism.
1992 June: Václav Klaus, leader of the Czech-based CDP, became prime minister; Havel resigned following Slovak gains in assembly elections. Aug: creation of separate Czech and Slovak states agreed.
1993 Jan: Czech Republic became sovereign state, with Klaus as prime minister. Havel elected president of the new republic. Admitted into United Nations, Conference on Security and Cooperation in Europe, and Council of Europe.

cystitis inflammation of the bladder, usually caused by bacterial infection, and resulting in frequent and painful urination. Treatment is by antibiotics and copious fluids with vitamin C.

cytology the study of ◊cells and their functions. Major advances have been made possible in this field by the development of ◊electron microscopes.

cytoplasm the part of the cell outside the ◊nucleus. Strictly speaking, this includes all the ◊organelles (mitochondria, chloroplasts, and so on), but often cytoplasm refers to *cytosol*, the jellylike matter in which the organelles are embedded.

cytotoxic drug any drug used to kill the cells of a malignant tumor, or as an ◊immunosuppressive following organ transplant; it may also damage healthy cells. Side effects include nausea, vomiting, hair loss, and bone-marrow damage.

czar alternate spelling of ◊*tsar*, an emperor of Russia.

Czechoslovakia former country in E central Europe, which came into existence as an independent republic 1918 after the breakup of the ◊Austro-Hungarian empire at the end of World War I.

Czech Republic country in E central Europe, bounded NE by Poland, E by the Slovak Republic, SW by Austria, and W by Germany.

Makhachkala; area 19,421 sq mi/50,300 sq km; population (1982) 1,700,000. It is mountainous, with deep valleys, and its numerous ethnic groups speak a variety of distinct languages. Annexed 1723 from Iran, which strongly resisted Russian conquest, it became an autonomous republic 1921.

Daguerre Louis Jacques Mande 1789–1851. French pioneer of photography. Together with Joseph Niépce, he is credited with the invention of photography (though others were reaching the same point simultaneously). In 1838 he invented the daguerreotype, a single image process superseded ten years later by ◊Talbot's negative/positive process.

daguerreotype in photography, a single-image process using mercury vapor and an iodine-sensitized silvered plate; it was invented by Louis Daguerre 1838.

Dahl Roald 1916–1990. British writer, celebrated for short stories with a twist, for example, *Tales of the Unexpected* 1979, and for children's books, including *Charlie and the Chocolate Factory* 1964. He also wrote the screenplay for the James Bond film *You Only Live Twice* 1967.

dahlia any perennial plant of the genus *Dahlia*, family Compositae, comprising 20 species and many cultivated forms. Dahlias are stocky plants with showy flowers that come in a wide range of colors. They are native to Mexico and Central America.

Dahomey former name (until 1975) of the People's Republic of ◊Benin.

Daimler Gottlieb 1834–1900. German engineer who pioneered the modern automobile. In 1886 he produced his first motor vehicle and a motor-bicycle. He later joined forces with Karl ◊Benz and was one of the pioneers of the high-speed four-stroke gasoline engine.

daisy any of numerous species of perennial plants in the family Compositae, especially the field daisy of Europe and North America *Chrysanthemum leucanthemum* and the English common daisy *Bellis perennis*, with a single white or pink flower rising from a rosette of leaves.

Dakar capital and chief port (with artificial harbor) of Senegal; population (1984) 1,000,000. It is an industrial center, and there is a university, established 1957.

Dakhla port in Western Sahara; population (1982) 17,800. First established as a Spanish trading port 1476, it was known as *Villa Cisneros*.

Daladier Edouard 1884–1970. French Radical politician. As prime minister April 1938–March 1940, he signed the ◊Munich Agreement 1938 (by which the Sudeten districts of Czechoslovakia were ceded to Germany) and declared war on Germany 1939. He resigned 1940 because of his unpopularity for failing to assist Finland against Russia. He was arrested on the fall of France 1940 and was a prisoner in Germany 1943–45. Following the end of World War II he was reelected to the Chamber of Deputies 1946–58.

Dalai Lama 14th incarnation 1935– . Spiritual and temporal head of the Tibetan state until 1959, when he went into exile in protest against Chinese annexation and oppression. His people have continued to demand his return.

Daley Richard Joseph 1902–1976. US politician and controversial mayor of Chicago 1955–76. He built a formidable political machine and ensured a Democratic presidential victory 1960 when J F Kennedy was elected. He hosted the turbulent national Democratic convention 1968.

D abbreviation for *500* in the Roman numeral system.

DA abbreviation for *district attorney*.

Dacca alternate name for ◊Dhaka, the capital of Bangladesh.

Dachau site of a Nazi ◊concentration camp during World War II, in Bavaria, Germany.

dachshund small dog of German origin, bred originally for digging out badgers. It has a long body and short legs. Several varieties are bred: standard size (up to 22 lb/10 kg), miniature (11 lb/5 kg or less), long-haired, smooth-haired, and wire-haired.

Dacia ancient region forming much of modern Romania. The various Dacian tribes were united around 60 BC, and for many years posed a threat to the Roman Empire; they were finally conquered by the Roman emperor Trajan AD 101–06, and the region became a province of the same name. It was abandoned to the invading Goths about 275.

Dada or *Dadaism* artistic and literary movement founded 1915 in Zürich, Switzerland, by the Romanian poet Tristan Tzara (1896–1963) and others in a spirit of rebellion and disillusionment during World War I. Other Dadaist groups were soon formed by the artists Marcel ◊Duchamp and ◊Man Ray in New York and Francis Picabia in Barcelona. Dada had a considerable impact on early 20th-century art, questioning established artistic rules and values.

Dadra and Nagar Haveli since 1961, a Union Territory of W India; capital Silvassa; area 189 sq mi/490 sq km; population (1991) 138,500. It was formerly part of Portuguese Daman. It produces rice, wheat, millet, and timber.

Daedalus in Greek mythology, an Athenian artisan supposed to have constructed for King Minos of Crete the labyrinth in which the ◊Minotaur was imprisoned. When Minos became displeased with him, Daedalus fled from Crete with his son ◊Icarus using wings made by them from feathers fastened with wax.

daffodil any of several Old World species of the genus *Narcissus*, family Amaryllidaceae, distinguished by their trumpet-shaped flowers. The common daffodil of N Europe *N. pseudonarcissus* has large yellow flowers and grows from a large bulb. There are numerous cultivated forms.

Dagestan autonomous republic of S Russia, situated E of the ◊Caucasus, bordering the Caspian Sea; capital

Dali Salvador 1904–1989. Spanish painter. In 1928 he collaborated with Luis Buñuel on the film *Un chien andalou*. In 1929 he joined the Surrealists and became notorious for his flamboyant eccentricity. Influenced by the psychoanalytic theories of Freud, he developed a repertoire of dramatic images, such as the distorted human body, limp watches, and burning giraffes in such pictures as *The Persistence of Memory* 1931 (Museum of Modern Art, New York). They are painted with a meticulous, polished clarity. He also used religious themes and painted many portraits of his wife Gala.

Dallas commercial city in Texas, population (1990) 1,006,900, metropolitan area (with Fort Worth) 3,885,400. Industries include banking, insurance, oil, aviation, aerospace, and electronics. Dallas–Fort Worth Regional Airport (opened 1973) is one of the world's largest. John F ◊Kennedy was assassinated here 1963.

Dalmatia region divided among Croatia, Montenegro in Yugoslavia, and Bosnia-Herzegovina. The capital is Split. It lies along the E shore of the Adriatic Sea and includes a number of islands. The interior is mountainous. Important products are wine, olives, and fish. Notable towns in addition to the capital are Zadar, Sibenik, and Dubrovnik.

history Dalmatia became Austrian 1815 and by the treaty of Rapallo 1920 became part of the kingdom of the Serbs, Croats, and Slovenes (Yugoslavia from 1931), except for the town of Zadar (Zara) and the island of Lastovo (Lagosta), which, with neighboring islets, were given to Italy until transferred to Yugoslavia 1947.

Dalmatian breed of dog, about 2 ft/60 cm tall at the shoulder, white with spots that are black or brown. Dalmatians are born white; the spots appear later. They were formerly used as coach dogs, walking beside horse-drawn carriages to fend off highwaymen.

Dalton John 1766–1844. English chemist who proposed the theory of atoms, which he considered to be the smallest parts of matter. He produced the first list of atomic weights in *Absorption of Gases* 1805 and put forward the law of partial pressures of gases (Dalton's law).

He was one of the first scientists to note and record color blindness (he was himself color blind).

dam structure built to hold back water in order to prevent flooding, to provide water for irrigation and storage, and to provide hydroelectric power. The biggest dams are of the earth- and rock-fill type, also called *embankment dams*. Early dams had a core made from puddled clay (clay which has been mixed with water to make it impermeable). Such dams are generally built on broad valley sites. Deep, narrow gorges dictate a *concrete dam*, where the strength of reinforced concrete can withstand the water pressures involved.

Dam (Henrik) Carl (Peter) 1895–1976. Danish biochemist who discovered vitamin K. For his success in this field he shared the 1943 Nobel Prize for Medicine with US biochemist Edward ◊Doisy (1893–1986).

Damascus (Arabic *Dimashq*) capital of Syria, on the river Barada, SE of Beirut; population (1981) 1,251,000. It produces silk, wood products, and brass and copper ware. Said to be the oldest continuously inhabited city in the world, Damascus was an ancient city even in Old Testament times. Most notable of the old buildings is the Great Mosque, completed as a Christian church in the 5th century.

Damocles lived 4th century BC. In Classical legend, a courtier of the elder Dionysius, ruler of Syracuse, Sicily. When Damocles made too much of his sovereign's good fortune, Dionysius invited him to a feast where he symbolically hung a sword over Damocles' head to demonstrate the precariousness of the happiness of kings.

dance Korean farmers in traditional costume dancing in celebration of the harvest thanksgiving festival, Chusok.

damper any device that deadens or lessens vibrations or oscillations; for example, one used to check vibrations in the strings of a piano. The term is also used for the movable plate in the flue of a stove or furnace for controlling the draft.

damson cultivated variety of plum tree *Prunus domestica* var. *institia*, distinguished by its small, oval, edible fruits, which are dark purple or blue to black in color.

Dana Richard Henry 1815–1882. US author and lawyer who went to sea and worked for his passage around Cape Horn to California and back, then wrote an account of the journey *Two Years before the Mast* 1840. He also published *The Seaman's Friend* 1841, a guide to maritime law.

Danbury city in SW Connecticut, NW of Bridgeport; population (1980) 60,470. Long a center for the manufacturing of hats, Danbury's newer industries include electronics, publishing, chemicals, and furniture.

dance rhythmic movement of the body, usually performed in time to music. Its primary purpose may be religious, magical, martial, social, or artistic—the last two being characteristic of nontraditional societies. The pre-Christian era had a strong tradition of ritual dance, and ancient Greek dance still exerts an influence on dance movement today. Although Western folk and social dances have a long history, the Eastern dance tradition long predates the Western. The European Classical tradition dates from the 15th century in Italy, the first printed dance text from 16th-century France, and the first dance school in Paris from the 17th century. The 18th century saw the development of European Classical ballet as we know it today, and the 19th century saw the rise of Romantic ballet. In the 20th century Modern dance firmly established itself as a separate dance idiom, not based on Classical ballet, and many divergent styles and ideas have grown from a willingness to explore a variety of techniques and amalgamate different traditions. *See illustration p. 257*

dandelion plant *Taraxacum officinale* belonging to the Compositae family. The stalk rises from a rosette of leaves that are deeply indented like a lion's teeth, hence the name (from French *dent de lion*). The flower heads are bright yellow. The fruit is surmounted by the hairs of the calyx which constitute the familiar dandelion "puff."

Dandelions, introduced from Europe, now grow throughout North America.

Dandie Dinmont breed of ◊terrier that originated in the Scottish border country. It is about 10 in/25 cm tall, short-legged and long-bodied, with drooping ears and a long tail. Its hair, about 2 in/5 cm long, can be grayish or yellowish. It is named after the character Dandie Dinmont in Walter Scott's novel *Guy Mannering* 1815.

Dane person of Danish culture from Denmark and N Germany. There are approximately 5 million speakers of Danish (including some in the US), a Germanic language belonging to the Indo-European family. The Danes are known for their seafaring culture, which dates back to the Viking age of expansion between the 8th and 10th centuries.

Daniel 6th century BC. Jewish folk hero and prophet at the court of Nebuchadnezzar; also the name of a book of the Old Testament, probably compiled in the 2nd century BC. It includes stories about Daniel and his companions Shadrach, Meshach, and Abednego, set during the Babylonian captivity of the Jews.

Danish language member of the North Germanic group of the Indo-European language family, spoken in Denmark and Greenland and related to Icelandic, Faroese, Norwegian, and Swedish. It has had a particularly strong influence on Norwegian. As one of the languages of the Vikings, who invaded and settled in parts of Britain during the 9th to 11th centuries, Old Danish had a strong influence on English.

Dante Alighieri 1265–1321. Italian poet. His masterpiece *La divina commedia/The Divine Comedy* 1307–21 is an epic account in three parts of his journey through Hell, Purgatory, and Paradise, during which he is guided part of the way by the poet Virgil; on a metaphorical level the journey is also one of Dante's own spiritual development. Other works include the philosophical prose treatise *Convivio/The Banquet* 1306–08, the first major work of its kind to be written in Italian rather than Latin; *Monarchia/On World Government* 1310–13, expounding his political theories; *De vulgari eloquentia/Concerning the Vulgar Tongue* 1304–06, an original Latin work on Italian, its dialects, and kindred languages; and *Canzoniere/ Lyrics*, containing his scattered lyrics.

Danton Georges Jacques 1759–1794. French revolutionary. Originally a lawyer, during the early years of the Revolution he was one of the most influential people in Paris. He organized the uprising Aug 10, 1792, that overthrew Louis XVI and the monarchy, roused the country to expel the Prussian invaders, and in April 1793 formed the revolutionary tribunal and the *Committee of Public Safety*, of which he was the leader until July of that year. Thereafter he lost power to the ◊Jacobins, and, when he attempted to recover it, was arrested and guillotined.

Danube (German *Donau*) second longest of European rivers, rising on the E slopes of the Black Forest, and flowing 1,776 mi/2,858 km across Europe to enter the Black Sea in Romania by a swampy delta.

Danville city in S Virginia, just above the North Carolina border, on the Dan River, SE of Roanoke; seat of Averett County; population (1990) 53,100. Danville is situated in a tobacco-growing area. Industries include tobacco processing and marketing and the manufacture of tools, textiles, and building materials.

The Confederate government moved from Richmond to Danville during the last days of the Civil War 1865.

Danelaw extent of Danish rule in England by 886

▨ area subject to Norsemen

Danzig German name for the Polish port of ◊Gdańsk.

Daphne in Greek mythology, a ◊nymph who was changed into a laurel tree to escape from ◊Apollo's amorous pursuit.

Dardanelles (ancient name *Hellespont*, Turkish name *Canakkale Boğazi*) Turkish strait connecting the Sea of Marmara with the Aegean Sea; its shores are formed by the ◊Gallipoli peninsula on the NW and the mainland of Anatolia on the SE. It is 47 mi/75 km long and 3–4 mi/5–6 km wide.

Dare Virginia 1587–?. First English child born in America. She was the granddaughter of John White, the governor of Roanoke colony (now in North Carolina). White returned to England soon after her birth, leaving Dare in Roanoke with the rest of her settler family. English communication with Roanoke was cut off for nearly four years during the war with Spain 1585–88. In 1591 the crew of an English ship found the colony deserted.

The enigmatic inscription "Croatan" carved in a tree led to speculation that the settlers, fearful of hostile Indians, had perhaps taken refuge with the friendly Croatan.

Dar es Salaam chief seaport in Tanzania, on the Indian Ocean, and capital of Tanzania until its replacement by ◊Dodoma 1974; population (1985) 1,394,000.

Darius I *the Great* c. 558–486 BC. King of Persia 521–48 BC. A member of a younger branch of the Achaemenid dynasty, he won the throne from the usurper Gaumata (died 522 BC) and reorganized the government. In 512 BC he marched against the Scythians, a people north of the Black Sea, and subjugated Thrace and Macedonia.

Darnley Henry Stewart or Stuart, Lord Darnley 1545–1567. British aristocrat, second husband of Mary Queen of Scots from 1565, and father of James I of England (James VI of Scotland). On the advice of her secretary, David Rizzio, Mary refused Darnley the crown matrimonial; in revenge, Darnley led a band of nobles who murdered Rizzio in Mary's presence. Darnley was assassinated 1567.

Darrow Clarence (Seward) 1857–1938. US lawyer, born in Ohio, a champion of liberal causes and defender of the underdog. He defended many labor-union leaders, including Eugene ◊Debs 1894. He was counsel for the defense in the Nathan Leopold and Richard Loeb murder trial in Chicago 1924, and in the Scopes monkey trial. Darrow matched wits in the latter trial with prosecution attorney William Jennings ◊Bryan. He was an opponent of capital punishment.

darts indoor game played on a circular board. Darts (like small arrow shafts) about 5 in/13 cm long are thrown at segmented targets and score points according to their landing place.

Darwin capital and port in Northern Territory, Australia, in NW Arnhem Land; population (1986) 69,000. It serves the uranium mining site at Rum Jungle to the south. Destroyed 1974 by a cyclone, the city was rebuilt on the same site.

Darwin Charles Robert 1809–1882. English scientist who developed the modern theory of ◊evolution and proposed, with Alfred Russel Wallace, the principle of ◊natural selection. After research in South America and the Galápagos Islands as naturalist on HMS *Beagle* 1831–36, Darwin published *On the Origin of Species by Means of Natural Selection or the Preservation of Favoured Races in the Struggle for Life* 1859. This explained the evolutionary process through the

Danube river

principles of natural and sexual selection. It aroused bitter controversy because it disagreed with the literal interpretation of the Book of Genesis in the Bible.

Darwinism, social in US history, an influential but contentious social theory, based on the work of Charles Darwin and Herbert Spencer, which claimed to offer a scientific justification for late-19th-century *laissez-faire* capitalism (the principle of unrestricted freedom in commerce).

Das Kapital Karl Marx's exposition of his theories on economic production, published in three volumes 1867–95. It focuses on the exploitation of the worker and appeals for a classless society where the production process and its rewards are shared equally.

data facts, figures, and symbols, especially as stored in computers. The term is often used to mean raw, unprocessed facts, as distinct from information, to which a meaning or interpretation has been applied.

Darwin Cartoon of Charles Darwin by Linley Sambourne, suggesting that he had been led astray by the serpent representing Satan.

CHARLES ROBERT DARWIN, LL.D., F.R.S.

IN HIS *DESCENT OF MAN* HE BROUGHT HIS OWN SPECIES DOWN AS LOW AS POSSIBLE—*I.E.*, TO: "A HAIRY QUADRUPED FURNISHED WITH A TAIL AND POINTED EARS, AND PROBABLY *ARBOREAL* IN ITS HABITS"—WHICH IS A REASON FOR THE VERY GENERAL INTEREST IN A "FAMILY TREE." HE HAS LATELY BEEN TURNING HIS ATTENTION TO THE "POLITIC WORM."

rock was formed, using the process of ◊radiometric dating.

dative in the grammar of certain inflected languages (see ◊language) such as Latin, the dative case is the form of a noun, pronoun, or adjective used for the indirect object of a verb. It is also used with some prepositions.

dauphin title of the eldest son of the kings of France, derived from the personal name of a count, whose lands, known as the *Dauphiné*, traditionally passed to the heir to the throne from 1349 to 1830.

Davenport city in SE Iowa, S of Dubuque, directly across from Rock Island, Illinois, on the Mississippi River; seat of Scott County; population (1990) 95,300. It forms the "Quad Cities" metropolitan area with the Illinois cities of Rock Island, Moline, and East Moline. Industries include aluminum, agriculture, and machinery parts.

David c. 1060–970 BC. Second king of Israel. According to the Old Testament he played the harp for King Saul to banish Saul's melancholy; he later slew the Philistine giant Goliath with a sling and stone. After Saul's death David was anointed king at Hebron, took Jerusalem, and made it his capital.

David sent Uriah (a soldier in his army) to his death in the front line of battle so that he might marry his widow, Bathsheba. David and Bathsheba's son Solomon became the third king.

David probably wrote a few of the psalms (of the Book of Psalms) and was celebrated as a secular poet. In both Jewish and Christian belief, the messiah would be a descendant of David; Christians hold this prophecy to have been fulfilled by Jesus Christ.

David Jacques Louis 1748–1825. French painter in the Neo-Classical style. He was an active supporter of and unofficial painter to the republic during the French Revolution, for which he was imprisoned 1794–95. In his *Death of Marat* 1793, he turned political murder into a Classical tragedy. Later he devoted himself to the empire in paintings such as the enormous, pompous *Coronation of Napoleon* 1805–07 (Louvre, Paris).

David I 1084–1153. King of Scotland from 1124. The youngest son of Malcolm III Canmore and St ◊Margaret, he was brought up in the English court of Henry I, and in 1113 married Matilda, widow of the 1st earl of Northampton. He invaded England 1138 in support of Queen Matilda, but was defeated at Northallerton in the Battle of the Standard, and again 1141.

David, St or *Dewi* 5th–6th century. Patron saint of Wales, Christian abbot and bishop. According to legend he was the son of a prince of Dyfed and uncle of King Arthur; he was responsible for the adoption of the leek as the national emblem of Wales, but his own emblem is a dove. Feast day March 1.

da Vinci see ◊Leonardo da Vinci, Italian Renaissance artist.

Davis Angela 1944– . US left-wing activist for black rights, prominent in the student movement of the 1960s. In 1970 she went into hiding after being accused of supplying guns used in the murder of a judge who had been seized as a hostage in an attempt to secure the release of three black convicts. She was captured, tried, and acquitted. At the University of California she studied under Herbert ◊Marcuse, and was assistant professor of philosophy at UCLA 1969–70. In 1980 she was the Communist vice-presidential candidate.

David The Death of Marat *(1793) by* Jacques-Louis David.

database in computing, a structured collection of data, which may be manipulated to select and sort desired items of information. For example, an accounting system might be built around a database containing details of customers and suppliers. In larger computers, the database makes data available to the various programs that need it, without the need for those programs to be aware of how the data are stored. The term is also sometimes used for simple record-keeping systems, such as mailing lists, in which there are facilities for searching, sorting, and producing records.

data processing (DP) use of computers for performing clerical tasks such as stock control, payroll, and dealing with orders. DP systems are typically batch systems, running on mainframe computers. DP is sometimes called EDP (electronic data processing).

date palm tree of the genus *Phoenix*. The female tree produces the fruit, dates, in bunches weighing 20–25 lb/9–11 kg. Dates are an important source of food in the Middle East, being rich in sugar; they are dried for export. The tree also supplies timber, and materials for baskets, rope, and animal feed.

dating science of determining the age of geological structures, rocks, and fossils, and placing them in the context of geological time. The techniques are of two types: relative dating and absolute dating. *Relative dating* can be carried out by identifying fossils of creatures that lived only at certain times (marker fossils), and by looking at the physical relationships of rocks to other rocks of a known age. *Absolute dating* is achieved by measuring how much of a rock's radioactive elements have changed since the

Davis Bette 1908–1989. US actress. She entered films in 1930, and established a reputation as a forceful dramatic actress with *Of Human Bondage* 1934. Later films included *Dangerous* 1935 and *Jezebel* 1938, both winning her Academy Awards; *All About Eve,* which won the 1950 Academy Award for best picture; and *Whatever Happened to Baby Jane?* 1962. She continued to make films throughout the 1980s such as *How Green Was My Valley* for television, and *The Whales of August* 1987, in which she co-starred with Lillian Gish.

Davis Jefferson 1808–1889. US politician, president of the short-lived Confederate States of America 1861–65. He was a leader of the Southern Democrats in the US Senate from 1857, and a defender of "humane" slavery; in 1860 he issued a declaration in favor of secession from the US. During the Civil War he assumed strong political leadership, but often disagreed with military policy. He was imprisoned for two years after the war, one of the few cases of judicial retribution against Confederate leaders.

Davis Miles (Dewey, Jr) 1926–1991. US jazz trumpeter, composer, and bandleader, one of the most influential and innovative figures in jazz. He pioneered bebop with Charlie Parker 1945, cool jazz in the 1950s, and jazz-rock fusion from the late 1960s. His albums include *Birth of the Cool* 1957 (recorded 1949 and 1950), *Sketches of Spain* 1959, *Bitches Brew* 1970, and *Tutu* 1985.

Davis Sammy, Jr 1925–1990. US entertainer. His starring role in the Broadway show *Mr Wonderful* 1956, his television work, and his roles in films with Frank Sinatra's "rat pack"—among them, *Ocean's Eleven* 1960 and *Robin and the Seven Hoods* 1964—made him a national celebrity. He also appeared in the film version of the opera *Porgy and Bess* 1959. He published two memoirs, *Yes I Can* 1965 and *Why Me?* 1989.

Davis Cup annual lawn tennis tournament for men's international teams, first held 1900 after Dwight Filley Davis (1879–1945) donated the trophy.

Davos town in an Alpine valley in Grisons canton, Switzerland 5,115 ft/1,559 m above sea level; population (1990) 10,400.

Davy Humphry 1778–1829. English chemist. He discovered, by electrolysis, the metallic elements sodium and potassium in 1807, and calcium, boron, magnesium, strontium, and barium in 1808. In addition, he established that chlorine is an element and proposed that hydrogen is present in all acids. He invented the "safety lamp" for use in mines where methane was present, enabling miners to work in previously unsafe conditions.

As a laboratory assistant in Bristol in 1799, he discovered the respiratory effects of laughing gas (nitrous oxide).

dawn raid in business, sudden and unexpected buying of a significant proportion of a company's shares, usually as a prelude to a takeover bid. The aim is to prevent the target company from having time to organize opposition to the takeover.

day time taken for the Earth to rotate once on its axis. The ***solar day*** is the time that the Earth takes to rotate once relative to the Sun. It is divided into 24 hours, and is the basis of our civil day. The ***sidereal day*** is the time that the Earth takes to rotate once relative to the stars. It is 3 minutes 56 seconds shorter than the solar day, because the Sun's position against the background of stars as seen from Earth changes as the Earth orbits it.

Davis US politician Jefferson Davis who became president of the American Confederacy 1861–65 during the Civil War.

Day Doris. Adopted name of Doris von Kappelhoff 1924– . US film actress and singing star of the 1950s and early 1960s, mostly in musicals and, later, coy sex comedies. Her films include *Tea for Two* 1950, *Calamity Jane* 1953, *Love Me or Leave Me* 1955, and Hitchcock's *The Man Who Knew Too Much* 1956. With *Pillow Talk* 1959, *Lover Come Back* 1962, and other 1960s light sex comedies, she played a self-confident but coy woman who manipulated some of the biggest male stars to capitulate.

Dayan Moshe 1915–1981. Israeli general and politician. As minister of defense 1967 and 1969–74, he was largely responsible for the victory over neighboring Arab states in the 1967 Six-Day War, but he was criticized for Israel's alleged unpreparedness in the 1973 October War and resigned along with Prime Minister Golda Meir. Foreign minister from 1977, Dayan resigned 1979 in protest over the refusal of the Begin government to negotiate with the Palestinians.

daylight saving time legal time for a given zone that is one hour later than the standard time based on universal coordinated time (see ◊time). It is used to provide additional daylight during the summer at the end of the usual working day.

Dayton city in Ohio; population (1990) 182,000. It produces precision machinery, household appliances, and electrical equipment. It has an aeronautical research center and a Roman Catholic university and was the home of aviators Wilbur and Orville Wright. The Aviation Hall of Fame is in the city, and Wright-Patterson Air Force Base, which has an aviation museum, is nearby. Dayton was settled in 1796.

Daytona Beach city on the Atlantic coast of Florida; population (1990) 62,000. Economic activities include printing, commercial fishing, and manufacture of electronic equipment and metal products. It is also a resort. The Daytona International Speedway for automobile racing is here.

dBASE family of microcomputer programs used for manipulating large quantities of data; also, a related ◊fourth-generation language. The first version, dBASE II, appeared in 1981; it has since become the basis for a recognized standard for database applications, known as Xbase.

DC in music, abbreviation for ***da capo*** (Italian "from the beginning"); in physics, abbreviation for ***direct current*** (electricity); abbreviation for the ***District of Columbia***.

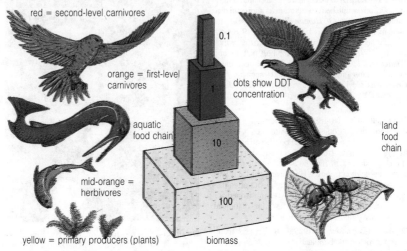

red = second-level carnivores

0.1

orange = first-level carnivores

dots show DDT concentration

aquatic food chain

land food chain

mid-orange = herbivores

1

10

100

yellow = primary producers (plants)

biomass

D-day June 6, 1944, the day of the Allied invasion of Normandy under the command of General Eisenhower, with the aim of liberating Western Europe from German occupation. The Anglo-American invasion fleet landed on the Normandy beaches on the stretch of coast between the Orne River and St Marcouf. Artificial harbors known as "Mulberries" were constructed and towed across the Channel so that equipment and armaments could be unloaded onto the beaches. After overcoming fierce resistance the allies broke through the German defenses; Paris was liberated on Aug 25, and Brussels on Sept 2.

DDT abbreviation for ***dichloro-diphenyl-trichloroethane*** ($CIC_6H_5)_2$ $CHCHCl_2$), an insecticide discovered 1939 by Swiss chemist Paul Müller. It is useful in the control of insects that spread malaria, but resistant strains develop. DDT is highly toxic and persists in the environment and in living tissue. Its use is now banned in most countries, but it continues to be used on food plants in Latin America.

DE abbreviation for the state of ◊**Delaware**.

deacon in the Roman Catholic and Anglican churches, an ordained minister who ranks immediately below a priest. In the Protestant churches, a deacon is in training to become a minister or is a lay assistant.

Dead Sea large lake, partly in Israel and partly in Jordan, lying 1,293 ft/394 m below sea level; area 394 sq mi/1,020 sq km. The chief river entering it is the Jordan; it has no outlet and the water is very salty.

Dead Sea Scrolls collection of ancient scrolls (rolls of writing) and fragments of scrolls found 1947–56 in caves on the W side of the Jordan, 7 mi/12 km S of Jericho and 2 km/1 mi from the N end of the Dead Sea, at ◊Qumran. They include copies of Old Testament books a thousand years older than those previously known to be extant. The documents date mainly from about 150 BC–AD 68, when the monastic community that owned them, the Essenes, was destroyed by the Romans because of its support for a revolt against their rule.

dean in education, in universities and medical schools, the head of administration; in the colleges of Oxford and Cambridge, UK, the member of the teaching staff charged with the maintenance of discipline; in Roman Catholicism, senior cardinal bishop, head of the college of cardinals; in the Anglican Communion, head of the chapter of a cathedral or collegiate church (a rural dean presides over a division of an archdeaconry).

Dean Dizzy (Jay Hanna) 1911–1974. US baseball player. He joined the St Louis Cardinals 1930 and made his major-league pitching debut 1932. Winning 30 games and leading the Cardinals to a World Series win, he was voted the National League's most valuable player 1934. Following an injury in the 1937 All-Star Game, his pitching suffered. He was traded to the Chicago Cubs, for whom he pitched until his retirement 1941.

Dean was elected to the Baseball Hall of Fame 1953.

Dean James (Byron) 1931–1955. US actor. Killed in an automobile accident after the public showing of his first film, *East of Eden* 1955, he posthumously became a cult hero with *Rebel Without a Cause* 1955 and *Giant* 1956.

He has become a symbol of teenage rebellion against American middle-class values.

Deane Silas 1737–1789. American public leader and diplomat. He served in the Continental Congress 1774–76 and was dispatched to Paris to gain support from the French government during the American Revolution (1775–83), recruiting French soldier Marie Lafayette, among others, for the Continental army. Falsely accused of financial improprieties, Deane was discharged from his post; he was exonerated posthumously by Congress 1842.

Dearborn city in Michigan, on the Rouge River 10 mi/16 km SW of Detroit; population (1990) 89,300. Settled 1795, it was the birthplace and home of Henry ◊Ford, who built his first automobile factory here. Automobile manufacturing is still the main industry. Dearborn also makes aircraft parts, steel, and bricks.

death permanent ending of all the functions that keep an organism alive. Death used to be pronounced when a person's breathing and heartbeat stopped. The advent of mechanical aids has made this point sometimes difficult to determine, and in controversial cases a person is now pronounced dead when the brain ceases to control the vital functions even if breath and heartbeat are maintained.

death cap fungus *Amanita phalloides*, the most poisonous mushroom known. The fruiting body has a scaly white cap and a collarlike structure near the base of the stalk.

Death Valley depression 140 mi/225 km long and 4–16 mi/6–26 km wide, in SE California. At 280 ft/85 m below sea level, it is the lowest point in the W hemisphere. Bordering mountains rise to 10,000 ft/3,000 m. It is one of the world's hottest and driest places, with temperatures sometimes exceeding 125° F/51° C and an annual rainfall of less than 2 in/5.1 cm. Borax, iron ore, tungsten, gypsum, and salts are extracted.

Debrecen third largest city in Hungary, 120 mi/193 km E of Budapest, in the Great Plain (*Alföld*) region; population (1988) 217,000. It produces tobacco, agricultural machinery, and pharmaceuticals. Lajos Kossuth declared Hungary independent of the ◊Habsburgs here 1849. It is a commercial center and has a university founded 1912.

Debs Eugene V(ictor) 1855–1926. US labor leader and socialist who organized the Social Democratic Party 1897. He was the founder and first president of the American Railroad Union 1893, and was imprisoned for six months in 1894 for defying a federal injunction to end the Pullman strike in Chicago. He was socialist candidate for the presidency in every election from 1900 to 1920, except that of 1916.

His powerful oratory and his evocation of homespun American ideals were the source of his appeal rather than any doctrinaire adherence to socialist theory.

debt something that is owed by a person or organization, usually money, goods, or services, usually as a result of borrowing. Debt servicing is the payment of interest on a debt. The national debt of a country is the total money owed by the national government to private individuals, banks, and so on; international debt, the money owed by one country to another, began on a large scale with the investment in foreign countries by newly industrialized countries in the late 19th–early 20th centuries. International debt became a global problem as a result of the oil crisis of the 1970s.

debt-for-nature swap agreement under which a proportion of a country's debts are written off in exchange for a commitment by the debtor country to undertake projects for environmental protection. Debt-for-nature swaps were set up by environment groups in the 1980s in an attempt to reduce the debt problem of poor countries, while simultaneously promoting conservation.

Debussy (Achille-) Claude 1862–1918. French composer. He broke with the dominant tradition of German Romanticism and introduced new qualities of melody and harmony based on the whole-tone scale, evoking oriental music. His work includes *Prélude à l'après-midi d'un faune* 1894 and the opera *Pelléas et Mélisande* 1902.

decagon in geometry, a ten-sided ◊polygon.

Decameron, The collection of tales by the Italian writer Giovanni Boccaccio, brought together 1348–53. Ten young people, fleeing plague-stricken Florence, amuse their fellow travelers by each telling a story on the ten days they spend together. The work had a great influence on English literature, particularly on Chaucer's *Canterbury Tales*.

decathlon two-day athletic competition for men consisting of ten events: 100 meters long jump, shot put, high jump, 400 meters (day one); 110 meters hurdles, discus, pole vault, javelin, 1,500 meters (day two).

Points are awarded for performances, and the winner is the athlete with the greatest aggregate score. The decathlon is an Olympic event.

Decatur city in central Illinois, on Lake Decatur; population (1990) 83,900. It has engineering, food processing, and plastics industries. It was founded 1829 and named after the US naval hero, Stephen Decatur.

Decatur Stephen 1779–1820. US naval hero, who distinguished himself in the war with the Barbary pirates at Tripoli 1801–05 when he succeeded in boarding and burning the *Philadelphia*, a US frigate captured by the enemy. During the War of 1812, he commanded three vessels, captured the British frigate *Macedonian*, and was blockaded by the British. Then in Jan 1815, unaware that the war was over, he battled four British ships, taking one but surrendering to the three pursuers. In 1815 he was again sent to the Barbary Coast, where he forced the bey of Algiers to sign the treaty ending US tribute to Algeria.

decibel unit (symbol dB) of measure used originally to compare sound intensities and subsequently electrical or electronic power outputs; now also used to compare voltages. An increase of 10 dB is equivalent to a 10-fold increase in intensity or power, and a 20-fold increase in voltage. A whisper has an intensity of 20 dB; 140 dB (a jet aircraft taking off nearby) is the threshold of pain.

deciduous of trees and shrubs, that shed their leaves at the end of the growing season or during a dry season to reduce ◊transpiration, the loss of water by evaporation.

Examples of deciduous trees are oak and maple.

decimal fraction a ◊fraction in which the denominator is any higher power of 10. Thus $3/10$, $51/100$ and $23/1,000$ are decimal fractions and are normally expressed as 0.3, 0.51, 0.023. The use of decimals greatly simplifies addition and multiplication of fractions, though not all fractions can be expressed exactly as decimal fractions.

decimal number system or ***denary number system*** the most commonly used number system, to the base ten. Decimal numbers do not necessarily contain a decimal point; 563, 5.63, and −563 are all decimal numbers. Other systems are mainly used in computing and include the binary number system, octal number system, and hexadecimal number system.

Declaration of Independence historic US document stating the theory of government on which the US was founded, based on the right "to life, liberty, and the pursuit of happiness." The statement was issued by the ◊Continental Congress July 4, 1776, renouncing all allegiance to the British crown and ending the political connection with Britain.

The declaration enumerated the grievances the colonists harbored against the king, which included his use of Indians to attack colonists, taxation without representation, and denial of civil liberties.

decolonization gradual achievement of independence by former colonies of the European imperial powers which began after World War I. The process of decolonization accelerated after World War II and the movement affected every continent: India and Pakistan gained independence from Britain 1947; Algeria gained independence from France 1962.

decomposer in biology, any organism that breaks down dead matter. Decomposers play a vital role in the ◊ecosystem by freeing important chemical substances, such as nitrogen compounds, locked up in dead organisms or excrement. They feed on some of

Degas The Man and the Puppet *(c. 1880), Gulbenkian Museum, Lisbon.*

deed legal document that passes an interest in property or binds a person to perform or abstain from some action. Deeds are of two kinds: indenture and deed poll. *Indentures* bind two or more parties in mutual obligations. A *deed poll* is made by one party only, such as when a person changes his or her name.

Bargain sale deeds convey title to property by contract but do not guarantee title unless they include a specific covenant to that effect; quitclaim deeds convey a grantor's interest but do not guarantee title; warranty deeds convey interest and guarantee title to the subject property.

deer any of various ruminant, even-toed, hoofed mammals belonging to the family Cervidae. The male typically has a pair of antlers, shed and regrown each year. Most species of deer are forest-dwellers and are distributed throughout Eurasia and North America, but are absent from Australia and Africa S of the Sahara.

Native to North America are white-tailed deer *Odocoileus viginianus*, mule deer *O. hemionus*, wapiti or elk *Cervus canadensis*, moose *Alces alces*, and caribou or reindeer *Rangifer tarandus*. The last two also occur in Eurasia. Red deer *Cervus elaphus*, roe deer *Capreolus capreolus*, and fallow deer *Dama dama* are typical Eurasian species.

deerhound large, rough-coated dog, formerly used for hunting and killing deer. Slim and long-legged, it grows to 2.5 ft/75 cm or more, usually with a bluish gray coat.

defamation in law, an attack on a person's reputation by libel or slander.

defibrillation use of electrical stimulation to restore a chaotic heartbeat to a rhythmical pattern. In fibrillation, which may occur in most kinds of heart disease, the heart muscle contracts irregularly; the heart is no longer working as an efficient pump. Paddles are applied to the chest wall, and one or more electric shocks are delivered to normalize the beat.

deficit financing in economics, a planned excess of expenditure over income, dictated by government policy, creating a shortfall of public revenue which is met by borrowing. The decision to create a deficit is made to stimulate an economy by increasing consumer purchasing and at the same time to create more jobs.

deflation in economics, a reduction in the level of economic activity, usually caused by an increase in interest rates and reduction in the money supply, increased taxation, or a decline in government expenditure.

Defoe Daniel 1660–1731. English writer. His *Robinson Crusoe* 1719, though purporting to be a factual account of shipwreck and solitary survival, was influential in the development of the novel. The fictional *Moll Flanders* 1722 and the partly factual *A Journal of the Plague Year* 1724 are still read for their concrete realism. A prolific journalist and pamphleteer, he was imprisoned 1702–04 for the ironic *The Shortest Way with Dissenters* 1702.

de Forest Lee 1873–1961. US inventor who held more than 300 patents, including the triode tube called by him the audion in 1906, precursor to the radio tube and one of the most influential inventions of the century. It generated, detected, and amplified radio waves. He also developed a movie-sound system and contributed to the phonograph, telephone, television, radar, and diathermy.

deforestation destruction of forest for timber, fuel, charcoal burning, and clearing for agriculture and extractive industries, such as mining, without plant-

the released organic matter, but leave the rest to filter back into the soil or pass in gas form into the atmosphere. The principal decomposers are bacteria and fungi, but earthworms and many other invertebrates are often included in this group. The ◊nitrogen cycle relies on the actions of decomposers.

decomposition process whereby a chemical compound is reduced to its component substances. In biology, it is the destruction of dead organisms either by chemical reduction or by the action of decomposers.

decompression sickness illness brought about by a sudden and substantial change in atmospheric pressure. It is caused by a too rapid release of nitrogen that has been dissolved into the bloodstream under pressure; when the nitrogen bubbles it causes the ◊bends. The condition causes breathing difficulties, joint and muscle pain, and cramps, and is experienced mostly by deep-sea divers who surface too quickly.

decretum collection of papal decrees. The best known is that collected by Gratian (died 1159) about 1140, comprising some 4,000 items. The decretum was used as an authoritative source of canon law (the rules and regulations of the church).

dedicated computer computer built into another device for the purpose of controlling or supplying information to it. Its use has increased dramatically since the advent of the ◊microprocessor: washing machines, digital watches, automobiles, and video recorders all now have their own processors.

ing new trees to replace those lost (reafforestation) or working on a cycle that allows the natural forest to regenerate. Deforestation causes fertile soil to be blown away or washed into rivers, leading to ◊soil erosion, drought, flooding, and loss of wildlife.

Degas (Hilaire Germain) Edgar 1834–1917. French Impressionist painter and sculptor. He devoted himself to lively, informal studies, often using pastels, of ballet, horse racing, and young women working. From the 1890s he turned increasingly to sculpture, modeling figures in wax in a fluent, naturalistic style.

de Gaulle Charles André Joseph Marie 1890–1970. French general and first president of the Fifth Republic 1958–69. He organized the ◊Free French troops fighting the Nazis 1940–44, was head of the provisional French government 1944–46, and leader of his own Gaullist party. In 1958 the national assembly asked him to form a government during France's economic recovery and to solve the crisis in Algeria. He became president at the end of 1958, having changed the constitution to provide for a presidential system, and served until 1969.

Reelected president 1965, he violently quelled student demonstrations May 1968 when they were joined by workers. The Gaullist party, reorganized as Union des Democrats pour la Cinquième République, won an overwhelming majority in the elections of the same year. In 1969 he resigned after the defeat of the government in a referendum on constitutional reform. He retired to the village of Colombey-les-Deux-Eglises in NE France.

degree in mathematics, a unit (symbol °) of measurement of an angle or arc. A circle or complete rotation is divided into 360°. A degree may be subdivided into 60 minutes (symbol '), and each minute may be subdivided in turn into 60 seconds (symbol "). *Temperature* is also measured in degrees, which are divided on a decimal scale. See also ◊Celsius, and ◊Fahrenheit.

De Havilland Geoffrey 1882–1965. British aircraft designer who designed and whose company produced the Moth biplane, the Mosquito fighter-bomber of World War II, and the postwar Comet, the world's first jet-driven airliner to enter commercial service.

De Havilland Olivia 1916– . US actress, a star in Hollywood from the age of 19, when she appeared in *A Midsummer Night's Dream* 1935. She later successfully played more challenging dramatic roles in *Gone With the Wind* 1939, *To Each His Own* (Academy Award) and *Dark Mirror* 1946, and *The Snake Pit* 1948. She won her second Academy Award for *The Heiress* 1949, and played in *Lady in a Cage* and *Hush, Hush, Sweet Charlotte*, both 1964.

dehydration process to preserve food. Moisture content is reduced to 10–20% in fresh produce, and this provides good protection against molds. Bacteria are not inhibited by drying, so the quality of raw materials is vital.

Deighton Len 1929– . British author of spy fiction, including *The Ipcress File* 1963 and the trilogy *Berlin Game, Mexico Set,* and *London Match* 1983–85, featuring the spy Bernard Samson. Samson was also the main character in Deighton's second trilogy *Spy Hook* 1989, *Spy Line* 1989, and *Spy Sinker* 1990.

Deimos one of the two moons of Mars. It is irregularly shaped, $9 \times 7.5 \times 7$ mi/$15 \times 12 \times 11$ km, orbits at a height of 15,000 mi/24,000 km every 1.26 days, and is not as heavily cratered as the other moon, Phobos. Deimos was discovered 1877 by US astronomer Asaph Hall (1829–1907), and is thought to be an asteroid captured by Mars's gravity.

Deirdre in Celtic legend, the beautiful intended bride of Conchobar. She eloped with Noisi, and died of sorrow when Conchobar killed him and his brothers.

deism belief in a supreme being; but the term usually refers to a movement of religious thought in the 17th and 18th centuries, characterized by the belief in a rational "religion of nature" as opposed to the orthodox beliefs of Christianity. Deists believed that God is the source of natural law but does not intervene directly in the affairs of the world, and that the only religious duty of humanity is to be virtuous.

de Klerk F(rederik) W(illem) 1936– . South African National Party politician, president 1989–94. Trained as a lawyer, he entered the South African parliament 1972. He served in the cabinets of B J Vorster and P W Botha 1978–89, and replaced Botha as National Party leader Feb 1989 and as state president Aug 1989. Projecting himself as a pragmatic conservative who sought gradual reform of the apartheid system, he won the Sept 1989 elections for his party, but with a reduced majority. In Feb 1990 he ended the ban on the ◊African National Congress opposition movement and released its effective leader, Nelson Mandela. In Feb 1991 de Klerk promised the end of all apartheid legislation and a new multiracial constitution, and by June of the same year had repealed all racially discriminating laws. In March 1992 a nationwide, whites-only referendum gave de Klerk a clear mandate to

de Gaulle French general, leader of the Free French in England during World War II, and president of France 1958–69, Charles de Gaulle.

de Klerk South African state president and National Party leader F W De Klerk, who oversaw the liberation of South Africa from apartheid.

proceed with plans for major constitutional reform to end white minority rule. In Feb 1993 he and Nelson Mandela agreed to form of a government of national unity after free, nonracial elections 1994. He and Mandela were co-recipients of the Nobel peace prize 1993. After the elections, de Klerk became vice president May 1994 in Mandela's government.

de Kooning Willem 1904– . Dutch-born US painter who immigrated to the US 1926 and worked as a commercial artist. After World War II he became, together with Jackson Pollock, one of the leaders of the Abstract Expressionist movement. His *Women* series, exhibited 1953, was criticized for its grotesque figurative style.

De Kooning joined the faculty of the Yale Art School and became a member of the National Institute of Arts 1960 and received the Presidential Medal of Freedom 1964. His paintings were commissioned for numerous Work Projects Administration (WPA) projects, and he won praise for his mural in the Hall of Pharmacy at the 1939 New York World's Fair.

Delacroix Eugène 1798–1863. French Romantic painter. His prolific output included religious and historical subjects and portraits of friends, among them the musicians Paganini and Chopin. Against French academic tradition, he evolved a highly colored, fluid style, as in *The Death of Sardanapalus* 1827.

de la Mare Walter 1873–1956. English poet, known for his verse for children, such as *Songs of Childhood* 1902, and the novels *The Three Royal Monkeys* 1910 for children and, for adults, *The Memoirs of a Midget* 1921.

Delaunay Robert 1885–1941. French painter, a pioneer in abstract art. With his wife Sonia Delaunay-Terk, he invented Orphism, an early variation on Cubism, focusing on the effects of pure color.

De Laurentiis Dino 1919– . Italian producer. His early films, including Fellini's *La strada/The Street* 1954, brought more acclaim than later epics such as *Waterloo* 1970. He then produced a series of Hollywood films: *Death Wish* 1974, *King Kong* (remake) 1976, and *Dune* 1984.

Delaware state in NE US; nickname First State/Diamond State
area 2,046 sq mi/5,300 sq km
capital Dover
cities Wilmington, Newark
physical two main divisions: (1) hilly and wooded; (2) gently undulating to the sea
features one of the most industrialized states; headquarters of the Du Pont chemical firm; Rehoboth Beach; Winterthur Museum
products dairy, poultry, and market-garden produce; chemicals; motor vehicles; textiles
population (1990) 666,200
famous people Du Pont family, J P Marquand

Delaware

history the first settlers were Dutch 1631 and Swedes 1638, but in 1664 the area was captured by the British and transferred to William Penn. A separate colony from 1704, it fought in the American Revolution as a state 1776, was one of the original 13 states, and was the first state to ratify the US Constitution, Dec 7, 1787. In 1802 the Du Pont gunpowder mill was established near Wilmington. Completion of the Philadelphia-Baltimore railroad line 1838, through Wilmington, fostered development. Delaware was famous as a chemical center by the early 1900s. Two auto-assembly plants and an oil refinery were built after World War II.

Delbruck Max 1906–1981. German-born US biologist who pioneered techniques in molecular biology, studying genetic changes occurring when viruses invade bacteria. He was awarded the Nobel Prize for Medicine 1969 which he shared with Salvador Luria (1912–1951) and Alfred Hershey (1908–).

Delhi Union Territory of the Republic of India from 1956; capital Delhi; area 579 sq mi/1,500 sq km; population (1991) 9,370,400. It produces grain, sugar cane, fruit, and vegetables.

Delhi capital of India, comprising the walled city of *Old Delhi*, situated on the W bank of the river Jumna, and *New Delhi* to the S, largely designed by British architect Edwin Lutyens and chosen to replace Calcutta as the seat of government 1912 (completed 1929; officially inaugurated 1931). Delhi is the administrative center of the Union Territory of Delhi and India's largest commercial and communications center; population (1991) 9,370,400.

delirium in medicine, a state of temporary confusion in which the subject is incoherent, frenzied, and out of touch with reality. It is often accompanied by delusions or hallucinations.

della Robbia Italian family of artists; see ◊Robbia, della.

Delphi city of ancient Greece, situated in a rocky valley north of the gulf of Corinth, on the southern slopes of Mount Parnassus, site of a famous ◊oracle in the temple of Apollo. The site was supposed to be the center of the Earth and was marked by a conical stone, the *omphelos*. The oracle was interpreted by priests from the inspired utterances of the Pythian priestess until it was closed down by the Roman emperor Theodosius I AD 390.

delphinium any plant of the genus *Delphinium* belonging to the buttercup family Ranunculaceae. There are some 250 species, including the great flowered larkspur *D. grandiflorum*, an Asian form and one of the ancestors of the garden delphinium. Most species have blue, purple, or white flowers in a long spike.

Delray Beach city in SE Florida, on the Atlantic Ocean, N of Fort Lauderdale; population (1990) 47,200. A tourist resort, it also relies economically on the cultivation of flowers.

del Sarto Andrea 1486–1531. Italian Renaissance painter; see ◊Andrea del Sarto.

delta tract of land at a river's mouth, composed of silt deposited as the water slows on entering the sea. Familiar examples of large deltas are those of the Mississippi, Ganges and Brahmaputra, Rhône, Po, Danube, and Nile; the shape of the Nile delta is like the Greek letter *delta* Δ, and thus gave rise to the name.

Delta Force US antiguerrilla force, based at Fort Bragg, North Carolina, and modeled on the British Special Air Service.

delta wing aircraft wing shaped like the Greek letter *delta* Δ. Its design enables an aircraft to pass through the ◊sound barrier with little effect. The supersonic airliner ◊Concorde and the US ◊space shuttle have delta wings.

dementia mental deterioration as a result of physical changes in the brain. It may be due to degenerative change, circulatory disease, infection, injury, or chronic poisoning. *Senile dementia*, a progressive loss of mental abilities such as memory and orientation, is typically a problem of old age, and can be accompanied by ◊depression.

Demeter in Greek mythology, the goddess of agriculture (Roman Ceres), daughter of Cronus and Rhea, and mother of Persephone by Zeus. Demeter and Persephone were worshiped in a sanctuary at Eleusis, where one of the foremost ◊mystery religions of Greece was celebrated. She was later identified with the Egyptian goddess ◊Isis.

De Mille Agnes George 1905–1989. US choreographer. After becoming a member of the Ballet Theater, she choreographed a long string of Broadway hits, including *Oklahoma!* 1943, *Carousel* 1945, *Brigadoon* 1947, *Gentlemen Prefer Blondes* 1949, and *Paint Your Wagon* 1951. She founded the Agnes De Mille Dance Theater 1953.

DeMille Cecil B(lount) 1881–1959. US film director and producer. He entered films 1913 with Jesse L Lasky (with whom he later established Paramount Pictures), and was one of the founders of Hollywood. He specialized in biblical epics, such as *The Sign of the Cross* 1932 and *The Ten Commandments* 1923; remade 1956. He also made the 1952 Academy-Award-winning *The Greatest Show on Earth*.

Demirel Suleyman 1924– . Turkish politician. Leader from 1964 of the Justice Party, he was prime minister 1965–71, 1975–77, and 1979–80. He favored links with the West, full membership in the European Community, and foreign investment in Turkish industry.

democracy (Greek *demos* "the community," *Kratos* "sovereign power") government by the people, usually through elected representatives. In the modern world, democracy has developed from the American and French revolutions.

Democratic Party one of the two main political parties of the US. It tends to be the party of the working person, as opposed to the Republicans, the party of big business, but the divisions between the two are not clear cut. Its stronghold since the Civil War has traditionally been industrial urban centers and the Southern states, but conservative Southern Democrats were largely supportive of Republican positions and helped elect President Reagan.

demography study of the size, structure, dispersement, and development of human populations to establish reliable statistics on such factors as birth and death rates, marriages and divorces, life expectancy, and migration.

Demosthenes *c.* 384–322 BC. Athenian orator and politician. From 351 BC he led the party that advocated resistance to the growing power of ◊Philip of Macedon, and in his *Philippics* incited the Athenians to war. This policy resulted in the defeat of Chaeronea 338, and the establishment of Macedonian supremacy. After the death of Alexander he organized a revolt; when it failed, he took poison to avoid capture by the Macedonians.

Delphi Tholos in the Sanctuary of Athena "Marmaria" in Delphi, Greece.

demotic script cursive (joined) writing derived from Egyptian hieratic script, itself a cursive form of ◊hieroglyphic. Demotic documents are known from the 6th century BC to about AD 470. It was written horizontally, from right to left.

Dempsey Jack (William Harrison) 1895–1983. US heavyweight boxing champion, nicknamed "the Manassa Mauler." He beat Jess Willard 1919 to win the title and held it until 1926, when he lost it to Gene Tunney. He engaged in the "Battle of the Long Count" with Tunney 1927.

dendrite part of a ◊nerve cell or neuron. The dendrites are slender filaments projecting from the cell body. They receive incoming messages from many other nerve cells and pass them on to the cell body. If the combined effect of these messages is strong enough, the cell body will send an electrical impulse along the axon (the threadlike extension of a nerve cell). The tip of the axon passes its message to the dendrites of other nerve cells.

dendrochronology analysis of the ◊annual rings of trees to date past events. Samples of wood are obtained by means of a narrow metal tube that is driven into a tree to remove a core extending from the bark to the center. Samples taken from timbers at an archeological site can be compared with a master core on file for that region or by taking cores from old, living trees; the year when they were felled can be determined by locating the point where the rings of the two samples correspond and counting back from the present.

Dene term used in Canada since the 1970s to describe the Native Americans (Athabaskan Indians) in the Northwest Territories. The official body representing them is called the Dene Nation.

Deneb or *Alpha Cygni* brightest star in the constellation Cygnus, and the 19th brightest star in the sky. It is one of the greatest supergiant stars known, with a true luminosity of about 60,000 times that of the Sun. Deneb is about 1,800 light-years from Earth.

Deneuve Catherine 1943– . French actress acclaimed for her poise and her performance in

Deng Xiaoping
Deng Xiaoping,
paramount ruler in
effective charge of
China throughout the
1980s.

Roman Polanski's film *Repulsion* 1965. She also appeared in *Les Parapluies de Cherbourg/Umbrellas of Cherbourg* 1964 (with her sister Françoise Dorléac [1942–1967]). *Belle de jour* 1967, *Hustle* 1975, *Le Dernier métro/The Last Metro* 1980, *The Hunger* 1983, and *Indochine* 1993.

Deng Xiaoping or *Teng Hsiao-ping* 1904– . Chinese political leader. A member of the Chinese Communist Party (CCP) from the 1920s, he took part in the Long March 1934–36. He was in the Politburo from 1955 until ousted in the Cultural Revolution 1966–69. Reinstated in the 1970s, he gradually took power and introduced a radical economic modernization program. He retired from the Politburo 1987 and from his last official position (as chair of State Military Commission) March 1990, but remained influential behind the scenes.

De Niro Robert 1943– . US actor. He won Oscars for his performances in *The Godfather Part II* 1974 and *Raging Bull* 1979, for which role he put on weight in the interests of authenticity as the boxer gone to seed, Jake LaMotta. His other films include *Mean Streets* 1973, *Taxi Driver* 1976, *The Deer Hunter* 1978, *The Untouchables* 1987, *Midnight Run* 1988, and *Cape Fear* 1992. He showed his versatility in *The King of Comedy* 1982 and other Martin Scorsese vehicles.

Denison city in NE Texas, near the Red River and the Oklahoma border, N of Dallas; population (1990) 21,500. A distribution center for grain and dairy products, its industries include textiles, wood products, and food processing.

Denmark peninsula and islands in N Europe, bounded N by the Skagerrak, E by the Kattegat, S by Germany, and W by the North Sea.

Denpasar capital city of Bali in the Lesser Sunda Islands of Indonesia; population (1980) 88,100. Industries include food processing, machinery, papermaking and printing, and handicrafts. There is a university (1962) and, housed in the temple and palace, a museum of Balinese art.

density measure of the compactness of a substance; it is equal to its mass per unit volume and is measured in lb per cubic foot/kg per cubic meter. Density is a ◊scalar quantity. The density D of a mass m occupying a volume V is given by the formula:

$$D = m/V.$$

◊Relative density is the ratio of the density of a substance to that of water at 39.2°F/4°C.

dentistry care and treatment of the teeth and gums. *Orthodontics* deals with the straightening of the teeth for aesthetic and clinical reasons, and *periodontics* with care of the supporting tissue (bone and gums).

The earliest dental school was opened in Baltimore, Maryland, 1839. An International Dental Federation was founded 1900.

depression A soup
kitchen in Chicago
during the Great
Depression of the
1930s.

Denmark
Kingdom of
(*Kongeriget Danmark*)

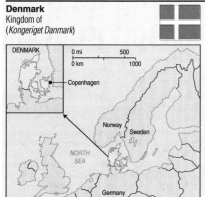

area 16,627 sq mi/43,075 sq km
capital Copenhagen
cities Aarhus, Odense, Aalborg, Esbjerg, all ports
physical comprises the Jutland peninsula and about 500 islands (100 inhabited) including Bornholm in the Baltic Sea; the land is flat and cultivated; sand dunes and lagoons on the W coast and long inlets (fjords) on the E; the main island is Sjælland (Zealand), where most of Copenhagen is located (the rest is on the island of Amager)
territories the dependencies of Faeroe Islands and Greenland
features Kronborg Castle in Helsingør (Elsinore); Tivoli Gardens (Copenhagen); Legoland Park in Sillund
head of state Queen Margrethe II from 1972
head of government Poul Nyrup Rasmussen from 1993
political system liberal democracy

political parties Social Democrats (SD), left of center; Conservative People's Party (KF), moderate center-right; Liberal Party (V), center-left; Socialist People's Party (SF), moderate left-wing; Radical Liberals (RV), radical internationalist, left of center; Center Democrats (CD), moderate centrist; Progress Party (FP), radical antibureaucratic; Christian People's Party (KrF), interdenominational, family values
exports bacon, dairy produce, eggs, fish, mink pelts, automobile and aircraft parts, electrical equipment, textiles, chemicals
currency kroner
population (1992) 5,167,000; growth rate 0% p.a.
life expectancy men 72, women 78
languages Danish (official); there is a German-speaking minority
religion Lutheran 97%
literacy 99% (1983)
GDP $142.1 bn (1992)

chronology
1940–45 Occupied by Germany.
1945 Iceland's independence recognized.
1947 Frederik IX succeeded Christian X.
1948 Home rule granted for Faeroe Islands.
1949 Became a founding member of NATO.
1960 Joined European Free Trade Association (EFTA).
1972 Margrethe II became Denmark's first queen in nearly 600 years.
1973 Left EFTA and joined EEC.
1979 Home rule granted for Greenland.
1985 Strong non-nuclear movement in evidence.
1990 General election; another coalition government formed.
1992 Rejection of Maastricht Treaty in national referendum.
1993 Poul Schlüter resigned; replaced by Poul Nyrup Rasmussen at head of Social Democrat-led coalition government. Second referendum approved the Maastricht Treaty after modifications.

dentition type and number of teeth in a species. Different kinds of teeth have different functions; a grass-eating animal will have large molars for grinding its food, whereas a meat-eater will need powerful canines for catching and killing its prey. The teeth that are less useful may be reduced in size or missing altogether. An animal's dentition is represented diagramatically by a dental formula.

Denver city and capital of Colorado, on the South Platte River, near the foothills of the Rocky Mountains; population (1990) 467,600, Denver–Boulder metropolitan area 1,848,300. It is a processing and distribution center for a large agricultural area and for natural resources (minerals, oil, gas). It was the center of a gold and silver boom in the 1870s and 1880s, and for oil in the 1970s.

De Palma Brian 1941– . US film director, especially of thrillers. His technical mastery and enthusiasm for spilling blood are shown in films such as *Sisters* 1973, *Carrie* 1976, and *The Untouchables* 1987.

Depardieu Gérard 1948– . French actor renowned for his imposing physique and screen presence. His films include *Deux hommes dans la ville* 1973, *Le camion* 1977, *Mon oncle d'Amérique* 1980, *The Moon in the Gutter* 1983, *Jean de Florette* 1985, *Cyrano de Bergerac* 1990. His English-speaking films include the US romantic comedy *Green Card* 1990, *1492–Conquest of Paradise* 1992, and *My Father the Hero* 1994.

deposit account in banking, an account in which money is left to attract interest, sometimes for a fixed term. Unlike a current account, the deposit account does not give constant access.

depreciation in economics, the decline of a currency's value in relation to other currencies. Depreciation also describes the fall in value of an asset (such as factory machinery) resulting from age, wear and tear, or other circumstances. It is an important factor in assessing company profits and tax liabilities.

depression in economics, a period of exceptionally low output and investment, with high unemployment. Specifically, the term describes two periods of crisis in world economy 1873–96 and 1929–39, also known as panics.

depression or *cyclone* or *low* in meteorology, a region of low atmospheric pressure. A depression forms as warm, moist air from the tropics mixes with cold, dry polar air, producing warm and cold boundaries (◊fronts) and unstable weather—low cloud and drizzle, showers, or fierce storms. The warm air, being less dense, rises above the cold air to produce the area of low pressure on the ground. Air spirals in toward the center of the depression in a counterclockwise direction in the northern hemisphere, clockwise in the southern hemisphere, generating winds up to gale force. Depressions tend to travel eastward and can remain active for several days.

A deep depression is one in which the pressure at the center is very much lower than that round about; it produces very strong winds, as opposed to a shallow depression in which the winds are comparatively light. A severe depression in the tropics is called a ◊hurricane, tropical cyclone, or typhoon, and is a great danger to shipping; a ◊tornado is a very intense, rapidly swirling depression, with a diameter of only a few hundred feet or so.

depression emotional state characterized by sadness, unhappy thoughts, apathy, and dejection. Sadness is a normal response to major losses such as bereavement or unemployment. After childbirth, postnatal depression is common. However, clinical depression, which is prolonged or unduly severe, often requires treatment, such as antidepressant medication, ◊cognitive therapy, or, in very rare cases, electroconvulsive therapy (ECT), in which an electrical current is passed through the brain.

De Quincey Thomas 1785–1859. English author whose works include *Confessions of an English Opium-Eater* 1821 and the essays "On the Knocking at the Gate in Macbeth" 1823 and "On Murder Considered as One of the Fine Arts" 1827. He was a friend of the poets Wordsworth and Coleridge.

Derbyshire county in N central England
area 1,015 sq mi/2,630 sq km
cities Matlock (administrative headquarters), Derby, Chesterfield, Ilkeston
features Peak District National Park (including Kinder Scout 2,088 ft/636 m); rivers: Derwent, Dove, Rother, Trent; Chatsworth House, Bakewell (seat of Duke of Devonshire); Haddon Hall
products cereals; dairy and sheep farming.

deregulation action to abolish or reduce government controls and supervision over private economic activities, as with the deregulation of the US airline industry 1978. Its purpose is to improve competition. Increased competition had the effect, in some areas, of driving smaller companies out of business. A tremendous increase in mergers, acquisitions, and bankruptcies followed deregulation as the stronger companies consumed the weaker. A wider array of services and lower prices in some industries also have resulted; see also ◊monetarism; ◊privatization.

derivative or *differential coefficient* in mathematics, the limit of the gradient of a chord linking two points on a curve as the distance between the points tends to zero; for a function with a single variable, $y = f'(x)$, it is denoted by $f'(x)$, $Df(x)$, or dy/dx, and is equal to the gradient of the curve.

dermatitis inflammation of the skin (see ◊eczema), usually related to allergy. *Dermatosis* refers to any skin disorder and may be caused by contact or systemic problems.

dermatology science of the skin, its nature and diseases. It is a rapidly expanding field owing to the proliferation of industrial chemicals affecting workers, and the universal use of household cleaners, cosmetics, and sunscreens.

derrick simple lifting machine consisting of a pole carrying a block and tackle. Derricks are commonly used on ships that carry freight. In the oil industry the tower used for hoisting the drill pipes is known as a derrick.

Derry county of Northern Ireland
area 799 sq mi/2,070 sq km
cities Derry (county town, formerly Londonderry), Coleraine, Portstewart
features rivers Foyle, Bann, and Roe; borders Lough Neagh
products mainly agricultural, but farming is hindered by the very heavy rainfall; flax, cattle, sheep, food processing, textiles, light engineering
population (1981) 187,000
famous people Joyce Cary.

dervish in Iran and Turkey, a religious mendicant; throughout the rest of Islam a member of an Islamic religious brotherhood, not necessarily mendicant in character. The Arabic equivalent is *fakir*. There are various orders of dervishes, each with its rule and special ritual. The "whirling dervishes" claim close communion with the deity through ecstatic dancing; the "howling dervishes" gash themselves with knives to demonstrate the miraculous feats possible to those who trust in Allah.

Derwent river in North Yorkshire, NE England; length 70 mi/112 km. Rising in the North Yorkshire moors, it joins the river Ouse SE of Selby.

desalination removal of salt, usually from sea water, to produce fresh water for irrigation or drinking. Distillation has usually been the method adopted, but in the 1970s a cheaper process, using certain polymer materials that filter the molecules of salt from the water by reverse osmosis, was developed.

Descartes René 1596–1650. French philosopher and mathematician. He believed that commonly accepted knowledge was doubtful because of the subjective nature of the senses, and attempted to rebuild human knowledge using as his foundation *cogito ergo sum* ("I think, therefore I am"). He also believed that the entire material universe could be explained in terms of mathematical physics, and founded coordinate geometry as a way of defining and manipulating geometrical shapes by means of algebraic expressions. ◊Cartesian coordinates, the means by which points are represented in this system, are named after him. Descartes also established the science of optics, and helped to shape contemporary theories of astronomy and animal behavior.

desert arid area without sufficient rainfall and, consequently, vegetation to support human life. The term includes the ice areas of the polar regions (known as cold deserts). Almost 33% of the Earth's land surface is desert, and this proportion is increasing.

Desert Storm, Operation code name of the military action to eject the Iraqi army from Kuwait 1991. The buildup phase was code-named *Operation Desert Shield* and lasted from Aug 1990, when Kuwait was first invaded by Iraq, to Jan 1991 when Operation Desert Storm was unleashed, starting the ◊Gulf War. Desert Storm ended with the defeat of the Iraqi army in the Kuwaiti theater of operations late Feb 1991. The cost of the operation was $53 billion.

De Sica Vittorio 1901–1974. Italian director and actor. He won his first Oscar with *The Bicycle Thief* 1949, a film of subtle realism. Later films included *Umberto D* 1955, *Two Women* 1960, and *The Garden of the Finzi-Continis* 1971. His considerable acting credits include *The Earnings of Madame de...* 1953 and *The Millionaires* 1960.

desktop publishing (DTP) use of microcomputers for small-scale typesetting and page makeup. DTP systems are capable of producing camera-ready pages (pages ready for photographing and printing), made up of text and graphics, with text set in different typefaces and sizes. The page can be previewed on the screen before final printing on a laser printer.

Des Moines capital and largest city in Iowa, on the Des Moines River, a tributary of the Mississippi; population (1990) 193,200. It is a major road, railroad, and air center. Industries include printing, banking, insurance, and food processing.

Drake University is here. The Des Moines Art Center was designed by Eliel Saarinen. Incorporated 1851, Des Moines became the state capital 1857.

desert

desert regions

continental

rain shadow

tropical

inselberg

Following erosion, rounded cores of old mountains may stand as inselbergs.

The main desert belts lie along the tropics where hot air descends, after rising and dropping its water over the equatorial forests. Other deserts lie in the centers of continents, far from the moist influence of the sea. Rain-shadow deserts lie in the lee of mountain ranges, where all rain falls on the windward side.

Any region that has very little rainfall can be regarded as a desert. Most desert areas have less than 12 in/30 cm of rain per year, and all this falls at once, leaving the land totally dry for the rest of the year. The lack of moisture means that few plants and animals can live in a desert environment. The soil does not have the vegetable matter needed to hold it together and dry particles are blown about in the wind, eroding bare rock and producing sand and dust.

saltpan

alluvial fan

When it does rain, flash floods wash sand and rocks out of surrounding valleys and deposit them on flatter ground, creating alluvial fans. The temporary lakes, or playas, dry out leaving salt flats.

cactus

Desert soil is a mixture of coarse and fine material. The fine surface sand and dust are blown away, leaving a crust of coarse stones, known as a desert pavement or deflation surface.

cactus

Plants must withstand prolonged periods of drought, either by storing moisture like the cactus, or by lying dormant like the sage bush.

Sand, hurled by the wind, erodes exposed rocks into strange shapes. The surface of the rocks may also flake off due to the intense heat.

lizard

sage bush

Most animals only come out at sunset and sunrise, avoiding the heat of the day and the chill of the night in burrows.

rodent

snake

wren

Desmoulins Camille 1760–1794. French revolutionary who summoned the mob to arms on July 12, 1789, so precipitating the revolt that culminated in the storming of the Bastille. A prominent left-wing ◊Jacobin, he was elected to the National Convention 1792. His *Histoire des Brissotins* was largely responsible for the overthrow of the right-wing Girondins, but shortly after he was sent to the guillotine as too moderate.

de Soto Hernando *c.* 1496–1542. Spanish explorer who sailed with d'Avila (*c.* 1400–1531) to Darien, Central America, 1519, explored the Yucatán Peninsula 1528, and traveled with Francisco Pizarro in Peru 1530–35. In 1538 he was made governor of Cuba and Florida. In his expedition of 1539, he explored Florida, Georgia, and the Mississippi River.

Desprez Josquin Franco-Flemish composer.

Dessalines Jean Jacques *c.* 1758–1806. Emperor of Haiti 1804–06. Born in Guinea, he was taken to Haiti as a slave, where in 1802 he succeeded ◊Toussaint L'Ouverture as leader of the black revolt against the French. After defeating the French, he proclaimed Haiti's independence and made himself emperor. He was killed when trying to suppress an uprising provoked by his cruelty.

destroyer small, fast warship designed for antisubmarine work. Destroyers played a critical role in the convoy system in World War II.

Modern destroyers often carry guided missiles and displace 3,700–5,650 tons.

détente (French) reduction of political tension and the easing of strained relations between nations, for example, the ending of the Cold War 1989–90, although it was first used in the 1970s to describe the easing East–West relations, trade agreements, and cultural exchanges.

detergent surface-active cleansing agent. The common detergents are made from ◊fats (hydrocarbons) and sulfuric acid, and their long-chain molecules have a type of structure similar to that of ◊soap molecules: a salt group at one end attached to a long hydrocarbon "tail." They have the advantage over soap in that they do not produce scum by forming insoluble salts with the calcium and magnesium ions present in hard water.

determinism in philosophy, the view that denies human freedom of action. Everything is strictly governed by the principle of cause and effect, and human action is no exception. It is the opposite of free will, and rules out moral choice and responsibility.

deterrence underlying conception of the nuclear arms race: the belief that a potential aggressor will be discouraged from launching a "first strike" nuclear attack by the knowledge that the adversary is capable of inflicting "unacceptable damage" in a retaliatory strike. This doctrine is widely known as that of *mutual assured destruction (MAD)*. Three essential characteristics of deterrence are the "capability to act," "credibility," and the "will to act."

detonator or *blasting cap* or *percussion cap* small explosive charge used to trigger off a main charge of high explosive. The relatively unstable compounds mercury fulminate and lead acid are often used in detonators, being set off by a lighted fuse or, more commonly, an electric current.

Detroit city in Michigan, situated on Detroit River; population (1990) 1,028,000, metropolitan area 4,665,200. It is an industrial center with the headquarters of Ford, Chrysler, and General Motors, hence its nickname, Motown (from "motor town"). Other manufactured products include metal products, machine tools, chemicals, office machines, and pharmaceuticals. During the 1960s and 1970s Detroit became associated with the "Motown Sound" of rock and soul music.

deuterium naturally occurring heavy isotope of hydrogen, mass number 2 (one proton and one neutron), discovered by Harold Urey 1932. It is sometimes given the symbol D. In nature, about one in evey 6,500 hydrogen atoms is deuterium. Combined with oxygen, it produces "heavy water" (D_2O), used in the nuclear industry.

deuteron nucleus of an atom of deterium (heavy hydrogen). It consists of one proton and one neutron, and is used in the bombardment of chemical elements to synthesize other elements.

de Valera Eámon 1882–1975. Irish nationalist politician, prime minister of the Irish Free State/Eire/Republic of Ireland 1932–48, 1951–54, and 1957–59, and president 1959–73. Repeatedly imprisoned, he participated in the Easter Rising 1916 and was leader of the nationalist ◊Sinn Féin party 1917–26, when he formed the republican Fianna Fáil party; he directed negotiations with Britain 1921 but refused to accept the partition of Ireland until 1937.

He was sentenced to death for his part in the Easter Rising, but the sentence was commuted, and he was released under an amnesty 1917. He directed the negotiations of 1921 but refused to accept the ensuing treaty that divided Ireland into the Free State and the North. Civil war followed. De Valera formed a new party, Fianna Fáil 1926, which secured a majority 1932. De Valera became prime minister and foreign minister of the Free State. Throughout World War II he maintained a strict neutrality, rejecting an offer by Churchill 1940 to recognize the principle of a united Ireland in return for Eire's entry into the war. He resigned after his defeat at the 1948 elections but was again prime minister in the 1950s and then president of the republic.

devaluation in economics, the lowering of the official value of a currency against other currencies, so that exports become cheaper and imports more expensive. Used when a country is badly in deficit in its balance of trade, it results in the goods the country produces being cheaper abroad, so that the economy is stimulated by increased foreign demand.

developing in photography, the process that produces a visible image on exposed photographic film. Developing involves treating the emulsion with chemical developer, a reducing agent that changes the light-altered salts into dark metallic silver. The developed image is a negative: darkest where the strongest light hit the emulsion, lightest where the least light hit it.

development in the social sciences, the acquisition by a society of industrial techniques and technology; hence the common classification of the "developed" nations of the First and Second Worlds and the poorer, "developing" or "underdeveloped" nations of the Third World. The assumption that development in the sense of industrialization is inherently good has been increasingly questioned since the 1960s.

deviance abnormal behavior; that is, behavior that deviates from the norms or the laws of a society or group, and so invokes social sanctions, controls, or stigma.

devil in Jewish, Christian, and Muslim theology, the supreme spirit of evil (*Beelzebub, Lucifer, Iblis*), or an evil spirit generally.

Devil's Island (French *Ile du Diable*) smallest of the Iles du Salut, off French Guiana, 27 mi/43 km NW of Cayenne. The group of islands was collectively and popularly known by the name Devil's Island and formed a penal colony notorious for its terrible conditions.

Devolution, War of war waged unsuccessfully 1667–68 by Louis XIV of France to gain Spanish territory in the Netherlands, of which ownership had allegedly "devolved" on his wife Maria Theresa.

Devon or *Devonshire* county in SW England *area* 2,594 sq mi/6,720 sq km *cities* Exeter (administrative headquarters), Plymouth; resorts: Paignton, Torquay, Teignmouth, and Ilfracombe *features* rivers: Dart, Exe, Tamar; National Parks: Dartmoor, Exmoor; Lundy bird sanctuary and marine nature preserve in the Bristol Channel *products* mainly agricultural, with sheep and dairy farming; cider and clotted cream; kaolin in the S; Honiton lace; Dartington glass *population* (1991) 1,008,300 *famous people* Francis Drake, John Hawkins, Charles Kingsley, Robert F Scott.

Devonian period of geological time 408–360 million years ago, the fourth period of the Paleozoic era. Many desert sandstones from North America and Europe date from this time. The first land plants flourished in the Devonian period, corals were abundant in the seas, amphibians evolved from air-breathing fish, and insects developed on land.

De Vries Hugo 1848–1935. Dutch botanist who conducted important research on osmosis in plant cells and was a pioneer in the study of plant evolution. His work led to the rediscovery of ◊Mendel's laws and the discovery of spontaneously occurring ◊mutations.

dew precipitation in the form of moisture that collects on the ground. It forms after the temperature of the ground has fallen below the ◊dew point of the air in contact with it. As the temperature falls during the night, the air and its water vapor become chilled, and condensation takes place on the cooled surfaces.

Dewar James 1842–1923. Scottish chemist and physicist who invented the vacuum flask (Thermos) 1872 during his research into the properties of matter at extremely low temperatures.

Dewey George 1837–1917. US naval officer. He was appointed chief of the Bureau of Equipment 1889 and of the Board of Inspection and Survey 1895. As commodore, Dewey was dispatched to the Pacific 1896. He destroyed the Spanish fleet in Manila harbor at the outbreak of the Spanish-American War 1898. Dewey was promoted to the rank of admiral of the navy (the highest naval rank ever awarded) 1899. He retired from active service 1900.

Dewey Melvil 1851–1931. US librarian. In 1876, he devised the Dewey decimal system of classification for accessing, storing, and retrieving books, widely used in libraries. The system uses the numbers 000 to 999 to designate the major fields of knowledge, then breaks these down into more specific subjects by the use of decimals.

Dewey founded the American Library Association 1876 and the first school of library science, at Columbia University, 1887.

Dewey Thomas Edmund 1902–1971. US public official. He was Manhattan district attorney 1937–38 and served as governor of New York 1942–54. Dewey was twice the Republican presidential candidate, losing to F D Roosevelt 1944 and to Truman 1948, the latter race being one of the greatest electoral upsets in US history.

dew point temperature at which the air becomes saturated with water vapor. At temperatures below the dew point, the water vapor condenses out of the air as droplets. If the droplets are large they become deposited on the ground as dew; if small they remain in suspension in the air and form mist or fog.

Dhaka or *Dacca* capital of Bangladesh from 1971, in Dhaka region, W of the river Meghna; population (1984) 3,600,000. It trades in jute, oilseed, sugar, and tea and produces textiles, chemicals, glass, and metal products.

Dhaulagiri mountain in the ◊Himalayas of W central Nepal, rising to 26,811 ft/8,172 m.

Dhofar mountainous western province of ◊Oman, on the border with Yemen; population (1982) 40,000. South Yemen supported guerrilla activity here in the 1970s, while Britain and Iran supported the government's military operations. The capital is Salalah, which has a port at Rasut.

diabase igneous rock formed below the Earth's surface, a form of basalt, containing relatively little silica (basic in composition).

diabetes disease *diabetes mellitus* in which a disorder of the islets of Langerhans in the ◊pancreas prevents the body producing the hormone ◊insulin, so that sugars cannot be used properly. Treatment is by strict dietary control and oral or injected insulin, depending on the type of diabetes.

Sugar accumulates first in the blood, then in the urine. The patient experiences thirst, weight loss, and copious voiding, along with degenerative changes in the capillary system. Without treatment, the patient may go blind, ulcerate, lapse into diabetic coma, and die. Early- onset diabetes tends to be more severe than that developing in later years. Before the discovery of insulin by Frederick ◊Banting and Charles Best, severe diabetics did not survive. Today, it is seldom fatal. A continuous infusion of insulin can be provided via a catheter implanted under the skin, which is linked to an electric pump. This more accurately mimics the body's natural secretion of insulin than injections or oral doses, and can provide better control of diabetes. It is, however, very dangerous if the pump should malfunction.

Much rarer, *diabetes insipidus* is due to a deficiency of a hormone secreted by the ◊pituitary gland to regulate the body's water balance. It is controlled by hormone therapy. In 1989, it was estimated that 4% of the world's population had diabetes, and that there were 12 million sufferers in Canada and the US.

Diaghilev Sergei Pavlovich 1872–1929. Russian ballet impresario who in 1909 founded the Ballets Russes/Russian Ballet (headquarters in Monaco), which he directed for 20 years. Through this company he brought Russian ballet to the West, introducing and encouraging a dazzling array of dancers, choreographers, and composers, such as Anna Pavlova, Vaslav Nijinsky, Mikhail Fokine, Léonide Massine, George Balanchine, Igor Stravinsky, and Sergey Prokofiev.

dialect variation of a spoken language shared by those in a particular area or a particular social group or both. The term is used to indicate a geographical area ("northern dialects") or social group ("black dialect").

Dickens Born into a family on the fringes of gentility, English author Charles Dickens was always acutely conscious of the social and economic abysses of Victorian society.

dialectic Greek term, originally associated with the philosopher Socrates' method of argument through dialogue and conversation. *Hegelian dialectic*, named after the German philosopher ◊Hegel, refers to an interpretive method in which the contradiction between a thesis and its antithesis is resolved through synthesis.

dialectical materialism political, philosophical, and economic theory of the 19th-century German thinkers Karl Marx and Friedrich Engels, also known as ◊Marxism.

dialysis in medicine, the process used to mimic the effects of the kidneys. It may be life-saving in some types of poisoning. Dialysis is usually performed to compensate for failing kidneys; there are two main methods, hemodialysis and peritoneal dialysis.

diamond generally colorless, transparent mineral, the hard crystalline form of carbon. It is regarded as a precious gemstone, and is the hardest substance known (10 on the ◊Mohs' scale). Industrial diamonds, which may be natural or synthetic, are used for cutting, grinding, and polishing.

Diamond v Chakrabarty a US Supreme Court decision 1980 that defined human-engineered microorganisms as patentable products.

Diana in Roman mythology, the goddess of chastity, hunting, and the Moon, daughter of Jupiter and twin of Apollo. Her Greek equivalent is the goddess ◊Artemis.

Diana Princess of Wales 1961– . The daughter of the 8th Earl Spencer, she married Prince Charles 1981, the first English bride of a royal heir since 1659. She is descended from the only sovereigns from whom Prince Charles is not descended, Charles II and James II. She had two sons, William and Henry before her separation from Charles 1992.

diaphragm muscular sheet separating the thorax from the abdomen in mammals. Its rhythmical movements affect the size of the thorax and cause the pressure changes within the lungs that result in breathing.

diaphragm barrier ◊contraceptive that is inserted into the vagina and fits over the cervix (neck of the uterus), preventing sperm from entering the uterus. For it to be effective, a ◊spermicide must be used and the diaphragm left in place for 6–8 hours after intercourse. This method is 97% effective if practiced correctly.

diarrhea excessive action of the bowels so that the feces are fluid or semifluid. It is caused by intestinal irritants (including some drugs and poisons), infection with harmful organisms (as in ◊dysentery, salmonella, or cholera), or allergies.

diary informal record of day-to-day events, observations, or reflections, usually not intended for a general readership. One of the earliest diaries extant is that of a Japanese noblewoman, the *Kagerō Nikki* 954–974, and the earliest known diary in English is that of Edward VI (ruled 1547–53). Notable diaries include those of Samuel Pepys and Anne Frank.

Diaspora dispersal of the Jews, initially from Palestine after the Babylonian conquest 586 BC, and then following the Roman sack of Jerusalem AD 70 and their crushing of the Jewish revolt of 135. The term has come to refer to all the Jews living outside Israel.

diatonic in music, a scale consisting of the seven notes of any major or minor key.

Diaz Bartolomeu *c.* 1450–1500. Portuguese explorer, the first European to reach the Cape of Good Hope 1488, and to establish a route around Africa. He drowned during an expedition with Pedro Cabral.

Díaz Porfirio 1830–1915. Dictator of Mexico 1877–80 and 1884–1911. After losing the 1876 election, he overthrew the government and seized power. He was supported by conservative landowners and foreign capitalists, who invested in railroads and mines. He centralized the state at the expense of the peasants and Indians, and dismantled all local and regional leadership. He faced mounting and revolutionary opposition in his final years and was forced into exile 1911.

Dickens Charles 1812–1870. English novelist, popular for his memorable characters and his portrayal of the social evils of Victorian England. In 1836 he published the first number of the *Pickwick Papers*, followed by *Oliver Twist* 1838, the first of his "reforming" novels; *Nicholas Nickleby* 1839; *Barnaby Rudge* 1840; *The Old Curiosity Shop* 1841; and *David Copperfield* 1849. Among his later books are *A Tale of Two Cities* 1859 and *Great Expectations* 1861.

Dickinson Emily Elizabeth 1830–1886. US poet. Dickinson wrote most of her poetry between 1850 and the late 1860s and was particularly prolific during the Civil War years, when she lived at home in Amherst, Massachusetts, in seclusion. She experimented with poetic rhythms, rhymes, and forms, as well as language and syntax. Her work is characterized by a wittiness and boldness that seem to contrast sharply with the quiet, reclusive life she led.

dictatorship term or office of an absolute ruler, overriding the constitution. (In ancient Rome a dictator was a magistrate invested with emergency powers for six months.) Although dictatorships were common in Latin America during the 19th century, the only European example during this period was the rule of Napoleon III. The crises following World War I produced many dictatorships, including the regimes of Atatürk and Piłsudski (nationalist); Mussolini, Hitler, Primo de Rivera, Franco, and Salazar (all right-wing); and Stalin (Communist).

Diderot Denis 1713–1784. French philosopher. He is closely associated with the Enlightenment, the European intellectual movement for social and scientific progress, and was editor of the enormously influential ◊*Encyclopédie* 1751–80.

Didion Joan 1934– . US author and journalist. She is known for her terse yet eloquent views of modern American society, especially California, where she grew up. Her works include the essays *Slouching toward Bethlehem* 1968 and *The White Album* 1979 and the novels *Run River* 1963, *Play It As It Lays* 1970, *A Book of Common Prayer* 1977, and *Democracy* 1984, which depict the cultural disintegration of modern life. She reported on current events in *Salvador* 1983 and the state of affairs in the city in *Miami* 1987.

Dido Phoenician princess, legendary founder of Carthage, N Africa, who committed suicide to avoid marrying a local prince. In the Latin epic "Aeneid," Virgil represents her death as the result of her desertion by the Trojan hero ◊Aeneas.

diecasting form of ◊casting in which molten metal is injected into permanent metal molds or dies.

Diefenbaker John George 1895–1979. Canadian Progressive Conservative politician, prime minister 1957–63. In 1958, seeking to increase his majority in the House of Commons, Diefenbaker called for new elections; his party won the largest majority in Canadian history. In 1963, however, Diefenbaker refused to accept atomic warheads for missiles supplied by the US, and the Progressive Conservative Party was ousted after losing a no-confidence vote in parliament.

Dien Bien Phu, Battle of decisive battle in the ◊Indochina War at a French fortress in North Vietnam, near the Laotian border. French troops were besieged March 13–May 7, 1954, by the communist Vietminh. The fall of Dien Bien Phu resulted in the end of French control of Indochina.

Diesel Rudolf 1858–1913. German engineer who patented the diesel engine. He began his career as a refrigerator engineer and, like many engineers of the period, sought to develop a more efficient power source than the conventional steam engine. Able to operate with greater efficiency and economy, the diesel engine soon found a ready market.

diesel engine ◊internal-combustion engine that burns a lightweight fuel oil. The diesel engine operates by compressing air until it becomes sufficiently hot to ignite the fuel. It is a piston-in-cylinder engine, like the ◊petrol engine, but only air (rather than an air-and-fuel mixture) is taken into the cylinder on the first piston stroke (down). The piston moves up and compresses the air until it is at a very high temperature. The fuel oil is then injected into the hot air, where it burns, driving the piston down on its power stroke. For this reason the engine is called a compression-ignition engine.

diet a particular selection of food, or the overall intake and selection of food for a particular person or people. A special diet may be recommended for medical reasons, to balance, limit, or increase certain nutrients; undertaken to lose weight, by a reduction in calorie intake or selection of specific foods; or observed on religious, moral, or emotional grounds. An adequate diet is one that fulfills the body's nutritional requirements and gives an energy intake proportional to the person's activity level (the average daily requirement is 2,400 calories for men, less for women, more for active children). In the Third World and in famine or poverty areas some 450 million people in the world subsist on fewer than 1,500 calories per day, whereas in the developed countries the average daily intake is 3,300 calories.

diet meeting or convention of the princes and other dignitaries of the Holy Roman (German) Empire, for example, the Diet of Worms 1521 which met to consider the question of Luther's doctrines and the governance of the empire under Charles V.

Dietrich Marlene (Maria Magdalene) 1904–1992. German-born US actress and singer who appeared with Emil Jannings in both the German and American versions of the film *The Blue Angel* 1930, directed by Josef von Sternberg. She stayed in Hollywood, becoming a US citizen 1937. Her husky, sultry singing voice added to her appeal. Her other films include *Blonde Venus* 1932, *Destry Rides Again* 1939, and *Just a Gigolo* 1978.

Dickens: major works

title	date	well-known characters
The Pickwick Papers	1837	Mr Pickwick, Sam Weller, Mr Snodgrass, Mr Jingle, Mr and Mrs Bardell
Oliver Twist	1838	Oliver Twist, Fagin, Mr Bumble, The Artful Dodger
Nicholas Nickleby	1839	Nicholas Nickleby, Wackford Squeers, Madame Mantalini, Smike, Vincent Crummles
The Old Curiosity Shop	1841	Little Nell, Dick Swiveller, Daniel Quilp
Barnaby Rudge	1841	Simon Tappertit (Sim), Miss Miggs, Gashford
A Christmas Carol	1843	Ebenezer Scrooge, Bob Cratchit, Marley's Ghost, Tiny Tim
Martin Chuzzlewit	1844	Martin Chuzzlewit (Junior), Mr Pecksniff, Mrs Gamp, Tom Pinch
Dombey and Son	1848	Dombey, Paul and Florence Dombey, Edith Granger, James Carker, Major Bagstock
David Copperfield	1850	David Copperfield, Mr Micawber, Mr Dick, Uriah Heep, Little Em'ly, Betsey Trotwood
Bleak House	1853	John Jarndyce, Esther Summerson, Harold Skimpole, Lady Dedlock, Mrs Jellyby
Hard Times	1854	Gradgrind, Tom and Louisa Gradgrind, Josiah Bounderby, Bitzer, Cissy Jupe
Little Dorrit	1857	Amy Dorrit, Flora Finching, Mr Merille
A Tale of Two Cities	1859	Dr Manette, Charles Darnay, Sydney Carton, Jerry Cruncher, Madame Defarge
Great Expectations	1861	Pip, Estella, Miss Havisham, Joe Gargery, Wemmick, Magwitch
Our Mutual Friend	1865	Noddy Boffin, Silas Wegg, Mr Podsnap, Betty Higden, Bradley Headstone, Reginald Wilfer
The Mystery of Edward Drood (unfinished)	1870	Rosa Bud, John Jasper

digestive system
The human digestive system.

digestive system

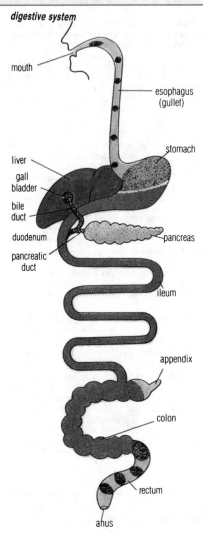

mouth

esophagus (gullet)

stomach

liver

gall bladder

bile duct

duodenum

pancreas

pancreatic duct

ileum

appendix

colon

rectum

anus

diffusion spontaneous and random movement of molecules or particles in a fluid (gas or liquid) from a region in which they are at a high concentration to a region in which they are at a low concentration, until a uniform concentration is achieved throughout. No mechanical mixing or stirring is involved. For instance, if a drop of ink is added to water, its molecules will diffuse until their color becomes evenly distributed throughout.

digestion process whereby food eaten by an animal is broken down physically, and chemically by ◊enzymes, usually in the ◊stomach and ◊intestines, to make the nutrients available for absorption and cell metabolism.

digestive system mouth, stomach, intestine, and associated glands of animals, which are responsible for digesting food. The food is broken down by physical and chemical means in the ◊stomach; digestion is completed, and most nutrients are absorbed in the small intestine; what remains is stored and concentrated into feces in the large intestine. In birds, additional digestive organs are the crop and ◊gizzard.

digit in mathematics, any of the numbers from 0 to 9 in the decimal system. Different bases have different ranges of digits. For example, the hexadecimal system has digits 0 to 9 and A to F, whereas the binary system has two digits (or ◊bits), 0 and 1.

digital in electronics and computing, a term meaning "coded as numbers." A digital system uses two-state, either on/off or high/low voltage pulses, to encode, receive, and transmit information. A *digital display* shows discrete values as numbers (as opposed to an analog signal, such as the continuous sweep of a pointer on a dial).

digital audio tape (DAT) digitally recorded audio tape produced in cassettes that can carry two hours of sound on each side and are about half the size of standard cassettes. DAT players/recorders were developed 1987. Prerecorded cassettes are copy-protected. The first DAT for computer data was introduced 1988.

digital computer computing device that operates on a two-state system, using symbols that are internally coded as binary numbers (numbers made up of combinations of the digits 0 and 1); see ◊computer.

digital data transmission in computing, a way of sending data by converting all signals (whether pictures, sounds, or words) into numeric (normally binary) codes before transmission, then reconverting them on receipt. This virtually eliminates any distortion or degradation of the signal during transmission, storage, or processing.

digitalis drug that increases the efficiency of the heart by strengthening its muscle contractions and slowing its rate. It is derived from the leaves of the common European woodland plant *Digitalis purpurea* (foxglove).

digital recording technique whereby the pressure of sound waves is sampled more than 30,000 times a second and the values converted by computer into precise numerical values. These are recorded and, during playback, are reconverted to sound waves.

dilatation and curettage (D and C) common gynecological procedure in which the cervix (neck of the womb) is widened, or dilated, giving access so that the

differential arrangement of gears in the final drive of a vehicle's transmission system that allows the driving wheels to turn at different speeds when cornering. The differential consists of sets of bevel gears and pinions within a cage attached to the crown wheel. When cornering, the bevel pinions rotate to allow the outer wheel to turn faster than the inner.

differentiation in embryology, the process whereby cells become increasingly different and specialized, giving rise to more complex structures that have particular functions in the adult organism. For instance, embryonic cells may develop into nerve, muscle, or bone cells.

diffraction the slight spreading of a light beam into a pattern of light and dark bands when it passes through a narrow slit or past the edge of an obstruction. A *diffraction grating* is a plate of glass or metal ruled with close, equidistant parallel lines used for separating a wave train such as a beam of incident light into its component frequencies (white light results in a spectrum).

lining of the womb can be scraped away (curettage). It may be carried out to terminate a pregnancy, treat an incomplete miscarriage, discover the cause of heavy menstrual bleeding, or for biopsy.

dill herb *Anethum graveolens* of the carrot family Umbelliferae, whose bitter seeds and aromatic leaves are used for culinary and medicinal purposes.

DiMaggio Joe 1914– . US baseball player with the New York Yankees 1936–51. In 1941 he set a record by getting hits in 56 consecutive games. He was an outstanding fielder, played center field, hit 361 home runs, and had a career average of .325. DiMaggio was married to the actress Marilyn Monroe. He was elected to the Baseball Hall of Fame 1955.

dime novel melodramatic paperback novel of a series started in the US in the 1850s, published by Beadle and Adams of New York, which frequently dealt with Deadwood Dick and his frontier adventures. Authors included Edward L Wheeler, E Z C Judson, Prentiss Ingraham, and J R Coryell. The "Nick Carter" Library added detective stories to the genre. Like British "penny dreadfuls," dime novels attained massive sales and were popular with troops during the American Civil War and World War I.

dimension in science, any directly measurable physical quantity such as mass (M), length (L), and time (T), and the derived units obtainable by multiplication or division from such quantities. For example, acceleration (the rate of change of velocity) has dimensions (LT^{-2}), and is expressed in such units as km s^{-2}. A quantity that is a ratio, such as relative density or humidity, is dimensionless.

diminishing returns, law of in economics, the principle that additional application of one factor of production, such as an extra machine or employee, at first results in rapidly increasing output but eventually yields declining returns, unless other factors are modified to sustain the increase.

Dimitrov Georgi 1882–1949. Bulgarian communist, prime minister from 1946. He was elected a deputy in 1913 and from 1919 was a member of the executive of the Comintern, an international communist organization (see the ◊International). In 1933 he was arrested in Berlin and tried with others in Leipzig for allegedly setting fire to the parliament building (see Reichstag fire). Acquitted, he went to the USSR, where he became general secretary of the Comintern until its dissolution in 1943.

Dinesen Isak 1885–1962. Adopted name of Danish writer Karen ◊Blixen, born Karen Christentze Dinesen.

Dingaan Zulu chief who obtained the throne in 1828 by murdering his predecessor, Shaka, and became notorious for his cruelty. In warfare with the Boer immigrants into Natal he was defeated on Dec 16, 1838—"Dingaan's Day." He escaped to Swaziland, where he was deposed by his brother Mpande and subsequently assassinated.

dingo wild dog of Australia. Descended from domestic dogs brought from Asia by Aborigines thousands of years ago, it belongs to the same species *Canis familiaris* as other domestic dogs. It is reddish brown with a bushy tail, and often hunts at night. It cannot bark.

Dinka member of the Dinka culture from S Sudan. The Dinka, numbering approximately 1 million, are a group of ◊Negroid tribes, primarily cattle herders, and inhabit the lands around the river system that flows into the White Nile. Their language belongs to the Chari-Nile family.

Dinkins David 1927– . Mayor of New York City 1990–94, a Democrat. He won a reputation as a moderate and consensual community politician and was Manhattan borough president before succeeding Edward I Koch to become New York's first black mayor. He lost his reelection bid 1993.

dinosaur (Greek *deinos* "terrible," *sauros* "lizard") any of a group (sometimes considered as two separate orders) of extinct reptiles living between 215 million and 65 million years ago. Their closest living relations are crocodiles and birds, the latter perhaps descended from the dinosaurs. Many species of dinosaur evolved over the millions of years during which they were the dominant large land animals. Most were large (up to 90 ft/27 m), but some were as small as birds and lizards, into which some evolved. Most became extinct 65 million years ago for reasons not fully understood, although many paleontological, astronomical, and ecological theories exist. They never coexisted with the ◊human species, which began to evolve only some 6 million years ago.

Dio Cassius AD 150–235. Roman historian. He wrote, in Greek, a Roman history in 80 books (of which 26 survive), covering the period from the founding of the city to AD 229, including the only surviving account of the invasion of Britain by Claudius 43 BC.

Diocletian Gaius Valerius Diocletianus 245–313. Roman emperor 284–305, when he abdicated in favor of Galerius. He reorganized and subdivided the empire, with two joint and two subordinate emperors, and in 303 initiated severe persecution of Christians.

diode combination of a cold anode and a heated cathode (or the semiconductor equivalent, which incorporates a *p–n* junction). Either device allows the passage of direct current in one direction only, and so is commonly used in a ◊rectifier to convert alternating current (AC) to direct current (DC).

Diogenes c. 412–323 BC. Ascetic Greek philosopher of the ◊Cynic school. He believed in freedom and self-sufficiency for the individual, and that the virtuous life was the simple life; he did not believe in social mores. His writings do not survive.

Dionysius two tyrants of the ancient Greek city of Syracuse in Sicily. *Dionysius the Elder* (432–367 BC) seized power 405 BC. His first two wars with Carthage further extended the power of Syracuse, but in a third (383–378 BC) he was defeated. He was a patron of ◊Plato. He was succeeded by his son, *Dionysius the Younger*, who was driven out of Syracuse by Dion 356; he was tyrant again 353, but in 343 returned to Corinth.

Dionysus in Greek mythology, the god of wine (son of Semele and Zeus), and also of orgiastic excess, who was attended by women called maenads, who were believed to be capable of tearing animals to pieces with their bare hands when under his influence. He was identified with the Roman ◊Bacchus, whose rites were less savage.

Dior Christian 1905–1957. French couturier. He established his own Paris salon 1947 and made an impact with the "New Look"—long, cinch-waisted, and full-skirted—after wartime austerity.

Diouf Abdou 1935– . Senegalese left-wing politician, president from 1980. He became prime minister 1970 under President Leopold Senghor and, on his retirement, succeeded him, being reelected in 1983, 1988, and 1993. His presidency has been characterized by authoritarianism.

dioxin any of a family of over 200 organic chemicals, all of which are heterocyclic hydrocarbons (see cyclic compounds). The term is commonly applied, however, to only one member of the family, 2,3,7,8-tetra-chlorodibenzo-*p*-dioxin (2,3,7,8-TCDD), a highly toxic chemical that occurs, for example, as an impurity in the defoliant Agent Orange, used in the Vietnam War, and sometimes in the weedkiller 2,4,5-T. It has been associated with a disfiguring skin complaint (chloracne), birth defects, miscarriages, and cancer.

diphtheria acute infectious disease in which a membrane forms in the throat (threatening death by ⟡asphyxia), along with the production of a powerful neurotoxin that poisons the system. The organism responsible is a bacterium (*Corynebacterium diphtheriae*). Its incidence has been reduced greatly by immunization.

diplodocus plant-eating sauropod dinosaur that lived about 145 million years ago, the fossils of which have been found in the W US. Up to 88 ft/27 m long, most of which was neck and tail, it weighed about 11 tons. It walked on four elephantine legs, had nostrils on top of the skull, and peglike teeth at the front of the mouth.

diploid having two sets of ⟡chromosomes in each cell. In sexually reproducing species, one set is derived from each parent, the ⟡gametes, or sex cells, of each parent being ⟡haploid (having only one set of chromosomes) due to ⟡meiosis (reduction cell division).

Disney Mickey Mouse, Disney's first and most famous cartoon character, made his debut in Plane Crazy 1928.

diplomacy process by which states attempt to settle their differences through peaceful means such as negotiation or ⟡arbitration. See ⟡foreign relations.

dip, magnetic angle at a particular point on the Earth's surface between the direction of the Earth's magnetic field and the horizontal. It is measured using a *dip circle*, which has a magnetized needle suspended so that it can turn freely in the vertical plane of the magnetic field. In the northern hemisphere the needle dips below the horizontal, pointing along the line of the magnetic field toward its north pole. At the magnetic north and south poles, the needle dips vertically and the angle of dip is 90°.

dipper any of various passerine birds of the family Cinclidae, found in hilly and mountainous regions across Eurasia and North America, where there are clear, fast-flowing streams. It can swim, dive, or walk along the bottom, using the pressure of water on its wings and tail to keep it down, while it searches for insect larvae and other small animals.

The American dipper *Cinclus mexicanus* of W North America, is about 8 in/20 cm long, sooty gray overall, and resembles a wren.

Dirac Paul Adrien Maurice 1902–1984. British physicist who worked out a version of quantum mechanics consistent with special ⟡relativity. The existence of the positron (positive electron) was one of its predictions. He shared the Nobel Prize for Physics 1933 with Austrian physicist Erwin Schrödinger (1887–1961).

direct current (DC) electric current that flows in one direction, and does not reverse its flow as ⟡alternating current does. The electricity produced by a battery is direct current.

disarmament reduction of a country's weapons of war. Most disarmament talks since World War II have been concerned with nuclear-arms verification and reduction, but biological, chemical, and conventional weapons have also come under discussion at the United Nations and in other forums. Attempts to limit the arms race (initially between the US and the USSR and since 1992 between the US and Russia) have included the ⟡Strategic Arms Limitation Talks (SALT) of the 1970s and the ⟡Strategic Arms Reduction Talks (START) of the 1980s–90s.

discharge in a river, the volume of water passing a certain point per unit of time. It is usually expressed in cubic meters per second (cumecs). The discharge of a particular river channel may be calculated by multiplying the channel's cross-sectional area (in square meters) by the velocity of the water (in meters per second).

discharge tube device in which a gas conducting an electric current emits visible light. It is usually a glass tube from which virtually all the air has been removed (so that it "contains" a near vacuum), with electrodes at each end. When a high-voltage current is passed between the electrodes, the few remaining gas atoms in the tube (or some deliberately introduced ones) ionize and emit colored light as they conduct the current along the tube. The light originates as electrons change energy levels in the ionized atoms.

disciple follower, especially of a religious leader. The word is used in the Bible for the early followers of Jesus. The 12 disciples closest to him are known as the ⟡apostles.

discount rate the rate that banks are charged to borrow money from the Federal Reserve Bank. One of the tools of ◊monetary policy, the discount rate allows the Federal Reserve System to govern consumer interest rates and the amount of money in circulation.

discrete data data that can take only whole-number or fractional values. The opposite is ◊continuous data, which can take all in-between values. Examples of discrete data include frequency and population data. However, measurements of time and other dimensions can give rise to continuous data.

discrimination distinction made (social, economic, political, legal) between individuals or groups such that one has the power to treat the other unfavorably. *Negative discrimination*, often based on ◊stereotype, includes anti-Semitism, apartheid, caste, racism, sexism, and slavery. *Positive discrimination*, or "affirmative action," is sometimes practiced in an attempt to counteract the effects of previous long-term discrimination. Minorities and, in some cases, majorities have been targets for discrimination.

discus circular disk thrown by athletes who rotate the body to gain momentum from within a circle 8 ft/2.5 m in diameter. The men's discus weighs 4.4 lb/2 kg and the women's 2.2 lb/1 kg. Discus throwing was a competition in ancient Greece at gymnastic contests, such as those of the Olympic Games. It is an event in the modern Olympics and athletics meetings.

disease any condition that impairs the normal state of an organism, and usually alters the functioning of one or more of its organs or systems. A disease is usually characterized by a set of specific symptoms and signs, although these may not always be apparent to the sufferer. Diseases may be inborn (see ◊congenital disease) or acquired through infection, injury, or other cause. Many diseases have unknown causes.

disinvestment withdrawal of investments in a country for political reasons. The term is also used in economics to describe non-replacement of stock as it wears out.

disk in computing, a common medium for storing large volumes of data (an alternative is ◊magnetic tape.) A magnetic disk is rotated at high speed in a disk-drive unit as a read/write (playback or record) head passes over its surfaces to record or "read" the magnetic variations that encode the data. There are several types, including ◊floppy disks, ◊hard disks, and ◊CD-ROM.

disk drive mechanical device that reads data from and writes data to a magnetic ◊disk.

disk formatting in computing, preparing a blank magnetic disk so that data can be stored on it. Data are recorded on a disk's surface on circular tracks, each of which is divided into a number of sectors. In formatting a disk the computer's operating system adds control information such as track and sector numbers, which enables the data stored to be accessed correctly by the disk-drive unit.

Disney Walt (Walter Elias) 1901–1966. US filmmaker who became a pioneer of family entertainment. He and his brother established an animation studio in Hollywood in 1923, and his first Mickey Mouse animated cartoon (*Plane Crazy*) appeared in black and white 1928. *Steamboat Willie* 1928 was his first Mickey Mouse cartoon in color. He developed the "Silly Symphony," a type of cartoon based on the close association of music with the visual image, such as *Fantasia* 1940. His many feature-length cartoons include *Snow White and the Seven Dwarfs* 1938 (his first), *Pinocchio* 1939, *Dumbo* 1941, *Bambi* 1942, *Cin-*

Disraeli *As prime minister under Queen Victoria, Benjamin Disraeli combined the ideals of "church, crown and national greatness" with a radical concern about poverty.*

derella 1950, *Alice in Wonderland* 1952, and *Peter Pan* 1953. Published materials such as books, magazines, comic books, and records accompanied his films and helped make his animated characters beloved throughout the world.

dispersion in optics, the splitting of white light into a spectrum; for example, when it passes through a prism or a diffraction grating. It occurs because the prism (or grating) bends each component wavelength to a slightly different extent. The natural dispersion of light through raindrops creates a rainbow.

Disraeli Benjamin, Earl of Beaconsfield 1804–1881. British Conservative politician and novelist. Elected to Parliament 1837, he was chancellor of the Exchequer under Lord ◊Derby 1852, 1858–59, and 1866–68, and prime minister 1868 and 1874–80. His imperialist policies brought India directly under the crown, and he was personally responsible for purchasing control of the Suez Canal. The central Conservative Party organization is his creation. His popular, political novels reflect an interest in social reform and include *Coningsby* 1844 and *Sybil* 1845.

Entering Parliament in 1837 after four unsuccessful attempts, he was laughed at as a dandy; when his maiden speech was shouted down, he said: "The time will come when you will hear me."

Excluded from Peel's government of 1841–46, Disraeli formed his Young England group to keep a critical eye on Peel's Conservatism and gradually came to be recognized as the leader of the Conservative Party in the Commons. During the next 20 years the Conservatives formed short-lived minority governments in 1852, 1858–59, and 1866–68, with Lord Derby as prime minister and Disraeli as chancellor of the Exchequer and leader of the Commons. On Lord Derby's retirement in 1868 Disraeli became prime minister, but a few months later he was defeated by William Gladstone in a general election. In 1874 Disraeli took office for the second time. Some useful reform measures were carried, but the outstanding feature of the government's policy was its imperialism: Disraeli purchased from the Khedive of Egypt a controlling interest in the Suez Canal, conferred on the Queen the title of Empress of India, and sent the Prince of Wales on the first royal tour of that country.

Dissenter former name for a Protestant refusing to conform to the established Christian church. For example, Baptists, Presbyterians, and Independents (now known as Congregationalists) were Dissenters.

Djibouti
Republic of
(*Jumhouriyya Djibouti*)

area 8,955 sq mi/23,200 sq km
capital (and chief port) Djibouti
cities Tadjoura, Obock, Dikhil
physical mountains divide an inland plateau from a coastal plain; hot and arid
features terminus of railroad link with Ethiopia; Lac Assal salt lake is the second lowest point on Earth (-471 ft/-144 m)
head of state and government Hassan Gouled Aptidon from 1977

political system authoritarian nationalism
political party People's Progress Assembly (RPP), nationalist
exports acts mainly as a transit port for Ethiopia
currency Djibouti franc
population (1992) 557,000 (Issa 47%, Afar 37%, European 8%, Arab 6%); growth rate 3.4% p.a.
life expectancy 50
languages French (official), Somali, Afar, Arabic
religion Sunni Muslim
literacy 20% (1988)
GDP $378 million (1987); $1,016 per head

chronology
1884 Annexed by France as part of French Somaliland.
1967 French Somaliland became the French Territory of the Afars and the Issas.
1977 Independence achieved from France; Hassan Gouled was elected president.
1979 All political parties combined to form the People's Progress Assembly (RPP).
1981 New constitution made RPP the only legal party. Gouled reelected. Treaties of friendship signed with Ethiopia, Somalia, Kenya, and Sudan.
1984 Policy of neutrality reaffirmed.
1987 Gouled reelected for a third term.
1991 Amnesty International accused secret police of brutality.
1992 Djibouti elected member of UN Security Council 1993–95; new constitution approved.
1993 Gouled reelected for a fourth term.

dissident in one-party states, a person intellectually dissenting from the official line. Dissidents have been sent into exile, prison, labor camps, and mental institutions, or deprived of their jobs. In the USSR the number of imprisoned dissidents declined from more than 600 in 1986 to fewer than 100 in 1990, of whom the majority were ethnic nationalists. In China the number of prisoners of conscience increased after the 1989 Tiananmen Square massacre, and in South Africa, despite the release of Nelson Mandela in 1990, numerous political dissidents remained in jail.

distance ratio in a machine, the distance moved by the input force, or effort, divided by the distance moved by the output force, or load. The ratio indicates the movement magnification achieved, and is equivalent to the machine's ◊velocity ratio.

distemper any of several infectious diseases of animals characterized by catarrh, cough, and general weakness. Specifically, it refers to a virus disease in young dogs, also found in wild animals, which can now be prevented by vaccination. In 1988 an allied virus killed over 10,000 common seals in the Baltic and North seas.

distillation technique used to purify liquids or to separate mixtures of liquids possessing different boiling points. *Simple distillation* is used in the purification of liquids (or the separation of substances in solution from their solvents)—for example, in the production of pure water from a salt solution.

distributor device in the ignition system of a piston engine that distributes pulses of high-voltage electricity to the spark plugs in the cylinders. The electricity is passed to the plug leads by the tip of a rotor arm, driven by the engine camshaft, and current is fed to the rotor arm from the ignition coil. The distributor also houses the contact point or breaker, which opens and closes to interrupt the battery current to the coil, thus triggering the high-voltage pulses. With electronic ignition it is absent.

District of Columbia seat of the federal government of the US, conterminous with the city of Washington, DC; area 69 sq mi/179 sq km. A rectangle along the Potomac River, donated by Maryland and Virginia, was selected as the federal seat of government 1791. For many years the District of Columbia included other local entities besides Washington. At the request of its residents, the portion donated by Virginia was returned to the state 1846, thus confining the District of Columbia to the E shore of the Potomac River. Residents elect a mayor and city council and a nonvoting delegate to the US Congress.

diuretic any drug that rids the body of fluid accumulated in the tissues by increasing the output of urine by the kidneys. It may be used in the treatment of heart disease, high blood pressure, kidney or liver disease, and some endocrine disorders. A potassium supplement is prescribed where potassium loss would be dangerous.

diverticulitis inflammation of diverticula (pockets of herniation) in the large intestine. It is usually controlled by diet and antibiotics.

dividend in business, the amount of money that company directors decide should be taken out of net profits for distribution to stockholders. It is usually declared as a percentage or fixed amount per share.

Most companies pay dividends quarterly; others once a year.

divination art of ascertaining future events or eliciting other hidden knowledge by supernatural or nonrational means. Divination played a large part in the ancient civilizations of the Egyptians, Greeks (see ◊oracle), Romans, and Chinese (see ◊*I Ching*), and is still practiced throughout the world.

Divine Comedy, The epic poem 1307–21 by Dante Alighieri, describing a journey through Hell, Purgatory, and Paradise. The poet Virgil is Dante's guide through Hell and Purgatory; to each of the three realms, or circles, Dante assigns historical and contemporary personages according to their moral (and also political) worth. In Paradise Dante finds his lifelong love Beatrice. The poem makes great use of symbolism and allegory, and influenced many English writers including Milton, Byron, Shelley, and T S Eliot.

Divine Light Mission religious movement founded in India in 1960, which gained a prominent following in the US in the 1970s. It proclaims *Guru Maharaj Ji* as the present age's successor to the gods or religious leaders Krishna, Buddha, Jesus, and Mohammed. He is believed to be able to provide his followers with the knowledge required to attain salvation.

divine right of kings Christian political doctrine that hereditary monarchy is the system approved by God, hereditary right cannot be forfeited, monarchs are accountable to God alone for their actions, and rebellion against the lawful sovereign is therefore blasphemous.

diving the sport of entering the water either from a springboard (3 ft/1 m or 10 ft/3 m) above the water, or from a platform (33 ft/10 m) above the water. Various differing starts are adopted, facing forward or backward, and somersaults, twists, and other positions or combinations thereof are performed in midair before entering the water. Pool depths of 20 ft/6 m are needed for high or platform diving, but 10 ft/3 m-deep pools may accommodate 1-or-3-meter-diving. Points are awarded and the level of difficulty of each dive is used as a multiplying factor.

diving apparatus any equipment used to enable a person to spend time underwater. Diving bells were in use in the 18th century, the diver breathing air trapped in a bell-shaped chamber. This was followed by cumbersome diving suits in the early 19th century. Complete freedom of movement came with the ◊aqualung, invented by Jacques ◊Cousteau in the early 1940s. For work at greater depths the technique of saturation diving was developed in the 1970s by which divers live for a week or more breathing a mixture of helium and oxygen at the pressure existing on the seabed where they work (as in tunnel building).

division of labor the separation of tasks in processing or producing goods, especially in industrial or factory settings, but also in traditional societies where males and females perform gender-related tasks (a sexual division of labor). See also ◊factory system.

divorce legal dissolution of a lawful marriage. It is distinct from an annulment, which is a legal declaration that the marriage was invalid. The ease with which a divorce can be obtained in different countries varies considerably and is also affected by different religious practices.

Dix Dorothea Lynde 1802–1887. US educator and medical reformer. From 1841 she devoted herself to a campaign for the rights of the mentally ill, helping to improve conditions and treatment in public institutions for the insane in the US, Canada, and Japan. During the American Civil War 1861–65, she served as superintendent of nurses.

Dixieland jazz name given to a jazz style that originated in New Orleans in the early 20th century and worked its way up the Mississippi. It is characterized by improvisation and the playing back and forth of the cornet, trumpet, clarinet, and trombone. The steady background beat is supplied by the piano, bass, and percussion instrument players, who also have their turns to solo. It is usually played by bands of four to

DNA How the DNA molecule divides.

1 original double helix
2 forms ladder
3 unzips
4 new bases join onto opened zip teeth
5 two identical double strands

Key
S sugars G guanine
P phosphates A adenine
C cytosine T thymine

eight members. Noted Dixieland musicians were King Oliver, Jelly Roll ◊Morton, and Louis ◊Armstrong.

Djakarta variant spelling of ◊Jakarta, the capital of Indonesia.

Djibouti country on the E coast of Africa, at the S end of the Red Sea, bounded E by the Gulf of Aden, SE by Somalia, and S and W by Ethiopia, and N by Eritrea.

Djibouti chief port and capital of the Republic of Djibouti, on a peninsula 149 mi/240 km SW of Aden and 351 mi/565 km NE of Addis Ababa; population (1988) 290,000.

DNA (*deoxyribonucleic acid*) complex giant molecule that contains, in chemically coded form, all the information needed to build, control, and maintain a living organism. DNA is a ladderlike double-stranded nucleic acid that forms the basis of genetic inheritance in all organisms, except for a few viruses that have only ◊RNA. In organisms other than bacteria it is organized into ◊chromosomes and contained in the cell nucleus.

Dnepropetrovsk city in Ukraine, on the right bank of the river Dnieper; population (1987) 1,182,000. It is the center of a major industrial region, with iron, steel, chemical, and engineering industries. It is linked with the Dnieper Dam, 37 mi/60 km downstream.

Dnieper or **Dnepr** river rising in the Smolensk region of Russia and flowing S through Belarus and Ukraine to enter the Black Sea E of Odessa; total length 1,400 mi/2,250 km.

Dobermann or **Dobermann pinscher** smooth-coated dog with a docked tail, much used as a guard dog. It stands up to 2.2 ft/70 cm tall, has a long head with a flat, smooth skull, and is often black with brown markings. It takes its name from the man who bred it in 19th-century Germany.

Dobzhansky Theodosius 1900–1975. US geneticist of Ukrainian origin. A pioneer of modern genetics and evolutionary theory, he showed that genetic variability between individuals of the same species is very high and that this diversity is vital to the process of evolution. His book *Genetics and the Origin of Species* was published in 1937.

Doctorow E(dgar) L(awrence) 1931– . US writer. He is noted for novels in which he weaves history and fiction together. His first novel, *The Book of Daniel* 1971, about the ◊Rosenbergs' trial and execution, won him instant fame. His other works include *Ragtime* 1975, *Loon Lake* 1980, *Lives of the Poets* 1984, *World's Fair* 1985, and *Billy Bathgate* 1989.

document in computing, data associated with a particular application. For example, a **text document** might be produced by a ◊word processor and a **graphics document** might be produced with a ◊CAD package. An **OMR** or **OCR** document is a paper document containing data that can be directly input to the computer using a document reader.

documentation in computing, the written information associated with a computer program or applications package. Documentation is usually divided into two categories: program documentation and user documentation.

dodecahedron regular solid with 12 pentagonal faces and 12 vertices. It is one of the five regular ◊polyhedra, or Platonic solids.

dodecaphonic in music, the ◊twelve-tone system of composition.

Dodgson Charles Lutwidge. Real name of writer Lewis ◊Carroll.

dodo extinct bird *Raphus cucullatus* formerly found on the island of Mauritius, but exterminated before the end of the 17th century. Although related to the pigeons, it was larger than a turkey, with a bulky body and very short wings and tail. Flightless and trusting, it was easy prey to humans.

Dodoma capital (replacing Dar es Salaam 1974) of Tanzania; 3,713 ft/1,132 m above sea level; population (1985) 85,000. It is a center of communications, linked by rail with Dar es Salaam and Kigoma on Lake Tanganyika, and by road with Kenya to the N and Zambia and Malawi to the S.

Doe Samuel Kenyon 1950–1990. Liberian politician and soldier, head of state 1980–90. He seized power in a coup. Having successfully put down an uprising April 1990, Doe was deposed and killed by rebel forces Sept 1990.

dog any carnivorous mammal of the family Canidae, including wild dogs, wolves, jackals, coyotes, and foxes. Specifically, the domestic dog *Canis familiaris*, the earliest animal descended from the wolf or jackal. Dogs were first domesticated over 10,000 years ago, and migrated with humans to all the continents. They have been selectively bred into many different varieties for use as working animals and pets.

doge chief magistrate in the ancient constitutions of Venice and Genoa. The first doge of Venice was appointed 697 with absolute power (modified 1297), and from his accession dates Venice's prominence in history. The last Venetian doge, Lodovico Manin, retired 1797 and the last Genoese doge 1804.

Dōgen 1200–1253. Japanese Buddhist monk, pupil of Eisai; founder of the Sōtō school of Zen. He did not reject study, but stressed the importance of *zazen*, seated meditation, for its own sake.

dogfish any of several small sharks found in the NE Atlantic, Pacific, and Mediterranean.
   The spiny dogfish *Squalus acanthius* of the Pacific and Atlantic grows to about 4 ft/1.2 m long. It is a common subject for dissection in biology laboratories.

dogwood any of a genus *Cornus* of trees and shrubs of the dogwood family (Cornaceae), native to temperate regions of North America and Eurasia. The flowering dogwood *C. florida* of the E US is often cultivated as an ornamental for its beautiful blooms consisting of clusters of small greenish flowers surrounded by four large white or pink petallike ◊bracts.

Doha (Arabic *Ad Dawḥah*) capital and chief port of Qatar; population (1986) 217,000. Industries include oil refining, refrigeration plants, engineering, and food processing. It is the center of vocational training for all the Persian Gulf states.

Doisy Edward 1893–1986. US biochemist. In 1939 he succeeded in synthesizing vitamin K, a compound earlier discovered by Carl ◊Dam, with whom he shared the 1943 Nobel Prize for Medicine.

doldrums area of low atmospheric pressure along the equator, in the intertropical convergence zone where the NE and SE trade winds converge. The doldrums are characterized by calm or very light winds, during which there may be sudden squalls and stormy weather. For this reason the areas are avoided as far as possible by sailing ships.

dollar monetary unit of several countries. In the US the dollar, which contains 100 cents, was adopted 1785 and is represented by the symbol "$." US dollars originally were issued as gold or silver coins; today both metal and paper dollars circulate, but paper predominates. Australia, Canada, and Hong Kong are among the other countries that use the dollar unit, but none of these dollars is equivalent in value to the US dollar.

Dollfuss Engelbert 1892–1934. Austrian Christian Socialist politician. He was appointed chancellor in 1932, and in 1933 suppressed parliament and ruled by decree. In Feb 1934 he crushed a protest by the socialist workers by force, and in May Austria was declared a "corporative" state. The Nazis attempted a coup d'état on July 25; the Chancellery was seized and Dollfuss murdered.

foxhound

Pekinese

pug

cocker spaniel

working collie

Labrador retriever

Egyptian greyhound

Jack Russell terrier

Chihuahua

Doberman pinscher

bloodhound

Old English sheepdog

dolphin The bottlenosed dolphin lives in groups of up to 15 individuals.

dolmen prehistoric monument in the form of a chamber built of large stone slabs, roofed over by a flat stone which they support. Dolmens are grave chambers of the Neolithic period, found in Europe and Africa, and occasionally in Asia as far east as Japan.

dolomite white mineral with a rhombohedral structure, calcium magnesium carbonate ($CaMg(CO_3)_2$). The term also applies to a type of limestone rock where the calcite content is replaced by the mineral dolomite. Dolomite rock may be white, gray, brown, or reddish in color, commonly crystalline. It is used as a building material. The region of the Alps known as the Dolomites is a fine example of dolomite formation.

dolphin any of various highly intelligent aquatic mammals of the family Delphinidae, which also includes porpoises. There are about 60 species. The name "dolphin" is generally applied to species having a beaklike snout and slender body, whereas the name "porpoise" is reserved for the smaller species with a blunt snout and stocky body. Dolphins use sound (echolocation) to navigate, to find prey, and for communication.

Domagk Gerhard 1895–1964. German pathologist, discoverer of antibacterial sulfonamide drugs. He found in 1932 that a coal-tar dye called Prontosil red contains chemicals with powerful antibacterial properties. Sulfanilamide became the first of the sulfonamide drugs, used before ◊antibiotics were discovered to treat a wide range of conditions, including pneumonia and septic wounds. Domagk was awarded the 1939 Nobel Prize for Physiology and Medicine.

dome a geologic feature that is the reverse of a basin. It consists of anticlinally folded rocks that dip in all directions from a central high point, like an inverted but usually irregular cup.

Domenichino real name Domenico Zampieri 1582–1641. Italian Baroque painter and architect, active in Bologna, Naples, and Rome. He began as an assistant to the ◊Carracci family of painters and continued the early Baroque style in, for example, frescoes 1624–28 in the choir of S Andrea della Valle, Rome.

Dome of the Rock building in Jerusalem dating from the 7th century AD that enshrines the rock from which, in Muslim tradition, Mohammed ascended to heaven on his ◊Night Journey. It stands on the site of the Jewish national Temple and is visited by pilgrims.

Domesday Book record of the survey of England carried out 1086 by officials of William the Conqueror in order to assess land tax and other dues, ascertain the value of the crown lands, and enable the king to estimate the power of his vassal barons. The name is derived from the belief that its judgment was as final as that of Doomsday.

dominance in genetics, the masking of one allele (an alternate form of a gene) by another allele. For example, if a heterozygous person has one allele for blue eyes and one allele for brown eyes, his or her eye color will be brown. The allele for blue eyes is described as ◊recessive and the allele for brown eyes as dominant.

Domingo Placido 1937– . Spanish tenor who excels in romantic operatic roles. He made his debut 1960 as

Dominica
Commonwealth of

area 290 sq mi/751 sq km
capital Roseau, with a deepwater port
cities Portsmouth, Marigot
physical second largest of the Windward Islands, mountainous central ridge with tropical rain forest
features of great beauty, it has mountains of volcanic origin rising to 5,317 ft/1,620 m; Boiling Lake (an effect produced by escaping subterranean gas)
head of state Clarence Seignoret from 1983
head of government Eugenia Charles from 1980
political system liberal democracy
political parties Dominica Freedom Party (DFP), centrist; Labor Party of Dominica (LPD), left-of-center coalition
exports bananas, coconuts, citrus, lime, bay oil
currency Eastern Caribbean dollar, pound sterling, French franc
population (1992) 71,500 (mainly black African in origin, but with a small Carib reserve of some 500); growth rate 1.3% p.a.
life expectancy men 57, women 59
language English (official), but the Dominican patois reflects earlier periods of French rule
media one independent weekly newspaper
religion Roman Catholic 80%
literacy 80%
GDP $91 million (1985); $1,090 per head

chronology
1763 Became British possession.
1978 Independence achieved from Britain. Patrick John, leader of Dominica Labor Party (DLP), elected prime minister.
1980 Dominica Freedom Party (DFP), led by Eugenia Charles, won convincing victory in general election.
1981 Patrick John implicated in plot to overthrow government.
1982 John tried and acquitted.
1985 John retried and found guilty. Regrouping of left-of-center parties resulted in new Labor Party of Dominica (LPD). DFP, led by Eugenia Charles, reelected.
1990 Charles elected to a third term.
1991 Integration into Windward Islands confederation proposed.

Dominican Republic
(*República Dominicana*)

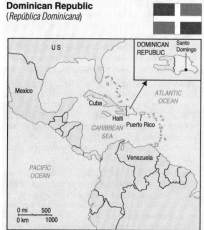

area 18,700 sq mi/48,442 sq km
capital Santo Domingo
cities Santiago de los Caballeros, San Pedro de Macoris
physical comprises eastern two-thirds of island of Hispaniola; central mountain range with fertile valleys
features Pico Duarte 10,417 ft/3,174 m, highest point in Caribbean islands; Santo Domingo is the oldest European city in the western hemisphere
head of state and government Joaquín Ricardo Balaguer from 1986
political system democratic republic
political parties Dominican Revolutionary Party (PRD), moderate, left of center; Christian Social Reform Party

(PRSC), independent socialist; Dominican Liberation Party (PLD), nationalist
exports sugar, gold, silver, tobacco, coffee, nickel
currency peso
population (1992) 7,471,000; growth rate 2.3% p.a.
life expectancy men 61, women 65
language Spanish (official)
religion Roman Catholic 95%
literacy men 78%, women 77% (1985 est)
GDP $4.9 bn (1987); $731 per head

chronology
1492 Visited by Christopher Columbus.
1844 Dominican Republic established.
1930 Military coup established dictatorship of Rafael Trujillo.
1937 Army massacred 19–20,000 Haitians living in the Dominican provinces adjoining the frontier.
1961 Trujillo assassinated.
1962 First democratic elections resulted in Juan Bosch, founder of the PRD, becoming president.
1963 Bosch overthrown in military coup.
1965 US Marines intervened to restore order and protect foreign nationals.
1966 New constitution adopted. Joaquín Balaguer, leader of PRSC, became president.
1978 PRD returned to power, with Silvestre Antonio Guzmán as president.
1982 PRD reelected, with Jorge Blanco as president.
1985 Blanco forced by International Monetary Fund to adopt austerity measures to save the economy.
1986 PRSC returned to power, with Balaguer elected president.
1990 Balaguer reelected by a small majority.
1991 Balaguer announced he would not run again in 1994.

Alfredo in Verdi's *La Traviata*, then spent four years with the Israel National Opera. He sang at the New York City Opera 1965 and has since perfomed diverse roles in opera houses worldwide. In 1986 he starred in the film version of *Otello*.

Dominica island in the E Caribbean, between Guadeloupe and Martinique, the largest of the Windward Islands, with the Atlantic Ocean to the E and the Caribbean Sea to the W.

Dominican order Roman Catholic order of friars founded 1215 by St Dominic. The Dominicans are also known as Friars Preachers, Black Friars, or Jacobins. The order is worldwide and there is also an order of contemplative nuns; the habit is black and white.

Dominican Republic country in the West Indies (E Caribbean), occupying the eastern two-thirds of the island of Hispaniola, with Haiti covering the western third; the Atlantic Ocean is to the E and the Caribbean Sea to the W.

Dominic, St 1170–1221. Founder of the Roman Catholic Dominican order of preaching friars. Feast day Aug 7.

Domino "Fats" (Antoine) 1928– . US rock-and-roll pianist, singer, and songwriter, exponent of the New Orleans style. His hits include "Ain't That a Shame" 1955 and "Blueberry Hill" 1956.

domino theory idea popularized by US president Eisenhower in 1954 that if one country came under communist rule, adjacent countries were likely to fall to communism as well.

Initially used to justify US intervention in SE Asia, the domino theory has also been invoked in reference to Central America.

Domitian Titus Flavius Domitianus AD 51–96. Roman emperor from AD 81. He finalized the conquest of Britain (see ◊Agricola), strengthened the Rhine–Danube frontier, and suppressed immorality as well as freedom of thought in philosophy (see ◊Epictetus) and religion (Christians were persecuted). His reign of terror led to his assassination.

Don river in Russia, rising to the S of Moscow and entering the NE extremity of the Sea of Azov; length 1,180 mi/1,900 km. In its lower reaches the Don is 1 mi/1.5 km wide, and for about four months of the year it is closed by ice. Its upper course is linked with the river Volga by a canal.

Donatello (Donato di Niccolo) 1386–1466. Italian sculptor of the early Renaissance, born in Florence. He was instrumental in reviving the Classical style, as in his graceful bronze statue of the youthful *David* (Bargello, Florence) and his equestrian statue of the general *Gattamelata* 1443 (Padua). The course of Florentine art in the 15th century was strongly influenced by his style.

Donegal mountainous county in Ulster province in the NW of the Republic of Ireland, surrounded on three sides by the Atlantic Ocean; area 1,864 sq mi/ 4,830 sq km; population (1991) 127,900. The county town is Lifford; the market port city of Donegal is at the head of Donegal Bay in the SW. Commercial activities include sheep and cattle raising, tweed and linen manufacture, and some deep-sea fishing. The river Erne hydroelectric project (1952) involved the building of large power stations at Ballyshannon.

Donen Stanley 1924– . US film director, formerly a dancer, who co-directed two of Gene Kelly's best musicals, *On the Town* 1949 and *Singin' in the Rain* 1952.

His other films include *Charade* 1963 and *Two for the Road* 1968.

Donetsk city in Ukraine; capital of Donetsk region, situated in the Donets Basin, a major coal-mining area, 372 mi/600 km SE of Kiev; population (1987) 1,090,000. It has blast furnaces, rolling mills, and other heavy industries.

Dönitz Karl 1891–1980. German admiral, originator of the wolf-pack submarine technique, which sank 15 million metric tons of Allied shipping in World War II. He succeeded Hitler in 1945, capitulated, and was imprisoned 1946–56.

Donizetti Gaetano 1797–1848. Italian composer who created more than 60 operas, including *Lucrezia Borgia* 1833, *Lucia di Lammermoor* 1835, *La Fille du régiment* 1840, *La Favorite* 1840, and *Don Pasquale* 1843. They show the influence of Rossini and Bellini, and are characterized by a flow of expressive melodies.

Don Juan character of Spanish legend, Don Juan Tenorio, supposed to have lived in the 14th century and notorious for his debauchery. Tirso de Molina, Molière, Mozart, Byron, and George Bernard Shaw have featured the legend in their works.

donkey another name for ◊ass.

Donne John 1571–1631. English metaphysical poet. His work consists of love poems, religious poems, verse satires, and sermons, most of which were first published after his death. His religious poems show the same passion and ingenuity as his love poetry. A Roman Catholic in his youth, he converted to the Church of England and finally became dean of St Paul's Cathedral, where he is buried.

Donovan William Joseph 1883–1959. US military leader and public official. Donovan served as US district attorney 1922–24 and as assistant to the US attorney general 1925–29. He was national security adviser to Presidents Hoover and F D Roosevelt and founded the Office of Strategic Services (OSS) 1942. As OSS director 1942–45, Donovan coordinated US intelligence during World War II.

Don Quixote de la Mancha satirical romance by the Spanish novelist Miguel de Cervantes, published in two parts 1605 and 1615. Don Quixote, a self-styled knight, embarks on a series of chivalric adventures accompanied by his servant Sancho Panza. Quixote's imagination leads him to see harmless objects as enemies to be fought, as in his tilting at windmills.

Dooley Thomas Anthony 1927–1961. US medical missionary. He founded Medico, an international welfare organization, 1957, after tending refugees in Vietnam who were streaming south after the partition of the country 1954. As well as Medico, he established medical clinics in Cambodia, Laos, and Vietnam.

Doolittle Hilda. Adopted name *HD* 1886–1961. US poet who went to Europe 1911, and was associated with Ezra Pound and the British writer Richard Aldington (to whom she was married 1913–37) in founding the ◊Imagist school of poetry, advocating simplicity, precision, and brevity. Her work includes the *Sea Garden* 1916 and *Helen in Egypt* 1916.

Doolittle James Harold 1896–1993. US aviation pioneer known for his participation in the development of new aircraft designs and more efficient aircraft fuel. During World War II he saw active service and in 1942 led a daring bombing raid over Tokyo. He later participated in the invasion of North Africa and the intensive bombing of Germany.

Doors, the US psychedelic rock group formed 1965 in Los Angeles by Jim Morrison (1943–1971, vocals), Ray Manzarek (1935– , keyboards), Robby Krieger (1946– , guitar), and John Densmore (1944– , drums). Their first hit was "Light My Fire" from their debut album *The Doors* 1967. They were noted for Morrison's poetic lyrics and flamboyant performance.

doo-wop US pop-music form of the 1950s, a style of harmony singing without instrumental accompaniment or nearly so, almost exclusively by male groups. The name derives from the practice of having the lead vocalist singing the lyrics against a backing of nonsense syllables from the other members of the group. Many of the doo-wop groups were named after birds; for example, the Ravens and the Orioles.

dopamine neurotransmitter, hydroxytyramine $C_8H_{11}NO_2$, an intermediate in the formation of adrenaline. There are special nerve cells (neurons) in the brain that use dopamine for the transmission of nervous impulses. One such area of dopamine neurons lies in the basal ganglia, a region that controls movement. Patients suffering from the tremors of Parkinson's disease show nerve degeneration in this region. Another dopamine brain area lies in the limbic system, a region closely involved with emotional responses. It has been found that schizophrenic patients respond well to drugs that act on limbic dopamine receptors in the brain.

doppelgänger (German "double-goer") apparition of a living person, a person's double, or a guardian spirit. The German composer and writer E T A Hoffman wrote a short story called *Die Doppelgänger* in 1821. English novelist Charles Williams used the idea to great effect in his novel *Descent into Hell* 1937.

Doppler effect change in the observed frequency (or wavelength) of waves due to relative motion between the wave source and the observer. The Doppler effect is responsible for the perceived change in pitch of a siren as it approaches and then recedes, and for the red shift of light from distant stars. It is named after the Austrian physicist Christian Doppler (1803–1853).

Dordogne river in SW France, rising in Puy-de-Dôme *département* and flowing 300 mi/490 km to join the river Garonne 14 mi/23 km N of Bordeaux. It gives its name to a *département* and is a major source of hydroelectric power.

Doré Gustave 1832–1883. French artist, chiefly known as a prolific illustrator, and also active as a painter, etcher, and sculptor. He produced closely worked engravings of scenes from, for example, Rabelais, Dante, Cervantes, the Bible, Milton, and Poe.

Dorian people of ancient Greece. They entered Greece from the north and took most of the Peloponnese from the Achaeans, perhaps destroying the ◊Mycenaean civilization; this invasion appears to have been completed before 1000 BC. Their chief cities were Sparta, Argos, and Corinth.

Doric in Classical architecture, one of the five types of column; see ◊order.

dormancy in botany, a phase of reduced physiological activity exhibited by certain buds, seeds, and spores. Dormancy can help a plant to survive unfavorable conditions, as in annual plants that pass the cold winter season as dormant seeds, and plants that form dormant buds.

dormouse small rodent, of the family Gliridae, with a hairy tail. There are about ten species, living in

Europe, Asia, and Africa. They are arboreal (live in trees) and nocturnal, and they hibernate during winter in cold regions.

Dorset county in SW England
area 1,023 sq mi/2,650 sq km
cities Dorchester (administrative headquarters), Poole, Shaftesbury, Sherborne; resorts: Bournemouth, Lyme Regis, Weymouth
features Chesil Bank, a shingle bank along the coast 11 mi/19 km long; Isle of Purbeck, a peninsula where kaolinite and Purbeck "marble" are quarried, and which includes Corfe Castle and the vacation resort of Swanage; Dorset Downs; Cranborne Chase; rivers Frome and Stour; Maiden Castle; Tank Museum at Royal Armored Corps Center, Bovington, where the cottage of T E ◊Lawrence is a museum
products Wytch Farm is the largest onshore oil field in the UK
population (1987) 649,000
famous people Thomas Hardy, the novelist, born at Higher Bockhampton (Dorchester is "Casterbridge," the heart of Hardy country).

Dorsey Tommy 1905–1956 and Jimmy 1904–1957. US bandleaders, musicians, and composers during the ◊swing era. They worked together in the Dorsey Brothers Orchestra 1934–35 and 1953–56, but led separate bands in the intervening period. The Jimmy Dorsey band was primarily a dance band; the Tommy Dorsey band was more jazz-oriented and featured the singer Frank Sinatra 1940–42. Both Dorsey bands featured in films in the 1940s, and the brothers appeared together in *The Fabulous Dorseys* 1947.

Dortmund industrial center in the ◊Ruhr, Germany, 36 mi/58 km NE of Düsseldorf; population (1988) 568,000. It is the largest mining town of the Westphalian coal field and the southern terminus of the Dortmund–Ems Canal. The enlargement of the Wesel–Datteln Canal 1989, connecting Dortmund to the Rhine River, allows barges to travel between Dortmund and Rotterdam in the Netherlands. Industries include iron, steel, engineering, and brewing.

dory any of several marine fishes of the order Zeiformes. The American John Dory *Zenopsis ocellata*, to 2 ft/60 cm long, is deep-bodied with long spines on the dorsal and ventral fins. It lives in depths of 300 ft/90 m to 1,200 ft/365 m.

DOS (acronym for *disk operating system*) computer ◊operating system specifically designed for use with disk storage; also used as an alternate name for a particular operating system, ◊MS-DOS.

Dos Santos José Eduardo 1942– . Angolan left-wing politician, president from 1979, a member of the People's Movement for the Liberation of Angola (MPLA). By 1989, he had negotiated the withdrawal of South African and Cuban forces, and in 1991 a peace agreement to end the civil war. In Sept 1992 his victory in multiparty elections was disputed by UNITA rebel leader Jonas Savimbi, and fighting resumed.

Dostoevsky Fyodor Mihailovich 1821–1881. Russian novelist. Remarkable for their profound psychological insight, Dostoevsky's novels have greatly influenced Russian writers, and since the beginning of the 20th century have been increasingly influential abroad. In 1849 he was sentenced to four years' hard labor in Siberia, followed by army service, for printing socialist propaganda. *The House of the Dead* 1861 recalls his prison experiences, followed by his major works *Crime and Punishment* 1866, *The Idiot* 1868–69, and *The Brothers Karamazov* 1880.

Dothan city in the SE of Alabama, SE of Montgomery; seat of Houston County; population (1990) 53,589. Its industries include fertilizer, clothing, furniture, vegetable oils, and hosiery. It is an agricultural and livestock marketing center.

Douala or *Duala* chief port and industrial center (aluminium, chemicals, textiles, pulp) of Cameroon, on the Wouri river estuary; population (1981) 637,000. Known as Kamerunstadt until 1907, it was capital of German Cameroon 1885–1901.

double bass large bowed four-stringed musical instrument, the bass of the ◊violin family, tuned in fourths, and descended from the violone of the ◊viol family.

Doubleday Abner 1819–1893. American Civil War military leader and reputed inventor of baseball. He served as major general in the Shenandoah Valley campaign and at the Battles of Bull Run and Antietam 1862, and Gettysburg 1863. He retired from active service 1873. In an investigation into the origins of baseball 1907, testimony was given that Doubleday invented the game 1839 in Cooperstown, New York, a claim refuted by sports historians ever since.

dough mixture consisting primarily of flour, water, and yeast, which is used in the manufacture of bread.

Douglas Kirk. Adopted name of Issur Danielovitch Demsky 1916– . US film actor. Usually cast as a dynamic and intelligent hero, as in *Spartacus* 1960, he was a major star of the 1950s and 1960s in such films as *Ace in the Hole* 1951, *The Bad and the Beautiful* 1953, *Lust for Life* 1956, *The Vikings* 1958, *Seven Days in May* 1964, and *The War Wagon* 1967. He continues to act and produce, along with his son Michael Douglas.

Douglas Michael 1944– . US film actor and producer. One of the biggest box-office draws of the late 1980s and 1990s, Douglas won an Academy Award for his portrayal of a ruthless corporate raider in *Wall Street* 1987. His acting range includes both romantic and heroic leads in films such as *Romancing the Stone* 1984 and *Jewel of the Nile* 1985, both of which he produced. Among his other films are *Fatal Attraction* 1987 and *Basic Instinct* 1991.

Douglas Stephen Arnold 1813–1861. US politician. He served in the US House of Representatives 1843–47 and as US senator from Illinois 1847–61. An active Democrat, he urged a compromise on slavery, and debated Abraham Lincoln during the 1858 Senate race, winning that election. After losing the 1860 presidential race to Lincoln, Douglas pledged his loyal support to the latter's administration 1861–65.

Douglas fir any of some six species of coniferous evergreen tree of the family Pinaceae. The most common is *Pseudotsuga menziesii*, native to W North America and E Asia. It grows 200–300 ft/60–90 m, has long, flat, spirally arranged needles and hanging cones, and produces hard, strong timber. *P. glauca* has shorter, bluish needles and grows to 100 ft/30 m in mountainous areas.

Douglas-Home Alec Douglas-Home, Baron Home of the Hirsel 1903– . British Conservative politician. He was foreign secretary 1960–63, and succeeded Harold Macmillan as prime minister 1963. He renounced his peerage (as 14th Earl of Home) to fight (and lose) the general election 1964, and resigned as party leader 1965. He was again foreign secretary 1970–74, when he received a life peerage. The playwright William Douglas-Home was his brother.

Douglass Frederick 1817–1895. US antislavery campaigner active during the American Civil War 1861–65. He issued a call to blacks to take up arms against the South and helped organize two black regiments. After the Civil War, he held several US government posts, including minister to Haiti 1889–91. He published appeals for full civil rights for blacks and also campaigned for women's suffrage.

Doulton Henry 1820–1897. English ceramicist. He developed special wares for the chemical, electrical, and building industries, and established the world's first stoneware-drainpipe factory 1846. From 1870 he created art pottery and domestic tablewares in Lambeth, S London, and Burslem, near Stoke-on-Trent.

Douro (Spanish *Duero*) river rising in N central Spain and flowing through N Portugal to the Atlantic at Porto; length 500 mi/800 km. Navigation at the river mouth is hindered by sandbars. There are hydroelectric installations. Vineyards (port and Mateus rosé) are irrigated with water from the river.

dove another name for ◊pigeon.

Dover city in SE New Hampshire, on the Cocheco River, NW of Portsmouth; seat of Strafford County; population (1990) 25,000. Industries include lumber, electronics, rubber, and aluminum products.

Dover capital of Delaware, located in the central part of the state, on the St Jones River, S of Wilmington; population (1990) 27,600. Industries include synthetic materials, adhesives, latex, resins, chemicals, food products, and space equipment.

Dover, Strait of (French *Pas-de-Calais*) stretch of water separating England from France, and connecting the English Channel with the North Sea. It is about 22 mi/35 km long and 21 mi/34 km wide at its narrowest part. It is one of the world's busiest sea lanes.

Dow Jones average New York Stock Exchange index, the most widely used indicator of US stock market prices. The average (no longer simply an average but today calculated to take into account changes in the constituent companies) is based on prices of 30 major companies, such as IBM and Walt Disney. It was first compiled 1884 by Charles Henry Dow, cofounder of Dow Jones & Co., publishers of the *Wall Street Journal.*

Down county in SE Northern Ireland, facing the Irish Sea on the E; area 953 sq mi/2,470 sq km; population (1981) 339,200. To the S are the Mourne Mountains, to the E Strangford sea lough. The county town is Downpatrick; the main industry is dairying.

Down syndrome chromosomal abnormality that manifests itself by slowing the person's mental abilities and motor skills; the leading clinical cause of mental disabilities. The incidence is approximately 1 in every 800 to 1,000 live births, and it has no predetermination to race, sex, or national origin. The extra chromosome material can come from either the mother or the father. With special education, these children can reach a level, in many cases, on a par with their non-disabled peers, but may do so at a slower pace. The syndrome is named after English physician J L H Down (1828–1896).

dowry property or money given by the bride's family to the groom or his family as part of the marriage agreement; the opposite of ◊bridewealth. In 1961 dowries were made illegal in India; however, in 1992 the Indian government reported more than 15,000 murders or suicides between 1988 and 1991 that were a direct result of insufficient dowries.

dowsing ascertaining the presence of water or minerals beneath the ground with a forked twig or pendulum. Unconscious muscular action by the dowser is thought to move the twig, usually held with one fork in each hand, possibly in response to a local change in the pattern of electrical forces. The ability has been known since at least the 16th century and, though not widely recognized by science, it has been used commercially and in archeology.

Doyle Arthur Conan 1859–1930. British writer, creator of the detective Sherlock Holmes and his assistant Dr Watson, who first appeared in *A Study in Scarlet* 1887 and featured in a number of subsequent stories, including *The Hound of the Baskervilles* 1902. Conan Doyle also wrote historical romances (*Micah Clarke* 1889 and *The White Company* 1891) and the scientific romance *The Lost World* 1912.

Drabble Margaret 1939– . British writer. Her novels include *The Millstone* 1966 (filmed as *The Touch of Love*), *The Middle Ground* 1980, *The Radiant Way* 1987, and *A Natural Curiosity* 1989. She edited the 1985 edition of the *Oxford Companion to English Literature.*

Draco 7th century BC. Athenian politician, the first to codify the laws of the Athenian city-state. These were notorious for their severity; hence *draconian*, meaning particularly harsh.

Draco in astronomy, a large but faint constellation, representing a dragon coiled around the north celestial pole. The star Alpha Draconis (Thuban) was the pole star 4,800 years ago.

Dracula in the novel *Dracula* 1897 by Bram ◊Stoker, the caped count who, as a ◊vampire, drinks the blood of beautiful women. The original Dracula is thought to have been Vlad Țepeș, or Vlad the Impaler, ruler of medieval Wallachia, who used to impale his victims and then mock them.

draft compulsory military service; also known as ◊conscription.

drag resistance to motion a body experiences when passing through a fluid—gas or liquid. The aerodynamic drag aircraft experience when traveling through the air represents a great waste of power, so they must be carefully shaped, or streamlined, to reduce drag to a minimum. Automobiles benefit from ◊streamlining, and aerodynamic drag is used to slow down spacecraft returning from space. Boats traveling through water experience hydrodynamic drag on their hulls, and the fastest vessels are ◊hydrofoils, whose hulls lift out of the water while cruising.

dragon Euro-Asian mythical reptilian beast, often portrayed as breathing fire. The name is popularly given to various sorts of lizard. These include the flying dragon *Draco volans* of SE Asia; the komodo dragon *Varanus komodoensis* of Indonesia, at over 10 ft/3 m the largest living lizard; and some Australian lizards with bizarre spines or frills.

dragonfly any of numerous insects of the order Odonata, including the damselfly. They all have long narrow bodies, two pairs of almost equal-sized, glassy wings with a network of veins; short, bristlelike antennae; powerful, "toothed" mouthparts; and very large compound eyes which may have up to 30,000 facets. They hunt other insects by sight, both as adults and as aquatic nymphs.

dragoon mounted soldier who carried an infantry weapon such as a "dragon," or short musket, as used by the French army in the 16th century. The name was retained by some later regiments after the original meaning became obsolete.

drag racing motor sport popular in the US. High-powered single-seater automobiles with large rear and small front wheels are timed over a 440 yd/402.2 m strip. Speeds of up to 280 mph/450 kph have been attained.

Drake Francis *c.* 1545–1596. English buccaneer and explorer. Having enriched himself as a pirate against Spanish interests in the Caribbean 1567–72, he was sponsored by Elizabeth I for an expedition to the Pacific, sailing around the world 1577–80 in the *Golden Hind*, robbing Spanish ships as he went. This was the second circumnavigation of the globe (the first was by the Portuguese explorer Ferdinand Magellan). Drake also helped to defeat the Spanish Armada 1588 as a vice admiral in the *Revenge*.

drama in theater, any play performed by actors for an audience. The term is also used collectively to group plays into historical or stylistic periods—for example, Greek drama, Restoration drama—as well as referring to the whole body of work written by a dramatist for performance. Drama is distinct from literature in that it is a performing art open to infinite interpretation, the product not merely of the playwright but also of the collaboration of director, designer, actors, and technical staff. See also ◊comedy, ◊tragedy, ◊mime, and pantomime.

Dravidian group of non-Indo-European peoples of the Deccan region of India and in N Sri Lanka. The Dravidian language family is large, with about 20 languages spoken in S India; the main ones are Tamil, which has a literary tradition 2,000 years old; Kanarese; Telugu; Malayalam; and Tulu.

Dreadnought class of battleships built for the British navy after 1905 and far superior in speed and armaments to anything then afloat. The first modern battleship to be built, it was the basis of battleship design for more than 50 years. The first Dreadnought was launched 1906, with armaments consisting entirely of big guns.

dream series of events or images perceived through the mind during sleep. Their function is unknown, but Sigmund ◊Freud saw them as wish fulfillment (nightmares being failed dreams prompted by fears of "repressed" impulses). Dreams occur in periods of rapid eye movement (REM) by the sleeper, when the cortex of the brain is approximately as active as in waking hours. Dreams occupy about a fifth of sleeping time.

Drenthe low-lying northern province of the Netherlands
area 1,027 sq mi/2,660 sq km
capital Assen
cities Emmen, Hoogeveen
physical fenland and moors; well-drained clay and peat soils
products livestock, arable crops, horticulture, petroleum
population (1988) 437,000
history governed in the Middle Ages by provincial nobles and by bishops of Utrecht, Drenthe was eventually acquired by Charles V of Spain 1536. It developed following land drainage initiated in the mid-18th century and was established as a separate province of the Netherlands 1796.

Dresden capital of the state of Saxony, Germany; population (1990) 520,000. Industries include chemicals, machinery, glassware, and musical instruments. It was one of the most beautiful German cities until its devastation by Allied fire-bombing 1945. Dresden county has an area of 2,602 sq mi/6,740 sq km and a population of 1,772,000.

Dreyer Carl Theodor 1889–1968. Danish film director. His wide range of films include the austere silent classic *La Passion de Jeanne d'Arc/The Passion of Joan of Arc* 1928 and the Expressionist horror film *Vampyr* 1932, after the failure of which Dreyer made no full-length films until *Vredens Dag/Day of Wrath* 1943. His two late masterpieces are *Ordet/The Word* 1955 and *Gertrud* 1964.

Dreyfus Alfred 1859–1935. French army officer, victim of miscarriage of justice, anti-Semitism, and coverup. Employed in the War Ministry, in 1894 he was accused of betraying military secrets to Germany, court-martialled, and sent to the penal colony on ◊Devil's Island, French Guiana. When his innocence was discovered 1896 the military establishment tried to conceal it, and the implications of the Dreyfus affair were passionately discussed in the press until he was exonerated in 1906.

drilling common woodworking and metal machinery process that involves boring holes with a drill ◊bit. The commonest kind of drill bit is the fluted drill, which has spiral grooves around it to allow the cut material to escape. In the oil industry, rotary drilling is used to bore oil wells. The drill bit usually consists of a number of toothed cutting wheels, which grind their way through the rock as the drill pipe is turned, and mud is pumped through the pipe to lubricate the bit and flush the ground-up rock to the surface.

Dreyfus French army officer Alfred Dreyfus, imprisoned on spurious charges of espionage.

dromedary The dromedary, domesticated since 400 BC, is superbly adapted for life in hot, dry climates.

driver in computing, a program that controls a peripheral device. Every device connected to the computer needs a driver program. The driver ensures that communication between the computer and the device is successful.

dromedary variety of Arabian ◊camel. The dromedary or one-humped camel has been domesticated since 400 BC. During a long period without water, it can lose up to one-quarter of its body weight without ill effects.

drug abuse the abuse of narcotic and hallucinogenic substances and stimulants.

drug, generic any drug produced without a brand name that is identical to a branded product. Usually generic drugs are produced when the patent on a branded drug has expired, and are cheaper than their branded equivalents.

Druidism religion of the Celtic peoples of the pre-Christian British Isles and Gaul. The word is derived from Greek *drus* "oak." The Druids regarded this tree as sacred; one of their chief rites was the cutting of mistletoe from it with a golden sickle. They taught the immortality of the soul and a reincarnation doctrine, and were expert in astronomy. The Druids are thought to have offered human sacrifices.

drum percussion instrument, essentially a piece of skin (parchment, plastic, or nylon) stretched over a resonator and struck with a stick or the hands; one of the oldest instruments. Electronic drums, first marketed 1980, are highly touch- and force-sensitive and can also be controlled by computer.

drumlin geologic feature formed in formerly glaciated areas. It consists of long, streamlined hills formed from glacial till or unstratified glacial drift of clay, sand, boulders, and gravel. A drumlin's long axis is oriented in the direction of glacial flow, and its blunt nose points upstream, with the gentler slope trailing off downstream.

Druse or *Druze* religious sect in the Middle East of some 500,000 people. They are monotheists, preaching that the Fatimid caliph al-Hakim (996–1021) is God; their scriptures are drawn from the Bible, the Koran, and Sufi allegories. Druse militia groups form one of the three main factions involved in the Lebanese civil war (the others are Amal Shiite Muslims and Christian Maronites). The Druse military leader (from the time of his father's assassination 1977) is Walid Jumblatt.

Dryden John 1631–1700. English poet and dramatist, noted for his satirical verse and for his use of the heroic couplet. His poetry includes the verse satire *Absalom and Achitophel* 1681, *Annus Mirabilis* 1667, and "St Cecilia's Day" 1687. Plays include the comedy *Mar-*

riage à la Mode 1672 and *All for Love* 1678, a reworking of Shakespeare's *Antony and Cleopatra*.

dry ice solid carbon dioxide (CO_2), used as a refrigerant. At temperatures above −110.2°F/−79°C, it sublimes (turns into vapor without passing through a liquid stage) to gaseous carbon dioxide.

dry rot infection of timber in damp conditions by fungi, such as *Merulius lacrymans*, that form a thread-like surface. Whitish at first, the fungus later reddens as reproductive spores are formed. Fungoid tentacles also enter the fabric of the timber, rendering it dry-looking and brittle. Dry rot spreads rapidly through a building.

Dual Entente alliance between France and Russia that lasted from 1893 until the Bolshevik Revolution of 1917.

dualism in philosophy, the belief that reality is essentially dual in nature. The French philosopher René ◊Descartes, for example, referred to thinking and material substance. These entities interact but are fundamentally separate and distinct.

Dualism is contrasted with ◊monism, the theory that reality is made up of only one substance.

Duarte José Napoleon 1925–1990. El Salvadorean politician, president 1980–82 and 1984–88. He was mayor of San Salvador 1964–70, and was elected president 1972, but exiled by the army 1982. On becoming president again 1984, he sought a negotiated settlement with the left-wing guerrillas 1986, but resigned on health grounds.

Dubai one of the ◊United Arab Emirates.

du Barry Marie Jeanne Bécu, Comtesse 1743–1793. Mistress of ◊Louis XV of France from 1768. At his death 1774 she was banished to a convent, and during the Revolution fled to London. Returning to Paris 1793, she was guillotined.

Dubček Alexander 1921–1992. Czechoslovak politician, chair of the federal assembly 1989–92. He was a member of the Slovak ◊resistance movement during World War II, and became first secretary of the Communist Party 1967–69. He launched a liberalization campaign (called the Prague Spring) that was opposed by the USSR and led to the Soviet invasion of Czechoslovakia 1968. He was arrested by Soviet troops and expelled from the party 1970. In 1989 he gave speeches at prodemocracy rallies, and after the fall of the hardline regime, he was elected speaker of the National Assembly in Prague, a position to which he was reelected 1990. He was fatally injured in an automobile crash Sept 1992.

Dublin (Gaelic *Baile Atha Cliath*) capital and port on the E coast of the Republic of Ireland, at the mouth of the river Liffey, facing the Irish Sea; population (1986 est) 502,700, Greater Dublin (including Dún Laoghaire) 921,000. It is the site of one of the world's largest breweries (Guinness); other industries include textiles, pharmaceuticals, electrical goods, and machine tools.

Du Bois W(illiam) E(dward) B(urghardt) 1868–1963. US educator and social critic. Du Bois was one of the early leaders of the National Association for the Advancement of Colored People (NAACP) and the editor of its journal *Crisis* 1909–32. As a staunch advocate of black American rights, he came into conflict with Booker T ◊Washington opposing the latter's policy of compromise on the issue of slavery.

Dubuffet Jean 1901–1985. French artist. He originated *l'art brut*, "raw or brutal art," in the 1940s. He

used a variety of materials in his paintings and sculptures (plaster, steel wool, straw, and so on) and was inspired by graffiti and children's drawings.

Dubuque city in E central Iowa, NE of Iowa City, just across the Mississippi River from the Wisconsin–Illinois border; population (1990) 57,546. An important port, it has shipbuilding and agricultural marketing facilities; industries include meatpacking, lumber, metals, and machinery.

Duccio di Buoninsegna c. 1255–1319. Italian painter, a major figure in the Sienese school. His greatest work is his altarpiece for Siena Cathedral, the *Maestà* 1308–11; the figure of the Virgin is Byzantine in style, with much gold detail, but Duccio also created a graceful linear harmony in drapery hems, for example, and this proved a lasting characteristic of Sienese style.

Duce (Italian "leader") title bestowed on the fascist dictator Benito ◊Mussolini by his followers and later adopted as his official title.

Duchamp Marcel 1887–1968. US artist, born in France. He achieved notoriety with his *Nude Descending a Staircase* 1912 (Philadelphia Museum of Art), influenced by Cubism and Futurism. An active exponent of ◊Dada, he invented "ready-mades," everyday items like a bicycle wheel on a kitchen stool, which he displayed as works of art.

duck any of several short-legged waterbirds with webbed feet and flattened bills, of the family Anatidae, which also includes the larger geese and swans. Ducks were domesticated for eggs, meat, and feathers by the ancient Chinese and the ancient Maya (see ◊poultry). Most ducks live in fresh water, feeding on worms and insects as well as vegetable matter. They are generally divided into dabbling ducks and diving ducks.

duel fight between two people armed with weapons. A duel is usually fought according to pre-arranged rules with the aim of settling a private quarrel.

due process of law legal principle, dating from the ◊Magna Carta, the charter of rights granted by King John of England 1215, and now enshrined in the fifth and fourteenth amendments to the US Constitution, that no person shall be deprived of life, liberty, or property without due process of law (a fair legal procedure). In the US, the provisions have been given a wide interpretation, to include, for example, the right to representation by an attorney.

Dufourspitze second highest of the alpine peaks, 15,203 ft/4,634 m high. It is the highest peak in the Monte Rosa group of the Pennine Alps on the Swiss-Italian frontier.

Du Fu another name for the Chinese poet Tu Fu.

Dufy Raoul 1877–1953. French painter and designer. He originated a fluent, brightly colored style in watercolor and oils, painting scenes of gaiety and leisure, such as horse racing, yachting, and life on the beach. He also designed tapestries, textiles, and ceramics.

Duisburg river port and industrial city in North Rhine–Westphalia, Germany, at the confluence of the Rhine and Ruhr rivers; population (1987) 515,000. It is the largest inland river port in Europe. Heavy industries include oil refining and the production of steel, copper, zinc, plastics, and machinery.

Dukas Paul (Abraham) 1865–1935. French composer. His orchestral scherzo *L'Apprenti sorcier/The Sorcerer's Apprentice* 1897 is full of the color and energy that characterizes much of his work.

duke highest title in the English peerage. It originated in England 1337, when Edward III created his son Edward, Duke of Cornwall.

dulcimer musical instrument consisting of a shallow soundbox strung with many wires that are struck with small wooden hammers. In Hungary it is called a cimbalom.

Also an oval-shaped stringed instrument of the Appalachian Mountains that is played in the lap or on a surface by plucking the strings with a quill or plectrum.

Dulles John Foster 1888–1959. US lawyer and politician. Senior US adviser at the founding of the United Nations, he largely drafted the Japanese peace treaty of 1951. As secretary of state 1952–59 he was critical of Britain in the ◊Suez Crisis. He was the architect of US ◊Cold War foreign policy, securing ◊SEATO and US intervention in support of South Vietnam following the expulsion of the French in 1954.

Duluth port on Lake Superior; by the mouth of the St Louis River, Minnesota; population (1990) 85,500. It manufactures steel, flour, timber, and dairy products. The westernmost port on the St Lawrence Seaway, Duluth ships iron ore, grain, coal, oil, and timber. Permanent settlement on what had been a fur-trading post began 1852.

Dumas Alexandre 1802–1870. French author, known as Dumas *père* (the father). He is remembered for his romances, the reworked output of a "fiction-factory" of collaborators. They include *Les trois mousquetaires/The Three Musketeers* 1844 and its sequels. Dumas *fils* was his son.

Dumas Alexandre 1824–1895. French author, known as Dumas *fils* (the son of Dumas *père*) and remembered for the play *La Dame aux camélias/The Lady of the Camellias* 1852, based on his own novel and the source of Verdi's opera *La Traviata*.

Du Maurier Daphne 1907–1989. British novelist whose romantic fiction includes *Jamaica Inn* 1936, *Rebecca* 1938, and *My Cousin Rachel* 1951. *Jamaica Inn*, *Rebecca*, and her short story "The Birds" were made into films by the English director Alfred Hitchcock.

dump in computing, the process of rapidly transferring data to external memory or to a printer. It is usually done to help with debugging or as part of an error-recovery procedure.

dumping in international trade, when one country sells goods to another at below marginal cost or at a price below that in its own country. Countries dump to sell off surplus produce or to improve their competitive positions in the recipient country. The practice is deplored by ◊free trade advocates because of the artificial, unfair advantage it yields. Dumping is also used by protectionists to justify retaliatory measures.

Duncan Isadora 1878–1927. US dancer and teacher. An influential pioneer of Modern dance, she adopted an expressive free form, dancing barefoot and wearing a loose tunic, inspired by the ideal of Hellenic beauty. She toured extensively, often returning to Russia after her initial success there 1905.

dune mound or ridge of wind-drifted sand. Loose sand is blown and bounced along by the wind, up the windward side of a dune. The sand particles then fall to rest on the lee side, while more are blown up from the windward side. In this way a dune moves gradually downwind.

Dunne Finley Peter 1867–1936. US humorist and social critic. His fictional character "Mr Dooley," the Irish saloonkeeper and sage, gained a national readership. Written in dialect, Mr Dooley's humorous yet pointed reflections on US politics and society appeared 1892–1915. From 1900 the "Mr Dooley columns" appeared in such national magazines as *Collier's* and *Metropolitan*.

duodecimal system system of arithmetic notation using 12 as a base, at one time considered superior to the decimal number system in that 12 has more factors (2, 3, 4, 6) than 10 (2, 5).

duodenum in vertebrates, a short length of alimentary canal found between the stomach and the small intestine. Its role is in digesting carbohydrates, fats, and proteins. The smaller molecules formed are then absorbed, either by the duodenum or the ileum.

duralumin lightweight aluminum ◊alloy widely used in aircraft construction, containing copper, magnesium, and manganese.

Durand Asher Brown 1796–1886. US painter and engraver. His paintings expressed communion with nature, as in *Kindred Spirits* 1849, a tribute to Thomas Cole, William Cullen Bryant, and the Catskill mountains. The founding of the Hudson River School of landscape art is ascribed to Cole and Durand.

Duras Marguerite 1914– . French author. Her work includes short stories (*Des Journées entières dans les arbres* 1954, stage adaption *Days in the Trees* 1965), plays (*La Musica* 1967), and film scripts (*Hiroshima mon amour* 1960). She also wrote novels including *Le Vice-Consul* 1966, evoking an existentialist world from the setting of Calcutta, and *Emily L.* 1989. *La Vie materielle* 1987 appeared in England as *Practicalities* 1990. Her autobiographical novel, *La Douleur* 1986, is set in Paris in 1945.

Durban principal port of Natal, South Africa, and second port of the republic; population (1985) 634,000, urban area 982,000. It exports coal, corn, and wool; imports heavy machinery and mining equipment; and is also a holiday resort.

Dürer Albrecht 1471–1528. German artist, the leading figure of the northern Renaissance. He was born in Nuremberg and traveled widely in Europe. Highly skilled in drawing and a keen student of nature, he perfected the technique of woodcut and engraving, producing woodcut series such as the *Apocalypse* 1498 and copperplate engravings such as *The Knight, Death, and the Devil* 1513 and *Melancholia* 1514; he may also have invented etching. His paintings include altarpieces and meticulously observed portraits, including many self-portraits.

Durham city in N central North Carolina, NW of Raleigh; seat of Durham County; population (1990) 136,600. Tobacco is the main industry, and other products include precision instruments, textiles, furniture, and lumber. Duke University is here.

Durkheim Emile 1858–1917. French sociologist, one of the founders of modern sociology, who also influenced social anthropology. He worked to establish sociology as a respectable and scientific discipline, capable of diagnosing social ills and recommending possible cures.

Durrell Lawrence (George) 1912–1990. British novelist and poet. Born in India, he joined the foreign service and lived mainly in the E Mediterranean, the setting of his novels, including the Alexandria Quartet: *Justine, Balthazar, Mountolive*, and *Clea* 1957–60; he also wrote travel books. He was the brother of the naturalist Gerald Durrell.

Dürrenmatt Friedrich 1921–1991. Swiss dramatist, author of grotesquely farcical tragicomedies, for example *The Visit* 1956 and *The Physicists* 1962.

Durrës chief port of Albania; population (1983) 72,000. It is a commercial and communications center, with flour mills, soap and cigarette factories, distilleries, and an electronics plant. It was the capital of Albania 1912–21.

Dushanbe formerly (1929–69) *Stalinabad* capital of Tajikistan, 100 mi/160 km N of the Afghan frontier; population (1987) 582,000. It is a road, rail, and air center. Industries include cotton mills, tanneries, meat-packing factories, and printing works. It is the seat of Tajik state university. A curfew was imposed Feb 1990–Jan 1991 in response to antigovernment rioting and pogroms; a state of emergency remained in force after Jan. In March–May 1992 antigovernment protests left more than 100 dead and in Aug protestors stormed the presidential palace demanding President Nabiyev's resignation. Nabiyev was seized while trying to flee the capital and resigned.

Düsseldorf industrial city of Germany, on the right bank of the river Rhine, 16 mi/26 km NW of Cologne, capital of North Rhine–Westphalia; population (1988) 561,000. It is a river port and the commercial and financial center of the Ruhr area, with food processing, brewing, agricultural machinery, textile, and chemical industries.

dust bowl area in the Great Plains region of North America (Texas to Kansas) that suffered extensive wind erosion as the result of drought and poor farming practice in once-fertile soil. Much of the topsoil was blown away in the droughts of the 1930s and the 1980s.

Dutch East Indies former Dutch colony, which in 1945 became independent as ◊Indonesia.

Dutch elm disease disease of elm trees *Ulmus*, principally Dutch, English, and American elm, caused by the fungus *Certocystis ulmi*. The fungus is usually spread from tree to tree by the elm-bark beetle, which lays its eggs beneath the bark. The disease has no cure, and control methods involve injecting insecticide into the trees annually to prevent infection, or the destruction of all elms in a broad band around an infected area, to keep the beetles out.

Dutch Guiana former Dutch colony, which in 1975 became independent as ◊Surinam.

Dutch language member of the Germanic branch of the Indo-European language family, often referred to by scholars as Netherlandic and taken to include the standard language and dialects of the Netherlands (excluding Frisian) as well as Flemish (in Belgium and N France) and, more remotely, its offshoot Afrikaans in South Africa.

Duvalier François 1907–1971. Right-wing president of Haiti 1957–71. Known as *Papa Doc*, he ruled as a dictator, organizing the Tontons Macoutes ("bogey-men") as a private security force to intimidate and assassinate opponents of his regime. He rigged the 1961 elections in order to have his term of office extended until 1967, and in 1964 declared himself president for life. He was excommunicated by the Vatican for harassing the church, and was succeeded on his death by his son Jean-Claude Duvalier.

Duvalier Jean-Claude 1951– . Right-wing president of Haiti 1971–86. Known as *Baby Doc*, he succeeded his father François Duvalier, becoming, at the age of 19, the youngest president in the world. He continued to receive support from the US but was pressured into moderating some elements of his father's regime, yet still tolerated no opposition. In 1986, with Haiti's economy stagnating and with increasing civil disorder, Duvalier fled to France, taking much of the Haitian treasury with him.

Dvořák Antonin (Leopold) 1841–1904. Czech composer. International recognition came with his series of *Slavonic Dances* 1877–86, and he was director of the National Conservatory, New York, 1892–95. Works such as his *New World Symphony* 1893 reflect his

Dyck Samson and Delilah *(c. 1618–20).*

interest in American folk themes, including black and native American. He wrote nine symphonies; tone poems; operas, including *Rusalka* 1900; large-scale choral works; the *Carnival* 1891–92 and other overtures; violin and cello concertos; chamber music; piano pieces; and songs. His Romantic music extends the Classical tradition of Beethoven and Brahms and displays the influence of Czech folk music.

Dyck Anthony Van 1599–1641. Flemish painter. Born in Antwerp, Van Dyck was an assistant to Rubens 1618–20, then briefly worked in England at the court of James I, and moved to Italy 1622. In 1626 he returned to Antwerp, where he continued to paint religious works and portraits. From 1632 he lived in England and produced numerous portraits of royalty and aristocrats, such as *Charles I on Horseback* about 1638 (National Gallery, London). *See illustration p. 293*

dye substance that, applied in solution to fabrics, imparts a color resistant to washing. *Direct dyes* combine with the material of the fabric, yielding a colored compound; *indirect dyes* require the presence of another substance (a mordant), with which the fabric must first be treated; *vat dyes* are colorless soluble substances that on exposure to air yield an insoluble colored compound.

dyke in earth science, a sheet of ◊igneous rock created by the intrusion of magma (molten rock) across layers of pre-existing rock. (By contrast, a sill is intruded *between* layers of rock.) It may form a ridge when exposed on the surface. A dyke is also a human-made embankment built along a coastline (for example, in the Netherlands) to prevent the flooding of lowland coastal regions.

Dylan Bob. Adopted name of Robert Allen Zimmerman 1941– . US singer and songwriter whose lyrics provided catchphrases for a generation and influenced innumerable songwriters. He began in the folk-music tradition. His early songs, as on his albums *Freewheelin'* 1963 and *The Times They Are A-Changin'* 1964, were associated with the US civil-rights movement and antiwar protest. From 1965 he worked in an individualistic rock style, as on the albums *Highway 61 Revisited* 1965 and *Blonde on Blonde* 1966.

dynamics or *kinetics* in mechanics, the mathematical and physical study of the behavior of bodies under the action of forces that produce changes of motion in them.

dynamite explosive consisting of a mixture of nitroglycerine and diatomaceous earth (diatomite, an absorbent, chalklike material). It was first devised by Alfred Nobel.

dynamo former name for ◊generator.

dysentery infection of the large intestine causing abdominal cramps and painful ◊diarrhea with blood. There are two kinds of dysentery: *amebic* (caused by a protozoan), common in the tropics, which may lead to liver damage; and *bacterial*, the kind most often seen in the temperate zones.

dyslexia (Greek "bad," "pertaining to words") malfunction in the brain's synthesis and interpretation of sensory information, popularly known as "word blindness." It results in poor ability to read and write, though the person may otherwise excel, for example, in mathematics. A similar disability with figures is called dyscalculus.

dysprosium (Greek *dysprositos* "difficult to get near") silver-white, metallic element of the ◊lanthanide series, symbol Dy, atomic number 66, atomic weight 162.50. It is among the most magnetic of all known substances. It is important in nuclear reactors because of its great capacity to absorb neutrons.

eagle *The bald eagle of N America lives along coasts, rivers, and lakes, where food is plentiful.*

eagle any of several genera of large birds of prey of the family Accipitridae, including the golden eagle *Aquila chrysaetos* of Eurasia and North America, which has a 6 ft/2 m wingspan and is dark brown.

Eakins Thomas 1844–1916. US painter. A trained observer of human anatomy and a devotee of photography. Eakins attempted to achieve a strong sense of visual realism. His work is characterized by strong contrasts between light and shade, as in *The Gross Clinic* 1875 (Jefferson Medical College, Philadelphia), a group portrait of a surgeon, his assistants, and students.

Eanes António dos Santos Ramalho 1935– . Portuguese politician. He helped plan the 1974 coup that ended the Caetano regime, and as army chief of staff put down a left-wing revolt Nov 1975. He was president 1976–86.

ear organ of hearing in animals. It responds to the vibrations that constitute sound, and these are translated into nerve signals and passed to the brain. A mammal's ear consists of three parts: outer ear, middle ear, and inner ear. The outer ear is a funnel that collects sound, directing it down a tube to the ***eardrum*** (tympanic membrane), which separates the outer and middle ear. Sounds vibrate this membrane, the mechanical movement of which is transferred to a smaller membrane leading to the inner ear by three small bones, the auditory ossicles. Vibrations of the inner ear membrane move fluid contained in the snail-shaped cochlea, which vibrates hair cells that stimulate the auditory nerve connected to the brain. Three fluid-filled canals of the inner ear detect changes of position; this mechanism, with other sensory inputs, is responsible for the sense of balance.

Earhart Amelia 1898–1937. US aviation pioneer and author, who in 1928 became the first woman to fly

ear *The structure of the human ear.*

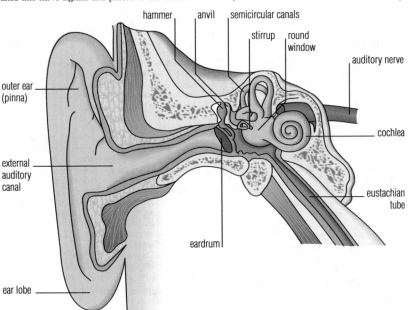

hammer anvil semicircular canals
stirrup round window
auditory nerve
outer ear (pinna)
cochlea
external auditory canal
eustachian tube
eardrum
ear lobe

Earth View of the Earth rising above the surface of the Moon, taken by the Apollo 11 spacecraft.

across the Atlantic. With copilot Frederick Noonan, she attempted a round-the-world flight 1937. Somewhere over the Pacific their plane disappeared.

earl in the British peerage, the third title in order of rank, coming between marquess and viscount; it is the oldest of British titles, being of Scandinavian origin. An earl's wife is a countess.

Early Jubal Anderson 1816–1894. American Confederate military leader. Although long a supporter of the Union, he joined the Confederate army at the outbreak of the American Civil War 1861. After the Battle of Bull Run 1862 he was made general in the Army of Northern Virginia, leading campaigns in the Shenandoah Valley 1862 and threatening Washington, DC, 1864.

Earp Wyatt 1848–1929. US frontier law officer. With his brothers Virgil and Morgan, Doc Holliday, and the legendary Bat ◊Masterson he was involved in the famous gunfight at the OK Corral in Tombstone, Arizona, on Oct 26, 1881. Famous as a scout and buffalo hunter, he also gained a reputation as a gambler and brawler. After leaving Tombstone 1882, he traveled before settling in Los Angeles.

Earth third planet from the Sun. It is almost spherical, flattened slightly at the poles, and is composed of three concentric layers: the ◊core, the ◊mantle, and the ◊crust. About 70% of the surface (including the north and south polar icecaps) is covered with water. The Earth is surrounded by a life-supporting atmosphere and is the only planet on which life is known to exist.

mean distance from the Sun 92,860,000 mi/149,500,000 km

equatorial diameter 7,923 mi/12,756 km
circumference 24,900 mi/40,070 km
rotation period 23 hr 56 min 4.1 sec
year (complete orbit, or sidereal period) 365 days 5 hr 48 min 46 sec. Earth's average speed around the Sun is 18.5 mps/30 kps; the plane of its orbit is inclined to its equatorial plane at an angle of 23.5°, the reason for the changing seasons.
atmosphere nitrogen 78.09%; oxygen 20.95%; argon 0.93%; carbon dioxide 0.03%; and less than 0.0001% neon, helium, krypton, hydrogen, xenon, ozone, radon
surface land surface 57,500,000 sq mi/150,000,000 sq km (greatest height above sea level 29,118 ft/8,872 m Mount Everest); water surface 139,400,000 sq mi/361,000,000 sq km (greatest depth 36,201 ft/11,034 m ◊Mariana Trench in the Pacific). The interior is thought to be an inner core about 1,600 mi/2,600 km in diameter, of solid iron and nickel; an outer core about 1,400 mi/2,250 km thick, of molten iron and nickel; and a mantle of mostly solid rock about 1,800 mi/2,900 km thick, separated by the ◊Mohorovičić discontinuity from the Earth's crust. The crust and the topmost layer of the mantle form about 12 major moving plates, some of which carry the continents. The plates are in constant, slow motion, called tectonic drift.
satellite the ◊Moon
age 4.6 billion years. The Earth was formed with the rest of the Solar System by consolidation of interstellar dust. Life began 3.5–4 billion years ago.

earthenware pottery made of porous clay and fired to temperatures of up to 2,101°F/1,150°C. Earthenware may be unglazed (flowerpots, wine coolers) or

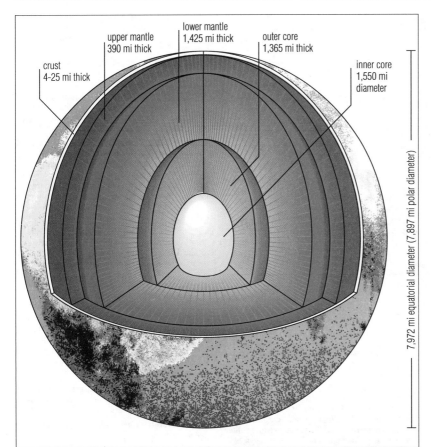

crust
4-25 mi thick

upper mantle
390 mi thick

lower mantle
1,425 mi thick

outer core
1,365 mi thick

inner core
1,550 mi
diameter

7,972 mi equatorial diameter (7,897 mi polar diameter)

Earth *Inside the Earth.*

glazed (most tableware); the glaze and body characteristically form quite separate layers.

earthquake shaking of the Earth's surface as a result of the sudden release of stresses built up in the Earth's crust. The study of earthquakes is called ◊seismology. Most earthquakes occur along ◊faults (fractures or breaks) in the crust. ◊Plate tectonic movements generate the major proportion: as two plates move past each other they can become jammed and deformed, and a series of shock waves (seismic waves) occur when they spring free. Their force (magnitude) is measured on the ◊Richter scale, and their effect (intensity) on the Mercalli scale. The point at which an earthquake originates is the ***sesmic focus***; the point on the Earth's surface directly above this is the ***epicenter***. *See table p. 298*

earth science scientific study of the planet Earth as a whole, a synthesis of several traditional subjects such as ◊geology, ◊meteorology, oceanography, ◊geophysics, ◊geochemistry, and ◊paleontology.

Earth Summit (official name ***United Nations Conference on Environment and Development***) international meeting in Rio de Janeiro, Brazil, June 1992, which drew up measures toward world environmental protection. Treaties were made to combat global warming and protect wildlife ("biodiversity") (the latter was not signed by the US).

earthworm ◊annelid worm of the class Oligochaeta. Earthworms are hermaphroditic and deposit their eggs in cocoons. They live by burrowing in the soil,

earthquake *Mexico City, Sept 19, 1985.*

major 20th-century earthquakes

date	place	magnitude (Richter scale)	number of deaths
1906	San Francisco, US	8.3	450
1908	Messina, Italy	7.5	83,000
1915	Avezzano, Italy	7.5	29,980
1920	Gansu, China	8.6	100,000
1923	Tokyo, Japan	8.3	99,330
1927	Nan-Shan, China	8.3	200,000
1932	Gansu, China	7.6	70,000
1935	Quetta, India	7.5	30,000
1939	Erzincan, Turkey	7.9	30,000
1939	Chillán, Chile	8.3	28,000
1948	USSR	7.3	110,000
1970	N Peru	7.7	66,794
1976	Tangshan, China	8.2	242,000
1978	NE Iran	7.7	25,000
1980	El Asnam, Algeria	7.3	20,000
1985	Mexico	8.1	25,000
1988	Armenia, USSR	6.9	25,000
1989	San Francisco, US	7.1	300
1990	NW Iran	7.7	50,000
1994	Los Angeles, US	6.6	55

feeding on the organic matter it contains. They are vital to the formation of humus, aerating the soil and leveling it by transferring earth from the deeper levels to the surface as castings.

earwig nocturnal insect of the order Dermaptera. The forewings are short and leathery and serve to protect the hind wings, which are large and are folded like a fan when at rest. Earwigs seldom fly. They have a pincerlike appendage in the rear. The male is distinguished by curved pincers; those of the female are straight. Earwigs are regarded as pests because they feed on flowers and fruit, but they also eat other insects, dead or alive. Eggs are laid beneath the soil, and the female cares for the young even after they have hatched. The male dies before the eggs have hatched.

Forficula is the common genus in North America.

easement in law, rights that a person may have over the land of another. A common example is a right of way; others are the right to bring water over another's land and the right to a sufficient quantity of light.

east one of the four cardinal points of the compass, indicating that part of the horizon where the Sun rises; when facing north, east is to the right.

East Anglia region of E England, formerly a Saxon kingdom, including Norfolk, Suffolk, and parts of Essex and Cambridgeshire. Norwich is the principal city of East Anglia. The University of East Anglia (UEA) was founded in Norwich 1962, and includes the Sainsbury Center for Visual Arts, opened 1978, which has a collection of ethnographic art and sculpture. East Anglian ports such as Harwich and Felixstowe have greatly developed as trade with the rest of Europe has increased.

Easter spring feast of the Christian church, commemorating the Resurrection of Jesus. It is a moveable feast, falling on the first Sunday following the full moon after the vernal equinox (March 21), that is, between March 22 and April 25.

Easter Island or *Rapa Nui* Chilean island in the S Pacific Ocean, part of the Polynesian group, about 2,200 mi/3,500 km W of Chile; area about 64 sq mi/166 sq km; population (1985) 2,000. It was first reached by Europeans on Easter Sunday 1722.

On it stand over 800 huge carved statues (moai) and the remains of boat-shaped stone houses, the work of neolithic peoples of unknown origin. The chief center is Hanga-Roa.

Easter Rising or *Easter Rebellion* in Irish history, a republican insurrection that began on Easter Monday, April 1916, in Dublin. It was inspired by the Irish Republican Brotherhood (IRB) in an unsuccessful attempt to overthrow British rule in Ireland. It was led by Patrick Pearce of the IRB and James Connolly of Sinn Féin.

East India Company, Dutch (*VOC*, or *Vereenigde Oost-Indische Compagnie*) trading company chartered by the States General (parliament) of the Netherlands, and established in the N Netherlands 1602. It was given a monopoly on Dutch trade in the Indonesian archipelago, and certain sovereign rights such as the creation of an army and a fleet.

Eastman George 1854–1932. US entrepreneur and inventor who founded the Eastman Kodak photographic company 1892. From 1888 he marketed his patented daylight-loading flexible roll films (to replace the glass plates used previously) and portable cameras. By 1900 his company was selling a pocket camera for as little as one dollar.

The films first worked with chemicals fixed to a paper base 1884 and later on celluloid 1889. In 1928 he perfected a film process for color photography and development, an important service offered on fine papers. He was known for his contributions to education and music.

East Pakistan former province of ◊Pakistan, now Bangladesh.

East Indies the Malay Archipelago; the Philippines are sometimes included. The term is also used to refer more generally to SE Asia.

East Pakistan former province of ◊Pakistan, now Bangladesh.

East Sussex county in SE England
area 695 sq mi/1,800 sq km
cities Lewes (administrative headquarters), Newhaven (cross-channel port), Brighton, Eastbourne, Hastings, Bexhill, Winchelsea, Rye
features Beachy Head, highest headland on the S coast at 590 ft/180 m, the E end of the South Downs; the Weald (including Ashdown Forest); Friston Forest; rivers: Ouse, Cuckmere, East Rother; Romney Marsh; the "Long Man" chalk hill figure at Wilmington, near Eastbourne; Herstmonceux, with a 15th-century castle (conference and exhibition center) and adjacent modern buildings, site of the Greenwich Royal Observatory 1958–90; other castles at Hastings, Lewes, Pevensey, and Bodiam; Battle Abbey and the site of the Battle of Hastings; Michelham Priory; Sheffield Park garden; University of Sussex at Falmer, near Brighton, founded 1961
products electronics, gypsum, timber
population (1988 est) 698,000

East Timor disputed territory on the island of ◊Timor in the Malay Archipelago; prior to 1975, it was a Portuguese colony for almost 460 years
area 5,706 sq mi/14,874 sq km
capital Dili
products coffee
population (1980) 555,000
history Following Portugal's withdrawal 1975, East Timor was left with a literacy rate of under 10% and no infrastructure. Civil war broke out and the left-wing Revolutionary Front of Independent East Timor

(Fretilin) occupied the capital, calling for independence. In opposition, troops from neighboring Indonesia invaded the territory, declaring East Timor (*Loro Sae*) the 17th province of Indonesia July 1976. This claim is not recognized by the United Nations. (It has long been the aim of Indonesian military rulers to absorb the remaining colonial outposts in the East Indies.) The war and its attendant famine are thought to have caused more than 100,000 deaths, but starvation had been alleviated by the mid-1980s, and the Indonesian government had built schools, roads, and hospitals. Fretilin guerrillas remained active, claiming to have the support of the population. In Nov 1991, at least 19 people were killed and 91 injured when Indonesian troops fired on pro-independence demonstrators.

Eastwood Clint 1930– . US film actor and director. As the "Man with No Name" in *A Fistful of Dollars* 1964, he started the vogue for "spaghetti Westerns." Later Westerns include *The Good, the Bad, and the Ugly* 1966, *High Plains Drifter* 1973, *The Outlaw Josey Wales* 1976, and *Unforgiven* 1992. His numerous other films include *In the Line of Fire* 1993.

Eau Claire city in W central Wisconsin, N of LaCrosse, on the Chippewa River; seat of Eau Claire County; population (1990) 56,850. It is a processing and marketing center for the region's dairy farmers. Industries include machine parts, electronics, printing, and brewing. Tourism is important to the economy.

ebony any of a group of hardwood trees of the ebony family Ebenaceae, especially some tropical persimmons of the genus *Diospyros*, native to Africa and Asia.

Their very heavy, hard, black timber polishes well and is used in cabinetmaking and inlaying; for piano keys and violin fingerboards, chin rests, and pegs; and for sculpture.

EC abbreviation for ◊*European Community*.

ECG abbreviation for ◊electrocardiogram.

echidna or *spiny anteater* toothless, egg-laying, spiny mammal of the order Monotremata, found in Australia and New Guinea. There are two species: *Tachyglossus aculeatus*, the short-nosed echidna, and the rarer *Zaglossus bruijni*, the long-nosed echidna. They feed entirely upon ants and termites, which they dig out with their powerful claws and lick up with their prehensile tongues. When attacked, an echidna rolls itself into a ball, or tries to hide by burrowing in the earth.

echo repetition of a sound wave, or of a ◊radar or ◊sonar signal, by reflection from a surface. By accurately measuring the time taken for an echo to return to the transmitter, and by knowing the speed of a radar signal (the speed of light) or a sonar signal (the speed of sound in water), it is possible to calculate the range of the object causing the echo (echolocation).

A similar technique is used in echo sounders to estimate the depth of water under a ship's keel or the depth of a school of fish.

Echo in Greek mythology, a ◊nymph who pined away until only her voice remained, after being rejected by Narcissus.

echo sounder or *sonar device* device that detects objects under water by means of ◊sonar—by using reflected sound waves. Most boats are equipped with echo sounders to measure the water depth beneath them. An echo sounder consists of a transmitter, which emits an ultrasonic pulse (see ◊ultrasound), and

echidna The short-nosed echidna is found throughout Australia.

a receiver, which detects the pulse after reflection from the seabed. The time between transmission and receipt of the reflected signal is a measure of the depth of water. Fishing boats also use echo sounders to detect shoals of fish.

eclipse passage of an astronomical body through the shadow of another. The term is usually employed for solar and lunar eclipses, which may be either partial or total, but also, for example, for eclipses by Jupiter of its satellites. An eclipse of a star by a body in the Solar System is called an occultation. *See panel p. 300*

Eco Umberto 1932– . Italian writer, semiologist, and literary critic. His works include *The Role of the Reader* 1979, the "philosophical thriller" *The Name of the Rose* 1983, and *Foucault's Pendulum* 1988.

ecology study of the relationship among organisms and the environments in which they live, including all living and nonliving components. The term was coined by the biologist Ernst Haeckel 1866.

Economic Community of West African States (ECOWAS, *Communauté Economique des Etats de l'Afrique de l'Ouest*) organization for the promotion of economic cooperation and development, established 1975 by the Treaty of Lagos. Its members include Benin, Burkina Faso, Cape Verde, Gambia, Ghana, Guinea, Guinea-Bissau, Ivory Coast, Liberia, Mali, Mauritania, Niger, Nigeria, Senegal, Sierra Leone, and Togo. Its headquarters are in Lagos, Nigeria.

economic growth rate of growth of output of all goods and services in an economy, usually measured as the percentage increase in gross domestic product or gross national product from one year to the next. It is regarded as an indicator of the rate of increase or decrease (if economic growth is negative) in the standard of living.

economics social science devoted to studying the production, distribution, and consumption of wealth. It consists of the disciplines of ◊*microeconomics*, the study of individual producers, consumers, or markets, and ◊*macroeconomics*, the study of whole economies or systems (in particular, areas such as taxation and public spending).

eclipse

The Sun is much larger than the Moon, but is at such a distance from the Earth that their diameters appear the same. One of nature's most awesome events occurs when the Moon passes in front of the Sun, hiding our parent star from view.

solar eclipses

Total solar eclipses occur if the Sun, Moon, and Earth are exactly aligned and the Sun is completely hidden; a partial eclipse takes place if only part of the Sun is obscured. Annular eclipses occur during an exact alignment if the Moon is at its furthest point from us. Its apparent diameter will be less, the Sun being seen as a ring around the Moon.

During a total solar eclipse the Sun's corona can be seen surrounding the lunar disk.

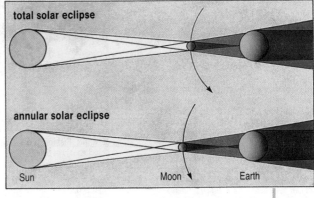

total solar eclipse

annular solar eclipse

Sun   Moon   Earth

☐ sunlight   ■ umbra   ▨ penumbra

lunar eclipses

Lunar eclipses take place when the Moon passes into the Earth's shadow. When this happens the lunar surface is plunged into darkness, although it is only very rarely that the Moon disappears completely from view. A small amount of sunlight is usually bent toward the lunar surface by the Earth's atmosphere.

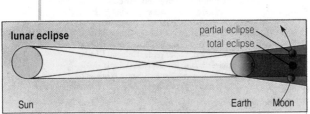

lunar eclipse

partial eclipse
total eclipse

Sun   Earth   Moon

☐ sunlight

■ umbra

▨ penumbra

Total solar eclipses (top) occur if the Moon passes through the umbra of the Earth's shadow. A partial eclipse (bottom) takes place when only part of the Moon enters this region. During a lunar eclipse, the curved shadow of the Earth can be seen crossing the lunar disk.

Ecuador
Republic of
(*República del Ecuador*)

area 104,479 sq mi/270,670 sq km
capital Quito
cities Cuenca; chief port Guayaquil
physical coastal plain rises sharply to Andes Mountains, which are divided into a series of cultivated valleys; flat, low-lying rain forest in E
environment about 25,000 species became extinct 1965–90 as a result of environmental destruction
features Ecuador is crossed by the equator, from which it derives its name; Galápagos Islands; Cotopaxi is world's highest active volcano; rich wildlife in rain forest of Amazon basin
head of state and government Sixto Duran Ballen from 1992
political system emergent democracy
political parties Social Christian Party (PSC), right-wing; United Republican Party (PUR), right-of-center coalition; Ecuadorean Roldosist Party (PRE)
exports bananas, cocoa, coffee, sugar, rice, fruit, balsa wood, fish, petroleum
currency sucre
population (1992) 10,607,000; (mestizo 55%, Indian 25%, European 10%, black African 10%); growth rate 2.9% p.a.
life expectancy men 62, women 66
languages Spanish (official), Quechua, Jivaro, and other Indian languages
religion Roman Catholic 95%
literacy men 85%, women 80% (1985 est)
GDP $10.6 bn (1987); $1,069 per head

chronology
1830 Independence achieved from Spain.
1925–48 Great political instability; no president completed his term of office.
1948–55 Liberals in power.
1956 First conservative president in 60 years.
1960 Liberals returned, with José Velasco as president.
1961 Velasco deposed and replaced by the vice president.
1962 Military junta installed.
1968 Velasco returned as president.
1972 A coup put the military back in power.
1978 New democratic constitution adopted.
1979 Liberals in power but opposed by right- and left-wing parties.
1982 Deteriorating economy provoked strikes, demonstrations, and a state of emergency.
1983 Austerity measures introduced.
1984–85 No party with a clear majority in the national congress; Febres Cordero narrowly won the presidency for the Conservatives.
1988 Rodrigo Borja Cevallos elected president for moderate left-wing coalition.
1989 Guerrilla left-wing group *Alfaro Vive, Carajo* ("Alfaro lives, damn it"), numbering about 1,000, laid down arms after nine years.
1992 PUR leader Sixto Duran Ballen elected president; PSC became largest party in congress.

ecosystem in ◊ecology, an integrated unit consisting of the ◊community of living organisms and the physical environment in a particular area. The relationships among species in an ecosystem are usually complex and finely balanced, and removal of any one species may be disastrous. The removal of a major predator, for example, can result in the destruction of the ecosystem through overgrazing by herbivores.

ECOWAS acronym from ◊*Economic Community of West African States*.

ecstasy or *MDMA* (3,4-methylenedioxymethamphetamine) illegal drug in increasing use from the 1980s. It is a modified amphetamine with mild psychedelic effects, and works by depleting serotonin (a neurotransmitter) in the brain.

ectopic in medicine, term applied to an anatomical feature that is displaced or found in an abnormal position. An *ectopic pregnancy* is one occurring outside the womb, usually in a Fallopian tube.

ECU for *European Currency Unit*, the official monetary unit of the European Community. It is based on the value of the different currencies used in the ◊European Monetary System (EMS).

Ecuador country in South America, bounded N by Colombia, E and S by Peru, and W by the Pacific Ocean.

ecumenical movement movement for reunification of the various branches of the Christian church. It began in the 19th century with the extension of missionary work to Africa and Asia, where the divisions created in Europe were incomprehensible; the movement gathered momentum from the need for unity in the face of growing secularism in Christian countries and of the challenge posed by such faiths as Islam. The *World Council of Churches* was founded 1948.

eczema inflammatory skin condition, a form of dermatitis, marked by dryness, rashes, itching, the formation of blisters, and the exudation of fluid. It may be allergic in origin and is sometimes complicated by infection.

Edberg Stefan 1966– . Swedish tennis player. He won the junior Grand Slam 1983 and his first Grand Slam title, the Australian Open, 1985, repeated 1987. Other Grand Slam singles titles include Wimbledon 1988, 1990 and the US Open 1991 and 1992.

Edda two collections of early Icelandic literature that together constitute our chief source for Old Norse mythology. The term strictly applies to the *Younger* or *Prose Edda*, compiled by Snorri Sturluson, a priest, about AD 1230.

Eddy Mary Baker 1821–1910. US founder of the Christian Science movement.

Edison Pioneering scientist and inventor Thomas Edison.

edelweiss perennial alpine plant *Leontopodium alpinum*, family Compositae, with a white, woolly, star-shaped bloom, found in the high mountains of Eurasia.

edema any abnormal accumulation of fluid in tissues or cavities of the body; waterlogging of the tissues due to excessive loss of ◊plasma through the capillary walls. It may be generalized (the condition once known as dropsy) or confined to one area, such as the ankles.

Eden Anthony, 1st Earl of Avon 1897–1977. British Conservative politician, foreign secretary 1935–38, 1940–45, and 1951–55; prime minister 1955–57, when he resigned after the failure of the Anglo-French military intervention in the ◊Suez Crisis.

Eden, Garden of in the Old Testament book of Genesis and in the Koran, the "garden" in which Adam and Eve lived after their creation, and from which they were expelled for disobedience.

Edgar the Peaceful 944–975. King of all England from 959. He was the younger son of Edmund I, and strove successfully to unite English and Danes as fellow subjects.

Edinburgh capital of Scotland and administrative center of the region of Lothian, near the S shores of the Firth of Forth; population (1988 est) 433,500. A cultural center, it holds a major annual festival of music and the arts. The university was established 1583. Industries include printing, publishing, banking, insurance, chemical manufactures, distilling, brewing, and some shipbuilding.

Edison Thomas Alva 1847–1931. US scientist and inventor, with over 1,000 patents. In Menlo Park, New Jersey, 1876–87, he produced his most important inventions, including the electric light bulb 1879. He constructed a system of electric power distribution for consumers, the telephone transmitter, and the phonograph.

In 1869 he invented an automatic vote recorder and the improved stock ticker in 1871, which earned him enough to found his manufacturing plant in Newark, New Jersey. He moved to Menlo Park in 1876 and from there to West Orange, New Jersey, where he invented the movie camera, mimeograph, fluoroscope, and an improved battery. In 1889 he began the Edison Light Co., which became the General Electric Co.

Edmonton capital of Alberta, Canada, on the North Saskatchewan River; population (1986) 576,200. It is the center of an oil and mining area to the N and also an agricultural and dairying region. Petroleum pipelines link Edmonton with Superior, Wisconsin, and Vancouver, British Columbia.

The city is on the Alaska Highway. Manufactured goods include processed foods, petrochemicals, plastic and metal products, lumber, and clothing. The University of Alberta, Athabasca University, and the Provincial Museum of Alberta are here. Fort Edmonton, a Hudson's Bay Company fur-trading post, was built in 1795. It was incorporated as a town soon after the arrival of the Canadian Pacific Railroad in 1891. It flourished as an outfitting point for prospectors seeking gold in the Klondike region of the Yukon in the late 1890s. Edmonton grew rapidly as a center for the rapidly growing Alberta oil industry after 1950.

Edmund II Ironside *c.* 989–1016. King of England 1016, the son of Ethelred II the Unready. He led the resistance to ◊Canute's invasion 1015, and on Ethelred's death 1016 was chosen king by the citizens of London, whereas the Witan (the king's council) elected Canute. In the struggle for the throne, Edmund was defeated by Canute at Assandun (Ashington), Essex, and they divided the kingdom between them; when Edmund died the same year, Canute ruled the whole kingdom.

education the process, beginning at birth, of developing intellectual capacity, manual skill, and social awareness, especially through instruction. In its more restricted sense, the term refers to the process of imparting literacy, numeracy, and a generally accepted body of knowledge.

Edward (full name Edward Antony Richard Louis) 1964– . Prince of the UK, third son of Queen Elizabeth II. He is seventh in line to the throne after Charles, Charles's two sons, Andrew, and Andrew's two daughters.

Edward the *Black Prince* 1330–1376. Prince of Wales, eldest son of Edward III of England. The epithet (probably posthumous) may refer to his black armor. During the Hundred Years' War he fought at the Battle of Crécy 1346 and captured the French king at Poitiers 1356. He ruled Aquitaine 1360–71; during the revolt that eventually ousted him, he caused the massacre of Limoges 1370.

Edward I 1239–1307. King of England from 1272, son of Henry III. Edward led the royal forces against Simon de Montfort in the ◊Barons' War 1264–67, and was on a crusade when he succeeded to the throne. He established English rule over all Wales 1282–84, and secured recognition of his overlordship from the Scottish king, although the Scots (under Wallace and Bruce) fiercely resisted actual conquest. In his reign Parliament took its approximate modern form with the ◊Model Parliament 1295. He was succeeded by his son Edward II.

Edward II 1284–1327. King of England from 1307. Son of Edward I and born at Caernarvon Castle, he was created the first Prince of Wales 1301. His invasion of Scotland 1314 to suppress revolt resulted in defeat at Bannockburn. He was deposed 1327 by his wife Isabella (1292–1358), daughter of Philip IV of France, and her lover Roger de ◊Mortimer, and murdered in Berkeley Castle, Gloucestershire. He was succeeded by his son Edward III.

In addition to military disasters, his reign was troubled by his extravagance and the unpopularity of his favorites.

Edward III 1312–1377. King of England from 1327, son of Edward II. He assumed the government 1330 from his mother, through whom in 1337 he laid claim to the French throne and thus began the ◊Hundred Years' War. He was succeeded by his grandson Richard II.

Edward VI 1537–1553. King of England from 1547, son of Henry VIII and Jane Seymour. The government was entrusted to his uncle the Duke of Somerset (who fell from power 1549), and then to the Earl of Warwick, later created Duke of Northumberland. He was succeeded by his sister, Mary I.

Edward VII 1841–1910. King of Great Britain and Ireland from 1901. As Prince of Wales he was a prominent social figure, but his mother Queen Victoria considered him too frivolous to take part in political life. In 1860 he made the first tour of Canada and the US ever undertaken by a British prince.

He took a close interest in politics and was on good terms with party leaders. He succeeded to the throne 1901 and was crowned 1902. Although he overrated his political influence, he contributed to the Entente Cordiale 1904 with France and the Anglo-Russian agreement 1907.

Edward VIII 1894–1972. King of Great Britain and Northern Ireland Jan–Dec 1936, when he renounced the throne to marry Wallis Warfield ◊Simpson (see ◊abdication crisis). He was created Duke of Windsor and was governor of the Bahamas1940–45, subsequently settling in France. Edward was extremely popular as prince of Wales, and he made fashion statements that changed the way men dressed throughout the 20th century in the Western world—soft collars, tweed sports jackets, cuffed trousers, low shoes, the Windsor knotted tie, and V-necked sweaters freed men from the starched look that characterized the turn of the century. He succeeded his father George V on Jan 20, 1936, and on Dec 11 he abdicated. A divorcee, Mrs Simpson was not acceptable consitutionally as queen. They were married in France in May 1937.

Edward the Confessor c. 1003–1066. King of England from 1042, the son of Ethelred II. He lived in Normandy until shortly before his accession. During his reign power was held by Earl Godwin and his son ◊Harold, while the king devoted himself to religion, including the rebuilding of Westminster Abbey (consecrated 1065), where he is buried. His childlessness led ultimately to the Norman Conquest 1066. He was canonized 1161.

Edward the Elder c. 870–924. King of the West Saxons. He succeeded his father ◊Alfred the Great 899. He reconquered SE England and the Midlands from the Danes, uniting Wessex and ◊Mercia with the help of his sister, Athelflad. By the time Edward died, his kingdom was the most powerful in the British Isles. He was succeeded by his son ◊Athelstan.

Edward the Martyr c. 963–978. King of England from 975. Son of King Edgar, he was murdered at Corfe Castle, Dorset, probably at his stepmother Aelfthryth's instigation (she wished to secure the crown for her son, Ethelred). He was canonized 1001.

EEC abbreviation for *European Economic Community*, see ◊European Community.

EEG abbreviation for ◊*electroencephalogram*.

eel any fish of the order Anguilliformes. Eels are snakelike, with elongated dorsal and anal fins. They include the freshwater eels of Europe and North America (which breed in the Atlantic), the marine conger eels, and the morays of tropical coral reefs.

efficiency output of a machine (work done by the machine) divided by the input (work put into the machine), usually expressed as a percentage. Because of losses caused by friction, efficiency is always less than 100%, although it can approach this for electrical machines with no moving parts (such as a transformer).

EFTA acronym for ◊*European Free Trade Association*.

EFTPOS (acronym for *electronic funds transfer at point of sale*) transfer of funds from one bank account to another by electronic means. For example, a customer inserts a plastic card into a point-of-sale computer terminal in a supermarket, and telephone lines are used to make an automatic debit from the customer's bank account to settle the bill.

egalitarianism belief that all citizens in a state should have equal rights and privileges. Interpretations of this can vary, from the notion of equality of opportunity to equality in material welfare and political decision-making. Some states clearly reject any thought of egalitarianism; most accept the concept of equal opportunities but recognize that people's abilities vary widely. Even those states which claim to be socialist find it necessary to have hierarchical structures in the political, social, and economic spheres. Egalitarianism was one of the principles of the French Revolution.

egg in animals, the ovum, or female ◊gamete (reproductive cell). After fertilization by a sperm cell, it begins to divide to form an embryo. Eggs may be deposited by the female (ovipary) or they may develop within her body (◊vivipary and ovovivipary). In the oviparous reptiles and birds, the egg is protected by a shell, and well supplied with nutrients in the form of yolk. *See illustration p. 304*

eggplant perennial plant, *Solanum melongena*, a member of the nightshade family (Solanaceae), originally native to tropical Asia. Its purple-skinned fruits are eaten as a vegetable.

ego in psychology, a general term for the processes concerned with the self and a person's conception of himself or herself, encompassing values and attitudes.

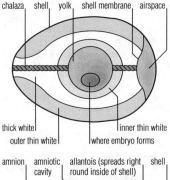

egg Section through a fertilized bird egg.

chalaza   shell   yolk   shell membrane   airspace

thick white
outer thin white

inner thin white
where embryo forms

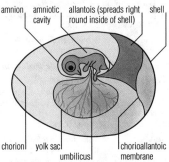

amnion   amniotic   allantois (spreads right   shell
            cavity   round inside of shell)

chorion   yolk sac   chorioallantoic
            umbilicus   membrane

In Freudian psychology, the term refers specifically to the element of the human mind that represents the conscious processes concerned with reality, in conflict with the ◊id (the instinctual element) and the ◊superego (the ethically aware element).

egret any of several herons with long feathers on the head or neck.

The snowy egret *Egretta thula* of North America, about 2 ft/60 cm long, was almost hunted to extinction for its graceful plumes before the practice was made illegal. The little egret *E. garzetta* 2 ft/60 cm long, is found in Asia, Africa, S Europe, and Australia.

Egypt country in NE Africa, bounded N by the Mediterranean Sea, E by the Suez Canal and Red Sea, S by Sudan, and W by Libya.

Egyptian religion in the civilization of ancient Egypt, totemic animals, believed to be the ancestors of the clan, were worshiped. Totems later developed into

Einstein Physicist Albert Einstein, 1944; he formulated the theories of relativity and his unified field theory.

gods, represented as having animal heads. One of the main cults was that of ◊Osiris, the god of the underworld. Immortality, conferred by the magical rite of mummification, was originally the sole prerogative of the king, but was extended under the New Kingdom to all who could afford it; they were buried with the Book of the Dead.

Egyptology the study of ancient Egypt. Interest in the subject was aroused by the Napoleonic expedition's discovery of the ◊Rosetta Stone 1799. Various excavations continued throughout the 19th century and gradually assumed a more scientific character, largely as a result of the work of the British archeologist Flinders Petrie from 1880 onward and the formation of the Egyptian Exploration Fund 1892. In 1922 another British archeologist, Howard Carter, discovered the tomb of Tutankhamen, the only royal tomb with all its treasures intact.

Ehrlich Paul 1854–1915. German bacteriologist and immunologist who produced the first cure for ◊syphilis. He developed the arsenic compounds, in particular Salvarsan, that were used in the treatment of syphilis prior to the discovery of antibiotics. He shared the 1908 Nobel Prize for Medicine with Ilya ◊Mechnikov for his work on immunity.

Eichmann (Karl) Adolf 1906–1962. Austrian Nazi. As an ◊SS official during Hitler's regime (1933–45), he was responsible for atrocities against Jews and others, including the implementation of genocide. He managed to escape at the fall of Germany 1945, but was discovered in Argentina 1960, abducted by Israeli agents, tried in Israel 1961 for ◊war crimes, and executed.

eider large marine ◊duck, *Somateria mollissima*, highly valued for its soft down, which is used in quilts and cushions for warmth. The adult male has a black cap and belly and a green nape. The rest of the plumage is white with pink breast and throat while the female is a mottled brown. The bill is large and flattened. It is found on the N coasts of the Atlantic and Pacific Oceans.

Eiffel (Alexandre) Gustave 1832–1923. French engineer who constructed the *Eiffel Tower* for the 1889 Paris Exhibition. The tower, made of iron, is 1,050 ft/320 m high, and stands in the Champ de Mars, Paris.

Einstein Albert 1879–1955. German-born US physicist who formulated the theories of ◊relativity, and worked on radiation physics and thermodynamics. In 1905 he published the special theory of relativity, and in 1915 issued his general theory of relativity. He received the Nobel Prize for Physics 1921. His latest conception of the basic laws governing the universe was outlined in his ◊unified field theory, made public 1953.

einsteinium synthesized, radioactive, metallic element of the actinide series, symbol Es, atomic number 99, atomic weight 254.

Eire Gaelic name for the Republic of ◊Ireland.

Eisai 1141–1215. Japanese Buddhist monk who introduced Zen and tea from China to Japan and founded the ◊Rinzai school.

Eisenhower Dwight David ("Ike") 1890–1969. 34th president of the US 1953–61, a Republican. A general in World War II, he commanded the Allied forces in Italy 1943, then the Allied invasion of Europe, and from Oct 1944 all the Allied armies in the West. As president he promoted business interests at home and conducted the ◊Cold War abroad. His vice president was Richard Nixon. *See illustration p. 307*

Egypt
Arab Republic of
(*Jumhuriyat Misr al-Arabiya*)

area 386,990 sq mi/1,001,450 sq km
capital Cairo
cities Gîza; ports Alexandria, Port Said, Suez, Damietta
physical mostly desert; hills in E; fertile land along Nile valley and delta; cultivated and settled area is about 13,700 sq mi/35,500 sq km
environment the building of the Aswan Dam (opened 1970) on the Nile has caused widespread salinization and an increase in waterborne diseases in villages close to Lake Nasser. A dramatic fall in the annual load of silt deposited downstream has reduced the fertility of cropland and has led to coastal erosion and the consequent loss of sardine shoals
features Aswan High Dam and Lake Nasser; Sinai; remains of ancient Egypt (pyramids, Sphinx, Luxor, Karnak, Abu Simbel, El Faiyum)
head of state and government Hosni Mubarak from 1981
political system democratic republic
political parties National Democratic Party (NDP), moderate left of center; Socialist Labor Party, right of center; Socialist Liberal Party, free-enterprise; New Wafd Party, nationalist
exports cotton and textiles, petroleum, fruit and vegetables
currency Egyptian pound
population (1992) 55,979,000; growth rate 2.4% p.a.
life expectancy men 57, women 60
languages Arabic (official); ancient Egyptian survives to some extent in Coptic

media there is no legal censorship, but the largest publishing houses, newspapers, and magazines are owned and controlled by the state, as is all television. Questioning of prevalent values, ideas, and social practices is discouraged
religions Sunni Muslim 95%, Coptic Christian 5%
literacy men 59%, women 30% (1985 est)
GDP $34.5 bn (1987); $679 per head
chronology
1914 Egypt became a British protectorate.
1936 Independence achieved from Britain. King Fuad succeeded by his son Farouk.
1946 Withdrawal of British troops except from Suez Canal Zone.
1952 Farouk overthrown by army in bloodless coup.
1953 Egypt declared a republic, with General Neguib as president.
1956 Neguib replaced by Col Gamal Nasser. Nasser announced nationalization of Suez Canal; Egypt attacked by Britain, France, and Israel. Cease-fire agreed because of US intervention.
1958 Short-lived merger of Egypt and Syria as United Arab Republic (UAR). Subsequent attempts to federate Egypt, Syria, and Iraq failed.
1967 Six-Day War with Israel ended in Egypt's defeat and Israeli occupation of Sinai and Gaza Strip.
1970 Nasser died suddenly; succeeded by Anwar Sadat.
1973 Attempt to regain territory lost to Israel led to fighting; cease-fire arranged by US secretary of state Henry Kissinger.
1977 Sadat's visit to Israel to address the Israeli parliament was criticized by Egypt's Arab neighbors.
1978–79 Camp David talks in the US resulted in a treaty between Egypt and Israel. Egypt expelled from the Arab League.
1981 Sadat assassinated, succeeded by Hosni Mubarak.
1983 Improved relations between Egypt and the Arab world; only Libya and Syria maintained a trade boycott.
1984 Mubarak's party victorious in the people's assembly elections.
1987 Mubarak reelected. Egypt readmitted to Arab League.
1988 Full diplomatic relations with Algeria restored.
1989 Improved relations with Libya; diplomatic relations with Syria restored. Mubarak proposed a peace plan.
1990 Gains for independents in general election.
1991 Participation in Gulf War on US-led side. Major force in convening Middle East peace conference in Spain.
1992 Outbreaks of violence between Muslims and Christians. Earthquake devastated Cairo.

He was well-liked and had a talent for administration.

EKG abbreviation for ◊*electrocardiogram*.

elastic collision in physics, a collision between two or more bodies in which the total ◊kinetic energy of the bodies is conserved (remains constant); none is converted into any other form of energy. ◊Momentum also is conserved in such collisions. The molecules of a gas may be considered to collide elastically, but large objects may not because some of their kinetic energy will be converted on collision to heat and sound.

elasticity in physics, the ability of a solid to recover its shape once deforming forces (stresses modifying its dimensions or shape) are removed. An elastic material obeys ◊Hooke's law: that is, its deformation is proportional to the applied stress up to a certain point, called the *elastic limit*, beyond which additional stress will deform it permanently. Elastic materials include metals and rubber; however, all materials have some degree of elasticity.

E layer (formerly called the Kennelly–Heaviside layer) the lower regions of the ◊ionosphere, which refract radio waves, allowing their reception around the surface of the Earth. The E layer approaches the Earth by day and recedes from it at night.

Elbe one of the principal rivers of Germany, 725 mi/1,166 km long, rising on the S slopes of the Riesengebirge, Czech Republic, and flowing NW across the German plain to the North Sea.

Elbruz or *Elbrus* highest mountain (18,510 ft/5,642 m) on the continent of Europe, in the Caucasus, Georgia.

elder in botany, small tree or shrub of the genus *Sambucus*, of the honeysuckle family (Caprifoliaceae), native to North America, Eurasia, and N Africa. Some are grown as ornamentals for their showy yellow or white flower clusters and their colorful black or scarlet berries. The American elder *S. canadensis* attains tree size and has blue berries.

Egypt, ancient
Egyptian mask from the Ptolemaic period, 3rd–2nd centuries BC.

elder in the Presbyterian church, a lay member who assists the minister (or teaching elder) in running the church.

El Dorado fabled city of gold believed by the 16th-century Spanish and other Europeans to exist somewhere in the area of the Orinoco and Amazon rivers.

Eleanor of Aquitaine *c.* 1122–1204. Queen of France 1137–51 as wife of Louis VII, and of England from 1154 as wife of Henry II. Henry imprisoned her 1174–89 for supporting their sons, the future Richard I and King John, in revolt against him.

Eleanor of Castile *c.* 1245–1290. Queen of Edward I of England, the daughter of Ferdinand III of Castile. She married Prince Edward 1254, and accompanied him on his crusade 1270. She died at Harby, Nottinghamshire, and Edward erected stone crosses in towns where her body rested on the funeral journey to London. Several *Eleanor Crosses* are still standing, for example at Northampton.

elector (German *Kurfürst*) any of originally seven (later ten) princes of the Holy Roman Empire who had the prerogative of electing the emperor (in effect, the king of Germany). The electors were the archbishops of Mainz, Trier, and Cologne, the court palatine of the Rhine, the Duke of Saxony, the Margrave of Brandenburg, and the king of Bohemia (in force to 1806). Their constitutional status was formalized 1356 in the document known as the *Golden Bull*, which granted them extensive powers within their own domains, to act as judges, issue coins, and impose tolls.

electoral college in the US government, the indirect system of voting for the president and vice president. The people of each state officially vote not for the presidential candidate, but for a list of electors nominated by each party. The whole electoral-college vote of the state then goes to the winning party (and candidate). A majority is required for election.

electric arc a continuous electric discharge of high current between two electrodes, giving out a brilliant light and heat. The phenomenon is exploited in the carbon-arc lamp, once widely used in film projectors. In the electric-arc furnace an arc struck between very large carbon electrodes and the metal charge provides the heating. In arc ◊welding an electric arc provides the heat to fuse the metal. The discharges in low-pressure gases, as in neon and sodium lights, can also be broadly considered as electric arcs.

electric charge property of some bodies that causes them to exert forces on each other. Two bodies both with positive or both with negative charges repel each other, whereas bodies with opposite or "unlike" charges attract each other, since each is in the ◊electric field of the other. In atoms, ◊electrons possess a negative charge, and ◊protons an equal positive charge. The ◊SI unit of electric charge is the coulomb (symbol C).

electric current the flow of electrically charged particles through a conducting circuit due to the presence of a potential difference. The current at any point in a circuit is the amount of charge flowing per second; its SI unit is the ampere (coulomb per second).

electric field in physics, the electrically charged region of space surrounding an electrically charged body. In this region, an electric charge experiences a force owing to the presence of another electric charge.

electricity all phenomena caused by ◊electric charge, whether static or in motion. Electric charge is caused by an excess or deficit of electrons in the charged substance, and an electric current by the movement of electrons around a circuit. Substances may be electrical conductors, such as metals, which allow the passage of electricity through them, or insulators, such as rubber, which are extremely poor conductors. Substances with relatively poor conductivities that can be improved by the addition of heat or light are known as ◊semiconductors.

electrocardiogram (ECG) or (EKG) graphic recording of the electrical changes in the heart muscle, as detected by electrodes placed on the chest. Electrocardiography is used in the diagnosis of heart disease.

electrochemistry the branch of science that studies chemical reactions involving electricity. The use of electricity to produce chemical effects, ◊electrolysis, is employed in many industrial processes, such as the manufacture of chlorine and the extraction of aluminum. The use of chemical reactions to produce electricity is the basis of electrical ◊cells, such as the dry cell and the ◊Leclanché cell.

electroconvulsive therapy (ECT) or *electroshock therapy* treatment for ◊schizophrenia and ◊depression, given under anesthesia and with a muscle relaxant. An electric current is passed through the brain to induce alterations in the brain's electrical activity. The treatment can cause distress and loss of concentration and memory, and so there is much controversy about its use and effectiveness.

electrocution death caused by electric current. It is used as a method of execution in some US states. The condemned person is strapped into a special chair and a shock of 1,800–2,000 volts is administered. See ◊capital punishment.

electrode any terminal by which an electric current passes in or out of a conducting substance; for example, the anode or cathode in a battery or the carbons in an arc lamp. The terminals that emit and collect the flow of electrons in thermionic ◊valves (electron tubes) are also called electrodes: for example, cathodes, plates, and grids.

electrodynamics the branch of physics dealing with electric currents and associated magnetic forces. ◊Quantum electrodynamics (QED) studies the interaction between charged particles and their emission and absorption of electromagnetic radiation. This field combines quantum theory and relativity theory, making accurate predictions about subatomic processes involving charged particles such as electrons and protons.

electroencephalogram (EEG) graphic record of the electrical discharges of the brain, as detected by electrodes placed on the scalp. The pattern of electrical activity revealed by electroencephalography is helpful in the diagnosis of some brain disorders, such as epilepsy.

electrolysis in chemistry, the production of chemical changes by passing an electric current through a solution or molten salt (the electrolyte), resulting in the migration of ions to the electrodes: positive ions (cations) to the negative electrode (cathode) and negative ions (anions) to the positive electrode (anode).

electrolyte a solution or molten substance in which an electric current is made to flow by the movement and discharge of ions in accordance with Faraday's laws of ◊electrolysis.

electromagnet an iron bar with coils of wire around it, which acts as a magnet when an electric current flows through the wire. Electromagnets have many uses: in switches, electric bells, solenoids, and metal-lifting cranes.

electromagnetic field in physics, the region in which a particle with an ◊electric charge experiences a force. If it does so only when moving, it is in a pure *magnetic field*; if it does so when stationary, it is in an *electric field*. Both can be present simultaneously.

electromagnetic force one of the four fundamental ◊forces of nature, the other three being gravity, the strong nuclear force, and the weak nuclear force. The ◊elementary particle that is the carrier for the electromagnetic (em) force is the photon.

electromagnetic induction in electronics, the production of an ◊electromotive force (emf) in a circuit by a change of magnetic flux through the circuit or by relative motion of the circuit and the magnetic flux. In a closed circuit an induced current will be produced. All dynamos and generators make use of this effect. When magnetic tape is driven past the playback head (a small coil) of a tape-recorder, the moving magnetic field induces an emf in the head, which is then amplified to reproduce the recorded sounds.

electromagnetic waves oscillating electric and magnetic fields traveling together through space at a speed of nearly 186,000 mi/300,000 km per second. The (limitless) range of possible wavelengths or ◊frequencies of electromagnetic waves, which can be thought of as making up the *electromagnetic spectrum*, includes radio waves, infrared radiation, visible light, ultraviolet radiation, X-rays, and gamma rays. *See illustration p. 308*

electromotive force (emf) in physics, the greatest potential difference that can be generated by a source of current. This is always greater than the measured potential difference generated, due to the resistance of the wires and components, in the circuit.

Eisenhower US soldier and Republican president Dwight D Eisenhower.

electron stable, negatively charged ◊elementary particle; it is a constituent of all atoms, and a member of the class of particles known as leptons. The electrons in each atom surround the nucleus in groupings called shells; in a neutral atom the number of electrons is equal to the number of protons in the nucleus. This electron structure is responsible for the chemical properties of the atom (see ◊atomic structure).

electronic mail or *E-mail* ◊telecommunications system that enables the users of a computer network to send messages to other users. Telephone wires are used to send the signals from terminal to terminal.

electronic music a form of studio-based serial music composed entirely of electronically generated and modified tones, as opposed to *concrete music*, which arranges pre-recorded sounds by intuition. The term was later broadened to include pre-recorded vocal and instrumental sounds, although always implying a serial basis. Maderna, ◊Stockhausen, and ◊Babbitt were among the pioneers of electronic music in the 1950s.

electronics branch of science that deals with the emission of ◊electrons from conductors and ◊semiconductors, with the subsequent manipulation of these electrons, and with the construction of electronic devices. The first electronic device was the thermionic ◊valve, or vacuum tube, in which electrons moved in a vacuum, and led to such inventions as ◊radio, ◊television, ◊radar, and the digital ◊computer. Replacement of valves with the comparatively tiny and reliable transistor from 1948 revolutionized electronic development. Modern electronic devices are based on minute integrated circuits (silicon chips), wafer-thin crystal slices holding tens of thousands of electronic components.

electron microscope instrument that produces a magnified image by using a beam of ◊electrons instead of light rays, as in an optical ◊microscope. An *electron lens* is an arrangement of electromagnetic coils that control and focus the beam. Electrons are not visible to the eye, so instead of an eyepiece there is a fluorescent screen or a photographic plate on which the electrons form an image. The wavelength of the electron beam is much shorter than that of light, so much greater magnification and resolution (ability to distinguish detail) can be achieved. The development of the

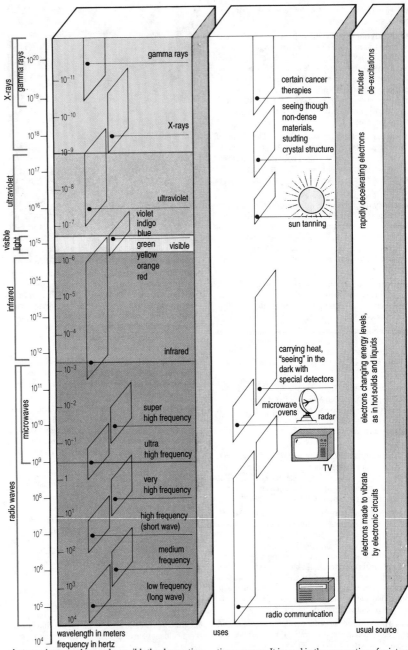

electromagnetic waves Frequencies are progressively higher from those of radio waves to the highest, gamma rays.

electron microscope has made possible the observation of very minute organisms, viruses, and even large molecules.

electron volt unit (symbol eV) for measuring the energy of a charged particle (◊ion or ◊electron) in terms of the energy of motion an electron would gain from a potential difference of one volt. Because it is so small, more usual units are mega- (million) and giga- (billion) electron volts (MeV and GeV).

electroplating deposition of metals upon metallic surfaces by electrolysis for decorative and/or protec-

tive purposes. It is used in the preparation of printers' blocks, "master" audio disks, and in many other processes.

electroporation in biotechnology, a technique of introducing foreign ◊DNA into pollen with a strong burst of electricity, used in creating genetically engineered plants.

electroscope an apparatus for detecting ◊electric charge. The simple gold-leaf electroscope consists of a vertical conducting (metal) rod ending in a pair of rectangular pieces of gold foil, mounted inside and insulated from an earthed metal case. An electric charge applied to the end of the metal rod makes the gold leaves diverge, because they each receive a similar charge (positive or negative) and so repel each other.

electrovalent bond another name for an ◊ionic bond, a chemical bond in which the combining atoms lose or gain electrons to form ions.

element substance that cannot be split chemically into simpler substances. The atoms of a particular element all have the same number of protons in their nuclei (their atomic number). Elements are classified in the periodic table (see ◊periodic table of the elements). Of the 109 known elements, 95 are known to occur in nature (those with atomic numbers 1–95). Those from 96 to 109 do not occur in nature and are synthesized only, produced in particle accelerators. Eighty-one of the elements are stable; all the others, which include atomic numbers 43, 61, and from 84 up, are radioactive.

elementary particle or *fundamental particle* any of those particles that combine to form ◊atoms and all ◊matter, the most familiar being the electron, proton, and neutron. More than 200 particles have now been identified by physicists, categorized into several classes as characterized by their mass, electric charge, spin, magnetic moment, and interaction. Although many particles were thought to be nondivisible and permanent, now most are known to be combinations of a small number of basic particles.

elephant mammal belonging to either of two surviving species of the order Proboscidea: the Asian elephant *Elephas maximus* and the African elephant *Loxodonta africana*. Elephants can grow to 13 ft/4 m and weigh up to 8 tons; they have a thick, gray, wrinkled skin, a large head, a long trunk used to obtain food and water, and upper incisors or tusks, which grow to a considerable length. The African elephant has very large ears and a flattened forehead, and the Asian species has smaller ears and a convex forehead. In India, Myanmar (Burma), and Thailand, Asiatic elephants are widely used for transport and logging.

elephantiasis in the human body, a condition of local enlargement and deformity, most often of a leg, the scrotum, a labium of the vulva, or a breast, caused by the blocking of lymph channels.

elevator any mechanical device for raising or lowering people or materials. It usually consists of a platform or boxlike structure suspended by motor-driven cables with safety ratchets along the sides of the shaft. US inventor Elisha Graves ◊Otis developed the first passenger safety elevator 1852, installed 1857. This invention permitted the development of skyscrapers from the 1880s. At first steam powered the movement, but hydraulic and then electric elevators were common from the early 1900s. Elevator operators worked controls and gates within the cab until the automatic, or self-starter, was introduced.

Elgin city in NE Illinois, NW of Chicago, on the Fox River; population (1990) 77,000. Industries include electrical machinery and dairy products. The city was once the home of Elgin watches.

Elgin marbles collection of ancient Greek sculptures, including the famous frieze and other sculptures from the Parthenon at Athens, assembled by the 7th Earl of Elgin. Sent to England 1812, and bought for the nation 1816 for £35,000, they are now in the British Museum. Greece has repeatedly asked for them to be returned to Athens.

Asiatic Elephant

African Elephant

elephant The elephant is the largest and most powerful land mammal.

Elijah *c.* mid-9th century BC. In the Old Testament, a Hebrew prophet during the reigns of the Israelite kings Ahab and Ahaziah. He came from Gilead. He defeated the prophets of ◊Baal, and was said to have been carried up to heaven in a fiery chariot in a whirlwind. In Jewish belief, Elijah will return to Earth to herald the coming of the Messiah.

Eliot Charles William 1834–1926. US educator credited with establishing the standards of modern American higher education. He was appointed professor at the Massachusetts Institute of Technology (MIT) 1865 and was named president of Harvard University 1869. Under Eliot's administration, the college and its graduate and professional schools were reorganized and the curriculum and admission requirements standardized. He retired 1909.

Eliot George. Adopted name of Mary Ann Evans 1819–1880. English novelist whose works include the pastoral *Adam Bede* 1859; *The Mill on the Floss* 1860, with its autobiographical elements; *Silas Marner* 1861, which contains elements of the folktale; and *Daniel Deronda* 1876. *Middlemarch*, published serially in 1871–72, is considered her greatest novel for its confident handling of numerous characters and central social and moral issues. Her work is pervaded by a penetrating and compassionate intelligence.

Eliot T(homas) S(tearns) 1888–1965. US poet, playwright, and critic who lived in London from 1915. His first volume of poetry, *Prufrock and Other Observations* 1917, introduced new verse forms and rhythms; further collections include *The Waste Land* 1922, *The Hollow Men* 1925, and *Old Possum's Book of Practical Cats* 1939. His plays include *Murder in the Cathedral* 1935 and *The Cocktail Party* 1949. His critical works include *The Sacred Wood* 1920. He was awarded the Nobel Prize for Literature 1948.

Elisabethville former name of ◊Lubumbashi, a city in Zaire.

Elizabeth city in NE New Jersey; population (1990) 110,000. Established 1664, it was the first English settlement in New Jersey. It has automobile, sewing-

Scots, executed 1587. Her conflict with Roman Catholic Spain led to the defeat of the ◊Spanish Armada 1588. The Elizabethan age was expansionist in commerce and geographical exploration, and arts and literature flourished. The rulers of many European states made unsuccessful bids to marry Elizabeth, and she used these bids to strengthen her power. She was succeeded by James I.

Elizabeth II 1926– . Queen of Great Britain and Northern Ireland from 1952, the elder daughter of George VI. She married her third cousin, Philip, the Duke of Edinburgh, 1947. They have four children: Charles, Anne, Andrew, and Edward.

Elizabeth 1709–1762. Empress of Russia from 1741, daughter of Peter the Great. She carried through a palace revolution and supplanted her cousin, the infant Ivan VI (1730–1764), on the throne. She continued the policy of westernization begun by Peter and allied herself with Austria against Prussia.

Elizabethan literature literature produced during the reign of Elizabeth I of England (1558–1603). This period saw a remarkable florescence of the arts in England, and the literature of the time is characterized by a new energy, richness, and confidence. Renaissance humanism, Protestant zeal, and geographical discovery all contributed to this upsurge of creative power. Drama was the dominant form of the age, and ◊Shakespeare and ◊Marlowe were popular with all levels of society. Other writers of the period include Edmund Spenser, Sir Philip Sidney, Francis Bacon, Thomas Lodge, Robert Greene, and John Lyly.

elk or **wapiti** North American deer *Cervus canadensis*, closely related to the red ◊deer of Eurasia. Head and body length is about 8 ft/2.5 m, and shoulder height is about 5 ft/1.5 m. They are grayish-brown with a yellow rump patch. Males carry magnificent antlers up to 5.8 ft/1.8 m along the beam. In Europe, moose are called elk.

Elkhart city in N Indiana, E of South Bend, where the Elkhart River meets the St Joseph River; population (1990) 43,600. Its factories produce mobile homes, firefighting apparatus, recreational vehicles, pharmaceuticals, and musical instruments.

Ellice Islands former name of ◊Tuvalu, a group of islands in the W Pacific Ocean.

Ellington Duke (Edward Kennedy) 1899–1974. US pianist who had an outstanding career as a composer and arranger of jazz. He wrote numerous pieces for his own jazz orchestra, accentuating the strengths of individual virtuoso instrumentalists, and became one of the leading figures in jazz over a 55-year period. Some of his most popular compositions include "Mood Indigo," "Sophisticated Lady," "Solitude," and "Black and Tan Fantasy." He was one of the founders of big band jazz.

ellipse curve joining all points (loci) around two fixed points (foci) such that the sum of the distances from those points is always constant. The diameter passing through the foci is the major axis, and the diameter bisecting this at right angles is the minor axis. An ellipse is one of a series of curves known as conic sections. A slice across a cone that is not made parallel to, and does not pass through, the base will produce an ellipse.

Ellis Island island in New York Harbor; area 27 acres/11 hectares. A former reception center for steerage-class immigrants during the immigration waves between 1892 and 1943 (12 million people passed

Elizabeth I Portrait miniature (c. 1595) by Nicholas Hilliard, Victoria and Albert Museum, London.

machine, and tool factories; oil refineries; and chemical works.

Elizabeth in the New Testament, mother of John the Baptist. She was a cousin of Jesus' mother Mary, who came to see her shortly after the Annunciation; on this visit (called the Visitation), Mary sang the hymn of praise later to be known as the "Magnificat."

Elizabeth the *Queen Mother* 1900– . Wife of King George VI of England. She was born Lady Elizabeth Angela Marguerite Bowes-Lyon, and on April 26, 1923, she married Albert, Duke of York, who became King George VI in 1936. Their children are Queen Elizabeth II and Princess Margaret.

Elizabeth I 1533–1603. Queen of England 1558–1603, the daughter of Henry VIII and Anne Boleyn. Through her Religious Settlement of 1559 she enforced the Protestant religion by law. She had ◊Mary, Queen of

elm The typical elm leaf is oval, toothed, and distinctly lopsided.

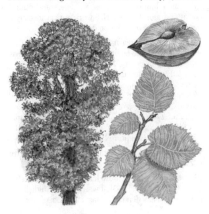

through it 1892–1924), it was later used as a detention center for nonresidents without documentation, or for those who were being deported. It is a National Historic Site (1964) and has the Museum of Immigration (1989).

Ellsworth Oliver 1745–1807. US jurist and chief justice of the US Supreme Court 1796–1800. As a Connecticut delegate to the Constitutional Convention 1777, he was instrumental in effecting the "Connecticut Compromise," which balanced large and small state interests. He was selected as US senator from Connecticut in 1787. Appointed chief justice by President Washington, his opinions shaped admiralty law and treaty law.

elm tree of the genus *Ulmus* of the family Ulmaceae, found in temperate regions of the N hemisphere and in mountainous parts of the tropics. All have doubly-toothed leaf margins and bear clusters of small flowers. The American elm *U. americana* and slippery elm *U. rubra* are native to E North America.

Elmira city in S central New York, on the Chemung River, W of Binghamton, just below the Finger Lakes region; seat of Chemung County; population (1990) 33,700. It is the processing and marketing center for the area's dairy and poultry farms. Other industries include business machinery, machine parts, airplanes, and fire engines. Elmira College (1853) is located here.

El Niño warm ocean surge of the ◊Peru Current, so called because it tends to occur at Christmas, recurring every 5–8 years or so in the E Pacific off South America. It involves a change in the direction of ocean currents, which prevents the upwelling of cold, nutrient-rich waters along the coast of Ecuador and Peru, killing fishes and plants. It is an important factor in global weather.

Elizabeth II Queen Elizabeth II of the United Kingdom and head of the Commonwealth.

El Salvador
Republic of
(*República de El Salvador*)

area 8,258 sq mi/21,393 sq km
capital San Salvador
cities Santa Ana, San Miguel
physical narrow coastal plain, rising to mountains in N with central plateau
features smallest and most densely populated Central American country; Mayan archeological remains
head of state and government Alfredo Cristiani from 1989
political system emergent democracy
political parties Christian Democrats (PDC), anti-imperialist; National Republican Alliance (ARENA), right-wing; National Conciliation Party (PCN), right-wing; Farabundo Marti Liberation Front (FMLN), left-wing
exports coffee, cotton, sugar

currency colón
population (1992) 5,460,000 (mainly of mixed Spanish and Indian ancestry; 10% Indian); growth rate 2.9% p.a.
life expectancy men 63, women 66
languages Spanish, Nahuatl
religion Roman Catholic 97%
literacy men 75%, women 69% (1985 est)
GDP $4.7 bn (1987); $790 per head

chronology
1821 Independence achieved from Spain.
1931 Peasant unrest followed by a military coup.
1932 30,000 peasants slaughtered following unrest, virtually eliminating native Salvadoreans.
1961 Following a coup, PCN established and in power.
1969 "Soccer" war with Honduras.
1972 Allegations of human-rights violations; growth of left-wing guerrilla activities. General Carlos Romero elected president.
1979 A coup replaced Romero with a military-civilian junta.
1980 Archbishop Oscar Romero assassinated; country on verge of civil war. José Duarte became first civilian president since 1931.
1981 Mexico and France recognized the guerrillas as a legitimate political force, but the US actively assisted the government in its battle against them.
1982 Assembly elections boycotted by left-wing parties and held amid considerable violence.
1986 Duarte sought a negotiated settlement with the guerrillas.
1988 Duarte resigned.
1989 Alfredo Cristiani (ARENA) became president in rigged elections; rebel attacks intensified.
1991 United Nations-sponsored peace accord signed by representatives of the government and the socialist guerrilla group, the FMLN.
1992 Peace accord validated; FMLN became political party.

embryo The development of a bird and a human embryo.

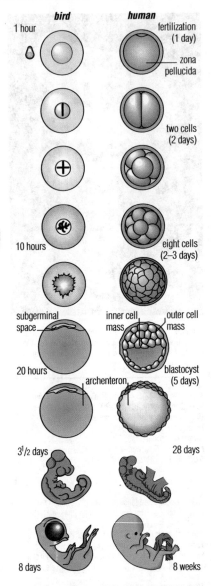

bird — **human**

1 hour — fertilization (1 day)

zona pellucida

two cells (2 days)

eight cells (2–3 days)

10 hours

subgerminal space — inner cell mass / outer cell mass

20 hours — blastocyst (5 days)

archenteron

3½ days — 28 days

8 days — 8 weeks

El Paso city in Texas, situated at the base of the Franklin Mountains, on the Rio Grande, opposite the Mexican city of Ciudad Juárez; population (1990) 515,300. It is the center of an agricultural and cattle-raising area, and there are electronics, food processing, packing, and leather industries, as well as oil refineries and industries based on local iron and copper mines.

There are several military installations in the area.

El Salvador country in Central America, bounded N and E by Honduras, S and SW by the Pacific Ocean, and NW by Guatemala. *See panel p. 311*

Ely Richard Theodore 1854–1943. US economist and an early advocate of government economic intervention, central planning, and the organization of the labor force. He was appointed professor of political economy at Johns Hopkins University 1881 and in 1885 founded the American Economic Association. In 1892 he became chair of the department of economics at the University of Wisconsin before joining the faculty of Northwestern University 1925.

Elyria city in N Ohio, on the Black River, W of Cleveland; seat of Lorain County; population (1990) 56,700. Industries include tools, electric motors, chromium hardware, chemicals, and automotive parts.

Elysée Palace *(Palais de l'Elysée)* building in Paris erected 1718 for Louis d'Auvergne, Count of Evreux. It was later the home of Mme de Pompadour, Napoleon I, and Napoleon III, and became the official residence of the presidents of France 1870.

Elysium in Greek mythology, originally another name for the Islands of the Blessed, to which favored heroes were sent by the gods to enjoy a life after death. Later a region in ◊Hades.

Emancipation Proclamation in US history, President Lincoln's Civil War announcement, Sept 22, 1862, stating that from the beginning of 1863 all black slaves in states still engaged in rebellion against the federal government would be emancipated. Slaves in border states still remaining loyal to the Union were excluded.

Lincoln had read a preliminary proclamation to his cabinet, who urged him to wait until a major Union victory before delivering it publicly.

embargo the legal prohibition by a government of trade with another country, forbidding foreign ships to leave or enter its ports. Trade embargoes may be imposed on a country seen to be violating international laws.

embezzlement in law, theft by an employee of property entrusted to him or her by an employer.

embolism blockage of a blood vessel by an obstruction called an embolus (usually a blood clot, fat particle, or bubble of air).

embossing relief decoration on metals, which can be cast, chased, or repoussé, and executed by hand or machine. In the 16th century the term was also used for carved decorations on wood. Embossed bindings for books were developed from the early 19th century; the leather is embossed before binding.

embroidery the art of decorating cloth with a needle and thread. It includes broderie anglaise, gros point, and petit point, all of which have been used for the adornment of costumes, gloves, book covers, furnishings, and ecclesiastical vestments.

embryo early development stage of an animal or a plant following fertilization of an ovum (egg cell), or activation of an ovum by ◊parthenogenesis. In humans, the term embryo describes the fertilized egg during its first seven weeks of existence; from the eighth week onward it is referred to as a fetus.

embryology study of the changes undergone by an organism from its conception as a fertilized ovum (egg) to its emergence into the world at hatching or birth. It is mainly concerned with the changes in cell organization in the embryo and the way in which these lead to the structures and organs of the adult (the process of ◊differentiation).

encomienda in colonial Spanish America, the granting of Indian people to individual conquistadors (settlers) by the Spanish crown.

emerald a clear, green gemstone variety of the mineral ◊beryl. It occurs naturally in Colombia, the Ural Mountains, in Russia, Zimbabwe, and Australia.

Emerson Ralph Waldo 1803–1882. US philosopher, essayist, and poet. He settled in Concord, Massachusetts, which he made a center of transcendentalism, and wrote *Nature* 1836, which states the movement's main principles emphasizing the value of self-reliance and the Godlike nature of human souls. His two volumes of *Essays* (1841, 1844) made his reputation: "Self-Reliance" and "Compensation" are among the best known.

emery grayish-black opaque metamorphic rock consisting of ◊corundum and magnetite, together with other minerals such as hematite. It is used as an ◊abrasive.

emetic any substance administered to induce vomiting. Emetics are used to empty the stomach in many cases of deliberate or accidental ingestion of a poison. The most frequently used is ipecacuanha.

Emilia-Romagna region of N central Italy including much of the Po Valley; area 8,531 sq mi/22,100 sq km; population (1988) 3,924,000. The capital is Bologna; other cities include Reggio, Rimini, Parma, Ferrara, and Ravenna. Agricultural produce includes fruit, wine, sugar beet, beef, and dairy products; oil and natural-gas resources have been developed in the Po Valley.

eminent domain in the US, the right of federal and state government and other authorized bodies to compulsorily purchase land that is needed for public purposes. The owner is entitled to receive a fair price for the land.

Empedocles *c.* 490–430 BC. Greek philosopher and scientist. He lived at Acragas (Agrigentum) in Sicily, and proposed that the universe is composed of four elements—fire, air, earth, and water—which through the action of love and discord are eternally constructed, destroyed, and constructed anew. According to tradition, he committed suicide by throwing himself into the crater of Mount Etna.

emphysema incurable lung condition characterized by disabling breathlessness. Progressive loss of the thin walls dividing the air spaces (alveoli) in the lungs reduces the area available for the exchange of oxygen and carbon dioxide, causing the lung tissue to expand. The term "emphysema" can also refer to any abnormal swelling of body tissues caused by the accumulation of air.

empiricism in philosophy, the belief that all knowledge is ultimately derived from sense experience. It is suspicious of metaphysical schemes based on ◊a priori propositions, which are claimed to be true irrespective of experience. It is frequently contrasted with ◊rationalism.

EMS abbreviation for ◊European Monetary System.

emu flightless bird *Dromaius novaehollandiae* native to Australia. It stands about 6 ft/1.8 m high and has coarse brown plumage, small rudimentary wings, short feathers on the head and neck, and powerful legs, well adapted for running and kicking. The female has a curious bag or pouch in the windpipe that enables her to emit the characteristic loud booming note.

emulsifier food ◊additive used to keep oils dispersed and in suspension, in products such as mayonnaise and peanut butter. Egg yolk is a naturally occurring emulsifier, but most of the emulsifiers in commercial use today are synthetic chemicals.

emulsion a stable dispersion of a liquid in another liquid—for example, oil and water in some cosmetic lotions.

enamel vitrified (glasslike) coating of various colors used for decorative purposes on a metallic or porcelain surface. In ◊cloisonné the various sections of the design are separated by thin metal wires or strips. In *champlevé* the enamel is poured into engraved cavities in the metal surface.

encaustic painting an ancient technique of painting, commonly used by the Egyptians, Greeks, and Romans, in which colored pigments were mixed with molten wax and painted on panels.

encephalitis inflammation of the brain, nearly always due to virus infection but also to parasites, fungi, or malaria. It varies widely in severity, from short-lived, relatively slight effects of headache, drowsiness, and fever to paralysis, coma, and death. One such type of viral infection is also sometimes called "sleeping sickness."

Encke's comet comet with the shortest known orbital period, 3.3 years. It is named after German mathematician and astronomer Johann Franz Encke (1791–1865), who calculated its orbit in 1819 from earlier sightings.

encyclopedia work of reference covering either all fields of knowledge or one specific subject. Although most encyclopedias are alphabetical, with cross-references, some are organized thematically with indexes, to keep related subjects together.

Encyclopédie encyclopedia in 35 volumes written 1751–77 by a group of French scholars (Encyclopédistes) including D'Alembert and Diderot, inspired by the English encyclopedia produced by Ephraim Chambers 1728. Religious skepticism and ◊Enlightenment social and political views were a feature of the work.

endangered species plant or animal species whose numbers are so few that it is at risk of becoming extinct. Officially designated endangered species are listed by the International Union for the Conservation of Nature (IUCN).

endive cultivated annual plant *Cichorium endivia*, family Compositae, the leaves of which are used in salads and cooking. One variety has narrow, curled leaves; another has wide, smooth leaves.

endocrine gland gland that secretes hormones into the bloodstream to regulate body processes. Endocrine glands are most highly developed in vertebrates, but are also found in other animals, notably insects. In humans the main endocrine glands are the pituitary, thyroid, parathyroid, adrenal, pancreas, ovary, and testis.

endocrine gland gland that secretes hormones into the bloodstream to regulate body processes. Endocrine glands are most highly developed in vertebrates, but are also found in other animals, notably insects. In humans the main endocrine glands are the pituitary, thyroid, parathyroid, adrenal, pancreas, ovary, and testis.

endometriosis common gynecological complaint in which patches of endometrium (the lining of the womb) are found outside the uterus.

endorphin natural substance (a polypeptide) that modifies the action of nerve cells. Endorphins are produced by the pituitary gland and hypothalamus of vertebrates. They lower the perception of pain by reducing the transmission of signals between nerve cells.

endoscopy examination of internal organs or tissues by an instrument allowing direct vision. An endoscope is equipped with an eyepiece, lenses, and its own light source to illuminate the field of vision. The endoscope that examines the alimentary canal is a flexible fiber-optic instrument swallowed by the patient.

endoskeleton the internal supporting structure of vertebrates, made up of cartilage or bone. It provides support, and acts as a system of levers to which muscles are attached to provide movement. Certain parts of the skeleton (the skull and ribs) give protection to vital body organs.

endosperm nutritive tissue in the seeds of most flowering plants. It surrounds the embryo and is produced by an unusual process that parallels the ◊fertilization of the ovum by a male gamete. A second male gamete from the pollen grain fuses with two female nuclei within the ◊embryo sac. Thus endosperm cells are triploid (having three sets of chromosomes); they contain food reserves such as starch, fat, and protein that are utilized by the developing seedling.

endotherm "warm-blooded," or homeothermic, animal. Endotherms have internal mechanisms for regulating their body temperatures to levels different from the environmental temperature.

Endymion in Greek mythology, a beautiful young man loved by Selene, the Moon goddess. He was granted eternal sleep in order to remain forever young. Keats's poem "Endymion" 1818 is an allegory of searching for perfection.

energy capacity for doing ◊work. Potential energy (PE) is energy deriving from position; thus a stretched spring has elastic PE, and an object raised to a height above the Earth's surface, or the water in an elevated reservoir, has gravitational PE. A lump of coal and a tank of gasoline, together with the oxygen needed for their combustion, have chemical energy. Other sorts of energy include electrical and nuclear energy, and light and sound. Moving bodies possess kinetic energy (KE). Energy can be converted from one form to another, but the total quantity stays the same (in accordance with the conservation of energy principle). For example, as an apple falls, it loses gravitational PE but gains KE. Although energy is never lost, after a number of conversions it tends to finish up as the kinetic energy of random motion of molecules (of the air, for example) at relatively low temperatures. This is "degraded" energy in that it is difficult to convert it back to other forms.

energy level or **shell** or **orbital** the permitted energy that an electron can have in any particular system. Energy levels can be calculated using ◊quantum theory. The permitted energy levels depend mainly on the distance of the electron from the nucleus.

energy of reaction energy released or absorbed during a chemical reaction, also called **enthalpy of reaction** or **heat of reaction**. In a chemical reaction, the energy stored in the reacting molecules is rarely the same as that stored in the product molecules. Depending on which is the greater, energy is either released (an exothermic reaction) or absorbed (an endothermic reaction) from the surroundings. The amount of energy released or absorbed by the quantities of substances represented by the chemical equation is the energy of reaction.

Engels Friedrich 1820–1895. German social and political philosopher, a friend of, and collaborator with, Karl ◊Marx on *The Communist Manifesto* 1848 and other key works. His later interpretations of Marxism, and his own philosophical and historical studies such as *Origins of the Family, Private Property, and the State* 1884 (which linked patriarchy with the development of private property), developed such concepts as historical materialism. His use of positivism and Darwinian ideas gave Marxism a scientific and deterministic flavor which was to influence Soviet thinking.

engine device for converting stored energy into useful work or movement. Most engines use a fuel as their energy store. The fuel is burned to produce heat energy—hence the name "heat engine"—which is then converted into movement. Heat engines can be classified according to the fuel they use (◊gasoline engine or ◊diesel engine), or according to whether the fuel is burned inside (◊internal combustion engine) or outside (◊steam engine) the engine, or according to whether they produce a reciprocating or rotary motion (◊turbine or ◊Wankel engine).

engineering the application of science to the design, construction, and maintenance of works, machinery, roads, railroads, bridges, harbor installations, engines, ships, aircraft and airports, spacecraft and space stations, and the generation, transmission, and use of electrical power. The main divisions of engineering are aerospace, chemical, civil, electrical, electronic, gas, marine, materials, mechanical, mining, production, radio, and structural.

England largest division of the ◊United Kingdom.
area 50,318 sq mi/130,357 sq km
capital London
cities Birmingham, Coventry, Leeds, Leicester, Manchester, Newcastle-upon-Tyne, Nottingham, Sheffield; ports Bristol, Dover, Liverpool, Portsmouth, Southampton
features variability of climate and diversity of scenery; among European countries, only the Netherlands is more densely populated
exports agricultural (cereals, rape, sugar beet, potatoes); meat and meat products; electronic (software), and telecommunications equipment; scientific instruments; textiles and fashion goods; North Sea oil and gas, petrochemicals, and pharmaceuticals; film and television programs; sound recordings. Tourism is important. There are worldwide banking and insurance interests
currency pound sterling
population (1986) 47,255,000
language English, with more than 100 minority languages
religion Christian, with the Church of England as the established church; Jewish; Muslim
For *government* and *history*, see ◊Britain, ancient; ◊England: history; ◊United Kingdom.

England: history for pre-Roman history, see ◊Britain, ancient.
5th–7th centuries Anglo-Saxons overran all England except Cornwall and Cumberland, forming independent kingdoms including Northumbria, Mercia, Kent, and Wessex.
c. 597 England converted to Christianity by St Augustine.
829 Egbert of Wessex accepted as overlord of all England.
878 Alfred ceded N and E England to the Danish invaders but kept them out of Wessex.
1066 Norman Conquest; England passed into French hands under William the Conqueror.
1172 Henry II became king of Ireland and established a colony there.
1215 King John forced to sign Magna Carta.
1284 Conquest of Wales, begun by the Normans, completed by Edward I.
1295 Model Parliament set up.
1338–1453 Hundred Years' War with France.
1348–49 Black Death killed about 30% of the population.
1381 Social upheaval led to the Peasants' Revolt, which was brutally repressed.
1399 Richard II deposed by Parliament for absolutism.
1414 Lollard revolt repressed.
1455–85 Wars of the Roses.
1497 Henry VII ended the power of the feudal nobility with the suppression of the Yorkist revolts.
1529 Henry VIII became head of the Church of England after breaking with Rome.
1536–43 Acts of Union united England and Wales after conquest.
1547 Edward VI adopted Protestant doctrines.

English sovereigns from 900

name	date of accession	relationship
West Saxon Kings		
Edward the Elder	901	son of Alfred the Great
Athelstan	925	son of Edward I
Edmund	940	half-brother of Athelstan
Edred	946	brother of Edmund
Edwy	955	son of Edmund
Edgar	959	brother of Edwy
Edward the Martyr	975	son of Edgar
Ethelred II	978	son of Edgar
Edmund Ironside	1016	son of Ethelred
Danish Kings		
Canute	1016	son of Sweyn
Hardicanute	1040	son of Canute
Harold I	1035	son of Canute
West Saxon Kings (restored)		
Edward the Confessor	1042	son of Ethelred II
Harold II	1066	son of Godwin
Norman Kings		
William I	1066	
William II	1087	son of William I
Henry I	1100	son of William I
Stephen	1135	son of Adela (daughter of William I)
House of Plantagenet		
Henry II	1154	son of Matilda (daughter of Henry I)
Richard I	1189	son of Henry II
John	1199	son of Henry II
Henry III	1216	son of John
Edward I	1272	son of Henry III
Edward II	1307	son of Edward I
Edward III	1327	son of Edward II
Richard II	1377	son of the Black Prince (son of Edward III)
House of Lancaster		
Henry IV	1399	son of John of Gaunt
Henry V	1413	son of Henry IV
Henry VI	1422	son of Henry V
House of York		
Edward IV	1461	son of Richard, Duke of York
Richard III	1483	brother of Edward IV
Edward V	1483	son of Edward IV
House of Tudor		
Henry VII	1485	son of Edmund Tudor, Earl of Richmond
Henry VIII	1509	son of Henry VII
Edward VI	1547	son of Henry VIII
Mary I	1553	daughter of Henry VIII
Elizabeth I	1558	daughter of Henry VIII
House of Stuart		
James I	1603	great-grandson of Margaret (daughter of Henry VII)
Charles I	1625	son of James I
The Commonwealth		
House of Stuart (restored)		
Charles II	1660	son of Charles I
James II	1685	son of Charles I
William III and Mary	1689	son of Mary (daughter of Charles I)/ daughter of James II
Anne	1702	daughter of James II

1553 Reversion to Roman Catholicism under Mary I.
1558 Elizabeth I adopted a religious compromise with Protestant state religion.
1588 Attempted invasion of England by the Spanish Armada.
1603 James I united the English and Scottish crowns; parliamentary dissidence increased.
1642–52 Civil War between royalists and parliamentarians, resulting in victory for Parliament.
1649 Charles I executed and the Commonwealth set up.
1653 Oliver Cromwell appointed Lord Protector.
1660 Restoration of Charles II.
1685 Monmouth's rebellion.
1688 William of Orange invited to take the throne; flight of James II.
1707 Act of Union between England and Scotland. For further history, see ◊United Kingdom.

English native to or an inhabitant of England, part of Britain, as well as their descendants, culture, and language. The English have a mixed cultural heritage combining Celtic, Anglo-Saxon, Norman, and Scandinavian elements.

English architecture the main styles in English architecture are Saxon, Norman, Early English (of which Westminster Abbey is an example), Decorated, Perpendicular (15th century), Tudor (a name chiefly applied to domestic buildings of about 1485–1558), Jacobean, Stuart (including the Renaissance and Queen Anne styles), Georgian, the Gothic revival of the 19th century, Modern, and Postmodern. Notable architects include Christopher Wren, Inigo Jones, John Vanbrugh, Nicholas Hawksmoor, Charles Barry, Edwin Lutyens, Hugh Casson, Basil Spence, Frederick Gibberd, Denys Lasdun, and Richard Rogers.

English Channel stretch of water between England and France, leading in the W to the Atlantic Ocean, and in the E via the Strait of Dover to the North Sea; it is also known as *La Manche* (French "the sleeve") from its shape.

English horn alternate name for ◊cor anglais, musical instrument of the oboe family.

English language member of the Germanic branch of the Indo-European language family. It is traditionally described as having passed through four major stages over about 1,500 years: *Old English* or *Anglo-Saxon* (c. 500–1050), rooted in the dialects of invading settlers (Jutes, Saxons, Angles, and Frisians); *Middle English* (c. 1050–1550), influenced by Norman French after the Conquest 1066 and by ecclesiastical Latin; *Early Modern English* (c. 1550–1700), including a standardization of the diverse influences of Middle English; and *Late Modern English* (c. 1700 onward), including in particular the development and spread of current Standard English. Through extensive exploration, colonization, and trade, English spread worldwide from the 17th century onward and remains the most important international language of trade and technology. It is used in many variations, for example, British, American, Canadian, West Indian, Indian, Singaporean, and Nigerian English, and many pidgins and Creoles.

English law one of the major European legal systems, ◊Roman law being the other. English law has spread to many other countries, including former English colonies such as the US, Canada, Australia, and New Zealand.

engraving art of creating a design by means of inscribing blocks of metal, wood, or some other hard material with a point. *Intaglio prints* are made mainly on metal by dry point and ◊etching.

Enid city in N central Oklahoma, N of Oklahoma City, seat of Garfield County; population (1990) 45,300. It is a processing and marketing center for the surrounding region's poultry, cattle, dairy farms, and oil wells. Enid was founded 1893, when land in the Cherokee Strip region, which was originally put aside for Indian tribes, was opened to white settlement.

Enlightenment European intellectual movement that reached its high point in the 18th century. Enlightenment thinkers were believers in social progress and in the liberating possibilities of rational and scientific knowledge. They were often critical of existing society and were hostile to religion, which they saw as keeping the human mind chained down by superstition.

enosis movement, developed from 1980, for the union of ◊Cyprus with Greece. The Campaign (led by ◊EOKA and supported by Archbishop Makarios) intensified from the 1950s. In 1960 independence from Britain, without union, was granted, and increased demands for union led to its proclamation 1974. As a result, Turkey invaded Cyprus, ostensibly to protect the Turkish community, and the island was effectively partitioned.

Entebbe city in Uganda, on the NW shore of Lake Victoria, 12 mi/20 km SW of Kampala, the capital; 3,728 ft/1,136 m above sea level; population (1983) 21,000. Founded 1893, it was the administrative center of Uganda 1894–1962.

enterprise zone special zone designated by government to encourage industrial and commercial activity, usually in economically depressed areas. Investment is attracted by means of tax reduction and other financial incentives.

entomology study of ◊insects.

entrepreneur in business, a person who successfully manages and develops an enterprise through personal skill and initiative. Examples include John D ◊Rockefeller, Henry ◊Ford, Anita Roddick, and Richard Branson.

entropy in ◊thermodynamics, a parameter representing the state of disorder of a system at the atomic, ionic, or molecular level; the greater the disorder, the higher the entropy. Thus the fast-moving disordered molecules of water vapor have higher entropy than those of more ordered liquid water, which in turn have more entropy than the molecules in solid crystalline ice.

Enver Pasha 1881–1922. Turkish politician and soldier. He led the military revolt 1908 that resulted in the Young Turks' revolution (see ◊Turkey). He was killed fighting the Bolsheviks in Turkestan.

environment in ecology, the sum of conditions affecting a particular organism, including physical surroundings, climate, and influences of other living organisms. See also ◊biosphere and ◊habitat.

Environmental Protection Agency (EPA) US agency set up 1970 to control water and air quality, industrial and commercial wastes, pesticides, noise, and radiation.

enzyme biological ◊catalyst produced in cells, and capable of speeding up the chemical reactions necessary for life by converting one molecule (substrate) into another. Enzymes are not themselves destroyed by this process. They are large, complex ◊proteins, and are highly specific, each chemical reaction requiring its own particular enzyme. The enzyme fits into a "slot" (active site) in the substrate molecule, forming an enzyme–substrate complex that lasts until the substrate is altered or split, after which the enzyme can fall away. The substrate may therefore be compared to a lock, and the enzyme to the key required to open it.

Eocene second epoch of the Tertiary period of geological time, 56.5–35.5 million years ago. Originally considered the earliest division of the Tertiary, the name means "early recent," referring to the early forms of mammals evolving at the time, following the extinction of the dinosaurs.

EOKA acronym for *Ethnikí Organósis Kipriakóu Agónos* (National Organization of Cypriot Struggle) an underground organization formed by General George Grivas 1955 to fight for the independence of Cyprus from Britain and ultimately its union (*enosis*) with Greece. In 1971, 11 years after the independence of Cyprus, Grivas returned to the island to form EOKA B and to resume the fight for *enosis*, which had not been achieved by the Cypriot government.

Eos in Greek mythology, the goddess of the dawn (Roman Aurora).

ephedrine drug that acts like adrenaline on the sympathetic ◊nervous system (sympathomimetic). Once used to relieve bronchospasm in ◊asthma, it has been superseded by safer, more specific drugs. It is contained in some cold remedies as a decongestant. Side effects include rapid heartbeat, tremor, dry mouth, and anxiety.

Ephesus ancient Greek seaport in Asia Minor, a center of the ◊Ionian Greeks, with a temple of Artemis destroyed by the Goths AD 262. Now in Turkey, it is one of the world's largest archeological sites. St Paul visited the city and addressed a letter (◊epistle) to the Christians there.

epic narrative poem or cycle of poems dealing with some great deed—often the founding of a nation or the forging of national unity—and often using religious or cosmological themes. The two major epic poems in the Western tradition are *The Iliad* and *The Odyssey*, attributed to Homer, and which were probably intended to be chanted in sections at feasts.

epicenter the point on the Earth's surface immediately above the seismic focus of an ◊earthquake. Most damage usually takes place at an earthquake's epicenter. The term sometimes refers to a point directly above or below a nuclear explosion ("at ground zero").

Epictetus *c.* AD 55–135. Greek Stoic philosopher who encouraged people to refrain from self-interest and to promote the common good of humanity. He believed that people were in the hands of an all-wise providence and that they should endeavor to do their duty in the position to which they were called.

Epicureanism system of philosophy that claims soundly based human happiness is the highest good, so that its rational pursuit should be adopted. It was named after the Greek philosopher Epicurus. The most distinguished Roman Epicurean was ◊Lucretius.

Epicurus 341–270 BC. Greek philosopher, founder of Epicureanism, who taught at Athens from 306 BC.

Epidaurus or *Epidavros* ancient Greek city and port on the E coast of Argolis, in the NE Peloponnese. The site contains a well-preserved theater of the 4th century BC; nearby are the ruins of the temple of Asclepius, the god of healing.

epidemic outbreak of infectious disease affecting large numbers of people at the same time. A widespread epidemic that sweeps across many countries (such as the ◊Black Death in the late Middle Ages) is known as a *pandemic*.

epidermis outermost layer of ◊cells on an organism's body. In plants and many invertebrates such as insects, it consists of a single layer of cells. In vertebrates, it consists of several layers of cells.

epiglottis small flap found in the throats of mammals. It moves during swallowing to prevent food from passing into the windpipe and causing choking.

epigram short, witty, and pithy saying or short poem. The epigram form was common among writers of ancient Rome, including Catullus and Martial. In English, the epigram has been employed by Ben Jonson, George Herrick, Alexander Pope, Jonathan Swift, W B Yeats, and Ogden Nash. An epigram was originally a religious inscription.

epilepsy medical disorder characterized by a tendency to develop fits, which are convulsions or abnormal feelings caused by abnormal electrical discharges in the cerebral hemispheres of the ◊brain. Epilepsy can be controlled with a number of ◊anticonvulsant drugs.

Epiphany festival of the Christian church, held Jan 6, celebrating the coming of the Magi (the three Wise Men) to Bethlehem with gifts for the infant Jesus, and symbolizing the manifestation of Jesus to the world. It is the 12th day after Christmas, and marks the end of the Christmas festivities.

Epirus (Greek *Ipiros*) region of NW Greece; area 3,551 sq mi/9,200 sq km; population (1981) 325,000. Its capital is Yannina, and it consists of the provinces (nomes) of Arta, Thesprotia, Yannina, and Preveza. There is livestock farming.

episcopacy in the Christian church, a system of government in which administrative and spiritual power over a district (diocese) is held by a bishop.

Episcopalianism US term for the Anglican Communion.

epistemology branch of philosophy that examines the nature of knowledge and attempts to determine the limits of human understanding. Central issues include how knowledge is derived and how it is to be validated and tested.

epistle in the New Testament, any of the 21 letters to individuals or to the members of various churches written by Christian leaders, including the 13 written by St ◊Paul. The term also describes a letter with a suggestion of pomposity and literary affectation, and a letter addressed to someone in the form of a poem, as in the epistles of ◊Horace and ◊Pope.

epoch subdivision of a geological period in the geological time scale. Epochs are sometimes given their own names (such as the Paleocene, Eocene, Oligocene, Miocene, and Pliocene epochs comprising the Tertiary period), or they are referred to as the late, early, or middle portions of a given period (as the Late Cretaceous or the Middle Triassic epoch).

epoxy resin synthetic ◊resin used as an ◊adhesive and as an ingredient in paints. Household epoxy resin adhesives come in component form as two separate tubes of chemical, one tube containing resin, the other a curing agent (hardener). The two chemicals are mixed just before application, and the mix soon sets hard.

Epsom salts $MgSO_4 \cdot 7H_2O$ hydrated magnesium sulfate, used as a relaxant and laxative and added to baths to soothe the skin. The name is derived from a bitter saline spring at Epsom, Surrey, England, which contains the salt in solution.

equation in mathematics, expression that represents the equality of two expressions involving constants and/or variables, and thus usually includes an equals sign (=). For example, the equation $A = \pi r^2$ equates the area A of a circle of radius r to the product πr^2. The algebraic equation $y = mx + c$ is the general one in coordinate geometry for a straight line.

equator the *terrestrial equator* is the great circle whose plane is perpendicular to the Earth's axis (the line joining the poles). Its length is 24,901.8 mi/40,092 km, divided into 360 degrees of longitude. The equator encircles the broadest part of the Earth, and represents

0° latitude. It divides the Earth into two halves, called the northern and the southern hemispheres.

Equatorial Guinea country in W central Africa, bounded N by Cameroon, E and S by Gabon, and W by the Atlantic Ocean; also five offshore islands including Bioko, off the coast of Cameroon.

equestrianism skill in horse riding, as practiced under International Equestrian Federation rules. An Olympic sport, there are three main branches of equestrianism: show jumping, dressage, and three-day eventing.

equilateral of a geometrical figure, having all sides of equal length.

For example, a rhombus is an equilateral parallelogram. An equilateral triangle is also equiangular, which means that all three angles are equal as well.

equilibrium in physics, an unchanging condition in which the forces acting on a particle or system of particles (a body) cancel out, or in which energy is distributed among the particles of a system in the most probable way; or the state in which a body is at rest or moving at constant velocity. A body is in ***thermal equilibrium*** with its surroundings if no heat enters or leaves it, so that all its parts are at the same temperature as the surroundings.

equinox the points in spring and autumn at which the Sun's path, the ecliptic, crosses the celestial equator, so that the day and night are of approximately equal length. The ***vernal equinox*** occurs about March 21 and the ***autumnal equinox***, Sept 23.

equity a company's assets, less its liabilities, which are the property of the owner or stockholders. Popularly, equities are stocks and shares which do not pay interest at fixed rates but pay dividends based on the company's performance. The value of equities tends to rise over the long term, but in the short term they are a

---

Equatorial Guinea
Republic of
(*República de Guinea Ecuatorial*)

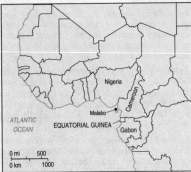

area 10,828 sq mi/28,051 sq km
capital Malabo (Bioko)
cities Bata, Mbini (Río Muni)
physical comprises mainland Río Muni, plus the small islands of Corisco, Elobey Grande and Elobey Chico, and Bioko (formerly Fernando Po) together with Annobón (formerly Pagalu)
features volcanic mountains on Bioko
head of state and government Teodoro Obiang Nguema Mbasogo from 1979
political system one-party military republic

political party Democratic Party of Equatorial Guinea (PDGE), militarily controlled
exports cocoa, coffee, timber
currency ekuele; CFA franc
population (1992) 367,000 (plus 110,000 estimated to live in exile abroad); growth rate 2.2% p.a.
life expectancy men 44, women 48
languages Spanish (official); pidgin English is widely spoken, and on Annobón (whose people were formerly slaves of the Portuguese) a Portuguese dialect; Fang and other African dialects spoken on Río Muni
religions nominally Christian, mainly Catholic, but in 1978 Roman Catholicism was banned
literacy 55% (1984)
GDP $90 million (1987); $220 per head

chronology
1778 Fernando Po (Bioko Island) ceded to Spain.
1885 Mainland territory came under Spanish rule; colony known as Spanish Guinea.
1968 Independence achieved from Spain. Francisco Macias Nguema became first president, soon assuming dictatorial powers.
1979 Macias overthrown and replaced by his nephew, Teodoro Obiang Nguema Mbasogo, who established a military regime. Macias tried and executed.
1982 Obiang elected president unopposed for another seven years. New constitution adopted.
1989 Obiang reelected president.
1992 New constitution adopted; elections held, but president continued to nominate candidates for top government posts.

risk investment because prices can fall as well as rise. Equity is also used to refer to the paid value of mortgaged real property, most commonly a house.

Equity a shortened term for the American Actors' Equity Association, the labor union for professional actors in the theater.

era any of the major divisions of geological time, each including several periods, but smaller than an eon. The currently recognized eras all fall within the Phanerozoic eon—or the vast span of time, starting about 570 million years ago, when fossils are found to become abundant. The eras in ascending order are the Paleozoic, Mesozoic, and Cenozoic. We are living in the Recent epoch of the Quaternary period of the Cenozoic era.

Erastianism belief that the church should be subordinated to the state. The name is derived from Thomas Erastus (1534–1583), a German-Swiss theologian and opponent of Calvinism, who maintained in his writings that the church should not have the power of excluding people as a punishment for sin.

Eratosthenes *c.* 276–194 BC. Greek geographer and mathematician whose map of the ancient world was the first to contain lines of latitude and longitude, and who calculated the Earth's circumference with an error of about 10%. His mathematical achievements include a method for duplicating the cube, and for finding ◊prime numbers (Eratosthenes' sieve).

erbium soft, lustrous, grayish, metallic element of the ◊lanthanide series, symbol Er, atomic number 68, atomic weight 167.26. It occurs with the element yttrium or as a minute part of various minerals. It was discovered 1843 by Carl Mosander (1797–1858), and named after the town of Ytterby, Sweden, near which the lanthanides (rare-earth elements) were first found.

Erebus, Mount the world's southernmost active volcano, 12,452 ft/3,794 m high, on Ross Island, Antarctica.

Erebus in Greek mythology, the god of darkness; also the intermediate region between upper Earth and ◊Hades.

ergonomics study of the relationship between people and the furniture, tools, and machinery they use at work. The object is to improve work performance by removing sources of muscular stress and general fatigue: for example, by presenting data and control panels in easy-to-view form, making office furniture comfortable, and creating a generally pleasant environment.

Erhard Ludwig 1897–1977. West German Christian Democrat politician, chancellor of the Federal Republic 1963–66. The "economic miracle" of West Germany's recovery after World War II is largely attributed to Erhard's policy of social free enterprise which he initiated during his period as federal economics minister (1949–63).

Ericsson John 1803–1889. Swedish-born US engineer who took out a patent to produce screw-propeller–powered paddle-wheel ships 1836. He built a number of such ships, including the *Monitor*, which was successfully deployed during the American Civil War.

Ericsson Leif *c.* 970. Norse explorer, son of Eric the Red, who sailed west from Greenland *c.* 1000 to find a country first sighted by Norsemen 986. He visited Baffin Island then sailed along the Labrador coast to Newfoundland, which was named "Vinland" (Wine Land), alledgedly because grapes grew there.

Eric the Red *c.* 950–1010. Allegedly the first European to find Greenland. According to a 13th-century saga, he was the son of a Norwegian chieftain, and was banished from Iceland about 982 for murder. He

---

Eritrea State of

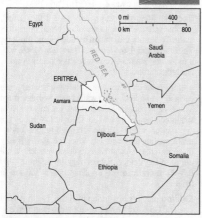

area 48,250 sq mi/125,000 sq km
capital Asmara
cities Keren, Adigrat; ports: Asab, Massawa
physical coastline along the Red Sea 620 mi/1,000 km; narrow coastal plain that rises to an inland plateau
features Dahlak Islands
head of state and government Issaias Afwerki from 1993

political system emergent democracy
political parties Eritrean People's Liberation Front (EPLF), militant nationalist; Eritrean National Pact Alliance (ENPA), moderate, centrist
products coffee, salt, citrus fruits, grains, cotton
currency birr
population (1993) 4,000,000
languages Amharic (official), Tigrinya (official), Arabic, Afar, Bilen, Hidareb, Kunama, Nara, Rashaida, Saho, and Tigre
media one bi-weekly newspaper (*Hadas Eritra*), government- owned, published in Tigrinya and Arabic, circulation (1993) 30,000; three monthly newssheets, all owned by Christian churches and published in Tigrinya. The national radio station broadcasts in six languages
religions Muslim, Coptic Christian

chronology
1962 Annexed by Ethiopia; secessionist movement began.
1974 Ethiopian emperor Haile Selassie deposed by military; Eritrean People's Liberation Front (EPLF) continued struggle for independence.
1990 Port of Massawa captured by Eritrean forces.
1991 Ethiopian president Mengistu Haile Mariam overthrown. EPLF secured the whole of Eritrea. Ethiopian government acknowledged Eritrea's right to secede. Issaias Afwerki became secretary general of provisional government.
1992 Transitional ruling council established.
1993 National referendum supported independence. Transitional government established for four-year period. Issaias Afwerki elected chairman of state council and president. UN membership granted.

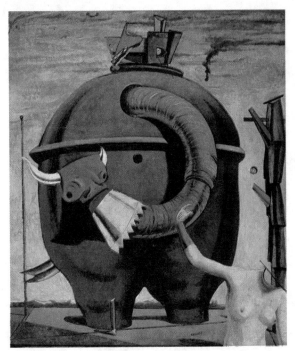

Ernst The Elephant Celébés *(1921), Tate Gallery, London.*

rock or soil (by contrast, ◊weathering does not involve transportation). Agents of erosion include the sea, rivers, glaciers, and wind. Water, consisting of sea waves and currents, rivers, and rain; ice, in the form of glaciers; and wind, hurling sand fragments against exposed rocks and moving dunes along, are the most potent forces of erosion. People also contribute to erosion by bad farming practices and the cutting down of forests, which can lead to the formation of dust bowls.

Ershad Hussain Mohammad 1930– . Military ruler of Bangladesh 1982–90. He became chief of staff of the Bangladeshi army 1979 and assumed power in a military coup 1982. As president from 1983, Ershad introduced a successful rural-oriented economic program. He was reelected 1986 and lifted martial law, but faced continuing political opposition, which forced him to resign Dec 1990. In 1991 he was formally charged with the illegal possession of arms, convicted, and sentenced to ten years' imprisonment. He received a further sentence of three years' imprisonment Feb 1992 after being convicted of corruption.

erythromycin an antibiotic with the chemical formula $C_{37}H_{67}NO_{13}$, isolated from a red-pigmented soil bacterium, *Streptomyces erythreus*. It is used in the treatment of a wide range of bacterial diseases and usually administered orally in the form of various salts and esters.

Esaki Leo 1925– . Japanese physicist who in 1957 noticed that electrons could sometimes "tunnel" through the barrier formed at the junctions of certain semiconductors. The effect is now widely used in the electronics industry. For this early discovery Esaki shared the 1973 Nobel Prize for Physics with British physicist Brian Josephson and Norwegian-born US physicist Ivar Giaever (1929–).

escalator automatic moving staircase that carries people between floors or levels. It consists of treads linked in an endless belt arranged to form strips (steps), powered by an electric motor that moves both steps and handrails at the same speed. Toward the top and bottom the steps flatten out for ease of passage. The first escalator was exhibited in Paris 1900.

Escher M(aurits) C(ornelis) 1902–1972. Dutch graphic artist. His prints are often based on mathematical concepts and contain paradoxes and illusions. The lithograph *Ascending and Descending* 1960, with interlocking staircases creating a perspective puzzle, is a typical work.

esker geological feature of formerly glaciated areas consisting of a long, steep-walled narrow ridge, often sinuous and sometimes branching. Eskers consist of stratified glacial drift and are thought to form by the deposits of streams running through tunnels underneath melting stagnant ice. When the glacier finally disappeared, the old stream deposits were left standing as a high ridge. Eskers vary in height 10–100 ft/3–30 m and can run to about 100 mi/160 km in length.

Eskimo member of a group of Asian, North American, and Greenland Arctic peoples who migrated east from Siberia about 2,000 years ago, exploiting the marine coastal environment and the tundra.

Eskişehir city in Turkey, 125 mi/200 km W of Ankara; population (1985) 367,000. Products include meerschaum, chromium, magnesite, cotton goods, tiles, and aircraft.

esophagus the passage by which food travels from mouth to stomach. The human esophagus is about 9

then sailed westward and discovered a land that he called Greenland.

Erie, Lake fourth largest of the Great Lakes of North America, connected to Lake Ontario by the Niagara River and bypassed by the Welland Canal; area 9,930 sq mi/25,720 sq km.

Erin poetic name for Ireland, derived from the dative case Érinn of the Gaelic name Ériu, possibly derived from Sanskrit "western."

Eritrea country in NE Africa, bounded W by Sudan, S by Ethiopia, SE by Djibouti, and E by the Red Sea. *See panel p. 319*

ermine short-tailed weasel *Mustela erminea*, of the N hemisphere. In N latitudes the coat becomes completely white, except for a black tip to the tail, but in warmer regions the back may remain brownish. The Eurasian name "stoat" is used especially during the summer, when the coat is brown. The fur is used commercially.

Ernst Max 1891–1976. German artist who worked in France 1922–38 and in the US from 1941. He was an active Dadaist, experimenting with collage, photomontage, and surreal images, and helped found the Surrealist movement 1924. His paintings are highly diverse.

Eros in Greek mythology, boy-god of love, traditionally armed with bow and arrows. He was the son of ◊Aphrodite, and fell in love with ◊Psyche. He is identified with the Roman Cupid.

Eros in astronomy, an asteroid, discovered 1898, that can pass 14 million mi/22 million km from the Earth, as observed in 1975. Eros was the first asteroid to be discovered that has an orbit coming within that of Mars. It is elongated, measures about 22×7 mi/36×12 km, rotates around its shortest axis every 5.3 hours, and orbits the Sun every 1.8 years.

erosion wearing away of the Earth's surface, caused by the breakdown and transportation of particles of

in/23 cm long. Its upper end is at the bottom of the ◊pharynx, immediately behind the windpipe.

ESP abbreviation for ◊extrasensory perception.

Esperanto language devised 1887 by Polish philologist Ludwig L Zamenhof (1859–1917) as an international auxiliary language. For its structure and vocabulary it draws on Latin, the Romance languages, English, and German.

espionage the practice of spying; a way to gather ◊intelligence.

Esquipulas pilgrimage town in Chiquimula department, SE Guatemala; seat of the "Black Christ," which is a symbol of peace throughout Central America. In May 1986 five Central American presidents met here to discuss a plan for peace in the region.

essay short piece of nonfiction, often dealing from a personal point of view with some particular subject. The essay became a recognized genre with French writer Montaigne's *Essais* 1580 and in English with Francis Bacon's *Essays* 1597. Today the essay is a part of journalism: articles in the broadsheet newspapers are in the essay tradition.

Essen city in North Rhine–Westphalia, Germany; population (1988) 615,000. It is the administrative center of the Ruhr region, situated between the rivers Emscher and Ruhr, and has textile, chemical, and electrical industries. Its 9th–14th-century minster is one of the oldest churches in Germany.

Essene member of an ancient Jewish religious sect located in the area near the Dead Sea c. 200 BC–AD 200, whose members lived a life of denial and asceticism, as they believed that the day of judgment was imminent.

Essequibo longest river in Guyana, South America, rising in the Guiana Highlands of S Guyana; length 630 mi/1,014 km. Part of the district of Essequibo, which lies to the W of the river, is claimed by Venezuela.

Essex county in SE England
area 1,417 sq mi/3,670 sq km
cities Chelmsford (administrative headquarters), Colchester; ports: Harwich, Tilbury; resorts: Southend, Clacton
features former royal hunting ground of Epping Forest (controlled from 1882 by the City of London); the marshy coastal headland of the Naze; since 1111 at Great Dunmow the Dunmow flitch (side of cured pork) can be claimed every four years by any couple proving to a jury they have not regretted their marriage within the year (winners are few); Stansted, London's third airport
products dairying, cereals, fruit
population (1988 est) 1,529,500.

estate in law, the rights that a person has in relation to any property. *Real estate* is an interest in any

Estonia Republic of

area 17,000 sq mi/45,000 sq km
capital Tallinn
cities Tartu, Narva, Kohtla-Järve, Pärnu
physical lakes and marshes in a partly forested plain; 481 mi/774 km of coastline; mild climate
features Lake Peipus and Narva River forming boundary with Russian Federation; Baltic islands, the largest of which is Saaremaa Island
head of state Lennart Meri from 1992
head of government Mart Laar from 1992
political system emergent democracy
political parties Estonian Popular Front (Rahvarinne), nationalist; Association for a Free Estonia, nationalist; Fatherland Group, right-wing; International Movement, ethnic Russian; Estonian Green Party, environmentalist
products oil and gas (from shale), wood products, flax, dairy and pig products
currency kroon
population (1992) 1,592,000 (Estonian 62%, Russian 30%, Ukrainian 3%, Byelorussian 2%)

language Estonian, allied to Finnish
religion traditionally Lutheran

chronology
1918 Estonia declared its independence. March: Soviet forces, who had tried to regain control from occupying German forces during World War I, were overthrown by German troops. Nov: Soviet troops took control after German withdrawal.
1919 Soviet rule overthrown with help of British navy; Estonia declared a democratic republic.
1934 Fascist coup replaced government.
1940 Estonia incorporated into USSR.
1941–44 German occupation during World War II.
1944 USSR regained control.
1980 Beginnings of nationalist dissent.
1988 Adopted own constitution, with power of veto on all centralized Soviet legislation. Popular Front (Rahvarinne) established to campaign for democracy. Estonia's supreme soviet (state assembly) voted to declare the republic "sovereign" and autonomous in all matters except military and foreign affairs; rejected by USSR as unconstitutional.
1989 Estonian replaced Russian as main language.
1990 Feb: Communist Party monopoly of power abolished; multiparty system established. March: proindependence candidates secured majority after republic elections; coalition government formed with Popular Front leader Edgar Savisaar as prime minister; Arnold Rüütel became president. May: prewar constitution partially restored.
1991 March: independence plebiscite overwhelmingly approved. Aug: full independence declared after abortive anti-Gorbachev coup; Communist Party outlawed. Sept: independence recognized by Soviet government and Western nations; admitted into United Nations and Conference on Security and Cooperation in Europe (CSCE).
1992 Jan: Savisaar resigned owing to his government's inability to alleviate food and energy shortages; new government formed by Tiit Vähi. June: New constitution approved. Sept: presidential election inconclusive; right-wing Fatherland Group did well in general election. Oct: Fatherland leader Lennart Meri chosen by parliament to replace Rüütel.

land; **personal estate** is an interest in any other kind of property. Estate property refers to the assets of a deceased person.

estate in European history, an order of society that enjoyed a specified share in government. In medieval theory, there were usually three estates—the **nobility**, the **clergy**, and the **commons**—with the functions of, respectively, defending society from foreign aggression and internal disorder, attending to its spiritual needs, and working to produce the base with which to support the other two orders.

ester organic compound formed by the reaction between an alcohol and an acid, with the elimination of water. Unlike ◊salts, esters are covalent compounds.

Estonia country in N Europe, bounded E by Russia, S by Latvia, and N and W by the Baltic Sea. *See panel p. 321*

Estonian member of the largest ethnic group in Estonia. There are 1 million speakers of the Estonian language, a member of the Finno-Ugric branch of the Uralic family. Most live in Estonia.

Estoril fashionable resort on the coast 13 mi/20 km W of Lisbon, Portugal; population (1981) 16,000. There is a Grand Prix motor-racing circuit.

estrogen any of a group of hormones produced by the ◊ovaries of vertebrates; the term is also used for various synthetic hormones that mimic their effects. (Some estrogens are also secreted by the cortex of the ◊adrenal glands.) The principal estrogen in mammals is estradiol. Estrogens promote the development of female secondary sexual characteristics; stimulate egg production; and, in mammals, prepare the lining of the uterus for pregnancy.

estuary river mouth widening into the sea, where fresh water mixes with salt water and tidal effects are felt.

Estuaries are extremely rich in life forms and are breeding grounds for thousands of species. Water pollution threatens these ◊ecosystems.

etching a ◊printmaking technique in which the design is made from a metal plate (usually copper or zinc), which is covered with a waxy overlayer (ground) and then drawn on with an etching needle. The exposed areas are then "etched," or bitten into, by a corrosive agent (acid), so that they will hold ink for printing.

ethanoic acid common name **acetic acid** CH_3CO_2H one of the simplest fatty acids (a series of organic acids). In the pure state it is a colorless liquid with an unpleasant pungent odor; it solidifies to an ice-like mass of crystals at 62.4°F/16.7°C, and hence is often called glacial ethanoic acid. Vinegar contains 5% or more ethanoic acid, produced by fermentation.

ethanol common name **ethyl alcohol** C_2H_5OH alcohol found in beer, wine, cider, spirits, and other alcoholic drinks. When pure, it is a colorless liquid with a pleasant odor, miscible with water or ether; it burns in air with a pale blue flame. The vapor forms an explosive mixture with air and may be used in high-compression internal combustion engines. It is produced naturally by the fermentation of carbohydrates by yeast cells. Industrially, it can be made by absorption of ethene and subsequent reaction with water, or by the reduction of ethanal in the presence of a catalyst, and is widely used as a solvent.

Ethelred II *the Unready* c. 968–1016. King of England from 978. He tried to buy off the Danish raiders by paying Danegeld. In 1002, he ordered the massacre of the Danish settlers, provoking an invasion by Sweyn I

of Denmark. War with Sweyn and Sweyn's son, Canute, occupied the rest of Ethelred's reign. He was nicknamed the "Unready" because of his apparent lack of foresight.

ethene common name **ethylene** C_2H_4 colorless, flammable gas, the first member of the ◊alkene series of hydrocarbons. It is the most widely used synthetic organic chemical and is used to produce the plastics polyethene (polyethylene), polychloroethene, and polyvinyl chloride (PVC). It is obtained from natural gas or coal gas, or by the dehydration of ethanol.

ether in chemistry, any of a series of organic chemical compounds having an oxygen atom linking the carbon atoms of two hydrocarbon radical groups (general formula R-O-R'); also the common name for ethoxyethane $C_2H_5OC_2H_5$ (also called diethyl ether). This is used as an anesthetic and as an external cleansing agent before surgical operations. It is also used as a solvent, and in the extraction of oils, fats, waxes, resins, and alkaloids.

ethics area of ◊philosophy concerned with human values, which studies the meanings of moral terms and theories of conduct and goodness; also called **moral philosophy**. It is one of the three main branches of contemporary philosophy.

Ethiopia country in E Africa, bounded NE by Djibouti and Eritrea, E and SE by Somalia, S by Kenya, and W and NW by Sudan.

ethnicity people's own sense of cultural identity; a social term that overlaps with such concepts as race, nation, class, and religion.

ethnology the branch of anthropology that deals with the comparative study of contemporary cultures, acculturation, and human ecology.

ethyl alcohol common name for ◊ethanol.

ethylene glycol alternate name for ◊glycol.

ethyne common name **acetylene** CHCH colorless inflammable gas produced by mixing calcium carbide and water. It is the simplest member of the alkyne series of hydrocarbons. It is used in the manufacture of the synthetic rubber neoprene, and in oxyacetylene welding and cutting.

Etna volcano on the E coast of Sicily, 10,906 ft/3,323 m, the highest in Europe. About 90 eruptions have been recorded since 1800 BC, yet because of the rich soil, the cultivated zone on the lower slopes is densely populated, including the coastal town of Catania. The most recent eruption was in Dec 1985.

Tours of this smoking volcano are conducted.

Etruscan member of an ancient people inhabiting Etruria, Italy (modern-day Tuscany and part of Umbria) from the 8th to 4th centuries BC. The Etruscan dynasty of the Tarquins ruled Rome 616–509 BC. At the height of their civilization, in the 6th century BC, the Etruscans achieved great wealth and power from their maritime strength. They were driven out of Rome 509 BC and eventually dominated by the Romans.

etymology study of the origin and history of words within and across languages. It has two major aspects: the study of the phonetic and written forms of words, and of the semantics or meanings of those words.

Euboea (Greek *Evvoia*) mountainous island off the E coast of Greece, in the Aegean Sea; area 1,450 sq mi/3,755 sq km; about 110 mi/177 km long; population (1981) 188,410. Mount Delphi reaches 5,721 ft/1,743 m. The chief town, Chalcis, is connected by a bridge to the mainland.

Ethiopia
People's Democratic Republic of
(*Hebretesebawit Ityopia,*
formerly also known as **Abyssinia**)

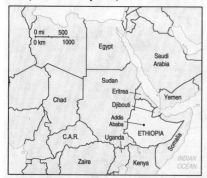

area 435,493 sq mi/1,128,221 sq km
capital Addis Ababa
cities Jimma, Dire Dawa
physical a high plateau with central mountain range divided by Rift Valley; plains in E; source of Blue Nile River
environment more than 90% of the forests of the Ethiopian highlands have been destroyed since 1900
features Danakil and Ogaden deserts; ancient remains (in Aksum, Gondar, Lalibela, among others); only African country to retain its independence during the colonial period
head of state and government Meles Zenawi from 1991
political system transition to democratic socialist republic
political parties Ethiopian People's Revolutionary Democratic Front (EPRDF), nationalist, left of center; Tigré People's Liberation Front (TPLF); Ethiopian People's Democratic Movement (EPDM); Oromo People's Democratic Organization (OPDO)
exports coffee, pulses, oilseeds, hides, skins
currency birr
population (1992) 50,345,000 (Oromo 40%, Amhara 25%, Tigré 12%, Sidamo 9%); growth rate 2.5% p.a.

life expectancy 38
languages Amharic (official), Tigrinya, Orominga, Arabic
religions Sunni Muslim 45%, Christian (Ethiopian Orthodox Church, which has had its own patriarch since 1976) 40%
literacy 35% (1988)
GDP $4.8 bn (1987); $104 per head. The country's debt-service payments 1993–95 will be $2 billion. obs 930502

chronology
1889 Abyssinia reunited by Menelik II.
1930 Haile Selassie became emperor.
1962 Eritrea annexed by Haile Selassie; resistance movement began.
1974 Haile Selassie deposed and replaced by a military government led by General Teferi Benti. Ethiopia declared a socialist state.
1977 Teferi Benti killed and replaced by Col Mengistu Haile Mariam.
1977–79 "Red Terror" period in which Mengistu's regime killed thousands of innocent people.
1981–85 Ethiopia spent at least $2 billion on arms.
1984 WPE (Workers' Party of Ethiopia) declared the only legal political party.
1985 Worst famine in more than a decade; Western aid sent and forcible internal resettlement programs undertaken.
1987 New constitution adopted, Mengistu Mariam elected president. New famine; food aid hindered by guerrillas.
1988 Mengistu agreed to adjust his economic policies in order to secure IMF assistance. Influx of refugees from Sudan.
1989 Coup attempt against Mengistu foiled. Peace talks with Eritrean rebels mediated by former US president Carter reported some progress.
1990 Rebels captured port of Massawa.
1991 Mengistu overthrown; transitional government set up by EPRDF. EPLF secured Eritrea; Eritrea's right to secede recognized. Meles Zenawi elected Ethiopia's new head of state and government.
1993 Eritrean independence recognized after referendum.

eucalyptus any tree of the genus *Eucalyptus* of the myrtle family Myrtaceae, native to Australia and Tasmania, where they are commonly known as gum trees. About 90% of Australian timber belongs to the eucalyptus genus, which comprises about 500 species. The trees have dark hardwood timber which is used principally for heavy construction as in railroad and bridge building. They are tall, aromatic, evergreen trees with pendant leaves and white, pink, or red flowers.

Eucharist chief Christian sacrament, in which bread is eaten and wine drunk in memory of the death of Jesus. Other names for it are the **Lord's Supper**, **Holy Communion**, and (among Roman Catholics, who believe that the bread and wine are transubstantiated, that is, converted to the body and blood of Christ) the **Mass**. The doctrine of transubstantiation was rejected by Protestant churches during the Reformation.

Euclid c. 330–c. 260 BC. Greek mathematician, who lived in Alexandria and wrote the *Stoicheia/Elements* in 13 books, of which 9 deal with plane and solid geometry and 4 with number theory. His great achievement lay in the systematic arrangement of previous discoveries, based on axioms, definitions, and theorems.

Eudoxus of Cnidus c. 390–c. 340 BC. Greek mathematician and astronomer. He devised the first system to account for the motions of celestial bodies, believing

them to be carried around the Earth on sets of spheres. Probably Eudoxus regarded these spheres as a mathematical device for ease of computation rather than as physically real, but the idea of celestial spheres was taken up by ◊Aristotle and became entrenched in astronomical thought until the time of Tycho ◊Brahe. Eudoxus also described the constellations in a work called *Phaenomena*, providing the basis of the constellation system still in use today.

Eugene city in W central Oregon, S of Portland, on the Willamette River; population (1990) 112,700. It is a processing and shipping center for agricultural products from the surrounding region; wood products are also manufactured.

The University of Oregon 1872 is here.

Eugène Prince of Savoy 1663–1736. Austrian general who had many victories against the Turkish invaders (whom he expelled from Hungary 1697 in the Battle of Zenta) and against France in the War of the ◊Spanish Succession (battles of Blenheim, Oudenaarde, and Malplaquet).

eugenics study of ways in which the physical and mental quality of a people can be controlled and improved by selective breeding, and the belief that this should be done. The idea was abused by the Nazi Party in Germany during the 1930s to justify the attempted extermination of entire groups of people.

Europe

Arctic Circle

Reykjavik • ICELAND

NORWEGIAN
SEA

Faroe Is.
(to Denmark)

ATLANTIC

OCEAN

N O R W A Y

S W E D E N

Gulf of Bothnia

Glittertind
8103ft/2470m

•Oslo

•Stockholm

BALTIC SEA A

N
IRELAND

IRELAND

Dublin •

UNITED

KINGDOM

NORTH

SEA

DENMARK

•Copenhagen

(to

English Channel

Amsterdam•
The Hague• NETHER-
London•   LANDS

•Brussels
BELGIUM

Paris•

LUXEMBOURG

Elbe

Berlin

North

GERMANY

Oder

Vistula

Wa

POLA

Loire

Seine

Rhine

Danube

Prague• CZECH
REPUBLIC

Tatra ▲
8,710ft/265

SLOVA
REPUBLIC

Bay of Biscay

F R A N C E

Vosges

Vienna•
•Bern
SWITZERLAND LIECHT.

AUSTRIA

Bratislava

•Buda

HUNGARY

Cantabrian Mts

Pico de Aneto
11,168ft/3404m ▲
Pyrenees

Garonne

Central
Massif

Rhône

Mt Blanc
15,770ft/4807m ▲

A l p s

Po

SLOVENIA
•Ljubljana
•Zagreb
CROATIA

Sava

D i n a r i c A l p s

BOSNIA-HERZ. Belg

Sarajevo

YUGO

ANDORRA   Marseille•

Ligurian Sea

MONACO

SAN MARINO

A
D
R
I
A
T
I
C
S
E
A

MAC

PORTUGAL

Madrid•

Ebro

•Barcelona

Corsica

I
T
A
L
Y

Apennines

Gran Sasso ▲
8,620ft/2655m

Tirane•

A
L
B
A
N
I
A

Lisbon•

SPAIN

Andalusia
Seville•

Strait of Gibraltar   Gibraltar (to UK)

Balearic Is.

Sardinia

Rome•

Tyrrhenian
Sea

Ionian
Sea

M E D I T E R R A N E A N   S E A

Sicily

MOROCCO

ALGERIA

TUNISIA

MALTA

| 0 | 250 | 500 | 750 | 1000 miles |
| 0 | 500 | 1000 | 1500 km |

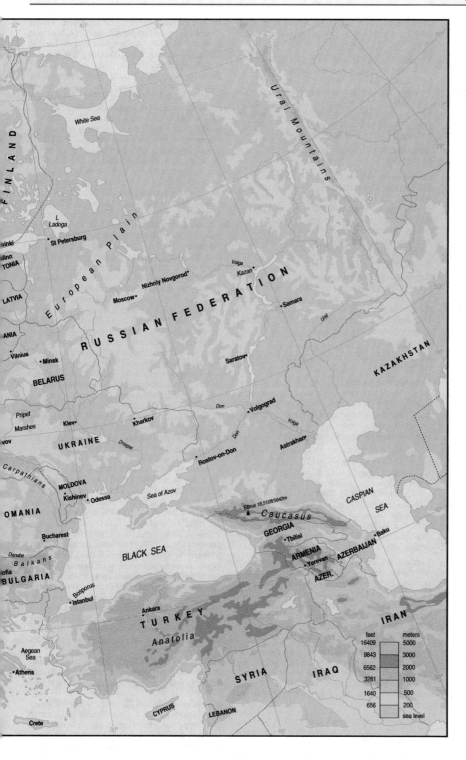

F I N L A N D

White Sea

L. Ladoga

St Petersburg

sinki

llinn
TONIA

LATVIA

ANIA

Vilnius

Minsk

BELARUS

European Plain

RUSSIAN FEDERATION

Ural Mountains

Moscow

Nizhniy Novgorod

Volga

Kazan

Samara

Saratov

Ural

KAZAKHSTAN

Pripet
Marshes

Kiev

Kharkov

Don

Volgograd

Volga

Astrakhan

UKRAINE

Dnieper

Don

Rostov-on-Don

Carpathians

ov

MOLDOVA

Kishinev

Odessa

Sea of Azov

CASPIAN

SEA

OMANIA

Bucharest

Danube

Balkans

ofia

BULGARIA

BLACK SEA

Elbrus 18,510ft/5642m

Caucasus

GEORGIA

Tbilisi

Baku

ARMENIA

Yerevan

AZERBAIJAN

AZER.

Bosporus

Istanbul

Ankara

T U R K E Y

Anatolia

IRAN

Aegean
Sea

Athens

SYRIA

IRAQ

feet	meters
16409	5000
9843	3000
6562	2000
3281	1000
1640	500
656	200
sea level	

CYPRUS

LEBANON

Crete

Eugenics can try to control the spread of inherited genetic abnormalities by counseling prospective parents.

Eugénie Marie Ignace Augustine de Montijo 1826–1920. Empress of France, daughter of the Spanish count of Montijo. In 1853 she married Louis Napoleon, who had become emperor as ◊Napoleon III. She encouraged court extravagance, Napoleon III's intervention in Mexico, and urged him to fight the Prussians. After his surrender to the Germans at Sedan, NE France, 1870, she fled to England.

Eumenides in Greek mythology, appeasing name for the ◊Furies.

eunuch castrated man. Originally eunuchs were bed-chamber attendants in harems in the East, but as they were usually castrated to keep them from taking too great an interest in their charges, the term became applied more generally. In China, eunuchs were employed within the imperial harem from some 4,000 years ago and by medieval times wielded considerable political power. Eunuchs often filled high offices of state in India and Persia.

Euphrates (Arabic *Furat*) river, rising in E Turkey, flowing through Syria and Iraq and joining the river Tigris above Basra to form the river Shatt-al-Arab, at the head of the Persian/Arabian Gulf; 2,240 mi/3,600 km in length. The ancient cities of Babylon, Eridu, and Ur were situated along its course.

Eurasian a person of mixed European and Asian parentage; also, native to or an inhabitant of both Europe and Asia.

eurhythmics practice of coordinated bodily movement as an aid to musical development. It was founded about 1900 by the Swiss musician Emil Jaques-Dalcroze, professor of harmony at the Geneva conservatoire. He devised a series of "gesture" songs, to be sung simultaneously with certain bodily actions.

Euripides c. 485–c. 406 BC. Athenian tragic dramatist, ranked with ◊Aeschylus and ◊Sophocles as one of the three great tragedians. He wrote about 90 plays, of which 18 and some long fragments survive. These include "Alcestis" 438 BC, "Medea" 431, "Hippolytus" 428, the satyr-drama "Cyclops" about 424–423, "Electra, Trojan Women" 415, "Iphigenia in Tauris" 413, "Iphigenia in Aulis" about 414–412, and "The Bacchae" about 405 (the last two were produced shortly after his death).

Eurodollar EB in finance, US currency deposited outside the US and held by individuals and institutions, not necessarily in Europe. Eurodollars originated in the 1960s when East European countries deposited their US dollars in West European banks, usually to finance trade, and often redeposit with other foreign banks. The practice is a means of avoiding credit controls and exploiting interest rate differentials.

Europa in astronomy, the fourth-largest moon of the planet Jupiter, diameter 1,950 mi/3,140 km, orbiting 417,000 mi/671,000 km from the planet every 3.55 days. It is covered by ice and criss-crossed by thousands of thin cracks, each some 30,000 mi/50,000 km long.

Europa in Greek mythology, the daughter of the king of Tyre, carried off by Zeus (in the form of a bull); she personifies the continent of Europe.

Europe second-smallest continent, occupying 8% of the Earth's surface
area 4,000,000 sq mi/10,400,000 sq km

largest cities (population over 1.5 million) Athens, Barcelona, Berlin, Birmingham, Bucharest, Budapest, Hamburg, Istanbul, Kharkov, Kiev, Lisbon, London, Madrid, Manchester, Milan, Moscow, Paris, Rome, St Petersburg, Vienna, Warsaw
physical conventionally occupying that part of Eurasia to the W of the Ural Mountains, N of the Caucasus Mountains and N of the Sea of Marmara; Europe lies entirely in the northern hemisphere between 36°N and the Arctic Ocean. About two-thirds of the continent is a great plain which covers the whole of European Russia and spreads westward through Poland to the Low Countries and the Bay of Biscay. To the north lie the Scandinavian highlands rising to 8,110 ft/2,470 m at Glittertind in the Jotenheim Range of Norway. To the south, a series of mountain ranges stretch from east to west (Caucasus, Balkans, Carpathians, Apennines, Alps, Pyrenees, and Sierra Nevada). The most westerly point of the mainland is Cape Roca in Portugal; the most southerly location is Tarifa Point in Spain; the most northerly point on the mainland is Nordkynn in Norway. A line from the Baltic to the Black Sea divides Europe between an eastern continental region and a western region characterized by a series of peninsulas that include Scandinavia (Norway, Sweden, and Finland), Jutland (Denmark and Germany), Iberia (Spain and Portugal), and Italy and the Balkans (Greece, Albania, Yugoslavia, Bulgaria, and European Turkey). Because of the large number of bays, inlets, and peninsulas, the coastline is longer in proportion to its size than that of any other continent. The largest islands adjacent to continental Europe are the British Isles, Novaya Zemlya, Sicily, Sardinia, Crete, Corsica, Gotland (in the Baltic Sea), and the Balearic Islands; other more distant islands associated with Europe include Iceland, Svalbard, Franz Josef Land, Madeira, the Azores, and the Canary Islands. The greater part of Europe falls within the N temperate zone which is modified by the Gulf Stream in the northwest; Central Europe has warm summers and cold winters; the Mediterranean coast has comparatively mild winters and hot summers
features Mount Elbruz 18,517 ft/5,642 m in the Caucasus mountains is the highest peak in Europe; Mont Blanc 15,772 ft/4,807 m is the highest peak in the Alps; lakes (over 2,000 sq mi/5,100 sq km) include Ladoga, Onega, Vänern; rivers (over 500 mi/800 km) include the Volga, Danube, Dnieper Ural, Don, Pechora, Dniester, Rhine, Loire, Tagus, Ebro, Oder, Prut, Rhône
products nearly 50% of the world's automobiles are produced in Europe(Germany, France, Italy, Spain, Russia, Georgia, Ukraine, Latvia, Belarus, UK); the rate of fertilizer consumption on agricultural land is four times greater than that in any other continent; Europe produces 43% of the world's barley (Germany, Spain, France, UK), 41% of its rye (Poland, Germany), 31% of its oats (Poland, Germany, Sweden, France), and 24% of its wheat (France, Germany, UK, Romania); Italy, Spain, and Greece produce more than 70% of the world's olive oil
population (1992) 727 million (excluding Turkey and the ex-Soviet republics); annual growth rate (1985–90) 0.45%, projected population of 762 million by 2010
language mostly Indo-European, with a few exceptions, including Finno-Ugrian (Finnish and Hungarian), Basque and Altaic (Turkish); apart from a fringe of Celtic, the NW is Germanic; Letto-Lithuanian languages separate the Germanic from the Slavonic tongues of E Europe; Romance languages spread E–W from Romania through Italy and France to Spain and Portugal

religion Christianity (Protestant, Roman Catholic, Eastern Orthodox), Muslim (Turkey, Albania, Yugoslavia, Bulgaria), Judaism.

European native to or an inhabitant of the continent of Europe and their descendants. Europe is multicultural and, although most of its languages belong to the Indo-European family, there are also speakers of Uralic (such as Hungarian) and Altaic (such as Turkish) languages, as well as Basque.

European Community political and economic alliance consisting of the European Coal and Steel Community (1952), European Economic Community (EEC, popularly called the Common Market, 1957), and the European Atomic Energy Commission (Euratom, 1957). The original six members—Belgium, France, West Germany, Italy, Luxembourg, and the Netherlands—were joined by the UK, Denmark, and the Republic of Ireland 1973; Greece 1981; and Spain and Portugal 1986. Association agreements—providing for free trade within ten years and the possibility of full EC membership—were signed with Czechoslovakia, Hungary, and Poland 1991, subject to ratification, and with Romania 1992. The aims of the EC include the expansion of trade, reduction of competition, the abolition of restrictive trading practices, the encouragement of free movement of capital and labor within the community, and the establishment of a closer union among European people. The Maastricht Treaty provides the framework for closer economic and political union. It was ratified 1993 by all member states.

European Court of Justice the court of the European Community (EC), which is responsible for interpreting Community law and ruling on breaches by member states and others of such law. It sits in Luxembourg with judges from the member states.

European Economic Community (EEC) popularly called the **Common Market** organization established 1957 with the aim of crating a single European market for the products of member states by the abolition of tariffs and other restrictions on trade.

European Free Trade Association (EFTA) organization established 1960 consisting of Austria, Finland, Iceland, Norway, Sweden, Switzerland, and (from 1991) Liechtenstein, previously a nonvoting associate member. There are no import duties between members.

European Monetary System (EMS) attempt by the European Community to bring financial cooperation and monetary stability to Europe. It was established 1979 in the wake of the 1974 oil crisis, which brought growing economic disruption to European economies because of floating exchange rates. Central to the EMS is the Exchange Rate Mechanism (ERM), a voluntary system of semifixed exchange rates based on the European Currency Unit (ECU).

European Monetary Union (EMU) the proposed European Community (EC) policy for a single currency and common economic policies. The proposal was announced by a European Community committee headed by EC Commission president Jacques Delors April 1989.

European Parliament the parliament of the European Community, which meets in Strasbourg to comment on the legislative proposals of the Commission of the European Communities. Members are elected for a five-year term. The European Parliament has 518 seats, apportioned on the basis of population, of which

Europe: history	
BC 3000	Bronze Age civilizations: Minoan, Mycenaean.
1000	Iron Age.
6th–4th centuries	Greek civilization at its height; Alexander the Great advances E to India.
3rd century	Rome in control of the Italian peninsula.
146	Greece a Roman province, and Carthage destroyed.
1st century	Augustus made the Rhine and Danube the Roman Empire's northern frontiers; see ◊Celts.
AD 1st century	Britain brought within the Roman Empire
2nd century	Roman Empire ceased to expand.
4th century	Christianity the established religion of the Roman Empire, which halved into E and W empires (see ◊Byzantine empires).
4th–6th centuries	W Europe overrun by Anglo Saxons, Franks, Goths, Lombards. W Roman empire fell 476. Middle Ages begin; feudalism prevails.
7th–8th centuries	Christendom threatened by the Moors (Muslim Arabs) via the Mediterranean countries.
800	Charlemagne given title of emperor by the Pope; Holy Roman empire begins.
1073	Gregory VII began 200 years of conflict between the powers of the empire and papacy.
1096–1272	Crusades to take Jerusalem.
12th century	Setting up of German, Flemish, and Italian city-states, which in the 14th–15th centuries fostered the Renaissance.
1453	Byzantine empire falls to the Turks.
16th–17th centuries	Dominated by rivalry of France and the Hapsburgs, the Protestant Reformation, and the Catholic Counter Reformation.
17th century	Absolute monarchy came to prevail (Louis XIV) in Europe, although in Britain supremacy of Parliament established.
18th century	War of the Austrian Succession and Seven Years' War ended in the loss of the French colonial empire to Britain and the establishment of Prussia as Europe's military power.
1789–95	French Revolution led to the Revolutionary and Napoleonic wars.
1821–29	Greek War of Independence marked the end of Turkish control of the Balkans.
1848	Year of revolutions (see ◊Louis Philippe, ◊Metternich, ◊Risorgimento).
1914–18	World War I arose from the Balkan question, Franco–German rivalry, and colonial differences; it destroyed the Austrian, Russian, and Turkish empires and paved the way for the Russian Revolution and the formation of the USSR.
1933	Hitler came to power in a defeated, impoverished Germany. His geopolitical aggression caused World War II.
1939–45	World War II resulted in decline of European colonial rule in Africa and Asia; emergence of Soviet power, and most of Western Europe under the military aegis of the US (NATO); the Cold War begins.
1957	Establishment of the European Economic Community.
1973	Enlargement of the European Community to include Britain, Denmark, and the Irish Republic.
1989–90	Beginning of democratization of Eastern bloc, including USSR, Poland, Romania, Czechoslovakia, East Germany. Unification of Germany.
1991	Baltic republics of Estonia, Latvia, and Lithuania regain independence; other Soviet republics follow.
1991–92	Yugoslavia splits into five nations.
1992	European Community becomes a single market.
1993	Czech Republic and Slovakia created by division of Slovakia.

the UK, France, Germany, and Italy have 81 each; Spain 60; the Netherlands 25; Belgium, Greece, and Portugal 24 each; Denmark 16; the Republic of Ireland 15; and Luxembourg 6.

European Space Agency (ESA) an organization of European countries (Austria, Belgium, Denmark, France, Germany, Ireland, Italy, the Netherlands,

Norway, Spain, Sweden, Switzerland, and the UK) that engages in space research and technology. It was founded 1975, with headquarters in Paris.

europium soft, grayish, metallic element of the ◊lanthanide series, symbol Eu, atomic number 63, atomic weight 151.96. It is used in lasers and as the red phosphor in color televisions; its compounds are used to make control rods for nuclear reators. It was named in 1901 by French chemist Eugène Demarçay (1852–1904) after the continent of Europe, where it was first found.

Eurydice in Greek mythology, the wife of ◊Orpheus. She was a dryad, or forest nymph, and died from a snake bite. Orpheus attempted unsuccessfully to fetch her back from the realm of the dead.

eustachian tube small air-filled canal connecting the middle ◊ear with the back of the throat. It is found in all land vertebrates and equalizes the pressure on both sides of the eardrum.

eustatic change worldwide rise or fall in sea level caused by a change in the amount of water in the oceans (by contrast, isostasy involves a rising or sinking of the land). During the last ice age, sea level fell because water became "locked-up" in the form of ice and snow, and less water reached the oceans.

euthanasia in medicine, mercy killing of someone with a severe and incurable condition or illness. The Netherlands legalized voluntary euthanasia 1983, but is the only country to have done so.

evangelicalism the beliefs of some Protestant Christian movements that stress biblical authority, faith, and the personal commitment of the "born again" experience.

evangelist person traveling to spread the Christian gospel, in particular the authors of the four Gospels in the New Testament: Matthew, Mark, Luke, and John. See also ◊televangelist.

Evans Arthur John 1851–1941. English archeologist. His excavation of ◊Knossos on Crete resulted in the discovery of pre-Phoenician Minoan script and proved the existence of the legendary Minoan civilization.

Evans Edith 1888–1976. English character actress who performed on the London stage and on Broadway. Her many imposing performances include the film role of Lady Bracknell in Oscar Wilde's comedy *The Importance of Being Earnest* 1952. Among her other films are *Tom Jones* 1963 and *Crooks and Coronets* 1969.

Evans Walker 1903–1975. US photographer best known for his documentary photographs of people in the rural American South during the Great Depression. Many of his photographs appeared in James Agee's book *Let Us Now Praise Famous Men* 1941.

Evansville industrial city in SW Indiana, on the Ohio River; population (1990) 126,300. Industries include pharmaceuticals and plastics. The University of Evansville is here.   The community, which dates to 1812, grew after the 1853 completion of the Wabash and Erie canal linking the Ohio at Evansville with Lake Erie.

evaporation process in which a liquid turns to a vapor without its temperature reaching boiling point. A liquid left to stand in a saucer eventually evaporates because, at any time, a proportion of its molecules will be fast enough (have enough kinetic energy) to escape through the attractive intermolecular forces at the liquid surface into the atmosphere. The temperature of the liquid tends to fall because the evaporating molecules remove energy from the liquid. The rate of evaporation rises with increased temperature because as the mean kinetic energy of the liquid's molecules rises, so will the number possessing enough energy to escape.

Eve in the Old Testament, the first woman, wife of ◊Adam. She was tempted by Satan (in the form of a snake) to eat the fruit of the Tree of Knowledge of Good and Evil, and then tempted Adam to eat of the fruit as well, thus bringing about their expulsion from the Garden of Eden.

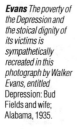

Evans *The poverty of the Depression and the stoical dignity of its victims is sympathetically recreated in this photograph by Walker Evans, entitled* Depression: Bud Fields and wife; Alabama, 1935.

evening primrose any plant of the genus *Oenothera*, family Onagraceae. Some 50 species are native to North America, several of which now also grow in Europe. Some are cultivated for their oil, which is used in treating eczema, premenstrual tension, and chronic fatigue syndrome.

Everest, Mount the world's highest mountain above sea level, in the ◊Himalayas, on the China–Nepal frontier; height 29,118 ft/8,872 m (recently measured by satellite to this new height from the former official height of 29,028 ft/8,848 m). It was first climbed by New Zealand mountaineer Edmund Hillary and Sherpa Tenzing Norgay 1953. More than 360 climbers have reached the summit; over 100 have died during the ascent.

Everett Edward 1794–1865. US religious leader, educator, and public figure. He served in the US House of Representatives 1825–35, as governor of Massachusetts 1835–39, and as US minister to England 1841–45.

He was president of Harvard University 1846–49. His four-month role as President Fillmore's secretary of state 1852–53 was followed by a short tenure in the US Senate 1853–54.

Everglades area of swamps, marsh, and lakes in S ◊Florida; area 5,000 sq mi/12,950 sq km. A national park covers the S tip.

evergreen in botany, a plant such as pine, spruce, or holly, that bears its leaves all year round. Most ◊conifers are evergreen. Plants that shed their leaves in autumn or during a dry season are described as ◊deciduous.

Evert Chris(tine) 1954– . US tennis player. She won her first Wimbledon title 1974, and has since won 21 Grand Slam titles. She became the first woman tennis player to win $1 million in prize money. She has an outstanding two-handed backhand and is a great exponent of baseline technique. Evert retired from competitive tennis 1989.

evolution slow process of change from one form to another, as in the evolution of the universe from its formation in the ◊Big Bang to its present state, or in the evolution of life on Earth. Some Christians and Muslims deny the theory of evolution as conflicting with the belief that God created all things (see ◊creationism). *See illustration p. 330*

exchange rate the price at which one currency is bought or sold in terms of other currencies, gold, or accounting units such as the special drawing right (SDR) of the ◊International Monetary Fund. Exchange rates may be fixed by international agreement or by government policy; or they may be wholly or partly allowed to "float" (that is, find their own level) in world currency markets.

excise taxes imposed on goods, usually considered luxury items or those items quickly consumed. The taxes are paid prior to sale, the cost being passed on to the consumer.

exclamation point punctuation mark (!) used to indicate emphasis or strong emotion ("That's terrible!"). It is appropriate after interjections ("Rats!"), emphatic greetings ("Yo!"), and orders ("Shut up!"), as well as those sentences beginning *How* or *What* that are not questions ("How embarrassing!", "What a surprise!").

exclusion principle in physics, a principle of atomic structure originated by Austrian–US physicist Wolfgang ◊Pauli. It states that no two electrons in a single atom may have the same set of ◊quantum numbers. Hence, it is impossible to pack together certain elementary particles, such as electrons, beyond a certain critical density, otherwise they would share the same location and quantum number. A white dwarf star is thus prevented from contracting further by the exclusion principle and never collapses.

excommunication in religion, exclusion of an offender from the rights and privileges of the Roman Catholic Church; King John, Henry VIII, and Elizabeth I were all excommunicated.

excretion in biology, the removal of waste products from the cells of living organisms. In plants and simple animals, waste products are removed by diffusion, but in higher animals they are removed by specialized organs. In mammals, for example, carbon dioxide and water are removed via the lungs, and nitrogenous compounds and water via the liver, the kidneys, and the rest of the urinary system.

executor in law, a person appointed in a will to carry out the instructions of the deceased. A person so named has the right to refuse to act. The executor also has a duty to bury the deceased, prove the will, and obtain a grant of probate (that is, establish that the will is genuine and obtain official approval of his or her actions).

existentialism branch of philosophy based on the concept of an absurd universe where humans have free will. Existentialists argue that philosophy must begin from the concrete situation of the individual in such a world, and that humans are responsible for and the sole judge of their actions as they affect others, though no one else's existence is real to the individual. The origin of existentialism is usually traced back to the Danish philosopher Kierkegaard; among its proponents were Martin Heidegger in Germany and Jean-Paul ◊Sartre in France.

exocrine gland gland that discharges secretions, usually through a tube or a duct, onto a surface. Examples include sweat glands which release sweat onto the skin, and digestive glands which release digestive juices onto the walls of the intestine. Some animals also have ◊endocrine glands (ductless glands) that release hormones directly into the bloodstream.

Exodus second book of the Old Testament, which relates the departure of the Israelites from slavery in Egypt, under the leadership of ◊Moses, for the Promised Land of Canaan. The journey included the miraculous parting of the Red Sea, with the Pharaoh's pursuing forces being drowned as the waters returned.

The Exodus is also recorded in the *Hagadda*, which is read at the Seder (during the Jewish festival of Passover) to commemorate the deliverance. During the 40 years of wandering in the wilderness, Moses brought the Ten Commandments down from Mt. Sinai.

exorcism rite used in a number of religions for the expulsion of so-called evil spirits. In Christianity it is employed, for example, in the Roman Catholic and Pentecostal churches.

exoskeleton the hardened external skeleton of insects, spiders, crabs, and other arthropods. It provides attachment for muscles and protection for the internal organs, as well as support. To permit growth it is periodically shed in a process called ecdysis.

Ex parte McCardle US Supreme Court decision 1869 dealing with the power of Congress to deprive the Supreme Court of jurisdiction over appeals. William McCardle, a Mississippi journalist convicted of sedi-

*evolution The
progress of evolution.*

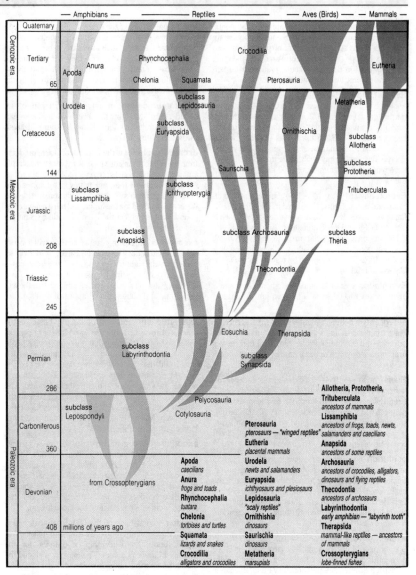

tion by a military court and refused a writ of habeas corpus by the federal circuit court, appealed his case to the Supreme Court. Afraid that the military Reconstruction governments would be found unconstitutional, Congress revoked the Court's jurisdiction over appeals. The Court ruled unanimously that this was fully within the constitutional right of Congress to make exceptions to the Supreme Court's right to hear appeals; furthermore, it was not the Court's job to discern the political motives of restrictions imposed by Congress.

Ex parte Merryman circuit court decision 1861 dealing with the right of the US president to restrict the civilian court under martial law for secessionist activities. Merryman, a Baltimore citizen, received a writ of habeas corpus from the acting circuit court judge, Chief Justice Taney. Taney ordered that Merryman be brought to trial or released and found the military in contempt of court when, under the authority of Presi-

dent Lincoln, it refused to comply. Taney declared that Lincoln was in violation of the Constitution, saying only Congress had the right to suspend habeas corpus. The case never reached the US Supreme Court.

Ex parte Milligan US Supreme Court decision 1866 that attended to the issue of the jurisdiction of military tribunals in areas where civilian courts are operating. Milligan, an Indiana citizen sentenced by a military tribunal to hang for secessionist activities, petitioned for a writ of habeas corpus on the grounds that as a civilian he was not subject to military law. The Court ruled 5–4 in favor of Milligan, holding that neither the US president nor Congress had the right to impose martial law outside of a war zone.

expectorant any substance, often added to cough mixture, intended to help expel mucus from the airways. It is debatable whether expectorants have an effect on lung secretions.

experiment in science, a practical test designed with the intention that its results will be relevant to a particular theory or set of theories. Although some experiments may be used merely for gathering more information about a topic that is already well understood, others may be of crucial importance in confirming a new theory or in undermining long-held beliefs.

experimental psychology application of scientific methods to the study of mental processes and behavior.

Explorer series of US scientific satellites. *Explorer 1*, launched Jan 1958, was the first US satellite in orbit and discovered the Van Allen radiation belts around the Earth.

explosive any material capable of a sudden release of energy and the rapid formation of a large volume of gas, leading when compressed to the development of a high-pressure wave (blast).

exponent or *index* in mathematics, a number that indicates the number of times a term is multiplied by itself; for example $x^2 = x \times x$, $4^3 = 4 \times 4 \times 4$.

exponential in mathematics, descriptive of a ◊function in which the variable quantity is an exponent (a number indicating the power to which another number or expression is raised).

export goods or service produced in one country and sold to another. Exports may be visible (goods physically exported) or invisible (services provided in the exporting country but paid for by residents of another country).

export credit loan, finance, or guarantee provided by a government or a financial institution enabling companies to export goods and services in situations where payment for them may be delayed or subject to risk.

exposure meter instrument used in photography for indicating the correct exposure—the length of time the camera shutter should be open under given light conditions. Meters use substances such as cadmium sulfide and selenium as light sensors. These materials change electrically when light strikes them, the change being proportional to the intensity of the incident light. Many cameras have a built-in exposure meter that sets the camera controls automatically as the light conditions change.

Expressionism style of painting, sculpture, and literature that expresses inner emotions; in particular, a movement in early 20th-century art in N and central Europe. Expressionists tended to distort or exaggerate natural appearance in order to create a reflection of an inner world; the Norwegian painter Edvard Munch's *Skriket/The Scream* 1893 (National Gallery, Oslo) is perhaps the most celebrated example. Expressionist writers include August Strindberg and Frank Wedekind.

extinction in biology, the complete disappearance of a species. In the past, extinctions are believed to have occurred because species were unable to adapt quickly enough to a naturally changing environment. Today, most extinctions are due to human activity. Some species, such as the ◊dodo of Mauritius, the moas of New Zealand, and the passenger ◊pigeon of North America, were exterminated by hunting. Others became extinct when their habitat was destroyed. See also ◊endangered species.

extracellular matrix strong material naturally occurring in animals and plants, made up of protein and long-chain sugars (polysaccharides) in which cells are embedded. It is often called a "biological glue" and forms part of ◊connective tissues such as bone and skin.

extradition surrender, by one state or country to another, of a person accused of a criminal offense in the state or country to which that person is extradited.

extrasensory perception (ESP) form of perception beyond and distinct from the known sensory processes. The main forms of ESP are clairvoyance (intuitive perception or vision of events and situations without using the senses); precognition (the ability to foresee events); and telepathy or thought transference (communication between people without using any known visible, tangible, or audible medium). Verification by scientific study has yet to be achieved.

Extremadura autonomous region of W Spain including the provinces of Badajoz and Cáceres; area 16,058 sq mi/41,600 sq km; population (1986) 1,089,000. Irrigated land is used for growing wheat; the remainder is either oak forest or used for pig or sheep grazing.

extroversion or *extraversion* personality dimension described by ◊Jung and later by Eysenck. The typical extrovert is sociable, impulsive, and carefree. The opposite of extroversion is introversion; the typical introvert is quiet and inward-looking.

extrusion common method of shaping metals, plastics, and other materials. The materials, usually hot, are forced through the hole in a metal die and take its cross-sectional shape. Rods, tubes, and sheets may be made in this way.

Eyck *Jan van Eyck's* Arnolfini Wedding *(1434) National Gallery, London.*

eye The human eye.

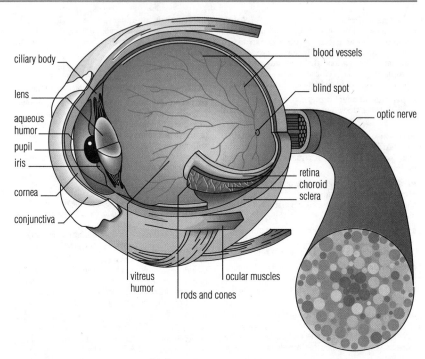

ciliary body

lens

aqueous humor

pupil

iris

cornea

conjunctiva

blood vessels

blind spot

optic nerve

retina
choroid
sclera

vitreus humor

ocular muscles

rods and cones

extrusive rock or *volcanic rock* ◊igneous rock formed on the surface of the Earth; for example, basalt. It is usually fine-grained (having cooled quickly), unlike the more coarse-grained intrusive rocks (igneous rocks formed under the surface). The magma (molten rock) that cools to form extrusive rock may reach the surface through a crack, such as the constructive margin at the Mid-Atlantic Ridge, or through the vent of a ◊volcano.

Eyck Jan van *c.* 1390–1441. Flemish painter of the early northern Renaissance, one of the first to work in oils. His paintings are technically brilliant and sumptuously rich in detail and color. In his *Arnolfini Wedding* 1434 (National Gallery, London) the bride and groom appear in a domestic interior crammed with disguised symbols, as a kind of pictorial marriage certificate.

Little is known of his brother *Hubert van Eyck* (died 1426), who is supposed to have begun the massive and complex altarpiece in St Bavo's cathedral, Ghent, *The Adoration of the Mystical Lamb*, completed by Jan 1432. *See illustration p. 331*

eye the organ of vision. In the human eye, the light is focused by the combined action of the curved *cornea*, the internal fluids, and the *lens*. The insect eye is compound—made up of many separate facets—known as ommatidia, each of which collects light and directs it separately to a receptor to build up an image. Invertebrates have much simpler eyes, with no lenses. Among

mollusks, cephalopods have complex eyes similar to those of vertebrates. The mantis shrimp's eyes contain ten color pigments with which to perceive color; some flies and fishes have five, while the human eye has only three.

eye, defects of the abnormalities of the eye that impair vision. Glass or plastic lenses, in the form of glasses or contact lenses, are the usual means of correction. Common optical defects are nearsightedness or myopia; farsightedness or hypermetropia; lack of accommodation or presbyopia; and ◊astigmatism. Other eye defects include ◊color blindness.

eyeglasses pair of lenses fitted in a frame and worn in front of the eyes to correct or assist defective vision. Common defects of the eye corrected by such lenses are nearsightedness (myopia), corrected by using concave (spherical) lenses; farsightedness (hypermetropia), corrected by using convex (spherical) lenses; and astigmatism, corrected by using cylindrical lenses. Spherical and cylindrical lenses may be combined in one lens. Bifocal glasses correct vision both at a distance and for reading by combining two lenses of different curvatures in one piece of glass. Today, lightweight plastic lenses are common instead of glass.

Eyre, Lake Australia's largest lake, in central South Australia, which frequently runs dry, becoming a salt marsh in dry seasons; area up to 3,500 sq mi/9,000 sq km. It is the continent's lowest point, 39 ft/12 m below sea level.

°F symbol for degrees ◊Fahrenheit.

Fabergé Peter Carl 1846–1920. Russian goldsmith and jeweler. Among his masterpieces was a series of jeweled Easter eggs, the first of which was commissioned by Alexander III for the tsarina 1884.

Fabius Laurent 1946– . French politician, leader of the Socialist Party from 1992. As prime minister 1984–86, he introduced a liberal, free-market economic program, but his career was damaged by the 1985 ◊Greenpeace sabotage scandal.

fable story, in either verse or prose, in which animals or inanimate objects are given the mentality and speech of human beings to point out a moral. Fables are common in folklore and children's literature, and range from the short fables of the ancient Greek writer Aesop to the modern novel *Animal Farm* 1945 by George Orwell

Fabricius Geronimo 1537–1619. Italian anatomist and embryologist. He made a detailed study of the veins and discovered the valves that direct the blood flow toward the heart. He also studied the development of chick embryos.

factor a number that divides into another number exactly. For example, the factors of 64 are 1, 2, 4, 8, 16, 32, and 64. In algebra, certain kinds of polynomials (expressions consisting of several or many terms) can be factorized. For example, the factors of $x^2 + 3x + 2$ are $x + 1$ and $x + 2$, since $x^2 + 3x + 2 = (x + 1)(x + 2)$. This is called factorization. See also ◊prime number.

factorial of a positive number, the product of all the whole numbers (integers) inclusive between 1 and the number itself. A factorial is indicated by the symbol "!." Thus $6! = 1 \times 2 \times 3 \times 4 \times 5 \times 6 = 720$. Factorial zero, 0!, is defined as 1.

factoring lending money to a company on the security of money owed to that company; this is often done on the basis of collecting those debts. The lender is known as the factor. Factoring may also describe acting as a commission agent for the sale of goods.

factory system the basis of manufacturing in the modern world. In the factory system workers are employed at a place where they carry out specific tasks, which together result in a product. This is called the division of labor. Usually these workers will perform their tasks with the aid of machinery. Such mechanization is another feature of the factory system, which leads to mass production.

Fadiman Clifton Paul 1904– . US editor and media personality. Following his appointment as book reviewer for the *New Yorker* 1933, Fadiman became moderator of the national radio program "Information Please" 1938–48. In 1944 he was appointed to the editorial board of the Book of the Month Club. From the 1950s, he published literary anthologies and continued to be a popular radio and television personality.

Fagatogo capital of American ◊Samoa, situated on Pago Pago Harbor, Tutuila Island; population (1980) 30,124.

Fahd 1921– . King of Saudi Arabia from 1982, when he succeeded his half brother Khalid. As head of government, he has been active in trying to bring about a solution to the Middle East conflicts.

Fahrenheit scale temperature scale invented 1714 by Gabriel Fahrenheit which was commonly used in English-speaking countries up until the 1970s, after which the ◊Celsius scale was generally adopted, in line with the rest of the world. In the Fahrenheit scale, intervals are measured in degrees (°F); °F = (°C × ⅑) + 32.

fainting sudden, temporary loss of consciousness caused by reduced blood supply to the brain. It may be due to emotional shock or physical factors, such as pooling of blood in the legs from standing still for long periods.

Fairbanks town in central Alaska, situated on the Chena Slough, a tributary of the Tanana River; population (1990) 30,800. Founded 1902, it became a gold-mining and fur-trading center and the terminus of the Alaska Railroad and the Pan-American highway.

It functions as a service center for the mineral development of central and N Alaska. Fort Wainwright, Eielson Air Force Base, and the main campus of the University of Alaska are outside the city limits.

Fairbanks Douglas, Sr. Adopted name of Douglas Elton Ulman 1883–1939. US actor. He played acrobatic

Fabergé *The Fabergé cuckoo egg (1900), presented by Tsar Nicholas II to his wife as an Easter egg.*

swashbuckling heroes in silent films such as *The Mark of Zorro* 1920, *The Three Musketeers* 1921, *Robin Hood* 1922, *The Thief of Bagdad* 1924, and *Don Quixote* 1925. He was married to film star Mary Pickford ("America's Sweetheart") 1920–33. In 1919 they founded United Artists with Charlie Chaplin and D W Griffith.

Fairbanks Douglas, Jr 1909– . US actor who appeared in the same type of swashbuckling film roles as his father, Douglas Fairbanks; for example, in *Catherine the Great* 1934 and *The Prisoner of Zenda* 1937.

Fair Deal the policy of social improvement advocated by Harry S Truman, president of the US 1945–53. The Fair Deal proposals, first mooted in 1945 after the end of World War II, aimed to extend the ◊New Deal on health insurance, housing development, and the laws to maintain farming prices. Although some bills became law—for example a Housing Act, a higher minimum wage, and wider social security benefits— the main proposals were blocked by a hostile Congress.

Fairfax Thomas, 3rd Baron Fairfax of Cameron 1612–1671. English general, commander in chief of the Parliamentary army in the English Civil War. With Oliver Cromwell he formed the New Model Army and defeated Charles I at Naseby. He opposed the king's execution, resigned in protest 1650 against the invasion of Scotland, and participated in the restoration of Charles II after Cromwell's death.

fairy tale magical story, usually a folk tale in origin. Typically in European fairy tales, a poor, brave, and resourceful hero or heroine goes through testing adventures to eventual good fortune.

Faisal Ibn Abdul Aziz 1905–1975. King of Saudi Arabia from 1964. He was the younger brother of King Saud, on whose accession 1953 he was declared crown prince. He was prime minister 1953–60 and 1962–75. In 1964 he emerged victorious from a lengthy conflict with his brother and adopted a policy of steady modernization of his country. He was assassinated by his nephew.

Faisal I 1885–1933. King of Iraq 1921–33. An Arab nationalist leader during World War I, he was instrumental in liberating the Near East from Ottoman control and was declared king of Syria in 1918 but deposed by the French in 1920. The British then installed him as king in Iraq, where he continued to foster pan-Arabism.

Falkland Islands

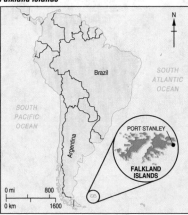

fakir originally a Muslim mendicant of some religious order, but in India a general term for an ascetic.

Falange Española former Spanish Fascist Party, founded 1933 by José Antonio Primo de Rivera (1903–1936), son of military ruler Miguel ◊Primo de Rivera. It was closely modeled in program and organization on the Italian fascists and on the Nazis. In 1937, when ◊Franco assumed leadership, it was declared the only legal party, and altered its name to Traditionalist Spanish Phalanx.

Falasha member of a small community of black Jews in Ethiopia. They suffered discrimination there, and, after being accorded Jewish status by Israel 1975, began a gradual process of resettlement in Israel. In the early 1980s only about 30,000 Falashim remained in Ethiopia.

falcon any bird of prey of the genus *Falco*, family Falconidae, order Falconiformes. Falcons are the smallest of the hawks (6–24 in/15–60 cm). They nest in high places and kill their prey by "stooping" (swooping down at high speed). They include the peregrine and kestrel.

falconry the use of specially trained falcons and hawks to capture birds or small mammals. Practiced since ancient times in the Middle East, falconry was introduced from continental Europe to Britain in Saxon times.

Faldo Nick 1957– . English golfer who was the first Briton in 54 years to win three British Open titles, and the only person after Jack ◊Nicklaus to win two successive US Masters titles (1989 and 1990). He is one of only six golfers to win the Masters and British Open in the same year.

Since turning professional in 1976 he has won more than 25 tournaments worldwide.

Falkland Islands (Argentine *Islas Malvinas*) British crown colony in the S Atlantic
area 4,700 sq mi/12,173 sq km, made up of two main islands: East Falkland 2,610 sq mi/6,760 sq km, and West Falkland 2,090 sq mi/5,413 sq km
capital Stanley; new port facilities opened 1984, Mount Pleasant airport 1985
features in addition to the two main islands, there are about 200 small islands, all with wild scenery and rich bird life
products wool, alginates (used as dyes and as a food additive) from seaweed beds
population (1986) 1,916

Falklands War war between Argentina and Britain over disputed sovereignty of the Falkland Islands initiated when Argentina invaded and occupied the islands April 2, 1982. On the following day, the United Nations Security Council passed a resolution calling for Argentina to withdraw. A British task force was immediately dispatched, and, after a fierce conflict in which more than 1,000 Argentine and British lives were lost, 12,000 Argentine troops surrendered and the islands were returned to British rule June 14–15, 1982.

Fallopian tube or *oviduct* in mammals, one of two tubes that carry eggs from the ovary to the uterus. An egg is fertilized by sperm in the Fallopian tubes, which are lined with cells whose ◊cilia move the egg toward the uterus.

fallout harmful radioactive material released into the atmosphere in the debris of a nuclear explosion (see ◊nuclear warfare) and descending to the surface of the Earth. Such material can enter the food chain, cause

◊radiation sickness, and last for hundreds of thousands of years (see ◊half-life).

Fall River city and port in Massachusetts; population (1990) 92,700. It stands at the mouth of the Taunton River, over the Little Fall River, which gave it its name. Textiles and clothing, rubber, paper, and plastics are among the goods produced. It was founded 1656 and was one of the nation's most important textile-mill centers in the 19th century. Lizzie Borden was acquitted here of murdering her father and stepmother 1892.

false-color imagery graphic technique that displays images in false (not true-to-life) colors so as to enhance certain features. It is widely used in displaying electronic images taken by spacecraft; for example, Earth-survey satellites such as *Landsat*. Any colors can be selected by a computer processing the received data.

family in biological classification, a group of related genera (see ◊genus). Family names are not printed in italic (unlike genus and species names), and by convention they all have the ending -idae (animals) or -aceae (plants and fungi). For example, the genera of hummingbirds are grouped in the hummingbird family, Trochilidae. Related families are grouped together in an ◊order.

family group of people related to each other by blood or by marriage.

Families are usually described as either "extended" (a large group of relations living together or in close contact with each other) or "nuclear" (a family consisting of two parents and their children).

family planning spacing or preventing the birth of children. Access to family-planning services (see ◊contraceptive) is a significant factor in women's health as well as in limiting population growth. If all those women who wished to avoid further childbirth were able to do so, the number of births would be reduced by 27% in Africa, 33% in Asia, and 35% in Latin America; and the number of women who die during pregnancy or childbirth would be reduced by about 50%.

famine severe shortage of food affecting a large number of people. Almost 750 million people (equivalent to double the population of Europe) worldwide suffer from hunger and malnutrition. The *food availability deficit* (FAD) theory explains famines as being caused by insufficient food supplies. A more recent theory is that famines arise when one group in a society loses its opportunity to exchange its labor or possessions for food.

fantasia *fantasy* or *fancy* in music, a free-form instrumental composition of improvised character.

farad SI unit (symbol F) of electrical capacitance (how much electricity a ◊capacitor can store for a given voltage). One farad is a capacitance of one ◊coulomb per volt. For practical purposes the microfarad (one millionth of a farad) is more commonly used.

Faraday Michael 1791–1867. English chemist and physicist. In 1821 he began experimenting with electromagnetism, and ten years later discovered the induction of electric currents and made the first dynamo. He subsequently found that a magnetic field will rotate the plane of polarization of light (see ◊polarized light). Faraday also investigated electrolysis.

Faraday's constant constant (symbol *F*) representing the electric charge carried on one mole of electrons. It is found by multiplying Avogadro's constant by the charge carried on a single electron, and is equal to

Fallopian tube The auricle (trumpet-shaped ending) of the female Fallopian tube, which catches the eggs released from the ovary.

9.648×10^4 coulombs per mole. One **faraday** is this constant used as a unit. The constant is used to calculate the electric charge needed to discharge a particular quantity of ions during ◊electrolysis.

Faraday's laws three laws of electromagnetic induction, and two laws of electrolysis, all proposed originally by English scientist Michael Faraday:

induction (1) a changing magnetic field induces an electromagnetic force in a conductor; (2) the electromagnetic force is proportional to the rate of change of the field; (3) the direction of the induced electromagnetic force depends on the orientation of the field.

electrolysis (1) the amount of chemical change during electrolysis is proportional to the charge passing through the liquid; (2) the amount of chemical change produced in a substance by a given amount of electricity is proportional to the electrochemical equivalent of that substance.

Far East geographical term for all Asia east of the Indian subcontinent.

Fargo city in SE North Dakota, across the Red River from Moorhead, Minnesota; seat of Cass County; population (1990) 74,100. The largest city in the state, it is a center for processing and distributing agricultural products and farm machinery. Chemicals and building materials are also manufactured.

Fargo William George 1818–1881. US long-distance transport pioneer. In 1844 he established with Henry Wells (1805–1878) and Daniel Dunning the first express company to carry freight west of Buffalo. Its success led to his appointment 1850 as secretary of the newly established American Express Company, of which he was president 1868–81. He also established *Wells, Fargo & Company* 1851, carrying goods express between New York and San Francisco via Panama.

Faroe Islands or *Faeroe Islands* or *Faeroes* (Danish *Faerøerne* "Sheep Islands") island group (18 out of 22 inhabited) in the N Atlantic, between the Shetland Islands and Iceland, forming an outlying part of ◊Denmark

area 540 sq mi/1,399 sq km; largest islands are Strømø, Østerø, Vagø, Suderø, Sandø, and Bordø *capital* Thorshavn on Strømø, population (1986) 15,287

products fish, crafted goods

currency Danish krone

population (1986) 46,000

languages Faeroese, Danish

government since 1948 the islands have had full self-government; they do not belong to the EC

history first settled by Norsemen in the 9th century, the Faroes were a Norwegian province 1380–1709. Their parliament was restored 1852. They withdrew from the European Free Trade Association 1972.

Farouk 1920–1965. King of Egypt 1936–52. He succeeded his father ◊Fuad I. In 1952 a coup headed by General Muhammed Neguib and Colonel Gamal Nasser compelled him to abdicate, and his son Fuad II was temporarily proclaimed in his place.

Farragut David (Glasgow) 1801–1870. US admiral, born near Knoxville, Tennessee. During the US Civil War he took New Orleans 1862, after destroying the Confederate fleet, and in 1864 effectively put an end to blockade-running at Mobile. The ranks of vice admiral (1864) and admiral (1866) were created for him by Congress.

Farrow Mia 1945– . US film and television actress. Popular since the late 1960s, she was associated with the director Woody Allen, both on and off screen 1982–92. She starred in his films *Zelig* 1983, *Hannah and Her Sisters* 1986, and *Crimes and Misdemeanors* 1990, as well as in Roman Polanski's *Rosemary's Baby* 1968.

Fars province of SW Iran, comprising fertile valleys among mountain ranges running NW–SE; population (1982) 2,035,600; area 51,487 sq mi/133,300 sq km. The capital is Shiraz, and there are imposing ruins of Cyrus the Great's city of Parargardae and of ◊Persepolis.

Farsi or *Persian* language belonging to the Indo-Iranian branch of the Indo-European family, and the official language of Iran (formerly Persia). It is also spoken in Afghanistan, Iraq, and Tajikistan.

fascism political ideology that denies all rights to individuals in their relations with the state; specifically, the totalitarian nationalist movement founded in Italy 1919 by ◊Mussolini and followed by Hitler's Germany 1933.

Fassbinder Rainer Werner 1946–1982. West German film director who began as a fringe actor and founded his own "anti-theater" before moving into films. His works are mainly stylized indictments of contemporary German society. He made more than 40 films, including *Die bitteren Tränen der Petra von Kant/The Bitter Tears of Petra von Kant* 1972, *Angst essen Seele auf/Fear Eats the Soul* 1974, and *Die Ehe von Maria Braun/The Marriage of Maria Braun* 1979.

fat in the broadest sense, a mixture of ◊lipids—chiefly triglycerides (lipids containing three ◊fatty acid molecules linked to a molecule of glycerol). More specifically, the term refers to a lipid mixture that is solid at room temperature (68°F/20°C); lipid mixtures that are liquid at room temperature are called **oils**. The higher the proportion of saturated fatty acids in a mixture, the harder the fat.

Fatah, al- Palestinian nationalist organization founded 1956 to bring about an independent state of Palestine. Also called the Palestine National Liberation Movement, it is the main component of the ◊Palestine Liberation Organization. Its leader is Yassir ◊Arafat.

Fates in Greek mythology, the three female figures who determined the destiny of human lives. They were envisaged as spinners: Clotho spun the thread of life, Lachesis twisted the thread, and Atropos cut it off. They are analogous to the Roman Parcae and Norse Norns.

Father's Day a day set apart in many countries for honoring fathers, observed on the third Sunday in June in the US, UK, and Canada. The idea for a father's day originated with Sonora Louise Smart Dodd of Spokane, Washington, in 1909 (after hearing a sermon on Mother's Day), and through her efforts the first Father's Day was celebrated there in 1910.

fathom in mining, seafaring, and handling timber, a unit of depth measurement (6 ft/1.83 m) used prior to metrication; it approximates to the distance between an adult man's hands when the arms are outstretched.

Fatimid dynasty of Muslim Shiite caliphs founded 909 by Obaidallah, who claimed to be a descendant of Fatima (the prophet Mohammed's daughter) and her husband Ali, in N Africa. In 969 the Fatimids conquered Egypt, and the dynasty continued until overthrown by Saladin 1171.

fatty acid or *carboxylic acid* organic compound consisting of a hydrocarbon chain, up to 24 carbon atoms long, with a carboxyl group (–COOH) at one end. The covalent bonds between the carbon atoms may be single or double; where a double bond occurs the carbon atoms concerned carry one instead of two hydrogen atoms. Chains with only single bonds have all the hydrogen they can carry, so they are said to be *saturated* with hydrogen. Chains with one or more double bonds are said to be *unsaturated* (see ◊polyunsaturate).

Faulkner William 1897–1962. US novelist who wrote in an experimental stream-of-consciousness style, often considered the finest 20th-century American writer. His works include *The Sound and the Fury* 1929, dealing with a favorite topic—the Southern family in decline; *As I Lay Dying* 1930; and *The Hamlet* 1940, *The Town* 1957, and *The Mansion* 1959, a trilogy covering the rise of the materialistic Snopes family. He was awarded the Nobel Prize for Literature in 1949.

fault in geology, a fracture in the Earth's crust along which the two sides have moved as a result of differing strains in the adjacent rock bodies. Displacement of

Faulkner US novelist, pioneer of the stream-of-consciousness literary style, William Faulkner.

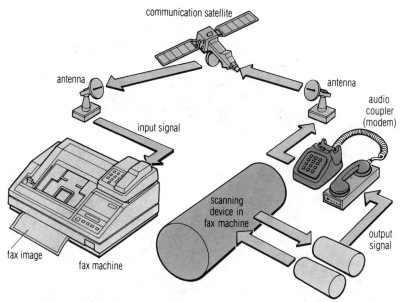

communication satellite

antenna

antenna

audio
coupler
(modem)

input signal

scanning
device in
fax machine

output
signal

fax image

fax machine

rock masses horizontally or vertically along a fault may be microscopic, or it may be massive, causing major ◊earthquakes.

Faunus in Roman mythology, the god of fertility and prophecy, with goat's ears, horns, tail, and hind legs, identified with the Greek ◊Pan.

Fauré Gabriel (Urbain) 1845–1924. French composer of songs, chamber music, and a choral *Requiem* 1888. He was a pupil of Saint-Saëns, became professor of composition at the Paris Conservatoire 1896 and was director from 1905 to 1920.

Faust legendary magician who sold his soul to the Devil. The historical Georg Faust appears to have been a wandering scholar and conjurer in Germany at the start of the 16th century. Goethe, Heine, Thomas Mann, and Paul Valéry all used the legend, and it inspired musical works by Schumann, Berlioz, Gounod, Boito, and Busoni.

Fauvism style of painting with a bold use of vivid colors inspired by van Gogh, Cézanne, and Gaugin. A short-lived but influential art movement, Fauvism originated in Paris 1905 with the founding of the Salon d'Automne by Henri ◊Matisse and others, when the critic Louis Vauxcelles called their gallery *"une cage aux fauves"* (a cage of wild beasts).

Fawkes Guy 1570–1606. English conspirator in the ◊Gunpowder Plot to blow up King James I and the members of both Houses of Parliament. Fawkes, a Roman Catholic convert, was arrested in the cellar underneath the House Nov 4, 1605, tortured, and executed. The event is still commemorated in Britain and elsewhere every Nov 5 with bonfires, fireworks, and the burning of the "guy," an effigy.

fax (common name for *facsimile transmission* or *telefax*) the transmission of images over a ◊telecommunications link, usually the telephone network. When placed on a fax machine, the original image is scanned by a transmitting device and converted into coded signals, which travel via the telephone lines to the receiving fax machine, where an image is created that is a copy of the original. Photographs as well as printed text and drawings can be sent. The standard

transmission takes place at 4,800 or 9,600 bits of information per second.

Fayetteville city in the NW corner of Arkansas, SE of Fort Smith; seat of Washington County; population (1990) 42,100. It is an agricultural trading center. Its main industry is poultry processing; others include lumber, clothing, and tools.

The University of Arkansas 1871 is here.

Fayetteville city in S central North Carolina, on the Cape Fear River, S of Durham and Chapel Hill and SW of Raleigh; population (1990) 75,700. Its industries include processing of the area's agricultural products, tools, textiles, and lumber. It was named after the Marquis de Lafayette.

FBI abbreviation for ◊Federal Bureau of Investigation, agency of the US Department of Justice.

fealty in feudalism, the loyalty and duties owed by a vassal to his lord. In the 9th century fealty obliged the vassal not to take part in any action that would endanger the lord or his property, but by the 11th century the specific duties of fealty were established and included financial obligations and military service. Following an oath of fealty, an act of allegiance and respect (homage) was made by the vassal; when a fief was granted by the lord, it was formalized in the process of investiture.

feather rigid outgrowth of the outer layer of the skin of birds, made of the protein keratin. Feathers provide insulation and facilitate flight. There are several types, including long quill feathers on the wings and tail, fluffy down feathers for retaining body heat, and contour feathers covering the body. The coloring of feathers is often important in camouflage or in courtship and other displays. Feathers are replaced at least once a year. *See illustration p. 338*

February Revolution the first of the two political uprisings of the ◊Russian revolution in 1917 that led to the overthrow of the tsar and the end of the ◊Romanov dynasty.

feces remains of food and other debris passed out of the digestive tract of animals. Feces consist of quanti-

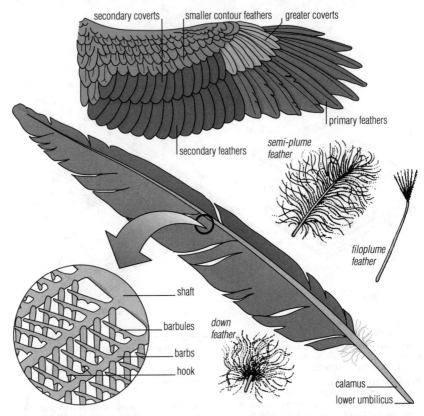

feather Types of feather.

secondary coverts   smaller contour feathers   greater coverts

primary feathers

secondary feathers

semi-plume feather

filoplume feather

shaft

barbules

barbs

hook

down feather

calamus

lower umbilicus

ties of fibrous material, bacteria and other microorganisms, rubbed-off lining of the digestive tract, bile fluids, undigested food, minerals, and water.

fecundity the rate at which an organism reproduces, as distinct from its ability to reproduce (◊fertility). In vertebrates, it is usually measured as the number of offspring produced by a female each year.

Federal Aviation Administration (FAA) agency of the US Department of Transportation that controls air traffic. Its responsibilities include regulating air transportation, aviation safety, developing and operating a system of air traffic control, requiring airports and airlines to provide antihijacking security, and conducting aviation research. The agency is also responsible for investigating airplane accidents. It was established in 1958 as the Federal Aviation Agency and was renamed upon its assignment to Transportation in 1967. It is directed by an administrator was appointed directly by the president.

Federal Bureau of Investigation (FBI) agency of the US Department of Justice that investigates violations of federal law not specifically assigned to other agencies, being particularly concerned with internal security. The FBI was established 1908 and built up a position of powerful autonomy during the autocratic directorship of J Edgar Hoover 1924–72. Louis J Freeh was appointed director Aug 1993.

federalism system of government in which two or more separate states unite under a common central government while retaining a considerable degree of local autonomy. A federation should be distinguished from a *confederation*, a looser union of states for

mutual assistance. Switzerland, the US, Canada, Australia, and Malaysia are all examples of federal government, and many supporters of the European Community see it as the forerunner of a federal Europe.

Federalist in US history, one who advocated the ratification of the US Constitution 1787–88 in place of the Articles of ◊Confederation. The Federalists became in effect the ruling political party during the presidencies of George Washington and John Adams 1789–1801, legislating to strengthen the authority of the newly created federal government.

The Federalists advocated reconciliation with Britain and were urban, educated, and vaguely antidemocratic.

Federal Reserve System (the "Fed") US central banking system and note-issuing authority, established 1913 to regulate the country's credit and ◊monetary policy. The Fed consists of the 12 federal reserve banks, their 25 branches and other facilities throughout the country; it is headed by a board of governors in Washington, DC, appointed by the president with Senate approval.

The Fed plays a major role in the formulation and implementation of monetary policy. It is independent and autonomous in its decisions. Inflation, interest rates, and overall economic activity can be governed by the Fed's decision to expand or restrict the supply of money to the economy. The ◊discount rate is the rate the Fed charges member banks to borrow money. By raising or lowering that rate, the Fed regulates credit. By requiring member banks to keep larger or smaller amounts of their deposits on hand as reserves, the Fed can apply another control. For these reasons, the chairman of the Federal Reserve is one of the most powerful figures in government. The decisions of the board of governors concerning discount and other rates are reached under exceptionally tight security and are eagerly awaited.

feedback general principle whereby the results produced in an ongoing reaction become factors in modifying or changing the reaction; it is the principle used in self-regulating control systems, from a simple thermostat and steam-engine ◊governor to automatic computer-controlled machine tools. A fully computerized control system, in which there is no operator intervention, is called a ***closed-loop feedback*** system. A system that also responds to control signals from an operator is called an ***open-loop feedback*** system.

feedback in music, a continuous tone, usually a high-pitched squeal, caused by the overloading of circuits between electric guitar and amplifier as the sound of the speakers is fed back through the guitar pickup. Deliberate feedback is much used in rock music.

feldspar one of a group of rock-forming minerals; the chief constituents of ◊igneous rock. Feldspars all contain silicon, aluminum, and oxygen, linked together to form a framework; spaces within this structure are occupied by sodium, potassium, calcium, or occasionally barium, in various proportions. Feldspars form white, gray, or pink crystals and rank 6 on the Mohs' scale of hardness.

Feller Bob (Robert William Andrew) 1918– . US baseball pitcher. He made his major-league debut 1936 and went on to a brilliant pitching career that lasted for the next 20 years. He led the American League six times by winning 20 or more games in a season; he pitched 3 no-hitters and 12 one-hitters and posted 266 career wins. Feller was famed for his powerful fastball and pinpoint control.

Fellini Federico 1920–1993. Italian film director and script writer whose films combine dream and fantasy sequences with satire and autobiographical details. His films include *I vitelloni/The Young and the Passionate* 1953, *La Strada/The Street* 1954, *La dolce vita* 1960, *Otto e mezzo/delete8½* 1963, *Giulietta degli spiriti/Juliet of the Spirits* 1965, *Satyricon* 1969, and *La città delle donne/City of Women* 1980.

felony in ◊criminal law, former term for an offense that is more serious than a misdemeanor; in the US, a felony is a crime generally punishable by imprisonment for a year or more.

feminism an active belief in equal rights and opportunities for women; see ◊women's movement.

femur the ***thigh-bone***; also the upper bone in the hind limb of a four-limbed vertebrate.

fencing sport of fighting with swords including the ***foil***, derived from the light weapon used in practice duels; the ***épée***, a heavier weapon derived from the dueling sword proper; and the ***saber***, with a curved handle and narrow V-shaped blade. In saber fighting, cuts count as well as thrusts. Masks and protective jackets are worn, and hits are registered electronically in competitions. Men's fencing has been part of every Olympic program since 1896; women's fencing was included from 1924 but only using the foil.

Fenian movement Irish-American republican secret society, founded 1858 and named after the ancient Irish legendary warrior band of the Fianna. The collapse of the movement began when an attempt to establish an independent Irish republic by an uprising in Ireland 1867 failed, as did raids into Canada 1866 and 1870, and England 1867.

fennel any of several varieties of a perennial plant *Foeniculum vulgare* with feathery green leaves, of the carrot family Umbelliferae. Fennels have an aniseed flavor, and the leaves and seeds are used in seasoning. The thickened leafstalks of sweet fennel *F. vulgare dulce* are eaten.

Ferdinand 1861–1948. King of Bulgaria 1908–18. Son of Prince Augustus of Saxe-Coburg-Gotha, he was elected prince of Bulgaria 1887 and, in 1908, proclaimed Bulgaria's independence of Turkey and assumed the title of tsar. In 1915 he entered World War I as Germany's ally, and in 1918 abdicated.

Ferdinand I *the Great* c. 1016–1065. King of Castile from 1035. He began the reconquest of Spain from the Moors and united all NW Spain under his and his brothers' rule.

Ferdinand II 1578–1637. Holy Roman emperor from 1619, when he succeeded his uncle Matthias; king of Bohemia from 1617 and of Hungary from 1618. A zealous Catholic, he provoked the Bohemian revolt that led to the Thirty Years' War. He was a grandson of Ferdinand I.

Ferdinand III 1608–1657. Holy Roman emperor from 1637 when he succeeded his father Ferdinand II; king of Hungary from 1625. Although anxious to conclude the Thirty Years' War, he did not give religious liberty to Protestants.

Ferghana city in Uzbekistan, in the fertile Ferghana Valley; population (1987) 203,000. It is the capital of the major cotton- and fruit-growing Ferghana region; nearby are petroleum fields. The Ferghana Valley is divided between the republics of Uzbekistan, Kyrgyzstan, and Tajikistan, causing interethnic violence among Uzbek, Meskhetian, and Kyrgyz communities.

Fermanagh county in the S part of Northern Ireland
area 648 sq mi/1,680 sq km
cities Enniskillen (county town), Lisnaskea, Irvinestown
physical in the center is a broad trough of low-lying land, in which lie Upper and Lower Lough Erne
products mainly agricultural; livestock, tweeds, clothing
population (1989 est) 52,000.

fermentation the breakdown of sugars by bacteria and yeasts using a method of respiration without oxygen (anaerobic). Fermentation processes have long been utilized in baking bread, making beer and wine, and producing cheese, yogurt, soy sauce, and many other foodstuffs.

Fermi Enrico 1901–1954. Italian-born US physicist who proved the existence of new radioactive elements produced by bombardment with neutrons, and discovered nuclear reactions produced by low-energy neutrons. His theoretical work included study of the weak nuclear force, one of the fundamental forces of nature, and (with Paul Dirac) of the quantum statistics of fermion particles. He was awarded a Nobel Prize 1938.

fermium synthesized, radioactive, metallic element of the ◊actinide series, symbol Fm, atomic number 100, atomic weight 257. Ten isotopes are known, the longest-lived of which, Fm-257, has a half-life of 80 days. Fermium has been produced only in minute quantities in particle accelerators.

fern The life cycle of a fern.

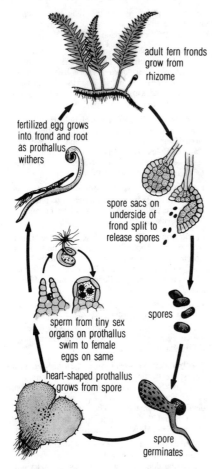

adult fern fronds grow from rhizome

fertilized egg grows into frond and root as prothallus withers

spore sacs on underside of frond split to release spores

spores

sperm from tiny sex organs on prothallus swim to female eggs on same

heart-shaped prothallus grows from spore

spore germinates

fern plant of the class Filicineae, related to ◊gymnosperms and ◊angiosperms; however, ferns reproduce by spores and not seed. Most are perennial, spreading by low-growing roots. The leaves, known as fronds, vary widely in size and shape. Some taller types, such as tree-ferns, grow in the tropics. There are over 7,000 species.

Ferrari Enzo 1898–1988. Italian founder of the Ferrari automobile manufacturing company, which specializes in Grand Prix racing automobiles and high-quality sports automobiles. He was a racing driver for Alfa Romeo in the 1920s, went on to become one of their designers, and in 1929 took over their racing division. In 1947 the first "true" Ferrari was seen. The Ferrari automobile has won more world championship Grands Prix than any other automobile.

ferret domesticated variety of the Old World ◊polecat. About 1.2 ft/35 cm long, it usually has yellowish-white fur and pink eyes, but may be the dark brown color of a wild polecat. Ferrets may breed with wild polecats. They have been used since ancient times to hunt rabbits and rats.

ferro-alloy alloy of iron with a high proportion of elements such as manganese, silicon, chromium, and molybdenum. Ferro-alloys are used in the manufacture of alloy steels. Each alloy is generally named after the added metal—for example, ferrochromium.

ferromagnetic material material that acquires very strong magnetism when placed in an external magnetic field. It may therefore be said to have a high magnetic permeability and susceptibility (which depends upon temperature). Examples are iron, cobalt, nickel, and their alloys. Some ferromagnetic materials retain their magnetism when the external magnetic field is removed and hence are used to make permanent magnets.

fertility an organism's ability to reproduce, as distinct from the rate at which it reproduces (see ◊fecundity). Individuals become infertile (unable to reproduce) when they cannot generate gametes (eggs or sperm) or when their gametes cannot yield a viable ◊embryo after fertilization.

fertility drug any of a range of drugs taken to increase a female's fertility, developed in Sweden in the mid-1950s. They increase the chances of a multiple birth.

fertilization in ◊sexual reproduction, the union of two ◊gametes (sex cells, often called egg and sperm) to produce a ◊zygote, which combines the genetic material contributed by each parent. In self-fertilization the male and female gametes come from the same plant; in cross-fertilization they come from different plants. Self-fertilization rarely occurs in animals; usually even ◊hermaphrodite animals cross-fertilize each other.

fertilizer substance containing some or all of a range of about 20 chemical elements necessary for healthy plant growth, used to compensate for the deficiencies of poor or depleted soil. Fertilizers may be *organic*, for example farmyard manure, composts, bonemeal, blood, and fishmeal; or *inorganic*, in the form of compounds, mainly of nitrogen, phosphate, and potash, which have been used on a very much increased scale since 1945.

Fès or *Fez* former capital of Morocco 808–1062, 1296–1548, and 1662–1912, in a valley N of the Great Atlas Mountains, 100 mi/160 km E of Rabat; population (1982) 563,000. Textiles, carpets, and leather are manufactured, and the *fez*, a brimless hat worn in S and E Mediterranean countries, is traditionally said to have originated here. Kairwan Islamic University dates from 859; a second university was founded 1961.

fescue any grass of the widely distributed genus *Festuca*. Many are used in temperate regions for lawns and pasture. Many upland species are viviparous.

fetishism in anthropology, belief in the supernormal power of some inanimate object that is known as a fetish. Fetishism in some form is common to most cultures, and often has religio-magical significance.

fetus stage in mammalian ◊embryo development. The human embryo is usually termed a fetus after the eighth week of development, when the limbs and external features of the head are recognizable.

feudalism main form of social organization in medieval Eu⌣ ⌣. A system based primarily on land, it involved a hierarchy of authority, rights, and power that extended from the monarch downward. An intricate network of duties and obligations linked royalty, nobility, lesser gentry, free tenants, villeins, and serfs. Feudalism was reinforced by a complex legal system and supported by the Christian church. With the growth of commerce and industry from the 13th century, feudalism gradually gave way to the class system as the dominant form of social ranking.

Feynman Richard P(hillips) 1918–1988. US physicist whose work laid the foundations of quantum electrodynamics. As a member of the committee investigating the *Challenger* space-shuttle disaster 1986, he demonstrated the lethal faults in rubber seals on the shuttle's booster rocket. For his work on the theory of radiation he shared the Nobel Prize for Physics 1965 with Julian Schwinger and Sin-Itiro Tomonaga (1906–1979).

fiber, dietary or *roughage* plant material that cannot be digested by human digestive enzymes; it consists largely of cellulose, a carbohydrate found in plant cell walls. Fiber adds bulk to the gut contents, assisting the muscular contractions that force food along the intestine. A diet low in fiber causes constipation and is believed to increase the risk of developing diverticulitis, diabetes, gall-bladder disease, and cancer of the large bowel—conditions that are rare in nonindustrialized countries, where the diet contains a high proportion of unrefined cereals.

fiberglass glass that has been formed into fine fibers, either as long continuous filaments or as a fluffy, short-fibered glass wool. Fiberglass is heat- and fire-resistant and a good electrical insulator. It has applications in the field of fiber optics and as a strengthener for plastics in ◊GRP (glass-reinforced plastics).

fiber optics branch of physics dealing with the transmission of light and images through glass or plastic fibers known as ◊optical fibers.

Fibonacci Leonardo, also known as *Leonardo of Pisa* c. 1175–c. 1250. Italian mathematician. He published *Liber abaci* in Pisa 1202, which was instrumental in the introduction of Arabic notation into Europe. From 1960, interest increased in *Fibonacci numbers*, in their simplest form a sequence in which each number is the sum of its two predecessors (1, 1, 2, 3, 5, 8, 13, ...). They have unusual characteristics with possible applications in botany, psychology, and astronomy (for example, a more exact correspondence than is given by Bode's law to the distances between the planets and the Sun).

fibrin an insoluble blood protein used by the body to stop bleeding. When an injury occurs fibrin is deposited around the wound in the form of a mesh, which dries and hardens, so that bleeding stops. Fibrin is developed in the blood from a soluble protein, fibrinogen.

fibula the rear lower bone in the hind leg of a vertebrate. It is paired and often fused with a smaller front bone, the tibia.

fiction in literature, any work in which the content is completely or largely invented. The term describes imaginative works of narrative prose (such as the novel or the short story), and is distinguished from *nonfiction* (such as history, biography, or works on practical subjects) and *poetry*.

Fiedler Arthur 1894–1979. US orchestra conductor. Concerned to promote the appreciation of music among the public, he founded the Boston Sinfonetta chamber-music group 1924. He reached an even wider audience with the Esplanade concerts along the Charles River from 1929. Fiedler's greatest fame was as founder and conductor of the Boston Pops Orchestra 1930, dedicated to popularizing light classical music through live and televised concert appearances.

field in physics, a region of space in which an object exerts a force on another separate object because of certain properties they both possess. For example, there is a force of attraction between any two objects that have mass when one is in the gravitational field of the other.

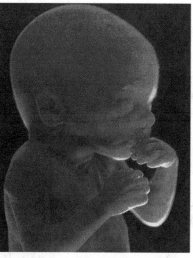

fetus Human fetus, about five months old.

field hockey a game played with hooked sticks and a ball, the object being to hit the ball into the goal. It is played between two teams, each of not more than 11 players. Hockey has been an Olympic sport for men since 1908 and for women since 1980. *See panel p. 342*

Fielding Henry 1707–1754. English novelist. His greatest work, *The History of Tom Jones, a Foundling* 1749 (which he described as "a comic epic in prose"), realized for the first time in English the novel's potential for memorable characterization, coherent plotting, and perceptive analysis. In youth a prolific playwright, he began writing novels with *An Apology for the Life of Mrs Shamela Andrews* 1741, a merciless parody of Samuel ◊Richardson's *Pamela*.

field marshal the highest rank in many European armies. A British field marshal is equivalent to a US general (of the army).

Fields W C. Adopted name of William Claude Dukenfield 1879–1946. US actor and screenwriter. His distinctive speech and professed attitudes such as hatred of children and dogs gained him enormous popularity in such films as *David Copperfield* 1935, *My Little Chickadee* (co-written with Mae West) and *The Bank Dick* both 1940, and *Never Give a Sucker an Even Break* 1941.

field studies study of ecology, geography, geology, history, archeology, and allied subjects, in the natural environment as opposed to the laboratory.

fife a type of small flute. Originally from Switzerland, it was known as the Swiss pipe and has long been played by military bands.

Fife region of E Scotland (formerly the county of Fife), facing the North Sea and Firth of Forth
area 502 sq mi/1,300 sq km
cities administrative headquarters Glenrothes; Dunfermline, St Andrews, Kirkcaldy, Cupar
physical the only high land is the Lomond Hills, in the NW; chief rivers Eden and Leven
features Rosyth naval base and dockyard (used for nuclear submarine refits) on N shore of the Firth of Forth; Tentsmuir, possibly the earliest settled site in Scotland. The ancient palace of the Stuarts was at Falkland, and eight Scottish kings are buried at Dunfermline

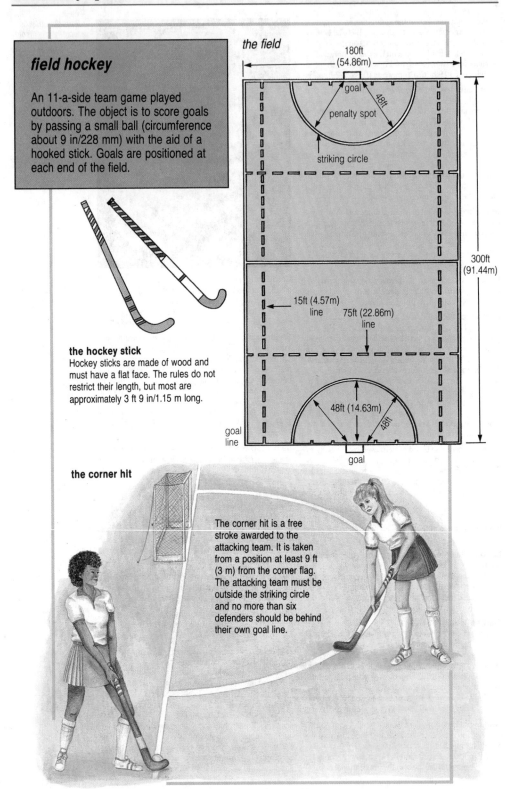

field hockey

An 11-a-side team game played outdoors. The object is to score goals by passing a small ball (circumference about 9 in/228 mm) with the aid of a hooked stick. Goals are positioned at each end of the field.

the field

180ft
(54.86m)

goal

48ft

penalty spot

striking circle

300ft
(91.44m)

15ft (4.57m)
line

75ft (22.86m)
line

48ft (14.63m)

48ft

goal
line

goal

the hockey stick
Hockey sticks are made of wood and must have a flat face. The rules do not restrict their length, but most are approximately 3 ft 9 in/1.15 m long.

the corner hit

The corner hit is a free stroke awarded to the attacking team. It is taken from a position at least 9 ft (3 m) from the corner flag. The attacking team must be outside the striking circle and no more than six defenders should be behind their own goal line.

products potatoes, cereals, electronics, petrochemicals (Mossmorran), light engineering
population (1991) 339,200.

fifth column group within a country secretly aiding an enemy attacking from without. The term originated 1936 during the Spanish Civil War, when General Mola boasted that Franco supporters were attacking Madrid with four columns and that they had a "fifth column" inside the city.

fifth-generation computer anticipated new type of computer based on emerging microelectronic technologies with high computing speeds and parallel processing. The development of very large-scale integration (VLSI) technology, which can put many more circuits on to an integrated circuit (chip) than is currently possible, and developments in computer hardware and software design may produce computers far more powerful than those in current use.

fig any tree of the genus *Ficus* of the mulberry family Moraceae, including the many cultivated varieties of *F. carica*, originally from W Asia. They produce two or three crops of fruit a year. Eaten fresh or dried, figs have a high sugar content and laxative properties.

The only native US fig is the Florida strangler fig *F. aurea*, which starts off as an epiphyte before developing its own root system.

figwort any Old World plant of the genus *Scrophularia* of the figwort family, which also includes foxgloves and snapdragons. Members of the genus have square stems, opposite leaves, and open two-lipped flowers in a cluster at the top of the stem.

Fiji country comprising 844 islands and islets in the SW Pacific Ocean, about 100 of which are inhabited.

file in computing, a collection of data or a program stored in a computer's external memory (for example, on ◊disk). It might include anything from information on a company's employees to a program for an adventure game. *Serial files* hold information as a sequence of characters, so that, to read any particular item of data, the program must read all those that precede it. *Random-access files* allow the required data to be reached directly.

Filene Edward Albert 1860–1937. US businessman renowned for his innovative retailing methods. One of his most imaginative merchandising ideas was the "bargain basement," where prices were dramatically lowered on certain goods. Incorporating his father's dry goods store in Boston as William Filene's Sons 1891, Filene was committed to employee profit-sharing and for that reason was removed by his partners 1928.

Fillmore Millard 1800–1874. 13th president of the US 1850–53, a Whig. Born into a poor farming family in New Cayuga County, New York State, he was Zachary Taylor's vice-president from 1849, and succeeded him on Taylor's death, July 9, 1850. Fillmore supported a compromise on slavery 1850 to reconcile North and South.

film noir (French "dark film") a term originally used by French critics to describe films characterized by pessimism, cynicism, and a dark, somber tone. It has been used to describe black-and-white Hollywood films of the 1940s and 1950s that portrayed the seedy side of life.

film, photographic strip of transparent material (usually cellulose acetate) coated with a light-sensitive emulsion, used in cameras to take pictures. The emulsion contains a mixture of light-sensitive silver halide

---

Fiji
Republic of

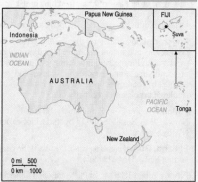

area 7,078 sq mi/18,333 sq km
capital Suva
cities ports Lautoka and Levuka
physical comprises 844 Melanesian and Polynesian islands and islets (about 110 inhabited), the largest being Viti Levu (4,028 sq mi/10,429 sq km) and Vanua Levu (2,146 sq mi/5,550 sq km); mountainous, volcanic, with tropical rain forest and grasslands
features almost all islands surrounded by coral reefs; high volcanic peaks; crossroads of air and sea services between N America and Australia
head of state Ratu Sir Penaia Ganilau from 1987
head of government Col Sitiveni Rabuka from 1992

political system democratic republic
political parties Alliance Party (AP), moderate centrist Fijian; National Federation Party (NFP), moderate left-of-center Indian; Fijian Labor Party (FLP), left-of-center Indian; United Front, Fijian
exports sugar, coconut oil, ginger, timber, canned fish, gold; tourism is important
currency Fiji dollar
population (1992) 748,000 (46% Fijian, holding 80% of the land communally, and 49% Indian, introduced in the 19th century to work the sugar crop); growth rate 2.1% p.a.
life expectancy men 67, women 71
languages English (official), Fijian, Hindi
religions Hindu 50%, Methodist 44%
literacy men 88%, women 77% (1980 est)
GDP $1.2 bn (1987); $1,604 per head

chronology
1874 Fiji became a British crown colony.
1970 Independence achieved from Britain; Ratu Sir Kamisese Mara elected as first prime minister.
1987 April: general election brought to power an Indian-dominated coalition led by Dr Timoci Bavadra. May: military coup by Col Sitiveni Rabuka removed new government at gunpoint; Governor General Ratu Sir Penaia Ganilau regained control within weeks. Sept: second military coup by Rabuka proclaimed Fiji a republic and suspended the constitution. Oct: Fiji ceased to be a member of the Commonwealth. Dec: civilian government restored with Rabuka retaining control of security as minister for home affairs.
1990 New constitution, favoring indigenous Fijians, introduced.
1992 General election produced coalition government; Col Rabuka named as president.

Finland
Republic of
(*Suomen Tasavalta*)

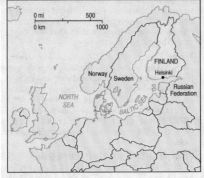

area 130,608 sq mi/338,145 sq km
capital Helsinki
cities Tampere, Rovaniemi, Lahti; ports Turku, Oulu
physical most of the country is forest, with low hills and about 60,000 lakes; one-third is within the Arctic Circle; archipelago in S; includes Åland Islands
features Helsinki is the most northerly national capital on the European continent; at the 70th parallel there is constant daylight for 73 days in summer and 51 days of uninterrupted night in winter
head of state Mauno Koivisto from 1982
head of government Esko Aho from 1991
political system democratic republic
political parties Social Democratic Party (SDP), moderate left of center; National Coalition Party (KOK), moderate right of center; Center Party (KP), centrist, rural-oriented; Finnish People's Democratic League (SKDL), left-wing; Swedish People's Party (SFP), independent Swedish-oriented; Finnish Rural Party (SMP), farmers and small businesses; Democratic Alternative, left-wing; Green Party
exports metal, chemical, and engineering products (ice-breakers and oil rigs), paper, sawn wood, clothing, fine ceramics, glass, furniture
currency markka
population (1992) 5,033,000; growth rate 0.5% p.a.
life expectancy men 70, women 78
languages Finnish 93%, Swedish 6% (both official), small Saami- and Russian-speaking minorities
religions Lutheran 97%, Eastern Orthodox 1.2%
literacy 99%
GDP $109.6 bn (1992)

chronology
1809 Finland annexed by Russia.
1917 Independence declared from Russia.
1920 Soviet regime acknowledged independence.
1939 Defeated by USSR in Winter War.
1941 Allowed Germany to station troops in Finland to attack USSR; USSR bombed Finland.
1944 Concluded separate armistice with USSR.
1948 Finno-Soviet Pact of Friendship, Cooperation, and Mutual Assistance signed.
1955 Finland joined the United Nations and the Nordic Council.
1956 Urho Kekkonen elected president; reelected 1962, 1968, 1978.
1973 Trade treaty with European Economic Community signed.
1977 Trade agreement with USSR signed.
1982 Mauno Koivisto elected president; reelected 1988.
1989 Finland joined Council of Europe.
1991 Big swing to the center in general election. New coalition government formed.
1992 Formal application for European Community membership.

salts (for example, bromide or iodide) in gelatin. When the emulsion is exposed to light, the silver salts are invisibly altered, giving a latent image, which is then made visible by the process of ◊developing. Films differ in their sensitivities to light, this being indicated by their speeds. Color film consists of several layers of emulsion, each of which records a different color in the light falling on it.

filter in chemistry, a porous substance, such as blotting paper, through which a mixture can be passed to separate out its solid constituents. In optics, a filter is a piece of glass or transparent material that passes light of one color only.

filter in electronics, a circuit that transmits a signal of some frequencies better than others. A low-pass filter transmits signals of low frequency and direct current; a high-pass filter transmits high-frequency signals; a band-pass filter transmits signals in a band of frequencies.

filtration technique by which suspended solid particles in a fluid are removed by passing the mixture through a filter, usually porous paper, plastic, or cloth. The particles are retained by the filter to form a residue and the fluid passes through to make up the filtrate. For example, soot may be filtered from air, and suspended solids from water.

final solution (to the Jewish question; German *Endlosung der Judenfrage*) euphemism used by the Nazis to describe the extermination of Jews (and other racial groups and opponents of of the regime) before and during World War II. See ◊Holocaust.

finch any of various songbirds of the family Fringillidae, in the order Passeriformes (perching birds).

They are seed-eaters with stout conical beaks and include goldfinches, crossbills, redpolls, and canaries.

fingerprint ridge pattern of the skin on a person's fingertips; this is constant through life and no two are exactly alike. Fingerprinting was first used as a means of identifying crime suspects in India, and was adopted by the English police 1901; it is now widely employed in police and security work.

Finland country in Scandinavia, bounded N by Norway, E by Russia, S and W by the Baltic Sea, and NW by Sweden.

Finland, Gulf of eastern arm of the ◊Baltic Sea, separating Finland from Estonia.

Finney Albert 1936– . English stage and film actor. He created the title roles in Keith Waterhouse's stage play *Billy Liar* 1960 and John Osborne's *Luther* 1961, and was artistic director of the Royal Court Theatre from 1972 to 1975. His films include *Saturday Night and Sunday Morning* 1960, *Tom Jones* 1963, *Murder on the Orient Express* 1974, and *The Dresser* 1984.

Finnish language member of the Finno-Ugric language family, the national language of Finland and closely related to neighboring Estonian, Livonian, Karelian, and Ingrian languages. At the beginning of the 19th century Finnish had no official status, since Swedish was the language of education, government, and literature in Finland. The publication of the *Kalevala*, a national epic poem, in 1835, contributed greatly to the arousal of Finnish national and linguistic feeling.

Finno-Ugric group or family of more than 20 languages spoken by some 22 million people in scattered communities from Norway in the west to Siberia in the east and to the Carpathian mountains in the south. Members of the family include Finnish, Lapp, and Hungarian.

fiord alternate spelling of ◊fjord.

fir any ◊conifer of the genus *Abies* in the pine family Pinaceae. The true firs include the balsam fir of N North America and the Eurasian silver fir *A. alba*. Douglas firs of the genus *Pseudotsuga* are native to W North America and the Far East.

Firdausi Abdul Qasim Mansur *c.* 935–1020. Persian poet, whose epic *Shahnama/The Book of Kings* relates the history of of Persia in 60,000 verses.

firearm weapon from which projectiles are discharged by the combustion of an explosive. Firearms are generally divided into two main sections: ◊artillery (ordnance or cannon), with a bore greater than 1 in/2.54 cm, and ◊small arms, with a bore of less than 1 in/2.54 cm. Although gunpowder was known in Europe 60 years previously, the invention of guns dates from 1300 to 1325, and is attributed to Berthold Schwartz, a German monk.

fire clay a ◊clay with refractory characteristics (resistant to high temperatures), and hence suitable for lining furnaces (firebrick). Its chemical composition consists of a high percentage of silicon and aluminum oxides, and a low percentage of the oxides of sodium, potassium, iron, and calcium.

firefly any winged nocturnal beetle of the family Lampyridae. They all emit light through the process of ◊bioluminescence.

Firenze Italian form of ◊Florence, a city in Italy.

fire protection methods available for fighting fires. Industrial and commercial buildings are often protected by an automatic sprinkler system: heat or smoke opens the sprinkler heads on a network of water pipes which spray the source of the fire. In circumstances where water is ineffective and may be dangerous; for example, for oil and gasoline storage-tank fires, foam systems are used; for industrial plants containing flammable vapors, carbon dioxide is used; where electricity is involved, vaporizing liquids create a nonflammable barrier; for some chemicals only various dry powders can be used.

Firestone Harvey Samuel 1868–1938. US industrialist who established a tire-manufacturing firm, the Firestone Tire and Rubber Co., in Akron, Ohio, in 1900. He pioneered the principle of the detachable rim and, from 1906, was the major supplier of tires to the Ford Motor Co.

First Legal Tender Case a US Supreme Court case (*Hepburn* v *Griswold*) 1870 that reviewed Congress's right to pay its debts with unbacked paper money. The case was one of numerous suits protesting the use of $450 million issued under the Legal Tender Acts (1862, 1863) to repay loans. The Court found the acts unconstitutional because they made the paper money legal tender for the payment of all debts, including ones contracted before the passage of the acts, a violation of the obligation of contracts. The Court also noted that the Constitution prohibits payment of public debts with anything but gold and silver.

fiscal policy that part of government policy devoted to achieving the desired level of revenue, notably through taxation, and deciding the priorities and purposes governing its expenditure.

fiscal year the financial year, which does not necessarily coincide with the calendar year.

For the US government, the budget year runs from Oct 1 to Sept 30. For businesses and financial institutions, it generally runs July 1 to June 30.

Fischer Bobby (Robert James) 1943– . US chess champion. In 1958, after proving himself in international competition, he became the youngest grand master in history. He was the author of *Games of Chess* 1959, and was also celebrated for his unorthodox psychological tactics. He won the world title from Boris Spassky in Reykjavik, Iceland, 1972 but retired the same year without defending his title. He returned to competitive chess 1992.

Fischer Emil Hermann 1852–1919. German chemist who produced synthetic sugars and from these various enzymes. His descriptions of the chemistry of the carbohydrates and peptides laid the foundations for the science of biochemistry. Nobel Prize 1902.

Fischer Hans 1881–1945. German chemist awarded a Nobel Prize 1930 for his discovery of hemoglobin in blood.

fish aquatic vertebrate that uses gills for obtaining oxygen from fresh or sea water. There are three main groups, not closely related: the bony fishes or Oste-

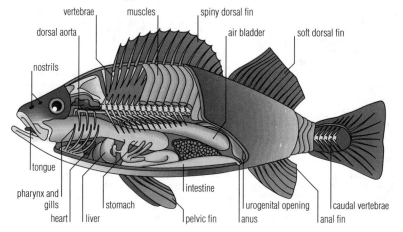

fish The anatomy of a fish.

fish classification

superclass Agnatha (jawless fishes)

order	no of species	examples
Petromyzoniformes	30	lamprey
Myxiniformes	15	hagfish

superclass Gnathostomata (jawed fishes) class Chondrichthyes (cartilaginous fishes) subclass Elasmobranchii (sharks and rays)

Hexanchiformes	6	frilled shark, comb-toothed shark
Heterodontiformes	10	Port Jackson shark
Lamniformes	200	typical shark
Rajiformes	300	skate, ray

subclass Holocephali (rabbitfishes)

Chimaeriformes	20	chimaera, rabbitfish

class Osteichthyes (bony fishes) subclass Sarcopterygii (fleshy-finned fishes)

Coelacanthiformes	1	coelacanth
Ceratodiformes	1	Australian lungfish
Lepidosireniformes	4	South American and African lungfish

subclass Actinopterygii (ray-finned fishes) superorder Chondrostei

Polypteriformes	11	bichir, reedfish
Acipensiformes	25	paddlefish, sturgeon

superorder Holostei

Amiiformes	8	bowfin, garpike

superorder Teleostei

Elopiformes	12	tarpon, tenpounder
Anguilliformes	300	eel
Notacanthiformes	20	spiny eel
Clupeiformes	350	herring, anchovy
Osteoglossiformes	16	arapaima, African butterfly fish
Mormyriformes	150	elephant-trunk fish, featherback
Salmoniformes	500	salmon, trout, smelt, pike
Gonorhynchiformes	15	milkfish
Cypriniformes	350	carp, barb, characin, loache
Siluriformes	200	catfish
Myctophiformes	300	deep-sea lantern fish, Bombay duck
Percopsiformes	10	pirate perch, cave-dwelling amblyopsid
Batrachoidiformes	10	toadfish
Gobiesociformes	100	clingfish, dragonets
Lophiiformes	150	anglerfish
Gadiformes	450	cod, pollack, pearlfish, eelpout
Atheriniformes	600	flying fish, toothcarp, halfbeak
Lampridiformes	50	opah, ribbonfish
Beryciformes	150	squirrelfish
Zeiformes	60	John Dory, boarfish
Gasterosteiformes	150	stickleback, pipefish, seahorse
Channiformes	5	snakeshead
Synbranchiformes	7	cuchia
Scorpaeniformes	700	gurnard, miller's thumb, stonefish
Dactylopteriformes	6	flying gurnard
Pegasiformes	4	sea-moth
Pleuronectiformes	500	flatfish
Tetraodontiformes	250	puffer fish, triggerfish, sunfish
Perciformes	6,500	perch, cichlid, damsel fish, gobie, wrass, parrotfish, gourami, marlin, mackerel, tuna, swordfish, spiny eel, mullet, barracuda, sea bream, croaker, ice fish, butterfish

ichthyes (goldfish, cod, tuna); the cartilaginous fishes or Chondrichthyes (sharks, rays); and the jawless fishes or Agnatha (hagfishes, lampreys).

Fish Hamilton 1808–1893. US public figure and diplomat. He held office in the US Senate 1851–57, by which time he had become a member of the Republican party. As secretary of state under President Grant 1869–77, his office was marked by moderation in his pursuit of US claims against the UK in the *Alabama* case and in averting war with Spain over Cuba.

Fisher John, St *c.* 1469–1535. English bishop, created bishop of Rochester 1504. He was an enthusiastic supporter of the revival in the study of Greek, and a friend of the humanists Thomas More and Desiderius Erasmus. In 1535 he was tried on a charge of denying the royal supremacy of Henry VIII and beheaded.

fish farming or *aquaculture* raising fish (including mollusks and crustaceans) under controlled conditions in tanks and ponds, sometimes in offshore pens. It has been practiced for centuries in the Far East, where Japan today produces some 100,000 tons of fish a year; the US, Norway, and Canada are also big producers. In the 1980s 10% of the world's consumption of fish was farmed, notably trout, Atlantic salmon, turbot, eel, mussels, and oysters.

fishing and fisheries fisheries can be classified by (1) type of water: freshwater (lake, river, pond); marine (inshore, midwater, deep sea); (2) catch: for example salmon fishing; (3) fishing method: diving, stunning or poisoning, harpooning, trawling, drifting.

marine fishing The greatest proportion of the world's catch comes from the oceans. The primary production area is the photic zone, the relatively thin surface layer (164 ft/50 m) of water that can be penetrated by light, allowing photosynthesis by plant ◊plankton to take place. Plankton-eating fish tend to be small in size and include herrings and sardines. Demersal fishes, such as haddock, halibut, and cod, live primarily near the ocean floor, and feed on various invertebrate marine animals. Over 20 million metric tons of them are caught each year by trawling. Pelagic fish, such as tuna, live in the open sea, near the surface, and purse seine nets are used to catch them; the annual catch is over 30 million metric tons a year.

freshwater fishing There is large demand for salmon, trout, carp, eel, bass, pike, perch, and catfish. These inhabit ponds, lakes, rivers, or swamps, and some species have been successfully cultivated (◊fish farming).

methods Lines, seine nets, and lift nets are the common commercial methods used. Purse seine nets, which close like a purse and may be as long as 30 nautical miles, have caused a crisis in the S Pacific where Japan, Taiwan, and South Korea fish illegally in other countries' fishing zones.

history Until the introduction of refrigeration, fish was too perishable to be exported, and fishing met local needs only. Between 1950 and 1970, the global fish catch increased by an average of 7% each year. On refrigerated factory ships, filleting and processing can be done at sea. Japan evolved new techniques for locating shoals (by sonar and radar) and catching them (for example, with electrical charges and chemical baits). By the 1970s, indiscriminate overfishing had led to serious depletion of stocks, and heated confrontations between countries using the same fishing grounds. A partial solution was the extension of fishing limits to 200 mi/320 km. The North Sea countries have experimented with the artificial breeding of fish eggs and release of small fry into the sea. In 1988, overfishing of the NE Atlantic led to hundreds of thousands of starving seals on the N coast of Norway. Marine pollution is blamed for the increasing number (up to 30%) of diseased fish in the North Sea. A United Nations resolution was passed 1989 to end drift-net fishing by June 1992.

ancillary industries These include the manufacture of nets, the processing of oil and fishmeal (nearly 25% of the fish caught annually are turned into meal for animal feed), pet food, glue, manure, and drugs such as insulin and other pharmaceutical products.

fission in physics, the splitting of a heavy atomic nucleus into two or more major fragments. It is accompanied by the emission of two or three neutrons and the release of large amounts of energy (see ◊nuclear energy).

fistula in medicine, an abnormal pathway developing between adjoining organs or tissues, or leading to the exterior of the body. A fistula developing between the bowels and the bladder, for instance, may give rise to urinary-tract infection by intestinal organisms.

Fitch John 1743–1798. US inventor and early experimenter with steam engines and steamships. In 1786 he designed the first steamboat to serve the Delaware River. His venture failed, so Robert ◊Fulton is erroneously credited with the invention of the steamship.

Fitchburg city in N Massachusetts, on the Nashua River, N of Worcester; population (1990) 41,200. Industries include paper, textiles, furniture, clothing, and foundry products.

fitness in genetic theory, a measure of the success with which a genetically determined character can spread in future generations. By convention, the normal character is assigned a fitness of one, and variants (determined by other alleles) are then assigned fitness values relative to this. Those with fitness greater than one will spread more rapidly and will ultimately replace the normal allele; those with fitness less than one will gradually die out.

Fitzgerald Ella 1918– . US jazz singer, recognized as one of the finest, most lyrical voices in jazz, both in solo work and with big bands. She is celebrated for her smooth interpretations of of George and Ira Gershwin and Cole Porter songs.

Fitzgerald F(rancis) Scott (Key) 1896–1940. US novelist and short-story writer. His early autobiographical novel *This Side of Paradise* 1920 made him known in the postwar society of of the East Coast, and *The Great Gatsby* 1925 epitomizes the Jazz Age.

Fitzgerald was born in Minnesota. His first book, *This Side of Paradise*, reflected his experiences at Princeton University. In 1920 he married Zelda Sayre (1900–1948). His second novel, *The Beautiful and the Damned* 1922, tells of a glamorous couple (resembling the Fitzgeralds) and of their unhappy decline. In 1924 the Fitzgeralds moved to the French Riviera, where they became members of a fashionable group of expatriates. In *The Great Gatsby* 1925 the narrator resembles the author, and Gatsby, the self-made millionaire, is lost in the soulless society he enters. Zelda Fitzgerald, a schizophrenic, entered an asylum in 1930. Her descent into mental illness forms the subject of *Tender Is the Night* 1934. After her confinement Fitzgerald went to Hollywood to write screenplays and earn enough to pay Zelda's medical bills. He fell in love with Sheilah Graham but declined into alcoholism. His other works include numerous short stories and his novel *The Last Tycoon*, about the film business, which was unfinished at his death but was made into a major motion picture 1976.

Fitzsimmons Robert Prometheus 1862–1917. English prizefighter best known for his US fights. He won the middleweight title in New Orleans 1891. Although he weighed only 160 lb/73 kg, he also competed as a heavyweight and in 1897 won the title from James J ("Gentleman Jim") Corbett in Carson City, Nevada. He lost that title to James J Jeffries in New York 1899.

five pillars of Islam the five duties required of every Muslim: repeating the *creed*, which affirms that Allah is the one God and Mohammed is his prophet; daily *prayer* or salat; giving *alms*; *fasting* during the month of Ramadan; and, if not prevented by ill health or poverty, the hajj, or *pilgrimage* to Mecca, once in a lifetime.

flamingo The greater, or roseate, flamingo may seem strangely built but it is, in fact, perfectly adapted to its environment.

fixed point temperature that can be accurately reproduced and used as the basis of a temperature scale. In the Celsius scale, the fixed points are the temperature of melting ice, which is 0°C (32°F), and the temperature of boiling water (at standard atmospheric pressure), which is 100°C (212°F).

fjord or **fiord** narrow sea inlet enclosed by high cliffs. Fjords are found in Norway, New Zealand, and W parts of Scotland. They are formed when an overdeepened U-shaped glacial valley is drowned by a rise in sea-level. At the mouth of the fjord there is a characteristic lip causing a shallowing of the water. This is due to reduced glacial erosion and the deposition of moraine at this point.

flaccidity in botany, the loss of rigidity (turgor) in plant cells, caused by loss of water from the central vacuole so that the cytoplasm no longer pushes against the cellulose cell wall. If this condition occurs throughout the plant then wilting is seen.

flagellant religious person who uses a whip on him- or herself as a means of penance. Flagellation was practiced in many religions from ancient times; notable outbreaks of this type of extremist devotion occurred in Christian Europe in the 11th–16th centuries.

flagellum small hairlike organ on the surface of certain cells. Flagella are the motile organs of certain protozoa and single-celled algae, and of the sperm cells of higher animals. Unlike ◊cilia, flagella usually occur singly or in pairs; they are also longer and have a more complex whiplike action.

Flagler Henry Morrison 1830–1913. US entrepreneur. He founded a salt factory in Saginaw, Michigan 1862, but when that failed moved to Cleveland and entered the oil-refining business with John D Rockefeller 1867. Flagler served as a director of Standard Oil 1870–1911 and invested in the Florida tourist industry. He established the Florida East Coast Railroad 1886 and built a string of luxury hotels.

Flaherty Robert 1884–1951. US film director, the father of documentary filmmaking. He exerted great influence through his pioneer documentary of Inuit life, *Nanook of the North* 1922, a critical and commercial success.

flamenco music and dance of the Andalusian gypsies of S Spain, evolved from Andalusian and Arabic folk music. The *cante* (song) is sometimes performed as a solo but more often accompanied by guitar music and passionate improvised dance. Hand clapping, finger clicking (castanets are a more recent addition), and enthusiastic shouts are all features.

Male flamenco dancers excel in powerful, rhythmic footwork while the female dancers place emphasis on the graceful and erotic movements of their hands and bodies.

flamingo long-legged and long-necked wading bird, family Phoenicopteridae, of the stork order Ciconiiformes. Largest of the family is the greater or roseate flamingo *Phoenicopterus ruber*, found in Africa, the Caribbean, and South America, with delicate pink plumage and 4 ft/1.25 m tall. They sift the mud for food with their downbent bills, and build colonies of high, conelike mud nests, with a little hollow for the eggs at the top.

Flanders region of the Low Countries that in the 8th and 9th centuries extended from Calais to the Scheldt and is now covered by the Belgian provinces of Oost Vlaanderen and West Vlaanderen (East and West Flanders), the French *département* of Nord, and part of the Dutch province of Zeeland. The language is Flemish. East Flanders, capital Ghent, has an area of 1,158 sq mi/3,000 sq km and a population (1991) of 1,335,700. West Flanders, capital Bruges, has an area of 1,197 sq mi/3,100 sq km and a population (1991) of 1,106,800.

flare, solar brilliant eruption on the Sun above a ◊sunspot, thought to be caused by release of magnetic energy. Flares reach maximum brightness within a few minutes, then fade away over about an hour. They eject a burst of atomic particles into space at up to 600 mps/1,000 kps. When these particles reach Earth they can cause radio blackouts, disruptions of the Earth's magnetic field, and ◊auroras.

flash point in physics, the lowest temperature at which a liquid or volatile solid heated under standard conditions gives off sufficient vapor to ignite on the application of a small flame.

flatfish bony fishes of the order Pleuronectiformes, having a characteristically flat, asymmetrical body with both eyes (in adults) on the upper side. Species include flounders, turbots, halibuts, plaice, and the European soles.

flatworm invertebrate of the phylum Platyhelminthes. Some are free-living, but many are parasitic (for example, tapeworms and flukes). The body is simple and bilaterally symmetrical, with one opening to the intestine. Many are hermaphroditic (with both male and female sex organs) and practice self-fertilization.

Flaubert Gustave 1821–1880. French novelist, author of *Madame Bovary* 1857, *Salammbô* 1862, *L'Education sentimentale/Sentimental Education* 1869, and *La Tentation de Saint Antoine/The Temptation of St Anthony* 1874. Flaubert also wrote the short stories *Trois contes/Three Tales* 1877. His dedication to art resulted in a meticulous prose style, realistic detail, and psychological depth, which is often revealed through interior monologue.

flax any plant of the genus *Linum*, family Linaceae. The species *L. usitatissimum* is the cultivated strain; *linen* is produced from the fiber in its stems. The seeds yield *linseed oil*, used in paints and varnishes. The plant, of almost worldwide distribution, has a stem up to 24 in/60 cm high, small leaves, and bright blue flowers.

flea wingless insect of the order Siphonaptera, with blood-sucking mouthparts. Fleas are parasitic on warm-blooded animals. Some fleas can jump 130 times their own height.

Fleming Alexander 1881–1955. Scottish bacteriologist who discovered the first antibiotic drug, ◊penicillin, in 1928. In 1922 he had discovered lysozyme, an antibacterial enzyme present in saliva, nasal secretions, and tears. While studying this, he found an unusual mold growing on a neglected culture dish, which he isolated and grew into a pure culture; this led to his discovery of penicillin. It came into use in 1941. In 1945 he won the Nobel Prize for Physiology and Medicine with Howard W Florey and Ernst B Chain, whose research had brought widespread realization of the value of penicillin.

Fleming Ian 1908–1964. English author of suspense novels featuring the ruthless, laconic James Bond, British Secret Service agent No 007. Most of the novels were made into successful films.

Fleming's rules memory aids used to recall the relative directions of the magnetic field, current, and motion in an electric generator or motor, using one's fingers. The three directions are represented by the thu*m*b (for *m*otion), *f*orefinger (for *f*ield), and se*c*ond finger (for *c*urrent), all held at right angles to each other. The right hand is used for generators and the left for motors. The rules were devised by the English physicist John Fleming.

Flemish member of the W Germanic branch of the Indo-European language family, spoken in N Belgium and the Nord *département* of France. It is closely related to Dutch.

Flemish art the style of painting developed and practiced in ◊Flanders. A Flemish style emerged in the early 15th century. Paintings are distinguished by keen observation, minute attention to detail, bright colors, and superb technique—oil painting was a Flemish invention. Apart from portraits, they depict religious scenes, often placed in contemporary Flemish landscapes, townscapes, and interiors. Flemish sculpture shows German and French influence.

fleur-de-lis (French "flower of the lily") heraldic device in the form of a stylized iris flower, borne on coats of arms since the 12th century and adopted by the French royal house of Bourbon.

Flevoland (formerly *IJsselmeerpolders*) low-lying province of the Netherlands established 1986.
area 544 sq mi/1,410 sq km
capital Lelystad
cities Dronten, Almere
population (1988) 194,000
history created 1986 out of land reclaimed from the IJsselmeer 1950–68.

flexor any muscle that bends a limb. Flexors usually work in opposition to other muscles, the extensors, an arrangement known as antagonistic.

flight or *aviation* people first took to the air in lighter-than-air craft such as balloons 1783 and began powered flight in 1852 in airships, but the history of aviation focuses on heavier-than-air craft called ◊airplanes. Developed from glider design, with wings, a tail, and a fuselage, the first successful flight of a powered, heavier-than-air craft was in 1896 by S P Langley's unmanned plane (*Model No 5*), for ¾ of a mile near the Potomac River; then, in 1903, the ◊Wright brothers flew the first piloted plane at Kitty Hawk. In 1903, Glenn ◊Curtiss publicized flight in the US and began the first flying school in 1909. A competition for the development of airplanes was inspired by a series of flights and air races in the US and Europe, and planes came into their own during World War I, being used by both sides. Biplanes were generally succeeded by monoplanes in the 1920s and 1930s, and they used runways or water (seaplanes and flying boats) for takeoffs and landings at airfields that soon became airports. In these decades airlines were formed for international travel, airmail, and cargo. The first jet plane was produced in Germany in 1939, the Heinkel He-178, but conventional prop planes were used for most of the destruction and transport of World War II. The 1950s brought economical passenger air travel on turboprops and jet airliners, which by the 1970s flew transatlantic in about 6 hours. The Concorde, a supersonic jetliner, flies passengers over that route in about 3 hours.

flint compact, hard, brittle mineral (a variety of chert), brown, black, or gray in color, found in nodules in limestone or shale deposits. It consists of fine grained silica, SiO_2 (usually ◊quartz), in cryptocrystalline form. Flint tools were widely used in prehistory.

flocculation in soils, the artificially induced coupling together of particles to improve aeration and drainage. Clay soils, which have very tiny particles and are difficult to work, are often treated in this way. The method involves adding more lime to the soil.

Flood, the in the Old Testament, the Koran, and *The Epic of Gilgamesh* (an ancient Sumerian legend), a deluge lasting 40 days and nights, a disaster alleged to have obliterated all humanity except a chosen few (in the Old Testament, the survivors were the family of ◊Noah and the pairs of animals sheltered on his ark).

floppy disk in computing, a storage device consisting of of a light, flexible disk enclosed in a cardboard or plastic jacket. The disk is placed in a disk drive, where it rotates at high speed. Data are recorded magnetically on one or both surfaces.

Florence city in NW Alabama, on the Tennessee River near the Tennessee Valley Authority's Wilson Dam, NW of Birmingham; seat of Lauderdale County; population (1990) 36,400. Industries include agricultural and poultry products, building materials, lumber, and fertilizers.

Florence city in NE South Carolina, NW of Myrtle Beach; seat of Florence County; population (1990) 29,800. It is a center of of the trucking industry, serving as a terminus for many companies. Other industries include dairy products, fertilizers, film, furniture, machined goods, and clothing.

Florence (Italian *Firenze*) capital of ◊Tuscany, N Italy, 55 mi/88 km from the mouth of the river Arno; population (1988) 421,000. It has printing, engineering, and optical industries; many crafts, including leather, gold and silver work, and embroidery; and its art and architecture attract large numbers of tourists. Notable medieval and Renaissance citizens included the writers Dante and Boccaccio, and the artists Giotto, Leonardo da Vinci, and Michelangelo. *See illustration p. 350*

floret small flower, usually making up part of a larger, composite flower head. There are often two different types present on one flower head: disk florets in the central area, and ray florets around the edge which usually have a single petal known as the ligule. In the common daisy, for example, the disk florets are yellow, while the ligules are white.

Florey Howard Walter, Baron Florey 1898–1968. Australian pathologist whose research into lysozyme, an antibacterial enzyme discovered by Alexander ◊Fleming, led him to study penicillin (another of Fleming's discoveries), which he and Ernst ◊Chain isolated and

Florence The cathedral of Santa Maria del Fiore (1314), Florence.

prepared for widespread use. With Fleming, they were awarded the Nobel Prize for Physiology or Medicine 1945.

Florida southeasternmost state of the US; mainly a peninsula jutting into the Atlantic, which it separates from the Gulf of Mexico; nickname Sunshine State
area 58,672 sq mi/152,000 sq km
capital Tallahassee
cities Miami, Tampa, Jacksonville
population (1990) 12,937,900, one of the fastest-growing of the states; including 15% nonwhite; 10% Hispanic, (especially Cuban)
physical 50% forested; lakes (including Okeechobee 695 sq mi/1,800 sq km; Everglades National Park (1,930 sq mi/5,000 sq km), with birdlife, cypresses, alligators
features Palm Beach island resort, between the lagoon of Lake Worth and the Atlantic; Florida Keys; John F Kennedy Space Center at Cape Canaveral; Disney World theme park; beach resorts on Gulf and on Atlantic; Daytona International Speedway
products citrus fruits, melons, vegetables, fish, shellfish, phosphates, chemicals, electrical and electronic equipment, aircraft, fabricated metals
famous people Chris Evert, Henry Flagler, James Weldon Johnson, Sidney Poitier, Philip Randolph, Joseph Stilwell
history discovered by Ponce de Leon and under Spanish rule from 1513 until its cession to England 1763; returned to Spain 1783 and purchased by the US 1819, becoming a state 1845.

It grew rapidly in the early 1920s, stimulated by

Florida

feverish land speculation. Despite the 1926 collapse of the boom, migration continued, especially of retirees from the North. After World War II, resorts, agriculture, and industry grew in importance. The space center at Cape Canaveral also contributed to the state economy. More recently, Florida has become a banking center, a development often partially attributed to the sizable inflow of cash derived from the traffic in illegal drugs from Latin America. Because of its proximity to Caribbean nations, the state became a haven for refugees from such countries as Cuba and Haiti.

flotation process common method of preparing mineral ores for subsequent processing by making use of the different wetting properties of various components. The ore is finely ground and then mixed with water and a specially selected wetting agent. Air is bubbled through the mixture, forming a froth; the desired ore particles attach themselves to the bubbles and are skimmed off, while unwanted dirt or other ores remain behind.

flounder any of a number of ◊flatfishes of several genera. A common North American species is the S flounder *Paralichthys lethostigma*, a valuable food fish about 20 in/50 cm long.

flow chart diagram, often used in computing, to show the possible paths that data can take through a system or program.

flower the reproductive unit of an ◊angiosperm or flowering plant, typically consisting of four whorls of modified leaves: ◊sepals, ◊petals, ◊stamens, and ◊carpels. These are borne on a central axis or receptacle. The many variations in size, color, number, and arrangement of parts are closely related to the method of of pollination. Flowers adapted for wind pollination typically have reduced or absent petals and sepals and long, feathery ◊stigmas that hang outside the flower to trap airborne pollen. In contrast, the petals of of insect-pollinated flowers are usually conspicuous and brightly colored.

flower power youth movement of the 1960s; see ◊hippie.

flugelhorn alto brass instrument, similar in appearance to the ◊cornet.

fluid any substance, either liquid or gas, in which the molecules are relatively mobile and can "flow."

fluid mechanics the study of the behavior of fluids (liquids and gases) at rest and in motion. Fluid mechanics is important in the study of the weather, the design of aircraft and road vehicles, and in industries, such as the chemical industry, which deal with flowing liquids or gases.

fluke any of various parasitic flatworms of the classes Monogenea and Digenea, that as adults live in and destroy the lives of sheep, cattle, horses, dogs, and humans. Monogenetic flukes can complete their life cycle in one host; digenetic flukes require two or more hosts, for example a snail and a human being, to complete their life cycle.

fluorescence in scientific usage, very short-lived ◊luminescence (a glow not caused by high temperature). Generally, the term is used for any luminescence regardless of the persistence. See ◊phosphorescence.

fluoridation addition of small amounts of fluoride salts to drinking water by certain water authorities to help prevent tooth decay. Experiments in Britain, the US, and elsewhere have indicated that a concentration of fluoride of 1 part per million in tap water retards the decay of teeth in children by more than 50%.

fluoride negative ion (Fl⁻) formed when hydrogen fluoride dissolves in water; compound formed between fluorine and another element in which the fluorine is the more electronegative element.

fluorine pale yellow, gaseous, nonmetallic element, symbol F, atomic number 9, atomic weight 19. It is the first member of of the halogen group of elements, and is pungent, poisonous, and highly reactive, uniting directly with nearly all the elements. It occurs naturally as the minerals fluorite (CaF_2) and cryolite (Na_3AlF_6). Hydrogen fluoride is used in etching glass, and the freons, which all contain fluorine, are widely used as refrigerants.

fluorite or *fluorspar* a glassy, brittle mineral, calcium fluoride CaF_2, forming cubes and octahedra; colorless when pure, otherwise violet or green.

fluorocarbon compound formed by replacing the hydrogen atoms of a hydrocarbon with fluorine. Fluorocarbons are used as inert coatings, refriger-

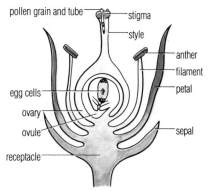

flower Cross section of a typical flower showing its basic components: sepals, petals, stamens (anthers and filaments), and carpel (ovary and stigma).

ants, synthetic resins, and as propellants in aerosols.

flute member of a group of ◊woodwind musical instruments (although usually made of metal), including the piccolo, the concert flute, and the bass or alto flute. Flutes are cylindrical in shape, with a narrowed end, containing a shaped aperture, across which the player blows. The air vibrations produce the note, which can be altered by placing fingers over lateral holes. Certain keys can be depressed to extend the range of the flute to three octaves.

flux in smelting, a substance that combines with the unwanted components of the ore to produce a fusible slag, which can be separated from the molten metal. For example, the mineral fluorite, CaF_2, is used as a flux in iron smelting; it has a low melting point and will form a fusible mixture with substances of higher melting point such as silicates and oxides.

flux in soldering, a substance that improves the bonding properties of solder by removing contamination from metal surfaces and preventing their oxidation, and by reducing the surface tension of the molten solder alloy. For example, with solder made of lead-tin alloys, the flux may be resin, borax, or zinc chloride.

fly any insect of the order Diptera. A fly has a single pair of wings, antennae, and compound eyes; the hind wings have become modified into knoblike projections (halteres) used to maintain equilibrium in flight. There are over 90,000 species.

flying squirrel Giant flying squirrels can glide over 440 yd/400 m between trees by stretching the broad, fur-covered membranes that extend from the sides of the body to the toes.

flying fish any of a family, Exocoetidae, of marine bony fishes of the order Beloniformes, best represented in tropical waters. They have winglike pectoral fins that can be spread to glide over the water.

flying squirrel any of numerous species of squirrel, not closely related to the true squirrels. They are characterized by a membrane along the side of the body from forelimb to hindlimb (in some species running to neck and tail) which allows them to glide through the air. Several genera of flying squirrel are found in the Old World; the New World has the genus *Glaucomys*. Most species are E Asian. *See illustration p. 351*

Flynn Errol. Adopted name of Leslie Thompson 1909–1959. Australian-born US film actor. He is renowned for his portrayal of swashbuckling heroes in such films as *Captain Blood* 1935, *Robin Hood* 1938, *The Charge of the Light Brigade* 1938, *The Private Lives of Elizabeth and Essex* 1939, *The Sea Hawk* 1940, and *The Master of Ballantrae* 1953.

flystrike or *blowfly strike* or *sheep strike* infestation of the flesh of living sheep by blowfly maggots, especially those of the blue blowfly. It is one of the most costly sheep diseases in Australia, affecting all the grazing areas of New South Wales. Control has mainly been by insecticide, but non-chemical means, such as docking of tails and mulesing, are increasingly being encouraged. Mulesing involves an operation to remove the wrinkles of skin which trap moisture and lay the sheep open to infestation.

flywheel heavy wheel in an engine that helps keep it running and smooths its motion. The ◊crankshaft in a gasoline engine has a flywheel at one end, which keeps the crankshaft turning in between the intermittent power strokes of the pistons. It also comes into contact with the ◊clutch, serving as the connection between the engine and the car's transmission system.

FM in physics, symbol for *frequency ◊modulation*, or the variation of the frequency of a carrier wave in accordance with the signal to be transmitted. Used in radio, FM is constant in amplitude and has much better signal-to-noise ratio than AM (amplitude modulation).

focal length or *focal distance* the distance from the center of a lens or curved mirror to the focal point. For a concave mirror or convex lens, it is the distance at which parallel rays of light are brought to a focus to form a real image (for a mirror, this is half the radius of curvature). For a convex mirror or concave lens, it is the distance from the center to the point at which a virtual image (an image produced by diverging rays of light) is formed.

Foch Ferdinand 1851–1929. Marshal of France during World War I. He was largely responsible for the Allied victory at the first battle of the ◊Marne Sept 1914, and commanded on the NW front Oct 1914–Sept 1916. He was appointed commander in chief of the Allied armies in the spring of 1918, and launched the Allied counteroffensive in July that brought about the negotiation of an armistice to end the war.

fog cloud that collects at the surface of the Earth, composed of water vapor that has condensed on particles of dust in the atmosphere. Cloud and fog are both caused by the air temperature falling below ◊dew point. The thickness of fog depends on the number of water particles it contains.

Fokine Mikhail 1880–1942. Russian dancer and choreographer, born in St Petersburg. He was chief choreographer to the Ballets Russes 1909–14, and with ◊Diaghilev revitalized and reformed the art of ballet, promoting the idea of artistic unity among dramatic, musical, and stylistic elements.

fold in geology, a bend in ◊beds or layers of rock. If the bend is arched in the middle it is called an *anticline*; if it sags downward in the middle it is called a *syncline*.
The line along which a bed of rock folds is called its axis. The axial plane is the plane joining the axes of successive beds.

folic acid a ◊vitamin of the B complex. It is found in legumes, green leafy vegetables, and whole grains, and is also synthesized by intestinal bacteria. It is essential for growth, and plays many other roles in the body. Lack of folic acid causes anemia, diarrhea, and a red tongue.

folk dance dance characteristic of a particular people, nation, or region. Many European folk dances are derived from the dances accompanying the customs and ceremonies of pre-Christian times. Some later became ballroom dances (for example, the minuet and waltz). Once an important part of many rituals, folk dance has tended to die out in industrialized countries. Examples of folk dance are Morris dance, farandole, and jota.

folklore the oral traditions and culture of a people, expressed in legends, riddles, songs, tales, and proverbs. The term was coined 1846 by W J Thoms (1803–85), but the founder of the systematic study of the subject was Jacob Grimm; see also ◊oral literature.

folk music body of traditional music, originally transmitted orally. Many folk songs originated as a rhythmic accompaniment to manual work or to mark a specific ritual. Folk song is usually melodic, not harmonic, and the modes used are distinctive of the country of origin; see ◊world music.

follicle in zoology, a small group of cells that surround and nourish a structure such as a hair (hair follicle) or a cell such as an egg (Graafian follicle; see ◊menstrual cycle).

follicle-stimulating hormone (FSH) a ◊hormone produced by the pituitary gland. It affects the ovaries in women, triggering off the production of an egg cell.

fold The folding of rock strata occurs where compression causes them to buckle.

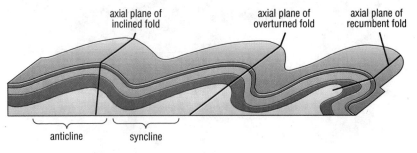

axial plane of inclined fold

axial plane of overturned fold

axial plane of recumbent fold

anticline   syncline

Luteinizing hormone is needed to complete the process. In men, FSH stimulates the testes to produce sperm.

Fonda Henry 1905–1982. US actor whose engaging style made him ideal in the role of the American pioneer and honorable man. His many films include the Academy Award–winning *The Grapes of Wrath* 1940, *My Darling Clementine* 1946, and *On Golden Pond* 1981, for which he won the Academy Award for best actor. He was the father of of actress Jane Fonda and actor and director Peter Fonda (1939–).

Fonda Jane 1937– . US actress. Her early films include *Cat Ballou* 1965, *Barefoot in the Park* 1967, *Barbarella* 1968, *They Shoot Horses, Don't They?* 1969, *Julia*, 1977, *The China Syndrome* 1979, *On Golden Pond* 1981 (in which she appeared with her father, Henry Fonda), *Agnes of God* 1985, *The Morning After* 1986, *Old Gringo* 1989, and *Stanley and Iris* 1990. She won Academy Awards for *Klute* 1971 and *Coming Home* 1979. She is active in promoting physical fitness and is married to businessman Ted Turner.

Fontainebleau school French school of Mannerist painting and sculpture. It was established at the court of Francis I, who brought Italian artists to Fontainebleau near Paris to decorate his hunting lodge: Rosso Fiorentino (1494–1540) arrived 1530, Francesco Primaticcio (1504/5–1570) came 1532. They evolved a distinctive decorative style using a combination of stucco sculpture and painting.

Fonteyn Margot. Adopted name of Margaret Hookham 1919–1991. English ballet dancer. She made her debut with the Vic-Wells Ballet in *Nutcracker* 1934 and first appeared as Giselle 1937, eventually becoming prima ballerina of the Royal Ballet, London. Renowned for her perfect physique, musicality, and interpretive powers, she created many roles in Frederick ◊Ashton's ballets and formed a legendary partnership with Rudolf ◊Nureyev. She did not retire from dancing until 1979.

food anything eaten by human beings and other animals to sustain life and health. The building blocks of food are nutrients, and humans can utilize the following nutrients: *carbohydrates*, as starches found in bread, potatoes, and pasta; as simple sugars in sucrose and honey; as fibers in cereals, fruit, and vegetables; *proteins* as from nuts, fish, meat, eggs, milk, and some vegetables; *fats* as found in most animal products (meat, lard, dairy products, fish), also in margarine, nuts and seeds, olives, and edible oils; vitamins are found in a wide variety of foods, except for vitamin B_{12}, which is mainly found in animal foods; minerals are found in a wide variety of foods; good sources of calcium are milk and broccoli, for example; iodine from seafood; iron from liver and green vegetables; water is ubiquitous in nature; alcohol is found in fermented distilled beverages, from more than 40% in liquor to 0.01% in low-alcohol beers.

Food and Agriculture Organization (FAO) United Nations agency that coordinates activities to improve food and timber production and levels of nutrition throughout the world. It is also concerned with investment in agriculture and dispersal of emergency food supplies. It has headquarters in Rome and was founded 1945.

food chain in ecology, a sequence showing the feeding relationships between organisms in a particular ◊ecosystem. Each organism depends on the next lowest member of the chain for its food. *See illustration p. 354*

Fonda US actor Henry Fonda receiving Hollywood's Life Achievement Award, photographed with his children Jane and Peter.

food irradiation the exposure of food to low-level ◊irradiation to kill microorganisms; a technique used in ◊food technology. Irradiation is highly effective, and does not make the food any more radioactive than it is naturally. Irradiated food is used for astronauts and immunocompromised patients in hospitals. Some vitamins are partially destroyed, such as vitamin C, and it would be unwise to eat only irradiated fruit and vegetables.

food poisoning any acute illness characterized by vomiting and diarrhea and caused by eating food contaminated with harmful bacteria (for example, listeriosis), poisonous food (for example, certain mushrooms, puffer fish), or poisoned food (such as lead or arsenic introduced accidentally during processing). A frequent cause of food poisoning is ◊salmonella bacteria. These come in many forms, and strains are found in cattle, pigs, poultry, and eggs.

food technology the application of science to the commercial processing of foodstuffs. Food is processed to make it more palatable or digestible, for which the traditional methods include boiling; frying; flour-milling; bread-, yogurt-, and cheese-making; and brewing, or to preserve it from spoilage caused by the action of ◊enzymes within the food that change its chemical composition, or the growth of bacteria, molds, yeasts, and other microorganisms. Fatty or oily foods also suffer oxidation of the fats, which makes them rancid. Traditional forms of *food preservation*, include salting, smoking, pickling, drying, bottling, and preserving in sugar. Modern food technology also uses many novel processes and ◊additives, which allow a wider range of foodstuffs to be preserved.

foot imperial unit of length (symbol ft), equivalent to 0.3048 m, in use in Britain since Anglo-Saxon times. It originally represented the length of a human foot. One foot contains 12 inches and is one-third of a yard.

foot-and-mouth disease contagious eruptive viral disease of cloven-hoofed mammals, characterized by blisters in the mouth and around the hooves. In cattle it causes deterioration of milk yield and abortions. It is an airborne virus which makes its eradication extremely difficult.

Inoculation with a vaccine is practiced in the US as a preventive measure.

food chain The complex interrelationships between animals and plants in a food chain.

food chain

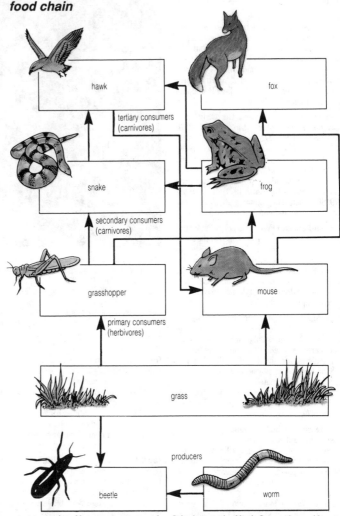

hawk

fox

tertiary consumers (carnivores)

snake

frog

secondary consumers (carnivores)

grasshopper

mouse

primary consumers (herbivores)

grass

producers

beetle

worm

football a contact sport played between two teams of 11 players with an inflated, pointed-oval ball. It is played on a field 100 yd/91 m long from goal line to goal line, with a goal posts on each of these lines, followed by a 10-yd/9-m end zone. The field is 53.3 yd/48.8 m wide. The team that scores the most points wins. Points are scored by running or passing the ball across the goal line (touchdown), by kicking it over the goal's crossbar after a touchdown (conversion or point after touchdown) or from the field during regular play (field goal), or by tackling an offensive player who has the ball in the end zone or blocking an offensive team's kick so it goes out of bounds from the end zone (safety). A touchdown counts 6 points, a field goal 3, a safety 2, and a conversion 1. Except in professional football, teams may attempt a 2-point conversion after a touchdown by running or passing the ball into the end zone. College and professional games consist of four 15-min quarters; high-school quarters are 12 min long. Players wear padded uniforms and helmets.

footrot contagious disease of sheep caused by a bacterium and spreading easily in warm, wet conditions. It is characterized by inflammation and lameness and is controlled by vaccination, foot-bathing, and segregation.

force any influence that tends to change the state of rest or the uniform motion in a straight line of a body. The action of an unbalanced or resultant force results in the acceleration of a body in the direction of action of the force, or it may, if the body is unable to move freely, result in its deformation (see ◊Hooke's law). Force is a vector quantity, possessing both magnitude and direction; its SI unit is the newton.

force ratio the magnification of a force by a machine.

Ford Gerald R(udolph) 1913– . 38th president of the US 1974–77, a Republican. He was elected to the House of Representatives 1949, was nominated to the vice-presidency by Richard Nixon 1973 following the resignation of Spiro ◊Agnew, and became president 1974, when Nixon was forced to resign following the ◊Watergate scandal. He pardoned Nixon and gave amnesty to those who had resisted the draft for the Vietnam War. *See illustration p. 356*

football

A game played by 11 men per team. The aim is, through a series of passing or running plays, to score touchdowns which are worth six points, plus one for the "point-after" (conversion). In college and high school football, conversions of one (kicking) or two (running or passing) points may be scored. Field goals (3 points) and safeties (2 points) are other ways of scoring.

the playing field

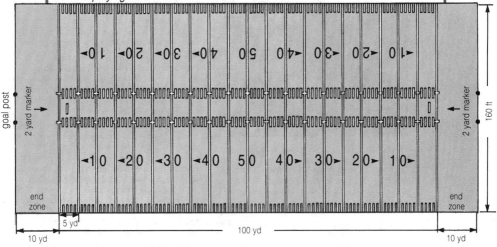

series of plays (*downs*)

The tactics of football depend upon a series of pre-planned plays. Once in possession of the ball, the attacking side (the offense) must head for the opposing goal line by either running with the ball, or by passing the ball to upfield players. In each series of downs the offense must gain at least ten yards in four plays or it loses possession of the ball.

the snap

The snap is the first move made by the center to his quarterback, who then sets up the offensive play.

key:
B   running back
QB quarterback
E   end
T   tackle
G   guard
C   center
E   end
LB line backer
DE defensive end
DT defensive tackle
DB defensive back

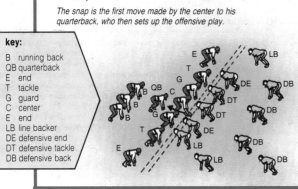

the football uniform

Football is a rough game, and players need maximum protection. They wear a helmet, and underneath their outer uniform, numerous chest-, arm- and leg-pads:

helmet
face mask
chin guard
shoulder pad
shoulder pad extension
elbow pad
arm guard
protective gloves
athletic support
thigh pad
knee pad
liner
rib pad
hip pad
shoes with cleats

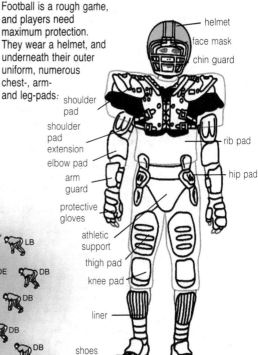

Ford *The 38th president of the United States of America, Gerald R Ford, a Republican, 1974–77.*

Ford Henry 1863–1947. US automobile manufacturer, who built his first automobile 1896 and founded the Ford Motor Company 1903. His Model T (1908–27) was the first automobile to be constructed solely by assembly-line methods and to be mass marketed; 15 million of these automobiles were made and sold.

Born in Dearborn, Michigan, Ford was apprenticed to a Detroit machinist 1878 before he started his own company. His innovative policies, such as a $5 daily minimum wage and a five-day work week, revolutionized employment practices. In 1928 he introduced the Model A, a stepped-up version of the Model T.

Ford John. Adopted name of Sean O'Feeney 1895–1973. US film director. Active from the silent film era, he was one of the original creators of the "Western," directing *The Iron Horse* 1924; *Stagecoach* 1939 became his masterpiece. He won Academy Awards for *The Informer* 1935, *The Grapes of Wrath* 1940, *How Green Was My Valley* 1941, and *The Quiet Man* 1952.

foreclosure in law, the transfer of title of a mortgaged property from the mortgagor (borrower, usually a home owner) to the mortgagee (loaner, for example a bank) if the mortgagor is in breach of of the mortgage agreement, usually by failing to make a number of payments on the mortgage (loan).

Foreign Legion volunteer corps of foreigners within a country's army. The French *Légion Etrangère*, 1831, is one of a number of such forces. Enlisted volunteers are of any nationality (about half are now French), but the officers are usually French. Headquarters until 1962 was in Sidi Bel Abbés, Algeria; the main base is now Corsica, with reception headquarters at Aubagne, near Marseille, France.

foreign relations a country's dealings with other countries. Specialized diplomatic bodies first appeared in Europe during the 18th century. After 1818 diplomatic agents were divided into: *ambassadors*, papal legates, and nuncios; *envoys* extraordinary, *ministers* plenipotentiary, and other ministers accredited to the head of state; ministers resident; and *chargés d'affaires*, who may deputize for an ambassador or minister, or be themselves the representative accredited to a minor country. Other diplomatic staff may include counselors and attachés (military, labor, cultural, press). *Consuls* are state agents with commercial and political responsibilities in foreign towns.

forensic science the use of scientific techniques to solve criminal cases. A multidisciplinary field embracing chemistry, physics, botany, zoology, and medicine, forensic science includes the identification of human bodies or traces. Traditional methods such as fingerprinting (see ◊fingerprint) are still used, assisted by computers; in addition, blood analysis, forensic dentistry, voice and speech spectograms, and ◊genetic fingerprinting are increasingly applied. Chemicals, such as poisons and drugs, are analyzed by ◊chromatography. Ballistics (the study of projectiles, such as bullets), another traditional forensic field, makes use of tools such as the comparison microscope and the ◊electron microscope.

Forester C(ecil) S(cott) 1899–1966. English novelist, born in Egypt. He wrote a series of historical novels set in the Napoleonic era that, beginning with *The Happy Return* 1937, cover the career—from midshipman to admiral—of Horatio Hornblower.

forestry the science of forest management. Recommended forestry practice aims at multipurpose crops, allowing the preservation of varied plant and animal species as well as human uses (lumbering, recreation). Forestry has often been confined to the planting of a single species, such as a rapid-growing conifer providing softwood for paper pulp and construction timber, for which world demand is greatest. In tropical countries, logging contributes to the destruction of ◊rain forests, causing global environmental problems. Small unplanned forests are ◊woodland.

forget-me-not any marsh plant of the genus *Myosotis* of the borage family. These plants have hairy leaves; bear clusters of small blue, white, or red flowers; and are considered a symbol of fidelity and friendship. The European true forget-me-not *M. scorpioides*, 12–28 in/30–70 cm in height, now grows widely in North America.

forging one of the main methods of shaping metals, which involves hammering or a more gradual application of pressure. A blacksmith hammers red-hot metal into shape on an anvil, and the traditional place of work is called a forge. The blacksmith's mechanical equivalent is the drop forge. The metal is shaped by the blows from a falling hammer or ram, which is usually accelerated by steam or air pressure. Hydraulic presses forge by applying pressure gradually in a squeezing action.

formaldehyde common name for ◊methanal.

formic acid common name for ◊methanoic acid.

formula in chemistry, a representation of a molecule, radical, or ion, in which the component chemical elements are represented by their symbols. An *empirical formula* indicates the simplest ratio of the elements in a compound, without indicating how many of them there are or how they are combined. A *molecular formula* gives the number of each type of element present in one molecule. A *structural formula* shows the relative positions of the atoms and the bonds between them. For example, for ethanoic acid, the empirical formula is CH_2O, the molecular formula is $C_2H_4O_2$, and the structural formula is CH_3COOH.

Formula is also another name for ◊chemical equation.

formula in mathematics, a set of symbols and numbers that expresses a fact or rule. $A = \pi r^2$ is the formula for calculating the area of a circle. Einstein's famous formula relating energy and mass is $E = mc^2$.

Forrest Nathan Bedford 1821–1877. American Confederate military leader and founder of the Ku Klux Klan 1866, a secret and sinister society dedicated to white supremacy. At the outbreak of the American Civil War 1861, Forrest escaped from Union troops before the fall of of Fort Donelson in Tennessee 1862. After the Battle of Shiloh 1862, he was promoted to the rank of brigadier general.

Forster E(dward) M(organ) 1879–1970. English novelist, concerned with the interplay of personality and the conflict between convention and instinct. His novels include *A Room with a View* 1908, *Howard's End* 1910, and *A Passage to India* 1924. He also wrote short stories, for example "The Eternal Omnibus" 1914; criticism, including *Aspects of the Novel* 1927; and essays, including *Abinger Harvest* 1936.

Forsyth Frederick 1938– . English thriller writer. His books include *The Day of the Jackal* 1970, *The Dogs of War* 1974, and *The Fourth Protocol* 1984.

forsythia any temperate E Asian shrub of the genus *Forsythia* of the olive family Oleaceae, which bear yellow bell-shaped flowers in early spring before the leaves appear.

Fort Collins city in N Colorado, on the Cache de la Poudre River, NE of Boulder; seat of Larimer County; population (1990) 87,800. It is the processing and marketing center for the surrounding agricultural area. Industries include engines, cement, plastics, film, and prefabricated metal buildings. The city was established as a fort 1864 for the protection of travelers on the Overland Trail.

Fort Knox US army post and gold depository in Kentucky, established 1917 as a training camp. The US Treasury gold-bullion vaults were built 1937.

Fort Lauderdale city in SE coastal Florida, just N of Miami; seat of Broward County; population (1990) 149,400. The city's main industry is tourism. Channels for boating cross the city, Atlantic Ocean beaches line it on the E, and deep-water Port Everglades to the S allows oceangoing vessels to dock. A fort was built here 1837 during the Seminole War.

Fort Myers city in SW Florida, on the Caloosahatchee River, SE of St Petersburg; seat of Lee County; population (1990) 45,200. It is a shipping center for its fish, fruit, and vegetable products. Tourism is also an important industry. The surrender of Holatto-Micco, the last Seminole chief, took place here 1858.

Fort Pierce city in E central Florida, where the Indian River flows into the Atlantic Ocean; seat of St Lucie County; population (1990) 36,800. It is an important transportation center for the fruit and vegetable crops of the surrounding area. Fishing and tourism are significant industries.

FORTRAN (acronym for *formula translation*) high-level computer-programming language suited to mathematical and scientific computations. Developed 1956, it is one of the earliest computer languages still in use. A recent version, Fortran 90, is now being used on advanced parallel computers. ◊BASIC was strongly influenced by FORTRAN and is similar in many ways.

Fort Smith city in W Arkansas, on the Arkansas River where it crosses the Oklahoma–Arkansas border, SW of Fayetteville; population (1990) 72,800. The site of coal and natural-gas mines, the city's industries include furniture, automobiles, paper, plastics, and metals. Fort Smith national historic site is here.

Fort Sumter fort in ◊Charleston Harbor, South Carolina, 4 mi/6.5 km SE of Charleston. The first shots of the US Civil War were fired here April 12, 1861, after its commander had refused the call to surrender made by the Confederate General Beauregard.

The attack was successful, with the South holding the fort until 1865; it had been prompted by President Lincoln's refusal to evacuate the fort and his decision instead to send reinforcements. Southern leaders felt

Ford *Henry Ford in his first car, a model F Ford, built 1896.*

they must attack to lend weight to their claims of independence.

Fort Ticonderoga fort in New York State, near Lake Champlain. It was the site of battles between the British and the French 1758–59, and was captured from the British May 10, 1775, by Benedict ◊Arnold and Ethan Allen (leading the ◊Green Mountain Boys).

Fortune 500 the 500 largest publicly owned US industrial corporations, a list compiled by the US business magazine *Fortune*. An industrial corporation is defined as one that derives at least 50% of its revenue from manufacturing or mining.

Fort Walton Beach city in the NW panhandle of Florida, on the Gulf of Mexico, E of Pensacola; population (1990) 21,500.

Fort Worth city in NE Texas; population (1990) 447,600. Formerly an important cattle area, it is now a grain, petroleum, aerospace, and railroad center serving the S US.

Manufactured products include aerospace equipment, motor vehicles, and refined petroleum. Carswell Air Force Base, Texas Christian University, and the Kimbell Art Museum are here. Fort Worth developed from an army post 1849 and was a stop on the Chisholm cattle trail. The arrival of the railroad 1876 fostered economic development that was furthered by the discovery of oil nearby in 1920.

fossil remains of an animal or plant preserved in rocks. Fossils may be formed by refrigeration (for example, Arctic ◊mammoths in ice); carbonization (leaves in coal); formation of a cast (dinosaur or human footprints in mud); or mineralization of bones, more generally teeth or shells. The study of fossils is called ◊paleontology.

fossil fuel fuel, such as coal, oil, and natural gas, formed from the fossilized remains of plants that lived hundreds of millions of years ago. Fossil fuels are a ◊nonrenewable resource and will eventually run out. Extraction of coal and oil causes considerable environmental pollution, and burning coal contributes to problems of ◊acid rain and the ◊greenhouse effect.

Foster Jodie. Adopted name of Alicia Christian Foster 1962– . US film actress and director who began as a child in a great variety of roles. She starred in *Taxi Driver* and *Bugsy Malone* both 1976, when only 14. Subsequent films include *The Accused* 1988 and *The Silence of the Lambs* 1991, for both of which she won the Academy Award for best actress.

Foster Stephen Collins 1826–1864. US songwriter, composer of "The Old Folks at Home" 1851, "My Old Kentucky Home" 1853, and others, which mostly drew from the black minstrel style.

Foucault Jean Bernard Léon 1819–1868. French physicist who used a pendulum to demonstrate the rotation of the Earth on its axis, and invented the gyroscope.

Foucault Michel 1926–1984. French philosopher who rejected phenomenology and existentialism. He was concerned with how forms of of knowledge and forms of human subjectivity are constructed by specific institutions and practices.

four-color process color ◊printing using four printing plates, based on the principle that any color is made up of differing proportions of the primary colors blue, red, and green. The first stage in preparing a color picture for printing is to produce separate films, one each for the blue, red, and green respectively in the

picture (color separations). From these separations three printing plates are made, with a fourth plate for black (for shading or outlines). Ink colors complementary to those represented on the plates are used for printing—yellow for the blue plate, cyan for the red, and magenta for the green.

Fourier Jean Baptiste Joseph 1768–1830. French applied mathematician whose formulation of heat flow 1807 contains the proposal that, with certain constraints, any mathematical function can be represented by trigonometrical series. This principle forms the basis of *Fourier analysis*, used today in many different fields of physics. His idea, not immediately well received, gained currency and is embodied in his *Théorie analytique de la chaleur/The Analytical Theory of Heat* 1822.

Four Noble Truths in Buddhism, a summary of the basic concepts: life is suffering (Sanskrit *duhkha*); suffering has its roots in desire (*tanha*, clinging or grasping); the cessation of desire is the end of suffering, *nirvana*; and this can be reached by the Noble Eightfold Path of *dharma* (truth).

four-stroke cycle the engine-operating cycle of most gasoline and ◊diesel engines. The "stroke" is an upward or downward movement of a piston in a cylinder. In a gasoline engine the cycle begins with the induction of a fuel mixture as the piston goes down on its first stroke. On the second stroke (up) the piston compresses the mixture in the top of the cylinder. An electric spark then ignites the mixture, and the gases produced force the piston down on its third, power, stroke. On the fourth stroke (up) the piston expels the burned gases from the cylinder into the exhaust.

Fourteen Points the terms proposed by President Wilson of the US in his address to Congress Jan 8, 1918, as a basis for the settlement of World War I. The creation of the League of Nations was one of the points.

The terms included: open diplomacy; freedom of the seas; removal of economic barriers; international disarmament; adjustment of colonial claims; German evacuation of Russian, Belgian, French, and Balkan territories; the restoration of Alsace-Lorraine to France; autonomy for the various ethnic groups in Austria, Hungary and the Ottoman Empire; an independent Poland; and a general association of nations (which was to become the League of Nations).

fourth estate another name for the press. The term was coined by the British politician Edmund Burke in analogy with the traditional three estates.

fourth-generation language in computing, a type of programming language designed for the rapid programming of ◊applications but often lacking the ability to control the individual parts of the computer. Such a language typically provides easy ways of designing screens and reports, and of using databases. Other "generations" (the term implies a class of language rather than a chronological sequence) are machine code (first generation); ◊assembly languages, or low-level languages (second); and conventional high-level languages such as ◊BASIC and ◊PASCAL (third).

Fourth of July in the US, the anniversary of the day in 1776 when the ◊Declaration of Independence was adopted by the Continental Congress. It is a public holiday, officially called *Independence Day*, commemorating independence from Britain.

Fourth Republic the French constitutional regime that was established between 1944 and 1946 and lasted until Oct 4, 1958: from liberation after Nazi

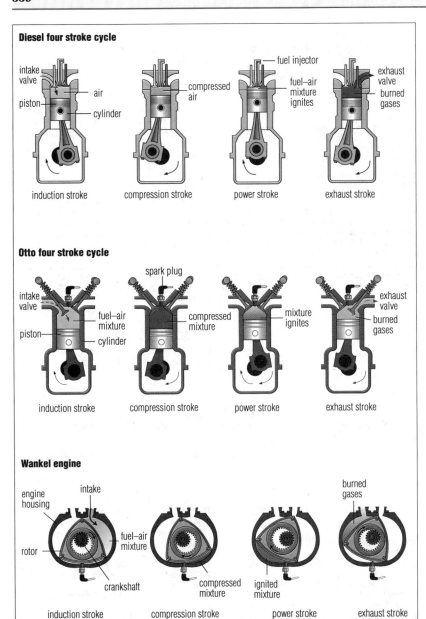

Diesel four stroke cycle

intake valve
air
piston
cylinder

compressed air

fuel injector
fuel–air mixture ignites

exhaust valve
burned gases

induction stroke · compression stroke · power stroke · exhaust stroke

Otto four stroke cycle

spark plug

intake valve
fuel–air mixture
piston
cylinder

compressed mixture

mixture ignites

exhaust valve
burned gases

induction stroke · compression stroke · power stroke · exhaust stroke

Wankel engine

engine housing
intake
rotor
fuel–air mixture
crankshaft

compressed mixture

ignited mixture

burned gases

induction stroke · compression stroke · power stroke · exhaust stroke

four-stroke cycle
The four-stroke cycle of modern engine types.

occupation during World War II to the introduction of of a new constitution by General de Gaulle.

fowl chicken or chickenlike bird. Sometimes the term is also used for ducks and geese. The red jungle fowl *Gallus gallus* is the ancestor of all domestic chickens. It is a forest bird of of Asia, without the size or egg-laying ability of many domestic strains. Guinea fowl are of African origin.

fox member of the smaller species of wild dog of the family Canidae, which live in Africa, Asia, Europe, North America, and South America. Foxes feed on a wide range of animals from worms to rabbits, scavenge for food, and also eat berries. They are very adaptable, maintaining high populations close to urban areas. *See illustration p. 360*

Fox George 1624–1691. English founder of the Society of ◊Friends. After developing his belief in a mystical "inner light," he became a traveling preacher 1647, and in 1650 was imprisoned for blasphemy at Derby, where the name Quakers was first applied derogatorily to him and his followers, supposedly because he enjoined Judge Bennet to "quake at the word of the Lord."

foxglove any flowering plant of the genus *Digitalis*, family Scrophulariaceae, found in Europe and the Mediterranean region. It bears showy spikes of bell-like flowers, and grows up to 5 ft/1.5 m high.

fox The common or red fox is versatile, intelligent, and a skillful hunter.

foxhound small, keen-nosed hound, up to 2 ft/60 cm tall and black, tan, and white in color. There are two recognized breeds: the English foxhound, bred for some 300 years to hunt foxes, and the American foxhound, not quite as stocky, used for foxes and other game.

foxtrot ballroom dance originating in the US about 1914. It has alternating long and short steps, supposedly like the movements of the fox.

fraction (from Latin *fractus* "broken") in mathematics, a number that indicates one or more equal parts of a whole. Usually, the number of equal parts into which the unit is divided (denominator) is written below a horizontal line, and the number of parts comprising the fraction (numerator) is written above; thus ⅔ or ¾. Such fractions are called vulgar or simple fractions. The denominator can never be zero.

fractionation or *fractional distillation* process used to split complex mixtures (such as crude oil) into their components, usually by repeated heating, boiling, and condensation; see ◊distillation.

Fragonard Jean Honoré 1732–1806. French painter, the leading exponent of the Rococo style (along with his master Boucher).

France country in W Europe, bounded NE by Belgium and Germany, E by Germany, Switzerland, and Italy, S by the Mediterranean Sea, SW by Spain and Andorra, and W by the Atlantic Ocean. *See maps pp. 361–62 and table p. 363*

France Anatole. Adopted name of Jacques Anatole Thibault 1844–1924. French writer renowned for the wit, urbanity, and style of his works. His earliest novel was *Le Crime de Sylvestre Bonnard/The Crime of Sylvester Bonnard* 1881; later books include the autobiographical series beginning with *Le Livre de mon*

France French Republic
(*République Française*)

area (including Corsica) 209,970 sq mi/543,965 sq km
capital Paris
cities Lyons, Lille, Bordeaux, Toulouse, Nantes, Strasbourg; ports Marseille, Nice, Le Havre
physical rivers Seine, Loire, Garonne, Rhône, Rhine; mountain ranges Alps, Massif Central, Pyrenees, Jura, Vosges, Cévennes; the island of Corsica
territories Guadeloupe, French Guiana, Martinique, Réunion, St Pierre and Miquelon, Southern and Antarctic Territories, New Caledonia, French Polynesia, Wallis and Futuna
features Ardennes forest, Auvergne mountain region, Riviera, Mont Blanc (15,781 ft/4,810 m), caves of Dordogne with relics of early humans; largest W European nation
head of state François Mitterrand from 1981
head of government Edouard Balladur from 1993
political system liberal democracy
political parties Socialist Party (PS), left of center; Rally for the Republic (RPR), neo-Gaullist conservative; Union for French Democracy (UDF), center-right; Republican Party (RP), center-right; French Communist Party (PCF), Marxist-Leninist; National Front, far right; Greens, environmentalist
exports fruit (especially apples), wine, cheese, wheat, automobiles, aircraft, iron and steel, petroleum products, chemi-

cals, jewelry, silk, lace; tourism is very important
currency franc
population (1992) 57,289,000 (including 4,500,000 immigrants, chiefly from Portugal, Algeria, Morocco, and Tunisia); growth rate 0.3% p.a.
life expectancy men 71, women 79
language French (regional languages include Basque, Breton, Catalan, and the Provençal dialect)
religions Roman Catholic 90%, Protestant 2%, Muslim 1%
literacy 99% (1984)
GNP $1,324.9 bn (1992)

chronology
1944–46 Provisional government headed by General Charles de Gaulle; start of Fourth Republic.
1954 Indochina achieved independence.
1956 Morocco and Tunisia achieved independence.
1957 Entry into European Economic Community.
1958 Recall of de Gaulle after Algerian crisis; start of Fifth Republic.
1959 De Gaulle became president.
1962 Algeria achieved independence.
1966 France withdrew from military wing of NATO.
1968 "May events" uprising of students and workers.
1969 De Gaulle resigned after referendum defeat; Georges Pompidou became president.
1974 Giscard d'Estaing elected president.
1981 François Mitterrand elected Fifth Republic's first socialist president.
1986 "Cohabitation" experiment, with the conservative Jacques Chirac as prime minister.
1988 Mitterrand reelected. Moderate socialist Michel Rocard became prime minister. Matignon Accord on future of New Caledonia approved by referendum.
1989 Greens gained 11% of vote in elections to European Parliament.
1991 French forces were part of the US-led coalition in the Gulf War. Edith Cresson became prime minister; Mitterrand's popularity rating fell rapidly.
1992 March: Socialist Party humiliated in regional and local elections; Greens and National Front polled strongly. April: Cresson replaced by Pierre Bérégovoy. Sept: referendum narrowly endorsed Maastricht Treaty.
1993 Socialist Party suffered heavy defeat in National Assembly elections. Edouard Balladur appointed prime minister; "cohabitation" government reestablished.

France

Regions and Départements

PARIS ■ 75

93
92
94

62
NORD
59
HAUTE 80
NORMANDIE PICARDIE 08
50 76 60 02
BASSE- 14 55 57
NORMANDIE 27 95 51 LORRAINE
29 22 78 77 54 67
BRETAGNE 61 91 ÎLE DE
35 53 FRANCE CHAMPAGNE 88 ALSACE
56 72 28 ARDENNE 68
PAYS DE LA 41 45 89 52 70 90
44 LOIRE 37 21 25
49 CENTRE 18 FRANCHE-
85 BOURGOGNE COMTE
79 86 36 58 71 39
POITOU- 87 23 03
CHARENTES LIMOUSIN 01 74
17 16 63 42 69 73
19
24 RHÔNE-ALPES
33 AUVERGNE 38
46 15 43 07 26 05
AQUITAINE 47 48
40 82 12 84 04 06
MIDI-PYRÉNÉES 30 PROVENCE-ALPES- 20B
64 32 31 81 34 13 COTE D'AZUR CORSE
65 LANGUEDOC- 83
09 ROUSSILLON 20A
11
66

0   100 mi
├──────────┤
0   150 km   *Départements* are numbered by the standard French alphabetical system

---

ami/My Friend's Book 1885, the satiric *L'Île des pingouins/Penguin Island* 1908, and *Les Dieux ont soif/The Gods Are Athirst* 1912. He was awarded the Nobel Prize for Literature 1921.

Francesca Piero della. See ◊Piero della Francesca, Italian painter.

Franche-Comté region of E France; area 6,253 sq mi/16,200 sq km; population (1987) 1,086,000. Its capital is Besançon, and it includes the *départements* of Doubs, Jura, Haute Saône, and Territoire de Belfort. In the mountainous Jura, there is farming and forestry, and elsewhere there are engineering and plastics industries.

Francis I 1494–1547. King of France from 1515. He succeeded his cousin Louis XII, and from 1519 European politics turned on the rivalry between him and the Holy Roman emperor Charles V, which led to war 1521–29, 1536–38, and 1542–44. In 1525 Francis was defeated and captured at Pavia and released only after signing a humiliating treaty. At home, he developed absolute monarchy.

Francis II 1544–1560. King of France from 1559 when he succeeded his father, Henri II. He married Mary Queen of Scots 1558. He was completely under the influence of his mother, ◊Catherine de' Medici.

Francis II 1768–1835. Holy Roman emperor 1792–1806. He became Francis I, Emperor of Austria 1804, and abandoned the title of Holy Roman emperor 1806. During his reign Austria was five times involved in war with France, 1792–97, 1798–1801, 1805, 1809, and 1813–14. He succeeded his father, Leopold II.

Franciscan order Catholic order of friars, *Friars Minor* or *Grey Friars*, founded 1209 by Francis of Assisi. Subdivisions were the strict Observants; the Conventuals, who were allowed to own property corporately; and the ◊Capuchins, founded 1529.

Francis of Assisi, St 1182–1226. Italian founder of the Roman Catholic Franciscan order of friars 1209 and, with St Clare, of the Poor Clares 1212. In 1224 he is said to have undergone a mystical experience during which he received the *stigmata* (five wounds of Jesus). Many stories are told of his ability to charm wild animals, and he is the patron saint of ecologists. His feast day is Oct 4.

fracium radioactive metallic element, symbol Fr, atomic number 87, atomic weight 223. It is one of the ◊alkali metals and occurs in nature in small amounts as a decay product of actinium. Its longest-lived isotope has a half-life of only 21 minutes. Fracium was discovered and named in 1939 by Margúrte Perey to honor her country.

Franck James 1882–1964. US physicist. He was awarded a Nobel Prize 1925 for his experiments of 1914 on the energy transferred by colliding electrons to mercury atoms, showing that the transfer was governed by the rules of ◊quantum theory.

Franco Francisco (Paulino Hermenegildo Teódulo Bahamonde) 1892–1975. Spanish dictator from 1939. As a general, he led the insurgent Nationalists to victory in the Spanish ◊Civil War 1936–39, supported by Fascist Italy and Nazi Germany, and established a dictatorship. In 1942 Franco reinstated a Cortes (Spanish parliament), which in 1947 passed an act by which he became head of state for life.

Franco-Prussian War 1870–71. The Prussian chancellor Bismarck put forward a German candidate for the vacant Spanish throne with the deliberate, and successful, intention of provoking the French emperor Napoleon III into declaring war. The Prussians defeated the French at Sedan, then besieged Paris. The Treaty of Frankfurt May 1871 gave Alsace, Lorraine, and a large French indemnity to Prussia. The war established Prussia, at the head of a newly established German empire, as Europe's leading power.

Frank member of a group of Germanic peoples prominent in Europe in the 3rd to 9th centuries. Believed to have originated in Pomerania on the Black Sea, they had settled on the Rhine by the 3rd century, spread into the Roman Empire by the 4th century, and gradu-

ally conquered most of Gaul, Italy, and Germany under the ◊Merovingian and ◊Carolingian dynasties. The kingdom of the W Franks became France, the kingdom of the E Franks became Germany.

Frank Anne 1929–1945. German diarist who fled to the Netherlands with her family 1933 to escape Nazi anti-Semitism (the ◊Holocaust). During the German occupation of Amsterdam, they and two other families remained in a sealed-off room, protected by Dutch sympathizers 1942–44, when betrayal resulted in their deportation and Anne's death in Belsen concentration camp. Her diary of her time in hiding was published 1947.

Frankenstein or *The Modern Prometheus* Gothic horror story by Mary Shelley, published in England 1818. Frankenstein, a scientist, discovers how to bring inanimate matter to life, and creates a man-monster. When Frankenstein fails to provide a mate to satisfy the creature's human emotions, it seeks revenge by killing Frankenstein's brother and bride. Frankenstein dies in an attempt to destroy his creation.

Frankenthaler Helen 1928– . US Abstract Expressionist painter, inventor of the color-staining technique whereby the unprimed, absorbent canvas is stained or soaked with thinned-out paint, creating deep, soft veils of translucent color.

Frankfort capital of Kentucky, located in the N central part of the state, on the Kentucky River, E of

France: rulers

title of ruler	name	date of accession	title of ruler	name	date of accession
kings	Pepin III/Childerich III	751	kings	Henri IV	1574
	Pepin III	752		Louis XIII	1610
	Charlemagne/Carloman	768		Louis XIV	1643
	Louis I	814		Louis XVI	1774
	Lothair I	840		National Convention	1792
	Charles II (the Bald)	843		Directory (five members)	1795
	Louis II	877	first consul	Napoléon Bonaparte	1799
	Louis III	879	emperor	Napoléon I	1804
	Charles III (the Fat)	882	king	Louis XVIII	1814
	Odo	888	emperor	Napoléon I	1815
	Charles III (the Simple)	893	kings	Louis XVIII	1815
	Robert I	922		Charles X	1824
	Rudolf	923		Louis XIX	1830
	Louis IV	936		Henri V	1830
	Lothair II	954		Louis-Philippe	1830
	Louis V	986	heads of state	Philippe Buchez	1848
	Hugues Capet	987		Louis Cavaignac	1848
	Robert II	996	president	Louis Napoléon Bonaparte	1848
	Henri I	1031	emperor	Napoléon III	1852
	Philippe I	1060	presidents	Adolphe Thiers	1871
	Louis VI	1108		Patrice MacMahon	1873
	Louis VII	1137		Jules Grevy	1879
	Philippe II	1180		François Sadui-Carnot	1887
	Louis VIII	1223		Jean Casimir-Périer	1894
	Louis IX	1226		François Faure	1895
	Philippe III	1270		Emile Loubet	1899
	Philippe IV	1285		Armand Fallières	1913
	Louis X	1314		Raymond Poincaré	1913
	Jean I	1316		Paul Deschanel	1920
	Philippe V	1328		Alexandre Millerand	1920
	Charles IV	1322		Gaston Doumergue	1924
	Philippe VI	1328		Paul Doumer	1931
	Jean II	1350		Albert Le Brun	1932
	Charles V	1356		Philippe Pétain (Vichy	
	Charles VI	1380		government)	1940
	Charles VII	1422		provisional government	1944
	Louis XI	1461		Vincent Auriol	1947
	Charles VIII	1483		René Coty	1954
	Louis XII	1498		Charles de Gaulle	1959
	François I	1515		Alain Poher	1969
	Henri II	1547		Georges Pompidou	1969
	François II	1559		Alain Poher	1974
	Charles IX	1560		Valéry Giscard d'Estaing	1974
	Henri III	1574		François Mitterrand	1981

Louisville; population (1990) 26,000. Industries include bourbon (whiskey), electronic equipment, furniture, and footwear. Frankfort became the capital of Kentucky 1786.

Frankfurt-am-Main city in Hessen, Germany, 45 mi/ 72 km NE of Mannheim; population (1988) 592,000. It is a commercial and banking center, with electrical and machine industries, and an inland port on the river Main. An international book fair is held here annually.

Frankfurter Felix 1882–1965. Austrian-born US jurist and Supreme Court justice. As a supporter of liberal causes, Frankfurter was one of the founders of the American Civil Liberties Union 1920. Appointed to the US Supreme Court 1939 by F D Roosevelt, he opposed the use of the judicial veto to advance political ends. He received the Presidential Medal of Freedom 1963.

frankincense resin of various African and Asian trees of the genus *Boswellia*, family Burseraceae, burned as incense. Costly in ancient times, it is traditionally believed to be one of the three gifts brought by the Magi to the infant Jesus.

Franklin Benjamin 1706–1790. US printer, publisher, author, scientist, and statesman. He proved that lightning is a form of electricity, distinguished between positive and negative electricity, and invented the lightning conductor. He was the first US ambassador to France 1776–85, and negotiated peace with Britain 1783. As a delegate to the ♦Continental Congress from Pennsylvania 1785–88, he helped to draft the ♦Declaration of Independence and the US ♦Constitution. *See illustration p. 364*

Franz Ferdinand or Francis Ferdinand 1863–1914. Archduke of Austria. He became heir to his uncle, Emperor Franz Joseph, in 1884, but while visiting Sarajevo June 28, 1914, he and his wife were assassinated by a Serbian nationalist. Austria used the episode to make unreasonable demands on Serbia that ultimately precipitated World War I.

Franz Joseph or Francis Joseph 1830–1916. Emperor of Austria-Hungary from 1848, when his uncle, Ferdinand I, abdicated. After the suppression of the 1848 revolution, Franz Joseph tried to establish an absolute monarchy but had to grant Austria a parliamentary constitution 1861 and Hungary equality with

Franklin Portrait of US politician and scientist Benjamin Franklin after a portrait by Joseph Siffred Duplessis 1783, National Portrait Gallery, London.

cities, headed by Milan, took advantage of this to establish their independence of imperial control. Frederick joined the Third Crusade, and was drowned while crossing a river in Anatolia.

Frederick II 1194–1250. Holy Roman emperor from 1212, called "the Wonder of the World." He led a crusade 1228–29 that recovered Jerusalem by treaty, without fighting. He quarreled with the pope, who excommunicated him three times, and a feud began that lasted with intervals until the end of his reign. Frederick, who was a religious septic, is often considered the most cultured man of his age. He was the son of Henry VI.

Frederick II *the Great* 1712–1786. King of Prussia from 1740, when he succeeded his father Frederick William I. In that year he started the War of the ◊Austrian Succession by his attack on Austria. In the peace of 1745 he secured Silesia. The struggle was renewed in the ◊Seven Years' War 1756–63. He acquired West Prussia in the first partition of Poland 1772 and left Prussia as Germany's foremost state. He was an efficient and just ruler in the spirit of the Enlightenment and a patron of the arts.

Frederick William 1620–1688. Elector of Brandenburg from 1640, "the Great Elector." By successful wars against Sweden and Poland, he prepared the way for Prussian power in the 18th century.

Frederick William I 1688–1740. King of Prussia from 1713, who developed Prussia's military might and commerce.

Frederick William III 1770–1840. King of Prussia from 1797. He was defeated by Napoleon 1806, but contributed to his final overthrow 1813–15 and profited by being allotted territory at the Congress of Vienna.

Frederick William IV 1795–1861. King of Prussia from 1840. He upheld the principle of the ◊divine right of kings, but was forced to grant a constitution 1850 after the Prussian revolution 1848. He suffered two strokes 1857 and became mentally debilitated. His brother William (later emperor) took over his duties.

Frederiction capital of New Brunswick, on the St John River; population (1986) 44,000. It was known as *St Anne's Point* until 1785 whne it was named after Prince Frederick, second son of George III.

Freedom, Presidential Medal of the highest peacetime civilian honor in the US. Instituted by President Kennedy 1963, it is awarded to those "who contribute significantly to the quality of American life." A list of recipients is published each Independence Day and often includes unknown individuals as well as artists, performers, and politicians.

free enterprise or *free market* economic system where private capital is used in business with profits going to private companies and individuals. The term has much the same meaning as ◊capitalism.

free fall the state in which a body is falling freely under the influence of ◊gravity, as in free-fall parachuting. The term *weightless* is normally used to describe a body in free fall in space.

Free French in World War II, movement formed by General Charles ◊de Gaulle in the UK June 1940, consisting of French soldiers who continued to fight against the Axis after the Franco-German armistice. They took the name *Fighting France* 1942 and served in many campaigns, among them General Leclerc's advance from Chad to Tripolitania 1942, the Syrian campaigns 1941, the campaigns in the Western

Austria 1867. He was defeated in the Italian War 1859 and the Prussian War 1866. In 1914 he made the assassination of his heir and nephew Franz Ferdinand the excuse for attacking Serbia, thus precipitating World War I.

Fraser Antonia 1932– . English author of biographies, including *Mary Queen of Scots* 1969; historical works, such as *The Weaker Vessel* 1984; and a series of detective novels featuring investigator Jemima Shore.

fraternity and sorority student societies (fraternity for men; sorority for women) in some US and Canadian universities and colleges. Although mainly social and residential, some are purely honorary, membership being on the basis of scholastic distinction; Phi Beta Kappa, the earliest of the fraternities, was founded at the College of William and Mary, Virginia in 1776.

fraud in law, an act of deception resulting in injury to another. To establish fraud it has to be demonstrated that (1) a false representation (for example, a factually untrue statement) has been made, with the intention that it should be acted upon; (2) the person making the representation knows it is false or does not attempt to find out whether it is true or not; and (3) the person to whom the representation is made acts upon it to his or her detriment.

Frederick IX 1899–1972. King of Denmark from 1947. He was succeeded by his daughter who became Queen ◊Margrethe II.

Frederick I *Barbarossa* ("red-beard") *c.* 1123–1190. Holy Roman emperor from 1152. Originally duke of Swabia, he was elected emperor 1152, and was engaged in a struggle with Pope Alexander III 1159–77, which ended in his submission; the Lombard

Desert, the Italian campaign, the liberation of France, and the invasion of Germany. Their emblem was the Cross of Lorraine, a cross with two bars.

Freemasonry the beliefs and practices of a group of linked national organizations open to men over the age of 21, united by a common code of morals and certain traditional "secrets." Modern Freemasonry began in 18th-century Europe. Freemasons do much charitable work, but have been criticized in recent years for their secrecy, their male exclusivity, and their alleged use of influence within and between organizations (for example, the police or local government) to further each other's interests. There are approximately 6 million members.

free port port or sometimes a zone within a port, where cargo may be accepted for handling, processing, and reshipment without the imposition of tariffs or taxes. Duties and tax become payable only if the products are for consumption in the country to which the free port belongs.

Freetown capital of Sierra Leone, W Africa; population (1988) 470,000. It has a naval station and a harbor. Industries include cement, plastics, footwear, and oil refining. Platinum, chromite, diamonds, and gold are traded. It was founded as a settlement for freed slaves in the 1790s.

free trade economic system where governments do not interfere in the movement of goods between countries; there are thus no taxes on imports. In the modern economy, free trade tends to hold within economic groups such as the European Community (EC), but not generally, despite such treaties as ◊GATT 1948 and subsequent agreements to reduce tariffs. The opposite of free trade is ◊protectionism.

free verse poetry without metrical form. At the beginning of the 20th century, many poets believed that the 19th century had accomplished most of what could be done with regular meter, and rejected it, in much the same spirit as John Milton in the 17th century had rejected rhyme, preferring irregular meters that made it possible to express thought clearly and without distortion.

free will the doctrine that human beings are free to control their own actions, and that these actions are not fixed in advance by God or fate. Some Jewish and Christian theologians assert that God gave humanity free will to choose between good and evil; others that God has decided in advance the outcome of all human choices (◊predestination), as in Calvinism.

freeze-drying method of preserving food; see ◊food technology. The product to be dried is frozen and then put in a vacuum chamber that forces out the ice as water vapor, a process known as sublimation.

freezing change from liquid to solid state, as when water becomes ice. For a given substance, freezing occurs at a definite temperature, known as the *freezing point*, that is invariable under similar conditions of pressure, and the temperature remains at this point until all the liquid is frozen. The amount of heat per unit mass that has to be removed to freeze a substance is a constant for any given substance, and is known as the latent heat of fusion.

Frelimo (acronym for *Front for the Liberation of Mozambique*) nationalist group aimed at gaining independence for Mozambique from the occupying Portuguese. It began operating from S Tanzania 1963 and continued until victory 1975.

French Guiana

Frémont John Charles 1813–1890. US soldier and politician who explored much of the Far West, was influential in the US acquisition of California, and ultimately saw his military career overshadowed by his political ambitions.

French Community former association consisting of France and those overseas territories joined with it by the constitution of the Fifth Republic, following the 1958 referendum. Many of the constituent states withdrew during the 1960s, and it no longer formally exists, but in practice all former French colonies have close economic and cultural as well as linguistic links with France.

French Guiana (French *Guyane Française*) French overseas *département* from 1946, and administrative region from 1974, on the N coast of South America, bounded W by Suriname and E and S by Brazil.
area 32,230 sq mi/83,500sq km
capital Cayenne
cities St Laurent features Eurospace rocket launch pad at Kourou; Iles du Salut, which include ◊Devil's Island
products timber, shrimps, gold
currency franc
population (1987) 89,000
languages 90% Creole, French, Amerindian
famous people Alfred ◊Dreyfus
history first settled by France 1604, the territory became a French possession 1817; penal colonies, including Devil's Island, were established from 1852; by 1945 the shipments of convicts from France ceased.

French horn musical ◊brass instrument.

French language member of the Romance branch of the Indo-European language family, spoken in France, Belgium, Luxembourg, Monaco, and Switzerland in Europe; also in Canada (principally in the province of Québec), various Caribbean and Pacific Islands (including overseas territories such as Martinique and French Guiana), and certain N and W African countries (for example, Mali and Senegal).

French Polynesia French Overseas Territory in the S Pacific, consisting of five archipelagos: Windward Islands, Leeward Islands (the two island groups comprising the ◊Society Islands), ◊Tuamotu Archipelago (including ◊Gambier Islands), ◊Tubuai Islands, and ◊Marquesas Islands
total area delete1,521 sq mi/3,940 sq km
capital Papeete on Tahiti
products cultivated pearls, coconut oil, vanilla; tourism is important
population (1990) 199,100

French Revolution 1789–99

1789	(May) Meeting of Estates-General called by Louis XIV to discuss reform of state finances. Nobility oppose reforms. (June) Third (commoners) estate demanded end to system where First (noble) estate and Second (church) estate could outvote them; rejected by Louis. Third estate declared themselves a National Assembly and *tennis court oath* pledged them to draw up new constitution. (July) Rumors of royal plans to break up the Assembly led to riots in Paris and the storming of the Bastille. Revolutionaries adopted the *tricolore* as their flag. Peasant uprisings occurred throughout the country.
1789–91	National Assembly reforms included abolition of noble privileges, dissolution of religious orders, appropriation of church lands, centralization of governments, and limits on the king's power.
1791	(June) King Louis attempted to escape from Paris in order to unite opposition to the Assembly, but was recaptured. (Sept) The king agreed to a new constitution. (Oct) New Legislative Assembly met, divided between moderate Girondists and radical Jacobins.
1792	(Jan) Girondists formed a new government but their power in Paris was undermined by the Jacobins. Foreign invasion led to the breakdown of law and order. Hatred of the monarchy increased. (Aug) The king was suspended from office and the government dismissed. (Sept) National Convention elected on the basis of universal suffrage; dominated by Jacobins. A republic was proclaimed. (Dec) The king was tried and condemned to death.
1793	(Jan) The king was guillotined. (April) The National Convention delegated power to the Committee of Public Safety, dominated by Robespierre. The Reign of Terror began.
1794	(July) Robespierre became increasingly unpopular, was deposed and executed.
1795	Moderate Thermidoreans took control of the Convention and created a new executive Directory of five members.
1795–99	Directory failed to solve France's internal or external problems and became increasingly unpopular.
1799	Coup d'état overthrew the Directory and a Consulate of three was established, including Napoleon as Chief Consul with special powers.

languages Tahitian (official), French
government a high commissioner (Alain Ohrel) and Council of Government; two deputies are returned to the National Assembly in France
history first visited by Europeans 1595; French Protectorate 1843; annexed to France 1880–82; became an Overseas Territory, changing its name from French Oceania 1958; self-governing 1977. Following demands for independence in ◊New Caledonia 1984–85, agitation increased also in Polynesia.

French Revolution the period 1789–1799 that saw the end of the French monarchy. Although the revolution began as an attempt to create a constitutional monarchy, by late 1792 demands for long-overdue reforms resulted in the proclamation of the First Republic. The violence of the revolution, attacks by other nations, and bitter factional struggles, riots, and counterrevolutionary uprisings consumed the republic. This helped bring the extremists to power, and the bloody Reign of Terror followed. French armies then succeeded in holding off their foreign enemies and one of the generals, ◊Napoleon, seized power 1799.

French Sudan former name (1898–1959) of ◊Mali.

French West Africa group of French colonies administered from Dakar 1895–1958. They are now Senegal, Mauritania, Sudan, Burkina Faso, Guinea, Niger, Ivory Coast, and Benin.

frequency in physics, the number of periodic oscillations, vibrations, or waves occurring per unit of time. The unit of frequency is the hertz (Hz), one hertz being equivalent to one cycle per second.

frequency in statistics, the number of times an event occurs. For example, when two dice are thrown repeatedly and the two scores added together, each of the numbers 2 to 12 may have a frequency of occurrence. The set of data including the frequencies is called a *frequency distribution*, usually presented in a frequency table or shown diagrammatically, by a frequency polygon.

frequency modulation see ◊FM.

fresco mural painting technique using water-based paint on wet plaster. Some of the earliest frescoes (about 1750–1400 BC) were found in Knossos, Crete (now preserved in the Heraklion Museum). Fresco reached its finest expression in Italy from the 13th to the 17th centuries. Giotto, Masaccio, Michelangelo, and many other artists worked in the medium.

Fresnel Augustin 1788–1827. French physicist who refined the theory of ◊polarized light. Fresnel realized in 1821 that light waves do not vibrate like sound waves longitudinally, in the direction of their motion, but transversely, at right angles to the direction of the propagated wave.

Fresno city in central California, SE of San Jose, seat of Fresno County; population (1990) 354,200. It is the processing and marketing center for the fruits and vegetables of the San Joaquin Valley. Industries include glass, machinery, fertilizers, and vending machines.
Fresno was originally a stop on the Central Pacific Railroad.

Freud Anna 1895–1982. Austrian-born founder of child psychoanalysis in the UK. Her work was influenced by the theories of her father, Sigmund Freud. She held that understanding of the stages of psychological development was essential to the treatment of children, and that this knowledge could only be obtained through observation of the child.

Freud Sigmund 1865–1939. Austrian physician who pioneered the study of the unconscious mind. He developed the methods of free association and interpretation of dreams that are basic techniques of ◊psychoanalysis, and formulated the concepts of the ◊id, ◊ego, and ◊superego. His books include *Die Traumdeutung/The Interpretation of Dreams* 1900, *Totem and Taboo* 1913, and *Das Unbehagen in der Kultur/Civilization and its Discontents* 1930.

Freya in Scandinavian mythology, the goddess of married love and the hearth, wife of Odin and mother of Thor. Friday is named after her.

friar a monk of any order, but originally the title of members of the mendicant (begging) orders, the chief of which were the Franciscans or Minors (Grey Friars), the Dominicans or Preachers (Black Friars), the Carmelites (White Friars), and Augustinians (Austin Friars).

friction in physics, the force that opposes the relative motion of two bodies in contact. The *coefficient of friction* is the ratio of the force required to achieve this relative motion to the force pressing the two bodies together.

Friedan Betty 1921– . US liberal feminist. Her book *The Feminine Mystique* 1963 started the contemporary women's movement, both in the US and the UK. She was a founder of the National Organization for Women (NOW) 1966 (and its president 1966–70), the National Women's Political Caucus 1971, and the First Women's Bank 1973. Friedan also helped to organize the Women's Strike for Equality 1970 and called the First International Feminist Congress 1973.

Born in Peoria, Illinois, her other works include *It Changed My Life* 1976 and *The Second Stage* 1981, a call for a change of direction in the movement.

Friedman Milton 1912– . US economist. The foremost exponent of ◊monetarism, he argued that a country's economy, and hence inflation, can be controlled through its money supply, although most governments lack the "political will" to control inflation by cutting government spending and thereby increasing unemployment. He was awarded the Nobel Prize for Economics 1976.

Friendly Islands another name for ◊Tonga, a country in the Pacific.

Friends, Society of or *Quakers* Christian Protestant sect founded by George ◊Fox in England in the 17th century. They were persecuted for their nonviolent activism, and many emigrated to form communities elsewhere, for example in Pennsylvania and New England. They now form a worldwide movement of about 200,000. Their worship stresses meditation and the freedom of all to take an active part in the service (called a meeting, held in a meeting house). They have no priests or ministers.

frigate escort warship smaller than a destroyer. Before 1975 the term referred to a warship larger than a destroyer but smaller than a light cruiser. In the 18th and 19th centuries a frigate was a small, fast sailing warship.

Frisch Karl von 1886–1982. Austrian zoologist, founder with Konrad ◊Lorenz of ethology, the study of animal behavior. He specialized in bees, discovering how they communicate the location of sources of nectar by movements called "dances." He was awarded the Nobel Prize for Medicine 1973 together with Lorenz and Nikolaas ◊Tinbergen.

Friuli-Venezia Giulia autonomous agricultural and wine-growing region of NE Italy, bordered to the E by Slovenia; area 3,011 sq mi/7,800 sq km; population (1990) 1,201,000. Cities include Udine (the capital), Gorizia, Pordenone, and Trieste.

Frobisher Martin 1535–1594. English navigator. He made his first voyage to Guinea, West Africa, 1554. In 1576 he set out in search of the Northwest Passage, and visited Labrador, and Frobisher Bay, Baffin Island. Second and third expeditions sailed 1577 and 1578.

frog any amphibian of the order Anura (Greek "tailless"). There are no clear rules for distinguishing

Freud *The Austrian psychiatrist and pioneer of psychoanalysis, Sigmund Freud.*

between frogs and toads. Frogs usually have squat bodies, hind legs specialized for jumping, and webbed feet for swimming. Many frogs use their long, extensible tongues to capture insects. Frogs vary in size from the tiny North American little grass frog *Limnaoedus ocularis*, 0.5 in/12 mm long, to the giant aquatic frog *Telmatobius culeus*, 20 in/50 cm long, of Lake Titicaca, South America.

Fromm Erich 1900–1980. German psychoanalyst who moved to the US 1933 to escape the Nazis. His *The Fear of Freedom* 1941 and *The Sane Society* 1955 were source books for alternative lifestyles.

frond large leaf or leaflike structure; in ferns it is often pinnately divided. The term is also applied to the leaves of palms and less commonly to the plant bodies of certain seaweeds, liverworts, and lichens.

Fronde French revolts 1648–53 against the administration of the chief minister ◊Mazarin during Louis XIV's minority. In 1648–49 the Paris *parlement* attempted to limit the royal power, its leaders were arrested, Paris revolted, and the rising was suppressed by the royal army under Louis II Condé. In 1650 Condé led a new revolt of the nobility, but this was suppressed by 1653. The defeat of the Fronde enabled Louis to establish an absolutist monarchy in the later 17th century.

front in meteorology, the boundary between two air masses of different temperature or humidity. A *cold front* marks the line of advance of a cold air mass from below, as it displaces a warm air mass; a *warm front* marks the advance of a warm air mass as it rises up over a cold one. Frontal systems define the weather of the mid-latitudes, where warm tropical air is constantly meeting cold air from the poles.

frost condition of the weather that occurs when the air temperature is below freezing, 32°F/0°C. Water in the atmosphere is deposited as ice crystals on the ground or exposed objects. As cold air is heavier than warm, ground frost is more common than hoar frost, which is formed by the condensation of water particles in the same way that ◊dew collects.

Frost Robert (Lee) 1874–1963. US poet whose verse, in traditional form, is written with an individual voice and penetrating vision. His poems include "Mending Wall" ("Something there is that does not love a wall"), "The Road Not Taken," and "Stopping by Woods on a Snowy Evening" and are collected in *A Boy's Will* 1913, *North of Boston* 1914, *New Hampshire* 1924, *Collected Poems* 1930, *A Further Range* 1936, and *A Witness Tree* 1942.

frog

The life cycle of frogs, and of their close relatives, the toads, comprises several distinct stages. The young, or larvae, look unlike the adults and are said to undergo a complete metamorphosis "change of form." The adult common frog mates in water. From the fertilized eggs emerge the larvae, which at first breathe solely with gills and have no legs. As they grow, they become more adult-like and eventually are able to live and breathe on land.

Adult frogs breathe using their lungs, through the moist skin, and through the lining of their mouths. They feed on worms, beetles, and flies. The aquatic tadpoles at first feed on weeds and algae, but then change to a meat diet.

Parental care in some species of frogs and toads involves carrying the eggs or tadpoles (larvae) on the back. 1. Male stream frog with tadpoles. 2. Female Surinam toad with young. 3. Male midwife toad carrying eggs.

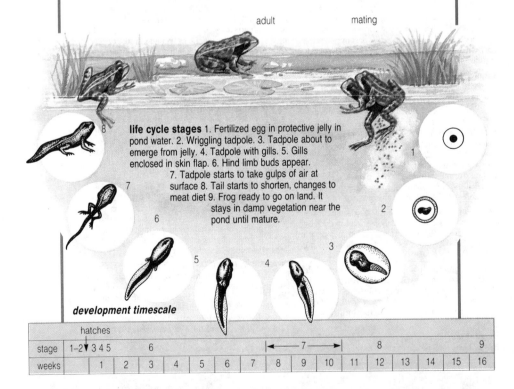

adult   mating

life cycle stages 1. Fertilized egg in protective jelly in pond water. 2. Wriggling tadpole. 3. Tadpole about to emerge from jelly. 4. Tadpole with gills. 5. Gills enclosed in skin flap. 6. Hind limb buds appear. 7. Tadpole starts to take gulps of air at surface 8. Tail starts to shorten, changes to meat diet 9. Frog ready to go on land. It stays in damp vegetation near the pond until mature.

development timescale

stage	hatches ↓ 1–2 3 4 5			6					7			8				9
weeks	1	2	3	4	5	6	7	8	9	10	11	12	13	14	15	16

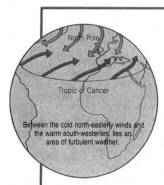

Between the cold north-easterly winds and the warm south-westerlies, lies an area of turbulent weather.

front

The weather in North America and northern Europe is highly variable because both areas lie along the boundary between the cold air mass of the Arctic and the warm air mass at the Tropic of Cancer. Due to the rotation of the Earth, the polar winds blow from the north east and the tropical winds blow from the south west. Where they meet they spiral around one another, producing complex weather systems.

development of a frontal system

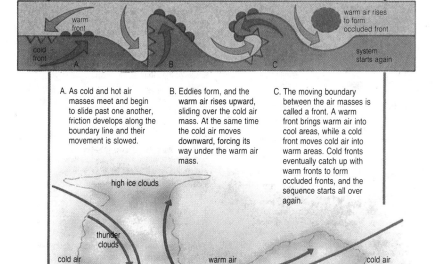

A. As cold and hot air masses meet and begin to slide past one another, friction develops along the boundary line and their movement is slowed.

B. Eddies form, and the warm air rises upward, sliding over the cold air mass. At the same time the cold air moves downward, forcing its way under the warm air mass.

C. The moving boundary between the air masses is called a front. A warm front brings warm air into cool areas, while a cold front moves cold air into warm areas. Cold fronts eventually catch up with warm fronts to form occluded fronts, and the sequence starts all over again.

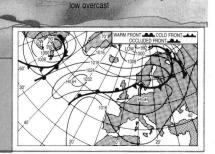

Different cloud and rain patterns occur along the moving fronts of hot and cold air masses.

On weather maps, cold and warm fronts are marked by different symbols.

The changeable weather patterns of northern Europe result from a succession of fronts.

fruit A fruit contains the seeds of a plant; there are several types.

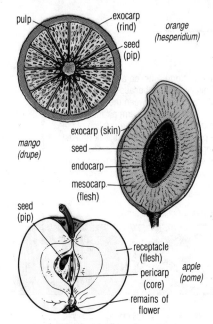

pulp
exocarp (rind)
seed (pip)
orange (hesperidium)

mango (drupe)
exocarp (skin)
seed
endocarp
mesocarp (flesh)

seed (pip)
receptacle (flesh)
pericarp (core)
remains of flower
apple (pome)

frostbite the freezing of skin or flesh, with formation of ice crystals leading to tissue damage. The treatment is slow warming of the affected area; for example, by skin-to-skin contact or with lukewarm water. Frostbitten parts are extremely vulnerable to infection, with the risk of gangrene.

fructose $C_6H_{12}O_6$ a sugar that occurs naturally in honey, the nectar of flowers, and many sweet fruits; it is commercially prepared from glucose.

fruit in botany, the ripened ovary in flowering plants that develops from one or more seeds or carpels and encloses one or more seeds. Its function is to protect the seeds during their development and to aid in their dispersal. Fruits are often edible, sweet, juicy, and colorful. When eaten they provide vitamins, minerals, and enzymes, but little protein. Most fruits are borne by perennial plants. When fruits are eaten by animals the seeds pass through the alimentary canal unharmed, and are passed out with the feces.

Fuad two kings of Egypt, including:

Fuad I 1868–1936. King of Egypt from 1922. Son of the Khedive Ismail, he succeeded his elder brother Hussein Kiamil as sultan of Egypt 1917; when Egypt was declared independent 1922 he assumed the title of king.

Fuchs Klaus (Emil Julius) 1911–1988. German spy who worked on atom-bomb research in the US in World War II, and subsequently in the UK. He was

fuchsia Fuchsia flowers are bell-like and hang downward.

imprisoned 1950–59 for passing information to the USSR and resettled in eastern Germany.

fuchsia any shrub or herbaceous plant of the genus *Fuchsia* of the evening-primrose family Onagraceae. Species are native to South and Central America and New Zealand, and bear red, purple, or pink bell-shaped flowers that hang downward.

fuel any source of heat or energy, embracing the entire range of materials that burn (combustibles). A *nuclear fuel* is any material that produces energy by nuclear fission in a nuclear reactor.

fuel cell cell converting chemical energy directly to electrical energy. It works on the same principle as a battery but is continually fed with fuel, usually hydrogen. Fuel cells are silent and reliable (no moving parts) but expensive to produce.

fuel injection injecting fuel directly into the cylinders of an internal combustion engine, instead of by way of a carburetor. It is the standard method used in ◊diesel engines, and is now becoming standard for gasoline engines. In the diesel engine, oil is injected into the hot compressed air at the top of the second piston stroke and explodes to drive the piston down on its power stroke. In the gasoline engine, fuel is injected into the cylinder at the start of the first induction stroke of the ◊four-stroke cycle.

Fuentes Carlos 1928– . Mexican novelist, lawyer, and diplomat whose first novel *La región más transparente/Where the Air Is Clear* 1958 encompasses the history of the country from the Aztecs to the present day.

fugue in music, a contrapuntal form (with two or more melodies) for a number of parts or "voices," which enter successively in imitation of each other. It was raised to a high art by J S ◊Bach.

Führer or *Fuehrer* title adopted by Adolf ◊Hitler as leader of the Nazi Party.

Fujairah or *Fujayrah* one of the seven constituent member states of the ◊United Arab Emirates; area 450 sq mi/1,150 sq km; population (1985) 54,000.

Fujian or *Fukien* province of SE China, bordering Taiwan Strait, opposite Taiwan
area 47,517 sq mi/123,100 sq km
capital Fuzhou
physical dramatic mountainous coastline
features being developed for tourists; designated as a pace-setting province for modernization 1980
products sugar, rice, special aromatic teas, tobacco, timber, fruit
population (1990) 30,048,000.

Fujimori Alberto 1939– . President of Peru from July 1990. As leader of the newly formed Cambio 90 (Change 90) he campaigned on a reformist ticket and defeated his more experienced Democratic Front opponent. With no assembly majority, and faced with increasing opposition to his policies, he imposed military rule early 1992.

Fujiyama or *Mount Fuji* Japanese volcano and highest peak, on Honshu Island, near Tokyo; height 12,400 ft/3,778 m.
  Extinct since 1707, it has a ◊Shinto shrine and a weather station on its summit. Fuji has long been revered for its picturesque cone-shaped crater peak, and figures prominently in Japanese art, literature, and religion.

Fula W African empire founded by people of predominantly Fulani extraction. The Fula conquered the Hausa states in the 19th century.

Fulani member of a W African culture from the S Sahara and Sahel. Traditionally nomadic pastoralists and traders, Fulani groups are found in Senegal, Guinea, Mali, Burkina Faso, Niger, Nigeria, Chad, and Cameroon. The Fulani language is divided into four dialects and belongs to the W Atlantic branch of the Niger-Congo family; it has more than 10 million speakers.

Fulbright (James) William 1905– . US Democratic politician. A US senator 1945–75, he was responsible for the *Fulbright Act* 1946, which provided grants for thousands of Americans to study abroad and for overseas students to study in the US. Fulbright chaired the Senate Foreign Relations Committee 1959–74, and was a strong internationalist and supporter of the ◊United Nations.

Fuller (Richard) Buckminster 1895–1983. US architect, engineer, and futurist social philosopher who embarked on an unorthodox career in an attempt to maximize energy resources through improved technology. In 1947 he invented the lightweight geodesic dome, a half-sphere of triangular components independent of buttress or vault.

He also invented a Dymaxion (a combination of the words "dynamics" and "maximum") house 1928 and automobile 1933 that was inexpensive and utilized his concept of using the least amount of energy output to gain maximum interior space and efficiency, respectively. Among his books are *Ideas and Integrities* 1963, *Utopia or Oblivion* 1969, and *Critical Path* 1981.

Fuller Margaret 1810–1850. US author and reformer. She was the editor of *The Dial*, the Transcendentalist magazine 1839–44, and noted for her public "conversations" for the edification of the women of Boston during the same period. She became the literary critic for the *New York Tribune* 1844. Later, while on assignment in Italy, she joined Giuseppe Mazzini's doomed nationalist revolt 1848. Fuller was lost at sea while returning to the US 1850.

Fuller Melville Weston 1833–1910. US jurist and chief justice of the US Supreme Court 1888–1910. Fuller

endorsed court options that limited state and federal strengths to regulate private business. He sided with the majority of the Court in *Pollack* v *Farmers Loan and Trust Co* 1895, which held invalid a flat-rate US income tax leading to passage of the 16th Amendment to the Constitution in 1913, authorizing an income tax.

fullerene form of carbon, discovered 1985, based on closed cages of carbon atoms. The molecules of the most symmetrical of the fullerenes are called ◊buckminsterfullerenes. They are perfect spheres made up of 60 carbon atoms linked together in 12 pentagons and 20 hexagons fitted together like those of a spherical football. Other fullerenes with 28, 32, 50, 70, and 76 carbon atoms have also been identified.

fuller's earth a soft, greenish-gray rock resembling clay, but without clay's plasticity. It is formed largely of clay minerals, rich in montmorillonite, but a great deal of silica is also present. Its absorbent properties make it suitable for removing oil and grease, and it was formerly used for cleaning fleeces ("fulling"). It is still used in the textile industry, but its chief application is in the purification of oils. Beds of fuller's earth are found in the S US, Germany, Japan, and the UK.

Fullilove v Klutznick a US Supreme Court decision 1980 dealing with the constitutionality of Congressional legislation allocating a certain percentage of public works contracts to minority-owned businesses. Fullilove, a white business owner, filed suit against the government, arguing that the Public Works Employment Act, a bill that required states to use at least 10% of federal public works funds to hire minority businesses, was racially discriminatory. The Court found that the act was not a violation of the 14th Amendment but a remedial measure intended to enforce the equal protection clause. Congress, according to a 6–3 decision, was within its rights to use control over federal funds for the legitimate goal of reversing racial discrimination.

Fulton Robert 1745–1815. US gunsmith, artist, engineer, and inventor. He designed steamships based on

Fujiyama Gaily decorated boats gather on a lake below Fujiyama.

fusion Electrical coils, weighing 12 tons each, used in Europe's first large thermonuclear fusion experiment at the Joint European Torus (JET) laboratory, Culham, Oxfordshire, England.

those invented by James Rumsey 1787 and John ◊Fitch 1790. With French support he built the first submarine, the *Nautilus* 1801. Combining the British-built steam engine with his own design of riverboat, a side-wheeler, he built and registered the *North River Steam Boat* 1807 (now erroneously known as the *Clermont*).

Funchal capital and chief port of the Portuguese island of Madeira, on the S coast; population (1980) 100,000. Tourism and Madeira wine are the main industries.

function in mathematics, a function *f* is a non-empty set of ordered pairs $(x, f(x))$ of which no two can have the same first element. Hence, if $f(x) = x^2$, two ordered pairs are (–2,4) and (2,4). The set of all first elements in a function's ordered pairs is called the **domain**, the set of all second elements is the **range**. In the algebraic expression $y = 4x^3 + 2$, the dependent variable *y* is a function of the independent variable *x*, generally written as $f(x)$.

Functionalism in architecture and design, a 20th-century school, also called Modernism or International Style, characterized by the ideal of excluding everything that serves no practical purpose. It developed as a reaction against the 19th-century practice of imitating and combining earlier styles, and its finest achievements are in the realm of industrial architecture and office furnishings.

fundamental forces in physics, the four fundamental interactions believed to be at work in the physical universe. There are two long-range forces: *gravity*, which keeps the planets in orbit around the Sun, and acts between all ◊particles that have mass; and the *electromagnetic force*, which stops solids from falling apart, and acts between all particles with ◊elec-tric charge. There are two very short-range forces: the *weak force*, responsible for radioactive decay and for other subatomic reactions; and the *strong force*, which binds together the protons and neutrons in the nuclei of atoms.

fundamentalism in religion, an emphasis on basic principles or articles of faith. *Christian fundamentalism* emerged in the US just after World War I (as a reaction to theological modernism and the historical criticism of the Bible) and insisted on belief in the literal truth of everything in the Bible. *Islamic fundamentalism* insists on strict observance of Muslim Shari'a law.

fungicide any chemical ◊pesticide used to prevent fungus diseases in plants and animals. Inorganic and organic compounds containing sulfur are widely used.

fungus (plural *fungi*) any of a group of organisms in the kingdom Fungi. Fungi are not considered plants. They lack leaves and roots; they contain no chlorophyll and reproduce by spores. Molds, yeasts, rusts, smuts, mildews, and mushrooms are all types of fungi.

fur the ◊hair of certain animals.

Furies in Greek mythology, the Erinyes, appeasingly called the Eumenides ("kindly ones"). They were the daughters of Earth or of Night, represented as winged maidens with serpents twisted in their hair. They punished such crimes as filial disobedience, murder, inhospitality, and oath-breaking, but were also associated with fertility.

furlong unit of measurement, originating in Anglo-Saxon England, equivalent to 220 yd/201.168 m.

furnace structure in which fuel such as coal, coke, gas, or oil is burned to produce heat for various purposes. Furnaces are used in conjunction with ◊boilers for heating, to produce hot water, or steam for driving turbines—in ships for propulsion and in power stations for generating electricity. The largest furnaces are those used for smelting and refining metals, such as the ◊blast furnace, electric furnace, and ◊open-hearth furnace.

fuse in electricity, a wire or strip of metal designed to melt when excessive current passes through. It is a safety device to stop at that point in the circuit when surges of current would otherwise damage equipment and cause fires. In explosives, a fuse is a cord impregnated with chemicals so that it burns slowly at a predetermined rate. It is used to set off a main explosive charge, sufficient length of fuse being left to allow the person lighting it to get away to safety.

fusion in physics, the fusing of the nuclei of light elements, such as hydrogen, into those of a heavier element, such as helium. The resultant loss in their combined mass is converted into energy. Stars and thermonuclear weapons work on the principle of ◊nuclear fusion.

So far no successful fusion reactor—one able to produce the required energy and contain the reaction—has been built. See ◊energy and ◊cold fusion.

future in business, a contract to buy or sell a specific quantity of a particular commodity or currency (or even a purely notional sum, such as the value of a particular stock index) at a particular date in the future. There is usually no physical exchange between buyer and seller. It is only the difference between the ground value and the market value that changes. Such transactions are a function of the *futures market*.

Futurism literary and artistic movement 1909–14, originating in Paris. The Italian poet Marinetti published the *Futurist Manifesto* 1909 urging Italian artists to join him in Futurism. In their works the Futurists eulogized the modern world and the "beauty of speed and energy."

Combining the shifting geometric planes of Cubism with vibrant colors, they aimed to capture the dynamism of a speeding automobile or train by the simultaneous repetition of forms. As a movement Futurism died out during World War I, but the Futurists' exultation in war and violence was seen as an early manifestation of ◊fascism.

Fuzhou or *Foochow* industrial port and capital of Fujian province, on Min River in SE China; population (1989) 1,270,000. It is a center for shipbuilding and steel production; rice, sugar, tea, and fruit pass through the port. There are joint foreign and Chinese factories.

G

Mutiny on the Bounty 1935, and *The Misfits* 1960. He was nicknamed the "King of Hollywood."

Gabo Naum. Adopted name of Naum Neemia Pevsner 1890–1977. US abstract sculptor, born in Russia. One of the leading exponents of ◊Constructivism, he left the USSR in 1922 for Germany and taught at the Bauhaus in Berlin (a key center of modern design). He lived in Paris and England in the 1930s, then settled in the US in 1946. He was one of the first artists to make kinetic (moving) sculpture and often used transparent colored plastics.

Gabon country in central Africa, bounded N by Cameroon, E and S by the Congo, W by the Atlantic Ocean, and NW by Equatorial Guinea.

Gaborone capital of Botswana, mainly an administrative and government-service center; population (1990) 341,100. The University of Botswana and Swaziland (1976) is here. The city developed after it replaced Mafikeng as the country's capital 1965.

Gabriel in the New Testament, the archangel who foretold the birth of John the Baptist to Zacharias and of Jesus to the Virgin Mary. He is also mentioned in the Old Testament in the book of Daniel. In Muslim belief, Gabriel revealed the Koran to Mohammed and escorted him on his ◊Night Journey.

Gaddafi alternate form of ◊Khaddhafi, Libyan leader.

Gaddi family of Italian painters in Florence: *Gaddo Gaddi* (c. 1250–1330); his son *Taddeo Gaddi* (c. 1300–1366), who was inspired by Giotto and painted the fresco cycle *Life of the Virgin* in Santa Croce, Florence; and grandson *Agnolo Gaddi* (active 1369–96), who also painted frescoes in Santa Croce, *The Story of the Cross* 1380s, and produced panel paintings in characteristic pale pastel colors.

gadolinium silvery-white metallic element of the lanthanide series, symbol Gd, atomic number 64, atomic weight 157.25.

g symbol for ◊gram.

G7 or *Group of Seven* the seven wealthiest nations in the world: the US, Japan, Germany, France, the UK, Italy, and Canada. Since 1975 their heads of government have met once a year to discuss economic and, increasingly, political matters.

GA abbreviation for the state of ◊Georgia.

gabbro basic (low-silica) igneous rock formed deep in the Earth's crust. It contains pyroxene and calcium-rich feldspar, and may contain small amounts of olivine and amphibole. Its coarse crystals of dull minerals give it a speckled appearance.

Gable (William) Clark 1901–1960. US actor. A star for more than 30 years in 90 films, he played romantic roles such as Rhett Butler in *Gone With the Wind* 1939. His other films include *The Painted Desert* 1931 (his first), *It Happened One Night* 1934 (Academy Award),

---

Gabon
Gabonese Republic
(*République Gabonaise*)

ATLANTIC OCEAN

Equatorial Guinea
São Tomé and Príncipe
Libreville
GABON
Cameroon
Zaire
Congo

0 mi 500
0 km 1000

area 103,319 sq mi/267,667 sq km
capital Libreville
cities Port-Gentil and Owendo (ports); Masuku (Franceville)
physical virtually the whole country is tropical rain forest; narrow coastal plain rising to hilly interior with savanna in E and S; Ogooué River flows N–W
features Schweitzer hospital at Lambaréné; Trans-Gabonais railroad
head of state and government Omar Bongo from 1967

political system emergent democracy
political parties Gabonese Democratic Party (PDG), nationalist; Morena Movement of National Recovery, left of center
exports petroleum, manganese, uranium, timber
currency CFA franc
population (1992) 1,253,000 including 40 Bantu groups; growth rate 1.6% p.a.
life expectancy men 47, women 51
languages French (official), Bantu
religions Christian 96% (Roman Catholic 65%), small Muslim minority 1%, animist 3%
literacy men 70%, women 53% (1985 est)
GDP $3.5 bn (1987); $3,308 per head

chronology
1889 Gabon became part of the French Congo.
1960 Independence from France achieved; Léon M'ba became the first president.
1964 Attempted coup by rival party foiled with French help. M'ba died; he was succeeded by his protégé Albert-Bernard Bongo.
1968 One-party state established.
1973 Bongo reelected; converted to Islam, he changed his first name to Omar.
1986 Bongo reelected.
1989 Coup attempt against Bongo defeated.
1990 PDG won first multiparty elections since 1964 amid allegations of ballot rigging.
1993 Hosted second African/African-American Summit.

Gadsden city in NE Alabama, on the Coosa River, SE of Huntsville; seat of Etowah County; population (1990) 42,500.

It is a distribution center for the area's livestock, poultry, and dairy products. Industries include manganese, bauxite, coal, timber, steel, rubber products, electrical machinery parts, and farm equipment.

Gadsden James 1788–1858. US military leader and diplomat. In 1823 he was appointed by President Monroe to supervise the forced resettlement of the North American Seminole Indians to S Florida and participated in the ensuing Seminole Wars. He was appointed US minister to Mexico 1853 and negotiated the Gadsden Purchase, acquiring for the US from Mexico what is now New Mexico and Arizona.

Gadsden Purchase in US history, the purchase of approximately 30,000 sq mi/77,700 sq km in what is now New Mexico and Arizona by the US 1853. The land was bought from Mexico for $10 million in a treaty negotiated by James Gadsden (1788–1858) of South Carolina, to construct a transcontinental railroad route, the Southern Pacific, completed in the 1880s.

Gaelic language member of the Celtic branch of the Indo-European language family, spoken in Ireland, Scotland, and (until 1974) the Isle of Man. Gaelic has been in decline for several centuries, discouraged until recently within the British state. There is a small Gaelic-speaking community in Nova Scotia.

Gagarin Yuri (Alexeyevich) 1934–1968. Soviet cosmonaut who in 1961 became the first human in space aboard the spacecraft *Vostok 1*.

Gaia or *Ge* in Greek mythology, the goddess of the Earth. She sprang from primordial Chaos and herself produced Uranus, by whom she was the mother of the ◊Cyclops and ◊Titans.

Gaia hypothesis theory that the Earth's living and nonliving systems form an inseparable whole that is regulated and kept adapted for life by living organisms themselves. The planet therefore functions as a single organism, or a giant cell. Since life and environment are so closely linked, there is a need for humans to understand and maintain the physical environment and living things around them. The Gaia hypothesis was elaborated by British scientist James (Ephraim) Lovelock in the 1970s.

Gainesville city in N Florida, SW of Jacksonville; seat of Alachua County; population (1990) 84,700. Its industries include electronic parts, concrete, and wooden products. The University of Florida 1853 is here.

Gainsborough Thomas 1727–1788. English landscape and portrait painter. In 1760 he settled in Bath and painted society portraits. In 1774 he went to London and became one of the original members of the Royal Academy. He was one of the first British artists to follow the Dutch in painting realistic landscapes rather than imaginative Italianate scenery.

gal or *galileo* unit of acceleration, used in geological surveying. One gal is one centimeter per second per second. The Earth's gravitational field often differs by several milligals (thousandths of a gal) in different places, because of the varying densities of the rocks beneath the surface.

Galahad in Arthurian legend, one of the knights of the Round Table. Galahad succeeded in the quest for the ◊Holy Grail because of his virtue. He was the son of ◊Lancelot of the Lake.

Gainsborough The Linley Sisters *(1772).*

Galápagos Islands (official name *Archipiélago de Colón*) group of 15 islands in the Pacific, belonging to Ecuador; area 3,000 sq mi/7,800 sq km; population (1982) 6,120. The capital is San Cristóbal on the island of the same name. The islands are a nature preserve. Their unique fauna (including giant tortoises, iguanas, penguins, flightless cormorants, and Darwin's finches), which inspired Charles ◊Darwin to formulate the principle of evolution by natural selection, is under threat from introduced species.

galaxy congregation of millions or billions of stars, held together by gravity. *Spiral galaxies,* such as the ◊Milky Way, are flattened in shape, with a central bulge of old stars surrounded by a disk of younger stars, arranged in spiral arms like a Catherine wheel. *Barred spirals* are spiral galaxies that have a straight bar of stars across their center, from the ends of which the spiral arms emerge. The arms of spiral galaxies contain gas and dust from which new stars are still forming. *Elliptical galaxies* contain old stars and very little gas. They include the most massive galaxies known, containing a trillion stars. At least some elliptical galaxies are thought to be formed by mergers between spiral galaxies. There are also irregular galaxies. Most galaxies occur in clusters, containing anything from a few to thousands of members. *See illustration p. 376*

Galbraith John Kenneth 1908– . Canadian-born US economist; he became a US citizen 1937. His major works include the *Affluent Society* 1958, in which he documents the tendency of the "invisible hand" of free-market capitalism to create private splendor and public squalor, *Economics and the Public Purpose* 1974, and *The Culture of Containment* 1992.

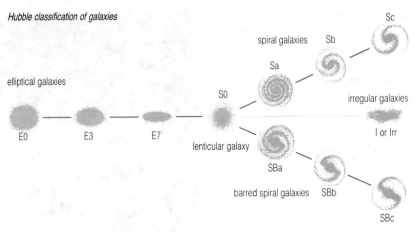

galaxy Galaxies were classified by US astronomer Edwin Hubble in 1925.

Hubble classification of galaxies

spiral galaxies   Sb   Sc

Sa

elliptical galaxies

S0   irregular galaxies

E0   E3   E7   I or Irr

lenticular galaxy

SBa

barred spiral galaxies   SBb

SBc

Galen c. 130–c. 200. Greek physician whose ideas dominated Western medicine for almost 1,500 years. Central to his thinking were the theories of humors and the threefold circulation of the blood. He remained the highest medical authority until Andreas Vesalius and William Harvey exposed the fundamental errors of his system.

Galicia mountainous but fertile autonomous region of NW Spain, formerly an independent kingdom; area 11,348 sq mi/29,400 sq km; population (1986) 2,785,000. It includes La Coruña, Lugo, Orense, and Pontevedra. Industries include fishing and the mining of tungsten and tin. The language is similar to Portuguese.

Galilee, Sea of alternate name for Lake Tiberias in N Israel.

Galileo spacecraft launched from the space shuttle *Atlantis* Oct 1989, on a six-year journey to Jupiter. It flew past Venus Feb 1990 and passed within 600 mi/970 km of Earth Dec 1990, using the gravitational

Galileo The Galileo spacecraft about to be detached from the Earth-orbiting space shuttle Atlantis at the beginning of its six-year journey to Jupiter.

fields of these two planets to increase its velocity. The craft flew past Earth again 1992 to receive its final boost toward Jupiter.

Galileo properly Galileo Galilei 1564–1642. Italian mathematician, astronomer, and physicist. He developed the astronomical telescope and was the first to see sunspots, the four main satellites of Jupiter, mountains and craters on the Moon, and the appearance of Venus going through "phases," thus proving it was orbiting the Sun. In mechanics, Galileo discovered that freely falling bodies, heavy or light, had the same, constant acceleration (although the story of his dropping cannonballs from the Leaning Tower of Pisa is questionable) and that a body moving on a perfectly smooth horizontal surface would neither speed up nor slow down.

Gall c. 1840–1894. American Sioux Indian leader. He became a noted warrior of the Hunkpapa Sioux and a protégé of Chief Sitting Bull. Gall accompanied Sitting Bull to Montana 1876 and led the encirclement and annihilation of General ◊Custer's force at Little Bighorn.

Gallatin Albert 1761–1849. Swiss-born US political leader and diplomat. He served in the US House of Representatives 1795–1801 and was secretary of the treasury 1801–13 during the administrations of Jefferson and Madison. He negotiated the treaty ending the War of 1812 and served as US minister to France 1815–22 and to England 1826–27.

gall bladder small muscular sac, part of the digestive system of most, but not all, vertebrates. In humans, it is situated on the underside of the liver and connected to the small intestine by the bile duct. It stores bile from the liver.

galley ship powered by oars, and usually also equipped with sails. Galleys typically had a crew of hundreds of oarsmen arranged in rows; they were used in warfare in the Mediterranean from antiquity until the 18th century.

Gallipoli port in European Turkey, giving its name to the peninsula (ancient name *Chersonesus*) on which it stands. In World War I, at the instigation of Winston Churchill, an unsuccessful attempt was made Feb 1915–Jan 1916 by Allied troops to force their way through the Dardanelles and link up with Russia. The campaign was fought mainly by Australian and New Zealand (◊ANZAC) forces, who suffered heavy losses. An estimated 36,000 Commonwealth troops died during the nine-month campaign.

gallium gray metallic element, symbol Ga, atomic number 31, atomic weight 69.75. It is liquid at room temperature. Gallium arsenide (GaAs) crystals are used in microelectronics, since electrons travel a thousand times faster through them than through silicon. The element was discovered in 1875 by Lecoq de Boisbaudran (1838–1912).

Gallo Robert Charles 1937– . US scientist credited with identifying the virus responsible for ◊AIDS. Gallo discovered the virus, now known as human immunodeficiency virus (HIV), in 1984; the French scientist Luc Montagnier (1932–) of the Pasteur Institute, Paris, discovered the virus, independently, in 1983. The sample in which Gallo discovered the virus was supplied by Montagnier, and it has been alleged that this may have been contaminated by specimens of the virus isolated by Montagnier a few months earlier.

gallon unit of liquid measure, equal to 3.785 liters, and subdivided into four quarts or eight pints. The UK and Canadian imperial gallon is equivalent to 4.546 liters.

gallstone pebblelike, insoluble accretion formed in the human gall bladder or bile ducts from cholesterol or calcium salts present in bile. Gallstones may be symptomless or they may cause pain, indigestion, or jaundice. They can be dissolved with medication or removed, along with the gall bladder, in an operation known as cholecystectomy.

Gallup George Horace 1901–1984. US journalist and statistician, who founded in 1935 the American Institute of Public Opinion and devised the Gallup Poll, in which public opinion is sampled by questioning a number of representative individuals.

Galsworthy John 1867–1933. English novelist and dramatist whose work examines the social issues of the Victorian period. He wrote *The Forsyte Saga* 1922 and its sequel *A Modern Comedy* 1929. His other novels include *The Country House* 1907 and *Fraternity* 1909; plays include *The Silver Box* 1906.

Galtieri Leopoldo 1926– . Argentine general, president 1981–82. A leading member from 1979 of the ruling right-wing military junta and commander of the army; Galtieri became president in 1981. Under his leadership the junta ordered the seizure 1982 of the Falkland Islands (Malvinas), a British colony in the SW Atlantic claimed by Argentina. After the surrender of his forces he resigned as army commander and was replaced as president. He and his fellow junta members were tried for abuse of human rights and court-martialed for their conduct of the war; he was sentenced to 12 years in prison in 1986.

galvanizing process for rendering iron rustproof, by plunging it into molten zinc (the dipping method), or by electroplating it with zinc.

Galveston Gulf of Mexico port on Galveston Island in Texas; population (1990) 59,000. It exports cotton, petroleum, wheat, annd timber and has chemical works and petroleum refineries. In 1900, 8,000 people died in one of the hurricanes that periodically hit the region. The city dates from an 1817 settlement by the pirate Jean Lafitte. Fishing is important, and the city has long been a resort for the island's sandy beaches.

Galway county on the W coast of the Republic of Ireland, in the province of Connacht; area 2,293 sq mi/5,940 sq km; population (1991) 180,300. Towns include Galway (county town), Ballinasloe, Tuam, Clifden, and Loughrea (near which deposits of lead, zinc, and copper were found 1959).

Galileo Italian mathematician, astronomer, and physicist Galileo Galilei.

Gama Vasco da *c.* 1469–1524. Portuguese navigator who commanded an expedition in 1497 to discover the route to India around the Cape of Good Hope in modern South Africa. On Christmas Day 1497 he reached land, which he named Natal. He then crossed the Indian Ocean, arriving at Calicut May 1498, and returning to Portugal Sept 1499. In 1502 he founded a Portuguese colony at Mozambique.

Gambia, The country in W Africa, bounded N, E, and S by Senegal and W by the Atlantic Ocean. *See panel p. 378*

Gambier Islands island group, part of ◊French Polynesia, administered with the Tuamotu Archipelago; area 14 sq mi/36 sq km; population (1983) 582. It includes four coral islands and many small islets. The main island is Mangareva, with its town Rikitea.

gambling or *gaming* staking of money or anything else of value on the outcome of a competition. Forms of gambling include betting on sports results, casino games like blackjack and roulette, card games such as poker and bridge, slot machines, or lotteries.

gamete cell that functions in sexual reproduction by merging with another gamete to form a ◊zygote. Examples of gametes include sperm and egg cells. In most organisms, the gametes are haploid (they contain half the number of chromosomes of the parent), owing to reduction division or ◊meiosis.

game theory a group of mathematical theories, developed in 1944 by Oscar Morgenstern (1902–1977) and John von Neumann, that seeks to abstract from invented game-playing scenarios and their outcome the essence of situations of conflict and/or cooperation in the real political, business, and social world.

gamma radiation very-high-frequency electromagnetic radiation, similar in nature to X-rays but of shorter wavelength, emitted by the nuclei of radioactive substances during decay or by the interactions of high-energy electrons with matter. Cosmic gamma rays have been identified as coming from pulsars, radio galaxies, and quasars, although they cannot penetrate the Earth's atmosphere.

gamma-ray astronomy the study of gamma rays from space. Much of the radiation detected comes from collisions between hydrogen gas and cosmic rays in our galaxy. Some sources have been identified, including the Crab nebula and the Vela pulsar (the most powerful gamma-ray source detected).

Gandhi Indira (born Nehru) 1917–1984. Indian politician, prime minister of India 1966–77 and 1980–84,

Gambia
Republic of The

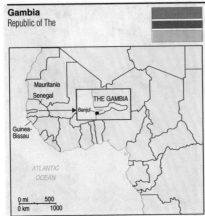

area 4,018 sq mi/10,402 sq km
capital Banjul
cities Serekunda, Bakau, Georgetown
physical banks of the river Gambia flanked by low hills
features smallest state in black Africa; stone circles; Karantaba obelisk marking spot where Mungo Park began his journey to the Niger River 1796
head of state and government Dawda K Jawara from 1970
political system liberal democracy
political parties Progressive People's Party (PPP), moderate centrist; National Convention Party (NCP), left of center
exports groundnuts, palm oil, fish
currency dalasi
population (1992) 921,000; growth rate 1.9% p.a.
life expectancy 42 (1988 est)
languages English (official), Mandinka, Fula and other native tongues
media no daily newspaper; two official weeklies sell about 2,000 copies combined and none of the other independents more than 700
religions Muslim 90%, with animist and Christian minorities
literacy men 36%, women 15% (1985 est)
GDP $189 million (1987); $236 per head

chronology
1843 Gambia became a crown colony.
1965 Independence achieved from Britain as a constitutional monarchy within the Commonwealth, with Dawda K Jawara as prime minister.
1970 Declared itself a republic, with Jawara as president.
1972 Jawara reelected.
1981 Attempted coup foiled with the help of Senegal.
1982 Formed with Senegal the Confederation of Senegambia; Jawara reelected.
1987 Jawara reelected.
1989 Confederation of Senegambia dissolved.
1990 Gambian troops contributed to the stabilizing force in Liberia.

and leader of the Congress Party 1966–77 and subsequently of the Congress (I) party. She was assassinated 1984 by members of her Sikh bodyguard, resentful of her use of troops to clear malcontents from the Sikh temple at ◊Amritsar.

Gandhi Mohandas Karamchand, called *Mahatma* ("Great Soul") 1869–1948. Indian nationalist leader. A pacifist, he led the struggle for Indian independence from the UK by advocating nonviolent noncooperation (*satyagraha*, defense of and by truth) from 1915. He was imprisoned several times by the British authorities and was influential in the nationalist Congress Party and in the independence negotiations 1947. He was assassinated by a Hindu nationalist in the violence that followed the partition of British India into India and Pakistan.

Gandhi Rajiv 1944–1991. Indian politician, prime minister from 1984 (following his mother Indira Gandhi's assassination) to Nov 1989. As prime minister, he faced growing discontent with his party's elitism and lack of concern for social issues. He was assassinated by a bomb at an election rally.

Gandhi Indira Gandhi, Nehru's daughter, had a controversial political career, during which she was twice prime minister of India.

Ganesh Hindu god, son of Siva and Parvati; he is represented as elephant-headed and is worshiped as a remover of obstacles.

Ganges (Hindi *Ganga*) major river of India and Bangladesh; length 1,560 mi/2,510 km.
It is the most sacred river for Hindus.

ganglion (plural *ganglia*) solid cluster of nervous tissue containing many cell bodies and ◊synapses, usually enclosed in a tissue sheath; found in invertebrates and vertebrates.

Gang of Four in Chinese history, the chief members of the radical faction that played a key role in directing the ◊Cultural Revolution and tried to seize power after the death of the communist leader Mao Zedong 1976. It included his widow, ◊Jiang Qing; the other members were three young Shanghai politicians: Zhang Chunqiao, Wang Hongwen, and Yao Wenyuan. The coup failed and the Gang of Four were arrested. Publicly tried in 1980, they were found guilty of treason.

gangrene death and decay of body tissue (often of a limb) due to bacterial action; the affected part gradually turns black and causes blood poisoning.

Gansu or *Kansu* province of NW China
area 204,580 sq mi/530,000 sq km
capital Lanzhou
features subject to earthquakes; the "Silk Road" (now a motor road) passed through it in the Middle Ages, carrying trade to central Asia
products coal, oil, hydroelectric power from the Huang He (Yellow) River
population (1990) 22,371,000, including many Muslims.

Ganymede in Greek mythology, a youth so beautiful he was chosen as cupbearer to Zeus.

Ganymede in astronomy, the largest moon of the planet Jupiter, and the largest moon in the Solar System, 3,270 mi/5,260 km in diameter (larger than the planet Mercury). It orbits Jupiter every 7.2 days at a distance of 700,000 mi/1.1 million km. Its surface is a mixture of cratered and grooved terrain.

Garbo Greta. Adopted name of Greta Lovisa Gustafsson 1905–1990. Swedish-born US film actress. She went to the US in 1925, and her captivating beauty and leading role in *The Torrent* 1926 made her one of Hollywood's first stars in silent films. Her later films include *Mata Hari* 1931, *Grand Hotel* 1932, *Queen Christina* 1933, *Anna Karenina* 1935, *Camille* 1936, and *Ninotchka* 1939. Her qualities of ethereality and romantic mystery on the screen intermingled with her seclusion in private life. She retired 1941.

García Lorca Federico, Spanish poet. See ◊Lorca, Federico García.

García Márquez Gabriel 1928– . Colombian novelist. His sweeping novel *Cien años de soledad/One Hundred Years of Solitude* 1967 (which tells the story of a family over a period of six generations) is an example of magic realism, a technique used to heighten the intensity of realistic portrayal of social and political issues by introducing grotesque or fanciful material. His later work includes *Love in the Time of Cholera* 1988. Nobel Prize for Literature 1982.

García Perez Alan 1949– . Peruvian politician, leader of the moderate, left-wing APRA party; president 1985–90. He inherited an ailing economy and was forced to trim his socialist program.

gardenia subtropical and tropical trees and shrubs of Africa and Asia, genus *Gardenia*, of the madder family Rubiaceae, with evergreen foliage and flattened rosettes of fragrant waxen-looking blooms, often white in color.

Garfield James A(bram) 1831–1881. 20th president of the US 1881, a Republican. A compromise candidate for the presidency, he held office for only four months before being assassinated in a Washington, DC, railroad station by a disappointed office-seeker. His short tenure was marked primarily by struggles within the Republican party over influence and cabinet posts.

Garibaldi Giuseppe 1807–1882. Italian soldier who played a central role in the unification of Italy by conquering Sicily and Naples 1860. From 1834 a member of the nationalist Mazzini's ◊Young Italy society, he was forced into exile until 1848 and again 1849–54. He fought against Austria 1848–49, 1859, and 1866, and led two unsuccessful expeditions to liberate Rome from papal rule in 1862 and 1867.

Garland Judy. Adopted name of Frances Gumm 1922–1969. US singer and actress whose performances are marked by a compelling intensity. Her films include *The Wizard of Oz* (which featured the tune that was to become her theme song, "Over the Rainbow") 1939, *Babes in Arms* 1939, *Strike Up the Band* 1940, *Meet Me in St Louis* 1944, *Easter Parade* 1948, *A Star Is Born* 1954, and *Judgment at Nuremberg* 1961.

garlic perennial plant *Allium sativum* of the lily family Liliaceae, with white flowers. The bulb, made of small segments, or cloves, is used in cooking, and its pungent essence has an active medical ingredient, allyl methyl trisulphide, which prevents blood clotting.

Garner John Nance 1868–1967. US political leader and vice president of the US 1933–41. He served in the US House of Representatives 1903–33. A Democratic leader in the House, he was chosen as Speaker 1931. He later served as vice president during Franklin Roosevelt's first two terms. Opposing Roosevelt's reelection in 1940, Garner retired from public life.

garnet group of silicate minerals with the formula $X_3Y_2(SiO_4)_3$, when X is calcium, magnesium, iron, or

manganese, and Y is iron, aluminum, or chromium. Garnets are used as semiprecious gems (usually pink to deep red) and as abrasives. They occur in metamorphic rocks such as gneiss and schist.

Garrick David 1717–1779. British actor and theater manager. He was a pupil of Samuel ◊Johnson. From 1747 he became joint licensee of the Drury Lane theater with his own company, and instituted a number of significant theatrical conventions including concealed stage lighting and banishing spectators from the stage. He played Shakespearean characters such as Richard III, King Lear, Hamlet, and Benedick, and collaborated with George Colman (1732–1794) in writing the play *The Clandestine Marriage* 1766. He retired from the stage 1766, but continued as a manager.

Garter, Order of the senior British order of knighthood, founded by Edward III in about 1347. Its distinctive badge is a garter of dark blue velvet, with the

Gandhi Mahatma Gandhi with his granddaughters.

García Márquez The power of Gabriel García Márquez's works lies in their innocence, their epic range, and his calm acceptance of the fantastic.

motto of the order, *Honi soit qui mal y pense* ("Shame be to him who thinks evil of it"), in gold letters.

Garvey Marcus (Moziah) 1887–1940. Jamaican political thinker and activist, an early advocate of black nationalism. He founded the UNIA (Universal Negro Improvement Association) in 1914, and moved to the US in 1916, where he established branches in New York and other northern cities. Aiming to achieve human rights and dignity for black people through black pride and economic self-sufficiency, he was considered one of the first militant black nationalists. He led a Back to Africa movement for black Americans to establish a black-governed country in Africa. The Jamaican cult of ◊Rastafarianism is based largely on his ideas.

Gary city in NW Indiana; population (1990) 116,600. It contains the steel and cement works of the US Steel Corporation and was named after E H Gary (1846–1927), its chairman. Cutbacks in steel production have left the city economically depressed.

gas in physics, a form of matter, such as air, in which the molecules move randomly in otherwise empty space, filling any size or shape of container into which the gas is put.

Gascony ancient province of SW France. With Guienne it formed the duchy of Aquitaine in the 12th century; Henry II of England gained possession of it through his marriage to Eleanor of Aquitaine in 1152, and it was often in English hands until 1451. It was then ruled by the king of France until it was united with the French royal domain 1607 under Henry IV.

gasohol motor fuel that is 90% gasoline and 10% ethanol (alcohol). The ethanol is usually obtained by fermentation, followed by distillation, using corn, wheat, potatoes, or sugar cane. It was used in early automobiles before gasoline became economical, and its use was revived during the 1940s war shortage and the energy shortage of the 1970s, for example in Brazil.

gasoline mixture of hydrocarbons derived from petroleum, whose main use is as a fuel for internal combustion engines. It is colorless and highly volatile.

gasoline engine or *piston engine* the most commonly used source of power for motor vehicles, introduced by the German engineers Gottlieb Daimler and Karl Benz 1885. The gasoline engine is a complex piece of machinery made up of about 150 moving parts. It is a reciprocating piston engine (see ◊internal-combustion engine), in which a number of pistons move up and down in cylinders. The motion of the pistons rotates a crankshaft, at the end of which is a heavy flywheel. From the flywheel the power is transferred to the car's driving wheels via the transmission system of clutch, gearbox, and final drive.

Gastonia city in SW North Carolina, directly W of Charlotte; seat of Gaston County; population (1990) 54,700. Its most important industry is textiles. It was the site of a violent labor strike 1929.

gastroenteritis inflammation of the stomach and intestines, giving rise to abdominal pain, vomiting, and diarrhea. It may be caused by food or other poisoning, allergy, or infection, and is dangerous in babies.

gas turbine engine in which burning fuel supplies hot gas to spin a ◊turbine. The most widespread application of gas turbines has been in aviation. All jet engines (see under ◊jet propulsion) are modified gas turbines, and some locomotives and ships also use gas turbines as a power source.

They are also used in industry for generating and pumping purposes.

Gates Horatio *c.* 1727–1806. British-born American military leader. George Washington appointed him brigadier general in the Continental army 1775 at the outbreak of the American Revolution. In command of the Northern Department, Gates won a tide-turning victory at the Battle of Saratoga 1777 after several American losses and retreats.

Gatling Richard Jordan 1818–1903. US inventor of a rapid-fire gun. Patented in 1862, the Gatling gun had ten barrels arranged as a cylinder rotated by a hand crank. Cartridges from an overhead hopper or drum dropped into the breech mechanism, which loaded, fired, and extracted them at a rate of 320 rounds per minute.

It was used in the US Civil War and in the Indian Wars that followed the settling of the American West. It was the precursor of the ◊machine gun.

GATT acronym for ◊General Agreement on Tariffs and Trade.

gauge any scientific measuring instrument—for example, a wire gauge or a pressure gauge. The term is also applied to the width of a railroad or trolley track.

Gauguin Paul 1848–1903. French Post-Impressionist painter. Going beyond the Impressionists' notion of reality, he sought a more direct experience of life in the magical rites of the people and rich colors of the South Sea islands. He disliked theories and rules of painting, and his pictures are Expressionist compositions characterized by his use of pure, unmixed colors. Among his paintings is *Le Christe Jaune* 1889 (Albright-Knox Art Gallery, Buffalo, New York).

Gaul member of the Celtic-speaking peoples who inhabited France and Belgium in Roman times; also their territory. Certain Gauls invaded Italy around 400 BC, sacked Rome 387 BC, and settled between the Alps and the Apennines; this district, known as Cisalpine Gaul, was conquered by Rome in about 225 BC.

gauss unit (symbol Gs) of magnetic induction or magnetic flux density, replaced by the SI unit, the

Gauguin Te Rerioa/The Dream *(1897), Courtauld Collection, London.*

◊tesla, but still commonly used. It is equal to one line of magnetic flux per square centimeter. The Earth's magnetic field is about 0.G s 5, and changes to it over time are measured in gammas (one gamma equals 10^{-5} gauss).

Gaviria (Trujillo) Cesar 1947– . Colombian Liberal Party politician, president from 1990; he was finance minister 1986–87 and minister of government 1987–89. He has supported the extradition of drug traffickers wanted in the US and has sought more US aid in return for stepping up the drug war.

Gawain in Arthurian legend, one of the knights of the Round Table who participated in the quest for the ◊Holy Grail. He is the hero of the 14th-century epic poem *Sir Gawayne and the Greene Knight.*

Gay John 1685–1732. British poet and dramatist. He wrote *Trivia* 1716, a verse picture of 18th-century London. His *The Beggar's Opera* 1728, a "Newgate pastoral" using traditional songs and telling of the love of Polly for highwayman Captain Macheath, was an extraordinarily popular success. Its satiric political touches led to the banning of *Polly,* a sequel.

Gaye Marvin 1939–1984. US soul singer and songwriter whose hits, including "Stubborn Kinda Fellow" 1962, "I Heard It Through the Grapevine" 1968, and "What's Goin' On" 1971, exemplified the Detroit ◊Motown sound.

He was killed by his father.

Gazankulu ◊Black National State in Transvaal province, South Africa, with self-governing status from 1971; population (1985) 497,200.

Gaza Strip strip of land on the Mediterranean Sea, under Israeli administration; capital Gaza; area 140 sq mi/363 sq km; population (1989) 645,000 of which 446,000 are refugees. In 1993 a preliminary accord was signed with Israel, outlining principles for interim Palestinian self-rule in the Gaza Strip.

gazelle any of a number of species of lightly built, fast-running antelopes found on the open plains of Africa and S Asia, especially those of the genus *Gazella.*

Gdan´sk (German *Danzig*) Polish port; population (1990) 465,100. Oil is refined, and textiles, televisions, and fertilizers are produced. In the 1980s there were repeated antigovernment strikes at the Lenin shipyards.

GDP abbreviation for ◊gross domestic product.

gear a toothed wheel that transmits the turning movement of one shaft to another shaft. Gear wheels may be used in pairs, or in threes if both shafts are to turn in the same direction. The gear ratio—the ratio of the number of teeth on the two wheels—determines the torque ratio, the turning force on the output shaft compared with the turning force on the input shaft. The ratio of the angular velocities of the shafts is the inverse of the gear ratio.

gecko any lizard of the family Gekkonidae. Geckos are common worldwide in warm climates, and have large heads and short, stout bodies. Many have no eyelids. Their adhesive toe pads enable them to climb vertically and walk upside down on smooth surfaces in their search for flies, spiders, and other prey. The Texas banded gecko *Coleonyx brevis,* 4.5in/12cm long, is unusual in that it has no toe pads. *See illustration p. 382*

Gehenna another name for ◊hell; in the Old Testament, a valley S of Jerusalem where children were sac-

gazelle Thomson's gazelle from the open plains of Sudan, Kenya, and N Tanzania has a distinctive dark stripe along its sides.

gecko The tokay gecko is one of the largest and most common geckos— 11 in/28 cm long.

rificed to the Phoenician god Moloch and fires burned constantly.

Gehrig Lou (Henry Louis) 1903–1941. US baseball player. Nicknamed "The Iron Horse" for his incomparable stamina and strength, he was signed by the New York Yankees 1923. Voted the American League's most valuable player 1927, 1931, 1934, and 1936, he achieved a remarkable lifetime 493 home runs, a .340 lifetime batting average, and a record 2,130 consecutive games played.

He was elected to the Baseball Hall of Fame 1939.

Geiger Hans 1882–1945. German physicist who produced the Geiger counter. After studying in Germany, he spent the period 1907–12 in Manchester, England, working with Ernest Rutherford on radioactivity. In 1908 they designed an instrument to detect and count ◊alpha particles, positively charged ionizing particles produced by radioactive decay.

In 1928 Geiger and Walther Müller produced a more sensitive version of the counter, which could detect all kinds of ionizing radiation.

Geiger counter any of a number of devices used for detecting nuclear radiation and/or measuring its intensity by counting the number of ionizing particles produced (see ◊radioactivity). It detects the momentary current that passes between ◊electrodes in a suitable gas when a nuclear particle or a radiation pulse causes the ionization of that gas. The electrodes are connected to electronic devices that enable the number of particles passing to be measured. The increased frequency of measured particles indicates the intensity of radiation. It is named after Hans Geiger.

Geisel Theodor Seuss; better known as **Dr Seuss**. 1904–1991. US author of children's books including *And to Think that I Saw It on Mulberry Street* 1937 and the classic *Horton Hatches the Egg* 1940. After winning Academy Awards for documentary films 1946 and 1947, he returned to writing children's books, including *Horton Hears a Who* 1954 and *The Cat in the Hat* 1957.

geisha female entertainer (music, singing, dancing, and conversation) in Japanese teahouses and at private parties. Geishas survive mainly as a tourist attraction. They are apprenticed from childhood and highly skilled in traditional Japanese arts and graces. There are now only approximately 20,000 geishas in Japan compared to 100,000 before World War II.

gel solid produced by the formation of a three-dimensional cage structure, commonly of linked large-molecular-mass polymers, in which a liquid is trapped. It is a form of ◊colloid. A gel may be a jellylike mass (pectin, gelatin) or have a more rigid structure (silica gel).

gelatin water-soluble protein prepared from boiled hide and bone, used in cooking to set jellies, and in glues and photographic emulsions.

Gell-Mann Murray 1929– . US physicist. In 1964 he formulated the theory of the ◊quark as one of the fundamental constituents of matter. In 1969 he was awarded a Nobel Prize for his work on elementary particles and their interaction.

gem mineral valuable by virtue of its durability (hardness), rarity, and beauty, cut and polished for ornamental use, or engraved. Of 120 minerals known to have been used as gemstones, only about 25 are in common use in jewelry today; of these, the diamond, emerald, ruby, and sapphire are classified as precious, and all the others semiprecious, for example the topaz, amethyst, opal, and aquamarine.

Gemayel Amin 1942– . Lebanese politician, a Maronite Christian; president 1982–88. He succeeded his brother, president-elect **Bechir Gemayel** (1947–1982), on his assassination on Sept 14, 1982. The Lebanese parliament was unable to agree on a successor when his term expired, so separate governments were formed under rival Christian and Muslim leaders.

Gemini prominent zodiacal constellation in the northern hemisphere represented as the twins Castor and Pollux. Its brightest star is ◊Pollux; Castor is a system of six stars. The Sun passes through Gemini from late June to late July. Each Dec, the Geminid meteors radiate from Gemini. In astrology, the dates for Gemini are between about May 21 and June 21.

gender in grammar, one of the categories into which nouns are divided in many languages, such as masculine, feminine, and neuter (as in Latin, German, and Russian), masculine and feminine (as in French, Italian, and Spanish), or animate and inanimate (as in some North American Indian languages).

gene unit of inherited material, encoded by a strand of ◊DNA, and transcribed by ◊RNA. In higher organisms, genes are located on the ◊chromosomes. The term "gene," coined 1909 by the Danish geneticist Wilhelm Johannsen (1857–1927), refers to the inherited factor that consistently affects a particular character in an individual—for example, the gene for eye color. Also termed a Mendelian gene, after Austrian biologist Gregor ◊Mendel, it occurs at a particular point or ◊locus on a particular chromosome and may have several variants or alleles, each specifying a particular form of that character—for example, the alleles for blue or brown eyes. Some alleles show ◊dominance. These mask the effect of other alleles known as ◊recessive.

gene amplification technique by which selected DNA from a single cell can be repeatedly duplicated until there is a sufficient amount to analyze by conventional genetic techniques.

gene bank collection of seeds or other forms of genetic material, such as tubers, spores, bacterial or yeast cultures, live animals and plants, frozen sperm and eggs, or frozen embryos. These are stored for possible future use in agriculture, plant and animal breeding, or in medicine, genetic engineering, or the restocking of wild habitats where species have become extinct. Gene banks will be increasingly used as the rate of extinction increases, depleting the Earth's genetic variety (biodiversity).

gene pool total sum of alleles (variants of ◊genes) possessed by all the members of a given population or species alive at a particular time.

General Agreement on Tariffs and Trade (GATT) organization within the United Nations founded 1948 with the aim of encouraging ◊free trade between nations through low tariffs, abolitions of quotas, and curbs on subsidies.

general strike refusal to work by employees in several key industries, with the intention of paralyzing the economic life of a country. In British history, the General Strike was a nationwide strike called by the Trade Union Congress on May 3, 1926, in support of the miners' union. Elsewhere, the general strike was used as a political weapon by anarchists and others (see ◊syndicalism), especially in Spain and Italy.

generator machine that produces electrical energy from mechanical energy, as opposed to an electric motor, which does the opposite. A simple generator (dynamo) consists of a wire-wound coil (◊armature) that is rotated between the poles of a permanent magnet. The movement of the wire in the magnetic field induces a current in the coil by ◊electromagnetic induction, which can be fed by means of a commutator as a continuous direct current into an external circuit. Slip rings instead of a commutator produce an alternating current, when the generator is called an alternator.

Genesis first book of the Old Testament, which includes the stories of the creation of the world, Adam and Eve, the Flood, and the history of the Jewish patriarchs Abraham, Isaac, Jacob, and Joseph (who brought his people to Egypt).

gene-splicing technique for inserting a foreign gene into laboratory cultures of bacteria to generate commercial biological products, such as synthetic insulin, hepatitis-B vaccine, and interferon. It was invented 1973 by the US scientists Stanley Cohen and Herbert Boyer, and patented in the US 1984. See ◊genetic engineering.

Cohen was working at Stanford University and Boyer at the University of California. Cohen shared a 1989 Nobel Prize for Physiology or Medicine for his work in cell growth.

genet small, nocturnal, meat-eating mammal, genus *Genetta*, in the mongoose and civet family (Viverridae). Most species live in Africa, but *G. genetta* is also found in Europe and the Middle East. It is about 1.6 ft/50 cm long with a 1.5 ft/45 cm tail, and grayish yellow with rows of black spots. It climbs well.

Genet Jean 1910–1986. French dramatist, novelist, and poet, an exponent of the Theater of ◊Cruelty. His turbulent life and early years spent in prison are reflected in his drama, characterized by ritual, role-play, and illusion, in which his characters come to act out their bizarre and violent fantasies. His plays include *Les Bonnes/The Maids* 1947, *Le Balcon/The Balcony* 1957, and two plays dealing with the Algerian situation: *Les Nègres/The Blacks* 1959 and *Les Paravents/The Screens* 1961.

genetic code the way in which instructions for building proteins, the basic structural molecules of living matter, are "written" in the genetic material ◊DNA. This relationship between the sequence of bases (the subunits in a DNA molecule) and the sequence of ◊amino acids (the subunits of a protein molecule) is the basis of heredity. The code employs codons of three bases each; it is the same in almost all organisms, except for a few minor differences recently discovered in some protozoa.

genetic disease any disorder caused at least partly by defective genes or chromosomes. In humans there are some 3,000 genetic diseases, including cleft palate, cystic fibrosis, Down syndrome, hemophilia, Huntington's chorea, some forms of anemia, spina bifida, and Tay-Sachs disease.

genetic engineering deliberate manipulation of genetic material by biochemical techniques. It is often achieved by the introduction of new ◊DNA, usually by means of a virus or ◊plasmid. This can be for pure research or to breed functionally specific plants, animals, or bacteria. These organisms with a foreign gene added are said to be transgenic.

genetic fingerprinting technique used for determining the pattern of certain parts of the genetic material ◊DNA that is unique to each individual. Like skin fingerprinting, it can accurately distinguish humans from one another, with the exception of identical siblings from multiple births.

genetics study of inheritance and of the units of inheritance (◊genes). The founder of genetics was Austrian biologist Gregor ◊Mendel, whose experiments with plants, such as peas, showed that inheritance takes place by means of discrete "particles," which later came to be called genes.

Geneva (French *Genève*) Swiss city, capital of Geneva canton, on the shore of Lake Geneva; population (1990) city 167,200; canton 376,000. It is a point of convergence of natural routes and is a cultural and commercial center. Industries include the manufacture of watches, scientific and optical instruments, foodstuffs, jewelry, and musical boxes.

Geneva Convention international agreement 1864 regulating the treatment of those wounded in war, and later extended to cover the types of weapons allowed, the treatment of prisoners and the sick, and the protection of civilians in wartime. The rules were revised at conventions held 1906, 1929, and 1949, and by the 1977 Additional Protocols.

Geneva, Lake (French *Lac Léman*) largest of the central European lakes, between Switzerland and France; area 225 sq mi/580 sq km.

Geneva Protocol international agreement 1925 designed to prohibit the use of poisonous gases, chemical weapons, and bacteriological methods of warfare. It came into force 1928 but was not ratified by the US until 1974.

Genghis Khan *c.* ?1167–1227. Mongol conqueror, ruler of all Mongol peoples from 1206. He began the conquest of N China 1213, overran the empire of the shah of Khiva 1219–25, and invaded N India, while his lieutenants advanced as far as the Crimea. When he died, his empire ranged from the Yellow Sea to the Black Sea; it continued to expand after his death to extend from Hungary to Korea. Genghis Khan controlled probably a larger area than any other individual in history. He was not only a great military leader, but the creator of a stable political system.

Genoa (Italian *Genova*) historic city in NW Italy, capital of Liguria; population (1989) 706,700. It is Italy's largest port; industries include oil-refining, chemicals, engineering, and textiles.

genocide deliberate and systematic destruction of a national, racial, religious, or ethnic group defined by the exterminators as undesirable. The term is commonly applied to the policies of the Nazis during World War II (what they called the "final solution"—the extermination of all "undesirables" in occupied Europe, particularly the Jews). *See* ◊Holocaust.

genome the full complement of ◊genes carried by a single (haploid) set of ◊chromosomes. The term may be applied to the genetic information carried by an individual or to the range of genes found in a given species.

genotype the particular set of alleles (variants of genes) possessed by a given organism. The term is usually used in conjunction with phenotype, which is the product of the genotype and all environmental effects. See also ◊nature–nurture controversy.

genre painting (French *genre* "kind," "type") painting scenes from everyday life. Genre paintings were enormously popular in the Netherlands and Flanders in the 17th century (Vermeer, de Hooch, and Brouwer were great exponents). The term "genre" is also used more broadly to mean a category in the arts, such as landscape painting, or literary forms, such as the detective novel.

Genscher Hans-Dietrich 1927– . German politician, chair of the West German Free Democratic Party (FDP) 1974–85, foreign minister 1974–92. A skilled and pragmatic tactician, Genscher became the reunified Germany's most popular politician.

Gentile da Fabriano *c.* 1370–1427. Italian painter of frescoes and altarpieces in the International Gothic style. Gentile was active in Venice, Florence, Siena, Orvieto, and Rome and collaborated with the artists Pisanello and Jacopo Bellini. *The Adoration of the Magi* 1423 (Uffizi, Florence) is typically rich in detail and crammed with courtly figures.

gentry the lesser nobility, particularly in England and Wales, not entitled to sit in the House of Lords. By the later Middle Ages, it included knights, esquires, and gentlemen, and after the 17th century, baronets.

genus (plural *genera*) group of ◊species with many characteristics in common. Thus all doglike species (including dogs, wolves, and jackals) belong to the genus *Canis* (Latin "dog"). Species of the same genus are thought to be descended from a common ancestor species. Related genera are grouped into ◊families.

geochemistry science of chemistry as it applies to geology. It deals with the relative and absolute abundances of the chemical elements and their ◊isotopes in the Earth, and also with the chemical changes that accompany geologic processes.

geode in geology, a subspherical cavity into which crystals have grown from the outer wall into the center. Geodes often contain very well-formed crystals of quartz (including amethyst), calcite, or other minerals.

geodesy methods of surveying the Earth for making maps and correlating geological, gravitational, and magnetic measurements. Geodesic surveys, formerly carried out by means of various measuring techniques on the surface, are now commonly made by using radio signals and laser beams from orbiting satellites.

geography the study of the Earth's surface; its topography, climate, and physical conditions, and how these factors affect people and society. It is usually divided into *physical geography*, dealing with landforms and climates, and *human geography*, dealing with the distribution and activities of peoples on Earth.

geological time time scale embracing the history of the Earth from its physical origin to the present day. Geological time is traditionally divided into eons (Phanerozoic, Proterozoic, and Archaean), which in turn are divided into eras, periods, epochs, ages, and finally chrons.

geology science of the Earth, its origin, composition, structure, and history. It is divided into several branches: *mineralogy* (the minerals of Earth), *petrology* (rocks), *stratigraphy* (the deposition of successive beds of sedimentary rocks), *paleontology* (fossils), and *tectonics* (the deformation and movement of the Earth's crust).

geometric mean in mathematics, the *n*th root of the product of *n* positive numbers. The geometric mean m of two numbers p and q is such that $m = \sqrt{p \times q}$. For example, the mean of 2 and 8 is $\sqrt{2 \times 8} = \sqrt{16} = \pm 4$.

geometric progression or *geometric sequence* in mathematics, a sequence of terms (progression) in which each term is a constant multiple (called the *common ratio*) of the one preceding it. For example, 3, 12, 48, 192, 768, ... is a geometric progression with a common ratio 4, since each term is equal to the previous term multiplied by 4. Compare ◊arithmetic progression.

geometry branch of mathematics concerned with the properties of space, usually in terms of plane (two-dimensional) and solid (three-dimensional) figures. The subject is usually divided into *pure geometry*, which embraces roughly the plane and solid geometry dealt with in Euclid's *Elements*, and *analytical* or

geological time chart					
eon	era	period	epoch	millions of years ago	life forms
			Holocene	0.01	
		Quaternary	Pleistocene	1.64	humans appeared
			Pliocene	5.2	
	Cenozoic		Miocene	23.5	
		Tertiary	Oligocene	35.5	
			Eocene	56.5	
			Palaeocene	65	mammals flourished
Phanerozoic		Cretaceous		146	heyday of dinosaurs
	Mesozoic	Jurassic		208	first birds
		Triassic		245	first mammals and dinosaurs
		Permian		290	reptiles expanded
		Carboniferous		363	first reptiles
	Palaeozoic	Devonian		409	first amphibians
		Silurian		439	first land plants
		Ordovician		510	first fish
		Cambrian		570	first fossils
	Precambrian	Proterozoic		3,500	earliest living things
		Archaean		4,600	

◊coordinate geometry, in which problems are solved using algebraic methods. A third, quite distinct, type includes the non-Euclidean geometries.

geophysics branch of earth science using physics to study the Earth's surface, interior, and atmosphere. Studies also include winds, weather, tides, earthquakes, volcanoes, and their effects.

George I 1660–1727. King of Great Britain and Ireland from 1714. He was the son of the first elector of Hanover, Ernest Augustus (1629–1698), and his wife ◊Sophia, and a great-grandson of James I. He succeeded to the electorate 1698, and became king on the death of Queen Anne. He attached himself to the Whigs, and spent most of his reign in Hanover, never having learned English.

George II 1683–1760. King of Great Britain from 1727, when he succeeded his father, George I, whom he detested. He married Caroline of Anspach 1705. She supported Robert ◊Walpole's position as adviser, and Walpole rallied support for George during the ◊Jacobite rebellions against him.

George III 1738–1820. King of Great Britain and Ireland from 1760, when he succeeded his grandfather George II. His rule was marked by intransigence resulting in the loss of the American colonies, for which he shared the blame with his chief minister Lord North, and the emancipation of Catholics in England. Possibly suffering from ◊porphyria, he had repeated attacks of insanity, permanent from 1811. He was succeeded by his son George IV.

He was virtually blind in his later years, giving rise to suspicions and misunderstandings concerning documents and decrees for his signature.

George IV 1762–1830. King of Great Britain and Ireland from 1820, when he succeeded his father George III, for whom he had been regent during the king's period of insanity 1811–20. In 1785 he secretly married a Catholic widow, Maria Fitzherbert, but in 1795 also married Princess Caroline of Brunswick, in return for payment of his debts. He was a patron of the arts. His prestige was undermined by his treatment of Caroline (they separated 1796), his dissipation, and his extravagance. He was succeeded by his brother, the duke of Clarence, who became William IV.

George V 1865–1936. King of Great Britain from 1910, when he succeeded his father Edward VII. He was the second son, and became heir 1892 on the death of his elder brother Albert, Duke of Clarence. In 1893, he married Princess Victoria Mary of Teck (Queen Mary), formerly engaged to his brother. During World War I he made several visits to the front. In 1917, he abandoned all German titles for himself and his family. The name of the royal house was changed from Saxe-Coburg-Gotha (popularly known as Brunswick or Hanover) to Windsor.

George VI 1895–1952. King of Great Britain from 1936, when he succeeded after the abdication of his brother Edward VIII, who had succeeded their father George V. Created Duke of York 1920, he married in 1923 Lady Elizabeth Bowes-Lyon (1900–   ), and their children are Elizabeth II and Princess Margaret. During World War II, he visited the Normandy and Italian battlefields.

George I 1845–1913. King of Greece 1863–1913. The son of Christian IX of Denmark, he was nominated to the Greek throne and, in spite of early unpopularity, became a highly successful constitutional monarch. He was assassinated by a Greek, Schinas, at Salonika.

Georgia

George II 1890–1947. King of Greece 1922–23 and 1935–47. He became king on the expulsion of his father Constantine I 1922 but was himself overthrown 1923. Restored by the military 1935, he set up a dictatorship under Joannis Metaxas, and went into exile during the German occupation 1941–45.

George, St patron saint of England. The story of St George rescuing a woman by slaying a dragon, evidently derived from the ◊Perseus legend, first appears in the 6th century. The cult of St George was introduced into W Europe by the Crusaders. His feast day is April 23.

Georgetown capital and port of Guyana, situated at the mouth of the Demerara River on the Caribbean coast; population (1983) 188,000. There is food processing and shrimp fishing.

Georgetown or *Penang* chief port of the Federation of Malaysia, and capital of Penang, on the island of Penang; population (1980) 250,600. It produces textiles and toys.

Georgia state in SE US; nicknames Empire State of the South/Peach State
area 58,904 sq mi/152,600 sq km
capital Atlanta
cities Columbus, Savannah, Macon
features Okefenokee National Wildlife Refuge (656 sq mi/1,700 sq km), Sea Islands, historic Savannah
products poultry, livestock, tobacco, corn, peanuts, cotton, soybeans, kaolinite, crushed granite, textiles, carpets, aircraft, paper products
population (1990) 6,478,200
famous people Jim Bowie; Erskine Caldwell; Jimmy Carter; Ray Charles; Ty Cobb; Bobby Jones; Martin Luther King, Jr; Margaret Mitchell; James Oglethorpe; Jackie Robinson
history explored 1540 by Hernando de Soto; claimed by the British and named after George II of England; founded 1733 as a colony for the industrious poor by James Oglethorpe, a philanthropist; one of the original 13 states of the US.

In 1864, during the Civil War, General W T Sherman's Union troops cut a wide swath of destruction as they marched from Atlanta to the sea. The state benefited after World War II from the growth of Atlanta as the financial and transportation center of the SE US.

Georgia, Republic of country in the Caucasus of SE Europe, bounded N by Russia, E by Azerbaijan, S by Armenia, and W by the Black Sea. *See panel p. 386*

Georgian period of English architecture, furniture making, and decorative art between 1714 and 1830. The architecture is mainly Classical in style, although external details and interiors were often rich in Rococo carving. Furniture was frequently made of mahogany and satinwood, and mass production became increasingly common; designers included Thomas Chippendale, George Hepplewhite, and Thomas Sheraton. The

Georgia
Republic of

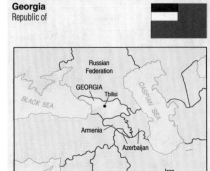

area 26,911 sq mi/69,700 sq km
capital Tbilisi
cities Kutaisi, Rustavi, Batumi, Sukhumi
physical largely mountainous with a variety of landscape from the subtropical Black Sea shores to the ice and snow of the crest line of the Caucasus; chief rivers are Kura and Rioni
features holiday resorts and spas on the Black Sea; good climate; two autonomous republics, Abkhazia and Adzharia; one autonomous region, South Ossetia
head of state Eduard Shevardnadze from 1992
head of government Tengiz Sigua from 1992
political system emergent democracy
political parties Georgian Popular Front, nationalist; Democratic National Party of Georgia, left of center; National Independence Party, nationalist
products tea, citrus and orchard fruits, tung oil, tobacco, vines, silk, hydroelectricity
population (1992) 5,482,000 (Georgian 70%, Armenian 8%, Russian 8%, Azeri 6%, Ossetian 3%, Abkhazian 2%)

language Georgian
religion Georgian Church, independent of the Russian Orthodox Church since 1917
GNP $24,030,000 (1990); $4,410 per head

chronology
1918–21 Independent republic.
1921 Uprising quelled by Red Army, and Soviet republic established.
1922–36 Linked with Armenia and Azerbaijan as the Transcaucasian Republic.
1936 Became separate republic within USSR.
1972 Drive against corruption by Georgian Communist Party (GCP) leader Eduard Shevardnadze.
1978 Outbreaks of violence by nationalists.
1981–88 Increasing demands for autonomy, spearheaded from 1988 by the Georgian Popular Front.
1989 March–April: Abkhazians demanded secession from Georgia, provoking interethnic clashes. April: GCP leadership purged. July: state of emergency imposed in Abkhazia; interethnic clashes in South Ossetia. Nov: economic and political sovereignty declared.
1990 March: GCP monopoly ended. Oct: nationalist coalition triumphed in supreme-soviet elections. Nov: Zviad Gamsakhurdia became president. Dec: GCP seceded from Communist Party of USSR; calls for Georgian independence.
1991 April: declared independence. May: Gamsakhurdia popularly elected president. Aug: GCP outlawed and all relations with USSR severed. Sept: anti-Gamsakhurdia demonstrations; state of emergency declared. Dec: Georgia failed to join new Commonwealth of Independent States (CIS).
1992 Jan: Gamsakhurdia fled to Armenia; Tengiz Sigua appointed prime minister; Georgia admitted into Conference on Security and Cooperation in Europe. Eduard Shevardnadze appointed interim president. July: admitted into United Nations. Aug: fighting started between Georgian troops and Abkhazian separatists in Abkhazia in NW. Oct: Shevardnadze elected chair of new parliament. Clashes in South Ossetia and Abkhazia continued.
1993 Increased fighting with separatists. Georgia joined CIS.

silver of this period is particularly fine, and ranges from the earlier, simple forms to the ornate, and from the Neo-Classical style of Robert Adam to the later, more decorated pre-Victorian taste.

geothermal energy energy extracted for heating and electricity generation from natural steam, hot water, or hot dry rocks in the Earth's crust. Water is pumped down through an injection well where it passes through joints in the hot rocks. It rises to the surface through a recovery well and may be converted to steam or run through a heat exchanger. Dry steam may be directed through turbines to produce electricity. It is a important source of energy in volcanically active areas such as Iceland and New Zealand.

geranium or cranesbill, plant of the genus *Geranium*, family Geraniaceae, which contains about 400 species. The plants are named after the long, beaklike process attached to the seed vessels. When ripe, this splits into coiling spirals, which jerk the seeds out, assisting in their distribution.

gerbil any of numerous rodents of the family Cricetidae with elongated back legs and good hopping or jumping ability. Gerbils range from mouse- to rat-size, and have hairy tails. Many of the 13 genera live in dry, sandy, or sparsely vegetated areas of Africa and Asia.

Géricault Théodore (Jean Louis André) 1791–1824. French Romantic painter. *The Raft of the Medusa* 1819 (Louvre, Paris) was notorious for exposing a rel-

atively recent scandal in which shipwrecked sailors had been cut adrift and left to drown. He painted *The Derby at Epsom* 1821 (Louvre, Paris) and pictures of cavalry. He also painted portraits.

germ colloquial term for a microorganism that causes disease, such as certain ◊bacteria and ◊viruses. Formerly, it was also used to mean something capable of developing into a complete organism (such as a fertilized egg, or the ◊embryo of a seed).

German native to or an inhabitant of Germany and their descendants, as well as their culture and language. In eastern Germany the Sorbs comprise a minority population who, in addition to German, speak a Slavic language. The Austrians and Swiss Germans speak German, although they are ethnically distinct. German-speaking minorities are found in France (Alsace-Lorraine), Romania (Transylvania), Czech Republic, Siberian Russia, Central Asia, Poland, Italy (Tyrol), and in areas that once belonged to the German Empire abroad.

Germanic languages branch of the Indo-European language family, divided into *East Germanic* (Gothic, now extinct), *North Germanic* (Danish, Faroese, Icelandic, Norwegian, Swedish), and *West Germanic* (Afrikaans, Dutch, English, Flemish, Frisian, German, Yiddish).

Germanicus Caesar 15 BC–AD 19. roman general. He was the adopted son of the emperor ◊Tiberius and married the emperor ◊Augustus' granddaughter Agrippina. Although he refused the suggestion of his troops that he claim the throne on the death of Augustus, his military victories in Germany made Tiberius jealous. Sent to the Middle East, he died near Antioch, possibly murdered at the instigation of Tiberius. He was the father of ◊Caligula and Agrippina, mother of ◊Nero.

germanium brittle, gray-white, weakly metallic (◊metalloid) element, symbol Ge, atomic number 32, atomic weight 72.6. It belongs to the silicon group, and has chemical and physical properties between those of silicon and tin. Germanium is a semiconductor material and is used in the manufacture of transistors and integrated circuits. The oxide is transparent to

infrared radiation, and is used in military applications. It was discovered 1886 by German chemist Clemens Winkler (1838–1904).

German language member of the Germanic group of the Indo-European language family, the national language of Germany and Austria, and an official language of Switzerland. There are many spoken varieties of German, including High German (*Hochdeutsch*) and Low German (*Plattdeutsch*).

German measles or *rubella* mild, communicable virus disease, usually caught by children. It is marked by a sore throat, pinkish rash, and slight fever, and has an incubation period of two to three weeks. If a woman contracts it in the first three months of pregnancy, it may cause serious damage to the unborn child.

Germany
Federal Republic of
(*Bundesrepublik Deutschland*)

area 137,853 sq mi/357,041 sq km
capital Berlin
cities Cologne, Munich, Essen, Frankfurt-am-Main, Dortmund, Stuttgart, Düsseldorf, Leipzig, Dresden, Chemnitz, Magdeburg; ports Hamburg, Kiel, Cuxhaven, Bremerhaven, Rostock
physical flat in N, mountainous in S with Alps; rivers Rhine, Weser, Elbe flow N, Danube flows SE, Oder, Neisse flow N along Polish frontier; many lakes, including Müritz
environment acid rain causing *Waldsterben* (tree death) affects more than half the country's forests; industrial E Germany has the highest sulfur-dioxide emissions in the world per head of population
features Black Forest, Harz Mountains, Erzgebirge (Ore Mountains), Bavarian Alps, Fichtelgebirge, Thüringer Forest
head of state Richard von Weizsäcker from 1984
head of government Helmut Kohl from 1982
political system liberal democratic federal republic
political parties Christian Democratic Union (CDU), right of center; Christian Social Union (CSU), right of center; Social Democratic Party (SPD), left of center; Free Democratic Party (FDP), liberal; Greens, environmentalist; Republicans, far right; Party of Democratic Socialism (PDS), reform-communist (formerly Socialist Unity Party: SED)
exports machine tools (world's leading exporter), automobiles, commercial vehicles, electronics, industrial goods, textiles, chemicals, iron, steel, wine, lignite (world's largest producer), uranium, coal, fertilizers, plastics
currency Deutschmark
population (1992) 80,293,000 (including nearly 5,000,000 "guest workers," *Gastarbeiter*, of whom 1,600,000 are Turks;

the rest are Yugoslav, Italian, Greek, Spanish, and Portuguese); growth rate –0.7% p.a.
life expectancy men 68, women 74
languages German, Sorbian
religions Protestant 42%, Roman Catholic 35%
literacy 99% (1985)
GNP $1,775.1 bn (1992)

chronology
1945 Germany surrendered; country divided into four occupation zones (US, French, British, Soviet).
1948 Blockade of West Berlin.
1949 Establishment of Federal Republic under the "Basic Law" Constitution with Konrad Adenauer as chancellor; establishment of the German Democratic Republic as an independent state.
1953 Uprising in East Berlin suppressed by Soviet troops.
1954 Grant of full sovereignty to both West Germany and East Germany.
1957 West Germany was a founder-member of the European Economic Community; recovery of Saarland from France.
1961 Construction of Berlin Wall.
1963 Retirement of Chancellor Adenauer.
1964 Treaty of Friendship and Mutual Assistance signed between East Germany and USSR.
1969 Willy Brandt became chancellor of West Germany.
1971 Erich Honecker elected SED leader in East Germany.
1972 Basic Treaty between West Germany and East Germany; treaty ratified 1973, normalizing relations between the two.
1974 Resignation of Brandt; Helmut Schmidt became chancellor.
1975 East German friendship treaty with USSR renewed for 25 years.
1982 Helmut Kohl became West German chancellor.
1987 Official visit of Honecker to the Federal Republic.
1988 Death of Franz-Josef Strauss, leader of the West German Bavarian CSU.
1989 West Germany: rising support for far right in local and European elections, declining support for Kohl. East Germany: mass exodus to West Germany began. Honecker replaced by Egon Krenz. National borders opened in Nov, including Berlin Wall. Reformist Hans Modrow appointed prime minister. Krenz replaced.
1990 March: East German multiparty elections won by a coalition led by the right-wing CDU. Oct 3: official reunification of East and West Germany. Dec 2: first all-German elections since 1932, resulting in a victory for Kohl.
1991 Kohl's popularity declined after tax increase. The CDU lost its Bundesrat majority to the SPD. Racism continued with violent attacks on foreigners.
1992 Neo-Nazi riots against immigrants continued.
1993 Unemployment exceeded 7%; severe recession. Outbreaks of racist violence. Restrictions on refugee admission introduced.

Germany

North Sea

Baltic Sea

Flensburg

Heligoland

Frisian Islands

Kiel

SCHLESWIG-
HOLSTEIN

Rügen

Stralsund

Rostock

Lübeck

Wismar

Bremerhaven

Hamburg

Schwerin

MECKLENBURG-WEST POMERANIA

Neubrandenburg

Groningen

Oldenburg

Bremen

NETHERLANDS

LOWER SAXONY

Osnabrück

Hanover

Wolfsburg

Berlin

Hildesheim

Brunswick

Brandenburg

Potsdam

Magdeburg

BRANDENBURG

NORTH RHINE-
WESTPHALIA

Bielefeld

Paderborn

Salzgitter-Bad

SAXONY-
ANHALT

Dessau

Cottbus

Hamm

Harz Mts

Göttingen

Halle

Leipzig

Essen

Dortmund

Duisburg

Hagen

Düsseldorf

Wuppertal

Kassel

Meissen

Dresden

Mönchengladbach

Cologne

Bonn

Siegen

Marburg

Weimar

Erfurt

Jena

Gera

SAXONY

Chemnitz

BELGIUM

Giessen

Fulda

THURINGIA

Koblenz

HESSE

Wiesbaden

Frankfurt

Mainz

LUX.

Trier

RHINELAND-
PALATINATE

Darmstadt

Würzburg

Bayreuth

Prague

SAARLAND

Mannheim

Saarbrücken

Heilbronn

Erlangen

Nuremberg

CZECH REPUBLIC

FRANCE

N

Pforzheim

Stuttgart

Tübingen

BADEN-WÜRTTEMBERG

Ulm

Augsburg

Ingolstadt

BAVARIA

Regensburg

Munich

Freiburg

Lake
Constance

Danube

Bavarian Alps

Salzburg

Zurich

AUSTRIA

SWITZERLAND

POLAND

Oder

Elbe

Weser

Spree

Neisse

Thuringian Forest

Bohemian Forest

Moselle

Rhine

Black Forest

For this reason immunization is recommended for girls.

German Shepherd see ◊Alsatian, a breed of dog.

German Spring offensive Germany's final offensive on the Western Front during World War I. By early 1918, German forces outnumbered the Allies on the Western Front. Germany staged three offensives, culminating in the Second Battle of the Marne, fought between July 15 and Aug 6. It marked the turning point of World War I. After winning the battle the Allies advanced steadily. By Sept Germany had lost all the territory it had gained during the Spring.

Germany Federal Republic of; country in central Europe, bounded N by the North and Baltic Seas and Denmark, E by Poland and the Czech Republic, S by Austria and Switzerland, and W by France, Luxembourg, Belgium, and the Netherlands. *See panel p. 387*

Germany, East (German Democratic Republic, GDR) country 1949–90, formed from the Soviet zone of occupation in the partition of Germany following World War II. East Germany became a sovereign state 1954, and was reunified with West Germany Oct 1990.

Germany, West (Federal Republic of Germany) country 1949–90, formed from the British, US, and French occupation zones in the partition of Germany following World War II; reunified with East Germany Oct 1990.

germination in botany, the initial stages of growth in a seed, spore, or pollen grain. Seeds germinate when they are exposed to favorable external conditions of moisture, light, and temperature, and when any factors causing dormancy have been removed.

Geronimo 1829–1909. Chief of the Chiricahua Apache Indians and war leader. From 1875 to 1885, he fought US federal troops, as well as settlers encroach-

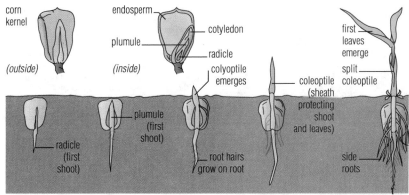

ing on tribal reservations in the Southwest, especially in SE Arizona and New Mexico. Geronimo fell from his horse following a drinking spree and lay on the cold ground overnight, resulting in his death from pneumonia. *See illustration p. 390*

Gershwin George 1898–1937. US composer who wrote both "serious" music, such as the tone poem "Rhapsody in Blue" 1924 and "An American in Paris" 1928, and popular musicals and songs, many with lyrics by his brother *Ira Gershwin* (1896–1983), including "I Got Rhythm," "'S Wonderful," and "Embraceable You."

His opera *Porgy and Bess* 1935 was an ambitious work that incorporated jazz rhythms and popular song styles in an operatic format.

Although his scores to musicals made him famous, his "serious" work earned him much critical acclaim. *Of Thee I Sing* 1931, a collaboration between the Gershwin brothers, was the first musical to win a Pulitzer prize.

gerund in the grammar of certain languages, such as Latin, a noun formed from a verb and functioning as a noun to express an action or state. In English, gerunds end in *-ing.*

Gesell Arnold Lucius 1880–1961. US psychologist and educator. He founded the Yale Clinic of Child Development which he directed 1911–48. Among the first to study the stages of normal development, he worked as a consultant to The Gesell Institute of Child Development, New Haven, Connecticut, which was founded 1950 to promote his educational ideas.

gestalt concept of a unified whole that is greater than, or different from, the sum of its parts; that is, a complete structure whose nature is not explained simply by analyzing its constituent elements. A chair, for example, will generally be recognized as a chair despite great variations between individual chairs in such attributes as size, shape, and color. The term was first used in psychology in Germany about 1910. It has been adopted from German because there is no exact equivalent in English.

Gestapo (contraction of *Geheime Staatspolizei*) Nazi Germany's secret police, formed 1933, and under the direction of Heinrich Himmler from 1936.

gestation in all mammals except the monotremes (duck-billed platypus and spiny anteaters), the period from the time of implantation of the embryo in the uterus to birth. This period varies among species; in humans it is about 266 days, in elephants 18–22 months, in cats about 60 days, and in some species of marsupial (such as opossum) as short as 12 days.

Gethsemane site of the garden where Judas Iscariot, according to the New Testament, betrayed Jesus. It is on the Mount of Olives, E of Jerusalem. When Jerusalem was divided between Israel and Jordan 1948, Gethsemane fell within Jordanian territory.

Getty J(ean) Paul 1892–1976. US oil billionaire, president of the Getty Oil Company from 1947, and founder of the Getty Museum (housing the world's highest-funded art gallery) in Malibu, California.

Gettysburg site in Pennsylvania of a decisive battle of the American ◊Civil War 1863, won by the North. The site is now a national cemetery, at the dedication of which President Lincoln delivered the *Gettysburg Address* Nov 19, 1863, a speech in which he reiterated the principles of freedom, equality, and democracy embodied in the US Constitution.

Getz Stan(ley) 1927–1991. US tenor saxophonist of the 1950s cool jazz school, closely identified with the Latin American bossa nova sound, which gave him a hit single, "The Girl from Ipanema" 1964. He is regarded as one of the foremost tenor-sax players of his generation.

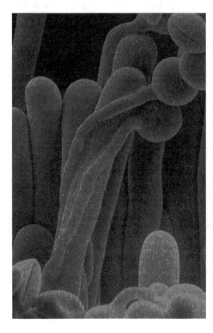

germination *False-color electron-microscope view of pollen grains germinating on the stigma of the opium poppy.*

Geronimo Apache Indian chief Geronimo, who led his people against white settlers in Arizona for over ten years, shown here after his surrender 1886.

geyser natural spring that intermittently discharges an explosive column of steam and hot water into the air due to the buildup of steam in underground chambers. One of the most remarkable geysers is Old Faithful, in Yellowstone National Park, Wyoming. Geysers also occur in New Zealand and Iceland.

G-force force that pilots and astronauts experience when their craft accelerate or decelerate rapidly. One G is the ordinary pull of gravity. Early astronauts were subjected to launch and reentry forces of up to six G or more; in the Space Shuttle, more than three G is experienced on liftoff. Pilots and astronauts wear G-suits that prevent their blood "pooling" too much under severe G-forces, which can lead to unconsciousness.

geyser Old Faithful, Yellowstone National Park, Wyoming.

Ghana country in W Africa, bounded N by Burkina Faso, E by Togo, S by the Gulf of Guinea, and W by the Ivory Coast.

Ghana, ancient trading empire that flourished in NW Africa between the 5th and 13th centuries. Founded by the Soninke people, the Ghana Empire was based, like the ◊Mali Empire that superseded it, on the Saharan gold trade. Trade consisted mainly of the exchange of gold from inland deposits for salt from the coast. At its peak in the 11th century, it occupied an area that includes parts of present-day Mali, Senegal, and Mauritania. Wars with the Berber tribes of the Sahara led to its fragmentation and collapse in the 13th century, when much of its territory was absorbed into Mali.

Ghats, Eastern and Western twin mountain ranges in S India, E and W of the central plateau; a few peaks reach about 9,800 ft/3,000 m. The name is a European misnomer, the Indian word *ghat* meaning "pass," not "mountain."

gherkin young or small green ◊cucumber, used for pickling.

ghetto (Old Venetian *gèto* "foundry") any deprived area occupied by a minority group, whether voluntarily or not. Originally a ghetto was the area of a town where Jews were compelled to live, decreed by a law enforced by papal bull 1555. The term came into use 1516 when the Jews of Venice were expelled to an island within the city which contained an iron foundry. Ghettos were abolished, except in E Europe, in the 19th century, but the concept and practice were revived by the Germans and Italians 1940–45.

Ghirlandaio Domenico *c.* 1449–1494. Italian fresco painter, head of a large and prosperous workshop in Florence. His fresco cycle 1486–90 in Sta Maria Novella, Florence, includes portraits of many Florentines and much contemporary domestic detail. He also worked in Pisa, Rome, and San Gimignano, and painted portraits.

GI abbreviation for *government issue*; hence (in the US) a common soldier.

Giacometti Alberto 1901–1966. Swiss sculptor and painter who trained in Italy and Paris. In the 1930s, in his Surrealist period, he began to develop his characteristic spindly constructions. His mature style of emaciated single figures, based on wire frames, emerged in the 1940s.

Giambologna (Giovanni da Bologna or Jean de Boulogne) 1529–1608. Flemish-born sculptor active mainly in Florence and Bologna. In 1583 he completed his public commission for the Loggia dei Lanzi in Florence, *The Rape of the Sabine Women*, a dynamic group of muscular figures and a prime example of Mannerist sculpture.

gibbon any of several small S Asian apes of the genus *Hylobates*, including the subgenus *Symphalangus*. The common or lar gibbon *H. lar* is about 2 ft/ 60 cm tall, with a body that is hairy except for the buttocks, which distinguishes it from other types of apes. Gibbons have long arms and no tail. They are arboreal in habit, being very agile when swinging from branch to branch. On the ground they walk upright, and are easily caught by predators.

Gibbon Edward 1737–1794. British historian, author of *The History of the Decline and Fall of the Roman Empire* 1776–88.

Gibbons v Ogden US Supreme Court decision 1824 dealing with states' intervention in the regulation of

Ghana
Republic of

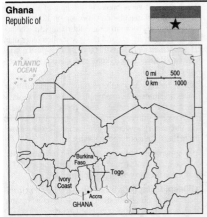

area 91,986 sq mi/238,305 sq km
capital Accra
cities Kumasi, and ports Sekondi-Takoradi, Tema
physical mostly tropical lowland plains; bisected by river Volta
environment forested areas shrank from 3.17 million sq mi/8.2 million sq km at the beginning of the 20th century to 730,000 sq mi/1.9 million sq km by 1990
features world's largest artificial lake, Lake Volta; relics of traditional kingdom of Ashanti: 32,000 chiefs and kings
head of state and government Jerry Rawlings from 1981
political system emergent democracy
exports cocoa, coffee, timber, gold, diamonds, manganese, bauxite

currency cedi
population (1992) 15,237,000; growth rate 3.2% p.a.
life expectancy men 50, women 54
languages English (official) and African languages
media all media are government-controlled and the two daily newspapers are government-owned
religion animist 38%, Muslim 30%, Christian 24%
literacy men 64%, women 43% (1985 est)
GNP $3.9 bn (1983); $420 per head

chronology
1957 Independence achieved from Britain, within the Commonwealth, with Kwame Nkrumah as president.
1960 Ghana became a republic.
1964 Ghana became a one-party state.
1966 Nkrumah deposed and replaced by General Joseph Ankrah.
1969 Ankrah replaced by General Akwasi Afrifa, who initiated a return to civilian government.
1970 Edward Akufo-Addo elected president.
1972 Another coup placed Col Acheampong at the head of a military government.
1978 Acheampong deposed in a bloodless coup led by Frederick Akuffo; another coup put Flight-Lt Jerry Rawlings in power.
1979 Return to civilian rule under Hilla Limann.
1981 Rawlings seized power again, citing the incompetence of previous governments. All political parties banned.
1989 Coup attempt against Rawlings foiled.
1992 New multiparty constitution approved. Partial lifting of ban on political parties. Nov: Rawlings won presidency in national elections.
1993 Fourth republic of Ghana formally inaugurated in Rawlings's presence.

---

interstate commerce. The conflict arose when New York State issued an injunction against Gibbons prohibiting his steamboat operation between New York and New Jersey. Although Gibbons was federally licensed, his business was in violation of a state law that granted to Ogden a monopoly on all steamboat operation in New York. Gibbons appealed to the US Supreme Court, which ruled that the New York law was de facto interference with the federal regulation of interstate commerce and therefore was unconstitutional.

Gibraltar British dependency, situated on a narrow rocky promontory in S Spain
area 2.5 sq mi/6.5 sq km
features strategic naval and air base, with NATO underground headquarters and communications center; colony of Barbary apes; the frontier zone is adjoined by the Spanish port of La Línea
exports mainly a trading center for the import and reexport of goods
population (1988) 30,000
history captured from Spain 1704 by English admiral George Rooke (1650–1709), it was ceded to Britain under the Treaty of Utrecht 1713. A referendum 1967 confirmed the wish of the people to remain in association with the UK, but Spain continues to claim sovereignty and closed the border 1969–85. In 1989, the UK government announced it would reduce the military garrison by half. Ground troop withdrawals began March 1991, but navy and airforce units remained.

Gibraltar, Strait of strait between N Africa and Spain, with the Rock of Gibraltar to the N and Jebel Musa to the S, the so-called Pillars of Hercules.

Gibson Althea 1927– . US tennis player, the first black American woman to compete at the US Champi-

onships at Forest Hills 1950 and at Wimbledon 1951. In 1957 she took both the women's singles and doubles titles at Wimbledon and the singles at Forest Hills. In 1958 she successfully defended all three titles.

Gide André 1869–1951. French novelist, born in Paris. His work is largely autobiographical and concerned with the dual themes of self-fulfilment and renunciation. It includes *L'Immoraliste/The Immoralist* 1902, *La Porte étroite/Strait Is the Gate* 1909, *Les Caves du Vatican/The Vatican Cellars* 1914, and *Les Faux-monnayeurs/The Counterfeiters* 1926; and an almost lifelong *Journal*. Nobel Prize for Literature 1947.

Gideon v Wainwright US Supreme Court decision 1963 dealing with the right of accused persons who are unable to afford legal assistance to a court-appointed lawyer. Prior to this case, only those defendants being tried for capital offenses were guaranteed counsel. Clarence Gideon, a Florida man accused only of a felony, was forced by poverty to defend himself. He was convicted but appealed his conviction, arguing that his constitutional right to a lawyer had been denied. The Court ordered a retrial, ruling that states must provide counsel for felony-case defendants who are too poor to provide their own.

Gielgud John 1904– . English actor and director, renowned as one of the greatest Shakespearean actors of his time. He made his debut at the Old Vic 1921, and his numerous stage appearances ranged from roles in works by Chekhov and Sheridan to those of Alan Bennett, Harold Pinter, and David Story.
  Gielgud's films include *Becket* 1964, *Oh! What a Lovely War* 1969, *Providence* 1977, and *Prospero's Books* 1991. He won an Academy Award for his role as a butler in *Arthur* 1981.

Giffard Henri 1825–1882. French inventor of the first passenger-carrying powered and steerable airship, called a dirigible, built 1852. The hydrogen-filled airship was 144 ft/43 m long, had a 3-hp steam engine that drove a three-bladed propeller, and was steered using a saillike rudder. It flew at an average speed of 3 mph/5 kph.

The first flight was on Sept 24, 1852.

gila monster lizard *Heloderma suspectum* of SW US and Mexico. It is one of the only two existing venomous lizards, the other being the Mexican beaded lizard of the same genus. It has poison glands in its lower jaw, but its bite is not usually fatal to humans.

Gilbert Cass 1859–1934. US architect, major developer of the ◊skyscraper. He designed the Woolworth Building, New York, 1913, the highest building in America (868 ft/265 m) when built and famous for its use of Gothic decorative detail.

He was also architect of the US Supreme Court building in Washington, DC, the Minnesota state capitol in St Paul, and the US Customs House in New York City.

Gilbert W(illiam) S(chwenk) 1836–1911. British humorist and dramatist who collaborated with composer Arthur ◊Sullivan, providing the libretti for their series of light comic operas from 1871; they include *HMS Pinafore* 1878, *The Pirates of Penzance* 1879, and *The Mikado* 1885.

Gilbert Walter 1932– . US molecular biologist who studied genetic control, seeking the mechanisms that switch genes on and off. By 1966 he had established the existence of the *lac* repressor, the molecule that suppresses lactose production. Further work on the sequencing of ◊DNA nucleotides won him a share of the 1980 Nobel Prize for Chemistry, with Frederick Sanger and Paul Berg.

Gilbert William 1544–1603. English scientist and physician to Elizabeth I and (briefly) James I. He studied magnetism and static electricity, deducing that the Earth's magnetic field behaves as if a bar magnet joined the North and South poles. His book on magnets, published 1600, is the first printed scientific book based wholly on experimentation and observation.

Gilbert and Ellice Islands former British colony in the Pacific, known since independence 1978 as the countries of ◊Tuvalu and ◊Kiribati.

Gilgamesh hero of Sumerian, Hittite, Akkadian, and Assyrian legend, and lord of the Sumerian city of

Uruk. The 12 verse books of the *Epic of Gilgamesh* were recorded in a standard version on 12 cuneiform tablets by the Assyrian king Ashurbanipal's scholars in the 7th century BC, and the epic itself is older than Homer's *Iliad* by at least 1,500 years. One-third mortal and two-thirds divine, Gilgamesh is lord of the Sumerian city of Uruk.

gill in biology, the main respiratory organ of most fishes and immature amphibians, and of many aquatic invertebrates. In all types, water passes over the gills, and oxygen diffuses across the gill membranes into the circulatory system, while carbon dioxide passes from the system out into the water.

gill imperial unit of volume for liquid measure, equal to one-quarter of a pint or four fluid ounces (0.118 liter). It is used in selling alcoholic drinks.

Gillespie Dizzy (John Birks) 1917–1993. US jazz trumpeter who, with Charlie ◊Parker, was the chief creator and exponent of the ◊bebop style (*Groovin' High* is a CD reissue of their seminal 78-rpm recordings).

Gillespie influenced many modern jazz trumpeters, including Miles Davis.

gin (Dutch *jenever* "juniper") alcoholic drink made by distilling a mash of corn, malt, or rye, with juniper flavoring. It was first produced in the Netherlands.

ginger SE Asian reedlike perennial *Zingiber officinale*, family Zingiberaceae; the hot-tasting underground root is used as a condiment and in preserves.

ginger ale sweetened, carbonated drink containing ginger flavoring, sugar, and syrup.

Ginsberg Allen 1926– . US poet. His "Howl" 1956, an influential poem of the ◊Beat Generation, criticizes the materialism of contemporary US society. In the 1960s Ginsberg traveled widely in Asia and was a key figure in introducing Eastern thought to students of that decade.

ginseng plant *Panax ginseng*, family Araliaceae, with a thick, forked aromatic root used in medicine as a tonic.

Giolitti Giovanni 1842–1928. Italian liberal politician, born in Mondovi. He was prime minister 1892–93, 1903–05, 1906–09, 1911–14, and 1920–21. He opposed Italian intervention in World War I and pursued a policy of broad coalitions, which proved ineffective in controlling Fascism after 1921.

Giorgione del Castelfranco *c.* 1475–1510. Italian Renaissance painter, active in Venice, probably trained by Giovanni Bellini. His work influenced Titian and other Venetian painters. His subjects are imbued with a sense of mystery and treated with a soft technique, reminiscent of Leonardo da Vinci's later works, as in *The Tempest* 1504 (Accademia, Venice).

Giotto space probe built by the European Space Agency to study ◊Halley's comet. Launched by an Ariane rocket in July 1985, *Giotto* passed within 375 mi/600 km of the comet's nucleus on March 13, 1986. On July 2, 1990, it flew 14,000 mi/23,000 km from Earth, which diverted its path to encounter another comet, Grigg-Skjellerup, on July 10, 1992.

Giotto di Bondone 1267–1337. Italian painter and architect. He broke away from the conventional Gothic style of the time, and introduced a naturalistic style, painting saints as real people. He painted cycles of frescoes in churches at Assisi, Florence, and Padua.

giraffe world's tallest mammal, *Giraffa camelopardalis*, belonging to the ruminant family Giraffidae. It stands over 18 ft/5.5 m tall, the neck accounting for

giraffe The giraffe is a specialized offshoot of the deer family.

nearly half this amount. The giraffe has two to four small, skin-covered, hornlike structures on its head and a long, tufted tail. The skin has a mottled appearance and is reddish brown and cream. Giraffes are found only in Africa, south of the Sahara Desert.

Giscard d'Estaing Valéry 1926– . French conservative politician, president 1974–81. He was finance minister to de Gaulle 1962–66 and Pompidou 1969–74. As leader of the Union pour la Démocratie Française, which he formed in 1978, Giscard sought to project himself as leader of a "new center."

Gish Lillian. Adopted name of Lillian de Guiche 1896–1993.

US film and stage actress who worked with the director D W Griffith, playing virtuous heroines in *Way Down East* and *Orphans of the Storm* both 1920. Deceptively fragile, she made a notable Hester in Victor Sjöström's *The Scarlet Letter* (based on the novel by Nathaniel Hawthorne). Her career continued well into the 1980s with movies such as *The Whales of August* 1987. She was the sister of the actress *Dorothy Gish* (1898–1968).

Gîza, El or *al-Jizah* site of the Great Pyramids and Sphinx; a suburb of ⬦Cairo, Egypt; population (1983) 1,500,000. It has textile and film industries.

gizzard muscular grinding organ of the digestive tract, below the crop of birds, earthworms, and some insects, and forming part of the ⬦stomach. The gizzard of birds is lined with a hardened horny layer of the protein keratin, preventing damage to the muscle layer during the grinding process. Most birds swallow sharp grit which aids maceration of food in the gizzard.

glacial trough or *U-shaped valley* steep-sided, flat-bottomed valley formed by a glacier. The erosive action of the glacier and of the debris carried by it results in the formation not only of the trough itself but also of a number of associated features, such as truncated spurs (projections of rock that have been sheared off by the ice) and hanging valleys (smaller glacial valleys that enter the trough at a higher level than the trough floor). Features characteristic of glacial deposition, such as drumlins and eskers, are

commonly found on the floor of the trough, together with linear lakes called ribbon lakes.

glacier tongue of ice, originating in mountains in snowfields above the snowline, which moves slowly downhill and is constantly replenished from its source. The scenery produced by the erosive action of glaciers is characteristic and includes ⬦glacial troughs (U-shaped valleys), corries, and arêtes. In lowlands, the laying down of ⬦moraine (rocky debris once carried by glaciers) produces a variety of landscape features.

Glackens William James 1870–1938. American painter. He was a member of the Ashcan school and one of "The Eight," a group of realists who exhibited at New York's Macbeth Gallery 1908. Glackens's painting eventually evolved into a realism that was strongly influenced by Impressionism. He painted subjects from everyday urban life, as well as those from fashionable society.

glacier Features of glaciers.

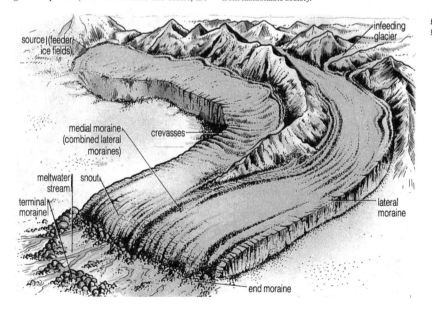

source (feeder ice fields)

infeeding glacier

medial moraine (combined lateral moraines)

crevasses

meltwater stream

snout

terminal moraine

lateral moraine

end moraine

Gladstone 19th-century British Liberal prime minister William Gladstone.

gladiator in ancient Rome, a trained fighter, recruited mainly from slaves, criminals, and prisoners of war, who fought to the death in arenas for the entertainment of spectators. The custom was introduced into Rome from Etruria in 264 BC and continued until the 5th century AD.

gladiolus any plant of the genus *Gladiolus* of S European and African cultivated perennials of the iris family Iridaceae, with brightly colored, funnel-shaped flowers, borne in a spike; the swordlike leaves spring from a corm.

Gladstone William Ewart 1809–1898. British Liberal politician, repeatedly prime minister. He entered Parliament as a Tory in 1833 and held ministerial office, but left the party 1846 and after 1859 identified himself with the Liberals. He was chancellor of the Exchequer 1852–55 and 1859–66, and prime minister 1868–74, 1880–85, 1886, and 1892–94. He introduced elementary education 1870 and vote by secret ballot 1872 and many reforms in Ireland, although he failed in his efforts to get a Home Rule Bill passed.

In Gladstone's first term as prime minister he carried through a series of reforms, including the disestablishment of the Church of Ireland, the Irish Land Act, and the abolition of the purchase of army commissions and of religious tests in the universities.

Glamorgan (Welsh *Morgannwg*) three counties of S Wales—Mid Glamorgan, South Glamorgan, and West Glamorgan—created 1974 from the former county of Glamorganshire. All are on the Bristol Channel.

gland specialized organ of the body that manufactures and secretes enzymes, hormones, or other chemicals. In animals, glands vary in size from small (for example, tear glands) to large (for example, the pancreas), but in plants they are always small, and may consist of a single cell. ◊*Endocrine glands*, discharge their products internally, and others, ◊*exocrine glands*, externally. Lymph nodes are sometimes wrongly called glands.

glandular fever or *infectious mononucleosis* viral disease characterized at onset by fever and painfully swollen lymph nodes (in the neck); there may

also be digestive upset, sore throat, and skin rashes. Lassitude persists for months and even years, and recovery can be slow. It is caused by the Epstein-Barr virus.

Glaser Donald Arthur 1926– . US physicist who invented the ◊bubble chamber in 1952, for which he received the Nobel Prize for Physics in 1960.

Born in Cleveland, Ohio, he was educated at the Case Institute of Technology, did research at the University of Michigan, and in 1960 became professor at the University of California.

Glasgow city and administrative headquarters of Strathclyde, Scotland; population (1991) 654,500. Industries include engineering, chemicals, printing, and distilling.

glasnost former Soviet leader Mikhail ◊Gorbachev's policy of liberalizing various aspects of Soviet life, such as introducing greater freedom of expression and information and opening up relations with Western countries. *Glasnost* was introduced and adopted by the Soviet government 1986.

glass transparent or translucent substance that is physically neither a solid nor a liquid. Although glass is easily shattered, it is one of the strongest substances known. It is made by fusing certain types of sand (silica); this fusion occurs naturally in volcanic glass (see ◊obsidian).

Glass Philip 1937– . US composer. As a student of Nadia ◊Boulanger, he was strongly influenced by Indian music; his work is characterized by repeated rhythmic figures that are continually expanded and modified. His compositions include the operas *Einstein on the Beach* 1975, *Akhnaten* 1984, and *The Making of the Representative for Planet 8* 1988.

glaucoma condition in which pressure inside the eye (intraocular pressure) is raised abnormally as excess fluid accumulates. It occurs when the normal flow of intraocular fluid out of the eye is interrupted. As pressure rises, the optic nerve suffers irreversible damage, leading to a reduction in the field of vision and, ultimately, loss of eyesight.

Glendower Owen c. 1359–c. 1416. (Welsh *Owain Glyndwr*) Welsh nationalist leader of a successful revolt against the English in N Wales, who defeated Henry IV in three campaigns 1400–02, although Wales was reconquered 1405–13. Glendower disappeared 1416 after some years of guerrilla warfare.

Glenn John (Herschel), Jr 1921– . US astronaut and politician. On Feb 20, 1962, he became the first American to orbit the Earth, doing so three times in the Mercury spacecraft *Friendship 7*, in a flight lasting 4 hr 55 min. After retiring from ◊NASA, he was elected to the US Senate as a Democrat from Ohio 1974; reelected 1980 and 1986. He unsuccessfully sought the Democratic presidential nomination 1984.

As a senator, he advocated nuclear-arms-production limitations and increased aid to education and job-skills programs.

Glens Falls city in E central New York, N of Albany and S of lakes George and Champlain; population (1990) 15,000. Situated in Warren County by a waterfall in the Hudson River, its industries include clothing, paper, machinery parts, insurance, and tourism.

gliding the art of using air currents to fly unpowered aircraft. Technically, gliding involves the gradual loss of altitude; gliders designed for soaring flight (utilizing air rising up a cliff face or hill, warm air rising as a "thermal" above sun-heated ground, and so on) are known as sailplanes. The sport of ◊hang-gliding was developed in the 1970s.

globefish another name for puffer fish.

Globe Theatre 17th-century London theater, octagonal and open to the sky, near Bankside, Southwark, where many of Shakespeare's plays were performed by Richard Burbage and his company. Built 1599 by Cuthbert Burbage, it was burned down 1613 after a cannon, fired during a performance of *Henry VIII*, set light to the thatch. It was rebuilt in 1614 but pulled down in 1644.

glockenspiel percussion instrument of light metal keys mounted on a carrying frame for use in military bands or on a standing frame for use in an orchestra (in which form it resembles a small xylophone or celesta).

Gloucester city in NE Massachusetts, on Cape Ann, NE of Boston; population (1990) 28,700. A famous fishing port, its industries include tourism and fish processing, especially lobster, whiting, and cod.

Gloucestershire county in SW England
area 1,019 sq mi/2,640 sq km
cities Gloucester (administrative headquarters), Stroud, Cheltenham, Tewkesbury, Cirencester
features Cotswold Hills; river Severn and tributaries; Berkeley Castle, where Edward II was murdered; Prinknash Abbey, where pottery is made; Cotswold Farm Park, near Stow-on-the-Wold, which has rare and ancient breeds of farm animals
products cereals, fruit, dairy products; engineering, coal in the Forest of Dean
population (1991) 520,600.

glow-worm wingless female of some luminous beetles (fireflies) in the family Lampyridae. The luminous organs situated under the abdomen serve to attract winged males for mating. There are about 2,000 species, distributed worldwide.

Gluck Christoph Willibald von 1714–1787. German composer who settled in Vienna as kapellmeister to Maria Theresa in 1754. In 1762 his *Orfeo ed Euridice/Orpheus and Eurydice* revolutionized the 18th-century conception of opera by giving free scope to dramatic effect. *Orfeo* was followed by *Alceste/Alcestis* 1767 and *Paride ed Elena/Paris and Helen* 1770.

glucose or *dextrose* or *grape-sugar* $C_6H_{12}O_6$ sugar present in the blood, and found also in honey and fruit juices. It is a source of energy for the body, being produced from other sugars and starches to form the "energy currency" of many biochemical reactions also involving ◊ATP.

glue-sniffing or *solvent misuse* inhalation of the fumes from organic solvents of the type found in paints, lighter fuel, and glue, for their hallucinatory effects. As well as being addictive, solvents are dangerous for their effects on the user's liver, heart, and lungs. It is believed that solvents produce hallucinations by dissolving the cell membrane of brain cells, thus altering the way the cells conduct electrical impulses.

gluten protein found in cereal grains, especially wheat. Gluten enables dough to stretch during rising. It has to be avoided by sufferers from celiac disease.

glyceride ◊ester formed between one or more acids and glycerol (propan-1,2,3-triol). A glyceride is termed a mono-, di-, or triglyceride, depending on the number of hydroxyl groups from the glycerol that have reacted with the acids.

glycerol or *glycerine* or *propan-1,2,3-triol* $HOCH_2CH(OH)CH_2OH$ thick, colorless, odorless, sweetish liquid. It is obtained from vegetable and animal oils and fats (by treatment with acid, alkali, superheated steam, or an enzyme), or by fermentation of glucose, and is used in the manufacture of high explosives, in antifreeze solutions, to maintain moist conditions in fruits and tobacco, and in cosmetics.

glycogen polymer (a polysaccharide) of the sugar ◊glucose made and retained in the liver as a carbohydrate store, for which reason it is sometimes called animal starch. It is a source of energy when needed by muscles, where it is converted back into glucose by the hormone ◊insulin and metabolized.

glycol or *ethylene glycol* or *ethane-1,2-diol* $(CH◊2 OH◊)2$ thick, colorless, odotless, sweetish liquid. It is used in antifreeze solutions, in the preparation of ethers and esters (used for explosives), as a solvent, and as a substitute for glycerol.

GMT abbreviation for ◊Greenwich Mean Time.

gnat any of various small flies of the order Diptera, that sometimes suck blood. In Britain, mosquitoes are often called gnats.

gneiss coarse-grained ◊metamorphic rock, formed under conditions of increasing temperature and pressure, and often occurring in association with schists and granites. It has a foliated, laminated structure, consisting of thin bands of micas and/or amphiboles alternating with granular bands of quartz and feldspar. Gneisses are formed during regional metamorphism; *paragneisses* are derived from sedimentary rocks and *orthogneisses* from igneous rocks. Garnets are often found in gneiss.

Gnosticism esoteric cult of divine knowledge (a synthesis of Christianity, Greek philosophy, Hinduism, Buddhism, and the mystery cults of the Mediterranean), which flourished during the 2nd and 3rd centuries and was a rival to, and influence on, early Christianity. The medieval French Cathar heresy and the modern *Mandean* sect (in S Iraq) descend from Gnosticism.

GNP abbreviation for ◊gross national product.

gnu or *wildebeest* either of two species of African ◊antelope, genus *Connochaetes*, with a cowlike face, a beard and mane, and heavy curved horns in both sexes. The body is up to 4.2 ft/1.3 m at the shoulder and slopes away to the hindquarters.

Goa state of India
area 1,428 sq mi/3,700 sq km
capital Panaji
population (1991) 1,168,600
history captured by the Portuguese 1510; the inland area was added in the 18th century. Goa was incorporated into India as a Union Territory with Daman and Diu 1961 and became a state 1987.

goat ruminant mammal of the genus *Capra* in the family Bovidae, closely related to the sheep. Both males and females have horns and beards. They are sure-footed animals, and feed on shoots and leaves more than on grass.

Gobelins French tapestry factory, originally founded as a dyeworks in Paris by Gilles and Jean Gobelin about 1450. The firm began to produce tapestries in the 16th century, and in 1662 the establishment was bought for Louis XIV by his minister Colbert. With the support of the French government, it continues to make tapestries.

Gogh Self Portrait with Bandaged Ear (1889), Courtauld Galleries, London.

Gobi Desert Asian desert divided between the Mongolian People's Republic and Inner Mongolia, China; 500 mi/800 km N–S, and 1,000 mi/1,600 km E–W. It is rich in fossil remains of extinct species.

Gobind Singh 1666–1708. Indian religious leader, the tenth and last guru (teacher) of Sikhism, 1675–1708, and founder of the Sikh brotherhood known as the ◊Khalsa. On his death, the Sikh holy book, the *Guru Granth Sahib*, replaced the line of human gurus as the teacher and guide of the Sikh community.

God the concept of a supreme being, a unique creative entity, basic to several monotheistic religions (for example Judaism, Christianity, Islam); in many polytheistic cultures (for example Norse, Roman, Greek), the term "god" refers to a supernatural being who personifies the force behind an aspect of life (for example Neptune, Roman god of the sea).

Godard Jean-Luc 1930– . French film director, one of the leaders of ◊New Wave cinema. His works are often characterized by experimental editing techniques and an unconventional dramatic form. His films include *A bout de souffle* 1959, *Vivre sa Vie* 1962, *Weekend* 1968, and *Je vous salue, Marie* 1985.

Goddard Robert Hutchings 1882–1945. US rocket pioneer. His first liquid-fueled rocket was launched at Auburn, Massachusetts, in 1926. By 1935 his rockets had gyroscopic control and carried cameras to record instrument readings. Two years later a Goddard rocket gained the world altitude record with an ascent of 1.9 mi/3 km.

Godiva Lady c. 1040–1080. Wife of Leofric, earl of Mercia (died 1057). Legend has it that her husband promised to reduce the heavy taxes on the people of Coventry if she rode naked through the streets at noon. The grateful citizens remained indoors as she did so, but "Peeping Tom" bored a hole in his shutters and was struck blind.

Godthaab (Greenlandic *Nuuk*) capital and largest town of Greenland; population (1982) 9,700. It is a storage center for oil and gas, and the chief industry is fish processing.

Godunov Boris 1552–1605. Tsar of Russia from 1598, elected after the death of Fyodor I, son of Ivan the Terrible. He was assassinated by a pretender to the throne who professed to be Dmitri, a brother of Fyodor

and the rightful heir. The legend that has grown up around this forms the basis of Pushkin's play *Boris Godunov* 1831 and Mussorgsky's opera of the same name 1874.

Goebbels (Paul) Josef 1897–1945. German Nazi leader. As minister of propaganda from 1933, he brought all cultural and educational activities under Nazi control and built up sympathetic movements abroad to carry on the "war of nerves" against Hitler's intended victims. On the capture of Berlin by the Allies, he poisoned himself.

Goering (German *Göring*) Hermann Wilhelm 1893–1946. Nazi leader, German field marshal from 1938. He was part of Hitler's inner circle, and with Hitler's rise to power was appointed commissioner for aviation from 1933 and built up the Luftwaffe (air force). He built a vast economic empire in occupied Europe, but later lost favor and was expelled from the party in 1945. Tried at Nuremberg for war crimes, he poisoned himself before he could be executed.

Goes Hugo van der, died 1482. Flemish painter, chiefly active in Ghent. His *Portinari altarpiece* about 1475 (Uffizi, Florence) is a huge oil painting of the Nativity, full of symbolism and naturalistic detail, and the *Death of the Virgin* about 1480 (Musée Communale des Beaux Arts, Bruges) is remarkable for the varied expressions on the faces of the apostles.

Goethe Johann Wolfgang von 1749–1832. German poet, novelist, and dramatist, generally considered the founder of modern German literature, and leader of the Romantic ◊Sturm und Drang movement. His works include the autobiographical *Die Leiden des Jungen Werthers/The Sorrows of the Young Werther* 1774 and *Faust* 1808, his masterpiece. A visit to Italy 1786–88 inspired the Classical dramas *Iphigenie auf Tauris/Iphigenia in Tauris* 1787 and *Torquato Tasso* 1790.

Gogh Vincent van 1853–1890. Dutch Post-Impressionist painter. He tried various careers, including preaching, and began painting in the 1880s. He met Paul ◊Gauguin in Paris, and when he settled in Arles, Provence, 1888, Gauguin joined him there. After a quarrel van Gogh cut off part of his own earlobe, and in 1889 he entered an asylum; the following year he committed suicide. The Arles paintings vividly testify to his intense emotional involvement in his art; among them are *The Yellow Chair* and several *Sunflowers* 1888 (National Gallery, London).

Gogol Nicolai Vasilyevich 1809–1852. Russian writer. His first success was a collection of stories, *Evenings on a Farm near Dikanka* 1831–32, followed by *Mirgorod* 1835. Later works include *Arabesques* 1835, the comedy play *The Inspector General* 1836, and the picaresque novel *Dead Souls* 1842, which satirizes Russian provincial society.

goiter enlargement of the thyroid gland seen as a swelling on the neck. It is most pronounced in simple goiter, which is caused by iodine deficiency. Much more common is toxic goiter or thyrotoxicosis, caused by overactivity of the thyroid gland.

Golan Heights (Arabic *Jawlan*) plateau on the Syrian border with Israel, bitterly contested in the ◊Arab-Israeli Wars and annexed by Israel Dec 14, 1981.

gold shiny, yellow, ductile and very malleable, metallic element, symbol Au (from Latin *aurum*, "gold"), atomic number 79, atomic weight 197. It occurs in nature frequently as a free metal (see ◊native metal) and is highly resistant to acids, tarnishing, and corrosion. Pure gold is the most malleable of all metals and is used as gold leaf or powder, where small amounts cover vast surfaces, such as gilded domes and statues. The elemental form is so soft that it is alloyed for strength with a number of other metals, such as silver, copper, and platinum. Its purity is then measured in ◊carats on a scale of 24 (24K = pure gold; 18K = 75% gold). It is used mainly for decorative purposes (jewelry, gilding) but also for coinage, dentistry, and conductivity in electronic devices.

Goldberg Rube 1883–1970. US cartoonist whose most famous and widely read of his strips featured ridiculously complicated inventions. He produced several popular comic strips that were nationally syndicated from 1915. Goldberg also devoted time to political cartooning, winning a Pulitzer Prize 1948.

Golden Fleece in Greek legend, the fleece of the winged ram Chrysomallus, which hung on an oak tree at Colchis and was guarded by a dragon. It was stolen by ◊Jason and the Argonauts.

goldenrod one of several tall, leafy perennials of the North American genus *Solidago*, in the daisy family Compositae. Flower heads are mostly composed of yellow florets.

goldfinch songbird of the genus *Carduelis*, found in Eurasia, N Africa, and North America.
The American goldfinch *C. tristis* is about 5 in/13 cm long and golden-brownish on top and underside, with white-barred wings and tail.

goldfish fish *Carassius auratus* of the ◊carp family, found in E Asia. Greenish-brown in its natural state, it has for centuries been bred by the Chinese, taking on highly colored and sometimes freakishly shaped forms. Goldfish can see a greater range of colors than any other animal tested.

Golding William 1911–1993. English novelist. His first book, *Lord of the Flies* 1954, was about savagery taking over among a group of English schoolboys marooned on a Pacific island. Later novels include *The Spire* 1964, *Rites of Passage* 1980 (Booker prize), and *The Paper Men* 1984. He was awarded the Nobel Prize for Literature in 1983.

Goldman Emma 1869–1940. US political organizer, feminist and co-editor of the anarchist monthly *Mother Earth* 1906–17. In 1908 her citizenship was revoked and in 1919 she was deported to Russia. Breaking with the Bolsheviks 1921, she spent the rest of her life in exile. Her writings include *My Disillusionment in Russia* 1923 and *Living My Life* 1931.

gold rush large influx of gold prospectors to an area where gold deposits have recently been discovered. The result is a dramatic increase in population. Cities such as Johannesburg, Melbourne, and San Francisco either originated or were considerably enlarged by gold rushes. Melbourne's population trebled from 77,000 to some 200,000 between 1851 and 1853.

Goldsmith Oliver 1728–1774. Irish writer whose works include the novel *The Vicar of Wakefield* 1766; the poem "The Deserted Village" 1770; and the play *She Stoops to Conquer* 1773. In 1761 Goldsmith met Samuel Johnson, and became a member of his "club." *The Vicar of Wakefield* was sold (according to Johnson's account) to save him from imprisonment for debt.

gold standard system under which a country's currency is exchangeable for a fixed weight of gold on demand at the central bank. It was almost universally applied 1870–1914, but by 1937 no single country was on the full gold standard. Britain abandoned the gold standard 1931; the US abandoned it 1971. Holdings of gold are still retained because it is an internationally recognized commodity, which cannot be legislated upon or manipulated by interested countries.

Goldwater Barry 1909– . US Republican politician; presidential candidate in the 1964 election, when he was overwhelmingly defeated by Lyndon ◊Johnson. As a US senator 1953–86, he voiced the views of his party's right-wing conservative faction. Many of Goldwater's conservative ideas were later adopted by the Republican right, especially the Reagan administration.

Goldwyn Samuel. Adopted name of Samuel Goldfish 1882–1974. US film producer. Born in Poland, he emigrated to the US 1896.
He founded the Goldwyn Pictures Corporation 1917, which eventually merged into Metro-Goldwyn-Mayer (MGM) 1924, although he was not part of the deal. He remained a producer for many years, making classics such as *Wuthering Heights* 1939, *The Little Foxes* 1941, *The Best Years of Our Lives* 1946, and *Guys and Dolls* 1955.

golf outdoor game in which a small rubber-cored ball is hit with a wooden- or iron-faced club into a series of holes using the least number of shots. On the first shot for each hole, the ball is hit from a tee, which elevates the ball slightly off the ground; subsequent strokes are played off the ground. Most courses have 18 holes and are approximately 6,000 yd/5,500 m in length.

Goliath in the Old Testament, champion of the ◊Philistines, who was said to have been slain by a stone from a sling by the young ◊David in single combat in front of their opposing armies.

Gómez Juan Vicente 1864–1935. Venezuelan dictator 1908–35. The discovery of oil during his rule attracted US, British, and Dutch oil interests and made Venezuela one of the wealthiest countries in Latin America. Gómez amassed a considerable personal fortune and used his well-equipped army to dominate the civilian population.

Gompers Samuel 1850–1924. US labor leader. His early career in the Cigarmakers' Union led him to found and lead the American Federation of Labor 1886. Gompers advocated nonpolitical activity within the existing capitalist system to secure improved wages and working conditions for members.

Gomułka Władysław 1905–1982. Polish Communist politician, party leader 1943–48 and 1956–70. He introduced moderate reforms, including private farming and tolerance for Roman Catholicism.

gonad the part of an animal's body that produces the sperm or egg cells (ova) required for sexual reproduction. The sperm-producing gonad is called a ◊testis, and the ovule-producing gonad is called an ◊ovary.

Goncharov Ivan Alexandrovitch 1812–1891. Russian novelist. His first novel, *A Common Story* 1847, was followed in 1858 by his humorous masterpiece *Oblomov*, which satirized the indolent Russian landed gentry.

Goncourt, de the brothers Edmond 1822–1896 and Jules 1830–1870. French writers. They collaborated in producing a compendium, *L'Art du XVIIIème siècle/18th-Century Art* 1859–75, historical studies, and a *Journal* published 1887–96 that depicts French literary life of their day. Edmond de Goncourt founded the Académie Goncourt, opened 1903, which awards

Gorbachev Mikhail Gorbachev was president of the USSR from 1985 to 1991.

an annual prize, the Prix Goncourt, to the author of the best French novel of the year.

Gond member of a heterogenous people of central India, about half of whom speak unwritten languages belonging to the Dravidian family. The rest speak Indo-European languages. There are over 4 million Gonds, most of whom live in Madhya Pradesh, E Maharashtra, and N Andra Pradesh, although some live in Orissa. Traditionally, many Gonds practiced shifting cultivation; agriculture and livestock remain the basis of the economy.

Gondwanaland or *Gondwana* southern landmass formed 200 million years ago by the splitting of the single world continent ◊Pangaea. (The northern landmass was ◊Laurasia.) It later fragmented into the continents of South America, Africa, Australia, and Antarctica, which then drifted slowly to their present positions. The baobab tree found in both Africa and Australia is a relic of this ancient landmass.

gonorrhea common sexually transmitted disease arising from infection with the bacterium *Neisseria gonorrhoeae*, which causes inflammation of the genito-urinary tract. After an incubation period of two to ten days, infected men experience pain while urinating and a discharge from the penis; infected women often have no external symptoms.

González Márquez Felipe 1942– . Spanish socialist politician, leader of the Socialist Workers' Party (PSOE), prime minister from 1982. Although reelected in the 1989 election, his popularity suffered from economic upheaval and allegations of corruption.

Good Friday in the Christian church, the Friday before Easter, which is observed in memory of the Crucifixion (the death of Jesus on the cross).

Goodman Benny (Benjamin David) 1909–1986. US clarinetist, nicknamed the "King of Swing" for the new jazz idiom he introduced with arranger Fletcher Henderson (1897–1952). In 1934 he founded his own 12-piece band, which combined the expressive improvisatory style of black jazz with disciplined precision ensemble playing. He is associated with such numbers as "Blue Skies" and "Let's Dance."

Good Neighbor policy the efforts of US administrations between the two World Wars to improve relations with Latin American and Caribbean states. The

phrase was first used by President F D Roosevelt in his inaugural speech March 1933 to describe the foreign policy of his ◊New Deal.

Goodyear Charles 1800–1860. US inventor who developed rubber coating 1837 and vulcanized rubber 1839, a method of curing raw rubber to make it strong and elastic.

goose aquatic bird of several genera (especially *Anser*) in the family Anatidae, which also includes ducks and swans. Both genders are similar in appearance: they have short, webbed feet, placed nearer the front of the body than in other members of the order Anatidae, and the beak is slightly hooked. They feed entirely on grass and plants.

gooseberry several prickly shrubs of the genus *Ribes* in the saxifrage family, native to Eurasia and North America, and closely related to currants in the same genus. The fleshy, red, blackish or green fruits are edible. The pasture gooseberry *R. cyanosbati* is native to North America. The European gooseberry *R. grossalaria* is cultivated in gardens.

gopher burrowing rodent of the genus *Citellus*, family Sciuridae. It is a kind of ground squirrel represented by some 20 species distributed across W North America and Eurasia. Length ranges from 6 in/15 cm to 16 in/90 cm, excluding the furry tail; coloring ranges from plain yellowish to striped and spotted species. The name *pocket gopher* is applied to the eight genera of the North American family Geomyidae.

Gorbachev Mikhail Sergeyevich 1931– . Soviet president, in power 1985–91. He was a member of the Politburo from 1980. As general secretary of the Communist Party (CPSU) 1985–91, and president of the Supreme Soviet 1988–91, he introduced liberal reforms at home (◊perestroika and ◊glasnost), proposed the introduction of multiparty democracy, and attempted to halt the arms race abroad. He became head of state 1989.

He was awarded the Nobel Peace Prize 1990 but his international reputation suffered in the light of harsh state repression of nationalist demonstrations in the Baltic states. Following an abortive coup attempt by hard-liners Aug 1991, international acceptance of independence for the Baltic states, and accelerated moves toward independence in other republics, Gorbachev's power base as Soviet president was greatly weakened and in Dec 1991 he resigned.

Gordian knot in Greek legend, the knot tied by King Gordius of Phrygia that—so an oracle revealed—could be unraveled only by the future conqueror of Asia. According to tradition, Alexander the Great, unable to untie it, cut it with his sword in 334 BC.

Gordimer Nadine 1923– . South African novelist, an opponent of apartheid. Her first novel, *The Lying Days*, appeared in 1953; her other works include *The Conservationist* 1974, the volume of short stories *A Soldier's Embrace* 1980, and *July's People* 1981. She was awarded the Nobel Prize for Literature in 1991.

Gordon Charles (George) 1833–1885. British general sent to Khartoum in the Sudan 1884 to rescue English garrisons that were under attack by the Mahdi, Mohammed Ahmed; he was himself besieged for ten months by the Mahdi's army. A relief expedition arrived Jan 28, 1885, to find that Khartoum had been captured and Gordon killed two days before.

Gore Al (Albert Arnold, Jr) 1948– . US vice president 1993– under President Bill Clinton. A Democrat, he served in the House of Representatives 1977–85 and the Senate 1985–93 and became noted for his concern for the environment.

Gorgon in Greek mythology, any of three sisters, Stheno, Euryale, and Medusa, who had wings, claws, enormous teeth, and snakes for hair. Medusa, the only one who was mortal, was killed by ◊Perseus, but even in death her head was still so frightful that it turned the onlooker to stone.

gorilla largest of the apes, *Gorilla gorilla*, found in the dense forests of West Africa and mountains of central Africa. The male stands about 6 ft/1.8 m, and weighs about 450 lbs/200 kg. Females are about half the size. The body is covered with blackish hair, silvered on the back in older males. Gorillas live in family groups; they are vegetarian, highly intelligent, and will attack only in self-defense. They are dwindling in numbers, being shot for food by some local people, or by poachers taking young for zoos, but protective measures are having some effect.

Göring Hermann. German spelling of ◊Goering, Nazi leader.

Gorky (Russian *Gor'kiy*) name 1932–90 of Nizhny Novgorod, a city in central Russia.

Gorky Maxim. Adopted name of Alexei Peshkov 1868–1936. Russian writer. Born in Nizhni Novgorod (named Gorky 1932–90 in his honor), he was exiled 1906–13 for his revolutionary principles. His works, which include the play *The Lower Depths* 1902 and the memoir *My Childhood* 1913–14, combine realism with optimistic faith in the potential of the industrial proletariat.

Goshen city in N Indiana, on the Elkhart River, SE of South Bend; seat of Elkhart County; population (1990) 23,700.

It is situated in an agricultural area and serves as a market town. Industries include steel, rubber, electrical, and building products.

Gospel in the New Testament generally, the message of Christian salvation; in particular the four written accounts of the life of Jesus by Matthew, Mark, Luke, and John. Although the first three give approximately the same account or synopsis (thus giving rise to the name "Synoptic Gospels"), their differences from John have raised problems for theologians.

gospel music vocal music developed in the 1920s in the black Baptist churches of the US South from spirituals. Outstanding among the early gospel singers was Mahalia Jackson, but from the 1930s to the mid-1950s male harmony groups predominated, among them the Dixie Hummingbirds, the Swan Silvertones, and the Five Blind Boys of Mississippi.

Gossaert Jan, Flemish painter, known as Mabuse.

Göteborg (German *Gothenburg*) port and industrial city (ships, vehicles, chemicals) on the W coast of Sweden, at the mouth of the Göta River; population (1990) 433,000. It is Sweden's second-largest city and is linked with Stockholm by the Göta Canal (built 1832).

Goth E Germanic people who settled near the Black Sea around AD 2nd century. There are two branches, the eastern Ostrogoths and the western Visigoths. The *Ostrogoths* were conquered by the Huns 372. They regained their independence 454 and under ◊Theodoric the Great conquered Italy 488–93; they disappeared as a nation after the Byzantine emperor ◊Justinian I reconquered Italy 535–55.

The *Visigoths* migrated to Thrace. Under ◊Alaric they raided Greece and Italy 395–410, sacked Rome,

gorilla The gorilla is a gentle, intelligent, and sociable animal.

and established a kingdom in S France. Expelled from there by the Franks, they established a Spanish kingdom which lasted until the Moorish conquest of 711.

Gothic architecture style of architecture that flourished in Europe from the mid-12th century to the end of the 15th century. It is characterized by vertical lines of tall pillars, spires, greater height in interior spaces, the pointed arch, rib vaulting, and the flying buttress.

Gothic art style of painting and sculpture that dominated European art from the late 12th century until the early Renaissance. The great Gothic church façades held hundreds of sculpted figures and profuse ornamentation, and manuscripts were lavishly decorated. Stained glass replaced mural painting to some extent in N European churches. The *International Gothic* style in painting emerged in the 14th century, characterized by delicate and complex ornamentation and increasing realism.

Gould Stephen Jay 1941– . US paleontologist and author. In 1972 he proposed the theory of punctuated equilibrium, suggesting that the evolution of species did not occur at a steady rate but could suddenly accelerate, with rapid change occurring over a few hundred thousand years. His books include *Ever Since Darwin* 1977, *The Panda's Thumb* 1980, *The Flamingo's Smile* 1985, and *Wonderful Life* 1990.

Gounod Charles François 1818–1893. French composer. His operas include *Sappho* 1851, *Faust* 1859, *Philémon et Baucis* 1860, and *Roméo et Juliette* 1867. He also wrote sacred songs, masses, and an oratorio, *The Redemption* 1882. His music inspired many French composers of the late 19th century.

gourd names applied to various members of the family Cucurbitaceae, including melons, squashes, and pumpkins. In a narrower sense, the name is applied to an inedible, ornamental variety of pumpkin *Cucurbita pepa*.

gout disease, a hereditary form of ◊arthritis, marked by an excess of uric acid crystals in the tissues, causing pain and inflammation in one or more joints (usually of the feet or hands). Acute attacks are treated with ◊anti-inflammatories.

government any system whereby political authority is exercised. Modern systems of government distinguish between liberal democracies, totalitarian (one-party) states, and autocracies (authoritarian, relying on force rather than ideology). The Greek philosopher Aristotle was the first to attempt a systematic classification of governments. His main distinctions were between government by one person, by few, and by many (monarchy, oligarchy, and democracy), although the characteristics of each may vary between states

Goya A Picnic *(late 1780s), National Gallery, London.*

Gracchus the brothers *Tiberius Sempronius* 163–133 BC and *Gaius Sempronius* 153–121 BC. Roman agrarian reformers. As ◊tribune (magistrate) 133 BC, Tiberius tried to redistribute land away from the large slave-labor farms in order to benefit the poor as well as increase the number of those eligible for military service. He was murdered by a mob of senators. Gaius, tribune 123–122 BC, revived his brother's legislation, and introduced other reforms, but was outlawed by the Senate and killed in a riot.

Graces in Greek mythology, three goddesses (Aglaia, Euphrosyne, Thalia), daughters of Zeus and Hera, personifications of pleasure, charm, and beauty; the inspirers of the arts and the sciences.

Graf Steffi 1969– . German lawn-tennis player who brought Martina ◊Navratilova's long reign as the world's number-one female player to an end. Graf reached the semifinal of the US Open 1985 at the age of 16, and won five consecutive Grand Slam singles titles 1988–89.

graffiti inscriptions or drawings carved, scratched, or drawn on public surfaces, such as walls, fences, or public-transport vehicles. *Tagging* is the act of writing an individual logo on surfaces with spray paint or large felt-tip pens.

grafting in medicine, the operation by which a piece of living tissue is removed from one organism and transplanted into the same or a different organism where it continues growing. In horticulture, it is a technique widely used for propagating plants, especially woody species. A bud or shoot on one plant, termed the *scion*, is inserted into another, the *stock*, so that they continue growing together, the tissues combining at the point of union. In this way some of the advantages of both plants are obtained.

Graham Billy (William Franklin) 1918– . US Protestant evangelist, known for the dramatic staging and charismatic eloquence of his preaching. Graham has preached to millions during worldwide crusades and on television, bringing many thousands to a "decision for Christ."

Graham Martha 1893–1991. US dancer, choreographer, teacher, and director. A leading exponent of modern dance in the US, she developed a distinctive vocabulary of movement, the *Graham Technique*, now taught worldwide. Her pioneering technique, designed to express inner emotion and intention through dance forms, represented the first real alternative to Classical ballet.

Graham Thomas 1805–1869. Scottish chemist who laid the foundations of physical chemistry (the branch of chemistry concerned with changes in energy during a chemical transformation) by his work on the diffusion of gases and liquids. *Graham's Law* 1829 states that the diffusion rate of a gas is inversely proportional to the square root of its density.

Grahame Kenneth 1859–1932. Scottish author. The early volumes of sketches of childhood, *The Golden Age* 1895 and *Dream Days* 1898, were followed by his masterpiece *The Wind in the Willows* 1908, an animal fantasy created for his young son, which was dramatized by A A Milne as *Toad of Toad Hall* 1929.

grain the smallest unit of mass in the three English systems (avoirdupois, troy, and apothecaries' weights) used in the UK and US, equal to 0.0648 g. It was reputedly the weight of a grain of wheat. One pound avoirdupois equals 7,000 grains; one pound troy or apothecaries' weight equals 5,760 grains.

and each may degenerate into tyranny (rule by an oppressive elite in the case of oligarchy or by the mob in the case of democracy).

governor in engineering, any device that controls the speed of a machine or engine, usually by regulating the intake of fuel or steam.

Goya Francisco José de Goya y Lucientes 1746–1828. Spanish painter and engraver. He painted portraits of four successive kings of Spain, and his etchings include *The Disasters of War*, depicting the French invasion of Spain 1810–14. Among his later works are the "black paintings" (Prado, Madrid), with horrific images such as *Saturn Devouring One of His Sons* c. 1822.

Graaf Regnier de 1641–1673. Dutch physician and anatomist who discovered the ovarian follicles, which were later named *Graafian follicles*. He named the ovaries and gave exact descriptions of the testicles. He was also the first to isolate and collect the secretions of the pancreas and gall bladder.

Grable Betty (Elizabeth Ruth) 1916–1973. US actress, singer, and dancer, who starred in *Moon over Miami* 1941, *I Wake Up Screaming* 1941, and *How to Marry a Millionaire* 1953. As a publicity stunt, her legs were insured for a million dollars. Her popularity peaked during World War II when US soldiers voted her their number-one pin-up girl.

gram metric unit of mass; one-thousandth of a kilogram.

grammar Greek *grammatike tekhne* "art of letters" the principles of the correct use of language, dealing with the rules of structuring words into phrases, clauses, sentences, and paragraphs in an accepted way. Emphasis on the standardizing impact of print has meant that spoken or colloquial language is often perceived as less grammatical than written language, but all forms of a language, standard or otherwise, have their own grammatical systems of differing complexity. People often acquire several overlapping grammatical systems within one language; for example, one formal system for writing and standard communication and one less formal system for everyday and peer-group communication.

Grampian region of Scotland
area 3,320 sq mi/8,600 sq km
cities Aberdeen (administrative headquarters)
features part of the Grampian Mountains (the Cairngorm Mountains); valley of the river Spey, with its whiskey distilleries; Balmoral Castle (royal residence on the river Dee near Braemar, bought by Prince Albert 1852, and rebuilt in Scottish baronial style); Braemar Highland Games in Aug
products beef cattle (Aberdeen Angus and Beef Shorthorn), fishing, North Sea oil service industries, tourism (winter skiing)
population (1991) 493,200
famous people John Barbour, James Ramsay MacDonald, Alexander Cruden.

Granada city in the Sierra Nevada in Andalusia, S Spain; population (1986) 281,000. It produces textiles, soap, and paper. The *Alhambra*, a fortified hilltop palace, was built in the 13th and 14th centuries by the Moorish kings.

Gran Chaco large lowland plain in N Argentina, W Paraguay, and SE Bolivia; area 251,000 sq mi/650,000 sq km. It consists of swamps, forests (a source of quebracho timber), and grasslands. There is cattle-raising.

Grand Banks continental shelf in the N Atlantic off SE Newfoundland, where the shallow waters are rich fisheries, especially for cod.

Grand Canal (Chinese *Da Yune*) the world's longest canal. It is 1,000 mi/1,600 km long and runs N from Hangzhou to Tianjin, China; it is 100–200 ft/30–61 m wide, and reaches depths of over 1 mi/1.5 km. The earliest section was completed 486 BC, and the northern section was built AD 1282–92, during the reign of Kublai Khan.

Grand Canyon gorge of multicolored rock strata cut by and containing the Colorado River, N Arizona. It is 217 mi/350 km long, 4–18 mi/6–29 km wide, and reaches depths of over 1.1 mi/1.7 km. It was made a national park 1919. Millions of tourists visit the canyon each year.

John Wesley Powell and ten companions first traveled down the river through the gorge 1869. *See illustration p. 402*

Grande Dixence dam the world's highest dam, located in Switzerland, which measures 935 ft/285 m from base to crest. Completed in 1961, it contains 8 million cu yd/6 million cu m of concrete.

Grand Forks city in E central North Dakota, on the Minnesota border, on the Red River, N of Fargo; seat of Grand Forks County; population (1990) 49,400. It serves the surrounding agricultural area; most of its industries, such as food-processing

Graf German tennis player Steffi Graf at Wimbledon 1989, where she won the ladies' singles title.

mills and fertilizer plants, are associated with agriculture.

The University of North Dakota 1883 is located here.

Grand Old Party (GOP) popular name for US ◊Republican Party.

grand opera type of opera without any spoken dialogue (unlike the *opéra-comique*), as performed at the Paris Opéra 1820s–80s. Using the enormous resources of the state-subsidized opera house, grand operas were extremely long (five acts), and included incidental music and a ballet.

grand slam in tennis, the four major tournaments: the Australian Open, the French Open, Wimbledon, and the US Open. In golf, it is also the four major tournaments: the US Open, the British Open, the Masters, and the PGA (Professional Golfers Association). In baseball, a grand slam is a home run with runners on all the bases. A grand slam in bridge is when all 13 tricks are won by one team.

Grange Red (Harold Edward). Nickname "the Galloping Ghost." 1903–1991. US American football player. He joined the Chicago Bears professional football team 1925, becoming one of the first superstars of the newly

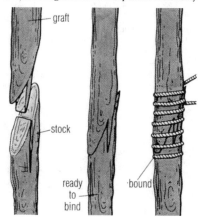

grafting Grafting, a method of artificial propagation in plants, is commonly used in the propagation of roses and fruit trees.

Grand Canyon The silt-laden Colorado River cuts through the lowest point of the Grand Canyon, Arizona.

founded National Football League. In both the 1923 and 1924 seasons he was chosen All-American halfback and won his nickname for his extraordinary open-field running ability.

Grange Movement in US history, a farmers' protest in the South and Midwest states against economic hardship and exploitation. The National Grange of the Patrons of Husbandry, formed 1867, was a network of local organizations, employing cooperative practices and advocating "granger" laws. The movement petered out in the late 1870s, to be superseded by the ◊Greenbackers.

Granger (James) Stewart 1913–1993. British film actor. After several leading roles in British romantic films during World War II, he moved to Hollywood in 1950 and subsequently appeared in such fanciful films as *Scaramouche* 1952, *The Prisoner of Zenda* 1952, and *The Wild Geese* 1978.

granite coarse-grained ◊igneous rock, typically consisting of the minerals quartz, feldspar, and mica. It may be pink or gray, depending on the composition of the feldspar. Granites are chiefly used as building materials.

Granite City city in SW Illinois, across the Mississippi River from St Louis, Missouri; population (1990)

granite Hay Tor (1,490 ft/453 m) is one of Dartmoor's granite tors.

32,800. An industrial city with its own port on the Chain of Rocks Canal, it manufactures steel products, automobile frames, and building materials.

Grant Cary. Adopted name of Archibald Leach 1904–1986. British-born actor who became a US citizen 1942. His witty, debonair personality made him a screen favorite for more than three decades. He was directed by Alfred ◊Hitchcock in *Suspicion* 1941, *Notorious* 1946, *To Catch a Thief* 1955, and *North by Northwest* 1959. He received a 1970 Academy Award for general excellence.

Grant Ulysses S(impson) 1822–1885. American Civil War general in chief for the Union and 18th president of the US 1869–77. As a Republican president, he carried through a liberal ◊Reconstruction policy in the South. He failed to suppress extensive political corruption within his own party and cabinet, which tarnished the reputation of his second term.

Born Hiram Ulysses Grant in Point Pleasant, Ohio, he graduated from West Point 1843 and had an unsuccessful career in the army 1839–54 and in business. At the outbreak of the Civil War he received a commission on the Mississippi front. His military career nearly ended in failure when Confederate forces surprised him at the Battle of Shiloh 1862, but Abraham ◊Lincoln's support was unwavering and Grant quickly redeemed himself, showing an aggressive fighting spirit. By his capture of Vicksburg in 1863 he brought the whole Mississippi front under Northern control and slowly wore down the Confederate general Lee's resistance, receiving his surrender at Appomattox 1865. He was elected president 1868 and reelected 1872. As president, he reformed the civil service and ratified the Treaty of Washington with the UK 1871. His two-volume *Memoirs* were very successful and restored his finances.

grape fruit of any vine of the genus *Vitis*, especially *V. vinifera*, of the Vitaceae family. The woody grapevine has small greenish flowers that produce clusters of large, juicy green, red, or black berries. Grapes are eaten as a dessert fruit, the juice is made into wines, and grape seed oil is extracted from the pips. They are also dried as raisins, or sultanas and currants if seedless. Grapes have been cultivated throughout the Old World for thousands of years and were successfully introduced to South America and the W coast of North America.

grapefruit round, yellow, juicy, sharp-tasting fruit of the evergreen tree *Citrus paradisi* of the Rutaceae family. The tree grows to about 30 ft/10 m and has dark shiny leaves and large white flowers. The large fruits grow in grapelike clusters (hence the name). Grapefruits were first established in the West Indies and subsequently cultivated in Florida by the 1880s; they are now also grown in Israel and South Africa. Some varieties have pink flesh.

graphical user interface (GUI) or *WIMP* in computing, a type of user interface in which programs and files appear as icons (small pictures), user options are selected from pull-down menus, and data are displayed in windows (rectangular areas), which the operator can manipulate in various ways. The operator uses a pointing device, typically a ◊mouse, to make selections and initiate actions.

graphite blackish-gray, laminar, crystalline form of ◊carbon. It is used as a lubricant and as the active component of pencil lead.

grass plant of the large family Gramineae of monocotyledons, with about 9,000 species distributed worldwide except in the Arctic regions. The majority are perennial, with long, narrow leaves and jointed, hollow stems; hermaphroditic flowers are borne in spikelets; the fruits are grainlike. Included are bluegrass, wheat, rye, corn, sugarcane, and bamboo. *See illustration p. 404*

Grass Günter 1927– . German writer. The grotesque humor and socialist feeling of his novels *Die Blechtrommel/The Tin Drum* 1959 and *Der Butt/The Flounder* 1977 are also characteristic of his poems.

grasshopper insect of the order Orthoptera, usually with strongly developed hind legs, enabling it to leap. The femur of each hind leg in the male usually has a row of protruding joints that produce the characteristic chirping when rubbed against the hard wing veins. Members of the order include ◊locusts, ◊crickets, and katydids.

gravel coarse ◊sediment consisting of pebbles or small fragments of rock, originating in the beds of lakes and streams or on beaches. Gravel is quarried for use in road building, railroad ballast, and for an aggregate in concrete. It is obtained from quarries known as gravel pits, where it is often found mixed with sand or clay. Some gravel deposits also contain metal ores (chiefly tin) or free metals (such as gold and silver).

gravitational force one of the four ◊fundamental forces of nature, the other three being the ◊electromagnetic force, the ◊strong force, and the ◊weak force. The gravitational force is the weakest of the four forces, but it acts over great distances. The particle that is postulated as the carrier of the gravitational force is the ◊graviton.

gravitational lensing bending of light by a gravitational field, predicted by Einstein's general theory of

Grant Hollywood film actor Cary Grant played romantic leading roles in the early 1930s.

relativity. The effect was first detected 1917 when the light from stars was found to be bent as it passed the totally eclipsed Sun. More remarkable is the splitting of light from distant quasars into two or more images by intervening galaxies. In 1979 the first double image of a quasar produced by gravitational lensing was discovered and a quadruple image of another quasar was later found.

graviton in physics, the gauge boson that is the postulated carrier of gravity.

gravity force of attraction that arises between objects by virtue of their masses. On Earth, gravity is the force of attraction between any object in the Earth's gravitational field and the Earth itself. It is regarded

Grant General Ulysses S Grant at City Point, near Hopewell, Virginia, June 1864.

grass The parts of a grass flower.

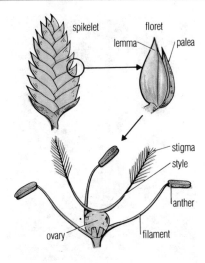

spikelet floret
lemma palea
stigma
style
anther
ovary filament

as one of the four ◊fundamental forces of nature, the other three being the ◊electromagnetic force, the ◊strong nuclear force, and the ◊weak nuclear force. The gravitational force is the weakest of the four forces, but it acts over great distances. The particle that is postulated as the carrier of the gravitational force is the ◊graviton.

gravure one of the three main ◊printing methods, in which printing is done from a plate etched with a pattern of recessed cells in which the ink is held. The greater the depth of a cell, the greater the strength of the printed ink. Gravure plates are expensive to make, but the process is economical for high-volume printing and reproduces illustrations well.

Gray Asa 1810–1888. US botanist and taxonomist who became America's leading expert in the field. His major publications include *Elements of Botany* 1836 and the definitive *Flora of North America* 1838, 1843. He based his revision of the Linnaean system of plant classification on fruit form rather than gross morphology.

Gray Thomas 1716–1771. English poet whose "Elegy Written in a Country Churchyard" 1751 is one of the most quoted poems in English. Other poems include "Ode on a Distant Prospect of Eton College," "The Progress of Poesy," and "The Bard"; these poems are now seen as the precursors of Romanticism.

Graz capital of Styria province, and second-largest city in Austria; population (1981) 243,400. Industries include engineering, chemicals, iron, and steel. It has a 15th-century cathedral and a university founded 1573. Lippizaner horses are bred near here.

Great Artesian Basin the largest area of artesian water in the world. It underlies much of Queensland, New South Wales, and South Australia, and in prehistoric times formed a sea. It has an area of 676,250 sq mi/1,750,000 sq km.

Great Australian Bight broad bay of the Indian Ocean in S Australia, notorious for storms.

Great Barrier Reef chain of coral reefs and islands about 1,250 mi/2,000 km long, off the E coast of Queensland, Australia, at a distance of 10–30 mi/15–45 km. It is believed to be the world's largest living organism and forms an immense natural breakwater, the coral rock forming a structure larger than all

human-made structures on Earth combined. The reef is in danger from large numbers of starfish, which are reported to have infested 35% of the reef. Some scientists fear the entire reef will disappear within 50 years.

Great Bear Lake lake on the Arctic Circle, in the Northwest Territories, Canada; area 12,275 sq mi/31,800 sq km.

Great Britain official name for ◊England, ◊Scotland, and ◊Wales, and the adjacent islands (except the Channel Islands and the Isle of Man) from 1603, when the English and Scottish crowns were united under James I of England (James VI of Scotland). With Northern ◊Ireland it forms the ◊United Kingdom.

Great Dane large, short-haired breed of dog, usually fawn in color, standing up to 30 in/76 cm tall, and weighing up to 154 lb/70 kg. It has a long head, a large nose, and small, erect ears. It was used in Europe for hunting boar and stags.

Great Dividing Range E Australian mountain range, extending 2,300 mi/3,700 km N–S from Cape York Peninsula, Queensland, to Victoria. It includes the Carnarvon Range, Queensland, which has many Aboriginal cave paintings, the Blue Mountains in New South Wales, and the Australian Alps.

Great Exhibition world fair held in Hyde Park, London, UK, in 1851, proclaimed by its originator Prince Albert as "the Great Exhibition of the Industries of All Nations." In practice, it glorified British manufacture: over half the 100,000 exhibits were from Britain or the British Empire. Over 6 million people attended the exhibition. The exhibition hall, popularly known as the Crystal Palace, was constructed of glass with a cast-iron frame, and designed by Joseph Paxton.

Great Falls city in central Montana, on the Missouri River, NE of Helena; seat of Cascade County; population (1990) 55,000. Its main industries are involved with the processing of copper and zinc from nearby mines. The processing of agricultural products and oil refining is also important. The city is named after nearby waterfalls, first discovered 1805 by Meriwether Lewis and William Clark.

Great Lakes series of five freshwater lakes along the US–Canadian border: Lakes Superior, Michigan, Huron, Erie, and Ontario; total area 94,600 sq mi/245,000 sq km. Interconnecting canals make them navigable by large ships, and they are drained by the ◊St Lawrence River. The whole forms the St Lawrence Seaway. They are said to contain 20% of the world's surface fresh water.

Great Leap Forward change in the economic policy of the People's Republic of China introduced by ◊Mao Zedong under the second five-year plan of 1958–62. The aim was to achieve rapid and simultaneous agricultural and industrial growth through the creation of large new agro-industrial communes. The inefficient and poorly planned allocation of state resources led to the collapse of the strategy by 1960 and the launch of a "reactionary program," involving the use of rural markets and private subsidiary plots. More than 20 million people died in the Great Leap famines of 1959–61.

Great Plains semiarid region to the E of the Rocky Mountains, stretching as far as the 100th meridian of longitude through Oklahoma, Kansas, Nebraska, and the Dakotas. The plains, which cover one-fifth of the US, extend from Texas in the S over 1,500 mi/2,400 km

N to Canada. Ranching and wheat farming have resulted in over-use of water resources to such an extent that available farmland has been reduced by erosion.

Great Red Spot prominent oval feature, 8,500 mi/14,000 km wide and some 20,000 mi/30,000 km long, in the atmosphere of the planet ◊Jupiter, S of the equator. It was first observed in the 19th century. Space probes show it to be a counterclockwise vortex of cold clouds, colored possibly by phosphorus.

Great Schism in European history, the period 1378–1417 in which rival popes had seats in Rome and in Avignon; it was ended by the election of Martin V during the Council of Constance 1414–17.

Great Slave Lake lake in the Northwest Territories, Canada; area 10,980 sq mi/28,450 sq km. It is the deepest lake (2,020 ft/615 m) in North America.

Great Trek in South African history, the movement of 12,000–14,000 Boer (Dutch) settlers from Cape Colony 1835 and 1845 to escape British rule. They established republics in Natal and the Transvaal. It is seen by many white South Africans as the main event in the founding of the present republic and also as a justification for continuing whites-only rule.

Great Wall of China continuous defensive wall stretching from W Gansu to the Gulf of Liaodong (1,450 mi/2,250 km). It was once even longer. It was built under the Qin dynasty from 214 BC to prevent incursions by the Turkish and Mongol peoples. Some 25 ft/8 m high, it consists of a brick-faced wall of earth and stone and a series of square watchtowers. It is so large that it can be seen from space.

Great War another name for ◊World War I.

Greco, El (Doménikos Theotokópoulos) 1541–1614. Spanish painter called "the Greek" because he was born in Crete. He studied in Italy, worked in Rome from about 1570, and by 1577 had settled in Toledo. He painted elegant portraits and intensely emotional religious scenes with increasingly distorted figures and

flickering light; for example, *The Burial of Count Orgaz* 1586 (Toledo).

Greece country in SE Europe, comprising the S Balkan peninsula, bounded N by Macedonia and Bulgaria, NW by Albania, NE by Turkey, E by the Aegean Sea, S by the Mediterranean Sea, and W by the Ionian Sea. *See panel p. 406 and maps pp. 407 and 409*

Greek native to or an inhabitant of ancient or modern Greece or person of Greek descent; also the language and culture. Modern Greek is an Indo-European language, spoken in Greece and by Greek Cypriots; also by people of Greek descent, especially in Canada, the US, and Australia.

Greek art sculpture, mosaic, and crafts of ancient Greece (no large-scale painting survives). It is usually divided into three periods: *Archaic* (late 8th century–480 BC), showing Egyptian influence; *Classical* (480–323 BC), characterized by dignified realism; and *Hellenistic* (323–27 BC), more exuberant or dramatic. Sculptures of human figures dominate all periods, and vase painting was a focus for artistic development for many centuries. *See illustration p. 409*

Greek language member of the Indo-European language family, which has passed through at least five distinct phases since the 2nd millennium BC: *Ancient Greek* 14th–12th centuries BC; *Archaic Greek*, including Homeric epic language, until 800 BC; *Classical Greek* until 400 BC; *Hellenistic Greek*, the common language of Greece, Asia Minor, W Asia, and Egypt to the 4th century AD, and *Byzantine Greek*, used until the 15th century and still the ecclesiastical language of the Greek Orthodox Church. *Modern Greek* is principally divided into the general vernacular (*Demotic Greek*) and the language of education and literature (*Katharevousa*).

Greek Orthodox Church see ◊Orthodox Church.

Greeley city in N Colorado, at the point where the Cache de Poudre River flows into the South Platte

Great Wall of China A derelict section of the Great Wall of China near Badaling, built from 214 BC to repel Turkish and Mongol invaders.

Greece
Hellenic Republic
(*Elliniki Dimokratia*)

area 50,935 sq mi/131,957 sq km
capital Athens
cities Larisa; ports Piraeus, Thessaloníki, Patras, Iráklion
physical mountainous; a large number of islands, notably Crete, Corfu, and Rhodes
environment acid rain and other airborne pollutants are destroying the Classical buildings and ancient monuments of Athens
features Corinth canal; Mount Olympus; the Acropolis; many Classical archeological sites; the Aegean and Ionian Islands
head of state Constantine Karamanlis from 1990
head of government Andreas Papandreou from 1993
political system democratic republic
political parties Panhellenic Socialist Movement (PASOK), democratic socialist; New Democracy Party (ND), center-right; Democratic Renewal (DR); Communist Party; Greek Left Party; Political Spring, moderate, left of center
exports tobacco, fruit, vegetables, olives, olive oil, textiles, aluminum, iron and steel
currency drachma
population (1992) 10,288,000; growth rate 0.3% p.a.
life expectancy men 72, women 76
language Greek

religion Greek Orthodox 97%
literacy men 96%, women 89% (1985)
GDP $79.2 bn (1992)

chronology
1829 Independence achieved from Turkish rule.
1912–13 Balkan Wars; Greece gained much land.
1941–44 German occupation of Greece.
1946 Civil war between royalists and communists; communists defeated.
1949 Monarchy reestablished with Paul as king.
1964 King Paul succeeded by his son Constantine.
1967 Army coup removed the king; Col George Papadopoulos became prime minister. Martial law imposed, all political activity banned.
1973 Republic proclaimed, with Papadopoulos as president.
1974 Former premier Constantine Karamanlis recalled from exile to lead government. Martial law and ban on political parties lifted; restoration of the monarchy rejected by a referendum.
1975 New constitution adopted, making Greece a democratic republic.
1980 Karamanlis resigned as prime minister and was elected president.
1981 Greece became full member of European Economic Community. Andreas Papandreou elected Greece's first socialist prime minister.
1983 Five-year military and economic cooperation agreement signed with US; ten-year economic cooperation agreement signed with USSR.
1985 Papandreou reelected.
1988 Relations with Turkey improved. Major cabinet reshuffle after mounting criticism of Papandreou.
1989 Papandreou defeated. Tzannis Tzannetakis became prime minister; his all-party government collapsed. Xenophon Zolotas formed new unity government. Papandreou charged with corruption.
1990 New Democracy Party (ND) won half of parliamentary seats in general election but no outright majority; Constantine Mitsotakis became premier; formed new all-party government. Karamanlis reelected president.
1992 Papandreou acquitted. Greece opposed recognition of independence of the Yugoslav breakaway republic of Macedonia. Decisive parliamentary vote to ratify Maastricht Treaty.
1993 Parliament ratified the Maastricht Treaty. PASOK won general election and Papandreou returned as prime minister.

River, NE of Boulder; population (1990) 60,500. A distribution center for the surrounding agricultural area, its main industry is the processing of sugar beet. It is named after Horace Greeley, one of its founders.

Greeley Horace 1811–1872. US editor, publisher, and politician. He founded the *New York Tribune* 1841 and, as a strong supporter of the Whig party, advocated many reform causes in his newspaper—among them, feminism and abolitionism. He was an advocate of American westward expansion, and is remembered for his advice "Go west, young man." One of the founders of the Republican party 1854, Greeley was the unsuccessful presidential candidate of the breakaway Liberal Republicans 1872.

Born in Amherst, New Hampshire, Greeley was trained as a printer and moved to New York City 1831. He worked on a variety of publications before founding the *New York Tribune*.

Greenbacker in US history, a supporter of an alliance of agrarian and industrial organizations, known as the Greenback Labor Party, which campaigned for currency inflation by increasing the paper dollars ("greenbacks") in circulation. In 1880 the

party's presidential nominee polled only 300,000 votes; the movement was later superseded by ◊Populism.

Green Bay city in NE Wisconsin, where the Little Fox River flows into Green Bay on Lake Michigan; seat of Brown County; population (1990) 96,400. It is a port of entry to the US through the St Lawrence Seaway and serves as a distribution center. Industries include paper and food products.

The Green Bay Packers team of the National Football League was organized here 1919.

Greene (Henry) Graham 1904–1991. English writer whose novels of guilt, despair, and penitence are set in a world of urban seediness or political corruption in many parts of the world. They include *Brighton Rock* 1938, *The Power and the Glory* 1940, *The Heart of the Matter* 1948, *The Third Man* 1950, *The Honorary Consul* 1973, and *Monsignor Quixote* 1982.

Greene Nathanael 1742–1786. American military leader. During the American Revolution 1775–83 he was commander of the Rhode Island regiments and later brigadier general in the Continental army, seeing action at the Battle of Long Island 1776 and in Washington's New Jersey campaigns 1777. He commanded

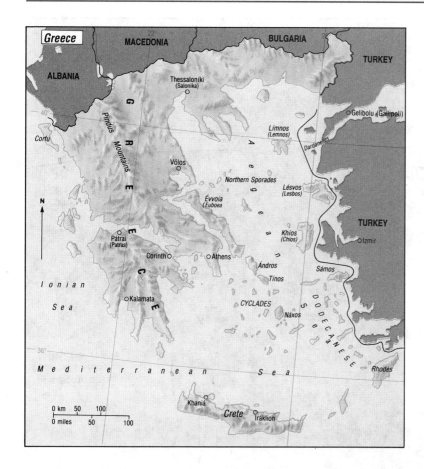

Greece

the successful American offensive in the South that ended the war.

greenhouse effect phenomenon of the Earth's atmosphere by which solar radiation, trapped by the Earth and re-emitted from the surface, is prevented from escaping by various gases in the air. The result is a rise in the Earth's temperature. The main greenhouse gases are carbon dioxide, methane, and ◊chlorofluorocarbons (CFCs). Fossil-fuel consumption and forest fires are the main causes of carbon-dioxide buildup; methane is a byproduct of agriculture (rice, cattle, sheep). Water vapor is another greenhouse gas. *See panel p. 408*

Greenland (Greenlandic *Kalaalit Nunaat*) world's largest island, lying between the North Atlantic and Arctic Oceans E of North America
area 840,000 sq mi/2,175,600 sq km
capital Godthaab (Greenlandic *Nuuk*) on the W coast
features the whole of the interior is covered by a vast ice sheet (the remnant of the last glaciation, part of the N Polar icecap); the island has an important role strategically and in civil aviation, and shares military responsibilities with the US; there are lead and cryolite deposits, and offshore oil is being explored
economy fishing and fish-processing
population (1990) 55,500; Inuit (Ammassalik Eskimoan), Danish, and other European
language Greenlandic (Ammassalik Eskimoan)

history Greenland was discovered about 982 by Eric the Red, who founded colonies on the W coast soon after Eskimos from the North American Arctic had made their way to Greenland. Christianity was introduced to the Vikings about 1000. In 1261 the Viking colonies accepted Norwegian sovereignty, but early in the 15th century all communication with Europe ceased, and by the 16th century the colonies had died out, but the Eskimos had moved on to the E coast. It became a Danish colony in the 18th century, and following a referendum 1979 was granted full internal self-government 1981.

greenmail payment made by a target company to avoid a takeover; for example, buying back a portion of its own shares from a potential predator (either a person or a company) at an inflated price.

Green Mountain Boys in US history, irregular troops who fought to protect the Vermont part of what was then New Hampshire colony from land claims made by neighboring New York. In the American Revolution they captured ◊Fort Ticonderoga from the British. Their leader was Ethan Allen (1738–1789), who was later captured by the British. Vermont declared itself an independent republic, refusing to join the Union until 1791. It is popularly known as the Green Mountain State.

Green Party political party aiming to "preserve the planet and its people," based on the premise that inces-

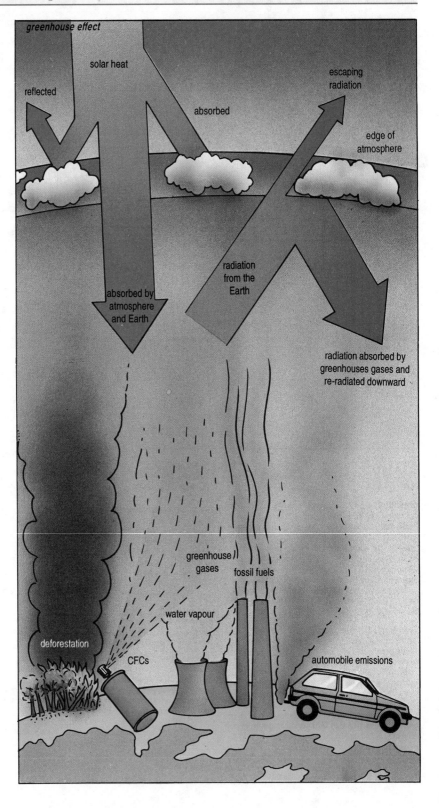

greenhouse effect
The warming effect of
the Earth's
atmosphere is called
the greenhouse effect.

greenhouse effect

solar heat

reflected

escaping
radiation

absorbed

edge of
atmosphere

absorbed by
atmosphere
and Earth

radiation
from the
Earth

radiation absorbed by
greenhouses gases and
re-radiated downward

greenhouse
gases

fossil fuels

water vapour

deforestation

CFCs

automobile emissions

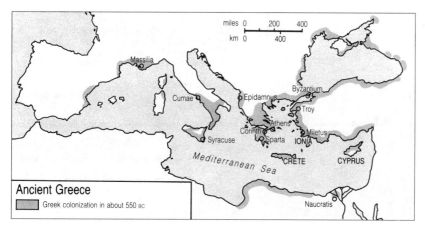

Ancient Greece

▨ Greek colonization in about 550 BC

sant economic growth is unsustainable. The leaderless party structure reflects a general commitment to decentralization. Green parties sprang up in W Europe in the 1970s and in E Europe from 1988. Parties in different countries are linked to one another but unaffiliated with any pressure group. The party had a number of parliamentary seats in 1992: Austria 9, Belgium 13, Finland 8, Italy 20, Luxembourg 2, Republic of Ireland 1, Greece 1, and Germany 2; and 29 members in the European Parliament (Belgium 3, France 8, Italy 7, the Netherlands 2, Spain 1, and Germany 8).

Greenpeace international environmental pressure group, founded 1971, with a policy of nonviolent direct action backed by scientific research. During a protest against French atmospheric nuclear testing in the S Pacific 1985, its ship *Rainbow Warrior* was sunk by French intelligence agents, killing a crew member.

green revolution in agriculture, a popular term for the change in methods of arable farming in Third World countries. The intent is to provide more and better food for their populations, albeit with a heavy reliance on chemicals and machinery. It was instigated in the 1940s and 1950s, but abandoned by some countries in the 1980s. Much of the food produced is exported as ◊cash crops, so that local diet does not always improve.

Greensboro city in N central North Carolina, W of Durham; seat of Guilford County; population (1990) 183,500. It is noted for its textile, chemical, and tobacco industries. Many schools are located here, including Guilford College (1834) and the University of North Carolina at Greensboro (1891). The Battle of Guilford Courthouse (1781) was fought nearby.

Greenstreet Sydney 1879–1954. British character actor. He made an impressive film debut in *The Maltese Falcon* 1941 and became one of the cinema's best-known villains. His other films include *Casablanca* 1943 and *The Mask of Dimitrios* 1944.

Greenville city in NW South Carolina, on the Reedy River, near the foothills of the Blue Ridge Mountains, SW of Spartanburg; seat of Greenville County; population (1990) 44,900. It is known as a major textile manufacturing center. Other industries include lumber and chemicals.

Greenwich inner borough of Greater London, England. Greenwich landmarks include the *Queen's House* 1637, designed by Inigo Jones, the first Palladian-style building in England; the *Royal Naval*

College, designed by Christopher Wren 1694; the *Royal Observatory* (founded here 1675). The source of Greenwich Mean Time has been moved to Cambridge 1990, but the Greenwich meridian (0°) remains unchanged. The *Cutty Sark*, one of the great tea clippers, is preserved as a museum of sail.

Greenwich Mean Time (GMT) local time on the zero line of longitude (the *Greenwich meridian*), which passes through the Old Royal Observatory at Greenwich, London. It was replaced 1986 by coordinated universal time (UTC), but continued to be used to measure longitudes and the world's standard time zones; see ◊time.

Greenwich Village in New York City, a section of lower Manhattan (from 14th Street south to Houston Street and from Broadway west to the Hudson River), which from the late 19th century became the bohemian and artistic quarter of the city and, despite expensive rentals, remains so.

Greer Germaine 1939– . Australian feminist who became widely known on the publication of her book *The Female Eunuch* 1970. Later works include *The*

Greek art Marble sculpture of the Venus de Milo, the Louvre, Paris.

Grenada

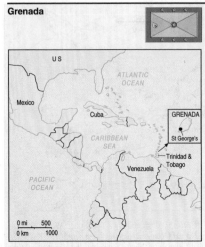

area (including the Grenadines, notably Carriacou) 131 sq mi/340 sq km
capital St George's
cities Grenville, Hillsborough (Carriacou)
physical southernmost of the Windward Islands; mountainous
features Grand-Anse beach; Annandale Falls; the Great Pool volcanic crater
head of state Elizabeth II from 1974, represented by governor-general
head of government Nicholas Braithwaite from 1990
political system emergent democracy
political parties New National Party (NNP), centrist; Grenada United Labor Party (GULP), nationalist, left of center; National Democratic Congress (NDC), centrist
exports cocoa, nutmeg, bananas, mace
currency Eastern Caribbean dollar
population (1992) 90,900, 84% of black African descent; growth rate –0.2% p.a.
life expectancy 69
language English (official); some French patois spoken
religion Roman Catholic 60%
literacy 85% (1985)
GDP $139 million (1987); $1,391 per head

chronology
1974 Independence achieved from Britain; Eric Gairy elected prime minister.
1979 Gairy removed in bloodless coup led by Maurice Bishop; constitution suspended and a People's Revolutionary Government established.
1982 Relations with the US and Britain deteriorated as ties with Cuba and the USSR strengthened.
1983 After Bishop's attempt to improve relations with the US, he was overthrown by left-wing opponents. A coup established the Revolutionary Military Council (RMC), and Bishop and three colleagues were executed. The US invaded Grenada, accompanied by troops from other E Caribbean countries; RMC overthrown, 1974 constitution reinstated.
1984 The newly formed NNP won 14 of the 15 seats in the house of representatives and its leader, Herbert Blaize, became prime minister.
1989 Herbert Blaize lost leadership of NNP, remaining as head of government; he died and was succeeded by Ben Jones.
1990 Nicholas Braithwaite of the NDC became prime minister.
1991 Integration into Windward Islands confederation proposed.

Obstacle Race 1979, a study of contemporary women artists, and *Sex and Destiny: The Politics of Human Fertility* 1984. She is also a speaker and activist.

Gregorian chant any of a body of plainsong choral chants associated with Pope Gregory the Great (540–604), which became standard in the Roman Catholic church.

Gregory I St, *the Great* c. 540–604. Pope from 590 who asserted Rome's supremacy and exercised almost imperial powers. In 596 he sent St ◊Augustine to England. He introduced the choral *Gregorian chant* into the liturgy. Feast day March 12.

Gregory VII or *Hildebrand* c. 1023–1085. Chief minister to several popes before his election to the papacy 1073. In 1077 he forced the Holy Roman emperor Henry IV to wait in the snow at Canossa for four days, dressed as a penitent, before receiving pardon. He was driven from Rome and died in exile. His feast day is May 25.

Gregory XIII 1502–1585. Pope from 1572 who introduced the reformed *Gregorian calendar*, still in use, in which a century year is not a leap year unless it is divisible by 400.

Gregory of Tours, St 538–594. French Christian bishop of Tours from 573, author of a *History of the Franks*. His feast day is Nov 17.

Grenada island country in the Caribbean, the southernmost of the Windward Islands.

Grenadines chain of about 600 small islands in the Caribbean Sea, part of the group known as the Windward Islands. They are divided between St Vincent and ◊Grenada.

Grenville George 1712–1770. British Whig politician, prime minister, and chancellor of the Exchequer, whose introduction of the ◊Stamp Act 1765 to raise revenue from the colonies was one of the causes of the American Revolution. His government was also responsible for prosecuting the radical John ◊Wilkes.

Grenville Richard 1542–1591. English naval commander and adventurer who died heroically aboard his ship *The Revenge* when attacked by Spanish warships. Grenville fought in Hungary and Ireland 1566–69, and was knighted about 1577. In 1585 he commanded the expedition that founded Virginia, for his cousin Walter ◊Raleigh. From 1586 to 1588 he organized the defense of England against the Spanish Armada.

Gretzky Wayne 1961– . Canadian ice-hockey player, probably the best in the history of the National Hockey League (NHL). Gretzky played with the Edmonton Oilers 1979–88 and with the Los Angeles Kings from 1988. He took just 11 years to break the NHL scoring record of 1,850 points (accumulated by Gordie Howe over 26 years) and won the Hart Memorial Trophy as the NHL's most valuable player of the season a record nine times (1980–87, 1989).

Grey Lady Jane 1537–1554. Queen of England for nine days, July 10–19 1553, the great-granddaughter of Henry VII. She was married 1553 to Lord Guildford Dudley (died 1554), son of the Duke of Northumberland. Edward VI was persuaded by Northumberland to set aside the claims of his sisters Mary and Elizabeth. When Edward died on July 6, 1553, Jane reluctantly accepted the crown and was proclaimed queen four days later. Mary, although a Roman

Catholic, had the support of the populace, and the Lord Mayor of London announced that she was queen July 19. Grey was executed on Tower Green.

Grey Zane 1875–1939. US author of Westerns, such as *Riders of the Purple Sage* 1912. He wrote more than 80 books and was primarily responsible for the creation of the Western as a literary genre.

greyhound ancient breed of dog, with a long narrow muzzle, slight build, and long legs, renowned for its swiftness. It is up to 2.6 ft/78 cm tall, and can exceed 40 mph/60 kph. Greyhound racing is a popular spectator sport.

grid network by which electricity is generated and distributed over a region or country. It contains many power stations and switching centers and allows, for example, high demand in one area to be met by surplus power generated in another.

Grieg Edvard Hagerup 1843–1907. Norwegian composer. Much of his music is small-scale, particularly his songs, dances, sonatas, and piano works. Among his orchestral works are the *Piano Concerto* 1869 and the incidental music for Ibsen's *Peer Gynt* 1876.

griffin mythical monster, the supposed guardian of hidden treasure, with the body, tail, and hind legs of a lion, and the head, forelegs, and wings of an eagle.

Griffith D(avid) W(ark) 1875–1948. US film director, an influential figure in the development of cinema as an art. He made hundreds of "one-reelers" 1908–13, in which he pioneered the techniques of masking, fade-out, flashback, crosscut, close-up, and long shot. After much experimentation with photography and new techniques he directed *The Birth of a Nation* 1915, about the aftermath of the Civil War, later criticized as degrading to blacks.

griffon small breed of dog originating in Belgium; red, black, or black and tan in color and weighing up to 11 lb/5 kg. Griffons are square-bodied and round-headed, and there are rough- and smooth-coated varieties.

Gris Juan 1887–1927. Spanish abstract painter, one of the earliest Cubists. He developed a distinctive geometrical style, often strongly colored. He experimented with paper collage and made designs for Diaghilev's Ballet Russes 1922–23.

Griswold v Connecticut a US Supreme Court decision 1965 dealing with state bans on the use of birth control. Griswold, the state director of the Planned Parenthood League, was convicted under a Connecticut anticontraceptive law for giving medical advice about birth control to a married couple. The Court overturned the conviction on appeal, ruling that the law was an illegitimate imposition of state police power on marital privacy guaranteed by the 1st, 3rd, 5th, 9th, and 14th Amendments.

Gromyko Andrei 1909–1989. President of the USSR 1985–88. As ambassador to the US from 1943, he took part in the Tehran, Yalta, and Potsdam conferences; as United Nations representative 1946–49, he exercised the Soviet veto 26 times. He was foreign minister 1957–85. It was Gromyko who formally nominated Mikhail Gorbachev as Communist Party leader 1985.

Groningen most northerly province of the Netherlands
area 907 sq mi/2,350 sq km
capital Groningen
cities Hoogezand-Sappemeer, Stadskanaal, Veendam, Delfzijl, Winschoten
physical Ems estuary, innermost W Fresian Islands
products natural gas, arable crops, dairy produce, sheep, horses
population (1991) 554,600
history under the power of the bishops of Utrecht from 1040, Groningen became a member of the Hanseatic League 1284. Taken by Spain 1580, it was recaptured by Maurice of Nassau 1594.

grooming in biology, the use by an animal of teeth, tongue, feet, or beak to clean fur or feathers. Grooming also helps to spread essential oils for waterproofing. In many social species, notably monkeys and apes, grooming of other individuals is used to reinforce social relationships.

Gropius Walter Adolf 1883–1969. German architect who lived in the US from 1937. He was an early exponent of the international modern style defined by glass curtain walls, cubic blocks, and unsupported corners—for example, the model factory and office building at the 1914 Cologne Werkbund exhibition. A founder-director of the ◊Bauhaus school in Weimar 1919–28, he advocated teamwork in design and artistic standards in industrial production.

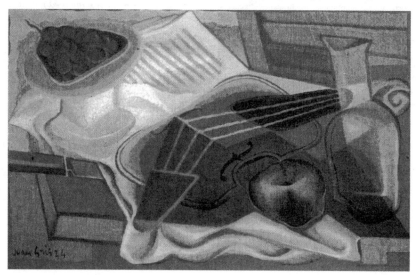

Gris Violin and Fruit Dish *1924, Tate Gallery, London.*

Grosz Suicide (1916), Tate Gallery, London, by German satirical artist Georg Grosz.

grosbeak any of various thick-billed finches of the family Fringillidae. The *pine grosbeak* *Pinicola enucleator* breeds in Arctic forests. Its plumage is similar to that of the pine crossbill.

gross domestic product (GDP) value of the output of all goods and services produced within a nation's borders, normally given as a total for the year. It thus includes the production of foreign-owned firms within the country, but excludes the income from domestically owned firms located abroad. See also ◊gross national product.

gross national product (GNP) the most commonly used measurement of the wealth of a country. GNP is defined as the total value of all goods and services produced by firms owned by the country concerned. It is measured as the ◊gross domestic product plus income from abroad, minus income earned during the same period by foreign investors within the country; see also ◊national income.

Grosvenor Gilbert Hovey 1875–1966. US publisher. Born in Constantinople to missionary parents, Grosvenor was educated at Amherst College and named editor of *National Geographic Magazine* 1899. Its financial status was shaky, but Grosvenor soon transformed it to a mass circulation periodical through the use of color photography from 1910.

Grosz Georg 1893–1959. German Expressionist painter and illustrator, a founder of the Berlin group of the Dada movement 1918. Grosz excelled in savage satirical drawings criticizing the government and the military establishment. After numerous prosecutions he fled his native Berlin 1932 and became a naturalized American 1938.

Grotefend George Frederick 1775–1853. German scholar. Although a student of the Classical rather than the oriental languages, he nevertheless solved the riddle of the wedgelike ◊cuneiform script as used in ancient Persia: decipherment of Babylonian cuneiform followed from his work.

Grotius Hugo 1583–1645. Dutch jurist and politician, born in Delft. He became a lawyer, and later received political appointments. In 1618 he was arrested as a republican and sentenced to imprisonment for life. His wife contrived his escape 1620, and he settled in France, where he composed the *De Jure Belli et Pacis/On the Law of War and Peace* 1625, the foundation of international law. He was Swedish ambassador in Paris 1634–45.

ground an electrical connection between an appliance and the ground, which becomes part of the circuit. In the event of a fault in an electrical appliance (for example, involving connection between the live part of the circuit and the outer casing) the current flows to earth, causing no harm to the user.

ground water water collected underground in porous rock strata and soils; it emerges at the surface as springs and streams. The groundwater's upper level is called the *water table*. Sandy or other kinds of beds that are filled with groundwater are called *aquifers*. Recent estimates are that usable ground water amounts to more than 90% of all the fresh water on Earth; however, keeping such supplies free of pollutants entering the recharge areas is a critical environmental concern.

grouper any of several species of large sea bass, especially the genera *Mycteroperca* and *Epinephelus*, found in warm waters.

grouse fowl-like game bird of the subfamily Tetraonidae, in the pheasant family, Phasianidae. The subfamily also includes quail, ptarmigan, and prairie chicken. Grouse are native to North America and N Europe. They are mostly ground-living. During the mating season the males undertake elaborate courtship displays in small individual territories (leks).

Grove City v Bell a US Supreme Court decision 1984 dealing with sexual discrimination in publicly funded schools. Grove City College, a private school in Pennsylvania, refused to comply officially with laws prohibiting sex discrimination. Although as a whole it was not a direct recipient of federal funds, certain programs in the school received federal scholarship money. The government moved to withhold funds from Grove City under the Education Amendments 1972. On appeal, the Court ruled 6–3 that restrictions on sex discrimination could be applied only to programs and not to the school as a whole; federal action was to be taken only on a "program-specific" basis.

GRP abbreviation for *glass-reinforced plastic*, a plastic material strengthened by glass fibers, usually erroneously known as ◊fiberglass. GRP is a favored material for boat hulls and for the bodies and some structural components of performance automobiles; it is also used in the manufacture of passenger automobiles.

GU abbreviation for *Guam*, the largest of the Mariana Islands.

Guadalajara industrial city (textiles, glass, soap, pottery), capital of Jalisco state, W Mexico; population (1990) 2,847,000. It is a key communications center. It has a 16th–17th-century cathedral, the Governor's Palace, and an orphanage with murals by the Mexican painter José Orozco (1883–1949).

Guadalcanal largest of the ◊Solomon Islands; area 2,510 sq mi/6,500 sq km; population (1987) 71,000. Gold, copra, and rubber are produced. During World War II it was the scene of a battle that was won by US forces after six months of fighting.

Guadeloupe island group in the Leeward Islands, West Indies, an overseas *département* of France; area 658 sq mi/1,705 sq km; population (1990) 387,000. The main islands are Basse-Terre, on which is the chief

town of the same name, and Grande-Terre. Sugar refining and rum distilling are the main industries.

Guam largest of the ◊Mariana Islands in the W Pacific, an unincorporated territory of the US
area 208 sq mi/540 sq km
capital Agaña
cities Apra (port), Tamuning
features major US air and naval base, much used in the Vietnam War; tropical, with much rain
products sweet potatoes, fish; tourism is important
currency US dollar
population (1990) 132,800
languages English, Chamorro (basically Malay-Polynesian)
religion 96% Roman Catholic
government popularly elected governor (Ricardo Bordallo from 1985) and single-chamber legislature
recent history ceded by Spain to the US 1898; occupied by Japan 1941–44. Guam achieved full US citizenship and self-government from 1950.

Guangdong or *Kwantung* province of S China
area 89,320 sq mi/231,400 sq km
capital ◊Guangzhou
features tropical climate; Hainan, Leizhou peninsula, and the foreign enclaves of Hong Kong and Macao in the Pearl river delta
products rice, sugar, tobacco, minerals, fish
population (1990) 62,829,000.

Guangxi or *Kwangsi Chuang* autonomous region in S China
area 85,074 sq mi/220,400 sq km
capital Nanning
products rice, sugar, fruit
population (1990) 42,246,000, including the Zhuang people, allied to the Thai, who form China's largest ethnic minority.

Guangzhou or *Kwangchow* or *Canton* capital of Guangdong province, S China; population (1989) 3,490,000. Industries include shipbuilding, engineering, chemicals, and textiles.

Guantánamo capital of a province of the same name in SE Cuba; population (1989) 200,400. It is a trading center in a fertile agricultural region producing sugar. Iron, copper, chromium, and manganese are mined nearby. There is a US naval base, for which the Cuban government has refused to accept rent since 1959.

Guaraní member of a South American Indian people who formerly inhabited the area that is now Paraguay, S Brazil, and Bolivia. The Guarani live mainly in reserves; few retain the traditional ways of hunting in the tropical forest, cultivation, and ritual warfare. About 1 million speak Guarani, a member of the Tupian language group.

Guardi Francesco 1712–1793. Italian painter. He produced souvenir views of his native Venice that were commercially less successful than Canaletto's but are now considered more atmospheric, with subtler use of reflected light.

Guare John 1938– . US playwright best known for his screenplay of Louis Malle's *Atlantic City* 1980. His stage plays include *House of Blue Leaves* 1971 and *Six Degrees of Separation* 1990.

Guarneri family of stringed-instrument makers of Cremona, Italy. Giuseppe "del Gesù" Guarneri (1698–1744) produced the finest models.

Guatemala country in Central America, bounded N and NW by Mexico, E by Belize and the Caribbean Sea, SE by Honduras and El Salvador, and SW by the Pacific Ocean. *See panel p. 414*

Guatemala City capital of Guatemala; population (1983) 1,300,000. It produces textiles, tires, footwear, and cement. It was founded 1776 when its predecessor (Antigua) was destroyed in an earthquake. It was severely damaged by another earthquake 1976.

guava tropical American tree *Psidium guajava* of the myrtle family Myrtaceae; the astringent yellow pear-shaped fruit is used to make guava jelly, or it can be stewed or canned. It has a high vitamin-C content.

Guangxi The limestone hills near Guilin in the Chinese province of Guangxi.

Guayaquil largest city and chief port of ◊Ecuador; population (1986) 1,509,100. The economic center of Ecuador, Guayaquil manufactures machinery and consumer goods, processes food, and refines petroleum. It was founded 1537 by the Spanish explorer Francisco de Orellana.

Guderian Heinz 1888–1954. German general in World War II. He created the Panzer (German "armor") divisions that formed the ground spearhead of Hitler's *Blitzkrieg* attack strategy, achieving a significant breakthrough at Sedan in Ardennes, France 1940, and leading the advance to Moscow 1941.

Guérin Camille 1872–1961. French bacteriologist who, with ◊Calmette, developed the *bacille* Calmette-Guérin (◊BCG) vaccine for tuberculosis.

Guernsey second largest of the ◊Channel Islands; area 24.3 sq mi/63 sq km; population (1986) 55,500. The capital is St Peter Port. Products include electronics, tomatoes, flowers, and, more recently, butterflies; from 1975 it has been a major financial center. Guernsey cattle, which are a distinctive pale fawn color and give rich creamy milk, originated here.

guerrilla irregular soldier fighting in a small unofficial unit, typically against an established or occupying power, and engaging in sabotage, ambush, and the like, rather than pitched battles against an opposing army. Guerrilla tactics have been used both by resistance armies in wartime (for example, the Vietnam War) and in peacetime by national liberation groups and militant political extremists (for example the ◊PLO; Tamil Tigers).

Guest Edgar Albert 1881–1959. US journalist and poet. From 1900 he wrote "Breakfast Table Chat" for the *Detroit Free Press*. The column combined light verse and folksy wisdom and was later nationally syndicated. Guest's best-selling collections of verse include *A Heap o' Livin'* 1916 and *Harbor Lights of Home* 1928.

Guevara "Che" Ernesto 1928–1967. Latin American revolutionary. He was born in Argentina and trained there as a doctor, but left his homeland 1953 because of his opposition to the right-wing president Perón. In effecting the Cuban revolution of 1959, he was second only to Castro and Castro's brother Raúl. In 1965 he went to the Congo to fight against white mercenaries, and then to Bolivia, where he was killed in an unsuccessful attempt to lead a peasant rising. He was an orthodox Marxist and renowned for his guerrilla techniques.

Guiana NE part of South America that includes ◊French Guiana, ◊Guyana, and ◊Surinam.

Guido Reni. Italian painter, see ◊Reni.

Guienne ancient province of SW France which formed the duchy of Aquitaine with Gascony in the 12th century. Its capital was Bordeaux. It became English 1154 and passed to France 1453.

guild or *gild* medieval association, particularly of artisans or merchants, formed for mutual aid and protection and the pursuit of a common purpose, religious

---

Guatemala
Republic of
(*República de Guatemala*)

area 42,031 sq mi/108,889 sq km
capital Guatemala City
cities Quezaltenango, Puerto Barrios (naval base)
physical mountainous; narrow coastal plains; limestone tropical plateau in N; frequent earthquakes
environment between 1960 and 1980 nearly 57% of the country's forest was cleared for farming
features Mayan archeological remains, including site at Tikal
head of state and government Ramiro de Leon Carpio from 1993
political system democratic republic
political parties Guatemalan Christian Democratic Party (PDCG), Christian center-left; Center Party (UCN), centrist; National Democratic Cooperation Party (PDCN), center-right; Revolutionary Party (PR), radical; Movement of National Liberation (MLN), extreme right-wing; Democratic

Institutional Party (PID), moderate conservative; Solidarity Action Movement (MAS), right-wing
exports coffee, bananas, cotton, sugar, beef
currency quetzal
population (1992) 9,442,000 (Mayaquiche Indians 54%, mestizos (mixed race) 42%); growth rate 2.8% p.a. (87% of under-fives suffer from malnutrition)
life expectancy men 57, women 61
languages Spanish (official); 40% speak 18 Indian languages
religion Roman Catholic 80%, Protestant 20%
literacy men 63%, women 47% (1985 est)
GDP $7 bn (1987); $834 per head

chronology
1839 Independence achieved from Spain.
1954 Col Carlos Castillo became president in US-backed coup, halting land reform.
1963 Military coup made Col Enrique Peralta president.
1966 Cesar Méndez elected president.
1970 Carlos Araña elected president.
1974 General Kjell Laugerud became president. Widespread political violence precipitated by the discovery of falsified election returns in March.
1978 General Fernando Romeo became president.
1981 Growth of antigovernment guerrilla movement.
1982 General Angel Anibal became president. Army coup installed General Ríos Montt as head of junta and then as president; political violence continued.
1983 Montt removed in coup led by General Mejía Victores, who declared amnesty for the guerrillas.
1985 New constitution adopted; PDCG won congressional elections; Vinicio Cerezo elected president.
1989 Coup attempt against Cerezo foiled. Over 100,000 people killed and 40,000 reported missing since 1980.
1991 Jorge Serrano Elías of the Solidarity Action Movement elected president. Diplomatic relations with Belize established.
1993 President Serrano deposed; Ramiro de Leon Carpio elected president by assembly.

Guinea
Republic of
(*République de Guinée*)

area 94,901 sq mi/245,857 sq km
capital Conakry
cities Labé, Nzérékoré, Kankan
physical flat coastal plain with mountainous interior;
sources of rivers Niger, Gambia, and Senegal; forest in SE
environment large amounts of toxic waste from industrialized countries have been dumped in Guinea
features Fouta Djallon, area of sandstone plateaus, cut by deep valleys
head of state and government Lansana Conté from 1984

political system military republic
political parties none since 1984
exports coffee, rice, palm kernels, alumina, bauxite, diamonds
currency syli or franc
population (1992) 7,232,000 (chief peoples are Fulani, Malinke, Susu); growth rate 2.3% p.a.
life expectancy men 39, women 42
languages French (official), African languages
media state-owned, but some criticism of the government tolerated; no daily newspaper
religions Muslim 85%, Christian 10%, local 5%
literacy men 40%, women 17% (1985 est)
GNP $1.9 bn (1987); $369 per head

chronology
1958 Full independence achieved from France; Sékou Touré elected president.
1977 Strong opposition to Touré's rigid Marxist policies forced him to accept return to mixed economy.
1980 Touré returned unopposed for fourth seven-year term.
1984 Touré died. Bloodless coup established a military committee for national recovery, led by Col Lansana Conté.
1985 Attempted coup against Conté while he was out of the country was foiled by loyal troops.
1990 Sent troops to join the multinational force that attempted to stabilize Liberia.
1991 Antigovernment general strike by National Confederation of Guinea Workers (CNTG).

---

or economic. Guilds became politically powerful in Europe but after the 16th century their position was undermined by the growth of capitalism.

Guilin or *Kweilin* principal tourist city of S China, on the Li River, Guangxi province; population (1984 est) 446,900. The dramatic limestone mountains are a tourist attraction.

guillotine beheading device consisting of a metal blade that descends between two posts. It was common in the Middle Ages and was introduced 1791 in an improved design by physician Joseph Ignace Guillotin (1738–1814) in France. It was subsequently used for executions during the French Revolution. It is still in use in some countries.

Guinea country in W Africa, bounded N by Senegal, NE by Mali, SE by the Ivory Coast, S by Liberia and Sierra Leone, W by the Atlantic Ocean, and NW by Guinea-Bissau. *See panel p. 416*

Guinea-Bissau country in W Africa, bounded N by Senegal, E and SE by Guinea, and SW by the Atlantic Ocean.

guinea pig species of cavy, a type of rodent.

Guinevere Welsh *Gwenhwyfar* in British legend, the wife of King ◊Arthur. Her adulterous love affair with the knight ◊Lancelot of the Lake led ultimately to Arthur's death.

Guinness Alec 1914– . English actor of stage and screen. His films include *Kind Hearts and Coronets* 1949 (in which he played eight parts), *The Bridge on the River Kwai* 1957 (Academy Award), and *Star Wars* 1977.

guitar six-stringed, or twelve-stringed, flat-bodied musical instrument, plucked or strummed with the fingers. The *Hawaiian guitar*, laid across the lap, uses a metal bar to produce a distinctive gliding tone; the solid-bodied *electric guitar*, developed in the

1950s, mixes and amplifies vibrations from microphone contacts at different points to produce a range of tone qualities.

Guiyang or *Kweiyang* capital and industrial city of Guizhou province, S China; population (1989) 1,490,000. Industries include metals and machinery.

Guizhou or *Kweichow* province of S China
area 67,164 sq mi/174,000 sq km
capital Guiyang
products rice, corn, nonferrous minerals
population (1990) 32,392,000.

Gujarat or *Gujerat* state of W India
area 75,656 sq mi/196,000 sq km
capital Ahmedabad
features heavily industrialized; includes most of the Rann of Kutch; the Gir Forest (the last home of the wild Asian lion)
products cotton, petrochemicals, oil, gas, rice, textiles
languages Gujarati (Gujerati), Hindi
population (1991) 41,174,000.

Gujarati inhabitant of Gujarat on the NW coast of India. The Gujaratis number approximately 30 million and speak their own Indo-European language, Gujarati, which has a long literary tradition. They are predominantly Hindu (90%), with Muslim (8%) and Jain (2%) minorities.

Gujarati language member of the Indo-Iranian branch of the Indo-European language family, spoken in and around the state of Gujarat in W India. It is written in its own script, a variant of the Devanagari script used for Sanskrit and Hindi.

gulag Russian term for the system of prisons and labor camps used to silence dissidents and opponents of the Soviet regime.

Gulfport city in SE Mississippi, on the Gulf of Mexico, W of Biloxi and E of New Orleans, Louisiana; seat of Harrison County and a port of entry to the US;

Guinea-Bissau

Republic of

(República da Guiné- Bissau)

area 13,944 sq mi/36,125 sq km

capital Bissau

cities Mansôa, São Domingos

physical flat coastal plain rising to savanna in E

features the archipelago of Bijagós

head of state and government João Bernardo Vieira from 1980 and 1984 respectively

political system emergent democracy

political party African Party for the Independence of Portuguese Guinea and Cape Verde (PAIGC), nationalist socialist

exports rice, coconuts, peanuts, fish, timber

currency peso

population (1992) 1,015,000; growth rate 2.4% p.a.

life expectancy 42; 1990 infant mortality rate was 14.8%

languages Portuguese (official), Crioulo (Cape Verdean dialect of Portuguese), African languages

religions animism 54%, Muslim 38%, Christian 8%

literacy men 46%, women 17% (1985 est)

GDP $135 million (1987); $146 per head

chronology

1956 PAIGC formed to secure independence from Portugal.

1973 Two-thirds of the country declared independent, with Luiz Cabral as president of a state council.

1974 Independence achieved from Portugal.

1980 Cape Verde decided not to join a unified state. Cabral deposed, and João Vieira became chair of a council of revolution.

1981 PAIGC confirmed as the only legal party, with Vieira as its secretary-general.

1982 Normal relations with Cape Verde restored.

1984 New constitution adopted, making Vieira head of government as well as head of state.

1989 Vieira reelected.

1991 Other parties legalized.

1992 Multiparty electoral commission established.

1993 Death penalty abolished for all offenses.

population (1990) 40,700. It is a major shipping point for lumber, cotton, and food products.

Gulf States oil-rich countries sharing the coastline of the ◊Persian Gulf (Bahrain, Iran, Iraq, Kuwait, Oman, Qatar, Saudi Arabia, and the United Arab Emirates). In the US, the term refers to those states bordering the Gulf of Mexico (Alabama, Florida, Louisiana, Mississippi, and Texas).

Gulf Stream warm ocean ◊current that flows north from the warm waters of the Gulf of Mexico. Part of the current is diverted east across the Atlantic, where it is known as the *North Atlantic Drift*, and warms what would otherwise be a colder climate in the British Isles and NW Europe.

Gulf War war Jan 16–Feb 28, 1991, between Iraq and a coalition of 28 nations led by the US. (It is also another name for the ◊Iran–Iraq War). The invasion and annexation of Kuwait by Iraq on Aug 2, 1990, provoked a buildup of US troops in Saudi Arabia, eventually totaling over 500,000. The UK subsequently deployed 42,000 troops, France 15,000, Egypt 20,000, and other nations smaller contingents. An air offensive lasting six weeks, in which "smart" weapons came of age, destroyed about one-third of Iraqi equipment and inflicted massive casualties. A 100-hour ground war followed, which effectively destroyed the remnants of the 500,000-strong Iraqi army in or near Kuwait.

gull seabird of the family Laridae, especially the genus *Larus*. Gulls are usually 10–30 in/25–75 cm long, white with gray or black on the back and wings, and have large beaks.

gum in botany, complex polysaccharides (carbohydrates) formed by many plants and trees, particularly by those from dry regions. They form four main groups: plant exudates (gum arabic); marine plant extracts (agar); seed extracts; and fruit and vegetable extracts. Some are made synthetically.

gum arabic substance obtained from certain species of ◊acacia, with uses in medicine, confectionery, and adhesive manufacture.

gun any kind of firearm or any instrument consisting of a metal tube from which a projectile is discharged; see also ◊artillery, ◊machine gun, ◊pistol, and ◊small arms.

gun metal type of ◊bronze, an alloy high in copper (88%), also containing tin and zinc, so-called because it was once used to cast cannons. It is tough, hard-wearing, and resists corrosion.

gunpowder or *black powder* the oldest known ◊explosive, a mixture of 75% potassium nitrate (saltpeter), 15% charcoal, and 10% sulfur. Sulfur ignites at a low temperature, charcoal burns readily, and the potassium nitrate provides oxygen for the explosion. Although progressively replaced since the late 19th century by high explosives, gunpowder is still widely used for quarry blasting, fuses, and fireworks.

Gunpowder Plot in British history, the Catholic conspiracy to blow up James I and his parliament on Nov 5, 1605. It was discovered through an anonymous letter. Guy ◊Fawkes was found in the cellar beneath the Palace of Westminster, ready to fire a store of explosives. Several of the conspirators were killed, and Fawkes and seven others were executed.

Guomindang Chinese National People's Party, founded 1894 by ◊Sun Yat-sen, which overthrew the Manchu Empire 1912. From 1927 the right wing, led by ◊Chiang Kai-shek, was in conflict with the left, led by Mao Zedong until the Communist victory 1949 (except for the period of the Japanese invasion 1937–45). It survives as the dominant political party of Taiwan, where it is still spelled *Kuomintang*.

guru Hindi *gurū* Hindu or Sikh leader, or religious teacher.

Gush Emunim Israeli fundamentalist group, founded 1973, which claims divine right to settlement of the West Bank, Gaza Strip, and Golan Heights as part of Israel. The claim is sometimes extended to the Euphrates.

Gustavus Adolphus (Gustavus II) 1594–1632. King of Sweden from 1611, when he succeeded his father

Charles IX. He waged successful wars with Denmark, Russia, Poland, and in the ◊Thirty Years' War became a champion of the Protestant cause. Landing in Germany 1630, he defeated the German general Wallenstein at Lützen, SW of Leipzig Nov 6, 1632, but was killed in the battle. He was known as the "Lion of the North."

Gustavus Vasa (Gustavus I) 1496–1560. King of Sweden from 1523, when he was elected after leading the Swedish revolt against Danish rule. He united and pacified the country and established Lutheranism as the state religion.

gut or **alimentary canal** in the ◊digestive system, the part of an animal responsible for processing food and preparing it for entry into the blood.

Gutenberg Johann c. 1400–1468. German printer, the inventor of printing from movable metal type, based on the Chinese wood-block-type method (although Laurens Janszoon ◊Coster has a rival claim).

Guthrie Woody (Woodrow Wilson) 1912–1967. US folk singer and songwriter whose left-wing protest songs, "dustbowl ballads," and "talking blues" influenced, among others, Bob Dylan; they include "Deportees," "Hard Travelin'," and "This Land Is Your Land."

Guyana country in South America, bounded N by the Atlantic Ocean, E by Suriname, S and SW by Brazil, and NW by Venezuela.

Guzmán Blanco Antonio 1829–1899. Venezuelan dictator and military leader (*caudillo*), who seized power 1870 and remained absolute ruler until 1889. He modernized Caracas to become the political capital; committed resources to education, communications, and agriculture; and encouraged foreign trade.

Gwyn Nell (Eleanor) 1651–1687. English comedy actress from 1665, formerly an orange-seller at Drury Lane Theatre, London. The poet Dryden wrote parts for her, and from 1669 she was the mistress of Charles II.

Gwynedd county in NW Wales
area 1,494 sq mi/3,870 sq km
cities Caernarvon (administrative headquarters), Bangor
features Snowdonia National Park including Snowdon, the highest mountain in Wales 3,561 ft/1,085 m, and the largest Welsh lake, Llyn Tegid (Bala Lake); Caernarvon Castle.

gymnastics physical exercises, originally for health and training (so-called from the way in which men of ancient Greece trained: *gymnos* "naked"). The *gymnasia* were schools for training competitors for public games. *Men's gymnastics* includes high bar, parallel bars, horse vault, rings, pommel horse, and floor exercises. *Women's gymnastics* includes asymmetrical bars, side horse vault, balance beam, and floor exercises. Also popular are sports acrobatics, performed by gymnasts in pairs, trios, or fours to music, where the emphasis is on dance, balance, and timing, and *rhythmic gymnastics*, choreographed to music and performed by individuals or six-girl teams, with small hand apparatus such as a ribbon, ball, or hoop.

gymnosperm in botany, any plant whose seeds are exposed, as opposed to the structurally more advanced ◊angiosperms, where they are inside an ovary. The group includes conifers and related plants such as cycads and ginkgos, whose seeds develop in ◊cones. Fossil gymnosperms have been found in rocks about 350 million years old.

Guyana
Cooperative Republic of

area 82,978 sq mi/214,969 sq km
capital (and port) Georgetown
cities New Amsterdam, Mabaruma
physical coastal plain rises into rolling highlands with savanna in S; mostly tropical rain forest
features Mount Roraima; Kaietur National Park, including Kaietur Fall on the Potaro (tributary of Essequibo) 821 ft/ 250 m
head of state and government Cheddi Jagan from 1992
political system democratic republic
political parties People's National Congress (PNC), Afro-Guyanan nationalist socialist; People's Progressive Party (PPP), Indian Marxist-Leninist

exports sugar, rice, rum, timber, diamonds, bauxite, shrimps, molasses
currency Guyanese dollar
population (1992) 748,000 (51% descendants of workers introduced from India to work the sugar plantations after the abolition of slavery, 30% black, 5% Amerindian); growth rate 2% p.a.
life expectancy men 66, women 71
languages English (official), Hindi, Amerindian
media one government-owned daily newspaper; one independent paper published three times a week, on which the government puts pressure by withholding foreign exchange for newsprint; one weekly independent in the same position. There is also legislation that restricts exchange of information between public officials, government, and the press
religions Christian 57%, Hindu 33%, Sunni Muslim 9%
literacy men 97%, women 95% (1985 est)
GNP $359 million (1987); $445 per head

chronology
1831 Became British colony under name of British Guiana.
1953 Assembly elections won by left-wing PPP; Britain suspended constitution and installed interim administration, fearing communist takeover.
1961 Internal self-government granted; Cheddi Jagan became prime minister.
1964 PNC leader Forbes Burnham led PPP–PNC coalition.
1966 Independence achieved from Britain.
1970 Guyana became a republic within the Commonwealth.
1981 Forbes Burnham became first executive president under new constitution.
1985 Burnham died; succeeded by Desmond Hoyte.
1992 PPP had decisive victory in assembly elections; Jagan became president.

gyroscope High-speed photograph of a gyroscope in motion.

gynecology in medicine, a specialist branch concerned with disorders of the female reproductive system.

gypsum common ◊mineral, composed of hydrous calcium sulfate, $CaSO_4 \cdot 2H_2O$. It ranks 2 on the Mohs' scale of hardness. Gypsum is used for making casts and molds, and for blackboard chalk.

Gypsy English name for a member of the ◊Romany people.

gyroscope mechanical instrument, used as a stabilizing device and consisting, in its simplest form, of a heavy wheel mounted on an axis fixed in a ring that can be rotated about another axis, which is also fixed in a ring capable of rotation about a third axis. Applications of the gyroscope principle include the gyrocompass, the gyropilot for automatic steering, and gyro-directed torpedoes.

Haakon seven kings of Norway, including:

Haakon IV 1204–1263. King of Norway from 1217, the son of Haakon III. Under his rule, Norway flourished both militarily and culturally; he took control of the Faroe Islands, Greenland 1261, and Iceland 1262–64. His court was famed throughout N Europe.

Haakon VII 1872–1957. King of Norway from 1905. Born Prince Charles, the second son of Frederick VIII of Denmark, he was elected king of Norway on separation from Sweden, and in 1906 he took the name Haakon. In World War II he carried on the resistance from Britain during the Nazi occupation of his country. He returned 1945.

habanera or *havanaise* slow dance in two-four time, originating in Havana, Cuba, which was introduced into Spain during the 19th century. There is a celebrated example of this dance in Bizet's opera *Carmen*.

habeas corpus in law, a writ directed to someone who has custody of a person, ordering him or her to bring the person before the court issuing the writ and to justify why the person is detained in custody.

Haber Fritz 1868–1934. German chemist whose conversion of atmospheric nitrogen to ammonia opened the way for the synthetic fertilizer industry. His study of the combustion of hydrocarbons led to the commercial "cracking" or fractional distillation of natural oil (petroleum) into its components (for example, diesel, gasoline, and paraffin). In electrochemistry, he was the first to demonstrate that oxidation and reduction take place at the electrodes; from this he developed a general electrochemical theory.

habitat in ecology, the localized ◊environment in which an organism lives. Habitats are often described by the dominant plant type or physical feature, such as a grassland habitat or rocky seashore habitat.

Habsburg European royal family; see ◊Hapsburg.

hacking unauthorized access to a computer, either for fun or for malicious or fraudulent purposes. Hackers generally use microcomputers and telephone lines to obtain access. In computing, the term is used in a wider sense to mean using software for enjoyment or self-education, not necessarily involving unauthorized access. See also computer ◊virus.

Hackman Gene 1931– . US actor. He became a star as "Popeye" Doyle in *The French Connection* 1971 and continued to play major combative roles in such films as *The Conversation* 1974, *The French Connection II* 1975, and *Mississippi Burning* 1988.

haddock marine fish *Melanogrammus aeglefinus* of the cod family found off the N Atlantic coast. It is brown with silvery underparts and black markings above the pectoral fins. It can grow to a length of 3 ft/1 m. Haddock are important food fish; about 100 million lb/45 million kg are taken annually off the New England fishing banks alone.

Hades in Greek mythology, the underworld where spirits went after death, usually depicted as a cavern

Hadrian's Wall A section of Hadrian's Wall leading eastward to Housesteads Fort.

Haile Selassie
Haile Selassie, former emperor of Ethiopia, who Westernized the institutions of his country.

or pit underneath the Earth, the entrance of which was guarded by the three-headed dog Cerberus. It was presided over by the god Pluto or Hades (Roman Dis). Pluto was the brother of Zeus and married ◊Persephone, daughter of Demeter and Zeus.

Hadrian AD 76–138. Roman emperor from 117. Born in Spain, he was adopted by his relative, the emperor Trajan, whom he succeeded. He abandoned Trajan's conquests in Mesopotamia and adopted a defensive policy, which included the building of Hadrian's Wall in Britain.

Hadrian's Wall Roman fortification built AD 122–126 to mark England's N boundary and abandoned about 383; its ruins run 115 mi/185 km from Wallsend on the river Tyne to Maryport, W Cumbria. In some parts, the wall was covered with a glistening, white coat of mortar. The fort at South Shields, Arbeia, built to defend the E end, is being reconstructed.

Hâfiz Shams al-Din Mohammed *c.* 1326–1390. Persian lyric poet who was born in Shiraz and taught in a Dervish college there. His *Diwan*, a collection of short odes, extols the pleasures of life and satirizes his fellow Dervishes.

hafnium silvery, metallic element, symbol Hf, atomic number 72, atomic weight 178.49. It occurs in nature in ores of zirconium, the properties of which it resembles. Hafnium absorbs neutrons better than most metals, so it is used in the control rods of nuclear reactors; it is also used for light-bulb filaments.

Haganah Zionist military organization in Palestine. It originated under the Turkish rule of the Ottoman Empire before World War I to protect Jewish settlements, and many of its members served in the British forces in both world wars. After World War II it condemned guerrilla activity, opposing the British authorities only passively. It formed the basis of the Israeli army after Israel was established 1948.

Hagerstown city in NW Maryland, on Antietam Creek, NW of Baltimore and just S of the Pennsylvania border; population (1980) 34,132. Industries include engine and missile parts and furniture.

Haggadah in Judaism, the part of the Talmudic literature not concerned with religious law (the *Halakah*), but devoted to folklore and legends of heroes.

Haggard H(enry) Rider 1856–1925. English novelist. He used his experience in the South African colonial service in his romantic adventure tales, including *King Solomon's Mines* 1885 and *She* 1887.

haggis Scottish dish made from a sheep's or calf's heart, liver, and lungs, minced with onion, oatmeal, suet, spices, and salt, mixed with stock, and traditionally boiled in the animal's stomach for several hours.

Hagia Sophia Byzantine building in Istanbul, Turkey, built 532–37 as an Eastern Orthodox cathedral, replacing earlier churches. From 1204 to 1261 it was a Catholic cathedral; 1453–1934 an Islamic mosque; and in 1934 it became a museum.

Hague, The (Dutch *'s-Gravenhage* or *Den Haag*) capital of the province of South Holland and seat of the Netherlands government, linked by canal with Rotterdam and Amsterdam; population (1991) 444,200.

Hahn Otto 1879–1968. German physical chemist who discovered nuclear fission (see ◊nuclear energy). In 1938 with Fritz Strassmann (1902–1980), he discovered that uranium nuclei split when bombarded with neutrons, which led to the development of the atomic bomb. He was awarded the Nobel Prize for Chemistry 1944.

Haifa port in NE Israel, at the foot of Mount Carmel; population (1988) 222,600. Industries include oil refining and chemicals. It is the capital of a district of the same name.

Haig Alexander (Meigs) 1924– . US general and Republican politician. He became President Nixon's White House chief of staff at the height of the ◊Watergate scandal, was NATO commander 1974–79, and secretary of state to President Reagan 1981–82.

haiku seventeen-syllable Japanese verse form, usually divided into three lines of five, seven, and five syllables. ◊Bashō popularized the form in the 17th century. It evolved from the 31-syllable *tanka* form dominant from the 8th century.

hail precipitation in the form of pellets of ice (hailstones). It is caused by the circulation of moisture in strong convection currents, usually within cumulonimbus ◊clouds.

Haile Selassie Ras (Prince) Tafari ("the Lion of Judah") 1892–1975. Emperor of Ethiopia 1930–74. He pleaded unsuccessfully to the League of Nations against Italian conquest of his country 1935–36, and lived in the UK until his restoration 1941. He was deposed by a military coup 1974 and died in captivity the following year. Followers of the Rastafarian religion (see ◊Rastafarianism) believe that he was the Messiah, the incarnation of God (Jah).

Hainan island in the South China Sea; area 13,124 sq mi/34,000 sq km; population (1990) 6,557,000. The capital is Haikou. In 1987 Hainan was designated a Special Economic Zone; in 1988 it was separated from Guangdong and made a new province. It is China's second-largest island.

Haiphong industrial port in N Vietnam; population (1989) 456,000. Among its industries are shipbuilding and the making of cement, plastics, phosphates, and textiles.

hair threadlike structure growing from mammalian skin. Each hair grows from a pit-shaped follicle of the outer skin layer (epidermal cells). Hair consists of dead cells impregnated with the protein keratin.

Haiti country in the Caribbean, occupying the W part of the island of Hispaniola; to the E is the Dominican Republic.

hajj pilgrimage to ◊Mecca that should be undertaken by every Muslim at least once in a lifetime, unless he or she is prevented by financial or health difficulties. A Muslim who has been on hajj may take the additional name Hajji. Many of the pilgrims on hajj also visit Medina, where the prophet Mohammed is buried.

hake any of various marine fishes of the cod family, found in N European, African, and American waters. They have silvery, elongated bodies and attain a length of 3 ft/1 m. They have two dorsal fins and one long anal fin. The silver hake *Merluccius bilinearis* is an important food fish.

halal conforming to the rules laid down by Islam. The term can be applied to all aspects of life, but usually refers to food permissible under Muslim dietary laws, including meat from animals that have been slaughtered in the correct ritual fashion.

Halas George Stanley 1895–1983. US athlete and sports promoter. He was founder of the Chicago Bears of the National Football League and was an active player until 1929. He acted as coach until retirement

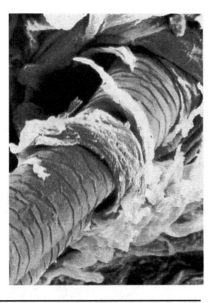

hair False-color electron-microscope view of a human hair, showing the surface layer of highly flattened and partly overlapping cells.

Haiti
Republic of
(*République d'Haïti*)

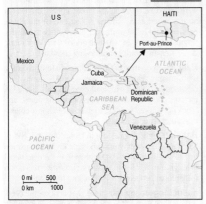

area 10,712 sq mi/27,750 sq km
capital Port-au-Prince
cities Cap-Haïtien, Gonaïves, Les Cayes
physical mainly mountainous and tropical; occupies W third of Hispaniola Island in Caribbean Sea; seriously deforested
features oldest black republic in the world; only French-speaking republic in the Americas; island of La Tortuga off N coast was formerly a pirate lair
head of state (interim) Joseph Nerette from 1991
head of government (interim) Robert Malval from 1993
political system transitional
political party National Progressive Party (PNP), right-wing military
exports coffee, sugar, sisal, cotton, cocoa, bauxite
currency gourde
population (1992) 6,764,000; growth rate 1.7% p.a.; one of highest population densities in the world; about 1.5 million Haitians live outside Haiti (in US and Canada); about 400,000 live in virtual slavery in the Dominican Republic, where they went or were sent to cut sugar cane

life expectancy men 51, women 54
languages French (official, spoken by literate 10% minority), Creole (spoken by 90% black majority)
media No official censorship, but journalists critical of the government have been beaten and killed. There are three daily papers, the largest of which has a circulation of (1993) 6,000, and four weekly newspapers. Only one of these (*Libète*) is in Creole, the majority language, and its circulation (1993) is 12,000. Radio is more important than the press since most of the population are illiterate. There are many small radio stations and news is also circulated on cassette.
religion Christian 95% of which 80% Roman Catholic, voodoo 4%
literacy men 40%, women 35% (1985 est)
GDP $2.2 bn (1987); $414 per head

chronology
1804 Independence achieved from France.
1915 Haiti invaded by US; remained under US control until 1934.
1957 Dr François Duvalier (Papa Doc) elected president.
1964 Duvalier pronounced himself president for life.
1971 Duvalier died, succeeded by his son, Jean-Claude (Baby Doc); thousands murdered during Duvalier era.
1986 Duvalier deposed; replaced by Lt Gen Henri Namphy as head of a governing council.
1988 Feb: Leslie Manigat became president. Namphy staged a military coup in June, but another coup in Sept led by Brig- Gen Prosper Avril replaced him with a civilian government under military control.
1989 Coup attempt against Avril foiled; US aid resumed.
1990 Opposition elements expelled; Ertha Pascal-Trouillot acting president.
1991 Jean-Bertrand Aristide elected president but later overthrown in military coup led by Brig Gen Raoul Cedras. Efforts to reinstate Aristide failed. Joseph Nerette became interim head of state.
1992 Economic sanctions imposed since 1991 were eased by the US but increased by the Organization of American States. Marc Bazin appointed premier.
1993 Bazin resigned. Robert Malval nominated as prime minister. UN blockade introduced in an effort to force Aristide's return.

1967, introducing the T-formation and giving special emphasis to the passing offense.

He became a charter member of the Football Hall of Fame 1963.

Hale George Ellery 1868–1938. US astronomer who made pioneer studies of the Sun and founded three major observatories. In 1889 he invented the spectroheliograph, a device for photographing the Sun at particular wavelengths. In 1917 he established on Mount Wilson, California, a 100-in/2.5-m reflector, the world's largest telescope until superseded 1948 by the 200-in/5-m reflector on Mount Palomar, which Hale had planned just before he died.

Hale Nathan 1755–1776. American Revolutionary War hero, hanged by the British as a spy. He crossed British lines disguised as a teacher and told George ◊Washington that he wished "to be useful." He was sent behind enemy lines on Long Island to gather information about the British army. Captured, he was hanged. Reputedly his final words were "I only regret that I have but one life to lose for my country."

Haley Bill 1927–1981. US pioneer of rock and roll who was originally a western-swing musician. His songs "Rock Around the Clock" 1954 (recorded with his group the Comets and featured in the 1955 film *Blackboard Jungle*) and "Shake, Rattle and Roll" 1955 were big hits of the early rock-and-roll era.

half-life during radioactive decay, the time in which the strength of a radioactive source decays to half its original value. In theory, the decay process is never complete, and there is always some residual radioactivity. For this reason, the half-life (the time taken for 50% of the isotope to decay) is measured, rather than the total decay time. It may vary from millionths of a second to billions of years.

halftone process technique used in printing to reproduce the full range of tones in a photograph or other illustration. The intensity of the printed color is varied from full strength to the lightest shades, even if one color of ink is used. The picture to be reproduced is photographed through a screen ruled with a rectangular mesh of fine lines, which breaks up the tones of the original into areas of dots that vary in frequency according to the intensity of the tone. In the darker areas the dots run together; in the lighter areas they have more space between them.

halibut any of several large flatfishes of the genus *Hippoglossus*, in the family Pleuronectidae, found in the Atlantic and Pacific oceans. The largest of the flatfishes, they may grow to 6 ft/2 m and weigh 200–300 lb/90–135 kg. They are very dark mottled brown or green above and pure white beneath. The Atlantic halibut *H. hippoglossus* is caught offshore at depths from 600 ft/180 m to 2,400 ft/730 m.

Halicarnassus ancient city in Asia Minor (now Bodrum in Turkey), where the tomb of Mausolus, built about 350 BC by widowed Queen Artemisia, was one of the Seven Wonders of the World. The Greek historian Herodotus was born there.

Halifax capital of Nova Scotia, E Canada's main port; population (1986) 296,000. Its industries include oil refining and food processing.

There are six military bases in Halifax and it is a major center of oceanography. It was founded by British settlers 1749.

halite mineral sodium chloride, NaCl, or common ◊salt. When pure it is colorless and transparent, but it is often pink, red, or yellow. It is soft and has a low density.

Haller Albrecht von 1708–1777. Swiss physician and scientist, founder of ◊neurology. He studied the muscles and nerves, and concluded that nerves provide the stimulus that triggers muscle contraction. He also showed that it is the nerves, not muscle or skin, that receive sensation.

Halley Edmond 1656–1742. English atronomer who not only identified 1705 the comet that was later to be known by his name, but also compiled a star catalog, detected the proper motion of stars using historical records, and began a line of research that—after his death—resulted in a reasonably accurate calculation of the astronomical unit.

Halley was also a pioneer geophysicist and meteorologist and worked in many other fields including mathematics. He was a friend of Isaac ◊Newton, whose *Principia* he financed.

Halley's comet comet that orbits the Sun about every 76 years, named after Edmond Halley who calculated its orbit. It is the brightest and most conspicuous of the periodic comets. Recorded sightings go back over 2,000 years. It travels around the Sun in the opposite direction to the planets. Its orbit is inclined at almost 20° to the main plane of the Solar System and ranges between the orbits of Venus and Neptune. It will next reappear 2061.

hallmark official mark stamped on British gold, silver, and (from 1913) platinum, instituted 1327 (royal charter of London Goldsmiths) in order to prevent fraud. After 1363, personal marks of identification were added. Now tests of metal content are carried out at authorized assay offices in London, Birmingham, Sheffield, and Edinburgh; each assay office has its distinguishing mark, to which is added a maker's mark, date letter, and mark guaranteeing standard.

Halloween evening of Oct 31, immediately preceding the Christian feast of Hallowmas or All Saints' Day. Customs associated with Halloween in the US and UK include children wearing masks or costumes, and "trick or treating"—going from house to house collecting candy, fruit, or money.

Hallstatt archeological site in Upper Austria, SW of Salzburg. The salt workings date from prehistoric times. In 1846 over 3,000 graves were discovered belonging to a 9th–5th century BC Celtic civilization transitional between the Bronze and Iron ages.

hallucinogen any substance that acts on the ◊central nervous system to produce changes in perception and mood and often hallucinations. Hallucinogens include ◊LSD, ◊peyote, and mescaline. Their effects are unpredictable and they are illegal in most countries.

halogen any of a group of five nonmetallic elements with similar chemical bonding properties: fluorine, chlorine, bromine, iodine, and astatine. They form a linked group in the ◊periodic table of the elements, descending from fluorine, the most reactive, to astatine, the least reactive. They combine directly with most metals to form salts, such as common salt (NaCl). Each halogen has seven electrons in its valence shell, which accounts for the chemical similarities displayed by the group.

Hals Frans c. 1581–1666. Flemish-born painter of lively portraits, such as the *Laughing Cavalier* 1624 (Wallace Collection, London), and large groups of military companies, governors of charities, and others (many examples in the Frans Hals Museum, Haarlem, the Netherlands). In the 1620s he experimented with genre (domestic) scenes.

Hamburg largest inland port of Europe, in Germany, on the river Elbe; population (1988) 1,571,000. Industries include oil, chemicals, electronics, and cosmetics.

Hamilton capital (since 1815) of Bermuda, on Bermuda Island; population about (1980) 1,617. It has a deep-sea harbor. Hamilton was founded 1612.

Hamilton port in Ontario; population (1986) 557,000. Linked with Lake Ontario by the Burlington Canal, it has a hydroelectric plant and steel, heavy machinery, electrical, chemical, and textile industries.

Hamilton city in the SW corner of Ohio, on the Great Miami River, NW of Cincinnati; seat of Butler County; population (1990) 61,400. Its industries include livestock processing, metal products, paper, and building materials.

The city was built on the site of Fort Hamilton, constructed 1791 by General Arthur St Clair and used as headquarters by General Anthony Wayne during his campaign in the Northwest Territory 1792–93.

Hamilton Alexander 1757–1804. US politician who influenced the adoption of a constitution with a strong central government and was the first secretary of the treasury 1789–95. He led the Federalist Party, and incurred the bitter hatred of Aaron ◊Burr when he voted against Burr in favor of Thomas Jefferson for the presidency 1801. Challenged to a duel by Burr, Hamilton was wounded and died the next day.

Hamilton, born in the West Indies, served during the American Revolution as captain and was George ◊Washington's secretary and aide-de-camp 1777–81. After the war he practiced as a lawyer. He was a member of the Constitutional Convention of 1787, and in the *Federalist* influenced public opinion in favor of the ratification of the Constitution. He was a strong advocate of the wealthy urban sector of American life and encouraged renewed ties with Britain, remaining distrustful of revolutionary France. As the first secretary of the treasury, he proved an able controller of the national finances.

Hamilton Edith 1867–1963. German-born US educator and Classical scholar, best remembered as a collector and translator of ancient myths. Her anthologies *Mythology* 1942 and *The Great Age of Greek Literature* 1943 became standard textbooks. Other important works include *The Greek Way* 1930 and *The Roman Way* 1932.

Hamito-Semitic language any of a family of languages spoken throughout the world. There are two main branches, the *Hamitic* languages of N Africa and the *Semitic* languages originating in Syria, Mesopotamia, Palestine, and Arabia, but now found from Morocco in the west to the Persian Gulf in the east.

Hamlin Hannibal 1809–1891. US political leader and vice-president 1861–65. Originally a Democrat, he served in the US House of Representatives 1843–47 and the US Senate 1848–61. Opposed to slavery, he joined the Republican Party 1856. He served as vice-president in Lincoln's first term. Returning to the Senate as a radical Republican 1868–80, he later served as US minister to Spain 1881–82.

Hammarskjöld Dag 1905–1961. Swedish secretary-general of the United Nations 1953–61. He opposed Britain over the ◊Suez Crisis 1956. His attempts to solve the problem of the Congo (now Zaire), where he was killed in a plane crash, were criticized by the USSR. He was awarded the Nobel Peace Prize 1961.

hammer in track and field athletics, a throwing event in which only men compete. The hammer is a spheri-

cal weight attached to a chain with a handle. The competitor spins the hammer over his head to gain momentum, within the confines of a circle, and throws it as far as he can. The hammer weighs 16 lb/7.26 kg and may originally have been a blacksmith's hammer.

Hammer Armand 1898–1990. US entrepreneur, one of the most remarkable business figures of the 20th century. A pioneer in trading with the USSR from 1921, he later acted as a political mediator. He was chair of the US oil company Occidental Petroleum until his death, and was also an expert on art.

hammerhead any of several species of shark of the genus *Sphyrna*, found in tropical seas, characterized by having eyes at the ends of flattened extensions of the skull. Hammerheads can grow to 13 ft/4 m.

Hammerstein Oscar, II 1895–1960. Lyricist and librettist who collaborated with Richard ◊Rodgers on some of the best-known American musicals, including *Oklahoma* 1943 (Pulitzer Prize), *Carousel* 1945, *South Pacific* 1949 (Pulitzer Prize), *The King and I* 1951, and *The Sound of Music* 1959.

Hammer v Dagenhart US Supreme Court decision 1918 dealing with Congress's power to regulate labor practices in the manufacture of goods for interstate trade. The father of a child who worked in a North Carolina cotton mill sued the mill for an infraction of the Child Labor Law 1916, which prohibited the interstate sale of products of child labor. The Court held that the law was invalid because it regulated local manufacturing under the guise of interstate commerce regulations. US v *Darby Lumber Co* overturned *Hammer*.

Hammett (Samuel) Dashiell 1894–1961. US crime novelist. His works, *The Maltese Falcon* 1930, *The Glass Key* 1931, and the *The Thin Man* 1932, introduced the "hard-boiled" detective character into fiction.

Hammond city in the NW corner of Indiana, on the Calumet River, just S of Chicago, Illinois; population (1990) 84,200. It is a major transportation center, connecting to Lake Michigan via the Calumet Canal. Industries include soap, cereal products, publishing, railroad equipment, and transportation facilities for the city's surrounding steel plants and oil refineries.

Hammond organ electric organ invented in the US by Laurens Hammond 1934 and widely used in gospel music. It was a precursor of the synthesizer.

Hampshire county of S England
area 1,455 sq mi/3,770 sq km
cities Winchester (administrative headquarters), Southampton, Portsmouth, Gosport
features New Forest, area 144 sq mi/373 sq km, a Saxon royal hunting ground
famous people Jane Austen, Charles Dickens, Gilbert White.

Hampton Lionel 1909– . US jazz musician, a top bandleader of the 1940s and 1950s. Originally a drummer, Hampton introduced the vibraphone, an electronically vibrated percussion instrument, to jazz music. With the Benny ◊Goodman band from 1936, he fronted his own big band 1941–65 and subsequently led small groups.

Hampton Wade 1818–1902. US politician and Confederate military leader. During the American Civil War 1861–65, he was appointed brigadier general in the cavalry 1862 and commander of the entire Confederate cavalry corps 1864. After the end of the war 1865 he returned to South Carolina, serving as governor 1876–79 and US senator 1879–91.

.Handel Portrait by
Thomas Hudson
(1756), National
Portrait Gallery,
London.

Appeals by President Coolidge 1924. He served as chief judge of that court 1939–51, handing down opinions in landmark copyright, antitrust, and the constitutional First Amendment cases.

Handel Georg Friedrich 1685–1759. German composer who became a British subject 1726. His first opera, *Almira*, was performed in Hamburg 1705. In 1710 he was appointed Kapellmeister to the elector of Hanover (the future George I of England). In 1712 he settled in England, where he established his popularity with such works as the *Water Music* 1717 (written for George I). His great choral works include the *Messiah* 1742 and the later oratorios *Samson* 1743, *Belshazzar* 1745, *Judas Maccabaeus* 1747, and *Jephtha* 1752.

Han dynasty Chinese ruling family 206 BC–AD 220 established by Liu Bang (256–195 BC) after he overthrew the ◊Qin dynasty and named after the Han River. There was territorial expansion to the W, SW, and N, including the conquest of Korea by emperor Wudi (Wu-ti, ruled 141–87 BC) and the suppression of the Xiongnu invaders. Under the Han, a Confucianist-educated civil service was established and Buddhism introduced.

Hangchow alternative transcription of ◊Hangzhou, a port in Zhejiang province, China.

hang-gliding technique of unpowered flying using air currents, perfected by US engineer Francis Rogallo in the 1970s. The aeronaut is strapped into a carrier, attached to a sail wing of nylon stretched on an aluminum frame like a paper dart, and jumps into the air from a high place, where updrafts of warm air allow soaring on the "thermals." See ◊gliding.

hanging execution by suspension, usually with a drop of 2–6 ft/0.6–2 m, so that the powerful jerk of the tightened rope breaks the neck. This was once a common form of ◊capital punishment in Europe and is still practiced in some states in the US.

Hangzhou or *Hangchow* port and capital of Zhejiang province, China; population (1989) 1,330,000. It has jute, steel, chemical, tea, and silk industries.

Hannibal 247–182 BC. Carthaginian general from 221 BC, son of Hamilcar Barca. His siege of Saguntum (now Sagunto, near Valencia) precipitated the Second ◊Punic War with Rome. Following a campaign in Italy (after crossing the Alps in 218), Hannibal was the victor at Trasimene in 217 and Cannae in 216, but he failed to take Rome. In 203 he returned to Carthage to meet a Roman invasion but was defeated at Zama in 202 and exiled in 196 at Rome's insistence.

Hanoi capital of Vietnam, on the Red River; population (1989) 1,088,900. Central Hanoi has one of the highest population densities in the world: 3,250 people per acre/1,300 per hectare. Industries include textiles, paper, and engineering.

Hanover industrial city, capital of Lower Saxony, Germany; population (1988) 506,000. Industries include machinery, vehicles, electrical goods, rubber, textiles, and oil refining.

Hanover German royal dynasty that ruled Great Britain and Ireland 1714–1901. Under the Act of Settlement 1701, the succession passed to the ruling family of Hanover, Germany, on the death of Queen Anne. On the death of Queen Victoria, the crown passed to Edward VII of the house of Saxe-Coburg.

Hanseatic League (German *Hanse* "group society") confederation of N European trading cities from

hamster rodent of the family Cricetidae with a thickset body, short tail, and cheek pouches to carry food. Several genera are found across Asia and in SE Europe. Hamsters are often kept as pets.

Hamsun Knut 1859–1952. Norwegian novelist whose first novel *Sult/Hunger* 1890 was largely autobiographical. Other works include *Pan* 1894 and *The Growth of the Soil* 1917, which won him a Nobel Prize 1920. His hatred of capitalism made him sympathize with Nazism, and he was fined in 1946 for collaboration.

Han member of the majority ethnic group in China, numbering about 990 million. The Hans speak a wide variety of dialects of the same monosyllabic language, a member of the Sino-Tibetan family. Their religion combines Buddhism, Taoism, Confucianism, and ancestor worship.

Hancock John 1737–1793. US politician and a leader of the American Revolution. As president of the Continental Congress 1775–77, he was the first to sign the Declaration of Independence 1776. Because he signed it in a large, bold hand (in popular belief, so that it would be big enough for George III to see), his name became a colloquial term for a signature in the US. He coveted command of the Continental Army, deeply resenting the selection of George ◊Washington. He was governor of Massachusetts 1780–85 and 1787–93.

Hand Learned Billings 1872–1961. US jurist. He became federal district judge under President Taft 1909 and was appointed to the Second Circuit Court of

the 12th century to 1669. At its height in the late 14th century the Hanseatic League included over 160 cities and towns, among them Lübeck, Hamburg, Cologne, Breslau, and Kraków. The basis of the league's power was its monopoly of the Baltic trade and its relations with Flanders and England. The decline of the Hanseatic League from the 15th century was caused by the closing and moving of trade routes and the development of nation states.

Hanukah or *Chanukah* Jewish festival of lights, which lasts eight days in December and celebrates the recapture of the Temple in Jerusalem by Judas Maccabaeus in 164 BC, and the "miracle" of one day's oil lasting for eight days when the Eternal Light was relit.

Hapsburg or *Habsburg* European royal family, former imperial house of Austria-Hungary. The name comes from the family castle in Switzerland. The Hapsburgs held the title Holy Roman emperor 1273–91, 1298–1308, 1438–1740, and 1745–1806. They ruled Austria from 1278, under the title emperor 1806–1918.

hara-kiri ritual suicide of the Japanese samurai (military caste) since the 12th century. Today it is illegal. It was carried out to avoid dishonor or to demonstrate sincerity, either voluntarily or on the order of a feudal lord. The correct Japanese term is *seppuku*, and, traditionally, the ritual involved cutting open one's stomach with a dagger before one's head was struck off by another samurai's sword.

Harare capital of Zimbabwe, on the Mashonaland plateau, about 5,000 ft/1,525 m above sea level; population (1982) 656,000. It is the center of a rich farming area (tobacco and corn), with metallurgical and food processing industries.

Harbin or *Haerhpin* or *Pinkiang* port on the Songhua River, NE China, capital of Heilongjiang province; population (1989) 2,800,000. Industries include metallurgy, machinery, paper, food processing, and sugar refining, and it is a major rail junction. Harbin was developed by Russian settlers after Russia was granted trading rights there 1896, and more Russians arrived as refugees after the October Revolution 1917.

hard disk in computing, a storage device consisting of a rigid metal ◊disk coated with a magnetic material. Data are read from and written to the disk by means of a unit called a disk drive. The hard disk may be permanently fixed into the drive or in the form of a disk pack that can be removed and exchanged with a different pack. Hard disks vary from large units with capacities of over 3,000 megabytes, intended for use with mainframe computers, to small units with capacities as low as 20 megabytes, intended for use with microcomputers.

Hardicanute *c.* 1019–1042. King of England from 1040. Son of Canute, he was king of Denmark from 1028. In England he was considered a harsh ruler.

Harding Warren G(amaliel) 1865–1923. 29th president of the US 1921–23, a Republican whose administration was known for its corruption. Harding entered the US Senate in 1914. As president he concluded the peace treaties with Germany, Austria, and Hungary, and in the same year called the Washington Conference. He opposed US membership in the ◊League of Nations, thus reinforcing the traditional US position of neutrality. There were charges of corruption among members of his cabinet (the ◊Teapot Dome Scandal), and Harding generally turned a benign eye to the activities of his close associates.

hardness physical property of materials that governs their use. Methods of heat treatment can increase the hardness of metals. A scale of hardness was devised by German–Austrian mineralogist Friedrich Mohs in the 1800s, based upon the hardness of certain minerals from soft talc (Mohs hardness 1) to diamond (10), the hardest of all materials.

See also ◊Brinell hardness test. The *hardness of water* refers to the presence of dissolved minerals in it that prevent soap lathering, particularly compounds of calcium and magnesium. Treatment with a water softener may remove or neutralize them.

Hardouin-Mansart Jules 1646–1708. French architect to Louis XIV from 1675. He designed the lavish Baroque extensions to the palace of Versailles (from 1678) and Grand Trianon. Other works include the Invalides Chapel (1680–91), the Place de Vendôme, and the Place des Victoires, all in Paris.

hardware the mechanical, electrical, and electronic components of a computer system, as opposed to the various programs, which constitute ◊software.

Hardy Thomas 1840–1928. English novelist and poet. His novels, set in rural "Wessex" (his native West Country), portray intense human relationships played out in a harshly indifferent natural world. They include *Far From the Madding Crowd* 1874, *The Return of the Native* 1878, *The Mayor of Casterbridge* 1886, *The Woodlanders* 1887, *Tess of the d'Urbervilles* 1891, and *Jude the Obscure* 1895. His poetry includes the *Wessex Poems* 1898, the blank-verse epic of the Napoleonic Wars *The Dynasts* 1904–08, and several volumes of lyrics.

hare mammal of the genus *Lepus* of the family Leporidae (which also includes rabbits) in the order Lagomorpha. Hares are larger than rabbits, with very long, black-tipped ears, long hind legs, and short, upturned tails.

Unlike rabbits, hares do not burrow. Their furred, open-eyed young (leverets) are cared for in a shallow depression rather than a specially prepared nest cavity. Jack rabbits and snowshoe rabbits are actually hares.

Hare Krishna popular name for a member of the ◊International Society for Krishna Consciousness, derived from their chant.

Hargobind 1595–1644. Indian religious leader, sixth guru (teacher) of Sikhism 1606–44. He encouraged Sikhs to develop military skills in response to growing persecution. At the festival of ◊Diwali, Sikhs celebrate his release from prison.

Hargreaves James died 1778. English inventor who co-invented a carding machine for combing wool 1760. About 1764 he invented his "spinning jenny," which enabled a number of threads to be spun simultaneously by one person.

Harlan John Marshall 1833–1911. US politician and jurist, associate justice of the US Supreme Court 1877–1911. Harlan supported the Union during the American Civil War 1861–65, serving as colonel in the 10th Kentucky Volunteer Infantry and elected Kentucky attorney general 1863. He was defeated as Republican candidate for governor of Kentucky 1871 and 1875.

Before embarking on his political career, Harlan practiced law in Kentucky. He was appointed associate justice by President Hayes after service on a federal Reconstruction Commission in Louisiana 1877 and held the office until his death.

Harlan John Marshall 1899–1971. US jurist and Supreme Court associate justice 1954–71. Chief counsel for the New York Crime Commission 1951–53, Harlan was appointed by President Eisenhower to the US Supreme Court 1954. As associate justice, he was a conservative, especially in the areas of free speech and civil and criminal rights.

Harlem commercial and residential district of Manhattan, New York City. The principal thoroughfare, 125th Street, runs E–W between the Hudson River and the East River. It was a Dutch settlement in 1658; it developed as a black population center from World War I. Harlem's heyday was the 1920s, when it established its reputation as the intellectual, cultural, and entertainment center of black America. Once noted for its music clubs and theaters, it retained the famed Apollo Theater; the Dance Theater and Theater of Harlem are also here.

Harlem Globetrotters US touring basketball team that plays exhibition matches worldwide. Comedy routines as well as their great skills are features of the games. They were founded 1927 by Abraham Saperstein (1903–1966).

Harlem Renaissance movement in US literature in the 1920s that used African-American life and black culture as its subject matter; it was an early manifestation of black pride in the US. The center of the movement was the Harlem section of New York City.

Harlingen city in the SE corner of Texas, S of Corpus Christi and just N of the Mexican border; population (1990) 48,735. Connected to the Rio Grande by an intracoastal waterway, it serves as the processing and marketing area for the lower Rio Grande Valley. Industries include citrus-fruit processing and cotton products.

Harlow Jean. Adopted name of Harlean Carpenter 1911–1937. US film actress, the first "platinum blonde" and the wisecracking sex symbol of the 1930s. Her films include *Hell's Angels* 1930, *Red Dust* 1932, *Platinum Blonde* 1932, *Dinner at Eight* 1933, *China Seas* 1935, and *Saratoga* 1937, during the filming of which she died (her part was completed by a double—with rear and long shots).

harmonica or *mouth organ* pocket-sized reed organ blown directly from the mouth; it was invented by Charles Wheatstone 1829.

harmonics in music, a series of partial vibrations that combine to form a musical tone. The number and relative prominence of harmonics produced determines an instrument's tone color (timbre). An oboe is rich in harmonics, the flute has few. Harmonics conform to successive divisions of the sounding air column or string: their pitches are harmonious.

harmony in music, any simultaneous combination of sounds, as opposed to melody, which is a succession of sounds. Although the term suggests a pleasant or agreeable sound, it is applied to any combination of notes, whether consonant or dissonant. Harmony deals with the formation of chords and their interrelation and logical progression.

Harold two kings of England:

Harold I died 1040. King of England from 1035. The illegitimate son of Canute, known as *Harefoot*, he claimed the throne 1035 when the legitimate heir Hardicanute was in Denmark. He was elected king 1037.

Harold II c. 1020–1066. King of England from Jan 1066. He succeeded his father Earl Godwin 1053 as earl of Wessex. In 1063 William of Normandy (◊William I) tricked him into swearing to support his claim to the English throne, and when the Witan (a council of high-ranking religious and secular men) elected Harold to succeed Edward the Confessor, William prepared to invade. Meanwhile, Harold's treacherous brother Tostig (died 1066) joined the king of Norway, Harald III Hardrada (1015–1066), in invading Northumbria. Harold routed and killed them at Stamford Bridge Sept 25. Three days later William landed at Pevensey, Sussex, and Harold was killed at the Battle of Hastings Oct 14, 1066.

harp plucked musical string instrument, with the strings stretched vertically within a wooden frame, normally triangular. The concert harp is now the largest musical instrument to be plucked by hand. It has up to 47 strings, and seven pedals set into the soundbox at the base to alter pitch.

Harper's Ferry village in W Virginia, where the Potomac and Shenandoah rivers meet. In 1859 antislavery leader John ◊Brown seized the federal government's arsenal here, an action that helped precipitate the Civil War.

During the war the strategically located settlement was the site of several engagements. In commemoration, Harper's Ferry National Historical Park is here.

harpsichord keyboard musical instrument common in the 16th–18th centuries, until superseded by the piano. The strings are plucked by quills. It was revived in the 20th century for the authentic performance of early music.

Harpy (plural *Harpies*) in early Greek mythology, a wind spirit; in later legend the Harpies have horrific women's faces and the bodies of vultures.

harrier breed of dog, a small hound originally used for hare-hunting.

Harriman (William) Averell 1891–1986. US diplomat. He was administrator of ◊lend-lease in World War II and warned of the Soviet Union's aggressive intentions from his post as ambassador to the USSR 1943–46. He became Democratic secretary of commerce 1946–48 in Truman's administration, governor of New York 1955–58, and negotiator of the Nuclear Test Ban Treaty with the USSR 1963. He served the L Johnson administration 1968–69 in the opening rounds of the Vietnam War peace talks at which he was chief negotiator.

Harris S part of Lewis with Harris, in the Outer ◊Hebrides Islands off Scotland; area 193 sq mi/500 sq km; population (1971) 2,900. It is joined to Lewis by a narrow isthmus. Harris tweeds are produced here.

Harris Joel Chandler 1848–1908. US author, born in Georgia. He wrote tales narrated by the former slave "Uncle Remus," based on black folklore, and involving the characters Br'er Rabbit and the Tar Baby.

Harrisburg capital city of Pennsylvania, located in the S central part of the state, on the Susquehanna River; seat of Dauphin County; population (1990) 52,400. Industries include steel, railroad equipment, food processing, printing and publishing, and clothing.

Harrison Benjamin 1833–1901. 23rd president of the US 1889–93, a Republican. He called the first Pan-American Conference, which led to the establishment of the Pan American Union, to improve inter-American cooperation, and develop commercial ties. In 1948 this became the ◊Organization of American States.

Harrison Rex (Reginald Carey) 1908–1990. English film and theater actor. He appeared in over 40 films and numerous plays, often portraying sophisticated and somewhat eccentric characters, such as the waspish Professor Higgins in *My Fair Lady* 1964, the musical version of Irish dramatist George Bernard Shaw's play *Pygmalion*.

His other films include *Blithe Spirit* 1945, *The Ghost and Mrs Muir* 1947, and *Dr Doolittle* 1967.

Harrison William Henry 1773–1841. 9th president of the US 1841. Elected 1840 as a Whig, he died one month after taking office. His political career was based largely on his reputation as an Indian fighter, and his campaign was constructed to give the impression that he was a man of the people with simple tastes and that the New Yorker, Martin ◊Van Buren, his opponent, was a "foppish" sophisticate.

harrow agricultural implement used to break up the furrows left by the ◊plow and reduce the soil to a fine consistency or tilth, and to cover the seeds after sowing. The traditional harrow consists of spikes set in a frame; modern harrows use sets of disks.

Hart Moss 1904–1961. US playwright. He collaborated with such major figures as Irving Berlin, Cole Porter, Kurt Weill, and Ira Gershwin.

Among Hart's most famous works are *The Man Who Came to Dinner* 1939 and the films *Gentlemen's Agreement* 1947 and *A Star is Born* 1954.

Harte (Francis) Bret 1839–1902. US writer and humorist of the American West. He founded *The Overland Monthly* 1868, in which he wrote short stories of the pioneer West, such as "The Outcasts of Poker Flat" and "The Luck of Roaring Camp," and poetry. In 1871, with his popularity at its height, he went East and signed a contract with *The Atlantic Monthly* for $10,000 for 12 stories a year, the most money then offered to a US writer. He entered a creative slump, however, and from 1878 to 1885 served as US consul in Germany and Scotland, where he entertained the literary circles. He then settled permanently in England.

hartebeest large African antelope *Alcelaphus buselaphus* with lyre-shaped horns set close on top of the head in both sexes. It may grow to 5 ft/1.5 m at the rather humped shoulders and up to 6 ft/2 m long. Although they are clumsy-looking runners, hartebeest can reach 40 mph/65 kph.

Hartford capital city of Connecticut, located in the N central part of the state, on the Connecticut River, NE of Waterbury; population (1990) 139,700. Industries include insurance, firearms, business office equipment, and tools. The Fundamental Orders of Connecticut, the first constitution that created a democratic government, was signed here 1639.

Hartly Marsden 1877–1943. US avant-garde painter. His works range from abstract, brightly colored representations of German soldiers and German military symbols, such as *Military* 1913, to New England landscapes, such as *Log Jam, Penobscot Bay* 1940–41.

Hartz Mountains range running N–S in Tasmania, Australia, with two remarkable peaks: Hartz Mountain (4,113 ft/1,254 m) and Adamsons Peak (4,017 ft/1,224 m).

Harvard University oldest educational institution in the US, founded 1636 at New Towne (later Cambridge), Massachusetts, and named after John Harvard (1607–1638), who bequeathed half his estate and his library to it. Women were first admitted 1969; the women's college of the university is *Radcliffe College*.

Harvey William 1578–1657. English physician who discovered the circulation of blood. In 1628 he published his book *De Motu Cordis/On the Motion of the Heart and the Blood in Animals*. He was court physician to James I and Charles I.

Haryana state of NW India
area 17,061 sq mi/44,200 sq km
capital Chandigarh
features part of the Ganges plain; a center of Hinduism
products sugar, cotton, oilseed, textiles, cement, iron ore
population (1991) 16,317,700
language Hindi.

Hasdrubal Barca died 207 BC. Carthaginian general, son of Hamilcar Barca and younger brother of Hannibal. He remained in command in Spain when Hannibal invaded Italy during the Second Punic War and, after fighting there against Scipio until 208, marched to Hannibal's relief. He was defeated and killed in the Metaurus valley, NE Italy.

hashish drug made from the resin contained in the female flowering tops of hemp (cannabis).

Hasidism or *Chasidism* religious sect of Orthodox Judaism, founded by Ba'al Shem Tov (*c.* 1700–1760), based on study of ◊kabbala and popular piety. It spread against strong opposition throughout E Europe during the 18th and 19th centuries, led by charismatic leaders, the *zaddikim*. They stressed piety and ecstatic prayer, denouncing the academic approach of Talmudic academies (see ◊Talmud). A later, more intellectual approach was instituted by the Lubavitch rabbi of Russia, now based in New York City. Hasidic men dress in the black suits and broad-brimmed hats of 18th-century European society, which they conservatively maintain.

Hassan II 1929– . King of Morocco from 1961. From 1976 he undertook the occupation of Western Sahara when it was ceded by Spain.

The result was a long and damaging guerrilla war against the Polisario fighters. Hassan is a moderate Arab leader, having met with Israeli leaders.

Hastings resort in East Sussex, England; population (1981) 74,800. The chief of the ◊Cinque Ports, it has ruins of a Norman castle.

Hastings, Battle of battle Oct 14, 1066, at which William the Conqueror, Duke of Normandy, defeated Harold, King of England. The site is 6 mi/10 km inland from Hastings, at Senlac, Sussex; it is marked by Battle Abbey.

Hathor in ancient Egyptian mythology, the sky goddess, later identified with ◊Isis.

Hatshepsut *c.* 1540–*c.* 1481 BC. Queen of Egypt during the 18th dynasty. She was the daughter of Thothmes I, with whom she ruled until the accession to the throne of her husband and half brother Thothmes II. Throughout his reign real power lay with Hatshepsut, and she continued to rule after his death, as regent for her nephew Thothmes III.

Hatteras cape on the coast of North Carolina, where the waters of the North Atlantic meet the Gulf Stream, causing great turbulence; it therefore is noted for shipwrecks (more than 700 are said to have occurred here) and is nicknamed "the Graveyard of the Atlantic."

Cape Hatteras National Seashore has both natural and historical interest, including a lighthouse and sea life typical of both the temperate and tropical zones.

Haughey Charles 1925– . Irish Fianna Fáil politician of Ulster descent. Dismissed 1970 from Jack Lynch's cabinet for alleged complicity in IRA gun-running, he was afterward acquitted. He was prime minister 1979–81, March–Nov 1982, and 1986–92, when he was replaced by Albert Reynolds.

Hausa member of an agricultural Muslim people of NW Nigeria, numbering 9 million. The Hausa language belongs to the Chadic subfamily of the Afro-Asiatic language group. It is used as a trade language throughout W Africa.

Haute-Normandie or *Upper Normandy* coastal region of NW France lying between Basse-Normandie and Picardy and bisected by the river Seine; area 4,757 sq mi/12,300 sq km; population (1986) 1,693,000. It comprises the *départements* of Eure and Seine-Maritime; its capital is Rouen. Major ports include Dieppe and Fécamp. The area has many beech forests.

Havana capital and port of Cuba, on the NW coast of the island; population (1989) 2,096,100. Products include cigars and tobacco, sugar, coffee, and fruit. The palace of the Spanish governors and the stronghold of La Fuerza (1583) survive. Tourism, formerly a major source of revenue, ended when Fidel Castro came to power 1959.

Havel Václav 1936– . Czech playwright and politician, president of Czechoslovakia 1989–92 and president of the Czech Republic from 1993. His plays include *The Garden Party* 1963 and *Largo Desolato* 1985, about a dissident intellectual. Havel became widely known as a human-rights activist. He was imprisoned 1979–83 and again 1989 for support of Charter 77, a human-rights manifesto. As president of Czechoslovakia he sought to preserve a united republic, but resigned in recognition of the breakup of the federation 1992. In 1993 he became president of the newly independent Czech Republic.

Haverhill city in NE Massachusetts, on the Merrimac River, N of Boston; population (1990) 51,418. Products include paints, chemicals, machine tools, and shoes.

Havel Playwright and political dissident Václav Havel, who became president of Czechoslovakia after the fall of the communist regime 1989.

Hawaii Pacific state of the US; nickname Aloha State
area 6,485 sq mi/16,800 sq km
capital Honolulu on Oahu
cities Hilo
physical Hawaii consists of a chain of some 20 volcanic islands, of which the chief are (1) *Hawaii*, noted for Mauna Kea (13,788 ft/4,201 m), the world's highest island mountain (site of a UK infrared telescope) and Mauna Loa (13,686 ft/4,170 m), the world's largest active volcanic crater; (2) *Maui*, the second largest of the islands; (3) *Oahu*, the third largest, with the greatest concentration of population and tourist attractions—for example, Waikiki beach and the Pearl Harbor naval base; (4) *Kauai*; and (5) *Molokai*, site of a historic leper colony
products sugar, coffee, pineapples, flowers, women's clothing
population (1990) 1,108,200; 34% European, 25% Japanese, 14% Filipino, 12% Hawaiian, 6% Chinese
language English
religion Christianity; Buddhist minority
famous people Father Joseph Damien, Kamehameha I, Queen Liliuokalani, Sanford Dole
history a Polynesian kingdom from the 6th century until 1893; Hawaii became a republic 1894; ceded itself to the US 1898, and became a US territory 1900. Japan's air attack on Pearl Harbor Dec 7, 1941, crippled the US Pacific fleet and turned the territory into an armed camp, under martial law, for the remainder of the war. Hawaii became a state 1959. Tourism is the chief source of income.

hawk any of various small to medium-sized birds of prey of the family Accipitridae, other than eagles, kites, ospreys, and vultures. The name is used especially to describe the genera *Accipiter* and *Buteo*. Hawks have short, rounded wings compared with falcons, and keen eyesight.

hawk person who believes in the use of military action rather than mediation as a means of solving a political dispute. The term first entered the political language of the US during the 1960s, when it was applied metaphorically to those advocating continuation and escalation of the Vietnam War. Those with moderate, or even pacifist, views were known as doves. In general usage today, a hawk is associated with conservative policies.

Hawke Bob (Robert) 1929– . Australian Labor politician, prime minister 1983–91, on the right wing of the party. He was president of the Australian Council of Trade Unions 1970–80. He announced his retirement from politics 1992.

Hawking Stephen 1942– . English physicist who has researched ◊black holes and gravitational field theory. His books include *A Brief History of Time* 1988, in which he argues that our universe is only one small part of a "super-universe" that has existed forever and that comprises an infinite number of universes like our own.

Hawks Howard 1896–1977. US director, writer, and producer of a wide range of classic films, swift-moving and immensely accomplished, including *Scarface* 1932, *Bringing Up Baby* 1938, *The Big Sleep* 1946, and *Gentlemen Prefer Blondes* 1953.

Hawthorne Nathaniel 1804–1864. US author who wrote about Puritan New England and won fame with *The Scarlet Letter* 1850, a powerful novel set in Boston 200 years earlier. He wrote three other novels (*The House of the Seven Gables* 1851, *The Blithedale Romance* 1852, and *The Marble Faun* 1860), many volumes of short stories, and *Tanglewood Tales* 1853, classic Greek legends retold for children. His short stories, which include "My Kinsman, Major Molineux" and "Young Goodman Brown," helped to establish the short story as an art form.

Haydn Franz Joseph 1732–1809. Austrian composer. A teacher of Mozart and Beethoven, he was a major exponent of the Classical sonata form in his numerous chamber and orchestral works (he wrote more than 100 symphonies). He also composed choral music, including the oratorios *The Creation* 1798 and *The Seasons* 1801. He was the first great master of the string quartet.

Hayes Rutherford Birchard 1822–1893. 19th president of the US 1877–81, a Republican. Born in Ohio, he was a major general on the Union side in the Civil War. During his presidency federal troops (see ◊Reconstruction) were withdrawn from the Southern states and the Civil Service reformed.

He was noted for his honesty, and his integrity was viewed by many as a way to overcome the aura of corruption that had surrounded the ◊Grant administration. Under Hayes, the political role of federal employees was curtailed.

hay fever allergic reaction to pollen, causing sneezing, inflammation of the eyes, and asthmatic symptoms. Sufferers experience irritation caused by powerful body chemicals related to ◊histamine produced at the site of entry. Treatment is by antihistamine drugs.

Hays Office film regulation body in the US 1922–45. Officially known as the Motion Picture Producers and Distributors of America, it was created by the major film companies to improve the industry's image and provide internal regulation, including a strict moral code.

Haywood William Dudley 1869–1928. US labor leader. One of the founders of the Industrial Workers of the World (IWW, "Wobblies") 1905, Haywood was arrested for conspiracy to murder an antiunion politician. His acquittal in 1907 made him a labor hero. Arrested again for sedition during World War I, he spent his later years in exile in the Soviet Union.

Hayworth Rita. Adopted name of Margarita Carmen Cansino 1918–1987. US dancer and film actress who gave vivacious performances in 1940s musicals and steamy, erotic roles in *Gilda* 1946 and *Affair in Trinidad* 1952. She was known as Hollywood's "Goddess" during the height of her career. She was married to Orson Welles 1943–48 and appeared in his films, including *The Lady from Shanghai* 1948. She was perfectly cast in *Pal Joey* 1957 and *Separate Tables* 1958.

Her later appearances were intermittent and she retired in 1972, a victim of Alzheimer's disease.

hazardous substance waste substance, usually generated by industry, which represents a hazard to the environment or to people living or working nearby. Examples include radioactive wastes, acidic resins, arsenic residues, residual hardening salts, lead, mercury, nonferrous sludges, organic solvents, and pesticides. Their economic disposal or recycling is the subject of research.

hazel shrub or tree of the genus *Corylus*, family Corylaceae, including the European common hazel or cob *C. avellana*, of which the filbert is the cultivated variety. North American species include the American hazel *C. americana*.

Hazlitt William 1778–1830. English essayist and critic whose work is characterized by invective,

Hawaii

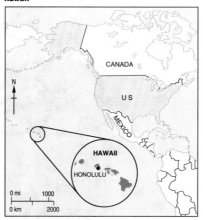

scathing irony, and a gift for epigram. His critical essays include *Characters of Shakespeare's Plays* 1817–18, *Lectures on the English Poets* 1818–19, *English Comic Writers* 1819, and *Dramatic Literature of the Age of Elizabeth* 1820. Other works are *Table Talk* 1821–22, *The Spirit of the Age* 1825, and *Liber Amoris* 1823.

health service government provision of medical care on a national scale.

State and local governments provide some public health services. The US provides care through private physicians and hospitals who are paid by the federally subsidized schemes *Medicare* and *Medicaid*. The Medicare health-insurance plan provides outpatient care for the elderly and disabled (toward which patients pay a share), and since 1985, fees for Medicare patients to join health-maintenance organizations (HMOs, covering visits to a group of doctors and hospital fees). The Medicaid state plan is paid to the state by the federal government for people unable to afford private care. US private health schemes include Blue Cross (established 1929) and Blue Shield (established 1917), as well as other insurance companies' plans.

hearing aid any device to improve the hearing of partially deaf people. Hearing aids usually consist of a battery-powered transistorized microphone/amplifier unit and earpiece. Some miniaturized aids are compact enough to fit in the ear or be concealed in the frame of eyeglasses.

Hearst William Randolph 1863–1951. US newspaper publisher, celebrated for his introduction of banner headlines, lavish illustration, and the sensationalist approach known as "yellow journalism."

heart muscular organ that rhythmically contracts to force blood around the body of an animal with a circulatory system. Annelid worms and some other invertebrates have simple hearts consisting of thickened sections of main blood vessels that pulse regularly. An earthworm has ten such hearts. Vertebrates have one heart. A fish heart has two chambers—the thin-walled *atrium* (once called the auricle) that expands to receive blood, and the thick-walled *ventricle* that pumps it out. Amphibians and most reptiles have two atria and one ventricle; birds and mammals have two atria and two ventricles. The beating of the heart is controlled by the autonomic nervous system and an internal control center or pacemaker, the sinoatrial node.

heart The structure of the human heart.

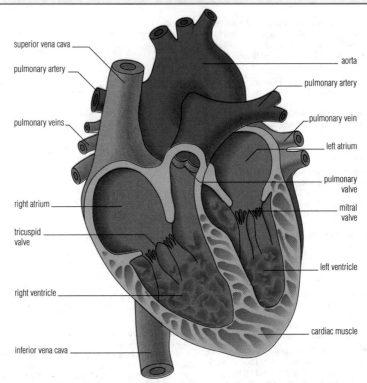

- superior vena cava
- pulmonary artery
- pulmonary veins
- right atrium
- tricuspid valve
- right ventricle
- inferior vena cava
- aorta
- pulmonary artery
- pulmonary vein
- left atrium
- pulmonary valve
- mitral valve
- left ventricle
- cardiac muscle

heart attack sudden onset of gripping central chest pain, often accompanied by sweating and vomiting, caused by death of a portion of the heart muscle following obstruction of a coronary artery by thrombosis (formation of a blood clot). Half of all heart attacks result in death within the first two hours, but in the remainder survival has improved following the widespread use of streptokinase and aspirin to treat heart-attack victims.

heartbeat the regular contraction and relaxation of the heart, and the accompanying sounds. As blood passes through the heart a double beat is heard. The first is produced by the sudden closure of the valves between the atria and the ventricles. The second, slightly delayed sound, is caused by the closure of the valves found at the entrance to the major arteries leaving the heart. Diseased valves may make unusual sounds, known as heart murmurs.

heart disease disorder affecting the heart; for example, ischaemic heart disease, in which the blood supply through the coronary arteries is reduced by ◊atherosclerosis; valvular heart disease, in which a heart valve is damaged; and cardiomyopathy, where the heart muscle itself is diseased.

heart–lung machine apparatus used during heart surgery to take over the functions of the heart and the lungs temporarily. It has a pump to circulate the blood around the body and is able to add oxygen to the blood and remove carbon dioxide from it. A heart–lung machine was first used for open-heart surgery in the US 1953.

heat form of internal energy possessed by a substance by virtue of the kinetic energy in the motion of its molecules or atoms. Heat energy is transferred by conduction, convection, and radiation. It always flows from a region of higher ◊temperature (heat intensity) to one of lower temperature. Its effect on a substance may be simply to raise its temperature, or to cause it to expand, melt (if a solid), vaporize (if a liquid), or increase its pressure (if a confined gas).

Heath Edward (Richard George) 1916– . British Conservative politician, party leader 1965–75. As prime minister 1970–74 he took the UK into the European Community but was brought down by economic and industrial relations crises at home. He was replaced as party leader by Margaret Thatcher 1975, and became increasingly critical of her policies and her opposition to the UK's full participation in the EC. In 1990 he undertook a mission to Iraq in an attempt to secure the release of British hostages.

heather low-growing evergreen shrub of the heath family, common on sandy or acid soil. The common heather *Calluna vulgaris* is a carpet-forming shrub, growing up to 24 in/60 cm high and bearing pale pink-purple flowers. It is found over much of Europe and has been introduced to North America.

heat shield any heat-protecting coating or system, especially the coating (for example, tiles) used in spacecraft to protect the astronauts and equipment inside from the heat of reentry when returning to Earth. Air friction can generate temperatures of up to 2,700°F/1,500°C on reentry into the atmosphere.

heat storage any means of storing heat for release later. It is usually achieved by using materials that undergo phase changes, for example, Glauber's salt and sodium pyrophosphate, which melts at 158°F/70°C. The latter is used to store off-peak heat in the home: the salt is liquefied by cheap heat during the night and then freezes to give off heat during the day.

heatstroke or *sunstroke* rise in body temperature caused by excessive exposure to heat. Mild heatstroke is experienced as feverish lassitude, sometimes with simple fainting; recovery is prompt following rest and replenishment of salt lost in sweat. Severe heatstroke causes collapse akin to that seen in acute ◊shock, and is potentially lethal without prompt treatment of cooling the body carefully and giving fluids to relieve dehydration.

heaven in Christianity and some other religions, the abode of God and the destination of the virtuous after death. Theologians now usually describe it as a place or state in which the soul experiences the full reality of God.

heavy metal in music, a style of rock characterized by histrionic guitar solos and a macho swagger. Heavy metal developed out of the hard rock of the late 1960s and early 1970s, was performed by such groups as Led Zeppelin and Deep Purple, and enjoyed a resurgence in the late 1980s. Bands include Van Halen (formed 1974), Def Leppard (formed 1977), and Guns 'n' Roses (formed 1987).

heavy metal in chemistry, a metallic element of high atomic weight, such as platinum, gold, and lead. Many heavy metals are poisonous and tend to accumulate and persist in living systems—for example, high levels of mercury (from industrial waste and toxic dumping) accumulate in shellfish and fish, which are in turn eaten by humans.

Treatment of heavy-metal poisoning is difficult because available drugs are not able to distinguish between the heavy metals that are essential to living cells (zinc, copper) and those that are poisonous.

heavy water or *deuterium oxide* D_2O water containing the isotope deuterium instead of hydrogen (relative molecular mass 20 as opposed to 18 for ordinary water).

Hebei or *Hopei* or *Hupei* province of N China
area 78,242 sq mi/202,700 sq km
capital Shijiazhuang
features includes special municipalities of Beijing and Tianjin
products cereals, textiles, iron, steel
population (1990) 61,082,000.

Hebrew member of the Semitic people who lived in Palestine at the time of the Old Testament and who traced their ancestry to ◊Abraham of Ur, a city of Sumer.

Hebrew Bible the sacred writings of Judaism (some dating from as early as 1200 BC), called by Christians the ◊Old Testament. It includes the Torah (the first five books, ascribed to Moses), historical and prophetic books, and psalms, originally written in Hebrew and later translated into Greek (◊Pentateuch) and other languages.

Hebrew language member of the ◊Hamito-Semitic language family spoken in SW Asia by the ancient Hebrews, sustained for many centuries in the Diaspora as the liturgical language of Judaism, revived by the late-19th-century Haskala movement, and developed in the 20th century as Israeli Hebrew, the national language of the state of Israel. It is the original language of the Old Testament of the Bible.

Hebrides group of more than 500 islands (fewer than 100 inhabited) off W Scotland; total area 1,120 sq mi/2,900 sq km. The Hebrides were settled by Scandinavians during the 6th–9th centuries and passed under Norwegian rule from about 890–1266.

Hecate in Greek mythology, the goddess of witchcraft and magic, sometimes identified with ◊Artemis and the Moon.

Hecht Ben 1894–1964. US journalist, author, and playwright. A collection of his newspaper feature stories, *1001 Nights in Chicago*, appeared 1922. Hecht's greatest success came in his 1928 collaboration with Charles MacArthur on the popular play *The Front Page*. He then went to Hollywood and wrote many successful screenplays, including *Twentieth Century* 1934 and *Wuthering Heights* 1939, and became known as a script-doctor for others' screenplays. Hecht's autobiography, *Child of the Century*, was published 1954.

hectare metric unit of area equal to 10,000 square meters (2.47 acres), symbol ha.

Hector in Greek legend, a Trojan prince, son of King Priam and husband of Andromache, who, in the siege of ◊Troy, was the foremost warrior on the Trojan side until he was killed by ◊Achilles.

hedge or *hedgerow* row of closely planted shrubs or low trees, generally acting as a land division and windbreak. Hedges also serve as a source of food and as a refuge for wildlife, and provide a ◊habitat not unlike the understory of a natural forest. Generally, the older the hedge, the more species are found contained in a given length, roughly one species per century for a 30-yd length. About 309 species of plant occur only in hedgerows. Hedges are a part of the landscape in Britain, N France, Ireland, and New England, but many have been destroyed to accommodate altered farming practices and larger machinery.

hedgehog insectivorous mammal of the genus *Erinaceus*, native to Europe, Asia, and Africa. The body, including the tail, is 1 ft/30 cm long. It is grayish-brown in color, has a piglike snout, and is covered with sharp spines. When alarmed it can roll itself into a ball. Hedgehogs feed on insects, slugs, and carrion. Long-eared hedgehogs and desert hedgehogs are placed in different genera.

hedonism ethical theory that pleasure or happiness is, or should be, the main goal in life. Hedonist sects in ancient Greece were the Cyrenaics, who held that pleasure of the moment is the only human good, and the ◊Epicureans, who advocated the pursuit of pleasure under the direction of reason. Modern hedonistic philosophies, such as those of the British philosophers Jeremy Bentham and J S Mill, regard the happiness of society, rather than that of the individual, as the aim.

Hefei or *Hofei* capital of Anhui province, China; population (1989) 980,000. Products include textiles, chemicals, and steel.

Hefner Hugh Marston 1926– . US publisher, founder of *Playboy* magazine 1953. With its distinctive rabbit logo, monthly "Playmate" centerfolds of nude women, and columns and interviews of opinion, fashion, and personal advice on sex and other topics, *Playboy* helped reshape the social attitudes of the postwar generation. In the early 1960s, the magazine's huge success led to the creation of a national chain of Playboy clubs and resorts.

Hegel Georg Wilhelm Friedrich 1770–1831. German philosopher who conceived of consciousness and the external object as forming a unity in which neither factor can exist independently, mind and nature being two abstractions of one indivisible whole. He believed development took place through dialectic: thesis and antithesis (contradiction) and synthesis, the resolution of contradiction. For Hegel, the task of philosophy was to comprehend the rationality of what already exists; leftist followers, including Karl Marx, used Hegel's

hedgerow

In Northern Europe, and especially in Britain, hedgerows are a traditional feature of the landscape. Hawthorn, blackthorn, elm and beech bushes were grown around the edges of farms and grazing land to define boundaries and to enclose cattle and sheep. With mechanized agriculture came the destruction of many hedgerows, along with the wildlife they support.

The dense growth and tough, thorny branches of hawthorn bushes are effective barriers to large mammals. But their foliage and flowers, and, those of the plants that grow around and beneath them, provide food for many caterpillars, butterflies, aphids and bees. The fruits are eaten by many birds and by voles and wood mice. Carnivorous birds feed on the insects and other small animals.

Life in the hedgerow

1. peacock butterfly 2. blackbird's nest
3. seven-spot ladybird 4. hollybush
5. comma butterfly 6. tiger moth
7. field mouse 8. warbler 9. dog rose
10. nettle 11. orange-tip butterfly
12. hawthorn 13. wren
14. hogweed 15. bramble bush
16. hawfinch 17. wood mouse
18. hedgehog 19. primrose
20. chickweed

dialectic to attempt to show the inevitability of radical change and to attack both religion and the social order of the European Industrial Revolution. He wrote *The Phenomenology of Spirit* 1807, *Encyclopaedia of the Philosophical Sciences* 1817, and *Philosophy of Right* 1821.

hegemony (Greek *hegemonia* "authority") political dominance of one power over others in a group in which all are supposedly equal. The term was first used for the dominance of Athens over the other Greek city-states, later applied to Prussia within Germany, and, in more recent times, to the US and the USSR with regard to the rest of the world.

Hegira the flight of the prophet Mohammed; see ◊Hijrah.

Heidegger Martin 1889–1976. German philosopher. In *Sein und Zeit/Being and Time* 1927 (translated 1962) he used the methods of Edmund Husserl's phenomenology to explore the structures of human existence. His later writings meditated on the fate of a world dominated by science and technology.

Heinkel Ernst 1888–1958. German aircraft designer who pioneered jet aircraft. He founded his firm 1922 and built the first jet aircraft 1939. During World War II his company was Germany's biggest producer of warplanes, mostly propeller-driven.

Heinlein Robert A(nson) 1907– . US science-fiction writer, associated with the pulp magazines of the 1940s, who wrote the militaristic novel *Starship Troopers* 1959 and the utopian cult novel *Stranger in a Strange Land* 1961. His work helped to increase the legitimacy of science fiction as a literary genre.

Heisenberg Werner Carl 1901–1976. German physicist who developed ◊quantum theory and formulated the ◊uncertainty principle, which concerns matter, radiation, and their reactions, and places absolute limits on the achievable accuracy of measurement. He was awarded a Nobel Prize 1932.

Hejaz former independent kingdom, merged 1932 with Nejd to form ◊Saudi Arabia; population (1970) 2,000,000. The capital is Mecca.

Hel or *Hela* in Norse mythology, the goddess of the underworld.

Helen in Greek mythology, the daughter of Zeus and Leda, and the most beautiful of women. She married ◊Menelaus, King of Sparta, but during his absence was abducted by Paris, Prince of Troy. This precipitated the Trojan War. Afterward she returned to Sparta with her husband.

Helena capital of Montana, located in the W central part of the state, near the Big Belt Mountains, S of the Missouri River; population (1990) 24,600. It was settled after gold was discovered 1864. Industries include agricultural products, machine parts, ceramics, paints, sheet metal, and chemicals.

Helios in Greek mythology, the sun god—thought to make his daily journey across the sky in a chariot—and father of ◊Phaethon.

helium (Greek *helios* "Sun") colorless, odorless, gaseous, nonmetallic element, symbol He, atomic number 2, atomic weight 4.0026. It is grouped with the ◊inert gases, is nonreactive, and forms no compounds. It is the second-most abundant element (after hydrogen) in the universe, and has the lowest boiling ($-452°F/-268.9°C$) and melting points ($-458°F/-272.2°C$) of all the elements. It is present in small quantities in the Earth's atmosphere from gases issu-

ing from radioactive elements (from alpha decay) in the Earth's crust; after hydrogen it is the second lightest element.

helix in mathematics, a three-dimensional curve resembling a spring, corkscrew, or screw thread. It is generated by a line that encircles a cylinder or cone at a constant angle.

hell in various religions, a place of posthumous punishment. In Hinduism, Buddhism, and Jainism, hell is a transitory stage in the progress of the soul, but in Christianity and Islam it is eternal (◊purgatory is transitory). Judaism does not postulate such punishment.

Hellenic period (from *Hellas*, Greek name for Greece) Classical period of ancient Greek civilization, from the first Olympic Games 776 BC until the death of Alexander the Great 323 BC.

Hellenistic period period in Greek civilization from the death of Alexander 323 BC until the accession of the Roman emperor Augustus 27 BC. Alexandria in Egypt was the center of culture and commerce during this period, and Greek culture spread throughout the Mediterranean region and the near East.

Heller Joseph 1923– . US novelist. He drew on his experiences in the US air force in World War II to write *Catch-22* 1961, satirizing war and bureaucratic methods. A film based on the book appeared 1970.

Hellespont former name of the ◊Dardanelles, the strait that separates Europe from Asia.

Hellman Lillian 1907–1984. US playwright whose work is concerned with contemporary political and social issues. *The Children's Hour* 1934, *The Little Foxes* 1939, and *Toys in the Attic* 1960 are all examples of the "well-made play."

Helmholtz Hermann Ludwig Ferdinand von 1821–1894. German physiologist, physicist, and inventor of the ophthalmoscope for examining the inside of the eye. He was the first to explain how the cochlea of the inner ear works, and the first to measure the speed of nerve impulses. In physics he formulated the law of conservation of energy, and worked in thermodynamics.

Héloïse 1101–1164. Abbess of Paraclete in Champagne, France, correspondent and lover of ◊Abelard. She became deeply interested in intellectual study in her youth and was impressed by the brilliance of Abelard, her teacher, whom she secretly married. After her affair with Abelard, and the birth of a son, Astrolabe, she became a nun 1129, and with Abelard's assistance, founded a nunnery at Paraclete. Her letters show her strong and pious character and her devotion to Abelard.

Helsinki (Swedish *Helsingfors*) capital and port of Finland; population (1990) 492,400, metropolitan area 978,000. Industries include shipbuilding, engineering, and textiles. The homes of the architect Eliel Saarinen and the composer Jean Sibelius outside the town are museums.

Helsinki Conference international meeting 1975 at which 35 countries, including the USSR and the US, attempted to reach agreement on cooperation in security, economics, science, technology, and human rights. This established the Conference on Security and Cooperation in Europe (CSCE).

Helvetius Claude Adrien 1715–1771. French philosopher. In *De l'Esprit* 1758 he argued, following David ◊Hume, that self-interest, however disguised, is the

Hemingway Nobel prize-winning American author Ernest Hemingway.

mainspring of all human action and that since conceptions of good and evil vary according to period and locality there is no absolute good or evil. He also believed that intellectual differences are only a matter of education.

hematite principal ore of iron, consisting mainly of iron (III) oxide, Fe_2O_3. It occurs as *specular hematite* (dark, metallic luster), *kidney ore* (reddish radiating fibers terminating in smooth, rounded surfaces), and a red earthy deposit.

hematology branch of medicine concerned with disorders of the blood.

Hemingway Ernest 1898–1961. US writer. War, bullfighting, and fishing are used symbolically in his work to represent honor, dignity, and primitivism—prominent themes in his short stories and novels, which include *A Farewell to Arms* 1929, *For Whom the Bell Tolls* 1940, and *The Old Man and the Sea* 1952. His deceptively simple writing styles attracted many imitators. He received the Nobel Prize for Literature 1954.

hemlock plant *Conium maculatum* of the carrot family Umbelliferae, native to Europe, W Asia, and N Africa. Reaching up to 6 ft/2 m high, it bears umbels of small white flowers. The whole plant, especially the root and fruit, is poisonous, causing paralysis of the nervous system. The name hemlock is also applied to members of the genus *Tsuga* of North American and Asiatic conifers of the pine family.

hemoglobin protein that carries oxygen. In vertebrates it occurs in red blood cells, giving them their color. Oxygen attaches to hemoglobin in the lungs or gills where the amount dissolved in the blood is high. This process effectively increases the amount of oxygen that can be carried in the bloodstream. The oxygen is later released in the body tissues where it is at low concentration. Hemoglobin also works in carrying carbon dioxide away from tissues to the lungs or gills.

hemophilia any of several inherited diseases in which normal blood clotting is impaired. The sufferer experiences prolonged bleeding from the slightest wound, as well as painful internal bleeding without apparent cause.

hemorrhage loss of blood from the circulatory system. It is "manifest" when the blood can be seen, as when it flows from a wound, and "occult" when the bleeding is internal, as from an ulcer or internal injury.

hemorrhoids distended blood vessels (◊varicose veins) in the area of the anus, popularly called piles.

hemp annual plant *Cannabis sativa*, family Cannabaceae. Originally from Asia, it is cultivated in most temperate countries for its fibers, produced in the outer layer of the stem, and used in ropes, twines, and, occasionally, in a type of linen or lace. Cannabis is obtained from certain varieties of hemp.

Henan or *Honan* province of E central China
area 64,462 sq mi/167,000 sq km
capital Zhengzhou
features river plains of the Huang He (Yellow River); ruins of Xibo, the 16th-century BC capital of the Shang dynasty, were discovered here in the 1980s
products cereals, cotton
population (1990) 85,510,000.

Hench Philip Showalter 1896–1965. US physician who introduced cortisone treatment for rheumatoid arthritis for which he shared the 1950 Nobel Prize for Medicine with Edward Kendall and Tadeus Reichstein.

Hendrix Jimi (James Marshall) 1942–1970. US rock guitarist, songwriter, and singer, legendary for his virtuoso experimental technique and flamboyance. *Are You Experienced?* 1967 was his first album.

His performance at the 1969 Woodstock festival included a memorable version of "The Star-Spangled Banner" and is recorded in the film *Woodstock*. He greatly expanded the vocabulary of the electric guitar and influenced both rock and jazz musicians.

Henlein Konrad 1898–1945. Sudeten-German leader of the Sudeten Nazi Party in Czechoslovakia, and closely allied with Hitler's Nazis. He was partly responsible for the destabilization of the Czechoslovak state 1938, which led to the ◊Munich Agreement and secession of the Sudetenland to Germany.

henna small shrub *Lawsonia inermis* of the loosestrife family Lythraceae, found in Iran, India, Egypt, and N Africa. The leaves and young twigs are ground to a powder, mixed to a paste with hot water, and applied to fingernails and hair, giving an orange-red hue. The color may then be changed to black by applying a preparation of indigo.

Henri Robert. Adopted name of Robert Henry Cozad 1865–1929. US landscape and portrait painter. Although he executed a number of noted works, such as *Himself* and *Herself* 1913, he is best known as a teacher, profoundly influencing such artists as George ◊Bellows, William ◊Glackens, Edward ◊Hopper, Rockwell Kent, and George ◊Luks.

Henrietta Maria 1609–1669. Queen of England 1625–49. The daughter of Henry IV of France, she married Charles I of England 1625. By encouraging him to aid Roman Catholics and make himself an absolute ruler, she became highly unpopular and was exiled 1644–60. She returned to England at the Restoration but retired to France 1665.

henry SI unit (symbol H) of inductance (the reaction of an electric current against the magnetic field that surrounds it). One henry is the inductance of a circuit that produces an opposing voltage of one volt when the current changes at one ampere per second.

Henry Joseph 1797–1878. US physicist, inventor of the electromagnetic motor 1829 and of a telegraphic apparatus. He also discovered the principle of electromagnetic induction, roughly at the same time as

Michael ◊Faraday, and the phenomenon of self-induction. A unit of inductance (henry) is named after him.

Henry Patrick 1736–1799. US politician who in 1775 supported the arming of the Virginia militia against the British by a speech ending, "Give me liberty or give me death!" He was governor of Virginia 1776–79 and 1784–86.

Henry William 1774–1836. British chemist. In 1803 he formulated *Henry's law*, which states that when a gas is dissolved in a liquid at a given temperature, the mass that dissolves is in direct proportion to the pressure of the gas.

Henry eight kings of England:

Henry I 1068–1135. King of England from 1100. Youngest son of William I, he succeeded his brother William II. He won the support of the Saxons by granting them a charter and marrying a Saxon princess. An able administrator, he established a professional bureaucracy and a system of traveling judges. He was succeeded by Stephen.

Henry II 1133–1189. King of England from 1154, when he succeeded ◊Stephen. He was the son of ◊Matilda and Geoffrey of Anjou (1113–1151). He curbed the power of the barons, but his attempt to bring the church courts under control had to be abandoned after the murder of Thomas à ◊Becket. During his reign the English conquest of Ireland began. He was succeeded by his son Richard I.

Henry III 1207–1272. King of England from 1216, when he succeeded John, but he did not rule until 1227. His financial commitments to the papacy and his foreign favorites led to de ◊Montfort's revolt 1264. Henry was defeated at Lewes, Sussex, and imprisoned. He was restored to the throne after the royalist victory at Evesham 1265. He was succeeded by his son Edward I.

Henry IV (Bolingbroke) 1367–1413. King of England from 1399, the son of ◊John of Gaunt. In 1398 he was banished by ◊Richard II for political activity but returned 1399 to head a revolt and be accepted as king by Parliament. He was succeeded by his son Henry V.

Henry V 1387–1422. King of England from 1413, son of Henry IV. Invading Normandy 1415 (during the Hundred Years' War), he captured Harfleur and defeated the French at ◊Agincourt. He invaded again 1417–19, capturing Rouen. His military victory forced the French into the Treaty of Troyes 1420, which gave Henry control of the French government. He married ◊Catherine of Valois 1420 and gained recognition as heir to the French throne by his father-in-law Charles VI, but died before him. He was succeeded by his son Henry VI.

Henry VI 1421–1471. King of England from 1422, son of Henry V. He assumed royal power 1442 and sided with the party opposed to the continuation of the Hundred Years' War with France. After his marriage 1445, he was dominated by his wife, ◊Margaret of Anjou. The unpopularity of the government, especially after the loss of the English conquests in France, encouraged Richard, Duke of ◊York, to claim the throne, and though York was killed 1460, his son Edward IV proclaimed himself king 1461 (see Wars of the ◊Roses). Henry was captured 1465, temporarily restored 1470, but again imprisoned 1471 and then murdered.

Henry VII 1457–1509. King of England from 1485, son of Edmund Tudor, Earl of Richmond (c. 1430–1456), and a descendant of John of Gaunt. He spent his early life in Brittany until 1485, when he landed in Britain to lead the rebellion against Richard III which ended with Richard's defeat and death at Bosworth. By his

marriage to Elizabeth of York 1486, he united the houses of York and Lancaster. Yorkist revolts continued until 1497, but Henry restored order after the Wars of the ◊Roses by the Star Chamber and achieved independence from Parliament by amassing a private fortune through confiscations. He was succeeded by his son Henry VIII.

Henry VIII 1491–1547. King of England from 1509, when he succeeded his father Henry VII and married Catherine of Aragon, the widow of his brother. During the period 1513–29 Henry pursued an active foreign policy, largely under the guidance of his Lord Chancellor, Cardinal Wolsey, who shared Henry's desire to make England stronger. Wolsey was replaced by Thomas More 1529 for failing to persuade the pope to grant Henry a divorce. After 1532 Henry broke with papal authority, proclaimed himself head of the church in England, dissolved the monasteries, and divorced Catherine. His subsequent wives were Anne Boleyn, Jane Seymour, Anne of Cleves, Catherine Howard, and Catherine Parr. He was succeeded by his son Edward VI.

Henry four kings of France, including:

Henry III 1551–1589. King of France from 1574. He fought both the ◊Huguenots (headed by his successor, Henry of Navarre) and the Catholic League (headed by the Third Duke of Guise). Guise expelled Henry from Paris 1588 but was assassinated. Henry allied with the Huguenots under Henry of Navarre to besiege the city, but was assassinated by a monk.

Henry VIII Portrait by Hans Holbein (1536), Thyssen Bornemisz̧ Collection, Lugano, Switzerland.

Henry IV 1553–1610. King of France from 1589. Son of Antoine de Bourbon and Jeanne, Queen of Navarre, he was brought up as a Protestant and from 1576 led the ◊Huguenots. On his accession he settled the religious question by adopting Catholicism while tolerating Protestantism. He restored peace and strong government to France and brought back prosperity by measures for the promotion of industry and agriculture and the improvement of communications. He was assassinated by a Catholic extremist.

Henry seven Holy Roman emperors, including:

Henry I *the Fowler* c. 876–936. King of Germany from 919, and duke of Saxony from 912. He secured the frontiers of Saxony, ruled in harmony with its nobles, and extended German influence over the Danes, the Hungarians, and the Slavonic tribes. He was about to claim the imperial crown when he died.

Henry III *the Black* 1017–1056. King of Germany from 1028, Holy Roman emperor from 1039 (crowned 1046). He raised the empire to the height of its power, and extended its authority over Poland, Bohemia, and Hungary.

Henry IV 1050–1106. Holy Roman emperor from 1056, who was involved from 1075 in a struggle with the papacy (see ◊Gregory VII). Excommunicated twice (1076 and 1080), Henry deposed Gregory and set up the antipope Clement III (died 1191) by whom he was crowned Holy Roman emperor 1084.

Henry VI 1165–1197. Holy Roman emperor from 1190. As part of his plan for making the empire universal, he captured and imprisoned Richard I of England and compelled him to do homage.

Henry the Lion 1129–1195. Duke of Bavaria 1156–80, duke of Saxony 1142–80, and duke of Lüneburg 1180–85. He was granted the Duchy of Bavaria by the Emperor Frederick Barbarossa. He founded Lübeck and Munich. In 1162 he married Matilda, daughter of Henry II of England. His refusal in 1176 to accompany Frederick Barbarossa to Italy led in 1180 to his being deprived of the duchies of Bavaria and Saxony. Henry led several military expeditions to conquer territory in the East.

Henry the Navigator 1394–1460. Portuguese prince, the fourth son of John I. He set up a school for navigators 1419 and under his patronage Portuguese sailors explored and colonized Madeira, the Cape Verde Islands, and the Azores; they sailed down the African coast almost to Sierra Leone.

Henson Jim (James Maury) 1936–1990. US puppeteer who created the television Muppet characters, including Kermit the Frog, Miss Piggy, and Fozzie Bear. The Muppets became popular on the children's educational TV series "Sesame Street," which first appeared in 1969 and soon became regular viewing in over 80 countries. In 1976 Henson created "The Muppet Show," which ran for five years and became one of the world's most widely seen TV programs, reaching 235 million viewers in 100 countries. Three Muppet movies followed. In 1989 the Muppets became part of the ◊Disney empire.

Henze Hans Werner 1926– . German composer whose large and varied output includes orchestral, vocal, and chamber music. He uses traditional symphony and concerto forms, and incorporates a wide range of styles including jazz. Operas include *Das Verratene Meer* (Berlin 1992) based on Yukio Mishima's *The Sailor Who Fell from Grace with the Sea*.

hepatitis any inflammatory disease of the liver, usually caused by a virus. Other causes include alcohol, drugs, gallstones, lupus erythematosus, and amebic dysentery. Symptoms include weakness, nausea, and jaundice.

Hepburn Audrey (Audrey Hepburn-Rushton) 1929–1993. British actress of Anglo-Dutch descent who often played innocent, childlike characters. Slender and doe-eyed, she set a different style from the more ample women stars of the 1950s. After playing minor parts in British films in the early 1950s, she became a Hollywood star in such films as *Funny Face* 1957, *My Fair Lady* 1964, *Wait Until Dark* 1968, and *Robin and Marian* 1976.

Hepburn Katharine 1909– . US actress who made feisty self-assurance her trademark. She appeared in such films as *Morning Glory* 1933 (Academy Award), *Little Women* 1933, *Bringing Up Baby* 1938, *The Philadelphia Story* 1940, *Woman of the Year* 1942, *The African Queen* 1951, *Pat and Mike* 1952 (with her frequent partner Spencer Tracy), *Guess Who's Coming to Dinner* 1967 (Academy Award), *Lion in Winter* 1968 (Academy Award), and *On Golden Pond* 1981 (Academy Award). She also had a distinguished stage career.

Hephaestus in Greek mythology, the god of fire and metalcraft (Roman Vulcan), son of Zeus and Hera, and husband of Aphrodite. He was lame.

Hepplewhite George died 1786. English furniture maker. He developed a simple, elegant style, working mainly in mahogany or satinwood, adding delicately inlaid or painted decorations of feathers, shells, or ears of wheat. His book of designs, *The Cabinetmaker and Upholsterer's Guide* 1788, was published posthumously.

heptathlon multi-event athletics discipline for women consisting of seven events over two days: 100-meters hurdles, high jump, shot put, 200 meters (day one); long jump, javelin, 800 meters (day two). Points are awarded for performances in each event in the same way as the ◊decathlon. It replaced the pentathlon (five events) in international competition 1981.

Hera in Greek mythology, the goddess of women and marriage (Roman Juno), sister-consort of Zeus, mother of Hephaestus, Hebe, and Ares.

Heracles in Greek mythology, a hero (Roman Hercules), son of Zeus and Alcmene, famed for strength. While serving Eurystheus, King of Argos, he performed 12 labors, including the cleansing of the ◊Augean stables. Driven mad by the goddess Hera, he murdered his first wife Megara and their children, and was himself poisoned by mistake by his second wife Deianira.

Heraclius c. 575–641. Byzantine emperor from 610. His reign marked a turning point in the empire's fortunes. Of Armenian descent, he recaptured Armenia 622, and other provinces 622–28 from the Persians, but lost them to the Muslims 629–41.

Heraklion alternate name for ◊Iráklion, a Greek port.

Herat capital of Herat province, and the largest city in W Afghanistan, on the N banks of the Hari Rud River; population (1980) 160,000. A principal road junction, it was a great city in ancient and medieval times.

herb any plant (usually a flowering plant) tasting sweet, bitter, aromatic, or pungent, used in cooking, medicine, or perfumery; technically, a herb is any plant in which the aerial parts do not remain above ground at the end of the growing season.

herbaceous plant plant with very little or no wood, dying back at the end of every summer. The herbaceous perennials survive winters as underground storage organs such as bulbs and tubers.

Herbert Victor 1859–1924. Irish-born US conductor and composer. In 1893 he became conductor of the 22nd Regiment Band, also composing light operettas for the New York stage. He was conductor of the Pittsburgh Philharmonic 1898–1904, returning to New York to help found the American Society of Composers, Authors, and Publishers (ASCAP) 1914.

herbicide any chemical used to destroy plants or check their growth; see ◊weedkiller.

herbivore animal that feeds on green plants (or photosynthetic single-celled organisms) or their products, including seeds, fruit, and nectar. The most numerous type of herbivore is thought to be the zooplankton, tiny invertebrates in the surface waters of the oceans that feed on small photosynthetic algae. Herbivores are more numerous than other animals because their food is the most abundant. They form a vital link in the food chain between plants and carnivores.

Herblock popular name Herbert Lawrence Block. 1909– . US cartoonist who gained a national reputation during the 1950s with his syndicated cartoons. He won Pulitzer Prizes 1942 and 1952 and published several collections of his work. He played a leading role in the public campaign against the communist witch-hunting tactics of Senator Joseph ◊McCarthy.

Herculaneum ancient city of Italy between Naples and Pompeii. Along with Pompeii, it was buried when Vesuvius erupted AD 79. It was excavated from the 18th century onward.

Hercules Roman form of ◊Heracles.

Hercules in astronomy, the fifth-largest constellation, lying in the northern hemisphere. Despite its size it contains no prominent stars. Its most important feature is a globular cluster of stars 22,500 light-years from Earth, one of the best examples in the sky.

Hereford and Worcester county in W central England
area 1,517 sq mi/3,930 sq km
cities Worcester (administrative headquarters), Hereford, Kidderminster, Evesham, Ross-on-Wye, Ledbury
features rivers: Wye, Severn; Malvern Hills (high point Worcester Beacon 1,395 ft/425 m) and Black Mountains; fertile Vale of Evesham.

heresy (Greek *hairesis* "parties" of believers) doctrine opposed to orthodox belief, especially in religion. Those holding ideas considered heretical by the Christian church have included Gnostics, Arians, Pelagians, Montanists, Albigenses, Waldenses, Lollards, and Anabaptists.

Herman Woody (Woodrow) 1913–1987. US bandleader and clarinetist. A child prodigy, he was leader of his own orchestra at 23, and after 1945 formed his Thundering Herd band. Soloists in this or later versions of the band included Lester Young and Stan ◊Getz.

hermaphrodite organism that has both male and female sex organs. Hermaphroditism is the norm in species such as earthworms and snails, and is common in flowering plants. Cross-fertilization is the rule among hermaphrodites, with the parents functioning as male and female simultaneously, or as one or the other sex at different stages in their development.

Hermaphroditus in Greek mythology, the son of Hermes and Aphrodite. He was loved by a ◊nymph who prayed for eternal union with him, so that they became one body with dual sexual characteristics, hence the term hermaphrodite.

Hermes in Greek mythology, a god, son of Zeus and Maia; messenger of the gods. He wore winged sandals, a wide-brimmed hat, and carried a staff around which serpents coiled. Identified with the Roman Mercury and ancient Egyptian Thoth, he protected thieves, travelers, and merchants.

hernia or *rupture* protrusion of part of an internal organ through a weakness in the surrounding muscular wall, usually in the groin or navel. The appearance is that of a rounded soft lump or swelling.

Hero and Leander in Greek legend, a pair of lovers. Hero was a priestess of Aphrodite at Sestos on the Hellespont, in love with Leander on the opposite shore at Abydos. When he was drowned while swimming across during a storm, she threw herself into the sea.

Herod *the Great* 74–4 BC. King of the Roman province of Judea, S Palestine, from 40 BC. With the aid of Mark Antony, he established his government in Jerusalem 37 BC. He rebuilt the Temple in Jerusalem, but his Hellenizing tendencies made him suspect to orthodox Jewry. His last years were a reign of terror, and in the New Testament, Matthew alleges that he ordered the slaughter of all the infants in Bethlehem to ensure the death of Jesus, whom he foresaw as a rival. He was the father of Herod Antipas.

Herod Agrippa I 10 BC–AD 44. Ruler of Palestine from AD 41. His real name was Marcus Julius Agrippa, erroneously called "Herod" in the Bible. Grandson of Herod the Great, he was made tetrarch (governor) of Palestine by the Roman emperor Caligula and king by Emperor Claudius AD 41. He put the apostle James to death and imprisoned the apostle Peter. His son was Herod Agrippa II.

Herod Agrippa II *c.* 40–AD 93. King of Chalcis (now S Lebanon), son of Herod Agrippa I. He was appointed by the Roman emperor Claudius about AD 50, and in AD 60 tried the apostle Paul. He helped the Roman commander Titus (subsequently emperor) take and sack Jerusalem AD 70, then went to Rome, where he died.

Herod Antipas 21 BC–AD 39. Tetrarch (governor) of the Roman province of Galilee, N Palestine, 4 BC–AD 39, son of Herod the Great. He divorced his wife to marry his niece Herodias, and was responsible for the death of John the Baptist. Jesus was brought before him on Pontius Pilate's discovery that he was a Galilean and hence of Herod's jurisdiction, but Herod returned him without giving any verdict. In AD 38 Herod Antipas went to Rome to try to persuade Emperor Caligula to give him the title of king, but was instead banished.

Herodotus *c.* 484–424 BC. Greek historian. After four years in Athens, he traveled widely in Egypt, Asia, and the Black Sea region of E Europe, before settling at Thurii in S Italy 443 BC. He wrote a nine-book history of the Greek-Persian struggle that culminated in the defeat of the Persian invasion attempts 490 and 480 BC. Herodotus was the first historian to apply critical evaluation to his material, while also recording divergent opinions.

heroin or *diamorphine* powerful opiate analgesic, an acetyl derivative of ◊morphine. It is more addictive than morphine but causes less nausea and is one of the most abused drugs in the US.

Because of its powerful habit-forming qualities, its manufacture and import are forbidden in the US, even for medical use.

heron large to medium-sized wading bird of the family Ardeidae, which also includes bitterns, egrets, night herons, and boatbills. Herons have sharp bills, broad wings, long legs, and soft plumage. They are found mostly in tropical and subtropical regions, but also in temperate zones.

The great blue heron *Ardea herodias* is native to North America. Gray-blue overall, breeding adults have yellowish bills and ornate plumes on the head, neck, and back. A wader, it feeds mainly on fish and frogs.

herpes any of several infectious diseases caused by viruses of the herpes group. *Herpes simplex I* is the causative agent of a common inflammation, the cold sore. *Herpes simplex II* is responsible for genital herpes, a highly contagious, sexually transmitted disease characterized by painful blisters in the genital area. It can be transmitted in the birth canal from mother to newborn. *Herpes zoster* causes ◊shingles; another herpes virus causes chickenpox.

The Epstein–Barr virus of infectious ◊mononucleosis also belongs to this group.

Herrick Robert 1591–1674. English poet and cleric, born in Cheapside, London. He published *Hesperides* 1648, a collection of sacred and pastoral poetry admired for its lyric quality, including "Gather ye rosebuds" and "Cherry ripe."

herring any of various marine fishes of the herring family (Clupeidae), but especially the important food fish *Clupea harengus*. A silvered greenish-blue, it swims close to the surface, and may be 10–16 in/25–40 cm long. Herring travel in schools several miles long and wide. They are found in large quantities off the E coast of North America, and the shores of NE Europe. Overfishing and pollution have reduced their numbers.

Herriot Edouard 1872–1957. French Radical socialist politician. An opponent of Poincaré, who as prime minister carried out the French occupation of the Ruhr, Germany, he was briefly prime minister 1924–25, 1926, and 1932. As president of the chamber of deputies 1940, he opposed the policies of the right-wing Vichy government and was arrested and later taken to Germany; he was released 1945 by the Soviets.

Herschel William 1738–1822. German-born English astronomer. He was a skilled telescope maker, and pioneered the study of binary stars and nebulae. He discovered the planet Uranus 1781 and infrared solar rays 1801. He cataloged over 800 double stars, and found over 2,500 nebulae, cataloged by his sister Caroline Herschel; this work was continued by his son John Herschel. By studying the distribution of stars, William established the basic form of our Galaxy, the Milky Way.

Hertfordshire county in SE England
area 629 sq mi/1,630 sq km
cities Hertford (administrative headquarters), St Albans, Watford, Hatfield, Hemel Hempstead, Bishop's Stortford, Letchworth (the first garden city, followed by Welwyn 1919 and Stevenage 1947)
features rivers: Lea, Stort, Colne; part of the Chiltern Hills; Hatfield House; Knebworth House (home of Lord Lytton); Brocket Hall (home of Palmerston and Melborne); home of G B ◊Shaw at Ayot St Lawrence; Berkhamsted Castle (Norman); Rothamsted agricultural experimental station
products engineering, aircraft, electrical goods, paper and printing; general agricultural goods

population (1991) 951,500
famous people Graham Greene was born at Berkhamsted.

hertz SI unit (symbol Hz) of frequency (the number of repetitions of a regular occurrence in one second). Radio waves are often measured in megahertz (MHz), millions of hertz, and the clock rate of a computer is usually measured in megahertz. The unit is named after Heinrich Hertz.

Hertzsprung–Russell diagram in astronomy, a graph on which the surface temperatures of stars are plotted against their luminosities. Most stars, including the Sun, fall into a narrow band called the main sequence. When a star grows old it moves from the main sequence to the upper right part of the graph, into the area of the giants and the supergiants. At the end of its life, as the star shrinks to become a white dwarf, it moves again, to the bottom left area. It is named after the Dane Ejnar Hertzsprung (1873–1967) and the American Henry Norris Russell (1877–1957), who independently devised it in the years 1911–13.

Herzegovina or *Hercegovina* part of ◊Bosnia-Herzegovina (which was formerly, until 1991, a republic of Yugoslavia).

Herzl Theodor 1860–1904. Austrian founder of the *Zionist* movement. He was born in Budapest and became a successful playwright and journalist, mainly in Vienna. The ◊Dreyfus case convinced him that the only solution to the problem of anti-Semitism was the resettlement of the Jews in a state of their own. His book *Jewish State* 1896 launched political ◊Zionism, and he became the first president of the World Zionist Organization 1897.

Hess (Walter Richard) Rudolf 1894–1987. German Nazi leader. Imprisoned with Hitler 1924–25, he became his private secretary, taking down *Mein Kampf* from his dictation. In 1932 he was appointed deputy *Führer* to Hitler. On May 10, 1941, he landed by air in the UK with his own compromise peace proposals and was held a prisoner of war until 1945, when he was tried at Nuremberg as a war criminal and sentenced to life imprisonment. He died in ◊Spandau prison, Berlin.

Hess Victor 1883–1964. Austrian physicist who emigrated to the US shortly after sharing a Nobel Prize in 1936 for the discovery of cosmic radiation.

He was professor at Fordham University, New York, from 1938.

Hesse Hermann 1877–1962. German writer who became a Swiss citizen 1923. A conscientious objector in World War I and a pacifist opponent of Hitler, he published short stories, poetry, and novels, including *Peter Camenzind* 1904, *Siddhartha* 1922, and *Steppenwolf* 1927. Later works, such as *Das Glasperlenspiel/The Glass Bead Game* 1943, tend toward the mystical. He was awarded the Nobel Prize for Literature 1946.

Hessen administrative region (German *Land*) of Germany
area 8,145 sq mi/21,100 sq km
capital Wiesbaden
cities Frankfurt-am-Main, Kassel, Darmstadt, Offenbach-am-Main
features valleys of the rivers Rhine and Main; Taunus Mountains, rich in mineral springs, as at Homburg and Wiesbaden; see also ◊Swabia
products wine, timber, chemicals, automobiles, electrical engineering, optical instruments
population (1988) 5,550,000
religion Protestant 61%, Roman Catholic 33%
history until 1945, Hessen was divided in two by a

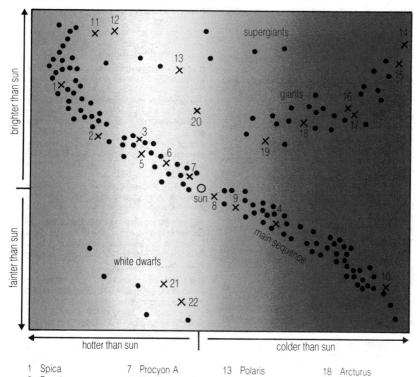

***Hertzsprung–
Russell diagram***
*Stars are plotted as
dots against a vertical
axis showing the
brightness (or
luminosity) of the star
and a horizontal axis
showing the star's
temperature.*

1	Spica	7	Procyon A	13	Polaris	18	Arcturus
2	Regulus	8	Tau Ceti	14	Betelgeuse	19	Pollux
3	Vega	9	61 Cygni A	15	Antares	20	Capella
4	61 Cygni B	10	Proxima Centauri	16	Mira	21	Sirius B
5	Sirius A	11	Rigel	17	Aldebaran	22	Procyon B
6	Altair	12	Deneb				

strip of Prussian territory, the S portion consisting of the valleys of the rivers Rhine and the Main, the N being dominated by the Vogelsberg Mountains (2,442 ft/744 m). Its capital was Darmstadt.

Hestia in Greek mythology, the goddess of the hearth (Roman Vesta), daughter of Kronos and Rhea.

Heston Charlton. Adopted name of Charles Carter 1924– . US film actor who often starred in biblical and historical epics (as Moses, for example, in *The Ten Commandments* 1956, and in the title role in *Ben-Hur* 1959).

heterosexuality sexual preference for, or attraction mainly to, persons of the opposite sex.

Hewish Antony 1924– . British radio astronomer who was awarded, with Martin ◊Ryle, the Nobel Prize for Physics 1974 for his work on ◊pulsars, rapidly rotating neutron stars that emit pulses of energy.

Heydrich Reinhard 1904–1942. German Nazi, head of the party's security service and Heinrich ◊Himmler's deputy. He was instrumental in organizing the ◊final solution, the policy of genocide used against Jews and others. "Protector" of Bohemia and Moravia from 1941, he was ambushed and killed the following year by three members of the Czechoslovak forces in Britain, who had landed by parachute. Reprisals followed, including several hundred executions and the massacre in Lidice.

Heyerdahl Thor 1914– . Norwegian ethnologist. He sailed on the ancient-Peruvian-style raft ◊*Kon-Tiki*

from Peru to the Tuamotu Archipelago along the Humboldt Current 1947, and in 1969–70 used ancient-Egyptian-style papyrus reed boats to cross the Atlantic. His experimental approach to historical reconstruction is not regarded as having made any important scientific contribution.

Hezbollah or *Hizbollah* (Party of God) extremist Muslim organization founded by the Iranian Revolutionary Guards who were sent to Lebanon after the 1979 Iranian revolution. Its aim is to spread the Islamic revolution of Iran among the Shiite population of Lebanon. Hezbollah is believed to be the umbrella movement of the groups that held many of the Western hostages taken since 1984.

HI abbreviation for ◊Hawaii.

Hialeah city in SE Florida, just NW of Miami; population (1990) 188,000. Industries include clothing, furniture, plastics, and chemicals. Hialeah Park racetrack is a center for horse racing.

Hiawatha 16th-century North American Indian teacher and Onondaga chieftain. He is said to have welded the Five Nations (later joined by a sixth) of the ◊Iroquois into the league of the *Long House*, as the confederacy was known in what is now upper New York State. Hiawatha is the hero of H W Longfellow's epic poem *The Song of Hiawatha*.

hibernation state of ◊dormancy in which certain animals spend the winter. It is associated with a dramatic reduction in all metabolic processes, including body temperature, breathing, and heart rate. It is a fallacy that animals sleep throughout the winter.

hibiscus any plant of the genus *Hibiscus* of the mallow family. Hibiscuses range from large herbaceous plants to trees. Popular as ornamental plants because of their brilliantly colored, red to white, bell-shaped flowers, they include *H. syriacus* and *H. rosa-sinensis* of Asia and the rose mallow *H. palustris* of North America.

Hickok "Wild Bill" (James Butler) 1837–1876. US pioneer and law enforcer, a legendary figure in the West. In the Civil War he was a sharpshooter and scout for the Union army. He then served as marshal in Kansas, killing as many as 27 people. He was a prodigious gambler and was fatally shot from behind while playing poker in Deadwood, South Dakota.

He established his reputation as a gunfighter when he killed a fellow scout, turned traitor.

hickory tree of the genus *Carya* of the walnut family, native to North America and Asia. It provides a valuable timber, and all species produce nuts, although some are inedible. The pecan *C. illinoensis* is widely cultivated in the S US, and the shagbark *C. ovata* in the N US.

Hickory city in W central North Carolina, in the foothills of the Blue Ridge Mountains, NW of Charlotte; population (1990) 28,300. The city's main industry is hosiery manufacture. Other products include rope, cotton, and wagons.

hieroglyphic Egyptian writing system of the mid-4th millennium BC–3rd century AD, which combines picture signs with those indicating letters. The direction of writing is normally from right to left, the signs facing the beginning of the line. It was deciphered 1822 by the French Egyptologist J F Champollion (1790–1832) with the aid of the ◊Rosetta Stone, which has the same inscription carved in hieroglyphic, demotic, and Greek.

hi-fi (abbreviation for *high-fidelity*) faithful reproduction of sound from a machine that plays recorded music or speech. A typical hi-fi system includes a turntable for playing vinyl records, a cassette tape deck to play magnetic tape recordings, a tuner to pick up radio broadcasts, an amplifier to serve all the equipment, possibly a compact-disk player, and two or more loudspeakers.

high-definition television (HDTV) ◊television system offering a significantly greater number of scanning lines, and therefore a clearer picture, than that provided by conventional systems. The Japanese HDTV system, or Vision as it is trade-named in Japan, uses 1,125 scanning lines and an aspect ratio of 16:9 instead of the squarish 4:3 which conventional television uses. A European HDTV system, called HD-MAC, using 1,250 lines, is under development. In the US, a standard incorporating digital techniques is being discussed.

higher education in most countries, education beyond the age of 18 leading to a university or college degree or similar qualification.

Highland Region administrative region of Scotland
area 10,077 sq mi/26,100 sq km
cities Inverness (administrative headquarters), Thurso, Wick
features comprises almost half the country; Grampian Mountains; Ben Nevis (highest peak in the UK); Loch Ness, Caledonian Canal; Inner Hebrides; the Queen Mother's castle of Mey at Caithness; John O'Groats' House; Dounreay (with Atomic Energy Authority's prototype fast reactor, and a nuclear processing plant)
products oil services, winter sports, timber, livestock, grouse and deer hunting, salmon fishing
population (1991) 209,400

high-level language in computing, a programming language designed to suit the requirements of the programmer; it is independent of the internal machine code of any particular computer. High-level languages are used to solve problems and are often described as *problem-oriented languages*—for example, ◊BASIC was designed to be easily learned by first-time programmers; ◊COBOL is used to write programs solving business problems; and ◊FORTRAN is used for programs solving scientific and mathematical problems. In contrast, low-level languages, such as ◊assembly languages, closely reflect the machine codes of specific computers, and are therefore described as *machine-oriented languages*.

High Point city in N central North Carolina, SW of Greensboro; population (1990) 69,500. The furniture industry is very important to the economy; the Southern Furniture Market is held four times a year. Hosiery is also manufactured.

high tech (abbreviation for *high technology*) in architecture, buildings that display technical innovation of a high order and celebrate structure and services to create exciting forms and spaces. The Hong Kong and Shanghai Bank, Hong Kong, is a masterpiece of this approach.

highway any road used for automobile traffic open to the public, especially a main road or thoroughfare.

hijacking illegal seizure or taking control of a vehicle and/or its passengers or goods. The term dates from 1923 and originally referred to the robbing of freight trucks. In recent times it (and its derivative, "skyjacking") has been applied to the seizure of aircraft, usually in flight, by an individual or group, often with some political aim.

International treaties (Tokyo 1963, The Hague 1970, and Montreal 1971) encourage cooperation against hijackers and make severe penalties compulsory.

Hijrah or *Hegira* the trip from Mecca to Medina of the prophet Mohammed, which took place AD 622 as a result of the persecution of the prophet and his followers. The Muslim calendar dates from this event, and the day of the Hijrah is celebrated as the Muslim New Year.

Hill Joe c. 1872–1915. Swedish-born US labor organizer. A member of the Industrial Workers of the World (IWW, "Wobblies"), he was convicted of murder on circumstantial evidence in Salt Lake City, Utah, 1914. Despite calls by President Wilson and the Swedish government for a retrial, Hill was executed 1915, becoming a martyr for the labor movement.

Hillary Edmund Percival 1919– . New Zealand mountaineer. In 1953, with Nepalese Sherpa mountaineer Tenzing Norgay, he reached the summit of Mount Everest, the first to climb the world's highest peak. As a member of the Commonwealth Transantarctic Expedition 1957–58, he was the first person since Scott to reach the South Pole overland, on Jan 3, 1958.

Hilton Conrad Nicholson 1887–1979. US entrepreneur, founder of the Hilton Hotel Corporation 1946. During the 1930s he steadily expanded his chain of luxury hotels and resorts and reorganized it as the Hilton Hotel Corporation 1946. He based the firm's marketing appeal on its recognizable name and high-quality standardized service.

Himachal Pradesh state of NW India
area 21,500 sq mi/55,700 sq km
capital Simla
features mainly agricultural state, one-third forested, with softwood timber industry
products timber, grain, rice, fruit
population (1991) 5,111,000; mainly Hindu
language Pahari
history created as a Union Territory 1948, it became a full state 1971.

Himalayas vast mountain system of central Asia, extending from the Indian states of Kashmir in the W to Assam in the E, covering the S part of Tibet, Nepal, Sikkim, and Bhutan. It is the highest mountain range in the world. The two highest peaks are *Mount ◊Everest* and Kangchenjunga. Other major peaks include Makalu, Annapurna, and Nanga Parbat, all over 26,000 ft/8,000 m.

Himmler Heinrich 1900–1945. German Nazi leader, head of the ◊SS elite corps from 1929, the police and the ◊Gestapo secret police from 1936, and supervisor of the extermination of the Jews in E Europe. During World War II he replaced Goering as Hitler's second-in-command. He was captured May 1945 and committed suicide.

Hindemith Paul 1895–1963. German composer. His Neo-Classical, contrapuntal works include chamber ensemble and orchestral pieces, such as the *Symphonic Metamorphosis on Themes of Carl Maria von Weber* 1944, and the operas *Cardillac* 1926, revised 1952, and *Mathis der Maler/Mathis the Painter* 1938.

Hindenburg Paul Ludwig Hans von Beneckendorf und Hindenburg 1847–1934. German field marshal and right-wing politician. During World War I he was supreme commander and, with Ludendorff, practically directed Germany's policy until the end of the war. He was president of Germany 1925–33.

Hindenburg Line German western line of World War I fortifications built 1916–17.

Hindi language member of the Indo-Iranian branch of the Indo-European language family, the official language of the Republic of India, although resisted as such by the Dravidian-speaking states of the south. Hindi proper is used by some 30% of Indians, in such northern states as Uttar Pradesh and Madhya Pradesh.

Hinduism (Hindu *sanatana dharma* "eternal tradition") religion originating in N India about 4,000 years ago, which is superficially and in some of its forms polytheistic, but has a concept of the supreme spirit, ◊Brahman, above the many divine manifestations. These include the triad of chief gods (the Trimurti): Brahma, Vishnu, and Siva (creator, preserver, and destroyer). Central to Hinduism are the beliefs in reincarnation and ◊karma; the oldest scriptures are the *Vedas.* Temple worship is almost universally observed and there are many festivals. There are over 805 million Hindus worldwide. Women are not regarded as the equals of men but should be treated with kindness and respect. Muslim influence in N India led to the veiling of women and the restriction of their movements from about the end of the 12th century.

Hindu Kush mountain range in central Asia, length 500 mi/800 km, greatest height Tirich Mir, 25,239 ft/ 7,690 m, in Pakistan. The narrow *Khyber Pass* (33 mi/ 53 km long) separates Pakistan from Afghanistan and was used by ◊Zahir and other invaders of India. The

Hinduism
Prambanan, on Indonesia's island of Java, was completed about AD 900; the three principal Hindu temples are dedicated to Brahma, Siva, and Vishnu.

present road was built by the British in the Afghan Wars.

Hindustan ("land of the Hindus") the whole of India, but more specifically the plain of the Ganges and Jumna rivers, or that part of India N of the Deccan.

Hindustani member of the Indo-Iranian branch of the Indo-European language family, closely related to Hindi and Urdu and originating in the bazaars of Delhi. It is a ◊lingua franca in many parts of the Republic of India.

Hine Lewis 1874–1940. US sociologist and photographer. His dramatic photographs of child labor conditions in US factories at the beginning of the 20th century led to changes in state and local labor laws.

Hines Duncan 1880–1959. US travel author and publisher. He published restaurant and hotel reviews such as *Adventures in Good Eating* 1936 and *Lodging for a Night* 1939. A pioneer travel critic, Hines helped raise the standard of travel accommodation in the US.
   He later licensed his name to a line of prepackaged cake mixes and founded his own publishing house for cookbooks and entertainment and travel guides.

hip-hop popular music originating in New York in the early 1980s, created with scratching (a percussive effect obtained by manually rotating a vinyl record) and heavily accented electronic drums behind a ◊rap vocal. Within a decade, ◊digital sampling had largely superseded scratching. The term "hip-hop" also comprises break dancing and graffiti.

Hipparchus *c.* 190–*c.* 120 BC. Greek astronomer who invented trigonometry, calculated the lengths of the solar year and the lunar month, discovered the precession of the equinoxes, made a catalog of 800 fixed stars, and advanced Eratosthenes' method of determining the situation of places on the Earth's surface by lines of latitude and longitude.
   A native of Nicaea in Bithynia, he lived in Rhodes, and possibly in Alexandria.

hippie member of a youth movement of the late 1960s, also known as *flower power*, which originated in San Francisco, California, and was characterized by nonviolent anarchy, concern for the environment, and rejection of Western materialism. The hippies formed a politically outspoken, antiwar, artistically prolific counterculture in North America and Europe. Their colorful psychedelic style, inspired by drugs such as ◊LSD, emerged in fabric design, graphic art, and music by bands such as Love (1965–71), the Grateful Dead, Jefferson Airplane (1965–74), and ◊Pink Floyd.

Hippocrates c. 460–c. 370 BC. Greek physician, often called the father of medicine. Important Hippocratic ideas include cleanliness (for patients and physicians), moderation in eating and drinking, letting nature take its course, and living where the air is good. He believed that health was the result of the "humors" of the body being in balance; imbalance caused disease. These ideas were later adopted by ◊Galen.

Hippolytus in Greek mythology, the son of Theseus. When he rejected the love of his stepmother, Phaedra, she falsely accused him of making advances to her and turned Theseus against him. Killed by Poseidon at Theseus' request, he was in some accounts of the legend restored to life when his innocence was proven.

hippopotamus (Greek "river horse") large herbivorous, even-toed hoofed mammal of the family Hippopotamidae. The common hippopotamus *Hippopotamus amphibius* is found in Africa. It averages over 13 ft/4 m long, 5 ft/1.5 m high, weighs about 5 tons/ 4,500 kg, and has a brown or slate-gray skin. It is an endangered species.

Hirabayashi v US US Supreme Court decision 1943 dealing with wartime legislation restricting the rights of citizens based on national origin. The case was brought in response to special curfews for Japanese-Americans on the US west coast. Hirabayashi charged that this and the forced relocation of Japanese-Americans during World War II was a violation of Fifth-Amendment rights. The Court refused to rule on relocation measures (◊*Korematsu* v *US* 1944) but upheld Congress's curfew, judging that danger of internal sabotage in the war with Japan warranted this extraordinary measure.

Hirohito (regnal era name *Shōwa*) 1901–1989. Emperor of Japan from 1926, when he succeeded his father Taishō (Yoshihito). After the defeat of Japan in World War II 1945, he was made a figurehead monarch by the US-backed 1946 constitution. He is believed to have played a reluctant role in General

◊Tōjō's prewar expansion plans. He was succeeded by his son ◊Akihito.

Hiroshima industrial city and port on the S coast of Honshu Island, Japan, destroyed by the first wartime use of an atomic bomb Aug 6, 1945. The city has largely been rebuilt since the war; population (1990) 1,085,700.

Hispanic person of Latin American descent from the Spanish-speaking nations, either native-born or an immigrant.

histamine inflammatory substance normally released in damaged tissues, which also accounts for many of the symptoms of ◊allergy. Substances that neutralize its activity are known as ◊antihistamines.

histology in medicine, the laboratory study of cells and tissues.

historical novel fictional prose narrative set in the past. Literature set in the historic rather than the immediate past has always abounded, but in the West, Walter Scott began the modern tradition by setting imaginative romances of love, impersonation, and betrayal in a past based on known fact; his use of historical detail, and subsequent imitations of this technique by European writers, gave rise to the genre.

The less serious possibilities of the historical novel were exploited by writers including Kenneth Roberts, James Michener, Jeffery Farnol, Stanley Weyman, and Rafael Sabatini in the early 20th century in the form of the *historical romance*; Dorothy Dunnett and George MacDonald Fraser revived the historical romance with some success in the late 1960s. Subgenres of the historical novel have developed, with their own conventions. Examples include the *Western*, many of which draw on Owen Wister's classic *The Virginian*; and the novels of the South in the period of the Civil War, notably Margaret Mitchell's *Gone With the Wind*. In the late 20th century, generational series of novels about families, often industrialists of the early 19th century, became popular.

Hitchcock Alfred 1899–1980. British film director who became a US citizen in 1955. A master of the suspense thriller, he was noted for his meticulously drawn storyboards that determined his camera angles and for his cameo "walk-ons" in his own films. His *Blackmail* 1929 was the first successful British talking film; *The Thirty-Nine Steps* 1935 and *The Lady Vanishes* 1939 are British suspense classics. He went to Hollywood 1940, where he made *Rebecca* 1940, *Notorious* 1946,

Hiroshima The total devastation caused by the atom bomb on Hiroshima toward the end of World War II.

Strangers on a Train 1951, *Rear Window* 1954, *Vertigo* 1958, *Psycho* 1960, and *The Birds* 1963. He also hosted two US television mystery series, "Alfred Hitchcock Presents" 1955–62 and "The Alfred Hitchcock Hour" 1963–65.

Hitler Adolf 1889–1945. German Nazi dictator, born in Austria. He was *Führer* (leader) of the Nazi Party from 1921 and author of *Mein Kampf/My Struggle* 1925–27. As chancellor of Germany from 1933 and head of state from 1934, he created a dictatorship by playing party and state institutions against each other and continually creating new offices and appointments. His position was not seriously challenged until the "Bomb Plot" July 20, 1944 to assassinate him. In foreign affairs, he reoccupied the Rhineland and formed an alliance with the Italian Fascist Mussolini 1936, annexed Austria 1938, and occupied the Sudetenland under the ◊Munich Agreement. The rest of Czechoslovakia was annexed March 1939. The Hitler–Stalin pact was followed in Sept by the invasion of Poland and the declaration of war by Britain and France (see ◊World War II). He committed suicide as Berlin fell.

Hitler–Stalin pact nonaggression treaty signed by Germany and the USSR Aug 23, 1939. Under the terms of the treaty both countries agreed to remain neutral and to refrain from acts of aggression against each other if either went to war. Secret clauses allowed for the partition of Poland—Hitler was to acquire western Poland, Stalin the eastern part. On Sept 1, 1939, Hitler invaded Poland. The pact ended when Hitler invaded Russia on June 22, 1941. See also ◊World War II.

Hittite member of any of a succession of peoples who inhabited Anatolia and N Syria from the 3rd millennium to the 1st millennium BC. The city of Hattusas (now Boğazköy in central Turkey) became the capital of a strong kingdom which overthrew the Babylonian Empire. After a period of eclipse the Hittite New Empire became a great power (about 1400–1200 BC), which successfully waged war with Egypt. The Hittite language is an Indo-European language.

HIV abbreviation for *human immunodeficiency virus*, the infectious agent that causes ◊AIDS.

hoatzin tropical bird *Opisthocomus hoatzin* found only in the Amazon, resembling a small pheasant in size and appearance. The bill is thick and the facial skin blue. Adults are olive with white markings above and red-brown below.

Hoban James C 1762–1831. Irish-born architect who emigrated to the US. He designed the White House, Washington, DC; he also worked on the Capitol and other public buildings.

Hobart capital and port of Tasmania, Australia; population (1986) 180,000. Products include zinc, textiles, and paper. Founded 1804 as a penal colony, it was named after Lord Hobart, then secretary of state for the colonies.

Hobbes Thomas 1588–1679. English political philosopher and the first thinker since Aristotle to attempt to develop a comprehensive theory of nature, including human behavior. In *The Leviathan* 1651, he advocates absolutist government as the only means of ensuring order and security; he saw this as deriving from the ◊social contract.

Ho Chi Minh adopted name of Nguyen Tat Thanh 1890–1969. North Vietnamese communist politician, premier and president 1954–69. Having trained in Moscow shortly after the Russian Revolution, he

Hitler German Nazi leader Adolf Hitler at Berchtesgaden, Bavaria.

headed the communist ◊Vietminh from 1941 and fought against the French during the ◊Indochina War 1946–54, becoming president and prime minister of the republic at the armistice. Aided by the communist bloc, he did much to develop industrial potential. He relinquished the premiership 1955, but continued as president. In the years before his death, Ho successfully led his country's fight against US-aided South Vietnam in the ◊Vietnam War 1954–75.

Ho Chi Minh City (until 1976 *Saigon*) chief port and industrial city of S Vietnam; population (1989) 3,169,100. Industries include shipbuilding, textiles, rubber, and food products. Saigon was the capital of the Republic of Vietnam (South Vietnam) from 1954 to 1976, when it was renamed.

Hockney David 1937– . English painter, printmaker, and designer, resident in California. He exhibited at the Young Contemporaries Show of 1961 and contributed to the Pop art movement. He developed an individual figurative style, as in his portrait *Mr and Mrs Clark and Percy* 1971, Tate Gallery, London, and has prolifically experimented with technique. His views of swimming pools reflect a preoccupation with surface pattern and effects of light. He has also produced drawings, etchings, photo collages, and sets for opera.

Hodgkin's disease rare form of cancer (also known as *lymphoadenoma*), mainly affecting the lymph nodes and spleen. It undermines the immune system,

Ho Chi Minh President Ho Chi Minh of Vietnam was, like Mao Zedong, an able strategist, poet, and patriotic hero.

leaving the sufferer susceptible to infection. However, it responds well to radiotherapy and ◊cytotoxic drugs, and long-term survival is usual.

Hoffa James Riddle "Jimmy" 1913–1975. notorious US labor union leader. A member of the Teamsters' (trucking) Union since 1931, he became its ruthless president 1957. In 1964 he effected the first national contract for the truckers but was also convicted in two trials of fraud and jury tampering. He went to prison 1967 and retained his presidency until 1971, when President Nixon commuted his sentence on condition that he should not engage in union activity until 1980. Hoffa disappeared 1975, however, and is considered to have been murdered.

Hoffman Dustin 1937– . US actor, icon of the anti-heroic 1960s. He won Academy Awards for his performances in *Kramer vs Kramer* 1979 and *Rain Man* 1988. His other films include *The Graduate* 1967, *Midnight Cowboy* 1969, *Little Big Man* 1970, *All the President's Men* 1976, *Tootsie* 1982, and *Hook* 1991. He appeared on Broadway in the 1984 revival of *Death of a Salesman*, which was also produced for television 1985.

Hoffmann E(rnst) T(heodor) A(madeus) 1776–1822. German composer and writer. He composed the opera *Undine* 1816 and many fairy stories, including *Nussknacker/Nutcracker* 1816. His stories inspired ◊Offenbach's *Tales of Hoffmann*.

Hofstadter Robert 1915–1990. US high-energy physicist who revealed the structure of the atomic nucleus. He demonstrated that the nucleus is composed of a high-energy core and a surrounding area of decreasing density. He shared the 1961 Nobel Prize for Physics with Rudolf Mössbauer.

Educated in New York and Princeton, Hofstadter did his research in California after 1950. He helped to construct a new high-energy accelerator at Stanford University, with which he showed that the proton and the neutron have complex structures and cannot be considered elementary particles. See also ◊quark.

hog member of the ◊pig family.

Hogan Paul 1940– . Australian TV comic, film actor, and producer. The box-office hit *Crocodile Dundee* (considered the most profitable film in Australian history) 1986 and *Crocodile Dundee II* 1988 (of which he was cowriter, star, and producer) brought him international fame.

Hogarth William 1697–1764. English painter and engraver who produced portraits and moralizing genre scenes, such as the series *A Rake's Progress* 1735. His portraits are remarkably direct and full of character, for example *Heads of Six of Hogarth's Servants* c. 1750–55 (Tate Gallery, London).

Hohenstaufen German family of princes, several members of which were Holy Roman emperors 1138–1208 and 1214–54. They were the first German emperors to make use of associations with Roman law and tradition to aggrandize their office, and included Conrad III; Frederick I (Barbarossa), the first to use the title Holy Roman emperor (previously the title Roman emperor was used); Henry VI; and Frederick II.

Hohenzollern German family, originating in Württemberg, the main branch of which held the titles of ◊elector of Brandenburg from 1415, king of Prussia from 1701, and German emperor from 1871. The last emperor, Wilhelm II, was dethroned 1918 after the disastrous course of World War I. Another branch of the family were kings of Romania 1881–1947.

Hohhot or *Huhehot* city and capital of Inner Mongolia (Nei Mongol) autonomous region, China; population (1989) 870,000. Industries include textiles, electronics, and dairy products. There are Lamaist monasteries and temples here.

Hokkaido (formerly until 1868 *Yezo* or *Ezo*) northernmost of the four main islands of Japan, separated from Honshu to the S by Tsugaru Strait and from Sakhalin to the N by Soya Strait; area 32,231 sq mi/83,500 sq km; population (1986) 5,678,000, including 16,000 ◊Ainus. The capital is Sapporo. Natural resources include coal, mercury, manganese, oil and natural gas, timber, and fisheries. Coal mining and agriculture are the main industries.

Holbein Hans, *the Elder* c. 1464–1524. German painter, active in Augsburg. His works include altarpieces, such as that of *St Sebastian* 1516 (Alte Pinakothek, Munich). He also painted portraits and designed stained glass.

Holbein Hans, *the Younger* 1497/98–1543. German painter and woodcut artist; the son and pupil of Hans Holbein the Elder. Holbein was born in Augsburg. In 1515 he went to Basel, where he became friendly with Erasmus; he painted three portraits of him in 1523, which were strongly influenced by Quentin Massys. He traveled widely in Europe and was court painter to England's Henry VIII from 1536. He also painted portraits of Thomas More and Thomas Cromwell; a notable woodcut series is *Dance of Death* about 1525. He designed title pages for Luther's New Testament and More's *Utopia*.

Holden William. Adopted name of William Franklin Beedle 1918–1981. US film actor, a star in the late 1940s and 1950s. He played leading roles in *Sunset Boulevard* 1950, *Stalag 17* 1953, *The Wild Bunch* 1969, and *Network* 1976.

holding company company with a controlling stockholding in one or more subsidiaries.

Holiday Billie. Adopted name of Eleanora Gough McKay 1915–1959. US jazz singer, also known as "Lady Day." She made her debut in Harlem clubs and became known for her emotionally charged delivery and idiosyncratic phrasing; she brought a blues feel to performances with swing bands. Songs she made her own include "Stormy Weather," "Strange Fruit," and "I Cover the Waterfront."

Holinshed Ralph c. 1520–c. 1580. English historian who published two volumes of the *Chronicles of England, Scotland and Ireland* 1578, on which Shakespeare based his history plays.

holistic medicine umbrella term for an approach that virtually all alternative therapies profess, which considers the overall health and lifestyle profile of a patient, and treats specific ailments not primarily as conditions to be alleviated but rather as symptoms of more fundamental disease.

Holland John Philip 1840–1914. Irish engineer who developed some of the first submarines. He began work in Ireland in the late 1860s and emigrated to the US 1873. His first successful boat was launched 1881 and, after several failures, he built the *Holland* 1893, which was bought by the US Navy two years later.

holly tree or shrub of the genus *Ilex*, family Aquifoliaceae, generally with glossy, sharp-pointed leaves and red berries. American holly *I. opaca* of the E US is used for Christmas decorations. Leaves of the Brazilian holly *I. paraguayensis* are used to make the tea yerba maté.

Holly Buddy. Adopted name of Charles Hardin Holley 1936–1959. US rock-and-roll singer, guitarist, and songwriter, born in Lubbock, Texas. Holly had a distinctive, hiccuping vocal style and was an early experimenter with recording techniques. Many of his hits with his band, the Crickets, such as "That'll Be the Day" 1957, "Peggy Sue" 1957, and "Maybe Baby" 1958, have become classics. He died in a plane crash.

hollyhock plant of the genus *Althaea* of the mallow family Malvaceae. *A. rosea*, originally a native of Asia, produces spikes of large white, yellow, or red flowers, 10 ft/3 m high when cultivated as a biennial.

Hollywood district in the city of Los Angeles, California; the center of the US film industry from 1911. It is the home of legendary film studios such as 20th Century Fox, MGM, Paramount, Columbia Pictures, United Artists, Disney, and Warner Brothers. Many film stars' homes are situated nearby in Beverly Hills and other communities adjacent to Hollywood.

Hollywood city in SE Florida, on the Atlantic Ocean, S of Fort Lauderdale and N of Miami; population (1990) 121,700. Famous as the center of the film industry, its principal industry is tourism.

Holmes, Sherlock fictitious private detective, created by the English writer Arthur Conan ◊Doyle in *A Study in Scarlet* 1887 and recurring in novels and stories until 1914. Holmes's ability to make inferences from slight clues always astonishes the narrator, Dr Watson.

Holmes Oliver Wendell 1841–1935. US jurist and Supreme Court justice 1902–32, noted for the elegance of his written opinions. He was appointed to the US Supreme Court by President T Roosevelt, and during his office handed down landmark decisions in a number of antitrust, constitutional First Amendment, and labor law cases. He retired from the Court 1932.

holmium (Latin *Holmia* "Stockholm") silvery, metallic element of the ◊lanthanide series, symbol Ho, atomic number 67, atomic weight 164.93. It occurs in combination with other rare-earth metals and in various minerals such as gadolinite. Its compounds are highly magnetic.

Holocaust, the the annihilation of an estimated 6 million Jews by the Hitler regime 1933–45 in the numerous extermination and ◊concentration camps, most notably Auschwitz, Sobibor, Treblinka, and Maidanek in Poland, and Belsen, Buchenwald, and Dachau in Germany. An additional 10 million people died during imprisonment or were exterminated; among them were Ukrainian, Polish, and Russian civilians and prisoners of war, gypsies, socialists, homosexuals, and others (labeled "defectives"). Victims were variously starved, tortured, experimented on, and worked to death. Millions were executed in gas chambers, shot, or hanged. It was euphemistically termed the ◊final solution (of the Jewish question).

Holocaust museums and memorial sites have been established in Israel and in other countries.

Holocene epoch of geological time that began 10,000 years ago, the second and current epoch of the Quaternary period. The glaciers retreated, the climate became warmer, and humans developed significantly.

holography method of producing three-dimensional (3-D) images by means of ◊laser light. Holography uses a photographic technique (involving the splitting of a laser beam into two beams) to produce a picture, or hologram, that contains 3-D information about the object photographed. Some holograms show meaningless patterns in ordinary light and produce a 3-D image only when laser light is projected through them, but reflection holograms produce images when ordinary light is reflected from them (as found on credit cards).

Holy Alliance "Christian Union of Charity, Peace, and Love" initiated by Alexander I of Russia 1815 and signed by every crowned head in Europe. The alliance became associated with Russian attempts to preserve autocratic monarchies at any price, and served as an excuse to meddle in the internal affairs of other states.

Holy Communion another name for the ◊Eucharist, a Christian sacrament.

Holy Grail in medieval Christian legend, the dish or cup used by Jesus at the Last Supper, supposed to have supernatural powers. Together with the spear with which he was wounded at the Crucifixion, it was an object of quest by King Arthur's knights in certain stories incorporated in the Arthurian legend.

Holy Land Christian term for ◊Israel, because of its association with Jesus and the Old Testament.

holy orders Christian priesthood, as conferred by the laying on of hands by a bishop. It is held by the Roman Catholic, Eastern Orthodox, and Anglican

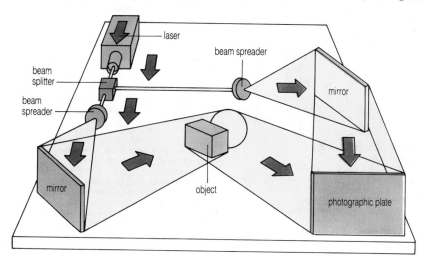

holography
Recording a transmission hologram.

laser

beam spreader

beam splitter

beam spreader

mirror

mirror

object

photographic plate

churches to have originated in Jesus' choosing of the apostles.

Holy Roman Empire empire of ◊Charlemagne and his successors, and the German Empire 962–1806, both being regarded as the Christian (hence "holy") revival of the Roman Empire. At its height it comprised much of western and central Europe. See ◊Germany, history and ◊Habsburg.

Holy See the diocese of the ◊pope.

Holy Spirit third person of the Christian ◊Trinity, also known as the Holy Ghost or the Paraclete, usually depicted as a white dove.

Holy Week in the Christian church, the last week of ◊Lent, when Christians commemorate the events that led up to the crucifixion of Jesus. Holy Week begins on Palm Sunday and includes Maundy Thursday, which commemorates the Last Supper.

Homelands Policy South Africa's apartheid policy which set aside ◊Black National States for black Africans.

homeopathy or **homoeopathy** system of medicine based on the principle that symptoms of disease are part of the body's self-healing processes, and on the practice of administering extremely diluted doses of natural substances found to produce in a healthy person the symptoms manifest in the illness being treated. Developed by German physician Samuel Hahnemann (1755–1843), the system is widely practiced today as an alternative to allopathic medicine, and many controlled tests and achieved cures testify its efficacy.

Homer according to ancient tradition, the author of the Greek narrative epics, the ◊*Iliad* and the ◊*Odyssey* (both derived from oral tradition). Little is known about the man, but modern research suggests that both poems should be assigned to the 8th century BC, with the *Odyssey* the later of the two. The predominant dialect in the poems indicates that Homer may have come from an Ionian Greek settlement, such as Smyrna or Chios, as was traditionally believed.

Homer Winslow 1836–1910. US painter and lithographer, known for his seascapes, both oils and watercolors, which date from the 1880s and 1890s.

Home Rule, Irish movement to repeal the Act of ◊Union 1801 that joined Ireland to Britain and to establish an Irish parliament responsible for internal affairs. In 1870 Isaac Butt (1813–1879) formed the Home Rule Association and the movement was led in Parliament from 1880 by Charles ◊Parnell. After 1918 the demand for an independent Irish republic replaced that for home rule.

Homestead Act in US history, an act of Congress 1862 to encourage settlement of land in the west by offering 160-acre/65-hectare plots cheaply or even free to those willing to cultivate and improve the land for a stipulated amount of time. By 1900 about 80 million acres/32 million hectares had been distributed. Homestead lands are available to this day.

homicide in law, the killing of a human being. This may be unlawful, lawful, or excusable, depending on the circumstances. Unlawful homicides include ◊murder, ◊manslaughter, ◊infanticide, and causing death by dangerous driving (vehicular homicide). Lawful homicide occurs where, for example, a police officer is justified in killing a criminal in the course of apprehension. Excusable homicide occurs when a person is killed in self-defense or by accident.

homonymy aspect of language in which, through historical accident, two or more words may sound and look alike (**homonymy** proper, as in a farmer's *bull* and a papal *bull*), may sound the same but look differ-

---

Honduras
Republic of
(*República de Honduras*)

area 43,282 sq mi/112,100 sq km
capital Tegucigalpa
cities San Pedro Sula; ports La Ceiba, Puerto Cortés
physical narrow tropical coastal plain with mountainous interior, Bay Islands
features archeological sites; Mayan ruins at Copán
head of state and government Rafael Leonardo Callejas from 1990
political system democratic republic

political parties Liberal Party of Honduras (PLH), center-left; National Party (PN), right-wing
exports coffee, bananas, meat, sugar, timber (including mahogany, rosewood)
currency lempira
population (1992) 4,996,000 (mestizo, or mixed, 90%; Indians and Europeans 10%); growth rate 3.1% p.a.
life expectancy men 58, women 62
languages Spanish (official), English, Indian languages
religion Roman Catholic 97%
literacy men 61%, women 58% (1985 est)
GDP $3.5 bn (1987); $758 per head

chronology
1838 Independence achieved from Spain.
1980 After more than a century of mostly military rule, a civilian government was elected, with Dr Roberto Suazo as president; the commander in chief of the army, General Gustavo Alvarez, retained considerable power.
1983 Close involvement with the US in providing naval and air bases and allowing Nicaraguan counterrevolutionaries ("Contras") to operate from Honduras.
1984 Alvarez ousted in coup led by junior officers, resulting in policy review toward US and Nicaragua.
1985 José Azcona elected president after electoral law changed, making Suazo ineligible for presidency.
1989 Government and opposition declared support for Central American peace plan to demobilize Nicaraguan Contras based in Honduras; Contras and their dependents in Honduras in 1989 thought to number about 55,000.
1990 Rafael Callejas (PN) inaugurated as president.
1992 Border dispute with El Salvador dating from 1861 finally resolved.

ent (**homophony**, as in *air* and *heir*; *gilt* and *guilt*), or may look the same but sound different (**homography**, as in the *wind* in the trees and roads that *wind*).

homosexuality sexual preference for, or attraction to, persons of one's own sex; in women it is referred to as ◊lesbianism. Both sexes use the term "gay." Men and women who are attracted to both sexes are referred to as bisexual. The extent to which homosexual behavior is caused by biological or psychological factors is an area of disagreement among experts.

Homs or **Hums** city, capital of Homs district, W Syria, near the Orontes River; population (1981) 355,000. Silk, cereals, and fruit are produced in the area, and industries include silk textiles, oil refining, and jewelry. ◊Zenobia, Queen of Palmyra, was defeated at Homs by the Roman emperor ◊Aurelian 272.

Honan alternate name for ◊Henan, a province of China.

Honduras country in Central America, bounded N by the Caribbean Sea, SE by Nicaragua, S by the Pacific Ocean, SW by El Salvador, and W and NW by Guatemala.

Honecker Erich 1912– . German communist politician, in power 1973–89, elected chair of the council of state (head of state) 1976. He governed in an outwardly austere and efficient manner and, while favoring East–West détente, was a loyal ally of the USSR. In Oct 1989, following a wave of prodemocracy demonstrations, he was replaced as leader of the Socialist Unity Party (SED) and head of state by Egon Krenz, and in Dec expelled from the Communist Party. Following revelations of corruption during his regime, he was placed under house arrest, awaiting trial on charges of treason, corruption, and abuse of power. In 1993 he was allowed to go into exile in Chile.

honey sweet syrup produced by honey ◊bees from the nectar of flowers. It is stored in honeycombs and made in excess of their needs as food for the winter. Honey comprises various sugars, mainly levulose and dextrose, with enzymes, coloring matter, acids, and pollen grains. It has antibacterial properties and was widely used in ancient Egypt, Greece, and Rome as a wound salve. It is still popular for sore throats, in hot drinks or lozenges.

honeysuckle vine or shrub of the genus *Lonicera*, family Caprifoliaceae. The common honeysuckle or woodbine *L. periclymenum* of Europe is a climbing plant with sweet-scented flowers, reddish and yellow-tinted outside and creamy-white inside; it now grows in the NE US.

Hong Kong British crown colony SE of China, in the South China Sea, comprising Hong Kong Island; the Kowloon Peninsula; many other islands, of which the largest is Lantau; and the mainland New Territories. It is due to revert to Chinese control 1997.
area 413 sq mi/1,070 sq km
capital Victoria (Hong Kong City)
cities Kowloon, Tsuen Wan (in the New Territories)
features an enclave of Kwantung province, China, it has one of the world's finest natural harbors; Hong Kong Island is connected with Kowloon by undersea railroad and ferries; a world financial center, its stock market has four exchanges; across the border of the New Territories in China itself is the Shenzhen special economic zone
exports textiles, clothing, electronic goods, clocks, watches, cameras, plastic products; a large proportion

Hong Kong

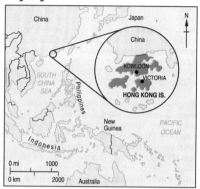

of the exports and imports of S China are transshipped here; tourism is important
currency Hong Kong dollar
population (1986) 5,431,000; 57% Hong Kong Chinese, most of the remainder refugees from the mainland
languages English, Chinese
media Hong Kong has the most free press in Asia but its freedoms are not enshrined in law
religions Confucianist, Buddhist, Taoist, with Muslim and Christian minorities

Hong Kong Chinese junk in Victoria Harbour, Hong Kong.

government Hong Kong is a British dependency administered by a crown-appointed governor (Chris Patten from 1992) who presides over an unelected executive council, composed of 4 ex-officio and 11 nominated members, and a legislative council composed of 3 ex-officio members, 29 appointees, and 24 indirectly elected members

history formerly part of China, Hong Kong Island was occupied by Britain 1841, during the first of the ◊Opium Wars, and ceded by China under the 1842 Treaty of Nanking. The Kowloon Peninsula was acquired under the 1860 Beijing (Peking) Convention and the New Territories secured on a 99-year lease from 1898. The colony, which developed into a major center for Sino-British trade during the late 19th and early 20th centuries, was occupied by Japan 1941–45. The restored British administration promised, after 1946, to increase self-government. These plans were shelved, however, after the 1949 Communist revolution in China. During the 1950s almost 1 million Chinese (predominantly Cantonese) refugees fled to Hong Kong. Immigration continued during the 1960s and 1970s, raising the colony's population from 1 million in 1946 to 5 million in 1980. From 1975, 160,000 Vietnamese ◊boat people fled to Hong Kong. The UK government began forced repatriation of some from 1989. Hong Kong's economy expanded rapidly during the corresponding period and the colony became one of Asia's major commercial, financial, and industrial centers boasting the world's busiest container port from 1987. As the date (1997) for the termination of the New Territories' lease approached, negotiations on Hong Kong's future were opened between Britain and China 1982. These culminated in a unique agreement, signed in Beijing 1984, in which Britain agreed to transfer full sovereignty of the islands and New Territories to China 1997 in return for Chinese assurance that Hong Kong's social and economic freedom and capitalist lifestyle would be preserved for at least 50 years. As plans for the transfer became more detailed, fears that China would exert more control than agreed led to tensions between the UK and China.

Honiara port and capital of the Solomon Islands, on the NW coast of Guadalcanal Island, on the river Mataniko; population (1985) 26,000.

Honolulu (Hawaiian "sheltered bay") capital city and port of Hawaii, on the south coast of Oahu; population (1990) 365,300. It is a holiday resort, noted for its beauty and tropical vegetation, with some industry.

The University of Hawaii's main campus is here, and there is an innovative state capitol building, dating from 1959. Pearl Harbor and Hickam Air Force Base are 7 mi/11 km to the NW. William Brown, a British sea captain, was the first European to see Honolulu, in 1794. It became the Hawaiian royal capital in the 19th century.

Honshu principal island of Japan. It lies between Hokkaido to the NE and Kyushu to the SW; area 89,205 sq mi/231,100 sq km, including 382 smaller islands; population (1990) 99,254,194. A chain of volcanic mountains runs along the island, which is subject to frequent earthquakes. The main cities are Tokyo, Yokohama, Osaka, Kobe, Nagoya, and Hiroshima.

Honthorst Gerrit van 1590–1656. Dutch painter who used extremes of light and shade, influenced by Caravaggio; helped form the **Utrecht School.**

Hooch Pieter de 1629–1684. Dutch painter, active in Delft and, later, Amsterdam. The harmonious domestic interiors and courtyards of his Delft period were influenced by Vermeer.

Hooke Robert 1635–1703. English scientist and inventor, originator of ◊Hooke's law, and considered the foremost mechanic of his time. His inventions included a telegraph system, the spirit level, marine barometer, and sea gauge. He coined the term "cell" in biology.

Hooker Joseph Dalton 1817–1911. English botanist who traveled to the Antarctic and made many botanical discoveries. His works include *Flora Antarctica* 1844–47, *Genera Plantarum* 1862–83, and *Flora of British India* 1875–97.

Hooker Thomas 1586–1647. British colonial religious leader in America. A Puritan, he opposed the religious leadership of Cambridge colony, and led a group of his followers westward to the Connecticut Valley, founding Hartford 1636. He became the de facto leader of the colony and in 1639 helped to formulate Connecticut's first constitution, the Fundamental Orders.

Hooke's law law stating that the deformation of a body is proportional to the magnitude of the deforming force, provided that the body's elastic limit (see ◊elasticity) is not exceeded. If the elastic limit is not reached, the body will return to its original size once the force is removed. It was discovered by Robert Hooke 1676.

hookworm parasitic roundworm (see ◊worm), of the genus *Necator*, with hooks around the mouth. It lives mainly in tropic and subtropic regions, but also in humid areas in temperate climates. The eggs are hatched in damp soil, and the larvae bore into the host's skin, usually through the soles of the feet. They make their way to the small intestine, where they live by sucking blood. The eggs are expelled with feces, and the cycle starts again. The human hookworm causes anemia, weakness, and abdominal pain. It is common in areas where defecation occurs outdoors.

Hoover Herbert Clark 1874–1964. 31st president of the US 1929–33, a Republican. He was secretary of commerce 1921–28. Hoover lost public confidence after the stock-market crash of 1929, when he opposed direct government aid for the unemployed in the Depression that followed.

Hoover was called upon to administer the European Food Program 1947, and in the late 1950s he headed two Hoover commissions that recommended reforms in government structure and operations.

Hoover J(ohn) Edgar 1895–1972. US lawyer and director of the Federal Bureau of Investigation (FBI) from its start 1924, where he built a powerful network for the detection of organized crime, including a national fingerprint collection.

Hoover William Henry 1849–1932. US manufacturer who developed the vacuum cleaner. "Hoover" soon became a generic name for vacuum cleaner.

Hoover Dam highest concrete dam in the US, 726 ft/ 221 m, on the Colorado River at the Arizona–Nevada border. It was begun during the Hoover administration, built 1931–36. Known as Boulder Dam 1933–47, under the F D Roosevelt administration, its name was restored by President Truman since Hoover was serving the Truman administration in postwar organization. The dam created Lake Meade, and has a hydroelectric power capacity of 1,300 megawatts.

Hope Bob. Adopted name of Leslie Towne Hope. 1903– . British-born US comedian, brought to the US in 1907. His earliest success was on Broadway and as a radio star in the 1930s. His film appearances include seven "Road" films made from 1940 with Bing Crosby and Dorothy Lamour. These include *The Road to*

Singapore 1940, *The Road to Zanzibar* 1941, *The Road to Morocco* 1942, *The Road to Utopia* 1946, *The Road to Rio* 1946, *The Road to Bali* 1952, and *The Road to Hong Kong* 1953. He made other films, such as *Paleface* 1948, a comic western.

Hopewell North American Indian agricultural culture of the central US, dated about AD 200. The Hopewell built burial mounds up to 40 ft/12 m high and structures such as Serpent Mound in Ohio; see also ◊Moundbuilder.

Hopi member of a North American Indian people, presently numbering approximately 9,000, who live mainly in pueblos in the SW US, especially NE Arizona. They live in stone and adobe houses, forming small towns on rocky plateaus, farm, and herd sheep. Their language belongs to the Uto-Aztecan family.

Hopkins Anthony 1937– . Welsh actor. Among his stage appearances are *Equus, Macbeth, Pravda,* and the title role in *King Lear.* His films include *The Lion in Winter* 1968, *A Bridge Too Far* 1977, *The Elephant Man* 1980, *84 Charing Cross Road* 1986, and *The Silence of the Lambs* (Academy Award) 1991.

Hopkins Gerard Manley 1844–1889. English poet and Jesuit priest. His work, marked by its religious themes and use of natural imagery, includes "The Wreck of the Deutschland" 1876 and "The Windhover" 1877. His employment of "sprung rhythm" greatly influenced later 20th-century poetry. His poetry was written in secret, and published 30 years after his death by his friend Robert Bridges.

Hopkins Mark 1802–1887. US educator and religious leader, president of Williams College 1836–72 and of the American Board of Commissioners for Foreign Missions 1857–87. He was also known as a popular lecturer and author on religious subjects.

Hopkinsville city in SW Kentucky, SW of Louisville; population (1990) 29,800. It is a marketplace for tobacco and livestock.

Hopper Dennis 1936– . US film actor and director who caused a sensation with the antiestablishment *Easy Rider* 1969, the archetypal "road" film, but whose *The Last Movie* 1971 was poorly received by the critics. He made a comeback in the 1980s. His work as an actor includes *Rebel Without a Cause* 1955, *The American Friend/Der amerikanische Freund* 1977, and *Blue Velvet* 1986.

Hopper Edward 1882–1967. US painter and etcher. His views of New England and New York in the 1930s and 1940s captured the loneliness and superficial glamour of city life, as in *Nighthawks* 1942 (Art Institute, Chicago).

Hopper was a realist who never followed avant-garde trends.

hops female fruit-heads of the hop plant *Humulus lupulus,* family Cannabiaceae; these are dried and used as a tonic and in flavoring beer. In designated areas in Europe, no male hops may be grown, since seedless hops produced by the unpollinated female plant contain a greater proportion of the alpha acid that gives beer its bitter taste.

Horace 65–8 BC. Roman lyric poet and satirist. He became a leading poet under the patronage of Emperor Augustus. His works include *Satires* 35–30 BC; the four books of *Odes,* about 25–24 BC; *Epistles,* a series of verse letters; and an influential critical work, *Ars poetica.* They are distinguished by their style, wit, discretion, and patriotism.

Horae in Greek mythology, the goddesses of the seasons, daughters of Zeus and Themis, three or four in number, sometimes personified.

horizon the limit to which one can see across the surface of the sea or a level plain, that is, about 3 mi/5 km at 5 ft/1.5 m above sea level, and about 40 mi/65 km at 1,000 ft/300 m.

hormone product of the ◊endocrine glands, concerned with control of body functions. The main glands are the thyroid, parathyroid, pituitary, adrenal, pancreas, uterus, ovary, and testis. Hormones bring about changes in the functions of various organs according to the body's requirements. The pituitary gland, at the base of the brain, is a center for overall coordination of hormone secretion; the thyroid hormones determine the rate of general body chemistry; the adrenal hormones prepare the organism during stress for "fight or flight"; and the sexual hormones such as estrogen govern reproductive functions.

hormone-replacement therapy (HRT) use of oral ◊oestrogen and progestogen to help limit the effects of the menopause in women. The treatment was first used in the 1970s.

Hormuz or *Ormuz* small island, area 16 sq mi/41 sq km, in the Strait of Hormuz, belonging to Iran. It is strategically important because oil tankers leaving the Persian Gulf for Japan and the West have to pass through the strait to reach the Arabian Sea.

horn one of a family of wind instruments, of which the French horn is the most widely used. See ◊brass instrument.

hornbill bird of the family of Bucerotidae, found in Africa, India, and Malaysia. Omnivorous, it is about 3 ft/1 m long, and has a powerful bill, usually surmounted by a bony growth or casque. During the breeding season, the female walls herself into a hole in a tree and does not emerge until the young are hatched.

hornet kind of ◊wasp.

Hornsby Rajah (Rogers) 1896–1963. US baseball player. He won the National League batting title in six consecutive seasons 1920–25. His .424 batting average 1924 is the highest achieved in the National League and he was voted the National League's most valuable player 1925. His lifetime batting average of .358 is the second-highest in history.

Hornsby was elected to the Baseball Hall of Fame 1942.

horoscope in Western astrology, a chart of the position of the Sun, Moon, and planets relative to the ◊zodiac at the moment of birth, used to assess a person's character and forecast future influences.

Horowitz Vladimir 1904–1989. Russian-born US pianist. He made his debut in the US 1928 with the New York Philharmonic Orchestra. Noted for his commanding virtuoso style, he was a leading interpreter of Liszt, Schumann, and Rachmaninov.

horror genre of fiction and film, devoted primarily to scaring the reader or audience, but often also aiming to be cathartic through their exaggeration of the bizarre and grotesque. Dominant figures in the horror tradition are Mary Shelley (*Frankenstein* 1818), Edgar Allan Poe, Bram Stoker, H P Lovecraft and, among contemporary writers, Stephen King and Clive Barker.

horse hoofed, odd-toed, grazing mammal *Equus caballus* of the family Equidae, which also includes zebras and asses. The many breeds of domestic horse

horse Horses have been domesticated from early in the 2nd millennium BC, probably at first to provide food.

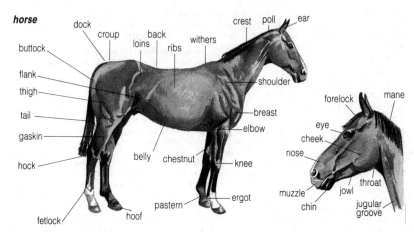

horse

dock
croup
back
withers
loins
ribs
buttock
crest poll ear
flank
shoulder
thigh
forelock mane
tail
breast
eye
gaskin
elbow
cheek
nose
belly chestnut
knee
hock
throat
ergot
muzzle jowl
pastern
chin
jugular groove
fetlock
hoof

of Euro-Asian origin range in color from white to gray, brown, and black. The yellow-brown Mongolian wild horse or Przewalski's horse *E. przewalskii*, named after its Polish "discoverer" about 1880, is the only surviving species of wild horse.

Breeds include the *Arab*, small and agile; *thoroughbred*, derived from the Arab via English mares, used in horse racing for its speed (the present stock is descended from three Arab horses introduced to Britain in the 18th century); *quarter horse*, used by cowboys for herding; *Lippizaner*, a pure white horse, named after its place of origin in Slovenia; *shire*, the largest draft horse in the world at 17 hands (1 hand = 4 in/10.2 cm), descended from the medieval war horses that carried knights in armor. Ponies combine the qualities of various types of horses with a smaller build (under 14.2 hands, or 58 in/1.47 m). The smallest is the hardy *Shetland*, about 10.5 hands, or 27 in/70 cm high. The *mule*, a hardy pack-animal, is the usually sterile offspring of a female horse and a male ass; the *hinny* is a similarly sterile offspring of a male horse and a female ass, but less useful as a beast of burden.

horsefly any of over 2,500 species of fly, belonging to the family Tabanidae. The females suck blood from horses, cattle, and humans; males live on plants and suck nectar. The larvae are carnivorous.

horsepower imperial unit (abbreviation hp) of power, now replaced by the ◊watt. It was first used by the engineer James ◊Watt, who employed it to compare the power of steam engines with that of horses.

horse racing sport of racing mounted or driven (hitched) horses. Two popular forms in the US are *flat racing*, in which thoroughbred horses are guided over a flat course by a rider called a jockey, and *harness racing*, in which a driver in a two-wheeled cart called a sulky drives a horse in one of two gaits: pacing (both legs on the same side are off the ground at the same time); trotting (diagonal legs are off the ground at the same time).

horseradish hardy perennial *Armoracia rusticana*, native to SE Europe but naturalized elsewhere, family Cruciferae. The thick, cream-colored root is strong-tasting and is often made into a condiment.

horseshoe crab marine arthropod of the order Xiphosura, class Merostomata, distantly related to spiders, which lives on the Atlantic coast of North America and the coasts of Asia. The upper side of the body is entirely covered with a rounded shell, and it has a long,

spinelike tail. Horseshoe crabs grow up to 2 ft/60 cm long. They crawl along the bottom in coastal waters and lay their eggs in the sand at the high water mark.

Horthy Nicholas Horthy de Nagybánya 1868–1957. Hungarian politician and admiral. Leader of the counterrevolutionary White government, he became regent 1920 on the overthrow of the communist Bela Kun regime by Romanian and Czechoslovak intervention. He represented the conservative and military class, and retained power until World War II, trying (although allied to Hitler) to retain independence of action. In 1944 he tried to negotiate a surrender to the USSR but Hungary was taken over by the Nazis and he was deported to Germany. He was released from German captivity the same year by the Western Allies and allowed to go to Portugal, where he died.

horticulture art and science of growing flowers, fruit, and vegetables. Horticulture is practiced in gardens and orchards, along with millions of acres of land devoted to vegetable farming. Some areas, like California, have specialized in horticulture because they have the mild climate and light fertile soil most suited to these crops.

Horus in ancient Egyptian mythology, the hawk-headed sun god, son of Isis and Osiris, of whom the pharaohs were declared to be the incarnation.

hospice residential facility specializing in palliative care for terminally ill patients and their relatives.

host organism that is parasitized by another. In commensalism, the partner that does not benefit may also be called the host.

hostage person taken prisoner as a means of exerting pressure on a third party, usually with threats of death or injury.

hot spot in geology, a hypothetical region of high thermal activity in the Earth's ◊mantle. It is believed to be the origin of many chains of ocean islands, such as Polynesia and the Galápagos.

Hottentot ("stammerer") South African term for a variety of different African peoples; it is nonscientific and considered derogatory by many. The name Khoikhol is preferred.

Houdini Harry. Adopted name of Erich Weiss 1874–1926. US escapologist and conjurer. He was renowned for his escapes from ropes and handcuffs, from trunks under water, from straitjackets and prison cells.

Houma city in S Louisiana, on the gulf intracoastal waterway, SW of New Orleans; population (1990) 30,500. The seat of Terrebonne parish, it is a supply center for offshore oil rigs in the Gulf of Mexico. Industries include shellfish processing and sugar refining.

Houphouët-Boigny Félix 1905–1993. Ivory Coast political leader. He held posts in French ministries, and became president of the Republic of the Ivory Coast on independence 1960, maintaining close links with France, which helped to boost an already thriving economy and encourage political stability. Pro-Western and opposed to communist intervention in Africa, Houphouët-Boigny was strongly criticized for maintaining diplomatic relations with South Africa. He was reelected for a seventh term 1990 in multiparty elections, amid allegations of ballot rigging and political pressure.

hour period of time comprising 60 minutes; 24 hours make one calendar day.

Hours, Book of in medieval Europe, a collection of liturgical prayers for the use of the faithful.

Books of Hours contained short prayers and illustrations, with each prayer suitable for a different hour of the day, in honor of the Virgin Mary. The enormous demand for Books of Hours was a stimulus for the development of Gothic illumination. A celebrated example is the *Très Riches Heures du Duc de Berry*, illustrated in the early 15th century by the Limbourg brothers.

House Edward Mandell 1858–1938. US politician and diplomat. He was instrumental in obtaining the presidential nomination for Woodrow Wilson 1912 and later served as Wilson's closest adviser. During World War I 1914–1918, House served as US liaison with Great Britain and was an important behind-the-scenes participant in the 1919 Versailles Peace Conference.

housefly fly of the genus *Musca*, found in and around dwellings, especially *M. domestica*, a common worldwide species. Houseflies are gray and have mouthparts adapted for drinking liquids and sucking moisture from food and manure.

House of Representatives, US lower chamber of the Congress. Revenue bills and impeachment charges must originate in the House, which also elects the president (as it did in 1800 and 1824) if there is no majority in the electoral college. Once bills are passed in the House, they are sent to the Senate for consideration.

House Un-American Activities Committee (HUAC) Congressional committee, established 1938, noted for its public investigating into alleged subversion, particularly of communists. First headed by Martin Dies, it achieved its greatest notoriety during the 1950s through its hearings on communism in the movie industry. It was later renamed the House Internal Security Committee.

Housman A(lfred) E(dward) 1859–1936. English poet and Classical scholar. His *A Shropshire Lad* 1896, a series of deceptively simple, nostalgic, ballad-like poems, was popular during World War I. This was followed by *Last Poems* 1922 and *More Poems* 1936.

Houston port in Texas; linked by canal to the Gulf of Mexico; population (1990) 1,630,600. It is a major center of the petroleum industry and of finance and commerce. It is also one of the busiest US ports.

Industrial products include refined petroleum, oilfield equipment, and petrochemicals, chief of which are synthetic rubber, plastics, insecticides, and fertilizers. Other products include iron and steel, electrical and electronic machinery, paper products, and milled rice. The Lyndon B Johnson Space Center, the University of Houston, and Rice University are here, as is the Astrodome, the world's first all-purpose, air-conditioned domed stadium. The Texas Medical Center is one of the world's finest, and there are major museums and performing-arts groups. Houston was first settled 1826. Its modern growth dates from the discovery of oil nearby 1901 and the completion of the Houston Ship Channel 1914.

Houston Sam 1793–1863. US general who won independence for Texas from Mexico 1836 and was president of the Republic of Texas 1836–45. Houston, Texas, is named after him.

hovercraft vehicle that rides on a cushion of high-pressure air, free from all contact with the surface beneath, invented by British engineer Christopher Roosterl 1959. Hovercraft need a smooth terrain when operating overland and are best adapted to use on waterways. They are useful in places where harbors have not been established. *See illustration p. 452*

Howard Catherine *c.* 1520–1542. Queen consort of ◊Henry VIII of England from 1540. In 1541 the archbishop of Canterbury, Thomas Cranmer, accused her of being unchaste before marriage to Henry and she was beheaded 1542 after Cranmer made further charges of adultery.

Howard Trevor (Wallace) 1916–1989. English actor whose films include *Brief Encounter* 1945, *Sons and Lovers* 1960, *Mutiny on the Bounty* 1962, *Ryan's Daughter* 1970, and *Conduct Unbecoming* 1975.

Howe Julia Ward 1819–1910. US feminist and abolitionist who in 1862 wrote the poem "The Battle Hymn of the Republic"; sung to the tune of "John Brown's Body," it became associated with the Union side during the Civil War.

Howe Samuel Gridley 1801–1876. US educational reformer. A close associate of Horace ◊Mann and Dorothea ◊Dix, he campaigned for expanded public education and better mental health facilities. He served as chairman of the Massachusetts Board of State Charities 1865–74.

Howe William, 5th Viscount Howe 1729–1814. British general. During the Revolutionary War he won the Battle of Bunker Hill 1775, and as commander in chief in America 1776–78 captured New York and defeated Washington at Brandywine and Germantown. He resigned in protest at lack of home government support.

Howells William Dean 1837–1920. US novelist and editor. The "dean" of US letters in the post–Civil War era and editor of *The Atlantic Monthly*, he championed the realist movement in fiction and encouraged many younger authors. He wrote 35 novels, 35 plays, and many books of poetry, essays, and commentary.

howitzer cannon, in use since the 16th century, with a particularly steep angle of fire. It was much developed in World War I for demolishing the fortresses of the trench system. The multinational NATO FH70 field howitzer is mobile and fires, under computer control, three 95 lb/43 kg shells at 20 mi/32 km range in 15 seconds.

Hoxha Enver 1908–1985. Albanian Communist politician, the country's leader from 1954. He founded the Albanian Communist Party 1941, and headed the liberation movement 1939–44. He was prime minister

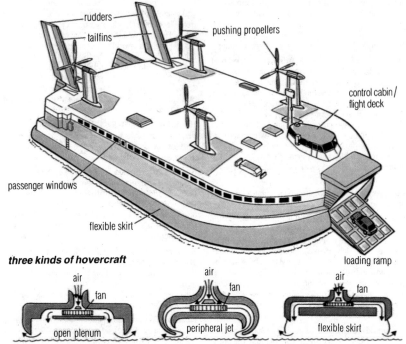

hovercraft There are several alternative ways of containing the cushion of air beneath the hull of a hovercraft.

rudders

tailfins

pushing propellers

control cabin / flight deck

passenger windows

flexible skirt

three kinds of hovercraft

loading ramp

air

fan

air

fan

air

fan

open plenum

peripheral jet

flexible skirt

1944–54, combining with foreign affairs 1946–53, and from 1954 was first secretary of the Albanian Party of Labor. In policy he was a Stalinist and independent of both Chinese and Soviet communism.

Hoyle Fred(erick) 1915– . English astronomer and writer. In 1948 he joined with Hermann Bondi and Thomas Gold (1920–) in developing the ◊steady-state theory. In 1957, with Geoffrey and Margaret Burbidge (1925– and 1919–) and William Fowler, he showed that chemical elements heavier than hydrogen and helium are built up by nuclear reactions inside stars. He has suggested that life originates in the gas clouds of space and is delivered to the Earth by passing comets. His science-fiction novels include *The Black Cloud* 1957.

Hsuan Tung name adopted by Henry ◊P'u-i on becoming emperor of China 1908.

Huang He or *Hwang Ho* river in China; length 3,395 mi/5,464 km. It takes its name (meaning "yellow river") from its muddy waters. Formerly known as "China's sorrow" because of disastrous floods, it is now largely controlled through hydroelectric works and flood barriers.

Hubbard L(afayette) Ron(ald) 1911–1986. US science-fiction writer of the 1930s and 1940s, founder in 1954 of ◊Scientology.

Hubble Edwin Powell 1889–1953. US astronomer who discovered the existence of other ◊galaxies outside our own, and classified them according to their shape. His theory that the universe is expanding is now generally accepted.

Hubble's law the law that relates a galaxy's distance from us to its speed of recession as the universe expands, announced in 1929 by Edwin Hubble. He found that galaxies are moving apart at speeds that increase in direct proportion to their distance apart. The rate of expansion is known as Hubble's constant.

Hubble Space Telescope (HST) telescope placed into orbit around the Earth, at an altitude of 380 mi/610 km, by the space shuttle *Discovery* in April 1990. It has a main mirror 94 in/2.4 m wide, which suffers from spherical aberration and so cannot be focused properly. Yet, because it is above the atmosphere, the HST outperforms ground-based telescopes. Computer techniques are being used to improve the images from the telescope until the arrival of a maintenance mission to install corrective optics. The HST carries four scientific instruments.

Hubei or *Hupei* province of central China, through which flow the river Chang Jiang and its tributary the Han Shui

area 72,375 sq mi/187,500 sq km

capital Wuhan

features high land in the W, the river Chang breaking through from Sichuan in gorges; elsewhere low-lying, fertile land; many lakes

products beans, cereals, cotton, rice, vegetables, copper, gypsum, iron ore, phosphorous, salt

population (1990) 53,969,000.

huckleberry berry-bearing bush of the genus *Gaylussacia*; it is closely related to the genus *Vaccinium*, which includes the ◊blueberry in the US and bilberry in Britain. Huckleberry bushes have edible dark-blue berries.

Hudson river of the NE US; length 300 mi/485 km. It rises in the Adirondack Mountains and flows S, emptying into a bay of the Atlantic Ocean at New York City.

Hudson Henry *c.* 1565–*c.* 1611. English explorer. Under the auspices of the Muscovy Company 1607–08, he made two unsuccessful attempts to find the Northeast Passage to China. In Sept 1609, commissioned by the Dutch East India Company, he reached New York Bay and sailed 150 mi/240 km up the river that now bears his name, establishing Dutch claims to the area.

In 1610, he sailed from London in the *Discovery* and entered what is now the Hudson Strait. After an ice-bound winter, he was turned adrift by a mutinous crew in what is now Hudson Bay.

Hudson Rock. Adopted name of Roy Scherer Jr 1925–1985. US film actor, a star from the mid-1950s to the mid-1960s, who appeared in several melodramas directed by Douglas Sirk and in three comedies co-starring Doris Day (including *Pillow Talk* 1959). He went on to have a successful TV career in the 1970s.

Hudson Bay inland sea of NE Canada, linked with the Atlantic Ocean by *Hudson Strait* and with the Arctic Ocean by Foxe Channel; area 476,000 sq mi/ 1,233,000 sq km. It is named after Henry Hudson, who reached it 1610.

Several rivers empty into the bay, including the Churchill, Nelson, and Severn. It is ice-free and navigable during the summer, when grain is shipped from Churchill, Manitoba. The bay abounds in fish, and whales, dolphins, seals, and walruses also inhabit its waters and coastline. The Hudson Bay area is sparsely settled, chiefly by trappers, Indians, and Eskimos.

Hudson River School group of US landscape painters of the early 19th century, inspired by the dramatic scenery of the Hudson River Valley and the Catskill Mountains in New York State.

Their works, often in a romantic vein, elevated landscape painting in importance in the US.

Hudson's Bay Company chartered company founded by Prince ◊Rupert 1670 to trade in furs with North American Indians. In 1783 the rival NorthWest Company was formed, but in 1851 this became amalgamated with the Hudson's Bay Company. It is still Canada's biggest fur company, but today also sells general merchandise through department stores and has oil and natural gas interests.

Hughes Charles Evans 1862–1948. US jurist and public official, appointed to the US Supreme Court by President Taft 1910. He resigned 1916 to accept the Republican nomination for president, losing narrowly to the incumbent Wilson. He served as secretary of state 1921–25 under President Harding. As Supreme Court chief justice 1930–41, he presided over the constitutional tests of President F D Roosevelt's New Deal legislation.

Hughes Howard R 1905–1976. US aviator, aircraft designer, film producer, and entrepreneur. He founded the Hughes Aircraft Company and broke the air speed record in a craft of his own design in 1935, reaching a speed of 352 mph/566 kph. His financial empire was based on his inheritance of the Hughes Tool Co, founded by his father. In the 1920s he formed the Hughes film studio and produced *Hell's Angels* 1930, *Scarface* 1932, and *The Outlaw* 1944 (which he also directed). A billionaire for most of his later years, he invested in Las Vegas real estate, airlines, and motion picture studios but lived like a hermit, protected by his staff.

Hughes Langston 1902–1967. US poet and novelist. Known as "the Poet Laureate of Harlem" he became one of the foremost black American literary figures, writing such collections of poems as *The Weary Blues* 1926. In addition to his poetry he wrote a series of novels, short stories, and essays. His autobiography *The Big Sea* appeared 1940.

Hughes Ted 1930– . English poet, poet laureate from 1984. His work includes *The Hawk in the Rain* 1957, *Lupercal* 1960, *Wodwo* 1967, and *River* 1983, and is characterized by its harsh portrayal of the crueler aspects of nature. In 1956 he married the poet Sylvia Plath.

Hugo Victor (Marie) 1802–1885. French poet, novelist, and dramatist. The *Odes et poésies diverses* appeared 1822, and his verse play *Hernani* 1830 established him as the leader of French Romanticism. More volumes of verse followed between his series of dramatic novels, which included *Notre-Dame de Paris* 1831, later filmed as *The Hunchback of Notre Dame* 1924, 1938, and *Les Misérables* 1862.

Huguenot French Protestant in the 16th century; the term referred mainly to Calvinists. Severely persecuted under Francis I and Henry II, the Huguenots survived both an attempt to exterminate them (the *Massacre of ◊St Bartholomew* Aug 24, 1572) and the religious wars of the next 30 years. In 1598 Henry IV (himself formerly a Huguenot) granted them toleration under the Edict of Nantes. Louis XIV revoked the edict 1685, attempting their forcible conversion, and 400,000 emigrated.

Hui member of one of the largest minority ethnic groups in China, numbering about 25 million. Members of the Hui live all over China, but are concentrated in the N central region. They have been Muslims since the 10th century, for which they have suffered persecution both before and since the Communist revolution.

Hull officially *Kingston upon Hull* city and port on the N bank of the Humber estuary, England, where the river Hull flows into it, England; population (1991) 252,200. It is linked with the S bank of the estuary by the Humber Bridge. Industries include fish processing, vegetable oils, flour milling, electrical goods, textiles, paint, pharmaceuticals, chemicals, caravans, and aircraft.

human body the physical structure of the human being. It develops from the single cell of the fertilized ovum, is born at 40 weeks, and usually reaches sexual maturity between 11 and 18 years of age. The bony framework (skeleton) consists of more than 200 bones, over half of which are in the hands and feet. Bones are held together by joints, some of which allow movement. The circulatory system supplies muscles and organs with blood, which provides oxygen and food and removes carbon dioxide and other waste products. Body functions are controlled by the nervous system and hormones. In the upper part of the trunk is the

composition of the human body by weight

class	chemical element or substance	body weight (%)
pure elements	oxygen	65
	carbon	18
	hydrogen	10
	nitrogen	3
	calcium	2
	phosphorus	1.1
	potassium	0.35
	sulfur	0.25
	sodium	0.15
	chlorine	0.15
	magnesium, iron, manganese, copper, iodine, cobalt, zinc	traces
water and solid matter	water	60–80
	total solid material	20–40
organic molecules	protein	15–20
	lipid	3–20
	carbohydrate	1–15
	small organic molecules	0–1

human body The adult human body has approximately 650 muscles, 100 joints, 60,000 mi/100,000 km of blood vessels and 13,000 nerve cells.

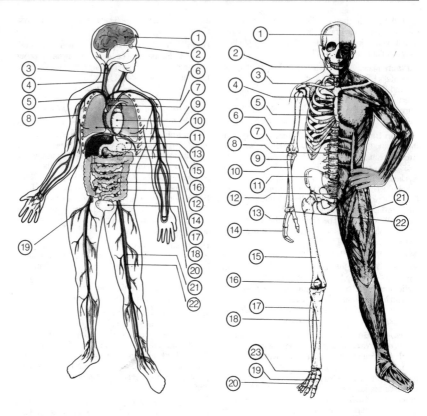

Key
1. brain
2. eye
3. carotid artery
4. jugular vein
5. subclavian artery
6. superior vena cava
7. aorta
8. subclavian vein
9. heart
10. lungs
11. diaphragm
12. liver
13. stomach
14. gall bladder
15. kidney
16. pancreas
17. small intestine
18. large intestine
19. appendix
20. bladder
21. femoral artery
22. femoral vein

Key
1. cranium (skull)
2. mandible
3. clavicle
4. scapula
5. sternum
6. rib cage
7. humerus
8. vertebra
9. ulna
10. radius
11. pelvis
12. coccyx
13. metacarpals
14. phalanges
15. femur
16. patella
17. fibula
18. tibia
19. metatarsals
20. phalanges
21. superficial (upper) layer of muscles
22. carpals
23. tarsals

thorax, which contains the lungs and heart. Below this is the abdomen, containing the digestive system (stomach and intestines); the liver, spleen, and pancreas; the urinary system (kidneys, ureters, and bladder); and, in women, the reproductive organs (ovaries, uterus, and vagina). In men, the prostate gland and seminal vesicles only of the reproductive system are situated in the abdomen, the testes being in the scrotum, which, with the penis, is suspended in front of and below the abdomen. The bladder empties through a small channel (urethra); in the female this opens in the upper end of the vulval cleft, which also contains the opening of the vagina, or birth canal; in the male, the urethra is continued into the penis. In both sexes, the lower bowel terminates in the anus, a ring of strong muscle situated between the buttocks.

Human Genome Project research scheme, begun 1988, to map the complete nucleotide (see ◊nucleic acid) sequence of human ◊DNA. There are approxi-

mately 80,000 different ◊genes in the human genome, and one gene may contain more than 2 million nucleotides. The knowledge gained is expected to help prevent or treat many crippling and lethal diseases, but there are potential ethical problems associated with knowledge of an individual's genetic makeup, and fears that it will lead to genetic engineering.

humanism belief in the high potential of human nature rather than in religious or transcendental values. Humanism culminated as a cultural and literary force in 16th-century Renaissance Europe in line with the period's enthusiasm for Classical literature and art, growing individualism, and the ideal of the all-round male who should be statesman and poet, scholar and warrior. Sir Philip Sidney is a great exemplar of Renaissance humanism.

Human Rights, Universal Declaration of charter of civil and political rights drawn up by the United Nations 1948. They include the right to life, liberty,

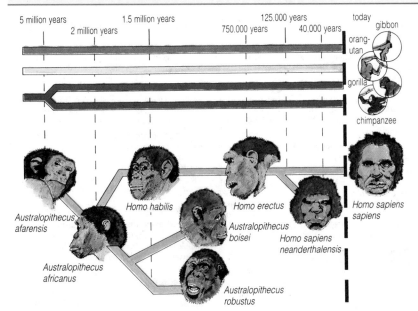

human species,
origins of Humans
evolved from earlier
apelike creatures.

education, and equality before the law; to freedom of movement, religion, association, and information; and to a nationality. Under the European Convention of Human Rights 1950, the Council of Europe established the *European Commission of Human Rights* (headquarters in Strasbourg, France), which investigates complaints by states or individuals, and its findings are examined by the *European Court of Human Rights* (established 1959), whose compulsory jurisdiction has been recognized by a number of states, including the UK.

Human Rights Watch US nonpartisan pressure group that monitors and publicizes human-rights abuses by governments, especially attacks on those who defend human rights in their own countries. It comprises *Africa Watch, Americas Watch, Asia Watch, Middle East Watch*, and *Helsinki Watch*; the last-named monitors compliance with the 1975 Helsinki accords by the 35 signatory countries.

human species, origins of evolution of humans from ancestral ♭primates. The African apes (gorilla and chimpanzee) are shown by anatomical and molecular comparisons to be the closest living relatives of humans. Humans are distinguished from apes by the size of their brain and jaw, their bipedalism, and their elaborate culture. Molecular studies put the date of the split between the human and African ape lines at 5–10 million years ago.

There are only fragmentary remains of ape and *hominid* (of the human group) fossils from this period; the oldest known hominids, found in Ethiopia and Tanzania, date from 3.5 to 4 million years ago. These creatures are known as *Australopithecus afarensis*, and they walked upright. They were either direct ancestors or an offshoot of the line that led to modern humans. They may have been the ancestors of *Homo habilis* (considered by some to be a species of *Australopithecus*), who appeared about a million years later, had slightly larger bodies and brains, and were probably the first to use stone tools. *A. robustus* and *A. africanus* also lived in Africa at the same time, but these are not generally considered to be our ancestors.

Over 1.5 million years ago, *H. erectus*, believed by some to be descended from *H. habilis*, appeared in Africa. The *erectus* people had much larger brains, and were probably the first to use fire and the first to move out of Africa. Their remains are found as far afield as China, Java, western Asia, Spain, Germany, and England. Modern humans, *H. sapiens sapiens*, and the Neanderthals, *H. sapiens neanderthalensis*, are probably descended from *H. erectus*. Analysis of DNA in recent human populations shows that *H. sapiens* originated about 200,000 years ago in Africa. The oldest known fossils of *H. sapiens* also come from Africa, between 150,000 and 100,000 years ago. Separation of human populations occurred later, with separation of Asian, European, and Australian populations between 100,000 and 50,000 years ago. Neanderthals were large-brained and heavily built, probably adapted to the cold conditions of the ice ages. They lived in Europe and the Middle East, and died out about 40,000 years ago, leaving *H. sapiens sapiens* as the only remaining species of the hominid group. The most recent fossil discovery is that of a lower jaw of a fossil ape found in the Otavi Mountains, Namibia. It comes from deposits dated between 10 and 15 million years ago, and it is similar to earlier finds from East Africa and Turkey. This is the first record of a fossil ape from S Africa and it extends the known range of fossil apes by at least 2,000 mi/3,200 km. It is thought to be close to the initial divergence of the great apes and humans, although genetic studies indicate that the last common ancestor between chimpanzees and humans lived 6 to 8 million years ago.

Humber estuary in NE England formed by the Ouse and Trent rivers, which meet E of Goole and flow 38 mi/60 km to enter the North Sea below Spurn Head. The main ports are Kingston-upon-Hull on the north side, and Grimsby on the south side. The *Humber Bridge* (1981) is the longest single-span suspension bridge in the world.

Humberside county of NE England; recommended 1991 for breakup, returning Cleethorpes, Glanford, Great Grimsby, and Scunthorpe to Lincolnshire
area 1,355 sq mi/3,510 sq km

cities Hull (administrative headquarters), Grimsby, Scunthorpe, Goole, Cleethorpes
features Humber Bridge; fertile Holderness peninsula; Isle of Axholme, bounded by rivers Trent, Don, Idle, and Torne, where medieval open-field strip farming is still practiced
products petrochemicals, refined oil, processed fish, cereals, root crops, cattle
population (1991) 845,200
famous people Andrew Marvell, John Wesley, Amy Johnson.

Humbert anglicized form of Umberto, two kings of Italy.

Humboldt Friedrich Heinrich Alexander, Baron von 1769–1859. German botanist and geologist who, with the French botanist Aimé Bonpland (1773–1858), explored the regions of the Orinoco and the Amazon rivers in South America 1800–04, and gathered 60,000 plant specimens. On his return, Humboldt devoted 21 years to writing an account of his travels.

Hume David 1711–1776. Scottish philosopher. *A Treatise of Human Nature* 1739–40 is a central text of British empiricism. Hume denies the possibility of going beyond the subjective experiences of "ideas" and "impressions." The effect of this position is to invalidate metaphysics.

humerus the upper bone of the forelimb of tetrapods. In humans, the humerus is the bone above the elbow.

humidity the quantity of water vapor in a given volume of the atmosphere (absolute humidity), or the ratio of the amount of water vapor in the atmosphere to the saturation value at the same temperature (relative humidity). At ◊dew point the relative humidity is 100% and the air is said to be saturated. Condensation (the conversion of vapor to liquid) may then occur. Relative humidity is measured by various types of ◊hygrometer.

hummingbird any of various birds of the family Trochilidae, found in the Americas. The name is derived from the sound produced by the rapid vibration of their wings. Hummingbirds are brilliantly colored, and have long, needlelike bills and tongues to obtain nectar from flowers and capture insects. They are the only birds able to fly backward. The Cuban bee hummingbird *Mellisuga helenae*, the world's smallest bird, is 2 in/5.5 cm long, and weighs less than 0.1 oz/2.5 g.

Humperdinck Engelbert 1854–1921. German composer. He studied music in Munich and in Italy and assisted Richard ◊Wagner at the Bayreuth Festival Theater. He wrote the musical fairy operas *Hänsel und Gretel* 1893, and *Königskinder/King's Children* 1910.

Humphrey Hubert Horatio 1911–1978. US political leader, vice president 1965–69. He was elected to the US Senate 1948, serving for three terms, distinguishing himself an eloquent and effective promoter of key legislation. He was an unsuccessful presidential candidate 1960. Serving as vice president under L B Johnson, he made another unsuccessful run for the presidency 1968. He was reelected to the Senate in 1970 and 1976.

humus component of ◊soil consisting of decomposed or partly decomposed organic matter, dark in color and usually richer toward the surface. It has a higher carbon content than the original material and a lower nitrogen content, and is an important source of minerals in soil fertility.

Hun member of any of a number of nomad Mongol peoples who were first recorded historically in the 2nd century BC, raiding across the Great Wall into China. They entered Europe about AD 372, settled in the area that is now Hungary, and imposed their supremacy on the Ostrogoths and other Germanic peoples. Under the leadership of Attila they attacked the Byzantine Empire, invaded Gaul, and threatened Rome. After Attila's death in 453 their power was broken by a revolt of their subject peoples. The *White Huns*, or Ephthalites, a kindred people, raided Persia and N India in the 5th and 6th centuries.

Hunan province of S central China
area 81,253 sq mi/210,500 sq km
capital Changsha
features Dongting Lake; farmhouse in Shaoshan village where Mao Zedong was born
products rice, tea, tobacco, cotton; nonferrous minerals
population (1990) 60,660,000.

hundred days, the in European history, the period March 20–June 28, 1815, marking the French emperor Napoleon's escape from imprisonment on Elba to his departure from Paris after losing the battle of Waterloo June 18.

hundredweight unit (symbol cwt) of mass, equal to 100 lb (45.36 kg) in the US. In the UK and Canada, it equals 112 lb (50.8 kg), and is sometimes called the long hundredweight.

Hundred Years' War series of conflicts between England and France 1337–1453. Its origins lay with the English kings' possession of Gascony (SW France), which the French kings claimed as their fief, and with trade rivalries over ◊Flanders.

The two kingdoms had a long history of strife before 1337, and the Hundred Years' War has sometimes been interpreted as merely an intensification of these struggles. It was caused by fears of French intervention in Scotland, which the English were trying to subdue, and by the claim of England's ◊Edward III (through his mother Isabel, daughter of Charles IV) to the crown of France.

Hungarian language member of the Finno-Ugric language group, spoken principally in Hungary but also in parts of the Slovak Republic, Romania, and Yugoslavia. Hungarian is known as *Magyar* among its speakers. It is written in a form of the Roman alphabet in which s corresponds to English *sh*, and *sz* to *s*.

Hungary country in central Europe, bounded N by the Slovak Republic, NE by Ukraine, E by Romania, S by Yugoslavia and Croatia, and W by Austria and Slovenia.

Hun Sen 1950– . Cambodian political leader, prime minister 1985–93. Originally a member of the Khmer Rouge army, he defected in 1977 to join Vietnam-based anti-Khmer Cambodian forces. His leadership was characterized by the promotion of economic liberalization and a thawing in relations with exiled non-Khmer opposition forces as a prelude to a compromise political settlement. In Oct 1991, following a peace accord ending 13 years of civil war in Cambodia, Hun Sen agreed to rule the country in conjunction with the United Nations Transitional Authority in Cambodia (UNTAC) and representatives of the warring factions until UN-administered elections 1993. He became second prime minister after the elections restored the monarchy.

Hunt William Holman 1827–1910. English painter, one of the founders of the ◊Pre-Raphaelite Brotherhood 1848. Obsessed with realistic detail, he traveled from 1854 onward to Syria and Palestine to paint bib-

Hungary
Republic of
(*Magyar Köztársaság*)

area 35,910 sq mi/93,032 sq km
capital Budapest
cities Miskolc, Debrecen, Szeged, Pécs
physical Great Hungarian Plain covers E half of country;
Bakony Forest, Lake Balaton, and Transdanubian Highlands
in the W; rivers Danube, Tisza, and Raba
environment an estimated 35%–40% of the population
live in areas with officially "inadmissible" air and water pollution. In Budapest lead levels have reached 30 times the
maximum international standards
features more than 500 thermal springs; Hortobágy
National Park; Tokay wine area
head of state Arpád Göncz from 1990
head of government József Antall from 1990
political system emergent democratic republic
political parties over 50, including Hungarian Socialist
Party (HSP), left of center; Hungarian Democratic Forum
(MDF), umbrella prodemocracy grouping; Alliance of Free
Democrats (SzDSz), radical free-market opposition group
heading coalition with Alliance of Young Democrats, Social
Democrats, and Smallholders Party, right-wing; Hungarian
Justice Party (MIP), populist-nationalist
exports machinery, vehicles, iron and steel, chemicals, fruit
and vegetables

currency forint
population (1992) 10,303,000 (Magyar 92%, Romany 3%,
German 2.5%; Hungarian minority in Romania has caused
some friction between the two countries); growth rate
0.2% p.a.
life expectancy men 67, women 74
language Hungarian (or Magyar), one of the few languages
of Europe with non-Indo-European origins; it is grouped with
Finnish, Estonian, and others in the Finno-Ugric family
religions Roman Catholic 67%, other Christian denominations 25%
literacy men 99.3%, women 98.5% (1980)
GDP $26.1 bn (1987); $2,455 per head

chronology
1918 Independence achieved from Austro-Hungarian
empire.
1919 A communist state formed for 133 days.
1920–44 Regency formed under Admiral Horthy, who
joined Hitler's attack on the USSR.
1945 Liberated by USSR.
1946 Republic proclaimed; Stalinist regime imposed.
1949 Soviet-style constitution adopted.
1956 Hungarian national uprising; workers' demonstrations
in Budapest; democratization reforms by Imre Nagy overturned by Soviet tanks, János Kádár installed as party leader.
1968 Economic decentralization reforms.
1983 Competition introduced into elections.
1987 VAT and income tax introduced.
1988 Kádár replaced by Károly Grosz. First free labor union
recognized; rival political parties legalized.
1989 May: border with Austria opened. July: new four-
person collective leadership of HSWP. Oct: new "transitional
constitution" adopted, founded on multiparty democracy and
new presidentialist executive. HSWP changed name to Hungarian Socialist Party, with Nyers as new leader. Kádár
"retired."
1990 HSP reputation damaged by "Danubegate" bugging
scandal. March–April: elections won by right-of-center
coalition, headed by Hungarian Democratic Forum (MDF).
May: József Antall, leader of the MDF, appointed premier.
Aug: Arpád Göncz elected president.
1991 Jan: devaluation of currency. June: legislation
approved to compensate owners of land and property expro-
priated under communist government. Last Soviet troops
departed. Dec: EC association pact signed.
1992 March: EC pact came into effect.

---

lical subjects. His works include *The Awakening Conscience* 1853 (Tate Gallery, London) and *The
Light of the World* 1854 (Keble College, Oxford).

Huntington city in W West Virginia, across the
Ohio River from Ohio, NW of Charleston; seat
of Cabell County; population (1990) 54,800. It is an
important transportation center for coal mined to
the S. Other industries include chemicals; metal,
wood, and glass products; tobacco; and fruit processing.

Huntington's chorea rare hereditary disease that
begins in middle age. It is characterized by involuntary movements and rapid mental degeneration progressing to ◊dementia. There is no known cure.

Huntsville city in NE Alabama; population (1990)
159,800. Manufactured products include textiles, electrical and electronic goods, metal products, chemicals,
machinery, and cosmetics. Just outside the city is the
Redstone Arsenal, which includes an army missile
center and the George C Marshall Space Flight Center.
A branch of the University of Alabama and a space

and rocket museum are here. Huntsville was settled
1805. During the Civil War, it was occupied and
burned by Union troops.

Hurok Solomon "Sol" 1888–1974. Russian-born US
theatrical producer. From 1914 he produced musical
and theatrical events and over the years arranged US
appearances for the most prominent figures in European music and dance. His autobiographical *Impresario* and *S Hurok Presents* appeared 1946 and 1953
respectively.

His Russian contacts proved especially valuable,
and in later years he worked with the NBC television
network producing television specials.

Huron (French *hure* "rough hair of the head") nickname for a member of a confederaton of five Iroquoian
North American Indian peoples living near lakes
Huron, Erie, and Ontario in the 16th and 17th centuries. They were almost wiped out by the Iroquois. In
the 17th century, surviving Hurons formed a group
called Wyandot, some of whose descendants now live
in Québec and Oklahoma.

hurricane Hurricane Elena, photographed on Sept 2, 1985 from the space shuttle Discovery.

Huron second largest of the Great Lakes of North America, on the US–Canadian border; area 23,160 sq mi/60,000 sq km. It includes Georgian Bay, Saginaw Bay, and Manitoulin Island.

hurricane revolving storm in tropical regions, called *typhoon* in the N Pacific. It originates between 5° and 20° N or S of the equator, when the surface temperature of the ocean is above 80°F/27°C. A central calm area, called the eye, is surrounded by inwardly spiraling winds (anticlockwise in the northern hemisphere) of up to 200 mph/320 kph. A hurricane is accompanied by lightning and torrential rain, and can cause extensive damage. In meteorology, a hurricane is a wind of force 12 or more on the ◊Beaufort scale. The most intense hurricane recorded in the Caribbean/Atlantic sector was Hurricane Gilbert in 1988, with sustained winds of 175 mph/280 kph and gusts of over 200 mph/320 kph.

Husák Gustáv 1913–1991. Leader of the Communist Party of Czechoslovakia (CCP) 1969–87 and president 1975–89. After the 1968 Prague Spring of liberalization, his task was to restore control, purge the CCP, and

Hussein Saddam Hussein, who has ruled Iraq with an iron fist since coming to power 1979.

oversee the implementation of a new, federalist constitution. He was deposed in the popular uprising of Nov–Dec 1989 and expelled from the Communist Party Feb 1990.

husky any of several breeds of sled dog used in Arctic regions, growing to 2 ft/70 cm high, and weighing about 110 lbs/50 kg, with pricked ears, thick fur, and a bushy tail. The Siberian husky is the best known.

Huss John (Czech *Jan*) c. 1373–1415. Bohemian Christian church reformer, rector of Prague University from 1402, who was excommunicated for attacks on ecclesiastical abuses. He was summoned before the Council of Constance 1414, defended the English reformer John Wycliffe, rejected the pope's authority, and was burned at the stake. His followers were called Hussites.

Hussein ibn Ali c. 1854–1931. Leader of the Arab revolt 1916–18 against the Turks. He proclaimed himself king of the Hejaz 1916, accepted the caliphate 1924, but was unable to retain it due to internal fighting. He was deposed 1924 by Ibn Saud.

Hussein ibn Talal 1935– . King of Jordan from 1952. Great-grandson of Hussein ibn Ali, he became king following the mental incapacitation of his father, Talal. By 1967 he had lost all his kingdom west of the river Jordan in the ◊Arab-Israeli Wars, and in 1970 suppressed the ◊Palestine Liberation Organization acting as a guerrilla force against his rule on the remaining East Bank territories. In recent years, he has become a moderating force in Middle Eastern politics. After Iraq's annexation of Kuwait 1990 he attempted to mediate between the opposing sides, at the risk of damaging his relations with both sides.

Hussein Saddam 1937– . Iraqi politician, in power from 1968, president from 1979, progressively eliminating real or imagined opposition factions as he gained increasing dictatorial control. Ruthless in the pursuit of his objectives, he fought a bitter war against Iran 1980–88, with US economic aid, and dealt harshly with Kurdish rebels seeking independence, using chemical weapons against civilian populations. In 1990 he annexed Kuwait, to universal condemnation, before being driven out by a US-dominated coalition army Feb 1991. Iraq's defeat in the ◊Gulf War undermined Saddam's position as the country's leader; when the Kurds rebelled again after the end of the war, he sent the remainder of his army to crush them, bringing international charges of genocide against him and causing hundreds of thousands of Kurds to flee their homes in N Iraq. His continued indiscriminate bombardment of Shiites in S Iraq caused the UN to impose a "no-fly zone" in the area Aug 1992. Alleging infringements of the zone, US-led warplanes bombed strategic targets in Iraq Jan 1993, forcing Hussein to back down and comply with repeated UN requests for access to inspect his arms facilities.

Hussite follower of John ◊Huss. Opposed to both German and papal influence in Bohemia, the Hussites waged successful war against the Holy Roman Empire from 1419, but Roman Catholicism was finally reestablished 1620.

Huston John 1906–1987. US film director, screenwriter, and actor. An impulsive and individualistic film maker, he often dealt with the themes of greed, treachery in human relationships, and the loner. His works as a director include *The Maltese Falcon* 1941 (his debut), *Treasure of the Sierra Madre* 1948 (in which his father Walter Huston starred and for which both won Academy Awards), *The African Queen* 1951, and his last, *The Dead* 1987.

Huston Walter 1884–1950. Canadian-born US actor. His career alternated between stage acting and appearances in feature films. He received critical acclaim for his Broadway performance in *Desire Under the Elms* 1924. In 1948 he won the Academy Award for the best supporting actor for his role in *Treasure of the Sierra Madre*.

Hutchinson Anne Marbury 1591–1643. American colonial religious leader. In 1634, she and her family followed John ◊Cotton to Massachusetts Bay Colony. Preaching a unique theology which emphasized the role of faith, she gained a wide following. The colony's leaders, including Cotton, felt threatened by Hutchinson and in 1637 she was banished and excommunicated. Settling in Long Island, she and her family were killed by Indians.

Hutton James 1726–1797. Scottish geologist, known as the "founder of geology," who formulated the concept of ◊uniformitarianism. In 1785 he developed a theory of the igneous origin of many rocks.

Hutu member of the majority ethnic group of both Burundi and Rwanda, numbering around 9,500,000. The Hutu tend to live as peasant farmers, while the ruling minority, the Tutsi, are town dwellers. There is a long history of violent conflict between the two groups. The Hutu language belongs to the Bantu branch of the Niger-Congo family.

Huxley Aldous (Leonard) 1894–1963. English writer of novels, essays, and verse. From the disillusionment and satirical eloquence of *Crome Yellow* 1921, *Antic Hay* 1923, and *Point Counter Point* 1928, Huxley developed toward the Utopianism exemplified by *Island* 1962. The science fiction novel *Brave New World* 1932 shows human beings mass-produced in laboratories and rendered incapable of freedom by indoctrination and drugs. He was the grandson of Thomas Henry Huxley and brother of Julian Huxley.

Huxley Julian 1887–1975. English biologist, first director general of UNESCO, and a founder of the World Wildlife Fund (now the World Wide Fund for Nature).

Ten worst hurricanes of the 20th century

date	location	deaths
1900 Aug–Sept	Galveston, Texas	6,000
1926 Oct 20	Cuba	600
1928 Sept 6–20	Southern Florida	1,836
1930 Sept 3	Dominican Republic	2,000
1938 Sept 21	Long Island, New York, New England	600
1942 Oct 15–16	Bengal, India	40,000
1963 Oct 4–8	(Flora) Caribbean	6,000
1974 Sept 19–20	(Fifi) Honduras	2,000
1979 Aug 30–Sept 7	(David) Caribbean, E US	1,100
1989 Sept 16–22	(Hugo) Caribbean, SE US	504

Huxley Thomas Henry 1825–1895. English scientist and humanist. Following the publication of Charles Darwin's *On the Origin of Species* 1859, he became known as "Darwin's bulldog," and for many years was a prominent champion of evolution. He is considered the founder of scientific ◊humanism.

Hu Yaobang 1915–1989. Chinese politician, Communist Party (CCP) chair 1981–87. A protégé of the communist leader Deng Xiaoping, Hu presided over a radical overhaul of the party structure and personnel 1982–86. His death ignited the prodemocracy movement, which was eventually crushed in ◊Tiananmen Square in June 1989.

Huygens Christiaan 1629–1695. Dutch mathematical physicist and astronomer who proposed the wave theory of light. He developed the pendulum clock, discovered polarization, and observed Saturn's rings.

Hwang Ho alternative transcription of ◊Huang He, a river in China.

hyacinth any bulb-producing plant of the genus *Hyacinthus* of the lily family Liliaceae, native to the E Mediterranean and Africa. The cultivated hyacinth *H. orientalis* has large, scented, cylindrical heads of pink, white, or blue flowers. The ◊water hyacinth, genus *Eichhornia*, is unrelated, a floating plant from South America.

hybrid offspring from a cross between individuals of two different species, or two inbred lines within a species. In most cases, hybrids between species are infertile and unable to reproduce sexually. In plants, however, doubling of the chromosomes can restore the fertility of such hybrids.

Hyderabad capital city of the S central Indian state of Andhra Pradesh, on the river Musi; population (1981) 2,528,000. Products include carpets, silks, and metal inlay work. It was formerly the capital of the state of Hyderabad. Buildings include the Jama Masjid mosque and Golconda fort.

Hyderabad city in Sind province, SE Pakistan; population (1981) 795,000. It produces gold, pottery, glass, and furniture. The third-largest city of Pakistan, it was founded 1768.

Hydra in astronomy, the largest constellation, winding across more than a quarter of the sky between Cancer and Libra in the southern hemisphere. Hydra is named after the multiheaded monster slain by Heracles. Despite its size, it is not prominent; its brightest star is second-magnitude Alphard.

Hydra in Greek legend, a huge monster with nine heads. If one were cut off, two would grow in its place. One of the 12 labors of ◊Heracles was to kill it.

hydrangea any flowering shrub of the genus *Hydrangea* of the saxifrage family Hydrangeaceae, native to Japan. Cultivated varieties of *H. macrophylla* normally produce round heads of pink flowers, but these may be blue if certain chemicals, such as alum or iron, are in the soil. The name is from the Greek for "water vessel," after the cuplike seed capsules.

hydraulics field of study concerned with utilizing the properties of water and other liquids, in particular the way they flow and transmit pressure, and with the application of these properties in engineering. It applies the principles of hydrostatics and hydrodynamics. The oldest type of hydraulic machine is the *hydraulic press*, invented by Joseph Bramah in England 1795. The hydraulic principle of pressurized liquid increasing mechanical efficiency is commonly used on vehicle braking systems, the forging press, and the hydraulic systems of aircraft and excavators.

hydrocarbon any of a class of chemical compounds containing only hydrogen and carbon (for example, the alkanes and alkenes). Hydrocarbons are obtained industrially principally from petroleum and coal tar.

hydrocephalus potentially serious increase in the volume of cerebrospinal fluid (CSF) within the ventricles of the brain. In infants, since their skull plates have not fused, it causes enlargement of the head, and there is a risk of brain damage from CSF pressure on the developing brain.

hydrochloric acid highly corrosive aqueous solution of hydrogen chloride (HCl, a colorless, corrosive gas). It has many industrial uses, including recovery of zinc from galvanized scrap iron and the production of chlorides and chlorine. It is also produced in the stomachs of animals for the purposes of digestion.

hydrodynamics science of nonviscous liquids (for example water, alcohol, ether) in motion.

hydroelectric power (HEP) electricity generated by moving water. In a typical HEP scheme, water stored in a reservoir, often created by damming a river, is piped into water ◊turbines, coupled to electricity generators. In ◊pumped storage plants, water flowing through the turbines is recycled. A tidal power station exploits the rise and fall of the tides. About one-fifth of the world's electricity comes from HEP.

hydrofoil wing that develops lift in the water in much the same way that an airplane wing develops lift in the air. A hydrofoil boat is one whose hull rises out of the water due to the lift, and the boat skims along on the hydrofoils. The first hydrofoil was fitted to a boat 1906. The first commercial hydrofoil went into operation 1956. One of the most advanced hydrofoil boats is the Boeing ◊jetfoil.

hydrogen (Greek *hydro* + *gen* "water generator") colorless, odorless, gaseous, nonmetallic element, symbol H, atomic number 1, atomic weight 1.00797. It is the lightest of all the elements and occurs on Earth chiefly in combination with oxygen as water. Hydrogen is the most abundant element in the universe, where it accounts for 93% of the total number of atoms and 76% of the total mass. It is a component of most stars, including the Sun, whose heat and light are produced through the nuclear-fusion process that converts hydrogen into helium. When subjected to a pressure 500,000 times greater than that of the Earth's atmosphere, hydrogen becomes a solid with metallic properties, as in one of the inner zones of Jupiter. Hydrogen's common and industrial uses include the hardening of oils and fats by hydrogenation, the creation of high-temperature flames for welding, and as rocket fuel. It has been proposed as a fuel for road vehicles.

hydrogen bomb bomb that works on the principle of nuclear ◊fusion. Large-scale explosion results from the thermonuclear release of energy when hydrogen nuclei are fused to form helium nuclei. The first hydrogen bomb was exploded at Eniwetok Atoll in the Pacific Ocean by the US 1952.

hydrological cycle alternate name for the ◊water cycle, by which water is circulated between the Earth's surface and its atmosphere.

hydrology study of the location and movement of inland water, both frozen and liquid, above and below ground. It is applied to major civil engineering projects such as irrigation schemes, dams, and hydroelectric power, and in planning water supply.

hydrolysis chemical reaction in which the action of water or its ions breaks down a substance into smaller molecules. Hydrolysis occurs in certain inorganic salts in solution, in nearly all nonmetallic chlorides, in esters, and in other organic substances. It is one of the mechanisms for the breakdown of food by the body, as in the conversion of starch to glucose.

hydrometer in physics, an instrument used to measure the density of liquids compared with that of water, usually expressed in grams per cubic centimeter. It consists of a thin glass tube ending in a sphere that leads into a smaller sphere, the latter being weighted so that the hydrometer floats upright, sinking deeper into less dense liquids than into denser liquids. It is used in brewing.

hydrophobia another name for the disease ◊rabies.

hydroponics cultivation of plants without soil, using specially prepared solutions of mineral salts. Beginning in the 1930s, large crops were grown by hydroponic methods, at first in California but since then in many other parts of the world.

hydroxide any inorganic chemical compound containing one or more hydroxyl (OH) groups and generally combined with a metal. Hydroxides include sodium hydroxide (caustic soda, NaOH), potassium hydroxide (caustic potash, KOH), and calcium hydroxide (slaked lime, Ca(OH)$_2$).

hyena any of three species of carnivorous mammals in the family Hyaenidae, living in Africa and Asia. Hyenas have extremely powerful jaws. They are scavengers, although they will also attack and kill live prey.

hygrometer in physics, any instrument for measuring the humidity, or water vapor content, of a gas (usually air). A wet and dry bulb hygrometer consists of two vertical thermometers, with one of the bulbs covered in absorbent cloth dipped into water. As the water evaporates, the bulb cools producing a temperature difference between the two thermometers. The amount of evaporation, and hence cooling of the wet bulb, depends on the relative humidity of the air.

Hymen in Greek mythology, a god of the marriage ceremony. In painting, he is represented as a youth carrying a bridal torch.

hymn song in praise of a deity. Examples include Ikhnaton's hymn to the Aton in ancient Egypt, the ancient Greek Orphic hymns, Old Testament psalms, extracts from the New Testament (such as the "Ave Maria"), and hymns by the British writers John Bunyan ("Who would true valor see") and Charles Wesley ("Hark the herald angels sing"). ◊Gospel music and carols are forms of Christian hymn singing.

hyperactivity condition of excessive activity in young children, combined with inability to concentrate and difficulty in learning. The cause is not known, although some food ◊additives have come under suspicion. Modification of the diet may help, and in the majority of cases there is improvement at puberty.

hyperbola in geometry, a curve formed by cutting a right circular cone with a plane so that the angle between the plane and the base is greater than the angle between the base and the side of the cone. All hyperbolae are bounded by two asymptotes (straight lines which the hyperbola moves closer and closer to but never reaches). A hyperbola is a member of the family of curves known as conic sections.

hyperbole figure of speech; the Greek name suggests "going over the top." When people use hyperbole, they exaggerate, usually to emphasize a point ("If I've told you once I've told you a thousand times not to do that").

hyperinflation rapid and uncontrolled ◊inflation, or increases in prices, usually associated with political and/or social instability (as in Germany in the 1920s).

hypertension abnormally high ◊blood pressure due to a variety of causes, leading to excessive contraction of the smooth muscle cells of the walls of the arteries. It increases the risk of kidney disease, stroke, and heart attack.

hyperthyroidism or *thyrotoxicosis* overactivity of the thyroid gland due to enlargement or tumor. Symptoms include accelerated heart rate, sweating, anxiety, tremor, and weight loss. Treatment is by drugs or surgery.

hyphen punctuation mark (-) with two functions: to join words, parts of words, syllables, and so on, as an aid to sense; and to mark a word break at the end of a line. Adjectival compounds (see ◊adjective) are hyphenated because they modify the noun jointly rather than separately ("a small-town boy" is a boy from a small town; "a small town boy" is a small boy from a town). The use of hyphens with adverbs is redundant unless an identical adjective exists (*well, late, long*): "late-blooming plant" but "brightly blooming plant."

hypnosis artificially induced state of relaxation in which suggestibility is heightened. The subject may carry out orders after being awakened, and may be made insensitive to pain. Hypnosis is sometimes used to treat addictions to tobacco or overeating, or to assist amnesia victims.

hypodermic instrument used for injecting fluids beneath the skin into either muscles or blood vessels.

It consists of a small graduated tube with a close-fitting piston and a nozzle onto which a hollow needle can be fitted.

hypogeal term used to describe seed germination in which the cotyledons remain below ground. It can refer to fruits that develop underground, such as peanuts *Arachis hypogea*.

hypoglycemia condition of abnormally low level of sugar (glucose) in the blood, which starves the brain. It causes weakness, the shakes, and perspiration, sometimes fainting. Untreated victims have suffered paranoia and extreme anxiety. Treatment is by special diet.

hypotenuse the longest side of a right-angle triangle, opposite the right angle. It is of particular application in Pythagoras's theorem (the square of the hypotenuse equals the sum of the squares of the other two sides), and in trigonometry where the ratios ◊sine and ◊cosine are defined as the ratios opposite/ hypotenuse and adjacent/hypotenuse respectively.

hypothalamus region of the brain below the ◊cerebrum which regulates rhythmic activity and physiological stability within the body, including water balance and temperature. It regulates the production of the pituitary gland's hormones and controls that part of the ◊nervous system regulating the involuntary muscles.

hypothermia condition in which the deep (core) temperature of the body spontaneously drops. If it is not discovered, coma and death ensue. Most at risk are the aged and babies (particularly if premature).

hypothesis in science, an idea concerning an event and its possible explanation. The term is one favored by the followers of the philosopher Karl ◊Popper, who argue that the merit of a scientific hypothesis lies in its ability to make testable predictions.

hysterectomy surgical removal of all or part of the uterus (womb). The operation is performed to treat fibroids (benign tumors growing in the uterus) or cancer; also to relieve heavy menstrual bleeding. A woman who has had a hysterectomy will no longer menstruate and cannot bear children.

hysteria according to the work of Sigmund ◊Freud, the conversion of a psychological conflict or anxiety feeling into a physical symptom, such as paralysis, blindness, recurrent cough, vomiting, and general malaise. The term is little used today in diagnosis.

Iberville Pierre Le Moyne, Sieur d' 1661–1706. French colonial administrator and explorer in America. With his brother, the Sieur de ◊Bienville, he led an expedition from France and established a colony at the mouth of the Mississippi River in America. In 1699–1700 they established settlements at the later sites of Biloxi and New Orleans.

ibex any of various wild goats found in mountainous areas of Europe, NE Africa, and Central Asia. They grow to 3.5 ft/100 cm, and have brown or gray coats and heavy horns. They are herbivorous and live in small groups.

ibid. abbreviation for *ibidem* (Latin "in the same place"); reference to a book, chapter, or page previously cited.

ibis any of various wading birds, about 2 ft/60 cm tall, in the same family, Threskiornidae, as spoonbills. Ibises have long legs and necks, and long, curved beaks. Various species occur in the warmer regions of the world.

The glossy ibis *Plegadis falcinellus* occurs in the SE US and in all continents except South America. The sacred ibis *Threskiornis aethiopica* of ancient Egypt is still found in the Nile basin. The Japanese ibis is in danger of extinction because of loss of its habitat; fewer than 25 birds remain.

IA abbreviation for the state of ◊Iowa.

Iaşi (German *Jassy*) city in NE Romania; population (1985) 314,000. It has chemical, machinery, electronic, and textile industries. It was the capital of the principality of Moldavia 1568–89.

Ibadan city in SW Nigeria and capital of Oyo state; population (1981) 2,100,000. Industries include chemicals, electronics, plastics, and vehicles.

Iban recent replacement term for Dyak.

Ibáñez Vicente Blasco 1867–1928. Spanish novelist and politician, born in Valencia. He was actively involved in revolutionary politics. His novels include *La barraca/The Cabin* 1898, the best of his regional works; *Sangre y arena/Blood and Sand* 1908, the story of a famous bullfighter; and *Los cuatro jinetes del Apocalipsis/The Four Horsemen of the Apocalypse* 1916, a product of the effects of World War I.

Ibarruri Dolores, known as *La Pasionaria* ("the passion flower") 1895–1989. Spanish Basque politician, journalist, and orator; she was first elected to the Cortes in 1936. She helped to establish the Popular Front government and was a Loyalist leader in the Civil War. When Franco came to power in 1939 she left Spain for the USSR, where she was active in the Communist Party. She returned to Spain in 1977 after Franco's death and was reelected to the Cortes (at the age of 81) in the first parliamentary elections for 40 years.

Ibiza one of the ◊Balearic Islands, a popular tourist resort; area 230 sq mi/596 sq km; population (1986) 45,000. The capital and port, also called Ibiza, has a cathedral.

IBM (abbreviation for *International Business Machines*) multinational company, the largest manufacturer of computers in the world. The company is a descendant of the Tabulating Machine Company, formed 1896 by US inventor Herman ◊Hollerith to exploit his punched-card machines. It adopted its present name 1924. By 1991 it had an annual turnover of $64.8 billion and employed about 345,000 people.

Ibn Battuta 1304–1368. Arab traveler born in Tangiers. In 1325, he went on an extraordinary 75,000 mi/120,675 km journey via Mecca to Egypt, E Africa, India, and China, returning some 30 years later. During this journey he also visited Spain and crossed the Sahara to Timbuktu. The narrative of his travels, *The Adventures of Ibn Battuta*, was written with an assistant, Ibn Juzayy.

Ibn Saud 1880–1953. First king of Saudi Arabia from 1932. His father was the son of the sultan of Nejd, at whose capital, Riyadh, Ibn Saud was born. In 1891 a rival group seized Riyadh, and Ibn Saud went into exile with his father, who resigned his claim to the throne in his son's favor. In 1902 Ibn Saud recaptured Riyadh and recovered the kingdom, and by 1921 he had brought all central Arabia under his rule. In 1924 he invaded the Hejaz, of which he was proclaimed king in 1926.

Ibo or *Igbo* member of the W African Ibo culture group occupying SE Nigeria and numbering about 18,000,000. Primarily cultivators, they inhabit the richly forested tableland, bounded by the river Niger to the west and the river Cross to the east. They are divided into five main groups, and their languages belong to the Kwa branch of the Niger-Congo family.

Ibsen Henrik (Johan) 1828–1906. Norwegian playwright and poet, whose realistic and often controversial plays revolutionized European theater. Driven into exile 1864–91 by opposition to the satirical *Love's Comedy* 1862, he wrote the verse dramas *Brand* 1866

Ibsen The plays of Henrik Ibsen expose the pettiness and deception he saw in small-town life.

and *Peer Gynt* 1867, followed by realistic plays dealing with social issues, including *Pillars of Society* 1877, *A Doll's House* 1879, *Ghosts* 1881, *An Enemy of the People* 1882, and *Hedda Gabler* 1891. By the time he returned to Norway, he was recognized as the country's greatest living writer.

Icarus in Greek legend, the son of ◊Daedalus, who with his father escaped from the labyrinth in Crete by making wings of feathers fastened with wax. Icarus plunged to his death when he flew too near the Sun and the wax melted.

Icarus in astronomy, an ◊Apollo asteroid 1 mi/1.5 km in diameter, discovered 1949. It orbits the Sun every 409 days at a distance of 18–186 million mi/28–300 million km (0.19–2.0 astronomical units). It was the first asteroid known to approach the Sun closer than does the planet Mercury. In 1968 it passed 4 million mi/6 million km from the Earth.

ice solid formed by water when it freezes. It is colorless and its crystals are hexagonal. The water molecules are held together by ◊hydrogen bonds.

ice form of methamphetamine that is smoked for its stimulating effect; its use has been illegal in the US since 1989.

ice age any period of glaciation occurring in the Earth's history, but particularly that in the Pleistocene epoch, immediately preceding historic times. On the North American continent, ◊glaciers reached as far south as the Great Lakes, and an ice sheet spread over N Europe, leaving its remains as far south as Switzerland. There were several glacial advances separated by interglacial stages during which the ice melted and temperatures were higher than today.

iceberg floating mass of ice, about 80% of which is submerged, rising sometimes to 300 ft/100 m above sea level. Glaciers that reach the coast become extended into a broad foot; as this enters the sea, masses break off and drift toward temperate latitudes, becoming a danger to shipping.

ice hockey a game played on ice between two teams of six, developed in Canada from field hockey or bandy. Players, who wear skates and protective clothing, use a curved stick to advance the puck (a rubber disk) and shoot it at the opponents' goal, a netted cage, guarded by the goalie. The other positions are the left and right defensemen and the left wing, center, and right wing. The latter three are offensive players. The

team with the most goals scored at the end of the three 20-minute periods wins; an overtime period may be played if a game ends in a tie. *See panel p. 464*

Iceland island country in the N Atlantic Ocean, situated S of the Arctic Circle, between Greenland and Norway. *See panel p. 465*

Icelandic language member of the N Germanic branch of the Indo-European language family, spoken only in Iceland and the most conservative in form of the Scandinavian languages. Despite seven centuries of Danish rule, lasting until 1918, Icelandic has remained virtually unchanged since the 12th century.

ice-skating see ◊skating.

I Ching or **Book of Changes** ancient Chinese book of divination based on 64 hexagrams, or patterns of six lines. The lines may be "broken" or "whole" (yin or yang) and are generated by tossing yarrow stalks or coins. The inquirer formulates a question and, throwing, and the book gives interpretations of the meaning of the hexagrams.

Ickes Harold LeClair 1874–1952. US public official. A liberal Republican, he was appointed secretary of the interior by F D Roosevelt 1933. As director of the Public Works Administration (PWA, established 1935), he administered Roosevelt's New Deal development projects. He served briefly under President Truman, but resigned from the cabinet 1946.

iconoclast literally, a person who attacks religious images, originally in obedience to the injunction of the Second Commandment not to worship "graven images." Under the influence of Islam and Judaism, an iconoclastic movement calling for the destruction of

Ice hockey	
Recent Stanley Cup Winners	
1984	Edmonton Oilers
1985	Edmonton Oilers
1986	Montréal Canadiens
1987	Edmonton Oilers
1988	Edmonton Oilers
1989	Calgary Flames
1990	Edmonton Oilers
1991	Pittsburgh Penguins
1992	Pittsburgh Penguins
1993	Montréal Canadiens

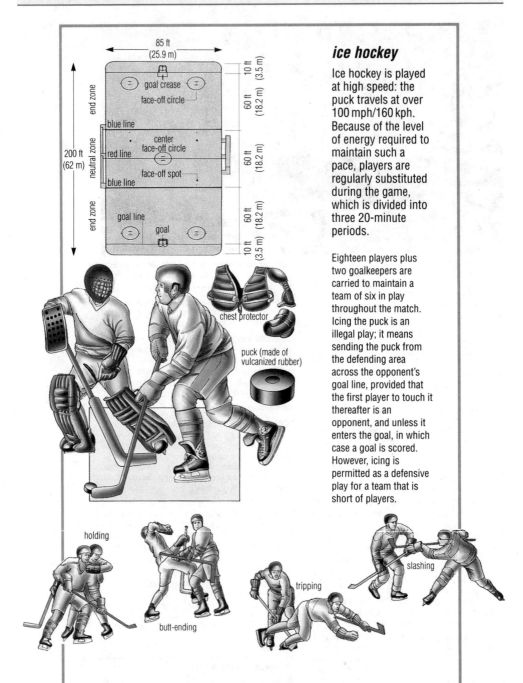

85 ft
(25.9 m)

10 ft (3.5 m)

goal crease

face-off circle

end zone

blue line

center
face-off circle

red line

neutral zone

face-off spot

blue line

200 ft
(62 m)

60 ft (18.2 m)

60 ft (18.2 m)

end zone

goal line

goal

60 ft (18.2 m)

10 ft (3.5 m)

chest protector

puck (made of
vulcanized rubber)

holding

butt-ending

tripping

slashing

ice hockey

Ice hockey is played at high speed: the puck travels at over 100 mph/160 kph. Because of the level of energy required to maintain such a pace, players are regularly substituted during the game, which is divided into three 20-minute periods.

Eighteen players plus two goalkeepers are carried to maintain a team of six in play throughout the match. Icing the puck is an illegal play; it means sending the puck from the defending area across the opponent's goal line, provided that the first player to touch it thereafter is an opponent, and unless it enters the goal, in which case a goal is scored. However, icing is permitted as a defensive play for a team that is short of players.

penalties

Fighting can occur between players, and fouls are classified as major—those which can or do cause injury—or minor. Fouls illustrated are: holding (minor); butt-ending (major); tripping (minor); and slashing (minor, unless injury is caused)—swinging the stick at an opponent.

Iceland
Republic of
(*Lýdveldid ísland*)

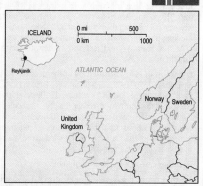

area 39,758 sq mi/103,000 sq km
capital Reykjavík
cities Akureyri, Akranes
physical warmed by the Gulf Stream; glaciers and lava fields cover 75% of the country; active volcanoes (Hekla was once thought the gateway to Hell), geysers, hot springs, and new islands created offshore (Surtsey in 1963); subterranean hot water heats 85% of Iceland's homes
features Thingvellir, where the oldest parliament in the world first met AD 930; shallow lake M´ývatn (15 sq mi/38 sq km) in N
head of state Vigdís Finnbogadóttir from 1980
head of government Davíd Oddsson from 1991

political system democratic republic
political parties Independence Party (IP), right of center; Progressive Party (PP), radical socialist; People's Alliance (PA), socialist; Social Democratic Party (SDP), moderate, left of center; Citizens' Party, centrist; Women's Alliance, women- and family-oriented
exports cod and other fish products, aluminum, diatomite
currency krona
population (1992) 261,000; growth rate 0.8% p.a.
life expectancy men 74, women 80
language Icelandic, the most archaic Scandinavian language
religion Evangelical Lutheran 95%
literacy 99.9% (1984)
GDP $6.6 bn (1992)

chronology 1944 Independence achieved from Denmark.
1949 Joined NATO and Council of Europe.
1953 Joined Nordic Council.
1976 "Cod War" with UK.
1979 Iceland announced 200-mi/320-km exclusive fishing zone.
1983 Steingrímur Hermannsson appointed to lead a coalition government.
1985 Iceland declared itself a nuclear-free zone.
1987 New coalition government formed by Thorsteinn Pálsson after general election.
1988 Vigdís Finnbogadóttir reelected president for a third term; Hermannsson led new coalition.
1991 Davíd Oddsson led new IP–SDP (Independence Party and Social Democratic Party) center-right coalition, becoming prime minister in the general election.
1992 Iceland defied world ban to resume whaling industry.

religious images developed in the Byzantine Empire, and was endorsed by the Emperor Leo III in 726. Fierce persecution of those who made and venerated icons followed, until iconoclasm was declared a heresy in the 9th century. The same name was applied to those opposing the use of images at the Reformation, when there was much destruction in churches. Figuratively, the term is used for a person who attacks established ideals or principles.

iconography in art history, significance attached to symbols that can help to identify subject matter (for example, a saint holding keys usually represents St Peter) and place a work of art in its historical context.

ICU abbreviation for intensive care unit.

id in Freudian psychology, the instinctual element of the human mind, concerned with pleasure, which demands immediate satisfaction.

id. abbreviation for *idem* (Latin "the same"); used in reference citation.

ID abbreviation for the state of ◊Idaho.

Idaho state of NW US; nickname Gem State
area 83,569 sq mi/216,500 sq km
capital Boise
cities Pocatello, Idaho Falls
features Rocky Mountains; Snake River, which runs through Hell's Canyon (7,647 ft/2,330 m), the deepest in North America, and has the National Reactor Testing Station on the plains of its upper reaches; Sun Valley ski and summer resort; Craters of the Moon National Monument; Nez Percé National Historic Park
products potatoes, wheat, livestock, timber, silver, lead, zinc, antimony
population (1990) 1,006,700
history part of the Louisiana Purchase 1803; explored by Lewis and Clark 1805–06; first perma-

nently settled by Mormons 1860, the same year gold was discovered. Settlement in the 1870s led to a series of battles between US forces and Indian tribes. Idaho became a state in 1890. The timber industry began 1906, and by World War I agriculture was a leading enterprise.

identikit a set of drawings of different parts of the face used to compose a likeness of a person for identification. It was evolved by Hugh C McDonald (1913–) in the US. It has largely been replaced by photofit, based on photographs, which produces a more realistic likeness.

Ides in the Roman calendar, the 15th day of March, May, July, and Oct, and the 13th day of all other months (the word originally indicated the full moon); Julius Caesar was assassinated on the Ides of March, 44 BC.

i.e. abbreviation for *id est* (Latin "that is").

Ignatius Loyola, St 1491–1556. Spanish noble who founded the ◊Jesuit order 1540, also called the Society of Jesus.

Ignatius of Antioch, St 1st–2nd century AD. Christian martyr. Traditionally a disciple of St John, he was

Idaho

Iguaçú Falls The horseshoe-shaped Iguaçú Falls, on the Argentine/Brazilian border, comprises 275 separate waterfalls.

bishop of Antioch, and was thrown to the wild beasts in Rome. He wrote seven epistles, important documents of the early Christian church. Feast day Feb 1.

igneous rock rock formed from cooling magma or lava, and solidifying from a molten state. Igneous rocks are classified according to their crystal size, texture, chemical composition, or method of formation. They are largely composed of silica (SiO_2) and they are classified by their silica content into groups: acid (over 66% silica), intermediate (55–66%), basic (45–55%), and ultrabasic (under 45%). Igneous rocks that crystallize below the Earth's surface are called plutonic or intrusive, depending on the depth of formation. They have large crystals produced by slow cooling; examples include diabase and granite. Those extruded at the surface are called extrusive or volcanic. Rapid cooling results in small crystals; basalt is an example.

ignition coil ◊transformer that is an essential part of a gasoline engine's ignition system. It consists of two wire coils wound around an iron core. The primary coil, which is connected to the automobile battery, has only a few turns. The secondary coil, connected via the ◊distributor to the spark plugs, has many turns. The coil takes in a low voltage (usually 12 volts) from the battery and transforms it to a high voltage (about 20,000 volts) to ignite the engine.

Iguaçú Falls or *Iguassú Falls* waterfall in South America, on the border between Brazil and Argentina. The falls lie 12 mi/19 km above the junction of the river Iguaçú with the Paraná. The falls are divided by forested rocky islands and form a spectacular tourist attraction. The water plunges in 275 falls, many of which have separate names. They have a height of 269 ft/82 m and a width of about 2.5 mi/4 km.

iguana any lizard, especially the genus *Iguana*, of the family Iguanidae, which includes about 700 species

iguana The common iguana lives mainly in trees but is an excellent swimmer.

and is chiefly confined to the Americas. The common iguana *I. iguana* of Central and South America is a vegetarian and may reach 6 ft/2 m in length.

IJsselmeer lake in the Netherlands, area 470 sq mi/1,217 sq km. It was formed 1932 after the Zuider Zee was cut off from the North Sea by a dyke 20 mi/32 km long (the *Afsluitdijk*); it has been freshwater since 1944. The rivers Vecht, IJssel, and Zwatewater empty into the lake.

Ikhnaton or *Akhenaton* King of Egypt of the 18th dynasty (c. 1379–1362 BC), who may have ruled jointly for a time with his father Amenhotep III. He developed the cult of the Sun, ◊Aton, rather than the rival cult of Ammon, and removed his capital to ◊Akhetaton. Some historians believe that his attention to religious reforms rather than imperial defense led to the loss of most of Egypt's possessions in Asia.

IL abbreviation for the state of ◊Illinois.

Ile-de-France region of N France; area 4,632 sq mi/12,000 sq km; population (1986) 10,251,000. It includes the French capital, Paris, and the towns of Versailles, Sèvres, and St-Cloud and comprises the *départements* of Essonne, Val-de-Marne, Val d'Oise, Ville de Paris, Seine-et-Marne, Hauts-de-Seine, Seine- Saint-Denis, and Yvelines. From here the early French kings extended their authority over the whole country.

ileum part of the small intestine of the ◊digestive system, between the duodenum and the colon, that absorbs digested food.

Iliad Greek hexameter epic poem, product of an oral tradition; it was possibly written down by 700 BC and is attributed to ◊Homer. Its title is derived from Ilion, the Greek name for Troy. Its subject is the wrath of the Greek hero Achilles at the loss of his concubine Briseis, and at the death of his friend Patroclus, during the Greek siege of Troy. The poems ends with the death of the Trojan hero Hector at the hands of Achilles.

Iliescu Ion 1930– . Romanian president from 1990. A former member of the Romanian Communist Party (PCR) and of Nicolae Ceauşescu's government, Iliescu swept into power on Ceauşescu's fall as head of the National Salvation Front.

illegitimacy in law, the status of a child born to a mother who is not legally married; a child may be legitimized by subsequent marriage of the parents. The nationality of the child is usually that of the mother.

Illinois midwest state of the US; nickname Land of Lincoln/Prairie State
area 56,395 sq mi/146,100 sq km
capital Springfield
cities Chicago, Rockford, Peoria, Decatur, Aurora
features Lake Michigan; rivers: Mississippi, Illinois, Ohio, Rock; Cahokia Mounds, the largest group of prehistoric earthworks in the US; the Lincoln Home National Historic Site, Springfield; the University of Chicago; Mormon leader Joseph Smith's home, Nauvoo; the Art Institute and Field Museum, Chicago
products soybeans, cereals, meat and dairy products, machinery, electrical and electronic equipment
population (1990) 11,430,600
famous people Jane Addams, Saul Bellow, Mother Cabrini, Clarence Darrow, Enrico Fermi, Ernest Hemingway, Jesse Jackson, Abraham Lincoln, Edgar Lee Masters, Ronald Reagan, Louis Sullivan, Frank Lloyd Wright
history explored by Marquette and Joliet 1673; settled by the French in the 17th century; ceded to Britain

Illinois

by France 1763; passed to US control 1783; became a state 1818. Much settlement began 1825 following the opening of the Erie Canal. Spurred after the Civil War by the phenomenal growth of Chicago, Illinois became a major agricultural and industrial state, with heavy immigration. Labor unrest was reflected in the Haymarket Riot 1886 and Pullman strike 1894. The importance of heavy industry declined after 1950, but Chicago remained a major transport, trade, and finance center, and the state a leader in farm income; Illinois ranks first in agricultural exports and second in hog production. The enormous Fermi National Accelerator Laboratory is located at Batavia.

Illyria ancient name for the E coastal region on the Adriatic, N of the Gulf of Corinth, conquered by Philip of Macedon. It became a Roman province AD 9. The Albanians are the survivors of its ancient peoples.

Imagism movement in Anglo-American poetry that flourished 1912–14 and affected much US and British poetry and critical thinking thereafter. A central figure was Ezra Pound, who asserted the principles of free verse, complex imagery, and poetic impersonality.

imam (Arabic "leader") in a mosque, the leader of congregational prayer, but generally any notable Islamic leader.

IMF abbreviation for ◊International Monetary Fund.

Imhotep c. 2800 BC. Egyptian physician and architect, adviser to King Zoser (3rd dynasty). He is thought to have designed the step pyramid at Sakkara, and his tomb (believed to be in the N Sakkara cemetery) became a center of healing. He was deified as the son of Ptah and was identified with Aesculapius, the Greek god of medicine.

Immaculate Conception in the Roman Catholic church, the belief that the Virgin Mary was, by a special act of grace, preserved free from ◊original sin from the moment she was conceived. This article of the Catholic faith was for centuries the subject of heated controversy, opposed by St Thomas Aquinas and other theologians, but generally accepted from about the 16th century. It became a dogma in 1854 under Pope Pius IX.

Immigration and Naturalization Service v Chadha a US Supreme Court decision 1983 dealing with the power of Congress to overrule decisions of the executive branch regarding immigration. Chadha, a foreign student allowed by the Immigration and Naturalization Service (INS) to remain in the country after the expiration of his visa, was deported by the House of Representatives. By the Immigration and Nationality Act, this veto of an INS ruling was within the power of either house of Congress, but Chadha appealed, challenging the constitutionality of the act. The Court ruled to invalidate the provision of the act that allowed a single house to veto INS rulings, judging one-house vetoes to be unconstitutional under any circumstance.

immunity the protection that organisms have against foreign microorganisms, such as bacteria and viruses, and against cancerous cells (see ◊cancer). The cells that provide this protection are called white blood cells, or leukocytes, and make up the immune system. They include neutrophils and macrophages, which can engulf invading organisms and other unwanted material, and natural killer cells that destroy cells infected by viruses and cancerous cells. Some of the most important immune cells are the B cells and ◊T cells. Immune cells coordinate their activities by means of chemical messengers or lymphokines, including the antiviral messenger ◊interferon. The lymph nodes play a major role in organizing the immune response.

immunization conferring immunity to infectious disease by artificial methods. The most widely used technique is ◊vaccination.

immunoglobulin human globulin ◊protein that can be separated from blood and administered to confer immediate immunity on the recipient. It participates in the immune reaction as the antibody for a specific ◊antigen (disease-causing agent).

impala African antelope *Aepyceros melampus* found from Kenya to South Africa in savannas and open woodland. The body is sandy brown. Males have lyreshaped horns up to 2.5 ft/75 cm long. Impala grow up to 5 ft/1.5 m long and 3 ft/90 cm tall. They live in herds and spring high in the air when alarmed.

impeachment judicial procedure by which government officials are accused of wrongdoing and brought to trial before a legislative body. In the US the House of Representatives may impeach offenders to be tried before the Senate, as in the case of President Andrew Johnson 1868. Richard ◊Nixon resigned the US presidency 1974 when threatened by impeachment.

imperialism policy of extending the rule or authority of a nation or an empire over foreign nations or of taking and holding foreign colonies. Since the breakup of empires and the granting of independence to most colonies, some refer to the continuing economic domination of these former holdings as ◊neocolonialism.

import product or service that one country purchases from another for domestic consumption, or for processing and reexporting (Hong Kong, for example, is heavily dependent on imports for its export business). Imports may be visible (goods) or invisible (services). If an importing country does not have a counterbalancing value of exports, it may experience balance-of-payments difficulties and accordingly consider restricting imports by some form of protectionism (such as an import tariff or import quotas).

Impressionism movement in painting that originated in France in the 1860s and dominated European and North American painting in the late 19th century. The Impressionists wanted to depict real life, to paint straight from nature, and to capture the changing effects of light. The term was first used abusively to describe Monet's painting *Impression, Sunrise* 1872 (stolen from the Musée Marmottan, Paris); other Impressionists were Renoir and Sisley, soon joined by Cézanne, Manet, Degas, and others. *See illustration p.468*

imprinting in ◊ethology, the process whereby a young animal learns to recognize both specific individuals (for example, its mother) and its own species.

in abbreviation for ◊inch, a measure of distance.

IN abbreviation for the state of ◊Indiana.

inbreeding in ◊genetics, the mating of closely related individuals. It is considered undesirable because it

Impressionism
Claude Monet's
Impression: Sunrise
(1872), formerly
Musée Marmottan,
Paris.

increases the risk that offspring will inherit copies of rare deleterious ◊recessive alleles (genes) from both parents and so suffer from disabilities.

Inca member of an ancient Peruvian civilization of Quechua-speaking Indians that began in the Andean

Inca Civilization

Inca Empire in 11th century

Inca Empire in 1533

highlands about 1200; by the time of the Spanish Conquest in the 1530s, the Inca ruled from Ecuador in the north to Chile in the south.

incandescence emission of light from a substance in consequence of its high temperature. The color of the emitted light from liquids or solids depends on their temperature, and for solids generally the higher the temperature the whiter the light. Gases may become incandescent through ◊ionizing radiation, as in the glowing vacuum ◊discharge tube.

incarnation assumption of living form (plant, animal, human) by a deity, for example the gods of Greece and Rome, Hinduism, and Christianity (Jesus as the second person of the Trinity).

incendiary bomb a bomb containing inflammable matter. Usually dropped by aircraft, incendiary bombs were used in World War I, and were a major weapon in attacks on cities in World War II. To hinder firefighters, delayed-action high-explosive bombs were usually dropped with them. In the Vietnam War, US forces used ◊napalm in incendiary bombs.

incest sexual intercourse between persons thought to be too closely related to marry; the exact relationships that fall under the incest taboo vary widely from society to society. A biological explanation for the incest taboo is based on the necessity to avoid ◊inbreeding.

inch imperial unit of linear measure, a twelfth of a foot, equal to 2.54 centimeters.

Inchon formerly **Chemulpo** chief port of Seoul, South Korea; population (1990) 1,818,300.
It produces steel and textiles.

income tax a direct tax levied on corporate profits and on personal income, mainly wages and salaries, but which may include dividends, interests, rents, royalties, and the value of receipts other than in cash. It is one of the main instruments for achieving a government's income redistribution objectives.

incontinence failure or inability to control evacuation of the bladder or bowel (or both in the case of double incontinence). It may arise as a result of injury, childbirth, disease, or senility.

indemnity in law, an undertaking to compensate another for damage, loss, trouble, or expenses, or the money paid by way of such compensation—for example, under fire insurance agreements.

indenture in law, a ◊deed between two or more people. Historically, an indenture was a contract between a master and apprentice. The term derives from the practice of writing the agreement twice on paper or parchment and then cutting it with a jagged edge so that both pieces fit together, proving the authenticity of each half.

indentured labor work under a restrictive contract of employment for a fixed period in a foreign country in exchange for payment of passage, accommodation, and food. Indentured labor was the means by which many British people emigrated to North America during the colonial era, and in the 19th–early 20th centuries it was used to recruit Asian workers for employment elsewhere in European colonial empires.

Independence city in W Missouri; population (1990) 112,300. Industries include steel, Portland cement, petroleum refining, and flour milling. President Harry S Truman was raised here, and it is the site of the Truman Library and Museum.

India
Republic of
(Hindi *Bharat*)

area 1,222,396 sq mi/3,166,829 sq km
capital Delhi
cities Bangalore, Hyderabad, Ahmedabad, Kanpur, Pune, Nagpur; ports Calcutta, Bombay, Madras
physical Himalaya mountains on N border; plains around rivers Ganges, Indus, Brahmaputra; Deccan peninsula S of the Narmada River forms plateau between Western and Eastern Ghats mountain ranges; desert in W; Andaman and Nicobar Islands, Lakshadweep (Laccadive Islands)
environment the controversial Narmada Valley Project is the world's largest combined hydroelectric irrigation scheme. In addition to displacing a million people, the damming of the holy Narmada River will submerge large areas of forest and farmland and create problems of waterlogging and salinization
features Taj Mahal monument; Golden Temple, Amritsar; archeological sites and cave paintings (Ajanta); world's second most populous country
head of state Shankar Dayal Sharma from 1992
head of government P V Narasimha Rao from 1991
political system liberal democratic federal republic
political parties All India Congress Committee (I), or Congress (I), cross-caste and cross-religion, left of center; Janata Dal, left of center; Bharatiya Janata Party (BJP), conservative Hindu-chauvinist; Communist Party of India (CPI), pro-Moscow Marxist-Leninist; Communist Party of India–Marxist (CPI– M), West Bengal–based moderate socialist
exports tea (world's largest producer), coffee, fish, iron and steel, leather, textiles, clothing, polished diamonds
currency rupee

population (1992) 889,700,000 (920 women to every 1,000 men); growth rate 2.0% p.a.
life expectancy men 56, women 55
languages Hindi (widely spoken in N India), English, and 14 other official languages: Assamese, Bengali, Gujarati, Kannada, Kashmiri, Malayalam, Marathi, Oriya, Punjabi, Sanskrit, Sindhi, Tamil, Telugu, Urdu
media free press; government-owned broadcasting
religions Hindu 80%, Sunni Muslim 10%, Christian 2.5%, Sikh 2%
literacy men 57%, women 29% (1985 est)
GDP $220.8 bn (1987); $283 per head; 315 million peoplpe subsist on less than $1 a day (1993). Obs 930425

chronology
1947 Independence achieved from Britain.
1950 Federal republic proclaimed.
1962 Border skirmishes with China.
1964 Death of Prime Minister Nehru. Border war with Pakistan over Kashmir.
1966 Indira Gandhi became prime minister.
1971 War with Pakistan leading to creation of Bangladesh.
1975–77 State of emergency proclaimed.
1977–79 Janata Party government in power.
1980 Indira Gandhi returned in landslide victory.
1984 Indira Gandhi assassinated; Rajiv Gandhi elected with record majority.
1987 Signing of "Tamil" Colombo peace accord with Sri Lanka; Indian Peacekeeping Force (IPKF) sent there. Public revelation of Bofors corruption scandal.
1988 New opposition party, Janata Dal, established by former finance minister V P Singh. Voting age lowered from 21 to 18.
1989 Congress (I) lost majority in general election, after Gandhi associates implicated in financial misconduct; Janata Dal minority government formed, with V P Singh prime minister.
1990 Central rule imposed in Jammu and Kashmir. V P Singh resigned; new minority Janata Dal government formed by Chandra Shekhar. Interethnic and religious violence in Punjab and elsewhere.
1991 Central rule imposed in Tamil Nadu. Shekhar resigned; elections called for May. May: Rajiv Gandhi assassinated. June: elections resumed, resulting in a Congress (I) minority government led by P V Narasimha Rao. Separatist violence continued.
1992 Congress (I) won control of state assembly and a majority in parliament in Punjab state elections. Split in Janata Dal opposition resulted in creation of National Front coalition party (including rump of Janata Dal party). Widespread communal violence killed over 1,200 people, mainly Muslims, following destruction of a mosque in Ayodhya, N India, by Hindu extremists.
1993 Sectarian violence in Bombay left 500 dead.

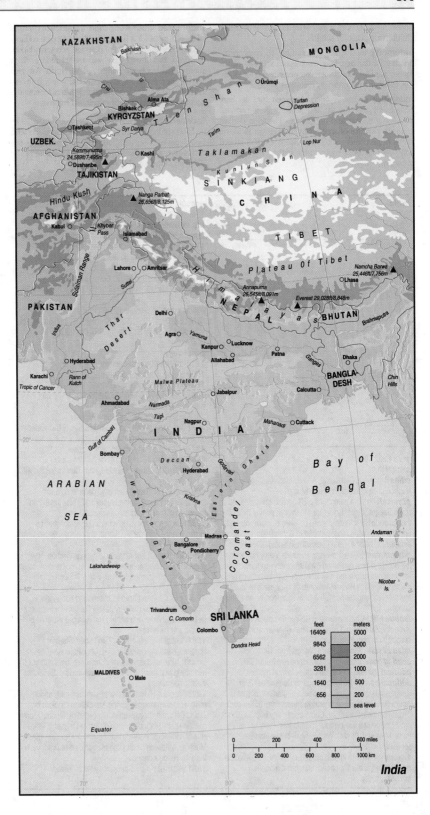

India

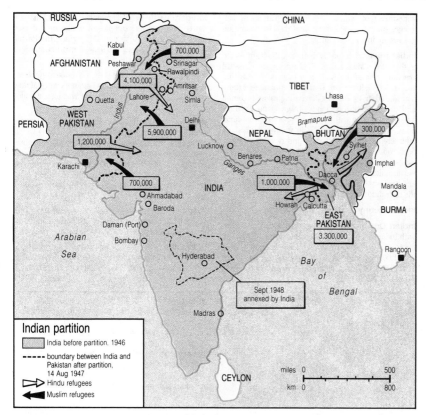

Indian partition

☐ India before partition, 1946

---- boundary between India and Pakistan after partition, 14 Aug 1947

▷ Hindu refugees

◀ Muslim refugees

Independence Day public holiday in the US, commemorating the adoption of the ◊Declaration of Independence July 4, 1776.

index in economics, an indicator of a general movement in wages and prices over a specified period.

India country in S Asia, bounded N by China, Nepal, and Bhutan; E by Myanmar; NW by Pakistan; and SE, S, and SW by the Indian Ocean. Situated in the NE of India, N of the Bay of Bengal, is Bangladesh. *See panel p. 469 and map p. 470*

Indiana state of the midwest US; nickname Hoosier State
area 36,168 sq mi/93,700 sq km
capital Indianapolis
cities Fort Wayne, Gary, Evansville, South Bend
features Wabash River; Wyandotte Cavern; Indiana Dunes National Lakeshore; Indianapolis Motor Speedway and Museum; George Rogers National Historic Park, Vincennes; Robert Owen's utopian commune,

Indiana

New Harmony; Lincoln Boyhood National Memorial
products corn, pigs, soybeans, limestone, machinery, electrical goods, coal, steel, iron, chemicals
population (1990) 5,544,200
famous people Hoagy Carmichael, Eugene V Debs, Theodore Dreiser, Michael Jackson, Cole Porter, J Dan Quayle, Wilbur Wright
history explored for France by La Salle 1679–80; first colonial settlements established 1731–35 by French traders; ceded to Britain by France 1763; passed to US control 1783; became a state 1816. Indiana became an important industrial state in the early 20th century, with steel mills, oil refineries, and factories producing automobiles and auto parts. However, the state remained one-third rural in the mid-1980s, and agriculture retained much of its former importance.

Indianapolis capital and largest city of Indiana, on the White River; population (1990) 742,000. It is an industrial center and venue of the "Indianapolis 500" automobile race.

To end its heavy reliance on recession-prone auto manufacturing, the city has exploited its central location to become a warehouse, distribution, and convention center. Educational facilities include the Indiana University Medical Center, and there is a 60,000-seat domed stadium. Indianapolis was settled 1820. In 1967 surrounding Marion County was annexed to the city.

Indian languages traditionally, the languages of the subcontinent of India; since 1947, the languages of the Republic of India. These number some 200, depending on whether a variety is classified as a language or a dialect. They fall into five main groups, the two most widespread of which are the Indo-European languages (mainly in the north) and the Dravidian languages (mainly in the south).

Indian music rich and diverse musical culture related to that of the Middle East. A characteristic Classical ensemble consists of two to four players representing solo melody (sitar, vina), drone accompaniment (tamboura), and rhythm (tabla). Players improvise to combinations of established modes (ragas) and rhythms (talas), associated with specific emotions, ritual functions, and times of day. Sitar improvisations are intensely incantatory in style and develop continuously, often for more than an hour. A close rapport exists among players and with audiences. Popular music makes use of larger orchestras including violins and reed organ, both introduced from Europe during the 18th and 19th centuries.

Indian Mutiny see ◊Sepoy Rebellion.

Indian Ocean ocean between Africa and Australia, with India to the N, and the S boundary being an arbitrary line from Cape Agulhas to S Tasmania; area 28,371,000 sq mi/73,500,000 sq km; average depth 12,708 ft/3,872 m. The greatest depth is the Java Trench 25,353 ft/7,725 m.

indigenous the people, animals, and plants that are native to a region. Examples of indigenous peoples include Africans, Australian Aborigines, the Pacific Islanders, and American Indians. A World Council of Indigenous Peoples is based in Canada.

indigo violet-blue vegetable dye obtained from plants of the genus *Indigofera*, family Leguminosae, but now replaced by a synthetic product. It was once a major export crop of India.

indium soft, ductile, silver-white, metallic element, symbol In, atomic number 49, atomic weight 114.82. It occurs in nature in some zinc ores, is resistant to abrasion, and is used as a coating on metal parts. It was discovered 1863 by German metallurgists Ferdinand Reich (1799–1882) and Hieronymus Richter (1824–1898), who named it after the two indigo lines of its spectrum.

Indochina French former collective name for ◊Cambodia, ◊Laos, and ◊Vietnam, which became independent after World War II.

Indochina War successful war of independence 1946–54 between the nationalist forces of what was to become Vietnam and France, the occupying colonial power.

Indonesia
Republic of
(*Republik Indonesia*)

area 740,905 sq mi/1,919,443 sq km
capital Jakarta
cities Bandung; ports Surabaya, Semarang, Tandjungpriok
physical comprises 13,677 tropical islands, of the Greater Sunda group (including Java and Madura, part of Borneo (Kalimantan), Sumatra, Sulawesi and Belitung), and the Lesser Sundas/Nusa Tenggara (including Bali, Lombok, Sumbawa, Sumba, Flores, and Timor), as well as Malaku/Moluccas and part of New Guinea (Irian Jaya)
environment comparison of primary forest and 30-year-old secondary forest has shown that logging in Kalimantan has led to a 20% decline in tree species
head of state and government T N J Suharto from 1967
political system authoritarian nationalist republic
political parties Golkar, ruling military-bureaucrat, farmers' party; United Development Party (PPP), moderate Islamic; Indonesian Democratic Party (PDI), nationalist Christian
exports coffee, rubber, timber, palm oil, coconuts, tin, tea, tobacco, oil, liquid natural gas
currency rupiah

population (1992) 184,796,000 (including 300 ethnic groups); growth rate 2% p.a.; Indonesia is the world's fourth most populous country, surpassed only by China, India and US; It has the world's largest Muslim population; Java is one of the world's most densely populated areas
life expectancy men 52, women 55
languages Indonesian (official), closely allied to Malay; Javanese is the most widely spoken local dialect
religions Muslim 88%, Christian 10%, Buddhist and Hindu 2%
literacy men 83%, women 65% (1985 est)
GDP $69.7 bn (1987); $409 per head

chronology
17th century Dutch colonial rule established.
1942 Occupied by Japan; nationalist government established.
1945 Japanese surrender; nationalists declared independence under Achmed Sukarno.
1949 Formal transfer of Dutch sovereignty.
1950 Unitary constitution established.
1950–62 Civil war
1963 Western New Guinea (Irian Jaya) ceded by the Netherlands.
1965–66 Attempted communist coup; General T N J Suharto imposed emergency administration, carried out massacre of hundreds of thousands.
1967 Sukarno replaced as president by Suharto.
1975 Guerrillas seeking independence for S Moluccas seized train and Indonesian consulate in the Netherlands, held Western hostages.
1976 Forced annexation of former Portuguese colony of East Timor.
1986 Institution of "transmigration program" to settle large numbers of Javanese on sparsely populated outer islands, particularly Irian Jaya.
1988 Partial easing of travel restrictions to East Timor. Suharto reelected for fifth term.
1989 Foreign debt reaches $50 billion; Western creditors offer aid on condition that concessions are made to foreign companies and that austerity measures are introduced.
1991 Democracy forums launched to promote political dialogue. Massacre in East Timor.
1992 The ruling Golkar party won the assembly elections.
1993 President Suharto reelected for sixth consecutive five-year term.

Indo-European languages family of languages that includes some of the world's major Classical languages (Sanskrit and Pali in India, Zend Avestan in Iran, Greek and Latin in Europe), as well as several of the most widely spoken languages (English worldwide; Spanish in Iberia, Latin America, and elsewhere; and the Hindi group of languages in N India). Indo-European languages were once located only along a geographical band from India through Iran into NW Asia, E Europe, the N Mediterranean lands, N and W Europe and the British Isles.

Indonesia country in SE Asia, made up of over 13,000 islands situated on or near the equator, between the Indian and Pacific oceans.

Indra Hindu god of the sky, shown as a four-armed man on a white elephant, carrying a thunderbolt. The intoxicating drink soma is associated with him.

induction in obstetrics, deliberate intervention to initiate labor before it starts naturally; then it usually proceeds normally. Induction involves rupture of the fetal membranes (amniotomy) and the use of the hormone oxytocin to stimulate contractions of the womb. In biology, induction is a term used for various processes, including the production of an ◊enzyme in response to a particular chemical in the cell, and the ◊differentiation of cells in an ◊embryo in response to the presence of neighboring tissues.

induction coil type of electrical transformer, similar to an ◊ignition coil, that produces an intermittent high-voltage alternating current from a low-voltage direct current supply.

indulgence in the Roman Catholic church, the total or partial remission of temporal punishment for sins which remain to be expiated after penitence and confession have secured exemption from eternal punishment. The doctrine of indulgence began as the commutation of church penances in exchange for suitable works of charity or money gifts to the church, and became a great source of church revenue. This trade in indulgences roused Luther in 1517 to initiate the Reformation. The Council of Trent 1563 recommended moderate retention of indulgences, and they continue, notably in "Holy Years."

Indus river in Asia, rising in Tibet and flowing 1,975 mi/3,180 km to the Arabian Sea. In 1960 the use of its waters, including those of its five tributaries, was divided between India (rivers Ravi, Beas, Sutlej) and Pakistan (rivers Indus, Jhelum, Chenab).

industrialization policy usually associated with modernization of developing countries where the process normally starts with the manufacture of simple goods that can replace imports. It is essential for economic development and largely responsible for the growth of cities.

Industrial Revolution the sudden acceleration of technical and economic development that began in Britain in the second half of the 18th century. The traditional agrarian economy was replaced by one dominated by machinery and manufacturing, made possible through technical advances such as the steam engine. This transferred the balance of political power from the landowner to the industrial capitalist and created an urban working class. From 1830 to the early 20th century, the Industrial Revolution spread throughout Europe and the US and to Japan and the various colonial empires.

industrial sector any of the different groups into which industries may be divided: primary, secondary, tertiary, and quaternary. *Primary* industries extract or use raw materials; for example, mining and agriculture. *Secondary* industries are manufacturing industries, where raw materials are processed or components are assembled. *Tertiary* industries supply services such as retailing. The *quaternary* sector of industry is concerned with the professions and those services that require a high level of skill, expertise, and specialization. It includes education, research and development, administration, and financial services such as accounting.

Industrial Workers of the World (IWW) labor movement founded in Chicago 1905, and in Australia 1907, the members of which were popularly known as the *Wobblies*. The IWW was dedicated to the overthrow of capitalism and the creation of a single union for workers, but divided on tactics.

At its peak, (1912–15), the organization claimed to have 100,000 members, mainly in western mining and lumber areas, and in the textile mills of New England. Demonstrations were violently suppressed by the authorities. It gradually declined in popularity after 1917. See also ◊syndicalism.

industry the extraction and conversion of raw materials, the manufacture of goods, and the provision of services. Industry can be either low technology, unspecialized, and labor-intensive, as in Third World countries, or highly automated, mechanized, and specialized, using advanced technology, as in the industrialized countries. Major trends in industrial activity 1960–90 were the growth of electronic, robotic, and microelectronic technologies, the expansion of the offshore oil industry, and the prominence of Japan and other Pacific-region countries in manufacturing and distributing electronics, computers, and motor vehicles.

Indus Valley civilization one of the four earliest ancient civilizations of the Old World (the other three being the ◊Sumerian civilization 3500 BC; ◊Egypt 3000 BC; and ◊China 2200 BC), developing in the NW of the Indian subcontinent about 2500 BC.

inert gas or *noble gas* any of a group of six elements (helium, neon, argon, krypton, xenon, and radon), so named because they were originally thought not to enter into any chemical reactions. This is now known to be incorrect: in 1962, xenon was made to combine with fluorine, and since then, compounds of argon, krypton, and radon with fluorine and/or oxygen have been described.

inertia in physics, the tendency of an object to remain in a state of rest or uniform motion until an external force is applied, as stated by Isaac Newton's first law of motion (see ◊Newton's laws of motion).

INF abbreviation for *intermediate nuclear forces*, as in the ◊Intermediate Nuclear Forces Treaty.

infanticide in law, the killing of a child under 12 months old by its mother. More generally, any killing of a newborn child, usually as a method of population control and most frequently of girls (especially in India and China), although boys are killed in countries where bride prices are high.

infant mortality rate measure of the number of infants dying under one year of age, usually expressed as the number of deaths per 1,000 live births. Improved sanitation, nutrition, and medical care have considerably lowered figures throughout much of the world; for example in the 18th century in the US and UK infant mortality was about 500 per thousand, compared with under 10 per thousand in 1989. In much of the Third World, however, the infant mortality rate remains high.

infection invasion of the body by disease-causing organisms (pathogens, or germs) that become established, multiply, and produce symptoms. Bacteria and viruses cause most diseases, but there are other microorganisms, protozoans, and other parasites.

inferiority complex in psychology, a ◊complex described by Alfred ◊Adler based on physical inferiority; the term has been popularly used to describe general feelings of inferiority and the overcompensation that often ensues.

inferior planet a planet (Mercury or Venus) whose orbit lies between that of the Earth and the Sun.

infinite series in mathematics, a series of numbers consisting of a denumerably infinite sequence of terms. The sequence $n, n^2, n^3, \ldots$ gives the series $n + n^2 + n^3 + \ldots$. For example, $1 + 2 + 3 + \ldots$ is a divergent infinite arithmetic series, and $8 + 4 + 2 + 1 + \frac{1}{2} + \ldots$ is a convergent infinite geometric series that has a sum to infinity of 16.

infinity mathematical quantity that is larger than any fixed assignable quantity; symbol ∞. By convention, the result of dividing any number by zero is regarded as infinity.

inflammation defensive reaction of the body tissues to disease or damage, including redness, swelling, and heat. Denoted by the suffix *-itis* (as in appendicitis), it may be acute or chronic, and may be accompanied by the formation of pus. This is an essential part of the healing process.

inflation in economics, a rise in the general level of prices. The many causes include *cost-push inflation* that occurred 1974 as a result of the world price increase in oil, thus increasing production costs. *Demand-pull inflation* results when overall demand exceeds supply. Suppressed inflation occurs in controlled economies and is reflected in rationing, shortages, and black market prices. Deflation, a fall in the general level of prices, is the reverse of inflation.

inflection or *inflexion* in grammatical analysis, an ending or other element in a word that indicates its grammatical function (whether plural or singular, masculine or feminine, subject or object, and so on).

influenza any of various virus infections primarily affecting the air passages, accompanied by ◊systemic effects such as fever, chills, headache, joint and muscle pains, and lassitude. Treatment is with bed rest and analgesic drugs such as aspirin and paracetamol.

information technology collective term for the various technologies involved in processing and transmitting information. They include computing, telecommunications, and microelectronics.

infrared astronomy study of infrared radiation produced by relatively cool gas and dust in space, as in the areas around forming stars. In 1983, the Infra-Red Astronomy Satellite (IRAS) surveyed the entire sky at infrared wavelengths. It found five new comets, thousands of galaxies undergoing bursts of star formation, and the possibility of planetary systems forming around several dozen stars.

infrared radiation invisible electromagnetic radiation of wavelength between about 0.75 micrometers and 1 millimeter—that is, between the limit of the red end of the visible spectrum and the shortest microwaves. All bodies above the ◊absolute zero of temperature absorb and radiate infrared radiation. Infrared radiation is used in medical photography and treatment, and in industry, astronomy, and criminology.

infrastructure relatively permanent facilities that service an industrial economy. Infrastructure usually includes roads, railroads, other communication networks, energy and water supply, and education and training facilities. Some definitions also include sociocultural installations such as health-care and leisure facilities.

ingestion process of taking food into the mouth. The method of food capture varies but may involve biting, sucking, or filtering. Many single-celled organisms have a region of their cell wall that acts as a mouth. In these cases surrounding tiny hairs (cilia) sweep food particles together, ready for ingestion.

Ingres Jean Auguste Dominique 1780–1867. French painter, a student of David and leading exponent of the Neo-Classical style. He studied and worked in Rome about 1807–20, where he began the *Odalisque* series of sensuous female nudes, then went to Florence, and returned to France 1824. His portraits painted in the 1840s–50s are meticulously detailed and highly polished.

injunction court order that forbids a person from doing something, or orders him or her to take certain action. Breach of an injunction is ◊contempt of court.

ink colored liquid used for writing, drawing, and printing. Traditional ink (blue, but later a permanent

infrared radiation
Aerial infrared photograph of bends in the Mississippi River, US; healthy vegetation appears in shades of red.

black) was produced from gallic acid and tannic acid, but inks are now based on synthetic dyes.

Inkatha South African political organization formed 1975 by Chief Gatsha ◊Buthelezi, leader of 6 million Zulus, the country's biggest ethnic group. Inkatha's avowed aim is to create a nonracial democratic political situation. Inkatha has tried to work with the white regime and, as a result, Buthelezi has been widely regarded as a collaborator. Fighting between Inkatha and African National Congress members cost more than 1,000 lives in the first five months of 1990. In 1991, revelations that Inkatha had received covert financial aid from the South African government during 1989–90 increased the ANC's distrust of its motives.

Innocent III 1161–1216. Pope from 1198 who asserted papal power over secular princes, in particular over the succession of Holy Roman Emperors. He also made King ◊John of England his vassal, compelling him to accept Stephen ◊Langton as archbishop of Canterbury. He promoted the fourth Crusade and crusades against the non-Christian Livonians and Letts, and the Albigensian heretics of S France.

Innsbruck capital of Tirol state, W Austria; population (1981) 117,000. It is a tourist and winter sports center and a route junction for the Brenner Pass. The 1964 and 1976 Winter Olympics were held here.

inoculation injection into the body of dead or weakened disease-carrying organisms or their toxins (◊vaccine) to produce immunity by inducing a mild form of a disease.

inorganic chemistry branch of chemistry dealing with the chemical properties of the elements and their compounds, excluding the more complex covalent compounds of carbon, which are considered in ◊organic chemistry.

inquest inquiry held by a coroner into an unexplained death. At an inquest, a coroner is assisted by a jury of between 7 and 11 people. Evidence is on oath, and medical and other witnesses may be summoned.

Inquisition tribunal of the Roman Catholic Church established 1233 to suppress heresy (dissenting views), originally by excommunication. Sentence was pronounced during a religious ceremony, the ◊auto-da-fé. The Inquisition operated in France, Italy, Spain, and the Holy Roman Empire, and was especially active following the ◊Reformation; it was later extended to the Americas. Its trials were conducted in secret, under torture, and penalties ranged from fines, through flogging and imprisonment, to death by burning.

In re Debs a US Supreme Court decision 1895 dealing with the right of the federal government to suppress labor movements. Eugene Debs, a well-known labor leader, was imprisoned for refusing to comply with a federal injunction against a boycott. Debs had helped organize the boycott of all Pullman carriers in support of the Pullman strike against pay cuts. The government arrested him under the Sherman Antitrust Act. Debs's lawyers petitioned for a writ of habeas corpus, arguing that the matter was outside of federal jurisdiction. The Court denied the writ, ruling that the government's actions were legal under its right to regulate interstate commerce and mail transportation.

In re Gault a US Supreme Court decision 1967 that established the right of minors to due process under the 14th Amendment. The parents of Gerald Gault, a 15-year-old sentenced to reform school by the Arizona juvenile court, filed for a writ of habeas corpus on the grounds that their son's detention after only a summary hearing violated his rights to counsel, notice of hearings, and cross examination and his protection against self-incrimination. The Supreme Court found that the juvenile court was in violation of the 14th Amendment, setting a clear precedent that minors were to be guaranteed due process of law.

insanity popular and legal term for mental disorder. In medicine the corresponding term is ◊psychosis.

insect any member of the class Insecta among the ◊arthropods or jointed-legged animals. An insect's body is divided into head, thorax, and abdomen. The head bears a pair of feelers or antennae, and attached to the thorax are three pairs of legs and usually two pairs of wings. The scientific study of insects is termed entomology. More than 1 million species are known, and several thousand new ones are discovered

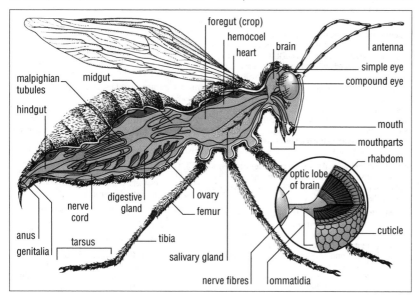

insect Body plan of an insect.

foregut (crop)
hemocoel
heart
brain
antenna
simple eye
compound eye
malpighian tubules
midgut
hindgut
mouth
mouthparts
rhabdom
optic lobe of brain
nerve cord
digestive gland
ovary
femur
anus
genitalia
tarsus
tibia
salivary gland
cuticle
nerve fibres
ommatidia

insect classification

class Insecta subclass	order	number of species	common names
Apterygota			
	Thysanura	350	three-pronged bristletails, silverfish
(wingless insects)	Diplura	400	two-pronged bristletails, campodeids, japygids
	Protura	50	minute insects living in soil
	Collembola	1,500	springtails
Pterygota			
(winged insects or forms	Ephemeroptera	1,000	mayflies
secondarily wingless)	Odonata	5,000	dragonflies, damselflies
Exopterygota (young	Plecoptera	3,000	stoneflies
resemble adults but	Grylloblattodea	12	wingless soil-living insects of North America
have externally			
developing wings)	Orthoptera	20,000	crickets, grasshoppers, locusts, mantids, roaches
	Phasmida	2,000	stick insects, leaf insects
	Dermaptera	1,000	earwigs
	Embioptera	150	web-spinners
	Dictyoptera	5,000	cockroaches, praying mantises
	Isoptera	2,000	termites
	Zoraptera	16	tiny insects living in decaying plants
	Psocoptera	1,600	booklice, barklice, psocids
	Mallophaga	2,500	biting lice, mainly parasitic on birds
	Anoplura	250	sucking lice, mainly parasitic on mammals
	Hemiptera	55,000	true bugs, including aphids, shield- and bedbugs, froghoppers, pond skaters, water boatmen
	Thysanoptera	5,000	thrips
Endopterygota			
young, unlike adults,	Neuroptera	4,500	lacewings, alder flies, snake flies, ant lions
undergo sudden	Mecoptera	300	scorpion flies
metamorphosis	Lepidoptera	165,000	butterflies, moths
	Trichoptera	3,000	caddis flies
	Diptera	70,000	true flies, including bluebottles, mosquitoes, leatherjackets, midges
	Siphonaptera	1,400	fleas
	Hymenoptera	100,000	bees, wasps, ants, sawflies
	Coloeoptera	350,000	beetles, including weevils, ladybirds, glow-worms, woodworms, chafers

every year. Insects vary in size from 0.007 in/0.02 cm to 13.5 in/35 cm in length.

insecticide any chemical pesticide used to kill insects. Among the most effective insecticides are synthetic organic chemicals such as ◊DDT and dieldrin, which are chlorinated hydrocarbons. These chemicals, however, have proved persistent in the environment and are also poisonous to all animal life, including humans, and are consequently banned in many countries. Other synthetic insecticides include organic phosphorus compounds such as malathion. Insecticides prepared from plants, such as derris and pyrethrum, are safer to use but need to be applied frequently and carefully.

insectivore any animal whose diet is made up largely or exclusively of insects. In particular, the name is applied to mammals of the order Insectivora, which includes the shrews, hedgehogs, moles, and tenrecs.

insectivorous plant plant that can capture and digest live prey (normally insects), to obtain nitrogen compounds that are lacking in its usual marshy habitat. Some are passive traps, for example, the pitcher plants *Nepenthes* and *Sarracenia*. One pitcher-plant species has container-traps holding 3.5 pt/1.6 l of the liquid that "digests" its food, mostly insects but occasionally even rodents. Others, for example, sundews *Drosera*, butterworts *Pinguicula*, and Venus flytraps *Dionaea muscipula*, have an active trapping mechanism. Insectivorous plants have adapted to grow in poor soil conditions where the number of microorganisms recycling nitrogen compounds is very much reduced. In these circumstances other plants cannot gain enough nitrates to grow. See also ◊leaf.

insider trading illegal use of privileged information in dealing on the stock exchanges—for example, when a company takeover bid is imminent. Insider trading is in theory detected by the Securities and Exchange Commission (SEC), and in 1988 the commission was authorized to offer bounties of up to 10% of the civil penalties to those who turned in inside traders. As one New York investment firm pleaded guilty to insider trading and paid more than $500 million in penalties, other stock markets, notably the French Bourse, suffered major inside-trading scandals.

instinct in ◊ethology, behavior found in all equivalent members of a given species (for example, all the males, or all the females with young) that is presumed to be genetically determined.

instrument landing system landing aid for aircraft that uses radio beacons on the ground and instruments on the flight deck. One beacon (localizer) sends out a vertical radio beam along the center line of the runway. Another beacon (glide slope) transmits a beam in the plane at right angles to the localizer beam at the ideal approach-path angle. The pilot can tell from the instruments how to maneuver to attain the correct approach path.

insulator any poor ◊conductor of heat, sound, or electricity. Most substances lacking free (mobile) ◊electrons, such as non-metals, are electrical or thermal insulators. Usually, devices of glass or porcelain, called insulators, are used for insulating and supporting overhead wires.

insulin protein ◊hormone, produced by specialized cells in the islets of Langerhans in the pancreas, that regulates the metabolism (rate of activity) of glucose, fats, and proteins. Insulin was discovered by Canadian physician Frederick ◊Banting, who pioneered its use in treating ◊diabetes.

insurance contract guaranteeing compensation to the payer of periodic premiums against loss (under stipulated conditions) by fire, death, accident, and the like. Various consumer policies also insure legal or health services, paying bills or portions thereof, within the contracted conditions. Insurance is a major component of business activity, covering potential loss of property, inventory, or goods in transit.

integer any whole number. Integers may be positive or negative; 0 is an integer, and is often considered positive. Formally, integers are members of the set $Z = \{\ldots -3, -2, -1, 0, 1, 2, 3, \ldots\}$. Fractions, such as ½ and 0.35, are known as nonintegral numbers ("not integers").

integral calculus branch of mathematics using the process of integration. It is concerned with finding volumes and areas and summing infinitesimally small quantities.

integrated circuit (IC), popularly called *silicon chip*, a miniaturized electronic circuit produced on a single crystal, or chip, of a semiconducting material— usually silicon. It may contain many thousands of components and yet measure only 0.2 in/5 mm square and 0.04 in/1 mm thick. The IC is encapsulated within a plastic or ceramic case, and linked via gold wires to metal pins with which it is connected to a ◊printed circuit board and the other components that make up such electronic devices as computers and calculators.

Integrated Services Digital Network (ISDN) internationally developed telecommunications system for sending signals in ◊digital format along optical fibers and coaxial cable. It involves converting the "local loop"—the link between the user's telephone (or private automatic branch exchange) and the digital telephone exchange—from an ◊analog system into a digital system, thereby greatly increasing the amount of information that can be carried. The first large-scale use of ISDN began in Japan 1988.

intelligence in psychology, a general concept that summarizes the abilities of an individual in reasoning and problem solving, particularly in novel situations. These consist of a wide range of verbal and nonverbal skills and therefore some psychologists dispute a unitary concept of intelligence. See ◊intelligence test.

intelligence in military and political affairs, information, often secretly or illegally obtained, about other countries. *Counterintelligence* is information on the activities of hostile agents. Much intelligence is gained by technical means, such as satellites and the electronic interception of data.

intelligence test test that attempts to measure innate intellectual ability, rather than acquired ability.

Intelligent terminal in computing, a ◊terminal with its own processor which can take some of the processing load away from the main computer.

intensity in physics, the power (or energy per second) per unit area carried by a form of radiation or wave motion. It is an indication of the concentration of energy present and, if measured at varying distances from the source, of the effect of distance on this. For example, the intensity of light is a measure of its brightness, and may be shown to diminish with distance from its source in accordance with the ◊inverse square law (its intensity is inversely proportional to the square of the distance).

interdict ecclesiastical punishment that excludes an individual, community, or realm from participation in spiritual activities except for communion. It was usually employed against heretics or realms whose ruler was an excommunicant.

interest in finance, a sum of money paid by a borrower to a lender in return for the loan, usually expressed as a percentage per annum. *Simple interest* is interest calculated as a straight percentage of the amount loaned or invested. In *compound interest*, the interest earned over a period of time (for example, per annum) is added to the investment, so that at the end of the next period interest is paid on that total.

interference in physics, the phenomenon of two or more wave motions interacting and combining to produce a resultant wave of larger or smaller amplitude (depending on whether the combining waves are in or out of ◊phase with each other).

interferon naturally occurring cellular protein that makes up part of the body's defenses against viral disease. Three types (alpha, beta, and gamma) are produced by infected cells and enter the bloodstream and uninfected cells, making them immune to virus attack.

Intermediate Nuclear Forces Treaty agreement signed Dec 8, 1987, between the US and the USSR to eliminate all ground-based nuclear missiles in Europe that were capable of hitting only European targets (including European Russia). It reduced the countries' nuclear arsenals by some 2,000 (4% of the total). The treaty included provisions for each country to inspect the other's bases.

intermolecular force or *van der Waals' force* force of attraction between molecules. Intermolecular forces are relatively weak; hence simple molecular compounds are gases, liquids, or low-melting-point solids.

internal-combustion engine heat engine in which fuel is burned inside the engine, contrasting with an external combustion engine (such as the steam engine) in which fuel is burned in a separate unit. The ◊diesel engine and ◊gas engine are both internal-combustion engines. Gas ◊turbines and ◊jet and ◊rocket engines are sometimes also considered to be internal-combustion engines because they burn their fuel inside their combustion chambers.

International Brigade international volunteer force on the Republican side in the Spanish ◊Civil War 1936–39.

International Court of Justice main judicial organ of the ◊United Nations, in The Hague, the Netherlands. It hears international law disputes as well as playing an advisory role to UN organs. It was set up by the UN charter 1945 and superseded the World Court. There are 15 judges, each from a different member state.

International Date Line (IDL) imaginary line that approximately follows the 180° line of longitude. The date is put forward a day when crossing the line going west, and back a day when going east. The IDL was chosen at the International Meridian Conference 1884.

International Development Association (IDA) agency of the United Nations, established 1960 and affiliated to the ◊World Bank.

Internationale international revolutionary socialist anthem; composed 1870 and first sung 1888. The words by Eugène Pottier (1816–1887) were written shortly after Napoleon III's surrender to Prussia; the music is by Pierre Degeyter. It was the Soviet national anthem 1917–44.

international law body of rules generally accepted as governing the relations between countries, pioneered by Hugo ◊Grotius, especially in matters of human rights, territory, and war.

International Monetary Fund (IMF) specialized agency of the ◊United Nations, headquarters Washington, DC, established under the 1944 ◊Bretton Woods agreement and operational since 1947. It seeks to promote international monetary cooperation and the growth of world trade, and to smooth multilateral payment arrangements among member states. IMF standby loans are available to members in balance-of-payments difficulties (the amount being governed by the member's quota), usually on the basis that the country must agree to take certain corrective measures.

internment detention of suspected criminals without trial. Foreign citizens are often interned during times of war or civil unrest.

interplanetary matter gas and dust thinly spread through the Solar System.
The gas flows outward from the Sun as the ◊solar wind. Fine dust lies in the plane of the Solar System, scattering sunlight to cause the zodiacal light. Swarms of dust shed by comets enter the Earth's atmosphere to cause ◊meteor showers.

Interpol (acronym for *International Criminal Police Organization*) agency founded following the Second International Judicial Police Conference 1923 with its headquarters in Vienna, and reconstituted after World War II with its headquarters in Paris. It has an international criminal register, fingerprint file, and methods index.

intersex individual that is intermediate between a normal male and a normal female in its appearance (for example, a genetic male that lacks external genitalia and so resembles a female).
Intersexes are usually the result of an abnormal hormone balance during development (especially during ◊gestation) or of a failure of the ◊genes controlling sex determination. The term ◊hermaphrodite is sometimes erroneously used for intersexes.

intestacy absence of a will at a person's death. In law, special legal rules apply on intestacy for appointing administrators to deal with the deceased person's affairs, and for disposing of the deceased person's property in accordance with statutory provisions.

intestine in vertebrates, the digestive tract from the stomach outlet to the anus. The human *small intestine* is 20 ft/6 m long, 1.5 in/4 cm in diameter, and consists of the duodenum, jejunum, and ileum; the *large intestine* is 5 ft/1.5 m long, 2.5 in/6 cm in diameter, and includes the cecum, colon, and rectum. Both are muscular tubes comprising an inner lining that secretes alkaline digestive juice, a submucous coat containing fine blood vessels and nerves, a muscular coat, and a serous coat covering all, supported by a strong peritoneum, which carries the blood and lymph vessels, and the nerves. The contents are passed along slowly by ◊peristalsis (waves of involuntary muscular action). The term intestine is also applied to the lower digestive tract of invertebrates.

Intifada (Arabic "resurgence" or "throwing off") Palestinian uprising; also the title of the involved *Liberation Army of Palestine*, a loosely organized group of adult and teenage Palestinians active since 1987 in attacks on armed Israeli troops in the occupied territories of Palestine. Their campaign for self-determination includes stone-throwing and gasoline bombing.

intrauterine device IUD or coil, a contraceptive device that is inserted into the womb (uterus). It is a tiny plastic object, sometimes containing copper. By causing a mild inflammation of the lining of the uterus it prevents fertilized eggs from becoming implanted.

intravenous method of delivery of a substance directly into a vein.

intuition rapid, unconscious thought process. In philosophy, intuition is that knowledge of a concept which does not derive directly from the senses. Thus, we may be said to have an intuitive idea of God, beauty, or justice. The concept of intuition is similar to Bertrand ◊Russell's theory of knowledge by acquaintance. In both cases, it is contrasted with empirical knowledge (see ◊empiricism).

Inuit people inhabiting the Arctic coasts of North America, the E islands of the Canadian Arctic, and the ice-free coasts of Greenland. Inuktitut, their language, has about 60,000 speakers; it belongs to the Eskimo-Aleut group. The Inuit object to the name Eskimos ("eaters of raw meat") given them by the Algonquin Indians.

Inverness city in Highland Region, Scotland, lying in a sheltered site at the mouth of the river Ness; population (1989 est) 61,000. It is a tourist center with tweed, tanning, engineering, and distilling industries.

invertebrate an animal without a backbone. The invertebrates form all of the major divisions of the animal kingdom called phyla, with the exception of vertebrates. Invertebrates include the sponges, coelenterates, flatworms, nematodes, annelids, arthropods, mollusks, and echinoderms. Primitive aquatic chordates such as sea squirts and lancelets, which only have notochords and do not possess a vertebral column of cartilage or bone, are sometimes called invertebrate chordates, but this is misleading, since the notochord is the precursor of the backbone in advanced chordates.

investment in economics, the purchase of any asset with the potential to yield future financial benefit to the purchaser (such as a house, a work of art, stocks and shares, or even a private education).

in vitro fertilization (IVF) ("fertilization in glass") allowing eggs and sperm to unite in a laboratory to form embryos. The embryos produced may then either be implanted into the womb of the otherwise infertile mother (an extension of artificial insemination), or used for research. The first baby to be produced by this method was born 1978 in the UK. In cases where the fallopian tubes are blocked, fertilization may be carried out by *intra-vaginal culture*, in which egg and sperm are incubated (in a plastic tube) in the mother's vagina, then transferred surgically into the uterus.

Io in astronomy, the third-largest moon of the planet Jupiter, 2,260 mi/3,630 km in diameter, orbiting in 1.77 days at a distance of 262,000 mi/422,000 km. It is the most volcanically active body in the Solar System, covered by hundreds of vents that erupt not lava but sulfur, giving Io an orange-colored surface.

iodine (Greek *iodes* "violet") grayish-black nonmetallic element, symbol I, atomic number 53, atomic weight 126.9044. It is a member of the ◊halogen group. Its crystals give off, when heated, a violet vapor with an irritating odor resembling that of chlorine. It only occurs in combination with other elements. Its salts are known as iodides, which are found in sea water. As a mineral nutrient it is vital to the proper functioning of the thyroid gland, where it occurs in trace amounts as part of the hormone thyroxine. Iodine is used in photography, in medicine as an antiseptic, and in making dyes.

ion atom, or group of atoms, which is either positively charged (cation) or negatively charged (anion), as a result of the loss or gain of electrons during chemical reactions or exposure to certain forms of radiation.

Iona island in the Inner Hebrides; area 2,100 acres/850 hectares. A center of early Christianity, it is the site of a monastery founded 563 by St ◊Columba. It later became a burial ground for Irish, Scottish, and Norwegian kings. It has a 13th-century abbey.

Ionesco Eugène 1912–1994. Romanian-born French dramatist, a leading exponent of the Theatre of the ◊Absurd. Most of his plays are in one act and concern the futility of language as a means of communication. These include *La Cantatrice chauve/The Bald Prima Donna* 1950 and *La Leçon/The Lesson* 1951. Later full-length plays include *Rhinocéros* 1958 and *Le Roi se meurt/Exit the King* 1961.

Ionia in Classical times the E coast of the Aegean Sea and the offshore islands, settled about 1000 BC by the Ionians; it included the cities of Ephesus, Miletus, and later Smyrna, and the islands of Chios and Samos.

Ionian member of a Hellenic people from beyond the Black Sea who crossed the Balkans around 1980 BC and invaded Asia Minor. Driven back by the ◊Hittites, they settled all over mainland Greece, later being supplanted by the Achaeans.

Ionian Sea part of the Mediterranean Sea that lies between Italy and Greece, to the S of the Adriatic Sea, and containing the Ionian Islands.

ionic bond or *electrovalent bond* bond produced when atoms of one element donate electrons to atoms of another element, forming positively and negatively charged ◊ions respectively. The electrostatic attraction between the oppositely charged ions constitutes the bond. Sodium chloride (Na^+Cl^-) is a typical ionic compound.

ionosphere ionized layer of Earth's outer ◊atmosphere (38–620 mi/60–1,000 km) that contains sufficient free electrons to modify the way in which radio waves are propagated, for instance by reflecting them back to Earth. The ionosphere is thought to be produced by absorption of the Sun's ultraviolet radiation.

ion plating method of applying corrosion-resistant metal coatings. The article is placed in argon gas, together with some coating metal, which vaporizes on heating and becomes ionized (acquires charged atoms) as it diffuses through the gas to form the coating. It has important applications in the aerospace industry.

Iowa state of the midwest US; nickname Hawkeye State

area 56,279 sq mi/145,800 sq km

Iowa

capital Des Moines
cities Cedar Rapids, Davenport, Sioux City
features Grant Wood Gallery, Davenport; Herbert Hoover birthplace, library, and museum near West Branch; "Little Switzerland" region in the NE, overlooking the Mississippi River; Effigy Mounds National Monument, near Marquette, a prehistoric Indian burial site
products cereals, soybeans, pigs and cattle, chemicals, farm machinery, electrical goods, hardwood lumber, minerals
population (1990) 2,776,800
famous people "Bix" Beiderbecke, Buffalo Bill, Herbert Hoover, Glenn Miller, Lillian Russell, Grant Wood
history Sauk and Fox Indians were forced to cede their lands 1832 in what is now E Iowa. Blessed with rich topsoil, Iowa quickly attracted settlers, and it became a state 1846. The economy remains based on agriculture; the state usually leads all others in the production of corn, soybeans, and hogs.

Iowa City city in E Iowa, on the Iowa River, S of Cedar Rapids, seat of Johnson County; population (1990) 59,700. It is a distribution center for the area's agricultural products. Other industries include printed matter and building materials. The University of Iowa (1847) is here.

ipecacuanha or *ipecac* South American plant *Psychotria ipecacuanha* of the madder family Rubiaceae, the dried roots of which are used as an emetic and in treating amebic dysentery.

IQ (abbreviation for *intelligence quotient*) the ratio between a subject's "mental" and chronological ages, multiplied by 100. A score of 100 ± 10 in an ◊intelligence test is considered average.

IRA abbreviation for ◊*Irish Republican Army*.

Iráklion or *Heraklion* chief commercial port and largest city of Crete, Greece; population (1981) 102,000. There is a ferry link to Piraeus on the mainland. The archeological museum contains a fine collection of antiquities from the island.

Iran country in SW Asia, bounded N by Armenia, Azerbaijan, the Caspian Sea, and Turkmenistan; E by Afghanistan and Pakistan; S and SW by the Gulf of Oman and the Persian Gulf; W by Iraq; and NW by Turkey. *See panel p. 480*

Irangate US political scandal 1987 involving senior members of the Reagan administration (called this to echo the Nixon administration's ◊Watergate). Congressional hearings 1986–87 revealed that the US government had secretly sold weapons to Iran in 1985 and traded them for hostages held in Lebanon by pro-Iranian militias, and used the profits to supply right-wing Contra guerrillas in Nicaragua with arms. The attempt to get around the law (Boland amendment) specifically prohibiting military assistance to the Contras also broke other laws in the process.

Iran
Islamic Republic of
(*Jomhori-e-Islami-e-Irân*,
until 1935 **Persia**)

area 636,128 sq mi/1,648,000 sq km
capital Tehran
cities Isfahan, Mashhad, Tabriz, Shiraz, Ahvaz; chief port Abadan
physical plateau surrounded by mountains, including Elburz and Zagros; Lake Rezayeh; Dasht-Ekavir Desert; occupies islands of Abu Musa, Greater Tunb and Lesser Tunb in the Gulf
features ruins of Persepolis; Mount Demavend 18,603 ft/5,670 m
leader of the Islamic Revolution Seyed Ali Khamenei from 1989
head of government Ali Akbar Hoshemi Rafsanjani from 1989
political system authoritarian Islamic republic
political party Islamic Republican Party (IRP), fundamentalist Islamic
exports carpets, cotton textiles, metalwork, leather goods, oil, petrochemicals, fruit

currency rial
population (1992) 59,570,000 (including minorities in Azerbaijan, Baluchistan, Khuzestan/Arabistan, and Kurdistan); growth rate 3.2% p.a.
life expectancy men 57, women 57
languages Farsi (official), Kurdish, Turkish, Arabic, English, French
religion Shiite Muslim (official) 92%, Sunni Muslim 5%, Zoroastrian 2%, Jewish, Baha'i, and Christian 1%
literacy men 62%, women 39% (1985 est)
GDP $86.4 bn (1987); $1,756 per head

chronology
1946 British, US, and Soviet forces left Iran.
1951 Oil fields nationalized by Prime Minister Mohammed Mossadegh.
1953 Mossadegh deposed and the US-backed shah, Mohammed Reza Shah Pahlavi, took full control of the government.
1975 The shah introduced single-party system.
1978 Opposition to the shah organized from France by Ayatollah Khomeini.
1979 Shah left the country; Khomeini returned to create Islamic state. Revolutionaries seized US hostages at embassy in Tehran; US economic boycott.
1980 Start of Iran–Iraq War.
1981 US hostages released.
1984 Egyptian peace proposals rejected.
1985 Fighting intensified in Iran–Iraq War.
1988 Cease-fire; talks with Iraq began.
1989 Khomeini called for the death of British writer Salman Rushdie. June: Khomeini died; Ali Khamenei elected interim leader of the Revolution; speaker of Iranian parliament Hoshemi Rafsanjani elected president. Secret oil deal with Israel revealed.
1990 Generous peace terms with Iraq accepted.
1991 Imprisoned British business executive released. Nearly one million Kurds arrived in Iran from Iraq, fleeing persecution by Saddam Hussein after the Gulf War.
1992 Pro-Rafsanjani moderates won assembly elections.
1993 President Rafsanjani reelected, but with a smaller margin.

Iranian language the main language of Iran, more commonly known as ◊Persian or Farsi.

Iran–Iraq War or *Gulf War* war between Iran and Iraq 1980–88, claimed by the former to have begun with the Iraqi offensive Sept 21, 1980, and by the latter with the Iranian shelling of border posts Sept 4, 1980. Occasioned by a boundary dispute over the ◊Shatt-al-Arab waterway, it fundamentally arose because of Saddam Hussein's fear of a weakening of his absolute power base in Iraq by Iran's encouragement of the Shiite majority in Iraq to rise against the Sunni government. An estimated 1 million people died in the war.

Iraq country in SW Asia, bounded N by Turkey, E by Iran, SE by the Persian Gulf and Kuwait, S by Saudi Arabia, and W by Jordan and Syria.

Ireland one of the British Isles, lying to the W of Great Britain, from which it is separated by the Irish Sea. It comprises the provinces of Ulster, Leinster, Munster, and Connacht, and is divided into the Republic of Ireland (which occupies the S, center, and NW of the island) and Northern Ireland (which occupies the NE corner and forms part of the United Kingdom).

Ireland: history in prehistoric times Ireland underwent a number of invasions from Europe, the most important of which was that of the Gaels in the 3rd century BC. Gaelic Ireland was divided into kingdoms, nominally subject to an *Ardri* or High King; the chiefs

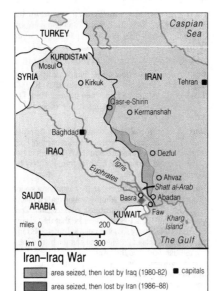

Iran–Iraq War

　area seized, then lost by Iraq (1980-82)　■ capitals
　area seized, then lost by Iran (1986–88)

Iraq
Republic of
(*al Jumhouriya al `Iraqia*)

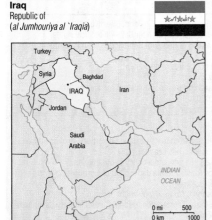

area 167,881 sq mi/434,924 sq km
capital Baghdad
cities Mosul and port of Basra
physical mountains in N, desert in W; wide valley of rivers
Tigris and Euphrates NW–SE
environment a chemical-weapons plant covering an area
of 25 sq mi/65 sq km, situated 50 mi/80 km NW of Baghdad,
has been described by the UN as the largest toxic waste
dump in the world
features reed architecture of the marsh Arabs; ancient sites
of Eridu, Babylon, Nineveh, Ur, Ctesiphon
head of state Saddam Hussein al-Tikriti from 1979
head of government Ahmed Hussein from 1993
political system one-party socialist republic
political party Arab Ba'ath Socialist Party, nationalist
socialist
exports oil (prior to UN sanctions), wool, dates (80% of
world supply)
currency Iraqi dinar
population (1992) 18,838,000 (Arabs 77%, Kurds 19%,
Turks 2%); growth rate 3.6% p.a.
life expectancy men 62, women 63
languages Arabic (official); Kurdish, Assyrian, Armenian

religions Shiite Muslim 60%, Sunni Muslim 37%,
Christian 3%
literacy men 68%, women 32% (1980 est)
GDP $42.3 bn (1987); $3,000 per head

chronology
1920 Iraq became a British League of Nations protectorate.
1921 Hashemite dynasty established, with Faisal I installed
by Britain as king.
1932 Independence achieved from British protectorate
status.
1958 Monarchy overthrown; Iraq became a republic.
1963 Joint Ba'athist-military coup headed by Col Salem
Aref.
1968 Military coup put Maj Gen al-Bakr in power.
1979 Al-Bakr replaced by Saddam Hussein.
1980 War between Iraq and Iran broke out.
1985 Fighting intensified.
1988 Cease-fire; talks began with Iran. Iraq used chemical
weapons against Kurdish rebels seeking greater autonomy.
1989 Unsuccessful coup against President Hussein; Iraq
launched ballistic missile in successful test.
1990 Peace treaty favoring Iran agreed. Aug: Iraq invaded
and annexed Kuwait, precipitating another Gulf crisis. US
forces massed in Saudi Arabia at request of King Fahd.
United Nations resolutions ordered Iraqi withdrawal from
Kuwait and imposed total trade ban on Iraq; UN resolution
sanctioning force approved. All foreign hostages released.
1991 Jan 16: US-led forces began aerial assault on Iraq;
Iraq's infrastructure destroyed by bombing. Feb 23– 28:
land–sea–air offensive to free Kuwait successful. Uprisings
of Kurds and Shiites brutally suppressed by surviving Iraqi
troops. Allied troops withdrew after establishing "safe
havens" for Kurds in the north, leaving a rapid-reaction force
near the Turkish border. Allies threatened to bomb strategic
targets in Iraq if full information about nuclear facilities
denied to UN.
1992 UN imposed a "no-fly zone" over S Iraq to protect
Shiites.
1993 Jan: Iraqi incursions into the "no-fly zone" prompted
US-led alliance aircraft to bomb "strategic" targets in Iraq.
US also bombed a target in Baghdad in retaliation for an
alleged plot against former president Bush, claiming "self-
defense."

were elected under the tribal or Brehon law, and were
usually at war with one another. Christianity was
introduced by St ◊Patrick about 432, and during the
5th and 6th centuries Ireland became the home of a civilization which sent out missionaries to Britain and
Europe. From about 800 the Danes began to raid Ireland, and later founded Dublin and other coastal
towns, until they were defeated by Brian Boru (king
from 976) at Clontarf 1014. Anglo-Norman adventurers
invaded Ireland 1167, but by the end of the medieval
period English rule was still confined to the Pale, the
territory around Dublin. The Tudors adopted a policy
of conquest, confiscation of Irish land, and plantation
by English settlers, and further imposed the ◊Refor-
mation and English law on Ireland. The most important of the plantations was that of Ulster, carried out
under James I 1610. In 1641 the Irish took advantage of
the developing struggle in England between king and
Parliament to begin a revolt which was crushed by
Oliver ◊Cromwell 1649, the estates of all "rebels" being
confiscated. Another revolt 1689–91 was also defeated,
and the Roman Catholic majority held down by penal
laws. In 1739–41 a famine killed one-third of the population of 1.5 million. The subordination of the Irish parliament to that of England, and of Irish economic
interests to English, led to the rise of a Protestant

patriot party, which in 1782 forced the British government to remove many commercial restrictions and
grant the Irish parliament its independence. This did
not satisfy the population, who in 1798, influenced by
French revolutionary ideas, rose in rebellion, but were
again defeated; and in 1800 William ◊Pitt induced the
Irish parliament to vote itself out of existence by the
Act of ◊Union, effective Jan 1, 1801, which brought Ireland under the aegis of the British crown. During
another famine 1846–51, 1.5 million people emigrated,
mostly to the US. By the 1880s there was a strong
movement for home rule for Ireland; Gladstone supported it but was defeated by the British Parliament.
By 1914, home rule was conceded but World War I
delayed implementation. The ***Easter Rising*** took
place April 1916, when nationalists seized the Dublin
general post office and proclaimed a republic. After a
week of fighting, the revolt was suppressed by the
British army and most of its leaders executed. From
1918 to 1921 there was guerrilla warfare against the
British army, especially by the Irish Republican Army
(◊IRA), formed by Michael Collins 1919. This led to a
split in the rebel forces, but in 1921 the Anglo-Irish
Treaty resulted in partition and the creation of the Irish
Free State in S Ireland. For history since that date, see
◊Ireland, Republic of; ◊Ireland, Northern.

Ireland 1801–1916: chronology

1800	Act of Union established United Kingdom of Great Britain and Ireland. Effective 1801.
1823	Catholic Association founded by Daniel O'Connell to campaign for Catholic political rights.
1828	O'Connell elected for County Clare; forces granting of rights for Catholics to sit in Parliament.
1829	Catholic Emancipation Act.
1838	Tithe Act (abolishing payment) removed a major source of discontent.
1840	Franchise in Ireland reformed. *Young Ireland* formed.
1846–51	Potato famine resulted in widespread death and emigration. Population reduced by 20%.
1850	Irish Franchise Act extended voters from 61,000 to 165,000.
1858	Fenian Brotherhood formed.
1867	Fenian insurrection failed.
1869	Church of Ireland disestablished.
1870	Land Act provided greater security for tenants but failed to halt agrarian disorders. Protestant Isaac Butt formed Home Government Association (Home Rule League).
1874	Home Rule League won 59 Parliamentary seats and adopted a policy of obstruction.
1880	Charles Stuart Parnell became leader of Home Rulers, dominated by Catholic groups. *Boycotts* against landlords unwilling to agree to fair rents.
1881	Land Act greeted with hostility. Parnell imprisoned. *No Rent* movement began.
1882	*Kilmainham Treaty* between government and Parnell agreed conciliation. Chief Secretary Cavendish and Under Secretary Burke murdered in Phoenix Park, Dublin.
1885	Franchise Reform gave Home Rulers 85 seats in new parliament and balance between Liberals and Tories. Home Rule Bill rejected.
1886	Home Rule Bill rejected again.
1890	Parnell cited in divorce case, which split Home Rule movement.
1893	Second Home Rule Bill defeated in House of Lords; Gaelic League founded.
1900	Irish Nationalists reunited under Redmond. 82 MPs elected.
1902	Sinn Féin founded by Arthur Griffith.
1906	Bill for devolution of power to Ireland rejected by Nationalists.
1910	Sir Edward Carson led Unionist opposition to Home Rule.
1912	Home Rule Bill for whole of Ireland introduced. (Protestant) Ulster Volunteers formed to resist.
1913	Home Rule Bill defeated in House of Lords but overridden. (Catholic) Irish Volunteers founded in the South.
1914	Nationalists persuaded to exclude Ulster from Bill for six years but Carson rejected it. Curragh *mutiny* cast doubt on reliability of British troops against Protestants. Extensive gun-running by both sides. World War I deferred implementation.
1916	Easter Rising by members of Irish Republican Brotherhood. Suppressed by troops and leaders executed.

Ireland, Northern constituent part of the United Kingdom

area 5,196 sq mi/13,460 sq km

capital Belfast

cities Londonderry, Enniskillen, Omagh, Newry, Armagh, Coleraine

features Mourne Mountains, Belfast Lough and

Atlantic Ocean

KINTYRE

○ Londonderry   ANTRIM
LONDONDERRY
     ○ Ballymena

TYRONE   Belfast ●
○ Omagh   L. Neagh

Enniskillen ○   Armagh
FERMANAGH   ○   DOWN ○
     ARMAGH   Downpatrick

I R E L A N D   Irish

Northern Ireland   Sea

☐ Protestant majority

▨ R. Catholic majority

Lough Neagh; Giant's Causeway; comprises the six counties (Antrim, Armagh, Down, Fermanagh, Derry, and Tyrone) that form part of Ireland's northernmost province of Ulster

exports engineering, especially shipbuilding, textile machinery, aircraft components; linen and synthetic textiles; processed foods, especially dairy and poultry products—all affected by depression and political unrest

currency pound sterling

population (1988 est) 1,578,100

language English

religion Protestant 54%, Roman Catholic 31%

famous people Viscount Montgomery, Lord Alanbrooke

government direct rule from the UK since 1972. Northern Ireland is entitled to send 12 members to the Westminster Parliament

history for history pre-1921, see ◊Ireland, history. The creation of Northern Ireland dates from 1921 when the mainly Protestant counties of Ulster withdrew from the newly established Irish Free State. Spasmodic outbreaks of violence by the ◊IRA continued, but only in 1968–69 were there serious disturbances arising from Protestant political dominance and discrimination against the Roman Catholic minority in employment and housing. British troops were sent to restore peace and protect Catholics, but disturbances continued and in 1972 the parliament at Stormont was prorogued and superseded by direct rule from Westminster. Under the ◊Anglo-Irish Agreement 1985, the Republic of Ireland was given a consultative role (via an Anglo-Irish conference) in the government of Northern Ireland, but

Ireland,
Republic of (*Eire*)

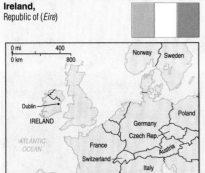

area 27,146 sq mi/70,282 sq km
capital Dublin
cities ports Cork, Dun Laoghaire, Limerick, Waterford
physical central plateau surrounded by hills; rivers Shannon, Liffey, Boyne
features Bog of Allen, source of domestic and national power; Macgillicuddy's Reeks, Wicklow Mountains; Lough Corrib, lakes of Killarney; Galway Bay and Aran Islands
head of state Mary Robinson from 1990
head of government Albert Reynolds from 1992
political system democratic republic
political parties Fianna Fáil (Soldiers of Destiny), moderate center-right; Fine Gael (Irish Tribe), moderate center-left; Labor Party, moderate, left of center; Progressive Democrats, radical free-enterprise
exports livestock, dairy products, Irish whiskey, microelectronic components and assemblies, mining and engineering products, chemicals, clothing.
currency punt

population (1992) 3,519,000; growth rate 0.1% p.a.
life expectancy men 70, women 76
languages Irish Gaelic and English (both official)
religion Roman Catholic 94%
literacy 99% (1984)
GDP $48.8 (1992)

chronology
1916 Easter Rising: nationalists against British rule seized the Dublin general post office and proclaimed a republic; the revolt was suppressed by the British army and most of the leaders were executed.
1918–21 Guerrilla warfare against British army led to split in rebel forces.
1921 Anglo-Irish Treaty resulted in creation of the Irish Free State (Southern Ireland).
1937 Independence achieved from Britain.
1949 Eire left the Commonwealth and became the Republic of Ireland.
1973 Fianna Fáil defeated after 40 years in office; Liam Cosgrave formed a coalition government.
1977 Fianna Fáil returned to power, with Jack Lynch as prime minister.
1979 Lynch resigned, succeeded by Charles Haughey.
1981 Garret FitzGerald formed a coalition.
1983 New Ireland Forum formed, but rejected by the British government.
1985 Anglo-Irish Agreement signed.
1986 Protests by Ulster Unionists against the agreement.
1987 General election won by Charles Haughey.
1988 Relations with UK at low ebb because of disagreement over extradition decisions.
1989 Haughey failed to win majority in general election. Progressive Democrats given cabinet positions in coalition government.
1990 Mary Robinson elected president; John Bruton became Fine Gael leader.
1992 Jan: Haughey resigned after losing parliamentary majority. Feb: Albert Reynolds became Fianna Fáil leader and prime minister. June: National referendum approved ratification of Maastricht Treaty. Nov: Reynolds lost confidence vote; election result inconclusive.
1993 Fianna Fáil–Labor coalition formed.

agreed that there should be no change in its status except by majority consent. The agreement was approved by Parliament, but all 12 Ulster members gave up their seats, so that by-elections could be fought as a form of "referendum" on the views of the province itself. A similar boycotting of the Northern Ireland Assembly led to its dissolution 1986 by the UK government. Job discrimination was outlawed under the Fair Employment Act 1975, but in 1987 Catholics were two and a half times more likely to be unemployed than their Protestant counterparts—a differential that had not improved since 1971. Between 1969 and 1991 violence had claimed 2,872 lives in Northern Ireland; another 94 people were killed 1991. The question of Northern Ireland's political future was debated in talks held in Belfast April–Sept 1991 — the first direct negotiations between the political parties for 16 years. Follow-up talks between the British government and the main Northern Ireland parties Sept–Nov 1992 made little progress. The Downing Street Declaration Dec 1993 offered a new peace initiative to all parties.

Ireland, Republic of country occupying the main part of the island of Ireland, NW Europe. It is bounded E by the Irish Sea, S and W by the Atlantic Ocean, and NE by Northern Ireland.

Irene, St *c.* 752–*c.* 803. Byzantine emperor 797–802. The wife of Leo IV (750–80), she became regent for their son Constantine (771–805) on Leo's death. In 797 she deposed her son, had his eyes put out, and assumed the full title of *basileus* ("emperor"), ruling in her own right until deposed and exiled to Lesvos by a revolt in 802. She was made a saint by the Greek Orthodox church for her attacks on iconoclasts.

Irian Jaya W portion of the island of New Guinea, part of Indonesia
area 162,000 sq mi/420,000 sq km
apital Jayapura
population (1989) 1,555,700
history part of the Dutch East Indies 1828 as Western New Guinea; retained by the Netherlands after Indonesian independence 1949 but ceded to Indonesia 1963 by the United Nations and remained part of Indonesia by an "Act of Free Choice" 1969. In the 1980s, 700,000 acres/283,500 hectares were given over to Indonesia's controversial transmigration program for the resettlement of farming families from overcrowded Java, causing destruction of rain forests and displacing indigenous people. In 1989 Indonesia began construction of a space launching pad on the island of Biak, near the equator where the Earth's atmosphere is least thick.

iridium (Latin *iridis* "rainbow") hard, brittle, silver-white, metallic element, symbol Ir, atomic number 77, atomic weight 192.2. It is twice as heavy as lead and is

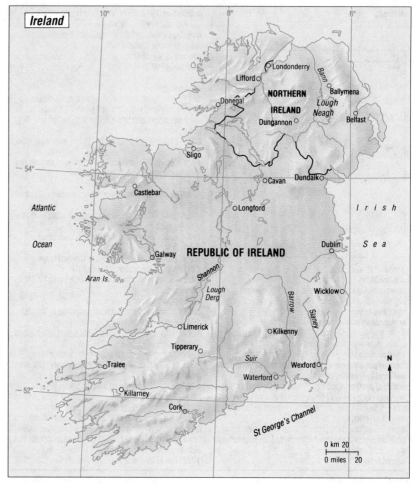

Ireland

resistant to tarnish and corrosion. It is one of the so-called platinum group of metals; it occurs in platinum ores and as a free metal (♢native metal) with osmium in osmiridium, a natural alloy that includes platinum, ruthenium, and rhodium.

iris in anatomy, the colored muscular diaphragm that controls the size of the pupil in the vertebrate eye. It contains radial muscle that increases the pupil diameter and circular muscle that constricts the pupil diameter. Both types of muscle respond involuntarily to light intensity.

iris in botany, perennial northern temperate flowering plants of the genus *Iris*, family Iridaceae. The leaves are usually sword-shaped; the purple, white, or yellow flowers have three upright inner petals and three outward- and downward-curving sepals. The wild iris is called flag.

Irish person of Irish culture from Ireland or person of Irish descent. The Irish mainly speak English, though there are approximately 30,000–100,000 speakers of Irish Gaelic, a Celtic language belonging to the Indo-European family.

Irish Republican Army (IRA) militant Irish nationalist organization whose aim is to create a united Irish socialist republic including Ulster. The paramilitary

wing of ♢Sinn Féin, it was founded 1919 by Michael ♢Collins and fought a successful war against Britain 1919–21. It came to the fore again 1939 with a bombing campaign in Britain, having been declared illegal in 1936. Its activities intensified from 1968 onward, as the civil-rights disorders ("the Troubles") in Northern Ireland developed. In 1970 a group in the north broke away to become the ***Provisional IRA***; its objective is the expulsion of the British from Northern Ireland.

iron (Germanic *eis* "strong") a hard, malleable and ductile, silver-gray metallic element, symbol Fe (from Latin ***ferrum***), atomic number 26, atomic weight 55.847. It is the fourth-most abundant element (the second-most abundant metal after aluminum) in the Earth's crust. The central core of the Earth, the radius of which is believed to be 2,200 miles, is held to consist principally of iron with some nickel. When the amounts in the crust and core are combined, iron is probably the most abundant constituent element of the planet.

Iron Age developmental stage of human technology when weapons and tools were made from iron. Iron was produced in Thailand by about 1600 BC but was considered inferior in strength to bronze until about 1000 when metallurgical techniques improved and the alloy steel was produced by adding carbon during the smelting process.

ironclad wooden warship covered with armor plate. The first to be constructed was the French *Gloire* 1858, but the first to be launched was the British HMS *Warrior* 1859. The first battle between ironclads took place during the American Civil War, when the Union *Monitor* fought the Confederate *Virginia* (formerly the *Merrimack*) March 9, 1862. The design was replaced by battleships of all-metal construction in the 1890s.

The US Navy's Great White Fleet was especially well known.

Iron Curtain in Europe after World War II, the symbolic boundary of the ◊Cold War between capitalist West and communist East. The term was popularized by the UK prime minister Winston Churchill from 1945.

Iron Guard profascist group controlling Romania in the 1930s. To counter its influence, King Carol II established a dictatorship 1938 but the Iron Guard forced him to abdicate 1940.

iron ore any mineral from which iron is extracted. The chief iron ores are ◊*magnetite*, a black oxide; ◊*hematite*, or kidney ore, a reddish oxide; *limonite*, brown, impure oxyhydroxides of iron; and *siderite*, a brownish carbonate.

iron pyrites or *pyrite* FeS_2 common iron ore. Brassy yellow, and occurring in cubic crystals, it is often called "fool's gold," since only those who have never seen gold would mistake it.

irony literary technique that achieves the effect of "saying one thing and meaning another," through the use of humor or mild sarcasm. It can be traced through all periods of literature, from Classical Greek and Roman epics and dramas to the good-humored and subtle irony of ◊Chaucer to the 20th-century writer's method for dealing with nihilism and despair, as in Samuel Beckett's *Waiting for Godot.*

Iroquois member of a confederation of NE North American Indians, the Six Nations (Cayuga, Mohawk, Oneida, Onondaga, and Seneca, with the Tuiscarora after 1723), traditionally formed by Hiawatha (actually a priestly title) 1570.

The Iroquois lived in upstate New York, and their descendants live in New York, Ontario, Québec, and Oklahoma, on reservations and among the general public. The Mohawk steelworkers are famous for constructing the girders of skyscrapers such as the Empire State Building.

irradiation in technology, subjecting anything to radiation, including cancer tumors. See also ◊food irradiation.

In optics, the term refers to the apparent enlargement of a brightly lit object when seen against a dark background.

irrational number a number that cannot be expressed as an exact ◊fraction. Irrational numbers include some square roots (for example, $\sqrt{2}$, $\sqrt{3}$, and $\sqrt{5}$ are irrational) and numbers such as π (the ratio of the circumference of a circle to its diameter, which is approximately equal to 3.14159) and e (the base of natural logarithms, approximately 2.71828).

Irrawaddy (Myanmar *Ayeryarwady*) chief river of Myanmar (Burma), flowing roughly N–S for 1,300 mi/2,090 km across the center of the country into the Bay of Bengal. Its sources are the Mali and N'mai rivers; its chief tributaries are the Chindwin and Shweli.

irrigation artificial water supply for dry agricultural areas by means of dams and channels. Drawbacks are that it tends to concentrate salts, ultimately causing infertility, and that rich river silt is retained at dams, to

the impoverishment of the land and fisheries below them.

Isaac in the Old Testament, Hebrew patriarch, son of ◊Abraham and Sarah, and father of Esau and Jacob.

Isaacs Alick 1921–1967. Scottish virologist who, with Jean Lindemann, in 1957 discovered ◊interferon, a naturally occurring antiviral substance produced by cells infected with viruses. The full implications of this discovery are still being investigated.

Isabella I *the Catholic* 1451–1504. Queen of Castile from 1474, after the death of her brother Henry IV. By her marriage with Ferdinand of Aragon 1469, the crowns of two of the Christian states in the Moorish-held Spanish peninsula were united. In her reign, during 1492, the Moors were driven out of Spain. She introduced the ◊Inquisition into Castile, expelled the Jews, and gave financial encouragement to ◊Columbus. Her youngest daughter was Catherine of Aragon, first wife of Henry VIII of England.

Isabella II 1830–1904. Queen of Spain from 1833, when she succeeded her father Ferdinand VII (1784–1833). The Salic Law banning a female sovereign had been repealed by the Cortes (parliament), but her succession was disputed by her uncle Don Carlos de Bourbon (1788–1855). After seven years of civil war, the Carlists were defeated. She abdicated in favor of her son Alfonso XII in 1868.

Isaiah 8th century BC. In the Old Testament, the first major Hebrew prophet. The son of Amos, he was probably of high rank, and lived largely in Jerusalem.

He was influential in the court of ancient Judah until the Assyrian invasion of 701 BC.

ISBN (abbreviation for *International Standard Book Number*) code number used for ordering or classifying book titles.

ISDN abbreviation for ◊Integrated Services Digital Network, a telecommunications system.

Isfahan or *Eşfahan* industrial city (steel, textiles, carpets) in central Iran; population (1986) 1,001,000. It was the ancient capital (1598–1722) of ◊Abbas I, and its features include the Great Square, Grand Mosque, and Hall of Forty Pillars.

Isherwood Christopher (William Bradshaw) 1904–1986. English novelist. He lived in Germany 1929–33 just before Hitler's rise to power, a period that inspired *Mr Norris Changes Trains* 1935 and *Goodbye to Berlin* 1939, creating the character of Sally Bowles (the basis of the musical *Cabaret* 1968). Returning to England, he collaborated with W H ◊Auden in three verse plays.

Ishiguro Kazuo 1954– . Japanese-born British novelist. His novel *An Artist of the Floating World* won the 1986 Whitbread Prize, and *The Remains of the Day*

iris *The iris is a plant of northern temperate regions.*

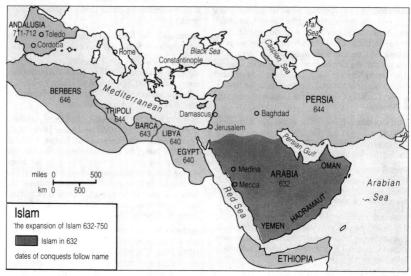

ANDALUSIA
711-712 ○ Toledo
○ Córdoba
○ Rome
Constantinople
Black Sea
Aral Sea
Caspian Sea
BERBERS 646
Mediterranean
TRIPOLI 644
Damascus○
○ Baghdad
PERSIA 644
BARCA 643
LIBYA 640
○ Jerusalem
Persian Gulf
EGYPT 640
miles 0 500
km 0 500
○ Medina
○ Mecca
ARABIA 632
OMAN
Arabian Sea
Red Sea
HADRAMAUT
YEMEN
ETHIOPIA

Islam
the expansion of Islam 632-750

Islam in 632

dates of conquests follow name

won the 1989 Booker Prize. His work is characterized by a sensitive style and subtle structure.

Ishtar Mesopotamian goddess of love and war, worshiped by the Babylonians and Assyrians, and personified as the legendary queen Semiramis.

isinglass pure form of gelatin obtained from the internal membranes of the swim bladder of various fishes, particularly the sturgeon. Isinglass is used in the clarification of wines and beer, and in cooking.

Isis the principal goddess of ancient Egypt. She was the daughter of Geb and Nut (Earth and Sky), and as the sister-wife of Osiris searched for his body after his death at the hands of his brother, Set. Her son Horus

then defeated and captured Set, but cut off his mother's head because she would not allow Set to be killed. She was later identified with ◊Hathor. The cult of Isis ultimately spread to Greece and Rome.

Islam (Arabic "submission," that is, to the will of Allah) religion founded in the Arabian peninsula in the early 7th century AD. It emphasizes the oneness of God, his omnipotence, benificence, and inscrutability. The sacred book is the *Koran* of the prophet Muhammad, the Prophet or Messenger of Allah. There are two main Muslim sects: ◊Sunni and ◊Shi'ite. Other schools include *Sufism*, a mystical movement originating in the 8th century.

Islamabad capital of Pakistan from 1967, in the Potwar district, at the foot of the Margala Hills and immediately NW of Rawalpindi; population (1981) 201,000. The city was designed by Constantinos Doxiadis in the 1960s. The Federal Capital Territory of Islamabad has an area of 350 sq mi/907 sq km and a population (1985) of 379,000.

Islamic art art and design of Muslim nations and territories. Because the Koran forbids figurative representation in art, Islamic artistry was channeled into calligraphy and ornament. Despite this, there was naturalistic Persian painting, which inspired painters in the Mogul and Ottoman empires. Ceramic tiles decorated mosques and palaces from Spain (Alhambra, Granada) to S Russia and Mogul India (Taj Mahal, Agra). Wood, stone, and stucco sculpture ornamented buildings. Islamic artists produced intricate metalwork and, in Persia in the 16th–17th centuries, woven textiles and carpets.

island area of land surrounded entirely by water. Australia is classed as a continent rather than an island, because of its size.

Ismail 1830–1895. Khedive (governor) of Egypt 1866–79. A grandson of Mehemet Ali, he became viceroy of Egypt in 1863 and in 1866 received the title of khedive from the Ottoman sultan. He amassed huge foreign debts and in 1875 Britain, at Prime Minister Disraeli's suggestion, bought the khedive's Suez Canal shares for nearly £4 million, establishing Anglo-French control of Egypt's finances. In 1879 the UK and France persuaded the sultan to appoint Tewfik, his

major islands

name and location	sq mi	sq km
Greenland (North Atlantic)	840,000	2,175,600
New Guinea (SW Pacific)	309,000	800,000
Borneo (SW Pacific)	287,300	744,100
Madagascar (Indian Ocean)	227,000	587,000
Baffin (Canadian Arctic)	195,928	507,258
Sumatra (Indian Ocean)	182,860	473,600
Honshu (NW Pacific)	89,176	230,966
Great Britain (N Atlantic)	88,795	229,978
Victoria (Canadian Arctic)	83,896	217,206
Ellesmere (Canadian Arctic)	75,767	196,160
Sulawesi (Indian Ocean)	73,057	189,216
South Island, New Zealand (SW Pacific)	57,870	149,883
Java (Indian Ocean)	48,900	126,602
North Island, New Zealand (SW Pacific)	44,274	114,669
Cuba (Caribbean Sea)	44,800	110,800
Newfoundland (NW Atlantic)	42,030	108,860
Luzon (W Pacific)	40,420	104,688
Iceland (N Atlantic)	39,800	103,000
Mindanao (W Pacific)	36,537	94,630
Ireland—N and the Republic (N Atlantic)	32,600	84,400
Hokkaido (NW Pacific)	32,245	83,515
Sakhalin (NW Pacific)	29,500	76,400
Hispaniola—Dominican Republic and Haiti (Caribbean Sea)	29,300	76,000
Banks (Canadian Arctic)	27,038	70,000
Tasmania (SW Pacific)	26,200	67,800
Sri Lanka (Indian Ocean)	24,900	64,600
Devon (Canadian Arctic)	21,331	55,247

son, khedive in his place.

Ismail I 1486–1524. Shah of Persia from 1501, founder of the *Safavi dynasty*, who established the first national government since the Arab conquest and Shiite Islam as the national religion.

Isma'ili member of an Islamic group, the second-largest ◊Shi'ite community in Islam (after the Twelver Shi'is). Isma'ilis comprise several smaller groups, the most important of which are the Nizari Isma'ilis, from 1094; the Da'udi Isma'ilis; the Musta'li Isma'ilis; and the Sulaymani Isma'ilis.

isobar line drawn on maps and weather charts linking all places with the same atmospheric pressure (usually measured in millibars). When used in weather forecasting, the distance between the isobars is an indication of the barometric gradient.

Israel
State of
(*Medinat Israel*)

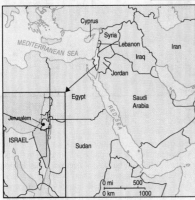

area 8,029 sq mi/20,800 sq km (as at 1949 armistice)
capital Jerusalem (not recognized by the United Nations)
cities ports Tel Aviv/Jaffa, Haifa, Acre, Eilat; Bat-Yam, Holon, Ramat Gan, Petach Tikva, Beersheba
physical coastal plain of Sharon between Haifa and Tel Aviv noted since ancient times for fertility; central mountains of Galilee, Samariq, and Judea; Dead Sea, Lake Tiberias, and river Jordan Rift Valley along the E are below sea level; Negev Desert in the S; Israel occupies Golan Heights, West Bank, and Gaza
features historic sites: Jerusalem, Bethlehem, Nazareth, Masada, Megiddo, Jericho; caves of the Dead Sea scrolls
head of state Ezer Weizman from 1993
head of government Yitzhak Rabin from 1992
political system democratic republic
political parties Israel Labor Party, moderate, left of center; Consolidation Party (Likud), right of center
exports citrus and other fruit, avocados, chinese leaves, fertilizers, diamonds, plastics, petrochemicals, textiles, electronics (military, medical, scientific, industrial), electro-optics, precision instruments, aircraft and missiles
currency shekel
population (1992) 5,239,000 (including 750,000 Arab Israeli citizens and over 1 million Arabs in the occupied territories); under the Law of Return 1950, "every Jew shall be entitled to come to Israel as an immigrant"; those from the East and E Europe are Ashkenazim, and those from Mediterranean Europe (Spain, Portugal, Italy, France, Greece) and Arab N Africa are Sephardim (over 50% of the population is now of Sephardic descent). Between Jan 1990 and April 1991, 250,000 Soviet Jews emigrated to Israel. An Israeli-born Jew is a Sabra. About 500,000 Israeli Jews are resident in the US. Growth rate 1.8% p.a.
life expectancy men 73, women 76
languages Hebrew and Arabic (official); Yiddish, European and W Asian languages
religions Israel is a secular state, but the predominant faith is Judaism 83%; also Sunni Muslim, Christian, and Druse
literacy Jewish 88%, Arab 70%
GDP $35 bn (1987); $8,011 per head

chronology
1948 Independent State of Israel proclaimed with David Ben-Gurion as prime minister; attacked by Arab nations, Israel won the War of Independence. Many displaced Arabs settled in refugee camps in the Gaza Strip and West Bank.
1952 Col Gamal Nasser of Egypt stepped up blockade of Israeli ports and support of Arab guerrillas in Gaza.
1956 Israel invaded Gaza and Sinai.
1959 Egypt renewed blockade of Israeli trade through Suez Canal.
1963 Ben-Gurion resigned, succeeded by Levi Eshkol.
1964 Palestine Liberation Organization (PLO) founded with the aim of overthrowing the state of Israel.
1967 Nasser calls for destruction of Israel. Arab nations mobilize forces. Israel victorious in the Six-Day War. Gaza, West Bank, E Jerusalem, Sinai, and Golan Heights captured.
1968 Israel Labor Party formed, led by Golda Meir.
1969 Golda Meir became prime minister.
1973 Yom Kippur War: Israel attacked by Egypt and Syria.
1974 Golda Meir succeeded by Yitzhak Rabin.
1975 Suez Canal reopened.
1977 Menachem Begin elected prime minister. Egyptian president addressed the Knesset.
1978 Camp David talks.
1979 Egyptian-Israeli agreement signed. Israel agreed to withdraw from Sinai.
1980 Jerusalem declared capital of Israel.
1981 Golan Heights formally annexed.
1983 Peace treaty between Israel and Lebanon signed but not ratified.
1985 Formation of government of national unity with Labor and Likud ministers.
1986 Yitzhak Shamir took over from Peres under power-sharing agreement.
1987 Outbreak of Palestinian uprising (Intifada) in West Bank and Gaza.
1988 Criticism of Israel's handling of Palestinian uprising in occupied territories; PLO acknowledged Israel's right to exist.
1989 New Likud–Labor coalition government formed under Shamir. Limited progress achieved on proposals for negotiations leading to elections in occupied territories.
1990 Coalition collapsed due to differences over peace process; international condemnation of Temple Mount killings. New Shamir right-wing coalition formed.
1991 Shamir gave cautious response to Middle East peace proposals. Some Palestinian prisoners released. Peace talks began in Madrid.
1992 Jan: Shamir lost majority in Knesset when ultra-orthodox party withdrew from coalition. June: Labor Party, led by Yitzhak Rabin, won elections; coalition formed under Rabin. Aug: US-Israeli loan agreement signed. Dec: 400 Hamas Islamic fundamentalists summarily expelled in the face of international criticism.
1993 Jan: Ban on contacts with PLO formally lifted. Feb: 100 of the expelled allowed to return. March: Ezer Weizman elected president; Binyamin "Bibi" Netanyahu elected leader of Likud party. Middle East peace talks restarted. July: Israel launched attacks against Hezbollah in S Lebanon. Sept: historic accord of mutual recognition agreed between Israel and PLO, to result in partial autonomy for Palestinians and phased Israeli withdrawal from parts of occupied territories

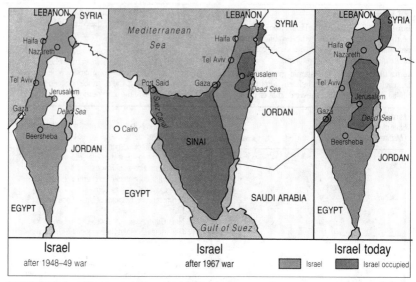

Israel	Israel	Israel today
after 1948–49 war	after 1967 war	□ Israel ■ Israel occupied

isolationism in politics, concentration on internal rather than foreign affairs; a foreign policy having no interest in international affairs that do not affect the country's own interests.

isomer chemical compound having the same molecular composition and mass as another, but with different physical or chemical properties owing to the different structural arrangement of its constituent atoms. For example, the organic compounds butane $(CH_3(CH_2)_2CH_3)$ and methyl propane $(CH_3CH(CH_3)CH_3)$ are isomers, each possessing four carbon atoms and ten hydrogen atoms but differing in the way that these are arranged with respect to each other.

isotherm line on a map linking all places having the same temperature at a given time.

isotope one of two or more atoms that have the same atomic number (same number of protons), but which contain a different number of neutrons, thus differing in their atomic masses. They may be stable or radioactive, naturally occurring or synthesized. The term was coined by English chemist Frederick Soddy, pioneer researcher in atomic disintegration.

Israel country in SW Asia, bounded N by Lebanon, E by Syria and Jordan, S by the Gulf of Aqaba, and W by Egypt and the Mediterranean Sea. *See panel p. 487*

Istanbul city and chief seaport of Turkey; population (1990) 6,620,200.

It produces textiles, tobacco, cement, glass, and leather. Founded as *Byzantium* about 660 BC, it was renamed *Constantinople* AD 330 and was the capi-

Istanbul The Topkapi Palace overlooking the Golden Horn, Istanbul.

tal of the ◊Byzantine Empire until captured by the Turks 1453. As *Istamboul* it was capital of the Ottoman Empire until 1922.

Itagaki Taisuke 1837–1919. Japanese military and political leader, the founder of Japan's first political party, the Jiyūtō (Liberal Party) 1875–81. Involved in the overthrow of the ◊Tokugawa shogunate and the ◊Meiji restoration 1866–68, Itagaki became a champion of democratic principles while continuing to serve in the government for short periods.

Itaipu world's largest hydroelectric plant, situated on the Paraná River, SW Brazil. A joint Brazilian-Paraguayan venture, it came into operation 1984; it supplies hydroelectricity to a wide area.

Italian native to or an inhabitant of Italy and their descendants, culture, and language. The language belongs to the Romance group of Indo-European languages.

Italian is spoken in S Switzerland and in areas of Italian settlement in the US, Argentina, the UK, and Australia.

Italian architecture architecture of the Italian peninsula after the fall of the Roman Empire. In the earliest styles—Byzantine, Romanesque, and Gothic—the surviving buildings are mostly churches. From the Renaissance and Baroque periods there are also palaces, town halls, and so on.

Italian language member of the Romance branch of the Indo-European language family, the most direct descendant of Latin. Broadcasting and films have standardized the Italian national tongue, but most Italians speak a regional dialect as well as standard Italian. The Italian language is also spoken in Switzerland and by people of Italian descent especially in the US, Australia, the UK, and Argentina.

Italian Somaliland former Italian trust territory on the Somali coast of Africa extending to 194,999 sq mi/502,300 sq km. Established 1892, it was extended 1925 with the acquisition of Jubaland from Kenya; administered from Mogadishu; under British rule 1941–50. Thereafter it reverted to Italian authority before uniting with British

---

Italy
Republic of
(*Repubblica Italiana*)

area 116,332 sq mi/301,300 sq km
capital Rome
cities Milan, Turin; ports Naples, Genoa, Palermo, Bari, Catania, Trieste
physical mountainous (Maritime Alps, Dolomites, Apennines) with narrow coastal lowlands; rivers Po, Adige, Arno, Tiber, Rubicon; islands of Sicily, Sardinia, Elba, Capri, Ischia, Lipari, Pantelleria; lakes Como, Maggiore, Garda
environment Milan has the highest recorded level of sulfur-dioxide pollution of any city in the world. The Po River, with pollution ten times higher than officially recommended levels, is estimated to discharge around 250 metric tons of arsenic into the sea each year
features continental Europe's only active volcanoes: Vesuvius, Etna, Stromboli; historic towns include Venice, Florence, Siena, Rome; Greek, Roman, Etruscan archeological sites
head of state Oscar Luigi Scalfaro from 1992
head of government Carlo Azeglio Ciampi from 1993
political system democratic republic
political parties Christian Democratic Party (DC), Christian, centrist; Democratic Party of the Left (PDS), pro- European socialist; Italian Socialist Party (PSI), moderate socialist; Italian Social Movement–National Right (MSI–DN), neofascist; Italian Republican Party (PRI), social

democratic, left of center; Italian Social Democratic Party (PSDI), moderate left of center; Liberals (PLI), right of center
exports wine (world's largest producer), fruit, vegetables, textiles (Europe's largest silk producer), clothing, leather goods, motor vehicles, electrical goods, chemicals, marble (Carrara), sulfur, mercury, iron, steel
currency lira
population (1992) 57,103,000; growth rate 0.1% p.a.
life expectancy men 73, women 80 (1989)
language Italian; German, French, Slovene, and Albanian minorities
religion Roman Catholic 100% (state religion)
literacy 97% (1989)
GDP $1,223.6 bn (1992)

chronology
1946 Monarchy replaced by a republic.
1948 New constitution adopted.
1954 Trieste (claimed by Yugoslavia after World War II), was divided between Italy and Yugoslavia.
1976 Communists proposed establishment of broad-based, left–right government, the "historic compromise"; rejected by Christian Democrats.
1978 Christian Democrat Aldo Moro, architect of the historic compromise, kidnapped and murdered by Red Brigade guerrillas infiltrated by Western intelligence agents.
1983 Bettino Craxi, a Socialist, became leader of broad coalition government.
1987 Craxi resigned; succeeding coalition fell within months.
1988 Christian Democrats' leader Ciriaco de Mita established a five-party coalition including the Socialists.
1989 De Mita resigned after disagreements within his coalition government; succeeded by Giulio Andreotti. De Mita lost leadership of Christian Democrats; Communists formed "shadow government."
1991 Referendum approved electoral reform.
1992 April: ruling coalition lost its majority in general election; President Cossiga resigned, replaced by Oscar Luigi Scalfaro in May. Giuliano Amato, deputy leader of PDS, accepted premiership. Sept: lira devalued and Italy withdrew from the Exchange Rate Mechanism.
1993 Investigation of corruption network exposed Mafia links with several notable politicians, including Craxi and Andreotti. Craxi resigned Socialist Party leadership; replaced by Giorgio Benvenuto and then Ottaviano del Turro. Referendum supported ending the proportional-representation electoral system. Amato resigned premiership; Carlo Ciampi, with no party allegiance, named as his successor.

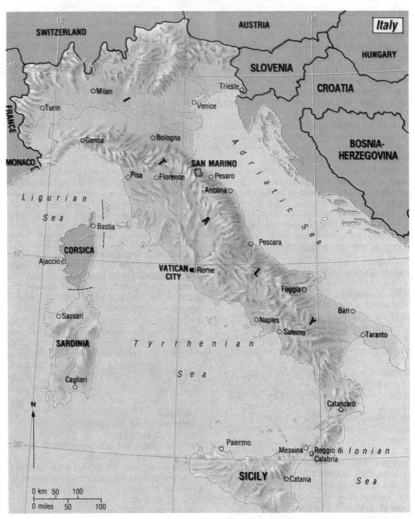

Somaliland 1960 to form the independent state of Somalia.

italic style of printing in which the letters slope to the right *like this*, introduced by the printer Aldus Manutius of Venice in 1501. It is usually used side by side with the erect Roman type to distinguish titles of books, films, and so on, and for purposes of emphasis and citation. The term "italic" is also used for the handwriting style developed for popular use in 1522 by Vatican chancery scribe Ludovico degli Arrighi, which became the basis for modern italic script.

Italy country in S Europe, bounded N by Switzerland and Austria, E by Slovenia, Croatia, and the Adriatic Sea, S by the Ionian and Mediterranean seas, and W by the Tyrrhenian and Ligurian seas and France. It includes the Mediterranean islands of Sardinia and Sicily. *See panel p. 489*

Ithaca (Greek *Itháki*) Greek island in the Ionian Sea, area 36 sq mi/93 sq km. Important in pre-Classical Greece, Ithaca was (in Homer's poem) the birthplace of ◊Odysseus, though this is sometimes identified with the island of Leukas (some archeologists have equated ancient Ithaca with Leukas rather than modern Ithaca).

Itō Hirobumi, Prince 1841–1909. Japanese politician, prime minister 1887, 1892–96, 1898, 1900–01. He was a key figure in the modernization of Japan and was involved in the ◊Meiji restoration 1866–68 and in official missions to study forms of government in the US and Europe in the 1870s and 1880s. As minister for home affairs, he helped draft the Meiji constitution of 1889.

Ivan III Ivan the Great 1440–1505. Grand duke of Muscovy from 1462, who revolted against Tatar overlordship by refusing tribute to Grand Khan Ahmed 1480. He claimed the title of tsar, and used the double-headed eagle as the Russian state emblem.

Ivan IV *the Terrible* 1530–1584. Grand duke of Muscovy from 1533; he assumed power 1544 and was crowned as first tsar of Russia 1547. He conquered Kazan 1552, Astrakhan 1556, and Siberia 1581. He reformed the legal code and local administration 1555 and established trade relations with England. In his last years he alternated between debauchery and religious austerities, executing thousands and, in rage, his own son.

Ives Charles (Edward) 1874–1954. US composer who experimented with ◊atonality, quarter tones, clashing

Ivory Coast
Republic of
(*République de la Côte d'Ivoire*)

area 124,471 sq mi/322,463 sq km
capital Yamoussoukro
cities Bouaké, Daloa, Man; ports Abidjan, San-Pédro
physical tropical rain forest (diminishing as exploited) in S; savanna and low mountains in N
environment an estimated 85% of the country's forest has been destroyed by humans

features Vridi canal, Kossou dam, Monts du Toura
head of state and government Henri Konan Bedie from 1993
political system emergent democratic republic
political party Democratic Party of the Ivory Coast (PDCI), nationalist, free-enterprise
exports coffee, cocoa, timber, petroleum products
currency franc CFA
population (1992) 12,951,000; growth rate 3.3% p.a.
life expectancy men 52, women 55 (1989)
languages French (official), over 60 native dialects
media the government has full control of the media
religions animist 65%, Muslim 24%, Christian 11%
literacy 35% (1988)
GDP $7.6 bn (1987); $687 per head

chronology
1904 Became part of French West Africa.
1958 Achieved internal self-government.
1960 Independence achieved from France, with Félix Houphouët-Boigny as president of a one-party state.
1985 Houphouët-Boigny reelected, unopposed.
1986 Name changed officially from Ivory Coast to Côte d'Ivoire.
1990 Houphouët-Boigny and PDCI reelected.
1993 Death of Houphouët-Boigny in Dec triggered political unrest.

time signatures, and quotations from popular music of the time. He wrote five symphonies, inlcuding *Holidays Symphony* 1904–13; chamber music, including the *Concord Sonata*; and the orchestral *Three Places in New England* 1903–14 and *The Unanswered Question* 1908.

Ives Frederic Eugene 1856–1937. US inventor who developed the ◊halftone process of printing photographs in 1878. The process uses a screen to break up light and dark areas into dots. By 1886 he had evolved the halftone process now generally in use. Among his many other inventions was a three-color printing process (similar to the ◊four-color process).

IVF abbreviation for ◊in vitro fertilization.

ivory the hard white substance of which the teeth and tusks of certain mammals are composed. Among the most valuable are elephants' tusks, which are of unusual hardness and density. Ivory is used in carving and other decorative work, and is so valuable that poachers continue to destroy the remaining wild elephant herds in Africa to obtain it illegally.

Ivory Coast (French *Côte d'Ivoire*) country in W Africa, bounded N by Mali and Burkina Faso, E by Ghana, S by the Gulf of Guinea, and W by Liberia and Guinea.

ivy any tree or shrub of the genus *Hedera* of the ginseng family Araliaceae. English or European ivy *H. helix* has shiny, evergreen, triangular or oval-shaped leaves, and clusters of small, yellowish-green flowers, followed by black berries. It climbs by means of rootlike suckers put out from its stem, and is injurious to trees.

Iwo Jima largest of the Japanese Volcano Islands in the W Pacific Ocean, 760 mi/1,222 km S of Tokyo; area 8 sq mi/21 sq km. Annexed by Japan 1891, it was captured by the US 1945 after fierce fighting. It was returned to Japan 1968.

IWW abbreviation for ◊Industrial Workers of the World.

Ixion in Greek mythology, a king whom Zeus punished for his crimes by binding him to a fiery wheel rolling endlessly through the underworld.

Izmir (formerly *Smyrna*) port and naval base in Turkey; population (1990) 1,757,400. Products include steel, electronics, and plastics. The largest annual trade fair in the Middle East is held here. It is the headquarters of ◊North Atlantic Treaty Organization SE Command.

Iznik modern name of ancient ◊Nicaea, a city in Turkey noted for the richly decorated pottery and tiles produced there in the 15th and 16th centuries.

J

jacana one of seven species of wading birds, family Jacanidae, with very long toes and claws enabling it to walk on the flat leaves of river plants, hence the name "lily trotter." Jacanas are found in Mexico, Central America, South America, Africa, S Asia and Australia. The female pheasant-tailed jacana *Hydrophasianus chirurgus* of Asia has a "harem" of two to four males.

jack tool or machine for lifting, hoisting, or moving heavy weights, such as motor vehicles. A ***screw jack*** uses the principle of the screw to magnify an applied effort; in an automobile jack, for example, turning the handle many times causes the lifting screw to rise slightly, and the effort is magnified to lift heavy weights. A ***hydraulic jack*** uses a succession of piston strokes to increase pressure in a liquid and force up a lifting ram.

jackal any of several wild dogs of the genus *Canis*, found in S Asia, S Europe, and N Africa. Jackals can grow to 2.7 ft/80 cm long, and have grayish-brown fur and a bushy tail.

Jackson city in S Michigan, on the Grand River, S of Lansing; seat of Jackson County; population (1990) 37,400. Its industries include motor-vehicle and air-

jacana The American jacana, or lily trotter, is a common water bird of lagoons and marshes in Mexico and Central America.

craft parts, tools, plastics, and air-conditioning equipment. The Republican Party was formed here 1854.

Jackson largest city and capital of Mississippi, on the Pearl River; population (1990) 196,600. It produces furniture, cottonseed oil, and iron and steel castings, and owes its prosperity to the discovery of gas fields to the S in the 1930s. Named after Andrew Jackson, later president, it dates from 1821 and was virtually destroyed by Union troops 1863, during the American Civil War.

Jackson Andrew 1767–1845. 7th president of the US 1829–37, a Democrat. A major general in the War of 1812, he defeated a British force at New Orleans in 1815 (after the official end of the war in 1814) and was involved in the war that led to the purchase of Florida in 1819. The political organization he built as president, with Martin Van Buren, was the basis for the modern ◊Democratic Party.

Jackson Glenda 1936– . English actress and politician. She has made many stage appearances, including *Marat/Sade* 1966, and her films include the Oscar-winning *Women in Love* 1969, *Sunday Bloody Sunday* 1971, and *A Touch of Class* 1973. On television she played Queen Elizabeth I in *Elizabeth R* 1971. In 1992 she was elected to Parliament as a Labour Party member.

Jackson Howell Edmunds 1832–1895. US jurist. Elected to the US Senate 1880, he was named federal district judge 1886 by Grover Cleveland and chief judge of the circuit court of appeals 1891 by Benjamin Harrison. In 1893 Jackson was appointed to the US Supreme Court, but illness prevented him from carrying out his duties.

Jackson Jesse 1941– . US Democratic politician, a cleric and campaigner for minority rights. He contested his party's 1984 and 1988 presidential nominations in an effort to increase voter registration and to put black issues on the national agenda. He is an eloquent public speaker.

Jackson Mahalia 1911–1972. US gospel singer. She made her first recording in 1934, and her version of the gospel song "Move on Up a Little Higher" was a com-

Jackson The 7th president of the United States, Andrew Jackson, a Democrat, 1829–37.

mercial success 1945. Jackson became a well-known radio and television performer in the 1950s and was invited to sing at the presidential inauguration of John F Kennedy.

Jackson Michael 1958– . US rock singer and songwriter whose videos and live performances are meticulously choreographed. His first solo hit was "Got to Be There" 1971; his worldwide popularity peaked with the albums *Thriller* 1982 and *Bad* 1987. The follow-up was *Dangerous* 1991.

Jackson Stonewall (Thomas Jonathan) 1824–1863. US Confederate general in the American Civil War. He acquired his nickname and his reputation at the Battle of Bull Run, from the firmness with which his brigade resisted the Northern attack. In 1862 he organized the Shenandoah Valley campaign and assisted Robert E ◊Lee's invasion of Maryland. He helped to defeat General Joseph E Hooker's Union army at the battle of Chancellorsville, Virginia, but was fatally wounded by one of his own soldiers in the confusion of battle.

A West Point graduate, after serving in the Mexican War 1846–48, he became professor of military tactics at the Virginia military institute.

Jacksonville port, resort, and commercial center in NE Florida; population (1990) 673,000. The port has naval installations and ship-repair yards. To the N the Cross-Florida Barge Canal links the Atlantic with the Gulf of Mexico. Manufactured goods include wood and paper products, chemicals, and processed food.

Jack the Ripper popular name for the unidentified mutilator and murderer of at least five women prostitutes in the Whitechapel area of London in 1888.

Several suspects have been suggested in extensive studies of the case, including members of the royal household.

Jacob in the Old Testament, Hebrew patriarch, son of Isaac and Rebecca, who obtained the rights of seniority from his twin brother Esau by trickery. He married his cousins Leah and Rachel, serving their father Laban seven years for each, and at the time of famine in Canaan joined his son Joseph in Egypt. His 12 sons were the traditional ancestors of the 12 tribes of Israel.

Jacob François 1920– . French biochemist who, with Jacques Monod, pioneered research into molecular genetics and showed how the production of proteins from ◊DNA is controlled. He shared the Nobel Prize for Medicine in 1965.

Jacobin member of an extremist republican club of the French Revolution founded at Versailles 1789, which later used a former Jacobin (Dominican) friary as its headquarters in Paris. Helped by ◊Danton's speeches, they proclaimed the French republic, had the king executed, and overthrew the moderate Girondins 1792–93. Through the Committee of Public Safety, they began the Reign of Terror, led by ◊Robespierre. After his execution 1794, the club was abandoned and the name "Jacobin" passed into general use for any left-wing extremist.

Jacobite in Britain, a supporter of the royal house of Stuart after the deposition of James II in 1688. They include the Scottish Highlanders, who rose unsuccessfully under Claverhouse in 1689; and those who rose in Scotland and N England under the leadership of James Edward Stuart, the ◊Old Pretender, in 1715, and followed his son ◊Charles Edward Stuart in an invasion of England that reached Derby in 1745–46. After the defeat at Culloden, Jacobitism disappeared as a political force.

Jackson US rock singer and songwriter Michael Jackson, whose success and popularity reached a peak with the Thriller album 1982.

Jacuzzi Candido 1903–1986. Italian-born US engineer who invented the Jacuzzi, a pump that produces a whirlpool effect in a bathtub. The Jacuzzi was commercially launched as a health and recreational product in the mid-1950s.

jade semiprecious stone consisting of either jadeite, $NaAlSi_2O_6$ (a pyroxene), or nephrite, $Ca_2(Mg,Fe)_5Si_8O_{22}(OH,F)_2$ (an amphibole), ranging from colorless through shades of green to black according to the iron content. Jade ranks 5.5–6.5 on the Mohs' scale of hardness.

Jaffa (biblical name *Joppa*) port in W Israel, part of ◊Tel Aviv from 1950.

Jagan Cheddi (Berrat) 1918– . Guyanese left-wing politician, president from 1992. He led the People's Progressive Party (PPA) from 1950, and was the first prime minister of British Guyana 1961–64. As candidate for president Aug 1992, he opposed privatization as leading to "recolonization."

The PPA won a decisive victory, and Jagan as veteran leader replaced Desmond Hoyte.

jaguar largest species of ◊cat *Panthera onca* in the Americas, formerly ranging from the SW US to S South America, but now extinct in most of North America. It can grow up to 8 ft/2.5 m long including the tail. The background color of the fur varies from

Jackson Confederate general Thomas Jackson, whose tactics in resisting Union forces at the Battle of Bull Run during the American Civil War earned him the nickname "Stonewall."

jaguar The jaguar has been hunted for its beautiful coat.

creamy white to brown or black, and is covered with black spots. The jaguar is usually solitary.

Jahangir "Holder of the World."

Adopted name of Salim 1569–1627. Third Mogul emperor of India 1605–27, succeeding his father ◊Akbar the Great. The first part of his reign was marked by peace, prosperity and a flowering of the arts, but the latter half by rebellion and succession conflicts.

Jahweh another spelling of ◊*Jehovah*, the Lord (meaning God) in the Hebrew Bible, used by some writers instead of *Adonai* (Lord) or *Hashem* (the Name)—all names used to avoid the representation of God in any form.

jai alai or *pelota* very fast ball game of Basque derivation, popular in Latin American countries and in the US where it is a betting sport. It is played by two, four, or six players, in a walled court, or *cancha*, and somewhat resembles squash, but each player uses a long, curved, wickerwork basket, or *cesta*, strapped to the hand, to hurl the ball, or *pelota* (about the size of a baseball), against the walls.

Jainism (Hindi *jaina* "person who overcomes") ancient Indian religion, sometimes regarded as an off-shoot of Hinduism. Jains emphasize the importance of not injuring living beings, and their code of ethics is based on sympathy and compassion for all forms of life. They also believe in ◊karma but not in any deity. It is a monastic, ascetic religion. There are two main sects: the Digambaras and the Swetambaras. Jainism practices the most extreme form of nonviolence (*ahimsā*) of all Indian sects, and influenced the philosophy of Mahatma Gandhi. Jains number approximately 6 million; there are Jain communities throughout the world but the majority live in India.

Jaipur capital of Rajasthan, India; population (1981) 1,005,000. It was formerly the capital of the state of Jaipur, which was merged with Rajasthan 1949. Products include textiles and metal products.

Jakarta or *Djakarta* (former name until 1949 *Batavia*) capital of Indonesia on the NW coast of Java; population (1980) 6,504,000. Industries include textiles, chemicals, and plastics; a canal links it with its port of Tanjung Priok where rubber, oil, tin, coffee, tea, and palm oil are among its exports; also a tourist center. Jakarta was founded by Dutch traders 1619.

Jakeš Miloš 1922– . Czech communist politician, a member of the Politburo from 1981 and party leader 1987–89. A conservative, he supported the Soviet invasion of Czechoslovakia in 1968. He was forced to resign in Nov 1989 following a series of prodemocracy mass rallies.

Jalalabad capital of Nangarhar province, E Afghanistan, on the road from Kabul to Peshawar in Pakistan; population (1984 est) 61,900 (numbers swelled to over 1 million during the civil war). The city was besieged by mujaheddin rebels after the withdrawal of Soviet troops from Afghanistan 1989.

Jamaica island in the Caribbean Sea, S of Cuba and W of Haiti.

James Henry 1843–1916. US novelist, who lived in Europe from 1875 and became a naturalized British

---

Jamaica

area 4,230 sq mi/10,957 sq km
capital Kingston
cities Montego Bay, Spanish Town, St Andrew
physical mountainous tropical island
features Blue Mountains (so called because of the haze over them) renowned for their coffee; partly undersea ruins of pirate city of Port Royal, destroyed by an earthquake 1692
head of state Elizabeth II from 1962, represented by governor-general
head of government P J Patterson from 1992

political system constitutional monarchy
political parties Jamaica Labor Party (JLP), moderate, centrist; People's National Party (PNP), left of center
exports sugar, bananas, bauxite, rum, cocoa, coconuts, liqueurs, cigars, citrus
currency Jamaican dollar
population (1992) 2,445,000 (African 76%, mixed 15%, Chinese, Caucasian, East Indian); growth rate 2.2% p.a.
life expectancy men 75, women 78 (1989)
languages English, Jamaican Creole
media one daily newspaper 1834–1988 (except 1973–82), privately owned; sensational evening and weekly papers
religions Protestant 70%, Rastafarian
literacy 82% (1988)
GDP $2.9 bn; $1,187 per head (1989)

chronology
1494 Columbus reached Jamaica.
1509–1655 Occupied by Spanish.
1655 Captured by British.
1944 Internal self-government introduced.
1962 Independence achieved from Britain, with Alexander Bustamante of the JLP as prime minister.
1967 JLP reelected under Hugh Shearer.
1972 Michael Manley of the PNP became prime minister.
1980 JLP elected, with Edward Seaga as prime minister.
1983 JLP reelected, winning all 60 seats.
1988 Island badly damaged by Hurricane Gilbert.
1989 PNP won a decisive victory with Michael Manley returning as prime minister.
1992 Manley resigned, succeeded by P J Patterson.
1993 Landslide victory for PNP in general election.

subject 1915. His novels deal with the impact of sophisticated European culture on the innocent American. They include *The Portrait of a Lady* 1881, *Washington Square* 1881, *The Bostonians* 1886, *The Ambassadors* 1903, and *The Golden Bowl* 1904. He also wrote more than a hundred shorter works of fiction, notably the supernatural tale *The Turn of the Screw* 1898.

He is assessed, both in the US and Europe, as one of the most significant and influential American writers. His career spanned more than half a century. Other major works include *Roderick Hudson* 1876, *The American* 1877, *The Tragic Muse* 1890, *The Spoils of Poynton* 1897, *The Awkward Age* 1899, *The Wings of the Dove* 1902. His mastery of the novel set the standard for many 20th-century writers.

James Jesse 1847–1882. US bank and train robber, born in Missouri and a leader, with his brother Frank (1843–1915), of the Quantrill raiders, a Confederate guerrilla band in the Civil War. Frank later led his own gang. Jesse was killed by Bob Ford, an accomplice; Frank remained unconvicted and became a farmer.

James William 1842–1910. US psychologist and philosopher, brother of the novelist Henry James. He turned from medicine to psychology and taught at Harvard 1872–1907. His books include *Principles of Psychology* 1890, *The Will to Believe* 1897, and *Varieties of Religious Experience* 1902, one of the most important works on the psychology of religion.

James I *the Conqueror* 1208–1276. King of Aragon from 1213, when he succeeded his father. He conquered the Balearic Islands and took Valencia from the ◊Moors, dividing it with Alfonso X of Castile by a treaty of 1244. Both these exploits are recorded in his autobiography *Libre dels feyts/Chronicle*. He largely established Aragon as the dominant power in the Mediterranean.

James I 1566–1625. King of England from 1603 and Scotland (as *James VI*) from 1567. The son of Mary Queen of Scots and Lord Darnley, he succeeded on his mother's abdication from the Scottish throne, assumed power 1583, established a strong centralized authority, and in 1589 married Anne of Denmark (1574–1619). As successor to Elizabeth I in England, he alienated the Puritans by his High Church views and Parliament by his assertion of ◊divine right, and was generally unpopular because of his favorites, such as Buckingham, and his schemes for an alliance with Spain. He was succeeded by his son Charles I.

James II 1633–1701. King of England and Scotland (as *James VII*) from 1685, second son of Charles I. He succeeded Charles II. James married Anne Hyde 1659 (1637–1671, mother of Mary II and Anne) and Mary of Modena 1673 (mother of James Edward Stuart). He became a Catholic 1671, which led first to attempts to exclude him from the succession, then to the rebellions of ◊Monmouth and Argyll, and finally to the Whig and Tory leaders' invitation to William of Orange to take the throne in 1688. James fled to France, then led an uprising in Ireland 1689, but after defeat at the Battle of the ◊Boyne 1690 remained in exile in France.

James I 1394–1437. King of Scotland 1406–37, who assumed power 1424. He was a cultured and strong monarch whose improvements in the administration of justice brought him popularity among the common people. He was assassinated by a group of conspirators led by the Earl of Atholl.

James III 1451–1488. King of Scotland from 1460, who assumed power 1469. His reign was marked by

James US outlaw Jesse James became a frontier legend for his daring robberies.

rebellions by the nobles, including his brother Alexander, Duke of Albany. He was murdered during a rebellion supported by his son, who then ascended the throne as James IV.

James IV 1473–1513. King of Scotland from 1488, who married Margaret (1489–1541, daughter of Henry VII) in 1503. He came to the throne after his followers murdered his father, James III, at Sauchieburn. His reign was internally peaceful, but he allied himself with France against England, invaded 1513 and was defeated and killed at the Battle of Flodden. James IV was a patron of poets and architects as well as a military leader.

James VI of Scotland. See ◊James I of England.

James, St several Christian saints, including:

James, St *the Great* died AD 44. A New Testament apostle, originally a Galilean fisher, he was the son of Zebedee and brother of the apostle John. He was put to death by ◊Herod Agrippa. James is the patron saint of Spain. Feast day July 25.

James, St *the Just* 1st century AD. The New Testament brother of Jesus, to whom Jesus appeared after the Resurrection. Leader of the Christian church in Jerusalem, he was the author of the biblical Epistle of James.

Jamestown first permanent British settlement in North America, established by Captain John Smith 1607. It was capital of Virginia 1624–99.

Jammu and Kashmir state of N India
area 39,102 sq mi/101,300 sq km
capital Jammu (winter); Srinagar (summer)
cities Leh
products timber, grain, rice, fruit, silk, carpets
population (1991) 7,718,700 (Indian-occupied territory)
history part of the Mogul Empire from 1586, Jammu came under the control of Gulab Singh 1820. In 1947 Jammu was attacked by Pakistan and chose to become part of the new state of India. Dispute over the area (see ◊Kashmir) caused further hostilities 1971 between India and Pakistan (ended by the Simla agreement 1972). Since then, separatist agitation has developed, complicating the territorial dispute between India and Pakistan.

Janáček Leoš 1854–1928. Czech composer. He became director of the Conservatoire at Brno in 1919 and professor at the Prague Conservatoire in 1920. His music, highly original and influenced by Moravian folk music, includes arrangements of folk songs, operas (*Jenůfa* 1904, *The Cunning Little Vixen* 1924), and the choral *Glagolitic Mass* 1926.

Janata alliance of political parties in India formed 1971 to oppose Indira Gandhi's Congress Party. Victory in the election brought Morarji Desai to power as prime minister but he was unable to control the various groups within the alliance and resigned 1979. His successors fared little better, and the elections of 1980 overwhelmingly returned Indira Gandhi to office.

Janesville city in S Wisconsin, on the Rock River, SE of Madison; seat of Rock County; population (1990) 52,100. Industries include automobiles and automobile parts, building materials, and electronic equip-ment. It is a processing and marketing center for the area's agricultural products.

Jansen Cornelius 1585–1638. Dutch Roman Catholic theologian, founder of ◊Jansenism with his book *Augustinus* 1640.

Jansenism Christian teaching of Cornelius Jansen, which divided the Roman Catholic church in France in the mid-17th century. Emphasizing the more predestinatory approach of Augustine's teaching, as opposed to that of the Jesuits, Jansenism was supported by the philosopher Pascal and Antoine Arnauld (a theologian linked with the abbey of Port Royal). Jansenists were excommunicated 1719.

Janus in Roman mythology, the god of doorways and passageways, patron of the beginning of the day, month, and year, after whom January is named; he is represented as having two faces, one looking forward and one back. In Roman ritual, the doors of Janus in the Forum were closed when peace was established.

Japan (*Nippon*)

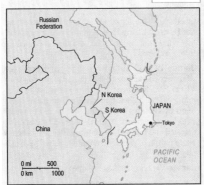

area 145,822 sq mi/377,535 sq km
capital Tokyo
cities Fukuoka, Kitakyushu, Kyoto, Sapporo; ports Osaka, Nagoya, Yokohama, Kobe, Kawasaki
physical mountainous, volcanic; comprises over 1,000 islands, the largest of which are Hokkaido, Honshu, Kyushu, and Shikoku
features Mount Fuji, Mount Aso (volcanic), Japan Alps, Inland Sea archipelago
head of state (figurehead) Emperor Akihito (Heisei) from 1989
head of government Morihito Hosokawa from 1993
political system liberal democracy
political parties Liberal Democratic Party (LDP), right of center; New Japan party, centrist; Social Democratic Party of Japan (SDJP), former Socialist Party, left of center; Komeito (Clean Government Party), Buddhist, centrist; Democratic Socialist Party, centrist; Japanese Communist Party (JCP), socialist; Nihon Shinto, centrist reformist; Shinsei, right-wing reformist
exports televisions, cassette and video recorders, radios, cameras, computers, robots, other electronic and electrical equipment, motor vehicles, ships, iron, steel, chemicals, textiles
currency yen
population (1992) 124,310,000; growth rate 0.5% p.a.
life expectancy men 76, women 82 (1989)
language Japanese
religions Shinto, Buddhist (often combined), Christian; 30% claim a personal religious faith
literacy 99% (1989)
GDP $3,674.5 bn (1992)

chronology
1867 End of shogun rule; executive power passed to emperor. Start of modernization of Japan.
1894–95 War with China; Formosa (Taiwan) and S Manchuria gained.
1902 Formed alliance with Britain.
1904–05 War with Russia; Russia ceded southern half of Sakhalin.
1910 Japan annexed Korea.
1914 Joined Allies in World War I.
1918 Received German Pacific islands as mandates.
1931–32 War with China; renewed 1937.
1941 Japan attacked US fleet at Pearl Harbor Dec 7.
1945 World War II ended with Japanese surrender. Allied control commission took power. Formosa and Manchuria returned to China.
1946 Framing of "peace constitution." Emperor Hirohito became figurehead ruler.
1952 Full sovereignty regained.
1958 Joined United Nations.
1968 Bonin and Volcano Islands regained.
1972 Ryukyu Islands regained.
1974 Prime Minister Tanaka resigned over Lockheed bribes scandal.
1982 Yasuhiro Nakasone elected prime minister.
1985 Yen revalued.
1987 Noboru Takeshita chosen to succeed Nakasone.
1988 Recruit scandal cast shadow over government and opposition parties.
1989 Emperor Hirohito (Shōwa) died; succeeded by his son Akihito. Many cabinet ministers implicated in Recruit scandal and Takeshita resigned; succeeded by Sosuke Uno. Aug: Uno resigned after sex scandal; succeeded by Toshiki Kaifu.
1990 Feb: new house of councillors' elections won by LDP. Public-works budget increased by 50% to encourage imports.
1991 Japan contributed billions of dollars to the Gulf War and its aftermath. Kaifu succeeded by Kiichi Miyazawa.
1992 Over 100 politicians implicated in new financial scandal. Emperor Akihito made first Japanese imperial visit to China. Trade surpluses reached record levels.
1993 Worst recession of postwar era; trade surpluses, however, again reached record levels. Government lost no-confidence vote over electoral reform; general election in July results in defeat of LDP after 38 years in power. Morihito Hosokawa of New Japan Party forms governing coalition.

Japan country in NE Asia, occupying a group of islands of which the four main ones are Hokkaido, Honshu, Kyushu, and Shikoku. Japan is situated between the Sea of Japan (to the W) and the N Pacific (to the E), E of North and South Korea.

Japanese art the painting, sculpture, and design of Japan. Early Japanese art was influenced by China. Painting later developed a distinct Japanese character, bolder and more angular, with the spread of Zen Buddhism in the 12th century. Ink painting and calligraphy flourished, followed by book illustration and decorative screens. Japanese prints developed in the 17th century, with multicolor prints invented around 1765. Buddhist sculpture proliferated from 580, and Japanese sculptors excelled at portraits. Japanese pottery stresses simplicity.

Japan Current or *Kuroshio* warm ocean ◊current flowing from Japan to North America.

Jaruzelski Wojciech 1923– . Polish general, communist leader from 1981, president 1985–90. He imposed martial law for the first year of his rule, suppressed the opposition, and banned labor-union activity, but later released many political prisoners. In 1989, elections in favor of the free labor union Solidarity forced Jaruzelski to speed up democratic reforms, overseeing a transition to a new form of "socialist pluralist" democracy and stepping down as president 1990.

Jarvik 7 the first successful artificial heart intended for permanent implantation in a human being. Made from polyurethane plastic and aluminum, it is powered by compressed air. Barney Clark became the first person to receive a Jarvik 7, in Salt Lake City, Utah, in Dec 1982; it kept him alive for 112 days.

The US Food and Drug Administration subsequently withdrew approval for artificial heart transplants because of evidence of adverse reactions.

jasmine any subtropical plant of the genus *Jasminum* of the olive family Oleaceae, with fragrant white or yellow flowers, and yielding jasmine oil, used in perfumes. The common jasmine *J. officinale* has pure white flowers; the Chinese winter jasmine *J. nudiflorum* has bright yellow flowers that appear before the leaves.

Jason in Greek legend, the leader of the Argonauts who sailed in the *Argo* to Colchis in search of the ◊Golden Fleece. He eloped with ◊Medea, daughter of the king of Colchis, who had helped him achieve his goal, but later deserted her.

Jat member of an ethnic group living in Pakistan and N India, and numbering about 11 million; they are the largest group in N India. The Jat are predominantly farmers. They speak Punjabi, a language belonging to the Iranian branch of the Indo-European family. They are thought to be related to the Romany people.

jaundice yellow discoloration of the skin and whites of the eyes caused by an excess of bile pigment in the bloodstream. Mild jaundice is common in newborns, but a serious form occurs in rhesus disease (see ◊rhesus factor).

Java or *Jawa* most important island of Indonesia, situated between Sumatra and Bali
area (with the island of Madura) 51,000 sq mi/132,000 sq km
capital Jakarta (also capital of Indonesia)
cities ports include Surabaya and Semarang
physical about half the island is under cultivation, the rest being thickly forested. Mountains and sea breezes keep temperatures down, but humidity is

Japanese art Bando Hikozaburo *(c. 1850) by Kunisada Utagawa, private collection.*

high, with heavy rainfall from Dec to March
features a chain of mountains, some of which are volcanic, runs along the center, rising to 9,000 ft/2,750 m. The highest mountain, Semeru (12,060 ft/3,676 m), is in the E
products rice, coffee, cocoa, tea, sugar, rubber, quinine, teak, petroleum
population (with Madura; 1989) 107,513,800, including people of Javanese, Sundanese, and Madurese origin, with differing languages
religion predominantly Muslim
history fossilized early human remains (*Homo erectus*) were discovered 1891–92. In central Java there are ruins of magnificent Buddhist monuments and of the Sivaite temple in Prambanan. The island's last Hindu kingdom, Majapahit, was destroyed about 1520 and followed by a number of short-lived Javanese kingdoms. The Dutch East India company founded a factory 1610. Britain took over during the Napoleonic period, 1811–16, and Java then reverted to Dutch control. Occupied by Japan 1942–45, Java then became part of the republic of ◊Indonesia.

Javanese member of the largest ethnic group in the Republic of Indonesia. There are more than 50 million speakers of Javanese, which belongs to the western branch of the Austronesian family. Although the Javanese have a Hindu-Buddhist heritage, they are today predominantly Muslim, practicing a branch of Islam known as *Islam Jawa*, which contains many Sufi features.

javelin spear used in athletics events. The men's javelin is about 8.5 ft/260 cm long, weighing 28 oz/800 g; the women's 7.5 ft/230 cm long, weighing 21 oz/600 g. It is thrown from a scratch line at the end of a run-up. The center of gravity on the men's javelin was altered 1986 to reduce the vast distances (100 yd/90 m) that were being thrown.

jaw one of two bony structures that form the framework of the mouth in all vertebrates except lampreys and hagfishes (the agnathous or jawless vertebrates). They consist of the upper jawbone (maxilla), which is fused to the skull, and the lower jawbone (mandible), which is hinged at each side to the bones of the temple by ◊ligaments.

Jefferson The 3rd president of the United States of America, Thomas Jefferson, a Democratic Republican 1801–09.

jay any of several birds of the crow family Corvidae, generally brightly colored and native to Eurasia and the Americas. In the Eurasian common jay *Garrulus glandarius*, the body is fawn with patches of white, blue, and black on the wings and tail.

Jay John 1745–1829. US diplomat and jurist, a member of the Continental Congress 1774–89 and its president 1779. With Benjamin Franklin and John Adams, he negotiated the Peace of Paris 1783, which concluded the American Revolution. President Washington named him first chief justice of the US 1789. He negotiated Jay's Treaty with England 1795, averting another war. He was governor of New York 1795–1801.

jazz polyphonic, syncopated music characterized by solo virtuosic improvisation, which developed in the US at the turn of the 20th century. Initially music for dancing, often with a vocalist, it had its roots in black American and other popular music. As jazz grew increasingly complex and experimental, various distinct forms evolved. Seminal musicians include Louis Armstrong, Charlie Parker, and John Coltrane.

jazz dance dance based on African techniques and rhythms, developed by black Americans around 1917. It entered mainstream dance in the 1920s, mainly in show business, and from the 1960s the teachers and choreographers Matt Mattox and Luigi expanded its vocabulary. Contemporary choreographers as diverse as Jerome ◊Robbins and Alvin Ailey used it in their work.

Jefferson Thomas 1743–1826. 3rd president of the US 1801–09, founder of the Democratic Republican Party. He published *A Summary View of the Rights of America* 1774 and as a member of the Continental Congresses of 1775–76 was largely responsible for the drafting of the ◊Declaration of Independence. He was governor of Virginia 1779–81, ambassador to Paris 1785–89, secretary of state 1789–93, and vice president 1797–1801.

Jefferson City capital of Missouri, located in the central part of the state, W of St Louis, on the Mississippi River; population (1990) 35,500. Industries include agricultural products, shoes, electrical appliances, and cosmetics.

Jeffreys Alec John 1950– . British geneticist who discovered the DNA probes necessary for accurate

◊genetic fingerprinting so that a murderer or rapist could be identified by, for example, traces of blood, tissue, or semen.

Jehol former name for the city of Chengde in NE Hebei province, N China.

Jehosophat 4th king of Judah *c.* 873–849 BC; he allied himself with Ahab, king of Israel, in the war against Syria.

Jehovah also *Jahweh* in the Old Testament the name of God, revealed to Moses; in Hebrew texts of the Old Testament the name was represented by the letters YHVH (without the vowels "a o a") as it was regarded as too sacred to be pronounced.

Jehovah's Witness member of a religious organization originating in the US 1872 under Charles Taze Russell (1852–1916). Jehovah's Witnesses attach great importance to Christ's second coming, which Russell predicted would occur 1914, and which Witnesses still believe is imminent. All Witnesses are expected to take part in house-to-house preaching; there are no clergy.

Jehu king of Israel *c.* 842–815 BC. He led a successful rebellion against the family of ◊Ahab and was responsible for the death of Jezebel.

jellyfish marine invertebrate of the phylum Cnidaria (coelenterates) with an umbrella-shaped body composed of a semitransparent gelatinous substance, with a fringe of stinging tentacles. Most adult jellyfishes move freely, but during parts of their life cycle many are polyplike and attached. They feed on small animals that are paralyzed by stinging cells in the jellyfishes' tentacles.

Jenner Edward 1749–1823. English physician who pioneered vaccination. In Jenner's day, smallpox was a major killer. His discovery 1796 that inoculation with cowpox gives immunity to smallpox was a great medical breakthrough. He coined the word "vaccination" from the Latin word for cowpox, *vaccina*.

Jeremiah 7th–6th century BC. Old Testament Hebrew prophet, whose ministry continued 626–586 BC. He was imprisoned during ◊Nebuchadnezzar's siege of Jerusalem on suspicion of intending to desert to the enemy. On the city's fall, he retired to Egypt.

Jericho Israeli-administered city in Jordan, N of the Dead Sea. It was settled by 8000 BC, and by 6000 BC had become a walled city with 2,000 inhabitants. In the Old Testament it was the first Canaanite stronghold captured by the Israelites, and its walls, according to the Book of ◊Joshua, fell to the blast of Joshua's trumpets. Successive archeological excavations since 1907 show that the walls of the city were destroyed many times.

Jeroboam 10th century BC. First king of Israel *c.* 922–901 BC after it split away from the kingdom of Judah.

Jerome, St *c.* 340–420. One of the early Christian leaders and scholars known as the Fathers of the Church. His Latin versions of the Old and New Testaments form the basis of the Roman Catholic Vulgate. He is usually depicted with a lion. Feast day Sept 30.

Jersey largest of the ◊Channel Islands; capital St Helier; area 45 sq mi/117 sq km; population (1990) 57,500.

It is governed by a lieutenant-governor representing the English crown and an assembly. Jersey cattle were originally bred here. Jersey gave its name to a woolen garment.

Jet Propulsion

jet propulsion Two
forms of jet engine.

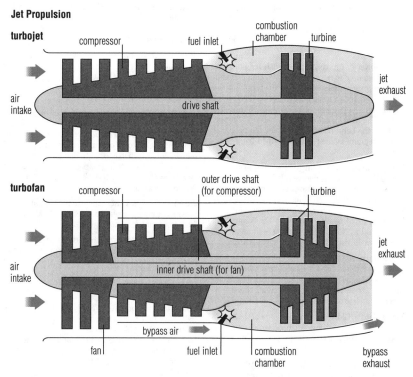

turbojet

combustion
chamber

compressor   fuel inlet   turbine

jet
exhaust

air
intake

drive shaft

turbofan

outer drive shaft
(for compressor)

compressor   turbine

jet
exhaust

air
intake

inner drive shaft (for fan)

bypass air

fan   fuel inlet   combustion   bypass
                               chamber   exhaust

Jersey City city of NE New Jersey; population (1990) 228,500. It faces Manhattan Island, to which it is connected by tunnels.

Jerusalem ancient city of Palestine, divided 1948 between Jordan and the new republic of Israel; area (pre-1967) 14.5 sq mi/37.5 sq km, (post-1967) 42 sq mi/108 sq km, including areas of the West Bank; population (1989) 500,000, about 350,000 Israelis and 150,000 Palestinians. In 1950 the western New City was proclaimed as the Israeli capital, and, having captured from Jordan the eastern Old City 1967, Israel affirmed 1980 that the united city was the country's capital; the United Nations does not recognize the claim.

Jesuit member of the largest and most influential Roman Catholic religious order (also known as the *Society of Jesus*) founded by Ignatius ◊Loyola 1534, with the aims of protecting Catholicism against the Reformation and carrying out missionary work. During the 16th and 17th centuries Jesuits were missionaries in Japan, China, Paraguay, and among the North American Indians. The order had (1991) about 29,000 members (15,000 priests plus students and lay members), and their schools and universities are renowned.

Jesus *c.* 4 BC–AD 29 or 30. Hebrew preacher on whose teachings Christianity was founded. According to the accounts of his life in the four Gospels, he was born in Bethlehem, Palestine, son of God and the Virgin Mary, and brought up by Mary and her husband Joseph as a carpenter in Nazareth. After adult baptism, he gathered 12 disciples, but his preaching antagonized the Roman authorities and he was executed by crucifixion. Three days later there came reports of his resurrection and, later, his ascension to heaven.

jet hard, black variety of lignite, a type of coal. It is cut and polished for use in jewelry and ornaments. Articles made of jet have been found in Bronze Age tombs.

jeté (French "thrown") in dance, a jump from one foot to the other. A *grand jeté* is a big jump in which the dancer pushes off on one foot, holds a brief pose in midair, and lands lightly on the other foot.

jetfoil advanced type of ◊hydrofoil boat built by Boeing, propelled by water jets. It features horizontal, fully submerged hydrofoils fore and aft and has a sophisticated computerized control system to maintain its stability in all waters.

jet lag the effect of a sudden switch of time zones in air travel, resulting in tiredness and feeling "out of step" with day and night. In 1989 it was suggested that use of the hormone melatonin helped to lessen the effect of jet lag by resetting the body clock. See also ◊circadian rhythm.

jet propulsion method of propulsion in which an object is propelled in one direction by a jet, or stream of gases, moving in the other. This follows from Isaac ◊Newton's third law of motion: "To every action, there is an equal and opposite reaction." The most widespread application of the jet principle is in the jet engine, the most common kind of aircraft engine.

Jet Propulsion Laboratory NASA installation at Pasadena, California, operated by the California Institute of Technology. It is the command center for NASA's deep-space probes such as the ◊Voyager, ◊Magellan, and ◊Galileo missions, with which it communicates via the Deep Space Network of radio telescopes at Goldstone, California; Madrid, Spain; and Canberra, Australia.

jet stream narrow band of very fast wind (velocities of over 95 mph/150 kph) found at altitudes of 6–10 mi/10–16 km in the upper troposphere or lower stratosphere. Jet streams usually occur about the latitudes of the Westerlies (35°–60°).

Jew follower of ◊Judaism, the Jewish religion. The term is also used to refer to those who claim descent from the ancient Hebrews, a Semitic people of the Middle East. Today, some may recognize their ethnic heritage but not practice the religious or cultural traditions. The term came into use in medieval Europe, based on the Latin name for Judeans, the people of Judah. Prejudice against Jews is termed ◊anti-Semitism.

Jewish-American writing US writing in English shaped by the Jewish experience. It was produced by the children of Eastern European Immigrants who came to the US at the end of the 19th century, and by the 1940s second- and third-generation Jewish-American writers had become central to US literary and intellectual life. Nobel Prize-winning authors include Saul Bellow 1976 and Isaac Bashevis Singer 1978.

Jew's harp musical instrument consisting of a two-pronged metal frame inserted between the teeth, and a springlike tongue plucked with the finger. The resulting drone excites resonances in the mouth that can be varied in pitch to produce a melody.

Jezebel in the Old Testament, daughter of the king of Sidon. She married King Ahab of Israel, and was brought into conflict with the prophet Elijah by her introduction of the worship of Baal.

Jiang Qing or **Chiang Ching** 1914–1991. Chinese communist politician, third wife of the party leader Mao Zedong. In 1960 she became minister for culture, and played a key role in the 1966–69 Cultural Revolution as the leading member of the Shanghai-based Gang of Four, who attempted to seize power 1976. Jiang was imprisoned 1981.

Jiangsu or **Kiangsu** province on the coast of E China
area 39,449 sq mi/102,200 sq km
capital Nanjing
features the swampy mouth of the river Chang Jiang; the special municipality of Shanghai
products cereals, rice, tea, cotton, soybeans, fish, silk, ceramics, textiles, coal, iron, copper, cement
population (1990) 67,057,000
history Jiangsu was originally part of the Wu kingdom, and Wu is still a traditional local name for the province. Jiangsu's capture by Japan in 1937 was an important step in that country's attempt to conquer China.

Jiangxi or **Kiangsi** province of SE China
area 63,613 sq mi/164,800 sq km
capital Nanchang
products rice, tea, cotton, tobacco, porcelain, coal, tungsten, uranium
population (1990) 37,710,000
history the province was Mao Zedong's original base in the first phase of the Communist struggle against the Nationalists.

Jiang Zemin 1926–   . Chinese political leader, state president 1993–   .
He succeeded ◊Zhao Ziyang as Communist Party leader after the Tiananmen Square massacre of 1989. Jiang is a cautious proponent of economic reform who held with unswerving adherence to the party's "political line."

Jiddah or **Jedda** port in Hejaz, Saudi Arabia, on the E shore of the Red Sea; population (1986) 1,000,000. Industries include cement, steel, and oil refining. Pilgrims pass through here on their way to Mecca.

Jilin or **Kirin** province of NE China in central ◊Manchuria
area 72,182 sq mi/187,000 sq km
capital Changchun
population (1990) 24,659,000.

Jim Crow the systematic practice of segregating black Americans, which was common in the South until the 1960s. *Jim Crow laws* are laws designed to deny civil rights to blacks or to enforce the policy of segregation, which existed until Supreme Court decisions and civil-rights legislation of the 1950s and 1960s (Civil Rights Act 1964, Voting Rights Act 1965) denied their legality.

Jinan or **Tsinan** city and capital of Shandong province, China; population (1989) 2,290,000. It has food-processing and textile industries.

jingoism blinkered, war-mongering patriotism. The term originated in 1878, when the British prime minister Disraeli developed a pro-Turkish policy, which nearly involved the UK in war with Russia. His supporters' war song included the line "We don't want to fight, but by jingo if we do."

Jinnah Mohammed Ali 1876–1948. Indian politician, Pakistan's first governor-general from 1947. He was president of the ◊Muslim League 1916, 1934–48, and by 1940 was advocating the need for a separate state of Pakistan; at the 1946 conferences in London he insisted on the partition of British India into Hindu and Muslim states.

Jinsha Jiang river that rises in SW China and forms the ◊Chang Jiang (Yangtze) at Yibin.

jive energetic American dance that evolved from the jitterbug, popular in the 1940s and 1950s; a forerunner of rock and roll.

Joan of Arc, St 1412–1431. French military leader. In 1429 at Chinon, NW France, she persuaded Charles VII that she had a divine mission to expel the occupying English from N France (see ◊Hundred Years' War) and secure his coronation. She raised the siege of Orléans, defeated the English at Patay, north of Orléans, and Charles was crowned in Reims. However, she failed to take Paris and was captured May 1430 by the Burgundians, who sold her to the English. She was found guilty of witchcraft and heresy by a tribunal of French ecclesiastics who supported the English. She was burned to death at the stake in Rouen May 30, 1431. In 1920 she was canonized.

Job *c.* 5th century BC. In the Old Testament, Hebrew leader who in the **Book of Job** questioned God's infliction of suffering on the righteous while enduring great sufferings himself.

Jodrell Bank site in Cheshire, England, of the Nuffield Radio Astronomy Laboratories of the University of Manchester. Its largest instrument is the 250 ft/76 m radio dish (the Lovell Telescope), completed 1957 and modified 1970. A 125 × 82 ft/38 × 25 m elliptical radio dish was introduced 1964, capable of working at shorter wave lengths.

Joffre Joseph Jacques Césaire 1852–1931. Marshal of France during World War I. He was chief of general staff 1911. The German invasion of Belgium 1914 took him by surprise, but his stand at the Battle of the ◊Marne resulted in his appointment as supreme commander of all the French armies 1915. His failure to make adequate preparations at Verdun 1916 and the military disasters on the ◊Somme led to his replacement by Nivelle in Dec 1916.

Johannesburg largest city of South Africa, situated on the Witwatersrand River in Transvaal; population (1985) 1,609,000. It is the center of a large gold-mining industry; other industries include engineering works, meat-chilling plants, and clothing factories.

John Elton. Adopted name of Reginald Kenneth Dwight 1947– . English pop singer, pianist, and composer, noted for his melodies and elaborate costumes and glasses. His best-known LP, *Goodbye Yellow Brick Road* 1973, includes the hit "Bennie and the Jets." His output is prolific and his hits continued intermittently into the 1990s; for example, "Nikita" 1985.

John II 1319–1364. King of France from 1350. He was defeated and captured by the Black Prince at Poitiers 1356 and imprisoned in England. Released 1360, he failed to raise the money for his ransom and returned to England 1364, where he died.

John XXII 1249–1334. Pope 1316–34. He spent his papacy in Avignon, France, engaged in a long conflict with the Holy Roman emperor, Louis of Bavaria, and the Spiritual Franciscans, a monastic order who preached the absolute poverty of the clergy.

John XXIII Angelo Giuseppe Roncalli 1881–1963. Pope from 1958. He improved relations with the USSR in line with his encyclical *Pacem in Terris/Peace on Earth* 1963, established Roman Catholic hierarchies in newly emergent states, and summoned the Second Vatican Council, which reformed church liturgy and backed the ecumenical movement.

John III Sobieski 1624–1696. King of Poland from 1674. He became commander in chief of the army 1668 after victories over the Cossacks and Tatars. A victory over the Turks 1673 helped to get him elected to the Polish throne, and he saved Vienna from the besieging Turks 1683.

John I 1357–1433. King of Portugal from 1385. An illegitimate son of Pedro I, he was elected by the Cortes (parliament). His claim was supported by an English army against the rival king of Castile, thus establishing the Anglo-Portuguese Alliance 1386. He married Philippa of Lancaster, daughter of John of Gaunt.

John IV 1603–1656. King of Portugal from 1640. Originally duke of Braganza, he was elected king when the Portuguese rebelled against Spanish rule. His reign was marked by a long war against Spain, which did not end until 1668.

John Bull imaginary figure who is a personification of England, similar to the American Uncle Sam. He is represented in cartoons and caricatures as a prosperous farmer of the 18th century.

John Paul II Karol Wojtyla 1920– . Pope from 1978, the first non-Italian to be elected pope since 1522. He was born near Kraków, Poland. He has upheld the tradition of papal infallibility and has condemned artificial contraception, women priests, married priests, and modern dress for monks and nuns—views that have aroused criticism from liberalizing elements in the church.

Johns Jasper 1930– . US painter and printmaker who rejected the abstract in favor of such simple subjects as flags, maps, and numbers. He uses pigments mixed with wax (encaustic) to create a rich surface with unexpected delicacies of color.

Johns Zero Through Nine *(1961), Tate Gallery, London.*

He has also created collages and lithographs.

Born in Augusta, Georgia, he moved to New York City in 1952. In the 1960s his works became more abstract before veering toward abstract expressionism in the mid-1970s. He was influenced by Marcel ◊Duchamp.

John, St 1st century AD. New Testament apostle. Traditionally, he wrote the fourth Gospel and the Johannine Epistles (when he was bishop of Ephesus), and the Book of Revelation (while exiled to the Greek island of Patmos). His emblem is an eagle; his feast day Dec 27.

Johnson Alvin Saunders 1874–1971. US social scientist and educator. He was a founder and an editor of the *New Republic* 1917. Joining with some of America's greatest scholars, Johnson was one of the founders of the New School for Social Research in New York City, serving as its director 1923–45. Johnson's memoir, *Progress: An Autobiography*, was published 1952.

Johnson Andrew 1808–1875. 17th president of the US 1865–69, a Democrat. He was a congressman from Tennessee 1843–53, governor of Tennessee 1853–57, senator 1857–62, and vice president 1865. He succeeded to the presidency on Lincoln's assassination (April 15, 1865). His conciliatory policy to the defeated South after the Civil War involved him in a feud with the Radical Republicans, culminating in his impeachment 1868 before the Senate, which failed to convict him by one vote.

Johnson Earvin ("Magic") 1959– . US basketball player. He played 1979–91 for the Los Angeles Lakers, winners of the National Basketball Association (NBA) championship 1980, 1982, 1985, 1987, and 1988. He was named the NBA's most valuable player 1980, 1982, and 1987. He played in the 1992 All-Star game and in the victorious 1992 US Olympic basketball team in Barcelona, Spain. He retired 1991 after discovering that he had HIV virus.

Johnson Jack 1878–1968. US heavyweight boxer. He overcame severe racial prejudice to become the first black heavyweight champion of the world 1908 when he traveled to Australia to challenge Tommy Burns. The US authorities wanted Johnson "dethroned" because of his color but could not find suitable challengers until 1915, when he lost the title in a dubious fight decision to the giant Jess Willard.

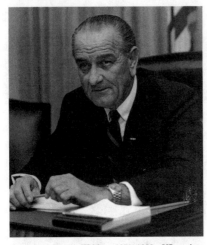

Johnson Lyndon B Johnson became president of the US after Kennedy's assassination in 1963.

Johnson James Weldon 1871–1938. US writer, lawyer, diplomat, and social critic. He was a strong supporter of Theodore Roosevelt and served him and Taft as US consul in Venezuela and Nicaragua 1906–12. He was editor of *New York Age* 1912–22 and was active in the National Association for the Advancement of Colored People (NAACP). As poet and anthropologist, he became one of the chief figures of the Harlem Renaissance of the 1920s. His autobiography *Along This Way* was published 1933.

Johnson Lyndon Baines 1908–1973. 36th president of the US 1963–69, a Democrat. He was elected to Congress 1937–49 and the Senate 1949–60. Born in Texas, he brought critical Southern support as J F Kennedy's vice-presidential running mate 1960, and became president on Kennedy's assassination. After the ◊Tonkin Gulf Incident, which escalated US involvement in the ◊Vietnam War, support won by Johnson's Great Society legislation (civil rights, education, alleviation of poverty) dissipated, and he declined to run for reelection 1968.

Johnson Philip (Cortelyou) 1906– . US architect who coined the term "international style." Originally designing in the style of ◊Mies van der Rohe, he later became an exponent of ◊Post-Modernism. He designed the giant AT&T building in New York 1978, a pink skyscraper with a Chippendale-style cabinet top.

Johnson Samuel, known as "Dr Johnson," 1709–1784. English lexicographer, author, and critic, also a brilliant conversationalist and the dominant figure in 18th-century London literary society. His *Dictionary*, published 1755, remained authoritative for over a century, and is still remarkable for the vigor of its definitions. In 1764 he founded the Literary Club, whose members included the painter Joshua Reynolds, the political philosopher Edmund Burke, the playwright Oliver Goldsmith, the actor David Garrick, and James ◊Boswell, Johnson's biographer.

Johnson City city in NE Tennessee, just below the Virginia border, in the Appalachian Mountains NE of Knoxville; population (1990) 49,400. Industries include tobacco, furniture, building materials, metals, textiles, and food processing.

Johnston Joseph Eggleston 1807–1891. US military leader during the American Civil War 1861–65. Joining the Confederacy, he commanded the Army of Ten-

nessee 1863. After the war, Johnston returned to private life, later serving in the US House of Representatives 1879–81 and as federal railroad commissioner 1887–91.

Johnstown city in SW Pennsylvania, on the Conemaugh River, E of Pittsburgh; population (1990) 28,100. Industries include steel, coal and coal byproducts, chemicals, building materials, and clothing. Johnstown was the victim of disastrous floods 1889.

John the Baptist, St *c.* 12 BC–*c.* AD 27. In the New Testament, an itinerant preacher. After preparation in the wilderness, he proclaimed the coming of the Messiah and baptized Jesus in the river Jordan. He was later executed by ◊Herod Antipas at the request of Salome, who demanded that his head be brought to her on a platter.

joint in any animal with a skeleton, a point of movement or articulation. In vertebrates, it is the point where two bones meet. Some joints allow no motion (the sutures of the skull), others allow a very small motion (the sacroiliac joints in the lower back), but most allow a relatively free motion. Of these, some allow a gliding motion (one vertebra of the spine on another), some have a hinge action (elbow and knee), and others allow motion in all directions (hip and shoulder joints), by means of a ball-and-socket arrangement. The ends of the bones at a moving joint are covered with cartilage for greater elasticity and smoothness, and enclosed in an envelope (capsule) of tough white fibrous tissue lined with a membrane which secretes a lubricating and cushioning ◊synovial fluid. The joint is further strengthened by ligaments.

In invertebrates with an ◊exoskeleton, the joints are places where the exoskeleton is replaced by a more flexible outer covering, the arthrodial membrane, which allows the limb (or other body part) to bend at that point.

Joliet city in NE Illinois, on the Des Plaines River, SW of Chicago; seat of Will County; population (1990) 76,800.

It is a center for barge traffic. Industries include building materials, chemicals, oil refining, heavy construction machinery, and paper. The city is named after the explorer Louis Joliet.

Joliet (or *Jolliet*) Louis 1645–1700. French-born Canadian explorer. He and Jesuit missionary Jacques ◊Marquette were the first to successfully chart the course of the Mississippi River down to its junction with the Arkansas River. They returned to Canada by way of the Illinois territory.

Joliot-Curie Irène (born Curie) 1897–1956 and Frédéric (born Joliot) 1900–1958. French physicists who made the discovery of artificial radioactivity, for which they were jointly awarded the 1935 Nobel Prize for Chemistry.

Jolson Al. Adopted name of Asa Yoelson 1886–1950. Russian-born US singer and entertainer. Popular in Broadway theater and vaudeville, he was chosen to star in the first talking picture, *The Jazz Singer* 1927.

Jolson, who got his start in vaudeville, was also a popular recording star.

Jonah 7th century BC. Hebrew prophet whose name is given to a book in the Old Testament. According to this, he fled by ship to evade his mission to prophesy the destruction of Nineveh. The crew threw him overboard in a storm, as a bringer of ill fortune, and he spent three days and nights in the belly of a whale before coming to land.

Jonathan Chief (Joseph) Leabua 1914–1987. Lesotho politician. A leader in the drive for independence, Jonathan became prime minister of Lesotho in 1965. His rule was ended by a coup in 1986.

Jones Inigo 1573–*c.* 1652. English Classical architect. Born in London, he studied in Italy and was influenced by the works of Palladio. He was employed by James I to design scenery for Ben Jonson's masques. He designed the Queen's House, Greenwich, 1616–35 and his English Renaissance masterpiece, the Banquet House in Whitehall, London, 1619–22.

Jones John Luther "Casey" 1864–1900. US railroad engineer and folk hero. His death on the "Cannonball Express," while on an overnight run 1900, is the subject of popular legend. Colliding with a stalled freight train, he ordered his fireman to jump to safety and rode the "Cannonball" to his death. The folk song "Casey Jones" is an account of the event.

Jonestown commune of the *People's Temple Sect*, NW of Georgetown, Guyana, established 1974 by the American Jim Jones (1933–1978), who originally founded the sect among San Francisco's black community. After a visiting US congressman was shot dead, Jones enforced mass suicide on his followers by instructing them to drink cyanide; 914 died, including over 240 children.

jonquil species of small daffodil *Narcissus jonquilla*, family Amaryllidaceae, with yellow flowers. Native to Spain and Portugal, it is cultivated elsewhere.

Jonson Ben(jamin) 1572–1637. English dramatist, poet, and critic. *Every Man in his Humour* 1598 established the English "comedy of humors," in which each character embodies a "humor," or vice, such as greed, lust, or avarice. This was followed by *Cynthia's Revels* 1600 and *Poetaster* 1601. His first extant tragedy is *Sejanus* 1603, with Burbage and Shakespeare as members of the original cast. The plays of his middle years include *Volpone, or The Fox* 1606, *The Alchemist* 1610, and *Bartholomew Fair* 1614.

Joplin city in SW Missouri, W of Springfield; population (1990) 41,000. Industries include zinc and lead smelting, leather goods, and furniture.

Joplin Janis 1943–1970. US blues and rock singer, born in Texas. She was lead singer with the San Francisco group Big Brother and the Holding Company 1966–68. Her biggest hit, Kris Kristofferson's "Me and Bobby McGee," was released on the posthumous *Pearl* LP 1971.

She died of a drug overdose.

Joplin Scott 1868–1917. US ♭ragtime pianist and composer, active in Chicago. His "Maple Leaf Rag" 1899 was the first instrumental sheet music to sell a million copies, and "The Entertainer," as the theme tune of the film *The Sting* 1973, revived his popularity. He was an influence on Jelly Roll Morton and other early jazz musicians.

Jordaens Jacob 1593–1678. Flemish painter, born in Antwerp. His style follows Rubens, whom he assisted

---

Jordan

Hashemite Kingdom of
(*Al Mamlaka al Urduniya al Hashemiyah*)

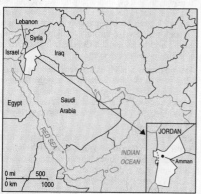

area 34,434 sq mi/89,206 sq km (West Bank 2,269 sq mi/5,879 sq km)
capital Amman
cities Zarqa, Irbid, Aqaba (the only port)
physical desert plateau in E; rift valley separates E and W banks of the river Jordan
features lowest point on Earth below sea level in the Dead Sea (–1,299 ft/–396 m); archeological sites at Jerash and Petra
head of state King Hussein ibn Talai from 1953
head of government Mudar Badran from 1989
political system constitutional monarchy
political parties none
exports potash, phosphates, citrus, vegetables
currency Jordanian dinar
population (1992) 3,636,000; West Bank (1988) 866,000; growth rate 3.6% p.a.

life expectancy men 67, women 71
languages Arabic (official), English
religions Sunni Muslim 92%, Christian 8%
literacy 71% (1988)
GDP $4.3 bn (1987); $1,127 per head (1988)

chronology
1946 Independence achieved from Britain as Transjordan.
1949 New state of Jordan declared.
1950 Jordan unilaterally annexed West Bank.
1953 Hussein ibn Talai officially became king of Jordan.
1958 Jordan and Iraq formed Arab Federation that ended when the Iraqi monarchy was deposed.
1967 Following Jordanian military offensive, Israel captured and occupied West Bank. Martial law imposed.
1976 Lower house dissolved, political parties banned, elections postponed until further notice.
1982 Hussein tried to mediate in Arab-Israeli conflict.
1984 Women voted for the first time.
1985 Hussein and Yassir Arafat put forward framework for Middle East peace settlement. Secret meeting between Hussein and Israeli prime minister.
1988 Hussein announced decision to cease administering the West Bank as part of Jordan, passing responsibility to Palestine Liberation Organization, and the suspension of parliament.
1989 Prime Minister Zaid al-Rifai resigned; Hussein promised new parliamentary elections following criticism of economic policies. Riots over price increases up to 50% following fall in oil revenues. First parliamentary elections for 22 years; Muslim Brotherhood won 25 of 80 seats but exiled from government; martial law lifted; Mudar Badran appointed prime minister.
1990 Hussein unsuccessfully tried to mediate after Iraq's invasion of Kuwait. Massive refugee problems as thousands fled to Jordan from Kuwait and Iraq.
1991 24 years of martial law ended; ban on political parties lifted.
1993 King Hussein publicly distanced himself from Iraqi leader Saddam Hussein. Abdul-Salam-al-Mujali appointed as new prime minister. Peace accord with Israel.

in various commissions. Much of his work is exuberant and on a large scale, including scenes of peasant life, altarpieces, portraits, and mythological subjects.

Jordan river rising on Mount Hermon, Syria, at 1,800 ft/ 550 m above sea level and flowing S for about 200 mi/320 km via the Sea of Galilee to the Dead Sea, 1,290 ft/390 m below sea level. It occupies the northern part of the Great Rift Valley; its upper course forms the boundary of Israel with Syria and the kingdom of Jordan; its lower course runs through Jordan; the West Bank has been occupied by Israel since 1967.

Jordan country in SW Asia, bounded N by Syria, NE by Iraq, E, SE and S by Saudi Arabia, S by the Gulf of Aqaba, and W by Israel. *See panel p. 503*

Jordan Michael 1963– . US basketball player. Playing for the Chicago Bulls 1984–93, he led them to NBA championship 1991, 1992 and 1993. As a rookie he led the National Basketball Association (NBA) in points scored (2,313). During the 1986–87 season he scored 3,000 points, the second player in NBA history to do so. He unexpectedly retired after the 1993 championship.

Joseph in the New Testament, the husband of the Virgin Mary, a descendant of King David of the Tribe of Judah, and a carpenter by trade. Although Jesus was not the son of Joseph, Joseph was his legal father. According to Roman Catholic tradition, he had a family by a previous wife, and was an elderly man when he married Mary.

Joseph in the Old Testament, the 11th and favorite son of ◊Jacob, sold into Egypt by his jealous half brothers. After he had risen to power there, they and his father joined him to escape from famine in Canaan.

Joseph Chief c. 1840–1904. American Indian chief of the Nez Percé people. After initially agreeing to leave tribal lands 1877, he later led his people in armed resistance. Defeated, Joseph ordered a mass retreat to Canada, but the Nez Percé were soon caught by General Nelson Miles. They were sent to the Colville Reservation, Washington 1885.

Joseph II 1741–1790. Holy Roman emperor from 1765, son of Francis I (1708–1765). The reforms he carried out after the death of his mother, ◊Maria Theresa, in 1780, provoked revolts from those who lost privileges.

Josephine Marie Josèphe Rose Tascher de la Pagerie 1763–1814. As wife of ◊Napoleon Bonaparte, she was empress of France 1804–1809. Born on Martinique, she married in 1779 Alexandre de Beauharnais, who played a part in the French Revolution, and in 1796 Napoleon, who divorced her in 1809 because she had not produced children.

Joseph of Arimathaea, St 1st century AD. In the New Testament, a wealthy Hebrew, member of the Sanhedrin (supreme court), and secret supporter of Jesus. On the evening of the Crucifixion he asked the Roman procurator Pilate for Jesus' body and buried it in his own tomb. Feast day March 17.

Josephson Brian 1940– . British physicist, a leading authority on superconductivity. In 1973 he shared a Nobel Prize for his theoretical predictions of the properties of a supercurrent through a tunnel barrier (the Josephson effect), which led to the development of the Josephson junction.

Josephson junction device used in "superchips" (large and complex integrated circuits) to speed the passage of signals by a phenomenon called "electron tunneling."

Although these superchips respond a thousand times faster than the ◊silicon chip, they have the disadvantage that the components of the Josephson junctions operate only at temperatures close to ◊absolute zero. They are named after English theoretical physicist Brian Josephson.

Josephus Flavius AD 37–c. 100. Jewish historian and general, born in Jerusalem. He became a Pharisee and commanded the Jewish forces in Galilee in their revolt against Rome from AD 66 (which ended with the mass suicide at Masada). When captured, he gained the favor of the Roman emperor Vespasian and settled in Rome as a citizen. He wrote *Antiquities of the Jews*, an early history to AD 66; *The Jewish War*, and an autobiography.

Joshua 13th century BC. In the Old Testament, successor of Moses, who led the Jews in their return to and conquest of the land of Canaan. The city of Jericho was the first to fall—according to the Book of Joshua, the walls crumbled to the blast of his trumpets.

joule SI unit (symbol J) of work and energy, replacing the ◊calorie (one joule equals 4.2 calories).

It is defined as the work done (energy transferred) by a force of one newton acting over one meter and equal to 10^7 ergs. It can also be expressed as the work done in one second by a current of one ampere at a potential difference of one volt. One ◊watt is equal to one joule per second.

Joule James Prescott 1818–1889. English physicist whose work on the relations between electrical, mechanical, and chemical effects led to the discovery of the first law of ◊thermodynamics.

Joule–Kelvin effect in physics, the fall in temperature of a gas as it expands adiabatically (without loss or gain of heat to the system) through a narrow jet. It can be felt when, for example, compressed air escapes through the valve of an inflated bicycle tire. Only hydrogen does not exhibit the effect. It is the basic principle of most refrigerators.

journeyman a man who served his apprenticeship in a trade and worked as a fully qualified employee. The term originated in the regulations of the medieval trade ◊guilds; it derives from the French *journée* ("a day") because journeymen were paid daily.

Joyce James (Augustine Aloysius) 1882–1941. Irish writer, born in Dublin, who revolutionized the form of the English novel with his "stream of consciousness" technique. His works include *Dubliners* 1914 (short stories), *Portrait of the Artist as a Young Man* 1916, *Ulysses* 1922, and *Finnegans Wake* 1939.

joystick in computing, an input device that signals to a computer the direction and extent of displacement of a hand-held lever. It is similar to the joystick used to control the flight of an aircraft.

Juan Carlos 1938– . King of Spain. The son of Don Juan, pretender to the Spanish throne, he married Princess Sofia in 1962, eldest daughter of King Paul of Greece. In 1969 he was nominated by ◊Franco to succeed on the restoration of the monarchy intended to follow Franco's death; his father was excluded because of his known liberal views. Juan Carlos became king in 1975.

Juárez Benito 1806–1872. Mexican politician, president 1861–65 and 1867–72. In 1861 he suspended repayments of Mexico's foreign debts, which prompted a joint French, British, and Spanish expedition to exert pressure. French forces invaded and created an empire for ◊Maximilian, brother of the Austrian emperor. After their withdrawal in 1867, Maximilian was executed, and Juárez returned to the presidency.

He won popularity for nationalizing church property in his first year in office. He was the first Indian (non-Spanish) president of Mexico.

Judah or **Judea** district of S Palestine. After the death of King Solomon 937 BC, Judah adhered to his son Rehoboam and the Davidic line, whereas the rest of Israel elected Jeroboam as ruler of the northern kingdom. In New Testament times, Judah was the Roman province of Judea, and in current Israeli usage it refers to the southern area of the West Bank.

Judaism: history

c. 2000 BC	Led by Abraham, the ancient Hebrews emigrated from Mesopotamia to Canaan.
18th century–1580	Some settled on the borders of Egypt and were put to forced labor.
13th century	They were rescued by Moses, who aimed at their establishment in Palestine. Moses received the Ten Commandments from God and brought them to the people. The main invasion of Canaan was led by Joshua about 1274.
12th–11th centuries	During the period of Judges, ascendancy was established over the Canaanites. *c.* 1000. Complete conquest of Palestine and the union of all Judea was achieved under David, and Jerusalem became the capital.
10th century	Solomon succeeded David and enjoyed a reputation for great wealth and wisdom; but his lack of a constructive policy led, after his death, to the secession of the north of Judea (Israel) under Jeroboam, with only the tribe of Judah remaining under the house of David as the southern kingdom of Judah.
9th–8th centuries	Assyria became the dominant power in the Middle East. Israel purchased safety by tribute, but the basis of the society was corrupt, and prophets such as Amos, Isaiah, and Micah predicted destruction. At the hands of Tiglathpileser and his successor Shalmaneser IV, the northern kingdom (Israel) was made into Assyrian provinces after the fall of Samaria 721, although the southern kingdom of Judah was spared as an ally.
586–458	Nebuchadnezzar took Jerusalem and carried off the major part of the population to Babylon. Judaism was retained during exile, and was reconstituted by Ezra on the return to Jerusalem.
520	The Temple, originally built by Solomon, was restored. *c.* 444 Ezra promulgated the legal code that was to govern the future of the Jewish people.
4th–3rd centuries	After the conquest of the Persian Empire by Alexander the Great, the Syrian Seleucid rulers and the Egyptian Ptolemaic dynasty struggled for Palestine, which came under the government of Egypt, although with a large measure of freedom.
2nd century	With the advance of Syrian power, Antiochus IV attempted intervention in the internal quarrels of the Hebrews, even desecrating the Temple, and a revolt broke out 165 led by the Maccabee family.
63	Judea's near-independence ended when internal dissension caused the Roman general Pompey to intervene, and Roman suzerainty was established.
1st century AD	A revolt led to the destruction of the Temple 66–70 by the Roman emperor Titus. Judean national sentiment was encouraged by the work of Rabbi Johanan ben Zakkai (*c.*20–90), and following him the president of the Sanhedrin (supreme court) was recognized as the patriarch of Palestinian Jewry.
2nd–3rd centuries	Greatest of the Sanhedrin presidents was Rabbi Judah (*c.* 135–220), who codified the traditional law in the *Mishna*. The Palestinian *Talmud* (*c.* 375) added the *Gemara* to the *Mishna*.
4th–5th centuries	The intellectual leadership of Judaism passed to the descendants of the 6th-century exiles in Babylonia, who compiled the Babylonian *Talmud*.
8th–13th centuries	Judaism enjoyed a golden era, producing the philosopher Saadiah, the poet Jehudah Halevi (*c.* 1075–1141), the codifier Moses Maimonides, and others.
14th–17th centuries	Where Christianity became the dominant or state religion, the Jews were increasingly segregated from mainstream life and trade by the Inquisition, anti-Semitic legislation, or by expulsion. The Protestant and Islamic states, and their colonies, allowed for refuge. Persecution led to messianic hopes, strengthened by the 16th-century revival of Kabbalism, culminating in the messianic movement of Shabbatai Sevi in the 17th century.
18th–19th centuries	Outbreaks of persecution increased with the rise of European nationalism. Reform Judaism, a rejection of religious orthodoxy and an attempt to interpret it for modern times, began in Germany 1810 and soon was established in England and the US. In the late 19th century, large numbers of Jews fleeing persecution (*pogrom*) in Russia and E Europe emigrated to the US, leading to the development of large Orthodox, Conservative, and Reform communities there. Many became Americanized and lost interest in religion.
20th century	Zionism (founded 1896) is a nationalist movement dedicated to achieving a secure homeland where the Jewish people would be free from persecution; this led to the establishment of the state of Israel 1948. Liberal Judaism (more radical than Reform) developed in the US. In 1911 the first synagogue in the UK was founded. The Nazi German regime 1933–45 exterminated 6 million European Jews. Hundreds of thousands of survivors take refuge with preexisting Jewish settlements in what eventually became the new state of Israel. Although most Israeli and American Jews were not affiliated with synagogues after the 1950s, they continued to affirm their Jewish heritage. Both Orthodox and Hasidic Judaism, however, flourished in their new homes and grew rapidly in the 1970s and 1980s.

Judaism the religion of the ancient Hebrews and their descendants the Jews, based, according to the Old Testament, on a covenant between God and Abraham about 2000 BC, and the renewal of the covenant with Moses about 1200 BC. It rests on the concept of one eternal invisible God, whose will is revealed in the *Torah* and who has a special relationship with the Jewish people. The Torah comprises the first five books of the Bible (the Pentateuch), which contains the history, laws, and guide to life for correct behavior. Besides those living in Israel, there are large Jewish populations today in the US, the former USSR (mostly Russia, Ukraine, Belarus, and Moldova), the UK and Commonwealth nations, and in Jewish communities throughout the world. There are approximately 18 million Jews, with about 9 million in the Americas, 5 million in Europe, and 4 million in Asia, Africa, and the Pacific.

Judas Iscariot 1st century AD. In the New Testament, the disciple who betrayed Jesus Christ. Judas was the treasurer of the group. At the last Passover supper, he arranged, for 30 pieces of silver, to point out Jesus to the chief priests so that they could arrest him. Afterward Judas was overcome with remorse and committed suicide.

Jude, St 1st century AD. Supposed half brother of Jesus and writer of the Epistle of Jude in the New Testament; patron saint of lost causes. Feast day Oct 28.

judicial review in the US, the power of a court to decide whether legislative acts or executive actions are constitutional. The ultimate authority for judicial review is the Supreme Court, which established its right to review executive and legislative actions in the ◊*Marbury* v *Madison* decision.

judiciary in constitutional terms, the system of courts and body of judges in a country. The independence of the judiciary from other branches of the central authority is generally considered to be an essential feature of a democratic political system. This independence is often written into a nation's constitution and protected from abuse by politicians.

Judith in Biblical legend, a Jewish widow, the heroine of Bethulia, who saved her community from a Babylonian siege by killing the enemy general Holofernes. The Book of Judith is part of the Apocrypha, a section of the Old Testament. Her story is much represented in Western art.

judo (Japanese *jūdo*, "gentle way") form of wrestling of Japanese origin. The two combatants wear loose-fitting, belted jackets and trousers to facilitate holds, and falls are broken by a square mat; when one has established a painful hold that the other cannot break, the latter signifies surrender by slapping the ground with a free hand. Degrees of proficiency are indicated by the color of the belt: for novices, white; after examination, brown (three degrees); and finally, black (nine degrees).

Judson Edward Zane Carroll, better known by his adopted name "Ned Buntline" 1823–1886. US author. Specializing in short adventure stories, he developed a stereotyped frontier hero in the pages of his own periodicals *Ned Buntline's Magazine* and *Buntline's Own*. In his dime novels in the 1870s, he immortalized Buffalo Bill Cody.

Juggernaut or *Jagannath* a name for Vishnu, the Hindu god, meaning "Lord of the World." His temple is in Puri, Orissa, India. A statue of the god, dating from about 318, is annually carried in procession on a large vehicle (hence the word "juggernaut"). Devotees formerly threw themselves beneath its wheels.

jugular vein one of two veins in the necks of vertebrates; they return blood from the head to the superior (or anterior) vena cava and thence to the heart.

jujitsu or *jujutsu* traditional Japanese form of self-defense; the modern form is ◊judo.

Julian *the Apostate* c. 331–363. Roman emperor. Born in Constantinople, the nephew of Constantine the Great, he was brought up as a Christian but early in life became a convert to paganism. Sent by Constantius to govern Gaul in 355, he was proclaimed emperor by his troops in 360, and in 361 was marching on Constantinople when Constantius' death allowed a peaceful succession. He revived pagan worship and refused to persecute heretics. He was killed in battle against the Persians of the Sassanid empire.

Juliana 1909– . Queen of the Netherlands 1948–80. The daughter of Queen Wilhelmina (1880–1962), she married Prince Bernhard of Lippe-Biesterfeld in 1937. She abdicated 1980 and was succeeded by her daughter ◊Beatrix.

Julius II 1443–1513. Pope 1503–13. A politician who wanted to make the Papal States the leading power in Italy, he formed international alliances first against Venice and then against France. He began the building of St Peter's Church in Rome 1506 and was the patron of the artists Michelangelo and Raphael.

July Revolution revolution July 27–29, 1830, in France that overthrew the restored Bourbon monarchy of Charles X and substituted the constitutional monarchy of Louis Philippe, whose rule (1830–48) is sometimes referred to as the July Monarchy.

jumbo jet popular name for a generation of huge wide-bodied airliners including the *Boeing 747*, which is 232 ft/71 m long, has a wingspan of 196 ft/60 m, a maximum takeoff weight of nearly 400 tons, and can carry more than 400 passengers.

Juneau ice-free port and state capital of Alaska, on Gastineau Channel in the S Alaska panhandle; population (1980) 19,528. Juneau is the commercial and distribution center for the fur-trading and mining of the Panhandle region; also important are salmon fishing, fish processing, and lumbering.

juneberry or *serviceberry* any tree or shrub of the genus *Amelanchier* of the rose family, having simple leaves, showy white flowers, and purple-black fruits. The Allegheny serviceberry *A. laevis*, native to the NE US, grows to a height of 40 ft/12 m and has edible fruit. Several species are grown as ornamentals.

Jung Carl Gustav 1875–1961. Swiss psychiatrist who collaborated with Sigmund ◊Freud until their disagreement in 1912 over the importance of sexuality in

Jupiter Jupiter, the largest planet in the Solar System, together with four of its moons: Io, Europa, Ganymede, and Callisto.

causing psychological problems. Jung studied religion and dream symbolism, saw the unconscious as a source of spiritual insight, and distinguished between introversion and extroversion. His books include *Modern Man in Search of a Soul* 1933.

jungle popular name for ◊rain forest.

juniper aromatic evergreen tree or shrub of the genus *Juniperus* of the cypress family Cupressaceae, found throughout temperate regions. Its berries are used to flavor gin. Some junipers are erroneously called ◊cedars.

junk bond derogatory term for a security officially rated as "below investment grade." It is issued in order to raise capital quickly, typically to finance a takeover to be paid for by the sale of assets once the company is acquired. Junk bonds have a high yield, but are a high-risk investment.

In the US securities market, junk bonds probably diminish since they must now pay an average of more than 5% more than the prevailing treasury bond rate in order to attract investors. Studies suggest that more than 35% of junk-bond issues may default.

Junkers Hugo 1859–1935. German airplane designer. In 1919 he founded in Dessau the aircraft works named after him. Junkers planes, including dive bombers, night fighters, and troop carriers, were used by the Germans in World War II.

Juno in Roman mythology, the principal goddess, identified with the Greek ◊Hera. The wife of Jupiter and queen of heaven, she was concerned with all aspects of women's lives.

Jupiter or *Jove* in Roman mythology, the chief god, identified with the Greek ◊Zeus. He was god of the sky, associated with lightning and thunderbolts; protector in battle; and bestower of victory. The son of Saturn, he married his sister Juno, and reigned on Mount Olympus as lord of heaven. His most famous temple was on the Capitoline Hill in Rome.

Jupiter the fifth planet from the Sun, and the largest in the Solar System (equatorial diameter 88,700 mi/142,800 km), with a mass more than twice that of all the other planets combined, 318 times that of the Earth's. It takes 11.86 years to orbit the Sun, at an average distance of 484 million mi/778 million km, and has at least 16 moons. It is largely composed of hydrogen and helium, liquefied by pressure in its interior, and probably with a rocky core larger than the Earth. Its main feature is the Great Red Spot, a cloud of rising gases, revolving counterclockwise, 8,500 mi/14,000 km wide and some 20,000 mi/30,000 km long.

Jura Mountains series of parallel mountain ranges running SW–NE along the French-Swiss frontier between the rivers Rhône and Rhine, a distance of 156 mi/250 km. The highest peak is ***Crête de la Neige***, 5,650 ft/1,723 m.

Jurassic period of geological time 208–146 million years ago; the middle period of the Mesozoic era. Climates worldwide were equable, creating forests of conifers and ferns; dinosaurs were abundant, birds evolved, and limestones and iron ores were deposited.

jurisprudence the science of law in the abstract— that is, not the study of any particular laws or legal system, but of the principles upon which legal systems are founded.

jury body of lay people (usually 12, sometimes 6) sworn to decide the facts of a case and reach a verdict in a court of law. Juries, used mainly in English-speak-

ing countries, are implemented primarily in criminal cases, but also sometimes in civil cases. The members of the jury are carefully selected by both prosecution and defense attorneys.

justification in printing and word processing, the arrangement of text so that it is aligned with either the left or right margin, or both.

Justinian I 483–565. Byzantine emperor from 527. He recovered N Africa from the Vandals, SE Spain from the Visigoths, and Italy from the Ostrogoths, largely owing to his great general Belisarius. He ordered the codification of Roman law, which has influenced European jurisprudence; he built the church of Sta Sophia in Constantinople, and closed the university in Athens in 529.

Justin, St *c.* 100–*c.* 163. One of the early Christian leaders and writers known as the Fathers of the Church. Born in Palestine of a Greek family, he was converted to Christianity and wrote two *Apologies* in its defense. He spent the rest of his life as an itinerant missionary, and was martyred in Rome. Feast day June 1.

Jute member of a Germanic people who originated in Jutland but later settled in Frankish territory. They occupied Kent, SE England, about 450, according to tradition under Hengist and Horsa, and conquered the Isle of Wight and the opposite coast of Hampshire in the early 6th century.

Jurassic Contorted Jurassic limestone strata in Jura, Switzerland.

jute fiber obtained from two plants of the genus *Corchorus* of the linden family: *C. capsularis* and *C. olitorius*. Jute is used for sacks and sacking, upholstery, webbing, twine, and stage canvas. The world's largest producer of jute is Bangladesh.

Jutland (Danish *Jylland*) peninsula of N Europe; area 11,400 sq mi/29,500 sq km. It is separated from Norway by the Skagerrak and from Sweden by the Kattegat, with the North Sea to the W. The larger N part belongs to Denmark, the S part to Germany.

Jutland, Battle of naval battle of World War I, fought between England and Germany on May 31, 1916, off the W coast of Jutland. Its outcome was indecisive, but the German fleet remained in port for the rest of the war.

Juvenal c. AD 60–140. Roman satirical poet. His 16 surviving satires give an explicit and sometimes brutal picture of the corrupt Roman society of his time. He may have lived in exile under the emperor Domitian, and remained very poor.

juvenile delinquency offenses against the law that are committed by young people. The American judicial system provides special status and treatment for juvenile offenders. Their identities are protected and their records barred from public view. Judicial proceedings are less formal than those of criminal courts. Incarceration may not extend beyond a defendant's majority. Sentencing is tailored to the developmental needs of defendants and may consist of probation, counseling, community service, supervision, or placement in homes for youthful offenders.

K symbol for *kelvin*, a scale of temperature.

K2 or *Chogori* second highest mountain above sea level, 28,261 ft, in/8,611 m the Karakoram range, Kashmir, N India. It was first climbed 1954 by an Italian expedition.

kabbala or *cabbala* (Hebrew "tradition") ancient esoteric Jewish mystical tradition of philosophy containing strong elements of pantheism yet akin to Neoplatonism. Kabbalistic writing reached its peak between the 13th and 16th centuries. It is largely rejected by current Judaic thought as medieval superstition, but is basic to the ◊Hassid sect.

kabuki drama originating in late 16th-century Japan, drawing on ◊Nō, puppet plays, and folk dance. Its colorful, lively spectacle became popular in the 17th and 18th centuries. Many kabuki actors specialize in particular types of character, female impersonators (*onnagata*) being the biggest stars.

Kabul capital of Afghanistan, 6,900 ft/2,100 m above sea level, on the river Kabul; population (1984) 1,179,300. Products include textiles, plastics, leather, and glass. It commands the strategic routes to Pakistan via the ◊Khyber Pass.

Kádár János 1912–1989. Hungarian Communist leader, in power 1956–88, after suppressing the national uprising. As Hungarian Socialist Workers' Party (HSWP) leader and prime minister 1956–58 and 1961–65, Kádár introduced a series of market-socialist economic reforms, while retaining cordial political relations with the USSR.

He was ousted as party general secretary May 1988 and forced into retirement May 1989.

Kafka Franz 1883–1924. Czech novelist, born in Prague, who wrote in German. His three unfinished allegorical novels *Der Prozess/The Trial* 1925, *Der Schloss/The Castle* 1926, and *Amerika/America* 1927 were posthumously published despite his instructions that they should be destroyed. His short stories include "Die Verwandlung/The Metamorphosis" 1915, in which a man turns into a huge insect. His vision of lonely individuals trapped in bureaucratic or legal labyrinths can be seen as a powerful metaphor for modern experience.

Kahn Louis 1901–1974. US architect, born in Estonia. A follower of Mies van de Rohe, he developed a Classically romantic style, in which functional "servant" areas, such as stairwells and air ducts, featured promi-

nently, often as towerlike structures surrounding the main living and working, or "served," areas. His projects are characterized by an imaginative use of concrete and brick and include the Salk Institute for Biological Studies, La Jolla, California, and the British Art Center at Yale University.

Kaifu Toshiki 1932– . Japanese conservative politician, prime minister 1989–91. A protégé of former premier Takeo Miki, he was selected as a compromise choice as Liberal Democratic Party (LDP) president and prime minister Aug 1989, following the resignation of Sosuke Uno. Kaifu resigned Nov 1991, having lost the support of important factional leaders in the LDP, and was replaced by Klichi Miyazawa.

Kaiser title formerly used by the Holy Roman emperors, Austrian emperors 1806–1918, and German emperors 1871–1918. The word, like the Russian "tsar," is derived from the Latin *Caesar*.

kakapo nocturnal, flightless parrot *Strigops habroptilus* that lives in burrows in New Zealand. It is green, yellow, and brown and weighs up to 7.5 lb/3.5 kg. When in danger, its main defense is to keep quite still. Because of the introduction of predators such as dogs, cats, rats, and ferrets, it is in danger of extinction, there being only about 40 birds left.

Kalahari Desert semidesert area forming most of Botswana and extending into Namibia, Zimbabwe, and South Africa; area about 347,400 sq mi/900,000 sq km. The only permanent river, the Okavango, flows into a delta in the NW forming marshes rich in wildlife. Its inhabitants are the nomadic Kung.

Kalamazoo city in SW Michigan, on the Kalamazoo River, SW of Lansing; seat of Kalamazoo County; population (1990) 80,300. Its industries include the processing of the area's agricultural products, automobile and transportation machinery parts, chemicals, and metal and paper products.

kale type of ◊cabbage.

Kalevala Finnish national epic poem compiled from legends and ballads by Elias Lönnrot 1835; its hero is Väinämöinen, god of music and poetry.

kakapo The kakapo is a nocturnal ground-living parrot of New Zealand.

Kandinsky
Battle/Cossacks
(1910), Tate Gallery,
London.

Kalgan city in NE China, now known as ◊Zhangjiakou.

Kali in Hindu mythology, the goddess of destruction and death. She is the wife of ◊Siva.

Kalimantan province of the republic of Indonesia occupying part of the island of Borneo
area 210,000 sq mi/543,900 sq km
cities Banjermasin and Balikpapan
physical mostly low-lying, with mountains in the N
products petroleum, rubber, coffee, copra, pepper, timber
population (1989 est) 8,677,500.

Kaltenbrunner Ernst 1901–1946. Austrian Nazi leader. After the annexation of Austria 1938 he joined police chief Himmler's staff, and as head of the Security Police (SD) from 1943 was responsible for the murder of millions of Jews (see the ◊Holocaust) and Allied soldiers in World War II. After the war, he was tried at Nuremberg for war crimes and hanged.

Kamchatka mountainous peninsula separating the Bering Sea and Sea of Okhotsk, forming (together with the Chukchi and Koryak national districts) a region of E Siberian Russia. Its capital, Petropavlovsk, is the only town; agriculture is possible only in the S. Most of the inhabitants are fishers and hunters.

Kamenev Lev Borisovich 1883–1936. Russian leader of the Bolshevik movement after 1917 who, with Stalin and Zinoviev, formed a ruling triumvirate in the USSR after Lenin's death 1924. His alignment with the Trotskyists led to his dismissal from office and from the Communist Party by Stalin 1926. Arrested 1934 after Kirov's assassination, Kamenev was secretly tried and sentenced, then retried, condemned, and shot 1936 for allegedly plotting to murder Stalin.

kamikaze pilots of the Japanese air force in World War II who deliberately crash-dived their planes, loaded with bombs, usually onto ships of the US Navy.

Kampala capital of Uganda, on Lake Victoria; population (1983) 455,000. It is linked by rail with Mom-

basa. Products include tea, coffee, textiles, fruit, and vegetables.

Kampuchea former name (1975–89) of ◊Cambodia.

Kandinsky Wassily 1866–1944. Russian painter, a pioneer of abstract art. Born in Moscow, he traveled widely, settling in Munich 1896. Around 1910 he produced the first known examples of purely abstract work in 20th-century art. He was an originator of the ◊Blaue Reiter movement 1911–12. From 1921 he taught at the ◊Bauhaus school of design. He moved to Paris 1933, becoming a French citizen 1939.

Kandy city in central Sri Lanka, on the Mahaweli River; capital of a district of the same name; population (1990) 104,000. Products include tea. One of the most sacred Buddhist shrines, the Dalada Maligawa, is situated in Kandy; it contains an alleged tooth of the Buddha.

kangaroo any marsupial of the family Macropodidae found in Australia, Tasmania, and New Guinea. Kangaroos are plant-eaters and most live in groups. They are adapted to hopping, the vast majority of species having very large back legs and feet compared with the small forelimbs. The larger types can jump 30 ft/9 m at a single bound. Most are nocturnal. Species vary from small rat kangaroos, only 1 ft/30 cm long, through the medium-sized wallabies, to the large red and great gray kangaroos, which are the largest living marsupials. These may be 5.9 ft/1.8 m long with 3.5 ft/1.1 m tails.

Ka Ngwane black homeland in Natal province, South Africa; population (1985) 392,800. It achieved self-governing status 1971.

Kankakee city in NE Illinois, on the Kankakee River, S of Chicago; seat of Kankakee County; population (1990) 27,600. It is a distribution center for corn. Industries also include building materials, furniture, pharmaceuticals, and farm machinery.

Kano capital of Kano state in N Nigeria, trade center of an irrigated area; population (1983) 487,100. Products include bicycles, glass, furniture, textiles, and chemicals. Founded about 1000 BC, Kano is a walled city, with New Kano extending beyond the walls.

Kanpur formerly *Cawnpore* capital of Kanpur district, Uttar Pradesh, India, SW of Lucknow, on the river Ganges; a commercial and industrial center (cotton, wool, jute, chemicals, plastics, iron, steel); population (1981) 1,688,000.

Kansas state in central US; nickname Sunflower State
area 82,296 sq mi/213,200 sq km
capital Topeka
cities Kansas City, Wichita, Overland Park
features Dodge City, once "cowboy capital of the world"; Eisenhower Center, Abilene; Fort Larned and Fort Scott; Pony Express station, Hanover; Wichita Cowtown, a frontier-era reproduction
products wheat, cattle, coal, petroleum, natural gas, aircraft, minerals
population (1990) 2,477,600
famous people Amelia Earhart; Dwight D Eisenhower; William Inge; Buster Keaton; Carry Nation; Charlie Parker
history explored by Francisco de Coronado for Spain 1541 and La Salle for France 1682; ceded to the US 1803 as part of the Louisiana Purchase.

The first permanent settlements were forts Leavenworth 1827, Scott 1842, and Riley 1853, outposts to protect the Santa Fe and Oregon trails. In the 1850s it was the scene of bloody warfare between pro- and antislavery settlers. It became a state 1861. By 1872 two railroads had crossed Kansas, and such towns as Dodge City and Abilene filled with cowboys driving cattle from Texas. Hardy winter wheat was brought to the state by Russian Mennonites. Kansas was hard hit by the Great Depression and dust-bowl soil erosion of the 1930s, but aircraft, oil, and gas industries provided the basis for economic recovery and expansion.

Kansas City city in Kansas, at the confluence of the Kansas and Missouri rivers, adjacent to Kansas City, Missouri; population (1990) 149,800. Food processing, electronics, and automobile-assembly plants are here, as well as the University of Kansas Medical Center. It was laid out in 1857 as Wyandotte and expanded in 1886.

Kansas City city in Missouri, at the confluence of the Kansas and Missouri rivers, adjacent to Kansas City, Kansas; population (1990) 435,100. Industries include steel and electronics manufactures, motor-vehicle assembly, and oil refining, and it is the financial, marketing, and distribution center of the region. The University of Missouri-Kansas City and the Kansas City Art Institute are among the schools here. The site was settled as a trading post by French fur trappers in 1821. It was dominated by boss Tom Pendergast (Democrat) in the 1920s and 1930s, and under his "protection" jazz musicians such as Lester Young, Count Basie, and Charlie Parker performed. Crown Center, a gigantic office, condominium, and shopping complex was completed in the 1970s.

Kant Immanuel 1724–1804. German philosopher who believed that knowledge is not merely an aggregate of sense impressions but is dependent on the conceptual apparatus of the human understanding, which is itself not derived from experience. In ethics, Kant argued that right action cannot be based on feelings or inclinations but conforms to a law given by reason, the *categorical imperative*.

Kanto flat, densely populated region of E Honshu Island, Japan; area 12,505 sq mi/32,377 sq km; population (1988) 37,867,000. The chief city is Tokyo.

kangaroo The great grey kangaroo may reach a weight of 200 lb/90 kg and a height of over 5 ft/1.5 m.

kaolinite or *kaolin* ◊clay mineral, hydrous aluminum silicate, $Al_2Si_2O_5(OH)_4$, formed mainly by the chemical weathering of ◊feldspar. It is important in the manufacture of porcelain and other ceramics, paper, rubber, paint, textiles, and medicines. It is mined in France, the UK, Germany, China, and the US.

kapok silky hairs that surround the seeds of certain trees, particularly the *kapok tree Bombax ceiba* of India and Malaysia, and the *silk-cotton tree Ceiba pentandra*, a native of tropical America. Kapok is used for stuffing cushions and mattresses and for sound insulation; oil obtained from the seeds is used in food and soap preparation.

Karachi largest city and chief seaport of Pakistan, and capital of Sind province, NW of the Indus delta; population (1981) 5,208,000. Industries include engineering, chemicals, plastics, and textiles. It was the capital of Pakistan 1947–59.

Karakoram mountain range in central Asia, divided among China, Pakistan, and India. Peaks include K2, Masharbrum, Gasharbrum, and Mustagh Tower. *Ladakh* subsidiary range is in NE Kashmir on the Tibetan border.

Karamanlis Constantinos 1907– . Greek politician of the New Democracy Party. A lawyer and an anticommunist, he was prime minister Oct 1955–March 1958, May 1958–Sept 1961, and Nov 1961–June 1963 (when he went into self-imposed exile because of a military coup). He was recalled as prime minister on the fall of the regime of the "colonels" in July 1974, and was president 1980–85.

karaoke amateur singing in public to prerecorded backing tapes. Karaoke originated in Japan and spread to other parts of the world in the 1980s. Karaoke machines are jukeboxes of backing tracks to well-known popular songs, usually with a microphone attached and lyrics displayed on a video screen.

karat or *carat* the unit of purity in gold in the US. Pure gold is 24-karat; 22-karat (the purest used in jew-

Kansas

elry) is 22 parts gold and two parts alloy (to give greater strength).

karate one of the ◊martial arts. Karate is a type of unarmed combat derived from kempo, a form of the Chinese Shaolin boxing. It became popular in the West in the 1930s.

Karelia autonomous republic of NW Russia
area 66,550 sq mi/172,400 sq km
capital Petrozavodsk
cities Vyborg
physical mainly forested
features Lake Ladoga
products fishing, timber, chemicals, coal
population (1989) 792,000
history Karelia was annexed to Russia by Peter the Great 1721 as part of the grand duchy of Finland. In 1917 part of Karelia was retained by Finland when it gained its independence from Russia. The remainder became an autonomous region 1920 and an autonomous republic 1923 of the USSR. Following the wars of 1939–40 and 1941–44, Finland ceded 18,000 sq mi/46,000 sq km of Karelia to the USSR. Part of this territory was incorporated in the Russian Soviet Republic and part in the Karelian autonomous republic. A movement for the reunification of Russian and Finnish Karelia emerged in the late 1980s.

Karen member of a group of SE Asian peoples, numbering 1.9 million. They live in E Myanmar (formerly Burma), Thailand, and the Irrawaddy delta. Their language belongs to the Thai division of the Sino-Tibetan family. In 1984 the Burmese government began a large-scale military campaign against the Karen National Liberation Army (KNLA), the armed wing of the Karen National Union (KNU).

Karl-Marx-Stadt former name (1953–90) of Chemnitz, a city in Germany.

Karloff Boris. Adopted name of William Henry Pratt 1887–1969. English-born US actor best known for his work in the US. He achieved Hollywood stardom with his role as the monster in the film *Frankenstein* 1931. Several popular sequels followed as well as starring appearances in other horror films including *Scarface* 1932, *The Lost Patrol* 1934, and *The Body Snatcher* 1945.

karma (Sanskrit "fate") in Hinduism, the sum of a human being's actions, carried forward from one life to the next, resulting in an improved or worsened fate. Buddhism has a similar belief, except that no permanent personality is envisaged, the karma relating only to the physical and mental elements carried on from birth to birth, until the power holding them together disperses in the attainment of nirvana.

Karmal Babrak 1929– . Afghani communist politician, president 1979–86. In 1965 he formed what

became the banned People's Democratic Party of Afghanistan (PDPA) 1977. As president, with Soviet backing, he sought to broaden the appeal of the PDPA but encountered wide resistance from the ◊Mujaheddin Muslim guerrillas.

Karnataka formerly (until 1973) *Mysore* state in SW India
area 74,035 sq mi/191,800 sq km
capital Bangalore
products mainly agricultural; minerals include manganese, chromite, and India's only sources of gold and silver
population (1991) 44,817,400
language Kannada
famous people Hyder Ali, Tippu Sultan.

Karpov Anatoly 1951– . Russian chess player. He succeeded Bobby Fischer of the US as world champion 1975, and held the title until losing to Gary Kasparov 1985. He lost to Kasparov again in 1990.

Kashmir former part of Jammu state in the north of British India with a largely Muslim population, ruled by a Hindu maharajah, who joined it to the republic of India 1947. There was fighting between pro-India and pro-Pakistan factions, the former being the Hindu ruling class and the latter the Muslim majority, and open war between the two countries 1965–66 and 1971. It is today divided between the Pakistani area of Kashmir and the Indian state of ◊Jammu and Kashmir. Since 1990 it has been riven by Muslim separatist violence.

Kashmir Pakistan-occupied
area 30,445 sq mi/78,900 sq km, in the NW of the former state of Kashmir, now ◊Jammu and Kashmir. Azad ("free") Kashmir in the W has its own legislative assembly based in Muzaffarabad while Gilgit and Baltistan regions to the N and E are governed directly by Pakistan. The Northern Areas are claimed by India and Pakistan
population 1,500,000
cities Gilgit, Skardu
features W Himalayan peak Nanga Parbat 26,660 ft/8,126 m, Karakoram Pass, Indus River, Baltoro Glacier.

Kasparov Gary 1963– . Russian chess player. When he beat his compatriot Anatoly Karpov to win the world title 1985, he was the youngest ever champion at 22 years 210 days.

Katmai active volcano in Alaska, 6,715 ft/2,046 m. Its major eruption 1912 created the "Valley of Ten Thousand Smokes." Katmai National Park, area 6,922 sq mi/17,928 sq km, was designated 1980. The lake-filled crater formed from the eruption is lined with glaciers.

Katmandu or *Kathmandu* capital of Nepal; population (1981) 235,000. Founded in the 8th century on an ancient pilgrim and trade route from India to Tibet and China, it has a royal palace, Buddhist temples, and monasteries.

Katyn Forest forest near Smolensk, SW of Moscow, Russia, where 4,500 Polish officer prisoners of war (captured in the German-Soviet partition of Poland 1940) were shot; 10,000 others were killed elsewhere. In 1989 the USSR accepted responsibility for the massacre.

Kaunda Kenneth (David) 1924– . Zambian politician, president 1964–91. Imprisoned in 1958–60 as founder of the Zambia African National Congress, he became in 1964 the first prime minister of Northern Rhodesia, then the first president of independent

Zambia. In 1973 he introduced one-party rule. He supported the nationalist movement in Southern Rhodesia, now Zimbabwe, and survived a coup attempt 1980 thought to have been promoted by South Africa. He was elected chair of the Organization of African Unity 1987. In 1990 he was faced with wide antigovernment demonstrations, leading to the acceptance of a multiparty political system. He lost the first multiparty election, in Nov 1991, to Frederick Chiluba.

Kawabata Yasunari 1899–1972. Japanese novelist, translator of Lady ◊Murasaki, and author of *Snow Country* 1947 and *A Thousand Cranes* 1952. His novels are characterized by melancholy and loneliness. He was the first Japanese to win the Nobel Prize for Literature, in 1968.

Kawasaki industrial city (iron, steel, shipbuilding, chemicals, textiles) on Honshu Island, Japan; population (1990) 1,173,600.

Kaye Danny. Adopted name of David Daniel Kaminski 1913–1987. US actor, comedian, and singer. He appeared in many films, including *Wonder Man* 1944, *The Secret Life of Walter Mitty* 1946, and *Hans Christian Andersen* 1952.

Kayseri (ancient name *Caesarea Mazaca*) capital of Kayseri province, central Turkey; population (1990) 421,400. It produces textiles, carpets, and tiles. In Roman times it was capital of the province of Cappadocia.

Kazakh or *Kazak* member of a pastoral Kyrgyz people of Kazakhstan. Kazakhs also live in China (Xinjiang, Gansu, and Qinghai), Mongolia, and Afghanistan. There are 5–7 million speakers of Kazakh, a Turkic language belonging to the Altaic family. They are predominantly Sunni Muslim, although pre-Islamic customs have survived.

Kazakhstan country in central Asia, bounded N by Russia, W by the Caspian Sea, E by China, and S by Turkmenistan, Uzbekistan, and Kyrgyzstan.

Kazan capital of Tatarstan, central Russia, on the river Volga; population (1989) 1,094,000. It is a transport, commercial, and industrial center (engineering, oil refining, petrochemicals, textiles, large fur trade). Formerly the capital of a Tatar khanate, Kazan was captured by Ivan IV "the Terrible" 1552.

Kazan Elia 1909– . US stage and film director, a founder of the ◊Actors Studio 1947. Plays he directed include *The Skin of Our Teeth* 1942, *A Streetcar Named Desire* 1947, and *Cat on a Hot Tin Roof* 1955; films include *Gentlemen's Agreement* 1948, *East of Eden* 1954, and *The Visitors* 1972.

Kazantzakis Nikos 1885–1957. Greek writer whose works include the poem *I Odysseia/The Odyssey* 1938 (which continues Homer's *Odyssey*) and the novels *Zorba the Greek* 1946, *The Greek Passion* 1951, and *The Last Temptation of Christ* 1951.

kazoo simple wind instrument adding a buzzing quality to the singing voice on the principle of "comb and paper" music.

kcal symbol for *kilocalorie* (see ◊calorie).

Kearny Philip 1814–1862. US military leader. In 1859 he served in the army of Napoleon III in Italy and received the French Croix de Guerre for his actions. With the outbreak of the American Civil War 1861, Kearny returned to the US and was named brigadier general of the New Jersey militia. He was killed in action near Chantilly, Virginia.

Kearny Stephen Watts 1794–1848. US military leader. As brigadier general he was given command of the Army of the West 1846. During the Mexican War

Kazakhstan
Republic of

area 1,049,150 sq mi/2,717,300 sq km
capital Alma-Ata
cities Karaganda, Semipalatinsk, Petropavlovsk
physical Caspian and Aral seas, Lake Balkhash; Steppe region
features Baikonur Cosmodrome (space launch site at Tyuratam, near Baikonur)

head of state Nursultan Nazarbayev from 1990
head of government Sergey Tereshchenko from 1991
political system emergent democracy
political parties Independent Socialist Party of Kazakhstan (SPK)
products grain, copper, lead, zinc, manganese, coal, oil
population (1992) 17,008,000 (Kazakh 40%, Russian 38%, German 6%, Ukrainian 5%)
language Russian; Kazakh, related to Turkish
religion Sunni Muslim
chronology
1920 Autonomous republic in USSR.
1936 Joined the USSR and became a full union republic.
1950s Site of Nikita Khrushchev's ambitious "Virgin Lands" agricultural extension program.
1960s A large influx of Russian settlers turned the Kazakhs into a minority in their own republic.
1986 Riots in Alma-Alta after Mikhail Gorbachev ousted local communist leader.
1989 Nursultan Nazarbayev became leader of the Kazakh Communist Party (KCP) and instituted economic and cultural reform programs.
1990 Nazarbayev became head of state.
1991 March: support pledged for continued union with USSR; Aug: Nazarbayev condemned attempted anti-Gorbachev coup; KCP abolished and replaced by Independent Socialist Party of Kazakhstan. Dec: joined new Commonwealth of Independent States; independence recognized by US.
1992 Admitted into United Nations and Conference on Security and Cooperation in Europe. Trade agreement with US.
1993 New constitution adopted, increasing the authority of the president and making Kazakh the state language.

1846–48, he was the military governor of New Mexico and joined in the conquest of California 1847 becoming military governor.

Keating Paul 1954– . Australian politician, Labor Party (ALP) leader and prime minister from 1991. He was treasurer and deputy leader of the ALP 1983–91.

Keaton Buster (Joseph Frank) 1896–1966. US comedian, actor, and film director. After being a star in vaudeville, he took up a career in "Fatty" Arbuckle comedies, and became one of the great comedians of the silent film era, with an inimitable deadpan expression (the "Great Stone Face") masking a sophisticated acting ability. His films include *One Week* 1920, *The Navigator* 1924, *The General* 1927, and *The Cameraman* 1928.

Keats John 1795–1821. English Romantic poet who produced work of the highest quality and promise before dying at the age of 25. *Poems* 1817, *Endymion* 1818, the great odes (particularly "Ode to a Nightingale" and "Ode on a Grecian Urn" 1819), and the narratives "Lamia," "Isabella," and "The Eve of St Agnes" 1820, show his lyrical richness and talent for drawing on both Classical mythology and medieval lore.

Kefauver (Carey) Estes 1903–1963. US Democratic politician. He was elected to the US House of Representatives 1939 and served in the US Senate 1948 until his death. He was an unsuccessful candidate for the Democratic presidential nomination 1952 and 1956.

Keillor Garrison 1942– . US writer and humorist. His hometown Anoka, Minnesota, in the American Midwest, inspired his stories about Lake Wobegon, including *Lake Wobegon Days* 1985 and *Leaving Home* 1987, which often started as radio monologues about "the town that time forgot, that the decades cannot improve."

Keller Helen Adams 1880–1968. US author and campaigner for the blind. She became blind and deaf after an illness when she was only 19 months old, but the teaching of Anne Sullivan, her lifelong companion, enabled her to learn the names of objects and eventually to speak. Keller graduated with honors from Radcliffe College in 1904; published several books, including. *The Story of My Life* 1902; and toured the

world, lecturing to raise money for the blind. She was born in Alabama.

Kellogg Frank Billings 1856–1937. US political leader and diplomat. Elected to the US Senate 1916, he was appointed US ambassador to Great Britain by President Harding 1922 and secretary of state 1925. He formulated the Kellogg–Briand Pact 1927, the international antiwar resolution, for which he was awarded the Nobel Peace Prize 1929.

Kellogg–Briand pact agreement negotiated 1927 between the US and France to renounce war and seek settlement of disputes by peaceful means. It took its name from the US secretary of state Frank B Kellogg (1856–1937) and the French foreign minister Aristide Briand. Most other nations subsequently signed. Some successes were achieved in settling South American disputes, but the pact made no provision for measures against aggressors and became ineffective in the 1930s, with Japan in Manchuria, Italy in Ethiopia, and Hitler in central Europe.

Kells, Book of 8th-century illuminated manuscript of the Gospels produced at the monastery of Kells in County Meath, Ireland. It is now in Trinity College library, Dublin.

Kelly Gene (Eugene Curran) 1912– . US film actor, dancer, choreographer, and director. He was a major star of the 1940s and 1950s in a series of MGM musicals, including *On the Town* 1949, *An American in Paris* 1951, and *Singin' in the Rain* 1952.

He also acted in nonmusicals, such as *Marjorie Morningstar* 1958 and *Inherit the Wind* 1960.

Kelly Grace (Patricia) 1928–1982. US film actress who retired from acting after marrying Prince Rainier III of Monaco 1956. She starred in *High Noon* 1952, *The Country Girl* 1954, for which she received an Academy Award, and *High Society* 1955. She also starred in three Hitchcock classics—*Dial M for Murder* 1954, *Rear Window* 1954, and *To Catch a Thief* 1955.

keloid in medicine, overgrowth of fibrous tissue, usually produced at the site of a scar. Black skin produces more keloid than does white skin; it has a puckered appearance caused by clawlike offshoots. Surgical removal is often unsuccessful, because the keloid returns.

kelp collective name for large brown seaweeds, such as those of the Fucaceae and Laminariaceae families. Kelp is also a term for the powdery ash of burned seaweeds, a source of iodine.

Kelvin William Thomson, 1st Baron Kelvin 1824–1907. Irish physicist who introduced the *kelvin scale*, the absolute scale of temperature. His work on the conservation of energy 1851 led to the second law of ◊thermodynamics.

kelvin scale temperature scale used by scientists. It begins at ◊absolute zero (−273.15°C) and increases by the same degree intervals as the Celsius scale; that is, 0°C is the same as 273 K and 100°C is 373 K.

Kempis Thomas à. Medieval German monk and religious writer; see ◊Thomas à Kempis.

kendo Japanese armed ◊martial art in which combatants fence with bamboo replicas of samurai swords. Masks and padding are worn for protection. The earliest recorded reference to kendo is from AD 789.

Keneally Thomas (Michael) 1935– . Australian novelist who won the Booker Prize with *Schindler's Ark* 1982, a novel based on the true account of Polish Jews saved from the gas chambers in World War II by a German industrialist. Other works include *Woman of the Inner Sea* 1992.

Kennedy Anthony 1936– . US jurist, appointed associate justice of the US Supreme Court 1988. A conservative, he wrote the majority opinion in *Washington* v *Harper* 1990 that the administration of medication for mentally ill prisoners, without the prisoner's consent, is permissible.

Kennedy Edward (Moore) "Ted" 1932– . US Democratic politician. He aided his brothers John and Robert Kennedy in their presidential campaigns of 1960 and 1968 respectively, and entered politics as a senator from Massachusetts 1962. He failed to gain the presidential nomination 1980, largely because of questions about his delay in reporting an automobile crash at Chappaquiddick Island, near Cape Cod, Massachusetts, in 1969, in which his passenger, Mary Jo Kopechne, was drowned.

He is a spokesman for liberal causes including national health and gun control.

Kennedy John F(itzgerald) "Jack" 1917–1963. 35th president of the US 1961–63, a Democrat; the first Roman Catholic and the youngest person to be elected president. In foreign policy he carried through the unsuccessful ◊Bay of Pigs invasion of Cuba, and in 1963 secured the withdrawal of Soviet missiles from the island. His program for reforms at home, called the *New Frontier*, was posthumously executed by Lyndon Johnson. Kennedy was assassinated while on a visit to Dallas, Texas, on Nov 22, 1963, by Lee Harvey Oswald (1939–1963), who was within a few days shot dead by Jack Ruby (1911–1967).

He created the Peace Corps, volunteers who give various types of health, agricultural, and educational aid overseas, and he proposed the Alliance for Progress for aid to Latin America. In the view of many, style was more important than substance in the Kennedy White House, but he inspired a generation of idealists and created an aura of positive activism. His wit and charisma combined with political shrewdness to disarm many critics. A number of conspiracy theories have developed around the Kennedy assassination, which was investigated by a special commission headed by Chief Justice Earl ◊Warren. The commission determined that Oswald acted alone. Oswald was a malcontent who had gone to live in the USSR in 1959 and later returned. Ruby was a Dallas nightclub owner.

Kennedy Joseph Patrick 1888–1969. US industrialist and diplomat; ambassador to the UK 1937–40. A self-made millionaire, he ventured into the film industry, then set up the Securities and Exchange Commission (SEC) for F D Roosevelt. He groomed each of his sons—Joseph Patrick Kennedy Jr (1915–1944), John F ◊Kennedy, Robert ◊Kennedy, and Edward ◊Kennedy—for a career in politics. His eldest son, Joseph, was killed in action with the naval air force in World War II.

Kennedy Robert (Francis) 1925–1968. US Democratic politician and lawyer. He was presidential campaign manager for his brother John F ◊Kennedy 1960, and as attorney general 1961–64 pursued a racket-busting policy and promoted the Civil Rights Act of 1964. He was also a key aide to his brother. When John Kennedy's successor, Lyndon Johnson, preferred Hubert H Humphrey for the 1964 vice-presidential nomination, Kennedy resigned and was elected senator from New York. In 1968 he campaigned for the Democratic Party's presidential nomination, but during a campaign stop in California was assassi-

Kennedy The 35th president of the US, John F Kennedy, a Democrat, and the youngest person to hold the office.

nated by Sirhan Bissara Sirhan (1944–), a Jordanian.

Kennedy Space Center ◊NASA launch site on Merritt Island, near Cape Canaveral, Florida, used for Apollo and space-shuttle launches. The first flight to land on the Moon (1969) and *Skylab*, the first orbiting laboratory (1973), were launched here.

The Center is dominated by the Vehicle Assembly Building, 525 ft/160 m tall, used for assembly of ◊Saturn rockets and space shuttles. It is named for Pres John F Kennedy.

Kenneth I *MacAlpin* died 858. King of Scotland from *c.* 844. Traditionally, he is regarded as the founder of the Scottish kingdom (Alba) by virtue of his final defeat of the Picts about 844. He invaded Northumbria six times, and drove the Angles and the Britons over the river Tweed.

Kennewick city in SE Washington, on the Columbia River, SE of Seattle; population (1990) 42,200. Dams built on the Columbia and Snake rivers provide irrigation for the area's grape, sugar beet, alfalfa, and corn crops.

Kenosha (Indian "pike" or "pickerel") city in the SE corner of Wisconsin, on Lake Michigan, SE of Milwaukee, seat of Kenosha County; population (1980) 77,685. Its industries include food-processing equipment, fertilizers, motor vehicles, textiles and clothing, and food products.

Kent county in SE England, nicknamed the "garden of England"
area 1,440 sq mi/3,730 sq km
cities Maidstone (administrative headquarters), Canterbury, Chatham, Rochester, Sheerness, Tunbridge Wells; resorts: Folkestone, Margate, Ramsgate
features traditionally, a "man of Kent" comes from E of the Medway and a "Kentish man" from W Kent; New Ash Green, a new town; Romney Marsh; the Isles of Grain, Sheppey (on which is the resort of Sheerness, formerly a royal dockyard) and Thanet; Weald (agricultural area); rivers: Darent, Medway, Stour; Leeds Castle (converted to a palace by Henry VIII); Hever Castle (where Henry VIII courted Anne Boleyn); Chartwell (Churchill's country home), Knole, Sissinghurst Castle and gardens; the Brogdale Experimental Horticulture Station at Faversham has the world's finest collection of apple and other fruit trees; the former RAF Manston became Kent International Airport 1989

Kentucky

products hops, apples, soft fruit, coal, cement, paper
population (1991) 1,485,600
famous people Edward Heath, Christopher Marlowe.

Kentucky state in S central US; nickname Bluegrass State
area 40,414 sq mi/104,700 sq km
capital Frankfort
cities Louisville, Lexington, Owensboro, Covington, Bowling Green
features bluegrass country; horse racing at Louisville (Kentucky Derby); Mammoth Cave National Park (main cave 4 mi/6.5 km long, up to 125 ft/38 m high, where Indian councils were once held); Abraham Lincoln's birthplace at Hodgenville; Fort Knox, US gold-bullion depository
products tobacco, cereals, textiles, coal, whiskey, horses, transport vehicles
population (1990) 3,365,300
famous people Mohammed Ali, Daniel Boone, Louis D Brandeis, Kit Carson, Henry Clay, D W Griffith, Thomas Hunt Morgan, Harland "Colonel" Sanders, Robert Penn Warren
history Kentucky was the first region W of the Alleghenies settled by American pioneers. James Harrod founded Harrodsburg 1774; in 1775 Daniel Boone, who blazed his Wilderness Trail 1767, founded Boonesboro. Originally part of Virginia, Kentucky became a state 1792. Badly divided over the slavery question, the state was racked by guerrilla warfare and partisan feuds during the Civil War.

In 1900, Kentucky ranked first among Southern states in per-capita income, but wealth was divided unevenly, and the Great Depression of the 1930s hit hard; by 1940, Kentucky was last among states in per-capita income. Although it remains one of the poorest states, better roads, education, television, and government programs have relieved the isolation of its rural communities.

Kenya country in E Africa, bounded N by Sudan and Ethiopia, E by Somalia, SE by the Indian Ocean, SW by Tanzania, and W by Uganda.

Kenya
Republic of
(*Jamhuri ya Kenya*)

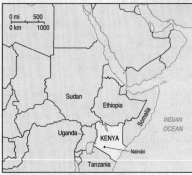

area 224,884 sq mi/582,600 sq km
capital Nairobi
cities Kisumu, port Mombasa
physical mountains and highlands in W and center; coastal plain in S; arid interior and tropical coast
environment the elephant faces extinction as a result of poaching
features Great Rift Valley, Mount Kenya, Lake Nakuru (salt lake with world's largest colony of flamingos), Lake Turkana (Rudolf), national parks with wildlife, Malindini Marine Reserve, Olduvai Gorge
head of state and government Daniel arap Moi from 1978
political system authoritarian nationalism
political parties Kenya African National Union (KANU), nationalist, centrist; National Democratic Party (NDP), centrist (launched 1991, not accepted by government)
exports coffee, tea, pineapples, petroleum products
currency Kenya shilling
population (1992) 26,985,000 (Kikuyu 21%, Luo 13%, Luhya 14%, Kelenjin 11%; Asian, Arab, European); growth rate 4.2% p.a.
life expectancy men 59, women 63 (1989)
languages Kiswahili (official), English; there are many local dialects
religions Protestant 38%, Roman Catholic 28%, indigenous beliefs 26%, Muslim 6%
literacy 50% (1988)
GDP $6.9 bn (1987); $302 per head (1988)

chronology
1895 British East African protectorate established.
1920 Kenya became a British colony.
1944 African participation in politics began.
1950 Mau Mau campaign began.
1953 Nationalist leader Jomo Kenyatta imprisoned by British authorities.
1956 Mau Mau campaign defeated, Kenyatta released.
1963 Achieved internal self-government, with Kenyatta as prime minister.
1964 Independence achieved from Britain as a republic within the Commonwealth, with Kenyatta as president.
1967 East African Community (EAC) formed with Tanzania and Uganda.
1977 Collapse of EAC.
1978 Death of Kenyatta. Succeeded by Daniel arap Moi.
1982 Attempted coup against Moi foiled.
1983 Moi reelected unopposed.
1984 Over 2,000 people massacred by government forces at Wajir.
1985–86 Thousands of forest villagers evicted and their homes destroyed to make way for cash crops.
1988 Moi reelected. 150,000 evicted from state-owned forests.
1989 Moi announced release of all known political prisoners. Confiscated ivory burned in attempt to stop elephant poaching.
1990 Despite antigovernment riots, Moi refused multiparty politics.
1991 Increasing demands for political reform; Moi promised multiparty politics.
1992 Constitutional amendment passed. Dec: Moi reelected in first direct elections despite allegations of fraud.

Kenyatta Jomo. Assumed name of Kamau Ngengi *c.* 1894–1978. Kenyan nationalist politician, prime minister from 1963, as well as the first president of Kenya from 1964 until his death. He led the Kenya African Union from 1947 (*KANU* from 1963) and was active in liberating Kenya from British rule.

Kepler Johannes 1571–1630. German mathematician and astronomer. He formulated what are now called *Kepler's laws* of planetary motion: (1) the orbit of each planet is an ellipse with the Sun at one of the foci; (2) the radius vector of each planet sweeps out equal areas in equal times; (3) the squares of the periods of the planets are proportional to the cubes of their mean distances from the Sun.

Kerala state of SW India, formed 1956 from the former princely states of Travancore and Cochin
area 15,015 sq mi/38,900 sq km
capital Trivandrum
features most densely populated, and most literate (60%), state of India; strong religious and caste divisions make it politically unstable
products tea, coffee, rice, oilseed, rubber, textiles, chemicals, electrical goods
population (1991) 29,011,200
languages Kannada, Malayalam, Tamil.

keratin fibrous protein found in the ◊skin of vertebrates and also in hair, nails, claws, hooves, feathers, and the outer coating of horns in animals such as cows and sheep.

Kerensky Alexandr Feodorovich 1881–1970. Russian revolutionary politician, prime minister of the second provisional government before its collapse Nov 1917, during the ◊Russian Revolution. He was overthrown by the Bolshevik revolution and fled to France 1918 and to the US 1940.

Kern Jerome (David) 1885–1945. US composer. Many of Kern's songs have become classics, notably "Smoke Gets in Your Eyes" from his musical *Roberta* 1933. He wrote the operetta *Show Boat* 1927, which includes the song "Ol' Man River."

Based on Edna Ferber's novel, *Show Boat* was the first example of serious musical theater in the US. Kern wrote dozens of hit songs and musicals from 1904 and Hollywood movies from the beginning of the sound era 1927. He worked mainly with lyricist Otto Harbach but also with Ira Gershwin, Oscar Hammerstein II, Dorothy Fields, and Johnny Mercer.

kernel the inner, softer part of a ◊nut, or of a seed within a hard shell.

kerosene thin oil obtained from the distillation of petroleum; a highly refined form is used in jet aircraft fuel. Kerosene is a mixture of hydrocarbons of the ◊paraffin series.

Kerouac Jack 1923–1969. US novelist who named and epitomized the ◊Beat Generation of the 1950s. His books, all autobiographical, include *On the Road* 1957, *Big Sur* 1963, and *Desolation Angel* 1965.

Kerry county of Munster province, Republic of Ireland, E of Cork
area 1,814 sq mi/4,700 sq km
county town Tralee
physical W coastline deeply indented; N part lowlying, but in the S are the highest mountains in Ireland, including Carrantuohill 3,417 ft/1,041 m, the highest peak in Ireland; many rivers and lakes
features Macgillycuddy's Reeks, Lakes of Killarney

products engineering, woolens, shoes, cutlery; tourism is important
population (1991) 121,700.

Kesselring Albert 1885–1960. German field marshal in World War II, commander of the Luftwaffe (air force) 1939–40, during the invasions of Poland and the Low Countries and the early stages of the Battle of Britain. He later served under Field Marshal Rommel in N Africa, took command in Italy 1943, and was commander in chief on the western front March 1945. His death sentence for war crimes at the Nuremberg trials 1947 was commuted to life imprisonment, but he was released 1952.

Kew Gardens popular name for the Royal Botanic Gardens, Kew, Surrey, England. They were founded 1759 by the mother of King George III as a small garden and passed to the nation by Queen Victoria 1840. By then they had expanded to almost their present size of 368 acres/149 hectares and since 1841 have been open daily to the public. They contain a collection of over 25,000 living plant species and many fine buildings. The gardens are also a center for botanical research.

key in music, the ◊diatonic scale around which a piece of music is written; for example, a passage in the key of C major will mainly use the notes of the C major scale. The term is also used for the lever activated by a keyboard player, such as a piano key.

keyboard in computing, an input device resembling a typewriter keyboard, used to enter instructions and data. There are many variations on the layout and labeling of keys. Extra numeric keys may be added, as may special-purpose function keys, whose effects can be defined by programs in the computer.

Keynes John Maynard, 1st Baron Keynes 1883–1946. English economist, whose *The General Theory of Employment, Interest, and Money* 1936 proposed the prevention of financial crises and unemployment by adjusting demand through government control of credit and currency. He is responsible for that part of economics now known as ◊macroeconomics.

Keynesian economics the economic theory of English economist John Maynard Keynes, which argues that a fall in national income, lack of demand for goods, and rising unemployment should be countered by increased government expenditure to stimulate the economy. It is opposed by monetarists (see ◊monetarism).

Key West town at the tip of the Florida peninsula; population (1980) 24,400. As a tourist resort, it was popularized by the novelist Ernest Hemingway.

kg symbol for ◊kilogram.

KGB secret police of the USSR, the *Komitet Gosudarstvennoy Bezopasnosti*/Committee of State Security, which was in control of frontier and general security and the forced-labor system. KGB officers held key appointments in all fields of daily life, reporting to administration offices in every major town The KGB was superseded by the Russian Federal Security Agency on the demise of the Soviet Union 1991.

Khabarovsk territory of SE Siberian Russia, bordering the Sea of Okhotsk and drained by the Amur River; area 318,501 sq mi/824,600 sq km; population (1985) 1,728,000. The capital is Khabarovsk. Mineral resources include gold, coal, and iron ore.

Khachaturian Aram Il'yich 1903–1978. Armenian composer. His use of folk themes is shown in the ballets *Gayaneh* 1942, which includes the "Saber Dance," and *Spartacus* 1956.

Khaddhafi Libyan leader Colonel Moamar al Khaddhafi has been accused by many countries of supporting international terrorism.

Khaddhafi or *Gaddafi* or *Qaddafi*, Moamer al 1942– . Libyan revolutionary leader. Overthrowing King Idris 1969, he became virtual president of a republic, although he nominally gave up all except an ideological role 1974. He favors territorial expansion in N Africa reaching as far as Zaire, has supported rebels in Chad, and has proposed mergers with a number of countries. During the ◊Gulf War, however, he advocated diplomacy rather than war. His theories, based on those of the Chinese communist leader Mao Zedong, are contained in a *Green Book*.

Khalistan projected independent Sikh state. See ◊Sikhism.

Khardungla Pass road linking the Indian town of Leh with the high-altitude military outpost on the Siachen Glacier at an altitude of 1,744 ft/5,662 m in the Karakoram range, Kashmir. It is thought to be the highest road in the world.

Kharkov capital of the Kharkov region, E Ukraine, 250 mi/400 km E of Kiev; population (1987) 1,587,000. It is a railroad junction and industrial city (engineering, tractors), close to the Donets Basin coalfield and Krivoy Rog iron mines. Kharkov was founded 1654 as a fortress town.

Khomeini The former Iranian Shiite Muslim leader held the title ayatollah, which means sign of Allah, when he became the chief teacher of Islamic philosophy and law.

Khartoum capital and trading center of Sudan, at the junction of the Blue and White Nile; population (1983) 476,000, and of Khartoum North, across the Blue Nile, 341,000. ◊Omdurman is also a suburb of Khartoum, giving the urban area a population of over 1.3 million.

khedive title granted by the Turkish sultan to his Egyptian viceroy 1867, retained by succeeding rulers until 1914.

Khmer or *Kmer* member of the largest ethnic group in Cambodia, numbering about 7 million. Khmer minorities also live in E Thailand and S Vietnam. The Khmer language belongs to the Mon-Khmer family of Austro-Asiatic languages.

Khmer Rouge communist movement in Cambodia (Kampuchea) formed in the 1960s. Controlling the country 1974–78, it was responsible for mass deportations and executions under the leadership of ◊Pol Pot. Since then it has conducted guerrilla warfare, and in 1991 gained representation in the governing body. The leader of the Khmer Rouge from 1985 is Khieu Samphan.

Khomeini Ayatollah Ruhollah 1900–1989. Iranian Shiite Muslim leader, born in Khomein, central Iran. Exiled for opposition to the Shah from 1964, he returned when the Shah left the country 1979, and established a fundamentalist Islamic republic. His rule was marked by a protracted war with Iraq, and suppression of opposition within Iran, executing thousands of opponents.

Khorana Har Gobind 1922– . Indian-born US biochemist who in 1976 led the team that first synthesized a biologically active gene. In 1968 he shared the Nobel Prize for Medicine for research on the interpretation of the genetic code and its function in protein synthesis.

Khrushchev Nikita Sergeyevich 1894–1971. Soviet politician, secretary-general of the Communist Party 1953–64, premier 1958–64. He emerged as leader from the power struggle following Stalin's death and was the first official to denounce Stalin, in 1956. His de-Stalinization program gave rise to revolts in Poland and Hungary 1956. Because of problems with the economy and foreign affairs (a breach with China 1960; conflict with the US in the Cuban missile crisis 1962), he was ousted by Leonid Brezhnev and Alexei Kosygin.

Khufu c. 2600 BC. Egyptian king of Memphis, who built the largest of the pyramids, known to the Greeks as the pyramid of Cheops (the Greek form of Khufu).

Khulna capital of Khulna region, SW Bangladesh, situated close to the Ganges delta; population (1981) 646,000. Industry includes shipbuilding and textiles; it trades in jute, rice, salt, sugar, and oilseed.

Khwārizmī, al- Mohammed ibn-Mūsā c. 780–c. 850. Persian mathematician from Khwarizm (now Khiva, Uzbekistan), who lived and worked in Baghdad. He wrote a book on algebra, from part of whose title (*al-jabr*) comes the word "algebra," and a book in which he introduced to the West the Hindu-Arabic decimal number system. The word "algorithm" is a corruption of his name.

Khyber Pass pass 33 mi/53 km long through the mountain range that separates Pakistan from Afghanistan. The Khyber Pass was used by invaders of India. The present road was constructed by the British during the Afghan Wars.

Kiangsi alternate spelling of ◊Jiangxi, a province of China.

Kiangsu alternate spelling of ◊Jiangsu, a province of China.

kibbutz Israeli communal collective settlement with collective ownership of all property and earnings, collective organization of work and decision-making, and communal housing for children. A modified version, the *Moshav Shitufi*, is similar to the ◊collective farms that were typical of the former USSR. Other Israeli cooperative rural settlements include the *Moshav Ovdim*, which has equal opportunity, and the similar but less strict *Moshav* settlement.

Kidd "Captain" (William) *c.* 1645–1701. Scottish pirate. He spent his youth privateering for the British against the French off the North American coast, and in 1695 was given a royal commission to suppress piracy in the Indian Ocean. Instead, he joined a group of pirates in Madagascar. On his way to Boston, Massachusetts, he was arrested 1699, taken to England, and hanged.

kidney in vertebrates, one of a pair of organs responsible for water regulation, excretion of waste products, and maintaining the ionic composition of the blood. The kidneys are situated on the rear wall of the abdomen. Each one consists of a number of long tubules; the outer parts filter the aqueous components of blood, and the inner parts selectively reabsorb vital salts, leaving waste products in the remaining fluid (urine), which is passed through the ureter to the bladder. *See panel p. 520*

Kiev capital of Ukraine, industrial center (chemicals, clothing, leatherwork), on the confluence of the Desna and Dnieper rivers; population (1987) 2,554,000. It was the capital of Russia in the Middle Ages.

Kigali capital of Rwanda, central Africa, 50 mi/80 km E of Lake Kivu; population (1981) 157,000. Products include coffee, hides, shoes, paints, and varnishes; there is tin mining.

Kikuyu member of Kenya's dominant ethnic group, numbering about three million. The Kikuyu are primarily cultivators, although many are highly educated and have entered the professions. Their language belongs to the Bantu branch of the Niger-Congo family.

Kildare county of Leinster province, Republic of Ireland, S of Meath
area 652 sq mi/1,690 sq km
county town Naas
physical wet and boggy in the N
features part of the Bog of Allen; the village of Maynooth, with a training college for Roman Catholic priests; the Curragh, a plain that is the site of the national stud and headquarters of Irish horse racing
products oats, barley, potatoes, cattle
population (1991) 122,516.

Kilimanjaro volcano in ◊Tanzania, the highest mountain in Africa, 19,364 ft/5,900 m.

Kilkenny county of Leinster province, Republic of Ireland, E of Tipperary
area 795 sq mi/2,060 sq km
county town Kilkenny
features river Nore
products agricultural, coal
population (1991) 73,600.

Killeen city in central Texas, S of Fort Worth and N of Austin; population (1990) 63,500. Although some concrete is produced here, the economy relies heavily on the nearby army base, Fort Hood.

Khrushchev Soviet politician Nikita Khrushchev at the Quai d'Orsay, Paris.

killer whale or *orca* toothed whale *Orcinus orca* of the dolphin family, found in all seas of the world. It is black on top, white below, and grows up to 30 ft/9 m long. It is the only whale that has been observed to prey on other whales, as well as on seals and seabirds.

It has been tamed and trained to perform in sea circuses and has proved to be gentle, friendly, intelligent, and hard working, thus prompting use of its alternate name orca in the US.

Kilmer Joyce 1886–1918. US poet. His first collection of poems *Summer of Love* was published 1911. He later gained an international reputation with the title work of *Trees and Other Poems* 1914.

kiln high-temperature furnace used commercially for drying timber, roasting metal ores, or for making cement, bricks, and pottery. Oil- or gas-fired kilns are used to bake ceramics at up to 3,200°F/1,760°C; electric kilns do not generally reach such high temperatures.

kilobyte (K or KB) in computing, a unit of memory equal to 1,024 ◊bytes. It is sometimes used, less precisely, to mean 1,000 bytes.

kilogram SI unit (symbol kg) of mass equal to 1,000 grams (2.24 lb). It is defined by scientists as a mass equal to that of the international prototype, a platinum-iridium cylinder held at the International Bureau of Weights and Measures at Sèvres, France.

kilometer unit (symbol km) of length equal to 1,000 meters (3,280.89 ft).

kilowatt unit (symbol kW) of power equal to 1,000 watts or about 1.34 horsepower.

kilowatt-hour commercial unit of electrical energy (symbol kWh), defined as the work done by a power of 1,000 watts in one hour. It is used to calculate the cost of electrical energy taken from utility-company supplies.

kimberlite an igneous rock that is ultrabasic (containing very little silica); a type of alkaline ◊peridotite containing mica in addition to olivine and other minerals. Kimberlite represents the world's principal source of diamonds.

Kim Il Sung 1912– . North Korean communist politician and marshal. He became prime minister 1948 and president 1972, retaining the presidency of the Communist Workers' party. He likes to be known as the "Great Leader" and has campaigned constantly for the reunification of Korea. His son *Kim Jong Il* (1942–), known as the "Dear Leader," has been named as his successor.

kidney

Blood enters the kidney through the renal artery. The blood is filtered through the glomeruli to extract the urine. The urine flows through the ureter to the bladder; the cleaned blood flow leaves the kidney along the renal vein.

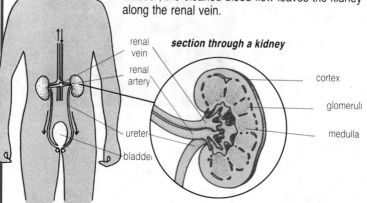

renal vein

renal artery

ureter

bladder

section through a kidney

cortex

glomeruli

medulla

The kidney machine is a copy of the glomerulus which acts as a coarse filtering mechanism in the kidney. Blood is pumped from the patient's body into an artificial kidney where it flows over a thin membrane placed between the blood and a cleaning fluid, called the dialysis fluid. There is a natural tendency, called dialysis, for impurities in the blood to flow across the membrane into the dialysis fluid.

A man undergoing continuous ambulatory peritoneal dialysis, allowing a membrane inside the body to take over the kidney's function.▼

artificial kidney (hemodializer)

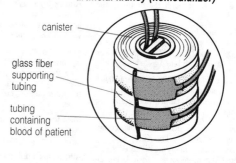

canister

glass fiber supporting tubing

tubing containing blood of patient

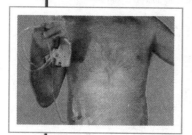

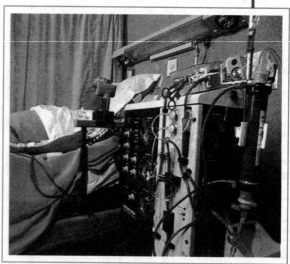

Elderly man undergoing renal dialysis on a kidney machine.

kimono traditional Japanese costume. Already worn in the Heian period (more than 1,000 years ago), it is still used by women for formal wear and informally by men.

Kim Young Sam 1927– . South Korean democratic politician, president from 1993. A member of the National Assembly from 1954 and president of the New Democratic Party (NDP) from 1974, he lost his seat and was later placed under house arrest because of his opposition to President Park Chung Hee. In 1983 he led a prodemocracy hunger strike but in 1987 failed to defeat Roh Tae-Woo in the presidential election. In 1990 he merged the NDP with the ruling party to form the new Democratic Liberal Party (DLP). In the Dec 1992 presidential election he captured 42% of the national vote, defeating Kim Dae Jung (34%) and Chung Ju Yung (16%), and assumed office Feb 1993.

kinetic energy the energy of a body resulting from motion. It is contrasted with ◊potential energy.

kinetics the branch of chemistry that investigates the rates of chemical reactions.

kinetics alternate name for ◊dynamics. It is distinguished from **kinematics**, which deals with motion without reference to force or mass.

kinetic theory theory describing the physical properties of matter in terms of the behavior—principally movement—of its component atoms or molecules. The temperature of a substance is dependent on the velocity of movement of its constituent particles, increased temperature being accompanied by increased movement. A gas consists of rapidly moving atoms or molecules and, according to kinetic theory, it is their continual impact on the walls of the containing vessel that accounts for the pressure of the gas. The slowing of molecular motion as temperature falls, according to kinetic theory, accounts for the physical properties of liquids and solids, culminating in the concept of no molecular motion at ◊absolute zero (0K/−273°C). By making various assumptions about the nature of gas molecules, it is possible to derive from the kinetic theory the various gas laws (such as ◊Avogadro's hypothesis, ◊Boyle's law, and ◊Charles's law).

King B B (Riley) 1925– . US blues guitarist, singer, and songwriter, one of the most influential electric-guitar players, who became an international star in the 1960s. His albums include *Blues Is King* 1967, *Lucille Talks Back* 1975, and *Blues 'n' Jazz* 1983.

King Billie Jean (born Moffitt) 1943– . US tennis player. She won a record 20 Wimbledon titles 1961–79 and 39 Grand Slam titles. She won the Wimbledon singles title six times, the US Open singles title four times, the French Open once, and the Australian Open once.

King Martin Luther Jr 1929–1968. US civil-rights campaigner, black leader, and Baptist minister. He first came to national attention as leader of the ◊Montgomery, Alabama, bus boycott 1955, and was one of the organizers of the massive (200,000 people) march on Washington, DC, 1963 to demand racial equality. An advocate of nonviolence, he was awarded the Nobel Peace Prize 1964. He was assassinated in Memphis, Tennessee, by James Earl Ray (1928–).

King Stephen 1946– . US writer of best-selling horror novels with small-town or rural settings. Many of his works have been filmed, including *Carrie* 1974, *The Shining* 1978, and *Christine* 1983.

His recent novels include *It* and *The Tommyknockers* (both 1987) *The Dark Half* 1989, and *Dolores Clai-*

King *Civil-rights campaigner Martin Luther King marching in 1965.*

borne 1992. He has also published three volumes of short stories, several screenplays, and a number of novels under the pseudonym Richard Bachman.

King William Lyon Mackenzie 1874–1950. Canadian Liberal prime minister 1921–26, 1926–30, and 1935–48. He maintained the unity of the English- and French-speaking populations, and was instrumental in establishing equal status for Canada with Britain.

king crab or *Alaskan king crab* large, edible crab *Paralithodes camtschatica*, of the N Pacific. The term "king crab" is sometimes used as another name for the ◊horseshoe crab.

kingdom the primary division in biological ◊classification. At one time, only two kingdoms were recognized: animals and plants. Today most biologists prefer a five-kingdom system, even though it still involves grouping together organisms that are probably unrelated. One widely accepted scheme is as follows: *Kingdom Animalia* (all multicellular animals); *Kingdom Plantae* (all plants, including seaweeds and other algae); *Kingdom Fungi* (all fungi, including the unicellular yeasts, but not slime molds); *Kingdom Protista* or *Protoctista* (protozoa, diatoms, dinoflagellates, slime molds, and various other lower organisms with eukaryotic cells); and *Kingdom Monera* (all prokaryotes—the bacteria and cyanobacteria, or ◊blue-green algae). The first four of these kingdoms make up the eukaryotes.

kingfisher heavy-billed bird of the worldwide family Alcedinidae, found near streams, ponds, and coastal areas. Kingfishers plunge-dive for fish and aquatic insects. The nest is usually a burrow in a riverbank.

kingfisher *The kingfisher, with its brilliantly colored plumage and daggerlike beak, is unmistakable.*

Kiribati
Republic of

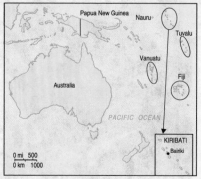

0 mi 500
0 km 1000

area 277 sq mi/717 sq km
capital (and port) Bairiki (on Tarawa Atoll)
physical comprises 33 Pacific coral islands: the Kiribati (Gilbert), Rawaki (Phoenix), Banaba (Ocean Island), and three of the Line Islands including Kiritimati (Christmas Island)
environment the islands are threatened by the possibility of a rise in sea level caused by global warming. A rise of approximately 1 ft/30 cm by the year 2040 will make existing fresh water brackish and undrinkable
features island groups crossed by equator and International Date Line

head of state and government Teatao Teannaki from 1991
political system liberal democracy
political parties National Progressive Party, governing faction; opposition parties: Christian Democratic Party and the Kiribati United Party
exports copra, fish
currency Australian dollar
population (1992) 74,700 (Micronesian); growth rate 1.7% p.a.
languages English (official), Gilbertese
religions Roman Catholic 48%, Protestant 45%
literacy 90% (1985)
GDP $26 million (1987); $430 per head (1988)

chronology
1892 Gilbert and Ellice Islands proclaimed a British protectorate.
1937 Phoenix Islands added to colony.
1950s UK tested nuclear weapons on Kiritimati (formerly Christmas Island).
1962 US tested nuclear weapons on Kiritimati.
1975 Ellice Islands separated to become Tuvalu.
1977 Gilbert Islands granted internal self-government.
1979 Independence achieved from Britain, within the Commonwealth, as the Republic of Kiribati, with Ieremia Tabai as president.
1982 and 1983 Tabai reelected.
1985 Fishing agreement with Soviet state-owned company negotiated, prompting formation of Kiribati's first political party, the opposition Christian Democrats.
1987 Tabai reelected.
1991 Tabai reelected but not allowed under constitution to serve further term; Teatao Teannaki elected president.

Kingsport city in NE Tennessee, on the Holston River, NE of Knoxville, near the Virginia border; population (1990) 36,400. Products include plastics, chemicals, textiles, paper and printing, and cement. Fort Patrick Henry, built here 1776, protected the Wilderness Road.

Kingston capital and principal port of Jamaica, West Indies, the cultural and commercial center of the island; population (1983) 101,000, metropolitan area 525,000. Founded 1693, Kingston became the capital of Jamaica 1872.

Kingston city in E Ontario, on Lake Ontario; population (1981) 60,300. Industries include shipbuilding yards, engineering works, and grain elevators. It grew from 1782 around the French Fort Frontenac, was captured by the English 1748, and renamed in honor of George III.

Kingston upon Hull official name of ◊Hull, a city NE England.

Kingstown capital and principal port of St Vincent and the Grenadines, West Indies, in the SW of the island of St Vincent; population (1989) 29,400.

Kinki region of S Honshu Island, Japan; population (1988) 22,105,000; area 12,773 sq mi/33,070 sq km. The chief city is Osaka.

Kinsey Alfred 1894–1956. US researcher whose studies of male and female sexual behavior 1948–53, based on questionnaires, were the first serious published research on this topic.

Kinshasa formerly *Léopoldville* capital of Zaire on the river Zaïre, 250 mi/400 km inland from the port of Matadi; population (1984) 2,654,000. Industries include chemicals, textiles, engineering, food processing, and furniture. It was founded by the explorer Henry Stanley 1887.

kinship in anthropology, human relationship based on blood or marriage, and sanctified by law and custom. Kinship forms the basis for most human societies and for such social groupings as the family, clan, or tribe.

Kipling (Joseph) Rudyard 1865–1936. English writer, born in India. *Plain Tales from the Hills* 1888, about Anglo-Indian society, contains the earliest of his masterly short stories. His books for children, including *The Jungle Books* 1894–95, *Just So Stories* 1902, *Puck of Pook's Hill* 1906, and the novel *Kim* 1901, reveal his imaginative identification with the exotic. Poems such as "Danny Deever," "Gunga Din," and "If–" express an empathy with common experience, which contributed to his great popularity, together with a vivid sense of "Englishness" (sometimes denigrated as a kind of jingoist imperialism). His work is increasingly valued for its complex characterization and subtle moral viewpoints. Nobel Prize 1907.

Kirghiz member of a pastoral people numbering approximately 1.5 million. They inhabit the central Asian region bounded by the Hindu Kush, the Himalayas, and the Tian Shan mountains. The Kirghiz are Sunni Muslims, and their Turkic language belongs to the Altaic family.

Kiribati republic in the W central Pacific Ocean, comprising three groups of coral atolls: the 16 Gilbert Islands, 8 uninhabited Phoenix Islands, 8 of the 11 Line Islands, and the volcanic island of Banaba.

Kirkland Gelsey 1952– . US ballerina of effortless technique and innate musicality. She joined the New York City Ballet 1968, where George Balanchine staged a new *Firebird* for her 1970 and Jerome Robbins chose her for his *Goldberg Variations* 1971 and other ballets. In 1974 Mikhail Baryshnikov sought her out and she joined the American Ballet Theater, where they danced in partnership, for example in *Giselle*.

Kishinev Russian name for Chişinău, the capital of Moldova.

Kissinger Henry 1923– . German-born US diplomat. After a brilliant academic career at Harvard University, he was appointed national security adviser 1969 by President Nixon, and was secretary of state 1973–77. His missions to the USSR and China improved US relations with both countries, and he took part in negotiating US withdrawal from Vietnam 1973 and in Arab-Israeli peace negotiations 1973–75. Nobel Peace Prize 1973.

Kitakyushu industrial port city (coal, steel, chemicals, cotton thread, plate glass, alcohol) in Japan, on the Hibiki Sea, N Kyushu Island, formed 1963 by the amalgamation of Moji, Kokura, Tobata, Yawata, and Wakamatsu; population (1990) 1,026,500. A tunnel (1942) links it with Honshu.

Kitasato Shibasaburo 1852–1931. Japanese bacteriologist who discovered the ◊plague bacillus while investigating an outbreak of plague in Hong Kong. Kitasato was the first to grow the tetanus bacillus in pure culture. He and the German bacteriologist Behring discovered that increasing nonlethal doses of tetanus toxin give immunity to the disease.

Kitchener city in SW Ontario; population (1986) 151,000, metropolitan area (with Waterloo) 311,000. Manufacturing includes agricultural machinery and tires. Settled by Germans from Pennsylvania in the 1800s, it was known as Berlin until 1916.

Kitchener Horatio Herbert, Earl Kitchener of Khartoum 1850–1916. British soldier and administrator. He defeated the Sudanese dervishes at Omdurman 1898 and reoccupied Khartoum. In South Africa, he was Chief of Staff 1900–02 during the Boer War, and commanded the forces in India 1902–09. He was appointed war minister on the outbreak of World War I, and drowned when his ship was sunk on the way to Russia.

kite one of about 20 birds of prey in the family Accipitridae, found in all parts of the world.

Kites have long, pointed wings and, usually, a forked tail. North America has five species, including the American swallow-tailed kite *Elanoides forficartus* of the SE US, which catches insects in flight as well as dropping down on snakes and lizards.

kite quadrilateral with two pairs of adjacent equal sides. The geometry of this figure follows from the fact that it has one axis of symmetry.

kiwi flightless bird *Apteryx australis* found only in New Zealand. It has long, hairlike brown plumage and

kiwi The little spotted kiwi is one of three species of kiwi found in New Zealand.

a very long beak with nostrils at the tip. It is nocturnal and insectivorous. The egg is larger in relation to the bird's size (similar to a domestic chicken) than that of any other bird.

kiwi fruit or *Chinese gooseberry* fruit of a vinelike plant *Actinidithia chinensis*, family Actinidiaceae, commercially grown on a large scale in New Zealand. Kiwi fruits are egg-sized, oval, and of similar flavor to a gooseberry, with a fuzzy brown skin.

Bright-green fuzzless varieties are now available.

Klaproth Martin Heinrich 1743–1817. German chemist who first identified the elements uranium, zirconium, cerium, and titanium.

Klee Paul 1879–1940. Swiss painter. He settled in Munich 1906, joined the ◊Blaue Reiter group 1912, and worked at the Bauhaus school of art and design 1920–31, returning to Switzerland 1933. His style in the 1920s and 1930s was dominated by humorous linear fantasies.

kleptomania (Greek *kleptēs* "thief") behavioral disorder characterized by an overpowering desire to possess articles for which one has no need. In klepto-

Klee Sun and Moon (1929), private collection.

mania, as opposed to ordinary theft, there is no obvious need or use for what is stolen and sometimes the sufferer has no memory of the theft.

Klondike former gold-mining area in ◊Yukon, named after the river valley where gold was found 1896. About 30,000 people moved there during the following 15 years. Silver is still mined there.

km symbol for ◊kilometer.

Knesset the Israeli parliament, consisting of a single chamber of 120 deputies elected for a period of four years.

knighthood, order of fraternity carrying with it the rank of knight, admission to which is granted as a mark of royal favor or as a reward for public services. During the Middle Ages in Europe such fraternities fell into two classes, religious and secular. The first class, including the ◊Templars and the *Knights of St John*, consisted of knights who had taken religious vows and devoted themselves to military service against the Saracens (Arabs) or other non-Christians. The secular orders probably arose from bands of knights engaged in the service of a prince or great noble.

knitting method of making fabric by looping and knotting yarn with two needles. Knitting may have developed from ◊crochet, which uses a single hooked needle, or from *netting*, using a shuttle.

Knossos chief city of ◊Minoan Crete, near present-day Iráklion, 4 mi/6 km SE of Candia. The archeological site excavated by Arthur ◊Evans 1899–1935, dates from about 2000–1400 BC, and includes the palace throne room, the remains of frescoes, and a labyrinth, legendary home of the ◊Minotaur.

knot in navigation, unit by which a ship's speed is measured, equivalent to one ◊nautical mile per hour (one knot equals about 1.15 miles per hour). It is also sometimes used in aviation.

Knox John *c.* 1505–1572. Scottish Protestant reformer, founder of the Church of Scotland. He spent several years in exile for his beliefs, including a period in Geneva where he met John ◊Calvin. He returned to Scotland 1559 to promote Presbyterianism. His books include *First Blast of the Trumpet Against the Monstrous Regiment of Women* 1558.

Knoxville city in E Tennessee; population (1990) 165,100. It is the center of a mining and agricultural region, and the administrative headquarters of the ◊Tennessee Valley Authority. The University of Tennessee, founded 1794, is here, and Oak Ridge National Laboratory, one of the world's largest nuclear research facilities, is nearby.

koala marsupial *Phascolarctos cinereus* of the family Phalangeridae, found only in E Australia. It feeds almost entirely on eucalyptus shoots. It is about 2 ft/60 cm long, and resembles a bear. The popularity of its grayish fur led to its almost complete extermination by hunters. Under protection since 1936, it has rapidly increased in numbers.

Kobe deep-water port in S Honshu, Japan; population (1990) 1,477,400. *Port Island*, created 1960–68 from the rock of nearby mountains, area 2 sq mi/5 sq km, is one of the world's largest construction projects.

Knossos *The palace of Minos in Knossos, Crete, showing the grand staircase in the east wing (the domestic quarter).*

Koch Robert 1843–1910. German bacteriologist. Koch and his assistants devised the techniques to culture bacteria outside the body, and formulated the rules for showing whether or not a bacterium is the cause of a disease. Nobel Prize for Medicine 1905.

Kodály Zoltán 1882–1967. Hungarian composer. With Béla ◊Bartók, he recorded and transcribed Magyar folk music, the scales and rhythm of which he incorporated in a deliberately nationalist style. His works include the cantata *Psalmus Hungaricus* 1923, a comic opera *Háry János* 1925–27, and orchestral dances and variations.

Kodiak island off the S coast of Alaska, site of a US naval base; area 3,670 sq mi/9,505 sq km. It is the home of the Kodiak bear, the world's largest bear. The town of Kodiak is one of the largest US fishing ports (mainly salmon).

Koestler Arthur 1905–1983. Hungarian author. Imprisoned by the Nazis in France 1940, he escaped to England. His novel *Darkness at Noon* 1940, regarded as his masterpiece, is a fictional account of the Stalinist purges, and draws on his experiences as a prisoner under sentence of death during the Spanish Civil War. He also wrote extensively about creativity, parapsychology, politics, and culture. He endowed Britain's first chair of parapsychology at Edinburgh, established 1984.

Kohl Helmut 1930– . German conservative politician, leader of the Christian Democratic Union (CDU) from 1976, West German chancellor (prime minister) 1982–90. He oversaw the reunification of East and West Germany 1989–90 and in 1990 won a resounding victory to become the first chancellor of reunited Germany. His miscalculation of the true costs of reunification and their subsequent effects on the German economy led to a dramatic fall in his popularity.

Kokomo city in N central Indiana, on Wildcat Creek, N of Indianapolis and SW of Fort Wayne; seat of Howard County; population (1990) 45,000. The city's industries produce automobile, radio, and plumbing parts; steel and wire; and electrical machinery. The first automobile to use gasoline was invented and tested here 1893.

Kolchak Alexander Vasilievich 1875–1920. Russian admiral, commander of the White forces in Siberia after the Russian Revolution. He proclaimed himself Supreme Ruler of Russia 1918, but was later handed over to the Bolsheviks by his own men and shot.

Kommunizma, Pik or *Communism Peak* highest mountain in the ◊Pamirs, a mountain range in Tajikistan; 24,599 ft/7,495 m. As part of the former USSR, it was known as *Mount Garmo* until 1933 and *Mount Stalin* 1933–62.

Kongur Shan mountain peak in China, 25,325 ft/7,719 m high, part of the Pamir range (see ◊Pamirs). The 1981 expedition that first reached the summit was led by British climber Chris Bonington.

Königsberg bridge problem long-standing puzzle that was solved by topology (the geometry of those properties of a figure which remain the same under distortion). In the city of Königsberg (now Kaliningrad in Russia), seven bridges connect the banks of the River Pregol'a and the islands in the river. For many years, people were challenged to cross each of the bridges in a single tour and return to their starting point. In 1736 Swiss mathematician Leonhard Euler converted the puzzle into a topological network, in which the islands and river banks were represented as

koala The koala lives in eucalyptus trees, and comes down only to pass from one tree to another.

nodes (junctions), and the connecting bridges as lines. By analyzing this network he was able to show that it is not traversible—that is, it is impossible to cross each of the bridges once only and return to the point at which one started.

Konoe Fumimaro, Prince 1891–1946. Japanese politician and prime minister 1937–39 and 1940–41. Entering politics in the 1920s, Konoe was active in trying to curb the power of the army in government and preventing an escalation of the war with China. He helped to engineer the fall of the ◊Tōjō government 1944 but committed suicide after being suspected of war crimes.

Kon-Tiki legendary creator god of Peru and sun king who ruled the country later occupied by the ◊Incas and was supposed to have migrated out into the Pacific. The name was used by explorer Thor ◊Heyerdahl for his raft (made of nine balsawood logs), which he sailed from Peru to the Tuamotu Islands, near Tahiti, on the Humboldt current 1947, in an attempt to show that ancient inhabitants of South America might have reached Polynesia. He sailed from April 28 to Aug 7, 1947, with five companions, over about 5,000 mi/8,000 km. The Tuamotu Archipelago was in fact settled by Austronesian seafarers, and Heyerdahl's theory is largely discounted by anthropologists.

kookaburra or *laughing jackass* largest of the world's ◊kingfishers *Dacelo novaeguineae*, found in Australia, with an extraordinary laughing call. It feeds on insects and other small creatures. The body and tail measure 18 in/45 cm, the head is grayish with a dark eye stripe, and the back and wings are flecked brown with gray underparts. Its laugh is one of the most familiar sounds of the bush of E Australia.

Koonalda Cave cave in SW South Australia below the Nullarbor Plain. Anthropologists in the 1950s and 1960s discovered evidence of flint-quarrying and human markings that have been dated as 20,000 years old.

Koran (alternatively transliterated as *Quran*) sacred book of ◊Islam. Written in the purest Arabic, it contains 114 *suras* (chapters), and is stated to have been divinely revealed to the prophet Mohammed about 616.

Korda Alexander 1893–1956. Hungarian-born British film producer and director, a dominant figure during the 1930s and 1940s. His films include *The Private Life of Henry VIII* 1933, *The Third Man* 1950, and *Richard III* 1956.

Korea peninsula in E Asia, divided into north and south; see ◊Korea, North, and ◊Korea, South.

Korea: history *2333 bc* The foundation of the Korean state traditionally dates back to the *Tangun dynasty. 1122–4th century* The Chinese Kija dynasty. *AD 688–1000* Korean peninsula unified by

Buddhist Shilla kingdom. *10th century* After centuries of internal war and invasion, Korea was united within its present boundaries. *1392* Chosun (Yi) dynasty established and Korea became a vassal of China. *16th century* Japan invaded Korea for the first time, later withdrawing from a country it had devastated. *1905* Japan began to treat Korea as a protectorate. *1910* Annexed by Japan. Many Japanese colonists settled in Korea, introducing both industrial and agricultural development. However, the enforced adoption of the Japanese language and customs was resented by Koreans. *1945* At the end of World War II, the Japanese in Korea surrendered, but the occupying forces at the cease-fire—the USSR north of the ◊38th parallel, and the US south of it—created a lasting division of the country as North and South Korea (see ◊Korea, North, and ◊Korea, South, for history since 1945).

Korean language language of Korea, written from the 5th century AD in Chinese characters until the invention of an alphabet by King Sejong 1443. The linguistic affiliations of Korean are unclear, but it may be distantly related to Japanese.

Korea, North country in E Asia, bounded NE by Russia, N and NW by China, E by the Sea of Japan, S by South Korea, and W by the Yellow Sea.

Korea, South country in E Asia, bounded N by North Korea, E by the Sea of Japan, S by the Korea Strait, and W by the Yellow Sea.

Korean War war 1950–53 between North Korea (supported by China) and South Korea, aided by the United Nations (the troops were mainly US). North Korean forces invaded the South June 25, 1950, and the Security Council of the United Nations, owing to a walk-out by the USSR, voted to oppose them. The North Koreans held most of the South when US reinforcements arrived Sept 1950 and forced their way through to the North Korean border with China. The Chinese retaliated, pushing them back to the original boundary Oct 1950; truce negotiations began 1951, although the war did not end until 1953.

Korematsu v US a US Supreme Court decision 1944 dealing with congressional measures forcing the relocation of citizens of certain national origins. Korematsu, a Japanese-American, filed suit to challenge a 1942 law excluding Americans of Japanese descent from living on the US W coast. Those Japanese-Americans already living on the coast were removed to inland internment camps. This, Korematsu argued, was a discriminatory violation of Fifth-Amendment rights. Citing the danger of domestic sabotage in the war against Japan, the Court ruled

---

Korea, North
Democratic People's Republic of
(*Chosun Minchu-chui Inmin Konghwa-guk*)

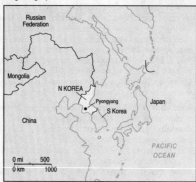

area 46,528 sq mi/120,538 sq km
capital Pyongyang
cities Chongjin, Nampo, Wonsan
physical wide coastal plain in W rising to mountains cut by deep valleys in interior
environment the building of a hydroelectric dam at Kumgangsan on a tributary of the Han River has been opposed by South Korea as a potential flooding threat to central Korea
features separated from South Korea by a military demarcation line; the richer of the two Koreas in mineral resources (copper, iron ore, graphite, tungsten, zinc, lead, magnesite, gold, phosphor, phosphates)
head of state Kim Il Sung from 1972 (also head of Korean Workers' Party)
head of government Kang Song San from 1992
political system communism
political parties Korean Workers' Party (KWP), Marxist-Leninist-Kim Il Sungist (leads Democratic Front for the Reunification of the Fatherland, including North Korean Democratic Party and Religious Chungwoo Party)
exports coal, iron, copper, textiles, chemicals

currency won
population (1992) 22,227,000; growth rate 2.5% p.a.
life expectancy men 67, women 73 (1989)
language Korean
religions traditionally Buddhist, Confucian, but religious activity curtailed by the state
literacy 99% (1989)
GNP $20 bn; $3,450 per head (1988)

chronology
1910 Korea formally annexed by Japan.
1945 Russian and US troops entered Korea, forced surrender of Japanese, and divided the country in two. Soviet troops occupied North Korea.
1948 Democratic People's Republic of Korea declared.
1950 North Korea invaded South Korea to unite the nation, beginning the Korean War.
1953 Armistice agreed to end Korean War.
1961 Friendship and mutual assistance treaty signed with China.
1972 New constitution, with executive president, adopted. Talks took place with South Korea about possible reunification.
1980 Reunification talks broke down.
1983 Four South Korean cabinet ministers assassinated in Rangoon, Burma (Myanmar), by North Korean army officers.
1985 Increased relations with the USSR.
1989 Increasing evidence shown of nuclear-weapons development.
1990 Diplomatic contacts with South Korea and Japan suggested the beginning of a thaw in North Korea's relations with the rest of the world.
1991 Became a member of the United Nations. Signed nonaggression agreement with South Korea; agreed to ban nuclear weapons.
1992 Signed Nuclear Safeguards Agreement, allowing international inspection of its nuclear facilities. Also signed a pact with South Korea for mutual inspection of nuclear facilities. Passed legislation making foreign investment in the country attractive. Yon Hyong Muk replaced by Kang Song San.
1993 Threatened to withdraw from Nuclear Non-Proliferation Treaty.

Korea, South
Republic of Korea
(*Daehan Minguk*)

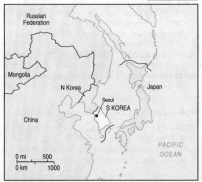

area 38,161 sq mi/98,799 sq km
capital Seoul
cities Taegu, ports Pusan, Inchon
physical southern end of a mountainous peninsula separating the Sea of Japan from the Yellow Sea
features Chomsongdae (world's earliest observatory); giant Popchusa Buddha; granite peaks of Soraksan National Park
head of state Kim Young Sam from 1992
head of government Hwang In Sung from 1993
political system emergent democracy
political parties Democratic Liberal Party (DLP), right of center; Democratic Party, left of center; Unification National Party (UNP), right of center
exports steel, ships, chemicals, electronics, textiles and clothing, plywood, fish
currency won
population (1992) 43,663,000; growth rate 1.4% p.a.
life expectancy men 66, women 73 (1989)
language Korean

media freedom of the press achieved 1987; large numbers of newspapers with large circulations. It is prohibited to say anything favorable about North Korea
religions traditionally Buddhist, Confucian, and Chondokyo; Christian 28%
literacy 92% (1989)
GNP $171bn (1988); $2,180 per head (1986)

chronology
1910 Korea formally annexed by Japan.
1945 Russian and US troops entered Korea, forced surrender of Japanese, and divided the country in two. US military government took control of South Korea.
1948 Republic proclaimed.
1950–53 War with North Korea.
1960 President Syngman Rhee resigned amid unrest.
1961 Military coup by General Park Chung-Hee. Industrial growth program.
1979 Assassination of President Park.
1980 Military takeover by General Chun Doo Hwan.
1987 Adoption of more democratic constitution after student unrest. Roh Tae Woo elected president.
1988 Former president Chun, accused of corruption, publicly apologized and agreed to hand over his financial assets to the state. Seoul hosted Summer Olympic Games.
1989 Roh reshuffled cabinet, threatened crackdown on protesters.
1990 Two minor opposition parties united with Democratic Justice Party to form ruling Democratic Liberal Party. Diplomatic relations established with the USSR.
1991 Violent mass demonstrations against the government. New opposition grouping, the Democratic Party, formed. Prime Minister Ro Jai Bong replaced by Chung Won Shik. Entered United Nations. Nonaggression and nuclear pacts signed with North Korea.
1992 DLP lost absolute majority in March general election; substantial gains made by Democratic Party and newly formed UNP, led by Chung Ju Wong. Diplomatic relations with China established. Dec: Kim Young Sam, DLP candidate, won the presidential election.
1993 Hwang In Sung appointed prime minister.

against Korematsu 6–3. The decision to uphold exclusion and relocation laws as legitimate exercises of war powers stood until 1983, when the Korematsu decision was reversed.

Korolev Sergei Pavlovich 1906–1966. Soviet designer of the first Soviet intercontinental missile, used to launch the first ◊Sputnik satellite and the Vostok spacecraft, also designed by Korolev, in which Yuri Gagarin made the world's first space flight.

Born in Zhitomir, Ukraine, Korolev became an aircraft designer before turning to rocketry.

Kościusko highest mountain in Australia (7,316 ft/2,229 m), in New South Wales.

Kościuszko Tadeusz 1746–1817. Polish general and nationalist who served with George Washington in the American Revolution (1776–83). He returned to Poland 1784, fought against the Russian invasion that ended in the partition of Poland, and withdrew to Saxony. He returned 1794 to lead the revolt against the occupation, but was defeated by combined Russian and Prussian forces and imprisoned until 1796.

kosher (Hebrew "appropriate") conforming to religious law with regard to the preparation and consumption of food; in Judaism, conforming to the Mosaic law of the Book of Deuteronomy. For example, only animals that chew the cud and have cloven hooves (cows and sheep, but not pigs) may be eaten. There are rules governing their humane slaughter

and their preparation (such as complete draining of blood) which also apply to fowl. Only fish with scales and fins may be eaten; shellfish may not. Milk products may not be cooked or eaten with meat or poultry, or until four hours after eating them. Utensils for meat must be kept separate from those for milk as well.

Kosovo autonomous region (1974–90) in S Serbia, Yugoslavia; capital Priština; area 4,207 sq mi/10,900 sq km; population (1986) 1,900,000, consisting of about 200,000 Serbs and about 1.7 million Albanians. Products include wine, nickel, lead, and zinc. Since it is largely inhabited by Albanians and bordering on

Korean War US soldiers entrenched at the top of "Old Baldy," Korea, Sept 1952.

Kraków Kraków's 14th-century Gothic cathedral.

Albania, there have been demands for unification with that country, while in the late 1980s Serbians agitated for Kosovo to be merged with the rest of Serbia. A state of emergency was declared Feb 1990 after fighting broke out between ethnic Albanians, police, and the Slavonic minority. The parliament and government were dissolved July 1990 and the Serbian parliament formally annexed Kosovo Sept 1990.

The Serbian invasion brought Kosovo to the brink of civil war. Albanian institutions and media were supressed, and "emergency legislation" used to rid industry of Albanian employees at all levels. In 1991 the Kosovo assembly, though still technically dissolved, organized a referendum on sovereignty which received 99% support. It elected a provisional government, headed by Bujar Bukoshi, which was recognized by Albania Oct 1991.

Kosygin Alexei Nikolaievich 1904–1980. Soviet politician, prime minister 1964–80. He was elected to the Supreme Soviet 1938, became a member of the Politburo 1946, deputy prime minister 1960, and succeeded Khrushchev as premier (while Brezhnev succeeded him as party secretary). In the late 1960s Kosygin's influence declined.

koto Japanese musical instrument; a long zither of ancient Chinese origin, having 13 silk strings supported by movable bridges. It rests on the floor and the strings are plucked with ivory plectra, producing a brittle sound.

Kourou river and second-largest town of French Guiana, NW of Cayenne, site of the Guiana Space Center of the European Space Agency.

Situated near the equator, it is an ideal site for launches of satellites into geosynchronous orbit.

Koussevitsky Serge 1874–1951. Russian musician and conductor, well known for his work in the US. He established his own orchestra in Moscow 1909, introducing works of Sergey Prokofiev, Sergey Rachmaninoff, and Igor Stravinsky. Although named director of the State Symphony after the Bolshevik Revolution 1917 Koussevitsky left the USSR for the US, becoming director of the Boston Symphony Orchestra 1924.

Kowloon peninsula on the Chinese coast forming part of the British crown colony of Hong Kong; the town of Kowloon is a residential area.

Kow Swamp area in N Victoria, Australia, W of the town of Echuca, where the remains of about 40 humans have been found, buried in shallow graves. These bones have mostly been dated at 9,000–14,000 years BP and were accompanied by human artifacts and objects such as shells. They are of a larger and more robust group of humans than those found from an earlier period at Lake Mungo and are similar to other finds from widely scattered sites in Australia such as Talgai in Queensland.

kph or *km/h* symbol for *kilometers per hour*.

Kraków or *Cracow* city in Poland, on the river Vistula; population (1990) 750,500. It is an industrial center producing freight cars, paper, chemicals, and tobacco. It was capital of Poland about 1300–1595.

Krasnodar territory of SW Russia, in the N Caucasus Mountains, adjacent to the Black Sea; area 32,290 sq mi/83,600 sq km; population (1985) 4,992,000. The capital is Krasnodar. In addition to stock rearing and the production of grain, rice, fruit, and tobacco, oil is refined.

Krasnoyarsk territory of Russia in central Siberia stretching N to the Arctic Ocean; area 927,617 sq mi/2,401,600 sq km; population (1985) 3,430,000. The capital is Krasnoyarsk. It is drained by the Yenisei River. Mineral resources include gold, graphite, coal, iron ore, and uranium.

Krebs Hans 1900–1981. German-born British biochemist who discovered the citric acid cycle, also known as the *Krebs cycle*, the final pathway by which food molecules are converted into energy in living tissues. For this work he shared with Fritz Lipmann the 1953 Nobel Prize for Medicine.

Krebs cycle or *citric acid cycle* or *tricarboxylic acid cycle* final part of the chain of biochemical reactions by which organisms break down food using oxygen to release energy (respiration). It takes place within structures called ◊mitochondria in the body's cells, and breaks down food molecules in a series of small steps, producing energy-rich molecules of ◊ATP.

Kreisler Fritz 1875–1962. Austrian violinist and composer, renowned as an interpreter of Brahms and Beethoven. From 1911 he was one of the earliest recording artists of Classical music, including records of his own compositions.

kremlin citadel or fortress of Russian cities. The Moscow kremlin dates from the 12th century, and the name "the Kremlin" was once synonymous with the Soviet government.

Krishna incarnation of the Hindu god ◊Vishnu. The devotion of the bhakti movement is usually directed toward Krishna; an example of this is the ◊International Society for Krishna Consciousness. Many stories are told of Krishna's mischievous youth, and he is the charioteer of Arjuna in the ◊*Bhagavad-Gītā*.

Kristallnacht "night of (broken) glass" Nov 9–10, 1938, when the Nazi Sturmabteilung (SA) militia in Germany and Austria mounted a concerted attack on Jews, their synagogues, homes, and shops. It followed the assassination of a German embassy official in Paris by a Polish-Jewish youth. Subsequent measures included German legislation against Jews owning businesses or property, and restrictions on their going to school or leaving Germany. It was part of the ◊Holocaust.

Kroeber Alfred Louis 1876–1960. US anthropologist. His extensive research into and analysis of the culture of California, Plains, Mexican, and South American Indians dramatically broadened the scope of anthropological studies. His textbook *Anthropology* 1923, 1948 remains a classic and influential work.

Krupp German steelmaking armaments firm, founded 1811 by *Friedrich Krupp* (1787–1826) and developed by *Alfred Krupp* (1812–1887) by pioneering the Bessemer steelmaking process. The company developed the long-distance artillery used in World War I, and supported Hitler's regime in preparation for World War II, after which the head of the firm, *Alfred Krupp* (1907–1967), was imprisoned.

krypton (Greek *kryptos* "hidden") colorless, odorless, gaseous, nonmetallic element, symbol Kr, atomic number 36, atomic weight 83.80. It is grouped with the inert gases and was long believed not to enter into reactions, but it is now known to combine with fluorine under certain conditions; it remains inert to all other reagents. It is present in very small quantities in the air (about 114 parts per million). It is used chiefly in fluorescent lamps, lasers, and gas-filled electronic valves.

KS abbreviation for the state of ◊Kansas.

Kuala Lumpur capital of the Federation of Malaysia; area 93 sq mi/240 sq km; population (1990) 1,237,900. The city developed after 1873 with the expansion of tin and rubber trading; these are now its main industries. Formerly within the state of Selangor, of which it was also the capital, it was created a federal territory 1974.

Kublai Khan 1216–1294. Mongol emperor of China from 1259. He completed his grandfather ◊Genghis Khan's conquest of N China from 1240, and on his brother Mungo's death 1259 established himself as emperor of China. He moved the capital to Beijing and founded the Yuan dynasty, successfully expanding his empire into Indochina, but was defeated in an attempt to conquer Japan 1281.

Kubrick Stanley 1928– . US-born British film director, producer, and screenwriter. His films include *Paths of Glory* 1957, *Dr Strangelove* 1964, *2001: A Space Odyssey* 1968, *A Clockwork Orange* 1971, and *The Shining* 1979, and *Full Metal Jacket* 1987.

Kuhn Thomas S 1922– . US historian and philosopher of science, who showed that social and cultural conditions affect the directions of science. *The Structure of Scientific Revolutions* 1962 argued that even scientific knowledge is relative, dependent on the paradigm (theoretical framework) that dominates a scientific field at the time.

Ku Klux Klan US secret society dedicated to white supremacy, founded 1866 in the southern states of the US to oppose ◊Reconstruction after the American ◊Civil War and to deny political rights to the black population. Members wore hooded white robes to hide their identities, and burned crosses at their nighttime meetings. Today the Klan has evolved into a paramilitary extremist group that has forged loose ties with other white supremacist groups.

It was originally headed by former Confederate general Nathan Bedford ◊Forrest and was disbanded in 1869 under pressure from members who opposed violence. Scattered groups continued a campaign of lynching and flogging, prompting anti-Klan laws in 1871. The group reemerged in 1915 as an antiblack, anti-Semitic, anti-Catholic, right-wing group that portrayed itself as fervently patriotic. It was publicized in the 1960s for terrorizing civil-rights activists and organizing racist demonstrations.

Ku Klux Klan Case a US Supreme Court decision (*Ex parte Yarbrough*) 1884 dealing with federal enforcement of the 15th Amendment. Jasper Yarbrough, a Georgia Klansman, was convicted under the Enforcement Act 1870 of harassing a black voter. He appealed to the US Supreme Court on the grounds that the 15th Amendment grants only the right to vote; it does not give Congress the power to protect that right. The Court unanimously upheld the Enforcement Act, ruling that the federal government had legitimate power to protect citizens from racial discrimination in all circumstances surrounding voting in federal elections.

Kumasi second-largest city in Ghana, W Africa, capital of Ashanti region, with trade in cocoa, rubber, and cattle; population (1984) 376,200.

Kundera Milan 1929– . Czech writer, born in Brno. His first novel, *The Joke* 1967, brought him into official disfavor in Prague, and, unable to publish further works, he moved to France. Other novels include *The Book of Laughter and Forgetting* 1979 and *The Unbearable Lightness of Being* 1984.

Kung (formerly *Bushman*) member of a small group of hunter-gatherer peoples of the NE Kalahari, southern Africa, still living to some extent nomadically. Their language belongs to the Khoisan family.

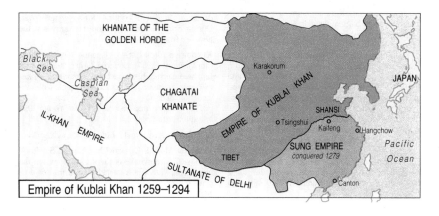

Empire of Kublai Khan 1259–1294

Kuwait
State of
(*Dowlat al Kuwait*)

area 6,878 sq mi/17,819 sq km
capital Kuwait (also chief port)
cities Jahra, Ahmadi, Fahaheel
physical hot desert; islands of Failaka, Bubiyan, and Warba at NE corner of Arabian Peninsula
environment during the Gulf War 1990–91, 650 oil wells were set ablaze and about 300,000 metric tons of oil were released into the waters of the Gulf leading to pollution haze, photochemical smog, acid rain, soil contamination, and water pollution
features there are no rivers and rain is light; the world's largest desalination plants, built in the 1950s
head of state and government Jabir al-Ahmad al-Jabir al-Sabah from 1977
political system absolute monarchy
political parties none
exports oil
currency Kuwaiti dinar
population (1992) 1,190,000 (Kuwaitis 40%, Palestinians 30%); growth rate 5.5% p.a.
life expectancy men 72, women 76 (1989)
languages Arabic 78%, Kurdish 10%, Farsi 4%
religion Sunni Muslim 45%, Shiite minority 30%
literacy 71% (1988)
GNP $19.1 bn; $10,410 per head (1988)

chronology
1914 Britain recognized Kuwait as an independent sovereign state.
1961 Full independence achieved from Britain, with Sheik Abdullah al-Salem al-Sabah as emir.
1965 Sheik Abdullah died; succeeded by his brother, Sheik Sabah.
1977 Sheik Sabah died; succeeded by Crown Prince Jabir.
1983 Shiite guerrillas bombed targets in Kuwait; 17 arrested.
1986 National assembly suspended.
1987 Kuwaiti oil tankers reflagged, received US Navy protection; missile attacks by Iran.
1988 Aircraft hijacked by pro-Iranian Shiites demanding release of convicted guerrillas; Kuwait refused.
1989 Two of the convicted guerrillas released.
1990 Prodemocracy demonstrations suppressed. Aug: Kuwait annexed by Iraq. Emir set up government in exile in Saudi Arabia.
1991 Feb: Kuwait liberated by US-led coalition forces; extensive damage to property and environment. New government omitted any opposition representatives. Trials of alleged Iraqi collaborators criticized.
1992 Reconstituted national assembly elected on restricted franchise, with opposition party winning majority of seats.
1993 Jan: incursions by Iraq into Kuwait again created tension; US-led air strikes reassured Kuwaitis.

kung fu Chinese art of unarmed combat (Mandarin *ch'üan fa*), one of the ◊martial arts. It is practiced in many forms, the most popular being *wing chun*, "beautiful springtime."

The basic principle is to use attack as a form of defense.

Kunming formerly *Yunnan* capital of Yunnan province, China, on Lake Dian Chi, about 6,500 ft/2,000 m above sea level; population (1989) 1,500,000. Industries include chemicals, textiles, and copper smelted with nearby hydroelectric power.

Kuomintang original spelling of the Chinese nationalist party, now known (outside Taiwan) as ◊Guomindang.

Kurd member of the Kurdish culture, living mostly in the Taurus and Sagros mountains of W Iran and N Iraq in the region called Kurdistan. Although divided among more powerful states, the Kurds have nationalist aspirations; there are some 8 million in Turkey (where they suffer from discriminatory legislation), 5 million in Iran, 4 million in Iraq, 500,000 in Syria, and 500,000 in Azerbaijan, Armenia, and Georgia. Several million live elsewhere in Europe. Some 1 million Kurds were made homeless and 25,000 killed as a result of chemical-weapon attacks by Iraq 1984–89, and in 1991 more than 1 million were forced to flee their homes in N Iraq. The Kurdish languages (Kurmanji, Sorani Kurdish, Guraní, and Zaza) are members of the Indo-Iranian branch of the Indo-European family, and the Kurds are a non-Arab, non-Turkic ethnic group. The Kurds are predominantly Sunni Muslims, although there are some Shiites in Iran.

Kurdistan or *Kordestan* hilly region in SW Asia near Mount Ararat, where the borders of Iran, Iraq, Syria, Turkey, Armenia, and Azerbaijan meet; area 74,600 sq mi/193,000 sq km; total population around 18 million.

Kuril Islands or *Kuriles* chain of about 50 small islands stretching from the NE of Hokkaido, Japan, to the S of Kamchatka, Russia; area 5,700 sq mi/14,765 sq km; population (1990) 25,000. Some of them are of volcanic origin. Two of the Kurils (Etorofu and Kunashiri) are claimed by Japan and Russia.

Kuropatkin Alexei Nikolaievich 1848–1921. Russian general. He distinguished himself as chief of staff during the Russo-Turkish War 1877–78, was commander in chief in Manchuria 1903, and resigned after his defeat at Mukden 1905 in the ◊Russo-Japanese War. During World War I he commanded the armies on the northern front until 1916.

Kurosawa Akira 1929– . Japanese director whose film *Rashōmon* 1950 introduced Western audiences to Japanese cinema. Epics such as *Shichinin no samurai/Seven Samurai* 1954 combine spectacle with intimate human drama.

The nostalgic and visionary *Yume/Dreams* 1990 has autobiographical elements.

al Kūt alternative term for Kūt-al-Imāra, a city in Iraq.

Kutuzov Mikhail Larionovich, Prince of Smolensk 1745–1813. Commander of the Russian forces in the Napoleonic Wars. He commanded an army corps at ◊Austerlitz and the army in its reatreat 1812. After the burning of Moscow that year, he harried the French throughout their retreat and later took command of the united Prussian armies.

Kuwait country in SW Asia, bounded N and NW by Iraq, E by the Persian Gulf, and S and SW by Saudi Arabia.

Kuwait City (Arabic *Al Kuwayt*) formerly *Qurein* chief port and capital of the state of Kuwait, on the S shore of Kuwait Bay; population (1985) 44,300, plus the suburbs of Hawalli, population (1985) 145,100, Jahra, population (1985) 111,200, and as-Salimiya, population (1985) 153,400. Kuwait is a banking and investment center. It was heavily damaged during the Gulf War.

Kuznets Simon 1901–1985. Russian-born economist who emigrated to the US 1922. He developed theories of national income and economic growth, used to forecast the future, in *Economic Growth of Nations* 1971. He won the Nobel Prize for Economics 1971.

Kuznetsov Anatoli 1930–1979. Russian writer. His novels *Babi Yar* 1966, describing the wartime execution of Jews at Babi Yar, near Kiev, and *The Fire* 1969, about workers in a large metallurgical factory, were seen as anti-Soviet. He lived in Britain from 1969, adopting the pseudonym A Anatoli

kW symbol for ◊kilowatt.

Kwa Ndebele black homeland in Transvaal province, South Africa; population (1985) 235,800. It achieved self-governing status 1981.

Kwangchu or *Kwangju* capital of South Cholla province, SW South Korea; population (1990) 1,144,700. It is at the center of a rice-growing region. A museum in the city houses a large collection of Chinese porcelain dredged up 1976 after lying for over 600 years on the ocean floor.

Kwa Zulu black homeland in Natal province, South Africa; population (1985) 3,747,000. It achieved self-

governing status 1971.

KY abbreviation for the state of ◊Kentucky.

Kyd Thomas *c.* 1557–1595. English dramatist, author in about 1588 of a bloody revenge tragedy, *The Spanish Tragedy*, which anticipated elements present in Shakespeare's *Hamlet*.

Kyoto former capital of Japan 794–1868 (when the capital was changed to Tokyo) on Honshu Island, linked by canal with Biwa Lake; capital of Kyoto prefecture; population (1989) 1,407,300. Industries include electrical, chemical, and machinery plants; silk weaving; and the manufacture of porcelain, bronze, and lacquerware.

Kyprianou Spyros 1932– . Cypriot politician, president 1977–88. Foreign minister 1961–72, he founded the federalist, center-left Democratic Front (DIKO) 1976.

Kyrgyzstan or *Kirghizia* country in central Asia, bounded N by Kazakhstan, E by China, W by Uzbekistan, and S by Tajikistan.

Kyushu southernmost of the main islands of Japan, separated from Shikoku and Honshu islands by Bungo Channel and Suo Bay, but connected to Honshu by bridge and rail tunnel
area 16,270 sq mi/42,150 sq km, including about 370 small islands
capital Nagasaki
cities Fukuoka, Kumamoto, Kagoshima
physical mountainous, volcanic, with subtropical climate
features the active volcano Aso-take (5,225 ft/ 1,592 m), with the world's largest crater
products coal, gold, silver, iron, tin, rice, tea, timber
population (1986) 13,295,000.

Kyrgyzstan
Republic of

area 76,641 sq mi/198,500 sq km
capital Bishkek (formerly Frunze)
cities Osh, Przhevalsk, Kyzyl-Kiya, Tormak
physical mountainous, an extension of the Tian Shan range
head of state Askar Akayev from 1990

head of government Tursunbek Chyngyshev from 1991
political system emergent democracy
political parties Democratic Kyrgyzstan, nationalist reformist; Asaba (Banner) Party and Free Kyrgyzstan Party, both opposition groupings
products cereals, sugar, cotton, coal, oil, sheep, yaks, horses
population (1992) 4,533,000 (Kyrgyz 52%, Russian 22%, Uzbek 13%, Ukrainian 3%, German 2%)
language Kyrgyz, a Turkic language
religion Sunni Muslim

chronology
1917–1924 Part of an independent Turkestan republic.
1924 Became autonomous republic within USSR.
1936 Became full union republic within USSR.
1990 June: ethnic clashes resulted in state of emergency being imposed in Bishkek. Nov: Askar Akayev, founder of Democratic movement, chosen as state president.
1991 March: Kyrgyz voters endorsed maintenance of Union in USSR referendum. Aug: President Akayev condemned anti-Gorbachev attempted coup in Moscow; Kyrgyz Communist Party, which supported the coup, suspended. Oct: Akayev directly elected president. Dec: joined new Commonwealth of Independent States and independence recognized by US.
1992 Joined the United Nations and Conference on Security and Cooperation in Europe. Supreme Soviet (parliament) renamed the Uluk Kenesh.

L Roman numeral for 50.

LA abbreviation for the state of ◊Louisiana.

Labanotation comprehensive system of accurate dance notation (***Kinetographie Laban***) devised 1928 by Rudolf von Laban (1879–1958), dancer, choreographer, and dance theorist.

labellum lower petal of an orchid flower; it is a different shape from the two lateral petals and gives the orchid its characteristic appearance. The labellum is more elaborate and usually larger than the other petals. It often has distinctive patterning to encourage ◊pollination by insects; sometimes it is extended backward to form a hollow spur containing nectar.

Labor Day legal national holiday in honor of workers. In Canada and the US, Labor Day is celebrated on the first Monday in September. In many countries it coincides with ◊May Day.

Labor, Knights of in US history, a national labor organization founded by Philadelphia tailor Uriah Stephens in 1869 and committed to cooperative enterprise, equal pay for both sexes, and an eight-hour day. The Knights grew rapidly in the mid-1880s under Terence V Powderly (1849–1924) but gave way to the American Federation of Labor after 1886.

labor union organization of employed workers formed to undertake collective bargaining with employers and to try to achieve improved working conditions for its members. Attitudes of government to unions and of unions to management vary greatly from country to country. Probably the most effective labor-union system is that of Sweden, and the most internationally known is the Polish ◊Solidarity.

Labor Day legal holiday in honor of workers. In Canada and the US, *Labor Day* is celebrated on the first Monday in September. In many countries it coincides with ◊May Day, the first day of May.

Labour Party UK political party based on socialist principles, originally formed to represent workers. It was founded in 1900 and first held office in 1924. The first majority Labour government 1945–51 introduced ◊nationalization and the National Health Service, and expanded ◊social security. Labour was again in power 1964–70 and 1974–79.

The party leader is elected by Labour members of Parliament.

Labrador area of NE Canada, part of the province of Newfoundland, lying between Ungava Bay on the NW,

the Atlantic Ocean on the E, and the Strait of Belle Isle on the SE; area 102,699 sq mi/266,060 sq km; population (1986) 28,741. It consists primarily of a gently sloping plateau with an irregular coastline of numerous bays, fjords, inlets, and cliffs (200–400 ft/60–120 m high). Industries include fisheries, timber and pulp, and many minerals. Hydroelectric resources include Churchill Falls on Churchill River, where one of the world's largest underground power houses is situated.

Labyrinth in Greek legend, the maze designed by the Athenian artisan Daedalus at Knossos in Crete for King Minos, as a home for the Minotaur—a monster, half man and half bull. After killing the Minotaur, Theseus, the prince of Athens, was guided out of the Labyrinth by a thread given to him by the king's daughter, Ariadne.

lace delicate, decorative, openwork textile fabric. Lace is a European craft with centers in Belgium, Italy, France, Germany, and England.

lacquer waterproof resinous varnish obtained from Oriental trees *Toxicodendron verniciflua*, and used for decorating furniture and art objects. It can be applied to wood, fabric, leather, or other materials, with or without added colors. The technique of making and carving small lacquerwork objects was developed in China, probably as early as the 4th century BC, and was later adopted in Japan.

La Crosse city in SW Wisconsin, at the confluence of the Black, La Crosse, and Mississippi rivers, NW of Madison; seat of La Crosse County; population (1990) 51,000. The processing and marketing center for the area's agricultural products, it also manufactures plastics, rubber products, and electrical machinery. The city began as a French trading post and grew as a lumber town.

lacrosse Canadian ball game, adopted from the North American Indians, and named after a fancied resemblance of the lacrosse stick (crosse) to a bishop's crosier. Thongs across the curved end of the crosse form a pocket to carry the small rubber ball. The field is approximately 110 yd/100 m long and a minimum of 60 yd/55 m wide in the men's game, which is played with ten players per side; the women's field is larger, and there are twelve players per side. The goals are just under 6 ft/2 m square, with loose nets. The world championship games were first held in 1967 for men, and in 1969 for women.

lactation secretion of milk from the mammary glands of mammals. In late pregnancy, the cells lining the lobules inside the mammary glands begin extracting substances from the blood to produce milk. The supply of milk starts shortly after birth with the production of colostrum, a clear fluid consisting largely of water, protein, antibodies, and vitamins. The production of milk continues practically as long as the infant continues to suck.

lactic acid or *2-hydroxypropanoic acid* $CH_3CHOHCOOH$ organic acid, a colorless, almost odorless liquid, produced by certain bacteria during fermentation and by active muscle cells when they are exercised hard and are experiencing oxygen debt. It occurs in yogurt, buttermilk, sour cream, poor wine, and certain plant extracts, and is used in food preservation and in the preparation of pharmaceuticals.

lactose white sugar, found in solution in milk; it forms 5% of cow's milk. It is commercially prepared from the whey obtained in cheese-making. Like table sugar (sucrose), it is a disaccharide, consisting of two basic sugar units (monosaccharides), in this case, glucose and galactose. Unlike sucrose, it is tasteless.

Ladoga (Russian *Ladozhskoye*) largest lake on the continent of Europe, in Russia, just NE of St Petersburg; area 7,100 sq mi/18,400 sq km. It receives the waters of several rivers, including the Svir, which drains Lake Onega and runs to the Gulf of Finland by the river Neva.

ladybird or *ladybug* beetle of the family Coccinellidae, generally red or yellow in color, with black spots. There are numerous species which, as larvae and adults, feed on aphids and scale-insect pests.

Laënnec René Théophile Hyacinthe 1781–1826. French physician, inventor of the ◊stethoscope 1814. He introduced the new diagnostic technique of auscultation (evaluating internal organs by listening with a stethoscope) in his book *Traité de l'auscultation médiaté* 1819, which quickly became a medical classic.

Lafayette city in W central Indiana, on the Wabash River, NW of Indianapolis, seat of Tippecanoe County; population (1990) 43,760. A distribution center for the area's agricultural products, its industries also include building materials, chemicals, wire, pharmaceuticals, and automobile parts.

Purdue University 1865 is nearby. The Battle of Tippecanoe was fought here 1811.

Lafayette city in S Louisiana, on the Vermilion River, W of New Orleans and SW of Baton Rouge; seat of Lafayette parish; population (1990) 94,440. Its economy centers around the area's oil industry. Settled by Acadians from Nova Scotia in the late 1700s, Lafayette is in the heart of the area of Louisiana that is associated with French-speaking "Cajuns."

Lafayette Marie Joseph Gilbert de Motier, Marquis de Lafayette 1757–1834. French soldier and politician. He fought against Britain in the American Revolution 1777–79 and 1780–82. During the French Revolution he sat in the National Assembly as a constitutional royalist and in 1789 presented the Declaration of the Rights of Man. After the storming of the ◊Bastille, he was given command of the National Guard. In 1792 he fled the country after attempting to restore the monarchy and was imprisoned by the Austrians until 1797. He supported Napoleon Bonaparte in 1815, sat in the chamber of deputies as a Liberal from 1818, and played a leading part in the revolution of 1830.

Lafitte Jean *c.* 1780–*c.* 1825. Pirate in America. Suspected of complicity with the British, he was attacked by American forces soon after the outbreak of the Anglo-American War 1812. He proved his loyalty to General Andrew Jackson by his heroic participation in the Battle of New Orleans 1815.

La Follette Robert Marion 1855–1925. US political leader. A US senator 1906–25, he was a leader of the national progressive reform movement and unsuccessfully ran for president on the Progressive ticket 1924. His memoirs *Autobiography, A Personal Narrative of Political Experiences* appeared in 1913.

La Fontaine Jean de 1621–1695. French poet. He was born at Château-Thierry, and from 1656 lived largely in Paris, the friend of the playwrights Molière and Racine, and the poet Boileau. His works include *Fables* 1668–94 and *Contes* 1665–74, a series of witty and bawdy tales in verse.

Lagash Sumerian city N of Shatra, Iraq, under independent and semiindependent rulers from about 3000–2700 BC. Besides objects of high artistic value, it has provided about 30,000 clay tablets giving detailed information on temple administration. Lagash was discovered in 1877 and excavated by Ernest de Sarzec, then French consul in Basra.

lager type of light ◊beer.

Lagerkvist Pär 1891–1974. Swedish author of lyric poetry, dramas (including *The Hangman* 1935), and novels, such as *Barabbas* 1950. He was awarded the 1951 Nobel Prize for Literature.

Lagerlöf Selma 1858–1940. Swedish novelist. Her first work was the romantic historical novel *Gösta Berling's Saga* 1891. The children's fantasy *Nils Holgerssons underbara resa/The Wonderful Voyage of Nils Holgersson* 1906–07 grew from her background as a schoolteacher. She was the first woman to receive a Nobel Prize, in 1909.

lagoon coastal body of shallow salt water, usually with limited access to the sea. The term is normally used to describe the shallow sea area cut off by a ◊coral reef or barrier islands.

Lagos chief port and former capital of Nigeria, located at the W end of an island in a lagoon and linked by bridges with the mainland via Iddo Island; population (1983) 1,097,000. Industries include chemicals, metal products, and fish. One of the most important slaving ports, Lagos was bombarded and occupied by the British 1851, becoming the colony of Lagos 1862.

Abuja was designated the new capital 1982 (officially recognized as such 1992).

Lagrange Joseph Louis 1736–1813. French mathematician. His *Mécanique analytique* 1788 applied mathematical analysis, using principles established by Newton, to such problems as the movements of planets when affected by each other's gravitational force. He presided over the commission that introduced the metric system in 1793.

La Guardia Fiorello (Henrico) 1882–1947. US Republican politician; congressman 1917, 1919, 1923–33; mayor of New York 1933–45. Elected against the opposition of the powerful Tammany Hall Democratic Party organization, he improved the administration, suppressed racketeering, and organized unemployment relief, slum-clearance schemes, and social services. Although nominally a Republican, he supported the Democratic president F D Roosevelt's ◊New Deal. La Guardia Airport, in New York City, is named after him.

Lahore capital of the province of Punjab and second city of Pakistan; population (1981) 2,920,000. Industries include engineering, textiles, carpets, and chemicals. It is associated with the Mogul rulers Akbar, Jahangir, and Aurangzeb, whose capital it was in the 16th and 17th centuries.

Laing R(onald) D(avid) 1927–1989. Scottish psychoanalyst, originator of the "social theory" of mental illness, for example that schizophrenia is promoted by family pressure for its members to conform to standards alien to themselves. His books include *The Divided Self* 1960 and *The Politics of the Family* 1971.

laissez faire (French "let alone") theory that the state should not intervene in economic affairs, except to break up a monopoly. The phrase originated with the Physiocrats, 18th-century French economists whose maxim was *laissez faire et laissez passer* (literally, "let go and let pass"—that is, leave the individual alone and let commodities circulate freely). The degree to which intervention should take place is still one of the chief problems of economics. The Scottish econo-

major lakes

name and location	sq mi	sq km
Caspian Sea (Azerbaijan/Russia/Kazakhstan/Turkmenistan/Iran)	143,240	370,990
Superior (US/Canada)	31,700	82,071
Victoria (Tanzania/Kenya/Uganda)	26,820	69,463
Aral Sea (Kazakhstan/Uzbekistan)	24,904	64,500
Huron (US/Canada)	23,000	59,547
Michigan (US)	22,300	57,735
Tanganyika (Malawi/Zaire/Zambia/Burundi)	12,700	32,880
Baikal (Russia)	12,150	31,456
Great Bear (Canada)	12,096	31,316
Malawi (Tanzania/Malawi/Mozambique)	11,150	28,867
Great Slave (Canada)	11,031	28,560
Erie (US/Canada)	9,910	25,657
Winnipeg (Canada)	9,417	25,380
Ontario (US/Canada)	7,550	19,547
Balkhash (Kazakhstan)	7,115	18,421
Ladoga (Russia)	6,835	17,695
Chad (Chad/Niger/Nigeria)	6,300	16,310
Maracaibo (Venezuela)	5,217	13,507

mist Adam ◊Smith justified the theory in *The Wealth of Nations*.

lake body of still water lying in depressed ground without direct communication with the sea. Lakes are common in formerly glaciated regions, along the courses of slow rivers, and in low land near the sea. The main classifications are by origin: *glacial lakes*, formed by glacial scouring; *barrier lakes*, formed by landslides and glacial moraines; *crater lakes*, found in volcanoes; and *tectonic lakes*, occurring in natural fissures.

Lake Veronica. Adopted name of Constance Frances Marie Ockelman 1919–1973. US film actress who was almost as celebrated for her much imitated "peekaboo" hairstyle as for her acting. She co-starred with Alan Ladd in several films during the 1940s, including *This Gun for Hire* and *The Glass Key* both 1942, and *The Blue Dahlia* 1946. She also appeared in *Sullivan's Travels* 1942 and *I Married a Witch* 1942.

Lake Charles city in SW Louisiana, on the Calcasieu River, SW of Baton Rouge, seat of Calcasieu parish; population (1990) 70,580. It is a port of entry on the Gulf of Mexico via a deep-water channel in the Calcasieu River. Most of the city's industries are related to the area's oil and gas resources and major crop, rice.

Lake District region in Cumbria, England; area 700 sq mi/1,800 sq km. It contains the principal English lakes, which are separated by wild uplands rising to many peaks, including Scafell Pike (3,210 ft/978 m).

Lakeland city in W central Florida, NE of Tampa and SW of Orlando, in the lake region and citrus belt; population (1990) 70,576. It serves as a center for the area's citrus products, but its economy depends mainly on its reputation as a winter resort.

Lakshadweep group of 36 coral islands, 10 inhabited, in the Indian Ocean, 200 mi/320 km off the Malabar coast; area 12 sq mi/32 sq km; population (1991) 51,700. The administrative headquarters are on Kavaratti Island. Products include coir, copra, and fish. The religion is Muslim. The first Western visitor was Vasco da Gama 1499. The islands were British from 1877 until Indian independence and were created a Union Territory of the Republic of India 1956. Formerly known as the Laccadive, Minicoy, and Amindivi Islands, they were renamed Lakshadweep 1973.

Lalique René 1860–1945. French designer and manufacturer of ◊Art Nouveau glass, jewelry, and house interiors. The Lalique factory continues in production at Wingen-sur-Moder, Alsace, under his son Marc and granddaughter Marie-Claude.

Lam Wilfredo 1902–1982. Cuban abstract painter. Influenced by Surrealism in the 1930s (he lived in Paris 1937–41), he created a semiabstract style using mysterious and sometimes menacing images and symbols, mainly taken from Caribbean tradition. His *Jungle* series, for example, contains voodoo elements. He visited Haiti and Martinique in the 1940s, Paris 1952, and also made frequent visits to Italy.

Lamaism religion of Tibet and Mongolia, a form of Mahāyāna Buddhism. Buddhism was introduced into Tibet in AD 640, but the real founder of Lamaism was the Indian missionary Padma Sambhava who began his activity about 750. The head of the church is the ◊Dalai Lama, who is considered an incarnation of the Bodhisattva Avalokiteśvara. On the death of the Dalai Lama great care is taken in finding the infant in whom he has been reincarnated.

Lamar Lucius Quintus Cincinnatus 1825–1893. US jurist and public official. He was a member of the US Senate 1877–85 and served as President Cleveland's secretary of the interior 1885–87. He sat on the US Supreme Court 1888–93.

Lamarck Jean Baptiste de 1744–1829. French naturalist whose theory of evolution, known as *Lamarckism*, was based on the idea that acquired characteristics (changes acquired in an individual's lifetime) are inherited, and that organisms have an intrinsic urge to evolve into better-adapted forms. His works include *Philosophie Zoologique/Zoological Philosophy* 1809 and *Histoire naturelle des animaux sans vertèbres/Natural History of Invertebrate Animals* 1815–22.

Lamb Charles 1775–1834. English essayist and critic. He collaborated with his sister *Mary Lamb* (1764–1847) on *Tales from Shakespeare* 1807, and his *Specimens of English Dramatic Poets* 1808 helped to revive interest in Elizabethan plays. As "Elia" he contributed essays to the *London Magazine* from 1820 (collected 1823 and 1833).

Lamb Willis 1913– . US physicist who revised the quantum theory of Paul ◊Dirac. The hydrogen atom was thought to exist in either of two distinct states carrying equal energies. More sophisticated measurements by Lamb in 1947 demonstrated that the two energy levels were not equal. This discrepancy, since known as the *Lamb shift* won him the 1955 Nobel Prize for Physics.

lamprey any of various eel-shaped jawless fishes belonging to the family Petromyzontidae. A lamprey feeds on other fish by fixing itself by its round mouth to its host and boring into the flesh with its toothed tongue. Lampreys breed in fresh water, and the young live as larvae for about five years before migrating to the sea.

Lancaster city in Pennsylvania, 70 mi/115 km W of Philadelphia; population (1990) 55,550. It produces textiles and electrical goods. It was capital of the US briefly 1777, and was the state capital 1799–1812.

Lancaster Burt (Burton Stephen) 1913– . US film actor, formerly an acrobat. A star from his first film, *The Killers* 1946, he proved himself adept both at action roles and more complex character parts as in such films as *From Here to Eternity* 1953, *The Rose*

Tattoo 1955, *Elmer Gantry* 1960, and *The Leopard/Il Gattopardo* 1963.

He was one of the first stars to produce, forming Hecht-Hill-Lancaster. His later films include *The Swimmer* 1968 and *Atlantic City* 1981.

Lancaster, House of English royal house, a branch of the Plantagenets.

Lancelot of the Lake in British legend, one of King Arthur's knights, the lover of Queen Guinevere. Originally a folk hero, he first appeared in the Arthurian cycle of tales in the 12th century.

Land Edwin Herbert 1909–1991. US inventor of the ◊Polaroid Land camera 1947, which developed the film in one minute inside the camera and produced an "instant" photograph.

While a student at Harvard, Land became interested in polarized light and invented the sheet polarizer, which imbedded lined-up crystals in a clear plastic sheet. This tremendous advance had implications for camera filters, sunglasses and other optical equipment, and related products. Land set up a laboratory 1932, then established the Polaroid Corporation 1937–80. His research also led to a process for 3-D pictures, "instant" color film, "instant" motion pictures, and a new theory of color perception, the "retinex" theory 1977.

Landis Kenesaw Mountain 1866–1944. US judge and baseball commissioner. He was judge in the fraud trial of the infamous "Black Sox" who conspired with gamblers to deliberately lose the 1919 World Series. Appointed as the first commissioner of major-league baseball 1921 he established strict standards against players' involvement with betting.

landlord and tenant in law, the relationship that exists between an owner of land or buildings (the landlord) and a person granted the right to occupy them (the tenant). The landlord grants a lease or tenancy, which may be for a year, a term of years, a week, or any other definite, limited period.

The relationship is known as lessor and lessee, and the lease agreement gives both parties legal rights and obligations.

Landon Alf(red Mossman) 1887–1987. US public official. As a popular liberal Republican, Landon ran for president against the incumbent F D Roosevelt 1936 but was overwhelmingly defeated. He later accepted a presidential appointment as US delegate to the 1938 Pan-American Conference.

Landsbergis Vytautas 1932– . President of Lithuania 1990–1993. He became active in nationalist politics in the 1980s, founding and eventually chairing the anticommunist Sajudis independence movement 1988.

When Sajudis swept to victory in the republic's elections March 1990, Landsbergis chaired the Supreme Council of Lithuania becoming, in effect, president. He immediately drafted the republic's declaration of independence from the USSR which, after initial Soviet resistance, was recognized Sept 1991.

Landseer Edwin Henry 1802–1873. English painter, sculptor, and engraver of animal studies. Much of his work reflects the Victorian taste for sentimental and moralistic pictures, for example *Dignity and Impudence* 1839 (Tate Gallery, London). The *Monarch of the Glen* (John Dewar and Sons Ltd) 1850, depicting a highland stag, was painted for the House of Lords. His sculptures include the lions at the base of Nelson's Column in Trafalgar Square, London, 1857–67.

Land's End promontory of W Cornwall, 9 mi/15 km WSW of Penzance, the westernmost point of England.

landslide sudden downward movement of a mass of soil or rocks from a cliff or steep slope. Landslides happen when a slope becomes unstable, usually because the base has been undercut or because materials within the mass have become wet and slippery.

Landsteiner Karl 1868–1943. Austrian-born immunologist who discovered the ABO ◊blood group system 1900–02, and aided in the discovery of the Rhesus blood factors 1940. He also discovered the polio virus.

He was awarded a Nobel Prize in 1930.

Lang Fritz 1890–1976. Austrian film director whose films are characterized by a strong sense of fatalism and alienation. His German films include *Metropolis* 1927, the sensational *M* 1931, in which Peter Lorre starred as a child-killer, and the series of Dr Mabuse films, after which he fled from the Nazis to Hollywood in 1936. His US films include *Fury* 1936, *You Only Live Once* 1937, *Scarlet Street* 1945, *Rancho Notorious* 1952, and *The Big Heat* 1953. He returned to Germany and directed a third picture in the Dr Mabuse series in 1960.

Lange David (Russell) 1942– . New Zealand Labor prime minister 1983–89. Lange, a lawyer, was elected to the House of Representatives 1977. Labor had a decisive win in the 1984 general election on a non-nuclear military policy, which Lange immediately put into effect, despite criticism from the US. He introduced a free-market economic policy and was reelected 1987. He resigned Aug 1989 over a disagreement with his finance minister.

Langton Stephen c. 1150–1228. English priest who was mainly responsible for drafting the charter of rights, the ◊Magna Carta.

Langtry Lillie. Adopted name of Emilie Charlotte le Breton 1853–1929. English actress, mistress of the future Edward VII. She was known as the "Jersey Lily" from her birthplace in the Channel Islands and considered to be one of the most beautiful women of her time.

language human communication through speech, writing, or both. Different nationalities or ethnic groups typically have different languages or variations on particular languages; for example, Armenians speaking the Armenian language and the British and Americans speaking distinctive varieties of the English language. One language may have various ◊dialects, which may be seen by those who use them as languages in their own right. The term is also used for systems of communication with languagelike qualities, such as *animal language* (the way animals communicate), *body language* (gestures and expressions used to communicate ideas), *sign language* (gestures for the deaf or for use as a ◊lingua franca, as among American Indians), and *computer languages* (such as BASIC and COBOL).

Languedoc former province of S France, bounded by the river Rhône, the Mediterranean Sea, and the regions of Guienne and Gascony.

Languedoc-Roussillon region of S France, comprising the *départements* of Aude, Gard, Hérault, Lozère, and Pyrénées-Orientales; area 10,576 sq mi/27,400 sq km; population (1986) 2,012,000. Its capital is Montpellier, and products include fruit, vegetables, wine, and cheese.

Lansing capital of Michigan, at the confluence of the Grand and Red Cedar rivers; population (1990) 127,300. Manufacturing includes motor vehicles, diesel engines, and pumps. General Motors automobile plants are here, and Michigan State University is the adjoining city of East Lansing. Lansing was settled in the 1840s and has been the state capital since 1847.

Lanthanide any of a series of 15 metallic elements (also known as rare earths) with atomic numbers 57 (lanthanum) to 71 (lutetium). One of its members, promethium, is radioactive. All occur in nature. Lanthanides are group because of their chemical similarities (they are all bivalent), their properties differing only slightly with atomic number.

lanthanum (Greek *lanthanein* "to be hidden") soft, silvery, ductile and malleable, metallic element, symbol La, atomic number 57, atomic weight 138.91, th first of the lanthanide series.

Lanzhou or *Lanchow* capital of Gansu province, China, on the river Huang He, 120 mi/190 km S of the Great Wall; population (1989) 1,480,000. Industries include oil refining, chemicals, fertilizers, and synthetic rubber.

Laois or *Laoighis* county in Leinster province, Republic of Ireland
area 664 sq mi/1,720 sq km
county town Port Laoise
physical flat except for the Slieve Bloom Mountains in the NW
products sugar beet, dairy products, woolens, agricultural machinery
population (1991) 52,300.

Laos landlocked country in SE Asia, bounded N by China, E by Vietnam, S by Cambodia, W by Thailand, and NW by Myanmar.

Laotian member of an Indochinese people who live along the Mekong river system. There are approximately 9 million Laotians in Thailand and 2 million in Laos. The Laotian language is a Thai member of the Sino-Tibetan family.

Lao Zi or Lao Tzu *c.* 604–531 BC. Chinese philosopher, commonly regarded as the founder of ◊Taoism, with its emphasis on the Tao, the inevitable and harmonious way of the universe. Nothing certain is known of his life, and he is variously said to have lived in the 6th or the 4th century BC. The *Tao Tê Ching*, the Taoist scripture, is attributed to him but apparently dates from the 3rd century BC.

La Paz capital city of Bolivia, in Murillo province, 12,400 ft/3,800 m above sea level; population (1988) 1,049,800. Products include textiles and copper. Founded by the Spanish 1548 as Pueblo Nuevo de Nuestra Senõra de la Paz, it has been the seat of government since 1898.

lapis lazuli rock containing the blue mineral lazurite in a matrix of white calcite with small amounts of other minerals. It occurs in silica-poor igneous rocks and metamorphic limestones found in Afghanistan, Siberia, Iran, and Chile. Lapis lazuli was a valuable pigment of the Middle Ages, also used as a gemstone and in inlaying and ornamental work.

Laplace Pierre Simon, Marquis de Laplace 1749–1827. French astronomer and mathematician. In 1796, he theorized that the Solar System originated from a cloud of gas (the nebular hypothesis). He studied the motion of the Moon and planets, and published a five-volume survey of ◊celestial mechanics, *Traité de*

Laos
Lao People's Democratic Republic
(*Saathiaranagroat Prachhathippatay Prachhachhon Lao*)

area 91,400 sq mi/236,790 sq km
capital Vientiane
cities Luang Prabang (the former royal capital), Pakse, Savannakhet
physical landlocked state with high mountains in E; Mekong River in W; jungle covers nearly 60% of land
features Plain of Jars, where prehistoric people carved stone jars large enough to hold a person
head of state Nouhak Phoumsavan from 1992
head of government General Khamtay Siphandon from 1991
political system communism, one-party state

political party Lao People's Revolutionary Party (LPRP) (only legal party)
exports hydroelectric power from the Mekong is exported to Thailand, timber, teak, coffee, electricity
currency new kip
population (1992) 4,409,000 (Lao 48%, Thai 14%, Khmer 25%, Chinese 13%); growth rate 2.2% p.a.
life expectancy men 48, women 51 (1989)
languages Lao (official), French
religions Theravāda Buddhist 85%, animist beliefs among mountain dwellers
literacy 45% (1991)
GNP $500 million (1987); $180 per head (1988)

chronology
1893–1945 Laos was a French protectorate.
1945 Temporarily occupied by Japan.
1946 Retaken by France.
1950 Granted semiautonomy in French Union.
1954 Independence achieved from France.
1960 Right-wing government seized power.
1962 Coalition government established; civil war continued.
1973 Vientiane cease-fire agreement. Withdrawal of US, Thai, and North Vietnamese forces.
1975 Communist-dominated republic proclaimed with Prince Souphanouvong as head of state.
1986 Phoumi Vongvichit became acting president.
1988 Plans announced to withdraw 40% of Vietnamese forces stationed in the country.
1989 First assembly elections since communist takeover.
1991 Constitution approved. Kaysone Phomvihane elected president. General Khamtay Siphandon named as new premier.
1992 Nov: Phomvihane died; replaced by Nouhak Phoumsavan. Dec: new national assembly created, replacing supreme people's assembly, and general election held (effectively one-party).

méchanique céleste 1799–1825. Among his mathematical achievements was the development of probability theory.

Lapland region of Europe within the Arctic Circle in Norway, Sweden, Finland, and the Kola Peninsula of NW Russia, without political definition. Its chief resources are chromium, copper, iron, timber, hydro-electric power, and tourism. The indigenous population are the ◊Saami (formerly known as Lapps), a seminomadic herding people. Lapland has low temperatures, with three months' continuous daylight in summer and three months' continuous darkness in winter. There is summer agriculture.

laptop computer portable microcomputer, small enough to be used on the operator's lap. It consists of a single unit, incorporating a keyboard, ◊floppy disk or ◊hard disk drives, and a screen. The screen often forms a lid that folds back in use. It uses a liquid-crystal or gas-plasma display, rather than the bulkier and heavier cathode-ray tubes found in most display terminals. A typical laptop computer measures about 8.3 × 11.7 in/210 × 297 mm (A4), is 2 in/5 cm thick, and weighs less than 6 lb 9 oz/3 kg.

larch any tree of the genus *Larix*, of the family Pinaceae. The common larch *L. decidua* grows to 130 ft/40 m. It is one of the few ◊conifer trees to shed its leaves annually. The small needlelike leaves are replaced every year by new bright-green foliage, which later darkens.

Large Electron Positron Collider (LEP) the world's largest particle ◊accelerator, in operation from 1989 at the CERN laboratories near Geneva in Switzerland. It occupies a tunnel 12.5 ft/3.8 m wide and 16.7 mi/27 km long, which is buried 590 ft/180 m underground and forms a ring consisting of eight curved and eight straight sections. In 1989 the LEP was used to measure the mass and lifetime of the Z particle, carrier of the weak nuclear force.

La Rioja region of N Spain; area 1,930 sq mi/5,000 sq km; population (1986) 263,000. The river Ebro passes through the region, but it is a tributary, the Río Oja, which gives its name to the region. The capital is Logroño. La Rioja is known for its woody red and white wines.

lark songbird of the family Alaudidae, found mainly in the Old World, but also in North America. Larks are brownish-tan in color and usually about 7 in/18 cm long; they nest on the ground in the open. The skylark *Alauda arvensis* sings as it rises almost vertically in the air. It breeds in Britain; it is light-brown, and 7 in/18 cm long.

larkspur plant of the genus ◊delphinium.

La Rochefoucauld François, duc de La Rochefoucauld 1613–1680. French writer. His *Réflexions, ou sentences et maximes morales/Reflections, or Moral Maxims* 1665 is a collection of brief, epigrammatic, and cynical observations on life and society, with the epigraph "Our virtues are mostly our vices in disguise." He was a lover of Mme de Lafayette.

larva stage between hatching and adulthood in those species in which the young have a different appearance and way of life from the adults. Examples include tadpoles (frogs) and caterpillars (butterflies and moths). Larvae are typical of the invertebrates, some of which (for example, shrimps) have two or more distinct larval stages. Among vertebrates, it is only the amphibians and some fishes that have a larval stage.

La Paz La Paz, the seat of government in Bolivia.

laryngitis inflammation of the larynx, causing soreness of the throat, a dry cough, and hoarseness. The acute form is due to a virus or other infection, excessive use of the voice, or inhalation of irritating smoke, and may cause the voice to be completely lost. With rest, the inflammation usually subsides in a few days.

larynx in mammals, a cavity at the upper end of the trachea (windpipe), containing the vocal cords. It is stiffened with cartilage and lined with mucous membrane. Amphibians and reptiles have much simpler larynxes, with no vocal cords. Birds have a similar cavity, called the **syrinx**, found lower down the trachea, where it branches to form the bronchi. It is very complex, with well-developed vocal cords.

la Salle René Robert Cavelier, Sieur de la Salle 1643–1687. French explorer. He made an epic voyage through North America, exploring the Mississippi River down to its mouth, and in 1682 founded Louisiana. When he returned with colonists, he failed to find the river mouth again, and was eventually murdered by his mutinous men.

Lascaux cave system in SW France with prehistoric wall paintings. It is richly decorated with realistic and symbolic paintings of buffaloes, horses, and red deer of the Upper Paleolithic period, about 18,000 BC. The caves, near Montignac in the Dordogne, were discovered 1940. Similar paintings are found in ◊Altamira, Spain. The opening of the Lascaux caves to tourists

lapis lazuli The deep-blue mineral lapis lazuli is the source of the pigment ultramarine.

laser

The laser was invented by US scientist, Theodore Maiman, who followed up a suggestion made by Charles Townes.

A laser beam is used to check quartz windows (center) for cleanliness, used in electro-optical technology.

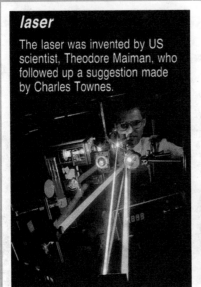

Technician working with a laser at an optical bench.

Mirrors reflecting the beam of an argon ion laser.

Gas laser

(1) In a gas laser, electrons moving between the electrodes pass energy to gas atoms. An energized atom emits a ray of light.

(2) The ray hits another energized atom causing it to emit a further ray of light.

(3) The rays bounce between the mirrors at each end causing a build-up of light. Eventually the beam becomes strong enough to pass through the half-silvered mirror at one end, producing a laser beam.

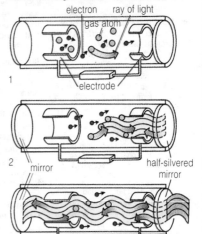

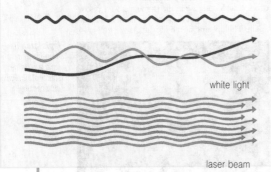

white light

laser beam

White light is a mixture of light waves of different wavelengths, corresponding to different colors. In a beam of white light, all the waves are out of step.

In a laser beam, all the waves are of the same wavelength, so the beam is a pure color. All the waves in a laser beam are in step.

led to deterioration of the paintings; the caves were closed 1963 and a facsimile opened 1983.

Las Cruces city in S New Mexico, on the Rio Grande, N of the Mexican border; population (1990) 62,120. It is a processing center for the area's crops, such as pecans, cotton, and vegetables. White Sands Missile Range is nearby.

laser (acronym for *light amplification by stimulated emission of radiation*) a device for producing a narrow beam of light, capable of traveling over vast distances without dispersion, and of being focused to give enormous power densities (10^8 watts per cm² for high-energy lasers). The laser operates on a principle similar to that of the ◊maser (a high-frequency microwave amplifier or oscillator). The uses of lasers include communications (a laser beam can carry much more information than can radio waves), cutting, drilling, welding, satellite tracking, medical and biological research, and surgery.

laser printer computer printer in which the image to be printed is formed by the action of a laser on a light-sensitive drum, then transferred to paper by means of an electrostatic charge. Laser printers are page printers, printing a complete page at a time. The printed image, which can take the form of text or pictures, is made up of tiny dots, or ink particles. The quality of the image generated depends on the fineness of these dots—most laser printers can print up to 300 dots per in/120 dots per cm across the page.

Las Palmas or *Las Palmas de Gran Canaria* tourist resort on the NE coast of Gran Canaria, Canary Islands; population (1991) 347,700. Products include sugar and bananas.

Lassa fever acute disease caused by a virus, first detected in 1969, and spread by a species of rat found only in W Africa. It is characterized by high fever and inflammation of various organs. There is no known cure, the survival rate being less than 50%.

Las Vegas city in Nevada, known for its nightclubs and gambling casinos; population (1990) 258,300. Las Vegas entertains millions of visitors each year and is an important convention center. Founded 1855 in a ranching area, the modern community developed with the coming of the railroad 1905. The first casino-hotel opened 1947.

The University of Nevada–Las Vegas is here, and Nellis Air Force Base, Hoover Dam, and Lake Mead National Recreation Area are nearby. An army base was established here 1864. The city's growth was helped by its proximity to S California population centers and the development of air conditioning.

La Tène prehistoric settlement at the east end of Lake Neuchâtel, Switzerland, which has given its name to a culture of the Iron Age. The culture lasted from the 5th century BC to the Roman conquest.

latent heat in physics, the heat absorbed or radiated by a substance as it changes state (for example, from solid to liquid) at constant temperature and pressure.

Lateran Treaties series of agreements that marked the reconciliation of the Italian state with the papacy in 1929. They were hailed as a propaganda victory for the Fascist regime. The treaties involved recognition of the sovereignty of the ◊Vatican City State, the payment of an indemnity for papal possessions lost during unification in 1870, and agreement on the role of the Catholic church within the Italian state in the form of a concordat between Pope Pius XI and the dictator Mussolini.

latex (Latin "liquid") fluid of some plants (such as the rubber tree and poppy), an emulsion of resins, proteins, and other organic substances. It is used as the basis for making rubber. The name is also applied to a suspension in water of natural or synthetic rubber (or plastic) particles used in rubber goods, paints, and adhesives.

Latimer Hugh 1490–1555. English Christian church reformer and bishop. After his conversion to Protestantism in 1524 he was imprisoned several times but was protected by Cardinal Wolsey and Henry VIII. After the accession of the Catholic Mary, he was burned for heresy.

Latin Indo-European language of ancient Italy. Latin has passed through four influential phases: as the language of (1) republican Rome, (2) the Roman Empire, (3) the Roman Catholic church, and (4) W European culture, science, philosophy, and law during the Middle Ages and the Renaissance. During the third and fourth phases, much Latin vocabulary entered the English language. It is the parent form of the ◊Romance languages, noted for its highly inflected grammar and conciseness of expression.

Latin America countries of South and Central America (also including Mexico) in which Spanish, Portuguese, and French are spoken.

Latter-day Saint member of the Christian sect the ◊Mormons.

Latvia country in N Europe, bounded E by Russia, N by Estonia, N and NW by the Baltic Sea, S by Lithuania, and SE by Belarus. *See panel p. 540*

Latvian language or *Lettish* language of Latvia; with Lithuanian it is one of the two surviving members of the Balto-Slavic branch of the Indo-European language family.

laudanum alcoholic solution (tincture) of the drug ◊opium.

laughing gas popular name for ◊nitrous oxide, an anesthetic.

Laughton Charles 1899–1962. English actor who became a US citizen in 1950. Initially a Classical stage actor, he joined the Old Vic 1933. His films were made in Hollywood and include such roles as the king in *The Private Life of Henry VIII* 1933 (Academy Award), Captain Bligh in *Mutiny on the Bounty* 1935, and Quasimodo in *The Hunchback of Notre Dame* 1939. In 1955 he directed *Night of the Hunter* and in 1961 appeared in *Judgment at Nuremberg.*

Laurasia northern landmass formed 200 million years ago by the splitting of the single world continent ◊Pangaea. (The southern landmass was ◊Gondwanaland.) It consisted of what was to become North America, Greenland, Europe, and Asia, and is believed to have broken up about 100 million years ago with the separation of North America from Europe.

laurel any evergreen tree of the European genus *Laurus*, family Lauraceae, with glossy, aromatic leaves, yellowish flowers, and black berries. The leaves of sweet bay or poet's laurel *L. nobilis* are used in cooking. Several species are cultivated worldwide.

California laurel *Umbellularia californica* of the W US belongs to a different genus in the laurel family.

Laurel and Hardy Stan Laurel (adopted name of Arthur Stanley Jefferson) (1890–1965) and Oliver Hardy (1892–1957). US film comedians who were one of the most successful comedy teams in film history

Latvia
Republic of

area 24,595 sq mi/63,700 sq km
capital Riga
cities Daugavpils, Liepāja, Jurmala, Jelgava, Ventspils
physical wooded lowland (highest point 1,024 ft/312 m), marshes, lakes; 293 mi/472 km of coastline; mild climate
features Western Dvina River; Riga is largest port on the Baltic after St Petersburg (formerly Leningrad)
head of state Guntis Ulmanis from 1993
head of government Valdis Birkavs from 1993
political system emergent democratic republic
political parties Latvian Popular Front, nationalist; Latvian Social-Democratic Workers' Party; Latvian Way
products electronic and communications equipment, electric railroad carriages, motorcycles, consumer durables, timber, paper and woolen goods, meat and dairy products
currency Latvian ruble
population (1990) 2,700,000 (Latvian 52%, Russian 34%, Byelorussian 5%, Ukrainian 3%)
language Latvian

religions mostly Lutheran Protestant, with a Roman Catholic minority

chronology
1917 Soviets and Germans contested for control of Latvia.
1918 Feb: Soviet forces overthrown by Germany. Nov: Latvia declared independence. Dec: Soviet rule restored after German withdrawal.
1919 Soviet rule overthrown by British naval and German forces May–Dec; democracy established.
1934 Coup replaced established government.
1939 German-Soviet secret agreement placed Latvia under Russian influence.
1940 Incorporated into USSR as constituent republic.
1941–44 Occupied by Germany.
1944 USSR regained control.
1980 Nationalist dissent began to grow.
1988 Latvian Popular Front established to campaign for independence. Prewar flag readopted; official status given to Latvian language.
1989 Popular Front swept local elections.
1990 Jan: Communist Party's (CP) monopoly of power abolished. March–April: Popular Front secured majority in elections. April: Latvian CP split into pro-independence and pro-Moscow wings. May: unilateral declaration of independence from USSR, subject to transitional period for negotiation.
1991 Jan: Soviet troops briefly seized key installations in Riga. March: overwhelming vote for independence in referendum. Aug: full independence declared at time of anti-Gorbachev coup; CP outlawed. Sept: independence recognized by Soviet government and Western nations; joined United Nations (UN) and Conference on Security and Cooperation in Europe.
1992 Russia began pull-out of ex-Soviet troops, to be completed 1994. July: curbing of rights of noncitizens in Latvia prompted Russia to request minority protection by UN.
1993 Latvian Way, led by former CP ideological secretary Anatolijs Gorbunov, won most seats in general election. Guntis Ulmanis elected president. Valdis Birkavs elected prime minister.

(Stan was slim, Oliver rotund). Their partnership began in 1927, survived the transition from silent films to sound, and resulted in more than 200 short and feature-length films, which were revived as a worldwide cult in the 1970s. Among these are *Pack Up Your Troubles* 1932, *Our Relations* 1936, and *A Chump at Oxford* 1940.

Lausanne resort and capital of Vaud canton, W Switzerland, above the N shore of Lake Geneva; population (1990) 123,200. Industries include chocolate, scientific instruments, and publishing.

lava Cooled lava of the pahoehoe type at Kilauea, Hawaii.

lava molten rock that erupts from a ◊volcano and cools to form extrusive ◊igneous rock. It differs from magma in that it is molten rock on the surface; magma is molten rock below the surface. Lava that is high in silica is viscous and sticky and does not flow far; it forms a steep-sided conical volcano. Low-silica lava can flow for long distances and forms a broad flat volcano.

Laval Pierre 1883–1945. French right-wing politician. He was prime minister and foreign secretary 1931–32, and again 1935–36. In World War II he joined Pétain's Vichy government as vice-premier in June 1940; dismissed in Dec 1940, he was reinstated by Hitler's orders as head of the government and foreign minister in 1942. After the war he was executed.

Laver Rod(ney George) 1938– . Australian lawn tennis player. He was one of the greatest left-handed players, and the only player to win the Grand Slam twice (1962 and 1969).

Lavoisier Antoine Laurent 1743–1794. French chemist. He proved that combustion needs only a part of the air, which he called oxygen, thereby destroying the theory of phlogiston (an imaginary "fire element" released during combustion). With Pierre de Laplace, the astronomer and mathematician, he showed that water is a compound of oxygen and hydrogen. In this way he established the basic rules of chemical combination.

law body of rules and principles under which justice is administered or order enforced in a state or nation. In western Europe there are two main systems: Roman law and English law. US law is a modified form of English law.

law courts bodies that adjudicate in legal disputes. Civil and criminal cases are usually dealt with by separate courts. In many countries there is a hierarchy of courts that provide an appeal system.

Many counties and municipalities also have courts, usually limited to minor offenses. There are also a number of federal and state specialized judicial and quasi-judicial bodies dealing with ◊administrative law. In the US, the head of the federal judiciary is the Supreme Court, which also hears appeals from the inferior federal courts and from the decisions of the highest state courts. The US Courts of Appeal—organized in circuits—deal with appeals from the US district courts in which civil and criminal cases are heard. State courts deal with civil and criminal cases involving state laws and usually consist of a Supreme Court or appeals court and courts in judicial districts.

Lawrence town in Massachusetts; population (1990) 70,200. Industries include textiles, clothing, paper, and radio equipment. The town was established 1845 to utilize power from the Merrimack Rapids on a site first settled 1655.

Lawrence city in NE Kansas, on the Kansas River between Topeka to the W and Kansas City to the E; seat of Douglas County; population (1990) 65,600. Its main industries are food processing and chemicals.

The University of Kansas 1863 is here. Lawrence was terrorized by Quantrill's Raiders 1863.

Lawrence D(avid) H(erbert) 1885–1930. English writer whose work expresses his belief in emotion and the sexual impulse as creative and true to human nature. The son of a Nottinghamshire miner, Lawrence studied at University College, Nottingham, and became a teacher. His writing first received attention after the publication of 1 the semiautobiographical *Sons and Lovers* 1913, which includes a portrayal of his mother (died 1911). Other novels include *The Rainbow* 1915, *Women in Love* 1921, and *Lady Chatterley's Lover* 1928. Lawrence also wrote short stories (for example "The Woman Who Rode Away") and poetry.

Lawrence Ernest O(rlando) 1901–1958. US physicist. His invention of the cyclotron particle ◊accelerator pioneered the production of artificial ◊radioisotopes.

Lawrence T(homas) E(dward), known as *Lawrence of Arabia* 1888–1935. British soldier and writer. Appointed to the military intelligence department in Cairo, Egypt, during World War I, he took part in negotiations for an Arab revolt against the Ottoman Turks, and in 1916 attached himself to the emir Faisal. He became a guerrilla leader of genius, combining raids on Turkish communications with the organization of a joint Arab revolt, described in *The Seven Pillars of Wisdom* 1926.

lawrencium synthesized, radioactive, metallic element, the last of the actinide series, symbol Lr, atomic number 103, atomic weight 262. Its only known isotope, Lr-257, has a half-life of 4.3 seconds and was originally synthesized at the University of California at Berkeley 1961 by bombarding californium with boron nuclei. The original symbol, Lw, was officially changed 1963.

Lawton city in SW Oklahoma, on Cache Creek, SW of Oklahoma City, seat of Comanche County; population

Lawrence English novelist, poet, and essayist D H Lawrence.

(1980) 80,054. Processing the area's agricultural products is the city's main industry. Fort Sill, an army base, is to the north.

lawyer a member of the legal profession who provides counsel to clients on matters of civil or criminal law and who represents clients on such matters in negotiations with others, before government agencies, and in civil and criminal courts. An ◊attorney.

laxative substance used to relieve constipation (infrequent bowel movement). Current medical opinion discourages regular or prolonged use. Regular exercise and a diet high in vegetable fiber is believed to be the best means of preventing and treating constipation.

Lazarus in the New Testament, the brother of Martha, a friend of Jesus, raised by him from the dead. Lazarus is also the name of a beggar in a parable told by Jesus (Luke 16).

Lazio (Roman *Latium*) region of W central Italy; area 6,639 sq mi/17,200 sq km; capital Rome; population (1990) 5,191,500. Products include olives, wine, chemicals, pharmaceuticals, and textiles. Home of the Latins from the 10th century BC, it was dominated by the Romans from the 4th century BC.

LCD abbreviation for ◊liquid-crystal display.

L-dopa chemical, normally produced by the body, which is converted by an enzyme to dopamine in the brain. It is essential for integrated movement of individual muscle groups.

Leacock Stephen Butler 1869–1944. Canadian humorist whose writings include *Literary Lapses* 1910, *Sunshine Sketches of a Little Town* 1912, and *Frenzied Fiction* 1918.

lead heavy, soft, malleable, gray, metallic element, symbol Pb (from Latin *plumbum*), atomic number 82, atomic weight 207.19. Usually found as an ore (most often in galena), it occasionally occurs as a free metal (◊native metal), and is the final stable product of the decay of uranium. Lead is the softest and weakest of the commonly used metals, with a low melting point; it is a poor conductor of electricity and resists acid cor-

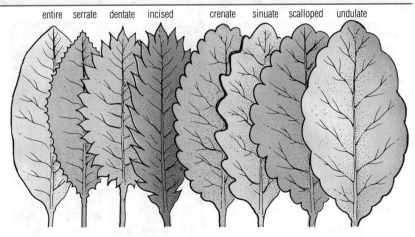

leaf Leaf shapes and arrangements on the stem are many and varied; in cross-section, a leaf is a complex arrangement of cells surrounded by the epidermis.

entire serrate dentate incised crenate sinuate scalloped undulate

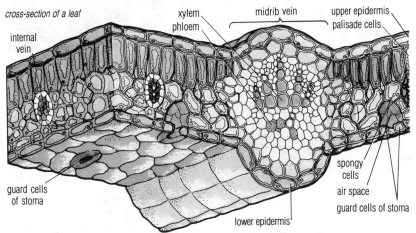

cross-section of a leaf

xylem
phloem

midrib vein

upper epidermis
palisade cells

internal
vein

guard cells
of stoma

spongy
cells

air space

guard cells of stoma

lower epidermis

rosion. As a cumulative poison, lead enters the body from lead water pipes, lead-based paints, and leaded gasoline. (In humans, exposure to lead shortly after birth is associated with impaired mental health between the ages of two and four.) The metal is an effective shield against radiation and is used in batteries, glass, ceramics, and alloys such as pewter and solder.

lead–acid cell type of ◊battery.

leaded gasoline gasoline containing the lead compound tetraethyllead, $(C_2H_5)_4Pb$, an antiknock agent. It improves the combustion of gasoline and the performance of an automobile engine. The lead from the exhaust fumes enters the atmosphere, mostly as simple lead compounds.

lead ore any of several minerals from which lead is extracted. The main primary ore is galena or lead sulfite PbS. This is unstable, and on prolonged exposure to the atmosphere it oxidizes into the minerals cerussite $PbCO_3$ and anglesite $PbSO_4$. Lead ores are usually associated with other metals, particularly silver—which can be mined at the same time—and zinc, which can cause problems during smelting.

leaf lateral outgrowth on the stem of a plant, and in most species the primary organ of ◊photosynthesis.

The chief leaf types are cotyledons (seed leaves), scale leaves (on underground stems), foliage leaves, and bracts (in the axil of which a flower is produced).

League of Nations international organization formed after World War I to solve international disputes by arbitration. Established in Geneva, Switzerland, 1920, the league included representatives from states throughout the world, but was severely weakened by the US decision not to become a member, and had no power to enforce its decisions. It was dissolved 1946. Its subsidiaries included the *International Labor Organization* and the *Permanent Court of International Justice* in The Hague, Netherlands, both now under the auspices of the ◊United Nations.

The formation of the league was first suggested by President ◊Wilson in his Fourteen Points as part of the peace settlement for World War I. The US did not become a member since it did not ratify the the Treaty of ◊Versailles. Although the league organized conferences, settled minor disputes, and did humanitarian work, it failed to handle the aggression of the 1930s—of Japan against China, Italy in Ethiopia, and Germany against neighboring countries.

Leakey Louis (Seymour Bazett) 1903–1972. British archeologist, born in Kenya. In 1958, with his wife

Mary Leakey, he discovered gigantic extinct-animal fossils in the ◊Olduvai Gorge in Tanzania, as well as many remains of an early human type.

Leakey Mary 1913– . British archeologist. In 1948 she discovered, on Rusinga Island, Lake Victoria, E Africa, the prehistoric ape skull known as *Proconsul*, about 20 million years old; and human remains at Laetoli, to the south, about 3,750,000 years old.

Leakey Richard 1944– . British archeologist. In 1972 he discovered at Lake Turkana, Kenya, an apelike skull, estimated to be about 2.9 million years old; it had some human characteristics and a brain capacity of 800 cu cm. In 1984 his team found an almost complete skeleton of *Homo erectus* some 1.6 million years old. He is the son of Louis and Mary Leakey.

Lean David 1908–1991. British film director. His films, noted for their atmospheric quality, include early work codirected with playwright Noël ◊Coward. *Brief Encounter* 1946 established Lean as a leading talent. Among his later films are such accomplished epics as *The Bridge on the River Kwai* 1957 (Academy Award), *Lawrence of Arabia* 1962 (Academy Award), and *Dr Zhivago* 1965. The unfavorable reaction to *Ryan's Daughter* 1970 caused him to withdraw from filmmaking for over a decade, but *A Passage to India* 1984 represented a return to form.

Lear Edward 1812–1888. English artist and humorist. His *Book of Nonsense* 1846 popularized the limerick (a five-line humorous verse). He first attracted attention by his paintings of birds, and later turned to land-

---

Lebanon
Republic of
(*al-Jumhouria al-Lubnaniya*)

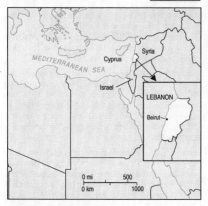

area 4,034 sq mi/10,452 sq km
capital and port Beirut
cities ports Tripoli, Tire, Sidon
physical narrow coastal plain; Bekka valley N–S between Lebanon and Anti-Lebanon mountain ranges
features Mount Hermon; Chouf Mountains; archeological sites at Baalbeck, Byblos, Tyre; until the civil war, the financial center of the Middle East
head of state Elias Hrawi from 1989
head of government Rafik al-Hariri from 1992
political system emergent democratic republic
political parties Phalangist Party, Christian, radical, right-wing; Progressive Socialist Party (PSP), Druse, moderate, socialist; National Liberal Party (NLP), Maronite, center-left; Parliamentary Democratic Front, Sunni Muslim, centrist; Lebanese Communist Party (PCL), nationalist, communist
exports citrus and other fruit, vegetables; industrial products to Arab neighbors
currency Lebanese pound
population (1990 est) 3,340,000 (Lebanese 82%, Palestinian 9%, Armenian 5%); growth rate –0.1% p.a.
life expectancy men 65, women 70 (1989)
languages Arabic, French (both official), Armenian, English
religions Muslim 57% (Shiite 33%, Sunni 24%), Christian (Maronite and Orthodox) 40%, Druse 3%
literacy 75% (1989)
GNP $1.8 bn; $690 per head (1986)

chronology
1920–41 Administered under French mandate.
1944 Independence achieved.

1948–49 Lebanon joined first Arab war against Israel. Palestinian refugees settled in the south.
1964 Palestine Liberation Organization (PLO) founded in Beirut.
1967 More Palestinian refugees settled in Lebanon.
1971 PLO expelled from Jordan; established headquarters in Lebanon.
1975 Outbreak of civil war between Christians and Muslims.
1976 Cease-fire agreed; Syrian-dominated Arab deterrent force formed to keep the peace but considered by Christians as a occupying force.
1978 Israel invaded S Lebanon in search of PLO forces shelling Israeli settlements on Lebanese border. International peacekeeping force established. Fighting broke out again.
1979 Part of S Lebanon declared an "independent free Lebanon."
1982 Bashir Gemayel became president but was assassinated before he could assume office; succeeded by his brother Amin Gemayel. Israel again invaded Lebanon. Palestinians withdrew from Beirut under supervision of international peacekeeping force. PLO moved its headquarters to Tunis.
1983 Agreement reached for the withdrawal of Syrian and Israeli troops but abrogated under Syrian pressure.
1984 Most of international peacekeeping force withdrawn. Muslim militia took control of W Beirut.
1985 Lebanon in chaos; many foreigners taken hostage.
1987 Syrian troops sent into Beirut.
1988 Agreement on a Christian successor to Gemayel failed; he established a military government; Selim al-Hoss set up rival government; threat of partition hung over the country.
1989 Christian leader General Michel Aoun declared "war of liberation" against Syrian occupation; Saudi Arabia and Arab League sponsored talks that resulted in new constitution recognizing Muslim majority; René Muhawad named president, assassinated after 17 days in office; Elias Hrawi named successor; Aoun occupied presidential palace, rejected constitution.
1990 Release of Western hostages began. General Aoun surrendered and legitimate government restored, with Umar Karami as prime minister.
1991 Government extended control to the whole country. Treaty of cooperation with Syria signed. More Western hostages released. General Aoun pardoned.
1992 Karami resigned as prime minister; succeeded by Rashid al-Solh. Remaining Western hostages released. General election boycotted by many Christians; pro-Syrian administration reelected; Rafik al-Hariri became prime minister.
1993 July: Israel launched attacks on S Lebanon against Hezbollah strongholds.

scapes. He traveled to Italy, Greece, Egypt, and India, publishing books on his travels with his own illustrations, and spent most of his later life in Italy.

learning theory in psychology, a theory about how an organism acquires new behaviors. Two main theories are Classical and operant ◊conditioning.

leather material prepared from the hides and skins of animals, by tanning with vegetable tannins and chromium salts. Leather is a durable and water-resistant material, and is used for bags, shoes, clothing, and upholstery. There are three main stages in the process of converting animal skin into leather: cleaning, tanning, and dressing. Tanning is often a highly polluting process.

Lebanon country in W Asia, bounded N and E by Syria, S by Israel, and W by the Mediterranean Sea. *See panel p. 543*

Lebanon city in SE Pennsylvania, NE of Harrisburg, seat of Lebanon County; population (1990) 24,800. Industries include iron and steel products, textiles, clothing, and chemicals.

Lebowa black homeland in Transvaal province, South Africa; population (1985) 1,836,000. It achieved self-governing status 1972.

Le Brun Charles 1619–1690. French artist, painter to Louis XIV from 1662. In 1663 he became director of the French Academy and of the Gobelins factory, which produced art, tapestries, and furnishings for the new palace of Versailles. In the 1640s he studied under the painter Poussin in Rome. Returning to Paris in 1646, he worked on large decorative schemes including the *Galerie des glaces* (Hall of Mirrors) at Versailles. He also painted portraits.

Le Carré John. Adopted name of David John Cornwell 1931– . English writer of thrillers. His low-key realistic accounts of complex espionage include *The Spy Who Came in from the Cold* 1963, *Tinker Tailor Soldier Spy* 1974, *Smiley's People* 1980, *The Russia House* 1989. and *The Night Manager* 1993. He was a member of the Foreign Service 1960–64.

lecithin lipid (fat), containing nitrogen and phosphorus, that forms a vital part of the cell membranes of plant and animal cells. The name is from the Greek *lekithos* "egg yolk", eggs are a major source of lecithin.

Leclanché Georges 1839–1882. French engineer. In 1866 he invented a primary electrical cell, the *Leclanché cell*, which is still the basis of most dry batteries. A Leclanché cell consists of a carbon rod (the ◊anode) inserted into a mixture of powdered carbon and manganese dioxide contained in a porous pot, which sits in a glass jar containing an ◊electrolyte (conducting medium) of ammonium chloride solution, into which a zinc ◊cathode is inserted. The cell produces a continuous current, the carbon mixture acting as a depolarizer; that is, it prevents hydrogen bubbles from forming on the anode and increasing resistance. In a dry battery, the electrolyte is made in the form of a paste with starch.

Le Corbusier assumed name of Charles-édouard Jeanneret 1887–1965. Swiss architect. His functionalist approach to town planning in industrial society was based on the interrelationship between machine forms and the techniques of modern architecture. His concept, *La Ville radieuse*, developed in Marseille, France (1945–50), and Chandigarh, India, placed buildings and open spaces with related functions in a circular formation, with buildings based on standard-sized units mathematically calculated according to the proportions of the human figure (see ◊Fibonacci).

LED abbreviation for ◊light-emitting diode.

Leda in Greek mythology, the wife of Tyndareus and mother of ◊Clytemnestra. Zeus, who came to her as a swan, was the father of her other children: ◊Helen of Troy and the twins Castor and Pollux.

Ledbetter Huddie, "Leadbelly" *c.* 1888–1949. US musician. Better known by his nickname, he was born in Mooringsport, Louisiana, and spent his early years as a farmhand. Drawn to music at an early age, he traveled throughout the South and became well known for his blues guitar playing. In 1934 he was "discovered" by visiting folklorists John and Alan Lomax, who helped him begin a professional concert and recording career. Ledbetter was an important source of inspiration for the urban folk movement of the 1950s. His rendition of "Good Night, Irene" became a folk classic.

Le Duc Tho 1911–1990. North Vietnamese diplomat who was joint winner (with US secretary of state Kissinger) of the 1973 Nobel Peace Prize for his part in the negotiations to end the Vietnam War. He indefinitely postponed receiving the award.

Ledyard John 1751–1789. American explorer and adventurer. As a British marine, he was sent to Long Island during the American Revolution 1775, but, refusing to fight against his own countrymen, he deserted in 1782. After an ill-fated journey through Siberia, he died in Cairo on his way to find the source of the Niger River.

Lee Bruce. Adopted name of Lee Yuen Kam 1941–1973. US "Chinese Western" film actor, an expert in ◊kung fu, who popularized the oriental martial arts in the West with pictures made in Hong Kong, such as *Fists of Fury* 1972 and *Enter the Dragon* 1973, his last film.

Lee Henry 1756–1818. American military and political leader. In the cavalry during the American Revolution 1775–83, he rose to the rank of major, winning the nickname "Light-Horse Harry" for his lightning attacks. After the war, he entered politics and served in the Continental Congress 1785–88, as governor of Virginia 1792–95, and as a member of the US House of Representatives 1799–1801.

Lee Robert E(dward) 1807–1870. US military leader, Confederate commander in the American ◊Civil War, and military strategist. In 1859 he suppressed John ◊Brown's raid on Harper's Ferry. Lee had freed his own slaves long before the war began, and he was opposed to secession, however his devotion to his native Virginia led him to join the Confederacy. At the outbreak of war he became military adviser to Jefferson ◊Davis, president of the Confederacy, and in 1862 commander of the Army of Northern Virginia. Lee actually had been offered command of the Union armies, but he resigned his commission to return to Virginia. During 1862–63 he made several raids into Northern territory but after his defeat at Gettysburg was compelled to take the defensive; he surrendered 1865 at Appomattox.

Lee Spike (Shelton Jackson) 1957– . US film director, actor and writer. His work presents the bitter realities of contemporary African-American life in an aggressive, often controversial manner. His films, in which he sometimes appears, include *She's Gotta Have It* 1986, *Do The Right Thing* 1989, *Jungle Fever* 1991, and *Malcolm X* 1992.

Lee and Yang Lee Tsung Dao (1926–) and Yang Chen Ning (1922–) Chinese physicists who studied how parity operates at the nuclear level. They found no proof for the claim, made by ◊Wigner, that nuclear processes were indistinguishable from their mirror images, and that elementary particles made no distinction between left and right. In 1956 they predicted that parity was not conserved in weak interactions. They shared a Nobel Prize 1957.

leech annelid worm forming the class Hirudinea. Leeches inhabit fresh water, and in tropical countries infest damp forests. As bloodsucking animals they are injurious to people and animals, to whom they attach themselves by means of a strong mouth adapted to sucking.

Leeds city in West Yorkshire, England, on the river Aire; population (1991 est) 674,400. Industries include engineering, printing, chemicals, glass, and woolens. Notable buildings include the Town Hall designed by Cuthbert Brodrick, Leeds University (1904), the Art Gallery (1844), Temple Newsam (birthplace of Henry Darnley 1545, now a museum), and the Cistercian Abbey of Kirkstall (1147). It is a center of communications where road, rail, and canal (to Liverpool and Goole) meet.

leek onionlike plant of the genus *Allium* of the lily family Liliaceae. The cultivated leek is a variety of the wild *A. ampeloprasum* of the Mediterranean area and Atlantic islands. The lower leaf parts form the bulb, which is eaten as a vegetable.

Lee Teng-hui 1923– . Taiwanese politician, vice president 1984–88, president and Kuomintang (see ◊Guomindang) party leader from 1988. Lee, the country's first island-born leader, is viewed as a reforming technocrat.

Leeuwenhoek Anton van 1632–1723. Dutch pioneer of microscopic research. He ground his own lenses, some of which magnified up to 200 times. With these he was able to see individual red blood cells, sperm, and bacteria, achievements not repeated for more than a century.

Leeward Islands (1) group of islands, part of the ◊Society Islands, in ◊French Polynesia, S Pacific; (2) general term for the N half of the Lesser ◊Antilles in the West Indies; (3) former British colony in the West Indies (1871–1956) comprising Antigua, Montserrat, St Christopher/St Kitts–Nevis, Anguilla, and the Virgin Islands.

left wing in politics, the socialist parties. The term originated in the French National Assembly of 1789, where the nobles sat in the place of honor to the right of the president, and the commons sat to the left. This arrangement has become customary in European parliaments, where the progressives sit on the left and the conservatives on the right. It is also usual to speak of the right, left, and center, when referring to the different elements composing a single party.

legacy in law, a gift of personal property made by a testator in a will and transferred on the testator's death to the legatee. *Specific legacies* are definite named objects; a *general legacy* is a sum of money or item not specially identified; a *residuary legacy* is all the remainder of the deceased's personal estate after debts have been paid and the other legacies have been distributed.

legend traditional or undocumented story about famous people. The term was originally applied to the books of readings designed for use in Christian religious service, and was extended to the stories of saints read in monasteries.

Lee US Confederate general Robert E Lee.

Léger Fernand 1881–1955. French painter, associated with ◊Cubism. From around 1909 he evolved a characteristic style, composing abstract and semiabstract works with cylindrical forms, reducing the human figure to constructions of pure shape. Mechanical forms are constant themes in his work, including his designs for the Swedish Ballet 1921–22, murals, and the abstract film *Ballet mécanique/Mechanical Ballet*.

legionnaire's disease pneumonialike disease, so called because it was first identified when it broke out at a convention of the American Legion in Philadelphia in 1976. Legionnaire's disease is caused by the bacterium *Legionella pneumophila*, which breeds in warm water (for example, in the cooling towers of airconditioning systems). It is spread in minute water droplets, which may be inhaled.

legislature lawmaking body or bodies in a political system. Some legislatures are unicameral (having one chamber), and some bicameral (with two).

Legnano, Battle of defeat of Holy Roman emperor Frederick I Barbarossa by members of the Lombard League in 1176 at Legnano, NW of Milan. It was a major setback to the emperor's plans for imperial domination over Italy and showed for the first time the power of infantry against feudal cavalry.

Le Guin Ursula K(roeber) 1929– . US writer of science fiction and fantasy. Her novels include *The Left Hand of Darkness* 1969, which questions sex roles; the *Earthsea* trilogy 1968–72; *The Dispossessed* 1974, which compares an anarchist and a capitalist society; *Orsinian Tales* 1976; and *Always Coming Home* 1985.

legume plant of the family Leguminosae, which has a pod containing dry seeds. The family includes peas, beans, lentils, clover, and alfalfa (lucerne). Legumes are important in agriculture because of their specialized roots, which have nodules containing bacteria capable of fixing nitrogen from the air and increasing the fertility of the soil. The edible seeds of legumes are called *pulses*.

Lehár Franz 1870–1948. Hungarian composer. He wrote many operettas, among them *The Merry Widow* 1905, *The Count of Luxembourg* 1909, *Gypsy Love* 1910, and *The Land of Smiles* 1929. He also composed songs, marches, and a violin concerto.

Le Havre industrial port (engineering, chemicals, oil refining) in Normandy, NW France, on the river Seine; population (1990) 197,200.

It is the largest port in Europe, and has transatlantic passenger links.

Lehman Herbert Henry 1878–1963. US political leader. In 1932 he became governor of New York, and his subsequent support of F D Roosevelt's reform policies earned his own administration the name "Little New Deal."

In 1942 Lehman was appointed director of the federal Office of Foreign Relief and Rehabilitation. He served in the US Senate 1949–57.

Leibniz Gottfried Wilhelm 1646–1716. German mathematician and philosopher. Independently of, but concurrently with, the British scientist Isaac Newton he developed the branch of mathematics known as ⟡calculus. In his metaphysical works, such as *The Monadology* 1714, he argued that everything consisted of innumerable units, *monads*, the individual properties of which determined each thing's past, present, and future. Monads, although independent of each other, interacted predictably; this meant that Christian faith and scientific reason need not be in conflict and that "this is the best of all possible worlds." His optimism is satirized in Voltaire's *Candide*.

Leicester Robert Dudley, Earl of Leicester *c.* 1532–1588. English courtier. Son of the Duke of Northumberland, he was created Earl of Leicester 1564. Queen Elizabeth I gave him command of the army sent to the Netherlands 1585–87 and of the forces prepared to resist the threat of Spanish invasion of 1588. His lack of military success led to his recall, but he retained Elizabeth's favor until his death.

Leicestershire county in central England
area 984 sq mi/2,550 sq km
cities Leicester (administrative headquarters), Loughborough, Melton Mowbray, Market Harborough
features Rutland district (formerly England's smallest county, with Oakham as its county town); Rutland Water, one of Europe's largest reservoirs; Charnwood Forest; Vale of Belvoir (under which are large coal deposits)
products horses, cattle, sheep, dairy products, coal
population (1991) 860,500
famous people C P Snow, Thomas Babington Macaulay, Titus Oates.

Leigh Vivien. Adopted name of Vivian Mary Hartley 1913–1967. English actress who appeared on the stage in London and New York, and won Academy Awards

lemur The fork-marked lemur is tree-dwelling, with large eyes that look forward over a small, pointed nose.

for her performances as Scarlett O'Hara in *Gone With the Wind* 1939 and as Blanche du Bois in *A Streetcar Named Desire* 1951.

Leinster SE province of the Republic of Ireland, comprising the counties of Carlow, Dublin, Kildare, Kilkenny, Laois, Longford, Louth, Meath, Offaly, Westmeath, Wexford, and Wicklow; area 7,577 sq mi/19,630 sq km; capital Dublin; population (1991) 1,860,000.

Leipzig city in W Saxony, Germany, 90 mi/145 km SW of Berlin; population (1986) 552,000. Products include furs, leather goods, cloth, glass, automobiles, and musical instruments.

Leisler Jacob 1640–1691. German-born colonial administrator in America. Taking advantage of the political instability caused by England's Glorious Revolution of 1688, he took command of New York in the name of William and Mary. Deposed in 1691 by troops dispatched from England, Leisler was tried and hanged for treason.

Leitrim county in Connacht province, Republic of Ireland, bounded NW by Donegal Bay
area 591 sq mi/1,530 sq km
county town Carrick-on-Shannon
features rivers: Shannon, Bonet, Drowes, and Duff
products potatoes, cattle, linen, woolens, pottery, coal, iron, lead
population (1991) 25,300.

Lemaître Georges Edouard 1894–1966. Belgian cosmologist who in 1927 proposed the ⟡Big Bang theory of the origin of the universe. He predicted that the entire universe was expanding, which the US astronomer Edwin ⟡Hubble confirmed. Lemaître suggested that the expansion had been started by an initial explosion, the Big Bang, a theory that is now generally accepted.

Le Mans industrial city in Sarthe *département*, W France; population (1990) 148,500, conurbation 191,000. It has a motor-racing circuit where the annual endurance 24-hour race (established 1923) for sports automobiles and their prototypes is held.

lemming small rodent of the family Cricetidae, especially the genus *Lemmus*, comprising four species worldwide in northern latitudes. It is about 5 in/12 cm long, with thick brownish fur, a small head, and a short tail. Periodically, when their population exceeds the available food supply, lemmings undertake mass migrations.

Lemmon Jack (John Uhler III) 1925– . US character actor, often cast as the lead in comedy films, such as *Some Like It Hot* 1959 but equally skilled in serious roles, as in *The China Syndrome* 1979 and *Dad* 1990. He won Academy Awards as best supporting actor (*Mr. Roberts*, 1955) and best actor (*Save the Tiger*, 1973).

lemon sour fruit of the small, evergreen, semitropical lemon tree *Citrus limon*. It may have originated in NW India, and was introduced into Europe by the Spanish Moors in the 12th or 13th century. It is now grown in Italy, Spain, California, Florida, South Africa, and Australia.

LeMond Greg 1961– . US racing cyclist, the first American to win the Tour de France 1986. He repeated his triumph 1989, 1990.

lemur prosimian ⟡primate of the family Lemuridae, inhabiting Madagascar and the Comoro Islands. There are about 16 species, ranging from mouse-sized to dog-sized animals. Lemurs are arboreal animals, and some species are nocturnal. They have long, bushy tails, and feed on fruit, insects, and small animals. Many are threatened with extinction owing to loss of their forest habitat and, in some cases, from hunting.

Lena longest river in Asiatic Russia, 2,730 mi/4,400 km, with numerous tributaries. Its source is near Lake Baikal, and it empties into the Arctic Ocean through a delta 240 mi/400 km wide. It is ice-covered for half the year.

Lendl Ivan 1960– . Czech-born American lawn-tennis player. He has won eight Grand Slam singles titles, including the US and French titles three times each. He has won more than $15 million in prize money.

lend-lease in US history, an act of Congress passed in March 1941 that gave the president power to order "any defense article for the government of any country whose defense the president deemed vital to the defense of the US." During World War II, the US negotiated many Lend-Lease agreements, notably with Britain and the Soviet Union.

Lenin Vladimir Ilyich. Adopted name of Vladimir Ilyich Ulyanov 1870–1924. Russian revolutionary, first leader of the USSR, and communist theoretician. Active in the 1905 Revolution, Lenin had to leave Russia when it failed, settling in Switzerland in 1914. He returned to Russia after the February revolution of 1917 (see ◊Russian Revolution). He led the ◊Bolshevik revolution in Nov 1917 and became leader of a Soviet government, concluded peace with Germany, and organized a successful resistance to White Russian (pro-tsarist) uprisings and foreign intervention 1918–20. His modification of traditional Marxist doctrine to fit conditions prevailing in Russia became known as *Marxism-Leninism*, the basis of communist ideology.

Leningrad former name (1924–91) of the Russian city ◊St Petersburg.

Lennon John (Ono) 1940–1980. UK rock singer, songwriter, and guitarist, in the US from 1971; a founder member of the ◊Beatles. Both before the band's breakup 1969 and in his solo career, he collaborated intermittently with his wife *Yoko Ono* (1933–). "Give Peace a Chance", a hit 1969, became an anthem of the peace movement. His solo work alternated between the confessional and the political, as on the album *Imagine* 1971. He was shot dead by a fan.

Le Nôtre André 1613–1700. French landscape gardener, creator of the gardens at Versailles and Les Tuileries, Paris.

lens in optics, a piece of a transparent material, such as glass, with two polished surfaces—one concave or convex, and the other plane, concave, or convex—that modifies rays of light. A convex lens brings rays of light together; a concave lens makes the rays diverge. Lenses are essential to glasses, microscopes, telescopes, cameras, and almost all optical instruments.

lensing, gravitational see ◊gravitational lensing.

Lent in the Christian church, the 40-day period of fasting that precedes Easter, beginning on Ash Wednesday, but omitting Sundays.

lentil annual Old World plant *Lens culinaris* of the pea family Leguminosae. The plant, which resembles vetch, grows 6–18 in/15–45 cm high and has white, blue, or purplish flowers. The seeds, contained in pods about 0.6 in/1.6 cm long, are widely used as food.

Lenz's law in physics, a law stating that the direction of an electromagnetically induced current (generated by moving a magnet near a wire or a wire in a magnetic field) will oppose the motion producing it. It is

Lenin Vladimir Ilyich Lenin with members of his family and friends in 1922.

named after the German physicist Heinrich Friedrich Lenz (1804–1865), who announced it in 1833.

Leo zodiacal constellation in the northern hemisphere represented as a lion. The Sun passes through Leo from mid-Aug to mid-Sept. Its brightest star is first-magnitude Regulus at the base of a pattern of stars called the Sickle. In astrology, the dates for Leo are between about July 23 and Aug 22.

Leo III *the Isaurian c.* 680–740. Byzantine emperor and soldier. He seized the throne in 717, successfully defended Constantinople against the Saracens 717–18, and attempted to suppress the use of images in church worship (see ◊iconoclast).

Leo I St *the Great c.* 390–461. Pope from 440 who helped to establish the Christian liturgy. Leo summoned the Chalcedon Council where his Dogmatical Letter was accepted as the voice of St Peter. Acting as ambassador for the emperor Valentinian III (425–455), Leo saved Rome from devastation by the Huns by buying off their king, Attila.

Leo III *c.* 750–816. Pope from 795. After the withdrawal of the Byzantine emperors, the popes had become the real rulers of Rome. Leo III was forced to flee because of a conspiracy in Rome and took refuge at the court of the Frankish king Charlemagne. He returned to Rome in 799 and crowned Charlemagne emperor on Christmas Day 800, establishing the secular sovereignty of the pope over Rome under the suzerainty of the emperor (who became the Holy Roman emperor).

Leo X Giovanni de' Medici 1475–1521. Pope from 1513. The son of Lorenzo the Magnificent of Florence, he was created a cardinal at 13. He bestowed on Henry VIII of England the title of Defender of the Faith. A patron of the arts, he sponsored the rebuilding of St Peter's Church, Rome. He raised funds for this by selling indulgences (remissions of punishment for sin), a sale that led the religious reformer Martin Luther to rebel against papal authority. Leo X condemned Luther in the bull *Exsurge domine* 1520 and excommunicated him in 1521.

Leominster city in N central Massachusetts, on the Nashua River, NE of Worcester; population (1990) 38,140. Industries include plastics, paper products, clothing, and chemicals.

Leonard Elmore (John, Jr) 1925– . US author of westerns and thrillers, marked by vivid dialogue, as in *City Primeval* 1980, *La Brava* 1983, *Stick* 1983, *Glitz* 1985, *Freaky Deaky* 1988, and *Get Shorty* 1990.

Leonardo da Vinci
The Virgin and Child
with St Anne and St
John the Baptist
(mid-1490s),
National Gallery,
London.

composing in his spare time, until the success of *Pagliacci* in 1892. His other operas include *La Bohème* 1897 (contemporary with Puccini's version) and *Zara* 1900.

Leone Sergio 1928–1989. Italian film director, responsible for popularizing "spaghetti" Westerns (Westerns made in Italy and Spain, usually with a US leading actor and a European supporting cast and crew) and making a world star of Clint Eastwood. His films include *Per un pugno di dollari/A Fistful of Dollars* 1964, *C'era una volta il West/Once Upon a Time in the West* 1968, and *C'era una volta il America/Once Upon a Time in America* 1984.

Leonidas died 480 BC. King of Sparta. He was killed while defending the pass of ◊Thermopylae with 300 Spartans, 700 Thespians, and 400 Thebans against a huge Persian army.

leopard or *panther* cat *Panthera pardus*, found in Africa and Asia. The background color of the coat is golden, and the black spots form rosettes, that differ according to the variety; black panthers are simply a color variation and retain the patterning as a "watered-silk" effect. The leopard is 5–8 ft/1.5–2.5 m long, including the tail, which may measure 3 ft/1 m.

Leopold I 1790–1865. King of the Belgians from 1831, having been elected to the throne on the creation of an independent Belgium. Through his marriage, when prince of Saxe-Coburg, to Princess Charlotte Augusta, he was the uncle of Queen Victoria of Great Britain and had considerable influence over her.

Leopold III 1901–1983. King of the Belgians 1934–51. He surrendered to the German army in World War II 1940. Postwar charges against his conduct led to a regency by his brother Charles and his eventual abdication 1951 in favor of his son Baudouin.

Léopoldville former name (until 1966) of ◊Kinshasa, a city in Zaire.

Lepanto, Battle of sea battle Oct 7, 1571, fought in the Mediterranean Gulf of Corinth off Lepanto (Italian name of the Greek port of *Naupaktos*), then in Turkish possession, between the Ottoman Empire and forces from Spain, Venice, Genoa, and the Papal States, jointly commanded by the Spanish soldier Don John of Austria. The combined western fleets overcame Muslim sea power. The Spanish writer Cervantes was wounded in the battle.

Le Pen Jean-Marie 1928– . French extreme right-wing politician. In 1972 he formed the French National Front, supporting immigrant repatriation and capital punishment; the party gained 14% of the national vote in the 1986 election. Le Pen was elected to the European Parliament in 1984.

leprosy or *Hansen's disease* chronic, progressive disease caused by a bacterium *Mycobacterium leprae* closely related to that of tuberculosis. The infection attacks the skin and nerves. Once common in many countries, leprosy is now confined almost entirely to the tropics. It is controlled with drugs.

Lerner Alan Jay 1918–1986. US lyricist, collaborator with Frederick ◊Loewe on musicals including *Brigadoon* 1947, *Paint Your Wagon* 1951, *My Fair Lady* 1956, *Gigi* 1958, and *Camelot* 1960.

lesbianism homosexuality (sexual attraction to one's own sex) between women, so called from the Greek island of Lesbos (now Lesvos), the home of ◊Sappho the poet and her followers to whom the behavior was attributed.

Leonard Sugar Ray 1956– . US boxer. In 1988 he became the first man to have won world titles at five officially recognized weights. In 1976 he was Olympic light-welterweight champion; he won his first professional title in 1979 when he beat Wilfred Benitez for the World Boxing Council (WBC) welterweight title. He later won titles at junior middleweight (World Boxing Association, WBA version) 1981, middleweight (WBC) 1987, light-heavyweight (WBC) 1988, and super-middleweight (WBC) 1988. In 1989 he drew with Thomas Hearns.

Leonardo da Vinci 1452–1519. Italian painter, sculptor, architect, engineer, and scientist. One of the greatest figures of the Italian Renaissance, he was active in Florence, Milan, and, from 1516, France. As state engineer and court painter to the duke of Milan, he painted the *Last Supper* mural about 1495 (Sta Maria delle Grazie, Milan), and on his return to Florence painted the *Mona Lisa* (Louvre, Paris) about 1503–06. His notebooks and drawings show an immensely inventive and inquiring mind, studying aspects of the natural world from anatomy to aerodynamics.

Leoncavallo Ruggiero 1857–1919. Italian operatic composer, born in Naples. He played in restaurants,

leopard The leopard
has exceptionally
acute hearing,
together with good
sight and sense of
smell.

Lesotho
Kingdom of

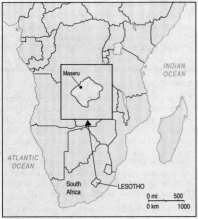

area 11,717 sq mi/30,355 sq km
capital Maseru
cities Teyateyaneng, Mafeteng, Roma, Quthing
physical mountainous with plateaus, forming part of South Africa's chief watershed
features Lesotho is an enclave within South Africa
political system constitutional monarchy
head of state King Letsie III from 1990
head of government Ntsu Mokhehle from 1993
political parties Basotho National Party (BNP), traditionalist, nationalist; Basutoland Congress Party (BCP); Basotho Democratic Alliance (BDA)

exports wool, mohair, diamonds, cattle, wheat, vegetables
currency maluti
population (1992) 1,854,000; growth rate 2.7% p.a.
life expectancy men 59, women 62 (1989)
languages Sesotho, English (official), Zulu, Xhosa
religions Protestant 42%, Roman Catholic 38%
literacy 59% (1988)
GNP $408 million; $410 per head (1988)

chronology
1868 Basutoland became a British protectorate.
1966 Independence achieved from Britain, within the Commonwealth, as the Kingdom of Lesotho, with Moshoeshoe II as king and Chief Leabua Jonathan as prime minister.
1970 State of emergency declared and constitution suspended.
1973 Progovernment interim assembly established; BNP won majority of seats.
1975 Members of the ruling party attacked by guerrillas backed by South Africa.
1985 Elections canceled because no candidates opposed BNP.
1986 South Africa imposed border blockade, forcing deportation of 60 African National Congress members. General Lekhanya ousted Chief Jonathan in coup. National assembly abolished. Highlands Water Project agreement signed with South Africa.
1990 Moshoeshoe II dethroned by military council; replaced by his son Mohato as King Letsie III.
1991 Lekhanya ousted in military coup led by Col Elias Tutsoane Ramaema. Political parties permitted to operate.
1992 Ex-king Moshoeshoe returned from exile.
1993 Free elections ended military rule; Ntsu Mokhehle of BCP became prime minister.

Lesbos alternate spelling of ◊Lesvos, an island in the Aegean Sea.

lesion any change in a body tissue that is a manifestation of disease or injury.

Lesotho landlocked country in S Africa, an enclave within South Africa.

less developed country (dc) any country late in developing an industrial base, and dependent on cash crops and unprocessed minerals. The Group of 77 was established in 1964 to pressure industrialized countries into giving greater aid to less developed countries.

Lesseps Ferdinand, Vicomte de Lesseps 1805–1894. French engineer, constructor of the ◊Suez Canal 1859–69; he began the ◊Panama Canal in 1879, but withdrew after failing to construct it without locks.

Lessing Doris (May) (née Taylor) 1919– . British novelist, born in Iran. Concerned with social and political themes, particularly the place of women in society, her work includes *The Grass is Singing* 1950, the five-novel series *Children of Violence* 1952–69, *The Golden Notebook* 1962, *The Good Terrorist* 1985, and *The Fifth Child* 1988. She has also written an "inner space fiction" series *Canopus in Argus Archives* 1979–83, and under the adopted name "Jane Somers," *The Diary of a Good Neighbour* 1981.

Lesvos Greek island in the Aegean Sea, near the coast of Turkey
area 831 sq mi/2,154 sq km
capital Mytilene
products olives, wine, grain

population (1981) 104,620
history ancient name Lesbos; an Aeolian settlement, the home of the poets Alcaeus and Sappho; conquered by the Turks from Genoa 1462; annexed to Greece 1913.

letterpress method of printing from raised type, pioneered by Johann ◊Gutenberg in Europe in the 1450s.

lettuce annual edible plant *Lactuca sativa*, family Compositae, believed to have been derived from the wild species *L. serriola*. There are many varieties, including the cabbage lettuce, with round or loose heads, and the Cos lettuce, with long, upright heads.

leukemia any one of a group of cancers of the blood cells, with widespread involvement of the bone marrow and other blood-forming tissue. The central feature of leukemia is runaway production of white blood cells that are immature or in some way abnormal. These rogue cells, which lack the defensive capacity of healthy white cells, overwhelm the normal ones, leaving the victim vulnerable to infection. Treatment is with radiotherapy and ◊cytotoxic drugs to suppress replication of abnormal cells, or by bone-marrow transplant.

leukocyte a white blood cell. Leukocytes are part of the body's defenses and give immunity against disease. There are several different types. Some (◊phagocytes and macrophages) engulf invading microorganisms, others kill infected cells, while ◊lymphocytes produce more specific immune responses. Human blood contains about 11,000 leukocytes to the cubic millimeter—about 1 to every 500 red cells.

Le Vau Louis 1612–1670. French architect who drafted the plan of Versailles, rebuilt the Louvre, and built Les Tuileries in Paris.

levee naturally formed raised bank along the side of a river channel. When a river overflows its banks, the rate of flow in the flooded area is less than that in the channel, and silt is deposited. After the waters have withdrawn the silt is left as a bank that grows with successive floods. Eventually the river, contained by the levee, may be above the surface of the surrounding flood plain. Notable levees are found on the lower reaches of the Mississippi in the US and the Po in Italy.

level or *spirit level* instrument for finding horizontal level, or adjusting a surface to an even level, used in surveying, building construction, and archeology. It has a glass tube of colored liquid, in which a bubble is trapped, mounted in an elongated frame.

Levelers democratic party in the English Civil War. The Levelers found wide support among Cromwell's New Model Army and the yeoman farmers, artisans, and small traders, and proved a powerful political force 1647–49. Their program included the establishment of a republic, government by a parliament of one house elected by male suffrage, religious toleration, and sweeping social reforms.

leveraged buyout in business, the purchase of a controlling proportion of the shares of a company by its own management, financed almost exclusively by borrowing. It is so called because the ratio of a company's long-term debt to its equity (capital assets) is known as its "leverage."

Lévesque René 1922–1987. French-Canadian politician. In 1968 he founded the Parti Québecois, with the aim of an independent Québec, but a referendum rejected the proposal in 1980. He was premier of Québec 1976–85.

Levi Primo 1919–1987. Italian novelist. He joined the anti-Fascist resistance during World War II, was captured, and sent to the concentration camp at Auschwitz. He wrote of these experiences in *Se questo è un uomo/If This Is a Man* 1947.

Levi-Montalcini Rita 1909– . Italian neurologist who discovered nerve-growth factor, a substance that controls how many cells make up the adult nervous system. She shared the 1986 Nobel Prize for Medicine with US biochemist Stanley Cohen (1922–).

Lévi-Strauss Claude 1908–1990. French anthropologist who sought to find a universal structure governing all societies, as reflected in the way their mythis are constructed. His work include *Tristes Tropiques* 1955 and *Mythologiques/Mythologies* 1964–71.

levitation counteraction of gravitational forces on a body. As claimed by medieval mystics, spiritualist mediums, and practitioners of transcendental meditation, it is unproven. In the laboratory it can be produced scientifically; for example, electrostatic force and acoustical waves have been used to suspend water drops for microscopic study. It is also used in technology, for example, in magnetic levitation as in ◊maglev trains.

Lewes, Battle of battle in 1264 caused by the baronial opposition to the English King Henry III, led by Simon de Montfort, earl of Leicester (1208–65). The king was defeated and captured at the battle.

Lewis (William) Arthur 1915– . British economist born on St Lucia, West Indies. He specialized in the economic problems of developing countries and created a model relating the terms of trade between less developed and more developed nations to their respective levels of labor productivity in agriculture. He shared the Nobel Prize for Economics with an American, Theodore Schultz, 1979. He wrote many books, including the *Theory of Economic Growth* 1955.

Lewis Carl (Frederick Carleton) 1961– . US track and field athlete who won eight gold medals and one silver in three successive Olympic Games. At the 1984 Olympic Games he equaled the performance of Jesse ◊Owens, winning gold medals in the 100 and 200 meters, 400-meter relay, and long jump.

Lewis Cecil Day. Irish poet; see ◊Day Lewis.

Lewis C(live) S(taples) 1898–1963. British academic and writer, born in Belfast. His books include the medieval study *The Allegory of Love* 1936 and the space fiction, *Out of the Silent Planet* 1938. He was a committed Christian and wrote essays in popular theology such as *The Screwtape Letters* 1942 and *Mere Christianity* 1952, the autobiographical *Surprised by Joy* 1955, and a series of books of Christian allegory for children, set in the magic land of Narnia, including *The Lion, the Witch, and the Wardrobe* 1950.

Lewis Jerry. Adopted name of Joseph Levitch 1926– . US comic actor and director. Formerly in partnership (1946–56) with Dean Martin, their film debut was in *My Friend Irma* 1949. He was revered as a solo performer by French critics ("Le Roi du Crazy"), but films that he directed such as *The Nutty Professor* 1963 were less well received in the US. He appeared with Robert De Niro in *The King of Comedy* 1982.

Lewis Jerry Lee 1935– . US rock-and-roll and country singer and pianist. His trademark was the boogie-woogie-derived "pumping piano" style in hits such as "Whole Lotta Shakin' Going On" and "Great Balls of Fire" 1957; later recordings include "What Made Milwaukee Famous" 1968.

Lewis John L(lewellyn) 1880–1969. US labor leader. President of the United Mine Workers (UMW) 1920–60, he was largely responsible for the adoption of national mining safety standards in the US. His militancy and the miners' strikes during and after World War II led to President Truman's nationalization of the mines in 1946.

He helped found the Congress of Industrial Organizations 1935, which unionized workers in mass-production industries.

Lewis (Harry) Sinclair 1885–1951. US novelist. He made a reputation with satirical novels: *Main Street* 1920, depicting American small-town life; *Babbitt* 1922, the story of a real-estate dealer of the Midwest caught in the conventions of his milieu; *Arrowsmith* 1925, a study of the pettiness in medical science; and *Elmer Gantry* 1927, a satiric portrayal of evangelical religion. *Dodsworth*, a gentler novel of a US industrialist, was published 1929. He was the first American to be awarded the Nobel Prize for Literature, in 1930.

Born in Sauk Center, Minnesota, Lewis graduated from Yale University. He stayed for a time at Upton Sinclair's socialist colony in New Jersey, then became a freelance journalist. His other works include *It Can't Happen Here* 1935, *Cass Timberlane* 1945, *Kingsblood Royal* 1947, and *The God-Seeker* 1949.

Lewis Meriwether 1774–1809. US explorer. He was commissioned by president Thomas Jefferson to find a land route to the Pacific with William Clark (1770–1838). They followed the Missouri River to its source, crossed the Rocky Mountains (aided by an Indian woman, Sacajawea) and followed the Columbia River to the Pacific, then returned overland to St Louis 1804–06.

Formerly private secretary to President Jefferson, he was rewarded for his expedition with the governorship of the Louisiana Territory. His death, near Nashville, Tennessee, has been ascribed to suicide, but was more probably murder.

The detailed journals kept of the expedition added to an understanding of the region and facilitated westward expansion.

Lewiston city in SW Maine, across the Androscoggin River from Auburn; population (1990) 39,750. It has textile, shoe, and clothing industries. Bates College 1855 is here.

Lexington city in Kentucky, center of the bluegrass country; population (1990) 225,400. Racehorses are bred in the area, and races and shows are held. There is a tobacco market and the University of Kentucky (1865).

Leyden Lucas van. See ◊Lucas van Leyden, Dutch painter.

Lhasa ("the Forbidden City") capital of the autonomous region of Tibet, China, at 16,400 ft/5,000 m; population (1982) 105,000. Products include handicrafts and light industry. The holy city of ◊Lamaism, Lhasa was closed to Westerners until 1904, when members of a British expedition led by Col Francis E Younghusband visited the city. It was annexed with the rest of Tibet 1950–51 by China, and the spiritual and temporal head of state, the Dalai Lama, fled in 1959 after a popular uprising against Chinese rule. Monasteries have been destroyed and monks killed, and an influx of Chinese settlers has generated resentment. In 1988 and 1989 nationalist demonstrators were shot by Chinese soldiers.

liability in accounting, a financial obligation. Liabilities are placed alongside assets on a balance sheet to show the wealth of the individual or company concerned at a given date.

Liaoning province of NE China
area 58,300 sq mi/151,000 sq km
capital Shenyang
cities Anshan, Fushun, Liaoyang
features one of China's most heavily industrialized areas
products cereals, coal, iron, salt, oil
population (1990) 39,460,000
history developed by Japan 1905–45, including the *Liaodong Peninsula*, whose ports had been conquered from the Russians.

Liaquat Ali Khan Nawabzada 1895–1951. Indian politician, deputy leader of the Muslim League 1940–47, first prime minister of Pakistan from 1947. He was assassinated by objectors to his peace policy with India.

liberalism political and social theory that favors representative government, freedom of the press, speech, and worship, the abolition of class privileges, the use of state resources to protect the welfare of the individual, and international ◊free trade. It is historically associated with the Liberal Party in the UK and the Democratic Party in the US.

Liberal Party British political party, the successor to the ◊Whig Party, with an ideology of liberalism. In the 19th century, it represented the interests of commerce and industry. Its outstanding leaders were Palmerston, Gladstone, and Lloyd George. From 1914 it declined, and the rise of the Labour Party pushed the

Liberia
Republic of

area 42,989 sq mi/111,370 sq km
capital and port Monrovia
cities ports Buchanan, Greenville
physical forested highlands; swampy tropical coast where six rivers enter the sea
features nominally the world's largest merchant marine as minimal registration controls make Liberia's a flag of convenience; the world's largest rubber plantations
head of state and government collective presidency from 1993
political system emergent democratic republic
political parties National Democratic Party of Liberia (NDLP), nationalist; Liberian Action Party (LAP); Liberian Unity Party (LUP); United People's Party (UPP); Unity Party (UP)
exports iron ore, rubber (Africa's largest producer), timber, diamonds, coffee, cocoa, palm oil
currency Liberian dollar
population (1992) 2,780,000 (95% indigenous); growth rate 3% p.a.
life expectancy men 53, women 56 (1989)
languages English (official), over 20 Niger-Congo languages
media two daily newspapers, one published under government auspices, the other independent and with the largest circulation (10,000 copies)
religions animist 65%, Muslim 20%, Christian 15%
literacy men 47%, women 23% (1985 est)
GNP $973 million; $450 per head (1988)

chronology
1847 Founded as an independent republic.
1944 William Tubman elected president.
1971 Tubman died; succeeded by William Tolbert.
1980 Tolbert assassinated in coup led by Samuel Doe, who suspended the constitution and ruled through a People's Redemption Council.
1984 New constitution approved. National Democratic Party of Liberia (NDPL) founded by Doe.
1985 NDPL won decisive victory in allegedly rigged general election. Unsuccessful coup against Doe.
1990 Rebels under former government minister Charles Taylor controlled nearly entire country by July. Doe killed during a bloody civil war between rival rebel factions. Amos Sawyer became interim head of government.
1991 Amos Sawyer reelected president. Rebel leader Charles Taylor agreed to work with Sawyer. Peace agreement failed but later revived; UN peacekeeping force drafted into republic.
1992 Monrovia under siege by Taylor's rebel forces.
1993 Peace agreement between opposing groups signed in Benin, under OAU/UN auspices. Interim collective presidency established prior to elections in 1994.

Liberals into the middle ground. The Liberals joined forces with the Social Democratic Party (SDP) as the Alliance for the 1983 and 1987 elections. In 1988, a majority of the SDP voted to merge with the Liberals to form the ◊Social and Liberal Democrats.

Liberia country in W Africa, bounded N by Guinea, E by the Ivory Coast, S and SW by the Atlantic Ocean, and NW by Sierra Leone. *See panel p. 551*

libido in Freudian psychology, the psychic energy, or life force, that is to be found even in a newborn child. The libido develops through a number of phases, identified by Freud as the *oral stage*, when a child tests everything by mouth, the *anal stage*, when the child gets satisfaction from control of its body, and the *genital stage*, when sexual instincts find pleasure in the outward show of love.

Libra faint zodiacal constellation in the southern hemisphere adjoining Scorpius, and represented as the scales of justice. The Sun passes through Libra during Nov. The constellation was once considered to be a part of Scorpius, seen as the scorpion's claws. In astrology, the dates for Libra are between about Sept 23 and Oct 23 (see ◊precession).

library collection of information (usually in the form of books) held for common use. The earliest was at Nineveh in Babylonian times. The first public library was opened in Athens in 330 BC. All ancient libraries were reference libraries: books could be consulted but not borrowed.

libretto the text of an opera or other dramatic vocal work, or the scenario of a ballet.

Libreville capital of Gabon, on the estuary of the river Gabon; population (1988) 352,000. Products include timber, oil, and minerals. It was founded 1849 as a refuge for slaves freed by the French. Since the 1970s the city has developed rapidly due to the oil trade.

Libya country in N Africa, bounded N by the Mediterranean Sea, E by Egypt, SE by Sudan, S by Chad and Niger, and W by Algeria and Tunisia.

license document issued by a government or other recognized authority conveying permission to the holder to do something otherwise prohibited and designed to facilitate accurate records, the maintenance of order, and collection of revenue.

lichen any organism of the group Lichenes, which consists of a specific fungus and a specific alga existing in a mutually beneficial relationship. Found as colored patches or spongelike masses adhering to trees, rocks, and other substrates, lichens flourish under adverse conditions.

Liechtenstein landocked country in W central Europe, bounded E by Austria and W by Switzerland.

lie detector instrument that records graphically certain body activities, such as thoracic and abdominal respiration, blood pressure, pulse rate, and galvanic skin response (changes in electrical resistance of the skin). Marked changes in these activities when a person answers a question may indicate that the person is lying.

life ability to grow, reproduce, and respond to such stimuli as light, heat, and sound. It is thought that life on Earth began about 4 billion years ago. The earliest

---

Libya
Great Socialist People's Libyan Arab-Jamahiriya
(*al-Jamahiriya al-Arabiya al-Libya al-Shabiya al-Ishtirakiya al-Uzma*)

area 679,182 sq mi/1,759,540 sq km
capital Tripoli
cities ports Benghazi, Misurata, Tobruk
physical flat-to-undulating plains with plateaus and depressions stretch S from the Mediterranean coast to an extremely dry desert interior
environment plan to pump water from below the Sahara to the coast risks rapid exhaustion of nonrenewable supply (Great Manmade River Project)
features Gulf of Sirte; rock paintings of about 3000 BC in the Fezzan; Roman city sites include Leptis Magna, Sabratha
head of state and government Moamer al-Khaddhafi from 1969

political system one-party socialist state
political party Arab Socialist Union (ASU), radical, left-wing
exports oil, natural gas
currency Libyan dinar
population (1992) 4,447,000 (including 500,000 foreign workers); growth rate 3.1% p.a.
life expectancy men 64, women 69 (1989)
language Arabic
religion Sunni Muslim 97%
literacy 60% (1989)
GNP $20 bn; $5,410 per head (1988)

chronology
1911 Conquered by Italy.
1934 Colony named Libya.
1942 Divided into three provinces: Fezzan (under French control); Cyrenaica, Tripolitania (under British control).
1951 Achieved independence as the United Kingdom of Libya, under King Idris.
1969 King deposed in a coup led by Col Moamer al-Khaddhafi. Revolution Command Council set up and the Arab Socialist Union (ASU) proclaimed the only legal party.
1972 Proposed federation of Libya, Syria, and Egypt abandoned.
1980 Proposed merger with Syria abandoned. Libyan troops began fighting in Chad.
1981 Proposed merger with Chad abandoned.
1986 US bombing of Khaddhafi's headquarters, following allegations of his complicity in terrorist activities.
1988 Diplomatic relations with Chad restored.
1989 US accused Libya of building a chemical-weapons factory and shot down two Libyan planes; reconciliation with Egypt.
1992 Khaddhafi under international pressure to extradite suspected Lockerbie and UTA (Union de Transports Aerians) bombers for trial outside Libya; sanctions imposed.

Liechtenstein
Principality of
(*Fürstentum Liechtenstein*)

area 62 sq mi/160 sq km
capital Vaduz
cities Balzers, Schaan, Ruggell
physical landlocked Alpine; includes part of Rhine Valley in W
features no airport or railroad station; easy tax laws make it an international haven for foreign companies and banks (some 50,000 companies are registered)
head of state Prince Hans Adam II from 1989

head of government Hans Brunhart from 1978
political system constitutional monarchy
political parties Fatherland Union (VU); Progressive Citizens' Party (FBP)
exports microchips, dental products, small machinery, processed foods, postage stamps
currency Swiss franc
population (1992) 29,600 (33% foreign); growth rate 1.4% p.a.
life expectancy men 78, women 83 (1989)
language German (official); an Alemannic dialect is also spoken
religions Roman Catholic 87%, Protestant 8%
literacy 100% (1989)
GNP $450 million (1986)
GDP $1 bn (1987); $32,000 per head

chronology
1342 Became a sovereign state.
1434 Present boundaries established.
1719 Former counties of Schellenberg and Vaduz constituted as the Principality of Liechtenstein.
1921 Adopted Swiss currency.
1923 United with Switzerland in a customs union.
1938 Prince Franz Josef II came to power.
1984 Prince Franz Joseph II handed over power to Crown Prince Hans Adam. Vote extended to women in national elections.
1989 Prince Franz Joseph II died; Hans Adam II succeeded him.
1990 Became a member of the United Nations (UN).
1991 Became seventh member of European Free Trade Association.

---

fossil evidence of life is threadlike chains of cells discovered in 1980 in deposits in NW Australia that have been dated as 3.5 billion years old.

It seems probable that the original atmosphere of Earth consisted of carbon dioxide, nitrogen, and water, and that complex organic molecules, such as ◊amino acids, were created when the then oxygen (and ozone-) free atmosphere was bombarded by ultraviolet radiation or by lightning. Attempts to replicate these conditions in the laboratory have successfully shown that amino acids, purine and pyrimidine bases (base pairs in DNA), and other vital molecules can be created in this way. It has also been suggested that life could have reached Earth from elsewhere in the universe in the form of complex organic molecules present in meteors or comets, but others argue that this is not really an alternative explanation because these primitive life forms must then have been created elsewhere by much the same process. Once the atmosphere changed to its present composition, life could only be created by living organisms (a process called biogenesis).

life cycle in biology, the sequence of developmental stages through which members of a given species pass. Most vertebrates have a simple life cycle consisting of ◊fertilization of sex cells or ◊gametes, a period of development as an ◊embryo, a period of juvenile growth after hatching or birth, an adulthood including ◊sexual reproduction, and finally death. Invertebrate life cycles are generally more complex and may involve major reconstitution of the individual's appearance (◊metamorphosis) and completely different styles of life. Plants have a special type of life cycle with two distinct phases, known as ◊alternation of generations. Many insects such as cicadas, dragonflies, and mayflies have a long larvae or pupae phase and a short adult phase. Dragonflies live an aquatic life

as larvae and an aerial life during the adult phase. In many invertebrates and protozoa there is a sequence of stages in the life cycle, and in parasites different stages often occur in different host organisms.

life sciences scientific study of the living world as a whole, a new synthesis of several traditional scientific disciplines including ◊biology, ◊zoology, and ◊botany, and newer, more specialized areas of study such as ◊biophysics and sociobiology.

ligament strong flexible connective tissue, made of the protein collagen, which joins bone to bone at moveable joints. Ligaments prevent bone dislocation (under normal circumstances) but permit joint flexion.

Ligeti György (Sándor) 1923– . Hungarian-born Austrian composer who developed a dense, highly chromatic, polyphonic style in which melody and rhythm are sometimes lost in shifting blocks of sound. He achieved international prominence with *Atmosphères* 1961 and *Requiem* 1965, which were used for Stanley Kubrick's film epic *2001: A Space Odyssey* 1968. Other works include an opera *Le Grand Macabre* 1978, and *Poème symphonique* 1962, for 100 metronomes (clockwork time-keeping devices).

light electromagnetic waves in the visible range, having a wavelength from about 400 nanometers in the extreme violet to about 770 nanometers in the extreme red. Light is considered to exhibit particle and wave properties, and the fundamental particle, or quantum, of light is called the photon. The speed of light (and of all electromagnetic radiation) in a vacuum is approximately 186,000 mi/300,000 km per second, and is a universal constant denoted by c.

light bulb incandescent filament lamp, first demonstrated by Joseph Swan in the UK 1878 and Thomas Edison in the US 1879. The present-day light bulb is a

lightning Lightning over wooded countryside, Derbyshire, England.

thin glass bulb filled with an inert mixture of nitrogen and argon gas. It contains a filament made of fine tungsten wire. When electricity is passed through the wire, it glows white hot, producing light.

light-emitting diode (LED) means of displaying symbols in electronic instruments and devices. An LED is made of ◊semiconductor material, such as gallium arsenide phosphide, that glows when electricity is passed through it. The first digital watches and calculators had LED displays, but many later models use ◊liquid-crystal displays.

lighthouse structure carrying a powerful light to warn ships or airplanes that they are approaching a place (usually land) dangerous or important to navigation. The light is magnified and directed out to the horizon or up to the zenith by a series of mirrors or prisms. Increasingly lighthouses are powered by electricity and automated rather than staffed; the more recent models also emit radio signals. Only a minority of the remaining staffed lighthouses still use dissolved acetylene gas as a source of power.

lightning high-voltage electrical discharge between two charged rainclouds or between a cloud and the Earth, caused by the buildup of electrical charges. Air in the path of lightning ionizes (becomes conducting), and expands; the accompanying noise is heard as thunder. Currents of 20,000 amperes and temperatures of 54,000°F/30,000°C are common.

light watt unit of radiant power (brightness of light). One light watt is the power required to produce a perceived brightness equal to that of light at a wavelength of 550 nanometers and 680 lumens.

light year in astronomy, the distance traveled by a beam of light in a vacuum in one year, approximately 5.88 trillion mi/9.46 trillion km.

lignite type of ◊coal that is brown and fibrous, with a relatively low carbon content. In Scandinavia it is burned to generate power.

Liguria coastal region of NW Italy, which includes the resorts of the Italian Riviera, lying between the W Alps and the Mediterranean Gulf of Genoa. The region comprises the provinces of Genova, La Spezia, Imperia, and Savona, with a population (1990) of 1,719,200 and an area of 2,093 sq mi/5,418 sq km. Genoa is the chief port city.

Likud alliance of right-wing Israeli political parties that defeated the Labor Party coalition in the May 1977 election and brought Menachem Begin to power. In 1987 Likud became part of an uneasy national coalition with Labor, formed to solve Israel's economic crisis. In 1989 another coalition was formed under Shamir.

lilac any flowering Old World shrub of the genus *Syringa* (such as *S. vulgaris*) of the olive family Oleaceae, bearing panicles (clusters) of small, sweetly scented, white or purplish flowers.

Lilongwe capital of Malawi since 1975, on the Lilongwe River; population (1987) 234,000. Products include tobacco and textiles. Capital Hill, 3 mi/5 km from the old city, is the site of government buildings and offices.

lily plant of the genus *Lilium*, family Liliaceae, of which there are some 80 species, most with showy, trumpet-shaped flowers growing from bulbs. The lily family includes hyacinths, tulips, asparagus, and plants of the onion genus. The term "lily" is also applied to many lilylike plants of allied genera and families.

lily of the valley plant *Convallaria majalis* of the lily family Liliaceae, growing in woods in Europe, N Asia, and North America. The small, pendant, white flowers are strongly scented. The plant is often cultivated.

Lima capital of Peru, an industrial city (textiles, chemicals, glass, cement) with its port at Callao; population (1988) 418,000, metropolitan area 4,605,000. Founded by the Spanish conquistador Francisco Pizarro 1535, it was rebuilt after destruction by an earthquake 1746.

Lima city in NW Ohio, US, on the Ottawa River, N of Dayton; seat of Allen County; population (1990) 45,550. Industries include motor-vehicle and aircraft parts, heavy machinery, electrical products, and oil processing.

limbo in Christian theology, a region for the souls of those who were not admitted to the divine vision. *Limbus infantum* was a place where unbaptized infants enjoyed inferior blessedness, and *limbus patrum* was where the prophets of the Old Testament dwelt. The word was first used in this sense in the 13th century by St Thomas Aquinas.

Limburg southernmost province of the Netherlands
area 838 sq mi/2,170 sq km
capital Maastricht
cities Heerlen, Roermond, Weert
physical river Maas (Meuse); sandy soils in river plain, marl soils in S; becomes hilly toward S

limestone
Carboniferous limestone pavement near Ballynahowan, Ireland, showing the patterns caused by rain wearing away joints in the rock.

features a monument marks the *Drielandenpunt*, where the Dutch, German, and Belgian borders meet
products chemicals, cement, fertilizer; mixed arable farming and horticulture are also important. The former coal industry is still remembered at Kerkrade, alleged site of the first European coal mine
population (1991) 1,109,900
history formerly part of the duchy of Limburg (which was divided 1839 into today's Dutch and Belgian provinces).

lime or *quicklime* CaO (technical name *calcium oxide*) white powdery substance used in making mortar and cement. It is made commercially by heating calcium carbonate ($CaCO_3$), obtained from limestone or chalk, in a lime kiln. Quicklime readily absorbs water to become calcium hydroxide (CaOH), known as slaked lime, which is used to reduce soil acidity.

Limerick county in the SW Republic of Ireland, in Munster province
area 1,038 sq mi/2,690 sq km
county town Limerick
physical fertile, with hills in the S
products dairy products
population (1991) 161,900.

Limerick county town of Limerick, Republic of Ireland, the main port of W Ireland, on the Shannon estuary; population (1991) 52,000. It was founded in the 12th century.

limestone sedimentary rock composed chiefly of calcium carbonate $CaCO_3$, either derived from the shells of marine organisms or precipitated from solution, mostly in the ocean. Various types of limestone are used as building stone.

Limousin former province and modern region of central France; area 6,544 sq mi/16,900 sq km; population (1986) 736,000. It consists of the *départements* of Corréze, Creuse, and Haute-Vienne. The chief town is Limoges. A thinly populated and largely unfertile region, it is crossed by the mountains of the Massif Central. Fruit and vegetables are produced in the more fertile lowlands. Kaolin is mined.

Limpopo river in SE Africa, rising in the Transvaal and reaching the Indian Ocean in Mozambique; length 1,000 mi/1,600 km.

Lin Biao or *Lin Piao* 1907–1971. Chinese politician and general. He joined the communists in 1927, became a commander of ◊Mao Zedong's Red Army, and led the Northeast People's Liberation Army in the civil war after 1945. He became defense minister in 1959, and as vice chair of the party in 1969 he was expected to be Mao's successor. But in 1972 the government announced that Lin had been killed in an airplane crash in Mongolia on Sept 17, 1971, while fleeing to the USSR following an abortive coup attempt.

Lincoln industrial city and capital of Nebraska; population (1990) 192,000. Industries include engineering, pharmaceuticals, electronic and electrical equipment, and food processing. It was known as *Lancaster* until 1867, when it was renamed after Abraham Lincoln and designated the state capital. Educational institutions include the main campus of the University of Nebraska and Nebraska Wesleyan University.

Lincoln President of the US during the Civil War, Abraham Lincoln.

Lincoln Abraham 1809–1865. 16th president of the US 1861–65, a Republican. In the American ◊Civil War, his chief concern was the preservation of the Union from which the Confederate (Southern) slave states had seceded on his election. In 1863 he announced the freedom of the slaves with the Emancipation Proclamation. He was reelected in 1864 with victory for the North in sight, but was assassinated at the end of the war.

Lincoln Benjamin 1733–1810. American military and political leader. As brigadier general in the Continental army during the American Revolution 1775–83, he aided the victory at Saratoga 1777 but was forced to surrender to the British at Charleston 1780. He was secretary of war for the Continental Congress 1781–83 and led the suppression of Shays' Rebellion 1787.

Lincolnshire county in E England
area 2,274 sq mi/5,890 sq km
cities Lincoln (administrative headquarters), Skegness
physical Lincoln Wolds; marshy coastline; the Fens in the SE; rivers: Witham, Welland

Lindbergh Pioneer US aviator Charles Lindbergh.

features 16th-century Burghley House; Belton House, a Restoration mansion
products cattle, sheep, horses, cereals, flower bulbs, oil
population (1991) 573,900
famous people Isaac Newton, Alfred Tennyson, Margaret Thatcher, John Wesley.

Lindbergh Charles A(ugustus) 1902–1974. US aviator who made the first solo nonstop flight in 33.5 hours across the Atlantic (Roosevelt Field, Long Island, New York, to Le Bourget airport, Paris) 1927 in the *Spirit of St Louis*, a Ryan monoplane designed by him.

Born in Detroit, Michigan, Lindbergh was a barnstorming pilot before attending the US Army School in Texas 1924 and becoming an officer in the Army Air Service Reserve 1925. His son, Charles, Jr (1930–1932), was kidnapped and killed, a crime for which Bruno Hauptmann was convicted and executed. Ensuing legislation against kidnapping was called the Lindbergh Act. Although he admired the Nazi air force and championed US neutrality in the late 1930s, he flew 50 combat missions in the Pacific theater in World War II. He wrote *The Spirit of St Louis* 1953 (Pulitzer Prize).

linear equation in mathematics, a relationship between two variables that, when plotted on Cartesian axes produces a straight-line graph; the equation has the general form $y = mx + c$, where m is the slope of the line represented by the equation and c is the y-intercept, or the value of y where the line crosses the y-axis in the ◊Cartesian coordinate system. Sets of linear equations can be used to describe the behavior of buildings, bridges, trusses, and other static structures.

linen yarn spun and the textile woven from the fibers of the stem of the ◊flax plant. Used by the ancient Egyptians, linen was introduced by the Romans to N Europe, where production became widespread. Religious refugees from the Low Countries in the 16th century helped to establish the linen industry in England, but here and elsewhere it began to decline in competition with cotton in the 18th century.

lingua franca any language that is used as a means of communication by groups who do not themselves normally speak that language; for example, English is a lingua franca used by Japanese doing business in Finland, or by Swedes in Saudi Arabia. The term comes from the mixture of French, Italian, Spanish, Greek, Turkish, and Arabic that was spoken around the Mediterranean from the time of the Crusades until the 18th century.

linguistics scientific study of language. Linguistics has many branches, such as origins (historical linguistics), the changing way language is pronounced (phonetics), derivation of words through various languages (etymology), development of meanings (semantics), and the arrangement and modifications of words to convey a message (grammar).

linkage in genetics, the association between two or more genes that tend to be inherited together because they are on the same chromosome. The closer together they are on the chromosome, the less likely they are to be separated by crossing over (one of the processes of ◊recombination) and they are then described as being "tightly linked."

Linnaeus Carolus 1707–1778. Swedish naturalist and physician. His botanical work *Systema naturae* 1735 contained his system for classifying plants into groups depending on shared characteristics (such as the number of stamens in flowers), providing a much-needed framework for identification. He also devised the concise and precise system for naming plants and animals, using one Latin (or Latinized) word to represent the genus and a second to distinguish the species.

linsang nocturnal, tree-dwelling, carnivorous mammal of the civet family, about 2.5 ft/75 cm long. The African linsang *Poiana richardsoni* is a long, low, and lithe spotted animal about 1.1 ft/33 cm long with a 1.25 ft/38 cm tail. The two species of oriental linsang, genus *Prionodon*, of Asia are slightly bigger.

linseed seeds of the flax plant *Linum usitatissimum*, from which linseed oil is expressed, the residue being used as cattle feed. The oil is used in paint, wood treatments, and varnishes, and in the manufacture of linoleum.

lion cat *Panthera leo*, now found only in Africa and NW India. The coat is tawny, the young having darker spot markings that usually disappear in the adult. The male has a heavy mane and a tuft at the end of the tail. Head and body measure about 6 ft/2 m, plus 3 ft/1 m of tail, the lioness being slightly smaller. Lions produce litters of two to six cubs, and often live in prides of several adult males and females with several young.

Lipchitz Jacques 1891–1973. Lithuanian-born sculptor, active in Paris from 1909; he emigrated to the US 1941. He was one of the first Cubist sculptors. The Barnes Foundation, Philadelphia, has many of his early works.

Li Peng 1928– . Chinese communist politician, a member of the Politburo from 1985, and head of government from 1987. During the prodemocracy demonstrations of 1989 he supported the massacre of students by Chinese troops and the subsequent execution of others. He sought improved relations with the USSR prior to its demise, and has favored maintaining firm central and party control over the economy.

lipid any of a large number of esters of fatty acids, commonly formed by the reaction of a fatty acid with glycerol (see ◊glycerides). They are soluble in alcohol but not in water. Lipids are the chief constituents of plant and animal waxes, fats, and oils.

Li Po 705–762. Chinese poet. He used traditional literary forms, but his exuberance, the boldness of his imagination, and the intensity of his feeling have won him recognition as perhaps the greatest of all Chinese poets. Although he was mostly concerned with higher themes, he is also remembered for his celebratory verses on drinking.

Lippershey Hans *c.* 1570–1619. Dutch lens maker, credited with inventing the telescope in 1608.

Lippi Filippino 1457–1504. Italian painter of the Florentine school, trained by Botticelli. He produced altarpieces and several fresco cycles, full of detail and drama, elegant and finely drawn. He was the son of Filippo Lippi.

Lippi Fra Filippo 1406–1469. Italian painter whose works include frescoes depicting the lives of St Stephen and St John the Baptist in Prato Cathedral 1452–66. He also painted many altarpieces of Madonnas and groups of saints.

Lippmann Gabriel 1845–1921. French doctor who invented the direct color process in photography. He was awarded the Nobel Prize for Physics in 1908.

liquefied petroleum gas (LPG) liquid form of butane, propane, or pentane, produced by the distillation of petroleum during oil refining. At room temperature these substances are gases, although they can be

linsang The banded linsang has a boldly marked coat that breaks up its body outline.

easily liquefied and stored under pressure in metal containers. They are used for heating and cooking where other fuels are not available: camping stoves and cigarette lighters, for instance, often use liquefied butane as fuel.

liquid state of matter between a ◊solid and a ◊gas. A liquid forms a level surface and assumes the shape of its container. Its atoms do not occupy fixed positions as in a crystalline solid, nor do they have freedom of movement as in a gas. Unlike gas, a liquid is difficult to compress since pressure applied at one point is equally transmitted throughout (Pascal's principle. ◊Hydraulics makes use of this property.

liquid air air that has been cooled so much that it has liquefied. This happens at temperatures below about −321°F/−196°C. The various constituent gases, including nitrogen, oxygen, argon, and neon, can be separated from liquid air by the technique of ◊fractionation.

liquidation In economics the winding up of a company by converting all its assets into money to pay off its liabilities.

liquid-crystal display (LCD) display of numbers (for example, in a calculator) or pictures (such as on a pocket television screen) produced by molecules of a substance in a semiliquid state with some crystalline properties, so that clusters of molecules align in parallel formations. The display is a blank until the application of an electric field, which "twists" the molecules so that they reflect or transmit light falling on them.

Lisbon (Portuguese *Lisboa*) city and capital of Portugal, in the SW of the country, on the tidal lake and estuary formed by the river Tagus; population (1984) 808,000. Industries include steel, textiles, chemicals, pottery, shipbuilding, and fishing. It has been the capital since 1260 and reached its peak of prosperity in the period of Portugal's empire during the 16th century. In 1755 an earthquake killed 60,000 people and destroyed much of the city.

Lister Joseph, 1st Baron Lister 1827–1912. English surgeon and founder of antiseptic surgery, influenced by Louis ◊Pasteur's work on bacteria. He introduced dressings soaked in carbolic acid and strict rules of hygiene to combat wound sepsis in hospitals.

Liszt Franz 1811–1886. Hungarian pianist and composer. An outstanding virtuoso of the piano, he was an established concert artist by the age of 12. His expressive, romantic, and frequently chromatic works include piano music (*Transcendental Studies* 1851), symphonies, piano concertos, and organ music. Much of his music is programmatic; he also originated the symphonic poem. Liszt was taught by his father, then by Carl Czerny (1791–1857). He traveled widely in Europe, producing an opera *Don Sanche* in Paris at the age of 14. As musical director and conductor at Weimar 1848–59, he championed the music of Berlioz and Wagner.

litany in the Christian church, a form of prayer or supplication led by a priest with set responses by the congregation.

liter metric unit of volume (symbol l), equal since 1964 to one cubic decimeter (61.025 cu in, 1.057 liquid qt, or 0.91 dry qt).

literacy ability to read and write. The level at which functional literacy is set rises as society becomes more complex, and it becomes increasingly difficult for an illiterate person to find work and cope with the other demands of everyday life.

literary criticism establishment of principles governing literary composition, and the assessment and interpretation of literary works. Contemporary criticism offers analyzes of literary works from structuralist, semiological, feminist, Marxist, and psychoanalytical perspectives, whereas earlier criticism tended to deal with moral or political ideas, or with a literary work as a formal object independent of its creator.

literature words set apart in some way from ordinary everyday communication. In the ancient oral traditions, before stories and poems were written down, literature had a mainly public function—mythic and religious. As literary works came to be preserved in writing, and, eventually, printed, their role became more private, serving as a vehicle for the exploration and expression of emotion and the human situation.

lithium soft, ductile, silver-white, metallic element, symbol Li, atomic number 3, atomic weight 6.941. It is one of the alkali metals, has a very low density (far less than most woods), and floats on water (specific gravity 0.57); it is the lightest of all metals. Lithium is

Lithuania
Republic of

area 25,174 sq mi/65,200 sq km
capital Vilnius
cities Kaunas, Klaipeda, Siauliai, Panevezys
physical central lowlands with gentle hills in W and higher terrain in SE; 25% forested; some 3,000 small lakes, marshes, and complex sandy coastline
features river Nemen; white sand dunes on Kursiu Marios lagoon
head of state Algirdas Brazauskas from 1993
head of government Adolfas Slezevicius from 1993
political system emergent democracy
political parties Sajudis (Lithuanian Restructuring Movement), nationalist; Democratic Party, centrist; Humanism and Progress Party, reformist; Social Democratic Party, left of center; Green Party, ecological; Christian Democratic Party, right of center; Democratic Labor Party, "reform communist"
products heavy engineering, electrical goods, shipbuilding, cement, food processing, bacon, dairy products, cereals, potatoes
currency Lithuanian ruble
population (1992) 3,802,000 (Lithuanian 80%, Russian 9%, Polish 7%, Byelorussian 2%)
language Lithuanian
religion predominantly Roman Catholic

chronology
1918 Independence declared following withdrawal of German occupying troops at end of World War I; USSR attempted to regain power.
1919 Soviet forces overthrown by Germans, Poles, and nationalist Lithuanians; democratic republic established.
1920–39 Province and city of Vilnius occupied by Poles.
1926 Coup overthrew established government; Antanas Smetona became president.
1939 Secret German-Soviet agreement brought most of Lithuania under Soviet influence.
1940 Incorporated into USSR as constituent republic.
1941 Lithuania revolted against USSR and established own government. During World War II Germany again occupied the country.
1944 USSR resumed rule.
1944–52 Lithuanian guerrillas fought USSR.
1972 Demonstrations against Soviet government.
1980 Growth in nationalist dissent, influenced by Polish example.
1988 Popular front formed, the Sajudis, to campaign for increased autonomy.
1989 Lithuanian declared the state language; flag of independent interwar republic readopted. Communist Party (CP) split into pro-Moscow and nationalist wings. Communist local monopoly of power abolished.
1990 Feb: nationalist Sajudis won elections. March: Vytautas Landsbergis became president; unilateral declaration of independence resulted in temporary Soviet blockade.
1991 Jan: Albertas Shiminas became prime minister. Soviet paratroopers briefly occupied key buildings in Vilnius. Sept: independence recognized by Soviet government and Western nations; Gediminas Vagnorius elected prime minister; CP outlawed; admitted into United Nations (UN) and Conference on Security and Cooperation in Europe (CSCE).
1992 July: Aleksandras Abisala became prime minister. Nov: DLP, led by Algirdas Brazauskas, won majority vote. Dec: Bronislovas Lubys appointed prime minister.
1993 Brazauskas elected president; Adolfas Slezevicius appointed prime minister.

used to harden alloys, and in batteries; its compounds are used in medicine to treat manic depression.

lithography printmaking technique originated in 1798 by Aloys Senefelder, based on the antipathy of grease and water. A drawing is made with greasy crayon on an absorbent stone, which is then wetted. The wet stone repels ink (which is greasy) applied to the surface and the crayon attracts it, so that the drawing can be printed. Lithographic printing is used in book production and has developed this basic principle into complex processes.

lithosphere topmost layer of the Earth's structure, forming the jigsaw of plates that take part in the movements of ◊plate tectonics. The lithosphere comprises the ◊crust and a portion of the upper ◊mantle. It is regarded as being rigid and moves about on the semi-molten ◊asthenosphere. The lithosphere is about 47 mi/75 km thick.

Lithuania country in N Europe, bounded N by Latvia, E by Belarus, S by Poland and the Kaliningrad area of Russia, and W by the Baltic Sea.

Lithuanian member of the majority ethnic group living in Lithuania, comprising 80% of the population.

Lithuanian language Indo-European language spoken by the people of Lithuania, which through its geographical isolation has retained many ancient features of the Indo-European language family. It acquired a written form in the 16th century, using the Latin alphabet, and is currently spoken by some 3–4 million people.

litmus dye obtained from various lichens and used in chemistry as an indicator to test the acidic or alkaline nature of aqueous solutions; it turns red in the presence of acid, and blue in the presence of alkali.

Little Bighorn, Battle of the engagement in Montana; Lieutenant Colonel George ◊Custer's defeat by the ◊Sioux Indians, June 25, 1876, under Chiefs ◊Crazy Horse and Sitting Bull, known as Custer's Last Stand. The battle was precipitated by the discovery of gold in the Black Hills and the subsequent violations of the 1868 treaty with the Sioux, which had granted them "sole use" of the area. Custer ignored scouting reports of an overwhelming Indian force and led a column of 265 soldiers into a ravine where thousands of Indian warriors lay in wait. Custer and every one of his command were killed. US reprisals against the Indians followed, abrogating the treaty, ending their rights, and driving them from the area.

Little Red Book book of aphorisms and quotations from the speeches and writings by ◊Mao Zedong, in which he adapted Marxist theory to Chinese conditions. Published 1966, the book was printed in huge numbers and read widely at the start of the ◊Cultural Revolution.

Little Richard Adopted name of Richard Penniman 1932– . US rock singer and pianist. He was one of the creators of rock and roll with his wildly uninhibited renditions of "Tutti Frutti" 1956, "Long Tall Sally" 1956, and "Good Golly Miss Molly" 1957. His subsequent career in soul and rhythm and blues was interrupted by periods as a Seventh-Day Adventist cleric.

Little Rock largest city and capital of Arkansas; population (1990) 175,800 Products include metal goods, oil-field and electronic equipment, chemicals, clothing, and processed food. Educational institutions include the University of Arkansas at Little Rock. A French trading post was built here 1722, and in 1821 it became the territorial capital. Union forces captured the city

1863, during the Civil War. Federal troops were sent here 1957 to enforce the integration of all-white Central High School.

liturgy in the Christian church, any service for public worship; the term was originally limited to the celebration of the ◊Eucharist.

liver large organ of vertebrates, which has many regulatory and storage functions. The human liver is situated in the upper abdomen, and weighs about 4.5 lb/2 kg. It receives the products of digestion, converts glucose to glycogen (a long-chain carbohydrate used for storage), and breaks down fats. It removes excess amino acids from the blood, converting them to urea, which is excreted by the kidneys. The liver also synthesizes vitamins, produces bile and blood-clotting factors, and removes damaged red cells and toxins such as alcohol from the blood.

Liverpool city, seaport, and administrative headquarters of Merseyside, NW England; population (1991 est) 448,300. In the 19th and early 20th centuries it exported the textiles of Lancashire and Yorkshire. Liverpool is the UK's chief Atlantic port with miles of specialized, mechanized quays on the river Mersey.

Livingston Robert R 1746–1813. American public official and diplomat. As secretary for foreign affairs 1781, he directed negotiations for the Paris Peace Treaty 1783. In 1801 he was named minister to France by President Jefferson. With James Monroe, Livingston secured the purchase of the Louisiana Territory 1803, acquiring a large part of North America from the French.

Livingstone David 1813–1873. Scottish missionary explorer. In 1841 he went to Africa, reached Lake Ngami 1849, followed the Zambezi to its mouth, saw the Victoria Falls 1855, and went to East and Central Africa 1858–64, reaching Lakes Shirwa and Malawi. From 1866, he tried to find the source of the river Nile, and reached Ujiji in Tanganyika in Oct 1871. British explorer Henry Stanley joined Livingstone in Ujiji.

Livonia former region in Europe on the E coast of the Baltic Sea comprising most of present-day Latvia and Estonia. Conquered and converted to Christianity in the early 13th century by the Livonian Knights, a crusading order, Livonia was independent until 1583, when it was divided between Poland and Sweden. In

Livingstone
Scottish doctor and missionary David Livingstone was the first European to explore many parts of Central and East Africa.

lizard The frilled lizard of N Australia and New Guinea has a rufflike erectile collar of skin—up to 10 in/ 25 cm across— around its neck.

1710 it was occupied by Russia, and in 1721 was ceded to Peter the Great, Tsar of Russia.

Livy Titus Livius 59 BC–AD 17. Roman historian, author of a *History of Rome* from the city's foundation to 9 BC, based partly on legend. It was composed of 142 books, of which 35 survive, covering the periods from the arrival of Aeneas in Italy to 293 BC and from 218 to 167 BC.

lizard reptile of the suborder Lacertilia, which together with snakes constitutes the order Squamata. Lizards are generally distinguishable from snakes by having four legs, moveable eyelids, eardrums, and a fleshy tongue, but some lizards are legless and snakelike in appearance. There are over 3,000 species of lizard worldwide.

Ljubljana (German *Laibach*) capital and industrial city (textiles, chemicals, paper, leather goods) of Slovenia, near the confluence of the rivers Ljubljanica and Sava; population (1981) 305,200. It has a nuclear research center and is linked with S Austria by the Karawanken road tunnel under the Alps (1979–83).

llama South American even-toed hoofed mammal *Lama glama* of the camel family, about 4 ft/1.2 m high at the shoulder. Llamas can be white, brown, or dark, sometimes with spots or patches. They are very hardy, and require little food or water. They spit profusely when annoyed.

Lloyd Harold 1893–1971. US film comedian, noted for his "trademark" of thick horn-rimmed glasses and straw hat, who invented the bumbling cliff-hanger and dangler. He appeared from 1913 in silent and talking films. His silent films include *Grandma's Boy* 1922, *Safety Last* 1923, and *The Freshman* 1925. His first talkie was *Movie Crazy* 1932. He produced films after 1938, including the reissued *Harold Lloyd's World of Comedy* 1962 and *Funny Side of Life* 1964.

Lloyd George David 1863–1945. Welsh Liberal politician, prime minister of Britain 1916–22. A pioneer of social reform, as chancellor of the Exchequer 1908–15 he introduced old-age pensions 1908 and health and unemployment insurance 1911. High unemployment, intervention in the Russian Civil War, and use of the military police force, the Black and Tans, in Ireland eroded his support as prime minister, and the creation of the Irish Free State in 1921 and his pro-Greek policy against the Turks caused the collapse of his coalition government.

Lloyd Webber Andrew 1948– . English composer. His early musicals, with lyrics by Time Rice, include *Joseph and the Amazing Technicolor Dreamcoat* 1968, *Jesus Christ Superstar* 1970, and *Evita* 1978, based on the life of the Argentine leader Eva Peron. He also wrote *Cats* 1981 and *The Phantom of the Opera* 1986.

lobby individual or pressure group that sets out to influence government action. The lobby is prevalent in the US, where the term originated in the 1830s from the practice of those wishing to influence state policy waiting for elected representatives in the lobby of the Capitol.

lobotomy in medicine, the cutting of a lobe. The term usually refers to the operation of *frontal lobotomy* (or *leucotomy*), where the frontal lobes are disconnected from the rest of the brain by cutting the white matter that joins them. This may alleviate the condition of patients with severe depression, anxiety states, or obsessive-compulsive disorders, but it is now rarely performed, and only on patients who have proved resistant to all other forms of treatment. It is irreversible and the degree of personality change is not predictable.

It was pioneered by A E Moniz (1874–1955), who shared the 1949 Nobel Prize for Medicine for his work in brain surgery.

lobster large marine crustacean of the order Decapoda. Lobsters are grouped with freshwater ◊crayfish in the suborder Reptantia ("walking"), although both lobsters and crayfish can also swim, using their fanlike tails. Lobsters have eyes on stalks and long antennae, and are mainly nocturnal. They scavenge and eat dead or dying fish.

local government that part of government dealing mainly with matters concerning the inhabitants of a particular area or town, usually financed at least in part by local taxes. In the US and UK, local government has comparatively large powers and responsibilities.

Locarno, Pact of series of diplomatic documents initialed in Locarno, Switzerland, Oct 16, 1925, and formally signed in London Dec 1, 1925. The pact settled the question of French security, and the signatories—Britain, France, Belgium, Italy, and Germany—guaranteed Germany's existing frontiers with France and Belgium. Following the signing of the pact, Germany was admitted to the League of Nations.

Lochner v New York a US Supreme Court decision 1905 dealing with the use of state police power to regulate working conditions. Lochner, an owner of a bakery convicted of violating a New York law that set maximum working hours for bakery workers, filed suit against the state. The US Supreme Court voted narrowly to overrule the New York law, ruling it an excessive use of state police power that violated the 14th-Amendment right to freedom of contract. Dissenting, Justice Holmes criticized the majority ruling for making its decision because of a belief in laissez-faire economics.

Loch Ness see ◊Ness, Loch

lock construction installed in waterways to allow boats or ships to travel from one level to another. The earliest form, the *flash lock*, was first seen in the East in 1st-century-AD China and in the West in 11th-century Holland. By this method barriers temporarily dammed a river and when removed allowed the flash flood to propel the waiting boat through any obstacle. This was followed in 12th-century China and 14th-century Holland by the *pound lock*. In this system the lock has gates at each end. Boats enter through one gate when the levels are the same both outside and inside. Water is then allowed in (or out of) the lock until the level rises (or falls) to the new level outside the other gate.

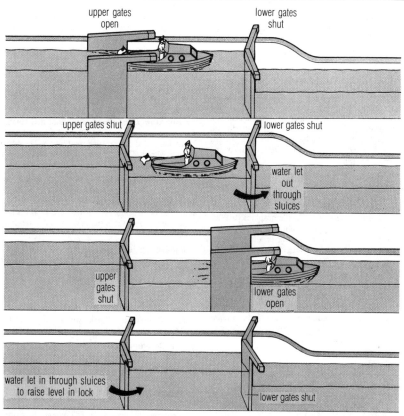

upper gates
open

lower gates
shut

upper gates shut

lower gates shut

water let
out
through
sluices

upper
gates
shut

lower gates
open

water let in through sluices
to raise level in lock

lower gates shut

lock *The operation of a lock as a boat passes through it.*

lock and key devices that provide security, usually fitted to a door of some kind. In 1778 English locksmith Robert Barron made the forerunner of the **mortise lock**, which contains levers that the key must raise to an exact height before the bolt can be moved. The **Yale lock**, a pin-tumbler cylinder design, was invented by US locksmith Linus Yale, Jr, in 1865. More secure locks include **combination locks**, with a dial mechanism that must be turned certain distances backward and forward to open, and **time locks**, which are set to be opened only at specific times.

Locke John 1632–1704. English philosopher. His *Essay concerning Human Understanding* 1690 maintained that experience was the only source of knowledge (empiricism), and that "we can have knowledge no farther than we have ideas" prompted by such experience. *Two Treatises on Government* 1690 helped to form contemporary ideas of liberal democracy.

lockjaw former name for ◊tetanus, a type of infection.

locomotive engine for hauling railroad trains. In 1804 Richard Trevithick built the first steam engine to run on rails. Locomotive design did not radically improve until British engineer George Stephenson built the *Rocket* 1829, which featured a multitube boiler and blastpipe, standard in all following **steam locomotives**. Today most locomotives are diesel or electric: **diesel locomotives** have a powerful diesel engine, and **electric locomotives** draw their power from either an overhead cable or a third rail alongside the ordinary track.

locus in mathematics, traditionally the path traced out by a moving point, but now defined as the set of all points on a curve satisfying given conditions. For example, the locus of a point that moves so that it is always at the same distance from another fixed point is a circle; the locus of a point that is always at the same distance from two fixed points is a straight line that perpendicularly bisects the line joining them.

locust swarming grasshopper, with short antennae and auditory organs on the abdomen, in the family Acrididae. As winged adults, flying in swarms, locusts may be carried by the wind hundreds of miles from their breeding grounds; on landing they devour all vegetation. Locusts occur in nearly every continent.

lode geological deposit rich in certain minerals, generally consisting of a large vein or set of veins containing ore minerals. A system of veins that can be mined directly forms a lode, for example the mother lode of the California gold rush.

lodestar or **loadstar** a star used in navigation or astronomy, often ◊Polaris, the Pole Star.

Łódź industrial city (textiles, machinery, dyes) in central Poland, 75 mi/120 km SW of Warsaw; population (1990) 848,300.

Loewe Frederick 1901–1988. US composer of musicals. In 1942 he joined forces with the lyricist Alan Jay Lerner (1918–1986), and their joint successes include *Brigadoon* 1947, *Paint Your Wagon* 1951, *My Fair Lady* 1956, *Gigi* 1958, and *Camelot* 1960.

loganberry hybrid between a ◊blackberry and a ◊raspberry with large, tart, dull-red fruit. It was developed by US judge James H Logan in 1881.

logarithm or *log* the ◊exponent or index of a number to a specified base—usually 10. For example, the logarithm to the base 10 of 1,000 is 3 because $10^3 = 1,000$; the logarithm of 2 is 0.3010 because $2 = 10^{0.3010}$. Before the advent of cheap electronic calculators, multiplication and division could be simplified by being replaced with the addition and subtraction of logarithms.

logic branch of philosophy that studies valid reasoning and argument. It is also the way in which one thing may be said to follow from, or be a consequence of, another (deductive logic). Logic is generally divided into the traditional formal logic of Aristotle and the symbolic logic derived from Friedrich Frege and Bertrand Russell.

LOGO high-level computer programming language designed to teach mathematical concepts. Developed about 1970 at the Massachusetts Institute of Technology, it became popular in schools and with home computer users because of its "turtle graphics" feature. This allows the user to write programs that create line drawings on a computer screen, or drive a small mobile robot (a "turtle" or "buggy") around the floor.

Loire longest river in France, rising in the Cévennes Mountains, at 4,430 ft/1,350 m and flowing for 650 mi/1,050 km first N then W until it reaches the Bay of Biscay at St Nazaire, passing Nevers, Orléans, Tours, and Nantes. It gives its name to the *départements* of Loire, Haute-Loire, Loire-Atlantique, Indre-et-Loire, Maine-et-Loire, and Saône-et-Loire. There are many châteaux and vineyards along its banks.

Loki in Norse mythology, one of the ◊Aesir (the principal gods), but the cause of dissension among the gods, and the slayer of ◊Balder. His children are the Midgard serpent Jörmungander, which girdles the Earth; the wolf Fenris; and Hela, goddess of death.

Lollard follower of the English religious reformer John ◊Wycliffe in the 14th century. The Lollards condemned the doctrine of the transubstantiation of the bread and wine of the Eucharist, advocated the diversion of ecclesiastical property to charitable uses, and denounced war and capital punishment. They were active from about 1377; after the passing of the statute *De heretico comburendo* ("The Necessity of Burning Heretics") 1401 many Lollards were burned, and in 1414 they raised an unsuccessful revolt in London, known as Oldcastle's rebellion.

Lombard Carole. Adopted name of Jane Alice Peters 1908–1942. US comedy film actress. A warm and witty actress, she starred in some of the best comedies of the 1930s: *Twentieth Century* 1934, *My Man Godfrey* 1936, and *To Be or Not to Be* 1942. She was married to Clark Gable in 1939.

Lombard or *Langobard* member of a Germanic people who invaded Italy in 568 and occupied Lombardy (named after them) and central Italy. Their capital was Monza. They were conquered by the Frankish ruler Charlemagne in 774.

Lombardi Vince(nt Thomas) 1913–1970. US football coach. As head coach of the Green Bay Packers 1959, he transformed a losing team into a major power, winning the first two Super Bowls 1967 and 1968. His last coaching position was with the Washington Redskins 1969–70.

Lombardy (Italian *Lombardia*) region of N Italy, including Lake Como; capital Milan; area 9,225 sq mi/23,900 sq km; population (1990) 8,939,400. It is the country's chief industrial area (chemicals, pharmaceuticals, engineering, textiles).

Lomé capital and port of Togo; population (1983) 366,000. It is a center for gold, silver, and marble crafts; industries include steel production and oil refining.

Lomé Convention convention in 1975 that established economic cooperation between the European Community and African, Caribbean, and Pacific countries. It was renewed 1979 and 1985.

Lomond, Loch largest freshwater Scottish lake, 21 mi/37 km long, area 27 sq mi/70 sq km, divided between Strathclyde and Central regions. It is overlooked by the mountain **Ben Lomond** (3,192 ft/973 m) and is linked to the Clyde estuary.

Lompoc city in SW California, near the Pacific Ocean, W of Santa Barbara; population (1990) 37,650. Industries include the processing of oil from the city's oil wells.

London The imposing keep of the Tower of London was built by Gundulf, William the Conqueror's bishop-architect.

London capital of England and the United Kingdom, on the river Thames; area 610 sq mi/1,580 sq km; population (1991) 6,378,600, larger metropolitan area about 9 million. The *City of London*, known as the "square mile," area 677 acres/274 hectares, is the financial and commercial center of the UK. *Greater London* from 1965 comprises the City of London and 32 boroughs. Popular tourist attractions include the Tower of London, St Paul's Cathedral, Buckingham Palace, and Westminster Abbey.

Roman *Londinium* was established soon after the Roman invasion AD 43; in the 2nd century London became a walled city; by the 11th century, it was the main city of England and gradually extended beyond the walls to link with the originally separate Westminster. Throughout the 19th century London was the largest city in the world (in population).

features The Tower of London, built by William the Conqueror on a Roman site, houses the crown jewels and the royal armories; 15th-century Guildhall; the Monument (a column designed by Christopher Wren) marks the site in Pudding Lane where the Great Fire of 1666 began; Mansion House (residence of the lord mayor); Barbican arts and conference center; Central Criminal Court (Old Bailey) and the Inner and Middle Temples; Covent Garden, once a vegetable market, is now a tourist shopping and entertainment area.

architecture London contains buildings in all styles of English architecture since the 11th century. *Norman:* the White Tower, Tower of London; St Bartholomew's, Smithfield; the Temple Church. *Gothic:* Westminster Abbey; Westminster Hall; Lambeth Palace; Southwark Cathedral. *Tudor:* St James's Palace; Staple Inn. *17th century:* Banqueting Hall, Whitehall (Inigo Jones); St Paul's, Kensington Palace; many City churches (Wren). *18th century:* Somerset House (Chambers); St Martin-in-the-Fields; Buckingham Palace. *19th century:* British Museum (Neo-Classical); Houses of Parliament; Law Courts (Neo-Gothic); Westminster Cathedral (Byzantine style). *20th century:* Lloyd's of London.

government There has since 1986 been no central authority for Greater London; responsibility is divided between individual boroughs and central government. The City of London has been governed by a corporation from the 12th century. Its structure and the electoral procedures for its common councillors and aldermen are medievally complex, and it is headed by the lord mayor (who is, broadly speaking, nominated by the former and elected annually by the latter). After being sworn in at the Guildhall, he or she is presented the next day to the lord chief justice at the Royal Courts of Justice in Westminster, and the *Lord Mayor's Show* is a ceremonial procession there in November.

commerce and industry From Saxon times the Port of London dominated the Thames from Tower Bridge to Tilbury; its activity is now centered outside the metropolitan area, and downstream Tilbury has been extended to cope with container traffic. The prime economic importance of modern London is as a financial center. There are various industries, mainly on the outskirts. There are also recording, broadcasting, television, and film studios; publishing companies; and the works and offices of the national press. Tourism is important. Some of the docks in the East End of London, once the busiest in the world, have been sold to the Docklands Development Corporation, which has built offices, houses, factories, and a railroad. Work on *Canary Wharf*, the world's largest office development project, was temporarily halted 1992 after its developers went into receivership.

education and entertainment Museums: British, Victoria and Albert, Natural History, Science museums; galleries: National and Tate. London University is the largest in Britain, while the Inns of Court have been the training school for lawyers since the 13th century. London has been the center of English drama since its first theater was built by James Burbage 1576.

London Jack (John Griffith) 1876–1916. US novelist, author of the adventure stories *The Call of the Wild* 1903, *The Sea Wolf* 1904, and *White Fang* 1906. By 1906 he was the most widely read writer in the US and had been translated into 68 languages.

Born in San Francisco, London was an adventurer himself, at various times a sailor, a hobo riding freight trains, and a gold prospector in the Klondike. Many of his works, which are uneven in quality, concern the human struggle against extreme natural forces for survival. His many short stories are collected in *The Son of the Wolf* 1900, *The God of His Fathers* 1901, *Children of the Frost* 1902, *Love of Life* 1907, and *Smoke Bellew* 1912. Among his other novels are *The People of the Abyss* 1903, *The Road* 1907, *The Iron Heel* 1907, and *Martin Eden* 1909.

Londonderry former name (until 1984) of the county and city of ◊Derry in Northern Ireland.

London, Treaty of secret treaty signed April 26, 1915, between Britain, France, Russia, and Italy. It promised Italy territorial gains (at the expense of Austria-Hungary) on condition that it entered World War I on the side of the Triple Entente (Britain, France, and Russia). Italy's intervention did not achieve the rapid victories expected, and the terms of the treaty (revealed by Russia 1918) angered the US. Britain and France refused to honor the treaty and, in the postwar peace treaties, Italy received far less territory than promised.

Long Huey 1893–1935. US Democratic politician, nicknamed "the Kingfish," governor of Louisiana 1928–31, US senator from Louisiana 1930–35, legendary for his political rhetoric. He was popular with poor white voters for his program of social and economic reform, which he called the "Share Our Wealth" program. It represented a significant challenge to F D Roosevelt's ◊New Deal economic program.

Born in Winnfield, Louisiana, he graduated from Tulane University with a law degree. He was fatally shot one month after announcing his intention to run for the presidency.

Longfellow Henry Wadsworth 1807–1882. US poet, remembered for ballads ("Excelsior," "The Village Blacksmith," "The Wreck of the Hesperus") and the mythic narrative epics *Evangeline* 1847, *The Song of ◊Hiawatha* 1855, and *The Courtship of Miles Standish* 1858.

Longford county of Leinster province, Republic of Ireland
area 401 sq mi/1,040 sq km
county town Longford
features rivers: Camlin, Inny, Shannon (the western boundary); several lakes
population (1991) 30,300.

Long Island island E of Manhattan and SE of Connecticut, separated from the mainland by Long Island Sound and the East River; 120 mi/193 km long by about 30 mi/48 km wide; area 1,400 sq mi/3,627 sq km; population (1984) 6,818,480.

The two New York City boroughs of Queens and Brooklyn are the western eighth of the island with a combined population of 4,165,090 (1984). East of them are the counties of Nassau and Suffolk. Along the N shore, facing the sound, are the wealthy Gold Coast communities, such as Great Neck and Oyster Bay. On the S shore, facing the Atlantic, are the popular summer-resort communities of the sandy barrier beaches, Coney Island, the Rockaways, Long Beach, Fire Island, and the Hamptons. The last glaciation of the ◊Ice Age came as far south as Long Island, leaving its rocky moraine to distinguish the cliffed and rolling north shore from the flat and sandy south; the westernmost extent of the moraine is in Jamaica, Queens.

Educational institutions include Adelphi, Hofstra, C W Post, Farmingdale and Stony Brook–SUNY, and various branches of the City University. La Guardia, Kennedy, and MacArthur airports service the region, and several bridges and tunnels connect the island to Manhattan and the Bronx. The island's many public and private facilities include museums, parks, parkways, beaches, marinas, nature preserves, golf, tennis, and country clubs; Jones Beach State Park, Shea Stadium, and Belmont and Aquaduct raceways are here. The largest employer is Grumman Aircraft, a major military contractor. Vegetable farms, orchards, vineyards, dairies, poultry, horse raising, fishing and shellfishing exist but are losing ground to suburban developments and pollution. Henry Hudson discovered the island 1609, and it was settled by the Dutch from New Amsterdam (in the W) and the English from New England (in the E) from the 1640s.

longitude see ◊latitude and longitude.

Long March in Chinese history, the 6,000 mi/10,000 km trek undertaken 1934–35 by ◊Mao Zedong and his communist forces from SE to NW China, under harassment from the Guomindang (nationalist) army.

Longmont city in N central Colorado, in the Rocky Mountain foothills, S of Fort Collins and NE of Boulder; population (1990) 51,550. Industries include business machinery, sugar-beet refining, and recreational vehicles.

Long Parliament English Parliament 1640–53 and 1659–60, which continued through the Civil War. After the Royalists withdrew in 1642 and the Presbyterian right was excluded in 1648, the remaining Rump ruled England until expelled by Oliver Cromwell in 1653. Reassembled 1659–60, the Long Parliament initiated the negotiations for the restoration of the monarchy.

Longview city in E Texas, E of Dallas; seat of Gregg County; population (1990) 70,310. In the heart of the oil fields of E Texas, Longview's industries are mainly oil and natural-gas processing.

loom any machine for weaving yarn or thread into cloth. The first looms were used to weave sheep's wool about 5000 BC. A loom is a frame on which a set of

Lorenz Austrian zoologist and biologist Konrad Lorenz, 1969.

lengthwise threads (warp) is strung. A second set of threads (weft), carried in a shuttle, is inserted at right angles over and under the warp.

loon any of various birds of the genus *Gavia*, family Gavidae, found in N regions of the N hemisphere. Loons are specialized for swimming and diving. Their legs are set so far back that walking is almost impossible, and they come to land only to nest, but loons are powerful swimmers and good flyers. They have straight bills and long bodies and feed on fish, crustaceans, and some water plants. There are just five species, the largest, the yellow-billed loon *G. adamsii*, being an Arctic species 2.5 ft/75 cm long.

Loos Anita 1888–1981. US writer, author of the humorous fictitious diary *Gentlemen Prefer Blondes* 1925. She became a screenwriter 1912 and worked on more than 60 films, including D W ◊Griffith's *Intolerance* 1916.

López Francisco Solano 1827–1870. Paraguayan dictator in succession to his father Carlos López. He involved the country in a war with Brazil, Uruguay, and Argentina, during which approximately 80% of the population died.

Lorain city in N central Ohio, on Lake Erie, NW of Akron and SW of Cleveland; population (1990) 71,240. An important Great Lakes port, it has shipbuilding yards and manufactures automobiles and heavy construction equipment.

Lorca Federico García 1898–1936. Spanish poet and playwright, born in Granada. His plays include *Bodas de sangre/Blood Wedding* 1933 and *La casa de Bernarda Alba/The House of Bernarda Alba* 1936. His poems include *Lament*, written for the bullfighter Mejías. Lorca was shot by the Falangists during the Spanish Civil War.

Lord in the UK, prefix used informally as alternative to the full title of a marquess, earl, or viscount; normally also in speaking of a baron, and as a courtesy title before the forename and surname of younger sons of dukes and marquesses.

Lords, House of upper house of the UK ◊Parliament.

Lorelei in Germanic folklore, a river ◊nymph of the Rhine who lures sailors onto the rock where she sits combing her hair. She features in several poems, including "Die Lorelei" by the German Romantic writer Heine. The *Lurlei* rock S of Koblenz is 430 ft/130 m high.

Loren Sophia. Adopted name of Sofia Scicolone 1934– . Italian film actress whose boldly sensual appeal was promoted by her husband, producer Carlo Ponti. Her work includes *Aida* 1953, *The Key* 1958, *La ciociara/Two Women* 1960, *Judith* 1965, and *Firepower* 1979.

Lorenz Konrad 1903–1989. Austrian ethologist. Director of the Max Planck Institute for the Physiology of Behavior in Bavaria 1955–73, he wrote the studies of ethology (animal behavior) *King Solomon's Ring* 1952 and *On Aggression* 1966. In 1973 he shared the Nobel Prize for Medicine with Nikolaas Tinbergen and Karl von Frisch.

Lorrain Claude. French painter; see ◊Claude Lorrain.

Lorraine region of NE France in the upper reaches of the Meuse and Moselle rivers; bounded N by Belgium, Luxembourg, and Germany and E by Alsace; area 9,095 sq mi/23,600 sq km; population (1986) 2,313,000. It comprises the *départements* of Meurthe-et-Moselle, Meuse, Moselle, and Vosges, and its capital is Nancy.

There are deposits of coal, iron ore, and salt; grain, fruit, and livestock are farmed. In 1871 the region was ceded to Germany as part of Alsace-Lorraine.

Lorre Peter. Adopted name of Lazlo Löwenstein 1904–1964. Hungarian character actor with bulging eyes, high voice, and melancholy mien. He made several films in Germany before moving to Hollywood in 1935. He appeared in *M* 1931, *Mad Love* 1935, *The Maltese Falcon* 1941, *Casablanca* 1942, *Beat the Devil* 1953, and *The Raven* 1963. His last film was *Patsy* 1964.

Los Alamos town in New Mexico, which has had a center for atomic and space research since 1942. In World War II the first atom (nuclear fission) bomb was designed there (under Robert ◊Oppenheimer), based on data from other research stations; the ◊hydrogen bomb was also developed there.

The town has a population of 12,000.

Los Angeles city and port in SW California; population (1990) 3,485,400, metropolitan area of Los Angeles–Long Beach 14,531,530. Industries include aerospace, electronics, motor vehicles, chemicals, clothing, printing, and food processing.

Features include Hollywood, center of the US film industry since 1911; the Hollywood Bowl concert arena; the Los Angeles Music Center; and the Los Angeles County Museum of Art. Educational institutions include the University of California at Los Angeles and the University of Southern California. Los Angeles was established as a Spanish settlement 1781, but it was a farming region with orange groves until the early 20th century, when it annexed neighboring communities and acquired distant water supplies, a deepwater port, and the film industry. In the 1920s large petroleum deposits were found in the area. The aircraft industry, with its need for year-round flying weather, developed here soon after and grew rapidly with the advent of World War II. In 1992, racial disturbances resulted in 50 deaths and heavy damage.

Lost Generation, the disillusioned US literary generation of the 1920s, members of which went to live in Paris. The phrase is attributed to the writer Gertrude Stein in Ernest Hemingway's early novel of 1920s Paris, *The Sun Also Rises* 1926.

lost-wax technique method of making sculptures.

Lothair 825–869. King of Lotharingia from 855, when he inherited the region from his father, the Holy Roman emperor Lothair I.

Lothair two Holy Roman emperors:

Lothair I 795–855. Holy Roman emperor from 817 in association with his father Louis I. On Louis's death in 840, the empire was divided between Lothair and his brothers; Lothair took N Italy and the valleys of the rivers Rhône and Rhine.

Lothair II c. 1070–1137. Holy Roman emperor from 1133 and German king from 1125. His election as emperor, opposed by the ◊Hohenstaufen family of princes, was the start of the feud between the ◊Guelph and Ghibelline factions, who supported the papal party and the Hohenstaufens' claim to the imperial throne respectively.

Lotharingia medieval region W of the Rhine, between the Jura mountains and the North Sea; the N portion of the lands assigned to Lothair I when the Carolingian empire was divided. It was called after his son King Lothair, and later corrupted to Lorraine; it is now part of Alsace-Lorraine, France.

Lothian region of Scotland
area 695 sq mi/1,800 sq km
cities Edinburgh (administrative headquarters), Livingston
features hills: Lammermuir, Moorfoot, Pentland; Bass Rock in the Firth of Forth, noted for seabirds
products bacon, vegetables, coal, whiskey, engineering, electronics
population (1991) 723,700
famous people Alexander Graham Bell, Arthur Conan Doyle, R L Stevenson.

lotus any of several different plants, especially the water lily *Nymphaea lotus*, frequent in Egyptian art, and *Nelumbo nucifera*, the pink Asiatic lotus, a sacred symbol in Hinduism and Buddhism, whose flower head floats erect above the water.

Lotus 1–2–3 ◊spreadsheet computer program, produced by Lotus Development Corporation. It first appeared in 1982 and its combination of spreadsheet, graphics display, and data management contributed to the rapid acceptance of the IBM Personal Computer in businesses.

Lotus Sūtra scripture of Mahāyāna Buddhism. It is Buddha Śākyamuni's final teaching, emphasizing that everyone can attain Buddhahood with the help of bodhisattvas. The original is in Sanskrit (*Saddharmapundarīka Sūtra*) and is thought to date from some time after 100 BC.

loudspeaker electromechanical device that converts electrical signals into sound waves, which are radiated into the air. The most common type of loudspeaker is the *moving-coil speaker*. Electrical signals from, for example, a radio are fed to a coil of fine wire wound around the top of a cone. The coil is surrounded by a magnet. When signals pass through it, the coil becomes an electromagnet, which by moving causes the cone to vibrate, setting up sound waves.

Louis Joe. Assumed name of Joseph Louis Barrow 1914–1981. US boxer, nicknamed "the Brown Bomber." He was world heavyweight champion between 1937 and 1949 and made a record 25 successful defenses (a record for any weight).

Louis Morris 1912–1962. US abstract painter. From Abstract Expressionism he turned to the color-staining technique developed by Helen ◊Frankenthaler, using thinned-out acrylic paints poured on rough canvas to create the illusion of vaporous layers of color. The *Veil* paintings of the 1950s are examples.

Louis I *the Pious* 788–840. Holy Roman emperor from 814, when he succeeded his father Charlemagne.

Louis III 863–882. King of N France from 879, while his brother Carloman (866–884) ruled S France. He was the son of Louis II. Louis countered a revolt of the nobility at the beginning of his reign, and his resistance to the Normans made him a hero of epic poems.

Louis VII c. 1120–1180. King of France from 1137, who led the Second ◊Crusade.

Louis IX St 1214–1270. King of France from 1226, leader of the 7th and 8th ◊Crusades. He was defeated in the former by the Muslims, spending four years in captivity. He died in Tunis. He was canonized 1297.

Louis X *the Stubborn* 1289–1316. King of France who succeeded his father Philip IV in 1314. His reign saw widespread discontent among the nobles, which he countered by granting charters guaranteeing seignorial rights, although some historians claim that by using evasive tactics, he gave up nothing.

Louis XIV Marble bust of the "Sun King" Louis XIV of France by Italian sculptor Bernini.

Louis XI 1423–1483. King of France from 1461. He broke the power of the nobility (headed by ◊Charles the Bold) by intrigue and military power.

Louis XIII 1601–1643. King of France from 1610 (in succession to his father Henry IV), he assumed royal power in 1617. He was under the political control of Cardinal ◊Richelieu 1624–42.

Louis XIV *the Sun King* 1638–1715. King of France from 1643, when he succeeded his father Louis XIII; his mother was Anne of Austria. Until 1661 France was ruled by the chief minister, Jules Mazarin, but later Louis took absolute power, summed up in his saying *L'Etat c'est moi* ("I am the state"). Throughout his reign he was engaged in unsuccessful expansionist wars—1667–68, 1672–78, 1688–97, and 1701–13 (the War of the ◊Spanish Succession)—against various European alliances, always including Britain and the Netherlands. He was a patron of the arts.

Louis XV 1710–1774. King of France from 1715, with the Duke of Orléans as regent until 1723. He was the great-grandson of Louis XIV. Indolent and frivolous, Louis left government in the hands of his ministers, the Duke of Bourbon and Cardinal Fleury (1653–1743). On the latter's death he attempted to rule alone but became entirely dominated by his mistresses, Madame de Pompadour and Madame ◊du Barry. His foreign policy led to French possessions in Canada and India being lost to England.

Louis XVI 1754–1793. King of France from 1774, grandson of Louis XV, and son of Louis the Dauphin. He was dominated by his queen, ◊Marie Antoinette, and French finances fell into such confusion that in 1789 the ◊States General (parliament) had to be summoned, and the ◊French Revolution began. Louis lost his personal popularity in June 1791 when he attempted to flee the country, and in Aug 1792 the Parisians stormed the Tuileries palace and took the royal family prisoner. Deposed in Sept 1792, Louis was tried in Dec, sentenced for treason in Jan 1793, and guillotined.

Louis XVIII 1755–1824. King of France 1814–24, the younger brother of Louis XVI. He assumed the title of king in 1795, having fled into exile in 1791 during the French Revolution, but became king only on the fall of Napoleon I in April 1814. Expelled during Napoleon's brief return (the "hundred days") in 1815, he resumed power after Napoleon's final defeat at Waterloo, pursuing a policy of calculated liberalism until ultra-royalist pressure became dominant after 1820.

Louisiana state in S US; nickname Pelican State
area 52,457 sq mi/135,900 sq km

capital Baton Rouge
cities New Orleans, Shreveport, Lafayette, Lake Charles
features New Orleans French Quarter: jazz, restaurants, Mardi Gras; Cajun country and the Mississippi River delta; Jean Lafitte National Park and Chalmette National Historical Park; plantation homes near Natchitoches
products rice, cotton, sugar, oil, natural gas, chemicals, sulfur, fish and shellfish, salt, processed foods, petroleum products, timber, paper
population (1990) 4,220,000; including Cajuns, descendants of 18th-century religious exiles from Canada, who speak a French dialect
famous people Louis Armstrong, P G T Beauregard, Huey Long
history explored by the Spanish Piñeda 1519, Cabeza de Vaca 1528, and De Soto 1541 and by the French explorer La Salle 1862, who named it after Louis XIV and claimed it for France. It became Spanish 1762–1800, then French, then passed to the US 1803 under the ◊Louisiana Purchase; admitted to the Union as a state 1812.

Louisiana Purchase purchase by the US from France 1803 of an area covering about 828,000 sq mi/2,144,000 sq km, including the present-day states of Louisiana, Missouri, Arkansas, Iowa, Nebraska, North Dakota, South Dakota, and Oklahoma.

Louis Philippe 1773–1850. King of France 1830–48. Son of Louis Philippe Joseph, Duke of Orléans 1747–93; both were known as *Philippe Egalité* from their support of the 1792 Revolution. Louis Philippe fled into exile 1793–1814, but became king after the 1830 revolution with the backing of the rich bourgeoisie. Corruption discredited his regime, and after his overthrow, he escaped to the UK and died there.

Louisville industrial city and river port on the Ohio River, Kentucky; population (1990) 269,000. Products include electrical goods, agricultural machinery, motor vehicles, tobacco, and whiskey. It is the home of the Kentucky Fair and Exposition Center, and the Kentucky Derby. The University of Louisville and the Actors Theater of Louisville are here. Louisville was founded 1778.

Lourdes town in Midi-Pyrénées region, SW France, on the Gave de Pau River; population (1982) 18,000. Its Christian shrine to St ◊Bernadette has a reputation for miraculous cures and Lourdes is an important Catholic pilgrimage center. The young peasant girl Bernadette Soubirous was shown the healing springs of the Grotte de Massabielle by a vision of the Virgin Mary 1858.

Lourenço Marques former name of ◊Maputo, the capital of Mozambique.

louse parasitic insect of the order Anoplura, which lives on mammals. It has a flat, segmented body with-

Louisiana

Louvre *US architect I M Pei designed the glass pyramid for the Louvre art gallery in Paris, constructed 1986–88.*

out wings, and a tube attached to the head, used for sucking blood from its host.

Louth smallest county of the Republic of Ireland, in Leinster province; county town Dundalk; area 317 sq mi/820 sq km; population (1991) 90,700.

Louvre French art gallery, former palace of the French kings, in Paris. It was converted to an art gallery in 1793 to house the royal collections. Today comprises seven sections: ancient, Oriental, Egyptian, painting, sculpture, applied arts and drawing. Its most famous items include the sculpture *Venus de Milo* and Leonardo da Vinci's painting *Mona Lisa*.

Lovelace Richard 1618–1658. English poet. Imprisoned in 1642 for petitioning for the restoration of royal rule, he wrote "To Althea from Prison," and in a second term in jail in 1648 revised his collection *Lucasta* 1649.

Loveland city in N central Colorado, S of Fort Collins; population (1990) 37,350. It is a processing and marketing center for the agricultural products of the area. Tourism is important to the economy, and Rocky Mountain National Park is to the W.

Low Juliette Gordon 1860–1927. Founder of the Girl Scouts in the US. She formed a troop of 16 "Girl Guides" in Savannah 1912, based on UK scouting organizations founded by Robert Baden-Powell. Establishing national headquarters in Washington, DC 1913, she changed the name of the organization to the Girl Scouts of America (GSA).

Low Countries region of Europe that consists of ◊Belgium and the ◊Netherlands, and usually includes ◊Luxembourg.

Lowell city in Massachusetts; population (1990) 103,400. Industries include electronics, plastics, and chemicals. Lowell was a textile center in the 19th century; a substantial part of the old city was designated a national park 1978 as a birthplace of the US industrial revolution. Wang Laboratories moved its headquarters here 1978.

Lowell Amy (Lawrence) 1874–1925. US poet who began her career by publishing the conventional *A Dome of Many-Colored Glass* 1912 but eventually succeeded Ezra Pound as leader of the ◊Imagists. Her works, in free verse, include *Sword Blades and Poppy Seed* 1916.

She was a controversial figure who demonstrated her scorn for conventionality by, for example, openly smoking cigars.

Lowell Francis Cabot 1775–1817. US industrialist who imported the new technology of English textile mills to America. With the cutoff of international trade during the Anglo-American War of 1812, Lowell established the Boston Manufacturing Co, a mechanized textile mill at Waltham, Massachusetts.

Lower Saxony (German *Niedersachsen*) administrative region (German *Land*) of N Germany
area 18,296 sq mi/47,400 sq km
capital Hanover
cities Brunswick, Osnabrück, Oldenburg, Göttingen, Wolfsburg, Salzgitter, Hildesheim
features Lüneburg Heath
products cereals, automobiles, machinery, electrical engineering
population (1988) 7,190,000
religion Protestant 75%, Roman Catholic 20%
history formed 1946 from Hanover, Oldenburg, Brunswick, and Schaumburg-Lippe.

Loy Myrna. Adopted name of Myrna Williams 1905–1993. US film actress who played Nora Charles in the *Thin Man* series (1934–47) costarring William Powell. Her other films include *The Mask of Fu Manchu* 1932 and *The Rains Came* 1939.

Loyalist member of approximately 30% of the US population remaining loyal to Britain in the ◊American Revolution. Many Loyalists went to E Ontario, Canada, after 1783.

Loyola founder of the Jesuits. See ◊Ignatius Loyola.

LSD abbreviation for *lysergic acid diethylamide*, a psychedelic drug and a hallucinogen, often producing states resembling those common in psychosis (for example, schizophrenia). It is derived from lysergic acid, originally extracted from poisonous ergot alkaloids. Its use is illegal.

Luanda (formerly *Loanda*) capital and industrial port (cotton, sugar, tobacco, timber, textiles, paper, oil) of Angola; population (1988) 1,200,000. Founded 1575, it became a Portuguese colonial administrative center as well as an outlet for slaves transported to Brazil.

Lubbers Rudolph Franz Marie (Ruud) 1939– . Dutch politician, prime minister of the Netherlands from 1982. Leader of the Christian Democratic Appeal (CDA), he is politically right of center. He became minister for economic affairs 1973.

Lubbock city in NW Texas, S of Amarillo; seat of Lubbock County; population (1990) 186,200. Industries include heavy farm and construction machinery, cotton, sorghum, and mobile homes. The rock-and-roll singer Buddy Holly was born here.

Lubitsch Ernst 1892–1947. German film director known for his stylish comedies, who worked in the US from 1921. His sound films include *Trouble in Paradise* 1932, *Design for Living* 1933, *Ninotchka* 1939, and *To Be or Not to Be* 1942.

lubricant substance used between moving surfaces to reduce friction. Carbon-based (organic) lubricants, commonly called grease and oil, are recovered from petroleum distillation.

Lucan (Marcus Annaeus Lucanus) AD 39–65. Latin poet, born in Córdoba, Spain, a nephew of the writer Seneca and favorite of Nero until the emperor became jealous of his verse. Lucan then joined a republican conspiracy and committed suicide on its failure. His epic poem "Pharsalia" deals with the civil wars of Caesar and Pompey, and was influential in the Middle Ages and Renaissance.

Lucas George 1944– . US film director and producer whose imagination was fired by the comic books in his father's store. He wrote and directed (in collaboration with Steven Spielberg) *Star Wars* 1977 and *The Empire Strikes Back* 1980. His other films include *THX 1138* 1971, *American Graffiti* 1973, *Raiders of the Lost Ark* 1981, *Indiana Jones and the Temple of Doom* 1984, *Willow* 1988, and *Indiana Jones and the Last Crusade* 1989, most of which were box-office hits.

Lucas van Leyden 1494–1533. Dutch painter and engraver, active in Leiden and Antwerp. He was a pioneer of Netherlandish genre scenes, for example *The Chess Players* (Staatliche Museen, Berlin). His woodcuts and engravings were inspired by Albrecht Dürer, whom he met in Antwerp in 1521.

Lucas's work influenced ◊Rembrandt.

Luce Clare Boothe 1903–1987. US journalist, playwright, and politician. She was managing editor of *Vanity Fair* magazine 1933–34, and wrote several successful plays, including *The Women* 1936 and *Margin for Error* 1940, both of which were made into films. She served as a Republican member of Congress 1943–47 and as ambassador to Italy 1953–57.

She was born in New York and married Time, Inc, founder Henry Robinson Luce in 1935.

Luce Henry Robinson 1898–1967. US publisher, founder of Time, Inc, which publishes the weekly news magazine *Time* 1923, the business magazine *Fortune* 1930, the pictorial magazine *Life* 1936, and the sports magazine *Sports Illustrated* 1954. He married Clare Boothe Luce in 1935.

Born of missionary parents in Tengchow, China, Luce was educated at Yale and Oxford universities. Other publications of Time, Inc, include *House and Home, Architectural Forum*, and Time-Life Books.

Lucerne (German *Luzern*) capital and tourist center of Lucerne canton, Switzerland, on the river Reuss where it flows out of Lake Lucerne; population (1990) city 59,400, canton 319,500. It developed around the Benedictine monastery, established about 750, and owes its prosperity to its position on the St Gotthard road and railroad.

Lucian c. 125–c. 190. Greek writer of satirical dialogues, in which he pours scorn on religions and mocks human pretensions. He was born at Samosata in Syria and for a time was an advocate at Antioch, but later traveled before settling in Athens about 165. He occupied an official post in Egypt, where he died.

Lucifer in Christian theology, another name for the ◊devil, the leader of the angels who rebelled against God. Lucifer is also another name for the morning star (the planet ◊Venus).

Lucknow capital and industrial city (engineering, chemicals, textiles, many handicrafts) of the state of Uttar Pradesh, India; population (1981) 1,007,000. During the Indian Mutiny against British rule, it was besieged July 2–Nov 16, 1857.

Lucretia Roman woman, the wife of Collatinus, said to have committed suicide after being raped by Sextus, son of Tarquinius Superbus, the last king of Rome. According to tradition, this incident led to the dethronement of Tarquinius and the establishment of the Roman Republic in 509 BC.

Lucretius (Titus Lucretius Carus) c. 99–55 BC. Roman poet and Epicurean philosopher whose *De Rerum natura/On the Nature of The Universe* envisaged the whole universe as a combination of atoms, and had some concept of evolutionary theory.

Lucullus Lucius Licinius 110–56 BC. Roman general and consul. As commander against Mithridates of Pontus 74–66 he proved to be one of Rome's ablest generals and administrators, until superseded by Pompey. He then retired from politics.

Lüda or *Lü-ta* or *Hüta* industrial port (engineering, chemicals, textiles, oil refining, shipbuilding, food processing) in Liaoning, China, on Liaodong Peninsula, facing the Yellow Sea; population (1986) 4,500,000. It comprises the naval base of Lüshun (known under 19th-century Russian occupation as Port Arthur) and the commercial port of Dalien (formerly Talien/Dairen).

Ludwig three kings of Bavaria, including:

Ludwig I 1786–1868. King of Bavaria 1825–48, succeeding his father Maximilian Joseph I. He made Munich an international cultural center, but his association with the dancer Lola Montez, who dictated his policies for a year, led to his abdication in 1848.

Ludwig II 1845–1886. King of Bavaria from 1864, when he succeeded his father Maximilian II. He supported Austria during the Austro-Prussian War 1866, but brought Bavaria into the Franco-Prussian War as Prussia's ally and in 1871 offered the German crown to the king of Prussia. He was the composer Richard Wagner's patron and built the Bayreuth theater for him. Declared insane 1886, he drowned himself soon after.

Luftwaffe German air force. In World War I and, as reorganized by the Nazi leader Hermann Goering in 1933, in World War II. The Luftwaffe also covered anti-aircraft defense and the launching of the flying bombs ◊V1 and V2.

luge a one- or two-person racing sled, on which riders lie face up. Luges are raced by both men and women in the winter Olympics.

Lugosi Bela. Adopted name of Bela Ferenc Blasko 1882–1956. Hungarian-born US film actor. Acclaimed for his performance in *Dracula* on Broadway 1927, Lugosi began acting in feature films in 1930. His appearance in the film version of *Dracula* 1931 marked the start of Lugosi's long career in horror films— among them, *Murders in the Rue Morgue* 1932, *The Raven* 1935, and *The Wolf Man* 1941.

Lukács Georg 1885–1971. Hungarian philosopher, one of the founders of "Western" or "Hegelian" Marxism, a philosophy opposed to the Marxism of the official communist movement.

Luke, St 1st century AD. Traditionally the compiler of the third Gospel and of the Acts of the Apostles in the New Testament. He is the patron saint of painters; his emblem is a winged ox, and his feast day Oct 18.

Luks George 1867–1933. US painter and graphic artist, a member of the ◊Ashcan School.

Lully Jean-Baptiste. Adopted name of Giovanni Battista Lulli 1632–1687. French composer of Italian origin who was court composer to Louis XIV. He composed music for the ballet, for Molière's plays, and established French opera with such works as *Alceste* 1674 and *Armide et Renaud* 1686. He was also a ballet dancer.

lumbago pain in the lower region of the back, usually due to strain or faulty posture. If it occurs with ◊sciatica, it may be due to pressure on spinal nerves by a displaced vertebra. Treatment includes rest, application of heat, and skilled manipulation. Surgery may be needed in rare cases.

lumen SI unit (symbol lm) of luminous flux (the amount of light passing through an area per second).

Lumet Sidney 1924– . US film director whose social conscience has sometimes prejudiced his invariably powerful films: *12 Angry Men* 1957, *Fail Safe* 1964, *Serpico* 1973, and *Dog Day Afternoon* 1975.

Lumière Auguste Marie 1862–1954 and Louis Jean 1864–1948. French brothers who pioneered cinematography. In 1895 they patented their cinematograph, a combined camera and projector operating at 16 frames per second, and opened the world's first cinema in Paris to show their films.

luminescence emission of light from a body when its atoms are excited by means other than raising its temperature. Short-lived luminescence is called fluorescence; longer-lived luminescence is called phosphorescence.

luminism method of painting, associated with the ◊Hudson River School in the 19th century, that emphasized the effects of light on water.
   Luminist painters included F H Lane, T Cole, A B Durand, M J Heade, and F E Church. They gave particular attention to the treatment of light in their paintings, stressing precision through technical accuracy.

luminosity or **brightness** in astronomy, the amount of light emitted by a star, measured in ◊magnitudes. The apparent brightness of an object decreases in proportion to the square of its distance from the observer. The luminosity of a star or other body can be expressed in relation to that of the sun.

Lumumba Patrice 1926–1961. Congolese politician, prime minister of Zaire 1960. Imprisoned by the Belgians, but released in time to attend the conference giving the Congo independence in 1960, he led the National Congolese Movement to victory in the subsequent general election. He was deposed in a coup d'état, and murdered some months later.

lung large cavity of the body, used for gas exchange. It is essentially a sheet of thin, moist membrane that is folded so as to occupy less space. Most tetrapod (four-limbed) vertebrates have a pair of lungs occupying the thorax. The lung tissue, consisting of multitudes of air sacs and blood vessels, is very light and spongy, and functions by bringing inhaled air into close contact with the blood so that oxygen can pass into the organism and waste carbon dioxide can be passed out. The efficiency of lungs is enhanced by ◊breathing movements, by the thinness and moistness of their surfaces, and by a constant supply of circulating blood. *See illustration p. 570*

lungfish three genera of fleshy-finned bony fishes of the subclass Dipnoi, found in Africa, South America, and Australia. They have elongated bodies, grow to about 6 ft/2 m, and in addition to gills have "lungs" allowing them to breathe air during periods of drought.

Luo member of the second-largest ethnic group of Kenya, living in the Lake Victoria region and in 1987 numbering some 2,650,000. The Luo traditionally live by farming livestock. The Luo language is of the Nilo-Saharan family.

lupus in medicine, any of various diseases characterized by lesions of the skin. One form (lupus vulgaris) is caused by the tubercle bacillus (see ◊tuberculosis). The organism produces ulcers that spread and eat away the underlying tissues. Treatment is primarily with standard antituberculous drugs, but ultraviolet light may also be used.

Lusaka capital of Zambia from 1964 (of Northern Rhodesia 1935–64), 230 mi/370 km NE of Livingstone; it is a commercial and agricultural center (flour mills, tobacco factories, vehicle assembly, plastics, printing); population (1988) 870,000.

Lusitania ocean liner sunk by a German submarine on May 7, 1915, with the loss of 1,200 lives, including some Americans; its destruction helped to bring the US into World War I.

lute family of stringed musical instruments of the 14th–18th century, including the plucked with the fingers. Members of the lute family were used both as solo instruments and for vocal accompaniment, and were often played in addition to, or instead of, keyboard instruments in larger ensembles and in opera.

lutetium (Latin *Lutetia* "Paris") silver-white, metallic element, the last of the ◊lanthanide series, symbol Lu, atomic number 71, atomic weight 174.97. It is used in the "cracking," or breakdown, of petroleum and in other chemical processes. It was named by its discoverer, French chemist Georges Urbain, (1872–1938) after his native city.

Luther Martin 1483–1546. German Christian church reformer, a founder of Protestantism. While he was a priest at the University of Wittenberg, he wrote an attack on the sale of indulgences (remissions of punishment for sin). The Holy Roman emperor Charles V summoned him to the Diet (meeting of dignitaries of

lung The human lungs contain 300,000 million tiny blood vessels which would stretch for 1,500 mi/2,400 km if laid end to end.

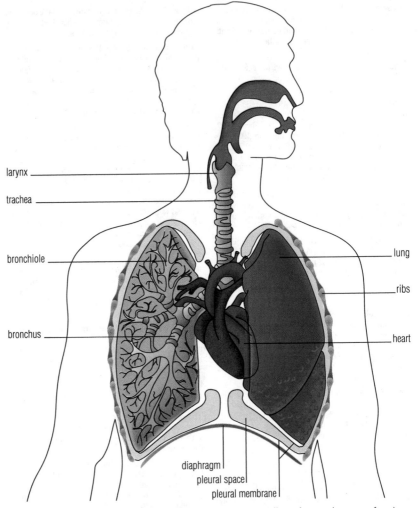

larynx

trachea

bronchiole

bronchus

lung

ribs

heart

diaphragm
pleural space
pleural membrane

the Holy Roman Empire) of Worms in Germany, in 1521, where he refused to retract his objections. Originally intending reform, his protest led to schism, with the emergence, following the ◊Augsburg Confession 1530 (a statement of the Protestant faith), of a new Protestant church. Luther is regarded as the instigator of the Protestant revolution, and Lutheranism is now the major religion of many N European countries, including Germany, Sweden, and Denmark.

Lutheranism form of Protestant Christianity derived from the life and teaching of Martin Luther; it is sometimes called Evangelical to distinguish it from the other main branch of European Protestantism, the Reformed. The most generally accepted statement of Lutheranism is that of the *Augsburg Confession* 1530 but Luther's Shorter Catechism also carries great weight. It is the largest Protestant body, including some 80 million persons, of whom 40 million are in Germany, 19 million in Scandinavia, 8.5 million in the US and Canada, with most of the remainder in central Europe.

lux SI unit (symbol lx) of illuminance or illumination (the light falling on an object). It is equivalent to one ◊lumen per square meter or to the illuminance of a sur-

face one meter distant from a point source of one ◊candela.

Luxembourg capital of the country of Luxembourg, on the Alzette and Petrusse rivers; population (1985) 76,000. The 16th-century Grand Ducal Palace, European Court of Justice, and European Parliament secretariat are situated here, but plenary sessions of the parliament are now held only in Strasbourg, France. Products include steel, chemicals, textiles, and processed food.

Luxembourg landlocked country in W Europe, bounded N and W by Belgium, E by Germany, and S by France.

Luxor (Arabic *al-Uqsur*) small town in Egypt on the E bank of the river Nile. The ancient city of Thebes is on the W bank, with the temple of Luxor built by Amenhotep III (*c.* 1411–1375 BC) and the tombs of the pharaohs in the Valley of the Kings.

Lu Xun Adopted name of Chon Shu-jêu 1881–1936. Chinese short-story writer. His three volumes of satirically realistic stories, *Call to Arms, Wandering*, and *Old Tales Retold*, reveal the influence of the Russian writer Nicolai Gogol.

He is one of the most popular of modern Chinese writers.

Luzern German name of ◊Lucerne, a city in Switzerland.

Luzon largest island of the ◊Philippines; area 41,750 sq mi/108,130 sq km; capital Quezon City; population (1970) 18,001,270. The chief city is Manila, capital of the Philippines. Products include rice, timber, and minerals. It has US military bases.

Lyceum ancient Athenian gymnasium and garden, with covered walks, where the philosopher Aristotle taught. It was SE of the city and named after the nearby temple of Apollo Lyceus.

lychee alternate spelling of litchi, a fruit-bearing tree.

Lycurgus Spartan lawgiver. He was believed to have been a member of the royal house of the ancient Greek city-state of Sparta, who, while acting as regent, gave the Spartans their constitution and system of education. Many modern scholars believe him to be purely mythical.

Lydia ancient kingdom in Anatolia (7th–6th centuries BC), with its capital at Sardis. The Lydians were the first Western people to use standard coinage. Their last king, Croesus, was defeated by the Persians in 546 BC.

Lyell Charles 1797–1875. Scottish geologist. In his *Principles of Geology* 1830–33, he opposed the French anatomist Georges Cuvier's theory that the features of the Earth were formed by a series of catastrophes, and

Luxor The temple of Queen Hatshepsut at Luxor, Egypt, showing a bust of the queen on one of the columns.

expounded the Scottish geologist James Hutton's view, known as ◊uniformitarianism, that past events were brought about by the same processes that occur today—a view that influenced Charles Darwin's theory of evolution.

Luxembourg
Grand Duchy of
(*Grand-Duché de Luxembourg*)

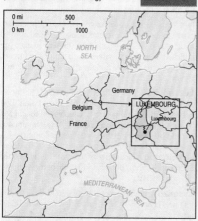

area 998 sq mi/2,586 sq km
capital Luxembourg
cities Esch-sur-Alzette, Dudelange
physical on the river Moselle; part of the Ardennes (Oesling) forest in N
features seat of the European Court of Justice, Secretariat of the European Parliament, international banking center; economically linked with Belgium
head of state Grand Duke Jean from 1964
head of government Jacques Santer from 1984
political system liberal democracy
political parties Christian Social Party (PCS), moderate, left of center; Luxembourg Socialist Workers' Party

(POSL), moderate, socialist; Democratic Party (PD), centre- left; Communist Party of Luxembourg, pro-European left-wing
exports pharmaceuticals, synthetic textiles, steel
currency Luxembourg franc
population (1992) 387,000; growth rate 0% p.a.
life expectancy men 71, women 78 (1989)
languages French (official), local Letzeburgesch, German
religion Roman Catholic 97%
literacy 100% (1989)
GNP $10.4 bn (1992)

chronology
1354 Became a duchy.
1482 Under Hapsburg control.
1797 Ceded, with Belgium, to France.
1815 Treaty of Vienna created Luxembourg a grand duchy, ruled by the king of the Netherlands.
1830 With Belgium, revolted against Dutch rule.
1890 Link with Netherlands ended with accession of Grand Duke Adolphe of Nassau-Weilburg.
1948 With Belgium and the Netherlands, formed the Benelux customs union.
1960 Benelux became fully effective economic union.
1961 Prince Jean became acting head of state on behalf of his mother, Grand Duchess Charlotte.
1964 Grand Duchess Charlotte abdicated; Prince Jean became grand duke.
1974 Dominance of Christian Social Party challenged by Socialists.
1979 Christian Social Party regained pre-eminence.
1991 Pact agreeing European free-trade area signed in Luxembourg.
1992 Voted in favor of ratification of Maastricht Treaty on European union.

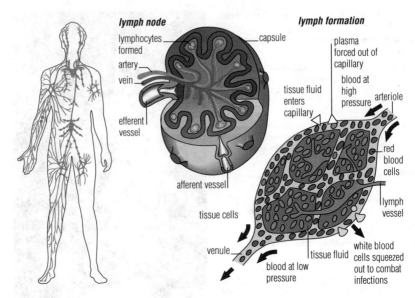

lymph Lymph is the fluid that carries nutrients, oxygen, and white blood cells to the tissues.

lymph node

lymphocytes formed

artery

vein

efferent vessel

afferent vessel

tissue cells

venule

lymph formation

capsule

plasma forced out of capillary

blood at high pressure

arteriole

tissue fluid enters capillary

red blood cells

lymph vessel

tissue fluid

blood at low pressure

white blood cells squeezed out to combat infections

Lyme disease disease transmitted by tick bites that affects all the systems of the body. First described in 1977 following an outbreak in children living around Lyme, Connecticut, it is caused by the microorganism *Borrelia burgdorferi*, isolated by Burgdorfer and Barbor in the US in 1982. Untreated, the disease attacks the nervous system, heart, liver, kidneys, eyes and joints, but responds to the antibiotic tetracycline. The tick that carries the disease, *Ixodes*, lives on deer, while *B. burgdorferi* relies on mice during its life cycle.

lymph fluid found in the lymphatic system of vertebrates.

lymph nodes small masses of lymphatic tissue in the body that occur at various points along the major lymphatic vessels. Tonsils and adenoids are large lymph nodes. As the lymph passes through them it is filtered, and bacteria and other microorganisms are engulfed by cells known as macrophages.

lymphocyte type of white blood cell with a large nucleus, produced in the bone marrow. Most occur in the ◊lymph and blood, and around sites of infection. *B-lymphocytes* or B cells are responsible for producing ◊antibodies. *T-lymphocytes* or ◊T-cells have several roles in the formation of ◊immunity.

Lynch "Jack" (John) 1917– . Irish politician, prime minister 1966–73 and 1977–79. A Gaelic footballer and a lawyer, in 1948 he entered the parliament of the republic as a Fianna Fáil member.

Lynchburg city in S central Virginia, on the James River, NE of Roanoke; population (1990) 66,050. Industries include clothing, paper and rubber products, and machine parts.

lynx cat *Felis lynx* found in rocky and forested regions of North America and Europe. About 3 ft/1 m in length, it has a short tail and tufted ears, and the long, silky fur is reddish brown or gray with dark spots. The North American bobcat or bay lynx *F. rufus* looks similar but is smaller. Some zoologists place the lynx, the bobcat, and the caracal in a separate genus, *Lynx*.

Lyon (English *Lyons*) industrial city (textiles, chemicals, machinery, printing) and capital of Rhône *département*, Rhône-Alpes region, and third largest city of France, at the confluence of the rivers Rhône and Saône, 170 mi/275 km NNW of Marseille; population (1990) 422,400, conurbation 1,221,000. Formerly a chief fortress of France, it was the ancient *Lugdunum*, taken by the Romans 43 BC.

Lyra small but prominent constellation of the northern hemisphere, representing the lyre of Orpheus. Its brightest star is ◊Vega.

lyre stringed instrument of great antiquity. It consists of a soundbox with two curved arms extended upward to a crosspiece to which four to ten strings are attached. It is played with a plectrum or the fingers. It originated in Asia, and was used in Greece and Egypt.

Lysander died 395 BC. Spartan general, politician and admiral. He brought the ◊Peloponnesian War between Athens and Sparta to a successful conclusion by capturing the Athenian fleet at Aegospotami 405 BC, and by starving Athens into surrender in the following year. He set up puppet governments in Athens and its former allies, and tried to secure for himself the Spartan kingship, but was killed in battle with the Thebans 395 BC.

Lysenko Trofim Denisovich 1898–1976. Soviet biologist who believed in the inheritance of ◊acquired characteristics (changes acquired in an individual's lifetime) and used his position under Joseph Stalin officially to exclude Gregor ◊Mendel's theory of inheritance. He was removed from office after the fall of Khrushchev in 1964.

Lysippus 4th century BC. Greek sculptor. He made a series of portraits of Alexander the Great (Roman copies survive, including examples in the British Museum and the Louvre) and also sculpted the *Apoxyomenos*, an athlete (copy in the Vatican), and a colossal *Hercules* (lost).

M Roman numeral for *1,000.*

MA abbreviation for *master of arts*, a degree of education; the state of ◊Massachusetts.

Mabuse Jan. Adopted name of Jan Gossaert *c.* 1478–*c.* 1533. Flemish painter, active chiefly in Antwerp. His common name derives from his birthplace, Maubeuge. His visit to Italy 1508 with Philip of Burgundy started a new vogue in Flanders for Italianate ornament and Classical detail in painting, including sculptural nude figures.

McAdam John Loudon 1756–1836. Scottish engineer, inventor of the macadam road surface. It originally consisted of broken granite bound together with slag or gravel, raised for drainage. Today, it is bound with tar or asphalt.

McAllen city in S Texas, just N of the Mexican border formed by the Rio Grande, SE of Laredo; population (1990) 84,000.

Industries include oil refining and the processing of agricultural products from the Rio Grande Valley. It is a US port of entry for Mexicans, and many of the city's inhabitants are Spanish-speaking.

Macao Portuguese possession on the S coast of China, about 40 mi/65 km W of Hong Kong, from which it is separated by the estuary of the Canton River; it consists of a peninsula and the islands of Taipa and Colôane
area 7 sq mi/17 sq km
capital Macao, on the peninsula

Macao

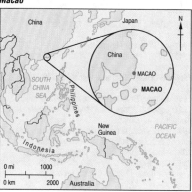

features the peninsula is linked to Taipa by a bridge and to Colôane by a causeway, both 1 mi/2 km long
currency pataca
population (1986) 426,000
languages Cantonese; Portuguese (official)
religions Buddhist, with 6% Catholic minority.

MacArthur Douglas 1880–1964. US general in World War II, commander of US forces in the Far East and, from March 1942, of the Allied forces in the SW Pacific. After the surrender of Japan he commanded the Allied occupation forces there. During 1950 he commanded the UN forces in Korea, but in April 1951, after expressing views contrary to US and UN policy, he was relieved of all his commands by President Truman.

Born in Little Rock, Arkansas, the son of an army officer, MacArthur graduated first in his class at West Point 1903, had a distinguished combat record in World War I, and rose to become chief of staff 1930–35. He defended the Philippines against the Japanese 1941–42 and escaped to Australia when his small force was overwhelmed and he was forced to surrender. He vowed at the time, "I shall return." He was responsible for the reconquest of New Guinea 1942–45 and of the Philippines 1944–45, being appointed General of the Army 1944. He retired from the army, but when North Korea crossed the 38th parallel and invaded South Korea 1950, he was asked to command UN forces to support the South's sovereignty. After a surprise landing at Inchon forced the North Koreans to retreat, MacArthur invaded the North until beaten back by Chinese troops. After he was removed from command, he received a hero's welcome on his return to the US.

Macbeth died 1057. King of Scotland from 1040. The son of Findlaech, hereditary ruler of Moray, he was commander of the forces of Duncan I, King of Scotia, whom he killed in battle 1040. His reign was prosperous until Duncan's son Malcolm III led an invasion and killed him at Lumphanan.

Maccabee or *Hasmonaean* member of an ancient Hebrew family founded by the priest Mattathias (died 166 BC) who, with his sons, led the struggle for independence against the Syrians in the 2nd century BC. Judas (died 161) reconquered Jerusalem 164 BC, and Simon (died 135) established its independence 142 BC. The revolt of the Maccabees lasted until the capture of Jerusalem by the Romans 63 BC. The story is told in four books of the ◊Apocrypha.

MacArthur US general Douglas MacArthur in 1945.

McCarthy Eugene (Joseph) 1916– . US politician. He was elected to the US House of Representatives 1948 and to the US Senate 1958. An early opponent of the Vietnam War, he ran for president 1968. Although his upset victory in the New Hampshire primary forced incumbent L B Johnson out of the race, McCarthy lost the Democratic nomination to Hubert Humphrey.

McCarthy Joe (Joseph Raymond) 1908–1957. US right-wing Republican politician. His unsubstantiated claim 1950 that the State Department and US army had been infiltrated by communists started a wave of anticommunist hysteria, wild accusations, and blacklists, which continued until he was discredited 1954. He was censured by the US Senate for misconduct.

McCarthy Mary (Therese) 1912–1989. US novelist and critic. Much of her work looks probingly and scathingly at US society, including the satirical novel *The Groves of Academe* 1952, which describes the early anticommunist "witch hunts" of the era, and *The Group* 1963 (film 1966), her best-known novel, which follows the lives of eight Vassar graduates into their thirties.

McCartney Paul 1942– . UK rock singer, songwriter, and bass guitarist; former member of the ◊Beatles, and leader of the pop group Wings 1971–81. His subsequent solo hits have included collaborations with Michael Jackson and Elvis Costello. Together with composer Carl Davis, McCartney wrote the *Liverpool Oratorio* 1991, his first work of Classical music.

McCauley Mary Ludwig Hays ("Molly Pitcher") 1754–1832. American war heroine. During the American Revolution, she accompanied her husband to the Battle of Monmouth 1778 and brought water in a pitcher to the artillerymen during the heat of the battle, thus gaining her nickname.

McClellan George Brinton 1826–1885. American Civil War general, the first general in chief of the Union forces 1861–62. He was dismissed twice by President Lincoln, for various delays in following up and attacking the Confederate army. Early in the Civil War he was replaced by General John Pope, but after the rout at the Second Battle of ◊Bull Run, Lincoln asked McClellan to rebuild and reorganize the Union's Army of the Potomac. He saved Washington, DC, from the threatening Confederate forces but delayed his offense until the opportunity was lost. He was dismissed again at this point, ran unsuccessfully for the presidency against Lincoln on the Democratic ticket 1864, and became governor of New Jersey 1878–81.

McClintock Barbara 1902–1992. US geneticist who worked at the Carnegie Institute, Cold Spring Harbor, New York, in the early days of chromosome mapping, and made some important contributions. She was awarded a Nobel Prize 1983.

McCullers Carson (Smith) 1917–1967. US novelist. Most of her writing, including her novels *The Heart Is a Lonely Hunter* 1940 and *Reflections in a Golden Eye* 1941, is set in the South, where she was born, and deals with spiritual isolation, containing elements of sometimes macabre violence.

MacDonald (James) Ramsay 1866–1937. British politician, first Labour prime minister Jan–Oct 1924 and 1929–31. Failing to deal with worsening economic conditions, he left the party to form a coalition government 1931, which was increasingly dominated by Conservatives, until he was replaced by Stanley Baldwin 1935.

Macdonald John Alexander 1815–1891. Canadian Conservative politician, prime minister 1867–73 and 1878–91. He was born in Glasgow but taken to Ontario as a child. In 1857 he became prime minister of Upper Canada. He took the leading part in the movement for federation, and in 1867 became the first prime minister of Canada. He was defeated 1873 but returned to office 1878 and retained it until his death.

Macedonia
Former Yugoslav Republic of

area 9,920 sq mi/25,700 sq km
capital Skopje
physical mountainous; rivers: Struma, Vardar; Mediterranean climate with hot summers
head of state Kiro Gligorov from 1990

head of government Branko Crvenkovski from 1992
political system emergent democracy
political parties Internal Macedonian Revolutionary Organization–Democratic Party for Macedonian National Unity (VMRO–DMPNE), centrist; League of Communists, left-wing
population (1990) 1,920,000
language Macedonian, closely allied to Bulgarian and written in Cyrillic
religion Macedonian Orthodox Christian

chronology
1913 Ancient country of Macedonia divided among Serbia, Bulgaria, and Greece.
1918 Serbian par included in what was to become Yugoslavia.
1941–44 Occupied by Bulgaria.
1945 Created a republic within Yugoslav Socialist Federation.
1980 Rise of nationalism after death of Yugoslav leader Tito.
1990 Multiparty election produced inconclusive result.
1991 "Socialist" dropped from republic's name. Referendum supported independence.
1992 Independence declared, but international recognition withheld because of objections to name by Greece.
1993 Sovereignty recognized by UK and Albania; won United Nations membership, with Greece's approval, under provisional name of Former Yugoslav Republic of Macedonia.

Macedonia region of the S Balkans, forming parts of modern Greece, Bulgaria, and Yugoslavia. Macedonia gained control of Greece after Philip II's victory at Chaeronea 338 BC. His son, ◊Alexander the Great, conquered a vast empire. Macedonia became a Roman province 146 BC.

Macedonia (Greek *Makedhonia*) mountainous region of N Greece, part of the ancient country of Macedonia which was divided between Serbia, Bulgaria, and Greece after the Balkan Wars of 1912–13. Greek Macedonia is bounded W and N by Albania and the Former Yugoslav Republic of Macedonia; area 13,200 sq mi/34,177 sq km; population (1991) 2,263,000. The chief city is Thessaloniki. Fertile valleys produce grain, olives, grapes, tobacco, and livestock. Mount Olympus rises to 9,570 ft/2,918 m on the border with Thessaly.

Macedonia country in SE Europe, bounded W by Albania, N by Yugoslavia, E by Bulgaria, and S by Greece.

Macedonian person of Macedonian culture from Macedonia (Yugoslavia) and the surrounding area, especially Greece, Albania, and Bulgaria. Macedonian, a Slavic language belonging to the Indo-European family, has 1–1.5 million speakers. The Macedonians are predominantly members of the Greek Orthodox Church and write with a Cyrillic script. They are known for their folk arts.

McEnroe John Patrick 1959– . US tennis player whose brash behavior and fiery temper on court dominated the men's game in the early 1980s. He was three times winner of Wimbledon 1981 and 1983–84. He also won three successive US Open titles 1979–81 and again in 1984. A fine doubles player, McEnroe also won ten Grand Slam titles, seven in partnership with Peter Flemming.

McGovern George (Stanley) 1922– . US politician. A Democrat, he was elected to the US House of Representatives 1956, served as an adviser to the Kennedy administration, and was a US senator 1962–80. He won the presidential nomination 1968, but was soundly defeated by the incumbent Richard Nixon.

McGraw John Joseph 1873–1934. US baseball manager. He became player-manager of the New York Giants 1902, and in this dual capacity led the team to two National League pennants and a World Series championship. After retiring as a player 1906, he managed the Giants to eight more pennants and two world championships.

McGuffey William Holmes 1800–1873. US educator. He is best remembered for his series the *Eclectic Readers,* which became standard reading textbooks throughout the US in the 19th century. He was president of Cincinnati College 1836–39 and Ohio University 1839–45.

Machel Samora 1933–1986. Mozambique nationalist leader, president 1975–86. Machel was active in the liberation front ◊Frelimo from its conception 1962, fighting for independence from Portugal. He became Frelimo leader 1966, and Mozambique's first president from independence 1975 until his death in a plane crash near the South African border.

Machiavelli Niccolò 1469–1527. Italian politician and author whose name is synonymous with cunning and cynical statecraft. In his most celebrated political writings, *Il principe/The Prince* 1513 and *Discorsi/Discourses* 1531, he discussed ways in which rulers can advance the interests of their states (and themselves)

through an often amoral and opportunistic manipulation of other people.

machine gun rapid-firing automatic gun. The Maxim (named after its inventor, US-born British engineer H S Maxim (1840–1916)) of 1884 was recoil-operated, but some later types have been gas-operated (Bren) or recoil assisted by gas (some versions of the Browning).

Mach number ratio of the speed of a body to the speed of sound in the undisturbed medium through which the body travels. Mach 1 is reached when a body (such as an aircraft) has a velocity greater than that of sound ("passes the sound barrier"), namely 1,087 ft/331 m per second at sea level. It is named after Austrian physicist Ernst Mach (1838–1916).

Machu Picchu ruined Inca city in Peru, built about AD 1500, NW of Cuzco, discovered 1911 by Hiram Bingham. It stands at the top of cliffs 1,000 ft/300 m high and contains the well-preserved remains of houses and temples. *See illustration p. 576*

Macintosh range of microcomputers produced by Apple Computers. The Apple Macintosh, introduced in 1984, was the first popular microcomputer with a ◊graphical user interface.

Macintosh Charles 1766–1843. Scottish manufacturing chemist who invented a waterproof fabric, lined with rubber, that was used for raincoats—hence *mackintosh.* Other waterproofing processes have now largely superseded this method.

Mack Connie. Adopted name of Cornelius McGillicuddy 1862–1956. US baseball manager. With the establishment of the American League 1901, he invested his own money in the Philadelphia Athletics ("A's") and became the team's first manager. In his record 50 years with the team 1901–51, he led them to nine American League pennants and five World Series championships.

Mackenzie Alexander c. 1755–1820. British explorer and fur trader. In 1789, he was the first European to see the river, now part of N Canada, named after him. In 1792–93 he crossed the Rocky Mountains to the Pacific coast of what is now British Columbia, making the first known crossing north of Mexico.

Mackenzie River river in the Northwest Territories, Canada, flowing NW from Great Slave Lake to the Arctic Ocean; about 1,120 mi/1,800 km long. It is the main channel of the Finlay-Peace-Mackenzie system, 2,635 mi/4,241 km long.

mackerel any of various fishes of the mackerel family Scombroidia, especially the common mackerel *Scomber Scombrus* found in the N Atlantic and Mediterranean. It weighs about 1.5 lb/0.7 kg, and is blue with irregular black bands down its sides, the latter and the under surface showing a metallic sheen. Like all mackerels, it has a deeply forked tail, and a sleek, streamlined body form.

McKinley, Mount or *Denali* peak in Alaska, the highest in North America, 20,320 ft/6,194 m; named after US president William McKinley.

The summit was first reached in 1913 by the Anglo-American explorer Hudson Stuck and three others. Mount McKinley, called Denali, "the high one," by the Indians, rises in the enlarged and renamed (1980) Denali National Park. See ◊Rocky Mountains.

MacLaine Shirley. Adopted name of Shirley MacLean Beaty 1934– . Versatile US actress whose films include Alfred Hitchcock's *The Trouble with*

Machu Picchu
Machu Picchu, lost city of the Incas, rediscovered in the Peruvian Andes by Hiram Bingham 1911.

Harry 1955 (her debut), *The Apartment* 1960, and *Terms of Endearment* 1983, for which she won an Academy Award.

Maclean Donald 1913–1983. British spy who worked for the USSR while in the UK civil service. He defected to the USSR 1951 together with Guy ◊Burgess.

McLean John 1785–1861. US jurist. In 1829 he was appointed to the US Supreme Court by President Jackson. During his Court tenure, McLean was an outspoken advocate of the abolition of slavery, writing a passionate dissent in the Dred Scott Case 1857.

McLuhan (Herbert) Marshall 1911–1980. Canadian theorist of communication, famed for his views on the effects of technology on modern society. He coined the phrase "the medium is the message," meaning that the form rather than the content of information has become crucial. His works include *The Gutenberg Galaxy* 1962 (in which he coined the phrase "the global village" for the worldwide electronic society then emerging), *Understanding Media* 1964, and *The Medium Is the Massage* (sic) 1967.

Macmillan (Maurice) Harold, 1st Earl of Stockton 1894–1986. British Conservative politician, prime minister 1957–63; foreign secretary 1955 and chancellor of the Exchequer 1955–57.

In 1963 he attempted to negotiate British entry into the European Economic Community, but was blocked by French president de Gaulle. Much of his career as prime minister was spent defending the retention of a UK nuclear weapon, and he was responsible for the purchase of US Polaris missiles 1962.

McMurtry Larry (Jeff) 1936– . US writer. Many of his works were made into films, including *Terms of Endearment* 1975, the film of which won the 1983 Academy Award for Best Picture. *Lonesome Dove* 1985 (Pulitzer Prize 1986; TV mini-series 1989) was followed by a sequel, *Streets of Laredo* 1993. He also

wrote *The Desert Rose* 1983, *Texasville* 1987, and *Buffalo Girls* 1990.

Macon city in central Georgia, on the Ocmulgee River, NE of Columbus; seat of Bibb County; population (1990) 106,600. An industrial city, Macon produces textiles, building materials, farm machinery, and chemicals; it processes fruits, pecans, and the special kaolin clay that is found nearby.

McPherson Aimee Semple 1890–1944. Canadian-born US religious leader. As a popular preacher, "Sister Aimee" reached millions through radio broadcasts of her weekly sermons, in which she emphasized the power of faith. She established the Church of the Four-Square Gospel in Los Angeles 1918.

McQueen Steve (Terrence Steven) 1930–1980. US actor, a film star of the 1960s and 1970s, admired for his portrayals of the strong, silent loner, and noted for performing his own stunt work. After television success in the 1950s, he became a film star with *The Magnificent Seven* 1960. His films include *The Great Escape* 1963, *Bullitt* 1968, *Papillon* 1973, and *The Hunter* 1980.

macramé art of making decorative fringes and lacework with knotted threads. The name comes from the Arabic word for "striped cloth," which is often decorated in this way.

macro in computer programming, a new command created by combining a number of existing ones. For example, if a programming language has separate commands for obtaining data from the keyboard and for displaying data on the screen, the programmer might create a macro that performs both these tasks with one command. A *macro key* on the keyboard combines the effects of pressing several individual keys.

macroeconomics division of economics concerned with the study of whole (aggregate) economies or systems, including such aspects as government income and expenditure, the balance of payments, fiscal policy, investment, inflation, and unemployment. It seeks to understand the influence of all relevant economic factors on each other and thus to quantify and predict aggregate national income.

Madagascar island country in the Indian Ocean, off the coast of E Africa, about 280 mi/400 km from Mozambique.

Madeira group of islands forming an autonomous region of Portugal off the NW coast of Africa, about 260 mi/420 km N of the Canary Islands. Madeira, the largest, and Porto Santo are the only inhabited islands. The Desertas and Selvagens are uninhabited islets. Their mild climate makes them a year-round resort
area 308 sq mi/796 sq km
capital Funchal, on Madeira
physical Pico Ruivo, on Madeira, is the highest mountain at 6,106 ft/1,861 m
products Madeira (a fortified wine), sugar cane, fruit, fish, handicrafts
population (1986) 269,500
history Portuguese from the 15th century; occupied by Britain 1801 and 1807–14. In 1980 Madeira gained partial autonomy but remains a Portuguese overseas territory.

Madhya Pradesh state of central India; the largest of the Indian states
area 170,921 sq mi/442,700 sq km
capital Bhopal
cities Indore, Jabalpur, Gwalior, Durg-Bhilainagar, Raipur, Ujjain
products cotton, oilseed, sugar, textiles, engineering, paper, aluminum
population (1991) 66,135,400
language Hindi
history formed 1950 from the former British province of Central Provinces and Berar and the princely states of Makrai and Chattisgarh; lost some southwestern districts 1956, including ◊Nagpur, and absorbed Bhopal, Madhya Bharat, and Vindhya Pradesh. In 1984 some 2,600 people died in ◊Bhopal from an escape of poisonous gas.

Madison capital of Wisconsin, 120 mi/193 km NW of Chicago, between lakes Mendota and Monona; population (1990) 191,300. Products include agricultural machinery and medical equipment.

The main campus of the University of Wisconsin and the US Forest Products Laboratory are here. The city was founded 1836 as the territorial capital and named after James Madison, fourth president of the US.

Madison James 1751–1836. 4th president of the US 1809–17. In 1787 he became a member of the Philadelphia Constitutional Convention and took a leading

---

Madagascar
Democratic Republic of
(*Repoblika Demokratika n`i Madagaskar*)

area 226,598 sq mi/587,041 sq km
capital Antananarivo
cities chief port Toamasina, Antseranana, Fianarantsoa, Toliary
physical temperate central highlands; humid valleys and tropical coastal plains; arid in S
environment according to 1990 UN figures, 93% of the forest area has been destroyed and about 100,000 species have been made extinct
features one of the last places to be inhabited, it evolved in isolation with unique animals (such as the lemur, now under threat from deforestation)
head of state Albert Zafy from 1993
head of government Francisque Raueny from 1993
political system emergent democratic republic
political parties National Front for the Defense of the Malagasy Socialist Revolution (FNDR); AKFM-Congress and

AKFM-Renewal, both left of center; Social Democratic Party (PSD), center-left
exports coffee, cloves, vanilla, sugar, chromite, shrimps
currency Malagasy franc
population (1992) 12,804,000, mostly of Malayo-Indonesian origin; growth rate 3.2% p.a.
life expectancy men 50, women 53 (1989)
languages Malagasy (official), French, English
religions animist 50%, Christian 40%, Muslim 10%
literacy 53% (1988)
GNP $2.1 bn (1987); $280 per head (1988)

chronology
1885 Became a French protectorate.
1896 Became a French colony.
1960 Independence achieved from France, with Philibert Tsiranana as president.
1972 Army took control of the government.
1975 Martial law imposed under a national military directorate. New Marxist constitution proclaimed the Democratic Republic of Madagascar, with Didier Ratsiraka as president.
1976 Front-Line Revolutionary Organization (AREMA) formed.
1977 National Front for the Defense of the Malagasy Socialist Revolution (FNDR) became the sole legal political organization.
1980 Ratsiraka abandoned Marxist experiment.
1983 Ratsiraka reelected, despite strong opposition from radical socialist National Movement for the Independence of Madagascar (MONIMA) under Monja Jaona.
1989 Ratsiraka reelected for third term after restricting opposition parties.
1990 Political opposition legalized; 36 new parties created.
1991 Antigovernment demonstrations; opposition to Ratsiraka led to general strike. Ratsiraka formed new unity government.
1992 Constitutional reform approved by referendum. First multiparty elections won by Democrat coalition.
1993 Albert Zafy, leader of coalition, elected president. Francisque Raueny appointed prime minister.

part in drawing up the US Constitution and the Bill of Rights. He allied himself firmly with Thomas ◊Jefferson against Alexander ◊Hamilton in the struggle between the more democratic views of Jefferson and the aristocratic, upper-class sentiments of Hamilton. As secretary of state in Jefferson's government 1801–09, Madison completed the ◊Louisiana Purchase negotiated by James Monroe. During his period of office the War of 1812 with Britain took place.

Born in Port Conway, Virginia, Madison graduated from the College of New Jersey (now Princeton) 1771. During his presidential administration, the nation was unprepared for the War of 1812, and there were threats of secession by New England states. Madison had long been an articulate champion of the federal structure of government, and as president, as he had done as a member of the Constitutional Convention, he regarded promotion of the Union as his paramount task. Although the War of 1812 ended in stalemate, Madison's fortunes rose with the national expansion that followed.

Madonna Adopted name of Madonna Louise Veronica Ciccone 1958– . US pop singer and actress who presents herself on stage and in videos with an exaggerated sexuality. Her first hit was "Like a Virgin" 1984; others include "Material Girl" 1985 and "Like a Prayer" 1989. Her films include *Desperately Seeking Susan* 1985, *Dick Tracy* 1990, and the documentary *In Bed with Madonna* 1991.

Madras industrial port (cotton, cement, chemicals, iron, and steel) and capital of Tamil Nadu, India, on the Bay of Bengal; population (1981) 4,277,000. Fort St George 1639 remains from the East India Company when Madras was the chief port on the E coast. Madras was occupied by the French 1746–48 and shelled by the German ship *Emden* 1914, the only place in India attacked in World War I.

Madrid industrial city (leather, chemicals, furniture, tobacco, paper) and capital of Spain and of Madrid province; population (1991) 2,984,600. Built on an elevated plateau in the center of the country, at 2,183 ft/655 m it is the highest capital city in Europe and has excesses of heat and cold. Madrid province has an area of 3,088 sq mi/8,000 sq km and a population of 4,855,000. Madrid began as a Moorish citadel captured by Castile 1083, became important in the times of

Charles V and Philip II, and was designated capital 1561.

madrigal form of secular song in four or five parts, usually sung without instrumental accompaniment. It originated in 14th-century Italy. Madrigal composers include Andrea Gabrieli, ◊Monteverdi, Thomas ◊Morley, and Orlando Gibbons.

Mafia secret society reputed to control organized crime such as gambling, loansharking, drug traffic, prostitution, and protection; connected with the ◊Camorra of Naples. It originated in Sicily in the late Middle Ages and now operates chiefly there and in countries to which Italians have emigrated, such as the US and Australia.

magazine a periodical publication, typically containing articles, essays, reviews, illustrations, and advertising. It is thought that the first magazine was *Le Journal des savants*, published in France 1665. The earliest illustrations were wood engravings; the halftone process was invented 1882 and photogravure was used commercially from 1895. ◊Printing and paper-manufacturing techniques made great progress during the 19th century, making larger print runs possible. Advertising began to appear in magazines around 1800; it was a moderately important factor by 1850 and crucial to most magazines' finances by 1880. Specialty magazines for various interests and hobbies appeared in the 20th century. In the US, subscriptions account for the majority of magazine sales. In Europe, distribution and sales are largely through newsdealers' shops and stands.

Magellan Ferdinand 1480–1521. Portuguese navigator. In 1519 he set sail in the *Victoria* from Seville with the intention of reaching the East Indies by a westerly route. He sailed through the **Strait of Magellan** at the tip of South America, crossed an ocean he named the Pacific, and in 1521 reached the Philippines, where he was killed in a battle with the islanders. His companions returned to Seville 1522, completing the voyage under del Cano.

Magellan NASA space probe to ◊Venus, launched May 1989; it went into orbit around Venus Aug 1990 to make a detailed map of the planet by radar. It revealed volcanoes, meteorite craters, and fold mountains on the planet's surface.

Magellanic Clouds in astronomy, the two galaxies nearest to our own galaxy. They are irregularly shaped, and appear as detached parts of the ◊Milky Way, in the southern constellations Dorado and Tucana.

Magellan, Strait of channel between South America and Tierra del Fuego, named after the Portuguese navigator Ferdinand ◊Magellan. It is 370 mi/595 km long, and joins the Atlantic and Pacific oceans.

maggot soft, plump, limbless larva of flies, a typical example being the larva of the blowfly which is deposited as an egg on flesh.

Maghreb name for NW Africa (Arabic "far west," "sunset"). The Maghreb powers—Algeria, Libya, Morocco, Tunisia, and Western Sahara—agreed on economic coordination 1964–65, with Mauritania cooperating from 1970. In 1989 these countries formed an economic union known as the Arab Maghreb Union. Chad and Mali are sometimes included. Compare ◊Mashraq, the Arab countries of the E Mediterranean.

magi (singular *magus*) priests of the Zoroastrian religion of ancient Persia, noted for their knowledge of astrology. The term is used in the New Testament of the Latin Vulgate Bible where the King James Version gives "wise men." The magi who came to visit the infant Jesus with gifts of gold, frankincense, and myrrh (the *Adoration of the Magi*) were in later tradition described as "the three kings"—Caspar, Melchior, and Balthazar.

magic art of controlling the forces of nature by supernatural means such as charms and ritual. The central ideas are that like produces like (*sympathetic magic*) and that influence carries by contagion or association; for example, by the former principle an enemy could be destroyed through an effigy, by the latter principle through personal items such as hair or nail clippings. See also ◊witchcraft.

Maginot Line French fortification system along the German frontier from Switzerland to Luxembourg built 1929–36 under the direction of the war minister, André Maginot. It consisted of semi underground forts joined by underground passages, and protected by antitank defenses; lighter fortifications continued the line to the sea. In 1940 German forces pierced the Belgian frontier line and outflanked the Maginot Line.

maglev (acronym for *magnetic levitation*) high-speed surface transport using the repellent force of superconductive magnets (see ◊superconductivity) to propel and support, for example, a train above a track.

magma molten rock material beneath the Earth's surface from which ◊igneous rocks are formed. ◊Lava is magma that has reached the surface and solidified, losing some of its components on the way.

Magna Carta in English history, the charter granted by King John 1215, traditionally seen as guaranteeing human rights against the excessive use of royal power. As a reply to the king's demands for excessive feudal dues and attacks on the privileges of the church, Archbishop Langton proposed to the barons the drawing-up of a binding document 1213. John was forced to accept this at Runnymede (now in Surrey) June 15, 1215.

magnesia common name for magnesium oxide.

magnesium lightweight, very ductile and malleable, silver-white, metallic element, symbol Mg, atomic number 12, atomic weight 24.305. It is one of the ◊al-kaline-earth metals, and the lightest of the commonly used metals. Magnesium silicate, carbonate, and chloride are widely distributed in nature. The metal is used in alloys and flash photography. It is a necessary trace element in the human diet, and green plants cannot grow without it since it is an essential constituent of the photosynthetic pigment ◊chlorophyll $(C_{55}H_{72}MgN_4O_5)$.

magnet any object that forms a magnetic field (displays ◊magnetism), either permanently or temporarily through induction, causing it to attract materials such as iron, cobalt, nickel, and alloys of these. It always has two ◊magnetic poles, called north and south.

magnetic field region around a permanent magnet, or around a conductor carrying an electric current, in which a force acts on a moving charge or on a magnet placed in the field. The field can be represented by lines of force, which by convention link north and south poles and are parallel to the directions of a small compass needle placed on them. Its magnitude and direction are given by the magnetic flux density, expressed in ◊teslas.

magnetic pole region of a magnet in which its magnetic properties are strongest. Every magnet has two poles, called north and south. The north (or north-seeking) pole is so named because a freely suspended magnet will turn so that this pole points toward the Earth's magnetic north pole. The north pole of one magnet will be attracted to the south pole of another, but will be repelled by its north pole. Like poles may therefore be said to repel, unlike poles to attract.

magnetic resonance imaging (MRI) diagnostic scanning system based on the principles of nuclear magnetic resonance. MRI yields finely detailed three-dimensional images of structures within the body without exposing the patient to harmful radiation. The technique is useful for imaging the soft tissues of the body, such as the brain and the spinal cord.

magnetic storm in meteorology, a sudden disturbance affecting the Earth's magnetic field, causing anomalies in radio transmissions and magnetic compasses. It is probably caused by ◊sunspot activity.

magnetic tape narrow plastic ribbon coated with an easily magnetizable material on which data can be recorded. It is used in sound recording, audiovisual systems (videotape), and computing. For mass storage on commercial mainframe computers, large reel-to-reel tapes are still used, but cartridges are coming in. Various types of cartridge are now standard on minis and PCs, while audio cassettes are sometimes used with home computers.

magnetism phenomena associated with ◊magnetic fields. Magnetic fields are produced by moving charged particles: in electromagnets, electrons flow through a coil of wire connected to a battery; in permanent magnets, spinning electrons within the atoms generate the field.

magnetite black iron ore, iron oxide (Fe_3O_4). Widely distributed, magnetite is found in nearly all igneous and metamorphic rocks. It is strongly magnetic and some deposits, called *lodestone*, are permanently magnetized. Lodestone has been used as a compass since the first millennium BC.

magnification measure of the enlargement or reduction of an object in an imaging optical system. *Linear magnification* is the ratio of the size (height) of the image to that of the object. *Angular magnification* is the ratio of the angle subtended at the observer's eye by the image to the angle subtended by the object when viewed directly.

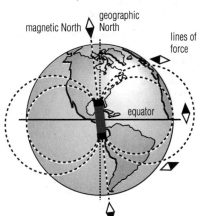

magnetic field The Earth's magnetic field is similar to that of a bar magnet with poles near, but not exactly at, the geographic poles.

magnolia In the magnolia's large flowers, the sepals are often indistinguishable from the petals and leaves.

magnitude in astronomy, measure of the brightness of a star or other celestial object. The larger the number denoting the magnitude, the fainter the object. Zero or first magnitude indicates some of the brightest stars. Still brighter are those of negative magnitude, such as Sirius, whose magnitude is −1.46. *Apparent magnitude* is the brightness of an object as seen from Earth; *absolute magnitude* is the brightness at a standard distance of 10 parsecs (32.6 light-years).

magnolia tree or shrub of the genus *Magnolia*, family Magnoliaceae, native to North America and E Asia. Magnolias vary in height from 2 ft/60 cm to 150 ft/30 m. The large, fragrant single flowers are white, rose, or purple. The southern magnolia *M. grandiflora* of the US grows up to 80 ft/24 m tall and has white flowers 9 in/23 cm across.

magpie any bird of a genus *Pica* in the crow family. It feeds on insects, snails, young birds, and carrion, and is found in Europe, Asia, N Africa, and W North America.

Magritte René 1898–1967. Belgian Surrealist painter whose paintings focus on visual paradoxes and everyday objects taken out of context. Recurring motifs include bowler hats, apples, and windows, for example *Golconda* 1953, where men in bowler hats are falling from the sky to a street below.

Magyar member of the largest ethnic group in Hungary, comprising 92% of the population. Magyars are of mixed Ugric and Turkic origin, and they arrived in Hungary toward the end of the 9th century. The Magyar language (see ◊Hungarian) belongs to the Uralic group.

Mahādevī (Sanskrit "great goddess") title given to Sakti, the consort of the Hindu god Siva. She is worshiped in many forms, including her more active manifestations as Kali or Durga and her peaceful form as Parvati.

Maharashtra state in W central India
area 118,811 sq mi/307,800 sq km
capital Bombay
cities Pune, Nagpur, Ulhasnagar, Sholapur, Nasik, Thana, Kolhapur, Aurangabad, Sangli, Amravati
features cave temples of Ajanta, containing 200 BC–7th century AD Buddhist murals and sculptures; Ellora cave temples 6th–9th century with Buddhist, Hindu, and Jain sculptures
products cotton, rice, groundnuts, sugar, minerals
population (1991) 78,706,700
language Marathi 50%
religions Hindu 80%, Parsee, Jain, and Sikh minorities
history formed 1960 from the southern part of the former Bombay state.

mahatma (Sanskrit "great soul") title conferred on Mohandas ◊Gandhi by his followers as the first great national Indian leader.

Mahāyāna (Sanskrit "greater vehicle") one of the two major forms of ◊Buddhism, common in N Asia (China, Korea, Japan, and Tibet). Veneration of bodhisattvas (those who achieve enlightenment but remain on the human plane in order to help other living beings) is a fundamental belief in Mahāyāna, as is the idea that everyone has within them the seeds of Buddhahood.

Mahfouz Naguib 1911– . Egyptian novelist and playwright. His novels, which deal with the urban working class, include the semiautobiographical *Khan al-Kasrain/The Cairo Trilogy* 1956–57. His *Children of Gebelawi* 1959 was banned in Egypt because of its treatment of religious themes. Nobel Prize for Literature 1988.

mah-jong or *mah-jongg* originally an ancient Chinese card game, dating from the Song dynasty 960–1279. It is now usually played by four people with 144 small ivory tiles, divided into six suits.

Mahler Gustav 1860–1911. Austrian composer and conductor whose work displays a synthesis of Romanticism and new uses of chromatic harmonies and musical forms. He composed 14 symphonies, including three unnumbered (as a student), nine massive repertoire symphonies, the titled *Das Lied von der Erde/Song of the Earth* 1909, and the incomplete *Symphony No. 10*. He also wrote song cycles.

Mahmud I 1696–1754. Ottoman sultan from 1730. After restoring order to the empire in Istanbul 1730, he suppressed the Janissary rebellion 1731 and waged war against Persia 1731–46. He led successful wars against Austria and Russia, concluded by the Treaty of Belgrade 1739. He was a patron of the arts and also carried out reform of the army.

Mahmud II 1785–1839. Ottoman sultan from 1808 who attempted to westernize the declining empire, carrying out a series of far-reaching reforms in the civil service and army. The pressure for Greek independence after 1821 led to conflict with Britain, France, and Russia, and he was forced to recognize Greek independence 1830.

mahogany timber from any of several genera of trees found in the Americas and Africa. Mahogany is a tropical hardwood obtained chiefly by rain-forest logging. It has a warm red color and takes a high polish.

Mailer Norman 1923– . US writer and journalist. He gained wide attention with his novel of World War II *The Naked and the Dead* 1948.

Maimonides Moses (Moses Ben Maimon) 1135–1204. Jewish rabbi and philosopher, born in Córdoba, Spain. Known as one of the greatest Hebrew scholars, he attempted to reconcile faith and reason.

Maine

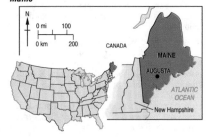

Maine northeasternmost state of the US, largest of the New England states; nickname Pine Tree State
area 33,273 sq mi/86,200 sq km
capital Augusta
cities Portland, Lewiston, Bangor
physical Appalachian Mountains; 80% of the state is forested
features Acadia National Park, including Bar Harbor and most of Mount Desert Island; Baxter State Park, including Mount Katahadin; Roosevelt's Campobello International Park; canoeing along the Allagush Wilderness Waterway
products dairy and market garden produce, paper, pulp, timber, footwear, textiles, fish, lobster; tourism is important
population (1990) 1,228,000
famous people Henry Wadsworth Longfellow, Kate Douglas Wiggin, Edward Arlington Robinson, Edna St Vincent Millay
history permanently settled by the British from 1623; absorbed by Massachusetts 1691; became a state 1820.

In colonial days, white-pine masts were built for the Royal Navy at Falmouth (now Portland). Maine produces 98% of the nation's blueberries and has the largest papermaking capacity of any of the 50 states but is generally economically depressed.

mainframe large computer used for commercial data processing and other large-scale operations. Because of the general increase in computing power, the differences between the mainframe, ◊supercomputer, minicomputer, and ◊microcomputer (personal computer) are becoming less marked.

majolica or *maiolica* tin-glazed ◊earthenware and the richly decorated enamel pottery produced in Italy in the 15th to 18th centuries. The name derives from the Italian form of Majorca, the island from where Moorish lusterware made in Spain was shipped to Italy. During the 19th century the word was used to describe molded earthenware with relief patterns decorated in colored glazes.

Major John 1943– . British Conservative politician, prime minister from Nov 1990.

He was foreign secretary 1989 and chancellor of the Exchequer 1989–90. His earlier positive approach to European Community (EC) matters was hindered during 1991 by divisions within the Conservative Party. Despite continuing public dissatisfaction with the poll tax, the National Health Service, and the recession, Major was returned to power in the April 1992 general election. His subsequent handling of a series of political crises called into question his ability to govern the country effectively.

Majorca (Spanish *Mallorca*) largest of the ◊Balearic Islands, belonging to Spain, in the W Mediterranean
area 1,405 sq mi/3,640 sq km
capital Palma
features the highest mountain is Puig Mayor, 4,741 ft/1,445 m
products olives, figs, oranges, wine, brandy, timber, sheep; tourism is the mainstay of the economy
population (1981) 561,215
history captured 797 by the Moors, it became the kingdom of Majorca 1276, and was united with Aragon 1343.

Makarios III 1913–1977. Cypriot politician, Greek Orthodox archbishop 1950–77. A leader of the Resistance organization ◊EOKA, he was exiled by the British to the Seychelles 1956–57 for supporting armed action to achieve union with Greece (*enosis*). He was president of the republic of Cyprus 1960–77

Major British prime minister John Major, who succeeded Margaret Thatcher 1990.

(briefly deposed by a Greek military coup July–Dec 1974).

Makua member of a people living to the north of the Zambezi River in Mozambique. With the Lomwe people, they make up the country's largest ethnic group. The Makua are mainly farmers, living in villages ruled by chiefs. The Makua language belongs to the Niger-Congo family, and has about 5 million speakers.

Malacca or *Melaka* state of W Peninsular Malaysia; capital Malacca; area 656 sq mi/1,700 sq km; population (1980) 465,000 (about 70% Chinese). Products include rubber, tin, and wire. The town originated in the 13th century as a fishing village frequented by pirates, and later developed into a trading port. Portuguese from 1511, then Dutch from 1641, it was ceded to Britain 1824, becoming part of the Straits Settlements.

malachite common ◊copper ore, basic copper carbonate, $Cu_2CO_3(OH)_2$. It is a source of green pigment and is polished for use in jewelry, ornaments, and art objects.

Málaga industrial seaport (sugar refining, distilling, brewing, olive-oil pressing, shipbuilding) and holiday resort in Andalusia, Spain; capital of Málaga province on the Mediterranean; population (1991) 524,800. Founded by the Phoenicians and taken by the Moors 711, Málaga was capital of the Moorish kingdom of Malaga from the 13th century until captured 1487 by the Catholic monarchs Ferdinand and Isabella.

Malagasy inhabitant of or native to Madagascar. The Malagasy language has about 9 million speakers; it belongs to the Austronesian family.

Malamud Bernard 1914–1986. US novelist and short-story writer. He first attracted attention with *The Natural* 1952, making a professional baseball player his hero. Later novels, often dealing with the Jewish immigrant tradition, include *The Assistant* 1957, *The Fixer* 1966, *Dubin's Lives* 1979, and *God's Grace* 1982.

Short story collections include *The Magic Barrel* 1958, *Rembrandt's Hat* 1973, and *The Stories of Bernard Malamud* 1983.

malaria The life cycle of the malaria parasite is split between mosquito and human hosts.

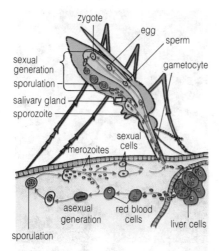

zygote

egg

sperm

sexual generation

gametocyte

sporulation

salivary gland

sporozoite

merozoites

sexual cells

asexual generation

red blood cells

liver cells

sporulation

malapropism amusing slip of the tongue, arising from the confusion of similar-sounding words; for example, "the pineapple [pinnacle] of perfection." The term derives from the French *mal à propos* (inappropriate); historically, it is associated with Mrs Malaprop, a character in Richard Sheridan's play *The Rivals* 1775.

malaria infectious parasitic disease of the tropics transmitted by mosquitoes, marked by periodic fever and an enlarged spleen. When a female mosquito of the *Anopheles* genus bites a human who has malaria, it takes in with the human blood one of four malaria protozoa of the genus *Plasmodium*. This matures within the insect and is then transferred when the mosquito bites a new victim. Malaria affects some 200 million people a year on a recurring basis.

Malawi country in SE Africa, bounded N and NE by Tanzania; E, S, and W by Mozambique; and W by Zambia.

Malawi, Lake or *Lake Nyasa* African lake, bordered by Malawi, Tanzania, and Mozambique, formed in a section of the Great ◊Rift Valley. It is about 1,650 ft/ 500 m above sea level and 350 mi/560 km long, with an area of 14,280 sq mi/37,000 sq km. It is intermittently drained to the S by the river Shiré into the Zambezi.

Malay a member of a large group of peoples comprising the majority population of the Malay Peninsula and Archipelago, also found in S Thailand and coastal Sumatra and Borneo. Their language belongs to the western branch of the Austronesian family.

Malayalam southern Indian language, the official language of the state of Kerala. Malayalam is closely related to Tamil, also a member of the Dravidian language family; it is spoken by about 20 million people. Written records in Malayalam date from the 9th century AD.

Malay language member of the Western or Indonesian branch of the Malayo-Polynesian language family, used in the Malay peninsula and many of the islands of Malaysia and Indonesia. The Malay language can be written in either Arabic or Roman scripts. The dialect of the S Malay peninsula is the basis of both Bahasa Malaysia and Bahasa Indonesia, the official languages of Malaysia and Indonesia. Bazaar Malay is a widespread pidgin variety used for trading and shopping.

Malayo-Polynesian family of languages spoken in Malaysia, better known as ◊Austronesian.

Malawi
Republic of
(*Malaŵi*)

area 45,560 sq mi/118,000 sq km
capital Lilongwe
cities Blantyre (largest city and commercial center), Mzuzu, Zomba
physical landlocked narrow plateau with rolling plains; mountainous W of Lake Malawi
features one-third is water, including lakes Malawi, Chilara, and Malombe; Great Rift Valley; Nyika, Kasungu, and Lengare national parks; Mulanje Massif; Shire River

head of state and government Hastings Kamusu Banda from 1966 for life
political system one-party republic
political party Malawi Congress Party (MCP), multiracial, right-wing
exports tea, tobacco, cotton, peanuts, sugar
currency kwacha
population (1992) 9,484,000 (nearly 1 million refugees from Mozambique); growth rate 3.3% p.a.
life expectancy men 46, women 50 (1989)
languages English, Chichewa (both official)
religions Christian 75%, Muslim 20%
literacy 25% (1989)
GNP $1.2 bn (1987); $160 per head (1988)

chronology
1891 Became the British protectorate Nyasaland.
1964 Independence achieved from Britain, within the Commonwealth, as Malawi.
1966 Became a one-party republic, with Hastings Banda as president.
1971 Banda was made president for life.
1977 Banda released some political detainees and allowed greater freedom of the press.
1986–89 Influx of nearly a million refugees from Mozambique.
1992 Calls for multiparty politics. Countrywide industrial riots caused many fatalities. Western aid suspended over human-rights violations.
1993 Referendum overwhelmingly supported the ending of one-party rule. Oct: Banda underwent brain surgery. Presidential council appointed.

Malaysia

area 127,287 sq mi/329,759 sq km
capital Kuala Lumpur
cities Johor Baharu, Ipoh, Georgetown (Penang), Kuching in Sarawak, Kota Kinabalu in Sabah
physical comprises Peninsular Malaysia (the nine Malay states—Johore, Kedah, Kelantan, Negri Sembilan, Pahang, Perak, Perlis, Selangor, Trengganu—plus Malacca and Penang); and E Malaysia (Sabah and Sarawak); 75% tropical jungle; central mountain range; swamps in E
features Mount Kinabalu (highest peak in SE Asia); Niah caves (Sarawak)
head of state Rajah Azlan Muhibuddin Shah (sultan of Perak) from 1989
head of government Mahathir bin Mohamad from 1981
political system liberal democracy

political parties New United Malays' National Organization (UMNO Baru), Malay-oriented nationalist; Malaysian Chinese Association (MCA), Chinese-oriented conservative; Gerakan Party, Chinese-oriented, left of center; Malaysian Indian Congress (MIC), Indian-oriented; Democratic Action Party (DAP), left of center, multiracial but Chinese-dominated; Pan-Malayan Islamic Party (PAS), Islamic; Semangat '46 (Spirit of 1946), moderate, multiracial
exports pineapples, palm oil, rubber, timber, petroleum (Sarawak), bauxite
currency ringgit
population (1992) 18,630,000 (Malaysian 47%, Chinese 32%, Indian 8%, others 13%); growth rate 2% p.a.
life expectancy men 65, women 70 (1989)
languages Malay (official), English, Chinese, Indian, and local languages
religions Muslim (official), Buddhist, Hindu, local beliefs
literacy 80% (1989)
GNP $34.3 bn; $1,870 per head (1988)

chronology
1786 Britain established control.
1826 Became a British colony.
1963 Federation of Malaysia formed, including Malaya, Singapore, Sabah (N Borneo), and Sarawak (NW Borneo).
1965 Secession of Singapore from federation.
1969 AntiChinese riots in Kuala Lumpur.
1971 Launch of *bumiputra* ethnic-Malay-oriented economic policy.
1981 Election of Dr Mahathir bin Mohamad as prime minister.
1982 Mahathir bin Mohamad reelected.
1986 Mahathir bin Mohamad reelected.
1987 Arrest of over 100 opposition activists, including DAP leader, as Malay-Chinese relations deteriorated.
1988 Split in ruling UMNO party over Mahathir's leadership style; new UMNO formed.
1989 Semangat '46 set up by former members of UMNO including ex-premier Tunku Abdul Rahman.
1990 Mahathir bin Mohamad reelected.
1991 New economic-growth program launched.

Malaysia country in SE Asia, comprising the Malay Peninsula, bounded N by Thailand, and surrounded E and S by the South China Sea and W by the Strait of Malacca; and the states of Sabah and Sarawak in the N part of the island of Borneo (S Borneo is part of Indonesia).

Malcolm III called *Canmore c.* 1031–1093. King of Scotland from 1058, the son of Duncan I (murdered by ◊Macbeth 1040). He fled to England when the throne was usurped by Macbeth, but recovered S Scotland and killed Macbeth in battle 1057. He was killed at Alnwick while invading Northumberland, England.

Malcolm X 1925–1965. US political leader. Born in Omaha, Nebraska, as Malcolm Little, he grew up in foster homes in Michigan, Massachusetts, and New York. Convicted of robbery 1946, he spent seven years in prison, becoming a follower of Black Muslim leader Elijah Mohammed and converting to Islam. In 1952 he officially changed his name to "Malcolm X" to signify his rootlessness in a racist society. Having become an influential national and international leader, Malcolm publicly broke with the Black Muslims 1964 and was assassinated in Harlem 1965. *The Autobiography of Malcolm X* appeared the same year. US director Spike Lee's movie *Malcolm X* was released 1992.

Maldives group of 1,196 islands in the N Indian Ocean, about 400 mi/640 km SW of Sri Lanka, only 203 of which are inhabited. *See panel p. 584*

Malé capital and chief atoll of the Maldives in the Indian Ocean; population (1990) 55,100.

Mali landlocked country in NW Africa, bounded to the NE by Algeria, E by Niger, SE by Burkina Faso, S by the Ivory Coast, SW by Senegal and Guinea, and W and N by Mauritania. *See panel p. 584*

Mali Empire Muslim state in NW Africa during the 7th–15th centuries. Thriving on its trade in gold, it reached its peak in the 14th century under Mansa Musa (reigned 1312–37), when it occupied an area covering present-day Senegal, Gambia, Mali, and S Mauritania. Mali's territory was similar to (though larger than) that of the Ghana Empire (see ◊Ghana, ancient), and gave way in turn to the ◊Songhai Empire.

mallard common wild duck *Anas platyrhynchos*, found almost worldwide, from which domestic ducks were bred. The male, which can grow to a length of 2 ft/60 cm, usually has a green head and brown breast, while the female is mottled brown. Mallards are omnivorous, dabbling ducks.

Mallarmé Stéphane 1842–1898. French poet who founded the Symbolist school with Paul Verlaine. His belief that poetry should be evocative and suggestive was reflected in *L'Après-midi d'un faune/Afternoon of a Faun* 1876, which inspired the composer Debussy.

Maldives
Republic of
(*Divehi Jumhuriya*)

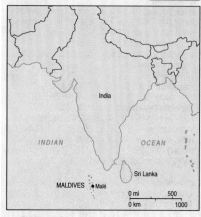

area 115 sq mi/298 sq km
capital Malé
cities Seenu
physical comprises 1,196 coral islands, grouped into 12 clusters of atolls, largely flat, none bigger than 5 sq mi/13 sq km, average elevation 6 ft/1.8 m; 203 are inhabited
environment the threat of rising sea level has been heightened by the frequency of flooding in recent years
features tourism developed since 1972

head of state and government Maumoon Abdul Gayoom from 1978
political system authoritarian nationalism
political parties none; candidates elected on the basis of personal influence and clan loyalties
exports coconuts, copra, bonito (fish related to tuna), garments
currency Rufiya
population (1992) 230,000; growth rate 3.7% p.a.
life expectancy men 60, women 63 (1989)
languages Divehi (Sinhalese dialect), English
religion Sunni Muslim
literacy 36% (1989)
GNP $69 million (1987); $410 per head (1988)

chronology
1887 Became a British protectorate.
1953 Long a sultanate, the Maldive Islands became a republic within the Commonwealth.
1954 Sultan restored.
1965 Achieved full independence outside the Commonwealth.
1968 Sultan deposed; republic reinstated with Ibrahim Nasir as president.
1978 Nasir retired; replaced by Maumoon Abdul Gayoom.
1982 Rejoined the Commonwealth.
1983 Gayoom reelected.
1985 Became a founder member of South Asian Association for Regional Cooperation (SAARC).
1988 Gayoom reelected. Coup attempt by mercenaries, thought to have the backing of former president Nasir, was foiled by Indian paratroops.

Mali
Republic of
(*République du Mali*)

area 478,695 sq mi/1,240,142 sq km
capital Bamako
cities Mopti, Kayes, Ségou, Timbuktu
physical landlocked state with river Niger and savanna in S; part of the Sahara in N; hills in NE; Senegal River and its branches irrigate the SW
environment a rising population coupled with recent droughts has affected marginal agriculture. Once in surplus, Mali has had to import grain every year since 1965
features ancient town of Timbuktu; railroad to Dakar is the only outlet to the sea
head of state Alpha Oumar Konare from 1992
head of government Abdoulaye Sekou Sow from 1993

political system emergent democratic republic
political parties Alliance for Democracy in Mali (ADEMA), centrist; National Committee for Democratic Initiative (CNID), center-left; Sudanese Union–African Democratic Rally (US–RDA), Sudanese nationalist
exports cotton, peanuts, livestock, fish
currency franc CFA
population (1992) 8,464,000; growth rate 2.9% p.a.
life expectancy men 44, women 47 (1989)
languages French (official), Bambara
religion Sunni Muslim 90%, animist 9%, Christian 1%
literacy 10% (1989)
GNP $1.6 bn (1987); $230 per head (1988)

chronology
1895 Came under French rule.
1959 With Senegal, formed the Federation of Mali.
1960 Became the independent Republic of Mali, with Modibo Keita as president.
1968 Keita replaced in an army coup by Moussa Traoré.
1974 New constitution made Mali a one-party state.
1976 New national party, the Malian People's Democratic Union, announced.
1983 Agreement between Mali and Guinea for eventual political and economic integration signed.
1985 Conflict with Burkina Faso lasted five days; mediated by International Court of Justice.
1991 Demonstrations against one-party rule. Moussa Traoré ousted in a coup led by Lt-Col Amadou Toumani Toure. New multiparty constitution agreed, subject to referendum.
1992 Referendum endorsed new democratic constitution. Alliance for Democracy in Mali (ADEMA) won multiparty elections; Alpha Oumar Konare elected president.
1993 Abdoulaye Sekou Sow appointed prime minister.

Malta
Republic of
(*Repubblika Ta'Malta*)

area 124 sq mi/320 sq km
capital and port Valletta
cities Rabat; port of Marsaxlokk
physical includes islands of Gozo 26 sq mi/67 sq km and
Comino 1 sq mi/2.5 sq km
features occupies strategic location in central Mediterranean; large commercial dock facilities
head of state Vincent Tabone from 1989
head of government Edward Fenech Adami from 1987
political system liberal democracy
political parties Malta Labor Party (MLP), moderate, left
of center; Nationalist Party, Christian, centrist, pro-European
exports vegetables, knitwear, handmade lace, plastics, electronic equipment

currency Maltese lira
population (1990 est) 373,000; growth rate 0.7% p.a.
life expectancy men 72, women 77 (1987)
languages Maltese, English
religion Roman Catholic 98%
literacy 90% (1988)
GNP $1.6 bn; $4,750 per head (1988)

chronology
1814 Annexed to Britain by the Treaty of Paris.
1947 Achieved self-government.
1955 Dom Mintoff of the Malta Labor Party (MLP) became
prime minister.
1956 Referendum approved MLP's proposal for integration
with the UK. Proposal opposed by the Nationalist Party.
1958 MLP rejected the British integration proposal.
1962 Nationalists elected, with Borg Olivier as prime
minister.
1964 Independence achieved from Britain, within the Commonwealth. Ten-year defense and economic-aid treaty with
UK signed.
1971 Mintoff reelected. 1964 treaty declared invalid and
negotiations began on leasing the NATO base in Malta.
1972 Seven-year NATO agreement signed.
1974 Became a republic.
1979 British military base closed.
1984 Mintoff retired and was replaced by Mifsud Bonnici as
prime minister and MLP leader.
1987 Edward Fenech Adami (Nationalist) elected prime
minister.
1989 Vincent Tabone elected president. US–USSR summit
held offshore.
1990 Formal application made for EC membership.
1992 Nationalist Party returned to power in general
election.

Mallorca Spanish form of ◊Majorca, an island in the
Mediterranean.

Malmö industrial port (shipbuilding, engineering,
textiles) in SW Sweden, situated across the öresund
from Copenhagen, Denmark; population (1990)
233,900. Founded in the 12th century, Malmö is
Sweden's third-largest city.

malnutrition the physical condition resulting from
dietary deficiencies. These may be caused by lack of
food resources (famine) or by lack of knowledge about
◊nutrition.

Malory Thomas 15th century. English author of the
prose romance *Le Morte d'Arthur* about 1470. It is a
translation from the French, modified by material
from other sources, and it deals with the exploits of
King Arthur's knights of the Round Table and the
quest for the ◊Holy Grail.

malpractice in law, ◊negligence by a professional
person, usually a doctor, that may lead to an action for
damages by the client. Such legal actions result in
doctors having high insurance costs that are reflected
in higher fees charged to their patients.

Malraux André 1901–1976. French writer. An
active antifascist, he gained international renown
for his novel *La Condition humaine/Man's
Estate* 1933, set during the Nationalist/Com-
munist Revolution in China in the 1920s. *L'Espoir/
Days of Hope* 1937 is set in Civil War Spain, where
he was a bomber pilot in the International Brigade.
In World War II he supported the Gaullist
resis-   tance, and was minister of cultural affairs
1960–69.

malt in brewing, grain (barley, oats, or wheat)
artificially germinated and then dried in a kiln.
Malts are fermented to make beers or lagers, or fermented and then distilled to produce spirits such as
whiskey.

Malta island in the Mediterranean Sea, S of Sicily, E of
Tunisia, and N of Libya.

Malta, Knights of another name for members of the
military-religious order of the Hospital of ◊St John of
Jerusalem.

Malthus Thomas Robert 1766–1834. English economist and cleric. His *Essay on the Principle of Population* 1798 (revised 1803) argued for population control,
since populations increase in geometric ratio and food
supply only in arithmetic ratio, and influenced Charles
◊Darwin's thinking on natural selection as the driving
force of evolution.

Maluku or *Moluccas* group of Indonesian islands
area 28,764 sq mi/74,500 sq km
capital Ambon, on Amboina
population (1989 est) 1,814,000
history as the Spice Islands, they were formerly part
of the Netherlands East Indies; the S Moluccas
attempted secession from the newly created Indonesian republic from 1949; exiles continue agitation in
the Netherlands.

Malvinas, Islas Argentine name for the ◊Falkland
Islands.

mamba one of two venomous snakes, genus
Dendroaspis, of the cobra family Elapidae, found in
Africa S of the Sahara. Unlike cobras, they are not
hooded.

mammals: classification

order	typical species
Monotremata	echidna, platypus

placental mammals:

Marsupiala	kangaroo, koala, opossum
Insectivora	shrew, hedgehog, mole
Chiroptera	bat
Primates	lemur, monkey, ape, human
Edentata	anteater, armadillo, sloth
Pholidota	pangolin
Dermoptera	flying lemur
Rodentia	rat, mouse, squirrel, porcupine
Lagomorpha	rabbit, hare, pika
Cetacea	whale, dolphin
Carnivora	cat, dog, weasel, bear
Pinnipedia	seal, walrus
Artiodactyla	pig, deer, cattle, camel, giraffe
Perissodactyla	horse, rhinoceros, tapir
Sirenia	dugong, manatee
Tubulidentata	aardvark
Hyracoidea	hyrax
Proboscidea	elephant

Mameluke member of a powerful political class that dominated Egypt from the 13th century until their massacre 1811 by Mehemet Ali.

Mamet David 1947– . US playwright. His plays, with their vivid, freewheeling language and sense of ordinary US life, include *American Buffalo* 1977, *Sexual Perversity in Chicago* 1978, *Glengarry Glen Ross* 1984 (filmed 1992), and *Oleanna* 1992, about a sexual harrassment case.

mammal animal characterized by having mammary glands in the female; these are used for suckling the young. Other features of mammals are ◊hair (very reduced in some species, such as whales); a middle ear formed of three small bones (ossicles); a lower jaw consisting of two bones only; seven vertebrae in the neck; and no nucleus in the red blood cells.

Mammals are divided into three groups: *placental mammals*, where the young develop inside the ◊uterus, receiving nourishment from the blood of the mother via the ◊placenta; *marsupials*, where the young are born at an early stage of development and develop further in a pouch on the mother's body; *monotremes*, where the young hatch from an egg outside the mother's body and are then nourished with milk. The monotremes are the least evolved and have been largely displaced by more sophisticated marsupials and placentals, so that there are only a few types surviving (platypus and echidna). Placentals are considered the most sophisticated and have spread to all parts of the globe. Where placentals have competed with marsupials, the placentals have in general displaced marsupial types. However, marsupials occupy many specialized niches in South America and, especially, Australasia.

mammary gland in female mammals, a milk-producing gland derived from epithelial cells underlying the skin, active only after the production of young. In all but monotremes (egg-laying mammals), the mammary glands terminate in teats which aid infant suckling. The number of glands and their position vary between species. In humans there are 2, in cows 4, and in pigs between 10 and 14.

mammography X-ray procedure used to detect breast cancer at an early stage, before the tumors can be seen or felt.

mammoth extinct elephant of genus *Mammuthus*, whose remains are found worldwide. Some were 50% taller than modern elephants.

Man, Isle of island in the Irish Sea, a dependency of the British crown, but not part of the UK
area 220 sq mi/570 sq km
capital Douglas
cities Ramsey, Peel, Castletown
features Snaefell 2,035 ft/620 m; annual TT (Tourist Trophy) motorcycle races, gambling casinos, Britain's first free port, tax haven; tailless Manx cat
products light engineering products; tourism, banking, and insurance are important
currency the island produces its own coins and notes in UK currency denominations
population (1986) 64,300
language English (Manx, nearer to Scottish than Irish Gaelic, has been almost extinct since the 1970s)
government crown-appointed lieutenant-governor, a legislative council, and the representative House of Keys, which together make up the Court of Tynwald, passing laws subject to the royal assent. Laws passed at Westminster only affect the island if specifically so provided
history Norwegian until 1266, when the island was ceded to Scotland; it came under UK administration 1765.

management buyout purchase of control of a company by its management, generally with debt funding, making it a ◊leveraged buyout.

Managua capital and chief industrial city of Nicaragua, on the lake of the same name; population (1985) 682,000. It has twice been destroyed by earthquake and rebuilt, 1931 and 1972; it was also badly damaged during the civil war in the late 1970s.

manatee any plant-eating aquatic mammal of the genus *Trichechus* constituting the family Trichechidae in the order Sirenia (sea cows). Manatees occur in marine bays and sluggish rivers, usually in turbid water.

Manaus capital of Amazonas, Brazil, on the Rio Negro, near its confluence with the Amazon; population (1991) 996,700. It can be reached by seagoing vessels, although it is 1,000 mi/1,600 km from the Atlantic. Formerly a center of the rubber trade, it developed as a tourist center in the 1970s.

Manchester city in NW England, on the river Irwell, 31 mi/50 km E of Liverpool. It is a manufacturing (textile machinery, chemicals, rubber, processed foods) and financial center; population (1991) 397,400. It is linked by the Manchester Ship Canal, built 1894, to the river Mersey and the sea.

Manchu last ruling dynasty in China, from 1644 until its overthrow 1912; its last emperor was the infant ◊P'u-i. Originally a nomadic people from Manchuria, they established power through a series of successful invasions from the north, then granted trading rights to the US and Europeans, which eventually brought strife and the ◊Boxer Rebellion.

Manchuria European name for the NE region of China, comprising the provinces of Heilongjiang, Jilin, and Liaoning. It was united with China by the Manchu dynasty 1644, but as the Chinese Empire declined, Japan and Russia were rivals for its control. The Russians were expelled after the ◊Russo-Japanese War 1904–05, and in 1932 Japan consolidated its position by creating a puppet state, *Manchukuo*, which disintegrated on the defeat of Japan in World War II.

Mandalay chief town of the Mandalay division of Myanmar (formerly Burma), on the river Irrawaddy, about 370 mi/495 km N of Yangon (Rangoon); population (1983) 533,000.

mandarin variety of the tangerine ◊orange *Citrus reticulata*.

Mandarin (Sanskrit *mantrin* "counsellor") standard form of the ◊Chinese language. Historically it derives from the language spoken by *mandarins*, Chinese imperial officials, from the 7th century onward. It is used by 70% of the population and taught in schools of the People's Republic of China.

mandate in history, a territory whose administration was entrusted to Allied states by the League of Nations under the Treaty of Versailles after World War I. Mandated territories were former German and Turkish possessions (including Iraq, Syria, Lebanon, and Palestine). When the United Nations replaced the League of Nations 1945, mandates that had not achieved independence became known as ◊trust territories.

Mandela Nelson (Rolihlahla) 1918– . South African politician and lawyer, president of the ◊African National Congress (ANC) from 1991. As organizer of the then banned ANC, he was imprisoned 1964. In prison he became a symbol of unity for the worldwide antiapartheid movement. In Feb 1990 he was released, the ban on the ANC having been lifted, and he entered into negotiations with the government about a multiracial future for South Africa. In Sept 1992, Mandela and President de Klerk agreed to hasten the creation of an interim government under which reforms could take place. In Feb 1993 they agreed to the formation of a government of national unity after free, nonracial elections in 1994. He and de Klerk were co-recipients of the Nobel Peace Prize 1993. Mandela won the 1994 elections easily and in May 1994 was sworn in as South Africa's president.

He was married 1955–92 to the South African civil-rights activist Winnie Mandela.

Mandela Winnie (Nomzamo) 1934– . Civil-rights activist in South Africa and former wife 1955–92 of Nelson Mandela. A leading spokesperson for the

Mandela The president of the African National Congress, Nelson Mandela.

African National Congress during her husband's imprisonment 1964–90, she has been jailed for a year and put under house arrest several times. In 1989 she was involved in the abduction of four youths, one of whom, Stompie Seipei, was later murdered. Winnie Mandela was convicted of kidnapping and assault, and given a six-year jail sentence May 1991, with the right to appeal. In April 1992 she and Nelson Mandela separated after 33 years of marriage. In the same year she resigned from her ANC leaderships posts.

mandolin musical instrument with four or five pairs of strings, tuned like a violin. It takes its name from its almond-shaped body (Italian *mandorla* "almond").

Manet Edouard 1832–1883. French painter, active in Paris. Rebelling against the academic tradition, he developed a clear and unaffected Realist style. His subjects were mainly contemporary, such as *Un Bar aux*

Manet A Bar at the Folies-Bergère (1882), the artist's last major painting.

Folies-Bergère/A Bar at the Folies-Bergère 1882 (Courtauld Art Gallery, London).

manganese hard, brittle, gray-white metallic element, symbol Mn, atomic number 25, atomic weight 54.9380.

It resembles iron (and rusts), but it is not magnetic and is softer. It is used chiefly in making steel alloys, also alloys with aluminum and copper. It is used in fertilizers, paints, and industrial chemicals. It is a necessary trace element in human nutrition. The name is old, deriving from the French and Italian forms of Latin for *magnesia* (MgO), the white tasteless powder used as an antacid from ancient times.

mango evergreen tree *Mangifera indica* of the cashew family Anacardiaceae, native to India but now widely cultivated for its oval fruits in other tropical and subtropical areas, such as the West Indies.

mangrove any of several shrubs and trees, especially of the mangrove family Rhizophoraceae, found in the muddy swamps of tropical coasts and estuaries. By sending down aerial roots from their branches, they rapidly form close-growing mangrove thickets. Their timber is impervious to water and resists marine worms. Mangrove swamps are rich breeding grounds for fish and shellfish. These habitats are being destroyed in many countries.

Manhattan island 12.5 mi/20 km long and 2.5 mi/4 km wide, lying between the Hudson and East rivers and forming a borough of the city of ◊New York. It includes the Wall Street business center, Broadway and its theaters Carnegie Hall (1891), the World Trade Center (1973), the Empire State Building (1931), the United Nations headquarters (1952), Madison Square Garden, and Central Park.

Manhattan Project code name for the development of the atom bomb in the US in World War II, to which the physicists Enrico Fermi and J Robert Oppenheimer contributed.

manic depression mental disorder characterized by recurring periods of ◊depression which may or may not alternate with periods of inappropriate elation (mania) or overactivity. Sufferers may be genetically predisposed to the condition. Some cases have been improved by taking prescribed doses of ◊lithium.

Manila industrial port (textiles, tobacco, distilling, chemicals, shipbuilding) and capital of the Philippines, on the island of Luzon; population (1990) 1,598,900, metropolitan area (including ◊Quezon City) 5,926,000.

Manipur state of NE India
area 8,646 sq mi/22,400 sq km
capital Imphal
features Loktak Lake; original Indian home of polo
products grain, fruit, vegetables, sugar, textiles, cement
population (1991) 1,826,700
language Hindi
religion Hindu 70%
history administered from the state of Assam until 1947 when it became a Union Territory. It became a state 1972.

Manitoba prairie province of Canada
area 250,900 sq mi/650,000 sq km
capital Winnipeg
features lakes Winnipeg, Winnipegosis, and Manitoba (area 1,814 sq mi/4,700 sq km); 50% forested
exports grain, manufactured foods, beverages, machinery, furs, fish, nickel, zinc, copper, and the world's largest cesium deposits
population (1991) 1,092,600
history trading posts and forts were built here by fur traders in the 18th century. What came to be known as the Red River settlement was first colonized 1811 by dispossessed Scottish Highlanders. The colony became the Canadian province of Manitoba 1870 after the Riel Rebellion 1869 ended. The area of the province was extended 1881 and 1912.

Manley Michael (Norman) 1924– . Jamaican politician, leader of the socialist People's National Party from 1969, and prime minister 1972–80 and 1989–92. He resigned the premiership because of ill health March 1992 and was succeeded by P J Patterson. Manley left parliament April 1992. His father, *Norman Manley* (1893–1969), was the founder of the People's National Party and prime minister 1959–62.

Mann Horace 1796–1859. US political leader and education reformer. Resigning from the Massachusetts state legislature 1937, he served as secretary of the state school board 1837–48. In that position he helped raise the level of funding and instruction for public education.

Manitoba

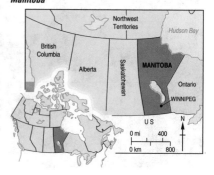

Mantegna The Agony in the Garden (c. 1455), National Gallery, London

Mann Thomas 1875–1955. German novelist and critic, concerned with the theme of the artist's relation to society. His first novel was *Buddenbrooks* 1901, which, followed by *Der Zauberberg/The Magic Mountain* 1924, led to a Nobel Prize 1929. Notable among his works of short fiction is *Der Tod in Venedig/Death in Venice* 1913.

manna sweetish exudation obtained from many trees such as the ash and larch, and used in medicine. The manna of the Bible is thought to have been from the tamarisk tree, or a form of lichen.

Mannerism in painting, sculpture, and architecture, a style characterized by a subtle but conscious breaking of the "rules" of Classical composition—for example, displaying the human body in an off-center, distorted pose, and using harsh, non-blending colors. The term was coined by Giorgio ◊Vasari and used to describe the 16th-century reaction to the peak of Renaissance Classicism. Strictly speaking, it refers to a style developed by painters and architects working in Italy (primarily Rome and Florence) during the years 1520 to 1575, beginning with, and largely derived from, the later works of Michelangelo in painting and architecture. It includes the works of the painters Giovanni Rosso and Parmigianino and the architect Giulio Romano.

Mannheim Karl 1893–1947. Hungarian sociologist who settled in the UK 1933. In *Ideology and Utopia* 1929 he argued that all knowledge, except in mathematics and physics, is ideological, a reflection of class interests and values; that there is therefore no such thing as objective knowledge or absolute truth.

manometer instrument for measuring the pressure of liquids (including human blood pressure) or gases. In its basic form, it is a U-tube partly filled with colored liquid; pressure of a gas entering at one side is measured by the level to which the liquid rises at the other.

Man Ray adopted name of Emmanuel Rudnitsky 1890–1977. US photographer, painter, and sculptor, active mainly in France; associated with the Dada movement. His pictures often showed Surrealist images like the photograph *Le Violon d'Ingres* 1924.

Mansfield industrial city (car parts, steel and rubber products) in N central Ohio, NE of Columbus, seat of Richland County; population (1990) 50,600.

Mantegna Andrea *c.* 1431–1506. Italian Renaissance painter and engraver, active chiefly in Padua and Mantua, where some of his frescoes remain. Paintings such as *The Agony in the Garden c.* 1455 (National Gallery, London) reveal a dramatic linear style, mastery of perspective, and strongly Classical architectural detail.

mantis any insect of the family Mantidae, related to cockroaches. Some species can reach a length of 8 in/20 cm. There are about 2,000 species of mantis, mainly tropical.

The 4 in/10 cm-long Chinese praying mantis, proficient at garden pest control, is now naturalized in North America.

mantle intermediate zone of the Earth between the crust and the core, accounting for 82% of the Earth's volume. It is thought to consist of silicate minerals such as olivine.

mantis The praying mantis is a superbly designed predator.

Mao Zedong Chairman Mao with vice chair Lin Biao, who is holding the Little Red Book of Mao's thoughts.

Mantle Mickey (Charles) 1931– . US baseball player. Signed by the New York Yankees, he broke into the major leagues 1951. A powerful switch-hitter (able to bat with either hand), he also excelled as a centerfielder. In 1956 he won baseball's Triple Crown, leading the American League in batting average, home runs, and runs batted in. He retired 1969 after 18 years with the Yankees and seven World Series championships.

mantra in Hindu or Buddhist belief, a word repeatedly intoned to assist concentration and develop spiritual power; for example, *om*, which represents the names of Brahma, Vishnu, and Siva. Followers of a guru may receive their own individual mantra.

Manu in Hindu mythology, the founder of the human race, who was saved by ◊Brahma from a deluge.

Maoism form of communism based on the ideas and teachings of the Chinese communist leader ◊Mao Zedong. It involves an adaptation of ◊Marxism to suit conditions in China and apportions a much greater role to agriculture and the peasantry in the building of socialism, thus effectively bypassing the capitalist (industrial) stage envisaged by Marx.

Maori member of the indigenous Polynesian people of New Zealand, who numbered 294,200 in 1986, about 10% of the total population. Their language, Maori, belongs to the eastern branch of the Austronesian family.

Mao Zedong or *Mao Tse-tung* 1893–1976. Chinese political leader and Marxist theoretician. A founder of the Chinese Communist Party (CCP) 1921, Mao soon emerged as its leader. He organized the ◊Long March 1934–35 and the war of liberation 1937–49, following which he established a People's Republic and communist rule in China; he headed the CCP and government until his death. His influence diminished with the failure of his 1958–60 ◊Great Leap Forward, but he emerged dominant again during the 1966–69 ◊Cultural Revolution. Mao adapted communism to Chinese conditions, as set out in the ◊Little Red Book.

maple Maples are typically deciduous with lobed leaves and winged fruit, or samaras.

map diagrammatic representation of an area—for example, part of the Earth's surface or the distribution of the stars. Modern maps of the Earth are made using satellites in low orbit to take a series of overlapping stereoscopic photographs from which a three-dimensional image can be prepared. The earliest accurate large-scale maps appeared about 1580.

maple deciduous tree of the genus *Acer*, family Aceraceae, with lobed leaves and green flowers, followed by two-winged fruits, or samaras. There are over 200 species, chiefly in northern temperate regions.

Mapplethorpe Robert 1946–1989. US art photographer known for his use of racial and homoerotic imagery in chiefly fine platinum prints. He developed a style of polished elegance in his gallery art works, whose often culturally forbidden subject matter caused controversy.

map projection ways of depicting the spherical surface of the Earth on a flat piece of paper. Traditional projections include the *conic*, *azimuthal*, and *cylindrical*. The most famous cylindrical projection is the ◊*Mercator projection*, which dates from 1569. The weakness of these systems is that countries in different latitudes are disproportionately large, and lines of longitude and latitude appear distorted. In 1973 German historian Arno Peters devised the *Peters projection* in which the countries of the world retain their relative areas.

Mapp v Ohio US Supreme Court decision 1961 dealing with the admission into criminal trials of evidence procured through illegal searches and seizures. Mapp, a Cleveland woman, was arrested for the possession of obscene materials discovered by police during an illegal search. Convicted by the state, Mapp appealed to the US Supreme Court, arguing that her Fourth-Amendment rights had been violated. The Court reversed Mapp's conviction, creating the rule that all illegally obtained evidence be excluded from state and federal trials.

Maputo formerly (until 1975) *Lourenço Marques* capital of Mozambique, and Africa's second-largest port, on Delagoa Bay; population (1987) 1,006,800. Linked by rail with Zimbabwe and South Africa, it is a major outlet for minerals, steel, textiles, processed foods, and furniture.

Maquis French ◊resistance movement that fought against the German occupation during World War II.

Maracaibo oil-exporting port in Venezuela, on the channel connecting Lake Maracaibo with the Gulf of Venezuela; population (1989) 1,365,308. It is the second-largest city in the country.

Maracaibo, Lake lake in NW Venezuela; area 5,400 sq mi/14,000 sq km. Oil was discovered here 1917.

Marat Jean Paul 1743–1793. French Revolutionary leader and journalist. He was elected to the National Convention 1792, where he carried on a long struggle with the right-wing Girondins, ending in their overthrow May 1793. In July he was murdered by Charlotte Corday, a member of the Girondins.

marathon athletics endurance race over 26 mi 385 yd/42.195 km. It was first included in the Olympic Games in Athens 1896. The distance varied until it was standardized 1924. More recently, races have been opened to wider participation, including social runners as well as those competing at senior level.

Marathon, Battle of 490 BC battle in which the Athenians and their allies from Plateae defeated the invading Persians on the plain of Marathon, NE of Athens.

azimuthal projection

North Pole

North Pole

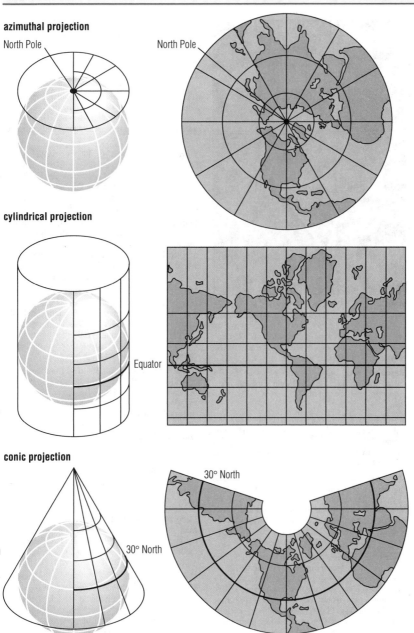

map projection
*Three widely used
map projections.*

cylindrical projection

Equator

conic projection

30° North

30° North

marble metamorphosed ◊limestone that takes and retains a good polish; it is used in building and sculpture. In its pure form it is white and consists almost entirely of calcite $CaCO_3$. Mineral impurities give it various colors and patterns. Carrara, Italy, is known for white marble.

Marbury v Madison US Supreme Court decision 1803 that affirmed the process of judicial review over Congressional acts. The plaintiff, William Marbury, had been appointed the District of Columbia's justice of the peace by President J Adams shortly before Jef-

ferson replaced Adams in office, but the new secretary of state, James Madison, withheld the letter of appointment. Marbury appealed to the Court to force Madison to produce the letter by issuing a writ of mandamus, a power granted by Congress in the Judiciary Act of 1789. The Court ruled unanimously that Congress did not have the right to expand judiciary powers. Since writs of mandamus were not provided for in the Constitution, the Court was not empowered to issue them. This was the first time the Court nullified an act of Congress on the basis of constitutionality.

Marconi Italian inventor Guglielmo Marconi, whose invention of radio "wireless telegraphy" earned him a Nobel Prize 1909.

Marc Franz 1880–1916. German Expressionist painter, associated with Wassily Kandinsky in founding the ◊Blaue Reiter movement. Animals played an essential part in his view of the world, and bold semi-abstracts of red and blue horses are characteristic of his work.

Marceau Marcel 1923– . French mime artist. He is the creator of the clown-harlequin Bip and mime sequences such as "Youth, Maturity, Old Age, and Death."

Marche, Le (English *the Marches*) region of E central Italy consisting of the provinces of Ancona, Ascoli Piceno, Macerata, and Pesaro e Urbino; capital Ancona; area 3,744 sq mi/9,700 sq km; population (1990) 1,435,600.

Marches boundary areas of England with Wales, and England with Scotland. In the Middle Ages these troubled frontier regions were held by lords of the Marches, sometimes called *marchiones* and later earls of March. The 1st Earl of March of the Welsh Marches was Roger de Mortimer (c. 1286–1330); of the Scottish Marches, Patrick Dunbar (died 1285).

March on Rome, the means by which Fascist leader Benito Mussolini came to power in Italy 1922. A protracted crisis in government and the threat of civil war enabled him to demand the formation of a Fascist government to restore order. On Oct 29, 1922, King Victor Emmanuel III invited Mussolini to come to Rome to take power. The "march" was a propaganda myth: Mussolini traveled overnight by train from Milan to Rome, where he formed a government the following day, Oct 30. Some 25,000 fascist Blackshirts were also transported to the city, where they marched in a ceremonial parade Oct 31.

Marciano Rocky (Rocco Francis Marchegiano) 1923–1969. US boxer, world heavyweight champion 1952–56. He retired after 49 professional fights, the only heavyweight champion to retire undefeated.

Marconi Guglielmo 1874–1937. Italian electrical engineer and pioneer in the invention and development of radio. In 1895 he achieved radio communication over more than a mile, and in England 1896 he conducted successful experiments that led to the formation of the company that became Marconi's Wireless Telegraph Company Ltd. He shared the Nobel Prize for Physics 1909.

Marco Polo see ◊Polo, Marco.

Marcos Ferdinand 1917–1989. Filipino right-wing politician, president from 1965 to 1986, when he was forced into exile in Hawaii by a popular front led by Corazon ◊Aquino. He was backed by the US when in power, but in 1988 US authorities indicted him and his wife Imelda Marcos for racketeering and embezzlement.

Marcos Imelda 1930– . Filipino politician and socialite, wife of Ferdinand Marcos, in exile 1986–91. She was acquitted 1990 of defrauding US banks. Under indictment for misuse of Philippine state funds, she returned to Manila in Nov 1991 and was an unsuccessful candidate in the 1992 presidential elections.

Marcus Aurelius Antoninus AD 121–180. Roman emperor from 161 and Stoic philosopher. He wrote the philosophical *Meditations*. Born in Rome, he was adopted by his uncle, the emperor Antoninus Pius, whom he succeeded in 161. He conceded an equal share in the rule to Lucius Verus (died 169).

Marcuse Herbert 1898–1979. US political philosopher, born in Germany. His theories, combining Marxism and Freudianism, greatly influenced the radicalism of the 1960s and 1970s. He preached the overthrow of the existing social order by using the system's very tolerance to ensure its defeat, but he was not an advocate of violent revolution.

Mardi Gras (French "fat Tuesday" from the custom of using up all the fat in the household before the beginning of ◊Lent) Shrove Tuesday. A festival was traditionally held on this day in Paris, and there are carnivals in many parts of the world, including New Orleans, Louisiana; Italy; and Brazil.

Margaret (Rose) 1930– . Princess of the UK, younger daughter of George VI and sister of Elizabeth II. In 1960 she married Anthony Armstrong-Jones, later created Lord Snowdon, but they were divorced 1978. Their children are *David, Viscount Linley* (1961–) and *Lady Sarah Armstrong-Jones* (1964–).

Margaret of Anjou 1430–1482. Queen of England from 1445, wife of ◊Henry VI of England. After the outbreak of the Wars of the ◊Roses 1455, she acted as the leader of the Lancastrians, but was defeated and captured at the battle of Tewkesbury 1471 by Edward IV.

Margaret, St 1045–1093. Queen of Scotland, the granddaughter of King Edmund Ironside of England. She went to Scotland after the Norman Conquest, and soon after married Malcolm III. The marriage of her daughter Matilda to Henry I united the Norman and English royal houses.

margarine butter substitute made from animal fats and/or vegetable oils. The French chemist Hippolyte Mège-Mouries invented margarine 1889. Today, margarines are usually made with vegetable oils, such as soy, corn, or sunflower oil, giving a product low in saturated fats (see ◊polyunsaturate) and fortified with vitamins A and D.

margin in finance, the difference between cost and selling price; also cash or collateral on deposit with a broker or lender to meet legal requirements against loss, as when stocks and other securities have been financed by funds supplied by the lender.

margrave German title (equivalent of marquess) for the "counts of the march," who guarded the frontier regions of the Holy Roman Empire from Charlemagne's time. Later the title was used by other territorial princes. Chief among these were the margraves of Austria and of Brandenburg.

Margrethe II 1940– . Queen of Denmark from 1972, when she succeeded her father Frederick IX. In 1967, she married the French diplomat Count Henri de Laborde de Monpezat, who took the title Prince Hendrik. Her heir is Crown Prince Frederick (1968–).

Marguerite of Navarre also known as *Margaret d'Angoulême* 1492–1549. Queen of Navarre from 1527, French poet, and author of the *Heptaméron* 1558, a collection of stories in imitation of Boccaccio's *Decameron*. The sister of Francis I of France, she was born in Angoulême. Her second husband 1527 was Henri d'Albret, king of Navarre.

Mariana Islands or *Marianas* archipelago in the NW Pacific E of the Philippines, divided politically into ◊Guam (an unincorporated territory of the US) and the ◊Northern Mariana Islands (a commonwealth of the US with its own internal government).

Mariana Trench lowest region on the Earth's surface; the deepest part of the sea floor. The trench is 1,500 mi/2,400 km long and is situated 200 mi/300 km E of the Mariana Islands, in the NW Pacific Ocean. Its deepest part is the gorge known as the Challenger Deep, which extends 36,210 ft/11,034 m below sea level.

Maria Theresa 1717–1780. Empress of Austria from 1740, when she succeeded her father, the Holy Roman emperor Charles VI; her claim to the throne was challenged and she became embroiled, first in the War of the ◊Austrian Succession 1740–48, then in the ◊Seven Years' War 1756–63; she remained in possession of Austria but lost Silesia. The rest of her reign was peaceful and, with her son Joseph II, she introduced social reforms.

Marie 1875–1938. Queen of Romania. She was the daughter of the duke of Edinburgh, second son of Queen Victoria of England, and married Prince Ferdinand of Romania in 1893 (he was king 1922–27). She wrote a number of literary works, notably *Story of My Life* 1934–35. Her son Carol became king of Romania, and her daughters, Elisabeth and Marie, queens of Greece and Yugoslavia respectively.

Marie Antoinette 1755–1793. Queen of France from 1774. She was the daughter of Empress Maria Theresa of Austria, and married ◊Louis XVI of France 1770. Her reputation for extravagance helped provoke the ◊French Revolution of 1789. She was tried for treason Oct 1793 and guillotined.

Marie de' Medici 1573–1642. Queen of France, wife of Henry IV from 1600, and regent (after his murder) for their son Louis XIII. She left the government to her favorites, the Concinis, until Louis XIII seized power and executed them 1617.

She was banished, but after she led a revolt 1619, ◊Richelieu effected her reconciliation with her son. When she attempted to oust him again 1630, she was exiled.

Marietta industrial town (plastics, metal products, chemicals, and office equipment) in SE Ohio; seat of Washington County; population (1990) 15,000. It lies where the Muskingum River flows into the Ohio River, SE of Columbus, and was the first permanent settlement (1788) in Ohio.

Mariana Islands

marigold any of several plants of the family Compositae, especially the genus *Tagetes*, including pot marigold *Calendula officinalis* and the tropical American *T. patula*, commonly known as French marigold.

marijuana the dried leaves and flowers of the ◊hemp plant (*Cannabis sativa*), used as a recreational but illegal drug. It is eaten or inhaled and causes euphoria, distortion of time, and heightened sensations of sight and sound.

Mariner spacecraft series of US space probes that explored the planets Mercury, Venus, and Mars 1962–75.

marines fighting force that operates both on land and at sea. The *US Marine Corps* (1775) is constituted as an arm of the US Navy. It is made up of infantry and air support units trained and equipped for amphibious landings under fire.

Marion Francis c. 1732–1795. American military leader. He waged a successful guerrilla war against the British after the fall of Charleston 1780 during the American Revolution. Establishing his field headquarters in inaccessible areas, he became popularly known as the "Swamp Fox." He played a major role in the American victory at Eutaw Springs 1781.

marionette type of ◊puppet, a jointed figure controlled from above by wires or strings. Intricately crafted marionettes were used in Burma (now Myanmar) and Ceylon (now Sri Lanka) and later at the courts of Italian princes in the 16th–18th centuries.

maritime law that part of the law dealing with the sea: in particular, fishing areas, ships, and navigation. Seas are divided into *internal waters* governed by a state's internal laws (such as harbors, inlets); *◊territorial waters* (the area of sea adjoining the coast over which a state claims rights); the *continental shelf* (the seabed and subsoil that the coastal state is entitled to exploit beyond the territorial waters); and the *high seas*, where international law applies.

marjoram aromatic herb of the mint family Labiatae. Wild marjoram *Origanum vulgare* is found both in Europe and Asia and has become naturalized in the Americas; the culinary sweet marjoram *O. majorana* is widely cultivated.

Mark Antony Antonius, Marcus 83–30 BC. Roman politician and soldier. He served under Julius ◊Caesar in Gaul, and was consul with him in 44, when he tried to secure for Caesar the title of king. After Caesar's assassination, he formed the Second Triumvirate with Octavian (◊Augustus) and Lepidus. In 42 he defeated

Marley Jamaican singer and guitarist Bob Marley, whose warm and expressive music gave reggae its earliest international currency.

Mars Mars as seen by a Viking space probe on its approach to the red planet.

Brutus and Cassius at Philippi. He took Egypt as his share of the empire and formed a liaison with ◊Cleopatra, but in 40 he returned to Rome to marry Octavia, the sister of Augustus. In 32 the Senate declared war on Cleopatra, and Antony was defeated by Augustus at the battle of Actium 31 BC. He returned to Egypt and committed suicide.

marketing promoting goods and services to consumers. In the 20th century, marketing has played an increasingly larger role in determining company policy, influencing product development, pricing, methods of distribution, advertising, and promotion techniques.

Markova Alicia. Adopted name of Lilian Alicia Marks 1910– . British ballet dancer. Trained by ◊Pavlova, she was ballerina with ◊Diaghilev's company 1925–29, was the first resident ballerina of the Vic-Wells Ballet 1933–35, partnered Anton ◊Dolin in their own Markova-Dolin Company 1935–37, and danced with the Ballets Russes de Monte Carlo 1938–41 and Ballet Theater 1941–46. She is associated with the great Classical ballets, such as *Giselle*.

Mark, St 1st century AD. In the New Testament, Christian apostle and evangelist whose name is given to the second Gospel. It was probably written AD 65–70, and used by the authors of the first and third Gospels. He is the patron saint of Venice, and his emblem is a winged lion; feast day April 25.

Marley Bob (Robert Nesta) 1945–1981. Jamaican reggae singer and songwriter, a Rastafarian whose songs, many of which were topical and political, popularized reggae worldwide in the 1970s. They include "Get Up, Stand Up" 1973 and "No Woman No Cry" 1974; his albums include *Natty Dread* 1975 and *Exodus* 1977.

Marlowe Christopher 1564–1593. English poet and dramatist. His work includes the blank-verse plays *Tamburlaine the Great* c. 1587, *The Jew of Malta* c. 1589, and *Edward II* and *Dr Faustus*, both c. 1592; the poem *Hero and Leander* 1598; and a translation of Ovid's *Amores*.

Marmara, Sea of small inland sea separating Turkey in Europe from Turkey in Asia, connected through the Bosporus with the Black Sea, and through the Dardanelles with the Aegean; length 170 mi/275 km, breadth up to 50 mi/80 km.

Marne, Battles of the in World War I, two unsuccessful German offensives. In the *First Battle* Sept 6–9, 1914, von Moltke's advance was halted by the British Expeditionary Force and the French under Foch; in the *Second Battle* July 15–Aug 4, 1918, Ludendorff's advance was defeated by British, French, and US troops under the French general Pétain, and German morale crumbled.

Maronite member of a Christian sect deriving from refugee Monothelites (Christian heretics) of the 7th century. They were subsequently united with the Roman Catholic church and number about 400,000 in Lebanon and Syria, with an equal number scattered in S Europe and the Americas.

Marquesas Islands (French *Iles Marquises*) island group in ◊French Polynesia, lying N of the Tuamotu Archipelago; area 490 sq mi/1,270 sq km; population (1988) 7,500. The administrative headquarters is Atuona on Hiva Oa. The islands were annexed by France 1842.

marquess or *marquis* title and rank of a nobleman who in the British peerage ranks below a duke and above an earl. The wife of a marquess is a marchioness.

marquetry inlaying of various woods, bone, or ivory, usually on furniture, to create ornate patterns and pictures. *Parquetry* is the term used for geometrical inlaid patterns. The method is thought to have originated in Germany or Holland.

Marquette Jacques 1637–1675. French Jesuit missionary and explorer. He went to Canada 1666, explored the upper lakes of the St Lawrence River, and in 1673 with Louis Jolliet (1645–1700), set out on a voyage down the Mississippi on which they made the first accurate record of its course.

In 1674 he and two companions camped near the site of present-day Chicago, making them the first Europeans to live there.

Márquez Gabriel Garcia. See ◊Garcia Márquez, Colombian novelist.

Marrakesh historic city in Morocco in the foothills of the Atlas Mountains, about 130 mi/210 km S of Casablanca; population (1982) 549,000. It is a tourist center, and has textile, leather, and food processing industries. Founded 1062, it has a medieval palace and mosques, and was formerly the capital of Morocco.

marriage legally or culturally sanctioned union of one man and one woman (monogamy); one man and two or more women (polygamy); one woman and two or more men (polyandry). The basis of marriage varies considerably in different societies (romantic love in the West; arranged marriages in some other societies), but most marriage ceremonies, contracts, or customs involve a set of rights and duties, such as care and protection, and there is generally an expectation that children will be born of the union to continue the family line, and maintain the family property.

Mars in Roman mythology, the god of war, depicted as a fearless warrior. The month of March is named after him. He is equivalent to the Greek Ares.

Mars fourth planet from the Sun, average distance 141.6 million mi/227.9 million km. It revolves around the Sun in 687 Earth days, and has a rotation period of 24 hr 37 min. It is much smaller than Venus or Earth, with a diameter 4,210 mi/6,780 km, and mass 0.11 that of Earth. Mars is slightly pearshaped, with a low, level northern hemisphere, which is comparatively uncratered and geologically "young," and a heavily cratered "ancient" southern hemisphere.

Marsalis Wynton 1961– . US trumpet player who has recorded both Classical and jazz music. He was a member of Art Blakey's Jazz Messengers 1980–82 and also played with Miles Davis before forming his own quintet. At one time this included his brother Branford Marsalis on saxophone.

Marseillaise, La French national anthem; the words and music were composed 1792 as a revolutionary song by the army officer Claude Joseph Rouget de Lisle (1760–1836).

Marseille (English *Marseilles*) chief seaport of France, industrial center (chemicals, oil refining, metallurgy, shipbuilding, food processing), and capital of the *département* of Bouches-du-Rhône, on the Golfe du Lion, Mediterranean Sea; population (1990) 807,700.

marsh low-lying wetland. Freshwater marshes are common wherever groundwater, surface springs, streams, or run-off causes frequent flooding or more or less permanent shallow water. A marsh is alkaline whereas a ◊bog is acid. Marshes develop on inorganic silt or clay soils. Rushes are typical marsh plants. Large marshes dominated by papyrus, cattail, and reeds, with standing water throughout the year, are commonly called ◊swamps. Near the sea, salt marshes may form.

Marshall George Catlett 1880–1959. US general and diplomat. He was army Chief of Staff in World War II, secretary of state 1947–49, and secretary of defense Sept 1950–Sept 1951. He initiated the ◊Marshall Plan 1947 and received the Nobel Peace Prize 1953.

Marshall John 1755–1835. US politician and jurist. He held office in the US House of Representatives 1799–1800 and was secretary of state 1800–01. As chief justice of the US Supreme Court 1801–35, he established the independence of the Court and the supremacy of federal over state law, and his opinions became universally accepted interpretations of the US Constitution.

Marshall Thurgood 1908–1993. US jurist and civil-rights leader. As US Supreme Court justice from 1967, he frequently presided over landmark civil-rights cases such as *Brown* v *Board of Education* 1954. The first black associate justice, he was a strong   voice for civil and individual rights throughout his career.

Marshall Islands country in SE Asia, consisting of the Radak (13 islands) and Ralik (11 islands) chains in the W Pacific Ocean. *See panel p. 596*

Marshall Plan program of US economic aid to Europe, set up at the end of World War II, totaling $13,000 billion 1948–52.

Officially known as the European Recovery Program, it was announced by Secretary of State George C ◊Marshall in a speech at Harvard June 1947, but it was in fact the work of a State Department group led by Dean ◊Acheson. The perceived danger of communist takeover in postwar Europe was the main reason for the aid effort.

marsh gas gas consisting mostly of ◊methane. It is produced in swamps and marshes by the action of bacteria on dead vegetation.

marsupial (Greek *marsupion* "little purse") mammal in which the female has a pouch where she carries her young (born tiny and immature) for a considerable time after birth. Marsupials include omnivorous, herbivorous, and carnivorous species, among them the kangaroo, wombat, opossum, phalanger, bandicoot, dasyure, and wallaby.

The marsupial anteater *Myrmecobius* has no pouch.

marten small bushy-tailed carnivorous mammal of the genus *Martes* in the weasel family Mustelidae. Martens live in North America, Europe, and temperate regions of Asia, and are agile climbers of trees.

Marshall Islands

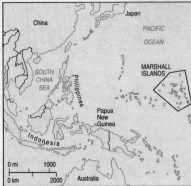

area 69 sq mi/180 sq km
capital Dalap-Uliga-Darrit (on Majuro atoll)
physical comprises the Radak (13 islands) and Ralik (11 islands) chains in the W Pacific
features include two atolls used for US atom-bomb tests 1946–63, Eniwetok and Bikini, where radioactivity will last

for 100 years; and Kwajal in atoll (the largest) which has a US intercontinental missile range
head of state and government Amata Kabua from 1991
political system liberal democracy
political parties no organized party system
products copra, phosphates, fish; tourism is important
currency US dollar
population (1990) 31,600
language English (official)
religions Christian, mainly Roman Catholic, and local faiths
GNP $512 million; $16,516 per head (1990)

chronology

1855 Occupied by Germany.
1914 Occupied by Japan.
1920–45 Administered by Japan under United Nations mandate.
1946–63 Eniwetok and Bikini atolls used for US atom-bomb tests; islanders later demanded rehabilitation and compensation for the damage.
1947 Became part of the UN Pacific Islands Trust Territory, administered by the US
1986 Compact of free association with US granted islands self- government, with US retaining military control and taking tribute.
1990 UN trust status terminated.
1991 Independence achieved; UN membership granted.

Martens Wilfried 1936– . Prime minister of Belgium 1979–92, member of the Social Christian Party. He was president of the Dutch-speaking CVP 1972–79 and, as prime minister, headed several coalition governments in the period 1979–92 when he was replaced by Jean-Luc Dehaene heading a new coalition.

Martial (Marcus Valerius Martialis) AD 41–104. Latin poet and epigrammatist. Born in Bilbilis, Spain, Martial settled in Rome AD 64, where he lived a life of poverty and dependence. His poetry, often obscene, is keenly observant of all classes in contemporary Rome.

martial arts any of several styles of armed and unarmed combat developed in the East from ancient techniques and arts. Common martial arts include ◊aikido, ◊judo, ◊jujitsu, ◊karate, ◊kendo, and ◊kung fu.

martial law replacement of civilian by military authorities in the maintenance of order.

In the US martial law is usually proclaimed by the president or the government of a state in areas of the country where the civil authorities have been rendered unable to act, or to act with safety. The legal position of martial law is neither well defined in the constitution nor laid down in statutes. In effect, when war or rebellion is in progress in an area, the military authorities are recognized as having the powers to maintain order by summary means.

martin any of several species of birds in the swallow family, Hirundinidae.

Only one species, the purple martin *Progne subis*, is native to North America. It is a dark, glossy purplish blue and about 8 in/20 cm long with a notched tail. It winters in South America.

Martinet Jean French inspector-general of infantry under Louis XIV whose constant drilling brought the army to a high degree of efficiency—hence the use of his name to mean a strict disciplinarian.

Martinmas in the Christian calendar, the feast of St Martin, Nov 11.

Martins Peter 1946– . Danish-born US dancer, choreographer, and ballet director, principal dancer with the New York City Ballet (NYCB) from 1965, its joint ballet master (with Anthony Tudor) from 1983, and its director from 1990. He trained with August Bournonville and brought that teacher's influence to the NYCB.

martyr (Greek "witness") one who voluntarily suffers death for refusing to renounce a religious faith. The first recorded Christian martyr was St Stephen, who was killed in Jerusalem shortly after Jesus' alleged ascension to heaven.

Marvin Lee 1924–1987. US film actor who began his career playing violent, often psychotic villains and progressed to playing violent, occasionally psychotic heroes. His work includes *The Big Heat* 1953, *The Killers* 1964, and *Cat Ballou* 1965.

Marx Karl (Heinrich) 1818–1883. German philosopher, economist, and social theorist whose account of change through conflict is known as historical, or dialectical, materialism (see ◊Marxism). His ◊Das Kapital/*Capital* 1867–95 is the fundamental text of Marxist economics, and his systematic theses on class struggle, history, and the importance of economic factors in politics have exercised an enormous influence on later thinkers and political activists.

Marx Brothers team of US film comedians: Leonard *Chico* (from the "chicks"—women—he chased) 1887–1961; Adolph, the silent *Harpo* (from the harp he played) 1888–1964; Julius *Groucho* (from his temper) 1890–1977; Milton *Gummo* (from his gumshoes, or galoshes) 1897–1977, who left the team before they began making films; and Herbert *Zeppo* (born at the time of the first zeppelins) 1901–1979, part of the team until 1935. They made a total of 13 zany films 1929–49 including *Animal Crackers* 1930, *Duck Soup* 1933, *A Night at the Opera* 1935, and *Go West* 1940.

Marxism philosophical system, developed by the 19th-century German social theorists ◊Marx and ◊Engels, also known as *dialectical materialism*, under which matter gives rise to mind (materialism) and all is subject to change (from dialectic; see ◊Hegel). As applied to history, it supposes that the succession of feudalism, capitalism, socialism, and finally the classless society is inevitable. The stubborn resistance of any existing system to change necessitates its complete overthrow in the *class struggle*—in the case of capitalism, by the proletariat—rather than gradual modification.

Mary in the New Testament, the mother of Jesus through divine intervention (see ◊Annunciation), wife of ◊Joseph. The Roman Catholic church maintains belief in her ◊Immaculate Conception and bodily assumption into heaven, and venerates her as a mediator. Feast day of the Assumption Aug 15.

Mary *Queen of Scots* 1542–1587. Queen of Scotland 1542–67. Also known as *Mary Stuart*, she was the daughter of James V. Mary's connection with the English royal line from Henry VII made her a threat to Elizabeth I's hold on the English throne, especially as she represented a champion of the Catholic cause. She was married three times. After her forced abdication she was imprisoned but escaped 1568 to England. Elizabeth I held her prisoner, while the Roman Catholics, who regarded Mary as rightful queen of England, formed many conspiracies to place her on the throne, and for complicity in one of these she was executed.

Mary I *Bloody Mary* 1516–1558. Queen of England from 1553. She was the eldest daughter of Henry VIII by Catherine of Aragon. When Edward VI died, Mary secured the crown without difficulty in spite of the conspiracy to substitute Lady Jane ◊Grey. In 1554 Mary married Philip II of Spain, and as a devout Roman Catholic obtained the restoration of papal supremacy and sanctioned the persecution of Protestants. She was succeeded by her half sister Elizabeth I.

When Mary died, the Protestant Elizabeth I gained the throne and settled the religious question, for the time, during her long, pivotal reign.

Maryland

Mary II 1662–1694. Queen of England, Scotland, and Ireland from 1688. She was the Protestant elder daughter of the Catholic ◊James II, and in 1677 was married to her cousin ◊William III of Orange. After the 1688 revolution she accepted the crown jointly with William.

Maryland state of eastern US; nickname Old Line State/Free State
area 12,198 sq mi/31,600 sq km
capital Annapolis
cities Baltimore, Silver Spring, Dundalk, Bethesda
features Chesapeake Bay, an inlet of the Atlantic Ocean; horse racing (the Preakness Stakes at Baltimore); yacht racing and the US Naval Academy at Annapolis; historic Fort McHenry; Fort Meade, a government electronic-listening center; Baltimore harbor
products poultry, dairy products, machinery, steel, automobiles and parts, electric and electronic equipment, chemicals, fish and shellfish
population (1990) 4,781,500
famous people Stephen Decatur, Francis Scott Key, Edgar Allan Poe, Frederick Douglass, Harriet Tubman, Upton Sinclair, H L Mencken, Babe Ruth, Billie Holiday
history one of the original 13 states, first settled 1634; it became a state 1788. In 1608 John Smith explored Chesapeake Bay, but the colony of Maryland, awarded by royal grant 1632 to Lord Baltimore for the settlement of English Catholics, dates from 1634. It ratified

Marx Brothers *US film and radio comedians; from left: Harpo, Groucho, Zeppo, and Chico.*

Masaccio The Virgin and Child *(from the Pisa polyptych, 1426), National Gallery, London.*

the federal Constitution 1788. During the British bombardment of Fort McHenry in the War of 1812, Francis Scott Key wrote the poem "The Star-Spangled Banner," which later became the lyrics to the US national anthem. Some Marylanders favored secession during the Civil War, during which the state was largely occupied by Union troops because of its strategic location near Washington, DC, and the Confederate armies three times invaded Maryland. In recent times the state has prospered from the growth of the federal government in nearby Washington and the redevelopment of Baltimore, whose port ranks second in handling foreign shipping. Between 1940 and 1980, Maryland's population more than tripled.

Mary Magdalene, St 1st century AD. In the New Testament, the woman whom Jesus cured of possession by evil spirits, was present at the Crucifixion and burial, and was the first to meet the risen Jesus. She is often identified with the woman of St Luke's gospel who anointed Jesus' feet, and her symbol is a jar of ointment; feast day July 22.

Masaccio (Tomaso di Giovanni di Simone Guidi) 1401–1428. Florentine painter, a leader of the early Italian Renaissance. His frescoes in Sta Maria del Carmine, Florence, 1425–28, which he painted with Masolino da Panicale (c. 1384–1447), show a decisive break with Gothic conventions. He was the first painter to apply the scientific laws of perspective, newly discovered by the architect Brunelleschi.

Masada rock fortress 1,300 ft/396 m above the western shore of the Dead Sea, Israel. Site of the Hebrews' final stand in their revolt against the Romans (AD 66–72). After withstanding a yearlong siege, the Hebrew population of 953 committed mass suicide rather than be conquered and enslaved.

Masaryk Tomáš (Garrigue) 1850–1937. Czechoslovak nationalist politician. He directed the revolutionary movement against the Austrian Empire, founding with Eduard Beneš and Stefanik the Czechoslovak National Council, and in 1918 was elected first president of the newly formed Czechoslovak Republic. Three times reelected, he resigned 1935 in favor of Beneš.

Maseru capital of Lesotho, S Africa, on the Caledon River; population (1986) 289,000. Founded 1869, it is a center for trade and diamond processing.

Mashraq (Arabic "east") the Arab countries of the E Mediterranean: Egypt, Sudan, Jordan, Syria, and Lebanon. The term is contrasted with ◊Maghreb, comprising the Arab countries of NW Africa.

Masire Quett Ketumile Joni 1925– . President of Botswana from 1980. In 1962, with Seretse ◊Khama, he founded the Botswana Democratic Party (BDP) and in 1965 was made deputy prime minister. After independence 1966, he became vice president and, on Khama's death 1980, president, continuing a policy of nonalignment.

Maskelyne Nevil 1732–1811. English astronomer who accurately measured the distance from the Earth to the Sun by observing a transit of Venus across the Sun's face 1769. In 1774 he measured the mass of the Earth by noting the deflection of a plumb line near Mount Schiehallion in Scotland.

masochism desire to subject oneself to physical or mental pain, humiliation, or punishment, for erotic pleasure, to alleviate guilt, or out of destructive impulses turned inward. The term is derived from Leopold von ◊Sacher-Masoch.

Mason James 1909–1984. English actor who portrayed romantic villains in British films of the 1940s. After *Odd Man Out* 1947 he worked in the US, playing intelligent but troubled, vulnerable men, notably in *A Star Is Born* 1954. He returned to Europe 1960, where he made *Lolita* 1962, *Georgy Girl* 1966, and *Cross of Iron* 1977.

Mason–Dixon Line in the US, the boundary line between Maryland and Pennsylvania (latitude 39° 43' 26.3' N), named after Charles Mason (1730–1787) and Jeremiah Dixon (died 1777), English astronomers and surveyors who surveyed it 1763–67. It was popularly seen as dividing the North from the South.

mass in physics, the quantity of matter in a body as measured by its inertia. Mass determines the acceleration produced in a body by a given force acting on it, the acceleration being inversely proportional to the mass of the body. The mass also determines the force exerted on a body by ◊gravity on Earth, although this attraction varies slightly from place to place. In the SI system, the base unit of mass is the kilogram.

Mass in Christianity, the celebration of the ◊Eucharist.

Massachusetts state of NE US; nickname Bay State/Old Colony State
area 8,299 sq mi/21,500 sq km

Massachusetts

capital Boston
cities Worcester, Springfield, New Bedford, Brockton, Cambridge
population (1990) 6,016,400
features Boston landmarks; Harvard University and the Massachusetts Institute of Technology, Cambridge; Cape Cod National Seashore; New Bedford and the islands of Nantucket and Martha's Vineyard, former whaling ports; Berkshire Hills with Tanglewood and other performing-arts centers; the battlefields of Lexington and Concord near Minute Man National Historical Park; Salem, site of witch trials; Plymouth Rock
products electronic, communications, and optical equipment; precision instruments; nonelectrical machinery; fish; cranberries; dairy products
famous people Samuel Adams, Louis Brandeis, Emily Dickinson, Ralph Waldo Emerson, Robert Goddard, Nathaniel Hawthorne, Oliver Wendell Holmes, Winslow Homer, William James, John F Kennedy, Robert Lowell, Paul Revere, Henry Thoreau, Daniel Webster
history one of the original 13 states, it was first settled 1620 by the Pilgrims at Plymouth. After the ◊Boston Tea Party 1773, the American Revolution began at Lexington and Concord April 19, 1775, and the British evacuated Boston the following year. Massachusetts became a state 1788.

In the early 19th century the first large-scale factories were built here to turn out textiles. The state also prospered from whaling and shipbuilding. Heavy immigration of Irish, Germans, and Italians greatly modified the Yankee character of Massachusetts by 1900. After World War II, high technology, sophisticated services, and tourism replaced textiles, footwear, and maritime activities as the mainspring of the economy.

massage manipulation of the soft tissue of the body, the muscles, ligaments, and tendons, either to encourage the healing of specific injuries or to produce the general beneficial effects of relaxing muscular tension, stimulating blood circulation, and improving the tone and strength of the skin and muscles.

Massasoit also known as Ousamequin, "Yellow Feather" c. 1590–1661. American chief of the Wampanoag, a people inhabiting the coasts of Massachusetts Bay and Cape Cod. He formed alliances with Plymouth Colony 1621 and Massachusetts Bay Colony 1638. After his death, his son Metacomet, known to the English as "King ◊Philip," took over his father's leadership.

mass–energy equation Albert ◊Einstein's equation $E = mc^2$, denoting the equivalence of mass and energy, where E is the energy in joules, m is the mass in kilograms, and c is the speed of light, in a vacuum, in meters per second.

Massif Central mountainous plateau region of S central France; area 36,000 sq mi/93,000 sq km, highest peak Puy de Sancy, 6,188 ft/1,886 m. It is a source of hydroelectricity.

mass number or *nucleon number* sum (symbol A) of the numbers of protons and neutrons in the nucleus of an atom. It is used along with the ◊atomic number (the number of protons) in ◊nuclear notation: in symbols that represent nuclear isotopes, such as $^{14}_{6}C$, the lower number is the atomic number, and the upper number is the mass number.

Massorah collection of philological notes on the Hebrew text of the Old Testament. It was at first an oral tradition, but was committed to writing in the Aramaic language at Tiberias, Palestine, between the 6th and 9th centuries.

mass production manufacture of goods on a large scale, a technique that aims for low unit cost and high output. In factories mass production is achieved by a variety of means, such as division and specialization of labor and ◊mechanization. These speed up production and allow the manufacture of near-identical, interchangeable parts. Such parts can then be assembled quickly into a finished product on an ◊assembly line.

Masterson Bat (William Barclay) 1853–1921. US marshal and sportswriter. In 1878 he succeeded his murdered brother, Edward, as marshal in Dodge City, Kansas, and gunned down his brother's killers in the famous gunfight at the OK Corral 1881 at Tombstone in Arizona. He moved to New York 1902, where he became a sportswriter for the *Morning Telegraph*.

mastiff breed of powerful dog, usually fawn in color, that was originally bred in Britain for hunting purposes. It has a large head, wide-set eyes, and broad muzzle. It can grow up to 3 ft/90 cm at the shoulder, and weigh 220 lb/100 kg.

mastodon any of an extinct family (Mastodontidae) of mammals of the elephant order (Proboscidae). They differed from elephants and mammoths in the structure of their grinding teeth. There were numerous species, among which the American mastodon *Mastodon americanum*, about 10 ft/3 m high, of the Pleistocene era, is well known. They were hunted by humans for food.

Mastroianni Marcello 1924– . Italian film actor, most popular for his carefully understated roles as an unhappy romantic lover in such films as Antonioni's *La notte/The Night* 1961. He starred in several films with Sophia Loren, including *Una giornata speciale/A Special Day* 1977, and worked with Fellini in *La dolce vita* 1960, *8 ½* 1963, *Roma* 1971, and *Ginger and Fred* 1986.

Mata Hari Adopted name of Gertrud Margarete Zelle 1876–1917. Dutch courtesan, dancer, and probable spy. In World War I she had affairs with highly placed military and government officials on both sides and told Allied secrets to the Germans. She may have been a double agent, in the pay of both France and Germany. She was shot by the French on espionage charges.

matamata South American freshwater turtle or terrapin *Chelys fimbriata* with a shell up to 15 in/40 cm long. The head is flattened, with a "snorkel" nose, and the neck has many projections of skin. The movement of these in the water may attract prey, which the matamata catches by opening its mouth suddenly to produce an inrush of water.

materialism philosophical theory that there is nothing in existence over and above matter and matter in motion. Such a theory excludes the possibility of deities. It also sees mind as an attribute of the physical, denying idealist theories that see mind as something independent of body; for example, Descartes' theory of "thinking substance."

mathematical induction formal method of proof in which the proposition $P(n + 1)$ is proved true on the hypothesis that the proposition $P(n)$ is true. The proposition is then shown to be true for a particular value of n, say k, and therefore by induction the proposition must be true for $n = k + 1, k + 2, k + 3, \ldots$. In many cases $k = 1$, so then the proposition is true for all positive integers.

mathematics science of spatial and numerical relationships. The main divisions of *pure mathematics* include geometry, arithmetic, algebra, calculus, and

---

mathematical symbols

$a \rightarrow b$	a implies b
∞	infinity
lim	limiting value
$a \sim b$	numerical difference between a and b
$a \approx b$	a approximately equal to b
$a = b$	a equal to b
$a = b$	a identical with b (for formulae only)
$a > b$	a greater than b
$a < b$	a less than b
$a \neq b$	a not equal to b
$b < a < c$	a greater than b and less than c, that is a lies between the values b & c but cannot equal either
$a \geqslant b$	a equal to or greater than b, that is, a at least as great as b
$a \leqslant b$	a equal to or less than b, that is, a at most as great as b
$a \leqslant b \leqslant c$	a lies between the values b & c and could take the values b and c
$\lvert a \rvert$	absolute value of a, this is always positive, for example $\lvert -5 \rvert = 5$
$+$	addition sign, positive
$-$	subtraction sign, negative
$\times$ or $\odot$	multiplication sign, times
$\div$ or $/$	division sign, divided by
$a + b = c$	$a + b$, read as "a minus b", denotes the addition of a and b. The result of the addition, c, is also known as the sum
$\int$	indefinite integral
$_a\int^b f(x)dx$	definite integral, or integral between $x = a$ and $x = b$
$a - b = c$	$a - b$, read as "a minus b," denotes subtraction of b from a $a - b$, or c, is the difference. Subtraction is the opposite of addition
$a \times b = c$ $ab = c$ $a \cdot b = c$	$\left\{ \begin{array}{l} a \times b, \text{ read as "}a \text{ multiplied by b," denotes multiplication of } a \text{ by } b \\ c \text{ is the product, } a \text{ and } b \text{ are factors of } c \end{array} \right.$
$a \div b = c$ $a/b = c$	$\left\{ \begin{array}{l} a \div c, \text{ read as "}a \text{ divided by b," denotes division. } a \text{ is the dividend, } b \text{ is the divisor; } c \text{ is the quotient} \\ \text{In fractions, } \frac{a}{b} \text{ or } a/b, a \text{ is the numerator (= dividend), } b \text{ the denominator (= divisor)} \end{array} \right.$
$a^b = c$	a^b, read as "a to the power b"; a is the base, b the exponent
$^b\sqrt{a} = c$	$^b\sqrt{a}$, is the bth root of a, b being known as the root exponent. In the special case of $^2\sqrt{a} = c$, $^2\sqrt{}$ a or c is known as the square root of a, and the root exponent is usually omitted, that is, $^2\sqrt{a} = \sqrt{a}$
e	exponential constant and is the base of natural (napierian) logarithms $= 2.7182818284...$
π	ratio of the circumference of a circle to its diameter $3.1415925535...$

---

trigonometry. Mechanics, statistics, numerical analysis, computing, the mathematical theories of astronomy, electricity, optics, thermodynamics, and atomic studies come under the heading of *applied mathematics*.

Mather Cotton 1663–1728. American theologian and writer. He was a Puritan minister in Boston, and wrote over 400 works of history, science, annals, and theology, including *Magnalia Christi Americana/The Great Works of Christ in America* 1702, a vast compendium of early New England history and experience. Mather appears to have supported the Salem witch-hunts.

Mather Increase 1639–1723. American colonial and religious leader. As a defender of the colonial right to self-government, he went to England 1688 to protest revocation of the Massachusetts charter. However, his silence during the Salem witch trials of 1692 lessened his public influence.

Mathewson Christy (Christopher) 1880–1925. US baseball player. He was signed by the New York Giants of the National League 1900 and during a 17-year major-league career, he amassed an impressive record of 373 wins and 188 losses. He retired from play 1916, becoming manager of the Cincinnati Reds 1916–18. Baseball Hall of Fame 1936.

Matisse Henri 1869–1954. French painter, sculptor, illustrator, and designer; one of the most original creative forces in early 20th-century art. His work concentrates on designs that emphasize curvaceous surface patterns, linear arabesques, and brilliant color. Subjects include odalisques (women of the harem), bathers, and dancers; later works include pure abstracts, as in his collages of colored paper shapes and the designs 1949–51 for the decoration of a chapel for the Dominican convent in Vence, near Nice.

Mato Grosso (Portuguese "dense forest") area of SW Brazil, now forming two states, with their capitals at Cuiaba and Campo Grande. The forests, now depleted, supplied rubber and rare timbers; diamonds and silver are mined.

matriarchy form of social organization in which the mother is recognized as head of the family or group, with descent and kinship traced to the mother, and where women rule or dominate the group's organization. See also ◊matriliny.

matrix in mathematics, a square ($n \times n$) or rectangular ($m \times n$) array of elements (numbers or algebraic variables). They are a means of condensing information about mathematical systems and can be used for, among other things, solving ◊simultaneous linear equations and transformations.

matter in physics, anything that has mass and can be detected and measured. All matter is made up of ◊atoms, which in turn are made up of ◊elementary particles; it exists ordinarily as a solid, liquid, or gas. The history of science and philosophy is largely taken up with accounts of theories of matter, ranging from the hard "atoms" of Democritus to the "waves" of modern quantum theory.

Matterhorn (French *le Cervin*, Italian *il Cervino*) mountain peak in the Alps on the Swiss-Italian border; 14,690 ft/4,478 m.

Matthau Walter. Adopted name of Walter Matuschanskavasky 1922– . US character actor, impressive in both comedy and dramatic roles. He gained film stardom in the 1960s after his stage success in *The Odd Couple* 1965. His many films include *Kotch* 1971, *Charley Varrick* 1973, and *The Sunshine Boys* 1975.

Matthews Stanley 1824–1889. US jurist. Appointed by President Garfield as associate justice of the US Supreme Court 1881–99, his most important decision, *Hurtado* v *California* 1888, was an important constitutional definition of due process of law.

Matthew, St 1st century AD. Christian apostle and evangelist, the traditional author of the first Gospel. He is usually identified with Levi, who was a tax collector in the service of Herod Antipas, and was called by Jesus to be a disciple as he sat by the Lake of Galilee receiving customs dues. His emblem is a man with wings; feast day Sept 21.

Matthias Corvinus 1440–1490. King of Hungary from 1458. His aim of uniting Hungary, Austria, and Bohemia involved him in long wars with Holy Roman emperor Frederick III and the kings of Bohemia and Poland, during which he captured Vienna (1485) and made it his capital. His father was János Hunyadi.

Maugham (William) Somerset 1874–1965. English writer. His work includes the novels *Of Human Bondage* 1915, *The Moon and Sixpence* 1919, and *Cakes and Ale* 1930; the short-story collections *The Trembling of a Leaf* 1921 and *Ashenden* 1928; and the plays *Lady Frederick* 1907 and *Our Betters* 1923.

Mau Mau Kenyan secret guerrilla movement 1952–60, an offshoot of the Kikuyu Central Association banned in World War II. Its aim was to end British colonial rule. This was achieved 1960 with the granting of Kenyan independence and the election of Jomo Kenyatta as Kenya's first prime minister.

Mauna Kea astronomical observatory in Hawaii, built on a dormant volcano at 13,784 ft/4,200 m above sea level. Because of its elevation high above clouds, atmospheric moisture, and artificial lighting, Mauna Kea is ideal for infrared astronomy. The first telescope on the site was installed 1970.

Mauritania
Islamic Republic of
(*République Islamique de Mauritanie*)

area 397,850 sq mi/1,030,700 sq km
capital Nouakchott
cities port of Nouadhibou, Kaédi, Zouérate
physical valley of river Senegal in S; remainder arid and flat
features part of the Sahara Desert; dusty sirocco wind blows in March
head of state and government Maaouia Ould Sid Ahmed Taya from 1984
political system emergent democratic republic
political parties Democratic and Social Republican Party (PRDS), center-left, militarist; Union of Democratic Forces (UFD), center-left; Rally for Democracy and National Unity (RDUN), centrist; Mauritian Renewal Party (PMR), centrist; Umma, Islamic fundamentalist; Socialist and Democratic Popular Front Union (UDSP), left of center

exports iron ore, fish, gypsum
currency ouguiya
population (1992) 2,108,000 (Arab-Berber 30%, black African 30%, Haratine—descendants of black slaves, who remained slaves until 1980—30%); growth rate 3% p.a.
life expectancy men 43, women 48 (1989)
languages French (official), Hasaniya Arabic, black African languages
religion Sunni Muslim 99%
literacy 17% (1987)
GNP $843 million; $480 per head (1988)

chronology
1903 Became a French protectorate.
1960 Independence achieved from France, with Moktar Ould Daddah as president.
1975 Western Sahara ceded by Spain. Mauritania occupied the southern area and Morocco the north. Polisario Front formed in Sahara to resist the occupation by Mauritania and Morocco.
1978 Daddah deposed in bloodless coup; replaced by Mohamed Khouna Ould Haidalla. Peace agreed with Polisario Front.
1981 Diplomatic relations with Morocco broken.
1984 Haidalla overthrown by Maaouia Ould Sid Ahmed Taya. Polisario regime formally recognized.
1985 Relations with Morocco restored.
1989 Violent clashes between Mauritanians and Senegalese. Arab-dominated government expelled thousands of Africans into N Senegal; governments had earlier agreed to repatriate each other's citizens (about 250,000).
1991 Amnesty for political prisoners. Multiparty elections promised. Calls for resignation of President Taya.
1992 First multiparty elections won by ruling PRDS. Diplomatic relations with Senegal resumed.

Mauna Loa active volcano rising to a height of 13,678 ft/4,169 m on the Pacific island of Hawaii; its craters include the second-largest active crater in the world.

Maundy Thursday in the Christian church, the Thursday before Easter. The ceremony of washing the feet of pilgrims on that day was instituted in commemoration of Jesus' washing of the apostles' feet and observed from the 4th century to 1754.

Maupassant Guy de 1850–1893. French author who established a reputation with the short story "Boule de Suif/Ball of Fat" 1880 and wrote some 300 short stories in all. His novels include *Une Vie/A Woman's Life* 1883 and *Bel-Ami* 1885. He was encouraged as a writer by Gustave ◊Flaubert.

Mauriac François 1885–1970. French novelist. His novel *Le Baiser au lépreux/A Kiss for the Leper* 1922 describes the conflict of an unhappy marriage. The irreconcilability of Christian practice and human nature is examined in *Fleuve de feu/River of Fire* 1923, *Le Désert de l'amour/The Desert of Love* 1925, and *Thérèse Desqueyroux* 1927. Nobel Prize for Literature 1952.

Mauritania country in NW Africa, bounded NE by Algeria, E and S by Mali, SW by Senegal, W by the Atlantic Ocean, and NW by Western Sahara. *See panel p. 601*

Mauritius island country in the Indian Ocean, E of Madagascar.

Maurois André. Adopted name of Emile Herzog 1885–1967. French novelist and writer whose works include the semiautobiographical *Bernard Quesnay* 1926 and fictionalized biographies, such as *Ariel* 1923, a life of Shelley.

Mauryan dynasty Indian dynasty *c.* 321–*c.* 185 BC, founded by *Chandragupta Maurya* (321–*c.* 279 BC).

Under Emperor ◊Asoka most of India was united for the first time, but after his death in 232 the empire was riven by dynastic disputes. Reliant on a highly organized aristocracy and a centralized administration, it survived until the assassination of Emperor Brihadratha 185 BC and the creation of the Sunga dynasty.

Maxim Hiram Stevens 1840–1916. US-born British inventor of the first automatic machine gun, in 1884.

Maximilian 1832–1867. Emperor of Mexico 1864–67. He accepted that title when the French emperor Napoleon III's troops occupied the country, but encountered resistance from the deposed president Benito ◊Juárez. In 1866, after the French troops withdrew on the insistence of the US, Maximilian was captured by Mexican republicans and shot.

Maximilian I 1459–1519. Holy Roman emperor from 1493, the son of Emperor Frederick III. He had acquired the Low Countries through his marriage to Mary of Burgundy 1477.

maxwell unit (symbol Mx) of magnetic flux (the strength of a ◊magnetic field in an area multiplied by the area). It is now replaced by the SI unit, the ◊weber (one maxwell equals 10^{-8} weber).

Maxwell (Ian) Robert (born Jan Ludvik Hoch) 1923–1991. Czech-born British publishing and newspaper proprietor who owned several UK national newspapers, including the *Daily Mirror*, the Macmillan Publishing Company, and the New York *Daily News*. At the time of his death the Maxwell domain carried debts of some $3.9 billion.

Maxwell James Clerk 1831–1879. Scottish physicist. His main achievement was in the understanding of ◊electromagnetic waves: *Maxwell's equations* bring together electricity, magnetism, and light in one

---

Mauritius
Republic of

area 720 sq mi/1,865 sq km; the island of Rodrigues is part of Mauritius; there are several small island dependencies
capital Port Louis
cities Beau Bassin-Rose Hill, Curepipe, Quater Bornes
physical mountainous, volcanic island surrounded by coral reefs
features unusual wildlife includes flying fox and ostrich; it was the home of the dodo (extinct from about 1680)
interim head of state Veerasamy Ringadoo from 1992
head of government Aneerood Jugnauth from 1982
political system liberal democratic republic
political parties Mauritius Socialist Movement (MSM),

moderate socialist-republican; Mauritius Labor Party (MLP), centrist, Hindu-oriented; Mauritius Social Democratic Party (PMSD), conservative, Francophile; Mauritius Militant Movement (MMM), Marxist-republican; Rodriguais People's Organization (OPR), left of center
exports sugar, knitted goods, tea
currency Mauritius rupee
population (1992) 1,081,000, 68% of Indian origin; growth rate 1.5% p.a.
life expectancy men 64, women 71 (1989)
languages English (official), French, Creole, Indian languages
religions Hindu 51%, Christian 30%, Muslim 17%
literacy 94% (1989)
GNP $1.4 bn (1987); $1,810 per head (1988)

chronology
1814 Annexed to Britain by the Treaty of Paris.
1968 Independence achieved from Britain within the Commonwealth, with Seewoosagur Ramgoolam as prime minister.
1982 Aneerood Jugnauth became prime minister.
1983 Jugnauth formed a new party, the Mauritius Socialist Movement. Ramgoolam appointed governor-general. Jugnauth formed a new coalition government.
1985 Ramgoolam died; succeeded by Veersamy Ringadoo.
1987 Jugnauth's coalition reelected.
1990 Attempt to create a republic failed.
1991 Jugnauth's ruling MSM–MMM–OPR coalition won general election; pledge to secure republican status by 1992.
1992 Mauritius became a republic while remaining a member of the Commonwealth. Ringadoo became interim president.

set of relations. He contributed to every branch of physical science—studying gases, optics, and the sensation of color. His theoretical work in magnetism prepared the way for wireless telegraphy and telephony.

Maya member of a group of Central American Indians who lived in agricultural villages in and around the Yucatán Peninsula and Guatemalan highlands from at least 3000 BC, and who developed a civilization of city-states that flourished from about AD 300 until about 900, when Toltecs from the Valley of Mexico moved south into the area, building new ceremonial centers of their own and dominating the local people. Nevertheless, Mayan sovereignty was maintained, for the most part, until late in the Spanish Conquest 1560s in some areas. The Maya had been ruled by a theocracy supported by taxation and tribute; they traded with their neighbors to the north and south; developed advanced mathematics, astronomy, art, and architecture; a glyph system of writing on stone, ceramics, and in book form; and they celebrated a complex religion with a calendar, many deities, and ceremonies that included a form of ball game and human sacrifice. Today they are Roman Catholic, live in farming and fishing villages, as well as the cities of Yucatán, Guatemala, Belize, and W Honduras. Many still speak Maya, a member of the Totonac-Mayan language family, as well as Spanish.

Mayan art art of the Central American civilization of the Maya, between about AD 300 and 900. Mayan figures have distinctive squat proportions and squared-off composition. Large, steeply inclined pyramids were built, such as those at ◊Chichen Itzá, decorated with sculpture and inscription.

May Day first day of May. In many countries it is a national holiday in honor of labor; see also ◊Labor Day.

Mayer Louis B(urt). Adopted name of Eliezer Mayer 1885–1957. Russian-born US film producer. Attracted to the entertainment industry, he became a successful theater-owner in New England and in 1914 began to buy the distribution rights to feature films. Mayer was soon involved in film production, moving to Los Angeles 1918 and becoming one of the founders of Metro-Goldwyn-Mayer (MGM) studios 1924. In charge of production, Mayer instituted the Hollywood "star" system. He retired from MGM 1951.

Mayflower the ship in which the ◊Pilgrims sailed 1620 from Plymouth, England, to found Plymouth plantation and Plymouth colony in present-day Massachusetts.

The *Mayflower* was one of two ships scheduled for departure in 1620. The second ship, the *Speedwell*, was deemed unseaworthy, so 102 people were crowded into the 90-foot *Mayflower*, which was bound for Virginia. Tension between Pilgrim and non-Pilgrim passengers threatened to erupt into a mutiny. Blown off course, the ship reached Cape Cod, Massachusetts, in December. The Mayflower Compact was drafted to establish self-rule for the Plymouth colony and to protect the rights of all the settlers.

Mayo county in Connacht province, Republic of Ireland
area 2,084 sq mi/5,400 sq km
cities Castlebar (administrative town)
features Lough Conn; wild Atlantic coast scenery; Achill Island; the village of Knock, where two women claimed a vision of the Virgin with two saints 1879, now a site of pilgrimage; Croagh Patrick 2,510 ft/765 m, the mountain where St Patrick spent the 40 days of Lent in 441; pilgrims climb the mountain on the last Sunday of July each year

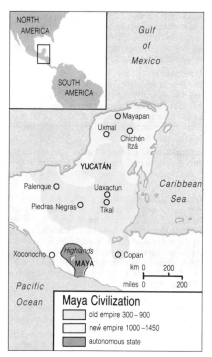

Maya Civilization
- [ ] old empire 300–900
- [ ] new empire 1000–1450
- [ ] autonomous state

products sheep and cattle farming; fishing
population (1991) 110,700.

mayor title of head of local administration for a town or city. Powers vary widely, although generally mayors oversee financial issues, local education, public safety, planning and zoning, taxation, and other aspects of municipal government.

Mays Willie (Howard Jr) 1931– . US baseball player who played with the New York (later San Francisco) Giants 1951–72 and the New York Mets 1973. He hit 660 career home runs, third best in baseball history, and was also an outstanding fielder and runner. He was the National League's Most Valuable Player 1954 and 1965.

Born in Westfield, Alabama, Mays was elected to the Baseball Hall of Fame 1979.

Mazarin Jules 1602–1661. French politician who succeeded Richelieu as chief minister of France 1642. His

Mayan art *A Chac Mool idol reclines at the center of a former sacrificial altar in the city of Chichen Itzá.*

attack on the power of the nobility led to the ◊Fronde and his temporary exile, but his diplomacy achieved a successful conclusion to the Thirty Years' War, and, in alliance with Oliver Cromwell during the British protectorate, he gained victory over Spain.

Mazowiecki Tadeusz 1927– . Polish politician, founder member of ◊Solidarity, and Poland's first postwar noncommunist prime minister 1989–90. Forced to introduce unpopular economic reforms, he was knocked out in the first round of the Nov 1990 presidential elections, resigning in favor of his former colleague Lech ◊Wałesa.

mazurka lively national dance of Poland from the 16th century. In triple time, it is characterized by footstamping and heel-clicking, together with a turning movement.

Mazzini Giuseppe 1805–1872. Italian nationalist. He was a member of the revolutionary society, the ◊Carbonari, and founded in exile the nationalist movement Giovane Italia (Young Italy) 1832. Returning to Italy on the outbreak of the 1848 revolution, he headed a republican government established in Rome, but was forced into exile again on its overthrow 1849. He acted as a focus for the movement for Italian unity (see ◊Risorgimento).

Mbabane capital (since 1902) of Swaziland, 100 mi/160 km W of Maputo, in the Dalgeni Hills; population (1986) 38,000. Mining and tourism are important.

McKinley William 1843–1901. 25th president of the US 1897–1901, a republican. His term as president was marked by the US's adoption of an imperialist policy, as exemplified by the Spanish-American War 1898 and the annexation of the Philippines. He was first elected to congress 1876. He was assassinated.

McKinley was born in Niles, Ohio, and became a lawyer. Throughout his political life, he was a trusted friend of business interests, supporting high tariffs for fledgling US industries. He sat in the House of Representatives 1877–83 and 1885–91, and was governor of Ohio 1892–96. As president he presided over a period of prosperity and was drawn into foreign conflicts largely against his will. He annexed the Philippine

Islands and implemented the ◊Open Door Policy with China. He was assassinated in Buffalo, New York, and was succeeded by Theodore Roosevelt.

MD abbreviation for *Doctor of Medicine*.

MD abbreviation for the state of ◊Maryland.

MDMA (3,4-methylenedio-xymethamphetamine) psychedelic drug, also known as ◊ecstasy.

ME abbreviation for the state of ◊Maine.

ME abbreviation for *myalgic encephalitis*, a debilitating condition also known as ◊chronic fatigue syndrome.

mead alcoholic drink made from honey and water fermented with yeast, often with added spices. It was known in ancient times and was drunk by the Greeks, Britons, and Norse.

Mead Margaret 1901–1978. US anthropologist who popularized cultural relativity and challenged the conventions of Western society with *Coming of Age in Samoa* 1928 and subsequent works. Her fieldwork was later criticized. She was a popular speaker on civil liberties, ecological sanity, feminism, and population control.

Meade George Gordon 1815–1872. US military leader. During the American Civil War, he commanded the Pennsylvania volunteers at the Peninsular Campaign, Bull Run, and Antietam 1862. He led the Army of the Potomac, and the Union forces at Gettysburg 1863. After the war, he served as military governor of Georgia, Alabama, and Florida 1868–69.

mean in mathematics, a measure of the average of a number of terms or quantities. The simple *arithmetic mean* is the average value of the quantities, that is, the sum of the quantities divided by their number. The *weighted mean* takes into account the frequency of the terms that are summed; it is calculated by multiplying each term by the number of times it occurs, summing the results and dividing this total by the total number of occurrences. The *geometric mean* of n quantities is the nth root of their product. In statistics, it is a measure of central tendency of a set of data.

meander The river Cuckmere, Sussex, England, meanders over the flood plain near its mouth.

meander loop-shaped curve in a river flowing across flat country. As a river flows, any curve in its course is accentuated by the current. The current is fastest on the outside of the curve where it cuts into the bank; on the curve's inside the current is slow and deposits any transported material. In this way the river changes its course across the flood plain.

A loop in a river's flow may become so accentuated that it becomes cut off from the normal course and forms an ◊oxbow lake. The word comes from the river Menderes in Turkey.

measles acute virus disease (rubeola), spread by airborne infection. Symptoms are fever, severe catarrh, small spots inside the mouth, and a raised, blotchy red rash appearing for about a week after two weeks' incubation. Prevention is by vaccination.

meat flesh of animals taken as food, in Western countries chiefly from domesticated herds of cattle, sheep, pigs, and poultry. Major exporters include Argentina, Australia, New Zealand, the US, and Denmark (chiefly bacon). The practice of cooking meat is at least 600,000 years old. More than 40% of the world's grain is now fed to animals.

Meath county in the province of Leinster, Republic of Ireland
area 903 sq mi/2,340 sq km
county town Trim
features Tara Hill, 509 ft/155 m high, was the site of a palace and coronation place of many kings of Ireland (abandoned in the 6th century) and St Patrick preached here
products sheep, cattle
population (1991) 105,600.

Mecca (Arabic *Makkah*) city in Saudi Arabia and, as birthplace of Mohammed, the holiest city of the Islamic world; population (1974) 367,000. In the center of Mecca is the Great Mosque, in the courtyard of which is the Kaaba, the sacred shrine containing the black stone believed to have been given to Abraham by the angel Gabriel.

mechanics branch of physics dealing with the motions of bodies and the forces causing these motions, and also with the forces acting on bodies in ◊equilibrium. It is usually divided into ◊dynamics and ◊statics.

mechanized infantry combat vehicle (MICV) tracked military vehicle designed to fight as part of an armored battle group; that is, with tanks. It is armed with a quick-firing cannon and one or more machine guns. MICVs have replaced armored personnel carriers.

Mechnikov Ilya 1845–1916. Russian scientist who discovered the function of white blood cells and ◊phagocytes. After leaving Russia and joining ◊Pasteur in Paris, he described how these "scavenger cells" can attack the body itself (autoimmune disease). He shared the Nobel Prize for Medicine 1908 with Paul ◊Ehrlich.

Mecklenburg–West Pomerania (German *Mecklenburg-Vorpommern*) administrative *Land* (state) of Germany
area 8,840 sq mi/22,887 sq km
capital Schwerin
cities Rostock, Wismar, Stralsund, Neubrandenburg
products fish, ships, diesel engines, electronics, plastics, chalk
population (1990) 2,100,000
history the state was formerly the two grand duchies of Mecklenburg-Schwerin and Mecklenburg-Strelitz, which became free states of the Weimar Republic 1918–34, and were joined 1946 with part of Pomerania to form a region of East Germany. In 1952 it was split into the districts of Rostock, Schwerin, and Neubrandenburg. Following German reunification 1990, the districts were abolished and Mecklenburg–West Pomerania was reconstructed as one of the five new states of the Federal Republic.

Medan seaport and economic center of the island of Sumatra, Indonesia; population (1980) 1,379,000. It trades in rubber, tobacco, and palm oil.

Medawar Peter (Brian) 1915–1987. Brazilian-born British immunologist who, with Macfarlane Burnet, discovered that the body's resistance to grafted tissue is undeveloped in the newborn child, and studied the way it is acquired.

Mede member of a people of NW Iran who in the 9th century BC were tributaries to Assyria, with their capital at Ecbatana (now Hamadán), in the ancient SW Asian country of Media. Allying themselves with Babylon, they destroyed the Assyrian capital of ◊Nineveh 612 BC, and extended their conquests into central Anatolia. In 550 BC they were overthrown by the Persians, with whom they rapidly merged.

Medea in Greek mythology, the sorceress daughter of the king of Colchis. When ◊Jason reached Colchis, she fell in love with him, helped him acquire the ◊Golden Fleece, and they fled together. When Jason later married Creusa, daughter of the king of Corinth, Medea killed his bride with the gift of a poisoned garment, and then killed her own two children by Jason.

Medellín industrial city (textiles, chemicals, engineering, coffee) in the Central Cordillera, Colombia, 5,048 ft/1,538 m above sea level; population (1985) 2,069,000. It is the second city of Colombia, and its drug capital, with 7,000 violent deaths in 1990.

Medford city in SW Oregon, S of Eugene; seat of Jackson County; population (1990) 47,000. It is a summer resort, and tourism is important to the economy. Other industries include processing of the area's agricultural crops and dairy products.

median in mathematics and statistics, the middle number of an ordered group of numbers. If there is no middle number (because there is an even number of terms), the median is the ◊mean (average) of the two middle numbers. For example, the median of the group 2, 3, 7, 11, 12 is 7; that of 3, 4, 7, 9, 11, 13 is 8 (the average of 7 and 9).

Medici noble family of Florence, the city's rulers from 1434 until they died out 1737. Family members included ◊Catherine de' Medici, Pope ◊Leo X, Pope ◊Clement VII, ◊Marie de' Medici.

Medici Cosimo de' 1389–1464. Italian politician and banker. Regarded as the model for Machiavelli's *The Prince*, he dominated the government of Florence from 1434 and was a patron of the arts. He was succeeded by his inept son *Piero de' Medici* (1416–1469).

Medici Lorenzo de', *the Magnificent* 1449–1492. Italian politician, ruler of Florence from 1469. He was also a poet and a generous patron of the arts.

medicine science of preventing, diagnosing, alleviating, or curing disease, both physical and mental; also any substance used in the treatment of disease. The basis of medicine is anatomy (the structure and form of the body) and physiology (the study of the body's functions).

medicine, alternative forms of medical treatment that do not use synthetic drugs or surgery in response

Western medicine: chronology

c. 400 BC	Hippocrates recognized that disease had natural causes.
c. AD 200	Galen consolidated the work of the Alexandrian doctors.
1543	Andreas Vesalius gave the first accurate account of the human body.
1628	William Harvey discovered the circulation of the blood.
1768	John Hunter began the foundation of experimental and surgical pathology.
1785	Digitalis was used to treat heart disease; the active ingredient was isolated 1904.
1798	Edward Jenner published his work on vaccination.
1877	Patrick Manson studied animal carriers of infectious diseases.
1882	Robert Koch isolated the bacillus responsible for tuberculosis.
1884	Edwin Klebs isolated the diphtheria bacillus.
1885	Louis Pasteur produced a vaccine against rabies.
1890	Joseph Lister demonstrated antiseptic surgery.
1895	Wilhelm Röntgen discovered X-rays.
1897	Martinus Beijerinck discovered viruses.
1899	Felix Hoffman developed aspirin; Sigmund Freud founded psychiatry.
1900	Karl Landsteiner identified the first three blood groups, later designated A, B, and O.
1910	Paul Ehrlich developed the first specific antibacterial agent, Salvarsan, a cure for syphilis.
1922	Insulin was first used to treat diabetes.
1928	Alexander Fleming discovered penicillin.
1932	Gerhard Domagk discovered the first antibacterial sulphonamide drug, Prontosil.
1937	Electro-convulsive therapy (ECT) was developed.
1940s	Lithium treatment for manic-depressive illness was developed.
1950s	Antidepressant drugs and beta-blockers for heart disease were developed. Manipulation of the molecules of synthetic chemicals became the main source of new drugs. Peter Medawar studied the body's tolerance of transplanted organs and skin grafts.
1950	Proof of a link between cigarette smoking and lung cancer was established.
1953	Francis Crick and James Watson announced the structure of DNA. Jonas Salk developed a vaccine against polio.
1958	Ian Donald pioneered diagnostic ultrasound.
1960s	A new generation of minor tranquilizers called benzodiazepines was developed.
1967	Christian Barnard performed the first human heart-transplant operation.
1971	Viroids, disease-causing organisms even smaller than viruses, were isolated outside the living body.
1972	The CAT scan, pioneered by Godfrey Hounsfield, was first used to image the human brain.
1975	César Milstein developed monoclonal antibodies.
1978	World's first *test-tube baby* was born in the UK.
1980s	AIDS (acquired immune-deficiency syndrome) was first recognized in the US. Barbara McClintock's discovery of the transposable gene was recognized.
1980	The World Health Organization reported the eradication of smallpox.
1983	The virus responsible for AIDS, now known as human immunodeficiency virus (HIV), was identified by Luc Montagnier at the Institut Pasteur, Paris; Robert Gallo at the National Cancer Institute, Maryland discovered the virus independently 1984.
1984	A vaccine against leprosy was developed.
1987	The world's longest-surviving heart-transplant patient died in France, 18 years after his operation.
1989	Grafts of fetal brain tissue were first used to treat Parkinson's disease.
1990	Gene for maleness discovered by UK researchers.
1991	First successful use of gene therapy (to treat severe combined immune deficiency) was reported in the US.
1993	First trials of gene therapy against cystic fibrosis occurred in the US.

to the symptoms of a disease, but aim to treat the patient as a whole (holism). The emphasis is on maintaining health (with diet and exercise) and on dealing with the underlying causes rather than just the symptoms of illness. It may involve the use of herbal remedies and techniques like ◊acupuncture, ◊homeopathy, and ◊chiropractic. Some alternative treatments are increasingly accepted by orthodox medicine, but the absence of enforceable standards in some fields has led to the proliferation of eccentric or untrained practitioners.

medieval art painting and sculpture of the Middle Ages in Europe and parts of the Middle East, dating roughly from the 4th century to the emergence of the Renaissance in Italy in the 1400s. This includes early Christian, Byzantine, Celtic, Anglo-Saxon, and Carolingian art. The Romanesque style was the first truly international style of medieval times, superseded by Gothic in the late 12th century. Religious sculpture, frescoes, and manuscript illumination proliferated; panel painting came only toward the end of the period.

Medina (Arabic **Madinah**) Saudi Arabian city, about 220 mi/355 km N of Mecca; population (1974) 198,000. It is the second-holiest city in the Islamic world, and is believed to contain the tomb of Mohammed. It produces grain and fruit.

meditation act of spiritual contemplation, practiced by members of many religions or as a secular exercise. It is a central practice in Buddhism. The Sanskrit term is *dhyāna*. See also ◊transcendental meditation (TM).

Mediterranean Sea inland sea separating Europe from N Africa, with Asia to the E; extreme length 2,300 mi/3,700 km; area 1,145,000 sq mi/2,966,000 sq km. It is linked to the Atlantic Ocean (at the Strait of Gibraltar), Red Sea, and Indian Ocean (by the Suez Canal), Black Sea (at the Dardanelles and Sea of Marmara). The main subdivisions are the Adriatic, Aegean, Ionian, and Tyrrhenian seas. It is highly polluted.

medulla central part of an organ. In the mammalian kidney, the medulla lies beneath the outer cortex and

Mediterranean Sea

is responsible for the reabsorption of water from the filtrate. In plants, it is a region of packing tissue in the center of the stem. In the vertebrate brain, the medulla is the posterior region responsible for the coordination of basic activities, such as breathing and temperature control.

Medusa in Greek legend, a mortal woman who was transformed into a ◊Gorgon. Medusa was slain by ◊Perseus; the winged horse ◊Pegasus was supposed to have sprung from her blood. Her head was so hideous—even in death—that any beholder was turned to stone.

megabyte (Mb) in computing, a unit of memory equal to 1,024 ◊kilobytes. It is sometimes used, less precisely, to mean 1 million bytes.

megalith prehistoric stone monument of the late Neolithic or early Bronze Age. Megaliths include single, large uprights (menhirs); rows; circles, generally with a central "altar stone" (for example Stonehenge); and the remains of burial chambers with the covering earth removed, looking like a hut (dolmens).

megaton one million (10^6) tons. Used with reference to the explosive power of a nuclear weapon, it is equivalent to the explosive force of one million tons of trinitrotoluene (TNT).

Meghalaya state of NE India
area 8,685 sq mi/22,500 sq km
capital Shillong
features mainly agricultural and comprises tribal hill districts
products potatoes, cotton, jute, fruit
minerals coal, limestone, white clay, corundum, sillimanite
population (1991) 1,760,600, mainly Khasi, Jaintia, and Garo
religion Hindu 70%
languages various.

Megiddo site of a fortress town in N Israel, where Thothmes III defeated the Canaanites about 1469 BC; the Old Testament figure Josiah was killed in battle about 609 BC; and in World War I the British field marshal Allenby broke the Turkish front 1918. It is identified with ◊Armageddon.

Mehemet Ali 1769–1849. Pasha (governor) of Egypt from 1805, and founder of the dynasty that ruled until 1953. An Albanian in the Ottoman service, he had originally been sent to Egypt to fight the French. As pasha, he established a European-style army and

navy, fought his Turkish overlord 1831 and 1839, and conquered Sudan.

Mehta Zubin 1936– . Indian conductor who became music director of the New York Philharmonic 1978. He is known for his flamboyant style of conducting and his interpretations of the Romantic composers.

Meiji Mutsuhito 1852–1912. Emperor of Japan from 1867, under the regnal era name Meiji ("enlightened"). During his reign Japan became a world industrial and naval power. His ministers abolished the feudal system and discrimination against the lowest caste, established state schools, reformed the civil service, and introduced the Western calendar and other modernizing measures, including a constitution 1889.

Meinhof Ulrike 1934–1976. West German urban guerrilla, member of the ◊Baader–Meinhof gang in the 1970s.

Mein Kampf (German "my struggle") book dictated by Adolf ◊Hitler to Rudolf Hess 1923–24 during Hitler's jail sentence for his part in the abortive 1923 Munich beer-hall putsch. Part autobiography, part political philosophy, the book presents Hitler's ideas of German expansion, anticommunism, and anti-Semitism. It was published in two volumes, 1925 and 1927.

meiosis in biology, a process of cell division in which the number of ◊chromosome in the cell is halved. It only occurs in eukaryotic cells, and is part of a life cycle that involves sexual reproduction because it allows the genes of two parents to be combined without the total number of chromosomes increasing. *See illustration p. 608*

Meir Golda 1898–1978. Israeli Labor (*Mapai*) politician. Born in Russia, she emigrated to the US 1906, and in 1921 went to Palestine. She was foreign minis-

Meir Golda Meir was prime minister of Israel from 1969 to 1974.

meiosis Meiosis is a type of cell division that produces gametes (sex cells, sperm and egg).

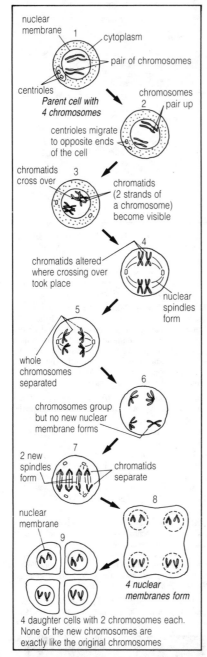

nuclear membrane 1
cytoplasm
pair of chromosomes
centrioles
Parent cell with 4 chromosomes

chromosomes 2 pair up

centrioles migrate to opposite ends of the cell

chromatids cross over 3
chromatids (2 strands of a chromosome) become visible

chromatids altered where crossing over took place 4
nuclear spindles form

5
whole chromosomes separated

6
chromosomes group but no new nuclear membrane forms

2 new spindles form 7
chromatids separate

nuclear membrane 9
8
4 nuclear membranes form

4 daughter cells with 2 chromosomes each. None of the new chromosomes are exactly like the original chromosomes

ter 1956–66 and prime minister 1969–74. Criticism of the Israelis' lack of preparation for the 1973 Arab-Israeli War led to election losses for Labor and, unable to form a government, she resigned.

Meistersinger (German "master singer") one of a group of German lyric poets, singers, and musicians of the 14th–16th centuries, who formed guilds for the revival of minstrelsy. Hans Sachs was a Meistersinger, and Richard Wagner's opera, *Die Meistersinger von Nürnberg* 1868, depicts the tradition.

Mekong river rising as the Za Qu in Tibet and flowing to the South China Sea, through a vast delta (about 77,000 sq mi/200,000 sq km); length 2,750 mi/4,425 km. It is being developed for irrigation and hydroelectricity by Cambodia, Laos, Thailand, and Vietnam.

Melanesia islands in the SW Pacific between Micronesia to the N and Polynesia to the E, embracing all the islands from the New Britain archipelago to Fiji.

melanoma mole or growth containing the dark pigment melanin. Malignant melanoma is a type of skin cancer developing in association with a pre-existing mole. Unlike other skin cancers, it is associated with brief but excessive exposure to sunlight.

Melbourne capital of Victoria, Australia, near the mouth of the river Yarra; population (1990) 3,080,000. Industries include engineering, shipbuilding, electronics, chemicals, food processing, clothing, and textiles.

Melbourne industrial city (food processing and electronic and aviation equipment) on the E coast of Florida, on the Indian River, SE of Orlando; population (1990) 59,600. Tourism is also important to the economy.

Melchite or *Melkite* member of a Christian church in Syria, Egypt, Lebanon, and Israel. The Melchite Church was founded in Syria in the 6th–7th centuries and is now part of the Eastern Orthodox Church.

melodrama play or film with romantic and sensational plot elements, often unsubtly acted. Originally it meant a play accompanied by music. The early melodramas used extravagant theatrical effects to heighten violent emotions and actions artificially. By the end of the 19th century, melodrama had become a popular genre of stage play.

melon any of several large, juicy (95% water), thick-skinned fruits of trailing plants of the gourd family Cucurbitaceae. The muskmelon *Cucumis melo* and the large red watermelon *Citrullus vulgaris* are two of the many edible varieties.

meltdown the melting of the core of a nuclear reactor, due to overheating. To prevent such accidents all reactors have equipment intended to flood the core with water in an emergency. The reactor is housed in a strong containment vessel, designed to prevent radiation escaping into the atmosphere. The result of a meltdown is an area radioactively contaminated for 25,000 years or more.

melting point temperature at which a substance melts, or changes from a solid to liquid form. A pure substance under standard conditions of pressure (usually one atmosphere) has a definite melting point. If heat is supplied to a solid at its melting point, the temperature does not change until the melting process is complete. The melting point of ice is 0°C or 32°F.

Melville Herman 1819–1891. US writer whose *Moby Dick* 1851 was inspired by his whaling experiences in the South Seas. These experiences were also the basis for earlier fiction, such as *Typee* 1846 and *Omoo* 1847. *Billy Budd* was completed just before his death and published 1924. Although most of his works were unappreciated during his lifetime, today he is one of the most highly regarded of US authors.

membrane in living things, a continuous layer, made up principally of fat molecules, that encloses a ◊cell or organelles within a cell. Certain small molecules can pass through the cell membrane, but most must enter or leave the cell via channels in the membrane made up of special proteins. The Golgi apparatus within the cell is thought to produce certain membranes.

Memling (or *Memlinc*) Hans *c.* 1430–1494. Flemish painter, born near Frankfurt-am-Main, Germany, but active in Bruges. He painted religious subjects and portraits. Some of his works are in the Hospital of St John, Bruges, including the *Adoration of the Magi* 1479.

memory in computing, the part of a system used to store data and programs either permanently or temporarily. There are two main types: immediate access memory and backing storage. Memory capacity is measured in ◊bytes or, more conveniently, in kilobytes (units of 1,024 bytes) or megabytes (units of 1,024 kilobytes).

memory ability to store and recall observations and sensations. Memory does not seem to be based in any particular part of the brain; it may depend on changes to the pathways followed by nerve impulses as they move through the brain. Memory can be improved by regular use as the connections between ◊nerve cells (neurons) become "well-worn paths" in the brain. Events stored in *short-term memory* are forgotten quickly, whereas those in *long-term memory* can last for many years, enabling recall of information and recognition of people and places over long periods of time. Research is just beginning to uncover the biochemical and electrical bases of the human memory.

Memphis ruined city beside the Nile, 12 mi/19 km S of Cairo, Egypt. Once the center of the worship of Ptah, it was the earliest capital of a united Egypt under King Menes about 3200 BC, but was superseded by Thebes under the new empire 1570 BC.

Memphis industrial port city (pharmaceuticals, food processing, cotton, timber, tobacco) on the Mississippi River, in Tennessee; population (1990) 610,300. The French built a fort here 1739, but Memphis was not founded until 1819. Its musical history includes Beale Street, home of the blues composer W C Handy, and Graceland, the home of Elvis Presley; its recording studios and record companies (Sun 1953–68, Stax 1960–75) made it a focus of the music industry.

Menander *c.* 342–291 BC. Greek comic dramatist, born in Athens. His work was virtually unknown until the discovery 1905 of substantial fragments of four of his plays in Egyptian papyri (many had been used as papier-mâché for Egyptian mummy cases). In 1957 the only complete Menander play, *Dyscholos/The Bad-Tempered Man*, was found.

Mencken H(enry) L(ouis) 1880–1956. US essayist and critic, known as "the sage of Baltimore." His unconventionally phrased, satiric contributions to the periodicals *The Smart Set* and *American Mercury* (both of which he edited) aroused controversy.

His critical reviews and essays were gathered in *Prejudices* 1919–27, comprising six volumes. He did not restrict himself to literary criticism, but took nearly every US institution to task in his writings. His book, *The American Language* 1918, is often revised.

Mende member of a W African people living in the rainforests of central east Sierra Leone and W Liberia. They number approximately 1 million. The Mende are farmers as well as hunter-gatherers, and each of their villages is led by a chief and a group of elders. The Mende language belongs to the Niger-Congo family.

Mendel Gregor Johann 1822–1884. Austrian biologist, founder of ◊genetics. His experiments with successive generations of peas gave the basis for his theory of particulate inheritance rather than blending, involving dominant and recessive characters; see ◊Mendelism. His results, published 1865–69, remained unrecognized until the early 20th century.

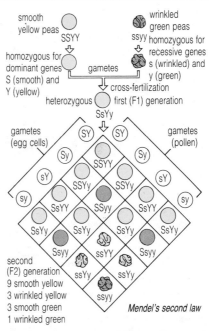

Mendel's second law

second (F2) generation
9 smooth yellow
3 wrinkled yellow
3 smooth green
1 wrinkled green

Mendelism
Mendel's laws explain the proportions of offspring having various characteristics.

Mendeleyev Dmitri Ivanovich 1834–1907. Russian chemist who framed the periodic law in chemistry 1869, which states that the chemical properties of the elements depend on their atomic weights. This law is the basis of the ◊periodic table of elements, in which the elements are arranged by atomic number and organized by their related groups.

Mendelism in genetics, the theory of inheritance originally outlined by Austrian biologist Gregor Mendel. He suggested that, in sexually reproducing species, all characteristics are inherited through indivisible "factors" (now identified with ◊genes) contributed by each parent to its offspring.

Mendelssohn (-Bartholdy) (Jakob Ludwig) Felix 1809–1847. German composer, also a pianist and conductor. As a child he composed and performed with his own orchestra and as an adult was helpful to ◊Schumann's career. Among his best-known works are *A Midsummer Night's Dream* 1827; the *Fingal's Cave* overture 1832; and five symphonies, which include the Reformation 1830, the Italian 1833, and the Scottish 1842. He was instrumental in promoting the revival of interest in J S Bach's music.

Mendes Chico (Filho Francisco) 1944–1988. Brazilian environmentalist and labor leader. Opposed to the destruction of Brazil's rain forests, he organized itinerant rubber tappers into the Workers' Party (PT) and was assassinated by Darci Alves, a cattle rancher's son. Of 488 similar murders in land conflicts in Brazil 1985–89, his was the first to come to trial.

Menelaus in Greek legend, king of Sparta, son of Atreus, brother of ◊Agamemnon, and husband of ◊Helen. With his brother he was joint leader of the Greek expedition against ◊Troy.

Menem Carlos (Saul) 1935– . Argentine politician, president from 1989; leader of the Peronist (Justicialist Party) movement. As president, he introduced sweeping privatization and public spending cuts, released hundreds of political prisoners jailed under the Alfonsín regime, and sent two warships to the Gulf to assist

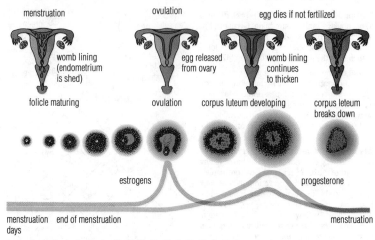

menstruation — ovulation — egg dies if not fertilized

womb lining (endometrium is shed) — egg released from ovary — womb lining continues to thicken

folicle maturing — ovulation — corpus luteum developing — corpus leteum breaks down

estrogens — progesterone

menstruation — end of menstruation — menstruation
days

1 2 3 4 5 6 7 8 9 10 11 12 13 14 15 16 17 18 19 20 21 22 23 24 25 26 27 28 1 2 3

start of menstruation — intercourse could result in fertilization

the US against Iraq in the 1992 Gulf War (the only Latin American country to offer support to the US).

He also improved relations with the UK.

Menéndez de Avilés Pedro 1519–1574. Spanish colonial administrator in America. Philip II of Spain granted him the right to establish a colony in Florida to counter French presence there. In 1565 he founded St Augustine and destroyed the French outpost at Fort Caroline.

Menes *c.* 3200 BC. Traditionally, the first king of the first dynasty of ancient Egypt. He is said to have founded Memphis and organized worship of the gods.

Mengistu Haile Mariam 1937– . Ethiopian soldier and socialist politician, head of state 1977–91 (president 1987–91). He seized power in a coup and was confronted with severe problems of drought and secessionist uprisings, but survived with help from the USSR and the West until his violent overthrow.

meningitis inflammation of the meninges (membranes) surrounding the brain, caused by bacterial or viral infection. Bacterial meningitis, though treatable by antibiotics, is the more serious threat. Diagnosis is by ◊lumbar puncture.

Menninger Karl Augustus 1893–1990. US psychiatrist, instrumental in reforming public mental-health facilities. With his father, prominent psychiatrist Charles Menninger, he founded the Menninger Clinic in Topeka 1920 and with his brother William, also a psychiatrist, established the Menninger Foundation 1941.

Mennonite member of a Protestant Christian sect, originating as part of the ◊Anabaptist movement in Zürich, Switzerland, 1523. Members refuse to hold civil office or do military service, and reject infant baptism. They were named Mennonites after Menno Simons (1496–1559), leader of a group in Holland. Persecution drove other groups to Russia and North America.

menopause in women, the cessation of reproductive ability, characterized by menstruation (see ◊menstrual cycle) becoming irregular and eventually ceasing. The onset is at about the age of 50, but varies greatly. Menopause is usually uneventful, but some women suffer from complications such as flushing,

excessive bleeding, and nervous disorders. Since the 1950s, ◊hormone replacement therapy (HRT), using ◊estrogen alone or with ◊progesterone, has been developed to counteract such effects.

menstrual cycle cycle that occurs in female mammals of reproductive age, in which the body is prepared for pregnancy. At the beginning of the cycle, a Graafian (egg) follicle develops in the ovary, and the inner wall of the uterus forms a soft spongy lining. The egg is released from the ovary, and the lining of the uterus becomes vascularized (filled with blood vessels). If fertilization does not occur, the corpus luteum (remains of the Graafian follicle) degenerates, and the uterine lining breaks down, and is shed. This is what causes the loss of blood that marks menstruation. The cycle then begins again. Human menstruation takes place from puberty to menopause, occurring about every 28 days.

mental handicap impairment of intelligence. It can be very mild, but in more severe cases, it is associated with social problems and difficulties in living independently. A person may be born with a mental handicap (for example, ◊Down's syndrome) or may acquire it through brain damage. There are between 90 and 130 million people in the world suffering such disabilities.

mental illness abnormal working of the mind. Since normal working cannot easily be defined, the borderline between mild mental illness and normality is a matter of opinion (not to be confused with normative behavior). Mild forms are known as *neuroses*, affecting the emotions, whereas more severe forms, *psychoses*, distort conscious reasoning.

menthol pungent, waxy, crystalline alcohol $C_{10}H_{19}OH$, derived from oil of peppermint and used in medicines and cosmetics.

menu in computing, a list of options, displayed on screen, from which the user may make a choice—for example, the choice of services offered to the customer by a bank cash dispenser: withdrawal, deposit, balance, or statement. Menus are used extensively in ◊graphical user-interface (GUI) systems, where the menu options are often selected using a pointing device called a ◊mouse.

Menuhin Yehudi 1916– . US-born violinist and conductor. A child prodigy, he achieved great depth of interpretation, and was often accompanied on the piano by his sister *Hephzibah* (1921–1981). He conducted his own chamber orchestra and founded schools in Surrey, England, and Gstaad, Switzerland, for training young musicians.

Menzies Robert Gordon 1894–1978. Australian politician, leader of the United Australia (now Liberal) Party and prime minister 1939–41 and 1949–66.

Mephistopheles or *Mephisto* another name for the ◊devil, or an agent of the devil, associated with the ◊Faust legend.

mercantilism economic theory, held in the 16th–18th centuries, that a nation's wealth (in the form of bullion or treasure) was the key to its prosperity. To this end, foreign trade should be regulated to create a surplus of exports over imports, and the state should intervene where necessary (for example, subsidizing exports and taxing imports). The bullion theory of wealth was demolished by Adam ◊Smith in Book IV of *The Wealth of Nations* 1776.

Mercator Gerardus 1512–1594. Latinized form of the name of the Flemish map-maker Gerhard Kremer. He devised the first modern atlas, showing *Mercator's projection* in which the parallels and meridians on maps are drawn uniformly at 90°. It is often used for navigational charts, because compass courses can be drawn as straight lines, but the true area of countries is increasingly distorted the further north or south they are from the equator. For other types, see ◊map projection.

Mercedes-Benz German car-manufacturing company created by a merger of the Daimler and Benz factories 1926. The first automobiles to carry the Mercedes name were those built by Gottlieb ◊Daimler 1901.

mercenary soldier hired by the army of another country or by a private army. Mercenary military service originated in the 14th century, when cash payment on a regular basis was the only means of guaranteeing soldiers' loyalty. In the 20th century mercenaries have been common in wars and guerrilla activity in Asia, Africa, and Latin America.

Merchant Ismail 1936– . Indian film producer, known for his stylish collaborations with James Ivory on films including *Shakespeare Wallah* 1965, *The Europeans* 1979, *Heat and Dust* 1983, *A Room with a View* 1985, *Maurice* 1987, and *Howard's End* 1992.

merchant bank financial institution that specializes in corporate finance and financial and advisory services for business. Originally developed in the UK in the 19th century, merchant banks now offer many of the services provided by the commercial banks.

merchant navy the passenger and cargo ships of a country. Most are owned by private companies. To avoid strict regulations on safety, union rules on crew wages, and so on, many ships are today registered under "flags of convenience," that is, flags of countries that do not have such rules.

Mercia Anglo-Saxon kingdom that emerged in the 6th century. By the late 8th century it dominated all England south of the Humber, but from about 825 came under the power of ◊Wessex. Mercia eventually came to denote an area bounded by the Welsh border, the river Humber, East Anglia, and the river Thames.

mercury or *quicksilver* heavy, silver-gray, metallic element, symbol Hg (from Latin *hydrargyrum*), atomic number 80, atomic weight 200.59. It is a dense, mobile liquid with a low melting point ($-37.96°F/-38.87°C$). Its chief source is the mineral cinnabar, HgS, but it sometimes occurs in nature as a free metal.

Mercury in astronomy, the closest planet to the Sun, at an average distance of 36 million mi/58 million km.

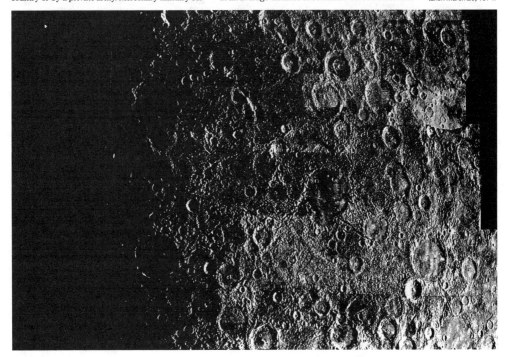

Mercury Mariner 10 spacecraft's photomosaic of the heavily cratered surface of Mercury, taken March 20, 1974.

Its diameter is 3,030 mi/4,880 km, its mass 0.056 that of Earth. Mercury orbits the Sun every 88 days, and spins on its axis every 59 days. On its sunward side the surface temperature reaches over 752°F/400°C, but on the "night" side it falls to −274°F/−170°C. Mercury has an atmosphere with minute traces of argon and helium. In 1974 the US space probe *Mariner 10* discovered that its surface is cratered by meteorite impacts. Mercury has no moons.

Mercury in Roman mythology, a god, identified with the Greek ◊Hermes, and like him represented with winged sandals and a winged staff entwined with snakes. He was the messenger of the gods, and was associated particularly with commerce.

Mercury project US project to put a human in space in the one-seat Mercury space craft 1961–63.

Mergenthaler Ottmar 1854–1899. German-born American who invented a typesetting method. He went to the US in 1872 and developed the first linotype machine (for casting hot-metal type in complete lines) 1876–86.

Mérida capital of Yucatán state, Mexico, a center of the sisal industry; population (1986) 580,000. It was founded 1542, and has a cathedral 1598. Its port on the Gulf of Mexico is Progreso.

Meriden industrial city (plastics, silver, and electronics) in S central Connecticut, E of Waterbury; population (1990) 59,500.

meridian half a great circle drawn on the Earth's surface passing through both poles and thus through all places with the same longitude. Terrestrial longitudes are usually measured from the Greenwich Meridian.

Mérimée Prosper 1803–1870. French author. Among his works are the short novels *Colomba* 1841, *Carmen* 1846, and the *Lettres à une inconnue/Letters to an Unknown Girl* 1873.

merino breed of sheep. Its close-set, silky wool is highly valued. The merino, originally from Spain, is now found all over the world, and is the breed on which the Australian wool industry is built.

Merlin legendary magician and counselor to King ◊Arthur. Welsh bardic literature has a cycle of poems attributed to him, and he may have been a real person.

mermaid mythical sea creature (the male is a *merman*), having a human head and torso and a fish's tail. The dugong and seal are among suggested origins for the idea.

Merovingian dynasty Frankish dynasty, named after its founder, *Merovech* (5th century AD). His descendants ruled France from the time of Clovis (481–511) to 751.

mesa (Spanish "table") flat-topped, steep-sided plateau, consisting of horizontal weak layers of rock topped by a resistant formation; in particular, those found in the desert areas of the US and Mexico. A small mesa is called a butte.

Mesmer Friedrich Anton 1734–1815. Austrian physician, an early experimenter in ◊hypnosis, which was formerly (and popularly) called *mesmerism* after him.

Mesolithic the Middle Stone Age developmental stage of human technology and of ◊prehistory.

Mesopotamia the land between the Tigris and Euphrates rivers, now part of Iraq. Here the civilizations of Sumer and Babylon flourished. Sumer (3500 BC) may have been the earliest urban civilization.

mesosphere layer in the Earth's ◊atmosphere above the stratosphere and below the thermosphere. It lies between about 31 mi/50 km and 50 mi/80 km above the ground.

Mesozoic era of geological time 245–65 million years ago, consisting of the Triassic, Jurassic, and Cretaceous periods. At the beginning of the era, the continents were joined together as Pangaea; dinosaurs and other giant reptiles dominated the sea and air; and ferns, horsetails, and cycads thrived in a warm climate worldwide. By the end of the Mesozoic era, the continents had begun to assume their present positions, flowering plants were dominant, and many of the large reptiles and marine fauna were becoming extinct.

Messerschmitt Willy 1898–1978. German airplane designer whose Me-109 was a standard Luftwaffe fighter in World War II, and whose Me-262 (1942) was the first mass-produced jet fighter.

Messiah (from Hebrew *māshīach* "anointed") in Judaism and Christianity, the savior or deliverer. Jews from the time of the Old Testament exile in Babylon have looked forward to the coming of the Messiah. Christians believe that the Messiah came in the person of ◊Jesus, and hence called him the Christ.

Messier Charles 1730–1817. French astronomer who discovered 15 comets and in 1781 published a list of 103 star clusters and nebulae. Objects on this list are given M (for Messier) numbers, which astronomers still use today, such as M1 (the Crab nebula) and M31 (the Andromeda galaxy).

Messina, Strait of channel in the central Mediterranean separating Sicily from mainland Italy; in Greek legend a monster (Charybdis), who devoured ships, lived in the whirlpool on the Sicilian side, and another (Scylla), who devoured sailors, in the rock on the Italian side. The Classical hero Odysseus passed safely between them.

metabolism the chemical processes of living organisms: a constant alternation of building up (*anabolism*) and breaking down (*catabolism*). For example, green plants build up complex organic substances from water, carbon dioxide, and mineral salts (photosynthesis); by digestion animals partially break down complex organic substances, ingested as food, and subsequently resynthesize them in their own bodies.

Metacomet Wampanoag leader better known as King ◊Philip.

metal any of a class of chemical elements with certain chemical characteristics (◊metallic character) and physical properties: they are good conductors of heat and electricity; opaque but reflect light well; malleable, which enables them to be cold-worked and rolled into sheets; and ductile, which permits them to be drawn into thin wires.

metal detector electronic device for detecting metal, usually below ground, developed from the wartime mine detector. In the head of the metal detector is a coil, which is part of an electronic circuit. The presence of metal causes the frequency of the signal in the circuit to change, setting up an audible note in the headphones worn by the user.

metallic bond the force of attraction operating in a metal that holds the atoms together. In the metal the ◊valency electrons are able to move within the crystal and these electrons are said to be delocalized. Their movement creates short-lived, positively charged ions. The electrostatic attraction between the delocalized electrons and the ceaselessly forming ions constitutes the metallic bond.

metallic character chemical properties associated with those elements classed as metals. These properties, which arise from the element's ability to lose electrons, are: the displacement of hydrogen from dilute acids; the formation of ◊basic oxides; the formation of ionic chlorides; and their reducing reaction, as in the ◊thermite process.

metalloid or **semimetal** any chemical element having some of but not all the properties of metals; metalloids are thus usually electrically semiconducting. They comprise the elements germanium, arsenic, antimony, and tellurium.

metallurgy the science and technology of producing metals, which includes extraction, alloying, and hardening. **Extractive**, or **process, metallurgy** is concerned with the extraction of metals from their ◊ores and refining and adapting them for use. **Physical metallurgy** is concerned with their properties and application. **Metallography** establishes the microscopic structures that contribute to hardness, ductility, and strength.

metamorphism geological term referring to the changes in rocks of the Earth's crust caused by increasing pressure and temperature. The resulting rocks are metamorphic rocks. All metamorphic changes take place in solid rocks. If the rocks melt and then harden, they become ◊igneous rocks.

metamorphosis period during the life cycle of many invertebrates, most amphibians, and some fish, during which the individual's body changes from one form to another through a major reconstitution of its tissues. For example, adult frogs are produced by metamorphosis from tadpoles, and butterflies are produced from caterpillars following metamorphosis within a pupa.

metaphor (Greek "transfer") figure of speech using an analogy or close comparison between two things that are not normally treated as if they had anything in common. Metaphor is a common means of extending the uses and references of words. See also ◊simile.

metaphysical poet member of a group of 17th-century English poets whose work is characterized by conciseness; ingenious, often highly intricate wordplay; and striking imagery. Among the exponents of this genre are John ◊Donne and George ◊Herbert.

metaphysics branch of philosophy that deals with first principles, in particular "being" (ontology) and "knowing" (◊epistemology), and that is concerned with the ultimate nature of reality. It has been maintained that no certain knowledge of metaphysical questions is possible.

meteor flash of light in the sky, popularly known as a **shooting** or **falling star**, caused by a particle of dust, a **meteoroid**, entering the atmosphere at speeds up to 45 mps/70 kps and burning up by friction at a height of around 60 mi/100 km. On any clear night, several **sporadic meteors** can be seen each hour.

meteorite piece of rock or metal from space that reaches the surface of the Earth, Moon, or other body. Most meteorites are thought to be fragments from asteroids, although some may be pieces from the heads of comets. Most are stony, although some are made of iron and a few have a mixed rock-iron composition.

Meteorites provide evidence for the nature of the Solar System and may be similar to the Earth's core and mantle, neither of which can be observed directly.

meteoroid chunk of rock in interplanetary space. There is no official distinction between meteoroids and asteroids, except that the term asteroid is generally reserved for objects larger than 1 mi/1.6 km in diameter, whereas meteoroids can range anywhere from pebble-size up.

meteorology scientific observation and study of the ◊atmosphere, so that weather can be accurately forecast. Data from meteorological stations and weather satellites are collated by computer at central agencies, and forecast and ◊weather maps based on current readings are issued at regular intervals. Modern analysis can give useful forecasts for up to six days ahead.

meter SI unit (symbol m) of length, equivalent to 1.093 yards or 39.37 inches. It is defined by scientists as the length of the path traveled by light in a vacuum during a time interval of 1/299,792,458 of a second.

methanal (common name **formaldehyde**) HCHO gas at ordinary temperatures, condensing to a liquid at $-5.8°F/-1°C$. It has a powerful, penetrating smell. Dissolved in water, it is used as a biological preservative. It is used in the manufacture of plastics, dyes, foam (for example urea-formaldehyde foam, used in insulation), and in medicine.

methane CH_4 the simplest hydrocarbon of the paraffin series. Colorless, odorless, and lighter than air, it burns with a bluish flame and explodes when mixed with air or oxygen. It is the chief constituent of natural gas and also occurs in the explosive firedamp of coal mines. Methane emitted by rotting vegetation forms marsh gas, which may ignite by spontaneous combustion to produce the pale flame seen over marshland and known as will-o'-the-wisp.

methanol (common name **methyl alcohol**) CH_3OH the simplest of the alcohols. It can be made by the dry

metamorphosis An adult green darner dragonfly perched on its empty larval skin after metamorphosis.

distillation of wood (hence it is also known as wood alcohol), but is usually made from coal or natural gas. When pure, it is a colorless, flammable liquid with a pleasant odor, and is highly poisonous.

Methodism evangelical Protestant Christian movement that was founded by John ◊Wesley 1739 within the Church of England, but became a separate body 1795. The Methodist Episcopal Church was founded in the US 1784. There are over 50 million Methodists worldwide.

Methuselah in the Old Testament, Hebrew patriarch who lived before the Flood; his life span of 969 years makes him a byword for longevity.

methyl alcohol common name for ◊methanol.

metonymy (Greek "transferred title") figure of speech that works by association, naming something closely connected with what is meant; for example, calling the theatrical profession "the stage," horse racing "the turf," or journalists "the press." It is related to ◊synecdoche.

metric system system of weights and measures developed in France in the 18th century and recognized by other countries in the 19th century. In 1960 an international conference on weights and measures recommended the universal adoption of a revised International System (Système International d'Unités, or SI), with seven prescribed "base units": the meter (m) for length, kilogram (kg) for mass, second (s) for time, ampere (A) for electric current, kelvin (K) for thermodynamic temperature, candela (cd) for luminous intensity, and mole (mol) for quantity of matter.

metric ton or **tonne** unit of mass (symbol t or T) equal to 2,205 lb/1,000 kg.

metronome clockwork device, invented by Johann Maelzel 1814, using a sliding weight to regulate the speed of a pendulum to assist in keeping time, particularly in music.

Metternich Klemens (Wenzel Lothar), Prince von Metternich 1773–1859. Austrian politician, the leading figure in European diplomacy after the fall of Napoleon. As foreign minister 1809–48 (as well as chancellor from 1821), he tried to maintain the balance of power in Europe, supporting monarchy and repressing liberalism.

Mexican War war between the US and Mexico 1846–48, begun in territory disputed between Texas (annexed by the US 1845 but claimed by Mexico) and Mexico. It began when General Zachary Taylor invaded New Mexico after efforts to purchase what are now California and New Mexico failed. Mexico City was taken 1847, and under the Treaty of Guadaloupe Hidalgo that ended the war, the US acquired New Mexico and California, as well as clear title to Texas in exchange for $15 million.

Mexico country in Central America, bounded N by the US, E by the Gulf of Mexico, SE by Belize and Guatemala, and SW and W by the Pacific Ocean.

Mexico City (Spanish **Ciudad de México**) capital, industrial (iron, steel, chemicals, textiles) city, and cultural center of Mexico, 7,400 ft/2,255 m above sea level on the S edge of the central plateau; population (1986) 18,748,000. It is thought to be one of the world's most

Mexico
United States of
(*Estados Unidos Mexicanos*)

area 756,198 sq mi/1,958,201 sq km
capital Mexico City
cities Guadalajara, Monterrey; port Veracruz
physical partly arid central highlands; Sierra Madre mountain ranges E and W; tropical coastal plains
environment during the 1980s, smog levels in Mexico City exceeded World Health Organization standards on more than 300 days of the year. Air is polluted by 130,000 factories and 2.5 million vehicles
features Rio Grande; 2,000 mi/3,218 km frontier with US; resorts Acapulco, Cancun, Mexicali, Tijuana; Baja California, Yucatán peninsula; volcanoes, including Popocatepetl; pre-Columbian archeological sites
head of state and government Carlos Salinas de Gortari from 1988

political system federal democratic republic
political parties Institutional Revolutionary Party (PRI), moderate, left-wing; National Action Party (PAN), moderate Christian socialist
exports silver, gold, lead, uranium, oil, natural gas, handicrafts, fish, shellfish, fruits and vegetables; cotton, machinery
currency peso
population (1992) 84,439,000 (mixed descent 60%, Indian 30%, Spanish descent 10%); 50% under 20 years of age; growth rate 2.6% p.a.
life expectancy men 67, women 73
languages Spanish (official) 92%, Nahuatl, Maya, Mixtec
religion Roman Catholic 97%
literacy men 92%, women 88% (1989)
GNP $126 bn (1987); $2,082 per head

chronology
1821 Independence achieved from Spain.
1846–48 Mexico at war with US; loss of territory.
1848 Maya Indian revolt suppressed.
1864–67 Maximilian of Austria was emperor of Mexico.
1917 New constitution introduced, designed to establish permanent democracy.
1983–84 Financial crisis.
1985 Earthquake in Mexico City.
1986 International Monetary Fund (IMF) loan agreement signed to keep the country solvent until at least 1988.
1988 PRI candidate Carlos Salinas de Gortari elected president. Debt reduction accords negotiated with US.
1991 PRI won general election. President Salinas promised constitutional reforms.
1993 North American Free Trade Agreement (NAFTA) signed.
1994 Dissatisfaction among peasants leads to serious uprising in S.

polluted cities because of its position in a volcanic basin 7,400 ft/2,000 m above sea level. Pollutants gather in the basin causing a smog cloud.

Meyerbeer Giacomo. Adopted name of Jakob Liebmann Beer 1791–1864. German composer of spectacular operas, including *Robert le Diable* 1831 and *Les Huguenots* 1836. From 1826 he lived mainly in Paris, returning to Berlin after 1842 as musical director of the Royal Opera.

mezuza in Judaism, a small box containing a parchment scroll inscribed with a prayer, the Shema from Deuteronomy 6:4–9; 11:13–21, which is found on the doorpost of every home and every room in a Jewish house, except the bathroom.

mezzanine (Italian *mezzano* "middle") architectural term for a story with a lower ceiling placed between two main stories, usually between the ground and first floors of a building.

mg symbol for *milligram*.

mi symbol for ◊mile.

MI abbreviation for the state of ◊Michigan.

Miami industrial city (food processing, transportation and electronic equipment, clothing, and machinery) and port in Florida; population (1990) 358,500. It is the hub of finance, trade, and air transport for the US, Latin America, and the Caribbean. There has been an influx of immigrants from Cuba, Haiti, Mexico, and South America since 1959.

mica group of silicate minerals that split easily into thin flakes along lines of weakness in their crystal structure (perfect basal cleavage). They are glossy, have a pearly luster, and are found in many igneous and metamorphic rocks. Their good thermal and electrical insulation qualities make them valuable in industry.

Michael in the Old Testament, an archangel, referred to as the guardian angel of Israel. In the New Testament Book of Revelation he leads the hosts of heaven to battle against Satan. In paintings, he is depicted with a flaming sword and sometimes a pair of scales. Feast day Sept 29 (Michaelmas).

Michael Mikhail Fyodorovich Romanov 1596–1645. Tsar of Russia from 1613. He was elected tsar by a national assembly, at a time of chaos and foreign invasion, and was the first of the Romanov dynasty, which ruled until 1917.

Michael 1921– . King of Romania 1927–30 and 1940–47. The son of Carol II, he succeeded his grandfather as king 1927 but was displaced when his father returned from exile 1930. In 1940 he was proclaimed king again on his father's abdication, overthrew 1944 the fascist dictatorship of Ion Antonescu (1882–1946), and enabled Romania to share in the victory of the Allies at the end of World War II. He abdicated and left Romania 1947.

Michelangelo Buonarroti 1475–1564. Italian sculptor, painter, architect, and poet, active in his native Florence and in Rome. His giant talent dominated the High Renaissance. The marble *David* 1501–04 (Accademia, Florence) set a new standard in nude sculpture. His massive figure style was translated into fresco in the Sistine Chapel 1508–12 and 1536–41 (Vatican). Other works in Rome include the dome of St Peter's basilica.

Michelson Albert Abraham 1852–1931. German-born US physicist. In conjunction with Edward

Mexico City The ornate Metropolitan Cathedral (1573), which stands at the center of Mexico City.

Morley, he performed in 1887 the **Michelson–Morley experiment** to detect the motion of the Earth through the postulated ether (a medium believed to be necessary for the propagation of light). The failure of the experiment indicated the nonexistence of the ether, and led ◊Einstein to his theory of ◊relativity. Michelson was the first American to be awarded a Nobel Prize, in 1907.

Michigan state in N central US; nickname Wolverine State/Great Lake State
area 58,518 sq mi/151,600 sq km

Michelangelo David (1501-04), Accademia, Florence.

Michigan

capital Lansing
cities Detroit, Grand Rapids, Flint
features Great Lakes: Superior, Michigan, Huron,
Erie; Porcupine Mountains; Muskegon, Grand, St
Joseph, and Kalamazoo rivers; over 50% forested; Isle
Royale National Park; Pictured Rocks and Sleeping
Bear national seashores; Henry Ford Museum and
Greenfield Village, Dearborn
products motor vehicles and equipment; nonelectrical machinery; iron and steel; chemicals; pharmaceuticals; dairy products
population (1990) 9,295,300
famous people Edna Ferber, Gerald Ford, Henry
Ford, Jimmy Hoffa, Iggy Pop, Diana Ross
history temporary posts established in early 17th
century by French explorers Brulé, Marquette, Joliet,
and La Salle; first settled 1668 at Sault Sainte Marie;
present-day Detroit settled 1701; passed to the British
1763 and to the US 1796; statehood achieved 1837.

Henry Ford's establishment of the moving assembly
line in 1913–14 made Detroit the motor-vehicle-pro-
duction capital of the world. Since then the state's fortunes have been closely tied to the fortunes of the
motor industry, prospering in the 1920s, 1940s, and
1950s, but badly hurt by the Great Depression of the
1930s and competition from Japanese manufacturers
since the 1970s.

Michigan, Lake lake in N central US, one of the
Great Lakes; area 22,390 sq mi/58,000 sq km. Chicago
and Milwaukee are its main ports.

Mickiewicz Adam 1798–1855. Polish revolutionary
poet, whose *Pan Tadeusz* 1832–34 is Poland's national
epic. He died in Constantinople while raising a Polish
corps to fight against Russia in the Crimean War.

micro- prefix (symbol μ) denoting a one-millionth
part. For example, a micrometer (μm), or micron, is
one-millionth of a meter.

microbe another name for ◊microorganism.

microbiological warfare use of harmful microorganisms as a weapon. See ◊biological warfare.

microbiology the study of organisms that can only
be seen under the microscope, mostly viruses and
single-celled organisms such as bacteria, protozoa,
and yeasts. The practical applications of microbiology
are in medicine (since many microorganisms cause
disease); in brewing, baking, and other food and
beverage processes, where the microorganisms carry
out fermentation; and in genetic engineering, which is
creating increasing interest in the field of microbiology.

microchip popular name for the silicon chip, or ◊in-
tegrated circuit.

microcomputer or *micro* or *personal computer* small desktop or portable computer, typically
designed to be used by one person at a time, although

individual computers can be linked in a network so
that users can share data and programs. Its central
processing unit is a ◊microprocessor, contained on a
single integrated circuit.

microeconomics the division of economics concerned with the study of individual decision-making
units within an economy: a consumer, firm, or industry. Unlike macroeconomics, it looks at how individual
markets work and how individual producers and consumers make their choices and with what consequences. This is done by analyzing how relevant
prices of goods are determined and the quantities that
will be bought and sold.

microform generic name for media on which text or
images are photographically reduced. The main
examples are *microfilm* (similar to the film in an
ordinary camera) and *microfiche* (flat sheets of film,
generally 4 in/105 mm × 6 in/148 mm, holding the
equivalent of 420 standard pages). Microform has the
advantage of low reproduction and storage costs, but
it requires special devices for reading the text. It is
widely used for archiving and for storing large volumes of text, such as library catalogs.

micrometer instrument for measuring minute
lengths or angles with great accuracy; different types
of micrometer are used in astronomical and engineering work.

micrometer or micron one-millionth of a meter.

Micronesia country in SE Asia, a group of islands in
the Pacific Ocean lying N of ◊Melanesia.

Micronesia, Federated States of island group in
the W Pacific comprising four constituent states—
Kosrae, Pohnpei, Chuuk (formerly Truk), and Yap;
capital Kolonia, on Pohnpei; area 270 sq mi/700 sq km;
population (1988) 86,000. Federal authority resides
with an executive president. Its people are Micronesian and Polynesian, and the main languages are
Kosrean, Ponapean, Trukese, and Yapese, although
the official language is English. Purchased by Germany from Spain 1898, the islands were occupied
1914 by Japan. They were captured by the US in
World War II, and part of the US Trust Territory of
the Pacific 1947–90. Micronesia became internally
self-governing from 1979, and in free association with
the US from 1986. Although independent from 1990,
the US controls its defense and foreign relations.
Micronesia became a member of the United Nations
1991.

Micronesian member of any of the indigenous Aus-
traloid and Polynesian peoples of Micronesia, including Pacific islands N of the equator, such as the
Caroline, Marshall, Mariana, and Gilbert islands.
Their languages belong to the Austronesian family.

microorganism or *microbe* living organism invisible to the naked eye but visible under a microscope.
Microorganisms include viruses and single-celled
organisms such as bacteria, protozoa, yeasts, and
some algae. The term has no taxonomic significance in
biology. The study of microorganisms is known as
microbiology.

microphone primary component in a sound-repro-
ducing system, whereby the mechanical energy of
sound waves is converted into electrical signals by
means of a ◊transducer. One of the simplest is the telephone receiver mouthpiece, invented by Scottish–US
inventor Alexander Graham Bell in 1876; other types
of microphone are used with broadcasting and sound-
film apparatus.

Micronesia
Federated States of (FSM)

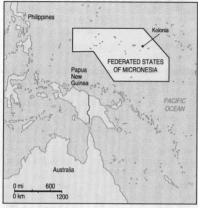

area 270 sq mi/700 sq km
capital Kolonia in Pohnpei state
cities Moen, in Chuuk state; Lelu, in Kosrae state; Colonia, in Yap state

physical an archipelago in the W Pacific
features equatorial, volcanic island chain, with extensive coral, limestone, and lava shores
head of state and government Bailey Olter from 1991
political system democratic federal state
political parties no formally organized political parties
products copra, fish products, tourism
currency US dollar
population (1985) 91,440
languages English (official) and local languages
religion Christianity

chronology
16th century Colonized by Spain.
1885 Purchased from Spain by Germany.
1914 Occupied by Japan.
1920 Administered by Japan under League of Nations mandate.
1944 Occupied by US.
1947 Became part of the UN Pacific Islands Trust Territory, administered by the US.
1982 Compact of Free Association signed with US.
1990 UN trust status terminated. Independent state established, with US responsible for defense and foreign affairs.
1991 First independent president elected. Entered into UN membership.

microprocessor complete computer ◊central processing unit contained on a single ◊integrated circuit, or chip. The appearance of the first microprocessor 1971 designed by Intel for a pocket calculator manufacturer heralded the introduction of the microcomputer. The microprocessor has led to a dramatic fall in the size and cost of computers, and ◊dedicated computers can now be found in washing machines, automobiles, and so on. Examples of microprocessors are the Intel 8086 family and the Motorola 68000 family.

microscope instrument for magnification with high resolution for detail. Optical and electron microscopes are the ones chiefly in use; other types include acoustic, scanning tunneling, and atomic force microscopes. In 1988 a scanning tunneling microscope was used to photograph a single protein molecule for the first time.

microsurgery surgical operation—rejoining a severed limb, for example—performed with the aid of a binocular microscope. Sewing of the nerves and blood vessels is done with a nylon thread so fine that it is only just visible to the naked eye. Restoration of movement and sensation in such cases may be comparatively limited.

microwave ◊electromagnetic wave with a wavelength in the range 0.1 in to 12 in/0.3 cm to 30 cm, or

microscope Scanning tunneling microscope (STM) image, magnified about 250,000 times, of a high-purity gold surface.

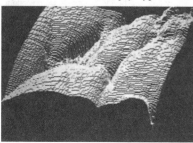

300–300,000 megahertz (between radio waves and ◊infrared radiation). They are used in radar, as carrier waves in radio broadcasting, and in microwave heating and cooking.

microscope Terms used to describe an optical microscope.

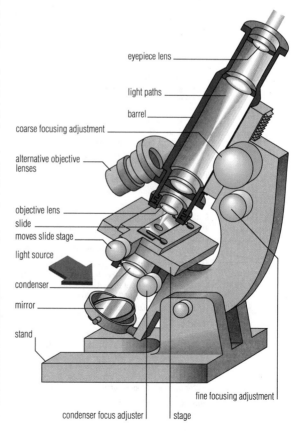

eyepiece lens

light paths

barrel

coarse focusing adjustment

alternative objective lenses

objective lens
slide
moves slide stage

light source

condenser

mirror

stand

condenser focus adjuster | stage

fine focusing adjustment

Mid-Atlantic Ridge
The Mid-Atlantic Ridge is the boundary between the crustal plates that form America, and Europe and Africa.

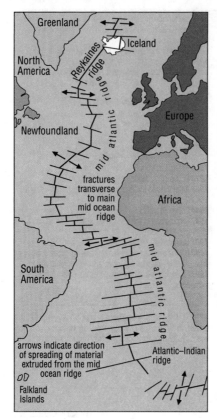

hand regions and between the treble and bass staves of printed music.

Middle East indeterminate area now usually taken to include the Balkan States, Egypt, and SW Asia. Until the 1940s, this area was generally called the Near East, and the term Middle East referred to the area from Iran to Burma (now Myanmar).

Middle English the period of the ◊English language from about 1050 to 1550.

Middle Kingdom period of Egyptian history embracing the 11th and 12th dynasties (roughly 2040–1786 BC); Chinese term for China and its empire until 1912, describing its central position in the Far East.

Middleton Thomas *c.* 1570–1627. English dramatist. He produced numerous romantic plays, tragedies, and realistic comedies, both alone and in collaboration, including *A Fair Quarrel* and *The Changeling* 1622 with Rowley; *The Roaring Girl* with Dekker; and *Women Beware Women* 1621.

Middletown city in S central Connecticut, on the Connecticut River, S of Hartford; population (1990) 42,800. Industries include insurance, banking, vehicle parts, electronics, hardware, and paper products. Wesleyan University is here.

Middletown industrial city (steel, paper products, and aircraft parts) in SW Ohio, on the Miami River, N of Cincinnati; population (1990) 46,000.

Middle Way the path to enlightenment, taught by Buddha, which avoids the extremes of indulgence and asceticism.

Mid Glamorgan (Welsh *Morgannwg Ganol*) county in S Wales
area 394 sq mi/1,020 sq km
cities Cardiff (administrative headquarters), Porthcawl, Aberdare, Merthyr Tydfil, Bridgend, Pontypridd
features includes a small area of the former county of Monmouthshire to the E; mountains in the N; Caerphilly Castle, with its water defenses
products the N was formerly a leading coal (Rhondda) and iron and steel area; Royal Mint at Llantrisant; agriculture in the S; Caerphilly mild cheese
population (1991) 534,100
languages Welsh 8.5%, English
famous people Geraint Evans.

Midi-Pyrénées region of SW France, comprising the *départements* of Ariège, Aveyron, Haute-Garonne, Gers, Lot, Haute-Pyrénées, Tarn, and Tarn-et-Garonne
area 17,486 sq mi/45,300 sq km
features several spa towns, winter resorts, and prehistoric caves
cities capital Toulouse; Montauban, Cahors, Rodez, Lourdes
products fruit, wine, livestock
population (1986) 2,355,000
history occupied by the Basques since prehistoric times, this region once formed part of the prehistoric province of Gascony that was taken by the English 1154, recaptured by the French 1453, inherited by Henry of Navarre, and reunited with France 1607.

Midland industrial city (chemicals and concrete) in central Michigan, on the Tittabawassee River, NW of Saginaw; population (1990) 38,100. There are oil and gas wells.

Midland city in W Texas, halfway between Fort Worth and El Paso; population (1990) 89,400. The city's economy depends on the oil companies located here after the discovery of oil 1923.

microwave heating heating by means of microwaves. Microwave ovens use this form of heating for the rapid cooking or reheating of foods, where heat is generated throughout the food simultaneously. If food is not heated completely, there is a danger of bacterial growth that may lead to food poisoning. Industrially, microwave heating is used for destroying insects in grain and enzymes in processed food, pasteurizing and sterilizing liquids, and drying timber and paper.

MICV abbreviation for ◊mechanized infantry combat vehicle.

Midas in Greek legend, a king of Phrygia who was granted the gift of converting all he touched to gold, and who, for preferring the music of Pan to that of Apollo, was given ass's ears by the latter.

Mid-Atlantic Ridge ◊ocean ridge, formed by the movement of plates described by ◊plate tectonics, that runs along the center of the Atlantic Ocean, parallel to its edges, for some 8,800 mi/14,000 km—almost from the Arctic to the Antarctic.

Middle Ages period of European history between the fall of the Roman Empire in the 5th century and the Renaissance in the 15th. Among the period's distinctive features were the unity of W Europe within the Roman Catholic church; the feudal organization of political, social, and economic relations; and the use of art for largely religious purposes.

middle C white note at the center of the piano keyboard, indicating the division between left- and right-

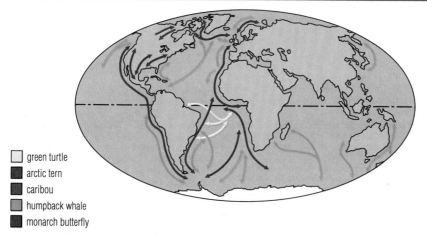

migration Map showing animal migratory patterns.

- ☐ green turtle
- ■ arctic tern
- ■ caribou
- ▨ humpback whale
- ■ monarch butterfly

Midlands area of England corresponding roughly to the Anglo-Saxon kingdom of ◊Mercia. The *East Midlands* comprises Derbyshire, Leicestershire, Northamptonshire, and Nottinghamshire. The *West Midlands* covers the former metropolitan county of West Midlands created from parts of Staffordshire, Warwickshire, and Worcestershire; and (often included) the *South Midlands* comprises Bedfordshire, Buckinghamshire, and Oxfordshire.

midsummer the time of the summer solstice, about June 21. Midsummer Day, June 24, is the Christian festival of St John the Baptist.

Midway Islands two islands in the Pacific, 1,120 mi/1,800 km NW of Honolulu; area 2 sq mi/5 sq km; population (1980) 500. They were annexed by the US 1867, and are now administered by the US Navy. The naval *Battle of Midway* June 3–6, 1942, between the US and Japan, was a turning point in the Pacific in World War II; the US victory marked the end of Japanese expansion in the Pacific.

Midwest or *Middle West* large area of the N central US. It is loosely defined, but is generally taken to comprise the states of Illinois, Iowa, Wisconsin, Minnesota, Nebraska, Kansas, Missouri, North Dakota, and South Dakota and the portions of Montana, Wyoming, and Colorado that lie E of the Rocky Mountains. Ohio, Michigan, and Indiana are often variously included, as well. Traditionally its economy is divided between agriculture and heavy industry. The main urban Midwest center is Chicago.

In its broadest sense, the Midwest has an area of 986,800 sq mi/2,556,000 sq km and a population of about 61.5 million—roughly one-fourth of the national total.

Mies van der Rohe Ludwig 1886–1969. German architect who practiced in the US from 1937. He succeeded Walter ◊Gropius as director of the ◊Bauhaus 1929–33. He designed the bronze-and-glass Seagram building in New York City 1956–59 and numerous apartment buildings.

Mifune Toshiro 1920– . Japanese actor who appeared in many films directed by Akira ◊Kurosawa, including *Rashomon* 1950, *Shichinin no samurai/Seven Samurai* 1954, and *Throne of Blood* 1957. He has also appeared in European and American films: *Grand Prix* 1966, *Hell in the Pacific* 1969.

migraine acute, sometimes incapacitating headache (generally only on one side), accompanied by nausea, that recurs, often with advance symptoms such as flashing lights. No cure has been discovered, but ◊ergotamine normally relieves the symptoms. Some sufferers learn to avoid certain foods, such as chocolate, which suggests an allergic factor.

migrant labor people who move from place to place to work or harvest seasonal crops. Economic or political pressures often cause people to leave their homelands to earn wages in this way, but some families live this way for several generations. Since the Great Depression of the 1930s, many families lost land and homes and took to the road. Since the 1960s, unions for migrant farm workers have been formed, principally by Cesar Chavez.

migration the movement, either seasonal or as part of a single life cycle, of certain animals, chiefly birds and fish, to distant breeding or feeding grounds.

mikado title until 1867 of the Japanese emperor, when it was replaced by the term *tennō* ("heavenly sovereign").

Milan (Italian *Milano*) industrial city (aircraft, automobiles, locomotives, textiles), financial and cultural center, capital of Lombardy, Italy; population (1988) 1,479,000.

mildew any fungus that appears as a destructive growth on plants, paper, leather, or wood when exposed to damp; such fungi usually form a thin white coating.

mile imperial unit of linear measure. A statute mile is equal to 1,760 yards (1.60934 km), and an international nautical mile is equal to 2,026 yards (1,852 m).

Milford industrial city (fabricated metal, writing pens, and electronics) in SW Connecticut, situated by the Housatonic River and Long Island Sound, W of New Haven; population (1990) 49,900.

milk secretion of the ◊mammary glands of female mammals, with which they suckle their young (during ◊lactation). Over 85% is water, the remainder comprising protein, fat, lactose (a sugar), calcium, phosphorus, iron, and vitamins. The milk of cows, goats, and sheep is often consumed by humans, but regular drinking of milk after infancy is principally a Western practice; for people in most of the world, milk causes flatulence and diarrhea.

Milky Way faint band of light crossing the night sky, consisting of stars in the plane of our Galaxy. The name Milky Way is often used for the Galaxy itself. It is a spiral ◊galaxy, about 100,000 light-years in diameter, containing at least 100 billion stars. The Sun is in one of its spiral arms, about 25,000 light-years from the center.

Mill James 1773–1836. Scottish philosopher and political thinker who developed the theory of ◊utilitarianism. He is remembered for his political articles, and for the rigorous education he gave his son John Stuart Mill.

Mill John Stuart 1806–1873. English philosopher and economist who wrote *On Liberty* 1859, the classic philosophical defense of liberalism, and *Utilitarianism* 1863, a version of the "greatest happiness for the greatest number" principle in ethics. His progressive views inspired *On the Subjection of Women* 1869.

Miller Arthur 1915– . US playwright. His plays deal with family relationships and contemporary American values, and include *Death of a Salesman* 1949 and *The Crucible* 1953, based on the Salem witch trials and reflecting the communist witch-hunts of Senator Joe ◊McCarthy. He was married 1956–61 to the film star Marilyn Monroe, for whom he wrote the film *The Misfits* 1960.

Miller Glenn 1904–1944. US trombonist and, as bandleader, exponent of the big-band swing sound from 1938. He composed his signature tune "Moonlight Serenade" (a hit 1939). Miller became leader of the US Army Air Force Band in Europe 1942, made broadcasts to troops throughout the world during World War II, and disappeared without a trace on a flight between England and France.

Miller Henry 1891–1980. US writer. From 1930 to 1940 he lived a bohemian life in Paris, where he wrote his novels *Tropic of Cancer* 1934 and *Tropic of Capricorn* 1938. They were so outspoken and sexually frank that they were banned in the US and England until the 1960s.

Born in New York City, Miller settled in Big Sur, California, in the 1940s and wrote the autobiographical *Rosy Crucifixion* trilogy, consisting of *Sexus* 1949, *Plexus* 1949, and *Nexus* 1957 (published as a whole in the US 1965). His bohemian image made him a favorite of the ◊Beat Generation. Other works include *The Colossus of Maroussi* 1941, *The Air-Conditioned Nightmare* 1945, and *Letters to Anais Nin* 1965.

Miller William 1782–1849. US religious leader. Ordained as a Baptist minister 1833, Miller predicted that the Second Advent would occur 1844. Many of his followers sold their property in expectation of the end of the world. Although Miller's movement disbanded soon after, his teachings paved the way for later Adventist sects.

millet any of several grasses, family Gramineae, of which the grains are used as a cereal food and the stems as fodder.

Millet Jean François 1814–1875. French artist, a leading member of the ◊Barbizon school, who painted scenes of peasant life and landscapes. *The Angelus* 1859 (Musée d'Orsay, Paris) was widely reproduced in his day.

Millett Kate 1934– . US radical feminist lecturer, writer, and sculptor whose book *Sexual Politics* 1970 was a landmark in feminist thinking. She was a founding member of the **National Organization of Women** (NOW). Later books include *Flying* 1974, *The Prostitution Papers* 1976, *Sita* 1977, and *The Loony Bin Trip* 1991, describing a period of manic depression and drug therapy.

millibar unit of pressure, equal to one-thousandth of a ◊bar.

milliliter one-thousandth of a liter (ml), equivalent to 1 cu cm (cc) or 0.0338 fluid ounce.

milling metal machining method that uses a rotating toothed cutting wheel to shape a surface. The term also applies to grinding grain, cacao, coffee, pepper, and other spices.

millipede any arthropod of the class Diplopoda. It has a segmented body, each segment usually bearing two pairs of legs, and the distinct head bears a pair of short clubbed antennae. Most millipedes are no more than 1 in/2.5 cm long; a few in the tropics are 12 in/30 cm.

Mills John 1908– . English actor who appeared in films such as *In Which We Serve* 1942, *The Rocking Horse Winner* 1949, *The Wrong Box* 1966, and *Oh! What a Lovely War* 1969. He received an Academy Award for *Ryan's Daughter* 1971. He is the father of the actresses Hayley Mills and Juliet Mills.

Millville city in SW New Jersey, on the Maurice River, SE of Philadelphia; population (1990) 26,000. Products include vegetables, poultry, and glass.

Milne A(lan) A(lexander) 1882–1956. English writer. His books for children were based on the teddy bear and other toys of his son Christopher Robin (*Winnie-the-Pooh* 1926 and *The House at Pooh Corner* 1928). He also wrote children's verse (*When We Were Very Young* 1924 and *Now We Are Six* 1927) and plays, including an adaptation of Kenneth Grahame's *The Wind in the Willows* as *Toad of Toad Hall* 1929.

Milosevic Slobodan 1941– . Serbian communist politician, party chief and president of Serbia from 1986; reelected Dec 1990 in multiparty elections and again reelected Dec 1992. Milosevic wielded considerable influence over the Serb-dominated Yugoslav federal army during the 1991–92 civil war and has continued to back Serbian militia in ◊Bosnia-Herzegovina 1992–93, although publicly disclaiming any intention to "carve up" the newly independent republic.

Milton John 1608–1674. English poet whose epic ◊Paradise Lost 1667 is one of the landmarks of English literature. Early poems including *Comus* (a masque performed 1634) and *Lycidas* (an elegy 1638) showed Milton's superlative lyric gift. Latin secretary to Oliver Cromwell during the Commonwealth period, he also wrote many pamphlets and prose works, including *Areopagitica* 1644, which opposed press censorship.

Milwaukee industrial port (meatpacking, brewing, engineering, machinery, electronic and electrical equipment, chemicals) in Wisconsin, on Lake Michigan; population (1990) 628,100. The site was settled 1818 and drew a large influx of German immigrants, beginning in the 1840s.

Educational institutions include Marquette University.

mime type of acting in which gestures, movements, and facial expressions replace speech. It has developed as a form of theater, particularly in France, where Marcel ◊Marceau and Jean Louis ◊Barrault have continued the traditions established in the 19th century by Deburau and the practices of the ◊commedia dell'arte in Italy. In ancient Greece, mime was a crude, realistic comedy with dialogue and exaggerated gesture.

mimicry imitation of one species (or group of species) by another. The most common form is **Batesian mimicry** (named after English naturalist H W Bates), where the mimic resembles a model that is poisonous or unpleasant to eat, and has aposematic, or warning, coloration; the mimic thus benefits from the fact that predators have learned to avoid the model. Hoverflies that resemble bees or wasps are an example. Appearance is usually the basis for mimicry, but calls, songs, scents, and other signals can also be mimicked.

Minamoto or **Genji** ancient Japanese clan, the members of which were the first ruling shoguns 1192–1219. Their government was based in Kamakura, near present-day Tokyo. After the death of the first shogun, Minamoto Yoritomo (1147–1199), the real power was exercised by the regent for the shogun; throughout the Kamakura period (1192–1333), the regents were of the Hōjō family, a branch of the ◊Taira.

minaret slender turret or tower attached to a Muslim mosque or to buildings designed in that style. It has one or more balconies, from which the *muezzin* calls the people to prayer five times a day.

mind in philosophy, the presumed mental or physical being or faculty that enables a person to think, will, and feel; the seat of the intelligence and of memory; sometimes only the cognitive or intellectual powers, as distinguished from the will and the emotions.

Mindanao second-largest island of the Philippines
area 36,526 sq mi/94,627 sq km
cities Davao, Zamboanga
physical mountainous rain forest
features an isolated people, the Tasaday, were reputedly first seen by others 1971 (this may be a hoax). The active volcano Apo reaches 9,600 ft/2,954 m, and Mindanao is subject to severe earthquakes. There is a Muslim guerrilla resistance movement
products pineapples, coffee, rice, coconut, rubber, hemp, timber, nickel, gold, steel, chemicals, fertilizer
population (1980) 10,905,250.

mine explosive charge on land or sea, or in the atmosphere, designed to be detonated by contact, vibration (for example, from an enemy engine), magnetic influence, or a timing device. Countermeasures include metal detectors (useless for plastic types), specially equipped helicopters, and (at sea) ◊minesweepers.

mineral naturally formed inorganic substance with a particlular chemical composition and a regularly repeating internal structure. Either in their perfect crystalline form or otherwise, minerals are the constituents of ◊rocks. In more general usage, a mineral is any substance economically valuable for mining (including coal and oil, despite their organic origins).
  Ice is also a mineral, the crystalline form of water, H_2O.

mineralogy study of minerals. The classification of minerals is based chiefly on their chemical composition and the kind of chemical bonding that holds these atoms together. The mineralogist also studies their crystallographic and physical characters, occurrence, and mode of formation.

mineral salt in nutrition, a simple inorganic chemical that is required by living organisms. Plants usually obtain their mineral salts from the soil, while animals get theirs from their food. Important mineral salts include iron salts (needed by both plants and animals), magnesium salts (needed mainly by plants, to make chlorophyll), and calcium salts (needed by animals to

make bone or shell). An element required only in tiny amounts is called a ◊trace element.

Minerva in Roman mythology, the goddess of intelligence, and of handicrafts and the arts, equivalent to the Greek ◊Athena. From the earliest days of ancient Rome, there was a temple to her on the Capitoline Hill, near the Temple of Jupiter.

minesweeper small naval vessel for locating and destroying mines at sea. A typical minesweeper weighs about 725 tons, and is built of reinforced plastic (immune to magnetic and acoustic mines). Remote-controlled miniature submarines may be used to lay charges next to the mines and destroy them.

Ming dynasty Chinese dynasty 1368–1644, based in Nanjing. During the rule 1402–24 of Yongle (or Yung-lo), there was territorial expansion into Mongolia and Yunnan in the SW. The administrative system was improved, public works were carried out, and foreign trade was developed. Art and literature flourished and distinctive blue and white porcelain was produced.

miniature painting (Latin *miniare* "to paint with minium" (a red color)) painting on a very small scale, notably early manuscript paintings, and later miniature portraits, sometimes set in jeweled cases. The art of manuscript painting was developed in Classical times in the West and revived in the Middle Ages. Several Islamic countries, for example Persia and India, developed strong traditions of manuscript art. Miniature portrait painting enjoyed a vogue in France and England in the 16th–19th centuries.

Minimalism movement in abstract art (mostly sculpture) and music toward severely simplified composition. Minimal art developed in the US in the 1950s in reaction to ◊Abstract Expressionism, shunning its emotive approach in favor of impersonality and elemental, usually geometric, shapes. It has found its fullest expression in sculpture, notably in the work of Carl Andre, who employs industrial materials in modular compositions. In music, from the 1960s, it has manifested itself in large-scale statements based on layers of imperceptibly shifting repetitive patterns; major Minimalist composers are Steve Reich and Philip ◊Glass.

mining extraction of minerals from under the land or sea for industrial or domestic uses. Exhaustion of traditionally accessible resources has led to development of new mining techniques; for example, extraction of oil from offshore deposits and from land shale reserves. Technology is also under development for the exploitation of minerals from entirely new sources such as mud deposits and mineral nodules from the sea bed.

mink two species of carnivores of the weasel family, genus *Mustela*, usually found in or near water. They have rich, brown fur, and are up to 1.6 ft/50 cm long with bushy tails 8 in/20 cm long. They live in Eurasia (*M. lutreola*) and North America (*M. vison*).

Minneapolis city in Minnesota, forming with St Paul the Twin Cities area; population (1990) 368,400, metropolitan area 2,464,100. It is at the head of navigation of the Mississippi River. Industries include food processing and the manufacture of machinery, electrical and electronic equipment, precision instruments, transport machinery, and metal and paper products.

Minnelli Liza 1946–   . US actress and singer, daughter of Judy ◊Garland and the director Vincente Minnelli. She achieved stardom in the Broadway musical *Flora, the Red Menace* 1965 and in the film *Cabaret*

1972. Her subsequent films include *New York, New York* 1977 and *Arthur* 1981.

Minnelli Vincente 1910–1986. US film director who specialized in musicals and occasional melodramas. His best films, such as *Meet Me in St Louis* 1944 and *The Band Wagon* 1953, display a powerful visual flair.

Minnesinger any of a group of German lyric poets of the 12th and 13th centuries who, in their songs, dealt mainly with the theme of courtly love without revealing the identity of the object of their affections. Minnesingers included Dietmar von Aist, Friedrich von Hausen, Heinrich von Morungen, Reinmar, and Walther von der Vogelweide.

Minnesota state in N midwest US; nickname Gopher State/North Star State
area 84,418 sq mi/218,700 sq km
capital St Paul
cities Minneapolis, Duluth, Bloomington, Rochester
features sources of the Mississippi River and the Red River of the North; Voyageurs National Park near the Canadian border; Minnehaha Falls at Minneapolis; Mayo Clinic at Rochester; more than 15,000 lakes
products cereals, soybeans, livestock, meat and dairy products, iron ore (about two-thirds of US output), nonelectrical machinery, electronic equipment
population (1990) 4,375,100
famous people F Scott Fitzgerald, Hubert H Humphrey, Sinclair Lewis, Charles and William Mayo
history first European exploration, by French fur traders, in the 17th century; region claimed for France by Daniel Greysolon, Sieur Duluth, 1679; part E of Mississippi River ceded to Britain 1763 and to the US 1783; part W of Mississippi passed to the US under the Louisiana Purchase 1803; became a territory 1849; statehood achieved 1858.

With the coming of the railroad in 1867, Minneapolis became the major US flour-milling center. Iron ore was discovered in the Mesabi, Cuyuna, and Vermilion ranges in the 1880s, and Duluth became a major Great Lakes port. In 1848 the value of manufactured products exceeded farm cash receipts for the first time as the state became increasingly urbanized and industrial.

minnow various small freshwater fishes of the carp family (Cyprinidae), found in streams and ponds worldwide. Most species are small and dully colored, but some are brightly colored. They feed on larvae and insects.

Red-bellied daces, genus *Chrosomus*, and cut-lipped minnows, genus *Exoglossum* are North American representatives.

Minoan civilization Bronze Age civilization on the Aegean island of Crete. The name is derived from Minos, the legendary king of Crete. The civilization is divided into three main periods: early Minoan, about 3000–2200 BC, middle Minoan, about 2200–1580 BC; and late Minoan, about 1580–1100 BC.

Minnesota

minor legal term for those under the age of majority, which varies from country to country but is usually between 18 and 21. In the US (from 1971 for voting, and in some states for nearly all other purposes) and certain European countries (in Britain since 1970) the age of majority is 18.

Minorca (Spanish *Menorca*) second largest of the ◊Balearic Islands in the Mediterranean
area 266 sq mi/689 sq km
cities Mahon, Ciudadela
products copper, lead, iron; tourism is important
population (1985) 55,500.

Minotaur in Greek mythology, a monster, half man and half bull, offspring of Pasiphaë, wife of King Minos of Crete, and a bull. It lived in the Labyrinth at Knossos, and its victims were seven girls and seven youths, sent in annual tribute by Athens, until ◊Theseus killed it, with the aid of Ariadne, the daughter of Minos.

Minsk or *Mensk* industrial city (machinery, textiles, leather; a center of the Russian computer industry) and capital of Belarus; population (1987) 1,543,000.

mint in botany, any aromatic plant, genus *Mentha*, of the family Labiatae, widely distributed in temperate regions. The plants have square stems, creeping rootstocks, and flowers, usually pink or purplish, that grow in a terminal spike. Mints include garden mint *M. spicata* and peppermint *M. piperita*.

mint in economics, a place where coins are stamped from metal under government authority.

In the US the official mint is the Bureau of the Mint, a division of the Treasury Department. The official Mint of the United States was established by the Coining Act 1792 in Philadelphia. The US Mint has general supervision of the four current coinage mints—in Denver, West Point, San Francisco, and Philadelphia—all of which are assay offices and bullion depositories. It directs the coinage of money, the manufacture of medals, and the custody of bullion.

Minton Thomas 1765–1836. English potter. He first worked under the potter Josiah Spode, but in 1789 established himself at Stoke-on-Trent as an engraver of designs (he originated the "willow pattern") and in the 1790s founded a pottery there, producing high-quality bone china, including tableware.

minuet European courtly dance of the 17th century, later used with the trio as the third movement in a Classical symphony.

Minuit Peter c. 1580–1638. Dutch colonial administrator in America. As a founder of New Amsterdam on Manhattan Island 1626 and its director general, he negotiated with the local Indians and supervised the construction of Fort Amsterdam. Ousted from his post 1631 by the Dutch Reformed Church, he helped found the Swedish colony of Fort Christina at the modern site of Wilmington, Delaware, 1638.

minute unit of time consisting of 60 seconds; also a unit of angle equal to one sixtieth of a degree.

Minuteman in weaponry, a US three-stage intercontinental ballistic missile (ICBM) with a range of about 5,000 mi/8,000 km. In US history the term was applied to members of the citizens' militia in the 1770s. These volunteer soldiers had pledged to be available for battle at a "minute's notice" during the ◊American Revolution.

Miocene fourth epoch of the Tertiary period of geological time, 23.5–5.2 million years ago. At this time

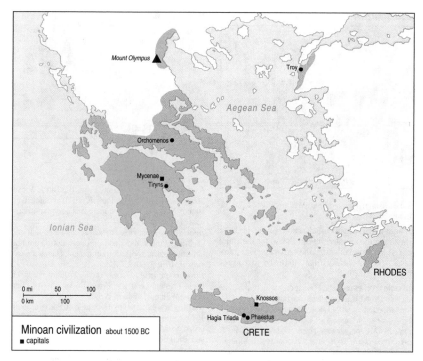

Mount Olympus ▲

Troy ●

Aegean Sea

Orchomenos ●

Mycenae ■
Tiryns ●

Ionian Sea

RHODES

0 mi   50   100
0 km   100

Knossos ■

Hagia Triada ●● Phaestus

Minoan civilization about 1500 BC
■ capitals

CRETE

grasslands spread over the interior of continents, and hoofed mammals rapidly evolved.

Mir (Russian "peace" or "world") Soviet space station, the core of which was launched Feb 20, 1986. *Mir* is intended to be a permanently occupied space station.

Mira or *Omicron Ceti* brightest long-period pulsating ◊variable star, located in the constellation ◊Cetus. Mira was the first star discovered to vary periodically in brightness.

Mirabeau Honoré Gabriel Riqueti, Comte de 1749–1791. French politician, leader of the National Assembly in the French Revolution. He wanted to establish a parliamentary monarchy on the English model. From May 1790 he secretly acted as political adviser to the king.

miracle play another name for ◊mystery play.

mirage illusion seen in hot climates of water on the horizon, or of distant objects being enlarged. The effect is caused by the ◊refraction, or bending, of light.

Miranda Carmen. Adopted name of Maria de Carmo Miranda da Cunha 1909–1955. Portuguese dancer and singer who lived in Brazil from childhood. Her Hollywood musicals include *Down Argentine Way* 1940 and *The Gang's All Here* 1943. Her hallmarks were extravagant costumes and headgear adorned with tropical fruits, a staccato singing voice, and fiery temperament.

Successful in Brazilian films, she went to Hollywood 1939 via Broadway and appeared in over a dozen musicals.

Miranda v Arizona US Supreme Court decision 1966 dealing with the admission into a trial of evidence obtained from suspects who are unaware of their rights. The petitioner, Ernesto Miranda, was convicted of kidnapping and rape after confessing to police interrogators. Miranda appealed the conviction, arguing that due process had been violated because he

had not been informed of his rights before his confession. The Court voted 5 to 4 to overturn Miranda's conviction. The ruling mandated that in order for testimony to be admissible in criminal trials, suspects must have been informed (1) of the right to remain silent, (2) that anything they do or say will be used against them in court, (3) of the right to an attorney, and (4) of the right to a court-appointed attorney if unable to afford one.

Miró Joan 1893–1983. Spanish Surrealist painter, born in Barcelona. In the mid-1920s he developed a distinctive abstract style with ameba shapes, some linear, some highly colored, generally floating on a plain background.

MIRV abbreviation for *multiple independently targeted reentry vehicle*, used in ◊nuclear warfare.

miscarriage spontaneous expulsion of a fetus from the womb before it is capable of independent survival. Often, miscarriages are due to an abnormality in the developing fetus.

Mishawaka industrial city (plastics, rubber, missiles, and vehicle and aircraft parts) in N central Indiana, E of South Bend; population (1990) 42,600.

Mishima Yukio 1925–1970. Japanese novelist whose work often deals with sexual desire and perversion, as in *Confessions of a Mask* 1949 and *The Temple of the Golden Pavilion* 1956. He committed hara-kiri (ritual suicide) as a protest against what he saw as the corruption of the nation and the loss of the samurai warrior tradition.

Mishna or *Mishnah* collection of commentaries on written Hebrew law, consisting of discussions between rabbis, handed down orally from their inception in AD 70 until about 200, when, with the Gemara (the main body of rabbinical debate on interpretations

Mississippi river

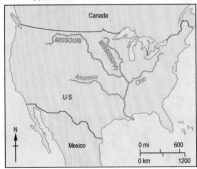

of the Mishna) it was committed to writing to form the Talmud.

missal in the Roman Catholic church, a service book containing the complete office of Mass for the entire year. A simplified missal in the vernacular was introduced 1969 (obligatory from 1971): the first major reform since 1570.

missile rocket-propelled weapon, which may be nuclear-armed (see ◊nuclear warfare). Modern missiles are often classified as surface-to-surface missiles (SSM), air-to-air missiles (AAM), surface-to-air missiles (SAM), or air-to-surface missiles (ASM). A *cruise missile* is in effect a pilotless, computer-guided aircraft; it can be sea-launched from submarines or surface ships, or launched from the air or the ground.

Mission city in S Texas, near the Rio Grande, W of McAllen; population (1990) 28,700. The economy is based on processing the area's citrus fruits and vegetables, and on nearby oil wells.

mission organized attempt to spread a religion. Throughout history, Christianity has been the most aggressive missionary religion; its activities during the colonization of what are now Third World nations was in some instances excessive, and it has frequently been criticized for obliterating both the beliefs and the people of some indigenous societies, as during the Spanish Conquest. During the 20th century, sects such as the Mormons and Jehovah's Witnesses proselytize regularly and systematically. Islam also has a history of militant missionizing, but in the 20th century has found ready converts in the Black Muslim movement of the US. Buddhism was spread both historically and recently by the teaching spirit of the wandering Buddha and his followers.

Mississippi river in the US, the main arm of the great river system draining the US between the Appalachian and the Rocky mountains. The length of the Mississippi is 2,350 mi/3,780 km; with its tributary the Missouri 3,740 mi/6,020 km.

Levees extend over more than 1,600 mi/2,575 km of its course because of the potentially dangerous spring flooding, as in 1993. St Louis is the chief central port on its banks. Waterborne commerce consists mainly of bulk commodities such as petroleum and petroleum products, grain, and iron ore. Passenger traffic was important during the 19th century, today excursion boats, especially paddle-wheel craft, provide day trips or longer cruises.

Mississippi state in SE US; nickname Magnolia State/Bayou State
area 47,710 sq mi/123,600 sq km

Mississippi state

capital Jackson
cities Biloxi, Meridian, Hattiesburg
features rivers: Mississippi, Pearl, Big Black; Vicksburg National Military Park (Civil War site); Gulf Islands National Seashore; mansions and plantations, many in the Natchez area
products cotton, rice, soybeans, chickens, fish and shellfish, lumber and wood products, petroleum and natural gas, transportation equipment, chemicals
population (1990) 2,573,200
famous people Jefferson Davis, William Faulkner, Elvis Presley, Leontyne Price, Eudora Welty, Tennessee Williams, Richard Wright
history first explored by Hernando de Soto for Spain 1540; settled by the French 1699, the English 1763; ceded to US 1798; statehood achieved 1817. After secession from the Union during the Civil War, it was readmitted 1870.

Mississippi was the scene of heavy fighting during the Civil War that left it devastated. Tenant farming replaced plantations, and only in the mid-1960s did manufacturing pass farming as a source of jobs. The legal segregation of blacks was dismantled during this period. Mississippi remains the poorest of the states in many respects, including personal income per head of population.

Missouri state in central US; nickname Show Me State/Bullion State
area 69,712 sq mi/180,600 sq km
capital Jefferson City
cities St Louis, Kansas City, Springfield, Independence
features rivers: Mississippi, Missouri; Pony Express Museum at St Joseph; birthplace of Jesse James; Mark Twain and Ozark state parks; Harry S Truman Library at Independence
products meat and other processed food, aerospace and transport equipment, lead, zinc
population (1990) 5,117,100
famous people George Washington Carver, T S Eliot, Jesse James, Joseph Pulitzer, Harry S Truman, Mark Twain
history explored by Hernando de Soto for Spain 1541; acquired by the US under the Louisiana Purchase 1803; achieved statehood 1821, following the Missouri Compromise of 1820.

Strong sympathy for both sides existed, but the state remained Union during the Civil War; many battles and skirmishes fostered a general lawlessness that continued in the postwar exploits of such bandits as Jesse and Frank James. While St Louis was eclipsed by Chicago as the commercial center of the Midwest, Kansas City benefited from the growth of the railroads. Increasingly urbanized and industrialized in the 20th century, Missouri is second to Michigan in producing automobiles and ranks high in aerospace production.

Missouri major river in the central US, a tributary of the Mississippi, which it joins N of St Louis; length 2,683 mi/4,320 km.

It is formed by the confluence of the Jefferson, Gallatin, and Madison rivers in SW Montana and flows SE through the states of Montana, North Dakota, and South Dakota to Sioux City, Iowa, where it turns S and forms the borders between Iowa and Nebraska and between Kansas and Missouri. Kansas City, Missouri, is the largest city on its banks. Since 1944 the muddy, turbulent river has been tamed by a series of locks and dams for irrigation and flood control.

Missouri Compromise in US history, the solution by Congress (1820–21) of a sectional crisis caused by the 1819 request from Missouri for admission to the union as a slave state, despite its proximity to existing nonslave states. The compromise was the simultaneous admission of Maine as a nonslave state to keep the same ratio.

mistletoe any of several parasitic evergreen shrubs of the genera *Viscum* and *Phoradendron* of the family Loranthaceae, especially American mistletoe *P. flavescens*, parasitic on broadleaved trees, and European mistletoe *V. album*. They grow on trees as branched bushes, with translucent white berries, and are used as Christmas decorations. See ◊Druidism. The seeds of the European mistletoe are dispersed by birds, but the dwarf mistletoe *Arceuthobium pusillum* of North America shoots its seeds at 60 mph/100 kph as far as 16 yd/15 m. Mistletoes lose water more than ten times as fast as other plants to draw nutrients to them.

mistral cold, dry, northerly wind that occasionally blows during the winter on the Mediterranean coast of France. It has been known to reach a velocity of 90 mph/145 kph.

Mitchell Margaret 1900–1949. US novelist, born in Atlanta, Georgia, which is the setting for her one book, the bestseller *Gone With the Wind* 1936, a story of the US Civil War. It was filmed starring Vivien Leigh and Clark Gable in 1939.

Mitchum Robert 1917– . US film actor, a star for more than 30 years as the big, strong, relaxed modern hero. His films include *Out of the Past* 1947, *The Night of the Hunter* 1955, and *The Friends of Eddie Coyle* 1973.

miter in the Christian church, the headdress worn by bishops, cardinals, and mitered abbots at solemn services. There are miters of many different shapes, but in the Western church they usually take the form of a tall cleft cap. The miter worn by the pope is called a tiara.

Mitford sisters the six daughters of British aristocrat Lord Redesdale, including: *Nancy* (1904–1973), author of the semiautobiographical *The Pursuit of Love* 1945 and *Love in a Cold Climate* 1949, and editor and part author of *Noblesse Oblige* 1956 elucidating

Missouri

"U" (upper-class) and "non-U" behavior; *Diana* (1910–), who married Oswald Mosley; *Unity* (1914–1948), who became an admirer of Hitler; *Jessica* (1917–), author of the autobiographical *Hons and Rebels* 1960 and *The American Way of Death* 1963.

Mithras in Persian mythology, the god of light. Mithras represented the power of goodness, and promised his followers compensation for present evil after death. He was said to have captured and killed the sacred bull, from whose blood all life sprang. Mithraism was introduced into the Roman Empire 68 BC. By about AD 250, it rivaled Christianity in strength.

Mithridates VI Eupator known as *the Great* 132–63 BC. King of Pontus (on the coast of modern Turkey, on the Black Sea), who became the greatest obstacle to Roman expansion in the E.

He massacred 80,000 Romans in overrunning the rest of Asia Minor and went on to invade Greece. He was defeated by ◊Sulla in the First Mithridatic War 88–84; by ◊Lucullus in the Second 83–81; and by ◊Pompey in the Third 74–64. He was killed by a soldier at his own order.

mitochondria (singular *mitochondrion*) membrane-enclosed organelles within eukaryotic cells, containing enzymes responsible for energy production during aerobic respiration. These rodlike or spherical bodies are thought to be derived from free-living bacteria that, at a very early stage in the history of life, invaded larger cells and took up a symbiotic way of life inside. Each still contains its own small loop of DNA called mitochondrial DNA, and new mitochondria arise by division of existing ones.

mitosis in biology, the process of cell division. The genetic material of eukaryotic cells is carried on a number of ◊chromosomes. To control their movements during cell division so that both new cells get a full complement, a system of protein tubules, known as the spindle, organizes the chromosomes into position in the middle of the cell before they replicate. The spindle then controls the movement of chromosomes as the cell goes through the stages of division: *interphase*, *prophase*, *metaphase*, *anaphase*, and *telophase*. See also ◊meiosis. *See illustration p. 626*

Mitre Bartólomé 1821–1906. Argentine president 1862–68. In 1852 he helped overthrow the dictatorial regime of Juan Manuel de Rosas, and in 1861 helped unify Argentina. Mitre encouraged immigration and favored growing commercial links with Europe. He is seen as a symbol of national unity.

Mitterrand François 1916– . French socialist politician, president from 1981. He held ministerial posts in 11 governments 1947–58, and founded the French Socialist Party (PS) 1971. In 1985 he introduced proportional representation, allegedly to weaken the growing opposition from left and right. Since 1982 his administrations have combined economic orthodoxy with social reform.

mixture in chemistry, a substance containing two or more compounds that still retain their separate physical and chemical properties. There is no chemical bonding between them and they can be separated from each other by physical means (compare ◊compound).

Miyazawa Kiichi 1920– . Japanese right-wing politician, prime minister 1991–93.. After holding a number of key government posts, he became leader of the ruling Liberal Democratic Party (LDP) and prime minister Nov 1991. He resigned July 1993 when the LDP lost its majority in a general election.

mitosis *The stages of mitosis, the process of cell division that takes place when a plant or animal cell divides for growth or repair.*

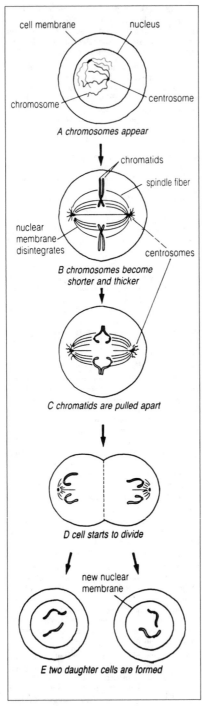

cell membrane

nucleus

chromosome

centrosome

A chromosomes appear

chromatids

spindle fiber

nuclear membrane disintegrates

centrosomes

B chromosomes become shorter and thicker

C chromatids are pulled apart

D cell starts to divide

new nuclear membrane

E two daughter cells are formed

Mizoram state of NE India
area 8,145 sq mi/21,100 sq km
capital Aizawl
products rice, hand-loom weaving
population (1991) 686,200
religion 84% Christian

history made a Union Territory 1972 from the Mizo Hills District of Assam. Rebels carried on a guerrilla war 1966–76, but 1976 acknowledged Mizoram as an integral part of India. It became a state 1986.

ml symbol for ***milliliter***.

mm symbol for ***millimeter***.

MN abbreviation for the state of ◊Minnesota.

mnemonic in computing, a short sequence of letters used in low-level programming languages to represent a machine-code instruction.

MO abbreviation for the state of ◊Missouri.

Moab ancient country in Jordan east of the southern part of the river Jordan and the Dead Sea. The inhabitants were closely akin to the Hebrews in culture, language, and religion, but were often at war with them, as recorded in the Old Testament. Moab eventually fell to Arab invaders. The ***Moabite Stone***, discovered 1868 at Dhiban, dates from the 9th century BC and records the rising of Mesha, king of Moab, against Israel.

Mobutu Sese Seko Kuku Ngbeandu Wa Za Banga 1930– . Zairean president from 1965. He assumed the presidency in a coup, and created a unitary state under a centralized government. The harshness of some of his policies and charges of corruption have attracted widespread international criticism. In 1991 opposition leaders forced Mobutu to agree formally to give up some of his powers, but the president continued to oppose constitutional reform. His decision Jan 1993 to pay his regular army with near worthless banknotes resulted in mutiny and the accidental shooting of the French ambassador by troops loyal to the president, causing French and Belgium governments to intervene and prepare to evacuate civilians.

mockingbird North American songbird *Mimus polyglottos* of the mimic thrush family Mimidae, found in the US and Mexico. About 10 in/25 cm long, it is brownish gray, with white markings on the black wings and tail. It is remarkable for its ability to mimic the songs of other species.

mode in mathematics, the element that appears most frequently in a given set of data. For example, the mode for the data 0, 0, 9, 9, 9, 12, 87, 87 is 9.

Model Parliament English parliament set up 1295 by Edward I; it was the first to include representatives from outside the clergy and aristocracy, and was established because Edward needed the support of the whole country against his opponents: Wales, France, and Scotland. His sole aim was to raise money for military purposes, and the parliament did not pass any legislation.

modem (acronym for ***modulator/demodulator***) device for transmitting computer data over telephone lines. Such a device is necessary because the ◊digital signals produced by computers cannot, at present, be transmitted directly over the telephone network, which uses ◊analog signals. The modem converts the digital signals to analog, and back again. Modems are used for linking remote terminals to central computers and enable computers to communicate with each other anywhere in the world.

modern dance 20th-century dance idiom that evolved in opposition to traditional ballet by those seeking a freer and more immediate means of dance expression. Leading exponents include Martha ◊Graham and Merce Cunningham in the US, Isadora ◊Duncan and Loie Fuller in Europe.

Modernism in the arts, a general term used to describe the 20th century's conscious attempt to break with the artistic traditions of the 19th century; it is based on a concern with form and the exploration of technique as opposed to content and narrative. In the visual arts, direct representationalism gave way to abstraction (see ◊abstract art); in literature, writers experimented with alternatives to orthodox sequential storytelling, such as ◊stream of consciousness; in music, the traditional concept of key was challenged by ◊atonality; and in architecture, Functionalism ousted decorativeness as a central objective.

Modesto city in central California, on the Tuolumne River, SE of San Francisco, on the fringes of the San Joaquin Valley; population (1990) 164,700. It is an agricultural center for wine, apricots, melons, beans, peaches, and livestock.

Modigliani Amedeo 1884–1920. Italian artist, active in Paris from 1906. He painted and sculpted graceful nudes and portrait studies. His paintings—for example, the portrait of *Jeanne Hebuterne* 1919 (Guggenheim Museum, New York)—have a distinctive elongated, linear style.

modulation in radio transmission, the intermittent change of frequency, or amplitude, of a radio carrier wave, in accordance with the audio characteristics of the speaking voice, music, or other signal being transmitted. See ◊pulse-code modulation, ◊AM (amplitude modulation), and ◊FM (frequency modulation).

module in construction, a standard or unit that governs the form of the rest. For example, Japanese room sizes are traditionally governed by multiples of standard tatami floor mats; today prefabricated buildings are mass-produced in a similar way. The components of a spacecraft are designed in coordination; for example, for the Apollo Moon landings the craft comprised a command module (for working, eating, sleeping), service module (electricity generators, oxygen supplies, maneuvering rocket), and lunar module (to land and return the astronauts).

modulus in mathematics, a number that divides exactly into the difference between two given numbers. Also, the multiplication factor used to convert a logarithm of one base to a logarithm of another base. Also, another name for ◊absolute value.

Mogadishu or *Mugdisho* capital and chief port of Somalia; population (1988) 1,000,000. It is a center for oil refining, food processing, and uranium mining. During the struggle to overthrow President Barre and the ensuing civil war 1991–92, much of the city was devastated and many thousands killed. In April 1992 the UN Security Council voted to send military observers to monitor a cease-fire in the city.

Mogul emperors N Indian dynasty 1526–1858, established by ◊Babur, Muslim descendant of Tamerlane, the 14th-century Mongol leader. The Mogul emperors ruled until the last one, ◊Bahadur Shah II, was dethroned and exiled by the British; they included Akbar, ◊Aurangzeb, and ◊Shah Jahan. The Moguls established a more extensive and centralized empire than their Delhi sultanate forebears, and the Mogul era was one of great artistic achievement as well as urban and commercial development.

Mohács, Battle of Austro-Hungarian defeat of the Turks 1687, which effectively marked the end of Turkish expansion into Europe. Named after the river port of that name on the Danube in Hungary, which is also the site of a Turkish victory 1526.

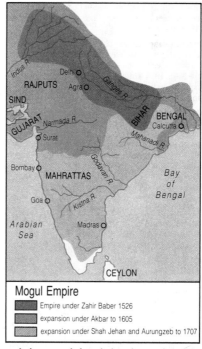

Mogul Empire

Empire under Zahir Baber 1526

expansion under Akbar to 1605

expansion under Shah Jehan and Aurungzeb to 1707

mohair yarn made from the long, lustrous hair of the ◊Angora goat or rabbit, loosely woven with cotton, silk, or wool to produce a fuzzy texture. It became popular for jackets, coats, and sweaters in the 1950s. Commercial mohair is now obtained from cross-bred animals, pure-bred supplies being insufficient to satisfy demand.

Mohamad Mahathir bin 1925– . Prime minister of Malaysia from 1981 and leader of the United Malays' National Organization (UMNO). His "look east" economic policy emulates Japanese industrialization.

Mohammed or *Muhammed, Mahomet c.* 570–632. Founder of Islam, born in Mecca on the Arabian peninsula. In about 616 he claimed to be a prophet and that the *Koran* was revealed to him by God (it was later written down by his followers). He fled from persecution to the town now known as Medina in 622: the flight, Hegira, marks the beginning of the Islamic era.

Mohave Desert arid region in S California, part of the Great Basin; area 15,000 sq mi/38,500 sq km.

Mohawk member of a North American Indian people, part of the ◊Iroquois confederation, who lived in the Mohawk Valley, New York, and now live on reservations in Ontario, Québec, and New York State, as well as among the general population. Their language belongs to the Macro-Siouan group. In 1990 Mohawks south of Montréal mounted a blockade in a dispute over land with the government of Québec province.

Mohenjo Daro ("mound of the dead") site of a city about 2500–1600 BC on the lower Indus River, Pakistan, where excavations from the 1920s have revealed the ◊Indus Valley civilization, to which the city of Harappa also belongs.

Mohican and Mohegan or *Mahican* two closely related North American Indian peoples, speaking an Algonquian language, who formerly occupied the Hudson Valley and parts of Connecticut, respectively.

The novelist James Fenimore ◊Cooper confused the two peoples in his fictional account *The Last of the Mohicans* 1826.

Moholy-Nagy Laszlo 1895–1946. US photographer, born in Hungary. He lived in Germany 1923–29, where he was a member of the Bauhaus school, and fled from the Nazis 1935. Through the publication of his illuminating theories and practical experiments, he had great influence on 20th-century photography and design.

Mohorovičić discontinuity also *Moho* or *M-discontinuity* boundary that separates the Earth's crust and mantle, marked by a rapid increase in the speed of earthquake waves. It follows the variations in the thickness of the crust and is found approximately 20 mi/32 km below the continents and about 6 mi/10 km below the oceans. It is named after the Yugoslav geophysicist Andrija Mohorovičić (1857–1936), who suspected its presence after analyzing seismic waves from the Kulpa Valley earthquake 1909.

Mohs' scale scale of hardness for minerals (in ascending order): 1 talc; 2 gypsum; 3 calcite; 4 fluorite; 5 apatite; 6 orthoclase; 7 quartz; 8 topaz; 9 corundum; 10 diamond.

Moi Daniel arap 1924– . Kenyan politician, president from 1978. Leader of Kenya African National Union (KANU), he became minister of home affairs 1964, vice president 1967, and succeeded Jomo Kenyatta as president. He enjoys the support of Western governments but has been widely criticized for Kenya's poor human-rights record. From 1988 his rule became increasingly authoritarian and in 1991, in the face of widespread criticism, he promised an eventual introduction of multiparty politics. In 1992 he was elected president in the first free elections amid widespread accusations of fraud.

molar one of the large teeth found toward the back of the mammalian mouth. The structure of the jaw, and the relation of the muscles, allows a massive force to be applied to molars. In herbivores the molars are flat with sharp ridges of enamel and are used for grinding, an adaptation to a diet of tough plant material. Carnivores have sharp powerful molars called carnassials, which are adapted for cutting meat.

molasses thick, usually dark, syrup obtained during the refining of sugar (either cane or beet) or made from varieties of sorghum. Fermented sugar-cane molasses produces rum; fermented beet-sugar molasses yields ethyl alcohol.

Unsulfured raw molasses, called blackstrap, is a nutritious food, containing in 1 tablespoon 585 mg of potassium.

mold mainly saprophytic ◊fungi living on foodstuffs and other organic matter, a few being parasitic on plants, animals, or each other. Many are of medical or industrial importance; for example, penicillin.

Moldavia former principality in E Europe, on the river Danube, occupying an area divided today between Moldova (formerly a Soviet republic) and Romania. It was independent between the 14th and 16th centuries, when it became part of the Ottoman Empire. In 1861 Moldavia was united with its neighboring principality Wallachia as Romania. In 1940 the eastern part, ◊Bessarabia, became part of the USSR, whereas the western part remained in Romania.

molding the use of a pattern, hollow form, or matrix to give a specific shape to something in a plastic or molten state. Molds are commonly used for shaping plastics, clays, and glass. In injection molding, molten plastic, for example, is injected into a water-cooled mold and takes the shape of the mold when it solidifies. In blow molding, air is blown into a blob of molten plastic inside a hollow mold. In compression molding, synthetic resin powder is simultaneously heated and pressed into a mold. When metals are used, the process is called ◊casting.

Moldova or *Moldavia* country in E central Europe, bounded N, S, and E by Ukraine, and W by Romania.

mole burrowing insectivore of the family Talpidae. Moles grow to 7 in/18 cm, and have acute senses of hearing, smell, and touch, but poor vision. They have shovellike, clawed front feet for burrowing, and eat insects, grubs, and worms.

mole SI unit (symbol mol) of the amount of a substance. It is defined as the amount of a substance that contains as many elementary entities (atoms, molecules, and so on) as there are atoms in 12 g of the ◊isotope carbon-12.

mole person working subversively within an organization. The term has come to be used broadly for someone who gives out ("leaks') secret information in the public interest; it originally meant a person who spends several years working for a government department or a company with the intention of passing secrets to an enemy or a rival.

molecular biology study of the molecular basis of life, including the biochemistry of molecules such as DNA, RNA, and proteins, and the molecular structure and function of the various parts of living cells.

molecule group of two or more ◊atoms bonded together. A molecule of an element consists of one or more like ◊atoms; a molecule of a compound consists of two or more different atoms bonded together. Molecules vary in size and complexity from the hydrogen molecule (H_2) to the large macromolecules of proteins. They are held together by ionic bonds, in which the atoms gain or lose electrons to form ◊ions, or by covalent bonds, where electrons from each atom are shared in a new molecular orbital.

The symbolic representation of a molecule is known as its formula. The presence of more than one atom is denoted by a subscript figure—for example, one molecule of the compound water, having two atoms of hydrogen and one atom of oxygen, is shown as H_2O.

Molière Adopted name of Jean Baptiste Poquelin 1622–1673. French satirical playwright from whose work modern French comedy developed. One of the founders of the Illustre Théâtre 1643, he was later its leading actor. In 1655 he wrote his first play, *L'Etourdi*, followed by *Les Précieuses Ridicules* 1659. His satires include *L'Ecole des femmes* 1662, *Le* Misanthrope 1666, *Le Bourgeois Gentilhomme* 1670, and *Le Malade imaginaire* 1673. Other satiric plays include *Tartuffe* 1664 (banned until 1697 for attacking the hypocrisy of the clergy), *Le Médecin malgré lui* 1666, and *Les Femmes savantes* 1672.

Moline industrial city (farm implements, furniture, and metal products) in NW Illinois, on the Mississippi River, W of Chicago; population (1990) 43,200.

Molise mainly agricultural region of S central Italy, comprising the provinces of Campobasso and Isernia; area 1,698 sq mi/4,400 sq km; population (1990) 336,500. Its capital is Campobasso.

mollusk any invertebrate of the phylum Mollusca with a body divided into three parts, a head, a foot, and a visceral mass. The majority of mollusks are marine animals, but some inhabit fresh water, and a few are

Moldova
Republic of

area 13,012 sq mi/33,700 sq km
capital Chişinău (Kishinev)
cities Tiraspol, Beltsy, Bendery
physical hilly land lying largely between the rivers Prut and Dniester; N Moldova comprises the level plain of the Beltsy Steppe and uplands; the climate is warm and moderately continental
features Black Earth region
head of state Mircea Snegur from 1989
head of government Andre Sangheli from 1992
political system emergent democracy
political parties Moldavian Popular Front (MRF), Romanian nationalist; Gagauz-Khalky People's Movement (GKPM), Gagauz separatist
products wine, tobacco, canned goods
population (1992) 4,394,000 (Moldavian 64%, Ukrainian 14%, Russian 13%, Gagauzi 4%, Bulgarian 2%)

language Moldavian, allied to Romanian
religion Russian Orthodox

chronology
1940 Bessarabia in the E became part of the Soviet Union whereas the W part remained in Romania.
1941 Bessarabia taken over by Romania–Germany.
1944 Red army reconquered Bessarabia.
1946–47 Widespread famine.
1988 A popular front, the Democratic Movement for Perestroika, campaigned for accelerated political reform.
1989 Jan–Feb: nationalist demonstrations in Chisinau. May: Moldavian Popular Front established. July: former Communist Party deputy leader Mircea Snegur became head of state. Aug: Moldavian language granted official status, triggering clashes between ethnic Russians and Moldavians. Nov: Gagauz-Khalky People's Movement formed to campaign for Gagauz autonomy.
1990 Feb: Popular Front polled strongly in supreme soviet elections. June: economic and political sovereignty declared; renamed Republic of Moldova. Oct: Gagauzi held unauthorized elections to independent parliament; state of emergency declared after interethnic clashes. Trans-Dniester region declared its sovereignty. Nov: state of emergency declared in Trans-Dniester region after interethnic killings.
1991 March: Moldova boycotted the USSR's constitutional referendum. Aug: independence declared after abortive anti-Gorbachev coup; Communist Party outlawed. Dec: Moldova joined new Commonwealth of Independent States.
1992 Admitted into United Nations and the Conference on Security and Cooperation in Europe; diplomatic recognition granted by US. Possible union with Romania discussed. Trans-Dniester region fighting intensified; Russian peacekeeping force reportedly deployed after talks between Moldova and Russia. Andrei Sangheli became premier.
1993 Secessionist unrest continued in Gagauz and Trans-Dniester regions.

---

terrestrial. They include bivalves, mussels, octopuses, oysters, snails, slugs, and squids. The body is soft, limbless, and coldblooded. There is no internal skeleton, but many species have a hard shell.

Moloch or *Molech* in the Old Testament, a Phoenician deity worshiped in Jerusalem in the 7th century BC, to whom live children were sacrificed by fire.

Molotov cocktail or *gasoline bomb* homemade weapon consisting of a bottle filled with gasoline, plugged with a rag as a wick, ignited, and thrown as a grenade. Resistance groups during World War II named them after the Soviet foreign minister Molotov.

molting the periodic shedding of the hair or fur of mammals, feathers of birds, or skin of reptiles. In mammals and birds, molting is usually seasonal and is triggered by changes of day length.

Moluccas another name for ◊Maluku, a group of Indonesian islands.

molybdenum (Greek *malybdos* "lead") heavy, hard, lustrous, silver-white, metallic element, symbol Mo, atomic number 42, atomic weight 95.94. The chief ore is the mineral molybdenite. The element is highly resistant to heat and conducts electricity easily. It is used in alloys, often to harden steels. It is a necessary trace element in human nutrition. It was named 1781 by Swedish chemist Karl Scheele, after its isolation by P J Hjelm (1746–1813), for its resemblance to lead ore.

Mombasa industrial port (oil refining, cement) in Kenya (serving also Uganda and Tanzania), built on Mombasa Island and adjacent mainland; population (1984) 481,000. It was founded by Arab traders in the 11th century and was an important center for ivory and slave trading until the 16th century.

Momoyama in Japanese history, the period 1568–1616 or 1573–1603. During this time three great generals, Oda Nobunaga (1534–1582), Toyotomi Hideyoshi (1537–1598), who invaded Korea 1592, and ◊Tokugawa Ieyasu, successively held power; Ieyasu established the Tokugawa shogunate. Portuguese missionaries and traders were an influence at this time, and ◊Japanese art, architecture (castles), and the tea ceremony flourished. The period is named after a castle built by Hideyoshi in Fushimi, central Honshu.

Monaco small sovereign state forming an enclave in S France, with the Mediterranean Sea to the south. *See panel p. 630*

Monaghan (Irish *Mhuineachain*) county of the NE Republic of Ireland, province of Ulster; area 498 sq mi/1,290 sq km; products include cereals, linen, potatoes, and cattle; population (1991) 51,300. The county town is Monaghan. The county is low and rolling, and includes the rivers Finn and Blackwater.

monasticism devotion to religious life under vows of poverty, chastity, and obedience, known to Judaism (for example ◊Essenes), Buddhism, and other religions, before Christianity. In Islam, the Sufis formed monastic orders from the 12th century.

Monaco
Principality of

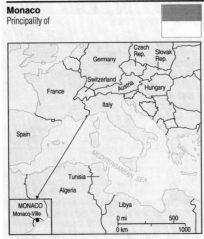

area 0.75 sq mi/1.95 sq km
capital Monaco-Ville
cities Monte Carlo, La Condamine; heliport Fontvieille
physical steep and rugged; surrounded landward by French territory; being expanded by filling in the sea

features aquarium and oceanographic center; Monte Carlo film festival, motor races, and casinos; world's second-smallest state
head of state Prince Rainier III from 1949
head of government Jean Ausseil from 1986
political system constitutional monarchy under French protectorate
political parties National and Democratic Union (UND); Democratic Union Movement; Monaco Action; Monégasque Socialist Party
exports some light industry; economy dependent on tourism and gambling
currency French franc
population (1989) 29,000; growth rate –0.5% p.a.
languages French (official), English, Italian
religion Roman Catholic 95%
literacy 99% (1985)

chronology
1861 Became an independent state under French protection.
1918 France given a veto over succession to the throne.
1949 Prince Rainier III ascended the throne.
1956 Prince Rainier married US actress Grace Kelly.
1958 Birth of male heir, Prince Albert.
1959 Constitution of 1911 suspended.
1962 New constitution adopted.
1963 Joined UN.

Mondale Walter "Fritz" 1928– . US Democrat politician, unsuccessful presidential candidate 1984. He was a senator 1964–76 from his home state of Minnesota, and vice president to Jimmy Carter 1977–81. After losing the 1984 presidential election to Ronald Reagan, Mondale retired from national politics to resume his law practice.

Mondrian Piet (Pieter Mondriaan) 1872–1944. Dutch painter, a pioneer of abstract art. He lived in Paris 1919–38, then in London, and from 1940 in New York. He was a founder member of the de ◊Stijl movement and chief exponent of Neo-Plasticism, a rigorous abstract style based on the use of simple geometric forms and pure colors. He typically painted parallel horizontal black lines which intersected vertical ones, creating square and rectangular blocks within the framework, some of which he filled with primary colors, midgray, or black, others being left white.

Monet Claude 1840–1926. French painter, a pioneer of Impressionism and a lifelong exponent of its ideals; his painting *Impression, Sunrise* 1872 gave the movement its name. In the 1870s he began painting the same subjects at different times of day to explore the effects of light on color and form; the *Haystacks* and *Rouen Cathedral* series followed in the 1890s, and from 1899 he painted a series of *Water Lilies* in the garden of his house at Giverny, Normandy (now a museum).

monetarism economic policy, advocated by the economist Milton Friedman and the Chicago school of economists, that proposes control of a country's money supply to keep it in step with the country's ability to produce goods, with the aim of curbing inflation. Cutting government spending is advocated, and the long-term aim is to return as much of the economy as possible to the private sector, allegedly in the interests of efficiency.

monetary policy economic policy aimed at controlling the amount of money in circulation, usually through controlling the level of lending or credit. Increasing interest rates is an example of a contractionary monetary policy, which aims to reduce infla-

tion by reducing the rate of growth of spending in the economy.

money any common medium of exchange acceptable in payment for goods or services or for the settlement of debts; legal tender. Money is usually coinage (invented by the Chinese in the second millennium BC) and paper notes (used by the Chinese from about AD 800). Developments such as the check and credit card fulfill many of the traditional functions of money.

money supply the quantity of money present in an economy at a given moment. Monetarists hold that a rapid increase in money supply inevitably provokes an increase in the rate of inflation.

Mongol member of any of the various Mongol (or Mongolian) ethnic groups of Central Asia. Mongols live in Mongolia, Russia, Inner Mongolia (China), Tibet, and Nepal. The Mongol language belongs to the Altaic family; some groups of Mongol descent speak languages in the Sino-Tibetan family, however.

Mongol Empire empire established by ◊Genghis Khan, who extended his domains from Russia to N China and became khan of the Mongol tribes 1206. His grandson ◊Kublai Khan conquered China and used foreigners (such as the Venetian traveler Marco Polo) as well as subjects to administer his empire. The Mongols lost China 1367 and suffered defeats in the west 1380; the empire broke up soon afterward.

Mongolia country in E Central Asia, bounded N by Russia and S by China. *See panel p. 632*

Mongolia, Inner (Chinese *Nei Mongol*) autonomous region of NE China from 1947
area 173,700 sq mi/450,000 sq km
capital Hohhot
features strategic frontier area with Russia; known for Mongol herders, now becoming settled farmers
physical grassland and desert
products cereals under irrigation; coal; reserves of rare earth oxides europium, and yttrium at Bayan Obo
population (1990) 21,457,000.

mongolism former name (now considered offensive) for ◊Down syndrome.

Monet The Luncheon in the Garden *(1873–74), Musée d'Orsay, Paris.*

Mongoloid referring to one of the three major varieties (see ◊races) of humans, *Homo sapiens sapiens*, including the indigenous peoples of Asia, the Indians of the Americas, Polynesians, and the Eskimos and Aleuts. General physical traits include dark eyes with epicanthic folds; straight to wavy dark hair; little beard or body hair; fair to tawny skin; low to medium-bridged noses; thin to medium lips. See also ◊Caucasoid, ◊Negroid.

mongoose any of various carnivorous mammals of the family Viverridae, especially the genus *Herpestes*. The Indian mongoose *H. mungo* is grayish in color and about 1.5 ft/50 cm long, with a long tail. It may be tamed and is often kept for its ability to kill snakes. The white-tailed mongoose *Ichneumia albicauda* of central Africa has a distinctive gray or white bushy tail.

monism in philosophy, the theory that reality is made up of only one substance. This view is usually contrasted with ◊dualism, which divides reality into two substances, matter and mind. The Dutch philosopher Baruch Spinoza saw the one substance as God or Nature. Monism is also sometimes used as a description of a political system in which only one party is permitted to operate.

monk man belonging to a religious order under the vows of poverty, chastity, and obedience, and living under a particular rule; see ◊monasticism.

Monk Thelonious (Sphere) 1917–1982. US jazz pianist and composer who took part in the development of ◊bebop. He had a highly idiosyncratic style, but numbers such as "Round Midnight" and "Blue Monk" have become standards. Monk worked in Harlem, New York, during the Depression, and became popular in the 1950s.

monkey any of the various smaller, mainly tree-dwelling anthropoid primates, excluding humans and the ◊apes. The 125 species live in Africa, Asia, and tropical Central and South America. Monkeys eat mainly leaves and fruit, and also small animals. Several species are endangered due to loss of forest habitat, for example the woolly spider monkey and black saki of the Amazonian forest.

monoculture farming system where only one crop is grown. In Third World countries this is often a ◊cash crop, grown on ◊plantations. Cereal crops in the industrialized world are also frequently grown on a monoculture basis; for example, wheat in the Canadian prairies.

monogamy practice of having only one husband or wife at a time in ◊marriage.

mononucleosis viral disease (also called "kissing disease," since it may be passed by body fluids, including saliva) characterized at onset by fever and painfully swollen lymph nodes (in the neck); there may also be digestive upset, sore throat, and skin rashes. Lassitude persists for months and even years, and recovery is often very slow. It is caused by the Epstein-Barr virus. A serious to fatal complication may be hepatitis.

Monophysite (Greek "one-nature") member of a group of Christian heretics of the 5th–7th centuries who taught that Jesus had one nature, in opposition to the orthodox doctrine (laid down at the Council of Chalcedon 451) that he had two natures, the human and the divine. Monophysitism developed as a reaction to ◊Nestorianism and led to the formal secession of the Coptic and Armenian churches from the rest of the Christian church. Monophysites survive today in Armenia, Syria, and Egypt.

monopoly in economics, the domination of a market for a particular product or service by a single company, which therefore has no competition and can keep prices high. In practice, a company can be said to have a monopoly when it controls a significant proportion of the market (technically an ◊oligopoly).

monorail railroad that runs on a single rail; the cars can be balanced on it or suspended from it. It was

Mongolia State of
(*Outer Mongolia* until 1924;
People's Republic of Mongolia
until 1991)

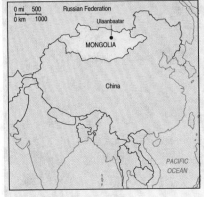

area 604,480 sq mi/1,565,000 sq km
capital Ulaanbaatar
cities Darhan, Choybalsan
physical high plateau with desert and steppe (grasslands)
features Altai Mountains in SW; salt lakes; part of Gobi Desert in SE; contains both the world's southernmost permafrost and northernmost desert.
head of state Punsalmaagiyn Ochirbat from 1990
head of government Puntsagiyn Jasray from 1992
political system emergent democracy
political parties Mongolian People's Revolutionary Party (MPRP), reform-communist; Mongolian Democratic Party (MDP), main opposition party; Mongolian Democratic Union

exports meat and hides, minerals, wool, livestock, grain, cement, timber
currency tugrik
population (1992) 2,182,000; growth rate 2.8% p.a.
life expectancy men 63, women 67 (1989)
languages Khalkha Mongolian (official), Chinese, Russian, and Turkic languages
religion officially none (Tibetan Buddhist Lamaism suppressed 1930s)
literacy 89% (1985)
GNP $3.6 bn; $1,820 per head (1986)

chronology
1911 Outer Mongolia gained autonomy from China.
1915 Chinese sovereignty reasserted.
1921 Chinese rule overthrown with Soviet help.
1924 People's Republic proclaimed.
1946 China recognized Mongolia's independence.
1966 20-year friendship, cooperation, and mutual-assistance pact signed with USSR. Relations with China deteriorated.
1984 Yumjaagiyn Tsedenbal, effective leader, deposed and replaced by Jambyn Batmonh.
1987 Soviet troops reduced; Mongolia's external contacts broadened.
1989 Further Soviet troop reductions.
1990 Democratization campaign launched by Mongolian Democratic Union. Punsalmaagiyn Ochirbat's MPRP elected in free multiparty elections. Mongolian script readopted.
1991 Massive privatization program launched as part of move toward a market economy. The word "Republic" dropped from country's name. GDP declined by 10%.
1992 Jan: New constitution introduced. Economic situation worsened; GDP again declined by 10%. Puntsagiyn Jasray appointed new prime minister.

---

invented 1882 to carry light loads, and when run by electricity was called a *telpher*.

monosodium glutamate (MSG) $NaC_5H_8NO_4$ a white, crystalline powder, the sodium salt of glutamic acid (an ◊amino acid found in proteins that plays a role in the metabolism of plants and animals). It is used to enhance the flavor of many packaged and "fast foods," and in Chinese cooking. Ill effects may arise from its overconsumption, and some people are very sensitive to it, even in small amounts. It is commercially derived from vegetable protein.

Monroe James Monroe, remembered for the Monroe Doctrine, his warning to European nations not to interfere with the countries of the Americas.

monotheism belief or doctrine that there is only one God; the opposite of polytheism.
It is the unifying theme of the Old Testament.

Monroe city in NE Louisiana, on the Ouachita River, E of Shreveport; population (1990) 54,900. Industries include furniture, chemicals, paper, natural gas, and soybeans.

Monroe James 1758–1831. 5th president of the US 1817–25, a Democratic Republican. He served in the American Revolution, was minister to France 1794–96, and in 1803 negotiated the ◊Louisiana Purchase. He was secretary of state 1811–17. His name is associated with the ◊Monroe Doctrine.
Monroe was born in Westmoreland County, Virginia. He attended the College of William and Mary and studied law under his lifelong friend Thomas ◊Jefferson. Monroe served in the Virginia legislature 1782, in the US Senate 1790–94, and as governor of Virginia 1799–1802. During the ◊Constitutional Convention he opposed ratification, fearing a central government with excessive power. As president, he presided over the so-called Era of Good Feeling, a period of domestic tranquility. He took no firm stand on the question of slavery, making his mark in foreign policy.

Monroe Marilyn. Adopted name of Norma Jean Mortenson or Baker 1926–1962. US film actress, the voluptuous blonde sex symbol of the 1950s, who made adroit comedies such as *Gentlemen Prefer Blondes* 1953, *How to Marry a Millionaire* 1953, *The Seven Year Itch* 1955, *Bus Stop* 1956, and *Some Like It Hot* 1959. Her second husband was baseball star Joe DiMaggio, and her third was playwright Arthur ◊Miller, who wrote *The Misfits* 1961 for her, a serious film that became her last. She committed suicide, taking an overdose of sleeping pills.

Monroe Doctrine declaration by US president James Monroe 1823 that any further European colonial ambitions in the western hemisphere would be threats to US peace and security, made in response to proposed European intervention against newly independent former Spanish colonies in South America. In return for the absence of such European ambitions, the US would not interfere in European affairs. The doctrine, subsequently broadened, has been a recurrent theme in US foreign policy, although it has no basis in US or international law.

Monrovia capital and port of Liberia; population (1985) 500,000. Industries include rubber, cement, and gasoline processing.

monsoon wind pattern that brings seasonally heavy rain to S Asia; it blows toward the sea in winter and toward the land in summer. The monsoon may cause destructive flooding all over India and SE Asia from April to Sept. Thousands of people are rendered homeless each year.

Montagu Ashley 1905– . British-born US anthropologist. As a critic of theories of racial determinism, he was a forceful defender of human rights and wrote such important works as *Man's Most Dangerous Myth: The Fallacy of Race* 1942. In 1950 he helped draft the definitive UNESCO "Statement on Race."

Montaigne Michel Eyquem de 1533–1592. French writer, regarded as the creator of the essay form. In 1580 he published the first two volumes of his *Essais*; the third volume appeared in 1588. Montaigne deals with all aspects of life from an urbanely skeptical viewpoint. Through the translation by John Florio in 1603, he influenced Shakespeare and other English writers.

Montana state in western US, on the Canadian border; nickname Treasure State
area 147,143 sq mi/318,100 sq km
capital Helena
cities Billings, Great Falls, Butte
physical mountainous forests in the W, rolling grasslands in the E
features rivers: Missouri, Yellowstone, Little Bighorn; Glacier National Park on the Continental Divide and Yellowstone National Park; Museum of the Plains Indian; Custer Battlefield National Monument; hunting and ski resorts
products wheat (under irrigation), cattle, coal, copper, oil, natural gas, lumber, wood products
population (1990) 799,100
famous people Gary Cooper, Myrna Loy
history explored for France by Verendrye early 1740s; passed to the US 1803 in the Louisiana Purchase; first settled 1809; W Montana obtained from Britain in the Oregon Treaty 1846; influx of gold-seeking immigrants mid-19th century; fierce Indian wars 1867–77, which included "Custer's Last Stand" at the Little Bighorn with the Sioux; achieved statehood 1889.

Energy production, in the form of oil, natural gas, and strip-mined coal, has replaced precious metals and copper in mineral exploitation. The plains area still produces grain crops, sheep, and cattle.

Montana Joe 1956– . US football player who has appeared in four winning Super Bowls as quarterback for the San Francisco 49ers 1982, 1985, 1989, and 1990, winning the Most Valuable Player award in 1982, 1985, and 1990. He threw a record five touchdown passes in the 1990 Super Bowl. He joined the Kansas City Chiefs 1993.

Monroe Legendary US film actress Marilyn Monroe.

Montand Yves 1921–1991. French actor and singer who achieved fame in the thriller *Le Salaire de la peur/The Wages of Fear* 1953 and continued to be popular in French and American films, including *Let's Make Love* 1960 (with Marilyn Monroe), *Le Sauvage/The Savage* 1976, *Jean de Florette* 1986, and *Manon des sources* 1986.

Mont Blanc (Italian *Monte Bianco*) highest mountain in the ◊Alps, between France and Italy; height 15,772 ft/4,807 m. It was first climbed 1786 by Jacques Balmat and Michel Paccard of Chamonix.

Montcalm Louis-Joseph de Montcalm-Gozon, Marquis de 1712–1759. French general, appointed military commander in Canada 1756. He won a succession of victories over the British during the French and Indian War, but was defeated in 1759 by James ◊Wolfe at Québec, where both he and Wolfe were killed; this battle marked the end of French rule in Canada.

Monte Carlo town and luxury resort in the principality of ◊Monaco, situated on a rocky promontory NE of Monaco town; population (1982) 12,000. It is known for its Casino (1878) designed by architect Charles Garnier, and the Monte Carlo automobile rally and Monaco Grand Prix.

Montenegro (Serbo-Croatian *Crna Gora*) constituent republic of Yugoslavia
area 5,327 sq mi/13,800 sq km
capital Titograd
cities Cetinje
features smallest of the republics; Skadarsko Jezero (Lake Scutari) shared with Albania
physical mountainous
population (1986) 620,000, including 400,000 Montenegrins, 80,000 Muslims, and 40,000 Albanians

Montana

Montréal *The Hotel de Ville in Montréal.*

language Serbian variant of Serbo-Croat
religion Serbian Orthodox
famous people Milovan Djilas
history part of ◊Serbia from the late 12th century, it became independent (under Venetian protection) after Serbia was defeated by the Turks 1389. It was forced to accept Turkish suzerainty in the late 15th century, but was never completely subdued by Turkey. It was ruled by bishop princes until 1851, when a monarchy was founded, and became a sovereign principality under the Treaty of Berlin 1878. The monarch used the title of king from 1910 with Nicholas I (1841–1921). Montenegro participated in the Balkan Wars 1912 and 1913. It was overrun by Austria in World War I, and in 1918 voted after the deposition of King Nicholas to become part of Serbia. In 1946 Montenegro became a republic of Yugoslavia. In a referendum March 1992 Montenegrins voted to remain part of the Yugoslav federation; the referendum was boycotted by Montenegro's Muslim and Albanian communities.

Monterrey industrial city (iron, steel, textiles, chemicals, food processing) in NE Mexico; population (1986) 2,335,000. It was founded 1597.

Montessori Maria 1870–1952. Italian educator. From her experience with mentally handicapped children, she developed the ***Montessori method***, an educational system for all children based on an informal approach, incorporating instructive play and allowing children to develop at their own pace.

Monteverdi Claudio (Giovanni Antonio) 1567–1643. Italian composer. He contributed to the development of the opera with *Orfeo* 1607 and *The Coronation of Poppea* 1642. He also wrote madrigals, ◊motets, and sacred music, notably the *Vespers* 1610.

Montevideo capital and chief port (grain, meat products, hides) of Uruguay, on the Río de la Plata; population (1985) 1,250,000. Industries include meat packing, tanning, footwear, flour milling, and textiles.

Montezuma II 1466–1520. Aztec emperor 1502–20. When the Spanish conquistador Cortés invaded Mexico, Montezuma was imprisoned and killed during the Aztec attack on Cortés's force as it tried to leave Tenochtitlán, the Aztec capital city.

Montgolfier Joseph Michel 1740–1810 and Étienne Jacques 1745–1799. French brothers whose hot-air balloon was used for the first successful human flight Nov 21, 1783.

Montgomery state capital of Alabama; population (1990) 187,100. The ***Montgomery Bus Boycott*** 1955 began here when a black passenger, Rosa Parks, refused to give up her seat to a white. Led by Martin Luther ◊King, Jr, the boycott was a landmark in the civil-rights campaign.

Two settlements on the site of the present-day city were consolidated 1819. Montgomery was the capital of the Confederacy in the first months of the American Civil War.

Montgomery Bernard Law, 1st Viscount Montgomery of Alamein 1887–1976. British field marshal. In World War II he commanded the 8th Army in N Africa in the Second Battle of El ◊Alamein 1942. As commander of British troops in N Europe from 1944, he received the German surrender 1945.

month unit of time based on the motion of the Moon around the Earth. The time from one new or full Moon to the next (the ***synodic*** or ***lunar month***) is 29.53 days. The time for the Moon to complete one orbit around the Earth relative to the stars (the ***sidereal month***) is 27.32 days. The ***solar month*** equals 30.44 days, and is exactly one-twelfth of the solar or tropical year, the time taken for the Earth to orbit the Sun. The ***calendar month*** is a human invention, devised to fit the calendar year.

Montpelier capital of Vermont, in the Green Mountains in the central part of the state, on the Winooski River; population (1990) 8,200. Industries include granite, insurance, and tourism.

Montréal inland port, industrial city (aircraft, chemicals, oil and petrochemicals, flour, sugar, brewing, meatpacking) of Québec, Canada, on Montréal Island at the junction of the Ottawa and St Lawrence rivers; population (1986) 2,921,000.

Montserrat volcanic island in the West Indies, one of the Leeward group, a British crown colony; capital Plymouth; area 42 sq mi/110 sq km; population (1985) 12,000. Practically all buildings were destroyed by Hurricane Hugo Sept 1989.

Moody Dwight Lyman 1837–1899. US evangelist. During the American Civil War 1861–65, he provided medical and moral support to the troops. In the 1870s he became a popular evangelist and founded the Northfield Seminary (now School) for girls 1879 and the Mount Hermon School for boys 1881, both in Massachusetts.

Moody Helen Wills married name of US tennis player Helen Newington Wills.

moon in astronomy, any natural ◊satellite that orbits a planet. Mercury and Venus are the only planets in the Solar System that do not have moons.

Moon natural satellite of Earth, 2,160 mi/3,476 km in diameter, with a mass 0.012 (approximately one-eightieth) that of Earth. Its surface gravity is only 0.16 (one-sixth) that of Earth. Its average distance from Earth is 238,855 mi/384,400 km, and it orbits in a west-to-east direction every 27.32 days (the ***sidereal month***). It spins on its axis with one side permanently turned toward Earth. The Moon has no atmosphere or water.

Moon Sun Myung 1920– . Korean industrialist and founder of the ◊Unification Church (***Moonies***) 1954. From 1973 he launched a major mission in the US and elsewhere. The church has been criticized for its manipulative methods of recruiting and keeping members. He was convicted of tax fraud in the US 1982.

Moon probe crewless spacecraft used to investigate the Moon. Early probes flew past the Moon or crash-landed on it, but later ones achieved soft landings or went into orbit. Soviet probes included the Luna/Lunik series. US probes (Ranger, Surveyor, Lunar Orbiter) prepared the way for the Apollo crewed flights.

The first space probe to hit the Moon was the Soviet *Lunik 2*, on Sept 13, 1959 (*Lunik 1* had missed the Moon eight months earlier). In Oct 1959, *Lunik 3* sent back the first photographs of the Moon's far side. *Lunik 9* was the first probe to soft-land on the Moon, on Feb 3, 1966, transmitting photographs of the surface to Earth. *Lunik 16* was the first probe to return automatically to Earth carrying Moon samples, in Sept 1970, although by then Moon rocks had already been brought back by US ◊Apollo astronauts who had landed on the Moon on July 20, 1969, and in Nov 1969. *Lunik 17* landed in Nov 1970 carrying a lunar rover, Lunokhod, which was driven over the Moon's surface by remote control from Earth. The first successful US Moon probe was *Ranger 7*, which took close-up photographs before it hit the Moon on July 31, 1964. *Surveyor 1*, on June 2, 1966, was the first US probe to soft-land on the lunar surface. It took photographs, and later Surveyors analyzed the surface rocks. Between 1966 and 1967 a series of five Lunar Orbiters photographed the entire Moon in detail, in preparation for the 1969 Apollo landings, when Neil Armstrong and Edwin Aldrin became the first men to walk on the Moon.

Moor any of the NW African Muslims, of mixed Arab and Berber origin, who conquered Spain and ruled its southern part from 711 to 1492. The name (English form of Latin *Maurus*) was originally applied to an inhabitant of the Roman province of Mauritania, in NW Africa.

Moore Dudley 1935– . English actor, comedian, and musician, formerly teamed with comedian Peter Cook. Moore became a Hollywood star after appearing in *10* 1979. His other films, mostly comedies, include *Bedazzled* 1968, *Arthur* 1981, and *Santa Claus* 1985.

He has played Classical piano concerts, including Carnegie Hall.

Moore Henry 1898–1986. British sculptor. His subjects include the reclining nude, mother and child groups, the warrior, and interlocking abstract forms. Many of his post–1945 works are in bronze or marble, including monumental semiabstracts such as *Reclining Figure* 1957–58 (outside the UNESCO building, Paris), and often designed to be placed in landscape settings.

Moore Roger 1928– . English actor who starred in the television series *The Saint* 1962–70, and assumed the film role of James Bond in 1973 in *Live and Let Die*.

His films include *Diane* 1955, *Gold* 1974, *The Wild Geese* 1978, and *Octopussy* 1983.

Moorhead city in W Minnesota, on the Red River, opposite Fargo, North Dakota; population (1990) 32,300. It is a center for an agricultural region that produces sugar beet, potatoes, grain, and dairy products.

moose large ◊deer *Alces alces* inhabiting N Asia and N Europe, where it is known as the elk. It is brown in color, stands about 6 ft/2 m at the shoulders, and has very large palmate antlers, a fleshy muzzle, a short neck, and long legs. It feeds on leaves and shoots.

moraine rocky debris or ◊till carried along and deposited by a ◊glacier. Material eroded from the side of a glaciated valley and carried along the glacier's edge is called lateral moraine; that worn from the valley floor and carried along the base of the glacier is called ground moraine. Rubble dropped at the foot of a melting glacier is called terminal moraine.

morality play didactic medieval European verse drama, in part a development of the ◊mystery play (or miracle play), in which human characters are replaced by personified virtues and vices, the limited humorous

elements being provided by the Devil. Morality plays, such as *Everyman*, flourished in the 15th century. They exerted an influence on the development of Elizabethan drama and comedy.

Moravia (Czech *Morava*) district of central Europe, forming two regions of the Czech Republic:
South Moravia (Czech *Jihomoravský*)
area 5,802 sq mi/15,030 sq km
capital Brno
population (1991) 2,048,900.
North Moravia (Czech *Severomoravský*)
area 4,273 sq mi/11,070 sq km
capital Ostrava
population (1991) 1,961,500.
features (N and S) river Morava; 25% forested
products corn, grapes, wine in the S; wheat, barley, rye, flax, sugar beet in the N; coal and iron
history part of the Avar territory since the 6th century; conquered by Charlemagne's Holy Roman Empire. In 874 the kingdom of Great Moravia was founded by the Slavic prince Sviatopluk, who ruled until 894. It was conquered by the Magyars 906, and became a fief of Bohemia 1029. It was passed to the Hapsburgs 1526, and became an Austrian crown land 1849. It was incorporated in the new republic of Czechoslovakia 1918, forming a province until 1949.

Moravia Alberto. Adopted name of Alberto Pincherle 1907–1991. Italian novelist. His first successful novel was *Gli indifferenti/The Time of Indifference* 1929, but its criticism of Mussolini's regime led to the government censoring his work until after World War II. Later books include *La romana/Woman of Rome* 1947, *La ciociara/Two Women* 1957, and *La noia/The Empty Canvas* 1961, a study of an artist's obsession with his model.

Moravian member of a Christian Protestant sect, the *Moravian Brethren*.

An episcopal church that grew out of the earlier Bohemian Brethren, it was established by the Lutheran Count Zinzendorf in Saxony 1722.

Mordvin Finnish people inhabiting the middle Volga Valley in W Asia. They are known to have lived in the region since the 1st century AD. There are 1 million speakers of Mordvin scattered throughout W Russia, about one-third of whom live in the Mordvinian republic. Mordvin is a Finno-Ugric language belonging to the Uralic family.

More (St) Thomas 1478–1535. English politician and author. From 1509 he was favored by ◊Henry VIII and employed on foreign embassies. He was a member of the privy council from 1518 and Lord Chancellor from 1529 but resigned over Henry's break with the pope. For refusing to accept the king as head of the church, he was executed. The title of his political book *Utopia* 1516 has come to mean any supposedly perfect society.

Before his execution More was imprisoned in the Tower of London for a year. He was canonized in 1935.

Moreau Jeanne 1928– . French actress who has appeared in international films, often in passionate, intelligent roles. Her work includes *Les Amants/The Lovers* 1958, *Jules et Jim/Jules and Jim* 1961, *Chimes at Midnight* 1966, and *Querelle* 1982.

Morgagni Giovanni Battista 1682–1771. Italian anatomist. As professor of anatomy at Padua, Morgagni carried out more than 400 autopsies, and developed the view that disease was not an imbalance of the body's humors but a result of alterations in the organs.

His work *On the Seats and Causes of Diseases as Investigated by Anatomy* 1761 formed the basis of ◊pathology.

Morgan Henry *c.* 1635–1688. Welsh buccaneer in the Caribbean. He made war against Spain, capturing and sacking Panama 1671. In 1674 he was knighted and appointed lieutenant governor of Jamaica.

Morgan J(ohn) P(ierpont) 1837–1913. US financier and investment banker whose company (sometimes criticized as "the money trust") became the most influential private banking house after the Civil War, being instrumental in the formation of many trusts to stifle competition. He set up the US Steel Corporation 1901 and International Harvester 1902.

Morgan Thomas Hunt 1866–1945. US geneticist, awarded the 1933 Nobel Prize for Medicine for his pioneering studies in Classical genetics. He was the first to work on the fruit fly *Drosophila*, which has since become a major subject of genetic studies. He helped establish that the genes were located on the chromosomes, discovered sex chromosomes, and invented the techniques of genetic mapping.

Morgan le Fay in the romance and legend of the English king ◊Arthur, an enchantress and healer, ruler of Avalon and sister of the king, whom she tended after his final battle. In some versions of the legend she is responsible for the suspicions held by the king of his wife ◊Guinevere.

Morley Edward 1838–1923. US physicist who collaborated with Albert ◊Michelson on the *Michelson–Morley experiment* 1887. In 1895 he established precise and accurate measurements of the densities of oxygen and hydrogen.

Morley Robert 1908–1992. English actor and playwright, who was active both in Britain and the US. His film work consisted mainly of character roles, in such movies as *Marie Antoinette* 1938, *The African Queen* 1952, and *Oscar Wilde* 1960.

Morley Thomas 1557–1602. English composer. A student of William ◊Byrd, he became organist at St Paul's Cathedral, London, and obtained a monopoly on music printing. A composer of the English madrigal school, he also wrote sacred music, songs for Shakespeare's plays, and a musical textbook.

Mormon or *Latter-day Saint* member of a Christian sect, the Church of Jesus Christ of Latter-day Saints, founded at Fayette, New York, 1830 by Joseph ◊Smith. According to Smith, Mormon was an ancient prophet in North America; his *Book of Mormon* is accepted by Mormons as part of the Christian scriptures. Smith said he found the book, inscribed on golden tablets, with the help of the angel Moroni in 1827, and that he translated it from "reformed Egyptian" by using special glasses. Originally persecuted, the Mormons migrated West under Brigham ◊Young's leadership and prospered. Today the worldwide membership in the Mormon church is about 6 million.

morning glory any twining or creeping plant of the genus *Ipomoea*, especially *I. purpurea*, family Convolvulaceae, native to tropical America, with dazzling

Morocco
Kingdom of
(*al-Mamlaka al-Maghrebia*)

area 177,070 sq mi/458,730 sq km (excluding Western Sahara)
capital Rabat
cities Marrakesh, Fez, Meknès; ports Casablanca, Tangier, Agadir
physical mountain ranges NE–SW; fertile coastal plains in W
features Atlas Mountains; the towns Ceuta (from 1580) and Melilla (from 1492) are held by Spain; tunnel crossing the Strait of Gibraltar to Spain proposed 1985
head of state Hassan II from 1961
head of government Mohamed Lawrani from 1992
political system constitutional monarchy
political parties Constitutional Union (UC), right-wing; National Rally of Independents (RNI), royalist; Popular Movement (MP), moderate socialist; Istiqlal, nationalist, right of center; Socialist Union of Popular Forces (USFP),

progressive socialist; National Democratic Party (PND), moderate, nationalist
exports dates, figs, cork, wood pulp, canned fish, phosphates
currency dirham (DH)
population (1992) 26,239,000; growth rate 2.5% p.a.
life expectancy men 62, women 65 (1989)
languages Arabic (official) 75%, Berber 25%, French, Spanish
religion Sunni Muslim 99%
literacy men 45%, women 22% (1985 est)
GNP $18.7 bn; $750 per head (1988)

chronology
1912 Morocco divided into French and Spanish protectorates.
1956 Independence achieved as the Sultanate of Morocco.
1957 Sultan restyled king of Morocco.
1961 Hassan II came to the throne.
1969 Former Spanish province of Ifni returned to Morocco.
1972 Major revision of the constitution.
1975 Western Sahara ceded by Spain to Morocco and Mauritania.
1976 Guerrilla war in Western Sahara with the Polisario Front. Sahrawi Arab Democratic Republic (SADR) established in Algiers. Diplomatic relations between Morocco and Algeria broken.
1979 Mauritania signed a peace treaty with Polisario.
1983 Peace formula for Western Sahara proposed by the Organization of African Unity (OAU); Morocco agreed but refused to deal directly with Polisario.
1984 Hassan signed an agreement for cooperation and mutual defense with Libya.
1987 Cease-fire agreed with Polisario, but fighting continued.
1988 Diplomatic relations with Algeria restored.
1989 Diplomatic relations with Syria restored.
1992 Mohamed Lawrani appointed prime minister; new constitution approved in referendum.
1993 Peace accord with Israel.

blue flowers. Small quantities of substances similar to the hallucinogenic drug ◊LSD are found in the seeds of some species.

Big-root morning glory *I. pandurata* is native to the E US.

Moro Aldo 1916–1978. Italian Christian Democrat politician. Prime minister 1963–68 and 1974–76, he was expected to become Italy's president, but he was kidnapped and shot by Red Brigade urban guerrillas.

Moroccan Crises two periods of international tension 1905 and 1911 following German objections to French expansion in Morocco. Their wider purpose was to break up the Anglo-French entente 1904, but both crises served to reinforce the entente and isolate Germany.

Morocco country in NW Africa, bounded N and NW by the Mediterranean Sea, E and SE by Algeria, and S by Western Sahara.

Moroni capital of the Comoros Republic, on Njazidja (Grand Comore); population (1980) 20,000. It has a small natural harbor from which coffee, cacao, and vanilla are exported.

Morpheus in Greek and Roman mythology, the god of dreams, son of Hypnos or Somnus, god of sleep.

morphine narcotic alkaloid $C_{17}H_{19}NO_3$ derived from ◊opium and prescribed only to alleviate severe pain. Its use produces serious side effects, including nausea, constipation, tolerance, and addiction, but it is highly valued for the relief of the terminally ill.

morphology in biology, the study of the physical structure and form of organisms, in particular their soft tissues.

Morris Robert 1734–1806. American political leader. A signatory of the Declaration of Independence 1776, he served in the Continental Congress 1775–78. In 1781 he was appointed superintendent of finance and dealt with the economic problems of the new nation. He served as one of Pennsylvania's first US senators 1789–95.

Morris William 1834–1896. English designer, a founder of the ◊Arts and Crafts movement, socialist, and writer who shared the Pre-Raphaelite painters' fascination with medieval settings. In 1861 he cofounded a firm that designed and produced furniture, carpets, and a wide range of decorative wallpapers, many of which are still produced today. His Kelmscott Press, set up 1890 to print beautifully designed books, influenced printing and book design. The prose romances *A Dream of John Ball* 1888 and *News from Nowhere* 1891 reflect his socialist ideology. He also lectured on socialism.

Morrison Toni 1931– . US novelist whose fiction records black life in the South. Her works include *Song of Solomon* 1978, *Tar Baby* 1981, *Beloved* 1987, based on a true story about infanticide in Kentucky, which won the Pulitzer Prize 1988, and *Jazz* 1992. She won the Nobel Prize for Literature 1993.

Morse Samuel (Finley Breese) 1791–1872. US inventor. In 1835 he produced the first adequate electric telegraph (see ◊telegraphy), and in 1843 was granted $30,000 by Congress for an experimental line between Washington, DC, and Baltimore. With his assistant Alexander Bain (1810–1877) he invented the Morse code.

Born in Charlestown, Massachusetts, Morse graduated from Yale 1810 and studied art in England. He served as the first president of the National Academy of Design 1826–45, which he helped to found, and

Morse Samuel Morse invented the electric telegraph and developed a code system (Morse code) to send messages.

taught at New York University from 1832. The first message 1844 transmitted between Washington and Baltimore was "What hath God wrought!"

Morse code international code for transmitting messages by wire or radio using signals of short (dots) and long (dashes) duration, originated by US inventor Samuel Morse for use on his invention, the telegraph (see ◊telegraphy).

mortar method of projecting a bomb via a high trajectory at a target up to 3–4 mi/6–7 km away. A mortar bomb is stabilized in flight by means of tail fins. The high trajectory results in a high angle of attack and makes mortars more suitable than artillery for use in built-up areas or mountains; mortars are not as accurate, however. Artillery also differs in firing a projectile through a rifled barrel, thus creating greater muzzle velocity.

Morte D'Arthur, Le series of episodes from the legendary life of King Arthur by Thomas ◊Malory, completed 1470, regarded as the first great prose work in English literature. Only the last of the eight books composing the series is titled *Le Morte D'Arthur*.

mortgage the pledging of real property—usually a building—as security for repayment of a loan. The loan and contracted interest is repaid over a contracted period of years, at which time ownership of the property reverts to the titleholder.

Mortimer John 1923– . English lawyer and writer. His works include the plays *The Dock Brief* 1958 and *A Voyage Round My Father* 1970, the novel *Paradise Postponed* 1985, and the television series "Rumpole of the Bailey," from 1978, centered on a fictional lawyer.

Mortimer Roger de, 8th Baron of Wigmore and 1st Earl of March *c.* 1287–1330. English politician and adventurer. He opposed Edward II and with Edward's queen, Isabella, led a rebellion against him 1326, bringing about his abdication. From 1327 Mortimer ruled England as the queen's lover, until Edward III had him executed.

Morton Jelly Roll. Adopted name of Ferdinand Joseph La Menthe 1885–1941. US New Orleans–style jazz pianist, singer, and composer. Influenced by Scott Joplin, he was a pioneer in the development of jazz from ragtime to swing by improvising and imposing his own personality on the music. His 1920s band was called the Red Hot Peppers.

mosaic design or picture, usually for a floor or wall, produced by inlaying small pieces of marble, glass, or other materials. Mosaic was commonly used by the Romans for their baths and villas (for example Hadrian's Villa at Tivoli) and by the Byzantines, especially for church decoration.

Moscow (Russian *Moskva*) industrial city, capital of Russia and of the Moskva region, and formerly (1922–91) of the USSR, on the Moskva River 400 mi/640 km SE of St Petersburg; population (1987) 8,815,000. Its industries include machinery, electrical equipment, textiles, chemicals, and many food products.

Moses *c.* 13th century BC. Hebrew lawgiver and judge who led the Hebrews out of slavery in Egypt (Exodus) and, after wandering 40 years in the desert, brought them to the border (E of the Jordan) of the promised land of Canaan. On Mount Sinai he claimed to have received from Jehovah the *Ten Commandments* engraved on tablets of stone. The first five books of the Old Testament—in Judaism, the ◊Torah—are called the *Five Books of Moses.*

Moses "Grandma" (born Anna Mary Robertson) 1860–1961. US painter. She was self-taught, and began full-time painting in about 1927, after many years as a farmer's wife. She painted naive and colorful scenes from rural American life.

Moses Ed(win Corley) 1955– . US track athlete and 400-meters hurdler. Between 1977 and 1987 he ran 122 races without defeat.

Moses Robert 1888–1981. US public official and urban planner. As parks commissioner for New York State 1924–64 and New York City 1934–60, he oversaw the development of bridges, highways, and public facilities. Serving as New York secretary of state 1927–28, he was the unsuccessful Republican candidate for New York governor 1934.

Mosley Oswald (Ernald) 1896–1980. British politician, founder of the British Union of Fascists (BUF) 1932. He was a member of Parliament 1918–31, then led the BUF until his internment 1940–43 during World War II. In 1946 Mosley was denounced when it became known that Italy had funded his prewar efforts to establish ◊fascism in Britain, but in 1948 he resumed fascist propaganda with his Union Movement, the revived BUF.

mosque (Arabic *mesjid*) in Islam, a place of worship. Chief features are: the dome; the minaret, a balconied turret from which the faithful are called to prayer; the *mihrab*, or prayer niche, in one of the interior walls, showing the direction of the holy city of Mecca; and an open court surrounded by porticoes.

mosquito any fly of the family Culicidae. The female mosquito has needlelike mouthparts and sucks blood before laying eggs. Males feed on plant juices. Some mosquitoes carry diseases such as ◊malaria.

Mosquito Coast Caribbean coast of Honduras and Nicaragua, characterized by swamp, lagoons, and tropical rain forest. The territory is inhabited by Miskito Indians, Garifunas, and Zambos, many of whom speak English. Between 1823 and 1860 Britain maintained a protectorate over the Mosquito Coast which was ruled by a succession of "Mosquito Kings."

moss small nonflowering plant of the class Musci (10,000 species), forming with the liverworts and the hornworts the order Bryophyta. The stem of each plant bears rhizoids that anchor it; there are no true roots. Leaves spirally arranged on its lower portion have sexual organs at their tips. Most mosses flourish best in damp conditions where other vegetation is thin. The peat or bog moss *Sphagnum* was formerly used for surgical dressings.

Mossadegh Mohammed 1880–1967. Iranian prime minister 1951–53. A dispute arose with the Anglo-Iranian Oil Company when he called for the nationalization of Iran's oil production, and when he failed in his attempt to overthrow the shah he was arrested by loyalist forces with support from the US. From 1956 he was under house arrest.

Mossi member of the majority ethnic group living in Burkina Faso. Their social structure, based on a monarchy and aristocracy, was established in the 11th century. The Mossi have been prominent traders, using cowrie shells as currency. There are about 4 million speakers of Mossi, a language belonging to the Gur branch of the Niger-Congo family.

Mostel Zero (Samuel Joel) 1915–1977. US comedian and actor, mainly in the theater. His films include *Panic in the Streets* 1950, *A Funny Thing Happened on the Way to the Forum* 1966, *The Producers* 1967, and *The Front* 1976.

motet sacred, polyphonic music for unaccompanied voices in a form that originated in 13th-century Europe.

moth any of the various families of mainly night-flying insects of the order Lepidoptera, which also includes the butterflies. Their wings are covered with microscopic scales. The mouthparts are formed into a sucking proboscis, but certain moths have no functional mouthparts, and rely upon stores of fat and other reserves built up during the caterpillar stage. At least 100,000 different species of moth are known.

mother-of-pearl or *nacre* the smooth lustrous lining in the shells of certain mollusks—for example pearl oysters, abalones, and mussels. When this layer is especially heavy it is used commercially for jewelry and decorations. Mother-of-pearl consists of calcium carbonate. See ◊pearl.

Mother's Day day set apart in the US, UK, and many European countries for honoring mothers. It is thought to have originated in Grafton, West Virginia, in 1908 when Anna Jarvis observed the anniversary of her mother's death.

In the US, Australia, and Canada, Mother's Day is observed on the second Sunday in May; in the UK it is known as Mothering Sunday and observed on the fourth Sunday of Lent.

Motherwell Robert 1915–1991. US painter associated with the New York school of ◊action painting. Borrowing from Picasso, Matisse, and the Surrealists, Motherwell's style of Abstract Expressionism retained some suggestion of the figurative. His works include the "Elegies to the Spanish Republic" 1949–76, a series of over 100 paintings devoted to the Spanish Revolution.

motion picture or *moving picture* see ◊cinema.

motion sickness nausea and vomiting caused by the motion of automobiles, boats, or aircraft. Constant vibration and movement sometimes stimulates changes in the fluid of the semicircular canals (responsible for balance) of the inner ear, to which the individual fails to adapt, and to which are added visual and psychological factors.

motor anything that produces or imparts motion; a machine that provides mechanical power, particularly an electric motor. Machines that burn fuel (gasoline, diesel) are usually called engines, but the internal-combustion engine that propels vehicles has long been called a motor, hence "motoring" and "motorcar" were used as early automotive terms. Actually the motor is a part of the ◊automobile engine.

motorboat small, waterborne craft for pleasure cruising or racing, powered by a gasoline, diesel, or gas-turbine engine. A boat not equipped as a motorboat may be converted by a detachable outboard motor. For increased speed, such as in racing, motorboat hulls are designed to skim the water (aquaplane) and reduce frictional resistance. Plastics, steel, and light alloys are now used in construction as well as the traditional wood.

motorcycle or **motorbike** two-wheeled vehicle propelled by a ◊gasoline engine. The motorbike is the lightweight version, with less power than the motorcycle, which may be equipped with a sidecar. The first successful motorized bicycle was built in France 1901, and British and US manufacturers first produced motorbikes 1903.

motorcycle racing speed contests on motorcycles. It has many different forms: **road racing** over open roads; **circuit racing** over purpose-built tracks; **speedway** over oval-shaped dirt tracks; **motocross** over natural terrain, incorporating hill climbs; and **trials**, also over natural terrain, but with the addition of artificial hazards.

Motown first black-owned US record company, founded in Detroit (Mo[tor] Town) 1959 by Berry Gordy, Jr (1929–). Its distinctive, upbeat sound (exemplified by the Four Tops and the Supremes) was a major element in 1960s pop music.

Mott Nevill Francis 1905– . English physicist who researched the electronic properties of metals, semiconductors, and noncrystalline materials. He shared the Nobel Prize for Physics 1977 with US physicists Philip Anderson (1923–) and John Van Vleck (1899–1980).

Moundbuilder member of any of the various North American Indian peoples of the Midwest and the South who built earth mounds, from about 300 BC. The mounds were linear and pictographic in form for tombs, such as the Great Serpent Mound in Ohio, and truncated pyramids and cones for the platforms of chiefs' houses and temples. The ◊Hopewell and ◊Natchez were Moundbuilders.

mountain natural upward projection of the Earth's surface, higher and steeper than a hill. The process of mountain building (orogeny) consists of volcanism, folding, faulting, and thrusting, resulting from the collision and welding together of two tectonic plates. *See panel p. 640*

mountain biking recreational sport that enjoyed increasing popularity in the 1990s. Mountain bikes first appeared on the mass market in the US in 1981, in the UK in 1984, and have been used in all aspects of cycling. However, it is also a competition sport, and the first world championship was held in France in 1987. The second world championship was held 1990 in Mexico. National mountain-bike championships have been held in the US since 1983 and in the UK since 1984. Mountain bikes have 10–15 gears, a toughened frame, and wider treads on the tires than ordinary bicycles.

highest mountains

name	height		location
	ft	m	
Everest	29,030	8,850	China–Nepal
K2	28,250	8,610	Kashmir–Jammu
Kangchenjunga	28,170	8,590	India–Nepal
Lhotse	27,890	8,500	China–Nepal
Kangchenjunga S Peak	27,800	8,470	India–Nepal
Makalu I	27,800	8,470	China–Nepal
Kangchenjunga W Peak	27,620	8,420	India–Nepal
Llotse E Peak	27,500	8,380	China–Nepal
Dhaulagiri	26,810	8,170	Nepal
Cho Oyu	26,750	8,150	China–Nepal
Manaslu	26,660	8,130	Nepal
Nanga Parbat	26,660	8,130	Kashmir–Jammu
Annapurna I	26,500	8,080	Nepal
Gasherbrum I	26,470	8,070	Kashmir–Jammu
Broad-highest	26,400	8,050	Kashmir–Jammu
Gasherbrum II	26,360	8,030	Kashmir–Jammu
Gosainthan	26,290	8,010	China
Broad-middle	26,250	8,000	Kashmir–Jammu
Gasherbrum III	26,090	7,950	Kashmir–Jammu
Annapurna II	26,040	7,940	Nepal
Nanda Devi	25,660	7,820	India
Rakaposhi	25,560	7,790	Kashmir
Kamet	25,450	7,760	India
Ulugh Muztagh	25,340	7,720	Tibet
Tirich Mir	25,230	7,690	Pakistan

* Heights are given to the nearest 10ft/m.

mountaineering art and practice of mountain climbing. For major peaks of the Himalayas it was formerly thought necessary to have elaborate support from Sherpas (local people), fixed ropes, and oxygen at high altitudes (**siege-style** climbing). In the 1980s the **Alpine style** was introduced. This dispenses with these aids, and relies on human ability to adapt, Sherpa-style, to high altitude.

mountain lion another name for ◊puma.

Mountbatten Louis, 1st Earl Mountbatten of Burma 1900–1979. British admiral and administrator. In World War II he became chief of combined operations 1942 and commander in chief in SE Asia 1943. As last viceroy of India 1947 and first governor-general of India until 1948, he oversaw that country's transition to independence. He was killed by an Irish Republican Army bomb aboard his yacht in the Republic of Ireland.

He was a favorite relative of the royal family and counselor to Prince Charles.

Mounties popular name for the **Royal Canadian Mounted Police**, known for their uniform of red jacket and broad-brimmed hat. Their Security Service, established 1950, was disbanded 1981 and replaced by the independent Canadian Security Intelligence Service.

Mount Palomar astronomical observatory, 50 mi/80 km NE of San Diego, California. It has a 200-in/5-m diameter reflector called the Hale. Completed 1948, it was the world's premier observatory during the 1950s.

mouse in computing, an input device used to control a pointer on a computer screen. It is a feature of ◊graphical user-interface (GUI) systems. The mouse is about the size of a pack of playing cards, is connected to the computer by a wire, and incorporates one or more buttons that can be pressed. Moving the mouse across a flat surface causes a corresponding movement of the pointer. In this way, the operator can

mountain

Animals and plants that live on mountains are adapted to cope with low temperatures, strong winds, a thin, poor soil, and air with little oxygen.

With increasing altitude, the climate becomes bleaker. Temperature, for example, falls by roughly 2°F/1°C for every 500ft/150m. On high mountains near the equator, this usually produces distinct zones of vegetation (shown right) similar to those found as one travels from the tropics to the North Pole.

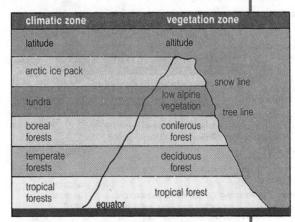

climatic zone	vegetation zone
latitude	altitude
arctic ice pack	snow line
tundra	low alpine vegetation / tree line
boreal forests	coniferous forest
temperate forests	deciduous forest
tropical forests	tropical forest
	equator

Alpine wildlife 1. brown bear 2. alpine marmot 3. chamois 4. peregrine falcon 5. golden eagle 6. ibex

7. Windflowers and gentians bloom in spring and last just a few weeks.

Plants of the alpine zone are small, compact and low-growing to survive the cold, strong winds. Most are perennial, continuing their growth over several years. Mountain animals tend to stay on the high slopes and peaks throughout the year. Many have a thick protective coat, and some of the hoofed mammals have soft pads on their feet that help them to cling to rocks.

manipulate objects on the screen and make menu selections.

mouse in zoology, one of a number of small rodents with small ears and a long, thin tail, belonging largely to the Old World family Muridae. The house mouse *Mus musculus* is distributed worldwide. It is 3 in/75 mm long, with a naked tail of equal length, and has a gray-brown body.

mouth cavity forming the entrance to the digestive tract. In land vertebrates, air from the nostrils enters the mouth cavity to pass down the trachea. The mouth in mammals is enclosed by the jaws, cheeks, and palate.

movie camera or *motion picture camera* camera that takes a rapid sequence of still photographs—24 frames (pictures) each second. When the pictures are projected one after the other at the same speed onto a screen, they appear to show movement, because our eyes hold onto the image of one picture before the next one appears.

Mozambique country in SE Africa, bounded N by Zambia, Malawi, and Tanzania; E and S by the Indian Ocean; SW by South Africa and Swaziland; and W by Zimbabwe.

Mozart Wolfgang Amadeus 1756–1791. Austrian composer and performer who showed astonishing precocity as a child and was an adult virtuoso. He was trained by his father, *Leopold Mozart* (1719–1787). From an early age he composed prolifically, his works including 27 piano concertos, 23 string quartets, 35 violin sonatas, and more than 50 symphonies including the E flat K543, G minor K550, and C major K551

("Jupiter") symphonies, all composed 1788. His operas include *Idomeneo* 1781, *Le Nozze di Figaro/The Marriage of Figaro* 1786, *Don Giovanni* 1787, *Così fan tutte/Thus Do All Women* 1790, and *Die Zauberflöte/The Magic Flute* 1791. Strongly influenced by ◊Haydn, Mozart's music marks the height of the Classical age in its purity of melody and form.

MP abbreviation for *member of Parliament*.

MS abbreviation for the state of ◊Mississippi.

MS-DOS (abbreviation for *Microsoft Disk Operating System*) computer ◊operating system produced by Microsoft Corporation, widely used on ◊microcomputers with Intel ×86 family microprocessors. A version called PC-DOS is sold by IBM specifically for its personal computers. MS-DOS and PC-DOS are usually referred to as DOS. MS-DOS first appeared 1981, and was similar to an earlier system from Digital Research called CP/M.

MT abbreviation for the state of ◊Montana.

Mubarak Hosni 1928– . Egyptian politician, president from 1981. Vice president to Anwar Sadat from 1975, Mubarak succeeded him on his assassination. He has continued to pursue Sadat's moderate policies, and has significantly increased the freedom of the press and of political association, while trying to repress the growing Islamic fundamentalist movement.

mucous membrane thin skin lining all animal body cavities and canals that come into contact with the air (for example, eyelids, breathing and digestive passages, genital tract). It secretes mucus, a moistening, lubricating, and protective fluid.

Mozambique
People's Republic of
(*República Popular de Moçambique*)

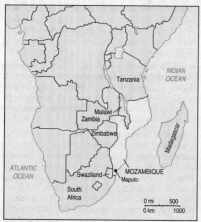

area 308,561 sq mi/799,380 sq km
capital and chief port Maputo
cities Beira, Nampula
physical mostly flat tropical lowland; mountains in W
features rivers Zambezi, Limpopo; "Beira Corridor" rail, road, and pipeline link with Zimbabwe
head of state and government Joaquim Alberto Chissano from 1986
political system emergent democratic republic
political parties National Front for the Liberation of Mozambique (Frelimo), Marxist-Leninist; Renamo, or

Mozambique National Resistance (MNR), former rebel movement
exports prawns, cashews, sugar, cotton, tea, petroleum products, copra
currency metical (replaced escudo 1980)
population (1992) 14,842,000 (mainly indigenous Bantu peoples; Portuguese 50,000); growth rate 2.8% p.a.; nearly 1 million refugees in Malawi
life expectancy men 45, women 48 (1989)
languages Portuguese (official), 16 African languages
religion animist 60%, Roman Catholic 18%, Muslim 16%
literacy men 55%, women 22% (1985 est)
GDP $4.7 bn; $319 per head (1987)

chronology
1505 Mozambique became a Portuguese colony.
1962 Frelimo (liberation front) established.
1975 Independence achieved from Portugal as a socialist republic, with Samora Machel as president and Frelimo as the sole legal party.
1977 Renamo resistance group formed.
1983 Reestablishment of good relations with Western powers.
1984 Nkomati accord of nonaggression signed with South Africa.
1986 Machel killed in airplane crash; succeeded by Joaquim Chissano.
1988 Tanzania announced withdrawal of its troops. South Africa provided training for Mozambican forces.
1989 Frelimo offered to abandon Marxist-Leninism; Chissano reelected. Renamo continued attacks on government facilities and civilians.
1990 One-party rule officially ended. Partial cease-fire agreed.
1991 Peace talks resumed in Rome, delaying democratic process. Attempted antigovernment coup thwarted.
1992 Peace accord signed, but fighting continued.

mucus lubricating and protective fluid, secreted by mucous membranes in many different parts of the body. In the gut, mucus smooths the passage of food and keeps potentially damaging digestive enzymes away from the gut lining. In the lungs, it traps airborne particles so that they can be expelled.

muezzin (Arabic) a person whose job is to perform the call to prayer five times a day from the minaret of a Muslim mosque.

muffler device in the exhaust system of automobiles and motorbikes. Gases leave the engine at supersonic speeds. The exhaust system and muffler are designed to slow them down, thereby silencing them.

Mugabe Robert (Gabriel) 1925– . Zimbabwean politician, prime minister from 1980 and president from 1987. He was in detention in Rhodesia for nationalist activities 1964–74, then carried on guerrilla warfare from Mozambique. As leader of ◊ZANU he was in an uneasy alliance with Joshua ◊Nkomo of ZAPU (Zimbabwe African People's Union) from 1976. The two parties merged 1987.

Muir John 1838–1914. Scottish-born US conservationist. From 1880 he headed a campaign that led to the establishment of Yosemite National Park. He was named adviser to the National Forestry Commission 1896 and continued to campaign for the preservation of wilderness areas for the rest of his life.

Mujaheddin (Arabic *mujahid* "fighters," from *jihad* "holy war") Islamic fundamentalist guerrillas of contemporary Afghanistan and Iran.

Mukden, Battle of taking of Mukden (now Shenyang), NE China, from Russian occupation by the Japanese 1905, during the ◊Russo-Japanese War. Mukden was later the scene of a surprise attack (the "Mukden incident") Sept 18, 1931, by the Japanese on the Chinese garrison, which marked the beginning of their invasion of China.

mulberry any tree of the genus *Morus*, family Moraceae, consisting of a dozen species, including the black mulberry *M. nigra*. It is native to W Asia and has heart-shaped, toothed leaves, and spikes of whitish flowers. It is widely cultivated for its fruit, which, made up of a cluster of small drupes, resembles a raspberry. The leaves of the Asiatic white mulberry *M. alba* are those used in feeding silkworms.

The red mulberry *M. rubra* of the E US also has large edible multiple fruit.

Muldoon Robert David 1921–1992. New Zealand National Party politician, prime minister 1975–84, during which time he pursued austere economic policies such as a wage-and-price policy to control inflation.

mule hybrid animal, usually the offspring of a male ass and a female horse.

mullah (Arabic "master") a teacher, scholar, or religious leader of Islam. It is also a title of respect given to various other dignitaries who perform duties connected with the sacred law.

Muller v Oregon a US Supreme Court decision 1908 dealing with the constitutionality of state laws regulating working conditions for women. Muller, an Oregon laundry owner, was convicted for requiring his female employees to work longer than 10 hours a day, exceeding the legal maximum for women according to state law. He appealed the conviction on the grounds that the state law violated the 14th-Amendment right to freedom of contracts. The Court upheld the conviction, ruling that the law legitimately promoted public health; since women were at greater risk in the workplace, they warranted state protection.

Mulliken Robert Sanderson 1896–1986. US chemist and physicist who received the 1966 Nobel Prize for Chemistry for his development of the molecular orbital theory.

He was professor at the University of Chicago 1931–61.

Mulroney Brian 1939– . Canadian politician. A former businessman, he replaced Joe Clark as Progressive Conservative Party leader 1983 and achieved a landslide in the 1984 election to become prime minister. He won the 1988 election on a platform of free trade with the US, and by the end of 1988 the Canada–US trade agreement was approved. Opposition within Canada to the Meech Lake agreement, a prerequisite to signing the 1982 Constitution, continued to plague Mulroney in his second term. A revised reform package Oct 1992 failed to gain voters' approval; and in early 1993 he was forced to resign the party leadership, although he remained prime minister until Kim Campbell was appointed his successor in June.

multilateralism trade among more than two countries without discrimination over origin or destination and regardless of whether a large trade gap is involved.

multinational corporation company or enterprise operating in several countries, usually defined as one that has 25% or more of its output capacity located outside its country of origin.

multiple birth in humans, the production of more than two babies from one pregnancy. Multiple births can be caused by more than two eggs being produced and fertilized (often as the result of hormone therapy to assist pregnancy), or by a single fertilized egg dividing more than once before implantation.

multiple independently targeted reentry vehicle (MIRV) nuclear-warhead-carrying part of a ballistic ◊missile that splits off in midair from the main body. Since each is individually steered and controlled, MIRVs can attack separate targets over a wide area.

multiple sclerosis (MS) incurable chronic disease of the central nervous system, occurring in young or middle adulthood. It is characterized by degeneration of the myelin sheath that surrounds nerves in the brain and spinal cord. It is also known as disseminated sclerosis. Its cause is unknown.

multiplier in economics, the theoretical concept, formulated by John Maynard Keynes, of the effect on national income or employment by an adjustment in overall demand. For example, investment by a company in a new plant will stimulate new income and expenditure, which will in turn generate new investment, and so on, so that the actual increase in national income may be several times greater than the original investment.

multistage rocket rocket launch vehicle made up of several rocket stages (often three) joined end to end. The bottom stage fires first, boosting the vehicle to high speed, then it falls away. The next stage fires, thrusting the now lighter vehicle even faster. The remaining stages fire and fall away in turn, boosting the vehicle's payload (cargo) to an orbital speed that can reach 17,500 mph/28,000 kph.

mummers' play or *St George play* British folk drama enacted in dumb show by a masked cast, performed on Christmas Day to celebrate the death of the old year and its rebirth as the new year. The plot usually consists of a duel between St George and an infidel knight, in which one of them is killed but later revived by a doctor. Mummers' plays are still performed in some parts of Britain.

mummy any dead body, human or animal, that has been naturally or artificially preserved. Natural mummification can occur through freezing (for example, mammoths in glacial ice from 25,000 years ago), drying, or preservation in bogs or oil seeps. Artificial mummification may be achieved by embalming (for example, the mummies of ancient Egypt) or by freeze-drying.

mumps virus infection marked by fever and swelling of the parotid salivary glands (such as those under the ears). It is usually minor in children, although meningitis is a possible complication. In adults the symptoms are severe and it may cause sterility in adult men.

Münchhausen Karl Friedrich, Freiherr (Baron) von 1720–1797. German soldier, born in Hanover. He served with the Russian army against the Turks, and after his retirement in 1760 told exaggerated stories of his adventures. This idiosyncrasy was utilized by the German writer Rudolph Erich Raspe (1737–1794) in his extravagantly fictitious *Adventures of Baron Munchausen* 1785, which he wrote in English while living in London.

Münchhausen's syndrome emotional disorder in which a patient feigns or invents symptoms to secure medical treatment. In some cases the patient will secretly ingest substances to produce real symptoms. It was named after the exaggerated tales of Baron Münchhausen.

Muncie city in E central Indiana, NE of Indianapolis; population (1990) 71,000. Industries include vehicle parts, livestock, dairy products, steel forgings, and wire. It was the subject of Robert and Helen Lynd's *Middletown*, a sociological study of a midwestern city.

Munda member of any one of several groups living in NE and central India, numbering about 5 million (1983). Their most widely spoken languages are Santali and Mundari, languages of the Munda group, an isolated branch of the Austro-Asiatic family. The Mundas were formerly nomadic hunter-gatherers, but now practice shifting cultivation. They are Hindus, but retain animist beliefs.

Munich (German *München*) industrial city (brewing, printing, precision instruments, machinery, electrical goods, textiles), capital of Bavaria, Germany, on the river Isar; population (1986) 1,269,400.

Munich Agreement pact signed on Sept 29, 1938, by the leaders of the UK (Neville ◊Chamberlain), France (Edouard ◊Daladier), Germany (Hitler), and Italy (Mussolini), under which Czechoslovakia was compelled to surrender its Sudeten-German districts (the **Sudetenland**) to Germany. Chamberlain claimed it would guarantee "peace in our time," but it did not prevent Hitler from seizing the rest of Czechoslovakia in March 1939.

Munro H(ugh) H(ector) English author who wrote under the adopted name Saki.

Munster southern province of the Republic of Ireland, comprising the counties of Clare, Cork, Kerry, Limerick, North and South Tipperary, and Waterford; area 9,318 sq mi/24,140 sq km; population (1991) 1,008,400.

Murakami Haruki 1949– . Japanese novelist and translator, one of Japan's best-selling writers, influ-

enced by 20th-century US writers and popular culture. His dreamy, gently surrealist novels include *A Wild Sheep Chase* 1982 and *Norwegian Wood* 1987.

Murasaki Shikibu *c.* 978–*c.* 1015. Japanese writer, a lady at the court. Her masterpiece of fiction, *The Tale of Genji*, is one of the classic works of Japanese literature, and may be the world's first novel.

Murat Joachim 1767–1815. King of Naples 1808–1815. An officer in the French army, he was made king by Napoleon, but deserted him in 1813 in the vain hope that Austria and Great Britain would recognize him. In 1815 he attempted unsuccessfully to make himself king of all Italy, but when he landed in Calabria in an attempt to gain the throne he was captured and shot.

Murcia autonomous region of SE Spain; area 4,362 sq mi/11,300 sq km; population (1986) 1,014,000. It includes the cities Murcia and Cartagena, and produces esparto grass, lead, zinc, iron, and fruit.

murder unlawful killing of one person by another. In the US, first-degree murder requires proof of premeditation; second-degree murder falls between first-degree murder and manslaughter.

If the killer can show provocation by the victim (action or words that would make a reasonable person lose self-control) or diminished responsibility (an abnormal state of mind caused by illness, injury, or mental subnormality), the charge may be reduced to a less serious one. See also ◊assassination and ◊homicide.

Murdoch (Keith) Rupert 1931– . Australian-born US media magnate with worldwide interests. His UK newspapers, generally right-wing, include the *Sun*, the *News of the World*, and *The Times*; in the US, he has a 50% share of 20th Century Fox, six Metromedia TV stations, and newspaper and magazine publishing companies. He purchased a 50% stake in a Hungarian tabloid, *Reform*, from 1989.

He became a US citizen in 1985.

Murdoch Iris 1919– . English novelist, born in Dublin. Her novels combine philosophical speculation with often outrageous situations and tangled human relationships. They include *The Sandcastle* 1957, *The Sea, The Sea* 1978, and *The Message to the Planet* 1990.

Murillo Bartolomé Estebán *c.* 1617–1682. Spanish painter, active mainly in Seville. He painted sentimental pictures of the Immaculate Conception; he also specialized in studies of street urchins.

Murmansk seaport in NW Russia, on the Barents Sea; population (1987) 432,000. It is the largest city in the Arctic, Russia's most important fishing port, and the base of naval units and the icebreakers that keep the Northeast Passage open.

Muromachi in Japanese history, the period 1392–1568, comprising the greater part of the rule of the ◊Ashikaga shoguns; it is named after the area of Kyoto where their headquarters were sited.

Murphy Eddie 1961– . US film actor and comedian. His first film, *48 Hours* 1982, introduced the streetwise, cocksure character that has become his specialty. Its great success, and that of his next two films, *Trading Places* 1983 and *Beverly Hills Cop* 1984, made him one of the biggest box-office draws of the 1980s.

Murray principal river of Australia, 1,600 mi/2,575 km long. It rises in the Australian Alps near Mount Kosciusko and flows W, forming the boundary between New South Wales and Victoria, and reaches

muscle Muscles make up 35–45% of the body weight; there are over 650 skeletal muscles.

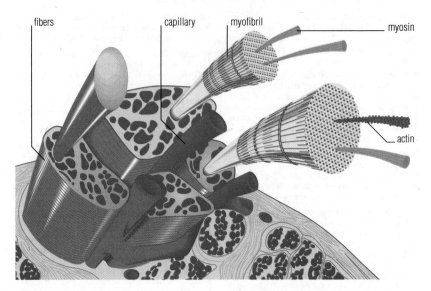

fibers   capillary   myofibril   myosin

actin

the sea at Encounter Bay, South Australia. With its main tributary, the Darling, it is 2,330 mi/3,750 km long.

Murrow Edward R(oscoe) 1908–1965. US broadcast journalist. Hired by the Columbia Broadcasting System (CBS) 1935 to plan its educational programs, Murrow was named director of its European Bureau 1937. From London he covered the events of World War II. Murrow hosted the popular radio show "Hear It Now" 1948–51 and television shows "See It Now" 1951–58, "Person to Person" 1953–58, and "Small World" 1958–60. After leaving CBS, he served as director of the US Information Agency 1961–64.

Musashi Miyamoto (1584–1645). Japanese samurai and painter also known as Niten.

Muscat or *Masqat* capital of Oman, E Arabia, adjoining the port of Matrah, which has a deep-water harbor; combined population (1982) 80,000. It produces natural gas and chemicals.

muscle contractile animal tissue that produces locomotion and maintains the movement of body substances. Muscle is made of long cells that can contract to between one-half and one-third of their relaxed length.

muscovite white mica, $KAl_2Si_3AlO_{10}(OH,F)_2$, a common silicate mineral. It is colorless to silvery white with shiny surfaces, and like all micas it splits into thin flakes along its one perfect cleavage. Muscovite is a metamorphic mineral occurring mainly in schists; it is also found in some granites, and appears as shiny flakes on bedding planes of some sandstones.

muscular dystrophy any of a group of inherited chronic muscle disorders marked by weakening and wasting of muscle. Muscle fibers degenerate, to be replaced by fatty tissue, although the nerve supply remains unimpaired. Death occurs in early adult life.

Muse in Greek mythology, one of the nine daughters of Zeus and Mnemosyne (goddess of memory) and inspirers of creative arts: Calliope, epic poetry; Clio, history; Erato, love poetry; Euterpe, lyric poetry; Melpomene, tragedy; Polyhymnia, sacred song; Terpsichore, dance; Thalia, comedy; and Urania, astronomy.

Museveni Yoweri Kaguta 1945– . Ugandan general and politician, president from 1986. He led the opposi-

tion to Idi Amin's regime 1971–78 and was minister of defense 1979–80 but, unhappy with Milton Obote's autocratic leadership, formed the National Resistance Army (NRA). When Obote was ousted in a coup in 1985, Museveni entered into a brief power-sharing agreement with his successor, Tito Okello, before taking over as president. Museveni leads a broad-based coalition government.

mushroom fruiting body of certain fungi, consisting of an upright stem and a spore-producing cap with radiating gills on the undersurface. There are many edible species belonging to the genus *Agaricus*. See also ◊fungus and ◊toadstool.

Musial Stan(ley Frank). Nicknamed "Stan the Man." 1920– . US baseball player. During his playing career of 22 years, he led the National League 6 times in hits, 8 times in doubles, 5 times in triples, and 7 times in batting average. He played his last season 1963 and was hired by the Cardinals as an executive.

music art of combining sounds into a coherent perceptual experience, typically in accordance with fixed patterns and for an aesthetic purpose. Music is generally categorized as Classical, ◊jazz, ◊pop music, ◊country and western, and so on.

musical 20th-century form of dramatic musical performance, combining elements of song, dance, and the spoken word, often characterized by lavish staging and large casts. It developed from the operettas and musical comedies of the 19th century.

music theater staged performance of vocal music that deliberately sets out to get away from the grandiose style and scale of traditional opera.

musk deer any of three species of small deer of the genus *Moschus*, native to the mountains of central and NE Asia. A solitary animal, the musk deer is about 30–40 in/80–100 cm in height, is sure-footed, and has large ears and no antlers. Males have long tusklike upper canine teeth. They are hunted and farmed for their musk (a waxy substance secreted by the male from an abdominal gland), which is used as medicine or perfume.

Muskegon city in W Michigan, on the Muskegon River where it enters Lake Michigan, NW of Grand

Music: great composers

Name	Dates	Nationality	Works
Giovanni Palestrina	c.1525–1594	Italian	motets, masses
Claudio Monteverdi	1567–1643	Italian	operas, vocal music
Henry Purcell	1659–1695	English	vocal music, operas
Antonio Vivaldi	1678–1741	Italian	concertos, chamber music
Georg Friedrich Handel	1685–1759	German	oratorios, operas, orchestra
Johann Sebastian Bach	1685–1750	German	keyboard choral music, concertos
Joseph Haydn	1732–1809	Austrian	symphonies, oratorios, chamber music
Wolfgang Mozart	1756–1791	Austrian	symphonies, operas, chamber music
Ludwig van Beethoven	1770–1827	German	symphonies, chamber music
Carl Maria von Weber	1786–1826	German	operas, concertos
Gioacchino Rossini	1792–1868	Italian	operas
Franz Schubert	1797–1828	Austrian	songs, symphonies, chamber music
Hector Berlioz	1803–1869	French	operas, symphonies
Felix Mendelssohn	1809–1847	German	symphonies, concertos
Frederik Chopin	1810–1849	Polish	piano music
Robert Schumann	1810–1856	German	piano, vocal music, concertos
Franz Liszt	1811–1886	Hungarian	piano, orchestral music
Richard Wagner	1813–1883	German	operas
Giuseppe Verdi	1813–1901	Italian	operas
César Franck	1822–1890	Belgian	symphony, organ works
Bedrich Smetana	1824–1884	Czech	symphonies, operas
Anton Bruckner	1824–1896	Austrian	symphonies
Johann Strauss II	1825–1899	Austrian	waltzes, operettas
Johannes Brahms	1833–1897	German	symphonies, concertos
Camille Saint Saëns	1835–1921	French	symphonies, concertos, operas
Modest Mussorgsky	1839–1881	Russian	operas, orchestral music
Peter Tchaikovsky	1840–1893	Russian	ballet music, symphonies
Antonin Dvořák	1841–1904	Czech	symphonies, operas
Edvard Grieg	1843–1907	Norwegian	concertos, orchestral music
Nikolai Rimsky-Korsakov	1844–1908	Russian	operas, orchestral music
Leos Janáček	1854–1928	Czech	operas, chamber music
Edward Elgar	1857–1934	English	orchestral music
Giacomo Puccini	1858–1924	Italian	operas
Gustav Mahler	1860–1911	Czech	symphonies
Claude Debussy	1862–1918	French	operas, orchestral music
Richard Strauss	1864–1949	German	operas, orchestral music
Carl Nielsen	1865–1931	Danish	symphonies
Jean Sibelius	1865–1957	Finnish	symphonies, orchestral music
Sergei Rachmaninov	1873–1943	Russian	symphonies, concertos
Arnold Schoenberg	1874–1951	Austrian	concertos, vocal, orchestral, and chamber music
Maurice Ravel	1875–1937	French	orchestral, piano, chamber music
Béla Bartók	1881–1945	Hungarian	operas, concertos, chamber music
Igor Stravinsky	1882–1971	Russian	ballets, operas, orchestral, chamber music
Anton Webern	1883–1945	Austrian	chamber, vocal music
Alban Berg	1885–1935	Austrian	operas, chamber music
Sergei Prokofiev	1891–1953	Russian	symphonies, operas, ballets, piano music
George Gershwin	1898–1937	American	musicals, operas
Dmitri Shostakovich	1906–1975	Russian	symphonies, chamber music
Oliver Messiaen	1908–1992	French	piano, organ, orchestral music
Benjamin Britten	1913–1976	English	vocal music, opera
Karlheinz Stockhausen	1928–	German	electronic, chamber music, music theater

Rapids; population (1990) 40,300. Industries include heavy machinery, metal products, vehicle parts, and sporting goods.

musk ox ruminant *Ovibos moschatus* of the family Bovidae, native to the Arctic regions of North America. It displays characteristics of sheep and oxen, is about the size of a small domestic cow, and has long brown hair. At certain seasons it exhales a musky odor. *See illustration p. 646*

muskrat rodent *Ondatra zibethicus* of the family Cricetidae, about 12in/30 cm long, living along streams, rivers, and lakes in North America. It has webbed hind feet, a side-to-side flattened tail, and shiny, light-brown fur. It builds up a store of food, plastering it over with mud, for winter consumption. It is hunted for its fur.

Muslim or *Moslem*, a follower of ◊Islam.

Muslim Brotherhood movement founded by members of the Sunni branch of Islam in Egypt in 1928. It aims at the establishment of a theocratic Islamic state and is headed by a "supreme guide." It is also active in Jordan, Sudan, and Syria.

mussel one of a number of bivalve mollusks, some of them edible, such as *Mytilus edulis*, found in clusters attached to rocks around the N Atlantic and American coasts. It has a blue-black shell.

musk ox *The musk ox once roamed throughout N Europe and America, but it now survives only in N Canada and Greenland.*

Mussolini Benito 1883–1945. Italian dictator 1925–43. As founder of the Fascist Movement (see ◊fascism) 1919 and prime minister from 1922, he became known as *Il Duce* ("the leader"). He invaded Ethiopia 1935–36, intervened in the Spanish Civil War 1936–39 in support of Franco, and conquered Albania 1939. In June 1940 Italy entered World War II supporting Hitler. Forced by military and domestic setbacks to resign 1943, Mussolini established a breakaway government in N Italy 1944–45, but was killed trying to flee the country.

Mussorgsky Modest Petrovich 1839–1881. Russian composer who was largely self-taught. His opera *Boris Godunov* was completed in 1869, although not produced in St Petersburg until 1874. Some of his works were "revised" by ◊Rimsky-Korsakov, and only recently has their harsh original beauty been recognized.

Mustafa Kemal Turkish leader who assumed the name of ◊Atatürk.

mustard any of several annual plants of the family Cruciferae, with sweet-smelling yellow flowers. Brown and white mustard are cultivated as a condiment in Europe and North America. The seeds of brown mustard *Brassica juncea* and white mustard *Sinapis alba* are used in the preparation of table mustard.

mutation in biology, a change in the genes produced by a change in the ◊DNA that makes up the hereditary material of all living organisms. Mutations, the raw material of evolution, result from mistakes during replication (copying) of DNA molecules. Only a few improve the organism's performance and are therefore favored by ◊natural selection. Mutation rates are increased by certain chemicals and by radiation.

mute in music, any device used to dampen the vibration of an instrument and so affect the tone. Brass instruments use plugs of metal or cardboard inserted in the bell, while orchestral strings apply a form of clamp to the bridge.

mutiny organized act of disobedience or defiance by two or more members of the armed services. In naval and military law, mutiny has always been regarded as one of the most serious of crimes, punishable in wartime by death.

mutual fund a company that invests its clients' funds in other companies, equities, or securities. The owner of stock in the investment company holds a proportional interest in the investment company based on the number of shares in the portfolio holdings of the company. In this way a small investor may benefit from professional judgment and a much broader range of investments than might be possible individually.

Muzorewa Abel (Tendekayi) 1925– . Zimbabwean politician and Methodist bishop. He was president of the African National Council 1971–85 and prime minister of Rhodesia/Zimbabwe 1979–80. He was detained for a year in 1983–84. He is leader of the minority United Africa National Council.

myalgic encephalomyelitis see ◊ME.

Myanmar formerly (until 1989) *Burma* country in SE Asia, bounded NW by India and Bangladesh, NE by China, SE by Laos and Thailand, and SW by the Bay of Bengal.

myasthenia gravis in medicine, an uncommon condition characterized by loss of muscle power, espe-

Mussolini *Benito Mussolini greeting Adolf Hitler at Florence railway station, Italy, Oct 1940.*

Myanmar
Union of
(*Thammada Myanmar Naingngandaw*)
(formerly **Burma**, until 1989)

area 261,228 sq mi/676,577 sq km
capital (and chief port) Yangon (formerly Rangoon)
cities Mandalay, Moulmein, Pegu
physical over half is rain forest; rivers Irrawaddy and Chindwin in central lowlands ringed by mountains in N, W, and E
environment landslides and flooding during the rainy season (June–Sept) are becoming more frequent as a result of deforestation
features ruined cities of Pagan and Mingun
head of state and government Than Shwe from 1992
political system military republic
political parties National Unity Party (NUP), military-socialist ruling party; National League for Democracy (NLD), pluralist opposition grouping
exports rice, rubber, jute, teak, jade, rubies, sapphires
currency kyat

population (1992) 43,466,000; growth rate 1.9% p.a. (includes Shan, Karen, Raljome, Chinese, and Indian minorities)
life expectancy men 53, women 56 (1989)
language Burmese
religions Hinayana Buddhist 85%, animist, Christian
literacy 66% (1989)
GNP $9.3 bn (1988); $210 per head (1989)

chronology
1886 United as province of British India.
1937 Became crown colony in the British Commonwealth.
1942–45 Occupied by Japan.
1948 Independence achieved from Britain. Left the Commonwealth.
1962 General Ne Win assumed power in army coup.
1973–74 Adopted presidential-style "civilian" constitution.
1975 Opposition National Democratic Front formed.
1986 Several thousand supporters of opposition leader Suu Kyi arrested.
1988 Government resigned after violent demonstrations. General Saw Maung seized power in military coup Sept; over 1,000 killed.
1989 Martial law declared; thousands arrested including advocates of democracy and human rights. Country renamed Myanmar and capital Yangon.
1990 Landslide victory for NLD in general election was ignored by military junta; opposition leader Aung San Suu Kyi placed under house arrest. Breakaway opposition group formed "parallel government" on rebel-held territory.
1991 Martial law and human-rights abuses continued. Military offensives continued. Suu Kyi awarded Nobel Prize for Peace but was not released.
1992 Jan–April: Pogrom against Muslim community in Arakan province, W Myanmar, carried out with army backing. April: Saw Maung replaced by Than Shwe. Several political prisoners liberated. Sept: martial law lifted, but restrictions on political freedom remained.
1993 Constitutional convention agreed on a more liberal constitution. Suu Kyi still being held.

---

cially in the face and neck. The muscles tire rapidly and fail to respond to repeated nervous stimulation. ◊Autoimmunity is the cause.

Mycenae ancient Greek city in the E Peloponnese, which gave its name to the Mycenaean (Bronze Age) civilization. Its peak was 1400–1200 BC, when the Cyclopean walls (using close-fitting stones) were erected. The city ceased to be inhabited after about 1120 BC.

Mycenaean civilization Bronze Age civilization that flourished in Crete, Cyprus, Greece, the Aegean Islands, and W Anatolia about 3000–1000 BC. During this period, magnificent architecture and sophisticated artifacts were produced.

myelin sheath insulating layer that surrounds nerve cells in vertebrate animals. It acts to speed up the passage of nerve impulses. Myelin is made up of fats and proteins and is formed from up to a hundred layers, laid down by special cells, the **Schwann cells**.

My Lai massacre killing of 109 civilians in My Lai, a village in South Vietnam, by US troops in March 1968. An investigation in 1969 was followed by the conviction of Lt William Calley, commander of the platoon.

myna or **mynah** any of various tropical starlings, family Sturnidae, of SE Asia. The glossy blackhill myna *Gracula religiosa* of India is a realistic mimic of sounds and human speech.

myoglobin globular protein, closely related to ◊hemoglobin and located in vertebrate muscle. Oxygen binds to myoglobin and is released only when the hemoglobin can no longer supply adequate oxygen to muscle cells.

myopia or **nearsightedness** defect of the eye in which a person can see clearly only those objects that are close up. It is caused either by the eyeball being too long or by the cornea and lens system of the eye being too powerful, both of which cause the images of distant objects to be formed in front of the retina instead of on it. Nearby objects are sharply perceived. Myopia can be corrected by suitable eyeglasses or contact lenses.

Mycenae The Lion Gate, the main entrance to the citadel.

myopia, low-luminance poor night vision. About 20% of people have poor vision in twilight and nearly 50% in the dark. Low-luminance myopia does not show up in normal optical tests, but in 1989 a method was developed of measuring the degree of blurring by projecting images on a screen using a weak laser beam.

Myron c. 500–440 BC. Greek sculptor. His *Discobolus/Discus-Thrower* and *Athene and Marsyas*, much admired in his time, are known through Roman copies. They confirm his ancient reputation for brilliant composition and naturalism.

myrrh gum resin produced by small trees of the genus *Commiphora* of the bursera family, especially *C. myrrha*, found in Ethiopia and Arabia. In ancient times it was used for incense and perfume and in embalming.

myrtle evergreen shrub of the Old World genus *Myrtus*, family Myrtaceae. The commonly cultivated Mediterranean myrtle *M. communis* has oval opposite leaves and white flowers followed by purple berries, all of which are fragrant.

The Oregon myrtle or California laurel *Umbellularia california* belongs to the ◊laurel family. The wax myrtles (genus *Myrica*) of the US bear wax-covered nuts collected for candle making.

mystery play or *miracle play* medieval religious drama based on stories from the Bible. Mystery plays were performed around the time of church festivals, reaching their height in Europe during the 15th and 16th centuries. A whole cycle running from the Creation to the Last Judgment was performed in separate scenes on mobile wagons by various town guilds.

mystery religion any of various cults of the ancient world, open only to the initiated; for example, the cults of Demeter (see ◊Eleusinian Mysteries), Dionysus, Cybele, Isis, and Mithras. Underlying some of them is a fertility ritual, in which a deity undergoes death and resurrection and the initiates feed on the flesh and blood to attain communion with the divine and ensure their own life beyond the grave. The influence of mystery religions on early Christianity was considerable.

mysticism religious belief or spiritual experience based on direct, intuitive communion with the divine. It does not always involve an orthodox deity, though it is found in all the major religions—for example, kabbalism in Judaism, Sufism in Islam, and the bhakti movement in Hinduism. The mystical experience is often rooted in asceticism and can involve visions, trances, and ecstasies; many religious traditions prescribe meditative and contemplative techniques for achieving mystical experience. Official churches fluctuate between acceptance of mysticism as a form of special grace, and suspicion of it as a dangerous deviation, verging on the heretical.

mythology study and interpretation of the stories symbolically underlying a given culture and of how they relate to similar stories told in other cultures. These stories describe gods and other supernatural beings, with whom humans may have relationships, and may be intended to explain the workings of the universe, nature, or human history.

myxedema thyroid-deficiency disease developing in adult life, most commonly in middle-aged women. The symptoms are loss of energy and appetite, inability to keep warm, mental dullness, and dry, puffy skin. It is completely reversed by giving the thyroid hormone known as thyroxine.

n. abbreviation for ◊*noun*, and *neuter*.

NAACP abbreviation for ◊National Association for the Advancement of Colored People, a US civil rights organization.

Nabokov Vladimir 1899–1977. US writer who left his native Russia 1917 and began writing in English in the 1940s. His most widely known book is *Lolita* 1955, the story of the middle-aged Humbert Humbert's infatuation with a precocious girl of 12. His other books include *Laughter in the Dark* 1938, *The Real Life of Sebastian Knight* 1945, *Pnin* 1957, and his memoirs *Speak, Memory* 1947.

nadir the point on the celestial sphere vertically below the observer and hence diametrically opposite the **zenith**. The term is used metaphorically to mean the low point of a person's fortunes.

Naga member of any of the various peoples who inhabit the highland region near the Indian/Myanmar (Burma) border; they number approximately 800,000. These peoples do not possess a common name; some of the main groups are Ao, Konyak, Sangtam, Lhota, Sema, Rengma, Chang, and Angami. They live by farming, hunting, and fishing. Their languages belong to the Sino-Tibetan family.

Nagaland state of NE India, bordering Myanmar (Burma) on the E
area 6,456 sq mi/16,721 sq km
capital Kohima
products rice, tea, coffee, paper, sugar
population (1991) 1,215,600
history formerly part of Assam, the area was seized by Britain from Burma (now Myanmar) 1826. The British sent 18 expeditions against the Naga peoples in the N 1832–87. After India attained independence 1947, there was Naga guerrilla activity against the Indian government; the state of Nagaland was established 1963 in response to demands for self-government, but fighting continued sporadically.

Nagasaki industrial port (coal, iron, shipbuilding) on Kyushu Island, Japan; population (1990) 444,600. Nagasaki was the only Japanese port open to European trade from the 16th century until 1859. An atomic bomb was dropped on it by the US Aug 9, 1945.

Nagorno-Karabakh autonomous region of ◊Azerbaijan
area 1,700 sq mi/4,400 sq km
capital Stepanakert
products cotton, grapes, wheat, silk
population (1987) 180,000 (76% Armenian, 23% Azeri), the Christian Armenians forming an enclave within the predominantly Shiite Muslim Azerbaijan
history an autonomous protectorate after the Russian Revolution 1917, Nagorno-Karabakh was annexed to Azerbaijan 1923 against the wishes of the largely Christian-Armenian population. Since the local, ethnic Armenian council declared its intention to transfer control of the region to Armenia 1989, the enclave has been racked by fighting between Armenian and Azeri troops, both attempting to assert control. By Feb 1992, the conflict had caused the loss of at least 1,000 lives (501 during 1991 alone) and the displacement of some 270,000 people, half of them Armenian and half Azeri.

Nagoya industrial seaport (cars, textiles, clocks) on Honshu Island, Japan; population (1990) 2,154,700. It has a shogun fortress 1610 and a notable Shinto shrine, Atsuta Jingu.

Nagpur industrial city (textiles, metals) in Maharashtra, India, on the river Pench; population (1981) 1,298,000. Pharmaceuticals, cotton goods, and hosiery are produced, and oranges are traded. Nagpur was founded in the 18th century, and was the former capital of Berar and Madhya Pradesh states.

Nagy Imre 1895–1958. Hungarian politician, prime minister 1953–55 and 1956. He led the Hungarian revolt against Soviet domination in 1956, for which he was executed.

Nahayan Sheik Sultan bin Zayed al- 1918– . Emir of Abu Dhabi from 1969, when he deposed his brother, Sheik Shakhbut. He was elected president of the supreme council of the United Arab Emirates 1971. In 1991 he was implicated, through his majority ownership, in the international financial scandals associated with the Bank of Commerce and Credit International.

Nahuatl member of any of a group of Mesoamerican Indian peoples (Mexico and Central America), of which the best-known group were the Aztecs. The Nahuatl are the largest ethnic group in Mexico, and their languages, which belong to the Uto-Aztecan (Aztec-Tanoan) family, are spoken by over a million people today.

nail in biology, a hard, flat, flexible outgrowth of the digits of primates (humans, monkeys, and apes). Nails are derived from the ◊claws of ancestral primates.

Nairobi capital of Kenya, in the central highlands at 5,450 ft/1,660 m; population (1985) 1,100,000. It has light industry and food processing and is the headquarters of the United Nations Environment Program. *See illustration p. 650*

Naismith James 1861–1939. Canadian-born inventor of basketball. He invented basketball as a game to be played indoors during the winter, while attending the Young Men's Christian Association (YMCA) Training School in Springfield, Massachusetts, 1891. Among his books is *Basketball, Its Origin and Development*, published posthumously 1941.

Nakasone Yasuhiro 1917– . Japanese conservative politician, leader of the Liberal Democratic Party (LDP) and prime minister 1982–87. He stepped up military spending and increased Japanese participation in international affairs, with closer ties to the US. He was forced to resign his party post May 1989 as a result of having profited from insider trading in the ◊Recruit scandal. After serving a two-year period of atonement, he rejoined the LDP April 1991.

Nairobi Nairobi is a modern city with broad thoroughfares and modern buildings of glass and concrete.

Nakhichevan autonomous republic forming part of Azerbaijan, even though it is entirely outside the Azerbaijan boundary, being separated from it by Armenia; area 2,120 sq mi/5,500 sq km; population (1986) 272,000. Taken by Russia in 1828, it was annexed to Azerbaijan in 1924. Some 85% of the population are Muslim Azeris who maintain strong links with Iran to the south. Nakhichevan has been affected by the Armenia–Azerbaijan conflict; many Azeris have fled to Azerbaijan, and in Jan 1990 frontier posts and border fences with Iran were destroyed. In May 1992 Armenian forces made advances in the region, but Azeri forces had regained control by Aug. The republic has sought independence from Azerbaijan.

Namath Joe (Joseph William) 1943– . US football player. In 1965 he signed with the New York Jets of the newly established American Football League and in 1969 led the team to a historic upset victory over the Baltimore Colts in Super Bowl III. After leaving the Jets 1977, he briefly played with the Los Angeles Rams.

Namib Desert coastal desert region in Namibia between the Kalahari Desert and the Atlantic Ocean. Its aridity is caused by the descent of dry air cooled by the cold Benguela current along the coast. The sand dunes of the Namib Desert are among the tallest in the world, reaching heights of 1,200 ft/370 m.

Namibia formerly (to 1968) *South West Africa* country in SW Africa, bounded N by Angola and Zambia, E by Botswana and South Africa, and W by the Atlantic Ocean. Walvis Bay, part of South Africa, forms an enclave in Namibia on the Atlantic coast.

Nanak 1469–c. 1539. Indian guru and founder of Sikhism, a religion based on the unity of God and the equality of all human beings. He was strongly opposed to caste divisions.

Nanchang industrial city (textiles, glass, porcelain, soap), capital of Jiangxi province, China, about 160 mi/260 km SE of Wuhan; population (1989) 1,330,000.

Nanjing or *Nanking* capital of Jiangsu province, China, 165 mi/270 km NW of Shanghai; center of industry (engineering, shipbuilding, oil refining), commerce, and communications; population (1989)

2,470,000. The bridge 1968 over the Chang Jiang River is the longest in China at 22,000 ft/6,705 m.

Nanning industrial river port, capital of Guangxi Zhuang autonomous region, China, on the You Jiang River; population (1989) 1,050,00. It was a supply town during the Vietnam War and the Sino-Vietnamese confrontation 1979.

nano- prefix used in ◊SI units of measurement, equivalent to a one-billionth part (10⁻⁹). For example, a nanosecond is one-billionth of a second.

nanotechnology the building of devices on a molecular scale. Micromachines, such as gears smaller in diameter than a human hair, have been made at the AT&T Bell laboratories in New Jersey. Building large molecules with useful shapes has been accomplished by research groups in the US. A robot small enough to travel through the bloodstream and into organs of the body, inspecting or removing diseased tissue, was under development in Japan 1990.

Nansen Fridtjof 1861–1930. Norwegian explorer and scientist. In 1893, he sailed to the Arctic in the *Fram*, which was deliberately allowed to drift north with an iceflow. Nansen, accompanied by F Hjalmar Johansen (1867–1923), continued north on foot and reached 86°14'6 N, the highest latitude then attained. After World War I, Nansen became League of Nations high commissioner for refugees. Nobel Peace Prize 1923.

Nantes, Edict of decree by which Henry IV of France granted religious freedom to the ◊Huguenots 1598. It was revoked 1685 by Louis XIV.

Nantucket island and resort in Massachusetts, S of Cape Cod, 46 sq mi/120 sq km. In the 18th–19th centuries, Nantucket was a whaling port; it is now a popular summer resort because of its excellent beaches.

napalm fuel used in flamethrowers and incendiary bombs. Produced from jellied gasoline, it is a mixture of *na*phthenic and *palm*itic acids. Napalm causes extensive burns because it sticks to the skin even when aflame. It was widely used by the US Army during the Vietnam War.

naphtha the mixtures of hydrocarbons obtained by destructive distillation of petroleum, coal tar, and shale oil. It is raw material for the petrochemical and

Namibia
Republic of
(formerly *South West Africa*)

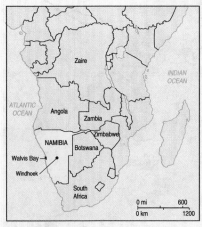

area 318,262 sq mi/824,300 sq km
capital Windhoek
cities Swakopmund, Rehoboth, Rundu
physical mainly desert
features Namib and Kalahari deserts; Orange River; Caprivi
Strip links Namibia to Zambezi River; includes the enclave of
Walvis Bay (area 432 sq mi/1,120 sq km)
head of state Sam Nujoma from 1990
head of government Hage Geingob from 1990
political system democratic republic
political parties South-West Africa People's Organization
(SWAPO), socialist Ovambo-oriented; Democratic Turnhalle
Alliance (DTA), moderate, multiracial coalition; United
Democratic Front (UDF), disaffected ex-SWAPO members;
National Christian Action (ACN), white conservative

exports diamonds, uranium, copper, lead, zinc
currency South African rand
population (1990 est) 1,372,000 (black African 85%,
European 6%)
life expectancy blacks 40, whites 69
languages Afrikaans (spoken by 60% of white population),
German, English (all official), several indigenous languages
religion Lutheran 51%, Roman Catholic 19%, Dutch 6%
Reformed Church, Anglican 6%
literacy whites 100%, nonwhites 16%
GNP $1.6 bn; $1,300 per head (1988)

chronology
1884 German and British colonies established.
1915 German colony seized by South Africa.
1920 Administered by South Africa, under League of Nations
mandate, as British South Africa.
1946 Full incorporation in South Africa refused by United
Nations (UN).
1958 South-West Africa People's Organization (SWAPO) set
up to seek racial equality and full independence.
1966 South Africa's apartheid laws extended to the country.
1968 Redesignated Namibia by UN.
1978 UN Security Council Resolution 435 for the granting of
full sovereignty accepted by South Africa and then rescinded.
1988 Peace talks between South Africa, Angola, and Cuba led
to agreement on full independence for Namibia.
1989 Unexpected incursion by SWAPO guerrillas from
Angola into Namibia threatened agreed independence.
Transitional constitution created by elected representatives;
SWAPO dominant party.
1990 Liberal multiparty "independence" constitution
adopted; independence achieved. Sam Nujoma elected
president.
1991 Agreement on joint administration of disputed port of
Walvis Bay reached with South Africa, pending final
settlement of dispute.
1992 Agreement on establishment of Walvis Bay Joint
Administrative Body.
1993 South Africa relinquished claim to Walvis Bay
sovereignty.

---

plastics industries. The term was originally applied to
naturally occurring liquid hydrocarbons.

naphthalene $CHC_{10}H_8$ a solid, white, shiny, aromatic
hydrocarbon obtained from coal tar. The smell of
moth-balls is due to their napthalene content. It is used
in making indigo and certain azo dyes, as a mild disinfectant, and as an insecticide.

Napier John 1550–1617. Scottish mathematician who
invented ◊logarithms 1614 and "Napier's bones," an
early mechanical calculating device for multiplication
and division.

Naples (Italian *Napoli*) industrial port (shipbuilding, automobiles, textiles, paper, food processing) and
capital of Campania, Italy, on the Tyrrhenian Sea; population (1988) 1,201,000. To the S is the Isle of Capri,
and behind the city is Mount Vesuvius, with the ruins
of Pompeii at its foot.

Naples, Kingdom of the southern part of Italy,
alternately independent and united with ◊Sicily in the
Kingdom of the Two Sicilies.

Napoleon I Bonaparte 1769–1821. Emperor of the
French 1804–14 and 1814–15. A general from 1796 in
the ◊Revolutionary Wars, in 1799 he overthrew the
ruling Directory (see ◊French Revolution) and made
himself dictator. From 1803 he conquered most of
Europe (the *Napoleonic Wars*) and installed his
brothers as puppet kings (see ◊Bonaparte). After the
Peninsular War and retreat from Moscow 1812, he was
forced to abdicate 1814 and was banished to the island

of Elba. In March 1815 he reassumed power but was
defeated by British forces at the Battle of ◊Waterloo
and exiled to the island of St Helena. His internal
administrative reforms and laws are still evident in
France.

Napoleon II 1811–1832. Title given by the Bona-
partists to the son of Napoleon I and Marie Louise;
until 1814 he was known as the king of Rome and after
1818 as the duke of Reichstadt. After his father's abdication 1814 he was taken to the Austrian court, where
he spent the rest of his life.

Napoleon III 1808–1873. Emperor of the French
1852–70, known as *Louis-Napoleon*. After two
attempted coups (1836 and 1840) he was jailed, then
went into exile, returning for the revolution of 1848,
when he became president of the Second Republic but
soon turned authoritarian. In 1870 he was
maneuvered by the German chancellor Bismarck into
war with Prussia (see ◊Franco-Prussian war); he was
forced to surrender at Sedan, NE France, and the
empire collapsed.
   He fled to England.

Napoleonic Wars 1803–15 a series of European
wars conducted by Napoleon I following the ◊Revolu-
tionary Wars, aiming for French conquest of Europe.
   1803 Britain renewed the war against France, following an appeal from the Maltese against Napoleon's
1798 seizure of the island. *1805* Napoleon's planned
invasion of Britain from Boulogne ended with Nelson's

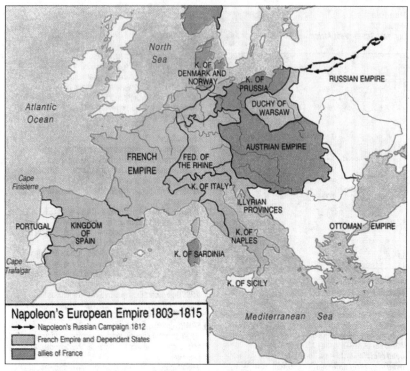

Napoleon's European Empire 1803–1815
➤➤ Napoleon's Russian Campaign 1812
French Empire and Dependent States
allies of France

victory at ◊Trafalgar. Coalition formed against France by Britain, Austria, Russia, and Sweden. Austria defeated at Ulm; Austria and Russia at ◊Austerlitz. *1806* Prussia joined the coalition and was defeated at Jena; Napoleon instituted an attempted blockade, the **Continental System**, to isolate Britain from Europe. *1807* Russia defeated at Eylau and Friedland and, on making peace with Napoleon under the **Treaty of Tilsit**, changed sides, agreeing to attack Sweden, but was forced to retreat. *1808* Napoleon's invasion of Portugal and strategy of installing his relatives as puppet kings led to the ◊Peninsular War. *1809* Revived Austrian opposition to Napoleon was ended by defeat at ◊Wagram. *1812* The Continental System finally collapsed on its rejection by Russia, and Napoleon made the fatal decision to invade; he reached **Moscow** but was defeated by the Russian resistance and by the bitter winter as he retreated through a countryside laid waste by the retreating Russians (380,000 French soldiers died). *1813* Britain, Prussia, Russia, Austria, and Sweden formed a new coalition, which defeated Napoleon at the **Battle of the Nations**, Leipzig, Germany. He abdicated and was exiled to Elba. *1814* Louis XVIII became king of France, and the Congress of Vienna met to conclude peace. *1815* Napoleon returned to Paris. On June 16 the British commander Wellington defeated the French marshal Ney at Quatre Bras (in Belgium, SE of Brussels), and Napoleon was finally defeated at **Waterloo**, S of Brussels, June 18.

narcissism in psychology, an exaggeration of normal self-respect and self-involvement which may amount to mental disorder when it precludes relationships with other people.

narcissus any bulbous plant of the genus *Narcissus*, family Amaryllidaceae. Species include the daffodil, jonquil, and narcissus.

Narcissus in Greek legend, a beautiful youth who rejected the love of the nymph ◊Echo and was condemned to fall in love with his own reflection in a pool. He pined away and in the place where he died a flower sprang up that was named after him.

narcotic pain-relieving and sleep-inducing drug. The chief narcotics induce dependency, and include opium, its derivatives and synthetic modifications (such as morphine and heroin); alcohols (such as ethanol); and barbiturates.

Narmada River river that rises in the Maikala range in Madhya Pradesh state, central India, and flows 778 mi/1,245 km WSW to the Gulf of Khambat, an inlet of the Arabian Sea. Forming the traditional boundary between Hindustan and Deccan, the Narmada is a holy river of the Hindus.

narwhal toothed whale *Monodon monoceros*, found only in the Arctic Ocean. It grows to 16 ft/5 m long, has a gray and black body, a small head, and short flippers. The male has a single spirally fluted tusk that may be up to 9 ft/2.7 m long.

NASA (acronym for **National Aeronautics and Space Administration**) US government agency, founded 1958, for spaceflight and aeronautical research. Its headquarters are in Washington, DC, and its main installation is at the ◊Kennedy Space Center in Florida. NASA's early planetary and lunar programs included Pioneer spacecraft from 1958, which gathered data for the later crewed missions, the most famous of which took the first people to the Moon in *Apollo 11* on July 16–24 1969. Other installations are located in Virginia (Langley Research Center and Wallops Station); California (Ames Research Center, Flight Research Center, and the Jet Propulsion Laboratory); Ohio (Lewis Research Center); Alabama (George C Marshall Space Flight Center); Maryland (Goddard

Space Flight Center), and Texas (Manned Spacecraft Center). The Office of Manned Space Flight is responsible for space missions with crews and for the spacestation and space-shuttle programs. The Office of Space Science and Applications deals with the scientific exploration of space. The Office of Advanced Research and Technology plans future flights and research. The Office of Tracking and Data Acquisition provides a network for tracking flights and accumulating data.

The agency was founded 1958 by the National Aeronautics and Space Act.

Nash (Frederic) Ogden 1902–1971. US poet and wit. He published numerous volumes of humorous, quietly satirical light verse, characterized by unorthodox rhymes and puns. They include *I'm a Stranger Here Myself* 1938, *Versus* 1949, and *Bed Riddance* 1970. Most of his poems first appeared in the *New Yorker*, where he held an editorial post and did much to establish the magazine's tone.

Born in Rye, New York, Nash also wrote children's books and lyrics for such musicals as *A Touch of Venus* 1943.

Nashua city in S New Hampshire, on the Nashua River where it meets the Merrimack River, just N of the Massachusetts border; population (1990) 79,600. Industries include electronics, asbestos, chemicals, and glass products.

Nashville port on the Cumberland River and capital of Tennessee; population (1990) 488,300. It is a banking and commercial center, and has large printing, music-publishing, and recording industries.

Most of the Bibles in the US are printed here, and it is the hub of the country-music business. It is the home of the Country Music Hall of Fame and Museum and Opryland. Educational institutions include Vanderbilt and Fisk universities. The Southern Baptist Convention is headquartered here.

Nashville dates from 1778, and the Confederate army was defeated here 1864 in the Civil War. In 1963 Nashville merged with surrounding Davidson county.

Nassau capital and port of the Bahamas, on New Providence Island; population (1980) 135,000.

A tourist center, it is known for fine beaches and the resort community of Paradise Island across the harbor. The College of the Bahamas is here. English settlers founded it in the 17th century, and it was a supply base for Confederate blockade runners during the American Civil War.

Nasser Gamal Abdel 1918–1970. Egyptian politician, prime minister 1954–56 and from 1956 president of Egypt (the United Arab Republic 1958–71). In 1952 he was the driving power behind the Neguib coup, which ended the monarchy. His nationalization of the Suez Canal 1956 led to an Anglo-French invasion and the ◊Suez Crisis, and his ambitions for an Egyptian-led union of Arab states led to disquiet in the Middle East (and in the West). Nasser was also an early and influential leader of the nonaligned movement.

nasturtium any plant of the genus *Nasturtium*, family Cruciferae, including watercress *N. officinale*, a perennial aquatic plant of Europe and Asia, grown as a salad crop. It also includes plants of the South American family Tropeolaceae, including the cultivated species *Tropaeolum majus*, with orange or scarlet flowers, and *T. minus*, which has smaller flowers.

Natal province of South Africa, NE of Cape Province, bounded on the east by the Indian Ocean
area 35,429 sq mi/91,785 sq km

Napoleon I
Napoleon Crossing the Alps *(1800)* by Jacques-Louis David, Charlottenburg Castle, Berlin.

capital Pietermaritzburg
cities Durban
physical slopes from the Drakensberg mountain range to a fertile subtropical coastal plain
features Ndumu Game Reserve, Kosi Bay Nature Preserve, Sodwana Bay National Park, Maple Lane Nature Preserve, and St Lucia National Park, which extends from coral reefs of the Indian Ocean north of Umfolozi River (whales, dolphins, turtles, crayfish), over forested sandhills to inland grasslands and swamps of Lake St Lucia, 125 sq mi/324 sq km (reedbuck, buffalo, crocodile, hippopotamus, black rhino, cheetah, pelican, flamingo, stork). It is under threat from titanium mining
products sugar cane, black wattle *Acacia mollissima*, corn, fruit, vegetables, tobacco, coal
population (1985) 2,145,000.

Natchez member of a North American Indian people of the Mississippi are, one of the Moundbuilder group of peoples. They had a highly developed caste system unusual in North America, headed by a ruler priest (the "Great Sun"). Members of the highest caste always married members of the lowest caste. The system lasted until French settlers colonized the area 1731. Only a few Natchez now survive in Oklahoma. Their Muskogean language is extinct.

Nation Carrie Amelia Moore 1846–1911. US Temperance Movement crusader during the Prohibition 1920–33. Protesting against Kansas state's flagrant disregard for the prohibition law, she marched into illegal saloons with a hatchet, lecturing the patrons on the abuses of alcohol and smashing bottles and bar.

National Association for the Advancement of Colored People (NAACP) US civil-rights organization dedicated to ending inequality and segregation for African-Americans through nonviolent protest.

Founded 1910, its first aim was to eradicate lynching. The NAACP campaigned to end segregation in state schools; it funded test cases that eventually led to the Supreme Court decision 1954 outlawing school segregation, although it was only through the ◊civil-rights movement of the 1960s that desegregation was achieved. In 1987 the NAACP had about 500,000 members, black and white.

national debt debt incurred by the central government of a country to its own people and institutions and also to overseas creditors. A government can borrow from the public by means of selling interest-bearing bonds, for example, or from abroad. Traditionally, a major cause of national debt was the cost of war but in recent decades governments have borrowed heavily in order to finance development or nationalization, to support an ailing currency, or to avoid raising taxes.

National Guard militia force recruited by each state of the US. The volunteer National Guard units are under federal orders in emergencies, and under the control of the governor in peacetime, and are now an integral part of the US Army.

national income the total income earned, not necessarily received, by all persons in a country over a specified time period. It consists of wages, interest, rent, profits, and the net income of the self-employed. Profits of government enterprises are not included.

nationalism in music, a 19th-century movement in which composers (such as Smetana and Grieg) included the folk material of their country in their works, projecting the national spirit and its expression.

nationalism in politics, a movement that consciously aims to unify a nation, create a state, or liberate it from foreign or imperialistic rule. Nationalist movements became a potent factor in European politics during the 19th century; since 1900 nationalism has become a strong force in Asia and Africa and in the late 1980s revived strongly in E Europe.

nationalization policy of bringing a country's essential services and industries under public ownership. It was pursued, for example, by the UK Labour government 1945–51. In recent years the trend toward nationalization has slowed and in many countries (the UK, France, and Japan) reversed (◊privatization). Assets in the hands of foreign governments or companies may also be nationalized; for example, Iran's oil industry, the ◊Suez Canal, and US-owned fruit plantations in Guatemala, all in the 1950s.

National Labor Relations Board v Jones and Laughlin Steel Co a US Supreme Court decision 1937 dealing with federal jurisdiction over intrastate trade. Jones and Laughlin appealed an NLRB order to reinstate several employees fired for union activities. The steel company argued that as an exclusively intrastate trader, it was immune to federal regulatory measures. The Court voted 5 to 4 to uphold the NLRB ruling, judging that since the steel industry was so intrinsically an interstate business the actions of Jones and Laughlin must have affected interstate commerce. The Court ruled that the "stream of commerce" placed local steel companies within federal jurisdiction.

national park land set aside and conserved for public enjoyment. The first was Yellowstone National Park, established 1872. National parks include not only the most scenic places, but also places distinguished for their historic, prehistoric, or scientific interest, or for their superior recreational assets. They range from areas the size of small countries to pockets of just a few acres.

national security adviser an appointee of the executive branch, the head of the ◊National Security Council, which, since the National Security Act 1947, coordinates the defense and foreign policy of the US. Anthony Lake was appointed to the post 1993.

National Security Agency (NSA) largest and most secret of US intelligence agencies. Established 1952 to intercept foreign communications as well as to safeguard US transmissions, the NSA collects and analyzes computer communications, telephone signals, and other electronic data, and gathers intelligence. Known as the Puzzle Palace, its headquarters are at Fort Meade, Maryland (with a major facility at Menwith Hill, England).

National Security Council US federal executive council that was established under the National Security Act of 1947. The membership includes the president, vice-president, and secretaries of state and defense. Their special advisers include the head of the Joint Chiefs of Staff and the director of the Central Intelligence Agency. The national security adviser heads the council's staff.

national security directive in the US, secret decree issued by the president that can establish national policy and commit federal funds without the knowledge of Congress, under the National Security Act 1947. The National Security Council alone decides whether these directives may be made public; most are not. The directives have been criticized as unconstitutional, since they enable the executive branch of government to make laws.

Native American the modern, politically conscious term used by North ◊American Indians, ◊Eskimos, and Aleuts to describe themselves as a group, although each society maintains its autonomy and its own name. See ◊Hopi, ◊Navaho, ◊Cherokee, ◊Sioux.

native metal or *free metal* any of the metallic elements that occur in nature in the chemically uncombined or elemental form (in addition to any combined form). They include bismuth, cobalt, copper, gold, iridium, iron, lead, mercury, nickel, osmium, palladium, platinum, ruthenium, rhodium, tin, and silver. Some are commonly found in the free state, such as gold; others occur almost exclusively in the combined state, but under unusual conditions do occur as native metals, such as mercury.

nativity Christian festival celebrating a birth: *Christmas* is celebrated Dec 25 from AD 336 in memory of the birth of Jesus in Bethlehem; *Nativity of the Virgin Mary* is celebrated Sept 8 by the Catholic and Eastern Orthodox churches; *Nativity of John the Baptist* is celebrated June 24 by the Catholic, Eastern Orthodox, and Anglican churches.

NATO abbreviation for ◊North Atlantic Treaty Organization.

natural gas mixture of flammable gases found in the Earth's crust (often in association with petroleum), now one of the world's three main fossil fuels (with coal and oil). Natural gas is a mixture of ◊hydrocarbons, chiefly methane, with ethane, butane, and propane.

natural selection the process whereby gene frequencies in a population change through certain individuals producing more descendants than others because they are better able to survive and reproduce in their environment. The accumulated effect of natural selection is to produce ◊adaptations such as the insulating coat of a polar bear or the spadelike forelimbs of a mole. The process is slow, relying first on random variation in the genes of an organism being produced by ◊mutation and secondly on the genetic ◊recombination of sexual reproduction. It was recognized by Charles Darwin and English naturalist Alfred Russel Wallace as the main process driving ◊evolution.

nature–nurture controversy or *environment–heredity controversy* long-standing dispute among philosophers and psychologists over the relative importance of environment, that is upbringing, experience and learning ("nurture"), and heredity, that is genetic inheritance ("nature"), in determining the makeup of an organism, as related to human personality and intelligence.

nature preserve area set aside to protect a habitat and the wildlife that lives within it, with only restricted admission for the public. A nature preserve often provides a sanctuary for rare species, and rare habitats, such as marshlands. The world's largest is Etosha Reserve, Namibia; area 38,415 sq mi/99,520 sq km.

Many state and local preserves have been established in the US since 1970. Some are called greenbelts and some are designated "forever wild," as well as those that are administered for limited or educational access.

Nauru island country in Polynesia, SW Pacific, W of Kiribati.

nautical mile formerly various units of distance used in navigation; since 1959, an internationally agreed-on standard equaling the average length of one minute of arc on a great circle of the Earth, or 6,076.12 ft/1,852 m.

Navaho member of a peaceable agricultural North American Indian people related to the ◊Apache; popu-

lation about 200,000. They were attacked by Kit ◊Carson and US troops 1864, and were rounded up and exiled. Their reservation, created 1868, is the largest in the US (25,000 sq mi/65,000 sq km), and is mainly in NE Arizona but extends into NW New Mexico and SE Utah. Many Navaho now herd sheep and earn an income from tourism, making and selling rugs, blankets, and silver and turquoise jewelry. Like the Apache, they speak a Southern Athabaskan language.

Navarre (Spanish *Navarra*) autonomous mountain region of N Spain
area 4,014 sq mi/10,400 sq km
capital Pamplona
features Monte Adi 4,933 ft/1,503 m; rivers: Ebro, Arga
population (1986) 513,000.

Navarre, Kingdom of former kingdom comprising the Spanish province of Navarre and part of what is now the French *département* of Basses-Pyrénées. It resisted the conquest of the ◊Moors and was independent until it became French 1284 on the marriage of Philip IV to the heiress of Navarre. In 1479 Ferdinand of Aragon annexed Spanish Navarre, with French Navarre going to Catherine of Foix (1483–1512), who kept the royal title. Her grandson became Henry IV of France, and Navarre was absorbed in the French crown lands 1620.

nave in architecture, the central part of a church, between the choir and the entrance.

navigation the science and technology of finding the position, course, and distance traveled by a ship, plane, or other craft. Traditional methods include the magnetic ◊compass and ◊sextant. Today the gyrocompass is usually used, together with highly sophisticated electronic methods, employing beacons of radio signals, such as Decca, Loran, and Omega. Satel-

---

Nauru
Republic of (*Naoero*)

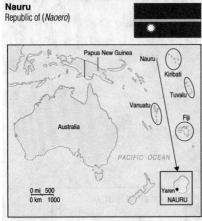

area 8 sq mi/21 sq km
capital (seat of government) Yaren District
physical tropical island country in SW Pacific; plateau encircled by coral cliffs and sandy beaches
features lies just S of equator; one of three phosphate rock islands in the Pacific
head of state and government Bernard Dowiyogo from 1989
political system liberal democracy
political party Democratic Party of Nauru (DPN), opposition to government

exports phosphates
currency Australian dollar
population (1990 est) 8,100 (mainly Polynesian; Chinese 8%, European 8%); growth rate 1.7% p.a.
languages Nauruan (official), English
religion Protestant 66%, Roman Catholic 33%
literacy 99% (1988)
GNP $160 million (1986); $9,091 per head (1985)

chronology
1888 Annexed by Germany.
1920 Administered by Australia, New Zealand, and UK until independence, except 1942–45, when it was occupied by Japan.
1968 Independence achieved from Australia, New Zealand, and UK with "special member" Commonwealth status. Hammer DeRoburt elected president.
1976 Bernard Dowiyogo elected president.
1978 DeRoburt reelected.
1986 DeRoburt briefly replaced as president by Kennan Adeang.
1987 DeRoburt reelected; Adeang established the Democratic Party of Nauru.
1989 DeRoburt replaced by Kensas Aroi, who was later succeeded by Dowiyogo.
1992 Dowiyogo reelected.
1993 Nauru filed lawsuit against Australian firm of lawyers for the recovery of $14 million of the island's trust fund. A claim against Australia for compensation for 60 years of environmental destruction was in progress at the International Court of Justice.

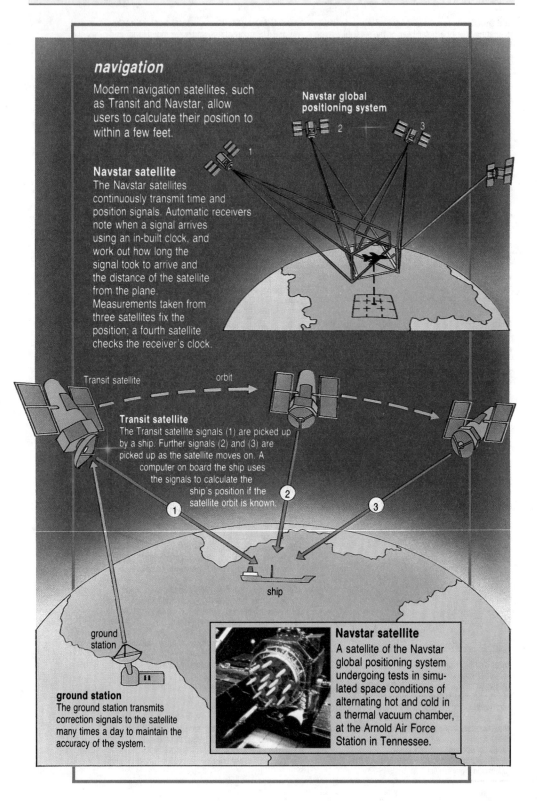

navigation

Modern navigation satellites, such as Transit and Navstar, allow users to calculate their position to within a few feet.

Navstar global positioning system

2   3

1

Navstar satellite

The Navstar satellites continuously transmit time and position signals. Automatic receivers note when a signal arrives using an in-built clock, and work out how long the signal took to arrive and the distance of the satellite from the plane. Measurements taken from three satellites fix the position; a fourth satellite checks the receiver's clock.

Transit satellite   orbit

Transit satellite

The Transit satellite signals (1) are picked up by a ship. Further signals (2) and (3) are picked up as the satellite moves on. A computer on board the ship uses the signals to calculate the ship's position if the satellite orbit is known.

1   2   3

ship

ground station

ground station

The ground station transmits correction signals to the satellite many times a day to maintain the accuracy of the system.

Navstar satellite

A satellite of the Navstar global positioning system undergoing tests in simulated space conditions of alternating hot and cold in a thermal vacuum chamber, at the Arnold Air Force Station in Tennessee.

lite navigation uses satellites that broadcast time and position signals.

Navigation Acts in British history, a series of acts of Parliament passed from 1381 to protect English shipping from foreign competition and to ensure monopoly trading between Britain and its colonies. The last was repealed 1849 (coastal trade exempt until 1853). The Navigation Acts helped to establish England as a major sea power, although they led to higher prices. They ruined the Dutch merchant fleet in the 17th century, and were one of the causes of the ◊American Revolution.

Navratilova Martina 1956– . Czech tennis player who became a naturalized US citizen 1981. The most outstanding woman player of the 1980s, she had 55 Grand Slam victories by 1991, including 18 singles titles. She won the Wimbledon singles title a record nine times, including six in succession 1982–87. She won the US Open in 1983–84 and 1986–87.

navy fleet of ships, usually a nation's warships and the organization to maintain them. The USSR had one of the world's largest merchant fleets and the world's largest fishing, hydrographic, and oceanographic fleets, in which all ships had intelligence-gathering equipment.

Nazareth town in Galilee, N Israel, SE of Haifa; population (1981) 64,000. According to the New Testament, it was the boyhood home of Jesus.

Nazism ideology based on racism, nationalism, and the supremacy of the state over the individual. The German Nazi party, the ***Nationalsozialistiche Deutsche Arbeiterpartei*** (National Socialist German Workers' Party), was formed from the German Workers' Party (founded 1919) and led by Adolf ◊Hitler 1921–45.

NC abbreviation for the state of ◊North Carolina.

ND abbreviation for the state of ◊North Dakota.

N'djamena capital of Chad, at the confluence of the Chari and Logone rivers, on the Cameroon border; population (1988) 594,000.

Ndola mining center and chief city of the Copperbelt province of central Zambia; population (1988) 442,700.

NE abbreviation for the state of ◊Nebraska; ◊New England.

Neagh, Lough lake in Northern Ireland, 15 mi/25 km W of Belfast; area 153 sq mi/396 sq km. It is the largest lake in the British Isles.

Neanderthal hominid of the Mid-Late Paleolithic, named after the Neander Thal (valley) near Düsseldorf, Germany, where a skeleton was found in 1856. *Homo sapiens neanderthalensis* lived from about 100,000 to 35,000 years ago and was similar in build to present-day people, but slightly smaller, stockier, and heavier-featured with a strong jaw and prominent brow ridges on a sloping forehead.

Recent evidence suggests their physical capacity for the sounds of speech. They were replaced throughout Europe by, or possibly interbred with, *Homo sapiens sapiens*.

nearsightedness alternate name for ◊myopia.

Nebr. abbreviation for the state of ◊Nebraska.

Nebraska state in central US; nickname Cornhusker State/Blackwater State
area 77,354 sq mi/200,400 sq km
capital Lincoln
cities Omaha, Grand Island, North Platte
population (1990) 1,578,400

Nebraska

features Rocky Mountain foothills; tributaries of the Missouri; Boys' Town for the homeless, near Omaha; the ranch of Buffalo Bill; the only unicameral legislature
products cereals, livestock, processed foods, fertilizers, oil, natural gas
famous people Fred Astaire, William Jennings Bryan, Johnny Carson, Willa Cather, Henry Fonda, Harold Lloyd, Malcom X
history exploited by French fur traders in the early 1700s; ceded to Spain by France 1763; retroceded to France 1801; part of the Louisiana Purchase 1803; explored by Lewis and Clark 1804–06; first settlement at Bellevue 1823; became a territory 1854 and a state 1867 after the Union Pacific began its transcontinental railroad at Omaha 1865.

Nebraska's farm economy was weakened in the 1930s by the Great Depression and dust storms, but World War II brought military airfields and war industries. Much of the industry developed since that time is related to agriculture.

Nebuchadnezzar or ***Nebuchadrezzar II*** king of Babylonia from 604 BC. Shortly before his accession he defeated the Egyptians at Carchemish and brought Palestine and Syria into his empire. Judah revolted, with Egyptian assistance, 596 and 587–586 BC; on both occasions he captured Jerusalem and took many Hebrews into captivity. He largely rebuilt Babylon and constructed the hanging gardens.

nebula cloud of gas and dust in space. Nebulae are the birthplaces of stars, but some nebulae are produced by

nebula *The Orion nebula is located 1,500 light-years from Earth and its fan-shaped cloud is 15 light-years across.*

Nehru Jawaharlal Nehru (left) with Muhammad Ali Jinnah, the founder of Pakistan.

gas thrown off from dying stars (see ◊supernova). Nebulae are classified depending on whether they emit, reflect, or absorb light.

necrosis death or decay of tissue in a particular part of the body, usually due to bacterial poisoning or loss of local blood supply.

nectar sugary liquid secreted by some plants from a nectary, a specialized gland usually situated near the base of the flower. Nectar often accumulates in special pouches or spurs, not always in the same location as the nectary. Nectar attracts insects, birds, bats, and other animals to the flower for ◊pollination and is the raw material used by bees in the production of honey.

nectarine smooth, shiny-skinned variety of ◊peach, usually smaller than other peaches and with firmer flesh. It arose from a natural mutation.

Neenah city in E Wisconsin, on the Fox River near Lake Winnebago, N of Oshkosh; population (1990) 23,200. To the E is Menasha, with which it forms one community. It is a processing and marketing center for the area's agricultural products.

Nefertiti or *Nofretete* queen of Egypt who ruled c. 1372–1350 BC; wife of the pharaoh ◊Ikhnaton.

Negev desert in S Israel that tapers to the port of Eilat. It is fertile under irrigation, and minerals include oil and copper.

negligence in law, doing some act that a "prudent and reasonable" person would not do, or omitting to do some act that such a person would do. Negligence may arise in respect of a person's duty toward an individual or toward other people in general. Breach of the duty of care that results in reasonably foreseeable damage is a tort.

Nelson British admiral Horatio Nelson, who was mortally wounded at the Battle of Trafalgar 1805.

Negroid referring to one of the three major varieties (see ◊races) of humans, *Homo sapiens sapiens*, mainly the indigenous peoples of Subsaharan Africa and some of the nearby islands in the Indian Ocean and the W Pacific. General physical traits include dark eyes, tightly curled dark hair, brown to very dark skin, little beard or body hair, low to medium-bridged wide noses, and wide or everted lips. See ◊Caucasoid, ◊Mongoloid.

Nehru Jawaharlal 1889–1964. Indian nationalist politician, prime minister from 1947. Before the partition (the division of British India into India and Pakistan), he led the socialist wing of the nationalist Congress Party, and was second in influence only to Mohandas Gandhi. He was imprisoned nine times by the British 1921–45 for political activities. As prime minister from the creation of the dominion (later republic) of India in Aug 1947, he originated the idea of nonalignment (neutrality toward major powers). His daughter was Prime Minister Indira Gandhi.

Nelson Horatio, Viscount Nelson 1758–1805. English admiral. He joined the navy in 1770. In the Revolutionary Wars against France he lost the sight in his right eye 1794 and lost his right arm 1797. He became a national hero, and rear admiral, after the victory off Cape St Vincent, Portugal. In 1798 he tracked the French fleet to Aboukir Bay and almost entirely destroyed it in the Battle of the Nile. In 1801 he won a decisive victory over Denmark at the Battle of ◊Copenhagen, and in 1805, after two years of blockading Toulon, another over the Franco-Spanish fleet at the Battle of ◊Trafalgar, near Gibraltar.

Nemesis in Greek mythology, the goddess of retribution, who especially punished hubris (Greek *hybris*), violent acts carried through in defiance of the gods and human custom.

Neo-Classicism movement in art and architecture in Europe and North America about 1750–1850, a revival of Classical Greek and Roman art. It superseded the Rococo style and was partly inspired by the excavation of the Roman cities of Pompeii and Herculaneum. The architect Piranesi was an early Neo-Classicist; in sculpture Antonio ◊Canova and in painting Jacques Louis ◊David were exponents.

neo-Darwinism the modern theory of ◊evolution, built up since the 1930s by integrating the 19th-century English scientist Charles ◊Darwin's theory of evolution through natural selection with the theory of genetic inheritance founded on the work of the Austrian biologist Gregor ◊Mendel.

neodymium yellowish metallic element of the ◊lanthanide series, symbol Nd, atomic number 60, atomic weight 144.24.

Its rose-colored salts are used in coloring glass, and neodymium is used in lasers.

Neo-Impressionism movement in French painting in the 1880s, an extension of the Impressionists' technique of placing small strokes of different color side by side. Seurat was the chief exponent; his minute technique became known as "pointillism."

Signac and Pissarro practiced the same style for a few years.

Neolithic last period of the ◊Stone Age, characterized by settled communities based on agriculture and domesticated animals, and identified by sophisticated, finely honed stone tools, and ceramic wares. The earliest Neolithic communities appeared about 9000 BC in the Middle East, followed by Egypt, India, and China. In Europe farming began in about 6500 BC in the Balkans and Aegean, spreading north and east by 1000 BC.

Nepal
Kingdom of
(*Nepal Adhirajya*)

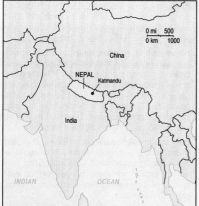

area 56,850 sq mi/147,181 sq km
capital Katmandu
cities Pátan, Moráng, Bhádgáon
physical descends from the Himalayan mountain range in N through foothills to the river Ganges plain in S
environment described as the world's highest rubbish dump, Nepal attracts 270,000 tourists, trekkers, and mountaineers each year. An estimated 1,100 lb/500 kg of rubbish is left by each expedition trekking or climbing in the Himalayas. Since 1952 the foothills of the Himalayas have been stripped of 40% of their forest cover
features Mount Everest, Mount Kangchenjunga; the only Hindu kingdom in the world; Lumbini, birthplace of the Buddha
head of state King Birendra Bir Bikram Shah Dev from 1972
head of government Girija Prasad Koirala from 1991
political system constitutional monarchy

political parties Nepali Congress Party (NCP), left- of-center; United Nepal Communist Party (UNCP), Marxist-Leninist-Maoist; United Liberation Torchbearers; Democratic Front, radical republican
exports jute, rice, timber, oilseed
currency Nepalese rupee
population (1992) 19,795,000 (mainly known by name of predominant clan, the Gurkhas; the Sherpas are a Buddhist minority of NE Nepal); growth rate 2.3% p.a.
life expectancy men 50, women 49 (1989)
language Nepali (official); 20 dialects spoken
religion Hindu 90%; Buddhist, Muslim, Christian
literacy men 39%, women 12% (1985 est)
GNP $3.1 bn (1988); $160 per head (1986)

chronology
1768 Nepal emerged as unified kingdom.
1815–16 Anglo-Nepali "Gurkha War"; Nepal became a British-dependent buffer state.
1846–1951 Ruled by the Rana family.
1923 Independence achieved from Britain.
1951 Monarchy restored.
1959 Constitution created elected legislature.
1960–61 Parliament dissolved by king; political parties banned.
1980 Constitutional referendum held following popular agitation.
1981 Direct elections held to national assembly.
1983 Overthrow of monarch-supported prime minister.
1986 New assembly elections returned a majority opposed to *panchayat* system of partyless government.
1988 Strict curbs placed on opposition activity; over 100 supporters of banned opposition party arrested; censorship imposed.
1989 Border blockade imposed by India in treaty dispute.
1990 *Panchayat* system collapsed after mass prodemocracy demonstrations; new constitution introduced; elections set for May 1991.
1991 Nepali Congress Party, led by Girija Prasad Koirala, won the general election.
1992 Communists led antigovernment demonstrations in Katmandu and Pátan.

neon (Greek *neon* "new") colorless, odorless, non-metallic, gaseous element, symbol Ne, atomic number 10, atomic weight 20.183. It is grouped with the ◊inert gases, is non-reactive, and forms no compounds. It occurs in small quantities in the Earth's atmosphere.

Neoplatonism school of philosophy that flourished during the declining centuries of the Roman Empire (3rd–6th centuries AD). Neoplatonists argued that the highest stage of philosophy is attained not through reason and experience, but through a mystical ecstasy. Many later philosophers, including Nicholas of Cusa, were influenced by Neoplatonism.

neoprene synthetic rubber, developed in the US 1931 from the polymerization of chloroprene. It is much more resistant to heat, light, oxidation, and petroleum than is ordinary rubber.

Nepal landlocked country in the Himalayan mountain range in Central Asia, bounded N by Tibet (an autonomous region of China), E, S, and W by India.

nephritis inflammation of the kidneys, caused by bacterial infection or, sometimes, by a body disorder that affects the kidneys, such as streptococcal infection of the throat. The degree of illness varies, and it may be acute or chronic, requiring a range of treatments from antibiotics to ◊dialysis. Acute nephritis is also known as *Bright's disease*.

nephron microscopic unit in vertebrate kidneys that forms **urine**. A human kidney is composed of over a million nephrons. Each nephron consists of a filter cup surrounding a knot of blood capillaries and a long narrow collecting tubule in close association with yet more capillaries. Waste materials and water pass from the bloodstream into the filter cup, and essential minerals and some water are reabsorbed from the tubule back into the blood. The urine that is left eventually passes out from the body.

Neptune in Roman mythology, the god of the sea, equivalent of the Greek ◊Poseidon.

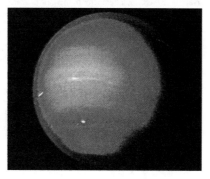

Neptune *False-color image of Neptune from* Voyager 2.

nerve cell The anatomy and action of a nerve cell.

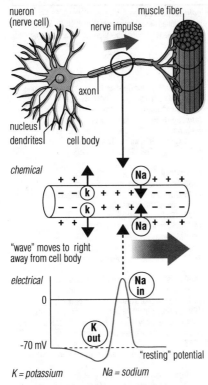

nueron
(nerve cell)

muscle fiber

nerve impulse

axon

nucleus
dendrites
cell body

chemical

+ +   Na + + +
− − k + + + − − −
− − k + + + − − −
+ +   Na + + +

"wave" moves to right
away from cell body

electrical

Na
in

0

K
out

−70 mV

"resting" potential

K = potassium   Na = sodium

Neptune in astronomy, the eighth planet in average distance from the Sun. Neptune orbits the Sun every 164.8 years at an average distance of 2.794 billion mi/ 4.497 billion km. It is a giant gas (hydrogen, helium, methane) planet, with a diameter of 30,200 mi/48,600 km and a mass 17.2 times that of Earth. Its rotation period is 16 hours 7 minutes. The methane in its atmosphere absorbs red light and gives the planet a blue coloring. It is believed to have a central rocky core covered by a layer of ice. Neptune has eight known moons.

neptunium silvery, radioactive metallic element of the ◊actinide series, symbol Np, atomic number 93, atomic weight 237.048. It occurs in nature in minute amounts in ◊pitchblende and other uranium ores, where it is produced from the decay of neutron-bombarded uranium in these ores. The longest-lived isotope, Np-237, has a half-life of 2.2 million years. The element can be produced by bombardment of U-238 with neutrons and is chemically highly reactive.

Nero AD 37–68. Roman emperor from 54. He poisoned ◊Britannicus, and murdered his own mother and his first wife Octavia. After the great fire of Rome 64, he persecuted the Christians, who were suspected of causing it. Military revolt followed 68; the Senate condemned Nero to death, and he committed suicide. He was fearful of the Senate, whose members he prosecuted (and executed) throughout his reign.

Neruda Pablo. Adopted name of Neftali Ricardo Reyes y Basualto 1904–1973. Chilean poet and diplomat. His work includes lyrics and the epic poem of the American continent *Canto General* 1950. He was awarded the Nobel Prize for Literature 1971. He served as consul and ambassador to many countries.

Nerva Marcus Cocceius Nerva AD *c.* 35–98. Roman emperor. He was proclaimed emperor on Domitian's death AD 96, and introduced state loans for farmers, family allowances, and allotments of land to poor citizens in his 16-month reign.

nerve strand of nerve cells enclosed in a sheath of connective tissue joining the ◊central and the ◊autonomic nervous systems with receptor and effector organs. A single nerve may contain both ◊motor and sensory nerve cells, but they act independently.

nerve cell or **neuron** elongated cell, part of the ◊nervous system, that transmits information rapidly between different parts of the body. When nerve cells are collected together in significant numbers (as in the ◊brain), they not only transfer information but also process it. The unit of information is the *nerve impulse*, a traveling wave of chemical and electrical changes affecting the membrane of the nerve cell.

nervous breakdown popular term for a reaction to overwhelming psychological stress. It has no equivalent in medicine: patients said to be suffering from a nervous breakdown may in fact be going through an episode of depression, manic depression, anxiety, or even schizophrenia.

nervous system the system of interconnected ◊nerve cells of most invertebrates and all vertebrates. It is composed of the ◊central and ◊autonomic nervous systems. It may be as simple as the nerve net of coelenterates (for example, jellyfishes) or as complex as the mammalian nervous system, with a central nervous system comprising brain and spinal cord, and a peripheral nervous system connecting up with sensory organs, muscles, and glands.

Ness, Loch lake in Highland region, Scotland; 22.5 mi/36 km long, 754 ft/229 m deep. There have been unconfirmed reports of a *Loch Ness monster* since the 15th century.

Nestorianism Christian doctrine held by the Syrian ecclesiastic Nestorius (died *c.* 457), patriarch of Constantinople 428–431. He asserted that Jesus had two natures, human and divine. He was banished for maintaining that Mary was the mother of the man Jesus only, and therefore should not be called the Mother of God. His followers survived as the Assyrian church in Syria, Iraq, Iran, and as the Christians of St Thomas in S India.

Netherlands, the country in W Europe on the North Sea, bounded E by Germany and S by Belgium. *See map p. 661 and panel p. 662*

Netherlands Antilles two groups of Caribbean islands, part of the Netherlands with full internal autonomy, comprising ◊Curaçao and Bonaire off the coast of Venezuela (◊Aruba is considered separately), and St Eustatius, Saba, and the southern part of St Maarten in the Leeward Islands, 500 mi/800 km to the NE
area 308 sq mi/797 sq km
capital Willemstad on Curaçao
products oil from Venezuela refined here; tourism is important
languages Dutch (official), Papiamento, English
population (1983) 193,000.

neuralgia sharp or burning pain originating in a nerve and spreading over its area of distribution. Trigeminal neuralgia, a common form, is a severe pain on one side of the face.

neuroleptic alternate name for antipsychotic.

neurology the branch of medicine concerned with the study and treatment of the brain, spinal cord, and peripheral nerves.

neuron another name for a ◊nerve cell.

Netherlands

neurosis in psychology, a general term referring to emotional disorders, such as anxiety, depression, and obsessions. The main disturbance tends to be one of mood; contact with reality is relatively unaffected, in contrast to the effects of ◊psychosis.

neurotransmitter chemical that diffuses across a ◊synapse, and thus transmits impulses between ◊nerve cells, or between nerve cells and effector organs (for example, muscles). Common neurotransmitters are norepinephrine (which also acts as a hormone) and acetylcholine, the latter being most frequent at junctions between nerve and muscle. Nearly 50 different neurotransmitters have been identified.

neutrality the legal status of a country that decides not to choose sides in a war. Certain states, notably Switzerland and Austria, have opted for permanent neutrality. Neutrality always has a legal connotation. In peacetime, neutrality toward the big power alliances is called *nonalignment* (see ◊nonaligned movement).

neutralization in chemistry, a process occurring when the excess acid (or excess base) in a substance is reacted with added base (or added acid) so that the resulting substance is neither acidic nor basic.

neutron one of the three main subatomic particles, the others being the proton and the electron. The neutron is a composite particle, being made up of three ◊quarks, and therefore belongs to the baryon group of the ◊hadrons. Neutrons have about the same mass as protons but no electric charge, and occur in the nuclei of all atoms except hydrogen. They contribute to the mass of atoms but do not affect their chemistry.

neutron bomb small hydrogen bomb for battlefield use that kills by radiation without destroying buildings and other structures. See ◊nuclear warfare.

neutron star very small, "superdense" star composed mostly of ◊neutrons. They are thought to form when massive stars explode as ◊supernovae, during which the protons and electrons of the star's atoms merge, owing to intense gravitational collapse, to make neutrons. A neutron star may have the mass of up to three Suns, compressed into a globe only 12 mi/20 km in diameter.

Nevada state in W US; nickname Silver State/Sagebrush State
area 110,550 sq mi/286,400 sq km
capital Carson City

Netherlands Kingdom of the (*Koninkrijk der Nederlanden*), popularly referred to as *Holland*

area 16,169 sq mi/41,863 sq km
capital Amsterdam
cities The Hague (seat of government), Utrecht, Eindhoven, Maastricht; chief port Rotterdam
physical flat coastal lowland; rivers Rhine, Scheldt, Maas; Frisian Islands
territories Aruba, Netherlands Antilles (Caribbean)
environment the country lies at the mouths of three of Europe's most polluted rivers, the Maas, Rhine, and Scheldt. Dutch farmers contribute to this pollution by using the world's highest concentrations of nitrogen-based fertilizer
features polders (reclaimed land) make up over 40% of the land area; dyke (*Afsluitdijk*) 20 mi/32 km long 1932 has turned the former Zuider Zee inlet into the freshwater

IJsselmeer; Delta Project series of dams 1986 forms sea defense in Zeeland delta of the Maas, Scheldt, and Rhine
head of state Queen Beatrix Wilhelmina Armgard from 1980
head of government Ruud Lubbers from 1982
political system constitutional monarchy
political parties Christian Democratic Appeal (CDA), Christian, right of center; Labor Party (PvdA), moderate, left of center; People's Party for Freedom and Democracy (VVD), free-enterprise, centrist
exports dairy products, flower bulbs, vegetables, petrochemicals, electronics
currency guilder
population (1992) 15,163,000 (including 300,000 of Dutch-Indonesian origin absorbed 1949–64 from former colonial possessions); growth rate 0.4% p.a.
life expectancy men 74, women 81 (1989)
language Dutch
religions Roman Catholic 40%, Protestant 31%
literacy 99% (1989)
GNP $320.4 bn (1992)

chronology
1940–45 Occupied by Germany during World War II.
1947 Joined Benelux customs union.
1948 Queen Juliana succeeded Queen Wilhelmina to the throne.
1949 Became a founding member of North Atlantic Treaty Organization (NATO).
1953 Dykes breached by storm; nearly 2,000 people and tens of thousands of cattle died in flood.
1958 Joined European Economic Community.
1980 Queen Juliana abdicated in favor of her daughter Beatrix.
1981 Opposition to cruise missiles averted their being sited on Dutch soil.
1989 Prime Minister Ruud Lubbers resigned; new Lubbers-led coalition elected.
1992 Maastricht Treaty on European political and monetary union ratified.

cities Las Vegas, Reno
population (1990) 1,201,800
physical Mohave Desert; lakes: Tahoe, Pyramid, Mead; mountains and plateaus alternating with valleys
features legal gambling and prostitution (in some counties); entertainment at Las Vegas and Reno casinos; Lehman Caves National Monument
products mercury, barite, gold
history explored by Kit Carson and John C Fremont 1843–45; ceded to the US after the Mexican War 1848; first permanent settlement a Mormon trading post 1848. Discovery of silver (the Comstock Lode) 1858 led to rapid population growth and statehood 1864. The building of the Hoover Dam in the 1930s provided the water and power needed for the growth of Las Vegas. In 1931 the state created two industries: divorce (Reno) and gambling (Las Vegas). Oil was discovered 1954, but gold exceeds all other mineral production.

Nevada

Tourism and gambling now generate more than half of the state's income.

new age movement of the late 1980s characterized by an emphasis on the holistic view of body and mind, alternative (or complementary) medicines, personal growth therapies, and a loose mix of theosophy, ecology, oriental mysticism, and a belief in the dawning of an astrological age of peace and harmony.

New Bedford city in SE Massachusetts, on the Acushnet River near Buzzards Bay, S of Boston; population (1990) 99,900. Industries include electronics, rubber and metal products, and fishing. During the 1800s it was a prosperous whaling town.

New Britain city in central Connecticut, SW of Hartford and NE of Waterbury; population (1990) 75,400. Long an industrial city, its industries include tools, hardware, and household appliances.

New Brunswick maritime province of E Canada
area 28,332 sq mi/73,400 sq km
capital Fredericton
cities St John, Moncton
features Grand Lake, St John River; Bay of Fundy
products cereals, wood, paper, fish, lead, zinc, copper, oil, natural gas
population (1991) 725,600; 37% French-speaking
history first reached by Europeans (Cartier) 1534; explored by Champlain 1604; remained a French colony as part of Nova Scotia until ceded to England 1713. After the American Revolution many United Empire Loyalists settled there, and it became a province of the Dominion of Canada 1867.

New Brunswick

Newfoundland and Labrador

New Caledonia island group in the S Pacific, a French overseas territory between Australia and the Fiji Islands
area 7,170 sq mi/18,576 sq km
capital Nouméa
physical fertile, surrounded by a barrier reef
products nickel (the world's third-largest producer), chrome, iron
currency CFP franc
population (1983) 145,300 (43% Kanak (Melanesian), 37% European, 8% Wallisian, 5% Vietnamese and Indonesian, 4% Polynesian)
language French (official)
religions Roman Catholic 60%, Protestant 30%
history New Caledonia was visited by Captain Cook 1774 and became French 1853. A general strike to gain local control of nickel mines 1974 was defeated. In 1981 the French socialist government promised moves toward independence. The 1985 elections resulted in control of most regions by Kanaks, but not the majority of seats. In 1986 the French conservative government reversed the reforms. The Kanaks boycotted a referendum Sept 1987 and a majority were in favor of remaining a French dependency. In 1989 the leader of the Socialist National Liberation front (the most prominent separatist group), Jean-Marie Tjibaou, was murdered.

New Deal in US history, the program introduced by President F D ◊Roosevelt 1933 to counter the ◊Depression of 1929, including employment on public works, farm loans at low rates, and social reforms such as old-age and unemployment insurance, prevention of child labor, protection of employees against unfair practices by employers, and loans to local authorities for slum clearance. In the first 100 days of Roosevelt's administration, he introduced and pushed through Congress hundreds of programs and economic initiatives. Critics from the right called his approach too socialistic, and the role of the federal government in the nation's economic life was strengthened to include policies that remain today. Some of his programs' provisions were declared unconstitutional by the Supreme Court 1935–36, and full employment was not established until the military-industrial needs of World War II.

New Delhi city adjacent to Old Delhi on the Yamuna River in the Union Territory of Delhi, N India; population (1991) 294,100. It is the administrative center of Delhi, and was designated capital of India by the British 1911. Largely designed by British architect Edwin Lutyens, New Delhi was officially inaugurated after its completion 1931. Chemicals, textiles, machine tools, electrical goods, and footwear are produced.

New England region of NE US, comprising the states of Maine, New Hampshire, Vermont, Massachu-

setts, Rhode Island, and Connecticut. It is a geographic region rather than a political entity, with an area of 66,672 sq mi/172,681 sq km. Boston is the principal urban center of the region, and Harvard and Yale its major universities.

Newfoundland and Labrador Canadian province on the Atlantic Ocean
area 156,600 sq mi/405,700 sq km
capital St John's
cities Corner Brook, Gander
physical Newfoundland island and ◊Labrador on the mainland on the other side of the Straits of Belle Isle; rocky
features Grand Banks section of the continental shelf rich in cod; home of the Newfoundland and Labrador dogs
products newsprint, fish products, hydroelectric power, iron, copper, zinc, uranium, offshore oil
population (1991) 571,600
history colonized by Vikings about AD 1000; Newfoundland reached by the English, under the Italian navigator Giovanni ◊Caboto, 1497. It was the first English colony, established 1583. French settlements made; British sovereignty was not recognized until 1713, although France retained the offshore islands of St Pierre and Miquelon. Internal self-government was achieved 1855. In 1934, as Newfoundland had fallen into financial difficulties, administration was vested in a governor and a special commission. A 1948 referendum favored federation with Canada and the province joined Canada 1949.

Newfoundland breed of dog, said to have originated in Newfoundland. Males can grow to 2.3 ft/70 cm tall, and weigh 145 lb/65 kg; the females are slightly smaller. They have an oily, water-repellent undercoat and are excellent swimmers. Gentle in temperament, their fur is dense, flat, and usually dull black. Newfoundlands that are black and white or brown and white are called *Landseers*.

New Guinea island in the SW Pacific, N of Australia, comprising Papua New Guinea and the Indonesian province of West Irian (Irian Jaya area); total area about 342,000 sq mi/885,780 sq km. Part of the Dutch East Indies from 1828, West Irian was ceded by the United Nations to Indonesia 1963.

New Hampshire state in NE US; nickname Granite State
area 9,264 sq mi/24,000 sq km
capital Concord
cities Manchester, Nashua
population (1990) 1,109,300
features White Mountains, including Mount Washington, the tallest peak east of the Rockies (with its cog

New Hampshire

railroad), and Mount Monadnock; the Connecticut River forms boundary with Vermont; earliest presidential-election party primaries every four years; no state income tax or sales tax; ski and tourist resorts
products dairy, poultry, fruits and vegetables; electrical and other machinery; pulp and paper
famous people Mary Baker Eddy, Robert Frost
history settled as a fishing colony near Rye and Dover 1623; separated from Massachusetts colony 1679. As leaders in the Revolutionary cause, its leaders received the honor of being the first to declare independence from Britain July 4, 1776. It became a state 1788, one of the original 13 states.

In the 19th century, abundant water power allowed textile mills to flourish, but the industry later declined. The state experienced rapid growth after 1970, as people and industry—especially high-technology businesses—moved N from the Boston area into S New Hampshire.

New Haven port town in Connecticut, on Long Island Sound; population (1990) 130,500. *Yale University*, third oldest in the US, was founded here 1701 and named after Elihu Yale (1648–1721), an early benefactor. New Haven was founded 1683 by English Protestants.

New Hebrides former name (until 1980) of ◊Vanuatu, a country in the S Pacific.

Ne Win adopted name of Maung Shu Maung 1911– . Myanmar (Burmese) politician, prime minister 1958–60, ruler from 1962 to 1974, president 1974–81, and chair until 1988 of the ruling Burma Socialist Program Party (BSPP). His domestic "Burmese Way to Socialism" policy program brought the economy into serious decline.

New Jersey state in NE US; nickname Garden State
area 7,797 sq mi/20,200 sq km
capital Trenton
cities Newark, Jersey City, Paterson, Elizabeth
population (1990) 7,730,200
features about 125 mi/200 km of seashore, including legalized gambling in Atlantic City and the Victorian beach resort of Cape May; Delaware Water Gap; Palisades along the west bank of the Hudson River;

New Jersey

Princeton University; Morristown National Historic Park; Edison National Historic Site, Menlo Park; Walt Whitman House, Camden; Statue of Liberty National Monument (shared with New York); the Meadowlands stadium
products fruits and vegetables, fish and shellfish, chemicals, pharmaceuticals, soaps and cleansers, transport equipment, petroleum refining
famous people Stephen Crane, Thomas Edison, Thomas Paine, Paul Robeson, Frank Sinatra, Bruce Springsteen, Woodrow Wilson
history colonized in the 17th century by the Dutch (New Netherlands); ceded to England 1664; became a state 1787. It was one of the original 13 states.

Wedged between the growing cities of Philadelphia and New York, New Jersey saw much fighting during the Revolution and became increasingly urban and industrial in the 19th century. In the 20th century, much of the state remains a farming region but also has experienced much air and water pollution as well as the dumping of toxic wastes in landfills. It remains a favored site for development, however, and ranks near the top among states in per-capita income; much urban renewal has occurred in the industrial port cities along the Hudson since the 1970s.

newly industrialized country (NIC) country that has in recent decades experienced a breakthrough into manufacturing and rapid export-led economic growth. The prime examples are Taiwan, Hong Kong, Singapore, and South Korea. Their economic development during the 1970s and 1980s was partly due to a rapid increase of manufactured goods in their exports.

Newman Barnett 1905–1970. US painter, sculptor, and theorist. His paintings are solid-colored canvases with a few sparse vertical stripes. They represent a mystical pursuit of simple or elemental art. His sculptures, such as *Broken Obelisk* 1963–67, consist of geometric shapes on top of each other.

Born in New York City, he was involved in the development of colorfield painting.

Newman John Henry 1801–1890. English Roman Catholic theologian. While still an Anglican, he wrote a series of *Tracts for the Times*, which gave their name to the Tractarian Movement (subsequently called the ◊Oxford Movement) for the revival of Catholicism. He became a Catholic 1845 and was made a cardinal 1879. In 1864 his autobiography, *Apologia pro vita sua*, was published.

Newman Paul 1925– . US actor and director, Hollywood's leading male star of the 1960s and 1970s. His films include *Somebody Up There Likes Me* 1956, *Cat on a Hot Tin Roof* 1958, *The Hustler* 1961, *Sweet Bird of Youth* 1962, *Hud* 1963, *Cool Hand Luke* 1967, *Butch Cassidy and the Sundance Kid* 1969, *The Sting* 1973, *The Verdict* 1983, *The Color of Money* 1986 (for which he won an Academy Award), and *Mr and Mrs Bridge* 1991.

New Mexico state in SW US; nickname Land of Enchantment
area 121,590 sq mi/315,000 sq km
capital Santa Fe
cities Albuquerque, Las Cruces, Roswell
population (1990) 1,515,100
physical more than 75% of the area lies over 3,900 ft/1,200 m above sea level; plains, mountains, caverns
features Great Plains; Rocky Mountains; Rio Grande; Carlsbad Caverns, the largest known; Los Alamos atomic and space research center; White Sands Missile Range (also used by space shuttle); Kiowa Ranch, site of D H Lawrence's stay in the Sangre de Christos

New Mexico

Mountains; Taos art colony; Santa Fe Opera Company; Navaho and Hopi Indian reservations; White Sands and Gila Cliff Dwellings national monuments
products uranium, potash, copper, oil, natural gas, petroleum and coal products; sheep farming; cotton; pecans; vegetables
famous people Billy the Kid, Kit Carson, Georgia O'Keeffe
history explored by Francisco de Coronado for Spain 1540–42; Spanish settlement 1598 on the Rio Grande; Santa Fe founded 1610; most of New Mexico ceded to the US by Mexico 1848; became a state 1912. The first atomic bomb, a test device, was exploded in the desert near Alamogordo July 16, 1945. Oil and gas development and tourism now contribute to the state economy.

New Orleans city and Mississippi River port in Louisiana; population (1980) 557,500. With an outlet to the Gulf of Mexico, New Orleans has led all US ports in shipping tonnage handled. It is a commercial and manufacturing center, with the chief products refined petroleum and petrochemicals. Educational institutions include Tulane University. In the 18th century New Orleans was the capital of Louisiana Territory. It passed to the US with the ◊Louisiana Purchase, and by 1852 it was the third-largest US city. It is the traditional birthplace of jazz.

Newport News industrial city (engineering, shipbuilding) and port of SE Virginia, at the mouth of the James River; population (1990) 170,000. With neighboring Chesapeake, Norfolk, and Portsmouth, it forms the Port of Hampton Roads, one of the chief US ports. It is the site of one of the world's largest shipyards.

news agency business handling news stories and photographs that are then sold to newspapers and magazines. International agencies include the Associated Press (AP, 1848), Agence France-Presse (AFP, 1944), United Press International (UPI, 1907), and ◊Reuters.

New South Wales state of SE Australia
area 309,418 sq mi/801,600 sq km
capital Sydney
cities Newcastle, Wollongong, Broken Hill
physical Great Dividing Range (including Blue Mountains) and part of the Australian Alps (including Snowy Mountains and Mount Kosciusko); Riverina district, irrigated by the Murray-Darling-Murrumbidgee river system; other main rivers Lachlan, Macquarie-Bogan, Hawkesbury, Hunter, Macleay, and Clarence
features a radio telescope at Parkes; Siding Spring Mountain 2,817 ft/859 m, NW of Sydney, with telescopes that can observe the central sector of the Galaxy. ◊Canberra forms an enclave within the state, and New South Wales administers the dependency of Lord Howe Island
products cereals, fruit, sugar, tobacco, wool, meat, hides and skins, gold, silver, copper, tin, zinc, coal; hydroelectric power from the Snowy River

population (1987) 5,570,000; 60% in Sydney
history called New Wales by English explorer Capt ◊Cook, who landed at Botany Bay 1770 and thought that the coastline resembled that of Wales. It was a convict settlement 1788–1850; opened to free settlement by 1819; achieved self-government 1856; and became a state of the Commonwealth of Australia 1901. Since 1973 there has been decentralization to counteract the pull of Sydney, and the New England and Riverina districts have separatist movements.

newspaper a daily or weekly publication in the form of folded sheets containing news, illustrations, timely comments, and advertising. Newsheets became commercial undertakings after the invention of printing and were introduced 1609 in Germany, 1616 in the Netherlands. In 1620, the first newspaper in English appeared in the Netherlands. In England, Addison and Steele published the *Tatler* 1709–11 and the *Spectator* 1711–12. The first newspaper in colonial America was *Publick Occurrences Both Forreign and Domestick*. It was planned as a monthly publication, but it was only published once, in Boston 1690. It was not until 1704 that another paper, the *News-Letter*, also published in Boston, appeared.

New Testament the second part of the ◊Bible, recognized by the Christian church from the 4th century as sacred doctrine. The New Testament includes the Gospels, which tell of the life and teachings of Jesus, the history of the early church, the teachings of St Paul, and mystical writings. It was written in Greek during the 1st and 2nd centuries AD, and the individual sections have been ascribed to various authors by Biblical scholars.

newton SI unit (symbol N) of ◊force. One newton is the force needed to accelerate an object with mass of one kilogram by one meter per second per second.

Newton Isaac 1642–1727. English physicist and mathematician who laid the foundations of physics as a modern discipline. He discovered the law of gravity, created calculus, discovered that white light is composed of many colors, and developed the three standard laws of motion still in use today. During 1665–66, he discovered the binomial theorem, and differential and integral calculus, and also began to investigate the phenomenon of gravitation. In 1685, he expounded his universal law of gravitation. His *Philosophiae naturalis principia mathematica*, usually referred to as *Principia*, was published in 1687, with the aid of Edmond ◊Halley.

Newton's laws of motion in physics, three laws that form the basis of Newtonian mechanics. (1) Unless acted upon by a net force, a body at rest stays at rest, and a moving body continues moving at the same speed in the same straight line. (2) A net force applied to a body gives it a rate of change of ◊momentum proportional to the force and in the direction of the force. (3) When a body A exerts a force on a body B, B exerts an equal and opposite force on A; that is, to every action there is an equal and opposite reaction.

Newton's rings in optics, an ◊interference phenomenon seen (using white light) as concentric rings of spectral colors where light passes through a thin film of transparent medium, such as the wedge of air between a large-radius convex lens and a flat glass plate. With monochromatic light (light of a single wavelength), the rings take the form of alternate light and dark bands. They are caused by interference (interaction) between light rays reflected from the plate and those reflected from the curved surface of the lens.

New Wave in pop music, a style that evolved parallel to punk in the second half of the 1970s. It shared the urban aggressive spirit of punk but was musically and lyrically more sophisticated; examples are the early work of Elvis Costello and Talking Heads.

New Wave (French *nouvelle vague*) French literary movement of the 1950s, a cross-fertilization of the novel, especially the ◊nouveau roman (Marguerite Duras, Alain Robbe-Grillet, Nathalie Sarraute), and film (directors Jean-Luc Godard, Alain Resnais, and François Truffaut).

New World the Americas, so called by the first Europeans who reached them. The term also describes animals and plants of the western hemisphere.

New York largest city in the US, industrial port (printing, publishing, clothing), cultural, financial, and commercial center, in S New York State, at the junction of the Hudson and East rivers and including New York Bay. It comprises the boroughs of the Bronx, Brooklyn, Manhattan, Queens, and Staten Island; population (1990) 7,322,600, white 43.2%, black 25.2%, Hispanic 24.4%. New York is also known as the Big Apple.

New York is the nation's corporate, financial, and media center. Real estate is one of its biggest businesses. It remains an important manufacturing center, although a declining one. It is the nation's center for book and magazine publishing and the visual and performing arts. It also ranks first among US cities in wholesale and retail trade. The two major airports are Kennedy International and La Guardia. The Port of New York is the nation's second-busiest harbor, although most active piers and harbors are now in New Jersey and Brooklyn. Tourism, conventions, and educational institutions are also important to the city's economy.

The Statue of Liberty stands on Liberty Island (called Bedloe's Island until 1956) in the inner harbor of New York Bay. Skyscrapers include the twin towers of the World Trade Center (1,350 ft/412 m) and the art deco Empire State Building (1,250 ft/381 m) and Chrysler building. St Patrick's Cathedral is 19th-century Gothic. Notable art museums include the Frick Collection, the Metropolitan Museum of Art (with a medieval department, the Cloisters), the Museum of Modern Art, the Guggenheim (designed by Frank Lloyd Wright), the Whitney, and the Morgan Library. Columbia University 1754 is the best known of a number of institutions of higher education. Other features include Central Park, Rockefeller Center, the United Nations complex, Carnegie Hall, Lincoln Center for the Performing Arts, the Broadway theater district, the New York Stock Exchange, Chinatown, Greenwich Village, and South Street Seaport. The Italian navigator Giovanni da Verrazano (?1485–?1528) reached New York Bay 1524, and Henry Hudson explored it 1609. The Dutch established a settlement on Manhattan 1624, named New Amsterdam, and on Governor's Island in New York Bay; they also settled in Brooklyn, Queens, and Staten Island by the 1640s; all this was captured by the English in 1664 and renamed New York. During the American Revolution, British troops occupied New York 1776–84. After the Revolution, New York was the capital of the US 1785–89. In the early 19th century, it passed Philadelphia to become the nation's largest city, and for the next 100 years it swelled with immigrants. In 1898 the five boroughs joined together to form the City of

New York The New York skyline, showing the twin towers of the World Trade Center.

New York

Greater New York. In the 1960s New York began declining in population, and its economy suffered because of high taxation (which led businesses to move to tax-free, nearby localities) and the departure of the middle class. In the 1970s a severe municipal financial crisis threatened, but in the 1980s the economy recovered, based on gains in service employment (particularly in financial services), office construction, and the cooperative real-estate market. From the late 1980s, the city's economy was once again threatened.

New York state in NE US; nickname Empire State/Excelsior State
area 49,099 sq mi/127,200 sq km
capital Albany
cities New York, Buffalo, Rochester, Yonkers, Syracuse
population (1990) 17,990,500
physical mountains: Adirondacks, Catskills; lakes: Champlain, Placid, Erie, Ontario; rivers: Mohawk, Hudson, St Lawrence (with Thousand Islands); Niagara Falls; Long Island; New York Bay
features West Point, site of the US Military Academy 1801; National Baseball Hall of Fame, Cooperstown; horse racing at Belmont, Aqueduct, Saratoga Springs; colleges: Colgate, Cornell, Columbia, New York University, CUNY, SUNY, Rensselaer Polytech, Pratt, Juilliard, and Vassar; Washington Irving's home at Philipsburg Manor; Fenimore House (J F ◊Cooper), Cooperstown; home of F D Roosevelt at Hyde Park, and the Roosevelt Library; home of Theodore Roosevelt, Oyster Bay; Statue of Liberty National Monument; Erie Canal; United Nations headquarters; New York City
products dairy products, apples, clothing, periodical and book printing and publishing, electronic components and accessories, office machines and computers, communications equipment, motor vehicles and equipment, pharmaceuticals, aircraft and parts
famous people Aaron Burr, Grover Cleveland, James Fenimore Cooper, George Gershwin, Alexander Hamilton, Fiorello La Guardia, Washington Irving, Henry James, Herman Melville, Arthur Miller, Nelson Rockefeller, Franklin D Roosevelt, Theodore Roosevelt, Peter Stuyvesant, Walt Whitman
history explored by the Italian navigator Giovanni da Verrazano for France 1524; explored by Samuel de Champlain for France and Henry Hudson for the Netherlands 1609; colonized by the Dutch from 1614; first permanent settlement at Albany (Fort Orange) 1624; Manhattan Island purchased by Peter Minuit 1625; New Amsterdam annexed by the English 1664. The first constitution was adopted 1777, when New York became one of the original 13 states. The Battle of Saratoga 1777, following which British troops surrendered, is considered the turning point of the American Revolution. By 1810 New York was the most populous of the states, a rank it maintained until the 1960s. The Erie Canal, completed 1825, fostered commerce by providing a link between the Atlantic and the Great Lakes. After the Civil War, New York was transformed from a chiefly agricultural state to an industrial giant. By 1970, however, the state was suffering economic decline, particularly in manufacturing. But it remains an important industrial state, and in New York City it contains the commercial, financial (Wall Street), and cultural capital of the country.

New York Times v Sullivan a US Supreme Court decision 1964 imposing limits on the power of public officials to bring libel suits against people who criticize

Niagara Falls
Canadian section of the Niagara River Falls.

New Zealand
Dominion of

area 103,777 sq mi/268,680 sq km
capital and port Wellington
cities Hamilton, Palmerston North, Christchurch, Dunedin; port Auckland
physical comprises North Island, South Island, Stewart Island, Chatham Islands, and minor islands; mainly mountainous
overseas territories Tokelau (three atolls transferred 1926 from former Gilbert and Ellice Islands colony); Niue Island (one of the Cook Islands, separately administered from 1903: chief town Alafi); Cook Islands are internally self-governing but share common citizenship with New Zealand; Ross Dependency in Antarctica
features Ruapehu in the North Island, 9,180 ft/2,797 m, highest of three active volcanoes; geysers and hot springs of the Rotorua district; Lake Taupo (238 sq mi/616 sq km), source of Waikato River; Kaingaroa state forest. In the South Island are the Southern Alps and Canterbury Plains
head of state Elizabeth II from 1952 represented by governor-general (Catherine Tizard from 1990)
head of government Jim Bolger from 1990
political system constitutional monarchy
political parties Labor Party, moderate, left of center; New

Zealand National Party, free-enterprise, center-right; Alliance Party, left of center, ecologists
exports lamb, beef, wool, leather, dairy products, processed foods, kiwi fruit, seeds and breeding stock, timber, paper, pulp, light aircraft
currency New Zealand dollar
population (1992) 3,481,000 (European, mostly British, 87%; Polynesian, mostly Maori, 12%); growth rate 0.9% p.a.
life expectancy men 72, women 78 (1989)
languages English (official), Maori
religions Protestant 50%, Roman Catholic 15%
literacy 99% (1989)
GNP $40.3 bn (1992)

chronology
1840 New Zealand became a British colony.
1907 Created a dominion of the British Empire.
1931 Granted independence from Britain.
1947 Independence within the Commonwealth confirmed by the New Zealand parliament.
1972 National Party government replaced by Labor Party, with Norman Kirk as prime minister.
1974 Kirk died; replaced by Wallace Rowling.
1975 National Party returned, with Robert Muldoon as prime minister.
1984 Labor Party returned under David Lange.
1985 Non-nuclear military policy created disagreements with France and the US.
1987 National Party declared support for the Labor government's non-nuclear policy. Lange reelected. New Zealand officially classified as a "friendly" rather than "allied" country by the US because of its non-nuclear military policy.
1988 Free-trade agreement with Australia signed.
1989 Lange resigned over economic differences with finance minister (he cited health reasons); replaced by Geoffrey Palmer.
1990 Palmer replaced by Mike Moore. Labor Party defeated by National Party in general election; Jim Bolger became prime minister.
1991 Formation of amalgamated Alliance Party set to challenge two-party system.
1992 Ban on visits by US warships lifted. Referendum aproved change in voting system from 1996.

their actions as public servants. The case was brought by Police Commissioner Sullivan of Montgomery, Alabama, in response to a paid advertisement in the *Times* that accused Sullivan's police force of brutality and repression. The Court ruled that Sullivan's case should not be sustained, finding unanimously that public officials cannot recover damages in libel suits without proof that defamatory falsehoods have been published intentionally and with actual malice.

New Zealand or *Aotearoa* country in the SW Pacific Ocean, SE of Australia, comprising two main islands, North Island and South Island, and other small islands.

NH abbreviation for the state of ◊New Hampshire.

niacin one of the "B group" ◊vitamins, deficiency of which gives rise to pellagra.

Niagara Falls two waterfalls on the Niagara River, on the Canada–US border, between lakes Erie and Ontario and separated by Goat Island. The *American Falls* are 167 ft/51 m high, 1,080 ft/330 m wide; *Horseshoe Falls*, in Canada, are 160 ft/49 m high, 2,600 ft/790 m across. *See illustration p. 667*

Niamey river port and capital of ◊Niger; population (1983) 399,000. It produces textiles, chemicals, pharmaceuticals, and foodstuffs.

Nibelungenlied *Song of the Nibelungs*, anonymous 12th-century German epic poem, derived from older sources. The composer Richard ◊Wagner made use of the legends in his *Ring* cycle.

Nicaea, Council of Christian church council held in Nicaea (now Iznik, Turkey) in 325, called by the Roman emperor Constantine. It condemned ◊Arianism as heretical and upheld the doctrine of the Trinity in the Nicene ◊Creed.

Nicaragua country in Central America, between the Pacific Ocean and the Caribbean Sea, bounded N by Honduras and S by Costa Rica.

Nice city on the French Riviera; population (1990) 345,700. Founded in the 3rd century BC, it repeatedly changed hands between France and the Duchy of Savoy from the 14th to the 19th century. In 1860 it was finally transferred to France.

Nicene Creed one of the fundamental ◊creeds of Christianity, promulgated by the Council of ◊Nicaea 325.

Nicholas I 1796–1855. Tsar of Russia from 1825. His Balkan ambitions led to war with Turkey 1827–29 and the Crimean War 1853–56.

Nicholas II 1868–1918. Tsar of Russia 1894–1917. He was dominated by his wife, Tsarina ◊Alexandra, who was under the influence of the religious charlatan ◊Rasputin. His mismanagement of the Russo-Japanese War and of internal affairs led to the revolution of 1905, which he suppressed, although he was forced to grant limited constitutional reforms. He took Russia into World War I in 1914, was forced to abdicate in 1917 after the ◊Russian Revolution, and was executed with his family.

Nicholas, St also known as *Santa Claus* 4th century AD. In the Christian church, patron saint of Russia, children, merchants, sailors, and pawnbrokers; bishop of Myra (now in Turkey). His legendary gifts of dowries to poor girls led to the custom of giving gifts to children on the eve of his feast day, Dec 6, still retained in some countries, such as the Netherlands; elsewhere the custom has been transferred to Christmas Day. His emblem is three balls.

Nicholson Ben 1894–1982. English abstract artist. After early experiments influenced by Cubism and de Stijl (see ◊Mondrian), Nicholson developed a style of geometrical reliefs, notably a series of white reliefs (from 1933).

Nicholson Jack 1937– . US film actor who, in the late 1960s, captured the mood of nonconformist, uncertain young Americans in such films as *Easy Rider* 1969 and *Five Easy Pieces* 1970. He subsequently became a mainstream Hollywood star, appearing in *Chinatown* 1974, *One Flew over the Cuckoo's Nest* (Academy Award) 1975, *The Shining* 1979, *Terms of Endearment* (Academy Award) 1983, *Batman* 1989, and *A Few Good Men* 1992.

nickel hard, malleable and ductile, silver-white metallic element, symbol Ni, atomic number 28, atomic weight 58.71. It occurs in igneous rocks and as a free metal (◊native metal), occasionally occurring in fragments of iron-nickel meteorites. It is a component of the Earth's core, which is held to consist principally of iron with some nickel. It has a high melting point, low electrical and thermal conductivity, and can be magnetized. It does not tarnish and therefore is much used for alloys, electroplating, and for coinage.

Nicklaus Jack (William) 1940– . US golfer, nicknamed "the Golden Bear." He won a record 20 major titles, including 18 professional majors between 1962 and 1986.

Nicobar Islands group of Indian islands, part of the Union Territory of ◊Andaman and Nicobar Islands.

Nicolle Charles 1866–1936. French bacteriologist whose discovery in 1909 that typhus is transmitted by the body louse made the armies of World War I introduce delousing as a compulsory part of the military routine. Nobel Prize for Medicine 1928.

Nicosia capital of Cyprus, with leather, textile, and pottery industries; population (1987) 165,000. Nicosia was the residence of Lusignan kings of Cyprus 1192–1475. The Venetians, who took Cyprus 1489, surrounded Nicosia with a high wall, which still

---

Nicaragua
Republic of
(*República de Nicaragua*)

area 49,363 sq mi/127,849 sq km
capital Managua
cities León, Granada; chief ports Corinto, Puerto Cabezas, El Bluff
physical narrow Pacific coastal plain separated from broad Atlantic coastal plain by volcanic mountains and lakes Managua and Nicaragua
features largest state of Central America and most thinly populated; Mosquito Coast, Fonseca Bay, Corn Islands
head of state and government Violeta Barrios de Chamorro from 1990
political system emergent democracy
political parties Sandinista National Liberation Front (FSLN), Marxist-Leninist; Democratic Conservative Party (PCD), centrist; National Opposition Union (UNO), loose, US-backed coalition

exports coffee, cotton, sugar, bananas, meat
currency cordoba
population (1992) 4,131,000 (mestizo 70%, Spanish descent 15%, Indian or black 10%); growth rate 3.3% p.a.
life expectancy men 61, women 63 (1989)
languages Spanish (official), Indian, English
religion Roman Catholic 95%
literacy 66% (1986)
GNP $2.1 bn; $610 per head (1988)

chronology
1838 Independence achieved from Spain.
1926–1933 Occupied by US marines.
1936 General Anastasio Somoza elected president; start of near-dictatorial rule by Somoza family.
1962 Sandinista National Liberation Front (FSLN) formed to fight Somoza regime.
1979 Somoza government ousted by FSLN.
1982 Subversive activity against the government by right-wing Contra guerrillas promoted by the US. State of emergency declared.
1984 The US mined Nicaraguan harbors. Action condemned by World Court 1986 and $17 billion in reparations ordered.
1985 Denunciation of Sandinista government by US president Reagan. FSLN won assembly elections.
1987 Central American peace agreement cosigned by Nicaraguan leaders.
1988 Peace agreement failed. Nicaragua held talks with Contra rebel leaders. Hurricane left 180,000 people homeless.
1989 Demobilization of rebels and release of former Somozan supporters; cease-fire ended.
1990 FSLN defeated by UNO, a US-backed coalition; Violeta Barrios de Chamorro elected president. Antigovernment riots.
1991 First presidential state visit to US for over fifty years.
1992 June: US aid suspended because of concern over role of Sandinista in Nicaraguan government. Sept: around 16,000 made homeless by earthquake.

Nijinsky The great Russian dancer and choreographer Vaslav Nijinsky as "Le Dieu Bleu" in 1912.

exists; the city fell to the Turks 1571. It was again partly taken by the Turks in the invasion 1974.

nicotine $C_{10}H_{14}N_2$ an alkaloid (nitrogenous compound) obtained from the dried leaves of the tobacco plant *Nicotiana tabacum* and used as an insecticide. A colorless oil, soluble in water, it turns brown on exposure to the air.

Niemeyer Oscar 1907– . Brazilian architect, joint designer of the United Nations headquarters in New York and of many buildings in Brasília, capital of Brazil.

Nietzsche Friedrick Wilhelm 1844–1900. German philosopher and writer. He rejected the absolute moral values and "slave morality" of Christianity. His ideal was the *übermensch*, or "Superman," who would impose his will on the weak and worthless. He published *Morgenröte/The Dawn* 1880–81, *Die fröhliche Wissenschaft/The Gay Science* 1881–82, *Also sprach Zarathustra/Thus Spake Zarathustra* 1883–85, *Jenseits von Gut und Böse/Between Good and Evil* 1885–86, *Zur Genealogie der Moral/Towards a Geneology of Morals* 1887, and *Ecce Homo* 1888.

Niger third-longest river in Africa, 2,600 mi/4,185 km. It rises in the highlands bordering Sierra Leone and Guinea, flows NE through Mali, then SE through Niger and Nigeria to an inland delta on the Gulf of Guinea. Its flow has been badly affected by the expansion of the Sahara Desert. It is sluggish and frequently floods its banks. It was explored by the Scotsman Mungo Park 1795–96.

Niger landlocked country in NW Africa, bounded N by Algeria and Libya, E by Chad, S by Nigeria and Benin, and W by Burkina Faso and Mali.

Niger-Congo languages the largest group of languages in Africa. It includes about 1,000 languages and covers a vast area south of the Sahara desert, from the W coast to the E, and down the E coast as far as South Africa. It is divided into groups and subgroups; the most widely spoken Niger-Congo languages are Swahili (spoken on the E coast), the members of the Bantu group (southern Africa), and Yoruba (Nigeria).

Nigeria country in W Africa on the Gulf of Guinea, bounded N by Niger, E by Chad and Cameroon, and W by Benin.

nightingale songbird of the thrush family with a song of great beauty, heard at night as well as by day. About 6.5 in/16.5 cm long, it is dull brown, lighter below, with a reddish brown tail. It migrates to Europe and winters in Africa. It feeds on insects and small animals.

Niger
Republic of
(*République du Niger*)

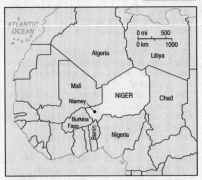

area 457,953 sq mi/1,186,408 sq km
capital Niamey
cities Zinder, Maradi, Tahoua
physical desert plains between hills in N and savanna in S; river Niger in SW, Lake Chad in SE
features part of the Sahara Desert and subject to Sahel droughts
head of state Mahamane Ousmane from 1993

head of government Mahamdou Issaufou from 1993
political system military republic
political parties Alliance for the Forces of Change (AFC), moderate left of center; National Movement for a Development Society (MNSD), right of center
exports peanuts, livestock, gum arabic, uranium
currency franc CFA
population (1992 8,281,000; growth rate 2.8% p.a.
life expectancy men 48, women 50 (1989)
languages French (official), Hausa, Djerma, and other minority languages
religions Sunni Muslim 85%, animist 15%
literacy men 19%, women 9% (1985 est)
GNP $2.2 bn; $310 per head (1987)

chronology
1960 Achieved full independence from France; Hamani Diori elected president.
1974 Diori ousted in army coup led by Seyni Kountché.
1977 Cooperation agreement signed with France.
1987 Kountché died; replaced by Col Ali Saibu.
1989 Ali Saibu elected president without opposition.
1990 Multiparty politics promised.
1991 Saibu stripped of executive powers; transitional government formed.
1992 Transitional government collapsed. Referendum endorsed the adoption of multiparty politics.
1993 Mahamane Ousmane elected president in multiparty elections; Mahamdou Issaufou appointed prime minister.

Nigeria
Federal Republic of

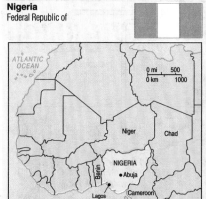

area 356,576 sq mi/923,773 sq km
capital Abuja
cities Ibadan, Ogbomosho, Kano; ports Lagos, Port Harcourt, Warri, Calabar
physical arid savanna in N; tropical rain forest in S, with mangrove swamps along the coast; river Niger forms wide delta; mountains in SE
environment toxic waste from northern industrialized countries has been dumped in Nigeria
features harmattan (dry wind from the Sahara); rich artistic heritage, for example, Benin bronzes
head of state and government (interim) Ernest Shonekan from 1993
political system military republic pending promised elections
political parties Social Democratic Party (SDP), left of center; National Republican Convention (NRC), right of center
exports petroleum (largest oil resources in Africa), cocoa, peanuts, palm oil (Africa's largest producer), cotton, rubber, tin
currency naira

population (1992) 89,666,00 (Yoruba in W, Ibo in E, and Hausa-Fulani in N); growth rate 3.3% p.a.
life expectancy men 47, women 49 (1989)
languages English (official), Hausa, Ibo, Yoruba
media all radio and television stations and almost 50% of all publishing owned by the federal government or the Nigerian states
religions Sunni Muslim 50% (in N), Christian 40% (in S), local religions 10%
literacy men 54%, women 31% (1985 est)
GNP $78 bn (1987); $790 per head (1984)

chronology
1914 N Nigeria and S Nigeria united to become Britain's largest African colony.
1954 Nigeria became a federation.
1960 Independence achieved from Britain within the Commonwealth.
1963 Became a republic, with Nnamdi Azikiwe as president.
1966 Military coup, followed by a counter-coup led by General Yakubu Gowon. Slaughter of many members of the Ibo tribe in north.
1967 Conflict over oil revenues led to declaration of an independent Ibo state of Biafra and outbreak of civil war.
1970 Surrender of Biafra and end of civil war.
1975 Gowon ousted in military coup; second coup put General Olusegun Obasanjo in power.
1979 Shehu Shagari became civilian president.
1983 Shagari's government overthrown in coup by Maj. Gen. Mohammedu Buhari.
1985 Buhari replaced in a bloodless coup led by Maj. Gen. Ibrahim Babangida.
1989 Two new political parties approved. Babangida promised a return to pluralist politics; date set for 1992.
1991 Nine new states created. Babangida confirmed his commitment to democratic rule for 1992.
1992 Multiparty elections won by Babangida's SDP.
1993 Results of presidential elections suspended by national commission, following complaints of ballot rigging. Babangida resigned in Aug. Military junta in power from Nov.

Nightingale Florence 1820–1910. English nurse, the founder of nursing as a profession. She took a team of nurses to Scutari (now Üsküdar, Turkey) in 1854 and reduced the ◊Crimean War hospital death rate from 42% to 2%. In 1856 she founded the Nightingale School and Home for Nurses in London.

Night Journey or **al-Miraj** (Arabic "the ascent") in Islam, the journey of the prophet Mohammed, guided by the archangel Gabriel, from Mecca to Jerusalem, where he met the earlier prophets, including Adam, Moses, and Jesus; he then ascended to paradise, where he experienced the majesty of Allah, and was also shown hell.

nightshade any of several plants in the family Solanaceae, which includes the black nightshade *Solanum nigrum*, bittersweet or woody nightshade *S. dulcamara*, and deadly nightshade or ◊belladonna.

Nihilist member of a group of Russian revolutionaries in the reign of Alexander II 1855–81. The name, popularized by the writer Turgenev, means "one who approves of nothing" (Latin *nihil*) belonging to the existing order. In 1878 the Nihilists launched a guerrilla campaign leading to the murder of the tsar 1881.

Nijinsky Vaslav 1890–1950. Russian dancer and choreographer. Noted for his powerful but graceful technique, he was a legendary member of ◊Diaghilev's Ballets Russes, for whom he ‵choreographed

Debussy's *Prélude à l'Après-midi d'un faune* 1912 and *Jeux* 1913, and Stravinsky's *The Rite of Spring* 1913.

Nile river in Africa, the world's longest, 4,160 mi/6,695 km. The *Blue Nile* rises in Lake Tana, Ethiopia, the *White Nile* at Lake Victoria, and they join at Khar-

Nile

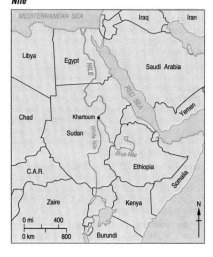

nitrogen cycle The nitrogen cycle is one of a number of cycles in which the chemicals necessary for life are recycled.

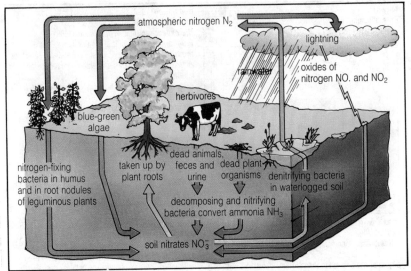

atmospheric nitrogen N₂

lightning

rainwater

oxides of nitrogen NO. and NO₂

herbivores

blue-green algae

nitrogen-fixing bacteria in humus and in root nodules of leguminous plants

taken up by plant roots

dead animals, feces and urine

dead plant organisms

denitrifying bacteria in waterlogged soil

decomposing and nitrifying bacteria convert ammonia NH₃

soil nitrates NO₃⁻

toum, Sudan. The river enters the Mediterranean Sea at a vast delta in N Egypt.

Nineveh capital of the Assyrian Empire from the 8th century BC until its destruction by the Medes under King Cyaxares in 612 BC. It was situated on the Tigris River (opposite the present city of Mosul, Iraq) and was adorned with palaces.

Ningxia or *Ningxia Hui* autonomous region (formerly *Ninghsia-Hui*) of NW China
area 65,620 sq mi/170,000 sq km
capital Yinchuan
physical desert plateau
products cereals and rice under irrigation; coal
population (1990) 4,655,000; including many Muslims and nomadic herders.

niobium soft, gray-white, somewhat ductile and malleable, metallic element, symbol Nb, atomic number 41, atomic weight 92.906. It occurs in nature with tantalum, which it resembles in chemical properties. It is used in making stainless steel and other alloys for jet engines and rockets and for making superconductor magnets.

Nippon English transliteration of the Japanese name for ◊Japan.

nirvana in Buddhism, the attainment of perfect serenity by the eradication of all desires. To some Buddhists it means complete annihilation, to others it means the absorption of the self in the infinite.

niter or *saltpeter* potassium nitrate, KNO₃, a mineral found on and just under the ground in desert regions; used in explosives. Niter occurs in Bihar, India; Iran; and Cape Province, South Africa. The salt was formerly used for the manufacture of gunpowder, but the supply of niter for explosives is today largely met by making the salt from nitratine (also called Chile saltpeter, NaNO₃). Saltpeter is a ◊preservative and is widely used for curing meats.

nitrate any salt of nitric acid, containing the NO₃⁻ ion. Nitrates of various kinds are used in explosives, in the chemical industry, in curing meat (see ◊niter), and as inorganic fertilizers. They are the most water-soluble salts known.

nitrate pollution the contamination of water by nitrates. Nitrates in the soil, whether naturally occur-

ring or from agricultural fertilizers, are used by plants to make proteins. However, increased use of artifical fertilizers and land cultivation means that higher levels of nitrates are being washed from the soil into rivers, lakes, and aquifers. There they cause an excessive enrichment of the water (eutrophication), leading to a rapid growth of algae, which in turn darkens the water and reduces its oxygen content. The water is expensive to purify and many plants and animals die.

nitric acid or *aqua fortis* HNO₃ fuming acid obtained by the oxidation of ammonia or the action of sulfuric acid on potassium nitrate. It is a highly corrosive acid, dissolving most metals, and a strong oxidizing agent. It is used in the nitration and esterification of organic substances, and in the making of sulfuric acid, nitrates, explosives, plastics, and dyes.

nitrite salt or ester of nitrous acid, containing the nitrite ion (NO₂⁻). Nitrites are used as preservatives (for example, to prevent the growth of botulism spores) and as coloring agents in cured meats such as bacon and sausages.

nitrogen (Greek *nitron* "native soda," sodium or potassium nitrate) colorless, odorless, tasteless, gaseous, nonmetallic element, symbol N, atomic number 7, atomic weight 14.0067. It forms almost 80% of the Earth's atmosphere by volume and is a constituent of all plant and animal tissues (in proteins and nucleic acids). Nitrogen is obtained for industrial use by the liquefaction and fractional distillation of air. Its compounds are used in the manufacture of foods, drugs, fertilizers, dyes, and explosives.

nitrogen cycle the process of nitrogen passing through the ecosystem. Nitrogen, in the form of inorganic compounds (such as nitrates) in the soil, is absorbed by plants and turned into organic compounds (such as proteins) in plant tissue. A proportion of this nitrogen is eaten by ◊herbivores, with some of this in turn being passed on to the carnivores, which feed on the herbivores. The nitrogen is ultimately returned to the soil as excrement and when organisms die and are converted back to inorganic form by ◊decomposers.

nitrogen oxide any chemical compound that contains only nitrogen and oxygen. All nitrogen oxides are gases. Nitrogen monoxide and nitrogen dioxide contribute to air pollution. See also ◊nitrous oxide.

nitroglycerine $C_3H_5(ONO_2)_3$ flammable, explosive oil produced by the action of nitric and sulfuric acids on glycerol. Although poisonous, it is used in cardiac medicine. It explodes with great violence if heated in a confined space and is used in the preparation of dynamite, cordite, and other high explosives.

nitrous oxide or *dinitrogen oxide* N_2O colorless, nonflammable gas that reduces sensitivity to pain. In higher doses it is an anesthetic. Well tolerated, but less potent than some other anesthetic gases, it is often combined with other drugs to allow lower doses to be used. It may be self-administered; for example, in childbirth. It is popularly known as "laughing gas."

Niven David 1909–1983. Scottish-born US film actor, in Hollywood from the 1930s. His films include *Wuthering Heights* 1939, *Separate Tables* 1958 (Academy Award), *The Guns of Navarone* 1961, and *The Pink Panther* 1964. He published two best-selling volumes of autobiography, *The Moon's a Balloon* 1972 and *Bring on the Empty Horses* 1975.

Nixon Richard (Milhous) 1913–1994. 37th president of the US 1969–74, a Republican. He attracted attention as a member of the Un-American Activities Committee 1948, and was vice president to Eisenhower 1953–61. As president he was responsible for US withdrawal from Vietnam, and forged new links with China, but at home his culpability in the cover-up of the ◊Watergate scandal and the existence of a "slush fund" for political machinations during his reelection campaign 1972 led to his resignation 1974 when threatened with ◊impeachment.

NJ abbreviation for the state of ◊New Jersey.

Nkomo Joshua 1917– . Zimbabwean politician, vice-president from 1988. As president of ZAPU (Zimbabwe African People's Union) from 1961, he was a leader of the black nationalist movement against the white Rhodesian regime. He was a member of Robert ◊Mugabe's cabinet 1980–82 and from 1987.

Nkrumah Kwame 1909–1972. Ghanaian nationalist politician, prime minister of the Gold Coast (Ghana's former name) 1952–57 and of newly independent Ghana 1957–60. He became Ghana's first president 1960 but was overthrown in a coup 1966. His policy of "African socialism" led to links with the communist bloc.

NM abbreviation for the state of ◊New Mexico.

Nō or *Noh* the Classical, aristocratic Japanese drama, which developed from the 14th to the 16th centuries and is still performed. There is a repertory of some 250 pieces, of which five, one from each of the several classes devoted to different subjects, may be put on in a performance lasting a whole day. Dance, mime, music, and chanting develop the mythical or historical themes. All the actors are men, some of whom wear masks and elaborate costumes; scenery is limited. Nō influenced ◊kabuki drama.

Noah in the Old Testament, the son of Lamech and father of Shem, Ham, and Japheth, who, according to God's instructions, built a ship, the ark, so that he and his family and specimens of all existing animals might survive the ◊Flood. There is also a Babylonian version of the tale, *The Epic of Gilgamesh*.

Nobel Alfred Bernhard 1833–1896. Swedish chemist and engineer. He invented ◊dynamite in 1867 and ballistite, a smokeless gunpowder, in 1889. He amassed a

Nixon *The 37th US president Richard Milhous Nixon, a Republican.*

large fortune from the manufacture of explosives and the exploitation of the Baku oil fields in Azerbaijan, near the Caspian Sea. He left this fortune in trust for the endowment of five ◊Nobel prizes.

nobelium synthesized, radioactive, metallic element of the ◊actinide series, symbol No, atomic number 102, atomic weight 259. It is synthesized by bombarding curium with carbon nuclei.

Nobel Prize annual international prize, first awarded 1901 under the will of Alfred Nobel, Swedish chemist, who invented dynamite. The interest on the Nobel endowment fund is divided annually among the persons who have made the greatest contributions in the fields of physics, chemistry, medicine, literature, and world peace. *See table p. 674*

noble gas alternate name for ◊inert gas.

nocturne in music, a lyrical, dreamy piece, often for piano, introduced by John Field (1782–1837) and adopted by Frédéric Chopin.

noise pollution unwanted and damaging sound. Permanent, incurable loss of hearing can be caused by prolonged exposure to high noise levels (above 85 decibels).

Noland Kenneth 1924– . US painter, associated with Abstract Expressionism. In the 1950s and early 1960s he painted targets, or concentric circles of color, in a clean, hard-edged style on unprimed canvas. His work centered on geometry, color, and symmetry. His later 1960s paintings experimented with the manipulation of color vision and afterimages, pioneering the field of ◊Op art.
    Noland was born in Asheville, North Carolina. In *Graded Exposure* 1967, he used large stripes to form a plaid.

nomadic pastoralism ◊farming system where animals (cattle, goats, camels) are taken to different locations in order to find fresh pastures. It is practiced in the developing world; for example, in central Asia and the Sahel region of W Africa. Increasing numbers of cattle may lead to overgrazing of the area and ◊desertification.

nominative in the grammar of some inflected languages—such as Latin, Russian, and Sanskrit—the form of a word used to indicate that a noun or pronoun is the subject of a finite verb.

Nobel Prizewinners: recent winners

Peace

1984 Bishop Desmond Tutu *(South Africa)*
1985 International Physicians for the Prevention of Nuclear War
1986 Elie Wiesel *(US)*
1987 President Oscar Arias Sanchez *(Costa Rica)*
1988 The United Nations peacekeeping forces
1989 The Dalai Lama *(Tibet)*
1990 President Mikhail Gorbachev *(USSR)*
1991 Aung San Suu Kyi *(Myanmar)*
1992 Rigoberta Menche *(Guatemala)*
1993 F W de Klerk *(South Africa)* and Nelson Mandela *(South Africa)*

Literature

1984 Jaroslav Seifert *(Czechoslovakia)*
1985 Claude Simon *(France)*
1986 Wole Soyinka *(Nigeria)*
1987 Joseph Brodsky *(USSR/US)*
1988 Naguib Mahfouz *(Egypt)*
1989 Camilo José Cela *(Spain)*
1990 Octavio Paz *(Mexico)*
1991 Nadine Gordimer *(South Africa)*
1992 Derek Walcott *(St Lucia)*
1993 Toni Morrison *(US)*

Economics

1984 Richard Stone *(UK)*
1985 Franco Modigliani *(US)*
1986 James Buchanan *(US)*
1987 Robert Solow *(US)*
1988 Maurice Allais *(France)*
1989 Trygve Haavelmo *(Norway)*
1990 Harry M Markowitz *(US)*, Merton H Miller *(US)*, and William F Sharpe *(US)*
1991 Ronald H Coase *(US)*
1992 Gary S Becker *(US)*
1993 Robert Fogel *(US)* and Douglass Worth *(US)*

Chemistry

1984 Bruce Merrifield *(US)*
1985 Herbert A Hauptman *(US)* and Jerome Karle *(US)*
1986 Dudley Herschbach *(US)*, Yuan Lee *(US)*, and John Polanyi *(Canada)*
1987 Donald Cram *(US)*, Jean-Marie Lehn *(France)*, and Charles Pedersen *(US)*

1988 Johann Deisenhofer *(West Germany)*, Robert Huber *(West Germany)*, and Hartmut Michel *(West Germany)*
1989 Sydney Altman *(US)* and Thomas Cech *(US)*
1990 Elias James Corey *(US)*
1991 Richard R Ernst *(Switzerland)*
1992 Rudolph A Marcus *(US)*
1993 Kary Mullis *(US)* and Michael Smith *(Canada)*

Physics

1984 Carlo Rubbia *(Italy)* and Simon van der Meer *(Netherlands)*
1985 Klaus von Klitzing *(West Germany)*
1986 Ernst Ruska *(West Germany)*, Gerd Binnig *(West Germany)*, and Heinrich Rohrer *(Switzerland)*
1987 Georg Bednorz *(West Germany)* and Alex Müller *(Switzerland)*
1988 Leon Lederman *(US)*, Melvin Schwartz *(US)*, and Jack Steinberger *(US)*
1989 Norman Ramsey *(US)*, Hans Dehmeit *(US)*, and Wolfgang Paul *(West Germany)*
1990 Richard E Taylor *(Canada)*, Jerome I Friedman *(US)*, and Henry W Kendall *(US)*
1991 Pierre-Gilles de Gennes *(France)*
1992 Georges Charpak *(France)*
1993 Joseph Taylor *(US)* and Russell Hulse *(US)*

Physiology or Medicine

1984 Niels Jerne *(Denmark)*, Georges Köhler *(West Germany)*, and César Milstein *(UK)*
1985 Michael Brown *(US)* and Joseph L Goldstein *(US)*
1986 Stanley Cohen *(US)* and Rita Levi-Montalcini *(Italy)*
1987 Susumu Tonegawa *(Japan)*
1988 James Black *(UK)*, Gertrude Elion *(US)*, and George Hitchings *(US)*
1989 Michael Bishop *(US)* and Harold Varmus *(US)*
1990 Joseph Murray *(US)* and Donnall Thomas *(US)*
1991 Erwin Neher *(Germany)* and Bert Sakmann *(Germany)*
1992 Edmond Fisher *(US)* and Edwin Krebs *(US)*
1993 Phillip Sharp *(US)* and Richard Roberts *(UK)*

nonaligned movement countries adopting a strategic and political position of neutrality ("nonalignment") toward major powers, specifically the US and former USSR. Although originally used by poorer states, the nonaligned position was later adopted by oil-producing nations. The 1989 summit in Belgrade was attended by 102 member states. With the ending of the Cold War, the movement's survival was in doubt.

non-cooperation movement or *satyagraha* in India, a large-scale civil disobedience campaign orchestrated by Mahatma ◊Gandhi 1920 following the ◊Amritsar massacre April 1919. Based on a policy of peaceful non-cooperation, the strategy was to bring the British administrative machine to a halt by the total withdrawal of Indian support. British-made goods were boycotted, as were schools, courts of law, and elective offices. The campaign made little impression on the British government, since they could ignore it when it was peaceful; when it became violent, Gandhi felt obliged to call off further demonstrations. Its most successful aspect was that it increased political awareness among the Indian people.

nonmetal one of a set of elements (around 20 in total) with certain physical and chemical properties opposite to those of metals. Nonmetals accept electrons (see ◊electronegativity) and are sometimes called electronegative elements.

Nono Luigi 1924–1990. Italian composer. His early vocal compositions have something of the spatial character of Gabrieli, for example *Il Canto Sospeso* 1955–56. After the opera *Intolleranza* 1960 his style moved away from ◊serialism to become increasingly expressionistic. His music is frequently polemical in subject matter, and a number of works incorporate tape-recorded elements.

nonrenewable resource natural resource, such as coal or oil, that takes thousands or millions of years to form naturally and can therefore not be replaced once it is consumed. The main energy sources used by humans are nonrenewable; renewable sources, such as solar, tidal, and geothermal power, have so far been less exploited.

nonsteroidal anti-inflammatory drug full name of NSAID.

Nordic ethnic designation for any of the various Germanic peoples, especially those of Scandinavia. The physical type of Caucasoid described under that term is tall, long-headed, blue-eyed, fair of skin and hair. The term is no longer in current scientific use.

Nord-Pas-de-Calais region of N France; area 4,786 sq mi/12,400 sq km; population (1990) 3,965,100. Its capital is Lille, and it consists of the *départements* of Nord and Pas-de-Calais.

Norfolk seaport in SE Virginia, on the Atlantic Ocean at the mouth of the James and Elizabeth rivers; population (1990) 261,200. It is the headquarters of the US Navy's Atlantic fleet, and the home of 22 other Navy commands. Industries include shipbuilding, chemicals, and motor-vehicle assembly.

Noriega Manuel (Antonio Morena) 1940– . Panamanian soldier and politician, effective ruler of Panama from 1982, as head of the National Guard, until deposed by the US 1989. An informer for the US Central Intelligence Agency, he was known to be involved in drug trafficking as early as 1972. He enjoyed US support until 1987. In the 1989 US invasion of Panama, he was forcibly taken to the US, tried, and convicted of trafficking in 1992.

Normal city in central Illinois, NE of Bloomington; population (1990) 40,000. It is a marketing center for the livestock and grains produced in the surrounding area. Illinois State University is here.

Norman any of the descendants of the Norsemen (to whose chief, Rollo, Normandy was granted by Charles III of France 911) who adopted French language and culture. During the 11th and 12th centuries they conquered England 1066 (under William the Conqueror), Scotland 1072, parts of Wales and Ireland, S Italy, Sicily, and Malta, and took a prominent part in the Crusades.

Normandy two regions of NW France: ◊Haute-Normandie and ◊Basse-Normandie. It was named after the Viking Norsemen (Normans), the people who conquered and settled in the area in the 9th century. As a French duchy it reached its peak under William the Conqueror and was renowned for its centers of learning established by Lanfranc and St Anselm. Normandy was united with England 1100–35. England and France fought over it during the Hundred Years' War, England finally losing it 1449 to Charles VII. In World War II the Normandy beaches were the site of the Allied invasion on D-day, June 6, 1944.

Norman French the form of French used by the Normans in Normandy from the 10th century, and by the Norman ruling class in England after the Conquest 1066. It remained the language of the English court until the 15th century, the official language of the law courts until the 17th century, and is still used in the Channel Islands.

Norris Frank 1870–1902. US novelist. A naturalist writer, he wrote *McTeague* 1899, about a brutish San Francisco dentist and the love of gold. He completed only two parts of his projected trilogy, the *Epic of Wheat: The Octopus* 1901, dealing with the struggles between wheat farmers, and *The Pit* 1903, describing the Chicago wheat exchange.

Norse or *Norseman* a member of any of the ancient Scandinavian peoples, also called ◊Vikings when they traded, explored, and raided far afield from their homelands during the 8th–11th centuries, settling in Iceland, Greenland, Russia, the British Isles, and N France. The term is sometimes used to refer specifically to W Scandinavians or just to Norwegians.

North Oliver 1943– . US Marine lieutenant colonel. In 1981 he joined the staff of the National Security Council (NSC), where he supervised the mining of Nicaraguan harbors 1983, an air-force bombing raid on Libya 1986, and an arms-for-hostages deal with Iran 1985, which, when uncovered 1986 (◊Irangate), forced his dismissal and trial.

North America third largest of the continents (when including Central America)
area 9,500,000 sq mi/24,000,000 sq km
largest cities (over 1 million) Mexico City, New York, Chicago, Toronto, Los Angeles, Montreal, Guadalajara, Monterrey, Philadelphia, Houston, Guatemala City, Vancouver, Detroit
population (1990) 395 million; the aboriginal American Indian, Eskimo, and Aleut peoples are now a minority within a population predominantly of European immigrant origin. Many Africans were brought in as laborers by the slave trade. Asians were also brought in as laborers, and today immigration from Asia and Latin America is on the increase
physical mountain belts to the E (Appalachians) and W (see ◊Cordilleras), the latter including the Rocky Mountains and the Sierra Madre; coastal plain on the Gulf of Mexico, into which the Mississippi River system drains from the central Great Plains; the St Lawrence River and the Great Lakes form a rough crescent with the Great Bear and Great Slave lakes and Lakes Athabasca and Winnipeg around the exposed rock of the great Canadian/Laurentian Shield, into which Hudson Bay breaks from the N
features wide climatic range, from arctic in Alaska and N Canada (only above freezing June–Sept) to the tropical in Central America, and arid in much of the W US; also, great extremes within the range, due to the vast size of the landmass
products the immensity of the US home market makes it less dependent on imports; the industrial and technological strengths of the US automatically tend to exert a pull on Canada, Mexico, and Central America. The continent is unique in being dominated in this way by a single power, which also exerts great influence over the general world economy
language predominantly English, Spanish, French
religion predominantly Christian
history according to archeological evidence, human settlement in North America began 100,000 to 40,000 years ago, when Mongoloid peoples from Asia migrated, over the Bering land bridge and E of the Brooks range in Alaska into the heart of the contin-ent. Settlement by these ancestors of the North American Indians then proceeded S and E. These Stone Age people lived by hunting, fishing, and harvesting fruits, nuts, and the seeds of wild plants. By 7000 BC, however, agriculture was known in Mexico and upper Central America, and by 1400 BC, ◊civilization had developed in these areas. Among the pre-Columbian civilizations were those of the Olmecs (1400–400 BC), Maya (1200 BC–AD 1521), and Aztecs (1325–1521).

The first-known European settlement in North America was by Vikings in what they called Vinland; a Norse settlement, dating from about 1000, has been found at L'Anse-aux-Meadows, Newfoundland. But permanent settlement came only after Christopher Columbus's voyage to the West Indies in 1492. In 1521 the Spanish, under Hernándo Cortés, destroyed the Aztec empire and imposed their rule on Mexico. The Spanish also colonized Central America and parts of what is now the S US, but most of the present US and Canada was claimed and explored by traders, trappers, and colonizers from the Netherlands, France, and England.

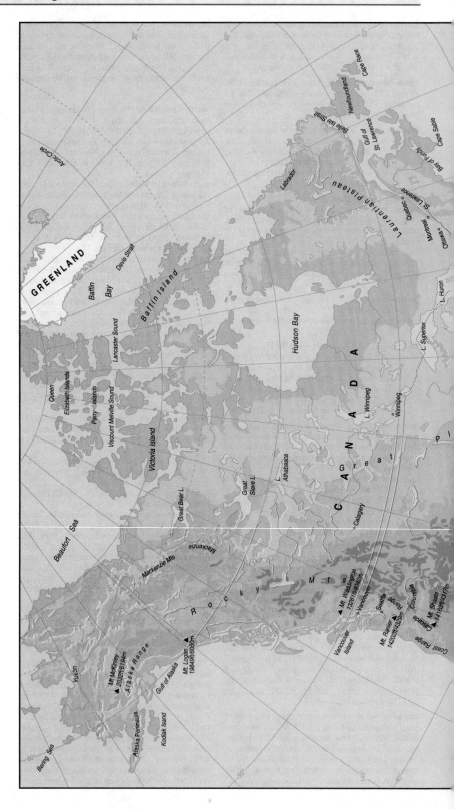

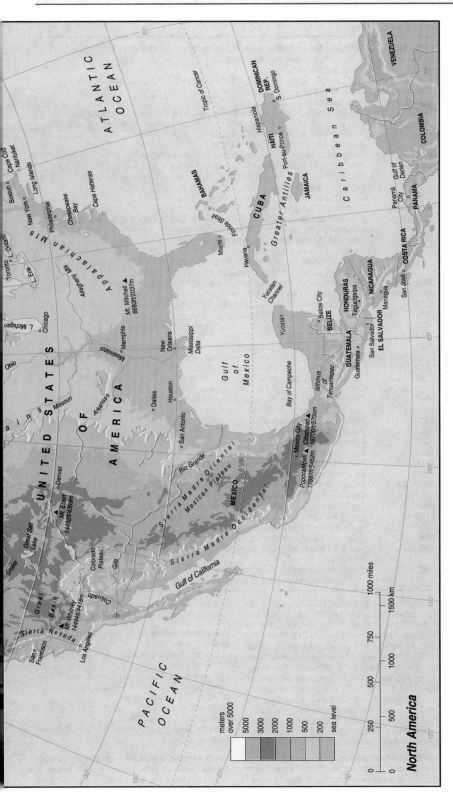

North America

North America: history

c. 100,000–40,000 BC	Mongoloid Asian peoples migrated into North America. Settlement spread south and east *c.* 7000–1400 BC civilization developed.
1400–400 BC	Period of Olmec civilization.
c. AD 1000	First known European settlement, of Norsemen in *Vinland*, a part of Newfoundland.
1200 BC–AD 1521	Mayan civilization.
AD 1325–1521	Aztec civilization.
1492	Columbus sailed from Spain to the West Indies, so named because he mistook them for the East Indies; for the same reason, the native Americans he encountered were called *Indians*. The permanent settlement of North America by Europeans began.
1497	John Cabot sailed from England to Canada.
1502	Columbus discovered the Mayan civilization in Central America.
1521	The Spanish adventurer Hernan Cortes, greeted at first by the Aztecs as a god, destroyed their capital city and their empire and took Mexico; he subsequently colonized other parts of Central and North America.
1534	Jacques Cartier began to colonize Canada for France.
17th century	England and France began to colonize Canada.
1756–63	France defeated in wars with Britain for control of Canada. Continuing hostility resulted in the country's division into British and French sectors.
1775	Beginning of American Revolution (War of Independence).
1776	Declaration of Independence.
1783	Britain recognized the independence of the 13 colonies in the Treaty of Paris, and the US now extended from the Atlantic seaboard to the Mississippi River.
1803	The Louisiana Purchase of land from France doubled the area of the US.
early 1800s	Central American Federation (CAF) formed.
1812–14	French trade blockade of British shipping sparked the Anglo-American War of 1812.
1819	The US bought Florida from Spain.
1821	Mexico and Central America won their independence from Spain.
1840	CAF disintegrated.
1841	Union of Upper (English) and Lower (French) Canada as Canada province; Dominion of Canada founded.
1848, 1851	The US won the Southwestern states from Mexico in the Mexican War.
1861	The US bought Alaska from Russia.
1861–65	The Civil War brought about the end of slavery.
1867	Canadian Confederation formed, with ties to Great Britain.
1898	Hawaii ceded itself to the US.
1903	The US leased the rights to the Panama Canal Zone.
1914	Panama Canal completed.
1948	Formation of OAS.
1949	Formation of NATO.
1961	The US backed the abortive invasion of Cuba by anti-Castro Cuban exiles.
1969	US space launch was the first to put a person on the Moon.
1960s–70s	Opposition to the Vietnam War caused domestic discord in the US.
1982	Canada gained its independence while remaining in the British Commonwealth.
1983	The US invaded Grenada to preserve the existing government.
1989	The US and Canada signed a free trade agreement. The US invaded Panama and took its leader, General Noriega, into custody.
1990	Collapse of Meech Lake accords, designed to resolve Canadian constitutional issues.
1990–91	Gulf War: US-led coalition, joined by Canada and other nations, drove the invader Iraq from Kuwait.
1992–93	The US, Canada, and Mexico reached accord on North American Free Trade Agreement (NAFTA), aimed at ending tariffs, and treaty was signed.

The American Revolution 1775–83 ended in the emergence of the US, stretching from the Atlantic west to the Mississippi River; its area was doubled by the Louisiana Purchase from France in 1803. Mexico and Central America won their independence from Spain in 1821. The US reached its present continental extent by acquiring its Southwest in 1848 and 1851 as a result of war with Mexico, and by purchasing Alaska from Russia in 1867. N of the US, a Canadian confederation, with continuing links to Great Britain, was formed in 1867. Geographically, North America (including the West Indies) now consists of 22 independent nations; several British, Dutch, French, and US island dependencies; and the Danish territory of Greenland.

North American Indian indigenous inhabitant of North America. Many describe themselves as "Native Americans" rather than "American Indians," the latter

term having arisen because Columbus believed he had reached the East Indies. See also ◊American Indian.

Northamptonshire county in central England
area 915 sq mi/2,370 sq km
cities Northampton (administrative headquarters), Kettering
features rivers Welland and Nene; Canons Ashby, Tudor house, home of the Drydens for 400 years; churches with broached spires
products cereals, cattle
population (1991) 568,900
famous people John Dryden, Richard III, Robert Browne.

North Atlantic Drift warm ocean ◊current in the N Atlantic Ocean; an extension of the ◊Gulf Stream. It flows east across the Atlantic and has a mellowing effect on the climate of NW Europe, particularly the British Isles and Scandinavia.

North Atlantic Treaty agreement signed April 4, 1949, by Belgium, Canada, Denmark, France, Iceland, Italy, Luxembourg, the Netherlands, Norway, Portugal, the UK, the US; Greece, Turkey 1952; West Germany 1955; and Spain 1982. They agreed that "an armed attack against one or more of them in Europe or North America shall be considered an attack against them all." The North Atlantic Treaty Organization (NATO) is based on this agreement.

North Atlantic Treaty Organization (NATO) association set up 1949 to provide for the collective defense of the major W European and North American states against the perceived threat from the USSR.

Its chief body is the Council of Foreign Ministers (who have representatives in permanent session), and there is an international secretariat in Brussels, Belgium, and also the Military Committee consisting of the Chiefs of Staff. The military headquarters SHAPE (Supreme Headquarters Allied Powers, Europe) is in Chièvres, near Mons, Belgium. After the E European ◊Warsaw Pact was disbanded 1991, an adjunct to NATO, the *North Atlantic Cooperation Council*, was established, including all the former Soviet republics, with the aim of building greater security in Europe.

North Brabant (Dutch *Noord Brabant*) southern province of the Netherlands, lying between the Maas (Meuse) River and Belgium
area 1,907 sq mi/4,940 sq km
capital 's-Hertogenbosch
cities Breda, Eindhoven, Tilburg
physical former heathland is now under mixed farming
products brewing, engineering, microelectronics, textile manufacture.

North Cape (Norwegian *Nordkapp*) cape in the Norwegian county of Finnmark; the most northerly point of Europe.

North Carolina state in E US; nickname Tar Heel State/Old North State
area 52,650 sq mi/136,400 sq km
capital Raleigh
cities Charlotte, Greensboro, Winston-Salem
features Appalachian Mountains (including Blue Ridge and Great Smoky mountains), site of Fort Raleigh on Roanoke Island, Wright Brothers National Memorial at Kitty Hawk, the Research Triangle established 1956 (Duke University, University of North Carolina, and North Carolina State University) for high-tech industries, Cape Hatteras and Cape Lookout national seashores
products tobacco, corn, soybeans, livestock, poultry, textiles, clothing, cigarettes, furniture, chemicals, machinery

population (1990) 6,628,600
famous people Billy Graham, O Henry, Jesse Jackson, Thomas Wolfe
history after England's Roanoke Island colony was unsuccessful 1585 and 1587, permanent settlement was made 1663; it was one of the original 13 states 1789.

In the Civil War, North Carolina was the last state to join the Confederacy but provided more troops than any other Southern state. After postwar recovery, textiles, tobacco products, and furniture came to dominate the economy. Per-capita income rose from 47% of the national average in 1930 to almost 83% in 1983. However, many of the state's industries offer predominantly low-skill, low-wage jobs and are, moreover, threatened by foreign competition. Tourism is important to the state's economy, and the mild climate has been attractive to retirement communities.

Walter Raleigh sent out 108 colonists from Plymouth, England, 1585 under his cousin Richard Grenville, who established the first English settlement in the New World on Roanoke Island; Virginia Dare was born there 1587, the first child of English parentage born in America; the survivors were taken home by Drake 1586. Further attempts failed there, since the settlers were found to have disappeared.

North Dakota state in N US; nickname Flickertail State/Sioux State
area 70,677 sq mi/183,100 sq km
capital Bismarck
cities Fargo, Grand Forks, Minot
features fertile Red River valley, Missouri Plateau; Garrison Dam on the Missouri River; Badlands, so called because the pioneers had great difficulty in crossing them (also site of Theodore Roosevelt's Elkhorn Ranch); International Peace Garden, on Canadian border; 90% of the land is cultivated
products cereals, meat products, farm equipment, oil, coal
population (1990) 638,800
famous people Maxwell Anderson, Louis L'Amour
history explored by La Verendrye's French Canadian expedition 1738–40; acquired by the US partly in the Louisiana Purchase 1803 and partly by treaty with Britain 1813. The earliest settlement was Pembina 1812, by Scottish and Irish families, and North Dakota became a state 1889, attracting many German and Norwegian settlers.

They and their descendants were hard hit by low prices in the 1920s and 1930s for the state's abundant wheat. Since 1950, North Dakota's oil, natural-gas, and lignite resources have contributed to a more diversified economic base, but it remains the most rural of all the states.

Northeast Passage sea route from the N Atlantic, around Asia, to the N Pacific, pioneered by Swedish explorer Nils Nordenskjöld 1878–79 and developed by

North Carolina

North Dakota

the USSR in settling N Siberia from 1935. Russia owns offshore islands and claims it as an internal waterway; the US claims that it is international.

northern lights common name for the ◊*aurora borealis*.

Northern Mariana Islands archipelago in the NW Pacific, with ◊Guam known collectively as the Mariana Islands. The Northern Marianas are a commonwealth in union with the US
area 182 sq mi/471 sq km
capital Garapan on Saipan
physical 16 islands and atolls extending 350 mi/560 km N of Guam
political system liberal democracy
political parties Democratic Party, center-left; Republican Party, right of center; Territorial Party, nationalist
currency US dollar
population (1990) 31,563
language English
religion mainly Roman Catholicism
history came under Spanish control 1565; sold to Germany 1899; came under Japanese control 1914 and Japanese rule under a League of Nations mandate 1921. Taken by US marines in World War II, the islands became a UN Trust Territory administered by the US 1947 and a US commonwealth territory 1978. Internal self-government and full US citizenship 1986. UN Trusteeship status ended Dec 22 1990.

Northern Rhodesia former name (until 1964) of ◊Zambia, a country in Africa.

Northern Securities Co v US a US Supreme Court decision 1904 dealing with the right of the federal government to restrict monopolistic business practices. Two competitors, the Great Northern and the Northern Pacific railroad companies, joined finances to form the Northern Securities holding company. Convicted under the Sherman Antitrust Act 1890, the holding company appealed to the Supreme Court, arguing that the financial merger was not illegal because it was not intended for the restraint of trade. The Court voted 5 to 4 to uphold the conviction, rejuvenating federal authority under the antitrust laws.

Northern Territory territory of Australia
area 519,633 sq mi/1,346,200 sq km
capital Darwin (chief port)
cities Alice Springs
features mainly within the tropics, although with wide range of temperature; very low rainfall, but artesian bores are used; Macdonnell Ranges (Mount Zeil 4,956 ft/1,510 m); ◊Cocos and ◊Christmas Islands included in the territory 1984; 50,000–60,000-year-old rock paintings of animals, birds, and fish in Kakadu National Park
products beef cattle, prawns, bauxite (Gove), gold and copper (Tennant Creek), uranium (Ranger)
population (1987) 157,000
government there is an administrator and a legislative assembly, and the territory is also represented in the federal parliament
history originally part of New South Wales, it was annexed 1863 to South Australia but from 1911 until 1978 (when self-government was introduced) was under the control of the Commonwealth of Australia government. Mineral discoveries on land occupied by Aborigines led to a royalty agreement 1979.

North Holland (Dutch *Noord Holland*) low-lying coastal province of the Netherlands occupying the peninsula jutting northward between the North Sea and the IJsselmeer
area 1,031 sq mi/2,670 sq km
population (1991) 2,397,000
capital Haarlem
cities Amsterdam, Hilversum, Den Helder, the cheese centers Alkmaar and Edam
physical most of the province is below sea level, protected from the sea by a series of sand dunes and artificial dykes
products flowers bulbs, grain, and vegetables
history once part of the former county of Holland that was divided into two provinces (North and South) 1840.

North Island smaller of the two main islands of ◊New Zealand.

North Pole the northern point where an imaginary line penetrates the Earth's surface by the axis about which it revolves; see also ◊Poles and ◊Arctic.

North Rhine–Westphalia (German *Nordrhein-Westfalen*) administrative *Land* of Germany
area 13,163 sq mi/34,100 sq km
capital Düsseldorf
cities Cologne, Essen, Dortmund, Duisburg, Bochum, Wuppertal, Bielefeld, Bonn, Gelsenkirchen, Münster, Mönchengladbach
features valley of the Rhine; Ruhr industrial district
products iron, steel, coal, lignite, electrical goods, fertilizers, synthetic textiles
population (1988) 16,700,000
religion 53% Roman Catholic, 42% Protestant
history see ◊Westphalia.

North Sea sea to the E of Britain and bounded by the coasts of Belgium, the Netherlands, Germany, Denmark, and Norway; area 202,000 sq mi/523,000 sq km; average depth 180 ft/55 m, greatest depth 2,165 ft/660 m. In the NE it joins the Norwegian Sea, and in the S it meets the Strait of Dover. It has fisheries, oil, and gas.

Northumberland county in N England
area 1,942 sq mi/5,030 sq km
cities Newcastle-upon-Tyne (administrative headquarters), Berwick-upon-Tweed, Hexham
features Cheviot Hills; rivers: Tweed, upper Tyne; Northumberland National Park in the west; Holy Island; the Farne island group; part of Hadrian's Wall and Housestead's Fort; Alnwick and Bamburgh castles; Thomas Bewick museum; large moorland areas are used for military maneuvers; Longstone Lighthouse from which Grace Darling rowed to the rescue is no longer inhabited, the crew having been replaced by an automatic light; wild white cattle of Chillingham
products sheep
population (1991) 300,600
famous people Thomas Bewick, Jack Charlton, Grace Darling.

Northumbria Anglo-Saxon kingdom that covered NE England and SE Scotland, comprising the 6th-century kingdoms of Bernicia (Forth–Tees) and Deira (Tees–Humber), united in the 7th century. It accepted the supremacy of Wessex 827 and was conquered by the Danes in the late 9th century.

Northwest Ordinances US Congressional legislation 1784–87 setting out procedures for the sale and settlement of lands still occupied by American Indians. The land, between the Great Lakes and the Mississippi and Ohio rivers, was to be formed into townships and sold at minimum $1 per acre. The sales revenue was the first significant source of income for the new federal government.

Northwest Passage Atlantic–Pacific sea route around the north of Canada. Canada, which owns offshore islands, claims it as an internal waterway; the US insists that it is an international waterway and sent an icebreaker through without permission 1985.

Northwest rebellion revolt against the Canadian government March–May 1885 by the métis (people of mixed French Canadian and North American Indian descent). Led by their political leader Louis Riel and his military lieutenant Gabriel Dumont (1838–1906), the métis population of what is now Saskatchewan rebelled after a number of economic and political grievances were ignored by the government.

Northwest Territories territory of Canada
area 1,322,552 sq mi/3,426,300 sq km
capital Yellowknife
physical extends to the North Pole, to Hudson's Bay in the E, and in the W to the edge of the Canadian Shield
features Mackenzie River; lakes: Great Slave, Great Bear; Miles Canyon
products oil, natural gas, zinc, lead, gold, tungsten, silver
population (1991) 54,000; over 50% native peoples (Indian, Inuit)
history the area was the northern part of Rupert's Land, bought by the Canadian government from the Hudson's Bay Company 1869. An act of 1952 placed the Northwest Territories under a commissioner acting in Ottawa under the Ministry of Northern Affairs and Natural Resources. In 1990 territorial control of over 135,000 sq mi/350,000 sq km of the Northwest Territo-

N W Territories

ries was given to the ◊Inuit, and in 1992 the creation of an Inuit autonomous homeland, Nunavut, was agreed to in a regional referendum..

North Yorkshire county in NE England
area 3,212 sq mi/8,320 sq km
cities Northallerton (administrative headquarters), York; resorts: Harrogate, Scarborough, Whitby
features England's largest county; including part of the Pennines, the Vale of York, and the Cleveland Hills and North Yorkshire Moors, which form a national park (within which is Fylingdales radar station to give early warning—4 minutes—of nuclear attack); and Rievaulx Abbey; Yorkshire Dales National Park (including Swaledale, Wensleydale, and Bolton Abbey in Wharfedale); rivers: Derwent, Ouse; Fountains Abbey near Ripon, with Studley Royal Gardens; York

Norway
Kingdom of
(*Kongeriket Norge*)

area 149,421 sq mi/387,000 sq km (includes Svalbard and Jan Mayen)
capital Oslo
cities Bergen, Trondheim, Stavanger
physical mountainous with fertile valleys and deeply indented coast; forests cover 25%; extends N of Arctic Circle
territories dependencies in the Arctic (Svalbard and Jan Mayen) and in Antarctica (Bouvet and Peter I Island, and Queen Maud Land)
environment an estimated 80% of the lakes and streams in the southern half of the country have been severely acidified by acid rain
features fjords, including Hardanger and Sogne, longest 115 mi/185 km, deepest 4,086 ft/1,245 m; glaciers in north; midnight sun and northern lights
head of state Harald V from 1991

head of government Gro Harlem Brundtland from 1990
political system constitutional monarchy
political parties Norwegian Labor Party (DNA), moderate left of center; Conservative Party, progressive, right of center; Christian People's Party (KrF), Christian, center-left; Center Party (SP), left of center, rural-oriented
exports petrochemicals from North Sea oil and gas, paper, wood pulp, furniture, iron ore and other minerals, high-tech goods, sports goods, fish
currency krone
population (1992) 4,283,000; growth rate 0.3% p.a.
life expectancy men 73, women 80 (1989)
languages Norwegian (official); there are Saami- (Lapp) and Finnish-speaking minorities
religion Evangelical Lutheran (endowed by state) 94%
literacy 100% (1989)
GNP $113.1 bn (1992)

chronology
1814 Became independent from Denmark; ceded to Sweden.
1905 Links with Sweden ended; full independence achieved.
1940–45 Occupied by Germany.
1949 Joined North Atlantic Treaty Organization (NATO).
1952 Joined Nordic Council.
1957 King Haakon VII succeeded by his son Olaf V.
1960 Joined European Free Trade Association (EFTA).
1972 Accepted into membership in European Economic Community; application withdrawn after a referendum.
1988 Gro Harlem Brundtland awarded Third World Prize.
1989 Jan P Syse became prime minister.
1990 Brundtland returned to power.
1991 King Olaf V died; succeeded by his son Harald V.
1992 Defied whaling ban to resume whaling industry. Brundtland relinquished leadership of the Labor Party. Formal application made for EC membership.
1993 Brundtland reelected. Growing opposition to EC membership.

nose *The structure of the human nose.*

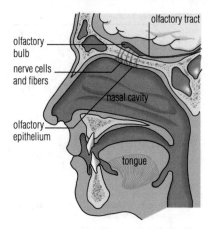

olfactory tract

olfactory bulb

nerve cells and fibers

nasal cavity

olfactory epithelium

tongue

detail of olfactory epithelium

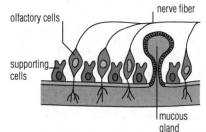

olfactory cells

nerve fiber

supporting cells

mucous gland

Minster; Castle Howard, designed by Vanbrugh, has Britain's largest collection of 18th–20th-century costume; largest accessible cavern in Britain, the Battlefield Chamber, Ingleton
products cereals, wool and meat from sheep, dairy products, coal, electrical goods
population (1991) 698,000
famous people Alcuin, W H Auden, Guy Fawkes.

Norwalk city in SW Connecticut, on the Norwalk River where it flows into Long Island Sound, NE of Stamford; population (1990) 78,300. Industries include electronic equipment, clothing, hardware, and furniture.

Norway country in NW Europe, on the Scandinavian peninsula, bounded E by Sweden, NE by Finland and Russia, S by the North Sea, W by the Atlantic Ocean, and N by the Arctic Ocean. *See panel p. 681*

Norwegian person of Norwegian culture. There are 4–4.5 million speakers of Norwegian (including some in the US), a Germanic language belonging to the Indo-European family. The seafaring culture of the Norwegians can be traced back to the Viking age from about AD 800–1050, when people of Norwegian descent settled Iceland and Greenland and undertook expeditions to Vinland (coast of Newfoundland).

Norwich cathedral city in Norfolk, E England; population (1991) 121,000. Industries include shoes, clothing, chemicals, confectionery, engineering, printing, and insurance. It has a Norman castle, a 15th-century Guildhall, medieval churches, Tudor houses, and a Georgian Assembly House.

Norwich city in SE Connecticut, at the confluence of the Yantic and Quinebaug rivers that form the Thames River, N of New London; seat of New London County; population (1990) 37,400. Industries include

leather, paper, and metal products; electronic equipment; and clothing.

nose in humans, the upper entrance of the respiratory tract; the organ of the sense of smell. The external part is divided down the middle by a septum of ◊cartilage. The nostrils contain plates of cartilage that can be moved by muscles and have a growth of stiff hairs at the margin to prevent foreign objects from entering. The whole nasal cavity is lined with a ◊mucous membrane that warms and moistens the air and ejects dirt. In the upper parts of the cavity the membrane contains 50 million olfactory receptor cells (cells sensitive to smell).

Nostradamus Latinized name of Michel de Nôtredame 1503–1566. French physician and astrologer who was consulted by Catherine de' Medici and was physician to Charles IX. His book of prophecies in rhyme, *Centuries* 1555, has had a number of interpretations.

notation in music, the use of symbols to represent individual sounds (such as the notes of the chromatic scale) so that they can be accurately interpreted and reproduced.

note in music, the written symbol indicating pitch and duration, the sound of which is a tone.

notebook computer small ◊laptop computer. Notebook computers became available in the early 1990s and, even complete with screen and hard-disk drive, are no larger than a standard classroom notebook.

Nottingham industrial city (engineering, coalmining, bicycles, textiles, knitwear, pharmaceuticals, tobacco, lace, electronics) and administrative headquarters of Nottinghamshire, England; population (1991) 261,500.

Nottinghamshire county in central England
area 834 sq mi/2,160 sq km
cities Nottingham (administrative headquarters), Mansfield, Worksop
features River Trent; the remaining areas of Sherwood Forest (home of ◊Robin Hood), formerly a royal hunting ground, are included in the "Dukeries"; Cresswell Crags (remains of prehistoric humans); D H Lawrence commemorative walk from Eastwood (where he lived) to Old Brinsley Colliery
products cereals, cattle, sheep, light engineering, footwear, limestone, ironstone, oil
population (1991) 980,600
famous people William Booth, D H Lawrence, Alan Sillitoe

Nouakchott capital of Mauritania; population (1985) 500,000. Products include salt, cement, and insecticides.

noun grammatical ◊part of speech that names a person, animal, object, quality, idea, or time. Nouns can refer to objects such as *house, tree (concrete nouns)*; specific persons and places such as *John Alden*, the *White House (proper nouns)*; ideas such as *love, anger (abstract nouns)*. In English many simple words are both noun and verb (*jump, reign, rain*). Adjectives are sometimes used as nouns ("a *local* man," "one of the *locals*").

nouveau roman (French "new novel") experimental literary form produced in the 1950s by French novelists of the ◊New Wave, including Alain Robbe-Grillet and Nathalie Sarraute. In various ways, these writers seek to eliminate character, plot, and authorial subjectivity in order to present the world as a pure, solid "thing in itself."

Nova Scotia

nouvelle cuisine (French "new cooking") contemporary French cooking style that avoids traditional rich sauces, emphasizing fresh ingredients and attractive presentation. The phrase was coined in the British magazine *Harpers & Queen* in June 1975.

nova (plural *novae*) faint star that suddenly erupts in brightness by 10,000 times or more. Novae are believed to occur in close ◊binary star systems, where gas from one star flows to a companion ◊white dwarf. The gas ignites and is thrown off in an explosion at speeds of 930 mps/1,500 kps or more. Unlike a ◊supernova, the star is not completely disrupted by the outburst. After a few weeks or months it subsides to its previous state; it may erupt many more times.

Nova Scotia maritime province of E Canada
area 21,423 sq mi/55,500 sq km
capital Halifax (chief port)
cities Dartmouth, Sydney
features Cabot Trail (Cape Breton Island); Alexander Graham Bell Museum; Fortress Louisbourg; Strait of Canso Superport, the largest deepwater harbor on the Atlantic coast of North America
products coal, gypsum, dairy products, poultry, fruit, forest products, fish products (including scallop and lobster)
physical comprising a peninsula with a highly indented coastline extending SE from New Brunswick into the Atlantic Ocean, and ◊Cape Breton Island which is linked to the mainland by the Canso Causeway
population (1991) 897,500
history Nova Scotia was visited by the Italian navigator Giovanni ◊Caboto 1497. A French settlement was established 1604, but expelled 1613 by English colonists from Virginia. The name of the colony was changed from *Acadia* to Nova Scotia 1621. England and France contended for possession of the territory until Nova Scotia (which then included present-day New Brunswick and Prince Edward Island) was ceded to Britain 1713; Cape Breton Island remained French until 1763. Nova Scotia was one of the four original provinces of the Dominion of Canada.

Noverre Jean-Georges 1727–1810. French choreographer, writer, and ballet reformer. He promoted ballet d'action (with a plot) and simple, free movement, and is often considered the creator of modern Classical ballet. *Les Petits Riens* 1778 was one of his works.

Novi Sad industrial and commercial city (pottery and cotton), capital of the autonomous province of Vojvodina in N Serbia, Yugoslavia, on the Danube River; population (1981) 257,700. Products include leather, textiles, and tobacco.

Novosibirsk industrial city (engineering, textiles, chemicals, food processing) in W Siberian Russia, on the Ob River; population (1987) 1,423,000. Winter lasts eight months here.

Noyes John Humphrey 1811–1886. US religious and communal leader. He formulated the "doctrine of free love" 1837 and in 1848 founded the Oneida Community in central New York which served as a forum for his social experiments. In 1879 Noyes was forced to move to Canada to avoid legal action against him. The former community, which made silverware and steel traps, became a joint stock company 1881.

Nu U (Thakin) 1907– . Myanmar politician, prime minister of Burma (now Myanmar) for most of the period from 1948 to the military coup of 1962. Exiled from 1966, U Nu returned to the country 1980 and, in 1988, helped found the National League for Democracy opposition movement.

Nuba member of a minority ethnic group living in S Sudan, numbering about 1 million (1991). They speak related dialects of Nubian, which belongs to the Chari-Nile family. Forced Islamization threatens their cultural identity, and thousands were killed in the Sudan civil war.

nuclear arms verification the process of checking the number and types of nuclear weapons held by a country in accordance with negotiated limits. The chief means are: *reconnaissance satellites* that detect submarines or weapon silos, using angled cameras to give three-dimensional pictures of installations, penetrating camouflage by means of scanners, and partially seeing through cloud and darkness by infrared devices; *telemetry*, or radio transmission of instrument readings; *interception* to get information on performance of weapons under test; *on-site inspection* by experts visiting bases, launch sites, storage facilities, and test sites in another country; *radar tracking* of missiles in flight; *seismic monitoring* of underground tests, in the same way as with earthquakes. This is not accurate and on-site inspection is needed. Tests in the atmosphere, space, or the oceans are forbidden, and the ban is accepted because explosions are not only dangerous to all but immediately detectable.

nuclear energy energy from the inner core or ◊nucleus of the atom, as opposed to energy released in chemical processes, which is derived from the electrons surrounding the nucleus.

nuclear fusion process whereby two atomic nuclei are fused, with the release of a large amount of energy. Very high temperatures and pressures are thought to be required in order for the process to happen. Under these conditions the atoms involved are stripped of all their electrons so that the remaining particles, which together make up ◊plasma, can come close together at very high speeds and overcome the mutual repulsion of the positive charges on the atomic nuclei. At very close range another nuclear force will come into play, fusing the particles together to form a larger nucleus. As fusion is accompanied by the release of large amounts of energy, the process might one day be harnessed to form the basis of commercial energy production. Methods of achieving controlled fusion are therefore the subject of research around the world.

nuclear physics the study of the properties of the nucleus of the ◊atom, including the structure of nuclei; nuclear forces; the interactions between particles and nuclei; and the study of radioactive decay. The study of elementary particles is ◊particle physics.

nuclear reactor device for producing ◊nuclear energy in a controlled manner. There are various types of reactor in use, all using nuclear fission. In a gas-cooled reactor, a circulating gas under pressure (such as carbon dioxide) removes heat from the core of the reactor, which usually contains natural uranium. The efficiency of the fission process is increased by slowing neutrons in the core by using a moderator such as carbon. The reaction is controlled with neutron-absorbing rods made of boron. An advanced gas-cooled reactor (AGR) generally has enriched uranium as its fuel. A water-cooled reactor, such as the steam-generating heavy water (deuterium oxide) reactor, has water circulating through the hot core. The water is converted to steam, which drives turbo-alternators for generating electricity. The most widely used reactor is the pressurized-water reactor, which contains a sealed system of pressurized water that is heated to form steam in heat exchangers in an external circuit. The ◊breeder reactor has no moderator and uses fast neutrons to bring about fission; it produces more fuel than it consumes.

nuclear safety the use of nuclear energy has given rise to concern over safety. Anxiety has been heightened by accidents such as those at Windscale (UK), Three Mile Island (US), and Chernobyl (Ukraine). There has also been mounting concern about the production and disposal of nuclear waste, the radioactive and toxic byproducts of the nuclear energy industry. Burial on land or at sea raises problems of safety, environmental pollution, and security. Nuclear waste has an active half-life of thousands of years and no guarantees exist for the safety of the various methods of disposal. Nuclear safety is still a controversial subject since governments will not recognize the hazards of ◊radiation and ◊radiation sickness. In 1990 a scientific study revealed an increased risk of leukemia in children whose fathers had worked at Sellafield between 1950 and 1985. Sellafield (UK) is the world's greatest discharger of radioactive waste, followed by Hanford, Washington (US).

nuclear warfare war involving the use of nuclear weapons. The worldwide total of nuclear weapons in 1990 was about 50,000, and the number of countries possessing nuclear weapons stood officially at five—US, USSR, UK, France, and China—although some other nations were thought either to have a usable stockpile of these weapons (Israel) or the ability to produce them quickly (Brazil, India, Pakistan, South Africa). Nuclear-weapons research began in Britain 1940, but was transferred to the US after it entered World War II. The research program, known as the Manhattan Project, was directed by J Robert Oppenheimer.

atom bomb The original weapon relied on use of a chemical explosion to trigger a chain reaction. The first test explosion was at Alamogordo, New Mexico, July 16, 1945; the first use in war was by the US against Japan Aug 6, 1945, over Hiroshima and three days later at Nagasaki.

hydrogen bomb A much more powerful weapon than the atomic bomb, it relies on the release of thermonuclear energy by the condensation of hydrogen nuclei to helium nuclei (as happens in the Sun). The first detonation was at Eniwetok Atoll, Pacific Ocean, 1952 by the US.

neutron bomb or *enhanced radiation weapon* (ERW) A very small hydrogen bomb that has relatively high radiation but relatively low blast, designed to kill (in up to six days) by a brief neutron radiation that leaves buildings and weaponry intact.

nuclear methods of attack now include aircraft bombs, missiles (long- or short-range, surface to surface, air to surface, and surface to air), depth charges, and high-powered landmines ("atomic demolition munitions") to destroy bridges and roads.

nuclear waste the radioactive and toxic byproducts of the nuclear-energy and nuclear-weapons industries. Nuclear waste may have an active life of several thousand years. Reactor waste is of three types: *high-level* spent fuel, or the residue when nuclear fuel has been removed from a reactor and reprocessed; *intermediate*, which may be long- or short-lived; and *low-level*, but bulky, waste from reactors, which has only short-lived radioactivity. Disposal, by burial on land or at sea, has raised problems of safety, environmental pollution, and security. In absolute terms, nuclear waste cannot be safely relocated or disposed of.

nuclear winter possible long-term effect of a widespread nuclear war. In the wake of the destruction caused by nuclear blasts and the subsequent radiation, it has been suggested that atmospheric pollution by dust, smoke, soot, and ash could prevent the Sun's rays from penetrating for a period of time sufficient to eradicate most plant life on which other life depends, and create a new Ice Age.

nucleic acid complex organic acid made up of a long chain of nucleotides. The two types, known as DNA (deoxyribonucleic acid) and RNA (ribonucleic acid), form the basis of heredity. The nucleotides are made up of a sugar (deoxyribose or ribose), a phosphate group, and one of four purine or pyrimidine bases. The order of the bases along the nucleic acid strand contains the genetic code.

nucleus in physics, the positively charged central part of an ◊atom, which constitutes almost all its mass. Except for hydrogen nuclei, which have only protons, nuclei are composed of both protons and neutrons. Surrounding the nuclei are electrons, which contain a negative charge equal to the protons, thus giving the atom a neutral charge.

nucleus in biology, the central, membrane-enclosed part of a ◊eukaryotic cell, containing the chromosomes.

nuisance in law, interference with enjoyment of, or rights over, land. There are two kinds of nuisance. *Private nuisance* affects a particular occupier of land, such as noise from a neighbor; the aggrieved occupier can apply for an ◊injunction and claim ◊damages. *Public nuisance* affects an indefinite number of members of the public, such as obstructing the highway; it is a criminal offense. In this case, individuals can claim damages only if they are affected more than the general public.

Nukua'lofa capital and port of Tonga on Tongatapu Island; population (1986) 29,000.

number symbol used in counting or measuring. In mathematics, there are various kinds of numbers. The everyday number system is the decimal ("proceeding by tens") system, using the base ten. ◊*Real numbers* include all *rational numbers* (integers, or whole numbers, and fractions) and *irrational numbers* (those not expressible as fractions). ◊*Complex numbers* include the real and unreal numbers (real-number multiples of the square root of −1). The binary number system, used in computers, has two as its base.

The ordinary numerals, 0, 1, 2, 3, 4, 5, 6, 7, 8, and 9, give a counting system that, in the decimal system, continues 10, 11, 12, 13, and so on. These are whole numbers (integers), with fractions represented as, for example, ¼, ½, ¾, or as decimal fractions (0.25, 0.5, 0.75).

Irrational numbers cannot be represented in this way and require symbols, such as $\sqrt{2}$, π, and e. They can be expressed numerically only as the (inexact) approximations 1.414, 3.142 and 2.718 (to three places of decimals) respectively. The symbols π and e are also examples of *transcendental numbers*, because they (unlike $\sqrt{2}$) cannot be derived by solving a polynomial equation (an equation with one ◊variable quantity) with rational ◊coefficients (multiplying factors). Complex numbers, which include the real numbers as well as unreal numbers, take the general form $a + b$i, where i = $\sqrt{-1}$ (that is, $i^2 = -1$), and a is the real part and bi the unreal part.

numismatics the study of ◊coins, and medals and decorations.

nun (Latin *nonna* "elderly woman") woman belonging to a religious order under the vows of poverty, chastity, and obedience, and living under a particular rule. Christian convents are ruled by a superior (often elected), who is subject to the authority of the bishop of the diocese or sometimes directly to the pope. See ◊monasticism.

Nunavut (Inuit "our land") semiautonomous Inuit homeland in Northwest Territories, Canada, extending over 772,000 sq mi/2,000,000 sq km. In a regional plebiscite May 1992, its creation in 1999 was approved by a narrow majority, after representatives of the 17,000 Inuit had negotiated hunting, fishing, and mineral rights in the area, as well as outright ownership of 135,100 sq mi/350,000 sq km.

Nuremberg (German *Nürnberg*) industrial city (electrical and other machinery, precision instruments, textiles, toys) in Bavaria, Germany; population (1988) 467,000. From 1933 the Nuremberg rallies were held here, and in 1945 the Nuremberg trials of war criminals.

Nuremberg trials after World War II, the trials of the 24 chief ◊Nazi war criminals Nov 1945–Oct 1946 by an international military tribunal consisting of four judges and four prosecutors: one of each from the US, UK, USSR, and France. An appendix accused the German cabinet, general staff, high command, Nazi leadership corps, ◊SS, Sturmabteilung, and ◊Gestapo of criminal behavior.

Nureyev Rudolf 1938–1993. Russian dancer and choreographer. A soloist with the Kirov Ballet, he defected to the West during a visit to Paris in 1961. Mainly associated with the Royal Ballet (London) and as Margot ◊Fonteyn's principal partner, he was one of the most brilliant dancers of the 1960s and 1970s. Nureyev danced in such roles as Prince Siegfried in *Swan Lake* and Armand in *Marguerite and Armand*, which was created specifically for Fonteyn and Nureyev. He also danced and acted in films and on television and choreographed several ballets.

nursing care of the sick, the very young, the very old, and the disabled. Organized training originated 1836 in Germany, and was developed in Britain by the work of Florence ◊Nightingale, who, during the Crimean War, established standards of scientific, humanitarian care in military hospitals. Nurses give day-to-day care and carry out routine medical and surgical procedures under the supervision of a physician.

nut any dry, single-seeded fruit that does not split open to release the seed, such as the chestnut. A nut is formed from more than one carpel, but only one seed becomes fully formed, the remainder aborting. The wall of the fruit, the pericarp, becomes hard and woody, forming the outer shell.

nuthatch small bird of the family Sittidae, with a short tail and pointed beak. Nuthatches climb head first up, down, and around tree trunks and branches, foraging for insects and their larvae.

The 5.5 in/14 cm long white-breasted nuthatch *Sitta carolinensis* of North America has a black cap, gray wings, and white underparts.

nutmeg kernel of the seed of the evergreen tree *Myristica fragrans*, native to the Moluccas. Both the nutmeg and its secondary covering, known as *mace*, are used as spice in cooking.

Nuuk Greenlandic for ◊Godthaab, the capital of Greenland.

NV abbreviation for the state of ◊Nevada.

NY abbreviation for the state of ◊New York.

Nyasa former name for Lake ◊Malawi.

Nyasaland former name (until 1964) for ◊Malawi.

Nyerere Julius (Kambarage) 1922– . Tanzanian socialist politician, president 1964–85. He devoted himself from 1954 to the formation of the Tanganyika African National Union and subsequent campaigning for independence. He became chief minister 1960, was prime minister of Tanganyika 1961–62, president of the newly formed Tanganyika Republic 1962–64, and first president of Tanzania 1964–85.

nylon synthetic long-chain polymer similar in chemical structure to protein. Nylon was the first all-synthesized fiber, made from petroleum, natural gas, air, and water by the Du Pont firm in 1938. It is used in the manufacture of molded articles, textiles, and medical sutures. Nylon fibers are stronger and more elastic than silk and are relatively insensitive to moisture and mildew. Nylon is used for hosiery and woven goods, simulating other materials such as silks and furs; it is also used for carpets.

nymph in Greek mythology, a guardian spirit of nature. *Hamadryads* or *dryads* guarded trees; *naiads*, springs and pools; *oreads*, hills and rocks; and *Nereids*, the sea.

nymph in entomology, the immature form of insects that do not have a pupal stage; for example, grasshoppers and dragonflies. Nymphs generally resemble the adult (unlike larvae), but do not have fully formed reproductive organs or wings.

white oak *Q. alba* of E US and the northern red oak *Q. rubra* are typical examples. The evergreen live oaks (such as *Q. virginiana*) form a subsection in the red oak group.

Oakland industrial port (vehicles, textiles, chemicals, food processing, shipbuilding) in California, on the E coast of San Francisco Bay; population (1990) 372,200. It is linked by a bridge (1936) with San Francisco. A major earthquake 1989 buckled the bay bridge and an Oakland freeway section, causing more than 60 deaths.

Oakley Annie (Phoebe Anne Oakley Mozee) 1860–1926. US sharpshooter, member of Buffalo Bill's Wild West Show (see William ◊Cody). Even though she was partially paralyzed in a train crash 1901, she continued to astound audiences with her ability virtually until her death. Kaiser Wilhelm of Germany had such faith in her talent that he allowed her to shoot a cigarette from his mouth.

oarfish any of a family *Regalecidae* of deep-sea bony fishes, found in warm parts of the Atlantic, Pacific, and Indian oceans. Oarfish are large, up to 30 ft/9 m long, elongated, and compressed, with a fin along the back and a manelike crest behind the head. They have a small mouth, no teeth or scales, and large eyes. They are often reported as sea serpents.

OAS abbreviation for ◊Organization of American States.

oasis area of land made fertile by the presence of water near the surface in an otherwise arid region. The occurrence of oases affects the distribution of plants, animals, and people in the desert regions of the world.

oat type of grass, genus *Avena*, a cereal food. The plant has long, narrow leaves and a stiff straw stem; the panicles of flowers, and later of grain, hang downward.

The cultivated oat *A. sativa* is produced for human and animal food.

Oates Joyce Carol 1938– . US writer. Her novels, often containing surrealism and violence, include *A Garden of Earthly Delights* 1967, *Them* 1969, *Unholy Loves* 1979, *A Bloodsmoor Romance* 1982, and *Because It Is Bitter, and Because It Is My Heart* 1990.

Born in Lockport, New York, Oates uses genres that range from romance to mystery to history, but most of her novels have supernatural elements. She also has written many short stories—notably, "Where Are You Going, Where Have You Been?"—poems, reviews, and critical essays. Her other works include *Goddess and Other Women* 1974, *The Assassions* 1975, *Bellefleur* 1980, *Angel of Light* 1981, *Last Days* 1984, *Marya: A Life* 1986, *You Must Remember This* 1987, *The Assignation* 1988, and *American Appetites* 1989.

oath solemn promise to tell the truth or perform some duty, combined with a declaration naming a deity or something held sacred. In the US witnesses raise their right hand in taking the oath.

OAU abbreviation for ◊Organization of African Unity.

Ob river in Asian Russia, flowing 2,100 mi/3,380 km from the Altai Mountains through the W Siberian Plain to the Gulf of Ob in the Arctic Ocean. With its main tributary, the *Irtysh*, it is 3,480 mi/5,600 km long.

obelisk tall, tapering column of stone, much used in ancient Egyptian and Roman architecture. Examples

Oahu island of Hawaii, in the N Pacific
area 589 sq mi/1,525 sq km
cities Honolulu (state capital)
physical formed by two extinct volcanoes
features Waikiki beach; Pearl Harbor naval base; Diamond Head; punchbowl craters
products sugar, pineapples; tourism is a major industry
history settled by Polynesians from other Pacific islands 300–600 AD. Kamehameha I, ruler 1824–54 of Hawaii, had taken Oahu by 1810. He made Honolulu the capital city of the Hawaiian kingdom.

oak any tree or shrub of the genus *Quercus* of the beech family Fagaceæ, with over 300 known species widely distributed in temperate zones. Oaks are valuable for timber, the wood being durable and straight-grained. Their fruits are called acorns.

The 60 species of North American oaks are divided into two groups: white oaks and red oaks. Most white oaks have leaves with rounded lobes, and their acorns are sweet and mature in one season. Red oaks characteristically have spiny, pointed lobes on their leaves, and their bitter acorns take two years to mature. The

oarfish The oarfish is a strange-looking deep-sea fish found in warm parts of the Atlantic, Pacific, and Indian oceans.

are Cleopatra's Needles 1475 BC, one of which is in London, the other in New York.

Oberammergau village in Bavaria, Germany, 45 mi/72 km SW of Munich; population (1980) 5,000. A Christian ◊passion play has been performed here every ten years since 1634 (except during the world wars) to commemorate the ending of the Black Death plague.

Oberon in folklore, king of the elves or fairies and, according to the 13th-century French romance *Huon of Bordeaux*, an illegitimate son of Julius Caesar. Shakespeare used the character in "A Midsummer Night's Dream."

obesity condition of being overweight (generally, 20% or more above the desirable weight for one's sex, build, and height). Obesity increases susceptibility to disease, strains the vital organs, and lessens life expectancy; it is remedied by healthy diet and exercise, unless caused by systemic (glandular) problems.

object program in computing, the ◊machine-code translation of a program written in a ◊source language.

oboe musical instrument of the ◊woodwind family. Played vertically, it is a wooden tube with a bell, is double-reeded, and has a yearning, poignant tone. Its range is almost three octaves. Oboe concertos have been composed by Vivaldi, Albinoni, Richard Strauss, and others.

Obote (Apollo) Milton 1924– . Ugandan politician who led the independence movement from 1961. He became prime minister 1962 and was president 1966–71 and 1980–85, being overthrown by first Idi ◊Amin and then by Lt Gen Tito Okello.

obscenity law law prohibiting the publishing of any material that tends to deprave or corrupt. Publication of any books, films, etc., that, when judged by contemporary standards, are found to have a prurient interest in sex, be patently offensive, and have no serious artistic, scientific, or social value is an offense.

observatory site or facility for observing astronomical or meteorological phenomena. The earliest recorded observatory was in Alexandria, N Africa, built by Ptolemy Soter in about 300 BC. The modern observatory dates from the invention of the telescope. Observatories may be ground-based, carried on aircraft, or sent into orbit as satellites, in space stations, and on the space shuttle.

obsession repetitive unwanted thought or compulsive action that is often recognized by the sufferer as being irrational, but which nevertheless causes distress. It can be associated with the irresistible urge of an individual to carry out a repetitive series of actions.

obsidian black or dark-colored glassy volcanic rock, chemically similar to ◊granite, but formed by cooling rapidly on the Earth's surface at low pressure.

obstetrics medical specialty concerned with the management of pregnancy, childbirth, and the immediate postnatal period.

Ocala city in N central Florida, SE of Gainesville; seat of Marion County; population (1990) 42,000. It is a marketing and shipping center for the citrus, poultry, cotton, and tobacco products grown in the surrounding area. Tourism is also vital to the economy.

O'Casey Sean. Adopted name of John Casey 1884–1964. Irish dramatist. His early plays are tragicomedies, blending realism with symbolism and poetic with vernacular speech: *The Shadow of a Gunman* 1922, *Juno and the Paycock* 1925, and *The Plough and the Stars* 1926. Later plays include *Red Roses for Me* 1946 and *The Drums of Father Ned* 1960.

occupational psychology study of human behavior at work. It includes dealing with problems in organizations, advising on management difficulties, and investigating the relationship between humans and machines (as in the design of aircraft controls; see also ◊ergonomics). Another area is psychometrics and the use of assessment to assist in selection of personnel.

ocean great mass of salt water. Strictly speaking three oceans exist—the Atlantic, Indian, and Pacific—to which the Arctic is often added. They cover approximately 70% or 140,000,000 sq mi/363,000,000 sq km of the total surface area of the Earth. Water levels recorded in the world's oceans have shown an increase of 4–6 in/10–15 cm over the past 100 years.

oceanography study of the oceans, their origin, composition, structure, history, and wildlife (seabirds, fish, plankton, and other organisms). Much oceanography uses computer simulations to plot the possible movements of the waters, and many studies are carried out by remote sensing.

ocean ridge mountain range on the seabed indicating the presence of a constructive plate margin (where tectonic plates are moving apart and magma rises to the surface; see ◊plate tectonics). Ocean ridges, such as the ◊Mid-Atlantic Ridge, consist of many segments offset along ◊faults, and can rise thousands of meters above the surrounding seabed.

ocean trench deep trench in the seabed indicating the presence of a destructive margin (produced by the movements of ◊plate tectonics). The subduction or dragging downward of one plate of the ◊lithosphere beneath another means that the ocean floor is pulled down. Ocean trenches are found around the edge of the Pacific Ocean and the NE Indian Ocean; minor ones occur in the Caribbean and near the Falkland Islands.

Oceanus in Greek mythology, one of the ◊Titans, the god of a river supposed to encircle the Earth. He was the ancestor of other river gods and the ◊nymphs of the seas and rivers.

ocelot wild cat *Felis pardalis* of the SW US, Mexico, and Central and South America, up to 3 ft/1 m long with a 1.5 ft/45 cm tail. It weighs about 40 lb/18 kg and has a pale yellowish coat marked with longitudinal stripes and blotches. Hunted for its fur, it is close to extinction.

O'Connell Daniel 1775–1847. Irish politician, called "the Liberator." Although ineligible, as a Roman Catholic, to take his seat, he was elected member of Parliament for County Clare 1828 and so forced the government to grant Catholic emancipation. In Parliament he cooperated with the Whigs in the hope of obtaining concessions until 1841, when he launched his campaign for repeal of the union.

In 1823 he founded the Catholic Association to press Roman Catholic claims.

O'Connor Flannery 1925–1964. US novelist and short-story writer. Her works have a great sense of evil and sin, and often explore the religious sensibility of the Deep South. Her short stories include *A Good Man Is Hard to Find* 1955, *Everything That Rises Must Converge* 1965, *The Habit of Being* 1979, and *Flannery O'Connor: Collected Works* 1988.

ocean

Wildlife in oceans ultimately depends on the tiny floating plants, the phytoplankton, that live in the lighted surface waters (the euphotic zone).

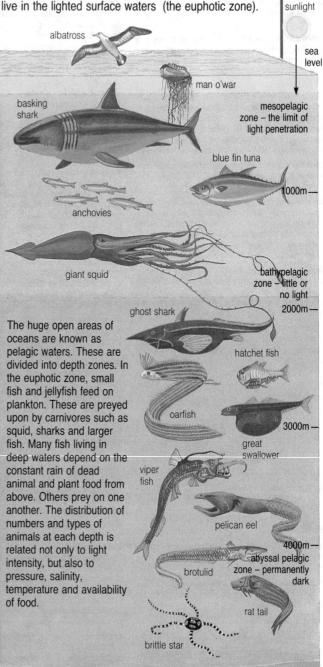

sunlight

sea level

albatross

man o'war

basking shark

mesopelagic zone – the limit of light penetration

blue fin tuna

1000m—

anchovies

giant squid

bathypelagic zone – little or no light

2000m—

ghost shark

hatchet fish

oarfish

3000m—

great swallower

viper fish

pelican eel

brotulid

4000m—
abyssal pelagic zone – permanently dark

rat tail

brittle star

seabed

---

dusk dawn

surface

copepod

Phytoplankton cease photosynthesizing at dusk and at night use the food they have produced for growth. By dawn each day, their mass may have doubled. Small floating animals, the zooplankton, such as copepods, migrate to the surface at dusk to feed on the plants when these are most nutritious. They return to deep water at dawn, allowing the phytoplankton to regenerate.

The huge open areas of oceans are known as pelagic waters. These are divided into depth zones. In the euphotic zone, small fish and jellyfish feed on plankton. These are preyed upon by carnivores such as squid, sharks and larger fish. Many fish living in deep waters depend on the constant rain of dead animal and plant food from above. Others prey on one another. The distribution of numbers and types of animals at each depth is related not only to light intensity, but also to pressure, salinity, temperature and availability of food.

Snaggle tooth fish, such as this, live in deep waters, where their luminous skin spots lure small fish, squid, and shrimps into their mouths.

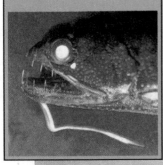

octane rating numerical classification of petroleum fuels indicating their combustion characteristics.

octave in music, a distance of eight notes as measured on the white notes of a piano keyboard. It corresponds to the consonance of first and second harmonics.

Octavian original name of ◊Augustus, the first Roman emperor.

October Revolution second stage of the ◊Russian Revolution 1917, when, on Oct 24 (Nov 6 in the Western calendar), the Bolshevik forces under Trotsky, and on orders from Lenin, seized the Winter Palace and arrested members of the Provisional Government. The following day the Second All-Russian Congress of Soviets handed over power to the Bolsheviks.

Octobrists group of Russian liberal constitutional politicians who accepted the reforming October Manifesto instituted by Tsar Nicholas II after the 1905 revolution and rejected more radical reforms.

octopus any of an order (Octopoda) of ◊cephalopods, genus *Octopus*, having a round or oval body and eight arms with rows of suckers on each. They occur in all temperate and tropical seas, where they feed on crabs and other small animals.

ode lyric poem of complex form. Odes originated in ancient Greece, where they were chanted to a musical accompaniment. Ancient Greek writers of odes include Sappho, Pindar, Horace, and Catullus. English poets who adopted the form include Edmund Spenser, John Milton, John Dryden, and John Keats.

Odessa seaport in Ukraine, on the Black Sea, capital of Odessa region; population (1989) 1,115,000. Products include chemicals, pharmaceuticals, and machinery.

Odessa city in W Texas, SW of Big Springs; seat of Ector County; population (1990) 89,700. It grew up among the oil fields located here.

Odets Clifford 1906–1963. US playwright, famous for his play about a taxi drivers' strike, *Waiting for Lefty* 1935. The most renowned of the Depression-era social-protest playwrights, he also wrote such plays as *Awake and Sing* 1935, perhaps his finest, and *Golden Boy* 1937. In the late 1930s he went to Hollywood and became a successful film writer and director, but he continued to write plays, including *The Country Girl* 1950.

Odin chief god of Scandinavian mythology, the **Woden** or **Wotan** of the Germanic peoples. A sky god, he lives in Asgard, at the top of the world-tree, and from the Valkyries (the divine maidens) receives the souls of heroic slain warriors, feasting with them in his great hall, Valhalla. The wife of Odin is Freya and Thor is their son. Wednesday is named after Odin.

Odysseus chief character of Homer's "Odyssey," king of the island of Ithaca; he is also mentioned in the "Iliad" as one of the leaders of the Greek forces at the siege of Troy. Odysseus was distinguished among Greek leaders for his cleverness and cunning. He appears in other later tragedies.

OE abbreviation for *Old English*; see ◊English language.

Oedipus in Greek legend, king of Thebes who unwittingly killed his father, Laius, and married his mother, Jocasta, in fulfillment of a prophecy. When he learned what he had done, he put out his eyes. His story was dramatized by the Greek tragedian ◊Sophocles.

octopus The octopus can swim by using its legs or squirting water backward to create a kind of jet propulsion.

Oedipus complex in psychology, term coined by Sigmund ◊Freud for the unconscious antagonism of a son to his father, whom he sees as a rival for his mother's affection. For a girl antagonistic to her mother, as a rival for her father's affection, the term is *Electra complex*.

O'Faolain Sean (John Whelan) 1900–1991. Irish novelist, short-story writer, and biographer. His first novel, *A Nest of Simple Folk* 1933, was followed by an edition of translated Gaelic, *The Silver Branch* 1938. His many biographies include *Daniel O'Connell* 1938 and *De Valera* 1939, about the nationalist whom he had fought beside in the Irish Republican Army.

Offa died 796. King of Mercia, England, from 757. He conquered Essex, Kent, Sussex, and Surrey; defeated the Welsh and the West Saxons; and established Mercian supremacy over all England south of the river Humber.

Offaly county of the Republic of Ireland, in the province of Leinster, between Galway on the W and Kildare on the E; area 772 sq mi/2,000 sq km; population (1991) 58,500.

Offa's Dyke defensive earthwork along the Welsh border, of which there are remains from the mouth of the river Dee to that of the river Severn. It represents the boundary secured by ◊Offa's wars with Wales.

Offenbach Jacques 1819–1880. French composer. He wrote light opera, initially for presentation at the *Bouffes parisiens*. Among his works are *Orphée aux enfers/Orpheus in the Underworld* 1858, *La belle Hélène* 1864, and *Les contes d'Hoffmann/The Tales of Hoffmann* 1881.

offset printing the most common method of ◊printing, which uses smooth (often rubber) printing plates. It works on the principle of ◊lithography: that grease and water repel one another.

O'Flaherty Liam 1897–1984. Irish author, best known for his short stories published in volumes such as *Spring Sowing* 1924, *The Tent* 1926, and *Two Lovely Beasts* 1948. His novels, set in County Mayo, include *The Neighbour's Wife* 1923, *The Informer* 1925, and *Land* 1946.

Ogden city in N Utah, on the Weber and Ogden rivers, N of Salt Lake City; population (1990) 63,900. It is a railroad, trading, and military supply center; Hill Air Force Base is nearby. Tourism is also important to the economy.

Oglethorpe James Edward 1696–1785. English soldier and colonizer of Georgia. He served in parliament for 32 years and in 1732 obtained a charter for the colony of Georgia, intended as a refuge for debtors and for European Protestants. The colony was also intended by the British to act as a buffer against Span-

Ohio

ish Florida. The colonists were selected carefully, and every aspect of life was planned and supervised.

Oglethorpe served as Georgia's first colonial governor 1733–34. In 1743, frustrated by settlers' complaints, he returned to England.

OH abbreviation for the state of ◊Ohio.

O Henry adopted name of US author William Sydney ◊Porter.

O'Higgins Bernardo 1778–1842. Chilean revolutionary, known as "the Liberator of Chile." He was a leader of the struggle for independence from Spanish rule 1810–17 and head of the first permanent national government 1817–23.

Ohio state in N central US; nickname Buckeye State
area 41,341 sq mi/107,100 sq km
capital Columbus
cities Cleveland, Cincinnati, Dayton, Akron, Toledo, Youngstown, Canton
population (1990) 10,847,100
features Ohio River; Lake Erie; Serpent Mound, a 1.3-m/4-ft embankment, 1,330 ft/405 m long and about 18 ft/5 m across (built by ◊Hopewell Indians about 2nd–1st centuries BC)
products coal, cereals, livestock, dairy foods, machinery, chemicals, steel, motor vehicles, automotive and aircraft parts, rubber products, office equipment, refined petroleum
famous people Sherwood Anderson, Neil Armstrong, Hart Crane, Thomas Edison, James Garfield, John Glenn, Ulysses S Grant, Zane Grey, Warren Harding, Benjamin Harrison, William H Harrison, Rutherford B Hayes, William McKinley, Paul Newman, Jesse Owens, John D Rockefeller, William T Sherman, William H Taft, James Thurber, Orville and Wilbur Wright
history explored for France by René La Salle 1669; ceded to Britain by France 1763; first settled at Marietta (capital of the Northwest Territory) by Europeans 1788; statehood 1803. By 1850 Ohio was the third-most populous state. In the Civil War, Ohio gave the Union

its greatest generals—U S Grant, W T Sherman, and P Sheridan. In the 1870s J D Rockefeller of Cleveland organized the Standard Oil Company, which soon controlled oil refining and distribution throughout the nation. At the same time, Akron became rubber capital of the world. For a century, Ohio remained a leader in heavy industry, but manufacturing peaked in 1969; agriculture and mining remain important. Seeking service and high-technology industries, the state needs to overcome an aging infrastructure and urban pollution and decay. Tourism continues as a valuable revenue producer.

ohm SI unit (symbol Ω) of electrical ◊resistance (the property of a substance that restricts the flow of electrons through it).

oil flammable substance, usually insoluble in water, and composed chiefly of carbon and hydrogen. Oils may be solids (fats and waxes) or liquids. The three main types are: *essential oils*, obtained from plants; *fixed oils*, obtained from animals and plants; and *mineral oils*, obtained chiefly from the refining of ◊petroleum.

oil spill leakage of oil from an oceangoing tanker, a pipeline, or other source. Oil spills are frequent and may cause enormous ecological harm. In Feb 1991 Iraqi military forces opened oil pipelines to leak into the Persian Gulf as part of military tactics during the Gulf War; the coalition forces also damaged oil facilities causing leakage. Together this damage caused the largest-ever oil spill, which pollutes the Gulf. In March 1989 the *Exxon Valdez* went aground, covering in oil 4,800 sq mi/1,850 sq km in Prince William Sound, Alaska, and killing sea birds, otters, and whales. The spill left pools of oil up to 3 ft/1 m deep on some beaches.

OK abbreviation for the state of ◊Oklahoma.

okapi ruminant *Okapia johnstoni* of the giraffe family, although with much shorter legs and neck, found in the tropical rain forests of central Africa. Purplish brown with a creamy face and black and white stripes on the legs and hindquarters, it is excellently camouflaged. Okapis have remained virtually unchanged for millions of years.

Okeechobee lake in the N Everglades, Florida; 40 mi/65 km long and 25 mi/40 km wide. It is the largest lake in the southern US, about 700 sq mi/1,800 sq km. Okeechobee has no single outlet but flows S through the Everglades.

O'Keeffe Georgia 1887–1986. US painter, based mainly in New York and New Mexico, known chiefly for her large, semiabstract studies of flowers and bones, such as *Black Iris* 1926 (Metropolitan Museum of Art, New York) and the *Pelvis Series* of the 1940s.

Okefenokee swamp in SE Georgia and NE Florida, rich in alligators, bears, deer, and birds. Much of its 660 sq mi/1,700 sq km forms a natural wildlife refuge. It is drained by the St Mary's and Suwannee rivers.

Okhotsk, Sea of arm of the N Pacific Ocean between the Kamchatka Peninsula and Sakhalin and bordered to the S by the Kuril Islands; area 361,700 sq mi/937,000 sq km. It is free of ice only in summer, and is often fogbound.

Okinawa group of islands, forming part of the Japanese ◊Ryukyu Islands in the W Pacific; the largest island is Okinawa
area 869 sq mi/2,250 sq km
capital Naha
features Okinawa, the largest island of the group (area 453 sq mi/1,176 sq km; population (1990) 105,852)

okapi The okapi has a prehensile tongue which it uses to pick tasty leaves.

oil drilling

Offshore rigs are used to extract oil from the seabed. These are some of the largest structures ever built and can contain living quarters for 300 workers.

The largest rigs are floating platforms called semi-submersible rigs. They are anchored to the seabed by cables and chains. Large air tanks below the surface keep the rig stable.

The simplest and earliest kind of rig is the fixed-leg platform. This stands on rigid legs which are fixed to the seabed. Some of these fixed-leg rigs are as tall as the Empire State Building in New York.

Trapped gas or water may exert sufficient pressure on oil-bearing rocks to force oil up to the surface. Pumps, such as "nodding donkey" pumps, may have to be used to raise the oil.

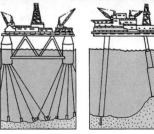

The gravity platform has large concrete tanks at its base. Oil from several wells is collected in the tanks. The great weight pins it to the seabed and no piles are needed to secure it.

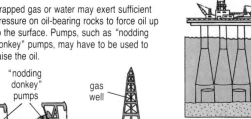

"nodding donkey" pumps

gas well

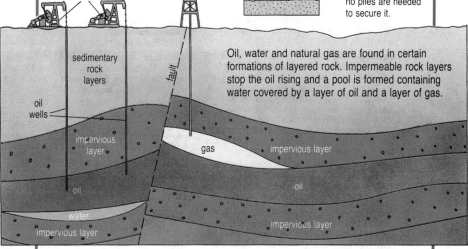

sedimentary rock layers

fault

oil wells

impervious layer

oil

water

impervious layer

gas

impervious layer

oil

impervious layer

Oil, water and natural gas are found in certain formations of layered rock. Impermeable rock layers stop the oil rising and a pool is formed containing water covered by a layer of oil and a layer of gas.

Oklahoma

population (1990) 3,145,500
history the principal island, Okinawa, was captured by the US in the *Battle of Okinawa* April 1–June 21 1945, with 47,000 US casualties (12,000 dead) and 60,000 Japanese (only a few hundred survived as prisoners). During the invasion over 150,000 Okinawans, mainly civilians, died; many were massacred by Japanese forces. The island was returned to Japan 1972.

Oklahoma state in S central US; nickname Sooner State
area 69,905 sq mi/181,100 sq km
capital Oklahoma City
cities Tulsa, Lawton, Norman, Enid
features Arkansas, Red, and Canadian rivers; Wichita and Ozark mountain ranges; the high plains have Indian reservations (Cherokee, Chickasaw, Choctaw, Creek, and Seminole); American Indian Hall of Fame; Chickasaw National Recreation Area
products cereals, peanuts, cotton, livestock, oil, natural gas, helium, machinery and other metal products
population (1990) 3,145,600
famous people John Berryman, Ralph Ellison, Woody Guthrie, Mickey Mantle, Will Rogers, Jim Thorpe
history explored for Spain by Francisco de Coronado 1541; most acquired by the US from France with the ◊Louisiana Purchase 1803.

The W Panhandle became US territory when Texas was annexed 1845. It was divided into Indian Territory and Oklahoma Territory 1890, part of which was thrown open to settlers with lotteries and other hurried distribution of land. Together with what remained of Indian Territory, it became a state 1907. Oil was struck 1897, and the state led all others in oil production until 1928. The 1930s brought drought, dust storms, and an exodus of many, especially to California. Economic growth resumed thereafter, particularly in the 1970s, when world oil prices rose.

Oklahoma City industrial city (oil refining, machinery, aircraft, telephone equipment), capital of Oklahoma, on the Canadian River; population (1990) 444,700. On April 22, 1889, a tent city of nearly 10,000 inhabitants was set up overnight as the area was opened to settlement. In 1910 Oklahoma City had 64,000 people and became the state capital.

Oil was discovered in 1928, and derricks are situated even on the state capitol grounds. A General Motors auto plant was established here 1979.

Olaf I Tryggvesson 969–1000. King of Norway from 995. He began the conversion of Norway to Christianity and was killed in a sea battle against the Danes and Swedes.

Olaf II Haraldsson 995–1030. King of Norway from 1015. He offended his subjects by his centralizing policy and zeal for Christianity, and was killed in battle by Norwegian rebel chiefs backed by ◊Canute of Denmark. He was declared the patron saint of Norway 1164.

Old Catholic one of various breakaway groups from Roman Catholicism—including those in Holland (such as the *Church of Utrecht*, who separated from Rome 1724 after accusations of ◊Jansenism) and groups in Austria, Czechoslovakia, Germany, and Switzerland—who rejected the proclamation of ◊papal infallibility of 1870. Old Catholic clergy are not celibate.

Oldenburg Claes 1929– . US Pop artist, known for "soft sculptures," gigantic replicas of everyday objects and foods, made of stuffed canvas or vinyl. One characteristic work is *Lipstick* 1969 (Yale University).

Old English general name for the range of dialects spoken by Germanic settlers in England between the 5th and 11th centuries AD, also known as ◊Anglo-Saxon. The literature of the period includes *Beowulf*, an epic in West Saxon dialect.

Oldfield Barney 1878–1946. US racing-car driver. Henry Ford employed him as a driver for his experimental race automobile 1902 and in the following year Oldfield set the world land speed record of 60 mph/96.6 kph. In 1910 he reached a speed in excess of 130 mph/209 kph.

Old Pretender nickname of James Edward Stuart, the son of James II of England.

Olds Ransom Eli 1864–1950. US automobile manufacturer. In 1895 he produced a gas-powered automobile and in the following year founded the Olds Motor Vehicle Company. Reorganizing the operation as the Olds Motor Works he produced his popular Oldsmobiles from 1899 in Detroit. He pioneered the assembly-line method of automobile production that would later be refined by Henry Ford.

Old Testament Christian term for the Hebrew ◊Bible, which is the first part of the Christian Bible. It contains 39 (according to Christianity) or 24 (according to Judaism) books, which include the origins of the world, the history of the ancient Hebrews and their covenant with God, prophetical writings, and religious poetry. The first five books (*The five books of Moses*) are traditionally ascribed to Moses and known as the Pentateuch (by Christians) or the Torah (by Jews).

Olduvai Gorge deep cleft in the Serengeti steppe, Tanzania, where Louis and Mary ◊Leakey found prehistoric stone tools in the 1930s. They discovered Pleistocene remains of prehumans and gigantic animals 1958–59. The gorge has given its name to the *Olduvai culture*, a simple stone-tool culture of prehistoric hominids, dating from 2–0.5 million years ago.

Old World the continents of the eastern hemisphere, so called because they were familiar to Europeans before the Americas. The term is used as an adjective to describe animals and plants that live in the eastern hemisphere.

oleander or *rose bay* evergreen Mediterranean shrub *Nerium oleander* of the dogbane family Apocynaceae, with pink or white flowers and aromatic leaves that secrete the poison oleandrin.

olefin common name for ◊alkene.

oligarchy rule of the few, in their own interests. It was first identified as a form of government by the Greek philosopher Aristotle. In modern times there have been a number of oligarchies, sometimes posing as democracies; the paramilitary rule of the ◊Duvalier family in Haiti, 1957–86, is an example.

Oligocene third epoch of the Tertiary period of geological time, 35.5–3.25 million years ago. The name, from Greek, means "a little recent," referring to the presence of the remains of some modern types of animals existing at that time.

oligopoly in economics, a situation in which a few companies control the major part of a particular market and concert their actions to perpetuate such control. This may include an agreement to fix prices (a ◊cartel).

olive evergreen tree *Olea europaea* of the family Oleaceae. Native to Asia but widely cultivated in Mediterranean and subtropical areas, it grows up to 50 ft/15 m high, with twisted branches and opposite, lance-shaped silvery leaves. The white flowers are followed by green oval fruits that ripen a bluish black. They are preserved in brine or oil, dried, or pressed to make olive oil.

olive branch ancient symbol of peace; in the Bible (Genesis 9), an olive branch is brought back by the dove to Noah to show that the flood has abated.

Olives, Mount of range of hills E of Jerusalem, associated with the Christian religion: a former chapel (now a mosque) marks the traditional site of Jesus' ascension to heaven, with the Garden of Gethsemane at its foot.

Olivier Laurence (Kerr), Baron Olivier 1907–1989. English actor and director. For many years associated with the Old Vic theater, he was director of the National Theatre company 1962–73.

His stage roles include Henry V, Hamlet, Richard III, and Archie Rice in John Osborne's *The Entertainer*. His acting and direction of filmed versions of Shakespeare's plays received critical acclaim for example, *Henry V* 1944 and *Hamlet* 1948.

olivine greenish mineral, magnesium iron silicate, $(Mg,Fe)_2SiO_4$. It is a rock-forming mineral, present in, for example, peridotite, gabbro, and basalt. Olivine is called *peridot* when pale green and transparent, and used in jewelry.

Olmec first civilization of Mesoamerica and thought to be the mother culture of the Mayans. It developed in the coastal zone S of Veracruz and in adjacent Tabasco 1200–400 BC. The Olmecs built a large clay pyramid and several smaller mounds on the island of La Venta. Some gigantic stone heads, vestiges of their religion, also remain. The naturalistic Olmec art had a distinctive and influential style, often using the "were-jaguar" motif of a sexless figure with fangs.

Olmstead v US a US Supreme Court decision 1928 dealing with the legality of telephone wiretapping in criminal investigations. The petitioner, a man convicted of selling alcohol illegally, appealed the case on the grounds that, in violation of the Fourth Amendment, the evidence against him had been obtained through telephone wiretaps. The Court upheld the conviction, ruling 5 to 4 that, since law enforcement officers made no actual entry into Olmstead's house, the surveillance was constitutional.

Olmsted Frederick Law 1822–1903. US landscape designer. Appointed superintendent of New York's Central Park 1857, Olmsted and his partner Calvert Vaux directed its design and construction. After the American Civil War 1861–65, he became a sought-after planner of public parks, designing the grounds of the World's Columbian Exposition 1893.

Olympia sanctuary in the W Peloponnese, ancient Greece, with a temple of Zeus, and the stadium (for foot races, boxing, wrestling) and hippodrome (for chariot and horse races), where the original Olympic Games were held.

Olympic venues

summer games/winter games

1896	Athens, Greece
1900	Paris, France
1904	St Louis, Missouri
1908	London, England
1912	Stockholm, Sweden
1920	Antwerp, Belgium
1924	Paris, France/Chamonix, France
1928	Amsterdam, Holland/St Moritz, Switzerland
1932	Los Angeles, California/Lake Placid, New York
1936	Berlin, Germany/Garmisch-Partenkirchen, Germany
1948	London, England/St Moritz, Switzerland
1952	Helsinki, Finland/Oslo, Norway
1956	Melbourne, Australia*/Cortina d'Ampezzo, Italy
1960	Rome, Italy/Squaw Valley, Colorado
1964	Tokyo, Japan/Innsbruck, Austria
1968	Mexico City, Mexico/Grenoble, France
1972	Munich, West Germany/Sapporo, Japan
1976	Montréal, Québec/Innsbruck, Austria
1980	Moscow, USSR/Lake Placid, New York
1984	Los Angeles, California/Sarajevo, Yugoslavia
1988	Seoul, South Korea/Calgary, Alberta
1992	Barcelona, Spain/Albertville, France
1994	Lillehammer, Norway (winter games)
1996	Atlanta, Georgia (summer games)

*Because of quarantine restrictions, equestrian events were held in Stockholm, Sweden.

Olympia capital of Washington, located in the W central part of the state, on the Deschutes River near Puget Sound; population (1990) 30,800. It is a deep-water port; fishing and tourism are important to the economy.

Olympic Games sporting contests originally held in Olympia, ancient Greece, every four years during a sacred truce; records were kept from 776 BC. Women were forbidden to be present, and the male contestants were naked. The ancient Games were abolished AD 394. The present-day Games have been held every four years since 1896. Since 1924 there has been a separate winter games program. From 1994 the winter and summer games will be held two years apart.

Olympus (Greek *Olimbos*) any of several mountains in Greece and elsewhere, one of which is **Mount Olympus** in N Thessaly, Greece, 9,577 ft/2,918 m high. In ancient Greece it was considered the home of the gods.

Om sacred word in Hinduism, used to begin prayers and placed at the beginning and end of books. It is composed of three syllables, symbolic of the Hindu Trimurti, or trinity of gods.

Omaha city in E Nebraska, on the Missouri River, population (1990) 335,800. It is a livestock-market center, with food-processing and meatpacking industries. Creighton University and the University of Nebraska Medical Center are here. Omaha was laid out in 1854. Its location at the E terminus of the Union Pacific Railroad (1869) spurred economic growth.

Oman country at the SE end of the Arabian peninsula, bounded W by the United Arab Emirates, Saudi Arabia, and Yemen, SE by the Arabian Sea, and NE by the Gulf of Oman. *See panel p. 694*

Omar 581–644. Adviser of the prophet Mohammed. In 634 he succeeded Abu Bakr as caliph (civic and religious leader of Islam), and conquered Syria, Palestine,

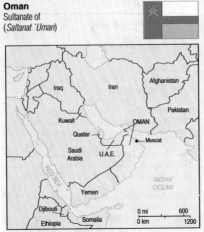

Oman
Sultanate of
(*Saltanat `Uman*)

area 105,000 sq mi/272,000 sq km
capital Muscat
cities Salalah, Nizwa
physical mountains to N and S of a high arid plateau;
fertile coastal strip
features Jebel Akhdar highlands; Kuria Muria islands;
Masirah Island is used in aerial reconnaissance of the

Arabian Sea and Indian Ocean; exclave on Musandam Peninsula controlling Strait of Hormuz
head of state and government Qaboos bin Said from 1970
political system absolute monarchy
political parties none
exports oil, dates, silverware, copper
currency rial Omani
population (1992) 1,640,000; growth rate 3.0% p.a.
life expectancy men 55, women 58 (1989)
languages Arabic (official), English, Urdu, other Indian
languages
religions Ibadhi Muslim 75%, Sunni Muslim, Shiite
Muslim, Hindu
literacy 20% (1989)
GNP $7.5 bn (1987); $5,070 per head (1988)

chronology
1951 The Sultanate of Muscat and Oman achieved full independence from Britain. Treaty of Friendship with Britain
signed.
1970 After 38 years' rule, Sultan Said bin Taimur replaced in
coup by his son Qaboos bin Said. Name changed to Sultanate of Oman.
1975 Left-wing rebels in south defeated.
1982 Memorandum of Understanding with UK signed, providing for regular consultation on international issues.
1985 Diplomatic ties established with USSR.
1991 Sent troops to Operation Desert Storm, as part of
coalition opposing Iraq's occupation of Kuwait.

Egypt, and Persia. He was assassinated by a slave.
The Mosque of Omar in Jerusalem is attributed to him.

Omar Khayyám *c.* 1050–1123. Persian astronomer,
mathematician, and poet. In the West, he is chiefly
known as a poet through Edward Fitzgerald's version
of *The Rubaiyat of Omar Khayyám* 1859.

Omayyad dynasty Arabian dynasty of the Islamic
empire who reigned as caliphs (civic and religious leaders of Islam) 661–750, when they were overthrown by
Abbasids. A member of the family, Abd Al-Rahma1 m,
escaped to Spain and in 756 assumed the title of emir of
Córdoba. His dynasty, which took the title of caliph in
929, ruled in Córdoba until the early 11th century.

ombudsman (Swedish "commissioner") official who
acts on behalf of the private citizen in investigating
complaints against the government. The post is of
Scandinavian origin; it was introduced in Sweden
1809, Denmark 1954, and Norway 1962, and spread to
other countries from the 1960s.

Hawaii was the first state to appoint an ombudsman
1967.

Omdurman, Battle of battle on Sept 2, 1898, in
which the Sudanese, led by the Khalifa, were defeated
by British and Egyptian troops under General Kitchener.

omnivore animal that feeds on both plant and
animal material. Omnivores have digestive adaptations intermediate between those of ◊herbivores and
◊carnivores, with relatively unspecialized digestive
systems and gut microorganisms that can digest a
variety of foodstuffs.

On occasion, when regular food supplies are low,
most mammals become omnivores.

Omsk industrial city (agricultural and other machinery, food processing, lumber mills, oil refining) in
Russia, capital of Omsk region, W Siberia; population
(1987) 1,134,000. Its oil refineries are linked with
Tuimazy in the Bashkir republic by a 1,000-mi/1,600-
km pipeline.

Onassis Aristotle (Socrates) 1906–1975. Turkish-
born Greek shipowner. In 1932 he started what
became the largest independent shipping line and
during the 1950s he was one of the first to construct
supertankers. In 1968 he married Jacqueline Kennedy,
widow of US president John F Kennedy.

oncogene gene carried by a virus that induces a cell
to divide abnormally, forming a ◊tumor. Oncogenes
arise from mutations in genes (proto-oncogenes) found
in all normal cells. They are usually also found in
viruses that are capable of transforming normal cells
to tumor cells. Such viruses are able to insert their
oncogenes into the host cell's DNA, causing it to divide
uncontrollably. More than one oncogene may be necessary to transform a cell in this way.

oncology branch of medicine concerned with the diagnosis and treatment of neoplasms, especially cancer.

Onega, Lake second-largest lake in Europe, NE of St
Petersburg, partly in Karelia, Russia; area 3,710 sq
mi/9,600 sq km. The *Onega Canal*, along its S shore,
is part of the Mariinsk system linking St Petersburg
with the river Volga.

O'Neill Eugene (Gladstone) 1888–1953. US playwright, widely regarded as the greatest US dramatist.
His plays, although tragic, are characterized by a
down-to-earth quality and are often experimental in
form, influenced by German expressionism, Strindberg, and Freud. They were a radical departure from
the romantic and melodramatic American theater
entertainments. They include the Pulitzer Prize-
winning plays *Beyond the Horizon* 1920 and *Anna
Christie* 1921, as well as *The Emperor Jones* 1920, *The
Hairy Ape* 1922, *Desire Under the Elms* 1924, *The
Iceman Cometh* 1946, and the posthumously produced
autobiographical drama *Long Day's Journey into
Night* 1956 (written 1940), also a Pulitzer Prize winner.
He was awarded the Nobel Prize for Literature 1936.

onion bulbous plant *Allium cepa* of the lily family Liliaceae. Cultivated from ancient times, it may have

originated in Asia. The edible part is the bulb, containing an acrid volatile oil and having a strong flavor.

on-line system in computing, originally a system that allows the computer to work interactively with its users, responding to each instruction as it is given and prompting users for information when necessary. Since almost all the computers people use now work this way, "on-line system" is now used to refer to large database, electronic mail, and conferencing systems accessed via a dial-up modem. These often have tens or hundreds of users from different places—sometimes from different countries—"on line" at the same time.

onomatopoeia (Greek "name-making") figure of speech that copies natural sounds. For example, the word "cuckoo" imitates the sound that the cuckoo makes.

Ontario province of central Canada
area 412,480 sq mi/1,068,600 sq km
capital Toronto
cities Hamilton, Ottawa (federal capital), London, Windsor, Kitchener, St Catharines, Oshawa, Thunder Bay, Sudbury
features Black Creek Pioneer Village; ◊Niagara Falls; richest, chief manufacturing, most populated, and leading cultural province of English-speaking Canada
products nickel, iron, gold, forest products, motor vehicles, iron, steel, paper, chemicals, copper, uranium
population (1986) 9,114,000
history first explored by the French in the 17th century, it came under British control 1763 (Treaty of Paris). An attempt 1841 to form a merged province with French-speaking Québec failed, and Ontario became a separate province of Canada 1867. Under the protectionist policies of the new federal government, Ontario gradually became industrialized and urban. Since World War II, more than 2 million immigrants, chiefly from Europe, have settled in Ontario.

Ontario map

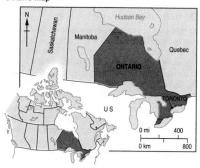

Ontario, Lake smallest and easternmost of the Great Lakes, on the US–Canadian border; area 7,400 sq mi/ 19,200 sq km. It is connected to Lake Erie by the Welland Canal and the Niagara River, and drains into the St Lawrence River. Its main port is Toronto.

onyx semiprecious variety of chalcedonic ◊silica (SiO_2) in which the crystals are too fine to be detected under a microscope, a state known as cryptocrystalline. It has straight parallel bands of different colors: milk-white, black, and red.

Oort Jan Hendrik 1900–1992. Dutch astronomer. In 1927, he calculated the mass and size of our Galaxy, the Milky Way, and the Sun's distance from its center,

from the observed movements of stars around the Galaxy's center. In 1950 Oort proposed that comets exist in a vast swarm, now called the *Oort cloud*, at the edge of the Solar System.

Oort cloud spherical cloud of comets beyond Pluto, extending out to about 100,000 astronomical units (1.5 light-years) from the Sun. The gravitational effect of passing stars and the rest of our Galaxy disturbs comets from the cloud so that they fall in toward the Sun on highly elongated orbits, becoming visible from Earth. As many as 10 trillion comets may reside in the Oort cloud, named after Dutch astronomer Jan Oort who postulated it 1950.

ooze sediment of fine texture consisting mainly of organic matter found on the ocean floor at depths greater than 6,600 ft/2,000 m. Several kinds of ooze exist, each named after its constituents.

opal form of ◊silica (SiO_2), often occurring as stalactites and found in many types of rock. The common opal is translucent, milk-white, yellow, red, blue, or green, and lustrous. Precious opal is opalescent, the characteristic play of colors being caused by close-packed silica spheres diffracting light rays within the stone.

Op art movement in modern art, popular in the 1960s. It uses scientifically based optical effects that confuse the spectator's eye. Precisely painted lines or dots are arranged in carefully regulated patterns that create an illusion of surface movement. Exponents include Victor Vasarely and Bridget Riley.

op. cit. abbreviation for *opere citato* (Latin "in the work cited"), used in reference citation.

OPEC acronym for ◊Organization of Petroleum-Exporting Countries.

open-hearth furnace method of steelmaking, now largely superseded by the basic–oxygen process. It was developed in 1864 in England by German-born William and Friedrich Siemens, and improved by Pierre and Emile Martin in France in the same year. In the furnace, which has a wide, saucer-shaped hearth and a low roof, molten pig iron and scrap are packed into the shallow hearth and heated by overhead gas burners using preheated air.

opera dramatic musical work in which singing takes the place of speech. In opera the music accompanying the action has paramount importance, although dancing and spectacular staging may also play their parts. Opera originated in late 16th-century Florence when the musical declamation, lyrical monologues, and choruses of Classical Greek drama were reproduced in current forms.

operating system (OS) in computing, a program that controls the basic operation of a computer. A typical OS controls the peripheral devices, organizes the filing system, provides a means of communicating with the operator, and runs other programs.

operetta light form of opera, with music, dance, and spoken dialogue. The story line is romantic and sentimental, often employing farce and parody. Its origins lie in the 19th-century *opéra comique* and is intended to amuse. Examples of operetta are Jacques Offenbach's *Orphée aux enfers/Orpheus in the Underworld* 1858, Johann's Strauss's *Die Fledermaus/The Bat* 1874, and Gilbert and Sullivan's *Pirates of Penzance* 1879 and *The Mikado* 1885.

Ophiuchus large constellation along the celestial equator, known as the serpent bearer because the constellation Serpens is wrapped around it. The Sun passes through Ophiuchus each Dec, but the constellation is not part of the zodiac. Ophiuchus contains ◊Barnard's star.

ophthalmia inflammation of the eyeball or conjunctiva. *Sympathetic ophthalmia* is the diffuse inflammation of the sound eye that is apt to follow septic inflammation of the other.

ophthalmology medical specialty concerned with diseases of the eye and its surrounding tissues.

opinion poll attempt to measure public opinion by taking a survey of the views of a representative sample of the electorate; the science of opinion sampling is called *psephology*. Most standard polls take random samples of around a thousand voters which gives results that should be accurate to within three percentage points, 95% of the time. The first accurately sampled opinion poll was carried out by George ◊Gallup during the US presidential election 1936.

opium drug extracted from the unripe seeds of the opium poppy *Papaver somniferum* of SW Asia. An addictive narcotic, it contains several alkaloids, including *morphine*, one of the most powerful natural painkillers and addictive narcotics known, and *codeine*, a milder painkiller.

Opium Wars two wars, the First Opium War 1839–42 and the Second Opium War 1856–60, waged by Britain against China to enforce the opening of Chinese ports to trade in opium. Opium from British India paid for Britain's imports from China, such as porcelain, silk, and, above all, tea.

opossum or *possum* any of a family (Didelphidae) of marsupials native to North and South America. Most opossums are tree-living, nocturnal animals, with prehensile tails, and hands and feet well adapted for grasping. They range from 4 in/10 cm to 20 in/50 cm in length and are insectivorous, carnivorous, or, more commonly, omnivorous.

Oppenheimer J(ulius) Robert 1904–1967. US physicist. As director of the Los Alamos Science Laboratory 1943–45, he was in charge of the development of the atomic bomb (the Manhattan Project). When later he realized the dangers of radioactivity, he objected to the development of the hydrogen bomb, and was alleged to be a security risk 1953 by the US Atomic Energy Commission (AEC).

Oppenheimer was the son of a German immigrant. Before World War II he worked with the physicist Ernest Rutherford in Cambridge. In 1963 the AEC, under G T Seaborg, granted him the Fermi award in physics.

optical fiber very fine, optically pure glass fiber through which light can be reflected to transmit an image or information from one end to the other. Optical fibers are increasingly being used to replace copper wire in telephone cables, the messages being coded as pulses of light rather than a fluctuating electric current.

optical illusion scene or picture that fools the eye. An example of a natural optical illusion is that the Moon appears bigger when it is on the horizon than when it is high in the sky, owing to the ◊refraction of light rays by the Earth's atmosphere.

optic nerve large nerve passing from the eye to the brain, carrying visual information. In mammals, it may contain up to a million nerve fibers, connecting the sensory cells of the retina to the optical centers in the brain. Embryologically, the optic nerve develops as an outgrowth of the brain.

optics branch of physics that deals with the study of ◊light and vision—for example, shadows and mirror images, lenses, microscopes, telescopes, and cameras. For all practical purposes light rays travel in straight lines, although Albert ◊Einstein demonstrated that they may be "bent" by a gravitational field. On striking a surface they are reflected or refracted with some absorption of energy, and the study of this is known as geometrical optics.

option in business, a contract giving the owner the right (as opposed to the obligation, as with futures contracts) to buy or sell a specific quantity of a particular commodity or currency at a future date and at an agreed price, in return for a premium. The buyer or seller can decide not to exercise the option if it would prove disadvantageous.

opus (Latin "work") in music, a term, used with a figure, to indicate the numbering of a composer's works, usually in chronological order.

Opus Dei Roman Catholic institution aimed at the dissemination of the ideals of Christian perfection. Founded in Madrid 1928, and still powerful in Spain, it is now international. Its members may be of either sex, and lay or clerical.

OR abbreviation for the state of ◊Oregon.

oracle Greek sacred site where answers (also called oracles) were given by priests of a diety to inquirers about personal affairs or state policy. These were often ambivalent. The earliest was probably at Dodona (in ◊Epirus), where priests interpreted the sounds made by the sacred oaks of ◊Zeus, but the most celebrated was that of Apollo at ◊Delphi.

oral literature stories that are or have been transmitted in spoken form, such as public recitation, rather than through writing or printing. Most preliterate societies have had a tradition of oral literature, including short folk tales, legends, myths, proverbs, and riddles as well as longer narrative works; and most of the ancient epics—such as the Greek *Odyssey* and the Mesopotamian *Gilgamesh*—seem to have been composed and added to over many centuries before they were committed to writing.

Oran (Arabic *Wahran*) seaport in Algeria; population (1983) 663,500. Products include iron, textiles, footwear, and processed food; the port trades in grain, wool, vegetables, and native esparto grass.

orange any of several evergreen trees of the genus *Citrus*, family Rutaceae, which bear blossom and fruit at the same time. Thought to have originated in SE Asia, orange trees are commercially cultivated in Spain, Israel, the US, Brazil, South Africa, and elsewhere. The sweet orange *C. sinensis* is the one com-

orchid The orchid belongs to one of the largest flowering-plant families: there are possibly as many as 20,000 species.

monly eaten fresh; the Jaffa, blood, and navel orange are varieties of this species.

Orange Free State province of the Republic of South Africa
area 49,405 sq mi/127,993 sq km
capital Bloemfontein
cities Springfontein, Kroonstad, Bethlehem, Harrismith, Koffiefontein
features plain of the High Veld; Lesotho forms an enclave on the Natal–Cape Province border
products grain, wool, cattle, gold, oil from coal, cement, pharmaceuticals
population (1987) 1,863,000; 82% ethnic Africans
history original settlements from 1810 were complemented by the ◊Great Trek, and the state was recognized by Britain as independent 1854. Following the South African, or Boer, War 1899–1902, it was annexed by Britain until it entered the union as a province 1910.

orangutan ape *Pongo pygmaeus*, found solely in Borneo and Sumatra. Up to 5.5 ft/1.65 m in height, it is covered with long, red-brown hair and mainly lives a solitary, arboreal life, feeding chiefly on fruit. Now an endangered species, it is officially protected because its habitat is being systematically destroyed by ◊deforestation.

oratorio dramatic, non-scenic musical setting of religious texts, scored for orchestra, chorus, and solo voices. Its origins lie in the *Laudi spirituali* performed by St Philip Neri's Oratory in Rome in the 16th century, followed by the first definitive oratorio in the 17th century by Cavalieri. The form reached perfection in such works as J S Bach's *Christmas Oratorio*, and Handel's *Messiah*.

Orbison Roy 1936–1988. US pop singer and songwriter specializing in slow, dramatic ballads, such as "Only the Lonely" 1960 and "Running Scared" 1961. His biggest hit was the jaunty "Oh, Pretty Woman" 1964.

orbit path of one body in space around another, such as the orbit of Earth around the Sun, or the Moon around Earth. When the two bodies are similar in mass, as in a ◊binary star, both bodies move around their common center of mass. The movement of objects in orbit follows Johann ◊Kepler's laws, which apply to artificial satellites as well as to natural bodies.

orca another name for ◊killer whale.

orchestra group of musicians playing together on different instruments. In Western music, an orchestra typically contains various bowed string instruments and sections of wind, brass, and percussion. The size and format may vary according to the needs of composers.

orchid any plant of the family Orchidaceae, which contains at least 15,000 species and 700 genera, distributed throughout the world except in the coldest areas, and most numerous in damp equatorial regions. The flowers are the most evolved of the plant kingdom, have three sepals and three petals and are sometimes solitary, but more usually borne in spikes, racemes, or panicles, either erect or drooping.

order in Classical ◊architecture, the ◊column (including capital, shaft, and base) and the entablature, considered as an architectural whole. The five orders are Doric, Ionic, Corinthian, Tuscan, and Composite.

order in biological classification, a group of related ◊families. For example, the horse, rhinoceros, and tapir families are grouped in the order Perissodactyla, the odd-toed ungulates, because they all have either one or three toes on each foot. The names of orders are

Oregon

not shown in italic (unlike genus and species names) and by convention they have the ending "-formes" in birds and fish; "-a" in mammals, amphibians, reptiles, and other animals; and "-ales" in fungi and plants. Related orders are grouped together in a ◊class.

ordination religious ceremony by which a person is accepted into the priesthood or monastic life in various religions. Within the Christian church, ordination authorizes a person to administer the sacraments.

Ordovician period of geological time 510–439 million years ago; the second period of the ◊Palaeozoic era. Animal life was confined to the sea: reef-building algae and the first jawless fish are characteristic.

ore body of rock, a vein within it, or a deposit of sediment, worth mining for the economically valuable mineral it contains. The term is usually applied to sources of metals. Occasionally metals are found uncombined (native metals), but more often they occur as compounds such as carbonates, sulfides, or oxides. The ores often contain unwanted impurities that must be removed when the metal is extracted.

Oregon state in NW US, on the Pacific coast; nickname Beaver State
area 97,079 sq mi/251,500 sq km
capital Salem
cities Portland, Eugene
population (1990) 2,842,300 *features* fertile Willamette river valley; rivers: Columbia, Snake; Crater Lake, deepest in the US (1,933 ft/589 m); mountains: Coast and Cascades; Oregon Dunes National Recreation Area, on Pacific coast
products wheat, livestock, timber, electronics
famous people Chief Joseph, Ursula LeGuin, Linus Pauling, John Reed
history coast sighted by Spanish and English sailors 16th-17th centuries; part of coastline charted by James Cook 1778 on his search for the Northwest Passage; claimed for the US 1792 by Robert Gray, whose ship *Columbia* sailed into the river now named for it; explored by Lewis and Clark 1805; Astoria, John Jacob Astor's fur depot, founded at the mouth of the Columbia 1811; boundary between US settlers and the Hudson's Bay Company fixed 1846 by Oregon Treaty. Oregon Territory included Washington until 1853; Oregon achieved statehood 1859. It remained relatively isolated until the completion of the first transcontinental railroad link 1883. Improved transportation helped make it the nation's leading lumber producer and a major exporter of food products. Development also was aided by hydroelectric projects, many of them undertaken by the federal government.

Orem city in N central Utah, SE of Salt Lake City; population (1990) 67,500. It was settled by Mormons 1861. Industries include electronics and steel.

Orestes in Greek legend, the son of ◊Agamemnon and ◊Clytemnestra, who killed his mother on the instructions of Apollo because she and her lover Aegisthus had murdered his father, and was then hounded by the ◊Furies until he was purified, and acquitted of the crime of murder.

organ musical wind instrument of ancient origin. It produces sound from pipes of various sizes under applied pressure and has keyboard controls. Apart from its continued use in serious compositions and for church music, the organ has been adapted for light entertainment.

organ in biology, part of a living body, such as the liver or brain, that has a distinctive function or set of functions.

organic chemistry branch of chemistry that deals with carbon compounds. Organic compounds form the chemical basis of life and are more abundant than inorganic compounds. In a typical organic compound, each carbon atom forms bonds covalently with each of its neighboring carbon atoms in a chain or ring, and additionally with other atoms, commonly hydrogen, oxygen, nitrogen, or sulfur.

organic farming farming without the use of synthetic fertilizers (such as ◊nitrates and phosphates) or ◊pesticides (herbicides, insecticides, and fungicides) or other agrochemicals (such as hormones, growth stimulants, or fruit regulators).

Organization for Economic Cooperation and Development (OECD) international organization of 24 industrialized countries that provides a forum for discussion and coordination of member states' economic and social policies. Founded 1961, with its headquarters in Paris, the OECD superseded the Organization for European Economic Cooperation, which had been established 1948 to implement the ◊Marshall Plan.

Organization of African Unity (OAU) association established 1963 to eradicate colonialism and improve economic, cultural, and political cooperation in Africa. Its membership expanded to 51 countries when Namibia joined after independence 1990. The secretary-general is Salim Ahmed Salim of Tanzania. Its headquarters are in Addis Ababa, Ethiopia.

The French-speaking Organisation Commune Africaine et Mauricienne/Joint African and Mauritian Organization (OCAM) works within the framework of the OAU for African solidarity.

Organization of American States (OAS) association founded 1948 by a charter signed by representatives of 30 North, Central, and South American states. It aims to maintain peace and solidarity within the hemisphere, and is also concerned with the social and economic development of Latin America.

Organization of Arab Petroleum Exporting Countries (OAPEC) body established 1968 to safeguard the interests of its members and encourage cooperation in economic activity within the petroleum industry. Its members are Algeria, Bahrain, Egypt, Iraq, Kuwait, Libya, Qatar, Saudi Arabia, Syria, and the United Arab Emirates; headquarters in Kuwait.

Organization of Central American States ODECA (*Organización de Estados Centroamericanos*) international association, first established 1951 and superseded 1962, promoting common economic, political, educational, and military aims in Central America. Its members are Costa Rica, El Salvador, Guatemala, Honduras, and Nicaragua,

provision being made for Panama to join at a later date. The permanent headquarters are in Guatemala City.

Organization of Petroleum-Exporting Countries (OPEC) body established 1960 to coordinate price and supply policies of oil-producing states. Its concerted action in raising prices in the 1970s triggered worldwide recession but also lessened demand so that its influence was reduced by the mid-1980s. OPEC members in 1991 were: Algeria, Ecuador, Gabon, Indonesia, Iran, Iraq, Kuwait, Libya, Nigeria, Qatar, Saudi Arabia, the United Arab Emirates, and Venezuela.

orienteering sport of cross-country running and route-finding. Competitors set off at one-minute intervals and have to find their way, using map and compass, to various checkpoints (approximately 0.5 mi/0.8 km apart), where their control cards are marked. World championships have been held since 1966.

original sin Christian doctrine that Adam's fall rendered humanity innately tainted and unable to achieve salvation except through divine grace.

Orinoco river in N South America, flowing for about 1,500 mi/2,400 km through Venezuela and forming for about 200 mi/320 km the boundary with Colombia; tributaries include the Guaviare, Meta, Apure, Ventuari, Caura, and Caroni. It is navigable by large steamers for 700 mi/1,125 km from its Atlantic delta; rapids obstruct the upper river.

oriole any of two families of brightly colored songbirds. The Old World orioles of Africa and Eurasia belong to the family Oriolidae. New World orioles belong to the family Icteridae.

Icteridae also includes blackbirds, bobolinks, grackles, meadowlarks, cowbirds, and tanagers. The northern oriole *Icterus galbula* of North America has a black head and wings and bright orange underparts.

Orion in astronomy, a very prominent constellation in the equatorial region of the sky, identified with the hunter of Greek mythology.

It contains the bright stars Betelgeuse and Rigel, as well as a distinctive row of three stars that make up Orion's belt. Beneath the belt, marking the sword of Orion, is the Orion nebula; nearby is one of the most distinctive dark nebulae, the Horsehead.

Orion in Greek mythology, a giant of ◊Boeotia, famed as a hunter.

Orissa state of NE India
area 60,139 sq mi/155,800 sq km
capital Bhubaneswar
cities Cuttack, Rourkela
features mainly agricultural; Chilka Lake with fisheries and game; temple of Jagannath or Juggernaut at Puri
products rice, wheat, oilseed, sugar, timber, chromite, dolomite, graphite, iron
population (1991) 31,512,000
language Oriya (official)
religion 90% Hindu
history administered by the British 1803–1912 as a subdivision of Bengal, it joined with Bihar to become a province. In 1936 Orissa became a separate province, and in 1948–49 its area was almost doubled before its designation as a state 1950.

Orlando industrial city in Florida; population (1990) 164,700. It is a winter resort and tourist center, with Walt Disney World and the Epcot Center nearby. Electronic and aerospace equipment are manufactured in the city, and citrus-fruit products are processed here. Educational institutions include the University of Central Florida. Orlando was settled 1843.

ornithology study of birds. It covers scientific aspects relating to their structure and classification, and their habits, song, flight, and value to agriculture as destroyers of insect pests. Worldwide scientific banding (or the fitting of coded rings to captured specimens) has resulted in accurate information on bird movements and distribution. There is an International Council for Bird Preservation with its headquarters at the Natural History Museum, London.

Interest in birds has led to the formation of societies for their protection, of which the Society for the Protection of Birds 1889 in Britain was the first. The Audubon Society 1905 in the US has similar aims; other countries now have similar societies.

Oromo a member of a group of E African peoples, especially of S Ethiopia, who speak a Hamito-Semitic (Afro-Asiatic) language.

Orpheus mythical Greek poet and musician. The son of Apollo and a muse, he married Eurydice, who died from the bite of a snake. Orpheus went down to Hades to bring her back and her return to life was granted on condition that he walk ahead of her without looking back. But he did look back and Eurydice was irretrievably lost. In his grief, he offended the ◊maenad women of Thrace, and was torn to pieces by them.

Orr Bobby (Robert) 1948– . Canadian ice-hockey player who played for the Boston Bruins 1967–76 and the Chicago Blackhawks 1976–79 of the National Hockey League. He was voted the best defenseman every year 1967–75, and was Most Valuable Player 1970–72. He was the first defenseman to score 100 points in a season, and was leading scorer 1970 and 1975.

orris root underground stem of a species of ◊iris grown in S Europe. Violet-scented, it is used in perfumery and herbal medicine.

Ortega Saavedra Daniel 1945– . Nicaraguan socialist politician, head of state 1981–90. He was a member of the Sandinista Liberation Front (FSLN), which overthrew the regime of Anastasio Somoza 1979. US-sponsored ◊Contra guerrillas opposed his government from 1982.

orthodontics branch of ◊dentistry, mainly dealing with correction of malocclusion (faulty position of teeth).

Orthodox Church or *Eastern Orthodox Church* or *Greek Orthodox Church* federation of self-governing Christian churches mainly found in E and SE Europe, the USSR, and parts of Asia. The center of worship is the Eucharist. There is a married clergy, except for bishops; the Immaculate Conception is not accepted. The highest rank in the church is that of Ecumenical Patriarch, or Bishop of Istanbul. There are approximately 130 million adherents.

orthopedics branch of medicine concerned with the surgery of bones and joints.

Orwell George. Adopted name of Eric Arthur Blair 1903–1950. English author. His books include the satire *Animal Farm* 1945, which included such sayings as "All animals are equal, but some are more equal than others," and the prophetic *Nineteen Eighty-Four* 1949, portraying the dangers of excessive state control over the individual. Other works include *Down and Out in Paris and London* 1933.

OS/2 single-user computer ◊operating system produced jointly by Microsoft Corporation and IBM for use on large microcomputers. Its main features are multitasking and the ability to access large amounts of internal ◊memory.

Osaka industrial port (iron, steel, shipbuilding, chemicals, textiles) on Honshu Island, Japan; population (1990) 2,623,800, metropolitan area 8,000,000. It is the oldest city of Japan and was at times the seat of government in the 4th–8th centuries.

Osborne John (James) 1929– . English dramatist. He became one of the first ◊Angry Young Men (anti-establishment writers of the 1950s) of British theater with his debut play, *Look Back in Anger* 1956. Other plays include *The Entertainer* 1957, *Luther* 1960, and *Watch It Come Down* 1976.

oscillator any device producing a desired oscillation (vibration). There are many types of oscillator for different purposes, involving various arrangements of thermionic ◊valves or components such as ◊transistors, ◊inductors, ◊capacitors, and ◊resistors.

oscilloscope or *cathode-ray oscilloscope* (CRO) instrument used to measure electrical voltages that vary over time and to display the waveforms of electrical oscillations or signals, by means of the deflection of a beam of ◊electrons. Readings are displayed graphically on the screen of a ◊cathode-ray tube.

Oshkosh city in E central Wisconsin, where the Fox River flows into Lake Winnebago, NW of Milwaukee; seat of Winnebago County; population (1990) 55,000. Industries include clothing, machinery, lumber, and electronics.

Osiris ancient Egyptian god, the embodiment of goodness, who ruled the underworld after being killed by ◊Set. The sister-wife of Osiris was ◊Isis or Hathor, and their son ◊Horus captured his father's murderer. The pharaohs were thought to be his incarnation.

Oslo capital and industrial port (textiles, engineering, timber) of Norway; population (1991) 461,600. The first recorded settlement was made in the 11th century by Harald III, but after a fire 1624, it was entirely replanned by Christian IV and renamed *Christiania* 1624–1924.

Osman I or *Othman I* 1259–1326. Turkish ruler from 1299. He began his career in the service of the Seljuk Turks, but in 1299 he set up a kingdom of his own in Bithynia, NW Asia, and assumed the title of sultan. He conquered a great part of Anatolia, so founding a Turkish empire. His successors were known as "sons of Osman," from which the term ◊Ottoman Empire is derived.

osmium hard, heavy, bluish-white, metallic element, symbol Os, atomic number 76, atomic weight 190.2. It is the densest of the elements, and is resistant to tarnish and corrosion. It occurs in platinum ores and as a free metal (see ◊native metal) with iridium in a natural alloy called osmiridium, containing traces of platinum, ruthenium, and rhodium. Its uses include pen points and light-bulb filaments; like platinum, it is a useful catalyst.

osmosis movement of solvent (liquid) through a semipermeable membrane separating solutions of different concentrations. The solvent passes from a less concentrated solution to a more concentrated solution until the two concentrations are equal. Applying external pressure to the solution on the more concentrated side arrests osmosis, and is a measure of the osmotic pressure of the solution.

osprey bird of prey *Pandion haliaetus*, the single member of the family Pandionidae; sometimes erro-

ostrich The ostrich cannot fly but it is the fastest animal on two legs.

neously called "fish hawk." To catch fish, it plunges feet first into the water. Dark brown above and a striking white below, the osprey measures 2 ft/60 cm with a 6 ft/2 m wingspan. Once on the verge of extinction in the US, it is now responding well to preservation programs.

Ossian (Celtic *Oisin*) legendary Irish hero, invented by the Scottish writer James Macpherson. He is sometimes represented as the son of Finn Mac Cumhaill, about 250, and as having lived to tell the tales of Finn and the Ulster heroes to St Patrick, about 400. The publication 1760 of Macpherson's poems, attributed to Ossian, made Ossian's name familiar throughout Europe.

ossification process whereby bone is formed in vertebrate animals by special cells (*osteoblasts*) that secrete layers of ◊extracellular matrix on the surface of the existing ◊cartilage. Conversion to bone occurs through the deposition of calcium phosphate crystals within the matrix.

osteomyelitis infection of bone, with spread of pus along the marrow cavity. Now quite rare, it may follow from a compound fracture (where broken bone protrudes through the skin), or from infectious disease elsewhere in the body.

osteoporosis disease in which the bone substance becomes porous and brittle. It is common in older people, affecting more women than men. It may be treated with calcium supplements and etidronate.

Ostia ancient Roman town near the mouth of the Tiber. Founded about 330 BC, it was the port of Rome and had become a major commercial center by the 2nd century AD. It was abandoned in the 9th century. The present-day seaside resort *Ostia Mare* is situated nearby.

otter Eurasian otters are among the fastest aquatic mammals, swimming at speeds of up to 6 mph/10 kph.

ostracism deliberate exclusion of an individual, or group, from society. It was an ancient Athenian political device to preserve public order. Votes on pieces of broken pot (Greek *ostrakon*) were used to exile unpopular politicians for ten years.

ostrich large flightless bird *Struthio camelus*, found in Africa. The male may be about 8 ft/2.5 m tall and weigh 300 lb/135 kg, and is the largest living bird. It has exceptionally strong legs and feet (two-toed) that enable it to run at high speed, and are also used in defense. It lives in family groups of one cock with several hens.

Ostrogoth member of a branch of the E Germanic people, the ◊Goths.

Oswald, St c. 605–642. King of Northumbria from 634, after killing the Welsh king Cadwallon. He became a Christian convert during exile on the Scottish island of Iona. With the help of St Aidan he furthered the spread of Christianity in N England.

Otago peninsula and coastal plain on South Island, New Zealand, constituting a district; area 25,220 sq mi/64,230 sq km; chief cities include Dunedin and Invercargill.

Othman c. 574–656. Third caliph (leader of the Islamic empire) from 644, a son-in-law of the prophet Mohammed. Under his rule the Arabs became a naval power and extended their rule to N Africa and Cyprus, but Othman's personal weaknesses led to his assassination. He was responsible for the compilation of the authoritative version of the Koran, the sacred book of Islam.

Otho I 1815–1867. King of Greece 1832–62. As the 17-year-old son of King Ludwig I of Bavaria, he was selected by the European powers as the first king of independent Greece. He was overthrown by a popular revolt.

Otis Elisha Graves 1811–1861. US engineer who developed an elevator that incorporated a safety device, making it acceptable for passenger use in the first skyscrapers. The device, invented 1852, consisted of vertical ratchets on the sides of the elevator shaft into which spring-loaded catches engage and "lock" the elevator into position in the event of cable failure.

O'Toole Peter 1932– . Irish-born English actor who made his name as *Lawrence of Arabia* 1962, and who then starred in such films as *Becket* 1964 and *The Lion in Winter* 1968. Subsequent appearances were few and poorly received by critics until *The Ruling Class* 1972, *The Stuntman* 1978, and *High Spirits* 1988.

otosclerosis overgrowth of bone in the middle ear causing progressive deafness. This inherited condition is gradual in onset, developing usually before middle age. It is twice as common in women as in men.

Ottawa capital of Canada, in E Ontario, on the hills overlooking the Ottawa River and divided by the Rideau Canal into the Upper (western) and Lower (eastern) towns; population (1986) 301,000, metropolitan area (with adjoining Hull, Québec) 819,000. Industries include timber, pulp and paper, engineering, food processing, and publishing. It was founded 1826–32 as Bytown, in honor of John By (1781–1836), whose army engineers were building the Rideau Canal. It was renamed 1854 after the Outaouac Indians.

otter any of various aquatic carnivores of the weasel family, found on all continents except Australia. Otters have thick, brown fur; short limbs; webbed

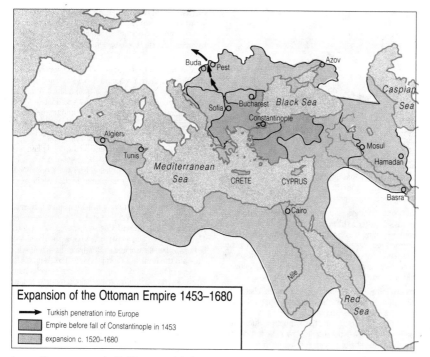

Expansion of the Ottoman Empire 1453–1680

➤ Turkish penetration into Europe

◼ Empire before fall of Constantinople in 1453

◻ expansion c. 1520–1680

toes; and long, compressed tails. They are social, playful, and agile.

Otto I 912–973. Holy Roman emperor from 936. He restored the power of the empire, asserted his authority over the pope and the nobles, ended the Magyar menace by his victory at the Lechfeld 955, and refounded the East Mark, or Austria, as a barrier against them.

Otto IV c. 1182–1218. Holy Roman emperor, elected 1198. He engaged in controversy with Pope Innocent III, and was defeated by the pope's ally, Philip of France, at Bouvines 1214.

Otto cycle alternate name for the ◊four-stroke cycle, introduced by the German engineer Nikolaus Otto (1832–1891) in 1876. It improved on existing piston engines by compressing the fuel mixture in the cylinder before it was ignited.

Ottoman Empire Muslim empire of the Turks 1300–1920, the successor of the ◊Seljuk Empire. It was founded by ◊Osman I and reached its height with ◊Suleiman in the 16th century. Its capital was Istanbul (formerly Constantinople).

Ouagadougou capital and industrial center of Burkina Faso; population (1985) 442,000. Products include textiles, vegetable oil, and soap. The city has the palace of Moro Naba, emperor of the Mossi people, a neo-Romanesque cathedral, and a central avenue called the Champs Elysées. It was the capital of the Mossi empire from the 15th century.

ounce another name for the snow ◊leopard.

ounce unit of mass, one-sixteenth of a pound ◊avoirdupois, equal to 437.5 grains (28.35 g); also one-twelfth of a pound troy, equal to 480 grains.

The *fluid ounce* is a measure of capacity, in the US equivalent to one-sixteenth of a pint, or eight fluid drams. In the UK and Canada, it equals one-twentieth of a pint.

outback the inland region of Australia. Its main inhabitants are Aborigines, miners (including opal miners), and cattle ranchers. Its harsh beauty has been recorded by such artists as Sidney Nolan.

ovary in female animals, the organ that generates the ◊ovum. In humans, the ovaries are two whitish rounded bodies about 1 in/25 mm by 1.5 in/35 mm, located in the abdomen near the ends of the ◊Fallopian tubes. Every month, from puberty to the onset of the menopause, an ovum is released from the ovary. This is called ovulation, and forms part of the ◊menstrual cycle. In botany, an ovary is the expanded basal portion of the ◊carpel of flowering plants, containing one or more ◊ovules. It is hollow with a thick wall to protect the ovules. Following fertilization of the ovum, it develops into the fruit wall or pericarp.

overhead in economics, fixed costs in a business that do not vary in the short term. These might include property rental, heating and lighting, insurance, and administration costs.

Overlord, Operation Allied invasion of Normandy June 6, 1944 (D-day), during World War II.

overtone note that has a frequency or pitch that is a multiple of the fundamental frequency, the sounding body's natural frequency. Each sound source produces a unique set of overtones, which gives the source its quality or timbre.

overture piece of instrumental music, usually preceding an opera. There are also overtures to suites, plays, and ballets, as well as "concert" overtures, such as Elgar's *Cockaigne* and John Ireland's descriptive *London Overture*.

Ovid (Publius Ovidius Naso) 43 BC–AD 17. Roman poet whose poetry deals mainly with the themes of love ("Amores" 20 BC, "Ars amatoria/The Art of Love" 1 BC), mythology ("Metamorphoses" AD 2), and exile ("Tristia" AD 9–12).

Owens US track and field athlete Jesse Owens during an exhibition of the long jump at White City, London, 1936.

ovulation in female animals, the process of releasing egg cells (ova) from the ◊ovary. In mammals it occurs as part of the ◊menstrual cycle.

ovule structure found in seed plants that develops into a seed after fertilization. It consists of an ◊embryo sac containing the female gamete (◊ovum or egg cell), surrounded by nutritive tissue, the nucellus. Outside this there are one or two coverings that provide protection, developing into the testa, or seed coat, following fertilization.

ovum (plural *ova*) female gamete (sex cell) before fertilization. In animals it is called an egg, and is produced in the ovaries. In plants, where it is also known as an egg cell or oosphere, the ovum is produced in an ovule. The ovum is nonmotile. It must be fertilized by a male gamete before it can develop further, except in cases of ◊parthenogenesis.

Owen Robert 1771–1858. British socialist, born in Wales. In 1800 he became manager of a mill at New Lanark, Scotland, where by improving working and housing conditions and providing schools he created a model community. His ideas stimulated the ◊cooperative movement (the pooling of resources for joint economic benefit).

Owens Jesse (James Cleveland) 1913–1980. US track and field athlete who excelled in the sprints, hurdles, and the long jump. At the 1936 Berlin Olympics he won four gold medals.

Owensboro city in NW Kentucky, on the Ohio River, SW of Louisville; seat of Davies County; population (1990) 53,500. Industries include bourbon (whiskey), electronics, tobacco, and steel.

owl any bird of the order Strigiformes, found worldwide. They are mainly nocturnal birds of prey, with mobile heads, soundless flight, acute hearing, and forward-facing immobile eyes, surrounded by "facial disks" of rayed feathers. All species lay white eggs, and begin incubation as soon as the first is laid. They regurgitate indigestible remains of their prey in pellets (castings).

owl The barn-owl family can be distinguished from other owl groups by the heart-shaped face, relatively small eyes, and long slender legs.

ox castrated male of domestic species of cattle, used in Third World countries for plowing and other agricultural purposes. Also the extinct wild ox or ◊aurochs of Europe, and extant wild species such as buffaloes and yaks.

oxalic acid $(COOH)_2 \cdot 2H_2O$ white, poisonous solid, soluble in water, alcohol, and ether. Oxalic acid is found in rhubarb, and its salts (oxalates) occur in wood sorrel (genus *Oxalis*, family Oxalidaceae) and other plants. It is used in the leather and textile industries, in dyeing and bleaching, ink manufacture, metal polishes, and for removing rust and ink stains.

oxbow lake curved lake found on the flood plain of a river. Oxbows are caused by the loops of ◊meanders being cut off at times of flood and the river subsequently adopting a shorter course. In the US, the term bayou is often used.

Oxford university city and administrative center of Oxfordshire in S central England, at the confluence of the rivers Thames and Cherwell; population (1991) 109,000. Oxford University has 40 colleges, the oldest being University College (1249). Other notable buildings are the Bodleian Library (1488), the Ashmolean Museum (1683), and Christopher Wren's Sheldonian Theatre (1664–68). Industries include motor vehicles at Cowley, steel products, electrical goods, paper, publishing, and English language schools. Tourism is important.

Oxford Movement also known as *Tractarian Movement* or *Catholic Revival* movement that attempted to revive Catholic religion in the Church of England. Cardinal Newman dated the movement from Keble's sermon in Oxford 1833. The Oxford Movement by the turn of the century had transformed the Anglican communion, and survives today as Anglo-Catholicism.

Oxfordshire county in S central England
area 1,007 sq mi/2,610 sq km
cities Oxford (administrative headquarters), Abingdon, Banbury, Henley-on-Thames, Witney, Woodstock
features river Thames and tributaries; Cotswolds and Chiltern Hills; Vale of the White Horse (chalk hill figure at Uffington, 374 ft/114 m long); Oxford University; Blenheim Palace, Woodstock (started 1705 by Vanbrugh with help from Nicholas Hawksmoor, completed 1722); Europe's major fusion project JET (Joint European Trust) at the UK Atomic Energy Authority's fusion laboratories at Culham
products cereals, automobiles, paper, bricks, cement
population (1991) 553,800
famous people William Davenant, Flora Thompson, Winston Churchill.

oxidation in chemistry, the loss of ◊electrons, gain of oxygen, or loss of hydrogen by an atom, ion, or molecule during a chemical reaction.

oxide compound of oxygen and another element, frequently produced by burning the element or a compound of it in air or oxygen.

Oxnard city in SW California, NW of Los Angeles; population (1990) 142,200. Industries include paper products, aircraft parts, and oil refining.

oxygen (Greek *oxys* "acid"; *genes* "forming") colorless, odorless, tasteless, nonmetallic, gaseous element, symbol O, atomic number 8, atomic weight 15.9994. It is the most abundant element in the Earth's crust (almost 50% by mass), forms about 21% by volume of the atmosphere, and is present in combined form in water and many other substances. Life on Earth

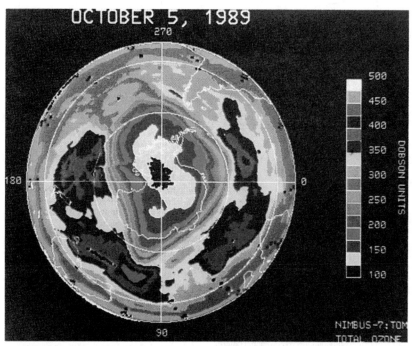

OCTOBER 5, 1989

ozone *Satellite map showing the hole in the ozone layer over Antarctica, Oct 5 1989.*

evolved using oxygen, which is a byproduct of ◊photosynthesis and the basis for ◊respiration in plants and animals.

oxyhemoglobin the oxygenated form of hemoglobin, the pigment found in the red blood cells. All vertebrates, and some invertebrates, use hemoglobin for oxygen transport because the two substances can combine reversibly. In mammals oxyhemoglobin forms in the lungs and is transported to the rest of the body, where the oxygen is released. The deoxygenated blood is then returned to the lungs. Hemoglobin will combine also with carbon monoxide, to form carboxyhemoglobin, but in this case the reaction is irreversible. Asphyxiation can result when oxyhemoglobin cannot form in sufficient quantities.

oyster bivalve ◊mollusk constituting the Ostreidae, or true oyster, family, having the upper valve flat, the lower concave, hinged by an elastic ligament. The mantle, lying against the shell, protects the inner body, which includes respiratory, digestive, and reproductive organs. Oysters commonly change their sex annually or more frequently; females may discharge up to a million eggs during a spawning period.

oz abbreviation for ◊ounce.

Özal Turgut 1927–1993. Turkish Islamic right-wing politician, prime minister 1983–89, president 1989–93. He was responsible for improving his country's relations with Greece, but his prime objective was to strengthen Turkey's alliance with the US.

Ozark Mountains area in the US (shared by Arkansas, Illinois, Kansas, Mississippi, Oklahoma) of ridges, valleys, and streams; highest point only 2,300 ft/700 m; area 50,000 sq mi/130,000 sq km. This heavily forested region between the Missouri and Arkansas rivers has agriculture and lead and zinc mines.

ozone O_3 highly reactive pale-blue gas with a penetrating odor. Ozone is an allotrope of oxygen (see ◊allotropy), made up of three atoms of oxygen. It is formed when the molecule of the stable form of oxygen (O_2) is split by ultraviolet radiation or electrical discharge. It forms a thin layer in the upper atmosphere, which protects life on Earth from ultraviolet rays, a cause of skin cancer. At lower atmospheric levels it is an air pollutant and contributes to the ◊greenhouse effect.

ozone depleter any chemical that destroys the ozone in the stratosphere. Most ozone depleters are chemically stable compounds containing chlorine or bromine, which remain unchanged for long enough to drift up to the upper atmosphere. The best known are ◊chlorofluorocarbons (CFCs), but many other ozone depleters are known, including halons, used in some fire extinguishers; methyl chloroform and carbon tetrachloride, both solvents; some CFC substitutes; and the pesticide methyl bromide.

p in music, abbreviation for **piano** (Italian "softly").

p(p). abbreviation for **page(s)**.

pacemaker or **sinoatrial node** (SAN) in vertebrates, a group of muscle cells in the wall of the heart that contracts spontaneously and rhythmically, setting the pace for the contractions of the rest of the heart. The pacemaker's intrinsic rate of contraction is increased or decreased, according to the needs of the body, by stimulation from the ♦autonomic nervous system. The term also refers to a medical device implanted under the skin of a patient whose heart beats irregularly. It delivers minute electric shocks to stimulate the heart muscles at regular intervals and restores normal heartbeat.

Pacific Ocean world's largest ocean, extending from Antarctica to the Bering Strait; area 64,170,000 sq mi/166,242,500 sq km; average depth 13,749 ft/4,188 m; greatest depth of any ocean 36,210 ft/11,034 m in the ♦Mariana Trench.

Pacific Security Treaty military alliance agreement between Australia, New Zealand, and the US, signed 1951. Military cooperation between the US and New Zealand has been restricted by the latter's policy of banning ships that might be carrying nuclear weapons or nuclear power sources.

Paine Radical author of The Rights of Man, *Thomas Paine.*

Pacific War war 1879–83 fought by an alliance of Bolivia and Peru against Chile. Chile seized Antofagasta and the coast between the mouths of the rivers Loa and Paposo, rendering Bolivia landlocked, and also annexed the S Peruvian coastline from Arica to the mouth of the Loa, including the nitrate fields of the Atacama Desert.

pacifism belief that violence, even in self-defense, is unjustifiable under any conditions and that arbitration is preferable to war as a means of solving disputes. In the East, pacifism has roots in Buddhism, and nonviolent action was used by Mahatma ♦Gandhi in the struggle for Indian independence.

Pacino Al(berto) 1940– . US film actor who played powerful, introverted but violent roles in films such as *The Godfather* 1972, *Serpico* 1973, *The Godfather, Part II* 1974, and *Scarface* 1983. *Dick Tracy* 1990 added comedy to his range of acting styles. He won an Academy Award for his portrayal of a retired blind army officer in *Scent of a Woman* 1992.

Padua (Italian **Padova**) city in N Italy, 28 mi/45 km W of Venice; population (1988) 224,000. The astronomer Galileo taught at the university, founded 1222.

Pagan archeological site in Myanmar, on the Irrawaddy River, with the ruins of the former capital (founded 847, taken by the Mongol leader Kublai Khan 1287). These include Buddhist pagodas, shrines, and temples with wall paintings of the great period of Burmese art (11th–13th centuries), during which the Pagan state controlled much of Burma (now Myanmar).

Paganini Niccolò 1782–1840. Italian violinist and composer, a virtuoso soloist from the age of nine. He invented all the virtuoso techniques that have since been included in violin composition. His works for the violin ingeniously exploit the potential of the instrument. His raffish appearance, wild amors, and virtuosity (especially on a single string) fostered a rumor of his being in league with the devil.

Pahang state of E Peninsular Malaysia; capital Kuantan; area 13,896 sq mi/36,000 sq km; population (1980) 799,000. It is mountainous and forested and produces rubber, tin, gold, and timber. There is a port at Tanjung Gelang. Pahang is ruled by a sultan.

Pahlavi dynasty Iranian dynasty founded by Reza Khan (1877–1944), an army officer who seized control of the government 1921 and was proclaimed shah 1925. During World War II, Britain and the USSR were nervous about his German sympathies and occupied Iran 1941–46. They compelled him to abdicate 1941 in favor of his son Mohammed Reza Shah Pahlavi, who took office in 1956, with US support, and was deposed in the Islamic revolution of 1979.

Paige Satchel (Leroy Robert) 1906–1982. US baseball player. As a pitcher, he established a near-legendary record, leading the Kansas City Monarchs of the Negro National League to the championship 1942. In 1948, with the end of racial segregation in the major leagues, Paige joined the Cleveland Indians. He later played with the St Louis Browns 1951–53.

pain sense that gives an awareness of harmful effects on or in the body. It may be triggered by stimuli such as trauma, inflammation, and heat. Pain is transmitted by specialized nerves and also has psychological components controlled by higher centers in the brain. Drugs that control pain are also known as analgesics.

Pakistan
Islamic Republic of

area 307,295 sq mi/796,100 sq km; one-third of Kashmir under Pakistani control
capital Islamabad
cities Karachi, Lahore, Rawalpindi, Peshawar
physical fertile Indus plain in E, Baluchistan plateau in W, mountains in N and NW
environment about 68% of irrigated land is waterlogged or suffering from salinization
features the "five rivers" (Indus, Jhelum, Chenab, Ravi, and Sutlej) feed the world's largest irrigation system; Tarbela (world's largest earthfill dam); K2 mountain; Khyber Pass; sites of the Indus Valley civilization
head of state Ghulam Ishaq Khan from 1993
head of government Benazir Bhutto from 1993
political system emergent democracy
political parties Pakistan People's Party (PPP), moderate, Islamic, socialist; Islamic Democratic Alliance (IDA), including the Pakistan Muslim League (PML), Islamic conservative; Mohajir National Movement (MQM),

Sind-based *mohajir* (Muslims previously living in India) settlers
exports cotton textiles, rice, leather, carpets
currency Pakistan rupee
population (1992) 130,129,000 (Punjabi 66%, Sindhi 13%); growth rate 3.1% p.a.
life expectancy men 54, women 55 (1989)
languages Urdu and English (official); Punjabi, Sindhi, Pashto, Baluchi, other local dialects
religion Sunni Muslim 75%, Shiite Muslim 20%, Hindu 4%
literacy men 40%, women 19% (1985 est)
GDP $39 bn (1988); $360 per head (1984)

chronology
1947 Independence achieved from Britain, Pakistan formed following partition of British India.
1956 Proclaimed a republic.
1958 Military rule imposed by General Ayub Khan.
1969 Power transferred to General Yahya Khan.
1971 Secession of East Pakistan (Bangladesh). After civil war, power transferred to Zulfiqar Ali Bhutto.
1977 Bhutto overthrown in military coup by General Zia ul-Haq; martial law imposed.
1979 Bhutto executed.
1981 Opposition Movement for the Restoration of Democracy formed. Islamization process pushed forward.
1985 Nonparty elections held, amended constitution adopted, martial law and ban on political parties lifted.
1986 Agitation for free elections launched by Benazir Bhutto.
1988 Zia introduced Islamic legal code, the Shari'a. He was killed in a military plane crash in Aug. Benazir Bhutto elected prime minister Nov.
1989 Pakistan rejoined the Commonwealth.
1990 Army mobilized in support of Muslim separatists in Indian Kashmir. Bhutto dismissed on charges of incompetence and corruption. Islamic Democratic Alliance (IDA), led by Nawaz Sharif, won Oct general election.
1991 Shari'a bill enacted; privatization and economic deregulation program launched.
1992 Sept: Floods devastated north of country. Oct: Pakistan elected to UN Security Council 1993–95.
1993 Oct: Benazir Bhutto elected prime minister.

Paine Thomas 1737–1809. English left-wing political writer, active in the American and French revolutions. His pamphlet *Common Sense* 1776 ignited passions in the American Revolution; others include *The Rights of Man* 1791 and *The Age of Reason* 1793. He advocated republicanism, deism, the abolition of slavery, and the emancipation of women.

painkiller agent for relieving pain. Types of painkiller include analgesics such as ◊aspirin and aspirin substitutes, ◊morphine, ◊codeine, paracetamol, and synthetic versions of the natural inhibitors, the encephalins and endorphins, which avoid the side effects of the others.

paint any of various materials used to give a protective and decorative finish to surfaces or for making pictures. A paint consists of a pigment suspended in a vehicle, or binder, usually with added solvents. It is the vehicle that dries and hardens to form an adhesive film of paint. Among the most common kinds are cellulose paints (or lacquers), oil-based paints, emulsion paints, and special types such as enamels and primers.

painting application of color, pigment, or paint to a surface. The chief methods of painting are *tempera* emulsion painting, with a gelatinous (for example, egg yolk) rather than oil base; known in ancient Egypt; *fresco* watercolor painting on plaster walls; the

palace of Knossos, Crete, contains examples from about 2,000 BC; *ink* developed in China from calligraphy in the Sung period and highly popular in Japan from the 15th century; *oil* ground pigments in linseed, walnut, or other oil; spread from N to S Europe in the 15th century; *watercolor* pigments combined with gum arabic and glycerol, which are diluted with water; the method was developed in the 15th–17th centuries from wash drawings; *acrylic* synthetic pigments developed after World War II; the colors are very hard and brilliant.

Pakistan country in S Asia, stretching from the Himalayas to the Arabian Sea, bounded W by Iran, NW by Afghanistan, NE by China, and E by India.

Palatinate (called the *Pfalz* in Germany) historic division of Germany, dating from before the 8th century. It was ruled by a *count palatine* (a count with royal prerogatives) and varied in size.

Palau former name (until 1981) of the Republic of ◊Belau.

Paleocene (Greek "old" + "recent") first epoch of the Tertiary period of geological time, 65–55 million years ago. Many types of mammals spread rapidly after the disappearance of the great reptiles of the Mesozoic.

Paleolithic earliest stage of human technology and development of the Stone Age; see ◊prehistory.

paleomagnetism science of the reconstruction of the Earth's ancient magnetic field and the former positions of the continents, from the evidence of what is called remanent magnetization in ancient rocks. Remanent magnetization is the record of magnetization acquired by igneous rocks as they cool past the point where they can be influenced by any later magnetization through the presence of the Earth's magnetic field. This permanent record of the direction of the Earth's magnetic field at the time of formation permits geologists to reconstruct the intervals at which the Earth's magnetic field has changed direction, or become reversed. Paleomagnetism shows that such events occur with some regularity—the magnetic north pole becoming the magnetic south pole, and vice versa at approximate half-million-year intervals, with shorter reversal periods in between the major spans.

paleontology in geology, the study of ancient life that encompasses the structure of ancient organisms and their environment, evolution, and ecology, as revealed by their ◊fossils.

Paleozoic era of geological time 590–248 million years ago. It comprises the Cambrian, ◊Ordovician, Silurian, Devonian, Carboniferous, and Permian periods. The Cambrian, Ordovician, and Silurian constitute the Lower Paleozoic; the Devonian, Carboniferous, and Permian make up the Upper Paleozoic. The era includes the evolution of hard-shelled multicellular life forms in the sea; the invasion of land by plants and animals; and the evolution of fish, amphibians, and early reptiles. The earliest identifiable fossils date from this era. The climate was mostly warm with short ice ages. The continents were very different from the present ones but, toward the end of the era, all were joined together as a single world continent called ◊Pangaea.

Palermo capital and seaport of Sicily; population (1988) 729,000. Industries include shipbuilding, steel, glass, and chemicals. It was founded by the Phoenicians in the 8th century BC.

Palestine (Arabic *Falastin* "Philistine") historic geographical area at the E end of the Mediterranean sea, also known as the Holy Land because of its historic and symbolic importance for Jews, Christians and Muslims. Early settlers included the Canaanites, Hebrews, and Philistines. Over the centuries it became part of the Egyptian, Assyrian, Babylonian, Macedonian, Ptolemaic, Seleucid, Roman, Byzantine, Arab, and Ottoman empires.

Today, it comprises parts of modern Israel, Ecgpt, and Jordan.

Palestine Liberation Organization (PLO) Arab organization founded 1964 to bring about an independent state in Palestine. It consists of several distinct groupings, the chief of which is al-◊Fatah, led by Yassir ◊Arafat, the president of the PLO from 1969. The PLO's original main aim was the destruction of the Israeli state, but over time it has changed to establishing a Palestinian state alongside that of Israel.

Palestine Wars another name for the ◊Arab–Israeli Wars.

Pali ancient Indo-European language of N India, related to Sanskrit, and a Classical language of Buddhism.

Palladio Andrea 1518–1580. Italian Renaissance architect noted for his harmonious and balanced Classical structures. He designed numerous country houses in and around Vicenza, Italy, making use of

Roman Classical forms, symmetry, and proportion. The Villa Malcontenta and the Villa Rotonda are examples of houses designed from 1540 for patrician families of the Venetian Republic. He also designed churches in Venice and published his studies of Classical form in several illustrated books.

His ideas were revived in England in the early 17th century by Inigo Jones and in the 18th century by Lord Burlington and later by architects in Italy, Holland, Germany, Russia, and the US, where his ideas were introduced by Thomas Jefferson and had wide influence on Federal-period architecture.

palladium lightweight, ductile and malleable, silver-white, metallic element, symbol Pd, atomic number 46, atomic weight 106.4.

It is one of the so-called platinum group of metals, and is resistant to tarnish and corrosion. It often occurs in nature as a free metal (see ◊native metal) in a natural alloy with platinum. Palladium is used as a catalyst, in alloys of gold (to make white gold) and silver, in electroplating, and in dentistry.

palliative in medicine, any treatment given to relieve symptoms rather than to cure the underlying cause. In conditions that will resolve of their own accord (for instance, the common cold) or that are incurable, the entire treatment may be palliative.

palm plant of the family Palmae, characterized by a single tall stem bearing a thick cluster of large palmate or pinnate leaves at the top. The majority of the numerous species are tropical or subtropical. Some, such as the coconut, date, sago, and oil palms, are important economically.

Several palms are native to Florida.

Palma (Spanish *Palma de Mallorca*) industrial port (textiles, cement, paper, pottery), resort, and capital of the Balearic Islands, Spain, on Majorca; population (1991) 308,600. Palma was founded 276 BC as a Roman colony. It has a Gothic cathedral, begun 1229.

Palme (Sven) Olof 1927–1986. Swedish social-democratic politician, prime minister 1969–76 and 1982–86. As prime minister he carried out constitutional reforms, turning the Riksdag into a single-chamber parliament and stripping the monarch of power, and was widely respected for his support of Third World Countries. He was assassinated Feb 1986.

Palmer Arnold (Daniel) 1929– . US golfer who helped to popularize the professional sport in the US in the 1950s and 1960s. He won the Masters 1958, 1960, 1962, and 1964; the US Open 1960; and the British Open 1961 and 1962.

Palm Sunday in the Christian calendar, the Sunday before Easter and first day of Holy Week, commemorating Jesus' entry into Jerusalem, when the crowd strewed palm leaves in his path.

Palmyra ancient city and oasis in the desert of Syria, about 150 mi/240 km NE of Damascus. Palmyra, the biblical *Tadmor*, was flourishing by about 300 BC. It was destroyed AD 272 after Queen Zenobia had led a revolt against the Romans. Extensive temple ruins exist, and on the site is a village called Tadmor.

Palo Alto city in California, situated SE of San Francisco at the center of the high-tech region known as "Silicon Valley"; population (1990) 55,900. It is the site of Stanford University.

Pamirs central Asian plateau mainly in Tajikistan, but extending into China and Afghanistan, traversed by mountain ranges. Its highest peak is Kommunizma

Pik (Communism Peak 24,600 ft/7,495 m) in the Akademiya Nauk range.

Pampas flat, treeless, Argentine plains, lying between the Andes Mountains and the Atlantic Ocean and rising gradually from the coast to the lower slopes of the mountains. The E Pampas contain large cattle ranches and the flax- and grain-growing area of Argentina; the W Pampas are arid and unproductive.

Pan in Greek mythology, the god of flocks and herds (Roman *Sylvanus*), shown as a man with the horns, ears, and hoofed legs of a goat, and playing a shepherd's panpipe (or syrinx).

Pan-Africanist Congress (PAC) militant black South African nationalist group, which broke away from the African National Congress (ANC) 1959. More radical than the ANC, the Pan-Africanist Congress has a black-only policy for Africa. PAC was outlawed from 1960 to 1990. Its military wing is called Poqo ("we alone").

Panama country in Central America, on a narrow isthmus between the Caribbean and the Pacific Ocean, bounded W by Costa Rica and E by Colombia.

Panama Canal canal across the Panama isthmus in Central America, connecting the Pacific and Atlantic oceans; length 50 mi/80 km, with 12 locks. Built by the US 1904–14 after an unsuccessful attempt by the French, it was formally opened 1920. The

Panama Canal Zone was acquired "in perpetuity" by the US 1903, comprising land extending about 3 mi/5 km on either side of the canal. The zone passed to Panama 1979, and control of the canal itself was ceded to Panama by the US Jan 1990 under the terms of the Panama Canal Treaty 1977. The Canal Zone has several US military bases. *See map p. 708*

Panama City capital of the Republic of Panama, near the Pacific end of the Panama Canal; population (1990) 584,800. Products include chemicals, plastics, and clothing. An earlier Panama, to the NE, founded 1519, was destroyed 1671, and the city was founded on the present site 1673.

Pan-American Union former name (1910–48) of the ♢Organization of American States.

Panchen Lama 10th incarnation 1935–1989. Tibetan spiritual leader, second in importance to the ♢Dalai Lama. A protégé of the Chinese since childhood, the present Panchen Lama is not universally recognized. When the Dalai Lama left Tibet 1959, the Panchen Lama was deputed by the Chinese to take over, but was stripped of power 1964 for refusing to denounce the Dalai Lama. He did not appear again in public until 1978.

pancreas in vertebrates, an accessory gland of the digestive system located close to the duodenum. When stimulated by the hormone secretin, it secretes enzymes into the duodenum that digest starches, pro-

---

Panama
Republic of
(*República de Panamá*)

area 29,768 sq mi/77,100 sq km
capital Panamá (Panama City)
cities Cristóbal, Balboa, Colón, David
physical coastal plains and mountainous interior; tropical rainforest in E and NW; Pearl Islands in Gulf of Panama
features Panama Canal; Barro Colorado Island in Gatún Lake (reservoir supplying the canal), a tropical forest reserve since 1923; Smithsonian Tropical Research Institute
head of state and government Guillermo Endara from 1989
political system emergent democratic republic
political parties Democratic Revolutionary Party (PRD), right-wing; Labor Party (PALA), right of center; Panamanian Republican Party (PPR), right-wing; Nationalist Liberal Republican Movement (MOLIRENA), left of center; Authentic Panamanian Party (PPA), centrist; Christian Democratic Party (PDC), center-left
exports bananas, petroleum products, copper, shrimps, sugar

currency balboa
population (1992) 2,515,000 (mestizo, or mixed race, 70%; West Indian 14%; European descent 10%; Indian (Cuna, Choco, Guayami) 6%); growth rate 2.2% p.a.
life expectancy men 71, women 75 (1989)
languages Spanish (official), English
religions Roman Catholic 93%, Protestant 6%
literacy 87% (1989)
GNP $4.2 bn (1988); $1,970 per head (1984)

chronology
1821 Achieved independence from Spain; joined confederacy of Gran Colombia.
1903 Full independence achieved on separation from Colombia.
1974 Agreement to negotiate full transfer of the Panama Canal from the US to Panama.
1977 US–Panama treaties transferred the canal to Panama, effective from 1990, with the US guaranteeing its protection and an annual payment.
1984 Nicolás Ardito Barletta elected president.
1985 Barletta resigned; replaced by Eric Arturo del Valle.
1987 General Noriega (head of the National Guard and effective ruler) resisted calls for his removal, despite suspension of US military and economic aid.
1988 Del Valle replaced by Manuel Solis Palma. Noriega, charged with drug smuggling by the US, declared a state of emergency.
1989 Opposition won election; Noriega declared results invalid; Francisco Rodríguez sworn in as president. Coup attempt against Noriega failed; Noriega declared head of government by assembly. "State of war" with the US announced. US invasion deposed Noriega; Guillermo Endara installed as president. Noriega sought asylum in Vatican embassy; later surrendered and taken to US for trial.
1991 Attempted antigovernment coup foiled. Army abolished.
1992 Noriega found guilty of drug offenses. Referendum voted down overwhelmingly government's constitutional changes, including abolition of a standing army.

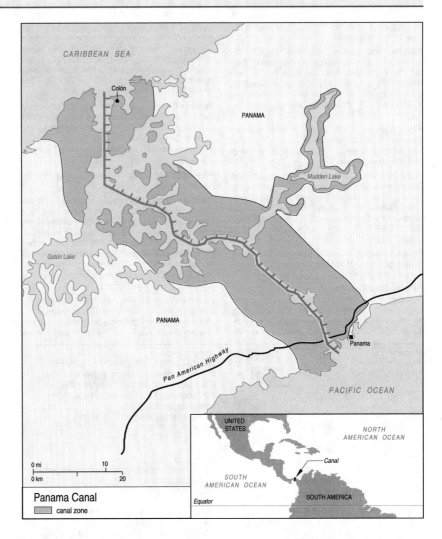

CARIBBEAN SEA

Colón

PANAMA

Madden Lake

Gatún Lake

PANAMA

Panama

Pan American Highway

PACIFIC OCEAN

UNITED STATES

NORTH AMERICAN OCEAN

Canal

SOUTH AMERICAN OCEAN

Equator

SOUTH AMERICA

0 mi   10

0 km   20

Panama Canal

canal zone

teins, and fats. In humans, it is about 7 in/18 cm long, and lies behind and below the stomach. It contains groups of cells called the *islets of Langerhans*, which secrete the hormones insulin and glucagon that regulate the blood sugar level.

panda one of two carnivores of different families, native to NW China and Tibet. The *giant panda Ailuropoda melanoleuca* has black-and-white fur with black eye patches, and feeds mainly on bamboo shoots. It can grow up to 4.5 ft/1.5 m long, and weigh up to 300 lb/140 kg. It is an endangered species. The *lesser, or red, panda Ailurus fulgens*, of the raccoon family, is about 1.5 ft/50 cm long, and is black and chestnut, with a long tail.

Pandora in Greek mythology, the first mortal woman. Zeus sent her to Earth with a box of evils (to counteract the blessings brought to mortals by ◊Prometheus' gift of fire); she opened the box, and the evils all flew out. Only hope was left inside as a consolation.

Pangaea or *Pangea* single landmass, made up of all the present continents, believed to have existed

between 250 and 200 million years ago; the rest of the Earth was covered by the Panthalassa ocean. Pangaea split into two landmasses—◊Laurasia in the north and ◊Gondwanaland in the south—which subsequently broke up into several continents. These then drifted slowly to their present positions (see ◊continental drift).

pansy cultivated violet derived from the European wild pansy *Viola tricolor*, and including many different varieties and strains. The flowers are usually purple, yellow, cream, or a mixture, and there are many highly developed varieties bred for size, color, or special markings. Several of the 400 different species are scented.

Panthalassa ocean that covered the surface of the Earth not occupied by the world continent ◊Pangaea between 250 and 200 million years ago.

pantheism (Greek *pan* "all"; *theos* "God") doctrine that regards all of reality as divine, and God as present in all of nature and the universe. It is expressed in Egyptian religion and Brahmanism; stoicism, Neoplatonism, Judaism, Christianity, and Islam can be interpreted in pantheistic terms. Pantheistic philosophers include Bruno, Spinoza, Fichte, Schelling, and Hegel.

pantheon originally a temple for worshiping all the gods, such as that in ancient Rome, rebuilt by the emperor Hadrian and still used as a church. In more recent times, the name has been used for a building where famous people are buried (as in the Panthéon, Paris).

panther another name for the ◊leopard.

pantothenic acid $C_9H_{17}NO_5$ one of the water-soluble B ◊vitamins, occurring widely throughout a normal diet. There is no specific deficiency disease associated with pantothenic acid but it is known to be involved in the breakdown of fats and carbohydrates.

panzer German mechanized divisions and regiments in World War II, used in connection with armored vehicles, mainly tanks.

papal infallibility doctrine formulated by the Roman Catholic Vatican Council 1870, which stated that the pope, when speaking officially on certain doctrinal or moral matters, was protected from error by God, and therefore such rulings could not be challenged.

Papal States area of central Italy in which the pope was temporal ruler from 756 until the unification of Italy 1870.

Papandreou Andreas 1919– . Greek socialist politician, founder of the Pan-Hellenic Socialist Movement (PASOK), and prime minister 1981–89, 1993– . He lost the 1989 election amid personal scandals and his implication in the alleged embezzlement and diver-

sion of funds to the Greek government of $200 million from the Bank of Crete In Jan 1992 a trial cleared Papandreou of all corruption charges, and in Oct 1993 he was reelected in a landslide.

papaya tropical tree *Carica papaya* of the family Caricaceae, native from Florida to South America. Varieties are grown throughout the tropics. The edible fruits resemble a melon, with orange-colored flesh and numerous blackish seeds in the central cavity; they may weigh up to 20 lb/9 kg.

Papeete capital and port of French Polynesia on the NW coast of Tahiti; population (1983) 79,000. Products include vanilla, copra, and mother-of-pearl.

paper thin, flexible material made in sheets from vegetable fibers (such as wood pulp) or rags and used for writing, drawing, printing, packaging, and various household needs. The name comes from papyrus, a form of writing material made from water reed, used in ancient Egypt. The invention of true paper, originally made of pulped fishing nets and rags, is credited to Tsai Lun, Chinese minister of agriculture, AD 105.

papier mâché craft technique that involves building up layer upon layer of pasted paper, which is then baked or left to harden. Used for trays, decorative objects, and even furniture, it is often painted, lacquered, or decorated with mother-of-pearl.

Papineau Louis Joseph 1786–1871. Canadian politician. He led a mission to England to protest against the planned union of Lower Canada (Québec) and Upper

---

Papua New Guinea

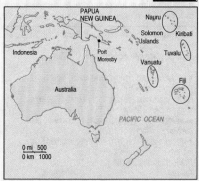

area 178,656 sq mi/462,840 sq km
capital Port Moresby (on E New Guinea)
cities Lae, Rabaul, Madang
physical mountainous; includes tropical islands of New Ireland, New Britain, and Bougainville; Admiralty Islands, D'Entrecasteaux Islands, and Louisiade Archipelago
features one of world's largest swamps on SW coast; world's largest butterfly, orchids; Sepik River
head of state Elizabeth II, represented by governor-general
head of government Paias Wingti from 1992
political system liberal democracy
political parties Papua New Guinea Party (Pangu Pati: PP), urban-and coastal-oriented nationalist; People's Democratic Movement (PDM), 1985 breakaway from the PP; National Party (NP), highlands-based; Melanesian Alliance (MA), Bougainville-based autonomy; People's Progress Party (PPP), conservative

exports copra, coconut oil, palm oil, tea, copper, gold, coffee
currency kina
population (1992) 3,834,000 (Papuans, Melanesians, Negritos, various minorities); growth rate 2.6% p.a.
life expectancy men 53, women 54 (1987)
languages English (official); pidgin English, 715 local languages
religions Protestant 63%, Roman Catholic 31%, local faiths
literacy men 55%, women 36% (1985 est)
GNP $2.5 bn; $730 per head (1987)

chronology
1883 Annexed by Queensland; became the Australian Territory of Papua.
1884 NE New Guinea annexed by Germany; SE claimed by Britain.
1914 NE New Guinea occupied by Australia.
1921–42 Held as a League of Nations mandate.
1942–45 Occupied by Japan.
1975 Independence achieved from Australia, within the Commonwealth, with Michael Somare as prime minister.
1980 Julius Chan became prime minister.
1982 Somare returned to power.
1985 Somare challenged by Paias Wingti, the deputy prime minister, who later formed a five-party coalition government.
1988 Wingti defeated on no-confidence vote and replaced by Rabbie Namaliu, who established a six-party coalition government.
1989 State of emergency imposed on Bougainville in response to separatist violence.
1991 Peace accord signed with Bougainville secessionists. Economic boom as gold production doubled. Wiwa Korowi elected as new governor-general. Deputy Prime Minister Ted Diro resigned, having been found guilty of corruption.
1992 April: killings by outlawed Bougainville secessionists reported. July: Wingti elected premier.

Canada (Ontario), and demanded economic reform and an elected provincial legislature. In 1835 he gained the cooperation of William Lyon ◊Mackenzie in Upper Canada, and in 1837 organized an unsuccessful rebellion of the French against British rule in Lower Canada. He fled the country, but returned 1847 to sit in the United Canadian legislature until 1854.

Papp Joseph 1921–1991. US theater director, and founder of the New York Shakespeare Festival 1954 held in an open-air theater in the city's Central Park. He also founded the New York Public Theater 1967, an off-Broadway forum for new talent, which staged the first productions of the musicals *Hair* 1967 and *A Chorus Line* 1975.

Pap test or *Pap smear* common name for ◊cervical smear.

Papua New Guinea country in the SW Pacific, comprising the E part of the island of New Guinea, the Bismarck Archipelago, and part of the Solomon Islands. *See panel p. 709*

papyrus type of paper made by the ancient Egyptians from the stem of the papyrus or paper reed *Cyperus papyrus*, family Cyperaceae.

parabola in mathematics, a curve formed by cutting a right circular cone with a plane parallel to the sloping side of the cone. A parabola is one of the family of curves known as ◊conic sections. The graph of $y = x^2$ is a parabola.

Paracelsus Adopted name of Theophrastus Bombastus von Hohenheim 1493–1541. Swiss physician, alchemist, and scientist. He developed the idea that minerals and chemicals might have medical uses (iatrochemistry). He introduced the use of ◊laudanum (which he named) for pain-killing purposes. Considered by some to be something of a charlatan, his books were also criticized because of their mystical content.

However, his rejection of the ancients and insistence on the value of experimentation make him a leading figure in early science.

parachute any canopied fabric device strapped to a person or a package, used to slow down descent from a high altitude, or returning spent missiles or parts to a safe speed for landing, or sometimes to aid (through braking) the landing of a plane or missile. Modern designs enable the parachutist to exercise considerable control of direction, as in ◊skydiving.

paradise (Persian "pleasure garden") in various religions, a place or state of happiness. Examples are the Garden of ◊Eden and the Messianic kingdom; the Islamic paradise of the Koran is a place of sensual pleasure.

Paradise Lost epic poem in 12 books, by John Milton, first published 1667. The poem describes the Fall of Man and the battle between God and Satan, as enacted through the story of Adam and Eve in the Garden of Eden. A sequel, *Paradise Regained*, was published 1671 and relates the temptation of Christ in the wilderness.

paraffin common name for ◊alkane, any member of the series of hydrocarbons with the general formula $CnH_{2}n_{+2}$. The lower members are gases, such as methane (marsh or natural gas). The middle ones (mainly liquid) form the basis of gasoline, kerosene, and lubricating oils, while the higher ones (paraffin waxes) are used in ointment and cosmetic bases.

Paraguay landlocked country in South America, bounded NE by Brazil, S by Argentina, and NW by Bolivia.

paralysis loss of voluntary movement due to failure of nerve impulses to reach the muscles involved. It may result from almost any disorder of the nervous system, including brain or spinal-cord injury, poliomyelitis,

---

Paraguay
Republic of
(*República del Paraguay*)

0 mi 500
0 km 1000

area 157,006 sq mi/406,752 sq km
capital Asunción
cities Puerto Presidente Stroessner, Pedro Juan Caballero; port Concepción
physical low marshy plain and marshlands; divided by Paraguay River; Paraná River forms SE boundary

features Itaipú dam on border with Brazil; Gran Chaco plain with huge swamps
head of state and government Juan Carlos Wasmosy from 1993
political system emergent democratic republic
political parties National Republican Association (Colorado Party), right of center; Liberal Party (PL), right of center; Radical Liberal Party (PLR), centrist
exports cotton, soybeans, timber, vegetable oil, maté
currency guaraní
population (1990 est) 4,660,000 (95% mixed Guarani Indian–Spanish descent); growth rate 3.0% p.a.
life expectancy men 67, women 72 (1989)
languages Spanish 6% (official), Guarani 90%
religion Roman Catholic 97%
literacy men 91%, women 85% (1985 est)
GNP $7.4 bn; $1,000 per head (1987)

chronology
1811 Independence achieved from Spain.
1865–70 War with Argentina, Brazil, and Uruguay; less than half the population survived and much territory lost.
1932–35 Territory won from Bolivia during the Chaco War.
1940–48 Presidency of General Higinio Morínigo.
1948–54 Political instability; six different presidents.
1954 General Alfredo Stroessner seized power.
1989 Stroessner ousted in coup led by General Andrés Rodríguez. Rodríguez elected president; Colorado Party won the congressional elections.
1991 Colorado Party successful in assembly elections.
1993 Colorado Party candidate Juan Carlos Wasmosy won presidential elections.

stroke, and progressive conditions such as a tumor or multiple sclerosis. Paralysis may also involve loss of sensation due to sensory-nerve disturbance.

Paramaribo port and capital of Suriname, South America, 15 mi/24 km from the sea on the river Surinamee; population (1980) 193,000. Products include coffee, fruit, timber, and bauxite. It was founded by the French on an Indian village 1540, made capital of British Suriname 1650, and placed under Dutch rule 1816–1975.

paranoia mental disorder marked by delusions of grandeur or persecution. In popular usage, paranoia means baseless or exaggerated fear and suspicion.

paraplegia paralysis of the lower limbs, involving loss of both movement and sensation; it is usually due to spinal injury.

parapsychology (Greek *para* "beyond") study of phenomena that are not within range of, or explicable by established science, for example, extra-sensory perception. The faculty allegedly responsible for such phenomena, and common to humans and other animals, is known as *psi*.

parasite organism that lives on or in another organism (called the "host"), and depends on it for nutrition, often at the expense of the host's welfare. Parasites that live inside the host, such as liver flukes and tapeworms, are called *endoparasites*; those that live on the outside, such as fleas and lice, are called *ectoparasites*.

parent–teacher association (PTA) group attached to a school consisting of parents and teachers who support the school by fund-raising and other activities. Throughout the US, PTAs are active as political pressure groups and as a way to involve parents in the public education process.

Paris port and capital of France, on the river Seine; *département* in the Ile de France region; area 40.5 sq mi/105 sq km; population (1990) 2,175,200. Products include metal, leather, and luxury goods and chemicals, glass, and tobacco.
features the river Seine is spanned by 32 bridges, the oldest of which is the Pont Neuf 1578. Churches include Notre Dame cathedral built 1163–1250; the Invalides, housing the tomb of Napoleon; the Gothic Sainte-Chapelle; and the 19th-century basilica of Sacré-Coeur, 410 ft/125 m high. Notable buildings include the Palais de Justice, the Hôtel de Ville, and the Luxembourg Palace and Gardens. The former palace of the Louvre (with its glass pyramid entrance by I M Pei 1989) is one of the world's major art galleries; the Musé d'Orsay 1986 has Impressionist and other paintings from the period 1848–1914; the Pompidou Center (Beauborg) 1977 exhibits modern art. Other landmarks are the Tuileries Gardens, the Place de la Concorde, the Eiffel Tower, and the Champs-Elysés avenue leading to the Arc de Triomphe. Central Paris was replanned in the 19th century by Baron Haussmann. To the W is the Bols de Boulogne and, beyond the river, La Défense business park with the Grande Arche 1989 by Danish architect Johan Otto von Sprekelsen; Montmarter is in the N of the city; the university, founded about 1150, is on the Left Bank.

Paris in Greek legend, a prince of Troy whose abduction of Helen, wife of King Menelaus of Sparta, caused the Trojan War. Helen was promised to him by the goddess Aphrodite as a bribe, in his Judgment between her beauty and that of two other goddesses, Hera and Athena. Paris killed the Greek hero Achilles by shooting an arrow into his heel, but was himself killed by Philoctetes before the capture of Troy.

Paris The Basilica of Sacré Coeur (1919).

Paris Commune two periods of government in France: *The Paris municipal government 1789–94* was established after the storming of the ◊Bastille and remained powerful in the French Revolution until the fall of Robespierre 1794. *The provisional national government March 18–May 1871* was formed while Paris was besieged by the Germans during the Franco-Prussian War. It consisted of socialists and left-wing republicans, and is often considered the first socialist government in history. Elected after the right-wing National Assembly at Versailles tried to disarm the National Guard, it fell when the Versailles troops captured Paris and massacred 20,000–30,000 people May 21–28.

parish in the US, the ecclesiastical unit committed to one minister or priest. In Britain, a subdivision of a county often coinciding with an original territorial subdivision in Christian church administration, served by a parish church.

Paris, Treaty of any of various peace treaties signed in Paris, including: *1763* ending the ◊Seven Years' War; *1783* recognizing American independence; *1814* and *1815* following the abdication and final defeat of ◊Napoleon I; *1856* ending the ◊Crimean War; *1898* ending the ◊Spanish-American War; *1919–20* the conference preparing the Treaty of ◊Versailles at the end of World War I was held in Paris; *1946* after World War II, the peace treaties between the ◊Allies and Italy, Romania, Hungary, Bulgaria, and Finland; *1951* treaty signed by France, West Germany, Italy, Belgium, Netherlands and Luxembourg, embodying the Schuman Plan to set up a single coal and steel authority; *1973* ending US participation in the ◊Vietnam War.

parity in economics, equality of price, rate of exchange, wages, and buying power. Parity ratios may be used in the setting of wages to establish similar status to different work groups. Parity in international exchange rates means that those on a par with each other share similar buying power. In the US, agricultural output prices are regulated by a parity system.

parity of a number, the state of being either even or odd. In computing, the term refers to the number of 1s in the binary codes used to represent data. A binary representation has *even parity* if it contains an even number of 1s and *odd parity* if it contains an odd number of 1s.

Park Mungo 1771–1806. Scottish explorer who traced the course of the Niger River 1795–97. He disappeared and probably drowned during a second African expedition 1805–06. He published *Travels in the Interior of Africa* 1799.

parrot The gray parrot of the lowland forest and savanna of Kenya and Tanzania.

Park Chung Hee 1917–1979. President of South Korea 1963–79. Under his rule South Korea had one of the world's fastest-growing economies, but recession and his increasing authoritarianism led to his assassination 1979.

Parker Charlie (Charles Christopher "Bird," "Yardbird") 1920–1955. US alto saxophonist and jazz composer, associated with the trumpeter Dizzy Gillespie in developing the ◊bebop style. His skillful improvisations inspired performers on all jazz instruments.

Parker Dorothy (born Rothschild) 1893–1967. US writer and wit, a leading member of the Algonquin Round Table. She reviewed for the magazines *Vanity Fair* and *The New Yorker*, and wrote wittily ironic verses, collected in several volumes including *Not So Deep As a Well* 1940, and short stories.

She also wrote screenplays in Hollywood, having moved there from New York City along with other members of her circle.

Parkersburg city in NW West Virginia, where the Little Kanawha River flows into the Ohio River, N of Charleston; population (1990) 33,900. Industries include chemicals, glassware, paper, and plastics.

Parkinson's disease or *parkinsonism* or *paralysis agitans* degenerative disease of the brain characterized by a progressive loss of mobility, muscular rigidity, tremor, and speech difficulties. The condition is mainly seen in people over the age of 50.

parliament (French "speaking") legislative body of a country. The world's oldest parliament is the Icelandic Althing which dates from about 930. The UK Parliament is usually dated from 1265. The legislature of the US is called ◊Congress and comprises the ◊House of Representatives and the ◊Senate.

Parliament, Houses of building where the UK legislative assembly meets. The present Houses of Parliament in London, designed in Gothic Revival style by the architects Charles Barry and A W Pugin, were built 1840–60, the previous building having burned down 1834. It incorporates portions of the medieval Palace of Westminster.

Parnassus mountain in central Greece, height 8,064 ft/2,457 m, revered by the ancient Greeks as the abode of Apollo and the Muses. The sacred site of Delphi lies on its southern flank.

Parnell Charles Stewart 1846–1891. Irish nationalist politician. He supported a policy of obstruction and

violence to attain ◊Home Rule, and became the president of the Nationalist Party 1877. In 1879 he approved the Land League, and his attitude led to his imprisonment 1881. His career was ruined 1890 when he was cited as corespondent in a divorce case.

parody in literature and the other arts, a work that imitates the style of another work, usually with mocking or comic intent; it is related to ◊satire.

Parr Catherine 1512–1548. Sixth wife of Henry VIII of England. She had already lost two husbands when in 1543 she married Henry VIII. She survived him, and in 1547 married Lord Seymour of Sudeley (1508–1549).

parrot any bird of the order Psittaciformes, abundant in the tropics, especially in Australia and South America. They are mainly vegetarian, and range in size from the 3.5 in/8.5 cm pygmy parrot to the 40 in/100 cm Amazon parrot. The smaller species are commonly referred to as parakeets. The plumage is often very colorful, and the call is usually a harsh screech. Several species are endangered.

Parry William Edward 1790–1855. English admiral and Arctic explorer. He made detailed charts during explorations of the Northwest Passage (the sea route between the Atlantic and Pacific oceans) 1819–20, 1821–23, and 1824–25.

parsec in astronomy, a unit (symbol pc) used for distances to stars and galaxies. One parsec is equal to 3.2616 ◊light-years, 2.063×10^5 ◊astronomical units, and 3.086×10^{13} km.

Parsee or *Parsi* follower of the religion Zoroastrianism. The Parsees fled from Persia after its conquest by the Arabs, and settled in India in the 8th century AD. About 100,000 Parsees now live mainly in Bombay State.

Parsifal in Germanic legend, one of the knights who sought the ◊Holy Grail; the father of Lohengrin.

parsley biennial herb *Petroselinum crispum* of the carrot family, Umbelliferae, cultivated for flavoring and its nutrient properties, being rich in vitamin C and minerals. Up to 1.5 ft/45 cm high, it has pinnate, aromatic leaves and yellow umbelliferous flowers.

parsnip temperate Eurasian biennial *Pastinaca sativa* of the carrot family Umbelliferae, with a fleshy edible root.

Parthenon temple of Athena Parthenos ("the Virgin") on the Acropolis at Athens; built 447–438 BC by Callicrates and Ictinus under the supervision of the sculptor Phidias, and the most perfect example of Doric architecture. In turn a Christian church and a Turkish mosque, it was then used as a gunpowder store, and reduced to ruins when the Venetians bombarded the Acropolis 1687. The ◊Elgin marbles were removed from the Parthenon in the early 19th century and are now in the British Museum, London.

Parthia ancient country in W Asia in what is now NE Iran, capital Ctesiphon. Parthian ascendancy began with the Arsacid dynasty in 248 BC, and reached the peak of its power under Mithridates I in the 2nd century BC; the region was annexed to Persia under the Sassanids AD 226.

participle in grammar, a form of the verb. English has two forms, a ***present participle*** ending in *-ing* (for example, "work*ing*" in "They were *working*," "*working* men," and "a hard-*working* team") and a ***past participle*** ending in *-ed* in regular verbs (for example, "train*ed*" in "They have been *trained* well," "*trained* soldiers," and "a well-*trained* team").

particle physics the study of the properties of ◊elementary particles and of fundamental interactions (see ◊fundamental forces).

particle, subatomic see ◊subatomic particle.

partisan member of an armed group that operates behind enemy lines or in occupied territories during wars. The name "partisans" was first given to armed bands of Russians who operated against Napoleon's army in Russia during 1812, but has since been used to describe Russian, Yugoslav, Italian, Greek, and Polish Resistance groups against the Germans during World War II. In Yugoslavia the communist partisans under their leader, Tito, played a major role in defeating the Germans.

partnership two or more persons carrying on a common business for shared profit. The business can be of any kind—for instance, lawyers, shop owners, or window cleaners. A partnership differs from a corporation in that the individuals remain separate in identity and are not protected by limited liability, so that each partner is personally responsible for any debts of the partnership.

part of speech grammatical function of a word, described in the grammatical tradition of the Western world, based on Greek and Latin. The four major parts of speech are the noun, verb, adjective, and adverb; the minor parts of speech vary according to schools of grammatical theory, but include the article, conjunction, preposition, and pronoun.

partridge any of various medium-sized ground-dwelling fowl of the family Phasianidae, which also includes pheasants, quail, and chickens.

Partridges are Old World birds, some of which have become naturalized in North America, especially the European gray partridge *Perdix perdix*, with mottled brown back, gray speckled breast, and patches of chestnut on the sides.

Parvati in Hindu mythology, the consort of Siva in one of her gentler manifestations, and the mother of Ganesa, the god of prophecy; she is said to be the daughter of the Himalayas.

Pasadena city in SW California, part of Greater ◊Los Angeles; population (1990) 131,600. Products include electronic equipment and precision instruments.

Pascagoula city in SE Mississippi, at the mouth of the Pascagoula River, E of Biloxi; population (1990) 25,900. Industries include fishing, shipbuilding, paper, petroleum, and chemicals. A French fort 1718, it was at other times owned by Britain, Spain, and the free state of West Florida.

PASCAL (French acronym for *program appliqué à la selection et la compilation automatique de la litterature*) a high-level computer-programming language. Designed by Niklaus Wirth (1934–) in the 1960s as an aid to teaching programming, it is still widely used as such in universities, but is also recognized as a good general-purpose programming language. It was named after 17th-century French mathematician Blaise Pascal.

pascal SI unit (symbol Pa) of pressure, equal to one newton per square meter. It replaces ◊bars and millibars (10^5 Pa equals one bar). It is named after the French scientist Blaise Pascal.

Pascal Blaise 1623–1662. French philosopher and mathematician. He contributed to the development of hydraulics, the ◊calculus, and the mathematical theory of ◊probability.

Pasco city in SE Washington, on the Columbia River, seat of Franklin County; population (1990) 20,300.

pas de deux dance for two performers. A *grand pas de deux* is danced by the prima ballerina and the premier danseur.

Pashto language or *Pushto* or *Pushtu* Indo-European language, the official language of Afghanistan, also spoken in N Pakistan.

Passaic city in NW New Jersey, on the Passaic River, N of Jersey City; population (1990) 58,000. Products include television cables, chemicals, plastics, pharmaceuticals, and clothing.

passion flower climbing plant of the tropical American genus *Passiflora*, family Passifloraceae. It bears distinctive flower heads comprising a saucer-shaped petal base, a fringelike corona, and a central stalk bearing the stamens and ovary. Some species produce edible fruit.

passion play play representing the death and resurrection of a god, such as Osiris, Dionysus, or Jesus; it has its origins in medieval ◊mystery plays. Traditionally, a passion play takes place every ten years at ◊Oberammergau, Germany.

pass laws South African laws that required the black population to carry passbooks (identity documents) at all times and severely restricted freedom of movement. The laws, a major cause of discontent, formed a central part of the policies of ◊apartheid. They were repealed 1986.

Passover also called *Pesach* in Judaism, an eight-day spring festival which commemorates the exodus of the Israelites from Egypt and the passing over by the Angel of Death of the Jewish houses, so that only the Egyptian firstborn sons were killed, redressing Pharaoh's murdering of all Jewish male infants.

The Last Supper was a Passover seder.

passport document issued by a national government authorizing the bearer to go abroad and guaranteeing the bearer the state's protection. Some countries require an intending visitor to obtain a special endorsement or visa.

Parthenon *The west front of the Parthenon, on the Acropolis in Athens, Greece.*

pasta food made from a dough of durum-wheat flour or semolina, water, and sometimes egg, and cooked in boiling water. It is usually served with a sauce. Pasta is available either fresh or dried, and comes in a wide variety of shapes. It may be creamy yellow or colored green with spinach or red with tomato. Pasta has been used in Italian cooking since the Middle Ages, but is now popular in many other countries.

Pasternak Boris Leonidovich 1890–1960. Russian poet and novelist. His novel *Dr Zhivago* 1957 was banned in the USSR as a "hostile act," and was awarded a Nobel Prize (which Pasternak declined). *Dr Zhivago* has since been unbanned and Pasternak has been posthumously rehabilitated.

Pasteur Louis 1822–1895. French chemist and microbiologist who discovered that fermentation is caused by microorganisms. He also developed a vaccine for ◊rabies, which led to the foundation of the Institut Pasteur in Paris 1888.

pasteurization treatment of food to reduce the number of microorganisms it contains and so protect consumers from disease. Harmful bacteria are killed and the development of others is delayed. For milk, the method involves heating it to 161°F/72°C for 15 seconds followed by rapid cooling to 50°F/10°C or lower. The process also kills beneficial bacteria and reduces the nutritive property of milk.

Patagonia geographic area of South America, S of latitude 40° S, with sheep farming, and coal and oil resources. Sighted by Ferdinand Magellan 1520, it was claimed by both Argentina and Chile until divided between them 1881.

patella or *knee cap* a flat bone embedded in the knee tendon of birds and mammals, which protects the joint from injury.

patent or *letters patent* documents conferring the exclusive right to make, use, and sell an invention for a limited period. Ideas are not eligible; neither is anything but new.

Paterson William 1745–1806. Irish-born US Supreme Court justice and political leader. A member of the Constitutional Convention 1787, he was elected one of New Jersey's first US senators 1789. After serving as New Jersey governor 1790–93, Paterson was appointed to the US Supreme Court by President Washington, serving as associate justice 1793–1806. He was noted for his vigorous prosecution of cases under the Sedition Act of 1798.

Pathan member of a people of NW Pakistan and Afghanistan, numbering about 14 million (1984). The majority are Sunni Muslims. The Pathans speak Pashto, a member of the Indo-Iranian branch of the Indo-European family.

Pathé Charles 1863–1957. French film pioneer who began his career selling projectors in 1896 and with the profits formed Pathé Frères with his brothers. In 1901 he embarked on film production and by 1908 had become the world's biggest producer, with branches worldwide. He also developed an early color process and established a weekly newsreel, *Pathé Journal.* World War I disrupted his enterprises and by 1918 he was gradually forced out of business by foreign competition.

pathogen in medicine, a bacterium or virus that causes disease. Most pathogens are ◊parasites, and the diseases they cause are incidental to their search for food or shelter inside the host. Nonparasitic organisms, such as soil bacteria or those living in the human gut and feeding on waste foodstuffs, can also become pathogenic to a person whose immune system or liver is damaged. The larger parasites that can cause disease, such as nematode worms, are not usually described as pathogens.

pathology medical specialty concerned with the study of disease processes and how these provoke structural and functional changes in the body and its tissues.

Paton Alan 1903–1988. South African writer. His novel *Cry, the Beloved Country* 1948 focused on racial inequality in South Africa. Later books include the study *Land and People of South Africa* 1956, *The Long View* 1968, and his autobiography *Towards the Mountain* 1980.

patriarch (Greek "ruler of a family") in the Old Testament, one of the ancestors of the human race, and especially those of the ancient Hebrews, from Adam to Abraham, Isaac, Jacob, and his sons (who became patriarchs of the Hebrew tribes). In the Eastern Orthodox Church, the term refers to the leader of a national church.

patrician member of a privileged class in ancient Rome, which originally dominated the ◊Senate. During the 5th and 4th centuries BC many of the rights formerly exercised by the patricians alone were extended to the plebeians, and patrician descent became a matter of prestige.

Patrick, St 389–c. 461. Patron saint of Ireland. Born in Britain, probably in S Wales, he was carried off by pirates to six years' slavery in Antrim, Ireland, before escaping either to Britain or Gaul—his poor Latin suggests the former—to train as a missionary. He is variously said to have landed again in Ireland 432 or 456, and his work was a vital factor in the spread of Christian influence there. His symbols are snakes and shamrocks; feast day March 17.

Patriot missile ground-to-air medium-range missile system used in air defense. It has high-altitude coverage, electronic jamming capability, and excellent mobility. US Patriot missiles were tested in battle against ◊Scud missiles fired by the Iraqis in the 1991 Gulf War.

patronage power to give a favored appointment to an office or position in politics, business, or the church; or ◊sponsorship of the arts. Patronage was for centuries bestowed mainly by individuals (in Europe often royal or noble) or by the church. In the 20th century, patrons have tended to be political parties, the state, and—in the arts—private industry and foundations.

Patton George (Smith) 1885–1945. US general in World War II, known as "Blood and Guts." He was appointed to command the 2nd Armored Division 1940 and became commanding general of the First Armored Corps 1941. In 1942 he led the Western Task Force that landed at Casablanca, Morocco. After commanding the 7th Army, he led the 3rd Army across France and into Germany, and in 1945 took over the 15th Army.

Patton was an outspoken advocate of mobility and armor. He played a central role in stopping the German counteroffensive at the Battle of the ◊Bulge Dec 1944–Jan 1945.

Paul Les. Adopted name of Lester Polfuss 1915– . US inventor of the solid-body electric guitar in the early 1940s, and a pioneer of recording techniques including overdubbing and electronic echo. The

Gibson Les Paul guitar was first marketed 1952 (the first commercial solid-body guitar was made by Leo Fender). As a guitarist in the late 1940s and 1950s he recorded with the singer Mary Ford (1928–1977).

Paul VI Giovanni Battista Montini 1897–1978. Pope from 1963. His encyclical *Humanae Vitae/Of Human Life* 1968 reaffirmed the church's traditional teaching on birth control, thus following the minority report of the commission originally appointed by Pope John rather than the majority view.

Pauli Wolfgang 1900–1958. Austrian physicist who originated the **exclusion principle**: in a given system no two fermions (electrons, protons, neutrons, or other elementary particles of half-integral spin) can be characterized by the same set of ◊quantum numbers. He also predicted the existence of neutrinos. He was awarded a Nobel Prize 1945 for his work on atomic structure.

Pauling Linus Carl 1901– . US chemist, author of fundamental work on the nature of the chemical bond and on the discovery of the helical structure of many proteins. He also investigated the properties and uses of vitamin C as related to human health. He won the Nobel Prize for Chemistry 1954. An outspoken opponent of nuclear testing, he also received the Nobel Peace Prize in 1962.

Paul, St *c.* AD 3–*c.* AD 68. Christian missionary and martyr; in the New Testament, one of the apostles and author of 13 epistles. Originally opposed to Christianity, he took part in the stoning of St Stephen. He is said to have been converted by a vision on the road to Damascus. After his conversion he made great missionary journeys, for example to Philippi and Ephesus, becoming known as the Apostle of the Gentiles (non-Jews). His emblems are a sword and a book; feast day June 29.

Pavarotti Luciano 1935– . Italian tenor whose operatic roles have included Rodolfo in *La Bohème*, Cavaradossi in *Tosca*, the Duke of Mantua in *Rigoletto*, and Nemorino in *L'Elisir d'amore*. His first performance in the title role of *Otello* was given in Chicago 1991.

Pavlov Ivan Petrovich 1849–1936. Russian physiologist who studied conditioned reflexes in animals. His work had a great impact on behavioral theory (see ◊behaviorism) and ◊learning theory. See also ◊conditioning. Nobel Prize for Medicine 1904.

Pavlova Anna 1881–1931. Russian dancer. Prima ballerina of the Imperial Ballet from 1906, she left Russia 1913, and went on to become one of the world's most celebrated exponents of Classical ballet. With London as her home, she toured extensively with her own company, influencing dancers worldwide with roles such as Mikhail ◊Fokine's *The Dying Swan* solo 1905.

Pawtucket city in NE Rhode Island, on the Blackstone River, NE of Providence; population (1990) 72,600. Industries include textiles, thread, machinery, and metal and glass products. It was the home of the first US water-powered cotton mill 1790.

Pays de la Loire agricultural region of W France, comprising the *départements* of Loire-Atlantique, Maine-et-Loire, Mayenne, Sarthe, and Vendée; capital Nantes; area 12,391 sq mi/32,100 sq km; population (1986) 3,018,000. Industries include shipbuilding and wine production.

Paz Octavio 1914– . Mexican poet and essayist. His works reflect many influences, including Marxism, surrealism, and Aztec mythology. His long poem *Piedra del sol/Sun Stone* 1957 uses contrasting images,

Patton An accomplished fencer, sailor, airplane pilot, and athlete, US Gen. George S Patton demanded rigorous standards of individual fitness and unit training of his troops during World War II.

centering upon the Aztec Calendar Stone (representing the Aztec universe), to symbolize the loneliness of individuals and their search for union with others. Nobel Prize for Literature 1990.

PCP abbreviation for **phencyclidine hydrochloride**, a drug popularly known as ◊angel dust.

pea climbing plant *Pisum sativum*, family Leguminosae, with pods of edible seeds, grown since prehistoric times for food. The pea is a popular vegetable and is eaten fresh, canned, dried, or frozen. The sweet pea *Lathyrus odoratus* of the same family is grown for its scented, butterfly-shaped flowers.

Peace Corps US organization of trained men and women, inspired by the British program Voluntary Service Overseas (VSO) and established by President Kennedy 1961. The Peace Corps provides skilled volunteer workers for Third World countries, especially in the fields of teaching, agriculture, and health, for a period of two years.

peace movement collective opposition to war. The Western peace movements of the late 20th century can trace their origins to the pacifists of the 19th century and conscientious objectors during World War I. The campaigns after World War II have tended to concentrate on nuclear weapons, but there are numerous organizations devoted to peace, some wholly pacifist, some merely opposed to escalation.

peach tree *Prunus persica*, family Rosaceae. It has ovate leaves and small, usually pink flowers. The yellowish edible fruits have thick velvety skins; the nectarine is a smooth-skinned variety.

peacock technically, the male of any of various large pheasants. The name is most often used for the common peacock *Pavo cristatus*, a bird of the pheasant family, native to S Asia. It is rather larger than a pheasant. The male has a large fan-shaped tail, brightly colored with blue, green, and purple "eyes" on a chestnut background. The female (peahen) is brown with a small tail.

Peale Norman Vincent 1898– . US religious leader. Through his radio program and book *The Art of*

Living 1948, he became one of the best-known religious figures in the US. His *The Power of Positive Thinking* 1952 became a national bestseller. Peale was elected president of the Reformed Church in America in 1969.

peanut or **groundnut** or **monkey nut** South American vinelike annual plant *Arachis hypogaea*, family Leguminosae. After flowering, the flower stalks bend and force the pods into the earth to ripen underground. The nuts are a staple food in many tropical countries and are widely grown in the S US. They yield a valuable edible oil and are the basis for numerous processed foods.

pear tree *Pyrus communis*, family Rosaceae, native to temperate regions of Eurasia. It has a succulent edible fruit, less hardy than the apple.

pearl shiny, hard, rounded abnormal growth composed of nacre (or mother-of-pearl), a chalky substance. Nacre is secreted by many mollusks, and deposited in thin layers on the inside of the shell around a parasite, a grain of sand, or some other irritant body. After several years of the mantle (the layer of tissue between the shell and the body mass) secreting this nacre, a pearl is formed.

Pearl Harbor an inlet of the Pacific Ocean where the US naval base is situated in Hawaii on Oahu Island. It was the scene of a Japanese surprise air attack on Dec 7, 1941, which brought the US into World War II. It took place while Japanese envoys were holding so-called peace talks in Washington. The local commanders Admiral Kimmel and Lieutenant General Short were relieved of their posts and held responsible for the fact that the base, despite warnings, was totally unprepared at the time of the attack. About 3,300 US military personnel were killed, 4 battleships were lost, and a large part of the US Pacific fleet was destroyed or damaged. The Japanese, angered by US embargoes of oil and other war matériel and convinced that US entry into the war was inevitable, opted to strike a major blow in hopes of forcing US concessions. Instead, it galvanized public opinion and raised anti-Japanese sentiment to a fever pitch, with war declared thereafter.

Pearson Drew 1897–1969. US newspaper columnist. Although his frank, anonymously published exposé *Washington Merry-Go-Round* 1931 became a bestseller, he was fired from the *Baltimore Sun* when his authorship became known. In 1932, however, he began openly publishing a syndicated column of the same name, working in conjunction with Robert Allen until 1942. Pearson continued the column alone until his death, after which it was taken over by newspaper columnist and writer, Jack Anderson (1922–   ).

Pearson Lester Bowles 1897–1972. Canadian politician, leader of the Liberal Party from 1958, prime minister 1963–68. As foreign minister 1948–57, he represented Canada at the United Nations, playing a key role in settling the ◊Suez Crisis 1956. Nobel Peace Prize 1957.

Peary Robert Edwin 1856–1920. US polar explorer who, after several unsuccessful attempts, became the first person to reach the North Pole on April 6, 1909. In 1988 an astronomer claimed Peary's measurements were incorrect.

peat fibrous organic substance found in bogs and formed by the incomplete decomposition of plants such as sphagnum moss. N Asia, Canada, Finland, Ireland, and other places have large deposits, which have been dried and used as fuel from ancient times. Peat can also be used as a soil additive.

pecan nut-producing ◊hickory tree *Carya illinoensis* or *C. pecan*, native to central US and N Mexico and now widely cultivated. The tree grows to over 150 ft/45 m, and the edible nuts are smooth-shelled, the kernel resembling a smoothly ovate walnut.

Peck (Eldred) Gregory 1916–   . US film actor specializing in strong, upright characters. His films include *Spellbound* 1945, *Duel in the Sun* 1946, *Gentleman's Agreement* 1947, *To Kill a Mockingbird* 1962, for which he won an Academy Award, and (cast against type as a Nazi doctor) *The Boys from Brazil* 1974.

Peckinpah Sam 1925–1985. US film director, often of Westerns, usually associated with slow-motion, blood-spurting violence. His best films, such as *The Wild Bunch* 1969, exhibit a thoughtful, if depressing, view of the world and human nature.

pectoral in vertebrates, the upper area of the thorax associated with the muscles and bones used in moving the arms or forelimbs. In birds, the *pectoralis major* is the very large muscle used to produce a powerful downbeat of the wing during flight.

pediatrics medical specialty concerned with the care of children.

pediment in architecture, the triangular part crowning the fronts of buildings in Classical styles. The pediment was a distinctive feature of Greek temples.

Pedro two emperors of Brazil, including:

Pedro I 1798–1834. Emperor of Brazil 1822–31. The son of John VI of Portugal, he escaped to Brazil on Napoleon's invasion, and was appointed regent 1821. He proclaimed Brazil independent 1822 and was crowned emperor, but abdicated 1831 and returned to Portugal.

Peel Robert 1788–1850. British Conservative politician. As home secretary 1822–27 and 1828–30, he founded the modern police force and in 1829 introduced Roman Catholic emancipation. He was prime minister 1834–35 and 1841–46, when his repeal of the ◊Corn Laws caused him and his followers to break with the party.

peer group in the social sciences, people who have a common identity based on such characteristics as similar social status, interests, age, or ethnic group. The concept has proved useful in analyzing the power and influence of co-workers, school friends, and ethnic and religious groups in socialization and social behavior.

Pegasus in astronomy, a constellation of the northern hemisphere, near Cygnus, and represented as the winged horse of Greek mythology.

It is the seventh-largest constellation in the sky, and its main feature is a square outlined by four stars, one of which (Alpherat) is actually part of the adjoining constellation Andromeda. Diagonally across is Markab (or Alpha Pegasi), about 100 light-years distant.

Pegasus in Greek legend, the winged horse that sprang from the blood of the Gorgon Medusa. He was transformed into a constellation.

Pei I(eoh) M(ing) 1917–   . Chinese-born American architect, noted for innovative modern design and high-technology structures, particularly the use of glass walls. His buildings include the Mile High Center in Denver, the National Airlines terminal (now owned by TWA) at Kennedy Airport in New York City, the John Hancock tower in Boston, the National Gallery extension in Washington, DC, the Bank of China Tower, Hong Kong, and the glass pyramid in front of the Louvre, Paris.

Peking alternative transcription of ◊Beijing, the capital of China.

pekingese breed of long-haired dog with a flat skull and flat face, typically less than 10 in/25 cm tall and weighing less than 11 lb/5 kg.

Peking man Chinese representative of an early species of human, found as fossils, 500,000–750,000 years old, in the cave of Choukoutien 1927 near Beijing (Peking). Peking man used chipped stone tools, hunted game, and used fire. Similar varieties of early human have been found in Java and E Africa. Their classification is disputed: some anthropologists classify them as *Homo erectus*, others as *Homo sapiens pithecanthropus*.

A skull found near Beijing 1927 was sent to the US 1941 but disappeared; others have since been found.

Pelagius 360–420. British theologian. He taught that each person possesses free will (and hence the possibility of salvation), denying Augustine's doctrines of predestination and original sin. Cleared of heresy by a synod in Jerusalem 415, he was later condemned by the pope and the emperor.

Pelé Adopted name of Edson Arantes do Nascimento 1940– . Brazilian soccer player. A prolific goal scorer, he appeared in four World Cup competitions 1958–70 and led Brazil to three championships (1958, 1962, 1970).

pelican any of a family (Pelecanidae) of large, heavy water birds remarkable for the pouch beneath the bill which is used as a fishing net and temporary store for catches of fish. Some species grow up to 6 ft/1.8 m and have wingspans of 10 ft/3 m.

Peloponnese (Greek *Peloponnesos*) peninsula forming the S part of Greece; area 8,318 sq mi/21,549 sq km; population (1991) 1,077,000. It is joined to the mainland by the narrow isthmus of Corinth and is divided into the nomes (administrative areas) of Argolis, Arcadia, Achaea, Elis, Corinth, Lakonia, and Messenia, representing its seven ancient states.

Peloponnesian War conflict between Athens and Sparta and their allies, 431–404 BC, originating in suspicions about the ambitions of the Athenian leader Pericles. It was ended by the Spartan general Lysander's capture of the Athenian fleet in 405, and his starving the Athenians into surrender in 404. Sparta's victory meant the destruction of the political power of Athens.

pelota see ◊jai alai.

pelvis in vertebrates, the lower area of the abdomen featuring the bones and muscles used to move the legs or hindlimbs. The ***pelvic girdle*** is a set of bones that allows movement of the legs in relation to the rest of the body and provides sites for the attachment of relevant muscles.

penance Roman Catholic sacrament, involving confession of sins and receiving absolution, and works performed (or punishment self-inflicted) in atonement for sin. Penance is worked out nowadays in terms of good deeds rather than routine repetition of prayers.

Penang (Malay *Pulau Pinang*) state in W Peninsular Malaysia, formed of Penang Island, Province Wellesley, and the Dindings on the mainland;
area 398 sq mi/1,030 sq km;
capital Penang (George Town);
population (1990) 1,142,200;
history Penang Island was bought by Britain from the ruler of Kedah 1785; Province Wellesley was acquired 1800.

penguin The male emperor penguin incubates a single egg on his feet, where the newly hatched chick will be protected by a flap of skin and feathers

Penderecki Krzystof 1933– . Polish composer. His expressionist works, such as the *Threnody for the Victims of Hiroshima* 1961 for strings, employ cluster and percussion effects. He later turned to religious subjects and a more orthodox style, as in the *Magnificat* 1974 and the *Polish Requiem* 1980–83. His opera *The Black Mask* 1986 explored a new vein of surreal humor.

pendulum weight (called a "bob") swinging at the end of a rod or cord. The regularity of a pendulum's swing was used in making the first really accurate clocks in the 17th century. Pendulums can be used for measuring the acceleration due to gravity (an important constant in physics), and in prospecting for oils and minerals.

Penelope in Greek legend, the wife of Odysseus, the king of Ithaca; their son was Telemachus. While Odysseus was absent at the siege of Troy she kept her many suitors at bay by asking them to wait until she had woven a shroud for her father-in-law, but unraveled her work each night. When Odysseus returned, after 20 years, he and Telemachus killed her suitors.

penguin any of an order (Sphenisciformes) of marine flightless birds, mostly black and white, found in the southern hemisphere. They range in size from 1.6 ft/40 cm to 4 ft/1.2 m tall, and have thick feathers to protect them from the intense cold. They are awkward on land, but their wings have evolved into flippers, making them excellent swimmers. Penguins congregate to breed in "rookeries," and often spend many months incubating their eggs while their mates are out at sea feeding.

penicillin any of a group of ◊antibiotic (bacteria killing) compounds obtained from filtrates of molds of the genus *Penicillium* (especially *P. notatum*) or produced synthetically. Penicillin was the first antibiotic to be discovered (by Alexander ◊Fleming); it kills a broad spectrum of bacteria, many of which cause disease in humans.

peninsula land surrounded on three sides by water but still attached to a larger landmass. Florida, is an example.

Peninsular War war 1808–14 caused by the French emperor Napoleon's invasion of Portugal and Spain. British expeditionary forces under Sir Arthur Wellesley (Duke of ◊Wellington), combined with Spanish and

Portuguese resistance, succeeded in defeating the French at Vimeiro 1808, Talavera 1809, Salamanca 1812, and Vittoria 1813. The results were inconclusive, and the war was ended by Napoleon's abdication.

penis male reproductive organ, used for internal fertilization; it transfers sperm to the female reproductive tract. In mammals, the penis is made erect by vessels that fill with blood, and in most mammals (but not humans) is stiffened by a bone. It also contains the urethra, through which urine is passed.

Penn William 1644–1718. English Quaker and founder of Pennsylvania, born in London. He joined the Quakers 1667 and was imprisoned several times for his beliefs. In 1681 he obtained a grant of land in America, in settlement of a debt owed by Charles II to his father, on which he established the colony of Pennsylvania as a refuge for the persecuted Quakers. Penn made religious tolerance a cornerstone of his administration of the colony. He maintained good relations with neighboring colonies and with the Indians in the area, but his utopian ideals were not successful for the most part.

Pennines mountain system, "the backbone of England," broken by a gap through which the river Aire flows to the E and the Ribble to the W; length (Scottish border to the Peaks in Derbyshire) 250 mi/400 km.

Pennsylvania state in NE US; nickname Keystone State
area 45,316 sq mi/117,400 sq km
capital Harrisburg
cities Philadelphia, Pittsburgh, Erie, Allentown, Scranton
features Allegheny Mountains; rivers: Ohio, Susquehanna, Delaware; Independence National Historic Park, Philadelphia; Valley Forge National Historic Park; Gettysburg Civil War battlefield; Pennsylvania Dutch country; Poconos resort region
products hay, cereals, mushrooms, cattle, poultry, dairy products, cement, coal, steel, petroleum products, pharmaceuticals, motor vehicles and equipment, electronic components, textiles
population (1990) 11,881,600
famous people Marian Anderson, Andrew Carnegie, Stephen Foster, Benjamin Franklin, Robert Fulton, Martha Graham, George C Marshall, Robert E Peary, Benjamin Rush, Gertrude Stein, John Updike
history disputed by Sweden, the Netherlands, and England early 17th century; granted to Quaker William ◊Penn 1682 by English King Charles II, after the 1664 capture of New Netherlands. The Declaration of Independence was proclaimed in Philadelphia, and many important Revolutionary War battles were fought here 1777–78. One of the original 13 states, Pennsylvania was a leader in both agriculture and industry. The Battle of Gettysburg 1863 was a turning point in the Civil War for the Union cause. Until 1920, Pennsylvania was dominant in oil, coal, iron, steel, and

Pennsylvania

textile production, but it already was losing its industrial lead when the Great Depression struck; by 1933, 37% of the work force was unemployed. Some areas never fully recovered, and the state now looks to agriculture, service-related industries, trade, and tourism for economic growth. There was a breakdown at the Three Mile Island nuclear reactor plant in Harrisburg 1979.

Pennsylvanian US term for the Upper or Late ◊Carboniferous period of geological time, 323–290 million years ago; it is named after the US state.

Pensacola port in NW Florida, on the Gulf of Mexico, with a large naval air-training station; population (1990) 58,200. Industries include chemicals, synthetic fibers, and paper.

pension a payment, not wages, made to a person (or his/her family) after fulfillment of certain conditions of service; an organized retirement plan. Pension plans vary widely, with some pensions calculated at a specified percentage of a worker's income, payable annually after retirement. Others provide lump-sum savings available for withdrawal at age 65. Employers sometimes match employee contributions; some plans are strictly employee contributions plus interest. Some plans are mandatory, others voluntary.

Pentagon the headquarters of the US Department of Defense, Arlington, Virginia. One of the world's largest office buildings (five-sided with a pentagonal central court), it houses the administrative and command headquarters for the US armed forces and has become synonymous with the military establishment bureaucracy.

Pentagon Papers Case US Supreme Court decision (*New York Times* v *US*; *US* v *Washington Post*) 1971 dealing with the right of the federal government to enjoin the publication of sensitive or classified material. The federal government filed the suit against the *Times* and the *Post* to discontinue publication of portions of "The Pentagon Papers," a set of classified documents about US involvement in Vietnam. The government argued that the threat to national security warranted the infringement on First Amendment rights. The Court ruled 6 to 3 to dismiss the government's suit, judging any suppression of the press, without proof of actual damage to national security, to be a violation of the First Amendment.

Pentateuch Greek (and Christian) name for the first five books of the Bible, ascribed to Moses, and called the *Torah* by Jews.

pentathlon five-sport competition. Pentathlon consists of former military training pursuits: swimming, fencing, running, horsemanship, and shooting. Formerly a five-event track and field competition for women, it was superseded by the seven-event heptathlon 1981.

Pentecost in Judaism, the festival of *Shavuot*, celebrated on the 50th day after ◊Passover in commemoration of the giving of the Ten Commandments to Moses on Mount Sinai, and the end of the grain harvest; in the Christian church, Pentecost is the day on which the apostles experienced inspiration of the Holy Spirit, commemorated on Whit Sunday.

Pentecostal movement Christian revivalist movement originating in the US 1906. Spiritual renewal is sought through baptism by the Holy Spirit, as experienced by the apostles on the first Pentecost. It represented a reaction against the rigid theology and formal worship of the traditional churches. Glossolalia, or speaking in tongues, often occurs. Pentecostalists believe in the literal word of the Bible and faith healing. They disapprove of alcohol, tobacco, dancing, the theater, gambling, and so on. It is an intensely missionary faith, and recruitment in person and on television has been very rapid since the 1960s: worldwide membership is more than 20 million, and it is the world's fastest growing sector of Christianity.

peony any perennial plant of the genus *Paeonia*, family Paeoniaceae, remarkable for their brilliant flowers. Most popular are the common peony *P. officinalis*, the white peony *P. lactiflora*, and the taller tree peony *P. suffruticosa*.

Peoria city in central Illinois, on the Illinois River; a transport, mining, and agriculture center; population (1990) 113,500. Fort Crève Coeur was built here by the French explorer Robert Cavalier de la Salle 1680 and became a trading center. The first US settlers arrived 1818, and the town was known as Fort Clark until 1825.

Pepin the Short c. 714–c. 768. King of the Franks from 751. The son of Charles Martel, he acted as Mayor of the Palace to the last Merovingian king, Childeric III, deposed him and assumed the royal title himself, founding the ◊Carolingian dynasty. He was ◊Charlemagne's father.

pepper climbing plant *Piper nigrum* native to the E Indies, of the Old World pepper family Piperaceae. When gathered green, the berries are crushed to release the seeds for the spice called black pepper. When the berries are ripe, the seeds are removed and their outer skin is discarded, to produce white pepper. Chili pepper, cayenne or red pepper, and the sweet peppers used as a vegetable come from ◊capsicums native to the New World.

peppermint perennial herb *Mentha piperita* of the mint family, native to Europe, with ovate, aromatic leaves and purple flowers. Oil of peppermint is used in medicine and confectionery.

pepsin enzyme that breaks down proteins during digestion. It requires a strongly acidic environment and is found in the stomach.

peptide molecule comprising two or more ◊amino acid molecules (not necessarily different) joined by **peptide bonds**, whereby the acid group of one acid is linked to the amino group of the other (–CO.NH). The number of amino acid molecules in the peptide is indicated by referring to it as a di-, tri-, or polypeptide (two, three, or many amino acids).

Pepys Samuel 1633–1703. English diarist. His diary 1659–69 was a unique record of both the daily life of the period and the intimate feelings of the man. Written in shorthand, it was not deciphered until 1825. Pepys was imprisoned 1679 in the Tower of London on suspicion of being connected with the Popish Plot.

Perak state of W Peninsular Malaysia; capital Ipoh; area 8,106 sq mi/21,000 sq km; population (1990) 2,222,200. It produces tin and rubber. The government is a sultanate. The other principal city is Taiping.

percentage way of representing a number as a ◊fraction of 100. Thus 45 percent (45%) equals 45 ÷ 100, and 45% of 20 is (45 ÷ 100) × 20 = 9.

perch any of the largest order of spiny-finned bony fishes, the Perciformes, with some 8,000 species. This order includes the sea basses, cichlids, damselfishes, mullets, barracudas, wrasses, and gobies. Perches of the freshwater genus *Perca* are found in Europe, Asia, and North America. They have varied shapes and are usually a greenish color. They are very prolific, spawning when about three years old, and have voracious appetites. The American yellow perch *P. flavescens*, to 12 in/30 cm, is abundant in lakes and streams, feeding on insects and other fishes.

percussion instrument musical instrument played by being struck with the hand or a beater. Percussion instruments can be divided into those that can be tuned to produce a sound of definite pitch, such as the kettledrum, tubular bells, glockenspiel, and xylophone and those without pitch, including bass drum, tambourine, triangle, cymbals, and castanets. *See illustration p. 720*

perennial plant plant that lives for more than two years. Herbaceous perennials have aerial stems and leaves that die each autumn. They survive the winter by means of an underground storage (perennating) organ, such as a bulb or rhizome. Trees and shrubs or woody perennials have stems that persist above ground throughout the year, and may be either ◊deciduous or ◊evergreen. See also ◊annual plant, ◊biennial plant.

Peres Shimon 1923– . Israeli socialist politician, prime minister 1984–86. Peres was prime minister, then foreign minister, under a power-sharing agreement with the leader of the Consolidation Party (Likud), Yitzhak ◊Shamir. From 1989 to 1990 he was finance minister in a new Labor–Likud coalition. As foreign minister 1993 he negotiated the peace agreement with the Palestine Liberation Organisation.

perestroika (Russian "restructuring") in Soviet politics, the wide-ranging economic and political reforms initiated from 1985 by Mikhail ◊Gorbachev, finally leading to the demise of the Soviet Union. Originally, in the economic sphere, *perestroika* was conceived as involving "intensive development" concentrating on automation and improved labor efficiency. It evolved to attend increasingly to market indicators and incentives ("market socialism") and the gradual dismantling of the Stalinist central-planning system, with decision-taking being devolved to self-financing enterprises.

Pérez de Cuéllar Javier 1920– . Peruvian diplomat, secretary-general of the United Nations 1982–91. He raised the standing of the UN by his successful diplomacy in ending the Iran–Iraq War 1988 and securing the independence of Namibia 1989.

perfume fragrant essence used to scent the body, cosmetics, and candles. More than 100 natural aromatic chemicals may be blended from a range of 60,000 flowers, leaves, fruits, seeds, woods, barks, resins, and roots, combined by natural animal fixatives and various synthetics. Favored ingredients include ◊balsam, ◊civet (from the African civet cat) hyacinth, jasmine, lily of the valley, musk (from the ◊musk deer), orange blossom, rose, and tuberose.

Pergamum ancient Greek city in W Asia Minor, which became the capital of an independent kingdom 283 BC under the ◊Attalid dynasty. As the ally of Rome it achieved great political importance in the 2nd century BC, and became a center of art and culture. Close to its site is the modern Turkish town of Bergama.

Peri Jacopo 1561–1633. Italian composer who served the Medici family, the rulers of Florence. His experimental melodic opera *Euridice* 1600 established the opera form and influenced Monteverdi. His first opera, *Dafine* 1597, is now lost.

percussion instrument Some of the most commonly used orchestral percussion instruments.

bass drum

kettle drum

tambourine

snare drum

glockenspiel

cymbals

tubular bells

castanets

triangle

pericarp wall of a ◊fruit. It encloses the seeds and is derived from the ◊ovary wall. In fruits such as the acorn, the pericarp becomes dry and hard, forming a shell around the seed. In fleshy fruits the pericarp is typically made up of three distinct layers. The *epicarp*, or *exocarp*, forms the tough outer skin of the fruit, while the *mesocarp* is often fleshy and forms the middle layers. The innermost layer or *endocarp*, which surrounds the seeds, may be membranous or thick and hard, as in the drupe (stone) of cherries, plums, and apricots.

Pericles *c.* 495–429 BC. Athenian politician who was effective leader of the city from 443 BC and under whom Athenian power reached its height. His policies helped to transform the Delian League into an Athenian empire, but the disasters of the ◊Peloponnesian War led to his removal from office 430 BC. Although quicky reinstated, he died soon after.

peridotite rock consisting largely of the mineral olivine; pyroxene and other minerals may also be present. Peridotite is an ultrabasic rock containing less than 45% silica by weight. It is believed to be one of the rock types making up the Earth's upper mantle, and is sometimes brought from the depths to the surface by major movements, or as inclusions in lavas.

perimeter or *boundary* line drawn around the edge of an area or shape. For example, the perimeter of a rectangle is the sum of its four sides; the perimeter of a circle is known as its *circumference*.

period punctuation mark (.). The term "period" is the preferred usage in North America; "full stop" is the preferred term in the UK. The period has two functions: to mark the end of a sentence and to indicate that a word has been abbreviated. It is also used in mathematics to indicate decimals and is then called a point.

periodic table of the elements classification of the elements to reflect the periodic law, namely that the properties of the chemical elements recur periodically when the elements are arranged in increasing order of their ◊atomic number and are shown in related groups. Today's arrangement is by atomic numbers as devised by Moseley in 1913–14; the original tables were set up by atomic weights (masses), first proposed by Newlands in 1863 and expanded on by Mendeleyev and Meyer in 1869. There are similarities in the chemical properties of the main elements in each of the main vertical groups and a gradation of properties along the horizontal periods. The periods correspond to the filling of successive electron shells, and the groups correspond to the number of valence electrons. *See table pp. 722–23*

periodontal disease (formerly known as *pyorrhea*) disease of the gums and bone supporting the teeth, caused by the accumulation of plaque and microorganisms; the gums recede, and the teeth eventually become loose and may drop out unless treatment is sought.

periscope optical instrument designed for observation from a concealed position such as from a submerged submarine. In its basic form it consists of a tube with parallel mirrors at each end, inclined at 45° to its axis. The periscope attained prominence in naval and military operations of World War I.

peristalsis wavelike contractions, produced by the contraction of smooth muscle, that pass along tubular organs, such as the intestines. The same term describes the wavelike motion of earthworms and other invertebrates, in which part of the body contracts as another part elongates.

periwinkle in botany, any of several trailing blue-flowered evergreen plants of the genus *Vinca* of the dogbane family Apocynaceae. They range in length from 8 in/20 cm to 3 ft/1 m.

perjury the offense of deliberately making a false statement on ◊oath (or affirmation) when appearing as a witness in legal proceedings, on a point material to the question at issue. In Britain and the US it is punishable by a fine, imprisonment, or both.

Perkins Anthony 1932–1992. US film actor who played the mother-fixated psychopath Norman Bates in Alfred Hitchcock's *Psycho* 1960 and *Psycho II* 1982. He played shy but subtle roles in *Friendly Persuasion* 1956, *The Trial* 1962, and *The Champagne Murders* 1967. He also appeared on the stage in London and New York.

Perkins Frances 1882–1965. US public official. She became the first female cabinet officer when she served as secretary of labor under F D Roosevelt 1933–45.

Under Truman she was a member of the federal civil service commission 1946–53.

Perm industrial city (shipbuilding, oil refining, aircraft, chemicals, lumber mills), and capital of Perm region, N Russia, on the Kama near the Ural Mountains; population (1987) 1,075,000. It was called Molotov 1940–57.

permafrost condition in which a deep layer of soil does not thaw out during the summer. Permafrost occurs under ◊periglacial conditions. It is claimed that 26% of the world's land surface is permafrost.

Permian period of geological time 290–245 million years ago, the last period of the Paleozoic era. Its end was marked by a significant change in marine life, including the extinction of many corals and trilobites. Deserts were widespread, and terrestrial amphibians and mammallike reptiles flourished. Cone-bearing plants (gymnosperms) came to prominence.

permutation in mathematics, a specified arrangement of a group of objects. It is the arrangement of *a* distinct objects taken *b* at a time in all possible orders. It is given by $a!/(a-b)!$, where "!" stands for ◊factorial. For example, the number of permutations of four letters taken from any group of six different letters is $6!/2! = (1 \times 2 \times 3 \times 4 \times 5 \times 6)/(1 \times 2) = 360$. The theoretical number of four-letter "words" that can be made from an alphabet of 26 letters is $26!/22! = 358,800$.

Perón (María Estela) Isabel (born Martínez) 1931– . President of Argentina 1974–76, and third wife of Juan Perón. She succeeded him after he died in office, but labor unrest, inflation, and political violence pushed the country to the brink of chaos. Accused of corruption, she was held under house arrest for five years. She went into exile in Spain.

Perón Juan Domingo 1895–1974. President of Argentina 1946–55 and 1973–74. A professional army officer, Perón took part in the right-wing military coup that toppled Argentina's government in 1943.

Perón María Eva (Evita) Duarte de 1919–1952. Argentinian populist leader, born in Buenos Aires. A successful film actress, she married Juan ◊Perón in 1945. When he became president the following year, she became his chief adviser and the unofficial minister of health and labor, devoting herself to helping the poor, improving education, and achieving women's suffrage. She was politically astute and sought the vice presidency in 1951 but was opposed by the army

and withdrew. After her death from cancer in 1952, Juan's political strength began to decline.

perpendicular in mathematics, at a right angle; also, a line at right angles to another or to a plane. For a pair of skew lines (lines in three dimensions that do not meet), there is just one common perpendicular, which is at right angles to both lines; the nearest points on the two lines are the feet of this perpendicular.

perpetual motion the idea that a machine can be designed and constructed in such a way that, once started, it will continue in motion indefinitely without requiring any further input of energy (motive power). Such a device contradicts the two laws of thermodynamics that state that (1) energy can neither be created nor destroyed (the law of conservation of energy) and (2) heat cannot by itself flow from a cooler to a hotter object. As a result, all practical (real) machines require a continuous supply of energy, and no heat engine is able to convert all the heat into useful work.

Perrault Charles 1628–1703. French author of the fairy tales *Contes de ma mère l'oye/Mother Goose's Fairy Tales* 1697, which include "Sleeping Beauty," "Little Red Riding Hood," "Blue Beard," "Puss in Boots," and "Cinderella."

Perrin Jean 1870–1942. French physicist who produced the crucial evidence that finally established the atomic nature of matter. Assuming the atomic hypothesis, Perrin demonstrated how the phenomenon of ◊Brownian motion could be used to derive precise values for ◊Avogadro's number. He was awarded the 1926 Nobel Prize for Physics.

Perry Matthew Calbraith 1794–1858. US naval officer, commander of the expedition of 1853 that reopened communication between Japan and the outside world after 250 years' isolation. A show of evident military superiority, the use of steamships (thought by the Japanese to be floating volcanoes), and an exhibition of US technical superiority enabled him to negotiate the Treaty of Kanagawa 1854, granting the US trading rights with Japan.

Perry Oliver Hazard 1785–1819. US naval officer. During the War of 1812 he played a decisive role in securing American control of Lake Erie. Ordered there in 1813, he was responsible for the decisive victory over the British at the Battle of Put-in-Bay and participated in the Battle of the Thames.

Persephone in Greek mythology, a goddess (Roman Proserpina), daughter of Zeus and Demeter. She was carried off to the underworld as the bride of Pluto, who later agreed that she should spend six months of the year above ground with her mother. The myth symbolizes the growth and decay of vegetation and the changing seasons.

Persepolis ancient royal city of the Persian Empire, 40 mi/65 km NE of Shiraz. It was burned down after its capture in 331 BC by Alexander the Great.

Perseus in Greek legend, son of Zeus and Danaë. He slew the ◊Gorgon Medusa and cut off her head, which he set in his shield. He then rescued and married ◊Andromeda, and became king of Tiryns.

Perseus in astronomy, a constellation of the northern hemisphere, near Cassiopeia, and represented as the mythological hero. The head of the decapitated Gorgon, Medusa, is marked by the variable star Algol. Perseus lies in the Milky Way and contains the Double Cluster, a twin cluster of stars. Every August the Perseid meteor shower radiates from its northern part.

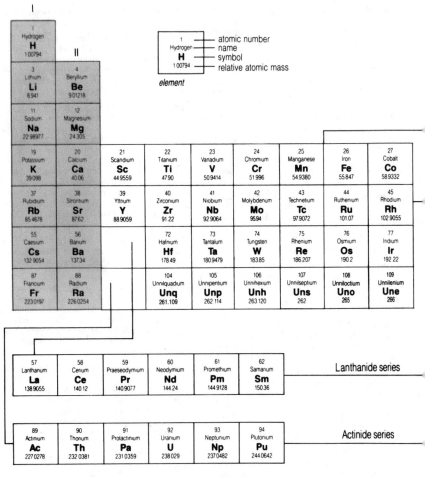

Pershing John Joseph 1860–1948. US general, who commanded the American Expeditionary Force sent to France 1917–18 during World War I. He was responsible for more than 2 million men and fought successfully to keep them a separate unit.

Persia, ancient kingdom in SW Asia. The early Persians were a nomadic ◊Aryan people who migrated through the Caucasus to the Iranian plateau.

7th century *BC* The Persians were established in the present region of Fars, which then belonged to the Assyrians. **550** *BC* Cyrus the Great overthrew the empire of the Medes, to whom the Persians had been subject, and founded the Persian Empire. **539** *BC* Having conquered all Anatolia, Cyrus added Babylonia (including Syria and Palestine) to his empire. **525** *BC* His son and successor Cambyses conquered Egypt. **521–485** *BC* Darius I organized an efficient centralized system of administration and extended Persian rule east into Afghanistan and NW India and as far north as the Danube, but the empire was weakened by internal dynastic struggles. **499–449** *BC* The Persian Wars with Greece ended Persian domination of the Aegean seaboard. **331** *BC* Alexander the Great drove the Persians under Darius III (died 330 *BC*) into retreat at Gaugmela on the Tigris, marking the end of the Persian Empire and the beginning of the Hellenistic period under the Seleucids. **250** *BC–AD* **230** The

Arsacid dynasty established Parthia as the leading power in the region. **224** The Sassanian Empire was established in Persia and annexed Parthia. **637** Arabs took the capital, Ctesiphon, and introduced Islam in place of Zoroastrianism. For modern history see ◊Iran.

Persian inhabitant of or native to Persia, now Iran, and referring to the culture and the language (see also ◊Persian language). The Persians are descended from central Asians of S Russia (◊Aryans), who migrated south into the region about 2000 BC.

Persian Gulf or ***Arabian Gulf*** large shallow inlet of the Arabian Sea; area 90,000 sq mi/233,000 sq km. It divides the Arabian peninsula from Iran and is linked by the Strait of Hormuz and the Gulf of Oman to the Arabian Sea. Oil fields surround it in the Gulf States of Bahrain, Iran, Iraq, Kuwait, Oman, Qatar, Saudi Arabia, and the United Arab Emirates.

Persian language member of the Indo-Iranian branch of the Indo-European language family and the official language of the state once known as Persia but now called Iran. Persian is known to its own speakers as ***Farsi***, the language of the province of Fars (Persia proper). It is written in a modified Arabic script, from right to left, and has a large mixture of Arabic religious, philosophical, and technical vocabulary.

								0
								2 Helium **He** 4.00260
			III	IV	V	VI	VII	
			5 Boron **B** 10.81	6 Carbon **C** 12.011	7 Nitrogen **N** 14.0067	8 Oxygen **O** 15.9994	9 Fluorine **F** 18.99840	10 Neon **Ne** 20.179
			13 Aluminium **Al** 26.98154	14 Silicon **Si** 28.086	15 Phosphorus **P** 30.97376P	16 Sulphur **S** 32.06	17 Chlorine **Cl** 35.453	18 Argon **Ar** 39.948
28 Nickel **Ni** 58.70	29 Copper **Cu** 63.546	30 Zinc **Zn** 65.38	31 Gallium **Ga** 69.72	32 Germanium **Ge** 72.59	33 Arsenic **As** 74.9216	34 Selenium **Se** 78.96	35 Bromine **Br** 79.904	36 Krypton **Kr** 83.80
46 Palladium **Pd** 106.4	47 Silver **Ag** 107.868	48 Cadmium **Cd** 112.40	49 Indium **In** 114.82	50 Tin **Sn** 118.69	51 Antimony **Sb** 121.75	52 Tellurium **Te** 127.75	53 Iodine **I** 126.9045	54 Xenon **Xe** 131.30
78 Platinum **Pt** 195.09	79 Gold **Au** 196.9665	80 Mercury **Hg** 200.59	81 Thallium **Tl** 204.37	82 Lead **Pb** 207.37	83 Bismuth **Bi** 207.2	84 Polonium **Po** 210	85 Astatine **At** 211	86 Radon **Rn** 222.0176

63 Europium **Eu** 151.96	64 Gadolinium **Gd** 157.25	65 Terbium **Tb** 158.9254	66 Dysprosium **Dy** 162.50	67 Holmium **Ho** 164.9304	68 Erbium **Er** 167.26	69 Thulium **Tm** 168.9342	70 Ytterbium **Yb** 173.04	71 Lutetium **Lu** 174.97

95 Americium **Am** 243.0614	96 Curium **Cm** 247.0703	97 Berkelium **Bk** 247.0703	98 Californium **Cf** 251.0786	99 Einsteinium **Es** 252.0828	100 Fermium **Fm** 257.0951	101 Mendelevium **Me** 258.0986	102 Nobelium **No** 259.1009	103 Lawrencium **Lr** 260.1054

Persian Wars series of conflicts between Greece and Persia 499–449 BC. The eventual victory of Greece marked the end of Persian domination of the ancient world and the beginning of Greek supremacy.

persimmon any tree of the genus *Diospyros* of the ebony family Ebenaceae, especially the common persimmon *D. virginiana* of the SE US. Up to 60 ft/19 m high, the persimmon has alternate oval leaves and yellow-green unisexual flowers. The small, sweet, orange fruits are edible.

personal computer (PC) another name for ◊microcomputer. The term is also used, more specifically, to mean the IBM Personal Computer and computers compatible with it.

personality individual's characteristic way of behaving across a wide range of situations. Two broad dimensions of personality are ◊extroversion and neuroticism. A number of more specific personal traits have also been described, including ◊psychopathy (antisocial behavior).

personification figure of speech (poetic or imaginative expression) in which animals, plants, objects, and ideas are treated as if they were human or alive ("Clouds chased each other across the face of the Moon"; "Nature smiled on their work and gave it her blessing"; "The future beckoned eagerly to them").

perspiration excretion of water and dissolved substances from the ◊sweat glands of the skin of mammals. Perspiration has two main functions: body cooling by the evaporation of water from the skin surface, and excretion of waste products such as salts.

Perth capital of Western Australia, with its port at nearby Fremantle on the Swan River; population (1990) 1,190,100. Products include textiles, cement, furniture, and vehicles. It was founded 1829 and is the commercial and cultural center of the state.

Peru country in South America, on the Pacific, bounded N by Ecuador and Colombia, E by Brazil and Bolivia, and S by Chile. *See panel p. 725*

Peru Current formerly known as *Humboldt Current* cold ocean ◊current flowing north from the Antarctic along the W coast of South America to S Ecuador, then west. It reduces the coastal temperature, making the W slopes of the Andes arid because winds are already chilled and dry when they meet the coast.

Perugino Pietro. Original name of Pietro Vannucci 1446–1523. Italian painter, active chiefly in Perugia. He taught Raphael who absorbed his soft and graceful figure style. Perugino produced paintings for the lower walls of the Sistine Chapel of the Vatican 1481 and in 1500 decorated the Sala del Cambio in Perugia.

Peshawar capital of North-West Frontier Province, Pakistan, 11 mi/18 km E of the Khyber Pass; population (1981) 555,000. Products include textiles, leather, and copper.

pest in biology, any insect, fungus, rodent, or other living organism that has a harmful effect on human beings, other than those that directly cause human diseases. Most pests damage crops or livestock, but the term also covers those that damage buildings, destroy food stores, and spread disease.

pesticide any chemical used in farming, gardening, or indoors to combat pests. Pesticides are of three main types: *insecticides* (to kill insects), *fungicides* (to kill fungal diseases), and *herbicides* (to kill plants, mainly those considered weeds). Pesticides cause a number of pollution problems through spray drift onto surrounding areas, direct contamination of users or the public, and as residues on food. The safest pesticides are those made from plants, such as the insecticides pyrethrum and derris.

Pétain Henri Philippe 1856–1951. French general and right-wing politician. His defense of Verdun 1916 during World War I made him a national hero. In World War II he became head of state June 1940 and signed an armistice with Germany. Removing the seat of government to Vichy, a health resort in central France, he established an authoritarian regime. He was imprisoned after the war.

With the Allied invasion he was taken to Germany, but returned 1945 and was sentenced to death for treason, the sentence being commuted to life imprisonment.

petal part of a flower whose function is to attract pollinators such as insects or birds. Petals are frequently large and brightly colored and may also be scented. Some have a nectary at the base and markings on the petal surface, known as honey guides, to direct pollinators to the source of the nectar. In wind-pollinated plants, however, the petals are usually small and insignificant, and sometimes absent altogether. Petals are derived from modified leaves, and are known collectively as a corolla.

Petaluma city in NW California, N of San Francisco, on the Petaluma River; population (1990) 43,200. It is an agricultural center for poultry and dairy products.

Peter three tsars of Russia, including:

Peter I *the Great* 1672–1725. Tsar of Russia from 1682 on the death of his brother Tsar Feodor; he assumed control of the government 1689. He attempted to reorganize the country on Western lines; the army was modernized, a fleet was built, the administrative and legal systems were remodeled, education was encouraged, and the church was brought under state control. On the Baltic coast, where he had conquered territory from Sweden, Peter built his new capital, St Petersburg.

Peter III 1728–1762. Tsar of Russia 1762. Weak-minded son of Peter I's eldest daughter, Anne, he was adopted 1741 by his aunt ◊Elizabeth, Empress of Russia, and at her command married the future Catherine II 1745. He was deposed in favor of his wife and probably murdered by her lover, Alexius Orlov.

Peter Pan or *The Boy Who Wouldn't Grow Up* play for children by James ◊Barrie, first performed in 1904. Peter Pan, an orphan with magical powers, arrives in the night nursery of the Darling children, Wendy, John, and Michael. He teaches them to fly and introduces them to the Never Never Land inhabited by fantastic characters, including the fairy Tinkerbell, the Lost Boys, and the pirate Captain Hook. The play was followed by a story, *Peter Pan in Kensington Gardens* 1906, and a book of the play 1911.

Peter, St Christian martyr, the author of two epistles in the New Testament and leader of the apostles. He is regarded as the first bishop of Rome, whose mantle the pope inherits. His real name was Simon, but he was nicknamed Kephas ("Peter," from the Greek for "rock") by Jesus, as being the rock upon which he would build his church. His emblem is two keys; feast day June 29.

Petersburg city in SE Virginia, on the Appomattox River, S of Richmond; population (1990) 38,400. Industries include tobacco products, textiles, leather products, boat building, and chemicals. It was the site of Fort Henry 1646, as well as of Revolutionary War and Civil War battles.

Petipa Marius 1818–1910. French choreographer who created some of the most important ballets in the Classical repertory. For the Imperial Ballet in Russia he created masterpieces such as *La Bayadère* 1877, *The Sleeping Beauty* 1890, *Swan Lake* 1895 (with Ivanov), and *Raymonda* 1898.

Petra (Arabic *Wadi Musa*) ancient city carved out of the red rock at a site in Jordan, on the E slopes of the Wadi el Araba, 56 mi/90 km S of the Dead Sea. An Edomite stronghold and capital of the Nabataeans in the 2nd century, it was captured by the Roman emperor Trajan 106 and destroyed by the Arabs in the 7th century. It was forgotten in Europe until 1812 when the Swiss traveler Jacob Burckhardt (1818–1897) came across it.

Petrarch (Italian *Petrarca*) Francesco 1304–1374. Italian poet, born in Arezzo, a devotee of the Classical tradition. His *Il Canzoniere* is composed of sonnets in praise of his idealized love, "Laura," whom he first saw 1327 (she was a married woman and refused to become his mistress).

petrochemical chemical derived from the processing of petroleum (crude oil). *Petrochemical industries* are those that obtain their raw materials from the processing of petroleum and natural gas. Polymers, detergents, solvents, and nitrogen fertilizers are all major products of the petrochemical industries. Inorganic chemical products include carbon black, sulfur, ammonia, and hydrogen peroxide.

petrodollars in economics, dollar earnings of nations that make up the ◊Organization of Petroleum-Exporting Countries (OPEC).

Petrograd former name (1914–24) of St Petersburg, a city in Russia.

petroleum or *crude oil* natural mineral oil, a thick greenish-brown flammable liquid found underground in permeable rocks. Petroleum consists of hydrocarbons mixed with oxygen, sulfur, nitrogen, and other elements in varying proportions. It is thought to be derived from ancient organic material that has been converted by, first, bacterial action, then heat and pressure (but its origin may be chemical also). From crude petroleum, various products are made by distillation and other processes; for example, fuel oil, gasoline, kerosene, diesel, lubricating oil, paraffin wax, and petroleum jelly.

petrology branch of geology that deals with the study of rocks, their mineral compositions, and their origins.

Peru
Republic of
(*República del Perú*)

area 496,216 sq mi/1,285,200 sq km
capital Lima, including port of Callao
cities Arequipa, Iquitos, Chiclayo, Trujillo
physical Andes mountains NW–SE cover 27% of Peru, separating Amazon river-basin jungle in NE from coastal plain in W; desert along coast N–S
environment an estimated 38% of the 3,100 sq mi/8,000 sq km of coastal lands under irrigation are either waterlogged or suffering from saline water. Only half the population has access to clean drinking water
features Lake Titicaca; Atacama Desert; Nazca lines, monuments of Machu Picchu, Chan Chan, Charín de Huantar
head of state and government Alberto Fujimori from 1990
political system democratic republic
political parties American Popular Revolutionary Alliance (APRA), moderate, left-wing; United Left (IU), left- wing; Change 90, centrist
exports coca, coffee, alpaca, llama and vicuña wool, fish meal, lead (largest producer in South America), copper, iron, oil
currency new sol

population (1992) 22,454,000 (Indian, mainly Quechua and Aymara, 46%; mixed Spanish–Indian descent 43%); growth rate 2.6% p.a.
life expectancy men 61, women 66
languages Spanish 68%, Quechua 27% (both official), Aymara 3%
religion Roman Catholic 90%
literacy men 91%, women 78% (1985 est)
GNP $19.6 bn (1988); $940 per head (1984)

chronology
1824 Independence achieved from Spain.
1849–74 Some 80,000–100,000 Chinese laborers arrived in Peru to fill menial jobs such as collecting guano.
1902 Boundary dispute with Bolivia settled.
1927 Boundary dispute with Colombia settled.
1942 Boundary dispute with Ecuador settled.
1948 Army coup, led by General Manuel Odría, installed a military government.
1963 Return to civilian rule, with Fernando Belaúnde Terry as president.
1968 Return of military government in a bloodless coup by General Juan Velasco Alvarado.
1975 Velasco replaced, in a bloodless coup, by General Morales Bermúdez.
1980 Return to civilian rule, with Fernando Belaúnde as president. Sendero Luminoso ("Shining Path") Maoist guerrilla group formed.
1981 Boundary dispute with Ecuador renewed.
1985 Belaúnde succeeded by Social Democrat Alan García Pérez.
1987 President García delayed the nationalization of Peru's banks after a vigorous campaign against the proposal.
1988 García pressured to seek help from the International Monetary Fund (IMF). Sendero Luminoso increased campaign of violence.
1989 Writer Mario Vargas Llosa entered presidential race; his Democratic Front won municipal elections Nov.
1990 Alberto Fujimori defeated Vargas Llosa in presidential elections. Assassination attempt on president failed.
1992 Two coup attempts against the government failed. US suspended humanitarian aid. Sendero Luminoso leader Abimael Guzman Reynoso was arrested and sentenced to life imprisonment after a show trial. Single-chamber legislature replaced two-chamber system.
1993 National congress voted to allow Fujimori to seek reelection in 1995.

Petronius Gaius, known as *Petronius Arbiter*, died *c.* AD 66. Roman author of the licentious romance *Satyricon*. He was a companion of the emperor Nero and supervisor of his pleasures.

pewter any of various alloys of mostly tin with varying amounts of lead, copper, or antimony. Pewter has been known for centuries and was once widely used for domestic utensils but is now used mainly for ornamental ware.

peyote spineless cactus *Lophopora williamsii* of N Mexico and the SW US. It has white or pink flowers. Its buttonlike tops contain the hallucinogen *mescaline*, which is used by American Indians in religious ceremonies.

pH scale from 0 to 14 for measuring acidity or alkalinity. A pH of 7.0 indicates neutrality, below 7 is acid, while above 7 is alkaline. Strong acids, such as those used in automobile batteries, have a pH of about 2; strong alkalis such as sodium hydroxide are pH 13.

Phaedra in Greek legend, a Cretan, daughter of Minos and Pasiphae, married to Theseus of Athens.

Her adulterous passion for her stepson, Hippolytus, led to her death. The story is told in plays by Euripides, Seneca, and Racine.

Phaethon in Greek mythology, the son of Helios, the Sun god, who was allowed for one day to drive the chariot of the Sun. Losing control of the horses, he almost set the Earth on fire and was killed by Zeus with a thunderbolt.

phagocyte type of white blood cell, or leukocyte, that can engulf a bacterium or other invading microorganism. Phagocytes are found in blood, lymph, and other body tissues, where they also ingest foreign matter and dead tissue. A macrophage differs in size and life span.

Phalangist member of a Lebanese military organization (*Phalanges Libanaises*), since 1958 the political and military force of the ◊Maronite Church in Lebanon. The Phalangists' unbending right-wing policies and resistance to the introduction of democratic institutions were among the contributing factors.

Phanerozoic (Greek *phanero* "visible") eon in Earth history, consisting of the most recent 570 million years. It comprises the Paleozoic, Mesozoic, and Cenozoic eras. The vast majority of fossils come from this eon, owing to the evolution of hard shells and internal skeletons. The name means "interval of well-displayed life."

Pharaoh Hebrew form of the Egyptian royal title Per-'o. This term, meaning "great house," was originally applied to the royal household, and after about 950 BC to the king.

Pharisee (Hebrew "separatist") member of an ancient Hebrew political party and sect of Judaism that formed in Roman-occupied Palestine in the 2nd century BC in protest against all movements favoring Hellenization. The Pharisees were the party of the common man, standing for rabbi, prayer, and synagogue. They were opposed by the aristocratic ◊Sadducees.

pharmacology study of the origins, applications, and effects of chemical substances on living organisms. Products of the pharmaceutical industry range from aspirin to anticancer agents.

pharynx interior of the throat, the cavity at the back of the mouth. Its walls are made of muscle strengthened with a fibrous layer and lined with mucous membrane. The internal nostrils lead backward into the pharynx, which continues downward into the esophagus and (through the epiglottis) into the windpipe. On each side, a Eustachian tube enters the pharynx from the middle ear cavity.

phase in physics, a stage in an oscillatory motion, such as a wave motion: two waves are in phase when their peaks and their troughs coincide. Otherwise, there is a *phase difference*, which has consequences in ◊interference phenomena and ◊alternating current electricity.

PhD abbreviation for the degree of *Doctor of Philosophy*.

pheasant any of various large, colorful Asiatic fowls of the family Phasianidae, which also includes grouse, quail, and turkey. The plumage of the male Eurasian ring-necked or common pheasant *Phasianus colchicus* is richly tinted with brownish-green, yellow, and red markings, but the female is a camouflaged brownish color. The nest is made on the ground. The male is polygamous.

phencyclidine hydrochloride (PCP) technical name for ◊angel dust.

phenomenology the philosophical perspective, founded by the German philosopher Edmund ◊Husserl, that concentrates on phenomena as objects of perception (rather than as facts or occurrences that exist independently) in attempting to examine the ways people think about and interpret the world around them. It has been practiced by the philosophers Martin Heidegger, Jean-Paul Sartre, and Maurice Merleau-Ponty.

Phidias mid-5th century BC. Greek Classical sculptor. He supervised the sculptural program for the Parthenon (most of it is preserved in the British Museum, London, and known as the *Elgin marbles*). He also executed the colossal statue of Zeus at Olympia, one of the Seven Wonders of the World.

Philadelphia industrial city and the world's largest freshwater port, on the Delaware River at the junction of the Schuylkill River, in Pennsylvania; population (1990) 1,585,600, metropolitan area 5,899,300. Products include refined oil, chemicals, textiles, processed food, printing and publishing, and transportation equipment. It is also a major port of entry and a financial, corporate, and research center. The University of Pennsylvania, the Franklin Institute, and Temple University are here, and the Philadelphia Orchestra and Museum of Art are among the nation's finest. Independence National Historic Park contains Independence Hall (1732–59), where the Declaration of Independence was adopted 1776, and the Liberty Bell.

philately the collection and study of postage stamps. It originated as a hobby in France about 1860.

Philby Kim (Harold) 1912–1988. British intelligence officer from 1940 and Soviet agent from 1933. He was liaison officer in Washington 1949–51, when he was confirmed to be a double agent and asked to resign. Named in 1963 as having warned Guy Burgess and Donald Maclean (similarly double agents) that their activities were known, he fled to the USSR and became a Soviet citizen and general in the KGB. A fourth member of the ring was Anthony Blunt.

Philip "King." Name given to Metacomet by the English c. 1639–1676. American chief of the Wampanoag people. During the growing tension over Indian versus settlers' land rights, Philip was arrested and his people were disarmed 1671. Full-scale hostilities culminated in "King Philip's War" 1675, and Philip was defeated and murdered 1676. Although costly to the English, King Philip's War ended Indian resistance in New England.

Philip Duke of Edinburgh 1921– . Prince of the UK, husband of Elizabeth II, a grandson of George I of Greece and a great-great-grandson of Queen Victoria. He was born in Corfu, Greece but brought up in England.

A naturalized British subject, taking the surname Mountbatten, he married Princess Elizabeth (from 1952 Queen Elizabeth II) in 1947, having the previous day received the title Duke of Edinburgh.

Philip six kings of France, including:

Philip II (Philip Augustus) 1165–1223. King of France from 1180. As part of his efforts to establish a strong monarchy and evict the English from their French possessions, he waged war in turn against the English kings Henry II, Richard I (with whom he also went on the Third Crusade), and John (against whom he won the decisive battle of Bouvines in Flanders 1214).

Philip IV *the Fair* 1268–1314. King of France from 1285. He engaged in a feud with Pope Boniface VIII and made him a prisoner 1303. Clement V (1264–1314), elected pope through Philip's influence 1305, moved the papal seat to Avignon 1309 and collaborated with Philip to suppress the ◊Templars, a powerful order of knights. Philip allied with the Scots against England and invaded Flanders.

Philip II of Macedon 382–336 BC. King of ◊Macedonia from 359 BC. He seized the throne from his nephew, for whom he was regent, defeated the Greek city-states at the battle of Chaeronea (in central Greece) 338 and formed them into a league whose forces could be united against Persia. He was assassinated while he was planning this expedition, and was succeeded by his son ◊Alexander the Great.

Philip five kings of Spain, including:

Philip II 1527–1598. King of Spain from 1556. He was born at Valladolid, the son of the Hapsburg emperor

Philippines
Republic of the
(*Republika ng Pilipinas*)

area 115,800 sq mi/300,000 sq km
capital Manila (on Luzon)
cities Quezon City (Luzon), Zamboanga (Mindanao); ports Cebu, Davao (on Mindanao), and Iloilo
physical comprises over 7,000 islands; volcanic mountain ranges traverse main chain N–S; 50% still forested. The largest islands are Luzon 41,754 sq mi/108,172 sq km and Mindanao 36,372 sq mi/94,227 sq km; others include Samar, Negros, Palawan, Panay, Mindoro, Leyte, Cebu, and the Sulu group
environment cleared for timber, tannin, and the creation of fish ponds, the mangrove forest was reduced from 1,930 sq mi/5,000 sq km to 146 sq mi/380 sq km between 1920 and 1988
features Luzon, site of Clark Field, US air base used as a logistical base in Vietnam War; Subic Bay, US naval base; Pinatubo volcano (5,770 ft/1,759 m); Mindanao has active volcano Apo (9,690 ft/2,954 m) and mountainous rain forest
head of state and government Fidel Ramos from 1992
political system emergent democracy
political parties People's Power, including the PDP–Laban Party and the Liberal Party, centrist pro-Aquino; Nationalist Party, Union for National Action (UNA), and Grand Alliance for Democracy (GAD), conservative opposition groupings; Mindanao Alliance, island-based decentralist body
exports sugar, copra (world's largest producer) and coconut oil, timber, copper concentrates, electronics, clothing
currency peso
population (1992) 63,609,000 (93% Malaysian); growth rate 2.4% p.a.
life expectancy men 63, women 69 (1989)
languages Tagalog (Filipino, official); English and Spanish
religions Roman Catholic 84%, Protestant 9%, Muslim 5%
literacy 88% (1989)
GNP $38.2 bn; $667 per head (1988)

chronology
1542 Named the Philippines (Filipinas) by Spanish explorers.
1565 Conquered by Spain.
1898 Ceded to the US after Spanish–American War.
1935 Granted internal self-government.
1942–45 Occupied by Japan.
1946 Independence achieved from US.
1965 Ferdinand Marcos elected president.
1983 Opposition leader Benigno Aquino murdered by military guard.
1986 Marcos overthrown by Corazon Aquino's People's Power movement.
1987 "Freedom constitution" adopted, giving Aquino mandate to rule until June 1992; People's Power won majority in congressional elections. Attempted right-wing coup suppressed. Communist guerrillas active. Government in rightward swing.
1988 Land Reform Act gave favorable compensation to holders of large estates.
1989 Referendum on southern autonomy failed; Marcos died in exile; Aquino refused his burial in Philippines. Sixth coup attempt suppressed with US aid; Aquino declared state of emergency.
1990 Seventh coup attempt survived by President Aquino.
1991 June: eruption of Mount Pinatubo, hundreds killed. US agreed to give up Clark Field airbase but keep Subic Bay naval base for ten more years. Sept: Philippines Senate voted to urge withdrawal of all US forces. US renewal of Subic Bay lease rejected. Nov: Imelda Marcos returned.
1992 Fidel Ramos elected to replace Aquino.

Charles V, and in 1554 married Queen Mary of England. On his father's abdication 1556 he inherited Spain, the Netherlands, and the Spanish possessions in Italy and the Americas, and in 1580 he annexed Portugal. His intolerance and lack of understanding of the Netherlanders drove them into revolt. Political and religious differences combined to involve him in war with England and, after 1589, with France. The defeat of the ◊Spanish Armada (the fleet sent to invade England in 1588) marked the beginning of the decline of Spanish power.

Philip V 1683–1746. King of Spain from 1700. A grandson of Louis XIV of France, he was the first Bourbon king of Spain. He was not recognized by the major European powers until 1713. See ◊Spanish Succession, War of the.

Philip Neri, St 1515–1595. Italian Roman Catholic priest who organized the Congregation of the Oratory. He built the oratory over the church of St Jerome, Rome, where prayer meetings were held and scenes from the Bible performed with music, originating the musical form ◊oratorio. Feast day May 26.

Philippi ancient city of Macedonia founded by Philip of Macedon 358 BC. Near Philippi, Mark Antony and Augustus defeated Brutus and Cassius 42 BC.

Philippines country in SE Asia, on an archipelago of more than 7,000 islands W of the Pacific Ocean and S of the SE Asian mainland.

Philip, St 1st century AD. In the New Testament, one of the 12 apostles. He was an inhabitant of Bethsaida (N Israel), and is said to have worked as a missionary in Anatolia. Feast day May 3.

Philistine member of a seafaring people of non-Semitic origin who founded city-states on the Palestinian coastal plain in the 12th century BC, adopting a Semitic language and religion. They were at war with the Israelites in the 11th–10th centuries BC. They were largely absorbed into the kingdom of Israel under King David, about 1000 BC, and later came under Assyrian rule.

Phillips Wendell 1811–1884. US reformer. After attending the World Anti-Slavery Convention in London 1840, he became an outspoken proponent of the abolition of slavery. In addition to abolition he espoused a variety of other social causes, including feminism, prohibition, unionization, and improved treatment of American Indians.

Philosophes the leading intellectuals of pre-revolutionary 18th-century France, including Condorcet,

Diderot, Rousseau, and Voltaire. Their role in furthering the principles of the enlightenment and extolling the power of human reason made them question the structures of the *ancien régime,* and they were held responsible by some for influencing the revolutionaries of 1789.

philosophy (Greek "love of wisdom") branch of learning that includes metaphysics (the nature of being), epistemology (theory of knowledge), logic (study of valid inference), ethics, and aesthetics. Philosophy is concerned with fundamental problems—including the nature of mind and matter, perception, self, free will, causation, time and space, and the existence of moral judgments—which cannot be resolved by a specific method.

phlebitis inflammation of a vein. It is sometimes associated with blockage by a blood clot (◊thrombosis), in which case it is more accurately described as thrombophlebitis.

phlox any plant of the genus *Phlox*, native to North America and Siberia. Phloxes are small with alternate leaves and showy white, pink, red, or purple flowers.
Woodland phlox *P. divaricata* is native to central US.

Phnom Penh capital of Cambodia, on the Mekong River, 130 mi/210 km NW of Saigon; population (1989) 800,000. Industries include textiles and food-processing.
On April 17, 1975, the entire population (about 3 million) was forcibly evacuated by the Khmer Rouge communist movement; survivors later returned.

phobia excessive irrational fear of an object or situation—for example, agoraphobia (fear of open spaces and crowded places), acrophobia (fear of heights), claustrophobia (fear of enclosed places). Behavior therapy is one form of treatment.

Phobos one of the two moons of Mars, discovered 1877 by the US astronomer Asaph Hall (1829–1907). It is an irregularly shaped lump of rock, cratered by ◊meteorite impacts. Phobos is $17 \times 13 \times 12$ mi/$27 \times 22 \times 19$ km across, and orbits Mars every 0.32 days at a distance of 5,840 mi/9,400 km from the planet's center. It is thought to be an asteroid captured by Mars' gravity.

Phoenicia ancient Greek name for N ◊Canaan on the E coast of the Mediterranean. The Phoenician civilization flourished from about 1200 until the capture of Tyre by Alexander the Great in 332 BC. Seafaring traders and artisans, they are said to have circumnavigated Africa and established colonies in Cyprus, N Africa (for example, Carthage), Malta, Sicily, and Spain. Their cities (Tyre, Sidon, and Byblos were the main ones) were independent states ruled by hereditary kings but dominated by merchant ruling classes.

phoenix mythical Egyptian bird that burned itself to death on a pyre every 500 years and rose rejuvenated from the ashes.

Phoenix capital of Arizona; industrial city (steel, aluminum, electrical goods, food processing) and tourist center on the Salt River; population (1990) 983,400.
Settled 1868, Phoenix became the territorial capital 1889. The completion of a dam 1912 provided the water and power needed for economic development. Tremendous growth, beginning in the 1940s, has transformed Phoenix from what was largely a health resort and retirement community into a major economic center.

phonetics identification, description, and classification of sounds used in articulate speech. These sounds are codified in the International Phonetic Alphabet (a highly modified version of the English/Roman alphabet).

phonograph alternate name for ◊record player.

phony war the period in World War II between Oct 1939, when the Germans had occupied Poland, and April 1940, when the invasions of Denmark and Norway took place. During this time there were few signs of hostilities in Western Europe; indeed, Hitler made some attempts to arrange a peace settlement with Britain and France.

phosphate salt or ester of ◊phosphoric acid. Incomplete neutralization of phosphoric acid gives rise to acid phosphates (see ◊acid salts and ◊buffer). Phosphates are used as fertilizers, and are required for the development of healthy root systems. They are involved in many biochemical processes, often as part of complex molecules, such as ◊ATP.

phosphor any substance that is phosphorescent, that is, gives out visible light when it is illuminated by a beam of electrons or ultraviolet light. The television screen is coated on the inside with phosphors that glow when beams of electrons strike them. Fluorescent lamp tubes are also phosphor-coated. Phosphors are also used in Day-Glo paints, and as optical brighteners in detergents.

phosphorescence in physics, the emission of light by certain substances after they have absorbed energy, whether from visible light, other electromagnetic radiation such as ultraviolet rays or X-rays, or cathode rays (a beam of electrons). When the stimulating energy is removed phosphorescence ceases, although it may persist for a short time after (unlike ◊fluorescence, which stops immediately).

phosphorus (Greek *phosphoros* "bearer of light") highly reactive, nonmetallic element, symbol P, atomic number 15, atomic weight 30.9738. It occurs in nature as phosphates (commonly in the form of the mineral ◊apatite), and is essential to plant and animal life. Compounds of phosphorus are used in fertilizers, various organic chemicals, for matches and fireworks, and in glass and steel.

photocell or *photoelectric cell* device for measuring or detecting light or other electromagnetic radiation, since its electrical state is altered by the effect of light. In a *photoemissive* cell, the radiation causes electrons to be emitted and a current to flow (photoelectric effect); a *photovoltaic* cell causes an ◊electromotive force to be generated in the presence of light across the boundary of two substances. A *photoconductive* cell, which contains a semiconductor, increases its conductivity when exposed to electromagnetic radiation.

photochemical reaction any chemical reaction in which light is produced or light initiates the reaction. Light can initiate reactions by exciting atoms or molecules and making them more reactive: the light energy becomes converted to chemical energy. Many photochemical reactions set up a ◊chain reaction and produce ◊free radicals.

photocopier machine that uses some form of photographic process to reproduce copies of documents or illustrations. Most modern photocopiers, as pioneered by the Xerox Corporation, use electrostatic photocopying, or ◊xerography ("dry writing"). This employs a drum coated with a light-sensitive material

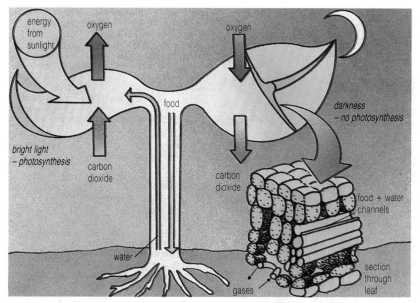

photosynthesis
Process by which green plants and some bacteria manufacture carbohydrates from water and atmospheric carbon dioxide, using the energy of sunlight.

such as selenium, which holds a pattern of static electricity charges corresponding to the dark areas of an image projected on to the drum by a lens. Finely divided pigment (toner) of opposite electric charge sticks to the charged areas of the drum and is transferred to a sheet of paper, which is heated briefly to melt the toner and stick it to the paper.

photography process for reproducing images on sensitized materials by various forms of radiant energy, including visible light, ultraviolet, infrared, X-rays, atomic radiations, and electron beams.

photogravure ◊printing process that uses a plate prepared photographically, covered with a pattern of recessed cells in which the ink is held. See ◊gravure.

photon in physics, the ◊elementary particle or "package" (quantum) of energy in which light and other forms of electromagnetic radiation are emitted. The photon has both particle and wave properties; it has no charge, is considered massless but possesses momentum and energy. It is one of the gauge bosons, a particle that cannot be subdivided, and is the carrier of the ◊electromagnetic force, one of the fundamental forces of nature.

photosynthesis process by which green plants trap light energy and use it to drive a series of chemical reactions, leading to the formation of carbohydrates. All animals ultimately depend on photosynthesis because it is the method by which the basic food (sugar) is created. For photosynthesis to occur, the plant must possess ◊chlorophyll and must have a supply of carbon dioxide and water. Actively photosynthesizing green plants store excess sugar as starch (this can be tested for in the laboratory using iodine).

phototropism movement of part of a plant toward or away from a source of light. Leaves are positively phototropic, detecting the source of light and orientating themselves to receive the maximum amount.

Phrygia former kingdom of W Asia covering the Anatolian plateau. It was inhabited in ancient times by an Indo-European people and achieved great prosperity in the 8th century BC under a line of kings bearing in turn the names Gordius and Midas, but then fell under Lydian rule. From Phrygia the cult of the Earth goddess Cybele was introduced into Greece and Rome.

Phyfe Duncan c. 1768–1854. Scottish-born US furniture maker. Establishing his own workshop in New York City 1792, he gained a national reputation. Although derived from earlier English and Greco-Roman designs, the Phyfe style was distinctive in its simplicity of line with elaborate ornamentation and carving. In 1837 he reorganized his firm as Duncan Phyfe and Sons.

phylum (plural *phyla*) major grouping in biological classification. Mammals, birds, reptiles, amphibians, fishes, and tunicates belong to the phylum Chordata; the phylum Molluska consists of snails, slugs, mussels, clams, squid, and octopuses; the phylum Porifera contains sponges; and the phylum Echinodermata includes sea stars, sea urchins, and sea cucumbers. Among plants there are between four and nine phyla (or divisions) depending on the classification used. Related phyla are grouped together in a ◊kingdom; phyla are subdivided into ◊classes.

physical chemistry branch of chemistry concerned with examining the relationships between the chemical compositions of substances and the physical properties that they display. Most chemical reactions exhibit some physical phenomenon (change of state, temperature, pressure, or volume, or the use or production of electricity), and the measurement and study of such phenomena has led to many chemical theories and laws.

physics branch of science concerned with the laws that govern the structure of the universe, and the forms of matter and energy and their interactions. For convenience, physics is often divided into branches such as nuclear physics, particle physics, solid- and liquid-state physics, electricity, electronics, magnetism, optics, acoustics, heat, and thermodynamics. Before the 20th century, physics was known as *natural philosophy*.

physiology branch of biology that deals with the functioning of living animals, as opposed to anatomy, which studies their structures.

Picasso The Three Dancers *(1925), Tate Gallery, London.*

Picardy (French *Picardie*) region of N France, including Aisne, Oise, and Somme *départements*
area 7,488 sq mi/19,400 sq km
population (1986) 1,774,000
products chemicals and metals
history in the 13th century the name Picardy was used to describe the feudal smallholdings N of Paris added to the French crown by Philip II. During the Hundred Years' War the area was hotly contested by France and England, but it was eventually occupied by Louis XI 1477. Picardy once more became a major battlefield in World War I.

picaresque (Spanish *pícaro* "rogue") novel consisting of a series of adventures befalling the central character, usually a lovable rogue. The genre originated in Spain and was popular in the 18th century in Britain. Daniel Defoe's *Moll Flanders*, Henry Fielding's *Tom Jones*, and Mark Twain's *Huckleberry Finn* are typical picaresque novels.

Picasso Pablo 1881–1973. Spanish artist, active chiefly in France, one of the most inventive and prolific talents in 20th-century art. His Blue Period 1901–04 and Rose Period 1905–06 preceded the revolutionary *Les Demoiselles d'Avignon* 1907 (Metropolitan Museum of Art, New York), which paved the way for Cubism. In the early 1920s he was considered a leader of the Surrealist movement. In the 1930s his work included metal sculpture, book illustration, and the mural *Guernica* 1937 (Casón del Buen Retiro, Madrid), a comment on the bombing of civilians in the Spanish Civil War. He continued to paint into his eighties.

piccolo woodwind instrument, the smallest member of the ◊flute family.

Pickett George Edward 1825–1875. US military leader. At the outbreak of the American Civil War 1861, he joined the Confederate army, rising to the rank of brigadier general 1862. Although he saw action in many battles, he is best remembered for leading the bloody, doomed "Pickett's Charge" at Gettysburg 1863.

Pickford Mary. Adopted name of Gladys Mary Smith. 1893–1979. Canadian-born US actress. The first star of the silent screen, she was known as "America's Sweetheart," and played innocent ingenue roles into her thirties. She and her second husband (from 1920), Douglas ◊Fairbanks, Sr, were known as "the world's sweethearts." With her husband and Charlie ◊Chaplin, she founded United Artists studio 1919. For many years she was the wealthiest and most influential woman in Hollywood.

Pict Roman term for a member of the peoples of N Scotland, possibly meaning "painted" (tattooed). Of pre-Celtic origin, and speaking a non-Celtic language, the Picts are thought to have inhabited much of England before the arrival of the Celtic Britons. They were united with the Celtic Scots under the rule of Kenneth MacAlpin 844.

pidgin English originally a trade jargon to establish contact between the British and the Chinese in the 19th century, but now commonly and loosely used to mean any kind of "broken" or "native" version of the English language.

pidgin language any of various trade jargons, contact languages, or ◊lingua francas arising in ports and markets where people of different linguistic backgrounds meet for commercial and other purposes. Usually a pidgin language is a rough blend of the vocabulary of one (often dominant) language with the syntax or grammar of one or more other (often depen-

physiotherapy treatment of injury and disease by physical means such as exercise, heat, manipulation, massage, and electrical stimulation.

Piaf Edith. Adopted name of Edith Gassion 1915–1963. French singer and songwriter, a cabaret singer in Paris from the late 1930s. She is remembered for the defiant song "Je ne regrette rien/I Regret Nothing" and "La Vie en rose" 1946.

Piaget Jean 1896–1980. Swiss psychologist distinguished by his studies of child development in relation to thought processes, and concepts of space, time, causality, and objectivity. Piaget believed this was a vital framework for studying human intelligence and he stressed the interaction of biological and environmental factors.

piano or *pianoforte* stringed musical instrument, played by felt-covered hammers activated from a keyboard, and capable of soft (piano) or loud (forte) tones, hence its name. The first piano was constructed 1704 and introduced 1709 by Bartolommeo Cristofori, a harpsichord-maker of Padua. It uses a clever mechanism to make the keyboard touch-sensitive. Extensively developed during the 18th century, the piano attracted admiration among many composers, although it was not until 1768 that Johann Christian Bach gave one of the first public recitals on the instrument.

Piano Renzo 1939– . Italian architect who designed (with Richard Rogers) the Pompidou Center, Paris, completed 1977. Among his other buildings are the Kansai Airport, Osaka, Japan and a sports stadium in Bari, Italy, both using new materials and making imaginative use of civil-engineering techniques.

dent) groups. Pidgin English in various parts of the world, *français petit negre*, and Bazaar Hindi or Hindustani are examples of pidgins that have served long-term purposes to the extent of being acquired by children as one of their everyday languages. At this point they become ◊creole languages.

Piedmont (Italian *Piemonte*) region of N Italy, bordering Switzerland to the N and France to the W, and surrounded, except to the E, by the Alps and the Apennines; area 9,804 sq mi/25,400 sq km; population (1990) 4,356,200. Its capital is Turin, and cities include Alessandria, Asti, Vercelli, and Novara. It also includes the fertile Po river valley. Products include fruit, grain, cattle, automobiles, and textiles. The movement for the unification of Italy started in the 19th century in Piedmont, under the house of Savoy.

Pierce Franklin 1804–1869. 14th president of the US, 1852–56. A Democrat, he held office in the US House of Representatives 1833–37, and the US Senate 1837–42. Chosen as a compromise candidate of the Democratic party, he was elected president 1852. Despite his expansionist foreign policy, North–South tensions grew more intense, and Pierce was denied renomination 1856.

Piero della Francesca *c.* 1420–1492. Italian painter, active in Arezzo and Urbino; one of the major artists of the 15th century. His work has a solemn stillness and unusually solid figures, luminous color, and compositional harmony. It includes a fresco series, *The Legend of the True Cross* (S Francesco, Arezzo), begun about 1452. Piero wrote two treatises, one on mathematics, one on the laws of perspective in painting.

Pierre capital of South Dakota, located in the central part of the state, on the Missouri River, near the geographical center of North America; population (1990) 12,900. Industries include tourism and grain and dairy products. As Fort Pierre in the early 1800s, it served as a fur-trading post; in the late 1800s it was a supply center for gold miners.

Pietism religious movement within Lutheranism in the 17th century which emphasized spiritual and devotional faith rather than theology and dogma. It was founded by Philipp Jakob Spener (1635–1705), a minister in Frankfurt, Germany, who emphasized devotional meetings for "groups of the Elect" rather than biblical learning; he wrote the *Pia Desideria* 1675. The movement was for many years associated with the University of Halle (founded 1694), Germany.

pig any even-toed hoofed mammal of the family Suidae. They are omnivorous, and have simple, non-ruminating stomachs and thick hides. The Middle Eastern *wild boar Sus scrofa* is the ancestor of domesticated breeds; it is 4.5 ft/1.5 m long and 3 ft/1 m high, with formidable tusks, but not naturally aggressive.

pigeon any bird of the family Columbidae, sometimes also called doves, distinguished by their large crops, which, becoming glandular in the breeding season, secrete a milky fluid ("pigeon's milk") that aids digestion of food for the young. They are found worldwide.

pigeon hawk another name for the merlin, a small ◊falcon.

pike any of a family Esocidae in the order Salmoniformes, of slender, freshwater bony fishes with narrow pointed heads and sharp, pointed teeth. The northern pike *Esox lucius*, of North America and Eurasia, may reach 7 ft/2.2 m and 20 lb/9 kg.

Piero della Francesca Baptism of Christ *by Piero della Francesca (c. 1439), National Gallery, London.*

Pike Zebulon Montgomery 1779–1813. US explorer and military leader. In 1806 he was sent to explore the Arkansas River and to contest Spanish presence in the area. After crossing Colorado and failing to reach the summit of the peak later named after him, he was captured by the Spanish, who released him 1807. Promoted to brigadier general, he was killed in action in the War of 1812.

Pilate Pontius early 1st century AD. Roman procurator of Judea AD 26–36. The New Testament Gospels describe his reluctant ordering of Jesus' crucifixion, but there has been considerable debate about his actual role in it.

pilgrimage journey to sacred places inspired by religious devotion. For Hindus, the holy places include Varanasi and the purifying river Ganges; for Buddhists, the places connected with the crises of Buddha's career; for the ancient Greeks, the shrines at Delphi and Ephesus among others; for Jews, the sanctuary at Jerusalem; and for Muslims, Mecca.

Pilgrims the emigrants who sailed from Plymouth, England, in the *Mayflower* on Sept 16, 1620, to found the first colony in New England at New Plymouth, Massachusetts. Of the 102 passengers, about a third were English Puritan refugees escaping religious persecution from Anglican England.

Pilgrim's Progress allegory by John Bunyan, published 1678–84, that describes the journey through life to the Celestial City of a man called Christian. On his way through the Slough of Despond, the House Beautiful, Vanity Fair, Doubting Castle, and other landmarks, he meets a number of allegorical figures.

This work was often the only other book an American pioneer family owned and read, besides the Bible.

Pill, the commonly used term for the contraceptive pill, based on female hormones. The combined pill, which contains synthetic hormones similar to estrogen and progesterone, stops the production of eggs, and makes the mucus produced by the cervix hostile to sperm. It is the most effective form of contraception apart from sterilization, being more than 99% effective.

pilotfish small marine fish *Naucrates ductor* of the family Carangidae, which also includes pompanos. It hides below sharks, turtles, or boats, using the shade as a base from which to prey on smaller fish. It is found in all warm oceans and grows to about 1.2 ft/36 cm.

pimento or *allspice* tree found in tropical parts of the New World. The dried fruits of the species *Pimenta dioica* are used as a spice. Also, a sweet variety of ◊capsicum pepper (more correctly spelled *pimiento*).

pimpernel any plant of the genus *Anagallis* of the primrose family Primulaceae comprising about 30 species mostly native to W Europe. The European scarlet pimpernel *A. arvensis* grows in cornfields, the flowers opening only in full sunshine. It is naturalized in North America.

Pinatubo, Mount active volcano on Luzon Island, the Philippines, 55 mi/88 km N of Manila. Dormant for 600 years, it erupted June 1991, killing 343 people and leaving as many as 200,000 homeless. Surrounding rice fields were covered with 10 ft/3 m of volcanic ash.

Pindling Lynden (Oscar) 1930– . Bahamian prime minister 1967–92. After studying law in London, he returned to the island to join the newly formed Progressive Liberal Party and then became the first black prime minister of the Bahamas.

pine any coniferous tree of the genus *Pinus*, family Pinaceae. There are 70–100 species, of which about 35 are native to North America. These are generally divided into two groupings: the soft pines and the hard pines. The former have needles in bundles of five and stalked cones without prickles; for example, eastern white pine *P. strobus*. Hard pines usually have needles in bundles of two or three and prickly cones; for example, jack pine *P. banksiana*. The oldest living species is probably the bristlecone pine *P. aristata*, native to California, of which some specimens are said to be 4,600 years old.

pineal body or *pineal gland* a cone-shaped outgrowth of the vertebrate brain. In some lower vertebrates, it develops a rudimentary lens and retina, which show it to be derived from an eye, or pair of eyes, situated on the top of the head in ancestral vertebrates. In fishes that can change color to match the background, the pineal perceives the light level and controls the color change. In birds, the pineal detects changes in daylight and stimulates breeding behavior as spring approaches. Mammals also have a pineal gland, but it is located deeper within the brain. It secretes a hormonelike substance, melatonin, thought to influence rhythms of activity. In humans, it is a small piece of tissue attached to the posterior wall of the third ventricle of the brain.

pineapple plant *Ananas comosus* of the bromeliad family, native to South and Central America, but now cultivated in many other tropical areas, such as Hawaii and Queensland, Australia. The mauvish flowers are produced in the second year, and subsequently consolidate with their bracts into a fleshy fruit.

Pine Bluff city in SE Arkansas, on the Arkansas River, SE of Little Rock, seat of Jefferson County; population (1990) 57,100.
Industries include paper, cotton, grain, and furniture.

pink any annual or perennial plant of the genus *Dianthus* of the family Carophyllaceae. The stems have characteristically swollen nodes, and the flowers range in color from white through pink to purple.

Members of the pink family include carnations, sweet williams, and baby's breath *Gypsophila paniculata*.

Pinkerton Allan 1819–1884. US detective, born in Glasgow, Scotland. He founded Pinkerton's National Detective Agency 1852 and built up the federal secret service from the espionage system he developed during the American Civil War. He thwarted an early assassination plot against Abraham ◊Lincoln and compiled the nation's most complete files on criminal activity. His agency became increasingly involved in the suppression of labor unrest. His men fought brutal battles against striking steelworkers 1892 and the ◊Molly Maguires.

Pink Floyd British psychedelic rock group, formed 1965. The original members were Syd Barrett (1946–), Roger Waters (1944–), Richard Wright (1945–), and Nick Mason (1945–). Their albums include *The Dark Side of the Moon* 1973 and *The Wall* 1979, with its spin-off film starring Bob Geldof.

pinnate leaf leaf that is divided up into many small leaflets, arranged in rows along either side of a midrib, as in ash trees (*Fraxinus*). It is a type of compound leaf. Each leaflet is known as a *pinna*, and where the pinnae are themselves divided, the secondary divisions are known as pinnules.

Pinocchio fantasy for children by Carlo Collodi, published in Italy 1883 and in an English translation 1892. It tells the story of a wooden puppet that comes to life and assumes the characteristics of a human boy. Pinocchio's nose grows longer every time he tells a lie. A Walt Disney cartoon film, based on Collodi's story, was released in 1940 and brought the character to a wider audience.

Pinochet (Ugarte) Augusto 1915– . Military ruler of Chile from 1973, when a coup backed by the US Central Intelligence Agency ousted and killed President Salvador Allende. Pinochet took over the presidency and governed ruthlessly, crushing all opposition. He was voted out of power when general elections were held in Dec 1989 but remains head of the armed forces until 1997.

pint liquid or dry measure of volume or capacity. A liquid pint is equal to 16 fluid ounces or half a liquid quart (0.473 liter), while a dry pint is equal to half a dry quart (0.551 liter).

Pinter Harold 1930– . English dramatist, originally an actor. He specializes in the tragicomedy of the breakdown of communication, broadly in the tradition of the Theatre of the ◊Absurd—for example, *The Birthday Party* 1958 and *The Caretaker* 1960. Later plays include *The Homecoming* 1965, *Old Times* 1971, *Betrayal* 1978, *Mountain Language* 1988, and *Moonlight* 1993.

pinworm nematode worm *Enterobius vermicularis*, an intestinal parasite of humans.

Pinyin Chinese phonetic alphabet approved 1956 by the People's Republic of China, and used since 1979 in transcribing all names of people and places from Chinese ideograms into other languages using the English/Roman alphabet. For example, the former transcription Chou En-lai became Zhou Enlai, Hua Kuo-feng became Hua Guofeng, Teng Hsiao-ping became Deng Xiaoping, Peking became Beijing.

piracy the taking of a ship, aircraft, or any of its contents, from lawful ownership, punishable under international law by the court of any country where the pirate may be found or taken. When the craft is taken over to alter its destination, or its passengers held to ransom, the term is ◊hijacking. Piracy is also used to describe infringement of ◊copyright.

Pirandello Luigi 1867–1936. Italian writer. His plays include *La morsa/The Vice* 1912, *Sei personaggi in cerca d'autore/Six Characters in Search of an Author* 1921, and *Enrico IV/Henry IV* 1922. The themes and treatment of his plays anticipated the work of Brecht, O'Neill, Anouilh, and Genet. Nobel Prize 1934.

piranha any South American freshwater fish of the genus *Serrusalmus*, in the same order as cichlids. They can grow to 2 ft/60 cm long, and have razor-sharp teeth; some species may rapidly devour animals, especially if attracted by blood.

Pisa city in Tuscany, Italy; population (1988) 104,000. It has an 11th–12th-century cathedral. Its famous campanile, the Leaning Tower of Pisa (repaired 1990), is 180 ft/55 m high and about 16.5 ft/5 m out of perpendicular. It has foundations only about 10 ft/3 m deep.

Pisces zodiac constellation, mainly in the northern hemisphere between Aries and Aquarius, near Pegasus. It is represented by two fish tied together by their tails. The Circlet, a delicate ring of stars, marks the head of the western fish in Pisces. The constellation contains the ***vernal equinox***, the point at which the Sun's path around the sky (the ***ecliptic***) crosses the celestial equator. The Sun reaches this point around March 21 each year as it passes through Pisces from mid-March to late April. In astrology, the dates for Pisces are between about Feb 19 and March 20.

Piscis Austrinus or ***Southern Fish*** constellation of the southern hemisphere near Capricornus. Its brightest star is Fomalhaut.

Pisistratus *c.* 605–527 BC. Athenian politician. Although of noble family, he assumed the leadership of the peasant party, and seized power 561 BC. He was twice expelled, but recovered power from 541 BC until his death. Ruling as a dictator under constitutional forms, he was the first to have the Homeric poems written down, and founded Greek drama by introducing the Dionysiac peasant festivals into Athens.

Pissarro Camille 1831–1903. French Impressionist painter, born in the West Indies. He went to Paris in 1855, met Jean-Baptist-Camille Corot, then Claude Monet, and became a leading member of the Impressionists. He experimented with various styles, including ◊Pointillism, in the 1880s.

pistachio deciduous Eurasian tree *Pistacia vera* of the cashew family Anacardiaceae, with green nuts, which are eaten salted or used to enhance and flavor foods.

pistil general term for the female part of a flower, either referring to one single ◊carpel or a group of several fused carpels.

pistol any small ◊firearm designed to be fired with one hand. Pistols were in use from the early 15th century.

piston barrel-shaped device used in reciprocating engines (steam, gasoline, diesel oil) to harness power. Pistons are driven up and down in cylinders by expanding steam or hot gases. They pass on their motion via a connecting rod and crank to a crankshaft, which turns the driving wheels. In a pump or compressor, the role of the piston is reversed, being used to move gases and liquids. See also ◊internal-combustion engine.

pit bull terrier or ***American pit bull terrier*** variety of dog that was developed in the US solely as a

piranha

piranha Red piranhas swim in shoals so large that they can devour even large animals quickly by their combined efforts.

fighting dog. It usually measures about 20 in/50 cm at the shoulder and weighs roughly 50 lb/23 kg, but there are no established criteria since it is not recognized as a breed by either the American or British Kennel Clubs. Selective breeding for physical strength and aggression has created a dog unsuitable for life in the modern community.

Pitcairn Islands British colony in Polynesia, 3,300 mi/5,300 km NE of New Zealand
area 10 sq mi/27 sq km
capital Adamstown
features the uninhabited Henderson Islands, an unspoiled coral atoll with a rare ecology, and tiny Ducie and Oeno islands, annexed by Britain 1902
products fruit and souvenirs to passing ships
population (1990) 52
language English
government the governor is the British high commissioner in New Zealand
history settled 1790 by nine mutineers from the British ship the *Bounty* together with some Tahitians; their occupation remained unknown until 1808.

pitch in chemistry, a black, sticky substance, hard when cold, but liquid when hot, used for waterproofing, roofing and paving. It is made by the destructive distillation of wood or coal tar, and has been used since antiquity for caulking wooden ships.

pitch in music, the position of a note in the scale, dependent on the frequency of the pedominant sound

Pisa The Leaning Tower of Pisa, Italy, is 180 ft/55 m high and about 16.5 ft/5 m out of perpendicular.

wave. In **standard pitch**, A above middle C has a frequency of 440 Hz. **Perfect pitch** is an ability to name or reproduce any note heard or asked for; it does not necessarily imply high musical ability.

pitch in mechanics, the distance between the adjacent threads of a screw or bolt. When a screw is turned through one full turn it moves up or down a distance equal to the pitch of its thread. A screw thread is a simple type of machine, acting like a rolled-up inclined plane, or ramp (as may be illustrated by rolling a long paper triangle around a pencil). A screw has a mechanical advantage greater than one.

pitchblende or **uraninite** brownish-black mineral, the major constituent of uranium ore, consisting mainly of uranium oxide (UO_2). It also contains some lead (the final, stable product of uranium decay) and variable amounts of most of the naturally occurring radioactive elements, which are products of either the decay or the fissioning of uranium isotopes. The uranium yield is 50–80%; it is also a source of radium, polonium, and actinium. Pitchblende was first studied by Pierre and Marie ◊Curie, who found radium and polonium in its residues in 1898.

Pitcher Molly. Nickname of Mary ◊McCauley.

Pitman Isaac 1813–1897. English teacher and inventor of Pitman's shorthand. He studied Samuel Taylor's scheme for shorthand writing, and in 1837 published his own system, *Stenographic Soundhand*, fast, accurate, and adapted for use in many languages.

Pitt William, **the Elder**, 1st Earl of Chatham 1708–1778. British Whig politician, "the Great Commoner." As paymaster of the forces 1746–55, he broke with tradition by refusing to enrich himself; he was dismissed for attacking the Duke of Newcastle, the prime minister. He served effectively as prime minister in coalition governments 1756–61 (successfully conducting the Seven Years' War) and 1766–68.

Pitt William, **the Younger** 1759–1806. British Tory prime minister 1783–1801 and 1804–06. He raised the importance of the House of Commons, clamped down on corruption, carried out fiscal reforms, and effected the union with Ireland. He attempted to keep Britain at peace but underestimated the importance of the French Revolution and became embroiled in wars with France from 1793; he died on hearing of Napoleon's victory at Austerlitz.

Pittsburgh industrial city (machinery, chemicals) in the NE US and the nation's largest inland port, where the Allegheny and Monongahela rivers join to form the Ohio River in Pennsylvania; population (1990) 369,900, metropolitan area 2,242,800.

Pittsfield city in W central Massachusetts, on the Housatonic River, just E of the New York border; population (1990) 48,600. Industries include electronics and tourism. Herman Melville wrote *Moby Dick* 1851 at his home here.

pituitary gland major ◊endocrine gland of vertebrates, situated in the center of the brain. The anterior lobe secretes hormones, some of which control the activities of other glands (thyroid, gonads, and adrenal cortex); others are direct-acting hormones affecting milk secretion and controlling growth. Secretions of the posterior lobe control body water balance and contraction of the uterus. The posterior lobe is regulated by nerves from the ◊hypothalamus, and thus forms a link between the nervous and hormonal systems.

Pius 12 popes, including:

Pius IV 1499–1565. Pope from 1559, of the ◊Medici family. He reassembled the Council of Trent (see Counter-Reformation under ◊Reformation) and completed its work 1563.

Pius V 1504–1572. Pope from 1566. He excommunicated Elizabeth I of England, and organized the expedition against the Turks that won the victory of ◊Lepanto.

Pius VII 1742–1823. Pope from 1800. He concluded a concordat (papal agreement) with France 1801 and took part in Napoleon's coronation, but relations became strained. Napoleon annexed the papal states, and Pius was imprisoned 1809–14. After his return to Rome 1814, he revived the Jesuit order.

Pius IX 1792–1878. Pope from 1846. He never accepted the incorporation of the Papal States and of Rome in the kingdom of Italy. He proclaimed the dogmas of the Immaculate Conception of the Virgin 1854 and papal infallibility 1870; his pontificate was the longest in history.

Pius XII (Eugenio Pacelli) 1876–1958. Pope from 1939. He was conservative in doctrine and politics, and condemned ◊Modernism. He proclaimed the dogma of the bodily assumption of the Virgin Mary 1950 and in 1951 restated the doctrine (strongly criticized by many) that the life of an infant must not be sacrificed to save a mother in labor. He was criticized for failing to speak out against atrocities committed by the Germans during World War II and has been accused of collusion with the Nazis.

Pizarro Francisco *c.* 1475–1541. Spanish conqueror of the Inca empire of Peru. Born in Spain, Pizarro traveled to the West Indies, where he met ◊Balboa and served as his lieutenant on the expedition that crossed Panama and resulted in their sighting of the Pacific Ocean 1513. While living in Panama, Pizarro heard of a wealthy Indian empire to the south, and beginning 1524 he explored the NW coast of South America, searching for gold and other riches. In 1531, with the permission of the king of Spain, he and 180 followers armed with cannon defeated the Inca king Atahualpa, later murdering him even though he gave them quantities of gold and silver they demanded. Pizarro founded Lima as the capital of Peru 1535. A feud then began among the Spanish leaders, and Pizarro was assassinated.

placebo (Latin "I will please") any harmless substance, often called a "sugar pill," that has no chemotherapeutic value and yet produces physiological changes.

placenta organ that attaches the developing ◊embryo or ◊fetus to the ◊uterus in placental mammals (mammals other than marsupials, platypuses, and echidnas). Composed of maternal and embryonic tissue, it links the blood supply of the embryo to the blood supply of the mother, allowing the exchange of oxygen, nutrients, and waste products. The two blood systems are not in direct contact, but are separated by thin membranes, with materials diffusing across from one system to the other. The placenta also produces hormones that maintain and regulate pregnancy. It is shed as part of the afterbirth.

plague disease transmitted by fleas (carried by the black rat) which infect the sufferer with the bacillus *Pasteurella pestis*. An early symptom is swelling of lymph nodes, usually in the armpit and groin; such swellings are called "buboes," hence **bubonic** plague. It causes virulent blood poisoning and the death rate is high.

plain

Animals of the plains depend on grasses and occasional trees for sustenance. Plant-eaters graze (feed on growing grass), browse (eat leaves, twigs and sparse vegetation), or forage (rummage for bulbs, roots and fruits). They are preyed upon by the meat-eaters.

African plain (savannah) wildlife and plants. 1. baboon 2. acacia tree 3. eland 4. low-growing shrubs 5. giraffe 6. elephant 7. steenbok 8. topi 9. warthog 10. weaver bird nests 11. termite mound 12. baobab tree 13. lions 14. rhinoceros

Russian plain (steppe) wildlife and plants. 1. shrubs and small trees 2. grass snake 3. lemmings 4. field voles 5. saiga antelope 6. suslik 7. marbled polecat 8. black-bellied hamster

In temperate grasslands, where winter temperatures can fall far below freezing and summer temperatures rise to 104°F/40°C, many of the animals survive by living underground in burrows. In tropical grasslands, the climate is less extreme. Here a great variety of plants grow, and provide food for many more types of animals. The African grasslands support the world's largest wildlife populations.

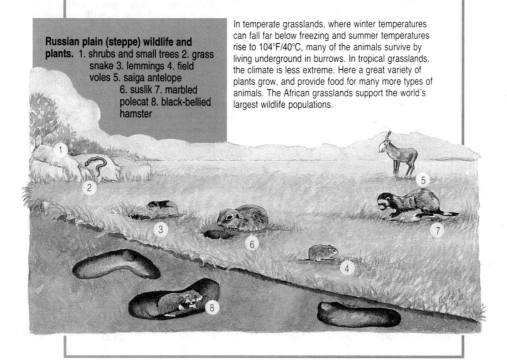

plain or *grassland* land, usually flat, upon which grass predominates. The plains cover large areas of the Earth's surface, especially between the deserts of the tropics and the rain forests of the equator, and have rain in one season only. In such regions the climate belts move north and south during the year, bringing rain forest conditions at one time and desert conditions at another. Temperate plains include the North European Plain, the High Plains of the US and Canada, and the Russian Plain also known as the steppe. *See panel p. 735*

Plains Indian member of any of the North American Indian peoples of the Great Plains, which extend over 2,000 mi/3,000 km from Alberta to Texas. The Plains Indians were drawn from diverse linguistic stocks fringing the Plains but shared many cultural traits, especially the nomadic hunting of bison herds once horses became available in the 18th century. The various groups include Blackfoot, Cheyenne, Comanche, Pawnee, and the Dakota or Sioux.

plainsong ancient chant of the Christian church first codified by Ambrose, bishop of Milan, and then by Pope Gregory in the 6th century. See ◊Gregorian chant.

Planck Max 1858–1947. German physicist who framed the quantum theory 1900. His research into the manner in which heated bodies radiate energy led him to report that energy is emitted only in indivisible amounts, called quanta, the magnitudes of which are proportional to the frequency of the radiation. His discovery ran counter to Classical physics and is held to have marked the commencement of the modern science. Nobel Prize for Physics 1918.

Planck's constant in physics, a fundamental constant (symbol *h*) that is the energy of one quantum of electromagnetic radiation (the smallest possible "packet" of energy; see ◊quantum theory) divided by the frequency of its radiation. Its value is 6.626196×10^{-34} joule seconds.

planet large celestial body in orbit around a star, composed of rock, metal, or gas. There are nine planets in the Solar System: Mercury, Venus, Earth, Mars, Jupiter, Saturn, Uranus, Neptune, and Pluto. The inner four, called the *terrestrial planets*, are small and rocky, and include the planet Earth. The outer planets, with the exception of Pluto, are called the *giant planets*, large balls of rock, liquid, and gas; the largest is Jupiter, which contains more than twice as much mass as all the other planets combined. Planets do not produce light, but reflect the light of their parent star.

plankton small, often microscopic, forms of plant and animal life that live in the upper layers of fresh

and salt water, and are an important source of food for larger animals. Marine plankton is concentrated in areas where rising currents bring mineral salts to the surface.

plant organism that carries out ◊photosynthesis, has cellulose cell walls and complex cells, and is immobile. A few parasitic plants have lost the ability to photosynthesize but are still considered to be plants.

Plantagenet English royal house, reigning 1154–1399, whose name comes from the nickname of Geoffrey, Count of Anjou (1113–1151), father of Henry II, who often wore in his hat a sprig of broom, *planta genista*. In the 1450s, Richard, Duke of York, took "Plantagenet" as a surname to emphasize his superior claim to the throne over Henry VI's.

plantain any plant of the genus *Plantago*, family Plantaginaceae. The great plantain *P. major* has oval leaves, grooved stalks, and spikes of green flowers with purple anthers followed by seeds, which are used in bird food.

plantation large farm or estate where commercial production of one crop—such as rubber (in Malaysia), palm oil (in Nigeria), or tea (in Sri Lanka)—is carried out. Plantations are usually owned by large companies, often ◊multinational corporations, and run by an estate manager. Many plantations were established in countries under colonial rule, using slave labor.

plant classification taxonomy or classification of plants. Originally the plant kingdom included bacteria, diatoms, dinoflagellates, fungi, and slime molds, but these are not now thought of as plants. The groups that are always classified as plants are the bryophytes (mosses and liverworts), pteridophytes (ferns, horsetails, and club mosses), gymnosperms (conifers, yews, cycads, and ginkgos), and angiosperms (flowering plants). The angiosperms are split into monocotyledons (for example, orchids, grasses, lilies) and dicotyledons (for example, oak, buttercup, geranium, and daisy).

plaque any abnormal deposit on a body surface, especially the thin, transparent film of sticky protein (called mucin) and bacteria on tooth surfaces. If not removed, this film forms tartar (calculus), promotes tooth decay, and leads to gum disease. Another form of plaque is a deposit of fatty or fibrous material in the walls of blood vessels that can block blood flow or break free to form blood clots.

plasma in biology, the liquid part of the ◊blood.

plasmid small, mobile piece of ◊DNA found in bacteria and used in ◊genetic engineering. Plasmids are separate from the bacterial chromosome but still multiply

planets

planet	main constituents	atmosphere	average distance from Sun in millions of mi	time for one orbit in Earth-years	diameter in thousands of mi	average density if density of water is one unit
Mercury	rocky, ferrous	—	36	0.241	3.03	5.4
Venus	rocky, ferrous	carbon dioxide	67	0.615	7.52	5.2
Earth	rocky, ferrous	nitrogen, oxygen	93	1.00	7.93	5.5
Mars	rocky	carbon dioxide	142	1.88	4.21	3.9
Jupiter	liquid hydrogen, helium	—	483	11.86	88.74	1.3
Saturn	hydrogen, helium	—	887	29.46	74.57	0.7
Uranus	icy, hydrogen, helium	hydrogen, helium	1,783	84.00	31.57	1.3
Neptune	icy, hydrogen, helium	hydrogen, helium	2,794	164.80	30.20	1.8
Pluto	icy, rocky	methane	3,666	248.50	1.39	about 2.0

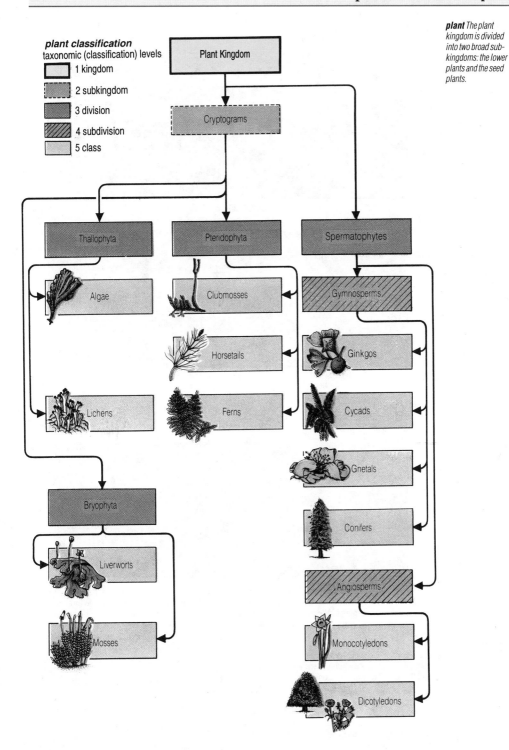

plant classification
taxonomic (classification) levels
1 kingdom
2 subkingdom
3 division
4 subdivision
5 class

Plant Kingdom

Cryptograms

Thallophyta

Pteridophyta

Spermatophytes

Algae

Clubmosses

Gymnosperms

Horsetails

Ginkgos

Lichens

Ferns

Cycads

Gnetals

Conifers

Bryophyta

Angiosperms

Liverworts

Monocotyledons

Mosses

Dicotyledons

plant The plant kingdom is divided into two broad sub-kingdoms: the lower plants and the seed plants.

plate tectonics The three main types of action in plate tectonics.

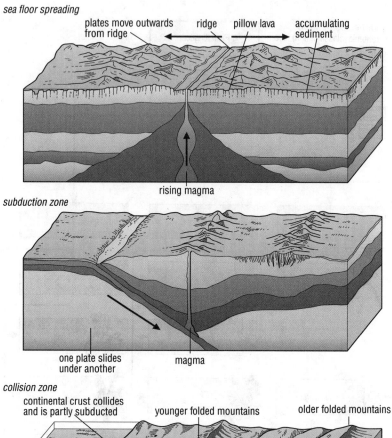

sea floor spreading

plates move outwards from ridge   ridge   pillow lava   accumulating sediment

rising magma

subduction zone

one plate slides under another   magma

collision zone

continental crust collides and is partly subducted   younger folded mountains   older folded mountains

during cell growth. Their size ranges from 3% to 20% of the size of the chromosome. There is usually only one copy of a single plasmid per cell, but occasionally several are found. Some plasmids carry "fertility genes" that enable them to move from one bacterium to another and transfer genetic information between strains. Plasmid genes determine a wide variety of bacterial properties including resistance to antibiotics and the ability to produce toxins.

plastic any of the stable synthetic materials that are fluid at some stage in their manufacture, when they can be shaped, and that later set to rigid or semirigid solids. Plastics today are chiefly derived from petroleum. Most are polymers, made up of long chains of identical molecules.

plastic surgery branch of surgery concerned with the repair of congenital disfigurement and the reconstruction of tissues damaged by disease or injury; and

cosmetic surgery undergone for reasons of vanity to conform to some esthetic norm or counter the effects of aging; for example, the removal of bags under the eyes or a double chin.

Plata, Río de la or *River Plate* estuary in South America into which the rivers Paraná and Uruguay flow; length 200 mi/320 km and width up to 150 mi/240 km. The basin drains much of Argentina, Bolivia, Brazil, Uruguay, and Paraguay, which all cooperate in its development.

plateau elevated area of fairly flat land, or a mountainous region in which the peaks are at the same height. An *intermontane plateau* is one surrounded by mountains. A *piedmont plateau* is one that lies between the mountains and low-lying land. A *continental plateau* rises abruptly from low-lying lands or the sea. Examples are the Tibetan Plateau and the Massif Central in France.

platelet tiny "cell" found in the blood, which helps it to clot. Platelets are not true cells, but membrane-bound cell fragments that bud off from large cells in the bone marrow.

plate tectonics theory formulated in the 1960s to explain the phenomena of ◊continental drift and seafloor spreading, and the formation of the major physical features of the Earth's surface. The Earth's outermost layer is regarded as a jigsaw of rigid major and minor plates up to 62 mi/100 km thick, which move relative to each other, probably under the influence of convection currents in the mantle beneath. Major landforms occur at the margins of the plates, where plates are colliding or moving apart—for example, volcanoes, fold mountains, ocean trenches, and ocean ridges.

Plath Sylvia 1932–1963. US poet and novelist whose powerful, highly personal poems, often expressing a sense of desolation, are distinguished by their intensity and sharp imagery. Her *Collected Poems* 1981 was awarded a Pulitzer Prize. Her autobiographical novel *The Bell Jar* 1961 deals with the events surrounding a young woman's emotional breakdown.

platinum (Spanish *platina* "little silver" (*plata* "silver")) heavy, soft, silver-white, malleable and ductile, metallic element, symbol Pt, atomic number 78, atomic weight 195.09.

It is the first of a group of six metallic elements (platinum, osmium, iridium, rhodium, ruthenium, and palladium) that possess similar traits, such as resistance to tarnish, corrosion, and attack by acid, and that often occur as free metals (◊native metals). They often occur in natural alloys with each other, the commonest of which is osmiridium. Both pure and as an alloy, platinum is used in dentistry, jewelry, and as a catalyst.

Plato c. 428–347 BC. Greek philosopher, pupil of Socrates, teacher of Aristotle, and founder of the Academy school of philosophy. He was the author of philosophical dialogues on such topics as metaphysics, ethics, and politics. Central to his teachings is the notion of Forms, which are located outside the everyday world—timeless, motionless, and absolutely real.

platoon in the army, the smallest infantry subunit. It contains 30–40 soldiers and is commanded by a lieutenant or second lieutenant. There are three or four platoons in a company.

platypus monotreme, or egg-laying, mammal *Ornithorhynchus anatinus*, found in Tasmania and E Australia. Semiaquatic, it has small eyes and no external ears, and jaws resembling a duck's beak. It lives in long burrows along river banks, where it lays two eggs in a rough nest. It feeds on water worms and insects, and when full-grown is 2 ft/60 cm long.

Plautus 3rd–2nd century BC. Roman comic dramatist, born in Umbria. He settled in Rome and was active before and after 200 BC, writing at least the 21 comedies that survive in his name, many of them based on Greek originals by playwrights such as ◊Menander. Shakespeare drew on his "Menaechmi" for "The Comedy of Errors."

Player Gary 1935– . South African golfer who won major championships in three decades and the first British Open 1959. A match-play specialist, he won the world title five times.

playing cards a set of small pieces of card with different markings, used in playing games. A standard set consists of a "deck" of 52 cards divided into four suits: hearts, clubs, diamonds, and spades. Within each suit there are 13 cards: 9 are numbered (two through ten), 3 are called face, picture (or court) cards (jack, queen, and king), and 1 is called the ace.

pleadings in law, documents exchanged between the parties to court actions, which set out the facts that form the basis of the case they intend to present in court, and (where relevant) stating what damages or other remedy they are claiming.

plebeian Roman citizen who did not belong to the privileged class of the ◊patricians. During the 5th–4th centuries BC, plebeians waged a long struggle to win political and social equality with the patricians, eventually securing admission to the offices formerly reserved for patricians.

plebiscite referendum or direct vote by all the electors of a country or district on a specific question. Since the 18th century plebiscites have been employed on many occasions to decide to what country a particular area should belong; for example, in Upper Silesia and elsewhere after World War I, and in the Saar 1935.

Pleiades in astronomy, a star cluster about 400 light-years away in the constellation Taurus, representing the Seven Sisters of Greek mythology. Its brightest stars (highly luminous, blue-white giants only a few million years old) are visible to the naked eye, but there are many fainter ones.

Pleiades in Greek mythology, the seven daughters of the giant Atlas who asked to be changed into a cluster of stars to escape the pursuit of the hunter Orion.

Pleistocene first epoch of the Quaternary period of geological time, beginning 1.64 million years ago and ending 10,000 years ago. The polar ice caps were extensive and glaciers were abundant during the ice age of this period, and humans evolved into modern *Homo sapiens sapiens* about 100,000 years ago.

plesiosaur prehistoric carnivorous marine reptile of the Jurassic and Cretaceous periods, which reached a length of 36 ft/12 m, and had a long neck and paddle-like limbs. The pliosaurs evolved from the plesiosaurs.

Plessy v Ferguson US Supreme Court decision 1896 dealing with state-imposed segregation laws. Homer Plessy brought this case to the Supreme Court to test Louisiana segregation laws after he was arrested for refusing to leave a whites-only train car. He argued that such discrimination was prohibited by the 13th and 14th Amendments, which granted equal protection under the law. The Court ruled 8 to 1 against Plessy, holding that the 13th Amendment only prohibited slavery and that the 14th Amendment guaranteed only political but not social rights. The Court accepted a doctrine of separate but equal accommodations, a standard for segregation maintained until 1954.

pleurisy inflammation of the pleura, the thin, secretory membrane that covers the lungs and lines the space in which they rest. Pleurisy is nearly always due to bacterial or viral infection, which can be treated with antibiotics. It renders breathing painful.

platypus When the platypus was discovered 200 years ago, scientists thought the first specimens were fakes.

Plexiglas trademark for a clear, lightweight, tough plastic first produced in the US 1930. It is widely used for watch glasses, advertising signs, domestic baths, motorboat windshields, aircraft canopies, and protective shields. Its chemical name is polymethylmethacrylate (PMMA).

Pliny the Elder (Gaius Plinius Secundus) *c.* AD 23–79. Roman scientific encyclopedist and historian; only his works on astronomy, geography, and natural history survive. He was killed in an eruption of Vesuvius, the volcano near Naples.

Pliny the Younger (Gaius Plinius Caecilius Secundus) *c.* AD 61–113. Roman administrator, nephew of Pliny the Elder, whose correspondence is of great interest. Among his surviving letters are those describing the eruption of Vesuvius, his uncle's death, and his correspondence with the emperor ◊Trajan.

Pliocene fifth and last epoch of the Tertiary period of geological time, 5.2–1.64 million years ago. The earliest hominid, the humanlike ape "australopithecines," evolved in Africa.

See also ◊human species.

pliosaur prehistoric carnivorous marine reptile, descended from the plesiosaurs, but with a shorter neck, and longer head and jaws. It was approximately 15 ft/5 m long. In 1989 the skeleton of one of a previously unknown species was discovered in N Queensland, Australia. A hundred million years ago, it lived in the sea which once covered the Great Artesian Basin.

PLO abbreviation for ◊Palestine Liberation Organization.

plover any shore bird of the family Charadriidae, found worldwide. Plovers are usually black or brown above, and white below, and have short bills. The largest of the ringed plovers is the killdeer *Charadrius vociferus*, called because of its cry.

plow the most important agricultural implement used for tilling the soil. The plow dates from about 3500 BC, when oxen were used to pull a simple wooden blade, or ard. In about 500 BC the iron share came into use.

plum tree *Prunus domestica*, bearing edible fruits that are smooth-skinned with a flat kernel. There are many varieties, including the Victoria, czar, egg-plum, greengage, and damson; the sloe *P. spinosa* is closely related. Dried plums are known as prunes.

pluralism in political science, the view that decision-making in contemporary liberal democracies is the outcome of competition among several interest groups in a political system characterized by free elections, representative institutions, and open access to the organs of power. This concept is opposed by corporatism and other approaches that perceive power to be centralized in the state and its principal elites (the Establishment).

Plutarch *c.* AD 46–120. Greek biographer and essayist, born in Chaeronea. His *Parallel Lives* comprise paired biographies of famous Greek and Roman soldiers and politicians, followed by comparisons between the two. Thomas North's 1579 translation inspired Shakespeare's Roman plays.

Pluto in astronomy, the smallest and, usually, outermost planet of the Solar System. The existence of Pluto was predicted by calculation by Percival Lowell and the planet was located by Clyde Tombaugh in 1930. It orbits the Sun every 248.5 years at an average distance of 3.6 billion mi/5.8 billion km. Its highly elliptical orbit occasionally takes it within the orbit of Neptune, as in 1979–99. Pluto has a diameter of about 1,400 mi/2,300 km, and a mass about 0.002 of that of Earth. It is of low density, composed of rock and ice, with frozen methane on its surface and a thin atmosphere.

Charon, Pluto's moon, was discovered 1978, revolving around Pluto with the same period as Pluto's rotation, remaining over the same point on Pluto's surface and showing the same face. The pair may be a double planet system.

Pluto in Greek mythology, the lord of the underworld (Roman Dis), sometimes known as Hades. He was the brother of Zeus and Poseidon.

plutonic rock igneous rock derived from magma that has cooled and solidified deep in the crust of the Earth; granites and gabbros are examples of plutonic rocks.

plutonium silvery-white, radioactive, metallic element of the ◊actinide series, symbol Pu, atomic number 94, atomic weight 239.13. It occurs in nature in minute quantities in ◊pitchblende and other ores, but is produced in quantity only synthetically. It has six allotropic forms and is one of three fissile elements (elements capable of splitting into other elements—the others are thorium and uranium). The element has awkward physical properties and is the most toxic substance known.

Plymouth city and seaport in Devon, England, at the mouth of the river Plym, with dockyard, barracks, and a naval base at Devonport; population (1981) 243,900.

plywood manufactured panel of wood widely used in building. It consists of several thin sheets, or plies, of wood, glued together with the grain (direction of the wood fibers) of one sheet at right angles to the grain of the adjacent plies. This construction gives plywood equal strength in every direction.

pneumatic drill drill operated by compressed air, used in mining and tunneling, for drilling shot holes (for explosives), and in road repairs for breaking up pavements. It contains an air-operated piston that delivers hammer blows to the drill bit many times a second. The French engineer Germain Sommeiller (1815–1871) developed the pneumatic drill 1861 for tunneling in the Alps.

pneumectomy surgical removal of all or part of the lung.

pneumonia inflammation of the lungs, generally due to bacterial or viral infection but also to particulate matter or gases. It is characterized by a buildup of fluid in the alveoli, the clustered air sacs (at the end of the air passages) where oxygen exchange takes place.

Pnom Penh alternate form of ◊Phnom Penh, the capital of Cambodia.

Po longest river in Italy, flowing from the Cottian Alps to the Adriatic Sea; length 415 mi/668 km. Its valley is fertile and contains natural gas. The river is heavily polluted with nitrates, phosphates, and arsenic.

Pocahontas *c.* 1595–1617. American Indian woman alleged to have saved the life of English colonist John Smith when he was captured by her father, Powhatan. Pocahontas was kidnapped 1613 by an Englishman, Samuel Argall, and she later married colonist John Rolfe (1585–1622) and was entertained as a princess at the English Court. Her marriage and conversion to Christianity brought about a period of peaceful relations between Indians and settlers, but she died of smallpox after her return to Virginia.

pod in botany, a type of fruit that is characteristic of legumes (plants belonging to the Leguminosae family), such as peas and beans. It develops from a single ◊carpel and splits down both sides when ripe to release the seeds.

podiatry the medical profession that deals with the specialized care of feet. Some podiatric treatments involve the use of orthopedic devices to correct fallen arches or improve improper positioning of feet during walking.

Poe Edgar Allan 1809–1849. US writer and poet. His short stories are renowned for their horrific atmosphere, as in "The Fall of the House of Usher" 1839 and "The Masque of the Red Death" 1842, and for their acute reasoning (ratiocination), as in "The Gold Bug" 1843 and "The Murders in the Rue Morgue" 1841 (in which the investigators Legrand and Dupin anticipate Conan Doyle's Sherlock Holmes). His poems include "The Raven" 1845.

poet laureate poet of the British royal household, so called because of the laurel wreath awarded to eminent poets in the Graeco-Roman world.
Early poets with unofficial status were Geoffrey Chaucer, John Skelton, Edmund Spenser, Samuel Daniel, and Ben Jonson. Ted Hughes was appointed poet laureate in 1984.
Other modern-day poet laureates include Wordsworth, Tennyson, Cecil Day Lewis, and John Betjeman.

poetry the imaginative expression of emotion, thought, or narrative, frequently in metrical form and often using figurative language. Poetry has traditionally been distinguished from prose (ordinary written language) by rhyme or the rhythmical arrangement of words (meter).

pogrom unprovoked violent attack on an ethnic group, particularly Jews, carried out with official sanction. The Russian pogroms against Jews began 1881, after the assassination of Tsar Alexander II, and again in 1903–06; persecution of the Jews remained constant until the Russian Revolution. Later there were pogroms in E Europe, especially in Poland after 1918, and in Germany under Hitler (see ◊Holocaust).

Poincaré Jules Henri 1854–1912. French mathematician who developed the theory of differential equations and was a pioneer in ◊relativity theory. He suggested that Isaac Newton's laws for the behavior of the universe could be the exception rather than the rule. However, the calculation was so complex and time-consuming that he never managed to realize its full implication.

Poincaré Raymond Nicolas Landry 1860–1934. French politician, prime minister 1912–13, president 1913–20, and again prime minister 1922–24 (when he ordered the occupation of the Ruhr, Germany) and 1926–29.

Poindexter John Marlan 1936– . US rear admiral and Republican government official. In 1981 he joined the Reagan administration's National Security Council (NSC) and became national security adviser 1985. As a result of the ◊Irangate scandal, Poindexter was forced to resign 1986, along with his assistant, Oliver North.

poinsettia or *Christmas flower* winter-flowering shrub *Euphorbia pulcherrima*, with large red leaves encircling small greenish-yellow flowers. It is native to Mexico and tropical America and is a popular houseplant in North America and Europe.

pointe (French "toe of shoe") in dance, the tip of the toe. A dancer *sur les pointes* is dancing on her toes in blocked shoes, as popularized by the Italian dancer Marie ◊Taglioni 1832.

Pointe-Noire chief port of the Congo, formerly (1950–58) the capital; population (1984) 297,000. Industries include oil refining and shipbuilding.

pointer breed of dog, often white mixed with black, tan, or dark brown, about 2 ft/60 cm tall, and weighing 62 lb/28 kg.

Pointillism technique in oil painting developed in the 1880s by the Neo-Impressionist Georges Seurat. He used small dabs of pure color laid side by side to create an impression of shimmering light when viewed from a distance. *See illustration p. 742*

poison or *toxin* any chemical substance that, when introduced into or applied to the body, is capable of injuring health or destroying life. The liver removes some poisons from the blood. The majority of poisons may be divided into *corrosives*, such as sulfuric, nitric, and hydrochloric acids; *irritants*, including arsenic and copper sulfate; *narcotics* such as opium, and carbon monoxide; and *narcotico-irritants* from any substances of plant origin including carbolic acid and tobacco.

poison ivy North American plant *Rhus radicans* of the cashew family, having leaves composed of three leaflets, yellowish flowers, and ivory-colored, berry-like fruit. The leaves are variable and may be dull or shiny, leathery or thin, toothed or smooth-edged. It can grow as an erect shrub, trailing vine, or climber. All parts of the plant contain a heavy, nonvolatile oil that causes inflammation of the skin with itching rash, blisters, and/or swelling in susceptible persons. Numerous birds feed on the berries.

poison oak any of several North American subspecies of poison ivy *Rhus radicans*. Poison oak always grows as an erect shrub (to 10 in/25 cm tall) with three-parted leaves that are usually blunt-tipped and hairy on both sides. The irritating effects to humans are similar to those of poison ivy.

poison pill in business, a tactic to avoid hostile takeover by making the target unattractive. For example, a company may give a certain class of stockholders the right to have their shares redeemed at a very good price in the event of the company being taken over, thus involving the potential predator in considerable extra cost.

poison sumac shrub or small tree *Rhus vernix* of the cashew family that thrives in a swampy habitat. Its large leaves are composed of 7–13 pointed leaflets, and it bears clusters of white globular fruit. All its parts contain a dangerous skin irritant more virulent than that of poison ivy or poison oak.

Poitier Sidney 1924– . US actor and film director, Hollywood's first black star. His films as an actor include *Something of Value* 1957, *Lilies of the Field* 1963, and *In the Heat of the Night* 1967, and *Sneakers* 1992, and as director *Stir Crazy* 1980.

Poitou-Charentes region of W central France, comprising the *départements* of Charente, Charente-Maritime, Deux-Sèvres, and Vienne
capital Poitiers
area 9,959 sq mi/25,800 sq km
products dairy products, wheat, chemicals, metal goods; brandy is made at Cognac
population (1986) 1,584,000

Pointillism Georges Seurat's Poseuses (1888), Henry P McIlhenny Collection, Luxembourg.

history once part of the Roman province of Aquitaine, this region was captured by the Visigoths in the 5th century and taken by the Franks AD 507. The area was contested by the English and French until the end of the Hundred Years' War 1453, when it was incorporated into France by Charles II.

poker card game of US origin, in which two to eight people play (usually for stakes) and try to obtain a "hand" of five cards ranking higher than those of their opponents. The best scoring hand wins the "pot."

pokeweed tall North American herbaceous plant *Phytolacca americana* of the family Phytolaccaceae. It has pale greenish flowers and purple berries, the seeds of which are poisonous. North American Indians used the juice of the berries for staining.

Poland country in E Europe, bounded N by the Baltic Sea, E by Lithuania, Belarus, and Ukraine, S by the Czech and Slovak Republics, and W by Germany.

Polanski Roman 1933– . Polish film director, born in Paris. His films include *Repulsion* 1965, *Cul de Sac* 1966, *Rosemary's Baby* 1968, *Tess* 1979, *Frantic* 1988, and *Bitter Moon* 1992.

He suffered a traumatic childhood in Nazi-occupied Poland, and later his wife, actress Sharon Tate, was the victim of murder by the Charles Manson "family."

He left the US for Europe and his tragic personal life is reflected in a fascination with horror and violence in his work.

polar coordinates in mathematics, a way of defining the position of a point in terms of its distance r from a fixed point (the origin) and its angle heta to a fixed line or axis. The coordinates of the point are $(r, heta)$.

Polaris or *Pole Star* or *North Star* the bright star closest to the north celestial pole, and the brightest star in the constellation Ursa Minor. Its position is indicated by the "pointers" in Ursa Major. Polaris is a yellow ♢supergiant about 500 light-years away.

polarized light light in which the electromagnetic vibrations take place in one particluar direction. In ordinary (unpolarized) light, the electric and magnetic fields vibrate in all directions perpendicular to the direction of propagation. After reflection from a polished surface or transmission through certain materials (such as Polaroid), the electric and magnetic fields are confined to one direction, and the light is said to be *plane polarized*. In *circularly polarized* and *elliptically polarized* light, the magnetic and electric fields are confined to one direction, but the direction rotates as the light propagates. Polarized light is used to test the strength of sugar solutions, to measure stresses in transparent materials, and to prevent glare.

Polaroid camera instant-picture camera, invented by Edwin Land in the US 1947. The original camera produced black-and-white prints in about one minute. Modern cameras can produce black-and-white prints in a few seconds, and color prints in less than a minute. An advanced model has automatic focusing and exposure. It ejects a piece of film on paper immediately after the picture has been taken.

pole either of the geographic north and south points of the axis about which the Earth rotates. The geographic poles differ from the magnetic poles, which are the points toward which a freely suspended magnetic needle will point.

Pole person of Polish culture from Poland and the surrounding area. There are 37–40 million speakers of Polish (including some in the US), a Slavic language belonging to the Indo-European family. The Poles are predominantly Roman Catholic, though there is an Orthodox Church minority. They are known for their distinctive cooking, folk festivals, and folk arts.

polecat Old World weasel *Mustela putorius* with a brown back and dark belly and two yellow face patches. The body is about 20 in/50 cm long and it has a strong smell from anal gland secretions. It is native to Asia, Europe, and N Africa. In North America,

◊skunks are sometimes called polecats. A ferret is a domesticated polecat.

Pole Star ◊Polaris, the northern pole star. There is no bright star near the southern celestial pole.

police civil law-and-order force. In the US, law enforcement is the responsibility of municipal and state government except for violations of specific federal laws or cases in which state borders have been crossed. Unlike many countries, there is no national police force. The ◊Federal Bureau of Investigation assists state and local law-enforcement authorities.

poliomyelitis or *polio* acute viral infection of the central nervous system affecting nerves that activate muscles. The disease used to be known as infantile paralysis since children were most often affected. The polio virus is a common one, and mostly, its effects are confined to the throat and intestine, as in flu or a mild digestive upset. There may also be muscle stiffness in the neck and back. Paralysis is seen in about 1% of cases, and the disease is life-threatening only if the muscles of the throat and chest are affected. Cases of this kind, once entombed in an "iron lung," are today maintained on a respirator. Two kinds of vaccine are available, one injected (see ◊Salk) and one given by mouth.

Polish Corridor strip of land designated under the Treaty of ◊Versailles 1919 to give Poland access to the Baltic. It cut off East Prussia from the rest of Germany. When Poland took over the southern part of East Prussia 1945, it was absorbed.

Polish language member of the Slavonic branch of the Indo-European language family, spoken mainly in Poland. Polish is written in the Roman and not the Cyrillic alphabet and its standard form is based on the dialect of Poznań in W Poland.

Poland
Republic of
(*Polska Rzeczpospolita*)

area 49,325 sq mi/127,886 sq km
capital Warsaw
cities Lódź, Kraków, Wrocław, Poznań, Katowice, Bydgoszcz, Lublin; ports Gdańsk, Szczecin, Gdynia
physical part of the great plain of Europe; Vistula, Oder, and Neisse rivers; Sudeten, Tatra, and Carpathian mountains on S frontier
environment atmospheric pollution derived from coal (producing 90% of the country's electricity), toxic waste from industry, and lack of sewage treatment have resulted in the designation of 27 ecologically endangered areas. Half the country's lakes have been seriously contaminated and three-quarters of its drinking water does not meet official health standards
features last wild European bison (only in protected herds)
head of state Lech Wałesa from 1990
head of government Waldemar Pawlak from 1993
political system emergent democratic republic
political parties Democratic Union, centrist, ex-Solidarity; Democratic Left Alliance, ex-communist; Center Alliance, right of center, Wałesa-linked; Social Democratic Party of the Polish Republic, 1990 successor to Polish United Workers' Party (PUWP), social democratic; Union of Social Democrats, radical breakaway from PUWP formed 1990; Solidarność (Solidarity) Parliamentary Club (OKP), anticommunist coalition
exports coal, softwood timber, chemicals, machinery, ships, vehicles, meat, copper (Europe's largest producer)

currency zloty
population (1992) 38,429,000; growth rate 0.6% p.a.
life expectancy men 66, women 74 (1989)
languages Polish (official), German
media broadcasters required by law to "respect Christian values"
religion Roman Catholic 95%
literacy 98% (1989)
GNP $276 billion (1988); $2,000 per head (1986)

chronology
1918 Poland revived as independent republic.
1939 German invasion and occupation.
1944 Germans driven out by Soviet forces.
1945 Polish boundaries redrawn at Potsdam Conference.
1947 Communist people's republic proclaimed.
1956 Poznań riots. Wladyslaw Gomułka installed as Polish United Workers' Party (PUWP) leader.
1970 Gomułka replaced by Edward Gierek after Gdańsk riots.
1980 Solidarity emerged as a free labor union following Gdańsk disturbances.
1981 Martial law imposed by General Wojciech Jaruzelski.
1983 Martial law ended.
1984 Amnesty for political prisoners.
1985 Zbigniew Messner became prime minister.
1987 Referendum on economic reform rejected.
1988 Solidarity-led strikes and demonstrations called off after pay increases. Messner resigned; replaced by the reformist Mieczysław F Rakowski.
1989 Solidarity relegalized. April: new "socialist pluralist" constitution formed. June: widespread success for Solidarity in assembly elections, the first open elections in 40 years. July: Jaruzelski elected president. Sept: "Grand coalition", first non-Communist government since World War II formed; economic restructuring undertaken on free-market lines; W Europe and US create $1 billion aid package.
1990 Jan: PUWP dissolved; replaced by Social Democratic Party and breakaway Union of Social Democrats. Lech Wałesa elected president; Dec: prime minister Mazowiecki resigned.
1991 Oct: Multiparty general election produced inconclusive result. Five-party center-right coalition formed under Jan Olszewski. Treaty signed agreeing to complete withdrawal of Soviet troops.
1992 June: Olszewski ousted on vote of no confidence; succeeded by Waldemar Pawlak. July: Hanna Suchocka replaced Pawlak.
1993 14% of work force (2.6 million) unemployed. Suchocka lost vote of confidence. Sept: general election; Pawlak appointed prime minister.

pollen Pollination, the process by which pollen grains transfer their male nuclei (gametes) to the ovary of a flower.

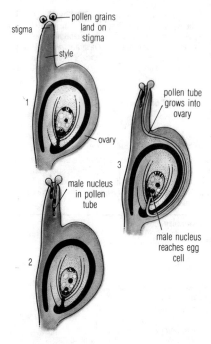

pollen grains land on stigma

stigma

style

1

pollen tube grows into ovary

ovary

3

male nucleus in pollen tube

male nucleus reaches egg cell

2

Politburo contraction of "political bureau," the executive committee (known as the Presidium 1952–66) of the Supreme Soviet in the USSR, which laid down party policy. It consisted of about 12 voting and 6 candidate (nonvoting) members.

political action committee (PAC) in the US, any organization that raises funds for political candidates and in return seeks to commit them to a particular policy. PACs also spend money on changing public opinion. In 1990, there were about 3,500 PACs, controlling some 25% of all funds spent in elections for ◊Congress. Donations to candidates amounted to $358.1 million, the largest PACs being the National Association of Realtors and the American Medical Association.

political correctness (PC) shorthand term for a set of liberal attitudes about education and society, and the terminology associated with them. To be politically correct is to be sensitive to unconscious racism and sexism and to display environmental awareness. However, the real or alleged enforcement of PC speech codes ("people of color" instead of "colored people," "differently abled" instead of "disabled," and so on) at more than 130 US universities by 1991 attracted derision and was criticized as a form of thought-policing.

political party association of like-minded people organized with the purpose of seeking and exercising political power. A party can be distinguished from an interest or ◊pressure group which seeks to influence governments rather than aspire to office, although some pressure groups, such as the Green movement, have over time transformed themselves into political parties.

Polk James Knox 1795–1849. 11th president of the US 1845–49, a Democrat, born in North Carolina. He allowed Texas admission to the Union, and forced the war on Mexico that resulted in the annexation of California and New Mexico.

Polk was an associate of Andrew ◊Jackson, who influenced his strongly expansionist policies. A believer in Manifest Destiny, Polk pursued war with Mexico but avoided armed conflict with Britain over the Oregon–Canada boundary.

polka folk dance in lively two-four time. The basic step is a hop followed by three short steps. The polka originated in Bohemia and spread with German immigrants to the US, becoming a style of Texas country music.

pollen the grains of ◊seed plants that contain the male gametes. In ◊angiosperms (flowering plants) pollen is produced within ◊anthers; in most ◊gymnosperms (cone-bearing plants) it is produced in male cones. A pollen grain is typically yellow and, when mature, has a hard outer wall. Pollen of insect-pollinated plants (see ◊pollination) is often sticky and spiny and larger than the smooth, light grains produced by wind-pollinated species.

pollination the process by which pollen is transferred from one plant to another. The male ◊gametes are contained in pollen grains, which must be transferred from the anther to the stigma in ◊angiosperms (flowering plants), and from the male cone to the female cone in ◊gymnosperms (cone-bearing plants). Fertilization (not the same as pollination) occurs after the growth of the pollen tube to the ovary. Self-pollination occurs when pollen is transferred to a stigma of the same flower, or to another flower on the same plant; cross-pollination occurs when pollen is transferred to another plant. This involves external pollen-carrying agents, such as wind, water, insects, birds, bats, and other small mammals.

Pollock Jackson 1912–1956. US painter, a pioneer of Abstract Expressionism and the foremost exponent of the technique of ◊action painting, a style he developed around 1946.

Pollock v Farmer's Loan and Trust Co US Supreme Court decision 1895 dealing with the right of Congress to levy a federal income tax. The Gorman Tariff Act 1894 imposed a 2% tax on all annual incomes over $4,000. The ensuing protests, including the test case, focused on three aspects of the tax: (1) it taxed income on state and municipal bonds, an infringement on states' rights; (2) it taxed income on land and private property, making it a direct tax not apportioned among the states according to population; and (3) it exempted certain people on the basis of personal income. The Court found 5 to 4 that these constitutional violations made the tax impermissible. This decision was rendered irrelevant in 1913 by the 16th Amendment, which empowered Congress to enact income taxes.

poll tax tax levied on every individual, without reference to his or her income or property. Being simple to administer, it was among the earliest sorts of tax (introduced in England 1377), but because of its indiscriminate nature (it is a regressive tax, in that it falls proportionately more heavily on poorer people) it has often proved unpopular.

pollution the harmful effect on the environment of by-products of human activity, principally industrial and agricultural processes—for example, noise, smoke, automobile emissions, chemical and radioactive effluents in air, seas, and rivers, pesticides, radiation, sewage (see ◊sewage disposal), and household waste. Pollution contributes to the ◊greenhouse effect.

Pollux in Greek mythology, the twin brother of Castor.

polo stick-and-ball game played between two teams of four on horseback. It originated in Iran, spread to

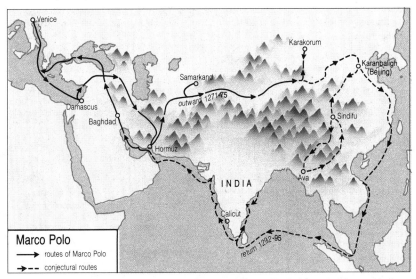

Marco Polo

→ routes of Marco Polo

→-- conjectural routes

India and was first played in England 1869. Polo is played on the largest field of any game, measuring up to 300 yd/274 m by 200 yd/182 m.

A small solid ball is struck with the side of a long-handled mallet through goals at each end of the field. A typical match lasts about an hour, and is divided into "chukkas" of 7.5 minutes each. No pony is expected to play more than two chukkas in the course of a day.

Polo Marco 1254–1324. Venetian traveler and writer. He traveled overland to China 1271–75, and served the emperor Kublai Khan until he returned to Europe by sea 1292–95. He was captured while fighting for Venice against Genoa, and, while in prison 1296–98, dictated an account of his travels.

polonaise Polish dance in stately three-four time, that was common in 18th-century Europe. The Polish composer Frédéric Chopin developed the polonaise as a pianistic form.

polonium radioactive, metallic element, symbol Po, atomic number 84, atomic weight 210. Polonium occurs in nature in small amounts and was isolated from ◊pitchblende. It is the element having the largest number of isotopes (27) and is 5,000 times as radioactive as radium, liberating considerable amounts of heat. It was the first element to have its radioactive properties recognized and investigated.

Pol Pot (also known as *Saloth Sar, Tol Saut,* and *Pol Porth*) 1925– . Cambodian politician and leader of the Khmer Rouge communist movement that overthrew the government 1975. After widespread atrocities against the civilian population, his regime was deposed by a Vietnamese invasion 1979. Pol Pot continued to help lead the Khmer Rouge despite officially resigning from all positions in 1989.

poltergeist (German "noisy ghost") unexplained phenomenon that invisibly moves objects or hurls them about, starts fires, or causes other mischief.

polyandry system whereby a woman is expected to have more than one husband at the same time. It is found in Tibet and certain parts of India, where polyandry takes the form of the marriage of one woman to several brothers, as a means of keeping intact a family's heritage and property. Although it is found in other areas, in practice, it is neither expected nor normative behavior.

Polybius *c.* 201–120 BC. Greek politician and historian. He was involved with the ◊Achaean League against the Romans and, following the defeat of the Macedonians at Pydna in 168 BC, he was taken as a political hostage to Rome. He returned to Greece in 151 and was present at the capture of Carthage by his friend Scipio in 146. The first part of his history of Rome in 40 books, covering the years 220–146, survives intact.

polychlorinated biphenyl (PCB) any of a group of chlorinated isomers of biphenyl ($C_6H_5)_2$. They are dangerous industrial chemicals, valuable for their fire-resisting qualities. They constitute an environmental hazard because of their persistent toxicity. Since 1973 their use has been limited by international agreement.

polyester synthetic resin formed by the ◊condensation of polyhydric alcohols (alcohols containing more than one hydroxyl group) with dibasic acids (acids containing two replaceable hydrogen atoms). Polyesters are thermosetting ◊plastics, used in making synthetic fibers, such as Dacron and Terylene, and constructional plastics. With fiberglass added as reinforcement, polyesters are used in automobile bodies and boat hulls.

polyethylene or *polyethene* polymer of the gas ethylene (technically called ethene, C_2H_4). It is a tough, white, translucent, waxy thermoplastic (which means it can be repeatedly softened by heating). It is used for packaging, bottles, toys, wood preservation, electric cable, pipes and tubing.

polygamy the practice of having more than one spouse at the same time. It is found among many peoples. Normally it has been confined to the wealthy and to chiefs and nobles who can support several women and their offspring, as among ancient Egyptians, Teutons, Irish, and Slavs. Islam limits the number of legal wives a man may have to four. Certain Christian sects—for example, the Anabaptists of Münster, Germany, and the Mormons—have practiced polygamy because it was the norm in the Old Testament.

polygon in geometry, a plane (two-dimensional) figure with three or more straight-line sides. Common polygons have names which define the number of sides (for example, triangle, quadrilateral, pentagon).

polyhedron in geometry, a solid figure with four or more plane faces. The more faces there are on a polyhedron, the more closely it approximates to a sphere. Knowledge of the properties of polyhedra is needed in crystallography and stereochemistry to determine the shapes of crystals and molecules.

There are only five types of regular polyhedron (with all faces the same size and shape), as was deduced by early Greek mathematicians; they are the tetrahedron (four equilateral triangular faces), cube (six square faces), octahedron (eight equilateral triangles), dodecahedron (12 regular pentagons) and icosahedron (20 equilateral triangles).

polymer compound made up of a large long-chain or branching matrix composed of many repeated simple units (*monomers*). There are many polymers, both natural (cellulose, chitin, lignin) and synthetic (polyethylene and nylon, types of plastic). Synthetic polymers belong to two groups: thermosoftening and thermosetting (see ◊plastic).

polymerization chemical union of two or more (usually small) molecules of the same kind to form a new compound. *Addition polymerization* produces simple multiples of the same compound. *Condensation polymerization* joins molecules together with the elimination of water or another small molecule.

polymorphism in genetics, the coexistence of several distinctly different types in a ◊population (groups of animals of one species). Examples include the different blood groups in humans, different color forms in some butterflies, and snail shell size, length, shape, color, and stripiness.

polymorphism in mineralogy, the ability of a substance to adopt different internal structures and external forms, in response to different conditions of temperature and/or pressure. For example, diamond and graphite are both forms of the element carbon, but they have very different properties and appearance.

Polynesia islands of Oceania E of 170° E latitude, including Hawaii, Kiribati, Tuvalu, Fiji, Tonga, Tokelau, Samoa, Cook Islands, and French Polynesia.

Polynesian a member of any of the seafaring peoples of Polynesia. They migrated by canoe from S Asia in about 2000 BC, peopling the islands of the S Pacific for about 2,000 years, and settling Hawaii last, from Tahiti. The Polynesian languages belong to the Oceanic branch of the Austronesian family.

Polynesian languages see ◊Malayo-Polynesian languages.

polyp or *polypus* small "stalked" benign tumor, most usually found on mucous membrane of the nose or bowels. Intestinal polyps are usually removed, since some have been found to be precursors of cancer.

polystyrene type of ◊plastic used in kitchen utensils or, in an expanded form, in insulation and ceiling tiles.

polytheism the worship of many gods, as opposed to monotheism (belief in one god). Examples are the religions of ancient Egypt, Babylon, Greece, Rome, Mexico, and modern Hinduism.

polyunsaturate type of ◊fat or oil containing a high proportion of triglyceride molecules whose ◊fatty-acid chains contain several double bonds. By contrast, the fatty-acid chains of the triglycerides in saturated fats (such as lard) contain only single bonds. Medical evidence suggests that polyunsaturated fats, used widely

in margarines and cooking fats, are less likely to contribute to cardiovascular disease than saturated fats, but there is also some evidence that they may have adverse effects on health.

pome type of pseudocarp, or false fruit, typical of certain plants belonging to the Rosaceae family. The outer skin and fleshy tissues are developed from the ◊receptacle (the enlarged end of the flower stalk) after fertilization, and the five ◊carpels (the true fruit) form the pome's core, which surrounds the seeds. Examples of pomes are apples, pears, and quinces.

pomegranate deciduous shrub or small tree *Punica granatum*, family Punicaceae, native to SW Asia but cultivated widely in tropical and subtropical areas. The round, leathery, reddish yellow fruit contains numerous seeds that can be eaten fresh or made into wine.

pomeranian small breed of dog, about 6 in/15 cm high, weighing about 6.5 lb/3 kg. It has long straight hair with a neck frill, and the tail is carried over the back.

Pompadour Jeanne Antoinette Poisson, Marquise de Pompadour 1721–1764. Mistress of ◊Louis XV of France from 1744, born in Paris. She largely dictated the government's ill-fated policy of reversing France's anti-Austrian policy for an anti-Prussian one. She acted as the patron of the Enlightenment philosophers Voltaire and Diderot.

Pompano Beach city in SE Florida, N of Fort Lauderdale, on the Atlantic Ocean; population (1990) 72,400. Tourism and fruit processing are important to the economy.

Pompeii ancient city in Italy, near the volcano ◊Vesuvius, 13 mi/21 km SE of Naples. In AD 63 an earthquake destroyed much of the city, which had been a Roman port and pleasure resort; it was completely buried beneath volcanic ash when Vesuvius erupted AD 79. Over 2,000 people were killed. Pompeii was rediscovered 1748 and the systematic excavation begun 1763 still continues.

Pompey the Great (Gnaeus Pompeius Magnus) 106–48 BC. Roman soldier and politician, consul 70–60 BC. From 60 BC to 53 BC, he was a member of the First Triumvirate with Julius ◊Caesar and Marcus Livius ◊Crassus, but took the opposite side in the civil war from 49 BC.

Pompidou Georges 1911–1974. French conservative politician, president 1969–74. He negotiated a settlement with the Algerians 1961 and, as prime minister 1962–68, with the students in the revolt of May 1968.

Ponce major city and industrial port (iron, textiles, sugar, rum) in S Puerto Rico, population (1980) 161,739. The Catholic University of Puerto Rico is here. The settlement, established in the late 17th century, was named after the Spanish explorer Juan Ponce de León.

Ponce de León Juan 1460–1521. Spanish explorer who discovered Florida. He sailed on Columbus's second voyage to the Americas 1493 and settled in the colony on Hispaniola, later conquering Puerto Rico 1508–09 and becoming its governor. In 1513, while searching for the legendary "fountain of youth," he discovered Florida, exploring much of its E coast and part of the W coast. Ponce de León returned to Florida in 1521 and was wounded in a battle with Indians. He died soon after in Cuba.

Pondicherry union territory of SE India; area 185 sq mi/480 sq km; population (1991) 789,400. Its capital is

Pompeii Forum Street and the Arch of Caligula, Pompeii.

Pondicherry, and products include rice, peanuts, cotton, and sugar. Pondicherry was founded by the French 1674 and changed hands several times among the French, Dutch, and British before being returned to France 1814 at the close of the Napoleonic Wars. Together with Karaikal, Yanam, and Mahé (on the Malabar Coast) it formed a French colony until 1954 when all were transferred to the government of India; since 1962 they have formed the Union Territory of Pondicherry. Languages spoken include French, English, Tamil, Telegu, and Malayalam.

Pontiac city in Michigan, 24 mi/38 km NW of Detroit, noted for motor manufacturing; population (1990) 71,200.

Pontiac c. 1720–1769. North American Indian, chief of the Ottawa from 1755. Allied with the French during the French and Indian War, Pontiac was hunted by the British after the French withdrawal. He led the "Conspiracy of Pontiac" 1763–64 in an attempt to resist British persecution. He achieved remarkable success against overwhelming odds but eventually signed a peace treaty 1766.

pony small horse under 4.5 ft/1.47 m (14.2 hands) shoulder height. Although of Celtic origin, all the pony breeds have been crossed with thoroughbred and Arab stock, except for the smallest—the hardy Shetland, which is less than 42 in/105 cm shoulder height.

Pony Express in the US, a system of mail-carrying by relays of horse riders that operated in the years 1860–61 between St Joseph, Missouri, and Sacramento, California, a distance of about 1,800 mi/2,900 km. The Pony Express was a private venture by a company called Russell, Majors, and Waddell. 157 stations were set up along the route and the riders, who included William Cody, (Buffalo Bill), needed several changes of horses between each station.

poodle breed of dog, including standard (above 15 in/38 cm at shoulder), miniature (below 15 in/38 cm), and toy (below 11 in/28 cm) varieties. The long, curly coat, usually cut into an elaborate style, is often either black or white, although grays and browns are also bred.

pool or **pocket billiards** game derived from ⟩billiards and played in many different forms. Originally popular in the US, it is now also played in Europe.

Pop art movement of young artists in the mid-1950s and 1960s, reacting against the elitism of abstract art. Pop art used popular imagery drawn from advertising, comic strips, film, and television. It originated in Britain 1956 with Richard Hamilton, Peter Blake (1932–), and others, and broke through in the US with the paintings of flags and numbers by Jasper Johns 1958 and Andy Warhol's first series of soup cans 1962.

pope the bishop of Rome, head of the Roman Catholic church, which claims he is the spiritual descendant of St Peter. Elected by the Sacred College of Cardinals, a pope dates his pontificate from his coronation with the tiara, or triple crown, at St Peter's Basilica, Rome. The pope had great political power in Europe from the early Middle Ages until the Reformation.

Popé Pueblo leader. Born in the Tewa Pueblo, Popé was a leader of native resistance to Spanish political control and missionary activity in the New Mexico–Arizona area. Establishing his residence in Taos (in present-day New Mexico) in the 1670s, he began to plot a general uprising against the Spanish authorities. In August 1680 the Pueblo rose simultaneously throughout the area, forcing the Spanish to abandon Santa Fe and flee to El Paso. Popé held control of the area until his death, restoring the traditional ways of life. However, raids by Ute and Apache and severe drought led to the Spanish reconquest of the area 1692.

porcupine A North American porcupine

Pope Alexander 1688–1744. English poet and satirist. He established his reputation with the precocious *Pastorals* 1709 and *Essay on Criticism* 1711, which were followed by a parody of the heroic epic *The Rape of the Lock* 1712–14 and "Eloisa to Abelard" 1717. Other works include a highly Neo-Classical translation of Homer's *Iliad* and *Odyssey* 1715–26.

poplar deciduous tree of the genus *Populus*, or cottonwood trees of the willow family Salicaceae. When ripe, the feathery seeds borne on elongated clusters are blown far and wide by the wind. Balsam poplar *P. balsamifera* and eastern cottonwood *P. deltoides* are native to North America. Eurasian white poplar *P. alba* and Lombardy poplar *P. nigra* are grown widely as ornamentals. Aspens belong to the same genus.

poplin strong fabric, originally with a warp of silk and a weft of worsted, but now usually made from cotton, in a plain weave with a finely ribbed surface.

pop music or *popular music* any contemporary music not categorizable as jazz or Classical. Pop became distinct from folk music with the advent of sound-recording techniques, and has incorporated blues, country and western, and music-hall elements; electronic amplification and other technological innovations have played a large part in the creation of new styles. The traditional format is a song of roughly three minutes with verse, chorus, and middle eight bars.

Popocatépetl (Aztec "smoking mountain") volcano in central Mexico, 30 mi/50 km SE of Mexico City; 17,526 ft/5,340 m. It last erupted 1920.

Popper Karl (Raimund) 1902– . Austrian philosopher of science. His theory of falsificationism says that although scientific generalizations cannot be conclusively verified, they can be conclusively falsified by a counterinstance; therefore, science is not certain knowledge but a series of "conjectures and refutations," approaching, though never reaching, a definitive truth. For Popper, psychoanalysis and Marxism are unfalsifiable and therefore unscientific.

poppy any plant of the genus *Papaver*, family Papaveraceae, that bears brightly colored, often dark-centered, flowers and yields a milky sap. Species include the crimson European field poppy *P. rhoeas* and the Asian ◊opium poppies. Closely related are the California poppy *Eschscholtzia californica* and the yellow horned or sea poppy *Glaucium flavum*.

population in biology and ecology, a group of animals of one species, living in a certain area and able to interbreed; the members of a given species in a ◊community of living things.

population the number of people inhabiting a country, region, area, or town.

Population statistics are derived from many sources; for example, through the registration of births and deaths, and from censuses of the population. The first US census was taken in 1790; other national censuses were taken in 1800 and 1801 and provided population statistics for Italy, Spain, the UK, and Ireland; and the cities of London, Paris, Vienna, and Berlin.

population control measures taken by some governments to limit the growth of their countries' populations by trying to reduce ◊birth rates. Propaganda, freely available contraception, and tax disincentives for large families are some of the measures that have been tried.

population explosion the rapid and dramatic rise in world population that has occurred over the last few hundred years. Between 1959 and 1990, the world's population increased from 2.5 billion to over 5 billion people. It is estimated that it will be at least 6 billion by the end of the century. Most of this growth is now taking place in the developing world, where rates of natural increase are much higher than in developed countries. Concern that this might lead to overpopulation has led some countries to adopt ◊population-control policies.

Populism in US history, a late 19th-century political movement that developed out of farmers' protests against economic hardship. The Populist (or People's) Party was founded 1892 and ran several presidential candidates.

porcupine any ◊rodent with quills on its body, belonging to either of two families: Old World porcupines (family Hystricidae), terrestrial in habit and having long black-and-white quills; or New World porcupines (family Erethizontidae), tree-dwelling, with prehensile tails and much shorter quills.

pornography obscene literature, pictures, photos, or films considered to be of no artistic merit and intended only to arouse sexual desire. Standards of what is obscene and whether a particular work has artistic value are subjective, hence there is often difficulty in determining whether a work violates the ◊obscenity laws. Opponents of pornography claim that it is harmful and incites violence to women and children. Others oppose its censorship claiming that it is impossible to distinguish pornography from art.

porphyria group of genetic disorders caused by an enzyme defect. Porphyria affects the digestive tract, causing abdominal distress; the nervous system, causing psychotic disorder, epilepsy, and weakness; the circulatory system, causing high blood pressure; and the skin, causing extreme sensitivity to light. No specific treatments exist.

porpoise any small whale of the family Delphinidae that, unlike dolphins, have blunt snouts without beaks. Common porpoises of the genus *Phocaena* can grow to 6 ft/1.8 m long; they feed on fish and crustaceans.

Porsche Ferdinand 1875–1951. German automotive engineer. The Volkswagen (German "people's car") was a Porsche product of the 1930s that became an international success (as the Beetle) in the 1950s–1970s.

port sweet red, tawny, or white dessert wine, fortified with brandy, made from grapes grown in the Douro basin of Portugal and exported from Oporto, hence the name.

port point where goods are loaded or unloaded from a water-based to a land-based form of transport. Most ports are coastal, though inland ports on rivers also exist. Ports often have specialized equipment to handle cargo in large quantities (for example, ◊container or roll on/roll off facilities).

Port Arthur industrial deepwater port (oil refining, shipbuilding, brass, chemicals) in Texas, 15 mi/24 km

SE of Beaumont; population (1990) 58,700. Founded 1895, it gained importance with the discovery of petroleum near Beaumont 1901.

Port Arthur former name (until 1905) of the port and naval base of Lüshun in NE China, now part of ◊Lüda.

Port-au-Prince capital and industrial port (sugar, rum, textiles, plastics) of Haiti; population (1982) 763,000.

Porter Cole (Albert) 1891–1964. US composer and lyricist of witty musical comedies. His shows include *The Gay Divorce* 1932, *Anything Goes* 1934, *Kiss Me, Kate* 1948, and *Silk Stockings* 1955. He also wrote movie musicals, such as *Born to Dance* 1936 and *High Society* 1956.

Porter Edwin Stanton 1869–1941. US director, a pioneer of silent films. His 1903 film *The Great Train Robbery* lasted an unprecedented 12 minutes and contained an early use of the close-up. More concerned with the technical than the artistic side of his films, which include *The Teddy Bears* 1907 and *The Final Pardon* 1912, Porter abandoned filmmaking 1916.

Porter Katherine Anne 1890–1980. US writer. She published three volumes of short stories (*Flowing Judas* 1930, *Pale Horse, Pale Rider* 1939, and *The Leaning Tower* 1944); a collection of essays, *The Days Before* 1952; and the allegorical novel *Ship of Fools* 1962 (made into a film 1965). Her *Collected Short Stories* 1965 won a Pulitzer Prize.

Porter William Sydney. Adopted name "O Henry." 1862–1910. US author. Born in Greensboro, North Carolina, Porter left home at an early age. Settling in Texas, he was convicted of embezzlement 1899 and served several years in prison. It was then that he began to write short stories under the distinctive adopted name "O Henry." After his release 1902, he moved to New York City, where he contributed stories, many with surprise endings, to the *New York World*. Among the published collections of O Henry's most famous stories are *The Four Million* (including "The Gift of the Magi") 1906, *The Voice of the City* 1908, and *Rolling Stones* 1913.

Porterville city in S central California, N of Bakersfield; population (1990) 29,600. Industries include citrus fruits and olive oil.

Portland industrial port (aluminum, paper, timber, lumber machinery, electronics) and capital of Multnomah Country, NW Oregon; on the Columbia River, 108 mi/173 km from the sea, at its confluence with the Willamette River; population (1990) 437,300.

Portland industrial port and largest city of Maine, on Casco Bay, SE of Sebago Lake; population (1990) 64,400. The University of Southern Maine is here. Portland was first settled in 1632. The home of the poet Henry Wadsworth Longfellow, who was born here, is now a museum.

Port Louis capital of Mauritius, on the island's NW coast; population (1987) 139,000. Exports include sugar, textiles, watches, and electronic goods.

Port Moresby capital and port of Papua New Guinea on the S coast of New Guinea; population (1987) 152,000.

Pôrto (English *Oporto*) industrial city (textiles, leather, pottery) in Portugal, on the river Douro, 3 mi/5 km from its mouth; population (1984) 327,000. It exports port wine; the suburb Vila Nova de Gaia on the south bank of the Douro is known for its port lodges.

Pôrto Alegre port and capital of Rio Grande do Sul state, S Brazil; population (1991) 1,254,600.

Port-of-Spain port and capital of Trinidad and Tobago, on the island of Trinidad; population (1988) 58,000. It has a cathedral (1813–28) and the San Andres Fort (1785).

Porto Novo capital of Benin, W Africa; population (1982) 208,258. It was a former Portuguese center for the slave and tobacco trade with Brazil and became a French protectorate 1863.

Port Said port in Egypt, on reclaimed land at the N end of the ◊Suez Canal; population (1983) 364,000. During the 1967 Arab-Israeli War the city was damaged and the canal blocked; Port Said was evacuated by 1969 but by 1975 had been largely reconstructed.

Portsmouth city and naval port in Hampshire, England, opposite the Isle of Wight; population (1991) 174,700. The naval dockyard was closed 1981 although some naval facilities remain.

Portsmouth port in Rockingham County, SE New Hampshire, on the estuary of the Piscataqua River; the state's only seaport; population (1990) 25,900.

Portsmouth port and independent city in SE Virginia, on the Elizabeth River, seat of a US navy yard and training center; population (1990) 103,900. Manufactured goods include electronic equipment, chemicals, clothing, and processed food.

Portugal country in SW Europe, on the Atlantic Ocean, bounded N and E by Spain.

Portugal
Republic of
(*República Portuguesa*)

area 35,521 sq mi/92,000 sq km (including the Azores and Madeira)
capital Lisbon
cities Coimbra; ports Pôrto, Setúbal
physical mountainous in N, plains in S
features rivers Minho, Douro, Tagus (Tejo), Guadiana; Serra da Estrêla mountains
head of state Mario Alberto Nober Lopes Soares from 1986
head of government Aníbal Cavaco Silva from 1985
political system democratic republic
political parties Social Democratic Party (PSD), moderate left of center; Socialist Party (PS), progressive socialist; Democratic Renewal Party (PRD), center-left; Democratic Social Center Party (CDS), moderate left of center

exports wine, olive oil, resin, cork, sardines, textiles, clothing, pottery, pulpwood
currency escudo
population (1992) 9,844,000; growth rate 0.5% p.a.
life expectancy men 71, women 78 (1989)
language Portuguese
religion Roman Catholic 97%
literacy men 89%, women 80% (1985)
GNP $83.9 bn (1992)

chronology
1928–68 Military dictatorship under António de Oliveira Salazar.
1968 Salazar succeeded by Marcello Caetano.
1974 Caetano removed in military coup led by General António Ribeiro de Spínola. Spínola replaced by General Francisco da Costa Gomes.
1975 African colonies became independent.
1976 New constitution, providing for return to civilian rule, adopted. Minority government appointed, led by Socialist Party leader Mario Soares.
1978 Soares resigned.
1980 Francisco Balsemão formed center-party coalition after two years of political instability.
1982 Draft of new constitution approved, reducing powers of presidency.
1983 Center-left coalition government formed.
1985 Aníbal Cavaco Silva became prime minister.
1986 Mario Soares elected first civilian president in 60 years. Portugal joined European Community.
1988 Portugal joined Western European Union.
1989 Constitution amended to allow major state enterprises to be denationalized.
1991 Mario Soares reelected president; Social Democrat (PSD) majority slightly reduced in assembly elections.

Portuguese inhabitant of Portugal. The Portuguese have a mixed cultural heritage that can be traced back to the Lusitanian Celts who were defeated by the Romans about 140 BC. In the 5th century AD the Suebi, a Germanic group, overran the Iberian peninsula, and were later subdued by the Visigoths. In the 8th century AD S Portugal was invaded by the Moors. The Portuguese are predominantly Roman Catholic.

Portuguese East Africa former name of ◊Mozambique in SE Africa.

Portuguese Guinea former name of ◊Guinea-Bissau in W Africa.

Portuguese language member of the Romance branch of the Indo-European language family; spoken by 120–135 million people worldwide, it is the national language of Portugal, closely related to Spanish and strongly influenced by Arabic. Portuguese is also spoken in Brazil, Angola, Mozambique, and other former Portuguese colonies.

Portuguese man-of-war any of a genus *Physalia* of phylum *Coelenterata* (see ◊coelenterate). They live in the sea, in colonies, and have a large air-filled bladder (or "float") on top and numerous hanging tentacles made up of feeding, stinging, and reproductive individuals. The float can be 1 ft/30 cm long.

Portuguese West Africa former name of ◊Angola in SW Africa.

Poseidon in Greek mythology, the chief god of the sea (Roman *Neptune*), brother of Zeus and Pluto. The brothers dethroned their father, Cronus, and divided his realm, Poseidon taking the sea; he was also worshiped as god of earthquakes. His sons were the merman sea god Triton and the Cyclops Polyphemus.

positivism theory that confines genuine knowledge within the bounds of science and observation. The theory is associated with the French philosopher Auguste Comte and ◊empiricism.

positron in physics, the antiparticle of the electron; an ◊elementary particle having the same magnitude of mass and charge as an electron but exhibiting a positive charge. The positron was discovered in 1932 by US physicist Carl Anderson at Caltech, its existence having been predicted by the British physicist Paul Dirac 1928.

possum another name for the ◊opossum, a marsupial animal with a prehensile tail found in North, Central and South America. The name is also used for many of the smaller marsupials found in Australia.

postcard card with space for a written message that can be sent through the mail without an envelope. The postcard's inventor was Emmanual Hermann, of Vienna, who in 1869 proposed a "postal telegram," sent at a lower fee than a normal letter with an envelope. The first picture postcard was produced 1894.

Post-Impressionism various styles of painting that followed ◊Impressionism in the 1880s and 1890s. The term was first used by the British critic Roger Fry in 1911 to describe the works of Paul Cézanne, Vincent van Gogh, and Paul Gauguin. These painters moved away from the spontaneity of Impressionism, attempting to give their work more serious meaning and permanence.

Postmodernism late 20th-century movement in the arts and architecture that rejects the preoccupation of

◊Modernism with purity of form and technique. Post-modern designers use an amalgam of style elements from the past, such as the Classical and the Baroque, and apply them to spare modern forms. Their slightly off-key familiarity creates a more immediate appeal than the austerities of Modernism.

post-mortem alternate name for ◊autopsy.

potash general name for any potassium-containing mineral, most often applied to potassium carbonate (K_2CO_3) or potassium hydroxide (KOH). Potassium carbonate, originally made by roasting plants to ashes in earthenware pots, is commercially produced from the mineral sylvite (potassium chloride, KCl) and is used mainly in making artificial fertilizers, glass, and soap.

potassium (Dutch *potassa* "potash") soft, waxlike, silver-white, metallic element, symbol K (Latin *kalium*), atomic number 19, atomic weight 39.0983. It is one of the ◊alkali metals and has a very low density—it floats on water, and is the second-lightest metal (after lithium). It oxidizes rapidly when exposed to air and reacts violently with water. Of great abundance in the Earth's crust, it is widely distributed with other elements and found in salt and mineral deposits in the form of potassium aluminum silicates.

potato perennial plant *Solanum tuberosum*, family Solanaceae, with edible tuberous roots that are rich in starch. Used by the Andean Indians for at least 2,000 years before the Spanish Conquest, the potato was introduced to Europe by the mid-16th century, and reputedly to England by the explorer Walter Raleigh.

Potemkin Grigory Aleksandrovich, Prince Potemkin 1739–1791. Russian politician. He entered the army and attracted the notice of Catherine II, whose friendship he kept throughout his life. He was an active administrator who reformed the army, built the Black Sea Fleet, conquered the Crimea 1783, developed S Russia, and founded the Kherson arsenal 1788 (the first Russian naval base on the Black Sea).

potential energy ◊energy possessed by an object by virtue of its relative position or state (for example, as in a compressed spring). It is contrasted with kinetic energy, the form of energy possessed by moving bodies.

Potomac river in West Virginia, Virginia, and Maryland states, rising in the Allegheny Mountains, and flowing SE through Washington, DC, into Chesapeake Bay. It is formed by the junction of the N Potomac, about 95 mi/153 km long, and S Potomac, about 130 mi/209 km long, and is itself 285 mi/459 km long.

Large ships can sail upstream as far as Washington. The Potomac is of little economic importance, but historic sites such as Mount Vernon, the home of George Washington, are on its banks.

Potsdam Conference conference held in Potsdam, Germany, July 17–Aug 2, 1945, between representatives of the US, the UK, and the USSR. They established the political and economic principles governing the treatment of Germany in the initial period of Allied control at the end of World War II, and sent an ultimatum to Japan demanding unconditional surrender on pain of utter destruction.

pottery and porcelain ◊ceramics in domestic and ornamental use including: *earthenware* made of porous clay and fired, whether unglazed (when it

Poseidon The Temple of Poseidon at Cape Sounion in Greece (northeastern corner).

remains porous, for example, flowerpots, winecoolers) or glazed (most tableware); *stoneware* made of nonporous clay with a high silica content, fired at high temperature, which is very hard; *bone china* (softpaste) semiporcelain made of 5% bone ash and china clay; first made in the West in imitation of Chinese porcelain; *porcelain* (hardpaste) characterized by its hardness, ringing sound when struck, translucence, and shining finish, like that of a cowrie shell (Italian *porcellana*); made of kaolin and petuntse (fusible ◊feldspar consisting chiefly of silicates reduced to a fine, white powder); first developed in China. Porcelain is high-fired at 2,552°F/1,400°C.

Poughkeepsie city in SE New York, on the Hudson River, N of New York City; population (1990) 28,900. Products include chemicals, ball bearings, and cough drops. Vassar College is here. Settled by the Dutch 1687, it was the temporary capital of New York 1717.

Poulenc Francis (Jean Marcel) 1899–1963. French composer and pianist. A self-taught composer of witty and irreverent music, he was a member of the group of French composers known as Les Six. Among his many works are the operas *Les Mamelles de Tirésias* 1947, and *Dialogues des Carmélites* 1957, and the ballet *Les Biches* 1923.

poultry domestic birds such as chickens, turkeys, ducks, and geese. They were domesticated for meat and eggs by early farmers in China, Europe, Egypt, and the Americas. Chickens were domesticated from the SE Asian jungle fowl *Gallus gallus* and then raised in the East as well as the West. Turkeys are New World birds, domesticated in ancient Mexico. Geese and ducks were domesticated in Egypt, China, and Europe.

pound British standard monetary unit, issued as a gold sovereign before 1914, as a note 1914–83, and as a circular yellow metal-alloy coin from 1983. The pound is also the name given to the unit of currency in Egypt, Lebanon, Malta, Sudan, and Syria.

pound imperial unit (symbol lb) of mass equal to 16 ounces (7,000 grains) avoirdupois, or 12 ounces (5,760 grains) troy; the metric equivalents are 0.45 kg and 0.37 kg respectively. It derives from the Roman *libra*, which weighed 0.327 kg.

Pound Ezra 1885–1972. US poet who lived in London from 1908. His *Personae* and *Exultations* 1909 established the principles of ◊Imagism. His largest work was the series of *Cantos* 1925–69 (intended to number 100), which attempted a massive reappraisal of history.

Poussin Nicolas 1594–1665. French painter, active chiefly in Rome; court painter to Louis XIII 1640–43. He was one of France's foremost landscape painters in the 17th century. He painted mythological and literary scenes in a strongly Classical style; for example, *Rape of the Sabine Women* about 1636–37 (Metropolitan Museum of Art, New York).

poverty condition that exists when the basic needs of human beings (shelter, food, and clothing) are not being met. Many different definitions of poverty exist, since there is little agreement on the standard of living considered to be the minimum adequate level (known as the *poverty level*) by the majority of people.

Powell Adam Clayton, Jr 1908–1972. US political leader. A leader of New York's black community, he was elected to the city council 1941. He was appointed to the US Congress 1944, and later became chairman of the House Education and Labor Committee. Following charges of corruption, he was denied his seat in Congress 1967. Reelected 1968, he won back his seniority by a 1969 decision of the US Supreme Court.

Powell Cecil Frank 1903–1969. English physicist. From the 1930s he and his team at Bristol University investigated the charged subatomic particles in cosmic radiation by using photographic emulsions carried in weather balloons. This led to his discovery of the pion (pi meson) 1946, a particle whose existence had been predicted by the Japanese physicist Hideki Yukawa 1935. Powell was awarded a Nobel Prize in 1950.

Powell Colin (Luther) 1937– . US general, chair of the Joint Chiefs of Staff 1989–93 and, as such, responsible for the overall administration of the Allied forces in Saudi Arabia during the ◊Gulf War 1991. A Vietnam War veteran, he first worked in government 1972 and was national security adviser 1987–89.

Powell Lewis Stanley 1907– . US jurist. He was associate justice of the US Supreme Court 1971–87. A conservative, Powell voted to restrict Fifth Amendment guarantees against self-incrimination and for capital punishment. In *United States* v *Nixon* 1974, he sided with the majority in limiting executive privilege.

power in physics, the rate of doing work or consuming energy. It is measured in watts (joules per second) or other units of work per unit time.

power of attorney in law, legal authority to act on behalf of another, for a specific transaction, or for a particular period.

Powys county in central Wales
area 1,961 sq mi/5,080 sq km
cities Llandrindod Wells (administrative headquarters)
features Brecon Beacons National Park; Black Mountains; rivers: Wye, Severn, which both rise on Plynlimon in Dyfed; Lake Vyrnwy, artificial reservoir supplying Liverpool and Birmingham; alternative technology center near Machynlleth
products agriculture, dairy cattle, sheep
population (1991) 117,500
languages Welsh 20%, English

Poznań (German *Posen*) industrial city (machinery, aircraft, beer) in W Poland; population (1985) 553,000. Founded 970, it was settled by German immigrants 1253 and passed to Prussia 1793; it was restored to Poland 1919.

pp abbreviation for *per procurationem* (Latin "by proxy"); in music, *pianissimo* (Italian "very softly").

praetor in ancient Rome, a magistrate, elected annually, who assisted the ◊consuls (the chief magistrates) and presided over the civil courts. After a year in office, a praetor would act as a provincial governor for a further year. The number of praetors was finally increased to eight. The office declined in importance under the emperors.

pragmatism philosophical tradition that interprets truth in terms of the practical effects of what is believed and, in particular, the usefulness of these effects. The US philosopher Charles Peirce is often accounted the founder of pragmatism; it was further advanced by William James.

Prague (Czech *Praha*) city and capital of the Czech Republic on the river Vltava; population (1991) 1,212,000. Industries include cars, aircraft, chemicals, paper and printing, clothing, brewing, and food processing. It became the capital 1918.

Prague Spring the 1968 program of liberalization, begun under a new Communist Party leader in Czechoslovakia. In Aug 1968 Soviet tanks invaded Czechoslovakia and entered the capital Prague to put down the liberalization movement initiated by the prime minister Alexander Dubček, who had earlier sought to assure the Soviets that his planned reforms would not threaten socialism. Dubček was arrested but released soon afterward. Most of the Prague Spring reforms were reversed.

Praia port and capital of the Republic of Cape Verde, on the island of São Tiago (Santiago); population (1980) 37,500. Industries include fishing and shipping.

prairie dog any of the North American genus *Cynomys* of burrowing rodents in the squirrel family (Sciuridae). They grow to 12 in/30 cm, plus a short 3 in/8 cm tail. Their "towns" can contain up to several thousand individuals. Their barking cry has given them their name. Persecution by ranchers has brought most of the five species close to extinction.

praseodymium (Greek *praseo* "leek-green" + *dymium*) silver-white, malleable, metallic element of the ◊lanthanide series, symbol Pr, atomic number 59, atomic weight 140.907. It occurs in nature in the minerals monzanite and bastnasite, and its green salts are used to color glass and ceramics. It was named in 1885 by Austrian chemist Carl von Welsbach (1858–1929).

prawn any of various ◊shrimps of the suborder Natantia ("swimming"), of the crustacean order Decapoda, as contrasted with lobsters and crayfishes, which are able to "walk." Species called prawns are generally larger than species called shrimps.

Praxiteles mid-4th century BC. Greek sculptor, active in Athens. His *Aphrodite of Knidos* about 350 BC (known through Roman copies) is thought to have initiated the tradition of life-size freestanding female nudes in Greek sculpture.

prayer address to divine power, ranging from a magical formula to attain a desired end, to selfless communication in meditation. Within Christianity the Catholic and Orthodox churches sanction prayer to the Virgin Mary, angels, and saints as intercessors, whereas Protestantism limits prayer to God alone.

Precambrian in geology, the time from the formation of Earth (4.6 billion years ago) up to 570 million years ago. Its boundary with the succeeding Cambrian period marks the time when animals first developed hard outer parts (exoskeletons) and so left abundant fossil remains. It comprises about 85% of geological time and is divided into two periods: the Archaean, in which no life existed, and the Proterozoic, in which there was life in some form.

precipitation in meteorology, water that falls to the Earth from the atmosphere. It includes rain, snow, sleet, hail, dew, and frost.

precipitation in chemistry, the formation of an insoluble solid in a liquid as a result of a reaction within the liquid between two or more soluble substances. If the solid settles, it forms a *precipitate*; if the particles of solid are very small, they will remain in suspension, forming a *colloidal precipitate* (see ◊colloid).

predestination in Christian theology, the doctrine asserting that God has determined all events beforehand, including the ultimate salvation or damnation of the individual human soul; see ◊free will.

prefix letter or group of letters that can be added to the beginning of a word to make a new word. For example, *over*time, *out*rage, *non*sense.

pregnancy in humans, the period during which an embryo grows within the womb. It begins at conception and ends at birth, and the normal length is 40 weeks. Menstruation usually stops on conception. About one in five pregnancies fails, but most of these failures occur very early on, so the woman may notice only that her period is late. After the second month, the breasts become tense and tender, and the areas round the nipples become darker. Enlargement of the uterus can be felt at about the end of the third month, and thereafter the abdomen enlarges progressively. Pregnancy in animals is called ◊gestation. *See illustration p. 754*

prehistoric life the diverse organisms that inhabited Earth from the origin of life about 3.5 billion years ago to the time when humans began to keep written records, about 3500 BC. During the course of evolution, new forms of life developed and many other forms, such as the dinosaurs, became extinct. Prehistoric life evolved over this vast timespan from simple bacterialike cells in the oceans to algae and protozoans and complex multicellar forms such as worms, mollusks, crustaceans, fishes, insects, land plants, amphibians, reptiles, birds, and mammals. On a geological timescale humans evolved relatively recently, about 4 million years ago, although the exact dating is a matter of some debate. See also ◊geological time.

prehistory human cultures before the use of writing. A classification system was devised 1816 by Danish archeologist Christian Thomsen, based on the predominant materials used by early humans for tools and weapons: ◊Stone Age, ◊Bronze Age, ◊Iron Age.

prelude in music, a composition intended as the preface to further music, to set a mood for a stage work, as in Wagner's *Lohengrin*; as used by Chopin, a short piano work.

premenstrual syndrome (PMS) a hormonal condition comprising a number of physical and emotional features that occur cyclically before menstruation, and which disappear with its onset. Symptoms include mood changes, breast tenderness, a feeling of bloatedness, and headache.

Preminger Otto (Ludwig) 1906–1986. Austrian-born US film producer, director, and actor. He directed *Margin for Error* 1942, *Laura* 1944, *The Moon Is Blue* 1953, *The Man with the Golden Arm* 1955, *Anatomy of a Murder* 1959, *Skidoo!* 1968, and *Rosebud* 1974. His films are characterized by an intricate technique of storytelling and a masterly use of the wide screen and the traveling camera.

Born in Vienna, Preminger went to the US 1935.

premolar in mammals, one of the large teeth toward the back of the mouth. In herbivores they are adapted for grinding. In carnivores they may be carnassials. Premolars are present in milk ◊dentition as well as permanent dentition.

preparatory school private high school that prepares students for entrance to a college or university.

preposition in grammar, a ◊part of speech coming before a noun or a pronoun to show a location (*in*, *on*), time (*during*), or some other relationship (for example, figurative relationships in phrases like "*by* heart" or "*on* time").

Pre-Raphaelite Brotherhood (PRB) group of British painters 1848–53; Dante Gabriel Rossetti, John Everett Millais, and Holman Hunt were founding members. They aimed to paint serious subjects, to study nature closely, and to shun the influence of the

pregnancy The development of a human embryo.

Pregnancy
not to scale

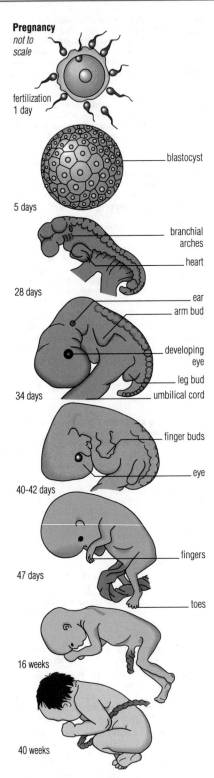

fertilization
1 day

blastocyst

5 days

branchial arches

heart

28 days

ear
arm bud

developing eye

leg bud
34 days   umbilical cord

finger buds

eye

40-42 days

fingers

47 days

toes

16 weeks

40 weeks

styles of painters after Raphael. Their subjects were mainly biblical and literary, painted with obsessive naturalism. Artists associated with the group include Edward Burne-Jones and William Morris.

Presbyterianism system of Christian Protestant church government, expounded during the Reformation by John Calvin in Geneva, which gives its name to the established church of Scotland and is also practiced in the US, England, the Netherlands, Switzerland, and elsewhere. There is no compulsory form of worship, and each congregation is governed by presbyters or elders (clerical or lay), who are of equal rank. Congregations are grouped in presbyteries, synods, and general assemblies.

prescription in medicine, an order written in a recognized form by a practitioner of medicine, dentistry, or veterinary surgery to a pharmacist for a preparation of medications to be used in treatment.

preservative substance (◊additive) added to a food in order to inhibit the growth of bacteria, yeasts, mold, and other microorganisms, and therefore extend its shelf-life. The term sometimes refers to ◊antioxidants (substances added to oils and fats to prevent their becoming rancid) as well. All preservatives are potentially damaging to health if eaten in sufficient quantity. Both the amount used, and the foods in which they can be used, are restricted by law.

president in government, the usual title of the head of state in a republic; the power of the office may range from diplomatic figurehead to the actual head of the government. For presidents of the US, who head the executive branch and its agencies, see ◊United States and entries by name.

Presley Elvis (Aron) 1935–1977. US singer and guitarist, the most influential performer of the rock-and-roll era. With his recordings for Sun Records in Memphis, Tennessee, 1954–55 and early hits such as "Heartbreak Hotel," "Hound Dog," and "Love Me Tender," all 1956, he created an individual vocal style, influenced by Southern blues, gospel music, country music, and rhythm and blues. His records continued to sell in their millions into the 1990s.

Presley was born in Tupelo, Mississippi. In the mid-1950s he met Colonel Tom Parker, who would manage his career for his entire life. In addition to selling millions of records, Presley acted in 33 motion pictures and made numerous television appearances. From the late 1960s, he took a Las Vegas-based touring act on the road. He died at Graceland, his mansion in Memphis, in 1977, the victim of drug dependence.

pressure in physics, the force acting normally (at right angles) to a body per unit surface area. The SI unit of pressure is the pascal (newton per square meter), equal to 0.01 millibars. In a fluid (liquid or gas), pressure increases with depth. At the edge of Earth's atmosphere, pressure is zero, whereas at sea level atmospheric pressure due to the weight of the air above is about 100 kilopascals (1,013 millibars or 1 atmosphere). Pressure is commonly measured by means of a ◊barometer, ◊manometer, or ◊Bourdon gauge.

pressure cooker closed pot in which food is cooked in water under pressure, where water boils at a higher temperature than normal boiling point (212°F/100°C) and therefore cooks food quickly. The modern pressure cooker has a quick-sealing lid and a safety valve that can be adjusted to vary the steam pressure inside.

pressure group or *interest group* or *lobby* association that puts pressure on governments or parties to ensure laws and treatment favorable to its own interest. Pressure groups have played an increasingly prominent role in contemporary Western democracies. In general they fall into two types: groups concerned with a single issue, such as nuclear disarmament, and groups attempting to promote their own interest, such as oil producers.

pretender claimant to a throne. In British history, the term is widely used to describe the Old Pretender (◊James Edward Stuart) and the Young Pretender (◊Charles Edward Stuart).

Pretoria administrative capital of the Union of South Africa from 1910 and capital of Transvaal province from 1860; population (1985) 741,300. Industries include engineering, chemicals, iron, and steel. Founded 1855, it was named after Boer leader Andries Pretorius (1799–1853).

Previn André (George) 1929– . US conductor and composer, born in Berlin. After a period working as a composer and arranger in the US film industry, he concentrated on conducting. He was principal conductor of the London Symphony Orchestra 1968–79. He was appointed music director of Britain's Royal Philharmonic Orchestra 1985 (a post he relinquished the following year, staying on as principal conductor), and of the Los Angeles Philharmonic in 1986.

He has done much on television and on stage to popularize Classical music.

Prévost d'Exiles Antoine François 1697–1763. French novelist, known as Abbé Prévost, who combined a military career with his life as a monk. His *Manon Lescaut* 1731 inspired operas by Massenet and Puccini.

Priam in Greek legend, the last king of Troy, husband of Hecuba and father of many sons and daughters, including ◊Cassandra, ◊Hector, and ◊Paris. He was killed by Pyrrhus, son of Achilles, when the Greeks entered the city of Troy concealed in a huge wooden horse which the Trojans believed to be a gift to the city.

Priapus in Greek mythology, the god of fertility, son of Dionysus and Aphrodite, represented as grotesquely ugly, with an exaggerated phallus. He was later a Roman god of gardens, where his image was frequently used as a scarecrow.

Price Leontyne 1927– . US opera singer. She played a leading singing role in Ira Gershwin's revival of his musical *Porgy and Bess* 1952–54. Gaining a national reputation, she made her operatic debut in San Francisco 1957. Price appeared at La Scala in Milan 1959 and became a regular member of the Metropolitan Opera in New York 1961.

Price Vincent 1911–1993. US actor who made his film debut in 1938 after a stage career. He is remembered for *Laura* 1944 and *Leave Her To Heaven* 1945 before becoming a star of horror films, including *Dragonwick* 1946, *House of Wax* 1953, the cult favorite *The Tingler* 1959, *The Fall of the House of Usher* 1960, and five more Roger Corman "campy" horrors through 1964. He is noted for hosting TV's "Mystery" series.

prickly pear cactus of the genus *Opuntia*, native to Central and South America, mainly Mexico and Chile, but naturalized in S Europe, N Africa, and Australia, where it is a pest. The common prickly pear *O. vulgaris* is low-growing, with flat, oval, stem joints, bright yellow flowers, and prickly, oval fruit; the flesh and seeds of the peeled fruit have a pleasant taste.

Priestley J(ohn) B(oynton) 1894–1984. English novelist and playwright. His first success was a novel about

Presley The "King of Rock and Roll," Elvis Presley, who created some of the most intense records of the period.

traveling theater, *The Good Companions* 1929. He followed it with a realist novel about London life, *Angel Pavement* 1930. As a playwright he was often preoccupied with theories of time, as in *An Inspector Calls* 1945.

primary in presidential election campaigns in the US, a statewide election to decide the candidates for the two main parties. Held in 35 states, primaries begin with New Hampshire in Feb and continue until June; they operate under varying complex rules.

primate in zoology, any member of the order of mammals that includes monkeys, apes, and humans (together called *anthropoids*), as well as lemurs, bushbabies, lorises, and tarsiers (together called *prosimians*). Generally, they have forward-directed eyes, gripping hands and feet, opposable thumbs, and big toes. They tend to have nails rather than claws, with gripping pads on the ends of the digits, all adaptations to the arboreal, climbing mode of life.

primate in the Christian church, the official title of an archbishop.

prime minister or *premier* head of a parliamentary government, usually the leader of the largest party. In countries with an executive president, the prime minister is of lesser standing, whereas in those with dual executives, such as France, power is shared with the president. *See table p. 756*

prime number number that can be divided only by 1 or itself, that is, having no other factors. There is an infinite number of primes, the first ten of which are 2, 3, 5, 7, 11, 13, 17, 19, 23, and 29 (by definition, the number 1 is excluded from the set of prime numbers). The number 2 is the only even prime because all other even numbers have 2 as a factor.

prime rate the interest rate charged by commercial banks to their best customers. It is the lowest interest or base rate on which other rates are calculated according to the risk involved. Only borrowers who have the highest credit rating qualify for the prime rate.

Primo de Rivera Miguel 1870–1930. Spanish soldier and politician, dictator from 1923 as well as premier from 1925. He was captain-general of Catalonia when he led a coup against the ineffective monarchy and became virtual dictator of Spain with the support of Alfonso XIII. He resigned 1930.

Primorye territory of Russia, SE Siberia, on the Sea of Japan; area 64,079 sq mi/165,900 sq km; population (1985) 2,136,000; capital Vladivostok. Timber and coal are produced.

prime ministers of Britain

Sir Robert Walpole	(Whig)	1721	Earl of Derby	(Conservative)	1866
Earl of Wilmington	(Whig)	1742	Benjamin Disraeli	(Conservative)	1868
Henry Pelham	(Whig)	1743	W E Gladstone	(Liberal)	1886
Duke of Newcastle	(Whig)	1754	Benjamin Disraeli	(Conservative)	1874
Duke of Devonshire	(Whig)	1756	W E Gladstone	(Liberal)	1880
Duke of Newcastle	(Whig)	1757	Marquess of Salisbury	(Conservative)	1885
Earl of Bute	(Tory)	1762	W E Gladstone	(Liberal)	1886
George Grenville	(Whig)	1763	Marquess of Salisbury	(Conservative)	1886
Marquess of Rockingham	(Whig)	1765	W E Gladstone	(Liberal)	1892
Duke of Grafton	(Whig)	1766	Earl of Roseberry	(Liberal)	1894
Lord North	(Tory)	1770	Marquess of Salisbury	(Conservative)	1895
Marquess of Rockingham	(Whig)	1782	Sir H Campbell-Bannerman	(Liberal)	1905
Earl of Shelbourne	(Whig)	1782	H H Asquith	(Liberal)	1908
William Pitt	(Tory)	1783	H H Asquith	(Coalition)	1915
Duke of Portland	(Coalition)	1783	D Lloyd George	(Coalition)	1916
Henry Addington	(Tory)	1801	A Bonar Law	(Conservative)	1922
William Pitt	(Tory)	1804	Stanley Baldwin	(Conservative)	1923
Lord Grenville	(Whig)	1806	Ramsay MacDonald	(Labour)	1924
Duke of Portland	(Tory)	1807	Stanley Baldwin	(Conservative)	1924
Spencer Percival	(Tory)	1809	Ramsay MacDonald	(Labour)	1929
Earl of Liverpool	(Tory)	1812	Ramsay MacDonald	(National)	1931
George Canning	(Tory)	1827	Stanley Baldwin	(National)	1935
Viscount Goderich	(Tory)	1827	N Chamberlain	(National)	1937
Duke of Wellington	(Tory)	1828	Sir Winston Churchill	(Coalition)	1940
Earl Grey	(Whig)	1830	Clement Attlee	(Labour)	1945
Viscount Melbourne	(Whig)	1834	Sir Winston Churchill	(Conservative)	1951
Sir Robert Peel	(Conservative)	1834	Sir Anthony Eden	(Conservative)	1955
Viscount Melbourne	(Whig)	1835	Harold Macmillan	(Conservative)	1957
Sir Robert Peel	(Conservative)	1841	Sir Alec Douglas-Home	(Conservative)	1963
Lord J Russell	(Liberal)	1846	Harold Wilson	(Labour)	1964
Earl of Derby	(Conservative)	1852	Edward Heath	(Conservative)	1970
Lord Aberdeen	(Peelite)	1852	Harold Wilson	(Labour)	1974
Viscount Palmerston	(Liberal)	1855	James Callaghan	(Labour)	1976
Earl of Derby	(Conservative)	1858	Margaret Thatcher	(Conservative)	1979
Viscount Palmerston	(Liberal)	1859	John Major	(Conservative)	1990
Lord J Russell	(Liberal)	1865			

primrose any plant of the genus *Primula*, family Primulaceae, with showy five-lobed flowers. The common primrose *P. vulgaris* is a woodland plant, native to Europe, bearing pale yellow flowers in spring. Related to it is the cowslip.

prince royal or noble title. In Rome and medieval Italy it was used as the title of certain officials, for example, *princeps senatus* (Latin "leader of the Senate"). The title was granted to the king's sons in 15th-century France, and in England from Henry VII's time.

Prince Adopted name of Prince Rogers Nelson 1960– . US pop musician who composes, arranges, and produces his own records and often plays all the instruments. His albums, including *1999* 1982 and *Purple Rain* 1984, contain elements of rock, funk,

and jazz. His stage shows are energetic and extravagant.

Prince Edward Island province of E Canada
area 2,200 sq mi/5,700 sq km
capital Charlottetown
features Prince Edward Island National Park; Summerside Lobster Carnival
products potatoes, dairy products, lobsters, oysters, farm vehicles
population (1991) 129,900
history first recorded visit by Cartier 1534, who called it Isle St-Jean; settled by French; taken by British 1758; annexed to Nova Scotia 1763; separate colony 1769; renamed after Prince Edward of Kent, father of Queen Victoria 1798; settled by Scottish 1803; joined Confederation 1873.

Prince William Sound channel in the Gulf of Alaska, extending 125 mi/200 km NW from Kayak Island. In March 1989 the oil tanker *Exxon Valdez* ran aground here, spilling 12 million gallons of crude oil in one of the world's greatest oil-pollution disasters.

printed circuit board (PCB) electrical circuit created by laying (printing) "tracks" of a conductor such as copper on one or both sides of an insulating board. The PCB was invented in 1936 by Austrian scientist Paul Eisler, and was first used on a large scale in 1948.

printer in computing, an output device for producing printed copies of text or graphics. Types include the *daisywheel printer*, which produces good-quality text but no graphics; the *dot-matrix printer*, which

Prince Edward Island

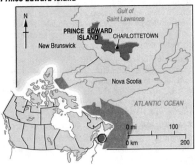

produces text and graphics by printing a pattern of small dots; the ***ink-jet printer***, which creates text and graphics by spraying a fine jet of quick-drying ink onto the paper; and the ◊***laser printer***, which uses electrostatic technology very similar to that used by a photocopier to produce high-quality text and graphics.

printing reproduction of text or illustrative material on paper, as in books or newspapers, or on an increasing variety of materials; for example, on plastic containers. The first printing used woodblocks, followed by carved wood type or molded metal type and hand-operated presses. Modern printing is effected by electronically controlled machinery. Current printing processes include electronic phototypesetting with ◊offset printing, and ◊gravure print.

printmaking creating a picture or design by printing from a plate (block, stone, or sheet) that holds ink or color. The oldest form of print is the woodcut, common in medieval Europe, followed by line ◊engraving (from the 15th century), and ◊etching (from the 17th); colored woodblock prints flourished in Japan from the 18th century. ◊Lithography was invented 1796.

prism in mathematics, a solid figure whose cross section is constant in planes drawn perpendicular to its axis. A cube, for example, is a rectangular prism with all faces (bases and sides) the same shape and size.

prism in optics, a triangular block of transparent material (plastic, glass, silica) commonly used to "bend" a ray of light or split a beam into its spectral colors. Prisms are used as mirrors to define the optical path in binoculars, camera viewfinders, and periscopes. The dispersive property of prisms is used in the spectroscope.

prison place of confinement for those accused of and/or convicted of contravening the law; after conviction most jurisdictions claim to aim at rehabilitation and deterrence as well as punishment. For major crimes, life imprisonment or death may be the sentence. Parole and probation programs exist, and "work-release" furlough programs allow convicts to work outside the prison or make family visits during their sentences.

privacy the right of the individual to be free from secret surveillance (by scientific devices or other means) and from the disclosure to unauthorized persons of personal data, as accumulated in computer data banks. Always an issue complicated by considerations of state security, public welfare (in the case of criminal activity), and other factors, it has been rendered more complex by present-day technology.

private enterprise sector of the economy in which economic activity is initiated through private capital and pursued for private profit. It is distinguished from ◊public spending, although public funds are often funneled into private enterprises, as with defense contractors or infrastructure development (public works contractors).

printed circuit board

A typical microcomputer PCB

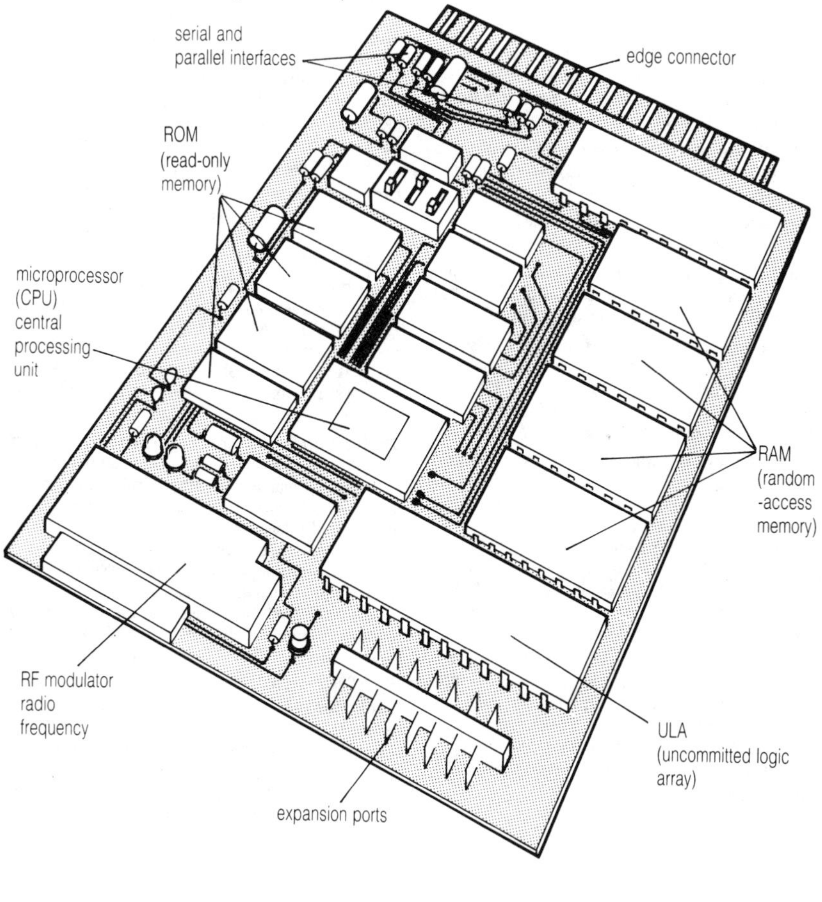

serial and parallel interfaces

edge connector

ROM (read-only memory)

microprocessor (CPU) central processing unit

RAM (random -access memory)

RF modulator radio frequency

ULA (uncommitted logic array)

expansion ports

printed circuit board *A typical microcomputer printed circuit board, or PCB.*

privateer privately owned and armed ship commissioned by a state to attack enemy vessels. The crews of such ships were, in effect, legalized pirates; they were not paid but received a share of the spoils. Privateering existed from ancient times until the 19th century, when it was declared illegal by the Declaration of Paris 1856.

privatization policy or process of selling or transferring state-owned or public assets and services (notably nationalized industries) to private investors. Privatization of services involves the government contracting private firms to supply services previously supplied by public authorities.

privet any evergreen shrub of the genus *Ligustrum* of the olive family Oleaceae, with dark green leaves, including the European common privet *L. vulgare*, with white flowers and black berries, naturalized in North America, and the native North American California privet *L. ovalifolium*, also known as hedge privet.

Prix Goncourt French literary prize for fiction, given by the Académie Goncourt (founded by Edmond de ◊Goncourt 1903).

probability likelihood, or chance, that an event will occur, often expressed as odds, or in mathematics, numerically as a fraction or decimal. In general, the probability that n particular events will happen out of a total of m possible events is n/m. A certainty has a probability of 1; an impossibility has a probability of 0. Empirical probability is defined as the number of successful events divided by the total possible number of events.

probate system for the administration of inheritance. Generally the function of probate (sometimes surrogate's) courts, probate determines the validity of wills, and the satisfaction of requirements of inheritance law. In the cases of persons dying without wills (intestacy), probate courts appoint administrators of estates.

probation in law, the placing of offenders under supervision of probation officers in the community, as an alternative to prison.

processor in computing, another name for the ◊central processing unit or ◊microprocessor of a computer.

Proconsul prehistoric ape skull found on Rusinga Island in Lake Victoria (Nyanza), E Africa, by Mary ◊Leakey. It is believed to be 20 million years old.

Procyon or *Alpha Canis Minoris* brightest star in the constellation Canis Minor and the eighth-brightest star in the sky. Procyon is a white star 11.4 light-years from Earth, with a mass of 1.7 Suns. It has a ◊white dwarf companion that orbits it every 40 years.

producer price index (PPI) measure of price changes. In 1978 the US government revised its reporting of wholesale price indexes to reflect separate price changes at three stages of the production process. Crude materials, intermediate goods, and finished goods were indexed separately, and each of these is a PPI. The finished goods index, the most cited PPI, and the ◊consumer price index are the two most common measures of inflation and cost of living.

productivity in economics, the output produced by a given quantity of labor, usually measured as output per person employed in the firm, industry, sector, or economy concerned. Productivity is determined by the quality and quantity of the fixed ◊capital used by labor, and the effort of the workers concerned.

profit-sharing system whereby an employer pays workers a share of the company's profits, which is often a percentage based on annual salary and invested by the employer in a retirement plan operated or overseen by the employer. It may be paid as cash or shares of stock in the firm. It originated in France in the early 19th century and was widely practiced for a time within the cooperative movement.

progesterone ◊steroid hormone that occurs in vertebrates. In mammals, it regulates the menstrual cycle and pregnancy. Progesterone is secreted by the corpus luteum (the ruptured Graafian follicle of a discharged ovum).

program in computing, a set of instructions that controls the operation of a computer. There are two main kinds: *applications programs*, which carry out tasks for the benefit of the user—for example, word processing; and ◊*systems programs*, which control the internal workings of the computer. A *utility program* is a systems program that carries out specific tasks for the user. Programs can be written in any of a number of ◊programming languages but are always translated into machine code before they can be executed by the computer.

programming language in computing, a special notation in which instructions for controlling a computer are written. Programming languages are designed to be easy for people to write and read, but must be capable of being mechanically translated (by a ◊compiler or an interpreter) into the machine code that the computer can execute. Programming languages may be classified as ◊high-level languages or low-level languages.

progression sequence of numbers each formed by a specific relationship to its predecessor. An *arithmetic progression* has numbers that increase or decrease by a common sum or difference (for example, 2, 4, 6, 8); a *geometric progression* has numbers each bearing a fixed ratio to its predecessor (for example, 3, 6, 12, 24); and a *harmonic progression* has numbers whose ◊reciprocals are in arithmetical progression, for example 1, ½, ⅓, ¼.

progressive education teaching methods that take as their starting point children's own aptitudes and interests, and encourage them to follow their own investigations and lines of inquiry.

Progressivism in US history, the name of both a reform movement and a political party, active in the two decades before World War I. Mainly middle-class and urban-based, Progressives secured legislation at national, state, and local levels to improve the democratic system, working conditions, and welfare provision.

Prohibition in US history, the period 1920–33 when the 18th Amendment to the US Constitution was in force, and the manufacture, transportation, and sale of intoxicating liquors were illegal. It represented the culmination of a long campaign by Populists, Progressives, temperance societies, and the Anti-Saloon League. This led to ◊bootlegging (the illegal distribution of liquor, often illicitly distilled), widespread disdain for the law, speakeasies, and greatly increased organized crime activity, especially in Chicago and towns near the Canadian border. Public opinion insisted on repeal 1933.

projector any apparatus that projects a picture on to a screen. In a *slide projector*, a lamp shines a light through the photographic slide or transparency, and a projection ◊lens throws an enlarged image of the slide onto the screen. A *film projector* has similar optics, but incorporates a mechanism that holds the film still while light is transmitted through each frame (picture). A shutter covers the film when it moves between frames.

Prokhorov Aleksandr 1916– . Russian physicist whose fundamental work on microwaves in 1955 led to the construction of the first practical ◊maser (the microwave equivalent of the laser) by Charles Townes, for which they shared the 1964 Nobel Prize for Physics.

Prokofiev Sergey (Sergeyevich) 1891–1953. Soviet composer. His music includes operas such as *The Love for Three Oranges* 1921; ballets for Sergei ◊Diaghilev, including *Romeo and Juliet* 1935; seven symphonies including the *Classical Symphony* 1916–17; music for films; piano and violin concertos; songs and cantatas (for example, that composed for the 30th anniversary of the October Revolution); and *Peter and the Wolf* 1936.

prolapse displacement of an organ due to the effects of strain in weakening the supporting tissues. The term is most often used with regard to the rectum (due to chronic bowel problems) or the uterus (following several pregnancies).

proletariat in Marxist theory, those classes in society that possess no property, and therefore depend on the sale of their labor or expertise (as opposed to the capitalists or bourgeoisie, who own the means of production, and the petty bourgeoisie, or working small-property owners). They are usually divided into the industrial, agricultural, and intellectual proletariat.

PROLOG (acronym for *programming in logic*) high-level computer-programming language based on logic. Invented in 1971 at the University of Marseille, France, it did not achieve widespread use until more than ten years later. It is used mainly for ◊artificial-intelligence programming.

PROM (acronym for *programmable read-only memory*) in computing, a memory device in the form of an integrated circuit (chip) that can be programmed after manufacture to hold information permanently. PROM chips are empty of information when manufactured, unlike ROM (read-only memory) chips, which have information built into them. Other memory devices are EPROM (erasable programmable read-only memory) and ◊RAM (random-access memory).

Prometheus in Greek mythology, a ◊Titan who stole fire from heaven for the human race. In revenge, Zeus had him chained to a rock where an eagle came each day to feast on his liver, which grew back each night, until he was rescued by the hero ◊Heracles.

promethium radioactive, metallic element of the ◊lanthanide series, symbol Pm, atomic number 61, atomic weight 145. It occurs in nature only in minute amounts, produced as a fission product/byproduct of uranium in ◊pitchblende and other uranium ores; for a long time it was considered not to occur in nature. The longest-lived isotope has a half-life of slightly more than 20 years.

pronghorn ruminant mammal *Antilocapra americana* constituting the family Antilocapridae, native to the W US. It is not a true antelope. It is light brown and about 3 ft/1 m high. It sheds its horns annually and can reach speeds of 60 mph/100 kph.

The loss of prairies to agriculture, combined with excessive hunting, has brought this unique animal close to extinction.

pronoun in grammar, a part of speech that is used in place of a noun, usually to save repetition of the noun.

For example: "The people arrived around nine o'clock. *They* behaved as though we were expecting *them*." Here, *they* and *them* are substitutes for repeating "the people."

pronunciation the way in which words are rendered into human speech sounds; either a language as a whole ("French pronunciation") or a particular word or name ("what is the pronunciation of *controversy?*"). The pronunciation of languages forms the academic subject of ◊phonetics.

propaganda systematic spreading (propagation) of information or disinformation, usually to promote a religious or political doctrine with the intention of instilling particular attitudes or responses. Examples of the use of propaganda are the racial doctrines put forth by Nazism in World War II, and some of the ideas and strategies propagated by the US and the USSR during the ◊Cold War (1945–90).

propane C_3H_8 gaseous hydrocarbon of the ◊alkane series, found in petroleum and used as fuel.

propanol or *propyl alcohol* third member of the homologous series of ◊alcohols. Propanol is usually a mixture of two isomeric compounds (see ◊isomer): 1-propanol ($CH_3CH_2CH_2OH$) and 2-propanol ($CH_3CHOHCH_3$). Both are colorless liquids that can be mixed with water and are used in perfumery.

propellant substance burned in a rocket for propulsion. Two propellants are used: oxidizer and fuel are stored in separate tanks and pumped independently into the combustion chamber. Liquid oxygen (oxidizer) and liquid hydrogen (fuel) are common propellants, used, for example, in the space-shuttle main engines. The explosive charge that propels a projectile from a gun is also called a propellant.

propeller screwlike device used to propel some ships and airplanes. A propeller has a number of curved blades that describe a helical path as they rotate with the hub, and accelerate fluid (liquid or gas) backward during rotation. Reaction to this backward movement of fluid sets up a propulsive thrust forward. The marine screw propeller was developed by Francis Pettit Smith in the UK and Swedish-born John Ericsson in the US and was first used 1839. The airscrew is used to propel piston or turboprop ◊airplanes.

Propertius Sextus *c.* 47–15 BC. Roman elegiac poet, a member of Maecenas' circle, who wrote of his love for his mistress "Cynthia."

property the right to title and to control the use of a thing (such as land, a building, a work of art, or a computer program). In US law, a distinction is made

pronghorn *The pronghorn is unique in that it sheds annually the sheaths that cover its horns.*

between real property, which involves a degree of geographical fixity, and personal property, which does not. Property is never absolute, since any society places limits on an individual's property (such as the right to transfer that property to another). Different societies have held widely varying interpretations of the nature of property and the extent of the rights of the owner to that property.

prophet person thought to speak from divine inspiration or one who foretells the future. In the Bible, the chief prophets were Elijah, Amos, Hosea, and Isaiah. In Islam, Muhammad is believed to be the last and greatest of a long line of prophets beginning with Adam and including Moses and Jesus.

prophylaxis any measure taken to prevent disease, including exercise and ◊vaccination. Prophylactic (preventive) medicine is an aspect of public-health provision that is receiving increasing attention.

proportion two variable quantities x and y are proportional if, for all values of x, $y = kx$, where k is a constant. This means that if x increases, y increases in a linear fashion.

prose spoken or written language without metrical regularity; in literature, prose corresponds more closely to the patterns of everyday speech than ◊poetry.

Proserpina in Roman mythology, the goddess of the underworld. Her Greek equivalent is ◊Persephone.

prostate gland gland surrounding and opening into the ◊urethra at the base of the ◊bladder in male mammals.

prosthesis replacement of a body part with an artificial substitute. Prostheses include artificial limbs, hearing aids, false teeth and eyes, and for the heart, a ◊pacemaker and plastic heart valves and blood vessels.

prostitution receipt of money for sexual acts. Society's attitude toward prostitution varies according to place and period. In some countries, tolerance is combined with licensing of brothels and health checks of the prostitutes (both male and female).

protactinium (Latin *proto* "before" + actinium) silver-gray, radioactive, metallic element of the ◊actinide series, symbol Pa, atomic number 91, atomic weight 231.036. It occurs in nature in very small quantities, in ◊pitchblende and other uranium ores. It has 14 known isotopes; the longest-lived, Pa-231, has a half-life of 32,480 years.

protectionism in economics, the imposition of heavy duties or import quotas by a government as a means of discouraging the import of foreign goods likely to compete with domestic products. Price controls, quota systems, and the reduction of surpluses are among the measures taken for agricultural products in the European Community (see ◊agriculture). The opposite practice is ◊free trade.

protectorate formerly in international law, a small state under the direct or indirect control of a larger one. The 20th-century equivalent was a ◊trust territory. In English history the rule of Oliver and Richard ◊Cromwell 1653–59 is referred to as *the Protectorate*.

protein complex, biologically important substance composed of ◊amino acids joined by ◊peptide bonds. Other types of bond, such as sulfur–sulfur bonds, hydrogen bonds, and cation bridges between acid sites, are responsible for creating the protein's characteristic three-dimensional structure, which may be fibrous, globular, or pleated.

protein engineering the creation of synthetic proteins designed to carry out specific tasks. For example, an enzyme may be designed to remove grease from soiled clothes and remain stable at the high temperatures in a washing machine.

pro tem abbreviation for *pro tempore* (Latin "for the time being").

Proterozoic eon of geological time, possible 3.5 billion to 570 million years ago, the second division of the Precambrian. It is defined as the time of simple life, since many rocks dating from this eon show traces of biological activity, and some contain the fossils of bacteria and algae.

Protestantism one of the main divisions of Christianity, which emerged from Roman Catholicism at the ◊Reformation. The chief Protestant denominations are the Episcopalian (Anglican Communion in the UK), Baptists, Christian Scientists, Congregationalists (United Church of Christ), Lutherans, Methodists, Pentecostals, and Presbyterians, with a total membership in about 300 million.

Proteus in Greek mythology, the warden of the sea beasts of the sea god Poseidon, who possessed the gift of prophecy and could transform himself into any form he chose to evade questioning.

protocol in computing, an agreed set of standards for the transfer of data between different devices. They cover transmission speed, format of data, and the signals required to synchronize the transfer. See also ◊interface.

proton positively charged ◊elementary particle, a constituent of the nucleus of all atoms. It belongs to the baryon group of hadrons and is composed of two up quarks and one down quark. A proton is extremely long-lived, with a life span of at least 10^{32} years. It carries a unit positive charge equal to the negative charge of an ◊electron. Its mass is almost 1,836 times that of an electron, or 1.673×10^{-24} g. The number of protons in the atom of an ◊element is equal to the atomic number of that element.

protoplasm contents of a living cell. Strictly speaking it includes all the discrete structures (organelles) in a cell, but it is often used simply to mean the jellylike material in which these float. The contents of a cell outside the nucleus are called ◊cytoplasm.

protozoan any of a group of single-celled, mainly heterotrophic organisms without rigid cell walls. Some, such as amebas, ingest other cells, but most are saprotrophs or parasites. They all require a fluid environment, and include ciliates, flagellates, rhizopods, and sporozoans.

protractor instrument used to measure a flat ◊angle.

Proudhon Pierre Joseph 1809–1865. French anarchist, born in Besançon. He sat in the Constituent Assembly of 1848, was imprisoned for three years, and had to go into exile in Brussels.

Proust Marcel 1871–1922. French novelist and critic. His immense autobiographical work *A la Recherche du temps perdu/Remembrance of Things Past* 1913–27, consisting of a series of novels, is the expression of his childhood memories coaxed from his subconscious; it is also a precise reflection of life in France at the end of the 19th century.

Provençal language member of the Romance branch of the Indo-European language family, spoken in and around Provence in SE France. It is now regarded as a dialect or patois.

Provence-Alpes-Côte d'Azur region of SE France, comprising the *départements* of Alpes-de-Haute-Provence, Hautes-Alpes, Alpes-Maritimes, Bouches-du-Rhône, Var, and Vaucluse; area 12,120 sq mi/31,400 sq km; capital Marseille; population (1986) 4,059,000. The *Côte d'Azur*, on the Mediterranean, is a tourist center. Provence was an independent kingdom in the 10th century, and the area still has its own language, Provençal.

Proverbs book of the Old Testament traditionally ascribed to the Hebrew king ◊Solomon. The Proverbs form a series of maxims on moral and ethical matters.

Providence industrial seaport (jewelry, silverware, textiles and textile machinery, watches, chemicals, meatpacking) and capital of Rhode Island, on Narragansett Bay and the Providence River, 27 mi/43 km from the Atlantic Ocean; population (1990) 160,700. Educational institutions include Brown University and the Rhode Island School of Design. Providence was founded 1636 by Roger William, who had been banished from Plymouth colony for his religious beliefs.

provitamin any precursor substance of a vitamin. Provitamins are injected substances that become converted to active vitamins within the organism. One example is ergosterol (provitamin D_2), which through the action of sunlight is converted to calciferol (vitamin D_2); another example is B-carotene, which is hydrolyzed in the liver to vitamin A.

Provo city in N central Utah, on the Provo River, SE of Salt Lake City; seat of Utah County; population (1990) 86,800.

Industries include iron and steel, food processing, and electronics. Brigham Young University is here.

Proxima Centauri the closest star to the Sun, 4.2 light-years away. It is a faint ◊red dwarf, visible only with a telescope, and is a member of the Alpha Centauri triple-star system.

proxy in law, a person authorized to stand in another's place; also the document conferring this right. The term usually refers to voting at meetings, but marriages by proxy are possible.

Prudhoe Bay a bay of the Arctic Ocean on the N coast (North Slope) of Alaska. An immense oil strike in the area in 1968 led to the construction of the 789-mi/1,270-km Trans-Alaska Pipeline, completed 1977, that carries oil from Prudhoe Bay to Valdez, on the S coast of Alaska. Almost 20% of US oil comes from the North Slope fields, although production has slowed.

Prussia N German state 1618–1945 on the Baltic coast. It was an independent kingdom until 1867, when it became, under Otto von ◊Bismarck, the military power of the North German Confederation and part of the German Empire 1871 under the Prussian king Wilhelm I. West Prussia became part of Poland under the Treaty of ◊Versailles, and East Prussia was largely incorporated into the USSR after 1945.

psalm sacred poem or song of praise. The Book of Psalms in the Old Testament is divided into five books containing 150 psalms. They are traditionally ascribed to David, the second king of Israel.

psi in parapsychology, a hypothetical faculty common to humans and other animals said to be responsible for extra-sensory perception (ESP) and telekinesis.

psoriasis chronic, recurring skin disease characterized by raised, red, scaly patches, usually on the scalp, back, arms, and/or legs. Tar preparations, steroid creams, and ultraviolet light are used to treat it, and sometimes it disappears spontaneously. Psoriasis may be accompanied by a form of arthritis (inflammation of the joints).

Psyche late Greek personification of the soul as a winged girl or young woman. The goddess Aphrodite was so jealous of Psyche's beauty that she ordered her son Eros, the god of love, to make Psyche fall in love with the worst of men. Instead, he fell in love with her himself.

psychedelic drug any drug that produces hallucinations or altered states of consciousness. Such sensory experiences may be in the auditory, visual, tactile, olfactory, or gustatory fields or in any combination. Among drugs known to have psychedelic effects are LSD (lysergic acid diethylamine), mescaline, and, to a mild degree, marijuana, along with a number of other plant-derived or synthetically prepared substances. Most of these drugs are known to cause temporary or recurring psychotic episodes.

psychedelic rock or *acid rock* pop music that usually involves advanced electronic equipment for both light and sound. The free-form improvisations and light shows that appeared about 1966, attempting to suggest or improve on mind-altering drug experiences, had by the 1980s evolved into stadium performances with lasers and other special effects.

psychiatry branch of medicine dealing with the diagnosis and treatment of mental disorder, normally divided into the areas of *neurotic conditions* including anxiety, depression, and hysteria and *psychotic* disorders such as schizophrenia. Psychiatric treatment consists of analysis, drugs, or electroconvulsive therapy.

psychoanalysis theory and treatment method for neuroses, developed by Sigmund ◊Freud. The main treatment method involves the free association of ideas, and their interpretation by patient and analyst. It is typically prolonged and expensive and its effectiveness has been disputed.

psychology systematic study of human and animal behavior. The first psychology laboratory was founded 1879 by Wilhelm Wundt at Leipzig, Germany. The subject includes diverse areas of study and application, among them the roles of instinct, heredity, environment, and culture; the processes of sensation, perception, learning and memory; the bases of motivation and emotion; and the functioning of thought, intelligence, and language. Significant psychologists have included Gustav Fechner (1801–1887) founder of psychophysics; Wolfgang Köhler (1887–1967), one of the ◊gestalt or "whole" psychologists; Sigmund Freud and his associates Carl Jung, Alfred Adler, and Hermann Rorschach (1884–1922); William James, Jean Piaget; Carl Rogers; Hans Eysenck; J B Watson, and B F Skinner.

psychopathy personality disorder characterized by chronic antisocial behavior (violating the rights of others, often violently) and an absence of feelings of guilt about the behavior.

psychosis or *psychotic disorder* general term for a serious mental disorder where the individual commonly loses contact with reality and may experience hallucinations (seeing or hearing things that do not exist) or delusions (fixed false beliefs). For example, in a paranoid psychosis, an individual may believe that others are plotting against him or her. A major type of psychosis is ◊schizophrenia (which may be biochemically induced).

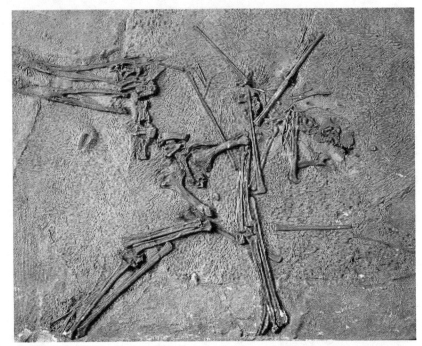

pterodactyl Fossil remains of a pterodactyl discovered in Württemberg, Germany.

psychosomatic a physical symptom or disease, thought to arise from emotional or mental factors.

psychosurgery operation to achieve some mental effect. For example, *lobotomy* is the separation of the white fibers in the prefrontal lobe of the brain, as a means of relieving a deep state of anxiety.

It is irreversible and the degree of personality change is not predictable. Some states strictly regulate its use.

psychotherapy treatment approaches for psychological problems involving talking rather than surgery or drugs. Examples include ◊cognitive therapy and ◊psychoanalysis.

pterodactyl genus of ◊pterosaur.

pterosaur extinct flying reptile of the order Pterosauria, existing in the Mesozoic age. They ranged from starling size to a 40 ft/12 m wingspan. Some had horns on their heads that, when in flight, made a whistling to roaring sound.

Ptolemy I *c.* 367–283 BC. Ruler of Egypt from 323 BC, king from 304. He was one of ◊Alexander the Great's generals, and established the dynasty and Macedonian organization of the state in Alexandria.

Ptolemy XIII 63–47 BC. Joint ruler of Egypt with his sister-wife ◊Cleopatra in the period preceding the Roman annexation of Egypt. He was killed fighting against Julius ◊Caesar.

puberty stage in human development when the individual becomes sexually mature. It may occur from the age of ten upward.

The sexual organs take on their adult form and pubic hair grows. In girls, menstruation begins, and the breasts develop; in boys, the voice breaks and becomes deeper, and facial hair develops.

pubes lowest part of the front of the human trunk, the region where the external generative organs are situated. The underlying bony structure, the pubic

arch, is formed by the union in the midline of the two pubic bones, which are the front portions of the hip bones. In women this is more prominent than in men, to allow more room for the passage of the child's head at birth, and it carries a pad of fat and connective tissue, the *mons veneris* (mountain of Venus), for its protection.

public corporation management and administrative structure, similar to a private ◊corporation, established to run state-owned or nationalized enterprises. They are governed by a board of directors, although some level of government is either the sole or controlling stockholder.

public school in the US and many English-speaking countries, "public" schools are maintained by the state, and "private" schools are independent institutions, supported by fees. In England, public schools are fee-paying independent schools.

public spending expenditure by government, covering the military, health, education, infrastructure, development projects, and the cost of servicing overseas borrowing.

Puccini Giacomo (Antonio Domenico Michele Secondo Maria) 1858–1924. Italian opera composer whose music shows a strong gift for melody and dramatic effect and whose operas combine exotic plots with elements of *verismo* (realism). They include *Manon Lescaut* 1893, *La Bohème* 1896, *Tosca* 1900, *Madame Butterfly* 1904, and the unfinished *Turandot* 1926.

Puebla (de Zaragoza) industrial city (textiles, sugar refining, metallurgy, hand-crafted pottery and tiles) and capital of Puebla state, S central Mexico; population (1986) 1,218,000. Founded 1535 as *Pueblo de los Angeles*, it was later renamed after General de Zaragoza, who defeated the French here 1862.

Pueblo city in S central Colorado, on the Arkansas River, SE of Colorado Springs; population (1990)

98,600. Industries include steel, coal, lumber, and livestock and other agricultural products.

Pueblo Indian (Spanish *pueblos*, villages) generic name for a member of any of the farming groups of the SW US and N Mexico, living in communal villages of flat-topped adobe or stone structures arranged in terraces. Surviving groups include the Hopi and the Zuni.

Puerto Rico the Commonwealth of, island of the West Indies (known as Porto Rico 1898–1932)
area 3,475 sq mi/9,000 sq km
capital San Juan
cities ports: Mayagüez, Ponce
features Old San Juan; nightclubs and casinos; rain forest of El Yunque; colonial-style San German; Arecibo Observatory
products apparel, textiles, pharmaceuticals, petroleum products, rum, refined sugar, coffee, computers, instruments, office machines, cattle, hogs, milk, cement
currency US dollar
population (1990) 3,522,000
language Spanish and English (official)
religion Roman Catholic
government under the constitution of 1952, similar to that of the US, with a governor elected for four years and a legislative assembly with a senate and house of representatives
famous people Roberto Clemente, José Ferrer, Eugenio María de Hostos, Raul Julia, Rita Moreno, Luís Muñoz Marín
history visited 1493 by Columbus; annexed by Spain 1509; ceded to the US after the ◊Spanish-American War 1898; achieved commonwealth status with local self-government 1952.

puff adder variety of ◊adder, a poisonous snake.

puffin any of various sea birds of the genus *Fratercula* of the ◊auk family, found in the N Atlantic and Pacific. The puffin is about 14 in/35 cm long, with a white face and front, red legs, and a large deep bill, very brightly colored in summer. Having short wings and webbed feet, puffins are poor fliers but excellent swimmers. They nest in rock crevices, or make burrows, and lay a single egg.

pug breed of small dog with short wrinkled face, chunky body, and tail curled over the hip. It weighs 13–18 lb/6–8 kg.

Puget Sound inlet of the Pacific Ocean on the W coast of Washington State.

Puglia (English *Apulia*) region of Italy, the SE "heel"; area 7,450 sq mi/19,300 sq km; capital Bari; population (1990) 4,081,500. Products include wheat, grapes, almonds, olives, and vegetables. The main industrial center is Taranto.

P'u-i (or *Pu-Yi*) Henry 1906–1967. Last emperor of China (as Hsuan Tung) from 1908 until his deposition 1912; he was restored for a week 1917. After his deposition he chose to be called Henry. He was president 1932–34 and emperor 1934–45 of the Japanese puppet state of Manchukuo (see ◊Manchuria).

Pulaski Casimir 1747–1779. Polish patriot and military leader. Hired by Silas ◊Deane and Benjamin Franklin in their campaign to recruit for the American Revolution 1775–83, he was placed in command of the Continental cavalry 1777. He saw action at Valley Forge 1777–78, and after a dispute with General Anthony Wayne, was given an independent cavalry command. He died in action in the siege of Savannah.

Pulitzer Joseph 1847–1911. Hungarian-born US newspaper publisher. He acquired *The World* 1883 in New York City and, as a publisher, his format set the style for the modern newspaper. After his death, funds provided in his will established 1912 the school of journalism at Columbia University and the annual Pulitzer Prizes in journalism, literature, and music (from 1917).

Pulitzer came to the US 1864 and became a citizen 1867. A Democrat, he merged two St Louis newspapers and published 1878 the successful St Louis *Post-Dispatch*. He made *The World* into a voice of the Democratic Party. During a circulation battle with rival publisher William Randolph ◊Hearst's papers, he and Hearst were accused of resorting to "yellow journalism," or sensationalism.

pull-down menu in computing, a list of options provided as part of a ◊graphical user interface. The presence of pull-down menus is normally indicated by a row of single words at the top of the screen. When the user points at a word with a ◊mouse, a full menu appears (is pulled down) and the user can then select the required option.

pulley simple machine consisting of a fixed, grooved wheel, sometimes in a block, around which a rope or chain can be run. A simple pulley serves only to change the direction of the applied effort (as in a simple hoist for raising loads). The use of more than

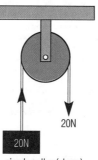

pulley The mechanical advantage of a pulley increases with the number of rope strands..

20N

20N

simple pulley (above)
pulley system used for
heavy weights (below)

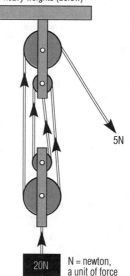

5N

20N   N = newton,
      a unit of force

one pulley results in a mechanical advantage, so that a given effort can raise a heavier load.

Pullman George 1831–1901. US engineer who developed the Pullman railroad automobile. In an attempt to improve the standard of comfort of rail travel, he built his first Pioneer Sleeping Automobile 1863. He formed the Pullman Palace Automobile Company 1867 and in 1881 the town of Pullman, Illinois, was built for his workers.

pulsar celestial source that emits pulses of energy at regular intervals, ranging from a few seconds to a few thousandths of a second. Pulsars are thought to be rapidly rotating ◊neutron stars, which flash at radio and other wavelengths as they spin. They were discovered in 1967 by Jocelyn Bell (now Burnell) and Antony Hewish at the Mullard Radio Astronomy Observatory, Cambridge, England. Over 500 radio pulsars are now known in our Galaxy, although a million or so may exist.

pulse crop such as peas and beans. Pulses are grown primarily for their seeds, which provide a concentrated source of vegetable protein, and make a vital contribution to human diets in poor countries where meat is scarce, and among vegetarians. Soybeans are the major temperate protein crop in the West; most are used for oil production or for animal feed. In Asia, most are processed into soy milk and beancurd. Groundnuts dominate pulse production in the tropical world and are generally consumed as human food.

pulse impulse transmitted by the heartbeat throughout the arterial systems of vertebrates. When the heart muscle contracts, it forces blood into the ◊aorta (the chief artery). Because the arteries are elastic, the sudden rise of pressure causes a throb or sudden swelling through them. The actual flow of the blood is about 2 ft/60 cm a second in humans. The pulse rate is generally about 70 per minute. The pulse can be felt where an artery is near the surface, for example in the wrist or the neck.

puma also called *cougar* or *mountain lion* large wild cat *Felis concolar* found in North and South America. Tawny-coated, it is 4.5 ft/1.5 m long with a 3 ft/1 m tail. Cougars live alone, with each male occupying a distinct territory; they eat deer, rodents, and cattle. They have been hunted nearly to extinction.

pumice light volcanic rock produced by the frothing action of expanding gases during the solidification of lava. It has the texture of a hard sponge and is used as an abrasive.

pump any device for moving liquids and gases, or compressing gases. Some pumps, such as the traditional *lift pump* used to raise water from wells, work by a reciprocating (up-and-down) action. Movement of a piston in a cylinder with a one-way valve creates a partial vacuum in the cylinder, thereby sucking water into it.

pumped storage hydroelectric plant that uses surplus electricity to pump water back into a high-level reservoir. In normal working conditions the water flows from this reservoir through the ◊turbines to generate power for feeding into the grid. At times of low power demand, electricity is taken from the grid to turn the turbines into pumps that then pump the water back again. This ensures that there is always a maximum "head" of water in the reservoir to give the maximum output when required.

pumpkin gourd *Cucurbita pepo* of the family Cucurbitaceae. The large, spherical fruit has a thick, orange rind, pulpy flesh, and many seeds.

pun figure of speech, a play on words, or double meaning that is technically known as *paronomasia* (Greek "adapted meaning"). Double meaning can be accidental, often resulting from homonymy, or the multiple meaning of words; puns, however, are deliberate, intended as jokes or as clever and compact remarks.

punctuation system of conventional signs (punctuation marks) and spaces employed to organize written and printed language in order to make it as readable, clear, and logical as possible.

Pune formerly *Poona* city in Maharashtra, India; population (1985) 1,685,000. Products include chemicals, rice, sugar, cotton, paper, and jewelry.

Punic (Latin *Punicus* "a Phoenician") relating to ◊Carthage, ancient city in N Africa founded by the Phoenicians.

Punic Wars three wars between ◊Rome and ◊Carthage: *First* 264–241 BC, resulted in the defeat of the Carthaginians under Hamilcar Barca and the cession of Sicily to Rome *Second* 218–201 BC, Hannibal invaded Italy, defeated the Romans at Trebia, Trasimene, and at Cannae (under Fabius Maximus), but was finally defeated himself by ◊Scipio Africanus Major at Zama (now in Algeria) *Third* 149–146 BC, ended in the destruction of Carthage, and its possessions becoming the Roman province of Africa.

Punjab (Sanskrit "five rivers": the Indus tributaries Jhelum, Chenab, Ravi, Beas, and Sutlej) former state of British India, now divided between India and Pakistan. Punjab was annexed by Britain 1849, after the Sikh Wars 1845–46 and 1848–49, and formed into a province with its capital at Lahore. Under the British, W Punjab was extensively irrigated, and land was granted to Indians who had served in the British army.

Punjab state of NW India
area 19,454 sq mi/50,400 sq km
capital Chandigarh
cities Amritsar, Jalandhar, Faridkot, Ludhiana
features mainly agricultural, crops chiefly under irrigation; longest life expectancy rates in India (59 for women, 64 for men); Harappa has ruins from the ◊Indus Valley civilization 2500 to 1600 BC
population (1991) 20,190,800
language Punjabi
religion 60% Sikh, 30% Hindu; there is friction between the two groups.

Punjab state of NE Pakistan
area 79,263 sq mi/205,344 sq km
capital Lahore
features wheat cultivation (by irrigation)
population (1981) 47,292,000
languages Punjabi, Urdu
religion Muslim.

Punjabi member of the majority ethnic group living in the Punjab. Approximately 37 million live in the Pakistan half of Punjab, while another 14 million live on the Indian side of the border. In addition to Sikhs, there are Rajputs in Punjab, some of whom have adopted Islam. The Punjabi language belongs to the Indo-Iranian branch of the Indo-European family. It is considered by some to be a variety of Hindi, by others to be a distinct language.

punk movement of disaffected youth of the late 1970s, manifesting itself in fashions and music designed to shock or intimidate. *Punk rock* began in the UK and stressed aggressive performance within a three-chord, three-minute format, as exemplified by the Sex Pistols.

pupa nonfeeding, largely immobile stage of some insect life cycles, in which larval tissues are broken down, and adult tissues and structures are formed.

puppet figure manipulated on a small stage, usually by an unseen operator. The earliest known puppets are from 10th-century BC China. The types include *finger* or *glove puppets* (such as Punch); *string marionettes* (which reached a high artistic level in ancient Burma and Sri Lanka and in Italian princely courts from the 16th to 18th centuries, and for which the composer Franz Joseph Haydn wrote his operetta *Dido* 1778); *shadow silhouettes* (operated byrods and seen on a lit screen, as in Java); and *bunraku* (devised in Osaka, Japan), in which three or four black-clad operators on stage may combine to work each puppet about 3 ft/1 m high.

During the 16th and 17th centuries, puppet shows became popular with European aristocracy, and puppets were extensively used as vehicles for caricature and satire until the 19th century, when they were offered as amusements for children in parks. In the 1920s Russian puppeteer Sergei Obraztsov founded the Puppet Theater in Moscow. Later in the 20th century interest was revived by television; for example, "The Muppet Show" in the 1970s.

Purana one of a number of sacred Hindu writings dealing with ancient times and events, and dating from the 4th century AD onward.

The 18 main texts include the *Vishnu Purāna* and *Bhāgavata*, which encourage devotion to Vishnu, above all in his incarnation as Krishna.

Purcell Henry 1659–1695. English Baroque composer. His work can be highly expressive, for example, the opera *Dido and Aeneas* 1689 and music for Dryden's *King Arthur* 1691 and for *The Fairy Queen* 1692. He wrote more than 500 works, ranging from secular operas and incidental music for plays to cantatas and church music.

purdah (Persian and Hindu "curtain") seclusion of women practiced by some Islamic and Hindu peoples. It had begun to disappear with the adoption of Western culture, but the fundamentalism of the 1980s revived it; for example, the wearing of the chador (an all-enveloping black mantle) in Iran.

The Koran actually requests only "modesty" in dress.

Pure Land Buddhism dominant form of Buddhism in China and Japan. It emphasizes faith in and love of Buddha, in particular Amitābha (Amida in Japan, Amituofo in China), the ideal "Buddha of boundless light," who has vowed that all believers who call on his name will be reborn in his Pure Land, or Western Paradise. This also applies to women, who had been debarred from attaining salvation through monastic life. There are over 16 million Pure Land Buddhists in Japan.

purgatory in Roman Catholic belief, a purificatory state or place where the souls of those who have died in a state of grace can expiate their venial sins, with a limited amount of suffering.

purge removal (for example, from a political party) of suspected opponents or persons regarded as undesirable (often by violent means). In 1934 the Nazis carried out a purge of their party and a number of party leaders were executed for an alleged plot against Adolf Hitler. During the 1930s purges were conducted in the USSR under Joseph Stalin, carried out by the secret police against political opponents, Communist Party members, minorities, civil servants, and large sections of the armed forces' officer corps. Some 10 million people were executed or deported to labor camps from 1934 to 1938.

Purim Jewish festival celebrated in Feb or March (the 14th of Adar in the Jewish calendar), commemorating Esther, who saved the Jews from destruction in 473 BC during the Persian occupation.

Puritan from 1564, a member of the Church of England who wished to eliminate Roman Catholic survivals in church ritual, or substitute a presbyterian for an episcopal form of church government. The term also covers the separatists who withdrew from the church altogether.

purpura condition marked by purplish patches on the skin or mucous membranes due to localized spontaneous bleeding. It may be harmless, as sometimes with the elderly, or linked with disease, allergy, or drug reactions.

pus yellowish liquid that forms in the body as a result of bacterial attack; it includes white blood cells (leukocytes) "killed in battle" with the bacteria, plasma, and broken-down tissue cells. An enclosed collection of pus is called an abscess.

Pusan or *Busan* chief industrial port (textiles, rubber, salt, fishing) of South Korea; population (1985) 3,797,600. It was invaded by the Japanese 1592 and opened to foreign trade 1883.

Pushkin Aleksandr 1799–1837. Russian poet and writer. His works include the novel in verse *Eugene Onegin* 1823–31 and the tragic drama *Boris Godunov* 1825. Pushkin's range was wide, and his willingness to experiment freed later Russian writers from many of the archaic conventions of the literature of his time.

Pushtu another name for the ◊Pashto language of Afghanistan and N Pakistan.

putrefaction decomposition of organic matter by microorganisms.

putsch a violent seizure of political power, such as Adolf Hitler and Erich von Ludendorff's abortive Munich beer-hall putsch Nov 1923, which attempted to overthrow the Bavarian government. The term is of Swiss–German origin.

Puttnam David (Terence) 1941– . English film producer who played a major role in reviving the British film industry internationally in the 1980s. Films include *Chariots of Fire* 1981, *The Killing Fields* 1984 (both of which won several Academy Awards), and *Memphis Belle* 1990.

Pushkin The greatest Russian poet, Alexandr Pushkin expressed his Romantic inspiration in a wide variety of lierary forms. He was fatally injured when fighting a duel arising from the indescretion of his beautiful wife.

Puvis de Chavannes Pierre Cécile 1824–1898. French Symbolist painter. His major works are vast decorative schemes in pale colors, mainly on mythological and allegorical subjects, for public buildings such as the Panthéon and Hôtel de Ville in Paris. His work influenced Paul Gauguin.

PVC abbreviation for *polyvinylchloride*, a type of plastic derived from vinyl chloride (CH_2=CHCl).

pyelitis inflammation of the renal pelvis, the central part of the kidney where urine accumulates before discharge. It is caused by bacterial infection and is more common in women than in men.

Pygmalion in Greek legend, a king of Cyprus who fell in love with an ivory statue he had carved. When Aphrodite brought it to life as a woman, Galatea, he married her.

Pygmy (sometimes *Negrillo*) member of any of several groups of small-statured, dark-skinned peoples of the rain forests of equatorial Africa. They were probably the aboriginal inhabitants of the region, before the arrival of farming peoples from elsewhere. They live nomadically in small groups, as hunter-gatherers; they also trade with other, settled people in the area.

Pylos port in SW Greece where the Battle of Navarino was fought 1827.

Pym John 1584–1643. English Parliamentarian, largely responsible for the petition of right 1628. As leader of the Puritan opposition in the ◊Long Parliament from 1640, he moved the impeachment of Charles I's advisers the Earl of Strafford and William Laud, drew up the Grand Remonstrance, and was the chief of five members of Parliament Charles I wanted arrested 1642. The five hid themselves and then emerged triumphant when the king left London.

Pynchon Thomas 1937– . US novelist who created a bizarre, labyrinthine world in his books, the first of which was *V* 1963. *Gravity's Rainbow* 1973 represents a major achievement in 20th-century literature, with its fantastic imagery and esoteric language, drawn from mathematics and science.

Born in Glen Cove, New York, Pynchon graduated from Cornell University. His other works include *The Crying of Lot 49* 1966 and *Vineland* 1990. He also published short stories in *Slow Learner* 1984.

Pyongyang capital and industrial city (coal, iron, steel, textiles, chemicals) of North Korea; population (1984) 2,640,000.

pyramid in geometry, a three-dimensional figure with triangular side-faces meeting at a common vertex (point) and with a ◊polygon as its base. The volume V of a pyramid is given by $V = Bh \div 13$, where B is the area of the base and h is the perpendicular height.

pyramid four-sided building with triangular sides. They were used in ancient Egypt to enclose a royal tomb; for example, the Great Pyramid of Khufu/Cheops at Gîza, near Cairo, 755 ft/230 m square and 481 ft/147 m high. In Babylon and Assyria broadly stepped pyramids (ziggurats) were used as the base for a shrine to a god: the Tower of ◊Babel was probably one of these.

Truncated pyramidal temple mounds were also built by the ancient Mexican and Peruvian civilizations, for example, at Teotihuacan and Cholula, near Mexico City, which is the world's largest in ground area (990 ft/300 m base, 195 ft/60 m high). Some New World pyramids were also used as royal tombs, for example, at the Mayan ceremonial center of Palenque.

pyramidal peak angular mountain peak with concave faces found in glaciated areas; for example, the Matterhorn in Switzerland. It is formed when three or four corries (steep-sided hollows) are eroded, back-to-back, around the sides of a mountain, leaving an isolated peak in the middle.

pyramid of numbers in ecology, a diagram that shows how many plants and animals there are at different levels in a ◊food chain.

pyramid The Great Pyramid was built for King Khufu of the 4th dynasty around 2650 BC, using almost two and a half million blocks of stone. To the east lie three small pyramids dedicated to members of Khufu's family.

Pyramus and Thisbe legendary Babylonian lovers whose story was retold by the Roman poet Ovid. Pursued by a lioness, Thisbe lost her veil, and when Pyramus arrived at their meeting place, he found it bloodstained. Assuming Thisbe was dead, he stabbed himself, and she, on finding his body, killed herself. In Shakespeare's *A Midsummer Night's Dream*, the "rude mechanicals" perform the story as a farce for the nobles.

Pyrenees (French *Pyrénées*, Spanish *Pirineos*) mountain range in SW Europe between France and Spain; length about 270 mi/435 km; highest peak Aneto (French Néthon) 11,172 ft/3,404 m. ◊Andorra is entirely within the range. Hydroelectric power has encouraged industrial development in the foothills.

pyrethrum popular name for some flowers of the genus *Chrysanthemum*, family Compositae. The ornamental species *C. coccineum*, and hybrids derived from it, are commonly grown in gardens. Pyrethrum powder, made from the dried flower heads of some species, is a powerful contact pesticide for aphids and mosquitoes.

pyridoxine or *vitamin B_6* $C_8H_{11}NO_3$ water-soluble ◊vitamin of the B complex. There is no clearly identifiable disease associated with deficiency but its absence from the diet can give rise to malfunction of the central nervous system and general skin disorders. Good sources are liver, meat, milk, and cereal grains. Related compounds may also show vitamin B_6 activity.

pyrite iron sulfide FeS_2; also called *fool's gold* because of its yellow metallic luster. Pyrite has a hard- ness of 6–6.5 on the Mohs' scale. It is used in the production of sulfuric acid.

Pyrrho *c.* 360–*c.* 270 BC. Greek philosopher, founder of ◊Skepticism, who maintained that since certainty was impossible, peace of mind lay in renouncing all claims to knowledge.

Pyrrhus *c.* 318–272 BC. King of ◊Epirus, Greece, from 307, who invaded Italy 280, as an ally of the Tarentines against Rome. He twice defeated the Romans but with such heavy losses that a *Pyrrhic victory* has come to mean a victory not worth winning. He returned to Greece 275 after his defeat at Beneventum, and was killed in a riot in Argos.

Pythagoras *c.* 580–500 BC. Greek mathematician and philosopher who formulated the Pythagorean theorem.

Pythagorean theorem in geometry, a theorem stating that in a right triangle, the square of the hypotenuse (the longest side) is equal to the sum of the squares of the other two sides (legs). If the hypotenuse is *c* units long and the lengths of the legs are *a* and *b*, then $c^2 = a^2 + b^2$.

python any constricting snake of the Old World subfamily Pythoninae of the family Boidae, which also includes ◊boas and the ◊anaconda. Pythons are found in the tropics of Africa, Asia, and Australia. Unlike boas, they lay eggs rather than produce living young. Some species are small, but the reticulated python *Python reticulatus* of SE Asia can grow to 33 ft/ 10 m.

greater central authority exerted over N central China, which was unified through a bureaucratic administrative system.

Qinghai or *Tsinghai* province of NW China
area 278,306 sq mi/721,000 sq km
capital Xining
features mainly desert, with nomadic herders
products oil, livestock, medical products
population (1990) 4,457,000; minorities include 900,000 Tibetans (mostly nomadic herders); Tibetan nationalists regard the province as being under colonial rule.

Qom or *Qum* holy city of Shiite Muslims, in central Iran, 90 mi/145 km S of Tehran; population (1986) 551,000. The Islamic academy of Madresseh Faizieh 1920 became the headquarters of Ayatollah ◊Khomeini.

quadrathon sports event in which the competitors must swim 2 miles, walk 30 miles, cycle 100 miles, and run 26.2 miles (a marathon) within 22 hours.

quadratic equation in mathematics, a polynomial equation of second degree (that is, an equation containing as its highest power the square of a variable, such as x^2). The general formula of such equations is $ax^2 + bx + c = 0$, in which a, b, and c are real numbers, and only the coefficient a cannot equal 0. In ◊coordinate geometry, a quadratic function represents a ◊parabola.

Quadruple Alliance in European history, three military alliances of four nations: *the Quadruple Alliance 1718* Austria, Britain, France, and the United Provinces (Netherlands) joined forces to prevent Spain from annexing Sardinia and Sicily; *the Quadruple Alliance 1813* Austria, Britain, Prussia, and Russia allied to defeat the French emperor Napoleon; renewed 1815 and 1818. See ◊Vienna, Congress of. *The Quadruple Alliance 1834* Britain, France, Portugal, and Spain guaranteed the constitutional monarchies of Spain and Portugal against rebels in the Carlist War.

quaestor Roman magistrate whose duties were mainly concerned with public finances. The quaestors

Qaboos bin Saidq 1940– . Sultan of Oman, the 14th descendant of the Albusaid family. Opposed to the conservative views of his father, he overthrew him 1970 in a bloodless coup and assumed the sultanship. Since then he has followed more liberal and expansionist policies, while maintaining his country's position of international nonalignment.

Qaddafi alternate form of ◊Khaddhafi, Libyan leader.

Qadisiya, Battle of battle fought in S Iraq 637. A Muslim Arab force defeated a larger Zoroastrian Persian army and ended the ◊Sassanian Empire. The defeat is still resented in Iran, where Muslim Arab nationalism threatens to break up the Iranian state.

Qatar country in the Middle East, occupying Qatar peninsula in the Arabian Gulf, bounded SW by Saudi Arabia and S by United Arab Emirates.

Qin dynasty China's first imperial dynasty 221–206 BC. It was established by ◊Shi Huangdi, ruler of the Qin, the most powerful of the Zhou era warring states. The power of the feudal nobility was curbed and

---

Qatar State of
(*Dawlat Qatar*)

area 4,402 sq mi/11,400 sq km
capital and chief port Doha
cities Dukhan, center of oil production
physical mostly flat desert with salt flats in S

features negligible rain and surface water; only 3% is fertile, but irrigation allows self-sufficiency in fruit and vegetables; extensive oil discoveries since World War II
head of state and government Sheik Khalifa bin Hamad al-Thani from 1972
political system absolute monarchy
political parties none
exports oil, natural gas, petrochemicals, fertilizers, iron, steel
currency riyal
population (1992) 520,000 (half in Doha; Arab 40%, Indian 18%, Pakistani 18%); growth rate 3.7% p.a.
life expectancy men 68, women 72 (1989)
languages Arabic (official), English
religion Sunni Muslim 95%
literacy 60% (1987)
GNP $5.9 bn (1983); $35,000 per head

chronology
1916 Qatar became a British protectorate.
1970 Constitution adopted, confirming the emirate as an absolute monarchy.
1971 Independence achieved from Britain.
1972 Emir Sheik Ahmad replaced in bloodless coup by his cousin, Crown Prince Sheik Khalifa.
1991 Forces joined UN coalition in Gulf War against Iraq.

originated as assistants to the consuls. Both urban and military quaestors existed, the latter being attached to the commanding generals in the provinces.

quail any of several genera of small ground-dwelling birds of the family Phasianidae, which also includes grouse, pheasants, bobwhites, and prairie chickens.

The California quail *Callipepla californiensis* is one of five species of quail native to North America.

Quaker popular name, originally derogatory, for a member of the Society of ◊Friends.

qualitative analysis in chemistry, a procedure for determining the identity of the component(s) of a single substance or mixture. A series of simple reactions and tests can be carried out on a compound to determine the elements present.

Quant Mary 1934– . British fashion designer who popularized the miniskirt in the UK. Her Chelsea boutique, Bazaar, revolutionized women's clothing and makeup in the "swinging London" of the 1960s. In the 1970s she extended into cosmetics and textile design.

quantitative analysis in chemistry, a procedure for determining the precise amount of a known component present in a single substance or mixture. A known amount of the substance is subjected to particular procedures. *Gravimetric analysis* determines the mass of each constituent present; volumetric analysis determines the concentration of a solution by titration against a solution of known concentration.

quantum chromodynamics (QCD) in physics, a theory describing the interactions of ◊quarks, the elementary particles that make up all hadrons (subatomic particles such as protons and neutrons). In quantum chromodynamics, quarks are considered to interact by exchanging particles called gluons, which carry the ◊strong nuclear force, and whose role is to "glue" quarks together. The mathematics involved in the theory is complex, and although a number of successful predictions have been made, as yet the theory does not compare in accuracy with ◊quantum electrodynamics, upon which it is modeled. See ◊elementary particles and ◊forces, fundamental.

quantum electrodynamics (QED) in physics, a theory describing the interaction of charged subatomic particles within electric and magnetic fields. It combines ◊quantum theory and ◊relativity, and considers charged particles to interact by the exchange of photons. QED is remarkable for the accuracy of its predictions—for example, it has been used to calculate the value of some physical quantities to an accuracy of ten decimal places, a feat equivalent to calculating the distance between New York and Los Angeles to within the thickness of a hair. The theory was developed by US physicists Richard Feynman and Julian Schwinger, and by Japanese physicist Sin-Itiro Tomonaga 1948.

quantum number in physics, one of a set of four numbers that uniquely characterize an ◊electron and its state in an ◊atom. The *principal quantum number n* defines the electron's main energy level. The *orbital quantum number l* relates to its angular momentum. The *magnetic quantum number m* describes the energies of electrons in a magnetic field. The *spin quantum number* m_s gives the spin direction of the electron.

quantum theory or *quantum mechanics* in physics, the theory that ◊energy does not have a continuous range of values, but is, instead, absorbed or radiated discontinuously, in multiples of definite, indivisible units called quanta. Just as earlier theory

quartz Well-formed crystals of quartz, which are pyramidal in shape.

showed how light, generally seen as a wave motion, could also in some ways be seen as composed of discrete particles (◊photons), quantum theory shows how atomic particles such as electrons may also be seen as having wavelike properties. Quantum theory is the basis of particle physics, modern theoretical chemistry, and the solid-state physics that describes the behavior of the silicon chips used in computers.

quarantine (from French *quarantaine* "40 days") any period for which people, animals, plants, or vessels may be detained in isolation when suspected of carrying contagious disease.

quark in physics, the ◊elementary particle that is the fundamental constituent of all hadrons (baryons, such as neutrons and protons, and mesons). There are six types, or "flavors": up, down, top, bottom, strange, and charmed, each of which has three varieties, or "colors": red, yellow, and blue (visual color is not meant, although the analogy is useful in many ways). To each quark there is an antiparticle, called an antiquark. See ◊quantum chromodynamics.

quart a unit of liquid or dry measure of volume or capacity. One liquid quart is equal to one-quarter of a gallon, or two pints, or 32 fluid ounces (0.946 liter), while a dry quart is equal to one-eighth of a peck, or two dry pints (1.101 liter).

quartz crystalline form of ◊silica SiO_2, one of the most abundant minerals of the Earth's crust (12% by volume). Quartz occurs in many different kinds of rock, including sandstone and granite. It ranks 7 on the Mohs' scale of hardness and is resistant to chemical or mechanical breakdown. Quartzes vary according to the size and purity of their crystals. Crystals of pure quartz are coarse, colorless, and transparent, and this form is usually called rock crystal. Impure colored varieties, often used as gemstones, include ◊agate, citrine quartz, and ◊amethyst. Quartz is used in ornamental work and industry, where its reaction to electricity makes it valuable in electronic instruments. Quartz can also be made synthetically.

quartzite ◊metamorphic rock consisting of pure quartz sandstone that has recrystallized under increasing heat and pressure.

quasar (from *quasi*-stellar object or QSO) one of the most distant extragalactic objects known, discovered 1964–65. Quasars appear starlike, but each emits more energy than 100 giant galaxies. They are thought to be at the center of galaxies, their brilliance emanating from the stars and gas falling toward an immense ◊black hole at their nucleus.

Quayle (James) Dan(forth) 1947– . US Republican politician, vice president 1989–93. A congressman for Indiana 1977–81, he became a senator 1981.

Quayle Chosen by George Bush as his running mate 1988, Dan Quayle was vice president of the US 1989–93.

Born into a rich and powerful Indianapolis newspaper-owning family, Quayle was admitted to the Indiana bar 1974, and was elected to the House of Representatives 1976 and to the Senate 1980. When George Bush ran for president 1988, he selected Quayle as his running mate, admiring his conservative views and believing that Quayle could deliver the youth vote. This choice encountered heavy critism because of Quayle's limited political experience.

Québec capital and industrial port (textiles, leather, timber, paper, printing, and publishing) of Québec province, on the St Lawrence River; population (1986) 165,000, metropolitan area 603,000.

Québec province of E Canada
area 594,710 sq mi/1,540,700 sq km
capital Quebec
cities Montréal, Laval, Sherbrooke, Verdun, Hull, Trois-Rivières
features immense water-power resources (for example, the James Bay project)
products iron, copper, gold, zinc, cereals, potatoes, paper, textiles, fish, maple syrup (70% of world's output)
population (1991) 6,811,800
language French (the only official language since 1974, although 17% speak English). Language laws 1989 prohibit the use of English on street signs
history known as New France 1534–1763; captured by the British and became province of Québec

Québec

1763–90, Lower Canada 1791–1846, Canada East 1846–67; one of the original provinces 1867. Nationalist feelings 1960s (despite existing safeguards for Québec's French-derived civil law, customs, religion, and language) were encouraged by French president de Gaulle's exclamation "*Vive le Québec libre/Long live free Québec*" on a visit to the province, and led to the foundation of the Parti Québecois by René Lévesque 1968. The Québec Liberation Front (FLQ) separatists had conducted a bombing campaign in the 1960s and fermented an uprising 1970; Parti Québecois won power 1976; a referendum on "sovereignty-association" (separation) was defeated 1980.

In 1982, when Canada severed its last legal ties with the UK, Québec opposed the new Constitution Act as denying the province's claim to an absolute veto over constitutional change. Robert Bourassa and Liberals returned to power 1985 and enacted restrictive English-language legislation. The right of veto was proposed for all provinces of Canada 1987, but the agreement failed to be ratified by its 1990 deadline and support for independence grew. The Parti Québecois was defeated by the Liberal Party 1989.

Quechua or *Quichua* or *Kechua* member of the largest group of South American Indians. The Quechua live in the Andean region. Their ancestors included the Inca, who established the Quechua language in the region. Quechua is the second official language of Peru and is widely spoken as a lingua franca in Ecuador, Bolivia, Columbia, Argentina, and Chile; it belongs to the Andean-Equatorial family.

Queen Anne style decorative art in England 1700–20, characterized by plain, simple lines, mainly in silver and furniture.

Queen Maud Land region of Antarctica W of Enderby Land, claimed by Norway since 1939.

Queens mainly residential borough and county at the west end of Long Island, New York City, population (1980) 1,891,300.

It has sports arenas (Shea Stadium, Forest Hills Tennis Club, and the National Tennis Center at Flushing Meadows), a botanical garden, a museum, and several branches of the City University of New York. Both La Guardia and Kennedy airports are here.

Queensberry John Sholto Douglas, 8th Marquess of Queensberry 1844–1900. British patron of boxing. In 1867 he formulated the *Queensberry Rules*, which form the basis of today's boxing rules.

Queensland state in NE Australia
area 666,699 sq mi/1,727,200 sq km
capital Brisbane
cities Townsville, Toowoomba, Cairns
features Great Dividing Range, including Mount Bartle Frere 5,438 ft/1,657 m; Great Barrier Reef (collection of coral reefs and islands about 1,250 mi/2,000 km long, off the E coast); Gold Coast, 20 mi/32 km long, S of Brisbane; Mount Isa mining area; Sunshine Coast, a 60-mi/100-km stretch of coast N of Brisbane, between Rainbow Beach and Bribie Island, including the resorts of Noosa Heads, Coolum Beach, and Caloundra
products sugar, pineapples, beef, cotton, wool, tobacco, copper, gold, silver, lead, zinc, coal, nickel, bauxite, uranium, natural gas
population (1987) 2,650,000
history part of New South Wales until 1859, when it became self-governing. In 1989 the ruling National Party was defeated after 32 years in power and replaced by the Labor Party.

question mark punctuation mark (?) used to indicate an inquiry, placed at the end of a direct question ("Who is coming?") or an implied question ("This is my reward?"). A question mark is never needed at the end of an indirect question ("He asked us who was coming"), since this is a statement. To express doubt, a writer or editor may insert a question mark ("born in ? 1235"), often in brackets.

quetzal long-tailed Central American bird *Pharomachus mocinno* of the trogon family. The male is brightly colored, with green, red, blue, and white feathers, and is about 4.3 ft/1.3 m long including tail. The female is smaller and lacks the tail and plumage.

Quetzalcoatl in pre-Columbian cultures of Central America, a feathered serpent god of air and water. In his human form, he was said to have been fair-skinned and bearded and to have reigned on Earth during a golden age. He disappeared across the eastern sea, with a promise to return; the Spanish conquistador Hernán ◊Cortés exploited the myth in his own favor when he invaded. Ruins of Quetzalcoatl's temples survive in various ancient Mesoamerican ceremonial centers including the one at Teotihuacán in Mexico. (See also ◊Aztec, ◊Mayan, and ◊Toltec civilizations).

Quezon City former capital of the Philippines 1948–76, NE part of metropolitan ◊Manila (the present capital), on Luzon Island; population (1990) 1,166,800. It was named after the Philippines' first president, Manuel Luis Quezon (1878–1944).

quietism a religious attitude, displayed periodically in the history of Christianity, consisting of passive contemplation and meditation to achieve union with God. The founder of modern quietism was the Spanish priest Molinos who published a *Guida Spirituale/ Spiritual Guide* 1675.

quince small tree *Cydonia oblonga*, family Rosaceae, native to W Asia. The bitter, yellow, pear-shaped fruit is used in preserves. Flowering quinces, genus *Chaenomeles*, are cultivated for their flowers.

Quincy Josiah 1772–1864. US public official. A staunch Federalist, he served in the US House of Representatives 1805–13, opposing the trade policies of the Jefferson administration and the Louisiana Purchase of 1803. As an opponent of US involvement in the Anglo-American War 1812–14, he resigned from Congress and returned to Boston, where he was mayor 1823–28.

quinine antimalarial drug extracted from the bark of the cinchona tree. Peruvian Indians taught French missionaries how to use the bark in 1630, but quinine was not isolated until 1820. It is a bitter alkaloid $C_{20}H_{24}N_2O_2$.

Quinn Anthony 1915– . Mexican-born US actor, in films from 1935. Famous for the title role in *Zorba the Greek* 1964, he later played variations on this larger-than-life character. Other films include Fellini's *La Strada* 1954.

Quintero Serafin Alvárez and Joaquin Alvárez. Spanish dramatists.

Quintilian (Marcus Fabius Quintilianus) *c.* AD 35–95. Roman rhetorician. He was born at Calgurris, Spain, taught rhetoric in Rome from AD 68, and composed the *Institutio Oratoria/The Education of an Orator*, in which he advocated a simple and sincere style of public speaking.

Quirinal one of the seven hills on which ancient Rome was built. Its summit is occupied by a palace built 1574 as a summer residence for the pope and occupied

quetzal The long-tailed quetzal of Mexico and Central America was considered sacred by the ancient Maya and Aztecs.

1870–1946 by the kings of Italy. The name Quirinal is derived from that of Quirinus, local god of the ◊Sabines.

Quisling Vidkun 1887–1945. Norwegian politician. Leader from 1933 of the Norwegian Fascist Party, he aided the Nazi invasion of Norway 1940 by delaying mobilization and urging non-resistance. He was made premier by Hitler 1942, and was arrested and shot as a traitor by the Norwegians 1945. His name became a generic term for a traitor who aids an occupying force.

Quito capital and industrial city (textiles, chemicals, leather, gold, silver) of Ecuador, about 9,850 ft/3,000 m above sea level; population (1986) 1,093,300. It was an ancient settlement, taken by the Incas about 1470 and by the Spanish 1534. It has a temperate climate all year round.

Quixote, Don novel by the Spanish writer ◊Cervantes; see ◊Don Quixote de la Mancha.

Qum alternate spelling of ◊Qom, a city of Iran.

Qumran or ***Khirbet Qumran*** archeological site in Jordan, excavated from 1951, in the foothills NW of the Dead Sea. Originally an Iron Age fort (6th century BC), it was occupied in the late 2nd century BC by a monastic community, the ◊Essenes, until the buildings were burned by Romans AD 68. The monastery library once contained the ◊Dead Sea Scrolls, which had been hidden in caves for safekeeping and were discovered 1947.

quorum minimum number of members required to the present for the proceedings of an assembly to be valid. The actual number of people required for a quorum may vary.

quota in international trade, a limitation on exports or imports. Restrictions may be imposed forcibly or voluntarily. The justification of quotas include protection of a home industry from an influx of cheap goods, prevention of a heavy outflow of goods (usually raw materials) because there are insufficient numbers to meet domestic demand, allowance for a new industry to develop before it is exposed to competition, or prevention of a decline in the world price of a particular commodity.

quo vadis? (Latin) where are you going?

qv abbreviation for *quod vide* (Latin "which see").

QwaQwa black homeland of South Africa that achieved self-governing status 1974; population (1985) 181,600.

R

Rabat capital of Morocco, industrial port (cotton textiles, carpets, leather goods) on the Atlantic coast, 110 mi/177 km W of Fez; population (1982) 519,000, Rabat-Salé 842,000. It is named after its original *ribat* or fortified monastery.

rabbi in Judaism, the chief religious leader of a synagogue or the spiritual leader (not a hereditary high priest) of a Jewish congregation; also, a scholar of Judaic law and ritual from the 1st century AD.

rabbit any of several genera of hopping mammals of the order Lagomorpha, which together with ◊hares constitute the family Leporidae. Rabbits differ from hares in bearing naked, helpless young and in occupying burrows.

Rabelais François 1495–1553. French satirist, monk, and physician whose name has become synonymous with bawdy humor.

rabies or *hydrophobia* disease of the central nervous system that can afflict all warm-blooded creatures. It is almost invariably fatal once symptoms have developed. Its transmission to humans is generally by a bite from an infected dog or, more recently, from a raccoon.

Rabin Yitzhak 1922– . Israeli Labor politician, prime minister 1974–77 and from 1992. Rabin was minister for defense under the conservative Likud coalition government 1984–90. His policy of favoring Palestinian self-government in the occupied territories contributed to the success of the center-left party in the 1992 elections and to a historic peace agreement with the Palestine Liberation Organizations in Oct 1993.

raccoon any of several New World species of carnivorous mammals of the genus *Procyon*, in the family Procyonidae. The common raccoon *P. lotor* is about 2 ft/60 cm long, with a gray-brown body, a black-and-white ringed tail, and a black "mask" around its eyes. The crab-eating raccoon *P. Cancrivorus* of South America is slightly smaller and has shorter fur.

race in anthropology, the term applied to the varieties of modern humans, *Homo sapiens sapiens*, having clusters of distinctive physical traits in common. The three major varieties are ◊Caucasoid, ◊Mongoloid, and ◊Negroid.

Rachmaninov Sergei (Vasilevich) 1873–1943. Russian composer, conductor, and pianist. After the 1917 Revolution he went to the US. His dramatically emotional Romantic music has a strong melodic basis and

includes operas, such as *Francesca da Rimini* 1906, three symphonies, four piano concertos, piano pieces, and songs.

Racine city and port of entry in SW Wisconsin, on the Root River where it flows into Lake Michigan; population (1990) 84,300.

Racine Jean 1639–1699. French dramatist and exponent of the Classical tragedy in French drama. His subjects came from Greek mythology and he observed the rules of Classical Greek drama. Most of his tragedies have women in the title role, for example *Andromaque* 1667, *Iphigénie* 1674, and *Phèdre* 1677.

racism belief in, or set of implicit assumptions about, the superiority of one's own ◊race or ethnic group, often accompanied by prejudice against members of an ethnic group different from one's own. Racism may be used to justify ◊discrimination, verbal or physical abuse, or even genocide, as in Nazi Germany, or as practiced by European settlers against American Indians in both North and South America.

rad unit of absorbed radiation dose, now replaced in the SI system by the ◊gray (one rad equals 0.01 gray), but still commonly used. It is defined as the dose when one kilogram of matter absorbs 0.01 joule of radiation energy (formerly, as the dose when one gram absorbs 100 ergs).

radar (acronym for *radio direction and ranging*) device for locating objects in space, direction finding, and navigation by means of transmitted and reflected high-frequency radio waves.

radiation in physics, emission of radiant ◊energy as particles or waves—for example, heat, light, alpha particles, and beta particles (see ◊electromagnetic waves and ◊radioactivity). See also ◊atomic radiation.

radiation sickness sickness resulting from exposure to radiation, including X-rays, gamma rays, neutrons, and other nuclear radiation, as from weapons and fallout. Such radiation ionizes atoms in the body and causes nausea, vomiting, diarrhea, and other symptoms.

radiation units units of measurement for radioactivity and radiation doses. Continued use of the units introduced earlier this century (the curie, rad, rem, and roentgen) has been approved while the derived SI units (becquerel, gray, sievert, and coulomb) become familiar.

radical in chemistry, a group of atoms forming part of a molecule, which acts as a unit and takes part in chemical reactions without disintegration yet often cannot exist alone; for example, the methyl radical $-CH_3$, or the carboxyl radical $-COOH$.

radical in politics, anyone with opinions more extreme than the main current of a country's major political party or parties.

radio transmission and reception of radio waves. In radio transmission a microphone converts ◊sound

raccoon Raccoons are good climbers and spend much of their time in trees, usually near water.

waves (pressure variations in the air) into ◊electromagnetic waves that are then picked up by a receiving aerial and fed to a loudspeaker, which converts them back into sound waves.

radioactive waste any waste that emits radiation in excess of the background level.

radioactivity spontaneous alteration of the nuclei of radioactive atoms, accompanied by the emission of radiation. It is the property exhibited by the radioactive ◊isotopes of stable elements and all isotopes of radioactive elements, and can be either natural orinduced.

radiocarbon dating or *carbon dating* method of dating organic materials (for example, bone or wood), used in archeology. Plants take up carbon dioxide gas from the atmosphere and incorporate it into their tissues, and some of that carbon dioxide contains the radioactive isotope of carbon, carbon-14. This decays at a known rate (half of it decays every 5,730 years); the time elapsed since the plant died can therefore be measured in a laboratory. Animals take carbon-14 into their bodies from eating plant tissues and their remains can be similarly dated. After 120,000 years so little carbon-14 is left that no measure is possible (see ◊half-life).

radio frequencies and wavelengths classification of, see ◊electromagnetic waves.

radio galaxy galaxy that is a strong source of electromagnetic waves of radio wavelengths. All galaxies, including our own, emit some radio waves, but radio galaxies are up to a million times more powerful.

radiography branch of science concerned with the use of radiation (particularly ◊X-rays) to produce images on photographic film or fluorescent screens. X-rays penetrate matter according to its nature, density, and thickness. In doing so they can cast shadows on photographic film, producing a radiograph.

radioisotope (contraction of *radioactive ◊isotope*) in physics, a naturally occurring or synthetic radioactive form of an element. Most radioisotopes are made by bombarding a stable element with neutrons in the core of a nuclear reactor. The radiations given off by radioisotopes are easy to detect (hence their use as ◊tracers), can in some instances penetrate substantial thicknesses of materials, and have profound effects (such as genetic ◊mutation) on living matter. Although dangerous, radioisotopes are used in the fields of medicine, industry, agriculture, and research.

Most natural isotopes of atomic mass below 208 are not radioactive. Those from 210 and up are all radioactive.

radioisotope scanning use of radioactive materials (radioisotopes or radionuclides) to pinpoint disease. It reveals the size and shape of the target organ and whether any part of it is failing to take up radioactive material, usually an indication of disease.

radiometric dating method of dating rock by assessing the amount of radioactive decay of naturally occurring ◊isotopes. The dating of rocks may be based on the gradual decay of uranium into lead. The ratio of the amounts of "parent" to "daughter" isotopes in a sample gives a measure of the time it has been decaying, that is, of its age. Different elements and isotopes are used depending on the isotopes present and the age of the rocks to be dated. Once-living matter can often be dated by ◊radiocarbon dating, employing the half-life of the isotope carbon-14, which is naturally present in organic tissue. Radiometric methods have been applied to the decay of long-lived isotopes, such as potassioum-40, rubidium-87, thorium-232, and uranium-238 which are found in rocks. These isotopes decay very slowly and this has enabled rocks as old as 3,800 million years to be dated accurately. Carbon dating can be used for material between 100,000 and 1,000 years old.

radio telescope instrument for detecting radio waves from the universe in radio astronomy. Radio telescopes usually consist of a metal bowl that collects and focuses radio waves the way a concave mirror collects and focuses light waves. Radio telescopes are much larger than optical telescopes, because the wavelengths they are detecting are much longer than the wavelength of light. The largest single dish is 1,000 ft/305 m across, at Arecibo, Puerto Rico.

radiotherapy treatment of disease by ◊radiation from X-ray machines or radioactive sources. Radiation, which reduces the activity of dividing cells, is of special value for its effect on malignant tissues, certain nonmalignant tumors, and some diseases of the skin.

radio wave electromagnetic wave possessing a long wavelength (ranging from about 10^{-3} to 10^4 m) and a low frequency (from about 10^5 to 10^{11} Hz). Included in the radio-wave part of the spectrum are ◊microwaves, used for both communications and for cooking; ultra high- and very high-frequency waves, used for television and FM (◊frequency modulation) radio communications; and short, medium, and long waves, used for AM (◊amplitude modulation) radio communications. Radio waves that are used for communications have all been modulated (see ◊modulation) to carry information.

radish annual herb *Raphanus sativus*, family Cruciferae.

radium (Latin *radius* "ray") white, radioactive, metallic element, symbol Ra, atomic number 88, atomic weight 226.02. It is one of the ◊alkaline-earth metals, found in nature in ◊pitchblende and other uranium ores. Of the 16 isotopes, the commonest, Ra-226, has a half-life of 1.622 years. The element was discovered and named in 1898 by Pierre and Marie ◊Curie, who were investigating the residues of pitchblende.

radon colorless, odorless, gaseous, radioactive, nonmetallic element, symbol Rn, atomic number 86, atomic weight 222. It is grouped with the ◊inert gases and was formerly considered non-reactive, but is now known to form some compounds with fluorine. Of the 20 known isotopes, only 3 occur in nature; the longest half-life is 3.82 days.

Rafsanjani Hojatoleslam Ali Akbar Hashemi 1934– . Iranian politician and cleric, president from 1989. When his former teacher Ayatollah ◊Khomeini returned after the revolution of 1979–80, Rafsanjani became the speaker of the Iranian parliament and, after Khomeini's death, state president and effective political leader.

Ragnarök (German *Götterdämmerung*) in Norse mythology, the ultimate cataclysmic battle between gods and forces of evil, from which a new order will come.

ragtime syncopated music ("ragged time") in 2/4 rhythm, usually played on piano. It developed in the US among black musicians in the late 19th century; it was influenced by folk tradition, minstrel shows, and marching bands, and was later incorporated into jazz. Scott ◊Joplin was a leading writer of ragtime pieces, called "rags."

Rahman Tunku Abdul 1903–1990. Malaysian politician, first prime minister of independent Malaya 1957–63 and of Malaysia 1963–70.

railroad method of transport in which trains convey passengers and goods along a twin rail track (at first made of wood but later of iron or steel with ties wedging them apart and relatively parallel). Following the work of English steam pioneers such as James ◊Watt, George ◊Stephenson built the first public steam railroad, from Stockton to Darlington, 1825. This heralded extensive railroad building in Britain, continental Europe, and North America, providing a fast and economical means of transport and communication. After World War II, steam engines were replaced by electric and diesel engines. At the same time, the growth of road building, air services, and automobile ownership destroyed the supremacy of the railroads.

rain form of ◊precipitation in which separate drops of water fall to the Earth's surface from clouds. The drops are formed by the accumulation of fine droplets that condense from water vapor in the air. The condensation is usually brought about by rising and subsequent cooling of air.

rainbow arch in the sky displaying the seven colors of the ◊spectrum in bands. It is formed by the refraction, reflection, and dispersion of the Sun's rays through rain or mist. Its cause was discovered by Theodoric of Freiburg in the 14th century.

rainbow coalition or *rainbow alliance* in politics, from the mid-1980s, a loose, left-of-center alliance of people from several different sections of society that are traditionally politically underrepresented, such as nonwhite ethnic groups. Its aims include promoting minority rights and equal opportunities.

rain forest dense forest usually found on or near the ◊equator where the climate is hot and wet. Heavy rainfall results as the moist air brought by the converging tradewinds rises because of the heat. Over half the tropical rain forests are in Central and South America, the rest in SE Asia and Africa. They provide the bulk of the oxygen needed for plant and animal respiration. Tropical rain forest once covered 14% of the Earth's land surface, but are now being destroyed at an increasing rate as their valuable timber is harvested and the land cleared for agriculture, causing problems of ◊deforestation. Although by 1991 over 50% of the world's rain forest had been removed, they still comprise about 50% of all growing wood on the planet, and harbor at least 40% of the Earth's species (plants and animals). *See panel p. 776*

Rainier III 1923– . Prince of Monaco from 1949. He was married to the US film actress Grace Kelly.

Rainier, Mount mountain in the ◊Cascade Range, Washington State; 14,415 ft/4,392 m, crowned by 14 glaciers and carrying dense forests on its slopes. It is a quiescent volcano. Mount Rainier national park was dedicated 1899.

raisin dried grape, used for eating, baking, and for confectionary. The chief kinds are the seedless raisin, the sultana, and the currant. The main producers are the Mediterranean area, California, Mexico, and Australia.

Rajasthan state of NW India
area 132,089 sq mi/342,200 sq km
capital Jaipur
features includes the larger part of the Thar Desert, where India's first nuclear test was carried out; in the SW is the Ranthambhor wildlife reserve, formerly the private hunting ground of the maharajahs of Jaipur, and rich in tiger, deer, antelope, wild boar, crocodile, and sloth bear
products oilseed, cotton, sugar, asbestos, copper, textiles, cement, glass
population (1991) 43,880,600
languages Rajasthani, Hindi
religions 90% Hindu, 3% Muslim
history formed 1948; enlarged 1956.

Raleigh industrial city (food processing, electrical machinery, textiles) and capital of North Carolina; population (1990) 208,000. It benefits from the nearby presence of the Research Triangle Park, a regional research and manufacturing center for high-technology products. Educational institutions include North Carolina State University. The present site was named for Sir Walter Raleigh, selected to be the state capital 1788, and laid out 1792.

Raleigh or *Ralegh* Walter *c.* 1552–1618. English adventurer. He made colonizing and exploring voyages to North America 1584–87 and South America 1595, and naval attacks on Spanish ports. His aggressive actions against Spanish interests brought him into conflict with the pacific James I. He was imprisoned for treason 1603–16 and executed on his return from an unsuccessful final expedition to South America.

RAM (acronym for *random-access memory*) in computing, a memory device in the form of a collection of integrated circuits (chips), frequently used in microcomputers. Unlike ◊ROM (read-only memory) chips, RAM chips can be both read from and written to by the computer, but their contents are lost when the power is switched off. Microcomputers of the 1990s may have 16–32 megabytes of RAM.

Rama incarnation of ◊Vishnu, the supreme spirit of Hinduism. He is the hero of the epic poem the Rāmāyana, and he is regarded as an example of morality and virtue.

Ramadan in the Muslim ◊calendar, the ninth month of the year. Throughout Ramadan a strict fast is observed during the hours of daylight; Muslims are encouraged to read the whole Koran in commemora-

Rafsanjani The president of Iran, Ali Akbar Rafsanjani.

rain forest

tropical rain forest habitat

Along the equator rising hot air draws winds in from the north and south. These winds, known as trade winds, are wet and their moisture falls as torrential rain as the air rises. The ensuing hot wet conditions encourage the prolific growth of thousands of plant species, giving rise to the tropical rain forest. The varied and abundant species of plants support many different species of animal. The rain runs off into huge rivers, such as the Amazon, the Zaïre, and the Mekong.

The tropical rain forest runs in a belt along the equator, broken only by mountain ranges.

The tallest trees, the emergents, may be 325 ft/100 m high. They have buttresses, or stilt roots, to keep them upright.

The forest floor is a dark place where little grows. When a large tree falls there is a temporary pool of light. Saplings grow rapidly toward the light and quickly take the tree's place. Growth is so vigorous that some plants, epiphytes, grow on the branches of others.

Many of the tree-living animals have forward-pointing eyes, enabling them to judge distances when jumping and climbing; others are gliders, moving rapidly from branch to branch. On the forest floor, pig-size creatures are most common as there is little room between the trunks for larger animals to pass.

There is a continuous canopy of branches, all interlocked and reaching up toward the light.

key
1 flying squirrel
2 spider monkey
3 Wallace's flying frog
4 tapir
5 gray parrot

Alongside rivers the leafy growth comes right down to water level.

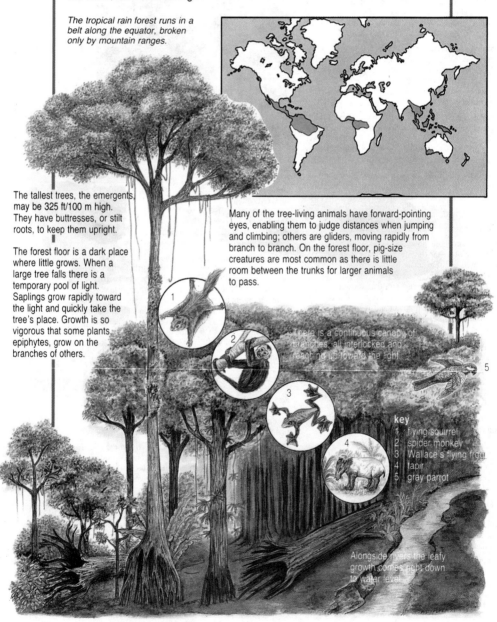

tion of the Night of Power (which falls during the month) when, it is believed, Mohammed first received his revelations from the angel Gabriel.

Ramakrishna 1834–1886. Hindu sage, teacher, and mystic (one dedicated to achieving oneness with or a direct experience of God or some force beyond the normal world). Ramakrishna claimed that mystical experience was the ultimate aim of religions, and that all religions which led to this goal were equally valid.

Ramsay William 1852–1916. Scottish chemist who, with Lord Rayleigh, discovered argon 1894. In 1895 Ramsay produced helium and in 1898, in cooperation with Morris Travers, identified neon, krypton, and xenon. In 1903, with Frederick Soddy, he noted the transmutation of radium into helium, which led to the discovery of the density and atomic weight of radium. Nobel Prize 1904.

Ramses II or **Rameses II** king of Egypt about 1304–1236 BC, the son of Seti I. He campaigned successfully against the Hittites, and built two rock temples at ◊Abu Simbel in Upper Egypt.

Ramses III or **Rameses III** king of Egypt about 1200–1168 BC. He won victories over the Libyans and the Sea Peoples and asserted his control over Palestine.

Rand Ayn Adopted name of Alice Rosenbaum 1905–1982. Russian-born US novelist. Her novel *The Fountainhead* 1943 (made into a film 1949), describing an idealistic architect who destroys his project rather than see it altered, displays her persuasive blend of vehement anticommunism and fervent philosophy of individual enterprise.

Rand Sally (Helen Gould Beck) 1904–1979. US exotic dancer. During the 1930s she worked as a dancer in Chicago and developed her trademark nude dance routine to Chopin and Debussy, which featured the coy use of huge ostrich fans. Playing a role in the 1965 burlesque revival on Broadway, she continued to dance until 1978.

Randolph Asa Philip 1889–1979. US labor and civil rights leader. Devoting himself to the cause of unionization, especially among black Americans, he was named a vice president of the American Federation of Labor and Congress of Industrial Organizations (AFL-CIO) 1957. He was one of the organizers of the 1963 civil rights march on Washington.

random number one of a series of numbers having no detectable pattern. Random numbers are used in ◊computer simulation and ◊computer games. It is impossible for an ordinary computer to generate true random numbers, but various techniques are available for obtaining pseudo-random numbers—close enough to true randomness for most purposes.

rangefinder instrument for determining the range or distance of an object from the observer; used to focus a camera or to sight a gun accurately. A *rangefinder camera* has a rotating mirror or prism that alters the image seen through the viewfinder, and a secondary window. When the two images are brought together into one, the lens is sharply focused.

Rangoon former name (until 1989) of ◊Yangon, the capital of Myanmar (Burma).

Ranjit Singh 1780–1839. Indian maharajah. He succeeded his father as a minor Sikh leader 1792, and created a Sikh army that conquered Kashmir and the Punjab. In alliance with the British, he established himself as "Lion of the Punjab," ruler of the strongest of the independent Indian states.

Ramses II The rock-cut temple of Ramses II at Abu Simbel.

Rao P(amulaparti) V(enkata) Narasimha 1921– . Indian politician.

rape in law, sexual intercourse without the consent of the subject. Most cases of rape are of women by men. In Islamic law a rape accusation requires the support of four independent male witnesses.

Some jurisdictions allow charges of rape to be brought against husbands replacing older legal doctrine asserting a wife's duty to submit to sex with her spouse. Sexual intercourse with a minor, not necessarily involving penetration, is defined as statutory rape (see ◊child abuse).

Raphael Sanzio (Raffaello Sanzio) 1483–1520. Italian painter, one of the greatest of the High Renaissance, active in Perugia, Florence, and Rome (from 1508), where he painted frescoes in the Vatican and for secular patrons. His religious and mythological scenes are harmoniously composed; his portraits enhance the character of his sitters and express dignity. Many of his designs were engraved. Much of his later work was the product of his studio. *See illustration p. 778*

rap music rapid, rhythmic chant over a prerecorded repetitive backing track. Rap emerged in New York 1979 as part of the ◊hip-hop culture, although the macho, swaggering lyrics that initially predominated have roots in ritual boasts and insults. Different styles were flourishing by the 1990s, such as jazz rap, gangsta rap, and reggae rap.

raspberry prickly cane plant of the genus *Rubus* of the Rosaceae family, native to Eurasia and North America, with white flowers followed by red fruits. These are eaten fresh and used for jam and wine.

Rasputin (Russian "dissolute") Grigory Efimovich 1871–1916. Siberian Eastern Orthodox mystic who acquired influence over the tsarina ◊Alexandra, wife of ◊Nicholas II, and was able to make political and ecclesiastical appointments. His abuse of power and notorious debauchery (reputedly including the tsarina) led to his murder by a group of nobles.

Rastafarianism religion originating in the West Indies, based on the ideas of Marcus ◊Garvey, who

Raphael Sanzio
The Bridgewater
*Madonna (1506–07),
National Gallery of
Scotland, Sutherland
loan.*

rattlesnake *The
diamondback
rattlesnake is the most
dangerous snake in
North America.*

called on black people to return to Africa and set up a black-governed country there. When Haile Selassie (*Ras Tafari*, "Lion of Judah") was crowned emperor of Ethiopia 1930, this was seen as a fulfillment of prophecy and some Rastafarians acknowledged him as an incarnation of God (*Jah*), others as a prophet. The use of ganja (marijuana) is a sacrament. There are no churches. There were about one million Rastafarians by 1990.

raster graphics computer graphics that are stored in the computer memory by using a map to record data (such as color and intensity) for every pixel that makes up the image. When transformed (enlarged, rotated, stretched, and so on), raster graphics become ragged and suffer loss of picture resolution, unlike ◊vector graphics. Raster graphics are typically used for painting applications, which allow the user to create artwork on a computer screen much as if they were painting on paper or canvas.

rat any of numerous long-tailed ◊rodents (especially of the families Muridae and Cricetidae) larger than mice and usually with scaly, naked tails. The genus

Rattus in the family Muridae includes the rats found in human housing.

ratio measure of the relative size of two quantities or of two measurements (in similar units), expressed as a proportion. For example, the ratio of vowels to consonants in the alphabet is 5:21; the ratio of 500 m to 2 km is 500:2,000, or 1:4.

rationalism in theology, the belief that human reason rather than divine revelation is the correct means of ascertaining truth and regulating behavior. In philosophy, rationalism takes the view that self-evident propositions deduced by reason are the sole basis of all knowledge (disregarding experience of the senses). It is usually contrasted with ◊empiricism, which argues that all knowledge must ultimately be derived from the senses.

rational number in mathematics, any number that can be expressed as an exact fraction (with a denominator not equal to 0), that is, as $a \div b$ where a and b are integers. For example, 2/1, 1/4, 15/4, $-3/5$ are all rational numbers, whereas π (which represents the constant 3.141592 . . .) is not. Numbers such as π are called ◊irrational numbers.

rattlesnake any of various New World pit ◊vipers of the genera *Crotalus* and *Sistrurus* (the massasaugas and pygmy rattlers), distinguished by horny flat segments of the tail, which rattle when vibrated as a warning to attackers. They can grow to 8 ft/2.5 m long. The venom injected by some rattlesnakes can be fatal.

Rauschenberg Robert 1925– . US Pop artist, a creator of happenings (art in live performance) and incongruous multimedia works such as *Monogram* 1959 (Moderna Museet, Stockholm), an automobile tire around the body of a stuffed goat daubed with paint. In the 1960s he returned to painting and used the silkscreen printing process to transfer images to canvas. He also made collages.

His works are spontaneous and use images and objects from everyday life.

Ravel (Joseph) Maurice 1875–1937. French composer. His work is characterized by its sensuousness, unresolved dissonances, and "tone color."

Examples are the piano pieces *Pavane pour une infante défunte* 1899 and *Jeux d'eau* 1901, and the ballets *Daphnis et Chloë* 1912 and *Boléro* 1928.

raven any of several large ◊crows (genus *Corvus*). The common raven *C. corax* is about 2 ft/60 cm long, and has black, lustrous plumage. It is a scavenger, and is found only in the northern hemisphere.

Rawalpindi city in Punjab province, Pakistan, in the foothills of the Himalayas; population (1981) 928,400. Industries include oil refining, iron, chemicals, and furniture.

ray any of several orders (especially Ragiformes) of cartilaginous fishes with a flattened body, winglike pectoral fins, and a whiplike tail.

Ray John 1627–1705. English naturalist who devised a classification system accounting for nearly 18,000 plant species. It was the first system to divide flowering plants into monocotyledons and dicotyledons, with additional divisions made on the basis of leaf and flower characters and fruit types.

Ray Nicholas. Adopted name of Raymond Nicholas Kienzle 1911–1979. US film director, critically acclaimed for his socially aware dramas such as *Rebel Without a Cause* 1955. His other films include *In a Lonely Place* 1950, *Johnny Guitar* 1954, and *55 Days at Peking* 1963.

Ray Satyajit 1921–1992. Indian film director, internationally known for his trilogy of life in his native Bengal: *Pather Panchali, Unvanquished*, and *The World of Apu* 1955–59. Later films include *The Music Room* 1963, *Charulata* 1964, *The Chess Players* 1977, and *The Home and the World* 1984.

Rayburn Samuel Taliaferro 1882–1961. US political leader. A Democrat, he was elected to the US Congress 1912. He supported President F D Roosevelt's New Deal program 1933, and was elected majority leader 1937 and Speaker of the House 1940. With the exception of two terms, he served as Speaker until his death. His tenure in the House 1912–61 was the longest on record.

rayon any of various shiny textile fibers and fabrics made from ◊cellulose. It is produced by pressing whatever cellulose solution is used through very small holes and solidifying the resulting filaments. A common type is ◊viscose, which consists of regenerated filaments of pure cellulose. Acetate and triacetate are kinds of rayon consisting of filaments of cellulose acetate and triacetate.

Rayon was originally made in the 1930s from the Douglas fir tree.

razorbill North Atlantic sea bird *Alca torda* of the auk family, which breeds on cliffs and migrates south in winter. It has a curved beak and is black above and white below. It uses its wings as paddles when diving. Razorbills are common off Newfoundland.

re abbreviation for Latin "with regard to."

reaction in chemistry, the coming together of two or more atoms, ions, or molecules with the result that a chemical change takes place. The nature of the reaction is portrayed by a chemical equation.

reaction principle principle stated by ◊Newton as his third law of motion: to every action, there is an equal and opposite reaction.

Reading industrial city (textiles, special steels) in E Pennsylvania; population (1990) 78,400. Reading was laid out 1748 and was an early iron- and steelmaking center, connected by canal and rail to nearby anthracite mines.

Reagan Ronald (Wilson) 1911– . 40th president of the US 1981–89, a Republican. He was governor of California 1966–74, and a former Hollywood actor.

Reagan Ronald Reagan, US president 1981–89.

Reagan was a hawkish and popular president. He adopted an aggressive policy in Central America, attempting to overthrow the government of Nicaragua, and invading Grenada 1983. In 1987, ◊Irangate was investigated by the Tower Commission; Reagan admitted that US–Iran negotiations had become an "arms for hostages deal," but denied knowledge of resultant funds being illegally sent to the Contras in Nicaragua. He increased military spending (sending the national budget deficit to record levels), cut social programs, introduced deregulation of domestic markets, and cut taxes. His ◊Strategic Defense Initiative, announced 1983, proved controversial owing to the cost and unfeasibility. He was succeeded by his vice president, George Bush.

realism in the arts and literature, an unadorned, naturalistic approach to subject matter. Realism also refers more specifically to a movement in mid-19th-century European art and literature, a reaction against Romantic and Classical idealization and a rejection of conventional academic themes (such as mythology, history, and sublime landscapes) in favor

Realism Gustave Courbet's The Stonebreakers *1849 (formerly Dresden State Museum, destroyed in World War II).*

of everyday life and carefully observed social settings. The movement was particularly important in France, where it had political overtones; the painters Gustave ◊Courbet and Honoré ◊Daumier, two leading Realists, both used their art to expose social injustice.

realism in medieval philosophy, the theory that "universals" have existence, not simply as names for entities but as entities in their own right. It is thus opposed to nominalism. In contemporary philosophy, the term stands for the doctrine that there is an intuitively appreciated reality apart from what is presented to the consciousness. It is opposed to idealism.

real number in mathematics, any of the ◊rational numbers (which include the integers) or ◊irrational numbers. Real numbers exclude imaginary numbers, found in ◊complex numbers of the general form $a + bi$ where $i = \sqrt{-1}$, although these do include a real component a.

real-time system in computing, a program that responds to events in the world as they happen. For example, an automatic-pilot program in an aircraft must respond instantly in order to correct deviations from its course. Process control, robotics, games, and many military applications are examples of real-time systems.

receiver in law, a person appointed by a court to collect and manage the assets of an individual, company, or partnership in serious financial difficulties. In the case of bankruptcy, the assets may be sold and distributed by a receiver to creditors.

recession in economics, a fall in business activity lasting more than a few months, causing stagnation in a country's output.

The average decline has been about 10% although some recessions, such as 1981–82, can be longer and more severe.

recessive gene in genetics, an allele (alternate form of a gene) that will show in the phenotype (observed characteristics of an organism) only if its partner allele on the paired chromosome is similarly recessive. Such an allele will not show if its partner is dominant, that is if the organism is heterozygous for a particular characteristic. Alleles for blue eyes in humans, and for shortness in pea plants are recessive. Most mutant alleles are recessive and therefore are only rarely expressed (see ◊sickle cell disease).

Recife industrial seaport (cotton textiles, sugar refining, fruit canning, flour milling) and naval base in Brazil; capital of Pernambuco state, at the mouth of the river Capibaribe; population (1991) 1,335,700. It was founded 1504.

reciprocal in mathematics, the result of dividing a given quantity into 1. Thus the reciprocal of 2 is 1/2; of 2/3 is 3/2; of x^2 is $1/x^2$ or x^{-2}. Reciprocals are used to replace division by multiplication, since multiplying by the reciprocal of a number is the same as dividing by that number.

recitative in opera, on-pitch speechlike declamation used in narrative episodes.

recombination in genetics, any process that recombines, or "shuffles," the genetic material, thus increasing genetic variation in the offspring. The two main processes of recombination both occur during meiosis (reduction division of cells). One is crossing over, in which chromosome pairs exchange segments; the other is the random reassortment of chromosomes that occurs when each gamete (sperm or egg) receives only one of each chromosome pair.

Reconstruction in US history, the period 1865–77 after the Civil War during which the nation was reunited under the federal government after the defeat of the Southern Confederacy.

recorder in music, a pure-toned instrument of the ◊woodwind family, in which the single reed is integrated with the mouthpiece. Recorders are played in a consort (ensemble) of matching tone and comprise sopranino, descant, treble, tenor, and bass.

recording the process of storing information, or the information store itself. Sounds and pictures can be stored on disks or tape. The phonograph record or ◊compact disk stores music or speech as a spiral groove on a plastic disk and the sounds are reproduced by a record player. In ◊tape recording, sounds are stored as a magnetic pattern on plastic tape. The best-quality reproduction is achieved using digital audio tape.

record player device for reproducing recorded sound stored as a spiral groove on a vinyl disk. A motor-driven turntable rotates the record at a constant speed, and a stylus or needle on the head of a pick-up is made to vibrate by the undulations in the record groove. These vibrations are then converted to electrical signals by a ◊transducer in the head (often a piezoelectric crystal). After amplification, the signals pass to one or more loudspeakers, which convert them into sound. Alternate formats are ◊compact disk and magnetic ◊tape recording.

Recruit scandal in Japanese politics, the revelation 1988 that a number of politicians and business leaders had profited from insider trading. It led to the resignation of several cabinet ministers, including Prime Minister Takeshita, whose closest aide committed suicide, and to the arrest of 20 people.

rectangle quadrilateral (four-sided plane figure) with opposite sides equal and parallel and with each interior angle a right angle (90°). Its area A is the product of the length l and height h; that is, $A = l \times h$. A rectangle with all four sides equal is a ◊square.

rectum lowest part of the digestive tract of animals, which stores feces prior to elimination (defecation).

recycling processing of industrial and household waste (such as paper, glass, and some metals and plastics) so that it can be reused. This saves expenditure on scarce raw materials, slows down the depletion of ◊nonrenewable resources, and helps to reduce pollution.

Red Army name of the army of the USSR until 1946; later known as the **Soviet Army**. It developed from the Red Guards, volunteers who carried out the Bolshevik revolution, and received its name because it fought under the red flag. The Chinese revolutionary army was also called the Red Army.

red blood cell or **erythrocyte** the most common type of blood cell, responsible for transporting oxygen around the body. It contains hemoglobin, which combines with oxygen from the lungs to form oxyhemoglobin. When transported to the tissues, these cells are able to release the oxygen because the oxyhemoglobin splits into its original constituents.

Red Cloud (Sioux name **Mahpiua Luta**) 1822–1909. American Sioux Indian leader. Paramount chief of the Oglala Sioux from 1860, he was advocate of accommodation with the US government and signed the Fort Laramie Treaty 1869 which gave the Indians a large area in the Black Hills of Dakota. He resisted any involvement in the war which culminated in the Battle of Little Bighorn 1876.

Red Cross international relief agency founded by the Geneva Convention 1864 at the instigation of the Swiss doctor Henri Dunant to assist the wounded and prisoners in war. Its symbol is a symmetrical red cross on a white ground. In addition to dealing with associated problems of war, such as refugees and the care of the disabled, the Red Cross is increasingly concerned with victims of natural disasters—floods, earthquakes, epidemics, and accidents.

red currant in botany, type of ◊currant.

red dwarf any star that is cool, faint, and small (about one-tenth the mass and diameter of the Sun). Red dwarfs burn slowly, and have estimated lifetimes of 100 billion years. They may be the most abundant type of star, but are difficult to see because they are so faint. Two of the closest stars to the Sun, ◊Proxima Centauri and ◊Barnard's Star, are red dwarfs.

Redford (Charles) Robert 1937– . US actor and film director. His first starring role was in *Barefoot in the Park* 1967, followed by *Butch Cassidy and the Sundance Kid* 1969 and *The Sting* 1973 (both with Paul ◊Newman).

His other films as an actor include *The Way We Were* 1973, *All the President's Men* 1976, *Out of Africa* 1985, *Havana* 1991, *Sneakers* 1992, and *Indecent Proposal* 1993. He directed *Ordinary People* 1980, *The Milagro Beanfield War* 1988, and *A River Runs Through It* 1992, and established the Sundance Institute in Utah for the development of theatrical talent.

red giant any large bright star with a cool surface. It is thought to represent a late stage in the evolution of a star like the Sun, as it runs out of hydrogen fuel at its center. Red giants have diameters between 10 and 100 times that of the Sun. They are very bright because they are so large, although their surface temperature is lower than that of the Sun, about 2,000–3,000K (3,000°–5,000°F/1,700–2,700°C).

Redgrave Michael 1908–1985. British actor. His stage roles included Hamlet and Lear (Shakespeare), Uncle Vanya (Chekhov), and the schoolmaster in Rattigan's *The Browning Version* (filmed 1951). On screen he appeared in *The Lady Vanishes* 1938, *The Importance of Being Earnest* 1952, and *Goodbye Mr Chips* 1959. He was the father of Vanessa and Lynn Redgrave, both actresses.

Redgrave Vanessa 1937– . British actress. She has played Shakespeare's Lady Macbeth and Cleopatra on the stage, and Olga in Chekhov's *Three Sisters* 1990. She won an Academy Award for the title role in the film *Julia* 1976; other films include *Howards End* 1992. She is active in left-wing politics.

Red Guard one of the school and college students, wearing red armbands, active in the ◊Cultural Revolution in China 1966–69. The armed workers who took part in the ◊Russian Revolution of 1917 were also called Red Guards.

Redon Odilon 1840–1916. French Symbolist painter and graphic artist. He used fantastic symbols and images, sometimes mythological. From the 1890s he painted still lifes and landscapes. His work was much admired by the Surrealists.

Redoubt, Mount active volcanic peak rising to 10,197 ft/3,140 m, W of Cook inlet in S Alaska. There were eruptions in 1966 and 1989.

Red River name of two rivers in the US. (1) The *Red River of the South* is a western tributary of the ◊Mississippi River 1,018 mi/1,638 km long; so called

because of the reddish soil sediment it carries. The stretch that forms the Texas–Oklahoma border is called Tornado Alley because of the storms caused by the collision in spring of warm air from the Gulf of Mexico with cold fronts from the N. The largest city on the river is Shreveport, Louisiana. (2) The *Red River of the North*, about 545 mi/877 km long, runs from North Dakota into Manitoba, and through Winnipeg, emptying into Lake Winnipeg. The fertile soil of the river valley produces large yields of wheat and other crops.

Red Scare in US history, campaign against radicals and dissenters which took place in the aftermath of World War I and the Russian Revolution, during a period of labor disorders in the US. A wave of strikes in 1919 was seen as a prelude to revolution and violently suppressed. Thousands of people were arrested on suspicion, and communists were banned from entry to the country.

Red Sea submerged section of the ◊Great Rift Valley (1,200 mi/2,000 km long and up to 200 mi/320 km wide). Egypt, Sudan, and Ethiopia (in Africa) and Saudi Arabia (Asia) are on its shores.

redwood giant coniferous tree, one of the two types of ◊sequoia.

reed any of various perennial tall, slender grasses of wet or marshy environments; in particular, species of the genera *Phragmites* and *Arundo*; also the stalk of any of these plants. The common reed *P. australis* attains a height of 10 ft/3 m, having stiff, erect leaves and straight stems bearing a plume of purplish flowers.

Reed Lou 1942– . US rock singer, songwriter, and guitarist; former member (1965–70) of the New York avant-garde group *The Velvet Underground*, perhaps the most influential band of the period. His solo work deals largely with urban alienation and angst, and includes the albums *Berlin* 1973, *Street Hassle* 1978, and *New York* 1989.

Reed Walter 1851–1902. US physician and medical researcher. His greatest work was carried out 1900–01 in Cuba, where a yellow-fever epidemic was ravaging US troops. His breakthrough isolation of the aedes mosquito as the sole carrier of yellow fever led to the eradication of the deadly disease.

reel in cinema, plastic or metal spool used for winding and storing film. As the size of reels became standardized it came to refer to the running time of the film: a standard 35-mm reel holds 900 ft/313 m of film, which runs for ten minutes when projected at 24 frames per second; hence a "two-reeler" was a film lasting 20 minutes. Today's projectors, however, hold bigger reels.

referee a quasi-judicial officer appointed by a court to take testimony or hear specified types of cases. These officials are sometimes called masters.

referendum procedure whereby a decision on proposed legislation is referred to the electorate for settlement by direct vote of all the people. It is most frequently employed in Switzerland, the first country to use it, but has become increasingly widespread. In 1992 several European countries (Ireland, Denmark, France) held referenda on whether or not to ratify the Maastricht Treaty on closer European economic and political union.

refining any process that purifies or converts something into a more useful form. Metals usually need refining after they have been extracted from their ores by such processes as smelting. Petroleum, or crude oil, needs refining before it can be used; the process involves fractional ◊distillation, the separation of the substance into separate components or "fractions."

reflection the throwing back or deflection of waves, such as ◊light or ◊sound waves, when they hit a surface. The *law of reflection* states that the angle of incidence (the angle between the ray and a perpendicular line drawn to the surface) is equal to the angle of reflection (the angle between the reflected ray and a perpendicular to the surface).

reflex in animals, a very rapid automatic response to a particular stimulus. It is controlled by the ◊nervous system. A reflex involves only a few nerve cells, unlike the slower but more complex responses produced by the many processing nerve cells of the brain.

reflex camera camera that uses a mirror and prisms to reflect light passing through the lens into the viewfinder, showing the photographer the exact scene that is being shot. When the shutter button is released the mirror springs out of the way, allowing light to reach the film. The most common type is the single-lens reflex (◊SLR) camera. The twin-lens reflex (TLR) camera has two lenses: one has a mirror for viewing, the other is used for exposing the film.

Reformation religious and political movement in 16th-century Europe to reform the Roman Catholic church, which led to the establishment of Protestant churches. Anticipated from the 12th century by the Waldenses, Lollards, and Hussites, it was set off by German priest Martin ◊Luther 1517, and became effective when the absolute monarchies gave it support by challenging the political power of the papacy and confiscating church wealth.

refraction the bending of a wave of light, heat, or sound when it passes from one medium to another. Refraction occurs because waves travel at different velocities in different media.

refractory (of a material) able to resist high temperature, for example ◊ceramics made from clay, minerals, or other earthy materials. Furnaces are lined with refractory materials such as silica and dolomite.

refrigeration use of technology to transfer heat from cold to warm, against the normal temperature gradient, so that a body can remain substantially colder than its surroundings. Refrigeration equipment is used for the chilling and deep-freezing of food in ◊food technology, and in air conditioners and industrial processes.

refugee person fleeing from oppressive or dangerous conditions (such as political, religious, or military persecution) and seeking refuge in a foreign country. In 1991 there were an estimated 17 million refugees worldwide, whose resettlement and welfare were the responsibility of the United Nations High Commission for Refugees (UNHCR). An estimated average of 3,000 people a day become refugees.

Regency style style of architecture and interior furnishings popular in England during the late 18th and early 19th centuries. The style is characterized by its restrained simplicity and its imitation of ancient Classical elements, often Greek.

regeneration in biology, regrowth of a new organ or tissue after the loss or removal of the original. It is common in plants, where a new individual can often be produced from a "cutting" of the original. In animals, regeneration of major structures is limited to lower organisms; certain lizards can regrow their tails if these are lost, and new flatworms can grow from a tiny fragment of an old one. In mammals, regeneration is limited to the repair of tissue in wound healing and the regrowth of peripheral nerves following damage.

regent person who carries out the duties of a sovereign during the sovereign's minority, incapacity, or lengthy absence from the country. In England since the time of Henry VIII, Parliament has always appointed a regent or council of regency when necessary.

Regents of the University of California v Bakke US Supreme Court decision 1978 dealing with "benign discrimination" in publicly funded schools. The case was a challenge to an affirmative-action program designed to remedy racial inequality in the University of California Medical School. Bakke, a white applicant denied admission to the school, sued the university on grounds of racial discrimination. He argued that his rejection was the result of a policy that accepted minority applicants at lower standards than those set for nonminorities. The Court sustained Bakke's complaint, ruling that any institution, regardless of motive, that discriminated solely because of race was in violation of the Civil Rights Act of 1964.

reggae predominant form of West Indian popular music of the 1970s and 1980s, characterized by a heavily accented offbeat and a thick bass line. The lyrics often refer to ◊Rastafarianism. Musicians include Bob Marley, Lee "Scratch" Perry (1940– , performer and producer), and the group Black Uhuru (1974–). Reggae is also played in the UK, South Africa, and elsewhere.

Regina industrial city (oil refining, cement, steel, farm machinery, fertilizers), and capital of Saskatchewan; population (1986) 175,000. It was founded 1882 as *Pile O'Bones*, and renamed in honor of Queen Victoria of England.

Rehnquist William Hubbs 1924– . US jurist; associate justice 1971–86 and chief justice 1986– of the US Supreme Court. As chief justice, he wrote the majority opinion for such cases as *Morrison* v *Olson* 1988, in which the court ruled that a special court can appoint special prosecutors to investigate crimes by high-ranking government officials, and *Hustler* v *Falwell* 1988, in which the Court ruled that public figures cannot be compensated for stress caused by parody that cannot possibly be taken seriously. Rehnquist dissented in *Texas* v *Johnson* 1989, in which the Court ruled that the burning of the US flag in protest is protected by individual rights set forth in the First Amendment. In 1990 Rehnquist dissented on the Court's ruling that it is unconstitutional for states to have the right to require a teenager to notify her parents before having an abortion.

Rehoboam king of Judah about 932–915 BC, son of Solomon. Under his rule the Jewish nation split into the two kingdoms of *Israel* and *Judah*. Ten of the tribes revolted against him and took Jeroboam as their ruler, leaving Rehoboam only the tribes of Judah and Benjamin.

Reich three periods in European history. The First Reich was the Holy Roman Empire 962–1806, the Second Reich the German Empire 1871–1918, and the ◊Third Reich Nazi Germany 1933–45.

Reims (English *Rheims*) capital of Champagne-Ardenne region, France; population (1990) 185,200. It is the center of the champagne industry and has textile industries. It was known in Roman times as *Durocorturum*. From 987 all but six French kings were crowned here. Ceded to England 1420 under the

Treaty of Troyes, it was retaken by Joan of Arc, who had Charles VII consecrated in the 13th-century cathedral. In World War II, the German High Command formally surrendered here to US general Eisenhower May 7, 1945.

reincarnation belief that after death the human soul or the spirit of a plant or animal may live again in another human or animal. It is part of the teachings of many religions and philosophies, for example ancient Egyptian and Greek (the philosophies of Pythagoras and Plato), Buddhism, Hinduism, Jainism, certain Christian heresies (such as the Cathars), and theosophy. It is also referred to as *transmigration* or *metempsychosis*.

reindeer or *caribou* deer *Rangifer tarandus* of Arctic and subarctic regions, common to North America and Eurasia. About 4 ft/120 cm at the shoulder, it has a thick, brownish coat and broad hooves well adapted to travel over snow. It is the only deer in which both sexes have antlers; these can grow to 5 ft/150 cm long, and are shed in winter.

relative density or *specific gravity* the density (at 68°F/20°C) of a solid or liquid relative to (divided by) the maximum density of water (at 39.2°F/4°C). The relative density of a gas is its density divided by the density of hydrogen (or sometimes dry air) at the same temperature and pressure.

relative humidity the concentration of water vapor in the air. It is expressed as the percentage that its moisture content represents of the maximum amount that the air could contain at the same temperature and pressure. The higher the temperature, the more water vapor the air can hold.

relativity in physics, the theory of the relative rather than absolute character of motion and mass, and the interdependence of matter, time, and space, as developed by German physicist Albert ◊Einstein in two phases:

special theory (1905) Starting with the premises that (1) the laws of nature are the same for all observers in unaccelerated motion, and (2) the speed of light is independent of the motion of its source, Einstein postulated that the time interval between two events was longer for an observer in whose frame of reference the events occur in different places than for the observer for whom they occur at the same place.

general theory of relativity (1915) The geometrical properties of space-time were to be conceived as modified locally by the presence of a body with mass. A planet's orbit around the Sun (as observed in three-dimensional space) arises from its natural trajectory in modified space-time; there is no need to invoke, as Isaac Newton did, a force of ◊gravity coming from the Sun and acting on the planet. Einstein's theory predicted slight differences in the orbits of the planets from Newton's theory, which were observable in the case of Mercury. The new theory also said light rays should bend when they pass by a massive object, owing to the object's effect on local space-time. The predicted bending of starlight was observed during the eclipse of the Sun 1919, when light from distant stars passing close to the Sun was not masked by sunlight.

relay in electrical engineering, an electromagnetic switch. A small current passing through a coil of wire wound around an iron core attracts an ◊armature whose movement closes a pair of sprung contacts to complete a secondary circuit, which may carry a large current or activate other devices. The solid-state equivalent is a thyristor switching device.

reindeer The reindeer ranges over the tundra of N Europe and Asia, Alaska, Canada, and Greenland.

relic part of some divine or saintly person, or something closely associated with them. Christian examples include the arm of St Teresa of Avila, the blood of St Januarius, and the True Cross. Buddhist relics include the funeral ashes of the historic Buddha, placed in a number of stupas or burial mounds.

relief in architecture, carved figures and other forms that project from the background. The Italian terms *basso-rilievo* (low relief), *mezzo-rilievo* (middle relief), and *alto-rilievo* (high relief) are used according to the extent to which the sculpture projects. The French term *bas-relief* is commonly used to mean low relief.

religion (Latin *religare* "to bind"; perhaps humans to God) code of belief or philosophy that often involves the worship of a ◊God or gods. Belief in a supernatural power is not essential (absent in, for example, Buddhism and Confucianism), but faithful adherence is usually considered to be rewarded, for example, by escape from human existence (Buddhism), by a future existence (Christianity, Islam), or by worldly benefit (Sōka Gakkai Buddhism). Among the chief religions are: *ancient and pantheist* religions of Babylonia, Assyria, Egypt, Greece, and Rome; *oriental* Hinduism, Buddhism, Jainism, Parseeism, Confucianism, Taoism, and Shinto; *"religions of a book"* Judaism, Christianity (the principal divisions are Roman Catholic, Eastern Orthodox, and Protestant), and Islam (the principal divisions are Sunni and Shiite); *combined derivation* such as Baha'ism, the Unification Church, and Mormonism. *See table p. 784*

REM US four-piece rock group formed 1980 in Georgia. Their songs are characterized by melodic bass lines, driving guitar, and evocative lyrics partly buried in the mix. Albums include *Reckoning* 1984, *Green* 1988, and the mass-market breakthrough *Out of Time* 1991.

rem acronym of *roentgen equivalent man* SI unit of radiation dose equivalent.

Some types of radiation do more damage than others for the same absorbed dose; the equivalent dose in rems is equal to the dose in rads multiplied by the relative biological effectiveness. One rem is approximately equivalent to the biological effect produced by one roentgen of X-ray or gamma-ray radiation. Humans can absorb up to 25 rems without immediate ill effects; 100 rems may produce radiation sickness; and more than 800 rems causes death.

Rembrandt Harmensz van Rijn 1606–1669. Dutch painter and etcher, one of the most prolific and significant artists in Europe of the 17th century. Between

religious festivals

date	festival	religion	event commemorated
Jan 6	Epiphany	Western Christian	coming of the Magi
Jan 6–7	Christmas	Orthodox Christian	birth of Jesus
Jan 18–19	Epiphany	Orthodox Christian	coming of the Magi
Jan–Feb	New Year	Chinese	Return of kitchen god to heaven
Feb–March	Shrove Tuesday	Christian	day before Lent
	Ash Wednesday	Christian	first day of Lent
	Purim	Jewish	story of Esther
	Mahashivaratri	Hindu	Siva
March–April	Palm Sunday	Western Christian	Jesus' entry into Jerusalem
	Good Friday	Western Christian	crucifixion of Jesus
	Easter Sunday	Western Christian	resurrection of Jesus
	Passover	Jewish	escape from slavery in Egypt
	Holi	Hindu	Krishna
	Holi Mohalla	Sikh	(coincides with Holi)
	Rama Naumi	Hindu	birth of Rama
	Ching Ming	Chinese	remembrance of the dead
April 13	Baisakhi	Sikh	founding of the Khalsa
April–May	Easter	Orthodox Christian	death and resurrection of Jesus
May–June	Shavuot	Jewish	giving of ten Commandments to Moses
	Pentecost (Whitsun)	Western Christian	Jesus' followers receiving the Holy Spirit
	Wesak	Buddhist	day of the Buddha's birth, enlightenment and death
	Martyrdom of Guru Arjan	Sikh	death of fifth guru of Sikhism
June	Dragon Boat Festival	Chinese	Chinese martyr
	Pentecost	Orthodox Christian	Jesus' followers receiving the Holy Spirit
July	Dhammacakka	Buddhist	preaching of Buddha's first sermon
Aug	Raksha Bandhan	Hindu	family
Aug–Sept	Janmashtami	Hindu	birthday of Krishna
Sept	Moon Festival	Chinese	Chinese hero
Sept–Oct	Rosh Hashana	Jewish	start of Jewish New Year
	Yom Kippur	Jewish	day of atonement
	Succot	Jewish	Israelites' time in the wilderness
Oct	Dusshera	Hindu	goddess Devi
Oct–Nov	Divali	Hindu	goddess Lakshmi
	Divali	Sikh	release of Guru Hargobind from prison
Nov	Guru Nanak's birthday	Sikh	founder of Sikhism
Nov–Dec	Bodhi Day	Buddhist (Mahayana)	Buddha's enlightenment
Dec	Hanukkah	Jewish	recapture of Temple of Jerusalem
	Winter Festival	Chinese	time of feasting
Dec 25	Christmas	Western Christian	birth of Christ
Dec–Jan	Birthday of Guru Gobind Sind	Sikh	last (tenth) human guru of Sikhism
	Martyrdom of Guru Tegh Bahadur	Sikh	ninth guru of Sikhism

1629 and 1669 he painted some 60 penetrating self-portraits. He also painted religious subjects, and produced about 300 etchings and over 1,000 drawings. His group portraits include *The Anatomy Lesson of Dr Tulp* 1632 (Mauritshuis, The Hague) and *The Night Watch* 1642 (Rijksmuseum, Amsterdam).

Remington Eliphalet 1793–1861. US inventor, gunsmith, and arms manufacturer and founder (with his father) of the Remington firm. He supplied the US army with rifles in the Mexican War 1846–48, then in 1856 the firm expanded into the manufacture of agricultural implements. His son Philo continued the expansion.

Remington Frederic 1861–1909. US artist and illustrator best known for his paintings, sculptures, and sketches of scenes of the American West, which he recorded during several trips to the region.

Remington Philo 1816–1889. US inventor and businessman, son of Eliphalet. He ran the arms business during the Civil War, when the firm had government contracts and later supplied several European armies with his new breech-loading rifles. In 1873 he became interested in the manufacture of typewriters, the first being demonstrated at the Centennial Exhibition in Philadelphia. By 1878, he produced the first typewriter with a shift key, which provided lower case as well as upper case letters. In 1879 his firm began making sewing machines.

REM sleep (acronym for *rapid-eye-movement* sleep) phase of sleep that recurs several times nightly in humans and is associated with dreaming. The eyes flicker quickly beneath closed lids.

Renaissance period and intellectual movement in European cultural history that is traditionally seen as ending the Middle Ages and beginning modern times. The Renaissance started in Italy in the 14th century and flourished in W Europe until about the 17th century.

The aim of Renaissance education was to produce the "complete human being" (***Renaissance man***), conversant in the humanities, mathematics and science (including their application in war), the arts and crafts, and athletics and sport; to enlarge the bounds of learning and geographical knowledge; to encourage the growth of skepticism and free thought, and the study and imitation of Greek and Latin literature and art. The revival of interest in Classical Greek and Roman culture inspired artists such as Leonardo da Vinci, Michelangelo, and Dürer, architects such as Brunelleschi and Alberti, writers such as Petrarch and Boccaccio. Scientists and explorers proliferated as well.

Renaissance art movement in European art of the 15th and 16th centuries. It began in Florence, Italy, with the rise of a spirit of humanism and a new appreciation of the Classical past. In painting and sculpture this led to greater naturalism and interest in anatomy and perspective. Renaissance art peaked around 1500 with the careers of Leonardo da Vinci, Raphael, Michelangelo, and Titian in Italy and Dürer in Germany.

René France-Albert 1935–   . Seychelles left-wing politician, the country's first prime minister after independence and president from 1977 after a coup. He has followed a nonnuclear policy of nonalignment.

Rennes industrial city (oil refining, chemicals, electronics, cars) and capital of Ille-et-Vilaine *département*, W France, at the confluence of the Ille and Vilaine, 35 mi/56 km SE of St Malo; population (1990) 203,500. It was the old capital of Brittany.

rennet extract, traditionally obtained from a calf's stomach, that contains the enzyme rennin, used to coagulate milk in the cheesemaking process. The enzyme can now be chemically produced.

Reno city in Nevada known for gambling and easy divorces; population (1990) 133,850. Products include building materials and electronic equipment. The University of Nevada-Reno is here. Reno was settled 1858 and grew quickly with the discovery nearby of the Comstock Lode, a large gold and silver deposit. The transcontinental railroad reached Reno 1868.

Renoir Jean 1894–1979. French director whose films, characterized by their humanism and naturalistic technique, include *Boudu sauvé des eaux/Boudu Saved from Drowning* 1932, *La grande Illusion* 1937, and *La Règle du jeu/The Rules of the Game* 1939. In 1975 he received an honorary Academy Award for his life's work. He was the son of the painter Pierre-Auguste Renoir.

Renoir Pierre-Auguste 1841–1919. French Impressionist painter. He met Monet and Sisley in the early 1860s, and together they formed the nucleus of the Impressionist movement. He developed a lively, colorful painting style with feathery brushwork and painted many voluptuous female nudes, such as *The Bathers* about 1884–87 (Philadelphia Museum of Art, US). In his later years he turned to sculpture.

replication in biology, production of copies of the genetic material DNA; it occurs during cell division (◊mitosis and ◊meiosis). Most mutations are caused by mistakes during replication.

repression in psychology, unconscious process said to protect a person from ideas, impulses, or memories that would threaten emotional stability were they to become conscious.

reprieve legal temporary suspension of the execution of a sentence of a criminal court. It is usually asso-

ciated with the death penalty. It is distinct from a pardon (extinguishing the sentence) and commutation (alteration) of a sentence (for example, from death to life imprisonment).

reproduction in biology, process by which a living organism produces other organisms similar to itself. There are two kinds: ◊asexual reproduction and ◊sexual reproduction.

Rembrandt Girl Leaning on a Windowsill *(1645),* Dulwich College Picture Gallery, London.

Renoir The French Impressionist Pierre-Auguste Renoir showed a more Classical approach in Les Parapluies/The Umbrellas c. 1881–84, painted after his visit to Italy 1881.

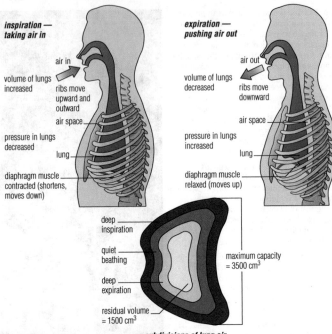

respiration The two phases of the process of respiration.

inspiration — taking air in

air in

volume of lungs increased

ribs move upward and outward

air space

pressure in lungs decreased

lung

diaphragm muscle contracted (shortens, moves down)

expiration — pushing air out

air out

volume of lungs decreased

ribs move downward

air space

pressure in lungs increased

lung

diaphragm muscle relaxed (moves up)

deep inspiration

quiet beathing

deep expiration

residual volume = 1500 cm³

maximum capacity = 3500 cm³

subdivisions of lung air

reptile any member of a class (Reptilia) of vertebrates. Unlike amphibians, reptiles have hard-shelled, yolk-filled eggs that are laid on land and from which fully formed young are born. Some snakes and lizards retain their eggs and give birth to live young. Reptiles are coldblooded and produced from eggs, and the skin is usually covered with scales. The metabolism is slow, and in some cases (certain large snakes) intervals between meals may be months. Reptiles date back over 300 million years.

republic country where the head of state is not a monarch, either hereditary or elected, but usually a president whose role may or may not include political functions.

Republican Party one of the US's two main political parties, formed 1854.

It is considered more conservative than the Democratic Party, favoring capital and big business and opposing state subvention and federal controls. In the late 20th century most presidents have come from the Republican Party, but in Congress Republicans have been outnumbered.

requiem in the Roman Catholic church, a mass for the dead. Musical settings include those by Palestrina, Mozart, Berlioz, and Verdi.

research the primary activity in science, a combination of theory and experimentation directed toward finding scientific explanations of phenomena. It is commonly classified into two types: *pure research*, involving theories with little apparent relevance to human concerns; and *applied research*, concerned with finding solutions to problems of social importance—for instance in medicine and engineering. The two types are linked in that theories developed from pure research may eventually be found to be of great value to society.

resin substance exuded from pines, firs, and other trees in gummy drops that harden in air. Varnishes are common products of the hard resins, and ointments come from the soft resins.

resistance in physics, that property of a substance that restricts the flow of electricity through it, associated with the conversion of electrical energy to heat; also the magnitude of this property. Resistance depends on many factors, such as the nature of the material, its temperature, dimensions, and thermal properties; degree of impurity; the nature and state of illumination of the surface; and the frequency and magnitude of the current. The SI unit of resistance is the ohm.

resistance movement opposition movement in a country occupied by an enemy or colonial power, especially in the 20th century; for example, the French resistance to Nazism in World War II.

resistor in physics, any component in an electrical circuit used to introduce ⃗resistance to a current. Resistors are often made from wire-wound coils or pieces of carbon. Rheostats and potentiometers are variable resistors.

resonance rapid and uncontrolled increase in the size of a vibration when the vibrating object is subject to a force varying at its natural frequency. In a trombone, for example, the length of the air column in the instrument is adjusted until it resonates with the note being sounded. Resonance effects are also produced by many electrical circuits. Tuning a radio, for example, is done by adjusting the natural frequency of the receiver circuit until it coincides with the frequency of the radio waves falling on the aerial.

resources materials that can be used to satisfy human needs. Because human needs are diverse and extend from basic physical requirements, such as food and shelter, to ill-defined aesthetic needs, resources encompass a vast range of items. The intellectual resources of a society—its ideas and technologies—determine which aspects of the environment meet that society's needs, and therefore become resources. For example, in the 19th century, uranium was used only in the manufacture of colored glass. Today, with the advent of nuclear technology, it is a military and energy resource. Resources are often categorized into *human resources*, such as labor, supplies, and skills, and *natural resources*, such as climate, fossil fuels, and water. Natural resources are divided into ◊nonrenewable resources and renewable resources.

respiration biochemical process whereby food molecules are progressively broken down (oxidized) to release energy in the form of ◊ATP. In most organisms this requires oxygen, but in some bacteria the oxidant is the nitrate or sulfate ion instead. In all higher organisms, respiration occurs in the ◊mitochondria. Respiration is also used to mean breathing, although this is more accurately described as a form of gas exchange.

Restoration in English history, the period when the monarchy, in the person of Charles II, was reestablished after the English Civil War and the fall of the ◊Protectorate 1660.

Restoration comedy style of English theater, dating from the Restoration. It witnessed the first appearance of women on the English stage, most notably in the "breeches part," specially created in order to costume the actress in male attire, thus revealing her figure to its best advantage. The genre placed much emphasis on sexual antics. Examples include Wycherley's *The Country Wife* 1675, Congreve's *The Way of the World* 1700, and Farquhar's *The Beaux' Stratagem* 1707.

restrictive trade practices agreements between people in a particular trade or business that keep the cost of goods or services artificially high (for example, an agreement to restrict output) or provide barriers to outsiders entering the trade or business.

Often, these practices are illegal.

resurrection in Christian, Jewish, and Muslim belief, the rising from the dead that all souls will experience at the Last Judgment. The Resurrection also refers to Jesus rising from the dead on the third day after his crucifixion, a belief central to Christianity and celebrated at Easter.

resuscitation steps taken to revive anyone on the brink of death. The most successful technique for life-threatening emergencies, such as electrocution, near-drowning, or heart attack, is mouth-to-mouth resuscitation. Medical and paramedical staff are trained in cardiopulmonary resuscitation: the use of specialized equipment and techniques to attempt to restart the breathing and/or heartbeat and stabilize the patient long enough for more definitive treatment.

retail sale of goods and services to a consumer. The retailer is the last link in the distribution chain. A retailer's purchases are usually made from a wholesaler, who in turn buys from a manufacturer.

retina light-sensitive area at the back of the ◊eye connected to the brain by the optic nerve. It has several layers and in humans contains over a million rods and cones, sensory cells capable of converting light into nervous messages that pass down the optic nerve to the brain.

retriever any of several breeds of hunting dogs, often used as guide dogs for the blind. The commonest breeds are the *Labrador retriever*, large, smooth-coated, and usually black or yellow; and the *golden retriever*, with either flat or wavy coat. They can grow to 2 ft/60 cm high and weigh 90 lb/40 kg.

Réunion French island of the Mascarenes group, in the Indian Ocean, 400 mi/650 km E of Madagascar and 110 mi/180 km SW of Mauritius
area 970 sq mi/2,512 sq km
capital St Denis
physical forested, rising in Piton de Neiges to 10,072 ft/3,069 m
features administers five uninhabited islands, also claimed by Madagascar
products sugar, corn, vanilla, tobacco, rum
population (1990) 597,800
history explored by Portuguese (the first European visitors) 1513; annexed by Louis XIII of France 1642; overseas *département* of France 1946; overseas region 1972.

Reuter Paul Julius, Baron de 1816–1899. German founder of the international news agency *Reuters*. He began a continental pigeon post 1849, and in 1851 set up a news agency in London. In 1858 he persuaded the press to use his news telegrams, and the service became worldwide. Reuters became a public company 1984.

Revelation last book of the New Testament, traditionally attributed to the author of the Gospel of St John but now generally held to be the work of another writer. It describes a vision of the end of the world, of the Last Judgment, and of a new heaven and earth ruled by God from Jerusalem.

Revere Paul 1735–1818. American revolutionary, a Boston silversmith, who carried the news of the approach of British troops to Lexington and Concord (see ◊American Revolution) on the night of April 18, 1775. On the next morning the first shots of the Revolution were fired at Lexington. Longfellow's poem "The Midnight Ride of Paul Revere" commemorates the event.

Revere, who took part in the ◊Boston Tea Party, was a courier for the Continental Congress, often riding from Boston to Philadelphia. In early 1775 he alerted rebels in New Hampshire that the British, under General Thomas Gage were transporting supplies from Fort William and Mary. The New Hampshire militiamen captured quantities of munitions that proved decisive at the Battle of Bunker Hill. Revere was active throughout the Revolution and printed the first continental money.

reverse takeover in business, a takeover where a company sells itself to another (a white knight) to avoid being the target of a purchase by an unwelcome predator.

revolution any rapid, theoretical, violent change in the political, social, or economic structure of society. It is usually applied to political change: examples include the American Revolution, where the colonists broke free from their colonial ties and established a sovereign, independent nation; the French Revolution, where an absolute monarchy was overthrown by opposition from inside the country and a popular uprising; and the Russian Revolution, where a repressive monarchy was overthrown by those seeking to institute widespread social and economic changes based on a socialist model. While political revolutions are often associated with violence, other types of change have just as much impact on society. Most notable is the Industrial Revolution of the mid-18th century. In the 1970s and 1980s a high-tech revolution could be identified, based on the increasing use of computers. In 1989–90 the ◊Eastern Bloc nations demonstrated against and voted out the ◊Communist party, in many cases creating a prodemocracy revolution.

Revolutionary Wars series of wars 1791–1802 between France and the combined armies of England, Austria, Prussia, and others during the period of the French Revolution, and on ◊Napoleon's ambition to conquer Europe.

revolutions of 1848 series of revolts in various parts of Europe against monarchical rule. While some of the revolutionaries had republican ideas, many more were motivated by economic grievances. The revolution began in France with the overthrow of Louis Philippe and then spread to Italy, the Austrian Empire, and Germany, where the short-lived ◊Frankfurt Parliament put forward ideas about political unity in Germany. None of the revolutions enjoyed any lasting success, and most were violently suppressed within a few months.

Some concessions were made to both liberal and nationalist movements, and 1848 is regarded as ending the conservative domination of ◊Metternich.

revue stage presentation involving short satirical and topical items in the form of songs, sketches, and monologues; it originated in the late 19th century.

Turn-of-the-century revues were spectacular entertainments, notably those of Florenz Ziegfeld, but the "intimate revue" became increasingly popular, employing writers such as Noël Coward.

Reye's syndrome rare disorder of the metabolism causing fatty infiltration of the liver and ◊encephalitis. It occurs mainly in children and has been linked with aspirin therapy, although its cause is still uncertain. The mortality rate is 50%.

Reykjavik capital (from 1918) and chief port of Iceland, on the SW coast; population (1988) 93,000. Fish processing is the main industry. Reykjavik is heated by underground mains fed by volcanic springs. It was a seat of Danish administration from 1801 to 1918.

Reynolds Burt 1936– . US film actor and director who excels in adventure films and comedies. He is known for doing his own stunts, since he started as a stuntman. His films include *Deliverance* 1972, the cult film *White Lightning* 1973, *Hustle* 1975, and *City Heat* 1984. He also appeared from 1991 as the lead in the television comedy series "Evening Shade."

Reynolds Joshua 1723–1792. English portrait painter, active in London from 1752. He became the first president of the Royal Academy 1768. His portraits display a facility for striking and characteristic compositions in a consciously grand manner. He often borrowed Classical poses, for example *Mrs Siddons as the Tragic Muse* 1784 (San Marino, California).

rhapsody in music, instrumental ◊fantasia, often based on folk melodies, such as Liszt's *Hungarian Rhapsodies* 1853–54.

Rhee Syngman 1875–1965. Korean right-wing politician. A rebel under Chinese and Japanese rule, he became president of South Korea from 1948 until riots forced him to resign and leave the country 1960.

rhinoceros The Sumatran rhinoceros is covered with thick, brown hair at birth, which gradually thins as the animal grows.

rhenium (Latin *Rhenus* "Rhine") heavy, silver-white, metallic element, symbol Re, atomic number 75, atomic weight 186.2. It has chemical properties similar to those of manganese and a very high melting point (5,756°F/3,180°C), which makes it valuable as an ingredient in alloys.

It was identified and named in 1925 by German chemists W Noddack (1893–1960), I Tacke, and O Berg.

rhesus factor ◊protein on the surface of red blood cells of humans, which is involved in the rhesus blood group system. Most individuals possess the main rhesus factor (Rh+), but those without this factor (Rh–) produce ◊antibodies if they come into contact with it. The name comes from rhesus monkeys, in whose blood rhesus factors were first found.

rhesus monkey macaque monkey *Macaca mulatta* found in N India and SE Asia. It has a pinkish face, red buttocks, and long, straight, brown-gray hair. It can grow up to 2 ft/60 cm long, with a 8 in/20 cm tail.

rhetoric (Greek *rhetor* "orator") traditionally, the art of public speaking and debate. Rhetorical skills are valued in such occupations as politics, teaching, law, religion, and broadcasting.

rhetorical question question, often used by public speakers and debaters, that either does not require an answer or for which the speaker intends to provide his or her own answer ("Does this government know what it is doing?").

rheumatic fever or *acute rheumatism* acute or chronic illness characterized by fever and painful swelling of joints. Some victims also experience involuntary movements of the limbs and head, a form of ◊chorea.

rheumatism nontechnical term for a variety of ailments associated with inflammation and stiffness of the joints and muscles.

Rhine (German *Rhein*, French *Rhin*) European river rising in Switzerland and reaching the North Sea via Germany and the Netherlands; length 820 mi/1,320 km. Tributaries include the Moselle and the Ruhr. The Rhine is linked with the Mediterranean by the Rhine–Rhône Waterway, and with the Black Sea by the Rhine–Main–Danube Waterway. It is the longest, and the dirtiest, river in Europe.

Rhineland province of Prussia from 1815. Its unchallenged annexation by Nazi Germany 1936 was a harbinger of World War II.

Rhineland-Palatinate (German *Rheinland-Pfalz*) administrative region (German *Land*) of Germany
area 7,643 sq mi/19,800 sq km
capital Mainz
cities Ludwigshafen, Koblenz, Trier, Worms
physical wooded mountain country, river valleys of Rhine and Moselle
products wine (75% of German output), tobacco, chemicals, machinery, leather goods, pottery
population (1992) 3,702,000

rhinoceros odd-toed hoofed mammal of the family Rhinocerotidae. The one-horned Indian rhinoceros *Rhinoceros unicornis* is up to 6 ft/2 m high at the shoulder, with a tubercled skin, folded into shieldlike pieces; the African rhinoceroses are smooth-skinned and two-horned. All are endangered.

Rhode Island (officially Rhode Island and Providence Plantations) state in NE US; the smallest state of the US; nickname Ocean State

Rhode Island

area 1,197 sq mi/3,100 sq km
capital Providence
cities Cranston, Woonsocket
population (1990) 1,003,464
features Narragansett Bay, with America's Cup yacht races; mansions of Newport; Block Island; Brown University; Rhode Island School of Design; University of Rhode Island
products poultry (Rhode Island Reds), jewelry, silverware, textiles, machinery, primary metals, rubber products, submarine assembly
famous people George M Cohan, Anne Hutchinson, Matthew C Perry, Oliver Hazard Perry, Gilbert Stuart, Roger Williams
history founded 1636 by Roger Williams, exiled from Massachusetts Bay Colony for religious dissent; one of the original 13 states and still the smallest one in area. The principle trends in the 19th century were industrialization, immigration, and urbanization. Rhode Island is the most industrialized state, and it suffers from high unemployment, low-wage manufacturing industries, and susceptibility to recessions.

Rhodes (Greek *Ródhos*) Greek island, largest of the Dodecanese, in the E Aegean Sea
area 545 sq mi/1,412 sq km
capital Rhodes
products grapes, olives
population (1981) 88,000
history settled by Greeks about 1000 BC; the ◊Colossus of Rhodes (fell 224 BC) was one of the ◊Seven Wonders of the World; held by the Knights Hospitallers of St John 1306–1522; taken from Turkish rule by the Italian occupation 1912; ceded to Greece 1947.

Rhodes Cecil (John) 1853–1902. South African politician, born in the UK, prime minister of Cape Colony 1890–96. Aiming at the formation of a South African federation and the creation of a block of British territory from the Cape to Cairo, he was responsible for the annexation of Bechuanaland (now Botswana) in 1885. He formed the British South Africa Company in 1889, which occupied Mashonaland and Matabeleland, thus forming *Rhodesia* (now Zambia and Zimbabwe).
The *Rhodes scholarships* were founded at Oxford University, UK, under his will, for students from the Commonwealth, the US, and Germany.

Rhodesia former name of ◊Zambia (Northern Rhodesia) and ◊Zimbabwe (Southern Rhodesia), in S Africa.

rhodium (Greek *rhodon* "rose") hard, silver-white, metallic element, symbol Rh, atomic number 45, atomic weight 102.905. It is one of the so-called platinum group of metals and is resistant to tarnish, corrosion, and acid. It occurs as a free metal in the natural alloy osmiridium and is used in jewelry, electroplating, and thermocouples.

rhododendron any of numerous shrubs of the genus *Rhododendron* of the heath family Ericaceae.

Most species are evergreen. The leaves are usually dark and leathery, and the large racemes of flowers occur in all colors except blue. They thrive on acid soils. ◊Azaleas belong to the same genus.

rhombus in geometry, an equilateral (all sides equal) ◊parallelogram. Its diagonals bisect each other at right angles, and its area is half the product of the lengths of the two diagonals. A rhombus whose internal angles are 90° is called a ◊square.

Rhône river of S Europe; length 500 mi/810 km. It rises in Switzerland and flows through Lake Geneva to Lyon in France, where at its confluence with the Saône the upper limit of navigation is reached. The river turns due S, passes Vienne and Avignon, and takes in the Isère and other tributaries. Near Arles it divides into the *Grand* and *Petit Rhône*, flowing respectively SE and SW into the Mediterranean W of Marseille. Here it forms a two-armed delta; the area between the tributaries is the marshy region known as the Camargue.

Rhône-Alpes region of E France in the upper reaches of the Rhône; area 16,868 sq mi/43,700 sq km; population (1992) 5,344,000. It consists of the *départements* of Ain, Ardèche, Drôme, Isère, Loire, Rhône, Savoie, and Haute-Savoie. The chief city is Lyon. There are several wine-producing areas, including Chenas, Fleurie, and Beaujolais. Industrial products include chemicals, textiles, and motor vehicles.

rhubarb perennial plant *Rheum rhaponticum* of the buckwheat family Polygonaceae, grown for its pink, edible leaf stalks. The leaves contain oxalic acid, and are poisonous. There are also wild rhubarbs native to Europe and Asia.

rhyme identity of sound, usually in the endings of lines of verse, such as *wing* and *sing*. Avoided in Japanese, it is a common literary device in other Asian and European languages. Rhyme first appeared in Europe in late Latin poetry but was not used in Classical Latin or Greek.

rhythm and blues (R & B) US popular music of the 1940s–60s, which drew on swing and jump-jazz rhythms and blues vocals, and was a progenitor of rock and roll. It diversified into soul, funk, and other styles. R & B artists include Bo Diddley, Jackie Wilson (1934–84), and Etta James (*c.* 1938–).

rhythm method method of natural contraception that works by avoiding intercourse when the woman is producing egg cells (ovulating). The time of ovulation can be worked out by the calendar (counting days from the last period), by temperature changes, or by inspection of the cervical mucus. All these methods are unreliable because it is possible for ovulation to occur at any stage of the menstrual cycle.

rib long, usually curved bone that extends laterally from the ◊spine in vertebrates. Most fishes and many reptiles have ribs along most of the spine, but in mammals they are found only in the chest area. In humans, there are 12 pairs of ribs. The ribs protect the lungs and heart, and allow the chest to expand and contract easily.

riboflavin or *vitamin B₂* ◊vitamin of the B complex whose absence in the diet causes stunted growth.

ribonucleic acid full name of ◊RNA.

ribosome in biology, the protein-making machinery of the cell. Ribosomes are located on the endoplasmic reticulum (ER) of eukaryotic cells, and are made of proteins and a special type of ◊RNA, ribosomal RNA.

They receive messenger RNA (copied from the ◊DNA) and ◊amino acids, and "translate" the messenger RNA by using its chemically coded instructions to link amino acids in a specific order, to make a strand of a particular protein.

rice principal cereal of the wet regions of the tropics; derived from grass of the species *Oryza sativa*, probably native to India and SE Asia. It is unique among cereal crops in that it is grown standing in water. The yield is very large, and rice is said to be the staple food of one-third of the world population.

Rice Grantland 1880–1954. US sports journalist. Gaining a reputation for vivid sports writing, he worked for the *New York Herald Tribune* 1914–30. After 1930 he wrote the column "The Sportlight," setting the standard for modern sports journalism. He succeeded Walter ◊Camp in selecting the annual All-America football team.

Richard I *the Lion-Heart* (French *Coeur-de-Lion*) 1157–1199. King of England from 1189, who spent all but six months of his reign abroad. He was the third son of Henry II, against whom he twice rebelled. In the third ◊Crusade 1191–92 he won victories at Cyprus, Acre, and Arsuf (against ◊Saladin), but failed to recover Jerusalem. While returning overland he was captured by the Duke of Austria, who handed him over to the emperor Henry VI, and he was held prisoner until a large ransom was raised. He then returned briefly to England, where his brother John I had been ruling in his stead. His later years were spent in warfare in France, where he was killed.

Richard II 1367–1400. King of England from 1377, effectively from 1389, son of Edward the Black Prince. He reigned in conflict with Parliament; they executed some of his associates 1388, and he executed some of the opposing barons 1397, whereupon he made himself absolute. Two years later, forced to abdicate in favor of ◊Henry IV, he was jailed and probably assassinated.

In 1399 his cousin Henry Bolingbroke, Duke of Hereford (later Henry IV), returned from exile to lead a revolt; Richard II was deposed by Parliament and imprisoned in Pontefract Castle, where he died mysteriously.

Richard III 1452–1485. King of England from 1483. The son of Richard, Duke of York, he was created Duke of Gloucester by his brother Edward IV, and distinguished himself in the Wars of the ◊Roses. On Edward's death 1483 he became protector to his nephew Edward V, and soon secured the crown for himself on the plea that Edward IV's sons were illegitimate. He proved a capable ruler, but the suspicion that he had murdered Edward V and his brother undermined his popularity. In 1485 Henry, Earl of Richmond (later ◊Henry VII), raised a rebellion, and Richard III was defeated and killed at Bosworth.

Richardson Samuel 1689–1761. English novelist, one of the founders of the modern novel. *Pamela* 1740–41, written in the form of a series of letters and containing much dramatic conversation, was sensationally popular all across Europe, and was followed by *Clarissa* 1747–48 and *Sir Charles Grandison* 1753–54.

Richardson Tony 1928–1991. English director and producer. With George Devine he established the English Stage Company 1955 at the Royal Court Theatre, with productions such as *Look Back in Anger* 1956. His films include *Saturday Night and Sunday Morning* 1960, *A Taste of Honey* 1961, *Tom Jones* 1963, and *Joseph Andrews* 1977.

Richelieu Armand Jean du Plessis de 1585–1642. French cardinal and politician, chief minister from 1624. He aimed to make the monarchy absolute; he ruthlessly crushed opposition by the nobility and destroyed the political power of the ◊Huguenots, while leaving them religious freedom. Abroad, he sought to establish French supremacy by breaking the power of the Hapsburgs; he therefore supported the Swedish king Gustavus Adolphus and the German Protestant princes against Austria and in 1635 brought France into the Thirty Years' War.

Richland city in SE Washington, on the Columbia River, NW of Walla Walla; population (1990) 33,300. It is a center for research for the US Department of Energy and a major producer of plutonium for nuclear weapons. It grew as a residential community for employees of the Hanford Engineer Works that helped to develop the atomic bomb from 1943.

Richler Mordecal 1931– . Canadian novelist, born in Montreal. His novels, written in a witty, acerbic style, include *The Apprenticeship of Duddy Kravitz* 1959 and *St Urbain's Horseman* 1971. Later works include *Joshua Then and Now* 1980 and *Home Sweet Home* 1984.

Richmond industrial city and port on the James River and capital of Virginia; population (1990) 219,000. It is a major tobacco market and distribution, commercial, and financial center of the surrounding region. Its diversified manufactures include tobacco products, chemicals, paper and printing, and textiles.

Educational institutions include the University of Richmond and Virginia Commonwealth University. The Museum of the Confederacy and Edgar Allan Poe Museum are here, as are the former homes of John Marshall and Robert E Lee and the graves of James Madison and Jefferson Davis. The first permanent colonial American settlement was established 1637. Richmond was the capital of the Confederacy 1861–65, and several Civil War battles were fought nearby.

Richter Burton 1931– . US high-energy physicist who, in the 1960s, designed the Stanford Positron Accelerating Ring (SPEAR). In 1974 Richter used SPEAR to produce a new particle, a hadeon, composed of a charmed quark and a charmed antiquark. The charmed quark had been first postulated by Sheldon Glashow in 1964. Richter shared the 1976 Nobel Physics Prize with Samuel Ting.

Richter Charles Francis 1900–1985. US seismologist, deviser of the ◊Richter scale used to measure the strength of the waves from earthquakes.

Richter scale scale based on measurement of seismic waves, used to determine the magnitude of an ◊earthquake at its epicenter. The magnitude of an earthquake differs from its intensity, measured by the ◊Mercalli scale, which is subjective and varies from place to place for the same earthquake. The scale is named after US seismologist Charles Richter.

Richthofen Manfred, Freiherr von (the "Red Baron") 1892–1918. German aviator. In World War I he commanded the 11th Chasing Squadron, known as *Richthofen's Flying Circus*, and shot down 80 aircraft before being killed in action.

Rickenbacker Edward Vernon 1890–1973. US racing-car driver, aviator, and airline executive. A race-car driver in his youth, by 1917 he had established a land speed record of 134 mph/216 kph. He purchased Eastern Airlines 1938 leaving briefly to serve as an adviser to the War Department during World War II. Taking on special missions, he ditched his plane in the

Pacific Ocean, drifting for 23 days before being rescued.

rickets defective growth of bone in children due to an insufficiency of calcium deposits. The bones, which do not harden adequately, are bent out of shape. It is usually caused by a lack of vitamin D and insufficient exposure to sunlight. Renal rickets, also a condition of malformed bone, is associated with kidney disease.

Rickey Branch Wesley 1881–1965. US baseball executive. As president of the Brooklyn Dodgers 1942–50, he made baseball history by signing Jackie Robinson, the first black American to play in the major leagues. As president of the St Louis Cardinals 1917 and manager 1919–25, he pioneered the minor-league system of developing talent.

Rickover Hyman George 1900–1986. Russian-born US naval officer. During World War II, he worked on the atomic bomb project, headed the navy's nuclear reactor division, and served on the Atomic Energy Commission. He was responsible for the development of the first nuclear submarine, the *Nautilus*, 1954. After retiring 1982, he became an outspoken critic of the dangers of nuclear research and development.

Riefenstahl Leni 1902– . German filmmaker. Her film of the Nazi rallies at Nuremberg, *Triumph des Willens/Triumph of the Will* 1934, vividly illustrated Hitler's charismatic appeal but tainted her career. After World War II her work was blacklisted by the Allies until 1952.

Riff member of a ◊Berber people of N Morocco, who under ◊Abd el-Krim long resisted the Spanish and French.

rifle ◊firearm that has spiral grooves (rifling) in its barrel. When a bullet is fired, the rifling makes it spin, thereby improving accuracy. Rifles were first introduced in the late 18th century.

rift valley valley formed by the subsidence of a block of the Earth's ◊crust between two or more parallel ◊faults. Rift valleys are steep-sided and form where the crust is being pulled apart, as at ◊ocean ridges, or in the Great Rift Valley of E Africa.

Rift Valley, Great volcanic valley formed 10–20 million years ago by a crack in the Earth's crust and running about 5,000 mi/8,000 km from the Jordan Valley through the Red Sea to central Mozambique in SE Africa. It is marked by a series of lakes, including Lake Turkana (formerly Lake Rudolf), and volcanoes, such as Mount Kilimanjaro.

At some points its traces have been lost by erosion, but elsewhere, as in S Kenya, cliffs rise thousands of feet.

Riga capital and port of Latvia; population (1987) 900,000. A member of the ◊Hanseatic League from 1282, Riga has belonged in turn to Poland 1582, Sweden 1621, and Russia 1710.

It was the capital of independent Latvia 1918–40 and was occupied by Germany 1941–44, before being annexed by the USSR. It again became independent Latvia's capital 1991.

Rigel or *Beta Orionis* brightest star in the constellation Orion. It is a blue-white supergiant, with an estimated diameter 50 times that of the Sun. It is 900 light-years from Earth, and is about 100,000 times more luminous than our Sun. It is the seventh-brightest star in the sky.

Rights of Man and the Citizen, Declaration of the historic French document. According to the statement of the French National Assembly 1789, these rights include representation in the legislature; equality before the law; equality of opportunity; freedom from arbitrary imprisonment; freedom of speech and religion; taxation in proportion to ability to pay; and security of property. In 1946 were added equal rights for women; right to work, join a union, and strike; leisure, social security, and support in old age; and free education.

right triangle triangle in which one of the angles is a right angle (90°). It is the basic form of triangle for defining trigonometrical ratios (for example, sine, cosine, and tangent) and for which the ◊Pythagorean theorem holds true. The longest side of a right triangle is called the hypotenuse.

right wing the more conservative or reactionary section of a political party or spectrum. It originated in the French national assembly 1789, where the nobles sat in the place of honor on the president's right, whereas the commons were on his left (hence ◊left wing).

rigor medical term for shivering or rigidity. *Rigor mortis* is the stiffness that ensues in a corpse soon after death, owing to the coagulation of muscle proteins.

Rig-Veda oldest of the ◊Vedas, the chief sacred writings of Hinduism. It consists of hymns to the Aryan gods, such as Indra, and to nature gods.

Riis Jacob August 1849–1914. Danish-born US journalist, photographer, and reformer. As police reporter for the *New York Evening Sun* 1888–99, he was exposed to the grim realities of urban life, and his photographic exposé of conditions in the New York slums, *How the Other Half Lives* 1890, made the American public aware of the poverty in its own midst.

Riley James Whitcomb 1849–1916. US poet. His first collection of poems, *The Old Swimmin' Hole*, was published 1883. His later collections include *Rhymes of Childhood* 1890 and *Home Folks* 1900. His use of the Midwestern vernacular and familiar themes earned him the unofficial title "The Hoosier Poet."

Rimbaud (Jean Nicolas) Arthur 1854–1891. French Symbolist poet. His verse was chiefly written before the age of 20, notably *Les Illuminations* published 1886. From 1871 he lived with ◊Verlaine.

Rimsky-Korsakov Nikolay Andreyevich 1844–1908. Russian composer. He used Russian folk idiom and rhythms in his Romantic compositions and published a text on orchestration. His operas include *The Maid of Pskov* 1873, *The Snow Maiden* 1882, *Mozart and Salieri* 1898, and *The Golden Cockerel* 1907, a satirical attack on despotism that was banned until 1909.

Ringling Charles 1863–1926. US circus promoter. With its three rings and large cast, the Ringlings' circus was touted as the "Greatest Show on Earth," the byword still most associated with the modern Ringling Brothers and Barnum and Bailey Circus (which the Ringling brothers acquired in 1907).

ringworm any of various contagious skin infections due to related kinds of fungus, usually resulting in circular, itchy, discolored patches covered with scales or blisters. The scalp and feet (athlete's foot) are generally involved. Treatment is with antifungal preparations.

Rio de Janeiro The Sugar Loaf peak in Rio de Janeiro.

Rio de Janeiro port and resort in E Brazil; population (1991) 5,487,300. The name (Portuguese "river of January") commemorates the arrival of Portuguese explorers Jan 1, 1502, but there is in fact no river. Sugar Loaf Mountain stands at the entrance to the harbor. Rio was the capital of Brazil 1763–1960.

Rio Grande river rising in the Rocky Mountains in S Colorado, and flowing S to the Gulf of Mexico, where it is reduced to a trickle by irrigation demands on its upper reaches; length 1,900 mi/3,050 km. Its last 1,500 mi/2,400 km form the US–Mexican border (Mexican name *Río Bravo del Norte*).

Río Muni the mainland portion of ◊Equatorial Guinea.

RIP abbreviation for *requiescat in pace* (Latin "may he/she rest in peace").

Risorgimento movement for Italian national unity and independence from 1815. Leading figures in the movement included ◊Cavour, ◊Mazzini, and ◊Garibaldi. Uprisings 1848–49 failed, but with help from France in a war against Austria—to oust it from Italian provinces in the north—an Italian kingdom was founded 1861. Unification was finally completed with the addition of Venetia 1866 and the Papal States 1870.

ritualization in ethology, a stereotype that occurs in certain behavior patterns when these are incorporated into displays. For example, the exaggerated and stylized head toss of the goldeneye drake during courtship is a ritualization of the bathing movement used to wet the feathers; its duration and form have become fixed. Ritualization may make displays clearly recognizable, so ensuring that individuals mate only with members of their own species.

river long water course that flows down a slope along a channel. It originates at a point called its *source*, and enters a sea or lake at its *mouth*. Along its length it may be joined by smaller rivers called *tributaries*. A river and its tributaries are contained within a drainage basin.

Rivera Diego 1886–1957. Mexican painter, active in Europe until 1921. He received many public commissions for murals exalting the Mexican revolution. A vast cycle on historical themes (National Palace, Mexico City) was begun 1929. In the 1930s he visited

the US and with Ben Shahn produced murals for the Rockefeller Center, New York (later overpainted because he included a portrait of Lenin).

Rivera Primo de. Spanish politician; see ◊Primo de Rivera.

Riverside city in California, on the Santa Ana River, E of Los Angeles; population (1990) 226,500. It was founded 1870. It is the center of a citrus-growing district and has a citrus research station; the seedless orange was developed at Riverside 1873.

riveting method of joining metal plates. A hot metal pin called a rivet, which has a head at one end, is inserted into matching holes in two overlapping plates, then the other end is struck and formed into another head, holding the plates tight. Riveting is used in building construction, boilermaking, and shipbuilding.

Riviera the Mediterranean coast of France and Italy from Marseille to La Spezia. The most exclusive stretch of the Riviera, with the finest climate, is the Côte d'Azur, from Menton to St Tropez, which includes Monaco.

Riyadh (Arabic *Ar Riyād*) capital of Saudi Arabia and of the Central Province, formerly the sultanate of Nejd, in an oasis, connected by rail with Dammam on the Arabian Gulf; population (1986) 1,500,000.

RNA *ribonucleic acid* nucleic acid involved in the process of translating ◊DNA, the genetic material, into proteins. It is usually single-stranded, unlike the double-stranded DNA, and consists of a large number of nucleotides strung together, each of which comprises the sugar ribose, a phosphate group, and one of four bases (uracil, cytosine, adenine, or guanine). RNA is copied from DNA by the assemblage of free nucleotides against an unwound portion (a single strand) of the DNA, with DNA serving as the template. In this process, uracil (instead of the thymine in DNA) is paired with adenine, and guanine with cytosine, forming base pairs that then separate. The RNA then travels to the ribosomes where it serves to assemble proteins from free amino acids. In a few viruses, such as retroviruses, RNA is the only hereditary material.

Roach Hal 1892–1992. US film producer, usually of comedies, who was active from the 1910s to the 1940s. He worked with ◊Laurel and Hardy, and also produced films for Harold Lloyd and Charley Chase. His work includes *The Music Box* 1932, *Way Out West* 1936, and *Of Mice and Men* 1939.

road specially constructed route for wheeled vehicles to travel on. Reinforced tracks became necessary with the invention of wheeled vehicles in about 3000 BC and most ancient civilizations had some form of road network. The Romans developed engineering techniques that were not equaled for another 1,400 years.

roadrunner crested North American ground-dwelling bird *Geococcyx californianus* of the ◊cuckoo family, found in the SW US and Mexico. It can run at a speed of 15 mph/25 kph.

Roanoke (American Indian "shell money") industrial city (railway repairs, chemicals, steel goods, furniture, textiles) in Virginia, on the Roanoke River; population (1980) 100,500. Founded 1834 as *Big Lick*, it was a small village until 1881 when the repair shops of the Virginia Rallroad were set up here, after which it developed rapidly.

Robbe-Grillet Alain 1922– . French writer, the leading theorist of *le nouveau roman* ("the new novel"), for example his own *Les Gommes/The Erasers* 1953,

river landscape

A river can be regarded as having three stages – a youthful stage, a mature stage, and an old stage. Over millions of years it can develop from one stage to the next, or all three stages may be visible at one time along its length. Each stage is recognizable by the distinctive landscape it forms.

youthful stage

The river begins its descent through a narrow V-shaped valley. Falling steeply over a short distance, it follows a zig-zag course and produces interlocking spurs.

The current is strong, cutting a deep channel and wearing potholes through exposed rocks. Waterfalls and rapids form where it runs over hard rocks.

mature stage

The river flows through a broad valley, floored with sediments, and changes course quite frequently. It cuts into the bank on the outsides of the curves where the current flows fast and deep. Along the inside of the curves, sand and gravel deposits build up. When the river washes against a valley spur it cuts it back into a steep bank, or bluff.

old age

The river meanders from side to side across a flat plain on which deep sediments lie.

Loops and oxbow lakes form where the changing course of a river cuts off a meander.

Often the water level is higher than that of the plain. This is caused by the deposition of sand forming high banks and levees, particularly during times of flood. Crevasse splay deposits are left wherever the river overflows its banks.

Sand and mud deposited at the river mouth form sand banks and may produce a delta.

major rivers

name and location	mi	km
Nile (NE Africa)	4,160	6,695
Amazon (South America)	4,080	6,570
Chang Jiang (China)	3,900	6,300
Mississippi–Missouri (US)	3,740	6,020
Ob–Irtysh (China/Kazakhstan /Russia)	3,480	5,600
Huang He (China)	3,395	5,464
Paraná (Brazil)	2,800	4,500
Zaïre (Africa)	2,800	4,500
Mekong (Asia)	2,750	4,425
Amur (Asia)	2,744	4,416
Lena (Russia)	2,730	4,400
Mackenzie (Canada)	2,635	4,241
Niger (Africa)	2,600	4,185
Yenisei (Russia)	2,550	4,100
Mississippi (US)	2,350	3,780
Murray–Darling (Australia)	2,330	3,750
Missouri (US)	2,328	3,725
Volga (Russia)	2,290	3,685
Euphrates (Iraq)	2,240	3,600
Madeira (Brazil)	2,013	3,240
São Francisco (Brazil)	1,988	3,199
Yukon (US/Canada)	1,979	3,185
Indus (Tibet/Pakistan)	1,975	3,180
Syrdar'ya (Kazakhstan)	1,913	3,078
Rio Grande (US/Mexico)	1,900	3,050
Purus (Brazil)	1,860	2,993
Danube (Europe)	1,776	2,858
Brahmaputra (Asia)	1,770	2,850
Japurá (Brazil)	1,750	2,816
Salween (Myanmar/China)	1,740	2,800
Tocantins (Brazil)	1,677	2,699
Zambezi (Africa)	1,650	2,650
Paraguay (Paraguay)	1,610	2,591
Nelson–Saskatchewan (Canada)	1,600	2,570
Orinoco (Venezuela)	1,600	2,600
Amu Darya (Tajikistan/ Turkmenistan/Uzbekistan)	1,578	2,540
Ural (Russia/Kazakhstan)	1,575	2,534
Kolyma (Russia)	1,562	2,513
Ganges (India/Bangladesh)	1,560	2,510
Orinoco (Venezuela)	1,490	2,400

La Jalousie/Jealousy 1957, and *Dans le labyrinthe/In the Labyrinth* 1959, which concentrates on the detailed description of physical objects. He also wrote the script for the film *L'Année dernière à Marienbad/Last Year in Marienbad* 1961.

robbery in law, a variety of theft: stealing from a person, using force, or the threat of force, to intimidate the victim.

Robbia, della Italian family of sculptors and architects, active in Florence. *Luca della Robbia* (1400–1482) created a number of major works in Florence, notably the marble *cantoria* (singing gallery) in the cathedral 1431–38 (Museo del Duomo), with lively groups of choristers. Luca also developed a characteristic style of glazed terracotta work.

Robbins Jerome 1918– . US dancer and choreographer, co-director of the New York City Ballet 1969–83 (with George Balanchine). His ballets are internationally renowned and he is considered the greatest US-born ballet choreographer. He also choreographed the musicals *The King and I* 1951, *West Side Story* 1957, and *Fiddler on the Roof* 1964.

Robert II *c.* 1054–1134. Eldest son of ◊William I (the Conqueror), succeeding him as Duke of Normandy

(but not on the English throne) 1087. His brother ◊William II ascended the English throne, and they warred until 1096, after which Robert took part in the First Crusade. When his other brother ◊Henry I claimed the English throne 1100, Robert contested the claim and invaded England unsuccessfully 1101. Henry invaded Normandy 1106, and captured Robert, who remained a prisoner in England until his death.

Robert three kings of Scotland:

Robert I *Robert the Bruce* 1274–1329. King of Scotland from 1306, and grandson of Robert de ◊Bruce. He shared in the national uprising led by William ◊Wallace, and, after Wallace's execution 1305, rose once more against Edward I of England, and was crowned at Scone 1306. He defeated Edward II at Bannockburn 1314. In 1328 the treaty of Northampton recognized Scotland's independence and Robert as king.

Robert II 1316–1390. King of Scotland from 1371. He was the son of Walter (1293–1326), steward of Scotland, who married Marjory, daughter of Robert I. He was the first king of the house of Stuart.

Robert III *c.* 1340–1406. King of Scotland from 1390, son of Robert II. He was unable to control the nobles, and the government fell largely into the hands of his brother, Robert, Duke of Albany (*c.* 1340–1420).

Robeson Paul 1898–1976. US bass singer and actor. He graduated from Columbia University as a lawyer, but limited opportunities for blacks led him instead to the stage. He appeared in *The Emperor Jones* 1924 and *Showboat* 1928, in which he sang "Ol' Man River." He played *Othello* in 1930, and his films include *Sanders of the River* 1935 and *King Solomon's Mines* 1937. An ardent advocate of black rights, he had his passport withdrawn 1950–58 because of his association with left-wing movements. He then left the US to live in England.

Robespierre Maximilien François Marie Isidore de 1758–1794. French politician in the ◊French Revolution. As leader of the ◊Jacobins in the National Convention, he supported the execution of Louis XVI and the overthrow of the right-wing republican Girondins, and in July 1793 was elected to the Committee of Public Safety. A year later he was guillotined; many believe that he was a scapegoat for the Reign of ◊Terror since he ordered only 72 executions personally.

robin one of two songbirds of the thrush family. (1) North American thrush, the robin *Turdus migratorius*, 10 in/25 cm long, gray brown with brick-red underparts. (2) Eurasian and African thrush *Erithacus rubecula*, 5 in/13 cm long, olive brown above with a red breast.

Robin Hood in English legend, an outlaw and champion of the poor against the rich, said to have lived in Sherwood Forest, Nottinghamshire, during the reign of Richard I (1189–99). He feuded with the sheriff of Nottingham, accompanied by Maid Marian and a band of followers known as his "merry men." He appears in ballads from the 13th century, but his first datable appearance is in Langland's *Piers Plowman* about 1377.

Robinson Edward G. Adopted name of Emanuel Goldenberg 1893–1973. US film actor, born in Romania, who emigrated with his family to the US 1903. He was noted for his gangster roles, such as *Little Caesar* 1930.

He also performed in dramatic and comedy roles in film and on the stage, and was a great art collector. He wrote two autobiographical volumes, *My Father, My Son* 1958 and *All My Yesterdays* 1973. His other films include *Dr Ehrlich's Magic Bullet* 1940, *Double Indemnity* 1944, *The Ten Commandments* 1956, and *Soylent Green* 1973.

Robinson Jackie (Jack Roosevelt) 1919–1972. US baseball player. In 1947 he became the first black American in the major leagues, playing second base for the Brooklyn Dodgers and winning rookie of the year honors. In 1949 he was the National League's batting champion and was voted the league's most valuable player. He had a career batting average of .311.

Robinson Mary 1944– . Irish Labour politician, president from 1990.

She became a professor of law at 25. A strong supporter of women's rights, she has campaigned for the liberalization of Ireland's laws prohibiting divorce and abortion.

Robinson Smokey (William) 1940– . US singer, songwriter, and record producer, associated with ◊Motown records from its conception. He was lead singer of the Miracles 1957–72 (hits include "Shop Around" 1961, "The Tears of a Clown" 1970) and his solo hits include "Cruisin'" 1979 and "Being With You" 1981. His light tenor voice and wordplay characterize his work.

Robinson Sugar Ray. Adopted name of Walker Smith 1920–1989. US boxer, world welterweight champion 1945–51; he defended his title five times. Defeating Jake LaMotta 1951, he took the middleweight title. He lost the title six times and won it seven times. He retired at the age of 45.

robot any computer-controlled machine that can be programmed to move or carry out work. Robots are often used in industry to transport materials or to perform repetitive tasks. For instance, robotic arms, fixed to a floor or workbench, may be used to paint machine parts or assemble electronic circuits. Other robots are designed to work in situations that would be dangerous to humans—for example, in defusing bombs or in space and deep-sea exploration.

Rochester industrial city in New York, on the Genesee River, S of Lake Ontario; population (1990) 231,600. Its manufactured products include photographic equipment and optical and other precision instruments. It was the birthplace of the Xerox copier, and the world headquarters of the Eastman Kodak Company are here.

Rochester commercial center with dairy and food-processing industries in Minnesota; population (1990) 70,745. Rochester is the home of the Mayo Clinic, part of a medical center established 1889.

rock constituent of the Earth's crust, composed of mineral particles and/or materials of organic origin consolidated into a hard mass as ◊igneous, ◊sedimentary, or ◊metamorphic rocks.

rock and roll pop music born of a fusion of rhythm and blues and country and western and based on electric guitar and drums. In the mid-1950s, with the advent of Elvis Presley, it became the heartbeat of teenage rebellion in the West and also had considerable impact on other parts of the world. It found perhaps its purest form in late-1950s rockabilly, the style of white Southerners in the US; the blanket term "rock" later came to comprise a multitude of styles.

The term rock and roll was popularized by US disk jockey Alan Freed (1922–1965) beginning in 1951 on radio and in stage shows hosted by him.

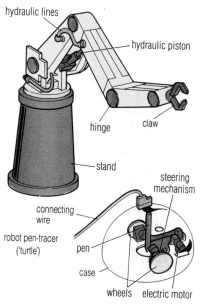

robot Two simple robots: the "robot arm" for industrial use, and the "turtle", used in teaching computing.

hydraulic lines

hydraulic piston

hinge   claw

stand

steering mechanism

connecting wire

robot pen-tracer ('turtle')

pen

case

wheels   electric motor

rock climbing sport originally an integral part of mountaineering. It began as a form of training for Alpine expeditions and is now divided into three categories: the *outcrop climb* for climbs of up to 100 ft/30 m; the *crag climb* on cliffs of 100–1,000 ft/30–300 m, and the *big wall climb*, which is the nearest thing to Alpine climbing, but without the hazards of snow and ice.

Rockefeller John D(avison) 1839–1937. US industrialist, founder of the Standard Oil Company of Ohio 1870 (which achieved monopolistic control of 90% of US refineries). He also founded the philanthropic Rockefeller Foundation 1913, to which his son John D Rockefeller, Jr (1874–1960) devoted his life.

rocket projectile driven by the reaction of gases produced by a fast-burning fuel. Unlike jet engines, which are also reaction engines, modern rockets carry their own oxygen supply to burn their fuel and do not require any surrounding atmosphere. For warfare, rocket heads carry an explosive device. *See illustration p. 796*

Rockford city in N Illinois, on the Rock River, NW of Chicago; population (1990) 139,400. Industries include automotive parts, furniture, machine tools, and food products.

Rock Hill city in N central South Carolina, S of Charlotte, North Carolina; population (1990) 41,600. Industries include chemicals, textiles, and paper products.

Rock Island city in NW Illinois, on the Mississippi River, W of Chicago; population (1990) 40,600. Industries include rubber and electronics. A US government arsenal is located here.

Rockne Knute Kenneth 1888–1931. Norwegian-born US American football coach. His greatest contribution to football was the extensive use of sophisticated formations and the forward pass. He established an unparalleled lifetime record of 105 wins, 12 losses, and 5 ties—with 5 undefeated, untied seasons.

Rockwell Norman 1894–1978. US painter and illustrator who designed magazine covers, mainly for *The Saturday Evening Post*, and cartoons portraying American life. His whimsical view of the ordinary

the Saturn V moon rocket

rocket *The three-stage Saturn V rocket used in the Apollo moonshots of the 1960s and 1970s.*

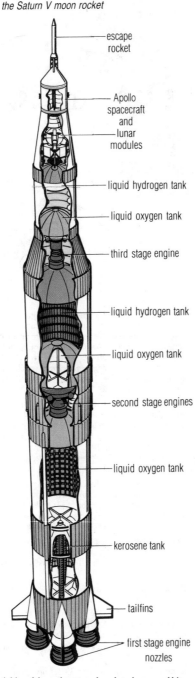

escape rocket

Apollo spacecraft and lunar modules

liquid hydrogen tank

liquid oxygen tank

third stage engine

liquid hydrogen tank

liquid oxygen tank

second stage engines

liquid oxygen tank

kerosene tank

tailfins

first stage engine nozzles

activities of the nation at work and at play earned him huge popularity.

Rocky Mountains or **Rockies** largest North American mountain system. They extend from the junction with the Mexican plateau, N through the W central states of the US, through Canada to the Alaskan border, and then form part of the Continental Divide, which separates rivers draining into the Atlantic or Arctic oceans from those flowing toward the Pacific Ocean. Mount Elbert is the highest peak, 14,433 ft/4,400 m. Some geographers consider the Yukon and Alaska ranges as part of the system, making the highest point Mount Mckinley (Denali) 20,320 ft/6,194 m.)

Rococo movement in the arts and architecture in 18th-century Europe, tending toward lightness, elegance, delicacy, and decorative charm. The term "Rococo" refers to **rocaille** (rock- or shell-work), a style of interior decoration based on S-curves and scroll-like forms. Watteau's paintings and Sèvres porcelain belong to the French Rococo vogue. In the 1730s the movement became widespread in Europe, notably in the churches and palaces of S Germany and Austria.

rodent any mammal of the worldwide order Rodentia, making up nearly half of all mammal species. Besides ordinary "cheek teeth," they have a single front pair of incisor teeth in both upper and lower jaw, which continue to grow as they are worn down.

rodeo originally a practical means of rounding up cattle in North America. It is now a professional sport in the US and Canada. Ranching skills such as bronco busting, bull riding, steer wrestling, and calf roping are all rodeo events. Because rodeo livestock is valuable, rules for its handling are laid out by the American Humane Association, yet criticism has been leveled at rodeos for cruel treatment of their animals.

Rodgers Richard (Charles) 1902–1979. US composer. He collaborated with librettist Lorenz Hart (1895–1943) on songs like "Blue Moon" 1934 and musicals like *On Your Toes* 1936, and with Oscar Hammerstein II (1895–1960) wrote many musicals, including *Oklahoma!* 1943, *South Pacific* 1949, *The King and I* 1951, and *The Sound of Music* 1959.

Rodin Auguste 1840–1917. French sculptor, often considered the greatest of his day. Through his work he freed sculpture from the idealizing conventions of the time by his realistic treatment of the human figure, introducing a new boldness of style and expression. Examples are *Le Penseur/The Thinker* 1880, *Le Baiser/The Kiss* 1886 (marble version in the Louvre, Paris), and *Les Bourgeois de Calais/The Burghers of Calais* 1884–86 (copy in Embankment Gardens, Westminster, London).

roentgen or **röntgen** unit (symbol R) of radiation exposure, used for X-rays and gamma rays. It is defined in terms of the number of ions produced in one cubic centimeter of air by the radiation. Exposure to 1,000 roentgens gives rise to an absorbed dose of about 870 rads (8.7 grays), which is a dose equivalent of 870 rems (8.7 sieverts).

Roe v Wade US Supreme Court decision 1973 dealing with the constitutionality of state antiabortion laws. The case challenged a Texas statute prohibiting the abortion of pregnancies that did not threaten the mother's life. The Court struck down the Texas law, ruling that state prohibition of abortion is unconstitutional on two grounds: (1) women are guaranteed the right to privacy by the 14th Amendment, and (2) unborn fetuses are not persons with the right to equal protection of the law. The highly controversial ruling limited state regulation to the prohibition of third-trimester abortions.

Rogers Ginger. Adopted name of Virginia Katherine McMath 1911– . US actress, dancer, and singer. She worked from the 1930s to the 1950s, often starring with Fred Astaire in such films as *Top Hat* 1935 and *Swing Time* 1936. Her later work includes *Bachelor Mother* 1939 and *Kitty Foyle* 1940.

Rogers Roy. Adopted name of Leonard Slye 1912– . US actor who moved to Hollywood from radio. He was a singing cowboy of the 1930s and 1940s, one of the Sons of the Pioneers. His first Roy Rogers film was *Under Western Stars* 1938, and he became "King of the Cowboys." He married his costar Dale Evans (who played in 20 of his films) in 1947. He played outside his own films in *Lake Placid Serenade* 1944, *Son of Paleface* 1952, *Alias Jesse James* 1959, and *Mackintosh and TJ* 1975.

Rogers Will (William Penn Adair) 1879–1935. US humorist. Born in Oologah Indian Territory (now Oklahoma), Rogers ended his formal education 1898 to work as a cowboy in Texas. He later traveled widely, performing in Wild West shows from 1902. In 1905 Rogers started his own vaudeville act of rope twirling and humorous banter. After beginning a Broadway career in 1915, which included Ziegfeld's Follies (1916–18, 1922, 1924–25), he moved to California to appear in motion pictures. From 1922 he wrote a humor column for *The New York Times*, and his wry comments on current affairs won him national popularity. Rogers was killed in a plane crash in Alaska with famed pilot Wiley Post.

Roget Peter Mark 1779–1869. English physician, one of the founders of the University of London, and author of a *Thesaurus of English Words and Phrases* 1852, a text constantly revised and still in print, offering synonyms.

Roh Tae-woo 1932– . South Korean right-wing politician and general. He held ministerial office from 1981 under President Chun, and became chair of the ruling Democratic Justice Party 1985. He was elected president 1987, amid allegations of fraud and despite being connected with the massacre of about 2,000 antigovernment demonstrators 1980.

Roland died 778. French hero whose real and legendary deeds of valor and chivalry inspired many medieval and later romances, including the 11th-century *Chanson de Roland* and Ariosto's *Orlando Furioso*. A knight of ◊Charlemagne, Roland was killed in 778 with his friend Oliver and the 12 peers of France at Roncesvalles (in the Pyrenees) by Basques. He headed the rearguard during Charlemagne's retreat from his invasion of Spain.

role in the social sciences, the part(s) a person plays in society, either in helping the social system to work or in fulfilling social responsibilities toward others. *Role play* refers to the way in which children learn adult roles by acting them out in play (mothers and fathers, cops and robbers). Everyone has a number of roles to play in a society: for example, a woman may be an employee, mother, and wife at the same time.

Rolling Stones, the British band formed 1962, once notorious as the "bad boys" of rock. Original members were Mick Jagger (1943–), Keith Richards (1943–), Brian Jones (1942–1969), Bill Wyman (1936–), Charlie Watts (1941–), and the pianist Ian Stewart (1938–1985). A rock-and-roll institution, the Rolling Stones were still performing and recording in the 1990s.

Rolls Charles Stewart 1877–1910. British engineer who joined with Henry ◊Royce in 1905 to design and produce automobiles.

Rolls had trained as a mechanical engineer and worked in railroad production and as an automobile dealer before joining up with Royce. Before the business could flourish he died in a flying accident.

ROM (acronym for *read-only memory*) in computing, a memory device in the form of a collection of integrated circuits (chips), frequently used in microcomputers. ROM chips are loaded with data and programs during manufacture and, unlike ◊RAM (random-access memory) chips, can subsequently only be read, not written to, by computer. However, the contents of the chips are not lost when the power is switched off, as happens in RAM.

Roman art sculpture and painting of ancient Rome, from the 4th century BC to the fall of the empire. Much Roman art was intended for public education, notably the sculpted triumphal arches and giant columns, such as *Trajan's Column* AD 106–113, and portrait sculptures of soldiers, politicians, and emperors. Surviving mural paintings (in Pompeii, Rome, and Ostia) and mosaic decorations show Greek influence. Roman art was to prove a lasting inspiration in the West.

Roman Britain period in British history from the mid-1st century BC to the mid-4th century AD. England was rapidly Romanized, but north of York fewer

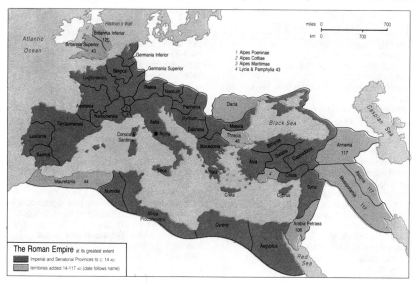

The Roman Empire at its greatest extent
Imperial and Senatorial Provinces to c. 14 AD
territories added 14–117 AD (date follows name)

remains of Roman civilization have been found. Roman towns include London, York, Chester, St Albans, Colchester, Lincoln, Gloucester, and Bath. The most enduring mark of the occupation was the system of military roads radiating from London.

Roman Catholicism one of the main divisions of the Christian religion, separate from the Eastern Orthodox church from 1054, and headed by the pope. For history and beliefs, see ◊Christianity. Membership is about 585 million worldwide, concentrated in S Europe, Latin America, and the Philippines.

romance in literature, tales of love and adventure, in verse or prose, that became popular in France about 1200 and spread throughout Europe. There were Arthurian romances about the legendary King Arthur and his knights, and romances based on the adventures of Charlemagne and on Classical themes. In the 20th century the term "romantic novel" is often used disparagingly, to imply a contrast with a realist novel.

Romance languages branch of Indo-European languages descended from the Latin of the Roman Empire ("popular" or "vulgar" as opposed to "classical" Latin).

The present-day Romance languages with national status are French, Italian, Portuguese, Romanian, and Spanish.

Roman Empire from 27 BC to the 5th century AD; see ◊Rome, ancient.

Romanesque style of W European ◊architecture of the 8th to 12th centuries, marked by rounded arches, solid volumes, and emphasis on perpendicular elements.

Romania country in SE Europe, bounded N and E by Ukraine, E by Moldova, SE by the Black Sea, S by Bulgaria, SW by Yugoslavia, and NW by Hungary.

Romanian person of Romanian culture from Romania, Yugoslavia, Moldova, and the surrounding area. There are 20–25 million speakers of the Romanian language.

Romanian language member of the Romance branch of the Indo-European language family, spoken in Romania, Macedonia, Albania, and parts of N Greece. It has been strongly influenced by the Slavonic languages and by Greek. The Cyrillic alphabet was used until the 19th century, when a variant of the Roman alphabet was adopted.

Romania

area 91,699 sq mi/237,500 sq km
capital Bucharest
cities Braşov, Timişoara, Cluj-Napoca, Iaşi; ports Galaţi, Constanta, Brăila
physical mountains surrounding a plateau, with river plains S and E
environment although sulfur-dioxide levels are low, only 20% of the country's rivers can provide drinkable water
features Carpathian Mountains, Transylvanian Alps; river Danube; Black Sea coast; mineral springs
head of state Ion Iliescu from 1989
head of government Nicolai Vacaroiu from 1992
political system emergent democratic republic
political parties National Salvation Front (NSF), reform socialist; Civic Alliance (CA), right of center; Convention for Democracy, umbrella organization for right-of-center National Liberal Party (NLP) and ethnic-Hungarian Magyar Democratic Union (UDM)
exports petroleum products and oil field equipment, electrical goods, automobiles, cereals
currency leu

population (1992) 23,332,000 (Romanians 89%, Hungarians 7.9%, Germans 1.6%); growth rate 0.5% p.a.
life expectancy men 67, women 73 (1989)
languages Romanian (official), Hungarian, German
media television is state-run; there are an estimated 900 newspapers and magazines, but only the progovernment papers have adequate distribution and printing facilities
religions Romanian Orthodox 80%, Roman Catholic 6%
literacy 98% (1988)
GNP $151 bn (1988); $6,400 per head

chronology
1944 Pro-Nazi Antonescu government overthrown.
1945 Communist-dominated government appointed.
1947 Boundaries redrawn. King Michael abdicated and People's Republic proclaimed.
1949 New Soviet-style constitution adopted. Joined Comecon.
1952 Second new Soviet-style constitution.
1955 Romania joined Warsaw Pact.
1958 Soviet occupation forces removed.
1965 New constitution adopted.
1974 Ceauşescu created president.
1985–86 Winters of austerity and power cuts.
1987 Workers demonstrated against austerity program.
1988–89 Relations with Hungary deteriorated over "systematization program."
1989 Announcement that all foreign debt paid off. Razing of villages and building of monuments to Ceauşescu. Communist orthodoxy reaffirmed; demonstrations violently suppressed; massacre in Timisoara. Army joined uprising; heavy fighting; bloody overthrow of Ceauşescu regime in "Christmas Revolution"; Ceauşescu and wife tried and executed; estimated 10,000 dead in civil warfare. Power assumed by new National Salvation Front, headed by Ion Iliescu.
1990 Securitate secret police replaced by new Romanian Intelligence Service; religious practices resumed; mounting strikes and protests against effects of market economy.
1991 April: treaty on cooperation and good neighborliness signed with USSR. Aug: privatization law passed. Sept: prime minister Peter Roman resigned following riots; succeeded by Theodor Stolojan heading a new cross-party coalition government. Dec: new constitution endorsed by referendum.
1992 Iliescu reelected president; Nicolai Vacaroiu appointed prime minister.

Roman law legal system of ancient Rome that is now the basis of ◊civil law, one of the main European legal systems.

Roman numerals ancient European number system using symbols different from Arabic numerals (the ordinary numbers 1, 2, 3, 4, 5, and so on). The seven key symbols in Roman numerals, as represented today, are I (1), V (5), X (10), L (50), C (100), D (500), and M (1,000). There is no zero, and therefore no place-value as is fundamental to the Arabic system. The first ten Roman numerals are I, II, III, IV (or IIII), V, VI, VII, VIII, IX, and X. When a Roman symbol is preceded by a symbol of equal or greater value, the values of the symbols are added (XVI = 16). When a symbol is preceded by a symbol of less value, the values are subtracted (XL = 40). A horizontal bar over a symbol indicates a multiple of 1,000 (X̄ = 10,000). Although addition and subtraction are fairly straightforward using Roman numerals, the absence of a zero makes other arithmetic calculations (such as multiplication) clumsy and difficult.

Although their role in mathematics is long obsolete, Roman numerals continue to enjoy a limited use as inscribed figures (for example, on timepiece faces, in the pagination of some written material, or as dates on buildings or motion pictures).

Romano Giulio. Italian painter and architect.

Romanov dynasty rulers of Russia from 1613 to the ◊Russian Revolution 1917. Under the Romanovs, Russia developed into an absolutist empire.

The first tsar was Michael; his most famous successors were ◊Peter the Great, ◊Catherine the Great, ◊Alexander I, ◊Nicholas I, and Alexander II.

Romanticism in literature, music, and the visual arts, a style that emphasizes the imagination, emotions, and creativity of the individual artist. Romanticism also refers specifically to late-18th- and early-19th-century European culture, as contrasted with 18th-century ◊Classicism.

Romany a nomadic Caucasoid people, also called ◊Gypsy (a corruption of "Egyptian," since they were erroneously thought to come from Egypt). They are now believed to have originated in NW India, and live throughout the world. The Romany language (spoken in different dialects in every country where Gypsies live) is a member of the Indo-European family. In the 14th century they settled in the Balkan peninsula, spread over Germany, Italy, and France, and arrived in England about 1500. During World War II, Nazi Germany tried to exterminate them, along with Jews, Slavs, and political prisoners (see ◊concentration camp).

Rome city in central New York, on the Mohawk River, NW of Albany; population (1990) 44,400. Industries include copper and brass products, paint, and household appliances. Construction of the Erie Canal began here 1817.

Rome (Italian **Roma**) capital of Italy and of Lazio region, on the river Tiber, 17 mi/27 km from the Tyrrhenian Sea; population (1987) 2,817,000.

Rome has few industries but is an important cultural, road, and rail center. A large section of the population finds employment in government offices. Remains of the ancient city include the Forum, Colosseum, and Pantheon.

Rome, ancient civilization based in Rome, which lasted for about 800 years. Traditionally founded 753 BC, Rome became a republic 510 BC. From then, its history is one of almost continual expansion until the murder of Julius ◊Caesar and foundation of the empire under ◊Augustus and his successors. At its peak under ◊Trajan, the Roman Empire stretched from Britain to Mesopotamia and the Caspian Sea. A long train of emperors ruling by virtue of military, rather than civil, power marked the beginning of Rome's long decline; under ◊Diocletian, the empire was divided into two parts—East and West—although temporarily reunited under ◊Constantine, the first emperor formally to adopt Christianity. The end of the Roman

Rome A view of the Forum of ancient Rome from the Capitoline Hill.

Ancient Rome: chronology

735 BC	According to tradition Rome was founded.	**82**	On his return Sulla established a dictatorship and ruled by terror.
510	The Etruscan dynasty of the Tarquins was expelled, and a republic was established, governed by two consuls, elected annually by the popular assembly, and a council of elders or Senate. The concentration of power in the hands of the aristocracy aroused the opposition of the plebeian masses.	**70**	His changes were reversed by Pompey and Crassus.
		66–62	Defeat of Mithridates and annexation of Syria and the rest of Asia Minor.
		60	Pompey formed an alliance with the democratic leaders Crassus and Caesar.
		51	Gaul conquered by Caesar as far as the Rhine.
390	Rome sacked by the Gauls.	**49**	Caesar's return to Italy (crossing the Rubicon) led to civil war between Caesar and Pompey.
367	The plebeians secured the right to elect tribunes, the codification of the laws, and the right to marry patricians; it was enacted that one consul must be a plebeian.	**48**	Defeat of Pompey at Pharsalus.
		44	Caesar's dictatorship ended by his assassination.
343–290	The Sabines to the N and the Samnites to the SE were conquered	**32**	The empire divided between Caesar's nephew Octavian in the west and Antony in the east; war between them.
338	The cities of Latium formed into a league under Roman control.	**31**	Defeat of Antony at Actium.
280–272	The Greek cities of the south were conquered.	**30**	With the deaths of Antony and Cleopatra, Egypt was annexed.
264–241	First Punic War, ending in a Roman victory and the annexation of Sicily.	**27**	Octavian took the name Augustus; he was now absolute ruler, although in title only *princeps* (first citizen).
238	Sardinia was seized from Carthage and became a Roman province.	**AD 43**	Claudius made the Rhine and the Danube the frontiers of the empire, and added Britain.
226–222	Roman conquest of Cisalpine Gaul (Lombardy); conflict with Carthage, which was attempting to conquer Sicily.	**96–180**	Under the Flavian emperors Nerva, Trajan, Hadrian, Antoninus Pius, and Marcus Aurelius Antoninus the empire enjoyed a golden age.
218	Hannibal invaded Italy and won a brilliant series of victories.	**115**	Trajan conquered Macedonia; peak of Roman territorial expansion.
202	Victory over Hannibal at Zama, followed by its conversion into a Roman province.	**180**	Death of Marcus Aurelius Antoninus was followed by a century of war and disorder; a succession of generals was placed on the throne by their armies.
146	After a revolt, Greece became in effect a Roman province. In the same year Carthage was annexed. On the death of the king of Pergamum, Rome succeeded to his kingdom in Asia Minor.	**284–305**	Diocletian reorganized the empire as a centralized autocracy.
133	Tiberius Gracchus put forward proposals for agrarian reforms and was murdered by the senatorial party.	**324–337**	Constantine I realized the political value of Christianity and became a convert.
123	Tiberius' policy was taken up by his brother Gaius Gracchus, who was also murdered.	**364**	Constantine removed the capital to Constantinople, and the empire was divided.
109–106	The leadership of the democrats passed to Marius.	**410**	The Goths overran Greece and Italy, sacked Rome, and finally settled in Spain. The Vandals conquered Italy.
91–88	Social War: a revolt of the Italian cities compelled Rome to grant citizenship to all Italians.	**451–452**	The Huns raided Gaul and Italy.
87–84	While Sulla was repelling an invasion of Greece by Mithridates, Marius seized power.	**476**	The last Western emperor was deposed.

Empire is generally dated by the sack of Rome by the Goths AD 410, or by the deposition of the last emperor in the west AD 476. The Eastern Empire continued until 1453 at ◊Constantinople.

Rome, Sack of invasion and capture of the city of Rome AD 140 by the Goths, generally accepted as marking the effective end of the Roman Empire.

Rome, Treaties of two international agreements signed March 25, 1957, by Belgium, France, West Germany, Italy, Luxembourg, and the Netherlands, which established the European Economic Community (◊European Community) and the European Atomic Energy Commission (EURATOM).

Rommel Erwin 1891–1944. German field marshal. He served in World War I, and in World War II he played an important part in the invasions of central Europe and France. He was commander of the N African offen-

sive from 1941 (when he was nicknamed "Desert Fox") until defeated in the Battles of El ◊Alamein.

Romney George 1734–1802. English portrait painter, active in London from 1762. He became, with Gainsborough and Reynolds, one of the most successful portrait painters of the late 18th century. He painted several portraits of Lady Hamilton, Admiral Nelson's mistress.

Romulus in Roman legend, founder and first king of Rome, the son of Mars and Rhea Silvia, daughter of Numitor, king of Alba Longa. Romulus and his twin brother Remus were thrown into the Tiber by their great-uncle Amulius, who had deposed Numitor, but were suckled by a she-wolf and rescued by a shepherd. On reaching adulthood they killed Amulius and founded Rome.

Romulus Augustulus born *c.* 461. last Roman emperor in the West. He was made emperor by his father the patrician Orestes, about 475 but was compelled to abdicate 476 by Odoacer, leader of the barbarian mercenaries, who nicknamed him Augustulus. Orestes was executed and Romulus Augustulus was sent to live on a pension in Campania. The date of his death is unknown.

rondo form of instrumental music in which the principal section returns like a refrain. Rondo form is often used for the last movement of a sonata or concerto.

Rondônia state in NW Brazil; the center of Amazonian tin and gold mining and of experiments in agricultural colonization; area 93,876 sq mi/243,044 sq km; population (1991) 1,373,700. Known as the Federal Territory of *Guaporé* until 1956, it became a state 1981.

Röntgen (or *Roentgen*) Wilhelm Konrad 1845–1923. German physicist who discovered X-rays 1895. While investigating the passage of electricity through gases, he noticed the ◊fluorescence of a barium platinocyanide screen. This radiation passed through some substances opaque to light, and affected photographic plates. Developments from this discovery have revolutionized medical diagnosis.

He received a Nobel Prize 1901. The unit of electromagnetic radiation (X-ray) is named roentgen or röntgen (r) after him.

rook gregarious European ◊crow *Corvus frugilegus*. The plumage is black and lustrous and the face bare; a rook can grow to 18 in/45 cm long. Rooks nest in colonies at the tops of trees.

Roosevelt (Anna) Eleanor 1884–1962. US social worker, lecturer, and First Lady; her newspaper column "My Day" was widely syndicated. She influenced ◊New Deal policies, especially supporting desegregation. She was a delegate to the UN general assembly and chair of the UN commission on human rights 1946–51, and helped to draw up the Declaration of Human Rights at the UN 1945. She was married to President Franklin Roosevelt.

Roosevelt Franklin D(elano) 1882–1945. 32nd president of the US 1933–45, a Democrat. He served as governor of New York 1929–33. Becoming president during the Great ◊Depression, he launched the ◊New Deal economic and social reform program, which made him popular with the people. After the outbreak of World War II he introduced ◊lend-lease for the supply of war materials and services to the Allies and drew up the ◊Atlantic Charter of solidarity. Once the US had entered the war 1941, he spent much time in meetings with Allied leaders (see ◊Tehran, and ◊Yalta conferences).

Roosevelt Theodore 1858–1919. 26th president of the US 1901–09, a Republican. After serving as governor of New York 1898–1900 he became vice president to ◊McKinley, whom he succeeded as president on McKinley's assassination 1901. He campaigned against the great trusts (associations of enterprises that reduce competition), while carrying on a jingoist foreign policy designed to enforce US supremacy over Latin America.

root the part of a plant that is usually underground, and whose primary functions are anchorage and the absorption of water and dissolved mineral salts. Roots usually grow downward and toward water (that is, they are positively geotropic and hydrotropic; see ◊tropism). Plants such as epiphytic orchids, which grow above ground, produce aerial roots that absorb moisture from the atmosphere. Others, such as ivy, have climbing

Roosevelt US president Franklin D Roosevelt led his country through the Depression of the 1930s and World War II, and was elected for an unprecedented fourth term of office 1944.

roots arising from the stems, which serve to attach the plant to trees and walls. *See illustration p. 802*

root of an equation, a value that satisfies the equality. For example, $x = 0$ and $x = 5$ are roots of the equation $x^2 - 5x = 0$.

root crop plant cultivated for its swollen edible root (which may or may not be a true root). Potatoes are the major temperate root crop; the major tropical root crops are cassava, yams, and sweet potatoes. Root crops are second in importance only to cereals as human food. Roots have a high carbohydrate content, but their protein content rarely exceeds 2%. Consequently, communities relying almost exclusively upon roots may suffer from protein deficiency. Food production for a given area from roots is greater than from cereals.

rope stout cordage with circumference over 1 in/2.5 cm. Rope is made similarly to thread or twine, by twisting yarns together to form strands, which are then in turn twisted around one another in the direc-

Roosevelt Teddy bears derive their name from Theodore Roosevelt, the 26th US president, a big-game hunter who, having killed its mother, refused to shoot a bear cub.

root Types of root.

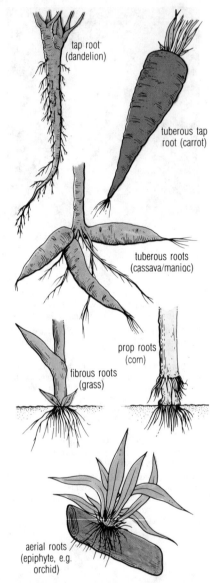

tap root
(dandelion)

tuberous tap
root (carrot)

tuberous roots
(cassava/manioc)

prop roots
(corn)

fibrous roots
(grass)

aerial roots
(epiphyte, e.g.
orchid)

tion opposite to that of the yarns. Although ◊hemp is still used to make rope, nylon is increasingly used.

Rorschach test in psychology, method of diagnosis involving the use of inkblot patterns that subjects are asked to interpret, to help indicate personality type, degree of intelligence, and emotional stability. It was invented by the Swiss psychiatrist Hermann Rorschach (1884–1922).

Rosario industrial river port (sugar refining, meat packing, maté processing) in Argentina, 175 mi/280 km NW of Buenos Aires, on the river Paraná; population (1991) 1,078,400. It was founded 1725.

rosary string of beads used in a number of religions, including Buddhism, Christianity, and Islam. The term also refers to a form of prayer used by Catholics, consisting of 150 ◊Ave Marias and 15 Paternosters

and Glorias, or to a string of 165 beads for keeping count of these prayers; it is linked with the adoration of the Virgin Mary.

Roscommon (originally Ros-Comain, "wood around a monastery") county of the Republic of Ireland in the province of Connacht
area 950 sq mi/2,460 sq km
cities Roscommon (county town)
physical bounded on the E by the river Shannon; lakes: Gara, Key, Allen; rich pastures
features remains of a castle put up in the 13th century by English settlers
population (1991) 51,900.

rose any shrub or climber of the genus *Rosa*, family Rosaceae, with prickly stems and fragrant flowers in many different colors. Numerous cultivated forms have been derived from the Eurasian sweetbrier or eglantine *R. rubiginosa* and dogrose *R. canina*. There are many climbing varieties, but the forms more commonly cultivated are bush roses and standards (cultivated roses grafted on to a briar stem).

Roseau formerly *Charlotte Town* capital of ◊Dominica, West Indies, on the SW coast of the island; population (1981) 20,000.

rosemary evergreen shrub *Rosemarinus officinalis* of the mint family Labiatae, native to the Mediterranean and W Asia, with small, scented leaves. It is widely cultivated as a culinary herb and for the aromatic oil extracted from the clusters of pale blue or purple flowers.

Rosenberg Julius 1918–53 and Ethel Greenglass 1915–53. US married couple, convicted of being leaders of a nuclear-espionage ring passing information from Ethel's brother via courier to the USSR. The Rosenbergs were executed after much public controversy and demonstration. They were the only Americans executed for espionage during peacetime.

Roses, Wars of the civil wars in England 1455–85 between the houses of ◊Lancaster (badge, red rose) and ◊York (badge, white rose), both of whom claimed the throne through descent from the sons of Edward III. As a result of ◊Henry VI's lapse into insanity 1453, Richard, Duke of York, was installed as protector of the realm. Upon his recovery, Henry forced York to take up arms in self-defense.

Rosetta Stone slab of basalt with inscriptions from 197 BC, found near the town of Rosetta, Egypt, 1799. Giving the same text in three versions—Greek, hieroglyphic, and demotic script—it became the key to deciphering other Egyptian inscriptions.

Rosh Hashanah two-day holiday that marks the start of the Jewish New Year (first new moon after the autumn equinox), traditionally announced by blowing a ram's horn (a shofar).

Rosicrucians group of early 17th-century philosophers who claimed occult powers and employed the terminology of ◊alchemy to expound their mystical doctrines (said to derive from ◊Paracelsus). The name comes from books published in 1614 and 1615, attributed to Christian Rosenkreutz ("rosy cross"), most probably a adopted name but allegedly a writer living around 1460. Several societies have been founded in Britain and the US that claim to be their successors, such as the Rosicrucian Fraternity (1614 in Germany, 1861 in the US).

Ross Betsy 1752–1836. American seamstress remembered as the maker of the first US flag. According to popular legend, she was approached 1776 by family acquaintance George Washington to create an official flag for the new nation. Despite little historical substantiation, it is believed by many that the familiar red and white stripes with white stars on a field of blue was Ross's original concept.

Ross James Clark 1800–1862. English explorer who discovered the magnetic North Pole 1831. He also went to the Antarctic 1839; Ross Island, Ross Sea, and Ross Dependency are named after him.

Ross Ronald 1857–1932. British physician and bacteriologist, born in India. From 1881 to 1899 he served in the Indian medical service, and during 1895–98 identified mosquitoes of the genus *Anopheles* as being responsible for the spread of malaria. Nobel Prize 1902.

Ross Dependency all the Antarctic islands and territories between 160° E and 150° W longitude and S of 60° S latitude; it includes Edward VII Land, Ross Sea and its islands, and parts of Victoria Land.

Rossellini Roberto 1906–1977. Italian film director. His World War II trilogy, *Roma città aperta/Rome, Open City* 1945, *Paisà/Paisan* 1946, and *Germania anno zero/Germany Year Zero* 1947, reflects his humanism, and is considered a landmark of European cinema.

Rossetti Christina (Georgina) 1830–1894. English poet, sister of Dante Gabriel Rossetti and a devout High Anglican (see ◊Oxford movement). Her verse includes *Goblin Market and Other Poems* 1862 and expresses unfulfilled spiritual yearning and frustrated love. She was a skillful technician and made use of irregular rhyme and line length.

Rossetti Dante Gabriel 1828–1882. British painter and poet, a founding member of the ◊Pre-Raphaelite Brotherhood (PRB) in 1848. As well as romantic medieval scenes, he produced many idealized portraits of women. His verse includes "The Blessed Damozel" 1850. His sister was the poet Christina Rossetti.

Rossetti was a friend of the critic ◊Ruskin, who helped establish his reputation as a painter, and of William Morris and his wife Jane, who became Rossetti's lover and the subject of much of his work.

Rossini Gioacchino (Antonio) 1792–1868. Italian composer. His first success was the opera *Tancredi* 1813. In 1816 his "opera buffa" *Il barbiere di Siviglia/ The Barber of Seville* was produced in Rome. During 1815–23 he produced 20 operas, and created (with ◊Donizetti and ◊Bellini) the 19th-century Italian operatic style.

Rostand Edmond 1869–1918. French dramatist, who wrote *Cyrano de Bergerac* 1897 and *L'Aiglon* 1900 (based on the life of Napoleon III), in which Sarah Bernhardt played the leading role.

Rostov-on-Don industrial port (shipbuilding, tobacco, automobiles, locomotives, textiles) in SW Russia, capital of Rostov region, on the river Don, 14 mi/23 km E of the Sea of Azov; population (1987) 1,004,000. Rostov dates from 1761 and is linked by river and canal with Volgograd on the river Volga.

Rostropovich Mstislav 1927– . Russian cellist and conductor, deprived of Soviet citizenship 1978 because of his sympathies with political dissidents. Prokofiev, Shostakovich, Khachaturian, and Britten wrote pieces for him. Since 1977 he has directed the National Symphony Orchestra, Washington, DC.

Roth Philip 1933– . US novelist whose portrayals of 20th-century Jewish-American life include *Goodbye*

Columbus 1959 and *Portnoy's Complaint* 1969. Psychosexual themes are prominent in his work. *Operation Shylock: A Confession* 1993, is a fantasy about his fictional double.

Rothko Mark 1903–1970. Russian-born US painter, an Abstract Expressionist and a pioneer of *Color Field* painting (abstract, dominated by areas of unmodulated, strong color). Rothko produced several series of paintings in the 1950s and 1960s, including one at Harvard University; one in the Tate Gallery, London; and one for a chapel in Houston, Texas, 1967–69.

Rothschild European family active in the financial world for two centuries. *Mayer Anselm Rothschild* (1744–1812) set up as a moneylender in Frankfurt-am-Main, Germany, and business houses were established throughout Europe by his ten children.

Rotterdam industrial port (brewing, distilling, shipbuilding, sugar and petroleum refining, margarine, tobacco) in the Netherlands and one of the foremost ocean cargo ports in the world, in the Rhine-Maas delta, linked by canal 1866–90 with the North Sea; population (1991) 582,266.

Rottweiler breed of dog originally developed in Rottweil, Germany, as a herding and guard dog, and subsequently used as a police dog. Powerfully built, the dog is about 25–27 in/63–66 cm high at the shoulder, black with tan markings, a short coat and docked tail.

Rouault Georges 1871–1958. French painter, etcher, illustrator, and designer. Early in his career he was associated with the Fauves but created his own style using heavy, dark colors and bold brushwork. His subjects included sad clowns, prostitutes, and evil lawyers; from about 1940 he painted mainly religious works.

roughage alternative term for dietary ◊fiber, material of plant origin that cannot be digested by enzymes normally present in the human ◊gut.

Rosetta Stone A basalt slab inscribed in 197 BC with a decree of the pharaoh Ptolemy Epiphanes in three scripts.

Roundhead member of the Parliamentary party during the English Civil War 1640–60, opposing the royalist Cavaliers. The term referred to the short hair then worn only by men of the lower classes.

Rousseau Henri "Le Douanier" 1844–1910. French painter, a self-taught naive artist. His subjects included scenes of the Parisian suburbs and exotic junglescapes, painted with painstaking detail; for example, *Surprised! Tropical Storm with a Tiger* 1891 (National Gallery, London).

Rousseau Jean-Jacques 1712–1778. French social philosopher and writer whose *Du Contrat social/Social Contract* 1762, emphasizing the rights of the people over those of the government, was a significant influence on the French Revolution. In the novel *Emile* 1762 he outlined a new theory of education.

Rousseau (Etienne-Pierre) Théodore 1812–1867. French landscape painter of the ◊Barbizon School. Born in Paris, he came under the influence of the British landscape painters Constable and Bonington, sketched from nature in many parts of France, and settled in Barbizon in 1848.

rowing propulsion of a boat by oars, either by one rower with two oars (sculling) or by crews (two, four, or eight persons) with one oar each, often with a coxswain. Major events include the world championship, first held 1962 for men and 1974 for women, and the Boat Race (between England's Oxford and Cambridge universities), first held 1829.

In the US the Harvard–Yale boat race is held on the Thames at New London, Connecticut, and National Championships are held annually.

Rozwi empire or **Changamire** highly advanced empire in SE Africa, located S of the Zambezi river and centered around the stone city of Great Zimbabwe. It replaced the gold-trading empire of Mwene Mutapa from the 15th century. The Rozwi empire survived until the Mfecane of the 1830s, when overpopulation to the south drove the Ngoni and Ndebele people northwards into Rozwi territory in search of more land.

Royal Greenwich Observatory the national astronomical observatory of the UK, founded 1675 at Greenwich, E London, England, to provide navigational information for sailors. After World War II it was moved to Herstmonceux Castle, Sussex; in 1990 it was transferred to Cambridge. It also operates telescopes on La Palma in the Canary Islands, including the 165-in/4.2-m William Herschel Telescope, commissioned 1987.

Royal Society oldest and premier scientific society in Britain, originating 1645 and chartered 1660; Christopher ◊Wren and Isaac ◊Newton were prominent early members. Its Scottish equivalent is the Royal Society of Edinburgh 1783.

royalty in law, payment to the owner for rights to use or exploit literary or artistic copyrights and patent rights in new inventions of all kinds.

Oil, gas, and other mineral deposits are also subject to royalty payments.

Royce (Frederick) Henry 1863–1933. British engineer, who so impressed Charles ◊Rolls by the automobile he built for his own personal use 1904 that Rolls-Royce Ltd was formed 1906 to produce automobiles and engines.

rpm abbreviation for *revolutions per minute*.

RSFSR abbreviation for *Russian Soviet Federal Socialist Republic*, the largest republic of the former Soviet Union; renamed the ◊Russian Federation 1991.

RSVP abbreviation for *répondez s'il vous plaît* (French "please reply").

Ruanda part of the former Belgian territory of Ruanda-Urundi until it achieved independence as ◊Rwanda, a country in central Africa.

rubber coagulated latex of a variety of plants, mainly from the New World. Most important is Para rubber, which derives from the tree *Hevea brasiliensis* of the spurge family. It was introduced from Brazil to SE Asia, where most of the world supply is now produced, the chief exporters being Peninsular Malaysia, Indonesia, Sri Lanka, Cambodia, Thailand, Sarawak, and Brunei. At about seven years the tree, which may grow to 60 ft/20 m, is ready for "tapping." Small incisions are made in the trunk and the latex drips into collecting cups. In pure form, rubber is white and has the formula $(C_5H_8)n$.

rubber plant Asiatic tree *Ficus elastica* of the mulberry family Moraceae, native to Asia and N Africa, producing latex in its stem. It has shiny, leathery, oval leaves, and young specimens are grown as house plants.

rubella technical term for ◊German measles.

Rubens The Descent from the Cross *(c. 1611), Antwerp Cathedral.*

Rubens Peter Paul 1577–1640. Flemish painter, who brought the exuberance of Italian Baroque to N Europe, creating, with an army of assistants, innumerable religious and allegorical paintings for churches and palaces. These show mastery of drama in large compositions, and love of rich color. He also painted portraits and, in his last years, landscapes.

Rubicon ancient name of the small river flowing into the Adriatic that, under the Roman Republic, marked the boundary between Italy proper and Cisalpine Gaul. By leading his army across it 49 BC, ◊Caesar declared war on the republic; hence to "cross the Rubicon" means to take an irrevocable step.

rubidium soft, silver-white, metallic element, symbol Rb, atomic number 37, atomic weight 85.47. It is one of the ◊alkali metals, ignites spontaneously in air, and reacts violently with water. It is used in photoelectric cells and vacuum-tube filaments.

Rubik Erno 1944– . Hungarian architect who invented the *Rubik cube*, a multicolored puzzle that can be manipulated and rearranged in only one correct way, but about 43 trillion wrong ones. Intended to help his students understand three-dimensional design, it became a fad that swept around the world.

Rubinstein Artur 1887–1982. Polish-born US pianist. He studied in Warsaw and Berlin and for 85 of his 95 years appeared with the world's major symphony orchestras, specializing in the music of Mozart, Chopin, Debussy, and the Spanish composers.

ruby the red transparent gem variety of the mineral ◊corundum Al_2O_3, aluminum oxide. Small amounts of chromium oxide, Cr_2O_3, substituting for aluminum oxide, give ruby its color. Natural rubies are found mainly in Myanmar (Burma), but rubies can also be produced artificially and such synthetic stones are used in ◊lasers.

Rudolf, Lake former name (until 1979) of Lake ◊Turkana in E Africa.

Rudolph 1858–1889. Crown prince of Austria, the only son of Emperor Franz Joseph. From an early age he showed progressive views that brought him into conflict with his father. He conceived and helped to write a history of the Austro-Hungarian empire. In 1881, he married Princess Stephanie of Belgium, and they had one daughter, Elizabeth. In 1889 he and his mistress, Baroness Marie Vetsera, were found shot in his hunting lodge at Mayerling, near Vienna. The official verdict was suicide, although there were rumors that it was perpetrated by Jesuits, Hungarian nobles, or the baroness's husband.

Rudolph two Holy Roman emperors:

Rudolph I 1218–1291. Holy Roman emperor from 1273. Originally count of Hapsburg, he was the first Hapsburg emperor and expanded his dynasty by investing his sons with the duchies of Austria and Styria.

Rudolph II 1552–1612. Holy Roman emperor from 1576, when he succeeded his father Maximilian II. His policies led to unrest in Hungary and Bohemia, which led to the surrender of Hungary to his brother Matthias 1608 and religious freedom for Bohemia.

rugby contact sport that originated at the Rugby boys' school, England, 1823, when a boy picked up the ball and ran with it while playing soccer. Rugby is played with an oval ball. It is now played in two forms: Rugby League (for professionals) and Rugby Union (for amateurs).

Ruhr river in Germany; it rises in the Rothaargebirge Mountains and flows W to join the Rhine at Duisburg. The *Ruhr Valley* (142 mi/228 km), a metropolitan industrial area (petrochemicals, automobiles; iron and steel at Duisburg and Dortmund) was formerly a coal-mining center.

ruminant any even-toed hoofed mammal with a rumen, the "first stomach" of its complex digestive system. Plant food is stored and fermented before being brought back to the mouth for chewing (chewing the cud) and then is swallowed to the next stomach. Ruminants include cattle, antelopes, goats, deer, and giraffes, all with a four-chambered stomach. Camels are also ruminants, but they have a three-chambered stomach.

rune character in the oldest Germanic script, chiefly adapted from the Latin alphabet, the earliest examples being from the 3rd century, and found in Denmark. Runes were scratched on wood, metal, stone, or bone.

Runyon (Alfred) Damon 1884–1946. US journalist, primarily a sports reporter, whose short stories in *Guys and Dolls* 1932 deal wryly with the seamier side of New York City life in his own invented jargon.

He reached the height of his popularity in the 1930s, writing a syndicated newspaper feature "As I See It."

rupture in medicine, another name for ◊hernia.

rush any grasslike plant of the genus *Juncus*, family Juncaceae, found in wet places in cold and temperate regions. The round stems and flexible leaves of some species have been used for making mats and baskets since ancient times.

Rush Benjamin 1745–1813. American physician and public official. Committed to the cause of the American Revolution 1775–83, he was a signatory of the Declaration of Independence 1776 and was named surgeon general of the Continental army 1777.

From 1797 to his death he was treasurer of the US Mint.

Rushdie (Ahmed) Salman 1947– . British writer, born in India of a Muslim family. His novel *The Satanic Verses* 1988 (the title refers to verses deleted from the Koran) offended many Muslims with alleged blasphemy. In 1989 the Ayatollah Khomeini of Iran called for Rushdie and his publishers to be killed.

Rushmore, Mount mountain in the Black Hills, South Dakota; height 6,203 ft/1,890 m. On its granite face are carved giant portrait heads of presidents Washington, Jefferson, Lincoln, and Theodore Roosevelt. The sculptor was Gutzon Borglum.

Rusk Dean 1909– . US Democrat politician. He was secretary of state to presidents J F Kennedy and L B Johnson 1961–69, and became unpopular through his involvement with the ◊Vietnam War.

Ruskin John 1819–1900. English art critic and social critic. He published five volumes of *Modern Painters* 1843–60 and *The Seven Lamps of Architecture* 1849, in which he stated his philosophy of art. His writings hastened the appreciation of painters considered unorthodox at the time, such as J M W ◊Turner and the ◊Pre-Raphaelite Brotherhood. His later writings were concerned with social and economic problems.

Russell Bertrand (Arthur William), 3rd Earl Russell 1872–1970. English philosopher and mathematician who contributed to the development of modern mathematical logic and wrote about social issues. His works include *Principia Mathematica* 1910–13 (with A N Whitehead), in which he attempted to show that math-

Russian rulers 1547–1917	
House of Rurik	
Ivan *the Terrible*	1547–84
Theodore I	1584–98
Irina	1598
House of Godunov	
Boris Godunov	1598–1605
Theodore II	1605
Usurpers	
Dimitri III	1605–06
Basil IV	1606–10
interregnum 1610–13	
House of Romanov	
Michael Romanov	1613–45
Alexis	1645–76
Theodore III	1676–82
Peter I *the Great*	
and Ivan V (brothers)	1682–96
Peter I, as tsar	1689–1721
Peter I, as emperor	1721–25
Catherine I	1725–27
Peter II	1727–30
Anna Ivanovna	1730–40
Ivan VI	1740–41
Elizabeth	1741–62
Peter III	1762
Catherine II *the Great*	1762–96
Paul I	1796–1801
Alexander I	1801–25
Nicholas I	1825–55
Alexander II	1855–81
Alexander III	1881–94
Nicholas II	1894–1917

ematics could be reduced to a branch of logic; *The Problems of Philosophy* 1912; and *A History of Western Philosophy* 1946. He was an outspoken liberal pacifist.

Russell Charles Taze 1852–1916. US founder of the ◊Jehovah's Witness sect 1872. Born in Pittsburgh, Russell, a successful businessman, began studying the Bible after encountering some Adventists and becoming convinced that Christ's return was imminent. On the basis of his studies he came to believe that Christ's "invisible return" had taken place in 1874 and that in 1914 a series of apocalyptic events would culminate in Christ's thousand-year reign on Earth. In 1879 he founded the journal that became *The Watchtower*, which spread his ideas. The movement under his leadership survived the failure of his prophecies in 1914, and it continued to grow rapidly after his death.

Russell Jane 1921– . US actress who was discovered by producer Howard Hughes. Her first film, *The Outlaw* 1943, was not properly released for several years because of censorship problems. Other films include *The Paleface* 1948, *Gentlemen Prefer Blondes* 1953, and *The Revolt of Mamie Stover* 1957.
She retired 1970.

Russell Ken 1927– . English film director whose work includes *Women in Love* 1969, *The Devils* 1971, and *Gothic* 1986. He has made television documentaries of the lives of the composers Elgar, Delius, and Richard Strauss.

Russia originally the pre-revolutionary Russian Empire (until 1917), now accurately restricted to the ◊Russian Federation.

Russian member of the majority ethnic group living in Russia. Russians are also often the largest minority in neighboring republics. The Russian language is a member of the East Slavonic branch of the Indo-European language family and was the official language of the USSR, with 130–150 million speakers. It is written in the Cyrillic alphabet. The ancestors of the Russians migrated from central Europe between the 6th and 8th centuries AD.

Russian Federation or *Russia* country in N Asia and E Europe, bounded N by the Arctic Ocean; E by the Bering Sea and the Sea of Okhotsk; W by Norway, Finland, the Baltic States, Belarus, and Ukraine; and S by China, Mongolia, Georgia, Azerbaijan, and Kazakhstan.

Russian Orthodox Church another name for the ◊Orthodox Church.

Russian Revolution two revolutions of Feb and Oct 1917 (Julian ◊calendar) that began with the overthrow of the Romanov dynasty and ended with the establishment of a communist soviet (council) state, the Union of Soviet Socialist Republics (USSR).

Russian Soviet Federal Socialist Republic (RSFSR) former name (until 1991) of the ◊Russian Federation.

Russo-Japanese War war between Russia and Japan 1904–05, which arose from conflicting ambitions in Korea and ◊Manchuria, specifically, the Russian occupation of Port Arthur (modern Dalian) 1896 and of the Amur province 1900. Japan successfully besieged Port Arthur May 1904–Jan 1905, took Mukden (modern Shenyang, see ◊Mukden, Battle of) on Feb 29–March 10, and on May 27 defeated the Russian Baltic fleet, which had sailed halfway around the world to Tsushima Strait. A peace was signed Aug 23, 1905. Russia surrendered its lease on Port Arthur, ceded S Sakhalin to Japan, evacuated Manchuria, and recognized Japan's interests in Korea.

rutabaga (or *swede*) annual or biennial plant *Brassica napus*, widely cultivated for its edible root, which is yellow, purple, or white. It is similar in taste to the turnip *B. rapa* but has more carbohydrates and sugars, is firmer fleshed, and longer keeping.

Ruth in the Old Testament, Moabite (see ◊Moab) ancestor of David (king of Israel) by her second marriage to Boaz. When her first husband died, she preferred to stay with her mother-in-law, Naomi, rather than return to her own people.

Ruth Babe (George Herman) 1895–1948. US baseball player, regarded by many as the greatest of all time. He played in ten World Series and hit 714 home runs, a record that stood from 1935 to 1974 and led to the nickname "Sultan of Swat."

Ruthenia or *Carpathian Ukraine* region of central Europe, on the S slopes of the Carpathian Mountains, home of the Ruthenes or Russniaks. Dominated by Hungary from the 10th century, it was part of Austria-Hungary until World War I. In 1918 it was divided between Czechoslovakia, Poland, and Romania; independent for a single day in 1938, it was immediately occupied by Hungary, captured by the USSR 1944, and 1945–47 became incorporated into Ukraine Republic, USSR. Ukraine became an independent republic 1991.

ruthenium hard, brittle, silver-white, metallic element, symbol Ru, atomic number 44, atomic weight 101.07. It is one of the so-called platinum group of metals; it occurs in platinum ores as a free metal and in the natural alloy osmiridium. It is used as a hardener

Russian Federation
formerly (until 1991)
Russian Soviet Federal Socialist
Republic (RSFSR)

area 6,591,100 sq mi/17,075,500 sq km
capital Moscow
cities St Petersburg (Leningrad), Nizhny-Novgorod (Gorky), Rostov-on-Don, Samara (Kuibyshev), Tver (Kalinin), Volgograd, Vyatka (Kirov), Ekaterinburg (Sverdlovsk)
physical fertile Black Earth district; extensive forests; the Ural Mountains with large mineral resources
features the heavily industrialized area around Moscow; Siberia; includes 16 autonomous republics (capitals in parentheses): Bashkir (Ufa); Buryat (Ulan-Ude); Checheno-Ingush (Grozny); Chuvash (Cheboksary); Dagestan (Makhachkala); Kabardino-Balkar (Nalchik); Kalmyk (Elista); Karelia (Petrozavodsk); Komi (Syktyvkar); Mari (Yoshkar-Ola); Mordovia (Saransk); Vladikavkaz (formerly Ordzhonikidze); Tatarstan (Kazan); Tuva (Kizyl); Udmurt (Izhevsk); Yakut (Yakutsk)
head of state Boris Yeltsin from 1990/91
head of government Viktor Chernomyrdin from 1992
political system emergent democracy
political parties Democratic Russia, liberal-radical, pro-Yeltsin; Congress of Civil and Patriotic Groups (CCDG), right-wing; Civic Union, right of center; Nashi (Ours), far-right, Russian imperialist coalition; Communist (Bolshevik) Party, Stalinist-communist
products iron ore, coal, oil, gold, platinum, and other minerals, agricultural produce
currency ruble

population (1992) 149,469,000 (82% Russian, Tatar 4%, Ukrainian 3%, Chuvash 1%)
language Great Russian
religion traditionally Russian Orthodox

chronology
1945 Became a founding member of United Nations (UN).
1988 Aug: Democratic Union formed in Moscow as political party opposed to totalitarianism. Oct: Russian- language demonstrations in Leningrad, tsarist flag raised.
1989 March: Boris Yeltsin elected to USSR Congress of People's Deputies. Sept: conservative-nationalist Russian United Workers' Front established in Sverdlovsk.
1990 May: anticommunist May Day protests in Red Square, Moscow; Yeltsin narrowly elected RSFSR president by Russian parliament. June: economic and political sovereignty declared; Ivan Silaev became Russian prime minister. Aug: Tatarstan declared sovereignty. Dec: rationing introduced in some cities; private land ownership allowed.
1991 June: Yeltsin directly elected president under a liberal-radical banner. July: Yeltsin issued a decree to remove Communist Party cells from workplaces; sovereignty of the Baltic republics recognized by the republic. Aug: Yeltsin stood out against abortive antiGorbachev coup, emerging as key power-broker within Soviet Union; national guard established and pre-revolutionary flag restored. Sept: Silaev resigned as Russian premier. Nov: Yeltsin named prime minister; Soviet and Russian Communist Parties banned; Yeltsin's goverment gained control of Russia's economic assets and armed forces. Oct: Checheno-Ingush declared its independence. Dec: Yeltsin negotiated formation of new confederal Commonwealth of Independent States; Russia admitted into UN; independence recognized by US and European Community.
1992 Jan: admitted into Conference on Security and Cooperation in Europe; assumed former USSR's permanent seat on UN Security Council; prices freed. Feb: demonstrations in Moscow and other cities as living standards plummeted. June: Yeltsin–Bush summit meeting. March: 18 out of 20 republics signed treaty agreeing to remain within loose Russian Federation; Tatarstan and Checheno-Ingush refused to sign. Dec: Victor Chernomyrdin elected prime minister; new constitution agreed in referendum. START II arms-reduction agreement signed with US.
1993 March: Power struggle between Yeltsin and Congress of People's Deputies. Yeltsin declared temporary presidential "special rule" pending referendum. Referendum gave vote of confidence in Yeltsin's presidency but did not support constitutional change. Sept: Yeltsin dissolved Supreme Soviet. Attempted coup by conservative opponents led to their arrest.

in alloys and as a catalyst; its compounds are used as coloring agents in glass and ceramics.

It was discovered in 1827 by Estonian chemist G W Osann, who produced it in impure form from residues of platinum ores, and named after 1828 for its place of discovery, the Ural mountains in Ruthenia (now part of the Ukraine). Pure ruthenium was isolated in 1845 by K K Klaus.

Rutherford Ernest 1871–1937. New Zealand physicist, a pioneer of modern atomic science. His main research was in the field of radioactivity, and he discovered alpha, beta, and gamma rays. He named the nucleus, and was the first to recognize the nuclear nature of the atom. Nobel Prize 1908.

Rutherford Margaret 1892–1972. English film and theater actress who specialized in formidable yet jovially eccentric roles.

One of the great character actresses, she became mildly successful in the mid-1930s but went on to her greatest success when she played Agatha Christie's Miss Marple, with her husband, actor Stringer Davis, in four films in the early 1960s and won an Academy Award for her role in *The VIPs* 1963. She was also seen in *Blithe Spirit* 1945, *Passport to Pimlico* 1949, *Mouse on the Moon* 1943, and Orson Welles's *Chimes at Midnight* 1966.

rutherfordium name proposed by US scientists for the element currently known as ♭unnilquadium (atomic number 104), to honor New Zealand physicist Ernest Rutherford.

Rutledge Wiley Blount, Jr 1894–1949. US jurist and associate justice of the US Supreme Court 1943–49. He was known as a liberal, often dissenting from conservative Court decisions, such as in *Wolf* v *Colorado* 1949, which allowed illegally obtained evidence to be used against a defendant in state courts.

Ruwenzori mountain range on the frontier between Zaire and Uganda, rising to 16,794 ft/5,119 m at Mount Stanley.

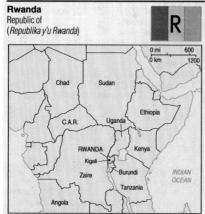

Rwanda
Republic of
(*Republika y'u Rwanda*)

area 10,173 sq mi/26,338 sq km
capital Kigali
cities Butare, Ruhengeri
physical high savanna and hills, with volcanic mountains in NW
features part of lake Kivu; highest peak Mount Karisimbi 14,792 ft/4,507 m; Kagera River (whose headwaters are the source of the Nile) and National Park
head of state Maj Gen Juvenal Habyarimana from 1973
head of government Agathe Uwilingiyimana from 1993
political system one-party military republic
political party National Revolutionary Movement for Development (MRND), nationalist, socialist

exports coffee, tea, pyrethrum
currency franc
population (1992) 7,347,000 (Hutu 90%, Tutsi 9%, Twa 1%); growth rate 3.3% p.a.
life expectancy men 49, women 53 (1989)
languages Kinyarwanda, French (official); Kiswahili
religions Roman Catholic 54%, animist 23%, Protestant 12%, Muslim 9%
literacy men 50% (1989)
GNP $2.3 bn (1987); $323 per head (1986)

chronology
1916 Belgian troops occupied Rwanda; League of Nations mandated Rwanda and Burundi to Belgium as Territory of Ruanda-Urundi.
1959 Interethnic warfare between Hutu and Tutsi.
1962 Independence from Belgium achieved, with Grégoire Kayibanda as president.
1972 Renewal of interethnic fighting.
1973 Kayibanda ousted in a military coup led by Maj-Gen Juvenal Habyarimana.
1978 New constitution approved; Rwanda remained a military-controlled state.
1980 Civilian rule adopted.
1988 Refugees from Burundi massacres streamed into Rwanda.
1990 Government attacked by Rwandan Patriotic Front (FPR), a Tutsi military-political organization based in Uganda.
1992 Peace accord with FPR.
1993 Power-sharing agreement with government repudiated by FPR. Peace accord formally signed. Agathe Uwilingiyimana became first femal prime minister.

Rwanda landlocked country in central Africa, bounded N by Uganda, E by Tanzania, S by Burundi, and W by Zaire.

Ryder Albert Pinkham 1847–1917. US painter who developed one of the most original styles of his time. He painted with broad strokes that tended to simplify form and used yellowish colors that gave his works an eerie, haunted quality. His works are poetic, romantic, and filled with unreality; *Death on a Pale Horse* 1910 (Cleveland Museum of Art) is typical.

rye Rye has been cultivated in Europe since Roman times.

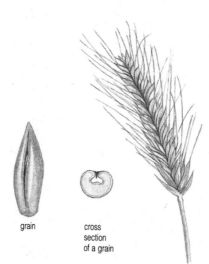

grain

cross section of a grain

Born in New Bedford, Massachusetts, he was self-taught and, as time passed, became more of a recluse.

Ryder Cup golf tournament for professional men's teams from the US and Europe. It is played every two years, and the match is made up of a series of singles, foursomes, and fourballs played over three days.

rye cereal *Secale cereale* grown extensively in N Europe and other temperate regions. The flour is used to make dark-colored ("black") breads. Rye is grown mainly as a forage crop, but the grain is also used to make whiskey and breakfast cereals.

Ryle Martin 1918–1984. English radioastronomer. At the Mullard Radio Astronomy Observatory, Cambridge, he developed the technique of sky-mapping using "aperture synthesis," combining smaller dish aerials to give the characteristics of one large one. His work on the distribution of radio sources in the universe brought confirmation of the ◊Big Bang theory. He won, with Antony ◊Hewish, the Nobel Prize for Physics 1974.

Ryukyu Islands southernmost island group of Japan, stretching toward Taiwan and including Okinawa, Miyako, and Ishigaki
area 870 sq mi/2,254 sq km
capital Naha, on Okinawa
features 73 islands, some uninhabited; subject to typhoons
products sugar, pineapples, fish
population (1985) 1,179,000
history originally an independent kingdom; ruled by China from the late 14th century until seized by Japan 1609 and controlled by the Satsuma feudal lords until 1868, when the Japanese government took over. Chinese claims to the islands were relinquished 1895. In World War II the islands were taken by US 1945 (see under ◊Okinawa); northernmost group, Oshima, restored to Japan 1953, the rest 1972.

Saami (or **Lapp**) member of a group of herding people living in N Scandinavia and the Kola Peninsula, and numbering about 46,000 (1983). Some are nomadic, others lead a more settled way of life. They live by herding reindeer, hunting, fishing, and producing handicrafts. Their language belongs to the Finno-Ugric family. Their religion is basically animist, but incorporates elements of Christianity.

Saarinen Eero 1910–1961. Finnish-born US architect. Son of Eliel ◊Saarinen. He is known for a wide range of innovative modern designs using a variety of creative shapes for buildings. His works include the TWA terminal at Kennedy Airport in New York City; Dulles Airport outside Washington, DC; the General Motors Technical Center in Warren, Michigan; the Thomas J Watson Research Center in Yorktown, New York; Ezra Stiles and Morse colleges and the ice-hockey rink at Yale University; Kresge Auditorium at the Massachusetts Institute of Technology; and US embassies in London and Oslo.

Saarinen Eliel 1873–1950. Finnish-born US architect and founder of the Finnish Romantic school. His most famous European work is the Helsinki railroad station. In the US he is particularly remembered for his designs for Cranbrook School in Bloomfield Hills, Michigan, and Christ Church in Minneapolis.

Saarland (French **Sarre**) *Land* (state) of Germany
area 992 sq mi/2,570 sq km
capital Saarbrücken
features one-third forest; crossed NW–S by the river Saar
products cereals and other crops; cattle, pigs, poultry. Former flourishing coal and steel industries survive only by government subsidy
population (1988) 1,034,000
history in 1919, the Saar district was administered by France under the auspices of the League of Nations; a plebiscite returned it to Germany 1935; Hitler gave it the name Saarbrücken. Part of the French zone of occupation 1945, it was included in the economic union with France 1947. It was returned to Germany 1957.

Sabbath the seventh day of the week, commanded by God in the Old Testament as a sacred day of rest; in Judaism, from sunset Friday to sunset Saturday; in Christianity, Sunday (or, in some sects, Saturday).

Sabine member of an ancient people of central Italy, conquered by the Romans and amalgamated with them in the 3rd century BC. The so-called **rape of the**

Sabine women—a mythical attempt by ◊Romulus in the early days of Rome to carry off the Sabine women to colonize the new city—is frequently depicted in art.

sable marten *Martes zibellina*, about 20 in/50 cm long and usually brown. It is native to N Eurasian forests, but now found mainly in E Siberia. The sable has diminished in numbers because of its valuable fur, which has long attracted hunters. Conservation measures and sable farming have been introduced to save it from extinction.

saccharin or *ortho-sulpho benzimide* $C_7H_5NO_3S$ sweet, white, crystalline solid derived from coal tar and substituted for sugar. Since 1977 it has been regarded as potentially carcinogenic. Its use is not universally permitted and it has been largely replaced by other sweetening agents.

Sacco-Vanzetti case murder trial in Massachusetts, 1920–21. Italian immigrants Nicola Sacco (1891–1927) and Bartolomeo Vanzetti (1888–1927) were convicted of murder during an alleged robbery. The conviction was upheld on appeal, with application for retrial denied. Prolonged controversy delayed execution until 1927. In 1977 the verdict was declared unjust because of the judge's prejudice against the accuseds' anarchist views.

Sacher-Masoch Leopold von 1836–1895. Austrian novelist. His books dealt with the sexual pleasure of having pain inflicted on oneself, hence ◊masochism.

sacrament in Christian usage, observances forming the visible sign of inward grace. In the Roman Catholic church there are seven sacraments: baptism, Holy Communion (Eucharist or mass), confirmation, rite of reconciliation (confession and penance), holy orders, matrimony, and the anointing of the sick.

Sacramento industrial port and capital (since 1854) of California, 80 mi/130 km NE of San Francisco; population (1990) 369,400, metropolitan area 1,481,100. It stands on the Sacramento River, which flows 382 mi/615 km through Sacramento Valley to San Francisco Bay. Industries include the manufacture of detergents and jet aircraft and food processing, including almonds, peaches, and pears.

Sadat Anwar 1918–1981. Egyptian politician. Succeeding ◊Nasser as president 1970, he restored morale by his handling of the Egyptian campaign in the 1973 attack upon Israel. In 1974 his plan for economic, social, and political reform to transform Egypt was

Sadat Anwar Sadat, president of Egypt from 1970 until he was assassinated by Islamic fundamentalists in Oct 1981.

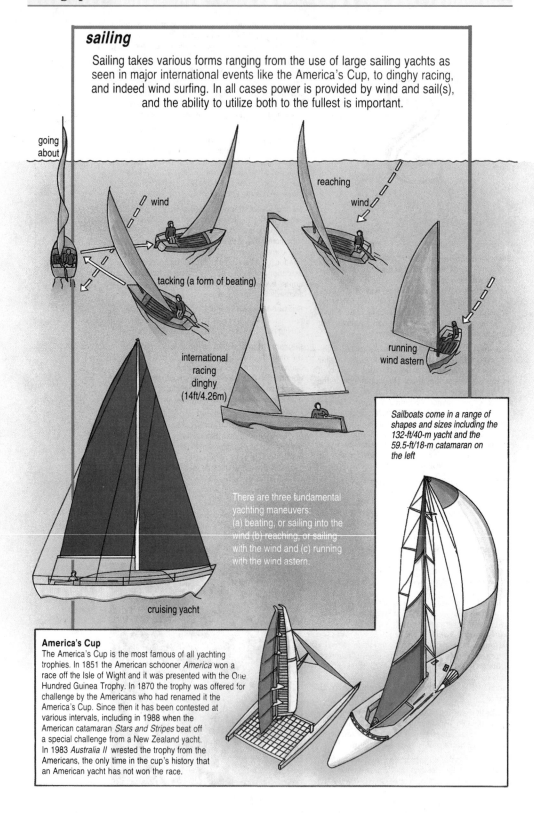

sailing

Sailing takes various forms ranging from the use of large sailing yachts as seen in major international events like the America's Cup, to dinghy racing, and indeed wind surfing. In all cases power is provided by wind and sail(s), and the ability to utilize both to the fullest is important.

going about

reaching

wind

wind

tacking (a form of beating)

international racing dinghy (14ft/4.26m)

running wind astern

Sailboats come in a range of shapes and sizes including the 132-ft/40-m yacht and the 59.5-ft/18-m catamaran on the left

There are three fundamental yachting maneuvers: (a) beating, or sailing into the wind (b) reaching, or sailing with the wind and (c) running with the wind astern.

cruising yacht

America's Cup
The America's Cup is the most famous of all yachting trophies. In 1851 the American schooner *America* won a race off the Isle of Wight and it was presented with the One Hundred Guinea Trophy. In 1870 the trophy was offered for challenge by the Americans who had renamed it the America's Cup. Since then it has been contested at various intervals, including in 1988 when the American catamaran *Stars and Stripes* beat off a special challenge from a New Zealand yacht. In 1983 *Australia II* wrested the trophy from the Americans, the only time in the cup's history that an American yacht has not won the race.

unanimously adopted in a referendum. In 1977 he visited Israel to reconcile the two countries, and shared the Nobel Peace Prize with Israeli prime minister Menachem Begin 1978. He was assassinated by Islamic fundamentalists.

Sadducee (Hebrew "righteous") member of the ancient Hebrew political party and sect of ◊Judaism that formed in pre-Roman Palestine in the first century BC. They were the group of priestly aristocrats in Jerusalem until the final destruction of the Temple AD 70.

Sade Donatien Alphonse François, Comte de, known as the *Marquis de Sade* 1740–1814. French author who was imprisoned for sexual offenses and finally committed to an asylum. He wrote plays and novels dealing explicitly with a variety of sexual practices, including ◊sadism.

sadism tendency to derive pleasure (usually sexual) from inflicting physical or mental pain on others. The term is derived from the Marquis de ◊Sade.

safflower Asian plant *Carthamus tinctorius*, family Compositae. It is thistlelike, and widely grown for the oil from its seeds, which is used in cooking, margarine, and paints and varnishes; the seed residue is used as cattle feed.

saffron plant *Crocus sativus* of the iris family, probably native to SW Asia, and formerly widely cultivated in Europe; also the dried orange-yellow ◊stigmas of its purple flowers, used for coloring and flavoring.

saga prose narrative written down in the 11th–13th centuries in Norway and Iceland. The sagas range from family chronicles, such as the *Landnamabok* of Ari (1067–1148), to legendary and anonymous works such as the *Njala* saga.

sage perennial herb *Salvia officinalis* with gray-green aromatic leaves used for flavoring. It grows up to 20 in/50 cm high and has bluish-lilac or pink flowers.

Saginaw city and port in E Michigan, on the Saginaw River, near Lake Huron, NW of Flint; population (1990) 69,500. Industries include automotive parts, metal products, salt, coal, and sugar beet. Saginaw was a lumber center until the late 19th century.

Sagittarius zodiac constellation in the southern hemisphere, represented as a centaur aiming a bow and arrow at neighboring Scorpius. The Sun passes through Sagittarius from mid-Dec to mid-Jan, including the winter solstice, when it is farthest south of the equator. The constellation contains many nebulae and globular clusters, and open ◊star clusters. Kaus Australis and Nunki are its brightest stars. The center of our Galaxy, the Milky Way, is marked by the radio source Sagittarius A. In astrology, the dates for Sagittarius are between about Nov 22 and Dec 21.

Sahara largest desert in the world, occupying 2,123,000 sq mi/5,500,000 sq km of N Africa from the Atlantic to the Nile, covering: W Egypt; part of W Sudan; large parts of Mauritania, Mali, Niger, and Chad; and southern parts of Morocco, Algeria, Tunisia, and Libya. Small areas in Algeria and Tunisia are below sea level, but it is mainly a plateau with a central mountain system, including the Ahaggar Mountains in Algeria, the Aïr Massif in Niger, and the Tibesti Massif in Chad, of which the highest peak is Emi Koussi, 11,208 ft/3,415 m. The area of the Sahara expanded by 251,000 sq mi/650,000 sq km 1940–90, but reforestation is being attempted in certain areas.

Saigon former name (until 1976) of ◊Ho Chi Minh City, Vietnam.

sailing pleasure cruising or racing a small and light vessel, whether sailing or power-driven. At the Olympic Games, seven categories exist: Soling, Flying Dutchman, Star, Finn, Tornado, 470, and Windglider or ◊windsurfing (boardsailing), which was introduced at the 1984 Los Angeles games. All these Olympic categories are sail-driven. The Finn and Windglider are solos events; the Soling class is for three-person crews; all other classes are for crews of two.

saint holy man or woman respected for his or her wisdom, spirituality, and dedication to his or her faith. Within the Roman Catholic church a saint is officially recognized through ◊canonization by the pope. Many saints are associated with miracles, and canonization usually occurs after a thorough investigation of the lives and miracles attributed to them. In the Orthodox church saints are recognized by the patriarch and Holy Synod after recommendation by local churches. The term is also used in Buddhism for individuals who have led a virtuous and holy life, such as Kūkai (775–835), founder of the Japanese Shingon sect of Buddhism. For individual saints, see under forename, for example ◊Paul, St.

St Bernard breed of large, heavily built dog 30 in/70 cm high at the shoulder, weight about 150 lb/70 kg. They have pendulous ears and lips, large feet, and drooping lower eyelids. They are usually orange and white.

St Christopher (St Kitts)–Nevis country in the West Indies, in the E Caribbean Sea, part of the Leeward Islands. *See panel p. 812*

St Elmo's fire bluish, flamelike electrical discharge that sometimes occurs above ships' masts and other pointed objects or about aircraft in stormy weather. Although high voltage, it is low current and therefore harmless. St Elmo (or St Erasmus) is the patron saint of sailors.

Saint-Exupéry Antoine de 1900–1944. French author who wrote the autobiographical *Vol de nuit/Night Flight* 1931 and *Terre des hommes/Wind, Sand, and Stars* 1939. His children's book *Le Petit Prince/The Little Prince* 1943 is also an adult allegory.

St George's port and capital of ◊Grenada, on the SW coast; population (1986) 7,500, urban area 29,000. It was founded 1650 by the French.

St Helena British island in the S Atlantic, 1,200 mi/1,900 km W of Africa, area 47 sq mi/122 sq km; population (1987) 5,600. Its capital is Jamestown, and it exports fish and timber. Ascension and Tristan da Cunha are dependencies.

St Helens, Mount volcanic mountain in Washington State. When it erupted 1980 after being quiescent since 1857, it devastated an area of 230 sq mi/600 sq km and its height was reduced from 9,682 ft/2,950 m to 8,402 ft/2,560 m.

Saint John largest city of New Brunswick, on the Saint John River, population (1986) 121,000. It is a fishing port and has shipbuilding, timber, fish-processing, petroleum, refining, and textile industries. Founded by the French as *Saint-Jean* 1635, it was taken by the British 1758.

St John, Order of (full title *Knights Hospitallers of St John of Jerusalem*) oldest order of Christian chivalry, named after the hospital at Jerusalem founded about 1048 by merchants of Amalfi for pilgrims, whose travel routes the knights defended from the Muslims. Today there are about 8,000 knights

St Christopher (St Kitts)–Nevis
Federation of

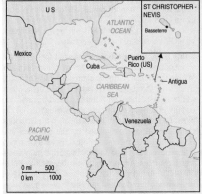

ST CHRISTOPHER - NEVIS
Basseterre

US
ATLANTIC OCEAN
Mexico
Cuba
Puerto Rico (US)
Antigua
CARIBBEAN SEA
Venezuela
PACIFIC OCEAN

0 mi 500
0 km 1000

area 104 sq mi/269 sq km (St Christopher 68 sq mi/176 sq km, Nevis 36 sq mi/93 sq km)
capital Basseterre (on St Christopher)
cities Charlestown (largest on Nevis)
physical both islands are volcanic
features fertile plains on coast; black beaches
head of state Elizabeth II from 1983 represented by governor-general
head of government Kennedy Simmonds from 1980

political system federal constitutional monarchy
political parties People's Action Movement (PAM), center-right; Nevis Reformation Party (NRP), Nevis-separatist; Labor Party, moderate left of center
exports sugar, molasses, electronics, clothing
currency Eastern Caribbean dollar
population (1992) 43,100; growth rate 0.2% p.a.
life expectancy men 69/women 72
language English
media no daily newspaper; two weekly papers, published by the governing and opposition party respectively—both receive advertising support from the government
religion Anglican 36%, Methodist 32%, other Protestant 8%, Roman Catholic 10% (1985 est)
literacy 90% (1987)
GNP $40 million (1983); $870 per head

chronology
1871–1956 Part of the Leeward Islands Federation.
1958–62 Part of the Federation of the West Indies.
1967 St Christopher, Nevis, and Anguilla achieved internal self-government, within the British Commonwealth, with Robert Bradshaw, Labor Party leader, as prime minister.
1971 Anguilla returned to being a British dependency.
1978 Bradshaw died; succeeded by Paul Southwell.
1979 Southwell died; succeeded by Lee L Moore.
1980 Coalition government led by Kennedy Simmonds.
1983 Full independence achieved within the Commonwealth.
1984 Coalition government reelected.
1989 Prime Minister Simmonds won a third successive term.

(male and female), and the Grand Master is the world's highest ranking Roman Catholic lay person.

St John's capital and chief port of Newfoundland; population (1986) 96,000, urban area 162,000. The main industry is fish processing; other products include textiles, fishing equipment, furniture, and machinery.

St John's port and capital of Antigua and Barbuda, on the NW coast of Antigua; population (1982) 30,000. It exports rum, cotton, and sugar.

St Kitts–Nevis contracted form of ◊St Christopher–Nevis.

Saint-Laurent Yves (Henri Donat Mathieu) 1936– . French fashion designer who has had an exceptional influence on fashion in the second half of the 20th century. He began working for Christian ◊Dior 1955 and succeeded him as designer on Dior's death 1957. He established his own label 1962 and went on to create the first "power-dressing" looks for men and women: Classical, stylish city clothes.

St Lawrence river in E North America. From ports on the ◊Great Lakes it forms, with linking canals (which also give great hydroelectric capacity to the river), the St Lawrence Seaway for oceangoing ships, ending in the Gulf of St Lawrence. It is 745 mi/1,200 km long and is icebound for four months each year.

The river's source is Lake Ontario. In its upper course the St Lawrence includes the scenic Thousand Islands and forms the border between the Canadian province of Ontario and the US state of New York. It then enters the province of Québec and flows past Montréal and the city of Québec. Below the latter, it broadens to a maximum width of 90 mi/145 km when it empties into the Gulf of St Lawrence, an arm of the Atlantic Ocean. French explorer Jacques Cartier discovered the river 1535, and the first permanent colonial settlement (city of Québec) was established 1608 by Samuel de Champlain.

St Louis city in Missouri, on the Mississippi River; population (1990) 396,700, metropolitan area 2,444,100. Its industries include aerospace equipment, aircraft, vehicles, chemicals, electrical goods, steel, food processing, and beer. Its central US location makes it a warehousing and distribution center and a hub of rail, truck, and airline transportation. St Louis and Washington universities are here, and the University of Missouri has a campus in the city.

St Lucia country in the West Indies, in the E Caribbean Sea, one of the Windward Islands.

St Moritz winter sports center in SE Switzerland; it contains the Cresta Run (built 1885) for toboggans, bobsleds, and luges. It was the site of the Winter Olympics 1928 and 1948.

St Paul capital and industrial city of Minnesota, adjacent to ◊Minneapolis; population (1990) 272,200. Industries include eletronics, publishing, printing, chemicals, refined petroleum, machinery, and processed food.

St Petersburg capital of the St Petersburg region, Russia, at the head of the Gulf of Finland; population (1989 est) 5,023,500. Industries include shipbuilding, machinery, chemicals, and textiles. It was renamed *Petrograd* 1914 and was called *Leningrad* from 1924 until 1991, when its original name was restored. Built on a low and swampy site, St Petersburg is split up by the mouths of the river Neva, which connects it with Lake Ladoga. The climate is severe. The city became a seaport when it was linked with the Baltic by a ship canal built 1875–93. It is also linked by canal and river with the Caspian and Black seas, and in 1975 a seaway connection was completed via lakes Onega and Ladoga with the White Sea near Belomorsk, allowing naval forces to reach the Barents Sea free of NATO surveillance.

St Petersburg seaside resort and industrial city (space technology), W Florida; population (1990) 238,600. It is across Tampa Bay from ◊Tampa.

St Lucia

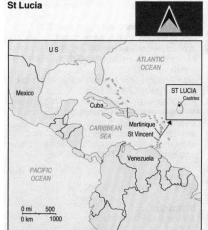

area 238 sq mi/617 sq km
capital Castries
cities Vieux-Fort, Soufrière
physical mountainous island with fertile valleys; mainly tropical forest
features volcanic peaks; Gros and Petit Pitons
head of state Elizabeth II from 1979, represented by governor-general
head of government John Compton from 1982

political system constitutional monarchy
political parties United Workers' Party (UWP), moderate left of center; St Lucia Labor Party (SLP), moderate left of center; Progressive Labor Party (PLP), moderate left of center
exports coconut oil, bananas, cocoa, copra
currency Eastern Caribbean dollar
population (1992) 135,000; growth rate 2.8% p.a.
life expectancy men 68, women 73 (1989)
languages English; French patois
media two independent biweekly newspapers
religion Roman Catholic 90%
literacy 78% (1989)
GNP $166 million; $1,370 per head (1987)

chronology
1814 Became a British crown colony following Treaty of Paris.
1967 Acquired internal self-government as a West Indies associated state.
1979 Independence achieved from Britain within the Commonwealth. John Compton, leader of the United Workers' Party (UWP), became prime minister. Allan Louisy, leader of the St Lucia Labor Party (SLP), replaced Compton as prime minister.
1981 Louisy resigned; replaced by Winston Cenac.
1982 Compton returned to power at the head of a UWP government.
1987 Compton reelected with reduced majority.
1991 Integration with Windward Islands proposed.
1992 UWP won general election.

St Pierre and Miquelon territorial dependency of France, eight small islands off the S coast of Newfoundland,
area St Pierre group 10 sq mi/26 sq km; Miquelon-Langlade group 83 sq mi/216 sq km
capital St Pierre
features the last surviving remnant of France's North American empire
products fish
currency French franc
population (1987) 6,300
language French
religion Roman Catholic
government French-appointed commissioner and elected local council; one representative in the National Assembly in France
history settled 17th century by Breton and Basque fisherfolk; French territory 1816–1976; overseas *département* until 1985; violent protests 1989 when France tried to impose its claim to a 200-mi/320-km fishing zone around the islands; Canada maintains that there is only a 12-mi/19-km zone.

Saint-Saëns (Charles) Camille 1835–1921. French composer, pianist and organist. Among his many lyrical Romantic pieces are concertos, the symphonic poem *Danse macabre* 1875, the opera *Samson et Dalila* 1877, and the orchestral *Carnaval des animaux/Carnival of the Animals* 1886.

Saint-Simon Claude Henri, Comte de 1760–1825. French socialist who fought in the American Revolution and was imprisoned during the French Revolution. He advocated an atheist society ruled by technicians and industrialists in *Du Système industrielle/The Industrial System* 1821.

St Valentine's Day Massacre the murder in Chicago of seven unarmed members of the "Bugs" Moran gang on Feb 14, 1929, by members of Al Capone's gang disguised as police. The killings testi-

fied to the intensity of gangland warfare for the control of the trade in illicit liquor during ◊Prohibition.

St Vincent and the Grenadines country in the West Indies, in the E Caribbean Sea, part of the Windward Islands. *See panel p. 814*

St Vitus's dance former name for ◊chorea, a nervous disorder. St Vitus, martyred under the Roman emperor Diocletian, was the patron saint of dancers.

sake Japanese wine made from rice. It is usually served heated but may also be drunk at room temperature. There are both dry and sweet types. Sake contains 14-18% alcohol.

Sakhalin (Japanese *Karafuto*) island in the Pacific, N of Japan, that since 1947, with the Kurils, forms a region of Russia; capital Yuzhno-Sakhalinsk (Japanese *Toyohara*); area 28,564 sq mi/74,000 sq km; population (1981) 650,000, including aboriginal ◊Ainu and Gilyaks. There are two parallel mountain ranges, rising to over 5,000 ft/1,525 m, which extend throughout its length, 600 mi/965 km.

Sakharov Andrei Dmitrievich 1921–1989. Soviet physicist, known both as the "father of the Soviet H-bomb" and as an outspoken human-rights cam-

St Petersburg St Isaac's cathedral, St Petersburg, Russia.

St Vincent and the Grenadines

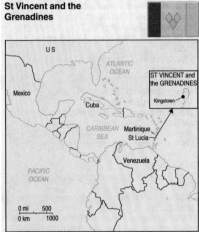

area 150 sq mi/388 sq km, including islets of the Northern Grenadines 17 sq mi/43 sq km
capital Kingstown
cities Georgetown, Chateaubelair
physical volcanic mountains, thickly forested
features Mustique, one of the Grenadines, a holiday resort; Soufrière volcano

head of state Elizabeth II from 1979, represented by governor-general
head of government James Mitchell from 1984
political system constitutional monarchy
political parties New Democratic Party (NDP), moderate, left of center; St Vincent Labor Party (SVLP), moderate, left of center
exports bananas, taros, sweet potatoes, arrowroot, copra
currency Eastern Caribbean dollar
population (1992) 109,000; growth rate –4% p.a.
life expectancy men 69, women 74 (1989)
languages English; French patois
media government-owned radio station; two privately owned weekly newspapers, subject to government pressure
religions Anglican 47%, Methodist 28%, Roman Catholic 13%
literacy 85% (1989)
GNP $188 million; $1,070 per head (1987)

chronology
1783 Became a British crown colony.
1958–62 Part of the West Indies Federation.
1969 Achieved internal self-government.
1979 Achieved full independence from Britain, within the Commonwealth, with Milton Cato as prime minister.
1984 James Mitchell replaced Cato as prime minister.
1989 Mitchell decisively reelected.
1991 Integration with Windward Islands proposed.

paigner. In 1948 he joined Igor Tamm in developing the hydrogen bomb; he later protested against Soviet nuclear tests and was a founder of the Soviet Human Rights Committee, winning the Nobel Peace Prize 1975. In 1980 he was sent to internal exile in Gorky (now Nizhni-Novgorod) for criticizing Soviet action in Afghanistan. At the end of 1986 he was allowed to return to Moscow and resume his place in the Soviet Academy of Sciences.

Saladin or *Sala-ud-din* 1138–1193. Born a Kurd, sultan of Egypt from 1175, in succession to the Atabeg of Mosul, on whose behalf he conquered Egypt 1164–74. He subsequently conquered Syria 1174–87 and precipitated the third ◊Crusade by his recovery of Jerusalem from the Christians 1187. Renowned for knightly courtesy, Saladin made peace with Richard I of England 1192.

Salamanca, Battle of victory of the British commander Wellington over the French army in the ◊Peninsular War, July 22, 1812.

salamander any tailed amphibian of the order *Urodela*. They are sometimes confused with lizards, but unlike lizards they have no scales or claws. Salamanders have smooth or warty moist skin. The order includes some 300 species, arranged in nine families, found mainly in the northern hemisphere. Salamanders include hellbenders, mudpuppies, waterdogs, sirens, mole salamanders, newts, and lungless salamanders (dusky, woodland, and spring salamanders).

Salamis ancient city on the E coast of Cyprus, the capital under the early Ptolemies until its harbor silted up about 200 BC, when it was succeeded by Paphos in the southwest.

Salamis, Battle of naval battle off the coast of the island of Salamis in which the Greeks defeated the Persians 480 BC.

Salazar Antonio de Oliveira 1889–1970. Portuguese prime minister 1932–68 who exercised a virtual dictatorship. During World War II he maintained Por-

tuguese neutrality but fought long colonial wars in Africa (Angola and Mozambique) that impeded his country's economic development as well as that of the colonies.

Salem city and manufacturing center in Massachusetts, 15 mi/24 km NE of Boston; population (1990) 38,100. Leather goods, electrical equipment, and machinery are manufactured here. Points of interest include Salem Maritime National Historic Site, the birthplace of Nathaniel Hawthorne, and the House of the Seven Gables 1668 that gave rise to his novel of the same name. Salem was settled 1626 and was the site of witchcraft trials 1692 that resulted in the execution of about 20 people.

Salem city in NW Oregon, settled about 1840 and made state capital 1859; population (1990) 107,800. It processes timber into wood products and has a prosperous fruit- and vegetable-canning industry. Williamette University is here. Salem was established by Methodist missionaries 1840–41 and became the territorial capital 1851.

salicylic acid HOC_6H_4COOH the active chemical constituent of aspirin, an analgesic drug. The acid and its salts (salicylates) occur naturally in many plants; concentrated sources include willow bark and oil of wintergreen.

Salinas city in W central California, S of San Jose; population (1990) 108,800. Fruits and vegetables, such as lettuce, are the economy's mainstay.

Salinas de Gortiari Carlos 1948– . Mexican politician, president from 1988, a member of the dominant Institutional Revolutionary Party (PRI).

Salinger J(erome) D(avid) 1919– . US writer, author of the classic novel of mid-20th-century adolescence *The Catcher in the Rye* 1951. He also wrote short stories about a Jewish family named Glass, including *Franny and Zooey* 1961.

Salisbury city and market town in Wiltshire, England, 84 mi/135 km SW of London; population (1983 est) 40,000. Salisbury is an agricultural center, and industries include brewing and carpet manufacture (in nearby Wilton). The cathedral of St Mary, built 1220–66, is an example of Early English architecture; its decorated spire 404 ft/123 m is the highest in England; its clock (1386) is one of the oldest still working. The cathedral library contains one of only four copies of the *Magna Carta*.

Salisbury former name (until 1980) of ◊Harare, the capital of Zimbabwe.

saliva in vertebrates, a secretion from the salivary glands that aids the swallowing and digestion of food in the mouth. In mammals, it contains the enzyme amylase, which converts starch to sugar. The salivary glands of mosquitoes and other blood-sucking insects produce ◊anticoagulants.

Salk Jonas Edward 1914– . US physician and microbiologist. In 1954 he developed the original vaccine that led to virtual eradication of paralytic ◊polio in industrialized countries. He was director of the Salk Institute for Biological Studies, University of California, San Diego, 1963–75.

salmon any of the various bony fishes of the family Salmonidae. More specifically the name is applied to several species of game fishes of the genera Salmo and Oncorhynchus of North America and Eurasia that mature in the ocean but, to spawn, return to the freshwater streams where they were born. Their normal color is silvery with a few dark spots, but the color changes at the spawning season.

Salmonella very varied group of bacteria. They can be divided into three broad groups. One of these causes typhoid and paratyphoid fevers, while a second group causes salmonella ◊food poisoning, which is characterized by stomach pains, vomiting, diarrhea, and headache. It can be fatal in elderly people, but others usually recover in a few days without antibiotics. Most cases are caused by contaminated animal products, especially poultry meat.

salsa Latin big-band dance music popularized by Puerto Ricans in New York City in the 1970s–80s and by, among others, the Panamanian singer Rubén Blades (1948–).

salt in chemistry, any compound formed from an acid and a base through the replacement of all or part of the hydrogen in the acid by a metal or electropositive radical. *Common salt* is sodium chloride (see ◊salt, common).

SALT abbreviation for ◊Strategic Arms Limitation Talks, a series of US–Soviet negotiations 1969–79.

salt, common or *sodium chloride* NaCl white crystalline solid, found dissolved in sea water and as rock salt (halite) in large deposits and salt domes. Common salt is used extensively in the food industry as a preservative and for flavoring, and in the chemical industry in the making of chlorine and sodium.

Salt Lake City capital of Utah, on the river Jordan, 11 mi/18 km SE of the Great Salt Lake; population (1990) 159,900.

Founded 1847, it is the headquarters of the Church of Jesus Christ of Latter-Day Saints (Mormon Church). The Mormon Tabernacle, Mormon Temple, and University of Utah are here. Products include refined petroleum, metal goods, processed food, and textiles; nearby mining adds to the city's economy. Salt Lake City became the territorial capital 1856.

salt marsh wetland with halophytic vegetation (tolerant to sea water). Salt marshes develop around estu-

aries and on the sheltered side of sand and shingle spits. Salt marshes usually have a network of creeks and drainage channels by which tidal waters enter and leave the marsh.

saltpeter former name for potassium nitrate (KNO_3), the compound used in making gunpowder (from about 1500). It occurs naturally, being deposited during dry periods in places with warm climates, such as India.

saluki breed of dog resembling the greyhound. It is about 26 in/65 cm high and has a silky coat, which is usually fawn, cream, or white.

Salvador port and naval base in Bahia state, NE Brazil, on the inner side of a peninsula separating Todos Santos Bay from the Atlantic Ocean; population (1991) 2,075,400. Products include cocoa, tobacco, and sugar. Founded 1510, it was the capital of Brazil 1549–1763.

Salvador, El republic in Central America; see ◊El Salvador.

Salvation Army Christian evangelical, social-service, and social-reform organization, originating 1865 in London, with the work of William Booth. It has military titles for its officials, is renowned for its brass bands, and it publishes the weekly journal *War Cry*. Originally called the Christian Revival Association, it has been known since 1878 as the Salvation Army. It provides food-and-shelter missions for social derelicts and runs "thrift shops," selling second-hand merchandise to raise funds.

Salyut series of seven space stations launched by the USSR 1971–82. Salyut was cylindrical in shape, 50 ft/15 m long, and weighed 21 tons/19 tonnes. It housed two or three cosmonauts at a time, for missions lasting up to eight months.

Salzburg capital of the state of Salzburg, W Austria, on the river Salzach; population (1981) 139,400. The city is dominated by the Hohensalzburg fortress. It is the seat of an archbishopric founded by St Boniface about 700 and has a 17th-century cathedral. Industries include stock rearing, dairy farming, forestry, and tourism. It is the birthplace of the composer Wolfgang Amadeus Mozart, and an annual music festival has been held here since 1920.

Salzburg federal province of Austria; area 2,779 sq mi/7,200 sq km; population (1987) 462,000. Its capital is Salzburg.

Samara capital of Kuibyshev region, W central Russia, and port at the junction of the rivers Samara and Volga, situated in the center of the fertile middle Volga plain; population (1987) 1,280,000. Industries include aircraft, locomotives, cables, synthetic rubber, textiles, fertilizers, petroleum refining, and quarrying. It was called *Kuibyshev* 1935–91, reverting to its former name Jan 1991.

Samaria region of ancient Israel. The town of Samaria (now Sebastiyeh) on the west bank of the river Jordan was the capital of Israel in the 10th–8th centuries BC. It was renamed Sebarte in the 1st century BC by the Roman administrator Herod the Great. Extensive remains have been excavated.

Samaritan member or descendant of the colonists forced to settle in Samaria (now N Israel) by the Assyrians after their occupation of the ancient kingdom of Israel 722 BC. Samaritans adopted a form of Judaism, but adopted only the Pentateuch, the five books of Moses of the Old Testament, and regarded their temple on Mount Gerizim as the true sanctuary.

samarium hard, brittle, gray-white, metallic element of the ◊lanthanide series, symbol Sm, atomic number 62, atomic weight 150.4. It is widely distributed in nature and is obtained commercially from the minerals monzanite and bastnasite. It is used only occasionally in industry, mainly as a catalyst in organic reactions. Samarium was discovered by spectroscopic analysis of the mineral samarskite and named in 1879 by French chemist Paul Lecoq de Boisbaudran (1838–1912) after its source.

Samarkand city in E Uzbekistan, capital of Samarkand region, near the river Zerafshan, 135 mi/ 217 km E of Bukhara; population (1987) 388,000. Industries include cotton-ginning, silk manufacture, and engineering.

samba Latin American ballroom dance; the music for this. Samba originated in Brazil and became popular in the West in the 1940s. There are several different samba rhythms; the bossa nova is a samba-jazz fusion.

Samoa volcanic island chain in the SW Pacific. It is divided into Western Samoa and American Samoa.

Samoa, American group of islands 2,610 mi/4,200 km S of Hawaii, administered by the US
area 77 sq mi/200 sq km
capital Fagatogo on Tutuila
features five volcanic islands, including Tutuila, Tau, and Swain's Island, and two coral atolls. National park (1988) includes prehistoric village of Saua, virgin rain forest, flying foxes
exports canned tuna, handicrafts
currency US dollar
population (1990) 46,800
languages Samoan and English
religion Christian
government as a non-self-governing territory of the US, under Governor A P Lutali, it is constitutionally

an unincorporated territory of the US, administered by the Department of the Interior
history the islands were acquired by the US Dec 1899 by agreement with Britain and Germany under the Treaty of Berlin. A constitution was adopted 1960 and revised 1967.

Samoa, Western country in the SW Pacific Ocean, in ◊Polynesia, NE of Fiji.

samoyed breed of dog, originating in Siberia. It weighs about 60 lb/25 kg and is 23 in/58 cm tall. It resembles a ◊chow chow, but has a more pointed face and a white or cream coat.

Samson 11th century BC. In the Old Testament, a hero of Israel. He was renowned for exploits of strength against the Philistines, which ended when his lover Delilah had his hair, the source of his strength, cut off, as told in the Book of Judges.

Samuel 11th–10th centuries BC. In the Old Testament, the last of the judges who ruled the ancient Hebrews before their adoption of a monarchy, and the first of the prophets; the two books bearing his name cover the story of Samuel and the reigns of kings Saul and David.

Samuelson Paul 1915– . US economist. He became professor at the Massachusetts Institute of Technology 1940 and was awarded a Nobel Prize 1970 for his application of scientific analysis to economic theory. His books include *Economics* 1948, a classic textbook, and *Linear Programming and Economic Analysis* 1958.

samurai member of the military caste in Japan from the mid-12th century until 1869, when the feudal system was abolished and all samurai pensioned off by the government. A samurai was an armed retainer of a *daimyō* (large landowner) with specific duties and privileges and a strict code of honor. A *rōnin* was a samurai without feudal allegiance.

Samoa, Western
Independent State of
(*Samoa i Sisifo*)

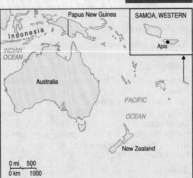

area 1,093 sq mi/2,830 sq km
capital Apia (on Upolu island)
physical comprises South Pacific islands of Savai'i and Upolu, with two smaller tropical islands and islets; mountain ranges on main islands
features lava flows on Savai'i
head of state King Malietoa Tanumafili II from 1962
head of government Tofilau Eti Alesana from 1988
political system liberal democracy
political parties Human Rights Protection Party (HRPP), led by Tofilau Eti Alesana; the Va'ai Kolone Group (VKG);

Christian Democratic Party (CDP), led by Tupua Tamasese Efi. All "parties" are personality-based groupings
exports coconut oil, copra, cocoa, fruit juice, cigarettes, timber
currency talà
population (1992) 160,000; growth rate 1.1% p.a.
life expectancy men 64, women 69 (1989)
languages English, Samoan (official)
religions Protestant 70%, Roman Catholic 20%
literacy 90% (1989)
GNP $110 million (1987); $520 per head

chronology
1899–1914 German protectorate.
1920–61 Administered by New Zealand.
1959 Local government elected.
1961 Referendum favored independence.
1962 Independence achieved within the Commonwealth, with Fiame Mata Afa Mulinu'u as prime minister.
1975 Mata Afa died.
1976 Tupuola Taisi Efi became first nonroyal prime minister.
1982 Va'ai Kolone became prime minister; replaced by Tupuola Efi. Assembly failed to approve budget; Tupuola Efi resigned; replaced by Tofilau Eti Alesana.
1985 Tofilau Eti resigned; head of state invited Va'ai Kolone to lead the government.
1988 Elections produced a hung parliament, with first Tupuola Efi as prime minister and then Tofilau Eti Alesana.
1990 Universal adult suffrage introduced.
1991 Tofilau Eti Alesana reelected. Fiame Naome became first woman in cabinet.

San'a capital of Yemen, SW Arabia, 200 mi/320 km N of Aden; population (1986) 427,000. A walled city, with fine mosques and traditional architecture, it is rapidly being modernized. Weaving and jewelry are local handicrafts.

San Andreas fault geological fault line stretching for 700 mi/1,125 km in a NW–SE direction through the state of California.

San Angelo city in W central Texas, where the North and Middle Concho rivers meet, SW of Abilene; population (1990) 84,500. Industries include wool, food processing, oil, livestock, and clay products.

San Antonio city in S Texas; population (1990) 935,900. It is a commercial and financial center; industries include aircraft maintenance, oil refining, and meat packing.

San Bernardino city in California, 50 mi/80 km E of Los Angeles; population (1990) 164,200. Products include processed food, steel, and aerospace and electronic equipment.

Sanctorius Sanctorius 1561–1636. Italian physiologist who pioneered the study of ◊metabolism and invented the clinical thermometer and a device for measuring pulse rate.

sanctuary the holiest area of a place of worship; also, a place of refuge from persecution or prosecution, usually in or near a place of worship. The custom of offering sanctuary in specific places goes back to ancient times and was widespread in Europe in the Middle Ages.

sand loose grains of rock, sized 0.0025–0.08 in/0.0625–2.00 mm in diameter, consisting chiefly of ◊quartz, but owing their varying color to mixtures of other minerals. Sand is used in cement-making, as an abrasive, in glass-making, and for other purposes.

Sand George. Adopted name of Amandine Aurore Lucie Dupin 1804–1876. French author whose prolific literary output was often autobiographical. In 1831 she left her husband after nine years of marriage and, while living in Paris as a writer, had love affairs with Alfred de Musset, ◊Chopin, and others. Her first novel *Indiana* 1832 was a plea for women's right to independence.

sandalwood fragrant heartwood of any of certain Asiatic and Australian trees of the genus *Santalum*, family Santalaceae, used for ornamental carving, in perfume, and burned as incense.

sandbar ridge of sand built up by the currents across the mouth of a river or bay. A sandbar may be entirely underwater or it may form an elongated island that breaks the surface. A sandbar stretching out from a headland is a *sand spit*.

Sandburg Carl August 1878–1967. US poet. He worked as a farm laborer and a bricklayer, and his poetry celebrates ordinary life in the US, as in *Chicago Poems* 1916, *The People, Yes* 1936, and *Complete Poems* 1951 (Pulitzer Prize). In free verse, it is reminiscent of Walt Whitman's poetry. Sandburg also wrote a monumental biography of Abraham Lincoln, *Abraham Lincoln: The Prairie Years* 1926 (two volumes) and *Abraham Lincoln: The War Years* 1939 (four volumes; Pulitzer Prize). *Always the Young Strangers* 1953 is his autobiography.

San Diego city and military and naval base in California; population (1990) 1,110,500, metropolitan area 2,498,000. It is an important Pacific Ocean fishing port. Manufacturing includes aerospace and elec-

tronic equipment, metal fabrication, printing and publishing, seafood canning, and shipbuilding.

The US Navy's largest operational complex is here. Educational institutions include the Salk Institute of Biological Studies, San Diego State University, the University of San Diego, and the University of California at San Diego, which includes the Scripps Institute of Oceanography in neighboring La Jolla. Attractions include the San Diego Zoo and Sea World. A 16-mi/26-km transit line opened 1981 connects to Tijuana, Mexico. San Diego's excellent deepwater harbor was discovered by Portuguese explorer Juan Rodriquez Cabrillo 1542. A Spanish mission and fort were established 1769. It passed to the US 1846 in the Mexican War. The coming of the railroad in 1884 began a period of rapid growth, particularly after 1940, with the establishment of military installations and defense-related industries.

Sandinista member of a Nicaraguan left-wing organization (Sandinist National Liberation Front, FSLN) named after Augusto César Sandino, a guerrilla leader killed in 1934. It was formed in 1962 and obtained widespread support from the labor unions, the church, and the middle classes, which enabled it to overthrow the regime of General Anastasio Somoza in July 1979. The FSLN dominated the Nicaraguan government and fought a civil war against American-backed Contra guerrillas until 1988. The FSLN was defeated in elections of 1990.

sandpiper any of various shorebirds belonging to the family Scolopacidae, which includes godwits, curlews, and ◊snipes.

sandstone ◊sedimentary rocks formed from the consolidation of sand, with sand-sized grains (0.0025–0.08 in/0.0625–2 mm) in a matrix or cement. Their principal component is quartz. Sandstones are commonly permeable and porous, and may form freshwater ◊aquifers. They are mainly used as building materials.

Sandwich Islands former name of ◊Hawaii, a group of islands in the Pacific.

San Francisco chief Pacific port of the US, in California; population (1990) 724,000, metropolitan area of San Francisco and Oakland 3,686,600. The city stands on a peninsula, on the south side of the Golden Gate Strait, spanned 1937 by the world's second-longest single-span bridge, 4,200 ft/1,280 m. The strait gives access to San Francisco Bay. Manufactured goods include textiles, fabricated metal products, electrical equipment, petroleum products, chemicals, and pharmaceuticals.

San Francisco is also a financial, trade, corporate, and diversified service center, and tourism is important to its economy as well. Points of interest include Chinatown, Fisherman's Wharf, Nob and Telegraph hills, and Golden Gate Park. Educational institutions include San Francisco State University, the University of San Francisco, and the University of California at San Francisco. It is also connected by bridge to Berkeley, with the University of California at Berkeley campus.

history In 1578 Sir Francis Drake's flagship, the *Golden Hind*, stopped near San Francisco on its voyage around the world. A Spanish fort and mission were established 1776. The original Spanish village was called Yerba Buena; its name was changed to San Francisco in 1846. In the same year the town was occupied during the war with Mexico. When gold was discovered in 1848 its population increased from about 800 to about 25,000 in two years. In 1906 the city was almost destroyed by an earthquake and subsequent fire that killed 452 people. It was the site of the drawing up of the United Nations Charter 1945 and of the signing of the

(1986) 602,000. Founded 1586 as a Franciscan mission, it became the colonial administrative headquarters and has fine buildings of the period.

San Marino small landlocked country within NE Italy.

San Martín José de 1778–1850. South American revolutionary leader. He served in the Spanish army during the Peninsular War, but after 1812 he devoted himself to the South American struggle for independence, playing a large part in the liberation of Argentina, Chile, and Peru from Spanish rule.

San Pedro Sula main industrial and commercial city in NW Honduras, the second-largest city in the country; population (1989) 300,900. It trades in bananas, coffee, sugar, and timber and manufactures textiles, plastics, furniture, and cement.

San Salvador capital of El Salvador 30 mi/48 km from the Pacific Ocean, at the foot of San Salvador volcano (8,360 ft/2,548 m); population (1984) 453,000. Industries include food processing and textiles. Since its foundation 1525, it has suffered from several earthquakes.

sans-culotte (French "without knee breeches") in the French Revolution, a member of the working classes, who wore trousers, as opposed to the aristocracy and bourgeoisie, who wore knee breeches.

Sanskrit the dominant Classical language of the Indian subcontinent, a member of the Indo-Iranian group of the Indo-European language family, and the sacred language of Hinduism. The oldest form of Sanskrit is *Vedic*, the variety used in the *Vedas* and *Upanishads* (about 1500–700 BC).

Santa Ana periodic warm Californian ◊wind.

Santa Anna Antonio López de 1795–1876. Mexican revolutionary who became general and dictator of Mexico for most of the years between 1824 and 1855. He led the attack on the ◊Alamo fort in Texas 1836.

A leader in achieving Mexican independence from Spain 1821, he led revolts against Emperor Agustin and two presidents, becoming president himself in 1833 and later assuming dictatorial powers. When the people of Texas, then part of Mexico, revolted against the Santa Anna government, he led the forces that captured the ◊Alamo in San Antonio 1836 but was wounded and captured later that year. Released after agreeing to independence for Texas, he returned to Mexico, where he regained political power. Defeated by US forces during the Mexican War 1846–48, Santa Anna was forced into exile, but he seized power again 1853, ruling as a dictator until he was forced from power for the last time 1855. For most of the next 20 years he lived in exile but returned to Mexico shortly before his death.

Santa Barbara oceanside city in S California; population (1990) 85,571. It is the site of a campus of the University of California. The Santa Ynez mountains are to the N. Manufactures include aircraft and aerospace equipment, precision instruments, and electronic components, but the city is better known for its wealthy residents and as a resort. A Spanish presidio and a mission (still in use) were built here in the 1780s, and the first American settler arrived 1816.

Santa Claus the American name, derived from the Dutch, for ◊St Nicholas. He is depicted as a fat, jolly old man with a long white beard, dressed in boots and a red hat and suit trimmed with white fur. He lives with Mrs Claus and his toy-making elves at the North Pole, and on Christmas Eve he travels in an airborne

San Francisco
Powell Street in San Francisco, California.

peace treaty between the Allied nations and Japan 1951. Another earthquake rocked the city 1989.

San Francisco conference conference attended by representatives from 50 nations who had declared war on Germany before March 1945; held in San Francisco, California. The conference drew up the United Nations Charter, which was signed June 26, 1945.

Sanger Frederick 1918– . English biochemist, the winner of two Nobel Prizes for Chemistry: one for his clarifying the structure of insulin, and the other, with two US scientists, for his work on the chemical structure of genes.

Sanger Margaret Higgins 1883–1966. US health reformer and crusader for birth control. In 1914 she founded the National Birth Control League. She founded and presided over the American Birth Control League 1921–28, the organization that later became the Planned Parenthood Federation of America, and the International Planned Parenthood Federation 1952.

San José capital of Costa Rica; population (1989) 284,600. Products include coffee, cocoa, and sugar cane. It was founded 1737 and has been the capital since 1823.

San José city in Santa Clara Valley, California; population (1990) 782,200. It is the center of "Silicon Valley," the site of many high-technology electronic firms turning out semiconductors and other computer components. There are also electrical, aerospace, missile, rubber, metal, and machine industries, and it is a commercial and transportation center for orchard crops and wines produced in the area.

San Juan capital of Puerto Rico; population (1990) 437,750. It is a port and industrial city. Products include chemicals, pharmaceuticals, machine tools, electronic equipment, textiles, plastics, and rum.

San Luis Potosí silver-mining city and capital of San Luis Potosí state, central Mexico; population

San Marino
Republic of
(*Repubblica di San Marino*)

area 24 sq mi/61 sq km
capital San Marino
cities Serravalle (industrial center)

physical on the slope of Mount Titano
features surrounded by Italian territory; one of the world's smallest states
heads of state and government two captains regent, elected for a six-month period
political system direct democracy
political parties San Marino Christian Democrat Party (PDCS), right of center; Democratic Progressive Party (PDP), Socialist Unity Party (PSU), and Socialist Party (PSS), all three left of center
exports wine, ceramics, paint, chemicals, building stone
currency Italian lira
population (1992) 23,600; growth rate 0.1% p.a.
life expectancy men 70, women 77
language Italian
religion Roman Catholic 95%
literacy 97% (1987)

chronology
1862 Treaty with Italy signed; independence recognized under Italy's protection.
1947–86 Governed by a series of left-wing and center-left coalitions.
1986 Formation of Communist and Christian Democrat "grand coalition."
1992 Joined the United Nations.

---

sleigh, drawn by eight reindeer, to deliver presents to good children, who are fast asleep when Santa arrives. The most popular legends claim that Santa lands his sleigh on rooftops, secretly entering homes through the chimney.

Santa Cruz city in W central California at the northern end of Monterey Bay, SW of San Jose; population (1990) 49,000. A division of the University of California is here. Industries include tourism, food processing, fishing, and electronics.

Santa Fe capital of New Mexico, on the Santa Fe River, 40 mi/65 km W of Las Vegas; population (1990) 55,900, many Spanish-speaking. A number of buildings date from the Spanish period, including a palace 1609–10; the cathedral 1869 is on the site of a monastery built 1622. Santa Fe produces American Indian jewelry and textiles; its chief industry is tourism.

Santa Fe Trail US trade route 1821–80 from Independence, Missouri, to Santa Fe, New Mexico.

Santa Maria city in SW California, NW of Santa Barbara; population (1990) 61,284. Industries include oil, food processing, and dairy products.

Santa Rosa city in NW California, N of San Francisco; population (1990) 113,300. Industries include wine, fruit, chemicals, and clothing.

Santayana George 1863–1952. Spanish-born US philosopher and critic. He developed his philosophy based on naturalism and taught that everything has a natural basis.

Santiago capital of Chile; population (1990) 4,385,500. Industries include textiles, chemicals, and food processing. It was founded 1541 and is famous for its broad avenues.

Santo Domingo capital and chief sea port of the Dominican Republic; population (1982) 1,600,000. Founded 1496 by Bartolomeo, brother of Christopher Columbus, it is the oldest colonial city in the Americas. Its cathedral was built 1515–40.

São Paulo city in Brazil, 45 mi/72 km NW of its port Santos; population (1991) 9,700,100, metropolitan area 15,280,000.

It is 3,000 ft/900 m above sea level, and 2°S of the Tropic of Capricorn. It is South America's leading industrial city, producing electronics, steel, and chemicals; it has meatpacking plants and is the center of Brazil's coffee trade. It originated as a Jesuit mission 1554.

São Tomé e Príncipe country in the Gulf of Guinea, off the coast of W Africa. *See panel p. 820*

sap the fluids that circulate through ◊vascular plants, especially woody ones. Sap carries water and food to plant tissues. Sap contains alkaloids, protein, and starch; it can be milky (as in rubber trees), resinous (as in pines), or syrupy (as in maples).

sapphire deep-blue, transparent gem variety of the mineral ◊corundum Al_2O_3, aluminum oxide. Small amounts of iron and titanium give it its color.
  A corundum gem of any color except red (which is a ruby) can be called a sapphire; for example, yellow sapphire.

Sappho *c.* 610–*c.* 580. Greek lyric poet, a native of Lesbos and contemporary of the poet ◊Alcaeus, famed for her female eroticism (hence lesbianism). The surviving fragments of her poems express a keen sense of loss, and delight in the worship of the goddess ◊Aphrodite.

Sapporo capital of ◊Hokkaido prefecture, Japan; population (1990) 1,671,800. Industries include rubber and food processing. It is a winter sports center and was the site of the 1972 Winter Olympics. Giant figures are sculpted in ice at the annual snow festival.

Saracen ancient Greek and Roman term for an Arab, used in the Middle Ages by Europeans for all Muslims. The equivalent term used in Spain was ◊Moor.

Saragossa English spelling of ◊Zaragoza, a city in Spain.

Sarajevo capital of ◊Bosnia-Herzegovina; population (1982) 449,000. Industries include engineering, brewing, chemicals, carpets, and ceramics. From April 1992 until early 1994 the city was the target of a siege by Serb militia units in their fight to carve up the newly independent republic.

São Tomé e Príncipe
Democratic Republic of

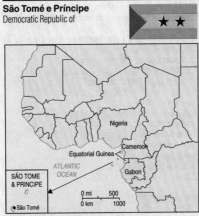

area 386 sq mi/1,000 sq km
capital São Tomé
cities Santo Antonio, Santa Cruz
physical comprises two main islands and several smaller ones, all volcanic; thickly forested and fertile
head of state and government Miguel Trovoada from 1991

political system emergent democratic republic
political parties Movement for the Liberation of São Tomé e Príncipe (MLSTP), nationalist socialist; Democratic Convergence Party–Reflection Group (PCD–EM), center-left
exports cocoa, copra, coffee, palm oil and kernels
currency dobra
population (1992) 126,000; growth rate 2.5% p.a.
life expectancy men 62, women 62
languages Portuguese (official), Fang (Bantu)
religions Roman Catholic 80%, animist
literacy men 73%, women 42% (1981)
GNP $32 million (1987); $384 per head (1986)

chronology
1471 Discovered by Portuguese.
1522–1973 A province of Portugal.
1973 Achieved internal self-government.
1975 Independence achieved from Portugal, with Manuel Pinto da Costa as president.
1984 Formally declared a nonaligned state.
1987 Constitution amended.
1988 Unsuccessful coup attempt against da Costa.
1990 New constitution approved.
1991 First multiparty elections held; Miguel Trovoada replaced Pinto da Costa.

Sarasota city in SW Florida, on the Gulf of Mexico, S of Tampa; population (1990) 51,000. It is a resort town specializing in food processing and electronics research. It is the winter home of Ringling Brothers and Barnum and Bailey Circus.

Saratoga Springs city and spa in New York State; population (1990) 25,000. In 1777 the British general John Burgoyne was defeated in two engagements nearby during the Revolutionary War.

Horse racing is popular during the summer.

Saratov Industrial port (chemicals, oil refining) on the river Volga in W central Russia; population (1987) 918,000. It was established in the 1590s as a fortress to protect the Volga trade route.

Sarawak state of Malaysia, on the NW corner of the island of Borneo
area 48,018 sq mi/124,400 sq km
capital Kuching
physical mountainous; the rain forest, which may be 10 million years old, contains several thousand tree species. A third of all its plant species are endemic to Borneo. Some 30% of the forest was cut down 1963–89; timber is expected to run out 1995–2001
products timber, oil, rice, pepper, rubber, and coconuts
population (1991) 1,669,000; 24 ethnic groups make up almost half this number

Saskatchewan

history Sarawak was granted by the Sultan of Brunei to English soldier James Brooke 1841, who became "Rajah of Sarawak."

It was a British protectorate from 1888 until captured by the Japanese in World War II. It was a crown colony 1946–63, when it became part of Malaysia.

sarcoma malignant ◊tumor arising from the fat, muscles, bones, cartilage, or blood and lymph vessels and connective tissues. Sarcomas are much less common than ◊carcinomas.

sardine common name for various small fishes (pilchards) in the herring family.

Sardinia (Italian *Sardegna*) mountainous island, special autonomous region of Italy; area 9,303 sq mi/24,100 sq km; population (1990) 1,664,400. Its capital is Cagliari, and it exports cork and petrochemicals. It is the second-largest Mediterranean island and includes Costa Smeralda (Emerald Coast) tourist area in the NE and *nuraghi* (fortified Bronze Age dwellings). After centuries of foreign rule, it became linked 1720 with Piedmont, and this dual kingdom became the basis of a united Italy 1861.

Sargasso Sea part of the N Atlantic (between 40° and 80°W and 25° and 30°N) left static by circling ocean currents, and covered with floating weed *Sargassum natans*.

Sargent John Singer 1856–1925. US portrait painter. Born in Florence of American parents, he studied there and in Paris, then settled in London around 1885. He was a fashionable and prolific painter.

Sargon two Mesopotamian kings:

Sargon I king of Akkad *c.* 2334–2279 BC, and founder of the first Mesopotamian empire. Like Moses, he was said to have been found floating in a cradle on the local river, in his case the Euphrates.

Sargon II died 705 BC. King of Assyria from 722 BC, who assumed the name of his predecessor. To keep conquered peoples from rising against him, he had whole populations moved from their homelands, including the Israelites from Samaria.

Sark one of the ◊Channel Islands, 6 mi/10 km E of Guernsey; area 2 sq mi/5 sq km; there is no town or village. It is divided into Great and Little Sark, linked by an isthmus, and is of great natural beauty. The Seigneurie of Sark was established by Elizabeth I, the ruler being known as Seigneur/Dame, and has its own parliament, the Chief Pleas. There is no income tax, and automobiles are forbidden; immigration is controlled.

Sarnoff David 1891–1971. Russian-born US broadcasting pioneer. Sarnoff immigrated with his family to New York 1900. After studying electrical engineering at the Pratt Institute, he was hired by the Marconi Wireless Co 1906. At first a telegraph operator, Sarnoff rose to become commercial manager of the company when it was taken over by the Radio Corporation of America (RCA) 1919. He was named general manager of RCA 1921 and founded the first radio network, the National Broadcasting Co (NBC), as a broadcast subsidiary 1926. Named RCA president 1930 and board chairman 1947, Sarnoff was an early promoter of television broadcasting during the 1940s and the first to manufacture color sets and to transmit color programs in the 1950s.

sarsaparilla drink prepared from the long twisted roots of several plants in the genus *Smilax* (family Liliaceae), native to Central and South America; it is used as a tonic.

Sartre Jean-Paul 1905–1980. French author and philosopher, a leading proponent of ◊existentialism. He published his first novel, *La Nausée/Nausea*, 1937, followed by the trilogy *Les Chemins de la Liberté/Roads to Freedom* 1944–45 and many plays, including *Huis Clos/In Camera* 1944. *L'Etre et le néant/Being and Nothingness* 1943, his first major philosophical work, sets out a radical doctrine of human freedom. In the later work *Critique de la raison dialectique/Critique of Dialectical Reason* 1960 he tried to produce a fusion of existentialism and Marxism.

Saskatchewan (Cree *Kis-is-ska-tche-wan* "swift flowing") province of W Canada
area 251,788 sq mi/652,300 sq km
capital Regina
cities Saskatoon, Moose Jaw, Prince Albert
physical prairies in the S; to the N, forests, lakes, and subarctic tundra; Prince Albert National Park
products more than 60% of Canada's wheat; oil, natural gas, uranium, zinc, potash (world's largest reserves), copper, helium (the only western reserves outside the US)
population (1991) 995,300
history once inhabited by Indians speaking Athabaskan, Algonquin, and Sioux languages, who depended on caribou and moose in the N and buffalo in the S. French trading posts established about 1750; owned by Hudson's Bay Company, first permanent settlement 1774; ceded to Canadian government 1870 as part of Northwest Territories; became a province 1905.

Saskatoon largest city in Saskatchewan; population (1986) 177,641. Industries include cement, oil refining, chemicals, metal goods, and processed food. The University of Saskatchewan is here. Saskatoon was settled 1882.

Sassanian Empire Persian empire founded AD 224 by Ardashir, a chieftain in the area of what is now Fars, in Iran, who had taken over ◊Parthia; it was named after his grandfather, Sasan. The capital was Ctesiphon, near modern ◊Baghdad, Iraq. After a rapid period of expansion, when it contested supremacy with Rome, it was destroyed in 637 by Muslim Arabs at the Battle of ◊Qadisiya.

satellite any small body that orbits a larger one, either natural or artificial. Natural satellites that orbit planets are called moons. The first *artificial satellite*, *Sputnik 1*, was launched into orbit around the Earth by the USSR 1957. Artificial satellites are used for scientific purposes, communications, weather forecasting, and military applications. The largest artificial satellites can be seen by the naked eye.

satire poem or piece of prose that uses wit, humor, or irony, often through ◊allegory or extended metaphor, to ridicule human pretensions or expose social evils. Satire is related to *parody* in its intention to mock, but satire tends to be more subtle and to mock an attitude

largest natural planetary satellites

planet	satellite	diameter in mi	mean distance from center of primary	orbital period in min days	reciprocal mass (planet = 1)
Jupiter	Ganymede	3,300	664,898	7.16	12,800
Saturn	Titan	3,200	759,227	15.95	4,200
Jupiter	Callisto	3,000	1,170,096	16.69	17,700
Jupiter	Io	2,240	261,982	1.77	21,400
Earth	Moon	2,160	238,866	27.32	81.3
Jupiter	Europa	1,900	416,897	3.55	39,700
Neptune	Triton	1,690	220,162	5.88	770

Saturn *A color-enhanced image of Saturn from the space probe* Voyager 1 *1980, at a range of 21 million mi/34 million km.*

or a belief, whereas parody tends to mock a particular work (such as a poem) by imitating its style, often with purely comic intent.

saturated fatty acid ◊fatty acid in which there are no double bonds in the hydrocarbon chain.

Saturn in astronomy, the second-largest planet in the Solar System, sixth from the Sun, and encircled by bright and easily visible equatorial rings. Viewed through a telescope it is ochre. Saturn orbits the Sun every 29.46 years at an average distance of 886,700,000 mi/1,427,000,000 km. Its equatorial diameter is 75,000 mi/120,000 km, but its polar diameter is 7,450 mi/12,000 km smaller, a result of its fast rotation and low density, the lowest of any planet.

Saturn in Roman mythology, the god of agriculture, whose period of rule was the ancient Golden Age; he was later identified with the Greek god Kronos. Saturn was dethroned by his sons Jupiter, Neptune, and Dis. At his festival, the Saturnalia in Dec, gifts were exchanged, and slaves were briefly treated as their masters' equals.

Saturn rocket family of large US rockets, developed by Wernher von Braun (1912–1977) for the ◊Apollo project. The two-stage Saturn IB was used for launching Apollo spacecraft into orbit around the Earth. The three-stage Saturn V sent Apollo spacecraft to the Moon, and launched the ◊*Skylab* space station. The lift-off thrust of a Saturn V was 3,850 tons. After Apollo and *Skylab*, the Saturn rockets were retired in favor of the ◊Space Shuttle.

satyr in Greek mythology, a lustful, drunken woodland creature characterized by pointed ears, two horns on the forehead, and a tail. Satyrs attended the god of wine, ◊Dionysus. Roman writers confused satyrs with goat-footed fauns.

Saudi Arabia country on the Arabian peninsula, stretching from the Red Sea in the W to the Arabian Gulf in the E, bounded N by Jordan, Iraq, and Kuwait; E by Qatar and United Arab Emirates; SE by Oman; and S by Yemen.

Saul in the Old Testament, the first king of Israel. He was anointed by Samuel and warred successfully against the neighboring Ammonites and Philistines, but fell from God's favor in his battle against the Amalekites. He became jealous and suspicious of David and turned against him and Samuel. After being wounded in battle with the Philistines, in which his three sons died, he committed suicide.

Sault Ste Marie twin industrial ports on the Canadian/US border, one in Ontario and one in Michigan; population (1981) 82,902 and (1990) 14,700, respectively. They stand at the falls (French *sault*) in St Mary's River, which links Lakes Superior and Huron. The falls are by passed by canals. Industries include steel, pulp, and agricultural trade.

sauna bath causing perspiration by means of dry heat. It consists of a small room in which the temperature is raised to about 200°F/90°C. The bather typically stays in it for only a few minutes and then follows it with a cold shower or swim. Saunas are popular in health clubs and sports centers.

savanna or *savannah* extensive open tropical grasslands, with scattered trees and shrubs. Savannas cover large areas of Africa, North and South America, and N Australia.

Savannah city and port of Georgia, 18 mi/29 km from the mouth of the Savannah River; population (1990) 137,600. Founded 1733, Savannah was the first city in the US to be laid out in geometrically regular blocks.

Savimbi Jonas 1934– . Angolan soldier and right-wing revolutionary, founder and leader of the National Union for the Total Independence of Angola (UNITA). From 1975 UNITA under Savimbi's leadership tried to overthrow the government. An agreement between the two parties was reached May 1991, but fighting broke out again following elections Sept 1992.

savings the amount of current income that is not spent on consumption. Distinct from ◊investments, which are considered expenditures for the production of goods for future consumption, savings usually takes the form of bank time deposits. The savings rate depends on many factors, such as interest rates, inflation rates, unemployment rates, and expectations for future earnings.

savings and loan association (*S&L*) a cooperative, mutual, savings organization that sells stock to its members. Created primarily to finance home mortgages, S&Ls at one time provided 40% of the funds for home purchases. From 1986, an industry-wide crisis developed when, in some parts of the US, declining real estate values and rising unemployment reduced the value of investments and the ability of borrowers to repay loans. For the first time, mergers were permitted across state lines in hopes that the healthier institutions could assume the debt of the weaker, but losses mounted. The Federal Home Loan Board (FHLB) and the Federal Savings and Loan Insurance Corporation (FSLIC) were unable to reverse the tide or cover the losses. By 1989 the losses were enormous, and a federal bailout pledging more than $100 billion in taxpayer funds was negotiated.

Savonarola Girolamo 1452–1498. Italian reformer, a Dominican friar and an eloquent preacher. His crusade against political and religious corruption won him popular support, and in 1494 he led a revolt in Florence that expelled the ruling Medici family and established a democratic republic. His denunciations of Pope ◊Alexander VI led to his excommunication in 1497, and in 1498 he was arrested, tortured, hanged, and burned for heresy.

Savoy area of France between the Alps, Lake Geneva, and the river Rhône. A medieval duchy, it was made into the *départements* of Savoie and Haute-Savoie, in the Rhône-Alpes region.

Saxe-Coburg-Gotha Saxon duchy. Albert, the Prince Consort of Britain's Queen Victoria, was a son of the 1st Duke, Ernest I (1784–1844), who was succeeded by Albert's elder brother, Ernest II (1818–1893). It remained the name of the British royal house until 1917, when it was changed to Windsor.

saxhorn family of brass musical instruments played with valves, invented by the Belgian Adolphe Sax (1814–1894) in 1845.

Saxon member of a Teutonic people who invaded Britain in the early Middle Ages; see ◊Anglo-Saxon.

Saxony (German *Sachsen*) administrative *Land* (state) of Germany
area 6,580 sq mi/17,036 sq km
capital Dresden
cities Leipzig, Chemnitz, Zwickau
physical on the plain of the river Elbe north of the Erzgebirge mountain range
products electronics, textiles, vehicles, machinery, chemicals, coal
population (1990) 5,000,000
history conquered by Charlemagne 792, Saxony became a powerful medieval German duchy. The electors of Saxony were also kings of Poland 1697–1763. Saxony was part of East Germany 1946–90, forming a region with Anhalt.

Saxony-Anhalt administrative *Land* (state) of Germany
area 10,000 sq mi/20,450 sq km
capital Magdeburg
cities Halle, Dessau
products chemicals, electronics, rolling stock, footwear, cereals, vegetables
population (1990) 3,000,000
history Anhalt became a duchy 1863 and a member of the North German Confederation 1866. Between 1946 and 1990 it was joined to the former Prussian province of Saxony as a region of East Germany.

Saudi Arabia
Kingdom of
(*al-Mamlaka al-'Arabiya as-Sa'udiya*)

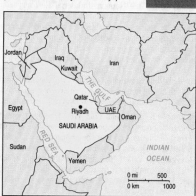

area 849,400 sq mi/2,200,518 sq km
capital Riyadh
cities Mecca, Medina, Taif; ports Jidda, Dammam
physical desert, sloping to the Persian Gulf from a height of 9,000 ft/2,750 m in the W
environment oil pollution caused by the Gulf War 1990–91 has affected 285 mi/460 km of the Saudi coastline, threatening desalination plants and damaging the wildlife of saltmarshes, mangrove forest, and mudflats
features Nafud Desert in N and the Rub'al Khali (Empty Quarter) in S, area 250,000 sq mi/650,000 sq km; with a ban on women drivers, there are an estimated 300,000 chauffeurs
head of state and government King Fahd Ibn Abdul Aziz from 1982

political system absolute monarchy
political parties none
exports oil, petroleum products
currency rial
population (1992) 15,267,000 (16% nomadic); growth rate 3.1% p.a.
life expectancy men 64, women 67 (1989)
language Arabic
religion Sunni Muslim; there is a Shiite minority
literacy men 34%, women 12% (1980 est)
GNP $70 bn (1988); $6,170 per head (1988)

chronology
1926–32 Territories of Nejd and Hejaz united and kingdom established.
1953 King Ibn Saud died and was succeeded by his eldest son, Saud.
1964 King Saud forced to abdicate; succeeded by his brother, Faisal.
1975 King Faisal assassinated; succeeded by his half brother, Khalid.
1982 King Khalid died; succeeded by his brother, Crown Prince Fahd.
1987 Rioting by Iranian pilgrims caused 400 deaths in Mecca; diplomatic relations with Iran severed.
1990 Iraqi troops invaded and annexed Kuwait and massed on Saudi Arabian border. King Fahd called for help from US and UK forces.
1991 King Fahd provided military and financial assistance in Gulf War. Calls from religious leaders for "consultative assembly" to assist in government of kingdom. Saudi Arabia attended Middle East peace conference.
1992 Formation of a "consultative council" seen as possible move toward representative government.

saxophone large family of wind instruments combining woodwind and brass features, the single reed of the clarinet and the wide bore of the bugle. Patented in 1846 by Adolphe Sax (1814–1894), a Belgian instrument maker, the saxophone is a lively and versatile instrument that has played a prominent part in the history of jazz. Four of the original eight sizes remain in common use: soprano, alto, tenor, and baritone. The soprano is usually straight, the others curved back at the mouthpiece end, and with an upturned bell.

Sayers Dorothy L(eigh) 1893–1957. English writer of crime novels featuring detective Lord Peter Wimsey and heroine Harriet Vane, including *Strong Poison* 1930, *The Nine Tailors* 1934, and *Gaudy Night* 1935. She also wrote religious plays for radio, and translations of Dante.

scabies contagious infection of the skin caused by the parasitic itch mite *Sarcoptes scaboi*, which burrows under the skin to deposit eggs. Treatment is by antiparasitic creams and lotions.

scalawag or *scallywag* in US history, a derogatory term for white Southerners who, during and after the Civil War of 1861–65, supported the Republican Party, and black emancipation and enfranchisement.

The reforms instituted by the scalawags were widely resented in the South, and their influence diminished with the rise of the Democratic party in the South.

scale in music, a sequence of pitches that establishes a key, and in some respects the character of a composition. A scale is defined by its starting note and may be *major* or *minor* depending on the order of intervals. A *chromatic* scale is the full range of 12 notes: it has no key because there is no fixed starting point.

Scalia Antonin 1936– . US jurist and associate justice of the US Supreme Court 1986– . He concurred with the majority in *Texas* v *Johnson* 1989, that ruled constitutional the burning of the US flag in protest. He dissented in *Edwards* v *Aguillard* 1987 when the Court ruled that states may not mandate the teaching of the theory of creationism to counteract the teaching of the theory of evolution.

scallop any marine bivalve ◊mollusk of the family Pectinidae, with a fan-shaped shell. There are two "ears" extending from the socketlike hinge. Scallops use water-jet propulsion to move through the water to escape predators such as starfish. The giant Pacific scallop found from Alaska to California can reach 8 in/20 cm width.

scaly anteater another name for the pangolin.

Scandinavia peninsula in NW Europe, comprising Norway and Sweden; politically and culturally it also includes Denmark, Iceland, the Faroe Islands, and Finland.

Scandinavian inhabitant of or native to Scandinavia (Denmark, Norway, Sweden, Iceland, and, often, Finland); also referring to the languages and cultures. The Scandinavian languages, including Faroese, belong to the Indo-European family.

scanning in medicine, the noninvasive examination of body organs to detect abnormalities of structure or function. Detectable waves—for example, ◊ultrasound, magnetic, or ◊X-rays—are passed through the part to be scanned. Their absorption pattern is recorded, analyzed by computer, and displayed pictorially on a screen.

scapula or *shoulder blade* large bone forming part of the pectoral girdle, assisting in the articulation of the arm with the chest region. Its flattened shape allows a large region for the attachment of muscles.

scarab any of a family Scarabaeidae of beetles, often brilliantly colored, and including cockchafers, June beetles, and dung beetles. The *Scarabeus sacer* was revered by the ancient Egyptians as the symbol of resurrection.

Scarlatti (Pietro) Alessandro (Gaspare) 1660–1725. Italian Baroque composer, Master of the Chapel at the court of Naples, who developed the opera form. He composed more than 100 operas, including *Tigrane* 1715, as well as church music and oratorios.

scarlet fever or *scarlatina* acute infectious disease, especially of children, caused by the bacterium *Streptococcus pyogenes*. It is marked by a sore throat and a bright red rash spreading from the upper to the lower part of the body. The rash is followed by the skin peeling in flakes. It is treated with antibiotics.

scatter diagram or *scattergram* a diagram whose purpose is to establish whether or not a relationship or ◊correlation exists between two variables; for example, between life expectancy and GNP (gross national product). Each observation is marked with a dot in a position that shows the value of both variables. The pattern of dots is then examined to see whether they show any underlying trend by means of a *line of best fit* (a straight line drawn so that its distance from the various points is as short as possible).

scent gland gland that opens onto the outer surface of animals, producing odorous compounds that are used for communicating between members of the same species (pheromones), or for discouraging predators.

Schechter v US a US Supreme Court decision 1935 dealing with the constitutionality of New Deal legislation over labor standards and trade practices. Found guilty under the National Industrial Recovery Act 1933 of violating minimum-wage and maximum-hours regulations, Schechter, a New York poultry dealer, appealed his case to the US Supreme Court. He argued that since he was a local dealer operating an exclusively intrastate trade, the case was outside federal jurisdiction. The Court found that Schechter's trade had no direct effect on interstate commerce and was therefore not subject to Congressional regulation. This was a serious blow to New Deal recovery policies.

Scheele Karl Wilhelm 1742–1786. Swedish chemist and pharmacist. In the book *Experiments on Air and Fire* 1777, he argued that the atmosphere was composed of two gases. One, which supported combustion (oxygen), he called "fire air," and the other, which inhibited combustion (nitrogen), he called "vitiated air." He thus anticipated Joseph ◊Priestley's discovery of oxygen by two years.

Scheherazade the storyteller in the ◊Arabian Nights.

Schenck v US a US Supreme Court decision 1919 dealing with Congress's power to revoke First-Amendment rights. Schenck, an outspoken antidraft activist, was convicted of providing aid and comfort to the enemy, in violation of the Espionage Act 1917. The Court unanimously upheld his conviction, ruling that Congress was obligated to interfere with the freedom of speech when it presented a "clear and present danger" to the well-being of the society.

Schenectady industrial city on the Mohawk River, New York State; population (1990) 65,600. It dates from 1662 and has long been a producer of electrical goods.

Schiller Johann Christoph Friedrich von 1759–1805. German dramatist, poet, and historian. He wrote *Sturm und Drang* ("storm and stress") verse and plays, including the dramatic trilogy *Wallenstein* 1798–99. Much of his work concerns the aspirations for political freedom and the avoidance of mediocrity.

schism formal split over a doctrinal difference between religious believers, as in the ◊Great Schism in the Roman Catholic church; over the doctrine of papal infallibility, as with the Old Catholics in 1879; and over the use of the Latin Tridentine mass 1988.

schist ◊metamorphic rock containing ◊mica or another platy or elongate mineral, whose crystals are aligned to give a foliation (planar texture) known as schistosity. Schist may contain additional minerals such as ◊garnet.

schizophrenia mental disorder, a psychosis of unknown origin, which can lead to profound changes in personality and behavior including paranoia and hallucinations. Contrary to popular belief, it does not involve a split personality. Modern treatment approaches include drugs, family therapy, stress reduction, and rehabilitation.

Schlesinger Arthur Meier, Jr 1917– . US historian. His first book, *The Age of Jackson*, won a Pulitzer Prize 1945. Becoming active in Democratic politics, he served as a speechwriter in the presidential campaigns of Adlai Stevenson 1956 and John Kennedy 1960.

Schleswig-Holstein *Land* (state) of Germany
area 6,060 sq mi/15,700 sq km
capital Kiel
cities Lübeck, Flensburg, Schleswig
features river Elbe, Kiel Canal, Heligoland
products shipbuilding, mechanical and electrical engineering, food processing
population (1988) 2,613,000
religions 87% Protestant; 6% Catholic
history Schleswig (Danish *Slesvig*) and Holstein were two duchies held by the kings of Denmark from 1460, but were not part of the kingdom; a number of the inhabitants were German, and Holstein was a member of the Confederation of the Rhine formed 1815. Possession of the duchies had long been disputed by Prussia, and when Frederick VII of Denmark died without an heir 1863, Prussia, supported by Austria, fought and defeated the Danes 1864, and in 1866 annexed the two duchies. A plebiscite held 1920 gave the northern part of Schleswig to Denmark, which made it the province of Haderslev and Aabenraa; the rest, with Holstein, remained part of Germany.

Schliemann Heinrich 1822–1890. German archeologist. He earned a fortune in business, retiring in 1863 to pursue his lifelong ambition to discover a historical basis for Homer's *Iliad*. In 1871 he began excavating at Hissarlik, Turkey, a site which yielded the ruins of nine consecutive cities and was indeed the site of Troy. His later excavations were at Mycenae 1874–76, where he discovered the ruins of the ◊Mycenaean civilization.

Schlüter Poul Holmskov 1929– . Danish right-wing politician, leader of the Conservative People's Party (KF) from 1974 and prime minister 1982–93. Having joined the KF in his youth, he trained as a lawyer and then entered the Danish parliament (Folketing) in 1964. His center-right coalition survived the 1990 election and was reconstituted, with Liberal support. In Jan 1993 Schlüter resigned, accused of dishonesty regarding his role in an incident involving Tamil

refugees. He was succeeded by Poul Nyrup Rasmussen.

Schmidt Helmut 1918– . German socialist politician, member of the Social Democratic Party (SPD), chancellor of West Germany 1974–83. As chancellor, Schmidt introduced social reforms and continued Brandt's policy of Ostpolitik. With the French president Giscard d'Estaing, he instigated annual world and European economic summits. He was a firm supporter of ◊NATO and of the deployment of US nuclear missiles in West Germany during the early 1980s.

Schoenberg Arnold (Franz Walter) 1874–1951. Austro-Hungarian composer, a US citizen from 1941. After Romantic early works such as *Verklärte Nacht/Transfigured Night* 1899 and the *Gurrelieder/Songs of Gurra* 1900–11, he experimented with ◊atonality (absence of key), producing works such as *Pierrot Lunaire* 1912 for chamber ensemble and voice, before developing the 12-tone system of musical composition. This was further developed by his pupils Alban ◊Berg and Anton Webern.

scholasticism the theological and philosophical systems that were studied in both Christian and Judaic schools in Europe in the medieval period. Scholasticism sought to integrate biblical teaching with Platonic and Aristotelian philosophy.

School District of Abington Township v Schempp a US Supreme Court decision 1963 dealing with mandatory religious worship in public schools. The case challenged the constitutionality of an Abington, Pennsylvania, statute that forced students to recite Bible verses and the Lord's Prayer in school. The Court ruled that such practice violated First-Amendment measures against establishing an official religion. Since the statute had no secular legislative purpose, it was declared invalid.

Schopenhauer Arthur 1788–1860. German philosopher whose *The World as Will and Idea* 1818 expounded an atheistic and pessimistic world view: an irrational will is considered as the inner principle of the world, producing an ever-frustrated cycle of desire, of which the only escape is esthetic contemplation or absorption into nothingness.

Schrödinger Erwin 1887–1961. Austrian physicist who advanced the study of wave mechanics (see ◊quantum theory). Born in Vienna, he became senior professor at the Dublin Institute for Advanced Studies 1940. He shared (with Paul Dirac) a Nobel Prize 1933.

Schubert Franz (Peter) 1797–1828. Austrian composer. His ten symphonies include the incomplete eighth in B minor (the "Unfinished") and the "Great" in C major. He wrote chamber and piano music, including the "Trout Quintet," and over 600 lieder (songs) combining the Romantic expression of emotion with pure melody. They include the cycles *Die schöne Müllerin/The Beautiful Maid of the Mill* 1823 and *Die Winterreise/The Winter Journey* 1827.

Schulz Charles Monroe 1922– . US cartoonist. His idea for the "Peanuts" cartoon strip was accepted by United Features Syndicate 1950. As the characters Snoopy, Charlie Brown, Lucy, and Linus became famous throughout the country, Schulz further promoted them through merchandise lines and television specials. In 1967 a musical based on the "Peanuts" characters, *You're a Good Man, Charlie Brown*, played on Broadway.

Schuman Robert 1886–1963. French politician. He was prime minister 1947–48, and as foreign minister

1948–53 he proposed in May 1950 a common market for coal and steel (the **Schuman Plan**), which was established as the European Coal and Steel Community 1952, the basis of the European Community.

Schumann Robert Alexander 1810–1856. German Romantic composer. His songs and short piano pieces show simplicity combined with an ability to portray mood and emotion. Among his compositions are four symphonies, a violin concerto, a piano concerto, sonatas, and song cycles, such as *Dichterliebe/Poet's Love* 1840. Mendelssohn championed many of his works.

Schurz Carl 1829–1906. German-born US editor and political leader. He held office in the US Senate 1869–75 and served as secretary of the interior under President Hayes 1877–81. He was editor of the *New York Evening Post* 1881–83.

A harsh critic of government corruption, he was president of the National Civil Service Reform League 1892–1901.

Schuyler Philip John 1733–1804. American public official. A member of the Continental Congress 1775–77, he was named general in command of the Department of New York at the outbreak of the American Revolution 1775. Replaced in 1777, he returned to the Continental Congress 1778–81. A supporter of the US Constitution, Schuyler became one of New York's first US senators 1789–91 and later served 1797–98.

Schwarzenegger Arnold 1947– . Austrian-born US film actor, one of the biggest box-office attractions of the late 1980s and early 1990s. He starred in sword-and-sorcery films such as *Conan the Barbarian* 1982 and later graduated to large-budget action movies such as *Terminator* 1984, *Predator* 1987, and *Terminator II* 1991.

Schwarzkopf (H) Norman (nicknamed "Stormin' Norman") 1934– . US general who was supreme commander of the Allied forces in the ◊Gulf War 1991. He planned and executed a blitzkrieg campaign, "Desert Storm," sustaining remarkably few casualties in the liberation of Kuwait. He was a battalion commander in the Vietnam War and deputy commander of the 1983 US invasion of Grenada.

Schweitzer Albert 1875–1965. French Protestant theologian, organist, and missionary surgeon. He founded the hospital at Lambaréné in Gabon in 1913, giving organ recitals to support his work there. He wrote a life of Bach and *Von reimarus zu Wrede/The Quest for the Historical Jesus* 1906 and was awarded the Nobel Peace Prize 1952 for his teaching of "reverence for life."

Schwinger Julian 1918– . US quantum physicist. His research concerned the behavior of charged particles in electrical fields. This work, expressed entirely through mathematics, combines elements from quantum theory and relativity theory. Schwinger shared

the Nobel Prize for Physics 1963 with Richard ◊Feynman and Sin-Itiro Tomonaga (1906–1979).

sciatica persistent pain in the leg, along the sciatic nerve and its branches. Causes of sciatica include inflammation of the nerve or pressure on, or inflammation of, a nerve root leading out of the lower spine.

science (Latin *scientia* "knowledge") any systematic field of study or body of knowledge that aims, through experiment, observation, and deduction, to produce reliable explanation of phenomena, with reference to the material and physical world.

science fiction or *speculative fiction* (also known as *SF* or *sci-fi*) genre of fiction and film with an imaginary scientific, technological, or futuristic basis. It is sometimes held to have its roots in the works of Mary Shelley, notably *Frankenstein* 1818. Often taking its ideas and concerns from current ideas in science and the social sciences, science fiction aims to shake up standard perceptions of reality.

Scientology "applied religious philosophy" based on dianetics, founded in California in 1954 by L Ron ◊Hubbard as the *Church of Scientology*. It claims to "increase man's spiritual awareness," but its methods of recruiting and retaining converts have been criticized.

Scilly, Isles of or *Scilly Isles/Islands*, or *Scillies* group of 140 islands and islets lying 25 mi/40 km SW of Land's End, England; administered by the Duchy of Cornwall; area 6.3 sq mi/16 sq km; population (1981) 1,850. The five inhabited islands are *St Mary's*, the largest, on which is Hugh Town, capital of the Scillies; *Tresco*, the second largest, with subtropical gardens; *St Martin's*, noted for beautiful shells; *St Agnes*, and *Bryher*.

Scipio Africanus Major 237–c. 183 BC. Roman general. He defeated the Carthaginians in Spain 210–206, invaded Africa 204, and defeated Hannibal at Zama 202.

Scipio Africanus Minor c. 185–129 BC. Roman general, the adopted grandson of Scipio Africanus Major, also known as *Scipio Aemilianus*. He destroyed Carthage 146, and subdued Spain 133. He was opposed to his brothers-in-law, the Gracchi (see ◊Gracchus).

scoliosis lateral curvature of the spine. Correction by operations to insert bone grafts (thus creating a straight but rigid spine) has been replaced by insertion of an electronic stimulative device in the lower back to contract the muscles adequately.

scorched earth in warfare, the policy of burning and destroying everything that might be of use to an invading army, especially the crops in the fields. It was used to great effect in Russia in 1812 against the invasion of the French emperor Napoleon and again during World War II to hinder the advance of German forces in 1941.

scorpion any arachnid of the order Scorpiones. Common in the tropics and subtropics, scorpions have large pincers and long tails ending in upcurved poisonous stings, though the venom is not usually fatal to a healthy adult human. Some species reach 10 in/25 cm. They produce live young rather than eggs, and hunt chiefly by night.

Scorpius zodiacal constellation in the southern hemisphere between Libra and Sagittarius, represented as a scorpion. The Sun passes briefly through Scorpius in the last week of Nov. The heart of the scor-

scorpion The scorpion belongs to an ancient group of animals.

pion is marked by the red supergiant star Antares. Scorpius contains rich Milky Way star fields, plus the strongest ◊X-ray source in the sky, Scorpius X-1. In astrology, the dates for Scorpius are between about Oct 24 and Nov 21.

Scorsese Martin 1942– . US director, screenwriter, and producer whose films concentrate on complex characterization and the themes of alienation and guilt. Drawing from his Italian-American Catholic background, his work often deals with sin and redemption, such as in his first major film, *Boxcar Bertha* 1972. His influential, passionate, and forceful movies includes *Mean Streets* 1973, *Taxi Driver* 1976, *Raging Bull* 1980, *The Last Temptation of Christ* 1988, *GoodFellas* 1990, and *Cape Fear* 1991.

Scotland the northernmost part of Britain, formerly an independent country, now part of the UK
area 30,297 sq mi/78,470 sq km
capital Edinburgh
cities Glasgow, Dundee, Aberdeen
features the Highlands in the N (with the ◊Grampian Mountains); central Lowlands, including valleys of the Clyde and Forth, with most of the country's population and industries; Southern Uplands (including the Lammermuir Hills); and islands of the Orkneys, Shetlands, and Western Isles; the world's greatest concentration of nuclear weapons are at the UK and US bases on the Clyde, near Glasgow; 8,000-year-old pinewood forests once covered 3,706,500 acres/1,500,000 hectares, now reduced to 30,900 acres/12,500 hectares
industry electronics, marine and aircraft engines, oil, natural gas, chemicals, textiles, clothing, printing, paper, food processing, tourism
currency pound sterling
population (1988 est) 5,094,000
languages English; Scots, a lowland dialect (derived from Northumbrian Anglo-Saxon); Gaelic spoken by 1.3%, mainly in the Highlands
religions Presbyterian (Church of Scotland), Roman Catholic
famous people Robert Bruce, Walter Scott, Robert Burns, Robert Louis Stevenson, Adam Smith
government Scotland sends 72 members to the UK Parliament at Westminster. Local government is on similar lines to that of England, but there is a differing legal system (see ◊Scots law). There is a movement for an independent or devolved Scottish assembly.

Scotland: history for early history, see also ◊Britain, ancient; ◊Celt; ◊Pict.

Scots language the form of the English language as traditionally spoken and written in Scotland, regarded by some scholars as a distinct language. Scots derives from the Northumbrian dialect of Anglo-Saxon or Old English, and has been a literary language since the 14th century.

Scott Ridley 1939– . English director and producer of some of the most visually spectacular and influential films of the 1980s and 1990s, such as *Alien* 1979, *Blade Runner* 1982, and *1492–The Search for Paradise* 1992. Criticized for sacrificing storyline and character development in favor of ornate sets, Scott replied with *Thelma and Louise* 1991, a carefully wrought story of female bonding and adventure.

Scott Robert Falcon (known as *Scott of the Antarctic*) 1868–1912. English explorer who commanded two Antarctic expeditions, 1901–04 and 1910–12. On Jan 18, 1912, he reached the South Pole, shortly after Norwegian Roald ◊Amundsen, but on the return journey he and his companions died in a bliz-

Scotland: history

1st millenium BC	Picts reached Scotland from mainland Europe.
6th century	St Columba founded a monastery on Iona and began conversion of Picts to Christianity.
***c.* 843**	Unification of Picts, Scots, Britons, and Angles under Kenneth I MacAlpine.
1018	At Battle of Carham, Malcolm II defeated Northumbrian army, bringing Lothian under Scottish rule.
1263	Battle of Largs: defeat of Scots by Norwegian king Haakon.
1296	Edward I of England invaded and declared himself King of Scotland.
1297	William Wallace and Andrew Moray defeated English at Battle of Stirling Bridge.
1314	Robert Bruce defeated English under Edward II at Battle of Bannockburn.
1328	Scottish independence under Robert Bruce recognized by England.
1371	Robert II, first Stuart king, crowned.
1513	Scots defeated by English and King James IV killed at Battle of Flodden.
1559	John Knox returned permanently to Scotland to participate in shift of Scottish church to Protestantism.
1567	Mary, Queen of Scots, forced to abdicate and the following year fled to England.
1603	Crowns of England and Scotland united under James VI who became James I of England.
1638	National Covenant condemned Charles I's changes in church ritual; Scottish rebellion.
1643	Solemn League and Covenant: Scottish Covenanters ally with English Parliament against Charles I.
1651	Cromwell invaded Scotland and defeated Scots at Dunbar and Inverkeithing.
1689	At Killiecrankie, Jacobite forces under Graham of Claverhouse, Viscount Dundee, defeated William of Orange's army but Dundee mortally wounded.
1692	Massacre of Glencoe: William of Orange ordered MacDonalds of Glencoe murdered in their sleep.
1707	Act of Union united Scottish and English parliaments.
1715	The *Fifteen*: Jacobite rebellion in support of James Edward Stuart, *James VII*.
1745	The *Fortyfive*: Charles Edward Stuart landed in Scotland and marched as far south as Derby before turning back.
1888	James Keir Hardie founded Scottish Labor Party.
1926	Secretary for Scotland became British cabinet post.
1928	National Party of Scotland formed (became Scottish National Party 1934)
1979	Referendum rejected proposal for directly elected Scottish assembly.
1989	Local rates replaced by *poll tax* despite wide opposition.
1990	350,000 warrants issued by March for nonpayment of poll tax.

zard only a few miles from their base camp. His journal was recovered and published in 1913.

Scott Walter 1771–1832. Scottish novelist and poet. His first works were translations of German ballads, followed by poems such as "The Lady of the Lake" 1810 and "Lord of the Isles" 1815. He gained a European reputation for his historical novels such as *Heart of Midlothian* 1818, *Ivanhoe* 1819, and *The Fair Maid of Perth* 1828. His last years were marked by frantic writing to pay off his debts, after the bankruptcy of his publishing company in 1826.

Scott Winfield 1786–1866. US military leader. During the Mexican War 1846–48 he led the capture of Veracruz and Mexico City. An unsuccessful Whig candidate for president 1852, Scott was still head of the army at the outbreak of the American Civil War 1861 but retired from active service in the same year.

Scout member of a worldwide youth organization that emphasizes character, citizenship, and outdoor life. It was founded (as the Boy Scouts) in England 1908 by Robert ◊Baden-Powell. His book *Scouting for Boys* 1908 led to the incorporation in the UK of the Boy Scout Association by royal charter in 1912.

The Boy Scouts of America was founded on the Baden-Powell model in 1910. There are about 3.5 million Boy Scouts in the US. Girl Scouts of the US was founded 1912, following the same model. There are about 2 million Girl Scouts.

screening or *health screening* the systematic search for evidence of a disease, or of conditions that may precede it, in people who are not suffering from any symptoms. The aim of screening is to try to limit ill health from diseases that are difficult to prevent and might otherwise go undetected. Examples are hypothyroidism and phenylketonuria, for which all newborn babies in Western countries are screened; breast cancer (◊mammography) and cervical cancer; and stroke, for which high blood pressure is a known risk factor.

screw in construction, cylindrical or tapering piece of metal or plastic (or formerly wood) with a helical groove cut into it. Each turn of a screw moves it forward or backward by a distance equal to the pitch (the spacing between neighboring threads).

Scriabin Alexander (Nikolayevich) 1872–1915. Russian composer and pianist born in Moscow, whose powerfully emotional piano works—tone poems, such as *Prometheus* 1911, and symphonies, such as *Divine Poem* 1903—employed unusual harmonies to express his musical feelings.

Scripps James Edmund 1835–1906. US newspaper publisher who established the *Detroit Evening News* 1873, and with his younger brother Edward (1854–1926) created the first US national newspaper chain 1880 with the *St Louis Evening Chronicle* and the *Cincinnati Post.*

scuba acronym for *self-contained underwater breathing apparatus*, another name for ◊aqualung.

Scud Soviet-produced surface-to-surface ◊missile that can be armed with a nuclear, chemical, or conventional warhead. The *Scud-B*, deployed on a mobile launcher, was the version most commonly used by the Iraqi army in the Gulf War 1991. It is a relatively inaccurate weapon.

sculpture the artistic shaping in relief or in the round of materials such as wood, stone, metal, and, more recently, plastic and other synthetics. The earliest sculptures are Paleolithic stone, bone, and ivory carvings. All ancient civilizations, including the Assyrian, Egyptian, Indian, Chinese, and Mayan, have left examples of sculpture. Traditional European sculpture descends from that of Greece, Rome, and Renaissance Italy. The indigenous tradition of sculpture in Africa, South America, and the Caribbean has inspired much contemporary sculpture.

scurvy disease caused by deficiency of vitamin C (ascorbic acid), which is contained in fresh vegetables and fruit. The signs are weakness and aching joints and muscles, progressing to bleeding of the gums and then other organs, and drying-up of the skin and hair. Treatment is by giving the vitamin.

Scylla and Charybdis in Greek legend, a sea monster and a whirlpool, between which Odysseus had to sail. Later writers located them in the Straits of Messina, between Sicily and Italy.

scythe harvesting tool with long wooden handle and sharp, curving blade. It is similar to a ◊sickle. The scythe was in common use in the Middle East and Europe from the dawn of agriculture until the early 20th century, by which time it had generally been replaced by machinery.

Scythia region north of the Black Sea between the Carpathian mountains and the river Don, inhabited by the Scythians 7th–1st centuries BC. From the middle of the 4th century, they were slowly superseded by the Sarmatians. The Scythians produced ornaments and vases in gold and electrum with animal decoration. Although there is no surviving written work, there are spectacular archeological remains, including vast royal burial mounds which often contain horse skeletons.

SDI abbreviation for ◊Strategic Defense Initiative.

sea anemone invertebrate marine animal of the phylum Cnidaria with a tubelike body attached by the base to a rock or shell. The other end has an open "mouth" surrounded by stinging tentacles, which capture crustaceans and other small organisms. Many sea anemones are beautifully colored, especially those in tropical waters.

sea bass any marine fish of the family Serranidae, of perchlike appearance. Striped bass *Roccus saxatilis* of the E North American coast, is the best known.

Seaborg Glenn Theodore 1912– . US nuclear chemist associated with the preparation and synthesis of all the ◊transuranic elements with atomic numbers 94–105 at the Lawrence Radiation Laboratory, University of California at Berkeley. With Edwin M McMillan he produced plutonium in 1940, for which both shared the 1951 Nobel Prize for Chemistry.

seafloor spreading growth of the ocean ◊crust outwards (sideways) from ocean ridges. The concept of seafloor spreading has been combined with that of continental drift and incorporated into ◊plate tectonics.

sea horse any marine fish of several related genera, especially *Hippocampus*, of the family Syngnathidae, which includes the pipefishes. The body is small and compressed and covered with bony plates raised into tubercles or spines. The tail is prehensile, and the tubular mouth sucks in small shellfish and larvae as food. The head and foreparts, usually carried upright, resemble those of a horse.

seal aquatic carnivorous mammal of the families Otariidae and Phocidae (sometimes placed in a separate order, the Pinnipedia). The eared seals or sea lions (Otariidae) have small external ears, unlike the true seals (Phocidae). Seals have a streamlined body with thick blubber for insulation, and front and hind flippers. They feed on fish, squid, or crustaceans, and are commonly found in Arctic and Antarctic seas, but also in Mediterranean, Caribbean, and Hawaiian waters.

In true seals, the hind flippers provide the thrust for swimming, but they cannot be brought under the body for walking on land. Among eared seals (and walruses), the front flippers are the most important for swimming and the hind flippers can be brought forward under the body for walking.

seal mark or impression made in a block of wax to authenticate letters and documents. Seals were used in ancient China and are still used in China, Korea, and Japan.

sea lion any of several genera of ◊seals of the family Otariidae (eared seals), which also includes the fur seals. These streamlined animals have large fore flippers which they use to row themselves through the water. The hind flippers can be turned beneath the body to walk on land.

seaplane airplane capable of taking off from, and landing on, water. There are two major types, floatplanes and flying boats. The floatplane is similar to an ordinary airplane but has floats in place of wheels; the flying boat has a broad hull shaped like a boat and may also have floats attached to the wing tips.

searching in computing, extracting a specific item from a large body of data, such as a file or table. The method used depends on how the data are organized. For example, a binary search, which requires the data to be in sequence, involves first deciding which half of the data contains the required item, then which quarter, then which eighth, and so on until the item is found.

Seaside city in W central California, on the S shore of Monterey Bay, S of San Francisco; population (1990) 38,900.

Industries include fruit processing.

season period of the year having a characteristic climate. The change in seasons is mainly due to the change in attitude of the Earth's axis in relation to the Sun, and hence the position of the Sun in the sky at a particular place. In temperate latitudes four seasons are recognized: spring, summer, autumn (fall), and winter. Tropical regions have two seasons—the wet and the dry. Monsoon areas around the Indian Ocean have three seasons: the cold, the hot, and the rainy.

seasonal affective disorder (SAD) recurrent depression characterized by an increased incidence at a particular time of year. One type of seasonal affective disorder increases in incidence in autumn and winter and is associated with increased sleeping and appetite.

SEATO abbreviation for ◊Southeast Asia Treaty Organization.

Seattle port (grain, timber, fruit, fish) of the state of Washington situated between Puget Sound and Lake Washington; population (1990) 516,300, metropolitan area (with Everett) 2,559,200. It is a center for the manufacture of jet aircraft (Boeing), and also has shipbuilding, food processing, and paper industries.

sea turtle any of various marine species of ◊turtles, some of which grow up to a length of up to 8 ft/2.5 m. They are excellent swimmers, having legs that are modified to oarlike flippers but make them awkward on land. The shell is more streamlined and lighter than that of other turtles. They often travel long distances to lay their eggs on the beaches where they were born.

sea urchin any of various orders of the class Echinoidea among the echinoderms. They all have a globular body enclosed with plates of lime and covered with spines. Sometimes the spines are anchoring organs, and they also assist in locomotion. Sea urchins feed on seaweed and the animals frequenting them, and some are edible.

seaweed any of a vast collection of marine and freshwater, simple, multicellular plant forms belonging to the ◊algae and found growing from about high-water mark to depths of 300–600 ft/100–200 m. Some have holdfasts, stalks, and fronds, sometimes with air bladders to keep them afloat, and are green, blue-green, red, or brown.

Sebastiano del Piombo c. 1485–1547. Italian painter, born in Venice, one of the great painters of the High Renaissance. Sebastiano was a pupil of ◊Gior-

gione and developed a similar style of painting. In 1511 he moved to Rome, where his friendship with Michelangelo (and rivalry with Raphael) inspired him to his greatest works, such as *The Raising of Lazarus* 1517–19 (National Gallery, London). He also painted powerful portraits.

Sebastian, St Roman soldier, traditionally a member of Emperor Diocletian's bodyguard until his Christian faith was discovered. He was martyred by being shot with arrows. Feast day Jan 20.

SEC abbreviation for ◊Securities and Exchange Commission, US government body.

secant in trigonometry, the function of a given angle in a right-angled triangle, obtained by dividing the length of the hypotenuse (the longest side) by the length of the side adjacent to the angle. It is the ◊reciprocal of the ◊cosine (sec = 1/cos).

secession (Latin *secessio*) in politics, the withdrawal from a federation of states by one or more of its members, as in the secession of the Confederate states from the Union in the US 1860.

second basic ◊SI unit (symbol sec or s) of time, onesixtieth of a minute. It is defined as the duration of 9,192,631,770 cycles of regulation (periods of the radiation corresponding to the transition between two hyperfine levels of the ground state) of the cesium-133 isotope. In mathematics, the second is a unit (symbol ') of angular measurement, equaling one-sixtieth of a minute, which in turn is one-sixtieth of a degree.

secondary emission in physics, an emission of electrons from the surface of certain substances when they are struck by high-speed electrons or other particles from an external source.

secondary sexual characteristic in biology, an external feature of an organism that is characteristic of its gender (male or female), but not the reproductive organs themselves. They include facial hair in men and breasts in women, combs in roosters, brightly colored plumage in many male birds, and manes in male lions. In many cases, they are involved in displays and contests for mates and have evolved by ◊sexual selection. Their development is stimulated by sex hormones.

secretary of state the title of the cabinet official with responsibility for conducting the foreign affairs of the US. It is the senior cabinet post and is fourth in line of succession to the presidency in the event of death or incapacitation.

secretin ◊hormone produced by the small intestine of vertebrates that stimulates the production of digestive secretions by the pancreas and liver.

secretion in biology, any substance (normally a fluid) produced by a cell or specialized gland, for example, sweat, saliva, enzymes, and hormones. The process whereby the substance is discharged from the cell is also known as secretion.

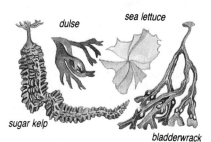

seaweed Some common seaweeds.

dulse

sea lettuce

sugar kelp

bladderwrack

seed *The structure of seeds.*

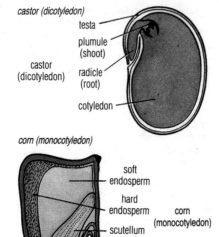

castor (dicotyledon)

- testa
- plumule (shoot)
- radicle (root)
- cotyledon

castor (dicotyledon)

corn (monocotyledon)

- soft endosperm
- hard endosperm
- scutellum
- plumule
- radicle

corn (monocotyledon)

secret police any state security force that operates internally, against political dissenters or subversives; for example, the US ◊Federal Bureau of Investigation and the UK ◊Special Branch.

Secret Service any government ◊intelligence organization. The US Secret Service is a law-enforcement unit of the Treasury Department. It is charged with combating counterfeiters and has responsibility for protecting the president and other senior members of the government.

sect small ideological group, usually religious in nature, that may have moved away from a main group, often claiming a monopoly of access to truth or salvation. Sects are usually highly exclusive. They demand strict conformity, total commitment to their code of behavior, and complete personal involvement, sometimes to the point of rejecting mainstream society altogether in terms of attachments, names, possessions, and family.

secularization the process through which religious thinking, practice, and institutions lose their religious and/or social significance. The concept is based on the theory, held by some sociologists, that as societies become industrialized their religious morals, values, and institutions give way to secular ones and some religious traits become common secular practices.

Securities and Exchange Commission (*SEC*) official US agency created 1934, under Joseph P ◊Kennedy, to ensure full disclosure to the investing public and protection against malpractice in the securities (stocks and bonds) and financial markets (such as ◊insider trading).

sedative any medication with the effect of lessening nervousness, excitement, or irritation. Sedatives will induce sleep in larger doses. Examples are ◊barbiturates, ◊narcotics, and benzodiazepines.

sediment any loose material that has "settled"— deposited from suspension in water, ice, or air, generally as the water current or wind speed decreases. Typical sediments are, in order of increasing coarseness, clay, mud, silt, sand, gravel, pebbles, cobbles, and boulders.

sedimentary rock rock formed by the accumulation and cementation of deposits that have been laid down by water, wind, ice, or gravity. Sedimentary rocks cover more than two-thirds of the Earth's surface and comprise three major categories: clastic, chemically precipitated, and organic (or biogenic). Clastic sediments are the largest group and are composed of fragments of pre-existing rocks; they include clays, sands, and gravels. Chemical precipitates include some limestones and evaporated deposits such as gypsum and halite (rock salt). Coal, oil shale, and limestone made of fossil material are examples of organic sedimentary rocks.

sedition the stirring up of discontent, resistance, or rebellion against the government in power.

seed the reproductive structure of higher plants (◊angiosperms and ◊gymnosperms). It develops from a fertilized ovule and consists of an embryo and a food store, surrounded and protected by an outer seed coat, called the testa. The food store is contained either in a specialized nutritive tissue, the ◊endosperm, or in the cotyledons of the embryo itself. In angiosperms the seed is enclosed within a ◊fruit, whereas in gymnosperms it is usually naked and unprotected, once shed from the female cone. Following ◊germination the seed develops into a new plant.

seed drill machine for sowing cereals and other seeds, developed by Jethro Tull in England 1701, although simple seeding devices were known in Babylon 2000 BC.

seed plant any seed-bearing plant; also known as a *spermatophyte*. The seed plants are subdivided into two classes: the ◊angiosperms, or flowering plants, and the ◊gymnosperms, principally the cycads and conifers. Together, they comprise the major types of vegetation found on land.

Seine French river rising on the Langres plateau NW of Dijon, and flowing 472 mi/774 km NW to join the English Channel near Le Havre, passing through Paris and Rouen.

seismology study of earthquakes and how their shock waves travel through the Earth. By examining the global pattern of waves produced by an earthquake, seismologists can deduce the nature of the materials through which they have passed. This leads to an understanding of the Earth's internal structure.

Selective Service Cases several US Supreme Court cases (including *Arver* v *US* 1918) dealing with the right of Congress to enact a mandatory military service law during wartime. The Court voted unanimously to uphold the Selective Service Act, the World War I conscription act. The decision was based on a judgment that the right to establish a military draft is implied in the Constitution in Congress's authority to declare war and maintain an army.

Selene in Greek mythology, the goddess of the Moon. She was the daughter of a ◊Titan, and the sister of Helios and Eos. In later times she was identified with ◊Artemis.

selenium (Greek *Selene* "Moon") gray, nonmetallic element, symbol Se, atomic number 34, atomic weight 78.96. It belongs to the sulfur group and occurs in several allotropic forms that differ in their physical and chemical properties. It is an essential trace element in human nutrition. Obtained from many sulfide ores and selenides, it is used as a red coloring for glass and enamel.

Seles Monica 1973– . Yugoslavian lawn-tennis player who won her first Grand Slam title, the French

Open, at the age of 16. She dominated the major events in 1991 but withdrew from Wimbledon and consequently missed the chance to achieve the Grand Slam. In 1991 she became the youngest woman player ever to achieve number-one ranking. In 1993 she was stabbed by a fan of her rival Steffi Graf and lost her number-one spot to Graf while recovering.

Seleucus I Nicator c. 358–280 BC. Macedonian general under Alexander the Great and founder of the **Seleucid Empire**. After Alexander's death 323 BC, Seleucus became governor and then (312 BC) ruler of Babylonia, founding the city of Seleucia on the river Tigris. He conquered Syria and had himself crowned king 306 BC, but his expansionist policies brought him into conflict with the Ptolemies of Egypt, and he was assassinated. He was succeeded by his son Antiochus I.

Seljuk Empire empire of the Turkish people (converted to Islam during the 7th century) under the leadership of the invading Tatars or Seljuk Turks. The Seljuk Empire 1055–1243 included Iran, Iraq and most of Anatolia and Syria. It was a loose confederation whose center was in Iran, jointly ruled by members of the family led by a great sultan exercising varying degrees of effective power. It was succeeded by the ◊Ottoman Empire.

Sellers Peter 1925–1980. English comedian and film actor. He made his name in the madcap British radio program "The Goon Show" 1949–60; his films include *The Ladykillers* 1955, *I'm All Right Jack* 1960, *Dr Strangelove* 1964, five *Pink Panther* films 1964–78 (as the bumbling Inspector Clouseau), and *Being There* 1979.

Selznick David O(liver) 1902–1965. US film producer whose early work includes *King Kong*, *Dinner at Eight*, and *Little Women* all 1933. His independent company, Selznick International (1935–40), made such lavish films as *Gone With the Wind* 1939, *Rebecca* 1940, and *Duel in the Sun* 1946.

semantics the branch of ◊linguistics dealing with the meaning of words.

semaphore visual signaling code in which the relative positions of two moveable pointers or hand-held flags stand for different letters or numbers. The system is used by ships at sea and for railroad signals.

Semarang port in N Java, Indonesia; population (1980) 1,027,000. There is a shipbuilding industry, and exports include coffee, teak, sugar, tobacco, kapok, and petroleum from nearby oil fields.

Semele in Greek mythology, the daughter of ◊Cadmus of Thebes and mother of Dionysus by Zeus. At Hera's suggestion she demanded that Zeus should appear to her in all his glory, but when he did so she was consumed by lightning.

semen see ◊sperm.

semicircular canal one of three looped tubes that form part of the labyrinth in the inner ◊ear. They are filled with fluid and detect changes in the position of the head, contributing to the sense of balance.

semicolon punctuation mark (;) with a function halfway between the separation of sentence from sentence by means of a period, or full stop, and the gentler separation provided by a comma. It also helps separate items in a complex list: "pens, pencils, and paper; staples, such as rice and beans; tools, various; and rope."

semiconductor crystalline material with an electrical conductivity between that of metals (good) and insulators (poor). The conductivity of semiconductors can usually be improved by minute additions of different substances or by other factors. Silicon, for example, has poor conductivity at low temperatures, but this is improved by the application of light, heat, or voltage; hence silicon is used in ◊transistors, rectifiers, and ◊integrated circuits (silicon chips).

semiology or **semiotics** the study of the function of signs and symbols in human communication, both in language and by various nonlinguistic means. Beginning with the notion of the Swiss linguist Ferdinand de Saussure that no word or other sign (**signifier**) is intrinsically linked with its meaning (**signified**), it was developed as a scientific discipline, especially by Claude ◊Lévi-Strauss and Roland ◊Barthes.

Semite member of any of the peoples of the Middle East originally speaking a Semitic language, and traditionally said to be descended from Shem, a son of Noah in the Bible. Ancient Semitic peoples include the Hebrews, Ammonites, Moabites, Edomites, Babylonians, Assyrians, Chaldaeans, Phoenicians, and Canaanites. The Semitic peoples founded the monotheistic religions of Judaism, Christianity, and Islam.

They speak languages of the Hamito-Semitic branch of the Afro-Asiatic family.

Senate in ancient Rome, the "council of elders." Originally consisting of the heads of patrician families, it was recruited from ex-magistrates and persons who had rendered notable public service, but was periodically purged by the censors. Although nominally advisory, it controlled finance and foreign policy.

The US Senate consists of 100 members, two from each state, elected for a six-year term. The term also refers to the upper house of the Canadian parliament and to the upper chambers of Italy and France. It is also given to the governing bodies in some universities, for example, the Faculty Senate.

Sendai city in Tōhoku region, NE Honshu Island, Japan; population (1990) 918,400. Industries include metal goods (a metal museum was established 1975), electronics, textiles, pottery, and food processing. It was a feudal castle town from the 16th century.

Sendak Maurice 1928– . US writer and book illustrator, whose children's books with their deliberately arch illustrations include *Where the Wild Things Are* 1963, *In the Night Kitchen* 1970, and *Outside Over There* 1981.

Born in Brooklyn, New York, he attended the Art Students League and illustrated books for other authors. *Kenny's Window* 1956 was the first book that he both wrote and illustrated. *Very Far Away* 1957 and *The Sign on Rosie's Door* 1960 soon followed. He also designed several works for the stage, including an operatic version of *Where the Wild Things Are* and a production of Mozart's *Magic Flute*.

Sendero Luminoso (Shining Path) Maoist guerrilla group active in Peru, formed 1980 to overthrow the government. Until 1988 its activity was confined to rural areas. By June 1988 an estimated 9,000 people had been killed in the insurgency, about half of them guerrillas. In 1992 attacks intensified in response to a government crackdown.

Seneca Lucius Annaeus c. 4 BC–AD 65. Roman Stoic playwright, author of essays and nine tragedies. He was tutor to the future emperor Nero but lost favor after the latter's accession to the throne and was ordered to commit suicide. His tragedies were accepted as Classical models by 16th-century dramatists.

Senegal
Republic of
(*République du Sénégal*)

area 75,753 sq mi/196,200 sq km
capital (and chief port) Dakar
cities Thiès, Kaolack
physical plains rising to hills in SE; swamp and tropical forest in SW
features river Senegal; Gambia forms an enclave within Senegal
head of state Abdou Diouf from 1981
head of government Habib Thiam from 1993
political system emergent socialist democratic republic
political parties Senegalese Socialist Party (PS), democratic socialist; Senegalese Democratic Party (PDS), left of center
exports peanuts, cotton, fish, phosphates

currency franc CFA
population (1992) 7,691,000; growth rate 3.1% p.a.
life expectancy men 51, women 54 (1989)
languages French (official); African dialects are spoken
religions Muslim 80%, Roman Catholic 10%, animist
literacy men 37%, women 19% (1985 est)
GNP $2 bn (1987); $380 per head (1984)

chronology
1659 Became a French colony.
1854–65 Interior occupied by French.
1902 Became a territory of French West Africa.
1959 Formed the Federation of Mali with French Sudan.
1960 Independence achieved from France, but withdrew from the federation. Léopold Sédar Senghor, leader of the Senegalese Progressive Union (UPS), became president.
1966 UPS declared the only legal party.
1974 Pluralist system reestablished.
1976 UPS reconstituted as Senegalese Socialist Party (PS). Prime Minister Abdou Diouf nominated as Senghor's successor.
1980 Senghor resigned; succeeded by Diouf. Troops sent to defend Gambia.
1981 Military help again sent to Gambia.
1982 Confederation of Senegambia came into effect.
1983 Diouf reelected. Post of prime minister abolished.
1988 Diouf decisively reelected.
1989 Violent clashes between Senegalese and Mauritanians in Dakar and Nouakchott killed more than 450 people; over 50,000 people repatriated from both countries. Senegambia federation abandoned.
1991 Constitutional changes outlined.
1992 Diplomatic links with Mauritania re-established.
1993 Diouf reelected. Habib Thiam appointed prime minister.

Senegal country in W Africa, on the Atlantic Ocean, bounded N by Mauritania, E by Mali, S by Guinea and Guinea-Bissau, and enclosing Gambia on three sides.

Senghor Léopold (Sédar) 1906– . Senegalese politician and writer, first president of independent Senegal 1960–80. He was Senegalese deputy to the French National Assembly 1946–58, and founder of the Senegalese Progressive Union. He was also a well-known poet and a founder of *négritude*, a black literary and philosophical movement.

senile dementia ◊dementia associated with old age, often caused by ◊Alzheimer's disease.

Sennacherib died 681 BC. King of Assyria from 705 BC. Son of ◊Sargon II, he rebuilt the city of Nineveh on a grand scale, sacked Babylon 689, and defeated Hezekiah, king of Judah, but failed to take Jerusalem. He was assassinated by his sons, and one of them, Esarhaddon, succeeded him.

Sennett Mack. Adopted name of Michael Sinnott 1880–1960. Canadian-born US film director. Born in Richmond, Québec, Sennett moved to New York 1904, where he began to perform in vaudeville. After working as an actor in Biograph Studio films under D W Griffith 1908–11, he founded his own film production company, the Keystone Company 1911. As director, Sennett made hundreds of short slapstick comedies, cast Charles ◊Chaplin in his first feature film (*Tillie's Punctured Romance* 1914), and started the career of Gloria Swanson. In the following years, Sennett developed the slapstick style of comedy, featuring the first flying custard pie and his Keystone Kops. Before his career ended, with the advent of sound films, he had directed most of Hollywood's major silent film stars. His studio closed 1933.

sense organ any organ that an animal uses to gain information about its surroundings. All sense organs have specialized receptors (such as light receptors in an eye) and some means of translating their response into a nerve impulse that travels to the brain. The main human sense organs are the eye, which detects light and color (different wavelengths of light); the ear, which detects sound (vibrations of the air) and gravity; the nose, which detects some of the chemical molecules in the air; and the tongue, which detects some of the chemicals in food, giving a sense of taste. There are also many small sense organs in the skin, including pain sensors, temperature sensors, and pressure sensors, contributing to our sense of touch.

Seoul or *Sŏul* capital of South ◊Korea (Republic of Korea), near the Han River, and with its chief port at Inchon; population (1985) 10,627,800. Industries include engineering, textiles, food processing, electrical and electronic equipment, chemicals, and machinery.

sepal part of a flower, usually green, that surrounds and protects the flower in bud. The sepals are derived from modified leaves, and collectively known as the calyx.

separation of powers an approach to limiting the powers of government by separating governmental functions into the executive, legislative, and judiciary. The concept has its fullest practical expression in the the US constitution (see ◊federalism).

Sephardi (plural *Sephardim*) Jew descended from those expelled from Spain and Portugal in the 15th century, or from those forcibly converted during the Inquisition to Christianity (Marranos). Many settled in N Africa and in the Mediterranean countries, as well as in the Netherlands, England, and Dutch colonies in the New World. Sephardim speak Ladino, a 15th-century Romance dialect, as well as the language of their nation.

Sepoy Indian soldier in the service of the British or Indian army in the days of British rule in India. The Indian Mutiny 1857–58 was thus also known as the ◊Sepoy Rebellion or Mutiny.

Sepoy Rebellion revolt 1857–58 of Indian soldiers (Sepoys) against the British in India; also known as the Sepoy, or Indian, Mutiny. The uprising was confined to the north, from Bengal to the Punjab, and central India. The majority of support came from the army and recently dethroned princes, but in some areas it developed into a peasant uprising and general revolt. It included the seizure of Delhi by the rebels, its siege and recapture by the British, and the defense of Lucknow by a British garrison. The mutiny led to the end of rule by the British East India Company and its replacement by direct British crown administration.

sepsis general term for infection; any poisoned state due to the introduction of disease-causing organisms from outside into the bloodstream.

septicemia technical term for blood poisoning.

septic shock life-threatening fall in blood pressure caused by blood poisoning (septicemia). Toxins produced by bacteria infecting the blood induce a widespread dilation of the blood vessels throughout the body, and it is this that causes the patient's collapse (see ◊shock). Septic shock can occur following bowel surgery, after a penetrating wound to the abdomen, or as a consequence of infection of the urinary tract. It is usually treated in an intensive care unit and has a high mortality rate.

sequoia two species of conifer in the redwood family Taxodiaceae, native to W US. The redwood *Sequoia sempervirens* is a long-lived timber tree, and one specimen, the Howard Libbey Redwood, is the world's tallest tree at 361 ft/110 m, with a circumference of 44 ft/13.4 m. The giant sequoia *Sequoiadendron giganteum* reaches up to 100 ft/30 m in circumference at the base, and grows almost as tall as the redwood. It is also (except for the bristlecone pine) the oldest living tree, some specimens being estimated at over 3,500 years of age.

seraph (plural **seraphim**) in Christian and Judaic belief, an ◊angel of the highest order. They are mentioned in the book of Isaiah in the Old Testament.

Serapis ancient Graeco-Egyptian god, a combination of Apis and Osiris, invented by the Ptolemies; his finest temple was the Serapeum in Alexandria.

Serb member of Yugoslavia's largest ethnic group, found mainly in Serbia, but also in the neighboring independent republics of Bosnia-Herzegovina and Croatia. Their language, generally recognized to be the same as Croat and hence known as Serbo-Croatian, belongs to the Slavic branch of the Indo-European family. It has more than 17 million speakers.

Serbia (Serbo-Croatian *Srbija*) constituent republic of Yugoslavia, which includes Kosovo and Vojvodina
area 34,122 sq mi/88,400 sq km
capital Belgrade
physical fertile Danube plains in the N, mountainous in the S
features includes the autonomous provinces of ◊Kosovo, capital Priština, of which the predominantly Albanian population demands unification with Albania, and ◊Vojvodina, capital Novi Sad, largest city Subotica, with a predominantly Serbian population

population (1986) 9,660,000
language the Serbian variant of Serbo-Croatian
religion Serbian Orthodox
history The Serbs settled in the Balkans in the 7th century and became Christians in the 9th century. They were united as one kingdom about 1169; the Serbian hero Stephan Dushan (1331–1355) founded an empire covering most of the Balkans. After their defeat at Kosovo 1389 they came under the domination of the Turks, who annexed Serbia 1459. Uprisings 1804–16, led by Kara George and Milosh Obrenovich, forced the Turks to recognize Serbia as an autonomous principality under Milosh. The assassination of Kara George on Obrenovich's orders gave rise to a long feud between the two houses. After a war with Turkey 1876–78, Serbia became an independent kingdom. On the assassination of the last Obrenovich 1903 the Karageorgevich dynasty came to the throne. The two Balkan Wars 1912–13 greatly enlarged Serbia's territory at the expense of Turkey and Bulgaria. Serbia's designs on Bosnia-Herzegovina, backed by Russia, led to friction with Austria, culminating in the outbreak of war 1914. Serbia was overrun 1915–16 and was occupied until 1918, when it became the nucleus of the new kingdom of the Serbs, Croats, and Slovenes, and subsequently ◊Yugoslavia. Rivalry between Croats and Serbs continued within the republic. During World War II Serbia was under a puppet government set up by the Germans; after the war it became a constituent republic of Yugoslavia. From 1986 Slobodan Milosević as Serbian party chief and president waged a populist campaign to end the autonomous status of the provinces of Kosovo and Vojvodina. Despite a violent Albanian backlash in Kosovo 1989–90 and growing pressure in Croatia and Slovenia to break away from the federation, Serbia formally annexed Kosovo Sept 1990. Milosević was reelected by a landslide majority Dec 1990, but in March 1991 there were anticommunist and anti-Milosević riots in Belgrade. The 1991 civil war in Yugoslavia arose from the Milosević nationalist government attempting the forcible annexation of Serb-dominated regions in Croatia, making use of the largely Serbian federal army. In Oct 1991 Milosević renounced territorial claims on Croatia pressured by threats of European Community (EC) and United Nations (UN) sanctions, but the fighting continued until a cease-fire was agreed upon Jan 1992. EC recognition of Slovenia's and Croatia's independence in Jan 1992 and Bosnia-Herzegovina's in April left Serbia dominating a greatly reduced "rump" Yugoslavia. A successor Yugoslavia, announced by Serbia and Montenegro April 1992, was rejected by the US and EC

Seurat The Neo-Impressionist Bathers at Asnières by Georges Seurat (1884), National Gallery, London.

because of concerns over serious human rights violations in Kosovo and Serbia's continued attempted partition of Bosnia-Herzegovina. In March 1992, and again in June, thousands of Serbs marched through Belgrade, demanding the ousting of President Milosević and an end to the war in Bosnia-Herzegovina.

serenade musical piece for chamber orchestra or wind instruments in several movements, originally intended for evening entertainment, such as Mozart's *Eine kleine Nachtmusik/A Little Night Music*.

serfdom the legal and economic status of peasants under ◊feudalism. Serfs could not be sold like slaves, but they were not free to leave their master's estate without his permission. They had to work the lord's land without pay for a number of days every week and pay a percentage of their produce to the lord every year. They also served as soldiers in the event of conflict. Serfs also had to perform extra labor at harvest time and other busy seasons; in return they were allowed to cultivate a portion of the estate for their own benefit.

Sergius, St of Radonezh 1314–1392. Patron saint of Russia, who founded the Eastern Orthodox monastery of the Blessed Trinity near Moscow 1334. Mediator among Russian feudal princes, he inspired the victory of Dmitri, Grand Duke of Moscow, over the Tatar khan Mamai at Kulikovo, on the upper Don, 1380.

serpentine group of minerals, hydrous magnesium silicate, $Mg_3Si_2O_5(OH)_4$, occurring in soft metamorphic rocks and usually dark green. The fibrous form *chrysotile* is a source of ◊asbestos; other forms are *antigorite* and *lizardite*. Serpentine minerals are formed by hydration of ultrabasic rocks during metamorphism. Rare snake-patterned forms are used in ornamental carving.

Serra Junipero 1713–1784. Spanish missionary and explorer in America. A Franciscan friar, he pursued a missionary career and served in Querétaro 1750–58. He was transferred to Baja California with the expulsion of the Jesuits from Mexico 1767 and in 1969 led a missionary expedition to Alta California. He subsequently established several missions throughout the region.

serum clear fluid that remains after blood clots. It is blood plasma with the anticoagulant proteins removed, and contains ◊antibodies and other proteins, as well as the fats and sugars of the blood. It can be produced synthetically, and is used to protect against disease.

Servetus Michael (Miguel Serveto) 1511–1553. Spanish Christian Anabaptist theologian and physician. He was a pioneer in the study of the circulation of the blood and found that it circulates to the lungs from the right chamber of the heart. He was burned alive by the church reformer Calvin in Geneva, Switzerland, for publishing attacks on the doctrine of the Trinity.

service industry commercial activity that provides and charges for various services to customers (as opposed to manufacturing or supplying goods), such as restaurants, the tourist industry, cleaning, hotels, and the retail trade (shops and supermarkets).

sesame annual plant *Sesamum indicum* of the family Pedaliaceae, probably native to SE Asia. It produces oily seeds used for food and soap making.

set or *class* in mathematics, any collection of defined things (elements), provided the elements are distinct and that there is a rule to decide whether an element is a member of a set. It is usually denoted by a capital letter and indicated by curly brackets.

Set in Egyptian mythology, the god of night, the desert, and of all evils. Portrayed as a grotesque animal, Set was the murderer of ◊Osiris.

Seton St Elizabeth Ann Bayley 1774–1821. US religious leader and social benefactor. A convert to Roman Catholicism, she founded schools for the poor. Known as "Mother Seton," she was proclaimed the first American saint 1975.

setter any of various breeds of gun dog, about 2.2 ft/ 66 cm high and weighing about 55 lb/25 kg. They have a long, smooth coat, feathered tails, and spaniellike faces. They are called "setters" because they were trained in crouching or "setting" on the sight of game to be pursued.

settlement out of court a compromise reached between the parties to a legal dispute. Most civil legal actions are settled out of court, reducing legal costs and avoiding the uncertainty of the outcome of a trial.

Seurat Georges 1859–1891. French artist. He originated, with Paul Signac, the Neo-Impressionist technique of ◊Pointillism (painting with small dabs rather than long brushstrokes). Examples of his work are *Bathers at Asnières* 1884 (National Gallery, London) and *Sunday on the Island of La Grande Jatte* 1886 (Art Institute of Chicago).

Seuss, Dr see ◊Geisel, Theodore Seuss.

seven deadly sins in Christian theology, anger, avarice, envy, gluttony, lust, pride, and sloth.

Seventh-Day Adventist or ◊Adventist member of the Protestant religious sect of the same name. It originated in the US in the fervent expectation of Christ's Second Coming, or advent, that swept across New York State following William Miller's prophecy that Christ would return on Oct 22, 1844. When this failed to come to pass, a number of Millerites, as his followers were called, reinterpreted his prophetic speculations and continued to maintain that the millennium was imminent. Adventists observe Saturday as the Sabbath and emphasize healing and diet; many are vegetarians. The sect has about 500,000 members in the US.

Seven Weeks' War war 1866 between Austria and Prussia, engineered by the German chancellor ◊Bismarck. It was nominally over the possession of ◊Schleswig-Holstein, but it was actually to confirm Prussia's superseding Austria as the leading German state. The Prussian victory at the Battle of Sadowa was the culmination of General von Moltke's victories.

Seven Wonders of the World in antiquity, the pyramids of Egypt, the hanging gardens of Babylon, the temple of Artemis at Ephesus, the statue of Zeus at Olympia, the Mausoleum at Halicarnassus, the Colossus of Rhodes, and the Pharos (lighthouse) at Alexandria.

Seven Years' War (in North America known as the *French and Indian War*) war 1756–63 arising from the conflict between Austria and Prussia, and between France and Britain over colonial supremacy. Britain and Prussia defeated France, Austria, Spain, and Russia; Britain gained control of India and many of France's colonies, including Canada. Spain ceded Florida to Britain in exchange for Cuba. Fighting against great odds, Prussia was eventually successful in becoming established as one of the great European powers. The war ended with the Treaty of Paris 1763, signed by Britain, France, and Spain.

Severn river of Wales and England, rising on the NE side of Plynlimmon, N Wales, and flowing 210 mi/338 km through Shrewsbury, Worcester, and Gloucester to the Bristol Channel. The *Severn bore* is a tidal wave up to 6 ft/2 m high.

Severus Lucius Septimus 146–211. Roman emperor. He held a command on the Danube when in 193 the emperor Pertinax was murdered. Proclaimed emperor by his troops, Severus proved an able administrator. He was born in N Africa, and was the only African to become emperor. He died at York while campaigning in Britain against the Caledonians.

Seville (Spanish *Sevilla*) city in Andalusia, Spain, on the Guadalquivir River, 60 mi/96 km N of Cadiz; population (1991) 683,500. Products include machinery, spirits, porcelain, pharmaceuticals, silk, and tobacco.

Sèvres fine porcelain produced at a factory in Sèvres, France, now a Paris suburb, since the early 18th century. It is characterized by the use of intensely colored backgrounds (such as pink and royal blue), against which flowers are painted in elaborately embellished frames, often in gold.

Sèvres, Treaty of the last of the treaties that ended World War I. Negotiated between the Allied powers and the Ottoman Empire, it was finalized Aug 1920 but never ratified by the Turkish government.

sewage disposal the disposal of human excreta and other waterborne waste products from houses, streets, and factories. Conveyed through sewers to sewage plants, sewage has to undergo a series of treatments to be acceptable for discharge into rivers or the sea, according to various local laws and ordinances. Raw sewage, or sewage that has not been treated adequately, is one serious source of water pollution and a cause of eutrophication.

Seward William Henry 1801–1872. US public official. A leader of the Republican party, he was appointed secretary of state by President Lincoln 1860. Although seriously wounded in the 1865 assassination of Lincoln, Seward continued to serve as secretary of state under President Andrew Johnson to 1868, purchasing Alaska for the US from Russia for $7.2 million 1867.

sewing machine apparatus for the mechanical sewing of cloth, leather, and other materials by a needle, powered by hand, treadle, or belted electric motor. The popular lockstitch machine, using a double thread, was invented independently in the US by both Walter Hunt 1834 and Elias ◊Howe 1846. Howe's machine was the basis of the machine patented 1851 by US inventor Isaac ◊Singer.

sex determination process by which the sex of an organism is determined. In many species, the sex of an individual is dictated by the two sex chromosomes (X and Y) it receives from its parents. In mammals, some plants, and a few insects, males are XY, and females XX; in birds, reptiles, some amphibians, and butterflies the reverse is the case. In bees and wasps, males are produced from unfertilized eggs, females from

Seville Seville cathedral (1401–1520), the largest medieval cathedral in Europe, occupies the site of a Moorish mosque.

sexual reproduction The human reproductive organs.

female reproductive system

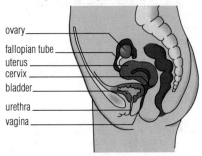

ovary

fallopian tube

uterus

cervix

bladder

urethra

vagina

male reproductive system

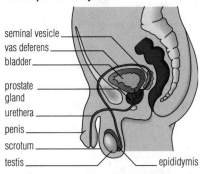

seminal vesicle

vas deferens

bladder

prostate gland

urethera

penis

scrotum

testis

epididymis

fertilized eggs. Environmental factors can affect some fish and reptiles, such as turtles, where sex is influenced by the temperature at which the eggs develop. In 1991 it was shown that maleness is caused by a single gene, 14 base pairs long, on the Y chromosome.

sexism belief in (or set of implicit assumptions about) the superiority of one's own sex, often accompanied by a ◊stereotype or preconceived idea about the opposite sex. Sexism may also be accompanied by ◊discrimination on the basis of sex, generally as practiced by men against women.

sex linkage in genetics, the tendency for certain characteristics to occur exclusively, or predominantly, in one sex only. Human examples include red-green color blindness and hemophilia, both found predominantly in males. In both cases, these characteristics are ◊recessive and are determined by genes on the ◊X chromosome.

sextant navigational instrument for determining latitude by measuring the angle between some heavenly body and the horizon. It was invented by John Hadley (1682–1744) in 1730 and can be used only in clear weather.

sexual reproduction reproductive process in organisms that requires the union, or ◊fertilization, of gametes (such as eggs and sperm). These are usually produced by two different individuals, although self-fertilization occurs in a few ◊hermaphrodites such as tapeworms. Most organisms other than bacteria and cyanobacteria (◊blue-green algae) show some sort of sexual process. Except in some lower organisms, the gametes are of two distinct types called eggs and sperm. The organisms producing the eggs are called females, and those producing the sperm, males. The

---

Seychelles
Republic of

India

INDIAN OCEAN

Somalia

Kenya

SEYCHELLES

Victoria

0 mi   500
0 km   1000

area 175 sq mi/453 sq km
capital Victoria (on Mahé island)
cities Cascade, Port Glaud, Misere
physical comprises two distinct island groups, one concentrated, the other widely scattered, totaling over 100 islands and islets
features Aldabra atoll, containing world's largest tropical lagoon; the unique "double coconut" (*coco de mer*); tourism is important
head of state and government France-Albert René from 1977
political system one-party socialist republic
political party Seychelles People's Progressive Front (SPPF), nationalist socialist

exports copra, cinnamon
currency Seychelles rupee
population (1992) 71,000; growth rate 2.2% p.a.
life expectancy 66 years (1988)
languages Creole (Asian, African, European mixture) 95%, English, French (all official)
religion Roman Catholic 90%
literacy 80% (1989)
GNP $175 million; $2,600 per head (1987)

chronology
1744 Became a French colony.
1794 Captured by British.
1814 Ceded by France to Britain; incorporated as a dependency of Mauritius.
1903 Became a separate British colony.
1975 Internal self-government agreed.
1976 Independence achieved from Britain as a republic within the Commonwealth, with James Mancham as president.
1977 France-Albert René ousted Mancham in an armed coup and took over presidency.
1979 New constitution adopted; Seychelles People's Progressive Front (SPPF) sole legal party.
1981 Attempted coup by South African mercenaries thwarted.
1984 René reelected.
1987 Coup attempt foiled.
1989 René reelected.
1991 Multiparty politics promised.
1992 Mancham returned from exile. Constitutional commission elected; constitutional reform received insufficient support in referendum.
1993 René defeated Mancham in multiparty presidential elections.

fusion of a male and female gamete produces a **zygote**, from which a new individual develops.

The alternatives to sexual reproduction are binary fission, budding, vegetative reproduction, parthenogenesis, and spore formation.

Seychelles country in the Indian Ocean, off E Africa, N of Madagascar.

Seyfert galaxy galaxy whose small, bright center is caused by hot gas moving at high speed around a massive central object, possibly a ◊black hole. Almost all Seyferts are spiral galaxies. They seem to be closely related to ◊quasars, but are about 100 times fainter. They are named after their discoverer Carl Seyfert (1911–1960).

Seymour Jane *c.* 1509–1537. Third wife of Henry VIII, whom she married in 1536. She died soon after the birth of her son Edward VI.

Sforza Italian family that ruled the duchy of Milan 1450–99, 1512–15, and 1522–35. Its court was a center of Renaissance culture and its rulers prominent patrons of the arts.

SFSR abbreviation for *Soviet Federal Socialist Republic*, administrative subdivision of the former USSR.

Shaanxi or *Shensi* province of NW China
area 75,579 sq mi/195,800 sq km
capital Xian
cities Yan'an
physical mountains; Huang He Valley, one of the earliest settled areas of China
products iron, steel, mining, textiles, fruit, tea, rice, wheat
population (1990) 32,882,000.

Shackleton Ernest 1874–1922. Irish Antarctic explorer. In 1907–09, he commanded an expedition that reached 88° 23' S latitude, located the magnetic South Pole, and climbed Mount ◊Erebus.

shad any of several marine fishes, especially the genus *Alosa*, the largest (2 ft/60 cm long and 6 lb/2.7 kg in weight) of the herring family (Clupeidae). They migrate in shoals to breed in rivers.

shah (more formally, *shahanshah* "king of kings") traditional title of ancient Persian rulers, and also of those of the recent ◊Pahlavi dynasty in Iran.

Shah Jahan 1592–1666. Mogul emperor of India from 1628, under whom the dynasty reached its zenith. Succeeding his father ◊Jahangir, he extended Mogul authority into the Deccan plateau (E India), subjugating Ahmadnagar, Bijapur, and Golconda 1636, but lost Kandahar in the NW to the Persians 1653. His reign marked the high point of Indo-Muslim architecture, with Delhi being rebuilt as Shahjahanabad, while the Taj Mahal and Pearl Mosque were constructed at Agra. On falling seriously ill 1658 he was dethroned and imprisoned by his son ◊Aurangzeb.

Shaka or *Chaka c.* 1787–1828. Zulu chief who formed a Zulu empire in SE Africa. He seized power from his half brother 1816 and then embarked on a bloody military campaign to unite the Zulu clans. He was assassinated by his two half brothers.

Shaker popular name for a member of the Christian sect of the United Society of Believers in Christ's Second Appearing (and an offshoot of the ◊Quakers). This was founded by James and Jane Wardley in England about 1747 and taken to North America 1774 by Ann Lee (1736–84), the wife of a Manchester blacksmith, known as Mother Ann. She founded a colony in New York, and eventually 18 colonies existed in several states. Separation from the world in self-regulating farm communities, prescribed modes of simple dress and living conditions, celibacy, and faith healing characterized their way of life. The name was applied because of their ecstatic trembling and shaking during worship.

Shakespeare William 1564–1616. English dramatist and poet. Established in London by 1589 as an actor and a playwright, he was England's unrivaled dramatist until his death, and is considered the greatest English playwright. His plays, written in blank verse, can be broadly divided into lyric plays, including *Romeo and Juliet* and *A Midsummer Night's Dream*; comedies, including *The Comedy of Errors, As You Like It, Much Ado About Nothing,* and *Measure For Measure*; historical plays, such as *Henry VI* (in three parts), *Richard III,* and *Henry IV* (in two parts), which often showed cynical political wisdom; and

Shakespeare: the plays

title	first performed
early plays	
Henry VI Part I	1589–92
Henry VI Part II	1589–92
Henry VI Part III	1589–92
The Comedy of Errors	1592–93
The Taming of the Shrew	1593–94
Titus Andronicus	1593–94
The Two Gentlemen of Verona	1594–95
Love's Labour's Lost	1594–95
Romeo and Juliet	1594–95
histories	
Richard III	1592–93
Richard II	1593–96
King John	1596–97
Henry IV Part I	1597–98
Henry IV Part II	1597–98
Henry V	1599
Roman plays	
Julius Caesar	1599–1600
Antony and Cleopatra	1607–08
Coriolanus	1607–08
the great or middle comedies	
A Midsummer Night's Dream	1595–96
The Merchant of Venice	1596–97
Much Ado About Nothing	1598–99
As You Like It	1599–1600
The Merry Wives of Windsor	1600–01
Twelfth Night	1601–02
the great tragedies	
Hamlet	1600–01
Othello	1604–05
King Lear	1605–06
Macbeth	1605–06
Timon of Athens	1607–08
the dark comedies	
Troilus and Cressida	1601–02
All's Well That Ends Well	1602–03
Measure for Measure	1604–05
late plays	
Pericles	1608–09
Cymbeline	1609–10
The Winter's Tale	1610–11
The Tempest	1611–12
Henry VIII	1612–13

Shakespeare This informal and romantic portrait of Shakespeare by John Taylor (c. 1610), National Portrait Gallery, London, is known as the "Chandos portrait."

tragedies, such as *Hamlet, Macbeth,* and *King Lear.* He also wrote numerous sonnets.

shale fine-grained and finely layered ◊sedimentary rock composed of silt and clay. It is a weak rock, splitting easily along bedding planes to form thin, even slabs (by contrast, mudstone splits into irregular flakes). Oil shale contains kerogen, a solid bituminous material that yields ◊petroleum when heated.

shallot small onion *Allium ascalonicum* in which bulbs are clustered like garlic; used for cooking and in pickles.

shaman (Tungu *samân*) ritual leader who acts as intermediary between society and the supernatural world in many indigenous cultures of Asia, Africa, and the Americas. Also known as a *medicine man, seer,* or *sorcerer,* the shaman is expected to use special powers to cure illness and control good and evil spirits. The term is used for any tribal sorcerer or medicine man regardless of geography.

Shamir Yitzhak 1915– . Polish-born Israeli right-wing politician; prime minister 1983–84 and 1986–92; leader of the Likud (Consolidation Party) until 1993. He was foreign minister under Menachem Begin 1980–83, and again foreign minister in the ◊Peres unity government 1984–86.

shamrock several trifoliate plants of the family Leguminosae, including ◊clovers. St Patrick is said to have used one to illustrate the doctrine of the Holy Trinity, and it was made the national badge of Ireland.

Shandong or *Shantung* province of NE China
area 59,174 sq mi/153,300 sq km
capital Jinan
cities ports: Yantai, Weihai, Qingdao, Shigiusuo
features crossed by the Huang He River and the ◊Grand Canal; Shandong Peninsula
products cereals, cotton, wild silk, varied minerals
population (1990) 84,393,000.

Shanghai port on the Huang-pu and Wusong rivers, Jiangsu province, China, 15 mi/24 km from the Chang Jiang estuary; population (1986) 6,980,000, the largest city in China. The municipality of Shanghai has an area of 2,239 sq mi/5,800 sq km and a population of 13,342,000. Industries include textiles, paper, chemicals, steel, agricultural machinery, precision instruments, shipbuilding, flour and vegetable-oil milling, and oil refining. It handles about 50% of China's imports and exports.

Shankar Ravi 1920– . Indian composer and musician. A virtuoso of the ◊sitar, he has composed film music and founded music schools in Bombay and Los Angeles.

Shannon longest river in Ireland, rising in County Cavan and flowing 240 mi/386 km through loughs Allen and Ree and past Athlone, to reach the Atlantic Ocean through a wide estuary below Limerick. It is also the greatest source of electric power in the republic, with hydroelectric installations at and above Ardnacrusha, 3 mi/5 km N of Limerick.

Shanxi or *Shansi* or *Shensi* province of NE China
area 60,641 sq mi/157,100 sq km
capital Taiyuan
cities Datong
features a drought-ridden plateau, partly surrounded by the ◊Great Wall
products coal, iron, fruit
population (1990) 28,759,000
history saw the outbreak of the Boxer Rebellion 1900.

SHAPE acronym for *Supreme Headquarters Allied Powers Europe,* situated near Mons, Belgium, and the headquarters of NATO's Supreme Allied Commander Europe (SACEUR).

sharecropping farming someone else's land, where the farmer gives the landowner a proportion of the crop instead of money. This system of rent payment was common in the US, especially the South, until after World War II. It is still common in parts of the developing world; for example, in India. Often the farmer is left with such a small share of the crop that he or she is doomed to poverty.

Shari'a the law of ◊Islam believed by Muslims to be based on divine revelation, and drawn from a number of sources, including the Koran, the Hadith, and the consensus of the Muslim community. Under this law, *qisās,* or retribution, allows a family to exact equal punishment on an accused; *diyat,* or blood money, is payable to a dead person's family as compensation.

Sharjah or *Shariqah* third largest of the seven member states of the ◊United Arab Emirates, situated on the Arabian Gulf NE of Dubai; area 1,004 sq mi/2,600 sq km; population (1985) 269,000. Since 1952 it has included the small state of Kalba. In 1974 oil was discovered offshore. Industries include ship repair, cement, paint, and metal products.

shark any member of various orders of cartilaginous fishes (class Chondrichthyes), found throughout the oceans of the world. There are about 400 known species of shark. They have tough, usually gray, skin covered in denticles (small toothlike scales). A shark's streamlined body has side pectoral fins, a high dorsal fin, and a forked tail with a large upper lobe. Five open gill slits are visible on each side of the generally pointed head. Most sharks are fish-eaters, and a few will attack humans. They range from several feet in length to the great *white shark Carcharodon carcharias,* 30 ft/9 m long, and the harmless plankton-feeding *whale shark Rhincodon typus,* over 50 ft/15 m in length.

Sharon city in W Pennsylvania, on the Shenango River, N of Pittsburgh, near the Ohio border; population (1990) 17,500. Industries include steel products and electronics.

Sharpeville black township in South Africa, 40 mi/65 km S of Johannesburg and N of Vereeniging; 69 people were killed here when police fired on a crowd of antiapartheid demonstrators March 21, 1960.

Shastri Lal Bahadur 1904–1966. Indian politician, prime minister 1964–66. He campaigned for national integration, and secured a declaration of peace with Pakistan at the Tashkent peace conference 1966.

Shatt-al-Arab (Persian *Arvand*) waterway formed by the confluence of the rivers ◊Euphrates and ◊Tigris; length 120 mi/190 km to the Persian Gulf. Basra, Khorramshahr, and Abadan stand on it.

Shaw George Bernard 1856–1950. Irish dramatist. He was also a critic and novelist, and an early member of the socialist ◊Fabian Society. His plays combine comedy with political, philosophical, and polemic aspects, aiming to make an impact on his audience's social conscience as well as their emotions. They include *Arms and the Man* 1894, *Devil's Disciple* 1897, *Man and Superman* 1905, *Pygmalion* 1913, and *St Joan* 1924. Nobel Prize 1925.

Shays Daniel *c.* 1747–1825. American political agitator. In 1786 he led Shays' Rebellion, an armed uprising of impoverished farmers, against the refusal of the state government to offer economic relief. The riot was suppressed 1787 by a Massachusetts militia force, but it drew public attention to the plight of the western farmers and the need for a stronger central government. Shays was pardoned 1788.

Sheba ancient name for S ◊Yemen (Sha'abijah). It was once renowned for gold and spices. According to the Old Testament, its queen visited Solomon; until 1975 the Ethiopian royal house traced its descent from their union.

Sheboygan city in E Wisconsin, on Lake Michigan, N of Milwaukee; population (1990) 50,000. Industries include wood, food, plastic, and enamel products.

Shechem ancient town in Palestine, capital of Samaria. In the Old Testament, it is the traditional burial place of Joseph; nearby is Jacob's well. Shechem was destroyed about AD 67 by the Roman emperor Vespasian; on its site stands Nablus (a corruption of Neapolis) built by the Roman emperor ◊Hadrian.

Sheeler Charles 1883–1965. US painter. He is best known for his paintings of factories and urban landscapes, such as *American Landscape* 1930. He was associated with precisionism, a movement that used sharply defined shapes to represent objects. His style was to photograph his subjects before painting them.

sheep any of several ruminant, even-toed, hoofed mammals of the family Bovidae. Wild species survive in the uplands of central and E Asia, N Africa, S Europe, and North America. The domesticated breeds are all classified as *Ovis aries*. Various breeds of sheep are reared worldwide for meat, wool, milk, and cheese, and for rotation on arable land to maintain its fertility.

sheepdog any of several breeds of dog, bred originally for herding sheep. The Old English sheepdog is gray or blue-gray, with white markings, and is about 22 in/56 cm tall at the shoulder. The Shetland sheepdog is much smaller, 14 in/36 cm tall, and shaped more like a long-coated collie. The dog now most commonly used by shepherds and farmers to tend sheep is the border collie.

Sheffield industrial city on the river Don, South Yorkshire, England; population (1991 est) 499,700. From the 12th century, iron smelting was the chief industry, and by the 14th century, Sheffield cutlery, silverware, and plate were made. During the Industrial Revolution the iron and steel industries developed rapidly. It now produces alloys and special steels, cutlery of all kinds, permanent magnets, drills, and precision tools. Other industries include electroplating, type-founding, and the manufacture of optical glass.

sheik leader or chief of an Arab family or village.

shellac resin derived from secretions of the lac insect.

Shelley Mary Wollstonecraft 1797–1851. English writer, the daughter of Mary Wollstonecraft and William Godwin. In 1814 she eloped with the poet Percy Bysshe Shelley, whom she married in 1816. Her novels include ◊*Frankenstein* 1818, *The Last Man* 1826, and *Valperga* 1823.

Shelley Percy Bysshe 1792–1822. English lyric poet, a leading figure in the Romantic movement. Expelled from Oxford University for atheism, he fought all his life against religion and for political freedom. This is reflected in his early poems such as *Queen Mab* 1813. He later wrote tragedies including *The Cenci* 1818, lyric dramas such as *Prometheus Unbound* 1820, and lyrical poems such as "Ode to the West Wind." He drowned while sailing in Italy.

shellfish popular name for mollusks and crustaceans, including the whelk and periwinkle, mussel, oyster, lobster, crab, and shrimp.

shell shock or *combat neurosis* or *battle fatigue* any of the various forms of mental disorder that affect soldiers exposed to heavy explosions or extreme ◊stress. Shell shock was first diagnosed during World War I.

Following the Vietnam War, many veterans were found to be suffering from post-traumatic shock syndrome, in which recurring "flashbacks" to combat experiences torment the sufferer.

Shenyang industrial city and capital of Liaoning province, China; population (1990) 4,500,000. It was the capital of the Manchu emperors 1644–1912; their tombs are nearby.

Shenzen special economic zone established 1980 opposite Hong Kong on the coast of Guangdong province, S China. Its status provided much of the driving force of its spectacular development in the 1980s when its population rose from 20,000 in 1980 to 600,000 in 1989. Part of the population is "rotated": newcomers from other provinces return to their homes after a few years spent learning foreign business techniques.

Shepard Alan Bartlett, Jr 1923– . US astronaut. He undertook the first manned US space flight, the suborbital *Mercury-Redstone 3* mission on board the *Freedom 7* capsule May 1961, and commanded the *Apollo 14* lunar landing mission 1971.

Shepard Sam 1943– . US dramatist and actor. His work combines colloquial American dialogue with striking visual imagery, and includes *The Tooth of Crime* 1972 and *Buried Child* 1978, for which he won a Pulitzer Prize. *Seduced* 1979 is based on the life of the recluse Howard Hughes. He has acted in a number of films, including *The Right Stuff* 1983, *Fool for Love* 1986, based on his play of the same name, and *Steel Magnolias* 1989.

shark The great white shark of the Atlantic, Pacific, and Indian oceans is a large and aggressive fish.

Sheraton Thomas *c.* 1751–1806. English designer of elegant inlaid furniture.

Sheridan Philip Henry 1831–1888. Union general in the American ◊Civil War. Recognizing Sheridan's aggressive spirit, General Ulysses S ◊Grant gave him command of his cavalry in 1864, and soon after of the Army of the Shenandoah Valley, Virginia. Sheridan laid waste to the valley, cutting off grain supplies to the Confederate armies. In the final stage of the war, Sheridan forced General Robert E ◊Lee to retreat to Appomattox and surrender.

Born in Albany, New York, Sheridan graduated from West Point 1853. Following the war, Sheridan led troops at the Mexican border and hastened the collapse of the regime of Emperor Maximilian. Sheridan served as military governor of Texas and Louisiana during ◊Reconstruction; his policies were so harsh that he was removed by President Andrew ◊Johnson. He was made general in chief of the US army 1883–88.

Sheridan Richard Brinsley 1751–1816. Irish dramatist and politician, born in Dublin. His social comedies include *The Rivals* 1775, celebrated for the character of Mrs Malaprop; *The School for Scandal* 1777; and *The Critic* 1779. In 1776 he became lessee of the Drury Lane Theatre. He became a member of Parliament in 1780.

sheriff (Old English *sctr* "shire," *gerēfa* "reeve") in the US, in all states but Rhode Island, the chief elected officer of a county law-enforcement agency, usually responsible for enforcement in unincorporated areas of the county and for the operation of the jail. The sheriff is also the officer of the local court who serves papers and enforces court orders.

Sherman city in NE Texas, N of Dallas; population (1990) 31,600. It is a processing and shipping center for agricultural products; textiles, electronics, and machinery are manufactured.

Sherman Roger 1721–1793. American public official. He was one of the signatories of the Declaration of Independence 1776, the Articles of Confederation 1781, and the US Constitution 1788. A supporter of American independence, he was a member of the Continental Congress 1774–81 and 1783–84. At the Constitutional Convention 1787 he introduced the "Connecticut Compromise," providing for a bicameral federal legislature. Sherman served in the US House of Representatives 1789–91 and the US Senate 1791–93.

Sherman William Tecumseh 1820–1891. Union general in the American ◊Civil War. In 1864 he captured and burned Atlanta; continued his march eastward, to the sea, laying Georgia waste; and then drove the Confederates northward. He was US Army chief of staff 1869–83.

Born in Lancaster, Ohio, Sherman graduated from West Point 1840. He served in the Mexican War and then became a banker. Early in the Civil War he served at the First Battle of Bull Run 1861 and Shiloh 1862. He replaced General U S ◊Grant as commander of the West 1864 and launched his Georgia campaign. Despite the ruthlessness of his campaign to capture Atlanta and the widespread destruction he inflicted as he marched to the sea, he was conciliatory in victory, offering terms that had to be repudiated by President A Johnson. Following the war, there was a move to nominate Sherman for president, but he announced that he would not run if nominated and would not serve if elected. He succeeded Grant as commander of the army 1869.

Sherpa member of a people in NE Nepal related to the Tibetans and renowned for their mountaineering skill.

They frequently work as support staff and guides for climbing expeditions. A Sherpa, Tensing Norgay, was one of the first two people to climb to the summit of Everest.

Sherwood Robert 1896–1955. US dramatist. His plays include *The Petrified Forest* 1934, *Idiot's Delight* 1936, *Abe Lincoln in Illinois* 1938, and *There Shall Be No Night* 1940. For each of the last three he received a Pulitzer prize.

Sherwood Forest hilly stretch of parkland in W Nottinghamshire, England, area about 200 sq mi/520 sq km. Formerly a royal forest, it is associated with the legendary outlaw ◊Robin Hood.

Shetland Islands islands off the N coast of Scotland, beyond the Orkneys
area 541 sq mi/1,400 sq km
cities Lerwick (administrative headquarters), on Mainland, largest of 19 inhabited islands
physical over 100 islands including Muckle Flugga (latitude 60° 51' N) the northernmost of the British Isles
products processed fish, handknits from Fair Isle and Unst, miniature ponies. Europe's largest oil port is Sullom Voe, Mainland
population (1988 est) 22,900
language dialect derived from Norse, the islands having been a Norse dependency from the 8th century until 1472.

Shevardnadze Edvard 1928– . Georgian politician, Soviet foreign minister 1985–91, head of state of Georgia from 1992. A supporter of ◊Gorbachev, he was first secretary of the Georgian Communist Party from 1972 and an advocate of economic reform. In 1985 he became a member of the Politburo, working for détente and disarmament. In July 1991, he resigned from the Communist Party (CPSU) and, along with other reformers and leading democrats, established the Democratic Reform Movement. In March 1992 he was chosen as chair of Georgia's ruling military council, and in Oct elected speaker of parliament.

shield in geology, alternate name for ◊craton, the ancient core of a continent.

shield in technology, any material used to reduce the amount of radiation (electrostatic, electromagnetic, heat, nuclear) reaching from one region of space to another, or any material used as a protection against falling debris, as in tunneling. Electrical conductors are used for electrostatic shields, soft iron for electromagnetic shields, and poor conductors of heat for heat shields. Heavy materials such as lead and concrete are used for protection against X-rays and nuclear radiation. See also ◊heat shield.

Shi Huangdi or *Shih Huang Ti* 259–210 BC. Emperor of China who succeeded to the throne of the state of Qin in 246 BC and reunited China as an empire by 228 BC. He burned almost all existing books in 213 BC to destroy ties with the past; rebuilt the ◊Great Wall of China; and was buried in Xian, Shaanxi province, in a tomb complex guarded by 10,000 life-size terracotta warriors (excavated in the 1980s).

Shiite or *Shiah* member of a sect of Islam that believes that ◊Ali was ◊Mohammed's first true successor. The Shiites are doctrinally opposed to the Sunni Muslims. They developed their own law differing only in minor directions, such as inheritance and the status of women. Holy men have greater authority in the Shiite sect than in the Sunni sect. They are prominent in Iran, Lebanon, and Indo-Pakistan, and are also found in Iraq and Bahrain.

Shikoku smallest of the four main islands of Japan, S of Honshu, E of Kyushu; area 7,257 sq mi/18,800 sq km; population (1986) 4,226,000; chief town Matsuyama. Products include rice, wheat, soybeans, sugar cane, orchard fruits, salt, and copper.

shingles common name for ◊herpes zoster, a disease characterized by infection of sensory nerves, with pain and eruption of blisters along the course of the affected nerves.

Shinto (Chinese *shin tao* "way of the gods") the indigenous religion of Japan. It combines an empathetic oneness with natural forces and loyalty to the reigning dynasty as descendants of the Sun goddess, Amaterasu-Omikami. Traditional Shinto followers stressed obedience and devotion to the emperor, and an aggressive nationalistic aspect was developed by the Meiji rulers. Today Shinto has discarded these aspects.

ship large seagoing vessel. The Greeks, Phoenicians, Romans, and Vikings used ships extensively for trade, exploration, and warfare. The 14th century was the era of European exploration by sailing ship, largely aided by the invention of the compass. In the 15th century Britain's Royal Navy was first formed, but in the 16th–19th centuries Spanish and Dutch fleets dominated the shipping lanes of both the Atlantic and Pacific. The ultimate sailing ships, the fast US and British tea clippers, were built in the 19th century. Also in the 19th century, iron was first used for some shipbuilding instead of wood. Steam-propelled ships of the late 19th century were followed by compound engine and turbine-propelled vessels from the early 20th century.

shire administrative area formed in Britain for the purpose of raising taxes in Anglo-Saxon times. By AD 1000 most of S England had been divided into shires with fortified strongholds at their centers. The Midland counties of England are still known as *the Shires*, for example Derbyshire, Nottinghamshire, and Staffordshire.

Shirer William L(awrence) 1904– . US journalist, author, and historian. A columnist and commentator for the Columbia Broadcasting System (CBS), from 1937 to 1941 he covered the events leading up World War II. He remained with CBS until 1947 and worked for the Mutual Broadcasting System 1947–49. His best-known book is *The Rise and Fall of the Third Reich* 1960.

shock in medicine, circulatory failure marked by a sudden fall of blood pressure and resulting in pallor, sweating, fast (but weak) pulse, and sometimes complete collapse. Causes include disease, injury, and psychological trauma.

Shockley William 1910–1989. US physicist and amateur geneticist who worked with John Bardeen and Walter Brattain on the invention of the ◊transistor. They were jointly awarded a Nobel Prize 1956. During the 1970s Shockley was criticized for his claim that blacks are genetically inferior to whites in terms of intelligence.

Shoemaker Willie (William Lee) 1931– . US jockey 1949–90. He rode 8,833 winners from 40,351 mounts and his earnings exceeded $123 million.

He was the leading US jockey 10 times. After his retirement he became a successful trainer before an automobile accident 1991 left him paralyzed. Standing 4 ft 11 in/1.5 m tall, he weighed about 95 lb/43 kg.

shogun in Japanese history, title of a series of military strongmen 1192–1868 who relegated the emperor's role to that of figurehead. Technically an imperial appointment, the office was treated as hereditary and was held by the ◊Minamoto clan 1192–1219, by the ◊Ashikaga 1336–1573, and by the ◊Tokugawa 1603–1868. The shogun held legislative, judicial, and executive power.

Sholes Christopher Latham 1819–1890. American printer and newspaper editor who, in 1867, invented the first practicable typewriter in association with Carlos Glidden and Samuel Soulé. In 1873, they sold their patents to ◊Remington & Sons, a firm of gunsmiths in New York, who developed and sold the machine commercially. In 1878 Sholes developed a shift-key mechanism that made it possible to touchtype.

Sholokhov Mikhail Aleksandrovich 1905–1984. Soviet novelist. His *And Quiet Flows the Don* 1926–40 depicts the Don Cossacks through World War I and the Russian Revolution. Nobel Prize 1965.

Shona member of a Bantu-speaking people of S Africa, comprising approximately 80% of the population of Zimbabwe. They also occupy the land between the Save and Pungure rivers in Mozambique, and smaller groups are found in South Africa, Botswana, and Zambia. The Shona are mainly farmers, living in scattered villages. The Shona language belongs to the Niger-Congo family.

shoot in botany, the parts of a ◊vascular plant growing above ground, comprising a stem bearing leaves, buds, and flowers. The shoot develops from the plumule of the embryo.

shooting star another name for a ◊meteor.

short circuit direct connection between two points in an electrical circuit. Its relatively low resistance means that a large current flows through it, bypassing the rest of the circuit, and this may cause the circuit to overheat dangerously.

shorthand any system of rapid writing, such as the abbreviations practiced by the Greeks and Romans. The first perfecter of an entirely phonetic system was Isaac ◊Pitman, by which system speeds of about 300 words a minute are said to be attainable.

Short Parliament the English Parliament that was summoned by Charles I on April 13, 1640, to raise funds for his war against the Scots. It was succeeded later in the year by the ◊Long Parliament.

short story short work of prose fiction, which typically either sets up and resolves a single narrative point or depicts a mood or an atmosphere. Short-story writers include Rudyard Kipling, Guy de Maupassant, Saki, Edgar Allan Poe, and Ernest Hemingway.

Shostakovich Dmitry (Dmitriyevich) 1906–1975. Soviet composer. His music is tonal, expressive, and sometimes highly dramatic; it was not always to official Soviet taste. He wrote 15 symphonies, chamber music, ballets, and operas, the latter including *Lady Macbeth of Mtsensk* 1934, which was suppressed as "too divorced from the proletariat," but revived as *Katerina Izmaylova* 1963.

shot put in track and field, the sport of throwing (or putting) overhand from the shoulder a metal ball (or shot). Standard shot weights are 16 lb/7.26 kg for men and 8.8 lb/4 kg for women.

Shrapnel Henry 1761–1842. British army officer who invented shells containing bullets, to increase the spread of casualties, first used 1804; hence the word *shrapnel* to describe shell fragments.

Shreveport port on the Red River, Louisiana; population (1990) 198,500. Industries include oil, natural gas, steel, telephone equipment, glass, and timber. It was founded 1836 and named after Henry Shreeve, a riverboat captain who cleared a giant logjam. The discovery of oil nearby 1906 stimulated economic growth.

shrew insectivorous mammal of the family Soricidae, found in Eurasia and the Americas. It is mouselike, but with a long nose and pointed teeth. Its high metabolic rate means that it must eat almost constantly. The common shrew *Sorex araneus* is about 3 in/7.5 cm long.

shrike "butcher-bird" of the family Laniidae, of which there are over 70 species, living mostly in Africa, but also in Eurasia and North America. They often impale insects and small vertebrates on thorns. They can grow to 14 in/35 cm long, and have gray, black, or brown plumage.

shrimp crustacean related to the ◊prawn. It has a cylindrical, semitransparent body, with ten jointed legs. Some shrimps grow as large as 10 in/25 cm long.

Shropshire county in W England. Sometimes abbreviated to **Salop**, it was officially known by this name from 1974 until local protest reversed the decision 1980
area 1,347 sq mi/3,490 sq km
cities Shrewsbury (administrative headquarters), Telford, Oswestry, Ludlow
physical bisected, on the Welsh border, NW–SE by the river Severn; Ellesmere, the largest of several lakes; the Clee Hills rise to about 1,800 ft/610 m in the SW
features Ironbridge Gorge open-air museum of industrial archeology, with the Iron Bridge (1779)
products chiefly agricultural: sheep and cattle
population (1991) 401,600
famous people Charles Darwin, A E Housman, Wilfred Owen, Gordon Richards.

shroud of Turin Christian relic; see ◊Turin shroud.

Shrove Tuesday in the Christian calendar, the day before the beginning of Lent. It is also known as *Mardi Gras*.

shrub perennial woody plant that typically produces several separate stems, at or near ground level, rather than the single trunk of most trees. A shrub is usually smaller than a tree, but there is no clear distinction between large shrubs and small trees.

Shultz George P 1920– . US Republican politician, economics adviser to President ◊Reagan 1980–82, and secretary of state 1982–89. Shultz taught as a labor economist at the University of Chicago before serving in the 1968–74 ◊Nixon administration, including secretary of labor 1969–70 and secretary of the treasury 1972–74.

shuttle diplomacy in international relations, the efforts of an independent mediator to achieve a compromise solution between belligerent parties, traveling back and forth from one to the other.

SI abbreviation for *Système International [d'Unités]* (French "International System [of Metric Units]"); see ◊SI units.

Sibelius Jean (Christian) 1865–1957. Finnish composer. His works include nationalistic symphonic poems such as *En saga* 1893 and *Finlandia* 1900, a violin concerto 1904, and seven symphonies.

Siberia Asian region of Russia, extending from the Ural Mountains to the Pacific Ocean
area 4,650,000 sq mi/12,050,000 sq km
cities Novosibirsk, Omsk, Krasnoyarsk, Irkutsk
features long and extremely cold winters
products hydroelectric power from rivers Lena, Ob, and Yenisei; forestry; mineral resources, including gold, diamonds, oil, natural gas, iron, copper, nickel, cobalt.

Sibyl in Roman legend, priestess of Apollo. She offered to sell ◊Tarquinius Superbus nine collections of prophecies, the *Sibylline Books*, but the price was too high. When she had destroyed all but three, he bought those for the identical price, and these were kept for consultation in emergency at Rome.

sic (Latin "thus," "so") sometimes found in brackets within a printed quotation to show that the original has been quoted accurately even though it contains an apparent error ("she wrote threatening to charge me with assult and batery [sic] if I did not apologize").

Sichuan or *Szechwan* province of central China
area 219,634 sq mi/569,000 sq km
capital Chengdu
cities Chongqing
features surrounded by mountains, it was the headquarters of the Nationalist government 1937–45, and China's nuclear research centersare here. It is China's most populous administrative area
products rice, coal, oil, natural gas
population (1990) 107,218,000.

Sicily (Italian *Sicilia*) the largest Mediterranean island, an autonomous region of Italy; area 9,920 sq mi/25,700 sq km; population (1990) 5,196,800. Its capital is Palermo, and towns include the ports of Catania, Messina, Syracuse, and Marsala. It exports Marsala wine, olives, citrus, refined oil and petrochemicals, pharmaceuticals, potash, asphalt, and marble. The region also includes the islands of Lipari, Egadi, Ustica, and Pantelleria. Etna, 10,906 ft/3,323 m high, is the highest volcano in Europe; its last major eruption was in 1971.

sickle harvesting tool of ancient origin characterized by a curving blade with serrated cutting edge and short wooden handle. It was widely used in the Middle East and Europe for cutting wheat, barley, and oats from about 10,000 BC to the 19th century.

sickle-cell disease
Scanning electron micrograph of the abnormal type of red blood cell that causes sickle-cell anemia.

sickle-cell disease hereditary chronic blood disorder common among people of black African descent; also found in the E Mediterranean, parts of the Persian Gulf, and in NE India. It is characterized by distortion and fragility of the red blood cells, which are lost too rapidly from the circulation. This often results in ◊anemia.

sidewinder rattlesnake *Crotalus cerastes* that lives in the deserts of the SW US and Mexico, and moves by throwing its coils into a sideways "jump" across the sand. It can grow up to 30 in/75 cm long.

SIDS acronym for *sudden infant death syndrome,* the technical name for ◊crib death.

Siegfried legendary Germanic and Norse hero. His story, which may contain some historical elements, occurs in the German ◊"Nibelungenlied/Song of the Nibelung" and in the Norse "Elder" or "Poetic" ◊"Edda" and the prose *Völsunga Saga* (in the last two works, the hero is known as Sigurd). Siegfried wins Brunhild for his liege lord and marries his sister, but is eventually killed in the intrigues that follow.

Siegfried Line in World War I, a defensive line established 1918 by the Germans in France; in World War II, the Allies' name for the West Wall, a German defensive line established along its western frontier, from the Netherlands to Switzerland.

siemens SI unit (symbol S) of electrical conductance, the reciprocal of the impedance of an electrical circuit. One siemens equals one ampere per volt. It was formerly called the mho or reciprocal ohm.

Siemens German industrial empire created by four brothers. The eldest, *Ernst Werner von Siemens*

(1812–1892), founded the original electrical firm of Siemens und Halske 1847 and made many advances in telegraphy. *William (Karl Wilhelm)* (1823–1883) moved to England; he perfected the open-hearth production of steel, pioneered the development of the electric locomotive and the laying of transoceanic cables, and improved the electric generator.

Siena city in Tuscany, Italy; population (1985) 60,670. Founded by the Etruscans, it has medieval architecture by ◊Pisano and Donatello, including a 13th-century Gothic cathedral, and many examples of the Sienese school of painting that flourished from the 13th to the 16th centuries. The *Palio* ("banner," in reference to the prize) is a dramatic and dangerous horse race in the main square, held annually (July 2 and August 16) since the Middle Ages.

Sierra Leone country in W Africa, on the Atlantic Ocean, bounded N and E by Guinea and SE by Liberia.

Sierra Madre chief mountain system of Mexico, consisting of three ranges, enclosing the central plateau of the country; highest point Pico de Orizaba 18,700 ft/5,700 m. The Sierra Madre del Sur ("of the south") runs along the SW Pacific coast.

Sierra Nevada mountain range in E California; higest point Mount Whitney 14,500 ft/4,418 m. The Sierra Nevada includes the King's Canyon, Sequoia, and Yosemite Valley national parks.

sievert SI unit (symbol Sv) of radiation dose equivalent. It replaces the rem (1 Sv equals 100 rem). Some types of radiation do more damage than others for the same absorbed dose—for example, the same absorbed

---

Sierra Leone
Republic of

area 27,710 sq mi/71,740 sq km
capital Freetown
cities Koidu, Bo, Kenema, Makeni
physical mountains in E; hills and forest; coastal mangrove swamps
features hot and humid climate (138 in/3,500 mm rainfall p.a.)
head of state and government military council headed by Capt Valentine Strasser from 1992
political system transitional
political parties All People's Congress (APC), moderate socialist; United Front of Political Movements (UNIFORM), center-left
media new press regulations from Feb 1993 threatened half the country's newspapers with closure.
exports palm kernels, cocoa, coffee, ginger, diamonds, bauxite, rutile

currency leone
population (1992) 4,373,000; growth rate 2.5% p.a.
life expectancy men 41, women 47 (1989)
languages English (official), local languages
media no daily newspapers; 13 weekly papers, of which 11 are independent but only one achieves sales of over 5,000 copies
religions animist 52%, Muslim 39%, Protestant 6%, Roman Catholic 2% (1980 est)
literacy men 38%, women 21% (1985 est)
GNP $965 million (1987); $320 per head (1984)

hronology
1808 Became a British colony.
1896 Hinterland declared a British protectorate.
1961 Independence achieved from Britain within the Commonwealth, with Milton Margai, leader of Sierra Leone People's Party (SLPP), as prime minister.
1964 Milton succeeded by his half brother, Albert Margai.
1967 Election results disputed by army, who set up a National Reformation Council and forced the governor-general to leave.
1968 Army revolt made Siaka Stevens, leader of the All People's Congress (APC), prime minister.
1971 New constitution adopted, making Sierra Leone a republic, with Stevens as president.
1978 APC declared only legal party. Stevens sworn in for another seven-year term.
1985 Stevens retired; succeeded by Maj Gen Joseph Momoh.
1989 Attempted coup against President Momoh foiled.
1991 Referendum endorsed multiparty politics.
1992 Military take-over; President Momoh fled. National Provisional Ruling Council (NPRC) established under Capt Valentine Strasser.

dose of alpha radiation causes 20 times as much biological damage as the same dose of beta radiation. The equivalent dose in sieverts is equal to the absorbed dose of radiation in rays multiplied by the relative biological effectiveness. Humans can absorb up to 0.25 Sv without immediate ill effects; 1 Sv may produce radiation sickness; and more than 8 Sv causes death.

sight the detection of light by an ◊eye, which can form images of the outside world.

Sigismund 1368–1437. Holy Roman emperor from 1411. He convened and presided over the council of Constance 1414–18, where he promised protection to the religious reformer ◊Huss, but imprisoned him after his condemnation for heresy and acquiesced in his burning. King of Bohemia from 1419, he led the military campaign against the ◊Hussites.

Signac Paul 1863–1935. French artist. In 1884 he joined with Georges Seurat in founding the Salon des Artistes Indépendants and developing the technique of ◊Pointillism.

signal any sign, gesture, sound, or action that conveys information. Examples include the use of flags (◊semaphore), light (traffic and railroad signals), radio telephony, radio telegraphy (◊Morse code), and electricity (telecommunications and computer networks).

Sigurd hero of Norse legend; see ◊Siegfried.

Sihanouk Norodom 1922– . Cambodian politician, king 1941–55 and from 1993, prime minister 1955–70, when his government was overthrown by a military coup led by Lon Nol. With Pol Pot's resistance front, he overthrew Lon Nol 1975 and again became prime minister 1975–76, when he was forced to resign by the ◊Khmer Rouge. He returned from exile Nov 1991 under the auspices of a United Nations–brokered peace settlement to head the Supreme National Council, a new coalition comprising all Cambodia's warring factions, including the Khmer Rouge.

Sikhism religion professed by 14 million Indians, living mainly in the Punjab. Sikhism was founded by Nanak (1469–c. 1539). Sikhs believe in a single God

silicon chip False-color microscope image of a computer memory chip.

who is the immortal creator of the universe and who has never been incarnate in any form, and in the equality of all human beings; Sikhism is strongly opposed to caste divisions.

Their holy book is the *Guru Granth Sahib*. Guru Gobind Singh (1666–1708) instituted the *Khanda-di-Pahul*, the baptism of the sword, and established the Khalsa ("pure"), the company of the faithful. The Khalsa wear the five Ks: *kes*, long hair; *kangha*, a comb; *kirpan*, a sword; *kachh*, short trousers; and *kara*, a steel bracelet. Sikh men take the last name "Singh" ("lion") and women "Kaur" ("princess").

Sikh Wars two wars in India between the Sikhs and the British: The *First Sikh War 1845–46* followed an invasion of British India by Punjabi Sikhs. The Sikhs were defeated and part of their territory annexed. The *Second Sikh War 1848–49* arose from a Sikh revolt in Multan. They were defeated, and the British annexed the Punjab.

Sikkim or *Denjong* state of NE India; formerly a protected state, it was absorbed by India 1975, the monarchy being abolished. China does not recognize India's sovereignty
area 2,818 sq mi/7,300 sq km
capital Gangtok
features Mount Kangchenjunga; wildlife including birds, butterflies, and orchids
products rice, grain, tea, fruit, soybeans, carpets, cigarettes, lead, zinc, copper
population (1991) 403,600
languages Bhutia, Lepecha, Khaskura (Nepali)—all official
religions Mahayana Buddhism, Hinduism
history ruled by the Namgyol dynasty from the 14th century to 1975, when the last chogyal, or king, was deposed. Allied to Britain 1886, Sikkim became a protectorate of India 1950 and a state of India 1975.

Sikorsky Igor 1889–1972. Ukrainian-born US engineer who built the first successful helicopter. He emigrated to the US 1918, where he first constructed multi-engined flying boats. His first helicopter (the VS300) flew 1939 and a commercial version (the R3) went into production 1943.

silage fodder preserved through controlled fermentation in a ◊silo, an airtight structure that presses green crops. It is used as a winter feed for livestock. The term also refers to stacked crops that may be preserved indefinitely.

Silesia region of Europe that has long been disputed because of its geographical position, mineral resources, and industrial potential; now in Poland and the Czech Republic. Dispute began in the 17th century with claims on the area by both Austria and Prussia. It was seized by Prussia's Frederick the Great, which started the War of the ◊Austrian Succession; this was finally recognized by Austria 1763, after the Seven Years' War. After World War I, it was divided in 1919 among newly formed Czechoslovakia, revived Poland, and Germany, which retained the largest part. In 1945, after World War II, all German Silesia east of the Oder-Neisse line was transferred to Polish administration; about 10 million inhabitants of German origin, both there and in Czechoslovak Silesia, were expelled.

silhouette profile or shadow portrait filled in with black or a dark color. A common pictorial technique in Europe in the late 18th and early 19th centuries, it was named after Etienne de Silhouette (1709–1767), a French finance minister who made paper cut-outs as a hobby.

silicon (Latin *silicium* "silica") brittle, nonmetallic element, symbol Si, atomic number 14, atomic weight 28.086. It is the second-most abundant element (after oxygen) in the Earth's crust and occurs in amorphous and crystalline forms. In nature it is found only in combination with other elements, chiefly with oxygen in silica (silicon dioxide, SiO_2) and the silicates. These form the mineral ◊quartz, which makes up most sands, gravels, and beaches.

silicon chip ◊integrated circuit with microscopically small electrical components on a piece of silicon crystal only a few millimeters square.

silicosis chronic disease of miners and stone cutters who inhale silica dust, which makes the lung tissues fibrous and less capable of aerating the blood. It is a form of pneumoconiosis.

silk fine soft thread produced by the larva of the ◊silkworm moth when making its cocoon. It is soaked, carefully unwrapped, and used in the manufacture of textiles. The introduction of synthetics originally harmed the silk industry, but rising standards of living have produced an increased demand for real silk. It is manufactured in China, India, Japan, and Thailand.

Silk Road ancient and medieval overland route of about 4,000 mi/6,400 km by which silk was brought from China to Europe in return for trade goods; it ran west via the Gobi Desert, Samarkand, and Antioch to Mediterranean ports in Greece, Italy, the Middle East, and Egypt. Buddhism came to China via this route, which was superseded from the 16th century by sea trade.

silk-screen printing or *serigraphy* method of ◊printing based on stencils. It can be used to print on most surfaces, including paper, plastic, cloth, and wood. An impermeable stencil (either paper or photographic) is attached to a finely meshed silk screen that has been stretched on a wooden frame, so that the ink passes through to the area beneath only where the image is required. The design can also be painted directly on the screen with varnish. A series of screens can be used to add successive layers of color to the design.

silkworm usually the larva of the *common silkworm moth Bombyx mori*. After hatching from the egg and maturing on the leaves of white mulberry trees (or a synthetic substitute), it spins a protective cocoon of fine silk thread 900 ft/275 m long. To keep the thread intact, the moth is killed before emerging from the cocoon, and several threads are combined to form the commercial silk thread woven into textiles.

Sills Beverly. Adopted name of Belle Silverman 1929– . US coloratura soprano. She was a child radio star who became one of the world's most dramatically gifted opera singers, making her debut at 17 in Philadelphia. She joined the New York City Opera 1955. She appeared at such European opera houses as La Scala, Milan 1969, and Covent Garden, London 1970. Her Metropolitan Opera debut was in 1975; in 1979 she became director of the New York City Opera, announcing her retirement in 1988. She wrote an autobiography, *Bubbles*, 1976.

silo in farming, an airtight tower in which ◊silage is made by the fermentation of freshly cut grass and other forage crops. In military technology, a silo is an underground chamber for housing and launching a ballistic missile.

Silurian period of geological time 439–409 million years ago, the third period of the Paleozoic era. Silurian sediments are mostly marine and consist of shales and limestone. Luxuriant reefs were built by corallike organisms. The first land plants began to evolve during this period, and there were many ostracoderms (armored jawless fishes). The first jawed fishes (called acanthodians) also appeared.

silver white, lustrous, extremely malleable and ductile, metallic element, symbol Ag (from Latin *argentum*), atomic number 47, atomic weight 107.868. It occurs in nature in ores and as a free metal; the chief ores are sulfides, from which the metal is extracted by smelting with lead. It is one of the best metallic conductors of both heat and electricity; its most useful compounds are the chloride and bromide, which darken on exposure to light and are the basis of photographic emulsions.

silverfish wingless insect, a type of bristletail.

Simenon Georges 1903–1989. Belgian crime writer. Initially a pulp fiction writer, in 1931 he created Inspector Maigret of the Paris Sûreté who appeared in a series of detective novels.

simile figure of speech that in English uses the conjunctions *like* and *as* to express comparisons ("run like the devil"; "as deaf as a post"). It is sometimes confused with ◊metaphor.

Simon (Marvin) Neil 1927– . US playwright. His stage plays (which were made into films) include the wryly comic *Barefoot in the Park* 1963, *The Odd Couple* 1965, and *The Sunshine Boys* 1972, and the more serious, autobiographical trilogy *Brighton Beach Memoirs* 1983, *Biloxi Blues* 1985, and *Broadway Bound* 1986. He has also written screenplays and co-written musicals.

Simon Herbert 1916– . US social scientist. He researched decision making in business corporations and argued that maximum profit was seldom the chief motive. He attempted to examine the psychological factors involved in decision making and created the concept of "satisfying behavior" as motivation for some decisions. He also was deeply involved in the effort to create artificial intelligence technology capable of analyzing the factors that influence human problem-solving processes. He was awarded the Nobel Prize for Economics 1978.

Simon Paul 1942– . US pop singer and songwriter. In a folk-rock duo with Art Garfunkel (1942–), he had such hits as "Mrs Robinson" 1968 and "Bridge Over Troubled Water" 1970. Simon's solo work includes the critically acclaimed album *Graceland* 1986, for which he drew on Cajun and African music.

simony in the Christian church, the buying and selling of church preferments, now usually regarded as a sin.

Simpson Wallis Warfield, Duchess of Windsor 1896–1986. US socialite, twice divorced. She married ◊Edward VIII 1937, who abdicated in order to marry her. He was given the title Duke of Windsor by his brother, George VI, who succeeded him.

sin transgression of the will of God or the gods, as revealed in the moral code laid down by a particular religion. In Roman Catholic theology, a distinction is made between *mortal sins*, which, if unforgiven, result in damnation, and *venial sins*, which are less serious. In Islam, the one unforgivable sin is *shirk*, denial that Allah is the only god.

Sinai Egyptian peninsula, at the head of the Red Sea; area 25,000 sq mi/65,000 sq km. Resources include oil, natural gas, manganese, and coal; irrigation water from the river Nile is carried under the Suez Canal.

Sinai, Mount (Arabic *Gebel Mûsa*) mountain near the tip of the Sinai Peninsula; height 7,500 ft/2,285 m. According to the Old Testament this is where ◊Moses received the Ten Commandments from God.

Sinatra Frank (Francis Albert) 1915– . US singer and film actor. Celebrated for his phrasing and emotion, especially on love ballads, he is particularly associated with the song "My Way." His films from 1941 include *From Here to Eternity* 1953 (Academy Award) and *Guys and Dolls* 1955.

Sinclair Upton 1878–1968. US novelist. His concern for social reforms is reflected in *The Jungle* 1906, an important example of naturalistic writing, which exposed the horrors of the Chicago meatpacking industry and led to a change in food-processing laws; *Boston* 1928; and his Lanny Budd series 1940–53, including *Dragon's Teeth* 1942, which won a Pulitzer Prize.

He was a committed Socialist who was actively involved in politics.

Sindhi member of the majority ethnic group living in the Pakistani province of Sind. The Sindhi language is spoken by about 15 million people. Since the partition of India and Pakistan 1947, large numbers of Urdu-speaking refugees have moved into the region from India, especially into the capital, Karachi.

sine in trigonometry, a function of an angle in a right-angled triangle which is defined as the ratio of the length of the side opposite the angle to the length of the hypotenuse (the longest side).

Singapore (Sanskrit *Singa pura* "city of the lion") country in SE Asia, off the tip of the Malay Peninsula.

Singer Isaac Bashevis 1904–1991. Polish-born US novelist and short-story writer, in the US from 1935. His works, written in Yiddish, often portray traditional Jewish life in Poland and the US, and the loneliness of old age. They include *The Family Moskat* 1950 and *Gimpel the Fool and Other Stories* 1957. Nobel Prize 1978.

Singer Isaac Merit 1811–1875. US inventor of domestic and industrial sewing machines. Within a few years of opening his first factory 1851, he became the world's largest manufacturer (despite charges of patent infringement by Elias Howe), and by the late 1860s more than 100,000 Singer sewing machines were in use in the US alone.

Singh Vishwanath Pratap 1931– . Indian politician, prime minister 1989–90. As a member of the Congress (I) Party, he held ministerial posts under Indira Gandhi and Rajiv Gandhi, and from 1984 led an anticorruption drive. When he unearthed an arms-sales scandal 1988, he was ousted from the government and party and formed a broad-based opposition alliance, the ◊Janata Dal, which won the Nov 1989 election. Mounting caste and communal conflict split the Janata Dal and forced him out of office Nov 1990.

Singh, Gobind see ◊Gobind Singh, Sikh guru.

Sinhalese member of the majority ethnic group of Sri Lanka (70% of the population). Sinhalese is the official language of Sri Lanka; it belongs to the Indo-Iranian branch of the Indo-European family, and is written in a script derived from the Indian Pali form. The Sinhalese are Buddhists. Since 1971 they have been involved in a violent struggle with the Tamil minority, who are seeking independence.

Singapore
Republic of

area 240 sq mi/622 sq km
capital Singapore City
cities Jurong, Changi
physical comprises Singapore Island, low and flat, and 57 small islands
features Singapore Island is joined to the mainland by causeway across Strait of Johore; temperature range 69°–93°F/21°–34°C
head of state Ong Teng Cheong from 1993
head of government Goh Chok Tong from 1990
political system liberal democracy with strict limits on dissent

political parties People's Action Party (PAP), conservative; Workers' Party (WP), socialist; Singapore Democratic Party (SDP), liberal pluralist
exports electronics, petroleum products, rubber, machinery, vehicles
currency Singapore dollar
population (1992) 2,792,000 (Chinese 75%, Malay 14%, Tamil 7%); growth rate 1.2% p.a.
life expectancy men 71, women 77 (1989)
languages Malay (national tongue), Chinese, Tamil, English (all official)
religions Buddhist, Taoist, Muslim, Hindu, Christian
literacy men 93%, women 79% (1985 est)
GDP $19.9 bn (1987); $7,616 per head

chronology
1819 Singapore leased to British East India Company.
1858 Placed under crown rule.
1942 Invaded and occupied by Japan.
1945 Japanese removed by British forces.
1959 Independence achieved from Britain; Lee Kuan Yew became prime minister.
1963 Joined new Federation of Malaysia.
1965 Left federation to become an independent republic.
1984 Opposition made advances in parliamentary elections.
1986 Opposition leader convicted of perjury and prohibited from running for election.
1988 Ruling conservative party elected to all but one of available assembly seats; increasingly authoritarian rule.
1990 Lee Kuan Yew resigned as prime minister; replaced by Goh Chok Tong.
1991 PAP and Goh Chok Tong reelected.
1992 Lee Kuan Yew surrendered PAP leadership to Goh Chok Tong.
1993 Ong Teng Cheong elected president.

sink hole funnel-shaped hollow in an area of limestone. A sink hole is usually formed by the enlargement of a joint, or crack, by ◊carbonation (the dissolving effect of water). It should not be confused with a swallow hole, or swallet, which is the opening through which a stream disappears underground when it passes onto limestone.

Sinn Féin ("We ourselves") Irish nationalist party founded by Arthur Griffith (1872–1922) in 1905; in 1917 Eamon ◊de Valera became its president. It is the political wing of the Irish Republican Army, and is similarly split between comparative moderates and extremists. In 1985 it gained representation in 17 out of 26 district councils in Northern Ireland.

Sino-Japanese Wars two wars waged by Japan against China 1894–95 and 1931–45 to expand to the mainland. Territory gained in the First Sino-Japanese War (Korea) and in the 1930s (Manchuria, Shanghai) was returned at the end of World War II.

Sino-Tibetan languages group of languages spoken in SE Asia. This group covers a large area, and includes Chinese and Burmese, both of which have numerous dialects. Some classifications include the Tai group of languages (including Thai and Lao) in the Sino-Tibetan family.

sinusitis painful inflammation of one of the sinuses, or air spaces, that surround the nasal passages. Most cases clear with antibiotics and nasal decongestants, but some require surgical drainage.

Sioux (or ***Dakota***) a member of a group of North American ◊Plains Indians, now living on reservations in South Dakota and Nebraska, and among the general public. Their language belongs to the Macro-Siouan family.

Sioux City city in NW Iowa, on the Missouri River, near Iowa's border with Nebraska and South Dakota; population (1990) 80,500. Industries include food processing, fabricated metals, fertilizer, and meatpacking. It is the head of navigation for the Missouri River.

Sioux Falls largest city in South Dakota; population (1990) 100,800. Its industry (electrical goods and agricultural machinery) is powered by the Big Sioux River over the Sioux Falls 100 ft/30 m.

siren in Greek legend, a sea ◊nymph who lured sailors to their deaths along rocky coasts by her singing. ◊Odysseus, in order to hear the sirens safely, tied himself to the mast of his ship and stuffed his crew's ears with wax.

Sirius or ***Dog Star*** or ***Alpha Canis Majoris*** the brightest star in the sky, 8.6 light-years from Earth in the constellation Canis Major. Sirius is a white star with a mass 2.3 times that of the Sun, a diameter 1.8 times that of the Sun, and a luminosity of 23 Suns. It is orbited every 50 years by a white dwarf, Sirius B, also known as the Pup.

sirocco hot, normally dry and dust-laden wind that blows from the deserts of N Africa across the Mediterranean into S Europe. It occurs mainly in the spring. The name "sirocco" is also applied to any hot oppressive wind.

sisal strong fiber made from various species of ◊agave, such as *Agave sisalina*.

Sistine Chapel chapel in the Vatican, Rome, begun under Pope Sixtus IV in 1473 by Giovanni del Dolci, and decorated by (among others) Michelangelo. It houses the conclave that meets to select a new pope.

Singapore
Singapore's city skyline.

Sisyphus in Greek mythology, a king of Corinth who, as punishment for his evil life, was condemned in the underworld to roll a huge stone uphill; it always fell back before he could reach the top.

Sita in Hinduism, the wife of Rama, an avatar (manifestation) of the god Vishnu; a character in the ◊Rāmāyana epic, characterized by chastity and kindness.

sitar Indian stringed instrument. It has a pear-shaped body, long neck, and an additional gourd resonator at the opposite end. A principal solo instrument, it has seven metal strings extending over movable frets and two concealed strings that provide a continuous singing drone.

Sitting Bull Sioux Indian chief Sitting Bull fought a rearguard action against white incursions into Indian lands.

Sitting Bull c. 1834–1893. North American Indian chief who agreed to ◊Sioux resettlement 1868. When the treaty was broken by the US, he led the Sioux against Lieutenant Colonel ◊Custer at the Battle of the ◊Little Bighorn 1876. *See illustration p. 847*

SI units (French *Système International d'Unités*) standard system of scientific units used by scientists worldwide. Originally proposed in 1960, it replaces the m.k.s., c.g.s., and f.p.s. systems. It is based on seven basic units: the meter (m) for length, kilogram (kg) for mass, second (s) for time, ampere (A) for electrical current, kelvin (K) for temperature, mole (mol) for amount of substance, and candela (cd) for luminosity.

Siva or **Shiva** in Hinduism, the third chief god (with Brahma and Vishnu). As Mahadeva (great lord), he is the creator, symbolized by the phallic *lingam*, who restores what as Mahakala he destroys. He is often sculpted as Nataraja, performing his fruitful cosmic dance. His consort or female principle (*sakti*) is Parvati, otherwise known as Durga or Kali.

Six-Day War another name for the third ◊Arab–Israeli War

skate any of several species of flatfish of the ray group. The common skate *Raja batis* is up to 6 ft/1.8 m long and grayish, with black specks. Its egg cases ("mermaids' purses") are often washed ashore by the tide.

skateboard single flexible board mounted on wheels and steerable by weight positioning. As a land alternative to surfing, skateboards developed in California in the 1960s and became a worldwide craze in the 1970s. Skateboarding is practiced in urban environments and has enjoyed a revival since the late 1980s.

skating self-propulsion on ice by means of bladed skates, or on other surfaces by skates with small rollers (wheels of wood, metal, or plastic). The chief competitive ice-skating events are figure skating, for singles or pairs, ice-dancing, and simple speed skating. The first world ice-skating championships were held in 1896.

skeleton the rigid or semirigid framework that supports an animal's body, protects its internal organs, and provides anchorage points for its muscles. The skeleton may be composed of bone and cartilage (vertebrates), chitin (arthropods), calcium carbonate (mollusks and other invertebrates), or silica (many protists).

skepticism ancient philosophical view that absolute knowledge of things is ultimately unobtainable, hence the only proper attitude is to suspend judgment. Its origins lay in the teachings of the Greek philosopher Pyrrho, who maintained that peace of mind lay in renouncing all claims to knowledge.

skiing self-propulsion on snow by means of elongated runners (skis) for the feet, slightly bent upward at the tip. It is a popular recreational sport, as cross-country ski touring or as downhill runs on mountain trails; events include downhill; slalom, in which a series of turns between flags have to be negotiated; cross-country racing; and ski jumping, when jumps of over 490 ft/150 m are achieved from ramps up to 295 ft/90 m high. Speed-skiing uses skis approximately one-third longer and wider than normal with which speeds of up to 125 mph/200 kph have been recorded. Recently, *snowboarding* (or monoboarding), the use of a single, very broad ski, similar to a surf board, used with the feet facing the front and placed together, has become increasingly popular.

SI units		
quantity	*SI unit*	*symbol*
absorbed radiation dose	gray	Gy
amount of substance	mole*	mol
electric capacitance	farad	F
electric charge	coulomb	C
electric conductance	siemens	S
electric current	ampere*	A
energy or work	joule	J
force	newton	N
frequency	hertz	Hz
illuminance	lux	lx
inductance	henry	H
length	meter*	m
luminous flux	lumen	lm
luminous intensity	candela*	cd
magnetic flux	weber	Wb
magnetic flux density	tesla	T
mass	kilogram*	kg
plane angle	radian	rad
potential difference	volt	V
power	watt	W
pressure	pascal	Pa
radiation dose equivalent	sievert	Sv
radiation exposure	roentgen	r
radioactivity	becquerel	Bq
resistance	ohm	Ω
solid angle	steradian	sr
sound intensity	decibel	dB
temperature	°Celsius	°C
temperature, thermodynamic	kelvin*	K
time	second*	s
*SI base unit		

skin the covering of the body of a vertebrate. In mammals, the outer layer (epidermis) is dead and protective, and its cells are constantly being rubbed away and replaced from below. The lower layer (dermis) contains blood vessels, nerves, hair roots, and sweat and sebaceous glands, and is supported by a network of fibrous and elastic cells.

Skinner B(urrhus) F(rederic) 1903–1990. US psychologist, a radical behaviorist who rejected mental concepts, seeing the organism as a "black box" where internal processes are not significant in predicting behavior. He studied operant conditioning and maintained that behavior is shaped and maintained by its consequences.

Skopje capital and industrial city of the Former Yugoslav Republic of Macedonia; population (1981) 506,547. Industries include iron, steel, chromium mining, and food processing.

skull in vertebrates, the collection of flat and irregularly shaped bones (or cartilage) that enclose the brain and the organs of sight, hearing, and smell, and provide support for the jaws. In mammals, the skull consists of 22 bones joined by sutures. The floor of the skull is pierced by a large hole for the spinal cord and a number of smaller apertures through which other nerves and blood vessels pass. *See illustration p. 850*

skunk North American mammal of the weasel family. The common skunk *Mephitis mephitis* has a long, arched body, short legs, a bushy tail, and black fur with white streaks on the back. In self-defense, it discharges a foul-smelling fluid.

skunk cabbage either of two disagreeably smelling North American plants of the arum family Araceae: *Symplocarpus foetidus*, of the E, growing in wet soils

skiing Swiss skier Pirmin Zurbriggen at the World Championships 1989.

and having large, cabbagelike leaves and a fleshy blunt spike of tiny flowers in a purple, hooded sheath; or *Lysichiton americanum* of the W, having similar appearance except that the sheath enclosing a more elongated flower spike is yellow.

skydiving sport of freefalling from an aircraft at a height of up to 12,000 ft/3,650 m, performing aerobatics, and opening a parachute when 2,000 ft/600 m from the ground.

Skye largest island of the Inner Hebrides, Scotland; area 672 sq mi/1,740 sq km; population (1987) 8,100. It is separated from the mainland by the Sound of Sleat. The chief port is Portree.

The economy is based on crofting, tourism, and livestock. A privately financed toll bridge to the island is due to be completed 1995.

Skylab US space station, launched May 14, 1973, made from the adapted upper stage of a Saturn V rocket. At 82.5 tons/75 tonnes, it was the heaviest object ever put into space, and was 84 ft/25.6 m long. *Skylab* contained a workshop for carrying out experiments in weightlessness, an observatory for monitoring the Sun, and cameras for photographing the Earth's surface.

skyscraper building so tall that it appears to "scrape the sky," developed 1868 in New York, where land

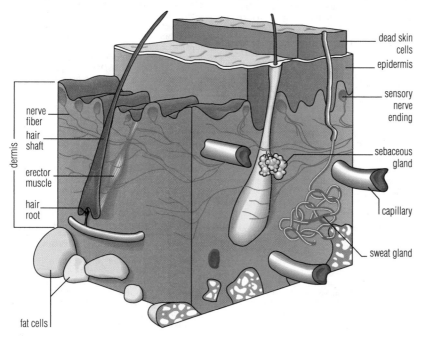

dead skin cells

epidermis

sensory nerve ending

sebaceous gland

capillary

sweat gland

nerve fiber

hair shaft

dermis

erector muscle

hair root

fat cells

skin The skin of an adult man covers about 20 sq ft/1.9 sq m; a woman's skin covers about 17 sq ft/1.6 sq m.

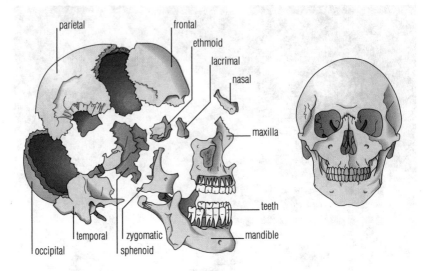

skull *The skull is a protective box for the brain, eyes, and hearing organs.*

parietal

frontal

ethmoid

lacrimal

nasal

maxilla

teeth

mandible

temporal

zygomatic

occipital

sphenoid

prices were high and the geology allowed such methods of construction. Skyscrapers are now found in cities throughout the world. The world's tallest free-standing structure is the CN (Canadian National) Tower, Toronto, 1,821 ft/555 m.

slag in chemistry, the molten mass of impurities that is produced in the smelting or refining of metals.

slaked lime Ca(OH)$_2$ (technical name *calcium hydroxide*) substance produced by adding water to quicklime (calcium oxide, CaO). Much heat is given out and the solid crumbles as it absorbs water. A solution of slaked lime is called limewater.

slang very informal language usage that often serves to promote a feeling of group membership. It is not usually accepted in formal speech or writing and includes expressions that may be impolite or taboo in conventional communication.

slash and burn simple agricultural method whereby natural vegetation is cut and burned, and the clearing then farmed for a few years until the soil loses its fertility, whereupon farmers move on and leave the area to regrow. Although this is possible with a small, widely dispersed population, it becomes unsustainable with more people and is now a form of ◊deforestation.

slate fine-grained, usually gray metamorphic rock that splits readily into thin slabs along its ◊cleavage planes. It is the metamorphic equivalent of ◊shale.

Slater Samuel 1768–1835. British-born US industrialist, whose knowledge of industrial technology and business acumen as a mill owner and banker made him a central figure in the New England textile industry. At first working for American firms, he established his own manufacturing company 1798.

Slaughterhouse Cases two related US Supreme Court cases (*The Butchers' Benevolent Association of New Orleans* v *The Crescent City Livestock Landing and Slaughter Co*; *Esteban* v *Louisiana*) 1873 brought against the Louisiana legislature for its law granting one slaughterhouse exclusive rights to operate in New Orleans. The suits claimed that this monopoly was in violation of the privileges and immunities clause of the 14th Amendment because it prevented citizens from pursuing the professions of their choice. The Court upheld the Louisiana monopoly statute by 5 to 4, implementing a narrow interpretation of the 14th Amendment that left the protection of most civil rights to state governments.

Slav member of an Indo-European people in central and E Europe, the Balkans, and parts of N Asia, speaking closely related ◊Slavonic languages. The ancestors of the Slavs are believed to have included the Sarmatians and ◊Scythians. Moving west from Central Asia, they settled in E and SE Europe during the 2nd and 3rd millennia BC.

The present Slavonic nations emerged around the 5th and 6th centuries AD. By the 7th century they were the predominant population of E and SE Europe.

slavery the enforced servitude of one person (a slave) to another or one group to another. A slave has no personal rights and is the property of another person through birth, purchase, or capture. Slavery goes back to prehistoric times but declined in Europe after the fall of the Roman Empire. During the imperialism of Spain, Portugal, and Britain in the 16th–18th centuries and in the American South in the 17th–19th centuries, slavery became a mainstay of an agricultural factory economy, with millions of Africans sold to work on plantations in North and South America. Millions more died in the process, but the profits from this trade were enormous. Slavery was abolished in the British Empire 1833 and in the US at the end of the Civil War 1863–65, but continues illegally in some countries.

Slavonic languages or *Slavic languages* branch of the Indo-European language family spoken in central and E Europe, the Balkans, and parts of N Asia. The family comprises the *southern group* (Slovene, Serbo-Croatian, Macedonian, and Bulgarian); the *western group* (Czech and Slovak, Sorbian in Germany, and Polish and its related dialects); and the *eastern group* (Russian, Ukrainian, and Belarusian).

sleep state of reduced awareness and activity that occurs at regular intervals in most mammals and birds, though there is considerable variation in the amount of time spent sleeping. Sleep differs from hibernation in that it occurs daily rather than seasonally, and involves less drastic reductions in metabolism. The function of sleep is unclear. People deprived

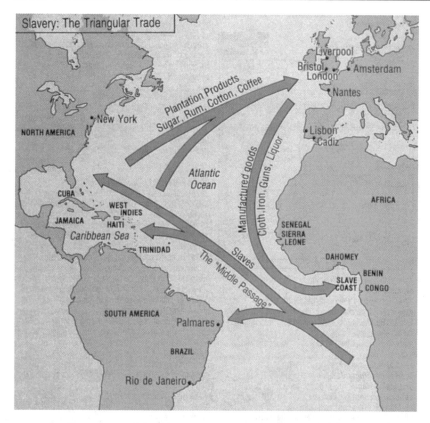

Slavery: The Triangular Trade

of sleep become irritable, uncoordinated, forgetful, hallucinatory, and even psychotic.

sleeping pill any pill or capsule that contains a drug (especially one of the ◊barbiturates) that induces sleep; in small doses, such drugs may relieve anxiety.

sleeping sickness or *trypanosomiasis* infectious disease of tropical Africa. Early symptoms include fever, headache, and chills, followed by ◊anemia and joint pains. Later, the disease attacks the central nervous system, causing drowsiness, lethargy, and, if left untreated, death. Sleeping sickness is caused by either of two ◊trypanosomes, *Trypanosoma gambiense* or *T. rhodiense*. Control is by eradication of the tsetse fly, which transmits the disease to humans.

Slidell John 1793–1871. American public official and diplomat. He was named minister to Mexico by President Polk 1845–48 and later served in the US Senate from 1853 to the outbreak of the American Civil War 1861, when he resigned and joined the Confederacy. He was captured and imprisoned by the US navy, living in exile in France after his release 1862.

slide rule mathematical instrument with pairs of logarithmic sliding scales, used for rapid calculations, including multiplication, division, and the extraction of square roots. It has been largely superseded by the electronic calculator.

Sligo county in the province of Connacht, Republic of Ireland, situated on the Atlantic coast of NW Ireland; area 695 sq mi/1,800 sq km; population (1991) 54,700. The county town is Sligo; there is livestock and dairy farming.

slime mold an extraordinary organism that shows some features of ◊fungus and some of ◊protozoa. Slime molds are not closely related to any other group, although they are often classed, for convenience, with the fungi.

Sloan John 1871–1951. US painter. Encouraged to paint by Robert ◊Henri, he later helped organize "The Eight," a group of realists who were against academic standards. He moved to New York 1904 and helped to organize the avant-garde Armory Show 1913. His paintings of working-class urban life pioneered the field of American realism.

sloth South American mammal, about 2.5 ft/70 cm long, of the order Edentata. Sloths are grayish brown and have small rounded heads, rudimentary tails, and prolonged forelimbs. Each foot has long curved claws adapted to clinging upside down from trees. They are vegetarian.

Slovakia one of the two republics that formed the Federative Republic of Czechoslovakia. Settled in the 5th–6th centuries by Slavs; it was occupied by the magyars in the 10th century, and was part of the kingdom of Hungary until 1918, when it became a province of Czechoslovakia. Slovakia was a puppet state under German domination 1939–45, and was abolished as an administrative division in 1949. Its capital and chief town is Bratislava. It was re-established as a sovereign state after the breakup of the Czechoslovak Republic in 1993.

Slovak Republic country in E central Europe, bounded N by Poland, W by Ukraine, S by Hungary, SW by Austria, and NW by the Czech Republic.

Slovak Republic

Slovak Republic
(*Slovenská Republika*)

area 18,940 sq mi/49,035 sq km
capital Bratislava
cities Košice, Nitra, Prešov, Banská Bystrica
physical W range of the Carpathian Mountains including
Tatra and Beskids in N; Danube plain in S; numerous lakes
and mineral springs
features fine beech and oak forests with bears and wild
boar
head of state Michal Kovak from 1993
head of government prime minister
political system emergent democracy
political parties Civic Democratic Union (CDU), center-
left; Movement for a Democratic Slovakia (HZDS), center-left,
nationalist; Christian Democratic Movement (KDH), right of
center; Slovak National Party, nationalist; Party of the
Democratic Left, left-wing, ex-communist; Coexistence and

Hungarian Christian Democratic Movement, both
representing Hungarian minority
exports iron ore, copper, mercury, magnesite, armaments,
chemicals, textiles, machinery
currency new currency based on koruna
population (1991) 5,268,900 (with Hungarian and other
minorities); growth rate 0.4% p.a.
life expectancy men 68, women 75
languages Slovak (official)
religions Roman Catholic (over 50%), Lutheran, Reformist,
Orthodox
literacy 100%
GDP $10,000 million (1990); $1,887 per head

chronology
906–1918 Under Magyar domination.
1918 Independence achieved from Austro-Hungarian
Empire; Slovaks joined Czechs in forming Czechoslovakia as
independent nation.
1948 Communists assumed power in Czechoslovakia.
1968 Slovak Socialist Republic created under new federal
constitution.
1989 Prodemocracy demonstrations in Bratislava; new
political parties formed, including Slovak-based People
Against Violence (PAV); Communist Party stripped of
powers. Dec: new government formed, including former
dissidents; political parties legalized; Václav Havel appointed
president of Czechoslovakia.
1991 Evidence of increasing Slovak separatism. March: PAV
splinter group formed under Slovak premier Vladimir Meciar.
April: Meciar dismissed, replaced by Jan Carnogursky.
1992 March: PAV renamed Civic Democratic Union (CDU).
June: Havel resigned following Slovak gains in assembly
elections. Aug: agreement on creation of separate Czech and
Slovak states.
1993 Jan: Slovak Republic became sovereign state, with
Meciar, leader of the MFDS, as prime minister. Feb: Michal
Kovak became president.
1994 Mar. No confidence vote in Parliament tumbles Meciar
regime from power.

Slovenia or *Slovenija* country in S central Europe,
bounded N by Austria, E by Hungary, W by Italy, and
S by Croatia.

slug air-breathing gastropod related to the snails, but
with absent or much reduced shell.

Sluis, Battle of (or *Sluys*) 1340 naval victory for
England over France which marked the beginning of
the Hundred Years' War. England took control of the
English Channel and seized 200 great ships from the
French navy of Philip IV; there were 30,000 French
casualties.

small arms one of the two main divisions of
firearms: guns that can be carried by hand. The first
small arms were portable handguns in use in the late
14th century, supported on the ground and ignited by
hand. Today's small arms range from breech-loading
single-shot rifles and shotguns to sophisticated automatic and semiautomatic weapons. In 1980, there were
11,522 deaths in the US caused by hand-held guns; in
the UK, there were 8. From 1988 guns accounted for
more deaths among teenage US males than all other
causes put together.

small claims court in the US, a court that deals with
small civil claims, using a simple procedure, often
without attorney intervention.

smallpox acute, highly contagious viral disease,
marked by aches, fever, vomiting, and skin eruptions
leaving pitted scars. Widespread vaccination programs have almost eradicated this often fatal disease.

smart card plastic card with an embedded microprocessor and memory. It can store, for example, personal data, identification, and bank-account details, to
enable it to be used as a credit or debit card. The card
can be loaded with credits, which are then spent electronically, and reloaded as needed. Possible other uses
range from hotel door "keys" to passports.

smell sense that responds to chemical molecules in
the air. It works by having receptors for particular
chemical groups, into which the airborne chemicals
must fit to trigger a message to the brain.

smelling salts or *sal volatile* a mixture of ammonium carbonate, bicarbonate, and carbonate together
with other strong-smelling substances, formerly used
as a restorative for dizziness or fainting.

smelt small fish, usually marine, although some
species are freshwater. They occur in Europe and
North America. The most common European smelt is
the sparling *Osmerus eperlanus*.

Smetana Bedřich 1824–1884. Czech composer whose
music has a distinct national character, as in, for
example, the operas *The Bartered Bride* 1866 and *Dal-
ibor* 1868, and the symphonic suite *My Country*
1875–80. He conducted the National Theater of Prague
1866–74.

Smith Adam 1723–1790. Scottish economist, often
regarded as the founder of political economy. His *The
Wealth of Nations* 1776 defined national wealth in
terms of labor. The cause of wealth is explained by the

division of labor—dividing a production process into several repetitive operations, each carried out by different workers. Smith advocated the free working of individual enterprise, and the necessity of "free trade."

Smith Al (Alfred Emanuel) 1873–1944. US political leader who served four terms as governor of New York but was unsuccessful as a candidate for the presidency. In 1928 he became the first Roman Catholic to receive a presidential nomination. In his lively, yet unsuccessful, campaign against Herbert Hoover he was called "The Happy Warrior."

Smith Bessie 1894–1937. US jazz and blues singer, born in Chattanooga, Tennessee. Known as the "Empress of the Blues," she established herself in the 1920s after she was discovered by Columbia Records. She made over 150 recordings accompanied by such greats as Louis Armstrong and Benny Goodman.

Her popularity waned in the Depression and she died after an auto accident.

Smith David 1906–1965. US sculptor and painter, whose work made a lasting impact on sculpture after World War II. He trained as a steel welder in an automobile factory. His pieces are large openwork metal abstracts.

Smith Ian (Douglas) 1919– . Rhodesian politician. He was a founder of the Rhodesian Front 1962 and prime minister 1964–79. In 1965 he made a unilateral declaration of Rhodesia's independence and, despite United Nations sanctions, maintained his regime with tenacity. In 1979 he was succeeded as prime minister by Bishop Abel Muzorewa, when the country was renamed Zimbabwe. He was suspended from the Zim-

babwe parliament April 1987 and resigned in May as head of the white opposition party.

Smith John 1580–1631. English colonist. After an adventurous early life he took part in the colonization of Virginia, acting as president of the North American colony 1608–09. He explored New England in 1614, which he named, and published pamphlets on America and an autobiography. His trade with the Indians may have kept the colonists alive in the early years.

Smith Joseph 1805–1844. US founder of the ♢Mormon religious sect.

Born in Vermont, he received his first religious call in 1820, and in 1827 claimed to have been granted the revelation of the **Book of Mormon** (an ancient American prophet), inscribed on gold plates and concealed a thousand years before in a hill near Palmyra, New York. He founded the Church of Jesus Christ of Latter-day Saints in Fayette, New York, 1830. The headquarters of the church was moved to Kirkland, Ohio, 1831; to Missouri 1838; and to Nauvoo, Illinois, 1840. Smith began the construction of a Mormon temple at Nauvoo, organized a private army to defend the sect from its enemies, and declared his candidacy for president. Hostility to Smith intensified when rumors that he had taken several wives began to circulate; Smith publicly opposed polygamy and acknowledged only one wife. He was jailed after some of his followers destroyed the printing press of a newspaper that had attacked him, and a mob stormed the jail and killed him.

Smith Maggie (Margaret Natalie) 1934– . English actress, notable for her commanding presence, fluting voice, and throwaway lines. Her films include *The*

Slovenia
Republic of

area 7,817 sq mi/20,251 sq km
capital Ljubljana
cities Maribor, Kranj, Celji; chief port: Koper
physical mountainous; Sava and Drava rivers
head of state Milan Kučan from 1990
head of government Janez Drnovšek from 1992
political system emergent democracy
political parties Christian Democratic Party, right of center; People's Party, right of center; Liberal Democratic Party, left of center; Democratic Party, left of center
products grain, sugarbeet, livestock, timber, cotton and woolen textiles, steel, vehicles
currency tolar

population (1992) 1,985,000 (Slovene 91%, Croat 3%, Serb 2%)
languages Slovene, resembling Serbo-Croat, written in Roman characters
religion Roman Catholic

chronology
1918 United with Serbia and Croatia.
1929 The kingdom of Serbs, Croats, and Slovenes took the name of Yugoslavia.
1945 Became a constituent republic of Yugoslav Socialist Federal Republic.
mid-1980s The Slovenian Communist Party liberalized itself and agreed to free elections. Yugoslav counterintelligence (KOV) began repression.
1989 Jan: Social Democratic Alliance of Slovenia launched as first political organization independent of Communist Party. Sept: constitution changed to allow secession from federation.
1990 April: nationalist DEMOS coalition secured victory in first multiparty parliamentary elections; Milan Kučan became president. July: sovereignty declared. Dec: independence overwhelmingly approved in referendum.
1991 June: independence declared; 100 killed after federal army intervened; cease-fire brokered by European Community (EC). July: cease-fire agreed between federal troops and nationalists. Oct: withdrawal of Yugoslav army completed. Dec: DEMOS coalition dissolved.
1992 Jan: EC recognized Slovenia's independence. April: Janez Drnovšek appointed prime minister; independence recognized by US. May: admitted into United Nations and Conference on Security and Cooperation in Europe. Dec: Liberal Democrats and Christian Democrats won assembly elections; Kučan reelected president.
1993 Drnovšek reelected prime minister.

Prime of Miss Jean Brodie 1969 (Academy Award), *California Suite* 1978, *A Private Function* 1984, and *A Room with a View* 1986.

Smithsonian Institution academic organization in Washington, DC, founded in 1846 with money left by British chemist and mineralogist James Smithson. The Smithsonian Institution undertakes scientific research but is also the parent organization of a collection of museums. These include the United States National Museum, the National Air and Space Museum, the National Gallery of Art, the Freer Gallery of Art, the National Portrait Gallery, and the National Collection of Fine Arts. The Smithsonian Institution also has a zoo and an astrophysical observatory.

smoking inhaling the fumes from burning substances, generally ◊tobacco in the form of ◊cigarettes. The practice can be habit-forming and is dangerous to health, since carbon monoxide and other toxic materials result from the combustion process. A direct link between lung cancer and tobacco smoking was established 1950; the habit is also linked to respiratory and coronary heart diseases. In the West, smoking is now forbidden in many public places because even *passive smoking*—breathing in fumes from other people's cigarettes—can be harmful.

Some illegal drugs, such as ◊crack and ◊opium, are also smoked.

smuggling the illegal import or export of prohibited goods or the evasion of customs duties on dutiable goods. Smuggling has a long tradition in most border and coastal regions; goods smuggled include tobacco, spirits, diamonds, gold, and illegal drugs.

Smuts Jan Christian 1870–1950. South African politician and soldier; prime minister 1919–24 and 1939–48. He supported the Allies in both world wars and was a member of the British imperial war cabinet 1917–18.

snail air-breathing gastropod mollusk with a spiral shell. There are thousands of species, on land and in water. The typical snails of the genus *Helix* have two species in Europe. The common garden snail *H. aspersa* is very destructive to plants.

snake reptile of the suborder Serpentes of the order Squamata, which also includes lizards. Snakes are characterized by an elongated limbless body, possibly evolved because of subterranean ancestors. One of the striking internal modifications is the absence or greatly reduced size of the left lung. The skin is covered in scales, which are markedly wider underneath where they form. There are 3,000 species found in the tropical and temperate zones, but none in New Zealand, Ireland, Iceland, and near the poles. Only three species are found in Britain: the adder, smooth snake, and grass snake.

Snake tributary of the Columbia River, in NW US; length 1,038 mi/1,670 km. It flows 40 mi/65 km through Hell's Canyon, one of the deepest gorges in the world.

snapdragon perennial herbaceous plant of the genus *Antirrhinum*, family Scrophulariaceae, with spikes of brightly colored two-lipped flowers.

snooker indoor game derived from ◊billiards (via ◊pool). It is played with 22 balls: 15 red, one each of yellow, green, brown, blue, pink, and black, and one white cueball. Red balls are worth one point when sunk, while the colored balls have ascending values from two points for the yellow to seven points for the black. The world professional championship was first held in 1927. The world amateur championship was first held 1963.

snoring loud noise during sleep made by vibration of the soft palate (the rear part of the roof of the mouth), caused by streams of air entering the nose and mouth at the same time. It is most common when the nose is partially blocked.

It is common in men, but women and children also snore.

snow precipitation in the form of soft, white, crystalline flakes caused by the condensation in air of excess water vapor below freezing point. Light reflecting in the crystals, which have a basic hexagonal (six-sided) geometry, gives snow its white appearance.

Snow C(harles) P(ercy), Baron Snow 1905–1980. English novelist and physicist. He held government scientific posts in World War II and 1964–66. His sequence of novels *Strangers and Brothers* 1940–64 portrayed English life from 1920 onward.

His *Two Cultures* (Cambridge Rede lecture 1959) discussed the absence of communication between literary and scientific intellectuals in the West, and added the phrase "the two cultures" to the language.

Snowdon (Welsh *Y Wyddfa*) highest mountain in Wales, 3,560 ft/1,085 m above sea level. It consists of a cluster of five peaks. At the foot of Snowdon are the Llanberis, Aberglaslyn, and Rhyd-ddu passes. A rack railroad ascends to the summit from Llanberis. *Snowdonia*, the surrounding mountain range, was made a national park 1951. It covers 845 sq mi/2,188 sq km of mountain, lakes, and forest land.

Snowdon Anthony Armstrong-Jones, Earl of Snowdon 1930– . English portrait photographer. In 1960 he married Princess Margaret; they were divorced 1978.

snuff finely powdered ◊tobacco for sniffing up the nostrils (or sometimes chewed or rubbed on the gums) as a stimulant or sedative. Snuff taking was common in 17th-century England and the Netherlands, and spread in the 18th century to other parts of Europe, but was largely superseded by cigarette smoking.

soap mixture of the sodium salts of various ◊fatty acids: palmitic, stearic, and oleic acid. It is made by the action of sodium hydroxide (caustic soda) or potassium hydroxide (caustic potash) on fats of animal or vegetable origin. Soap makes grease and dirt disperse in water in a similar manner to a ◊detergent.

soap opera television or radio melodrama. It originated in the US as a series of daytime programs sponsored by soap-powder and detergent manufacturers.

The popularity of the genre has led to soap operas being shown at peak viewing times in many languages and countries.

soapstone compact, massive form of impure ◊talc.

Soares Mario 1924– . Portuguese socialist politician, president from 1986. Exiled 1970, he returned to Portugal 1974, and, as leader of the Portuguese Socialist Party, was prime minister 1976–78. He resigned as party leader 1980, but in 1986 he was elected Portugal's first socialist president.

soccer or *football* ball game originating in the UK, popular in Europe, the Middle East, and North and South America. It is played between two teams each of 11 players, on a field 100–130 yd/90–120 m long and 50–100 yd/45–90 m wide, with a spherical, inflated (traditionally leather) ball, circumference 27 in/0.69 m. The object of the game is to send the ball with the feet or head into the opponents' goal, an area 8 yd/7.31 m wide and 8 ft/2.44 m high.

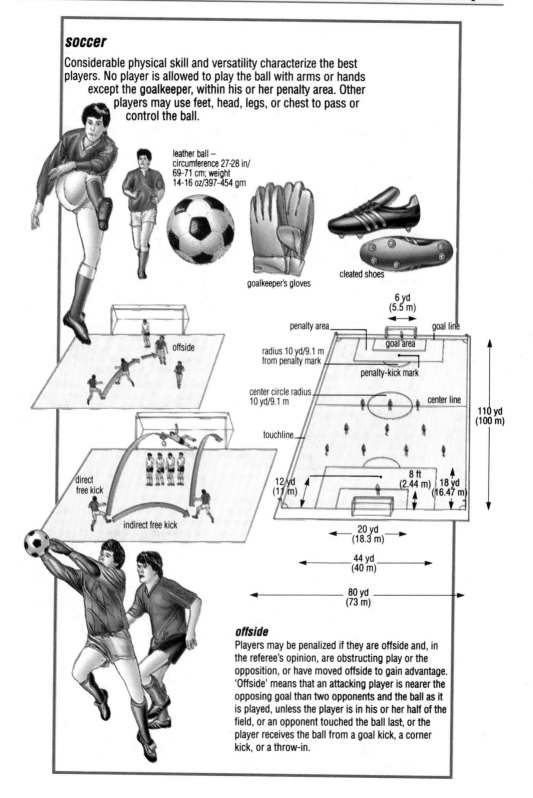

soccer

Considerable physical skill and versatility characterize the best players. No player is allowed to play the ball with arms or hands except the goalkeeper, within his or her penalty area. Other players may use feet, head, legs, or chest to pass or control the ball.

leather ball — circumference 27-28 in/ 69-71 cm; weight 14-16 oz/397-454 gm

goalkeeper's gloves

cleated shoes

offside

direct free kick

indirect free kick

6 yd (5.5 m)

penalty area

goal line

radius 10 yd/9.1 m from penalty mark

goal area

penalty-kick mark

center circle radius 10 yd/9.1 m

center line

touchline

110 yd (100 m)

12 yd (11 m)

8 ft (2.44 m)

18 yd (16.47 m)

20 yd (18.3 m)

44 yd (40 m)

80 yd (73 m)

offside

Players may be penalized if they are offside and, in the referee's opinion, are obstructing play or the opposition, or have moved offside to gain advantage. 'Offside' means that an attacking player is nearer the opposing goal than two opponents and the ball as it is played, unless the player is in his or her half of the field, or an opponent touched the ball last, or the player receives the ball from a goal kick, a corner kick, or a throw-in.

social contract the idea that government authority derives originally from an agreement between ruler and ruled in which the former agrees to provide order in return for obedience from the latter. It has been used to support both absolutism (◊Hobbes) and democracy (◊Locke, ◊Rousseau).

social democracy political ideology or belief in the gradual evolution of a democratic ◊socialism within existing political structures. The earliest was the German Sozialdemokratische Partei (SPD), today one of the two main German parties, created in 1875 from August Bebel's earlier German Social Democratic Workers' Party, founded 1869. Parties along the lines of the German model were founded in the last two decades of the 19th century in a number of countries, including Austria, Belgium, the Netherlands, Hungary, Poland, and Russia. The British Labour Party is in the social democratic tradition.

social history branch of history that documents the living and working conditions of people rather than affairs of state. In recent years television programs, books, and museums have helped to give social history a wide appeal.

socialism movement aiming to establish a classless society by substituting public for private ownership of the means of production, distribution, and exchange. The term has been used to describe positions as widely apart as anarchism and social democracy. Socialist ideas appeared in Classical times; in early Christianity; among later Christian sects such as the ◊Anabaptists and Diggers; and, in the 18th and early 19th centuries, were put forward as systematic political aims by Jean-Jacques Rousseau, Claude Saint-Simon, François Fourier, and Robert Owen, among others. See also Karl ◊Marx and Friedrich ◊Engels.

socialization process, beginning in childhood, by which a person becomes a member of a society, learning its norms, customs, laws, and ways of living. The main agents of socialization are the family, school, peer groups, work, religion, and the mass media. The main methods of socialization are direct instruction, rewards and punishment, imitation, experimentation, role play, and interaction.

social science the group of academic disciplines that investigate how and why people behave the way they do, as individuals and in groups. The term originated with the 19th-century French thinker Auguste ◊Comte. The academic social sciences are generally listed as sociology, economics, anthropology, political science, and psychology.

social security state provision of financial aid to alleviate poverty and to provide income to retired persons and disabled workers. The term "social security" was first applied officially in the US, in the Social Security Act 1935. The term usually refers specifically to old-age pensions, which have a contributory element, unlike "welfare." The federal government is responsible for social security (medicare, retirement, survivors', and disability insurance); unemployment insurance is covered by a joint federal-state system for industrial workers, but few in agriculture are covered; and welfare benefits are the responsibility of individual states, with some federal assistance. The program is an important source of income for the growing population of retired Americans. Politically sacrosanct, the benefits pose a growing burden for the working-age population.

Society Islands (French *Archipel de la Société*) archipelago in ◊French Polynesia, divided into the Windward Islands and the Leeward Islands; area 650 sq mi/1,685 sq km; population (1983) 142,000. The administrative headquarters is Papeete on ◊Tahiti. The *Windward Islands* (French *Iles du Vent*) have an area of 460 sq mi/1,200 sq km and a population (1983) of 123,000. They comprise Tahiti, Moorea (area 51 sq mi/132 sq km; population 7,000), Maio (or Tubuai Manu; 3.5 sq mi/9 sq km; population 200), and the smaller Tetiaroa and Mehetia. The *Leeward Islands* (French *Iles sous le Vent*) have an area of 156 sq mi/404 sq km and a population of 19,000. They comprise the volcanic islands of Raiatea (including the main town of Uturoa), Huahine, Bora-Bora, Maupiti, Tahaa, and four small atolls. Claimed by France 1768, the group became a French protectorate 1843 and a colony 1880.

sociology the systematic study of society, in particular of social order and social change, social conflict, and social problems. It studies institutions such as the family, law, and the church, as well as concepts such as norm, role, and culture. Sociology attempts to study people in their social environment according to certain underlying moral, philosophical, and political codes of behavior.

Socrates *c.* 469–399 BC. Athenian philosopher. He wrote nothing but was immortalized in the dialogues of his pupil Plato. In his desire to combat the skepticism of the ◊sophists, Socrates asserted the possibility of genuine knowledge. In ethics, he put forward the view that the good person never knowingly does wrong. True knowledge emerges through dialogue and systematic questioning and an abandoning of uncritical claims to knowledge.

Socratic method method of teaching used by Socrates, in which he aimed to guide pupils to clear thinking on ethics and politics by asking questions and then exposing their inconsistencies in cross-examination. This method was effective against the ◊sophists.

Soddy Frederick 1877–1956. English physical chemist who pioneered research into atomic disintegration and coined the term ◊isotope. He was awarded a Nobel Prize 1921 for investigating the origin and nature of isotopes.

sodium soft, waxlike, silver-white, metallic element, symbol Na (from Latin *natrium*), atomic number 11, atomic weight 22.898. It is one of the ◊alkali metals and has a very low density, being light enough to float on water. It is the sixth-most abundant element (the fourth-most abundant metal) in the Earth's crust. Sodium is highly reactive, oxidizing rapidly when exposed to air and reacting violently with water. Its most familiar compound is sodium chloride (common salt), which occurs naturally in the oceans and in salt deposits left by dried-up ancient seas.

sodium chloride or *common salt* or *table salt* NaCl white, crystalline compound found widely in nature. It is is a a typical ionic solid with a high melting point (1,474°F/801°C); it is soluble in water, insoluble in organic solvents, and is a strong electrolyte when molten or in aqueous solution. Found in concentrated deposits, it is widely used in the food industry as a flavoring and preservative, and in the chemical industry in the manufacture of sodium, chlorine, and sodium carbonate.

Sodom and Gomorrah two ancient cities in the Dead Sea area of the Middle East, recorded in the Old Testament (Genesis) as being destroyed by fire and brimstone for their wickedness.

Sofia or *Sofiya* capital of Bulgaria since 1878; population (1990) 1,220,900. Industries include textiles, rubber, machinery, and electrical equipment. It lies at the foot of the Vitosha Mountains.

softball bat-and-ball game similar to ◊baseball. Among the differences between the two sports are playing-field dimensions and equipment specifications; softball diamonds are smaller overall. The distance between bases is 60 ft/18.3 m; pitchers stand 46 ft/14 m from home plate; and the softball itself (which is about as hard as a baseball) is approximately 12 in/30.5 cm in circumference (a baseball is about 9 in/23 cm). In proportional terms of weight to size, a softball is lighter than a baseball and therefore, when pitched or batted, generally will not attain the speed and distance of a well-hit baseball. Softball bats can be no longer than 34 in/86.4 cm.

A regulation softball game is seven innings (for baseball it is nine), but actual play (rules, actions, and objectives) is so alike in both games that the technical differences cannot disguise the fact that softball is the legitimate offspring of baseball. The one element of play that is significantly distinct, however, is the execution of the pitch; a legally delivered softball must be thrown underhand. Pitching defines the two styles of softball play: fast pitch and slow pitch. Of the nearly 175,000 teams registered with the US Amateur Softball Association, more than 80% play slow-pitch softball. The slow-pitch game customarily is played with 10-player teams, the tenth being a fourth outfielder or a "short fielder" (covering the area between infield and outfield). The arc of a slow-pitched ball must not be less than 3 ft/0.9 m, and the ball must cross home plate in a downward motion. Both bunting and base stealing are illegal in slow-pitch games. Some slow-pitch teams use a ball that is as large as 16 in/40.6 cm in circumference. Bunting and stealing are allowed in fast-pitch games, but it is never legal in softball for a runner to leave the base before the ball is pitched.

software in computing, a collection of programs and procedures for making a computer perform a specific task, as opposed to ◊hardware, the physical components of a computer system. Software is created by programmers and is either distributed on a suitable medium, such as the ◊floppy disk, or built into the computer in the form of firmware. Examples of software include ◊operating systems, ◊compilers, and applications programs, such as payrolls. No computer can function without some form of software.

soil loose covering of broken rocky material and decaying organic matter overlying the bedrock of the Earth's surface. Various types of soil develop under different conditions: deep soils form in warm wet climates and in valleys; shallow soils form in cool dry areas and on slopes. *Pedology*, the study of soil, is significant because of the relative importance of different soil types to agriculture.

soil erosion the wearing away and redistribution of the Earth's soil layer. It is caused by the action of water, wind, and ice, and also by improper methods of ◊agriculture. If unchecked, soil erosion results in the formation of deserts (desertification). It has been estimated that 20% of the world's cultivated topsoil was lost between 1950 and 1990.

soil mechanics branch of engineering that studies the nature and properties of the soil. Soil is investigated during construction work to ensure that it has the mechanical properties necessary to support the foundations of dams, bridges, and roads.

solar energy Solar dishes at the Themis experimental solar-power station at Targassone in the French Pyrénées.

solar energy energy derived from the Sun's radiation. The amount of energy falling on just 0.3861 sq mi/1 sq km is about 4,000 megawatts, enough to heat and light a small town. In one second the Sun gives off 13 million times more energy than all the electricity used in the US in one year. *Solar heaters* have industrial or domestic uses. They usually consist of a black (heat-absorbing) panel containing pipes through which air or water, heated by the Sun, is circulated, either by thermal ◊convection or by a pump.

solar radiation radiation given off by the Sun, consisting mainly of visible light, ◊ultraviolet radiation, and ◊infrared radiation, although the whole spectrum of ◊electromagnetic waves is present, from radio waves to X-rays. High-energy charged particles such as electrons are also emitted, especially from solar ◊flares. When these reach the Earth, they cause magnetic storms (disruptions of the Earth's magnetic field), which interfere with radio communications.

solar system the sun and all the bodies orbiting it; the nine planets (Mercury, Venus, Earth, Mars, Jupiter, Saturn, Uranus, Neptune, and Pluto), their moons, the asteroids, and the comets. It is thought to have formed from a cloud of gas and dust in space about 4.6 billion years ago. The Sun contains 99% of the mass of the solar system. The edge of the solar system is not clearly defined, marked only by the limit of the Sun's gravitational influence, which extends about 1.5 light years, almost halfway to the nearest star, Alpha Centauri, 4.3 light years away. *See illustration p. 858*

solar wind stream of atomic particles, mostly protons and electrons, from the Sun's corona, flowing outward at speeds of between 200 mps/300 kps and 600 mps/1,000 kps.

solder any of various alloys used when melted for joining metals such as copper, its common alloys (brass and bronze), and tin-plated steel, as used for making food cans.

sole flatfish found in temperate and tropical waters. The *common sole Solea solea*, also called *Dover sole*, is found in the southern seas of NW Europe. Up to 20 in/50 cm long, it is a prized food fish, as is the *sand or French sole Pegusa lascaris* further south.

solenoid coil of wire, usually cylindrical, in which a magnetic field is created by passing an electric current through it (see ◊electromagnet). This field can be used to move an iron rod placed on its axis. Mechanical valves attached to the rod can be operated by switching the current on or off, so converting electrical energy into mechanical energy. Solenoids are used to relay energy from the battery of an automobile to the starter motor by means of the ignition switch.

solid in physics, a state of matter that holds its own shape (as opposed to a liquid, which takes up the shape of its container, or a gas, which totally fills its container). According to ◊kinetic theory, the atoms or mol-

solar system Most of the objects in the solar system lie close to the plane of the ecliptic.

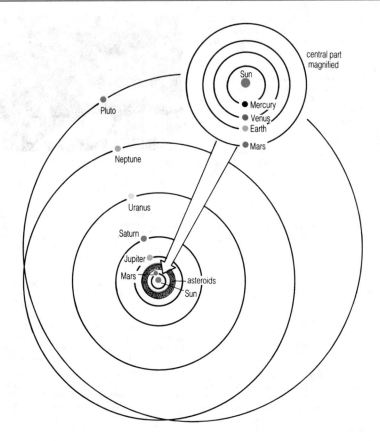

central part magnified

Pluto

Sun

Mercury
Venus
Earth
Mars

Neptune

Uranus

Saturn

Jupiter

Mars — asteroids

Sun

ecules in a solid are not free to move but merely vibrate about fixed positions, such as those in crystal lattices.

Solidarity (Polish *Solidarność*) national confederation of independent labor unions in Poland, formed under the leadership of Lech ◊Wałesa Sept 1980. An illegal organization from 1981 to 1989, it was then elected to head the Polish government. Divisions soon emerged in the leadership. Solidarity had 2.8 million members in 1991.

solid-state circuit electronic circuit where all the components (resistors, capacitors, transistors, and diodes) and interconnections are made at the same time, and by the same processes, in or on one piece of single-crystal silicon. The small size of this construction accounts for its use in electronics for space vehicles and aircraft.

Solomon *c.* 974–*c.* 937 BC. In the Old Testament, third king of Israel, son of David by Bathsheba. During a peaceful reign, he was famed for his wisdom and his alliances with Egypt and Phoenicia. The much later biblical Proverbs, Ecclesiastes, and Song of Songs are attributed to him. He built the temple in Jerusalem with the aid of heavy taxation and forced labor, resulting in the revolt of N Israel.

Solomon Islands country in the SW Pacific Ocean, E of New Guinea, comprising many hundreds of islands, the largest of which is Guadalcanal.

Solon *c.* 638–558 BC. Athenian statesman. As one of the chief magistrates about 594 BC, he carried out the cancellation of all debts from which land or liberty was the security and the revision of the constitution that laid the foundations of Athenian democracy.

Solti Georg 1912– . Hungarian-born British conductor. He was music director at the Royal Opera House, Covent Garden, London, 1961–71, and became director of the Chicago Symphony Orchestra 1969. He was also principal conductor of the London Philharmonic Orchestra 1979–83.

solubility in physics, a measure of the amount of solute (usually a solid or gas) that will dissolve in a given amount of solvent (usually a liquid) at a particular temperature. Solubility may be expressed as grams of solute per 100 grams of solvent or, for a gas, in parts per million (ppm) of solvent.

solution two or more substances mixed to form a single, homogenous phase. One of the substances is the *solvent* and the others (*solutes*) are said to be dissolved in it.

solvent substance, usually a liquid, that will dissolve another substance (see ◊solution). Although the commonest solvent is water, in popular use the term refers to low-boiling-point organic liquids, which are harmful if used in a confined space. They can give rise to

Solomon Islands

area 10,656 sq mi/27,600 sq km
capital Honiara (on Guadalcanal)
cities Gizo, Yandina
physical comprises all but the northernmost islands (which belong to Papua New Guinea) of a Melanesian archipelago stretching nearly 900 mi/1,500 km. The largest is Guadalcanal (area 2,510 sq mi/6,500 sq km); others are Malaita, San Cristobal, New Georgia, Santa Isabel, Choiseul; mainly mountainous and forested
features rivers ideal for hydroelectric power
head of state Elizabeth II represented by governor-general
head of government Francis Billy Hilly from 1993
political system constitutional monarchy
political parties People's Alliance Party (PAP), center-left; Solomon Islands United Party (SIUPA), right of center
exports fish products, palm oil, copra, cocoa, timber
currency Solomon Island dollar
population (1992) 339,000 (Melanesian 95%, Polynesian 4%); growth rate 3.9% p.a.
life expectancy men 66, women 71
languages English (official); there are some 120 Melanesian dialects
religions Anglican 34%, Roman Catholic 19%, South Sea Evangelical 17%
literacy 60% (1989)
GNP $141 million; $420 per head (1987)

chronology
1893 Solomon Islands placed under British protection.
1978 Independence achieved from Britain within the Commonwealth, with Peter Kenilorea as prime minister.
1981 Solomon Mamaloni of the People's Progressive Party (PPP) replaced Kenilorea as prime minister.
1984 Kenilorea returned to power, heading a coalition government.
1986 Kenilorea resigned after allegations of corruption; replaced by his deputy, Ezekiel Alebua.
1988 Kenilorea elected deputy prime minister. Joined Vanuatu and Papua New Guinea to form the Spearhead Group, aiming to preserve Melanesian cultural traditions and secure independence for the French territory of New Caledonia.
1989 Solomon Mamaloni, now leader of the People's Action Party (PAP), elected prime minister; formed PAP-dominated coalition.
1990 Mamaloni resigned as PAP party leader, but continued as head of a government of national unity.
1993 Francis Billy Hilly, an independent politician, elected prime minister.

respiratory problems, liver damage, and neurological complaints.

Solzhenitsyn Alexander (Isayevich) 1918– . Soviet novelist, a US citizen from 1974. He was in prison and exile 1945–57 for anti-Stalinist comments. Much of his writing is semiautobiographical and highly critical of the system, including *One Day in the Life of Ivan Denisovich* 1962, which deals with the labor camps under Stalin, and *The Gulag Archipelago* 1973, an exposé of the whole Soviet labor-camp network. This led to his expulsion from the USSR 1974.

Somalia country in NE Africa (the Horn of Africa), on the Indian Ocean, bounded NW by Djibouti, W by Ethiopia, and SW by Kenya. *See panel p. 860*

Somaliland region of Somali-speaking peoples in E Africa including the former British Somaliland Protectorate (established 1887) and Italian Somaliland (made a colony 1927, conquered by Britain 1941 and administered by Britain until 1950)—which both became independent 1960 as the Somali Democratic Republic, the official name for ◊Somalia—and former French Somaliland, which was established 1892, became known as the Territory of the Afars and Issas 1967, and became independent as ◊Djibouti 1977.

Somerset county in SW England
area 1,336 sq mi/3,460 sq km
cities administrative headquarters Taunton; Wells, Bridgwater, Glastonbury, Yeovil
physical rivers Avon, Parret, and Exe; marshy coastline on the Bristol Channel; Mendip Hills (including Cheddar Gorge and Wookey Hole, a series of limestone caves where Old Stone Age flint implements and bones of extinct animals have been found); the Quantock Hills; Exmoor

products engineering, dairy products, cider, Exmoor ponies
population (1991) 459,100
famous people Ernest Bevin, Henry Fielding, John Pym.

Somme, Battle of the Allied offensive in World War I July–Nov 1916 at Beaumont-Hamel-Chaulnes, on the river Somme in N France, during which severe losses were suffered by both sides. It was planned by the Marshal of France, Joseph Joffre, and UK commander in chief Douglas Haig; the Allies lost over 600,000 soldiers and advanced 20 mi/32 km. It was the first battle in which tanks were used. The German offensive around St Quentin March–April 1918 is sometimes called the Second Battle of the Somme.

Somoza Anastasio 1896–1956. Nicaraguan soldier and politician. As head of the Nicaraguan army, he deposed President Juan Bautista Sacasa, his uncle, 1936 and assumed the presidency the following year, ruling as a dictator until his assassination 1956. During his rule, Somoza exiled most of his political foes and amassed a fortune. He was succeeded by his sons Luis Somoza Debayle (1922–67), who was president 1957–63, and Anastasio Somoza Debayle (1925–80), who ruled 1963–79, when he was overthrown by the leftist Sandinista rebels (he, too, was later assassinated).

Somoza Debayle Anastasio 1925–1980. Nicaraguan soldier and politician, president 1967–72 and 1974–79. The second son of Anastasio Somoza García, he succeeded his brother Luis Somoza Debayle (1922–1967; president 1956–63) as president of Nicaragua in 1967, to head an even more oppressive regime. He was removed by Sandinista guerrillas in 1979, and assassinated in Paraguay 1980.

Somalia
Somali Democratic Republic
(*Jamhuriyadda Dimugradiga Somaliya*)

area 246,220 sq mi/637,700 sq km
capital Mogadishu
cities Hargeisa, Kismayu, port Berbera
physical mainly flat, with hills in N
environment destruction of trees for fuel and by grazing livestock has led to an increase in desert area
features occupies a strategic location on the Horn of Africa
head of state and government Ali Mahdi Mohammed from 1991
political system one-party socialist republic
political party Somali Revolutionary Socialist Party (SRSP), nationalist, socialist
exports livestock, skins, hides, bananas, fruit
currency Somali shilling
population (1992) 7,872,000 (including 350,000 refugees in Ethiopia and 50,000 in Djibouti); growth rate 3.1% p.a.
life expectancy men 53, women 53 (1989)
languages Somali, Arabic (both official), Italian, English
religion Sunni Muslim 99%

literacy 40% (1986)
GNP $1.5 bn; $290 per head (1987)

chronology
1884–87 British protectorate of Somaliland established.
1889 Italian protectorate of Somalia established.
1960 Independence achieved from Italy and Britain.
1963 Border dispute with Kenya; diplomatic relations broken with Britain.
1968 Diplomatic relations with Britain restored.
1969 Army coup led by Maj Gen Mohamed Siad Barre; constitution suspended, Supreme Revolutionary Council set up; name changed to Somali Democratic Republic.
1978 Defeated in eight-month war with Ethiopia. Armed insurrection began in north.
1979 New constitution for socialist one-party state adopted.
1982 Antigovernment Somali National Movement formed. Oppressive countermeasures by government.
1987 Barre reelected president.
1989 Dissatisfaction with government and increased guerrilla activity in north.
1990 Civil war intensified. Constitutional reforms promised.
1991 Mogadishu captured by rebels; Barre fled; Ali Mahdi Mohammed named president; free elections promised. Secession of NE Somalia, as the Somaliland Republic, announced. Cease-fire signed, but later collapsed. Thousands of casualties as a result of heavy fighting in capital.
1992 Relief efforts to ward off impending famine severely hindered by unstable political situation; relief convoys hijacked by "warlords." Dec: UN peacekeeping troops, mainly US Marines, sent in to protect relief operations; dominant warlords agreed truce.
1993 March: leaders of armed factions agreed to federal system of government, based on 18 autonomous regions. June: US-led UN forces destroyed headquarters of warlord Gen Mohammad Farah Aidid, following killing of Pakistani peacekeeping troops. US announced withdrawal of its troops in 1994.

sonar (acronym for *sound navigation and ranging*) method of locating underwater objects by the reflection of ultrasonic waves. The time taken for an acoustic beam to travel to the object and back to the source enables the distance to be found since the velocity of sound in water is known. Sonar devices, or *echo sounders*, were developed 1920.

sonata piece of instrumental music written for a soloist or a small ensemble and consisting of a series of related movements.

Sondheim Stephen (Joshua) 1930– . US composer and lyricist. He wrote the lyrics of Leonard Bernstein's *West Side Story* 1957 and composed witty and sophisticated musicals, including *A Little Night Music* 1973, *Pacific Overtures* 1976, *Sweeney Todd* 1979, *Into the Woods* 1987, and *Sunday in the Park with George* 1989.

song composition for one or more singers, often with instrumental accompaniment, such as madrigals and chansons. Common forms include folk song and ballad. The term "song" is used for secular music, whereas motet and cantata tend to be forms of sacred music.

Song dynasty or *Sung dynasty* Chinese imperial family 960–1279, founded by northern general Taizu (Zhao Kuangyin 928–76). A distinction is conventionally made between the Northern Song period 960–1126, when the capital lay at Kaifeng, and Southern Song 1127–1279, when it was at Hangzhou (Hangchow). A stable government was supported by a thoroughly centralized administration. The dynasty was eventually ended by Mongol invasion.

Songhai Empire former kingdom of NW Africa, founded in the 8th century, which developed into a powerful Muslim empire under the rule of Sonni Ali (reigned 1464–92). It superseded the ◊Mali Empire and extended its territory, occupying an area that included parts of present-day Guinea, Burkina Faso, Senegal, Gambia, Mali, Mauritania, Niger, and Nigeria. In 1591 it was invaded and overthrown by Morocco.

sonic boom noise like a thunderclap that occurs when an aircraft passes through the ◊sound barrier, or begins to travel faster than the speed of sound. It happens when the cone-shaped shock wave caused by the plane touches the ground.

sonnet fourteen-line poem of Italian origin introduced to England by Thomas Wyatt in the form used by Petrarch (rhyming *abba abba cdcdcd* or *cdecde*) and followed by Milton and Wordsworth; Shakespeare used the form *abab cdcd efef gg*.

Sons of Liberty in American colonial history, the name adopted by those colonists opposing the ◊Stamp Act of 1765. Merchants, lawyers, farmers, artisans, and laborers joined what was an early instance of concerted resistance to British rule, causing the repeal of the act in March 1766.

Sophia Electress of Hanover 1630–1714. Twelfth child of Frederick V, elector palatine of the Rhine and king of Bohemia, and Elizabeth, daughter of James I of England. She married the elector of Hanover in 1658. Widowed in 1698, she was recognized in the succession to the English throne in 1701, and when Queen

Anne died without issue in 1714, her son George I founded the Hanoverian dynasty.

sophist one of a group of 5th-century BC itinerant lecturers on culture, rhetoric, and politics. Skeptical about the possibility of achieving genuine knowledge, they applied bogus reasoning and were concerned with winning arguments rather than establishing the truth. ◊Plato regarded them as dishonest, and *sophistry* came to mean fallacious reasoning.

Sophocles c. 496–406 BC. Athenian dramatist, attributed with having developed tragedy by introducing a third actor and scene-painting, and ranked with ◊Aeschylus and ◊Euripides as one of the three great tragedians. He wrote some 120 plays, of which seven tragedies survive. These are *Antigone* 441 BC, *Oedipus the King, Electra, Ajax, Trachiniae, Philoctetes* 409 BC, and *Oedipus at Colonus* 401 BC (produced after his death).

Sopwith Thomas Octave Murdoch 1888–1989. English designer of the Sopwith Camel biplane, used in World War I, and joint developer of the Hawker Hurricane fighter plane used in World War II.

sorbic acid tasteless acid found in the fruit of the mountain ash (genus *Sorbus*) and prepared synthetically. It is widely used in the preservation of food—for example, cider, wine, soft drinks, animal feeds, bread, and cheese.

Sorbonne common name for the University of Paris, originally a theological institute founded 1253 by Robert de Sorbon, chaplain to Louis IX.

Sorel Georges 1847–1922. French philosopher who believed that socialism could only come about through a general strike; his theory of the need for a "myth" to sway the body of the people was used by fascists.

Sørensen Søren 1868–1939. Danish chemist who in 1909 introduced the concept of using the ◊pH scale as a measure of the acidity of a solution. On Sørensen's scale, still used today, a pH of 7 is neutral; higher numbers represent alkalinity, and lower numbers acidity.

sorghum or *great millet* or *Guinea corn* any cereal grass of the genus *Sorghum*, native to Africa but cultivated widely in India, China, the US, and S Europe. The seeds are used for making bread. Durra is a member of the genus.

sorrel any of several plants of the genus *Rumex* of the buckwheat family Polygonaceae. *R. acetosa* is grown for its bitter salad leaves. Dock plants are of the same genus.

sorting arranging data in sequence. When sorting a collection, or file, of data made up of several different ◊fields, one must be chosen as the *key field* used to establish the correct sequence. For example, the data in a company's mailing list might include fields for each customer's first names, surname, address, and telephone number. For most purposes, the company would wish the records to be sorted alphabetically by surname; therefore, the surname field would be chosen as the key field.

sorus in ferns, a group of sporangia, the reproductive structures that produce ◊spores. They occur on the lower surface of fern fronds.

SOS internationally recognized distress signal, using letters of the ◊Morse code (. . .—. . .).

Sōseki Natsume, adopted name of Natsume Kinnosuke 1867–1916. Japanese novelist whose works are deep psychological studies of urban intellectual lives.

Strongly influenced by English literature, his later works are somewhat reminiscent of Henry James; for example, the unfinished *Meian/Light and Darkness* 1916. Sōseki is regarded as one of Japan's greatest writers.

Sotho member of a large ethnic group in S Africa, numbering about 7 million (1987) and living mainly in Botswana, Lesotho, and South Africa. The Sotho are predominantly farmers, living in small village groups. They speak a variety of closely related languages belonging to the Bantu branch of the Niger-Congo family. With English, Sotho is the official language of Lesotho.

soul according to many religions, the intangible and immortal part of a human being that survives the death of the physical body.

soul music emotionally intense style of ◊rhythm and blues sung by, among others, Sam Cooke, Aretha Franklin, and Al Green (1946–). A synthesis of blues, gospel music, and jazz, it emerged in the 1950s. Sometimes all popular music made by African-Americans is labeled soul music.

sound physiological sensation received by the ear, originating in a vibration (pressure variation in the air) that communicates itself to the ear, and travels in every direction, spreading out as an expanding sphere. All sound waves in air travel with a speed dependent on the temperature; under ordinary conditions, this is about 1,070 ft/330 m per second. The pitch of the sound depends on the number of vibrations imposed on the air per second, but the speed is unaffected. The loudness of a sound is dependent primarily on the amplitude of the vibration of the air.

sound barrier concept that the speed of sound, or sonic speed (about 760 mph/1,220 kph at sea level), constitutes a speed limit to flight through the atmosphere, since a badly designed aircraft suffers severe buffeting at near sonic speed owing to the formation of shock waves. US test pilot Chuck Yeager first flew through the "barrier" in 1947 in a Bell X-1 rocket plane. Now, by careful design, such aircraft as Concorde can fly at supersonic speed with ease, though they create in their wake a ◊sonic boom.

soundtrack band at one side of a motion-picture film on which the accompanying sound is recorded. Usually it takes the form of an optical track (a pattern of light and shade). The pattern is produced on the film when signals from the recording microphone are made to vary the intensity of a light beam. During playback, a light is shone through the track on to a photocell, which converts the pattern of light falling on it into appropriate electrical signals. These signals are then fed to loudspeakers to recreate the original sounds.

Sousa John Philip 1854–1932. US bandmaster and composer of marches, such as "The Stars and Stripes Forever!" 1897.

He became known as a brilliant bandmaster during his tenure as leader of the Marine Band 1880–92. He went on to form the Sousa Band 1892 and toured internationally with this group until his death. In addition to about 140 stirring marches, he composed operettas, symphonic poems, suites, waltzes, and songs.

sousaphone large bass ◊tuba designed to wrap around the player in a circle and having a forward-facing bell. The form was suggested by US bandmaster John Sousa. Today they are largely fabricated in lightweight fiberglass.

South Africa
Republic of
(*Republiek van Suid-Afrika*)

area 472,148 sq mi/1,223,181 sq km (includes Walvis Bay and independent black homelands)
capital and port Cape Town (legislative), Pretoria (administrative), Bloemfontein (judicial)
cities Johannesburg; ports Durban, Port Elizabeth, East London
physical southern end of large plateau, fringed by mountains and lowland coastal margin
territories Marion Island and Prince Edward Island in the Antarctic
features Drakensberg Mountains, Table Mountain; Limpopo and Orange rivers; the Veld and the Karoo; part of Kalahari Desert; Kruger National Park
head of state and government Nelson Mandela from 1994
political system republic
political parties White: National Party (NP), right of center, racist; Conservative Party of South Africa (CPSA), extreme right, racist; Democratic Party (DP), left of center, multiracial. Coloureds: Labor Party of South Africa, left of center; People's Congress Party, right of center. Indian: National People's Party, right of center; Solidarity Party, left of center. Black: African national Congress.
exports corn, sugar, fruit, wool, gold (world's largest producer), platinum, diamonds, uranium, iron and steel, copper; mining and minerals are largest export industry, followed by arms manufacturing
currency rand
population (1992) 32,063,000 (73% black: Zulu, Xhosa, Sotho, Tswana; 18% white: 3% mixed, 3% Asian); growth rate 2.5% p.a.
life expectancy whites 71, Asians 67, blacks 58
languages Afrikaans and English (both official), Bantu
religions Dutch Reformed Church 40%, Anglican 11%, Roman Catholic 8%, other Christian 25%, Hindu, Muslim
literacy whites 99%, Asians 69%, blacks 50% (1989)
GNP $81 bn; $1,890 per head (1987)

chronology
1910 Union of South Africa formed from two British colonies and two Boer republics.
1912 African National Congress (ANC) formed.
1948 Apartheid system of racial discrimination initiated by Daniel Malan, leader of National Party (NP).
1955 Freedom Charter adopted by ANC.
1958 Malan succeeded as prime minister by Hendrik Verwoerd.
1960 ANC banned.
1961 South Africa withdrew from Commonwealth and became a republic.
1962 ANC leader Nelson Mandela jailed.
1964 Mandela, Walter Sisulu, Govan Mbeki, and five other ANC leaders sentenced to life imprisonment.
1966 Verwoerd assassinated; succeeded by B J Vorster.
1976 Soweto uprising.
1977 Death in custody of Pan African Congress activist Steve Biko.
1978 Vorster resigned and was replaced by Pieter W Botha.
1984 New constitution adopted, giving segregated representation to Coloureds and Asians and making Botha president. Nonaggression pact with Mozambique signed but not observed.
1985 Growth of violence in black townships.
1986 Commonwealth agreed on limited sanctions. US Congress voted to impose sanctions. Some major multinational companies closed down their South African operations.
1987 Government formally acknowledged the presence of its military forces in Angola.
1988 Botha announced "limited constitutional reforms." South Africa agreed to withdraw from Angola and recognize Namibia's independence as part of regional peace accord.
1989 Botha gave up NP leadership and state presidency. F W de Klerk became president. ANC activists released; beaches and public facilities desegregated. Elections held in Namibia to create independence government.
1990 ANC ban lifted; Nelson Mandela released from prison. NP membership opened to all races. ANC leader Oliver Tambo returned. Daily average of 35 murders and homicides recorded.
1991 Mandela and Zulu leader Mangosuthu Buthelezi urged end to fighting between ANC and Inkatha. Mandela elected ANC president. Revelations of government support for Inkatha threatened ANC cooperation. De Klerk announced repeal of remaining apartheid laws. South Africa readmitted to international sport; US lifted sanctions. PAC and Buthelezi withdrew from negotiations over new constitution.
1992 Constitution leading to all-races majority rule approved by whites-only referendum. Massacre of civilians at black township, threatened constitutional talks.
1993 Feb: de Klerk and Mandela agreed to formation of government of national unity after free elections. Buthelezi not consulted; he opposed such an arrangement. July: riots by groups seeking to wreck ANC negotiated constitutional changes following announcement of April 1994 date for nonracial elections.
1994 April: ANC emerges as dominant party in nation's first free, non racial elections. May: Mandela becomes president and de Klerk vice president in New government.

Souter David Hackett 1939– . US jurist, appointed as associate justice of the US Supreme Court by President Bush 1990.

South Africa country on the southern tip of Africa, bounded N by Namibia, Botswana, and Zimbabwe and NE by Mozambique and Swaziland.

South African Wars two wars between the Boers (settlers of Dutch origin) and the British; essentially fought for the gold and diamonds of the Transvaal. The *War of 1881* was triggered by the attempt of the Boers of the ◊Transvaal to reassert the independence surrendered 1877 in return for British aid against African peoples. The British were defeated at Majuba, and the Transvaal again became independent. The *War of 1899–1902*, also known as the *Boer War*, was preceded by the armed Jameson Raid into the Boer Transvaal; a failed attempt, inspired by the Cape

Colony prime minister Rhodes, to precipitate a revolt against Kruger, the Transvaal president. The *uitlanders* (non-Boer immigrants) were still not given the vote by the Boers, negotiations failed, and the Boers invaded British territory, besieging Ladysmith, Mafeking (now Mafikeng), and Kimberley. The war ended with the Peace of Vereeniging following the Boer defeat.

South America fourth largest of the continents, nearly twice as large as Europe, extending S from ◊Central America.
area 6,893,429 sq mi/17,854,000 sq km
largest cities (over 3.5 million inhabitants) Buenos Aires, São Paulo, Rio de Janeiro, Bogotá, Santiago, Lima, Caracas
features Andes in the W; Brazilian and Guiana highlands; central plains from the Orinoco basin to Patagonia; Parana-Paraguay-Uruguay system flowing to form the La Plata estuary; Amazon river basin, with its remaining great forests and their rich fauna and flora
products coffee; cocoa; sugar; bananas; oranges; wine; meat and fish products; cotton; wool; handicrafts; minerals incuding oil, silver, iron ore, copper
population (1988) 285,000,000: originally ◊American Indians, who survive chiefly in Bolivia, Peru, and Ecuador and are increasing in number. In addition there are many mestizo (people of mixed Spanish or Portuguese and Indian ancestry) elsewhere; many people originally from Europe, largely Spanish, Italian, and Portuguese; and many of African descent, originally imported as slaves
language Spanish, Portuguese (chief language in Brazil), many Indian languages
religion Roman Catholic, Indian beliefs

South Australia state of the Commonwealth of Australia
area 379,824 sq mi/984,000 sq km
capital Adelaide (chief port)
cities Whyalla, Mount Gambier
features Murray Valley irrigated area, including wine-growing Barossa Valley; lakes: ◊Eyre, Torrens; mountains: Mount Lofty, Musgrave, Flinders; parts of the Nullarbor Plain, and Great Victoria and Simpson deserts; experimental rocket range in the arid N at Woomera
products meat and wool (80% of area cattle and sheep grazing), wines and spirits, dried and canned fruit, iron (Middleback Range), coal (Leigh Creek), copper, uranium (Roxby Downs), oil and natural gas in the NE, lead, zinc, iron, opals, household and electrical goods, vehicles
population (1987) 1,388,000; 1% Aborigines
history possibly known to the Dutch in the 16th century; surveyed by Dutch navigator Abel Tasman 1644; first European settlement 1834; province 1836; became a state 1901. In 1963 British nuclear tests were made at Maralinga, in which Aborigines were said to have died.

South Carolina

South America: history

20,000 BC	Humans began to populate the continent.
c.1000–500 BC	Chavín civilization flourished in Peru.
1494	Treaty of Tordesillas assigned what is now Brazil to Portugal, the rest of South America to Spain.
15th century	The Inca civilization developed in Peru.
16th century	Spain and Portugal invaded and conquered South America, killing and enslaving the people.
1513	The Spanish explorer Balboa discovered the Pacific Ocean.
1532–35	Francisco Pizarro conquered Peru and the Incas for Spain.
1780	Peruvian Túpac Amaru (José Condorcanqui), who claimed descent from Inca chieftains, led a revolt against Spanish rule and was executed.
19th century	Simon Bolívar and José de San Martín liberated South America's Spanish colonies. Brazil gained independence without struggle. Massive European immigration.
1818	Chile declared independence.
1822	Bolívar and San Martín met but failed to agree on plans for South American independence.
1865–70	President F S Lopez involved Paraguay in a war with Brazil, Argentina, and Uruguay. Paraguay was defeated and over half its population killed, including Lopez.
1879–83	Pacific War, between Chile and the forces of Bolivia and Peru, ended with Chile's acquisition of all of Bolivia's coastal territory and part of Peru's southern coast. Bolivia still seeks access to the coast.
1889	Brazilian monarchy overthrown and republic established.
1932–35	Chaco war, between Paraguay and Bolivia; the territorial dispute which caused it was settled by arbitration 1938.
1930s	US Marines intervened in Nicaragua.
1952	Bolivian revolution, with nationalization of the tin mines.
1970–73	CIA-backed military coup ended the rule of Salvador Allende's elected socialist government in Chile.
1977	Panama and the US signed a treaty to give Panama control of the Panama Canal in 1999.
20th century	Rapid industrialization and population growth.
1980s	Widespread inability to meet interest payments on loans incurred from economically powerful countries to finance rapid industrialization and capture export markets.
1982	Argentina's invasion of the Falkland Islands triggered war with the UK; the UK regained the Islands.
1992	The first Earth Summit convened in Rio de Janeiro, Brazil, in an effort to cooperate in solving global environmental problems. Celebration of Columbus' first voyage to the New World; Native American representatives protested.
1993	Summit meeting of Latin American leaders calls for end of US embargo of Cuba.

South Bend city on the St Joseph River, N Indiana; population (1990) 105,500. Industries include the manufacture of agricultural machinery, automobiles, and aircraft equipment.

South Carolina state in SE US; nickname Palmetto State
area 31,112 sq mi/80,600 sq km
capital Columbia
cities Charleston, Greenville-Spartanburg
population (1990) 3,486,700
features large areas of woodland; subtropical climate in coastal areas; antebellum Charleston; Myrtle Beach and Hilton Head Island ocean resorts
products tobacco, soybeans, lumber, textiles, clothing, paper, wood pulp, chemicals, nonelectrical machinery, primary and fabricated metals
famous people John C Calhoun, "Dizzy" Gillespie, DuBose Heyward, Francis Marion, John B Watson
history explored first by De Gordillo for Spain 1521; Charles I gave the area (known as Carolina) to Robert Heath (1575–1649) in 1629, and the first English settlement was in 1670 at Albemarle Point, but poor condi-

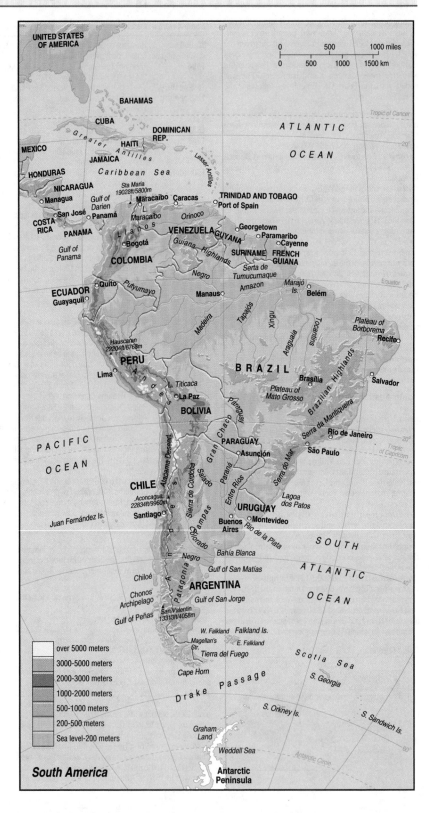

UNITED STATES
OF AMERICA

0   500   1000 miles
0   500   1000   1500 km

Tropic of Cancer

BAHAMAS

CUBA

DOMINICAN
REP.

ATLANTIC

MEXICO

Greater
HAITI
Antilles

OCEAN

JAMAICA

HONDURAS

Caribbean Sea

Lesser Antilles

NICARAGUA

Sta Maria
19028ft/5800m

Managua

Gulf of
Darien

Maracaibo   Caracas

TRINIDAD AND TOBAGO

San José

Panamá

Port of Spain

COSTA
RICA

Maracaibo
L.

Orinoco

Georgetown

PANAMA

Llanos

VENEZUELA
GUYANA

Paramaribo

Gulf of
Panama

Bogotá

Guiana Highlands

Cayenne

SURINAME
FRENCH
GUIANA

COLOMBIA

Negro

Serta de
Tumucumaque

Equator   0°

ECUADOR

Quito

Putumayo

Amazon

Marajó
Is.

Belém

Guayaquil

Manaus

Madeira

Tapajós

Xingu

Tocantins

Plateau of
Borborema

Hauscaran
22204ft/6768m

Araguaia

Recife

PERU

B R A Z I L

Lima

A

L. Titicaca

Brasília

Brazilian Highlands

Salvador

n

La Paz

Plateau of
Mato Grosso

d

BOLIVIA

Paraguay

Serra da Mantiqueira

PACIFIC

Gran Chaco

PARAGUAY

Rio de Janeiro

OCEAN

Atacama Desert

Asunción

São Paulo

Tropic
of Capricorn

CHILE

Sierra de Córdoba

Salado

Paraná

Serra do Mar

Aconcagua
22834ft/9960m

Entre Ríos

Lagoa
dos Patos

Juan Fernández Is.

Santiago

Pampas

URUGUAY

Buenos
Aires

Montevideo

Colorado

Río de la Plata

SOUTH

Negro

Bahía Blanca

ATLANTIC

Chiloé

Gulf of San Matías

OCEAN

Chonos
Archipelago

Patagonia

ARGENTINA

Gulf of San Jorge

Gulf of Peñas

San Valentin
13313ft/4058m

W. Falkland   Falkland Is.

over 5000 meters

Magellan's
Str.

E. Falkland

3000-5000 meters

Tierra del Fuego

Scotia Sea

2000-3000 meters

Cape Horn

S. Georgia

1000-2000 meters

Drake Passage

500-1000 meters

S. Orkney Is.

S. Sandwich Is.

200-500 meters

Sea level-200 meters

Graham
Land

South America

Antarctic
Peninsula

Weddell Sea

Antarctic Circle

tions drove the settlers to Charles Town (now Charleston). South Carolina, one of the original thirteen states, was the first state to secede from the Union 1860, and the first battle of the Civil War took place at Fort Sumter in Charleston Harbor, April 12, 1861. Union troops caused widespread destruction in the closing months of the war 1865, including the burning of Columbia. Under Reconstruction, the state was readmitted to the Union 1868, and federal troops left 1877. Tenant farming, or sharecropping, replaced plantation slave labor and, beginning around 1890, tobacco and soybeans replaced rice and cotton as the main crops. Textiles became the state's leading industry after 1900. After 1954, desegregation proceeded very slowly but peaceably. In 1989 Hurricane Hugo devastated coastal areas in the state.

South Dakota state in W US; nickname Coyote or Sunshine State
area 77,123 sq mi/199,800 sq km
capital Pierre
cities Sioux Falls, Rapid City, Aberdeen
physical Great Plains; Black Hills (which include granite Mount Rushmore, on whose face giant relief portrait heads of former presidents Washington, Jefferson, Lincoln, and T Roosevelt are carved); Badlands
products cereals, hay, livestock, gold (second-largest US producer), meat products
population (1990) 696,000
famous people Crazy Horse, Sitting Bull, Ernest O Lawrence
history first explored 1743 by Verendrye for France; claimed by France 18th century; passed to the US as part of the Louisiana Purchase 1803; explored by Lewis and Clark 1804–06; first permanent settlement, Fort Pierre 1817, reached by first Missouri River steamboat 1831. A gold rush brought thousands of prospectors and settlers to the Black Hills by railroad 1873–74, and South Dakota became a state 1889. In the 20th century, dam construction along the Missouri river, rural electrification, and reclamation of arid land helped raise the standard of living, but economic opportunities remain limited.

Southeast Asia Treaty Organization (SEATO) collective military system 1954–77 established by Australia, France, New Zealand, Pakistan, the Philippines, Thailand, the UK, and the US, with Vietnam, Cambodia, and Laos as protocol states. After the Vietnam War, SEATO was phased out.

Southern Christian Leadership Conference (SCLC) US civil-rights organization founded 1957 by Martin Luther ◊King, Jr, and led by him until his assassination 1968. It advocated nonviolence and passive resistance, and it sponsored the 1963 march on Washington, DC that focused national attention on the civil-rights movement. Its nonviolent philosophy was increasingly challenged by militants, and it lost its central position in the movement.

southern lights common name for the ◊aurora australis, colored light in southern skies.

South Georgia island in the S Atlantic, a British crown colony administered with the South Sandwich Islands; area 1,450 sq mi/3,757 sq km. South Georgia lies 800 mi/1,300 km SE of the Falkland Islands, of which it was a dependency until 1985. The British Antarctic Survey has a station on nearby Bird Island.

South Glamorgan (Welsh *De Morgannwg*) county in S Wales
area 161 sq mi/416 sq km
cities Cardiff (administrative headquarters), Barry, Penarth

South Dakota

features mixed farming in the fertile Vale of Glamorgan; Welsh Folk Museum at St Fagans, near Cardiff
products dairy farming, industry (steel, plastics, engineering) in the Cardiff area
population (1991) 392,800
languages 6.5% Welsh, English
famous people Sarah Siddons, Shirley Bassey, R S Thomas.

South Holland (Dutch *Zuid Holland*) low-lying coastal province of the Netherlands, between the provinces of North Holland and Zeeland
area 1,123 sq mi/2,910 sq km
capital The Hague
cities Rotterdam, Dordrecht, Leiden, Delft, Gouda
products bulbs, horticulture, livestock, dairy products, chemicals, textiles
population (1991) 3,245,300
history once part of the former county of Holland, which was divided into two provinces 1840.

South West Africa former name (until 1968) of ◊Namibia.

South Yorkshire metropolitan county of England, created 1976, originally administered by an elected council; its powers reverted to district councils from 1986
area 602 sq mi/1,560 sq km
cities Barnsley, Sheffield, Doncaster
features river Don; part of Peak District National Park
products metal work, coal, dairy, sheep, arable farming
population (1991) 1,269,300
famous people Ian Botham, Arthur Scargill.

Soutine Chaim 1894–1943. Lithuanian-born French Expressionist artist. He painted landscapes and portraits, including many of painters active in Paris in the 1920s and 1930s. He had a distorted style, using thick application of paint (impasto) and brilliant colors.

sovereignty absolute authority within a given territory. The possession of sovereignty is taken to be the distinguishing feature of the state, as against other forms of community. The term has an internal aspect, in that it refers to the ultimate source of authority within a state, such as a parliament or monarch, and an external aspect, where it denotes the independence of the state from any outside authority.

soviet originally a strike committee elected by Russian workers in the 1905 revolution; in 1917 these were set up by peasants, soldiers, and factory workers. The soviets sent delegates to the All-Russian Congress of Soviets to represent their opinions to a future government. They were later taken over by the ◊Bolsheviks.

Soviet Far East former name (until 1991) of a geographical division of Asiatic Russia, now known as Russian Far East.

---

space flight: chronology

1903	Russian scientist Konstantin Tsiolkovsky published the first practical paper on aeronautics.
1926	US engineer Robert Goddard launched the first liquid-fuel rocket.
1937–45	In Germany, Wernher von Braun developed the V2 rocket.
1957	Oct 4: The first space satellite, *Sputnik 1* (USSR, Russian "fellow-traveller"), orbited the Earth at a height of 142–558 mi/229–898 km in 96.2 min. Nov 3: *Sputnik 2* was launched carrying a dog, "Laika;" it died on board seven days later.
1958	Jan 31: *Explorer 1*, the first US satellite, discovered the Van Allen radiation belts.
1961	April 12: the first crewed spaceship, *Vostok 1* (USSR), with Yuri Gagarin on board, was recovered after a single orbit of 89.1 min at a height of 88–109 mi/142–175 km.
1962	Feb 20: John Glenn in *Friendship 7* (US) became the first American to orbit the Earth. *Telstar* (US), a communications satellite, sent the first live television transmission between the US and Europe.
1963	June 16–19: Valentina Tereshkova in *Vostok 1* (USSR) became the first woman in space.
1967	April 24: Vladimir Komarov was the first person to be killed in space research, when his ship, *Soyuz 1* (USSR), crash-landed on the Earth.
1969	July 20: Neil Armstrong of *Apollo 11* (US) was the first person to walk on the Moon.
1970	Nov 10: *Luna 17* (USSR) was launched; its space probe, *Lunokhod*, took photographs and made soil analyses of the Moon's surface.
1971	April 19: *Salyut 1* (USSR), the first orbital space station, was established; it was later visited by the *Soyuz 11* crewed spacecraft.
1973	*Skylab 2*, the first US orbital space station, was established.
1975	July 15–24: *Apollo 18* (US) and *Soyuz 19* (USSR) made a joint flight and linked up in space.
1979	The European Space Agency's satellite launcher, *Ariane 1*, was launched.
1981	April 12: The first reusable crewed spacecraft, the space shuttle *Columbia* (US), was launched.
1986	Space shuttle *Challenger* (US) exploded shortly after take-off, killing all seven crew members.
1988	US shuttle program resumed with launch of *Discovery*. Soviet shuttle *Buran* was launched from the rocket *Energiya*. Soviet cosmonauts Musa Manarov and Vladimir Titov in space station *Mir* spent a record 365 days 59 min in space.
1990	April: Hubble Space Telescope (US) was launched from Cape Canaveral. June 1: X-ray and ultraviolet astronomy satellite *ROSAT* (US/Germany/UK) was launched from Cape Canaveral. Dec 2: *Astro-1* ultraviolet observatory and the road Band X-ray Telescope were launched from the space shuttle *Columbia*. Japanese television journalist Toyohiro Akiyama was launched with Viktor Afanasyev and Musa Manarov to the space station *Mir*.
1991	April 5: The Gamma Ray Observatory was launched from the space shuttle *Atlantis* to survey the sky at gamma-ray wavelengths. May 18: Astronaut Helen Sharman, the first Briton in space, was launched with Anatoli Artsebarsky and Sergei Krikalek to *Mir* space station, returning to Earth May 26 in *Soyuz TM-11* with Viktor Afanasyev and Musa Manarov. Manarov set a record for the longest time spent in space, 541 days, having also spent a year aboard *Mir* 1988.
1992	European satellite *Hipparcos*, launched 1989 to measure the position of 120,000 stars, failed to reach geostationary orbit and went into a highly elliptical orbit, swooping to within 308 mi/500 km of the Earth every ten hours. The mission was later retrieved. May 16: Space shuttle *Endeavor* returned to Earth after its maiden voyage. During its mission, it circled the Earth 141 times and traveled 2.5 million mi/4 million km. Oct 23: *LAGEOS II* (Laser Geodynamics Satellite) was released from the space shuttle *Columbia* into an orbit so stable that it will still be circling the Earth in billions of years.
1993	December: Space Shuttle *Endeavor* successfully carried out mission to replace the Hubble Space Telescope's solar panels and repair its mirror.

Soviet Union alternate name for the former ◊Union of Soviet Socialist Republics (USSR).

Soweto (acronym for *South West Township*) racially segregated urban settlement in South Africa, SW of Johannesburg; population (1983) 915,872. It has experienced civil unrest because of the ◊apartheid regime.

soybean leguminous plant *Glycine max*, native to E Asia, in particular Japan and China. Originally grown as a forage crop, it is increasingly used for human consumption in cooking oils and margarine, as a flour, soy milk, soy sauce, or processed into tofu, miso, or textured vegetable protein.

Soyinka Wole 1934– . Nigerian author who was a political prisoner in Nigeria 1967–69. His works include the play *The Lion and the Jewel* 1963; his prison memoirs *The Man Died* 1972; *Aké, The Years*

of Childhood 1982, an autobiography, and *Isara*, a fictionalized memoir 1989. He was the first African to receive the Nobel Prize for Literature, in 1986.

Soyuz Soviet series of spacecraft, capable of carrying up to three cosmonauts. Soyuz spacecraft consist of three parts: a rear section containing engines; the central crew compartment; and a forward compartment that gives additional room for working and living space. They are now used for ferrying crews up to space stations, though they were originally used for independent space flight.

Soyuz 1 crashed on its first flight April 1967, killing the lone pilot, Vladimir Komarov. Yet in 1968 *Soyuz 3* had the first manned rendezvous and possible docking by a cosmonaut; in 1969 *Soyuz 6* had three spacecraft and seven men put into Earth orbit simultaneously for the first time; and in 1971 *Soyuz 11* linked up with the first space station, *Salyut 1*, although three cosmonauts died on reentry due to loss of pressure in the spacecraft.

Spaak Paul-Henri 1899–1972. Belgian socialist politician. From 1936 to 1966 he held office almost continuously as foreign minister or prime minister. He was an ardent advocate of international peace.

Spacelab small space station built by the European Space Agency, carried in the cargo bay of the US space shuttle, in which it remains throughout each flight, returning to Earth with the shuttle. Spacelab consists of a pressurized module in which astronauts can work, and a series of pallets, open to the vacuum of space, on which equipment is mounted.

space probe any instrumented object sent beyond Earth to collect data from other parts of the Solar System and from deep space. The first probe was the Soviet *Lunik 1*, which flew past the Moon 1959. The first successful planetary probe was the US *Mariner 2*, which flew past Venus 1962, using transfer orbit. The first space probe to leave the Solar System was *Pioneer 10* 1983. Space probes include *Galileo, Giotto, Magellan, Mars Observer, Ulysses*, the ◊Moon probes, and the Mariner, Pioneer, Viking, and Voyager series. Japan launched its first space probe 1990.

space shuttle reusable crewed spacecraft. The first was launched April 12, 1981, by the US. It was developed by NASA to reduce the cost of using space for commercial, scientific, and military purposes. After leaving its payload in space, the space-shuttle orbiter can be flown back to Earth to land on a runway, and is then available for reuse.

The space-shuttle orbiter, the part that goes into space, is 122 ft/37.2 m long and weighs 75 tons. Although most of its cargoes will be unmanned, two to eight crew members may occupy the orbiter's nose section for up to 30 days. In its cargo bay the orbiter can carry up to 32 tons of satellites, scientific equipment, ◊Spacelab, or military payloads. At launch, the shuttle's three main engines are fed with liquid fuel from a cylindrical tank attached to the orbiter; this tank is discarded shortly before the shuttle reaches orbit. Two additional solid-fuel boosters provide the main thrust for launch, but are jettisoned after two minutes.

space station any large structure designed for human occupation in space for extended periods of time. Space stations are used for carrying out astronomical observations and surveys of Earth, as well as for biological studies and the processing of materials in weightlessness. The first space station was ◊*Salyut 1*, and the US has launched ◊*Skylab*.

space–time in physics, combination of space and time used in the theory of ◊relativity. When developing relativity, Albert Einstein showed that time was in many respects like an extra dimension (or direction) to space. Space and time can thus be considered as entwined into a single entity, rather than two separate things.

Spain country in SW Europe, on the Iberian Peninsula between the Atlantic Ocean and the Mediterranean Sea, bounded N by France and W by Portugal.

spaniel any of several breeds of dog, characterized by large, drooping ears and a wavy, long, silky coat. The *Sussex spaniel* is believed to be the oldest variety, weighs 45 lb/20 kg, is 15 in/40 cm tall, and is a golden liver color.

Spanish an inhabitant of Spain or a person of Spanish descent, as well as the culture and Romance language of such persons. The standard Spanish

space shuttle Liftoff of the space shuttle Atlantis Oct 18, 1989.

language, Castilian, originated in the kingdoms of Castile and Aragon (Catalan and Basque languages are also spoken in Spain).

Spanish-American War brief war 1898 between Spain and the US over Spanish rule in Cuba and the Philippines; the complete defeat of Spain made the US a colonial power. The Treaty of Paris ceded the Philippines, Guam, and Puerto Rico to the US; Cuba became independent. The US paid $20 million to Spain. Thus ended Spain's colonial presence in the Americas.

Spanish Armada fleet sent by Philip II of Spain against England in 1588. Consisting of 130 ships, it sailed from Lisbon and carried on a running fight up the Channel with the English fleet of 197 small ships under Howard of Effingham and Francis ◊Drake. The Armada anchored off Calais but fireships forced it to put to sea, and a general action followed off Gravelines. What remained of the Armada escaped around the N of Scotland and W of Ireland, suffering many losses by storm and shipwreck on the way. Only about half the original fleet returned to Spain.

Spanish Civil War 1936–39. See ◊Civil War, Spanish.

Spanish Guinea former name of the Republic of ◊Equatorial Guinea.

Spanish language member of the Romance branch of the Indo-European language family, traditionally known as Castilian and originally spoken only in NE Spain. As the language of the court, it has been the standard and literary language of the Spanish state since the 13th century. It is now a world language, spoken in Mexico and all South and Central American countries (except Brazil, Guyana, Suriname, and French Guiana) as well as in the Philippines, Cuba, Puerto Rico, and much of the US.

Spanish Main common name for the Caribbean Sea in the 16th–17th centuries, but more properly the South American mainland between the river Orinoco and Panama.

Spanish Sahara former name for ◊Western Sahara.

Spanish Succession, War of the war 1701–14 of Britain, Austria, the Netherlands, Portugal, and Den-

Spain (*España*)

France

Andorra

SPAIN
• Madrid

MEDITERRANEAN SEA

Portugal

Morocco

0 mi   500
0 km   1000

area 194,960 sq mi/504,750 sq km
capital Madrid
cities Zaragoza, Seville, Murcia, Córdoba; ports Barcelona, Valencia, Cartagena, Málaga, Cádiz, Vigo, Santander, Bilbao
physical central plateau with mountain ranges; lowlands in S
territories Balearic and Canary Islands; in N Africa: Ceuta, Melilla, Alhucemas, Chafarinas Is, Peñón de Vélez
features rivers Ebro, Douro, Tagus, Guadiana, Guadalquivir; Iberian Plateau (Meseta); Pyrenees, Cantabrian Mountains, Andalusian Mountains, Sierra Nevada
head of state King Juan Carlos I from 1975
head of government Felipe González Márquez from 1982
political system constitutional monarchy
political parties Socialist Workers' Party (PSOE), democratic socialist; Popular Alliance (AP), center-right; Christian Democrats (DC), centrist; Liberal Party (PL), left of center

exports citrus fruits, grapes, pomegranates, vegetables, wine, sherry, olive oil, canned fruit and fish, iron ore, cork, vehicles, textiles, petroleum products, leather goods, ceramics
currency peseta
population (1992) 39,085,000; growth rate 0.2% p.a.
life expectancy men 74, women 80 (1989)
languages Spanish (Castilian, official), Basque, Catalan, Galician, Valencian, Majorcan
religion Roman Catholic 99%
literacy 97% (1989)
GNP $573.7 bn (1992)

chronology
1936–39 Civil war; General Francisco Franco became head of state and government; fascist party Falange declared only legal political organization.
1947 General Franco announced restoration of the monarchy after his death, with Prince Juan Carlos as his successor.
1975 Franco died; succeeded as head of state by King Juan Carlos I.
1978 New constitution adopted with Adolfo Suárez, leader of the Democratic Center Party, as prime minister.
1981 Suárez resigned; succeeded by Leopoldo Calvo Sotelo. Attempted military coup thwarted.
1982 Socialist Workers' Party (PSOE), led by Felipe González, won a sweeping electoral victory. Basque separatist organization (ETA) stepped up its guerrilla campaign.
1985 ETA's campaign spread to holiday resorts.
1986 Referendum confirmed NATO membership. Spain joined the European Economic Community.
1988 Spain joined the Western European Union.
1989 PSOE lost seats to hold only parity after general election. Talks between government and ETA collapsed and truce ended.
1992 ETA's "armed struggle" resumed. European Community's Maastricht Treaty ratified.
1993 Allegations of corruption within PSOE. González narrowly won general election and formed a new minority government, including independents in his cabinet.

mark (the Allies) against France, Spain, and Bavaria. It was caused by Louis XIV's acceptance of the Spanish throne on behalf of his grandson, Philip V of Spain, in defiance of the Partition Treaty of 1700, under which it would have passed to Archduke Charles of Austria (later Holy Roman emperor Charles VI).

sparrow any of a family (Passeridae) of small Old World birds of the order Passeriformes with short, thick bills, including the now worldwide house or English sparrow *Passer domesticus*. Many numbers of the New World family Emberizidae, which includes warblers, orioles, and buntings, are also called sparrows; for example, the North American song sparrow *Melospize melodia*.

Sparta ancient Greek city-state in the S Peloponnese (near Sparte), developed from Dorian settlements in the 10th century BC. The Spartans, known for their military discipline and austerity, took part in the ◊Persian and ◊Peloponnesian wars.

Spartacist member of a group of left-wing radicals in Germany at the end of World War I, founders of the *Spartacus League*, which became the German Communist Party in 1919. The league participated in the Berlin workers' revolt of Jan 1919, which was suppressed by the Freikorps on the orders of the socialist government. The agitation ended with the murder of Spartacist leaders Karl Liebknecht and Rosa Luxemburg.

Spartacus died 71 BC. Thracian gladiator who in 73 BC led a revolt of gladiators and slaves in Capua, near Naples and swept throuigh southern Italy and Cisalpine Gaul. He was eventually caught by Roman general ◊Crassus 71 BC and Spartacus and his followers were crucified.

Spartanburg city in NW South Carolina, NW of Columbia, in the foothills of the Blue Ridge Mountains; population (1990) 43,500. It is an agricultural center. Its industries include food products, furniture, textiles, paper, and plumbing supplies.

Speaker presiding officer in the US House of Representatives. The Speaker is second in line of succession to the presidency in the event of death or incapacitation.

special drawing right (SDR) the right of a member state of the ◊International Monetary Fund to apply for money to finance its balance of payments deficit. Originally, the SDR was linked to gold and the US dollar. After 1974 SDRs were defined in terms of a "basket" of the 16 currencies of countries doing 1% or more of the world's trade. In 1981 the SDR was simplified to a weighted average of US dollars, French francs, German marks, Japanese yen, and UK pounds sterling.

special education education, often in separate "special schools," for children with specific physical or mental problems or disabilities.

In the US, the federal department of education has been leading the recent movement toward "main-

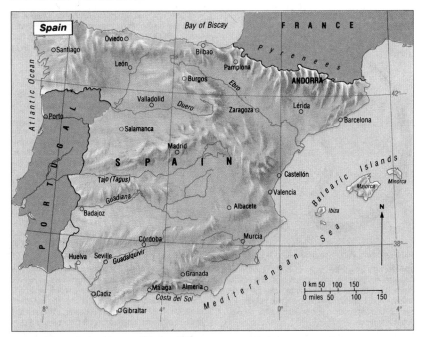

streaming," which calls for the integration of students with special needs into the normal school system whenever practical.

speciation emergence of a new species during evolutionary history. One cause of speciation is the geographical separation of populations of the parent species, followed by reproductive isolation and selection for different environments so that they no longer produce viable offspring when they interbreed. Other causes are assortative mating and the establishment of a polyploid population.

species in biology, a distinguishable group of organisms that resemble each other or consist of a few distinctive types (as in ◊polymorphism), and that can all interbreed to produce fertile offspring. Species are the lowest level in the system of biological classification.

specific gravity alternative term for ◊relative density.

specific heat capacity in physics, quantity of heat required to raise unit mass (1 kg) of a substance by one ◊kelvin (1°C). The unit of specific heat capacity in the SI system is the ◊joule per kilogram kelvin (J kg^{-1} K^{-1}).

spectrum (plural *spectra*) in physics, an arrangement of frequencies or wavelengths when electromagnetic radiations are separated into their constituent parts. Visible light is part of the ◊electromagnetic spectrum and most sources emit waves over a range of wavelengths that can be broken up or "dispersed"; white light can be separated into red, orange, yellow, green, blue, indigo, and violet. The visible spectrum was first studied by Isaac ◊Newton, who showed in 1672 how white light could be broken up into different colors.

speech recognition or *voice input* in computing, any technique by which a computer can understand ordinary speech. Spoken words are divided into "frames," each lasting about one-thirtieth of a second, which are converted to a wave form. These are then compared with a series of stored frames to determine the most likely word. Research into speech recognition started in 1938, but the technology did not become sufficiently developed for commercial applications until the late 1980s.

speech synthesis or *voice output* computer-based technology for generating speech. A speech synthesizer is controlled by a computer, which supplies strings of codes representing basic speech sounds (phonemes); together these make up words. Speech-synthesis applications include children's toys, automobile and aircraft warning systems, and talking books for the blind.

speed the rate at which an object moves. The average speed v of an object may be calculated by dividing the distance s it has traveled by the time t taken to do so, and may be expressed as: $v = s/t$ The usual units of speed are miles per second or miles per hour.

speed of light speed at which light and other ◊electromagnetic waves travel through empty space. Its value is 186,281 mi/299,792,458 m per second. The speed of light is the highest speed possible, according to the theory of ◊relativity, and its value is independent of the motion of its source and of the observer. It is impossible to accelerate any material body to this speed because it would require an infinite amount of energy.

speed of sound speed at which sound travels through a medium, such as air or water. In air at a temperature of 32°F/0°C, the speed of sound is 1,087 ft/331 m per second. At higher temperatures, the speed of sound is greater; at 64°F/18°C it is 1,123 ft/342 m per second. It is greater in liquids and solids; for example, in water it is around 4,724 ft/1,440 m per second, depending on the temperature.

Speer Albert 1905–1981. German architect and minister in the Nazi government during World War II. Commissioned by Hitler, Speer, like his counterparts in Fascist Italy, chose an overblown Classicism to glo-

sperm Only a single sperm is needed to fertilize a single egg or ovum, but up to 500 million may start the journey toward the egg.

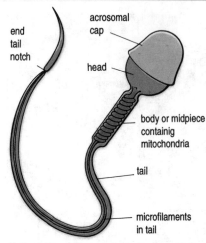

acrosomal cap

end tail notch

head

body or midpiece containig mitochondria

tail

microfilaments in tail

rify the state, as, for example, in his plan for the Berlin and Nuremberg Party Congress Grounds 1934.

speleology scientific study of caves, their origin, development, physical structure, flora, fauna, folklore, exploration, mapping, photography, cave-diving, and rescue work. *Potholing*, which involves following the course of underground rivers or streams, has become a popular sport.

Spender Stephen (Harold) 1909– . English poet and critic. His earlier poetry has a left-wing political content, as in *Twenty Poems* 1930, *Vienna* 1934, *The Still Centre* 1939, and *Poems of Dedication* 1946. Other works include the verse drama *Trial of a Judge* 1938, the autobiography *World within World* 1951, and translations. His *Journals 1939–83* were published 1985.

Sphinx The avenue of ram sphinxes at the temple of Karnak in Luxor, Egypt.

Spenser Edmund c. 1552–1599. English poet, who has been called the "poet's poet" because of his rich imagery and command of versification. His major

work is the moral allegory *The Faerie Queene*, of which six books survive (three published 1590 and three 1596). Other books include *The Shepheard's Calendar* 1579, *Astrophel* 1586, the love sonnets *Amoretti* and the *Epithalamion* 1595.

sperm or *semen* the fluid containing the male ◊gametes (sperm cells) of animals. Usually, each sperm cell has a head capsule containing a nucleus, a middle portion containing ◊mitochondria (which provide energy), and a long tail (flagellum).

spermicide any cream, jelly, pessary, or other preparation that kills the ◊sperm cells in semen. Spermicides are used for contraceptive purposes, usually in combination with a ◊condom or ◊diaphragm. Sponges impregnated with spermicide have been developed but are not yet in widespread use. Spermicide used alone is only 75% effective in preventing pregnancy.

sphere in mathematics, a perfectly round object with all points on its surface the same distance from the center. This distance is the radius of the sphere. For a sphere of radius r, the volume $V = 4 \div 3\pi r^3$ and the surface area $A = 4\pi r^2$.

sphincter ring of muscle found at various points in the alimentary canal, which contracts and relaxes to control the movement of food. The *pyloric sphincter*, at the base of the stomach, controls the release of the gastric contents into the duodenum. After release the sphincter contracts, closing off the stomach.

Sphinx mythological creature, represented in Egyptian, Assyrian, and Greek art as a lion with a human head. In Greek myth the Sphinx killed all those who came to her and failed to answer her riddle about what animal went first on four legs, then on two, and last on three: the answer is humanity (baby, adult, and old person with stick). She committed suicide when ◊Oedipus gave the right answer.

spice any aromatic vegetable substance used as a condiment and for flavoring food. Spices are mostly

obtained from tropical plants, and include pepper, nutmeg, ginger, and cinnamon. They have little food value but increase the appetite and may facilitate digestion.

spider any arachnid (eight-legged animal) of the order Araneae. There are about 30,000 known species. Unlike insects, the head and breast are merged to form the cephalothorax, connected to the abdomen by a characteristic narrow waist. There are eight legs, and usually eight simple eyes. On the undersurface of the abdomen are spinnerets, usually six, which exude a viscid fluid. This hardens on exposure to the air to form silky threads, used to make silken egg cases, silk-lined tunnels, or various kinds of webs and snares for catching prey that is then wrapped. The fangs of spiders inject substances to subdue and digest prey, the juices of which are then sucked into the stomach by the spider.

spider plant African plant of the genus *Chlorophytum* of the lily family. Two species, *C. comosum* and *C. elatum*, are popular house plants. They have long narrow variegated leaves and produce flowering shoots from which the new plants grow. The flowers are small and white. Spider plants absorb toxins from the air and therefore have a purifying action on the local atmosphere.

Spielberg Steven 1947– . US film director, writer, and producer. His highly successful films, including *Jaws* 1975, *Close Encounters of the Third Kind* 1977, *Raiders of the Lost Ark* 1981, and *ET* 1982 gave popular cinema a new "respectable" appeal. He also directed *Indiana Jones and the Temple of Doom* 1984, *The Color Purple* 1985, *Indiana Jones and the Last Crusade* 1989, and *Jurassic Park* 1993. *Schindler's List* 1993 is a fact-based account of a German businessman who manipulated the survival of some 1,000 Jews from Nazi extermination.

spin in physics, the intrinsic ◊angular momentum of a subatomic particle, nucleus, atom, or molecule, which continues to exist even when the particle comes to rest. A particle in a specific energy state has a particular spin, just as it has a particular electric charge and mass. According to ◊quantum theory, this is restricted to discrete and indivisible values, specified by a spin ◊quantum number. Because of its spin, a charged particle acts as a small magnet and is affected by magnetic fields.

spina bifida congenital defect in which part of the spinal cord and its membranes are exposed, due to incomplete development of the spine (vertebral column).

spinach annual plant *Spinacia oleracea* of the goosefoot family Chenopodiaceae. It is native to Asia and widely cultivated for its leaves, which are eaten as a vegetable.

spinal tap or ***lumbar puncture*** insertion of a hollow needle between two lumbar (lower back) vertebrae to withdraw a sample of cerebrospinal fluid (CSF) for testing. Normally clear and colorless, the CSF acts as a fluid buffer around the brain and spinal cord. Changes in its quantity, color, or composition may indicate neurological damage or disease.

spine the backbone of vertebrates. It consists of separate disk-shaped bony units (vertebrae), processes that enclose and protect the spinal cord. The spine connects with the skull, ribs, back muscles, and pelvis.

spinet plucking-action keyboard instrument similar to a ◊harpsichord but smaller, which has only one string for each note.

spinning art of drawing out and twisting fibers (originally wool or flax) into a long thread, or yarn, by hand or machine. Synthetic fibers are extruded as a liquid through the holes of a spinneret. Spinning was originally done by hand, then with the spinning wheel, and in about 1767 in England James ◊Hargreaves built the ***spinning jenny***, a machine that could spin 8, then

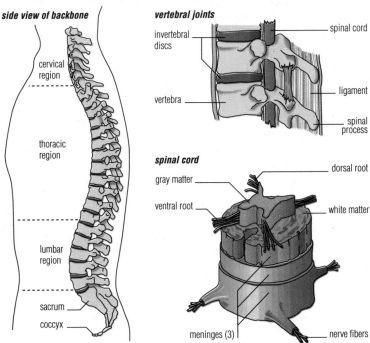

side view of backbone

cervical region

thoracic region

lumbar region

sacrum

coccyx

vertebral joints

invertebral discs

vertebra

spinal cord

ligament

spinal process

spinal cord

gray matter

ventral root

dorsal root

white matter

meninges (3)

nerve fibers

spine *The human spine extends every night during sleep.*

16, bobbins at once. Later, Samuel Crompton's **spinning mule** 1779 had a moving carriage carrying the spindles and is still in use today.

Spinoza Benedict or Baruch 1632–1677. Dutch philosopher who believed in a rationalistic pantheism that owed much to Descartes' mathematical appreciation of the universe. Mind and matter are two modes of an infinite substance that he called God or Nature, good and evil being relative. He was a determinist, believing that human action was motivated by self-preservation.

spiny anteater alternate name for ◊echidna.

spiral a plane curve formed by a point winding around a fixed point from which it distances itself at regular intervals, for example the spiral traced by a flat coil of rope. Various kinds of spirals can be generated mathematically—for example, an equiangular or logarithmic spiral (in which a tangent at any point on the curve always makes the same angle with it) and an involute. Spirals also occur in nature as a normal consequence of accelerating growth, such as the spiral shape of the shells of snails and some other mollusks.

spiritualism belief in the survival of the human personality and in communication between the living and those who have "passed on." The spiritualist movement originated in the US in 1848. Adherents to this religious denomination practice **mediumship**, which claims to allow clairvoyant knowledge of distant events and spirit healing. The writer Arthur Conan Doyle and the Victorian prime minister Gladstone were converts.

spit ridge of sand or shingle projecting from the land into a body of water. It is deposited by waves carrying material from one direction to another across the mouth of an inlet (longshore drift). Deposition in the brackish water behind a spit may result in the formation of a ◊salt marsh.

Spitsbergen mountainous island with a deeply indented coastline in the Arctic Ocean, the main island in the Norwegian archipelago of ◊Svalbard, 408 mi/657 km N of Norway; area 15,075 sq mi/39,043 sq km. Fishing, hunting, and coal mining are the chief economic activities. The Norwegian Polar Research Institute operates an all-year scientific station on the W coast. Mount Newton rises to 5,620 ft/1,713 m.

Spitz Mark Andrew 1950– . US swimmer. He won a record seven gold medals at the 1972 Olympic Games, all in world record times.

He won 11 Olympic medals in total (four in 1968) and set 26 world records between 1967 and 1972. His attempt to qualify for the 1992 Olympics failed.

spleen organ in vertebrates, part of the lymphatic system, which helps to process ◊lymphocytes. It also regulates the number of red blood cells in circulation by destroying old cells, and stores iron. It is situated behind the stomach.

Split (Italian **Spalato**) port in Croatia, on the Adriatic coast; population (1981) 236,000. Industries include engineering, cement, and textiles. Split was bombed during 1991 as part of Yugoslavia's blockade of the Croatian coast.

Spock Benjamin McLane 1903– . US pediatrician and writer on child care. His *Common Sense Book of Baby and Child Care* 1946 urged less rigidity in bringing up children than had been advised by previous generations of writers on the subject, but this was misunderstood as advocating permissiveness. He was also active in the peace movement, especially during the Vietnam War.

spoils system in the US, the granting of offices and favors among the supporters of a party in office. The spoils system, a type of ◊patronage, was used by President Jefferson and was enlarged in scope by the 1820 Tenure of Office Act, which gave the president and Senate the power to reappoint posts that were the gift of the government after each four-year election. The practice remained common in the 20th century in US local government.

Spokane city on the Spokane River, E Washington; population (1990) 177,200. It is situated in a mining, timber, and rich agricultural area, and is the seat of Gonzaga University (1887). Spokane was incorporated 1881 and was the site of Expo '74 (International Exposition of Environment 1974).

Spoleto town in Umbria, central Italy; population (1985) 37,000. There is an annual opera and drama festival (June–July) established by Gian Carlo ◊Menotti. It was a papal possession 1220–1860 and has Roman remains and medieval churches.

sponge any saclike simple invertebrate of the phylum Porifera, usually marine. A sponge has a hollow body, its cavity lined by cells bearing flagellae, whose whiplike movements keep water circulating, bringing in a stream of food particles. The body walls are strengthened with protein (as in the bath sponge) or small spikes of silica, or a framework of calcium carbonate.

spontaneous generation or **abiogenesis** erroneous belief that living organisms can arise spontaneously from non-living matter. This survived until the mid-19th century, when the French chemist Louis Pasteur demonstrated that a nutrient broth would not generate microorganisms if it was adequately sterilized. The theory of biogenesis holds that spontaneous generation cannot now occur; it is thought, however, to have played an essential role in the origin of ◊life on this planet 4 billion years ago.

spoonbill any of several large wading birds of the Ibis family (Threskiornithidae), characterized by a long, flat bill, dilated at the tip in the shape of a spoon. Spoonbills are white or pink, and up to 3 ft/90 cm tall.

The roseate spoonbill *Ajaia ajaja* of North and South America is found in shallow open water, which it sifts for food.

spoonerism exchange of elements in a flow of words. Usually a slip of the tongue, a spoonerism can also be contrived for comic effect (for example "a troop of Boy Scouts" becoming "a scoop of Boy Trouts"). William Spooner (1844–1930) gave his name to the phenomenon.

spore small reproductive or resting body, usually consisting of just one cell. Unlike a ◊gamete, it does not need to fuse with another cell in order to develop into a new organism. Spores are produced by the lower plants, most fungi, some bacteria, and certain protozoa. They are generally light and easily dispersed by wind movements. Plant spores are haploid and are produced by the sporophyte, following ◊meiosis.

spreadsheet in computing, a program that mimics a sheet of ruled paper, divided into columns and rows. The user enters values in the sheet, then instructs the program to perform some operation on them, such as totaling a column or finding the average of a series of numbers. Highly complex numerical analyses may be built up from these simple steps.

spring device, usually a metal coil, that returns to its original shape after being stretched or compressed. Springs are used in some machines (such as clocks) to store energy, which can be released at a controlled rate. In other machines (such as engines) they are used to close valves.

spring in geology, a natural flow of water from the ground, formed at the point of intersection of the water table and the ground's surface. The source of water is rain that has percolated through the overlying rocks. During its underground passage, the water may have dissolved mineral substances that may then be precipitated at the spring (hence, a mineral spring).

springbok South African antelope *Antidorcas marsupialis* about 30 in/80 cm at the shoulder, with head and body 4 ft/1.3 m long. It may leap 10 ft/3 m or more in the air when startled or playing, and has a fold of skin along the middle of the back which is raised to a crest in alarm. Springboks once migrated in herds of over a million, but are now found only in small numbers where protected.

Springdale city in NW Arkansas, NW of Little Rock; population (1990) 29,900. Industries include food and livestock processing.

Springfield capital and agricultural and mining center of Illinois; population (1990) 105,200. President Abraham Lincoln was born and is buried here. Lincoln lived and practiced law in Springfield from 1837 until he became president 1861. His home and tomb are historic sites. Sangamon State University is here. Springfield was settled 1818 and became the state capital 1837.

Springfield city in Massachusetts; population (1990) 157,000. It was the site (1794–1968) of the US arsenal and armory, known for the Springfield rifle. Basketball originated here 1891, and points of interest include the National Basketball Hall of Fame. The community dates from 1636.

Springfield city and agricultural center in Missouri; population (1990) 140,500. Industries include electronic equipment and processed food. The city is also a tourist center for the Ozark Mountains and the home of Southwest Missouri State University. Springfield was settled 1829.

Springfield city in W Oregon on the Willamette River, E of Eugene; population (1990) 45,000. Industries include lumber, animal feeds, and agricultural products.

Springsteen Bruce 1949– . US rock singer, songwriter, and guitarist, born in New Jersey. His music combines melodies in traditional rock idiom and reflective lyrics about working-class life and the pursuit of the American dream on such albums as *Born to Run* 1975, *Born in the USA* 1984, and *Human Touch* 1992.

Springsteen began his early career in the late 1960s playing small East Coast clubs, where he earned a cult following. In concerts with the E Street Band, playing long ambitious sets, his performance is electrifying. "The Boss" won many new fans in the mid-1980s performing in a series of sold-out concerts across the US.

spruce coniferous tree of the genus *Picea* of the pine family, found over much of the northern hemisphere. Pyramidal in shape, spruces have rigid, prickly needles and drooping, leathery cones. Some are important forestry trees, such as sitka spruce *P. sitchensis*, native to W North America, and the Norway spruce *P. abies*, now planted widely in North America.

Sputnik series of ten Soviet Earth-orbiting satellites. *Sputnik 1* was the first artificial satellite, launched Oct 4, 1957. It weighed 185 lb/84 kg, with a 23 in/58 cm diameter, and carried only a simple radio transmitter which allowed scientists to track it as it orbited Earth. It burned up in the atmosphere 92 days later. Sputniks were superseded in the early 1960s by the Cosmos series.

Squanto also known as Tisquantum *c.* 1580–1622. American Pawtuxet Indian ally of the Plymouth colonists. Kidnapped by the English and taken to England 1605, he returned to New England 1619 as a guide for Captain John Slaine. His own tribe having been wiped out by an epidemic, Squanto settled among the Wampanoag people, serving as interpreter for Chief ◊Massasoit in his dealings with the Pilgrims.

square in geometry, a quadrilateral (four-sided) plane figure with all sides equal and each angle a right angle. Its diagonals bisect each other at right angles. The area A of a square is the length l of one side multiplied by itself ($A = l \times l$).

Also, any quantity multiplied by itself is termed a square, represented by an ◊exponent of power 2; for example, $4 \times 4 = 4^2 = 16$ and $6.8 \times 6.8 = 6.8^2 = 46.24$.

square root in mathematics, a number that when squared (multiplied by itself) equals a given number. For example, the square root of 25 (written $\sqrt{25}$) is ± 5, because $5 \times 5 = 25$, and $(-5) \times (-5) = 25$. As an ◊exponent, a square root is represented by ½, for example, $16^{\frac{1}{2}} = 4$.

squash or *squash rackets* racket-and-ball game usually played by two people on an enclosed court, derived from ◊rackets. Squash became a popular sport in the 1970s and later gained competitive status. There are two forms of squash: the American form, which is played in North and some South American countries, and the English, which is played mainly in Europe and Commonwealth countries such as Pakistan, Australia, and New Zealand.

squint or *strabismus* common condition in which one eye deviates in any direction. A squint may be convergent (with the bad eye turned inward), divergent (outward), or, in rare cases, vertical. A convergent squint is also called *cross-eye*.

squirrel rodent of the family Sciuridae. Squirrels are found worldwide except for Australia, Madagascar, and polar regions. Some are tree dwellers; these generally have bushy tails, and some, with membranes between their legs, are called ◊flying squirrels. Others are terrestrial, generally burrowing forms called ground squirrels; these include chipmunks, gophers, marmots, and prairie dogs.

The small red squirrel *Tamia sciurus* of Alaska, the Rocky Mountains, and NE US, grows to 14 in/35 cm

spruce Spruces are evergreen trees of the pine family.

Sri Lanka
Democratic Socialist Republic of
(*Prajathanrika Samajawadi Janarajaya
Sri Lanka*)
(until 1972 *Ceylon*)

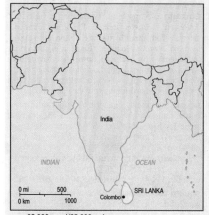

India

INDIAN   OCEAN

0 mi   500
0 km   1000   Colombo ● SRI LANKA

area 25,328 sq mi/65,600 sq km
capital (and chief port) Colombo
cities Kandy; ports Jaffna, Galle, Negombo, Trincomalee
physical flat in N and around the coast; hills and mountains
in S and central interior
features Adam's Peak (7,538 ft/2,243 m); ruined cities of
Anuradhapura, Polonnaruwa
head of state Dingiri Banda Wijetunge from 1993
head of government Ranil Wickremasinghe from 1993
political system liberal democratic republic
political parties United National Party (UNP), right of
center; Sri Lanka Freedom Party (SLFP), left of center;
Democratic United National Front (DUNF), center-left; Tamil
United Liberation Front (TULF), Tamil autonomy; Eelam
People's Revolutionary Liberation Front (EPLRF), Indian-
backed Tamil-secessionist "Tamil Tigers"
exports tea, rubber, coconut products, graphite, sapphires,
rubies, other gemstones

currency Sri Lanka rupee
population (1992) 17,464,000 (Sinhalese 74%, Tamils
17%, Moors 7%); growth rate 1.8% p.a.
life expectancy men 67, women 72 (1989)
languages Sinhala, Tamil, English
religions Buddhist 69%, Hindu 15%, Muslim 8%,
Christian 7%
literacy 87% (1988)
GNP $7.2 bn; $400 per head (1988)

chronology
1802 Ceylon became a British colony.
1948 Ceylon achieved independence from Britain within the
Commonwealth.
1956 Sinhala established as the official language.
1959 Prime Minister Solomon Bandaranaike assassinated.
1972 Socialist Republic of Sri Lanka proclaimed.
1978 Presidential constitution adopted by new government
headed by Junius Jayawardene of the UNP.
1983 Tamil guerrilla violence escalated; state of emergency
imposed.
1987 President Jayawardene and Indian prime minister Rajiv
Gandhi signed Colombo Accord. Violence continued despite
cease-fire policed by Indian troops.
1988 Left-wing guerrillas campaigned against Indo-Sri
Lankan peace pact. Prime Minister Ranasinghe Premadasa
elected president.
1989 Premadasa became president; D B Wijetunge, prime
minister. Leaders of the TULF and the banned Sinhala
extremist People's Liberation Front (JVP) assassinated.
1990 Indian peacekeeping force withdrawn. Violence
continued.
1991 March: defense minister Ranjan Wijeratne
assassinated; Sri Lankan army killed 2,552 Tamil Tigers at
Elephant Pass. Oct: impeachment motion against President
Premadasa failed. Dec: new party, the Democratic United
National Front (DUNF), formed by former members of the
UNP.
1992 35 Tamil civilians massacred by Sinhalese soldiers.
1993 DUNF leader assassinated; DUNF and SLFP leaders
held the government responsible. President Premadasa
assassinated; succeeded by Prime Minister Wijetunge. Ranil
Wickremasinghe became prime minister.

including the tail, builds large tree nests and accumulates the cones of spruce and other conifers for winter
use. The larger eastern gray squirrel *Sciurus carolinensis* of E North America grows to 20 in/50 cm
including tail, stores nuts and acorns, and is a
common sight in city parks and suburbs.

Sri Lanka island in the Indian Ocean, off the SE coast
of India.

SS Nazi elite corps (German *Schutz-Staffel* "protective
squadron") established 1925. Under ◊Himmler its
500,000 membership included the full-time *Waffen-
SS* (armed SS), which fought in World War II, and
spare-time members. The SS performed state police
duties and was brutal in its treatment of the Jews and
others in the concentration camps and occupied territories. It was condemned at the Nuremberg Trials of
war criminals.

stabilizer one of a pair of fins fitted to the sides of a
ship, especially one governed automatically by a ◊gy-
roscope mechanism, designed to reduce side-to-side
rolling of the ship in rough weather.

Staël Anne Louise Germaine Necker, Madame de
1766–1817. French author, daughter of the financier
Necker. She wrote semiautobiographical novels such
as *Delphine* 1802 and *Corinne* 1807, and the critical
work *De l'Allemagne* 1810, on German literature. She

was banished from Paris by Napoleon in 1803 because
of her advocacy of political freedom.

Staffordshire county in W central England
area 1,050 sq mi/2,720 sq km
cities Stafford (administrative headquarters), Stoke-
on-Trent
features largely flat, comprising the Vale of Trent
and its tributaries; Cannock Chase; Keele University
1962; Staffordshire bull terriers
products coal in the N; china and earthenware in the
Potteries and the upper Trent basin
population (1991) 1,020,300
famous people Arnold Bennett, Peter de Wint,
Robert Peel.

stagflation economic condition (experienced in the
US in the 1970s) in which rapid inflation is accompanied by stagnating, even declining, output and by
increasing unemployment. It is a recently coined term
to explain a condition that violates many of the suppo-
sitions of Classical economics. Under the Carter administration, interest rates skyrocketed, prices rose
dramatically, and a deep recession occurred. The
increase in ◊OPEC petroleum prices was a major contributing factor.

stainless steel widely used ◊alloy of iron, chromium,
and nickel that resists rusting. Its chromium content

also gives it a high tensile strength. It is used for cutlery and kitchen fittings.

stalactite and stalagmite cave structures formed by the deposition of calcite dissolved in ground water. *Stalactites* grow downward from the roofs or walls and can be icicle-shaped, straw-shaped, curtain-shaped, or formed as terraces. *Stalagmites* grow upward from the cave floor and can be conical, fir-cone-shaped, or resemble a stack of saucers. Growing stalactites and stalagmites may meet to form a continuous column from floor to ceiling.

Stalin Joseph. Adopted name (Russian "steel") of Joseph Vissarionovich Djugashvili 1879–1953. Soviet politician. A member of the October Revolution Committee 1917, Stalin became general secretary of the Communist Party 1922. After ◊Lenin's death 1924, Stalin sought to create "socialism in one country" and clashed with ◊Trotsky, who denied the possibility of socialism inside Russia until revolution had occurred in W Europe. Stalin won this ideological struggle by 1927, and a series of five-year plans was launched to collectivize industry and agriculture from 1928. All opposition was eliminated in the Great Purge 1936–38. During World War II, Stalin intervened in the military direction of the campaigns against Nazi Germany. His role was denounced after his death by Khrushchev and other members of the Soviet regime.

Stalingrad former name (1925–61) of the Russian city of ◊Volgograd.

Stallone Sylvester 1946– . US film actor, director, and screenwriter, a bit player who rocketed to fame as the boxer in *Rocky* (his screenplay; Best Picture Oscar) 1976 and its sequels. Other films include the violent *Rambo* series from 1982 and the comedy *Stop! Or My Momma Will Shoot* 1992.

stamen male reproductive organ of a flower. The stamens are collectively referred to as the ◊androecium. A typical stamen consists of a stalk, or filament, with an anther, the pollen-bearing organ, at its apex, but in some primitive plants, such as *Magnolia*, the stamen may not be markedly differentiated. *See illustration p. 876*

Stamford city in SW Connecticut, on Long Island Sound, NE of New York City; population (1990) 108,100. Industries include computers, hardware, rubber, plastics, and pharmaceuticals.

Stamp Act UK act of Parliament 1765 that sought to raise enough money from the American colonies to cover the cost of their defense. Refusal to use the required tax stamps and a blockade of British merchant shipping in the colonies forced repeal of the act the following year. It helped to precipitate the ◊American Revolution.

standard deviation in statistics, a measure (symbol σ or *s*) of the spread of data. The deviation (difference) of each of the data items from the mean is found, and their values squared. The mean value of these squares is then calculated. The standard deviation is the square root of this mean.

standard model in physics, the modern theory of ◊elementary particles and their interactions. According to the standard model, elementary particles are classified as leptons (light particles, such as electrons), hadrons (particles, such as neutrons and protons, that are formed from quarks), and gauge bosons. Leptons and hadrons interact by exchanging gauge bosons, each of which is responsible for a different fundamental force: photons mediate the electromagnetic force,

stalactite and stalagmite Large stalagmites with stalactites above in Ogof Ffynnon Dhu (Cave of the Black Spring), S Wales.

which affects all charged particles; gluons mediate the strong nuclear force, which affects quarks; gravitons mediate the force of gravity; and the weakons (intermediate vector bosons) mediate the weak nuclear force. See also ◊forces, fundamental, ◊quantum electrodynamics, and ◊quantum chromodynamics.

standard of living in economics, the measure of consumption and welfare of a country, community, class, or person. Individual standard-of-living expectations are heavily influenced by the income and consumption of other people in similar jobs.

Standard Oil Co of New Jersey et al v US US Supreme Court decision 1911 dealing with the dissolution of unreasonable corporate monopolies. The Standard Oil Co, ordered to dissolve after being convicted of an attempt to eliminate free competition in the industry, appealed to the Supreme Court. The Court upheld the conviction formulating a new subjective definition of an illegal trust as "an unreasonable attempt" to restrain competition in trade.

standard temperature and pressure (STP) in chemistry, a standard set of conditions for experimental measurements, to enable comparisons to be made between sets of results. Standard temperature is 0°C and standard pressure 1 atmosphere (101,325 Pa).

standard volume in physics, the volume occupied by one kilogram molecule (the molecular mass in kilograms) of any gas at standard temperature and pressure.

standing wave in physics, a wave in which the positions of nodes (positions of zero vibration) and anti-

Stalin Soviet leader Joseph Stalin taking the salute during a march past of workers in Red Square, Moscow, in May 1932.

stamen *The stamen is the male reproductive organ of a flower.*

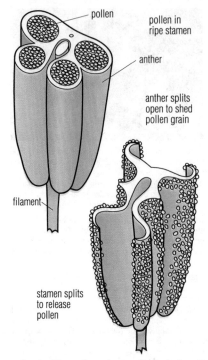

pollen

pollen in ripe stamen

anther

anther splits open to shed pollen grain

filament

stamen splits to release pollen

nodes (positions of maximum vibration) do not move. Standing waves result when two similar waves travel in opposite directions through the same space.

Standish Miles *c.* 1584–1656. American colonial military leader. As military adviser to the Pilgrim Fathers, he arrived in New England 1621 and obtained a charter for Plymouth colony from England 1925. Although one of the most influential figures in colonial New England, he is best remembered through American poet Henry Longfellow's *The Courtship of Miles Standish* 1863.

Stanford Leland 1824–1893. US public official and railroad developer. Elected governor of California 1861, he became president of the Central Pacific Railroad in the same year, and was one of the founders of the Southern Pacific Railroad 1870. He served in the US Senate 1885–93.

Stanislavsky Konstantin Sergeivich 1863–1938. Russian actor, director, and teacher of acting. He rejected the declamatory style of acting in favor of a more realistic approach, concentrating on the psychological basis for the development of character. The ◊Actors Studio is based on this approach.

Stanley Henry Morton. Adopted name of John Rowlands1841–1904. Welsh-born US explorer and journalist who made four expeditions to Africa. He and David ◊Livingstone met at Ujiji 1871 and explored Lake Tanganyika. He traced the course of the river Zaïre (Congo) to the sea 1874–77, established the Congo Free State (Zaire) 1879–84, and charted much of the interior 1887–89.

Stanton Edwin McMasters 1814–1869. US public official, secretary of war 1862–68. A lawyer and a Democrat, he was appointed US attorney general by President Buchanan 1860 and then secretary of war by Republican president Lincoln 1862.

Born in Steubenville, Ohio, Stanton attended Kenyon College, was admitted to the bar 1836, and gained a reputation as a skilled lawyer. As secretary of war he was an effective, if autocratic administrator. Although retained in office by President A Johnson, Stanton eventually broke with him over Reconstruction policies and was forced to resign 1868. He was named to the US Supreme Court 1869 by President Grant, but died before taking office.

Stanton Elizabeth Cady 1815–1902. US feminist who, with Susan B ◊Anthony, founded the National Woman Suffrage Association 1869, the first women's movement in the US, and was its first president. She and Anthony wrote and compiled the *History of Women's Suffrage* 1881–86. Stanton also worked for the abolition of slavery.

stanza (Italian "resting or stopping place") group of lines in a poem. A stanza serves the same function in poetry as a paragraph in prose. Stanzas are often of uniform length and separated by a blank line.

star luminous globe of gas, mainly hydrogen and helium, which produces its own heat and light by nuclear reactions. Although stars shine for a very long time—many billions of years—they are not eternal, and have been found to change in appearance at different stages in their lives.

starch widely distributed, high-molecular-mass ◊carbohydrate, produced by plants as a food store; main dietary sources are cereals, legumes, and tubers, including potatoes. It consists of varying proportions of two ◊glucose polymers (polysaccharides): straight-chain (amylose) and branched (amylopectin) molecules.

star cluster group of related stars, usually held together by gravity. Members of a star cluster are thought to form together from one large cloud of gas in space. *Open clusters* such as the Pleiades contain from a dozen to many hundreds of young stars,loosely scattered over several light-years. Globular clusters are larger and much more densely packed, containing perhaps 100,000 old stars.

starfish or *seastar* any echinoderm of the subclass Asteroidea with arms radiating from a central body. Usually there are five arms, but some species have more. They are covered with spines and small pincer-like organs. There are also a number of small tubular processes on the skin surface that assist in locomotion and respiration. Starfish are predators, and vary in size from 0.5/1.2 cm into 3 ft/90 cm.

Stark Johannes 1874–1957. German physicist. In 1902 he predicted, correctly, that high-velocity rays of positive ions (canal rays) would demonstrate the ◊Doppler effect, and in 1913 showed that a strong electric field can alter the wave length of light emitted by atoms (the *Stark effect*). He was awarded the Nobel Prize for Physics 1919.

starling any member of a large widespread Old World family (Sturnidae) of chunky, dark, generally gregarious birds of the order Passeriformes. The European starling *Sturnus vulgaris*, common in N Eurasia, has been naturalized in North America from the late 19th century. The black, speckled plumage is glossed with green and purple. Its own call is a bright whistle, but it is a mimic of the songs of other birds. It is about 8 in/20 cm long.

Star of David or *Magen David* six-pointed star (made with two equilateral triangles), a symbol of Judaism since the 17th century. It is the central motif on the flag of Israel, and, since 1897, the emblem of Zionism.

START acronym for ◊Strategic Arms Reduction Talks.

Star Wars popular term for the ◊Strategic Defense Initiative announced by US president Reagan in 1983.

state territory that forms its own domestic and foreign policy, acting through laws that are typically decided by a government and carried out, by force if necessary, by agents of that government. It can be argued that growth of regional international bodies such as the European Community means that states no longer enjoy absolute sovereignty.

State Department (Department of State) US government department responsible for ◊foreign relations, headed by the ◊secretary of state, the senior cabinet officer of the executive branch.

Staten Island island in New York harbor, part of New York City, comprising the county of Richmond and since 1975, the borough of Staten Island; area 60 sq mi/155 sq km.

States General former French parliament that consisted of three estates: nobility, clergy, and commons. First summoned 1302, it declined in importance as the power of the crown grew. It was not called at all 1614–1789 when the crown needed to institute fiscal reforms toavoid financial collapse. Once called, the demands made by the States General formed the first phase in the ◊French Revolution. States General is also the name of the Dutch parliament.

states of matter forms (solid, liquid, or gas) in which material can exist. Whether a material is solid, liquid, or gas depends on its temperature and the pressure on it. The transition between states takes place at definite temperatures, called melting point and boiling point.

States' Rights interpretation of the US constitution which emphasizes the powers retained by individual states and minimizes those given to the federal government. The dividing line between state and national sovereignty was left deliberately vague in the Philadelphia convention devising the constitution 1787.

static electricity ◊electric charge that is stationary, usually acquired by a body by means of electrostatic inductionor friction. Rubbing different materials can produce static electricity, as seen in the sparks produced on combing one's hair or removing a nylon shirt. In some processes static electricity is useful, as in paint spraying where the parts to be sprayed are charged with electricity of opposite polarity to that on the paint droplets, and in ◊xerography.

statics branch of mechanics concerned with the behavior of bodies at rest and forces in equilibrium, and distinguished from ◊dynamics.

statistics branch of mathematics concerned with the collection and interpretation of data. For example, to determine the ◊mean age of the children in a school, a statistically acceptable answer might be obtained by calculating an average based on the ages of a representative sample, consisting, for example, of a random tenth of the pupils from each class. ◊Probability is the branch of statistics dealing with predictions of events.

status in the social sciences, an individual's social position, or the esteem in which he or she is held by others in society. Both within and between most occupations or social positions there is a status hierarchy. *Status symbols*, such as insignia of office or an expensive automobile, often accompany high status.

Stauffenberg Claus von 1907–1944. German colonel in World War II who, in a conspiracy to assassinate Hitler, planted a bomb inthe dictator's headquarters conference room in the Wolf's Lair at Rastenburg, East Prussia, July 20, 1944. Hitler was merely injured, and Stauffenberg and 200 others were later executed by the Nazi regime.

STD abbreviation for *sexually transmitted disease*, a term encompassing not only traditional ◊venereal disease, but also a growing list of conditions, such as ◊AIDS and scabies, which are known to be spread by sexual contact. Other diseases sexual in origin include viral ◊hepatitis and cervical cancer.

steady-state theory in astronomy, a rival theory to that of the ◊Big Bang, which claims that the universe has no origin but is expanding because new matter is being created continuously throughout the universe. The theory was proposed 1948 by Hermann Bondi, Thomas Gold (1920–), and Fred ◊Hoyle, but was dealt a severe blow in 1965 by the discovery of ◊cosmic background radiation (radiation left over from the formation of the universe) and is now largely rejected.

steam in chemistry, a dry, invisible gas formed by vaporizing water. The visible cloud that normally forms in the air when water is vaporized is due to minute suspended water particles. Steam is widely used in chemical and other industrial processes and for the generation of power.

steam engine engine that uses the power of steam to produce useful work. It was the principal power source during the British Industrial Revolution in the 18th century. The first successful steam engine was built 1712 by English inventor Thomas Newcomen, and it was developed further by Scottish mining engineer James Watt from 1769 and by English mining engineer Richard Trevithick, whose high-pressure steam engine 1802 led to the development of the steam locomotive.

steel alloy or mixture of iron and up to 1.7% carbon, sometimes with other elements, such as manganese, phosphorus, sulfur, and silicon. The US, Russia, Ukraine, and Japan are the main steel producers. Steel has innumerable uses, including ship and automobile manufacture, skyscraper frames, and machinery of all kinds.

steel band musical ensemble common in the West Indies, mostly of percussion instruments made from oil drums that give a metallic ringing tone.

Steele Richard 1672–1729. Irish essayist who founded the journal *The Tatler* 1709–11, in which Joseph ◊Addison collaborated. They continued their joint work in *The Spectator*, also founded by Steele, 1711–12, and *The Guardian* 1713. Healso wrote plays, such as *The Conscious Lovers* 1722.

Steen Jan 1626–1679. Dutch painter. Born in Leiden, he was also active in The Hague, Delft, and Haarlem. He painted humorous everyday scenes, mainly set in taverns or bourgeois households, as well as portraits and landscapes.

Stefan–Boltzmann law in physics, a law that relates the energy, E, radiated away from a perfect emitter (a ◊black body), to the temperature, T, of that body. It has the form $M = \sigma\, T^4$, where M is the energy radiated per unit area per second, T is the temperature, and σ is the *Stefan–Boltzmann constant*. Its value is 5.6697×10^{-8} W m^{-2} K^{-4}. The law was derived by Austrian physicists Joseph Stefan and Ludwig Boltzmann.

Steffens Lincoln 1866–1936. US journalist. Born in San Francisco and educated at Berkeley, Steffens joined the staff of the *New York Evening Post* 1892. An expert in financial affairs, Steffens served as editor of the *New York Commercial Advertiser* 1897–1901 and later joined the staff of *McClure's Magazine*. Intent on exposing corruption and fraud in high places, he joined forces with writers Ida Tarbell and Ray Stannard Baker and initiated the style of investigative journalism since known as "muckraking." Steffens later covered the Mexican Revolution and befriended Lenin. His *Autobiography* appeared 1931.

Steichen Edward 1897–1973. Luxembourg-born US photographer, who with Alfred ◊Stieglitz helped to establish photography as an art form. His style evolved during his career from painterly impressionism to realism.

Stein Gertrude 1874–1946. US writer who influenced authors Ernest ◊Hemingway, Sherwood ◊Anderson, and F Scott ◊Fitzgerald with her conversational tone, cinematic technique, use of repetition, and absence of punctuation: devices intended to convey immediacy and realism. Her work includes the self-portrait *The Autobiography of Alice B Toklas* 1933.

Born in Allegheny, Pennsylvania, Stein went to Paris 1903 after medical school at Johns Hopkins University and lived there, writing and collecting art, for the rest of her life. She settled in with her brother, also a patron of the arts, and a companion/secretary, Alice B Toklas (1877–1967), and in her home she held court to a "lost generation" of expatriate US writers and modern artists (Picasso, Matisse, Braque, Gris). She also wrote *The Making of Americans* 1906–11, *Composition as Explanation* 1926, *Tender Buttons* 1941, *Mrs. Reynolds* 1952, and the operas (with composer Virgil Thomson) *Four Saints in Three Acts* 1929 and *The Mother of Us All* 1947. A tour of the US 1934 resulted in *Everybody's Autobiography* 1937.

Steinbeck John (Ernst) 1902–1968. US novelist. His realist novels, such as *In Dubious Battle* 1936, *Of Mice and Men* 1937, and *The Grapes of Wrath* 1939 (Pulitzer Prize 1940), portray agricultural life in his native California, where migrant farm laborers from the Oklahoma dust bowl struggled to survive. Nobel Prize 1962.

Born in Salinas, California, Steinbeck worked as a laborer to support his writing career, and his experiences supplied much authentic material for his books. He first achieved success with *Tortilla Flat* 1935, a humorous study of the lives of Monterey *paisanos* (farmers). His early naturalist works are his most critically acclaimed. Later books include *Cannery Row* 1944, *The Wayward Bus* 1947, *East of Eden* 1952, *Once There Was a War* 1958, *The Winter of Our Discontent* 1961, and *Travels with Charley* 1962. He also wrote screenplays for films, notably *Viva Zapata!* 1952. His best-known short story is the fable "The Pearl."

Steinberg Saul 1914– . Romanian-born US artist best known for cartoons contributed to the *New Yorker* and other magazines. His work portrays a childlike personal world with allusions to the irrational and absurd.

Steinem Gloria 1934– . US journalist and liberal feminist who emerged as a leading figure in the US women's movement in the late 1960s. She was also involved in radical protest campaigns against racism and the Vietnam War. She cofounded the Women's Action Alliance 1970 and *Ms* magazine. In 1983 a collection of her articles was published as *Outrageous Acts and Everyday Rebellions*.

Steiner Rudolf 1861–1925. Austrian philosopher, originally a theosophist, who developed his own mystic and spiritual teaching, anthroposophy, designed to develop the whole human being. A number of Steiner

schools follow a curriculum laid down by him with a strong emphasis on the arts, although the schools also include the possibilities for pupils to take state exams.

Stella Frank 1936– . US painter, a pioneer of the hard-edged geometric trend in abstract art that followed Abstract Expressionism. From around 1960 he also experimented with the shape of his canvases.

Stella Joseph 1877–1946. Italian-born US painter. With artist Max ◊Weber, he was America's leading Futurist. His cubistic and futuristic views of New York City are captured in such paintings as *Brooklyn Bridge* 1919–20 and *New York Interpreted* 1920–22. His works are mostly mechanical and urban scenes, although his later paintings include tropical landscapes.

stem main supporting axis of a plant that bears the leaves, buds, and reproductive structures; it may be simple or branched. The plant stem usually grows above ground, although some grow underground, including rhizomes, ◊corms, rootstocks, and ◊tubers. Stems contain a continuous vascular system that conducts water and food to and from all parts of the plant.

Stendhal adopted name of Marie Henri Beyle 1783–1842.

French novelist. His novels *Le Rouge et le noir/The Red and the Black* 1830 and *La Chartreuse de Parme/The Charterhouse of Parma* 1839 were pioneering works in their treatment of disguise and hypocrisy; a review of the latter by fellow novelist ◊Balzac in 1840 furthered Stendhal's reputation.

Stephen c. 1097–1154. King of England from 1135. A grandson of William I, he was elected king 1135, although he had previously recognized Henry I's daughter ◊Matilda as heiress to the throne. Matilda landed in England 1139, and civil war disrupted the country until 1153, when Stephen acknowledged Matilda's son, Henry II, as his own heir.

Stephen I, St 975–1038. King of Hungary from 997, when he succeeded his father. He completed the conversion of Hungary to Christianity and was canonized in 1803.

Stephens Alexander Hamilton 1812–1883. American public official. A leader of the Whig party, he served in the US House of Representatives 1843–59 and was an opponent of the Mexican War 1846–48 and a strong defender of slavery. In 1861 he was chosen as vice president of the Confederacy. Arrested and briefly imprisoned at the end of the American Civil War 1865, he served again as US Congressman 1872–82.

Stephen, St died c. AD 35. The first Christian martyr; he was stoned to death. Feast day Dec 26.

Stephenson George 1781–1848. English engineer who built the first successful steam locomotive, and who also invented a safety lamp in 1815. He was appointed engineer of the Stockton and Darlington Railroad, the world's first public railroad, in 1821, and of the Liverpool and Manchester Railroad in 1826. In 1829 he won a £500 prize with his locomotive *Rocket*.

steppe the temperate grasslands of Europe and Asia. Sometimes the term refers to other temperate grasslands and semiarid desert edges.

stereophonic sound system of sound reproduction using two complementary channels leading to two loud speakers, which gives a more natural depth to the sound. Stereo recording began with the introduction of two-track magnetic tape in the 1950s. See ◊hi-fi.

stereotype (Greek "fixed impression") in sociology, a fixed, exaggerated, and preconceived description about a certain type of person, group, or society. It is based on prejudice rather than fact, but by repetition and with time, stereotypes become fixed in people's minds, resistant to change or factual evidence to the contrary.

sterilization any surgical operation to terminate the possibility of reproduction. In women, this is normally achieved by sealing or tying off the ◊Fallopian tubes (tubal ligation) so that fertilization can no longer take place. In men, the transmission of sperm is blocked by ◊vasectomy.

sterilization the killing or removal of living organisms such as bacteria and fungi. A sterile environment is necessary in medicine, food processing, and some scientific experiments. Methods include heat treatment (such as boiling), the use of chemicals (such as disinfectants), irradiation with gamma rays, and filtration.

sterling silver ◊alloy containing 925 parts of silver and 75 parts of copper. The copper hardens the silver, making it more useful.

Sternberg Josef von 1894–1969. Austrian film director, in the US from childhood. He is best remembered for his seven films with Marlene Dietrich, including *The Blue Angel/Der blaue Engel* 1930, *Blonde Venus* 1932, and *The Devil Is a Woman* 1935, all of which are marked by his expressive use of light and shadow.

Sterne Laurence 1713–1768. Irish writer, creator of the comic antihero Tristram Shandy. *The Life and Opinions of Tristram Shandy, Gent* 1760–67, an eccentrically whimsical and bawdy novel, foreshadowed many of the techniques and devices of 20th-century novelists, including James Joyce. His other works include *A Sentimental Journey through France and Italy* 1768.

steroid in biology, any of a group of cyclic, unsaturated alcohols (lipids without fatty acid components), which, like sterols, have a complex molecular structure consisting of four carbon rings. Steroids include the sex hormones, such as ◊testosterone, the cortico steroid hormones produced by the ◊adrenal gland, bile acids, and ◊cholesterol. The term is commonly used to refer to ◊anabolic steroid.

sterol in biology, any of a group of solid, cyclic, unsaturated alcohols, with a complex structure that includes four carbon rings; cholesterol is an example. Steroids are derived from sterols.

stethoscope instrument used to ascertain the condition of the heart and lungs by listening to their action. It consists of two earpieces connected by flexible tubes to a small plate that is placed against the body. It was invented in 1819 in France by René Théophile Hyacinthe ◊Laënnec.

Steuben Friedrich Wilhelm von, Baron 1730–1794. Prussian military leader in the American Revolution 1775–83. After joining George Washington at Valley Forge 1778, he was named inspector general of the Continental army. He later saw action in the South and was present at the victory of Yorktown 1781.

Steubenville city in E Ohio, on the Ohio River, S of Youngstown, near the West Virginia border; population (1990) 22,100.
Industries include steel, coal, paper, and chemicals. Originally *Fort Steuben*, it was built 1786 to protect government land agents from the Indians.

Stevens John Paul 1920– . US jurist and associate justice of the US Supreme Court from 1975, appointed by President Ford. A moderate whose opinions and dissents were wide ranging, he opined that the death penalty is not by definition cruel and unusual punishment in *Jurek v Texas* 1976, and that the burning of the US flag in protest is unconstitutional in *Texas v Johnson*.

Stevens Wallace 1879–1955. US poet. An insurance company executive, he was not recognized as a major poet until late in life. His volumes of poems include *Harmonium* 1923, *The Man with the Blue Guitar* 1937, and *Transport to Summer* 1947. *The Necessary Angel* 1951 is a collection of essays. An elegant and philosophical poet, he won the Pulitzer Prize 1954 for his *Collected Poems*.

Stevenson Adlai 1900–1965. US Democratic politician. He is best known as the losing Democratic nominee in two presidential elections against Dwight ◊Eisenhower 1952 and 1956. He served in the F D ◊Roosevelt administration in the 1930s and 1940s and became a successful reform-minded governor of Illinois 1949–52. He was named ambassador to the UN by John ◊Kennedy 1961.

Stevenson Robert Louis 1850–1894. Scottish novelist and poet, author of the adventure novel *Treasure Island* 1883. Later works included the novels *Kidnapped* 1886, *The Master of Ballantrae* 1889, *Dr Jekyll and Mr Hyde* 1886, and the anthology *A Child's Garden of Verses* 1885.

Stewart James 1908– . US actor. He made his Broadway debut in 1932 and soon after worked in Hollywood. Speaking with a soft drawl, he specialized in the role of the stubbornly honest, ordinary American in such films as *Mr Smith Goes to Washington* 1939, *The Philadelphia Story* 1940 (Academy Award), *It's a Wonderful Life* 1946, *Harvey* 1950, *The Man from Laramie* 1955, and *The FBI Story* 1959. His films with director Alfred ◊Hitchcock include *Rope* 1948, *Rear Window* 1954, *The Man Who Knew Too Much* 1956, and *Vertigo* 1958.
Born in Indiana, Pennsylvania, he was an air force pilot in World War II.

Stewart Potter 1915–1985. US jurist and appointed associate justice of the US Supreme Court 1958–81 by President Eisenhower. Seen as a moderate, he is known for up holding civil rights for minorities and for opinions on criminal procedure. He dissented in both *Escabedo* v *Illinois* 1964 and in *In re Gault* 1967, which gave juveniles due process rights.

Stieglitz Alfred 1864–1946. US photographer who was mainly responsible for the recognition of photography as an art form. After forming the multimedia Photo-Secession Group at 291 Fifth Avenue, New York, with Edward ◊Steichen, he began the magazine *Camera Work* 1902–17. Through exhibitions, competitions, and publication at his galleries, he helped establish a photographic aesthetic.

stigma in a flower, the surface at the tip of a ◊carpel that receives the ◊pollen. It often has short outgrowths, flaps, or hairs to trap pollen and may produce a sticky secretion to which the grains adhere.

stigmata impressions or marks corresponding to the five wounds Jesus received at his crucifixion, which are said to have appeared spontaneously on St Francis and other saints.

Stijl, De (Dutch "the style") group of 20th-century Dutch artists and architects led by ◊Mondrian from 1917. They believed in the concept of the "designer"; that all life, work, and leisure should be surrounded by art; and that everything functional should also be aesthetic. The group had a strong influence on the ◊Bauhaus school.

Stilwell Joseph Warren 1883–1946. US general, nicknamed "Vinegar Joe." In 1942 he became US military representative in China, when he commanded the Chinese forces cooperating with the British (with whom he quarreled) in Burma (now Myanmar); he later commanded all US forces in the Chinese, Burmese, and Indian theaters until recalled to the US 1944 after differences over nationalist policy with ◊Chiang Kai-shek. Stilwell sought engagement of 30 divisions of Chinese nationalist troops in battle against the Japanese. Chiang Kai-shek refused, preferring to reserve his forces for use against the Chinese Communists in the anticipated Chinese civil war. At Chiang's insistence, President F D ◊Roosevelt recalled Stilwell, giving him command of the US 10th Army on the Japanese island of Okinawa.

stimulant any drug that acts on the brain to increase alertness and activity; for example, ◊amphetamine. When given to children, stimulants may have a paradoxical, calming effect. Stimulants cause liver damage, are habit-forming, have limited therapeutic value, and are now prescribed only to treat narcolepsy and to reduce the appetite in dieting.

Sting adopted name of Gordon Sumner 1951– .
English pop singer, song writer, actor, and bass player. As a member of the trio *the Police* 1977–83, he had UK number-one hits with "Message in a Bottle" 1979, "Walking on the Moon" 1979, and "Every Breath You Take" 1983. In his solo career he has often drawn on jazz, as on the albums *The Dream of Blue Turtles* 1985 and *Soul Cages* 1991.

stipule outgrowth arising from the base of a leaf or leaf stalk in certain plants. Stipules usually occur in pairs or fused into a single semicircular structure.

St Joseph city in NW Missouri, on the Missouri River, NW of Kansas City; population (1980) 76,691. Industries include food processing, dairy products, metal products, concrete, and steel. In the mid-1800s, it served as the eastern terminus for the Pony Express.

stock in the US, each share of stock represents proportional ownership in a corporation. Once offered by a corporation going public, stock can be bought and sold on a ◊stock exchange, but the corporation has no obligation to buy it back. Sold to raise capital, stock gives the holder specified rights, including the right to examine the books and the right to vote for the directors. Dividends can be paid, in cash or in stock, when the corporation declares a profit.

stock-car racing sport popular in the US. Stock cars are high-powered sports automobiles that race on specially built tracks at distances up to 400–500 mi/640–800 km. The sport is governed in the US by the National Associaton for Stock-Car Auto Racing (NASCAR) founded 1947.

stock exchange institution for the buying and selling of stock in publicly held corporations. An exchange trades in stocks that are already issued. Trading is done only by members who have purchased or inherited a "seat" on the exchange. They can act as brokers for nonmembers, on a commission basis, or as floor brokers, acting for other members. Registered traders have no contact with the public but trade only their private accounts. The world's largest exchanges are in New York, London, and Tokyo, and stock prices are watched carefully as indicators of confidence in the economy.

Stockhausen Karlheinz 1928– . German composer of avant-garde music who has continued to explore new musical sounds and compositional techniques since the 1950s. His major works include *Gesang der Jünglinge* 1956, and *Kontakte* 1960 (electronic music), and *Sirius* 1977.

Stockholm capital and industrial port of Sweden; population (1990) 674,500. It is built on a number of islands. Industries include engineering, brewing, electrical goods, paper, textiles, and pottery.

Stock Market Crash, 1929 Wall Street crash, 1929 a panic in the US following an artificial stock market boom 1927–29 fed by speculation of shares bought on 10% margin. On Oct 24, 1929, 13 million shares changed hands, with further heavy selling on Oct 28, and the disposal of 16 million shares on Oct 29. Many stock holders were ruined, banks and businesses failed, and unemployment rose to approximately 17 million during the Great Depression 1929–40 that ensued.

stocks wooden frame with holes used in Europe and the US until the 19th century to confine the legs and sometimes the arms of minor offenders, and expose them to public humiliation. The pillory had a similar purpose.

Stockton industrial river port (agricultural machinery, food processing) on the San Joaquin River in California; population (1990) 210,900.

stoicism (Greek *stoa* "porch") Greek school of philosophy, founded about 300 BC by Zeno of Citium. The stoics were pantheistic materialists who believed that happiness lay in accepting the law of the universe. They emphasized human brotherhood, denounced slavery, and were internationalist. The name is derived from the porch on which Zeno taught.

Stoker Bram (Abraham) 1847–1912. Irish novelist, actor, theater manager, and author. His novel ◊Dracula 1897 crystallized most aspects of the traditional vampire legend and became the source for all subsequent fiction and films on the subject.

Stokes George Gabriel 1819–1903. Irish physicist. During the late 1840s, he studied the ◊viscosity (resistance to relative motion) of fluids. This culminated in *Stokes' law*, $F = 6\pi\epsilon rv$, which applies to a force acting on a sphere falling through a liquid, where ϵ is the liquid's viscosity and r and v are the radius and velocity of the sphere.

STOL (acronym for *short take off and landing*) aircraft fitted with special devices on the wings (such as sucking flaps) that increase aerodynamic lift at low speeds. Small passenger and freight STOL craft may become common with the demand for small airports, especially in difficult terrain.

stoma (plural *stomata*) in botany, a pore in the epidermis of a plant. Each stoma is surrounded by a pair of guard cells that are crescent-shaped when the stoma is open but can collapse to an oval shape, thus closing off the opening between them. Stomata allow the exchange of carbon dioxide and oxygen (needed for ◊photosynthesis and ◊respiration) between the internal tissues of the plant and the outside atmosphere. They are also the main route by which water is lost from the plant, and they can be closed to conserve water, the movements being controlled by changes in turgidity of the guard cells.

Stomata occur in large numbers on the aerial parts of a plant, and on the under surface of leaves, where there may be as many as 300,000 per square inch.

stomach the first cavity in the digestive system of animals. In mammals it is a bag of muscle situated just below the diaphragm. Food enters it from the esophagus, is digested by the acid and ◊enzymes secreted by the stomach lining, and then passes into the duodenum. Some plant-eating mammals have multichambered stomachs that harbor bacteria in one of the chambers to assist in the digestion of ◊cellulose. The gizzard is part of the stomach in birds.

Stone Harlan Fiske 1872–1946. US jurist. He was associate justice to the US Supreme Court 1925–41 and chief justice 1941–46 under President Roosevelt. During World War II he authored opinions favoring federal war powers and regulation of aliens.

Stone Lucy 1818–1893. US feminist orator and editor. Married to the radical Henry Blackwell in 1855, she gained wide publicity when, after a mutual declaration rejecting the legal superiority of the man in marriage, she chose to retain her own surname despite her marriage. The term "Lucy Stoner" was coined to mean a woman who advocated doing the same.

stone plural *stone* British unit (symbol st) of mass (chiefly used to express body mass) equal to 14 pounds avoirdupois (6.35 kg).

Stone Age the developmental stage of humans in ◊prehistory before the use of metals, when tools and weapons were made chiefly of stone, especially flint. The Stone Age is subdivided into the Old or Paleolithic, the Middle or Mesolithic, and the New or Neolithic. The people of the Old Stone Age were hunters and gatherers, whereas the Neolithic people took the first steps in agriculture, the domestication of animals, weaving, and pottery.

stonefish any of a family (Synanceiidae) of tropical marine bony fishes with venomous spines and bodies resembling encrusted rocks.

Stonehenge megalithic monument dating from about 2000 BC on Salisbury Plain, Wiltshire, England. It consisted originally of a circle of 30 upright stones,

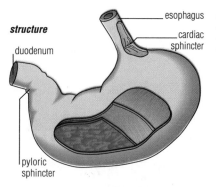

structure

esophagus — cardiac sphincter — duodenum — pyloric sphincter

stomach *The human stomach can hold about 2.6 pt/1.5 l of liquid.*

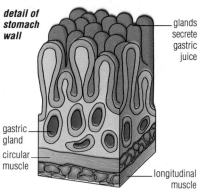

detail of stomach wall

glands secrete gastric juice — gastric gland — circular muscle — longitudinal muscle

their tops linked by lintel stones to form a continuous circle about 100 ft/30 m across. Within the circle was a horseshoe arrangement of five trilithons (two uprights plus a lintel, set as five separate entities), and a so-called "altar stone"—an upright pillar—on the axis of the horseshoe at the open, NE end, which faces in the direction of the rising sun. It has been suggested that it served as an observatory.

Stonehenge *Stonehenge, Salisbury Plain, England.*

Stoppard Tom 1937– . Czechoslovak-born British playwright whose works use wit and wordplay to explore logical and philosophical ideas. His play *Rosencrantz and Guildenstern Are Dead* 1966 was followed by comedies including *The Real Inspector Hound* 1968, *Jumpers* 1972, *Travesties* 1974, *Dirty Linen* 1976, *The Real Thing* 1982, and *Hapgood* 1988. He has also written for radio, television, and the cinema.

stork any of a family (Ciconiidea) of long-legged, long-necked wading birds with long, powerful wings, and long bills used for spearing prey. Some species grow up to 5 ft/1.5 m tall.

Story Joseph 1779–1845. US jurist and associate justice of the US Supreme Court 1811–45 under President Madison. He wrote several decisions defining the role of federal courts in admiralty law. The most notable was *United States* v *Schooner Amistad* 1841, in which the Court ordered black slaves who had seized a slaving ship repatriated to Africa.

Stowe Harriet Beecher 1811–1896. US suffragist, abolitionist, and author of the antislavery novel *Uncle Tom's Cabin*, first published serially 1851–52. The inspiration came to her in a vision in 1848, and the book brought immediate success.

STP abbreviation for ◊standard temperature and pressure.

Strachey (Giles) Lytton 1880–1932. English critic and biographer, a member of the ◊Bloomsbury Group of writers and artists. He wrote *Landmarks in French Literature* 1912. The mocking and witty treatment of Cardinal Manning, Florence Nightingale, Thomas Arnold, and General Gordon in *Eminent Victorians* 1918 won him recognition. His biography of *Queen Victoria* 1921 was more affectionate.

Stradivari Antonio (Latin form *Stradivarius*) 1644–1737. Italian stringed instrument maker, generally considered the greatest of all violin makers. He was born in Cremona and studied there with Niccolo Amati. He produced more than 1,100 instruments from the family workshops, over 600 of which survive. The secret of his mastery is said to be in the varnish but is probably a combination of fine proportioning and aging.

Straits Settlements former province of the East India Company 1826–58, a British crown colony 1867–1946; it comprised Singapore, Malacca, Penang, Cocos Islands, Christmas Island, and Labuan.

Strasbourg city on the river Ill, in Bas-Rhin *département*, capital of Alsace, France; population (1990)255,900. Industries include automobile manufacture, tobacco, printing and publishing, and preserves. The ◊Council of Europe meets here, and sessions of the European Parliament alternate between Strasbourg and Luxembourg.

Strategic Air Command (SAC) the headquarters commanding all US land-based strategic missile and bomber forces.

Strategic Arms Limitation Talks (SALT) series of US-Soviet discussions aimed at reducing the rate of nuclear-arms buildup. (See also ◊disarmament.) The talks, delayed by the Soviet invasion of Czechoslovakia 1968, began in 1969 between US president Lyndon Johnson and Soviet leader Brezhnev. Neither the SALT I accord (effective 1972–77) nor SALT II called for reductions in nuclear weaponry, merely a limit on the expansion of these forces. SALT II was mainly negoti-

ated by US president Ford before 1976 and signed by Soviet leader Brezhnev and President Carter in Vienna in 1979l. It was never fully ratified because of the Soviet occupation of Afghanistan, although the terms of the accord were respected by both sides until President ◊Reagan exceeded its limitations during his second term 1985–89. SALT talks were superseded by START (Strategic Arms Reduction Talks) negotiations under Reagan, and the first significant reductions began under Soviet President Gorbachev.

Strategic Arms Reduction Talks (START) a phase in US-Soviet peace discussions. START began with talks in Geneva 1983, leading to the signing of the ◊Intermediate Nuclear Forces Treaty (INF) 1987. In 1989 proposals for reductions in conventional weapons were added to the agenda. As the Cold War drew to a close from 1989, the two nations moved rapidly toward total agreement, and in July 1991 the START treaty was signed in Moscow. See also ◊disarmament. START II signed 1993.

Strategic Defense Initiative (SDI) also called *Star Wars* attempt by the US to develop a defense system against incoming nuclear missiles, based in part outside the Earth's atmosphere. It was announced by President Reagan in March 1983, and the research had by 1990 cost over $16.5 billion. In 1988, the Joint Chiefs of Staff announced that they expected to be able to intercept no more than 30% of incoming missiles. Some scientists maintain that the system is basically unworkable, and it was phased out 1993.

Stratford-upon-Avon market town on the river Avon, in Warwickshire, England; population (1986 est) 20,900. It is the birthplace of William ◊Shakespeare.

Strathclyde region of Scotland
area 5,367 sq mi/13,900 sq km
cities Glasgow (administrative headquarters), Paisley, Greenock, Kilmarnock, Clydebank, Hamilton, Coatbridge, Prestwick
features includes some of Inner ◊Hebrides; river Clyde; part of Loch Lomond; Glencoe, site of the massacre of the Macdonald clan; Breadalbane; islands: Arran, Bute, Mull
products dairy, pig, and poultry products; shipbuilding; engineering; coal from Ayr and Lanark; oil-related services
population (1991) 2,218,200, half the population of Scotland
famous people William Burrell, James Keir Hardie, David Livingstone.

stratigraphy branch of geology that deals with the sequence of formation of ◊sedimentary rock layers and the conditions under which they were formed. Its basis was developed by William Smith, a British canal engineer.

stratosphere that part of the atmosphere 6–25 mi/10–40 km from the Earth's surface, where the temperature slowly rises from a low of $-67°F/-55°C$ to around $32°F/0°C$.

The air is rarefied and at around 15 mi/25 km much ◊ozone is concentrated.

Strauss Johann (Baptist) 1825–1899. Austrian conductor and composer, the son of composer Johann Strauss (1804–1849). In 1872 he gave up conducting and wrote operettas, such as *Die Fledermaus* 1874, and numerous waltzes, such as *The Blue Danube* and *Tales from the Vienna Woods*, which gained him the title "the Waltz King."

Strauss Richard (Georg) 1864–1949. German composer and conductor. He followed the German Romantic tradition but had a strongly personal style, characterized by his bold, colorful orchestration. He first wrote tone poems such as *Don Juan* 1889, *Till Eulenspiegel's Merry Pranks* 1895, and *Also sprach Zarathustra* 1896. He then moved on to opera with *Salome* 1905 and *Elektra* 1909, both of which have elements of polytonality. He reverted to a more traditional style with *Der Rosenkavalier* 1911.

He spent his final years in the US, teaching and composing at the Eastman School of Music in New York.

Stravinsky Igor 1882–1971. Russian composer, later of French (1934) and US (1945) nationality. He studied under ◊Rimsky-Korsakov and wrote the music for the Diaghilev ballets *The Firebird* 1910, *Petrushka* 1911, and *The Rite of Spring* 1913 (controversial at the time for their unorthodox rhythms and harmonies). His versatile work ranges from his Neo-Classicalballet *Pulcinella* 1920 to the choral-orchestral *Symphony of Psalms* 1930. He later made use of serial techniques in such works as the *Canticum Sacrum* 1955 and the ballet *Agon* 1953–57.

strawberry low-growing perennial plant of the genus *Fragaria*, family Rosaceae, widely cultivated for its red, fleshy fruits, which are rich in vitamin C. Wild strawberry *F. virginiana* has small aromatic fruits and grows over much of the eastern half of North America. Cultivated strawberries are hybrids between North American wild species and European species.

stream of consciousness narrative technique in which a writer presents directly the uninterrupted flow of a character's thoughts, impressions, and feelings, without the conventional devices of dialogue and description. It first came to be widely used in the early 20th century. Leading exponents have included the novelists Virginia Woolf, James Joyce, and William Faulkner.

Streep Meryl 1949– . US actress known for her strong character roles. She became a leading star of the 1980s, winning numerous awards. Her films include *The Deer Hunter* 1978, *Kramer vs Kramer* 1979 (Academy Award), *The French Lieutenant's Woman* 1980, *Sophie's Choice* 1982 (Academy Award), *Out of Africa* 1985, *Ironweed* 1988, *A Cry in the Dark* 1989, and the comedy *Death Becomes Her* 1992.

Streisand Barbra (Barbara Joan) 1942– . US singer and actress who became a film star in *Funny Girl* 1968. Her subsequent films include *What's Up Doc?* 1972, *The Way We Were* 1973, and *A Star Is Born* 1979. She directed, scripted, composed, and starred in *Yentl* 1983 and *Prince of Tides* 1991.

streptomycin antibiotic drug discovered in 1944, used to treat tuberculosis, influenzal meningitis, and other infections, some of which are unaffected by ◊penicillin.

stress in psychology, any event or situation that makes demands on a person's mental or emotional resources. Stress can be caused by overwork, anxiety about exams, money, or job security, unemployment, bereavement, poor relationships, marriage breakdown, sexual difficulties, poor living or working conditions, and constant exposure to loud noise.

Many changes that are apparently "for the better," such as being promoted at work, going to a new school, moving to a new house, and getting married, are also a source of stress. Stress can cause, or aggravate, physical illnesses, among them psoriasis, eczema, asthma,

and stomach and mouth ulcers. Apart from removing the source of stress, acquiring some control over it and learning to relax when possible are the best treatments.

stridulatory organs in insects, organs that produce sound when rubbed together. Crickets rub their wings together, but grasshoppers rub a hind leg against a wing. Stridulation is thought to be used for attracting mates, but may also serve to mark territory.

Temperatures can be determined from the stridulations of crickets: adding 40 to the number of chirps counted in 15 seconds gives the approximate temperature in Fahrenheit.

strike stoppage of work by employees (with picketing), often as members of a labor union, to obtain or resist change in wages, hours, or conditions. A "lockout" is a weapon of an employer to thwart or enforce such change by preventing employees from working. Another measure is "work to rule," when production is virtually brought to a halt by strict observance of union rules.

Strindberg August 1849–1912. Swedish playwright and novelist. His plays, influential in the development of dramatic technique, are in a variety of styles including historical plays, symbolic dramas (the two-part *Dödsdansen/The Dance of Death* 1901) and "chamberplays" such as *Spöksonaten/The Ghost [Spook] Sonata* 1907. *Fadren/The Father* 1887 and *Fröken Julie/Miss Julie* 1888 are among his works.

stringed instrument musical instrument that produces a sound by making a stretched string vibrate. Today the strings are made of gut, metal, and Pearlon (a plastic). Types of sringed instruments include: *bowed* violin family, viol family; *plucked* guitar, ukelele, lute, sitar, harp, banjo, lyre; *plucked mechanically* harpsichord; *struck mechanically* piano, clavichord; *hammered* dulcimer.

string quartet ◊chamber music ensemble consisting of first and second violins, viola, and cello. The 18th-century successor to the domestic viol consort, the string quartet with its stronger and more rustic tone formed the basis of the symphony orchestra. Important composers for the string quartet include Haydn (more than 80 string quartets), Mozart (27), Schubert (20), Beethoven (17), Dvořák (8), and Bartók (6).

strip mining or *open-pit mining* mining from the surface rather than by tunneling underground. Coal, iron ore, and phosphates are often extracted by strip mining. Often the mineral deposit is covered by soil, which must first be stripped off, usually by large machines such as walking draglines and bucket-wheel excavators. The ore deposit is then broken up by explosives and collected from the surface.

Stroessner Alfredo 1912– . Military leader and president of Paraguay 1954–89. As head of the armed forces from 1951, he seized power in a coup in 1954 sponsored by the right-wing ruling Colorado Party. Accused by his opponents of harsh repression, his regime spent heavily on the military to preserve his authority. Despite criticisms of his government's civil-rights record, he was reelected seven times and remained in office until ousted in an army-led coup 1989.

Stroheim Erich von. Assumed name of Erich Oswald Stroheim 1885–1957. Austrian actor and director, in Hollywood from 1914. He was successful as an actor in villainous roles, but his career as a director was wrecked by his extravagance (*Greed* 1923) and he returned to acting in such international films as *La Grande Illusion* 1937 and *Sunset Boulevard* 1950.

He also directed *Queen Kelly* 1928 (unfinished).

stroke or *cerebrovascular accident* or *apoplexy* interruption of the blood supply to part of the brain due to a sudden bleed in the brain (cerebral hemhorrhage) or ◊embolism or ◊thrombosis. Strokes vary in severity from producing almost no symptoms to proving rapidly fatal. In between are those (often recurring) that leave a wide range of impaired function, depending on the size and location of the event.

strong force one of the four ◊fundamental forces of nature, the other three being the electromagnetic force, gravity, and the weak force. The strong force was first described by Japanese physicist Hideki Yukawa 1935. It is the strongest of all the forces, acts only over very small distances within the nucleus of the atom (10^{-13} cm), and is responsible for binding together ◊quarks to form hadrons, and for binding together protons and neutrons in the atomic nucleus. The particle that is the carrier of the strong force is the gluon, of which there are eight kinds, each with zero mass and zero charge.

strontium soft, ductile, pale-yellow, metallic element, symbol Sr, atomic number 38, atomic weight 87.62. It is one of the ◊alkaline-earth metals, widely distributed in small quantities only as a sulfate or carbonate. Strontium salts burn with a red flame and are used in fireworks and signal flares.

structuralism 20th-century philosophical movement that has influenced such areas as linguistics, anthropology, and literary criticism. Inspired by the work of the Swiss linguist Ferdinand de Saussure, structuralists believe that objects should be analyzed as systems of relations, rather than as positive entities.

strychnine $C_{21}H_{22}O_2N_2$ bitter-tasting, poisonous alkaloid. It is a poison that causes violent muscular spasms, and is usually obtained by powdering the seeds of plants of the genus *Strychnos* (for example *S. nux vomica*). Curare is a related drug.

Stuart Gilbert Charles 1755–1828. American artist. A protégé of the American painter Benjamin ◊West in London 1776–82, he gained fame as one of the foremost portraitists of the time. Returning to the US, he set up a studio in Philadelphia 1794. Best known for his portraits of George Washington, he produced portraits of various prominent public figures.

Stuart or *Stewart* royal family who inherited the Scottish throne in 1371 and the English throne in 1603, holding it until 1714, when Queen Anne died without heirs and the house was replaced by ◊Hanover.

sturgeon any of a family (Acipenseridae) of large, primitive, bony fishes with five rows of bony plates, small sucking mouths, and chin barbels used for exploring the bottom of the water for prey.

Sturluson Snorri 1179–1241. Icelandic author of the Old Norse poems called ◊Eddas and the *Heimskringla*, a saga chronicle of Norwegian kings until 1177.

Sturm und Drang German early Romantic movement in literature and music, from about 1775, concerned with the depiction of extravagant passions. Writers associated with the movement include Johann Gottfried von Herder, Johann Wolfgang von Goethe, and Friedrich von Schiller. The name is taken from a play by Friedrich von Klinger 1776.

Stuttgart capital of Baden-Württemberg, on the river Neckar, Germany; population (1988) 565,000. Industries include the manufacture of vehicles and electrical goods, foodstuffs, textiles, papermaking and publishing; it is a fruit-growing and wine-producing center. There are two universities. Stuttgart was founded in the 10th century.

Stuyvesant Peter 1610–1672. Dutch colonial leader in America. Appointed director general of New Netherland 1646, he arrived there in 1647. He reorganized the administration of the colony and established a permanent boundary with Connecticut by the Treaty of Hartford 1650. Forced to surrender the colony to the British 1664, Stuyvesant remained there for the rest of his life.

style in flowers, the part of the ◊carpel bearing the ◊stigma at its tip. In some flowers it is very short or completely lacking, while in others it may be long and slender, positioning the stigma in the most effective place to receive the pollen.

Usually the style withers after fertilization but in certain species, such as rock clematis *Clematis verticillaris*, it develops into a long feathery plume that aids dispersal of the fruit.

Styx in Greek mythology, the river surrounding the underworld.

subatomic particle any of the subdivisions of the atom, including those ◊elementary particles that combine to form all ◊matter. See also ◊particle physics.

submarine vessel capable of traveling and functioning under water, used in research and military operations. The first underwater boat was constructed for James I of England by the Dutch scientist Cornelius van Drebbel (1572–1633) in 1620. In the 1760s, the American David Bushnell (1742–1824) designed a submarine called *Turtle* for attacking British ships, and in 1800, Robert Fulton designed a submarine called *Nautilus* for Napoleon for the same purpose. John P Holland, an Irish emigrant to the US, designed a submarine about 1875, which was used by both the US and the British navies at the turn of the century. A naval submarine, or submersible torpedo boat, the *Gymnote*, was launched by France 1888. The conventional submarine of World War I was driven by diesel engine on the surface and by battery-powered electric motors underwater. The diesel engine also drove a generator that produced electricity to charge the batteries. In both world wars submarines, from the oceangoing to the midget type, played a vital role. The first nuclear-powered submarine, the *Nautilus*, was launched by the US 1954. In oceanography, salvage, and pipe-laying, smaller submarines called submersibles are used.

submersible vessel designed to operate under water, especially a small submarine used by engineers and research scientists as a ferry craft to support diving operations. The most advanced submersibles are the so-called lock-out type, which have two compartments: one for the pilot, the other to carry divers. The diving compartment is pressurized and provides access to the sea.

subpoena (Latin "under penalty") in law, an order requiring someone who might not otherwise come forward of his or her own volition to give evidence before a court or judicial official at a specific time and place. A witness who fails to comply with a subpoena is in ◊contempt of court.

substrate in biochemistry, a compound or mixture of compounds acted on by an enzyme. The term also refers to a substance such as ◊agar that provides the nutrients for the metabolism of microorganisms. Since the enzyme systems of microorganisms regulate their metabolism, the essential meaning is the same.

subway or *underground* rail service that runs underground. The first underground line in the world was in London. Opened 1863, it was essentially a roofed-in trench. The London Underground is still the longest, with over 250 mi/400 km of routes. Many major cities throughout the world have extensive systems; New York's subway system and Moscow's each handle millions of passengers a day.

succession in ecology, a series of changes that occur in the structure and composition of the vegetation in a given area from the time it is first colonized by plants (*primary succession*), or after it has been disturbed by fire, flood, or clearing (*secondary succession*).

Succot or *Sukkoth* in Judaism, a harvest festival celebrated in Oct, also known as the *Feast of Booths*, which commemorates the time when the Israelites lived in the wilderness during the ◊Exodus from Egypt. As a reminder of the shelters used in the wilderness, huts are built and used for eating and sleeping during the seven days of the festival.

succubus a female spirit.

succulent plant thick, fleshy plant that stores water in its tissues; for example, cacti and stonecrops *Sedum*. Succulents live either in areas where water is very scarce, such as deserts, or in places where it is not easily obtainable because of the high concentrations of

salts in the soil, as in salt marshes. Many desert plants are ◊xerophytes.

sucrase enzyme capable of digesting sucrose into its constituent molecules of glucose and fructose.

Sucre legal capital and judicial seat of Bolivia; population (1988) 95,600. It stands on the central plateau at an altitude of 9,320 ft/2,840 m.

Sucre Antonio José de 1795–1830. South American revolutionary leader. As chief lieutenant of Simón ◊Bolívar, he won several battles in freeing the colonies of Ecuador and Bolivia from Spanish rule, and in 1826 became president of Bolivia. After a mutiny by the army and invasion by Peru, he resigned in 1828 and was assassinated in 1830 on his way to join Bolívar.

sucrose or *cane sugar* or *beet sugar* $C_{12}H_{22}O_{10}$ a sugar found in the pith of sugar cane and in sugar beets. It is popularly known as ◊sugar.

Sudan country in NE Africa, bounded N by Egypt, NE by the Red Sea, E by Eritrea and Ethiopia, S by Kenya, Uganda, and Zaire, W by the Central African Republic and Chad, and NW by Libya. It is the largest country in Africa.

Sudan
Democratic Republic of
(*Jamhuryat es-Sudan*)

area 967,489 sq mi/2,505,800 sq km
capital Khartoum
cities Omdurman, Juba, Wadi Medani, al-Obeid, Kassala, Atbara, al-Qadarif, Kosti; chief port Port Sudan
physical fertile valley of river Nile separates Libyan Desert in W from high rocky Nubian Desert in E
environment the building of the Jonglei Canal to supply water to N Sudan and Egypt threatens the grasslands of S Sudan
features Sudd swamp; largest country in Africa
head of state and government General Omar Hassan Ahmed el-Bashir from 1989
political system military republic
political parties New National Umma Party (NNUP), Islamic, nationalist; Democratic Unionist Party (DUP), moderate, nationalist; National Islamic Front, Islamic, nationalist
exports cotton, gum arabic, sesame seed, peanuts, sorghum
currency Sudanese pound
population (1992) 29,971,000; growth rate 2.9% p.a.
life expectancy men 51, women 55 (1989)
languages Arabic 51% (official), local languages
religions Sunni Muslim 73%, animist 18%, Christian 9% (in south)
literacy 30% (1986)
GNP $8.5 bn (1988); $330 per head (1988)

chronology
1820 Sudan ruled by Egypt.
1885 Revolt led to capture of Khartoum by self-proclaimed Mahdi.
1896–98 Anglo-Egyptian offensive led by Lord Kitchener subdued revolt.
1899 Sudan administered as an Anglo-Egyptian condominium.
1955 Civil war between Muslim north and non-Muslim south broke out.
1956 Sudan achieved independence from Britain and Egypt as a republic.
1958 Military coup replaced civilian government with Supreme Council of the Armed Forces.
1964 Civilian rule reinstated.
1969 Coup led by Col Gaafar Mohammed Nimeri established Revolutionary Command Council (RCC); name changed to Democratic Republic of Sudan.
1970 Union with Egypt agreed in principle.
1971 New constitution adopted; Nimeri confirmed as president; Sudanese Socialist Union (SSU) declared only legal party.
1972 Proposed Federation of Arab Republics, comprising Sudan, Egypt, and Syria, abandoned. Addis Ababa conference proposed autonomy for southern provinces.
1974 National assembly established.
1983 Nimeri reelected. Shari'a (Islamic law) introduced.
1985 Nimeri deposed in a bloodless coup led by General Swar al-Dahab; transitional military council set up. State of emergency declared.
1986 More than 40 political parties fought general election; coalition government formed.
1987 Virtual civil war with Sudan People's Liberation Army (SPLA).
1988 Al-Mahdi formed a new coalition. Another flare-up of civil war between north and south created tens of thousands of refugees. Floods made 1.5 million people homeless. Peace pact signed with SPLA.
1989 Sadiq al-Mahdi overthrown in coup led by General Omar Hassan Ahmed el-Bashir.
1990 Civil war continued with new SPLA offensive.
1991 Federal system introduced, with division of country into nine states.
1993 March: SPLA leaders John Garang and Riek Machar announced unilateral cease-fire in ten years' war with government in Khartoum. April peace talks began between government and two factions of the SPLA.

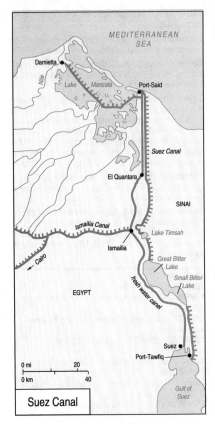

Suez Canal

MEDITERRANEAN SEA
Damietta
Nile
Lake Manzala
Port-Said
Suez Canal
El Quantara
SINAI
Ismailia Canal
Lake Timsah
Ismailia
Cairo
Great Bitter Lake
Small Bitter Lake
EGYPT
fresh water canal
Suez
Port-Tawfiq
Gulf of Suez

0 mi | 20
0 km | 40

sudden infant death syndrome (SIDS) in medicine, the technical term for ◊crib death.

Sudetenland mountainous region of the Czech Republic. As part of Czechoslovakia, the region was annexed by Germany under the ◊Munich Agreement 1938; it was returned to Czechoslovakia 1945.

Suetonius (Gaius Suetonius Tranquillus) *c.* AD 69–140. Roman historian, author of *Lives of the Caesars* (Julius Caesar to Domitian).

Suez Canal artificial waterway, 100 mi/160 km long, from Port Said to Suez, linking the Mediterranean and Red seas, separating Africa from Asia, and providing the shortest eastward sea route from Europe. It was opened 1869, nationalized 1956, blocked by Egypt during the Arab-Israeli War 1967, and not reopened until 1975.

Suez Crisis military confrontation Oct–Dec 1956 following the nationalization of the Suez Canal by President Nasser of Egypt. In an attempt to reassert international control of the canal, Israel launched an attack, after which British and French troops landed. Widespread international censure forced the withdrawal of the British and French. The crisis resulted in the resignation of British prime minister Eden.

suffix letter or group of letters added to the end of a word in order to show its tense ("pass*ed*"), form the plural ("child*ren*"), change the part of speech ("wonder*ful*" adjective; "wonder*ment*" noun), or to form a new word ("sex*ist*").

Suffolk county of E England
area 1,467 sq mi/3,800 sq km
cities Ipswich (administrative headquarters), Bury St Edmunds, Lowestoft, Felixstowe
physical low undulating surface and flat coastline; rivers: Waveney, Alde, Deben, Orwell, Stour; part of the Norfolk Broads
features Minsmere marshland bird reserve, near Aldeburgh; site of ◊Sutton Hoo (7th-century ship-burial); site of Sizewell B, Britain's first pressurized-water nuclear reactor plant (under construction)
products cereals, sugar beet, working horses (Suffolk punches), fertilizers, agricultural machinery
population (1991) 629,900.

suffragist a woman fighting for the right to vote. In the US, the suffragist movement officially began at the Seneca Falls Convention 1848. Elizabeth Cady ◊Stanton and Susan B ◊Anthony founded the National Woman Suffrage Association 1869. At about the same time, Lucy ◊Stone formed the American Woman Suffrage Association. The two groups merged 1890 as the National American Woman Suffrage Association. The perseverance of this group and others led to the ratification of the 19th Amendment 1920, which gave US women the right to vote.

Sufism mystical movement of ◊Islam that originated in the 8th century. Sufis believe that deep intuition is the only real guide to knowledge. The movement has a strong strain of asceticism. The name derives from Arabic *suf*, a rough woolen robe worn as an indication of disregard for material things. There are a number of groups or brotherhoods within Sufism, each with its own method of meditative practice, one of which is the whirling dance of the ◊dervishes.

sugar any sweet, soluble crystalline carbohydrate, either a monosaccharide or disaccharide. The major sources are tropical sugar cane *Saccharum officinarum*, which accounts for about two-thirds of production, and temperate sugar beet *Beta vulgaris*. ◊Honey also contains sugars.

Suharto Raden 1921– . Indonesian politician and general. He ousted Sukarno to become president 1967. He ended confrontation with Malaysia, invaded East Timor 1975, and reached a cooperation agreement with Papua New Guinea 1979. His authoritarian rule has met with domestic opposition from the left. He was reelected 1973, 1978, 1983, 1988, and 1993.

suicide the act of killing oneself intentionally; a person who does this.

It is often considered a crime in law, with consequences for a suicide's estate, or criminal prosecution for unsuccessful attempt. It is also a crime in terms of some religious laws. Aiding and abetting another's suicide is often considered illegal. Survivors of joint suicides may be charged with manslaughter. In some cultures, suicide is considered honorable behavior, such as suicide in ancient Rome, historic ◊hara-kiri in Japan, or historic suttee in India.

Sui dynasty Chinese ruling family 581–618 which reunited China after the strife of the Three Kingdoms era. There were two Sui emperors: Yang Qien (Yang Chien, 541–604), and Yangdi (Yang-ti, ruled 605–17). Though short-lived, the Sui reestablished strong centralized government, rebuilding the ◊Great Wall and digging canals which later formed part of the Grand Canal system. The Sui capital was Chang'an.

suite in music, formerly a grouping of old dance forms; later the term came to be used to describe a set of instrumental pieces, sometimes assembled from a stage work, such as Tchaikovsky's *Nutcracker Suite* 1891–92.

Sukarno Achmed 1901–1970. Indonesian nationalist, president 1945–67. During World War II he cooperated in the local administration set up by the Japanese, replacing Dutch rule. After the war he became the first president of the new Indonesian republic, becoming president-for-life in 1966; he was ousted by ♢Suharto.

Sulawesi formerly *Celebes* island in E Indonesia, one of the Sunda Islands; area (with dependent islands) 73,000 sq mi/190,000 km; population (1980) 10,410,000. It is mountainous and forested and produces copra and nickel.

Suleiman or *Solyman* 1494–1566. Ottoman sultan from 1520, known as **the Magnificent** and **the Lawgiver**. Under his rule, the Ottoman Empire flourished and reached its largest extent. He made conquests in the Balkans, the Mediterranean, Persia, and N Africa, but was defeated at Vienna in 1529 and Valletta (on Malta) in 1565. He was a patron of the arts, a poet, and an administrator.

sulfate SO_4^{2-} salt or ester derived from sulfuric acid. Most sulfates are water soluble (the exceptions are lead, calcium, strontium, and barium sulfates), and require a very high temperature to decompose them.

sulfide compound of sulfur and another element in which sulfur is the more electronegative element. Sulfides occur in a number of minerals. Some of the more volatile sulfides have extremely unpleasant odors (hydrogen sulfide smells of bad eggs).

sulfite SO_3^{2-} salt or ester derived from sulfurous acid.

sulfonamide any of a group of compounds containing the chemical group sulfonamide (SO_2NH_2) or its derivatives, which were, and still are in some cases, used to treat bacterial diseases. Sulfadiazine ($C_{10}H_{10}N_4O_2S$) is an example.

sulfur brittle, pale-yellow, nonmetallic element, symbol S, atomic number 16, atomic weight 32.064. It occurs in three allotropic forms: two crystalline (rhombic and monoclinic) and one amorphous. It burns in air with a blue flame and a stifling odor; it is insoluble in water but soluble in carbon disulfide. It is found abundantly in volcanic regions and occurs in nature in combination with metals and other substances, as well as a free, brittle, crystalline solid.

sulfur dioxide SO_2 a pungent gas, produced by burning sulfur in air or oxygen.

sulfuric acid H_2SO_4 (also called oil of vitriol) dense, oily, colorless liquid that gives out heat when added to water. It is used extensively in the chemical industry, in gasoline refining, and in manufacturing fertilizers, detergents, explosives, and dyes.

sulfurous acid H_2SO_3 solution of sulfur dioxide (SO_2) in water. It is a weak acid.

Sulla Lucius Cornelius 138–78 BC. Roman general and politician, a leader of the senatorial party. Forcibly suppressing the democrats by marching on Rome in 88 BC, he departed for a successful campaign against Mithridates VI of Pontus. The democrats seized power in his absence, but on his return in 82 Sulla captured Rome and massacred all opponents. The reforms he introduced as dictator, which strengthened the Senate, were conservative and short-lived. He retired 79 BC.

Sullivan Arthur (Seymour) 1842–1900. English composer who wrote operettas in collaboration with William Gilbert, including *HMS Pinafore* 1878, *The Pirates of Penzance* 1879, and *The Mikado* 1885. Their partnership broke down in 1896. Sullivan also composed serious instrumental, choral, and operatic works—for example, the opera *Ivanhoe* 1890—which he valued more highly than the operettas.

Sullivan John L(awrence) 1858–1918. US boxer. He won the heavyweight championship from Paddy Ryan 1882 and in the following years toured widely throughout the US and British Isles. In 1892 he lost his title to James "Gentleman Jim" Corbett in the first championship bout held according to the Marquis of Queensbury rules.

sumac any bush or tree of the genus *Rhus* of the cashew family, having pinnate compound leaves and clusters of small reddish fruits. Staghorn sumac *R. typhina*, growing to 36 ft/11 m tall, is common in North America. Included too are several poisonous plants (sometimes referred to collectively as the genus *Toxicodendron*), such as ♢poison ivy, ♢poison sumac, and certain Japanese sumacs.

Sumatra or *Sumatera* second-largest island of Indonesia, one of the Sunda Islands; area 182,800 sq mi/473,600 sq km; population (1989) 36,882,000. East of a longitudinal volcanic mountain range is a wide plain; both are heavily forested. Products include rubber, rice, tobacco, tea, timber, tin, and petroleum.

Sumerian civilization the world's earliest civilization, dated about 3500 BC, and located at the confluence of the Tigris and Euphrates rivers in lower Mesopotamia (present-day Iraq). It was a city-state with priests as secular rulers. Sumerian culture was based on the taxation of the surplus produced by agricultural villagers to support the urban ruling class and its public-works program, which included state-controlled irrigation. Cities included ♢Lagash, Eridu, and ♢Ur. Trade with Egypt and the Indus Valley led to the formation of the ancient Egyptian civilization and the ♢Indus Valley civilization.

summit or *summit conference* meeting of heads of government to discuss common interests, especially the US-Soviet summits 1959–90, of which there were 15. The term was first used during World War II, and the ♢Yalta Conference and ♢Potsdam Conference 1945 were summits that did much to determine the political structure of the postwar world. Later summits have been of varying importance, partly as public-relations exercises.

Sumner Charles 1811–1874. US political leader. Elected to the US Senate as a FreeSoil Democrat 1852, he was defeated by South Carolina congressman Preston Brooks 1856 for his uncompromising abolitionist views on the issue of slavery. During the American Civil War 1861–65, he was a Republican leader in Congress. A supporter of Radical Reconstruction, he opposed President Grant's renomination 1872.

Sumner James 1887–1955. US biochemist. In 1926 he succeeded in crystallizing the enzyme urease and demonstrating its protein nature. For this work Sumner shared the 1946 Nobel Prize for Chemistry with John Northrop and Wendell Stanley.

sumo wrestling national sport of Japan. Fighters of larger than average size (rarely less than 285 lb/130 kg) try to push, pull, or throw each other out of a circular ring.

Sun Ultraviolet image of the solar disk and solar prominence, recorded by the Skylab space station 1973.

Sun the ◊star at the center of the Solar System. Its diameter is 865,000 mi/1,392,000 km; its temperature at the surface is about 5,800K (9,980°F/5,530°C), and at the center 15,000,000K (27,000,000°F/15,000,000°C). It is composed of about 70% hydrogen and 30% helium, with other elements making up less than 1%. The Sun's energy is generated by nuclear fusion reactions that turn hydrogen into helium at its center. The gas core is far denser than mercury or lead on Earth. The Sun is about 4.7 billion years old, with a predicted lifetime of 10 billion years.

At the end of its life, it will expand to become a ◊red giant the size of Mars's orbit, then shrink to become a ◊white dwarf. The Sun spins on its axis every 25 days near its equator, but more slowly toward its poles. Its rotation can be followed by watching the passage of dark ◊sunspots across its disk. Sometimes bright eruptions called ◊flares occur near sunspots. Above the Sun's photosphere lies a layer of thinner gas called the chromosphere, visible only by means of special instruments or at eclipses. Tongues of gas called prominences extend from the chromosphere into the corona, a halo of hot, tenuous gas surrounding the Sun. Gas boiling from the corona streams outward through the Solar System, forming the ◊solar wind. Activity on the Sun, including sunspots, flares, and prominences, waxes and wanes during the *solar cycle*, which peaks every 11 years or so. The unmanned space probe *Pioneer 9* achieved solar orbit in 1968, and reported data on solar radiation.

Sunbelt popular name for the S and SW continental US because of the warm climate. The Sunbelt is growing much faster in population than the N US, with a steady migration of retirees and high-tech and service industries. The 20 states that, roughly, comprise the Sunbelt have a population of more than 110 million. The largest city in the Sunbelt is Los Angeles.

Sundanese member of the second-largest ethnic group in the Republic of Indonesia. There are more than 20 million speakers of Sundanese, a member of the western branch of the Austronesian family. Like their neighbors, the Javanese, the Sundanese are predominantly Muslim. They are known for their performing arts, especially *jaipongan* dance traditions, and distinctive batik fabrics.

sundial instrument measuring time by means of a shadow cast by the Sun. Almost completely superseded by the proliferation of clocks, it survives ornamentally in gardens. The dial is marked with the hours at graduated distances, and a style or gnomon (parallel to Earth's axis and pointing to the north) casts the shadow.

sunfish any of various small members of the North American family (Centrarchidae) of freshwater bony fishes with compressed, almost circular bodies ranging from 6 in/15 cm to 12 in/30 cm and including bluegills, pumpkinseeds, rock bass, and crappies. The considerably larger basses also belong to this family. Ocean sunfishes of the family Molidae have disk-shaped, abruptly truncated bodies. The 10 ft/3 m species *Mola mola* is found worldwide.

sunflower tall plant of the genus *Helianthus*, family Compositae. The common sunflower *H. annuus*, probably native to Mexico, grows to 15 ft/4.5 m in favorable conditions. It is commercially cultivated in central Europe, the US, Russia, Ukraine, and Australia for the oil-bearing seeds that follow the yellow-petaled flowers.

Sunni member of the larger of the two main sects of ◊Islam, with about 680 million adherents. Sunni Muslims believe that the first three caliphs were all legitimate successors of the prophet Mohammed, and that guidance on belief and life should come from the Koran and the Hadith, and from the Shari'a, not from a human authority or spiritual leader. Imams in Sunni Islam are educated lay teachers of the faith and prayer leaders. The name derives from the *Sunna*, Arabic "code of behavior," the body of traditional law evolved from the teaching and acts of Mohammed.

sunspot dark patch on the surface of the Sun, actually an area of cooler gas, thought to be caused by strong magnetic fields that block the outward flow of heat to the Sun's surface. Sunspots consist of a dark central *umbra*, about 4,000K (6,700°F/3,700°C), and a lighter surrounding *penumbra*, about 5,500K (9,400°F/5,200°C). They last from several days to over a month, ranging in size from 1,250 mi/2,000 km to groups stretching for over 62,000 mi/100,000 km. The number of sunspots visible at a given time varies from none to over 100 in a cycle averaging 11 years.

Sun Yat-sen or *Sun Zhong Shan* 1867–1925. Chinese revolutionary leader, founder of the ◊Guomindang (nationalist party) 1894, and provisional president of the Republic of China 1912 after playing a vital part in deposing the emperor. He was president of a breakaway government from 1921.

superactinide any of a theoretical series of super-heavy, radioactive elements, starting with atomic number 113, that extend beyond the ◊transactinide series in the periodic table. They do not occur in nature and none has yet been synthesized.

supercomputer the fastest, most powerful type of computer, capable of performing its basic operations in picoseconds (trillionths of a second), rather than nanoseconds (billionths of a second), like most other computers.

superconductivity in physics, increase in electrical conductivity at low temperatures. The resistance of some metals and metallic compounds decreases uniformly with decreasing temperature until at a critical temperature (the superconducting point), within a few degrees of absolute zero (0 K/–459.67°F/–273.16°C), the resistance suddenly falls to zero. The phenomenon was discovered by Dutch scientist Heike Kamerlingh-Onnes (1853–1926) in 1911.

supercooling in physics, the lowering in temperature of a saturated solution without crystallization taking place, forming a supersaturated solution. Usually crystallization rapidly follows the introduction of a small (seed) crystal or agitation of the supercooled solution.

superego in Freudian psychology, the element of the human mind concerned with the ideal, responsible for ethics and self-imposed standards of behavior. It is characterized as a form of conscience, restraining the ◊ego, and responsible for feelings of guilt when the moral code is broken.

supergiant the largest and most luminous type of star known, with a diameter of up to 1,000 times that of the Sun and absolute magnitudes of between −5 and −9.

Superior, Lake largest and deepest of the Great Lakes and the largest freshwater lake in the world; area about 31,700 sq mi/82,100 sq km. It is bordered by the Canadian province of Ontario and the US states of Minnesota, Wisconsin, and Michigan. As the western-most of the Great Lakes, Superior is at the western end of the St Lawrence Seaway. Duluth, Minnesota, is the largest US city on its shores, and with its sister city, Superior, Wisconsin, it is the busiest Great Lakes port, shipping grain and iron ore to the US and Europe. Also on Lake Superior is Canada's busiest Great Lakes port, Thunder Bay, Ontario, shipping coal and grain chiefly to points in E Canada.

supernova the explosive death of a star, which temporarily attains a brightness of 100 million Suns or more, so that it can shine as brilliantly as a small galaxy for a few days or weeks. Very approximately, it is thought that a supernova explodes in a large galaxy about once every 100 years. Many supernovae remain undetected because of obscuring by interstellar dust—astronomers estimate some 50%.

supersaturation in chemistry, the state of a solution that has a higher concentration of solute than would normally be obtained in a saturated solution.

supersonic speed speed greater than that at which sound travels, measured in ◊Mach numbers. In dry air at 32°F/0°C, sound travels at about 727 mph/1,170 kph, but decreases its speed with altitude until, at 39,000 ft/12,000 m, it is only 658 mph/1,060 kph.

Superstring Theory in physics and astronomy, the theory that attempts to link the four ◊fundamental forces. It postulates that each force emerged separately during the expansion of the very early universe from the ◊Big Bang. It also postulates viewing matter as tiny vibrating strings instead of particles within a universe of more than the currently known four dimensions. Continuing research pursues a model based on a ten-dimensional universe, present at singularity. At the Big Bang, the ten dimensions split into two components, with four dimensions expanded into the current observable universe while the other six dimensions contracted to a point in space.

supersymmetry in physics, a theory that relates the two classes of elementary particle, the fermions and the bosons. According to supersymmetry, each fermion particle has a boson partner particle, and vice versa. It has not been possible to marry up all the known fermions with the known bosons, and so the theory postulates the existence of other, as yet undiscovered fermions, such as the photinos (partners of the photons), gluinos (partners of the gluons), and gravitinos (partners of the gravitons). Using these ideas, it has become possible to develop a theory of gravity—called supergravity—that extends Einstein's work and considers the gravitational, nuclear, and electromagnetic forces to be manifestations of an underlying superforce. Supersymmetry has been incorporated into the ◊superstring theory, and appears to be a crucial ingredient in the "theory of everything" sought by scientists.

supply and demand one of the fundamental approaches to economics, which examines and compares the supply of a good with its demand (usually in the form of a graph of supply and demand curves plotted against price). For a typical good, the supply curve is upward-sloping (the higher the price, the more the manufacturer is willing to sell), while the demand curve is downward-sloping (the cheaper the good, the more demand there is for it). The point where the curves intersect is the equilibrium price at which supply equals demand.

supply-side economics school of economic thought advocating government policies that allow market forces to operate freely, such as privatization, cuts in public spending and income tax, reductions in labor-union power, and cuts in the ratio of unemployment benefits to wages. Supply-side economics developed as part of the monetarist (see ◊monetarism) critique of ◊Keynesian economics.

Supreme Court highest US judicial tribunal, composed since 1869 of a chief justice (William Rehnquist from 1986) and eight associate justices. Appointments are made for life by the president, with the advice and consent of the Senate, and justices can be removed only by impeachment.

The US Supreme Court hears appeals from decisions of the US Court of Appeals and from the state supreme courts. It also adjudicates questions of constitutional propriety and conflicts between the executive and legislative branches of the federal government. See also individual biographies and court decisions.

Surabaya port on the island of Java, Indonesia; population (1980) 2,028,000. It has oil refineries and shipyards and is a naval base.

surd an expression containing the root of an ◊irrational number that can never be exactly expressed—for example, √3 = 1.732050808....

surface-area-to-volume ratio the ratio of an animal's surface area (the area covered by its skin) to its total volume. This is high for small animals, but low for large animals such as elephants.

surface tension in physics, the property that causes the surface of a liquid to behave as if it were covered with a weak elastic skin; this is why a needle can float on water. It is caused by the exposed surface's tendency to contract to the smallest possible area because of unequal cohesive forces between ◊molecules at the surface. Allied phenomena include the formation of droplets, the concave profile of a meniscus, and the ◊capillary action by which water soaks into a sponge.

surfing sport of riding on the crest of large waves while standing on a narrow, keeled surfboard, usually of light synthetic material such as fiberglass, about 6 ft/1.8 m long (or about 8–9 ft/2.4–7 m known as the Malibu), as first developed in Hawaii and Australia. ◊Windsurfing is a recent development.

surgery in medicine, originally the removal of diseased parts or foreign substances from the body through cutting and other manual operations. It now includes such techniques as beamed high-energy ultrasonic waves, binocular magnifiers for microsurgery, and lasers.

Suriname country on the N coast of South America, bounded W by French Guiana, S by Brazil, E by Guyana, and N by the Atlantic Ocean. *See panel p. 890*

Surrealism movement in art, literature, and film that developed out of ◊Dada around 1922. Led by André

Suriname
Republic of
(*Republiek Suriname*)

area 63,243 sq mi/163,820 sq km
capital Paramaribo
cities Nieuw Nickerie, Brokopondo, Nieuw Amsterdam
physical hilly and forested, with flat and narrow coastal plain
features Surinamee River
head of state and government Ronald Venetiaan from 1991
political system emergent democratic republic
political parties Party for National Unity and Solidarity (KTPI)*, Indonesian, left of center; Suriname National Party (NPS)*, Creole, left of center; Progressive Reform Party (VHP)*, Indian, left of center; New Front for Democracy (NF)
*members of Front for Democracy and Development (FDD)

exports alumina, aluminum, bauxite, rice, timber
currency Suriname guilder
population (1990 est) 408,000 (Hindu 37%, Creole 31%, Javanese 15%); growth rate 1.1% p.a.
life expectancy men 66, women 71 (1989)
languages Dutch (official), Sranan (creole), English, others
religions Christian 30%, Hindu 27%, Muslim 20%
literacy 65% (1989)
GNP $1.1 bn (1987); $2,920 per head (1985)

chronology
1667 Became a Dutch colony.
1954 Achieved internal self-government as Dutch Guiana.
1975 Independence achieved from the Netherlands, with Dr Johan Ferrier as president and Henck Arron as prime minister; 40% of the population emigrated to the Netherlands.
1980 Arron's government overthrown in army coup; Ferrier refused to recognize military regime; appointed Dr Henk Chin A Sen to lead civilian administration. Army replaced Ferrier with Dr Chin A Sen.
1982 Army, led by Lt Col Desi Bouterse, seized power, setting up a Revolutionary People's Front.
1985 Ban on political activities lifted.
1986 Antigovernment rebels brought economic chaos to Suriname.
1987 New constitution approved.
1988 Ramsewak Shankar elected president.
1989 Bouterse rejected peace accord reached by President Shankar with guerrilla insurgents, vowed to continue fighting.
1990 Shankar deposed in army coup.
1991 Johan Kraag became interim president. New Front for Democracy won assembly majority. Ronald Venetiaan elected president.
1992 Peace accord with guerrilla groups.

◊Breton, who produced the *Surrealist Manifesto* 1924, the Surrealists were inspired by the thoughts and visions of the subconscious mind. They explored varied styles and techniques, and the movement became the dominant force in Western art between World Wars I and II.

Surrey county in S England
area 641 sq mi/1,660 sq km
cities Kingston upon Thames (administrative headquarters), Guildford, Woking
features rivers: Thames, Mole, Wey; hills: Box and Leith; North Downs; Runnymede, Thameside site of the signing of Magna Carta; Yehudi Menuhin School; Kew Palace and Royal Botanic Gardens; in 1989 it was the most affluent county in Britain—average income 40% above national average
products vegetables, agricultural products, service industries
population (1991) 997,000
famous people Eric Clapton, John Galsworthy, Aldous Huxley, Laurence Olivier.

surveying the accurate measuring of the Earth's crust, or of land features or buildings. It is used to establish boundaries, and to evaluate the topography for engineering work. The measurements used are both linear and angular, and geometry and trigonometry are applied in the calculations.

Sūrya in Hindu mythology, the sun god, son of the sky god Indra. His daughter, also named Sūrya, is a female personification of the Sun.

Susquehanna river rising in central New York State, and flowing 444 mi/715 km to Chesapeake Bay. It

is used for hydroelectric power. On the strentgh of its musical name, Samuel ◊Coleridge planned to establish a communal settlement here with his fellow poet Robert Southey.

Sussex former county of England, on the S coast, now divided into East Sussex and West Sussex.

Sutherland Joan 1926– . Australian soprano. She went to England in 1951, where she made her debut the next year in *The Magic Flute*; later roles included *Lucia di Lammermoor*, Donna Anna in *Don Giovanni*, and Desdemona in *Otello*. She retired from the stage in 1990.

She usually performed under the baton of her husband, conductor Richard Bonynge.

suttee Hindu custom whereby a widow committed suicide by joining her husband's funeral pyre, often under public and family pressure. Banned in the 17th century by the Mogul emperors, the custom continued even after it was made illegal under British rule 1829. There continue to be sporadic revivals.

Sutton Hoo archeological site in Suffolk, England, where in 1939 a Saxon ship burial was excavated. It is the funeral monument of Raedwald, King of the East Angles, who died about 624 or 625. The jewelry, armor, and weapons discovered were placed in the British Museum, London.

Suu Kyi Aung San 1945– . Myanmar (Burmese) politician and human rights campaigner, leader of the National League for Democracy (NLD), the main opposition to the military junta. When the NLD won the 1990 elections, the junta refused to surrender power, and placed Suu Kyi under house arrest. She was awarded the Nobel Peace Prize 1991 in recognition of her "non-violent struggle for democracy and human rights" in Myanmar. She is the daughter of former Burmese premier ◊Aung San.

Suzhou or *Soochow*, formerly *Wuhsien* 1912–49; city S of the Yangtze river delta and E of the ◊Grand Canal, in Jiangsu province, China; population (1983) 670,000. It has embroidery and jade-carving traditions and Shizilin and Zhuozheng gardens. The city dates from about 1000 BC, and the name Suzhou from the 7th century AD; it was reputedly visited by the Venetian Marco ◊Polo.

Svalbard Norwegian archipelago in the Arctic Ocean. The main island is Spitsbergen; other islands include North East Land, Edge Island, Barents Island, and Prince Charles Foreland.

Svedberg Theodor 1884–1971. Swedish chemist. In 1924 he constructed the first ultracentrifuge, a machine that allowed the rapid separation of particles by mass. He was awarded the Nobel Prize for Chemistry 1926.

Svengali person who molds another into a performer and masterminds his or her career. The original Svengali was a character in the novel *Trilby* 1894 by George ◊Du Maurier.

Swabia (German *Schwaben*) historic region of SW Germany, an independent duchy in the Middle Ages. It includes Augsburg and Ulm and forms part of the *Länder* (states) of Baden-Württemberg, Bavaria, and Hessen.

Swahili (Arabic *sawahil* "coasts") language belonging to the Bantu branch of the Niger-Congo family, widely used in east and central Africa. Swahili originated on the E African coast as a *lingua franca* used

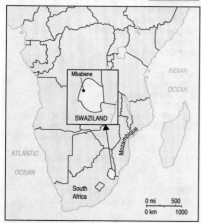

among traders, and contains many Arabic loan words. It is an official language in Kenya and Tanzania.

swallow any bird of the family Hirundinidae of small, insect-eating birds in the order Passeriformes, with long, narrow wings and deeply forked tails. Swallows feed while flying.

Species include the barn swallow *Hirundo rustica* and the purple martin *Progne subis*.

Suzhou *Tiger Hill Pagoda near Suzhou, China.*

Swaziland
Kingdom of
(*Umbuso weSwatini*)

area 6,716 sq mi/17,400 sq km
capital Mbabane
cities Manzini, Big Bend
physical central valley; mountains in W (Highveld); plateau in E (Lowveld and Lubombo plateau)
features landlocked enclave between South Africa and Mozambique
head of state and government King Mswati III from 1986
political system near-absolute monarchy
political party Imbokodvo National Movement (INM), nationalist monarchist
exports sugar, canned fruit, wood pulp, asbestos
currency lilangeni
population (1992) 826,000; growth rate 3% p.a.
life expectancy men 47, women 54 (1989)
languages Swazi 90%, English (both official)
religions Christian 57%, animist
literacy men 70%, women 66% (1985 est)
GNP $539 million; $750 per head (1987)

chronology
1903 Swaziland became a special High Commission territory.
1967 Achieved internal self-government.
1968 Independence achieved from Britain, within the Commonwealth, as the Kingdom of Swaziland, with King Sobhuza II as head of state.
1973 The king suspended the constitution and assumed absolute powers.
1978 New constitution adopted.
1982 King Sobhuza died; his place was taken by one of his wives, Dzeliwe, until his son, Prince Makhosetive, reached the age of 21.
1983 Queen Dzeliwe ousted by another wife, Ntombi.
1984 After royal power struggle, it was announced that the crown prince would become king at 18.
1986 Crown prince formally invested as King Mswati III.
1987 Power struggle developed between advisory council Liqoqo and Queen Ntombi over accession of king. Mswati dissolved parliament; new government elected with Sotsha Dlamini as prime minister.
1991 Calls for democratic reform.
1992 Mswati dissolved parliament, assuming "executive powers."

swamp region of low-lying land that is permanently saturated with water and usually overgrown with vegetation; for example, the everglades of Florida. A swamp often occurs where a lake has filled up with sediment and plant material. The flat surface so formed means that runoff is slow, and the water table is always close to the surface. The high humus content of swamp soil means that good agricultural soil can be obtained by draining.

swan any of several large, long-necked, aquatic, web-footed birds of the family Anatidae, which also includes ducks and geese.

Species include the Old World mute swan *Cygnus olor*, with all-white plumage, now introduced in parks worldwide, and the ***black swan*** of Australia, *C. atratus*. The North American ***trumpeter swan*** *C. buccinator* is the largest, with a wingspan of 8 ft/2.4 m. This species was nearly extinct by 1900, and although numbers have recovered, it is still endangered. Pairing is generally for life, and the young are called cygnets.

Swanson Gloria. Adopted name of Gloria Josephine Mae Svenson 1897–1983. US actress, a star of silent films who influenced American tastes and fashion for more than 20 years. She retired in 1932 but made several major comebacks. Her work includes *Sadie Thompson* 1928, *Queen Kelly* 1928 (unfinished), and *Sunset Boulevard* 1950.

She was second only to Mary Pickford in fame and in 1926 she formed her own production company with Joseph Kennedy as her financial backer.

swastika (Sanskrit *svastika*) cross in which the bars are extended at right angles in the same clockwise or a counterclockwise direction. An ancient good-luck symbol in both the New and the Old World and an Aryan and Buddhist mystic sign, it was adopted by Hitler as the emblem of the Nazi Party and incorporated into the German national flag 1935–45.

Swaziland country in SE Africa, bounded E by Mozambique and SE, S, W, and N by South Africa. *See panel p. 891*

sweat gland ◊gland within the skin of mammals that produces surface perspiration. In primates, sweat glands are distributed over the whole body, but in most other mammals they are more localized; for example, in cats and dogs, they are restricted to the feet and around the face. In humans, sweat glands occur in larger numbers in the male than the female.

sweatshop workshop or factory where employees work long hours under substandard conditions for low wages. Exploitation of labor in this way is associated with unscrupulous employers, who often employ illegal immigrants or children in their labor force.

At the turn of the century women were employed on a large scale since they would work for less money than men. Such exploitation led to the rise of labor unions and the labor movement.

Sweden country in N Europe, bounded W by Norway, NE by Finland and the Gulf of Bothnia, SE by the Baltic Sea, and SW by the Kattegat.

Sweden
Kingdom of
(*Konungariket Sverige*)

area 173,745 sq mi/450,000 sq km
capital Stockholm
cities Göteborg, Malmö, Uppsala, Norrköping, Västerås
physical mountains in W; plains in S; thickly forested; more than 20,000 islands off the Stockholm coast
environment of the country's 90,000 lakes, 20,000 are affected by acid rain; 4,000 are so severely acidified that no fish are thought to survive in them
features lakes, including Vänern, Vättern, Mälaren, Hjälmaren; islands of Öland and Gotland; wild elk
head of state King Carl XVI Gustaf from 1973
head of government Carl Bildt from 1991
political system constitutional monarchy
political parties Social Democratic Labor party (SAP), moderate, left of center; Moderate Party, right of center; Liberal Party, center-left; Centre Party, centrist; Christian Democratic Party, Christian, centrist; Left (Communist) Party, European, Marxist; Green, ecological

exports aircraft, vehicles, ballbearings, drills, missiles, electronics, petrochemicals, textiles, furnishings, ornamental glass, paper, iron and steel
currency krona
population (1992) 8,673,000 (including 17,000 Saami [Lapps] and 1.2 million immigrants from Turkey, Yugoslavia, Greece, Iran, Finland and other Nordic countries); growth rate 0.1% p.a.
life expectancy men 74, women 81 (1989)
languages Swedish; there are Finnish- and Saami-speaking minorities
religion Lutheran (official) 95%
literacy 99% (1989)
GNP $245.8 bn (1992)

chronology
12th century United as an independent nation.
1397–1520 Under Danish rule.
1914–45 Neutral in both world wars.
1951–76 Social Democratic Labor Party (SAP) in power.
1969 Olof Palme became SAP leader and prime minister.
1971 Constitution amended, creating a single-chamber Riksdag, the governing body.
1975 Monarch's last constitutional powers removed.
1976 Thorbjörn Fälldin, leader of the Center Party, became prime minister, heading center-right coalition.
1982 SAP, led by Palme, returned to power.
1985 SAP formed minority government, with Communist support.
1986 Olof Palme murdered. Ingvar Carlsson became prime minister and SAP party leader.
1988 SAP reelected with reduced majority; Green Party gained representation in Riksdag.
1990 SAP government resigned.
1991 Formal application for European Community (EC) membership submitted. Election defeat for SAP; Carlsson resigned. Coalition government formed; Carl Bildt became new prime minister.
1992 Cross-party collaboration to solve economic problems.

Switzerland
Swiss Confederation
(German *Schweiz*, French *Suisse*,
Romansch *Svizzera*)

area 15,946 sq mi/41,300 sq km
capital Bern
cities Zürich, Geneva, Lausanne; river port Basel (on the Rhine)
physical most mountainous country in Europe (Alps and Jura mountains); highest peak Dufourspitze 15,203 ft/4,634 m in Apennines
environment an estimated 43% of coniferous trees, particularly in the central Alpine region, have been killed by acid rain, 90% of which comes from other countries. Over 50% of bird species are classified as threatened
features winter sports area of the upper valley of the river Inn (Engadine); lakes Maggiore, Lucerne, Geneva, Constance

head of state and government Adolf Ogi from 1993
government federal democratic republic
political parties Radical Democratic Party (FDP), radical, center-left; Social Democratic Party (SPS), moderate, left of center; Christian Democratic Party (PDC), Christian, moderate, centrist; People's Party (SVP), center-left; Liberal Party (PLS), federalist, center-left; Green Party, ecological
exports electrical goods, chemicals, pharmaceuticals, watches, precision instruments, confectionery
currency Swiss franc
population (1992) 6,911,000; growth rate 0.2% p.a.
life expectancy men 74, women 82 (1989)
languages German 65%, French 18%, Italian 12%, Romansch 1% (all official)
religions Roman Catholic 50%, Protestant 48%
literacy 99% (1989)
GNP $240.5 bn (1992)

chronology
1648 Became independent of the Holy Roman Empire.
1798–1815 Helvetic Republic established by French revolutionary armies.
1847 Civil war resulted in greater centralization.
1874 Principle of the referendum introduced.
1971 Women given the vote in federal elections.
1984 First female cabinet minister appointed.
1986 Referendum rejected proposal for membership in United Nations.
1989 Referendum supported abolition of citizen army and military service requirements.
1991 18-year-olds allowed to vote for first time in national elections. Four-party coalition remained in power.
1992 René Felber elected president with Adolf Ogi as vice president. Closer ties with European Community rejected in national referendum.
1993 Ogi replaced Felber as head of state.

Swedenborg Emanuel 1688–1772. Swedish theologian and philosopher. He trained as a scientist, but from 1747 concentrated on scriptural study, and in *Divine Love and Wisdom* 1763 concluded that the Last Judgment had taken place in 1757, and that the **New Church**, of which he was the prophet, had now been inaugurated. His writings are the scriptures of the sect popularly known as Swedenborgians, and his works are kept in circulation by the Swedenborg Society, London.

Swedish language member of the Germanic branch of the Indo-European language family, spoken in Sweden and Finland and closely related to Danish and Norwegian.

sweet potato tropical American plant *Ipomoea batatas* of the morning-glory family Convolvulaceae; the white-orange tuberous root is used as a source of starch and alcohol and eaten as a vegetable.

sweet william biennial to perennial plant *Dianthus barbatus* of the pink family Caryophyllaceae, native to S Europe. It is grown for its fragrant red, white, and pink flowers.

swift any fast-flying, short-legged bird of the family Apodidae, of which there are about 75 species, found largely in the tropics. They are 4–11 in/9–23 cm long, with brown or gray plumage, long, pointed wings, and usually a forked tail. They are capable of flying 70 mph/110 kph.
   The chimney swift *Chaetura pelagica*, which breeds in North America, is 5.5 in/13 cm long, with a cigar-shaped body and a short, stubby, superficially unforked tail.

Swift Jonathan 1667–1745. Irish satirist and Anglican cleric, author of *Gulliver's Travels* 1726, an allegory describing travel to lands inhabited by giants, miniature people, and intelligent horses. Other works include *The Tale of a Tub* 1704, attacking corruption in religion and learning; contributions to the Tory paper *The Examiner*, of which he was editor 1710–11; the satirical *A Modest Proposal* 1729, which suggested that children of the poor should be eaten; and many essays and pamphlets.

Swift and Co v US US Supreme Court decision 1905 dealing with federal regulation of local business transactions. When the meatpacking industry colluded to fix the price of fresh meat in Chicago, the federal government issued an injunction against price fixing. The beef trust appealed, arguing that local commerce was outside of federal jurisdiction. The Court upheld the injunction, ruling that, since the local transaction affected businesses that participated in interstate trade, the federal government had the power to regulate it.

swimming self-propulsion of the body through water. As a competitive sport there are four strokes: crawl, breaststroke, backstroke, and butterfly. (In freestyle events, the crawl is usually used, since it is the "fastest" stroke for most swimmers; but any stroke may be used.) Distances of races vary from 25 yards up to the mile or more. Swimming meets are held in pools and at beach clubs (for the events longer than the mile).

Swinburne Algernon Charles 1837–1909. English poet. He attracted attention with the choruses of his

Greek-style tragedy *Atalanta in Calydon* 1865, but he and ◊Rossetti were attacked in 1871 as leaders of "the fleshly school of poetry," and the revolutionary politics of *Songs before Sunrise* 1871 alienated others.

swing music jazz style popular in the 1930s–40s, a big-band dance music with a simple harmonic base of varying tempo from the rhythm section (percussion, guitar, piano), harmonic brass and woodwind sections (sometimes strings), and superimposed solo melodic line from, for example, trumpet, clarinet, or saxophone. Exponents included Benny Goodman, Duke Ellington, and Glenn Miller, who introduced jazz to a mass white audience.

Switzerland landlocked country in W Europe, bounded N by Germany, E by Austria and Liechtenstein, S by Italy, and W by France. *See panel p. 893*

swordfish marine bony fish *Xiphias gladius*, the only member of its family (Xiphiidae), characterized by a long swordlike beak protruding from the upper jaw. It may reach 15 ft/4.5 m in length and weigh 1,000 lb/ 450 kg.

sycamore or *plane tree* any of several Eurasian trees of the genus *Platanus* of the family Plantanaceae. Species include the oriental plane tree *P. orientalis*, a favorite of the Greeks and Romans; the American sycamore *P. occidentalis* of the E US; and the Arizona sycamore *P. Wrightii*. All species have pendulous burrlike fruits and some grow to 100 ft/30 m high.

Sydenham Thomas 1624–1689. English physician, the first person to describe measles and to recommend the use of quinine for relieving symptoms of malaria. His original reputation as "the English Hippocrates" rested upon his belief that careful observation is more useful than speculation. His *Observationes medicae* was published in 1676.

Sydney capital and port of New South Wales, Australia; population (1990) 3,656,900. Industries include engineering, oil refining, electronics, scientific equipment, chemicals, clothing, and furniture. It is a financial center, and has three universities. The 19th-century Museum of Applied Arts and Sciences is the most popular museum in Australia.

Originally a British penal colony 1788, Sydney developed rapidly following the discovery of gold in the surrounding area. The main streets still follow the lines of the original wagon tracks, and the Regency Bligh House survives. Modern landmarks are the harbor bridge (single span 1,652 ft/503.5 m) 1923–32, Opera House 1959–73, and Center Point Tower 1980.

Sydow Max (Carl Adolf) von 1929– . Swedish actor associated with the director Ingmar Bergman. He made his US debut as Jesus in *The Greatest Story Ever Told* 1965. His other films include *The Seventh Seal* 1957, *The Exorcist* 1973, and *Hannah and Her Sisters* 1985.

syllogism set of philosophical statements devised by Aristotle in his work on logic. It establishes the conditions under which a valid conclusion follows or does not follow by deduction from given premises.

symbiosis any relationship between two organisms of different species, where both partners benefit from the association. A well-known example is the pollination relationship between insects and flowers, where the insects feed on nectar and carry pollen from one flower to another. This kind of relationship is better known as mutualism. Strictly speaking, symbiosis refers to continuous, intimate contact between mutually benefiting species, such as the fungus and alga in ◊lichen.

symbolism in the arts, the use of symbols as a device for concentrating or intensifying meaning. In particular, the term is used for a late 19th-century movement in French poetry, associated with Paul Verlaine, Stéphane Mallarmé, and Arthur Rimbaud, who used words for their symbolic rather than concrete meaning.

Symbolism movement in late 19th-century painting that emerged in France inspired by the trend in poetry. The subjects were often mythological, mystical, or fantastic. Gustave Moreau was a leading Symbolist painter.

symmetry exact likeness in shape about a given line (axis), point, or plane. A figure has symmetry if one half can be rotated and/or reflected onto the other. (Symmetry preserves length, angle, but not necessarily orientation.) In a wider sense, symmetry exits if a change in the system leaves the essential features of the system unchanged; for example, reversing the sign of electric charges does not change the electrical behavior of an arrangement of charges.

symphony musical composition for orchestra, traditionally in four separate but closely related movements. It developed from the smaller ◊sonata form, the Italian overture, and the dance suite of the 18th century.

synagogue Jewish place of worship, also called a temple by the non-Orthodox. As an institution it dates from the destruction of the Temple in Jerusalem AD 70, although it had been developing from the time of the Babylonian Exile as a substitute for the Temple. In antiquity it was a public meeting hall where the Torah was also read, but today it is used primarily for prayer and services. A service requires a quorum (*minyan*) of ten adult Jewish men.

synapse junction between two ◊nerve cells, or between a nerve cell and a muscle (a neuromuscular junction), across which a nerve impulse is transmitted. The two cells are separated by a narrow gap called the *synaptic cleft*. The gap is bridged by a chemical ◊neurotransmitter, released by the nerve impulse.

syncline geological term for a fold in the rocks of the Earth's crust in which the layers or ◊beds dip inward, thus forming a troughlike structure with a sag in the middle. The opposite structure, with the beds arching upward, is an anticline.

syncopation in music, the deliberate upsetting of rhythm by shifting the accent to a beat that is normally unaccented.

syndicalism (French *syndicat* "trade union") political movement in 19th-century Europe that rejected parliamentary activity in favor of direct action, culminating in a revolutionary general strike to secure worker ownership and control of industry. After 1918 syndicalism was absorbed in communism, although it continued to have an independent existence in Spain until the late 1930s.

syndrome in medicine, a set of signs and symptoms that always occur together, thus characterizing a particular condition or disorder.

synecdoche (Greek "accepted together") figure of speech that uses either the part to represent the whole ("There were some *new faces* at the meeting," rather than *new people*), or the whole to stand for the part ("The West Indies beat England at cricket," rather than naming the national teams in question).

synergy (Greek "combined action") in architecture, the augmented strength of systems, where the strength of a wall is greater than the added total of its individual units.

Sydney *Sydney Opera House, opened 1973.*

synergy in medicine, the "cooperative" action of two or more drugs, muscles, or organs; applied especially to drugs whose combined action is more powerful than their simple effects added together.

Synge J(ohn) M(illington) 1871–1909. Irish playwright, a leading figure in the Irish dramatic revival of the early 20th century. His six plays reflect the speech patterns of the Aran Islands and W Ireland. They include *In the Shadow of the Glen* 1903, *Riders to the Sea* 1904, and *The Playboy of the Western World* 1907, which caused riots at the Abbey Theatre, Dublin, when first performed.

Synge Richard 1914– . British biochemist who investigated paper ◊chromatography (a means of separating mixtures). By 1940 techniques of chromatography for separating proteins had been devised. Still lacking were comparable techniques for distinguishing the amino acids that constituted the proteins. By 1944, Synge and his colleague Archer Martin had worked out a procedure, known as ascending chromatography, which filled this gap and won them the 1952 Nobel Prize for Chemistry.

synonymy near or identical meaning between or among words. There are very few strict synonyms in any language, although there may be many near-synonyms, depending upon the contexts in which the words are used. Thus *brotherly* and *fraternal* are synonyms in English, but a *brotherhood* is not the same as a *fraternity*. People talk about the brotherhood of man but seldom if ever about the "fraternity of man." *Brotherhood* and *fraternity* are not therefore strictly synonymous.

synovial fluid viscous yellow fluid that bathes movable joints between the bones of vertebrates. It nourishes and lubricates the ◊cartilage at the end of each bone.

synthesis in chemistry, the formation of a substance or compound from more elementary compounds. The synthesis of a drug can involve several stages from the initial material to the final product; the complexity of these stages is a major factor in the cost of production.

synthesizer device that uses electrical components to produce sounds. In ***preset synthesizers***, the sound of various instruments is produced by a built-in computer-type memory. In ***programmable synthesizers*** any number of new instrumental or other sounds may be produced at the will of the performer. ***Speech synthesizers*** can break down speech into 128 basic elements (allophones), which are then combined into words and sentences, as in the voices of electronic teaching aids.

synthetic any material made from chemicals. Since the 1900s, more and more of the materials used in everyday life are synthetics, including plastics (polythene, polystyrene), ◊synthetic fibers (nylon, acrylics, polyesters), synthetic resins, and synthetic rubber. Most naturally occurring organic substances are now made synthetically, especially pharmaceuticals.

synthetic fiber fiber made by chemical processes, unknown in nature. There are two kinds. One is made from natural materials that have been chemically processed in some way; ◊rayon, for example, is made by processing the cellulose in wood pulp. The other type is the true synthetic fiber, made entirely from chemicals. ◊Nylon was the original synthetic fiber, made from chemicals obtained from petroleum (crude oil).

syphilis venereal disease caused by the spiral-shaped bacterium (spirochete) *Treponema pallidum.* Untreated, it runs its course in three stages over many years, often starting with a painless hard sore, or chancre, developing within a month on the area of infection (usually the genitals). The second stage, months later, is a rash with arthritis, hepatitis, and/or meningitis. The third stage, years later, leads eventually to paralysis, blindness, insanity, and death. The Wassermann test is a diagnostic blood test for syphilis.

Syracuse industrial city on Lake Onondaga, in New York State; population (1990) 163,900. Industries

Syria
Syrian Arab Republic
(*al-Jamhuriya al-Arabya as- Suriya*)

area 71,506 sq mi/185,200 sq km
capital Damascus
cities Aleppo, Homs, Hama; chief port Latakia
physical mountains alternate with fertile plains and desert areas; Euphrates River
features Mount Hermon, Golan Heights; crusader castles (including Krak des Chevaliers); Phoenician city sites (Ugarit), ruins of ancient Palmyra
head of state and government Hafez al-Assad from 1971
political system socialist republic
political parties National Progressive Front (NPF), pro-Arab, socialist; Communist Action Party, socialist
exports cotton, cereals, oil, phosphates, tobacco
currency Syrian pound
population (1992) 12,471,000; growth rate 3.5% p.a.
life expectancy men 67, women 69 (1989)
languages Arabic 89% (official), Kurdish 6%, Armenian 3%

religions Sunni Muslim 74%; ruling minority Alawite, and other Islamic sects 16%; Christian 10%
literacy men 76%, women 43% (1985 est)
GNP $17 bn (1986); $702 per head

chronology
1946 Achieved full independence from France.
1958 Merged with Egypt to form the United Arab Republic (UAR).
1961 UAR disintegrated.
1967 Six-Day War resulted in the loss of territory to Israel.
1970–71 Syria supported Palestinian guerrillas against Jordanian troops.
1971 Following a bloodless coup, Hafez al-Assad became president.
1973 Israel consolidated its control of the Golan Heights after the Yom Kippur War.
1976 Substantial numbers of troops committed to the civil war in Lebanon.
1978 Assad reelected.
1981–82 Further military engagements in Lebanon.
1982 Islamic militant uprising suppressed; 5,000 dead.
1984 Presidents Assad and Gemayel approved plans for government of national unity in Lebanon.
1985 Assad secured the release of 39 US hostages held in an aircraft hijacked by extremist Shiite group, Hezbollah. Assad reelected.
1987 Improved relations with US and attempts to secure the release of Western hostages in Lebanon.
1989 Diplomatic relations with Morocco restored. Continued fighting in Lebanon; Syrian forces reinforced in Lebanon; diplomatic relations with Egypt restored.
1990 Diplomatic relations with Britain restored.
1991 Syria fought against Iraq in Gulf War. President Assad agreed to US Middle East peace plan. Assad re elected president.
1993 Syria joined Iraq and other Arab countries in boycotting UN treaty outlawing production and use of chemical weapons.

include the manufacture of electrical and other machinery, paper, and food processing. There are canal links with the ◊Great Lakes, and the Hudson and St Lawrence rivers.

Syria country in W Asia, on the Mediterranean Sea, bounded N by Turkey, E by Iraq, S by Jordan, and SW by Israel and Lebanon.

Syriac language ancient Semitic language, originally the Aramaic dialect spoken in and around Edessa (now in Turkey) and widely used in W Asia from about 700 BC to AD 700. From the 3rd to 7th centuries it was a Christian liturgical and literary language.

systems analysis in computing, the investigation of a business activity or clerical procedure, with a view to deciding if and how it can be computerized. The analyst discusses the existing procedures with the people involved, observes the flow of data through the business, and draws up an outline specification of the required computer system (see also ◊systems design).

systems design in computing, the detailed design of an application package. The designer breaks the system down into component programs and designs the required input forms, screen layouts, and print-outs. Systems design forms a link between systems analysis and ◊programming.

Szczecin (German *Stettin*) industrial (shipbuilding, fish processing, synthetic fibers, tools, iron) port on the river Oder, in NW Poland; population (1990) 413,400.

Szilard Leo 1898–1964. Hungarian-born US physicist who, in 1934, was one of the first scientists to realize that nuclear fission, or atom splitting, could lead to a chain reaction releasing enormous amounts of instantaneous energy. He emigrated to the US in 1938 and there influenced ◊Einstein to advise President F D Roosevelt to begin the nuclear arms program. After World War II he turned his attention to the newly emerging field of molecular biology.

table tennis or *ping pong* indoor game played on a rectangular table by two or four players. It was developed in Britain about 1880 and derived from lawn tennis. World championships were first held 1926.

taboo (Polynesian *tabu*, "forbidden") prohibition applied to magical and religious objects. In psychology and the social sciences the term refers to practices that are generally prohibited because of religious or social pressures; for example, ◊incest is forbidden in most societies.

Tacitus Publius Cornelius *c.* AD 55–*c.* 120. Roman historian. A public orator in Rome, he was consul under Nerva 97–98 and proconsul of Asia 112–113. He wrote histories of the Roman Empire, *Annales* and *Historiae*, covering the years AD 14–68 and 69–97 respectively. He also wrote a *Life of Agricola* 97 (he married Agricola's daughter in 77) and a description of the German tribes, *Germania* 98.

Tacoma port in Washington State, on Puget Sound, 25 mi/40 km S of Seattle; population (1990) 176,700. It is a lumber and shipping center, with fishing and boatbuilding industries. Industries include primary metals, wood and paper products, chemicals, and processed foods.

Founded 1868, the city developed after being chosen as the terminus of the North Pacific Railroad 1873.

Taegu third-largest city in South Korea, situated between Seoul and Pusan; population (1990) 2,228,800. Nearby is the Haeinsa Temple, one of the country's largest monasteries and repository of the *Triptaka Koreana*, a collection of 80,000 wood blocks on which the Buddhist sculptures are carved. Grain, fruit, textiles, and tobacco are produced.

Taejon (Korean "large rice paddy") capital of South Chungchong province, central South Korea; population (1990) 1,062,100. Korea's tallest standing Buddha and oldest wooden building are found NE of the city at Popchusa in the Mount Songnisan National Park.

tae kwon do Korean ◊martial art similar to ◊karate, which includes punching and kicking. It was included in the 1988 Olympic Games as a demonstration sport.

Taft William Howard 1857–1930. 27th president of the US 1909–13, a Republican. He was secretary of war 1904–08 in Theodore Roosevelt's administration, but as president his conservatism provoked Roosevelt to stand against him in the 1912 election. Taft served as chief justice of the Supreme Court 1921–30.

Born in Cincinnati, Ohio, Taft graduated from Yale University and Cincinnati Law School. His first interest was always the judiciary, although he accepted a post as governor of the Philippines and took responsibility for the construction of the ◊Panama Canal. His single term as president was characterized by struggles against progressives, although he prosecuted more trusts than had his predecessor. As chief justice of the Supreme Court, he supported a minimum wage.

Tagalog member of the majority ethnic group living around Manila on the island of Luzon, in the Philippines, and numbering about 10 million (1988). The Tagalog live by fishing and trading. In its standardized form, known as Pilipino, Tagalog is the official language of the Philippines, and belongs to the Western branch of the Austronesian family. The Tagalogs' religion is a mixture of animism, Christianity, and Islam.

Taglioni Marie 1804–1884. Italian dancer. A ballerina of ethereal style and exceptional lightness, she was the first to use ◊pointe work, or dancing on the toes, as an expressive part of ballet rather than as sheer technique. She created many roles, including the title role in *La Sylphide* 1832, first performed at the Paris Opéra, and choreographed by her father *Filippo* (1771–1871).

Tagore Rabindranath 1861–1941. Bengali Indian writer, born in Calcutta, who translated into English his own verse *Gitanjali* ("song offerings") 1912 and his verse play *Chitra* 1896. Nobel Prize for Literature 1913.

Tahiti largest of the Society Islands, in ◊French Polynesia; area 402 sq mi/1,042 sq km; population (1983) 116,000. Its capital is Papeete. Tahiti was visited by Capt James ◊Cook 1769 and by Admiral ◊Bligh of the *Bounty* 1788. It came under French control 1843 and became a colony 1880.

Tai member of any of the groups of SE Asian peoples who speak Tai languages, all of which belong to the Sino-Tibetan language family. There are over 60 million speakers, the majority of whom live in Thailand. Tai peoples are also found in SW China, NW Myanmar (Burma), Laos, and N Vietnam.

T'ai Chi series of 108 complex, slow-motion movements, each named (for example, the White Crane Spreads Its Wings) and designed to ensure effective circulation of the *chi*, or intrinsic energy of the universe, through the mind and body. It derives partly

Taft *The 27th president of the United States of America, William H Taft, a Republican.*

Taiwan
Republic of China
(*Chung Hua Min Kuo*)

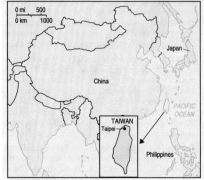

area 13,965 sq mi/36,179 sq km
capital Taipei
cities ports Kaohsiung, Keelung
physical island (formerly Formosa) off People's Republic of China; mountainous, with lowlands in W
environment industrialization has taken its toll: an estimated 30% of the annual rice crop is dangerously contaminated with mercury, cadmium, and other heavy metals
features Penghu (Pescadores), Jinmen (Quemoy), Mazu (Matsu) islands
head of state Lee Teng-hui from 1988
head of government Lien Chan from 1993
political system emergent democracy
political parties Nationalist Party of China (Kuomintang: KMT), anticommunist, Chinese nationalist; Democratic Progressive Party (DPP), centrist-pluralist, pro-self-determination grouping; Workers' Party (Kuntang), left of center
exports textiles, steel, plastics, electronics, foodstuffs

currency New Taiwan dollar
population (1992) 20,727,000 (Taiwanese 84%, mainlanders 14%); growth rate 1.4% p.a.
life expectancy 70 men, 75 women (1986)
languages Mandarin Chinese (official); Taiwan, Hakka dialects
religions officially atheist; Taoist, Confucian, Buddhist, Christian
literacy 90% (1988)
GNP $119.1 bn; $6,200 per head (1988)

chronology
1683 Taiwan (Formosa) annexed by China.
1895 Ceded to Japan.
1945 Recovered by China.
1949 Flight of Nationalist government to Taiwan after Chinese communist revolution.
1954 US-Taiwanese mutual defense treaty.
1971 Expulsion from United Nations.
1972 Commencement of legislature elections.
1975 President Chiang Kai-shek died; replaced as Kuomintang leader by his son, Chiang Ching-kuo.
1979 US severed diplomatic relations and annulled 1954 security pact.
1986 Democratic Progressive Party (DPP) formed as opposition to the nationalist Kuomintang.
1987 Martial law lifted; opposition parties legalized; press restrictions lifted.
1988 President Chiang Ching-kuo died; replaced by Taiwanese-born Lee Teng-hui.
1989 Kuomintang won assembly elections.
1990 Formal move toward normalization of relations with China. Hau Pei-tsun became prime minister.
1991 President Lee Teng-hui declared end to state of civil war with China. Constitution amended. Kuomintang won landslide victory in assembly elections.
1992 Diplomatic relations with South Korea broken. Dec: in first fully democratic elections Kuomintang lost support to DPP but still secured a majority of seats.
1993 Lien Chan appointed prime minister. Cooperation pact with China signed.

from the Shaolin ◊martial arts of China and partly from ◊Taoism.

taiga or ***boreal forest*** Russian name for the forest zone south of the ◊tundra, found across the northern hemisphere. Here, dense forests of conifers (spruces and hemlocks), birches, and poplars occupy glaciated regions punctuated with cold lakes, streams, bogs, and marshes. Winters are prolonged and very cold, but the summer is warm enough to promote dense growth.

Taipei or ***Taibei*** capital and commercial center of Taiwan; population (1990) 2,719,700. Industries include electronics, plastics, textiles, and machinery. The National Palace Museum 1965 houses the world's greatest collection of Chinese art, taken there from the mainland 1948.

Taira or ***Heike*** in Japanese history, a military clan prominent in the 10th–12th centuries and dominant at court 1159–85. Their destruction by their rivals, the ◊Minamoto, 1185 is the subject of the 13th-century literary classic *Heike Monogatari/The Tale of the Heike.*

Taiwan country in E Asia, officially the Republic of China, occupying the island of Taiwan between the E China Sea and the S China Sea, separated from the coast of China by the Formosa Strait.

Taiyuan capital of Shanxi province, on the river Fen He, NE China; industries include iron, steel, agricultural machinery, and textiles; population (1989)

1,900,000. It is a walled city, founded in the 5th century AD, and is the seat of Shanxi University.

Tajik or ***Tadzhik*** speaker of any of the Tajiki dialects that belong to the Iranian branch of the Indo-European family. The Tajiks have long been associated with neighboring Turkic peoples and their language contains Altaic loan words. The Tajiks inhabit Tajikistan, parts of Uzbekistan, and Afghanistan.

Tajikistan (formerly until 1991 ***Tadzhikistan***) country in central Asia, bounded N by Kyrgyzstan and Uzbekistan, E by China, and S by Afghanistan and Pakistan.

Taj Mahal white marble mausoleum built 1630–53 on the river Jumna near Agra, India. Erected by Shah Jahan to the memory of his favorite wife, it is a celebrated example of Indo-Islamic architecture, the fusion of Muslim and Hindu styles. *See illustration p. 900*

takahe flightless bird *Porphyrio mantelli* of the rail family, native to New Zealand. It is about 2 ft/60 cm tall, with blue and green plumage and a red beak. The takahe was thought to have become extinct at the end of the 19th century, but small numbers were rediscovered 1948 in a mountain valley on South Island.

Talbot William Henry Fox 1800–1877. English pioneer of photography. He invented the paper-based calotype process, the first negative/positive method.

Talbot made photograms several years before Louis Daguerre's invention was announced.

talc $Mg_3Si_4O_{10}(OH)_2$, mineral, hydrous magnesium silicate. It occurs in tabular crystals, but the massive impure form, known as *steatite* or *soapstone*, is more common. It is formed by the alteration of magnesium compounds and usually found in metamorphic rocks. Talc is very soft, ranked 1 on the Mohs' scale of hardness. It is used in powdered form in cosmetics, lubricants, and as an additive in paper manufacture.

Talgai skull cranium of a pre-adult male, dated from 10,000–20,000 years ago, found at Talgai station, S Queensland, Australia. It was one of the earliest human archeological finds in Australia, having been made in 1886. Its significance was not realized, however, until the work of Edgeworth David and others after 1914.

Tallahassee (Cree Indian "old town") capital of Florida; an agricultural and lumbering center; population (1990) 124,800. The Spanish explorer Hernando ◊de Soto founded an Indian settlement here 1539, and the site was chosen as the Florida territorial capital 1821.

Talleyrand Charles Maurice de Talleyrand-Périgord 1754–1838. French politician and diplomat. As bishop of Autun 1789–91 he supported moderate reform during the ◊French Revolution, was excommunicated by the pope, and fled to the US during the Reign of Terror (persecution of antirevolutionaries). He returned and became foreign minister under the Directory 1797–99 and under Napoleon 1799–1807. He represented France at the Congress of ◊Vienna 1814–15.

Tallinn (German *Reval*) naval port and capital of Estonia; population (1987) 478,000. Industries include electrical and oil-drilling machinery, textiles, and paper. Founded 1219, it was a member of the ◊Hanseatic League; it passed to Sweden 1561 and to Russia 1750. Vyshgorod castle (13th century) and other medieval buildings remain.

Talmud the two most important works of post-Biblical Jewish literature. The Babylonian and the Palestinian (or Jerusalem) Talmud provide a compilation of ancient Jewish law and tradition. The Babylonian Talmud was edited at the end of the 5th century AD and is the more authoritative version for later Judaism; both Talmuds are written in a mix of Hebrew and Ara-

takahe The takahe is a flightless member of the rail family, native to New Zealand.

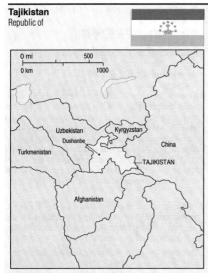

Tajikistan
Republic of

area 55,251 sq mi/143,100 sq km
capital Dushanbe
cities Khodzhent (formerly Leninabad), Kurgan-Tyube, Kulyab
physical mountainous, more than half of its territory lying above 10,000 ft/3,000 m; huge mountain glaciers, which are the source of many rapid rivers
features Pik Kommunizma (Communism Peak); health resorts and mineral springs
head of state Imamoli Rakhmanov from 1992
head of government Abdumalik Abdullajanov from 1992
political system emergent democracy
political parties Socialist (formerly Communist) Party of Tajikistan (SPT); Democratic Party; Islamic Revival Party
products fruit, cereals, cotton, cattle, sheep, silks, carpets, coal, lead, zinc, chemicals, oil, gas
population (1992) 5,568,000 (Tajik 63%, Uzbek 24%, Russian 8%, Tatar 1%, Kyrgyz 1%, Ukrainian 1%)
language Tajik, similar to Farsi (Persian)
religion Sunni Muslim

chronology
1921 Part of Turkestan Soviet Socialist Autonomous Republic.
1929 Became a constituent republic of USSR.
1990 Ethnic Tajik-Armenian conflict in Dushanbe resulted in rioting against Communist Party of Tajikistan (CPT); state of emergency and curfew imposed.
1991 Jan: curfew lifted in Dushanbe. March: maintenance of Soviet Union endorsed in referendum; President Makhkamov forced to resign after failed antiGorbachev coup; CPT broke links with Moscow. Sept: declared independence; Rakhman Nabiyev elected president; CPT renamed Socialist Party of Tajikistan; state of emergency declared. Dec: joined new Commonwealth of Independent States.
1992 Jan: admitted into Conference for Security and Cooperation in Europe. Nabiyev temporarily ousted; state of emergency lifted. Feb: joined the Muslim Economic Cooperation Organization. March: admitted into United Nations; US diplomatic recognition achieved. May: coalition government formed. Sept: Nabiyev forced to resign; replaced by Imamoli Rakhmanov; Abdumalik Abdullajanov became prime minister.
1993 Civil war between the forces of the country's communist former rulers and Islamic and prodemocracy groups continued to rage.

Taj Mahal Over 20,000 laborers were employed in the construction of the Taj Mahal (1630–53) near Agra, N India.

maic. They contain the commentary (*gemara*) on the ◊Mishna (early rabbinical commentaries compiled about AD 200), and the material can be generally divided into *halakhah*, consisting of legal and ritual matters, and *haggadah*, concerned with ethical, theological, and folklorist matters.

tamarind evergreen tropical tree *Tamarindus indica*, family Leguminosae, native to the Old World, with pinnate leaves and reddish-yellow flowers, followed by pods. The pulp surrounding the seeds is used medicinally and as a flavoring.

tamarisk any small tree or shrub of the genus *Tamarix*, flourishing in warm, salty, desert regions of Europe and Asia where no other vegetation is found. The common tamarisk *T. gallica* has scalelike leaves and spikes of very small, pink flowers.

tambourine musical percussion instrument of ancient origin, almost unchanged since Roman times, consisting of a shallow drum with a single skin and loosely set jingles in the rim that increase its effect.

Tamerlane or *Tamburlaine* or *Timur i Leng* ("Timur the Lame") 1336–1405. Mongol ruler of Samarkand, in Uzbekistan, from 1369 who conquered Persia, Azerbaijan, Armenia, and Georgia. He defeated the Golden Horde 1395, sacked Delhi 1398, invaded Syria and Anatolia, and captured the Ottoman sultan in Ankara 1402; he died invading China. He was a descendant of the Mongol leader Genghis Khan and the great-grandfather of Babur, founder of the Mogul Empire.

Tamil member of the majority ethnic group living in the Indian state of Tamil Nadu (formerly Madras). Tamils also live in S India, N Sri Lanka, Malaysia, Singapore, and South Africa, totaling 35–55 million worldwide. Tamil belongs to the Dravidian family of languages; written records in Tamil date from the 3rd century BC. The 3 million Tamils in Sri Lanka are predominantly Hindu, although some are Muslims, unlike the Sinhalese majority, who are mainly Buddhist. The

Tamil Tigers, most prominent of the various Tamil groupings, are attempting to create a separate homeland in N Sri Lanka through both political and military means.

Tamil Nadu formerly (until 1968) *Madras State* state of SE India
area 50,219 sq mi/130,100 sq km
capital Madras
products mainly industrial: cotton, textiles, silk, electrical machinery, tractors, rubber, sugar refining
population (1991) 55,638,300
language Tamil
history the present state was formed 1956. Tamil Nadu comprises part of the former British Madras presidency (later province) formed from areas taken from France and Tipu Sahib, the sultan of Mysore, in the 18th century, which became a state of the Republic of India 1950. The NE was detached to form Andhra Pradesh 1953; in 1956 other areas went to Kerala and Mysore (now Karnataka), and the Laccadive Islands (now Lakshadweep) became a separate Union Territory.

Tampa port and resort on Tampa Bay in W Florida; population (1990) 280,000. Industries include fruit and vegetable canning, shipbuilding, and the manufacture of fertilizers, clothing, beer, and cigars.

Tampere (Swedish *Tammerfors*) city in SW Finland; population (1990) 172,600, metropolitan area 258,000. Industries include textiles, paper, footwear, and turbines. It is the second-largest city in Finland.

Tampico port on the Rio Pánuco, 6 mi/10 km from the Gulf of Mexico, in Tamaulipas state, Mexico; population (1980) 268,000. Industries include oil refining and fishing.

tanager any of various New World passerine birds, of the family Emberizidae, which also includes ◊blackbirds, ◊orioles, and grackles. Tanagers that breed in N America all belong to the genus *Piranga* and include the scarlet tanager *P. olivacea*, about 7 in/18 cm long.

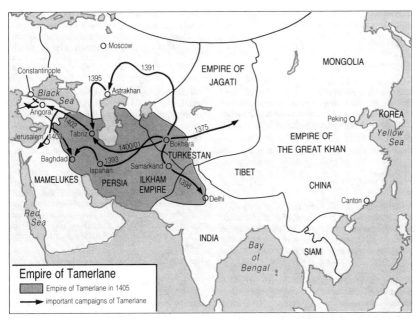

Empire of Tamerlane

▮ Empire of Tamerlane in 1405

➤ important campaigns of Tamerlane

There are about 230 species in forests of Central and South America; all males are brilliantly colored.

Tananarive former name for ◊Antananarivo, the capital of Madagascar.

Taney Roger Brooke 1777–1864. US lawyer. He was President Jackson's attorney general 1831, and US secretary of the treasury 1833–35. In 1835 he was appointed as chief justice of the US Supreme Court. In the Dred Scott case 1857 he ruled that Congress had no right to ban slavery in the territories, a decision that gravely aggravated sectional tensions.

Tanganyika former British colony in E Africa, which now forms the mainland of ◊Tanzania.

Tanganyika, Lake lake 2,534 ft/772 m above sea level in the Great Rift Valley, E Africa, with Zaire to the W, Zambia to the S, and Tanzania and Burundi to the E. It is about 400 mi/645 km long, with an area of about 12,000 sq mi/31,000 sq km, and is the deepest lake (4,710 ft/1,435 m) in Africa. The mountains around its shores rise to about 8,860 ft/2,700 m. The chief ports on the lake are Bujumbura (Burundi), Kigoma (Tanzania), and Kalémié (Zaire).

Tang dynasty the greatest of China's imperial dynasties, which ruled 618–907. Founded by the Sui official Li Yuan (566–635), it extended Chinese authority into central Asia, Tibet, Korea, and Annam, establishing what was then the world's largest empire. The dynasty's peak was reached during the reign (712–56) of Emperor Minghuang (Hsuan-tsung).

tangent in geometry, a straight line that touches a curve and gives the gradient of the curve at the point of contact. At a maximum, minimum, or point of inflection, the tangent to a curve has zero gradient. Also, in trigonometry, a function of an acute angle in a right-angled triangle, defined as the ratio of the length of the side opposite the angle to the length of the side adjacent to it; a way of expressing the gradient of a line.

Tangier or *Tangiers* or *Tanger* port in N Morocco, on the Strait of Gibraltar; population (1982) 436,227. It was a Phoenician trading center in the 15th century BC.

Captured by the Portuguese 1471, it passed to England 1662 as part of the dowry of Catherine of Braganza, but was abandoned 1684, and later became a lair of ◊Barbary Coast pirates. From 1923 Tangier and a small surrounding enclave became an international zone, administered by Spain 1940–45. In 1956 it was transferred to independent Morocco and became a free port 1962.

tank armored fighting vehicle that runs on tracks and is fitted with weapons systems capable of defeating other tanks and destroying life and property. The term was originally a code name for the first effective tracked and armored fighting vehicle, invented by the British soldier and scholar Ernest Swinton, and used in the battle of the Somme 1916.

tanager The male scarlet tanager is distinguished by its bright red plumage and black wings and tail.

Tannenberg, Battle of two battles, named after a village now in N Poland: *1410* the Poles and Lithuanians defeated the Teutonic Knights, establishing Poland as a major power; *1914* during World War I, when Tannenberg was part of East Prussia, ◊Hindenburg defeated the Russians.

tannic acid or *tannin* $C_{14}H_{10}O_9$ yellow astringent substance, composed of several phenol rings, occurring in the bark, wood, roots, fruits, and galls (growths) of certain trees, such as the oak. It precipitates gelatin to give an insoluble compound, used in the manufacture of leather from hides (tanning).

tanning treating animal skins to preserve them and make them into leather. In vegetable tanning, the prepared skins are soaked in tannic acid. Chrome tanning, which is much quicker, uses solutions of chromium salts.

tantalum hard, ductile, lustrous, gray-white, metallic element, symbol Ta, atomic number 73, atomic weight 180.948. It occurs with niobium in tantalite and other minerals. It can be drawn into wire with a very high melting point and great tenacity, useful for lamp filaments subject to vibration. It is also used in alloys, for corrosion-resistant laboratory apparatus and chemical equipment, as a catalyst in manufacturing synthetic rubber, in tools and instruments, and in rectifiers and capacitors.

Tantrism forms of Hinduism and Buddhism that emphasize the division of the universe into male and female forces that maintain its unity by their interaction; this gives women equal status with men. Tantric Hinduism is associated with magical and sexual yoga practices that imitate the union of Siva and Sakti, as described in religious books known as the *Tantras*. In Buddhism, the *Tantras* are texts attributed to the Buddha, describing methods of attaining enlightenment.

Tanzania country in E Africa, bounded N by Uganda and Kenya; S by Mozambique, Malawi, and Zambia; W by Zaire, Burundi, and Rwanda; and E by the Indian Ocean.

Taoism Chinese philosophical system, traditionally founded by the Chinese philosopher Lao Zi 6th century BC. He is also attributed authorship of the scriptures, *Tao Te Ching*, although these were apparently compiled 3rd century BC. The "tao" or "way" denotes the hidden principle of the universe, and less stress is laid on good deeds than on harmonious interaction with the environment, which automatically ensures right behavior. The magical side of Taoism is illustrated by the *I Ching* or *Book of Changes*, a book of divination.

tap dancing rapid step dance, derived from clog dancing. Its main characteristic is the tapping of toes and heels accentuated by steel taps affixed to the shoes. It was popularized in vaudeville and in 1930s films by such dancers as Fred Astaire and Bill "Bojangles" Robinson (1878–1949).

tape recording, magnetic method of recording electric signals on a layer of iron oxide, or other mag-

Tanzania
United Republic of
(*Jamhuri ya Muungano wa Tanzania*)

political system one-party socialist republic
political party Revolutionary Party of Tanzania (CCM), African, socialist
exports coffee, cotton, sisal, cloves, tea, tobacco, cashew nuts, diamonds
currency Tanzanian shilling
population (1992) 25,809,000; growth rate 3.5% p.a.
life expectancy men 49, women 54 (1989)
languages Kiswahili, English (both official)
religions Muslim 35%, Christian 35%, traditional 30%
literacy 85% (1987)
GNP $4.9 bn; $258 per head (1987)

chronology
16th–17th centuries Zanzibar under Portuguese control.
1890–1963 Zanzibar a British protectorate.
1920–46 Tanganyika administered as a British League of Nations mandate.
1946–62 Tanganyika under United Nations (UN) trusteeship.
1961 Tanganyika achieved independence from Britain, within the Commonwealth, with Julius Nyerere as prime minister.
1962 Tanganyika became a republic with Nyerere as president.
1964 Tanganyika and Zanzibar became the United Republic of Tanzania with Nyerere as president.
1967 East African Community (EAC) formed. Nyerere committed himself to building a socialist state (the Arusha Declaration).
1977 Revolutionary Party of Tanzania (CCM) proclaimed the only legal party. EAC dissolved.
1978 Ugandan forces repulsed after crossing into Tanzania.
1979 Tanzanian troops sent to Uganda to help overthrow the president, Idi Amin.
1985 Nyerere retired from presidency but stayed on as CCM leader; Ali Hassan Mwinyi became president.
1990 Nyerere surrendered CCM leadership; replaced by President Mwinyi.
1992 CCM agreed to abolish one-party rule. East African cooperation pact with Kenya and Uganda to be reestablished.

area 364,865 sq mi/945,000 sq km
capital Dodoma (since 1983)
cities Zanzibar Town, Mwanza; chief port and former capital Dar es Salaam
physical central plateau; lakes in N and W; coastal plains; lakes Victoria, Tanganyika, and Nyasa
environment the black rhino faces extinction as a result of poaching
features comprises islands of Zanzibar and Pemba; Mount Kilimanjaro, 19,340 ft/5,895 m, the highest peak in Africa; Serengeti National Park, Olduvai Gorge; Ngorongoro Crater, 9 mi/14.5 km across, 2,500 ft/762 m deep
head of state and government Ali Hassan Mwinyi from 1985

netic material, coating a thin plastic tape. The electrical signals from the microphone are fed to the electromagnetic recording head, which magnetizes the tape in accordance with the frequency and amplitude of the original signal. The impulses may be audio (for sound recording), video (for television), or data (for computer). For playback, the tape is passed over the same, or another, head to convert magnetic into electrical signals, which are then amplified for reproduction. Tapes are easily demagnetized (erased) for reuse, and come in cassette, cartridge, or reel form.

tapestry ornamental woven textile used for wall hangings, furniture, and curtains. The tapestry design is threaded into the warp with various shades of yarn. The great European centers of tapestry weaving were in Belgium, France, and England. The ◊Bayeux Tapestry is an embroidery rather than a true tapestry.

tapeworm any of various parasitic flatworms of the class Cestoda. They lack digestive and sense organs, can reach 50 ft/15 m in length, and attach themselves to the host's intestines by means of hooks and suckers. Tapeworms are made up of hundreds of individual segments, each of which develops into a functional hermaphroditic reproductive unit capable of producing numerous eggs. The larvae of tapeworms usually reach humans in imperfectly cooked meat or fish, causing anemia and intestinal disorders.

tapir any of the odd-toed hoofed mammals (perissodactyls) of the single genus *Tapirus*, now constituting the family Tapiridae. There are four species living in the American and Malaysian tropics. They reach 3 ft/1 m at the shoulder and weigh up to 770 lb/350 kg. Their survival is in danger because of destruction of the forests.

taproot in botany, a single, robust, main ◊root that is derived from the embryonic root, or radicle, and grows vertically downward, often to considerable depth. Taproots are often modified for food storage and are common in biennial plants such as the carrot *Daucus carota*, where they act as perennating organs.

tar dark brown or black viscous liquid obtained by the destructive distillation of coal, shale, and wood. Tars consist of a mixture of hydrocarbons, acids, and bases. ◊Creosote and ◊paraffin are produced from wood tar.

Taranto naval base and port in Puglia region, SE Italy; population (1988) 245,000. It is an important commercial center, and its steelworks are part of the new industrial complex of S Italy. It was the site of the ancient Greek *Tarentum*, founded in the 8th century BC by ◊Sparta, and was captured by the Romans 272 BC.

tarantula wolf spider *Lycosa tarantula* with a 1 in/2.5 cm body. It spins no web, relying on its speed in hunting to catch its prey. The name "tarantula" is also used for any of the numerous large, hairy spiders of the family Theraphosidae, with large poison fangs, native to the SW US and tropical America.

Tarbell Ida Minerva 1857–1944. US journalist whose exposés of corruption in high places made her one of the most prominent "muckrakers" in the US. She was an editor and contributor to *McClure's Magazine* 1894–1906. Her book *The History of the Standard Oil Company* 1904 sparked antitrust reform.

tariff tax or duty placed on goods when they are imported into a country or trading bloc (such as the European Community) from outside. The aim of tar-

tapeworm *Electron-microscope picture (x 200) of the head of a tapeworm, showing the hooks used to cling on to the host's tissues.*

iffs is to reduce imports by making them more expensive.

Tarkington Booth 1869–1946. US novelist. His novels for young people, which include *Penrod* 1914, are classics. He was among the best-selling authors of the early 20th century with works such as *Monsieur Beaucaire* 1900 and novels of the Midwest, including *The Magnificent Ambersons* 1918 (filmed 1941 by Orson Welles).

tarot cards fortune-telling aid consisting of 78 cards: the *minor arcana* in four suits (resembling playing cards) and the *major arcana*, 22 cards with densely symbolic illustrations that have links with astrology and the ◊Kabbala.

tarpon large silver-sided fish *Tarpon atlanticus* of the family Megalopidae. It reaches 6 ft/2 m and may weigh 300 lb/135 kg. It lives in warm W Atlantic waters.

Tarquinius Superbus lived 6th century BC. Last king of Rome 534–510 BC. He abolished certain rights of Romans, and made the city powerful. According to legend, he was deposed when his son Sextus raped ◊Lucretia.

tarragon perennial bushy herb *Artemisia dracunculus* of the daisy family Compositae, native to the Old World, growing to 5 ft/1.5 m, with narrow leaves and small green-white flower heads arranged in groups. Tarragon contains an aromatic oil; its leaves are used to flavor salads, pickles, and tartar sauce. It is closely related to wormwood.

Tarzan fictitious hero inhabiting the African rain forest, created by US writer Edgar Rice ◊Burroughs in *Tarzan of the Apes* 1914, with numerous sequels. He and his partner Jane have featured in films, comic strips, and television series.

Tasaday member of an indigenous people of the rain forests of Mindanao in the ◊Philippines, contacted in the 1960s. Some anthropologists doubt their claim to leading a hunter-gatherer way of life.

Tashkent capital of Uzbekistan; population (1990) 2,100,000. Industries include the manufacture of mining machinery, chemicals, textiles, and leather goods. Founded in the 7th century, it was taken by the Turks in the 12th century and captured by Tamerlane

1361. In 1865 it was taken by the Russians. It was severely damaged by an earthquake 1966.

Tasman Abel Janszoon 1603–1659. Dutch navigator. In 1642, he was the first European to see Tasmania. He also made the first European sightings of New Zealand, Tonga, and Fiji.

Tasmania former name (1642–1856) *Van Diemen's Land* island off the S coast of Australia; a state of the Commonwealth of Australia;
area 26,171 sq mi/67,800 sq km
capital Hobart
cities Launceston (chief port)
features an island state (including small islands in the Bass Strait, and Macquarie Island); Franklin River, a wilderness area saved from a hydroelectric scheme 1983, which also has a prehistoric site; unique fauna including the Tasmanian devil
products wool, dairy products, apples and other fruit, timber, iron, tin, coal, copper, silver
population (1987) 448,000
history the first European to visit here was Abel Tasman 1642; the last of the Tasmanian Aboriginals died 1876.
Tasmania joined the Australian Commonwealth as a state 1901.

Tasmanian devil carnivorous marsupial *Sarcophilus harrisii*, in the same family (Dasyuridae) as native "cats." It is about 2.1 ft/65 cm long with a 10 in/25 cm bushy tail. It has a large head, strong teeth, and is blackish with white patches on the chest and hind parts. It is nocturnal, carnivorous, and can be ferocious when cornered. It has recently become extinct in Australia and survives only in remote parts of Tasmania.

Tasmanian wolf or *thylacine* carnivorous marsupial *Thylacinus cynocephalus*, in the family Dasyuridae. It is doglike in appearance and can be nearly 2 m 6 ft/2 m from nose to tail tip. It was hunted to probable extinction in the 1930s, but there are still occasional unconfirmed reports of sightings.

Tasso Torquato 1544–1595. Italian poet, author of the romantic epic poem of the First Crusade *Gerusalemme Liberata/Jerusalem Delivered* 1574, followed by the *Gerusalemme Conquistata/Jerusalem Conquered*, written during the period from 1576 when he was mentally unstable.

taste sense that detects some of the chemical constituents of food. The human ◊tongue can distinguish only four basic tastes (sweet, sour, bitter, and salty) but it is supplemented by the nose's sense of smell. What we refer to as taste is really a composite sense made up of both taste and smell.

Tatar or *Tartar* member of a Turkic people, the descendants of the mixed Mongol and Turkic followers of ◊Genghis Khan, called the Golden Horde because of the wealth they gained by plunder. The vast Tatar state was conquered by Russia 1552. The Tatars now live mainly in the Russian autonomous republic of Tatarstan, W Siberia, Turkmenistan, and

Uzbekistan (where they were deported from the Crimea 1944). There are over 5 million speakers of the Tatar language, which belongs to the Turkic branch of the Altaic family. The Tatar people are mainly Muslim, although some have converted to the Orthodox Church.

Tatarstan formerly *Tatar Autonomous Republic* autonomous republic of E Russia;
area 26,250 sq mi/68,000 sq km
capital Kazan
products oil, chemicals, textiles, timber
population (1986) 3,537,000 (48% Tatar, 43% Russian)
history a territory of Volga-Kama Bulgar state from the 10th century when Islam was introduced; conquered by the Mongols 1236; the capital of the powerful Khanate of Kazan until conquered by Russia 1552; an autonomous republic from 1920. In recent years the republic (mainly Muslim and an important industrial and oil-producing area) has seen moves toward increased autonomy. In Aug 1990 the republic's assembly upgraded Tatarstan to full republic status, proclaiming its economic and political "sovereignty," and in April 1991 there were popular demonstrations in support of this action. In June 1991 it refused to participate in the Russian presidential election, and in March 1992 declined to be party to a federal treaty, signed in Moscow by 18 of Russia's other 20 main political subdivisions. A referendum March 21, 1992, favored Tatarstan becoming a sovereign state within Russia.

Taurus zodiacal constellation in the northern hemisphere near Orion, represented as a bull. The Sun passes through Taurus from mid-May to late June. Its brightest star is Aldebaran, seen as the bull's red eye. Taurus contains the Hyades and Pleiades open ◊star clusters, and the Crab nebula. In astrology, the dates for Taurus are between about April 20 and May 20.

tautology repetition of the same thing in different words. For example, it is tautologous to say that something is *most unique*, since something unique cannot, by definition, be comparative.

taxation the raising of money from individuals and organizations by state and local governments, to pay for the goods and services they provide. Taxation can be direct (a deduction from income) or indirect (added to the purchase price of goods or services—that is, a tax on consumption).

taxis (plural *taxes*) or *tactic movement* in botany, the movement of a single cell, such as a bacterium, protozoan, single-celled alga, or gamete, in response to an external stimulus. A movement directed toward the stimulus is described as positive taxis, and away from it as negative taxis. The alga *Chlamydomonas*, for example, demonstrates positive *phototaxis* by swimming toward a light source to increase the rate of photosynthesis. *Chemotaxis* is a response to a chemical stimulus, as seen in many bacteria that move toward higher concentrations of nutrients.

taxonomy another name for the ◊classification of living organisms.

Taylor Elizabeth 1932– . English-born US actress. Noted for both her beauty and acting skill, her films include *Lassie Come Home* 1942, *National Velvet* 1944, *Father of the Bride* 1950, *Giant* 1956, *Raintree County* 1957, *Cat on a Hot Tin Roof* 1958, *Butterfield 8* 1960 (Academy Award), *Cleopatra* 1963, and *Who's Afraid of Virginia Woolf?* 1966 (Academy Award). She appeared on Broadway in *The Little Foxes* 1981.

Tasmanian devil
The Tasmanian devil, despite its name, is no more vicious than any other carnivore.

Taylor Zachary 1784–1850. 12th president of the US 1849–50. A veteran of the War of 1812 and a hero of the Mexican War (1846–48), he was nominated for the presidency by the Whigs 1848 and was elected, but died less than one and a half years into his term. He was succeeded by Vice President Millard Fillmore.

Taylor was born in Virginia but grew up in frontier Kentucky. He began 40 years of army service 1808 and played a key role in Fort Harrison's defense during the War of 1812. Most of his military career was spent on the frontier, and he distinguished himself in campaigns against the Indians. In the Seminole Wars in Florida his successes led to his promotion to brigadier general and command of the Florida department (1838–40). By now known by his nickname "Old Rough and Ready," Taylor won his greatest fame in the Mexican War. While commander of the US forces occupying the recently annexed Texas, he opposed Mexican forces on President Polk's orders.

In spring 1846, Taylor advanced into Mexico and almost immediately won several battles and a promotion to major general. By fall he had taken Monterrey and in Feb 1847 defeated Santa Anna at Buena Vista. Having defeated his opponents Lewis Cass and Martin van Buren for the presidency, Taylor found his short term in office dominated by controversies over the slavery issue, with Taylor supporting the antislavery elements that were pushing for the admission to the Union of more free states. Taylor died unexpectedly of cholera while the Compromise of 1850 was being shaped.

Tay-Sachs disease inherited disorder, due to a defective gene, causing an enzyme deficiency that leads to blindness, retardation, and death in childhood. Because of their enforced isolation and inbreeding during hundreds of years, it is most common in people of E European Jewish descent.

Tayside region of Scotland
area 2,973 sq mi/7,700 sq km
cities Dundee (administrative headquarters), Perth, Arbroath, Forfar
features river Tay; ◊Grampian Mountains; Lochs Tay and Rannoch; hills: Ochil and Sidlaw; vales of the North and South Esk
products beef and dairy products, soft fruit from the fertile Carse of Gowrie (SW of Dundee)
population (1991) 385,300
famous people J M Barrie, John Buchan, Princess Margaret.

TB abbreviation for the infectious disease ◊tuberculosis.

Tbilisi formerly *Tiflis* capital of the Republic of Georgia; industries include textiles, machinery, ceramics, and tobacco; population (1987) 1,194,000. Dating from the 5th century, it is a center of Georgian culture, with fine medieval churches. Anti-Russian demonstrations were quashed here by troops 1981 and 1989; the latter clash followed rejected demands for autonomy from the Abkhazia enclave, and resulted in 19 or more deaths from poison gas (containing chloroacetophenone) and 100 injured. In Dec 1991 at least 50 people were killed as well-armed opposition forces attempted to overthrow President Gamsakhurdia, eventually forcing him to flee.

T cell or *T lymphocyte* immune cell (see ◊immunity and ◊lymphocyte) that plays several roles in the body's defenses. T cells are so called because they mature in the ◊thymus.

Tchaikovsky Pyotr Il'yich 1840–1893. Russian composer. His strong sense of melody, personal expres-

sion, and brilliant orchestration are clear throughout his many Romantic works, which include six symphonies, three piano concertos, a violin concerto, operas (for example, *Eugene Onegin* 1879), ballets (for example, *The Nutcracker* 1892), orchestral fantasies (for example, *Romeo and Juliet* 1870), and chamber and vocal music.

tea evergreen shrub *Camellia sinensis*, family Theaceae, of which the fermented, dried leaves are infused to make a beverage of the same name. Known in China as early as 2737 BC, tea was first brought to Europe AD 1610 and rapidly became a fashionable drink. In 1823 it was found growing wild in N India, and plantations were later established in Assam and Sri Lanka; producers today include Africa, South America, Georgia, Azerbaijan, Indonesia, and Iran.

teak tropical Asian timber tree *Tectona grandis*, family Verbenaceae, with yellowish wood used in furniture and shipbuilding.

teal any of various small, short-necked dabbling ducks of the genus *Anas*. The drakes generally have a bright head and wing markings. The green-winged teal *A. crecca* is about 14 in/35 cm long.

Teapot Dome Scandal US political scandal that revealed the corruption of President ◊Harding's administration. It centered on the leasing of naval oil reserves 1921 at Teapot Dome, Wyoming, without competitive bidding, as a result of bribing the secretary of the interior, Albert B Fall (1861–1944). Fall was tried and imprisoned 1929.

tear gas any of various volatile gases that produce irritation and tearing of the eyes, used by police against crowds and used in chemical warfare. The gas is delivered in pressurized, liquid-filled canisters or grenades, thrown by hand or launched from a specially adapted rifle. Gases (such as Mace) cause violent coughing and blinding tears, which pass when the victim breathes fresh air, and there are no lasting effects. Blister gases (such as mustard gas) and nerve gases are more harmful and may cause permanent injury or death.

technetium (Greek *technetos* "artificial") silver-gray, radioactive, metallic element, symbol Tc, atomic number 43, atomic weight 98.906. It occurs in nature only in extremely minute amounts, produced as a fission product from uranium in ◊pitchblende and other uranium ores. Its longest-lived isotope, Tc-99, has a half-life of 216,000 years. It is a superconductor and is used as a hardener in steel alloys and as a medical tracer.

technology the use of tools, power, and materials, generally for the purposes of production. Almost every human process for getting food and shelter depends on complex technological systems, which have been developed over a 3-million-year period. Significant milestones include the advent of the ◊steam engine 1712, the introduction of ◊electricity, and the ◊internal combustion engine in the mid-1800s, and recent developments in communications, ◊electronics, and the nuclear and space industries. The *advanced technology* (highly automated and specialized) on which modern industrialized society depends is frequently contrasted with the *low technology* (labor-intensive and unspecialized) that characterizes some developing countries. Intermediate technology is an attempt to adapt scientifically advanced inventions to less developed areas by using local materials and methods of manufacture.

tectonics in geology, the study of the movements of rocks on the Earth's surface. On a small scale tectonics involves the formation of ◊folds and ◊faults, but on a large scale ◊plate tectonics deals with the movement of the Earth's surface as a whole.

Tecumseh 1768–1813. North American Indian chief of the Shawnee. He attempted to unite the Indian peoples from Canada to Florida against the encroachment of white settlers, but the defeat of his brother Tenskwatawa, popularly known as "the Prophet," at the battle of Tippecanoe in Nov 1811 by then-governor of the Indiana Territory W H ◊Harrison, largely destroyed the confederacy built by Tecumseh. He allied himself with the British in the War of 1812, during which he helped take Detroit, fomented the Creek War 1813 in the South, and led an invasion of Ohio. He was killed in Canada at the Battle of the Thames 1813, a battle won by Harrison, who would campaign for the presidency 1840 largely on the strength of his military exploits against Tecumseh.

tefillin or *phylacteries* in Judaism, two small leather boxes containing scrolls from the Torah, that are strapped to the left arm and the forehead by Jewish men for daily prayer.

Tegucigalpa capital of Honduras; population (1989) 608,000. Industries include textiles and food-processing.

Tehran capital of Iran; population (1986) 6,043,000. Industries include textiles, chemicals, engineering, and tobacco. It was founded in the 12th century and made the capital 1788 by Mohammed Shah. Much of the city was rebuilt in the 1920s and 1930s. Tehran is the site of the Gulistan Palace (the former royal residence). There are three universities; the Shahyad Tower is a symbol of modern Iran.

Tehran Conference conference held 1943 in Tehran, Iran, the first meeting of World War II Allied leaders Churchill, Roosevelt, and Stalin. The chief subject discussed was coordination of Allied strategy in W and E Europe.

Teilhard de Chardin Pierre 1881–1955. French Jesuit theologian, paleontologist, and philosopher. He developed a creative synthesis of nature and religion, based on his fieldwork and fossil studies. Publication of his *Le Phénomène humain/The Phenomenon of Man*, written 1938–40, was delayed (due to his unorthodox views) until after his death by the embargo of his superiors. He saw humanity as being in a constant process of evolution, moving toward a perfect spiritual state.

Te Kanawa Kiri 1944– . New Zealand soprano. Te Kanawa's first major role was the Countess in Mozart's *The Marriage of Figaro* at Covent Garden, London, 1971. Her voice combines the purity and intensity of the upper range with an extended lower range of great richness and resonance. Apart from Classical roles, she has also featured popular music in her repertoire, such as the 1984 recording of Leonard Bernstein's *West Side Story*.

tektite (from *tektos* "molten") small, rounded glassy stone, found in certain regions of the Earth, such as Australasia. Tektites are probably the scattered drops of molten rock thrown out by the impact of a large ◊meteorite.

Tel Aviv officially *Tel Aviv–Jaffa* city in Israel, on the Mediterranean coast; population (1987) 320,000. Industries include textiles, chemicals, sugar, printing, and publishing. Tel Aviv was founded 1909 as a Jewish residential area in the Arab town of Jaffa, with which it was combined 1949; their ports were superseded 1965 by Ashdod to the S.

telecommunications communications over a distance, generally by electronic means. Long-distance voice communication was pioneered 1876 by US inventor Alexander Graham Bell, when he invented the telephone as a result of English chemist and physicist Michael Faraday's discovery of electromagnetism. Today it is possible to communicate with most countries by telephone cable, or by satellite or microwave link, with over 100,000 simultaneous conversations and several television channels being carried by the latest satellites. ◊Integrated Services Digital Network (ISDN) makes videophones and high-quality fax possible; the world's first large-scale center of ISDN began operating in Japan 1988. ISDN is a system that transmits voice and image data on a single transmission line by changing them into digital signals. The chief method of relaying long-distance calls on land is microwave radio transmission.

telegraphy transmission of coded messages along wires by means of electrical signals. The first modern form of telecommunication, it now uses printers for the transmission and receipt of messages. Telex is an international telegraphy network.

telephone instrument for communicating by voice over long distances, invented by US inventor Alexander Graham ◊Bell 1876. The transmitter (mouthpiece) consists of a carbon microphone, with a diaphragm that vibrates when a person speaks into it. The diaphragm vibrations compress grains of carbon to a greater or lesser extent, altering their resistance to an electric current passing through them. This sets up variable electrical signals, which travel along the telephone lines to the receiver of the person being called. There they cause the magnetism of an electromagnet to vary, making a diaphragm above the electromagnet vibrate and give out sound waves, which mirror those that entered the mouthpiece originally.

telephoto lens photographic lens of longer focal length than normal that takes a very narrow view and gives a large image through a combination of telescopic and ordinary photographic lenses.

teleprinter or *teletypewriter* transmitting and receiving device used in telecommunications to handle coded messages. Teleprinters are automatic typewriters keyed telegraphically to convert typed words into electrical signals (using a 5-unit Baudot code, see ◊baud) at the transmitting end, and signals into typed words at the receiving end.

telescope optical instrument that magnifies images of faint and distant objects; any device for collecting and focusing light and other forms of electromagnetic radiation. It is a major research tool in astronomy and is used to sight over land and sea; small telescopes can be attached to cameras and rifles. A telescope with a large aperture, or opening, can distinguish finer detail and fainter objects than one with a small aperture. The *refracting telescope* uses lenses, and the *reflecting telescope* uses mirrors. A third type, the *catadioptric telescope*, with a combination of lenses and mirrors, is used increasingly. See also ◊radio telescope.

televangelist in North America, a fundamentalist Christian minister, often of a Pentecostal church, who hosts a television show and solicits donations from viewers. Well-known televangelists include Jim Bakker, convicted 1989 of fraudulent misuse of donations, and Jimmy Swaggart.

television (TV) reproduction at a distance by radio waves of visual images. For transmission, a television camera converts the pattern of light it takes in into a pattern of electrical charges. This is scanned line by line by a beam of electrons from an electron gun, resulting in variable electrical signals that represent the visual picture. These vision signals are combined with a radio carrier wave and broadcast as magnetic waves. The TV aerial picks up the wave and feeds it to the receiver (TV set). This separates out the vision signals, which pass to a cathode-ray tube. The vision signals control the strength of a beam of electrons from an electron gun, aimed at the screen and making it glow more or less brightly. At the same time the beam is made to scan across the screen line by line, mirroring the action of the gun in the TV camera. The result is a recreation of the pattern of light that entered the camera. Thirty pictures are built up each second with interlaced scanning in North America (25 in Europe), with a total of 525 lines in North America and Japan (625 lines in Europe).

Tell Wilhelm (William) legendary 14th-century Swiss archer, said to have refused to salute the Hapsburg badge at Altdorf on Lake Lucerne. Sentenced to shoot an apple from his son's head, he did so, then shot the tyrannical Austrian ruler Gessler, symbolizing his people's refusal to submit to external authority.

Tell el Amarna site of the ancient Egyptian capital ◊Akhetaton. The ◊Amarna tablets were found there.

Teller Edward 1908– . Hungarian-born US physicist. Born in Budapest, Teller received his PhD from the University of Leipzig 1930. After a period of research at Göttingen 1931–33 and with Niels Bohr in 1934, he immigrated to the US and became a faculty member of George Washington University 1935. Teller joined the staff of Columbia University 1941 and the University of Chicago 1942 to work with Enrico Fermi on atomic fission. From 1941 to 1945 he was also a member of the Manhattan Project, which developed the first atomic bombs. In 1946 Teller was appointed professor at the University of Chicago and played a central role in the development and testing of the first hydrogen bomb 1952.

tellurium (Latin *Tellus* "Earth") silver-white, semi-metallic (◊metalloid) element, symbol Te, atomic number 52, atomic weight 127.60.

Chemically it is similar to sulfur and selenium, and it is considered as one of the sulfur group. It occurs naturally in telluride minerals, and is used in coloring glass blue–brown, in the electrolytic refining of zinc, in electronics, and as a catalyst in refining petroleum.

Telstar US communications satellite, launched July 10, 1962, which relayed the first live television transmissions between the US and Europe. *Telstar* orbited the Earth in 158 minutes, and so had to be tracked by ground stations, unlike the geostationary satellites of today.

tempera painting medium in which powdered pigments are bound together, usually with egg yolk and water. A form of tempera was used in ancient Egypt, and egg tempera was the foremost medium for panel painting in late medieval and early Renaissance Europe. It was gradually superseded by oils from the late 15th century onward.

temperature state of hotness or coldness of a body, and the condition that determines whether or not it will transfer heat to, or receive heat from, another body according to the laws of ◊thermodynamics. It is measured in degrees Celsius (before 1948 called centigrade), kelvin, or Fahrenheit.

The normal temperature of the human body is about 98.4°F/36.9°C. Variation by more than a degree or so indicates ill-health, a rise signifying excessive activity (usually due to infection), and a decrease signifying deficient heat production (usually due to lessened vitality).

Templar member of a Christian military order, founded in Jerusalem 1119, the *Knights of the Temple of Solomon*. The knights took vows of poverty, chastity, and obedience and devoted themselves to the recovery of Palestine from the Muslims.

Temple industrial city (building materials, steel, furniture, railroad supplies) in central Texas, S of Waco; population (1990) 46,100.

television
*Simplified block
diagram of a complete
color television
system—
transmitting and
receiving.*

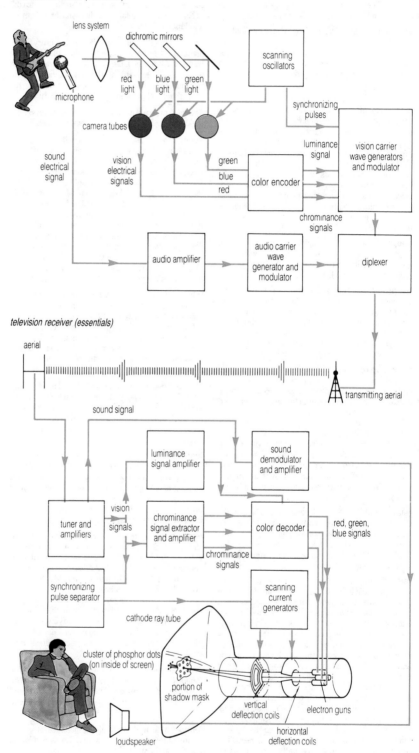

television transmitter (essentials)

lens system

dichromic mirrors

scanning oscillators

red light   blue light   green light

microphone

camera tubes

synchronizing pulses

luminance signal

vision carrier wave generators and modulator

sound electrical signal

vision electrical signals

green
blue
red

color encoder

chrominance signals

audio amplifier

audio carrier wave generator and modulator

diplexer

television receiver (essentials)

aerial

transmitting aerial

sound signal

luminance signal amplifier

sound demodulator and amplifier

vision signals

tuner and amplifiers

chrominance signal extractor and amplifier

color decoder

red, green, blue signals

chrominance signals

synchronizing pulse separator

scanning current generators

cathode ray tube

cluster of phosphor dots (on inside of screen)

portion of shadow mask

vertical deflection coils

electron guns

loudspeaker

horizontal deflection coils

Temple Shirley 1928– . US actress who became the most successful child star of the 1930s. The charming, curly-haired, dimpled tot's films include *Bright Eyes* 1934, in which she sang "On the Good Ship Lollipop"; *Little Miss Marker* 1934; *The Little Colonel* 1935; *Captain January* 1936; *Heidi* 1937; and *The Little Princess* 1939.

Temple of Jerusalem the center of Jewish national worship in both ancient and modern days. The Western or Wailing Wall is the surviving part of the western wall of the platform of the enclosure of the Temple. Solomon built the Temple *c.* 950 BC but it was destroyed by Nebuchadnezzer in 586 BC. It was rebuilt in the late 6th century BC, restored by the ◊Maccabees and later by Herod the Great, but destroyed by the Romans in AD 70. Since then, Jews have come here to pray, to mourn their dispersion and the loss of their homeland.

Ten Commandments in the Old Testament, the laws given by God to the Hebrew leader Moses on Mt Sinai, engraved on two tablets of stone. They are: to have no other gods besides Jehovah; to make no idols; not to misuse the name of God; to keep the sabbath holy; to honor one's parents; not to commit murder, adultery, or theft; not to give false evidence; not to be covetous. They form the basis of Jewish and Christian moral codes; the "tablets of the Law" given to Moses are also mentioned in the Koran. The giving of the Ten Commandments is celebrated in the Jewish festival of *Shavuot* (see ◊Pentecost).

tendon or *sinew* cord of tough, fibrous connective tissue that joins muscle to bone in vertebrates. Tendons are largely composed of the protein collagen, and because of their inelasticity are very efficient at transforming muscle power into movement.

tendril in botany, a slender, threadlike structure that supports a climbing plant by coiling around suitable supports, such as the stems and branches of other plants. It may be a modified stem, leaf, leaflet, flower, leaf stalk, or stipule (a small appendage on either side of the leaf stalk), and may be simple or branched. The tendrils of Virginia creeper *Parthenocissus quinquefolia* are modified flower heads with suckerlike pads at the end that stick to walls, while those of the grapevine *Vitis* grow away from the light and thus enter dark crevices where they expand to anchor the plant firmly.

Tenerife largest of the ◊Canary Islands, Spain; area 795 sq mi/2,060 sq km; population (1981) 557,000. *Santa Cruz* is the main town, and *Pico de Teide* is an active volcano.

Tennessee state in E central US; nickname Volunteer State
area 42,151 sq mi/109,200 sq km
capital Nashville
cities Memphis, Knoxville, Chattanooga, Clarksville

Tennessee

features Tennessee Valley Authority; Great Smoky Mountains National Park; Grand Old Opry, Nashville; Beale Street Historic District and Graceland, estate of Elvis Presley, Memphis; research centers including Oak Ridge National Laboratory
products cereals, cotton, tobacco, soybeans, livestock, timber, coal, zinc, copper, chemicals
population (1990) 4,877,200
famous people Davy Crockett, David Farragut, W C Handy, Cordell Hull, Andrew Jackson, Andrew Johnson, Dolly Parton, John Crowe Ransom, Bessie Smith
history settled by Europeans 1757; became a state 1796. Tennessee was deeply divided in the Civil War; the battles of Shiloh, Murfreesboro, Chattanooga, and Nashville were fought here.

tennis racket and ball game invented toward the end of the 19th century. It was introduced by Major Clopton Wingfield at a Christmas party at Nantclwyn, Wales, in 1873. His game was then called "Sphairistike." It derived from ◊court tennis. Although played on different surfaces (grass, wood, shale, clay, concrete), it is sometimes still called "lawn tennis."

The aim of the two or four players is to strike the ball into the prescribed area of the court, with oval-headed rackets (strung with gut or nylon), in such a way that it cannot be returned. The game is won by those first winning four points (called 15, 30, 40, game), unless both sides reach 40 (deuce), when two consecutive points are needed to win. A set is won by winning six games with a margin of two over opponents, although a tie-break system operates, that is, at six games to each side (or in some cases eight), except in the final set. Major events include the ◊Davis Cup, first contested in 1900 for international men's competition; Wimbledon (originating 1877), a UK open event; and the US, French, and Australian Opens.

Tennyson Alfred, 1st Baron Tennyson 1809–1892. English poet, poet laureate 1850–92, whose verse has a majestic, musical quality. His works include "The Lady of Shalott," "The Lotus Eaters," "Ulysses," "Break, Break, Break," "The Charge of the Light Brigade"; the longer narratives *Locksley Hall* 1832 and *Maud* 1855; the elegy *In Memoriam* 1850; and a long series of poems on the Arthurian legends *The Idylls of the King* 1857–85.

Tenochtitlán capital of the Mexican ◊Aztecs. Founded *c.* 1325 on an island among the lakes that occupied much of the Valley of Mexico, on the site of modern Mexico City. Its population reached about 150,000. Spanish conquistador Hernán ◊Cortés met Aztec ruler ◊Montezuma here Nov 1519. Welcomed as guests, the Spaniards captured Montezuma and forced him to recognize the sovereignty of ◊Charles V. Cortés destroyed Tenochtitlán 1521 and rebuilt it as a Spanish colonial city.

Teotihuacán huge ancient city in central Mexico, founded *c.* 300 BC about 20 mi/32 km N of modern Mexico City. Known as the "metropolis of the gods," it reached its zenith in the 5th–6th centuries. As a religious center of Mesoamerica, it contained two great pyramids and the temple of ◊Quetzalcóatl. It is one of the best-excavated archeological sites in Mexico.

tequila Mexican alcoholic liquor distilled from the ◊agave plant. It is named after the place, near Guadalajara, where the conquistadors first developed it from Aztec *pulque*, which would keep for only a day.

terbium soft, silver-gray, metallic element of the ◊lanthanide series, symbol Tb, atomic number 81, atomic

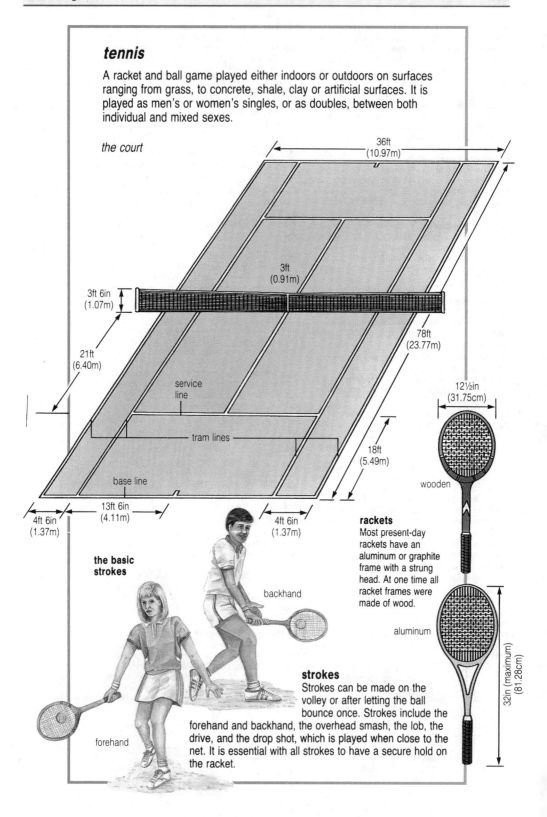

tennis

A racket and ball game played either indoors or outdoors on surfaces ranging from grass, to concrete, shale, clay or artificial surfaces. It is played as men's or women's singles, or as doubles, between both individual and mixed sexes.

the court

36ft
(10.97m)

3ft
(0.91m)

3ft 6in
(1.07m)

21ft
(6.40m)

78ft
(23.77m)

service line

tram lines

18ft
(5.49m)

base line

12½in
(31.75cm)

wooden

13ft 6in
(4.11m)

4ft 6in
(1.37m)

4ft 6in
(1.37m)

rackets
Most present-day rackets have an aluminum or graphite frame with a strung head. At one time all racket frames were made of wood.

the basic strokes

backhand

aluminum

32in (maximum)
(81.28cm)

strokes
Strokes can be made on the volley or after letting the ball bounce once. Strokes include the forehand and backhand, the overhead smash, the lob, the drive, and the drop shot, which is played when close to the net. It is essential with all strokes to have a secure hold on the racket.

forehand

weight 158.925. It occurs in gadolinite and other ores, with yttrium and ytterbium, and is used in lasers, semiconductors, and television tubes. It was named in 1843 by Swedish chemist Carl Mosander (1797–1858) for the town of Ytterby, Sweden, where it was first found.

Terence (Publius Terentius Afer) 190–159 BC. Roman dramatist, born in Carthage and taken as a slave to Rome, where he was freed and came under ◊Scipio Africanus Minor's patronage. His surviving six comedies (including "The Eunuch" 161 BC) are subtly characterized and based on Greek models. They were widely read and performed during the Middle Ages and Renaissance.

Teresa Mother. Born Agnes Bojaxhiu 1910– . Roman Catholic nun. She was born in Skopje, Albania, and at 18 entered a Calcutta convent and became a teacher. In 1948 she became an Indian citizen and founded the Missionaries of Charity, an order for men and women based in Calcutta that helps abandoned children and the dying. She was awarded the Nobel Peace Prize 1979.

Teresa, St 1515–1582. Spanish mystic who founded an order of nuns 1562. She was subject to fainting fits, during which she saw visions. She wrote *The Way to Perfection* 1583 and an autobiography, *Life of the Mother Theresa of Jesus*, 1611. In 1622 she was canonized, and in 1970 was made the first female Doctor of the Church. She was born in Avila.

termite any member of the insect order Isoptera. Termites are soft-bodied social insects living in large colonies which include one or more queens (of relatively enormous size and producing an egg every two seconds), much smaller kings, and still smaller soldiers, workers, and immature forms. Termites build galleried nests of soil particles that may be 20 ft/6 m high.

tern any of various lightly built seabirds placed in the same family (Laridae) as gulls and characterized by pointed wings and bill and usually a forked tail. Terns plunge-dive after aquatic prey. They are 8–20 in/20–50 cm long, and usually colored in combinations of white and black.

terracotta (Italian "baked earth") brownish-red baked clay, usually unglazed, used in building, sculpture, and pottery. The term is specifically applied to small figures or figurines, such as those found at Tanagra. Excavations at Xian, China, have revealed life-size terracotta figures of the army of the Emperor Shi Huangdi dating from the 3rd century BC.

terrapin general name for any turtle, that frequents fresh or brackish water. The name is sometimes specifically used for the tidewater diamondback terrapins (genus *Malaclemys*) of E North America.

Terre Haute city in W Indiana, on the Wabash River; population (1990) 57,500. Industries include plastics, chemicals, and glass. Terre Haute was laid out 1816.

terrier any of various breeds of highly intelligent, active dogs. They are usually small. Types include the bull, cairn, fox, Irish, Scottish, Sealyham, Skye, and Yorkshire terriers. They were originally bred for hunting rabbits and following quarry such as foxes down into burrows.

territorial behavior in biology, any behavior that serves to exclude other members of the same species from a fixed area or ◊territory. It may involve aggressively driving out intruders, marking the boundary (with dung piles or secretions from special scent glands), conspicuous visual displays, characteristic songs, or loud calls.

territorial waters area of sea over which the adjoining coastal state claims territorial rights. This is most commonly a distance of 12 nautical mi/22.2 km from the coast, but, increasingly, states claim fishing and other rights up to 200 mi/370 km.

territory in animal behavior, a fixed area from which an animal or group of animals excludes other members of the same species. Animals may hold territories for many different reasons; for example, to provide a constant food supply, to monopolize potential mates, or to ensure access to refuges or nest sites. The size of a territory depends in part on its function: some nesting and mating territories may be only a few square yards, whereas feeding territories may be as large as hundreds of square miles.

Terror, Reign of period of the ◊French Revolution when the Jacobins were in power (Oct 1793–July 1794) under ◊Robespierre and instituted mass persecution of their opponents. About 1,400 were executed, mainly by guillotine, until public indignation rose and Robespierre was overthrown in July 1794.

Terry Alfred Howe 1827–1890. US military leader. He served with distinction in the American Civil War 1861–65. After the war he commanded the Department of Dakota and also served in the Department of the South 1869–72. He was George ◊Custer's commander in the 1876 Sioux War and later negotiated with Sitting Bull, supervising the opening of the Northern Plains.

tertiary in the Roman Catholic church, a member of a "third order" (see under ◊holy orders); a lay person who, while marrying and following a normal employment, attempts to live in accordance with a modified version of the rule of one of the religious orders. The first such order was founded by St ◊Francis 1221.

Tertiary period of geological time 65–1.64 million years ago, divided into five epochs: Paleocene, Eocene, Oligocene, Miocene, and Pliocene. During the Tertiary, mammals took over all the ecological niches left vacant by the extinction of the dinosaurs, and became the prevalent land animals. The continents took on their present positions, and climatic and vegetation zones as we know them became established. Within the geological time column the Tertiary follows the Cretaceous period and is succeeded by the Quaternary period.

Tertullian Quintus Septimius Florens AD 155–222. Carthaginian Father of the Church, the first major Christian writer in Latin; he became a leading exponent of Montanism.

terza rima poetical meter used in Dante's *Divine Comedy*, consisting of three-line stanzas in which the second line rhymes with the first and third of the following stanza. The English poet Shelley's "Ode to the West Wind" is another example.

tesla SI unit (symbol T) of ◊magnetic flux density. One tesla represents a flux density of one ◊weber per square meter, or 10^4 gauss. It is named after the Croatian engineer Nikola Tesla.

Tesla Nikola 1856–1943. Croatian electrical engineer who emigrated to the US 1884. He invented fluorescent lighting, the Tesla induction motor, and the Tesla coil, and developed the ◊alternating current (AC) electrical supply system.

Test Ban Treaty agreement signed by the US, the USSR, and the UK Aug 5, 1963, contracting to test

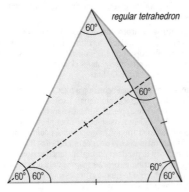

tetrahedron A regular tetrahedron is a pyramid on a triangular base with all its sides equal in length.

regular tetrahedron

nuclear weapons only underground. In the following two years 90 other nations signed the treaty, the only major nonsignatories being France and China, which continued underwater and ground-level tests.

testis (plural *testes*) the organ that produces ◊sperm in male (and hermaphrodite) animals. In vertebrates it is one of a pair of oval structures that are usually internal, but in mammals (other than elephants and marine mammals), the paired testes (or testicles) descend from the body cavity during development, to hang outside the abdomen in a scrotal sac.

testosterone in vertebrates, hormone secreted chiefly by the testes, but also by the ovaries and the cortex of the adrenal glands. It promotes the development of secondary sexual characteristics in males. In animals with a breeding season, the onset of breeding behavior is accompanied by a rise in the level of testosterone in the blood.

tetanus or *lockjaw* acute disease caused by the toxin of the bacillus *Clostridium tetani*, which usually enters the body through a wound. The bacterium is chiefly found in richly manured soil. Untreated, in seven to ten days tetanus produces muscular spasm and rigidity of the jaw spreading to the other muscles, convulsions, and death. There is a vaccine, and the disease may be treatable with tetanus antitoxin and antibiotics.

Tet Offensive in the Vietnam War, a prolonged attack mounted by the ◊Vietcong against Saigon (now Ho Chi Minh City) and other South Vietnamese cities and hamlets, beginning Jan 30, 1968. Although the Vietcong were finally forced to withdraw, the Tet Offensive brought into question the ability of the South Vietnamese army and their US allies to win the war and added fuel to the antiwar movement in both the US and Australia.

tetracycline one of a group of antibiotic substances having in common the four-ring structure of chlorte-

Texas

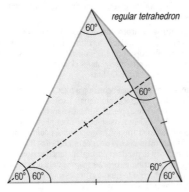

tracycline, the first member of the group to be isolated. They are prepared synthetically or obtained from certain bacteria of the genus *Streptomyces*. They are broad-spectrum antibiotics, effective against a wide range of disease-causing bacteria.

tetrahedron (plural *tetrahedra*) in geometry, a solid figure (◊polyhedron) with four triangular faces; that is, a ◊pyramid on a triangular base. A regular tetrahedron has equilateral triangles as its faces.

tetrapod (Latin "four-legged") type of ◊vertebrate. The group includes mammals, birds, reptiles, and amphibians. Birds are included because they evolved from four-legged ancestors, the forelimbs having become modified to form wings. Even snakes are tetrapods, because they are descended from four-legged reptiles.

Teutonic Knight member of a German Christian military order, the ***Knights of the Teutonic Order***, founded 1190 by Hermann of Salza in Palestine. They crusaded against the pagan Prussians and Lithuanians from 1228 and controlled Prussia until the 16th century. Their capital was Marienburg (now Malbork, Poland).

Texarkana twin cities that straddle the Texas–Arkansas border; population (1990) 22,600 (Texas), 31,700 (Arkansas). Industries include furniture, lumber, cotton, and sand and gravel.

Texas state in SW US; nickname Lone Star State
area 266,803 sq mi/691,200 sq km
capital Austin
cities Houston, Dallas-Fort Worth, San Antonio, El Paso, Corpus Christi, Lubbock
features rivers: Rio Grande, Red; arid Staked Plains, reclaimed by irrigation; the Great Plains; Gulf Coast resorts; Lyndon B Johnson Space Center, Houston; Alamo, San Antonio; Big Bend and Guadalupe Mountains national parks
products rice, cotton, sorghum, wheat, hay, livestock, shrimp, meat products, lumber, wood and paper products, petroleum (nearly one-third of US production), natural gas, sulfur, salt, uranium, chemicals, petrochemicals, nonelectrical machinery, fabricated metal products, transportation equipment, electric and electronic equipment
population (1990) 16,986,500
famous people James Bowie, George Bush, Buddy Holly, Sam Houston, Howard Hughes, Lyndon Johnson, Janis Joplin, Katherine Anne Porter, Patrick Swayze, Tina Turner
history settled by the Spanish 1682; part of Mexico 1821–36; Santa Anna massacred the Alamo garrison 1836, but was defeated by Sam Houston at San Jacinto the same year; Texas became an independent republic 1836–45, with Houston as president; in 1845 it became a state of the US. Texas is the only state in the US to have previously been an independent republic.

Texas City city in SE Texas, on Galveston Bay, SE of Houston; population (1990) 40,800. Industries include tin, chemicals, oil, and grains.

Texas v White a US Supreme Court decision 1869 that dealt with the legal status of Confederate and Reconstruction governments. The provisional Reconstruction government of Texas sued for the return of property sold by the Confederate government during the Civil War. The case raised the question of which, if either, of the two governments was the valid, legal representative of Texas with the power to control state finances. The Court ruled that since secession was unconstitutional the Confederate state government had never existed as a legal body. It therefore had no right to dispose of state property. The Court also ruled that the provisional postwar government was a valid legal state government with the right to sue in the name of the people of Texas.

Thackeray William Makepeace 1811–1863. English novelist and essayist, born in Calcutta, India. He was a regular contributor to *Fraser's Magazine* and *Punch*. *Vanity Fair* 1847–48 was his first novel, followed by *Pendennis* 1848, *Henry Esmond* 1852 (and its sequel *The Virginians* 1857–59), and *The Newcomes* 1853–55, in which Thackeray's tendency to sentimentality is most marked.

Thailand country in SE Asia on the Gulf of Siam, bounded E by Laos and Cambodia, S by Malaysia, and W by Myanmar (Burma).

thalassemia or *Cooley's anemia* any of a group of chronic hereditary blood disorders that are widespread in the Mediterranean countries, Africa, the Far East, and the Middle East. They are characterized by an abnormality of the red blood cells and bone marrow, with enlargement of the spleen. The genes responsible are carried by about 100 million people worldwide.

Thalberg Irving Grant 1899–1936. US film-production executive. At the age of 20 he was head of production at Universal Pictures, and in 1924 he became production supervisor of the newly formed Metro-Goldwyn-Mayer (MGM). He was responsible for such prestige films as *Ben-Hur* 1926 and *Mutiny on the Bounty* 1935. With Louis B Mayer he built up MGM into one of the biggest Hollywood studios of the 1930s.

Born in Brooklyn, New York, Thalberg was hired 1918 as assistant to Carl Laemmle, president of Universal Pictures Corporation in New York. Having moved to Hollywood 1919, Thalberg, "the boy genius," was named head of the studio 1923, leaving to become vice president in charge of production for MGM the following year. Throughout the rest of his brief career, he displayed an uncanny eye for talent and a consummate skill in business matters. Among his most memorable productions were *Grand Hotel* 1932 and *A Night at the Opera* 1935.

Thales 640–546 BC. Greek philosopher and scientist. He made advances in geometry, predicted an eclipse of the Sun 585 BC, and, as a philosophical materialist, theorized that water was the first principle of all things, that the Earth floated on water, and so proposed an explanation for earthquakes. He lived in Miletus in Asia Minor.

thalidomide hypnotic drug developed in the 1950s for use as a sedative. When taken in early pregnancy, it caused malformation of the fetus (such as abnormalities in the limbs) in over 5,000 recognized cases, and the drug was withdrawn.

Thailand
Kingdom of
(*Prathet Thai* or *Muang Thai*)

area 198,108 sq mi/513,115 sq km
capital and chief port Bangkok
cities Chiangmai, Nakhon Sawan river port
physical mountainous, semiarid plateau in NE, fertile central region, tropical isthmus in S
environment tropical rain forest was reduced to 18% of the land area 1988 (from 93% in 1961); logging was banned by the government 1988
features rivers Chao Phraya, Mekong, Salween; ancient ruins of Sukhothai and Ayurrhaya
head of state King Bhumibol Adulyadej from 1946
head of government Chuan Leekpai from 1992
media About 20 daily papers, the largest (*Thai Rath*) having a circulation of 1 million (1992). Self- censorship and some state interference. Six TV channels (two owned by the army and three state-controlled); 496 radio stations (1992), none privately owned.

political system military-controlled emergent democracy
political parties New Aspiration Party; Samakkhi Tham (Justice and Unity) Party, right of center, airforce-linked; Palang Dharma, anticorruption; Social Action Party (Kij Sangkhom), right of center; Thai Nation (Chart Thai), conservative, pro-business; Liberal Democratic Party
exports rice, textiles, rubber, tin, rubies, sapphires, corn, tapioca
currency baht
population (1992) 56,801,000 (Thai 75%, Chinese 14%); growth rate 2% p.a.
life expectancy men 62, women 68 (1989)
languages Thai and Chinese (both official); regional dialects
religions Buddhist 95%, Muslim 4%
literacy 89% (1988)
GNP $52 bn (1988); $771 per head (1988)

chronology
1782 Siam absolutist dynasty commenced.
1896 Anglo-French agreement recognized Siam as independent buffer state.
1932 Constitutional monarchy established.
1939 Name of Thailand adopted.
1941–44 Japanese occupation.
1947 Military seized power in coup.
1972 Withdrawal of Thai troops from South Vietnam.
1973 Military government overthrown.
1976 Military reassumed control.
1980 General Prem Tinsulanonda assumed power.
1983 Civilian government formed; martial law maintained.
1988 Prime Minister Prem resigned; replaced by Chatichai Choonhavan.
1989 Thai pirates continued to murder, pillage, and kidnap Vietnamese "boat people" at sea.
1991 Military seized power in coup. Interim civilian government formed under Anand Panyarachun. 50,000 demonstrated against new military-oriented constitution.
1992 General election produced five-party coalition; the subsequent appointment of General Suchinda Kraprayoon as premier provoked widespread riots, and Suchinda fled the country after army shooting of 100 demonstrators. New coalition government led by Chuan Leekpai.

thallium soft, bluish-white, malleable, metallic element, symbol Tl, atomic number 81, atomic weight 204.37. It is a poor conductor of electricity. Its compounds are poisonous and are used as insecticides and rodent poisons; some are used in the optical-glass and infrared-glass industries and in photoelectric cells.

Thames river in S England; length 210 mi/338 km. It rises in the Cotswold Hills above Cirencester and is tidal as far as Teddington. Below London there is protection from flooding by means of the Thames Barrier. The headstreams unite at Lechlade.

thanatology study of the psychological aspects of the experiences of death and dying and its application in counseling and assisting the terminally ill. It was pioneered by US psychiatrist Elizabeth Kübler-Ross in the 1970s.

Thanksgiving (Day) national holiday in the US (fourth Thursday in Nov) and Canada (second Monday in Oct), first celebrated by the Pilgrim settlers in Massachusetts after their first harvest 1621.

Thant, U 1909–1974. Burmese diplomat, secretary-general of the United Nations 1962–71. He helped to resolve the US-Soviet crisis over the Soviet installation of missiles in Cuba, and he made the controversial decision to withdraw the UN peacekeeping force from the Egypt–Israel border 1967 (see ◊Arab-Israeli Wars).

Thatcher Margaret Hilda (born Roberts), Baroness Thatcher of Kesteven 1925– . British Conservative politician, prime minister 1979–90. She was education minister 1970–74 and Conservative Party leader from 1975. In 1982 she sent British troops to recapture the Falkland Islands from Argentina. She confronted labor-union power during the miners' strike 1984–85, sold off majority stakes in many public utilities to the private sector, and reduced the influence of local government through such measures as the abolition of metropolitan councils, the control of expenditure through "rate-capping," and the introduction of the community charge, or ◊poll tax, from 1989. In 1990 splits in the cabinet over the issues of Europe and consensus government forced her resignation. An astute Parliamentary tactician, she tolerated little disagreement, either from the opposition or from within her own party.

theater performance by actors for an audience; it may include ◊drama, dancing, music, ◊mime, and ◊puppets. The term is also used for the place or building in which dramatic performances take place. Theater history can be traced to Egyptian religious ritualistic drama as long ago as 3200 BC. The first known European theaters were in Greece from about 600 BC.

Thatcher British Conservative politician and former prime minister Margaret Thatcher.

Thebes capital of Boeotia in ancient Greece. In the Peloponnesian War it was allied with Sparta against Athens. For a short time after 371 BC when Thebes defeated Sparta at Leuctra, it was the most powerful state in Greece. Alexander the Great destroyed it 336 BC and although it was restored, it never regained its former power.

Thebes Greek name of an ancient city (*Niut-Ammon*) in Upper Egypt, on the Nile. Probably founded under the first dynasty, it was the center of the worship of Ammon, and the Egyptian capital under the New Kingdom from about 1600 BC. Temple ruins survive near the villages of Karnak and Luxor, and in the nearby *Valley of the Kings* are buried the 18th–20th dynasty kings, including Tutankhamen and Amenhotep III.

theism belief in the existence of gods, but more specifically in that of a single personal God, at once immanent (active) in the created world and transcendent (separate) from it.

Themistocles c. 525–c. 460 BC. Athenian soldier and politician. Largely through his success in persuading the Athenians to build a navy, Greece was saved from Persian conquest. He fought with distinction in the Battle of ◊Salamis 480 BC during the Persian War. About 470 he was accused of embezzlement and conspiracy against Athens, banished and fled to Asia, where Artaxerxes, the Persian king, received him with favor.

Theocritus c. 310–c. 250 BC. Greek poet whose "Idylls" became models for later pastoral poetry. Probably born in Syracuse, he spent much of his life in Alexandria under the Greek dynasty of the Ptolemies.

Theodora 508–548. Byzantine empress from 527. She was originally the mistress of Emperor Justinian before marrying him in 525. She earned a reputation for charity, courage, and championing the rights of women.

Theodoric the Great c. 455–526. King of the Ostrogoths from 474 in succession to his father. He invaded Italy 488, overthrew King Odoacer (whom he murdered) and established his own Ostrogothic kingdom there, with its capital in Ravenna. He had no strong successor, and his kingdom eventually became part of the Byzantine Empire of Justinian.

Theodosius I "the Great" c. AD 346–395. Roman emperor. Appointed Emperor of the East in 379, he fought against the ◊Goths successfully, and established Christianity throughout the region. He invaded Italy in 393, restoring unity to the empire and died in Milan. He was buried in Constantinople.

theology study of God or gods, either by reasoned deduction from the natural world or through revelation, as in the scriptures of Christianity, Islam, or other religions.

theory in science, a set of ideas, concepts, principles, or methods used to explain a wide set of observed facts. Among the major theories of science are ◊relativity, ◊quantum theory, ◊evolution, and ◊plate tectonics.

theosophy any religious or philosophical system based on intuitive insight into the nature of the divine, but especially that of the Theosophical Society, founded in New York 1875 by Madame Blavatsky and H S Olcott. It was based on Hindu ideas of ◊karma and ◊reincarnation, with ◊nirvana as the eventual aim.

Theravāda one of the two major forms of ◊Buddhism, common in S Asia (Sri Lanka, Thailand, Cambodia, and Myanmar); the other is the later Mahāyāna.

therm unit of energy defined as 10^5 British thermal units; equivalent to 1.055×10^8 joules. It is no longer in scientific use.

Thermidor 11th month of the French Revolutionary calendar, which gave its name to the period after the fall of the Jacobins and the proscription of Robespierre by the National Convention on 9 Thermidor 1794.

thermocouple electric temperature-measuring device consisting of a circuit having two wires made of different metals welded together at their ends. A current flows in the circuit when the two junctions are maintained at different temperatures (Seebeck effect). The electromotive force generated—measured by a millivoltmeter—is proportional to the temperature difference.

thermodynamics branch of physics dealing with the transformation of heat into and from other forms of energy. It is the basis of the study of the efficient working of engines, such as the steam and internal-combustion engines. The three laws of thermodynamics are (1) energy can be neither created nor destroyed, heat and mechanical work being mutually convertible; (2) it is impossible for an unaided self-acting machine to convey heat from one body to another at a higher temperature; and (3) it is impossible by any procedure, no matter how idealized, to reduce any system to the ◊absolute zero of temperature (0K/–273°C) in a finite number of operations. Put into mathematical form, these laws have widespread applications in physics and chemistry.

thermography photographic recording of heat patterns. It is used medically as an imaging technique to identify "hot spots" in the body—for example, tumors, where cells are more active than usual.

Thermography was developed in the 1970s and 1980s by the military to assist night vision by detecting the body heat of an enemy or the hot engine of a tank. It uses a photographic method (using infrared radiation) employing infrared-sensitive films.

thermometer instrument for measuring temperature. There are many types, designed to measure different temperature ranges to varying degrees of accuracy. Each makes use of a different physical effect of temperature.

Expansion of a liquid is employed in common *liquid-in-glass thermometers*, such as those containing mercury or alcohol. The more accurate *gas thermometer* uses the effect of temperature on the pressure of a gas held at constant volume. A *resistance thermometer* takes advantage of the change in resistance of a conductor (such as a platinum wire) with variation in temperature. Another electrical thermometer is the ◊thermocouple. Mechanically, temperature change can be indicated by the change in curvature of a *bimetallic strip* (as commonly used in a thermostat).

Thermopylae, Battle of battle during the ◊Persian Wars 480 BC when Leonidas, king of Sparta, and 1,000 men defended the pass of Thermopylae to the death against a much greater force of Persians. The pass led from Thessaly to Phocis in central Greece.

thermosphere layer in the Earth's ◊atmosphere above the mesosphere and below the exosphere. Its lower level is about 50 mi/80 km above the ground, but its upper level is undefined. The ionosphere is located in the thermosphere. In the thermosphere the temperature rises with increasing height to several thousand degrees Celsius. However, because of the thinness of the air, very little heat is actually present.

thesaurus (Greek "treasure") collection of synonyms or words with related meaning. Thesaurus compilers include Francis ◊Bacon, Comenius (1592–1670), and Peter Mark ◊Roget, whose work was published 1852.

Theseus in Greek legend, a hero of ◊Attica, supposed to have united the states of the area under a constitutional government in Athens. Ariadne, whom he later abandoned on Naxos, helped him find his way through the Labyrinth to kill the ◊Minotaur. He also fought the Amazons and was one of the ◊Argonauts.

Thespis 6th century BC. Greek poet, born in Attica, said to have introduced the first actor into plays (previously presented by choruses only), hence the word *thespian* for an actor. He was also said to have invented tragedy and to have introduced the wearing of linen masks.

Thessaloníki (English *Salonika*) port in Macedonia, NE Greece, at the head of the Gulf of Thessaloníki, the second largest city of Greece; population (1981) 706,200. Industries include textiles, shipbuilding, chemicals, brewing, and tanning. It was founded from Corinth by the Romans 315 BC as *Thessalonica* (to whose inhabitants St Paul addressed two epistles), captured by the Saracens AD 904 and by the Turks 1430, and restored to Greece 1912.

Thessaly (Greek *Thessalia*) region of E central Greece, on the Aegean; area 5,367 sq mi/13,904 sq km; population (1991) 731,200. It is a major area of cereal production. It was an independent state in ancient Greece and later formed part of the Roman province of ◊Macedonia. It was Turkish from the 14th century until incorporated in Greece 1881.

thiamine or *vitamin B₁* a water-soluble vitamin of the B complex. It is found in seeds and grain. Its absence from the diet causes the disease beriberi.

Thiers Louis Adolphe 1797–1877. French politician and historian, first president of the Third Republic 1871–73. He held cabinet posts under Louis Philippe, led the parliamentary opposition to Napoleon III from 1863, and as head of the provisional government 1871 negotiated peace with Prussia and suppressed the briefly autonomous ◊Paris Commune.

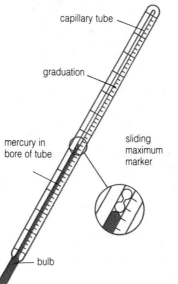

thermometer
Maximum and minimum thermometers are universally used in weather-reporting stations.

capillary tube

graduation

mercury in bore of tube

sliding maximum marker

bulb

Thirty Years' War

The Netherlands after the Peace of Westphalia 1648

█ United Provinces

█ The Generality, i.e. areas seized from the Spanish Netherlands by the United Provinces

□ Spanish Netherlands

His economic policies facilitated the nation's recovery after the Franco-Prussian War.

Third Reich (Third Empire) term used by the Nazis to describe Germany during the years of Hitler's dictatorship after 1933. The idea of the Third Reich was based on the existence of two previous German empires, the medieval Holy Roman Empire and the second empire 1871–1918.

Third World or *developing world* those countries that are less developed than the industrialized free-market countries of the West (First World) and the industrialized former Communist countries (Second World). Third World countries are the poorest, as measured by their income per head of population, and are concentrated in Asia, Africa, and Latin America.

Thirteen Colonies American 13 colonies that signed the ◊Declaration of Independence from Britain 1776. Led by George Washington, the Continental Army defeated the British army in the ◊American Revolution 1776–81 to become the original 13 United States of America: Connecticut, Delaware, Georgia, Maryland, Massachusetts, New Hampshire, New Jersey, New York, North Carolina, Pennsylvania, Rhode Island, South Carolina, and Virginia. They were united first under the Articles of ◊Confederation and from 1789, the US ◊constitution.

38th parallel demarcation line between North (People's Democratic Republic of) and South (Republic of) Korea, agreed at the Yalta Conference 1945 and largely unaltered by the Korean War 1950–53.

35 mm width of photographic film, the most popular format for the camera today. The 35-mm camera falls into two categories, the ◊SLR and the ◊rangefinder.

Thirty Years' War major war 1618–48 in central Europe. Beginning as a German conflict between Protestants and Catholics, it gradually became transformed into a struggle to determine whether the ruling Austrian Hapsburg family would gain control of all Germany. The war caused serious economic and demographic problems in central Europe.

thistle prickly plant of several genera, such as *Carduus, Carlina, Onopordum,* and *Cirsium,* in the family Compositae. The stems are spiny, the flower heads purple, white, or yellow and cottony, and the leaves deeply indented with prickly margins. The thistle is the Scottish national emblem.

Thomas Clarence 1948– . US Supreme Court justice (1991–). Born in Savannah, Georgia, he received a law degree from Yale University Law School (1974). President Reagan appointed him head of the civil rights division of the Department of Education 1981 and the head of the Equal Employment Opportunities Commission 1982. Thomas served there until 1990, when President Bush appointed him a justice on the US Court of Appeals. In 1991 he was nominated to the Supreme Court to succeed Thurgood Marshall, and after extremely bitter and sensational confirmation hearings, in which he was accused of sexual harassment by former colleague Anita Hill, Thomas was confirmed by the Senate and took his seat on the Court.

Thomas Dylan (Marlais) 1914–1953. Welsh poet. His poems include the celebration of his 30th birthday "Poem in October" and the evocation of his youth "Fern Hill" 1946. His "play for voices" *Under Milk Wood* 1954 describes with humor and compassion a day in the life of the residents of a small Welsh fishing village, Llareggub. The short stories of *Portrait of the Artist as a Young Dog* 1940 are autobiographical.

Thomas Norman Mattoon 1884–1968. US political leader, six times Socialist candidate for president 1928–48. One of the founders of the American Civil Liberties Union 1920, he also served as a director of the League for Industrial Democracy 1922–37. He was a brilliant speaker and published *A Socialist's Faith* 1951.

Thomas Seth 1785–1859. US clock manufacturer. Establishing his own firm 1812 he became enormously successful in the manufacture of affordable shelf clocks. In 1853 the firm was reorganized as the Seth Thomas Clock Company and continued to prosper into the 20th century.

Thomas à Kempis 1380–1471. German Augustinian monk who lived at the monastery of Zwolle. He took his name from his birthplace Kempen; his real surname was Hammerken. His *De Imitatio Christi/Imitation of Christ* is probably the most widely known devotional work ever written.

Thomas Aquinas medieval philosopher; see ◊Aquinas, St Thomas.

Thomas, St in the New Testament, one of the 12 Apostles, said to have preached in S India, hence the ancient churches there were referred to as the "Christians of St Thomas."

He is not the author of the Gospel of St Thomas, the ◊nostic collection of Jesus' sayings.

Thomson Elihu 1853–1937. US inventor. He founded, with E J Houston (1847–1914), the Thomson-Houston Electric Company 1882, later merging with the Edison Company to form the General Electric Company. He made advances into the nature of the ◊electric arc and invented the first high-frequency ◊dynamo and ◊transformer.

Thomson George Paget 1892–1975. English physicist whose work on ◊interference phenomena in the scattering of electrons by crystals helped to confirm the wavelike nature of particles. He shared a Nobel Prize with C J Davisson 1937.

Thomson J(oseph) J(ohn) 1856–1940. English physicist who discovered the ◊electron. He was responsible for organizing the Cavendish atomic research laboratory at Cambridge University. His work inaugurated the electrical theory of the atom and led to ◊Aston's discovery of ◊isotopes. Nobel Prize 1906.

Thor in Norse mythology, the god of thunder (his hammer), and represented as a man of enormous strength defending humanity against demons. He was the son of Odin and Freya, and Thursday is named after him.

thorax in tetrapod vertebrates, the part of the body containing the heart and lungs, and protected by the rib cage; in arthropods, the middle part of the body, between the head and abdomen.

Thoreau Henry David 1817–1862. US author and naturalist. His work *Walden, or Life in the Woods* 1854 stimulated the back-to-nature movement, and he completed some 30 volumes based on his daily nature walks. His essay "Civil Disobedience" 1849, prompted by his refusal to pay taxes, advocated peaceful resistance to unjust laws and had a wide impact, even in the 20th century.

thorium dark gray, radioactive, metallic element of the ◊actinide series, symbol Th, atomic number 90, atomic weight 232.038. It occurs throughout the world in small quantities in minerals such as thorite and is widely distributed in monazite beach sands. It is one of three fissile elements (the others are uranium and plutonium), and its longest-lived isotope has a half-life of 1.39×10^{10} years. Thorium is used to strengthen alloys. It was discovered by Jöns Berzelius 1828 and was named by him after the Norse god Thor.

Thorpe Jim (James Francis) 1888–1953. US athlete. A member of the 1912 US Olympic Team in Stockholm, he won gold medals for the decathlon and pentathlon but was forced to return when he admitted that he had played semiprofessional baseball. He played major-league baseball 1913–19 and was an outstanding player of professional football 1917–29. His Olympic medals were restored to him by the Amateur Athletic Union 1973.

Thousand Islands group of about 1,700 islands in the upper St Lawrence River, on the border between Canada and the US. Most of them are in Ontario; the rest are in the US state of New York. Some are in Canada's St Lawrence Islands National Park; many of the others are privately owned. The largest is Wolfe Island in Ontario, 49 sq mi/127 sq km. The islands are popular summer resorts.

Thrace (Greek *Thráki*) ancient region of the Balkans, SE Europe, formed by parts of modern Greece and Bulgaria. It was held successively by the Greeks, Persians, Macedonians, and Romans.

Three Mile Island island in the Shenandoah River near Harrisburg, Pennsylvania, site of a nuclear power station which was put out of action following a major accident March 1979. Opposition to nuclear power in the US was reinforced after this accident and safety standards reassessed.

threshing agricultural process of separating cereal grains from the plant. Traditionally, the work was carried out by hand in winter months using the flail, a jointed beating stick. Today, threshing is done automatically inside the combine harvester at the time of cutting.

thrips any of a number of tiny insects of the order Thysanoptera, usually with feathery wings. Many of the 3,000 species live in flowers and suck their juices, causing damage and spreading disease. Others eat fungi, decaying matter, or smaller insects.

throat in human anatomy, the passage that leads from the back of the nose and mouth to the ◊trachea and esophagus. It includes the ◊pharynx and the ◊larynx, the latter being at the top of the trachea. The word "throat" is also used to mean the front part of the neck, both in humans and other vertebrates; for example, in describing the plumage of birds. In engineering, it is any narrowing entry, such as the throat of a carburetor.

thrombosis condition in which a blood clot forms in a vein or artery, causing loss of circulation to the area served by the vessel. If it breaks away, it often travels to the lungs, causing pulmonary embolism.

throwing event field event. There are four at most major international track and field meets: ◊discus, ◊hammer, ◊javelin, and ◊shot put.

thrush any bird of the large family Turdidae, order Passeriformes, found worldwide and known for their song. Thrushes are usually brown with speckles of other colors. They are 5–12 in/12–30 cm long.

North American species include the hermit thrush *Catharus guttatus*, a beautiful songster; the wood thrush *Hylocichla mustelina*; and the American robin *Turdus migratorius*. European species include the song thrush *T. philomelos* and the mistle thrush *T. viscivorus*.

thrush infection usually of the mouth (particularly in infants), but also sometimes of the vagina, caused by a yeastlike fungus (genus *Candida*). It is seen as white patches on the mucous membranes.

Thucydides *c.* 455–400 BC. Athenian historian who exercised military command in the ◊Peloponnesian War with Sparta, but was banished from Athens in 424. In his *History of the Peloponnesian War*, he gave a detailed account of the conflict down to 411.

thulium soft, silver-white, malleable and ductile, metallic element, of the ◊lanthanide series, symbol Tm, atomic number 69, atomic weight 168.94. It is the least abundant of the rare-earth metals, and was first found in gadolinite and various other minerals. It is used in arc lighting.

Thunder Bay city and port on Lake Superior, Ontario, formed by the union of Port Arthur and its twin city of Fort William to the S; industries include shipbuilding, timber, paper, wood pulp, and export of wheat; population (1986) 122,000.

Thurber James (Grover) 1894–1961. US humorist. His short stories, written mainly for the *New Yorker* magazine, include "The Secret Life of Walter Mitty" 1932, and his doodle drawings include fanciful impressions of dogs.

Born in Columbus, Ohio, Thurber was partially blind as a result of an accident in childhood; he became totally blind in the last ten years of his life but continued to work. His stories and sketches are collected in *Is Sex Necessary?* (with E B White) 1929, *The Middle-Aged Man on the Flying Trapeze* 1935, *The Last Flower* 1939, and *My World and Welcome to It* 1942. He also wrote adult fairy tales—*Many Moons* 1943, *The Great Quillow* 1944, *The White Deer* 1945, *The 13*

Clocks 1950, and *The Wonderful O* 1957—and a play, *The Male Animal* 1940.

thyme herb, genus *Thymus*, of the mint family Labiatae. Garden thyme *T. vulgaris*, native to the Mediterranean, grows to 1 ft/30 cm high, and has pinkish flowers. Its aromatic leaves are used for seasoning.

thymus organ in vertebrates, situated in the upper chest cavity in humans. The thymus processes ◊lymphocyte cells to produce T-lymphocytes (T denotes "thymus-derived"), which are responsible for binding to specific invading organisms and killing them or rendering them harmless.

thyristor type of ◊rectifier, an electronic device that conducts electricity in one direction only. The thyristor is composed of layers of ◊semiconductor material sandwiched between two electrodes called the anode and cathode. The current can be switched on by using a third electrode called the gate.

thyroid ◊endocrine gland of vertebrates, situated in the neck in front of the trachea. It secretes several hormones, principally thyroxine, an iodine-containing hormone that stimulates growth, metabolism, and other functions of the body. The thyroid gland may be thought of as the regulator gland of the body's metabolic rate. If it is overactive, as in thyrotoxicosis, the sufferer feels hot and sweaty, has an increased heart rate, diarrhea, and weight loss. Conversely, an underactive thyroid leads to myxedema, a condition characterized by sensitivity to the cold, constipation, and weight gain. In infants, an underactive thyroid leads to cretinism, a form of mental retardation.

Tiananmen Square (Chinese "Square of Heavenly Peace") paved open space in central Beijing (Peking), China, the largest public square in the world (area 0.14 sq mi/0.4 sq km). On June 3–4, 1989, more than 1,000 unarmed protesters were killed by government troops in a massacre that crushed China's emerging prodemocracy movement.

tide The gravitational pull of the Moon is the main cause of the tides.

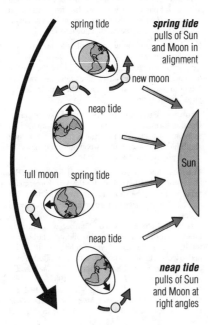

spring tide

spring tide pulls of Sun and Moon in alignment

new moon

neap tide

Sun

full moon   spring tide

neap tide

neap tide pulls of Sun and Moon at right angles

Tianjin or **Tientsin** port and industrial and commercial city in Hubei province, central China; population (1989) 5,620,000. The special municipality of Tianjin has an area of 1,544 sq mi/4,000 sq km and a population (1990) of 8,788,000. Its handmade silk and wool carpets are renowned. Dagan oil field is nearby. Tianjin was opened to foreign trade 1860 and occupied by the Japanese 1937.

Tian Shan (Chinese **Tien Shan**) mountain system in central Asia. **Pik Pobedy** on the Xinjiang-Kyrgyz border is the highest peak at 24,415 ft/7,440 m.

Tiberius Claudius Nero 42 BC–AD 37. Roman emperor, the stepson, adopted son, and successor of Augustus from AD 14. He was a cautious ruler whose reign was marred by the heavy incident of trials for treason or conspiracy. Tiberius fell under the influence of Sejanus who encouraged the emperor's fear of assassination and was instrumental in Tiberius's departure from Rome to Caprae. He never returned to Rome.

Tibet autonomous region of SW China (Pinyin form **Xizang**);
area 471,538 sq mi/1,221,600 sq km
capital Lhasa
features Tibet occupies a barren plateau bounded S and SW by the Himalayas and N by the Kunlun Mountains, traversed W to E by the Bukamagna, Karakoram, and other mountain ranges, and having an average elevation of 13,000–15,000 ft/4,000–4,500 m.
  The Sutlej, Brahmaputra, and Indus rivers rise in Tibet, which has numerous lakes, many of which are salty. The ◊yak is the main domestic animal
government Tibet is an autonomous region of China, with its own People's Government and People's Congress. The controlling force in Tibet is the Communist Party of China, represented locally by First Secretary Wu Jinghua from 1985. Tibetan nationalists regard the province as being under colonial rule
products wool, borax, salt, horn, musk, herbs, furs, gold, iron pyrites, lapis lazuli, mercury, textiles, chemicals, agricultural machinery
population (1991) 2,190,000 including 2,090,000 Tibetan nationalists (94.5%); many Chinese have settled in Tibet; 2 million Tibetans live in China outside Tibet
religion traditionally Lamaist (a form of Mahāyāna Buddhism)
history Tibet was an independent kingdom from the 5th century AD. It came under nominal Chinese rule about 1700. Independence was regained after a revolt 1912. China regained control 1951 when the historic ruler and religious leader, the ◊Dalai Lama, was driven from the country and the monks (who formed 25% of the population) were forced out of the monasteries. Between 1951 and 1959 the Chinese People's Liberation Army (PLA) controlled Tibet, although the Dalai Lama returned as nominal spiritual and temporal head of state. In 1959 a Tibetan uprising spread from bordering regions to Lhasa and was supported by Tibet's local government. The rebellion was suppressed by the PLA, prompting the Dalai Lama and 9,000 Tibetans to flee to India. The Chinese proceeded to dissolve the Tibet local government, abolish serfdom, collectivize agriculture, and suppress ◊Lamaism. In 1965 Tibet became an autonomous region of China. Chinese rule continued to be resented, however, and the economy languished.

tick any of an arachnid group (Ixodoidea) of large bloodsucking mites. Many carry and transmit diseases to mammals (including humans) and birds.

tide rise and fall of sea level due to the gravitational forces of the Moon and Sun. High tide occurs at an average interval of 12 hr 24 min 30 sec. The highest or **spring tides** are at or near new and full Moon; the lowest or **neap tides** when the Moon is in its first or third quarter. Some seas, such as the Mediterranean, have very small tides.

Tientsin alternate form of ◊Tianjin, an industrial city in NE China.

Tiepolo Giovanni Battista 1696–1770. Italian painter, born in Venice. He created monumental Rococo decorative schemes in palaces and churches in NE Italy, SW Germany, and Madrid (1762–70). The style is light-hearted, the palette light and warm, and he made great play with illusion.

Tierra del Fuego island group divided between Chile and Argentina. It is separated from the mainland of South America by the Strait of Magellan, and Cape Horn is at the southernmost point. The chief town, Ushuaia, Argentina, is the world's most southerly town. Industries include oil and sheep farming.

Tiffany Louis Comfort 1848–1933. US artist and glass-maker, son of Charles Louis Tiffany, who founded Tiffany and Company, the New York City jewelers. He produced stained-glass windows, iridescent Favrile (from Latin *faber* "craftsman") glass, and lampshades in the Art Nouveau style. He used glass that contained oxides of iron and other elements to produce rich colors.

In 1881 he founded his own decorating firm. By 1893, he began producing his glass art objects, which remained popular through the 1920s and enjoyed a resurgence of popularity from the 1950s on.

tiger largest of the great cats *Panthera tigris*, formerly found in much of central and S Asia but nearing extinction because of hunting and the destruction of its natural habitat. The tiger can grow to 12 ft/3.6 m long and weigh 660 lb/300 kg; it has a yellow-orange coat with black stripes. It is solitary, and feeds on large ruminants. It is a good swimmer.

Tigré or **Tigray** region in the N highlands of Ethiopia; area 25,444 sq mi/65,900 sq km. The chief town is Mekele. The region had an estimated population of 2.4 million in 1984, at a time when drought and famine were driving large numbers of people to fertile land in the S or into neighboring Sudan. Since 1978 a guerrilla group known as the Tigré People's Liberation Front (TPLF) has been fighting for regional autonomy. In 1989 government troops were forced from the province, and the TPLF advanced toward Addis Ababa, playing a key role in the fall of the Ethiopian government May 1991.

Tigris (Arabic **Shatt Dijla**) river flowing through Turkey and Iraq (see also ◊Mesopotamia), joining the ◊Euphrates above Basra, where it forms the ◊Shatt-al-Arab; length 1,000 mi/1,600 km.

Tijuana city and resort in NW Mexico; population (1990) 742,700.

It is known for horse races and casinos. ◊San Diego adjoins it across the US border.

Tilden Samuel Jones 1814–1886. US politician. A Democrat, he was governor of New York 1874–76, elected on a reform ticket. He received the Democratic presidential nomination 1876, and although he received a plurality of popular votes, the 1877 electoral college awarded the majority of electoral votes to Rutherford B Hayes.

till or **boulder clay** deposit of clay, mud, gravel, and boulders left by a ◊glacier. It is unsorted, with all sizes of fragments mixed up together, and shows no stratification; that is, it does not form clear layers or ◊beds.

Tillich Paul Johannes 1886–1965. Prussian-born US theologian, best remembered for his *Systematic Theology* 1951–63. Fleeing the Nazis, he arrived in the US 1933 and served as professor of theology at the Union Theological Seminary 1933–55, Harvard University 1955–62, and the University of Chicago 1962–65.

timber wood used in construction, furniture, and paper pulp. Hardwoods include tropical mahogany, teak, ebony, rosewood, temperate oak, elm, beech, and eucalyptus. All except eucalyptus are slow-growing, and world supplies are near exhaustion. Softwoods comprise the conifers (pine, fir, spruce, and larch), which are quick to grow and easy to work but inferior in quality of grain. White woods include ash, birch, and cottonwood; all have light-colored timber, are fast-growing, and can be used through modern methods as veneers on cheaper timber.

Timbuktu or **Tombouctou** town in Mali; population (1976) 20,500. A camel caravan center from the 11th century on the fringe of the Sahara, since 1960 it has been surrounded by the southward movement of the desert, and the former canal link with the river Niger is dry. Products include salt.

time continuous passage of existence, recorded by division into hours, minutes, and seconds. Formerly the measurement of time was based on the Earth's rotation on its axis, but this was found to be irregular. Therefore the second, the standard ◊SI unit of time, was redefined 1956 in terms of the Earth's annual orbit of the Sun, and 1967 in terms of a radiation pattern of the element cesium.

Universal time (UT), based on the Earth's actual rotation, was replaced by coordinated universal time (UTC) 1972, the difference between the two involving the addition (or subtraction) of leap seconds on the last day of June or Dec. National observatories make standard time available in various countries. From 1986 the term Greenwich Mean Time was replaced by UTC. However, the Greenwich meridian, adopted 1884, remains that from which all longitudes are measured, and the world's standard time zones are calculated from it.

time-sharing in computing, a way of enabling several users to access the same computer at the same time. The computer rapidly switches between user terminals and programs, allowing each user to work as if he or she had sole use of the system.

Timişoara capital of Timiş county, W Romania; population (1985) 319,000. Industries include electrical engineering, chemicals, pharmaceuticals, textiles, food processing, metal, and footwear. The revolt against the Ceauşescu regime began here Dec 1989 when demonstrators prevented the arrest and deportation of a popular Protestant minister who was promoting the rights of ethnic Hungarians. This soon led to large prodemocracy rallies.

Timor largest and most easterly of the Lesser Sunda Islands, part of Indonesia; area 12,973 sq mi/33,610 sq km. **West Timor** (capital Kupang) was formerly Dutch and was included in Indonesia on independence. ◊East Timor (capital Dili), an enclave on the NW coast, and the islands of Atauro and Jaco formed an overseas province of Portugal until it was seized by Indonesia 1975. The annexation is not recognized by the United Nations, and guerrilla warfare by local people seeking independence continues. Since 1975 over 500,000 Timorese have been killed by Indonesian troops or have resettled in West Timor, according to Amnesty International. Products include coffee, corn, rice, and coconuts.

Timothy in the New Testament, companion to St ◊Paul, both on his missionary journeys and in prison. Two of the Pauline epistles are addressed to him.

tin soft, silver-white, malleable and somewhat ductile, metallic element, symbol Sn (from Latin *stannum*), atomic number 50, atomic weight 118.69. Tin exhibits ◊allotropy, having three forms: the familiar lustrous metallic form above 55.8°F/13.2°C; a brittle form above 321.8°F/161°C; and a gray powder form below 55.8°F/13.2°C (commonly called tin pest or tin disease). The metal is quite soft (slightly harder than lead) and can be rolled, pressed, or hammered into extremely thin sheets; it has a low melting point. In nature it occurs rarely as a free metal. It resists corrosion and is therefore used for coating and plating other metals.

Tinbergen Jan 1903– . Dutch economist. He shared a Nobel Prize 1969 with Ragnar Frisch for his work on ◊econometrics (the mathematical-statistical expression of economic theory).

Tinbergen Niko(laas) 1907–1988. Dutch zoologist. He was one of the founders of ◊ethology, the scientific study of animal behavior in natural surroundings. Specializing in the study of instinctive behavior, he shared a Nobel Prize with Konrad ◊Lorenz and Karl von ◊Frisch 1973. He is the brother of Jan Tinbergen.

tinnitus in medicine, constant internal sounds, inaudible to others. The phenomenon may originate from noisy conditions (drilling, machinery, or loud music) or from infection of the middle or inner ear. The victim may become overwhelmed by the relentless noise in the head.

Tintoretto adopted name of Jacopo Robusti 1518–1594. Italian painter, active in Venice. His dramatic religious paintings are spectacularly lit and full of movement, such as his huge canvases of the lives of Christ and the Virgin in the Scuola di San Rocco, Venice, 1564–88.

Tipperary county in the Republic of Ireland, province of Munster, divided into north and south regions. *North Tipperary*: administrative headquarters Nenagh; area 772 sq mi/2,000 sq km; population (1991) 57,800. *South Tipperary*: administrative headquarters Clonmel; area 872 sq mi/2,260 sq km; population (1991) 74,800. It includes part of the Golden Vale, a dairy-farming region.

Tirana or *Tiranë* capital (since 1920) of Albania; population (1990) 210,000. Industries include metallurgy, cotton textiles, soap, and cigarettes. It was founded in the early 17th century by Turks when part of the Ottoman Empire. Although the city is now largely composed of recent buildings, some older districts and mosques have been preserved.

tire inflatable (pneumatic) rubber casing fitted to the wheel rims of bicycles and motor vehicles. The first pneumatic rubber tire was patented by R W Thompson 1845, but it was John Boyd Dunlop of Belfast who independently reinvented pneumatic tires for use with bicycles 1888–89. ◊Vulcanization, used in tire manufacture, was invented by Charles ◊Goodyear in 1844.

Tiresias or *Teiresias* in Greek legend, a man blinded by the gods and given the ability to predict the future.

Tirol federal province of Austria; area 4,864 sq mi/12,600 sq km; population (1989) 619,600. Its capital is Innsbruck, and it produces diesel engines, optical instruments, and hydroelectric power. Tirol was formerly a province (from 1363) of the Austrian Empire, divided 1919 between Austria and Italy (see ◊Trentino–Alto Adige).

Tirpitz Alfred von 1849–1930. German admiral. As secretary for the navy 1897–1916, he created the German navy and planned the World War I U-boat campaign.

tissue in biology, any kind of cellular fabric that occurs in an organism's body. Several kinds of tissue can usually be distinguished, each consisting of cells of a particular kind bound together by cell walls (in plants) or extracellular matrix (in animals). Thus, nerve and muscle are different kinds of tissue in animals, as are parenchyma and sclerenchyma in plants.

tissue culture process by which cells from a plant or animal are removed from the organism and grown under controlled conditions in a sterile medium containing all the necessary nutrients. Tissue culture can provide information on cell growth and differentiation, and is also used in plant propagation and drug production.

Titan in Greek mythology, any of the giant children of Uranus and Gaia, who included Cronus, Rhea, Themis, and Oceanus. Cronus and Rhea were in turn the parents of Zeus, who ousted Cronus as the ruler of the world.

titanium strong, lightweight, silver-gray, metallic element, symbol Ti, atomic number 22, atomic weight 47.90. The ninth-most abundant element in the Earth's crust, its compounds occur in practically all igneous rocks and their sedimentary deposits. It is very strong and resistant to corrosion, so it is used in building high-speed aircraft and spacecraft; it is also widely used in making alloys, as it unites with almost every metal except copper and aluminum. Titanium oxide is used in high-grade white pigments.

Titan rocket family of US space rockets, developed from the Titan intercontinental missile. Two-stage Titan rockets launched the Gemini crewed missions. More powerful Titans, with additional stages and strap-on boosters, were used to launch spy satellites and space probes, including the ◊Viking and ◊Voyager probes and Mars Observer.

Titian anglicized form of Tiziano Vecellio *c.* 1487–1576. Italian painter, active in Venice, one of the greatest artists of the High Renaissance. In 1533 he became court painter to Charles V, Holy Roman emperor, whose son Philip II of Spain later became his patron. Titian's work is richly colored, with inventive composition. He produced a vast number of portraits, religious paintings, and mythological scenes, including *Bacchus and Ariadne* 1520–23, *Venus and Adonis* 1554, and the *Entombment of Christ* 1559.

Titicaca lake in the Andes, 12,500 ft/3,810 m above sea level and 4,000 ft/1,220 m above the tree line; area 3,200 sq mi/8,300 sq km, the largest lake in South America. It is divided between Bolivia (port at Guaqui) and Peru (ports at Puno and Huancane). It has enormous edible frogs, and is one of the few places in the world where reed boats are still made (Lake Tana in Ethiopia is another).

titmouse any of a family (Paridae) of small birds of the order Passeriformes, found worldwide except in South America and Australia. There are 65 species, all agile and hardy, and often seen hanging upside down from twigs to feed. In North America many of the species are called chickadees.

Tito adopted name of Josip Broz 1892–1980. Yugoslav communist politician, in power from 1945. In World War II he organized the National Liberation Army to carry on guerrilla warfare against the German invasion 1941, and was created marshal 1943. As prime minister 1946–53 and president from 1953, he followed a foreign policy of "positive neutralism."

Titus Flavius Sabinus Vespasianus AD 39–81. Roman emperor from AD 79. Eldest son of ◊Vespasian, he captured Jerusalem 70 to end the Jewish revolt in Roman Palestine. He completed the Colosseum, and helped to mitigate the suffering from the eruption of Vesuvius in 79, which destroyed Pompeii and Herculaneum.

Titusville town in E Florida, on the Indian River, E of Orlando; population (1990) 39,400. Industries include citrus fruits and sport fishing. The Kennedy Space Center is nearby.

TN abbreviation for the state of ◊Tennessee.

TNT (abbreviation for ***trinitrotoluene***) $CH_3C_6H_2(NO_2)_3$, a powerful high explosive. It is a yellow solid, prepared in several isomeric forms from ◊toluene by using sulfuric and nitric acids.

toad any of the more terrestrial warty-skinned members of the tailless amphibians (order Anura). The name commonly refers to members of the genus *Bufo*, family Bufonidae, which are found worldwide, except for the Australian and polar regions.

The American toad *B. americanus* reaches 3.5 in/9 cm and is found from suburban backyards to mountain wildernesses throughout the NE US.

toadstool inedible or poisonous type of ◊fungus with a fleshy, gilled fruiting body on a stalk.

tobacco any large-leaved plant of the genus *Nicotiana* of the nightshade family Solanaceae, native to tropical parts of the Americas. *N. tabacum* is widely cultivated in warm, dry climates for use in cigars and cigarettes, and in powdered form as snuff.

Tobago island in the West Indies; part of the republic of ◊Trinidad and Tobago.

Tobin James 1918– . US Keynesian economist. He was awarded a Nobel Prize 1981 for his "general equilibrium" theory, which states that other criteria than monetary considerations are applied by households and firms when making decisions on consumption and investment. He is critical of monetarists for putting too much emphasis on a single asset—money—and he has analyzed the impact of changes in fiscal or monetary policy on the economy as a whole. He also has examined the process of portfolio selection, considering the trade-off between risk and yield across a broad range of assets.

Tobruk Libyan port; population (1984) 94,000. Occupied by Italy 1911, it was taken by Britain 1941 during World War II, and unsuccessfully besieged by Axis forces April–Dec 1941. It was captured by Germany June 1942 after the retreat of the main British force to Egypt, and this precipitated the replacement of Auchinleck by Montgomery as British commander.

Tocqueville Alexis de 1805–1859. French politician and political scientist, author of the first analytical study of the US constitution, *De la Démocratie en Amérique/Democracy in America* 1835, and of a penetrating description of France before the Revolution, *L'Ancien Régime et la Révolution/The Old Regime and the Revolution* 1856.

tofu or ***dofu*** or ***doufu*** pressed ◊soy bean curd derived from soy milk. It is a good source of protein and naturally low in fat.

Togo country in W Africa, on the Atlantic Ocean, bounded N by Burkina Faso, E by Benin, and W by Ghana. *See panel p. 922*

Tōjō Hideki 1884–1948. Japanese general and premier 1941–44 during World War II. Promoted to Chief of Staff of Japan's Guangdong army in Manchuria 1937, he served as minister for war 1940–41. He was held responsible for defeats in the Pacific 1944 and forced to resign. After Japan's defeat, he was hanged as a war criminal.

tokamak experimental machine designed by Soviet scientists to investigate controlled nuclear fusion. It consists of a doughnut-shaped chamber surrounded by electromagnets capable of exerting very powerful magnetic fields. The fields are generated to confine a very hot (millions of degrees) ◊plasma of ions and electrons, keeping it away from the chamber walls. See also ◊JET.

Tokugawa military family that controlled Japan as ◊shoguns 1603–1868. ***Tokugawa Ieyasu*** (1542–1616) was the Japanese general and politician who established the Tokugawa shogunate. The Tokugawa were feudal lords who ruled about one-quarter of Japan. Undermined by increasing foreign incursions, they were overthrown by an attack of provincial forces from Chōshū, Satsuma, and Tosa, who restored the ◊Meiji emperor to power.

Tokyo capital of Japan, on Honshu Island; population (1990) 8,163,100, metropolitan area over 12 million. The Sumida River delta separates the city from its suburb of Honjo. It is Japan's main cultural and industrial center (engineering, chemicals, textiles, electrical goods). Founded in the 16th century as ***Yedo*** (or ***Edo***), it was renamed when the emperor moved his court there from Kyoto 1868. An earthquake 1923 killed 58,000 people and destroyed much of the city, which was again severely damaged by Allied bombing in World War II. The subsequent rebuilding has made it into one of the world's most modern cities.

Toledo city on the river Tagus, Castilla–La Mancha, central Spain; population (1982) 62,000. It was the capital of the Visigoth kingdom 534–711 (see ◊Goth), then became a Moorish city, and was the Castilian capital 1085–1560.

Toledo port on Lake Erie, Ohio, at the mouth of the Maumee River; population (1990) 332,900. Industries include food processing and the manufacture of vehicles, electrical goods, and glass. A French fort was built 1700, but permanent settlement did not begin

Togo
Republic of
(*République Togolaise*)

currency franc CFA
population (1992) 3,701,000; growth rate 3% p.a.
life expectancy men 53, women 57 (1989)
languages French (official), Ewe, Kaber
religions animist 46%, Catholic 28%, Muslim 17%, Protestant 9%
literacy men 53%, women 28% (1985 est)
GNP $1.3 bn (1987); $240 per head (1985)

chronology
1885–1914 Togoland was a German protectorate until captured by Anglo-French forces.
1922 Divided between Britain and France under League of Nations mandate.
1946 Continued under United Nations trusteeship.
1956 British Togoland integrated with Ghana.
1960 French Togoland achieved independence from France as the Republic of Togo with Sylvanus Olympio as head of state.
1963 Olympio killed in a military coup. Nicolas Grunitzky became president.
1967 Grunitzky replaced by Lt Gen Etienne Gnassingbé Eyadéma in bloodless coup.
1973 Assembly of Togolese People (RPT) formed as sole legal political party.
1975 EEC Lomé convention signed in Lomé, establishing trade links with developing countries.
1979 Eyadéma returned in election. Further EEC Lomé convention signed.
1986 Attempted coup failed.
1991 Eyadéma legalized opposition parties. National conference elected Joseph Kokou Koffigoh head of interim government; troops loyal to Eyadéma failed to reinstate him.
1992 Overwhelming referendum support for multiparty politics.
1993 Feb: all-party talks to avoid civil war began in France but were suspended after disagreements among participants. July/August: President Eyadéma won multiparty election.

area 21,930 sq mi/56,800 sq km
capital Lomé
cities Sokodé, Kpalimé
physical two savanna plains, divided by range of hills NE–SW; coastal lagoons and marsh
environment the homes of thousands of people in Keto were destroyed by coastal erosion as a result of the building of the Volta dam
features Mono Tableland, Oti Plateau, Oti River
head of state Etienne Gnassingbé Eyadéma from 1967
head of government Joseph Kokou Koffigoh from 1991
political system emergent democracy
political parties Rally of the Togolese People (RPT), centrist nationalist; Alliance of Togolese Democrats (ADT), left of center; Togolese Movement for Democracy (MDT), left of center; Coordination of New Forces, left of center, broad coalition
exports phosphates, cocoa, coffee, coconuts

until after the War of 1812. The University of Toledo is here.

Tolkien J(ohn) R(onald) R(euel) 1892–1973. English writer who created the fictional world of Middle Earth in *The Hobbit* 1937 and the trilogy *The Lord of the Rings* 1954–55, fantasy novels peopled with hobbits, dwarves, and strange magical creatures. His work developed a cult following in the 1960s and had many imitators. At Oxford University he was professor of Anglo-Saxon 1925–45 and Merton professor of English 1945–59.

Tolstoy Leo Nikolaievich 1828–1910. Russian novelist who wrote War and Peace 1863–69 and Anna Karenina 1873–77. From 1880 Tolstoy underwent a profound spiritual crisis and took up various moral positions, including passive resistance to evil, rejection of authority (religious or civil) and private ownership, and a return to basic mystical Christianity. He was excommunicated by the Orthodox Church, and his later works were banned.

Toltec member of an ancient American Indian people who ruled much of Mexico in the 10th–12th centuries, with their capital and religious center at Tula, NE of Mexico City. They also constructed a similar city at Chichén Itzá in Yucatán. After the Toltecs' fall in the 13th century, the Aztecs took over much of their former territory, except for the regions regained by the Maya.

toluene or *methyl benzene* $C_6H_5CH_3$ colorless, inflammable liquid, insoluble in water, derived from petroleum. It is used as a solvent, in aircraft fuels, in preparing phenol (carbolic acid, used in making resins

for adhesives, pharmaceuticals, and as a disinfectant), and the powerful high explosive ◊TNT.

tomato annual plant *Lycopersicon esculentum* of the nightshade family Solanaceae, native to South America. It is widely cultivated for the many-seeded red fruit (technically a berry), used in salads and cooking.

ton unit (symbol t) of mass. The *short ton*, used in the US and Canada, is 2,000 lb/907 kg. The *long ton*, used in the UK, is 2,240 lb/1,016 kg. The *metric ton* or *tonne* is 2,205 lb/1,000 kg.

tonality in music, the observance of a key structure; that is, the recognition of the importance of a tonic or key note and of the diatonic scale built upon it. See also ◊atonality.

tone poem in music, another name for ◊symphonic poem as used, for example, by Richard Strauss.

Tonga country in the SW Pacific Ocean, in ◊Polynesia.

tongue in tetrapod vertebrates, a muscular organ usually attached to the floor of the mouth. It has a thick root anchored at the base to a skeletal system (the hyoid apparatus), formed from what were gill supports in fishes. The tongue is covered with a ◊mucous membrane containing nerves and "taste buds" in mammals. It directs food to the teeth and into the throat for chewing and swallowing. In humans, it is crucial for speech; in other animals, for lapping up water and for grooming. In some animals, such as frogs, it can be flipped forward to catch insects; in others, such as anteaters, it serves to reach for food found in deep holes.

Tonga
Kingdom of
(*Pule'anga Fakatu'i 'o Tonga*)
or *Friendly Islands*

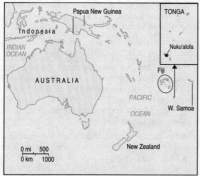

area 290 sq mi/750 sq km
capital Nuku'alofa (on Tongatapu island)
cities Pangai, Neiafu
physical three groups of islands in SW Pacific, mostly coral formations, but actively volcanic in W

features of 170 islands in the Tonga group, 36 are inhabited
head of state King Taufa'ahau Tupou IV from 1965
head of government Baron Vaea from 1991
political system constitutional monarchy
political parties none
currency Tongan dollar or pa'anga
population (1992) 97,300; growth rate 2.4% p.a.
life expectancy men 69, women 74 (1989)
languages Tongan (official), English
religions Wesleyan 47%, Roman Catholic 14%, Free Church of Tonga 14%, Mormon 9%, Church of Tonga 9%
literacy 93% (1988)
GNP $65 million (1987); $430 per head

chronology
1831 Tongan dynasty founded by Prince Taufa'ahau Tupou.
1900 Became a British protectorate.
1965 Queen Salote died; succeeded by her son, King Taufa'ahau Tupou IV.
1970 Independence achieved from Britain within the Commonwealth.
1990 Three prodemocracy candidates elected. Calls for reform of absolutist power.

Tonkin Gulf Incident clash that triggered US entry into the Vietnam War in Aug 1964. Two US destroyers (USS *C Turner Joy* and USS *Maddox*) reported that they were fired on by North Vietnamese torpedo boats. It is unclear whether hostile shots were actually fired, but the reported attack was taken as a pretext for making air raids against North Vietnam. On Aug 7 the US Congress passed the *Tonkin Gulf Resolution*, which formed the basis for the considerable increase in US military involvement in the Vietnam War.

tonsils in higher vertebrates, masses of lymphoid tissue situated at the back of the mouth and throat (palatine tonsils), and on the rear surface of the tongue (lingual tonsils). The tonsils contain many ◊lymphocytes and are part of the body's defense system against infection.

Tony award annual award by the League of New York Theaters to playwrights, performers, and technicians in ◊Broadway plays. It is named after the US actress and producer Antoinette Perry (1888–1946).

tool any implement that gives the user a mechanical advantage, such as a hammer or a saw; a *machine tool* is a tool operated by power. Tools are the basis of industrial production; the chief machine tool is the lathe. The industrial potential of a country is often calculated by the number of machine tools available. Automatic control of machine tools, a milestone in industrial development, is known as ◊automation, and electronic control is called robotics (see ◊robot).

tooth in vertebrates, one of a set of hard, bonelike structures in the mouth, used for biting and chewing food, and in defense and aggression. In humans, the first set (20 milk teeth) appear from age six months to two and a half years. The permanent ◊dentition replaces these from the sixth year onward; the wisdom teeth (third molars) sometimes not appearing until the age of 25 or 30. Adults have 32 teeth: 2 incisors, 1 canine (eye tooth), 2 premolars, and 3 molars on each side of each jaw. Each tooth consists of an enamel coat (hardened calcium deposits), dentine (a thick, bonelike layer), and an inner pulp cavity, housing nerves and blood vessels. Mammalian teeth have roots sur-

rounded by cementum, which fuses them into their sockets in the jawbones. The neck of the tooth is covered by the ◊gum, while the enamel-covered crown protrudes above the gum line.

topaz mineral, aluminum fluosilicate, $Al_2SiO_4(F,OH)_2$.
It is usually yellow, but pink if it has been heated, and is used as a gemstone when transparent. It ranks 8 on the Mohs' scale of hardness.

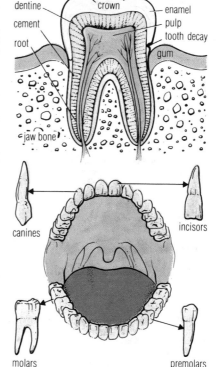

tooth Adults have 32 teeth: 2 incisors, 1 canine, 2 premolars, and 3 molars on each side of each jaw.

Topeka capital of Kansas; population (1990) 119,900. It is a center for agricultural trade, and its products include processed food, printed materials, and rubber and metal products. The Menninger Foundation, a noted psychiatric center, is here. The community was platted 1854 and developed as a railroad center. It was made the state capital 1861.

topi or *korrigum* antelope *Damaliscus korrigum* of equatorial Africa, head and body about 5.5 ft/1.7 m long, 3.5 ft/1.1 m high at the shoulder, with a chocolate-brown coat.

topography the surface shape and aspect of the land, and its study. Topography deals with relief and contours, the distribution of mountains and valleys, the patterns of rivers, and all other features, natural and artificial, that produce the landscape.

topology branch of geometry that deals with those properties of a figure that remain unchanged even when the figure is transformed (bent, stretched)—for example, when a square painted on a rubber sheet is deformed by distorting the sheet. Topology has scientific applications, as in the study of turbulence in flowing fluids. The map of a subway system is an example of the topological representation of a network; connectivity (the way the lines join together) is preserved, but shape and size are not.

topsoil the upper, cultivated layer of soil, which may vary in depth from 3 to 18 in/8 to 45 cm. It contains organic matter—the decayed remains of vegetation, which plants need for active growth—along with a variety of soil organisms, including earthworms.

Torah in ◊Judaism, the first five books of the Hebrew Bible (Christian Old Testament). It contains a traditional history of the world from the Creation to the death of Moses; it also includes the Hebrew people's covenant with their one God, rules for religious observance, and guidelines for social conduct, including the Ten Commandments.

Tordesillas, Treaty of agreement reached 1494 when Spain and Portugal divided the uncharted world between themselves. An imaginary line was drawn 370 leagues W of the Azores and the Cape Verde Islands, with Spain receiving all lands discovered to the W, and Portugal those to the E (in South America, Brazil).

tornado extremely violent revolving storm with swirling, funnel-shaped clouds, caused by a rising column of warm air propelled by strong wind. A tornado can rise to a great height, but with a diameter of only a few hundred yards or meters or less. Tornadoes move with wind speeds of 100–300 mph/160–480 kph, destroying everything in their path. They are common in the central US and Australia.

Toronto (North American Indian "place of meeting") known until 1834 as *York*. Port and capital of Ontario, on Lake Ontario; metropolitan population (1985) 3,427,000. It is Canada's main industrial and commercial center (banking, shipbuilding, automobiles, farm machinery, food processing, publishing) and also a cultural center, with theaters and a film industry. A French fort was established 1749, and the site became the provincial capital 1793.

torpedo self-propelled underwater missile, invented 1866 by British engineer Robert Whitehead. Modern torpedoes are homing missiles; some resemble mines in that they lie on the seabed until activated by the acoustic signal of a passing ship. A television camera enables them to be remotely controlled, and in the final stage of attack they lock on to the radar or sonar signals of the target ship.

torpedo or *electric ray* any species of the order Torpediniformes of mainly tropical rays (cartilaginous fishes), whose electric organs between the pectoral fin and the head can give a powerful shock. They can grow to 6 ft/180 cm in length.

torr unit of pressure equal to 1/760 of an ◊atmosphere, used mainly in high-vacuum technology.

Torreón industrial and agricultural city in Coahuila state, N Mexico, on the river Nazas at an altitude of 3,700 ft/1,127 m; population (1986) 730,000. Before the arrival of the railroad 1907 Torreón was the largest of the three Laguna cotton-district cities (with Gómez Palacio and Ciudad Lerdo).

tort in law, a wrongful act for which someone can be sued for damages in a civil court. It includes such acts as libel, trespass, injury done to someone (whether intentionally or by negligence), and inducement to break a contract (although breach of contract itself is not a tort).

tortoise any member of the family Testudinidae, the land-living members of the order Chelonia, which includes all ◊turtles, terrestrial or aquatic. The shell of tortoises is generally more domed than that of aquatic turtles; their hind legs are stumpy and columnar; the front legs are often shovel-shaped for digging. Tortoises are herbivorous and occur in the warmer regions of all continents except Australia. Tortoises range in size from 4 in/10 cm to 5 ft/150 cm, and some are known to live for 150 years.

Tory Party the forerunner of the British ◊Conservative Party about 1680–1830. It was the party of the squire and parson, as opposed to the Whigs (supported by the trading classes and Nonconformists). The name is still applied colloquially to the Conservative Party. In the US a Tory was an opponent of the break with Britain in the Revolutionary War 1775–83.

total internal reflection the complete reflection of a beam of light that occurs from the surface of an optically "less dense" material. For example, a beam from an underwater light source can be reflected from the surface of the water, rather than escaping through the surface. Total internal reflection can only happen if a light beam hits a surface at an angle greater than the ◊critical angle for that particular pair of materials.

totalitarianism government control of all activities within a country, overtly political or otherwise, as in fascist or communist dictatorships. Examples of totalitarian regimes are Italy under Benito ◊Mussolini 1922–45; Germany under Adolph ◊Hitler 1933–45; the USSR under Joseph ◊Stalin from the 1930s until his death in 1953; more recently Romania under Nicolae ◊Ceauşescu 1974–89.

totemism (Algonquin Indian "mark of my family") the belief in individual or clan kinship with an animal, plant, or object. This totem is sacred to those concerned, and they are forbidden to eat or desecrate it; marriage within the clan is usually forbidden. Totemism occurs among Pacific Islanders and Australian Aborigines, and was formerly prevalent throughout Europe, Africa, and Asia. Most North and South American Indian societies had totems as well.

toucan any South and Central American forest-dwelling bird of the family Ramphastidae. Toucans have very large, brilliantly colored beaks and often handsome plumage. They live in small flocks and eat fruits, seeds, and insects. They nest in holes in trees, where the female lays 2–4 eggs; both parents care for the eggs and young. There are 37 species, ranging from 1 ft/30 cm to 2 ft/60 cm in size.

touch sensation produced by specialized nerve endings in the skin. Some respond to light pressure, others to heavy pressure. Temperature detection may also contribute to the overall sensation of touch. Many animals, such as nocturnal ones, rely on touch more than humans do. Some have specialized organs of touch that project from the body, such as whiskers or antennae.

Toulon port and capital of Var *département*, SE France, on the Mediterranean Sea, 30 mi/48 km SE of Marseille; population (1990) 170,200. It is the chief Mediterranean naval station of France. Industries include oil refining, chemicals, furniture, and clothing. Toulon was the Roman *Telo Martius* and was made a port by Henry IV. It was occupied by the British 1793, and Napoleon first distinguished himself in driving them out. In World War II the French fleet was scuttled here to avoid its passing to German control.

Toulouse capital of Haute-Garonne *département*, SW France, on the river Garonne, SE of Bordeaux; population (1990) 365,900. The chief industries are textiles and aircraft construction (Concorde was built here). It was the capital of the Visigoths (see ◊Goth) and later of Aquitaine 781–843.

Toulouse-Lautrec Henri Marie Raymond de 1864–1901. French artist, associated with the Impressionists. He was active in Paris, where he painted entertainers and prostitutes. From 1891 his lithograph posters were a great success.

touraco any fruit-eating African bird of the family Musophagidae. They have long tails, erectile crests, and short, rounded wings. The largest are 28 in/70 cm long.

Tour de France French road race for professional cyclists held annually over approximately 3,000 mi/4,800 km of primarily French roads. The race takes about three weeks to complete and the route varies each year, often taking in adjoining countries, but always ending in Paris. A separate stage is held every day, and the overall leader at the end of each stage wears the coveted "yellow jersey" (French *maillot jaune*).

Toussaint L'Ouverture Pierre Dominique *c.* 1743–1803. Haitian revolutionary leader, born a slave. He joined the insurrection of 1791 against the French colonizers and was made governor by the revolutionary French government. He expelled the Spanish and British, but when the French emperor Napoleon reimposed slavery he revolted, was captured, and died in prison in France. In 1983 his remains were returned to Haiti.

Tower of London English fortress on the Thames bank to the east of the city of London. The keep, or White Tower, was built about 1078 by Bishop Gundulf on the site of British and Roman fortifications. It is surrounded by two strong walls and a moat (now dry), and was for centuries a royal residence and the principal state prison.

Today it is a barracks, an armory, and a museum.

toxemia condition in which poisons are spread throughout the body by the bloodstream, such as those produced by ◊pathogens or by localized cells in the body.

toxic poisonous or harmful. Radioactivity, air and water pollutants, and poisons ingested or inhaled— for example, lead from automobile exhausts, asbestos, and chlorinated solvents—are some toxic substances that occur in the environment; generally the effects take some time to become apparent (anything from a few hours to many years). The cumulative effects of toxic waste pose a serious threat to the ecological stability of the planet.

toxic shock syndrome rare condition marked by rapid onset of fever, vomiting, and low blood pressure, sometimes leading to death. It is caused by a toxin of the bacterium *Staphylococcus aureus*, normally harmlessly present in the body, which may accumulate, for example, if a tampon used by a woman during a period remains unchanged beyond four to six hours.

Toyotomi Hideyoshi. Adopted name of Kinoshita Tōkichirō 1537–1598. Japanese warlord, one of the three military leaders who unified Japan in the 16th century (◊Momoyama period). Successful military campaigns and alliances gave him control of central and SW Japan by 1587 and E Japan by 1590. His invasion of Korea 1592–98 was, however, defeated.

trace element chemical element necessary for the health of a plant or animal, but only in minute quantities. For example, iodine is need by the thyroid gland of mammals for making hormones that control growth and body chemistry, and for all metabolic processes.

tracer in science, a small quantity of a radioactive ◊isotope (form of an element) used to follow the path of a chemical reaction or a physical or biological process. The location (and possibly concentration) of the tracer is usually detected by using a Geiger–Muller counter.

trachea tube that forms an airway in air-breathing animals. In land-living ◊vertebrates, including humans, it is also known as the *windpipe* and runs from the larynx to the upper part of the chest. Its diameter is about 0.6 in/1.5 cm and its length 4 in/10 cm. It is strong and flexible, and reinforced by rings of ◊cartilage. In the upper chest, the trachea branches into two tubes: the left and right bronchi, which enter the lungs. Insects have a branching network of tubes called tracheae, which conduct air from holes (spira-

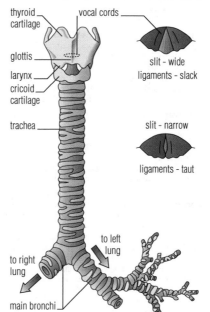

trachea The human trachea, or windpipe.

thyroid cartilage

vocal cords

glottis

larynx

cricoid cartilage

trachea

slit - wide
ligaments - slack

slit - narrow
ligaments - taut

to left lung

to right lung

main bronchi

cles) in the body surface to all the body tissues. The finest branches of the tracheae are called tracheoles.

tracheotomy surgical opening in the windpipe (trachea), usually created for the insertion of a tube to enable the patient to breathe. It is done either to bypass the airway impaired by disease or injury, or to safeguard it during surgery or a prolonged period of mechanical ventilation.

trachoma chronic eye infection, resembling severe ◊conjunctivitis. The conjunctiva becomes inflamed, with scarring and formation of pus, and there may be damage to the cornea. It is caused by a viruslike organism (◊chlamydia), and is a disease of dry tropical regions. Although it responds well to antibiotics, numerically it remains the biggest single cause of blindness worldwide.

tractor in agriculture, a powerful motor vehicle, commonly having large rear wheels or caterpillar tracks, used for pulling farm machinery and loads. It is usually powered by a diesel engine and has a power-take-off mechanism for driving machinery, and a hydraulic lift for raising and lowering implements.

Tracy Spencer 1900–1967. US actor distinguished for his understated, seemingly effortless, natural performances. His films include *Captains Courageous* 1937 and *Boys' Town* 1938 (for both of which he won Academy Awards), and he starred with Katharine Hepburn in nine films, including *Adam's Rib* 1949 and *Guess Who's Coming to Dinner* 1967, his final appearance.

His other films include *Bad Day at Black Rock* 1955, *The Last Hurrah* 1958, *The Old Man and the Sea* 1958, and *Inherit the Wind* 1960. He was one of Hollywood's most versatile performers.

trademark name or symbol that is distinctive of a marketed product. The owner may register the mark to prevent its unauthorized use.

tradescantia any plant of the genus *Tradescantia* of the family Commelinaceae, native to North and Central America. The spiderwort *T. virginiana* is a cultivated garden plant; the wandering jew *T. albiflora* is a common house plant, with green oval leaves tinged with pink or purple or silver-striped.

trade wind prevailing wind that blows toward the equator from the northeast and southeast. Trade winds are caused by hot air rising at the equator and the consequent movement of air from north and south to take its place. The winds are deflected toward the west because of the Earth's west-to-east rotation. The unpredictable calms known as the ◊doldrums lie at their convergence.

Trafalgar, Battle of battle Oct 21, 1805, in the ◊Napoleonic Wars. The British fleet under Admiral Nelson defeated a Franco-Spanish fleet; Nelson was mortally wounded. The victory laid the foundation for British naval supremacy throughout the 19th century. It is named after Cape Trafalgar, a low headland in SW Spain, near the western entrance to the Straits of Gibraltar.

tragedy in the theater, a play dealing with a serious theme, traditionally one in which a character meets disaster as a result either of personal failings or circumstances beyond his or her control. Historically the Greek view of tragedy, as defined by Aristotle and expressed by the great tragedians Aeschylus, Euripides, and Sophocles, has been predominant in the western tradition. In the 20th century tragedies in the narrow Greek sense of dealing with exalted personages in an elevated manner have virtually died out. Tragedy has been replaced by dramas with "tragic" implications or overtones, as in the work of Ibsen, O'Neill, Tennessee Williams, Pinter, and Osborne, for example, or by the hybrid tragicomedy.

tragicomedy drama that contains elements of tragedy and comedy; for example, Shakespeare's "reconciliation" plays, such as *The Winter's Tale*, which reach a tragic climax but then lighten to a happy conclusion. A tragicomedy is the usual form for plays in the tradition of the Theatre of the ◊Absurd, such as Samuel ◊Beckett's *En attendant Godot/Waiting for Godot* 1953 and Tom ◊Stoppard's *Rosencrantz and Guildenstern are Dead* 1967.

Trajan Marcus Ulpius (Trajanus) AD 52–117. Roman emperor and soldier, born in Seville. He was adopted as heir by ◊Nerva, whom he succeeded AD 98.

trance mental state in which the subject loses the ordinary perceptions of time and space, and even of his or her own body.

tranquilizer common name for any drug for reducing anxiety or tension (anxiolytic), such as benzodiazepines, barbiturates, antidepressants, and beta-blockers. The use of drugs to control anxiety is becoming much less popular, because most of the drugs used are capable of inducing dependence.

transactinide any of a series of nine radioactive, metallic elements with atomic numbers that extend beyond the ◊actinide series, those from 104 (rutherfordium) to 112 (unnamed). They are grouped because of their expected chemical similarities (they are all bivalent), the properties differing only slightly with atomic number. All have ◊half-lives that measure less than two minutes.

Trans-Alaskan Pipeline one of the world's greatest civil engineering projects, the construction of a pipeline to carry petroleum (crude oil) 800 mi/1,285 km from N Alaska to the ice-free port of Valdez. It was completed 1977 after three years' work and much criticism by ecologists.

Trans-Amazonian Highway or *Transamazonica* road in Brazil, linking Recife in the E with the provinces of Rondonia, Amazonas, and Acre in the W.

transcendental meditation (TM) technique of focusing the mind, based in part on Hindu meditation. Meditators are given a mantra (a special word or phrase) to repeat over and over to themselves; such meditation is believed to benefit the practitioner by relieving stress and inducing a feeling of well-being and relaxation. It was introduced to the West by Maharishi Mahesh Yogi and popularized by the Beatles in the late 1960s.

transducer device that converts one form of energy into another. For example, a thermistor is a transducer that converts heat into an electrical voltage, and an electric motor is a transducer that converts an electrical voltage into mechanical energy. Transducers are important components in many types of sensor, converting the physical quantity to be measured into a proportional voltage signal.

transformational grammar theory of language structure initiated by Noam ◊Chomsky, which proposes that below the actual phrases and sentences of a language (its **surface structure**) there lies a more basic layer (its **deep structure**), which is processed by various transformational rules when we speak and write.

transformer device in which, by electromagnetic induction, an alternating current (AC) of one voltage is transformed to another voltage, without change of ◊frequency. Transformers are widely used in electrical apparatus of all kinds, and in particular in power transmission where high voltages and low currents are utilized.

transfusion intravenous delivery of blood or blood products (plasma, red cells) into a patient's circulation to make up for deficiencies due to disease, injury, or surgical intervention. Cross-matching is carried out to ensure the patient receives the right type of blood. Because of worries about blood-borne disease, self-transfusion with units of blood "donated" over the weeks before an operation is popular.

transistor solid-state electronic component, made of ◊semiconductor material, with three or more ◊electrodes, that can regulate a current passing through it. A transistor can act as an amplifier, ◊oscillator, ◊photocell, or switch, and (unlike earlier electron tubes) usually operates on a very small amount of power. Transistors commonly consist of a tiny sandwich of ◊germanium or ◊silicon, alternate layers having different electrical properties. A crystal of pure germanium or silicon would act as an insulator (nonconductor).

transit in astronomy, the passage of a smaller object across the visible disk of a larger one. Transits of the inferior planets occur when they pass directly between the Earth and the Sun, and are seen as tiny dark spots against the Sun's disk.

transition metal any of a group of metallic elements that have incomplete inner electron shells and exhibit variable valency—for example, cobalt, copper, iron, and molybdenum. They are excellent conductors of electricity, and generally form highly colored compounds.

Transkei largest of South Africa's Bantustans, or homelands, extending NE from the Great Kei River, on the coast of Cape Province, to the border of Natal; area 16,910 sq mi/43,808 sq km; population (1985) 3,000,000, including small white and Asian minorities. It became self-governing 1963, and achieved full "independence" 1976. Its capital is Umtata, and it has a port at Mnganzana. It is one of the two homelands of the Xhosa people (the other is Ciskei), and products include livestock, coffee, tea, sugar, corn, and sorghum. It is governed by a military council since a 1987 coup (military leader Maj Gen H B Holomisa from 1987).

translation in living cells, the process by which proteins are synthesized. During translation, the information coded as a sequence of nucleotides in messenger ◊RNA is transformed into a sequence of amino acids in a peptide chain. The process involves the "translation" of the ◊genetic code.

translation in literature, the rendering of words from one language to another. The first recorded named translator was Livius Andronicus, who translated Homer's *Odyssey* from Greek to Latin in 240 BC.

translation program in computing, a program that translates another program written in a high-level language or assembly language into the machine-code instructions that a computer can obey. See ◊compiler.

transpiration the loss of water from a plant by evaporation. Most water is lost from the leaves through pores known as ◊stomata, whose primary function is to allow gas exchange between the plant's internal tissues and the atmosphere. Transpiration from the leaf surfaces causes a continuous upward flow of water from the roots via the ◊xylem, which is known as the transpiration stream.

A single corn plant has been estimated to transpire 64 gal/245 l of water in one growing season.

transplant in medicine, the transfer of a tissue or organ from one human being to another or from one part of the body to another (skin grafting). In most organ transplants, the operation is for life-saving purposes, though the immune system tends to reject foreign tissue. Careful matching and immunosuppressive drugs must be used, but these are not always successful.

transsexual person who identifies himself or herself completely with the opposite sex, believing that the wrong sex was assigned at birth. Unlike *transvestites*, who desire to dress in clothes traditionally worn by the opposite sex; transsexuals think and feel emotionally in a way typically considered appropriate to members of the opposite sex, and may undergo surgery to modify external sexual characteristics.

Trans-Siberian Railway railroad line connecting the cities of European Russia with Omsk, Novosibirsk, Irkutsk, and Khabarovsk, and terminating at Vladivostok on the Pacific. It was built 1891–1905; from Leningrad to Vladivostok is about 5,400 mi/8,700 km. A northern line, 1,928 mi/3,102 km long, was completed 1984 after ten years' work.

transubstantiation in Christian theology, the doctrine that the whole substance of the bread and wine changes into the substance of the body and blood of Jesus when consecrated in the ◊Eucharist.

transuranic any chemical element with atomic number greater than that of uranium (92). All are radioactive. Neptunium, plutonium, and perhaps americium occur in nature; the rest are synthesized elements only. The first were synthesized in 1940, neptunium and then plutonium.

Transvaal province of NE South Africa, bordering Zimbabwe to the N; area 101,325 sq mi/262,499 sq km; population (1985) 7,532,000. Its capital is Pretoria, and towns include Johannesburg, Germiston, Brakpan, Springs, Benoni, Krugersdorp, and Roodepoort. Products include diamonds, coal, iron ore, copper, lead, tin, manganese, meat, corn, tobacco, and fruit. The main rivers are the Vaal and Limpopo with their tributaries. Swaziland forms an enclave on the Natal border. It was settled by *Voortrekkers*, Boers who left Cape Colony in the Great Trek from 1831. Independence was recognized by Britain 1852, until the settlers' difficulties with the conquered Zulus led to British annexation 1877. It was made a British colony after the South African War 1899–1902, and in 1910 became a province of the Union of South Africa.

Transylvania mountainous area of central and NW Romania, bounded to the S by the Transylvanian Alps (an extension of the ◊Carpathian Mountains), formerly a province, with its capital at Cluj. It was part of Hungary from about 1000 until its people voted to unite with Romania 1918. It is the home of the vampire legends.

trapezium in geometry, a four-sided plane figure (quadrilateral) with no two sides parallel.

trapezoid in geometry, a four-sided plane figure (quadrilateral) with only two sides parallel. If the parallel sides have lengths a and b and the perpendicular distance between them is h (the height of the trapezoid), its area $A = \frac{1}{2}h(a + b)$.

transpiration

During photosynthesis, carbon dioxide enters the leaves of a plant through the stomata. A leaf that is permeable to carbon dioxide is also permeable to water vapor. Therefore, water is lost from the plant. The evaporation of water from the leaves is called transpiration. It produces a transpiration stream, which is a tension that draws water up the vessels of the stem. The tension can be sufficiently great to draw water up trees 325 ft/100 m tall

Transpiration rates can be measured using a potometer.

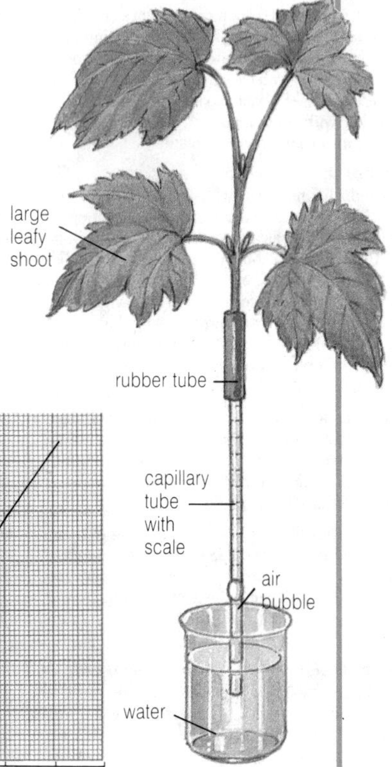

large leafy shoot

rubber tube

capillary tube with scale

air bubble

water

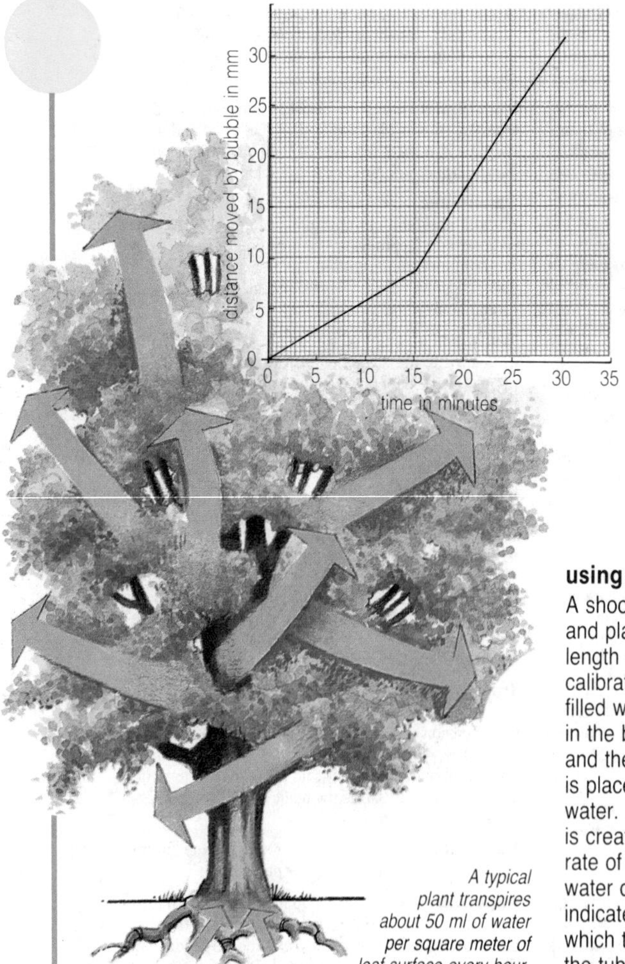

A typical plant transpires about 50 ml of water per square meter of leaf surface every hour.

using a potometer

A shoot is cut from a tree and placed in the top of a length of rubber tubing. A calibrated capillary tube, filled with water, is inserted in the bottom of the tubing and the whole arrangement is placed in a beaker of water. If a small air bubble is created in the tube, the rate of movement of the water due to transpiration is indicated by the speed with which the bubble moves up the tube.

treaty written agreement between two or more states. Treaties take effect either immediately on signature or, more often, on ratification. Ratification involves a further exchange of documents and usually takes place after the internal governments have approved the terms of the treaty. Treaties are binding in international law, the rules being laid down in the Vienna Convention on the Law of Treaties 1969.

tree perennial plant with a woody stem, usually a single stem or "trunk," made up of ◊wood and protected by an outer layer of ◊bark. It absorbs water through a ◊root system. There is no clear dividing line between ◊shrubs and trees, but sometimes a minimum height of 20 ft/6 m is used to define a tree.

tree diagram in probability theory, a branching diagram consisting only of arcs and nodes (but not loops curving back on themselves), which is used to establish probabilities.

Trent, Council of conference held 1545–63 by the Roman Catholic church at Trento, N Italy initiating the ◊Counter-Reformation; see also ◊Reformation.

Trentino–Alto Adige autonomous region of N Italy, comprising the provinces of Bolzano and Trento; capital Trento; chief towns Trento in the Italian-speaking southern area, and Bolzano-Bozen in the northern German-speaking area of South Tirol (the region was Austrian until ceded to Italy 1919); area 5,250 sq mi/13,600 sq km; population (1990) 891,400.

Trenton capital and industrial city (metalworking, ceramics) of New Jersey, on the Delaware River; population (1990) 88,700. It was first settled by Quakers 1679; George Washington defeated the British here 1776. It became the state capital 1790.

trespass going on to the land of another without authority. In law, a landowner has the right to eject a trespasser by the use of reasonable force and can sue for any damage caused.

Trevithick Richard 1771–1833. British engineer, constructor of a steam road locomotive 1801 and the first steam engine to run on rails 1804.

Triad secret society, founded in China as a Buddhist cult AD 36. It became known as the Triad because the triangle played a significant part in the initiation ceremony. Today it is reputed to be involved in organized crime (drugs, gambling, prostitution) among overseas Chinese. Its headquarters are alleged to be in Hong Kong.

trial by ordeal in the Middle Ages, a test of guilt or innocence.

triangle in geometry, a three-sided plane figure, the sum of whose interior angles is 180°. Triangles can be classified by the relative lengths of their sides. A *scalene triangle* has no sides of equal length; an *isosceles triangle* has at least two equal sides; an *equilateral triangle* has three equal sides (and three equal angles of 60°).

Triangles can also be classified by their angle measures: a *right triangle* has one right (90°) angle; an *acute triangle* has three acute (less than 90°) angles; an *obtuse triangle* has one obtuse (greater than 90°) angle; an *equiangular triangle* has three equal angles. (All equilateral triangles are equiangular, and vice versa.) If the length of one side of a triangle is *l* and the perpendicular distance from that side to the opposite corner is *h* (the height or altitude of the triangle), its area $A = \frac{1}{2}(l \times h)$.

triangulation technique used in surveying and navigation to determine distances, using the properties of

the triangle. To begin, surveyors measure a certain length exactly to provide a base line. From each end of this line they then measure the angle to a distant point, using a theodolite. They now have a triangle in which they know the length of one side and the two adjacent angles. By simple trigonometry they can work out the lengths of the other two sides.

Triassic period of geological time 245–208 million years ago, the first period of the Mesozoic era. The continents were fused together to form the world continent ◊Pangaea. Triassic sediments contain remains of early dinosaurs and other reptiles now extinct. By late Triassic times, the first mammals had evolved.

triathlon test of stamina involving three sports: swimming 2.4 mi/3.8 km, cycling 112 mi/180 km, and running a marathon 26 mi 385 yd/42.195 km, each one immediately following the last.

tribune Roman magistrate of ◊plebeian family, elected annually to defend the interests of the common people; only two were originally chosen in the early 5th century BC, but there were later ten. They could veto the decisions of any other magistrate.

triceratops any of a genus *Triceratops* of massive, horned dinosaurs of the order Ornithischia. They had three horns and a neck frill and were up to 25 ft/8 m long; they lived in the Cretaceous period.

Trident nuclear missile deployed on certain US nuclear-powered submarines and in the 1990s also being installed on four UK submarines. Each missile has 8 warheads (◊MIRVs) and each of the four submarines will have 16 Trident D-5 missiles. The Trident replaced the earlier Polaris and Poseidon missiles.

Trieste port on the Adriatic coast, opposite Venice, in Friuli-Venezia-Giulia, Italy; population (1988) 237,000, including a large Slovene minority. It is the site of the International Center for Theoretical Physics, established 1964.
history Trieste was under Austrian rule from 1382 (apart from Napoleonic occupation 1809–14) until transferred to Italy 1918. It was claimed after World War II by Yugoslavia, and the city and surrounding territory were divided 1954 between Italy and Yugoslavia.

trillium any of various perennial herbaceous woodland plants of the genus *Trillium* of the lily family. They have a whorl of three leaves around the erect stem. The single terminal flower has three green sepals and three usually maroon or white petals. The nodding trillium *T. cernuum* ranges across most of the eastern half of North America.

trilobite any of a large class (Trilobita) of extinct, marine, invertebrate arthropods of the Paleozoic era, with a flattened, oval body, 0.4–26 in/1–65 cm long. The hard-shelled body was divided by two deep furrows into three lobes.

Trinidad and Tobago country in the West Indies, off the coast of Venezuela. *See panel p. 930*

Trinity in Christianity, the union of three persons—Father, Son, and Holy Ghost/Spirit—in one godhead. The precise meaning of the doctrine has been the cause of unending dispute, and was the chief cause of the split between the Eastern Orthodox and Roman Catholic churches. *Trinity Sunday* occurs on the Sunday after Pentecost.

triode three-electrode thermionic tube containing an anode and a cathode (as does a ◊diode) with an additional negatively based control grid. Small variations in voltage on the grid bias result in large variations in the current. The triode was commonly used in ampli-

Trinidad and Tobago
Republic of

area Trinidad 1,864 sq mi/4,828 sq km and Tobago 116 sq mi/300 sq km
capital Port-of-Spain
cities San Fernando, Arima, Scarborough (Tobago)
physical comprises two main islands and some smaller ones; coastal swamps and hills E–W
features Pitch Lake, a self-renewing source of asphalt used by 16th-century explorer Walter Raleigh to repair his ships
head of state Noor Hassanali from 1987
head of government Patrick Manning from 1991
political system democratic republic
political parties National Alliance for Reconstruction

(NAR), nationalist, left of center; People's National Movement (PNM), nationalist, moderate, centrist; National Development Part (NDA), center-left
exports oil, petroleum products, chemicals, sugar, cocoa
currency Trinidad and Tobago dollar
population (1992) 1,261,000 (African descent 40%, Indian 40%, European 16%, Chinese and others 2%), 1.2 million on Trinidad; growth rate 1.6% p.a.
life expectancy men 68, women 72 (1989)
languages English (official), Hindi, French, Spanish
media freedom of press guaranteed by constitution and upheld by government; there are two independent morning newspapers and several weekly tabloids
religions Roman Catholic 32%, Protestant 29%, Hindu 25%, Muslim 6%
literacy 97% (1988)
GNP $4.5 bn; $3,731 per head (1987)

chronology
1888 Trinidad and Tobago united as a British colony.
1956 People's National Movement (PNM) founded.
1959 Achieved internal self-government, with PNM leader Eric Williams as chief minister.
1962 Independence achieved from Britain, within the Commonwealth, with Williams as prime minister.
1976 Became a republic, with Ellis Clarke as president and Williams as prime minister.
1981 Williams died and was succeeded by George Chambers, with Arthur Robinson as opposition leader.
1986 National Alliance for Reconstruction (NAR), headed by Arthur Robinson, won general election.
1987 Noor Hassanali became president.
1990 Attempted antigovernment coup defeated.
1991 General election saw victory for PNM, with Patrick Manning as prime minister.

fiers until largely superseded by the ◊transistor. The tube was invented by the US radio engineer Lee De Forest.

Triple Alliance pact from 1882 between Germany, Austria-Hungary, and Italy to offset the power of Russia and France. It was last renewed 1912, but during World War I Italy's initial neutrality gradually changed and it denounced the alliance 1915. The term also refers to other alliances: 1668—England, Holland, and Sweden; 1717—Britain, Holland, and France (joined 1718 by Austria); 1788—Britain, Prussia, and Holland; 1795—Britain, Russia, and Austria.

Triple Entente alliance of Britain, France, and Russia 1907–17. In 1911 this became a military alliance and formed the basis of the Allied powers in World War I against the Central Powers, Germany and Austria-Hungary.

The failure of the alliance system to create a stable balance of power, coupled with widespread horror of the carnage created by World War I, led to attempts to create international cooperation with the League of Nations.

triple jump field event in track and field comprising a hop, step, and jump sequence from a take-off board into a sandpit landing area measuring 26.25 ft/8 m (minimum) in length. The take-off board is usually 42.65 ft/13 m from the landing area. Each competitor has six attempts and the winner is the one with the longest jump.

Tripoli (Arabic *Tarabolus al-Gharb*) capital and chief port of Libya, on the Mediterranean coast; population (1982) 980,000. Products include olive oil, fruit, fish, and textiles.

history Tripoli was founded about the 7th century BC

by Phoenicians from Oea (now Tripoli in Lebanon). It was a base for Axis powers during World War II. In 1986 it was bombed by the US Air Force in retaliation for international guerrilla activity.

Tripura state of NE India since 1972, formerly a princely state, between Bangladesh and Assam;
area 4,053 sq mi/10,500 sq km
capital Agartala
features agriculture on a rotation system in the rain forest, now being superseded by modern methods
products rice, cotton, tea, sugar cane; steel, jute
population (1991) 2,744,800
language Bengali
religion Hindu.

trireme ancient Greek warship with three banks of oars as well as sails, 115 ft/38 m long. They were used at the battle of ◊Salamis and by the Romans until the 4th century AD.

Tristan legendary Celtic hero who fell in love with Isolde, the bride he was sent to win for his uncle King Mark of Cornwall; the story became part of the Arthurian cycle and is the subject of Wagner's opera *Tristan und Isolde*.

tritium radioactive isotope of hydrogen, three times as heavy as ordinary hydrogen, consisting of one proton and two neutrons. It has a half-life of 12.5 years.

triumvir one of a group of three administrators sharing power in ancient Rome, as in the *First Triumvirate* 60 BC: Caesar, Pompey, Crassus; and *Second Triumvirate* 43 BC: Augustus, Antony, and Lepidus.

Trois-Rivières port on the St Lawrence River, at the point where the St Maurice River enters the St Lawrence, Québec; population (1986) 129,000. The chief industry is the production of newsprint. It was founded by the French explorer Samuel de ◊Champlain 1634.

Trollope Anthony 1815–1882. English novelist who delineated provincial English middle-class society in a series of novels set in or around the imaginary cathedral city of Barchester. *The Warden* 1855 began the series, which includes *Barchester Towers* 1857, *Doctor Thorne* 1858, and *The Last Chronicle of Barset* 1867. His political novels include *Can You Forgive Her?* 1864, *Phineas Finn* 1867–69, and *The Prime Minister* 1875–76.

trombone ◊brass wind musical instrument developed from the sackbut. It consists of a tube bent double, varied notes being obtained by an inner sliding tube. Usual sizes of trombone are alto, tenor, bass, and contra-bass.

trompe l'oeil painting that gives a convincing illusion of three-dimensional reality. It has been common in most periods in the West, from Classical Greece through the Renaissance and later.

trophic level in ecology, the position occupied by a species (or group of species) in a ◊food chain. The main levels are *primary producers* (photosynthetic plants), *primary consumers* (herbivores), *secondary consumers* (carnivores), and *decomposers* (bacteria and fungi).

tropical disease any illness found mainly in hot climates. The most important tropical diseases worldwide are ◊malaria, schistosomiasis, ◊leprosy, and river blindness. Malaria kills about 1.5 million people each year, and produces chronic anemia and tiredness in 100 times as many, while schistosomiasis is responsible for 1 million deaths a year. All the main tropical diseases are potentially curable, but the facilities for diagnosis and treatment are rarely adequate in the countries where they occur.

tropics the area between the tropics of Cancer and Capricorn, defined by the parallels of latitude approximately 23°30' N and S of the equator. They are the limits of the area of Earth's surface in which the Sun can be directly overhead. The mean monthly temperature is over 68°F/20°C.

tropism or *tropic movement* the directional growth of a plant, or part of a plant, in response to an external stimulus such as gravity or light. If the movement is directed toward the stimulus it is described as positive; if away from it, it is negative. *Geotropism* for example, the response of plants to gravity, causes the root (positively geotropic) to grow downward, and the stem (negatively geotropic) to grow upward.

troposphere lower part of the Earth's ◊atmosphere extending about 6.5 mi/10.5 km from the Earth's surface, in which temperature decreases with height to about −76°F/−60°C except in local layers of temperature inversion. The *tropopause* is the upper boundary of the troposphere, above which the temperature increases slowly with height within the atmosphere. All of the Earth's weather takes place within the troposphere.

Trotsky Leon. Adopted name of Lev Davidovitch Bronstein 1879–1940. Russian revolutionary. He joined the Bolshevik party and took a leading part in the seizure of power 1917 and raising the Red Army that fought the Civil War 1918–20. In the struggle for power that followed ◊Lenin's death 1924, ◊Stalin defeated Trotsky, and this and other differences with the Communist Party led to his exile 1929. He settled in Mexico, where he was assassinated with an ice pick at Stalin's instigation. Trotsky believed in world revolution and in permanent revolution, and was an uncompromising, if liberal, idealist.

Trotskyism form of Marxism advocated by Leon Trotsky. Its central concept is that of *permanent revolution*. In his view a proletarian revolution, leading to a socialist society, could not be achieved in isolation, so it would be necessary to spark off further revolutions throughout Europe and ultimately worldwide. This was in direct opposition to the Stalinist view that socialism should be built and consolidated within individual countries.

Troy (Latin *Ilium*) ancient city (now Hissarlik in Turkey) of Asia Minor, just S of the Dardanelles, besieged in the ten-year Trojan War (mid-13th century BC), as described in Homer's *Iliad*. According to the legend, the city fell to the Greeks, who first used the stratagem of leaving behind, in a feigned retreat, a large wooden horse containing armed infiltrators to open the city's gates. Believing it to be a religious offering, the Trojans took it within the walls.

Troy city in E New York, E of Albany on the east bank of the Hudson River; seat of Rensselear County, incorporated 1816; population (1990) 54,300. Industries include clothing, abrasives, metals, paper, automobile and railroad parts, and processed foods.

troy system system of units used for precious metals and gems. The pound troy (0.37 kg) consists of 12 ounces (each of 120 carats) or 5,760 grains (each equal to 65 mg).

Trudeau Pierre (Elliott) 1919– . Canadian Liberal politician. He was prime minister 1968–79 and 1980–84. In 1980, having won again by a landslide on a platform opposing Qúebec separatism, he helped to defeat the Québec independence movement in a referendum. He repatriated the constitution from Britain 1982, but by 1984 had so lost support that he resigned.

Truffaut François 1932–1984. French New Wave film director and actor, formerly a critic. A popular, romantic, and intensely humane filmmaker, he wrote and directed a series of semiautobiographical films starring Jean-Pierre Léaud, beginning with *Les Quatre Cent Coups/The 400 Blows* 1959. His other films include *Jules et Jim* 1961, *Fahrenheit 451* 1966, *L'Enfant sauvage/The Wild Child* 1970, and *La Nuit américaine/Day for Night* 1973 (Academy Award).

His interest in cinema led to a job as film critic for *Cahiers du Cinema* during the 1950s before embarking on his career as director. His later work includes *The Story of Adèle H* 1975 and *The Last Metro* 1980. He was influenced by Alfred Hitchcock, and also drew on Surrealist and comic traditions. He played one of the leading roles in Steven Spielberg's *Close Encounters of the Third Kind* 1977.

truffle subterranean fungus of the order Tuberales. Certain species are valued as edible delicacies; in particular, *Tuber melanosporum*, generally found growing under oak trees. It is native to the Périgord region of France but cultivated in other areas as well. It is rounded, blackish brown, covered with warts externally, and with blackish flesh.

Truk group of about 55 volcanic islands surrounded by a coral reef in the E Caroline islands of the W Pacific, forming one of the four states of the Federated States of Micronesia. Fish and copra are the main products.

Truman Harry S 1884–1972. 33rd president of the US 1945–53, a Democrat. In Jan 1945 he became vice-pres-

Truman US politician and president Harry Truman.

ident to F D Roosevelt, and president when Roosevelt died in April that year. He played an important role at the ◊Potsdam Conference, used ◊atomic bombs against Japan to end World War II, launched the ◊Marshall Plan to restore Western Europe's postwar economy, and nurtured the European Community and NATO (including the rearmament of West Germany). He believed in the ◊United Nations (UN) and when South Korea was invaded by North Korea 1950, had US forces join the UN forces, with General ◊MacArthur at their head. He fired MacArthur 1951 when the general's war policy conflicted with UN aims.

Truman Doctrine US president Harry Truman's 1947 dictum that the US would "support free peoples who are resisting attempted subjugation by armed minorities or by outside pressures." It was used to justify sending a counterinsurgency military mission to Greece after World War II and sending US troops abroad (for example, to Korea).

trumpet small high-register ◊brass wind instrument; a doubled tube with valves. Before the 19th century, the trumpet had no valves and was restricted to harmonies.

tuber Tubers are produced underground from stems, as in the potato, or from roots, as in the dahlia.

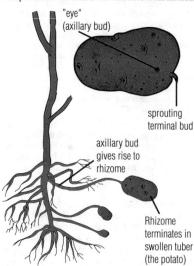

"eye" (axillary bud)

sprouting terminal bud

axillary bud gives rise to rhizome

Rhizome terminates in swollen tuber (the potato)

trust arrangement whereby a person or group of people (the trustee or trustees) hold property for others (the beneficiaries) entitled to the beneficial interest. A trust can be a legal arrangement under which A is empowered to administer property belonging to B for the benefit of C. A and B may be the same person; B and C may not.

A ◊unit trust holds and manages a number of marketable securities; by buying a "unit" in such a trust, the purchaser has a proportionate interest in each of the securities so that his or her risk is spread. Nowadays, an investment trust is not a trust, but a public company investing in marketable securities money subscribed by its stockholders who receive dividends from the income earned. A charitable trust, such as the Ford Foundation, administers funds for charitable purposes. A business trust is formed by linking several companies by transferring shares in them to trustees; or by the creation of a holding company, whose shares are exchanged for those of the separate companies. Competition is thus eliminated, and in the US both types were outlawed by the Sherman Antitrust Act 1890 (first fully enforced by "trust buster" Theodore ◊Roosevelt, as in the breakup of the Standard Oil Company of New Jersey by the Supreme Court 1911).

Trust Territory country or area formerly held under the United Nations trusteeship system to be prepared for independence, either former ◊mandates, territories taken over by the Allies in World War II, or those voluntarily placed under the UN by the administering state.

trypanosome any parasitic flagellate protozoan of the genus *Trypanosoma* that lives in the blood of vertebrates, including humans. They often cause serious diseases, called trypanosomiases, such as sleeping sickness or Chagas' disease, and are transmitted by the bite of such insects as tsetse flies or assassin bugs.

trypanosomiasis any of several debilitating longterm diseases caused by a trypanosome (protozoan of the genus *Trypanosoma*). They include sleeping sickness (nagana) in Africa, transmitted by the bites of ◊tsetse flies, and Chagas' disease in the Americas, spread by assassin bugs.

tsar the Russian imperial title 1547–1721 (although it continued in popular use to 1917), derived from Latin *caesar*.

tsetse fly any of a number of blood-feeding African flies of the genus *Glossina*, some of which transmit the disease nagana to cattle and sleeping sickness to human beings. Tsetse flies may grow up to 0.6 in/1.5 cm long.

tsunami (Japanese "harbor wave") wave generated by an undersea ◊earthquake or volcanic eruption. In the open ocean it may take the form of several successive waves, rarely in excess of a meter in height but traveling at speeds of 400–500 mph/650–800 kph. In the coastal shallows tsunamis slow down and build up, producing towering waves that can sweep inland and cause great loss of life and property. In 1983 an earthquake in the Pacific caused tsunamis up to 10ft/3 m high, which killed more than 100 people in Akita, northern Japan.

Tuareg a member of a nomadic Berber people of the west and central Sahara.

tuba large bass ◊brass wind musical instrument of the cornet family. The *Wagner tuba* combines features of the euphonium and french horn.

tube or *electron tube* in electronics, a glass tube containing gas at low pressure, which is used to control the flow of electricity in a circuit. Three or more metal electrodes are inset into the tube. By varying the voltage on one of them, called the grid electrode, the current through the tube can be controlled, and the tube can act as an amplifier. Tubes have been replaced for most applications by ◊transistors. However, they are still used in high-power transmitters and amplifiers, and in some hi-fi systems.

tuber swollen region of an underground stem or root, usually modified for storing food. The potato is a *stem tuber*, as shown by the presence of terminal and lateral buds, the "eyes" of the potato. *Root tubers*, for example dahlias, developed from adventitious roots (growing from the stem, not from other roots) lack these. Both types of tuber can give rise to new individuals and so provide a means of ◊vegetative reproduction.

tuberculosis (TB) formerly known as *consumption* or *phthisis* infectious disease caused by the bacillus *Mycobacterium tuberculosis*. It takes several forms, of which pulmonary tuberculosis is by far the most common. A vaccine, ◊BCG, was developed around 1920 and the first antituberculosis drug, streptomycin, in 1944.

Tubman US abolitionist. Born a slave in Maryland, she escaped to Philadelphia (where slavery was outlawed) 1849. She set up the *Underground Railroad*, a secret network of sympathizers, to help slaves escape to the North and Canada. During the American ◊Civil War she spied for the Union army. She spoke against slavery and for women's rights, and founded schools for emancipated slaves after the Civil War.

Tubuai Islands or *Austral Islands* chain of volcanic islands and reefs 800 mi/1,300 km long in ◊French Polynesia, S of the Society Islands; area 57 sq

mi/148 sq km; population (1983) 6,300. The main settlement is Mataura on Tubuai. They were visited by Capt Cook 1777 and annexed by France 1880.

Tucson resort city in the Sonora Desert in SE Arizona; population (1990) 405,400. It stands 2,500 ft/760 m above sea level, and the Santa Catalina Mountains to the NE rise to about 9,000 ft/2,750 m. Industries include aircraft, electronics, and copper smelting. Tucson passed from Mexico to the US 1853 and was the territorial capital 1867–77.

Tudor dynasty English dynasty 1485–1603, descended from the Welsh Owen Tudor (*c.* 1400–1461),

---

Tunisia
Tunisian Republic
(*al-Jumhuria at-Tunisiya*)

area 63,378 sq mi/164,150 sq km
capital and chief port Tunis
cities ports Sfax, Sousse, Bizerta
physical arable and forested land in N graduates toward desert in S
features fertile island of Jerba, linked to mainland by causeway (identified with island of lotus-eaters); Shott el Jerid salt lakes; holy city of Kairouan, ruins of Carthage
head of state and government Zine el-Abidine Ben Ali from 1987

political system emergent democratic republic
political party Constitutional Democratic Rally (RCD), nationalist, moderate, socialist
exports oil, phosphates, chemicals, textiles, food, olive oil
currency dinar
population (1992) 8,143,000; growth rate 2% p.a.
life expectancy men 68, women 71 (1989)
languages Arabic (official), French
media publications must be authorized; the offense of defamation is used to protect members of the government from criticism
religion Sunni Muslim 95%; Jewish, Christian
literacy men 68%, women 41% (1985 est)
GNP $9.6 bn (1987); $1,163 per head (1986)

chronology
1883 Became a French protectorate.
1955 Granted internal self-government.
1956 Independence achieved from France as a monarchy, with Habib Bourguiba as prime minister.
1957 Became a republic with Bourguiba as president.
1975 Bourguiba made president for life.
1985 Diplomatic relations with Libya severed.
1987 Bourguiba removed Prime Minister Rashed Sfar and appointed Zine el-Abidine Ben Ali. Ben Ali declared Bourguiba incompetent and seized power.
1988 Constitutional changes toward democracy announced. Diplomatic relations with Libya restored.
1989 Government party, RDC, won all assembly seats in general election.
1991 Opposition to US actions during the Gulf War. Crackdown on religious fundamentalists.

tundra habitat

The landscape around the ice caps at the North and South Poles consists of an open treeless plain called tundra, or muskeg in North America. Winters last for about eight or nine months and the temperature can fall to −85°F/−30°C. The ground is frozen for most of the year, and in the summer there is only time for the topmost layer of soil to thaw. The meltwater cannot drain away and this gives rise to a waterlogged landscape where only low stunted plants grow. Insects flourish during the short summer, and birds migrate into the area to feed on them. Other animals winter in the forests in warmer latitudes and migrate into the region in the summer.

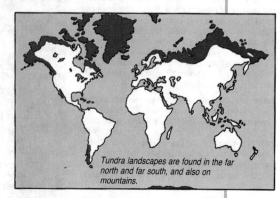

Tundra landscapes are found in the far north and far south, and also on mountains.

Herds of reindeer migrate into the area in the summer to feed on vegetation. Clouds of insects emerge from the ponds and lakes to take advantage of the brief period of sunlight.

reindeer

Water from a spring may freeze underground and eventually force up a dome-shaped hill of ice known as a a pingo.

Arctic hare

Arctic foxes

insects

Expansion and contraction of freezing soil produces wedges of ice that split the ground into polygonal shapes. The outlines of the polygons are marked by channels of rocks or by distinctive vegetation.

Some animals, such as Arctic foxes, develop a white coat in winter.

In the summer only the top several feet of soil can thaw. Below this the ground remains permanently frozen — a condition known as permafrost.

ducks

Canada geese

In winter, the low ground-hugging plants are blanketed and insulated by snow.

second husband of Catherine of Valois (widow of Henry V of England). Their son Edmund married Margaret Beaufort (1443–1509), the great-granddaughter of ◊John of Gaunt, and was the father of Henry VII, who became king by overthrowing Richard III 1485. The dynasty ended with the death of Elizabeth I 1603.

tulip plant of the genus *Tulipa*, family Liliaceae, usually with single goblet-shaped flowers on the end of an upright stem and leaves of a narrow oval shape with pointed ends. It is widely cultivated as a garden flower.

Tulsa city in NE Oklahoma, on the Arkansas River, NE of Oklahoma City; population (1990) 367,300. It is an oil-producing and aerospace center; other industries include mining, machinery, metals, and cement.

tumor overproduction of cells in a specific area of the body, often leading to a swelling or lump. Tumors are classified as benign or malignant (see ◊cancer).

tuna any of various large marine bony fishes of the mackerel family, especially the genus *Thunnus*, popular as food and game. Albacore *T. alalunga*, bluefin tuna *T. thynnus*, and yellowfin tuna *T. albacores* are commercially important.

tundra region of high latitude almost devoid of trees, resulting from the presence of ◊permafrost. The vegetation consists mostly of grasses, sedges, heather, mosses, and lichens. Tundra stretches in a continuous belt across N North America and Eurasia.

tungsten hard, heavy, gray-white, metallic element, symbol W (from German *Wolfram*), atomic number 74, atomic weight 183.85. It occurs in the minerals wolframite, scheelite, and hubertite. It has the highest melting point of any metal (6,170°F/3,410°C) and is added to steel to make it harder, stronger, and more elastic; its other uses include high-speed cutting tools, electrical elements, and thermionic couplings. Its salts are used in the paint and tanning industries.

Tunis capital and chief port of Tunisia; population (1984) 597,000. Industries include chemicals and textiles. Founded by the Arabs, it was captured by the Turks 1533, then occupied by the French 1881 and by the Axis powers 1942–43. The ruins of ancient ◊Carthage are to the NE.

Tunisia country in N Africa, on the Mediterranean Sea, bounded SE by Libya and W by Algeria. *See illustration and panel p. 933*

Turkey
Republic of
(*Türkiye Cumhuriyeti*)

area 300,965 sq mi/779,500 sq km
capital Ankara
cities ports Istanbul and Izmir
physical central plateau surrounded by mountains
environment only 0.3% of the country is protected by national parks and reserves compared with a global average of 7% per country
features Bosporus and Dardanelles; Mount Ararat; Taurus Mountains in SW (highest peak Kaldi Daĝ, 12,255 ft/3,734 m); sources of rivers Euphrates and Tigris in E; archeological sites include çatal Hüyük, Ephesus, and Troy; rock villages of Cappadocia; historic towns (Antioch, Iskenderun, Tarsus)
head of state Suleyman Demirel from 1993
head of government Tansu Ciller from 1993
political system democratic republic
political parties Motherland Party (ANAP), Islamic, nationalist, right of center; Social Democratic Populist Party (SDPP), moderate, left of center; True Path Party (TPP), centre-right
exports cotton, yarn, hazelnuts, citrus, tobacco, dried fruit, chromium ores
currency Turkish lira
population (1992) 58,584,000 (Turkish 85%, Kurdish

12%); growth rate 2.1% p.a.
life expectancy men 63, women 66 (1989)
languages Turkish (official), Kurdish, Arabic
religion Sunni Muslim 98%
literacy men 86%, women 62% (1985)
GNP $112.5 bn (1992)

chronology
1919–22 Turkish War of Independence provoked by Greek occupation of Izmir. Mustafa Kemal (Atatürk), leader of nationalist congress, defeated Italian, French, and Greek forces.
1923 Treaty of Lausanne established Turkey as independent republic under Kemal. Westernization began.
1950 First free elections; Adnan Menderes became prime minister.
1960 Menderes executed after military coup by General Cemal Gürsel.
1965 Suleyman Demirel became prime minister.
1971 Army forced Demirel to resign.
1973 Civilian rule returned under Bulent Ecevit.
1974 Turkish troops sent to protect Turkish community in Cyprus.
1975 Demirel returned to head of a right-wing coalition.
1978 Ecevit returned, as head of coalition, in the face of economic difficulties and factional violence.
1979 Demeril returned. Violence grew.
1980 Army took over, and Bulent Ulusu became prime minister. Harsh repression of political activists attracted international criticism.
1982 New constitution adopted.
1983 Ban on political activity lifted. Turgut Özal became prime minister.
1987 Özal maintained majority in general election.
1988 Improved relations and talks with Greece.
1989 Özal elected president; Yildirim Akbulut became prime minister. Application to join European Community (EC) rejected.
1991 Mesut Yilmaz became prime minister. Turkey sided with UN coalition against Iraq in Gulf War. Conflict with Kurdish minority continued. Coalition government formed under Suleyman Demirel after inconclusive election result.
1992 Earthquake claimed thousands of lives.
1993 Özal died and was succeeded by Demirel. Tansu Ciller became prime minister.

turkey The common turkey, native to wooded country in the US and Mexico, is a strong flier over short distances.

Tunney Gene 1898–1978. US boxer. As a professional he won the US light-heavyweight title 1922. He began to fight as a heavyweight in 1924 and was the upset winner over heavyweight champion Jack Dempsey 1926. Tunney retained the title against Dempsey in the famous "Long Count" bout 1927 and retired undefeated 1928.

After his retirement from boxing, he became successful in business and published *A Man Must Fight* 1932 and *Arms for Living* 1941.

turbine engine in which steam, water, gas, or air (see ◊windmill) is made to spin a rotating shaft by pushing on angled blades, like a fan. Turbines are among the most powerful machines. Steam turbines are used to drive generators in power stations and ships' propellers; water turbines spin the generators in hydroelectric power plants; and gas turbines (as jet engines; see ◊jet propulsion) power most aircraft and drive machines in industry.

turbot any of various flatfishes of the flounder group prized as food, especially *Scophthalmus maximus* found in European waters. It grows up to 3 ft/1 m long and weighs up to 30 lb/14 kg. It is brownish above and whitish underneath.

Turgenev Ivan Sergeievich 1818–1883. Russian writer, notable for poetic realism, pessimism, and skill in characterization. His works include the play *A Month in the Country* 1849, and the novels *A Nest of Gentlefolk* 1858, *Fathers and Sons* 1862, and *Virgin Soil* 1877. His series *A Sportsman's Sketches* 1852 criticized serfdom.

Turin (Italian *Torino*) capital of Piedmont, NW Italy, on the river Po; population (1988) 1,025,000. Industries include iron, steel, automobiles, silk and other textiles, fashion goods, chocolate, and wine. There is a university, established 1404, and a 15th-century cathedral. Features include the Palazzo Reale (Royal Palace) 1646–58 and several gates to the city. It was the first capital of united Italy 1861–64.

Turing Alan Mathison 1912–1954. English mathematician and logician. In 1936 he described a "universal computing machine" that could theoretically be programmed to solve any problem capable of solution by a specially designed machine. This concept, now called the *Turing machine*, foreshadowed the digital computer.

Turin shroud ancient piece of linen bearing the image of a body, claimed to be that of Jesus. Independent tests carried out 1988 by scientists in Switzerland, the US, and the UK showed that the cloth of the shroud dated from between 1260 and 1390. The shroud, property of the pope, is kept in Turin Cathedral, Italy.

Turk member of any of the Turkic-speaking peoples of Asia and Europe, especially the principal ethnic group of Turkey. Turkic languages belong to the Altaic family and include Uzbek, Ottoman, Turkish, Azeri, Turkoman, Tatar, Kirghiz, and Yakut.

Turkana, Lake formerly (to 1979) *Lake Rudolf* lake in the Great Rift Valley, 1,230 ft/375 m above sea level, with its northernmost end in Ethiopia and the rest in Kenya; area 3,475 sq mi/9,000 sq km. It is saline, and shrinking by evaporation. Its shores were an early human hunting ground, and valuable remains have been found that are accurately datable because of undisturbed stratification.

turkey any of several large game birds of the pheasant family, native to the Americas. The wild turkey *Meleagris galloparvo* reaches a length of 4.3 ft/1.3 m, and is native to North and Central American woodlands. The domesticated turkey derives from the wild species. The ocellated turkey *Agriocharis ocellata* is found in Central America; it has eyespots on the tail.

Turkey country between the Black Sea to the N and the Mediterranean Sea to the S, bounded E by Armenia, Georgia, and Iran, SE by Iraq and Syria, W by Greece and the Aegean Sea, and NW by Bulgaria.

Turkish language language of central and W Asia, the national language of Turkey. It belongs to the Altaic language family. Varieties of Turkish are spoken in NW Iran and several of the Central Asian Republics, and all have been influenced by Arabic and Persian. Originally written in Arabic script, it has been written within Turkey in a variant of the Roman alphabet since 1928.

Turkmenistan country in central Asia, bounded N by Kazakhstan and Uzbekistan, W by the Caspian Sea, and S by Iran and Afghanistan.

Turks and Caicos Islands British crown colony in the West Indies, the SE archipelago of the Bahamas
area 166 sq mi/430 sq km
capital Cockburn Town on Grand Turk
features a group of some 30 islands, of which six are inhabited. The largest is the uninhabited *Grand Caicos*; others include *Grand Turk* (population 3,100), *South Caicos* (1,400), *Middle Caicos* (400), *North Caicos* (1,300), *Providenciales* (1,000), and *Salt Cay* (300); since 1982 the Turks and Caicos have developed as a tax haven
government governor, with executive and legislative councils (chief minister from 1987 Michael John Bradley, Progressive National Party)
exports crayfish and conch (flesh and shell)
currency US dollar
population (1980) 7,500, 90% of African descent
languages English, French Creole
religion Christian
history secured by Britain 1766 against French and Spanish claims, the islands were a Jamaican dependency 1873–1962, and in 1976 attained internal self-government.

turmeric perennial plant *Curcuma longa* of the ginger family, native to India and the East Indies; also the ground powder from its tuberous rhizomes, used in curries to give a yellow color, and as a dyestuff.

Turner John Napier 1929– . Canadian Liberal politician, prime minister 1984. He was elected to the House of Commons 1962 and served in the cabinet of Pierre Trudeau until resigning 1975. He succeeded Trudeau as party leader and prime minister 1984, but lost the 1984 and 1988 elections. Turner resigned as leader 1989, and returned to his law practice.

Turkmenistan
Republic of

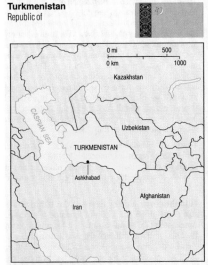

area 188,406 sq mi/488,100 sq km
capital Ashkhabad
cities Chardzhov, Mary (Merv), Nebit-Dag, Krasnovodsk
physical some 90% of land is desert including the Kara Kum "Black Sands" desert (area 120,000 sq mi/ 310,800 sq km)

features on the edge of the Kara Kum desert is the Altyn Depe, "golden hill", site of a ruined city with a ziggurat, or stepped pyramid; river Amu Darya; rich deposits of petroleum, natural gas, sulfur, and other industrial raw materials
head of state Saparmurad Niyazov from 1991
head of government Sakhat Muradov from 1992
political system socialist pluralist
products silk, karakul, sheep, astrakhan fur, carpets, chemicals, rich deposits of petroleum, natural gas, sulfur, and other industrial raw materials
population (1992) 3,859,000 (Turkmen 72%, Russian 10%, Uzbek 9%, Kazakh 3%, Ukrainian 1%)
language West Turkic, closely related to Turkish
religion Sunni Muslim

chronology
1921 Part of Turkestan Soviet Socialist Autonomous Republic.
1925 Became a constituent republic of USSR.
1991 Jan: Communist Party leader Saparmurad Niyazov became state president. Aug: Niyazov initially supported attempted anti-Gorbachev coup. Oct: independence declared. Dec: joined new Commonwealth of Independent States (CIS).
1992 Jan: admitted into Conference for Security and Cooperation in Europe. Feb: joined Muslim Economic Cooperation Organization. March: admitted into UN. May: new constitution adopted. Nov–Dec: 60-member assembly elected with Sakhat Muradov as prime minister.
1993 Dec: hosted CIS conference; signed agreement allowing Russian troops to patrol borders with Iran and Afganistan.

Turner Joseph Mallord William 1775–1851. English landscape painter. He traveled widely in Europe, and his landscapes became increasingly Romantic, with the subject often transformed in scale and flooded with brilliant, hazy light. Many later works anticipate Impressionism; for example, *Rain, Steam and Speed* 1844 (National Gallery, London).

Turner Nat 1800–1831. US slave, who led 60 slaves in the most serious US slave revolt—the Southampton Insurrection of 1831—to capture an armory in Southampton County, Virginia. Before he and 16 of the others were hanged, at least 55 people throughout the region, 24 of them children, had been killed. He thought himself divinely appointed to lead the slaves to freedom. He eluded capture for 6 weeks following the uprising, which so alarmed slave owners that repressive measures forbidding the educating of any blacks were swiftly enacted. Widespread torture and execution followed as owners exacted retribution,

Turner The Fighting Téméraire *(1838),* Tate Gallery, London.

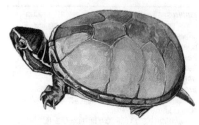

turtle *The common musk turtle lives in the slow, shallow, muddy streams of the US.*

and the abolition movement in the South was abandoned.

Turner Robert Edward III "Ted" 1938– . US businessman and sportsman who developed a conglomerate that includes WTBS, a sports and entertainment cable television channel; CNN, a cable television news network; MGM/UA Entertainment Company; the Atlanta Braves baseball team; and the Atlanta Hawks basketball team. He won the America's Cup 1977.

turnip biennial plant *Brassica rapa* cultivated in temperate regions for its edible white-or yellow-fleshed root and the young leaves, which are used as a green vegetable. Closely allied to it is the rutabaga *B. napus.*

turquoise mineral, hydrous basic copper aluminum phosphate. Blue-green, blue, or green, it is a gemstone. Turquoise is found in Iran, Turkestan, Mexico, and southwestern US.

turtle any member of the reptilian order Chelonia, characterized by a horn-covered bony shell consisting of an upper and lower portion joined along the sides. The main divisions are the hidden-necked turtles (Cryptodira) that withdraw their heads in an S-shaped vertical curve and the side-necked turtles (Pleurodira) that withdraw their heads in a horizontal, sideways curve. See also ◊terrapin, ◊tortoise, and ◊sea turtle.

Tuscaloosa city in W central Alabama, on the Black Warrior River, SW of Birmingham; population (1990) 77,800. Industries include chemicals, tires, paper, and lumber. It was originally founded by Creek Indians 1809.

The University of Alabama 1831 is here.

Tutu South African Anglican archbishop Desmond Tutu speaking at Nelson Mandela's 70th-birthday concert 1988.

Tuscany (Italian *Toscana*) region of N central Italy, on the W coast; area 8,878 sq mi/23,000 sq km; population (1990) 3,562,500. Its capital is Florence, and cities include Pisa, Livorno, and Siena. The area is mainly agricultural, with many vineyards, such as in the Chianti hills; it also has lignite and iron mines and marble quarries (Carrara marble is from here). The Tuscan dialect has been adopted as the standard form of Italian. Tuscany was formerly the Roman *Etruria*, and inhabited by Etruscans around 500 BC. In medieval times the area was divided into small states, united under Florentine rule during the 15th–16th centuries. It became part of united Italy 1861.

Tussaud Madame (Anne Marie Grosholtz) 1761–1850. French wax-modeler. In 1802 she established an exhibition of wax models of celebrities in London. It was destroyed by fire 1925, but reopened 1928.

Tutankhamen king of Egypt of the 18th dynasty, about 1360–1350 BC. A son of Ikhnaton (also called Amenhotep IV), he was about 11 at his accession. In 1922 his tomb was discovered by the British archeologists Lord Carnarvon and Howard Carter in the Valley of the Kings at Luxor, almost untouched by tomb robbers. The contents included many works of art and his solid-gold coffin, which are now displayed in a Cairo museum.

Tutsi member of a minority ethnic group living in Rwanda and Burundi. Although fewer in number, they have traditionally been politically dominant over the Hutu majority and the Twa (or Pygmies). The Tutsi are traditionally farmers; they also hold virtually all positions of importance in Burundi's government and army. They have carried out massacres in response to Hutu rebellions, notably in 1972 and 1988. In Rwanda the balance of power is more even.

Tutu Desmond (Mpilo) 1931– . South African priest, Anglican archbishop of Cape Town and general secretary of the South African Council of Churches 1979–84. One of the leading figures in the struggle against apartheid in the Republic of South Africa, he was awarded the 1984 Nobel Prize for Peace.

Tuva (Russian *Tuvinskaya*) autonomous republic (administrative unit) of Russia, NW of Mongolia;
area 65,813 sq mi/170,500 sq km
capital Kyzyl
features good pasture; gold, asbestos, cobalt
population (1986) 284,000
history part of Mongolia until 1911 and declared a Russian protectorate 1914; after the 1917 revolution it became the independent Tannu-Tuva republic 1920, until incorporated in the USSR as an autonomous region 1944. It was made the Tuva Autonomous Republic 1961.

Tuvalu country in the SW Pacific Ocean; formerly (until 1976) the Ellice Islands; part of ◊Polynesia.

Twain Mark. Adopted name of Samuel Langhorne Clemens 1835–1910. US writer. He established his reputation with the comic masterpiece *The Innocents Abroad* 1869 and two classic American novels, in dialect, *The Adventures of Tom Sawyer* 1876 and *The Adventures of Huckleberry Finn* 1885. He also wrote satire, as in *A Connecticut Yankee at King Arthur's Court* 1889.

tweed cloth made of woolen yarn, usually of several shades, but in its original form without a regular pattern and woven on a hand loom in the more remote parts of Ireland, Wales, and Scotland.

Tuvalu
South West Pacific State of
(formerly *Ellice Islands*)

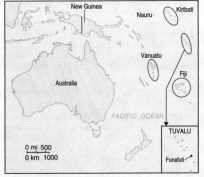

area 9.5 sq mi/25 sq km
capital Funafuti
physical nine low coral atolls forming a chain of 650 mi/
579 km in the SW Pacific
features maximum height above sea level 20 ft/6 m;
coconut palms are main vegetation
head of state Elizabeth II from 1978, represented by
governor-general

head of government Bikenibeu Paeniu from 1989
political system liberal democracy
political parties none; members are elected to parliament
as independents
exports copra, handicrafts, stamps
currency Australian dollar
population (1992) 9,500 (Polynesian 96%); growth rate
3.4% p.a.
life expectancy 60 men, 63 women (1989)
languages Tuvaluan, English
religion Christian (Protestant)
literacy 96% (1985)
GDP (1983) $711 per head

chronology
1892 Became a British protectorate forming part of the
Gilbert and Ellice Islands group.
1916 The islands acquired colonial status.
1975 The Ellice Islands were separated from the Gilbert
Islands.
1978 Independence achieved from Britain, within the
Commonwealth, with Toaripi Lauti as prime minister;
reverted to former name Tuvalu.
1981 Dr Tomasi Puapua replaced Lauti as premier.
1986 Islanders rejected proposal for republican status.
1989 Bikenibeu Paeniu elected new prime minister.

Tweed William Marcy ("Boss") 1823–1878. US politician. He held office in the US House of Representatives 1853–55. In various municipal offices, and from 1867 in New York state senate, he controlled government spending and accumulated a fortune estimated at somewhere between $45 million and $200 million. He was convicted of forgery and larceny and sent to jail 1873–75, when he escaped to Spain.

twelve-tone system or *twelve-note system* system of musical composition in which the 12 notes of the chromatic scale are arranged in a particular order, called a "series" or "tone-row." A work using the system consists of restatements of the series in any of its formations. Arnold ◊Schoenberg and Anton Webern were exponents of this technique.

twin one of two young produced from a single pregnancy. Human twins may be genetically identical, having been formed from a single fertilized egg that splits into two cells, both of which became implanted. Nonidentical twins are formed when two eggs are fertilized at the same time.

two-stroke cycle operating cycle for internal combustion piston engines. The engine cycle is completed after just two strokes (movement up or down) of the piston, which distinguishes it from the more common ◊four-stroke cycle. Power mowers and lightweight motorcycles use two-stroke gasoline engines, which are cheaper and simpler than four-strokes.

TX abbreviation for the state of ◊Texas.

Tyler city in NE Texas, SE of Dallas; population (1990) 75,508. Industries include oil, roses, vegetables, furniture, and plastics.

Tyler John 1790–1862. 10th president of the US 1841–45, succeeding William H ◊Harrison, who died after only one month in office. Tyler was the first US vice president to succeed to the presidency. Because he was not in favor of many of the Whig Party's policies, he was constantly at odds with the cabinet and Congress, until elections forced the Whigs from power and

enabled Tyler to reorganize his cabinet. His government negotiated the Webster–Ashburton Treaty, which settled the Maine–New Brunswick boundary dispute in Canada 1842 and annexed Texas 1845.

Tyler Wat died 1381. English leader of the Peasants' Revolt of 1381. He was probably born in Kent or Essex, and may have served in the French wars. After taking Canterbury he led the peasant army to Blackheath and occupied London. At Mile End King Richard II met the rebels and promised to redress their grievances, which included the imposition of a poll tax. At a further conference at Smithfield, Tyler was murdered.

Tyndale William 1492–1536. English translator of the Bible. The printing of his New Testament (the basis of the King James Version) was begun in Cologne 1525 and, after he had been forced to flee, completed in Worms. He was strangled and burned as a heretic at Vilvorde in Belgium.

Tyndall John 1820–1893. Irish physicist who 1869 studied the scattering of light by invisibly small sus-

Twain US novelist Mark Twain was the first American to write novels in the vernacular.

pended particles. Known as the *Tyndall effect*, it was first observed with colloidal solutions, in which a beam of light is made visible when it is scattered by minute colloidal particles (whereas a pure solvent does not scatter light). Similar scattering of blue wavelengths of sunlight by particles in the atmosphere makes the sky look blue (beyond the atmosphere, the sky is black).

Tyne and Wear metropolitan county in NE England, created 1974, originally administered by an elected metropolitan council; its powers reverted to district councils 1986;
area 208 sq mi/540 sq km
cities Newcastle-upon-Tyne, South Shields, Gateshead, Sunderland
features bisected by the rivers Tyne and Wear; includes part of ◊Hadrian's Wall; Newcastle and Gateshead, linked with each other and with the coast on both sides by the Tyne and Wear Metro (a light railroad using existing suburban lines, extending 34 mi/54 km)
products once a center of heavy industry, it is now being redeveloped and diversified
population (1991) 1,087,000

typesetting means by which text, or copy, is prepared for ◊printing, now usually carried out by computer. Text is keyed on a typesetting machine in a similar way to typing. Laser or light impulses are projected on to light-sensitive film that, when developed, can be used to make plates for printing.

typewriter keyboard machine that produces characters on paper. The earliest known typewriter design was patented by Henry Mills in England 1714. However, the first practical typewriter was built 1867 in Milwaukee, Wisconsin, by Christopher Sholes, Carlos Glidden, and Samuel Soulé. By 1873 Remington and Sons, US gunmakers, produced under contract the first machines for sale and 1878 patented the first with lower-case as well as upper-case (capital) letters.

typhoid fever acute infectious disease of the digestive tract, caused by the bacterium *Salmonella typhi*, and usually contracted through a contaminated water supply. It is characterized by bowel hemorrhage and damage to the spleen. Treatment is with antibiotics.

typhoon violently revolving storm, a ◊hurricane in the W Pacific Ocean.

typhus acute infectious disease, often fatal, caused by bacteria transmitted by lice, fleas, mites, and ticks.

Symptoms include fever, headache, and rash. Typhus is epidemic among people living in overcrowded conditions. Treatment is by antibiotics.

typography design and layout of the printed word. Typography began with the invention of writing and developed as printing spread throughout Europe after the invention of metal moveable type by Johann ◊Gutenberg about 1440. Hundreds of variations have followed since, but the basic design of the Frenchman Nicholas Jensen (about 1420–80), with a few modifications, is still the ordinary ("roman") type used in printing.

Tyr in Norse mythology, the god of battles, whom the Anglo-Saxons called Týw, hence "Tuesday."

tyrannosaurus any of a genus *Tyrannosaurus* of gigantic flesh-eating ◊dinosaurs, order Saurischia, which lived in North America and Asia about 70 million years ago. They had two feet, were up to 50 ft/15 m long, 20 ft/6.5 m tall, weighed 10 tons, and had teeth 6 in/15 cm long.

Tyre (Arabic *Sur* or *Soûr*) town in SW Lebanon, about 50 mi/80 km S of Beirut, formerly a port until its harbor silted up; population (1980 est) about 14,000. It stands on the site of the ancient city of the same name, a seaport of ◊Phoenicia.

Tyrone county of Northern Ireland;
area 1,220 sq mi/3,160 sq km
cities Omagh (county town), Dungannon, Strabane, Cookstown
features rivers: Derg, Blackwater, Foyle; Lough Neagh
products mainly agricultural
population (1981) 144,000.

Tyrrhenian Sea arm of the Mediterranean Sea surrounded by mainland Italy, Sicily, Sardinia, Corsica, and the Ligurian Sea. It is connected to the Ionian Sea through the Straits of Messina. Islands include Elba, Ustica, Capri, Stromboli, and the Lipari Islands.

Tyson Mike (Michael Gerald) 1966– . US heavyweight boxer, undisputed world champion from Aug 1987 to Feb 1990. He won the World Boxing Council heavyweight title 1986 when he beat Trevor Berbick to become the youngest world heavyweight champion. He beat James "Bonecrusher" Smith for the World Boxing Association title 1987 and later that year became the first undisputed champion since 1978 when he beat Tony Tucker for the International Boxing Federation title. He was in prison from 1992.

U-2 US military reconnaissance airplane, used in secret flights over the USSR from 1956 to photograph military installations. In 1960 a U-2 was shot down over the USSR and the pilot, Gary Powers, was captured and imprisoned. He was exchanged for a US-held Soviet agent two years later.

Uccello Paolo. Adopted name of Paolo di Dono 1397–1475. Italian painter, active in Florence, one of the first to use perspective. His surviving paintings date from the 1430s onward. Decorative color and detail dominate his later pictures. His works include *St George and the Dragon* about 1460 (National Gallery, London).

UDI acronym for *unilateral declaration of independence*.

Udmurt (Russian *Udmurtskaya*) autonomous republic in the W Ural foothills, central Russia
area 16,200 sq mi/42,100 sq km
capital Izhevsk
products timber, flax, potatoes, peat, quartz
population (1985) 1,559,000 (58% Russian, 33% Udmurt, 7% Tatar)
history conquered in the 15th–16th centuries; constituted the Votyak Autonomous Region 1920; name changed to Udmurt 1932; Autonomous Republic 1934; part of the independent republic of Russia from 1991.

Uganda landlocked country in E Africa, bounded N by Sudan, E by Kenya, S by Tanzania and Rwanda, and W by Zaire. *See panel p. 942*

UHF (abbreviation for *ultra high frequency*) referring to radio waves of very short wavelength, used, for example, for television broadcasting.

UK abbreviation for the ◊United Kingdom.

Ukraine country in E central Europe, bounded E by Russia, S by Moldova, Romania, and the Black Sea, and W by Poland, the Slovak Republic, and Hungary. *See panel p. 943*

Ukrainian member of the majority ethnic group living in Ukraine; there are minorities in Siberian Russia, Kazakhstan, Poland, the Slovak Republic, and Romania. There are 40–45 million speakers of Ukrainian, a member of the East Slavonic branch of the Indo-European family, closely related to Russian. Ukrainian-speaking communities are also found in Canada and the US.

Uccello *Florentine Renaissance painter Paolo Uccello's* St George and the Dragon *(c. 1460), National Gallery, London.*

Uganda
Republic of

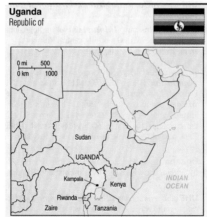

area 91,351 sq mi/236,600 sq km
capital Kampala
cities Jinja, M'Bale, Entebbe, Masaka
physical plateau with mountains in W; forest and grassland; arid in NE
features Ruwenzori Range (Mount Margherita, 16,765 ft/5,110 m); national parks with wildlife (chimpanzees, crocodiles, Nile perch to 160 lb/70 kg); Owen Falls on White Nile where it leaves Lake Victoria; Lake Albert in W
head of state and government Yoweri Museveni from 1986
political system emergent democratic republic
political parties National Resistance Movement (NRM), left of center; Democratic Party (DP), center-left; Conservative Party (CP), center-right; Uganda People's Congress (UPC), left of center; Uganda Freedom Movement (UFM), left of center
exports coffee, cotton, tea, copper
currency Uganda new shilling

population (1992) 17,194,000 (largely the Baganda, after whom the country is named; also Langi and Acholi, some surviving Pygmies); growth rate 3.3% p.a.
life expectancy men 49, women 51 (1989)
languages English (official), Kiswahili, Luganda, and other African languages
religions Roman Catholic 33%, Protestant 33%, Muslim 16%, animist
literacy men 70%, women 45% (1985 est)
GNP $3.6 bn (1987); $220 per head

chronology
1962 Independence achieved from Britain, within the Commonwealth, with Milton Obote as prime minister.
1963 Proclaimed a federal republic with King Mutesa II as president.
1966 King Mutesa ousted in coup led by Obote, who ended the federal status and became executive president.
1969 All opposition parties banned after assassination attempt on Obote.
1971 Obote overthrown in army coup led by Maj Gen Idi Amin Dada; ruthlessly dictatorial regime established; nearly 49,000 Ugandan Asians expelled; over 300,000 opponents of regime killed.
1978 Amin forced to leave country by opponents backed by Tanzanian troops. Provisional government set up with Yusuf Lule as president. Lule replaced by Godfrey Binaisa.
1978–79 Fighting broke out against Tanzanian troops.
1980 Binaisa overthrown by army. Elections held and Milton Obote returned to power.
1985 After opposition by National Resistance Army (NRA), and indiscipline in army, Obote ousted by Brig Tito Okello; power-sharing agreement entered into with NRA leader Yoweri Museveni.
1986 Agreement ended; Museveni became president, heading broad-based coalition government.
1992 Announcement made that East African cooperation pact with Kenya and Tanzania would be revived.
1993 King of Baganda reinstated as formal monarch.

ukulele type of small four-stringed ◊guitar.

Ulaanbaatar or *Ulan Bator*, formerly (until 1924) *Urga* capital of the Mongolian Republic; a trading center producing carpets, textiles, vodka; population (1991) 575,000.

ulcer any persistent breach in a body surface (skin or mucous membrane). It may be caused by infection, irritation, or tumor. Common ulcers include stomach, peptic, mouth (aphthous), intestinal (see ◊colitis), and varicose.

Ulster former kingdom in Northern Ireland, annexed by England 1461, from Jacobean times a center of English, and later Scottish, settlement on land confiscated from its owners; divided 1921 into Northern Ireland (counties Antrim, Armagh, Down, Fermanagh, Londonderry, and Tyrone) and the Republic of Ireland (counties Cavan, Donegal, and Monaghan).

ultrasound pressure waves similar in nature to sound waves but occurring at frequencies above 20,000 Hz (cycles per second), the approximate upper limit of human hearing (15–16 Hz is the lower limit). Ultrasonics is concerned with the study and practical application of these phenomena.

ultrasound scanning or *ultrasonography* in medicine, the use of ultrasonic pressure waves to create a diagnostic image. It is a safe, noninvasive technique that often eliminates the need for exploratory surgery.

ultraviolet astronomy study of cosmic ultraviolet emissions using artificial satellites. The US has

launched a series of satellites for this purpose, receiving the first useful data 1968. Only a tiny percentage of solar ultraviolet radiation penetrates the atmosphere, this being the less dangerous longer-wavelength ultraviolet. The dangerous shorter-wavelength radiation is absorbed by gases in the ozone layer high in the Earth's upper atmosphere.

ultraviolet radiation light rays invisible to the human eye, of wavelengths from about 4×10^{-4} to 5×10^{-6} millimeters(where the ◊X-ray range begins). Physiologically, they are important but also dangerous, causing the formation of vitamin D in the skin and producing sunburn in excess. They are strongly germicidal and may be produced artificially by mercury vapor and arc lamps for therapeutic use.

Ulysses Roman name for ◊Odysseus, the Greek mythological hero.

Ulysses space probe to study the Sun's poles, launched 1990 by a US space shuttle. It is a joint project by NASA and the European Space Agency. In Feb 1992, the gravity of Jupiter swung *Ulysses* on to a path that loops it first under the Sun's south pole in 1994 and then over the north pole in 1995 to study the Sun and solar wind at latitudes not observable from the Earth.

Umayyad alternate spelling of ◊Omayyad dynasty.

umbilical cord connection between the ◊embryo and the ◊placenta of placental mammals. It has one vein and two arteries, transporting oxygen and nutrients to the developing young, and removing waste

Ukraine

area 233,089 sq mi/603,700 sq km
capital Kiev
cities Kharkov, Donetsk, Odessa, Dnepropetrovsk, Lugansk (Voroshilovgrad), Lviv (Lvov), Mariupol (Zhdanov), Krivoi Rog, Zaporozhye
physical Russian plain; Carpathian and Crimean Mountains; rivers: Dnieper (with the Dnieper dam 1932), Donetz, Bug
features Askaniya-Nova Nature Preserve (established 1921); health spas with mineral springs
head of state Leonid Kravchuk from 1990
head of government Leonid Kravchuk from 1993
political system emergent democracy
political party Ukrainian People's Movement (Rukh), umbrella nationalist grouping, with three leaders
products grain, coal, oil, various minerals
currency grivna
population (1992) 52,135,000 (Ukrainian 73%, Russian 22%, Byelorussian 1%, Russian-speaking Jews 1%—some 1.5 million have emigrated to the US, 750,000 to Canada)

language Ukrainian (Slavonic)
famous people Ivan Kotlyarevsky and Taras Shevchenko
religions traditionally Ukrainian Orthodox; also Ukrainian Catholic

chronology
1918 Independent People's Republic proclaimed.
1920 Conquered by Soviet Red Army.
1921 Poland allotted charge of W Ukraine.
1932–33 Famine caused the deaths of more than 7.5 million people.
1939 W Ukraine occupied by Red Army.
1941–44 Under Nazi control; Jews massacred at Babi Yar; more than 5 million Ukrainians and Ukrainian Jews deported and exterminated.
1944 Soviet control reestablished.
1945 Became a founder member of the United Nations.
1946 Ukrainian Uniate Church proscribed and forcibly merged with Russian Orthodox Church.
1986 April: Chernobyl nuclear disaster.
1989 Ukrainian People's Movement (Rukh) established. Ban on Ukrainian Uniate Church lifted.
1990 July: voted to proclaim sovereignty; former Communist Party (CP) leader Leonid Kravchuk indirectly elected president; sovereignty declared.
1991 Aug: demonstrations against the abortive anti Gorbachev coup; independence declared, pending referendum; CP activities suspended. Oct: voted to create independent army. Dec: Kravchuk popularly elected president; independence overwhelmingly endorsed in referendum; joined new Commonwealth of Independent States; independence acknowledged by US and European Community.
1992 Jan: admitted into Conference on Security and Cooperation in Europe (CSCE); pipeline deal with Iran to end dependence on Russian oil; prices freed. Feb: prices "temporarily" re-regulated. March: agreed tactical arms shipments to Russia suspended. May: Crimean sovereignty declared, but subsequently rescinded. Aug: joint control of Black Sea fleet agreed with Russia. Oct: Leonid Kuchma became prime minister.
1993 Sept: President Kravchuk eliminated post of prime minister.

products. At birth, the umbilical cord drops off or is severed, leaving a scar called the navel.

Uncle Sam nickname for the US government. It was coined during the War of 1812 by opponents of US policy. It was probably derived from the initials "US" placed on government property.

Uncle Tom's Cabin best-selling US novel by Harriet Beecher Stowe, written 1851–52. A sentimental but powerful portrayal of the cruelties of slave life on Southern plantations, it promoted the call for abolition. The heroically loyal slave Uncle Tom has in the 20th century become a byword for black subservience.

unconformity in geology, a break in the sequence of ◊sedimentary rocks. It is usually seen as an eroded surface, with the ◊beds above and below lying at different angles. An unconformity represents an ancient land surface, where exposed rocks were worn down by erosion and later covered in a renewed cycle of deposition. *See illustration p. 944*

underground economy unofficial economy of a country, which includes undeclared earnings from a second job ("moonlighting") and enjoyment of undervalued goods and services (such as company "perks"), designed for tax evasion purposes. In industrialized countries, it has been estimated to equal about 10% of ◊gross domestic product.

Underground Railroad in US history, a network established in the North before the ◊American Civil War to provide sanctuary and assistance for escaped black slaves. Safe houses, transport facilities, and "conductors" existed to lead the slaves to safety in the North and Canada, although the number of fugitives who secured their freedom by these means may have been exaggerated.

unemployment lack of paid employment. The unemployed are usually defined as those out of work who are available for and actively seeking work. Unemployment is measured either as a total or as a percentage of those who are available for work, known as the working population or labor force. Periods of widespread unemployment in Europe and the US in the 20th century include 1929–1930s, and the years since the mid-1970s.

UNESCO (acronym for *United Nations Educational, Scientific, and Cultural Organization*) agency of the UN, established 1946, with its headquarters in Paris. The US, contributor of 25% of its budget, withdrew 1984 on grounds of its "overpoliticization and mismanagement," and Britain followed 1985.

ungulate general name for any hoofed mammal. Included are the odd-toed ungulates (perissodactyls) and the even-toed ungulates (artiodactyls), along with subungulates such as elephants.

unconformity The Great Unconformity—between the Hakatai shales and the overlying Tapeats sandstone—in the Grand Canyon, Arizona.

Uniate Church any of the ◊Orthodox churches that accept the Catholic faith and the supremacy of the pope and are in full communion with the Roman Catholic church, but retain their own liturgy and separate organization.

UNICEF acronym for *United Nations International Children's Emergency Fund.*

unicellular organism animal or plant consisting of a single cell. Most are invisible without a microscope but a few, such as the giant ◊ameba, may be visible to the naked eye. The main groups of unicellular organisms are bacteria, protozoa, unicellular algae, and unicellular fungi or yeasts. Some become disease-causing agents, ◊pathogens.

unicorn mythical animal referred to by Classical writers, said to live in India and resembling a horse, but with one spiraled horn growing from the forehead.

It was especially important in medieval Christian symbolism and lore.

unidentified flying object or *UFO* any light or object seen in the sky whose immediate identity is not apparent. Despite unsubstantiated claims, there is no evidence that UFOs are alien spacecraft. On investigation, the vast majority of sightings turn out to have been of natural or identifiable objects, notably bright stars and planets, meteors, aircraft, and satellites, or to have been perpetrated by pranksters. The term *flying saucer* was coined in 1947 and has been in use since.

Unification Church or *Moonies* church founded in Korea 1954 by the Reverend Sun Myung ◊Moon. The number of members (often called "moonies") is about 200,000 worldwide. The theology unites Christian and Taoist ideas and is based on Moon's book *Divine Principle*, which teaches that the original purpose of creation was to set up a perfect family, in a perfect relationship with God.

There are few other rituals, although there is a weekly pledge, which is a ceremony of rededication. Accusations that the church engages in a cultlike programming of members, together with its business,

political, and journalistic activities, have given it a persistently controversial and unsavory reputation.

unified field theory in physics, the theory that attempts to explain the four fundamental forces (strong nuclear, weak nuclear, electromagnetic, and gravity) in terms of a single unified force (see ◊particle physics).

uniformitarianism in geology, the principle that processes that can be seen to occur on the Earth's surface today are the same as those that have occurred throughout geological time. For example, desert sandstones containing sand-dune structures must have been formed under conditions similar to those present in deserts today. The principle was formulated by James ◊Hutton and expounded by Charles ◊Lyell.

Union, Act of 1707 Act of Parliament that brought about the union of England and Scotland; that of 1801 united England and Ireland. The latter was revoked when the Irish Free State was constituted 1922.

Union of Soviet Socialist Republics (USSR) former country in N Asia and E Europe that reverted to independent states 1991; see ◊Armenia, ◊Azerbaijan, ◊Belarus, ◊Estonia, ◊Georgia, ◊Kazakhstan, ◊Kyrgyzstan, ◊Latvia, ◊Lithuania, ◊Moldova, ◊Russian Federation, ◊Tajikistan, ◊Turkmenistan, ◊Ukraine, and ◊Uzbekistan. *See map pp. 946–47*

unit standard quantity in relation to which other quantities are measured. There have been many systems of units. Some ancient units, such as the day, the foot, and the pound, are still in use. ◊SI units, the latest version of the metric system, are widely used in science.

Unitarianism a Christian denomination that rejects the orthodox doctrine of the Trinity and gives a preeminent position to Jesus as a religious teacher, while denying his deity. Unitarians believe in individual conscience and reason as a guide to right action, rejecting the doctrines of original sin, the atonement, and eternal punishment. See also ◊Arianism and Socinianism.

United Arab Emirates (UAE)
(*Ittihad al-Imarat al-Arabiyah*)
federation of the emirates of Abu Dhabi,
Ajman, Dubai, Fujairah, Ras al
Khaimah,
Sharjah, Umm al Qaiwain

total area 32,292 sq mi/83,657 sq km
capital Abu Dhabi
cities (chief port) Dubai
physical desert and flat coastal plain; mountains in E
features linked by dependence on oil revenues

head of state and of government Sheik Sultan Zayed bin
al-Nahayan of Abu Dhabi from 1971
political system absolutism
political parties none
exports oil, natural gas, fish, dates
currency UAE dirham
population (1992) 1,989,000 (10% nomadic); growth rate
6.1% p.a.
life expectancy men 68, women 72 (1989)
languages Arabic (official), Farsi, Hindi, Urdu, English
religions Muslim 96%, Christian, Hindu
literacy 68% (1989)
GNP $22 bn (1987); $11,900 per head

chronology
1952 Trucial Council established.
1971 Federation of Arab Emirates formed; later dissolved.
Six Trucial States formed United Arab Emirates, with ruler of
Abu Dhabi, Sheik Zayed, as president.
1972 The seventh state, Ras al Khaimah, joined the
federation.
1976 Sheik Zayed threatened to relinquish presidency
unless progress toward centralization became more rapid.
1985 Diplomatic and economic links with USSR and China
established.
1987 Diplomatic relations with Egypt restored.
1990–91 Iraqi invasion of Kuwait opposed; UAE fights with
UN coalition.
1991 Bank of Commerce and Credit International (BCCI)
controlled by Abu Dhabi's ruler, collapsed.

Unitas John Constantine 1933– . US football player.
He was signed by the Baltimore Colts 1956 and led the
team to five NFL championship titles in the years
1958–71. Following his release from the Colts, Unitas
played for the San Diego Chargers 1973. He was one of
the greatest passers in the history of the game.

United Arab Emirates federation in SW Asia, on
the Arabian Gulf, bounded NW by Qatar, SW by Saudi
Arabia, and SE by Oman.

United Arab Republic union formed 1958, broken
1961, between ◊Egypt and ◊Syria. Egypt continued to
use the name after the breach up until 1971.

United Kingdom (UK) country in NW Europe off the
coast of France, consisting of England, Scotland,
Wales, and Northern Ireland. *See maps and panel
pp. 948–50*

United Nations (UN) association of states for
international peace, security, and cooperation, with
its headquarters in New York. The UN was established 1945 as a successor to the ◊League of Nations,
and has played a role in many areas, such as refugees,
development assistance, disaster relief, and cultural
cooperation. Boutros ◊Boutros-Ghali became secretary-general 1992. *See table pp. 952–53*

United Nations Security Council most powerful
body of the UN. It has five permanent members—the
US, Russia, the UK, France, and China—which exercise a veto in that their support is requisite for all decisions, plus ten others, elected for two-year terms by a
two-thirds vote of the General Assembly; retiring members are not eligible for reelection.

United States (US) officially *United States of
America* (USA) country in North America, extend-
ing from the Atlantic Ocean in the E to the Pacific
Ocean in the W, bounded N by Canada and S by
Mexico, and including the outlying states of Alaska
and Hawaii. *See panel, tables, and map pp. 954–59*

United States: architecture little survives of the
earliest native American architecture, although the
early settlers in each region recorded the house and village styles of the local Indians. The most notable prehistoric remains are the cliff dwellings in the
Southwest. Archeologists have also discovered traces
of structures associated with the moundbuilding peoples in the Mississippi river valley. Subsequent architectural forms are those that came with colonizers
from European cultures, those adapted to American
conditions and social development, and, most recently,
those that were developed and innovated by American
architects. *16th and 17th centuries* Earliest European architectural influences were those of the Spanish colonizers, coming N from their Mexican colony or
from early settlements in Florida; most were small or
transitory. Spanish influence in the Southwest and California grew through the 19th century and continued
in the 20th. The dominant American colonial architecture came to the E coast from 17th-century English
immigrants, but also from Dutch, Swedish, and
German settlers. Generally, new arrivals attempted to
reconstruct the architecture they had known in their
home countries, making adaptations to available materials and craftsmanship. Wood tended to be the material of choice in the northern colonies; wood, brick, and
stone in the middle colonies; and wood and brick in the
southern colonies. The earliest styles were primarily
for farm homes and some urban dwellings, churches,
and a few public buildings. Houses most often were
small, had massive chimney stacks, and were timber-
framed with brick, clapboard, or wattle-and-daub
walls. Early churches and civic buildings were like
large houses rather than imposing edifices. By the end
of the century, with more settlers, greater resources,
and more skilled builders, more elegant and elaborate
examples of Jacobean and Queen Anne style were
built, and more imposing public architecture was constructed, such as William and Mary College in
Williamsburg, Virginia. *18th century* Neo-Classical

The successor republics to the USSR

ARCTIC OCEAN

BALTIC SEA

Part of
Russian Federation

Lithuania

Estonia

Latvia

Belarus

Moscow

RUSSIAN

Moldova

Ukraine

BLACK SEA

Georgia

Armenia

Azerbaijan

CASPIAN SEA

Kazakhstan

ARAL
SEA

Uzbekistan

Turkmenistan

Kyrgyzstan

Tajikistan

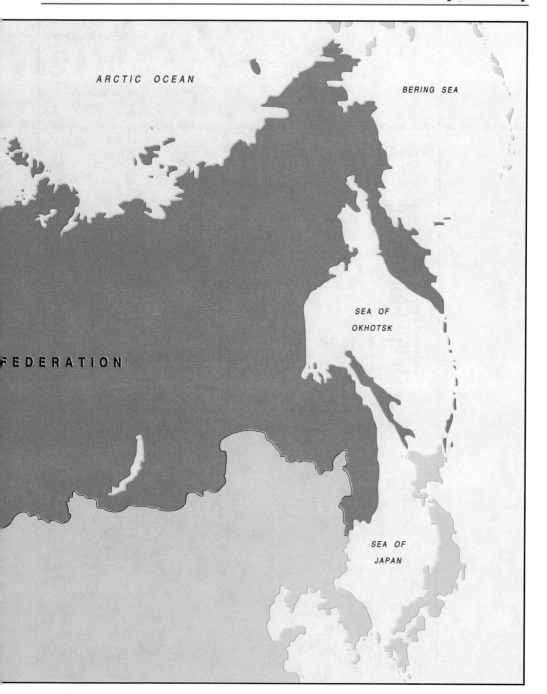

United Kingdom

ATLANTIC

OCEAN

SHETLAND

ORKNEY

NORTH

SEA

The districts of Northern Ireland
1 Londonderry
2 Limavady
3 Coleraine
4 Ballymoney
5 Moyle
6 Larne
7 Ballymena
8 Magherafelt
9 Cookstown
10 Strabane
11 Omagh
12 Fermanagh
13 Dungannon
14 Craigavon
15 Armagh
16 Newry and Mourne
17 Banbridge
18 Down
19 Lisburn
20 Antrim
21 Newtownabbey
22 Carrickfergus
23 North Down
24 Arda
25 Castlereagh
26 Belfast

WESTERN
ISLES

HIGHLAND

GRAMPIAN

S C O T L A N D

TAYSIDE

FIFE

CENTRAL

STRATHCLYDE

Edinburgh

LOTHIAN

BORDERS

NORTHUMBERLAND

DUMFRIES
AND GALLOWAY

TYNE AND WEAR

DURHAM

CLEVELAND

CUMBRIA

NORTH YORKSHIRE

ISLE
OF MAN

DONEGAL

LEITRIM

SLIGO

MAYO

ROSCOMMON

GALWAY

LONGFORD

CAVAN

MONAGHAN

WEST
MEATH

OFFALY

LOUTH

MEATH

KILDARE

DUBLIN

Dublin

I R E L A N D

LAOIS

CLARE

LIMERICK

TIPPERARY

KILKENNY

CARLOW

WICKLOW

WEXFORD

KERRY

CORK

WATERFORD

N

I R E L A N D

St. George's Channel

LANCASHIRE

GREATER MANCHESTER

MERSEYSIDE

W
YORKS

HUMBERSIDE

S
YORKS

NOTT

DERBYSHIRE

LINCOLNSHIRE

CHESHIRE

GWYNEDD

CLWYD

SHROP
SHIRE

STAFFORD
SHIRE

LEICESTERSHIRE

NORFOLK

WALES

POWYS

WEST MIDLANDS

WARWICK
SHIRE

NORTHAMPTON

CAMBRIDGE
SHIRE

SUFFOLK

HEREFORD
AND WORCESTER

BEDFORD
SHIRE

HERTFORD

ESSEX

DYFED

GLOUCESTER
SHIRE

OXFORD
SHIRE

BUCKS

GREATER
London LONDON

WEST GLAMORGAN
MID GLAMORGAN
SOUTH GLAMORGAN

GWENT

Cardiff

AVON

WILTSHIRE

BERKSHIRE

SURREY

KENT

E
N
G
L
A
N
D

SOMERSET

HAMPSHIRE

WEST
SUSSEX

EAST
SUSSEX

Str. of Dover

DEVON

DORSET

ISLE OF WIGHT

CORNWALL

ENGLISH CHANNEL

Isles of Scilly

Alderney

Guernsey

Channel Is.
(Br.)

Jersey

ATLANTIC   OCEAN

FRANCE

0   50   100   150 miles
0   100   200 km

United Kingdom
of Great Britain and Northern Ireland
(UK)

area 94,247 sq mi/244,100 sq km
capital London
cities Birmingham, Glasgow, Leeds, Sheffield, Liverpool, Manchester, Edinburgh, Bradford, Bristol, Belfast, Newcastle-upon-Tyne, Cardiff
physical became separated from European continent about 6000 BC; rolling landscape, increasingly mountainous toward the N, with Grampian Mountains in Scotland, Pennines in N England, Cambrian Mountains in Wales; rivers include Thames, Severn, and Spey
territories Anguilla, Bermuda, British Antarctic Territory, British Indian Ocean Territory, British Virgin Islands, Cayman Islands, Falkland Islands, Gibraltar, Hong Kong (until 1997), Montserrat, Pitcairn Islands, St Helena and Dependencies (Ascension, Tristan da Cunha), Turks and Caicos Islands
environment an estimated 67% (the highest percentage in Europe) of forests have been damaged by acid rain
features milder climate than N Europe because of Gulf Stream; considerable rainfall. Nowhere more than 74.5 mi/120 km from sea; indented coastline, various small islands
head of state Elizabeth II from 1952
head of government John Major from 1990
political system liberal democracy
political parties Conservative and Unionist Party, right of center; Labour Party, moderate left of center; Social and Liberal Democrats, center-left; Scottish National Party (SNP), Scottish nationalist; Plaid Cymru (Welsh Nationalist Party), Welsh nationalist; Official Ulster Unionist Party (OUP), Democratic Unionist Party (DUP), Ulster People's Unionist Party (UPUP), all Northern Ireland right of center, in favor of remaining part of United Kingdom; Social Democratic Labour Party (SDLP), Northern Ireland, moderate left of center; Sinn Féin, Northern Ireland, socialist, pro- united Ireland; Green Party, ecological
exports cereals, rape, sugar beet, potatoes, meat and meat products, poultry, dairy products, electronic and telecommunications equipment, engineering equipment and scientific instruments, oil and gas, petrochemicals, pharmaceuticals, fertilizers, film and television programs, aircraft
currency pound sterling (£)
population (1992) 57,561,000 (81.5% English, 9.6% Scottish, 1.9% Welsh, 2.4% Irish, 1.8% Ulster); growth rate 0.1% p.a.
religion Christian (55% Protestant, 10% Roman Catholic); Muslim, Jewish, Hindu, Sikh
life expectancy men 72, women 78 (1989)
languages English, Welsh, Gaelic
literacy 99% (1989)
GNP $1,040.5 bn (1992)

chronology
1707 Act of Union between England and Scotland under Queen Anne.
1721 Robert Walpole unofficially first prime minister, under George I.
1783 Loss of North American colonies that form US; Canada retained.
1801 Act of Ireland united Britain and Ireland.
1819 Peterloo massacre: cavalry charged a meeting of supporters of parliamentary reform.
1832 Great Reform Bill became law, shifting political power from upper to middle class.
1838 Chartist working-class movement formed.
1846 Corn Laws repealed by Robert Peel.
1851 Great Exhibition in London.
1867 Second Reform Bill, extending the franchise, introduced by Disraeli and passed.
1906 Liberal victory; program of social reform.
1911 Powers of House of Lords curbed.
1914 Irish Home Rule Bill introduced.
1914–18 World War I.
1916 Lloyd George became prime minister.
1920 Home Rule Act incorporated NE of Ireland (Ulster) into the United Kingdom of Great Britain and Northern Ireland.
1921 Ireland, except for Ulster, became a dominion (Irish Free State, later Eire, 1937).
1924 First Labour government led by Ramsay MacDonald.
1926 General Strike.
1931 Coalition government; unemployment reached 3 million.
1939 World War II began.
1940 Winston Churchill became head of coalition government.
1945 Labour government under Clement Attlee; welfare state established.
1951 Conservatives under Winston Churchill defeated Labour.
1956 Suez Crisis.
1964 Labour victory under Harold Wilson.
1970 Conservatives under Edward Heath defeated Labour.
1972 Parliament prorogued in Northern Ireland; direct rule from Westminster began.
1973 UK joined European Economic Community.
1974 Three-day week, coal strike; Wilson replaced Heath.
1976 James Callaghan replaced Wilson as prime minister.
1977 Liberal–Labour pact.
1979 Victory for Conservatives under Margaret Thatcher.
1981 Formation of Social Democratic Party (SDP). Riots occurred in inner cities.
1982 Unemployment over 3 million. Falklands War.
1983 Thatcher reelected.
1984–85 Coal strike, the longest in British history.
1986 Abolition of metropolitan counties.
1987 Thatcher reelected for third term.
1988 Liberals and most of SDP merged into the Social and Liberal Democrats, leaving a splinter SDP. Inflation and interest rates rose.
1989 The Green Party polled 2 million votes in the European elections.
1990 Riots as poll tax introduced in England. Troops sent to the Persian Gulf following Iraq's invasion of Kuwait. British hostages held in Iraq, later released. Britain joined European exchange rate mechanism (ERM). Thatcher replaced by John Major as Conservative leader and prime minister.
1991 British troops took part in US-led war against Iraq under United Nations umbrella. Severe economic recession and rising unemployment.
1992 Recession continued. April: Conservative Party won fourth consecutive general election, but with reduced majority. John Smith replaced Neil Kinnock as Labour leader. Sept: sterling devalued and UK withdrawn from ERM. Oct: drastic coal mine closure program encountered massive public opposition; subsequently reviewed. Major's popularity at unprecedentedly low rating. Nov: Maastricht Treaty on European union ratified. Revelations of past arms sales to Iraq implicated senior government figures, including the prime minister.
1993 Recession continued. The Conservatives placed third in a by-election, and the chancellor of the Exchequer was replaced. Maastricht Treaty formally ratified.

North

Shetland Is

Orkney Is

Pentland Firth

Outer Hebrides

North
Minch

Inner Hebrides

NORTH

Skye

Rhum

Coll

Tiree

Mull

Jura

Islay

Arran

West Highlands

North Highlands

Grampian Mts

Ness

Dee

Tay

Forth

Clyde

Tweed

▲ Ben Nevis
4402ft/1342m

SEA

ATLANTIC

OCEAN

Southern Uplands

Cheviot Hills

Tyne

Tees

Pennines

North York
Moors

Spernn Mts

L. Neagh

Mts of Antrim

North Channel

Cumbrian Mts

Scafell Pike
3208ft/978m

L. Erne

L. Mask

L. Corrib

Central Plain

Shannon

Barrow

Wicklow
Mts

Macgillycuddys Reeks
3415ft/1041m ▲
Mts of Kerry

Blackwater

St. George's Channel

I. of Man

IRISH SEA

Liverpool Bay

Ribble

Mersey

Trent

The
Wash

Snowdon ▲
3559ft/1085m

Cardigan Bay

Cambrian Mts

Severn

Avon

Welland

Ouse

The Fens

Cotswolds

Thames

London

Bristol Channel

Exmoor

Dartmoor

South Downs

North Downs

Str. of Dover

ENGLISH CHANNEL

Isles of Scilly

Alderney

Guernsey

*Channel Is.
(Br.)*

Jersey

FRANCE

| 0 | 50 | 100 | 150 miles |
| 0 | 100 | 200 km | |

style dominated and was referred to as Georgian architecture, although designs lagged behind English sources, and the scale of projects was generally modest. No architects set up offices, but itinerant master craftsmen with plan-and-model books, working for educated colonial sponsors, diffused European-style developments along the eastern seaboard. Many fine homes were built, with distinct variations preferred in each of the colonial regions. Many churches and public buildings were influenced by British architect Christopher Wren. As settlement moved inland, the rough-hewn timber or log cabin became an American architectural mainstay. Other, finer, buildings from this period include numerous plantation houses, such as Westover or Carter's Grove in Virginia; Dutch patroon mansions along the Hudson River in New York or in E Pennsylvania; the then Virginia capital of Williamsburg; churches with steeples, such as Old North Church in Boston, Christ Church in Philadelphia, Christ Church in Williamsburg; public buildings, such as the Old State House or Fanueil Hall in Boston, Independence Hall in Philadelphia, or Charles Bulfinch's new State House in Boston; and numerous urban structures. *19th century* Early in the century, Neo-Classical patterns were used to design the new republic's buildings, such as the Capitol and the ◊White House in Washington, DC. The style was given strong inspiration by Thomas Jefferson, especially after his stay in Europe. He introduced and promoted a revival of Renaissance architecture based on Andrea Palladio and otherwise helped define what is now known as Federal-period architecture. His own work is best seen in his Virginia home, Monticello (which started as an 18th-century Georgian project and which he transformed throughout his life); in his design for the Virginia state capitol in Richmond, adapted from the Roman Maison Carré at Nimes, France; and in his harmonious plan for the campus of the University of Virginia at Charlottesville. Other structures from the first half of the century include the Greek-revival work of Charles Bulfinch and Benjamin Latrobe (notably in their work on the US Capitol). After the Civil War, Romanesque forms in stone and brick were promoted by Henry Hobson Richardson. An appreciation for and adaptation of French Renaissance design emerged, as well as a Romantic revival of Gothic architecture in both domestic and public buildings. *20th century* Architecture in the early 20th century often combined the elements of earlier times and cultures; pseudo-English Tudor, French Provincial, and Spanish Mission models were built for residences, but Stanford White's Beaux Arts style dominated office buildings, clubs, mansions, and theaters, such as his Madison Square Garden in New York City. Most dramatically, this was the century of the modern architect, and Americans became internationally famous for innovative and creative design, since the ◊skyscraper became the fundamental US contribution to world architecture. Spare, functional Modernist form predominated by mid-century, but by the 1980s a return to softening elements was promoted by Post-Modernists. Notable 20th-century US architects include Frank Lloyd Wright, Louis Henry Sullivan, Walter Gropius, Ludwig Mies van der Rohe, Eliel and Eero Saarinen, I M Pei, Philip Johnson, Kevin Roche, Minoru Yamasaki, and Edward Durrell Stone.

United States: art painting and sculpture in the US from colonial times to the present. The unspoiled American landscapes romantically depicted in the 18th and 19th centuries gave way to realistic and Modernistic city scenes in the 20th. Modern movements have flourished in the US, among them Abstract Expressionism and Pop art. *colonial* The first American-born artist in the European tradition was the portraitist Robert Feke (1705–50). The historical painter Benjamin West, working mainly in England, encouraged the portraitist John Singleton Copley. Charles Willson Peale and Gilbert Stuart, a student of West's, painted the founders of the new nation. *19th century* The recording of the Indians' lifeways by George Catlin, the dramatic landscapes of Washington Allston, the nature pictures of Audubon, the seascapes of Winslow Homer, the art of the West of Frederic Remington, the realism of Thomas Eakins, and the Romantic landscapes of the Hudson River school found in the works of such artists as Thomas Cole, Asher B Durand, Martin Johnson Heade, and Frederick Edwin Church represent the vitality of US art in this century. The Impressionist-influenced James Whistler and Mary Cassatt and the society painter John Singer Sargent were active mainly in Europe. *early 20th century* The members of the Ashcan school, led by Robert Henri, introduced social realism in art; they depicted slum squalor and city life. The group was actually known as The Eight and also included John Sloan, George Luks, William Glackens, Everett Shinn, Maurice Prendergast, Ernest Lawson, and Arthur B Davies. The controversial New York Armory Show 1913 introduced Europe's most avant-garde styles, Cubism and Futurism; Dada arrived soon after, and New York City vied with Paris as the world capital of art. In the 1930s and 1940s, several major European artists emigrated to the US, notably Max Ernst, Max Beckmann, Piet Mondrian, Hans Hoffmann, and Lyonel Feininger. The giant heads of presidents were carved out of Mount Rushmore by G Borglum. *mid-20th century* Abstract Expressionism was practiced by the inventor of action painting, Jackson Pollock, his wife Lee Krasner, and the spiritual Mark Rothko. More politically concerned, Ben Shahn created influential graphics. The sculptor Alexander Calder invented mobiles. *late 20th century* The Pop-art movement, begun in the 1950s with Robert Rauschenberg and Jasper Johns and led by such artists as Andy Warhol, was a reaction against abstract art. It used precise and distorted images from the media, such as advertising, film, television, and comic strips. Andy Warhol painted soup cans 1962; Jasper Johns painted flags and numbers; Roy Lichtenstein used comic-strip characters to depict romance and heroism; Claes Oldenburg made soft sculptures of everyday items, many times their normal size. It led to multimedia works and performance art in the following decades. By the 1990s, extremely high prices were being paid at auction for works of art by well-known artists; museum facilities were expanded to house donated collections and traveling exhibitions; and the designs for art exhibitions, their catalogs, and posters had become, in some ways, art forms in themselves.

United States: literature early US literature falls into two distinct periods: colonial writing 1620–1776, largely dominated by the Puritans, and post-Revolutionary literature after 1787, when the ideal of US literature developed, and poetry, fiction, and drama began to evolve on national principles. *colonial period* 1607–1765 Literature of this period includes travel books and religious verse, but is mainly theological: Roger Williams, Cotton Mather, and Jonathan Edwards were typical Puritan writers. Benjamin Franklin's *Autobiography* is the first work of more than historical interest.

UN membership

country	year of admission	contribution (%) to UN budget	country	year of admission	contribution (%) to UN budget
Afghanistan	1946	0.01	Guinea-Bissau	1974	0.01
Albania	1955	0.01	Guyana	1966	0.01
Algeria	1962	0.16	Haiti†	1945	0.01
Angola	1976	0.01	Honduras†	1945	0.01
Antigua & Barbuda	1981	0.01	Hungary	1955	0.18
Argentina†	1945	0.57	Iceland	1946	0.03
Armenia	1992	***	India†	1945	0.36
Australia†	1945	1.51	Indonesia	1950	0.16
Austria	1955	0.75	Iran†	1945	0.77
Azerbaijan	1992	***	Iraq†	1945	0.13
Bahamas	1973	0.02	Ireland	1955	0.18
Bahrain	1971	0.03	Israel	1949	0.23
Bangladesh	1974	0.01	Italy	1955	4.29
Barbados	1966	0.01	Jamaica	1962	0.01
Belarus†	1945	0.31	Japan	1956	12.45
Belgium†	1945	1.06	Jordan	1955	0.01
Belize	1981	0.01	Kazakhstan	1992	***
Benin	1960	0.01	Kenya	1963	0.01
Bhutan	1971	0.01	Kuwait	1963	0.25
Bolivia†	1945	0.01	Kyrgyzstan	1992	***
Bosnia-Herzegovina	1992	***	Laos	1955	0.01
Botswana	1966	0.01	Latvia	1991	***
Brazil†	1945	1.59	Lebanon†	1945	0.01
Brunei	1984	0.03	Lesotho	1966	0.01
Bulgaria	1955	0.13	Liberia†	1945	0.01
Burkina Faso	1960	0.01	Libya	1955	0.24
Burundi	1962	0.01	Liechtenstein	1990	0.01
Cambodia	1955	0.01	Lithuania	1991	***
Cameroon	1960	0.01	Luxembourg†	1945	0.06
Canada†	1945	3.11	Macedonia	1993	0.01
Cape Verde	1975	0.01	Madagascar	1960	0.01
Central African Republic	1960	0.01	Malawi	1964	0.01
Chad	1960	0.01	Malaysia	1957	0.12
Chile†	1945	0.08	Maldives	1965	0.01
China†	1945	0.77	Mali	1960	0.01
Colombia†	1945	0.13	Malta	1964	0.01
Comoros	1975	0.01	Marshall Islands	1991	0.01
Congo	1960	0.01	Mauritania	1961	0.01
Costa Rica†	1945	0.01	Mauritius	1968	0.01
Côte d'Ivoire	1960	0.02	Mexico†	1945	0.88
Croatia	1992	***	Micronesia	1991	0.01
Cuba†	1945	0.09	Moldova	1992	***
Cyprus	1960	0.02	Monaco	1993	0.01
Czech Republic	1993	***	Mongolia	1961	0.01
Denmark†	1945	0.65	Morocco	1956	0.03
Djibouti	1977	0.01	Mozambique	1975	0.01
Dominica	1978	0.01	Myanmar (Burma)	1948	0.01
Dominican Republic†	1945	0.02	Namibia	1990	0.01
Ecuador†	1945	0.03	Nepal	1955	0.01
Egypt††	1945	0.07	Netherlands†	1945	1.50
El Salvador†	1945	0.01	New Zealand†	1945	0.24
Eritrea	1993	0.01	Nicaragua†	1945	0.01
Equatorial Guinea	1968	0.01	Niger	1960	0.01
Estonia	1991	***	Nigeria	1960	0.20
Ethiopia†	1945	0.01	North Korea	1991	0.05
Fiji	1970	0.01	Norway†	1945	0.55
Finland	1955	0.57	Oman	1971	0.03
France†	1945	6.00	Pakistan	1947	0.06
Gabon	1960	0.02	Panama†	1945	0.02
Gambia	1965	0.01	Papua New Guinea	1975	0.01
Georgia	1992	***	Paraguay†	1945	0.03
Germany **	1973/1990	8.93	Peru†	1945	0.06
Ghana	1957	0.01	Philippines†	1945	0.07
Greece†	1945	0.35	Poland†	1945	0.47
Grenada	1974	0.01	Portugal	1955	0.20
Guatemala†	1945	0.02	Qatar	1971	0.05
Guinea	1958	0.01	Romania	1955	0.17

UN membership (continued)

country	year of admission	contribution (%) to UN budget	country	year of admission	contribution (%) to UN budget
Russian Federation *	1945	9.41	Tunisia	1956	0.03
Rwanda	1962	0.01	Turkey†	1945	0.27
St Christopher–Nevis	1983	0.01	Turkmenistan	1992	***
St Lucia	1979	0.01	Uganda	1962	0.01
St Vincent & Grenadines	1980	0.01	Ukraine†	1945	1.18
San Marino	1992	***	United Arab Emirates	1971	0.21
São Tomé Principe	1975	0.01	United Kingdom†	1945	5.02
Saudi Arabia†	1945	0.96	United States of America†	1945	25.00
Senegal	1960	0.01	Uruguay†	1945	0.04
Seychelles	1976	0.01	Uzbekistan	1992	***
Sierra Leone	1961	0.01	Vanuatu	1981	0.01
Singapore	1965	0.12	Venezuela†	1945	0.49
Slovak Republic	1993	***	Vietnam	1977	0.01
Slovenia	1992	***	Western Samoa	1976	0.01
Solomon Isles	1978	0.01	Yemen **	1947	0.01
Somalia	1960	0.01	Yugoslavia†	1945	0.42
South Africa†	1945	0.41	Zaire	1960	0.01
South Korea	1991	0.69	Zambia	1964	0.01
Spain	1955	1.98	Zimbabwe	1980	0.02
Sri Lanka	1955	0.01			
Sudan	1956	0.01	† founder members		
Suriname	1975	0.01			
Swaziland	1968	0.01	*Became a separate member upon the demise of the		
Sweden	1946	1.11	USSR which was a founder member 1945		
Syria†	1945	0.04			
Tajikistan	1992	***	** represented by two countries until unification 1990		
Tanzania	1961	0.01	*** contributions to be determined		
Thailand	1946	0.11			
Togo	1960	0.01	The sovereign countries that are not UN members are		
Trinidad & Tobago	1962	0.05	Andorra, Kiribati, Nauru, Switzerland, Taiwan, Tonga, Tuvalu, and Vatican City.		

post-Revolutionary period 1785–1820 This period produced much political writing, by Thomas Paine, Thomas Jefferson, and Alexander Hamilton, and one noteworthy poet, Philip Freneau.

early 19th century The influence of English Romantics became evident, notably on the poems of William Cullen Bryant (1794–1878), Washington Irving's tales, Charles Brockden Brown's Gothic fiction, and James Fenimore Cooper's novels of frontier life. During 1830–60 intellectual life was centered in New England, which produced the essayists Ralph Waldo Emerson, Henry Thoreau, and Oliver Wendell Holmes; the poets Henry Wadsworth Longfellow, James Lowell, and John Whittier; and the novelists Nathaniel Hawthorne and Louisa May Alcott. Outside the New England circle were the novelists Edgar Allan Poe and Herman Melville.

post–Civil War period 1865–1900 The disillusionment of this period found expression in the realistic or psychological novel. Ambrose Bierce and Stephen Crane wrote realistic war stories; Mark Twain and Bret Harte dealt with western life; the growth of industrialism led to novels of social realism, notably the works of William Howells and Frank Norris; and Henry James and his disciple Edith Wharton developed the novel of psychological analysis among the well-to-do. The dominant poets were Walt Whitman and Emily Dickinson.

short story This form has attracted many of the major novelists from Hawthorne, Poe, and James onward, and was popularized as a form by O Henry; writers specializing in it have included Ring Lardner, Katherine Anne Porter, Flannery O'Connor, William Saroyan, Eudora Welty, Grace Paley, and Raymond Carver.

drama The US produced a powerful group of playwrights between the wars, including Eugene O'Neill, Maxwell Anderson, Lillian Hellman, Elmer Rice, Thornton Wilder, and Clifford Odets. They were followed by Arthur Miller and Tennessee Williams. A later generation includes Edward Albee, Neil Simon, David Mamet, John Guare, and Sam Shepard.

poetry Poets like Edwin Arlington Robinson, Carl Sandburg, Vachel Lindsay, Robert Frost, and Edna St Vincent Millay extended the poetic tradition of the 19th century, but after the ◊Imagist movement of 1912–14 an experimental modern tradition arose with Ezra Pound, T S Eliot, William Carlos Williams, Marianne Moore, "HD" (Hilda Doolittle), and Wallace Stevens. Attempts at writing the modern US epic include Pound's *Cantos*, Hart Crane's *The Bridge*, and William Carlos Williams's *Paterson*. Among the most striking post–World War II poets are Karl Shapiro, Theodore Roethke, Robert Lowell, Charles Olson, Sylvia Plath, Gwendolyn Brooks, Denise Levertov, John Ashbery, A R Ammons, and Allen Ginsberg.

literary criticism Irving Babbitt (1865–1933), George Santayana, H L Mencken, and Edmund Wilson (1895–1972) were dominant figures, followed by Lionel Trilling (1905–75), Van Wyck Brooks, Yvor Winters (1900–68), and John Crowe Ransom, author of *The New Criticism* 1941, which stressed structural and linguistic factors. More recently, US criticism has been influenced by French literary theory and the journalistic criticism of Gore Vidal, Tom Wolfe, George Plimpton, and Susan Sontag.

fiction since 1900 The main trends have been realism, as exemplified in the work of Jack London, Upton Sinclair, and Theodore Dreiser, and modernist experimentation. After World War I, Sherwood Anderson, Sinclair Lewis, Ernest Hemingway, William Faulkner, Thomas Wolfe, F Scott Fitzgerald, John Dos Passos, Henry Miller, and Richard Wright established the

United States of America

area 3,618,770 sq mi/9,368,900 sq km
capital Washington, DC
cities New York, Los Angeles, Chicago, Philadelphia, Detroit, San Francisco, Washington, Dallas, San Diego, San Antonio, Houston, Boston, Baltimore, Phoenix, Indianapolis, Memphis, Honolulu, San José
physical topography and vegetation from tropical (Hawaii) to arctic (Alaska); mountain ranges parallel with E and W coasts; the Rocky Mountains separate rivers emptying into the Pacific from those flowing into the Gulf of Mexico; Great Lakes in N; rivers include Hudson, Mississippi, Missouri, Colorado, Columbia, Snake, Rio Grande, Ohio
environment the US produces the world's largest quantity of annual municipal waste per person (1,900 lb/850 kg)
features see individual states
territories the commonwealths of Puerto Rico and Northern Marianas; the federated states of Micronesia; Guam, the US Virgin Islands, American Samoa, Wake Island, Midway Islands, Marshall Islands, Belau, and Johnston and Sand Islands
head of state and government Bill Clinton from 1993
political system liberal democracy
political parties Democratic Party, liberal center; Republican Party, center-right
currency US dollar
population (1992) 255,414,000 (white 80%, black 12%, Asian/Pacific islander 3%, American Indian, Inuit, and Aleut 1%, Hispanic [included in above percentages] 9%); growth rate 0.9% p.a.
life expectancy men 72, women 79 (1989)
languages English, Spanish
religions Christian 86.5% (Roman Catholic 26%, Baptist 19%, Methodist 8%, Lutheran 5%), Jewish 1.8%, Muslim 0.5%, Buddhist and Hindu less than 0.5%
literacy 99% (1989)
GNP $5,880.7 bn (1990)

chronology
1776 Declaration of Independence.
1787 US constitution drawn up.
1789 Washington elected as first president.
1803 Louisiana Purchase.
1812–14 War with England, arising from commercial disputes caused by Britain's struggle with Napoleon.
1819 Florida purchased from Spain.
1836 The battle of the Alamo, Texas, won by Mexico.
1841 First wagon train left Missouri for California.
1846 Mormons, under Brigham Young, founded Salt Lake City, Utah.
1846–48 Mexican War resulted in cession to US of Arizona, California, part of Colorado and Wyoming, Nevada, New Mexico, Texas, and Utah.

1848–49 California gold rush.
1860 Lincoln elected president.
1861–65 Civil War between North and South.
1865 Slavery abolished. Lincoln assassinated.
1867 Alaska bought from Russia.
1890 Battle of Wounded Knee, the last major battle between American Indians and US troops.
1898 War with Spain ended with the Spanish cession of Philippines, Puerto Rico, and Guam; it was agreed that Cuba be independent. Hawaii annexed.
1917–18 US entered World War I.
1919–21 Wilson's 14 Points became base for League of Nations.
1920 Women achieved the vote.
1924 American Indians made citizens by Congress.
1929 Wall Street stock-market crash.
1933 F D Roosevelt's New Deal to alleviate the Depression put into force.
1941 The Japanese attack on Pearl Harbor Dec 7 precipitated US entry into World War II.
1945 US ended war in the Pacific by dropping atomic bombs on Hiroshima and Nagasaki, Japan.
1950–53 US involvement in Korean War. McCarthy anticommunist investigations (HUAC) became a "witch hunt."
1954 Civil Rights legislation began with segregation ended in public schools.
1957 Civil Rights bill on voting.
1958 First US satellite in orbit.
1961 Abortive CIA-backed invasion of Cuba at the Bay of Pigs.
1963 President Kennedy assassinated; L B Johnson assumed the presidency.
1964–68 "Great Society" civil-rights and welfare measures in the Omnibus Civil Rights bill.
1964–75 US involvement in Vietnam War.
1965 US intervention in Dominican Republic.
1969 US astronaut Neil Armstrong was the first human on the Moon.
1973 OPEC oil embargo almost crippled US industry and consumers. Inflation began.
1973–74 Watergate scandal began in effort to reelect Richard Nixon and ended just before impeachment; Nixon resigned as president; replaced by Gerald Ford, who "pardoned" Nixon.
1975 Final US withdrawal from Vietnam.
1979 US–Chinese diplomatic relations normalized.
1979–80 Iranian hostage crisis; relieved by Reagan concessions and released on his inauguration day Jan 1981.
1981 Space shuttle mission was successful.
1983 US invasion of Grenada.
1986 "Irangate" scandal over secret US government arms sales to Iran, with proceeds to antigovernment Contra guerrillas in Nicaragua.
1987 Reagan and Gorbachev (for USSR) signed intermediate-range nuclear forces treaty. Wall Street stock-market crash caused by program trading.
1988 US became world's largest debtor nation, owing $532 billion. George Bush elected president.
1989 Bush met Gorbachev at Malta, end to Cold War declared; large cuts announced for US military; US invaded Panama; Noriega taken into custody.
1990 Bush and Gorbachev met again. Nelson Mandela freed in South Africa, toured US. US troops sent to Middle East following Iraq's invasion of Kuwait.
1991 Jan–Feb: US-led assault drove Iraq from Kuwait in Gulf War. US support was given to the USSR during the dissolution of communism and the recognition of independence of the Baltic republics. July: Strategic Arms Reduction Treaty (START) signed at US–Soviet summit in Moscow.
1992 Bush's popularity slumped as economic recession continued. Widespread riots in Los Angeles. Nov: Bill Clinton won presidential elections for the Democrats; independent candidate Ross Perot won nearly 20% of votes.
1993 Jan: Clinton inaugurated. He delayed executive order to suspend ban on homosexuals in the armed forces. Feb: medium-term economic plan passed by Congress to cut federal budget deficit. July: air strike on Baghdad, Iraq. Sept: Clinton pushed for his reform programs for medical insurance and government bureaucracy. Dec: Signed North American Free Trade Agreement (NAFTA) bill.

US: presidents and elections

year	president	party	losing candidate(s)	party
1789	1. George Washington	Federalist	no opponent	
1792	reelected		no opponent	
1796	2. John Adams	Federalist	Thomas Jefferson	Democrat–Republican
1800	3. Thomas Jefferson	Democrat–Republican	Aaron Burr	Democrat–Republican
1804	reelected		Charles Pinckney	Federalist
1808	4. James Madison	Democrat–Republican	Charles Pinckney	Federalist
1812	reelected		DeWitt Clinton	Federalist
1816	5. James Monroe	Democrat–Republican	Rufus King	Federalist
1820	reelected		John Quincy Adams	Democrat–Republican
1824	6. John Quincy Adams	Democrat–Republican	Andrew Jackson	Democrat–Republican
			Henry Clay	Democrat–Republican
			William H Crawford	Democrat–Republican
1828	7. Andrew Jackson	Democrat	John Quincy Adams	National Republican
1832	reelected		Henry Clay	National Republican
1836	8. Martin Van Buren	Democrat	William Henry Harrison	Whig
1840	9. William Henry Harrison	Whig	Martin Van Buren	Democrat
1841	10. John Tyler[1]	Whig		
1844	11. James K Polk	Democrat	Henry Clay	Whig
1848	12. Zachary Taylor	Whig	Lewis Cass	Democrat
1850	13. Millard Fillmore[2]	Whig		
1852	14. Franklin Pierce	Democrat	Winfield Scott	Whig
1856	15. James Buchanan	Democrat	John C Fremont	Republican
1860	16. Abraham Lincoln	Republican	Stephen Douglas	Democrat
			John Breckinridge	Democrat
			John Bell	Constitutional Union
1864	reelected		George McClellan	Democrat
1865	17. Andrew Johnson[3]	Democrat		
1868	18. Ulysses S Grant	Republican	Horatio Seymour	Democrat
1872	reelected		Horace Greeley	Democrat–Liberal Republican
1876	19. Rutherford B Hayes	Republican	Samuel Tilden	Democrat
1880	20. James A Garfield	Republican	Winfield Hancock	Democrat
1881	21. Chester A Arthur[4]	Republican		
1884	22. Grover Cleveland	Democrat	James Blaine	Republican
1888	23. Benjamin Harrison	Republican	Grover Cleveland	Democrat
1892	24. Grover Cleveland	Democrat	Benjamin Harrison	Republican
			James Weaver	People's
1896	25. William McKinley	Republican	William J Bryan	Democrat–People's
1900	reelected		William J Bryan	Democrat
1901	26. Theodore Roosevelt[5]	Republican		
1904	reelected		Alton B Parker	Democrat
1908	27. William H Taft	Republican	William J Bryan	Democrat
1912	28. Woodrow Wilson	Democrat	Theodore Roosevelt	Progressive
			William H Taft	Republican
1916	reelected		Charles E Hughes	Republican
1920	29. Warren G Harding	Republican	James M Cox	Democrat
1923	30. Calvin Coolidge[6]	Republican		
1924	reelected		John W Davis	Democrat
			Robert M LaFollette	Progressive
1928	31. Herbert Hoover	Republican	Alfred E Smith	Democrat
1932	32. Franklin D Roosevelt	Democrat	Herbert Hoover	Republican
			Norman Thomas	Socialist
1936	reelected		Alfred Landon	Republican
1940	reelected		Wendell Willkie	Republican
1944	reelected		Thomas E Dewey	Republican
1945	33. Harry S Truman[7]	Democrat		

main literary directions. Among the internationally known novelists since World War II have been John O'Hara, James Michener, Eudora Welty, Truman Capote, J D Salinger, Saul Bellow, John Updike, Norman Mailer, Vladimir Nabokov, Bernard Malamud, Philip Roth, Ralph Ellison, and James Baldwin. Recent US literature increasingly expresses the cultural pluralism, regional variety, and the historical and ethnic range of US life. Feminism and minority consciousness have been brought to the fore by authors such as Alice Walker, Toni Morrison (Nobel Prize 1993), and Maya Angelou. Best-selling authors of popular fiction include Judith Kravitz, Sidney Sheldon, Anne Rice, Stephen King and John Grisham.

US v American Tobacco Co a US Supreme Court decision 1911 dealing with the distinction between reasonable and unreasonable formations of trusts. The American Tobacco Co appealed to the Supreme Court after being convicted of monopolistic practices by the federal government. The federal district court had ordered the dissolution of the company, but the Supreme Court revised this decision on the grounds that the attempts to restrain trade had not been unreasonable. The Court ordered that the company be reorganized but not dissolved.

US v E C Knight Co a US Supreme Court decision 1895 dealing with the right of the federal government to restrict the formation of corporate monopolies. The American Sugar Co established a 98% monopoly on sugar manufacturing in the US when it purchased the E C Knight Sugar Co, its leading competitor. The Justice Department filed suit against Knight for conspiracy to violate federal antitrust legislation. The Court ruled 8 to 1 that manufacturing was distinct from commerce and therefore outside of federal regulatory jurisdiction. The charges against Knight were dropped, virtually nullifying an important provision of the Sherman Antitrust Act 1890.

US v Nixon a US Supreme Court decision 1974 dealing with the extent to which a US president may exercise executive privilege in a criminal investigation. During the ◊Watergate investigations, President Nixon cited this privilege in refusing to produce certain tape recordings that had been subpoenaed by Special Prosecutor Jaworski. The Court ruled unanimously that while the president had certain privileges, they were subject to definition by the judiciary, the final interpreters of the Constitution. According to the Court, given the circumstances of the criminal investigation, Jaworski had the power to overrule presidential autonomy, requiring Nixon to yield the tapes.

universal indicator in chemistry, a mixture of ◊pH indicators, used to gauge the acidity or alkalinity of a solution. Each component changes color at a different pH value, and so the indicator is capable of displaying a range of colors, according to the pH of the test solution, from red (at pH 1) to purple (at pH 13).

The pH of a substance may be found by adding a few drops of universal indicator and noting the color, or by dipping in an absorbent paper strip that has been impregnated with the indicator.

universal joint flexible coupling used to join rotating shafts; for example, the drive shaft in an automobile. In a typical universal joint the ends of the shafts to be joined end in U-shaped yokes. They dovetail into each other and pivot flexibly about an X-shaped spider. This construction allows side-to-side and up-and-down movement, while still transmitting rotary motion.

universe all of space and its contents, the study of which is called cosmology. The universe is thought to be between 10 billion and 20 billion years old, and is mostly empty space, dotted with ◊galaxies for as far as telescopes can see. The most distant detected galaxies and ◊quasars lie 10 billion light-years or more from Earth, and are moving farther apart as the universe expands. Several theories attempt to explain how the universe came into being and evolved, for example, the ◊Big Bang theory of an expanding universe originating in a single explosive event, and the contradictory ◊steady-state theory.

university institution of higher learning for those who have completed primary and secondary education.

In the US there are both state universities (funded by the individual states) and private universities. The oldest universities in the US are all private: Harvard 1636, William and Mary 1693, Yale 1701, Pennsylvania 1741, and Princeton 1746. Typically, a university offers advanced degrees in addition to the four-year bachelor's degree; is made up of colleges, such as liberal arts, sciences, law, medicine; and offers special degrees such as divinity, technical, and vocational as well.

unnilennium synthesized radioactive element of the ◊transactinide series, symbol Une, atomic number 109, atomic weight 266. It was first produced in 1982 at the Laboratory for Heavy Ion Research in Darmstadt, Germany, by fusing bismuth and iron nuclei; it took a week to obtain a single new, fused nucleus.

unnilhexium synthesized radioactive element of the ◊transactinide series, symbol Unh, atomic number 106, atomic weight 263. It was first synthesized in 1974 by two institutions, each of which claims priority. The University of California at Berkeley bombarded californium with oxygen nuclei to get isotope 263; the Joint Institute for Nuclear Research in Dubna, Russia, bombarded lead with chromium nuclei to obtain isotopes 259 and 260.

unniloctium synthesized, radioactive element of the ◊transactinide series, symbol Uno, atomic number 108, atomic weight 265. It was first synthesized in 1984 by the Laboratory for Heavy Ion Research in Darmstadt, Germany.

unnilpentium synthesized, radioactive, metallic element of the ◊transactinide series, symbol Unp, atomic number 105, atomic weight 262. Six isotopes have been synthesized, each with very short (fractions of a second) half-lives. Two institutions claim to have been the first to produce it: the Joint Institute for Nuclear Research in Dubna, Russia, in 1967 (proposed name *nielsbohrium*); and the University of California at Berkeley, who disputed the Soviet claim, in 1970 (proposed name *hahnium*).

unnilquadium synthesized, radioactive, metallic element, the first of the ◊transactinide series, symbol Unq, atomic number 104, atomic weight 262. It is produced by bombarding californium with carbon nuclei and has ten isotopes, the longest-lived of which, Unq-262, has a half-life of 70 seconds. Two institutions claim to be the first to have synthesized it: the Joint Institute for Nuclear Research in Dubna, Russia, in 1964 (proposed name *kurchatovium*); and the University of California at Berkeley, in 1969 (proposed name *rutherfordium*).

unnilseptium synthesized, radioactive element of the ◊transactinide series, symbol Uns, atomic number 107, atomic weight 262. It was first synthesized by the Joint Institute for Nuclear Research in Dubna, Russia, in 1976; in 1981 the Laboratory for Heavy Ion Research in Darmstadt, Germany, confirmed its existence.

Upanishad one of a collection of Hindu sacred treatises, written in Sanskrit, connected with the ◊Vedas but composed later, about 800–200 BC. Metaphysical and ethical, their doctrine equated the atman (self) with the Brahman (supreme spirit)—*"Tat tvam asi"* ("Thou art that")—and developed the theory of the transmigration of souls.

Updike John (Hoyer) 1932– . US writer. Associated with the *New Yorker* magazine from 1955, he soon established a reputation for polished prose, poetry, and criticism. His novels include *The Poorhouse Fair* 1959, *The Centaur* 1963, *Couples* 1968, *The Witches of Eastwick* 1984, *Roger's Version* 1986, and *S.* 1988, and deal with the tensions and frustrations of contemporary US middle-class life and their effects on love and marriage.

Upper Volta former name (until 1984) of ◊Burkina Faso.

Ur ancient city of the ◊Sumerian civilization, in modern Iraq. Excavations by the British archeologist Leonard Woolley show that it was inhabited from about 3500 BC. He discovered evidence of a flood that may have inspired the *Epic of* ◊Gilgamesh as well as the biblical account, and remains of ziggurats, or step pyramids.

Ural Mountains (Russian *Ural'skiy Khrebet*) mountain system running from the Arctic to the Caspian Sea, traditionally separating Europe from Asia. The highest peak is Naradnaya, 6,214 ft/1,894 m. It has vast mineral wealth.

uraninite uranium oxide, UO_2, an ore mineral of uranium, also known as *pitchblende* when occurring in massive form. It is black or brownish black, very dense, and radioactive. It occurs in veins and as massive crusts, usually associated with granite rocks.

uranium hard, lustrous, silver-white, malleable and ductile, radioactive, metallic element of the ◊actinide series, symbol U, atomic number 92, atomic weight

United States of America		
state	capital	date of joining the Union
Alabama	Montgomery	1819
Alaska	Juneau	1959
Arizona	Phoenix	1912
Arkansas	Little Rock	1836
California	Sacramento	1850
Colorado	Denver	1876
Connecticut	Hartford	1788
Delaware	Dover	1787
Florida	Tallahassee	1845
Georgia	Atlanta	1788
Hawaii	Honolulu	1959
Idaho	Boise	1890
Illinois	Springfield	1818
Indiana	Indianapolis	1816
Iowa	Des Moines	1846
Kansas	Topeka	1861
Kentucky	Frankfort	1792
Louisiana	Baton Rouge	1812
Maine	Augusta	1820
Maryland	Annapolis	1788
Massachusetts	Boston	1788
Michigan	Lansing	1837
Minnesota	St Paul	1858
Mississippi	Jackson	1817
Missouri	Jefferson City	1821
Montana	Helena	1889
Nebraska	Lincoln	1867
Nevada	Carson City	1864
New Hampshire	Concord	1788
New Jersey	Trenton	1787
New Mexico	Santa Fé	1912
New York	Albany	1788
North Carolina	Raleigh	1789
North Dakota	Bismarck	1889
Ohio	Columbus	1803
Oklahoma	Oklahoma City	1907
Oregon	Salem	1859
Pennsylvania	Harrisburg	1787
Rhode Island	Providence	1790
South Carolina	Columbia	1788
South Dakota	Pierre	1889
Tennessee	Nashville	1796
Texas	Austin	1845
Utah	Salt Lake City	1896
Vermont	Montpelier	1791
Virginia	Richmond	1788
Washington	Olympia	1889
West Virginia	Charleston	1863
Wisconsin	Madison	1848
Wyoming	Cheyenne	1890

238.029. It is the most abundant radioactive element in the Earth's crust, its decay giving rise to essentially all radioactive elements in nature; its final decay product is the stable element lead. Uranium combines readily with most elements to form compounds that are extremely poisonous. The chief ore is ◊pitchblende, in which the element was discovered by German chemist Martin Klaproth 1789; he named it after the planet Uranus, which had been discovered 1781.

uranium ore material from which uranium is extracted, often a complex mixture of minerals. The main ore is uraninite (or pitchblende) UO_2, which is commonly found with sulfide minerals. The US and South Africa are the main producers in the West.

Uranus in Greek mythology, the primeval sky god, whose name means "Heaven." He was responsible for

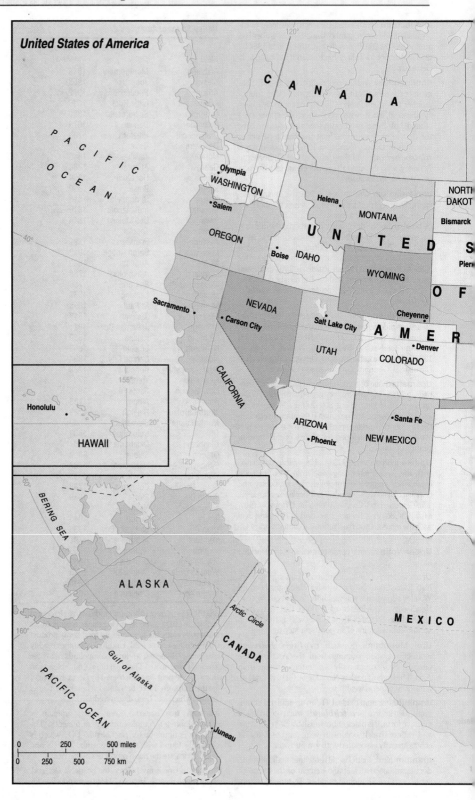

United States of America

CANADA

PACIFIC
OCEAN

120°

40°

WASHINGTON
•Olympia

•Salem

OREGON

Sacramento•

155°

Honolulu •

HAWAII

20°

120°

•Boise IDAHO

Helena•

MONTANA

NORTH
DAKOT

Bismarck

U N I T E D   S

Pier

WYOMING

NEVADA

•Carson City

CALIFORNIA

Salt Lake City•

Cheyenne
•

O F

A M E R

UTAH

•Denver

COLORADO

ARIZONA

•Phoenix

•Santa Fe

NEW MEXICO

160°

BERING SEA

ALASKA

140°

Arctic Circle

CANADA

160°

Gulf of Alaska

60°

PACIFIC OCEAN

•Juneau

140°

MEXICO

20°

0   250   500 miles
0   250   500   750 km

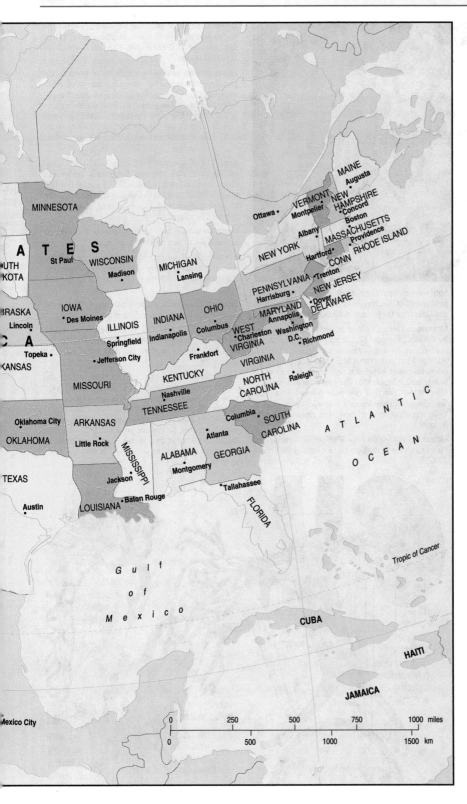

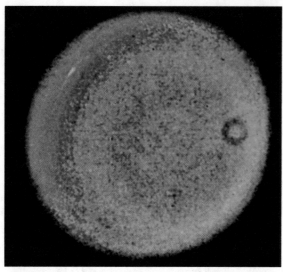

***Uranus** False-color image of clouds in the upper atmosphere of Uranus, seen from Voyager 2.*

Urbana industrial city (food processing, electronics, and metal products) in E central Illinois, E of Springfield; population (1990) 36,300. The University of Illinois 1867 is here.

urbanization process by which the proportion of a population living in or around towns and cities increases through migration as the agricultural population decreases. The growth of urban concentrations in the US and Europe is a relatively recent phenomenon, dating back only about 150 years to the beginning of the Industrial Revolution (although the world's first cities were built more than 5,000 years ago.)

urea $CO(NH_2)_2$ waste product formed in the mammalian liver when nitrogen compounds are broken down. It is excreted in urine. When purified, it is a white, crystalline solid. In industry it is used to make urea-formaldehyde plastics (or resins), pharmaceuticals, and fertilizers.

uremia excess of urea (a nitrogenous waste product) in the blood, caused by kidney damage.

ureter tube connecting the kidney to the bladder. Its wall contains fibers of smooth muscle, whose contractions aid the movement of urine out of the kidney.

urethra in mammals, a tube connecting the bladder to the exterior. It carries urine and, in males, semen.

Urey Harold Clayton 1893–1981. US chemist. In 1932 he isolated ◊heavy water and discovered ◊deuterium, for which he was awarded the 1934 Nobel Prize for Chemistry.

uric acid $C_5H_4N_4O_3$ nitrogen-containing waste substance, formed from the breakdown of food and body protein. It is only slightly soluble in water. Uric acid is the normal means by which most land animals that develop in a shell (birds, reptiles, insects, and land gastropods) deposit their waste products. The young are unable to get rid of their excretory products while in the shell and therefore store them in this insoluble form.

both the sunshine and the rain, and was the son and husband of ◊Gaia, the goddess of the Earth. Uranus and Gaia were the parents of Kronos and the ◊Titans.

Uranus the seventh planet from the Sun, discovered by William ◊Herschel 1781. It is twice as far out as the sixth planet, Saturn. Uranus has a diameter of 31,600 mi/50,800 km and a mass 14.5 times that of Earth. It orbits the Sun in 84 years at an average distance of 1.8 billion mi/2.9 billion km. The spin axis of Uranus is tilted at 98°, so that one pole points toward the Sun, giving extreme seasons. It has 15 moons, and in 1977 was discovered to have thin rings around its equator.

Urban II c. 1042–1099. Pope 1088–99. He launched the First ◊Crusade at the Council of Clermont in France 1095.

urinary system The human urinary system.

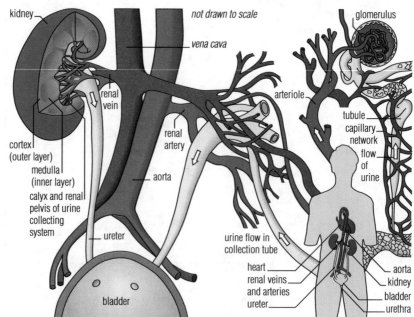

urinary system system of organs that removes nitrogenous waste products and excess water from the bodies of animals. In vertebrates, it consists of a pair of kidneys, which produce urine; ureters, which drain the kidneys; and (in bony fishes, amphibians, some reptiles, and mammals) a bladder, which stores the urine before its discharge. In mammals, the urine is expelled through the urethra; in other vertebrates, the urine drains into a common excretory chamber called a cloaca, and the urine is not discharged separately.

urine amber-colored fluid made by the kidneys from the blood. It contains excess water, salts, proteins, waste products in the form of urea, a pigment, and some acid.

Ursa Major the third largest constellation in the sky, in the north polar region. Its seven brightest stars make up the familiar shape of the *Big Dipper*. The second star of the "handle" of the dipper, called Mizar, has a companion star, Alcor. Two stars forming the far side of the "bowl" (one of them, Dubhe, being the constellation's brightest star) act as pointers to the north pole star, Polaris.

Ursa Minor constellation in the northern sky. It is shaped like a dipper, with the north pole star Polaris at the end of the handle.
It contains the orange subgiant Kochab, about 95 light-years from Earth.

Uruguay country in South America, on the Atlantic coast, bounded N by Brazil and W by Argentina.

Urumqi or *Urumchi* industrial city and capital of Xinjiang Uygur autonomous region, China, at the northern foot of the Tian Shan Mountains; population

Utah

(1989) 1,110,000. It produces cotton textiles, cement, chemicals, iron, and steel.

US abbreviation for the *United States* (popular and most frequent name used by speakers of American English for the nation).

USA abbreviation (official) for the ◊*United States of America*; *US Army*.

USDA abbreviation for the *US Department of Agriculture*.

USSR abbreviation for the former ◊*Union of Soviet Socialist Republics*.

UT abbreviation for the state of ◊Utah.

Utah state in western US; nickname Beehive State/Mormon State
area 84,881 sq mi/219,900 sq km
capital Salt Lake City
cities Provo, Ogden
physical Colorado Plateau to the E, mountains in center, Great Basin to the W, Great Salt Lake

---

Uruguay
Oriental Republic of
(*República Oriental del Uruguay*)

area 68,031 sq mi/176,200 sq km
capital Montevideo
cities Salto, Paysandú
physical grassy plains (pampas) and low hills
features rivers Negro, Uruguay, Río de la Plata
head of state and government Luis Lacalle Herrera from 1989
political system democratic republic
political parties Colorado Party (PC), progressive, center-

left; National (Blanco) Party (PN), traditionalist, right of center; Amplio Front (FA), moderate, left-wing
exports meat and meat products, leather, wool, textiles
currency nuevo peso
population (1992) 3,130,000 (Spanish, Italian; mestizo, mulatto, black); growth rate 0.7% p.a.
life expectancy men 68, women 75 (1989)
language Spanish
media the Ministry of Defense controls broadcasting licenses; press heavily dependent on official advertising. Four national and two Montevideo daily papers, combined circulation 500,000 copies per week (1993); all proprietors associated with political parties
religion Roman Catholic 66%
literacy 96% (1984)
GNP $7.5 bn; $2,470 per head (1988)

chronology
1825 Independence declared from Brazil.
1836 Civil war.
1930 First constitution adopted.
1966 Blanco party in power, with Jorge Pacheco Areco as president.
1972 Colorado Party returned, with Juan Maria Bordaberry Arocena as president.
1976 Bordaberry deposed by army; Dr Méndez Manfredini became president.
1984 Violent antigovernment protests after ten years of repressive rule.
1985 Agreement reached between the army and political leaders for return to constitutional government. Colorado Party won general election; Dr Julio Maria Sanguinetti became president.
1986 Government of national accord established under President Sanguinetti's leadership.
1989 Luis Lacalle Herrera elected president.

Utrillo French artist Maurice Utrillo's Street at Sannois (1913), Courtauld Collection, London.

features Great American Desert; Colorado river system; Dinosaur and Rainbow Bridge national monuments; five national parks: the Arches, Bryce Canyon, Canyonlands, Capitol Reef, Zion; auto racing at Bonneville Salt Flats; Mormon temple and tabernacle, Salt Lake City
products wool, gold, silver, copper, coal, salt, steel
population(1990) 1,722,850
famous people Brigham Young
history explored first by Franciscan friars for Spain

1776; Great Salt Lake discovered by US frontier scout Jim Bridger 1824; part of the area ceded by Mexico 1848; developed by Mormons, still by far the largest religious group in the state; territory 1850, but not admitted to statehood until 1896 because of Mormon reluctance to relinquish plural marriage.

uterus hollow muscular organ of female mammals, located between the bladder and rectum, and connected to the Fallopian tubes above and the vagina

Uzbekistan
Republic of

area 172,741 sq mi/447,400 sq km
capital Tashkent
cities Samarkand, Bukhara, Namangan
physical oases in the deserts; rivers: Amu Darya, Syr Darya; Fergana Valley; rich in mineral deposits
features more than 20 hydroelectric plants; three natural gas pipelines
head of state Islam Karimov from 1990
head of government Abdul Hashim Mutalov from 1991

political system socialist pluralist
political parties National Democratic (formerly Communist) Party, reform-socialist; Democratic Party, tolerated opposition
products rice, dried fruit, vines (all grown by irrigation); cotton, silk
population (1992) 21,363,000 (Uzbek 71%, Russian 8%, Tajik 5%, Kazakh 4%)
language Uzbek, a Turkic language
religion Sunni Muslim

chronology
1921 Part of Turkestan Soviet Socialist Autonomous Republic.
1925 Became constituent republic of the USSR.
1944 Some 160,000 Meskhetian Turks forcibly transported from their native Georgia to Uzbekistan by Stalin.
1989 Tashlak, Yaipan, and Ferghana were the scenes of riots in which Meskhetian Turks were attacked; 70 killed and 850 wounded.
1990 June: economic and political sovereignty declared; former Uzbek Communist Party (UCP) leader Islam Karimov became president.
1991 March: Uzbek supported "renewed federation" in USSR referendum. Aug: anti-Gorbachev coup in Moscow initially accepted by President Karimov; later, Karimov resigned from Soviet Communist Party (CPSU) Politburo; UCP broke with CPSU; prodemocracy rallies dispersed by militia; independence declared. Dec: joined new Commonwealth of Independent States.
1992 Jan: admitted into Conference on Security and Cooperation in Europe; violent food riots in Tashkent. March: joined the United Nations; US diplomatic recognition achieved.

below. The embryo develops within the uterus, and in placental mammals is attached to it after implantation via the ◊placenta and umbilical cord. The lining of the uterus changes during the ◊menstrual cycle. In humans and other higher primates, it is a single structure, but in other mammals it is paired.

U Thant Burmese diplomat; see ◊Thant, U.

Utopia any ideal state in literature, named after philosopher Thomas More's ideal commonwealth in his book *Utopia* 1516. Other versions include Plato's *Republic*, Francis Bacon's *New Atlantis* 1626, and *City of the Sun* by the Italian Tommaso Campanella (1568–1639). Utopias are a common subject in ◊science fiction.

Utrecht province of the Netherlands lying SE of Amsterdam, on the Kromme Rijn (Crooked Rhine)
area 513 sq mi/1,330 sq km
capital Utrecht
cities Amersfoort, Zeist, Nieuwegeun, Veenendaal
products chemicals, livestock, textiles, electrical goods
population (1991) 1,026,800
history ruled by the bishops of Utrecht in the Middle Ages, the province was sold to the emperor Charles V of Spain 1527. It became a center of Protestant resistance to Spanish rule and, with the signing of the Treaty of Utrecht, became one of the seven United Provinces of the Netherlands 1579.

Utrecht, Treaty of treaty signed 1713 that ended the War of the ◊Spanish Succession. Philip V was recog-nized as the legitimate king of Spain, thus founding the Spanish branch of the Bourbon dynasty and ending the French king Louis XIV's attempts at expansion; the Netherlands, Milan, and Naples were ceded to Austria; Britain gained Gibraltar; the duchy of Savoy was granted Sicily.

Utrillo Maurice 1883–1955. French artist. He painted townscapes of his native Paris, many depicting Mont-martre, often from postcard photographs.

Utrillo was the son of Suzanne Valadon, a trapeze-performer who was encouraged to become an artist herself after posing as a model for many painters of the day. His work from 1908 to 1914 is considered his best.

Uttar Pradesh state of N India
area 113,638 sq mi/294,400 sq km
capital Lucknow
cities Kanpur, Varanasi, Agra, Allahabad, Meerut
features most populous state; Himalayan peak Nanda Devi 25,655 ft/7,817 m
population (1991) 138,760,400
famous people Indira Gandhi, Ravi Shankar
language Hindi
religions 80% Hindu, 15% Muslim
history formerly the heart of the Mogul Empire and generating point of the ◊Indian Mutiny 1857 and sub-sequent opposition to British rule; see also ◊Agra.

Uzbekistan country in central Asia, bounded N by Kazakhstan and the Aral Sea, E by Kyrgyzstan and Tajikistan, S by Afghanistan, and W by Turk-menistan.

v in physics, symbol for *velocity*.

V1, V2 (German *Vergeltungswaffe* "revenge weapons") German flying bombs of World War II, launched against Britain in 1944 and 1945. The V1, also called the doodlebug and buzz bomb, was an uncrewed monoplane carrying a bomb, powered by a simple kind of jet engine called a pulse jet. The V2, a rocket bomb with a preset guidance system, was the first long-range ballistic ◊missile. It was 47 ft/14 m long, carried a 1-ton warhead, and hit its target at a speed of 3,000 mph/5,000 kph.

VA abbreviation for the state of ◊Virginia.

vaccination use of specially modified ◊pathogens (bacteria and viruses) to confer immunity to the diseases with which they are associated. When injected or taken by mouth, a vaccine stimulates the production of antibodies to protect against that particular disease. Vaccination is the oldest form of ◊immunization.

vaccine any preparation of modified viruses or bacteria that is introduced into the body, usually either orally or by a hypodermic syringe, to induce the specific ◊antibody reaction that produces ◊immunity against a particular disease.

vacuum in general, a region completely empty of matter; in physics, any enclosure in which the gas pressure is considerably less than atmospheric pressure (101,325 pascals).

Vaduz capital of the European principality of Liechtenstein; industries include engineering and agricultural trade; population (1984) 5,000.

vagina the front passage in female mammals, linking the uterus to the exterior. It admits the penis during sexual intercourse, and is the birth canal down which the fetus passes during delivery.

valence the combining capacity of an ◊atom or ◊radical, determined by the number of electrons that an atom will add, lose, or share when it reacts with another atom. Elements that lose electrons (such as hydrogen and the ◊metals) have a positive valence; those that add electrons (such as oxygen and other nonmetals) have a negative valence.

valence electron in chemistry, an electron in the outermost shell of an ◊atom. It is the valence electrons that are involved in the formation of ionic and covalent bonds (see ◊molecule). The number of electrons in this outermost shell represents the maximum possible valence for many elements and matches the number of the group that the element occupies in the ◊periodic table of the elements.

Valencia industrial city (wine, fruit, chemicals, textiles, ship repair) in Valencia region, E Spain; population (1991) 777,400. The Community of Valencia, consisting of Alicante, Castellón, and Valencia, has an area of 8,994 sq mi/23,300 sq km and a population of 3,772,000.

Valentine, St according to tradition a bishop of Terni martyred at Rome, now omitted from the calendar of saints' days as probably nonexistent. His festival was Feb 14, but the custom of sending "valentines" to a loved one on that day seems to have arisen because the day accidentally coincided with the Roman mid-February festival of Lupercalia.

Valéry Paul 1871–1945. French poet and mathematician. His poetry includes *La Jeune Parque/The Young Fate* 1917 and *Charmes/Enchantments* 1922.

Valhalla in Norse mythology, the hall in ◊Odin's palace where he feasted with the souls of heroes killed in battle.

Valkyrie in Norse mythology, any of the female attendants of ◊Odin. They selected the most valiant warriors to die in battle and escorted them to Valhalla.

Vallandigham Clement Laird 1820–1871. US political leader. He served in the US House of Representatives 1858–63. A staunch Democrat, he supported Stephen Douglas for president 1860 and opposed many of President Lincoln's war policies. He was arrested for sedition 1862 and deported to the Confederacy. Returning to Ohio 1864, he remained a strong foe of the radical Republicans until his death.

Vallejo industrial city (fruit and flour processing and petroleum refining) in NW California, on San Pablo Bay, NE of Berkeley; population (1990) 109,200. It was California's capital 1852–53.

Valletta capital and port of Malta; population (1987) 9,000; urban area 101,000.

Valley Forge site in Pennsylvania 20 mi/32 km NW of Philadelphia, where George Washington's army spent the winter of 1777–78 in great hardship during the ◊American Revolution. Of the 10,000 men there, 2,500 died of disease and the rest suffered from lack of rations and other supplies; many deserted.

During that winter, Washington introduced Prussian officers who trained the irregulars. The Franco-American alliance 1778 boosted morale and brought new recruits to the army, which emerged from the ordeal to inflict heavy losses on the British.

Valley of Ten Thousand Smokes valley in SW Alaska, on the Alaska Peninsula, where in 1912 Mount Katmai erupted in one of the largest volcanic explosions ever known, though without loss of human life since the area was uninhabited. The valley was filled with ash to a depth of 660 ft/200 m. It was dedicated as the Katmai National Monument 1918. Thousands of fissures on the valley floor continue to emit steam and gases.

Valley of the Kings burial place of ancient kings opposite ◊Thebes, Egypt, on the left bank of the Nile.

Valois branch of the Capetian dynasty, originally counts of Valois (see Hugh ◊Capet) in France, members of which occupied the French throne from Philip VI 1328 to Henry III 1589.

valve device that controls the flow of a fluid. Inside a valve, a plug moves to widen or close the opening through which the fluid passes. The valve was invented by US radio engineer Lee de Forest (1873–1961).

valve in animals, a structure for controlling the direction of the blood flow. In humans and other vertebrates, the contractions of the beating heart cause the correct blood flow into the arteries because a series of valves prevent back flow. Diseased valves, detected as "heart murmurs," have decreased efficiency. The tendency for low-pressure venous blood to collect at the base of limbs under the influence of gravity is counteracted by a series of small valves within the veins. It was the existence of these valves that prompted the 17th-century physician William Harvey to suggest that the blood circulated around the body.

vampire (Magyar *vampir*) in Hungarian and Slavonic folklore, an "undead" corpse that sleeps by day in its native earth, and by night, often in the form of a bat, sucks the blood of the living. ◊Dracula is a vampire in popular fiction.

vampire bat any South and Central American bat of the family Desmodontidae, of which there are three species. The *common vampire Desmodus rotundus* is found from N Mexico to central Argentina; its head and body grow to 3.5 in/9 cm. Vampires feed on the blood of birds and mammals; they slice a piece of skin from a sleeping animal with their sharp incisor teeth and lap up the flowing blood.

vanadium silver-white, malleable and ductile, metallic element, symbol V, atomic number 23, atomic weight 50.942. It occurs in certain iron, lead, and uranium ores and is widely distributed in small quantities in igneous and sedimentary rocks. It is used to make steel alloys, to which it adds tensile strength.

Van Allen radiation belts two zones of charged particles around the Earth's magnetosphere, discovered 1958 by US physicist James Van Allen. The atomic particles come from the Earth's upper atmosphere and the ◊solar wind, and are trapped by the Earth's magnetic field. The inner belt lies 620–3,100 mi/1,000–5,000 km above the equator, and contains ◊protons and ◊electrons. The outer belt lies 9,300–15,500 mi/15,000–25,000 km above the equator, but is lower around the magnetic poles. It contains mostly electrons from the solar wind.

Van Buren Martin 1782–1862. Eighth president of the US 1837–41, a Democrat, who had helped establish the ◊Democratic Party. He was secretary of state 1829–31, minister to Britain 1831–33, vice president 1833–37, and president during the Panic of 1837, the worst US economic crisis until that time, caused by land speculation in the West. Refusing to intervene, he advocated the establishment of an independent treasury, one not linked to the federal government, worsening the depression and losing the 1840 election.

Born of Dutch ancestry in Kinderhook, New York, Van Buren was a US senator from New York 1821–28, and governor of New York 1829, As president, he attempted to hold the Southern states in the Union by advocating a strict states' rights position on slavery, but his refusal to annex Texas alienated many Southerners. He adhered to Jeffersonian principles of nonintervention in economic affairs. He lost the 1844 Democratic nomination to Polk, and in 1848 ran unsuccessfully for president as a candidate of Free Soil, a small but influential political party opposed to the expansion of slavery in the western territories.

Vancouver industrial city (oil refining, engineering, shipbuilding, aircraft, timber, pulp and paper, textiles, fisheries) in Canada, its chief Pacific seaport, on the

mainland of British Columbia; population (1986) 1,381,000.

Vancouver city in SW Washington, on the Columbia River, N of Portland, Oregon; population (1990) 46,400. It is a manufacturing and shipping center for agriculture and timber. It began as a trading post for the Hudson's Bay Company 1825.

Vancouver Island island off the W coast of Canada, part of British Columbia
area 12,404 sq mi/32,136 sq km
cities Victoria, Nanaimo, Esquimalt (naval base)
products coal, timber, fish.

Vandal member of a Germanic people related to the ◊Goths. In the 5th century AD the Vandals invaded Roman ◊Gaul and Spain, many settling in Andalusia (formerly Vandalitia) and others reaching N Africa 429. They sacked Rome 455 and were defeated by Belisarius, general of the emperor ◊Justinian, in the 6th century.

van de Graaff Robert Jemison 1901–1967. US physicist who from 1929 developed a high-voltage generator, which in its modern form can produce more than a million volts. It consists of a continuous vertical conveyor belt that carries electrostatic charges (resulting from friction) up to a large hollow sphere supported on an insulated stand. The lower end of the belt is earthed, so that charge accumulates on the sphere. The size of the voltage built up in air depends on the radius of the sphere, but can be increased by enclosing the generator in an inert atmosphere, such as nitrogen.

Vanderbilt Cornelius 1794–1877. US industrialist who made a fortune in steamships and (from the age of 70) by financing railroads. He defeated stock raids and takeover attempts by other financiers in the process of amassing a fortune of more than $100 million. Despite his wealth, he did not engage in any philanthropic activities until near his death, when he gave $1 million to what would become Vanderbilt University. See also Jay ◊Gould.

Vanderbilt William Henry 1821–1885. US financier and railroad promoter. Given control of the Staten Island Railroad 1857, he was named vice president of the New York and Harlem Railroad 1864, acquired other railroads, and became president of the New York Central Railroad 1877. Vanderbilt was famous for his contemptuous phrase "The public be damned."

van der Waals Johannes Diderik 1837–1923. Dutch physicist who was awarded a Nobel Prize 1910 for his theoretical study of gases. He emphasized the forces of attraction and repulsion between atoms and molecules in describing the behavior of real gases, as opposed to the ideal gases dealt with in ◊Boyle's law and ◊Charles's law.

Van Devanter Willis 1859–1941. US jurist. He was appointed as US Supreme Court justice 1910–37 by President Taft. Active in Republican politics, he served as assistant US attorney general 1897–1903 and federal circuit judge 1903–10. A staunch conservative, Van Devanter was a bitter opponent of the New Deal until his retirement.

Van Diemen's Land former name (1642–1855) of ◊Tasmania, Australia. It was named by Dutch navigator Abel Tasman after the governor-general of the Dutch East Indies, Anthony van Diemen. The name Tasmania was used from the 1840s and became official 1855.

van Dyck Anthony. Flemish painter, see ◊Dyck, Anthony van.

Vane John 1927– . British pharmacologist who discovered the wide role of prostaglandins in the human body, produced in response to illness and stress. He shared the 1982 Nobel Prize for Medicine with Sune Bergström (1916–) and Bengt Samuelson (1934–) of Sweden.

van Eyck Jan. Flemish painter; see ◊Eyck, Jan van.

van Gogh Vincent. Dutch painter; see ◊Gogh, Vincent van.

vanilla any climbing orchid of the genus *Vanilla*, native to tropical America but cultivated elsewhere, with fragrant, large, white or yellow flowers. The dried and fermented fruit, or podlike capsules, of *V. planifolia* are the source of the vanilla flavoring used in cooking and baking.

Van Rensselaer Stephen 1764–1839. American public official and soldier. A commander during the War of 1812, he suffered a serious defeat at Queenstown. He was a US congressman 1822–29. As president of the New York Canal Commission 1825–39 he oversaw the construction of the Erie Canal.

Vanuatu group of islands in the SW Pacific Ocean, part of ◊Melanesia.

Varanasi or *Benares* holy city of the Hindus in Uttar Pradesh, India, on the river Ganges; population

(1981) 794,000. There are 1,500 golden shrines, and a 3 mi/5 km frontage to the Ganges with sacred stairways (ghats) for purification by bathing.

Vargas Llosa Mario 1937– . Peruvian novelist, author of *La ciudad y los perros/The Time of the Hero* 1963 and *La guerra del fin del mundo/The War at the End of the World* 1982.

variable in mathematics, a changing quantity (one that can take various values), as opposed to a ◊constant. For example, in the algebraic expression $y = 4x^3 + 2$, the variables are x and y, whereas 4 and 2 are constants.

variable quantity that can take different values. Variables play an important role in computer programming because they can be used to represent different items of data in the course of a program.

variable star in astronomy, a star whose brightness changes, either regularly or irregularly, over a period ranging from a few hours to months or even years. The Cepheid variables regularly expand and contract in size every few days or weeks.

variations in music, a form based on constant repetition of a simple theme, each new version being elaborated or treated in a different manner. The theme is easily recognizable, either as a popular tune or—as a gesture of respect—as the work of a fellow composer; for example, Brahms honors Bach in the *Variations on the St Antony Chorale*.

varicose veins or *varicosis* condition where the veins become swollen and twisted. The veins of the legs are most often affected; other vulnerable sites include the rectum (hemorrhoids) and testes.

variegation description of plant leaves or stems that exhibit patches of different colors. The term is usually applied to plants that show white, cream, or yellow on their leaves, caused by areas of tissue that lack the green pigment ◊chlorophyll. Variegated plants are bred for their decorative value, but they are often con-

---

Vanuatu
Republic of
(*Ripablik Blong Vanuatu*)

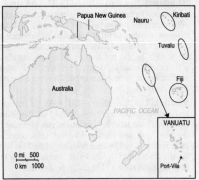

area 5,714 sq mi/14,800 sq km
capital Vila (on Efate)
cities Luganville (on Espíritu Santo)
physical comprises around 70 islands, including Espíritu Santo, Malekula, and Efate; densely forested, mountainous
features three active volcanoes
head of state Fred Timakata from 1989
head of government Maxime Carlot from 1991
political system democratic republic
political parties Union of Moderate Parties (UMP),

Francophone centrist; Vanuatu National United Party (VNUP), formed by Walter Lini; Vanua'aku Pati (VP), Anglophone centrist; Melanesian Progressive Party (MPP), Melanesian centrist; Fren Melanesian Party
exports copra, fish, coffee, cocoa
currency vatu
population (1992) 154,000 (90% Melanesian); growth rate 3.3% p.a.
life expectancy men 67, women 71 (1989)
languages Bislama 82%, English, French (all official)
literacy 53%
religions Presbyterian 40%, Roman Catholic 16%, Anglican 14%, animist 15%
GDP $125 million (1987); $927 per head

chronology
1906 Islands jointly administered by France and Britain.
1975 Representative assembly established.
1978 Government of national unity formed, with Father Gerard Leymang as chief minister.
1980 Revolt on the island of Espíritu Santo delayed independence but it was achieved within the Commonwealth, with George Kalkoa (adopted name Sokomanu) as president and Father Walter Lini as prime minister.
1988 Dismissal of Lini by Sokomanu led to Sokomanu's arrest for treason. Lini reinstated.
1989 Sokomanu sentenced to six years' imprisonment; succeeded as president by Fred Timakata.
1991 Lini voted out by party members; replaced by Donald Kalpokas. General election produced UMP–VNUP coalition under Maxime Carlot.

Vatican City State
(*Stato della Città del Vaticano*)

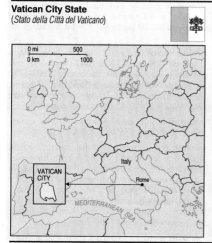

```
0 mi        500
0 km           1000
```

VATICAN CITY

Italy

Rome

MEDITERRANEAN SEA

area 0.4 sq km/109 acres
physical forms an enclave in the heart of Rome, Italy
features Vatican Palace, official residence of the pope; basilica and square of St Peter's; churches in and near Rome, the pope's summer villa at Castel Gandolfo; the world's smallest state
head of state and government John Paul II from 1978
political system absolute Catholicism
currency Vatican City lira; Italian lira
population (1985) 1,000
languages Latin (official), Italian
religion Roman Catholic

chronology
1929 Lateran Treaty recognized sovereignty of the pope.
1947 New Italian constitution confirmed the sovereignty of the Vatican City State.
1978 John Paul II became the first non-Italian pope for more than 400 years.
1985 New concordat signed under which Roman Catholicism ceased to be Italy's state religion.

siderably weaker than the normal, uniformly green plant. Many will not breed true and require ◊vegetative reproduction.

vascular bundle strand of primary conducting tissue (a "vein") in vascular plants, consisting mainly of water-conducting tissues, metaxylem and protoxylem, which together make up the primary ◊xylem, and nutrient-conducting tissue, phloem. It extends from the roots to the stems and leaves. Typically the phloem is situated nearest to the epidermis and the xylem toward the center of the bundle. In plants exhibiting secondary growth, the xylem and phloem are separated by a thin layer of vascular cambium, which gives rise to new conducting tissues.

vascular plant plant containing vascular bundles. Pteridophytes (ferns, horsetails, and club mosses), ◊gymnosperms (conifers and cycads), and ◊angiosperms (flowering plants) are all vascular plants.

vas deferens in male vertebrates, a tube conducting sperm from the testis to the urethra. The sperms are carried in a fluid secreted by various glands, and can be transported very rapidly when the smooth muscle in the wall of the vas deferens undergoes rhythmic contraction, as in sexual intercourse.

vasectomy male sterilization; an operation to cut and tie the ducts (see ◊vas deferens) that carry sperm from the testes to the penis. Vasectomy does not affect sexual performance, but the semen produced at ejaculation no longer contains sperm.

vassal in medieval Europe, a person who paid feudal homage to a superior lord (see ◊feudalism), and who promised military service and advice in return for a grant of land. The term was used from the 9th century.

Vassar Matthew 1792–1868. British-born US entrepreneur and educational philanthropist. A proponent of higher education for women, he endowed Vassar Female College in Poughkeepsie, New York, 1861. The school opened 1865 with a full college curriculum and became one of the finest women's educational institutions in the US.

Vatican City State sovereign area within the city of Rome, Italy.

Vatican Council either of two Roman Catholic ecumenical councils called by Pope Pius IX 1869 (which met 1870) and by Pope John XXIII 1959 (which met

1962). These councils deliberated over elements of church policy.

vaudeville variety entertainment in theaters, popular in the US from the 1890s to the 1920s. Consisting of 10 to 15 acts, ranging from singers and dancers to magicians, jugglers, acrobats, and comedians, it was the equivalent of the English music hall.

VDT abbreviation for visual display terminal.

Veblen Thorstein (Bunde) 1857–1929. US social critic. His insights on culture and economics were expressed in his books *The Theory of the Leisure Class* 1899 and *The Theory of Business Enterprise* 1904. He was a founder of the New School for Social Research in New York 1919.

vector graphics computer graphics that are stored in the computer memory by using geometric formulas. Vector graphics can be transformed (enlarged, rotated, stretched, and so on) without loss of picture resolution. It is also possible to select and transform any of the components of a vector-graphics display because each is separately defined in the computer memory. In these respects vector graphics are superior to ◊raster graphics.

vector quantity any physical quantity that has both magnitude and direction (such as the velocity or acceleration of an object) as distinct from ◊scalar quantity (such as speed, density, or mass), which has magnitude but no direction. A vector is represented either geometrically by an arrow whose length corresponds to its magnitude and points in an appropriate direction, or by a pair of numbers written vertically and placed within parentheses (*x y*).

Vectors can be added graphically by constructing a parallelogram of vectors (such as the ◊parallelogram of forces commonly employed in physics and engineering).

Veda (Sanskrit "divine knowledge") the most sacred of the Hindu scriptures, hymns written in an old form of Sanskrit; the oldest may date from 1500 or 2000 BC. The four main collections are: the *Rigveda* (hymns and praises); *Yajurveda* (prayers and sacrificial formulae); *Sâmaveda* (tunes and chants); and *Atharvaveda*, or Veda of the Atharvans, the officiating priests at the sacrifices.

Vega or *Alpha Lyrae* brightest star in the constellation Lyra and the fifth-brightest star in the sky. It is a blue-white star, 25 light-years from Earth, with a luminosity 50 times that of the Sun.

vegan vegetarian who eats no foods of animal origin, including fish, eggs, and milk.

vegetarian person who eats only foods obtained without slaughter, for humanitarian, aesthetic, political, or health reasons. Vegans abstain from all foods of animal origin.

vegetative reproduction type of ◊asexual reproduction in plants that relies not on spores, but on multicellular structures formed by the parent plant. Some of the main types are stolons and runners, gemmae, bulbils, sucker shoots produced from roots (such as in the creeping thistle *Cirsium arvense*), ◊tubers, ◊bulbs, ◊corms, and rhizomes. Vegetative reproduction has long been exploited in horticulture and agriculture, with various methods employed to multiply stocks of plants.

vein in animals with a circulatory system, any vessel that carries blood from the body to the heart. Veins contain valves that prevent the blood from running back when moving against gravity. They always carry deoxygenated blood, with the exception of the veins leading from the lungs to the heart in birds and mammals, which carry newly oxygenated blood.

Velázquez Diego Rodríguez de Silva y 1599–1660. Spanish painter, born in Seville, the outstanding Spanish artist of the 17th century. In 1623 he became court painter to Philip IV in Madrid, where he produced many portraits of the royal family as well as occasional religious paintings, genre scenes, and other subjects. *Las Meninas/The Ladies-in-Waiting* 1655

(Prado, Madrid) is a complex group portrait that includes a self-portrait, but nevertheless focuses clearly on the doll-like figure of the Infanta Margareta Teresa.

Velde, van de family of Dutch artists. Both *Willem van de Velde* the Elder (1611–93) and his son *Willem van de Velde* the Younger (1633–1707) painted sea battles for Charles II and James II (having settled in London 1672). Another son *Adriaen van de Velde* (1636–1672) painted landscapes.

veldt subtropical grassland in South Africa, equivalent to the ◊Pampas of South America.

vellum type of parchment, often rolled in scrolls, made from the skin of a calf, kid, or lamb. It was used from the late Roman Empire and Middle Ages for exceptionally important documents and the finest manuscripts. For example, *Torahs* (the five books of Moses) are always written in Hebrew on vellum. The modern term now describes thick, high-quality paper that resembles fine vellum parchment.

velocity speed of an object in a given direction. Velocity is a ◊vector quantity, since its direction is important as well as its magnitude (or speed).

velocity ratio (VR), or *distance ratio* in a machine, the ratio of the distance moved by an effort force to the distance moved by the machine's load in the same time. It follows that the velocities of the effort and the load are in the same ratio. Velocity ratio has no units.

velvet fabric of silk, cotton, nylon, or other textile, with a short, thick pile. Utrecht, Netherlands, and Genoa, Italy, are traditional centers of manufacture. It

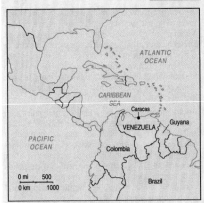

Venezuela
Republic of
(*República de Venezuela*)

area 352,162 sq mi/912,100 sq km
capital Caracas
cities Barquisimeto, Valencia; port Maracaibo
physical Andes Mountains and Lake Maracaibo in NW; central plains (llanos); delta of river Orinoco in E; Guiana Highlands in SE
features Angel Falls, world's highest waterfall
head of state and of government Ramon José Velasquez Mujica from 1993
government federal democratic republic
political parties Democratic Action Party (AD), moderate left of center; Social Christian Party (COPEI), Christian center-right; Movement toward Socialism (MAS), left of center

exports coffee, timber, oil, aluminum, iron ore, petrochemicals
currency bolívar
population (1992) 20,184,000 (mestizos 70%, white (Spanish, Portuguese, Italian) 20%, black 9%, Amerindian 2%); growth rate 2.8% p.a.
life expectancy men 67, women 73 (1989)
languages Spanish (official), Indian languages 2%
religions Roman Catholic 96%, Protestant 2%
literacy 88% (1989)
GNP $47.3 bn (1988); $2,629 per head (1985)

chronology
1961 New constitution adopted, with Rómulo Betancourt as president.
1964 Dr Raúl Leoni became president.
1969 Dr Rafael Caldera became president.
1974 Carlos Andrés Pérez became president.
1979 Dr Luis Herrera became president.
1984 Dr Jaime Lusinchi became president; social pact established between government, labor unions, and business; national debt rescheduled.
1987 Widespread social unrest triggered by inflation; student demonstrators shot by police.
1988 Carlos Andrés Pérez elected president. Payments suspended on foreign debts (increase due to drop in oil prices).
1989 Economic austerity program enforced by $4.3 billion loan from International Monetary Fund. Price increases triggered riots; 300 people killed. Feb: martial law declared. May: General strike. Elections boycotted by opposition groups.
1991 Protests against austerity program continued.
1992 Attempted antigovernment coups failed. Pérez promised constitutional changes.
1993 Pérez resigned, accused of corruption; Ramon José Velasquez succeeded him as interim head of state pending elections.

is woven on a double loom, then cut between the center pile to form velvet nap.

vena cava one of the large, thin-walled veins found just above the ◊heart, formed from the junction of several smaller veins. The *posterior vena cava* receives oxygenated blood returning from the lungs, and empties into the left atrium. The *anterior vena cava* collects deoxygenated blood returning from the rest of the body and passes it into the right side of the heart, from where it will be pumped into the lungs.

Venda ◊Black National State from 1979, near the Zimbabwe border, in South Africa
area 2,510 sq mi/6,500 sq km
capital Thohoyandou
cities MaKearela
features homeland of the Vhavenda people
government military council since a coup 1990 (military leader Ramushwana from 1990)
products coal, copper, graphite, construction stone
population (1980) 343,500
languages Luvenda, English.

vendetta any prolonged feud, in particular one in which the relatives of a dishonored or murdered person seek revenge on the wrongdoer or members of the family. The tradition is Mediterranean, known in Europe and the US as a way of settling wrongs in Corsica, Sardinia, and Sicily, as practiced by the ◊Mafia.

venereal disease (VD) any disease mainly transmitted by sexual contact, although commonly the term is used specifically for gonorrhea and syphilis, both occurring worldwide, and chancroid ("soft sore") and lymphogranuloma venerum, seen mostly in the tropics. The term *sexually transmitted diseases* (STDs) is more often used to encompass a growing list of conditions passed on primarily, but not exclusively, in this way.

Veneto region of NE Italy, comprising the provinces of Belluno, Padova (Padua), Treviso, Rovigo, Venezia (Venice), and Vicenza; area 7,102 sq mi/18,400 sq km; population (1990) 4,398,100. Its capital is Venice, and towns include Padua, Verona, and Vicenza. The Veneto forms part of the N Italian plain, with the delta of the river Po; it includes part of the Alps and Dolomites, and Lake Garda. Products include cereals, fruit, vegetables, wine, chemicals, ships, and textiles.

Venezuela country in N South America, on the Caribbean Sea, bounded E by Guyana, S by Brazil, and W by Colombia.

Venice (Italian *Venezia*) city, port, and naval base on the NE coast of Italy; population (1990) 79,000. It is the capital of Veneto region. The old city is built on piles on low-lying islands in a salt-water lagoon, sheltered from the Adriatic Sea by the Lido and other small strips of land. There are about 150 canals crossed by some 400 bridges. Apart from tourism (it draws 8 million tourists a year), industries include glass, jewelry, textiles, and lace. Venice was an independent trading republic from the 10th century, ruled by a doge, or chief magistrate, and was one of the centers of the Italian Renaissance.

veni, vidi, vici (Latin "I came, I saw, I conquered") Julius ◊Caesar's description of his victory over King Pharnaces II (63–47 BC) at Zela in 47 BC.

Venn diagram in mathematics, a diagram representing a ◊set or sets and the logical relationships between them. The sets are drawn as circles. An area of overlap between two circles (sets) contains elements that are common to both sets, and thus represents a third set.

Circles that do not overlap represent sets with no elements in common (disjoint sets). The method is named after the British logician John Venn (1834–1923).

Ventura city in SW California, on the Pacific Ocean, NW of Los Angeles; population (1980) 83,475. Industries include oil and agricultural products, such as citrus fruits and lima beans.

venture capital or *risk capital* financing provided by venture capital companies, individuals, and merchant banks for medium- or long-term business ventures that are not their own and in which there is a strong element of risk.

Venturi Robert 1925– . US architect. He pioneered Postmodernism through his books *Complexity and Contradiction in Architecture* 1967 (Pulitzer Prize 1991) and *Learning from Las Vegas* 1972. In 1986 he was commissioned to design the extension to the National Gallery, London, opened 1991.

Venus in Roman mythology, the goddess of love and beauty, equivalent to the Greek ◊Aphrodite. The patrician Romans believed that they were descended from Aeneas, the son of the goddess, and Anchises, a shepherd. She was venerated as the guardian of the Roman people.

Venus second planet from the Sun. It orbits the Sun every 225 days at an average distance of 67.2 million mi/108.2 million km and can approach the Earth to within 24 million mi/38 million km, closer than any other planet. Its diameter is 7,500 mi/12,100 km and its mass is 0.82 that of Earth. Venus rotates on its axis more slowly than any other planet, once every 243 days and from east to west, the opposite direction to the other planets (except Uranus and possibly Pluto). Venus is shrouded by clouds of sulfuric acid droplets that sweep across the planet from east to west every four days. The atmosphere is almost entirely carbon dioxide, which traps the Sun's heat by the ◊greenhouse effect and raises the planet's surface temperature to 900°F/480°C, with an atmospheric pressure of 90 times that at the surface of the Earth.

Venus flytrap insectivorous plant *Dionaea muscipula* of the sundew family, native to the SE US; its leaves have two hinged blades that close and entrap insects.

Veracruz port (trading in coffee, tobacco, and vanilla) in E Mexico, on the Gulf of Mexico; population (1980) 305,456. Products include chemicals, sisal, and tex-

Venus Venus photographed from a Pioneer probe.

Vermeer A Young Woman Standing at a Virginal (*c. 1670*), National Gallery, London, by Dutch painter Jan Vermeer.

tiles. It was founded by the Spanish conquistador Hernando Cortés as Villa Nueva de la Vera Cruz ("new town of the true cross") on a nearby site 1519 and transferred to its present site 1599.

verb grammatical part of speech for what someone or something does (*to go*), experiences (*to live*), or is (*to be*). Verbs involve the grammatical categories known as number (singular or plural: "He *runs*; they *run*"), voice (active or passive: "She *writes* books; it *is written*"), mood (statements, questions, orders, emphasis, necessity, condition), aspect (completed or continuing action: "She *danced*; she *was dancing*"), and tense (variation according to time: simple present tense, present progressive tense, simple past tense, and so on).

verbena any plant of the genus *Verbena*, family Verbenaceae, of about 100 species, mostly found in the American tropics. The leaves are fragrant and the tubular flowers arranged in close spikes in colors ranging from white to rose, violet, and purple. The garden verbena is a hybrid annual.

Vercingetorix Gallic chieftain. Leader of a revolt of all the tribes of Gaul against the Romans 52 BC; he lost, was captured, displayed in Julius Caesar's triumph 46 BC, and later executed. This ended the Gallic resistance to Roman rule.

Verdi Giuseppe (Fortunino Francesco) 1813–1901. Italian opera composer of the Romantic period, who took his native operatic style to new heights of dramatic expression. In 1842 he wrote the opera *Nabucco*, followed by *Ernani* 1844 and *Rigoletto* 1851. Other works include *Il Trovatore* and *La Traviata* both 1853, *Aïda* 1871, and the masterpieces of his old age, *Otello* 1887 and *Falstaff* 1893. His *Requiem* 1874 commemorates Alessandro Manzoni.

Verdun fortress town in NE France on the Meuse. During World War I it became the symbol of French resistance, withstanding a German onslaught 1916.

Verlaine Paul 1844–1896. French lyric poet who was influenced by the poets Baudelaire and ◊Rimbaud. His volumes of verse include *Poèmes saturniens/Saturnine Poems* 1866, *Fêtes galantes/Amorous Entertainments* 1869, and *Romances sans paroles/Songs without Words* 1874. In 1873 he was imprisoned for attempting to shoot Rimbaud. His later works reflect his attempts to lead a reformed life. He was acknowledged as leader of the ◊Symbolist poets.

Vermeer Jan 1632–1675. Dutch painter, active in Delft. Most of his pictures are ◊genre scenes, with a limpid clarity and distinct air of stillness, and a harmonious palette often focusing on yellow and blue. He frequently depicted solitary women in domestic settings, as in *The Lacemaker* (Louvre, Paris).

Vermont state in NE US; nickname Green Mountain State
area 9,611 sq mi/24,900 sq km
capital Montpelier
cities Burlington, Rutland, Barre
features brilliant autumn foliage and winter sports; Green Mountains; Lake Champlain
products apples, maple syrup, dairy products, kaolinite, granite, marble, slate, business machines, paper and allied products; tourism is important
population (1990) 562,800
famous people Chester A Arthur, Calvin Coolidge, John Dewey
history explored by the Frenchman Samuel de Champlain from 1609; settled 1724; became a state 1791.

vermouth sweet or dry white wine flavored with bitter herbs and fortified with alcohol.

Verne Jules 1828–1905. French author of tales of adventure that anticipated future scientific developments: *Five Weeks in a Balloon* 1862, *Journey to the Center of the Earth* 1864, *Twenty Thousand Leagues under the Sea* 1870, and *Around the World in Eighty Days* 1873.

Vernier Pierre 1580–1637. French mathematician who invented a means of making very precise measurements with what is now called the vernier scale. He was a French government official and in 1631 published *La construction, l'usage, et les propriétez du quadrant nouveau mathématique/ The construction, uses and properties of a new mathematical quadrant*, in which he explained his method.

Verona industrial city (printing, paper, plastics, furniture, pasta) in Veneto, Italy, on the Adige River; population (1988) 259,000. It also trades in fruit and vegetables.

Veronese Paolo *c*. 1528–1588. Italian painter, born in Verona, active mainly in Venice (from about 1553). He specialized in grand decorative schemes, such as his ceilings in the Doge's Palace in Venice, with *trompe l'oeil* effects and inventive detail. The subjects are religious, mythological, historical, and allegorical.

Versailles city in N France, capital of Les Yvelines *département*, on the outskirts of Paris; population (1990) 91,000. It grew up around the palace of Louis XV. Within the palace park are two small châteaux, Le Grand Trianon and Le Petit Trianon, built for Louis XIV (by Jules-Hardouin Mansart (1646–1708)) and Louis XV (by Jacques Gabriel (1698–1782)) respectively.

Versailles, Treaty of peace treaty after World War I between the Allies and Germany, signed June 28, 1919. It established the League of Nations. Germany surrendered Alsace-Lorraine to France, and large areas in the east to Poland, and made smaller cessions to Czechoslovakia, Lithuania, Belgium, and Denmark. The Rhineland was demilitarized, German rearmament was restricted, and Germany agreed to pay reparations for war damage. The treaty was never ratified by the US, which made a separate peace with Germany and Austria 1921.

verse arrangement of words in a rhythmic pattern, which may depend on the length of syllables (as in

Greek or Latin verse), or on stress, as in English. Classical Greek verse depended upon quantity, a long syllable being regarded as occupying twice the time taken up by a short syllable.

vertebrate any animal with a backbone. The 41,000 species of vertebrates include mammals, birds, reptiles, amphibians, and fishes. They include most of the larger animals, but in terms of numbers of species are only a tiny proportion of the world's animals. The zoological taxonomic group Vertebrata is a subgroup of the ◊phylum *Chordata*.

vertex (plural *vertices*) in geometry, a point shared by three or more sides of a solid figure; the point farthest from a figure's base; or the point of intersection of two sides of a plane figure or the two rays of an angle.

vertigo dizziness; a whirling sensation accompanied by a loss of any feeling of contact with the ground. It may be due to temporary disturbance of the sense of balance (as in spinning for too long on one spot), psychological reasons, disease such as labyrinthitis, or intoxication.

Very Large Array (VLA) largest and most complex single-site radio telescope in the world. It is located on the Plains of San Augustine, 50 mi/80 km west of Socorro, New Mexico. It consists of 27 dish antennae, each 82 ft/25 m in diameter, arranged along three equally spaced arms forming a Y-shaped array. Two of the arms are 13 mi/21 km long, and the third, to the north, is 11.8 mi/19 km long. The dishes are mounted on railroad tracks enabling the configuration and size of the array to be altered as required.

Vesalius Andreas 1514–1564. Belgian physician who revolutionized anatomy. His great innovations were to perform postmortem dissections and to make use of illustrations in teaching anatomy.

Vesey Denmark *c.* 1767–1822. American resistance leader. Buying his freedom for $600 in 1800, he became an outspoken and eloquent critic of the institution of slavery. Arrested 1822 on suspicion of fomenting a rebellion among local slaves, he and five other black leaders were hanged despite a lack of evidence against them.

Vespasian (Titus Flavius Vespasianus) AD 9–79. Roman emperor from AD 69. Proclaimed emperor by his soldiers while he was campaigning in Palestine, he reorganized the eastern provinces, and was a capable administrator. He was responsible for the construction of the Colosseum in Rome, which was completed by his son ◊Titus.

Vespucci Amerigo 1454–1512. Florentine merchant. The Americas were named after him as a result of the widespread circulation of his accounts of his explorations. His accounts of the voyage 1499–1501 indicate that he had been to places he could not possibly have reached (the Pacific Ocean, British Columbia, Antarctica).

Vesta in Roman mythology, the goddess of the hearth, equivalent to the Greek ◊Hestia. In Rome, the sacred flame in her shrine in the Forum was kept constantly lit by the six *Vestal Virgins.*

vestigial organ in biology, an organ that remains in diminished form after it has ceased to have any significant function in the adult organism. In humans, the appendix is vestigial, having once had a digestive function in our ancestors.

Vesuvius (Italian *Vesuvio*) active volcano SE of Naples, Italy; height 4,190 ft/1,277 m. In 79 BC it destroyed the cities of Pompeii, Herculaneum, and Oplonti.

veterinary science the study, prevention, and cure of disease in animals. More generally, it covers animal anatomy, breeding, and relations to humans.

The American Veterinary Medical Association was formed 1883.

veto (Latin "I forbid") exercise by a sovereign, branch of legislature, or other political power, of the right to prevent the enactment or operation of a law, or the taking of some course of action.

Under the US Constitution, the president may veto legislation, although that veto may, in turn, be overruled by a two-thirds majority in Congress. At the United Nations, members of the Security Council can exercise a veto on resolutions.

VHF (abbreviation for *very high frequency*) referring to radio waves that have very short wavelengths (10 m–1 m). They are used for interference-free ◊FM (frequency-modulated) transmissions. VHF transmitters have a relatively short range because the waves cannot be reflected over the horizon like longer radio waves.

Vico Giambattista 1668–1744. Italian philosopher, considered the founder of the modern philosophy of history. He argued that we can understand history more adequately than nature, since it is we who have made it. He believed that the study of language, ritual, and myth was a way of understanding earlier societies. His cyclical theory of history (the birth, development, and decline of human societies) was put forward in *New Science* 1725.

Victor Emmanuel II 1820–1878. First king of united Italy from 1861. He became king of Sardinia on the abdication of his father Charles Albert 1849. In 1855 he allied Sardinia with France and the UK in the Crimean War. In 1859 in alliance with the French he defeated the Austrians and annexed Lombardy. By 1860 most of Italy had come under his rule, and in 1861 he was proclaimed king of Italy. In 1870 he made Rome his capital.

Victor Emmanuel III 1869–1947. King of Italy from the assassination of his father, Umberto I, 1900. He acquiesced in the Fascist regime of Mussolini from 1922 and, after the dictator's fall 1943, relinquished power to his son Umberto II, who cooperated with the Allies. Victor Emmanuel formally abdicated 1946.

Victoria state of SE Australia
area 87,854 sq mi/227,600 sq km
capital Mebourne
cities Geelong, Ballarat, Bendigo
physical part of the Great Dividing Range, running E–W and including the larger part of the Australian Alps; Gippsland lakes; shallow lagoons on the coast; the mallee shrub region
products sheep, beef cattle, dairy products, tobacco, wheat, vines for wine and dried fruit, orchard fruits,

Vermont

Victoria Queen Victoria reading official dispatches at Frogmore, England, with an Indian servant in attendance, 1893.

vegetables, gold, brown coal (Latrobe Valley), oil and natural gas (Bass Strait)

population (1987) 4,184,000; 70% in the Melbourne area

history annexed for Britain by Capt Cook 1770; settled in the 1830s; after being part of New South Wales became a separate colony 1851, named after the queen; became a state 1901.

Victoria industrial port (shipbuilding, chemicals, clothing, furniture) on Vancouver Island, capital of British Columbia; population (1986) 66,303.

Victoria port and capital of the Seychelles, on Mahé Island; population (1987) 24,300. Industries include copra, vanilla, and cinnamon.

Victoria city in S Texas, on the Guadalupe River, near the Gulf of Mexico; population (1990) 55,100. It is a transportation center for oil, natural gas, chemicals, and dairy products.

Victoria 1819–1901. Queen of the UK from 1837, when she succeeded her uncle William IV, and empress of India from 1876. In 1840 she married Prince ◊Albert of Saxe-Coburg and Gotha. Her relations with her prime ministers ranged from the affectionate (Melbourne and Disraeli) to the stormy (Peel, Palmerston, and Gladstone). Her golden jubilee 1887 and diamond jubilee 1897 marked a waning of republican sentiment, which had developed with her withdrawal from public life on Albert's death 1861.

Only child of Edward, duke of Kent, fourth son of George III, she was born in London. She and Albert had four sons and five daughters. After Albert's death 1861 she lived mainly in retirement. Nevertheless, she kept control of affairs, refusing the prince of Wales (Edward VII) any active role.

Victoria Falls or *Mosi-oa-tunya* waterfall on the river Zambezi, on the Zambia–Zimbabwe border. The river is 5,580 ft/1,700 m wide and drops 400 ft/120 m to flow through a 100-ft/30-m wide gorge.

Victoria, Lake or *Victoria Nyanza* largest lake in Africa; area over 26,800 sq mi/69,400 sq km; length 255 mi/410 km. It lies on the equator at an altitude of 3,728 ft/1,136 m, bounded by Uganda, Kenya, and Tanzania. It is a source of the river Nile.

vicuna ◊ruminant mammal *Lama vicugna* of the camel family that lives in herds on the Andean plateau. It can run at speeds of 30 mph/50 kph. It has good eyesight, fair hearing, and a poor sense of smell. It was hunted close to extinction for its meat and soft brown fur, which was used in textile manufacture, but the vicuna is now a protected species; populations are increasing thanks to strict conservation measures. It is related to the ◊alpaca, the guanaco, and the ◊llama.

video cassette recorder (VCR) device for recording pictures and sound on cassettes or spools of magnetic tape. The first commercial VCR was launched 1956 for the television broadcasting industry, but from the late 1970s cheaper models developed for home use, to record broadcast programs for future viewing and to view rented or owned videocassettes of commercial films.

video game electronic game played on a visual-display screen or, by means of special additional or built-in components, on the screen of a television set. The first commercially sold was a simple bat-and-ball game developed in the US 1972, but complex variants are now available in color and with special sound effects.

Vienna (German *Wien*) capital of Austria, on the river Danube at the foot of the Wiener Wald (Vienna Woods); population (1986) 1,481,000. Industries include engineering and the production of electrical goods and precision instruments.

Vienna, Congress of international conference held 1814–15 that agreed the settlement of Europe after the Napoleonic Wars. National representatives included the Austrian foreign minister Metternich, Alexander I of Russia, the British foreign secretary Castlereagh and military commander Wellington, and the French politician Talleyrand.

Vientiane (Lao *Vieng Chan*) capital and chief port of Laos on the Mekong River; population (1985) 377,000. Noted for its pagodas, canals, and houses on stilts, it is a trading center for forest products and textiles. The Temple of the Heavy Buddha, the Pratuxai triumphal arch, and the Black Stupa are here. The Great Sacred Stupa to the NE of the city is the most important national monument in Laos.

Vietcong (Vietnamese "Vietnamese communists") in the Vietnam War 1954–75, the members of the National Front for the Liberation of South Vietnam, founded 1960, who fought the South Vietnamese and US forces. The name was coined by the South Viet-

vicuna The vicuna is a species of llama found in the high Andes.

namese government to differentiate these communist guerrillas from the ◊Vietminh.

Vietminh the Vietnam Independence League, founded 1941 to oppose the Japanese occupation of Indochina and later directed against the French colonial power. The Vietminh were instrumental in achieving Vietnamese independence through military victory at Dien Bien Phu 1954.

Vietnam
Socialist Republic of
(*Công Hòa Xã Hội Chu Nghĩa Việt Nam*)

area 127,259 sq mi/329,600 sq km
capital Hanoi
cities ports Ho Chi Minh City (formerly Saigon), Da Nang, Haiphong
physical Red River and Mekong deltas, center of cultivation and population; tropical rain forest; mountainous in N and NW
environment during the Vietnam War an estimated 5.4 million acres/2.2 million hectares of forest were destroyed. The country's National Conservation Strategy is trying to replant 500 million trees each year
features Karst hills of Halong Bay, Cham Towers
head of state Le Duc Anh from 1992
head of government Vo Van Kiet from 1991
political system communism
political party Communist Party
exports rice, rubber, coal, iron, apatite

currency dong
population (1992) 69,052,000 (750,000 refugees, majority ethnic Chinese left 1975–79, some settled in SW China, others fled by sea — the "boat people" — to Hong Kong and elsewhere); growth rate 2.4% p.a.
life expectancy men 62, women 66 (1989)
languages Vietnamese (official), French, English, Khmer, Chinese, local languages
media independent newspapers prohibited by law 1989; central government approval is required for appointment of editors
religions Buddhist, Taoist, Confucian, Christian
literacy 78% (1989)
GNP $12.6 bn; $180 per head (1987)

chronology
1945 Japanese removed from Vietnam at end of World War II.
1946 Commencement of Vietminh war against French.
1954 France defeated at Dien Bien Phu. Vietnam divided along 17th parallel.
1964 US troops entered Vietnam War.
1973 Paris cease-fire agreement.
1975 Saigon captured by North Vietnam.
1976 Socialist Republic of Vietnam proclaimed.
1978 Admission into Comecon. Vietnamese invasion of Cambodia.
1979 Sino-Vietnamese border war.
1986 Retirement of "old guard" leaders.
1987–88 Over 10,000 political prisoners released.
1988–89 Troop withdrawals from Cambodia continued.
1989 "Boat people" leaving Vietnam murdered and robbed at sea by Thai pirates. Troop withdrawal from Cambodia completed. Hong Kong forcibly repatriated some Vietnamese refugees.
1991 Vo Van Kiet replaced Do Muoi as prime minister. Cambodia peace agreement signed. Relations with China normalized.
1992 Sept: Le Duc Anh elected president. Dec: relations with South Korea normalized; US eased 30-year-old trade embargo.

Vietnam War
American troops of
the 1st Cavalry
Division (Airmobile),
Vietnam 1967.

Vietnam country in SE Asia, on the South China Sea, bounded N by China and W by Cambodia and Laos.

Vietnamese member of the majority group (90%) of peoples inhabiting Vietnam and referring to their language and culture, which is also called Annamese. Although Annamese is an independent language, it has been influenced by Chinese and there are Khmer loan words.

Vietnam War 1954–1975 war between communist North Vietnam and US-backed South Vietnam. Following the division of French Indochina into North and South Vietnam and the Vietnamese defeat of the French 1954, US involvement in Southeast Asia grew through the ◊SEATO pact. Noncommunist South Vietnam was viewed, in the context of the 1950s and the ◊cold war, as a bulwark against the spread of communism throughout SE Asia. Advisers and military aid were dispatched to the region at increasing levels because of the so-called domino theory, which contended that the fall of South Vietnam would precipitate the collapse of neighboring states. Corruption and inefficiency within the South Vietnamese government led the US to assume ever greater responsibility for the war effort, until more than 500,000 US troops were engaged.

vigilante in US history, originally a member of a "vigilance committee," a self-appointed group to maintain public order in the absence of organized authority, especially in Western frontier communities.

Early vigilante groups included the "Regulators" in South Carolina in the 1760s and in Pennsylvania 1794 during the Whiskey Rebellion. Many more appeared in the 19th century in frontier towns. Once authorized police forces existed, certain vigilante groups, such as the post–Civil War ◊Ku Klux Klan, operated outside the law, often as perpetrators of mob violence such as lynching.

Viking or *Norseman* medieval Scandinavian sea warrior. They traded with and raided Europe in the 8th–11th centuries, and often settled there. In France the Vikings were given ◊Normandy. Under Sweyn I they conquered England 1013, and his son Canute was king of England as well as Denmark and Norway. In the east they established the first Russian state and founded ◊Novgorod. They reached the Byzantine Empire in the south, and in the west sailed the seas to Ireland, Iceland, Greenland, and North America; see ◊Eric the Red, Leif ◊Ericsson, ◊Vinland.

Viking probes two US space probes to Mars, each one consisting of an orbiter and a lander. They were launched Aug 20 and Sept 9, 1975. They transmitted color pictures and analyzed the soil. No definite signs of life were found.

Viking 1 carried life detection labs and landed on July 20, 1976, for detailed research and photos. Designed to work for 90 days, it operated for six and a half years, going silent Nov 1982. *Viking 2* was similar in setup to *Viking 1*; it landed on Mars Sept 3, 1976, and functioned for three and a half years.

Villa-Lobos Heitor 1887–1959. Brazilian composer. His style was based on folk tunes collected on travels in his country; for example, in the *Bachianas Brasileiras* 1930–44, he treats them in the manner of Bach. His works range from guitar solos to film scores to opera; he produced 2,000 works, including 12 symphonies.

villeinage system of serfdom that prevailed in Europe in the Middle Ages. A villein was a peasant who gave dues and services to his lord in exchange for land. In France until the 13th century, "villeins" could refer to rural or urban non-nobles, but after this, it came to mean exclusively rural non-noble freemen. In Norman England, it referred to free peasants of relatively high status.

Villon François 1431–c. 1465. French poet who used satiric humor, pathos, and lyric power in works written in the slang of the time. Among the little of his work that survives, *Petit Testament* 1456 and *Grand Testament* 1461 are prominent (the latter includes the "Ballade des dames du temps jadis/Ballad of the Ladies of Former Times").

Vilnius capital of Lithuania; population (1987) 566,000. Industries include engineering and the manufacture of textiles, chemicals, and foodstuffs.

Vincent de Paul, St c. 1580–1660. French Roman Catholic priest and founder of the two charitable orders of Dazarists 1625 and Sisters of Charity 1634. After being ordained 1600, he was captured by Barbary pirates and held as a slave in Tunis until he escaped 1607. He was canonized 1737; feast day July 19.

vine or *grapevine* any of various climbing woody plants of the genus *Vitis*, family Vitaceae, especially *V. vinifera*, native to Asia Minor and cultivated from antiquity. Its fruit is eaten or made into wine or other fermented drinks; dried fruits of certain varieties are known as raisins and currants. Many other species of climbing plant are also termed vines.

Vietnam War: chronology

1954 Under the Geneva Convention the former French colony of Indochina was divided into the separate states of North and South Vietnam. Within South Vietnam the communist Vietcong, supported by North Vietnam and China, attempted to seize power. The US began to provide military advisers to support the South Vietnamese.
1964 The Tonkin Gulf Incident, when North Vietnamese torpedo boats allegedly attacked two US destroyers, prompted the US to send troops.
1967 Several large-scale invasion attempts by North Vietnam were defeated by indigenous and US forces.
1968 Tet Offensive in South Vietnam; My Lai massacre by US troops.
1973 In the US, the unpopularity of sending troops to an undeclared war led to the start of US withdrawal. A peace treaty was signed between North and South Vietnam.
1975 South Vietnam was invaded by North Vietnam in March.
1976 South Vietnam was annexed by North Vietnam, and the two countries were renamed the Socialist Republic of Vietnam.

Viking

In their narrow, shallow-drafted and highly maneuvrable longships, the Vikings spread from their Scandinavian homelands to fight, trade and settle through most of the coastal regions of 8th to 11th-century Europe. They established kingdoms in the British Isles, Normandy, and Russia. As Normans they founded a kingdom in Sicily and in 1066 achieved a second conquest of England. They are believed to have sailed to North America and as far south as the Byzantine Empire where Swedish Vikings (Varangians) formed the imperial guard.

A stone cross (below) from Middleton, Yorkshire, depicting a well-armed Viking warrior. His weapons include a spear, sword, axe, and dagger.

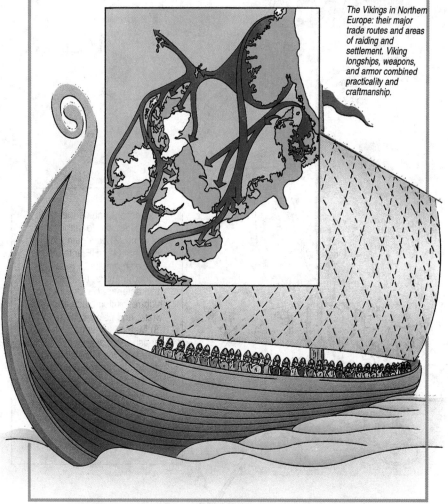

The Vikings in Northern Europe: their major trade routes and areas of raiding and settlement. Viking longships, weapons, and armor combined practicality and craftmanship.

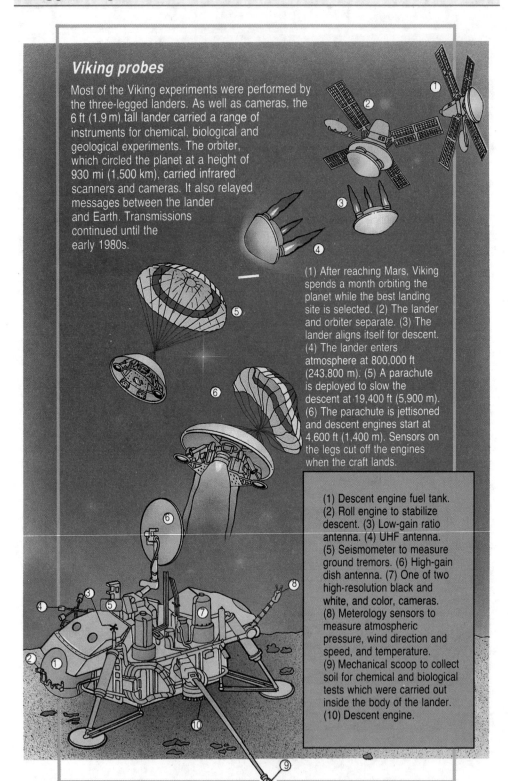

Viking probes

Most of the Viking experiments were performed by the three-legged landers. As well as cameras, the 6 ft (1.9 m) tall lander carried a range of instruments for chemical, biological and geological experiments. The orbiter, which circled the planet at a height of 930 mi (1,500 km), carried infrared scanners and cameras. It also relayed messages between the lander and Earth. Transmissions continued until the early 1980s.

(1) After reaching Mars, Viking spends a month orbiting the planet while the best landing site is selected. (2) The lander and orbiter separate. (3) The lander aligns itself for descent. (4) The lander enters atmosphere at 800,000 ft (243,800 m). (5) A parachute is deployed to slow the descent at 19,400 ft (5,900 m). (6) The parachute is jettisoned and descent engines start at 4,600 ft (1,400 m). Sensors on the legs cut off the engines when the craft lands.

(1) Descent engine fuel tank. (2) Roll engine to stabilize descent. (3) Low-gain ratio antenna. (4) UHF antenna. (5) Seismometer to measure ground tremors. (6) High-gain dish antenna. (7) One of two high-resolution black and white, and color, cameras. (8) Meterology sensors to measure atmospheric pressure, wind direction and speed, and temperature. (9) Mechanical scoop to collect soil for chemical and biological tests which were carried out inside the body of the lander. (10) Descent engine.

vinegar sour liquid consisting of a 4% solution of acetic acid produced by the oxidation of alcohol, used to flavor food and as a preservative in pickling. *Malt vinegar* is brown and made from malted cereals; *white vinegar* is distilled from it. Other sources of vinegar include cider, wine, and honey. *Balsamic vinegar* is wine vinegar aged in wooden barrels.

Vineland industrial city (foundry products, glassware, chemicals, and vegetables) in SW New Jersey, N of Millville; population (1990) 54,800.

Vinland Norse name for the area of North America, probably the coast of Nova Scotia or New England, which the Norse adventurer and explorer Leif ◊Ericsson visited about 1000. It was named after the wild grapes that grew there and is celebrated in an important Norse saga.

Vinson Frederick Moore 1890–1953. US jurist. He held office in the US House of Representatives 1924–28 and 1930–38 and was appointed chief justice of the US Supreme Court 1946–53 by President Truman. He defended federal intervention in social and economic matters, and dissented in *Youngstown Sheet and Tube Co v Sawyer* 1952, revoking presidential nationalization of the steel industry during the Korean War.

viol family of bowed stringed instruments prominent in the 16th–18th centuries, before their role was taken by the violins. Developed for close-harmony chamber music, they have a pure and restrained tone. Viols normally have six strings, a flat back, and narrow shoulders.

viola bowed, stringed musical instrument, alto member of the ◊violin family.

violet plant of the genus *Viola*, family Violaceae, with toothed leaves and mauve, blue, or white flowers, such as the Canada violet *V. canadensis* and primrose violet *V. primulifolia* of North America and the sweet violet *V. odorata* of Europe. The pansy is also a kind of violet.

violin bowed, four-stringed musical instrument, the smallest and highest pitched of the violin family. The strings are tuned in fifths (G, D, A, and E), with G as the lowest, tuned below middle C.

violin family family of bowed stringed instruments developed in 17th-century Italy, which eventually superseded the viols and formed the basis of the modern orchestra. There are four instruments: violin, viola, cello (or violoncello) and the double bass, which is descended from the double bass viol (or violone).

violoncello or *cello* bowed, stringed musical instrument, tenor member of the ◊violin family.

VIP abbreviation for *very important person.*

viper any front-fanged venomous snake of the family Viperidae. Vipers range in size from 1 ft/30 cm to 10 ft/

violin family All the members of the violin family share a common design with minor variations, except the double bass.

3 m, and often have diamond or jagged markings. Most give birth to live young.

Virgil (Publius Vergilius Maro) 70–19 BC. Roman poet who wrote the "Eclogues" 37 BC, a series of pastoral poems; the "Georgics" 30 BC, four books on the art of farming; and his epic masterpiece, the ◊Aeneid 29–19 BC. He was patronized by Maecenas on behalf of Octavian (later the emperor Augustus).

virginal in music, a small type of ◊harpsichord.

Virginia state in E US; nickname Old Dominion
area 40,762 sq mi/105,600 sq km
capital Richmond
cities Norfolk, Virginia Beach, Newport News, Hampton, Chesapeake, Portsmouth
features Blue Ridge Mountains, which include the Shenandoah National Park; Arlington National Cemetery; Mount Vernon (home of George Washington 1752–99); Monticello (Thomas Jefferson's home near Charlottesville); Stratford Hall (Robert E Lee's birthplace at Lexington); Williamsburg restoration; Jamestown and Yorktown historic sites
products sweet potatoes, corn, tobacco, apples, peanuts, coal, ships, trucks, paper, chemicals, processed food, textiles
population (1990) 6,187,400.

Virginia Beach city and resort in SE Virginia, on Chesapeake Bay, E of Norfolk; population (1990) 393,100. The colonists who settled Jamestown first landed here 1607.

Virginia creeper or *woodbine* E North American climbing vine *Parthenocissus quinquefolia* of the grape family, having tendrils, palmately compound leaves, green flower clusters, and blue berries consumed by numerous birds but inedible to humans.

Virgin Islands group of about 100 small islands, northernmost of the Leeward Islands in the Antilles, West Indies. Tourism is the main industry.

Virginia

[Map of Virginia and surrounding states showing Illinois, Indiana, Ohio, West Virginia, Kentucky, RICHMOND, VIRGINIA, Tennessee, North Carolina, South Carolina, Georgia, ATLANTIC OCEAN, with scale 0 mi 100 / 0 km 200, and an inset map of the United States]

Virgin Islands

They comprise the *US Virgin Islands* St Thomas (with the capital, Charlotte Amalie), St Croix, St John, and about 50 small islets; area 135 sq mi/350 sq km; population (1990) 101,800; and the *British Virgin Islands* Tortola (with the capital, Road Town), Virgin Gorda, Anegada, and Jost van Dykes, and about 40 islets; area 58 sq mi/150 sq km; population (1987) 13,250.

Christopher Columbus reached these islands 1493. They were divided between Britain and Denmark 1666. Denmark sold its islands to the US 1917; they form an unincorporated territory, with residents electing a governor and legislature. The British Virgin Islands have partial internal self-government.

Virgo zodiacal constellation, the second largest in the sky. It is represented as a maiden holding an ear of wheat. The Sun passes through Virgo from late Sept to the end of Oct. Virgo's brightest star is the first-magnitude Spica. Virgo contains the nearest large cluster of galaxies to us, 50 million light-years away, consisting of about 3,000 galaxies centered on the giant elliptical galaxy M87. Also in Virgo is the nearest ◊quasar, 3C 273, an estimated 3 billion light-years distant. In astrology, the dates for Virgo are between about Aug 23 and Sept 22.

virion the smallest unit of a mature ◊virus.

virtual in computing, without physical existence. Some computers have virtual memory, making their immediate-access memory seem larger than it is; some computers can also simulate *virtual devices*. For example, the Acorn A3000 and A5000 computers have only one floppy-disk drive but can behave as if they were equipped with two, using part of the ◊RAM to simulate the second drive.

◊Virtual reality is a computer simulation of a whole physical environment.

virtual reality advanced form of computer simulation, in which a participant has the illusion of being part of an artificial environment. The participant views the environment through two tiny television screens (one for each eye) built into a visor. Sensors detect movements of the participant's head or body, causing the apparent viewing position to change. Gloves (datagloves) fitted with sensors may be worn, which allow the participant seemingly to pick up and move objects in the environment.

virus infectious particle consisting of a core of nucleic acid (DNA or RNA) enclosed in a protein shell. Viruses are acellular and able to function and reproduce only if they can invade a living cell to use the cell's system to replicate themselves. In the process they may disrupt or alter the host cell's own DNA. The healthy human body reacts by producing an antiviral protein, ◊interferon, which prevents the infection spreading to adjacent cells.

virus in computing, a piece of ◊software that can replicate itself and transfer itself from one computer to another, without the user being aware of it. Some viruses are relatively harmless, but others can damage or destroy data. They are written by anonymous programmers, often maliciously, and are spread along telephone lines or on ◊floppy disks. Antivirus software can be used to detect and destroy well-known viruses, but new viruses continually appear and these may bypass existing antivirus programs.

Visalia city in central California, in the San Joaquin Valley, SE of Fresno; population (1990) 75,600. It is an agricultural center for grapes, citrus fruits, and dairy products.

Visby historic town and bishopric on the Swedish island of Gotland in the Baltic that became the center of the German ◊Hanseatic League.

Visconti dukes and rulers of Milan 1277–1447. They originated as north Italian feudal lords who attained dominance over the city as a result of alliance with the Holy Roman emperors. Despite papal opposition, by the mid-14th century they ruled 15 other major towns in northern Italy. The duchy was inherited by the ◊Sforzas 1447.

viscose yellowish, syrupy solution made by treating cellulose with sodium hydroxide and carbon disulfide. The solution is then regenerated as continuous filament for the making of ◊rayon and as cellophane.

viscosity in physics, the resistance of a fluid to flow, caused by its internal friction, which makes it resist flowing past a solid surface or other layers of the fluid. It applies to the motion of an object moving through a fluid as well as the motion of a fluid passing by an object.

Vishnu in Hinduism, the second in the triad of gods (with Brahma and Siva) representing three aspects of the supreme spirit. He is the *Preserver*, and is believed to have assumed human appearance in nine *avatāras*, or incarnations, in such forms as Rama and Krishna. His worshipers are the Vaishnavas.

vision defect any abnormality of the eye that causes less-than-perfect sight. In a *nearsighted* eye, the lens is fatter than normal, causing light from distant objects to be focused in front and not on the retina. A person with this complaint, called ◊myopia, cannot see clearly for distances over a few yards, and needs glasses with diverging lenses. *Farsightedness*, also called hypermetropia, is caused by an eye lens thinner than normal that focuses light from distant objects behind the retina. The sufferer cannot see close objects clearly, and needs converging-lens glasses. There are other vision defects, such as ◊color blindness and ◊astigmatism.

vitamin any of various chemically unrelated organic compounds that are necessary in small quantities for the normal functioning of the body. Many act as coenzymes, small molecules that enable ◊enzymes to function effectively. They are normally present in adequate amounts in a balanced diet. Deficiency of a vitamin will normally lead to a metabolic disorder ("deficiency disease"), which can be remedied by sufficient intake of the vitamin. They are generally classified as *water-soluble* (B and C) or *fat-soluble* (A, D, E, and K). See separate entries for individual vitamins, also nicotinic acid, ◊folic acid, and ◊pantothenic acid.

vitriol any of a number of sulfate salts. Blue, green, and white vitriols are copper, ferrous, and zinc sulfate, respectively. *Oil of vitriol* is sulfuric acid.

Vitus, St Christian saint, perhaps Sicilian, who was martyred in Rome early in the 4th century. Feast day June 15.

Vivaldi Antonio (Lucio) 1678–1741. Italian Baroque composer, violinist, and conductor. He wrote 23 symphonies; 75 sonatas; over 400 concertos, including the *Four Seasons* (about 1725) for violin and orchestra; over 40 operas; and much sacred music. His work was largely neglected until the 1930s.

Known as the Red Priest, because of his flaming hair color, Vivaldi spent much of his church career teaching music at a girls' orphanage. He wrote for them and for himself.

vivipary in animals, a method of reproduction in which the embryo develops inside the body of the female from which it gains nourishment (in contrast to ovipary and ovovivipary). Vivipary is best developed in placental mammals, but also occurs in some arthropods, fishes, amphibians, and reptiles that have placentalive structures. In plants, it is the formation of young plantlets or bulbils instead of flowers. The term also describes seeds that germinate prematurely, before falling from the parent plant.

vivisection literally, cutting into a living animal. Used originally to mean experimental surgery or dissection practiced on a live subject, the term is often used by ◊antivivisection campaigners to include any experiment on animals, surgical or otherwise.

Vladimir I St 956–1015. Russian saint, prince of Novgorod, and grand duke of Kiev. Converted to Christianity 988, he married Anna, Christian sister of the Byzantine emperor ◊Basil II, and established the Byzantine rite of Orthodox Christianity as the Russian national faith.

Vladivostok port (naval and commercial) in E Siberian Russia, at the Amur Bay on the Pacific coast; population (1987) 615,000. It is kept open by icebreakers during winter. Industries include shipbuilding and the manufacture of precision instruments.

Vlaminck Maurice de 1876–1958. French painter who began using brilliant color as an early member of the *Fauves* (see ◊Fauvism), mainly painting landscapes. He later abandoned Fauve color. He also wrote poetry, novels, and essays.

vodka strong colorless alcoholic liquor distilled from rye, potatoes, or barley.

voice sound produced through the mouth and by the passage of air between the ◊vocal cords. In humans the sound is much amplified by the hollow sinuses of the face, and is modified by the movements of the lips, tongue, and cheeks.

Vojvodina autonomous area in N, Yugoslavia; area 8,299 sq mi/21,500 sq km; population (1986) 2,050,000, including 1,110,000 Serbs and 390,000 Hungarians. Its capital is Novi Sad. In Sept 1990 Yugoslavia effectively stripped Vojvodina of its autonomous status, causing antigovernment and anticommunist riots in early 1991.

volcano crack in the Earth's crust through which hot magma (molten rock) and gases well up. The magma becomes known as lava when it reaches the surface. A volcanic mountain, usually cone shaped with a crater on top, is formed around the opening, or vent, by the buildup of solidified lava and ashes (rock fragments).

Most volcanoes arise on plate margins (see ◊plate tectonics), where the movements of plates generate magma or allow it to rise from the mantle beneath. However, a number are found far from plate-margin activity, on "hot spots" where the Earth's crust is thin.

Volga longest river in Europe; 2,290 mi/3,685 km, 2,200 mi/3,540 km of which are navigable. It drains most of the central and eastern parts of European Russia, rises in the Valdai plateau, and flows into the Caspian Sea 55 mi/88 km below the city of Astrakhan.

Volgograd formerly (until 1925) *Tsaritsyn* and (1925–61) *Stalingrad*, an industrial city (metal goods, machinery, lumber mills, oil refining) in SW Russia, on the river Volga; population (1987) 988,000.

volleyball indoor and outdoor team game played on a court between two teams of six players each. A net is placed across the center of the court, and players hit the ball with their hands over it, the aim being to ground it in the opponents' court.

volt SI unit (symbol V) of electromotive force or electric potential. A small battery usually has a potential of one or two volts; the domestic electricity supply in the US is 110 volts. A high-tension transmission line may carry up to 765,000 volts.

Volta main river in Ghana, about 1,000 mi/1,600 km long, with two main upper branches, the Black and White Volta. It has been dammed to provide power.

Volta Alessandro 1745–1827. Italian physicist who invented the first electric cell (the voltaic pile), the electrophorus (an early electrostatic generator), and an ◊electroscope.

Voltaire Adopted name of François-Marie Arouet 1694–1778. French writer who believed in ◊deism and devoted himself to tolerance, justice, and humanity. He was threatened with arrest for *Lettres philosophiques sur les Anglais/Philosophical Letters on the English* 1733 (essays in favor of English ways, thought, and political practice) and had to take refuge. Other writings include *Le Siècle de Louis XIV/The Age of Louis XIV* 1751; *Candide* 1759, a parody on ◊Leibniz's "best of all possible worlds"; and *Dictionnaire philosophique* 1764.

voltmeter instrument for measuring potential difference (voltage). It has a high internal resistance (so that it passes only a small current), and is connected in parallel with the component across which potential difference is to be measured. A common type is constructed from a sensitive current-detecting moving-coil galvanometer placed in series with a high-value resistor (multiplier). To measure an AC (◊alternating current) voltage, the circuit must usually include a rectifier; however, a moving-iron instrument can be used to measure alternating voltages without the need for such a device.

volume in geometry, the space occupied by a three-dimensional solid object. A prism (such as a cube) or a cylinder has a volume equal to the area of the base multiplied by the height. For a pyramid or cone, the volume is equal to one-third of the area of the base multiplied by the perpendicular height. The volume of a sphere is equal to $\frac{4}{3} \times \pi r^3$, where r is the radius. Volumes of irregular solids may be calculated by the technique of ◊integration.

vomiting expulsion of the contents of the stomach through the mouth. It may have numerous causes, including direct irritation of the stomach, severe pain, dizziness, and emotion. Sustained or repeated vomiting may indicate serious disease, and dangerous loss of water, salt, and acid may result (as in ◊bulimia).

volcanoes

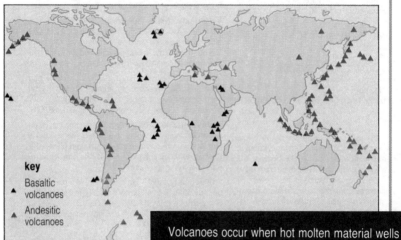

key

▲ Basaltic volcanoes

▲ Andesitic volcanoes

Andesitic volcanoes are found where areas of the Earth's surface are being pushed together. They take their name from the Andes mountains in South America. Basaltic volcanoes form where areas of the Earth's surface are pulling apart, and usually erupt from the ocean floor.

Volcanoes occur when hot molten material wells up from the interior of the Earth. The molten material is generated by the movements of plate tectonics and is known as lava when it appears at the surface. The volcanic mountain is formed by the buildup of solidified lava and ash around the vent or crack in the Earth's surface.

andesitic formation

ash and dust

built on contorted mountain rock layers

thick, slow lava

steep sides

There are two main types of volcano. The more violent is the andesitic volcano which is typical of island arcs and coastal mountain chains. The molten rock is mostly derived from plate material and is rich in silica. This makes it very stiff and it solidifies to form high, steep-sided volcanic mountains.

The stiff lava of an andesitic volcano often clogs the volcanic vent. Eruptions can be violent as the blockage is blasted free, as in the eruption of Mount Saint Helens in North America in 1980.

The black silica-poor lava from a basaltic volcano, such as those in Hawaii or Iceland, often forms wrinkled ropy surfaces before it sets.

The quieter type of volcano is the basaltic type which is found along rift valleys and ocean ridges, and also over "hot spots" beneath the Earth's crust. The molten material is derived from the Earth's mantle and is quite runny. It flows for some distance over the surface before it sets and so forms broad low volcanoes.

basaltic formation

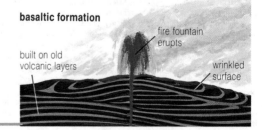

fire fountain erupts

built on old volcanic layers

wrinkled surface

von Braun Wernher 1912–1977. German rocket engineer who developed German military rockets (◊V1 and V2) during World War II and later worked for the space agency ◊NASA in the US.

Vonnegut Kurt, Jr 1922– . US writer whose work generally has surrealistic elements, satire, and fantasy and depicts the flaws of contemporary society. His novel *Slaughterhouse Five* 1969 mixes his World War II experience of the fire-bombing of Dresden, Germany, with a fantasy world on the planet Tralfamadore with the science-fiction element dominated by absurdism and earthly black humor.

Von Neumann John 1903–1957. Hungarian-born US scientist and mathematician, known for his pioneering work on computer design. He invented his "rings of operators" (called Von Neumann algebras) in the late 1930s, and also contributed to set theory, games theory, cybernetics (with his theory of self-reproducing automata, called *Von Neumann machines*), and the development of the atomic and hydrogen bombs.

voodoo set of magical beliefs and practices, followed in some parts of Africa, South America, and the West Indies, especially Haiti. It arose in the 17th century on slave plantations as a combination of Roman Catholicism and W African religious traditions; believers retain membership in the Roman Catholic church. Beliefs include the existence of *loa*, spirits who closely involve themselves in human affairs, and some of whose identities mesh with those of Christian saints. The loa are invoked by the priest (*houngan*) or priestess (*manbo*) at ceremonies, during which members of the congregation become possessed by the spirits and go into a trance.

vote expression of opinion by ballot, show of hands, or other means. For direct vote, see ◊plebiscite and ◊referendum. In parliamentary elections the results can be calculated in a number of ways.

Voyager probes two US space probes, originally ◊Mariners. *Voyager 1*, launched Sept 5, 1977, passed Jupiter March 1979, and reached Saturn Nov 1980. *Voyager 2* was launched earlier, Aug 20, 1977, on a slower trajectory that took it past Jupiter July 1979, Saturn Aug 1981, Uranus Jan 1986, and Neptune Aug 1989. Like the Pioneer probes, the Voyagers are on their way out of the Solar System. Their tasks now include helping scientists to locate the position of the heliopause, the boundary at which the influence of the Sun gives way to the forces exerted by other stars.

VSTOL (abbreviation for *vertical/short takeoff and landing*) aircraft capable of taking off and landing either vertically or using a very short length of runway (see ◊STOL). Vertical takeoff requires a vector-control system that permits the thrust of the aircraft engine to be changed from horizontal to vertical for takeoff and back again to horizontal to permit forward flight. An alternative VSTOL technology developed in the US involves tilting the wings of the aircraft from vertical to horizontal and along with them the aircraft propellers, thus changing from vertical lift to horizontal thrust.

Vulcan in Roman mythology, the god of fire and destruction, later identified with the Greek god ◊Hephaestus.

vulcanization technique for hardening rubber by heating and chemically combining it with sulfur. The process also makes the rubber stronger and more elastic. If the sulfur content is increased to as much as 30%, the product is the inelastic solid known as ebonite. More expensive alternatives to sulfur, such as selenium and tellurium, are used to vulcanize rubber for specialized products such as vehicle tires. The process was discovered accidentally by US inventor Charles ◊Goodyear 1839 and patented 1844.

Vulgate (Latin "common") the Latin translation of the Bible produced by St Jerome in the 4th century.

It is the oldest surviving version of the entire Bible and differs from earlier Latin translations in working from the Hebrew rather than the Greek. In 1546 it was adopted by the Council of Trent as the official Roman Catholic Bible and was later used for official English versions like the Douai.

vulture any of various carrion-eating birds of prey with naked heads and necks and with keen senses of sight and smell. Vultures are up to 3.3 ft/1 m long, with wingspans of up to 11.5 ft/3.5 m. The plumage is usually dark, and the head brightly colored.

Waco city in E central Texas, on the Brazos River, S of Fort Worth; population (1990) 103,600. It is an agricultural shipping center for cotton, grain, and livestock; industries include aircraft parts, glass, cement, tires, and textiles. Baylor University (1845) is here.

wadi in arid regions of the Middle East, a steep-sided valley containing an intermittent stream that flows in the wet season.

wafer in microelectronics, a "superchip" some 3–4 in/8–10 cm in diameter, for which wafer-scale integration (WSI) is used to link the equivalent of many individual ◊silicon chips, improving reliability, speed, and cooling.

Wagner Honus (John Peter) 1874–1955. US baseball player. He had an impressive lifetime batting average of .329. In addition to his fielding skills, he was a great runner; his career record of 722 stolen bases won him the nickname "the Flying Dutchman."

Wagner Richard 1813–1883. German opera composer. He revolutionized the 19th-century conception of opera, envisaging it as a wholly new art form in which musical, poetic, and scenic elements should be unified through such devices as the leitmotif. His operas include *Tannhäuser* 1845, *Lohengrin* 1850, and *Tristan und Isolde* 1865. In 1872 he founded the Festival Theater in Bayreuth; his masterpiece *Der Ring des Nibelungen/The Ring of the Nibelung*, a sequence of four operas, was first performed there in 1876. His last work, *Parsifal*, was produced in 1882.

Wagner German composer Richard Wagner occupies a permanent place in opera history for his innovative theories.

Wahabi puritanical Saudi Islamic sect founded by Mohammed ibn-Abd-al-Wahab (1703–1792), which regards all other sects as heretical. By the early 20th century it had spread throughout the Arabian peninsula; it still remains the official ideology of the Saudi Arabian kingdom.

Wailing Wall or (in Judaism) *Western Wall* the remaining part of the ◊Temple in Jerusalem, a sacred site of pilgrimage and rayer for Jews. There they offer prayers either aloud ("wailing") or on pieces of paper placed between the stones of the wall.

Waite Morrison Remick 1816–1888. US lawyer and chief justice of the US from 1874, appointed by President Grant. He presided over constitutional challenges to Reconstruction 1865–77, but is best remembered for his decisions upholding the right of states to regulate public utilities.

Waksman Selman Abraham 1888–1973. US biochemist, born in Ukraine. He coined the word "antibiotic" for bacteria-killing chemicals derived from microorganisms. Waksman was awarded a Nobel Prize in 1952 for the discovery of streptomycin, an antibiotic used against tuberculosis.

Walachia alternate spelling of ◊Wallachia, part of Romania.

Walcott Derek 1930– . St Lucian poet and playwright. His work fuses Caribbean and European, Classical and contemporary elements, and deals with the divisions within colonial society and his own search for cultural identity. His works include the long poem *Omeros* 1990, and his adaptation for the stage of Homer's *The Odyssey* 1992; his *Collected Poems* were published in 1986. He won the Nobel Prize for Literature 1992.

Wald Lillian D 1867–1940. US public health administrator and founder of New York City's Henry Street Settlement House 1895. In 1912 she founded the National Organization for Public Health Nursing and was also active in union and antiwar activities.

Her memoirs, *House on Henry Street*, appeared 1915.

Waldenses also known as *Waldensians* or *Vaudois* Protestant religious sect, founded c. 1170 by Peter Waldo, a merchant of Lyons. They were allied to the ◊Albigenses. They lived in voluntary poverty, refused to take oaths or take part in war, and later rejected the doctrines of transubstantiation, purgatory, and the invocation of saints. Although subjected to persecution until the 17th century, they spread in France, Germany, and Italy, and still survive in Piedmont.

Waldheim Kurt 1918– . Austrian politician and diplomat, president 1986–92. He was secretary-general of the United Nations 1972–81, having been Austria's representative there 1964–68 and 1970–71.

He was elected president of Austria despite revelations that during World War II he had been an intelligence officer in an army unit responsible for transporting Jews to death camps. His election therefore led to some diplomatic isolation of Austria, and in 1991 he announced that he would not run for reelection.

Wales (Welsh *Cymru*) Principality of; constituent part of the United Kingdom, in the west between the British Channel and the Irish Sea
area 8,021 sq mi/20,780 sq km
capital Cardiff
cities Swansea, Wrexham, Newport, Carmarthen
features Snowdonia mountains (Snowdon 3,561 ft/1,085 m, the highest point in England and Wales) in

the NW and in the SE the Black Mountains, Brecon Beacons, and Black Forest ranges; rivers Severn, Wye, Usk, and Dee

exports traditional industries (coal and steel) have declined, but varied modern and high-technology ventures are being developed. Tourism is important

currency pound sterling

population (1991) 2,835,073

language Welsh 19% (1991), English

religion Nonconformist Protestant denominations; Roman Catholic minority

government returns 38 members to the UK Parliament

history for ancient history, see also ◊Britain, ancient *c.* 400 BC Wales occupied by Celts from central Europe. AD *50–60* Wales became part of the Roman Empire. *c.* 200 Christianity adopted. *c.* 450–600 Wales became the chief Celtic stronghold in the west since the Saxons invaded and settled in S Britain. The Celtic tribes united against England. *8th century* Frontier pushed back to ◊Offa's Dyke. *9th–11th centuries* Vikings raided the coasts. At this time Wales was divided into small states organized on a clan basis, although princes such as Rhodri (844–878), Howel the Good (*c.* 904–949), and Griffith ap Llewelyn (1039–1063) temporarily united the country. *11th–12th centuries* Continual pressure on Wales from the Normans across the English border was resisted, notably by Llewelyn I and II. *1277* Edward I of England accepted as overlord by the Welsh. *1284* Edward I completed the conquest of Wales that had been begun by the Normans. *1294* Revolt against English rule put down by Edward I. *1350–1500* Welsh nationalist uprisings against the English; the most notable was that led by Owen Glendower. *1485* Henry Tudor, a Welshman, became Henry VII of England. *1536–43* Acts of Union united England and Wales after conquest under Henry VIII. Wales sent representatives to the English Parliament; English law was established in Wales; English became the official language. *18th century* Evangelical revival made Nonconformism a powerful factor in Welsh life. A strong coal and iron industry developed in the south. *19th century* The miners and ironworkers were militant supporters of Chartism, and Wales became a stronghold of labor unionism and socialism. *1893* University of Wales founded. *1920s–30s* Wales suffered from industrial depression; unemployment reached 21% 1937, and a considerable exodus of population took place. *post-1945* Growing nationalist movement and a revival of the language, earlier suppressed or discouraged. *1966* Plaid Cymru, the Welsh National Party, returned its first member to Westminster. *1979* Referendum rejected a proposal for limited home rule. *1988* Bombing campaign against estate agents selling Welsh properties to English buyers. For other history, see also ◊England, history; ◊United Kingdom.

Walesa Lech 1943– . Polish labor-union leader and president of Poland from 1990, founder of ◊Solidarity (Solidarność) in 1980, an organization, independent of the Communist Party, which forced substantial political and economic concessions from the Polish government 1980–81 until being outlawed. He was awarded the Nobel Prize for Peace 1983.

Wales, Prince of title conferred on the eldest son of the UK's sovereign. Prince ◊Charles was invested as 21st Prince of Wales at Caernarvon 1969 by his mother, Elizabeth II.

Walker Alice 1944– . US poet, novelist, critic, and essay writer. She was active in the US civil-

Wales: history

c. 400 BC	Wales occupied by Celts from central Europe.
AD 50–60	Wales became part of the Roman Empire.
c. 200	Christianity adopted. *c.* 450–600 Wales became the chief Celtic stronghold in the west since the Saxons invaded and settled in S Britain. The Celtic tribes united against England.
8th century	Frontier pushed back to ◊Offa's Dyke.
9th–11th centuries	Vikings raided the coasts. At this time Wales was divided into small states organized on a clan basis, although princes such as Rhodri (844–878), Howel the Good (*c.* 904–949), and Griffith ap Llewelyn (1039–1063) temporarily united the country.
11th–12th centuries	Continual pressure on Wales from the Normans across the English border was resisted, notably by ◊Llewelyn I and II.
1277	Edward I of England accepted as overlord by the Welsh.
1284	Edward I completed the conquest of Wales that had been begun by the Normans.
1294	Revolt against English rule put down by Edward I.
1350–1500	Welsh nationalist uprisings against the English; the most notable was that led by Owen Glendower.
1485	Henry Tudor, a Welshman, became Henry VII of England.
1536–43	Acts of Union united England and Wales after conquest under Henry VIII. Wales sent representatives to the English Parliament; English law was established in Wales; English became the official language.
18th century	Evangelical revival made Nonconformism a powerful factor in Welsh life. A strong coal and iron industry developed in the south.
19th century	The miners and ironworkers were militant supporters of Chartism, and Wales became a stronghold of trade unionism and socialism.
1893	University of Wales founded.
1920s–30s	Wales suffered from industrial depression; unemployment reached 21% 1937, and a considerable exodus of population took place.
post-1945	Growing nationalist movement and a revival of the language, earlier suppressed or discouraged.
1966	◊Plaid Cymru, the Welsh National Party, returned its first member to Westminster.
1979	Referendum rejected a proposal for limited home rule.
1988	Bombing campaign against estate agents selling Welsh properties to English buyers.

Walesa Lech Walesa won a landslide victory in his country's 1990 presidential election.

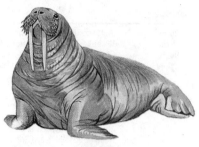

walrus The walrus is a member of the Odobenidae family.

rights movement in the 1960s and, as a black woman, wrote about the double burden of racist and sexist oppression that such women bear. Her novel *The Color Purple* 1983 (filmed 1985) won the Pulitzer Prize.

Born in Eatonton, Georgia, she also wrote the novels *The Third Life of Grange Copeland* 1970, *Meridian* 1976, and *The Temple of My Familiar* 1989. Walker's collections of poems include *Once* 1968 and *Revolutionary Petunias* 1973; her short stories and essays are collected in *Love and Trouble: Stories of Black Women* 1973 and *In Search of Our Mothers' Gardens: Womanist Prose* 1983.

wallaby any of various small and medium-sized members of the ◊kangaroo family.

Wallace George Corley 1919– . US politician who was opposed to integration; he was governor of Alabama 1963–67, 1971–79, and 1983–87. He contested the presidency in 1968 as an independent (the American Independent Party) and in 1972 campaigned for the Democratic nomination but was shot at a rally and became partly paralyzed.

Wallace was born in Clio, Alabama, and held various state jobs before being elected to the governorship for the first time. During the 1963 integration of the University of Alabama, he defied a court order and prevented access to black students; he later complied with the order. His wife served as governor 1967–71 when he was ineligible to run for a third consecutive term. Wallace moderated his staunchly antiintegration views and was elected for a fourth term as governor by a populist coalition of blacks and whites 1982. He retired 1987.

Wallace Henry Agard 1888–1965. US editor and public official. Appointed secretary of the treasury by Franklin Roosevelt 1933 he served as vice president during Roosevelt's third term 1941–45. He later broke with Truman and, after serving as editor of the *New Republic* 1946–47, was the unsuccessful Progressive Party candidate for president 1948.

Wallachia independent medieval principality, founded 1290, with allegiance to Hungary until 1330 and under Turkish rule 1387–1861, when it was united with the neighboring principality of Moldavia to form Romania.

Waller Fats (Thomas Wright) 1904–1943. US jazz pianist and composer with a forceful stride piano style. His songs, many of which have become jazz standards, include "Ain't Misbehavin'" 1929, "Honeysuckle Rose" 1929, and "Viper's Drag" 1934.

wallflower European perennial garden plant *Cheiranthus cheiri*, family Cruciferae, with fragrant red or yellow flowers in spring.

Walloon member of a French-speaking people of SE Belgium and adjacent areas of France. The name "Walloon" is etymologically linked to "Welsh."

walnut genus *Juglans* of trees of the family Juglandaceae, closely related to hickories. Walnuts have pinnately compound leaves and nuts enclosed in a thick leathery husk. Six species, including the black walnut *J. nigra* and the butternut *J. cinerea*, are native to the US. About 15 other species occur in South America and Eurasia. The English walnut *J. regia*, originally from SE Europe and Asia, is cultivated widely for its nut crop.

Walpole Horace, 4th Earl of Orford 1717–1797. English novelist, letter writer and politician, the son of Robert Walpole. He was a Whig member of Parliament 1741–67.

He converted his house at Strawberry Hill, Twickenham (then a separate town SW of London), into a Gothic castle; his *The Castle of Otranto* 1764 established the genre of the Gothic, or "romance of terror," novel. More than 4,000 of his letters have been published.

Walpole Robert, 1st Earl of Orford 1676–1745. British Whig politician, the first "prime minister" as First Lord of the Treasury and chancellor of the Exchequer 1715–17 and 1721–42. He encouraged trade and tried to avoid foreign disputes (until forced into the War of Jenkins's Ear with Spain 1739).

walrus Arctic marine carnivorous mammal *Odobenus rosmarus* of the family Odobenidae, similar to the eared ◊seals. It can reach 13 ft/4 m in length, and weigh up to 3,000 lb/1,400 kg. It has webbed flippers, a bristly moustache, and large tusks. It is gregarious except at breeding time and feeds mainly on mollusks. It has been hunted close to extinction for its ivory tusks, hide, and blubber. The Alaskan walrus is close to extinction.

Walton Izaak 1593–1683. English author of the classic fishing text *Compleat Angler* 1653. He was born in Stafford and settled in London as an ironmonger. He also wrote short biographies of the poets George Herbert and John Donne and the theologian Richard Hooker.

waltz ballroom dance in three-four time evolved from the Austrian *Ländler* (traditional peasants' country dance) and later made popular by the ◊Strauss family in Vienna.

Wanamaker John 1838–1922. US retailer who developed the modern department store. He established his own firm, John Wanamaker and Company, 1869. Renting an abandoned railroad depot 1876, he merchandised goods in distinct departments; he publicized his stores through extensive advertising.

Wandering Jew in medieval legend, a Jew named Ahasuerus, said to have insulted Jesus on his way to Calvary and to have been condemned to wander the world until the Second Coming.

Wankel engine rotary gasoline engine developed by the German engineer Felix Wankel (1902–) in the 1950s. It operates according to the same stages as the ◊four-stroke gasoline engine cycle, but these stages take place in different sectors of a figure-eight chamber in the space between the chamber walls and a triangular rotor. Power is produced once on every turn of the rotor. The Wankel engine is simpler in construction than the four-stroke piston gasoline engine, and produces rotary power directly (instead of via a crankshaft). Problems with rotor seals have prevented its widespread use.

wapiti alternate name for ◊elk.

war act of force, usually on behalf of the state, intended to compel a declared enemy to obey the will of the other. The aim is to render the opponent incapable of further resistance by destroying its capability and will to bear arms in pursuit of its own aims. War is therefore a continuation of politics carried on with violent and destructive means, as an instrument of policy.

Warburg Otto 1878–1976. German biochemist who in 1923 devised a manometer (pressure gauge) sensitive enough to measure oxygen uptake of respiring tissue. By measuring the rate at which cells absorb oxygen under differing conditions, he was able to show that enzymes called cytochromes enable cells to process oxygen. He was awarded the Nobel Prize for Medicine 1931. Warburg also demonstrated that cancerous cells absorb less oxygen than normal cells.

war crime offense (such as murder of a civilian or a prisoner of war) that contravenes the internationally accepted laws governing the conduct of wars, particularly The Hague Convention 1907 and the Geneva Convention 1949. A key principle of the law relating to such crimes is that obedience to the orders of a superior is no defense.

In practice, prosecutions are generally brought by the victorious side.

Ward Montgomery 1843–1913. US retailer who pioneered the mass marketing of clothing and personal items through the mails. Serving the needs of farm families in remote rural areas, he constantly expanded his catalog from its inception in 1872. He moved the firm's headquarters to the Ward Tower in Chicago 1900.

Warhol Andy. Adopted name of Andrew Warhola 1928–1987. US Pop artist and filmmaker. He made his name in 1962 with paintings of Campbell's soup cans, Coca-Cola bottles, and film stars. In his New York studio, the Factory, he produced series of garish silkscreen prints. His films include the semidocumentary *Chelsea Girls* 1966 and *Trash* 1970.

Warner Robins city in central Georgia, south of Macon; population (1990) 43,700. Industries include nuts, fruits, and airplane parts.

War of 1812 a war between the US and Britain caused by British interference with American trade (shipping) as part of Britain's economic warfare against Napoleonic France. US sailors were impressed from American ships, and a blockade was imposed on US shipping by Britain. Also, British assistance was extended to Indians harassing the NW settlements (see ◊Tecumseh). President Madison authorized the beginning of hostilities against the British on the high seas and in Canada. US forces failed twice in attempts to invade British-held Canada but achieved important naval victories, while in 1814 British forces occupied Washington, DC, and burned the White House and the Capitol. A treaty signed at Ghent, Belgium, in Dec 1814 ended the conflict. Before news of the treaty reached the US, American troops under Andrew ◊Jackson defeated the British at New Orleans 1815.

War Powers Act US Congressional legislation passed 1973, over President Nixon's veto, aimed at restricting the president's introduction of US forces into potentially hostile situations without Congressional declaration of war. The measure calls for notification of Congress by the president of plans to dispatch military forces and sets a time limit by which either Congress must approve or the forces must be withdrawn. The act has been considered unconstitutional by each president since its passage, and its provisions generally have been ignored by both Congress and presidents.

Warren industrial city (steel and iron products, tools, and paint) in NE Ohio, on the Mahoning River, NW of Youngstown; population (1990) 50,800.

Warren Earl 1891–1974. US jurist and chief justice of the US Supreme Court 1953–69. He served as governor of California 1943–53. As chief justice, he presided over a moderately liberal court, taking a stand against racial discrimination and ruling that segregation in schools was unconstitutional. He headed the commission that investigated 1963–64 President Kennedy's assassination.

Born in Los Angeles, Warren graduated from the University of California at Berkeley 1914 and practiced law in the San Francisco area. He became active in the Republican party and in 1938 was appointed California's attorney general, which paved the way for the governorship. He was appointed to the Supreme Court by President Eisenhower. His most important ruling was in *Brown* v *Board of Education* 1954, in which the Court unanimously ruled against segregation in public schools and made it illegal to classify races for discrimination purposes. The Warren Court oversaw the reapportionment by population of many election districts in cases such as *Reynolds* v *Sims* 1964. Other rulings involved individual rights, especially in criminal procedures, as in *Miranda* v *Arizona* 1966, which ruled in favor of a defendant being informed of his or her rights at the time of arrest. The Warren Commission 1963–64, appointed by President Johnson, reached the controversial conclusion that no conspiracy was involved in the assassination of President Kennedy. Warren retired from the Court 1969 and was succeeded by Warren Burger.

Warren Joseph 1741–1775. American colonial physician and revolutionary leader. Opposing British colonial rule in Massachusetts, he sent Paul ◊Revere and William Dawes to warn the countryside of the approach of the British 1775. Appointed major general of the Massachusetts militia, he was killed at the Battle of Bunker Hill 1775.

Warren Robert Penn 1905–1989. US poet and novelist, the only author to receive a Pulitzer prize for both prose and poetry. His novel *All the King's Men* 1946 was modeled on the career of Huey ◊Long, and he also won Pulitzer prizes for *Promises* 1968 and *Now and Then: Poems* 1976–78. He was the first official US poet laureate 1986–88.

Born in Guthrie, Kentucky, and educated at Vanderbilt University, Warren received an MA degree from Berkeley 1927 and became a leading figure in the Southern literary revival. A faculty member at Vanderbilt 1931–34; Louisiana State University 1934–42; the University of Minnesota 1942–50; and Yale University 1950–56, 1961–73, Warren was a respected critic. Among his collections of poems is *Brother to Dragons* 1953.

Warsaw (Polish *Warszawa*) capital of Poland, on the river Vistula; population (1990) 1,655,700. Industries include engineering, food processing, printing, clothing, and pharmaceuticals.

Warsaw Pact or *Eastern European Mutual Assistance Pact* military alliance 1955–91 between the USSR and East European communist states, originally established as a response to the admission of West Germany into NATO. Its military structures and agreements were dismantled early in 1991; a political organization remained until the alliance was officially dissolved July 1991.

wart protuberance composed of a local overgrowth of skin. The common wart (*Verruca vulgaris*) is due to a

wart hog The wart hog derives its name from two fleshy wartlike growths beneath its eyes.

virus infection. It usually disappears spontaneously within two years, but can be treated with peeling applications, burning away (cautery), or freezing (cryosurgery).

wart hog African wild ◊pig *Phacochoerus aethiopicus*, which has a large head with a bristly mane, fleshy pads beneath the eyes, and four large tusks. It has short legs and can grow to 2.5 ft/80 cm at the shoulder.

Warwick Richard Neville, Earl of Warwick 1428–1471. English politician, called *the King-maker*. During the Wars of the ◊Roses he fought at first on the Yorkist side against the Lancastrians, and was largely responsible for placing Edward IV on the throne. Having quarrelled with him, he restored Henry VI in 1470, but was defeated and killed by Edward at Barnet, Hertfordshire.

Wash, the bay of the North Sea between Norfolk and Lincolnshire, England. The rivers Nene, Ouse, Welland, and Witham drain into the Wash.

Washington state in NW US; nickname Evergreen State/Chinook State
area 68,206 sq mi/176,700 sq km
capital Olympia
cities Seattle, Spokane, Tacoma
features Columbia River; national parks: Olympic (Olympic Mountains), Mount Rainier (Cascade Range), North Cascades; 90 dams

Washington US teacher and reformer Booker T Washington was born a slave.

products apples and other fruits, potatoes, livestock, fish, timber, processed food, wood products, paper and allied products, aircraft and aerospace equipment, aluminum
population (1990) 4,866,700 (including 1.4% Indians, mainly of the Yakima people)
famous people Bing Crosby, Jimi Hendrix, Mary McCarthy, Theodore Roethke
history explored by Spanish, British, and Americans in the 18th century; settled from 1811; became a territory 1853 and a state 1889.

Rival American and British territorial claims threatened war in the early 1840s that was settled by the Oregon Treaty 1846. The transcontinental railroad arrived 1883. Radical labor activity repressed 1919. The New Deal era brought many public-works projects, and Boeing became the largest employer in World War II. Mount St Helens erupted here 1980, and many in the state are now fighting to close the antiquated and dangerous nuclear plant at Hanford.

Washington Booker T(aliaferro) 1856–1915. US educationist, pioneer in higher education for black people in the South. He was the founder and first principal of Tuskegee Institute, Alabama, in 1881, originally a training college for blacks, and now an academic institution. He maintained that economic independence was the way to achieve social equality.

Washington George 1732–1799. Commander of the American forces during the Revolutionary War and 1st president of the US 1789–97, known as "the father of his country." An experienced soldier, he had fought in campaigns against the French during the French and Indian War. He was elected to the Virginia House of Burgesses 1759 and was a leader of the Virginia militia, gaining valuable exposure to wilderness fighting. As a strong opponent of the British government's policy, he sat in the Continental Congresses of 1774 and 1775, and on the outbreak of the ◊American Revolution was chosen commander in chief of the Continental army. After many setbacks, he accepted the surrender of British general Cornwallis at Yorktown 1781.

After the war Washington retired to his Virginia estate, Mount Vernon, but in 1787 he reentered politics as president of the Constitutional Convention in Philadelphia and was elected US president 1789. Although he attempted to draw his ministers from all factions, his aristocratic outlook alienated his secretary of state, Thomas Jefferson, with whose resignation in 1793 the two-party system originated. Washington accepted the fiscal policy championed by Alexander ◊Hamilton and oversaw the payment of the foreign and domestic debt incurred by the new nation. He also shaped the powers of the presidency, assuming some implied powers not specified in the Constitution—among them, the power to create a national bank.

Washington, DC (District of Columbia) national capital of the US, on the Potomac River

Washington

area 69 sq mi/180 sq km

features designed by French engineer Pierre L'Enfant (1754–1825) and completed by Andrew Ellicott and Benjamin Banneker. Among buildings of architectural note are the Capitol, the Pentagon, the White House, the Washington Monument, and the Jefferson and Lincoln memorials. The National Gallery has an outstanding collection of paintings; libraries include the Library of Congress, the National Archives, and the Folger Shakespeare Library. The Smithsonian Institution and its several museums are on the National Mall.

population (1983) 606,900 (metropolitan area, extending outside the District of Columbia, 3,000,000)

history the District of Columbia, initially land ceded from Maryland 1788 and Virginia 1789, was established by an act of Congress 1790–91 and was first used as the seat of Congress Dec 1, 1800. The Virginia portion was returned 1846. The right to vote in national elections was not granted to residents until 1961. Local self-rule began 1975.

wasp any of several families of winged stinging insects of the order Hymenoptera, characterized by a thin stalk between the thorax and the abdomen. Wasps can be social or solitary. Among social wasps, the queens devote themselves to egg laying, the fertilized eggs producing female workers; the males come from unfertilized eggs and have no sting. The larvae are fed on insects, but the mature wasps feed mainly on fruit and sugar. In winter, the fertilized queens hibernate, but the other wasps die.

Washington The 1st president of the United States of America, George Washington, a federalist.

Paper wasps, family Vespidae, include the common paper wasp *Polistes annularis* and hornets and yellow jackets (both genus *Vespula*). Potter wasps, mason wasps, and mud daubers all use mud with which to construct their nests. *See illustration p. 988*

watch portable timepiece. In the early 20th century increasing miniaturization, mass production, and, in

Washington, DC the Capitol, Washington DC, national capital of the US.

wasp Wasps can be solitary or social in their habits.

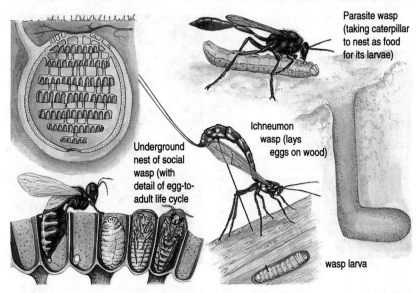

Parasite wasp (taking caterpillar to nest as food for its larvae)

Underground nest of social wasp (with detail of egg-to-adult life cycle

Ichneumon wasp (lays eggs on wood)

wasp larva

World War I, the advantages of the wristband led to the watch moving from the pocket to the wrist. Watches were also subsequently made waterproof, antimagnetic, self-winding, and shock-resistant. In 1957 the electric watch was developed, and in the 1970s came the digital watch, which dispensed with all moving parts.

water H_2O liquid without color, taste, or odor. It is an oxide of hydrogen. Water begins to freeze at 32°F/0°C, and to boil at 212°F/100°C. When liquid, it is virtually incompressible; frozen, it expands by $\frac{1}{11}$ of its volume. At 39.2°F/4°C, one cubic centimeter of water has a mass of one gram; this is its maximum density, forming the unit of specific gravity. It has the highest known specific heat, and acts as an efficient solvent, particularly when hot. Most of the world's water is in the sea; less than 0.01% is fresh water.

waterbuck any of several African ◊antelopes of the genus *Kobus* which usually inhabit swampy tracts and reedbeds. They vary in size from 6 ft/1.4 m to 7.25 ft/2.1 m long, are up to 4.5 ft/1.4 m tall at the shoulder, and have long brown fur. The large curved horns, normally carried only by the males, have corrugated surfaces. Some species have white patches on the buttocks. Lechwe, kor, and defassa are alternative names for some of the species.

Waterbury city in W Connecticut, on the Naugatuck River; population (1990) 109,000. Products include clocks, watches, brass and copper ware, and plastics. It was founded 1674.

watercolor painting method of painting with pigments mixed with water, known in China as early as the 3rd century. The art as practiced today began in England in the 18th century with the work of Paul Sandby and was developed by Thomas Girtin and J M W Turner. Other watercolorists were Raoul Dufy, Paul Cézanne, and John Marin. The technique of watercolor painting requires great skill since its transparency rules out overpainting.

watercress perennial aquatic plant *Nasturtium officinale* of the crucifer family, found in Europe and Asia, and cultivated as a salad crop.

water cycle or *hydrological cycle* in ecology, the natural circulation of water through the ◊biosphere.

Water is lost from the Earth's surface to the atmosphere either by evaporation from the surface of lakes, rivers, and oceans, or through the transpiration of plants. This atmospheric water forms clouds that condense to deposit moisture on the land and sea as rain or snow. The water that collects on land flows to the ocean in streams and rivers.

Watergate US political scandal, named after the building in Washington, DC, that housed the Democrats' campaign headquarters in the 1972 presidential election. Five men, hired by the Republican Committee to Reelect the President (CREEP), were caught after breaking into the Watergate with complex electronic surveillance equipment. Investigations revealed that the White House was implicated in the break-in, and that there was a "slush fund" used to finance unethical activities. In Aug 1974, President ◊Nixon was forced by the Supreme Court to surrender to Congress tape recordings of conversations he had held with administration officials, which indicated his complicity in a cover-up. Nixon resigned rather than face impeachment for obstruction of justice and other crimes.

water hyacinth tropical aquatic plant *Eichhornia crassipes* of the pickerelweed family Pontederiaceae. In one growing season 25 plants can produce 2 million new plants. It is liable to choke waterways, depleting the water of nutrients and blocking the sunlight, but can be used as a purifier of sewage-polluted water as well as in making methane gas, compost, concentrated protein, paper, and baskets. Originating in South America, it now grows in more than 50 countries.

water lily aquatic plant of the family Nymphaeaceae. The fleshy roots are embedded in mud and the large round leaves float on the water. The cup-shaped flowers may be white, pink, yellow, or blue.

The white water lily *Nymphaea odorata* is common in E North America as is the yellow-flowered spatterdock *Nuphar advena*. *Victoria regia*, with leaves about 6 ft/2 m in diameter, occurs in South America.

Waterloo, Battle of battle on June 18, 1815, in which British forces commanded by Wellington defeated the French army of Emperor Napoleon near the village of Waterloo, 8 mi/13 km S of Brussels, Belgium. Napoleon found Wellington's army isolated from his allies and began a direct offensive to smash them, but the British held on until joined by the Prussians under General Blücher. Four days later Napoleon abdicated for the second and final time.

watermelon large ◊melon *Citrullus vulgaris* of the gourd family, native to tropical Africa, with pink, white, or yellow flesh studded with black seeds and a green rind. It is widely cultivated in subtropical regions.

water pollution any addition to fresh or sea water that disrupts biological processes or causes a health hazard. Common pollutants include nitrate, pesticides, and sewage (see ◊sewage disposal), though a huge range of industrial contaminants, such as chemical byproducts and residues created in the manufacture of various goods, also enter water—legally, accidentally, and through illegal dumping.

water polo water sport developed in England 1869, originally called "soccer-in-water." The aim is to score goals, as in soccer, at each end of a swimming pool. It is played by teams of seven on each side (from squads of 13).

water skiing water sport in which a person is towed across water on a ski or skis, wider than those used for skiing on snow, by means of a rope (75 ft/23 m long) attached to a speedboat. Competitions are held for overall performances, slalom, tricks, and jumping.

water table the upper level of ground water (water collected underground in porous rocks). Water that is above the water table will drain downward; a spring forms where the water table cuts the surface of the ground. The water table rises and falls in response to rainfall and the rate at which water is extracted, for example, for irrigation and industry.

Watson James Dewey 1928–   . US biologist whose research on the molecular structure of DNA and the genetic code, in collaboration with Francis ◊Crick, earned him a shared Nobel Prize in 1962. Based on earlier works, they were able to show that DNA formed a double helix of two spiral strands held together by base pairs.

Watson John Broadus 1878–1958. US psychologist, founder of behaviorism. He rejected introspection (observation by an individual of his or her own mental processes) and regarded psychology as the study of observable behavior, within the scientific tradition.

Watson-Watt Robert Alexander 1892–1973. Scottish physicist who developed a forerunner of ◊radar. During a long career in government service (1915–52) he proposed in 1935 a method of radiolocation of aircraft—a key factor in the Allied victory over German aircraft in World War II.

watt SI unit (symbol W) of power (the rate of expenditure or consumption of energy). A light bulb may use, for example, 40, 100, or 150 watts of power; an electric heater will use several kilowatts (thousands of watts). The watt is named after the Scottish engineer James Watt.

Watteau Jean-Antoine 1684–1721. French Rococo painter. He developed a new category of genre painting known as the *fête galante*, scenes of a kind of aristocratic pastoral fantasy world. One of these pictures, *The Embarkation for Cythera* 1717 (Louvre, Paris), won him membership in the French Academy.

Waugh Evelyn (Arthur St John) 1903–1966. English novelist. His social satires include *Decline and Fall* 1928, *Vile Bodies* 1930, and *The Loved One* 1948. A

Roman Catholic convert from 1930, he developed a serious concern with religious issues in *Brideshead Revisited* 1945.

   The Ordeal of Gilbert Pinfold 1957 is largely autobiographical.

Wausau industrial city (dairy products, paper products, insurance, chemicals, and plastics) in central Wisconsin, on the Wisconsin River, NW of Green Bay; population (1990) 37,100.

wave in the oceans, a ridge or swell formed by wind or other causes. The power of a wave is determined by the strength of the wind and the distance of open water over which the wind blows (the fetch). Waves are the main agents of ◊coastal erosion and deposition: sweeping away or building up beaches, creating ◊spits and ◊berms, and wearing down cliffs by their hydraulic action and by the corrasion of the sand and shingle that they carry. A ◊tsunami (misleadingly called a "tidal wave") is formed after a submarine earthquake.

wave in physics, a disturbance consisting of a series of oscillations that propagate through a medium (or space). There are two types: in a *longitudinal wave* (such as a sound wave) the disturbance is parallel to the wave's direction of travel; in a *transverse wave* (such as an ◊electromagnetic wave) it is perpendicular. The medium only vibrates as the wave passes; it does not travel outward from the source with the waves.

wavelength the distance between successive crests of a ◊wave. The wavelength of a light wave determines its color; red light has a wavelength of about 700 nanometers for example. The complete range of wavelengths of electromagnetic waves is called the electromagnetic ◊spectrum.

Wavell Archibald, 1st Earl 1883–1950. British field marshal in World War II. As commander in chief Middle East, he successfully defended Egypt against Italy July 1939. He was transferred as commander in chief India in July 1941, and was viceroy 1943–47.

wax solid fatty substance of animal, vegetable, or mineral origin. Waxes are composed variously of ◊esters, ◊fatty acids, free ◊alcohols, and solid hydrocarbons.

Wayne Anthony ("Mad Anthony") 1745–1796. American Revolutionary War officer and Indian fighter. He secured a treaty 1795 that made possible the settlement of Ohio and Indiana. He built Fort Wayne, India.

Wayne John ("Duke"). Adopted name of Marion Morrison 1907–1979. US actor, the archetypal Western hero: plain-speaking, brave, and solitary. His films include *Stagecoach* 1939, *Red River* 1948, *She Wore a Yellow Ribbon* 1949, *The Searchers* 1956, *Rio Bravo* 1959, *The Man Who Shot Liberty Valance* 1962, and *True Grit* 1969 (Academy Award). He was active in conservative politics.

weak nuclear force or *weak interaction* one of the four fundamental forces of nature, the other three being gravity, the electromagnetic force, and the strong force. It causes radioactive decay and other subatomic reactions. The particles that carry the weak force are called ◊weakons (or intermediate vector bosons) and comprise the positively and negatively charged W particles and the neutral Z particle.

weakon or *intermediate vector boson* in physics, a gauge boson that carries the weak nuclear force, one of the fundamental forces of nature. There are three types of weakon, the positive and negative W particle and the neutral Z particle.

weathering

Frost, wind, rain and sunshine all have a part to play in the gradual wearing away of the landscape. As soon as an area of rock is exposed on the surface of the Earth, it is attacked over time by the weather, which reduces it to sand and rubble. This material is carried downward by gravity, rivers and glaciers and redeposited in low areas. Eventually it may be turned back into solid rock.

Frost shattering produces spiky peaks.

In mountainous areas the water that collects in rock cracks freezes regularly. As it does so, it expands, forcing the rocks apart.

A combination of temperature, moisture and chemical effects can wear away the outer skin of a rock. As a result it may peel off, layer by layer. This process is known as onion-skin weathering.

The debris broken off the peaks by the frost piles up as slopes of scree.

Soft soil may be washed away by the rain. Where a boulder provides protection, only the surrounding soil may be washed away, leaving the boulder on a soil pedestal.

The debris produced by weathering forms the basis of soil. It can work its way downhill in a process known as soil creep, causing trees to bend and posts to lean.

The carbon dioxide in rainwater produces weak carbonic acid. This reacts with some minerals, and causes spheroidal weathering of dolerite, the opening up of cracks called grykes in limestone, and the decay of granite into china clay.

Soil creep may give rise to a stepped appearance – terracettes – on a hillside.

weapon any implement used for attack and defense, from simple clubs, spears, and bows and arrows in prehistoric times to machine guns and nuclear bombs in modern times. The first revolution in warfare came with the invention of ◊gunpowder and the development of cannons and shoulder-held guns. Many other weapons now exist, such as grenades, shells, torpedoes, rockets, and guided missiles. The ultimate in explosive weapons are the atomic (fission) and hydrogen (fusion) bombs. They release the enormous energy produced when atoms split or fuse together (see ◊nuclear warfare). There are also chemical and bacteriological weapons.

weasel any of various small, short-legged, lithe carnivorous mammals with bushy tails, especially the genus *Mustela*, found worldwide except Australia. They feed mainly on small rodents although some, like the mink *M. vison*, hunt aquatic prey. Most are 5–10 in/12–25 cm long, excluding tail.

weather day-to-day variation of climatic and atmospheric conditions at any one place, or the state of these conditions at a place at any one time. Such conditions include humidity, precipitation, temperature, cloud cover, visibility, and wind. To a meteorologist the term "weather" is limited to the state of the sky, precipitation, and visibility as affected by fog or mist. A region's ◊climate is derived from the average weather conditions over a long period of time. See also ◊meteorology.

weaving the production of textile fabric by means of a loom. The basic process is the interlacing at right angles of longitudinal threads (the warp) and horizontal threads (the weft), the latter being carried across from one side of the loom to the other by a type of bobbin called a shuttle.

Webb (Martha) Beatrice (born Potter) 1858–1943 and Sidney (James), Baron Passfield 1859–1947. English social reformers, writers, and founders of the London School of Economics (LSE) 1895. They were early members of the socialist ◊Fabian Society, and were married in 1892. They argued for social insurance in their minority report (1909) of the Poor Law Commission, and wrote many influential books, including *The History of Trade Unionism* 1894, *English Local Government* 1906–29, and *Soviet Communism* 1935.

Sidney Webb was a member of the Labour Party executive 1915–25, entered Parliament in 1922, and held several government posts.

Webber Andrew Lloyd. English composer of musicals: see ◊Lloyd Webber.

weber SI unit (symbol Wb) of magnetic flux (the magnetic field strength multiplied by the area through which the field passes). It is named after German chemist Wilhelm Weber. One weber equals 10^8 ◊maxwells.

Weber Max 1864–1920. German sociologist, one of the founders of modern sociology. He emphasized cultural and political factors as key influences on economic development and individual behavior.

Weber Max 1881–1961. Russian-born US painter and sculptor. Influenced by Parisian avant-garde painters of the Cubist and Futurist schools, he was a prominent figure in importing these styles to the US and also created Futuristic sculpture.

Weber Wilhelm Eduard 1804–1891. German physicist who studied magnetism and electricity, brother of Ernst Weber. Working with Karl Gauss, he made sensitive magnetometers to measure magnetic fields, and instruments to measure direct and alternating currents. He also built an electric telegraph. The SI unit of magnetic flux, the *weber*, is named after him.

Webster Daniel 1782–1852. US politician and orator. He sat in the US House of Representatives 1813–27 and the Senate 1827–41, 1845–50, at first as a ◊Federalist and later as a ◊Whig. He was secretary of state 1841–43 and 1850–52, and negotiated the Webster-Ashburton Treaty 1842, which fixed the Maine–Canada boundary. His "seventh of March" speech in the Senate 1850 helped secure a compromise on the slavery issue. He argued that the Congress was powerless under the Constitution to interfere with slavery, and he maintained that the breakup of the Union would produce an even greater evil. He was born in Salisbury, New Hampshire.

Webster John c. 1580–1634. English dramatist who ranks after Shakespeare as the greatest tragedian of his time and is the Jacobean whose plays are most frequently performed today. His two great plays *The White Devil* 1608 and *The Duchess of Malfi* 1614 are dark, violent tragedies obsessed with death and decay and infused with poetic brilliance.

Webster Noah 1758–1843. US lexicographer whose books on grammar and spelling and *American Dictionary of the English Language* 1828 standardized US English.

Webster learned 26 languages and began the scientific study of ◊etymology. Following the American Revolution, he was prompted by patriotic sentiment to create schoolbooks that would impart that sentiment to young students. His *Blue-Backed Speller* sold nearly 100 million copies in a century.

Weddell Sea arm of the S Atlantic Ocean that cuts into the Antarctic continent SE of Cape Horn; area 3,000,000 sq mi/8,000,000 sq km. Much of it is covered with thick pack ice for most of the year.

wedge block of triangular cross-section that can be used as a simple machine. An axe is a wedge: it splits wood by redirecting the energy of the downward blow sideways, where it exerts the force needed to split the wood.

Wedgwood Josiah 1730–1795. English pottery manufacturer. He set up business in Staffordshire in the early 1760s to produce his agateware as well as unglazed blue or green stoneware (jasper) decorated with white Neo-Classical designs, using pigments of his own invention.

weedkiller or *herbicide* chemical that kills some or all plants. Selective herbicides are effective with cereal crops because they kill all broad-leaved plants without affecting grasslike leaves. Those that kill all plants include sodium chlorate and paraquat; see also ◊Agent Orange. The widespread use of weedkillers in agriculture has led to a dramatic increase in crop yield but also to pollution of soil and water supplies and killing of birds and small animals, as well as creating a health hazard for humans.

weevil any of a superfamily (Curculionoidea) of ◊beetles, usually less than 0.25 in/6 mm long, and with a head prolonged into a downward beak, which is used for boring into plant stems and trees for feeding.

Wegener Alfred Lothar 1880–1930. German meteorologist and geophysicist, whose theory of ◊continental drift, expounded in *Origin of Continents and Oceans* 1915, was originally known as Wegener's hypothesis. His ideas can now be explained in terms of

plate tectonics, the idea that the Earth's crust consists of a number of plates, all moving with respect to one another.

weight the force exerted on an object by ◊gravity. The weight of an object depends on its mass—the amount of material in it—and the strength of the Earth's gravitational pull, which decreases with height. Consequently, an object weighs less at the top of a mountain than at sea level. On the Moon, an object has only one-sixth of its weight on Earth, because the pull of the Moon's gravity is one-sixth that of the Earth.

weightlessness condition in which there is no gravitational force acting on a body, either because gravitational force is canceled out by equal and opposite acceleration, or because the body is so far outside a planet's gravitational field that it no force is exerted upon it.

weight lifting the sport of lifting the heaviest possible weight above one's head to the satisfaction of judges. In international competitions there are two standard lifts: *snatch* and *jerk*.

Weill Kurt (Julian) 1900–1950. German composer, US citizen from 1943. He wrote chamber and orchestral music and collaborated with Bertolt ◊Brecht on operas such as *Die Dreigroschenoper/The Threepenny Opera* 1928 and *Aufsteig und Fall der Stadt Mahagonny/The Rise and Fall of the City of Mahagonny* 1930, all attacking social corruption (*Mahagonny* caused a riot at its premiere in Leipzig). He tried to evolve a new form of ◊music theater, using subjects with a contemporary relevance and the simplest musical means. In 1935 he left Germany for the US where he wrote a number of successful scores for Broadway, among them the anti-war musical *Johnny Johnson* 1936 (including the often covered "September Song") and *Street Scene* 1947 based on an Elmer Rice play of the Depression.

Weimar Republic the constitutional republic in Germany 1919–33, which was crippled by the election of antidemocratic parties to the Reichstag (parliament), and then subverted by the Nazi leader Hitler after his appointment as chancellor 1933. It took its name from the city where in Feb 1919 a constituent assembly met to draw up a democratic constitution.

Weizmann Chaim 1874–1952. Zionist leader, the first president of Israel (1948–52), and chemist. Born in Russia, he became a naturalized British subject, and as director of the navy's laboratories 1916–19 discovered a process for manufacturing acetone, a solvent. He conducted the negotiations leading up to the Balfour Declaration, which favored a Jewish state. He

became head of the Hebrew University in Jerusalem, then in 1948 became the first president of the new republic of Israel.

Welch Robert H W, Jr 1899–1985. US anticommunist crusader and business executive. He founded the extreme right-wing John Birch Society 1958 in memory of the American Baptist missionary. A supporter of the losing Republican presidential candidate Barry Goldwater 1964, Welch later became increasingly venomous in his accusations against supposed communist agents and sympathizers.

welding joining pieces of metal (or nonmetal) at faces rendered plastic or liquid by heat or pressure (or both). The principal processes today are gas and arc welding, in which the heat from a gas flame or an electric arc melts the faces to be joined. Additional "filler metal" is usually added to the joint.

Welensky Roy 1907–1991. Rhodesian politician. He was instrumental in the creation of a federation of Northern Rhodesia (now Zambia), Southern Rhodesia (now Zimbabwe), and Nyasaland (now Malawi) in 1953 and was prime minister 1956–63, when the federation was disbanded. His Southern Rhodesian Federal Party was defeated by Ian Smith's Rhodesian Front in 1964. In 1965, following Smith's Rhodesian unilateral declaration of Southern Rhodesian independence from Britain, Welensky left politics.

Welles (George) Orson 1915–1985. US actor and film and theater director, whose first film was *Citizen Kane* 1941, which he produced, directed, and starred in. Using innovative lighting, camera angles and movements, it is a landmark in the history of cinema, yet he subsequently directed very few films in Hollywood. His performances as an actor include the character of Harry Lime in *The Third Man* 1949.

Welles Gideon 1802–1878. US politician, one of the founders of the Republican Party 1854. Welles was appointed secretary of the navy by President Lincoln 1861 and in that position supervised the expansion of the Union naval forces and advocated the development of ironclads (wooden, iron-plated warships). An opponent of President Grant, he joined the Liberal Republicans 1872.

Wellington capital and industrial port (woolen textiles, chemicals, soap, footwear, bricks) of New Zealand on North Island on the Cook Strait; population (1991) 149,600; urban area 324,800. The harbor was sighted by Capt James Cook 1773.

Wellington Arthur Wellesley, 1st Duke of Wellington 1769–1852. British soldier and Tory politician. As commander in the ◊Peninsular War, he expelled the French from Spain 1814. He defeated Napoleon Bonaparte at Quatre-Bras and Waterloo 1815, and was a member of the Congress of Vienna. As prime minister 1828–30, he was forced to concede Roman Catholic emancipation.

Wells H(erbert) G(eorge) 1866–1946. English writer of "scientific romances" such as *The Time Machine* 1895 and *The War of the Worlds* 1898. His later novels had an antiestablishment, anticonventional humor remarkable in its day, for example *Kipps* 1905 and *Tono-Bungay* 1909. His many other books include *Outline of History* 1920 and *The Shape of Things to Come* 1933, a number of his prophecies from which have since been fulfilled. He also wrote many short stories.

Welsh corgi breed of dog with a foxlike head and pricked ears. The coat is dense, with several varieties of coloring. Corgis are about 1 ft/30 cm at the shoulder, and weigh up to 27 lb/12 kg.

Welsh language in Welsh *Cymraeg* member of the Celtic branch of the Indo-European language family, spoken chiefly in the rural north and west of Wales; it is the strongest of the surviving Celtic languages, and in 1991 was spoken by 18.7% of the Welsh population.

Welty Eudora 1909– . US novelist and short-story writer, born in Jackson, Mississippi. Her works reflect life in the American South and are notable for their creation of character and accurate rendition of local dialect. Her novels include *Delta Wedding* 1946, *Losing Battles* 1970, and *The Optimist's Daughter* 1972.

Wenceslas, St 907–929. Duke of Bohemia who attempted to Christianize his people and was murdered by his brother. He is patron saint of the Czech Republic and the "good King Wenceslas" of a popular carol. Feast day Sept 28.

Wends NW Slavonic peoples who settled east of the rivers Elbe and Saale in the 6th–8th centuries. By the 12th century most had been forcibly Christianized and absorbed by invading Germans; a few preserved their identity and survive as the Sorbs of Lusatia (E Germany/Poland).

werewolf in folk belief, a human being either turned by spell into a wolf or having the ability to assume a wolf form. The symptoms of ◊porphyria may have fostered the legends.

Wesberry v Sanders a US Supreme Court decision 1964 dealing with apportionment of Congressional districts. After a suit against Georgia's apportionment statute was dismissed by the federal circuit court, the case was appealed to the Supreme Court. The Court ruled that all Congressional districts must be equal in size of voting population. The Georgia statute was declared invalid because its unequal apportionment gave greater voting power to residents of certain districts.

Wesley John 1703–1791. English founder of ◊Methodism. When the pulpits of the Church of England were closed to him and his followers, he took the gospel to the people. For 50 years he rode about the country on horseback, preaching daily, largely in the open air. His sermons became the doctrinal standard of the Wesleyan Methodist Church.

Wesley went to Oxford University together with his brother Charles, where their circle was nicknamed Methodists because of their religious observances. He was ordained in the Church of England 1728 and in 1735 he went to the American colony of Georgia as a missionary. On his return he experienced "conversion" 1738, and from being rigidly High Church developed into an ardent Evangelical.

Wessex the kingdom of the West Saxons in Britain, said to have been founded by Cerdic about AD 500, covering present-day Hampshire, Dorset, Wiltshire, Berkshire, Somerset, and Devon. In 829 Egbert established West Saxon supremacy over all England. Thomas ◊Hardy used the term Wessex in his novels for the SW counties of England.

West Benjamin 1738–1820. American Neo-Classical painter, active in London from 1763. He enjoyed the patronage of George III for many years and painted historical pictures.

West was born in Pennsylvania. His *Death of General Wolfe* 1770 (National Gallery, Ottawa) began a vogue for painting recent historical events in contemporary costume. Many early American artists studied with him, including Washington Allston, Gilbert Stuart, and J S Copely.

West Mae 1892–1980. US vaudeville, stage, and film actress. She wrote her own dialogue, setting herself up as a provocative sex symbol and the mistress of verbal innuendo. She appeared on Broadway in *Sex* 1926, *Drag* 1927, and *Diamond Lil* 1928, which was the basis of the film (with Cary Grant) *She Done Him Wrong* 1933. Her other films include *I'm No Angel* 1933, *Going to Town* 1934, *My Little Chickadee* 1944 (with W C Fields), *Myra Breckinridge* 1969, and *Sextette* 1977. Both her plays and her films led to legal battles over censorship.

West Rebecca. Adopted name of Cicely Isabel Fairfield 1892–1983. British journalist and novelist, an active feminist from 1911. *The Meaning of Treason* 1959 deals with the spies Burgess and Maclean. Her novels have political themes and include *The Fountain Overflows* 1956 and *The Birds Fall Down* 1966.

West African Economic Community international organization established 1975 to end barriers in trade and to achieve cooperation in development. Members include Burkina Faso, Ivory Coast, Mali, Mauritania, Niger, and Senegal; Benin and Togo have observer status.

West Bank area (2,270 sq mi/5,879 sq km) on the west bank of the river Jordan; population (1988) 866,000. The West Bank was taken by the Jordanian army 1948 at the end of the Arab-Israeli war that followed the creation of the state of Israel, and was captured by Israel during the Six-Day War June 5–10, 1967. The continuing Israeli occupation and settlement of the area has created tensions with the Arab population.

West Bengal state of NE India
area 33,929 sq mi/87,900 sq km
capital Calcutta
cities Asansol, Durgarpur
physical occupies the west part of the vast alluvial plain created by the rivers Ganges and Brahmaputra, with the Hooghly River; annual rainfall in excess of 100 in/250 cm
products rice, jute, tea, coal, iron, steel, automobiles, locomotives, aluminum, fertilizers
population (1991) 67,982,700

Western genre of popular fiction and film based on the landscape and settlement of the American West, with emphasis on the conquest of Indian territory. It developed in American ◊dime novels and frontier literature. The Western became established in written form with such novels as Owen Wister's *The Virginian* 1902 and Zane Grey's *Riders of the Purple Sage* 1912. From the earliest silent films, movies extended the Western mythology and, with Italian "spaghetti" Westerns and Japanese Westerns, established it as an international form.

Western European Union (WEU) organization established 1955 as a consultative forum for military issues among the W European governments: Belgium, France, the Netherlands, Italy, Luxembourg, the UK, Germany, and (from 1988) Spain and Portugal.

Western Sahara formerly *Spanish Sahara* disputed territory in NW Africa bounded to the N by Morocco, to the W and S by Mauritania, and to the E by the Atlantic Ocean
area 103,011 sq mi/266,800 sq km
capital Laâyoune (Arabic *El Aaiún*)
cities Dhakla
features electrically monitored fortified wall enclosing the phosphate area
exports phosphates
currency dirham

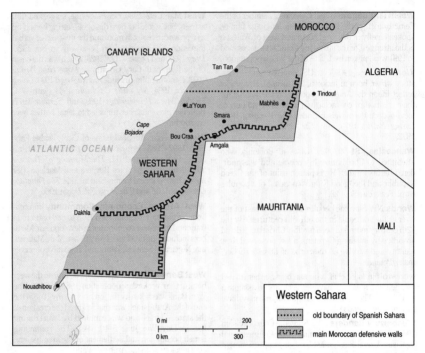

Western Sahara

········	old boundary of Spanish Sahara
ᴀᴘᴀᴘ	main Moroccan defensive walls

population (1988) 181,400; another estimated 165,000 live in refugee camps near Tindouf, SW Algeria. Ethnic composition: Sawrawis (traditionally nomadic herders)
language Arabic
religion Sunni Muslim
government administered by Morocco

West Indies archipelago of about 1,200 islands, dividing the Atlantic from the Gulf of Mexico and the Caribbean. The islands are divided into:
Bahamas; *Greater Antilles* Cuba, Hispaniola (Haiti, Dominican Republic), Jamaica, and Puerto Rico; *Lesser Antilles* Aruba, Netherlands Antilles, Trinidad and Tobago, the Windward Islands (Grenada, Barbados, St Vincent, St Lucia, Martinique, Dominica, Guadeloupe), the Leeward Islands (Montserrat, Antigua, St Christopher (St Kitts)–Nevis, Barbuda, Anguilla, St Martin, British and US Virgin Islands), and many smaller islands.

West Indies, Federation of the federal union 1958–62 comprising Antigua, Barbados, Dominica, Grenada, Jamaica, Montserrat, St Christopher (St Kitts)–Nevis and Anguilla, St Lucia, St Vincent, and Trinidad and Tobago. This federation came to an end when first Jamaica and then Trinidad and Tobago withdrew.

West Virginia

Westinghouse George 1846–1914. US inventor and manufacturer. The most profitable of his designs was an air brake for railroad automobiles, perfected 1869. Westinghouse later devised a system of railroad signals and an efficient means of distributing natural gas. His greatest success came with the establishment of the Westinghouse Electric Co 1886, through which he adapted alternating current for domestic and industrial use.

West Irian former name of ◊Irian Jaya, a province of Indonesia.

Westmoreland William (Childs) 1914– . US military leader who served as commander of US forces in Vietnam 1964–68. He was an aggressive advocate of expanded US military involvement there.

Weston Edward 1886–1958. US photographer. A founding member of the "f/64" group (after the smallest lens opening), a school of photography advocating sharp definition. He is noted for the technical mastery, composition, and clarity in his California landscapes, clouds, gourds, cacti, and nude studies.

West Palm Beach resort city on the SE coast of Florida, on the lagoon Lake Worth, N of Miami; population (1990) 67,600.
Industries include transistors, aircraft parts, building materials, and citrus fruits; tourism is important to the economy.

Westphalia independent medieval duchy, incorporated in Prussia by the Congress of Vienna 1815, and made a province 1816 with Münster as its capital. Since 1946 it has been part of the German *Land* (region) of ◊North Rhine–Westphalia.

Westphalia, Treaty of agreement 1648 ending the ◊Thirty Years' War. The peace marked the end of the supremacy of the Holy Roman Empire and the emergence of France as a dominant power. It recognized the sovereignty of the German states, Switzerland, and the

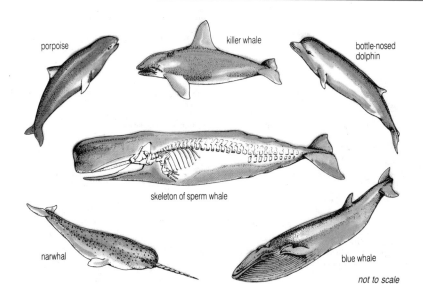

porpoise

killer whale

bottle-nosed dolphin

whale The ancestors of the whales were once land animals.

skeleton of sperm whale

narwhal

blue whale

not to scale

Netherlands; Lutherans, Calvinists, and Roman Catholics were given equal rights.

West Point former fort in New York State, on the Hudson River, 50 mi/80 km N of New York City, site of the US Military Academy (commonly referred to as West Point), established 1802. Women were admitted 1976. West Point has been a military post since 1778.

West Virginia state in E central US; nickname Mountain State
area 24,279 sq mi/62,900 sq km
capital Charleston
cities Huntington, Wheeling
physical Allegheny Mountains; Ohio River
features port of Harper's Ferry, restored as when John Brown seized the US armory 1859
products apples, corn, poultry, dairy and meat products, coal, natural gas, oil, chemicals, synthetic fibers, plastics, steel, glass, pottery
population (1990) 1,793,500
famous people Pearl S. Buck, Thomas "Stonewall" Jackson, Walter Reuther, Cyrus Vance
Long one of the poorest parts of the country, West Virginia reached its peak population in 1950. The decline of employment in coal mining and heavy industry has hampered the state's economic life.

wetland permanently wet land area or habitat. Wetlands include areas of ◊marsh, fen, ◊bog, flood plain, and shallow coastal areas. Wetlands are extremely fertile. They provide warm, sheltered waters for fisheries, lush vegetation for grazing livestock, and an abundance of wildlife. Estuaries and seaweed beds are more than 16 times as productive as the open ocean.

Weyden Rogier van der *c.* 1399–1464. Netherlandish painter, official painter to the city of Brussels from 1436. He painted portraits and religious subjects, such as *The Last Judgment* about 1450 (Hôtel-Dieu, Beaune). His refined style had considerable impact on Netherlandish painting.

whale any marine mammal of the order Cetacea, with front limbs modified into flippers and with internal vestiges of hind limbs. The order is divided into the toothed whales (Odontoceti) and the baleen whales

(Mysticeti). The toothed whales include ◊dolphins and ◊porpoises, along with large forms such as sperm whales. The baleen whales, with plates of modified mucous membrane called baleen in the mouth, are all large in size and include finback and right whales. There were hundreds of thousands of whales at the beginning of the 20th century, but they have been hunted close to extinction (see ◊whaling).

whaling the hunting of whales, largely discontinued 1986. Whales are killed for whale oil (made from the thick layer of fat under the skin called "blubber"), used for food and cosmetics; for the large reserve of oil in the head of the sperm whale, used in the leather industry; and for *ambergris*, a waxlike substance from the intestines, used in making perfumes. There are synthetic substitutes for all these products. Whales are also killed for their meat, which is eaten by the Japanese and was used as pet food in the US and Europe.

Wharton Edith (born Jones) 1862–1937. US novelist. Her work, known for its subtlety and form and influenced by her friend Henry James, was mostly set in New York society. It includes *The House of Mirth* 1905; the grim, uncharacteristic novel of New England *Ethan Frome* 1911; *The Custom of the Country* 1913; and *The Age of Innocence* 1920.

wheat cereal plant derived from the wild *Triticum*, a grass native to the Middle East. It is the chief cereal used in breadmaking and is widely cultivated in temperate climates suited to its growth. Wheat is killed by frost, and damp renders the grain soft, so warm, dry regions produce the most valuable grain. *See illustration p. 996*

Wheeling city in NW West Virginia, on the Ohio River, SW of Pittsburgh, Pennsylvania; population (1990) 34,900. Industries include coal and natural-gas processing, iron and steel, textiles, glass, pottery, paper, and chemicals. Fort Henry, site of the last battle 1782 of the American Revolution, is here.

whelk any of various families of large marine snails with a thick spiral shell, especially the family Buccinidae. Whelks are scavengers, and also eat other shellfish. The largest grow to 16 in/40 cm long. Tropi-

wheat As one of the most important cereals, wheat has been developed in many varieties to suit different growing conditions.

wheat

grain

cross section of a grain

cal species, such as the conches, can be very colorful.

The common northern whelk *Buccinum undatum* is widely distributed around the North Sea and the Atlantic.

Whig Party in the UK, predecessor of the Liberal Party. The name was first used of rebel Covenanters and then of those who wished to exclude James II from the English succession (as a Roman Catholic). They were in power continuously 1714–60 and pressed for industrial and commercial development, a vigorous foreign policy, and religious toleration. During the French Revolution, the Whigs demanded parliamentary reform in Britain, and from the passing of the Reform Bill in 1832 became known as Liberals.

Whistler Miss Cicely Alexander, Harmony in Grey and Green (1872), Tate Gallery, London.

Whig Party in the US, political party opposed to the autocratic presidency of Andrew Jackson from 1834. The Whig presidents were W H Harrison, Taylor, and Fillmore. The party diverged over the issue of slavery: the Northern Whigs joined the Republican party and the Southern or "Cotton" Whigs joined the Democrats. The title was taken from the British Whig Party which supported Parliament against the king. During the American Revolution, colonial patriots described themselves as Whigs, while those remaining loyal to Britain were known as Tories.

whippet breed of dog resembling a small greyhound. It grows to 22 in/56 cm at the shoulder, and 20 lb/9 kg in weight.

The whippet was developed in England for racing. It was probably produced by crossing a terrier and a greyhound.

whippoorwill North American nightjar *Caprimulgus vociferus*, so called from its cry.

whip snake any of the various species of nonpoisonous slender-bodied tree-dwelling snakes of the New World genus *Masticophis*, family Colubridae, also called *coachwhips*. They are closely allied to members of the genus *Coluber* of SW North America, Eurasia, Australasia, and N Africa, some of which are called whip snakes in the Old World, but racers in North America.

whiskey (Gaelic *uisge breatha*, water of life) a strong alcoholic liquor made from a fermented mash of various cereals: Scotch whiskey from malted barley; Irish whiskey usually from barley, and North American whiskey and bourbon from rye and corn. Scotch and other whiskeys are usually blended; pure malt whiskeys are more expensive. Whiskey is generally aged in wooden casks for 4–12 years.

Whistler James Abbott McNeill 1834–1903. US painter and etcher, active in London from 1859. His riverscapes and portraits show subtle composition and color harmonies: for example, *Arrangement in Grey and Black: Portrait of the Painter's Mother* 1871 (Louvre, Paris).

Whitby, Synod of council summoned by King Oswy of Northumbria 664, which decided to adopt the Roman rather than the Celtic form of Christianity for Britain.

White counterrevolutionary, especially during the Russian civil wars 1917–21. Originally the term described the party opposing the French Revolution, when the royalists used the white lily of the French monarchy as their badge.

White Byron Raymond 1917– . US jurist. He worked to elect John F Kennedy to the presidency 1960 and was appointed by him as associate justice of the Supreme Court, serving 1962–93. He was a moderate conservative, usually dissenting on the rights of criminals, but upholding the right of accused citizens to trial by jury.

He also played professional football, with the Pittsburgh Pirates (now Steelers) 1938 and for the Detroit Lions 1940–41. He was elected to the Football Hall of Fame 1954.

White Edward Douglass, Jr 1845–1921. US jurist. Elected to the US Senate 1891, President Cleveland nominated him as associate justice to the US Supreme Court 1893 and under President Taft he was nominated as chief justice 1911–21. During his office the Court made important decisions on US economic policy as in *United States* v *E C Knight and Co* 1895

White House The official residence of the president of the United States, in Washington, DC.

when he joined the majority in weakening the Sherman Antitrust Act by removing manufacture of goods from its purview.

White Patrick (Victor Martindale) 1912–1990. Australian writer who did more than any other to put Australian literature on the international map. His partly allegorical novels explore the lives of early settlers in Australia and often deal with misfits or inarticulate people. They include *The Aunt's Story* 1948, *The Tree of Man* 1955, and *Voss* 1957 (based on the ill-fated 19th-century explorer Leichhardt). Nobel Prize for Literature 1973.

White Stanford 1853–1906. US architect. One of the most prominent US architects of the 19th century, he specialized in the Renaissance style and designed, among many famous projects, the original Madison Square Garden and the Washington Square Arch, both in New York City. A flamboyant and arrogant personality, he was murdered in the rooftop restaurant of Madison Square Garden by the husband of a former lover.

white blood cell or *leukocyte* one of a number of different cells that play a part in the body's defenses and give immunity against disease. Some (◊phagocytes and macrophages) engulf invading microorganisms, others kill infected cells, while ◊lymphocytes produce more specific immune responses. White blood cells are colorless, with clear or granulated cytoplasm, and are capable of independent amoeboid movement. They occur in the blood, ◊lymph, and elsewhere in the body's tissues.

white-collar worker non-manual employee, such as an office worker or manager. With more mechanized production methods, the distinction between white- and blue-collar (manual) workers is becoming increasingly blurred.

white dwarf small, hot ◊star, the last stage in the life of a star such as the Sun. White dwarfs have a mass similar to that of the Sun, but only 1% of the Sun's diameter, similar in size to the Earth. Most have surface temperatures of 14,400° F/8,000° C or more, hotter than the Sun. Yet, being so small, their overall luminosities may be less than 1% of that of the Sun. The Milky Way contains an estimated 50 billion white dwarfs.

White dwarfs consist of degenerate matter in which gravity has packed the protons and electrons together as tightly as is physically possible, so that a spoonful of it weighs several tons. White dwarfs are thought to be the shrunken remains of stars that have exhausted their internal energy supplies. They slowly cool and fade over billions of years.

Whitefield George 1714–1770. British Methodist evangelist. He was a student at Oxford University and took orders in 1738, but was suspended for his unorthodox doctrines and methods. For many years he traveled through Britain and America, and by his preaching contributed greatly to the Great Awakening. He died while visiting New England.

Whitehorse capital of Yukon Territory; population (1986) 15,199. Whitehorse is on the NW Highway. It replaced Dawson as capital 1953.

White House official residence of the president of the US, in Washington, DC. It is a plain edifice of sandstone, built in the Italian Renaissance style 1792–99 to the designs of James Hoban, who also restored it after it was burned by the British 1814; it was then painted white to hide the scars.

Whitman Walt(er) 1819–1892. US poet who published *Leaves of Grass* 1855, which contains the symbolic "Song of Myself." It used unconventional free verse (with no rhyme or regular rhythm) and scandalized the public by its frank celebration of sexuality.

Born at West Hill (Huntington, Long Island), New York, as a young man Whitman worked as a printer,

whydah During the breeding season the male paradise whydah has elongated black tail feathers 11 in/28 cm long.

teacher, and journalist. In 1865 he published *Drum-Taps*, a volume inspired by his work as an army nurse during the Civil War. *Democratic Vistas* 1871 is a collection of his prose pieces. He also wrote an elegy for Abraham Lincoln, "When Lilacs Last in the Dooryard Bloom'd." He preached a particularly American vision of individual freedom and human brotherhood. Such poets as Ezra Pound, Wallace Stevens, and Allen Ginsberg show his influence in their work.

Whitney Eli 1765–1825. US inventor who in 1794 patented the cotton gin, a device for separating cotton fiber from its seeds. Also a manufacturer of firearms, he created a standardization system that was the precursor of the assembly line.

Whittier John Greenleaf 1807–1892. US poet who was a powerful opponent of slavery, as shown in the verse *Voices of Freedom* 1846. Among his other works are *Legends of New England in Prose and Verse, Songs of Labor* 1850, and the New England nature poem *Snow-Bound* 1866.

Whittle Frank 1907– . British engineer who patented the basic design for the turbojet engine 1930. In the Royal Air Force he worked on jet propulsion 1937–46. In May 1941 the Gloster E 28/39 aircraft first flew with the Whittle jet engine. Both the German (first operational jet planes) and the US jet aircraft were built using his principles.

WHO acronym for ◊World Health Organization.

Who, the English rock group, formed 1964, with a hard, aggressive sound, high harmonies, and a propensity for destroying their instruments on stage. Their albums include *Tommy* 1969, *Who's Next* 1971, and *Quadrophenia* 1973.

whooping cough or ***pertussis*** acute infectious disease, seen mainly in children, caused by colonization of the air passages by the bacterium *Bordetella pertussis*. There may be catarrh, mild fever, and loss of appetite, but the main symptom is violent coughing, associated with the sharp intake of breath that is the characteristic "whoop," and often followed by vomiting and severe nose bleeds. The cough may persist for weeks.

whydah any of various African birds of the genus *Vidua*, order Passeriformes, of the weaver family. They lay their eggs in the nests of waxbills, which rear the young. Young birds resemble young waxbills, but the adults do not resemble adult waxbills. Males have long tail feathers used in courtship displays.

Whymper Edward 1840–1911. English mountaineer. He made the first ascent of many Alpine peaks, including the Matterhorn 1865, and in the Andes scaled Chimborazo and other mountains.

Wichita industrial city (oil refining, aircraft, motor vehicles) in S Kansas; population (1990) 304,000. Wichita was founded about 1867.

It became a stopover on the Chisholm cattle-driving trail; when the railroad arrived 1872, the city became a major cattle-shipping point. Petroleum was discovered nearby 1915, and aircraft manufacture began 1920. Wichita State University is here.

Wichita Falls city in N Texas, on the Wichita River, S of the Oklahoma border; population (1990) 96,300. It is an important petroleum-processing center. Other industries include leather goods, textiles, foodstuffs, electronics, and pharmaceutical goods.

Wien's law in physics, a law of radiation stating that the wavelength carrying the maximum energy is inversely proportional to the body's absolute temperature: the hotter a body is, the shorter the wavelength. It has the form $\lambda_{max}T$ = constant, where λ_{max} is the wavelength of maximum intensity and T is the temperature. The law is named after German physicist Wilhelm Wien.

Wiesel Elie 1928– . US academic and human-rights campaigner, born in Romania. He was held in Buchenwald concentration camp during World War II, and has assiduously documented wartime atrocities against the Jews in an effort to alert the world to the dangers of racism and violence. Nobel Peace Prize 1986.

Wight, Isle of island and county in S England
area 147 sq mi/380 sq km
cities Newport (administrative headquarters), resorts: Ryde, Sandown, Shanklin, Ventnor

features the *Needles*, a group of pointed chalk rocks up to 100 ft/30 m high in the sea to the W; the *Solent*, the sea channel between Hampshire and the island (including the anchorage of *Spithead* opposite Portsmouth, used for naval reviews); *Cowes*, venue of Regatta Week and headquarters of the Royal Yacht Squadron; Osborne House, near Cowes, a home of Queen Victoria, for whom it was built 1845; Farringford, home of the poet Alfred Tennyson, near Freshwater

products chiefly agricultural; tourism

population (1991) 126,600

famous people Thomas Arnold, Robert Hooke

Wigner Eugene Paul 1902– . Hungarian-born US physicist who introduced the notion of parity into nuclear physics with the consequence that all nuclear processes should be indistinguishable from their mirror images. For this, and other work on nuclear structure, he shared the 1963 Nobel Prize for Physics with Maria Goeppert-Mayer and Hans Jensen (1906–1973).

Wilde Oscar (Fingal O'Flahertie Wills) 1854–1900. Irish writer. With his flamboyant style and quotable conversation, he dazzled London society and, on his lecture tour 1882, the US. He published his only novel, *The Picture of Dorian Gray*, 1891, followed by witty plays including *A Woman of No Importance* 1893 and *The Importance of Being Earnest* 1895. In 1895 he was imprisoned for two years for homosexual offenses; he died in exile.

wildebeest another name for ◊gnu.

Wilder Thornton (Niven) 1897–1975. US playwright and novelist. He won Pulitzer prizes for the novel *The Bridge of San Luis Rey* 1927, and for the plays *Our Town* 1938 and *The Skin of Our Teeth* 1942. His farce *The Matchmaker* 1954 was filmed 1958. In 1964 it was adapted into the hit stage musical *Hello, Dolly!*, also made into a film 1969.

Wilkes John 1727–1797. British Radical politician, imprisoned for his political views; member of Parliament 1757–64 and from 1774. He championed parliamentary reform, religious toleration, and US independence.

Wilkes Barre industrial city (furniture, textiles, wire, tobacco products, and heavy machinery) in NE Pennsylvania, on the Susquehanna River, SW of Scranton; population (1990) 47,500.

Wilkins Maurice Hugh Frederick 1916– . New Zealand–born British scientist. In 1962 he shared the Nobel Prize for Medicine with Francis ◊Crick and James ◊Watson for his work on the molecular structure of nucleic acids, particularly ◊DNA, using X-ray diffraction.

will in law, declaration of how a person wishes his or her property to be disposed of after death. It also appoints administrators of the estate (◊executors) and may contain wishes on other matters, such as place of burial or use of organs for transplant. Wills must comply with formal legal requirements of the local jurisdiction.

Willard Frances Elizabeth Caroline 1839–1898. US educator and campaigner. Committed to the cause of the prohibition of alcohol, culminating in the Prohibition 1920–33, she served as president of the Women's Christian Temperance Union 1879–98. She was also elected president of the National Council of Women 1888.

William I *the Conqueror* c. 1027–1087. King of England from 1066. He was the illegitimate son of Duke Robert the Devil and succeeded his father as duke of Normandy 1035. Claiming that his relative King Edward the Confessor had bequeathed him the English throne, William invaded the country 1066, defeating ◊Harold II at Hastings, Sussex, and was crowned king of England.

William II *Rufus, the Red* c. 1056–1100. King of England from 1087, the third son of William I. He spent most of his reign attempting to capture Normandy from his brother ◊Robert II, duke of Normandy. His extortion of money led his barons to revolt and caused confrontation with Bishop Anselm. He was killed while hunting in the New Forest, Hampshire, and was succeeded by his brother Henry I.

William III *William of Orange* 1650–1702. King of Great Britain and Ireland from 1688, the son of William II of Orange and Mary, daughter of Charles I. He was offered the English crown by the parliamentary opposition to James II. He invaded England 1688 and in 1689 became joint sovereign with his wife, ◊Mary II. He spent much of his reign campaigning, first in Ireland, where he defeated James II at the battle of the Boyne 1690, and later against the French in Flanders. He was succeeded by Mary's sister, Anne.

William IV 1765–1837. King of Great Britain and Ireland from 1830, when he succeeded his brother George IV; third son of George III. He was created duke of Clarence 1789, and married Adelaide of Saxe-Meiningen (1792–1849) 1818. During the Reform Bill crisis he secured its passage by agreeing to create new peers to overcome the hostile majority in the House of Lords. He was succeeded by Victoria.

William I 1797–1888. King of Prussia from 1861 and emperor of Germany from 1871; the son of Friedrich Wilhelm III. He served in the Napoleonic Wars 1814–15 and helped to crush the 1848 revolution. After he succeeded his brother Friedrich Wilhelm IV to the throne of Prussia, his policy was largely dictated by his chancellor ◊Bismarck, who secured his proclamation as emperor.

William II 1859–1941. Emperor of Germany from 1888, the son of Frederick III and Victoria, daughter of Queen Victoria of Britain. In 1890 he forced Chancellor Bismarck to resign and began to direct foreign policy himself, which proved disastrous. He encouraged warlike policies and built up the German navy. In 1914 he first approved Austria's ultimatum to Serbia and then, when he realized war was inevitable, tried in vain to prevent it. In 1918 he fled to Holland, after Germany's defeat and his abdication.

William I 1772–1844. King of the Netherlands 1815–40. He lived in exile during the French occupation 1795–1813 and fought against the emperor Napoleon at Jena and Wagram. The Austrian Netherlands were added to his kingdom by the Allies 1815, but secured independence (recognized by the major European states 1839) by the revolution of 1830. William's unpopularity led to his abdication 1840.

William II 1792–1849. King of the Netherlands 1840–49, son of William I. He served with the British army in the Peninsular War and at Waterloo. In 1848 he averted revolution by conceding a liberal constitution.

William *the Silent* 1533–1584. Prince of Orange from 1544. Leading a revolt against Spanish rule in the Netherlands from 1573, he briefly succeeded in uniting the Catholic south and Protestant northern provinces, but the former provinces submitted to Spain while the latter formed a federation 1579 (Union of Utrecht) which repudiated Spanish suzerainty 1581.

Wilson US president Woodrow Wilson, who took the US into World War I.

Williams Roger c. 1603–1683. American colonist, founder of the Rhode Island colony 1636, based on democracy and complete religious freedom. He tried to maintain good relations with the Indians of the region, although he fought against them in the Pequot War and King Philip's War.

He came to America as a Puritan minister in Massachusets 1631 but was banished from the colony 1635 for his "dangerous opinions"; he deplored theocracy and advocated separation of church and state. He then founded Providence 1636, disavowed Puritanism 1639, and returned to England to secure a patent with full religious freedom for his colony in the face of threats from the Puritans. He subsequently returned to Rhode Island and was the colony's president 1654–57; there he founded the first Baptist Church in America.

Williams Ted (Theodore Samuel) 1918– . US baseball player. Establishing a lifetime batting average of .344, he was six times the American League batting champion and twice won the most valuable player award. In 1947 he became the second player ever to twice win the Triple Crown (leading the league in batting, home runs, and runs batted in for a season).

Williams Tennessee (Thomas Lanier) 1911–1983. US playwright, born in Mississippi. His work is characterized by fluent dialogue and searching analysis of the psychological deficiencies of his characters. His plays, usually set in the Deep South against a background of decadence and degradation, include *The Glass Menagerie* 1945, *A Streetcar Named Desire* 1947, and *Cat on a Hot Tin Roof* 1955, the last two of which earned Pulitzer Prizes.

Many of his plays have been made into successful theatrical films, several of which were directed memorably by Elia Kazan. His other plays include *Suddenly Last Summer* 1958 and *Sweet Bird of Youth* 1959. After writing *The Night of the Iguana* 1961, also awarded the Pulitzer Prize, he entered a period of ill health, and none of his subsequent plays succeeded. However, his earlier work earned him a reputation as one of America's preeminent playwrights.

Williams William Carlos 1883–1963. US poet. His spare images and language reflect everyday speech. His epic poem *Paterson* 1946–58 celebrates his hometown in New Jersey. *Pictures from Brueghel* 1963 won him, posthumously, a Pulitzer prize. His vast body of prose work includes novels, short stories, and the play

A Dream of Love 1948. His work had a great impact on younger US poets.

Williamsburg historic city in Virginia; population (1990) 11,500. Founded 1632, capital of the colony of Virginia 1699–1779, much of it has been restored to its 18th-century appearance.

Williamsport industrial city (electronics, plastics, metals, lumber, textiles, and aircraft parts) in N central Pennsylvania, on the Susquehanna River, N of Harrisburg; population (1990) 31,900. It is the birthplace of Little League baseball (1939).

Willkie Wendell Lewis 1892–1944. US politician who was the Republican presidential candidate 1940. After losing to F D Roosevelt, he continued as a leader of the liberal wing of the Republican Party. Becoming committed to the cause of international cooperation, he published *One World* 1942.

willow any tree or shrub of the genus *Salix*, family Salicaceae. There are over 350 species, mostly in the northern hemisphere, and they flourish in damp places. The leaves are often lance-shaped, and the male and female catkins are found on separate trees.

North American species include black willow *S. nigra* and Pacific willow *S. lasiandra*. The weeping willow *S. babylonica* is a native of China, cultivated worldwide.

Wilmington industrial port and city (chemicals, textiles, shipbuilding, iron and steel goods; headquarters of Du Pont enterprises) in Delaware; population (1990) 71,500. Founded by Swedish settlers as **Fort Christina** 1638, it was taken from the Dutch and renamed by the British 1664.

Wilmington port and industrial city (textiles, tobacco, lumber, and chemicals) in SE North Carolina, on the Cape Fear River, near the Atlantic Ocean; population (1990) 55,500. Tourism is important to the economy.

Wilson Edmund 1895–1972. US critic and writer. Perhaps the foremost American social and literary critic of the 20th century, he was an editor of *Vanity Fair* 1920–21, the *New Republic* 1926–31, and *The New Yorker* 1944–48. Among his most influential works are *Axel's Castle* 1931, a survey of symbolism, and *The Wound and the Bow* 1941, a study of the relationship of neurosis to creativity.

Wilson (James) Harold, Baron Wilson of Rievaulx 1916– . British Labour politician, party leader from 1963, prime minister 1964–70 and 1974–76. His premiership was dominated by the issue of UK admission to membership in the European Community, the social contract (unofficial agreement with the labor unions), and economic difficulties.

Wilson (Thomas) Woodrow 1856–1924. 28th president of the US 1913–21, a Democrat. He kept the US out of World War I until 1917, and in Jan 1918 issued his "Fourteen Points" as a basis for a just peace settlement. At the peace conference in Paris he secured the inclusion of the ◊League of Nations in individual peace treaties, but these were not ratified by Congress, so the US did not join the League. Nobel Peace Prize 1919.

Wilson, born in Staunton, Virginia, was educated at Princeton University, of which he became president 1902–10. In 1910 he became governor of New Jersey. Elected US president 1912 against Theodore Roosevelt and William Howard Taft, he initiated antitrust legislation and secured valuable economic and social reforms in his progressive "New Freedom" program. Wilson also instituted a federal income tax, the first since the

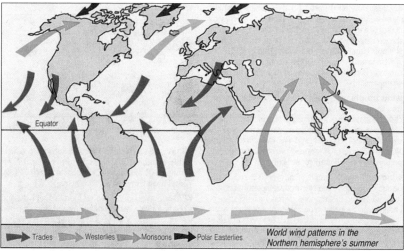

wind World wind patterns in the northern hemisphere's summer.

Trades Westerlies Monsoons Polar Easterlies

World wind patterns in the Northern hemisphere's summer

Civil War. He strove to keep the US neutral during World War I, but the unrestricted German U-boat campaign, sensationalized by the sinking of the British liner *Lusitania* (with 128 Americans lost), forced him to declare war 1917. His refusal to compromise on the text of the League of Nations' proposal contributed to its defeat in Congress. In 1919 Wilson suffered a stroke during a nationwide campaign to gain support for the League and retired from public life.

Wimbledon English lawn-tennis center used for international championship matches, situated in south London. There are currently 18 courts.

WIMP (acronym for *windows, icons, menus, pointing device*) in computing, another name for ◊graphical user interface (GUI).

wind the lateral movement of the Earth's atmosphere from high-pressure areas (anticyclones) to low-pressure areas (depression). Its speed is measured using an ◊anemometer or by studying its effects on, for example, trees by using the ◊Beaufort Scale. Although modified by features such as land and water, there is a basic worldwide system of ◊trade winds, ◊westerlies, and polar easterlies.

Windhoek capital of Namibia; population (1988) 115,000. It is just N of the Tropic of Capricorn, 180 mi/290 km from the W coast.

wind instrument musical instrument that uses the performer's breath, sometimes activating a reed or reeds, to make a column of air vibrate. The pitch of the note is controlled by the length of the column. The main types are ◊woodwind instruments and ◊brass instruments.

windmill mill with sails or vanes that, by the action of wind upon them, drive machinery for grinding corn or pumping water, for example. Wind turbines, designed to use wind power on a large scale, usually have a propeller-type rotor mounted on a tall shell tower. The turbine drives a generator for producing electricity.

window in computing, a rectangular area on the screen of a ◊graphical user interface. A window is used to display data and can be manipulated in various ways by the computer user.

wind power the harnessing of wind energy to produce power. The wind has long been used as a source of energy: sailing ships and windmills are ancient inventions. After the energy crisis of the 1970s ◊wind turbines began to be used to produce electricity on a large scale. By the year 2000, 10% of Denmark's energy is expected to come from wind power.

Windsor industrial lake port (car engines, pharmaceuticals, iron and steel goods, paint, bricks) in Ontario, SE Canada, opposite Detroit, Michigan; population (1986) 254,000. It was founded as a Hudson's Bay Company post 1853.

Windsor Duke of. Title of ◊Edward VIII.

Windsor, House of official name of the British royal family since 1917, adopted in place of Saxe-Coburg-Gotha. Since 1960 those descendants of Elizabeth II not entitled to the prefix HRH (His/Her Royal Highness) have borne the surname Mountbatten-Windsor.

windsurfing or *boardsailing* or *sailboarding* water sport combining elements of surfing and sail-

windsurfing French windsurfing champion Pascal Maka.

ing, first developed in the US 1968. The windsurfer stands on a board that is propelled and steered by means of a sail attached to a mast that is articulated at the foot. Since 1984 the sport has been included in the Olympic Games as part of the yachting events. From 1992 men and women have to compete in separate categories. There are also annual boardsailing world championships.

wind tunnel test tunnel in which air is blown over, for example, a stationary model aircraft, motor vehicle, or locomotive to simulate the effects of movement. Lift, drag, and airflow patterns are observed by the use of special cameras and sensitive instruments. Wind-tunnel testing assesses aerodynamic design, preparatory to full-scale construction.

wind turbine windmill of advanced aerodynamic design connected to an electricity generator and used in wind-power installations. Wind turbines can be either large propeller-type rotors mounted on a tall tower, or flexible metal strips fixed to a vertical axle at top and bottom. In 1990, over 20,000 wind turbines were in use throughout the world, generating 1,600 megawatts of power.

Windward Islands islands in the path of the prevailing wind, notably: *West Indies* see ◊Antilles; ◊Cape Verde Islands; and ◊*French Polynesia* (Tahiti, Moorea, Makatea).

wine alcoholic beverage, usually made from fermented grape pulp, although wines have also traditionally been made from many other fruits such as damsons and elderberries. *Red wine* is the product of the grape with the skin; *white wine* of the inner pulp of the grape. The sugar content is converted to ethyl alcohol by the yeast *Saccharomyces ellipsoideus*, which lives on the skin of the grape. The largest wine-producing countries are Italy, France, Russia, Georgia, Moldova, Armenia, and Spain; others include almost all European countries, Australia, South Africa, the US, and Chile.

For *dry wine* the fermentation is allowed to go on longer than for *sweet* or *medium*; ◊champagne (sparkling wine from the Champagne region of France) is bottled while still fermenting, but other sparkling wines are artificially carbonated. Some wines are fortified with additional alcohol obtained from various sources, and with preservatives. Some of the latter may cause dangerous side effects (see ◊additive). For this reason, organic wines, containing no preservatives, have recently become popular.

wing in biology, the modified forelimb of birds and bats, or the membranous outgrowths of the ◊exoskeleton of insects, which give the power of flight. Birds and bats have two wings. Bird wings have feathers attached to the fused digits ("fingers") and forearm bones, while bat wings consist of skin stretched between the digits. Most insects have four wings, which are strengthened by wing veins.

Winnipeg capital and industrial city (processed foods, textiles, transportation, and transportation equipment) in Manitoba, on the Red River, S of Lake Winnipeg; population (1986) 623,000. Established as Winnipeg 1870 on the site of earlier forts, the city expanded with the arrival of the Canadian Pacific Railroad 1881.

The city annexed several adjacent communities 1972 to become the largest Canadian city W of Toronto. The University of Manitoba and University of Winnipeg are here.

Winnipeg, Lake lake in S Manitoba, draining much of the Canadian prairies; area 9,460 sq mi/24,500 sq km.

Wisconsin

Winston-Salem industrial city (tobacco products, textiles, clothing, and furniture) in N central North Carolina, NE of Charlotte; population (1990) 143,500. Wake Forest University 1834 is here.

Winter Haven city in central Florida, E of Lakeland; a center for citrus-fruit processing and shipping; population (1990) 24,700. Other industries include tourism, cigars, and alcohol.

Winthrop John 1588–1649. American colonist and first governor of the Massachusetts Bay Colony. A devout Puritan and one of the founders of the Massachusetts Bay Company 1628, he served as Massachusetts governor or deputy governor until his death. He first arrived in New England with a large group of settlers 1630. He was a founder of the city of Boston the same year.

wire thread of metal, made by drawing a rod through progressively smaller-diameter dies. Fine-gauge wire is used for electrical power transmission; heavier-gauge wire is used to make load-bearing cables.

Wisconsin state in N central US; nickname Badger State
area 56,163 sq mi/145,500 sq km
capital Madison
cities Milwaukee, Green Bay, Racine
features lakes: Superior, Michigan; Mississippi River; Door peninsula
products leading US dairy state; corn, hay, industrial and agricultural machinery, engines and turbines, precision instruments, paper products, automobiles and trucks, plumbing equipment
population (1990) 4,891,800
famous people Edna Ferber, Harry Houdini, Joseph McCarthy, Spencer Tracy, Orson Welles, Thornton Wilder, Frank Lloyd Wright
history explored by Jean Nicolet for France 1634; originally settled near Ashland by the French; passed to Britain 1763; included in US 1783. Wisconsin became a territory 1836 and a state 1848.

Wise Stephen Samuel 1874–1949. Hungarian-born US religious leader. Ordained as a reform rabbi 1893, he served congregations in New York City 1893–1900 and Portland, Oregon, 1900–07, after which he became rabbi of the Free Synagogue in New York. He was president of the American Jewish Congress 1924–49.

wisteria any climbing shrub of the genus *Wisteria*, including *W. sinensis*, of the family Leguminosae, native to E US and E Asia. Wisterias have racemes of bluish, white, or pale mauve flowers, and pinnate leaves (leaves on either side of the stem).

witchcraft the alleged possession and exercise of magical powers—*black magic* if used with evil intent, and *white magic* if benign. Its origins lie in traditional beliefs and religions. Practitioners of witchcraft have often had considerable skill in, for example, herbal medicine and traditional remedies; this prompted the World Health Organization in 1976 to recommended the integration of traditional healers into the health teams of African states.

witch hazel any flowering shrub or small tree of the genus *Hamamelis* of the witch-hazel family, native to North America and E Asia, especially *H. virginiana*. An astringent extract prepared from the bark or leaves is used in medicine as an eye lotion and a liniment.

witness in law, a person who was present at some event (such as an accident, a crime, or the signing of a document) or has relevant special knowledge (such as a medical expert) and can be called on to give evidence in a court of law.

Wittelsbach Bavarian dynasty, who ruled Bavaria as dukes from 1180, electors from 1623, and kings 1806–1918.

Wittgenstein Ludwig 1889–1951. Austrian philosopher. His *Tractatus Logico-Philosophicus* 1922 postulated the "picture theory" of language: that words represent things according to social agreement. He subsequently rejected this idea, and developed the idea that usage was more important than convention.

Wodehouse P(elham) G(renville) 1881–1975. English novelist, a US citizen from 1955, whose humorous novels portray the accident-prone world of such characters as the socialite Bertie Wooster and his invaluable and impeccable manservant Jeeves, and Lord Emsworth of Blandings Castle with his prize pig, the Empress of Blandings.

wolf any of two species of large wild dogs of the genus *Canis*. The gray or timber wolf *C. lupus*, of North America and Eurasia, is highly social, measures up to 3 ft/90 cm at the shoulder, and weighs up to 100 lb/45 kg. It has been greatly reduced in numbers except for isolated wilderness regions.

Wolfe James 1727–1759. British soldier who served in Canada and commanded a victorious expedition against the French general Montcalm in Québec on the Plains of Abraham, during which both commanders were killed. The British victory established their supremacy over Canada.

Wolfe Thomas 1900–1938. US novelist. He wrote four long and hauntingly powerful autobiographical novels, mostly of the South: *Look Homeward, Angel* 1929, *Of Time and the River* 1935, *The Web and the Rock* 1939, and *You Can't Go Home Again* 1940 (the last two published posthumously).

Born in Asheville, North Carolina, Wolfe studied playwriting at the University of North Carolina and Harvard University. He settled in New York City, with hopes of becoming a playwright. His first novel, *Look Homeward, Angel*, was a realistic, brutal view of the South and Southern family life, the result of six years of work with Scribner's editor Maxwell Perkins. He also wrote *The Story of a Novel* 1936 and the short-story collections *From Death to Morning* 1935 and *The Hills Beyond* 1941.

Wolfe Tom. Adopted name of Thomas Kennerly, Jr 1931– . US journalist and novelist. In the 1960s he was a founder of the "New Journalism," which brought fiction's methods to reportage. Wolfe recorded US mores and fashions in pop-style essays in, for example, *The Kandy-Kolored Tangerine-Flake Streamline Baby* 1965. His sharp social eye is applied to the New York of the 1980s in his novel *The Bonfire of the Vanities* 1988.

Born in Richmond, Virginia, Wolfe graduated from Yale University and worked at newspaper and magazine reporting. He also wrote *The Electric Kool-Aid Acid Test* 1968; *Radical Chic and Mau-Mauing the Flak Catchers* 1970; *The Painted Word* 1975, about art; *The Right Stuff* 1979, about the first US astronauts; and *From Bauhaus to Our House* 1981, about modern architecture. *The Bonfire of the Vanities* was filmed 1990.

wolframite iron manganese tungstate, (Fe,Mn)WO$_4$, an ore mineral of tungsten. It is dark gray with a sub-metallic surface luster, and often occurs in hydrothermal veins in association with ores of tin.

Wollstonecraft Mary 1759–1797. British feminist, member of a group of radical intellectuals called the English Jacobins, whose book *A Vindication of the Rights of Women* 1792 demanded equal educational opportunities for women. She married William Godwin and died giving birth to a daughter, Mary (later Mary ◊Shelley).

Wolsey Thomas *c.* 1475–1530. English cleric and politician. In Henry VIII's service from 1509, he became archbishop of York 1514, cardinal and lord chancellor 1515, and began the dissolution of the monasteries. His reluctance to further Henry's divorce from Catherine of Aragon, partly because of his ambition to be pope, led to his downfall 1529. He was charged with high treason 1530 but died before being tried.

wolverine largest land member *Gulo gulo* of the weasel family (Mustelidae), found in Europe, Asia, and North America. It is stocky in build, about 3.3 ft/1 m long. Its long, thick fur is dark brown on the back and belly and lighter on the sides. It covers food that it cannot eat with an unpleasant secretion. Destruction of habitat and trapping for its fur have greatly reduced its numbers.

wombat any of a family (Vombatidae) of burrowing, herbivorous marsupials, native to Tasmania and S Australia. They are about 3.3 ft/1 m long, heavy, with a big head, short legs and tail, and coarse fur.

women's movement the campaign for the rights of women, including social, political, and economic equality with men. Early European campaigners of the 17th–19th centuries fought for women's right to own property, to have access to higher education, and to vote (see ◊suffragette). Once women's suffrage was achieved in the 20th century, the emphasis of the movement shifted to the goals of equal social and economic opportunities for women, including employment. A continuing area of concern in industrialized countries is the contradiction between the now generally accepted principle of equality and the demonstrable inequalities that remain between the sexes in state policies and in everyday life.

wood the hard tissue beneath the bark of many perennial plants; it is composed of water-conducting cells, or secondary ◊xylem, and gains its hardness and strength from deposits of lignin. *Hardwoods*, such as oak, and *softwoods*, such as pine, have commercial value as structural material and for furniture.

Wood Grant 1892–1942. US painter based mainly in his native Iowa. Though his work is highly stylized, he struck a note of hard realism in his studies of farmers, such as *American Gothic* 1930 (Art Institute, Chicago).

woodcock either of two species of wading birds, genus *Scolopax*, of the family Scolopacidae, which have barred plumage, long bills, and live in wet woodland areas.

The American woodcock *S. minor*, about 11 in/28 cm long, is shortlegged and short-necked, with a long,

woodland

Northern temperate woods support huge populations of insects, slugs, snails and worms, on which prey birds, amphibians and mammals.

In an oak wood, there are several distinct small environments, or micro-habitats. High among the foliage, in the tree canopy, are animals that feed on the leaves, flowers and fruits. The open branches and the tree trunk support beetles and warps that search for food or lay eggs in bark crevices. On the ground, in the shade of the trees grow various flowering plants, as well as ferns, mosses and fungi. A fallen tree provides a home for fungi and invertebrates. Within the soil live insect larvae, worms and ants.

1. jay 2. oak tortix
3. sparrowhawk 4. wren 5. purple hairstreak 6. gall warp 7. oak bush cricket 8. acorns 9. bumble bee 10. wood ant 11. tree creeper 12. beard lichen 13. grey squirrel 14. bluebell 15. centipede 19. wood anemone 20. violet 21. pot worm 22. tiger moth larva 23. cockchafer 24. wireworm 25. starling 26. primrose 27. hart's tongue fern 28. woodwarbler 29. red underwing 30. badger 31. longicorn larva 32. ground beetle 33. woodlouse 34. dogs mercury 35. fly agaric 36. horn of plenty

straight bill. It nests in moist woodlands and thickets throughout E North America. The Eurasian woodcock *S. rusticola*, somewhat larger, is similar in appearance and habits.

woodcut print made by a woodblock in which a picture or design has been cut in relief. The woodcut is the oldest method of ◊printing, invented in China in the 5th century AD. In the Middle Ages woodcuts became popular in Europe, illustrating early printed books and broadsides.

woodland area in which trees grow more or less thickly; generally smaller than a forest. Temperate climates, with four distinct seasons a year, tend to support a mixed woodland habitat, with some conifers but mostly broad-leaved and deciduous trees, shedding their leaves in autumn and regrowing them in spring. In the Mediterranean region and parts of the southern hemisphere, the trees are mostly evergreen.

woodlouse any of the several families of mostly terrestrial crustaceans of the order Isopoda (especially the sow bugs, genera *Onisais* and *Porcellio*) that live in damp places under rocks or fallen timber. They have rounded oval, evenly segmented bodies and flat undersides. Some species of sow bugs can roll up when threatened. The pillbugs (family Armadillidiidae) typically roll up. Rock slaters (family Ligiidae) are amphibious on ocean beaches.

woodpecker bird of the family Picidae, which drills holes in trees to obtain insects. There are about 200 species worldwide. The largest of these, the imperial woodpecker *Campephilus imperialis* of Mexico, is very rare and may already be extinct.

North American woodpeckers include four species of sapsuckers (genus *Sphyrapicus*), which drill and then tap holes in trees for sap and the attracted insects. The pileated woodpecker *Dryocopus pileatus* is the largest, about 17 in/43 cm long, with a red crest.

Woodstock the first free rock festival, held near Bethel, New York State, over three days in Aug 1969. It was attended by 400,000 people, and performers included the Band, Country Joe and the Fish, the Grateful Dead, Jimi Hendrix, Jefferson Airplane, and the Who. The festival was a landmark in the youth culture of the 1960s (see ◊hippie) and was recorded in the film *Woodstock* 1970.

woodpecker The green woodpecker is, in some areas, called the yaffle, a name supposedly resembling its call.

woodwind musical instrument from which sound is produced by blowing into a tube, causing the air within to vibrate. Woodwind instruments include those, like the flute, originally made of wood but now more commonly of metal. The saxophone, made of metal, is an honorary woodwind because it is related to the clarinet. The oboe, bassoon, flute, and clarinet make up the normal woodwind section of an orchestra.

woodworm common name for the larval stage of certain wood-boring beetles. Dead or injured trees are their natural target, but they also attack structural timber and furniture.

wool the natural hair covering of the sheep, and also of the llama, angora goat, and some other ◊mammals. The domestic sheep *Ovis aries* provides the great bulk of the fibers used in (textile) commerce. Lanolin is a byproduct.

Woolf Virginia (born Virginia Stephen) 1882–1941. English novelist and critic. Her first novel, *The Voyage Out* 1915, explored the tensions experienced by women who want marriage and a career. In *Mrs Dalloway* 1925 she perfected her "stream of consciousness" technique. Among her later books are *To the Lighthouse* 1927, *Orlando* 1928, and *The Years* 1937, which considers the importance of economic independence for women.

Woolworth Frank Winfield 1852–1919. US entrepreneur. He opened his first successful "five and ten cent" store in Lancaster, Pennsylvania, in 1879, and, together with his brother C S Woolworth (1856–1947), built up a chain of similar stores throughout the US, the UK, and Europe.

Woonsocket industrial city (rubber, chemicals, woolen goods) in N Rhode Island, on the Blackstone River, NW of Providence; population (1990) 43,900.

World War I US troops in Alsace during World War I.

World War I

1914 outbreak	On June 28 the heir to the Austrian throne was assassinated in Sarajevo, Serbia; on July 28 Austria declared war on Serbia; as Russia mobilized, Germany declared war on Russia and France, taking a shortcut in the west by invading Belgium; on Aug 4 Britain declared war on Germany; dominions within the British Empire, including Australia, were automatically involved.
Western Front	The German advance reached within a few miles of Paris, but an Allied counterattack at the Marne drove them back to the Aisne River; the opposing lines then settled into trench warfare.
Eastern Front	The German commander Hindenburg halted the Russian advance through the Ukraine and across Austria-Hungary at the Battle of Tannenberg in E Prussia.
Africa	By Sept most of Germany's African colonies were in Allied hands; guerrilla warfare centered in Cameroon until 1916 and military operations in German East Africa until Nov 1918.
Middle East	On Nov 1 Turkey entered the war on the side of the Central Powers and soon attacked Russia in the Caucasus Mountains.
1915 Western Front	Several offensives on both sides resulted in insignificant gains. At Ypres, Belgium, the Germans used poison gas for the first time.
Eastern Front	The German field marshals Mackensen and Hindenburg drove back the Russians and took Poland.
Middle East	British attacks against Turkey in Mesopotamia (Iraq), the Dardanelles, and at Gallipoli (where 7,600 Anzacs were killed) were all unsuccessful.
Italy	Italy declared war on Austria; Bulgaria joined the Central Powers.
war at sea	Germany declared all-out U-boat war, but the sinking of the British ocean liner *Lusitania* (with Americans among the 1,198 lost) led to demands that the US enter the war.
1916 Western Front	The German attack at Verdun was countered by the Allies on the river Somme, where tanks were used for the first time.
Eastern Front	Romania joined the Allies but was soon overrun by Germany.
Middle East	Kut-al-Imara, Iraq, was taken from the British by the Turks.
war at sea	The Battle of Jutland between England and Germany, although indecisive, put a stop to further German naval participation in the war.
1917	The US entered the war in April. British and British Empire troops launched the third battle at Ypres and by Nov had taken Passchendaele.
1918 Eastern Front	On March 3 Soviet Russia signed the Treaty of Brest-Litovsk with Germany, ending Russian participation in the war (the Russian Revolution 1917 led into their civil war 1918–21).
Western Front	Germany began a final offensive. In April the Allies appointed the French marshal Foch supreme commander, but by June (when the first US troops went into battle) the Allies had lost all gains since 1915, and the Germans were on the river Marne. The battle at Amiens marked the launch of the victorious Allied offensive.
Italy	At Vittorio Veneto the British and Italians finally defeated the Austrians.
German capitulation	This began with naval mutinies at Kiel, followed by uprisings in the major cities. Kaiser Wilhelm II abdicated, and on Nov 11 the armistice was signed.
1919	June 18, peace treaty of Versailles. (The US signed a separate peace accord with Germany and Austria 1921.)

Worcester industrial port (textiles, engineering, printing) in central Massachusetts, on the Blackstone River; population (1990) 169,800. It was permanently settled 1713. Educational institutions include Clark University and Worcester Polytechnic Institute.

word processor in computing, a program that allows the input, amendment, manipulation, storage, and retrieval of text; or a computer system that runs such software. Since word-processing programs became available to microcomputers, the method has been gradually replacing the typewriter for producing letters or other text.

Wordsworth William 1770–1850. English Romantic poet. In 1797 he moved with his sister Dorothy to Somerset to be near ◊Coleridge, collaborating with him on *Lyrical Ballads* 1798 (including "Tintern Abbey").

From 1799 he lived in the Lake District, and later works include *Poems* 1807 (including "Intimations of Immortality") and *The Prelude* (written by 1805, published 1850). He was appointed poet laureate in 1843.

work in physics, a measure of the result of transferring energy from one system to another to cause an object to move. Work should not be confused with ◊energy (the capacity to do work, which is also measured in joules) or with ◊power (the rate of doing work, measured in joules per second).

World Bank popular name for the *International Bank for Reconstruction and Development* specialized agency of the United Nations that borrows in the commercial market and lends on commercial terms. It was established 1945 under the 1944 Bretton Woods agreement, which also created the International Monetary Fund. The *International Development Association* is an arm of the World Bank.

World Council of Churches (WCC) international organization aiming to bring together diverse movements within the Christian church. Established 1945, it has a membership in more than 100 countries and more than 300 churches; headquarters in Geneva, Switzerland.

World Health Organization (WHO) agency of the United Nations established 1946 to prevent the spread of diseases and to eradicate them. It has a staff of about 4,500. Its headquarters are in Geneva, Switzerland.

World Intellectual Property Organization (WIPO) specialist agency of the United Nations established 1974 to coordinate the international protection (initiated by the Paris convention 1883) of inventions, trademarks, and industrial designs, and also literary and artistic works (as initiated by the Berne convention 1886).

World War I 1914–1918. War between the Central European Powers (Germany, Austria-Hungary, and allies) on one side and the Triple Entente (Britain and the British Empire, France, and Russia) and their allies, including the US (which entered 1917), on the other side. An estimated 10 million lives were lost and twice that number were wounded. It was fought on the eastern and western fronts, in the Middle East, in Africa, and at sea. Toward the end of the war Russia withdrew because of the Russian Revolution 1917. The peace treaty of Versailles 1919 was the formal end to the war. *See illustration p. 1005*

World War II 1939–1945. War between Germany, Italy, and Japan (the Axis powers) on one side, and Britain, the Commonwealth, France, the US, the USSR, and China (the Allied powers) on the other. An estimated 55 million lives were lost, 20 million of them citizens of the USSR. The war was fought in the Atlantic and Pacific theaters. In 1945, Germany surrendered (May) but Japan fought on until the US dropped atomic bombs on Hiroshima and Nagasaki (Aug). *See illustration p. 1008*

worm any of various elongated limbless invertebrates belonging to several phyla. Worms include the ◊flatworms, such as ◊flukes and ◊tapeworms; the roundworms or nematodes, such as the eelworm and the hookworm; the marine ribbon worms or nemerteans; and the segmented worms or ◊annelids.

WORM (acronym for *write once read many times*) in computing, a storage device, similar to ◊CD-ROM. The computer can write to the disk directly, but cannot later erase or overwrite the same area. WORMs are mainly used for archiving and backup copies.

Worms industrial city in Rhineland-Palatinate, Germany, on the river Rhine; population (1984) 73,000. The vineyards of the Liebfrauenkirche produced the original Liebfraumilch wine; it is now produced by many growers around Worms. The Protestant reformer Martin Luther appeared before the *Diet* (Assembly) *of Worms* 1521 and was declared an outlaw by the Roman Catholic church.

wormwood any plant of the genus *Artemisia*, family Compositae, especially the aromatic herb *A. absinthium*, the leaves of which are used in absinthe. ◊Tarragon is a member of this genus.

Wounded Knee site on the Oglala Sioux Reservation, South Dakota, of a confrontation between the US Army and American Indians. Chief Sitting Bull was killed, supposedly resisting arrest, on Dec 15, 1890, and on Dec 29 a group of Indians involved in the Ghost Dance Movement (aimed at resumption of Indian control of North America with the aid of the spirits of dead braves) were surrounded and 153 killed.

wrack any of the large brown ◊seaweeds characteristic of rocky shores. The bladder wrack *Fucus vesiculosus* has narrow, branched fronds up to 3.3 ft/1 m long, with oval air bladders, usually in pairs on either side of the midrib or central vein.

wren any of a family (Troglodytidae) of small birds of order Passeriformes, with slender, slightly curved bills, and uptilted tails.

The house wren of North America *Troglodytes aedon* is common in brush, farmyard, and park.

Wren Christopher 1632–1723. English architect, designer of St Paul's Cathedral, London, built 1675–1710; many London churches including St Bride's, Fleet Street, and St Mary-le-Bow, Cheapside; the Royal Exchange; Marlborough House; and the Sheldonian Theater, Oxford.

wrestling sport popular in ancient Egypt, Greece, and Rome, and included in the Olympics from 704 BC. The two main modern international styles are *Greco-Roman*, concentrating on above-waist holds, and *freestyle*, which allows the legs to be used; in both the aim is to throw the opponent to the ground.

Wright Frank Lloyd 1869–1959. US architect who rejected Neo-Classicist styles for "organic architecture," in which buildings reflected their natural surroundings. Among his buildings are his Wisconsin home Taliesin East 1925; Falling Water, near Pittsburgh, Pennsylvania, 1936, a house built straddling a waterfall; and the Guggenheim Museum, New York, 1959.

Wright Orville 1871–1948 and Wilbur 1867–1912. US inventors; brothers who pioneered piloted, powered

World War II

1939 Sept	German invasion of Poland; Britain and France declared war on Germany; the USSR invaded Poland; fall of Warsaw (Poland divided between Germany and USSR).
Nov	The USSR invaded Finland.
1940 March	Soviet peace treaty with Finland.
April	Germany occupied Denmark, Norway, the Netherlands, Belgium, and Luxembourg. In Britain, a coalition government was formed under Churchill.
May	Germany outflanked the defensive French Maginot Line.
May–June	Evacuation of 337,131 Allied troops from Dunkirk, France, across the Channel to England.
June	Italy declared war on Britain and France; the Germans entered Paris; the French prime minister Pétain signed an armistice with Germany and moved the seat of government to Vichy.
July–Oct	Battle of Britain between British and German air forces.
Sept	Japanese invasion of French ◊Indochina.
Oct	Abortive Italian invasion of Greece.
1941 April	Germany occupied Greece and Yugoslavia.
June	Germany invaded the USSR; Finland declared war on the USSR.
July	The Germans entered Smolensk, USSR.
Dec	The Germans came within 25 mi/40 km of Moscow, with Leningrad (now St Petersburg) under siege. First Soviet counteroffensive. Japan bombed Pearl Harbor, Hawaii, and declared war on the US and Britain. Germany and Italy declared war on the US.
1942 Jan	Japanese conquest of the Philippines.
June	Naval battle of Midway, the turning point of the Pacific War.
Aug	German attack on Stalingrad (now Volgograd), USSR.
Oct–Nov	Battle of El Alamein in N Africa, turn of the tide for the Western Allies.
Nov	Soviet counteroffensive on Stalingrad.
1943 Jan	The Casablanca Conference issued the Allied demand for unconditional surrender; the Germans retreated from Stalingrad.
March	The USSR drove the Germans back to the river Donetz.
May	End of Axis resistance in N Africa.
July	A coup by King Victor Emmanuel and Marshal Badoglio forced Mussolini to resign.
Aug	Beginning of the campaign against the Japanese in Burma (now Myanmar); US Marines landed on Guadalcanal, Solomon Islands.
Sept	Italy surrendered to the Allies; Mussolini was rescued by the Germans who set up a Republican Fascist government in N Italy; Allied landings at Salerno; the USSR retook Smolensk.
Oct	Italy declared war on Germany.
Nov	The US Navy defeated the Japanese in the Battle of Guadalcanal.
Nov–Dec	The Allied leaders met at the Tehran Conference.
1944 Jan	Allied landing in Nazi-occupied Italy: Battle of Anzio.
March	End of the German U-boat campaign in the Atlantic.
May	Fall of Monte Cassino, S Italy.
June 6	D-day: Allied landings in Nazi-occupied and heavily defended Normandy.
July	The bomb plot by German generals against Hitler failed.
Aug	Romania joined the Allies.
Sept	Battle of Arnhem on the Rhine; Soviet armistice with Finland.
Oct	The Yugoslav guerrilla leader Tito and Soviets entered Belgrade.
Dec	German counteroffensive, Battle of the Bulge.
1945 Feb	The Soviets reached the German border; Yalta conference; Allied bombing campaign over Germany (Dresden destroyed); the US reconquest of the Philippines was completed; the Americans landed on Iwo Jima, south of Japan.
April	Hitler committed suicide; Mussolini was captured by Italian partisans and shot.
May	German surrender to the Allies.
June	US troops completed the conquest of Okinawa (one of the Japanese Ryukyu Islands).
July	The Potsdam Conference issued an Allied ultimatum to Japan.
Aug	Atomic bombs were dropped by the US on Hiroshima and Nagasaki; Japan surrendered.

World War II USS
Bunker Hill *takes two*
Kamikazes in 30
seconds May 11,
1945, in the Leyte
Gulf.

flight. Inspired by Otto ◊Lilienthal's gliding, they perfected their piloted glider 1902. In 1903 they built a powered machine, a 12-hp 750-lb/341-kg plane, and became the first to make a successful powered flight, near Kitty Hawk, North Carolina. Orville flew 120 ft/36.6 m in 12 sec; Wilbur, 852 ft/260 m in 59 sec.

Both brothers were born in Dayton, Ohio, and became interested in flight at early ages. They devised a wing-control system and added a rudder and a balancing tail to existing gliders. By 1903 they had built and flown a power-driven plane; they received a patent in 1906 and in 1909 set up the American Wright Corp to produce planes for the War Department. After Wilbur's death Orville did research and served on the National Advisory Committee for Aeronautics 1915–48.

Wright Richard 1908–1960. US novelist. He was one of the first to depict the condition of black people in 20th-century US society with *Native Son* 1940 and the autobiography *Black Boy* 1945.

writ in law, a document issued by a court requiring performance of certain actions.

Examples include a writ of ◊habeas corpus, a writ of certiorari by which the US Supreme Court calls up cases from inferior courts for review, or a writ of attachment of property in civil litigation.

writing any written form of communication using a set of symbols: see ◊alphabet, ◊cuneiform, ◊hieroglyphic. The last two used ideographs (picture writing) and phonetic word symbols side by side, as does modern Chinese. Syllabic writing, as in Japanese, develops from the continued use of a symbol to represent the sound of a short word. Some 8,000-year-old

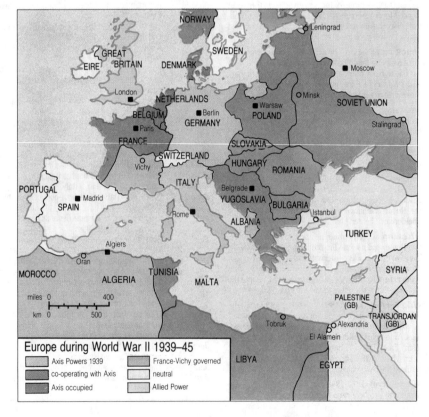

Europe during World War II 1939–45

- Axis Powers 1939
- co-operating with Axis
- Axis occupied
- France-Vichy governed
- neutral
- Allied Power

inscriptions, thought to be pictographs, were found on animal bones and tortoise shells in Henan province, China, at a Neolithic site at Jiahu. They are thought to predate by 2,500 years the oldest known writing (Mesopotamian cuneiform of 3,500 BC).

Wroclaw industrial river port in Poland, on the river Oder; population (1990) 643,200. Under the German name of **Breslau**, it was the capital of former German Silesia. Industries include shipbuilding, engineering, textiles, and electronics.

Wuhan river port and capital of Hubei province, China, at the confluence of the Han and Chang Jiang rivers, formed 1950 as one of China's greatest industrial areas by the amalgamation of Hankou, Hanyang, and Wuchang; population (1989) 3,710,000. It produces iron, steel, machine tools, textiles, and fertilizer.

Wycliffe John c. 1320–1384. English religious reformer. He attacked abuses in the church, maintaining that the Bible rather than the church was the supreme authority. He criticized such fundamental doctrines as priestly absolution, confession, and indulgences, and set disciples to work on translating the Bible into English. He sent out bands of traveling preachers, was denounced as a heretic, but died peacefully at Lutterworth.

Wyeth Andrew (Newell) 1917– . US painter. His portraits and landscapes, usually in watercolor or tempera, are naturalistic, minutely detailed, and often have a strong sense of the isolation of the countryside: for example, *Christina's World* 1948 (Museum of Modern Art, New York).

Born in Chadds Ford, Pennsylvania, the son of artist-illustrator N C ◊Wyeth, he is among the most popular of contemporary US artists. His paintings depict people of the land, especially Wyeth's own sur-

Wyoming

roundings in Chadds Ford and Maine, where his summer home is located. His son James Browning Wyeth (1946–) is also an artist.

Wyeth N(ewel) C(onvers) 1882–1944. US artist, the foremost US illustrator of his time as well as an accomplished muralist. He illustrated over 20 children's classics, including *Treasure Island*, *The Adventures of Tom Sawyer*, *Robin Hood*, and *The Yearling*.

Wyoming state in W US; nickname Equality State
area 97,812 sq mi/253,400 sq km
capital Cheyenne
cities Casper, Laramie
features Rocky Mountains; national parks: Yellowstone (including the geyser Old Faithful), Grand Teton
products oil, natural gas, sodium salts, coal, uranium, sheep, beef
population (1990) 453,600
famous people Buffalo Bill, Jackson Pollock
history acquired by US from France as part of the ◊Louisiana Purchase 1803; Fort Laramie, a trading post, settled 1834; women acheived the vote 1869; became a state 1890.

x in mathematics, an unknown quantity.

Xavier, St Francis 1506–1552. Spanish Jesuit missionary. He went to the Portuguese colonies in the East Indies, arriving at Goa 1542. He was in Japan 1549–51, establishing a Christian mission that lasted for 100 years. He returned to Goa in 1552, and sailed for China, but died of fever there. He was canonized 1622.

X chromosome larger of the two sex chromosomes, the smaller being the ◊Y chromosome. These two chromosomes are involved in sex determination. Genes carried on the X chromosome produce the phenomenon of ◊sex linkage.

xenon (Greek *xenos* "stranger") colorless, odorless, gaseous, non-metallic element, symbol Xe, atomic number 54, atomic weight 131.30. It is grouped with the ◊inert gases and was long believed not to enter into reactions, but is now known to form some compounds, mostly with fluorine. It is a heavy gas present in very small quantities in the air (about one part in 20 million).

Xenophon *c.* 430–354 BC. Greek historian, philosopher, and soldier. He was a disciple of ◊Socrates (described in Xenophon's *Symposium*). In 401 he joined a Greek mercenary army aiding the Persian prince Cyrus, and on the latter's death took command. His *Anabasis* describes how he led 10,000 Greeks on a 1,000-mi/1,600-km march home across enemy territory. His other works include *Memorabilia, Apology,* and *Hellenica/A History of My Times.*

xerography dry, electrostatic method of producing images, without the use of negatives or sensitized paper, invented in the US by Chester Carlson 1938 and applied in the Xerox ◊photocopier.

xerophyte plant adapted to live in dry conditions. Common adaptations to reduce the rate of ◊transpiration include a reduction of leaf size, sometimes to spines or scales; a dense covering of hairs over the leaf to trap a layer of moist air (as in edelweiss); and permanently rolled leaves or leaves that roll up in dry weather (as in vinemesquite grass). Many desert cacti are xerophytes.

Xerxes *c.* 519–465 BC. King of Persia from 485 BC when he succeeded his father Darius. In 480, at the head of a great army which was supported by the Phoenician navy, he crossed the Dardanelles over a bridge of boats. He captured and burned Athens, but the Persian fleet was defeated at Salamis and Xerxes was forced to retreat. His general Mardonius remained behind in Greece, but was defeated by the Greeks at Plataea 479. Xerxes was eventually murdered in a court intrigue.

Xhosa member of a Bantu people of southern Africa, living mainly in the Black National State of ◊Transkei. Traditionally, the Xhosa were farmers and pastoralists, with a social structure based on a monarchy. Many are now town-dwellers, and provide much of the unskilled labor in South African mines and factories. Their Bantu language belongs to the Niger-Congo family.

Xian industrial city and capital of Shaanxi province, China; population (1989) 2,710,000. It produces chemicals, electrical equipment, and fertilizers.

Xi Jiang or *Si-Kiang* river in China, that rises in Yunnan province and flows into the South China Sea; length 1,200 mi/1,900 km. Guangzhou lies on the northern arm of its delta, and Hong Kong island at its mouth. The name means "west river."

X-ray band of electromagnetic radiation in the wavelength range 10^{-11} to 10^{-9} m (between gamma rays and ultraviolet radiation; see ◊electromagnetic waves). Applications of X-rays make use of their short wavelength (as in ◊X-ray diffraction) or their penetrating power (as in medical X-rays of internal body tissues). X-rays are dangerous and can cause cancer.

X-ray astronomy detection of X-rays from intensely hot gas in the universe. Such X-rays are prevented from reaching the Earth's surface by the atmosphere, so detectors must be placed in rockets and satellites. The first celestial X-ray source, Scorpius X-1, was discovered by a rocket flight 1962.

X-ray diffraction method of studying the atomic and molecular structure of crystalline substances by using ◊X-rays. X-rays directed at such substances spread out as they pass through the crystals owing to ◊diffraction (the slight spreading of waves around the edge of an opaque object) of the rays around the atoms. By using measurements of the position and intensity of the diffracted waves, it is possible to calculate the shape and size of the atoms in the crystal. The method has been used to study substances such as ◊DNA that are found in living material.

xylem tissue found in ◊vascular plants, whose main function is to conduct water and dissolved mineral nutrients from the roots to other parts of the plant. Xylem is composed of a number of different types of cell, and may include long, thin, usually dead cells known as tracheids; fibers (schlerenchyma); thin-walled parenchyma cells; and conducting vessels.

xylophone musical ◊percussion instrument in which wooden bars of varying lengths are arranged according to graded pitch, or as a piano keyboard, over resonators to produce sounds when struck with hammers.

lic 1922–91. It remained an autonomous republic within the Russian Federation after the collapse of the Soviet Union 1991, since when it has agitated for greater independence.

Yalta Conference in 1945, a meeting at which the Allied leaders Churchill (UK), Roosevelt (US), and Stalin (USSR) completed plans for the defeat of Germany in World War II and the foundation of the United Nations. It took place in Yalta, a Soviet holiday resort in the Crimea.

yam any climbing plant of the genus *Dioscorea*, family Dioscoreaceae, cultivated in tropical regions; its starchy tubers are eaten as a vegetable. The Mexican yam *D. composita* contains a chemical used in the manufacture of the contraceptive pill.

Yamoussoukro capital of ◊Ivory Coast; population (1986) 120,000. The economy is based on tourism and agricultural trade.

Yanamamo or *Yanomamo* (plural *Yanamami*) a member of a seminomadic South American Indian people, numbering approximately 15,000, who live in S Venezuela and N Brazil. The Yanamamo language belongs to the Macro-Chibcha family. In Nov 1991 Brazil granted the Yanamami possession of their original land, 36,293 sq mi/58,395 km on its northern border.

Yangon since 1989 the name for *Rangoon* capital and chief port of Myanmar (Burma) on the Yangon River, 20 mi/32 km from the Indian Ocean; population (1983) 2,459,000. Products include timber, oil, and rice. The city *Dagon* was founded on the site AD 746; it was given the name Rangoon (meaning "end of conflict") by King Alaungpaya 1755.

Yang Shangkun 1907– . Chinese communist politician. He held a senior position in the party 1956–66 but was demoted during the Cultural Revolution. He was rehabilitated 1978, elected to the Politburo 1982, and served as state president 1988–93.

Yangtze-Kiang alternative transcription of ◊Chang Jiang, the longest river in China.

yak species of cattle *Bos grunniens*, family Bovidae, which lives in wild herds at high altitudes in Tibet. It stands about 6 ft/2 m at the shoulder and has long shaggy hair on the underparts. It has large, upward-curving horns and humped shoulders. It is in danger of becoming extinct.

Yakima city in S central Washington, on the Yakima River, SE of Seattle; population (1990) 54,800.

Yakut (Russian *Yakutskaya*) autonomous republic in Siberian Russia
area 1,197,760 sq mi/3,103,000 sq km
capital Yakutsk
features one of world's coldest inhabited places; river Lena
products furs, gold, natural gas, some agriculture in the S
population (1986) 1,009,000 (50% Russians, 37% Yakuts)
history the nomadic Yakuts were conquered by Russia in the 17th century; Yakut was a Soviet repub-

Yalta Conference
The Allied leaders Stalin, Roosevelt, and Churchill at the Yalta Conference, 1945.

Yankee initially, a disparaging term for a Dutch free-booter, later applied to English settlers by colonial Dutch in New York. Now it may be a colloquial term for a New Englander, any US northerner (used in the South), or any American (used outside the US).

Yao member of a people living in S China, N Vietnam, N Laos, Thailand, and Myanmar (Burma), and numbering about 4 million (1984). The Yao language may belong to either the Sino-Tibetan or the Thai language family. The Yao incorporate elements of ancestor worship in their animist religion.

Yaoundé capital of Cameroon, 130 mi/210 km E of the port of Douala; population (1984) 552,000. Industry includes tourism, oil refining, and cigarette manufacturing.

yard unit (symbol yd) of length, equivalent to three feet (0.9144 m).

It is sometimes used to denote a cubic yard (0.7646 cubic meters), as of topsoil.

yarrow or *milfoil* perennial herb *Achillea millefolium* of the family Compositae, with feathery, scented leaves and flat-topped clusters of white or pink flowers.

yd abbreviation for *yard*.

year unit of time measurement, based on the orbital period of the Earth around the Sun.

yeast one of various single-celled fungi (especially the genus *Saccharomyces*) that form masses of minute circular or oval cells by budding. When placed in a sugar solution the cells multiply and convert the sugar into alcohol and carbon dioxide. Yeasts are used as fermenting agents in baking, brewing, and the making of wine and spirits. Brewer's yeast *S. cerevisiae* is a rich source of vitamin B.

Yeats W(illiam) B(utler) 1865–1939. Irish poet. He was a leader of the Celtic revival and a founder of the Abbey Theatre in Dublin. His early work was romantic and lyrical, as in the poem "The Lake Isle of Innisfree" and plays *The Countess Cathleen* 1892 and *The Land of Heart's Desire* 1894. His later books of poetry include *The Wild Swans at Coole* 1917 and *The Winding Stair* 1929. He was a senator of the Irish Free State 1922–28. Nobel Prize for Literature 1923.

yellow fever or *yellow jack* acute tropical viral disease, prevalent in the Caribbean area, Brazil, and on the W coast of Africa. Its symptoms are a high fever and yellowish skin (jaundice, possibly leading to liver failure); the heart and kidneys may also be affected.

Yellowknife capital of Northwest Territories, on the N shore of Great Slave Lake; population (1986) 11,753. It was founded 1935 when gold was discovered in the area and became the capital 1967.

Yemen
Republic of
(*al Jamhuriya al Yamaniya*)

area 205,367 sq mi/531,900 sq km
capital San"ā
cities Ta"iz; and chief port Aden
physical hot moist coastal plain, rising to plateau and desert
features once known as *Arabia felix* because of its fertility, includes islands of Perim (in strait of Bab-el-Mandeb, at S entrance to Red Sea), Socotra, and Kamaran
head of state Ali Abdullah Saleh from 1990
head of government Haydar Abu Bakr al-Attas from 1993
political system emergent democratic republic
political parties Yemen Socialist Party (YSP), Democratic Unionist Party, National Democratic Front, Yemen Reform Group, General People's Congress
exports cotton, coffee, grapes, vegetables
currency rial
population (1992) 12,147,000; growth rate 2.7% p.a.
life expectancy men 47, women 50
language Arabic
religions Sunni Muslim 63%, Shiite Muslim 37%
literacy men 20%, women 3% (1985 est)
GNP $4.9 bn (1983); $520 per head

chronology
1918 Yemen became independent.
1962 North Yemen declared the Yemen Arab Republic (YAR), with Abdullah al-Sallal as president. Civil war broke out between royalists and republicans.
1967 Civil war ended with the republicans victorious. Sallal deposed and replaced by Republican Council. The People's Republic of South Yemen was formed.
1970 People's Republic of South Yemen renamed People's Democratic Republic of Yemen.
1971–72 War between South Yemen and the YAR; union agreement signed but not kept.
1974 Ibrahim al-Hamadi seized power in North Yemen and Military Command Council set up.
1977 Hamadi assassinated and replaced by Ahmed ibn Hussein al-Ghashmi.
1978 Constituent people's assembly appointed in North Yemen and Military Command Council dissolved. Ghashmi killed by envoy from South Yemen; succeeded by Ali Abdullah Saleh. War broke out again between the two Yemens. South Yemen president deposed and Yemen Socialist Party (YSP) formed.
1979 Cease-fire agreed with commitment to future union.
1983 Saleh elected president of North Yemen for a further five-year term.
1984 Joint committee on foreign policy for the two Yemens met in Aden.
1985 Ali Nasser reelected secretary-general of the YSP in South Yemen; removed his opponents. Three bureau members killed.
1986 Civil war in South Yemen; Ali Nasser dismissed. New administration under Haydar Abu Bakr al-Attas.
1988 President Saleh reelected in North Yemen.
1989 Draft constitution for single Yemen state published.
1990 Border between two Yemens opened; countries formally united May 22 as Republic of Yemen.
1991 New constitution approved.
1992 Antigovernment riots.
1993 General People's Congress won most seats in general elections but no overall majority; coalition government formed, led by Haydar Abu Bakr al-Attas. Five-man presidential council formed.

Yellow River English name for the ◊Huang He River, China.

Yellow Sea gulf of the Pacific Ocean between China and Korea; area 180,000 sq mi/466,200 sq km. It receives the Huang He (Yellow River) and Chang Jiang.

Yellowstone National Park largest US nature preserve, established 1872, on a broad plateau in the Rocky Mountains, chiefly in NW Wyoming, but also in SW Montana and E Idaho; area 3,469 sq mi/8,983 sq km. The park contains more than 3,000 geysers and hot springs, including periodically erupting Old Faithful. It is one of the world's greatest wildlife refuges. Much of the park was ravaged by forest fires 1988.

John Colter, a trapper, explored the area in 1807.

Yeltsin Boris Nikolayevich 1931– . Russian politician, president of the Russian Soviet Federative Socialist Republic (RSFSR) 1990–91, and president of the newly independent Russian Federation from 1991. He directed the Federation's secession from the USSR and the formation of a new, decentralized confederation, the ◊Commonwealth of Independent States (CIS), with himself as the most powerful leader. A referendum 1993 supported his policies of price deregulation and accelerated privatization, despite severe economic problems and civil unrest. He has consistently requested international aid to bring his country out of recession.

Yemen country in SW Asia, bounded N by Saudi Arabia, E by Oman, S by the Gulf of Aden, and W by the Red Sea.

Yenisei river in Asian Russia, rising in the Tuva region and flowing across the Siberian plain into the Arctic Ocean; length 2,550 mi/4,100 km.

Yerevan industrial city (tractor parts, machine tools, chemicals, bricks, bicycles, wine, fruit canning) and capital of Armenia, a few miles N of the Turkish border; population (1987) 1,168,000. It was founded in the 7th century and was alternately Turkish and Persian from the 15th century until ceded to Russia 1828. Armenia became an independent republic 1991.

Yevtushenko Yevgeny Aleksandrovich 1933– . Soviet poet, born in Siberia. He aroused controversy with his anti-Stalinist "Stalin's Heirs" 1956, published with Khrushchev's support, and "Babi Yar" 1961. His autobiography was published 1963.

yew any evergreen coniferous tree of the genus *Taxus* of the family Taxaceae, native to the northern hemisphere. The leaves and bright red berrylike seeds are poisonous; the wood is hard and close-grained.

Yiddish language member of the west Germanic branch of the Indo-European language family, deriving from 13th–14th-century Rhineland German and spoken by northern, central, and eastern European Jews, who have carried it to Israel, the US, and many other parts of the world. It is written in the Hebrew alphabet and has many dialects reflecting European areas of residence, as well as many borrowed words from Polish, Russian, Lithuanian, and other languages encountered.

yin and yang Chinese for "dark" and "bright" respectively, referring to the passive (characterized as feminine, negative, intuitive) and active (characterized as masculine, positive, intellectual) principles of nature. Their interaction is believed to maintain equilibrium and harmony in the universe and to be present in all things. In Taoism and Confucianism they are represented by two interlocked curved shapes within a circle, one white, one black, with a spot of the contrasting color within the head of each.

yoga (Sanskrit "union") Hindu philosophical system attributed to Patanjali, who lived about 150 BC at Gonda, Uttar Pradesh, India. He preached mystical union with a personal deity through the practice of self-hypnosis and a rising above the senses by abstract meditation, adoption of special postures, and ascetic practices. As practiced in the West, yoga is more a system of mental and physical exercise, and of induced relaxation as a means of relieving stress.

yogurt also called *yoghurt* or *yoghourt* semisolid curdlike dairy product made from milk fermented with bacteria. It was originally made by nomadic tribes of Central Asia, from mare's milk in leather pouches attached to their saddles. It spread to the Asian and Mediterranean regions, where it is drunk plain, but honey, sugar, and fruit were added in Europe and the US, and the product was made solid and creamy, to be eaten by spoon.

Yokohama Japanese port on Tokyo Bay; population (1990) 3,220,350.

Industries include shipbuilding, oil refining, engineering, textiles, glass, and clothing.

yolk store of food, mostly in the form of fats and proteins, found in the ◊eggs of many animals. It provides nourishment for the growing embryo.

Yom Kippur the Jewish Day of ◊Atonement.

Yom Kippur War the surprise attack on Israel October 1973 by Egypt and Syria; see ◊Arab-Israeli Wars. It is named after the Jewish national holiday on which it began, the holiest day of the Jewish year.

Yonkers city in Westchester County, New York, on the Hudson River, just N of the Bronx, New York City; population (1990) 188,100. Products include machinery, processed foods, chemicals, clothing, and electric and electronic equipment. Yonkers was a Dutch settlement from about 1650.

York English dynasty founded by Richard, Duke of York (1411–60). He claimed the throne through his descent from Lionel, Duke of Clarence (1338–1368), third son of Edward III, whereas the reigning monarch, Henry VI of the rival house of Lancaster, was descended from the fourth son. The argument was fought out in the Wars of the ◊Roses. York was killed at the Battle of Wakefield 1460, but next year his son became King Edward IV, in turn succeeded by his son Edward V and then by his brother Richard III, with whose death at Bosworth the line ended. The Lancastrian victor in that battle was crowned Henry VII and consolidated his claim by marrying Edward IV's eldest daughter, Elizabeth.

York city in S Pennsylvania, SE of Harrisburg; population (1990) 42,100. It is an agricultural processing center for the area and manufactures paper products, building materials, and heavy machinery. The Articles of Confederation were adopted here during the Continental Congress 1777–78.

York cathedral and industrial city (railroad rolling stock, scientific instruments, sugar, chocolate, and glass) in North Yorkshire, N England
population (1991) 100,600
features The Gothic York Minster, containing medieval stained glass. Much of the 14th-century city wall survives. Jorvik Viking Center, opened 1984 after excavation of a site at Coppergate, contains wooden remains of Viking houses. The National Railroad Museum and the 19th-century railroad station; and the university 1963.

Yosemite Half Dome Mountain in the Yosemite National Park, California.

none achieved much practical success; attempted uprisings by Young Italy 1834 and 1844 failed miserably. It was superseded in Italy by the ◊Risorgimento.

Youngstown industrial city (fabricated metals) in E Ohio, on the Mahoning River; population (1990) 95,700. Youngstown was laid out 1797. The city's first steel plant was established 1892, close to coal and iron deposits. Ten thousand workers lost their jobs when three steel plants shut down 1977.

Youngstown Sheet and Tube Co v Sawyer US Supreme Court decision 1952 dealing with the right of the US president to nationalize private industry during wartime. The case arose over President Truman's seizure of steel mills during the Korean War. A crucial part of the war effort, the steel industry had been on the brink of a national strike. The Court ruled that the president's actions were illegal because neither Congressional legislation nor the Constitution had empowered him to intervene in labor disputes or to nationalize property.

Young Turk member of a reformist movement of young army officers in the Ottoman Empire founded 1889. The movement was instrumental in the constitutional changes of 1908 and the abdication of Sultan Abdul-Hamid II 1909. It gained prestige during the Balkan Wars 1912–13 and encouraged Turkish links with the German empire. Its influence diminished after 1918. The term is now used for a member of any radical or rebellious faction within a party or organization.

Young Women's Christian Association *YWCA* organization for the welfare of women and girls, founded London 1855. The first YWCA in the US was formally established 1858 in New York City; another followed in Boston, Massachusetts, 1866. Both were in response to the effects of the Industrial Revolution on women. Its facilities and activities are similar to those of the YMCA.

Ypres (Flemish *Ieper*) Belgian town in W Flanders, 25 mi/40 km S of Ostend, a site of three major battles 1914–17 fought in World War I. The Menin Gate 1927 is a memorial to British soldiers lost in these battles.

ytterbium soft, lustrous, silvery, malleable, and ductile element of the ◊lanthanide series, symbol Yb, atomic number 70, atomic weight 173.04. It occurs with (and resembles) yttrium in gadolinite and other minerals, and is used in making steel and other alloys.

yttrium silver-gray, metallic element, symbol Y, atomic number 39, atomic weight 88.905. It is associated with and resembles the rare-earth elements (◊lanthanides), occurring in gadolinite, xenotime, and other minerals. It is used in color-television tubes and to reduce steel corrosion.

Yuba City city in N central California, on the Feather River, N of San Francisco; population (1990) 27,400. It is an agricultural trading center for nuts, fruits, rice, and dairy products.

Yucatán peninsula in Central America, divided among Mexico, Belize, and Guatemala; area 70,000 sq mi/180,000 sq km. Tropical crops are grown. It is inhabited by Maya Indians and contains the remains of their civilization.

yucca plant of the genus *Yucca*, family Liliaceae, with over 40 species found in Latin America and SW US. The leaves are stiff and sword-shaped and the flowers white and bell-shaped.

Yugoslavia country in SE Europe, with a SW coastline on the Adriatic Sea, bounded W by Bosnia-Herzegovina, NW by Croatia, E by Romania and Bulgaria, and S by Macedonia and Albania.

Yoruba member of the majority ethnic group living in SW Nigeria; there is a Yoruba minority in E Benin. They number approximately 20 million in all, and their language belongs to the Kwa branch of the Niger-Congo family. The Yoruba established powerful city-states in the 15th century, known for their advanced culture which includes sculpture, art, and music.

Yosemite area in the Sierra Nevada, E California, a national park from 1890; area 1,189 sq mi/3,079 sq km. It includes Yosemite Gorge, Yosemite Falls (2,425 ft/739 m in three leaps) with many other lakes and waterfalls, and groves of giant sequoia trees.

Young Brigham 1801–1877. US ◊Mormon religious leader, born in Vermont. He joined the Mormon Church, or Church of Jesus Christ of Latter-day Saints, 1832, and three years later was appointed an apostle. After a successful recruiting mission in Liverpool, England, he returned to the US and, as successor of Joseph Smith (who had been murdered), led the Mormon migration to the Great Salt Lake in Utah 1846, founded Salt Lake City, and headed the colony until his death.

Young Cy (Denton True) 1867–1955. US baseball player. As a pitcher of unequaled skill and stamina, he established a lifetime record of 511 victories. In 16 seasons, he finished with 20 or more wins, 5 times exceeding 30. He was nicknamed "Cy" for his "cyclone" pitch.

The Cy Young Award, given annually to the outstanding pitcher in both the American and National leagues, is named after him. He was elected to the Baseball Hall of Fame 1937.

Young Italy Italian nationalist organization founded 1831 by Giuseppe ◊Mazzini while in exile in Marseille. The movement, which was immediately popular, was followed the next year by Young Germany, Young Poland, and similar organizations. All the groups were linked by Mazzini in his Young Europe movement, but

Yugoslavia

area 34,100 sq mi/88,400 sq km
capital Belgrade
cities Kraljevo, Leskovac, Pristina, Novi Sad, Titograd
head of state Dobrica Cosic from 1992
head of government Radoje Kontic from 1993
political system socialist pluralist republic
political parties Socialist Party of Serbia, ex-communist; Serbian Renaissance Movement, pro-monarchist; Democratic Party, Serbia-based, liberal, free-market; Montenegro League of Communists; Democratic Coalition of Muslims; Alliance of Reform Forces, Montenegro-based; Internal Macedonian Revolutionary Organization–Democratic Party for Macedonian National Unity (VMRO–DMPNE), Macedonian nationalist; Macedonian League of Communists
exports machinery, electrical goods, chemicals, clothing, tobacco
currency dinar
population (1992) 10,394,000 (Serb 53%, Albanian 15%, Macedonian 11%, Montenegrin 5%, Muslim 3%, Croat 2%)
life expectancy men 69, women 75 (1989)
languages Serbian variant of Serbo-Croatian, Macedonian, Slovenian

religion Eastern Orthodox 41% (Serbs), Roman Catholic 12% (Croats), Muslim 3%
literacy 90% (1989)
GNP $154.1 bn; $6,540 per head (1988)

chronology
1918 Creation of Kingdom of the Serbs, Croats, and Slovenes.
1929 Name of Yugoslavia adopted.
1941 Invaded by Germany.
1945 Yugoslav Federal Republic formed under leadership of Tito; communist constitution introduced.
1948 Split with USSR.
1953 Self-management principle enshrined in constitution.
1961 Nonaligned movement formed under Yugoslavia's leadership.
1974 New constitution adopted.
1980 Tito died; collective leadership assumed power.
1987 Threatened use of army to curb unrest.
1988 Economic difficulties: 1,800 strikes, 250% inflation, 20% unemployment. Ethnic unrest in Montenegro and Vojvodina; party reshuffled and government resigned.
1989 Reformist Croatian Ante Marković became prime minister. Twenty-nine died in ethnic riots in Kosovo province, protesting against Serbian attempt to end autonomous status of Kosovo and Vojvodina; state of emergency imposed. May: inflation rose to 490%; tensions with ethnic Albanians rose.
1990 Multiparty systems established in Serbia and Croatia.
1991 June: Slovenia and Croatia declared independence, resulting in clashes between federal and republican armies; Slovenia accepted European Community (EC)- sponsored peace pact. Fighting continued in Croatia; repeated calls for cease-fires failed. Dec: President Stipe Mesic and Prime Minister Ante Marković resigned.
1992 Jan: EC-brokered cease-fire established in Croatia; EC and US recognized Slovenia's and Croatia's independence. Bosnia-Herzegovina and Macedonia declared independence. April: Bosnia-Herzegovina recognized as independent by EC and US amid increasing ethnic hostility. New Federal Republic of Yugoslavia (FRY) proclaimed by Serbia and Montenegro but not recognized externally. May: Western ambassadors left Belgrade. International sanctions imposed against Serbia and Montenegro. Hostilities continued. Jun: Dobrica Cosic became president. Jul: Milan Panic became prime minister. Sept: UN membership suspended. Oct: Panic lost vote of confidence and removed from office. Dec: Slobodan Milosevic reelected Serbian president.
1993 Radoje Kontic became prime minister.

Yukon territory of NW Canada
area 186,631 sq mi/483,500 sq km
capital Whitehorse
cities Dawson, Mayo
features named after its chief river, the Yukon; includes the highest point in Canada, Mount Logan, 19,850 ft/6,050 m; Klondike Gold Rush International Historical Park, which extends into Alaska
products gold, silver, lead, zinc, oil, natural gas, coal
population (1991) 26,500
history settlement dates from the gold rush 1896–1910, when 30,000 people moved to the ◊Klondike river valley (silver is now worked there). It became separate from the Northwest Territories 1898, with Dawson as the capital 1898–1951. Construction of the Alcan Highway during World War II helped provide the basis for further development.

Yukon River river in North America, 1,979 mi/3,185 km long, flowing from Lake Tagish in Yukon Territory into Alaska, where it empties into the Bering Sea.

Yunnan province of SW China, adjoining Myanmar (Burma), Laos, and Vietnam
area 168,373 sq mi/436,200 sq km

capital Kunming
physical rivers: Chang Jiang, Salween, Mekong; crossed by the Burma Road; mountainous and well forested
products rice, tea, timber, wheat, cotton, rubber, tin, copper, lead, zinc, coal, salt
population (1990) 36,973,000.

Yukon

Z

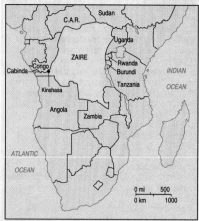

Zahir ud-din Muhammad Indian emperor, founder of Mogul dynasty. See ◊Babur.

Zaire country in central Africa, bounded W by Congo, N by the Central African Republic and Sudan, E by Uganda, Rwanda, Burundi, and Tanzania, SE by Zambia, and SW by Angola. There is a short coastline on the Atlantic Ocean.

Zaïre River formerly (until 1971) *Congo* second-longest river in Africa, rising near the Zambia–Zaire border (and known as the *Lualaba River* in the upper reaches) and flowing 2,800 mi/4,500 km to the Atlantic Ocean, running in a great curve that crosses the equator twice, and discharging a volume of water second only to the Amazon. The chief tributaries are the Ubangi, Sangha, and Kasai.

Zama, Battle of battle fought in 202 BC in Numidia (now Algeria), in which the Carthaginians under Hannibal were defeated by the Romans under Scipio, so ending the Second Punic War.

Zambezi river in central and SE Africa; length 1,650 mi/2,650 km from NW Zambia through Mozambique to the Indian Ocean, with a wide delta near Chinde. Major tributaries include the Kafue in Zambia. It is interrupted by rapids, and includes on the Zimbabwe–Zambia border the Victoria Falls (Mosi-oa-tunya) and Kariba Dam, which forms the reservoir of Lake Kariba with large fisheries.

Zagreb industrial city (leather, linen, carpets, paper, and electrical goods) and capital of Croatia, on the Sava River; population (1981) 1,174,512. Zagreb was a Roman city (*Aemona*) and has a Gothic cathedral. Its university was founded 1874. The city was damaged by bombing Oct 1991 during the Croatian civil war.

Zaire
Republic of (*République du Zaïre*)
(formerly *Congo*)

area 905,366 sq mi/2,344,900 sq km
capital Kinshasa
cities Lubumbashi, Kananga, Kisangani; ports Matadi, Boma
physical Zaïre River basin has tropical rainforest and savanna; mountains in E and W
features lakes Tanganyika, Mobutu Sese Seko, Edward; Ruwenzori mountains
head of state Mobutu Sese Seko Kuku Ngbendu wa Zabanga from 1965
head of government Faustin Birindwa from 1993
political system socialist pluralist republic
political parties Popular Movement of the Revolution (MPR), African socialist; numerous new parties registered 1991
exports coffee, copper, cobalt (80% of world output), industrial diamonds, palm oil

currency zaïre
population (1992) 41,151,000; growth rate 2.9% p.a.
life expectancy men 51, women 54 (1989)
languages French (official), Swahili, Lingala, other African languages; over 300 dialects
religions Christian 70%, Muslim 10%
literacy men 79%, women 45% (1985 est)
GNP $5 bn (1987); $127 per head

chronology
1908 Congo Free State annexed to Belgium.
1960 Independence achieved from Belgium as Republic of the Congo. Civil war broke out between central government and Katanga province.
1963 Katanga war ended.
1967 New constitution adopted.
1970 Col Mobutu elected president.
1971 Country became the Republic of Zaire.
1972 The Popular Movement of the Revolution (MPR) became the only legal political party. Katanga province renamed Shaba.
1974 Foreign-owned businesses and plantations seized by Mobutu and given in political patronage.
1977 Original owners of confiscated properties invited back. Mobutu reelected; Zairians invaded Shaba province from Angola, repulsed by Belgian paratroopers.
1978 Second unsuccessful invasion from Angola.
1988 Potential rift with Belgium avoided.
1990 Mobutu announced end of ban on multiparty politics, following internal dissent.
1991 Multiparty elections promised. Sept: after antigovernment riots, Mobutu agreed to share power with opposition; Etienne Tshisekedi appointed premier. Oct: Tshisekedi dismissed.
1992 Aug: Tshisekedi reinstated against Mobutu's wishes; interim opposition parliament formed. Oct: renewed rioting.
1993 Jan: army mutiny; France and Belgium prepared to evacuate civilians. March: Tshisekedi dismissed by Mobutu, replaced by Faustin Birindwa, but Tshisekedi still considered himself in office. He sought foreign military assistance in toppling Mobutu.

Zambia
Republic of

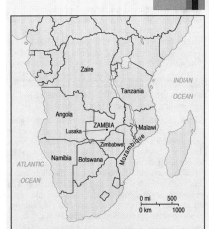

area 290,579 sq mi/752,600 sq km
capital Lusaka
cities Kitwe, Ndola, Kabwe, Chipata, Livingstone
physical forested plateau cut through by rivers
features Zambezi River, Victoria Falls, Kariba Dam
head of state and government Frederick Chiluba from 1991
political system socialist pluralist republic

political parties United National Independence Party (UNIP), African socialist; Movement for Multiparty Democracy (MMD), moderate, left of center; National Democratic Alliance (NADA), moderate centrist
exports copper, cobalt, zinc, emeralds, tobacco
currency kwacha
population (1992) 8,303,000; growth rate 3.3% p.a.
life expectancy men 54, women 57 (1989)
language English (official); Bantu dialects
religions Christian 66%, animist, Hindu, Muslim
literacy 54% (1988)
GNP $2.1 bn (1987); $304 per head (1986)

chronology
1899–1924 As Northern Rhodesia, under administration of the British South Africa Company.
1924 Became a British protectorate.
1964 Independence achieved from Britain, within the Commonwealth, as the Republic of Zambia with Kenneth Kaunda as president.
1972 United National Independence Party (UNIP) declared the only legal party.
1976 Support for the Patriotic Front in Rhodesia declared.
1980 Unsuccessful coup against President Kaunda.
1985 Kaunda elected chair of the African Front Line States.
1987 Kaunda elected chair of the Organization of African Unity (OAU).
1988 Kaunda reelected unopposed for sixth term.
1990 Multiparty system announced for 1991.
1991 Movement for Multiparty Democracy won landslide election victory; Frederick Chiluba became president.
1992 Food and water shortages caused by severe drought.

Zambia landlocked country in S central Africa, bounded N by Zaire and Tanzania, E by Malawi, S by Mozambique, Zimbabwe, Botswana, and Namibia, and W by Angola.

Zanzibar island region of Tanzania
area 640 sq mi/1,658 sq km (50 mi/80 km long)
cities Zanzibar
products cloves, copra
population (1985) 571,000
history settled by Arab traders in the 7th century; occupied by the Portuguese in the 16th century; became a sultanate in the 17th century; under British protection 1890–1963. Together with the island of Pemba, some nearby islets, and a strip of mainland territory, it became a republic 1963. It merged with Tanganyika as Tanzania 1964.

Zapata Emiliano 1879–1919. Mexican Indian revolutionary leader. He led a revolt against dictator Porfirio Díaz (1830–1915) from 1911 under the slogan "Land and Liberty," to repossess for the indigenous Mexicans the land taken by the Spanish. By 1915 he was driven into retreat, and was assassinated.

Zapotec member of a North American Indian people of S Mexico, now numbering approximately 250,000, living mainly in Oaxaca. The Zapotec language, which belongs to the Oto-Mangean family, has nine dialects. The ancient Zapotec built the ceremonial center of Monte Albán 1000–500 BC; developing one of the classic Mesoamerican civilizations by AD 300, but declined under pressure from the Mixtecs from 900 until the Spanish Conquest 1530s.

Zaragoza (English **Saragossa**) industrial city (iron, steel, chemicals, plastics, canned food, electrical goods) in Aragon, Spain; population (1991) 614,400. The medieval city walls and bridges over the river Ebro survive, and there is a 15th-century university.

zebra black and white striped member of the horse genus *Equus* found in Africa; the stripes serve as camouflage or dazzle and confuse predators. It is about 5 ft/1.5 m high at the shoulder, with a stout body and a short, thick mane. Zebras live in family groups and herds on mountains and plains, and can run up to 40 mph/60 kph. Males are usually solitary.

zebu any of a species of ♀cattle *Bos indicus* found domesticated in E Asia, India, and Africa. It is usually light-colored, with large horns and a large fatty hump near the shoulders. It is used for pulling loads, and is held by some Hindus to be sacred. There are about 30 breeds.

Zedekiah last king of Judah 597–586 BC. Placed on the throne by Nebuchadnezzar, he rebelled, was forced to witness his sons' execution, then was blinded and

zebra Burchell's zebras show great variation in stripe pattern, both between individuals and over the geographical range.

sent to Babylon. The witness to these events was the prophet Jeremiah, who describes them in the Old Testament.

Zeeland province of the SW Netherlands
area 691 sq mi/1,790 sq km
capital Middelburg
cities Vlissingen, Terneuzen, Goes
features mostly below sea level, Zeeland is protected by a system of dykes
products cereals, potatoes
population (1991) 357,000
history disputed by the counts of Flanders and Holland during the Middle Ages, Zeeland was annexed to Holland 1323 by Count William III.

Zeeman Pieter 1865–1943. Dutch physicist who discovered 1896 that when light from certain elements, such as sodium or lithium (when heated), is passed through a spectroscope in the presence of a strong magnetic field, the spectrum splits into a number of distinct lines. His discovery, known as the *Zeeman effect*, won him a share of the 1902 Nobel Prize for Physics.

Zen form of ◊Buddhism introduced from India to Japan via China in the 12th century. *Kōan* (paradoxical questions), tea-drinking, and sudden enlightenment are elements of Zen practice. Soto Zen was spread by the priest Dōgen (1200–1253), who emphasized work, practice, discipline, and philosophical questions to discover one's Buddha-nature in the "realization of self."

Zenger John Peter 1697–1746. American colonial printer and newspaper editor. In 1733 he founded the *New York Weekly Journal* through which he publicized his opposition to New York governor William Cosby. In 1734 he was arrested for seditious libel. Acquitted by a jury in 1735, he published *A Brief Narrative of the Case and Trial of John Peter Zenger* 1736 and remained a spokesman for the principle of freedom of the press.

zenith uppermost point of the celestial horizon, immediately above the observer; the ◊nadir is below, diametrically opposite. See ◊celestial sphere.

Zenobia queen of Palmyra AD 266–272. She assumed the crown as regent for her sons, after the death of her husband Odaenathus, and in 272 was defeated at Emesa (now Homs) by Aurelian and taken captive to Rome.

Zeno of Elea *c.* 490–430 BC. Greek philosopher who pointed out several paradoxes that raised "modern" problems of space and time. For example, motion is an illusion, since an arrow in flight must occupy a determinate space at each instant, and therefore must be at rest.

Zeppelin Ferdinand, Count von Zeppelin 1838–1917. German airship pioneer. On retiring from the army 1891, he devoted himself to the study of aeronautics, and his first airship was built and tested 1900. During World War I a number of Zeppelin airships bombed England. They were also used for luxury passenger transport but the construction of hydrogen-filled airships with rigid keels was abandoned after several disasters in the 1920s and 1930s. Zeppelin also helped to pioneer large multi-engine bomber planes.

Zeus in Greek mythology, the chief of the gods (Roman Jupiter). He was the son of Cronus, whom he overthrew; his brothers included Pluto and Poseidon, his sisters Demeter and Hera. As the supreme god he dispensed good and evil and was the father and ruler of all humankind. His emblems are the thunderbolt and aegis (shield), representing the thundercloud. The colossal ivory and gold statue of the seated god, made by Phidias for the temple of Zeus in the Peloponnese, was one of the ◊Seven Wonders of the World.

Zhangjiakou or *Changchiakow* historic city and trade center in Hebei province, China, 100 mi/160 km NW of Beijing, on the Great Wall; population (1980) 1,100,000. Zhangjiakou is on the border of Inner Mongolia (its Mongolian name is *Kalgan*, "gate") and on the road and railroad to Ulaanbaatar in Mongolia. It developed under the Manchu dynasty, and was the center of the tea trade from China to Russia.

Zhao Ziyang 1918– . Chinese politician, prime minister 1980–87 and secretary of the Chinese Communist Party 1987–89. His reforms included self-management and incentives for workers and factories. He lost his secretaryship and other posts after the Tiananmen Square massacre in Beijing June 1989.

Zhejiang or *Chekiang* province of SE China
area 39,295 sq mi/101,800 sq km
capital Hangzhou
features smallest of the Chinese provinces; the base of the Song dynasty 12th–13th centuries; densely populated
products rice, cotton, sugar, jute, corn; timber on the uplands
population (1990) 41,446,000.

Zhengzhou or *Chengchow* industrial city (light engineering, cotton textiles, foods) and capital (from 1954) of Henan province, China, on the Huang Ho River; population (1989) 1,660,000.

Zhivkov Todor 1911– . Bulgarian Communist Party leader 1954–89, prime minister 1962–71, president 1971–89. His period in office was one of caution and conservatism. In 1991 he was tried for gross embezzlement.

Zhou Enlai or *Chou En-lai* 1898–1976. Chinese politician. Zhou, a member of the Chinese Communist Party (CCP) from the 1920s, was prime minister 1949–76 and foreign minister 1949–58. He was a moderate Maoist and weathered the Cultural Revolution. He played a key role in foreign affairs.

Zhu De or *Chu Teh* 1886–1976. Chinese Red Army leader from 1931. He devised the tactic of mobile guerrilla warfare and organized the ◊Long March to Shaanxi 1934–36. He was made a marshal 1955.

Zhukov Georgi Konstantinovich 1896–1974. Marshal of the USSR in World War II and minister of defense 1955–57. As chief of staff from 1941, he defended

Zhou Enlai Chinese politician and prime minister Zhou Enlai, 1971.

Moscow 1941, counterattacked at Stalingrad (now Volgograd) 1942, organized the relief of Leningrad (now St Petersburg) 1943, and led the offensive from the Ukraine March 1944 which ended in the fall of Berlin.

Zia ul-Haq Mohammad 1924–1988. Pakistani general, in power from 1977 until his death, probably an assassination, in an aircraft explosion. He became army chief of staff 1976, led the military coup against Zulfikar Ali ◊Bhutto 1977, and became president 1978. Zia introduced a fundamentalist Islamic regime and restricted political activity.

Zimbabwe extensive stone architectural ruins near Victoria in Mashonaland, Zimbabwe. The structure was probably the work of the Shona people who established their rule about AD 1000 and who mined minerals for trading. The word *zimbabwe* means "house of stone" in Shona language. The new state of Zimbabwe took its name from these ruins.

Zimbabwe landlocked country in S central Africa, bounded N by Zambia, E by Mozambique, S by South Africa, and W by Botswana.

zinc (Germanic *zint* "point") hard, brittle, bluish-white, metallic element, symbol Zn, atomic number 30, atomic weight 65.37. The principal ore is sphalerite or zinc blende (zinc sulfide, ZnS). Zinc is little affected by air or moisture at ordinary temperatures; its chief uses are in alloys such as brass and in coating metals (for example, galvanized iron). Its compounds include zinc oxide, used in ointments (as an astringent) and cosmetics, paints, glass, and printing ink.

zinc ore mineral from which zinc is extracted, principally sphalerite $(Zn,Fe)S$, but also zincite, ZnO_2, and smithsonite, $ZnCO_3$, all of which occur in mineralized veins. Ores of lead and zinc often occur together, and are common worldwide; Canada, the US, and Australia are major producers.

Zimbabwe
Republic of

area 150,695 sq mi/390,300 sq km
capital Harare
cities Bulawayo, Gweru, Kwekwe, Mutare, Hwange
physical high plateau with central high veld and mountains in E; rivers Zambezi, Limpopo
features Hwange National Park, part of Kalahari Desert; ruins of Great Zimbabwe
head of state and government Robert Mugabe from 1987
political system effectively one-party socialist republic
political party Zimbabwe African National Union–Patriotic Front (ZANU–PF), African socialist; Forum Party, moderate centrist; United Front, a right of center coalition opposed to ZANU–PF, comprising the Zimbabwe United Movement (ZUM), the Zimbabwe African National Union (Ndongo) and the United African National Council (UANC).
exports tobacco, asbestos, cotton, coffee, gold, silver, copper
currency Zimbabwe dollar
population (1992) 9,871,000 (Shona 80%, Ndbele 19%; about 100,000 whites); growth rate 3.5% p.a.
life expectancy men 59, women 63 (1989)
languages English (official), Shona, Sindebele
religions Christian, Muslim, Hindu, animist
literacy men 81%, women 67% (1985 est)
GNP $5.5 bn (1988); $275 per head (1986)

chronology
1889–1923 As Southern Rhodesia, under administration of British South Africa Company.
1923 Became a self-governing British colony.
1961 Zimbabwe African People's Union (ZAPU) formed, with Joshua Nkomo as leader.
1962 ZAPU declared illegal.
1963 Zimbabwe African National Union (ZANU) formed, with Robert Mugabe as secretary-general.
1964 Ian Smith became prime minister. ZANU banned. Nkomo and Mugabe imprisoned.
1965 Smith declared unilateral independence.
1966–68 Abortive talks between Smith and UK prime minister Harold Wilson.
1974 Nkomo and Mugabe released.
1975 Geneva conference set date for constitutional independence.
1979 Smith produced new constitution and established a government with Bishop Abel Muzorewa as prime minister. New government denounced by Nkomo and Mugabe. Conference in London agreed independence arrangements (Lancaster House Agreement).
1980 Independence achieved from Britain, with Robert Mugabe as prime minister and Rev Canaan Banana as president.
1981 Rift between Mugabe and Nkomo.
1982 Nkomo dismissed from the cabinet, leaving the country temporarily.
1984 ZANU–PF party congress agreed to create a one-party state in future.
1985 Relations between Mugabe and Nkomo improved. Troops sent to Matabeleland to suppress rumored insurrection; 5,000 civilians killed.
1986 Joint ZANU–PF rally held amid plans for merger.
1987 White-roll seats in the assembly were abolished. President Banana retired; Mugabe combined posts of head of state and prime minister with the title executive president.
1988 Nkomo returned to the cabinet and was appointed vice president.
1989 Opposition party, the Zimbabwe Unity Movement, formed by Edgar Tekere; draft constitution drawn up, renouncing Marxism–Leninism; ZANU and ZAPU formally merged.
1990 ZANU–PF reelected. State of emergency ended. Opposition to creation of one-party state.
1992 United Front formed to oppose ZANU–PF. March: Mugabe declared dire drought and famine situation a national disaster.

zinnia any annual plant of the genus *Zinnia*, family Compositae, native to Mexico and South America, notably the cultivated hybrids of *Z. elegans*, with brightly colored, daisylike flowers.

Zion Jebusite (Amorites of Canaan) stronghold in Jerusalem captured by King David, and the hill on which he built the Temple, symbol of Jerusalem and of Jewish national life.

Zionism political movement advocating the reestablishment of a Jewish homeland in Palestine, the "promised land" of the Bible, with its capital Jerusalem, the "city of Zion."

zircon zirconium silicate, $ZrSiO_4$, a mineral that occurs in small quantities in a wide range of igneous, sedimentary, and metamorphic rocks. It is very durable and is resistant to erosion and weathering. It is usually colored brown, but can be other colors, and when transparent may be used as a gemstone.

zirconium (Germanic *zircon*, from Persian *zargun* "golden") lustrous, grayish-white, strong, ductile, metallic element, symbol Zr, atomic number 40, atomic weight 91.22. It occurs in nature as the mineral zircon (zirconium silicate), from which it is obtained commercially. It is used in some ceramics, alloys for wire and filaments, steel manufacture, and nuclear reactors, where its low neutron absorption is advantageous.

zither a member of a family of musical instruments that have strings attached across a flat sound-board and are plucked, bowed, or struck with a beater, to play a note. Examples are the ◊dulcimer, the Japanese ◊koto, and a 45-stringed folk instrument from Austria and Germany.

zodiac zone of the heavens containing the paths of the Sun, Moon, and planets. When this was devised by the ancient Greeks, only five planets were known, making the zodiac about 16° wide. In astrology, the zodiac is divided into 12 signs, each 30° in extent: Aries, Taurus, Gemini, Cancer, Leo, Virgo, Libra, Scorpio, Sagittarius, Capricorn, Aquarius, and Pisces. These do not cover the same areas of sky as the astronomical constellations.

Zog Ahmed Beg Zogu 1895–1961. King of Albania 1928–39. He became prime minister of Albania 1922, president of the republic 1925, and proclaimed himself king 1928. He was driven out by the Italians 1939 and settled in England.

Zola Émile Edouard Charles Antoine 1840–1902. French novelist and social reformer. With *La Fortune des Rougon/The Fortune of the Rougons* 1867 he began a series of some 20 naturalistic novels, portraying the fortunes of a French family under the Second Empire. They include *Le Ventre de Paris/The Underbelly of Paris* 1873, *Nana* 1880, and *La Débâcle/The Debacle* 1892. In 1898 he published *J'accuse/I Accuse*, a pamphlet indicting the persecutors of ◊Dreyfus, for which he was prosecuted for libel but later pardoned.

zone standard time or *standard time* the time in any of the 24 time zones, each an hour apart, into which the Earth is divided. The respective times depend on their distances, east or west of Greenwich, England. In North America the eight zones (Atlantic, Eastern, Central, Mountain, Pacific, Alaska, Hawaii-Aleutian, and Samoa) use the mean solar times of meridians 15° apart, starting with 60° longitude. (See also ◊time.)

zoo abbreviation for *zoological gardens*, a place where animals are kept in captivity. Originally created purely for visitor entertainment and education, zoos have become major centers for the breeding of endangered species of animals; a 1984 report identified 2,000 vertebrate species in need of such maintenance. The Arabian oryx has already been preserved in this way; it was captured 1962, bred in captivity, and released again in the desert 1972, where it has flourished.

zoology branch of biology concerned with the study of animals. It includes description of present-day animals, the study of evolution of animal forms, anatomy, physiology, embryology, behavior, and geographical distribution.

Zoroaster or *Zarathustra* 6th century BC. Persian prophet and religious teacher, founder of Zoroastrianism. Zoroaster believed that he had seen God, Ahura Mazda, in a vision. His first vision came at the age of 30 and, after initial rejection and violent attack, he converted King Vishtaspa. Subsequently, his teachings spread rapidly, becoming the official religion of the kingdom. According to tradition, Zoroaster was murdered at the age of 70 while praying at the altar.

Z particle in physics, an ◊elementary particle, one of the weakons responsible for carrying the ◊weak nuclear force.

Zuider Zee former sea inlet in the NW Netherlands, closed off from the North Sea by a 20-mi/32-km dyke 1932; much of it has been reclaimed as land. The remaining lake is called the ◊IJsselmeer.

Zulu member of a group of southern African peoples mainly from Natal, South Africa. Their present homeland, KwaZulu, represents the nucleus of the once extensive and militaristic Zulu kingdom. Today many Zulus work in the industrial centers around Johannesburg and Durban. The Zulu language, closely related to Xhosa, belongs to the Bantu branch of the Niger-Congo family.

Zürich financial center and industrial city (machinery, electrical goods, textiles) on Lake Zürich; population (1990) 341,300.

Situated at the foot of the Alps, it is the capital of Zürich canton and the largest city in Switzerland.

Zwingli Ulrich 1484–1531. Swiss Protestant, born in St Gallen. He was ordained a Roman Catholic priest 1506, but by 1519 was a Reformer and led the Reformation in Switzerland with his insistence on the sole authority of the Scriptures. He was killed in a skirmish at Kappel during a war against the cantons that had not accepted the Reformation.

Zworykin Vladimir Kosma 1889–1982. Russian-born US electronics engineer, in the US from 1919. He invented a television camera tube and the ◊electron microscope.

zygote ◊ovum (egg) after ◊fertilization but before it undergoes cleavage to begin embryonic development.